Entered according to Act of Congress, in the year 1858, by

S. FRENCH, L. C. PRATT, H. L. PRATT, J. B. HENSHAW,

in the Clerk's Office of the District Court of the United States, for the Southern District of New York.

S. W. BENEDICT, STEREOTYPER AND PRINTER,
16 Spruce Street, New York.

PUBLISHERS' NOTICE.

——◦——

BELIEVING as we did, that the business interests of New York demanded the publication of a work which would show at once its Mercantile, Manufacturing and Commercial resources, and present to business men, through each City, Town and Village, a medium of acquaintance with each other, we were induced to undertake the preparation and publication of the present volume. As we have progressed with the work, the universal approbation and support which it has received from an intelligent public, through every portion of the State, has confirmed us in the belief that we had correctly divined their wants.

In accordance with our plan, we have made a new Map of New York City, also one for the State, on which every Town in its appropriate County is laid down by number, which, taken in connection with the alphabetical list of Towns and their numbers, will be found more convenient, accurate and recent than any now in use. Our alphabetical List of Towns and Post Villages, it will be observed, makes what has been so much needed, a complete Post Office Directory for the State, as in every instance where the postmaster's name stands against any Town or Village, it indicates that a Post Office is located there. It will be observed by referring to the list, that there are very many Towns that contain no Post Office by the same name, and also that there are many important Villages, and some Cities, embraced in the limits of almost unheard-of Towns. This may, at first, cause some perplexity, as in the body of the work the arrangement is alphabetical by Towns. The difficulty may, however, be removed by observing in the list the name of the Town standing against each Village.

Other plans of arrangement will doubtless suggest themselves, as being preferable to the one which we have adopted, but we think, on reflection, it will be conceded, that its convenience as a reference book has been promoted by the present arrangement.

For the benefit of professional men and others who may be interested in that department, we have appended a Statistical Register, which, however, may not be as full as some works which have been published, giving statistical matters only; but, we trust, sufficiently so for all practical purposes.

To obtain our information, it was found necessary to canvass the State. To do this, experienced and trusty men were employed to visit each County and obtain the required lists. Owing to the fact that the State was canvassed by so many different men, each in a measure depending on his own judgment what items to record, it may be found that some branches of business are represented in a part of the counties and omitted in the rest, but the instructions being in the main the same, the business is as uniformly and fully represented as business purposes may require.

That it is difficult to make the orthography of proper names, and all other matters which compose a Directory, perfectly accurate, the experience of all Directory Publishers goes to prove, and as the errors usually lie on the surface, it is very natural that they should be criticised before the truths are appreciated. The present work may not be entirely free from unavoidable errors and omissions, but we cherish the belief, from the great care and labor bestowed upon its compilation, that it will be found a full and reliable source of present and future reference.

PUBLISHERS.

INDEX.

ERRATA, AND NAMES TOO LATE FOR INSERTION.

Artists' (Daguerrian) Materials.—Luther Robinson, (manufacturer) Chittenango *Sullivan.*

Attorneys.—Lewis Kingsley, S. C. Graves *Cincinnatus.* Edward C. Reed, Isaac A. Gates, Wm. W. Northrop, L. D. Dibble *Cortlandville.* White & Jones, M'Grawville Townsend Ross *Homer.* Alanson Coats, Amos L. Kinney *Truxton.*

Axle Manufacturer.—J. B. Mowry. 290 Pearl *New York.*

Band Leather Manufacturer.—Hugh Moffatt, 543 8th Av. *New York.*

Bank Note Reporters.—J. Thompson, 12 Spruce, Charles & Leonori, 35 Wall *New York.*

Carriage & Coach Makers.—Levi Adams, Charles Boice, I. Ford, Lockwood & Gillen *Harlem.* W. C. Dunn, John Flin, M'Cabe & Lenox, J. C. Parker *Yorkville.*

Druggists.—Bristol & Mason. James M'Carn, Newark *Arcadia.* Hood & Peck, L. Ely, Clyde *Galen.* Wm. H. Sisson, George C. Dean *Lyons.* A. G. Heminway, Wm. H. Bowman, Wm. H. Cuyler *Palmyra.*

Fringe and Tassel.—M. Horn. 579 Broadway *Albany.*

Gold and Silver Refiners.—Robert Langman. Marshall st. n. Jackson Ferry, Charles Langman, 164 Concord *Brooklyn.*

Paint Manufacturers.—J. C Bell, 166 Thompson. J. K. Marcher, W. 28th bet. 9th & 10th Avs. *New York.*

Tubular Filter.—W. Latting, (manufacturer,) (see advertisement) 149 Fulton *New York.*

Sheetings and Shirtings.—Charles H. Parsons, (wholesale) 65 Liberty *New York.*

Buffalo Savings Bank.—Russell H. Heywood, President, Robert Pomeroy, Secretary. Business hours from 9 to 12 A.M. & 2 to 4 P.M.—Office, Buffalo Bank Buildings, Main st. *Buffalo.*

LIST OF TOWNS AND POST VILLAGES

Accord, Rochester, *Ulster*..Moses J. Schoonmaker
Acra, Cairo, *Greene*...........Daniel S. Lennon
Adams, 5, *Jefferson*............Joseph D. Smith
Adams Basin, Ogden. *Monroe*......Marcus Adams
Adams Centre, Adams, *Jefferson*.Claudius Hubbard
Adamsville, Kingsbury, *Washington*..A.W.Harding
Addison, 4. *Steuben*...........Chas. E. Gillett
Adirondac. Newcomb, *Essex*....Andrew Porteous
Adriance, Fishkill, *Duchess*..Abra'm B. Stockholm
Akron, Newstead, *Erie*.........Elisha M. Adams
Alabama, 9, *Genesee*.........Reuben B. Warren
ALBANY, 9, *Albany*.............Lewis Benedict
Albion, 17, *Oswego*..............................
ALBION, Barre, *Orleans*........Harman Goodrich
Alden, 13, *Erie*...............Horace Stanley
Alder Creek, Boonville, *Oneida*...Henry White
Alexander, 2, *Genesee*........Elbridge G. Moulton
Alexandria, 21, *Jefferson*.....John W. Fuller
Alexandria Centre, Alexandria, *Jefferson*.. D. Howe
Alfred, 11, *Alleghany*.........Samuel Russell
Allen, 19. *Alleghany*.........John W. Stewart
Allen Centre, Allen, *Alleghany*...Chester Rotch
Allen's Hill, Richmond, *Ontario*...J. Tallmadge
Alloway, Lyons, *Wayne*....De Witt C. Van Slyck
Almond, 12, *Alleghany*.........Ira Cutler
Alps, Nassau, *Rensselaer*......Thomas Ten Eyck
Altay, *Steuben*...............Abel Kendall
Alton, Sodus, *Wayne*..........Thomas Forbes
Amagansett, East Hampton, *Suffolk*..D.B.Van Scoy
Amber, Otisco, *Onondaga*.........Albert Niles
Amboy, 7, *Oswego*............Robert G. Carter
Amenia, 11, *Duchess*............Hiram Vail
Amenia Union, Amenia, *Duchess*....A. Hitchcock
Ames, Canajoharie, *Montgomery*...C. G. Robinson
Amesville, *Ulster*............Thomas M. Holt
Amherst, 19. *Erie*..............................
Amity, 10, *Alleghany*...........................
Amity, Warwick, *Orange*...........Isaac Hoyt
Amsterdam, 8, *Montgomery*......James W. Phillips
Ansquascook, Jackson, *Washington*..J. Thompson
Ancram, 3, *Columbia*........Peter P. Rossman
Andes, 3, *Delaware*...........Daniel B. Shaver
Andover, 5, *Alleghany*.........David J. Hale
ANGELICA, 14, *Alleghany*...........Ezra Starr
Angola, Collins, *Erie*...........Caleb Taylor
Annsville, 18, *Oneida*..........................
Antwerp, 20, *Jefferson*.........Alonzo Chapin
Apalachin. Owego, *Tioga*........Ransom Steele
Appling, *Jefferson*..........Susan Howard
Apulia. Fabius, *Onondaga*.........Edwin Miles
Arcadia, 3, *Wayne*..............................
Argoesville, Sharon, *Schoharie*...John Simmons, jr.
Argyle, 8. *Washington*........John A. Pattison
Arkport, Hornellsville, *Steuben*.....Jas. Hurlburt
Arietta. 5. *Hamilton*...........................
Arkwright, 19, *Chautauque*.....Simeon Clinton
Arthursburgh, La Grange, *Duchess*....V. Brooks
Ashford, 25. *Cattaraugus*.....Daniel W. Wilson
Ashland, 2, *Greene*............Joshua Draper
Astoria, Newtown, *Queens*.......Edwin Mills
Athens, 4, *Greene*...........Orrin E. Osborn
Athol, 5, *Warren*...........John L. Gilpin
Attica, 15, *Wyoming*.........Alden S. Stevens
Attica. Attica, *Wyoming*..........Wm. Tanner
Attlebury, Stanford, *Duchess*...Phineas K. Sackett
Auburn, 12, *Cayuga*...........Ethan A. Warden
Augusta, 5, *Oneida*............Nelson Maxon
Aurelius, 12, *Cayuga*.........Alanson Partelow
Auriesville, Glen, *Montgomery*...J. C. Van Alstine
Aurora, 11, *Erie*...............................

Aurora, Ledyard, *Cayuga*.........Chas. Campbell
Ausable, 2, *Clinton*............................
Ausable Forks, Jay, *Essex*......Geo. C. Dickinson
Austerlitz, 11, *Columbia*.........Anson Brown
Ava, 28, *Oneida*..............Joshua Colman
Avoca, 26, *Steuben*..........John D. Griswold
Avon, 12, *Livingston*........Wm. A. Furman
Axeville, Conewango. *Cattaraugus*..H. W. Cowley
Babcock Hill. *Oneida*........John H. Champion
Babylon. Huntington, *Suffolk*...Walter W. Robbin
Bainbridge, 1, *Chenango*........Abram G. Owens
Baiting Hollow, Riverhead, *Suffolk*.Micha Howell
Baldwin. *Chemung*...........John G. Lowman
Baldwinsville, Lysander, *Onondaga*....L. B. Hall
Ballston, 5, *Saratoga*..........................
BALLSTON, Milton, *Saratoga*......Jas. Comstock
Ballston Centre, Ballston, *Saratoga*.Wm. O. Smith
Bangor, 6, *Franklin*...........Joshua Dickinson
Barbourville, Tompkins. *Delaware*.S. Van Schoyk
Barcelona, Westfield, *Chautauque*..Amos Whitten
Barker, 10, *Broome*.............................
Burkerville, *Saratoga*..........Ira J. Barker
Barnerville. Fulton, *Schoharie*...Clark B. Griggs
Barre, 2, *Orleans*..............................
Barre Centre, Barre, *Orleans*....Benj. Matison
Barrington, 8, *Yates*.........Samuel Lockwood
Barrytown, Redhook, *Duchess*...Augustus Martin
Barryville, Lumberland, *Sullivan*.Calvin P. Fuller
Barton, 1, *Tioga*............Samuel Mills
BATAVIA, 7, *Genesee*..........Chas. E. Ford
BATH, 18, *Steuben*..........Timothy Whiting
Battenville, Greenwich, *Washington*.Elijah Hyatt
Beach Hill, *Ulster*.........Samuel N. Hendrix
Bearsville, *Ulster*..........Christian Baehr
Beaver Brook, Lumberland, *Sullic*.C. S. Woodward
Beaver Dams, Dix, *Chemung*.....Almon Beecher
Beaver Kill, Rockland, *Sullivan*.Albert C. Babcock
Beaver Meadow, *Chenango*......Thomas Havens
BEDFORD, 15, *Westchester*.....Nehemiah S. Bates
Bedford Station. Bedford, *Westch*...G. W. Gardner
Beekman, 2, *Duchess*...........James Peters
Beekmantown, 7, *Clinton*.......Franklin Weaver
Belfast, 16, *Alleghany*......Thomas P. Alexander
Belle Isle, Camillus, *Onondaga*.....Ephm. Shead
Belleville, Ellisburgh, *Jefferson*.Bradf'd K. Hawes
Bellport, Brookhaven, *Suffolk*....William Raynor
Belmont. 4, *Franklin*...........................
Bemus Heights, Stillwater, *Saratoga*...E. Dunscomb
Bennett's Corners. Lenox, *Madison*.Prescott M'Doel
Bennett's Creek, *Steuben*..........John Coston
Bennettsville, Bainbridge, *Chenango*..D. Van Horn
Bennington, 16, *Wyoming*......George G. Hoskins
Benson, Hope, *Hamilton*..........John Harris
Benton, 6, *Yates*......Benjamin Coddington, jr.
Benton Centre, Benton, *Yates*......A. H. Savage
Bergen, 13, *Genesee*........William P. Munger
Bergholtz, *Niagara*...........Henry Kittel
Berkshire, 9, *Tioga*.........Carlisle P. Johnson
Berlin, 4, *Rensselaer*........John Whitford
Berne, 6, *Albany*............Datus E. Tyler
Bethany, 3, *Genesee*..........Ira R. Gifford
Bethel, 5, *Sullivan*.........Charles B. Roosa
Bethlehem, 4, *Albany*.........Nathaniel Adams
Big Brook, Western, *Oneida*....Chauncey Hayden
Big Eddy, Lumberland, *Sullivan*...John S. Hughes
Big Flats, 4, *Chemung*........Lauren A. Tuttle
Big Hollow, Windham, *Greene*....Erastus T. Peck
Big Stream Point. Starkey, *Yates*...L. G. Townsend
BINGHAMTON, 7, *Broome*........Benjamin T. Cooke
Birdsall, 20, *Alleghany*.......William C. Mathews
Black Brook, 1, *Clinton*.........John Rogers
Black Creek, New Hudson, *Alleghany*..E. F. Bard
Black River, Rutland, *Jefferson*.Geo. W. Hazelton
Black Rock, 16. *Erie*.........Morgan O. Lewis
Blauveltville, Orangetown, *Rockland*.I. M. Dederer
Bleecker, 8, *Fulton*........Theron A. Hamlen
Blenheim, 3. *Schoharie*........Philetus Reed
Blockville, Harmony, *Chautauque*.Alonzo Farrand
Blodgett Mills, *Cortland*........John H. Tanner
Bloomingburgh, Mam'k'g. *Sull*...J. W. Hasbrook
Blooming Grove, 4, *Orange*......Henry F. Breed
Bloomville, Kortright, *Delaware*.....John Peters

Bluff Point, Jerusalem, *Yates*......Robert Chissom
Bolivar, 2, *Alleghany*.................Nelson Hoyt
Bolton, 9, *Warren*...............Truman Lyman
Bombay, 10, *Franklin*..........Alonzo Robinson
Boonville, 27, *Oneida*...........John M. Lewis
Borodino,Spafford, *Onondaga*....Eleazer G. Fulton
Boston, 8, *Erie*.................John Churchill
Bouckville, Madison, *Madison*....Moses Maynard
Bovina, 6, *Delaware*...........Thomas M'Farland
Bovina Centre, Bovina, *Delaware*..Edw. M'Kenzie
Boylston, 21, *Oswego*...............
Bradford, 19, *Steuben*.... ....Edgar Munson
Brainard's Bridge, Nassau, *Renss*..Seth Hastings
Braman's Corner, Duanesburgh, *Schen*..J. Braman
Branchport, Jerusalem, *Yates*..Myron H. Weaver
Brandon 7, *Franklin*................
Brandt, 1, *Erie*................Simeon Brown
Brantingham, Greig, *Lewis*....David H. Higby
Brasher, 27, *St. Lawrence*................
Brasher Falls, Brasher, *St. Law*..Calvin T. Hubbard
Brasher Iron Works, Brasher, *St. Law*.I.W. Skinner
Breakabeen, Fulton, *Schoharie*..... ...Jonas Krum
Brewerton, Cicero, *Onondaga*......Asa W. Emmons
Bridgehampton, Southampton, *Suff*..L. L. Newton
Bridgeport, Sullivan, *Madison*..Spencer Marsh, jr.
Bridgeville, Thompson, *Sullivan*..Hen. W. Howell
Bridgewater, 2, *Oneida*.........David Mannering
Brighton, 12, *Monroe*.........Benj. B. Blossom
Bristol, 5, *Ontario*.............Stephen Francis
Bristol Centre, Bristol, *Ontario*....George Gooding
Broadalbin, 5, *Fulton*...........Laban Capron
Brockett's Bridge, Oppenheim, *Fult*..Z. Brockett
Brockport, Sweden, *Monroe*....Joshua Harrison
Brookfield, 5, *Madison*.......John T. G. Bailey
Brookhaven, 4, *Suffolk*...............
BROOKLYN, 1, *Kings*...........Gold S. Silliman
Brook's Grove, Mt. Morris. *Livings*..M. W. Brooks
Brookville, Alexander, *Genesee*..Lucius Farnham
Broome, 4, *Schoharie*................
Broome Centre, Broome, *Schoharie*..Henry Tibbitts
Brownville, 14, *Jefferson*.......Oliver Lawton
Brunswick, 9, *Rensselaer*............
Brush's Mills, *Tompkins*.........Henry A. Brush
Brutus, 16, *Cayuga*..................
Bruynswick, Shawangunk, *Ulster*..Dan. A. Taylor
Buck's Bridge, *St. Lawrence*.....Wm. H. Wilcox
Buckram, *Queens*................Lot Cornelius
Buck Tooth, Little Valley, *Cattar*.John Boardman
Buel, Canajoharie, *Montgomery*..Sam. C. Hamilton
BUFFALO, 17, *Erie*.........Isaac R. Harrington
Buffalo Plains, Black Rock, *Erie*...Joseph B. Scott
Bullville, Crawford, *Orange*.....W. W. Wallace
Burdett, Hector, *Tompkins*.......Joseph Carson
Burke, 14, *Franklin*.........Stephen M. Morse
Burlingham, Mamakating, *Sullivan*..Ammi Abbott
Burlington, 17, *Otsego*..............Henry Sill
Burlington Flatts, Burlington, *Ots*.G.W. Lawrence
Burns, 21, *Alleghany*.............P. S. Jones
Burnt Hills, Ballston, *Saratoga*.Samuel B. Edwards
Burr's Mills, Watertown, *Jefferson*..Foster Lewis
Burton, 5, *Cattaraugus*.........James G. Johnson
Burtonsville, Charleston, *Montgom*.David M. Scott
Bushnell's Basin, Perrinton, *Monroe*.Isaac Hastings
Bushnellsville, Lexington, *Greene*..Alvin Bushnell
Bushwick, 8, *Kings*..................
Buskirk's Bridge, Cambridge,*Wash*.G. Menchester
Busti, 4, *Chautauque*...........Lyman C. Fargo
Butler, 7, *Wayne*...............Lester Watson
Butterfly, New Haven, *Oswego*......John Parsons
Buttermilk Falls, Cornwall, *Orange*..Cor. Nelson
Butternuts, 4, *Otsego*........Harley Sergeant
Byersville, West Sparta, *Living*...Sam'l G. Stoner
Byron, 12, *Genesee*.............Charles B. Hall
Cabin Hill, Andes, *Delaware*...Andrew Marshall
Cadyville, Plattsburgh, *Clinton*....Hen K. Averill
Cairo, 5, *Greene*............Jonathan B. Webster
CALDWELL, 3, *Warren*............Hiram Wood
Caledonia, 14, *Livingston*.........Ged Blakeslee
Callikoon, Cochecton, *Sullivan*..Alpheus B. Royce
Callikoon Depot, Cochecton, *Sull*..Wm. L. Storke
Cambria, 12, *Niagara*......Charles Molyneaux
Cambridge, 2, *Washington*.......Clark M'Clellan
Camden, 16, *Oneida*............Wm. R. Paddock
Cameron, 11, *Steuben*............Hiram Averill
Camillus, 14, *Onondaga*.....Gaylord N. Sherwood
Campbell, 10, *Steuben*..............
Campbelltown, Campbell, *Steuben*..Aden J. Pratt
Campbellville, Pawling, *Duchess*..J.Wesley Stark
Campville, Owego, *Tioga*.......Joshua Mersereau
Canaan, 17, *Columbia*..........Samuel Frisbee
Canaan Centre, Canaan, *Col*..Norman W. Williams
Canaan Four Corners, Canaan, *Col*..A. D. Cornwell

Candice, 3, *Ontario*............Joseph S. Secor
Canajoharie, 1, *Montgomery*..Joseph W. Caldwell
Canal, Van Buren, *Onondaga*......Abel H. Toll
CANANDAIGUA, 6, *Ontario*....George L. Wheeler
Canastota, Lenox, *Madison*......Aaron B. Brush
Candor, 7, *Tioga*..............R. D. Willard
Caneadea, *Alleghany*.......Alanson B. Whitney
Canfield's Corners, Nichols, *Tioga*....Clark Hyatt
Canisteo, 14, *Steuben*......Nathaniel C. Taylor
Cannonsville, Tompkins, *Dela*..Ebenezer Adams
Canoga, Fayette, *Seneca*........Henry Hoskins
CANTON, 13, *St. Lawrence*......Ephraim C. Goff
Cape Vincent, 22, *Jefferson*..George A. Ainsworth
Cardiff, Lafayette, *Onondaga*........Isaac Garfield
Carlisle, 12, *Schoharie*..........George Rich
Carlton, 9, *Orleans*........Elmer H. Garbutt
CARMEL, 2, *Putnam*..........Augustus Hazen
Caroga, 9, *Fulton*..................
Caroline, 3, *Tompkins*........Hiram N. Roanceville
Caroline Centre, Caroline, *Tompkins*.Reub. Higgins
Carroll, 5, *Chautauque*......Benjamin T. Morgan
Carrollton, 4, *Cattaraugus*.... ..Abner O. Hurst
Carthage, Wilna, *Jefferson*...Harvey Ferrington
Cassadaga, Pomfret, *Chautauque*....James Beebe
Cassville, Paris, *Oneida*........Calvin A. Budlong
Castile, 5, *Wyoming*...........Andrew Cole
Castle Creek, *Broome*.........Moses Puffer
Castleton, Schodack, *Renss*.Jeremiah Van Hoesen
Castleton, 1, *Richmond*..............
Catharine, 10, *Chemung*......Jerome Thompson
Catlin, 8, *Chemung*.................
Cato, 17, *Cayuga*............Charles F. Allen
Cato Four Corners, Cato, *Cayuga*.....Abel West
Caton, 5, *Steuben*..........Naboth C. Babcock
CATSKILL, 3, *Greene*.............David Ely
Cayuga, Aurelius, *Cayuga*........Samuel Fitch
Cayuta, 6, *Chemung*.........Jacob Swartwood
Cayutaville, Hector, *Tompkins*.......John Beebe
Cazenovia, 10, *Madison*..........R. Jackson
Cedar Hill, Bethlehem, *Alb*...H. Y. Schoonmaker
Cedar Swamp, Oyster Bay, *Queens*.Jas. Luyster, jr.
Cedarville, Litchfield, *Herkimer*..Lorenzo Hesford
Central Bridge, Schoharie. *Schoharie*..Levi Totten
Central Square, Hastings, *Oswego*.Henry B. Conde
Centre Almond, Almond, *Alle*.Lazarus S. Rathbun
Centre Berlin, Berlin, *Renss*...Jeffroy W. Thomas
Centre Cambridge, Cambridge, *Wash*.A. Ingraham
Centerfield, Canandaigua, *Ontario*..Joseph White
Centre Independence, Independ'e *Alle*.Jabez Card
Centre Lisle, Lisle, *Broome*...Benj. B. Woodworth
Centreport, Huntington, *Suffolk*....S. M. Nichols
Centre Sherman, Sherman, *Chau*.Wm. L. Freeman
Centreville, 26, *Alleghany*......Lewis C. Veazey
Centre White Creek, Wh. Creek, *Was*.W. S. Pratt
Champion, 10, *Jefferson*.....Gustavus M. Spencer
Champion S. Roads, Champion, *Jeff*. C. J. Johnson
Champlain, 12, *Clinton*........Freeman B. Smith
Chapelsburgh, Humphrey, *Catt*....Russell Chapel
Chapinville, Hopewell, *Ont*..Rensselaer Gardner
Charleston, 3, *Montgomery*.....Elisha H. Bromley
Charleston 4 Cor., Charleston, *Montg*..Is. S. Frost
Charlotte, 16, *Chautauque*..............
Charlotte, Greece, *Monroe*......Ambrose Jones
Charlotte Centre, Charlotte, *Chaut*.Freeman Lake
Charlotteville, Summit, *Schoharie*..Jacob Hoffman
Charlton, 7, *Saratoga*.........Hiram Sabing
Chateaugay, 15, *Franklin*......Leander Douglass
Chautauque, 13, *Chautauque*............
Chetham, 16, *Columbia* . . ..Seth Daly
Chatham Centre, Chatham, *Col*..Chauncy A. King
Chatham 4 Corners, Chatham, *Col*. F. H. Rathbone
Chaumont, Lyme, *Jefferson*......Philip P. Gaige
Chazy, 8, *Clinton*.............Harry Graves
Cheektowaga, 15, *Erie*....Nathaniel Illingsworth
Chemeng, 2, *Chemung*........Jefferson B. Clark
Chenango, 2, *Broome*................
Chenango, *Cortland*...........Abijah T. Pierce
Chenango Forks, Chenango, *Broome*..J. B. Rogers
Cherry Creek, 17, *Chautauque*.......James Carr
Cherry Valley, 23, *Otsego*......Benjamin Davis
Cheshire, Canandaigua, *Ontario*..Robert Renwick
Chesterfield, 14, *Essex*.............
Chestnut, Ridge, *Duchess*........Edgar Vincent
Chester 5, *Orange*..........Daniel B. Foster
Chester 7, *Warren*.................
Chestertown, Chester, *Warren*....Wm. Hotchkiss
Chief Warrior, *Erie*.........Joseph R. Walton
Chill, 7, *Monroe* ....Pierpont Chapman
China, 1, *Wyoming*...........Lorenzo D. Davis
Chittenango, Sullivan, *Madison*.Benjamin Jenkins
Churchtown, Claverack, *Colum*..W. W. Van Ness
Churchville, Riga, *Monroe*.........Orson Tuller

Cicero, 28, *Onondaga*...........Isaac Garfield
Cincinnatus. 4, *Cortland*......Chaplin V. Perkins
City, Amenia. *Duchess*.......Wm. H. Boetwick
Clarence, 20, *Erie*...........Josiah B. Baily
Clarence Centre, Clarence, *Erie*..David Von Tine
Clarendon, 3, *Orleans*.....Thaddeus R. Sherwood
Clark's Factory, Middletown, *Delaw*..E. A. Clark
Clarkson, 19, *Monroe*...........Silas Walbridge
Clarkson Centre, Clarkson, *Monroe*.Henry Kimball
CLARKSTOWN, 2, *Rockland*.......Wm. H. Melick
Clarksville, 7, *Alleghany*
Clarksville, New Scotland, *Albany*...P. L. Houck
Claverack, 9, *Columbia*........Andrew Michael
Clay, 19, *Onondaga*..............Philander Childs
Clayton, 16, *Jefferson*...........Stephen Hale
Clayville, Paris. *Oneida*.........Eason Allen
Clear Creek, Ellington, *Chautauque*..T. G. Bailey
Clermont. 1, *Columbia*............Levi Leroy
Cleaveland, Constantia, *Oswego*...Abner H. Allen
Clifton Park, 1, *Saratoga*........Wm. B. Noxon
Clifton Springs, Manchester, *Ontario* Moses Parker
Clinton, 19, *Clinton*
Clinton, 14. *Duchess*
Clinton. Kirkland, *Oneida*...Samuel Brownell, jr.
Clintondale, *Ulster*.............Edwin S. Pierce
Clinton Hollow, Clinton, *Duchess*..Semca Crouse
Clintonville, Ausable, *Clinton*.Timothy Carpenter
Clockville, Lenox, *Madison*......Francis L. Bligh
Clove. Unionvale, *Duchess*......Daniel Lossing
Clovesville, Middletown, *Delaware*.Matth. Griffin
Clyde. Galen, *Wayne*.....a Jacob T. Van Buskirk
Clymer, 2, *Chautauque*.............Silas Terry
Cobleskill, 9, *Schoharie*..........Thos. Smith
Cochecton, 6, *Sullivan*.........Ellery T. Calkins
Coeymans, 3, *Albany*..........Noble T. Johnson
Coeymans Hollow, *Albany*........Platt A. Smith
Cohocton. 29, *Steuben*.........Walter M. Eldred
Cohoes, Watervliet, *Albany*.......Hezekiah Howe
Colchester. 2. *Delaware*.......Hezekiah Elwood
Cold Brook, Russia, *Herkimer*.....Cameron Moon
Colden. 7, *Erie*..................Chas. H. Baker
Coldenham, Newburgh, *Orange*....B. K. Johnson
Cold Spring, 2. *Cattaraugus*.
Cold Spring. Phillipstown, *Putnam*..Levi J. Mabl
Cold Spring Harbor, Oyst. Bay, *Suffolk*.S. A. Jones
Colesville, 6, *Broome*...........Jas. H. Cole
College Point, Flushing, *Queens*..John H. Storm
Collikoon, 7, *Sullivan*
Colliersville, Milford, *Otsego*....Jared Goodyear
Collins, 3, *Erie*..............Samuel C. Neyes
Collins Centre, Collins, *Erie*....Geo. H. Hodges
Collinsville, West Turin, *Lewis*....Homer Collins
Colosse, Mexico, *Oswego*......Alvin Richardson
Colton, 6, *St. Lawrence*
Columbia, 3, *Herkimer*..........Alonze Elwood
Columbus, 16, *Chenango*........Hiram E. Storrs
Commack. Smithtown. *Suffolk*....Chas. B. Velsor
Comstock's Landing, F't Ann, *Washington*.N. Long
Concord, 4, *Erie*
Conesus, 6, *Livingston*..........Justus Allen
Conesville, 2, *Schoharie*......Dewitt C. Stryker
Conewango, 12, *Cattaraugus*..Geo. A. S. Crooker
Conklin, 3, *Broome*...........Henry C. Bayless
Conquest, 16, *Cayuga*..........L. B. Phinney
Constable, 13, *Franklin*
Constableville, West Turin, *Lewis*....Seth Miller
Constantia. 6, *Oswego*..........Julian Carter
Cooper's Plains, *Steuben*........Alvin Corbyn
Cooperstown, Otsego, *Otsego*......Wm. Nichols
Coopersville. *Clinton*..........Horace Hayford
Copake. 4, *Columbia*.......Wm. Van Benschoten
Copenhagen, Denmark. *Lewis*..Horace Davenport
Coram. Brookhaven, *Suffolk*...Lewis R. Overton
Corbettsville, Conklin. *Broome*...Jos. Bowers, jr.
Corfu. Pembroke, *Genesee*...........Aaron Long
Coriath, 17, *Saratoga*........John R. Houghton
Corning, Painted Post, *Steuben*...Wm. B. Whiting
Cornwall, 3, *Orange*.......Henry F. Chedeayne
Cornwallsville, Durham, *Greene*....Elias P. Austin
Cortland, 22, *Westchester*
CORTLAND VILLAGE, 7, *Cortland*.Jebiel W. Taylor
County Line, *Niagara*...........Samuel Pease
Coventry, 2, *Chenango* ...Nicholas A. Eggleston
Coventryville, Coventry, *Chenango*...L. K. Foote
Covert, 2, *Seneca*............Erastus C. Gregg
Coveville, Northumberland, *Saratog*.G. W. Brazier
Covington, 13, *Wyoming*.......Lyman Broughton
Cowlesville, Bennington, *Wyoming*.H. W. Sargent
Coxsackie, 11, *Greene*.........Geo. N. Keith
Craigsville. Blooming Grove, *Orange*..H. Seeley
Crain's Corners, Warren, *Herkimer*..Job Bronson
Cranberry Creek, N'thampton, *Full*.F.C. Ingraham

Cranesville, Amsterdam, *Montgomery*.....J. Grost
Crawford, 15, *Orange*.........Cornelius Slott
Croghan, 19, *Lewis*.............Jos. Virkler
Cross River, Lewisborough, *Westchester*.W. Hunt
Croton, Franklin, *Delaware*......Sylvester Rich
Croton Falls, North Salem, *Westchester*..T. R. Lee
Croton Landing, *Westchester*.......Jas. M'Cord
Crown Point, 4, *Essex*.........Chauncey Fenton
Cram Elbow, Hyde Park, *Duchess*.Israel Marshall
Cuba, 8, *Alleghany*..............J. A. Story
Cuddebackville, Deerpark, *Orange*..P. Cuddeback
Cutchogue, Southold, *Suffolk*....Thos. J. Conklin
Cuyler, Truxton, *Cortland*..Wm. Blanchard, 2d
Cuylerville. Leicester, *Livingston*..N. L. Bowman
Dale, Middlebury, *Wyoming*...Sidney S. Monroe
Danby, 2, *Tompkins*..............Uri Clark
Dansville, 27, *Livingston*.......Chs. E. Lamport
Danube, 6, *Herkimer*...........Wm. Kritsinger
Darien, 1, *Genesee*..........Alfred C. Peters
Darien Centre, Darien, *Genesee*....Ashbel Stone
Davenport, 15, *Delaware*........John Sherman
Davenport Centre, Davenport, *Delaware*...J. Shue
Day, 20, *Saratoga*.........Joseph Rockwell
Dayton, 28, *Cattaraugus*........Ralph Johnson
Dean's Corners, Saratoga, *Saratoga*..G. Wright. jr.
Deansville, Marshall, *Oneida*.......John Dean
Decatur, 9, *Otsego*.........Jas. E. Lansing
Doepikill, *Rensselaer*.......George W. Grant
Deerfield, 23, *Oneida*.
Deer River, *Lewis*.........Edward E. Hulbert
Deer Park. 8, *Orange*.
De Friestville, Greenbush, *Renss*...R. A. Downs
DeKalb, 15, *St. Lawrence*.......John Rounds
Delavan, Yorkshire, *Cattaraugus*..P. B. Whitney
DELHI, 7, *Delaware*..........Norwood Bowne
Delphi, Pompey, *Onondaga*......Wm. A. Bates
Delta, Lee. *Oneida*...........Manair G. Phillips
Denmark, 11. *Lewis*.......Salmatius T. Bordwell
Denning, 8, *Ulster*
Dennison's Corners, *Herkimer*...Chas. Wightman
Depauville, Clayton, *Jeff*.....Sidney P. Johnson
De Peyster, 21, *St. Lawrence*........Levi Fay
Deposit, Tompkins, *Delaware*..Addison J. Wheeler
De Ruyter, 1, *Madison*.............B. Birdsall
Devereaux, *Herkimer*..........Henry Devereaux
De Witt, 11, *Onondaga*........Henry C. Goodell
De Wittville,Chautauque, *Chautau*..Hiram Russell
Dexter, Brownville, *Jeff*.........Nathan Bassett
Diana, 14, *Lewis*.............James Palmer
Dickinson, 8, *Franklin*....Simeon C. Harwood
Dix Hills, Huntington, *Suffolk*....Gilbert Carll
Dix, 9, *Chemung*.
Doansburgh, Southeast, *Putnam*....Benj. Doane
Dobbs' Ferry, *Westchester*.Edingham W.Walgrove
Dormansville. *Albany*......Detus E. Battershall
Doty's Corner, Dansville, *Steuben*..Geo.G.Babcock
Dover, 4, *Duchess*............James Ketcham
Dresden. 17. *Washington*.
Dryden, 4, *Tompkins*........Abraham Tanner
Duane, 3 *Franklin*..........Ezekiel Ladd
Duanesburgh, 1, *Schenectady*......Truman Case
Dundee. Starkey, *Yates*.......Samuel S. Benham
Dunkirk, Pomfret, *Chautauque*.....L. B.Brown
Dunnsville, Guilderland, *Albany*....Peter Foland
Durham, 9, *Greene*.............Urell Bradley
Durhamville, Verona, *Oneida*.....Warren Norton
Eagle, 2, *Wyoming*.............Cyril Rawson
Eagle Harbor. Gaines, *Orleans*..A.M.Starkweather
Eagle Mills, *Renss*...........J. H. Mambert
Eagle Village, Eagle, *Wyoming*...C. H. Denman
Earlville, Nelson, *Madison*........Daniel Wells
East Avon. Avon, *Livingston*..Gilbert T. Palmer
East Bergen. Bergen, *Genesee*..Gilbert Churchill
East Berne. Berne. *Albany*......And.ew Warner
East Bethany, Bethany, *Genesee*..Daniel R. Prindle
East Bloomfield, 17, *Ontario*..Edwin W. Fairchild
East Branch, Hancock, *Delaware*...H. B. Clauson
East Cameron, Cameron, *Steuben*..Alex. Campbell
East Canisteo, Canisteo, *Steuben*..Jeremiah Baker
East Carlton, Carlton, *Orleans*....Samuel Jacobs
East Chatham, Chatham. *Columbia*....O. Palmer
East Chester, 3, *Westchester*..Fisher W.Valentine
East China, China, *Wyoming*....Herman Wilson
East Cobleskill, Cobleskill, *Schoharis*..R. R. Earls
East Constable, Constable. *Franklin*..G.W.Darling
East Cutchogue, Suffolk. *Suffolk*..T. A. Tuthill
East Durham. Durham. *Greene*..Amos Cleaveland
East Evans, Evans, *Erie*..........Levi Aldrich
East Florence. Florence, *Oneida*..A. H. Thompson
East Gaines, Gaines, *Orleans*......S. C. Perry
East Genoa, Genoa. *Cayuga*.......Samuel Close
East Glenville, Glenville, *Schenec*...P. H. Dedrick

East Greenbush, Greenbush, Renss....S. Kimball
East Greene, Greene, Chenango......D. F. Smith
East Greenwich, Greenwich, Wash. ...Wm. Hall
East Groveland, Groveland, Livingston. .. E. Hunt
East Guilford, Guilford, Chenango... Sam'l Elwell
East Hamburgh, Hamburgh, Erie....M. Stillwell
East Hamilton, Hamilton, Madison W.T.Maunchester
East Hampton, 7, Suffolk......Thomas T. Parsons
East Hill, Nunda, Alleghany....Wm. Robinson
East Homer, Homer, Cortland....Luther R. Rose
East Java, Java, Wyoming......Nathan P. Currier
East Kill, Hunter, Greene........John P. Bench
East Koy, Pike, Alleghany.....Isaac Quackenbush
East Lansing, Lansing, Tompkins.....John Ludlow
East Leon, Leon, Cattaraugus......O. D. Waldron
East Lexington. Lexington, Greene.. West Chase
East Line, Ballston, Saratoga........R. A. Ogden
East Maine, Maine, Broome.... Moses W. Bennet
East M'Donough. M'Donough, Che..Horace Corbin
East Moriches, Brookhaven, Suff..Jacob H. Miller
East Nassau, Nassau, Rensselaer....Jas. Turner
East New York. Flatbush, Kings.Edwin M. Strong
East Norwich, Oys. Bay, Q'ns.P. A. Stoutenburgh
Easton, 1, Washington.........Aaron Barker
East Orangeville, Orangeville, Wyo..F. Fullington
East Otto. Otto, Cattaraugus.... Philander Griffith
East Painted Post, Painted Post, Steuben.A. Rowley
East Palmyra, Palmyra, Wayne....Jacob Sherman
East Pembroke. Pembroke, Genesee..G. W. Wright
East Peru, Peru, Clinton.........Silas Hinkley
East Pharsalia, Pharsalia. Chenango...Henry Baker
East Pierpont, Pierpont, St. Lawrence..Jos. Dinick
East Pike, Pike, Wyoming....Washington Wheeler
East Place, Clinton...........Silas Hinkley
East Rodman, Rodman. Jefferson....Thomas Wait
East Salem, Salem. Washington....Isaac Bininger
East Sandlake, Sandlake, Rens....E. S. Himes
East Schuyler, Schuyler, Herkimer.... P. M. Smith
East Solon, Solon, Cortland........Orrin Leonard
East Springfield, Springfield, Otsego.Davis Dutcher
East Springwater, Livingston....Wm. B. Peabody
East Virgil, Virgil, Cortland....H. J. Messenger
East Worcester, Worcester, Otsego..D. W. Thurber
Eaton, 7, Madison...............Alpheus Morse
Eatonville, Herkimer, Herkimer..B. Weatherwax
Eddyville. Mansfield, Cattaraugus...Wm. H. Eddy
Eden, 9, Erie.................Lyman Pratt
Edenville, Warwick, Orange.......Legrand Mead
Edgecomb's Corners. Galway, Sara..M. C. Bowers
Edinburgh, 16, Saratoga..........John Barker
Edinburgh Centre, Edinburgh, Sara...J. L. Snow
Edmeston, 15, Otsego........Harvey H. Waldo
Edwards, 8. St. Lawrence.........J. B. Pickit
Edwardsville, Edwards, St. Law...H. J. Pohlman
Egypt, Perrinton, Monroe......Josiah Q. Aldrich
Elba, 11, Genesee.........Wm. C. Raymond
Elbridge, 16, Onondaga..........John D. Rhodes
Elgin, Lyndon, Cattaraugus.........Wm. Little
ELIZABETHTOWN, 10, Essex.....Wm. W. Root
Elizaville, Columbia........Jacob Elkenburgh
Ellenburgh, 9, Clinton......Alvah S. Marshall
Ellenville, Wawarsing, Ulster..Rich. H. Brodhead
Ellery, 8. Chautauque...........Odin Benedict
Ellicott, 7, Chautauque.............
Ellicott Creek, Erie..........James M. Greeno
ELLICOTTVILLE, 17, Cattaraugus..J. King Skinner
Ellington, 22, Chautauque......J. F. Farman
Ellisburgh, 1, Jefferson..........Austin T. Fisk
Elliston, Onondaga.........Furman B. North
Elmira, 3, Chemung.......Henry H. Matthews
Elton, Freedom, Cattaraugus......Alonzo Pixley
Eminence, Schoharie..........Minard Garner
Enfield, 6, Tompkins......Carlos C. Applegate
Enfield Centre, Enfield, Tompkins...Elihu Dennis
Ephratah, 2, Fulton.......Peter G. Getman
Erieville, Nelson, Madison..Samuel J. Anderson
Erin, 5, Chemung............Joshua Baker
Erwin, 8, Steuben...............
Erwin Centre, Erwin, Steuben.....Ansel C. Smith
Esopus, 10, Ulster............Samuel Elmore
Esperance, 14, Schoharie.......John S. Frost
Essex, 12, Essex.........Charles G. Fancher
Etna, Dryden, Tompkins.......Walker Marsh
Euclid. Clay, Onondaga.........Wm. Coon
Evans, 2, Erie..................Orin Clark
Evansville, Le Ray, Jefferson..James H. Bowen
Exeter 22, Otsego............Wm. P. Jones
Fabius. 5, Onondaga......Elisha H. Sprague
Factoryville, Tioga........Benjamin H. Davis
Fairfield, 13.Herkimer.........Alden S. Gage
Fair Mount, Onondaga. ....Wheeler Truesdell
Fairport, Elmira, Chemung....George W. Seeley

Fair View, Farmersville, Cattar's.....Amos Pettit
Fairville. Arcadia, Wayne........Edwin Pultz
Falisburgh, 10. Sullivan...........Edward Palen
Farmer, Ovid, Seneca........Morgan Harris
Farmer's Mills, Kent, Putnam......H. Townsend
Farmersville, 21, Cattar........Luther Cross
Farmingdale, Queens........John Monfort
Farmington, Barre, Orleans........Charles Lee
Farmington, 12, Ontario....Daniel A. Robinson
Farrell Place, Clinton........Andrew Farrell
Fayette, 5, Seneca.........Lewis Goodyear
Fayetteville, Manlius, Onondaga...James Read
Federal Store, Duchess........James Hammond
Felt's Mills, Rutland, Jefferson....Orien Wheelock
Fenner. 11, Madison......William P. Barritt. 2d
Ferguson's Corners, Yates....William S. Ferguson
Finchville, New Hope, Orange....John K. Austin
Fine, 14, St. Lawrence..........
Fireplace, Brookhaven, Suffolk..Nathaniel Miller
Fishkill. 1, Duchess........William Pelham
Fishkill Landing. Fishkill. Duchess..James Mackin
Fishkill Plains. Fishkill, Duchess. .D. Van Bramer
Five Corners, Geneva, Cayuga....Samuel S. Lyon
Flackville, St. Lawrence........William H. Guest
Flanders, Southampton, Suffolk....Jesse Hallock
Flat Brook, Canaan, Columbia...W. S. Woodworth
Flatbush, 5, Kings........R. L. Schoonmaker
Flat Creek, Root, Montgomery....Isaac Folinsbee
Flatlands. 4, Kings.....John B. Hendrickson
Fleming, 11, Cayuga........Elias Thorne
Flemingsville, Owego, Tioga....David Fleming
Flint Creek, Seneca, Ontario... E. B. Woodworth
Florence, 17, Oneida........Junius A. Cowles
Florida, 5, Montgomery.........
Florida, Warwick, Orange... W. V. N. Armstrong
Floyd, 21, Oneida...........Linus L. Moulton
Flushing, 3, Queens.........Francis Bloodgood
Fluvanna,Ellicott, Chautauque.Samuel Whittemore
Fonda, Mohawk. Montgomery......Peter Fritcher
Forestburgh, 2, Sullivan....Daniel M. Broadhead
Fort Ann, 14, Washington......Isaac Clements
Fort Covington, 11, Franklin....Joseph Spencer
Fort Edward. 7, Washington.....Timo. Stoughton
Ft. Edward Centre, Ft. Edward, Wash..D. Roberts
Fort Hamilton. New Utrecht, Kings...Jos. Crocker
Fort Hunter, Florida. Montgomery....Peter Enders
Fort Miller, Ft. Edward, Wash....Isaac M. Grey
Fort Plain, Minden, Montgomery...Gilbert Warner
Fortsville, Moreau, Saratoga....Truman Wilcox
Fosterdale, Cochecton, Sullivan....Wm. Embley
Fosterville, Aurelius, Cayuga.Jonathan Foster, jr.
Fowler, 2. St. Lawrence. ....Jabez Glazier
Fowlersville, York, Livingston.....John P. Casey
Frankfort, 10, Herkimer........Chauncey Elwood
Frankfort Hill, Frankfort, Herk...E. Wetmore, jr.
Franklin, 13. Delaware........Willis C. Ripley
Franklin, 2, Franklin...........
Franklinton, Middleburgh, Schoharie...M. Mattice
Franklinville, 18, Cattaraugus........Silas Adams
Fredonia, Pomfret, Chautauque......Levi L. Pratt
Freedom, 23, Cattaraugus........Enoch Hurlitt
Freedom Plains, La Grange, Duchess...J. G. Smith
Freetown, 5, Cortland.........Mordecai Leach
Freetown Corners. Freetown,Cortland. S B. Pierce
French Creek, 1, Chautauque......Jesse Nason
Frowsburgh, Carroll, Chautauque......John Frew
Froysbush,Canajoharie. Montg...John I. Wendell
Friendship. 9, Alleghany........Alba Wellman
Frontier, Clinton.............John M'Coy
Fullerville Iron Works, St Law...C. G. Edgerton
Fulton, Volney. Owego.........George Mitchell
Fulton, 6, Schoharie...........
Fultonham, Fulton, Schoharie.....Levi Totten, jr.
Fultonville. Glen, Montgomery....John H. Strain
Gaines, 6, Orleans............John Hutchinson
Gainesville, 8, Wyoming........Barnabas Graves
Galen, 5. Wayne..............
Gales, Sullivan..............Alson Lord
Galesville, Greenwich, Washington.Hart Reynolds
Gallatin, 2, Columbia.........
Gallatinville, Gallatin, Columbia.....Eli Loomis
Gallupville. Wright, Schoharie.Weidman Dominick
Galway, 8, Saratoga.........Ezekiel O. Smith
Gansevoort, Northumberland, Sara..H. Lawrence
Gardnerville, Seward, Schoharie... D. B. Gardner
Garoga, Ephratah. Fulton........C. Hutchinson
Garrattsville, New Lisbon, Otsego..D. Herrington
Gates, 11, Monroe............Moses Gage
Gay Head, Greene...........Orson Howard
Geddes, 15, Onondaga........Simeon Spaulding
Genegantslet, Greene, Chenango......Alvin Gray
Genesee, 1, Alleghany..........

Genesee, 9, *Livingston*........Wallace R. Walker
Genesee Falls, 4, *Wyoming*........................
Geneva, Seneca, *Ontario*.......Barzillai Slosson
Genoa, 1, *Cay ga*........William J. Close
Georgetown, 2, *Madison*.....Epaphro Wetmore
German, 10, *Chenango*.......Franklin S. Barnes
German Flats, 5, *Herkimer*........................
Germantown, 7, *Columbia*....William Overbaugh
Gerry, 23, *Chautauque*........Emory F. Warren
Ghent, 12, *Columbia* ....Jacob D. Waltermire
Gibson. *Steuben*............Butler S. Wolcott
Gibson's Corners, *Tioga*....Amaziah Benjamin
Gibsonville, Leicester, *Livingston*...Amb. Halstead
Gilbert's Mills, Schroeppel, *Oswego*.....E. S. Cook
Gilbertsville, Butternuts, *Otsego*.Hervey Gatchell
Gilboa, 1. *Schoharie*.............John Reed
Gilman, 4, *Hamilton*..............E. P. Gilman
Glasco. Saugerties, *Ulster*.....Henry D. Martin
Glen, 4, *Montgomery*.............John Hanchet
Glen Cove, Oyster Bay, *Queens*...Sam'l M. Titus
Glenham. Fishkill, *Duchess*....James A. Townsend
Glenn's Falls. Queensbury, *Warren*..S. J. Williams
Glenville, 6, *Schenectady*.......Willis L. Calkins
Glen Wild, Thompson, *Sullivan*...Wm. M. Bowers
Gloversville. Johnstown, *Fulton*..Elisha L. Burton
Goff's Mills. Howard. *Steuben*..........Wm. Goff
Good Ground. Southampton, *Suffolk*..Alvin Squires
Gorham. 7, *Ontario*...........Josiah L. Yeckley
Goshen, 6, *Orange*............Virgil S. Seward
Gouverneur, 16, *St. Lawrence* ...Chauncey Dodge
Gowanda, Persia, *Cattaraugus*..Wm. Woodbury
Grafton, 10. *Rensselaer*......Paul Albertson
Grahamsville, Neversink, *Sull.*Stoddard Hammond
Granby, 2 *Oswego*................................
Granger, 23, *Alleghany*........Henry White
Grangerville, Saratoga, *Saratoga*..Calvin J. Reed
Granville. 13, *Washington*....James C. Hopkins
Gravesend. 7, *Kings*........M. Schoonmaker
Gravesville, *Herkimer*.......Wm. G. Graves
Great Bend, Le Ray, *Jefferson*.....Daniel Potter
Great Valley, 10, *Cattaraugus*..Daniel Farrington
Greece, 17, *Monroe*..........Erastus Walker
Greenboro. *Oswego*...........John H. Corey
Greenburgh. 11. *Westchester*....................
Greenbush, 7, *Rensselaer*....Joseph H. Mather
Greene, 3, *Chenango*..........Chester Bingham
Greenfield, 14, *Saratoga*........................
Greenfield Centre, Greenfield, *Sar.*.R. C. Weeden
Green Point, Bushwick, *Kings*....James H. Harris
Greenport, Southold, *Suffolk* ....John Lewis
Greenport. 8, *Columbia*..........................
Green River, Hillsdale, *Columbia*.Jerome Eastland
Green's Corners, *Oneida*........Philander Swan
Greenville, 10, *Greene*....Alexander N. Bentley
Greenwich, 6, *Washington*........Asa F. Holmes
Greenwood, 31, *Steuben*............Levi Davis
Greig, 4, *Lewis*................................
Greigsville, York, *Livingston*.....Henry Lawson
Griffin's Mills, Aurora, *Erie*......Orson B. Baker
Griswold's Mills, Ft. Ann, *Wash.*.Stephen P. Potter
Groom's Corners, *Saratoga*.......John Palmer
Groton, 10, *Tompkins* ......Sylvanus De Lano
Groton City, Groton, *Tompkins*... Lyman Warfield
Grove, 22, *Alleghany*............S. C. Jones
Groveland. 7, *Livingston*........Charles Goheen
Groveland Centre. Groveland, *Liv.*...E. P. Fuller
Guilderland. 8, *Albany*...........Henry Sloan
Guilderland Centre. Guilderland, *Alb.*J. D. Ogsbury
Guilford. 6, *Chenango*...........John Clark
Guilford Centre, Guilford, *Chen.*....Thos. P. Hicks
Hadley, 19, *Saratoga*........George Kenyon
Hagaman's Mills, Amsterdam, *Mont.*Heli. Pawling
Hague, 10, *Warren*.........Nathaniel Garfield
Haight, 16, *Alleghany*..........................
Half Moon, 2, *Saratoga*........Samuel Peters
Hall's Corners, Seneca, *Ontario*..George Renwick
Hall's Mills. Rensselaerville, *Alb.*Harvey C. Smith
Hallsville, Minden, *Montgomery* ..Abraham Toller
Halsey Valley, Tioga, *Tioga*.....Israel S. Hoyt
Hamburgh, 10, *Erie*...............John S. Weld
Hamburgh on Lake, Hamburgh,*Erie*.A. N. Winship
Hamden, 8, *Delaware*...........Smith M. Titus
Hamilton, 4, *Madison*........Samuel P. Russell
Hammond, 16, *St. Lawrence*.......Abel P. Morse
Hammond's Mills, Campbell, *Steu.*-Seth Hammond
Hampton, 16, *Washington*........Josiah Williams
Hamptonburgh, 11, *Orange*........A. B. Watkins
Hancock, 1, *Delaware*.........Marvin Wheeler
Hanford's Landing, Greece, *Monroe*...Nath. Hall
Hannibal, 1, *Oswego*...............Alfred Rice
Hannibal Centre, Hannibal, *Oswego*..And. Hulett
Hanover, 24, *Chautauque*.........Benajah Tubbs

Harford, 12, *Cortland*............Riley Stevens
Harlem, New York, *New York*.....John S. Kenyon
Harlemville. Claverack,*Columbia.*Fayette M. Blunt
Harmony, 3, *Chautauque*......Samuel S. Welch
Harpersfield, 17, *Delaware*.....Richard B. Gibbs
Harpersville, Colesville, *Broome*.....Elias Patrick
Harriettstown, 1, *Franklin*........................
Harriettstown, *Essex*.............A. B. Neal
Harrisburgh. 9, *Lewis*............Wm. Bush
Harris Hill. *Erie*.............Michael Shultz
Harrison, 8, *Westchester*.......James D. Merritt
Hartford, 12, *Washington*......Samuel D. Kidder
Hartland. 5, *Niagara*.......George L. Angevine
Hart's Village, Washington,*Duchess.*l. Haight, jr.
Hartsville, 15, *Steuben*..........................
Hartsville, Manlius, *Onondaga*..Pardon Thompson
Hartwick, 13, *Otsego*..........S. Hartington
Hartwick Seminary, Hartwick, *Otsego*..E. Chaffe
Hartwood, *Sullivan*...........Nathaniel Greene
Hasbrouck, Fallsburgh, *Sullivan*....Moses Dean
Haskenville. *Steuben*...........A. S. Phillips
Hastings, 4, *Oswego*.........Peter Devendorf
Hastings upon Hudson, *Westchester*.i. Lefurge, jr.
Havana, Catharine, *Chming...*.Geo. V. Hitchcock
Haverstraw, 4, *Rockland*.........John S. Gurnee
Haviland Hollow, Patterson, *Putnam.*Isaac J. Cowl
Hawkin's Creek, *Sullivan*.....Ezekiel G. Scott
Hebron, 9, *Washington*........Charles J. White
Hector, 7, *Tompkins*........Simeon P. Bradford
Heldorburgh. Guilderland. *Albany.*Cornelius Secor
Helena, Brasher, *St. Lawrence*.....Benj. Nevin
Hemlock Lake, Livonia, *Livings.*E. H. O. Meachem
Hempstead. 4. *Queens*.........John W. Smith
Hempstead Branch, Hempstead, *Queens.*J. S. Wood
Henderson, 6, *Jefferson*......Washington Bullard
Henrietta. 6, *Monroe*...........Joel B. Jones
Herkimer, 9, *Herkimer*..........Jas. A. Suitee
Hermitage. Wethersfield, *Wyoming*..B. K. Bronson
Hermon, 4, *St. Lawrence*.....Elisha Burnham
Hess Road, *Niagara*............Asahel Staples
Heuvelton, Oswegatchie, *St. Law*...Thos. Seaman
Hickory Corners, Lockport, *Niagara.*Dan. Pomroy
Higginsville, *Oneida*.........Thomas C. Howes
High Falls, Marbletown, *Ulster*...Jacob H. Depuy
Highland Mills, Monroe, *Orange*...Morgan Blunt
High Market, West Turin, *Lewis*..S. C. Thompson
Hillsboro', *Oneida*.............John Lamble
Hillsdale, 11, *Columbia*........Isaac Foster
Hindsburgh, Murray, *Orleans*....Dwight Harwood
Hinmansville. Schroeppel, *Oswego.*Nath'l Coburn
Hinsdale, 8, *Cattaraugus*......Nelson J. Norton
Hizerville, *Oneida*..............Adam Hizer
Hoag's Corner, Nassau, *Rens.*.....Wm. B. Hoag
Hobart, Stamford, *Delaware*....Robt. S. Marshall
Hobbieville, *Alleghany*..........A. S. Spencer
Hoffman's Ferry, Glenville, *Schen.*.Jas. J. Marlett
Hoffman's Gate, Claverack, *Col.*...W. B. Shelden
Hogansburgh, Bombay, *Franklin*....Fred. J. Mills
Holland, 8, *Erie*............Philip D. Riley
Holland Patent, Trenton, *Oneida.*...John Cande
Holley, Murray, *Orleans*........Hiram Frisbie
Homer, 8, *Cortland*...........Jacob T. Stone
Honeoye, Richmond, *Ontario*...Jedediah Briggs
Honeoye Falls, Mendon, *Monroe*...Edward Downs
Hoosick, 12, *Rensselaer*.......J. F. Armstrong
Hoosick Falls, Hoosick, *Rensselaer*...Adin Thayer
Hope, 1, *Hamilton*...............James Harris
Hope Centre, Hope, *Hamilton* ......Henry Denne
Hopewell, 10, *Ontario*........Nathaniel Lewis
Hopkinton, 9, *St. Lawrence*.....Zorobster Culver
Horicon, 9, *Warren*.............Benj. T. Wells
Hornby, 9, *Steuben*............John M. Bixby
Hornellsville, 15. *Steuben*.......Martin Adsit
Hounsfield, 7, *Jefferson*.........................
Houseville, Turin, *Lewis*......S. M. Van Namee
Howard, 17, *Steuben*..........Aaron M'Connell
Howell's Depot, Wallkill, *Orange*..Geo. W. Bell
Howlet Hill, Onondaga, *Onondaga.*.Leonard Caten
Hudson. 13, *Columbia*.......Robert H. Barnard
Huguenot, Deer Park, *Orange*..J. S. Van Inwegen
Hulburton, Murray, *O. leans*......Abijah Reed
Hull's Corners, Hannibal, *Oswego*.....Burr Hull
Hull's Mills, Stanford, *Duchess*..Edward P. Barton
Hume, 23, *Alleghany*...........Isaac Minard
Hunter, 2, *Greene*.........William W. Edwards
Hunter's Land, Middleburgh, *Scho.*.G. W. Tippets
Huntington, 1, *Suffolk*.........Henry S. Smith
Hunt's Hollow, Portage, *Livingston*..Horace Hunt
Hurley, 13, *Ulster*.............Hiram Patterson
Huron, 10, *Wayne*............Edward W. Bottum
Hyde, *Warren*.................John Parker
Hyde Park, 8, *Duchess*........J. A.   utenburgh

Hyde Settlement, Barker, *Broome*..Franklin Hyde
Hyndsville, Seward, *Schoharie*....Philip T. Hilton
Ilion, German Flats, *Herkimer*.Samuel Remington
Independence, 4, *Alleghany*........J. P. Livermore
Indian River, Watson, *Lewis*............D. G. Bent
Ira, 19, *Cayuga*.....................Joseph Earl
Irondequoit, 15, *Monroe*............C. K. Hubbie
Irving, Hanover, *Chautauque*....Henry J. Newton
Islip, 2, *Suffolk*................Henry Brewster
Italy, 1, *Yates*.............................
Italy Hill, Italy, *Yates*.........Luther B. Blood
Italy Hollow, Italy, *Yates*......Lewis B. Graham
Ithaca, 5, *Tompkins*............Julius M Ackley
Jackson, 4, *Washington*........Fredrick Newton
Jacksonburgh, *Herkimer*.........Sanford Rankin
Jackson Corners. Milan. *Duchess*....Jacob J. Stall
Jacksonville, Ulysses, *Tomp*.Wm C. Woodworth
Jack's Reef, Elbridge, *Onondaga*....Harvey Hall
Jamaica, 2, *Queens*.............Richard Brush
Jamesport, *Suffolk*......... David Williamson
Jamestown, Ellicott. *Chautauque*..Smith Seymour
Jamesville, De Witt, *Onondaga*......Samuel Hill
Jasper, 13, *Steuben*............Andrew Craig
Java, 8, *Wyoming*............Joseph Currier
Java Village, Java, *Wyoming*.....Barnard C. Ring
Jay, 15, *Essex*................Wm. H. Butrick
Jeddo, *Orleans*..............Samuel L. Hoag
Jefferson, 5, *Schoharie*........Adam F. Mattice
Jericho. Oyster Bay, *Queens*........A. G. Carll
Jerusalem, 2, *Yates*...........Henry Larzelere
Jerusalem South, Hempstead, *Queens*.John B. Post
Johnsburgh. 6, *Warren*...........Ira Russell
Johnsonburgh, Orangeville, *Wyo*.Geo. A. Johnson
Johnson's Creek, *Niagara*.......Hiram G. Dean
JOHNSTOWN, 3, *Fulton*..........Daniel B. Cady
Jonesville, Clifton Park, *Sara*..Smith L. Mitchell
Jordan. Elbridge, *Onondaga*.....Justus Hough
Jordanville, Warren, *Herkimer*....Phineas F. Hyde
Joy. *Wayne*...............Adam Tinckelpaugh
Junction, Schaghticoke, *Rens*........J. T. Grant
Junius, 9, *Seneca*...........Lucas E. Moore
Kattleville, *Broome*............Solomon Orcutt
Keene, 8, *Essex*...............Stephen Patridge
Keeney's Settlement, *Cortland*......Alvin Brown
Keeseville, Au Sable, *Essex*..Carlisle D. Beaumont
Kelloggsville, Niles, *Cayuga*.......Dwight Lee
Kendall, 10, *Orleans*.........Walter R. Sanford
Kendall Mills. *Orleans*.......Cassius S. Marvin
Kennedysville, Bath, *Steuben*.....Geo. A. Farnam
Kensico, *Westchester*..........Dwight Capron
Kent, 5, *Putnam*............. Stillman Boyd
Ketcham's Corners, Stillwater, *Sar*.John R. Myers
Kill Buck, Great Valley, *Cattar*....John Greene
Kinderhook, 15, *Columbia*....Charles Whiting. jr
Kingsboro', Johnstown, *Fulton*...Jonathan Wooster
King's Bridge, New York, *N. York*.John P. Dodge
Kingsbury, 11, *Washington*....Charles B. Vaughn
King's Ferry, Genoa, *Cayuga*.....Samuel Atwater
King's Settlement, Norwich, *Che*..Elijah K. Buell
Kingston, 11, *Ulster*.........Wm. H. Romeyn
Kinney's 4 Corners, Hannibal, *Osw*.Jas. Martin. jr.
Kirkland, 7, *Oneida*...........Nathan Thompson
Kirkville, Manlius, *Onondaga*.....Obadiah Hubbs
Kiskatom, *Greene*.............Jacob S. Bloom
Knowersville, Guilderland, *Alb*..Charles Thornton
Knowlesville, Ridgeway, *Orleans*....Oliver Davis
Knox, 7, *Albany*............Henry Barckley
Kortright, 16, *Delaware*..........Ezra T. Gibbs
Kyserike, Rochester, *Ulster*.....Isaac A. Robison
Kyserville, Springwater, *Liv*...Ab'm S. Thompson
Lackawack, Wawarsing, *Ulster*...James Benedict
Lafargeville, Orleans, *Jefferson*...Edgar W. Bedell
La Fayette, 7, *Onondaga*........Chester Baker
La Grange, Covington, *Wyoming*.Chas. E. Morgan
La Grange, 6, *Duchess*..............
Lairdsville, Westmoreland, *Oneida*..Peter Magher
Lake, Greenwich, *Wash*..Abraham Matthews.jr.
LAKE PLEASANT, 2, *Hamilton*......Lyman Holmes
Lakeport, *Madison*............John Breeze
Lake Ridge, *Tompkins*............John Moe
Lakeville, Livonia, *Livingston*... Horace Doolittle
Lamson's, *Onondaga*.........John H. Lamson
Lancaster, 14, *Erie*...........Elias H. M'Neal
Lansingburgh, 15, *Rensselaer*........S. D. Smith
Lansing, 9. *Tompkins*..................
Lansingville. Lansing, *Tompkins*. Aaron L. Palmer
Lapeer, 12, *Cortland*.................
Larned's Corners, Hopewell, *Ont*.Jacob Wormley
Lassellsville, Ephratah, *Fulton*...Wm. Lassell, jr.
Laurens, 5, *Otsego*............Elisha B. Steele
Lawrence, 10, *St. Lawrence*.................
Lawrenceville, Lawrence, *St. Law*....E. Whiting

Lawyersville, Cobleskill, *Schoha*..J.W. Redington
Lebanon, 3, *Madison*........Horace A. Campbell
Ledyard, 7, *Cayuga*.........Amaziah Underhill
Lee, 19, *Oneida*..............Asa D. Johnson
Leeds, Catskill, *Greene*........Sillock D. Smith
Leedsville, Amenia, *Duchess*....Joseph D. Hunt
Leesville, Sharon, *Schoharie*....Walter L. Judd
Leicester, 6, *Livingston*..................
Lenox. 14, *Madison*........Joseph W. Bruce
Leon. 14, *Cattar*.............Ira R. Jones
Leonardsville, Brookfield, *Mad*...Nathan V. Brand
Le Ray, 12, *Jefferson*.....................
Le Raysville, Le Ray, *Jefferson*.....Ennis Mosher
Le Roy. 5, *Genesee*..........Chas. B. Thompson
Levanna, Ledyard, *Cayuga*..........Otis Howe
Levant, *Chautauque*............John W. Winsor
Lewis, 9, *Essex*.............Alanson Wilder
Lewisboro, 18. *Westchester*.....Amos S. Northrop
Lewiston, 10, *Niagara*........Moses H. Fitts
Lexington, 1, *Greene*........Geo. W. Halcott
Lexington Heights, Lex'gton, *Green*.N. Hitchcock
Lyden, 15, *Lewis*.............Thomas Baker
Liberty, 8, *Sullivan*..........Gideon Wakis
Libertyville, New Paltz, *Ulst*..Isaac Schoonmaker
Lima, 11, *Livingston*.........Franklin Carter
Limerick, Brownville, *Jefferson*.......Ely Smith
Linden, *Genesee*..............A. G. Perry
Lindley, 5, *Steuben*.....................
Linklaen, 20, *Chenango*......John S. Blackman
Lisbon, 23, *St. Lawrence*......Wm. A. Campfield
Lisle, 12, *Broome*............Wm. H. Stoddard
Litchfield, 2, *Herkimer*.......Alanson Townsend
Lithgow, Washington, *Duchess*....Jacob Sisson
Little Britain, Hamptonb. *Orange*..G. A. Denniston
Little Falls, 7, *Herkimer*..........Joseph Lee
Little Genesee, Genesee, *Allegh*....Jabez Burdick
Little Sodus, Sodus, *Cayuga*......Wm. Wyman
Little Valley, 3, *Cattaraugus*.......Ira Gaylord
Little York, Homer. *Cortland*......J. E. Cushing
Liverpool, Salina, *Onondaga*.....John J. Forger
Livingston, 6, *Columbia*.......P. J. Bachman
Livingstonville, Broome, *Schoharie*..John Whiting
Livonia, 10, *Livingston*..........Andrew Sill
Lock Berlin, Galen, *Wayne*....Wm. A. Griswold
Locke, 2. *Cayuga*..............M. D. Murphy
LOCKPORT, 3, *Niagara*........Solomon Parmele
Locust Tree, *Niagara*.............L. B. Horton
Lodi, 1, *Seneca*..............Peter Himrod
Lodi Centre, Lodi, *Seneca*. Abraham La Tourette
Logan. Hector, *Tompkins*......Jabez S. Smith
Long Lake, 7, *Hamilton*.................
Lorraine, 2, *Jefferson*..........Moses Brown
Louisville, 26, *St. Lawrence*..........Levi Miller
Lowell, *Oneida*..............Joel H. Collins
Low Hampton, *Washington*.......Wm. S. Miller
Lowville, 7. *Lewis*........Cornelius P. Leonard
Lloyd, 9, *Ulster*..........James D. Terwilliger
Ludlowville, Lansing, *Tompkins*....Amasa Wood
Lumberland. 1, *Sullivan*........James Eldred
Luzerne, 1.*Warren*............Reuben Wells
Lyme, 15, *Jefferson*.....................
Lyndon, 20, *Cattaraugus*..................
Lyndonville, Yates, *Orleans*.....Joseph Babcock
LYONS, 4. *Wayne*...........James Satterlee
Lyonsdale, Greig. *Lewis*..........D. S. Howard
Lysander, 18, *Onondaga*.......Chauncey Betts
M'Connellsville, Vienna, *Oneida*..Francis M'Cune
M'Donough, 9, *Chenango*........Jacob P. Hill
M'Grawville, Cortlandtville, *Cortl*..P. H M'Graw
M'Lean, Groton, *Tompkins*.....Daniel B. Marsh
Mabbettsville, Washington, *Duch*..Sam. R. Wood
Macedon, 1, *Wayne*.........Wm. P. Hawkins
Macedon Centre, Macedon, *Wayne*.....Ira Odell
Machias, 22, *Cattaraugus*........R. L. Whitcher
Macomb, 20, *St. Lawrence*......Wm. Houghton
Madison, 5, *Madison*..........John S. Lucas
Madrid, 24, *St. Lawrence*......John T. Rutherford
Magnolia, Chautauque, *Chautauq*..Rich. Whitney
Mahopac, *Putnam*............Reuben D. Baldwin
Maine, 8, *Broome*............Abel H. Clark
Malden, Saugerties, *Ulster*..Duncan Livingston
Malden Bridge, Chatham, *Col*.L.VanValkenburgh
MALONE, 5, *Franklin*............Fred. P. Allen
Malta, 4, *Saratoga*............Chas. Moore
Maltaville, Malta, *Saratoga*.....Moses H. Hulin
Mamakating, 3, *Sullivan*.................
Mamaroneck, 7, *Westchester*.....John I. Marshall
Manchester, 11, *Ontario*.....Jefferson P. M'Cauley
Manchester Bridge, *Duchess*........Jacob Dolson
Manchester Centre, Manchester, *Ont*.J. Dewey, jr.
Mandana, Skaneateles, *Onondaga*....D. T. Fowler
Manhasset, *Queens*............R. H. Titus

Manheim, 14, *Herkimer* ....Alfred Snell
Manheim Centre, Manheim, *Herkimer*..J. Markell
Manlius, 10, *Onondaga*..................Horace Nims
Manlius Centre, Manlius, *Onondaga*....John Mable
Mannsville, Ellisburgh, *Jefferson*..Dexter Wilder
Manorville, Brookhaven, *Suffolk*......Seth Rayner
Mansfield, 16, *Cattaraugus*
Maple Grove, Butternutts, *Otsego*.Zenas Washbon
Marathon, 2, *Cortland*................Jesse Rodgers
Marbletown, 7, *Ulster*...........C. M. Van Buren
Marcellus, 9, *Onondaga*...........Elijah Rowley
Marcellus Falls, Marcellus, *Onond.*.G. P. Herring
Marcy, 22, *Oneida*...........Wm. M. Mayhew
Marengo, Galen, *Wayne*..........Morris D. Beadle
Margaretsville, Middletown, *Delaw.*.O. M. Allaben
Markville, Duanesburgh, *Schen.*.J. J. Quackenbush
Marietta, Marcellus, *Onondaga*....Alanson Hicks
Marion, 15, *Wayne*..............Elisha R. Wright
Marlboro, 3, *Ulster*..........Miles J. Fletcher
Marshall, 4, *Oneida*.........Edward E. Baxter
MARTINSBURGH, 6, *Lewis*.......David T. Martin
Martin's Hill, Catlin, *Chemung*....Abel Buckley
Martville, Sterling, *Cayuga*-Horace J. Kingsbury
Maryland, 7, *Otsego*............Geo. W. Chase
Masonville, 11, *Delaware*.....Fred. S. Freeman
Massena, 23, *St. Lawrence*..........Silas Joy
Matildaville, Parishville, *St. Lawre.*-Wm. R. Stark
Mattleawan, Fishkill, *Duchess*........David Davis
Mattituck, Southold, *Suffolk*......Jas. Shirley
Mayfield, 6, *Fulton*..............David Getman
Mayville, Chautauque, *Chautauque*..S. A. Beavis
Mechanicsville, Stillwater, *Saratoga*....Jas. Lee
Mecklenburgh, Hector, *Tompkins*..D. B. Wheeler
Medina, Ridgeway, *Orleans*.....Isaac W. Swan
Medway, *Greene*..............Samuel C. Titus
Mellenville, Claverack, *Columbia*.Jeremiah Groat
Mendon, 3, *Monroe*..........Albert Sherwood
Mentz, 15, *Cayuga*
Meredith, 14, *Delaware*..........Jos. H. Tyrrell
Merrick, *Queens*..............Carman Smith
Merrillsville, *Franklin*............J. R. Merrill
Mexico, 9, *Oswego*..........Rawson A. Butler
Middleburgh, 3, *Schoharie*....David B. Danforth
Middlebury, 14, *Wyoming*........Amos Walt
Middlefield, 11, *Otsego*.........L. M. Gilbert
Middlefield Centre, *Otsego*.....Geo. R. Fowler
Middle Granville, Granville, *Washingt.*G. N. Bates
Middle Hope, Newburgh, *Orange.*.E. S. Woolsey
Middle Island, Brookhaven, *Suff.*B. T. Hutchinson
Middleport, Royalton, *Niagara*....F. L. Taylor
Middletown, 4, *Delaware*
Middlesex, 9, *Yates*..........Oliver S. Williams
Middleville, Fairfield, *Herkim.*-Varnum S. Kinyon
Milan, 16, *Duchess*..........Rensselaer Case
Milford, 6, *Otsego*..........Albert Westcott
Military Road, Theresa, *Jefferson*-Thos. Robinson
Miller's Bay, Lyme, *Jefferson*........Jacob Jones
Miller's Place, Brookhaven, *Suffolk*.C. Woodhull
Mill Grove, *Erie*..............Hugh M. Case
Millport, Veteran, *Chemung*......Jos. C. Stott
Mill's Corners, Broadalbin, *Fulton*-Chas. Thatcher
Milltown, Kent, *Putnam*..........Hart Weed
Millville, Shelby, *Orleans*......Simeon Lyman
Milo, 5, *Yates*..............Jonathan Moore
Milo Centre, Milo, *Yates*........Abel B. Hunt
Milton, 9, *Saratoga*
Milton, Marlboro, *Ulster*..........Nancy Soper
Mina, 3, *Chautauque*............Isaac Relf
Minaville, Florida, *Montgomery*...Elias A. Brown
Minden, 11, *Montgomery*........Jacob H. Baum
Minerva, 1, *Essex*..............Anson West
Minetto, *Oswego*............Stanton S. Gillett
Minisink, 7, *Orange*............Ovil J. Brown
Modena, Plattekill, *Ulster*......Daniel Everett
Moffett's Store, New Lebanon, *Columb.*J. F. Hart
Mohawk, German Flats, *Herkimer*..C. Devendorf
Mohawk, 7, *Herkimer*
Moira, 9, *Franklin*.............Fred. H. Petit
Mongaup, *Sullivan*..........Francis Little
Mongaup Valley, *Sullivan*....Wynkoop Klersted
Monroe, 2, *Orange*............Daniel P. Fuller
Monroe Works, Monroe, *Orange*....John Coffey
Monsey, *Rockland*............Aaron Johnson
Montezuma, Mentz, *Cayuga*......S. W. Budlong
Montgomery, 14, *Orange*......Chris. S. Coleman
Monticello, Thompson, *Sullivan*..Fred. M. St. John
Mooers, 11, *Clinton*............Zetus Newell
Moravia, 5, *Cayuga*............Austin B. Hale
Moreau, 18, *Saratoga*........Luthena Reynolds
Morehouse, 6, *Hamilton*
Morehouseville, Morehouse, *Ham.*A. K. Morehouse
Moreland, *Chemung*..........Green Bennit
Moresville, Roxbury, *Delaware*....John L. More

Moriah, 5, *Essex*..........Nathaniel S. Storrs
Moriches, Brookhaven, *Suffolk*..James M. Fanning
Moringville, *Westchester*......Isaac H. Barker
Morley, Canton, *St. Lawrence*....Philo P. Gibson
Morristown, 19, *St. Lawrence*....Marshall Eager
MORRISVILLE, Eaton, *Madison*......Hiram Lewis
Morseville, *Schoharie*........Jeremiah Ruland
Moscow, Leicester, *Livingston*........Andrew Sill
Mott's Corners, Caroline, *Tomp.*..J. Hardenburgh
Mottville, Skaneateles, *Onondaga*..Howard Delano
Mount Cambria, Cambria, *Niagara*...John Hodge
Mount Hope, 9, *Orange*........John W. Martin
Mount Morris, 1, *Livingston*...Augustus Conkey
Mount Pleasant, 13, *Westchester*
Mount Pleasant, Saratoga.....Henry C. Granger
Mount Sinai, *Suffolk*........Charles Phillips
Mount Upton, Guilford, *Chen.*....Willis Gregory
Mount Vision, Laurens, *Otsego*....Harvey Keyes
Mount Washington, Urbana, *Steuben*..O. Longwell
Mud Creek, Bath, *Steuben*......David P. Graves
Mumford, *Monroe*............R. N. Havens
Murray, 6, *Orleans*........Henry M. Sinclair
Nanticoke Springs, Nanticoke, *Broome*..T. Carey
Nanticoke, 11, *Broome*
Nannet, *Rockland*............David De Clark
Napanoch, *Ulster*..........Gabriel W. Ladlum
Naples, 1, *Ontario*......Denison H. Chesebro
Napoli, 11, *Cattaraugus*........Orrie Marsh
Nashville, Hanover, *Chautauque*..Adlei S. Moss
Nassau, 2, *Rensselaer*.......Charles Waterbury
Natural Bridge, Wilna, *Jefferson*..Wm. Christian
Navarino, Onondaga, *Onondaga*....John T. Gillett
Nelson, 9, *Madison*..........John Donaldson
Neversink, 11, *Sullivan*........Amos Y. Grant
New Albion, 16, *Cattaraugus*..John R. Wescott
Newark, 8, *Tioga*
Newark, Arcadia, *Wayne*......Daniel H. Lusk
Newark Valley, Newark, *Tioga*..Wm. S. Lincoln
New Baltimore, 12, *Greene*....Irenus C. Sherman
New Berlin, 15, *Chenango*..George M. Williams
New Berlin Centre, New Berlin, *Chen.*A. Greene
New Bremen, 8, *Lewis*......Chs. G. Loomis, jr.
New Britain, New Lebanon, *Col.*....A. B. Davis
NEWBURGH, 13, *Orange*........Saml. W. Eager
New Castle, 14, *Westchester*......Moses W. Fish
Newcomb, 7, *Essex*
Newfane, 7, *Niagara*..........Henry Eshbaugh
Newfield, 1, *Tompkins*........Moses Crowell
New Hackensack, Fishkill, *Duchess*-Wm. Seward
New Hamburgh, Po'keepsie, *Duchess*..W. Millard
New Hampton, Wallkill, *Orange*..Hiram Phillips
New Hartford, 8, *Oneida*........James Groves
New Haven, 14, *Oswego*........S. G. Merriam
New Hudson, *Allegany*..........John M'Graw
New Hurley, Shawangunk, *Ulster*....J. Alsdorf
Newkirk's Mills, Bleecker, *Fulton*-G. A. Newkirk
New Lebanon, 18, *Columbia*........M. Y. Tilden
New Lebanon Centre, *Columbia*..F. W. Everest
New Lebanon Springs, *Columbia*...Benj. Nichols
New Lisbon, 13, *Otsego*........George J. Peck
New London, Verona, *Oneida*....James I. Carley
New Milford, Warwick, *Orange*....Thomas Gale
New Ohio, Colesville, *Broome*....E. S. Holcomb
New Paltz, 4, *Ulster*........Ezekiel S. Elting
New Paltz Landing, *Ulster*....Phillip J. Lefever
Newport, 12, *Herkimer*......Wm. H. Willard
New Road, Sidney, *Delaware*......Daniel Weed
New Rochelle, 5, *Westchester*..Jas. P. Huntington
New Salem, New Scotland, *Albany*.Ab'ham Mann
New Scotland, 2, *Albany*......Edmond Raynsford
Newstead, 21, *Erie*............Lewis Seaton
New Sweden, Au Sable, *Clinton*..J. C. Fitzgerald
Newton's Corners, *Fulton*........John Newton
Newtown, 1, *Queens*........John I. Burroughs
New Utrecht, 6, *Kings*......Wm. H. Cropsey
New Vernon, Mt. Hope, *Orange*....Gilbert Beebe
New Village, Brookhaven, *Suffolk*...Sam. B. Lee
Newville, Danube, *Herkimer*........Ezra Jones
New Windsor, 12, *Orange*....John D. Gildersleeve
New Woodstock, Cazenovia, *Mad.*.S. L. Hubbard
New York, *New York*..........Wm. V. Brady
N. Y. Mills, Whitestown, *Oneida*-Wm. D. Walcott
Niagara Falls, 11, *Niagara*......Genet Conger
Nichols, 3, *Tioga*..........John C. Barstow
Nicholville, Hopkinton, *St. Law.*-Edson J. Wilson
Nile, *Allegany*............Luther B. Whitwood
Niles, 9, *Cayuga*............C. D. De Witt
Nine Corners, *Cayuga*........Harrison Fowler
Ninevah, Colesville, *Broome*....Hial Edgerton
Niskayuna, 3, *Schenectady*....A. Van Hovenburgh
Niverville, *Columbia*..........Peter Dennis
Norfolk, 25, *St. Lawrence*......John Stocker
North Adams, Adams, *Jefferson*....Albert Rice

North Almond, Almond, *Alleghany*...James Ward
Northampton. 7, *Fulton*..........Wm. O. Fay
North Argyle, Argyle, *Wash*. Nicholas Robertson
North Bangor, Bangor, *Frank*. George H. Stevens
North Bay. *Oneida*.........Francis H. Conent
North Bergen, Bergen, *Genesee*...Den. F. Merrill
North Blenheim, *Schoharie*. ..Munson Morehouse
North Bloomfield, *Ontario*......A. H. Fairchild
North Boston, Boston. *Erie*......Jacob C. Cook
North Brookfield, Brookfield, *Mad*. Joseph Avery
North Castle, 16, *Westchester*......Sam. P. Smith
North Chatham, Chatham. *Columbia*...Wm. Carr
North Chemung. Chemung, *Chemung*. Jacob Tice
North Chili, Chili. *Monroe*......Robert Fulton
North Clarence, Clarence. *Erie*. ..Jacob Baxter
North Clymer, Clymer. *Chau*. ..Joseph R. Roads
North Cohocton, Cohocton. *Sten*.. John Nicholson
North Duanesburgh, *Schenectady*. ..James Donnan
North East. 12, *Duchess*........Wm. B. Reed
North East Centre, No. East. *Duch*. Lyman Bassett
North Easton, Easton. *Wash*.....Sanford R. Potter
Northfield, 4, *Richmond*......................
North Gage, Deerfield, *Oneida*. .Thomas Fell. jr
North Galway. Galway, *Saratoga*. ..E. S. Hanford
North Granville. Granville, *Wash*. .Jehiel Dayton
North Greenwich, Greenwich *Wash*...Wm. Reid
North Guilford. Guilford, *Chen*. Geo. H. Thompson
North Harpersfield, *Delaware*.....H. W. Hamilton
North Haverstraw. Haverstraw, *Rock*. Wm. Govan
North Hebron. Hebron. *Wash*.. ..Jonathan Allen
North Hector. Hector. *Tompkins*....Orren Wilcox
North Hempstead, 5. *Queens*.....Elias Lewis. jr
North Hoosick. Hoosick, *Renss*....Isaac Brownell
North Hudson. 6, *Essex*......................
North Java, Java, *Wyoming*. ...Merritt B. Lewis
North Kortright. Kortright. *Del*..Edmund Keeler
North Lansing. Lansing. *Tomp*. Roswell Beardsley
North Linklaen, Linklaen, *Chen*. ..Joshua C. Davis
North Middlesex, Middlesex, *Yates*..A. S. Thomas
North Norwich, 14. *Chenango*. Lewis E. Carpenter
North Perrysburgh. Perrysb. *Cattara*. C. Blackney
Northport, Huntington, *Suffolk*..........S.E. Busce
North Reading, Reading. *Steuben*. .James Masters
North Ridgeway. Ridgeway. *Orleans* E. W. Hawkins
North Russell. Russell. *St. Law*.....Linus A. Clark
North Salem, 19, *Westchester*....Nelson Grummon
North Sheldon. Sheldon, *Wyoming*. Elihu H. Persons
North Shore, Castleton. *Richmond*, N. P. H. Barrett
North Stephentown. Steph. *Renss*..H. T. Douglass
North Sterling. Sterling, *Cayuga*. W. T. Churchill
Northumberland, 12. *Saratoga*.....Joseph Finne
North Urbana, Urbana, *Steuben*...R. L. Chapman
Northville, Northampton, *Fulton*....Darius Moore
North Western. Western. *Oneida*......David Brill
North Wethersfield, *Wyoming*. ...Edwin Gardner
North White Creek, *Wash*.. Benjamin P. Crocker
North Wilna. Wilna. *Jefferson*....Jonathan Osborn
Norton's Mills. *Ontario*..........Zuriel Brown
Norway, 16. *Herkimer*..........David Du Bois
Norwich. 7, *Chenango*......Henry De Forest
Nunda, 16. *Livingston*.......Edgar M. Brown
Nyack. Orangetown. *Rockland*...Wm. B. Collins
Nyack Turnpike, Clarkstown, *Rock*. W. O. Blenis
Oakfield, 10. *Genesee*.......... George March
Oak Hill. Durham, *Greene*..........Henry J. Peck
Oakland. Portage. *Livingston*. ...Hiram A. Rider
Oak Orchard, Ridgeway, *Orleans*. .Mason Turner
Oak Point. *St. Lawrence*......James H. Consall
Oak's Corners, Phelps. *Ontario*...Henry C. Swift
Oaksville, Otsego, *Otsego*........Charles Childs
O'Connellville, Chili, *Monroe*.....M. M'N. Walsh
Ogden, 10. *Monroe*......................
Ogdensburgh. Oswegatchie, *St. Law*. G. Robinson
Ohio, 18. *Herkimer*........Reuben H. Wood
Olcott, Newfane, *Niagara*.....Thomas Armstrong
Olean, 6, *Cattaraugus*........Olcott P. Boardman
Olive, 14. *Ulster*..........John J. Tappen
Olive Bridge, Olive, *Ulster*........Wm. J. Davis
Omar. *Jefferson*..........T. R. Stackhouse
Oneida Castle, Vernon. *Oneida*....John Buswell
Oneida Depot, Lenox. *Madison*......Asa Smith
Oneida Lake, Lenox. *Madison*.....Calvin W. Hart
Oneida Valley, Lenox, *Madison*. .Geo. T. Kirkland
Oneonta, 3, *Otsego*........Samuel J. Cook
Onondaga. 8, *Onondaga*.......Charles D. Easton
Onondaga Hollow, *Onondaga*.....Arthur Pattison
Ontario, 13, *Wayne*........Joseph Patterson
Oppenheim, 1, *Fulton*........John P. House
Oran, Pompey *Onondaga*.........Julius Candee
Orange. 20. *Steuben*.........Thomas Shannon
Orange Port, *Niagara*..........S. R. Hart
Orangetown, 1, *Rockland*......................
Orangeville, 10, *Wyoming*..........Jerry Merrill

Oregon, Stockton, *Chautauqua*......A. Bloomfield
Orient. Southold. *Suffolk*..........Joseph Terry
Oriskany, Whitestown, *Oneida*......H. C. Balls
Oriskany Falls, Augusta, *Oneida*..Geo. W. Couch
Orleans, Phelps. *Ontario*........Kendal King
Orleans, 17. *Jefferson*..................
Orwell. 20. *Oswego*..........B. F. Mason
Osborne's Bridge, *Fulton*.....W. H. Van Ness
Osborne Hollow, Chenango, *Broome*. ..J. Carroll
Osceola. 1. *Lewis*......................
Ossian. 26. *Alleghany*........Francis Jewell
Ossining, 13. *Westchester*.................
Oswegatchie. 29. *St. Lawrence*..............
Oswego. 12. *Oswego*..............C. Ames
Otego, 2. *Otsego*..............H. E. Stone
Otisco. 4, *Onondaga*.........Ashbel Searl
Otisville, Mount Hope, *Orange*.....John Mullock
Otawa, Otego. *Otsego*........S. Osborne
Otsego, 18, *Otsego*......................
Otselic. 19. *Chenango*........Joel Buckingham
Otto, 26, *Cattaraugus*.........J. P. Darling
Ovin, 3, *Seneca*..........James Van Horn
Owasco, 10. *Cayuga*.........H. G. Tompkins
Owxco, 6, *Tioga*............C. R. Barstow
Ox Bow, Antwerp. *Jefferson*......E. Brainerd
Oxford. 5. *Chenango*..........L. M'Neil
Oxford Depot, *Orange*........Peter B. Taylor
Oyster Bay, 6, *Queens*......James Colwell
Page's Corners, Warren, *Herkimer*. ..John Lewis
Payne's Hollow, German Flats, *Herkimer*. .C. Paine
Painted Post. 7, *Steuben*........H. S. Brooks
Palatine. 9. *Montgomery*........Archibald Fox
Palatine Bridge, Palatine, *Mont*. Webster Wagnor
Palenville, *Greene*............C. H. Teal
Palermo, 10, *Oswego*........David Jennings
Palmyra, 2, *Wayne*..........Thomas Nince
Pamelia. 13. *Jefferson*..................
Pamelia 4 Corners, Pamelia. *Jeff*....C. G. Harger
Panama. Harmony, *Chautauqua*....John Stewart
Papakunk, *Delaware*..........Judah Kelley
Paris. 3. *Oneida*............D. R. Kelley
Parish, 3, *Oswego*..............E. E. Ford
Parishville, 8, *St. Lawrence*.....F. D. Brooks
Parksville, *Sullivan*..........Wm. Bradley
Parma, 18. *Monroe*..........Wm. Goodell
Parma Centre, Parma. *Monroe*........C. A. Knox
Partridge Island, Hancock, *Del*. .Jas. Wheeler. jr
Patchin's Mills, Cohocton. *Steuben*. .H. A. Weed
Patchogue, Brookhaven, *Suffolk*....J. B. Wilcox
Patten's Mills. Fort Ann, *Wash*.....J. W. Ha..rey
Patterson, 4. *Putnam*.........H. Crosby
Pawlings, 3, *Duchess*.........Robert Watts
Pavilion. 4, *Genesee*........Wm. M. Sprague
Pavilion Centre. Pavilion, *Genesee*, .Gilman Barnet
Peasleeville. *Clinton*.........E. A. Bigelow
Peekville. Fishkill. *Duchess*.....George Smith
Peekskill, Courtland , *Westchester*. .Jacob S. Odell
Pekin, Cambria, *Niagara*........S. S. Sage
Pelham, 4, *Westchester*........John Bolton
Peltonville, Pultney, *Steuben*....John Gload
Pembroke. 8, *Genesee*........Guy C. Clark
Pendleton. 2. *Niagara*.......Simon Bellinger
Penfield. 14. *Monroe*..........Henry Ward
Penn Yan. Milo, *Yates*.......J. C. Robinson
Peoria. *Wyoming*.............Jas. Gordon
Pepacton. Colchester. *Delaware*.....T. Shaver
Perch River, Brownville, *Jefferson*. .Hugh Smith
Perrinton. 4. *Monroe*........H. Van Buren
Perry, 12. *Wyoming*.........J. H. Bailey
Perry Centre, Perry, *Wyoming*.....J. Lathrop
Perrysburgh, 29. *Cattaraugus*.....H. C. Hurd
Perry's Mills. Champlain. *Clinton*. .Lucian Perry
Perryville, Fenner. *Madison*.......Silas Judd
Persia, 27, *Cattaraugus*..................
Perth, 4. *Fulton*............Alex. Stewart
Peru. 3. *Clinton*........Edgar Beckwith
Peruville, Groton. *Tompkins*.....Wm. Baldwin
Peterborough. Smithfield, *Madison*. ..O. Williams
Petersburgh, 11, *Rensselaer*....A. E. Reynolds
Petersburgh Four Corners, *Rensselaer*. S. Reynolds
Pharsalie, 12, *Chenango*........Ansel Brown
Phelps, 9, *Ontario*..........D. Stephenson
Philadelphia, 19, *Jefferson*......J. B. Carpenter
Phillipsport, Mamakating, *Sullivan*...J. Masten, Jr
Phillipstown, 8, *Putnam*..................
Phillipsville, Amity. *Alleghany*......A. Morris
Phillips' Creek, Alfred. *Alleghany*. S. W. Cartwright
Phœnix. Schroeppel. *Oswego*......J. M. Rice
Piermont. Orange. *Rockland*........David Clark
Pierpont, 7, *St. Lawrence*.....A. A. Crampton
Pierrepont Manor. Ellsburgh, *Jeff*...J. G. Pease
Piffard, York, *Livingston*......D. H. M'Pherson
Pike, 8, *Wyoming*..........Samuel Windsor

Filler Point, Brownville, *Jefferson*......J. L. Alger
Pinckney. 10. *Lewis*.................................
Pine, Vienna. *Oneida*.................C. Brodock
Pine Bush. Rochester, *Ulster*.........C. J. Deyo
Pine Grove. Tyrone, *Steuben*......E. Vanderhoof
Pine Hill, Shandaken, *Ulster*.........A. A. Scott
Pine Plains, 15, *Duchess*......Lewis D. Hedges
Pine's Bridge. Yorktown, *Westches.* Benj. D. Miller
Pineville. *Steuben*....................D. B. Bryan
Pitcairn. 1. *St Lawrence*..........John Sloper
Pitcher. 11. *Chenango*................E. C. Lyons
Pitcher Springs, Pitcher, *Chenango*...R. K. Bourne
Pittsfield. 14. *Otsego*..................O. Spafard
Pittsford. 5. *Monroe*........W. M. Huntington
Pittstown, 13, *Rensselaer*..........D. W. Hyde
Plainfield, 16, *Otsego*...........Luther Smith
Plainville. Lysander, *Onondaga*...B. B. Schenck
Plank Road. *Onondaga*.........Joseph Palmer
Pinto. *Cattaraugus*.................R. H. M'Coy
Plattekill. 2. *Ulster*...............Levi Bodine
PLATTSBURGH. 5, *Clinton*.........Levi Platt
Pleasant Plains, Clinton, *Duchess*.B. J. Vankeuron
Pleasant Valley, 9, *Duchess*........J. H. Traver
Pleasantville, Mount Pleasant, *Westch.*.J. R. Banks
Plesis. Alexandria. *Jefferson*......E. H. Turner
Plymouth. 13. *Chenango*.......Dennis Ballow
Poestenkill. 5. *Rensselaer*.......H. Vanderzee
Point Peninsula. Brownville, *Jeff*...Wm. J. Enders
Poland. Russia, *Herkimer*........S. S. Evans
Poland, 6. *Chautauque*..........................
Poland Centre, Poland, *Chau.*......N. E. Cheney
Polkville, *Onondaga*...........H. M'Kiernan
Pompey, 6, *Onondaga*........Calvin S. Ball
Pompey Centre, Pompey, *Onon.*...Judson Candee
Pomfret. 20. *Chautauque*..........................
Pond Eddy, *Sullivan*..........Moses De Witt
Pond Settlement, *Steuben*........A. Hoagland
Poolville. Hamilton, *Madison*.....Orman Beers
Pope's Corners, *Saratoga*......A. H. Pearsall
Pope's Mills, *St. Lawrence*.....Russell Covell
Poplar Ridge, Venice, *Cayuga*...Allen Mosher
Portage, 15. *Livingston*..........................
Portageville. Portage. *Wyoming*...Alvah S. Green
Port Byron. Mentz, *Cayuga*.......Eli Wilson
Port Chester. Rye, *Westchester*...Edward Field
Port Crane. *Broome*............W. C. Hopkins
Porter. 9. *Niagara*..............................
Porter's Corners, Greenfield, *Sara.*..F. V. Hewitt
Port Gibson. Manchester, *Ontario*.James Halladay
Port Glasgow. Huron, *Wayne*.....M. W. Gage
Port Henry, Moriah, *Essex*........J. Tarbell
Port Jackson. Florida. *Montgomery*.Jeremiah Snell
Port Jefferson, Brookhaven, *Suff.* H. K. Townsend
Port Jervis Deer Park, *Orange*......John Conklin
Port Kendall, *Essex*.............Levi Higby
Port Kent, Chesterfield, *Essex*....Charles P. Allen
Portland. 21, *Chautauque*.........Curtis Wilber
Portlandville. *Otsego*............Jesse Mumford
Port Leyden. Leyden, *Lewis*......J. H. Williams
Port Onta-io. Richland, *Oswego*....E. Chapman
Portville, 7, *Cattaraugus*.......H. Dusenbury
Post Creek. Southport, *Chemung*...Jacob Bucker
Postville, Russia. *Herkimer*........Z. Popple
Potsdam, 12. *St. Lawrence*.......W. L. Knowles
Potter, 8. *Yates*................Peleg Thomas
Potter Hill. *Rensselaer*........George Pierce
Potter Hollow. Rensselaerville, *Albany*.N. Laraway
Pottersville. Chester, *Warren*......M. Codman
Poughkeepsie. 7. *Duchess*...........Isaac Platt
Poughquag, Beekman, *Duchess*....S. V. Rogers
Poundridge, 17, *Westchester*....A. H. Lockwood
Prattsburgh, 30. *Steuben*..........Wm. B. Boyd
Pratt's Hollow. Eaton, *Madison*...O. Chamberlin
Prattsville, 7. *Greene*...........Thomas Fitch
Preble, 10, *Cortland*............J. B. Phelps
Preston. 8, *Chenango*...........Smith Johnson
Preston Hollow. Rens'ville, *Alb.*.H. T. Devereux
Princetown. 2, *Schenectady*......................
Prospect, Remsen, *Oneida*........G. B. Johnson
Prospect Hill. Pittstown, *Rensselaer*..James Grant
Providence. 16. *Saratoga*..........S. H. Brown
Pulteney. 31. *Steuben*...........J. T. Benton
Pultneyville. Williamson, *Wayne*..Geo. D. Phelps
Pulver's Corners, Pine Plains, *Duch.*.Jacob Pulver
Purdy Creek. Hornellsville, *Steuben*..B. S. Buskirk
Purdy's Station. *Westchester*.....Isaac H. Purdy
Purvis, Rockland, *Sullivan*......Jas. E. Sprague
Putnam, 13. *Washington*........Wm. G. Corbet
Putnam Valley, 1. *Putnam*..........................
Quaker Hill, Pawlings, *Duchess*....John P. Hayes
Quaker Springs, Saratoga, *Sarat*.Amos Reynolds
Quaker Street, Duanesburgh, *Schen*.Kirby Wilber
Queensbury, 2. *Warren*.........L. C. P. Seeley
Quogue, Southampton, *Suffolk*....J. P. Howell

Rackett River, Massena, *St. Law*...Allison Mears
Ramapo, 3. *Rockland*..........................
Ramapo Works, Ramapo. *Rockland*..Edw. H. Lord
Randolph. 13, *Cattaraugus*........T. S Sheldon
Ransomville, Porter, *Niagara*.....Wm. J. Moss
Rapids, *Niagara*..............A. J. Mansfield
Rathboneville, Addison. *Steub.*.Ransom Rathbone
Raynertown. Pittstown, *Rens.*....R. T. Cushman
Raymondville. *St Lawrence*......Giles J. Hall
Reading, 21. *Steuben*...........Hiram Chapman
Reading Centre. Reading. *Steuben*..A. Simmonds
Red Bridge. *Ulster*.............Lewis Wisner
Red Creek. Wolcott, *Wayne*......D. Underhill
Red Falls, *Greene*...........E. E. Millegan
Redfield, 19, *Oswego*..........H. Griswold
Redford. Saranac, *Clinton*........N. H. Lund
Red Hook, 18. *Duchess*..........John Bates
Red Mills, Carmel, *Putnam*........J. Whiting
Red Wood. Alexandria. *Jefferson*...J. Buckbee
Reed's Corners, *Ontario*..........Mason Reed
Reidsville. Berne. *Albany*......James Miller
Remsen. 25, *Oneida*...........James D. Ray
Rensselaerville. 1. *Albany*........J. T. Hnyck
Rexford Flats. Clifton Park, *Saratoga*..Nelson Cole
Reynale's Basin, Royalton, *Niagara*..Geo. Morse
Reynoldsville. Hector, *Tompkins*....Selah Sarles
Rhineheck. 17. *Duchess*.......Wm. B. Platt
Rice. 19. *Cattaraugus*.........W. S. Pitcher
Richburgh. Wirt, *Alleghany*......A. W. Miner
Richfield, 21, *Otsego*...........A. Churchill
Richfield Spring, Richfield, *Otsego*.Cyrus Osborn
Richford. 10, *Tioga*...........J. H. Deming
Richland, 15, *Oswego*..........J. T. Stevens
Richmond, 4. *Ontario*..........................
Richmond, Northfield. *Richmond*...John Johnson
Richmond Mills. Richmond. *Ont.*Joseph Morse. jr.
Richmond Valley, Westfield, *Richm.*...Henry Cole
Richmondville, 10, *Schoharie*......Silas Dickinson
Richville, De Kalb. *St. Lawrence*....A. B. Lynde
Ridge. Mount Morris, *Livingston*....Edwin Stilson
Ridgebury, Minisink, *Orange*......R. A. Elmer
Ridgeway. 7, *Orleans*...........W. H. Pells
Riga, 8, *Monroe*...............J. M'Pherson
Ripley, 11, *Chautauque*.........S. B. Northam
RIVERHEAD, 3, *Suffolk*..........................
River Road Forks, Mt. Morris, *Living.*..W. W. Deak
River Side. *Ulster*............David Wolley
Roanoke. Stafford. *Genesee*.......Joel P. Reed
Roberts' Corners. *Jefferson*......D. Spencer, jr.
ROCHESTER. 13. *Monroe*.........Darius Perrin
Rochester, 5, *Ulster*...........................
Rockaway. Hempstead. *Queens*....D. T. Jennings
Rock City, Milan. *Duchess*..........A. Shook
Rock City Mills. *Saratoga*.....H. Van Nostrand
Rockdale. *Chenango*...........Ransom Clark
Rockland, 12, *Sullivan*.........Chester Darbee
Rockland Lake, Clarkstown, *Rockl*...A. P. Stevens
Rock Stream. Starkey, *Yates*....H. A. Newcomb
Rookville, Belfast. *Alleghany*.....John Dort. jr.
Rockville Centre. Hempstead, *Queens.*.Rob. Pettit
Rodman, 4. *Jefferson*...........B. F. Hunt
Rome, 11, *Oneida*............B. G. Savary
Romulus, 4. *Seneca*...........Henry Swan
Rondout. Kingston, *Ulster*......John Hudlar
Roosevelt. *Oswego*............Geo. S. Bowen
Root, 2, *Montgomery*..........John Bowdish
Rose, 6, *Wayne*............Benj. Hendricks
Roseboom, *Otsego*.........Martin Dickinson
Rosendale. 12, *Ulster*.........J. A. Snyder
Roslyn, N. Hempstead, *Queens*....Wm Heicks
Rossie, 17, *St. Lawrence*.......Zacheus Gates
Roseville, Westfield, *Richmond*....B. F. Wynant
Rotterdam. 3, *Schenectady*........J. Burrows
Rouse's Point. Champlain, *Clinton*...E. M. Gates
Roxbury, 5, *Delaware*..........D. M. Smith
Royalton. 4, *Niagara*.......Jacob Shoemaker
Rush. 2. *Monroe*..........Nathan Dasschy
Rushford, 17, *Alleghany*.......Grover Leavens
Rushville. Gorham. *Ontario*.......Abijah Otis
Russell, 5, *St. Lawrence*........Benj. Smith
Russia, 17. *Herkimer*.........Henry Stanton
Rutland. 9, *Jefferson*..........Sam'l. Frink
Rye. 9. *Westchester*...........Wm. Smith
Sackett's Harbor. Hounsfield, *Jeff*..O. H. Harris
Sageville. *Hamilton*..........J. C. Holmes
Sag Harbor. Southampton, *Suffolk*...P. Fordham
St. Andrews. *Orange*............Lotan Kidd
St. Armand, 17, *Essex*.........................
St Johnsville. 10. *Montgomery*.....Lewis Averill
St. Lawrence. *Jefferson*.........D. E. Pierce
SALEM, 5, *Washington*...........Geo Allen
Salem Centre. N Salem. *Westches.*..Clark Stevens
Salem Cross Roads. Portland, *Chau.*.W. L. Mintura
Salina, 13, *Onondaga*........Wm. B. Whitmore

Salisbury, 15, *Herkimer*.............W. C. Ford
Salisbury Centre, Salis., *Herkimer*..Hiram Headley
Salisbury Mills, Blooming G., *Orange*.R.VanAllen
Salmon River, Albion, *Oswego*....Geo.W.Stillwell
Salt Point, Pleas.Val., *Duchess*.R.D.C.Vanderburgh
Salt Springville. *Otsego*..........J. Clearwater
Salubria, Dix, *Chemung*........W. C. Booth
Semmonsville, *Fulton*...........G. H Sholtus
Samsonville, Haverstraw, *Ulster*...H. A. Samson
Sand Bank, Albion, *Oswego*.........J. L. Taft
Sandburgh, Fallsburgh, *Sullivan*. Sturges Andrews
Sand Lake, 6. *Rensselaer*........Nathan Upham
Sandusky. Freedom. *Cattaraugus*....Eber Holmes
Sandy Creek, 22. *Oswego*........J. G. Ayer
SANDY HILL, Kingsbury, *Wash*....D. Doubleday
Sanford, 5, *Broome*..........John Pinney, jr.
Sanford's Cornors, Le Ray, *Jeff*...Phineas Hardy
Saugersfield. 1. *Oneida*........Daniel North
Saranac, 6, *Clinton*........Alfred Fling
Saratoga, 11. *Saratoga*.
Saratoga Springs, 10, *Saratoga*.....T. J. Marvin
Sardinia, 5, *Erie*............R. Simons
Saugerties, 17, *Ulster*........Geo. A. Gey
Sauquoit, Paris, *Oneida*.........J. Knight
Savannah. 6, *Wayne*...........J. J. Jolly
Sayville, Islip, *Suffolk*........J T. Howell
Schaghticoke. 14. *Rensselaer*.....S. L. Kenyon
SCHENECTADY, 4, *Schenectady*.....Peter Banker
Schenevus, Maryland, *Otsego*....Carlton Brown
Schodack, 1, *Rensselaer*.
Schodack Centre, Scho.. *Renss*..J.H.Vanderburgh
Schodack Depot, Schodack, *Renss*...Wm. Smith
Schodack Landing, Schodack, *Renss*..P. P. Huyck
Schoharie, 15. *Schoharie*........Rice Orcut
Schroon, 2. *Essex*.
Schroon Lake, Schroon, *Ess*.A.B.VanBenthuysen
Schroon River. Schroon, *Essex*....Russell Root
Schroeppel, 3, *Oswego*.
Schultzville. Clinton, *Duchess*.....D. H. Schultz
Schuyler, 11, *Herkimer*.
Schuyler's Falls, 4, *Clinton*......M. A. Barnes
Schuyler's Lake, Exeter, *Otsego*..Wm. C. Harp
Schuylersville, Saratoga, *Saratoga*...J. T. Smith
Scio, 3, *Allegany*............S. F. Blood
Sciota, *Clinton*............J. Ober
Scipio, 8. *Cayuga*...........J. E. Beardsley
Scipioville, Scipio, *Cayuga*....G. L Watkins
Sconondoa, Verona, *Oneida*......E. B. Stevens
Scotch Town, Wallkill, *Orange*....L. N. Moore
Scott, 9, *Cortland*...........D. F. Randolph
Scottsburgh, Sparta, *Livingston*...O. M. Hopkins
Scottsville, Wheatland, *Monroe*....W. G. Lacy
Scriba, 13. *Oswego*...........B. C. Turner
Searsburgh, Hector, *Tompkins*.....D. F. Sears
Seatuck, Brookhaven, *Suffolk*.....P. S. Robinson
Seely Creek, Southport, *Chemung*..W. R. Shepard
Seelysburgh, Napoli, *Cattaraugus*...E. L. Bussett
Sempronius, 4, *Cayuga*........Abel Heald
Seneca, *Tompkins*...........H. Milliman
Seneca, 8, *Ontario*.
Seneca Castle, Seneca, *Ontario*....Thomas Ottley
Seneca Falls. 7, *Seneca*.........D. C. Bloomer
Sennet, 14. *Cayuga*...........S. M. Spooner
Setauket, Brookhaven, *Suffolk*.....J. R. Satterly
Seward. 11, *Schoharie*.
Shandaken, 15, *Ulster*.........A. R. Whipple
Shandaken Centre, Shandaken, *Ulster*.Chas. Terry
Shannon, *Steuben*............T. B. Gold
Sharon, 12, *Schoharie*.........R. W. Brown
Sharon Centre, Sharon, *Schoharie*..Caleb B. Fox
Shaver Town, Andes, *Delaware*....Alfred Shaver
Shawangunk, 1. *Ulster*.........M. F. Deyo
Shawney, Wheatfield, *Niagara*....Edwin Cook
Shawsville. *Broome*...........C. S. Graves
Shelby, 1, *Orleans*...........James Gilson
Shelby Basin, Shelby, *Orleans*..Wm. F. Wilkinson
Sheldon, 9, *Wyoming*.........W. J. Humphrey
Sheldrake, Covert, *Seneca*.......John Harris
Shelter Island. 9. *Suffolk*......A. R. Havens
Shenandoah. Fishkill, *Duchess*.....A. Pulling
Sherburne, 17, *Chenango*........E. S. Lyman
Sheridan, 25, *Chautauqua*.......J. E. Acker
Sherman, 9, *Chautauqua*........E. Miller
Sherman's Hollow, *Yates*........Isaac Haight
Sherwood's Cornors, Scipio, *Cayuga*...A. Thomas
Shingle Creek, *St. Lawrence*......Alex. Wight
Shokan, Olive, *Ulster*..........Thos. Heill
Short Tract, Granger, *Allghany*....Jas. Platt
Shrub Oak, Yorktown, *Westchester*...Lewis Purdy
Shushan. Salem, *Washington*......Danl. Volintine
Sidney, 12, *Delaware*..........Thos. P. Williams
Sidney Centre, Sidney, *Delaware*.Chas. S. Heyatt
Sidney Plains, Sidney, *Delaware*....C. S. Rogers
Siloam, Smithfield, *Madison*......U. P. Strong

Silver Creek. Hanover, *Chautauqua*....C. C. Swift
Sing Sing, Ossining, *Westchester*...J. W. Robinson
Skaneateles, 1. *Onondaga*........John Snook, jr.
Slate Hill, Minisink, *Orange*......D. C. Hallock
Slaterville, Caroline. *Tompkins*......Jas. Heath
Sloansville, Esperance, *Schoharie*....J. Larkin
Sloatsburgh, Ramapo, *Rockland*......Jacob Sloat
Smith's Basin. Ft. Ann, *Washington*..L. C. Holmes
Smithsboro, Tioga. *Tioga*........A. F. Benjamin
Smithfield. 12, *Madison*.
Smith's Mills, Hanover, *Chautauqua*...R. B. Smith
Smithville, 3. *Suffolk*... ... ...Jas. Hallock
Smithville, Adams, *Jefferson*.....R. W. Dewey
Smithville, 4, *Chenango*.
Smithville Flats, Smithville, *Chen*...John S. Tarbell
Smoky Hollow, Claverack, *Columbia*..J. I. Planter
Smyrna, 18, *Chenango*.........F. E. Dimmick
Sociality, Dayton, *Cattaraugus*....Leander Bacon
Sodus, 11, *Wayne*...........John White
Sodus Centre, Sodus, *Wayne*......T. W. Lamson
Sodus Point, Sodus, *Wayne*......Wm. Wickham
Solon, 6, *Cortland*...........N. P. Emerson
Somers, 20, *Westchester*........F. J. Coffin
Somerset, 6, *Niagara*.........F. O. Pratt
Somerville, Rossie, *St. Lawrence*...Henry R. Albro
South Albion, Albion, *Oswego*.....D. V Thomas
South Amenia, Amenia, *Duchess*..M.F.Winchester
Southampton, 6. *Suffolk*........Chas. Parsons
South Argyle, Argyle, *Washington*..Wm.Congdon
South Avon. Avon, *Livingston*.....C. T. Isham
South Bainbridge, Bainbridge, *Chen*..Jas. H. Shutts
South Barre, Barre, *Orleans*......O. S. Church
South Berne, Berne, *Albany*......R. Lawrence
South Bradford, Bradford, *Steuben*..A. S. Gardner
South Bristol, 2, *Ontario*.......Allen Brown
South Butler, Butler, *Wayne*......G. S. Graves
South Byron, Byron, *Genesee*.....J. T. Boynton
South Cairo, Cairo, *Greene*......Zarak Ferry
South Cameron, Cameron, *Steuben*..Jas. Lawrence
South Canton, Canton, *St. Law*....A. Barrows, jr.
South Chemung. Chemung, *Che*....G. W. Roberts
South Chili, Chili. *Monroe*......Wm. R. Mudge
South Columbia, Columbia, *Herkimer*..N. Brown
South Corinth, Corinth, *Saratoga*....B. Martin
South Cortland, Cortland, *Cort*....Darius Sanders
South Danby, Danby, *Tompkins*....Aaron Bennett
South Dansville, 27. *Steuben*.....A. W. Beech
South Dickinson, Dickinson, *Frank*..Eldred Baker
South Dover, Dover, *Duchess*......S. Wheeler
South Durham, Durham, *Greene*....A. T. Renwick
South East, 3, *Putnam*.........Salamon Denton
South Easton, Easton, *Washington*..T. D. Beadle
South Edmeston, Edmeston, *Otsego*...D. H. Spurr
South Edwards, Edwards, *St. Law*...I. Winslow
Southfield, 3, *Richmond*.
South Franklin, Franklin, *Delaware*..G. H. Terry
South Granville, Granville, *Wash*...B. F. Potter
South Hammond, Hammond. *St. Law*..Henry King
South Hartford, Hartford, *Wash*....Jacob Allen
South Hill, *Steuben*..........C. D. Hubbard
South Kortright, Kortright, *Dela*....John M'Minn
South Lansing, Lansing, *Tompkins*..D. D. Minier
South Livonia, Livonia, *Livingston*..D. Bunnell
South Lodi, Lodi, *Seneca*.......John Ingersoll
South Marcellus, Marcellus, *Ononda*..C. N. Potter
South Middletown, Wallkill, *Orange*.O. P. Coleman
South New Berlin, N. Berlin, *Chenan*..N. Crandall
Southold, 9, *Suffolk*.........Franklin Tuthill
South Onondaga, Onondaga, *Onondu*..C. Amidon
South Otselic, Otselic, *Chenango*...S. E. Warren
South Owego, Owego, *Tioga*......Caleb Lamb
South Oyster Bay, O. Bay, *Queens*...T. Carman
South Plymouth, Plymouth, *Chenun*..Delos Janes
Southport, Southport. *Chemung*....R. T. Jones
South Pultney, Pultney, *Steuben*...Lebbeus Drew
South Richland, Richland, *Oswego*..Stephen Tinker
South Royalton, Royalton. *Niagara*..W. Furaman
South Rutland, Rutland, *Jefferson*..Oscar S. Oaks
South Salem, Lewisboro, *Westchester*..G. Hawley
South Schodack, Schodack, *Renss*...Jos. S. Hare
Southside, *Richmond*..........G. A. Cole
South Sodus, Sodus, *Wayne*......O. D. Warren
South Stephentown. Stephentown, *Renss*.C. Moffit
South Thurston, Thurston, *Steuben*..Henry Rising
South Trenton, Trenton, *Oneida*....J. D. Lewis
South Valley, Cherry Valley, *Otsego*..D. W. Rice
South Valley, 1, *Cattaraugus*.
South Venice, Venice, *Cayuga*....Wm. S. Tupper
Southville, Stockholm, *St. Law*....Rufus Mead, jr.
South Wales, Wales, *Erie*.......D. S. Warner
South Westerlo, Westerlo, *Albany*..Thos. Saxton
South Wilson, Wilson, *Niagara*...Micah Anderson
South Windsor, Windsor, *Broome*...A. W. Coburn

South Worcester, Worcester, Otsego....A. Becker
Spafford, Onondaga...............Wm. W Legg
Spafford Hollow, Spafford, Onondaga....Kelly Case
Sparta. 2. Livingston..............E. A. Janes
Speedsville, Caroline, Tompkins....S. P. Ashley
Spencer, 5, Tioga......,.........Henry Miller
Spencerport, Ogden. Monroe..........Henry Bell
Spencertown, Austerlitz, Columbia....J. P. Clark
Spoonk, Southampton, Suffolk......Luther Cook
Spraker's Basin. Root, Mont......E. B. Spraker
Spring Brook. Erie.............Zenas Colby
Springfield, 20, Otsego..........D. L. Keyes
Spring Mills, Independence, Alleghany...W. Cobb
Springport, 20, Cayuga
Springs. Easthampton, Suffolk....David D. Parsons
Spring Valley, Orangetown, Rockland...R. W. Coe
Springville, Concord, Erie......M. L. Badgley
Springwater, 5, Livingston........Thos. D. Dyer
Sprout Creek, Lagrange, Duchess...Hiram Montfort
Staatsburg. Hyde Park, Duchess....James Russell
Stafford, 6, Genesee.............John March
Stanford, 18, Delaware..........Charles Griffin
Stanford, 15, Duchess
Stanfordville, Stanford, Duchess......M. J. Miller
Stapleton, Southfield, Richmond....Edward Blake
Starkey, 4, Yates............Isaac Lanning
Stark, 5, Herkimer
Starkville, Stark. Herkimer.......E. Diefendorf
Stephentown, 3, Rensselaer........T. D. Platt
Sterling, 22, Cayuga..........Wm. F. Longley
Sterlingville, Philadelphia, Jeff....James Sterling
Steuben, 26, Oneida...........Merit Brooks
Stevensville, Liberty. Sullivan....O.D. Stephens
Stillwater. 6, Saratoga..........A. Palmer
Stittville, Trenton. Oneida........Wm. Grant
Stockbridge, 13. Madison........Horace Dexter
Stockholm, 11, St. Lawrence......C H. Holmes
Stockport, 19, Columbia.........Joseph Wild
Stockton. 15, Chautauque.......Milton Smith
Stokes, Lee. Oneida...........H. E. Gregory
Stone Arabia, Palatine, Mont.....John A. Lipe
Stone Church, Bergen. Genesee...Calvin Granger
Stone Mills, Orleans, Jefferson....Walter Schram
Stone Ridge, Marbletown, Ulster...J. Vandermark
Stony Brook, Brookhaven, Suffolk...J. N. Gould
Stony Creek, Athol, Warren......James Fuller
Stormville, Fishkill. Duchess.....Wm. R. Kelley
Stowell's Corners, Jefferson........Ira Hall
Stow's Square, Lowville, Lewis..Chas. Davenport
Stratford, 10, Fulton
Stratton's Fall, Delaware.......Lewis Stratton, jr.
Strykersville. Sheldon, Wyoming..Hez B. Rounds
Stuyvesant, 14, Columbia.........A. Bidwell
Stuyvesant Falls, Stuyvesant, Col..P. A. Van Allen
Success, Riverhead, Suffolk........John Luce
Suffolk, Riverhead, Suffolk.......Geo. Halsey
Sugar Hill, Orange, Steuben......David Webb
Sugar Loaf, Goshen, Orange. :...Edgar Wells
Sullivan, 15, Madison..........Wm. W. Clark
Summer Hill, 3, Cayuga........Ezra Hough
Summit, 7, Schoharie..........Wm. T. Moak
Susquehannah, Colesville, Broome....F. Doolittle
Sweden, 9, Monroe...........D. N. Glazier
SYRACUSE, Salina, Onondaga.....Wm. Jackson
Taberg, Annsville, Oneida.........J. C. Thorne
Taghkanic, 5, Columbia.........C. Whitbeck
Taylor, 14, Cortland
Tannersville, Hunter, Greene...Wm. E. Anthony
Tappantown, Orangetown, Rockland..J. I. Blauvelt
Tarrytown, Greenburgh, Westchester...M. H.Wilson
Taylorsville, Ontario..........John D. Feagles
Ten Mile Spring. Cold Spring, Cattar..T. Higgins
Texas, Mexico, Oswego..........Hiram Parker
The Corner, Ulster.............A. D. Ladew
The Glen, Warren.............C. Whittaker
The Purchase, Harrison, Westchest.J..T. Carpenter
Theresa, 48, Jefferson..........Silas L. George
The Square, Cayuga...........P. Van Keuren
Thompson's Station, Suffolk......F. M. A. Wicks
Thompson, 4, Sullivan.........Jona. Stratton
Thompsonville, Thompson. Sullivan
Three Mile Bay, Lyme. Jefferson....Russell Day
Throopsville, Mentz, Cayuga....Ludlow Williams
Thurston, 12, Steuben..........John Crawling
Ticonderoga, 3, Essex..........Alfred Weed
Tioga, 2, Tioga
Tioga Centre, Tioga, Tioga....William Ransom
Tivoli, Red Hook, Duchess.....Consider Clark
Tomhannock, Pittstown. Rensselaer...L. V. Reed
Tompkinsville. Castleton, Richmond..F. S. Jones
Tompkins, 10, Delaware
Tonawanda, 13, Erie............Jacob Kilber
Tontine, Steuben...........Timothy Kendall
Towlesville, Howard, Steuben....S.W. Stewart

Towner's, Patterson, Putnam....James Towner
Town Line, Lancaster, Erie.....Robert Neel
Townsend. Dix, Chemung.........S. C. Swim
Townsendville, Lodi, Seneca....Gilbert Ganong
Trenton, 24, Oneida...........John Billings
Trenton Falls, Trenton, Oneida....D.W. Bacon
Triangle. 18, Broome..........Israel Saxton
Tribe's Hill, Amsterdam, Mont....Fisher Putnam
Troupsburgh, 2. Steuben........Charles Card
Trout Creek, Delaware..........L. L. Teed
Troy, 8, Rensselaer..........Thos. Clowes
Trumansburgh, Ulysses, Tompkins..L. D. Branch
Trumbull Corners, Tompkins....A. C. Sherwood
Truxton, 11, Cortland.........Edw. Miller
Tuckahoe, Westchester.......Peter U. Morgan
Tully, 4. Onondaga...........John B. Hall
Tully Valley, Tully, Ononduga...Wm Salisbury
Turin 5. Lewis.............E. B. Holden
Turner's. Orange.............Elmore Earl
Tuscarora, Sparta, Livingston....Samuel Powers
Tuthill, Shawangunk, Ulster....J. L. Hasbrouck
Tyre, 10. Seneca............Simon P. Babcock
Tyrone, 22, Steuben...........L. Compton
Ulysses. 8, Tompkins
Ulsterville, Shawangunk, Ulster...Nelson Crist
Unadilla, 1, Otsego.........A. D. Williams
Unadilla Centre, Unadilla, Otsego..Simeon Lamb
Unadilla Forks, Unadilla, Otsego..H. H. Babcock
Union, 9, Broome............T. Twining
Union Centre, Union, Broome....Wm. A. Norton
Union Corners, Sparta, Livingston...Ruth Youngs
Union Falls, Black Brook, Clinton..J. T. Duncan
Union Mills, Broadalbin, Fulton....O. R. Ryder
Union Settlement, Oswego.......Silas Penoyer
Union Society, Windham, Greene...E. S. Bailey
Union Springs, Springport, Cayuga..J. C. Yawger
Union Square, Mexico, Oswego....A. Skinner
Union Vale, 3, Duchess
Union Valley, Cortland......De Grand Benjamin
Union Village, Lisle. Broome.....Rodney French
Unionville, Minisink, Orange.......L. L. Smith
Unitaria, Broome...........Robert Pike. jr.
Upper Aquebogue, Riverhead, Suffolk.B. F. Wells
Upper Jay, Jay, Essex..........Benj. Wells
Upper Lisle, Lisle, Broome......Darius Pratt
Upper Red Hook, Red Hook, Duchess.D. A. Cuck
Urbana, 24. Steuben..........S. B. Fairchild
UTICA, 9, Oneida...........J. A. Shearman
Vail's Mills, Mayfield, Fulton....J. V. Marselis
Valatie, Kinderhook, Columbia....Geo. Marshall
Vallona Springs, Colesville, Broome.Z.C. Wiswall
Van Buren, 17, Onondaga........H. R. Dow
Van Buren Centre. V. Buren, Onon.G. W. Marvin
Van Buren Harbor, Pomfret, Chaut.H. S. Stearns
Van Ettenville, Cayuta, Chemung...Chas. Patchin
Van Hornesville, Stark, Herkimer.J. H. Shumway
Varick, 5. Seneca...........J. Y. Gambee
Varna, Dryden, Tompkins......Wm. Scutt, 2d
Varysburgh. Sheldon, Wyoming..W. H. Ainsworth
Venice, 6, Cayuga..........A. P. Lawson
Verbank, Union Vale, Duchess....A. L. Colwell
Vermillion, Palermo, Oswego......Morris Place
Vermont, Gerry, Chautauque......S. E. Palmer
Vernal, Attica, Wyoming.........David Filkins
Vernon, 6, Oneida...........C. C. Bill
Vernon Centre, Vernon, Oneida..Elihu M. Foote
Verona, 13, Oneida...........A. Whaley
Verplank, Courtlandt, Westchest.Wm. Bleakley jr.
Versailles, Perrysburgh, Cattaraugus.A. H. Barker
Vesper, Tully, Onondaga.......C. M. Clark
Vestal, 1, Broome...........Lewis Wright
Veteran, 7, Chemung.........Wm. Van Duser
Victor, 18, Ontario...........A. P. Dickinson
Victory, 21, Cayuga..........L. Hooker
Vienna, 18, Oneida...........Linus Parker
Villenova, 18, Chautauque......Geo. Hopkins
Virgil, 1, Cortland...........A. E. Hebard
Vischer's Ferry, Clift. P'k, Sar.G. W. Van Vranken
Vista, Lewisborough, Westchester..W. M. Crissey
Volney, 11, Oswego.........Samuel Griswold
Volusia, Westfield. Chautauque....John Howard
Waddington, Madrid, St. Lawrence..S. J. Dewey
Wadham's Mills, Westport, Essex..J. R. Delano
Wading River, Riverhead, Suffolk....S. Miller
Walden, Montgomery, Orange....Marcus K. Hill
Waldensville, Schoharie........Hiram Walden
Wales. 13, Erie............Jas. Wood
Wales Centre, Wales, Erie........Ira Bell
Walesville, Whitestown, Oneida..W. H. Olmsted
Wallkill, 10. Orange
Walton, 9, Delaware.........G. S. Sawyer
Walworth, 14, Wayne.........B. Billings
Wampeville, Lenox, Madison.....B. M. Case
Wappinger's Falls, Fishkill, Duchess..E. D. Sweet

Wernerville, Richmondville, *Schohar.*8. Westcott
Warren. 4, *Herkimer*................F. Tunnicliff
Warren.burgh, 4, *Warren*.........Lewis Person
WARSAW. 11, *Wyoming*.............C. W. Bailey
Warwick. 1, *Orange*.................Joseph Roe
Washington, 10, *Duchess*............Wm. Frost
Washington Hollow, Washi'n. *Duch.* J. S. Simmons
Washin'n Mills. New Hartford, *Onei.* T W.McLane
Waterburgh, Hector, *Tompkins*....Levi H. Owen
Waterford, 3, *Saratoga*.............Jas. I. Scott
WATERLOO, 8. *Seneca*..............Wm. Knox
Waterport, *Orleans*..............Wm. Cochran
WATERTOWN. 8, *Jefferson*.........P. S. Johnson
Watervale, Pompey, *Onondaga*.........Wm. Ely
Water Valley, Hamburgh. *Erie.* J. J. Curlbertson
Waterville, Sangersfield, *Oneida.* W. B. Stafford
Waterville Corners, Concord. *Erie.* Abner Wilson
Watervliet, 10, *Albany*......................
Watervliet Centre, Watervliet, *Albany*..L. Morris
Watson. 13, *Lewis* ....Peter Kirley
Wawarsing, 6, *Ulster*...........J. M. Jackson
Wayland, 28, *Steuben*......................
Wayne, 23. *Steuben*.............J. B. Mitchell
Webster, 15, *Monroe*...........Wm. Corning
Weedsport. Brutus, *Cayuga*....M. Henderson
Wellington, Camillus, *Onondaga*....Loron Tyler
Wells, 3. *Hamilton*.............Wm. B. Peck
Wellsburgh. *Cemung*............Abner Wells
Wells Corners, Minisink, *Orange.* J. H. Sanderson
Wellsville. Scio, *Alleghany*.......C. L. Farnum
West Addison, Addison. *Steuben*....R. Saunders
West Almond, 13, *Alleghany*......J. G. Prentiss
West Amboy. Amboy, *Oswego*.....Henry Garber
West Bainbridge, Bainbridge, *Chenan.* T. Nichols
West Bergen, Bergen, *Genese.*...J. D. Doolittle
West Bloomfield, 19, *Ontario*.......Solon Peck
West Branch. Western. *Oneida*....Jas. Mitchell
West Brookville, Mamakating, *Sullivan.* D. Smith
West Brunswick, 1, *Herkimer*................
West Burlington, Burlington, *Otsego.* Truman Moss
Westbury, *Wayne*............E. E. Ingham
West Butler, Butler, *Wayne*.......Hiram Sears
West Camden, Camden. *Oneida*....A. W. Barnes
West Candor, Candor, *Tioga*......Ira Woodford
West Carlton, Carlton, *Orleans*......Geo. Kuck
West Cayuta, Cayuta, *Chemung*....Le Roy Wood
West Charlton, Charlton, *Saratoga*..F. McMartin
West Chazy, Chazy, *Clinton*....Ira F. Chamberlain
Westchester, 1. *Westchester*........M. S. Arnow
West Clarksville, C'ville. *Alleghany*..A. Congdon
West Colesville, Colesville, *Broome*...J. Pickering
West Concord, Concord, *Erie*......A. K. Ostrander
West Conesus, Conesus. *Livingston.* J. Huntington
West Constable, Constable, *Frank.* W. C. Gleason
West Davenport, Davenport, *Delaware*...C. Miller
West Day, Day, *Saratoga*..........Thos. Frost
West Dresden, Dresden. *Yates*........W. Holden
West Dryden, Dryden, *Tompkins*....J. S. Barber
West Edmeston, Edmeston. *Otsego*...John Gaskin
West Ellery, Ellery, *Chautauque*....A. S. Felton
Westerlo, 2, *Albany*..............Robt. S. Lay
Westernville, Western. *Oneida*....Erastus Ely
West Exeter, Exeter, *Otsego*....H. A. Matterson
West Farmington. Farmington, *Ontario*..W. Wood
West Farms, 2, *Westchester*.....Ralph H. Smith
West Fayette, Fayette, *Seneca*....Samuel Gambee
Westfield, 12, *Chautauque*..........Wm. Saxton
Westfield, 2, *Richmond*....................
Westford, 10, *Otsego*............Geo. Skinner
West Fulton. Fulton, *Schoharie*......Eli Settle
West Gaines, Gaines, *Orleans*........H. Noble
West Galway, Galway, *Fulton*.......Geo. Logan
West Genesee, Genesee, *Alleghany.* Jared Maxson
West Gilboa, Gilboa, *Schoharie*.....Edward Wood
West Greece, *Monroe*...........Edward Walker
West Greenfield, G'field, *Saratoga*....J. Satterley
West Greenwood, Greenwood, *Steuben*..A. Mead
West Groton, Groton, *Tompkins*....Cicero Phelps
West Hadley, Hadley, *Saratoga*......David Wait
West Hebron, Hebron, *Washington.* L. B. Wilson
West Henrietta, Henrietta. *Monroe.* J. M. Cutler
West Hills, Huntington, *Suffolk.* ...Ezra Oakley
West Hurley, Hurley, *Ulster*.........H. Jewell
West Junius, Junius. *Seneca*......J. S. Vandomark
West Kill. Lexington, *Greene*......C. Bushnell
West Laurens, Laurens, *Otsego*...R. H. Mulkin
West Lexington, Lexingt. *Greene*...Austin Chase
West Leyden. Leyden, *Lewis*........R. T. Hough
West Linklaen, Linklaen, *Chenango.* R. P. Turner
West Lowville, Lowville, *Lewis*...J. Windecker
West Martinsburgh, Martins., *Lewis*..Jer. Salmon
West Meredith, Meredith, *Delaware*...A. Stilson
West Milton, Milton, *Saratoga*......H. Crippen
West Monroe, 5, *Oswego*..........H. J. Jewell
Westmoreland, 12, *Oneida*.........Amos Barnes

West Moriah. Moriah. *Essex*........J. E. Mather
West Newark. *Toga*.............E. Richardson
West Niles, Niles. *Cayuga*.........Cyrus Ellis
West Oneonta, Oneonta, *Otsego*....Allen Tabor
West Perth, Perth, *Fulton*............Wm. Rob
West Plattsburgh, Plattsb. *Clinton*..N.A.Vaughan
West Point, Cornwall, *Orange*....Mary Berard
Westport. 11. *Essex*.............W. J. Cutting
West Potsdam, Potsdam, *St. Law.*....Benj. Lane
West Rush, Rush. *Monroe*...........E. Hoyt
West Sandlake, Sandlake. *Rense*....Jacob Boyce
West Schuyler, Schuyler, *Herkimer*..Ira Gordon
West Shaudaken, Shand., *Ulster*.....Geo. Brown
West Somers. Somers, *Westchester*......E. Frost
West Somerset, Somerset. *Niagara*....M. S. Hees
West Sparta. 2. *Livingston*..................
West Stephentown, Stephentown, *Rense.* Ira Tift
West Stockholm. Stock., *St. Law.* D. H. Chapman
West Taghkanic, Tagh., *Col*.....R. A. Rosaback
West Theresa, Theresa, *Jefferson*...John Rappole
Western. 20, *Oneida*......................
Westernville, Western. *Oneida*......Erastus Ely
West Town, Minisink. *Orange*......H. C. Halsey
West Troupsburgh, Tr'ps b.. *Steuben*..N. M Perry
West Troy, Watervliet, *Albany*....O. S. Brigham
West Turin, 2. *Lewis*......................
West Union. 1. *Steuben*..........David Sherman
West Vienna. Vienna. *Oneida*......Silas Jewell
Westville, 12, *Franklin*....................
Westville, Westford, *Otsego*.......Nelson Beach
West Walworth, Walworth, *Wayne.* S. L. Miller
West Webster. Webster, *Monroe*......S. C. Peet
West Windsor, Windsor, *Broome*....Lewis Riley
West Winfield, Winfield, *Herkimer*...Jas. M. Rose
Wethersfield, 7, *Wyoming*.......Joel S. Smith
Wethersfield Springs, Weth., *Wyoming*..B.Bancroft
Whallonsburgh. Essex. *Essex*....Jas. S. Whallon
Wheatfield, 1, *Niagara*...................
Wheatland, 1, *Monroe*..........John Murdock
Wheeler, 25, *Steuben*..........Ephraim Aulls
White Creek. 3. *Washington*......Stephen Barker
Whitehall, 15, *Washington*.........W. G. Walcott
White Lake, Bethel, *Sullivan*......J. P. Roosa
WHITE PLAINS, 10, *Westchester*....Elijah Guyon
Whiteside's Corners, *Saratoga*.....James Fuller
White's Store. Norwich, *Chenan.* David Westcott
Whitestown, 14, *Oneida*........W. C. Champlin
Whitesville. Independence, *Alleghany.* L. D. Brown
Whitlocksville. Bedford. *Westchester.* W. M. Beyes
Whitney's Point, Triangle, *Broome*...G. F. Osborn
Whitney's Valley, Burns, *Allegh.* ..Joseph Leonard
Willet. 3, *Cortland*.............Chauncy Bean
Williams' Bridge, West Farms. *Westch.* B.Valentine
Williamsburgh. 2. *Kings*........O. Longworth
Williamson. 12, *Wayne*..........S. C. Moody
Williamstown, 18, *Oswego*........Jacob Potts
Williamsville. Amherst, *Erie*.......J. S. Tefft
Willink, Aurora, *Erie*.............Joseph Riley
Willsborough, 13, *Essex*.........Chas. Sheldon
Wilseyville, Candor, *Tioga*........J. D. Smith
Wilmington, 16. *Essex*...........E. A. Adams
Wilmot, 19, *Herkimer*........Gardner Hinckley
Wilna, 11, *Jefferson*............Chas. Pierce
Wilson's, 8. *Niagara*............J. C. Brown
Wilton. 13. *Saratoga*.........R. F. Buckbee
Windfall, *Onondaga*.............David Preston
Windham, 5, *Greene*.............A. Parker
Windham Centre, Windham, *Greene*....B. Phelps
Windsor. 4, *Broome*............Jeremiah Hull
Winfield, 1, *Herkimer*............B. Carver
Wirt. 5. *Alleghany*...........J. B. Kenyon
Wiscoy, Hume, *Alleghany*.........John Todd
Wolcott. 9, *Wayne*...........I. Leavenworth
Woodbourne. Fallsburgh, *Sullivan*....M. T. Mares
Woodhull, 3, *Steuben*........S. V. Lattimore
Woodstock, 16, *Ulster*........S. A. De Forest
Woodville, Ellisburgh, *Jefferson*....M. A. Gray
Woodwardville, Schroon, *Essex*....John Reed
Worcester, 8, *Otsego*........H. B. Watermann
Worth. 3. *Jefferson*..................
Wright, 16, *Schoharie*...................
Wright's Corners, Newfane, *Niag.*...S. C.Wright
Wrightsville, *Clinton*..........Standish Gage
Wurtsboro, Mamakating, *Sullivan*....S. Henderson
Wynantskill. Greenbush. *Rensel.* ..Henry Frazee
Wyoming, Middlebury, *Wyoming.* ...Lewis W. Pray
Yaphank, Brookhaven, *Suffolk*....John P. Mills
Yates, 8, *Orleans*.................John Mead
Yatesville, Potter, *Westchester*....E. A. Bashford
York, 13, *Livingston*............James Frazer
Yorkshire. 24, *Cattaraugus*.........S. Lincoln
Yorktown, 21, *Westchester*........J. H. Purdy
Yorkville, New York, *New York*....Chas. Gaylor
Youngstown, Porter, *Niagara* ....Oliver Spencer
Zoar, Eden, *Erie*...................Jehiel Hill

NEW YORK

MERCANTILE UNION DIRECTORY.

Accountants.

Cheesman Morton, 373 Bowery *New York.*
Gellatly John, 71 Nassau
Hughes H. 98 Broadway
Isaacs M. 54 Wall. Savings Bank
Jones John. 33 West
Jones T. 247 Broadway
Loudon Wm. R. 223 Chrystie
Marsh Christopher C. 88 Cedar
Penny J. 5 Dey
Senior Richard, 78 Nassau
Townsend W. W. 1 South

Agents.

AGENTS—COMMERCIAL.

Cleveland Warren A. 60 William *New York.*
Congreve Charles, 59 Maiden L.
Durand J. V. 16 South William
Halliday Edward C. 7 Wall
Woodward & Dusenbery, 45 William

AGENTS—MERCANTILE.

Cleveland W. A. 60 William *New York.*
Tappan & Douglass, 70 Cedar & 22 Nassau

AGENTS—ADVERTISING.

Palmer Volney B. Tribune Buildings, opposite City Hall *New York.*
Pratt George, 116 Nassau

AGENTS—COLLECTING.

Carpenter H. 75 Greenwich *New York.*
Coles Willet, 14 Wall
Cutter William T. 1 Hanover
Dean Benjamin T. 95½ Cannon
Hickson John. 86 Centre
Jones W. B. 513 Broome
Lyons John, 13 Chambers & 225 Stanton
Marren Bernard, 74 Ludlow
Nisbet Andrew, 50 Robinson
Smith S. J. 249 W. 13th
Taylor C. G. & H. A. 88 Cedar
Temple Richard, 27 Fulton
Watts Charles F. 41 West Broadway
West Henry P. 159 Grand

AGENTS—FREIGHT. (See also Agents—Passage.)

Brish J. H. & Co. 123 Washington *New York.*
Carson W. B. 7 West
Chamberlain Stephen S. agent New York and Troy Steamboat Co. Pier 17 N. R.
Dickey T. H. & Co. 166 Maiden L.

Gebert J. F. 126 Greenwich *New York.*
Hall Amos C. agent for the Norwich and Worcester Steamboat Co. Pier 16, N. R.
Harnden & Co. 75 South
Holman P. 145 Washington
Johnson G. A. & F. 67 South
Littlejohn Frederick S. agent of the Old Oswego Line of Lake Boats, 100 Broad
Losche P. A. 74 Greenwich
McMurray J. 69 South
Newton Isaac, 144 Greenwich
Pierson H. & W. 61 South
Roche. Brothers & Masterson, 164 Maiden Lane
Schultz Peter C. agent People's Line Steamboats, Pier 16 N. R. and 28 South
Tapscott & Co. 86 South
Thomson Wm. H. Pier 1 N. R.
Tyson Wm. 10 West
Van Tobel I. 133 Washington

AGENTS—GENERAL.

Bancroft Wm. H. agent for Piano Forte legs, 189 E. 9th *New York.*
Bliss N. 5 John
Bradford H. 192 Broadway
Center Sylvester, 12 West
Dean Nicholas, 19 Centre & 74 Broadway
Douglass A. E. patent safety fuse, 89 Wall
Dyckman Jacob G. 127 Fulton
Gourgas J. J. J. 75 & 77 Nassau
Howes & Brown. 33 Nassau
Jacks James, 30 9th Av.
Hazard Robinson, agent for the celebrated Bergen ale, 35 Vesey
Hoffman Samuel, 102 Nassau
Hutchins John G. 277½ Division
Loomis & Lyman, 38 Broadway
Marvin A. S. 138½ Water
Mullany E. B. 42 Cliff
Norcross & Co. 60 Nassau
Perier Alphonse, agent of the Belgian glass co. 287 Pearl
Spencer & Matson, 1 Ann
Trimble Alanson S. 190 West
Warner Alexander, 107 John, for the Shakers
Wickham James, 190 West

AGENTS—HOUSE.

Attwater Elisha M. 12 Hammersley pl. & 32 Cliff *New York.*
Atridge J. 275 3d
Barnard E. W. 193 7th
Babeuf Henry F. 35 Desbrosses
Bailey John F. 232 Broome
Beare T. M. 6 Wall
Blanchet Francis, 291 6th Av.
Brush Philander, 119 Bedford
Buck Gurdon, 7 Broad
Busteed George W. 45 William

Covert J. 75 Wall *New York.*
Crevier J. 122 Church
Crommelin Alfred, 307 Bowery
Denham John, Av. 8 cor. W. 16th
Duncan J. A. 134 Water
Downs George, 284 E. 13th
Falconer Ed. 5 Mangin
Field David, 135 Delancy
Fisher Robert, 179 Essex
Galpin Geo. 7 Chatham square
Gamblo Benjamin F. 30 2d Av.
Giles J. F. 168 Walker
Hagedorn John, 45 Oak
Haines John L. 250 3d Av
Hallock George G. 221 Delancy
Harrison Hiram, 72 E. 19th
Health Francis, 20 Chambers
Haos P. S. 35 Wall
Holden Oliver, 25 John
Holley W. C. 12 Nassau
Jenkins Joseph, 49 Chambers
Le Roy Benjamin, 209 Spring
Levy Asa S. 41 Broome
Lewis R. E. 19 Centre
Mallory C. S. 306 8th st
M'Craken Francis, 177 Bleecker
Metz J. jr. 32 Cliff
Myers Myer S. 42 Reade
Nowton Wm. K. 10 Centre
Nexsen E. 7 Nassau
Oakley R. 3 Broad
Osgood G. P. 6 Wall
Pitkin J. R. 68 Broadway
Roe Nathaniel, 72 King
Russell John F. 34 Norfolk
Seaman John T. 120 Water
Sherridan Patrick, 181 7th
Storm Samuel, 11 King
Sutton Thomas W. 465 Pearl & 220 Division
Vanderpoel A. B. 23 Wall
Wandell John C. 162 7th
Ward Isaac, 112 2d
Watts C. F. 41 W. Broadway
Wells James N. 135 9th Av.
Wright T. 106 W. 11th
Zurn Casper, 297 Av. A

AGENTS—INSURANCE. (See also Insurance Companies.)

Albany County.

Ford J. W. 46 Broadway, *Albany.*
Groot P. W. 6 Douw's Building
Southwick & Comstock, 420 Broadway
Jenkins John F. 7 Commercial Building

Broome County.

Stowe W. W. *Binghamton.*
M'Kinney C.

Chautauque County.

Wells Austin S. *Westfield.*

2

Columbia County.

White J. W.   *Hillsdale*
Carpenter A. Franklin Square
                               Hudson.
Magoun S. L. Warren st

Duchess County.

Owen J. (Fire & Life) Fishkill
  Landing   *Fishkill.*
Bogardus E. R.
Frost S. V. (Agt for Howard Ins.
  Co. of New York) 302 Main
                     Poughkeepsie.
Morris H. W. (Life, Health and
  Fire) 22 Market
Corliss C. R. 16 Market

Erie County.

Hopkins T. A. Williamsville
                      Amherst.
Henshaw Jefferson, Willink
                      Aurora.
Lee J. R. 181 Main   *Buffalo.*
Davis George. Reed's Wharf
Hill & Clark, 152 Main
Smith A. M. C. Exchange
Brewster & Crittenden, 4 Mer-
  chants' Exchange
Welbridge O. B. cor. Washing-
  ton & Dock

Fulton County.

Hayes E. H.   *Broadalbin.*

Genesee County.

Richardson Wm.   *Stafford.*

Herkimer County.

Earl S. & B.   *Herkimer.*
Brooks Wm.   *Little Falls.*
Ashley Geo.
Reed Philo
Wait E. B.
Foot S. N.
Green F. L.

Kings County.

Underhill James E. (Fire) 50 Ful-
  ton   *Brooklyn.*
Crowell Stephen, (Fire and Life)
  30 Fulton
Bulkely Chas. E. (Fire) 16 Fulton
Requa James A. (Life and Health)
  206 Fulton
Suydam J. S. (Fire) 33 Fulton
Taylor J. Lewis, 45 Fulton
King J. S. (Fire) 11 S. 7th
                  Williamsourgh.
Payson, Henry (Fire) 79 1st

Livingston County.

Shepard Charles   *Dansville.*
Greene Nelson W.
Frazer & Abbott
Norton L. C.
Bouge H. V.
Brown Merritt
Bryant D. C.
Chapin B. J.
Poles P. E.
Lauderdale W. E.   *Geneseo.*
Hamilton Wm. J.
Hinman W. M.   *Mount Morris.*

Monroe County.

Ely Abraham P. Smith's Block,
  Buffalo   *Rochester.*
Ayrault Nicholas, (Fire) 4 Arcade
  Gallery
Hamilton Theodore B. (Fire and
  Life) 6 Arcade
Holmes W. T. (Life) 32 Exchange
Parsons S. & Co. (Fire) 18 Front

New York County.

Bigelow Asa, jr. 46 Pine *New York.*
Glover T. B. 194 Av. B

Hegeman Abraham, 23 Water
                     New York.
Hooker Edward, 39 Wall, 6 Jaun-
  cey court
Hopper John, 71 Cedar
Hosford F. J. 50 Wall
Newman Samuel L. 34 Av. C
Post Joel K. 292 Fifth

Niagara County.

Morse C. A.   *Lockport.*
Reed James W.
Moss Charles S.
Scoville H. W.
Child Wm. H.   *Niagara Falls.*
Grout Wm. P.   *Wilson.*

Oneida County.

Hathaway J.   *Rome.*
Boardman D. L. James st
Williams J. W. (Fire) 11 Whites-
  boro   *Utica.*

Ontario County.

Young Aaron, Geneva   *Seneca.*
Kidder N. B.   do
Dox J. L.   do
Mundy G. M.   do
Strong John C.   do
Folger Chas. J.   do
Barnard Edwin   do
White Henry E.   do

Orange County.

Lyon T. J. Port Jervis *Deer Park.*

Orleans County.

Harrington C. A. Albion *Barre.*
Clark Thomas S. do
Swan Isaac, Medina   *Ridgeway.*
Cole E. W. Knowlesville
Saxe Peter   *Yates.*

Oswego County.

Shumway Wm. H. (Fire, Marine
  and Life) Telegraph block. First
  st   *Oswego.*

Rensselaer County.

Tracy H. S. (Fire, Inland, Ma-
  rine, Life and Health) 294 State
                   Lansingburgh.
Ranson I. (Fire, Life and Health)
  corner Richard & State
Peck E. A. (Life) 173 River *Troy.*
Henderson A. G. (Fire, Marine,
  Life and Health) 193 River
Ball E. (Fire) 14 Boardman's
  Buildings
Hall Daniel (Fire) 9½ 1st
Wheeler A. F. (Fire) corner Con-
  gress & 2d
Lambert John T. Agent for Al-
  bany Ins. Co. 10 1st

Saratoga County.

Bullard E. F.   *Waterford.*
Lawrence John
Knickerbocker John

Tompkins County.

Schuyler G. W. (Fire)   *Ithaca.*
Drake C. B. (Life)
Dana F. R. (Fire)
Bruyn W. V. (Fire and Marine)
Ingersoll J. O. M. (Life and
  Health)
Bishop D. E. (Life)
Hopkins W. T. (Fire)

Ulster County.

Trumpbour J. H. Main st
                    Kingston.

Wayne County.

Taylor R. Newark   *Arcadia.*

Ketcham J. L. S. Clyde *Galen.*
Cornwell F. S.   *Lyons.*
Ashley R. W.
Parshall D. W.
Adams John
Aldrich Wm. F.   *Palmyra.*
Smith Frederick
Pardee R. G.

Westchester County.

Miller George W.   *Bedford.*
Hadden I. Peekskill   *Courtlandt.*
Brown Stephen, do
Creinar M. S.   do
Whitney T. A.   do
Bayles Nathaniel, Tarrytown
                    Greenburgh.
Cobb M. L (Hartford Protection)
  Sing Sing   *Ossining.*
Stanto.. George E. Sing Sing
Roscoe Caleb,   do
Smith Horace, Portchester *Rye*
Horton Elisha, (Westchester Mu-
  tual)   *White Plains.*
Farrington T. O, (Westchester
  Mutual)   *Yonkers.*

Wyoming County.

Smith L. W.   *Warsaw.*
Young A. W.
Hawley Alanson
Andrews E. W.

Yates County.

Bennett H. B. Penn Yan   *Milo.*
Reddy Leander do
Jones E. B.   do
Wells S. H.   do
Wolcott H. G. Dundee   *Starkey.*
Purdy Wm. S.

Agents—Miscellaneous.

Allen A. 111 Division *New York.*
Allen Tilly, 38 Wall
Andrews H. B. & Co. 205 South
Backmeister Gustavus, 161 Wil-
  liam
Beebe Jeremiah S. 5 Hanover
Bell Richard. Post's Buildings
Bronson Frederic, 64 Merchants'
  Exchange
Chadwick Wm. N. 102 Nassau
Collins Jas. jr. 52 Wall, Agent
  for the State of Indiana
Dando Stephen, 2 Monroe, Agent
  for the Christian Advocate and
  Journal
Davis W. H. 34 Liberty
Dayton Wm. G. 56 Merchants'
  Exchange
Hervey J. H. 42 Cliff
Hopper Isaac T. 16 Centre
Jackson P. 5 John
Laner Richard, 167 Cedar
LeRoy Wm. Henry, 34 Liberty
Luckey J. N. 44 Cortlandt
Maclachlan Wm. Post's Buildings
Peck Curtis, 205 South
Peck W. T. 98 John
Perkins 37 4th
Ransom H. E. Post's Buildings
Reed B. C. 27 South
Rich James B. 233 Washington
Rider John P. 497 Broadway
Seaman F. 190 Water
Sebring T. V. W. 112 Water
Seiferheld Julius, 133 Washington
Seton, Sam'] W. 148 Grand
Seymour William, 22 and 26 Wall
Shepard Geo. G. 143 Maiden Lane
Spoom & Hoffman, 114 Greenwich.
Tappan & Douglass, 76 Cedar
Tebbetts John H. 335 Pearl
Townsend C. A. 2 Washington
Townsend Walter W. 1 South
Turnbull & Ackerson, 157 Bl'kr
Vandercleek William, 479 Broad-
  way
Willis W. B. 53 Nassau
Wolf J. F. & W.

AGENTS—PASSENGER.

Adams Porter W. 106 Barclay
Allen John, 187 Cedar, American
Inland Passage line
Byrnes P. W. & Co. 88 South
Center & Co. 12 West
Havens Joseph H. 39 Burling slip
Johnson G. A. & F. 67 South
Lowe D. 20 Pine
Martin Joseph T. 27 South
Matthews Emery, Pier 17 N. R.
Mills John W. 109 West
O'Brien Thomas H. 37 Burling slip
Roche, Brothers & Co. 35 Fulton
Selover Isaiah, 157 Cedar
Shannon Robert T. 36 Park row
Spofford, Tileston & Co. 48 South
Tapscott W. & J. T. 86 South
Thompson Samuel & Nephew, 275
Pearl
Wolf & Rischmuller, 159 Washington and 97 Liberty

AGENTS—PATENT.

Erie County.

Howe Thomas P. 162 Main *Buffalo.*

New York County.

Bailey J. H. 28 Chambers
New York.
Douglas Thos. W. 2 John
Farnham Calvin H. 9 Nassau
Gilroy Clinton G. Tribune Buildings
Serrell William, 289 Broadway

Rensselaer County.

Smith Jason, *Troy.*
Brundage Edwin L. 16 Boardman's
Buildings

AGENTS—REAL ESTATE.

Apalachicola Land Co. 35 Wall
New York.
Attridge John, 275 3d
Beare Thos. M. 6 Wall
Brown Ebenezer H. 71 Wall and
278 Houston
Buck Gurdon, 7 Broad
Bull Jireh, 238 William
Chase Anson H. 2 Wall
Davis Ezra P. 49 Chambers
Fisher Robert, 20 Chambers
Galpin George. 7 Chatham square
Gamble Benj'n, 345 Bowery
Gellatly P. N. 71 Nassau
Giles John S. 168 Walker
Glover Thaddeus B. 194 Av. B
Hamlin John G. 172 Ludlow
Hardman Aaron. 142 Mulberry
Holden Oliver, jr. 25 John & 25
Greenwich Av.
Holley Philologus, 133 Amity &
10 Wall
Jackson A. H. 192 Broadway
Janes Walter R. 50 Wall
Jenkins E. 3 Nassau
Lewis Richard E. 19 Centre
Loomis Henry, 58 William
Mattison S. H. 3 Nassau
Miller Nehumiah, 216 7th
Morris Dewitt C. 50 Grove
Oakley Richard, 3 Broad
Overton John B. 2 Wall
Pakker Abram H. 75 Duane
Pinckney Charles C. 92 Stanton
Pugsley & Raynor, 551 6th Av.
Richardson Samuel, 11 Nassau
Storrow Thomas W. 34 Liberty
Upton James. 243 William
Wandell John C. 2 Roosevelt
Warner Effingham H. 5 Wall
Watkins Samuel. 32½ Madison
West Henry P. 159 Grand
Whitlock William H. 87 1st
Wright Finley. 108 11th
Refused, 35 Wall

AGENTS—THEATRICAL.

Corbyn & Martini, 4 Barclay
New York.

Agricultural Implement Manufacturers.

Albany County.

Wheeler M. & Co. *Albany.*

Cayuga County.

Roundtree, Anthony &
Everson, *Springport.*

Duchess County.

Arnold B. & Son, 173 Main
Poughkeepsia.

Kings County.

Moore John, S. 1st corner Water
Williamsburgh.

Livingston County.

Wiard Seth & H. *East Avon.*
Chandler W. H. & S.

Oneida County.

Millard D. J. Clayville *Paris.*
Millard S. A. do
Brainard W. G. Dominic st *Rome.*
Wheeler O. do

Orleans County.

King S. L. Albion *Barre.*

Rensselaer County.

Deyoe Geo. C. 294 State
Lansingburgh.

Wayne County.

Tracy R. *Arcadia.*

Agricultural Warehouses.

Albany County.

Emery Horace L. 369 & 371
Broadway *Albany.*

Columbia County.

Gifford F. A. Columbia st. *Hudson.*

Duchess County.

Armstrong C. & Co. 197 Main
Poughkeepsis.

Erie County.

Peters T. C. & Brothers, corner
Washington and Exchange
Buffalo.

Livingston County.

Gilman F. M. *Dansville.*
Hall & Summers *Mount Morris.*

Monroe County.

Rapaljie & Briggs, Irving Block
Rochester.
Holmes & Palmer, Brockport
Sweden.
Fitch, Bang & Co. do

New York County.

Allen A. B. & Co. 189 & 191 Water
New York.
Hills S. C. 48 Fulton
Mayher John & Co. 187 Water &
195 Front
Moore John, 193 Front
Spader J. V. 42 Fulton

Niagara County.

Marvin W. K. *Lockport.*

Oneida County.

Foster & Co. 135 Genesee *Utica.*
Tyrrel & Co. 47 do

Rensselaer County.

Starbuck N. B. 313 River *Troy.*
Warren Henry, 315 do
Rich John & Co. 437 do

Amusement, Places of.

American Museum, Broadway,
cor. Ann *New York.*
Astor Place Opera House, Astor
Place cor. 8th
Bowery Theatre, 46, 48 & 50
Bowery
Broadway Theatre, 328 & 330
Broadway
Burton's Theatre, 41 Chambers
Chatham Theatre, 143 Chatham
Chinese Assembly Rooms, G. H.
Andrews, 539 Broadway
Chinese Museum, 539 Broadway
French Joseph, 322 Broadway
Olympic Theatre, 442 Broadway
White Charles, 68 Bowery
Vauxhall Garden, 2 4th Av.
Zoological Hall, 37½ Bowery

Anatomical Models.

Hyatt J. C. & D. 449 Broadway
New York.

Architects.

Albany County.

Smith, Willard E. Exchange
Albany.
Penchard George L. 17 Dou w's
Building
Rector H. & Son, 83 Hudson
Woollet Wm. L. jr. 16 Steuben

Erie County.

Otis Calvin N. 190 Main *Buffalo.*

Genesee County.

Hart J. R. *Batavia.*

Kings County.

Beers S. A. Montague near Court
Brooklyn.
King Gamaliel, Fulton corner of
Orange
Funk John H. 271 Adams
Anderson C. F. 38 Stanton
Olmsted Wm. B. 61 Atlantic
Martens J. W. 127 Atlantic
Stebbins Asa, cor. Atlantic &
Henry
Hanford E. 11 S. 7th *Williamsburgh.*
Williams S. F. 41 S. 3d
Kingsland Thomas, 140 4th

Monroe County.

Searl Henry, 11 Arcade *Rochester.*

New York County.

Arnot David H. 50 Wall *New York.*
Berrian James, 224 8th Av.
Blesch & Eidlitz, 11 Wall
Brown Clarkson, 12 Wall
Caillouette David, 56 Lewis
Davis Alexander J. 93 Merchants' Exchange
Diaper Frederick, 60 Broadway
Forsyth John, 190 Water
Field & Correja, 95 Merchants
Exchange
Garney John, 618 Broadway
Gescheidt Morris, 11 Wall
Hanford Ebenezer, 50 Wall
Hatfield Oliver P. 23 Chambers
Hatfield Robert G. 23 Chambers

Hill Amzi, 11 Nassau *New York.*
Hurry Edmond, 14 Wall
Hurry William, 13 Wall
Hurry Wm. jr. 13 Wall
Jackson T. R. 170 Broadway
Lafever Minard, 247 Broadway
Long Robert Cary, 29 Wall
Lucas Isaac, 1 Cottage Place
Pearson I. Green, 56½ Merchants'
    Exchange
Pollard Calvin, 5 Broad
Ranlett William H. 70 Nassau
Rink John J. 196 Forsyth
Ritch John W. 257 Broadway
Ruess J. 209 Bleecker
Rogers John. 257 Broadway
Schmidt Frederick, 18 Wall
Shelden Richard A. 8 Wall
Thomas Thomas, 304 Broadway
Thomas Thomas & Son 37 Canal
Thomas William, 18 Wall
Trench Joseph & Co. 12 Chambers
Upjohn Richard, 64 Broadway
Warner C. L. & Son, 2 Wall
Warner Sem'l. A. 170 Broadway
Warren Owen G. 94 Merchants'
    Exchange
Webb Edward J. 25 Nassau
Wells Joseph C. 17 Wall
Wright Archibald, 609 Broadway
Wight A. 607 Broadway
Wills Frank, 156 Broadway
Winham Aldridge, 113 3d Av.

Rensselaer County.

Thayer H. 198 1st   *Troy.*

Westchester County.

Burwick W. A. Peekskill
                        Courtlandt.

**Artificial Arm and Leg
    Makers.**

Penniman A. D. 76½ Church
                        New York.
Selpho William, 24 Spring
Thomas John F. 79 Pike slip

Artificial Eye Makers.

Gray James, 157 Grand *New York.*
Powell James W. 261 Broadway,
    entrance 1½ Warren, oculist and
    aurist.

**Artificial Flowers — Im-
    porters of.**

Bazin Andrew, 3 Barclay
                        New York.
Christopher Richard, 181 William
Civette, Aimee & Co. 62 White
Eastwood Edward, 14 John
Helbronner, Leopold & Maurice,
    139 William
Hoguet Joseph, 10 John
Kahn N. 39 John, importer of
    French feathers, flowers, and
    materials for florists
Lemercier Gaston, 172 William,
    importer of French artificial
    flowers, feathers, and materials
    for flower-makers
Lowitz, Becker & Cludius, 56
    John
Pearson M. & C. 116 Hester
Perry T. 54 Canal
Pinchbeck William F. 265 Wil-
    liam
Simons W. G. 60 John
Strange Edwin B. & Brother, 18
    Murray and 21 Park place

**Artificial Flower Manu-
    facturers.**

Erie County.

Putnam M. A. 273 Main *Buffalo.*

Kings County.

Blake Charles F. Lawrence near
    Johnson   *Brooklyn.*

Monroe County.

Jones Mrs. 10 South Clinton
                        Rochester.
Scott M. 73½ State

New York County.

Ackerman Melancton B. D. 12
    West Broadway place *New York.*
Bassford Geo. W. 479 Pearl
Blanchi Frances. 175 Division
Christy Mary. 169 3d Av.
Christopher Richard. 257 William
Condon James, 355 Bowery
Doherty Mary A. 169 William
Dunovan Mary, 263 William
Gandon Jules. rear 122 Church
Hawk Mary, 110 Division
Holsworth E. 286 Pearl
Jacquemod, 65 Walker
Jueger Emma, 198 Broome
Jarvis A. F. 72 Canal
Kelly Elizabeth J. 156 William
Onderdonk William, 38 Roose-
    velt
Pearson M. & C. 116 Church
Perryman Hester. 88 Forsyth
Perryman George H. 256 Grand
Ranchbeck Wm. F. 265 William
Price Thomas, 177 William
Saxton Stephen R. 83 Division
Stuart Martha. 244 Grand
Refused, 173 3d Av.

Artists—Decorative.

New York.

Basham Frederick, 408 Broadway
Cailloutte & Jackson, 327 5th and
    136 Mercer
Chapman E. 289 Broadway
Chapman T. A. 289 Broadway
Coffee Thomas, 57 Canal
Decheaux Ed. 306 Broadway
Earl Joseph, 293 Broadway
Fanshan S. R. 1 Cortlandt
Ficht John H. 208 Spring
Gallier John. 548 Broadway
Garvey Denis. 689 Broadway
Garvey John. 813 Broadway
Gibson William, 77 White
Halpin John, 42 John
Heinbrook Ferdinand, 166 Hester
Johnson J. H. 465 Pearl
Kyle J. 334 Broome
Murphy & Gunning, 52 M'Dougal
Pellegorini Giuseppe, 414 B.way
Platt George, 60 Broadway
Shields C. 66 John
Spencer Mrs. L. M. 72 Crosby
Turner Aaron, 476 Broadway

Artists' Materials.

Albany County.

Gould J. S.   *Albany.*

Kings County.

Frothingham James, 141 Fulton,
                        Brooklyn

New York County.

Deckham E. 306 Broadway
                        New York.
Dodge Samuel N. 189 Chatham
Kelly Theodore, rear 35½ Woos-
    ter
Rand & Co., 342 Broadway
Ridner John P. 497   do

Artists—Scagliola.

Farley Henry S. 28 Canal,
                        New York.
Foutine Charles, rear 86 Duane

Artists—Sculptors.

Brunswick H. 245 Hester
                        New York.
Ellis S. 247 Broadway
Flaeschner Medardus, 262 W
    18th
Kolm Joseph & Co. 36 Great
    Jones
Launitz Robert E. 536 Broadway
Lazzoti Joseph, 8 Ludlow
Major J. & D 49 Wall
Mancini John, 55½ Beech
Page Wm. 247 Wall
Piatti Anthony. 36 Howard
Sence & Flagella. 289 Broadway
Swezey Nelson. 31 4th Av.
Weeks W. W. 68 Chatham
Whitfield John S. 62 White

Art Unions.

American, 497 Broadway, and 60
    Mercer
International, 289 Broadway
London, 497 Broadway

**Ashes, Pot, Pearl (and Sale-
    ratus.)**

Albany County.

Sarles W.   *Coeymans.*

Allegany County.

Brundage Morris   *Alfred.*
Green Luke
Fisk J.   *Allen.*
Angel I.   *Almond.*
Smith A. C. & I. B.
Hunt, Swink & Co.   *Andover.*
Hale D. J.
Rewick R.   *Belfast.*
Chamberlain, Hughes & Co.
Fay Lambert   *Clarksville.*
Skiff Wm. & E.   *Hume.*
White C. & D. C. Whitesville
                    Independence.
Haskins & Tollman
Green I. W. & Son   *Centre.*
Spalding I. C. Black Creek
                    New Hudson.
Jameson H. D.   do
Prentiss James E. *West Almond.*
Miner A. W.   *Wirt.*

Erie County.

Warren & Co.   *Clarence.*
Serman & Godfrey   *Collins.*
Smith C. Collins Center
Pratt Lyman   *Elden.*
Richard Sherman E.   *Evans.*
Fisk Thomas, Water Valley
                    Hamburgh.
Riley Philip L.   *Holland.*
Carpenter T.   *Lancaster.*
Hastings S. P.   *Sardinia.*

Essex County.

Noble H. R.   *Elizabethtown.*

Genesee County.

Merrill Daniel F. North Bergen
                        Bergen
Kendall Charles   *Bethany.*
Dixon Edward, East Bethany
Scovel L.   do
Sherman William   *Le Roy.*
Sprague W. M.   *Pavilion.*
March Samuel   *Stafford.*

Herkimer County.

Clark & Crine, Mohawk
                    German Flats.

Jefferson County.

Butterfield & White, Redwood
                    Alexandria.
Suits & Hosford, Plessis

Bell Geo. P.   *Brownville.*
Smith ——, Perch River
Smith Levi, Limerick
Ingles & Huntington, Depauville
                            Clayton.
Fisk A. T.   *Ellisburgh.*

Kings County.

Francis Norman, 20th corner 1st.
                        Williamsburgh.
Ely, N. C. & Co. cor. 1st & N. 4th
Coggswell. Crane & Co. cor. 1st
& N. 4th

Lewis County.

Miller & Duff, Constableville
                        West Turin.
Thompson S. C.

Madison County.

Lewis R. M. & H. Morrisville
                            Eaton.
Sims & Bates, Chittenango
                        Sullivan.
Crouse James,   do

Monroe County.

Crosby & Dauchy   *Rush.*
Edson F. M. Scottsville
                        Wheatland.

New York.

Andrews Thomas, 68 Washing-
ton ; also dealer in imported
sal. soda.carb. soda, and soda ash
Brower John. 7 Coenties slip
Brown & Lombard, 117 Front
Cassidy Palmer & Co. 48, 49 &
51 West
Cornell Thomas F. 7 Coenties slip
Degrauw A. J. S. 69 Washington
Earle & Co. 68 Washington
Latham D. H. 68 Washington

Niagara County.

Dayharsh John, Pekin *Lewiston.*
Mather Elijah, Middleport
                        Royalton.
Colwell & Sleeper, Gassport

Oneida County.

Graves H.   *Boonville.*

Ontario County.

Steele Hiram   *East Bloomfield.*

Cattaraugus County.

Barlow Foster D. Rutledge
                        Conewango.
M'Coy Stephen   *Ellicottville.*
Howard ——   *Freedom.*
Holmes E. & M.
Whitcomb J.   *New Albion.*
Rose Chester   *Otto*
Garfield E.   *Randolph.*
Holmes A. East Randolph

Orleans County.

Garbutt E. H.   *Carlton.*

Oswego County.

Merriam S. G.   *New Haven.*
Wright & Crawford, Pulaski
                        Richland.

Otsego County.

Lansing James E.   *Decatur.*

Rensselaer County.

Carpenter & Darling, 79 N. 2d
                        Troy.

Steuben County.

Burnham & Smith   *Avoca.*
Rogers W. C.   *Dansville.*
Newcomb A. S.   *Orange.*

Hastings W. & L. D.   *Urbana.*
Leach J. C.   *Woodhull.*

St. Lawrence County.

Pickett J. B.   *Edwards.*
Martin Wm.
Shaw E. South Edwards *Edwards.*
Abbott E. W.   *Fowler.*
Maddock & Learned   *Hermon.*
Cook & Bingham
Chittenden C. S. & A. H.
                        Hopkinton.
McMartin A.   *Louisville.*
Britton D.
Clark R.   *Massena.*
Phillips A. B.
Sackrider Norman   *Norfolk.*
Brooks E. D.   *Parishville.*
Gilbert & Flower
Welch. Martin & Russell *Pierpont.*
Paul E. R.   *Pitcairn.*
Clark Theodore   *Pottsdam.*
Skeeles Albert M. West Pottsdam
Hunt Truman, Crary's Mills

Wayne County.

Smith M. Newark   *Arcadia.*
Dewey & Wells   *Lyons.*
White John   *Sodus.*
Fish P. Alton

Wyoming County.

Reed John   *China.*
Currier J.   *Java.*
Currier N. P. East Java
Bronson James, North Java
King & Richardson, Java Village
Collar & Stevens, Wyoming
                        Middlebury.
Bailey J. H.   *Perry.*
Ayrault L.   *Pike.*
Platt J. L. & Co.
Gillespie J. C.
Choate A.   *Warsaw.*

Yates County.

Turner James   *Potter.*

**Attorneys and Counselors-
at-Law.**

Albany County.

Allen Otis, 5 Douw's B. *Albany.*
Austin & McMalin, 37 State
Beardslee R. Y. 55   do
Benedict Lewis, City Hall
Bingham R. H. 450 Broadway
Birdseye Lucien. 59 State
Blanchard Anthony, Blount's
Buildings
Bramhall C. H. 78 State
Brinsmade James B. 1 Douw's
Buildings
Burton J. S. 66 State
Callanan & Gibbs. 50 State
Cole John, 513 Broadway
Collier J. A. 542 do
Colvin A. J. 106 State
Courtney Samuel G. Exchange
Cross J. R.   do
Dean & Newland, 4 Commercial
Buildings
Delancy E. F. 44 State
De Forest De Witt C. Exchange
Dexter J. 3 N. Pearl
Dewitt R. V. 56 State
Douw John D. P.15 Douw'sB'd'gs
Downing Geo. 94 State
Edwards Isaac
Fairchild M. 66 State
Frothingham. Lansing & Pruyn,
513 Broadway
Gansevoort & Hill, 13 Douw's
Buildings
Holstein L. D. City Hall
Hammond, King & Barnes, 450
Broadway
Harris & Van Vorst. Exchange
Harris Ira.   do.
Hawley Gideon,   do.

Hawley N. 11 Douw's Buildings
                        Albany.
Hayden & Doolittle, 83 State
Hill. Cagger & Porter, 57 do
Hilton R. J. 78   do
Hilton & Van Vorst, 78   do
James Thomas D. 66   do
Jenkins & McMartin. 44   do
Kingsley & Wood, 59   do
Lansing L. 1. 450 Broadway
Lansing Henry Q. Exchange
Lansing J. 66 State
Learned Wm. L. 71 State
Livingston & Wyman. 94 do
McCall H. S. 5 Douw's Buildings
McHarg Wm. C.
Morange Wm. D. 57 State
Morou ——, 106   do
Nichols M. C. G. 11 Douw's
Building
Northup R. H. 8   do.
Paddock W. S. 71 State
Patterson John, 11 City Hall
Percy & Higgins, 75 State
Pruyn & Martin. 53   do
Reynolds, Van Schaack & Olcott,
8 Howard
Rhoades Julius, Exchange
Robinson & Taylor, 94 State
Saunders Jas. B. 9 Douw's
Buildings
Schuyler Wm. C. 420 Broadway
Settle J. M. City Hall
Sharp Alex'r. P. 71 State
Shepard & Bancroft, 3 Broadway
Sherman E. J. 496 Broadway
Stephens, Edwards & Meads, 480
Broadway
Sturtevant J. B. 3 North Pearl
Taber & Joice. 6 Com. Buildings
Tallman Charles M. 3 N. Pearl
Van Hoevenburgh T. S. 450 B'd'y
Van Vechten T. 44 State
Wells R. H. 9 Blount's Buildings
Werner J. I. 59 State
Wheaton & Hadley, 83 State
Whelpley J. 75 State
Whipple A. D. L. 81 State
White Edwards & Wilson, 1 Com-
mercial Buildings
Willet F. S. 78 State
Wood Bradford R. 59 State
Wright D. 3 North Pearl
Younglove T. G. 44 State
Young W. A. Exchange
Clark George W. Reedsville
                        Berne,
Settle Peter
Voorhees ——, Knowersville
                        Guilderland.
Jenkins J.   *Rensselaerville.*
Chittenden O. H.
Murphy R. W.
Falk L.
Brisbin J. H. West-Troy
                        Watervliet.
Himes L. L.   do
Clark R. S.   do
Hastings H. J.   do
Brigham H.   do
Van Miller & Van Sandvoord
                        Cohoes.
Hubbard M.

Allegany County.

Smith Joseph   *Almond.*
Wygant M. L.
Brundage Benj. C.   *Andover.*
Marston Peter
Angell Wm. G.   *Angelica.*
Lloyd Ransom
Grover & Simons
Weatherby & Angel
Hull Andrew J.
Nye A. S.
Collins Charles
Wilson Samuel C.
Norton E. E.
Snow & Tillotson   *Belfast.*
Champlin A.   *Cuba.*
Davidson ——
Hatch Wolcott

Hewett O. W.   *Friendship.*
Prindle F. W. Little Genesee
     Genesee.
Harding E. E.   *Hume*
Stewart W. A.
Hubbard M. G.
Butler W. B. Whitesville
    Independence.
Chase Amos
Laning A. P.   *Rushford.*
Leavens Grover
Walker O. L.
Jones George B.Wellsville *Scio.*
Foster Lewis
Jones Z. H.
Boorn Hiram *West Almond.*

Broome County.

Birdsall & Bartlett *Binghamton.*
Dickinsons & Tompkins
Belden L. O.
Hotchkiss & Seymour
Bates H. R.
Loomis B. N.
Hunt C. H.
Read R.
Morris J.
Mather E. C.
Kattel E. C.
Waterman William M.
Tyler C.
Griswold H. S.
Clapp John
Judd S.
Stewart William,
Stowe W. W.
Badger L. Harpersville *Colesville.*
Barlow J. A.
Hawley J. B.
Faulk J. Nineveh
M'Dowell A. Centre Lisle *Lisle.*
Northrup G. A.   *Union.*
Smith F. B.
Wheeler F. G.   *Windsor.*

Cattaraugus County.

Crocker George A. S. Rutledge
    Conewango.
Harmon & Wood *Ellicottville.*
Washburn C. P.
Fox C. J.
Angel & Crosby
Rice A. G.
Rice & Harrington
Gibbs Ansen
Spring Samuel S. *Franklinville*
M'Luer David
Jewel J. B.   *Machias.*
M'Kay C. G. Eddyville *Mansfield.*
Bunn R.
Fos Pliny L.   *New Albion.*
Howe Chester, Gowanda *Persia.*
Hurd A. H.
Torrence C. C.
Woodbury Wm.
Weeden Joseph E. *Randolph.*
Owen Robert, jr.
Williams Charles
Sheldon Alexander
Miller Wm. R. East Randolph
Chamberlain B. F.

Cayuga County.

Beardsley N. 67 Genesee *Auburn.*
Porter & Beardsley, 67 do
Hopkins P. W. 75 do
Rathbun George, 81 do
Rathbun G. Oscar, 81 do
Cook H. T.   79 do
Pomeroy T. M. 83 do
Wright & Allen, 87 do
Wright D.   87 do
Day F. G.   89 do
Goodwin S. A. 91 do
Warden W. T. 91 do
Andreus D.   91 do
Hall B. F.   95 do
Capron E. W. 95 do
Leland Z. & Co. 95 do
Bronson P.   105 do

How T. Y. jr. 103 Genesee *Auburn.*
Hulbert J. P. 103 do
Settser C. N. 94 do
Morgan & Blatchford, South
Seward Wm. H.   do
Clark & Underwood, 94 Genesee
Giles S. Weedsport *Brutus.*
Cornwell Wm. J. do
Young M.   *Cato.*
Ogden W.   *Conquest.*
Smith W.   *Genoa.*
Humphrey George *Ira.*
Rich G. R.
Stephens N. T. *Locke.*
White O.
Dewey —, Montezuma *Mentz.*
Budlong S. W. do
Robinson D. Port Byron
Bundy & Wells, do
King F. M.   do
Haynes C. W. do
Aikin L. O.   *Moravia.*
Van Auken D. J. *Niles.*
Woods A.   *Scipio.*
Winnegar C. *Springport.*

Chautauque County.

Fenton R. E. Frewsburgh *Carroll.*
Richmond A.   *Charlotte.*
Warren E. F.
Peck E. M.
Sears E. H.
Green W. Mayville, *Chautauque.*
Green G. A. do
Morris L.   do
Osborn T. A. do
Rop A.   *Clymer.*
Hazeltine A. Jamestown *Ellicott.*
Cook Orsell do
Waite F. H. do
Brown S. A. do
Burnell M.   do
Marvin Rich'd P. do
Waite Joseph do
Green Chas. B. *Ellington.*
Jacobs Horatio N.
Spencer E. Forestville *Hanover.*
Sherman D. do
Wilson W. T. do
Ward E. Silver Creek
McDonald J. R. do
Cook —,   do
Leland C. R. Irving
Sackett J.   do
Smith John, Panama *Harmony.*
Sessions Walter B. do
Cottle P. S. Fredonia *Pomfret.*
Barker Geo. do
Kertland E. do
Delvin J. S. do
Snow S.   do
Hoton J.   do
Matteson Chas. F. Fredonia
Grovener Thos. P. do
Risley H. A. do
Cram J.   do
Mullett E. Dunkirk
Strope M.   *Villenova.*
Smith & Chadwick *Westfield.*
Dixon, Parker & Marvin
Hinckley John G.
Hinckley Watson S.
Young Zenas

Chemung County.

Gibbs Wm. H. Havana *Catherine.*
Jackson Hiram W. do
Crawford Marcus do
Meguire J.   do
Quinn Edward, Salubria *Dix.*
Quinn Geo. E. do
Armitage Enoch do
Baskin C. J.   do
Brown Civilian *Elmira.*
Brooks Elijah P.
Brush Geo. A.
Diven Alexander L.
Dunn James
Dunn J. Davis
Fassett Newton C.
Gray Hiram

Gardner Geo. A.   *Elmira.*
Gregg Andrew K
Gregg Isaac B.
Hathaway Samuel G. jr.
Hart Erastus P.
Konkle Aaron
Konkle Wm. P.
Maxwell Thomas
Maxwell U.
North Theodore
Patterson Wm. H.
Robertson A.
Spalding Thomas S.
Simpson A. C.
Thurston Ariel S.
Vanderlyn Peter
Wisner John W.
Woods James L.
Carpenter E. Horse Heads
Jones —,   do
Daily Walter L. Millport *Veteran.*
Smith Gabriel L. do
Phelps Frederick do

Chenango County.

Banks James   *Bainbridge*
Seyer Wm. S.
Clark Henry A.
Maynard A. K. South Bainbridge
Storing Adam   *German.*
Monell & Squiers *Greene.*
Chase Lester
Johnson Alonzo
Foote Erastus E.
Ely Noah   *New Berlin.*
Hyde John
Bennett Henry
Sumner Geo. W
Southwick & Pritchard
Purdy Smith M. *Norwich.*
Cook Abial
Rexford Benjamin F.
Wait John
Smith Geo. M.
Clark Hiram C.
Merritt Sherwood S.
Hyde Henry M.
Carr James M. D.
Hubbard Harvey
Mason William N.
Rexford J. DeWitt
Newton Warren
Johnson Oscar W.
Phelps Hamilton
Grey Daniel
Thorp Charles A.
Prindle H. G.
Johnson E. jr.   *Otselic.*
Baldwin Rufus J. *Oxford.*
Balcom & Clarke
Clapp James
Clapp James jr.
Glover James W.
McKoon Samuel
Mygatt Henry R.
Parker Horace
Perkins G. H.
Tracy John
Van Der Lyn, Henry
Kenyon S. B.   *Pitcher.*
Bourne R. K. Pitcher Spa
Judson Roswell *Sherburne.*
Barnes Ira P.
Fay B W.

Clinton County.

Simmons George A. Keeseville
    Au Sable.
Tomlinson Thomas A.
Finch Martin
Tabor Charles F.
Seeley Frederick
Ames Samuel
M'Lean Campbell
Hubbell Silas   *Champlain.*
Averell Calvin H.
Hubbell Frederick A.
Robbins Horatio G.
Horton H. H. East Chazy *Chazy.*
Johnson —, West do
Armstrong —,   *Mooers*

Watson T. B. *Peru.*
M'Masters D. S. *Plattsburgh.*
Ellsworth P. G.
Averill James
Beckwith S. B. M.
Beckwith G. M.
Johnson H. S.
Stetson L.
Moore George
Moore A. C.
Brock L. D.
M'Neil D. B.
Skinner St. John B. L.
Sweetland Wm.
Nutting L. H.
Woodward J. D.
Hale Wm. F.
Sanborn John H.
Standish George A.
Palmer F. S.
Palmer G. W.
Jones Charles H.
Jones Wm. R.
Allen Horace, *Saranac*

Columbia County.

Snyder J. *Ancram.*
Holdridge A. P. Spencertown
Austerlitz.
Dutcher C. B. do
Babcock B. W. do
Clyde G. Chatham Centre
Chatham.
Bishop P. W. Chatham Four Corners
Hall C. M. do
Payne E. do
Benn E. H. *Claverack.*
Russell A. S.
Van Ness Wm. W. Churchtown
Gallop W. R. *Clermont.*
Hoysradt Wm. W. *Gallatin.*
Gilbert M. *Ghent.*
Payne E.
Baker T. K. *Hillsdale.*
Dorr R. G.
Newkirk J. C. Warren st *Hudson.*
Sanford M. do
Pechtel M. do
Gaul J. jr. 4th st
Stebbins S. L. Warren st
Miller D. cor. Warren & 4th
Miller H. do
Miller K. do
McClellan Robert, Warren st
Suthevlane Josiah, do
Rowley Alex. S. Public Square
Magoun S. L. Warren st
Storm R. B. 300 do
Clarke W. H. 300 do
Monell J. D. do
Monell C. L. do
Monell R. B. do
Miller T. do
Skinner R. P. do
Fairfield J. W. do
Hogeboom & Collier Warren st
Porter Wm. A. do
Peck Darius, do
Cowles E. P. do
Cowles D. S. do
Hoes E. Valatie *Kinderhook.*
Schermerhorn C. P. Valatie
Bulkley G. W. do
Van Schaack D. do
Van Santvoord, do
Toby W. H. do
Reynolds J. H. do
Wilcoxson J. do
Andrews R. E. *Livingston.*
Esselstyne & Welch
Benestell P. H. West Taghkanic
Taghkanic.

Cortland County.

Shankland Wm. H.
Cortland Village.
Hawks Daniel
Ballard H. & A. L.
Reynolds & Crandall
Conger & Thomas

Stephens & Duel *Cortland Village.*
Freer J. D. P.
Ferguson J. H.
Leach Jas. S.
Schamerhorn Jas. A.
Reynolds Lyman
Randall Henry S.
Leal E. M.
Gould Edwin F.

Delaware County.

Douglass A. B. *Andes.*
Morse Richard
King R. *Davenport.*
Becker A.
Murray Wm. jr. *Delhi.*
Allaben J. R.
Gorden Samuel
Edgarton Albert
Youmans Wm. jr.
Moore E. P.
Ten Broeck A. J.
Hatheway C.
Wright P. P.
Parker & Palmer
Parker A.
Palmer E.
Palmer J.
Moore E.
Hughston J. A.
Wheeler T. H.
Johnston S. C.
Mitchell H. L. *Franklin.*
Douglass A.
Wheeler E. F. *Hancock.*
Givens S. A. *Harpersfield.*
Law Samuel A. *Meredith.*
Ten Brouck W. A. Cloverville
Middletown.
Cowles J. C. *Roxbury.*
Monson L. Hobert *Stamford.*
Gleason Wm. jr. do
Champlin W. B. do
Holloway C. T. do
Wheeler W. R. Deposit *Tompkins.*
Lusk Simon do
Palmer F. do
Moores A. C. do
Curtis J. M. do
Wheeler N. K. do

Duchess County.

Sackett L. B. *Beekman.*
Wickam A. D. *Clinton.*
Swift E. M. *Dover.*
Liston J. K. *Fishkill.*
Opple J. W.
Thayer J. S.
Owen I. Mattawan,
Bogardus E. R. Fishkill Landing
Monell & Owen, do
Stoutenburgh J. A. *Hyde Park.*
Bowman O. T. Lafayette Corners
Milan.
Roe A. *North East.*
Peck R. *Pine Plains.*
Eno W.
Eno W. Stewart
Swift C. W. 39 Market
Poughkeepsie.
Swift Henry, 39 do
Varick & Eldridge, do
Buttolph E. A. do
Davis B. D. do
Thompson & Weeks, 24 do
Barnard F. W. & I. F. 18 Market
Corliss C. R. 16 do
Emott James, jr. 14 do
Mason L. 14 do
Dodge & Campbell, 14 do
Tallman John P. H. do
Northrop L. M. 29 do
Dean G. 29 do
Herrick A. R. 27 do
Swan C. 27 do
Forbus Alexander, 21 do
Ruggles Charles J. 21 do
Cole Ulysses, 21 do
Jewett Jacob B. 21 do
Barnard R. 7 Liberty
Street W. J. 9½ Garden

Heermans Benjamin M.
Poughkeepsia
Jackson J. H. 11 Garden
Paine G. W. 11 do
Angvine Henry, 8½ do
Coffin & Van Wyck, 10 Garden
Wilkinson R. & W. 10½ do
Elsheier J. *Red Hook*
Wager A. *Rhinebeck.*
McCarty J. C.
Armstrong J.
Conger M.
Brewer William, Stanfordville
Stanford.

Erie County.

Thayer — Williamsville, *Amherst.*
Paul James C. Willink, *Aurora.*
Johnson Wm. C. do
Carver Lafayette, do
Sawen Albert, do
Humphrey Jas. M. do
Graves Lewis W. do
Brown John F. do
Bull Absalom, *Black Rock.*
Hatch J. H. do
Clark S. S. *Boston.*
Austin & Scraggs, 162 Main
Buffalo.
Babcock & Welch, cor. Canal,
Dock & Lloyd
Baker A. L. 6 Seneca
Barton Hiram, 155 Main
Beattie D. C. 164 do
Bliss John H. 196 do
Brown John F. Post-office Buildings
Brown L. 147 Main
Burrows R. L. cor. Main and West
Seneca
Cameron Hugh, 163 Main
Chamberlain S. M. Spaulding's
Exchange
Clarke Charles E. Post-office
Building
Clinton & Tibbetts, 164 Main
Cook E. & E. 158 do
Crocker James, 162 do
Daniels Charles, 4 Exchange
Davis Cyrus E. 23 Spaulding's
Exchange
Davis Wm. 190 Main
Day H. C. Post-office Buildings
Dudley Thomas J. jr. Spaulding's
Exchange
Efner E. D. cor. Maine and West
Seneca
Evans Ellicott, Spaulding's Exchange
Fenner Channing G. 84 Exchange
Flanders H. 190 Main
Fobes G. P. Spaulding's Exchange
Ganson John, do
Germain Rollin, do
Gibbs A. 162 Main
Goodrich H. A. 230½ Main
Gold G. K. cor. Seneca and Main
Gould S. O. 162 Main
Graham James H. 156 do
Green & Sheldon, North Division
Haddock L. R. 190 Main
Halbert & Cass, 156 do
Hall & Bowen, Spaulding's Exc
Harris A. C. 162 Main
Hawley Elias S. 190 do
Hecox Wm. H. 190 do
Hill J. F. Spaulding's Exchange
Hoffman Phocion, 4 Exchange
Hopkins Nelson K. 4 do
Hopkins Timothy A. Court-house
Houghton & Sprague, 148 Main
Hubbell John, 27 Spaulding's Exchange
Hudson & Smith, over Post-office
Lapp C. N. 385 Main
Lewis L. L. 278½ do
Lockwood Stephen, 179 Main
Macomber C. S. cor Seneca &
Main
Mallory James A. 234½ Main
Mann Wm. W. 7 & 8 Spaulding's
Exchange

Marshall O. H. 163 Main *Buffalo.*
Marvin Le Grand & George L. 156 Main
Mason & Green, 190 do
Masten Joseph G. Spaulding's Exchange
M'Cumber Orlando, 156 Main
M'Nett A. J. 155   do
Metz & Harvey, Spaulding's Exchange
Miller Wm. F. 162 Main
Nichols A. P. 268½ do
Norton Charles D. 163 do
Parker & Baldwin, 152 do
Peacock Wm. W. 4 Exchange
Pool & Cutting, 155 Main
Potter & Howard. 258½ do
Putnam James O. 7 & 8 Spaulding's Exchange
Rogers & Cutting. 190 Main
Sanders & Coe, 4 Exchange
Seymour Horatio, jr. 234½ Main
Shepard C. E. 4 Exchange
Sizer Thomas J. Spaulding's Exchange
Smith & Verplank,   do.
Smith W L. G. 152 Main
Smith Wm. C. 26 Spaulding's Exchange
Spaulding E. G.   do
Stevens F. P.   do
Stewart & Stevens. 190 Main
Talcott & Love, 164   do
Tanner & Le Clear, 3 Terrace
Tillinghast Dyer, Spaulding's Exchange
Thompson A. H.   do
Thompson B. 175 Main
Vanderpool J. V. over Post-office
Vedder E. B. 4 Exchange
Viele Henry K. 26 Spaulding's Exchange
Vosburg P. M. Post-office Buildings
Wadsworth J. 163 Main
Walker Horatio N. 146 do
Wilbur J. B. 147   do
Wilcox H. N. 156 Main
Williams & Hibbard, 4 Exchange
Williams & Shumway, 13 Spaulding's Exchange
Hull Edmond   *Clarence.*
Severence Chas. C. Springville
          Concord.
Fosdick Morris,   do
Redfield H. J.   *Eden.*
Welch Nelson,
Thorn Abram, Center *Hamburgh.*
Irish J. E. Water Valley
Hunt ——
Bush Wm. T   *Tonawanda.*

Essex County.

Watson Winslow C. Port Kent
          Chesterfield.
Wilkins Joseph B. *Crown Point.*
Fenton Chauncy
Hand A. C.   *Elizabethtown.*
Kellogg & Hall
Mc Vine & Livingston
Cuyler Edward T.
Blanchard Cyrus L.
Dwyer Samuel C.
Higbee Wm.
Pond B. & A.
Nicholson Martin F.
Ross H. H.   *Essex.*
Shumway E. &.
Havens P. E.
Cheney Charles
Whitley Joseph, Ausable Forks
          Jay.
Trumbull T. D.
Butler James P. Moriah 4 corners
          Moriah.
Butler Philander,   do
Ravens J. F.   do
Waldo A. B. Port Henry
Tarbell Jonathan,   do
Crossett H. G. Schroon Lake
          Schroon.

Rawson B. P. Schroon Lake
          Schroon.
Potter J. F.   do
Burnet Jonathan, *Ticonderoga.*
Clough Moses T.
Haight Augustus
Andrews G. R.
Calkins Wm.
Aikins Asa   *Westport.*
Wicker J. C.

Franklin County.

Crary Nathan   *Bangor.*
Smith E. B.   *Chateaugay.*
Keeler E. A.
Douglass Landon,
Paddock Henry A.*Fort Covington.*
Parkhurst Jab'z
Wallace ——
Spencer J. C.
Fisk P. B.
Jackson Joseph H.   *Malone.*
Hutton John
Flanders Joseph R.
Wheeler W. A.
Foote R. G.
Parmelee A. B.
Fitch Edward
Conant Marshall
Miriam Horace
Seaver J. J.
Hobbs Albert
Taylor Horace
Wright Thomas, jr. West Constable   *Westville.*

Fulton County.

Johnson Nathan J.   *Broadalbin.*
McFarlan Wm.
Kennedy Wm.
Carrol J. M.
Montieth J. D. L.
Banker John   *Ephratah.*
Cady Daniel   *Johnstown.*
Wells John
Dodge William L
Frothingham John
Cady John W.
Haring Aaron
Brooks Peter
Cady Daniel B.
Fraser McIntyre
McMartin Martin
Stewart Duncan McIntyre
Cameron Daniel
Akin Ethan
Chamberlain Benj.
Cuyler Joseph
Wait Wm. Vails Mills *Mayfield.*
Kinnicutt James H. Mayfield Corners
Ayres A. Hamilton, Northville
          Northampton.
Grinnell C. S.
Gleason Wesley
Dudley J. M.   *Oppenheim.*

Genesee County.

Smith Richard   *Batavia.*
Tracy P. L.
Lay G. W.
Redfield H. J.
Brown J. L.
Glowackie H. J.
Wakeman S.
Fitch T.
Lay J. F.
Young B.
Pringle B.
Dibble E. C.
Tigart M.
Martindale J. H.
Bryon W. C.
Hewitt M. W.
Wilber H.
Soper H. U.
Robertson M. F.
Pringle E.
Kimberly J. H.
Bartow Alfred F.   *Le Roy.*
Skinner & Bissell

Hascall & Bangs   *Le Roy.*
Danforth Charles
Barton Charles
Olmstead J. R.
Hascall H. W.
Brown George W.   *Oakfield.*

Greene County.

Teshune W. F.   *Athens*
Mattoon Peleg   *Caire*
Day Caleb   *Catskill*
Van Vleck John & Pruyn
Adams & King
Murdock Alexander
Van Orden Wm. H.
Dorlon R.
Parker James
Beach Linley Z.
Powers & Day
Person Edward   *Coxsackie.*
Van Dyck Jacob C.
Silvester Peter H.
Cornwall Augustus
Leete William E.
Brouck John B.
Gilbert W. Cumming   *Durham.*
Tremaine Lyman
Winant Heman   *Prattsville.*
Fitch F. J. & J. S.
Olney D. K. & J.   *Windham.*

Herkimer County.

Judd Geo. B.   *Frankfort.*
Cleland E. T.
Macauley James
Marsh Ely T.
Judd Garwood L.
Hamilton Ira E. E. Ilion
          German Flats.
Owen Volney, Mohawk
Prescott Amos H.   do
Monk David F.   do
Wightman J. N.   do
Burton Chas. A.   *Herkimer.*
Rasbach John A.
Gray Chas.
Earl S. & R.
Graves Ezra
Hoffman Michael, jr.
Underwood John C.
Loomis A.   *Little Falls.*
Nolton & Brooks
Benton & Barrett
Lake J. N. & D.
Ford & Waterman
Capron & Link
Feeter Geo. H.
Cramer J. G.   *Russia.*
Smith E. W. Centre   *Salisbury.*
Buckingham C. Van Hornsville
          Stark.

Jefferson County.

Thompson W. C.   *Adams.*
Skinner C.
Saunders T. P.
Brown L. H.
Sherman & Maxson
Wright Benjamin
Rogers C. W.
Wager Western W.   *Brownville.*
Priest De Witt & Co.
Ainsworth S. R.   *Cape Vincent.*
Clarke Charles E.   *Champion.*
Hubbard Stephen J.
Hawes B. & C. Bellville
          Ellisburgh.
Davis A. A.   *Henderson.*
Ford A. Sacketts Harbor
          Houndsfield.
Ford C. W. Sacketts Harbor
Burnham D. N.   do
Van Vleck Isaac,   do
Dickey J. O.   do
Boyden N. B.   do
Clarke Chas. E. Great Bend
          Le Ray
Tamblin John W. Evans Mills
Nims Allen   do
Boyer Joseph   do
Brown Parley   *Lorraine.*

Bentley John   *Lorraine.*
Bagley & Wright, Watertown
      Pamelia.
Wager D. J.   *Philadelphia.*
Lewis E. W.   *Theresa.*
Gibbs A. C.
Mullin & Goodale   *Watertown.*
Sherman Geo. C.
Starbuck & Hungerford
Dutton John H.
Ingalls Lotus
Moore Joshua. jr.
Barnes Rodolphus
Darwin Luther J.
Wilson Alexander
Sherman Wooster
Clarke & Calvin
Chittenden Thomas C.
Chittenden Thomas C. jr.
Gilbert Albert B.
Emerson Frederick
Bucklin G. M. Carthage   *Wilna.*
Hammond T. S.

Kings County.

Callicott T. Cary, 339 Gold
      Brooklyn.
Campbell James L. 6 Montague
 Hall
Church R. S. 135 Hudson Av.
Cooper Geo. H. Montague Hall
Cortelyon John. 3 Front
Dawson Rodman B. 98 Fulton
Dikeman Frank H. 70   do
Dikeman John, Montague Hall
Dikeman John. jr.   do
Dunga G. & B. 3 Front
Garrison Samuel. Montague Hall
Greene W. A. City Hall
Greenwood Joseph M. 3 Front
Hammond Alonzo B. Montague
 Hall
Hammond Burton G. 3   do
Haynes & Stoddard, 3 Front
Ingraham Richard, Montague
 Hall
Johnson & Fonda, 1 Front
King John B. 6 Montague Hall
Kissam & Underhill, 14 Atlantic
Lewis & Curtis, 128   do
Lott, Murphy & Vanderbilt, 3
 Front
Lowry C. J. 83 Fulton
Lynde C. R. 211 do
Martense & Morse, 1 Front
Moore H. A. 83 Fulton
Morehouse B. S. 58 Atlantic
Robinson John O. Green Point
Rockwell Wm. 35 Willoughby
Rogers Sidney P. cor. Atlantic
 & Henry
Rolfe & Trembly, 3 Front
Smith C. P. 83 Fulton
Smith John C. 94 Myrtle Av.
Spooner Alden J. 3 Front
Stanton P. V. R. 3   do
Van Brunt N. 1 Front
Voorhees J. 45 Fulton
Wering N. F. 48 do
Winslow R. C. 3 Front
Berry John, 3 S. 7th
      Williamsburgh.
Boughton Joseph, 140 4th
Briggs C. M. 108 Grand
Egan Daniel, 38 S. 7th
Fish P. J. 137 4th
Hamilton P. 9th near 3d
Hodges Wm. H. 124 S. 1st
Jennings Ebenezer, 127 Grand
Maurice James, 163   do
Meeker S. M. 87 4th
Prime Wm. C. S. 9th
Richards Wm. 137 4th
Shapter P. 101   do
Soper A. D. 108 Grand
Stearns J.M. 95 4th
Thompson George, 108 Grand

Lewis County.

Merrill L. Copenhagen, *Denmark.*
Bennett D. M.   *Martinsburgh.*

Barnes A. H.   *Martinsburgh.*
Scovill C. P.
Brown Edward A.   *Turin.*
Lahe John, Constableville
      West Turin.

Livingston County.

Hosmer W. H. C. & G.   *Avon.*
Dann Amos
Cooley John B.
McMartin J.   *Caledonia.*
Alger James   *Conesus.*
Faulkner E.   *Dansville.*
Hubbard & Bulkley
Harwood & Wilkinson
Hicks R. F.
Van Derlip & Endrus
Frazer & Abbott
Dorr R. L.
O'Brien E.
Bryant D. C.
Bennett J. W
Bogue H. V.
Cook & Avery
Stevens M.
Proctor L. B.
Wood & Chamberlin   *Geneseo.*
Augell B. F.
Tracy F.
Hamilton Wm. J.
Lord Scott
Hendee & Guiteau
Kelsey W. H.
Bryan C. H.
Kershner J.
Wood H. J.   *Lima.*
Davidson C. C.
Smith Lewis E.   *Livonia.*
Northrop Sam'l H. Hemlock Lake
Wisner & Adams   *Mount Morris.*
Seymour McNiel
Hastings Geo.
Miller Anthony G.
Mills Wm.
Barto H. D. jr.
Peck Luther C.   *Nunda.*
Bagley Benedict
Barber Andrew
Chalker Henry
Bishop G. W.
Woodruff P. Scottsburgh *Sparta.*
Collins Wm. E.   *York.*

Madison County.

Gray Geo. W.   *Brookfield.*
Hinckley Geo. W. Leonardsville
Hough Wm. J.   *Cazenovia.*
Feirchild Sidney T.
Stobbins Chas.
Thomas Richard
Paddock H. Graves
Lincklaen Ledyard
Wendel B. Rush
Stebbins Chas. jr.
Miner H. C.   *De Ruyter.*
Bentley A. V.
Brown & Kennedy, Morrisville
      Eaton.
Holmes S. T.   do
Foote N.   do
Holmes E.   do
Bentley Z. T.   do
Sloan A. S.   do
Granger O. P   do
Kinney Wm. H.   do
Nye & Whittemore   *Hamilton.*
Foote John
Goodwin & Mitchell
Sheldon A. N.
Eldredge J. B.
Church S. E.
Mason Joseph
Mason Charles
Sloan J. C. Oneida Depot, *Lenox.*
Barlow & Snow, Canastota
Seber A. J.   do
Goodell Wm. W.   do
Fowler L.   do
Loomis T. T. Wampsville
De Ferriere C. J.   do
Seeber J. A.   do

Chapman B. F. Clockville, *Lenox.*
Chapman Stephen   do
Stone A. C. Peterboro *Smithfield.*
Huntington Nehemiah, Peterboro
Curtis G. T.   do
Temple M.   *Stockbridge.*
Lansing W. E. Chittenango
      Sullivan
Walrath D. D.   do
Stower John G.   do
Kennedy C. L.   do

Monroe County.

Jewett S. B. & Selden, Clarkson
 Corners   *Clarkson.*
Clarke J. L. Clarkson Corners
Shuart D.G.West Mendon *Mendon*
Polk Charles   do
Patterson John E.   *Parma.*
Townsend G. P.   *Penfield.*
Bellows Ira   *Pittsford.*
Goss E.
Abram James, 2 Arcade Exchange
      Rochester.
Adams H. B. 5 Buffalo
Adams L.   5 do
Beach Daniel B. 17 Buffalo
Bennett J. B. 32 Smith's Arcade
Bishop W. S. Smith's Arcade
Boughton Selleck. 83 do
Bowne, Benedict & Husbands, 2
 Arcade Exchange
Bowen John J. 7 Reynolds' Arcade
Breck William, 17 Buffalo
Bush J. S. 4 Reynolds' Arcade
Campbell James C. 15 Arcade
 Exchange
Chapin Moses, 37 Exchange
Chase Wm. 41 Main
Clarke Charles H. 6 Reynolds'
 Arcade
Clarke Charles L. 36 State
Clark R. B. 7 City Hall
Cogswell W. F. 16 Buffalo
Danforth Geo. F. 42 State
Davis Zimri L. 14 Arcade Ex-
 change
Dwinelle John W. 15   dc
Dwinello Samuel H. 16   do
Ely Alfred, Smith's Block, Buffalo
Ely Alexander,   do   do
Ely George,   do   do
Ferry Lorenzo, 8 Arcade Gallery
Fitzhugh Wm. A. 17 Buffalo
Frothingham F. 18 Arcade Ex-
 change
Gay Horace, Carthage Flats
Gibbons Washington, 14 Arcade
 Exchange
Griffin Ebenezer, 2 State
Haight Robert. 6 Arcade Gallery
Hamilton Theodore B. 6   do
Hastings & Newton, 42 State
Hastings Truman, 31 Buffalo
Hotch H. 25 State
Hopkins E. A. 86 Buffalo
Hovey L. H. 43 Main, Globe
 Buildings
Humphrey Harvey, 16 Buffalo
Hunter Henry, 3 Arcade Gallery
Husband Thomas B. 71 Buffalo
Huson & Porter,   4   do
Ide E. 33 Smith's Arcade
Jerome H. R. 2 State
Jordan Christopher, 71 Exchange
King & Hyde, 2 State
Laing D. Smith's Block. Buffalo
Lathrop A. Globe Buildings, Main
Lee & Farrar, Gould's Building,
 14½ State
M'Alpine B. D. 20 Buffalo
M'Alpine B. R. 20   dc
Matthews Selah, 71   dc
Miller Samuel,1 Reynolds' Arcade
Mudge A. G. 33 Smith's   do
Nash Chauncey, 37 do   do
Paine & Cochran, 8 City Hall
Perry Chauncey, 19 Arcade Gal-
 lery
Pomeroy E. 55 State
Sargent H. 86 Buffalo

Selden H. R. 5 Reynolds' Arcade *Rochester.*
Sherwood Anson, 83 Smith's do
Smith E. D. 2 State
Smith Hiram C. 3 Arcade Exchange
Smith L. W. 36 Smith's Arcade
Thompson J. jr. 5 Reynolds' do
Tryon James S. 6 Arcade Exchange
Ward L. 36 State
Wentworth A. N. 4 Stone's Block cor. Main & St. Paul
Wentworth D. N. do
Wheeler E. B. do
Whittlesey Frederick. 16 Buffalo
Wood Daniel, 1 Arcade Exchange
Fuller J. 10 Main, Brockport *Sweden.*
Downs Wm. T. 24 Main
Holmes E. B. do
Fuller Jerome, do
Palmer Isaac, 3d. do
Thomas H. J. do
Wheeler S. do
Norton H. P. do
Rogers Chas. M. *Webster.*
Brown D. D. S. Scottsville *Wheatland.*
Dorr J. do

Montgomery County.
Carey David P. *Amsterdam.*
Patterson Culver
Cochran Clark B.
Heath Solomon F.
Sheldon Alexander
Van Derveer John W.
Belding Samuel
Wilcox Lester *Canayoharie.*
Cook James H.
Riggs Hiram
Wetmore J. F.
Mitchell & Sacia
Smith George
Lathrop R. R.
Wetmore P.
Cummings John
Randall Phineas, Ames
Putnam C. H. *Glenn.*
Van Vectian Giles F. Fultonville
Fish F. do
Fish H. do
Adams Henry C. Fort Plain *Minden.*
Adams Henry do
Darrow John do
Yost & Lobdell do
Wendle Jacob do
Holt Daniel do
Crouse George do
Stocker William D. do
Wagnor Peter J. do
Webster Peter G. do
Webster Charles W. do
Cushney & Fergusson. Fonds *Mohawk.*
Schenck E. T. do
Semmons Stephen do
Degroff J. D. do
Loucks H. Palatine Bridge *Palatine.*
Loucks Samuel do
Hees Abraham do
Mitchell John A. *St. Johnsville.*
Baker H.

New York County.
Ackley Wm. B. 9 Wall *New York.*
Adams Francis, 11 Nassau
Adams Robert A. 11 Nassau
Adriance Isaac, 69 Nassau
Aitken John, 9 Nassau
Aitken William B. 6 Broad
Alexander Henry M. 11 Nassau
Alker Henry, 27 Beekman
Allen Augustus, 15 Wall
Allen William M. 87 Wall
Allen William M. 75 & 77 Nassau
Allen Horatio, 15 Wall

Allen William, 87 Wall *New York.*
Allen, Hudson & Campbell, 15 Wall
Alley John, 38 Wall
Amerman Jacob K. 52 John
Anderson Abel T. 142 Broadway
Anderson John, jr. 20 Beekman
Andrews John, 54 Wall
Andrews Robert W. 74 Wall
Androus G. P. 71 Wall
Angus Robert, 7 Nassau
Angus & Dubois. 7 Nassau
Anson Alonson. 33 Wall
Anthon John. 51 Liberty
Anthon William H. 51 Liberty
Appleby Charles Edgar, 51 Liberty
Armstrong William H. 79 Nassau
Arthur John, 4 Hanover
Arnould H. S. 2 Well
Ashley Joseph C. 54 Wall
Ashley Lucien S. 77 Nassau
Atwater Isaac, 75 & 77 Nassau
Auld J. B. 75 & 77 Nassau
Austin William, 79 Nassau
Austin & Campbell, 79 Nassau
Bade Albert, 4 New
Bagley S. V. rear 75 & 77 Nassau
Bailey John F. 9 Chambers & 221 Broome
Baker Daniel I. 11 Nassau
Baker Gookin, 10 Wall
Baker John, 76 Wall
Baldwin Daniel, 16 Wall
Baldwin James M 20 Nassau
Baldwin D. A. 9 Nassau
Balch Thomas, 5 Nassau
Balestier Joseph N. 2 Wall
Bangs Francis N. 20 Nassau
Banks William G. 15 Centre
Banta Matthias, 62 Wall
Barber William, 10 do
Barker Isaac O. 134 Nassau
Barker Smith. 15 Beekman
Barlow Jason H. 75 & 77 Nassau
Barlow Samuel L. M. 76 Merch. Exchange
Barnard Daniel P. 16 Wall
Barnard & Parsons, 16 do
Barney Hiram, 29 do
Barney & Butler, 29 do
Barrett William C. 10 do
Bayard William M. 10 do
Beadle Delos W. 74 Broadway
Beck Folker J. 64 Wall
Beckwith Henry. 62 do
Beebe Welcome R. 76 do
Beebe & Donohue, 76 do
Belknap Aaron B. 23 & 25 do
Belknap D. P. 64 John
Bell John, 52 Wall
Bell William H. 52 John
Bell Samuel P. 52 John
Bellows Charles T. 40 Wall
Benedict Abner. 27 do
Benedict Charles L. 70 do
Benedict Erastus C. 70 do
Benedict James L. 52 John
Benedict & Boardman, 25 Nassau
Benedict Jesse W. 25 do
Benedict & Belknap, 64 John
Benner Robert, 75 & 77 Nassau
Bennett William, 140 Broadway
Benton Lewis, 58 Wall
Betts William C. 52 do
Bidwell Marshall S. 66 do
Bigelow John, 61 do
Billinge Benjamin L. 110 Chambers & 95 Av. C
Bishop Edward E. 22 Chambers
Bishop Edward W. 22 do
Bissell John, 11 Wall
Black Charles N. 3 do
Blackford Wm. H. 75 Nassau
Blackwell William B. 78 do
Blake James C. 18 Chambers
Blatchford Edgecombe H. 1 Hanover
Blatchford Richard M. 1 do
Bliss Francis C. 136 Nassau
Bliss William, 90 do
Bloomer Elisha, 79 do
Bloomfield William, 90 do

Blunt Joseph, 11 Wall *New York.*
Blunt Nathaniel B. 25 Chambers
Boardman Andrew, 25 Nassau
Bogardus Alonzo, 75 & 77 Nassau
Bogardus Archibald R. 8 City Hall pl
Bogardus William H. 8 do
Bogert Cornelius, 192 Broadway
Bogert Henry A. 19 Wall
Bogert Horatio, 192 Broadway
Bonney Benjamin W. 36 Wall
Bonney & Roe, 38 do
Bosworth Joseph S. 51 Liberty
Boudinot Henry C. 140 Broadway
Boughton, Ward & Sparks, 62 John
Bovee Christian N. 36 Wall
Bowdoin George R. J. Merchants' Exchange
Bowdoin James & Barlow, 76 do
Bowen James, 8 Wall
Bowly Daniel, Law Department, City Hall & 75 & 77 Nassau
Bowman George, 4 Hanover
Bowman James F. 4 do
Bowne Richard H. 62 Wall
Boyd John. 23 do
Boyle Edward, 54 do
Brackett Joseph W. 11 do
Bradford Alexander W. 79 Nassau
Bradley Alvin C. 62 Wall
Bradley, Mills & Beckwith, 62 Wall
Bradshaw George, 52 John
Bradshaw Hamilton, 67 Wall
Brady Henry A. 37 do
Brady James T. 10 do
Brady John F. 4 New
Brady John R. 10 Wall
Brainard Roswell C. 16 Wall
Brewer Merwin R. 50 do
Brewster Henry, 75 & 77 Nassau
Brewster Mason S. 75 & 77 do
Bromley I. W. R. 49 William
Bronson Charles, 79 Nassau
Brown A. P. 47 Wall
Brooks Benj. S. 54 do
Broply Stephen B. 54 do
Brown Augustus L. 25 Chambers
Brown Daniel B. 20 Beekman
Brown Elias G. 40 Wall
Brown Franklin, 75 Nassau
Brown Samuel, 53 Wall
Brown David F. 16 do
Brown B. Franklin, 17 do
Bronson F. 38 William
Bronson A. 38 do
Brush David H. 116 do
Brush James H. 116 do
Bryan Frederick H. B. 28 Chambers
Bryan John A. 65 Wall
Buckham George. 5 do
Buckley T. C. T. 79 Nassau
Bulkeley Josh. 272 Pearl
Bulkeley Lucius E. 14 Wall
Burchard John D. 10 do
Burch Thos. H. 54 do
Burger T. P. 262 Broadway
Burke Frederick W. 127 Fulton
Burke Michael, 44 Wall
Burling Cornelius A. 34 Liberty
Burlock Horton H. 75 Nassau
Burr Edwin, 70 Wall
Burrall Charles, 96 Merchants' Exchange
Burrill Alexander M. 78 Nassau
Burrill John E. jr. 2 Nassau
Burrowes Philip, 44 Wall
Burt Addison M. 54 do.
Bushnell Charles I. 65 do
Bushnell George W. 5 Nassau
Bushnell & Dloesy, 5 do
Bushnell Orsamus, 20 do
Busteed Richard, 45 William
Busteed G. W. sen. 45 do
Butler Aaron, jr. 140 Nassau
Butler Benjamin F. 39 Wall
Butler Charles, 20 Nassau
Butler Charles E. 2 Hanover
Butler George B. 54 Wall
Butler Hiram, 140 Nassau

Butler William A. 29 Wall *New York.*
Butterworth J. F. 87 Merchants' Exchange
Butterworth S. F. 38 Exchange
Byrne Francis, 6 City Hall place
Byrne Henry H. 136 Nassau
Cady Francis, 19 Wall
Cady Howard C. 74 do
Callicot T. Carey, 43 William
Callaghan Patrick, 14½ Pine
Cambreleng Stephen, 18 Wall
Camp Enoch E. 89 Centre
Campbell Anthony P. 29 Wall
Campbell John D. 35 Wall
Campbell Matthew. 11 Wall
Campbell Robert B. 72 Wall
Campbell Robert G. 79 Nassau
Campbell Samuel, 11 Wall
Campbell William W. 52 John
Campbell & Hinsdale, 35 Wall
Capwell Albert B. 72 Wall
Carnes Fred. G. 66 Wall
Carpenter George, 12 Chambers
Carpentier Edward R. 136 Nassau
Carpentier James S. 20 Beekman
Carr Andrew S. 106 Broadway
Carter William B. 29 Wall
Cary Jeremiah C. 11 Wall
Casserly Eugene, 69 Nassau
Catlin Charles T. 14 Pine
Catlin George, 14 Pine
Chadwick Stephen F. 19 Wall
Channing William H. 136 Nassau
Chapman Lebbeus, jr. 38 Wall
Chase Nelson, 1 New
Chatfield David J. 61 Wall
Chedsey Nathan A. 176 Fulton
Chester Elisha W. 54 Wall
Chester Geo. F. 54 Wall
Child Asa, 11 Nassau
Christie & Mather, 43 Wall, Jauncey court
Chrystie William F. 51 William
Churchill Franklin H. 18 Wall
Claggett Rufus, 35 Wall
Clark Edward, 5 Nassau
Clark J. Farley, 69 Wall
Clark Edward P. 2 Wall
Clark Gerardus, 50 Wall
Clark Horace F. 55 Wall
Clark Lott C. 78 Mer. Exchange
Clark Alexander, 2 Wall
Clark Wm. F. 77 Mer. Exchange
Clarke Bayard. 8 Wall
Clarke Daniel W. 20 Chambers
Clarkson Samuel F. 75 & 77 Nassau
Clason & English, 23 and 25 Wall
Cleaveland John, 38 Wall
Cleaveland & Titus, 38 Wall
Clerke Thomas, 11 Wall
Clerke Thomas W. 11 Wall
Clift Smith, 44 Nassau
Clinton Charles A. 6 Broad
Clinton Henry L. 80 Nassau
Cochran John, 52 John
Cochran Robert, 64 John
Coddington David S. 17 Wall
Coddington Jonathan S. jr. 17 Wall
Codwise David, 51 Liberty
Coe Frederick A. 52 John
Coit Joshua, 11 Wall
Coit William, 9 Nassau
Cole Jacob, 140 Broadway and 757 Greenwich
Coles John B. jr. 76 Nassau
Comstock Nathan, jr. 9 Chambers
Cone Edward W. 61 Wall
Coalan C. J. 1 Nassau
Conger Abraham B. 20 Nassau
Cook Henry G. 16 Wall
Cook John, 20 Cliff
Cook William G. 142 Fulton
Cooper John M. 20 Chambers
Coppinger John B. 70 Wall and 64 Orchard
Coren A. E. 235 Broadway
Corlies Alfred W. 23 Wall
Cornell George J. 69 Wall
Corning Alfred H. 5 Nassau
Covington William B. 38 William
Covert Richard D. 74 Wall

Cowdrey David M. 13 Chambers *New York.*
Cowdrey Peter A. 67 Wall
Cowdrey Samuel F. 67 Wall
Cowenhoven William H. 36 Nassau
Cowles Edward E. 12 Wall
Cowles Henry B. 12 Wall
Craft William D. 79 Nassau
Craig D. Samuel, 20 Chambers
Cram Henry A. 69 Wall
Crane L. H. 14 Wall
Crapo Samuel A. 3 Hanover
Crawford Joseph, 42 John
Crist Abraham, 14 Wall
Cromwell Charles T. 68 Wall
Crooke Philip S. 29 Wall
Crosby Elisha, 27 Wall
Crosby John F. 1 Hanover
Cruger Henry D. 54 Broadway
Cudlipp Reuben H. 9 Chambers
Cummins J. S. Lane, 11 Nassau
Cummins & Alexander, 11 Nassau
Cunningham Frederick, 47 Wall
Cuppaldge James F. 27 Chambers
Curtis Edw. 9 Wall & 74 Broadw'y
Curtis George, 8 Wall
Curtis William E. 54 Wall
Cushman J. Newland, 73 Nassau
Cutler Peter Y. 77 Mer. Exchange
Cutler & Townsend, 77 Merchants' Exchange
Cutten Morris K. 54 Wall
Cutter William T. 2 Hanover
Cutting Francis B. 72 Wall
Cutting Walter L. 70 Wall
Dakin Samuel D. 2 Hanover
Daly Charles P. 20 Nassau
Dana Alexander H. 63 Wall
Daniels Byron G. 80 Nassau
Darlington Thomas, 14 Wall
Davidson Morris M. 49 William
Davies Henry E. 66 Wall
Davis Samuel, 35 Wall
Davison Charles A. 71 Wall
Day Henry, 83 Mer. Exchange
Dayton Isaac, 75 and 77 Nassau
Deagle Lorenzo D. P. 18 Bowery
Dean George, 64 Wall
De Forest Frederick L. 54 Wall
De Forest Henry G. 56 Wall
De Forest William H. 90 Wall
Deklyn Barent, 13 Chambers
Delany Charles Mc. C. 59 Nassau
Delaplaine John F. 7 New
Delaplaine John F. jr. 7 New
Delavan Edward C. 25 Nassau
Demotte Mortimer, 192 Broadway & 5 John
Dennison Robert, 27 Fulton
De Peyster Frederick, 11 Pine
Derry Edmond S. 142 Fulton
Develin John E. 11 Wall
Devereux John C. 76 Nassau
Dewey Horace M. 11 Nassau
Dewitt J. N. L. 29 Wall
Dewitt C. John 88 Nassau
Dewitt Edward, 88 Nassau
Dewitt C. Graham, 20 Beekman
Dewitt Peter 88 Nassau
Dey Anthony, 51 Liberty
Dibbles Frederick, 14 Wall
Diblee Thomas B. 76 Nassau
Dickinson Alfred, 70 Wall
Dill James, 49 William
Dillon John B. 45 William
Dillon Robert J. 30 Wall
Dillon Romaine, 30 Wall
Dinnies Chas. F. 184 Fulton
Diossy Addison S. 41 Wall
Disosway Cornelius R. 33 John
Ditmars Abraham D. 45 William
Dodd Thomas C. 2 Wall
Dodge Henry S. 19 Wall
Dodge & Van Santvoord 19 Wall
Dodge Robert 43 Wall
Dodge William, 72 Wall
Doherty C. H. 221 Cherry
Doherty John, 70 Wall
Dominick Francis, 4 Hanover
Donnelly Edward C. 12 Wall
Donohue Charles, 26 Beekman

Dorr Francis O. 9 Wall *New York.*
Dorr Francis F. 14 Wall
Dorr Henry C. 51 William
Dorr James A. 69 Wall
Dougherty C. H. 221 Cherry
Dowling George D. 140 Bowery
Doyle John T. 5 Wall
Dresser Horace, 79 Nassau
Drake John, 90 Merchants' Exchange
Drinker William W. 552 Greenwich & 65 Chambers
Duer John, 52 Wall
Dubois Jacob, 7 Nassau
Dunscomb William E. 27 Vesey
Dunlap S. F. 37 Wall, Jauncey court
Dusenbury E. 72 Wall
Dusenbury Wm. H. 8 Wall
Dustin D. H. 41 Wall
Duryees John T. 15 Wall
Dyckman William N. 127 Fulton
Dyett Anthony R. 7 Chambers
Dykers Francis H. 56 Wall
Ebbetts William H. 29 Wall
Eckel Christian G. 11 Wall
Eddy Lathrop S. 44 Wall
Edgar Jonathan, 25 Nassau
Edgerton Edward A. 64 John
Edson Clement M. 1 Hanover
Edwards Charles, 52 Wall
Edwards Jonathan, 74 Broadway
Edwards Ogden, 67 Wall
Edwards Walter, 64 Wall
Edwards & Moran, 64 Wall
Edwards Wm. H. 40 Wall
Egan Charles C. 36 Wall
Eldredge Nathaniel T. 49 William
Ellingwood N. Dane, 9 Nassau
Ellis Chesselden, 71 Wall
Ellsworth Judiah, 170 Broadway
Ellsworth & Letson, 170 Broadw.
Elmendorf Edmund, jr. 14½ Pine
Elting Wm. H. 75 and 77 Nassau
Ely Elias H. 68 Fulton
Evans David, 79 Nassau
Everett R. J. 85 Liberty
Everts Wm. M. 2 Hanover
Embree Robert C. 76 Nassau
Emerson Rockwell, 61 Wall
Emerson Wm. 10 Wall
Emerson & Prichard, 10 Wall
Emmet C. Temple, 45 William
Emmet Richard S. 45 William
Emmet Robert, 45 William
Emmet Thomas A. 45 William
English Wm. C. R. 47 Wall
Ewen Edward D. 9 Chambers
Fancher E. L. 86 Nassau
Farr E. F. 79 Nassau
Fayerweather R. 61 Wall
Ferguson Jordan G. 6 Wall
Ferres Marcus, 1 Hanover
Ferris Benjamin C. 20 Chambers
Fessenden Henry F. 81 Wall
Fessenden Thomas, 81 Wall
Field David Dudley, 8 Wall
Field Maunsell B. 90 Nassau
Field Stephen J. 41 Wall
Field Theodore W. 68 Fulton
Field Thomas C. 71 Cedar
Fish Hamilton, 76 Nassau
Flagg Wm. J. 12 Wall
Flanagan John R. 6 Wall
Fleetwood Stanley H. 20 Nassau
Floyd Augustus, 32 Wall
Folsom George, 6 Wall
Ford Gordon L. 41 Liberty
Foster J. F. Giraud, 69 Wall
Fowler Isaac V. 80 Nassau
Fowler John, jr. 124 Nassau
Fraser Charles, 2 Wall & 229 5th
Freeman Wm. C. 18 Centre
French Ulysses D. 69 Nassau
Frye Frederick, 54 Wall
Furman Henry H. 15 Wall
Gaines S. W. & R. A. 69 Nassau
Galbraith Benjamin, 25 Park pl.
Galligar Wm. 44 Wall
Gallatin Albert, jr. 44 Wall
Gardiner Abm. S. 54 Wall

Gardiner John B. r. 75 & 77 Nas. | New York.
Garniss James R. 35 Wall
Garniss David R. 35 Wall
Garretson E. T. 12 Wall
Garr Andrew S. 106 Broadway
Gay Calvin B. 156 Broadway
Geissenhainer Frederick W. jr. 14½ Pine
Genet G. C. 56 Wall
Genet Henry W. 35 Wall
Genet E. I. 56 Wall
Gerard James W. 79 Nassau
Gerard J. W. jr. 79 Nassau
Gibbs Alexander. 5 Nassau
Gibbs Geo. 69 Wall
Gifford George, 17 Wall
Gilbert Albert, 16 Wall
Gilbert George Y. 5 Wall
Gilbert Jasper W. 67 Wall
Gilford Thomas B. 127 Fulton
Glover Charles H. 35 Wall
Glover T. James, 14 Pine
Goddard George C. 12 Wall
Goff Amariah W. 34 Liberty
Gomez A. L. 127 Fulton
Goodman Richard, 106 Broadway
Gordon George, jr. 11 Wall
Gould David, 71 Cedar
Gouverneur Adolph N. 12 Wall
Graham De Witt C. 20 Beekman
Graham David, 20 Beekman
Graham Charles K. 20 Beekman
Graham James Lorimer,51 Liberty
Graham John, 20 Beekman
Graham John Lorimer, 40 Wall
Grant Gilbert A. 18 Wall
Gray Epenetus C. 64 John
Gray William Farley, 11 Pine
Green Andrew H. 11 Pine
Green J. Wilson, 27 Fulton & 203 Water
Green James, 127 Fulton
Gridley James, 59 Nassau
Griffen Abraham B. 20 Chambers
Griffin Charles A. 18 Wall
Griffin & Laroque, 65 Merchants' Exchange
Griffith H. Wharton, 12 Wall
Griffith G. William, 35 Wall,
Grim Charles F. 14½ Pine
Hackett John K. 14 Wall
Haight Nicholas, 51 William
Hale Alden J. 38 Wall
Hall Alexander O. 72 Wall
Hall Charles H. 235 Broadway
Hall David P. 2 Wall
Hall Gilbert B. 6 City Hall place
Hall J. Prescott, 2 Hanover
Hall Willis, 14 Wall
Hallett F. A. 54 Wall
Halsey George A. 28 William
Hulsted John O. 18 Wall
Hamersley A. Gordon, 5 Nassau
Hamersley Andrew S. 35 Wall
Hamersley John W. 35 Wall
Hamilton Alexander, jr. Jauncey court
Hamilton Charles A. 51 Liberty
Hamilton Philip, Jauncey court
Hammond John A. 95 Cedar
Hancock John, 177 Broadway
Hand John H. 53 Wall
Hanford Philander, 11 Wall
Hardenbrook John A. 15 Centre
Haring Clinton, 18 Wall
Harned William H. 15 Centre & 21 Horatio
Harrington Madison G. 72 Wall
Harrington Richard M. 42 John
Harrison David, jr. 26 Nassau
Harrison W. B. 65 Exchange
Harrison Thomas, 44 Wall
Hart Charles B. 2 Wall
Hart Felix, 13 Chambers
Hart Joseph C. 2 Wall
Hasbrock G. D. 1 Nassau
Haskett William J. 15 Centre
Haskin John B. 60 Nassau
Hastings Hiram P. 36 John
Havens Charles G. 89 Merchants' Exchange

Havens Henry W. 61 Wall | New York.
Hawley David, 20 Nassau
Hedley John H. 59 Nassau
Herdman H. P. 13 Chambers
Henry Thomas S. 136 Nassau
Henry Peter S. 5 Nassau
Hillyer William A. 140 Broadway & 187 2d
Hilton Archibald, 17 Wall
Hilton Henry, 44 Wall
Hilyer W. Ashly, 187 2d
Hinchman Augustus F. 63 Wall
Hinsdale Theodore, 39 Wall
Hitchcock Andrew H. 19 Wall
Hitchings Benjamin G. 35 Wall
Hoar Edward S. 10 Wall
Hobart Dayton, 11 Wall
Hoffman Edward, 64 John
Hoffman Francis S. 5 Wall
Hoffman Murray, 78 Nassau
Hoffman Murray, jr. 78 Nassau
Hoffman Ogden, 10 Wall
Hoffman Ogden. jr. 10 Wall
Hoffman Wickham, 68 Wall
Hogan Thomas R. 75 & 77 Nassau
Holden Horace, 18 Beekman
Holmes Leroy, 11 Wall
Holmes Robert D. 10 City Hall pl
Hone John, 69 Wall
Hopper John, 43 Wall
Hoppin William J. 54 Wall
Horn William T. 67 Wall
Hornfager William C. 3 Nassau
Hosford J. 34 Liberty
Hosford S. 1 Nassau
Howard James P. 7 Nassau
Howe Josiah, 41 Wall
Howe & Treadwell. 68 Broadway
Howland John, 1 New
Hoxie Nathaniel B. 27 Beekman
Hoyt Jesse, rear 35 Wall
Hoyt Lorenzo, 4 Hanover
Hudson Edward H. 192 Broadway
Hudson Ephm. H. 15 Wall
Hudson George, 87 Wall
Hudson W. Woodbridge, 20 Nassau
Huggins James S. 58 Wall
Hughson Frederick. 87 Wall
Humphrey James, 1 Hanover
Hunt Chas. H. 54 Wall
Hunt Hiram, 20 Chambers
Hunt James, 15 Centre
Hurd James M. 13 Chambers
Hurd John C. 11 Wall
Hurst Lewis, 6 Wall
Husson Joseph, rear 76 & 77 Nassau
Hutchins Waldo. 40 Wall
Hyatt James P. 61 Wall
Hyslop Thomas, 17 Wall
Inglis William, 36 John
Ireland George, jr. 7 Nassau
Ireland John B. 49 William
Irving John T. 7 Nassau
Irving Pierre M. 32 Wall
Isham Giles L. 68 Wall
Jack Charles U. 19 Centre
Janes Horace P. 55 Wall
Jansen William H. 62 John
Jaques David R. 127 Fulton
Jaques Eden S. 127 Fulton
Jarvis Nathaniel, jr. 20 Beekman
Jay John, 20 Nassau
Jennings R. jr. 131 Cherry
Jeremiah Pearson H. 4 City Hall place
Jesup James R. 54 Wall
Joachimsson P. J. 118 Nassau
Johnson & Southmayd, 60 Wall
Johnson Isaac A. 20 Nassau
Johnson William S. 74 Broadway
Johnson Alexander, 60 Wall
Johnson, Waters, & Edwards, 74 Broadway
Johnson W. Templeton, 51 William
Johnson John T. 5 Wall
Jones Alfred G. 20 Nassau
Jones Charles, 12 Wall
Jones Horace P. 65 Wall
Jones George A. 74 Broadway

Jones Samuel, Jauncey court. 41 Wall | New York.
Jones Samuel. jr. 41 Wall
Jones William A. 75 and 77 Nassau
Jordan Ambrose L. 5 Nassau
Jordan & Clark. 5 Nassau
Jordan Philip, 14½ Pine
Judah Charles D. 10 Wall
Judah George, 70 Wall
Judah S. B. H. 70 Wall
Judson Charles, 68 Fulton
Judson Samuel W. 8 Wall
Judson William. 98 Broadway
Kane Cornelius V. S. 76 Nassau
Kane Dionysius A. 8 North William
Kane J. G. 7 Nassau
Keller Charles M. 47 Wall. solicitor of American and Foreign patents.
Kendrick Charles E. 35 Wall, commissioner for Texas
Kennelly William, 45 William
Kent James, 29 Wall
Kent William. 66 Wall
Kent, Davies & Thomas, 66 Wall
Kernorhan William S. 20 Wall
Ketchum Edgar, 69 Nassau
Ketchum Hiram, 31 Wall
Ketchum & Fessenden. 31 Wall
Ketchum William, 87 Cedar
Ketchum & Waterman. 3 Nassau
Keteltas Eugene. 116 William
Kimball Elijah H. 53 Wall
Kimball Richard B. 53 Wall
King Charles C. 27 Wall
King Frederick I. 12 Wall
King Frederick W. 65 Wall
King James G. jr. 56 Wall
King John A. jr., 68 Wall
Kinney Franklin S. 84 Cedar
Kip Leonard W. 192 Broadway & 5 John
Kirkham Benjamin W. 83 Mer. Ex.
Kissam Benjamin F. 6 Wall
Kissam George B. 6 Wall
Knox John M. 20 Nassau
Knox & Mason, 20 Wall
Kortright N. Gouverneur, 84 Liberty
Kursheedt Alexander. 35 Wall
Labau N. Bergasse. 29 Beekman
L'Amoreux Andrew, 6 City Hall place
L'Amoreux Edwin R. 6 City Hall place
Lambertson Frederick W. 33 John
Lane Thaddeus H. 52 Wall
Lapugh Henry D. 54 Wall
Lapugh, Whittelsey & Dowing, 54 Wall
Larocque Jeremiah, 65 Merch. Ex.
Latson William, 80 Murray
Latson John W. 170 Broadway.
Latting John J. 59 Fulton
Law Stephen, 54 Wall
Lawrence John L. 67 Wall
Lawrence John S. 67 Wall
Lawrence Joseph C. 66 Wall
Lawrence E. L. 16 Wall
Lawrence S. A. 16 Wall
Lawrence William B. 44 Wall
Lawrence William B. jr. 44 Wall
Lawson William, 80 Murray
Lawton C. D. & C. 140 Nassau
Lawton William, 16 Wall
Learn William R. 6 Wall
Leatson J. W. 172 Broadway
Lee John H. 15 Centre
Lee & Van Wyck 15 Centre
Lee William P. 6 Wall
Leete Edgar J. 54 Wall
Leeds C. Carroll, 45 William
Leeds William B. 23 Wall
Leeds & Corlus, 50 Wall
Lent John A. 29 Wall
Leonard William H. 63 Wall
Leveridge Benjamin C. 331 Pearl
Leveridge John, 331 Pearl
Leveridge John W. C. 331 Pearl
Levi Asahel, 14 Wall
Lewis Edward Z. 69 Wall

Lewis Chas. D. 27 Wall *New York.*
Leyne Maurice. 12 Wall
Lies Eugene, 79 Merchs' Exch.
Litchfield ——. 62 Wall
Litchfield & Tracy, 62 Wall
Littell John D. 84 Cedar
Livingston Ansen, 52 John
Livingston Cambridge. 17 Wall
Livingston Charles L. 11 Wall
Livingston Clarence. 17 Wall
Livingston John. 54 Wall
Livingston John A. 18 Centre
Livingston John R. jr. 16 Wall
Livingston Livingston. 19 Wall
Living ton, Van Antwerp and Whitbeck, 19 Wall
Lockwood Levi A. 15 Beekman
Lockwood Ralph. 14 Wall
Loder Jeremiah, 66 Wall
Logan Adam D. 83 Merch. Exch.
Logan Edgar. 83 Merch. Exch.
Loomis J. V. 69 Nassau
Lord Daniel, 82 Merch. Exch.
Lord Daniel D. 82 Merchs' Exch.
Lovell Joseph. 68 Wall
Lowerre William, 78 Murray
Luckey Freeborn G. 75 & 77 Nassau
Ludewig Hermann E. 35 Wall, German law agency
Ludlow Thos. W. Jauncey court, Wall
Luff Martin H. 17 Wall
Lux Joseph, 61 Wall
Lyman Samuel P. 38 Broadway
Lynch Edward L. 25 Nassau
Lynch James, 25 Nassau
Lyne Morris, 12 Wall
Lyons J. 13 Chambers
M'Adam J. G. 27 Beekman
M'Adam Quentin, 27 Beekman
M'Ardle William M. 27 Beekman
M'Cahill John, 14 Wall
M'Carthy Florence, 33 Madison
M'Cullock J. S. 87 Wall
M'Cunn John H. 49 William
M'Cunn & Moncrief, 29 Wall
M'Coun Joseph H. 2 Well
M'Crea Alexander, 60 Nassau
M'Daniel William, 72 Wall
M'Donald Alexander L. 52 John
MacDonough A. R. 1 Nassau
M'Gay James, 20 Chambers
M'Gowan Henry P. 80 Nassau
M'Gregor John D. 44 Wall
M'Keag William, 10 City Hall pl
M'Keen James, 20 Chambers
M'Kinley Edward, 70 Wall
M'Kinstry Charles, 66 Wall
M'Knight Thomas. 84 Liberty
M'Lean George, 45 Wall
M'Mahon Dennis, jr. 13 Chambers
M'Murray William, 44 Wall
M'Murray & Hilton. 44 Wall
Maclay Moses B. 9 Nassau
Maclay William B. 54 Wall
Macgregor John D. 44 Wall
Mackay H. S. 59 Nassau
Major D. 248 8th Av.
Malcolm Jas. F. 9 Chambers
Man Albon P. 64 Wall
Mann Abijah, jr. 54 Wall
Manning J. Angus, 61 Wall
Manning R. 191 Broadway
Marbury Francis F. 29 Wall
Marselis Peter T. 6 City Hall pl
Marsh C. C. 61 Wall
Marsh Edward W. 61 Wall
Marsh John. jr. 53 Wall
Marsh Luther R. 6 Wall
Martin Edward. 78 Nassau
Martin Henry G. 29 Wall
Martin Isaac F. 29 Wall
Martin, Strong & Smith, 29 Wall
Martin John M. 10 Wall
Martin William R. 90 Exchange
Martindale Edward, 11 Pine
Martindale Stephen, jr. 12 Wall
Marvin Dan, 60 Nassau
Mason John, 56 Wall
Mason John M. 29 Nassau
Mason Michael P. 90 Chambers

Mather Frederick E. 74 Wall *New York.*
Mather & White. 74 Wall
Mathews Albert, 25 Chambers
Maurice James, 10 Wall
Maxwell Hugh, 11 Wall
Maxwell John S. 11 Wall
Maxwell William H. 41 Wall
Mayer Daniel, 8th Av. cor. 23d
Mead Charles D. 52 John
Meech William B. 170 Broadway
Meeker David E. 11 Wall
Meeker Samuel M. 11 Wall
Meeks Washington. 50 Wall
Meeks William H. 50 Wall
Megrath George. 11 Wall
Melville Allan, 14 Wall
Melville Alean. 12 Wall
Merch W. B. 141 Amos
Meredith Samuel, 16 Wall
Merrihew Stephen, 52 Wall
Merrill Nelson, 16 Wall
Millard A. B. 80 Nassau
Millard A. Orville, 50 Wall
Miledater William J. 69 Wall
Miller Jonathan, 12 Wall
Miller Sylvanus, 49 William
Miller Livingston K. 5 John & 192 Broadway
Mills Ethelbert S. 62 Wall
Mills & Beckworth, 62 Wall
Mills Joseph T. 131 Cherry
Milspaugh Philip, 28 Beekman
Miner Phineas L. 17 Wall
Minor Cornelius, 38 Wall
Mitchell John W. 5 Wall
Mitchell W. & J. F. 11 Wall
Mitchell William M. 49 William
Moffat John, 43 Wall, Jauncey court
Moncrief James, 29 Wall
Monell John D. 36 John
Moody John, 80 Nassau
Moore Charles B. 72 Wall
Moore & M'Daniel, 79 Wall
Moore William H. H. 104 Wall
Morange Henry H. 54 Wall
Morell George W. 91 Wall
Morey A. C. 471 6th Av.
Morrells J. 52 John
Morrill Augustus C. 9 Chambers
Morrill Elisha, 20 Chambers
Morris Andrew C. 20 Beekman
Morris Gerard W. 1 New
Morris Henry M. 1 New
Morris William L. 6 Broad
Morrison Henry, 6 City Hall pl.
Morrogh James. 70 Wall
Morse Coles, 2 Hanover
Mortimer W. G. 11 Wall
Mortimer R. 19 Wall
Morton Hamilton, 41 Wall, Jauncey court
Morton Washington, 2 Jauncey court
Mott Henry A. 25 Park place
Mott Richard, 11 Wall
Mott & Cary, 11 Wall
Mount Richd. E. jr. 75 & 77 Nassau
Mulock Charles, 60 Nassau
Mulock William, 79 Nassau
Mulvey Peter, 29 Chambers
Mumford S. Jones, 9 Nassau
Munson James. jr. 14½ Pine
Myers Peter H. 9 Nassau
Myers T. Bailey, 20 Nassau
Nagle Cornelius. 140 Nassau
Nash Alanson, 26 Beekman
Nash & Donohue, 26 Beekman
Nash Stephen F. Post's Buildings
Nathan Jonathan. 60 Wall
Neilson Joseph, 25 Wall
Nelson George P. 5 Wall
Nelson John W. 61 Wall
Nelson & Newton. 61 Wall
Newhouse John, 170 Broadway
Newman Clement D. 80 Nassau
Newton Charles W. 61 Wall
Nicholl George R. 75 & 77 Nassau
Nichols Effingham H. 7 Nassau
Nicoll Henry, 7 Nassau
Niles George W. 192 Broadway

Niles William W. 192 Broadway *New York.*
Nims Theodore. 29 Chambers
Norcross & Co. 60 Nassau
Norcom Fred. 78 Mer. Exchange
North Thomas M. 63 Wall
Norton Edward, 61 Wall
Norton William. 11 Nassau
Noyes Wm. Curtis. 50 Wall
Oakley Jesse. 19 Wall
O'Conor Charles. 95 Nassau
Ogden David B. 4 New
Ogden Richard H. 79 Merchants' Exchange
Onderdonk Henry G. 85 Nassau
O'Rourke John, 25   do
Osborn Charles F. 147 Mulberry
Owen Edward H. 72 Wall
Owen Samuel. 75 & 77 Nassau
Packard Windkoop. 18 Wall
Paddock Francis H. 54 do
Paget Charles, rear 75 & 77 Nassau
Paine Elijah, 51 Liberty
Paine William H. 53 Wall
Palmer Joseph E. 123 Cherry & 50 Nassau
Palmer Justus, 56 William
Panton John A. 61 Wall
Paris Irving. 9 Nassau
Parisen Richard F. 113 South & 23 Madison
Parish John H. 30 Wall
Parsons George W. 16 do
Parsons Samuel M. 56 do
Partridge George S. 2 do
Patten Joseph H. 68 do
Patterson J. M. 74 do
Patterson Peter E. 14 do
Paulding & Sweeney, 104½ Chambers
Payne Thatcher T. 61 Wall
Peabody Charles A. 6 do
Peet William, 75 do
Paile Thomas, 5 do
Poll Ferris, 3 Nassau
Pell John A. 51 Wall
Penniman A. D. 70½ Church
Perry Andrew J. 6 Wall
Peters John R. 62 do
Phelps James L. jr. 52 John
Phillips Alfred A. 6 City Hall place
Pierrepont Edwards, 61 Wall
Pierson Henry R. 6 do
Pike Robert G. 16 do
Pinckney John M. 49 William
Pinckney Thomas C. 78 Nassau
Pinney Ambrose L. 75 & 77 do
Pirsson John W. 75 & 77 do
Pitkin John R. 68 Broadway
Pitkin Lucius. 11 Wall
Platt James N. 79 Nassau
Platt John M. 44 do
Platt Zephania, 49 William
Pleasants M. F. 8 N. William
Porter Edmund J. 18 Centre
Porter M. 70 Wall
Porter William A. 2 do
Post Charles C. 7 Nassau
Potter Clarkson N. 18 Wall
Potter Ellis. 20 Nassau
Power John H. 129 Fulton
Powers Thomas J. 50 Wall
Powers William P. 5 Nassau
Powers & Tallmadge, 50 Wall
Preston Walter. 54 do
Prichard William M. 10 do
Prime William C. 25 do
Proudfit James, 61 William
Purroy J. B. 11 Wall
Radcliffe Jacob I. 14 do
Rankin John. jr. 5 Nassau
Rankin Robert. 87 Wall
Rankin & Morell, 90 do
Ransom Adam G. 5 Nassau
Rapallo Anthony, 11 Wall
Rapallo Charles A. 14 do
Ray Robert, 66 do
Raymond Jas. H. 8 do
Raymond Samuel G. 1 Nassau
Reed Lewis B. jr. 61 Wall

Reed Richard, 20 Chambers *New York.*
Reed Stephen. 95 Cedar
Remington Albert G. 20 Nassau
Remington J. H. C. 74 Wall
Remsen William. 74 Broadway
Reynolds J. N. 96 Exchange
Reynolds Gilbert U. 95 Cedar
Reynolds Philip, 11 Nassau
Rice Edwin T. 69 Wall
Richardson Henry J. 184 Fulton
Richardson Wm. P. 17 Wall
Rider & Tompkins, 39 Wall, Jauncey court
Ridgway J. S. 8 Wall
Riggs Elisha, 56 do
Riker D. Phœnix, 129 Fulton
Riker Elijah H. rear 35 Wall
Riker Henry L. 129 Fulton
Riker John H. 129 do
Riker John L. 129 do
Ring James J. 90 Beekman
Rives Francis R. 52 Wall
Roberts Nathaniel W. 75 Nassau
Robertson Anthony L. 45 William
Robinson Beverly, 52 Wall
Robinson Beverly, jr. 52 do
Robinson Hamilton W. 54 do
Robinson John O. 78 Nassau
Robinson Lucius. 51 Liberty
Rodgers & Woodman, 39 William
Rodman Thomas D. 54 Wall
Roe Alfred, 38 do
Roe Andrew J. 14 do
Roe Charles S. 38 do
Rogers A. Robertson, 39 do
Rogers Archibald G. 78 Nassau
Rogers N. P. 73 Wall
Romaine Charles N. 95 Cedar
Romaine Samuel B. 20 Nassau
Romaine Samuel B. jr. 20 do
Romaine Worthington 20 do
Romeyn Theodore, 4 New
Ronalds William R. 47 Wall
Roosevelt Clinton, 35 Wall & 23 Chambers
Roosevelt James H. 482 Broadway
Roosevelt James J. 25 Nassau
Roosevelt S. Weir, 25 do
Ross A. Mackenzie, 71 do
Rowan John J. B. 137 Greenwich Av.
Rowen Edwin H. 72 Wall
Rowland William S. 26 Beekman
Rowley Levi, 41 Wall
Rowley Reuben, 76 Nassau
Rowley Robert S. 76 do
Ruggles Henry J. 74 Broadway
Ruggles Philo T. 20 Nassau
Ruggles Saml. B. 74 Broadway
Russell Abraham D. 6 City Hall place
Russell William C. 8 Wall
Russell & Storrs, 6 Wall
Rutherfurd Lewis M. 76 Nassau
Rutherfurd Walter, 76 do
Ruthven James A. 25 do
Sackett C. D. 59 do
Sackett Granville A. 59 do
Sackman O. C. 106 Centre
Sambertson F. 33 John
Sanders Edward, 20 Cliff
Sanders John, 69 Wall
Sandford Charles H. 110 Chambers
Sandford Chas. W. 110 Chambers
Sanford Edward, 70 Wall
Sanford James S. 70 do
Sandfords & Porter, 70 do
Sanxay Skeffington, 8 do
Sayre Francis, 53 do
Sayres Gilbert, 52 do
Schell Augustus, 222 Grand & 60 Wall
Schermerhorn Wm. C. 68 Wall
Schieffelin Rich'd L. 20 Chambers
Scoles John B. 20 do
Scoles & Cooper, 20 do
Scovell Harris, rear 75 & 77 Nassau & 6 Wall
Scoville Charles E. 70 Wall

Scudder Isaac, 11 Nassau *New York.*
Sears William S. 28 Beekman
Sedgwick Henry D. 56 Wall
Sedgwick Theodore, 56 do
Sealey B T. 34 Liberty
Seeley Ebenezer, 61 Wall
Seely Bigelow, 61 do
Seely Edward H. 184 Fulton
Seely William A. 184 do
Seixas Daniel, 51 Wall
Senior R. 78 Nassau
Selden Dudley, 45 William
Seymour Edward, 23 & 25 Wall
Seymour Wm. 23 Wall
Shaffer Chauncey, 75 & 77 Nassau
Shaler William, 37 Chambers
Shankland Thos. 29 Wall
Shannon Robert H. 10 do
Sharot Henry D. 14 Chambers
Shaw J. E. 14 Wall
Shaw W. J. Tenney, 50 Wall
Shea Charles E. 34 Liberty
Sheldon Frederick, jr. 61 Wall
Shelden R. A. 8 Wall
Sheldon William E. 192 Broadway
Shelton & Flagg, 12 Wall
Shepard L. B 61 do
Shepard & Swan, 61 do
Shepherd Daniel, 61 do
Shepherd Edward H. 18 Wall
Shepherd & Melville, 14 do
Sherman Benjamin F. 11 do
Sherman Charles A. 5 do
Sherman Frederick R. 12 do
Sherman James A. 77 Grand
Sherwood John, 44 Wall
Sherwood John D. 5 do
Sherwood Geo. B 44 do
Sherwood L. & L. 156 Broadway
Sherwood Robert H. 44 Wall
Sherwood Samuel, 44 do
Shufeldt George A. 80 Nassau
Sickles Daniel E. 80 do
Sickles George G. 79 do
Sidell John A. 30 North William
Silberrad Lewis, 15 Wall
Silliman Benjamin D. 51 Wall
Silliman William, 15 Beekman
Simpson Dan'l L. 6 City Hall place
Sinclair William J. 11 Pine
Slosson E. 222 Grand & 40 Wall
Slosson John, 222 Grand & 40 Wall
Slosson & Schell, 40 Wall & 222 Grand
Sluyter James S. 41 Wall
Smales Henry, 5 do
Smidt John C. T. 18 do
Smith Augustus F. 29 do
Smith Alve, 140 Broadway
Smith C. Bainbridge, 116 William
Smith Charles Henry, 88 Wall
Smith Charles H. 116 William
Smith E. Delafield, 17 Wall
Smith E. Fitch, 71 do
Smith Fletcher, 35 do
Smith Jesse C. 74 do
Smith J. B. 39 do
Smith James M. 136 Nassau
Smith J. Lawrence, 7 do
Smith Russell, 54 Wall
Smith Sandford S. 34 Liberty
Smith Thomas W. 81 Nassau
Smith Wessell S. 127 Fulton
Smith William B. 16 Wall
Smith & Vanderpoel, 39 do
Smith & Woodward, 74 do
Snebly Chew, 12 City Hall place
Sniffen Allen M. 90 Chambers
Snow Augustin, 61 Liberty
Sommers Thomas S. 71 Cedar
Southard John H. 79 Nassau
Southmayd Chas. F. 60 Wall
Sparks Jared, 59 John
Sparks Thos. J. 18 City Hall place
Speir & Nash, Post's Buildings
Spooner & Paddock, 54 Wall
Spooner Alden J. 54 do
Spring Gardiner, jr. 7 Nassau
Stafford William R. 71 Wall
Stallknecht Frederick S. 25 Wall
Stanley Richard H. 47 do

Staples John B 16 Wall *New York*
Staples Seth P. 12 do
Starr Peter, jr. 1 Hanover
Stemmler John A. 15 Wall
Stephens Benjamin. 7 Nassau
Stephens John L. 67 Wall
Sterling Charles F. 68 do
Sterling William G. 7 Nassau
Stevens George, 27 Beekman
Stevens John B. 16 Wall
Stevenson George W. 27 Beekman
Stevenson G. 44 Nassau
Stevenson James L 19 Centre
Stewart Charles H. 49 William
Stewart Chas. 60 Nassau
Stewart Thomas E. 51 Liberty
Stewart J. Hopkins, 54 Wall
Stewart William P. 61 do
Stitt George S. 52 John
Stogdill William H. 14 Wall
Stone Daniel H. 5 Nassau
Stone Wm. H. 74 Wall
Stone John R. 31 do
Storrs James H. 9 do
Story Wm. H. 67 do
Stoughton Edwin W. 72 Wall.
Strahan Edward. 69 Nassau
Striker Garret H. jr. 70 Wall
Strong Charles E. 66 do
Strong Braddock E. 18 Bowery
Strong George T. 68 Wall
Strong George W. 68 do
Strong Peter R. 25 Nassau
Strong Robert M. 29 Wall
Stuart Charles, 60 Nassau
Stuart Homer H. 54 Wall
Sturtevant Oscar W. 6 do
Sturtevant & Marsh, 6 do
Stuyvesant Theodore, 20 Chambers
Sullivan George, 4 New
Summers Owen S. 8 Wall
Swan Edward S. 61 do
Sweeny Charles, 104 Chambers
Sweeny Peter B. 16 Wall
Taggard William H. 14 Wall
Taggard & Darlington, 14 do
Talcott Thomas G. 35 do
Tallmadge Frederick 8.50 do
Tallmadge James, 44 do
Talmage William M. 115 William
Tallman Harman C. 95 Nassau
Tappen Abraham B. 7 do
Taylor Charles K. 60 do
Taylor Daniel B. 142 do
Taylor James, 76 do
Taylor John N. 49 William
Taylor Thomas J. 95 Nassau
Taylor George. 29 Wall
Taylor & Carter, 29 do
Teller Peter W. 90 2d
Tenbroeck Rensselaer, 192 Broadway & 5 John
Terry Edmund, 44 Wall
Thatcher T. Payne. 61 Wall
Thayer James S. 7 Nassau
Thayer Stephen H. 18 Beekman
Therasson Louis F. 65 Wall
Thomas J. A. 66 do
Thomas Lewis S. 70 do
Thompson Albert A. 136 Nassau
Thompson Andrew, 25 do
Thompson George, 72 Wall
Thomson James, 17 do
Thomson James, 354 3d Av.
Thorn James, jr. 7 Nassau
Thorn William K. 29 Beekman
Thurston David, 7 Nassau
Tilden Samuel J. 11 Pine
Tillotson John H. 59 John
Tillou Francis R. 70 Wall
Tillou & Cutting, 70 do
Tillou Francis, 1 Nassau
Titus George N. 38 Wall
Topping D. H. 140 Nassau
Torbert J. B. 29 Wall
Towner H. C. 79 Nassau
Townsend Emery, 64 John
Townsend Henry D. 2 Wall
Townsend John, jr. 69 do
Townsend John J. 69 do
Townsend Randolph W. 64 Cedar
Tracy ——, 62 Water

Treadwell Edward E. 41 Wall
New York.
True Benjamin K. 51 do
Tucker Gideon J 18 do
Tucker Thomas W. 3 Hanover
Tuffs John. 54 Wall
Turk Edward, 34 Liberty
Turney Paschal W. 51 Liberty
Tysen Raymond M. 25 Nassau
Ullmann Daniel, 29 Wall
Ullmann John J. 27 do
Underhill Abraham, 19 Wall
Underhill Bailey, 19 do
Upton F. H. 72 do
Valentine Eugene, 87 do
Valentine T. 75 do
Valentine & Hughson, 87 do
Van Antwerp P. 19 do
Van Bergen Peter A. 78 Exchange
Van Buren John. 54 Wall
Van Buren & Robinson, 54 Wall
Van Cott Joshua M. 54 do
Van Cott William H. 345 Bowery
Vanderpoel Aaron J. 39 Wall
Van Hook William, 35 do
Van Hovenbergh M. 14 Chambers
Van Namee James, 15 Beekman
Van Pelt Reuben W. 79 Nassau
Vansantvoord Cornelius, 19 Wall
Vansantvoord & Dodge, 19 do
Van Schaick Henry, 11 Nassau
Vanslyke John K. 51 William
Van Voorhis C. W. 60 Nassau
Van Vranken Nicholas, 39 Wall
Van Wagenen G. C. 71 do
Van Wagenen Wm. W. 4 Hanover
Ven Winkle E. S. 90 Merchants'
  Exchange, entrance 38 William
Van Wyck William, 15 Centre
Varnum Joseph B. jr. 51 Liberty
Venvill William, 142 Broadway
Vermilye T. C. 69 Nassau
Verplanck Gulian C. 52 do
Verplanck Samuel, 11 Wall
Voorhees Richard, 35 Centre
Waddell Wm. C. H. 60 Broadway
Waddington Wm. D. 69 Wall
Wadsworth Louis F. 72 do
Wait W. Howard, 62 do
Waite & Delany, 69 Nassau
Wakeman Abram, 18 Beekman
Walgrove D. W. jr. 36 John
Walker Frederick W. 11 Nassau
Walker & Adams, 11 do
Walkins J. 1 do
Waller & Anderson, 142 Broadway
Wallis Alexander H. 52 John
Wallis John, 52 do
Wallis Joseph, 58 William
Wanmaker Henry P. 43 Wall,
  Jauncey court
Ward Albert, 19 Wall
Ward Elijah, 52 John
Ward Henry H. 54 Wall
Ward Richard R. 58 do
Ward Sylvester L. H. 95 Cedar
Ward Theodore A. 95 do
Warner Thos. 18 City Hall place
Warren H. E. 5 Wall
Waters Erastus G. 71 Nassau
Waters George G. 74 Broadway
Watkins Joseph, 1 Nassau
Watson Alex. 75 and 77 Nassau
Watson Robert D. 69 Wall
Watson William, 51 William
Webster Daniel, 6 Wall
Wedgewood Wm. B. 14 Wall
Weed Harvey A. 16 do
Weeks John A. 56 do
Welder John L. 35 do
Wells Alexander, 92 do
Wells Thomas L. 71 Wall
Wells & Van Wagenen, 71 Wall
Welsch Charles, 71 Nassau
Wendell I. rear 35 Wall
Wendell John L 35 Wall
Wendell & Talcott, 35 Wall
West Edward C. 35 Wall
West & Griffith, 35 Wall
Westbrook Frederick E. 75 Merchant's Exchange
Western Henry M. 235 Broadway

Westervelt Isaac Y. 75 & 77
  Nassau *New York.*
Westervelt Harman C. 52 Wall
Westlake Owen E. 51 Liberty
Wetmore Charles F. 33 John
Wetmore Charles J. 33 John
Wetmore William C. 61 Wall
Wetmore & Browne. 61 Wall
Wetmore & Dustin. 33 John
Weyant Michael, 25 Pine
Wheaton Wm. R. 146 East B.way
Whedon David P. 12 City Hall pl
Wheeler Alfred, 16 Wall
Wheeler Clark B. 15 Wall
Wheeler David E. 60 Wall
Wheeler H. Hill, 15 Wall
Wheeler John. jr. 67 William
White David L. 14 Wall
White George. 11 Wall
White James W. 11 Nassau
White John E. 11 Nassau
White John H. 74 Wall
White Joseph L. 14 Wall
White J. L. & D. L. 14 Wall
Whitehead Charles E. 20 Nassau
Whitehead John. 4 Mercha. Exch.
Whiting James R. 61 Wall
Whittlesey Henry M. 54 Wall
Wight Amherst. 96 Beekman
Wightman Stillman K. 9 Wall
Wightman & Clark, 9 Wall
Wilkes Edwin, 34 Liberty
Wilkes Henry, 34 Liberty
Willard Ammiel J. 14 Wall
Willett Edward M. 67 Wall
Williams Andrew, 56 William
Williams Samuel, 64 John
Williams Stephen C. 64 Wall
Williamson Richard, jr. 6 Wall
Wilmarth P. C. 16 Bowery
Willink John A. 75 & 77 Nassau
Wilson A. rear 75 and 77 Nassau
Wilson Edward J. 45 William
Wilson Harris, 10 Wall
Wilson James W. 1 Nassau
Wilson Peter, 80 Murray
Winans Joseph W. 64 John
Winne Richard, 8 Wall
Winslow Robert F. 26 Beekman
Winter Gabriel, 31 Wall
Winter William, 31 Wall
Winthrop Charles F. 11 Wall
Winthrop & Johnson, 51 William
Wolff George L. 14½ Pine
Wood George, 106 Broadway
Wood Gilbert B. 7 Nassau
Wood Loren. 142 Broadway
Wood Wm. G. 38 Wall
Woodbury Peter T. 18 Wall
Woodhull Caleb S. 59 Fulton
Woodman Aaron, 37 Wall, Jauncey court
Woodman W. H. 11 Wall
Woodruff L. B. 106 Broadway
Woodruff & Goodman, 106 B.way
Woodruff Samuel M. 63 Wall
Woodruff & Leonard, 63 Wall
Woodward & Dusenbury 45 Wm.
Wordsworth William, 7 Chambers
Wordsworth & Dyatt, 7 Chambers
Wright George Wm. 52 Wall
Wright J. Butler, 61 Wall
Yates Charles, 71 Cedar
Yenni Edmund, 14½ Pine
York Joseph S. 74 Broadway
Young Elisha S. 11 Nassau
Young Isaac, 192 Broadway
Zabriskie Martin R. 51 Liberty

Niagara County.

Sage S. S. Pekin *Cambria.*
Piper S. B. *Lewiston.*
Stow H. J.
Piper C. H.
Page James H.
Colton Isaac C. *Lockport.*
Walcott A.
Woods & Bowen
Chase E. L.
Dayton & Murray
Holmes & Moss

Southworth M. W. *Lockport.*
Webster T. M.
Parker & Burrell
Gardner & Curtenius
Caverno & Ely
Ransom E.
Stevens & Fithian,
Newton E.
La Mont G. D.
Nicholls L. H.
Brown Samuel
Seaman M. Middleport *Royalton.*
Hunting Moses S. *Somerset.*

Oneida County.

Chandler A. E. *Boonville.*
Frazier H. B.
Bamber Wm.
Ruger W. C. *Bridgewater.*
Cromwell S. *Camden.*
Monroe I.
Carroll K.
Roscoe S. R.
Thompson Aaron H. *Florence.*
Thompson Charles B.
Hoyt G. L.
Williams O. S. Clinton *Kirkland.*
J. V. Sweeting, do
Smith I. Delta *Lee.*
Dean J. Deansville *Marshall.*
Northrop K. do
Bagg G. W. Casville *Paris.*
Yoman G. A. *Remsen.*
Comstock & Beach, Dominick st.
  Rome.
Stryker J. do
Dennison C. do
Frost & Utley do
Fitch J. P. do
Roberts S. B. do
Barnes Wheeler, James st.
Griswold & Jones, do
Van Dresser & Elwood, do
Bennett Alanson, do
Foster, Bennett & Boardman, do
Parkhurst W. S. do
Johnson E. M. K. Dominick st.
Tallman Wm. M. do
Palmer D. D. Waterville
  Sangersfield.
Fowler George, do
Beardsley Samuel, 119 Genesee
  Utica.
Benedict & Mitchell, Exchange
Bond J. W. 88 Genesee
Bradish J. 179 do
Clark & Richardson 4 Main
Coburn A. Exchange Buildings
Coye J. G. 98 Genesee
Crafts & Bronson, 162 do
Davis P. 4 Main
Denio H. Washington Hall
Doolittle C. H. do
Garvin S. B. Exchange Buildings
Graham E. A. 86 Genesee
Harris J. P. 56 Hotel
Hatch J. M. 86 Genesee
Hackley A. Mechanics' Hall
Hogan J. Washington Hall
Hunt W. 15 Broad
Hurd & French 122 Genesee
Hurlburt H. 128 do
Kellogg & M'Intosh, 116 do
Kirkland & Bacon, 94 do
Little A. 86 do
Matteson, Jones & Congar, 69 do
Melhinch A. 66 do
Morehouse R. H. 96 do
Murphy G. 136 do
Palmer J. U. 122 do
Rathburn J. H. Washington Hall
Seymour & Johnson, 71 Genesee
Spencer & Kernan, 53 Hotel
Stoddard E. J. Exchange Building
Timan J. R. 136 Genesee
Tisdale D. 132 do
Tracy Wm. 54 Hotel
Tripp I. jr. 132 Genesee
Walker Thomas R. 129 do
Wetmore E. A. 88 do
Williams A. G. 96 do
Williams E. W. 96 do

Williams J. W. Whitesboro st. *Utica.*
Carroll J. New London *Verona.*
Stafford ——, Durhamville
Frazer P. L. Westerville *Western.*
Merrill Wm. O. Whitesboro *Whitestown.*
Flandreu & Spriggs, Whitesboro
White N. C. do

Onondaga County.

Weaver Z. *Cicero.*
Eager Wm. *De Witt.*
Brewster J. W. Jamesville
Porter Wm. jr. Jordan *Elbridge.*
Raymond L. B. do
Farnham R. do
Munroe J. do
Parker S. C. Baldwinsville *Lysander.*
Graves & Church, do
Stansbury G. A. do
Morgan & Kimball do
Wigent E. B. do
Kenedy N. G. *Marcellus.*
Edwards Samuel L. *Manlius.*
Van Schaack H. V.
Jerome A.
Watson I. Fayetteville
Worden H. do
Birdseye V. *Pompey.*
Gott D.
Ruger John, Salina st. Syracuse *Salina.*
Ruger O. J. do
Wilkinson & Bagg do
Sedgwick & Dillage do
Vanderburgh O. do
Rexford & Montgomery, Malcolm's Block do
Williams G. M. Genesee st.
Windsor H. P. do
Walter George B. do
Bridges Otis L. do
Green Wm. W. do
Gardiner & Burdick do
Trowbridge R. F. do
Lawrence C. Water st.
Raynor R. do
Forbes & Sheldon do
Hillis D. D. Genesee st.
Sessions John, do
Wells Henry, do
Davis & Andrews, Water st.
Lawrence James R. do
Sabin J. F. Water st. Syracuse
Baldwin H. do
Lawrence O. Journal Buildings
Judd S. C. City Hall
Lawrence & Brosnan, Salina st.
Johnson Q. A. do
Newcomb John L. do
Comstock George F. do
Noxon & Leavenworth do
Griswold A. C. Genesee st.
Giles Charles S. Salina st.
Page A. S. do
Hickox ——, Exchange
Graves & Wood, Church st.
Spencer & North, Genesee st.
Jewett W. H. *Skaneateles.*
Lee Benoni
Mosley D. T.
Jewett F. G.
Hiscock L. H. *Tully.*

Ontario County.

Fanrot & Collister *Canandaigua.*
Lapham & Peck
Wilson & Lester
Sibley Mark H.
Wilder Myron O.
Hubbell & Howell
Warden & Chester
Mallory & Drury
Mason J.
Taylor H. W.
Benjamin O.
Sibley John C.
Granger G.

Collins La Fayette *East Bloomfield.*
Wilson A *Manchester.*
Baldwin Samuel E. *Phelps.*
Stepherson Dolphin
Austin James G.
Kidder N. B. Geneva *Seneca.*
Park Nathan, do
Slosson B. do
Strong John C. do
Mundy Gideon M. do
Hudson David, do
Folger Charles J. do
Bradford J. M. do
Dox Peter M. do
Whiting John N. do
Whiting Bowen, do
Fellows Joseph, do
Woods James H. do
Horton George M. do
Sill Wm. E. do
Hudson David, do
Hurd E. H. do
White Henry H. do
Bean John E. do
Brown James C. do
Walker Silas, do
Dickinson John *West Bloomfield.*

Orange County.

Marvis Grant, Craigsville *Blooming Grove.*
Feagles David *Chester.*
Sullivan C. *Cornwall.*
Lyon T. J. Port Jervis *Deer Park.*
Van Inwegen George *Goshen.*
Swezey M.
Winfield C. H.
Sharp W. F.
Wilkin S. J.
Gott J. W.
Duryea B. F.
Dunning B. F.
Hoffman Jas. F
Westcott N.
Gidney D. F.
Strong S. H.
Monell C.
Wilkins A. J.
Jansen A. D.
Booth J. B.
Fullerton S. W. Slate Hill *Minisink.*
Borland Charles *Montgomery.*
Bull H. B.
Whelan Joseph V.
Monell John J. 2d st. *Newburgh.*
M'Coy Levi H. do
Fiste David W. do
Betts Geo. F. do
M'Kissock Thomas
Fullerton Wm. cor. Water & 2d
Brewster Eugene A. 3d st.
Brown John W. do
Reeve Nathan, — do
Proudfit Robert, do
Ringland David C. do
Hasbrouck W. C. do
Boice Daniel B. do
Mace Benjamin H. do
Eager Samuel W. do
Sherman M. 2d st
Betts Frederick J. 3d st.
Smith John A. do
George Thomas, cor. Water & 3d
Belknapp Chauncey F. 3d st.
Fowler James W. do
Pronk J. N. South Middletown *Wallkill.*
Wilkin J. G

Orleans County.

Ressac & Cole, Albion *Barre.*
Church & Davis, do
Bryant & White, do
Tucker & M'Allaster, do
Cole D. H. do
Goff H. S. do
Hard Gideon, do
Reynolds E. R. do

Ward A. Albion *Barre.*
Thomas Arad, do
Curtis H. R. do
Graves Nelson A. do
Garrison Andrew *Murray.*
Van Sick ——
Ferry L. D.
Burrows S. W Medina *Ridgway.*
Garter Reuben, do
Servoss A. do
Gilson James, Shelby

Oswego County.

Sanders William, Cleveland *Constantia.*
Van Denberg J. do
Gordon ——, do
Crombie James, Oswego Falls *Granby.*
Dudley Lord G. do
Darling ——, do
Gilson James M. Central Square *Hastings.*
Castle G. do
Higgins John B. *Mexico.*
Smith Luke D.
Downing Levi
Whitney Cyrus
Whitney O. H.
Martin & Cozzins, Bank Buildings, Bridge st. *Oswego.*
Brown James, Lawrence Buildings, Bridge st.
Lee Charles, Granite Block
Hathaway Jesse A. Bridge st.
Marsh. Wright & Perry, 2 Central Block, 1st st.
Burt Bradley B. 1st st.
Shumway Wm. H. Telegraph Block, 1st st.
Bancroft Dewitt C. do
Grant Abraham P. do
Robinson & Allen, do
Babcock & Rhoades, 1st st.
Talcott Enoch B. cor. Bridge & 1st
Ludington Archibald N. *Parish.*
M'Carty Andrew Z. Pulaski *Richland*
King Don Alonzo, Pulaski
Wardwell Samuel, do
Rhodes B. Franklin, do
M'Carty Daniel, do
Stevens Joseph T. do
Rhodes John, do
Watson John B. do
Huntington S. C. do
Getty A. B. Phœnix *Schroeppel.*
Burke S. W. do
Curtiss Wm. P. Fulton *Volney.*
Hull Ames G. do
Esmond Joseph, dc
Tyler Ransom H. do
Stephens Melvin F. do
Cromlie & Burton, do

Otsego County:

Gorham G. S. Burlington Green *Burlington.*
Brown L. D. do
Davis J. W. *Butternuts.*
Little D. H. *Cherry Valley*
Campbell H. J.
Hammond J. D.
Morse O. A.
Coleman D.
Dewey E.
Bates D. C.
Pomeroy Daniel E. *Edmeston.*
Smith Samuel T.
Smith —— *Exeter.*
M'Intosh Thomas *Hartwick.*
Baker J. H.
Chatfield S. S. *Laurens.*
Ferry Elijah E. Schenevus *Maryland.*
Bow Le Roy E. *Middlefield*
Ely Sumner S.
Morehouse John B.
Brown E. F. *Milford.*
Barringer F. W.

Brown E.   *Milford.*
Olin Wm. H.   *Oneonta.*
Shaw A. G.
Beach Samuel B.
Cook W. K.
Hunt Harvey   *Otego.*
Blakely Ebenezer
Starkweather G. A. Cooperstown
                    Otsego.
Crippen Schuyler,   do
Averill Wm. H.   do
Cooper Richard,   do
Walworth Lyman J.   do
Palmer Lewis R.   do
Field Cutler,   do
Wood Jerome B.   do
Nelson Rensselaer,   do
Ingalls Marshall,   do
Ingalls Lyman,   do
Smith Ezra,   do
Burditt Luther I.   do
Lathrop Horace,   do
Saxton Luther C.   do
Davenport J. S.   *Richfield.*
Andrus C.
Belknap E.
Elwood J. B.
Hyde Jay
Basinger S   *Springfield.*
Bragg Edward S.   *Unadilla.*
Belknap Ely C.
Gregory Jared C.
Hawes William B
Noble Chas. C.
Page Sherman
Waterman H. B.   *Worcester.*
Burnside S. S.
Grant S. H.
Teneyck A.
Waterman & Grant
Becker A. South Worcester
Crow Isaac,   do

Putnam County.

Ga Nun Charles   *Carmel.*
Miller J. G.
Bailey Benjamin
Dean Wm. A.
Ryder Ambrose
Feks Elijah
Dykman J. O. Cold Spring
                    Phillipstown.

Queens County.

Wood L.   *Flushing.*
Griffin Sydney L.   *Hempstead.*
Hadden A.
Potter Pierpont   *Jamaica.*
Lambersen J. G.
Cogswell W. I.
Maurice James   *Newtown.*
Eastman Henry W. Roslyn
                North Hempstead.
M'Cann Wm. T. & Wm. S.
                   Oyster Bay.

Rensselaer County.

Sanders L. R.   *Berlin.*
Filley M. L. 311 State
                Lansingburgh.
Lansing John V. 311 State
Storer Wm. D. 288   do
Knickerbocker J. F. 268 do
Ransom I. cor. Richard & State
Peck & Storer   *Nassau.*
Bingham Anson
Reynolds N. H. W.   *Petersburg.*
White J. D.
Van Every Michael
Ripley Thomas E.   *Schaghticoke.*
Wilbur Charles
Whales H. N.
Knickerbocker H.
Albertson John P. 10 2d   *Troy.*
Ball Marcus, 14 Boardman's
   Buildings
Blair G. T. Courthouse
Britton I. G. 21 1st
Brooks H. S. 254 Congress
Buell David. jr. 1st
Christie R. jr. 25 do

Day George, Courthouse   *Troy.*
Edson Henry. 9½ 1st
Fairbanks & Gale, cor. Congress
   & 2d
Fitch John, 27 Congress
Forsyth J. 7 1st
Freiot James, 3 Albany
Gardner D. 27¼ Congress
Gould George, 25½ do
Hadley Amos K. 21 1st
Hayner H. Z. 25½ Congress
Hunt & Patterson, 6¼ 1st
Huntington Samuel G. 9½ 1st
Jennys R. C. 87 2d
Kellogg Giles B. 14 Boardman's
   Buildings
Kendrick & Warren, 15 do
King E. R. 263 River
Lampost J. T. 10 1st
Lane Jacob L. 8½ do
Mann F. N. cor. Congress & 2d
M'Conihe I. 47 1st
Millard John A. 3 Albany
Miller N. cor. Congress & 2d
Neil James, 27 Congress
Olin A. B. & Geer A. C. 36 2d
Olin Job S. 25½ Congress
Parmeter R. A. 47 1st
Pearsou E. 227 River
Pierson Job, 87 2d
Potter Geo. J. cor. Congress & 2d
Richards Chas. E. 200 River
Robertson Gilbert, 200 do
Seymour & Romeyn, 25½ Congress
Seymour W. W. 23 do
Shelden C. D. 263 River
Smith Levi, 87 2d
Stow G. 3 Albany
Tibbitts Geo. 7 1st
Townsend R. M. U. I. 47 1st
Tracy & Taylor, 47   do
Van Wormer A. A. 25 1st
Viele John J. 47   do
Waite Geo. 47 1st
Warren Moses, 23½ Congress
Wells J. F. 11 4th
Wheeler & Percy, cor. of Congress & 2d
Willard & Raymond, 6 Cannon
   Place
Woodcock D. C. 1 Franklin sq.

Richmond County.

Clarke L. C. Port Richmond
                  Northfield.
Degrott A.   do
Headly H. E.   do
Wyman Charles   do

Rockland County.

Prall H. G.   *Haverstraw.*
Pye Edward, Nyack *Orangetown.*
Maxwell William Hugh
Blanch & Vervalen, Pierment

St. Lawrence County.

Russell John S.   *Canton.*
Russell Thomas V.
Cooke & Barker
Cooke William C.
Barker Winslow T.
Baldwin Silas
Brayton John D.   *Edwards.*
Anthony C.   *Gouverneur.*
Fowler E.
Dodge & Parker
Pooler Charles T.   *Hermon.*
Conant George C.   *Lisbon.*
Crary Edward, Columbia, *Madrid.*
M'Cleland Charles, Columbia
Redington James, Waddington
Chipman William
King C. J.   *Massena.*
Wright C. B.   *Morristown.*
Hutchins R.   *Norfolk.*
Lawrence William R.
Foote & Hanna   *Oswegatchie.*
James & Brown, Ogdensburgh
Chaplin David M.   do

Vary Bennett H. Ogdensburgh
                  Oswegatchie.
Reed Amos   Ogdensburgh
Robbins & Wright   do
M'Naughton Joseph   do
Brown Anthony C.   do
Foote H. G.   do
Finn John   do
Havens & Stilwell   do
Myers & Baldwin   do
Perkins Bishop   do
Morris George   do
Grant G. W.   do
Housbrouck D.   do
Hopkins James G.   do
Alten Horace,   *Potsdam.*
Knowles Liberty
Knowles & Reide
Knowles Henry L.
Dart & Baldwin
Wallace William H.

Saratoga County.

Ellsworth J.   *Corinth.*
Smith E. O.   *Galway.*
Whitlock F. J.
Scott George G. Ballston, *Milton.*
Culver & De Forest do
Brotherson John   do
Culver William   do
Odell William T.   do
Thompson John W.   do
Litch William B.   do
Young Thomas G.   do
Maxwell David   do
Metcalf John, Gansevoort
               Northumberland.
St. John Seymour   *Providence.*
Merrill H. W.   *Saratoga.*
Lewis John
Breabin John B.
Russell C. A.
Willard John, *Saratoga Springs.*
Booker A.
Hulbert John C.
Walworth R. H
Doe N. B.
Carr John T.
Marvin Thomas J.
Warren W. L. F.
Plunkett J. R.
Smith Alanson
Castle W. E.
Bartlett A. S.
Learing William M.
Hoag F.
Hoag Solomon
Briggs Joseph D.
Root F. S.
Lester C. S.
Avery P. J.
Avery William S.
Hay William
Beach W. A.
Wentworth John
Lincoln H. S.
Thayer B. C.
Walton C.
M'Gregor John R.
Maxwell A. S.
King William H.   *Waterford*
Mandeville Joshua
Lawrence & Scott
House James I.
Cramer John
Waldron F. S.
Bullard, Cramer & Ormsby
Todd J. M.
Kirtland & Seymour
Cramer John, 2d

Schenectady County.

Smith D.   *Glenville*
Fuller J. 132 State *Schenectady*
Johnson S. H. 59 do
Wright & Lima, 31 State
Palmer Thomas, 23 do
Fuller Henry, 130 do
M'Chesney J. @. 100 do
Chadsey D. M. 30   do
Baker S. L. 30   do

Smith D. C. 28 State *Schenectady.*
Harman J. D. 150 do
Potter P. P. 7 Union
Van Ingen T.H. 13 do
Rosa Edward do

Schoharie County.

Mahan Stephen L. *Blenheim.*
Baldwin Frederick J.
Matice John W. *Broome.*
Lawyer Thomas *Cobleskill.*
Miller G.
Lawyer Tiffany
Ramsey J. Henry
Smith Thomas
Lawyer Demosthenes
Smith Henry
Clark Charles G.
Hawse Jonah
Mowers Henry, East Cobleskill
Frost John S. *Esperance.*
Mann John E.
Jackson S. W. *Gilboa.*
Mackey Joseph
Sanford & Danforth *Middleburgh.*
Engle Wm. H.
Wells Wellington
Goodyear & Martin *Schoharie.*
Pond A. B. F.
Holliday Elias
Houck Jacob, jr.
Brewster Ralph
Gebhard Jacob
Gebhard John
Davis Wm. H.
Fox Jeremiah *Sharon.*
Eldridge B. B. Sharon Centre
Beekman Wm. Leesville
Ferguson Thomas *Summit.*
Boughton Seymour

Seneca County.

Halsey Charles *Lodi.*
Sabin John H.
Cutler Andrew J.
Seeley John E. *Ovid.*
Herron David
Gregory Alva
Sackett W. A. *Seneca Falls.*
Vide S. S.
Clark Wm.
Bellows M. L.
Bloomer D. C.
Bascom A.
Foot F.
Miller J. T.
Stanton H. B.
Knox John *Waterloo.*
M'Alister John
Richardson Jas. K.
Birdsall Samuel
Knox A. T.
Knox Wm.
Burton Wm. H.
Swift Chas. S.
Hawks Cyrus D.
Hadley Sterling G.

Steuben County.

Tininny F. E. & J. W. *Addison.*
Cornell F. R. E.
Herron D.
Baldwin W. W
Van Loon J. C.
Straight D. *Avoca.*
Reed L. H. *Bath.*
Howell & Co.
Barns & Bonham
Rumsey & Van Valkenburgh
Campbell Robert & Charles
Donaho P. S.
Ferris A P.
M'Dowell C. J. *Cohocton.*
Wheeler N. J.
Brayton Lyman *Dansville.*
Platt C. F. *Erwin.*
Gilbert W. J.
Reynolds Thomas U. *Hornellsville.*
Brundage Robe. t
Bennett Hiram

Hawley Wm. *Hornellsville.*
Finch Nathaniel
Babbitt J. F. *Orange.*
Spencer George T. *Painted Post.*
Irvine Wm.
Herron Joseph
Head Jonathan C.
Gray & Berry
Montgomery A. C. *Prattsburgh.*
Baldwin W.
Hill J. H. *Tyrone.*
Brown Morris *Urbana.*
Larrowe Jacob
Comstock H. L.
Bradley George *Woodhull.*

Suffolk County.

Strong Selah B. South *Brookhaven.*
Floyd Abraham do
Wickham W. jr. Patchogue
Buffett Wm. F. North Port
Huntington.
Skumaker John G. Babylon
Buffett Wm. J *Smithtown.*
Huntting J. R.
Goldsmith Joseph, Hull *Southold.*
Cady Francis N. do
Albertson Joseph C. do

Sullivan County.

Johnston J. W. Barryville
Lumberland.
Cox Geo. B. Bloomingburgh
Mamakating.
Dimmick Alpheus, do
Stewart James L. do
Lord G. W. Monticello *Thompson.*
Nivan A. C. do
Thompson J. A. do
Wilkins W. do
Ludington Clinton V. R
Fairchild Eli W. do
Wright Wm. B. do

Tioga County.

Matille H. T. Newark Valley
Newark.
Slosson W. de
M'Knight C.
Platt William *Owego.*
Parker John M.
Munger Alanson
Avery C. P.
Camp Geo. Sidney
Farrington Thomas
Taylor John J.
Strong Stephen
Sweet E. S.
Davis & Warner
Pert L. B,
Fay F. J.
Nichols John A. *Spencer.*
Wood George B.

Tompkins County.

Ring Elihu, Mecklenburg *Hector.*
Hamilton D. H. do
Drake C. B. 8 Tioga *Ithaca.*
Ferris & Cushing 16 do
Crittenden S. jr. 12 do
Linn Wm. 7 do
Dana Fitz Read, 21 do
Ackley J. M. 8 do
Dana & Beers, 21 do
Mack Stephen, do
Rowe J. 8 do
Smith S. W. 12 do
Love & Freer, 10 do
Dowe & Boardman, 53
Johnson A. S. 94 Owego
Humphrey Chas. 62 do
Humphrey Wm. R. 62 do
Day Chas. G. 51 do
Dewitt Wm. L. 59 do
Bruyn & Williams cor. Aurora &
Owego
Wells & Marsh 15 Aurora
Schuyler & Riggs 28 do
Wright M. R. 29 do
Sherrill & Spencer 8 Cayuga
Stockholm D. B. 2 Clinton House

Crowell Moses *Newfield.*
Garfield S. S.
Anderson John G.

Ulster County.

Forsyth & Husbrouck *Kingston.*
Westbrook T. R. Wall st
Westbrook C. R. do
Chipp Howard
Schoonmaker Marrius
Kenyon Wm. S.
Sudam H.
Ostrander Jonathan D.
Hartenburgh Jacob
M'Cauley Robert F
Dubois Jacob H.
Vangaasbeek Peter
Van Buren John
Pierce Samuel W.
Linderman Jas. O.
Steele J. B. Rondout
Craft J. L. Milton *Marlborough.*
Reynolds G. G. do
Soper Wm. do
Cole John, Modena *Plattekill.*
Westbrook Jacob, jr. *Rosendale.*
Livingston John Q.
Gates Theodore B. *Saugerties*
Whitaker Egbert
Lyon John, Jordanville
Shawangunk.
M'Kinney C. Tuthill
Gorham N. R. Ellenville
Wawarsing.
Broadhead Henry do

Warren County.

Green Wm. H. Chestertown
Chester.
Smith Wm. J. *Horiconville.*
Butler B. C. *Luzerne*
Baldwin L. H. Glenn's Falls
Queensbury.
Berrine M. W. & I. S. do
Mott Isaac do
Ferris Orange do
Paddock Ira A. do
Allen King do
Richards Geo. *Warrensburg.*

Washington County.

King Wm. H. *Argyle*
Coon James S.
Sharp & Martin *Cambridge.*
Thorn Geo. *Fort Ann.*
Pike Silas
Jacksway Teltish
Walt & Parry *Fort Edward.*
Boies Joseph *Greenwich*
Ingalls Chas. F.
Lawrie James J
Boies D. A.
Ingalls C. R.
Culver E. D.
Beaman Saml. S. *Hampton.*
Frasier Louson *West Hebron.*
Northrup Henry B. Sandy Hill
Kingsbury.
Hughes Chas. Sandy Hill
Parris U. G. do
Milliman N. B. do
Wait Luther. do
Clark Orville. do
Martindale H. C. do
Weston Frederick, do
Northup Lyman H do
Allen Cornelius L. *Salem.*
M'Farlane John H.
Gibson James
M'Dougal Archibald L.
Crary Charles
Blair B. *Salem.*
Russell David
Church Lemuel
Crocker John S. North White
Creek *White Creek.*
Howe L. J. do
Crocker B. K. do
Putman J. P. do
Cook M. E. do

Boyd J. H.   *Whitehall.*
Bush A. T.
Davis E.
Doig R.
Parker W. H.
Potter J.
Parks F.
Stevens J. J.

Wayne County.

Middleton George H. Newark
                          Arcadia.
Culver S. C.   do
Melvin John   do
Williams S. K.   do
Scott George W.   do
Ketcham J. L. L. Clyde, *Galen.*
Eldridge George,   do
Basford & Welling,   do
Stone W. S.   do
Sherwood & Mackenzie *Lyons.*
Smith & Cornwell
Clark Wm. jr.
Adams Wm. H. & Son
Olmsted George
Parshall D. W.
Vanmarter Wm.
Benton George W.
Strong & Palmer   *Palmyra.*
Aldrich & Hopkins
Peddie James
Nindee Thomas
Smith Franklin
Cuyler George W.
Clark Chauncey F.   *Wolcott.*
Merrill N. W.
Carey John W.   *Red Creek.*

Westchester County.

Hart Robert S.   *Bedford.*
Close Odell
Bates John S.
Roberts Wm. H.
Nelson Wm. Peekskill *Courtlandt.*
Nelson Thomas.   do
Nelson Wm. Rufus, do
Ferris J. Henry,   do
Frost Calvin,   do
Wells E.   do
Hunt Wm. A.   do
Travis David W.   do
Briggs Daniel C.   do
Beekman Gerard R. Tarrytown
                      Greenburgh.
Irving H. O.   do
Wildey E. H.   do
Coles Robert H.   *New Rochelle.*
Case George
Harrison D. & Son
Cobb M. L. Sing Sing *Ossining.*
Rockwood Albert, do
Reynolds Samuel F.do
Hoffman John T.   do
Larkin Francis,   do
Voris Richard R.   do
Beers James E. Portchester *Rye.*
Purdy Samuel   *West Farms.*
Purdy Charles A.   *White Plains.*
Mills John W.
Tompkins J. W.
Clapp Jno. A.
Mitchell Josiah S.
Lyon Samuel E.
Hay Thomas H.
Mitchell Minott
Platt L. C.
Winslow Robert F.
Scrugham W. W.   *Yonkers.*

Wyoming County.

Farnum Moulton,   *Attica.*
Putnam & Skinner,
Hoyt J. G.
Corlett Todd
Spring L.   *China.*
Flint Robert   *Genesee Falls.*
Moffit Miles
Cobb Nelson
Smith F. Carlos
Skinner & Fray, Wyoming
                      Middlebury.

Hayward L. A.   *Perry.*
Pettit J. J.
Gibbs Levi
Mitchell William
Lent Abram
Trall M.
Peck A.
Windsor J. H.
Kelly F.
Shepherd John N. Varysburg
                      Sheldon.
Thayer L. W.   *Warsaw.*
Doolittle J. R.
Crozier Wm. M.
Bailey C. W.
McKay F. C. D.
Smith W. Riley

Yates County.

Sunderland D. J.   *Barrington.*
Franklin B. W. Penn Yan *Milo.*
Van Allen J. V.   do
Harpending A. V.   do
Glover J. S.   do
Van Buren E.   do
Welles Henry,   do
Welles S. H.   do
Prosser David B.   do
Briggs Wm. S.   do
Lewis John L. jr.   do
Judd Charles G.   do
Oliver Andrew,   do
Taylor James,   do
Parsons Wm. C.   do
Morris Daniel, Rushville *Potter.*
Torry Samuel H.   do
Wolcott John, Dundee *Starkey*
Seeley James L. do
Hoogland Edward, do

Auctioneers.

New York.

Austens & Spicer, 36 William cor.
    Exchange place
Baker Jacob S. 7 Broad, auction
    and real estate
Baker Robert N. 173 Broadway
Sangs, Platt & Co. 204 Broadway
Bell Thomas. 11 Spruce
Bleecker Anthony J. 7 Broad
Boyle Terence, 185 Chatham
Brown Josiah W. 102 Broadway
Bushnell Samuel, 154 Pearl
Burling & Ebbetts, 36 Wall
Cady Jesse, 180 Broadway
Carter Wellington A. 7 New
Cassedy C. 400 Bowery
Catterfield & Topping, 39 William
Chesterman & Hoguet. 13 William
Cole & Chilton, 9 Wall
Cooley & Keese. 191 Broadway
Colton Francis, 59 Beekman
Corlies, Haydock & Co. 35 Wil-
    liam
Draper. Warrens & Montant, 55
    & 57 Beaver
Dumont & Hosack, 11 Wall
Ford James M. 87 Ann
Fosters & Livingston, 41 Broad
Francis John, 181 Chatham
Franklin William H., Son & Co. 5
    Broad
Gerard & Betts, 106 Wall
Greenough Walter & Co. 106 Wall
Groot John R. 152 Pearl
Haggerty, Draper & Jones, 54
    William
Hoffman L. M. & Co. 105 and 107
    Wall & 68 Broad
Hough & Boyd, 56 Ann
Hune Henry, 175½ Chatham
Kemp Rufus C. 12 Wall & 359
    Broadway
Leeds Henry H. & Co. 8 Wall
Lewis W. N. 187 Chatham
Mallaby T. 17 Wall
M'Carty W. D. 60 Broadway
M'Cormick John, 175 Chatham
M'Cormick William, 14 Spruce

M'Crea James A. 168 Pearl
                      New York.
M'Kee Alexander. 173 Chatham
Miller James M. 75 Maiden lane
Minturn & Co. 113 Wall
Mooney Benjamin, 14 Platt
Morgan Homer, 1 Pine
Moriarty John, 173 Chatham
Mortimer A. L. 33 Catherine
Muller Adrian H. 7 Wall
Murphy Joseph, 15 Spruce
Nash Daniel D. 139 Fulton
Newcomb William B. 28 B.way
Newmark J. 23 Bowery
O'Connor Joseph, 90 Broadway
Parks David, 178½ Pearl
Parks Peter, 11 Wall
Pells & Co. 109 Wall
Perry H. A. 145 Broadway
Platt Jacob S. 23 Platt
Power Lawrence, 5 James
Rollings G. B. & Co. 35 Wall
Rudderow John & Co. 163 Pearl
Ryan Cornelius H. 161 Greenwich
Sargeant & Sons, A. 15 Wall
Sayers & Winters, 5 William
Scanlan H. 215 Canal
Seixas Hyman L. 190 Broadway
Shirley W. W. 17 Nassau
Sniffen John, 53 Ann
Snow E. L. 51 Ann
Steward Edward, 205 Canal
Stocking A. Y. & H. 199 Broadway
Van Antwerp & Osgood, 68 B.way
Van Wyck & Kobbe, 17 William
Willard Henry E. 3 Broad
Wilmerdings, Priest & Mount, 51
    Beaver
Witters William, 211 Canal

**Augers, Bits, and Chisels—
Manufacturers.**

Monroe County.

Hinsdale B. M. (augers) 117 Buf-
    falo   *Rochester.*
Hughes Bernard, (augers) 56
    Asylum

Rensselaer County.

Allen J. H. River, near State,
    Dam   *Troy.*

Yates County.

Kimble William, Penn Yan, *Milo.*

Aurists.

Brown George, 382 Broome
                      New York.
Castle & Edwards, 518 Broadway
Powell James W. 261 Broadway,
    entrance 1½ Warren, & Oculist

**Awnings and Sacking Bot-
toms.**

Cheesman J. L. 113 Suffolk
                      New York.
Chester & Quackenbush, 154½
    Barrow
Johnson Charles. 197 Hester
Kenney & Evans 122 E. Broadw.
Parisen W. 548 Pearl & 191 South
Tyler James, 2 Mulberry

Awning and Tent Makers.

Kings County.

Hunter & McKennet, (tents) 136
    Fulton   *Brooklyn.*

Monroe County.

Williams E. C. 12 State *Rochester*

New York County.

Workman Wm. 181 Reade
New York.

Axe Helve Maker.

Goodwin John, 304 Stanton
New York.

Axe Dealers.

Clarke, Wooster & Co. 10 Broadw.
New York.
Collins & Co. 283 Canal
Tisdale S. T. & Co. 218 Water

Axe Manufacturers.

Albany County.

White Miles, Cohoes *Water vliet.*
Simmons D. & Co. do

Chenango County.

Packard A. *Bainbridge.*

Erie County.

White L. & I. J. 23 Ohio *Buffalo.*
Hagerman N. Hydraulics *Concord.*
Blaisdell H. Springville

Essex County.

Miller S. & E. . *Ticonderoga.*

Franklin County.

Earle W. & B. *Malone.*
Beardsley & Co.

Herkimer County.

Lauriat J. B. *Little Falls.*
Angell E. *Newport.*

Jefferson County.

Douglass Norton *Watertown.*
Hadcock Solomon
Matthews Pitt, Carthage *Wilna*
Davis S. J. do

Madison County.

Parker Samuel *Eaton.*

Ontario County.

Beardsley & Co. *Phelps.*

St. Lawrence County. .

Fowler T. *Russell.*

Seneca County.

Seeley Nathaniel *Ovid.*

Ulster County.

Wideman Henry *Saugerties.*
Davis S. N. & Co. Napanock
Wawarsing.

Axle (Patent) Makers.

Westchester County.

Saunders Wm. H. Hastings
Greenburgh.

Baby Jumpers.

Halstead G. 210 Canal *New York.*
Kurtz Ehl, 291 Bowery
Tuttle Geo. W. 311 Broadway

Bags and Bagging.

Kings County.

Tucker, Cooper & Co. New York
Hemp Co. cor. Grand between
Myrtle & Flushing Av's East
Brooklyn *Brooklyn.*

New York County.

Clessman E. L. 16 Platt *New York.*
Cole John V. 39 Burling slip
Forker & Brother, 2 do
Nash Charles, 84 Pike slip
Owens Edward, 249 Front
Philbin Michael, 40 South
Schenck & Brother, 80 & 82 Water
Warfield P. 4 Burling slip

Orange County.

Harrison & Brown, (seamless bags)
Newburgh.

Otsego County.

Laurens Cotton Bag Co. W. C.
Field, Agent *Laurens.*

Bags—Carpet.

Hall & Wilcox, Greenwich
New York.
Jaques Wm. C. 58 Nassau
Matthews & Hunt, 166 Pearl
Underwood B. 100 William

Bakers.

Albany County.

Hodge J. 663 Broadway *Albany.*
Stratton & Peterson,796 Broadway
Clark John, 870 do
Hamilton J. 14 Columbia
M'Carty O. 94 Water
Myers F. H. 29 Union
Turner J. 66 Hamilton
Graves J. C. 94 Green
Putnam C. 62 Lydius
Keeler J. N. 50 Ferry
Nusbaum ——, 118 S. Pearl
Arnold J. 203 do
M'Garvey D. 229 do
Stern M. 189 do
Clark J. 214 do
Burree A. 71 do
M'Cauley J. 66 Beaver
Paddock Stephen, 76 S. Pearl
Honeysett J. 194 Hamilton
Miller Henry, 48 Clinton
Mitchell F. 35 Steuben
Kendall Wm. 138 N. Pearl
M'Auley J. N. Pearl & Lumber
Pritchard & Packard, 166 Wash'tn
Hunter Robert, 36 do
Penden A. 76 do
Dunn P. 351 State
Brimhall H. 47 Canal
Gibson W. 270 Bowery
Mitchell F. 43 Washington
Goodell R. West Troy *Watervliet.*
Marks J.
Mallory W. *Cohoes.*

Broome County.

Hagaman D. *Binghamton.*
Tucker N.

Cayuga County

M'Crea A. State st. *Auburn*
King B. F. B. North st.
Vanalstine J. Weedsport *Brutus.*

Chautauque County.

Smithers ——, Fredonia *Pomfret.*

Chenango County.

Greenman & Co. *Norwich.*
Randolph & Frants *Oxford.*

Columbia County.

Burns R. H. Warren st. *Hudson.*
Hulme Wm. do
Martin Miss E. do
Paul C. 96 do
M'Crosson Mrs. Valatie *Kinderhook*

Duchess County.

Gildersleve Wm. H. *Fishkill.*
Chapman Wm. Wappinger's Falls
Capewell G. Fishkill Landing
Rowland P. S. *Hydepark.*
Bartlett J. 322 Main *Poughkeepsie.*
Luman & Sutton, 211 Main
Hawkins B. 362 do
Gausman Geo. & Son, 8 Liberty
Cole F. *Red Hook.*
Riggins C.
Marquartal C. *Rhinebeck.*

Erie County.

Hope J. cor. Mohawk & Morgan
Buffalo.
Piens Theodore, Genesee square
Dow W. F. 11 So. Division
Woodruff James, 30 E. Seneca
Payne T. Seneca near Chicago
Van Velzor Benjamin, 296 Main
Sprickman Louis, Water
Smith James, 11 Main

Genesee County.

Murry John *Alexander.*
Page B. C. & O. *Batavia.*

Greene County.

Ashley John *Catskill.*
Pennoye R. R.
Martin William H. *Coxsackie.*

Herkimer County.

Angel & Fowler *Little Falls*
Heath H.

Kings County.

Bell Hugh, 39 Hudson Av.
Brooklyn
Bithell Charles, Water near Jay
Bond A. F. 84 Myrtle Av.
Brant Henry. 166 York
Bridgins B. 116 Willoughby
Bridgins James, 217 Bridge
Brodie Alexander. 16 Hicks
Bromer John, corner Douglass &
Hoyt
Byrnes Joseph, 22 State
Callon John. Myrtle Av.
Campbell Joseph, Columbia st.
Carman Timothy, corner Tillary
& Lawrence
Chellborg Albert. 173 Jay
Cobb William A. Flushing Av.
East Brooklyn
Corwin Daniel. 167 Nassau
Darham James. 144 Concord
Deforest John & Isaac, Smith near
Warren
Drake William. 64 Main
Duff Patrick. 133 Tillary
Early Owen, 94 Front
Fronz F. cor. Livingston & Boerum
Glassey Nathan. 170 Myrtle Av.
Green Conrad, corner Smith &
Bergen
Griffing & Lewis, 59 Henry
Hoff J. 38 Hicks
Hahn William, Pacific near Court
Hamilton Henry, Carlton
Herlihy Jeremiah, 173 York
Hobbs H. 244 Henry
Hobbs John W. 363 Hudson Av.
Hoffner Charles
Hough John, 144 Johnson
Howell James, 47 Hudson Av.
Hunt Alfred, 203 Adams
Johnson John, 56 Main
Kerby Francis C. 103 Myrtle Av.
Kroushear Philip, 167 do
Langstaff John, 145 do
Laughlin John, 124 Hudson
Lessells William. 100 Prospect
Lindsay G. 12 Hudson Av.
M'Nish Robert. 84½ Atlantic
Mackin Charles, 46 Main
Mason John, 273 Fulton
Mellany P. 268 Hicks

Mooney S. B. Union, st. *Brooklyn.*
Mumby Robert, 159 Fulton
Nickson William, 231 Washington
Ohling C. R. cor. Smith & Baltic
Pearson James, Myrtle Av.
Phillips Anthony, 99½ Sands
Radford Henry, 68½ Fulton
Reid John, 54 Hudson Av.
Reinhardt John, 97 Bridge
Rhame Augustus, Classan Av. East
Riley Joseph A. jr. 111 High
Rugg M. F. 273 Hudson Av.
Sayrs J. 62 Atlantic
Seabury James M. 156 Sands
Simmerman Henry, 1 Linden row
Smith Isaac D. Prince cor. Johnson
Sueckner William, 206 Fulton
Spatz John F. 171 Tillary
Strattnn John B. 137 Atlantic
Swaney M. 74 Nassau
Swaney T. 155 Court
Sweet William F. 192 Nassau
Taylor Thomas, 349 Adams
Thorn William, 21 Atlantic
Varrick Robert, 211   do
Volckmer Henry E. 123 Fulton
Vollmer John A. cor. Boerum & Dean
Waldron S. Myrtle Av.
Warner John, 312 Atlantic
Warnock Andrew, 105 Pearl
Weber Henry, 142 Nassau
Westorer J. Hudson Av.
Woolsey Joseph, Myrtle Av.
Byrlof F. Green Point *Bushwick.*
Glander D. D. & Co. E. New York
                                    Flatbush.
Garnett Henry, S. 7th cor. 2d
                                    Williamsburgh.
Webb J. G. 57 4th
Malling Ronrad, Ewing st.
Hall J. W. 262 S. 3d
Reading Philip, 141 S. 2d
Flannagan Robert W. 201 do
Matthews Charles, 72 S. 1st
Van Velsor Chas. B. 45 Grand
Cocks John, 107   do
Harrison John, 161   do
Lindsay Thomas, 243   do
Waters Samuel L. 220   do
Richardson John. 206   do
Sexton Philip, 226 1st
Beam Henry, 85 N. 2d.
Burns W. H. 43   do
Keen Wm. H. 106 N. 3d
Taylor Israel, 34   do
Remsen A. Grand st. cor. Graham Av.
Cooper George, 98 Union
Bisson Ambrose, 96 Remsen
Gens John, 135 Ewing
Ormsbee D. B. Bushwick Av.

Livingston County.

Brown Wm.   *Dansville.*
Hilliard Rufus   *Mount Morris*
Warner ——   *Nunda.*

Madison County.

Lawson John L.   *Cazenovia.*
Curtis Saml.   *Hamilton.*

Monroe County.

Hemmel Augustus, 79 Clinton
                                    Rochester.
Yeoman Philip, cor. of Monroe & William
Lovell Robert, 212 Buffalo
Nagle & Yaman 113 Main
Miller L. 197   do
Serpell J. 111   do
Howe Jacob, 29 N. Fitzhugh
Paul Robert, 50 Exchange
Wadsworth Whiting, cor. Spring & Fitzhugh
Gibson B. 192 State
Braithwaite R. Mill st.
Cubros J. Vincent Park
Stevens J. C. 26 Fort
Caldwell J. S. 72 Troup

Flackanstaen V. cor. Brown & Maple   *Rochester.*

Montgomery County.

Matthews George   *Cunajoharie.*
Hanfield & Haven, Fort Plain
                                    Minden.

New York County.

Adams Sarah, 483 Pearl *New York.*
Adler David, 216 Stanton
Aikin Richard, 17 Perry
Aitken James G. 388 Broadway
Akin John, 415 Greenwich
Alhelt Adam, 72 Pike
Allen George, 51 Sullivan
Althouse Jacob, 128 Orchard
Anderson Charles. 260 Walker
Archer Moses, 253 Delancy
Arcularius George & Son, 319 Hudson
Arcularius George L. 805 Greenwich
Ardler David, 216 Stanton
Arthur John D. 125 Greenwich
Angen Louis F. 332 Houston
Bailey Phebe, 104 Mott
Baker Richard, 9th Av.
Baierlein F. 211 Houston
Baker Nicholas, 86 9th Av.
Baker Rd. 28th West
Banning A. 115 Spring
Barber William C. 370 6th
Barth Louis, 185 Av. B
Bassett E. 343 3d Av.
Baudau Joseph, 134 Reade
Bayar, Anthony J. 341 Greenwich
Beck Michael, 613 4th
Becker ——, 364 10th
Behlen A. 263 3d
Belknap Dayton C. 4 Jefferson & 360 Grand
Bell John, 248 Henry
Bell John, 366 Cherry
Bell Patrick, 115 Broome
Benker John C. 11 Forsyth
Berdan James, 748 Washington
Berg George, 9th Av.
Bersrem Jacob, 368 6th
Busley George. 229 6th
Beyer George B. 261 6th Av.
Beyer John, 129   do
Billings Jeremiah, 100 9th Av.
Bishop Savage, 251 3d Av.
Black James, 235 Bowery
Blacklaw Alexander, 9 Goerck
Bloom Henry, 326 Broome
Bohn Wm. 193 Houston
Boland Henry, 69½ Cannon
Bolton Thomas, 255 6th
Bonnell Stephen, 905 Broadway
Bonnell & Ten Eyck, 31 Madison
Born Jacob, 479 Washington
Bowman & Inglis, 28 W. 18th
Boyd Heman, 404 Cherry
Boyd Hugh, 187 Grand
Boyd John, 202 Elm
Boyd Joseph, 126 10th Av.
Boyle John, 302 Mott
Brack Geo. A. 196 Fulton
Brade Samuel, 233 Hudson
Breeze George, 79 Crosby
Brennemann Christian, 56 Av. A
Bresler George, 226 5th
Brert L. 118 Wooster
Brewster Abr. 5 Bedford
Bridge Samuel H. 358 Madison
Bridges J. 83 Pitt & 275 Houston
Bridges John. 186 Av. B
Bridges William, 118 Houston
Bridgins Charles W. 68 Carmine
Bridges C. 47 5th
Briggs Elijah P. 287 Front
Brockner Wash. 235 Bleecker
Brown John, 61 Vandam
Brown T. D. 18 Cherry
Brown P. W. 132 8th Av.
Brown P. S. 376 4th & 366 Bowery
Brown Thos. 28 West
Brues Joseph, 211 Delancy
Bryant Emma, 49 3d Av.

Bunny Charlotte, 71½ W. 13th
                                    New York.
Burdge H. 257 Spring
Burdge John W. 199 Bleecker
Burdge J. W. 543 Greenwich
Burgett J. 246½   do
Burns Arthur, 5 Bedford
Burrell George W. 80 3d
Burrell William, 124 Grand
Burrows Chester, 126 Cannon
Bushnell C. 381 Broome
Butcher W. 199 Varick
Butler Henry B. 53 Carmine
Calderhead John, 289 Spring
Campbell J. W. 27th st
Campbell & Moorhead. 126 W.21st
Carleton Joshua, 740 Broadway
Carnegie John, 364 3d Av.
Carstens Christian, 231 Walker
Cavanagh Peter, 390 Cherry
Chappell Thomas & Sons, 266 E. Broadway
Chick Christian, 45 Mulberry
Clarke Robert, 75 Greenwich Av.
Clauder Christian, 77 Norfolk
Claussen Fred. W. 132 8th Av.
Clink G. W. 126 Greenwich Av.
Clock Mary, 10 Av. D
Collins Franklin A. 8 Greenwich Av.
Coagan James, 94 Ridge
Cook Alexander, 263 Elizabeth
Cook George, 164 Perry
Coon Petor E. 44 Carmine
Cooper J. D. 494 6th Av.
Coulter Charles, 248 Canal
Cramsey James, 87 3d Av.
Cramer George, 123 W. 19th
Crasto A. G. 375 Houston
Crawford C. Mrs. 740 Broadway
Crennan John, 253 Mulberry
Cronenweth Jacob, 104 Centre
Cuche Charles, 67 Thompson
Currier John A. 191 Greenwich
Cushing James, 200 Hester
Daniells Charles, 29 Chrystie
Darrah Charles, 86 W. 18th
Daubern Nicholas, 27 Roosevelt
Davidson John, 93 Broad
Davidson & Young, 262 & 264 Front
Day Samuel W. 173 Walker
Dazet Jean, 213 Centre
Dean Mary E. 231 Madison
Deckelmann Philip, 468 4th
Decon Mrs. 296 8th Av.
Denmark & Jarvis, 92 James
Denner John, 33 Av. A
Dennison, Day & Co. 164 Madison
Devlin Charles, 44 Frankfort
Devoe Schmidt W. 16 1st Av.
Devoe Andrew, 863 4th Av.
Dhuerraf John, 203 Rivington
Didier M. 5 Centre market place
Dihl Martin, 22 Spring
Dobbs John, 650 Greenwich
Dobbs A. W. 550 Greenwich
Dominics ——, 734 Greenwich
Donegan James, 6 1st Av.
Dondel John D. 125 24th
Dowtel John D. 7th Av.
Duncan Walter, 169 Bowery
Early Jacob, 335 3d
Ebbets Edward A. 319 Hudson
Eberth Valentine, 191 1st Av.
Ehrhardt George, 251 Bowery
Eicks Hermann H. 655 Greenwich
Ellis C. C. 281 9th Av. Bloomingdale Bakery
Emeny John, 22 6th Av.
Emeny William, 724 Greenwich
Emmons Francis, 530 Pearl
Erhardt G. 251 Bowery
Eybel Henry, 292 10th
Fagan M. 84 Av. B
Farley John, 135 Houston
Farmer James, 270 Greenwich
Farrell William, 39 Mott
Farwell William, 43 do
Fass John, 232 Stanton
Fernau Henry, 101 Willet
Fernau John, 170 Amos

Ferrier Robert, 251 6th Av.
　　　　New York.
Fetter Jacob, 209 1st Av.
Fischer Jacob, 90 Morris
Fisher & Baldwin, 387 6th Av.
Fisher Samuel, jr. 313 Water
Flagg William, 54 Greenwich
Flannigan Richard, 555 Grand
Ford A. 8th Av.
Fowler B. 313 Water
Fox H. F. 181 Spring
Fox Jacob, 42 Broome
Fraser Alexander, 18 Clark
Frech Jacob, 86 Av. D
Freckleton John, 91 11th
Freeman James, 64 Suffolk
Fuechsel Augustus, 28 Hamersley
Fulmer Reinart, 58 Chrystie
Fuss John, 252 Stanton
Galligan James, 61 Walnut
Gardner John F. 186 N. William
Gaskin G. 50 James & 110 Cherry
Gedney Benjamin F. 128 Av. C
Geis Francis, 175 Broome
Genger Thomas, 110 7th Av.
Gettlemann Geo. P. 333 3d
Gibb Alexander, 75 Varick
Gibson George, 187 Church
Gibson James, 160 Spring
Gilfillan William, 86 Laurens
Gittelman George P. 333 3rd
Glander Henry, 6 Morton
Gleichman Charles, 248 2d
Goeller John M. 537 Broome
Goldsmith Raffield, 3 Av. B
Gonlak Daniel, 70 Broome
Goodwin James, 233 Rivington
Gordon Henry, 548 Broome
Graosers Bernhart, 22 Orange
Grannan John, 253 Mulberry
Griffin John, 12 Pitt
Groshlos Michael, 105 Orange
Grubber L. rear 14 W. Broadway
Guehlegh Jacob, 156 3d Av.
Gulak D. 70 Broome
Hagen Thomas J. 253 3d Av.
Hahan Martin, 6 Pearl
Haig Stephen, 3 5th
Hail Mrs. M. 236 6th Av.
Halle Jacob, 155½ Lewis
Halley Alexander, 164 W. 16th
Halley Robert, 304 W. 17th
Haloin Alexis, 93 Hudson, boulan-
　ger Français
Hamilton Mary, 123 3d Av.
Hamilton W. & J. 13 King
Hard Philip, Av. A. bet. E. 13th &
　E. 14th
Harper John, 80 Houston
Harrington N. 118　do
Harris Chas. J. 502　do
Harrison Mrs. 543 Greenwich
Haraler John, 146 Houston
Hart Philip, 28 Av. B
Hartmann Jacob, 132 Pitt
Harvey William, 87 Ridge
Hatherington Ellen, 324 Madison
Hauck Valentine, 488 Greenwich
Hawes John, 231 Washington
Hay Peter, W. 20th cor. 7th Av.
Hayes John, 87 Pitt
Hayter Richard, 155 Forsyth
Hecker & Brothers, 79 W. Broad-
　way, 482 Pearl & 58 Rutgers
Heidet Francois X. 137 Wooster
Heisenbuttle Christian, 48 Oak
Heisor Andrew, 252 5th
Heissenbuttle F. 298 William
Helmes Peter, 174 3d Av.
Hess Jacob, 37th 9th Av.
Hessler John, 656 Water
Hewes H. 135 Hammond
Hickinbottom Geo. 342 Madison
Hill M. 91 11th
Hill Martin, 12th. bet.1st & 2d Avs.
Hirsh Phillip, 182 Varick
Hitzelberger Christ'r. 159 8th Av.
Hoff Jacob, 55 Ridge
Hoffmire Henry, 100 Reade
Hoil William H. 105 Columbia
Holmes William, 32 Forsyth
Homer Henry, 11 Lispenard

Hons Claus H. 77 4th　New York.
Horsington R. 445 Greenwich
Hort William, 190 8th Av.
Houston William, 231 Delancy
Howe Benjamin F. 482 Broadway
Howe John W. 143 8th Av.
Hughes Bernard, 23 M'Dougal
Hughes Daniel, 236 W. 16th
Hughes Henry, 135 Hammond
Hughes Henry, 721 Washington
Hughes Mary, 13 M'Dougal
Hulse Paul, 174 Allen
Humbert William B. 220 Bowery
Hummel C. 488 Greenwich
Hunzelman John, 13 2d Av.
Huntington Hiram L. 67 Cortlandt
Huyler David, 43 Troy
Huyler David, 35 4th
Huyzer A. 245 5th
Immen John H. 197 Prince
Innes Charles, 698 Broadway
Jackson William, 285 Bleecker
Jacobs George F. 1 12th
Johnson Alice, 231 Av. B
Johnson Robert, 28½ Thompson
Johnson & Treadwell, 110 Beek'n
Jolley Richard, 26 Orchard
Jones Rebecca, 226 Division
Joy A. 36 Allen
Junes C. jr. 693½ Broadway
Kaler A. 36 Anthony
Karn John, 65 1st
Kashow Israel, 282 3d
Kaufman J. & Wm. C. 160 South
Kauth Peter, 133 Clinton
Kearney Michael, 237 E. 25th
Kehoe John, 1st Av. near 25th
Keizer John, 5 Chrystie
Kelling James F. 57 Anthony
Kelly James, 79 Beekman
Kelz Leonard, 227 E. 13th
Kern John, 65 1st
Killian Andrew, 24 Av. D
Kirk David, 144 6th Av.
Klingler Christian, 136 Sullivan
Klink Geo. W. 126 Greenwich Av.
Kloppenburg Otto, 160 South
Knapp William, 93 W. Broadway
Knowlton James R. 165 Rivington
Koan John, 65 1st
Kobbe Henry, 144 Laurens
Koellstadt Jacob, 26 Sullivan
Koeman John C. 282 Division
Kohler Adam, 36 Anthony
Kolb Francis, 188 Orchard
Kornarer John, 282 Division
Kopf Charles, 242 3d
Kran John, 65 1st
Krapp John, 63 Market
Kronethall William, 113 Houston
Kuhl George, 235 Av. B
Kummelstihl S. 179 Rivington
Lahr, Valentine, 467 Greenwich
Lance Mary, 109 Forsyth
Lang Alexander, 388 Pearl
Lang Gottlieb, 150 Washington
Lang Leonard, 256 Broome
Lang Philip, 267 Division
Lang Robert, 381 Broome
Lauer Jacob, 25 Av. C
Lawrence R. Y. 11½ 3d Av.
Leaycraft Daniel, 67 Bayard
Leopold George, 195 Division
Lescolt O. 196　　do
Lewis Elias, 62 Mulberry
Lindsay Richard, 169 Greene
Lockstand James, 51 Prince
Logan Alexander, 127 19th
Long William, 144 Walker
Lowe Joshua, 39th st.
Lower John, 95 Goerck
Luttrell William, 220 Mott
Luxford Edward, 180 Mulberry
Lyon George W. P. 4 Carmine
M'Ateer James, 71 Bayard
M'Bride Alexander,333 Thompson
M'Callum Cornelia, 382 Pearl
M'Connel F. 226 1st Av.
M'Cosker Maria, 230 1st Av.
M'Donald Henry, 82 Catharine
M'Donough T. R. 314 Bowery
M'Fadden Peter, 293 3d Av.

M'Fall H. jr. E. 27th st. New York.
M'Gey Isaac, 172 Mulberry
M'Gey James, 37 Charles
M'Ginnis Kennedy, 119 Hammond
M'Gnire James, 52 Cherry
M'Millan George, 34½ Oak
M'Nann Mary, 138 W. 20th
M'Quade Patrick, 32½ Catharine
Magee Isabella, 5 Cannon
Main Samuel R. 38 W. 13th
Manck V. 105 Christopher
Mander Henry, 32 2d Av.
Mann Charles, 34 Wooster
Manson Daniel, 194 6th Av.
Marks Isaac, 376 Grand
Marshall William, 74 Market
Martin Hahm, 6 Pearl
Marwede Frederick, 119 Orange
Masterton Wm. E. 334 Bleecker
Matthews Thomas, 418 Cherry
Maurege John, 595 Greenwich
Moany Peter, 78 Bayard
Meikle Wm. 187 Church
Meiser Andrew, 1 12th
Menhorn John L. 240 W. 16th
Menoll John, 175 Stanton
Metzer George, 298 Bowery
Meyer Henry, 229 Hudson
Meyer Frederick, 776 Washington
Meyerhoff Martin, 125 Stanton
Mexican George, 293 Bowery
Michel Frederick, 414 Broome
Middlehoff G. 537 6th Av.
Middleton Alexander, 8th Av.
Mildeberger Oliver, 22 Harrison
Miller John, 74 4th Av.
Milliken William N. 75 Lewis
Mills John, 186 3d Av. & 31 9th Av.
Milner Alfred A. 56 Jane
Mink Valentine, 105 Christopher
Mitchell Henry S. 79 Columbia
Mitchell Jacob F. 196 W. 21st
Mitchell Patrick, 67 Charlton
Moadinger John, jr. 586 Grand
Molitor Francis W. 45 Ludlow
Molitor Frederick, 290 Bowery
Moore Thomas H. 296 Greenwich
Moore Charles, 931 Broadway
Moyle William, 175 Av. A
Muhlbecker John, 243 Rivington
Munn Henry, 115 Lewis
Munson A. 196 E. 21st
Munson James H. 10 Beekman,
　& Connecticut Pie Depot
Myer Frederick, 776 Washington
Myers Bernard, 87 Hammond
Myers Henry, 214 6th Av.
Myers John, 84 Av. B
Naedhing John, 681 Water
Nelson Peter, 109 W. 20th
Neville Francis, 82 Orange
Newell Frederick, 202 2d Av.
Niess Joseph, 13 King
Oakley Wooster, 375 Houston
Ohlwaze Louis, 206 Greene
Oliver John, 34 Cherry
Orr Joseph, 74 Watts
Otten Hannah, 114½ Allen
Ougler Francis, 5 Av. C
Paar John, 33 1st Av. near E. 18th
Palmer Melancthon, 373½ Pearl
　& 11 Mott
Pangor John C. 11 Forsyth
Parr James, 77 Mott, ship bread
　& crackers
Parr John F. 495 Pearl
Peacock James, 619 Greenwich
Pennoyer William, 157 11th
Pennycook John 64 8th Av.
Petrie Alexander, 10th Av.
Pfeiffer William, 142 Forsyth
Pitman John, 26 Broome
Platt John E. 232 Canal
Platt Henry, 33 7th Av.
Pleignet J. C. 197 4th Av.
Plyow Geo. 1½ Carmine
Pohle Frederick, 124 Delancy
Post Sylvester O. 268 5th
Price James, 119 Av. C
Price William, 226 Houston
Pritchard W. 7th Av. cor. 19th
Pudney Wm. H. 108 Bleecker

Pullar Jas. 62 Stanton *New York*.
Pullar William, 19 6th Av.
Purdy Abraham B. 342 Hudson
Purdy Samuel V. 105 Hudson
Raab Henry, 6 Av. B
Ramsey J C. 87 2d Av. cor. 5th
Rauch Henry, 412 10th
Ray Francis A. & Allis, 367 Monroe
Ray John, 103 Bedford
Raynor Jacob, 55 Ludlow
Raynor Nathan, 400 Grand
Rebhann J. George, 169 7th
Reeds J. 94 Charles
Reid Alexander, Av. B cor. 12th
Reid John, 94 Charles
Reitinger John, 166 Walker
Reuch Conrad, 94 Sheriff
Rice John, 263 3d
Richter Daniel H. 215 Delancy
Rick John. 447 Washington
Ridabock A. H. 90 Hudson
Robertson John, 24 Rivington
Robertson John, 50 9th Av.
Rogers George W. 147 Division
Rogers William B. 17 Pike
Rooney James, 101 King
Rose Conrad, 30 Av. B
Rose Henry, 253 Centre
Rottman John F. 137½ Liberty
Rowlee J. B. 196 Av. C
Ruhnberg F. E. 74 University pl
Rusher John T. 19 Vandam
Rutherford David, 187 Church
Ryckman Samuel, rear 43 Dey
Sanford J. L. & Co. 154 South
Sang Alexander, 368 Pearl
Sauer N. 8th st
Saul William, 40 Lispenard
Sayre Isaac, 80 Chambers
Scanlon James, cor. 6th & Av. B
Schaaf George, 94 Lewis
Schaeffer Henry, 55 Av. B
Schafer Philip, 136 Hester
Scheierling George A. 46 Hester
Schenck Robert, 7 Lewis
Schleiger Adam, 601 Water
Schlinghuyde Adolph, 21 Anthony
Schmidt Ann, 182 6th Av.
Schnatz Peter, 4 Av. A
Schoonmaker J. H. & Co. 219 Fulton
Schwab Frederic, 295 Broome
Schwartz Frederick, 156 Reade
Schwartz G. 143 3d
Schwegler Frederick. 54 Av. C
Schweitzer Lauohert, 70 Walnut
Shiek Christian. 45 Mulberry
Seibe Hans L. 152 Greenwich
Semon Henry, 178 2d
Shaddle Henry V. 25 Barclay
Shaffer H. 55 Av. B
Shannon W. J. 367 Greenwich
Sheppard Henry, 115 Suffolk
Sheumen George. 304 Spring
Sheriff George, 1 9th Av.
Shnatz Peter, 4 Av. A
Shumway M. 99 Canal
Simpson & Kemp, 363 Bowery & 47 Christopher
Sinclair John. 104 Reade
Slater John. 506 Houston
Slipper Charity, 141 Delancy
Smith Jacob, 11 Essex
Smith Peter. 405 Av. B
Smith William, 378 Hudson
Sneckner John, 210 Bowery
Sour Nicholas, 328 8th
Sparks Frederick, 39 Vesey
Speir Robert. jr. 96 Pine
Spindler Peter, 48 Walnut
Sriner James, 9th Av.
Steel Henry, 69 Orange
Steel William. 111 Cherry
Stehr Louis, 77 4th
Steinle Frederick, 711 Greenwich
Steinseick Charles. 23 Marion
Stern, Morris & Rosenstein, 171 Broome
Stevens David, 145 Duane
Sthulte Theodore, 388 Monroe
Stiehl Adam, 200 Av. B
Stiehl Heinrich, 59 Orange

Stives John G. 36 Ludlow *New York*.
Stodola Samuel. 12 Mulberry
Stosser Frederick, 155 Forsyth
Strose Solomon, 230 Houston
Stubbins Thomas F. 106 8th Av.
Subbs William. 107½ 9th Av.
Suydam Cornelius, 117 Mott
Suydam Phebe, 136 Mott
Suydam William, 117 Mott
Swain Rinaldo R. 100 3d Av.
Swarts Geo. jr. cor. Av. A & 6th
Switzer L. 70 Walnut
Tag I. H. 8th Av.
Taylor David H. 42 Pearl
Taylor Hugh, 57 Hamersley
Taylor Joseph, 8th Av.
Taylor & Wilson, rear 73 Fulton
Thall John F. 528 Grand
Thayer Warren. 123 3d Av.
Thies Anthony, 648 Washington
Thomson Peter & Sons, 356 Greenwich
Thompson Robert, 43 Leonard
Thurauf John. 235 Stanton
Thompson James, 32½ Catharine & 343 6th Av.
Towner Samuel, 553 Hudson
Tracy Edward, 167 E. 11th
Treadwell's Ephraim Son, 106 Warren
Tritton Richard, 105 Bayard
Troughton Elisha, 96 Roosevelt
Trumpy Caspar, 91 Av. D
Trumpy Caspar. 238 7th
Trust Caspar, 122 W. 19th
Trust Conrad, 85 Sheriff
Trust George, 291 Rivington
Tubbs William, 107½ 9th Av.
Turnbull James, 643 Broome
Turner James, 9th Av. cor. 29th
Turner Thomas, 642 Hudson
Ungroch Henry, 366 Cherry
Ungrich M. 7th Av.
Ungrich M. 33d st
Vaniderstine Isaac M. 160 Orcha'd
Van Eaden Benjamin. 456 Hudson
Vermeule Jane H. 105 Clinton
Volckmer Catharine A. 182 Canal
Von Hagen Martin, 97½ Cedar
Vorrath John F. 88 Rivington
Wachter Conrad. 21 Hester
Wachter John. 292 E. 11th
Wagner John. 219 3d
Wagner John J. 252 Delancy
Walcott Joseph B. 279 Bleecker
Walduck Robert M. 96 6th Av.
Wall Jacob. 253 Grand
Walsh P. 42 Canal
Walter John. 27 Av. B
Walter Fred. & Co. 238 Broadway
Walters Gerard, 49 Beekman
Ward James, 39½ Vesey
Warren James. 201 Monroe
Waters John, 46 Laurens
Webb Joseph B. 20 Stanton
Webb Thomas, 476 Pearl & 105 Division
Webster William, 351 Hudson
Weitcher John. 292 11th
Welsh Patrick. 42 Canal
Wentworth M. B. & O. F. 103 & 220½ Greenwich
Wernig Jasper. 316 Rivington
West Zimri, 36 Hudson
Wether John, 116 Mulberry
Wettrau George W. 182 Delancy
White Alexander F. 21 Spring
White Jacob, 234 Stanton
White John, 19 Catharine
White & Gilbert, 9th Av.
Wick Jacob, 41st st.
Widmayer George. 9 James
Wieners John C. 114 Delancy
Williams Catharine H. 515 Huds'n
Williams Isaac, 226 8th Av.
Wilson Thomas C. 402 8th
Wilt Benjamin, 216 Division & 324 Grand
Wilt George W. 62 Ludlow
Wilt Henry, 15 Essex
Winthrop John, 63 Av. D

Wirt Jacob, 114 Willet *New York*.
Wirth George, 131 Willet
Wohlrabe Andrew, 131 Division
Wohlfort Frederick. 27 Av. B
Worth Jacob, 234 Stanton
Woods William H. 257 Grand
Woodward Richard, 2 Hall place
Woollatts Thomas, 71 9th Av.
Yohr Frederick J. 60 Allen
Young Adam, 154 Christopher
Young Walter J. 134 Church
Zeigler Lewis, 175 Stanton
Zimmer George, 26th West
Zimmerman Andrew, 75 6th Av.
Zimmerman William, 274 Madison

Niagara County.

Scott Robert   *Lewiston*.
Allen Isaac   *Lockport*.
Waggoner John
Schmeck William
Curtis A. H.   *Niagara Falls*.

Oneida County.

Scofil J. Dominick st.   *Rome*.
Mallery & Glover, do
Elmer L. K. & C. W.
Hackett William, 126 Genesee
                             Utica.
Williams L. 21 Liberty
Pomaroy & Crippen, 23 & 24 Fayette
Horsburgh A. 72 Bleeker
Wilkins L. 33 & 35 do

Onondaga County.

Dean G. W. Water st. Syracuse
                             Salina.
Ormsbee L. J. James st. do
Thurber P. & Co.   do
Wood S. Salina st.   do

Ontario County.

Anderson James   *Canandaigua*.
Stringham T.
Suidam H. L. & Co. Geneva *Seneca*.

Orange County.

Doer H. Buttermilk Falls *Cornwall*.
Daniels J.   do
Emsley James
Martin H. Port Jervis *Deer Park*.
Gasley W. M.   *Goshen*.
Pitts Samuel
Wilson Henry   *Montgomery*.
Chapman P. & Son, 51 Water
                         Newburgh.
Tartis John C. 103   do
Bonticour George. 116 do
Gravey Thomas, Colden st.
Hamilton Mrs.   do
Parrett J. South Middletown
                         Wallkill.

Orleans County.

Woolford & Wall. Albion *Barre*.
Smith E. & S. C. Medina *Ridgeway*.

Oswego County.

Kishner John, cor. 1st & Seneca
                         Oswego.
Worts M. C. 5 Phœnix Block, 1st st.
Blackwood Neil. 1st st.
Hempstead Charles, Pulaski
                         Richland.

Putnam County.

Daniels J. Cold Spring
                         Phillipstown
Leonard L.   do

Queens County.

Myee W. H.   *Flushing*.
Thorp F.
Irving C.
Pittman J. S.

Seabury R. S.   *Hempstead.*
Cane Phillip A.
Edwards G.   *Jamaica.*
Cornwell J. W.
Smith R. H. Astoria   *Newtown.*
Kirk Joshua, Jericho   *Oyster Bay.*

Rensselaer County.

Fox J. 273 State   *Lansingburgh.*
Corbins A. B. 89½ Richard
Miller Mrs. 6 Hoosick   *Troy.*
Heath Daniel   do
Hodge James, 3 N. 3d st.
Duncan David, 38 N. do
Morse E. 40   do 2d st.
Morse Warren C. 40 N. 2d
Bunnell A. 12 Federal
Taylor John W. 148 2d
Inwood Robert, 250 4th
Wickes J. 149   do
Dexter C. B. 141   do
Chase D. E. 76 Congress
Cheput Z. rear of 18 Division
Smith Thomas, 175 Front st. South

Richmond County.

Van Duzer T. H. Tompkinsville   *Castleton.*
Scott G., Stapleton   *Southfield.*

Rockland County.

Hawkins J. Nyack   *Orangetown.*
Styles D. Piermont

St. Lawrence County.

Barber John, Isabella st. Ogdensburgh   *Oswegatchie.*
Winslow Jehiel, Ford st.
Bull Henry   *Potsdam.*

Saratoga County.

Root Joel   *Saratoga Springs.*
White Henry
Titcomb Mary P.   *Waterford.*
Fletcher Edward

Schoharie County.

Parrot William   *Schoharie.*

Schenectady County.

Herbert J. State st.   *Schenectady.*
Moon G. W. 95 Ferry
Anthony W. H. 91 do

Suffolk County.

Handley C. D. Patchogue   *Brookhaven.*
Van Ansaull N.   do
Shepard George   *Huntington.*

Tompkins County.

Whiton J. L. 115 Owego   *Ithaca.*
Baker & Youngs, 7   do

Ulster County.

Pine James S.   *Kingston.*
Reading John
Allcorn J. Rondout
Stephen F.   do
Uhle Martin   do
Canfield George   *New Paltz.*
Suderly C. F.   *Saugerties.*
Devlin Mark
Wilber U. Ellenville   *Wawarsing.*

Washington County.

Colvin J. L. Sandy Hill *Kingsbury.*

Wayne County.

Mugridge Jos. Newark   *Arcadia.*
Hewlett William   *Lyons.*
Gardner Isaac   *Palmyra.*
Palmer Philip

Westchester County.

Polhill Jas. Peekskill *Cortlandt.*
Wood Samuel S. do
Webb John, Portchester   *Rye.*
Decasco J. P.   *West Farms.*
Morratt John
Trobe John
Palmer Lloyd
Mead H. A.   *White Plains.*
Conquagood Peter   *Yonkers.*
M'Farland D.

Wyoming County

Chase J. M.   *Warsaw.*

Yates County.

Wyman A. Penn Yan   *Milo.*
Jacobus & Kenyon, do

Balances and Scales.

Ayers Isaac, 83 Fulton *New York.*
Brown J. L. 234 Water
Chatillon John, 33 Cherry
Fairbanks & Co. 81 Water
Geralds Ashael, 120 Barrow
Johnston James, 67 Fulton
Kissam James A. 67 Fulton
Labarte Nathl. 44 & 46 Eldridge
Lewis John, 91 Fulton
McDougall S. T 103 Wall
Morton & Bremner, 61 Elizabeth
N. Y. Journeyman Scale Co. 43 Greene
Potter Samuel S. 209 Water
Ranche H. 412 10th
Scharfer H. 52 Av. B cor. 4th
Smith O. T. 50 West
Van Varick M. 213 Spring
Wade Ezekiel, jr. 17 Peck slip
Wilkie J. 8th Av.

Ballast.

Bertran Wm. R. 67 South
                       New York.

Bending—Patent Leather Machine.

Kumbel Wm. 33 Ferry *New York.*
Rees & Hoyt, 67 & 69 Frankfort

Rensselaer County.

Hillman Joseph, 173 River *Troy.*

Bankers.

Erie County.

Seymour H. R. & Co. 181 Main
  cor. Seneca   *Buffalo.*

Bankers. (See also Brokers.)

Augusta & Insurance Co.'s Bank, 96 Wall   *New York.*
Beebee, Ludlow & Co. 49 Wall
Belden C. & G. 60 Wall
Belmont August. 67 Wall
Brown, Brothers & Co. 59 Wall
Cammann & Whitehouse, 56 Wall
Comstock D. A. 43 Wall, Jauncey court
Corning & Co. 63 Wall
Dennistoun, Wood & Co. 59 Wall
Dixon Joshua & Co. 49 William
Dixon Thomas. 49   do
Draper & Glover, 54 Wall
De Rham & Moore, 24 Exchange place
Dykers, Alstyne & Co. 62 Wall
Fisher & Denny, 8 Jauncey court
Dunscomb & Beckwith, 50 Wall
Harmoy's Nephew & Co. 159 Bwy.

Jaudon S. & Co. 54 Wall *New York.*
Kennedy David S. 58 Wall
Ketchum, Rogers & Bement, 47 Wall
King James G. & Sons, 53 William
Kruger Richard, 28 Exchange pl.
Lahens J. & Co. 62 Wall
Little Jacob & Co. 44 Wall
Morgan Matthew, 56 Wall
Nevins R. H. & Co. 49 Merchants' Exchange
Pickersgil W. C. & Co. 49 Wall
Pilot & Lebarbier, 67 Wall
Prime Edward, 54 Wall
Prime Rufus, 54   do
Riggs Elisha, 56 Wall
Robbins G. S. & Son. 52 Wall
Roche, Brothers & Co. 35 Fulton
Speyers & Co. 51 Broad
Thayer Ebenezer, agent for Green & Co. Bankers, Paris, 6 Wall
Townsend T. & E. 24 Merchants' Exchange
Ward & Co. 54 Wall
Winslow, Lanier & Co. 62 Wall
Winter J. G. & Co. 54 Wall

Banks—Savings.

Albany County.

Savings Institution. John Townsend President, James Taylor Treasurer. 4 State *Albany.*

Cayuga County.

Auburn Savings Institution. Chas. B. Perry President, Charles P. Ward Treasurer. 63 Genesee *Auburn.*

Duchess County.

Savings Institution. Thomas W. Talmadge President, John B. Forbus Vice President, Josiah Burritt Treasurer. 277 Main *Poughkeepsie.*

Kings County.

Brooklyn Savings Institution. Hosea Webster President, William Hull Secretary, open Tuesdays, Thursdays & Saturdays from 5 to 7 P. M. Interest 5 per cent. Cor. Fulton & Concord *Brooklyn.*

Monroe County.

Rochester Savings Institution. Jacob Goul President, Hiram Wright Secretary, Edward Whalin Treasurer. State st. *Rochester.*

New York County.

Bank for Savings in the City of New York. Philip Hone President, James De Peyster Ogden Secretary, C. O. Halsted Treasurer. Open from 4 to 6 P. M. daily. 107 Chambers   *New York.*
Bowery. James Mills President, Giles H. Coggeshall Secretary. Open Mondays, Thursdays and Saturdays, from 5 to 7 P. M.   125 Bowery
East River Savings Institution. Elias G. Drake President, Thomas Williams jr., George M. Clearman Vice-Presidents, Charles A. Whitney Secretary. Open on Mondays, Thursdays and Saturdays, from 5 to 7 P. M. Interest payable January and July. 145 Cherry
Greenwich. Abraham Van Nest President, C. Gilbert and E. N. Pigot Secretaries, Lambert Suydam Treasurer. Open Mondays,

Wednesdays and Fridays, from 5
to 7 P. M. Interest payable January and July, 41 6th Av.
New York.
*Institution for the Savings of
Merchants' Clerks.* G. King President, J. I. Palmer Treasurer. T.
Spencer Kirby Secretary. Open
on Tuesdays, Thursday and Saturdays, from 6 to 8 P. M. 5 Beekman
Seaman's Bank for Savings.
Benjamin Strong President, Wm.
Nelson Secretary, Joseph W. Alsop, jr. Treasurer. Open daily
from 10 to 2 P. M. Interest payable 1st January and July. 82 Wall

Oneida County.

Utica Savings Institution. J.
Walker President. S. Williams
Secretary & Treasurer, 10 Bleek-
er *Utica.*

Rensselaer County.

Troy Savings Institution. G.
Corning President, F. Leake Ac-
countant *Troy.*

Basket Makers.

Rensselaer County.

Smith & Stephen, near State dam
Troy.

Baskets—Importers of.

Dufiot H. 69 William *New York.*
Johnston Robert R. 38 Catharine
Loreaux Remy, 82 John
Philopoteaux Etienne, 3 Maiden L.
Ward H. D. & E. 106 Maiden L.
Zinn Charles, 52 Maiden Lane.

Baskets—Dealers in.

Atkinson Wm. 5 Av. D *New York.*
Blohm Christian, 95 Renwick
Cameron James, 68 Catherine
Carr John, 58 Essex
Caverly Samuel L. 71 Vesey &
206 Greenwich
Dietrich Christian, 202 Grand
Engelhardt John B. 149 Greenw'h
Fagin James K. 297 Spring
Hancock George. 2 Centre mark't
Hartley David. 222 William
Haynes Nathaniel, 165 Stanton
Hopeman Lentman, 11 Thompson
Hutchings James. 194 6th Av.
Jackson Peter, 147 Mott
Johnson John, 240 Division
Kindon Henry, 296 Pearl
Lanke E. N. W. 30 College place
Mackey Elbert H. 94 Vesey
M'Gennis William. 216 Spring
Mills Wm. H. 225 Fulton
Myer Joseph, 108 Mott
O'Brien Timothy, 1 Centre mark't
Pfester Joseph, 211 2d
Randel J. & S. 241 Broadway
Rosenbauer Nicholas, 27 Delancy
Rowe William, 96 Vesey
Sakman George. 139 Houston
Spickermore Peter R. 28 Reade
Stoerte Andrew, rear 5 Walnut
Thompson John. 90 Mott
Tobin James, 306 2d
Topf John, 271 Bleecker
Wolf Solomon, 97 Division

Bathing Houses.

Albany County.

Dean N. S. 19 Norton *Albany.*

Kings County.

Hudson John, (salt water) 94 Co-
lumbia *Brooklyn.*
Gray E. (salt and warm) foot of
Fulton
Hanfield Harman, (salt and warm)
1st cor. Kent Av. *Williamsburgh.*

New York County.

Balloni Louis J. 41 Merchants'
Exchange *New York.*
Braman Jarvis, 4 Cortlandt
Burns T. H. 154 Crosby
Byrnes T. H. 600 Broadway
Carroll Edward J. 36 Barclay
Chatman A. F. 2 Franklin square
Ciprico George, 10 Frankfort
Duryer & Faulkner, 11 & 13 Cath.
George F. S. 235 Houston
Gomperts Benjamin. 101 Bowery
Harvey James, 61 Broadway
Jackson Charles H. 155 Grand
Locke John. 47 Ann
Miller Richard H. 41 Merchants'
Exchange
Phalon Edward. 197 Broadway
Rabineau H. C. 1 Vesey (Astor
House,) Battery swimming. Ir-
ving House. Carlton House, and
foot of Desbrosses
Stoppani Charles G. 398 Broadway
Sweet William H. 222 Canal
Timolat Louis J. 547 Pearl

Batting and Wicking.

Chenango County.

Whitmore John E. *Guilford.*

Jefferson County.

Sigourney John M. *Watertown.*

Oneida County.

Howell J. (yarn, wicking, twine
and batting) *New Hartford.*
Read J. (do do do)
Halbert ——, 2 Fulton *Utica.*

Rockland County.

Tallman J. D. Spring Valley
Orangetown.
Crum J. *Ramapo.*

Bedstead Manufacturers.

Albany County.

Meade John & Co. (patent right &
left screw bedstead) 41 James
Albany.
Tingley O.
Parkhurst & Still, Cohoes
Watervliet.

Duchess County.

Blake & Kenworthy, Mill st.
Poughkeepsie.

Erie County.

Utley Horace, (mahogany)13 Swan
Buffalo.
Atkins Joel, 46 Clinton

Greene County.

Gilbert & Tremaine *Hunter.*
Howard & Ingalls
Jackson Charles, Black Creek
Riga.

Kings County.

Wells Samuel, 86 Grand
Williamsburgh.

Monroe County.

Cowles James B. Curtis' Block,
Main st. *Rochester.*

Robinson O. Selye Buildings,
Brown's Race *Rochester.*

Oneida County.

M'Lean S. Whitesboro st. *Utica.*
Thomas Thos. do

Oswego County.

Bickford James, Crocker's Buildings, Bridge st. *Oswego.*

Rensselaer County.

Marble E. T. 279 River *Troy.*
Van Allen John, (patent)417 River

Tompkins County.

Jarvis J. S. 113 Owego *Ithaca.*

Beer Pump Makers.

Kimmel W. J. W. cor.13th st.& 4th
Av. *New York.*
Sealy Richard, 321 & 542 Pearl

Bell Hangers. (See also Lock-smiths.)

Albany County.

Woolensack J. 6 Liberty *Albany.*
Blackall J. & W. 100 Hamilton

Cayuga County.

Whipple E. H. Water st. *Auburn.*

Kings County.

Brown James, 55 Atlantic
Brooklyn.
M'Nully M. 40 Henry
Beckett H. Orange st. near Heavy
Dalton Wm. 255 Adams
Thomas T. Myrtle Av.

Monroe County.

Sherlock & Co. Curtis Block,
Main st. *Rochester.*

Bell Telegraph Manufac-turers.

Onondaga County.

Hudson L. A. Houghton's Bell
Tel. for Public Houses, Genesee st. Syracuse *Salina.*

Belting Manufacturers.

Duchess County.

Francis I. *Fishkill.*
Vanderwater A.

Bill Posters.

Collins Philip, 38 Elm *New York.*
Rielly Ann, 76 Ann

Billiard Saloons. (See also Porter Houses.)

Austin John S. 3 Park row
New York.
Bassford Abraham, 3 Ann
Bassford D. 149 Fulton
Denman W. P. 69 Vandam
Estephe Victor, 156 Fulton
Harting Wm. 193 William
Irving Rooms, 401 Broadway
Mayeram Bernard. 55 Barclay
Monteverde Francis, 5 do
Musso J. 178 Canal
Phelan Michael, 6½ Barclay
Robenson Adolph, 56 West

Seamans T. 355 4th Av. *New York.*
Venn Henry B. 298 Bowery

Billiard Table Makers.

Bassford & Field, 8 Ann
　　　　　　　New York.
Moore Strong V. 106 Fulton
O'Connor Tobias, 63 Ann
Winant Daniel D. 71 & 73 Gold

Bird and Beast Stuffer.

Bell John G. 299 Broadway
　　　　　　　New York.

Bird Cage Makers.

Brown James, rear 112 Division
　　　　　　　New York.
Beeoth Francis B. 297 Spring
Gailhard J. B. 456 Broadway
Grieve A. 5 John
Kelly Joseph, 25 Fulton
Pacaw John, 406 Broadway

Birds—Dealers in.

Demarest James, 332 Broadway
　　　　　　　New York.
Grieve A. 5 John
Harment M. 21 Clinton market
Heirinanze Garrett,　do
Keltas Edward. 236 Division
Martin William, 350 6th Av.
Messenger W. F. 564½ Broadway
Rouche Charles, 162 William
Roux Adeline, 26 Clinton market
Shaw Joseph, 21 Amos
Tobin Thomas, 129 Cherry
Wells James, gardens laid out
　and kept in order, conservato-
　ries and green-houses attended
　to, 37 W. 13th
Williams Charles, 48 Fulton
Williams Henry, 355 Bowery

Bit and Stirrup Makers.

Barrett William, 89 Reade
　　　　　　　New York.
Harvey George, rear 89 Elizabeth

Blacking Makers.

Albany County.

Rosecrans & Owens, 43 Dean
　　　　　　　Albany.

Kings County.

Blakley John, 57 Fulton *Brooklyn.*

Monroe County.

Woodruff R. 3 Scio　*Rochester.*

New York County.

Chapel John, 72 Fulton, basement
　　　　　　　New York.
Dare & Webb, 77 Catherine
Fatman Lewis & Co. 200 Front
Fraser & Everitt. 35 Gold
Jones Robert, 162 William
Lee Charles, 1 John
Lockwood R. G. 3 Cortlandt
Mooney & Parmenter, 76 Division
Van Dewenter John, 82 Dey

Black Lead Manufacturer.

Essex County.

Ives C. P.　　　*Ticonderoga.*

Blacksmiths.

Albany County.

Percival G. 196 Broadway
　　　　　　　Albany.
Cunliff S. jr. 18 Quay
Treadwell C. 14 do
Carroll William, 84 Montgomery
Graham John Q. 4 Spencer
Hogan E. 49 Water
M'Sheen P. 176 Montgomery
Wemple J. D. W. 53 Hamilton
Quim M. 86 Green
Concklin J. & A. 89 Green
Caldwell W. J. 90　do
Shaw L. 99　　do
Boyle J. 210 S. Pearl
Langrish ——, 171 do
Russ J. P. 6 Grand
Footman P. 4 do
Witt William. 243 State
Shaw E. 96 Canal
Rull N. 438 Lydius
O'Brien M. 25 Washington
O'Neill ——, 96　do
Lossing J. 17 Bowery
M'Donald H.
　　　　　　　Coeymans.
Carroll Wm. R. & Son
Cook Charles
Whitmore T.
Van Buren P.
Johnson John, Dunnsville
　　　　　　　Guilderland.
Pearl Isaac
Shouday John
Tigget Jacob
Shoudy Henry
Mesick George
Quackenbush ——
Champion B.　　*Knox.*
Weaver ——,
Fitzsimmons P. West Troy
　　　　　　　Watervliet.
O'Brien M.
Coghall S.
Mason J. West Troy
Derby A.　　do
Sullivan George, do
Saven J.　　do
Wilkinson J. L. Cohoes
Allerton G.　　*Westerlo.*
Disbrow H. C.

Allegany County.

Rhinevault & Crandall　*Alfred.*
Burdick & Palmeter
Burdick E. P.
Bell ——
Allen ——
Brown ——, Phillips' Creek
Warren David H.　　*Allen.*
Gregory E.
Brown E.　　*Almond.*
Ball N.
Kline T. R.
Beadle George　　*Amity.*
Brown S.
Sorter Jesse
Lee & Crane　　*Andover.*
Porter A. & J.
Carpenter Samuel　*Angelica.*
Fisk P. M.
Bell John
Miles Harvey
Shephard P. H.
Anderson A.　　*Belfast.*
Burr M. H.
Barnard ——
Orcutt H.
Clancey Michael　　*Birdsall.*
Dye Wm. E.
Young David
Burdick Franklin　　*Bolivar.*
Lewis George W.　　*Burns.*
Fitzgerald Wm.
Ingersoll Wm. Whitney Valley
Easterbrook A.　　*Caneadea.*
Madison ——
Drock S. B.
Currier & Gilbert　　*Cuba.*
Beard & Randolph

Allen Henry R.　　*Cuba.*
Scott David
Young Josiah　　*Clarksville.*
Dunn Levi
Peckham James
Hand M. B.　　*Friendshp.*
Atherton C.
Spear R.
Burritt T.
Fay G. B. W.
Flint M. H.
Gilbert C. D.
Clark J.
Darus B.
Navelin N.
Stannard A.
Emmons Levi　　*Granger*
Rodlon Benjamin
Holbrook H. J. Short Tract
Tibbals Peter,　do
Wells D. B & S. Little Genesee
　　　　　　　Genesee.
Wakeman A.　　*Hume.*
Avery Nathan M.
Kline James
Stockwell ——
Lochinard Luke
Kernis James
Minard L. L.　　*Wiscoy*
Cranston James,　do
Madison John,　do
Higgins Thomas, Whitesville
　　　　　　　Independence
Ainsworth Le Roy
Jackson ——,
Fisher & Fortner, Centre
Smith John D. Black Creek
　　　　　　　New Hudson.
Brown ——,　do　*Ossian.*
Wivel Samuel
Narregang J. & O.
Wilkins James
Dunham D. S.　　*Rushford.*
Osborn J. G.
Bresler A.
Howser Alpheus
Thompson Israel
Jenkins Jedediah　　*Scio.*
Finch E.
Richardson ——
Palmer S. & D. Wellsville
Wickham Aaron　*West Almond.*
M'Gibony Samuel
Smith W. B. & R. D.　　*Wirt.*
Lattimer Lorenzo

Broome County.

Hollister M. A. Chenango Forks
　　　　　　　Barker.
Palmer J.　　do
Wilson E. T.　　do
Smead J. W.　　*Binghamton.*
Hungerford G. F.
M'Collister C.
Stone A. F.
Curtiss M.
Curtiss B. C.
Demming A.
Jackson A. W.
Pine P. Susquehannah　*Colesville.*
Lyon & Ailsworth. Nineveh
Murven & Alexander, Harpers-
　ville
Dort E.　　do
Benedict E. Centre　　*Lisle.*
Collier N
Cady N.　　*Maine.*
De Lane M.
Chittenden A. D. Whitney's Point
　　　　　　　Triangle.
Mead J.　　do　*Union.*
Chatfield G.
Crocker C.
Gardiner L. B.
Bartle P. L.
Smith G. W.
Brigham U. Centre
Moore H. W.　do
Hull & Taylor　　*Windsor.*
Hulbert & Bird
Sleeper H. L.

Cattarangus County.

Coyle John — Ashford.
Balon David
Frank A. F.
Hopkins Edwin
Lamberton & Rockover — Burton.
Grover Ebenezer
Frink Albert — Conewango.
Leffingwell Edwin
Woodford Nelson
Northup Issac & Co.
Blackman G. R. — Ellicottville.
Fellows W. E.
Potter W. E.
Blackman J. & J.
Blackman Franklin — Farmersville.
Blackman James
Patterson James — Franklinville.
Graves Harvey
Miller Alexander
Tait William
Crandall Benjamin — Freedom.
Wells & Babcock, Sandusky
Wilder Barnard — do
Johnson Jerome — do
M'Intire Leonard, Elton
Armstrong Henry — do
Alexander John — Great Valley.
Lunton James
Conklin Samuel
Peabody L. — Little Valley.
Case Phineas — Lyndon.
Winslow Ira — Machias.
Jones Palmer
Thornton N. N.
Brown N. M.
Kirkpatrick William
Davis Hiram
Boom & Crapo, Eddyville
— Mansfield.
Haskins H. S. — New Albion.
Allen F.
Huntley J.
Niles N. S.
Ten Eyck S.
Gross S.
Benson & Ballard — Otto.
Morris C. H.
Vosburgh & Slingerland
Austin Henry, East Otto
Darling John — do
Patch Samuel — Perrysburgh.
Southworth James
Meacham —
Shepard J. M.
Davis Jacob, Gowanda — Persia.
Davis Benjamin, — do
Davis Joseph, — do
Darby Morgan, — do
Warden & Van Hart — Portville.
Langdon Massena
Langdon Mordica
Perry —
Litchfield O. — Randolph.
Giles E. F.
Nevins John
Eggleston S. L. East Randolph
Northup J. B. — do
Green Willis A. — South Valley.
Figals John W. — Yorkshire.
Runnion & Moshier
Robbins Alvah
House J. D.
Lowden Chas. F. Delavan
Van Slyke Lysander, do

Cayuga County.

Morris & Bench, Seminary Av.
— Auburn.
Stevens William, State st.
Phinney A. — Conquest.
Bush T. — Springport.
Fleming — — Summerhill.
Lawson A. P. — Venice.

Chautauque County.

Broadhead — — Busti.
Button & Darling
Osgood L. — Carroll.

King & Chase, Frewsburgh
— Carroll.
Bronson J. M. — Charlotte.
M'Naughton J.
Henderson R.
Chapman E.
Carver A. Mayville — Chautauque.
Rheabottom W. do
Mills & Smith, do
Barnes H. do
Brownell B. De Wittville
Norton C. W. do
Eddy W. A. — Cherry Creek.
Carr & Adams
Wilcox B. T.
Wilcox D. T.
Rice William — Clymer.
Wood D.
Simmons George — Ellery.
Culver S.
Eddy Safford, Jamestown Ellicott.
Garfield Samuel, do
Taft & Davis, do
Eigenbroadt & Case — Ellington.
Willis Leonard — French Creek.
Moore Ransom
Wilson & Co. Vermont — Gerry.
Barclay J. Irving — Hanover.
Hawkins —, do
Halfort J. Forestville
Phelps J. H. do
Suydam G. do
Delong O. do
M'Mannis —, do
Patney A. Nashville
Crop & Wolly, Smith's Mills
De Camp J. L. — Harmony.
Kelso William
Davis Reuben, Panama
Lawrence Ebenezer, do
Wilcox John S. do
Keith & Woodard, Silver Creek
Smith H. — Poland.
Gillett M. — Fredonia — Pomfret.
Dickinson & Mason, do
Doolittle R. N. do
Dickinson J. do
Jewett O. P — Portland.
Daily O.
Andrews A.
Skinner D., Salem Cross Roads
Heywood James — do
Utley L. — do
Murphy G. Ripley
Kendall H. do
Stonner J. do
Canning Stodard — Sheridan.
Phillips Orrin
Clark Miles J. — Sherman.
Hill Joel
Meriut J. C. & H. — Villenova.
Smith R. O. & Wm. C.
Taft H.
Macomber Lewis — Westfield.
Curtis Sidney
Wilcox & Clow
Wheeler Dexter
Phillips Elias M.
Rowley Alonzo
Gavit David W.

Chenango County.

Crandall W. B. — Linchlean.
Bolen A. F.
Fuller T.
White T — New Berlin.
Clark O.
Pike John
Lucas Wm.
Alesworth & Button, South New Berlin
Babcock & Burrell, — do
Cooke — — North Norwich.
North W.
Brown E.
Brookins C.
Ray L. jr. — Norwich.
Hill H. — Otselic.
Butts A.
Martin Wm.
Thompson L. & L.

Schermerhorn W. — Otselic.
Hackett & Hawley — Oxford.
M'Neil C. & F.
M'Calpin Charles
Roberts Wilmot
Wheeler John B.
Bacon A. — Pharsalia.
Greene T. J.
Carter Thomas — Pitcher.
Taylor Abial
Knowles Leonard
Monroe D. — Plymouth.
Degraff A. S.
Sarroll William. South Plymouth
Merriam J. D. — Preston.
Gerland R. — Sherburne.
Redfield & Crane
Brown H. & Co.
Wickham L.
Dart Geo.
Hatch W.
Mead G.C. — Smyrna.
Strew John
Hayward & Nearing
Smith & Ireland — Bainbridge.
Caswell M. South Bainbridge
French M. H. Bennettsville
Downing B. — Columbus.
Hoag C.
Moon & Minor — Coventry.
Tryon J. L.
Newcomb Wm. P. Livermore's Corners — German.
Wilson Joseph — Greene.
Davis Perry — Guilford.
Delevan Charles

Clinton County.

Dimham L. — Beekmantown.
Comer S.
Cross Loyal
Sherman & Wool, East — Chazy.
Chamberlain & Halburd, West
Richardson R. — Mooers.
Angell —
Soules Horace
Manning —
Roberts Levi — Plattsburgh.
Trombley L.
Grandy & Laport — Saranac.
Stevens A. G.
Myers Christian, Redford
Harris & Brown

Columbia County.

White J. — Ancram.
Drum A.
Scism S.
Brown L. C. Spencertown
— Austerlitz.
Carpenter O. L. Canaan 4 Corners
— Canaan.
Shaver G. Malden Bridge
— Chatham.
Beebe H. East Chatham
Carpenter A. S. do
Simpson W. H. North Chatham
Myer R. — Claverack.
Van Dusen C. & Co.
Neefus D. C. Smoky Hollow
Shaver G.
Washburn D.
Rivenburgh A. Mellenville
Anderson J. Churchtown
Raught W. — do
Anderson H. — Copake.
Fryman H.
Tin Brooks W
Williams J.
Hollenbeck A. J. — Gallatin.
Spalding M.
Miller C.
Mead W.
Messer J. — Ghent.
Coffin C. G.
M'Gibbon H.
Fritts P.
Ward H. — Hillsdale.
Harris John E.
Miller S. Franklin square Hudson.
Worth R. M. Water st.

Burger P. S. & J. C. Union st.
Hudson.

Blake S. N. State st.?
Baker J. Columbia st.
Traver Wm. I. 4th st.
Mesick J. Valatie *Kinderhook.*
Ostrander P. I. do
Miller A. do
Van Slike P. B.
Hoes J.
Riesdorph E.
Niver W. *Livingston.*
Ames N. C.
Smith Z. P.
Babcock L. S. *New Lebanon.*
Sloan F. W. •
Hayward E. •
Palmer A. •
Leggett J. *Stuyvesant.*
Mandville E.
Smith J. F *Taghkanic.*

Cortland County.

Allen Edward *Cortland Village.*
Jones Jedediah
Terry J. W.
Wheeler A.
Falmiter Erastus
Earl John R. *Preble.*
Hine William
Kiff William
Hamilton Alexander

Delaware County.

Becker D. *Andes.*
Holliday William *Colchester.*
Gun M. *West Davenport.*
Ganes J.
Hanvey J.
Penfield O. *Delhi.*
Carrington & Moore
Flower W.
Bill D. *Franklin.*
Rowe & Cobine
Baldwin W. M. & Co.
Groat J. E.
Tenant A.
Foot E.
Penfield E. B. *Harpersfield.*
Baird W.
Gregory J. Bloomville *Kortright.*
Rowe William *Meredith.*
Rowe S.
Johnson J.
Pierce W.
Maybee C.
M'Lean A. jr. Clark's Factory
Middletown.
Finn H. Margaretsville
Wallace H. G. *Stamford.*
Wilson Robert F. Hobart
Carrington J. do
Cause J. . do
M'Caughn William do
Beckwith S. Sidney Plains
Sidney.
Beckwith D. do
Demunder G. Deposit *Tompkins.*
Block J. do
Green T. J. do
Stoddard & Johnson *Walton.*
Ames J.

Duchess County.

Fish C. D. *Amenia.*
Andrews I. Union
Lounsbury L. do
Cronk S. *Beekman.*
Olivet D. *Clinton.*
Williams M.
Mirch A. G.
Abbey, R. B. Clinton Hollow
Thomas R. W. do
Thomas C. *Dover.*
Shelden D.
Worden M.
Record G.
Harris R.
Ferris J.
Burroughs J. M.

Cole Samuel, Wappinger's Falls
Fishkill.
Way F. do
Potter S. do
Brooks J. do
Vannorsdall H. do
Cook C.. Glenham
Southard J. do
Van Ostrand J. do
Howe R. do
Gore & Archibald, Fishkill Land-
ing
Stevenson William do
Quick A., Stormville
Harris E., Hopewell
Ballard C. Fishkill Plains
Jones Z. G. do
Vannosdall I. M. do
Wigg D. *Hyde Park.*
Fairchilds A. K.
Piersaul P.
Dennis W. Jackson's Corner
Milan.
Case R. Milanville
Killman H. Lafayette Corner
Hevenor J. G.
Hutchens H. Rock City
Caulkins J. G. Centre
North East.
Winchell W. Spencer Corner
Patterson & Roe, do
Lloyd G.
Stockwell R.
Thompson D.
Corbin I. *Pauling.*
Sherwood S.
Osborn E. N.
Stocking Reubin *Pine Plains.*
Hart W. jr. *Pleasant Valley.*
Place W. S.
Martin A.
Toby H. M. Salt Point
Wood W. do
Bobsen A. 206 Main
Poughkeepsie.
M'Cort George T. 377 Main
Vankuren M. 497 do
Johnson J. 5 Hamilton
Davis Charles, Academy st.
Heagney John, 21 Washington
Williams Joseph, 12 do
Vannosdall & St. John, New Ham-
burgh
Heavnor J. W.
Lee D.
Wilhelms ——, Upper Red Hook
Van Veadenburgh E.
Ellsworth G. H.
Barringer R. Barrytown
Thompson G.
Hevenor P.
Barringer F.
Traver A. *Rhinebeck.*
Traver J.
Noxon B.
Hevenor R. D.
Simpson A. *Stanford.*
Height L. C.
Hoffman N. & R.
Benedict A., Attlebury
Martin J.. Verbank *Union Vale.*
Degroff C.
Mory J. J.
Johnson W.
Dunkin M.
Mead S. *Washington.*
Mead G.
Lawrence Wm. /
Valentine J. Hart's Village
M'Cormick ——, Washington Hol-
low
Platt J. Salt Point
Williams W. Lithgow
Jackson E. Mabbettsville

Erie County.

Howe & Hendee *Alden.*
Vaughan P. W. T.
Crocker John, Williamsville
Amherst.

Klapp J. Williamsville, *Amherst.*
Irr Michael, do
Switzer David, do
Edwards W. Willink *Aurora.*
Burhans James, do
Rouse D. A. do
Cranes Thomas, do
Cranes John, do
Wilson John P. do
Love Levi *Black Rock.*
Jenks Perry *Boston.*
Brindley George
Atterley Edward
Washburn Salmon, North Boston
Sprague William *Brandt.*
Cook Philip *Cheektowaga.*
Shanocker Anthony
Shanocker Jacob
Bannister Reuben
Ott George
Hickman A. Illinois st. *Buffalo.*
Langdon G. W. Ohio st.
Raze & Dickey, Hydraulics
Trix & Roberts, do
Baker Moses, Washington st.
Bussemer John, 27 Genesee
Schmal Peter, do
Leak W. L. opposite No. Church
Woods J. cor. Main & Chippewa
Rand E. T. Hanover st.
Loomis A. *Clarence.*
Guise John
Goddard R.
Perin R. G. B.
Hodgkin Ira
Diller Jacob
Roberts J. S.
Fisher John
Whitmer Chas.
Chase A. *Colden.*
Farnsworth & Braman *Collins.*
Kerr & Kane
Van Dine James
Tripp Hiram
Curtiss ——
Turner O. Collins Centre
Palmer ——, Gowanda
Holman Joel, Springville *Concord.*
Collins S. do
Shultus Geo. do
Holden Chas. do
Ryther Solomon B. *Eden.*
Hills Russell
Archibald Asa
Hunt Wm.
Clark Philip *Evans.*
Holt S.
Trask David
Ensign & Conkwright *Hamburgh.*
Rowley Martin *Holland.*
Cheney J. & J. C
Rogers Aaron
Davis N. P.
Bancroft G. TownLine *Lancaster.*
Halsey Stephen T.
Grimes W. H.
Coats Chas.
Baldwin C. H. *Newstead.*
Stewart H. Akron
Ackerson & Brown, Akron
M'Arthur Alden *Sardinia.*
Stokes ——
Phillips John *Tonawanda.*
Stimpson E. B.
Bartlett Joseph C.
Smith James, South Wales *Wales.*
Myers Patrick
King Noah
Phelps Martin
Cole Reynold, Wales Centre
Wood Jesse do
Denison Dudley

Essex County.

Tenant John, Port Kent
Chesterfield.
Matthews E. L. *Elizabethtown.*
Lobdell James
Deyo Jacob
Fancher C. G. & Pierce *Essex.*
Rogers Lorenzo
Stephens John, Whallonsburg

Goff Levi — *Keene.*
Russell Edmond
Reynolds Reuben
Shattock Frederick — *Lewis.*
Bibby Thomas — *Minerva.*
Lawrence Noble
Foster B. D. Moriah 4 corners
— *Moriah.*
Tanner James do
Pierce Wm. do
Wetherell Albert, do
Green George, do
Kile Andrew, do
Foster Willis E. do
Sanford Daniel E. do
Crane Samuel, do
Vaughn Charles, do
Johnson Roswell, do
Conten B. do
Bunn Isaac, do
Swan Orlando, Port Henry
Wheelock George, do
Span H. D. do
Skiff David C. — *St. Armand.*
Skiff O.
Moody H.
Goodspeed Milton
Jacobs John — *Willsborough.*

Franklin County.

Dickinson J. & Sons — *Bangor.*
Bennett Thomas — *Chateaugay.*
Spoon Joseph
Holonback L. A.
Holonback Harrison
Blanchard Seth — *Fort Covington.*
Congor Wm. J. — *Moira.*
Kemball E. Brush's Mills
Pettee J. do
Steward Joel, West Constable
— *Westville.*
Martin Hollis
Stearns Wm.

Fulton County.

Sears Ira C. — *Broadalbin.*
Thayer Chas.
Shults John — *Ephratah.*
Brown P. P. — *Garoga.*
Rudd Lester
Seeley I.
Smith Jonas — *Johnstown.*
Smith David
Moore Frederick
Ferguson Alexander
Burr H. L. Gloversville
Mead Philip, Kingsboro
Bedingham Edward. do
Dickerson J. & H. Vail's Mills
— *Mayfield.*
Peck James, do
Barry & Wells, Mayfield Corners
Anthony O. & C. Riceville
Van Dyke Giles, Northville
— *Northampton.*
Van Arnam Wm. do
Bennett O. do
Brown J.
Morrison George
Wilsey W. B. Osborn's Bridge
Tomblinson A. do
Cook Jacob — *Oppenheim.*
Strous John
Hayes John P. S.
Smith Thomas
Neff Stewart — *Perth.*
Thorp Henry
Mead, Duncan & Co.
Pyre Augustus — *Stratford.*

Genesee County.

Combs J. E. — *Alabama.*
Stage H. H.
Winchel S.
Taber J. & Son
Flanders Wm., Oakfield
Chappel Henry — *Alexander.*
Lynn S. — *Batavia.*
Trumbull J. & Son
Gould Chester — *Bergen.*
Spafford Alonzo

Goodenough George — *Bergen.*
Gray ——, North Bergen
Oliver & Bradley — *Bethany.*
Voorhees J. East Bethany
Lyman Benjamin, do
Herrick Z. P., Linden
Brewer Cornelius, do
Voorhees J. & G. do
Gaines N. — *Byron.*
Robinson Elijah & Son — *Darien.*
Jones J. & A
Garrison Wm. C.
Dodson Peter
Thurston John, Centre
Bradley Wm. — *Elba.*
Silfridge C. — *Le Roy.*
Gardner J. & Co.
Pierce & Sanford
Arms W. B. — *Pavilion.*
Young Wm.
Bartholomew D. D.
Dickson Darius, Centre
Powers Ed. jr. — *East Pembroke.*
Kingdon John — *Stafford.*

Greene County.

Tuttle D. & Son — *Ashland*
Spoor Casper H. — *Athens.*
Lennon Daniel S. Acra — *Cairo.*
Utter Cyrus do
De Bois Wm. do
Plank Peter
Conover M. — *Catskill.*
Magilton William
Vedder J., Leeds
Conover D. do
Foster Theodore — *Coxsackie.*
Hallenbeck Nicholas
Hallenbeck Jacob L. V. H.
Rugg Datus E. — *Durham.*
Thorpe Ira
Chapman Robert W. — *Greenville.*
Haswell ——
Hisert Benjamin F.
Southard Smith
Carroll Bernard — *Hunter.*
Edwards W. H.
Trace Hiram W.
Winter David, East Kill
Campbell George, do
Peet Isaac W. — *Lexington.*
Martin Frederick V.
Van Valkenburgh Isaac T.
Beggs William, West Kill
Piedfer Joseph do
Johnson Samuel, East Lexington
Burley Nathaniel do
Turner Gideon — *New Baltimore.*
Turner William
Hyatt Jeremiah
Matthew William — *Prattsville.*
Jordan Michael
Clarke Daniel
Blish Roderick S.
Wixfield Simeon, Hensonville
— *Windham.*
Parsons Eli. Union Society
Bagley L. & Son do
Doty & Doty do

Hamilton County.

Abrams D. B. — *Wells.*
Whitman C.
De Forest Isaac

Herkimer County.

Hanner Philip — *Columbia.*
Canfield Wm.
Kinny S. H.
Stancliel Geo.
Moyer J. D. — *Danube.*
Miller Henry
Miller A.
Maaks J.
Clark ——
Woolcott & Lever
Bander M. C.
Shelden Wm. M. — *Fairfield.*
Mason W. C.
Hendrix J.
Castar Barney — *Frankfort.*

Dygert Jacob — *Frankfort.*
Thomas John
Pryne P.
Potter Smith, West Frankfort
Shyswack C. Centre do
Pruyne Henry, Frankfort Hill
Harter Benj. — *Herkimer.*
Webber David
Harter J. P.
M'Chesney & Ferman — *Little Falls.*
Harter & Lebart
Caster Robert
M'Chesney Henry
Keller Henry J.
Barney A. — *Newport.*
Angell W. W.
Longstaff Geo.
Broughton S. R.
Bullock Samuel — *Norway.*
Handcock John W.
Garett James M. — *Ohio.*
Cook Wm. — *Russia.*
Klinglin M. — *Salisbury Centre.*
Snell Edwin
Cain Peter — *Schuyler.*
Cain Warren
Hough M.
Stansel Paul — *Stark.*
Tahorsh Isaac
Shimmel J.
Wormuth Wm. Starkville
Diefendorff A. do
Bell Henry, Jordanville — *Warren.*
Lyman F. do
Petre Jonas, Page's Corners
Dawbey O. W. do
Purchase C. Crane's Corners
Luce & Stiles — *Winfield*
Davis ——
Stout & Walker, West Winfield
Harriss —— do

Jefferson County.

Graves S. — *Adams.*
Van Wormer R.
Morgan & Saunders
Hungerford L. P.
Worriner M. North
Elliott S. Adams Centre
Hall Geo. & Brother, do
Newville J., Redwood
— *Alexandria.*
Tassie Peter, Plessis
Comstock Wm. R. do
Elliott Justin, Alexandria Bay
Eddy Reuben, do
Smith C. do
Willis J. E. — *Antwerp.*
Arlow S.
Olmstead H. Ox Bow
Potter Hiram, do
Hamblin H. do
Lord & Lewis — *Brownville.*
Strong & Lewis
Robinson D.
Moyer Solomon, Dexter
Briggs I.
Wilson A. Perch River
Fredingbury Henry, Limerick
Forsyth John — *Cape Vincent.*
Hadley Ira
Davis Wm.
Smith William
Carter N. A. — *Champion.*
Gates & Hammond
Brocklin John V.
Earl Frank
Burton W. R. — *Clayton.*
Tabo J.
Manvill Edwin, Depauville
Osborn Schuyler, do
Hudson L. F. — *Ellisburgh.*
Hyde Levi
Ramsdill F. G.
Gray & Sons, Woodville
Freeman J. Belleville
Clark E. do
Hall J. do
Cook H. Mannsville
Wheeler Geo. do
Kates O. K. — *Henderson*

De Wolf D. D. Sackett's Harbor
Houndsfield.
Hunter T. do
Penye John do
Carter Nathan A. Great Bend
Le Ray.
Odell David, do
Himes L. R. Evans' Mills
Gillet Elisha *Lorraine.*
Mount Wilson, Three Mile Bay
Lyme.
Wilson A. do
Whaler Wm. do
Thorn R. do
Smith Frank, Millen's Bay
Bushnell George, Lafargeville
Orleans.
Miatt Wolcott R. do
Baxter H. *Philadelphia.*
Strong Wm.
Foster S.
Proctor H
Heustis D. *Rodman.*
Elliott A. East Rodman
Conway Alex. do
Chase C. South Rutland *Rutland.*
Prichard H. S. do
Butterfield F. Black River
Whaley James, do
Loomis Ashley, Felt's Mills
Babcock J. do
Ryther P. H. *Theresa.*
Brown Geo. T.
Ansted Andrew

Kings County.

Allen David, 5 Water *Brooklyn.*
Baldwin Platt R. foot Harrison
Bond Lewis, Bedford Av. corner
Flushing
Correll B. cor. Hamilton Av. &
Columbia st.
Dick John, Pearl near Tillary
Downey John, Hudson Av.
Duffy James, cor. Columbia &
Warren
Farrington Hiram, Flushing Av.
Fulon Samuel, cor. Smith & Pacific
Herbert Joseph, 45 Prospect
Hughes J., York near Pearl
Jeffers Wm. Pearl st.
Jenkins John, Myrtle Av. near
Spencer
Jennings M. 19 Willow
Jones Evan, Myrtle Av. n. Spencer
Jones John, Liberty n. Sprague
Place
Kiernan Francis, 203 Plymouth
Lacey John, 115 Front
Latimer W. S. & Co. Columbia n.
State
Learey E. D. Washington near
Front
Lihee Wm. Furman st.
M'Caffrey M. Atlantic st.
Marquis J. 190 Nassau
Morrison H. State st.
Nowlin Peter, Hoyt cor. Baltic
Owens John, 176 Tillary
Perrine Wm. T. Nevins n. Fulton
Pollard S. S. 146 Carll
Post Isaac, 9 Myrtle Av.
Remsen William, Doughty near
Columbia
Silk T. cor. Water & Fulton
Smith E. Bedford Av.
Sticsvere Henry, 203 Jay
Tigney Thomas. Everett n. Fulton
Wright Mott, Marshall
Parry William, Bushwick Av.
Bushwick.
Hicks Wm. Green Point
Evans T. M. do
Johnson Edward *Flatbush.*
Foster A.
Ditmas John I.
Wortman John 8 New Lots
Fleming Joseph *Flatlands.*
Anderson John, Flatlands Neck
Vanderveer John, do
Skidmore Isaac, Canarsie

Lake Daniel D. *Gravesend.*
Jackson John *New Utrecht.*
Church James C. Fort Hamilton
Hogan D. 1st st. *Williamsburgh.*
M'Elroy Patrick, 199 1st
Nishwitz Frederick, Water st.
near Grand
Wilkinson T. 2d st. near N. 1st
Bryant George do cor. 3d
M'Geviston H. 167 4th
Smith George, 74 N. 2d
Mitchell & Thompson, 13 N. 2d
Tuttle John, 249 2d
Smith Joseph, 3 N. 3d
Lake Cortlandt, 2d st. near N. 4th
Holland M. 1st st. cor. N. 8th
Dawber Lewis, Wither st.
Baird James, Bushwick Av.
Roussel Joseph, Stag st.
Stadtmulier Adam, 124 Wykoff

Lewis County.

Hartwell A. N. *Denmark.*
Lansing J. W.
Seymour William
Sherman W.
Smith & Symonds
Cheney E.
Vroomer J.
Riske T. *Copenhagen.*
Yeomans J.
Flanders H.
Hunt William *Diana.*
Cook J. I. *Lowville.*
Campbell L.
Batchelor S.
Dewey William
Botsford E. *Martinsburgh.*
Pible C.
Hess F. J. West Martinsburgh
Gillett Abiathar *Turin.*
Wallace E. B.
Hess Sanford
Claffey Thomas
Allen Hiram, Houseville
Sumley ——— Constableville
West Turin.
Peyster P. & A. D. do
Wescott & Sixley do

Livingston County.

Jackson Samuel *Avon.*
Waldo R. P.
Thrasher John, 2d
Smith John, East Avon
Bacon Elisha, South do
Renwick Archibald *Caledonia.*
Quailtrough Thomas
Smith James & Robert
Elyea Garrett
Knights M. *Conesus.*
Wells Isaac T.
Sherwood Stephen
Harrison & Porter *Dansville.*
Keshner Henry
Dildine Z.
Curtis E.
Carpenter F.
M'Andre J.
Ritter J.
Teasdale H. M.
Irons Bidkan
Dunklebury J
Sharp J. P.
Draper S.
Parsons C. *Geneseo.*
Tucker B.
Gill & M'Arthur
Farnham H.
Mills William A. *Groveland.*
Van Antwerp James
Whitney Leonard
Starner Gideon
Stone & Lord, Cuylerville
Leicester.
Grant William, Moscow
Anderson William, do
Flint Charles, do
Woodard William *Lima.*
Welch J.

Thurston William *Livonia.*
Bowen William, Hemlock Lake
Millard Henry A. do
Grugg Hugh, do
Wells John, do
Kennedy George, South Livonia
Bryant William, Lakeville
Richardson J. *Mount Morris.*
Holland & M'Arthur
Goodwin S.
Hall P. W. *Nunda.*
Holmes David
Patterson & Edgerly, Oakland
Portage.
Smith L. F. Hunt's Hollow
Baker & De Long, do
Thomas Joseph *Sparta.*
Hempsher John, Scottsburgh
Hendershott James, do
Hopkins Martin D. *Springwater.*
Hopkins Norman R.
Williams William, Dansville
West Sparta.
Jones ———, Kysorville
Naragan A. do
Povost Joseph, Union Corners
Holcomb Joseph, Byersville
Miller John *York.*
Stringham R., Greigsville
Bush William

Madison County.

Brond Samuel 2d *Brookfield.*
Green Asa
Merchant Hiram H.
Brown John
Cross L. W. West Brookfield
Worden Delosa, North do
Lawton & Co. do
Peet Eber *Cazenovia.*
Bordwell Mills
Bigelow Eli
Benson H.
Aldrich Uriah
Billings Fletcher
Mitchell John & Son
Ferguson C. & J. New Woodstock
Burgess & Tabor do
Morse, Savage &Co. do
Hart Chas. & Co. *De Ruyter.*
Maxson & Burdick
Crandall James
Maydole J. H. *Eaton.*
Henshaw D.
Clark Thomas
Allen E. E. Morrisville
Brigham Henry, do
Towsley Hiram, do
Nash L. Pratt's Hollow
Wormuth A. *Fenner.*
Kendall H. W.
Woodworth Martin
Jennings & Winchester
Georgetown.
Judd George W.
Rigby David
Utter R. C.
Hill D. P. *Hamilton.*
Barnard John
Eaton Stillman
Waters Lewis, Earlville
Howard Edmond
Colson S., Poolyille
Wood ——, Hubbard's Corners
Scott George, do
Bates B. *Lenox.*
Nellis S. K. Canastota
Roach Lansing, do
Ingraham W. do
Williams J. Oneida Depot
Phillips J. A. Wampsville
Webster R. Clockville
Simone H. do
Armstrong Jabez *Lebanon.*
Abbott Daniel
Winchester S.
Bills S.
Leonard A.
Baker Cornelius
House & Messenger *Madison.*
Shaw John

Davis J. E. Bouckville **Madison.**
Peckham M. & S. Solsville
Seaver John P. Erieville **Nelson**
Edgerton Leander, do
White Elijah, do
Rice Luther
Anderson James
Martindale Z. & Son, Peterboro
Smithfield.
Travis Nathan, do
Nash D. do
Clemons W. P. do
Evans George, do
Marquizee Timothy, do
Nash Lewis, Siloam
Lewis W. H. Chittenango
Sullivan.
Brosseau & Herrick, do
Tibbitts Obadiah, do
Chawgo Jacob, do
Severance David
Hyde J. R.
Hill D. S. Perryville
Culvier R.
Andrews Z. Bridgeport
Swartafagre J. L. do
Wheat J. D. do

Monroe County.

Caley Thomas **Brighton.**
Shelmire John
Bowen John
Turner G.
Lacoir Isaac
Gardinier T.
Patterson Aaron, North Chili **Chili.**
Harriman John do
Lowrie J. Clarkson Corners
Clarkson.
Atkins M. G. do
Irving G. Jenkin's Corners **Greece.**
Martin D. M. do
Cole S. do
Housten T. East **Henrietta.**
Tuttle N East Mendon **Mendon.**
Daggett A. R. do
M'Neal F. do
Hubbell F. do
Abby A. T. do
Turner & Co. Mendon Centre
Callen William, Honeoye Falls
Annis J. West Mendon
Stratton Samuel **Ogden.**
Van Deventer J. Spencer's Basin
Hancock P. R. do
Austin James C. Parma Corners
Parma.
Lowry Goan do
Denning H. C. Parma Centre
Bascom S. do
Mentor Dorman do
Haynes Robert **Penfield.**
Beebe & Markham
Walker G.
Howard L. T. Fairport **Perrinton.**
Norman H. H. do
M'Donald D. Bushnell's Basin
Walcott D. **Pittsford.**
Staines J.
Johnson J.
Ide Oliver **Riga.**
Spicer George
Baker James, Churchville
Tupper Marshall do
Jones David, Black Creek
M'Glachlin H. F. Court st.
Rochester.
Huntley R. B. 77 South
Wilson N. G. do
Masey J. cor. Achilles & North
Cutting Wm. 3 North
Smith N. H. cor. of Franklin &
North
Penney J. Ely st.
Walker L. 3 Minerva
Kavanagh & Hyland, cor. Buffalo
& Trowbridge
Sullivan Peter, 180 Buffalo
Malvin James, Pine st.
Goodrich J. M. 134 S. Sophia
Mead L. H. 143 do

Southwick M. Mill st. **Rochester.**
M'Bride C. Mumford st.
Thorn George. 22 Mill
Sharp Charles S. Front st.
Striker Lorenzo, Buffalo st.
Heath A. & A. **Rush.**
Morgan Michael, West Rush
Burnett Gilbert do
Wood A. Brockport **Sweden.**
Brown Hiram, do
M'Kee D. West Webster **Webster.**
Wicks B. R. do
Welcher Wm. do
Vallean & Deitz, Scottsville
Wheatland.
Hon George do
Sheridan Michael do
Connor J. do
Lewis George, Mumford
Robinson J. do

Montgomery County.

Zeller & Vanness **Amsterdam.**
Chase Cyrus B.
Nudt Wm. H.
Neff John
Shaw N. B.
Harvey John & Sons
Potter T. J. & Co.
Rowe Henry, Hagaman's Mills
Vosburgh J. E. do
Shaw John, Cranesville
Hunt Joseph, Tribes Hill
Longahure Richard, **Canajoharie.**
Hundermark Loudrick
Joslyn John, Ames
Winne C. I. Buel
Alpaugh P. do
Miller J. **Charleston.**
Chilson & Miller, Burtonville
Bailey Lewis **Florida.**
Nellis & Casey
Mead & Williamson, Minaville
Ferguson James, Port Jackson
Vanderhoff Cornelius, do
Wickerson A. do
Hilton Abraham, do
Huntly Gilbert, do
Van Vleck ——, do
Neff —— do
Mead A. do
Daley J. do
Hilton Alexander, Fort Hunter
Eldridge Nathan, Braman's Cors.
O'Brien H. **Glen.**
Conover David
Gulc Wm.
Putnam John R. Fultonville
M'Gee A. do
Horning Nicholas do
M'Crankee James H. Smith Town
Breeharnus James H. do
Firth G. Fultonville
Lasher Aaron, Fort Plain **Minden.**
Heidell Jacob, do
Coeler Henry, do
Burke John D. do
Failing John R. do
Sparks Abraham, do
Yates James, Fonda **Mohawk.**
Bohannon R. W. do
Groft P. P. G. do
Jeder & Kline, do
Hanson B. J. do
Hanson John, do
Nellis George, Palatine Bridge
Palatine.
England Joseph, Stone Arabia
Myers John, do
Bander James, do
Fox Jessie, do
Nellis Peter P. do
Nellis Peter, do
Dillenback Martimus, do
Nestle John, do
Tucker Joseph **Root.**
Formcrook Henry
Clute G. R.
Nolen Patrick
Antis John J.
Bond Edmond, Spraker's Basin

Dockstader J. M. Spraker's Basin
Root.
Allen Augustus **St. Johnsville.**
Crouse George
Kretser John
Fuller Henry
Yourman Jeremiah

New York County.

Ackerman A. 135 Christopher
Ackerman Geo. 875 Huison
Alexander William, 98 Grand
Anderson Peter G. 32 Spruce
Anderson W. J. C. 761 Washington
Ashton William, 306 Front
Atkinson Richard. 52 West
Austin, Requa & Co. 223 Canal
Banham Wm. 39 2d
Barden & Kay, 267 W. 16th
Barker John, 162 Maiden lane
Baxter Malcolm, 195 W. 15th
Beebe Richard W. 68 Willet
Beker D. 140 3d
Berly P. N. 114 Rivington
Benson Wm. J. 63 W. 18th
Biggart Robert, 122 Troy
Blanke & Gandell. 495 Water
Bogert Jas. S. 24th st.
Bourne J. 3d Av. cor. E. 14th
Bowne & Secord, 57 Willet
Brady Thomas, 7 Clinton
Brennan Charles, 32 Columbia
Brender Charles, 16 Jones
Burdett John A. 276 Chambers
Burke R. cor. 13th st. & 4th Av.
Burk Michal, rear 9 Orange
Burke William, 67 Columbia
Burnett John R. 181 Elm
Burns Thomas T. 231 South
Campbell Charles M. 50 E. 12th
Carlin John, 2 E. 21st
Carroll Thomas, 28th st. 10th Av.
Chamberlin Wm. H. 317 Madison
Chatterton Laurence, 139 Essex
Chittenden Stephen, 385 Bowery
Churchill & Timmons, 479 Broome
Clark James M. 33 Hamersley
Clarke Joseph, 486 Water
Clarkson W. S. 44 Eldridge
Clough James, 8th Av.
Coleman Henry, Jane near West
Colgan George, 35 Cross
Collins John, 34 Hamilton
Collins John G. 41 Wooster
Condin ——, 136 3d
Conner Matthew, 34 Cherry
Connor Thomas, 551 Washington
Conroy Timothy, 74 Allen
Convoy John, rear 58 Mulberry
Courtnay Eugene, rear 34 Pell
Creek J. 10th Av. bet. 14th & 15th
Crawford E. W. 16th st. cor. 10th
Av.
Crawford Matthew, 113¼ Elm
Cronkhyte Elizha H. 183 Prince
Crossgrove L. 106 19th
Cummins Patrick, cor. 1st Av.
Darling G. & Brothers, 92 W. 19th
Debevoise & Morris, 125 Essex
Decker T. B. 8th Av.
Dennis Wm. E. 64 E. 13th
Derby John C. 61 Gold
Devenport James, 22 E. 20th
Devoe David, 43 Harrison
Didier G. W. 19th st. bet. 7th & 8th
Avs.
Dixon Charles, W. 31st st.
Dogherty John. 22 11th
Downing Patrick, 113 Sheriff
Downs William, 162 Maiden lane
Drysdale Robert, 20 5th
Duncan & West, 55 Dey & 4 Liberty place
Dunn John, 102 Goerck
Duval Wm. 508 Greenwich
Eales Thos. cor. 22d st. & 1st Av.
Elderson John, 44 Crosby
Ewing George, 438 Broome
Fawcett John, 184 Mulberry
Ferguson Bailey N. 143 Essex
Finley John, 456 Wooster

Flender Thomas, 60 Thomas
New York.
Flood Edward, 90 Reade
Foot & Co. 280 11th
Forman J. G. 561 Washington
Foster Robert, E. 24th st.
Fox V. H 452 Water
Fox V. H. 187 Cherry
Freeman James C. 107 11th
Friend Frederick. 48 Eldridge
Furrey Patrick. 355 Washington
Gale John, 479 Broome
Gannon Patrick, 10 Albany
Gaul John, 1 Essex
German Philip, 182 Chrystie
Gildersleeve Benjamin, 405 Monroe
Cannon
Goings John R. 100 Chrystie
Goldie Joseph, 133 Attorney
Goulding Thomas, 35 Stone
Graham William, 284 11th
Graley James, 81 Elizabeth
Greene John. 126 Amity
Green Thos., W. 16th st.
Griffin & Fitzsimmons. 542 Wash.
Grosz Michael; 5 Greene
Guerin John 158 4th
Hach John, 218 3d
Harned & Rothery, E. 26th near
3d Av.
Harrigan John, 312 3d Av.
Haydon John, 13 Thames
Henderson P. G. 39 Spruce
Higgins Christopher, 216 2d
Higgins George, 70 Frankfort
Higgins H. 193 E. 11th
Hoban John. 187 W. 21st
Hobson Nathaniel, 171 Stanton
Hoey John, 72 & 74 Pitt
Hoey Joseph, 344 Madison
Hoey Peter, 385 Cherry
Holmes David B. 133 Attorney
Homberg Johann. 186 Chrystie
Horne John, 13 Cannon
Howarth John, 178 W. 20th
Howoy Thomas, 11 Downing
Hunt George W. 41 Gold
Hunt Wm. 231 Chrystie
Hyde Thomas, 20 Clinton
Hyland James, 50 Wooster
Irvin A. 83 E. 26th
Ingles John, E. 28th st.
Iteman & Lawrence, 174 Eldridge
Jackson Samuel. 30 W. 18th
Jeffers Richard, 160 Crosby
Jennings Peter, 107 Pitt
Jeremiah & Burgher, 83 1st Av.
Jinkins Richard, 296 Delancy
Johnston Andrew, 10th Av. cor.
E. 13th
Jonas Richard, 169 Varick
Jonas Robert, rear 281 Spring
Jonas William, 73 Laurens
Jones Henry & H. H. 44 West
Joost Nichols, 435 Houston
Jubb James N. 22 E. 21st
Kay & Barden, 267 W. 16th
Keiser Conrad, 53 Lewis
Kelly T. 21 Laurens & 50 Dey
Kennedy John, 31 S. William
Kenney Peter, 1st Av. cor. E. 13th
Kipp R. 165 Eldridge
Lafrenier Oliver, 149 Essex
Laforge Jacob, 7 Broome
Lancaster P. 137 16th
Laroe James G. 41 Cannon
Larrin John, 213 13th
Lavy Peter 8. 93 3d Av.
Lawson John, rear 35 Willet
Lay Michael, 54 Madison
Levison Henry. 291 Mott
Lewis James, 99 Lewis
Linehan Barthol. D. 164 Crosby
Lithgow St. Clair, 120 Church
Lonnargan L. 122 17th
M'Ardle Henry, 249 Delancy
M'Brien J. 126 Amity
M'Cabe John, 39 Chrystie
M'Carthy John, 301 Water
M'Carty Dennis, 652 Washington
M'Carty Patrick, 201 Mercer
M'Coy James, rear 111 Spring

M'Donald Thomas, 46 Jay
New York.
M'Donald Terry, 34 Hester
M'Donnell Edward, 79 Mulberry
M'Donnell ———, 355 Washington
M'Fadden Thomas, 289 Madison
M'Garr Hugh, 62 E. 13th
M'Ginnis ———, 385 3d Av.
M'Golrick Hugh, 3 Scott's alley
M'Guire Thomas, 17 Monroe
M'Kenna T. 3d Av. E. 26th
M'Lean Allan, 45 Gold
M'Manus Patrick, rear 122 Mott
M'Mullen A. 43 Broome
Madden John, 15 Dover
Macy M. B. 39 Dover
Martin Patrick, 102 2d
Mead John, 294 3d Av.
Miller & Hilliard, 33 S. William
Monahan James & Brine, 6th Av.
between 19th & 29th
Montgomery John, 270 Cherry
Moore Richard, 235 W. 16th
Moran P., W. 15th near 7th Av.
Morey & Van Beuren, 119 Prince
Morin John, 13 Cannon
Morris & Scofield, W. 29th
Morris William, 174 Laurens
Mulligan James, 197 Grand
Murray Thos. E. 22d cor. 5th Av.
Myers W. 68 Bank
Nelson Henry, 240 2d Av.
Nevin Samuel, 1 12th
Nuss G. 6th Av.
Oliver Samuel, 11th cor. 7th Av.
O'Neill Francis, 523 Hudson
O'Neill James, 796 Washington
O'Sullivan James, 126 Clinton pl.
Pales Henry, 32 W. Broadway
Parsel Henry A. 396 Bleecker
Patton William, 34 Spruce
Patton William, 96 James
Peterson Abram P. 6 3d
Pine Joseph, rear 119 Walker
Post John R. 586 Hudson
Powell Benjamin, 195 Delancy
Prentiss Watson B. 34 Av. C
Price Simeon, 366 Madison
Pullis Henry, 32 W. Broadway
Quin Matthew, 234 1st Av.
Requa A. 221 Canal
Reynolds John, 115 Elm
Richardson William, 223 Mott
Rieglemann John. 254 5th
Roach Patrick, 71 Watts
Rohr C. (refused) 183 Clinton
Rurk Patrick, 10 Pitt
Schalbie A. 506 Water
Schwartz Jacob, 218 2d
Seager Edwin, 134 Washington
Secor Francis, 28 Rector
Sharr Patrick, 31 S. William
Shear Abraham M. 658 Wash.
Sheridan John, 60 Walnut
Sherry Patrick, 799 Greenwich
Short Michael, 13th cor. 7th Av.
Smith George, 96 Troy
Smith Joseph, 485 Water
Smith Peter. 415 3d Av.
Smith T. 451 1st Av.
Snedden James, 24 Goerck
Speller Chas. 506 Washington
Statmiller A., W. 29th st.
Steward Jonas, 10 Christopher
Stivers William, 85 1st Av.
Stoddart J. 55 Washington
Stoddart Robert, 557 Washington
Storms R. 258 W. 17th
Strait David, 73½ Allen
Sullivan J. O. 126 8th
Thomas D. 346 Cherry
Thompson James, 37 Bridge
Thompson John G. 7 Henry
Thum Richard, 242 South
Troy Nicholas, 62 W. Broadway
Tweedy David. 3! S. William
Van Buren H. 8. 137 Christopher
Vanderbelt & Co. 73 Laurens
Vanderbeck & Archer, 230 W. 18th
Vanzant Andrew, 165 Christopher
Waldron James, 366 6th
Waldron & Oliver, 199 W. 11th

Wallace Thomas, 46 Gansevoort
New York.
Walsh Patrick, E. 18th cor. 5th Av.
Walsh Thomas, 186 Mott
Waters Jacob, 220 Cherry
Waters John, 8th Av.
Watson James, rear 22 4th Av.
Welch J. 71 West Broadway
Welch J. H. cor. Leonard & West
Broadway
Weldon Patrick M. 81 Broad
Westervelt J. L. 199 Greenwich
Westervelt William. 177 Prince
Wheeler Lucius. 319 W. 17th
Wheeler W. 49 1st
White John. W. 15th near 7 Av.
Whritner D. East bet. Delancy
& Broome
Wilkins Harvey, 96 Sullivan
Wilkinson G. rear 46 Elizabeth
Williams C. 133 Greenwich Av.
Williams Harris, 65 Hamersley
Wilson Henry. 427 Monroe
Wilson P. M. 117 Prince
Windle Peter. 53 Lewis
Wood & Gregory, 400 Water
Wright Horace, 34 Corlears
Yate Samuel, 71 Bank
Yermann Francis J. 40th st.
Yermann John, 104 West 18th

Niagara County.

Cook Bates   Lewiston.
Platt J. & W
Hasley Amos, Pekin
Dutton John   do
Perigo H.   Lockport.
Brown Samuel C. & Son Newfane.
Huie J. M. & Brother
Mohler John
Armstrong Thomas, Olcott
Marshall Francis H.   do
Gegan John   Niagara Falls.
Bonecher Jacob
Emerson J. W. Youngstown
Porter.
Clark Willard W.   do
Shaft David, Ransomville
Peckham & Pratt   Somerset.
Jenny Seth
Donaly Richard, Tonawanda
Wheatfield.
M'Kay & Wetmore   Wilson.
Johnson H. & R.
Bonested William

Oneida County.

Linkfield & Briggs   Annsville.
Simmons N. F.   Camden.
Jones J. J.   Deerfield.
Morgan ———
Barden A.
Roberts William   Florence.
Gartland Sylvester
Jones J. R.
Brandt J. B. Dominick st. Rome.
Higgins & Mills, James st.
Briggs A.   do
Pierce E. Holland Patent Trenton.
Bacon D. Trenton Falls
Cady B. F. So. Trenton
Timerman D. 48 Seneca   Utica.
Stevens J. W. 34 Water
Thomas William, 45 Whitesboro
Davis D. R. 6 Seneca
Bates J. W. 18 Fayette
Rose H.   do
Christian Nathan, Jay st.
Yale J. Broad st.
Foster William, 11 Bleeker
Slater & Brant, 34 John
White P. 8 Main
Glean F.   Whitestown.
Beebe J. H. Whitesboro

Onondaga County.

Cook William   Cicero.
Smith, R. D.   Marcellus.
Putnam G. D. Water st. Syracuse
Salina.

Phelps S. Orange st. *Syracuse*
 Salina.
Featherly J. & F. James st.
Hare B. & Co. do
Phillips William, Free st.
Sawyer S. & Co. Wolf st.

Ontario County.

Taylor N. C. *Bristol.*
Gooding R. B.
Everets S. R.
Worden S.
Bennett D. H.
Hoyt Charles *Canandaigua.*
Felton & Newman
Rockwell George
Billings B.
Baldwin M. *East Bloomfield.*
Hodge H. L.
Benton M.
Johnson J. *Manchester.*
Spencer Abel *Phelps.*
Cole William
Alger J. D. Honeoye *Richmond.*
Bishop Sheldon, do
Harris A. do
Smith Albert C. Allen's Hill
Hardy ——, do
M'Connell John, do
Hapgood John, Geneva *Seneca.*
Hand Moses B. do
Osman William, do
Ide John, do
Brondage William, do
Van Lew William, do
Johnson William, do
Dey M. M. do
Smith John, do
Doty William *South Bristol.*
Treat Homer H.
Seavey William *Victor.*
Moul Charles E.
Fetus Samuel
Morgan Nathan
Meddough Martin
Smith & Burke *West Bloomfield.*
Mackin & Webb
Huntington S.

Orange County.

Orr Hugh, Salisbury Mills
 Blooming Grove.
Thurston I. do
Robins G. Washingtonville
Kelley & Coleman, do
Owens E. Craigeville
Wood O. T. *Chester.*
Stewart R.
Fitzgerald S. S.
Tole John *Cornwall.*
Mandigo L. Buttermilk Falls
June & Gibbs do
Torry G.
Campbell Jacob B. *Crawford.*
Knight T.
Rhodes S Port Jervis *Deer Park.*
Skinner N. do
Jones A. J. *Goshen.*
Dodge R. Ridgebury *Minisink.*
Robins R. S. Slate Hill
Gardiner C. Wells Corners
Crawford A. S. do
Parsons I., Howell's Depot
Penny B. F. Wells Corners
Mathews N. do
Stevens D., West Town
Halsey J. M. Unionville
Chumar & Coleman *Montgomery.*
Jewell D.
Malone James
Millspaugh M. Walden
Burhans Wm. do
Earley Thos. J. *Monroe.*
Hudson Wm.
Harding W. S. Otisville
 Mount Hope.
Conklin C.
Ogden J.
Thorn L. Finchville
Boyd John, Water st. *Newburgh.*
M'Cann P 110 do

Frost C. Western Av. *Newburgh.*
Smith I. do
DeGroff James, Front st.
Montgomery Geo. 4th st.
Lynch John, Colden st.
DeForest D. R. Front st.
M'Cullough Thos. *New Winasor.*
M'Crean J. W. T. New Hampton
 Wallkill.
Cory H. D. do
Crane Wm. N. South Middletown
Crane G. B. do
Kain H. & Co. do
Brown T. do
DePuy & Schoonmaker do
Wright A. Amity *Warwick.*
Sayer H. G. do
Green H. Edenville
Sloan J. New Milford
Burroughs H. do
Wright E. Florida
Hunter Wm. Sugar Loaf
Sullivan J. do
Youmans J. do

Orleans County.

Blakesly & Washburn, Albion
 Barre.
Phillips Robert, do
Boardwell Joseph, do
Mead & Fisk, Barre Centre
Harwick J. do
Fish Solomon S. *Carlton.*
Powell Lyman C. Waterport
Williams John, East Carlton
Perry David, West do
Woodward S. *Clarendon.*
Martin Wm. jr.
Dewey M.
Childs L. S. *Gaines.*
Cradder Wm.
Bassett Wm. R. *Kendall.*
Shay J.
Smith Gideon
Williams Bradley F. Holley
 Murray.
Goff Sandford do
Bushnell S. do
Pease Elisha do
Davis ——, Sandy Creek
Utley Hiram, Hulburton
Morse Lucius, Knowlesville
 Ridgeway.
Douglass Beman do
Bigelow J. J. *Shelby.*
Bailey J.
Mead John *Yates.*
Clark Lambert
Jenkinson James
Lewis Isaiah
Olds Martin
Palmer J. M. Lyndonville
Handy W. P. do
Martin G. W. do
Harris P. L. do
Pinchin A. B. County Line
Harkway James, North Ridgeway

Oswego County.

Decker Peter *Albion.*
Whipple Windsor
Wilcox James
Mann M. O. Carterville *Amboy.*
Crandall Daniel S. Amboy Centre
Stanton Nathan, West Amboy
Webster J. *Constantia.*
Dakin S. J.
Raymore M.
Gage H. S.
Phillips B.
Cummins Charles, Cleaveland
Harris —— do
Abbott L. A. do
Baker J. Oswego Falls *Granby.*
Rice Aaron & Co. do
Rice —— do
Gardner S. H. & H. A. do
Northrop ——, do
Johnson —— *Hannibal.*
Brett William
Downing Jabin
Perkins W. Hannibal Centre

Church —— *Hastings.*
Clute ——
Green D. D. Central Square
Shepard T. do
Smith & Alfred *Mexico.*
Barrett W.
Stebbins Charles
Penfield A. & W
Markham S. D., Colosse
Blackman Daniel, Texas
Wilder W. R. *New Haven.*
Wilson John
Dugwell William H.
Babcock J. G.
Bracy William
Platt & Madison *Orwell.*
Hopper Andrew, 1st st. *Oswego.*
Davis & Gage do
Bryant Seneca V. do
Allen D. L. & Co. Canal
Yaw David W. do
Battis Andrew, Bridge st.
Clark M. do
Riley James do
Disbrow & Denton, 2d st.
Crolius G. A. & Co. (ship smiths)
 Water st.
Crolius J. M. & Co. (ship smiths)
 cor. 1st & Van Buren
Carter H. T. cor. 1st & Bridge
Gleason B. cor. 3d & Bridge
Wood G. H. cor. 2d & Cayuga
Lyon Cyrus L. *Parish.*
Bonner John *Redfield.*
Dale George, Pulaski *Richland.*
Thomas Luther B. do
Box William, do
Dillenback Isaac, do
Ingersoll R. L. do
Robbins Philip, do
Box John, do
Jones John, do
Crandall & Kenyon, do
Box John, Port Ontario
Cable C. & N. Phœnix *Schræppel.*
Beebe Nathan, do
Munger Curtis, do
Capron David, do
Ross H. Gilbert's Mills
Linbeck N. Hinmansville
Jones F. do
Newell & Abraham *Scriba.*
Loveridge Joel
Paul John, jr. *Williamstown.*
Freeman A. E.
Squiers John

Otsego County.

Cockburn T. West *Burlington.*
Breese L. do
Stockwell C. A. Burlington Flats
Hulbert A. do
Gossart J. Burlington Green
Frater William, do
Bacon D. *Butternuts.*
Barrett S.
Kynion J. P.
Winton M. T.
Wilkins D. *Cherry Valley.*
Bush G.
De Long H.
Millson G.
Dutcher G.
Vandyke A.
Tisdale G. A.
Davis L. D. *Decatur*
Brown Exre
Wright H.
Hopkins Samuel *Edmeston.*
Potter Timothy
Parmerter Wm. West Edmeston
Salisbury J. B. & H. *Exeter.*
Fisk H. D. West Exeter
Angell F. Cortes, do
Smith J. S. & W. B. Schuyler's
 Lake
Brewer David, do
Fenton S. C. *Laurens.*
Mead J.
Allen A.
Couse P.

Follett Jordon C.   *Middlefield.*
Briggs George L.
Jones James B.
Shipard A. C. J.
Kelso Spencer
Allen Reuben
Pratt Thomas
Murray Alexander
Briggs E. K.   *Milford.*
Goodrich R. A. & D
Newkirk D.
Schermerhorn T. G.
Barney J. H.
Wild James & William   *Oneonta.*
M'Crany John
Daly Samuel, West Oneonta
Packard J. M.   do
Benedict Alanson, do
Richardson Nelson & Ira, do
Pendleton James
Allen Nicholas
Baldwin S. & J.   *Otego.*
Sacket O. E.
Crane D. H.
Hall J.
Brand M.   *Plainfield.*
Stillman John B.
Weaver H.
Babcock ——
Hover Jacob   *Unadilla.*
Woodruff Levi B.
Potter Nathan   *Westford.*
Grant O. G.   *Worcester.*
Guile John
Preston Reuben
Dickinson O. H.
Boiling Michael
Groat Wm. D., East Worcester
Ten Brook Jeremiah, South do

Putnam County.

Sloat L. M.   *Carmel.*
Quick Norman
Phillips J. F.   *Kent.*
Lawrence C.
Hazzleton D. B. Farmers' Mills
  Kent.
Birch J. S.   *Patterson.*
Evans E.
Ellsworth A.
Kenny J. Cold Spring
  Phillipstown.
Coe T.   do
Warren J.   do
Dykeman D.   do
M'Gowan W.
Denny J.
Denny R.
Boice S.
Warren H.
Wallace H.   *Putnam Valley.*
Warren E.
Pratt N.
Trowbridge P. B.   *Southeast.*
Hope Wm.
Corbin ——

Queens County.

Parks A.   *Flushing.*
Bedell J.
Shore T., Rockville   *Hempstead.*
Abrams Oliver, Rockaway
Golden Christopher
Baldwin Thomas, Hick's Neck
Cornwell W. & J. Raynor Town
Abrams Alfred   do
Frost Isaac, Christian Hook
Abraham Smith, Rockaway
Watts H., Foster's Meadow
Losee Stephen,   do
Pearsall Clarkson
Hents Henry, jr.
Pettit John
Weeks Walter N.
Hicks Wm. Trimming Square
Pearsall T., Far Rockaway
Pearsall Jeremiah,   do
Doughty Samuel,   do
Allen Wm., Merrick
Lodge James H.   *Jamaica.*
Baylis Ephaim

Nostrand Zachariah,   *Jamaica*
Brush Wm A.
Knight Henry,
Dunn Jacob,
Nostrand Elijah & Nathaniel
M'Laughlin John
Doxey Solomon
Nostrand Peter
Rappelyea George   *Newtown.*
Tilton E.
Nass A.
Morris C. R.
Baxter Charles H., Roslyn
  North Hempstead.
Wright Daniel
Smith Wm. H.
Underhill Wm.. Manhasset
Place Wm. Cow Neck
Velson John, Lakeville
Ludiam Samuel Y.   *Oyster Bay.*
Hoagland C. East Norwich
Wright Wm. Jericho
Valentine J.   do
Coles J. & E.   do
Albertson Derrick, do
Davis Thomas,   do
Wright John,   do
Wright A.   do

Rensselaer County.

Clum J.   *Brunswick.*
Hyler G. W.   *Greenbush.*
Van Vleck F. B. 172 State
  Lansingburgh.
McMannas Thomas, Richard st.
Porter O.   do
Ahern J. Jay st.
Hunt E.   do
Edgar Alexander, Ferry st.
Clark W. W. East Nassau   *Nassau.*
Lucy Daniel. Front st.   *Troy.*
Purdy Nathan,   do
Simmon Benjamin. 360 River
Patten John V. 5 Jacob
Bates & Cammon, near the bridge
Hensbery Daniel, Maiden Lane
Hutchinson John, cor. Mechanic
  & Grand Division
Middleton David, 195 Fourth
Boyle J. 4 Fulton
Smith John, 6 do
Shelley T. 163 Congress
Roddy T. 154   do
Sealey E. A. 13 Ferry
Donnelly Peter. 9 do
M'Coy S., Adams near 2d
Tripp W. G. 6th near Ferry
Reilly J, Ida Hill
Hogan J. 42 Ferry
Fitzsimmons P. South Troy
Albert John, Nail Factory
Bowman J. 513 River
Faucher S. N. River near State
  dam
Shook J.

Richmond County.

Thompson & Fountain, Tompkins-
  ville   *Castleton.*
Marsh I., Richmond,   *Northfield*
Noble W. B., Stapleton   *Southfield.*
Journey D., Rossville   *Westfield.*

Rockland County.

Hennion R. Piermont   *Orangetown.*
Demerest J. T. Nyack
Dutcher J.   do
Harris W. H.   do
Burd D.   do
Onderdonk J.   do
Van Zant T. Spring Valley

St. Lawrence County.

Ertus Joseph   *Brasher.*
Lowel H.
Stowe Marshall   *Canton.*
Kipp Albert E.
Haynes, Wiley & Gurtin
Sherman & Jones

Smith Harry   *Canton.*
M'Ewen
Bailly Walter
Bassett Elijah
M'Kenzie Daniel
Finneman Wm.
Wells ——
Spaulding A.   *De Kalb.*
Welch & Nash, Richville
Thompson & Co.   do
Case L.   do
Monroe T.   do
Wood Wm. W.   do
Washburn Rufus   *Depeyster.*
Lathrop L. D.
Petrie Edward
Raymond James   *Edwards.*
Wood John, South Edwards
Wood Silas,   do
Abbot E. W.   *Fowler.*
Fuller & Peck
Root Caleb O.
Fosgate Edwin
Graves James N.
Whitney Nathaniel
Wheeler & Son   *Gouverneur.*
Marsh W.
M'Cain Wm.
Darley J.
Nicol John   *Hammond.*
Eustis Tobias
Wait Sidney S.
Lugton John
Cunningham John
Graves James
Comstock S. & F.   *Harmon.*
Merriam Samuel
Carter Henry
Ellis A. E.
Campbell ——
Snell Hiram,   *Hopkinton.*
Lawrence Ruel
Tinuff P. D.
Wright & Kellogg
Blake Henry
Doty B. T.   *Lisbon.*
Shelden Wm.
Corbin Benjamin
Northrop Wm.
Trust James   *Macomb.*
Taylor ——
Partridge ——
Hosford & Lovegrove, Columbia
  Madrid.
Wright James,   do
Read Wm.   do
Proctor & Ellis, Waddington
Rand John,   do
Rand J. P.   do
Carrigan & Myers,   do
M'Quade John,   do
Rand Festus G.   *Massena.*
Rankin Hugh
Crowley A. M.
Stafford S. Lewisville
M'Pherson ——,   do
Powers ——,   do
M'Pherson E.   *Louisville.*
Stafford S. J.
Power J.
Tobin J.
Harris E.
Marvin R. J.
Miller George   *Morristown.*
Brown Albert
Dunn Joseph, jr.
Marsean Simon
Fry John
Mundigo Charles, Edwardsville
Stiles John, jr.   do
Taylor Samuel,   do
Robinson Arby,   *Norfolk.*
Robinson Alba
Livingsworth Arza
Putnam D. C.
Kingsbury R. Raymondsville
Arnold ——
Chaney A. & Co. Ogdensburgh
  Oswegatchie.
Alden A. E. & W. C. do
Gordon Wm.   do
Lytle James W.   do

Northrep L. S. Ogdensburgh
Oswegatchie.
Burditt David, do
Jaques James Parishville.
Howe O.
Lucas John Pierpont.
Lucas Jerome
Shipman Adolph Pitcairn.
Putnam John C. Potsdum.
Hyde Henry H.
Drake James
Dayton Johnson W.
White Francis F.
Burton Benjamin
Salls Briggs, West Potsdam
Ross James do
Bailey Julius do
Mills P. Russell.
Flannigan —— Stockholm.
Rice Cornelius
Hudson Joshua C.
Stearns J.
Lowell M.

Saratoga County.

Gardiner L. Charlton.
Curtiss & Bell
Wilkinson James
Willis Robert
Edwards Henry
M'Gowan C. & A. West Charlton
Barruss Elisha Corinth.
Ellis Joseph
Carpenter Isaac
Eglin Henry Edinburgh.
Mead Alanson Galway.
Mead Amon
Irish S. W.
Lyon ——
Barrows T. Greenfield.
Ingerson Asa, South Greenfield
Eddy Samuel
Flynn John Halfmoon.
Rosekrans D.
Cole Frederick Malta.
Ogden R. A.
Smith & Parks, Glenn's Falls
Moreau.
Scovill Anson, do
Barton John, Ballston Spa Milton.
Selring Harrison, do
Lord Henry Providence.
Carpenter J. W.
Duel S.
Wooster George
Marshall Amos, Bakerville
Henry James Saratoga.
Shaw Edward
Oakley D. R.
Myres D.
Howland A.
Esmond C.
Wroath William
Wroath John
Deuel P.
Servier G.
Kelsey Benjamin
Terwilliger S. Saratoga Springs.
Cook Wm.
Hodgman John
Hodgman & Briggs
French B.
Clare John
Flanagan & Co.
Thompson I. & Co.
Blackall J. (whitesmith)
Dickinson Daniel Stillwater.
Bookman George
Vosburg J. P. Waterford.
Hurd George
Hale James
Stcenbrough David
Pearsall Thomas Wilton.
Lea Garret
Sawyer James
Buck Lyman
Jeffers Thomas

Schenectady County.

Clossan & Walling Glenville.

Mesick A. 1 Rotterdam
Schenectady.
Swits W. A. 14 do
Clute & Riggles, 217 State
Van Syce A. G. State st.
Barhydt & Greenhelgh, 20 Canal
Banker I. Liberty st.
Vedder J. I. Canal st.

Schoharie County.

Martin W. A. Blenheim.
Martin Geo. W.
Martin Almiron
Brown George Carlisle.
Rockefeler H.
Fero J. W.
Thrall George
Relyea David
Bellinger George Cobleskill.
Kromer C.
Harrison ——
Smith John J. Esperance.
Brownell F.
Wilber A
Quick D. C. Sloansville
Lown Isaac, do
Stratton C, do
Getter David, Fultonham Fulton.
Vanorman C. do
Crawford A. West Fulton
Hazelton L. Breakabeen
Decker A. do
Hunt Jacob Gilboa.
Fare David
Van Dusen James W.
Efner John Middleburgh.
Smith Hiram
Smith Sylvester
Bouck Thomas W.
Snyder Adam
Bourn L. G. Richmondville.
Zeh Stephen G
Zeh Hiram
Ochampanch Wm.
Handy J.
Warner Marcus, Warnerville
Westerhouse Geo. Central Bridge
Schoharie.
Feek J. J.
Spaulding Wm.
Rickett David
Calkins L. Hyndsville Seward.
Rowley Nelson, Gardinersville
Van Scoyck ——
Shaver Jacob, Gallupville Wright.

Seneca County.

Messinger Aaron Fayette.
Deal Jacob
Smith George Ovid.
Schooley William J.
Grisern Oscar
Church George
Munson J. & K. Farmer
Colton Firman do
Crane Thomas Romulus.
Burke Henry
Mooney John
Church Abijah R.

Steuben County.

Mills J. H. Cohocton.
Knapp Theodore
Johnson Benjamin
Dickinson Elon
Cramer J. North Cohocton
Cramer H. do
Webster Harvey Troupsburgh.
Fuller Rufus

Suffolk County.

Smith W., Setauket Brookhaven.
Mott Tuttle, Middle Island
Jayne Van Wycke T., Patchogue
Miller Charles do
Smith Floyd do
Smith Ellis do
Ireland George, Comac
Huntington.
Brewster A., North Port

Hawxhurst Solomon, Babylon
Huntington.
Hart Ezra do
Moore Mulford Riverhead,
Corwin Daniel
Smith John Smithtown.
Homedieu A. L.
Arthur Franklin O.
Arthur Erastus
Jayne Charles H.
Rose Henry S. Southampton.
Burnett John F.
Bennett Sylvanus
Halsey Alfred R.
Terry Daniel Southold.
Berseuger Adam
Buckingham Chatfield, East Cutchogue
Wisdom Wm. A. Greenport
Wells Daniel, do
Wells Henry, do

Sullivan County.

Lorgan P. M. Mongaup Valley
Bethel.
Garrett C. & R. Liberty.
Eaton B. Barryville Lumberland.
Stage J. W. Big Eddy
Sinsabaugh & Williams, Bloomingburgh Mamakating.
Anderson J. W. Bloomingburgh
Smith John W. do
Crane C. C. do
Hamilton Geo. Burlingham
Watts R. do
Lockwood S. B. Wurtsboro
Stanton D. T do
Horton T. do
Vernel Peleg S. Monticello
Orr Hugh, do

Tompkins County.

Tucker Ezra Enfield.
Laning J.
Baker Henry, Enfield Centre
Lord Ezra, do
Anderson B. B & D. C. Newfield.
Ramsey Isaac
Todd & Campbell

Ulster County.

Elmendorph Geo. Kingston.
Houghtailing N.
Masten Andrew N.
Houghtaling John H.
Dewey Edgar
Houghtaling John E. D.
Shaffer G. N. Rondout
Davis I. A. Eddyville
Hartenburgh J. R. High Falls
Marbletown.
Davis F. H., Stone Ridge
Palen John, do
Delamater S. do
Van Luren A. do
Quick W. New Paltz.
Coe E.
Du Bois C.
Frear M.
Dolson W. Libertyville
Broadhead I. Kyserike Rochester.
Bogardus Wm. H. Rosendale.
Burhans Geo. Saugerties.
Myer Peter T. B.
Post Wm. A. Glasco
Fundy Peter, do
Segandorph D. Pine Hill
Shandaken.
Hasbrouck J. do
Smith T. do
Germond T. do
M'Gowan S. Shawangunk.
Brundage F. T. Port Ben
Wawarsing.
Hoag & Gerard, Ellenville

Warren County.

Crandall S. W. Caldwell.
Nichols Isaac

Braley J. Chestertown *Chester.*
Dunn O. K.   do
Wallace Richard   *Hague.*
Hodkins P.
Leach J. H.   *Horiconville.*
May Horace
Shay Geo.
Shaw Benj.
Welch A. W. Glenn's Falls
        Queensbury.
Robins & Co.   do
Gager Wm. H.   do
Bullard James,   do
Corney Timothy,   do
Wills A. P.   *Warrensburgh.*
Glynn Geo.
Wilson ——,
Mixture John
White Josiah

Washington County.

Ketcham John   *Argyle.*
Michael John
Carswell Benjamin
Kilmer Simeon, North Argyle
Williams Simeon,   do
Bain Abram, South Argyle
Schermerhorn Simeon, do
Wilson Christopher   *Cambridge.*
Robertson Josiah
Fenton Zalmon, jr.
Twist Russell
Hyde Joseph
Robertson John B.
Beattie Alex. Cambridge Centre
Skellie William, North Cambridge
Wood Ira,   do
White James   *Easton.*
Mabb Henry
Rifenburgh David
Burdick William, Union Village
Potter Joel,   do
Fenton Francis, Galesville
Smith Albert M.   do
Briggs Warren North Easton
Burdick Ezra,   do
Hutchinson John,   do
Hill Enoch, South Easton
Sewell William P. do
Pike Hunter   *Fort Edward.*
Traver Andrew
Elmore Ora
Broughton P.
Wait Sidney, Fort Miller
Brown Joseph,   do
Prentiss & Richards,   *Greenwich.*
Billings Derick
Akin Amos, Centre Falls
Connell Richard O. do
Hyatt J. K. Battenville
Barnard Abner C. East Greenw'h
Henry William, Lake
Clark J. L.   do
Tefft Lewis, Galesville
Davison James, North Greenwich
Broughton Aaron   *Hampton.*
Rayden Abner
Moore James   *Hebron.*
Flack Nelson
Williamson Alexander
Scott Doty & Brother, N. Hebron
West Egbert,   East do
Turner James,   do
Clark & Son,   do
Barckley William,   do
Dixon Ebenezer,   West do
Conkey William T.   do
Elliott Daniel.   *Kingsbury.*
Pasco J.   Sandy Hill
Hall Seneca,   do
Prescott G. A.   do
Ogden L. D.   do
Hooper Peter H. do
Walker A.   do
Mead M. Smiths' Basin
Lilly Thomas   *Putnam.*
French Solomon
Huelett Arnold
Cramond Simon
Crown Eugene   *Salem.*

Hight Alvah   *Salem.*
M'Killip E. D.
Bartlett E. D.
Rider David
Smith Charles   *White Creek.*
Wakefield Wm. Centre Creek

Wayne County.

Riggs Joseph A. Newark *Arcadia.*
Riggs A.   do
Taylor S.   do
Brownell W.   do
Tracy S. R.   do
Whitlock L. L.   do
Dunwell A.
Van Innager, Fairville
Whitbeck A. J. do
Wakeman M. & J. Newark
Cornage ——,   do
M'Guire ——   *Butler.*
Condit John, Clyde   *Galen.*
Howard C.   do
Stratton & Brothers, Clyde
Gage M. W.   *Huron.*
Wesley John   *Lyons.*
Croul P. C.
Robinson John
Eyck John
Scott Wm.
Croul Columbus
Stuver James, Alloway
Howig E. K. Macedonville
        Macedon.
Bilbie Wm.   *Marion.*
Curtis Harvey
Ellsworth & Brothers   *Ontario.*
Bingham C. B.   *Palmyra.*
Soper F.
Warn Thomas M.   *Rose.*
Bassett John
Tindall & Alexander
Rineheart Martin
Chiller John   *Sodus.*
Hoyt & Brother   *Walworth.*
French Lewis   *Williamson.*
Dobbs ——, East Williamson
Flemming Wm. Pultneyville
Cripen Cyrus   *Wolcott.*
Crane Daniel H.

Westchester County.

Burgers I. Peekskill   *Courtlandt.*
Cavat James P.   do
Bennett F.   do
Lawrence A.   *East Chester.*
Riley Thomas
Milrose J. Tarrytown *Greenburgh.*
Culver Nathan L. Dobbs' Ferry
Boyd Wm.   *Mamaroneck.*
Devean W. F. P.   *New Rochelle.*
M'Cabe James
Redfield B.
Hatfield R.
Lounsbury J. W. Portchester *Rye.*
Mead David H.
Lewis Michael   *Westchester.*
Valentine Samuel
Doty Phillips
Shaw Wm.   *West Farms.*

Wyoming County.

Newton Levi   *Attica.*
Wright & Alexander
Tinker & Fox
Toms Parleman
Smith S. H.   *Bennington.*
Franklin S. Cowlesville
Conklin Wm. H.   *Castile.*
Knapp Wm. L.
Belden Simeon
Smith B. F.
Barton N.
Lemley Jacob   *Covington.*
Phero & Broughton, Peoria
Birdsall Asa, La Grange
David Henry   *Eagle.*
Windangle Jonas
Case & Patterson, Eagle Village
Yale James   do

Acker Samuel   *Genesee Falls*
Bristol Fayette
Humphrey James
Shaw Samuel
Blood John   *Java.*
Wait E.
Davis Gardner   *Middlebury.*
Smith & Ridge, Wyoming
Morse James H.   *Orangeville.*
Fullington F. East Orangeville
Dalbeer Wm. & Son   *Perry.*
Simmons P.
Prall Thomas
Stowell F.
Austin William, Perry Centre
M'Intire Wm.   *Pike.*
Cheeney & Stafford
Kendall H. G.
Robinson A.
Farmcrook C.
Crippin & Everest, East Pike
Stowe A. C.   do
Partridge A. L. East Koy
Doshant John,   *Sheldon.*
Bump Hiram. Varysburg
Cowding P. Strykersville
Potter Wm. E.   do
Jones H. & B. Johnsburg
Knapp & Whiting   *Warsaw.*
Buxton C. & T.
De Witt C.
Fiero Wm.

Yates County.

Robinson O.   *Barrington.*
Lyon S. C., Benton Centre, *Benton.*
Dickinson A.. Belona
Smith & Campbell do
Elliott C., Italy Hollow   *Italy.*
Thompson W., Italy Hill
Hilterbridle ——   *Jerusalem.*
Vanness & Pulver, Branchport
Harrington & Abeel   *Middlesex.*
Kilpatrick Jesse
Loncor Martin   *Milo.*
Jones E. B. Penn Yan
Hughs David,   do
Powell & Elliott, do
Kimble Wm.   do
Legg J. Milo Centre
Ide Wm. H. H.   *Potter.*
Peabody John A. Rushville
Wheeler Levi, Yatesville
Conley David R.   do
Dunn Warren, Dundee   *Starkey.*
Slocum B. F.   do
O'Neil Albert,   do
Green John.   do
Hurd Stephen, Rock Stream

Blank Book Manufactur-
ers. *(See also Binders.)*

Erie County.

Leavitt James L. 18 & 19 Merchants' Exchange   *Buffalo.*

Monroe County.

Drake Samuel, 12 Exchange
        Rochester.

Washington County.

Strong Marcellus, Sandy Hill
        Kingsbury.

Bleachers—Cotton Goods.

Martin R. 100 Troy   *New York.*
Ritchie William, 107 Troy
Waterbury C. A. 106 Broadway

Rensselaer County.

Marshall & Yourt, Ida Hill, *Troy.*

Bleachers—Embroidered
Muslins.

Dietz Rosa, 419 Broadway, bleaches laces, &c.   *New York.*
Robinson Elizabeth, 89 Mercer

Bleachers—Hat and Straw.

Albany County.

Ware F. A. 3 Union   Albany.
Cutler M. L. 542 Broadway
Cook Mrs. 162 S. Pearl

New York County.

Barrett J. G. 31 Ludlow New York.
Betts Samuel S. 410 Pearl
Berry Chas. H. 17 N. William
Gardner Ira C. 44 6th Av
Gowen H. K. 50 Division
Mason Coventon, 1 Division
Pearson M. & C. 116 Hester
M'Leod Jane, 36 Sheriff
Wilson Archibald, 236 Walker
Wilson Carington, 6th Av. n. 26th
Woolton C. L. 235 Division

Block Letter Signs.

Ackerman J. 101 & 105 Nassau
                    New York.
Brandon A. & G. 7 Tryon Row
Cragin B. F. 20 Nassau

Block and Pump Makers.

Baptist J. W. 271 South New York.
Beyea Benjamin, 229 West
Boyce Bartholomew D. 106 Le Roy
Bryant George W. 234 South
Burr Daniel, 60 Vesey
Chapman Benj. H. 35 Tompkins
Chapman W. T. foot Rivington
Coleman & Chapman, 22 South
Coger William, 247 South
Davidson John, 168   do
Dennis James M. 897 Broadway
Dewey James, 21 Coenties slip
Dillingham Wm. 246 Front
Hanson John C. 293   do
Harkness James, 232 South
Lewis Samuel, 289 West
Lord & Pinckney, 375 Front
Matsenger Henry, 230 2d
Mitchell John, 223 South
Morton Joseph T. 50 West
Munson James, 116 Wall
Munson & Stuyvesant, 44 West
Nicols S. 293 Stanton & 76 South
Nolan James, 23 Old Slip
Platt F. 96 Pike slip & 142 Monroe
Rogers Abel D. 164 Maiden lane
Rogers Isaiah, 500 Water
Sealy Richard, 521 Pearl
Simpson William, 19 Front
Staples G. W. 36 Burling slip
Stuyvesant Peter J. 44 West
Taylor & Wilson, 205 do
Tomlinson Isaac, 179 Lewis
Westcott & Ferguson, 242½ South
Whittemore Robert J. 225 Lewis
Williams Richard, 36 Depeyster

Boarding Houses.

Albons H. 26 West   New York.
Aldridge H. 22 City Hall place
Alexander J. B. 126 Av. C
Allason Mrs. 70 Greenwich
Allen Joseph, 218 Grand
Allison Margaret, 20 Harrison
Almgreen A. G. 100 Oliver
Ames Henry, 567 Greenwich
Anderson Charles, 390 Water
Anderson Oly, 302 Front
Andrew F. 141 W. Broadway
Andrews Ann, 129 Chambers
Ankers John, 157 Cherry
Anthony John. 36 Av. D
Archer William, 138 9th Av.
Arding Adeline, 4 Columbia place
Aristide Martin, 94 Church
Atfield John, 63 Washington
Becker Albert V. 198 Grand
Baker J. 90 King
Baldwin A. S. 7 Broadway

Ball William M. 212 Fulton
                    New York.
Bange John T. 611 Grand
Banks William, 159 Mott
Bant George, 380 Pearl
Bunta Sarah, 76 Grand
Barker Mrs. 13 Broadway
Barney Eliza A. 75 White
Barry Ann, 154 Walker
Barry John, 42 Cherry
Basset Elizabeth, 25 Marion
Batey John N. 546 Grand
Beach William, 176 Greenwich
Beak James, 1 Delancy
Beauchamp L. 151 Greenwich
Beach George, 306 Water
Beach Ezra, 247 Spring
Beckett Geo. 305 Water
Beck Hugh, 358 Greenwich
Beck L. & Co. 92 Fulton
Beckwith Belinda O. 26 Beekman
Bedford Donald, 101 Horatio
Beirne Henry, 31 Morris
Beirns Thos. 359 Water
Belcher Morrison, 199 Duane
Bell Hester, 179 Mulberry
Bennett George, 380 Pearl
Benstein Philip, 69 Broome
Bent George, 380 Pearl
Beran Edward, 329 Pearl
Bick H. 139 Liberty
Billings Catharine, 202 Greenwich
Birmingham Dorcas, 247 W. 21st
Blackburn J. 112 Greenwich
Blackstock Moses, 46 Harrison
Blackwell Jacob, 13 Sullivan
Blake Benjamin, 18 Thames
Blake Elizabeth, 544 Pearl
Blake Rufus, 29 Centre
Blauret & Gold, 89 W. Broadway
Bliss Diabold, rear 82 Wooster
Blonk George, 410 10th
Bogart Sarah, 335 Pearl
Bone Mary, 146 Orange
Boon James, 77 Hameraley
Booth Jeremiah, 24 St. Peter's. pl.
Boughton Henry, 566 Grand
Bouman Henry, 76 Roosevelt
Bourke C. 89 Cherry
Brady Michael, 111 W. 21st
Braidert George, 528 Pearl
Branin P. 105 Washington
Brannagan Terence, 120 Cedar
Brannigan Jane, 39 Frankfort
Breidert M. S. 528 Pearl
Brennan Thos. 48½ Cherry
Brewer Sarah, 210 Walker
Brock William, 98 Washington
Bromley Jane, 45 Beekman
Brooks Joseph, 250 West
Brooks William, 69 Fulton
Brower John, 407 West
Brown John H. 37 Oak
Brown James, 13th st.
Brown Letitia, 134 Av. C
Brown Joseph F. 13 Water
Bryan Levi, 35 Lispenard
Bryant Jane, 145 Lewis
Buel George M. 63 Fulton
Bunke Charles & Co. 99 Cedar
Burnes Mrs. 105 John
Burnet Hannah, 193 Mulberry
Burnet Mary, 190 Hester
Burus Robert, 141 Washington
Bursley George, 84 James
Burrows Michael. 368 Water
Burnham O. R. 175 Broadway
Busteed Anna, 86 Mott
Butenop & Co. 136 Cedar
Butenop John, 136 Greenwich
Buttner John, 5 Albany
Byrne James, 118 Mulberry
Byrnes Mary, 78 Gold
Byrnes Robert, 141 Washington
Callaghan Mary Ann, 45 Dey
Campbell Catharine, 131 W. 16th
Campbell Jane, 111 Chambers
Campbell Matthew, 139 W. 19th
Caradine Richard, 96 Oliver
Carle Caroline, 166 Bowery
Carman & Elbert, 385 Water

Carney Moses, 164 W. 17th
                    New York.
Carns Ann, 75 Market
Carpenter Wm. 66 Oliver
Carr Catharine, 90 Laurens
Carrs M. 335 Water
Carroll ——, 209 Allen
Cary Maria, 191 Hester
Cass William. 203 Bowery
Cast Jeune, 36 Rose
Catley Thomas, 100 Jane
Chesnut Margaret, 39 Cherry
Christian Mary, 64 Eldridge
Christman Caspar, 31 Bayard
Churchill Roswell, 96 Liberty
Clapper Elizabeth, 385 6th
Clark Margaret, 109 Greene
Clark Riley, 16 Laurens
Clarke Daniel, 75 Washington
Clanson & Suhr, 1 Peck slip
Clement Susan, 512 Broadway
Clements Nancy, 504 Grand
Clohecy Marks. 354 9th
Clousing Charles, 268 William
Coburn Margaret, 7 Dover
Cochran John C. 300 Madison
Cock A. L. 275 Grand
Coles Eliza, 43 Sullivan
Collier E. C. 102 Gold
Collins Harriet, 106 Av. C
Collins Joseph, 46 Trinity place
Colon Deborah, 314 2d
Conant Asa C. 53 Ludlow
Condit Sarah A. 201 Elm
Conover William, 48 Robinson
Constantine Mrs. 58 Broadway
Constable John G. 68 Oliver
Cook Catherine A. 81 Bayard
Cooke Thomas, 30 Pearl
Cooley Eli F. 274   do
Coon J. L. 65 Church
Corby Mary, 11 Washington
Cornell James, 26 Greenwich Av.
Corson Joseph, 87 Cherry
Coughlan Bridget, 74 6th Av.
Courter Nathan, 134 Elizabeth
Cowley Michael, 251 Pearl
Cox Jane, 115 3d Av.
Cranch John, 13 Dover
Crane Mary, 2 Rivington
Crane Thomas B. 136 Mott
Cranna George, 86 9th Av.
Cray Tamar, 16 Spring
Crocker Ann, 5 Forsyth
Cronin Cornelius, 157 Mulberry
Crooker Robert, 234 Broome
Cuddy James, 100 Cedar
Curry John, 174 Mott
Curry Samuel & R. 2 Stone
Curtin W. 18 Cherry
Curtis Thomas, 72 Mott
Dacker Charles, 63 Duane
Daily Michael, 323 Water
Dakin ——, 4 1st Av.
Dannerker Mary, 24 Thompson
Darcy Hugh, 171 Charles
Davis William, 261 8th Av.
Day Caleb, 553 Pearl
Decamp Maria, 253 Spring
Decker Chas. 76 Greenwich
Decker Mrs. 318   do
De Boas Rucine, 77 Wooster
Delancy Elizabeth, 98 W. 20th
Danny Thomas, 113 Bedford
Desmond John. 87 Cherry
Dessoye George, 62 Reade
Deuney Mrs. A. 306 Pearl
Devean Sarah, 185 Grand
Deveraux Elizabeth, 114 Mulberry
De Voe Ely, 132 Elizabeth
Donnelly T. 32½ Washington
Diefenbacher J. 84 Greenwich
Dohn William, 188 Liberty
Donaldson John, 135 Cherry
Donovan Mary. 18 Oak
Donovin Thomas, 35 Laurens
Dowry Philip J. 75 Roosevelt
Drake Mary, 133 Wooster
Draper W. D. 5 Mercer
Driscoll Daniel, 332 Water
Droger Geo. 128 Greenwich
Duffy Alice, 352 Madison

Duffy Bernard G. 560 4th st. & 31 Washington *New York.*
Duffy Maurice, 302 Pearl
Dulchete Anthony, 75 Oliver
Dunham J. 34 Cherry
Dunlap Hannah, 47 Robinson
Duryee Mary Ann C. 149 Chambers
Dutcher Catherine B. 198 Broadw.
Duvall Mary, 503 Greenwich
Dwyer Edward, 31 Depeyster
Dwyer Thomas, 22 Reade
Dyer Chas. C. 510 Greenwich
Eagan John, 107 Washington
Eames Eliza. 220 Centre
Eckel F. M. 330 Water
Eike Ernest, 52 Leonard
Ellert John, 73 Roosevelt
Elliott Charles C. 179 Reade
Ellis Mrs. 129 Av. D.
Ellison Deborah A. 304 Pearl
Evans John, 114 Hester
Fuller P. 151 Washington
Fahrbach Charles, 47 Greenwich
Farley J. 345 Water & 96 Cherry
Farmer Margaret, 89 Beekman
Favier Joseph. 94 Gold
Feguira Joseph G. 180 6th Av.
Ferguson Harriet, 14 Crosby
Ferris Governeur, 192 6th Av.
Feusier John P. 35 Dey
Field John. 73 Beekman
Finighty Martin, 33 Washington
Finley Robert I. 26 Peck slip
Finton John. 41 Laurens
Fisher Alexander, 97 Oliver
Fitzgerald John, 63 Cherry
Fitzpatrick Patrick, 479 Cherry
Flanagan Christopher A. 194 Beek.
Flack F. 1 Carlisle
Fleming Margaret, 223 Centre
Flinn Mary, 253 7th
Fleidner & Co. 82 Greenwich
Flint Daniel, 229 Water
Foerin Jacob & Co. 5 Carlisle
Foote C. B. 35 Chambers
Forde John. 71 Washington
Foster Mary Anne. 27 Hudson
Foster Roxana E. 49 East Broadw.
Fourcade Julia, 17 Front
Fowler Isaac F. 151 10th
Frahlich R. 101 Washington
Francis Frederick, 50 Allen
Fredinburgh Esther. 706 4th
French James M. 288 Greenwich
French John. 105 John
Frolick W. R. 58 Greenwich
Funk Augustus, 375 Broome
Gaffney James, 134 Mulberry
Ganon Patrick, 60 Greenwich
Garrison Francis. 86 Pike slip
Gautier Samuel, 195½ Forsyth
Geisler Frederick. 31 Albany
Geib Charlotte, 105 Pitt
George Stephen L. 358 8th
Geyer Jacob, 307 Houston
Gibbs James, 62 Oliver
Gildersleeve Eliza, 546 Broadway
Gililand Elizabeth, 216 W. 16th
Gillard J. 67 Cherry
Gilman Charlotte, 60 6th Av.
Gilmartin Henry, 10 Trinity pl
Gilpatrick Mrs. 66 Gold
Gilso Harriet, 25 Pitt
Giraud Joseph, 102 Oliver
Girod Jacques, 29 Spruce
Glen Elizabeth, 275 Bowery
Gombault Margaret, 534 Broadwy
Goodwin William M. 279 Pearl
Gould George, 32 Houston
Goward Eliza, 357 10th
Grant Joshua, 3 White
Gray ——, 33 Bowery
Gray Jane E. 233 Thompson
Gray Mrs. Mary, 267 Greenwich
Graves John, 343½ Water
Greenwood James, 106 Bowery
Gregit Sylvester, 7 Albany
Gregory Hester, 88 Rivington
Gribble Edward, 111 South
Griffin Hannah A. 63 Thompson
Griffith Ann, 64 Av. D
Gwynne Thomas, 5 Peck slip

Habermass L. 86 Greenwich
New York.
Hackett William, 34 Trinity pl
Hadfield J. 347 Canal
Haff Jane. 116 Chambers
Haley William, 396 Water
Hall J. N. & Co. 8 Carlisle
Hall Mrs. 339 Pearl
Hall Sarah T. 39 Canal
Hallett Hester A. 215 Bowery
Hallett Henry, 10 Elizabeth
Hallock Abigail, 84 Murray
Halsey Mrs 357 Water
Hambal Charles. 43 Water
Hamel James, 263 Rivington
Hammes John, 180 Greenwich
Hamilton & Wilson, 106
Hannagan James, 3 Monroe
Hanson John, 11 Rector
Harper Elizabeth, 154 Barrow
Harris Mrs. C. H. 326 Pearl
Harris Hiram, 202 Greenwich
Harris & Hall, 164 Church
Harrison Ann, 147 Chambers
Hart Mark, 423 10th
Harting Wm. 157 Washington
Hartley Mary, 60 James
Hatfield Jane, 59 Av. D
Heusler F. X. 78 Bayard
Hawke Andrew, 277 Front
Haydock Sarah A. 49 Cliff
Haywood Jane, 42 Warren
Hazard Sarah, 90 Henry
Heald Henry, 2 Front
Healy Jeremiah, 483 Pearl
Heath Frederick A. 106 Greenwh
Heath George W. 49 Bowery
Heath Jane, 49 Bayard
Helme John C. 630 4th
Henion John K. 121 Cannon
Hennell Frederick, 396 Pearl
Hermance Elizabeth, 75 Beekman
Hermann Adam, 606 Pearl
Hernberg Charles, 157½ Greenwich
Hibson James, 338 Pearl
Hickok Mary, 10 Greenwich Av.
Hicks Laurence, 39 3d Av.
Hill James R. 21 Catharine slip
Hinds, Elisha, 347 Pearl
Hoes Martha, 54 Vesey
Hoff William C. 41 Franklin
Holland Thomas, 79 Washington
Hollister Josep: , 52 Frankfort
Holmes Oliver. 434 Greenwich
Holt Henry A. 166 & 168 Duane
Holt Stephen, 85 Beekman
Hopkins Hannah. 77 Washington
Horen David. 395 Water
Horton A. 94 Norfolk
Horton Clarissa, 198 Spring
Hotten Gerhard & Co. 37 Elm
Howard Elizabeth, 21 Thomas
Howell Cornelia A. 447 Monroe
Howland Rebecca, 78 Essex
Hoyt Eliza. 196 South
Hoon G. 138 Greenwich
Hudeler Jacob, 216 Houston
Huggans James, 31 Corlears
Hughes William, 384 Cherry
Hurley Danis. 394 Water
Hurrell Elizabeth, 25 Oak
Hutchison Lucy, 191 Grand
Hutchison Matthew, 77 Barclay
Hutton Washington Q. 102 Mott
Hyslop Mary, 69 Beach
Ingersoll C. 698 Houston
Igo Edmund. 111 Washington
Irwin James, 347 Broome
Irwin Thomas. 318 Water
Ives Levi, 73 Oliver
Jacks Eliza, 630 Hudson
Jenks Mary, 83 Murray
Jennings Patrick, 25 Washington
Jesop Abigail Mrs. 375 Pearl
Jillard J. 67 Cherry
Johnson Andrew, 42 Cherry
Johnson Jacob, 85 Lewis
Johnson Mary, 296 Cherry
Jones Sarah, 49 Grand
Johnson Mrs. 375 Pearl
Jones Edward Mrs. 68 Cliff

Jordan Hannah, 29 Clark
New York.
Joyce Patrick, 9 Morris
Jung John, 29 Cross
Kampf Henry, 132 Greenwich
Karb Christophe, 113 Cedar
Kearney Francis, 28 Centre
Keatley Jane, 162 William
Kellogg M. Mrs. 475 Pearl
Kelehan Thomas, 23 Washington
Kelley Charles, 146 Christopher
Kelley William, 36 Hudson
Kelly Thomas, 30 Frankfort
Kelly Mary F. 8. 200 West
Kemp B. 883 Greenwich
Kenna Edmund, 253 Washington
Kennedy Morgan & Co. 107 Cherry
Kiefer Christian, 126 Greenwich
Kiersted Samuel, 280 5th
Kirk John, 36 Oliver
Kitzer J. 73 Cherry
Knapp Frances, 1 Oliver
Knack H. 103 Washington
Knott William, 98 William
Knox Hannah, 77 Canal
Krassiger John, 109 Greenwich
Kratzer Ann, 252 William
Krone Ann, 138 Greenwich
Kyte Catharine, 333 Hudson
Laforge Benjamin, 235 Delancy
Lamphier Levi, 156 Lewis
Lane Mary, 115 Liberty
Larkin John, 104 Oliver
Larkins Maria, 145 Stanton
Larue Mary, 89 Rutgers
Lang C. 30 E. 21st
Lawson John, 80 Greenwich
Leaycraft Gertrude, 274 Bowery
Lebner Leopold, 51 Clinton
Lee Rufus R. 139 10th Av.
Lefebvre Henry, 51 Dey
Leonard James, 73 Roosevelt
Levins ——, 144 Hester
Levy John, 3 Sullivan
Lewis Mary, 9 Dover
Lewis Mary, 133 Grand
Lonergan Catherine, 37 Mott
Lounsberry Mary, 256 William
Lyall Ann, 14 Ann
M'Arthy John, 301 Water
M'Colloh Elizabeth, 62 Watts
M'Daly ——, 333 Water
M'Ginnis James, 303 Water
M'Glenn Dominick, 24 Morris
M'Goon William, 117 Washington
M'Guire Ellen, 6 West
M'Guire ——, 305 Pearl
M'Laughlin John, 238 Water
M'Laughlin William. 91 Gold
M'Lellan John, 154 Cherry
M'Namara Berth. 73 Washington
M'Nair James, 330 Pearl
Madison William, 211 Fifth
Maher L. 93 Cherry
Mahoney Daniel, 249 W. 18th
Malmgrens Nils, 94 Roosevelt
Melouney P. 118 Washington
Maloy Hannah, 18 Mercer
Mamon D. 73 Washington
Maniort Antoine, 98 Duane
Manning Mrs. 391 Pearl
Mar Thomas, 390 Water
Marston Mary, 169 William
Martin Charles E. 282 Fifth
Martin Patrick, 202 Chambers
Martin Sarah. 60 Lispenard
Maslin William, 153 Elm
Mather Isaac R. 41 Norfolk
Maxwell Ann M. 191 Chambers
Mayne Mrs. F. 11 Barclay
Mayer H. 60 Cherry
Mead H. 76 Cherry
Medhurst Eliza A. 541 Houston
Meir C. H. 89 Washington
Meriam Francis W. 52 Beekman
Merrill Abraham, 151 Walker
Meyers F. 146 Greenwich
Meyers Joseph, 469 Water
Micheals Sarah, 316 Rivington
Mickell John F. 233 Walker
Middleton Mary, 10 Morris
Milgate Mesry, 197 Fulton

Miller R. 319 Water *New York.*
Miller Thomas S. 194 4th st.
Miller Martin, 233 Church
Miller William, 128 Liberty
Milles Luther J. 347 Madison
Mills Margaret, 136 Av. C.
Mix & Tripp, 8 Broadway
Moffatt J. 107 Cherry
Molowney James, 21½ Wash'ton
Molowney Patrick, 118 Wash'ton
Monaghan Owen, 46 Washington
Moon Mary A. 16 Beekman
Moore Matilda, 507 Broadway
Mott Elizabeth, 181 Mott
Mott Paulina, 114 Varick
Mudget Samuel, 166 Washington
Moultney P. 118 Washington
Muller William, 128 Liberty
Murphy Catharine, 46 Roosevelt
Murphy Martin, 24 Albany
Murray Ann, 5 Washington
Murray Frances, 21 Av. C
Murray James, 197 Mulberry
Murtland Margaret A. 177 Elm
Nafey Susannah, 10½ Front
Nathaway Elizabeth, 417 Cherry
Neale Bridget, 8 Clarkson
Nelson Sarah, 71 Essex
Nelson William, 412 10th
Nichol Martha, 249 6th Av.
Nichols Starr, 40 Warren
Nicholls Harry, 35 Madison
Nixon Abraham, 14 Washington
Noland Deborah, 261 West
Norris Wm. 4 Manhattan place
Nott William, 178 William
Oakley Phœbe, 20 Jay
Oberg Peter, 81 Market
Obeneauer John, 8 Duane
Odell Maria, 150 Sullivan
Oertel Conrad, 120 Greenwich
O'Herne William, 196 Chambers
O'Nell Mary, 67 Madison
O'Neill M. & Brother, 59 Wash.
O'Reilly Martin, 370 Water
O'Rourke Ellen, 218 Centre
Osborn Benjamin, 234 Cherry
Ostrander Isabella, 13 Orchard
Overin Fanny, 31 Catharine
Owens Patrick 442 Monroe
Palmer J. 202 8th Av.
Parker John B. 582 Grand
Wallace Parker, 53 Cherry
Parkinson E. 123 10th Av.
Partenheimer William, 9 Albany
Patton Ellen, 80 Bayard
Peet Caroline, 183 Bowery
Pelzea Sarah, 562 Grand
Penfold Nicholas B. 331 Pearl
Perrenot John F. 9 Barclay
Perry Alice, 22 Oak
Perry Henry, 230 Water
Peters John, 97 Orchard
Peterson Peter, 31½ Oak
Peterson & Co. 353 Water
Phillips Samuel, Cherry st.
Pierre Peter, 107 Reade
Pilkington Richard, 460 Water
Pinkerton Wm. P. 351 Water
Pitts Jacob, 49 Whitehall
Plummer Mrs. 63 Broadway
Plunkett P. W. 77 Washington
Plunkett T. 317 Water
Polegreen Mary, 550 Grand
Poole Jane, 112 Sullivan
Post Francis, 4 Bedford
Powell William F. 330 Pearl
Powers Mary, 57 Washington
Prentiss Thomas, 255 3d
Price Hannah, 242 Grand
Price Sophia C. 7 Roosevelt
Priel John, 20 Rector
Pritchard Thomas, 5 Hamilton
Pugh James, 344 Water
Purcell Henry, 40 Cherry
Py Piero, 119 Washington
Pyser Louis, 8 Dover
Quick Mrs. 38 Crosby
Quinn Charles, 3 Washington
Quinn, Patrick, 21 Batavia
Ray John, 102 James
Reed ——, 99 Bowery

Reinhardt J. & J. 134 Greenwich *New York.*
Renouf Francis, 35 Eldridge
Renwick Ellen, 400 Washington
Reynolds Archibald C. 1 Reade
Reynolds Ellen B. 14 Wooster
Rheutan John W. 158 Eldridge
Richard John & Co. 343 Water
Richardson Edward, 190 Cherry
Riddell Emeline B. 9 Roosevelt
Rikeman Richard, 359 6th
Riker Delia, 34 Eldridge
Ritter Mary, 50 Lispenard
Ritter P. 498 Broadway
Rivington John, 199 Bowery
Robbins Sarah, 141 Walker
Roberts George, 90 Crosby
Robertson Charles, 38 Oak
Robertson W. J. 7th Av.
Robinson Edward, 96 Carmine
Robinson William, 62 Greenwich
Rode Frederick G. 63 James
Roedenberger Jacob, 110 Liberty
Rogers Thomas, 13 & 15 Hudson
Rolfe Jane, 82 Frankfort
Romer Henry, 82 Essex
Ronner John, 66 Elm
Ronwick Ellen, 400 Washington
Rook Martin, 23 Laurens
Ross Marianna, 98 Leonard
Rose H. R. 339 Water
Ross Thomas, 75 Oliver
Rested Jane, 123 Beekman
Rowland T. 349 Spring
Rubinstein Abraham, 11 Albany
Rucastle John, 45 Whitehall
Rufner S. S. 559 Pearl
Runyon Ellen, 146 Grand
Rusher Elizabeth, 107 Broome
Ryder Catherine, 418 Pearl
Ryer Thomas, 86 Hester
Seuter Wilhelm, 119 Cedar
Scanlan Thomas, 31 City Hall place
Schneider George, 192 2d
Scholmhales ——, 121 Liberty
Schorfield T. S. & Co. 138 Greenwich
Schulmotz Theod. 118 Greenwich
Schulter F. 392 Water
Schuman Charles, 113 Greenwich
Schwartz, 150 Washington
Scott Thomas, 72 Broome
Seaman John, 369 10th
Seely John G. 7 Catharine slip
Sell William P. 104 Greenwich
Semon Ann, 146 Elm
Serveira John B. 31 Beekman
Sexsmith Cornelia, 92 Bowery
Shanley Patrick, 116 Mulberry
Sharp William, 271 Water
Sheridan Sarah, 46 Canal
Sherwood Benjamin, 98 John
Sherwood Cath. B. 136 Grand
Sigler Harriet, 251 Centre
Sloat Horace F. 237 Houston
Smith Albert L. 63 Barclay
Smith Andrew, 68 Oliver
Smith C. 379 Water
Smith Emanuel, 374 Water
Smith James, 159 Cherry
Smith James G. cor. Water
Smith John, 128 Ludlow
Smith Mary, 223 Washington
Smith Mary, 64 James
Smith Nathaniel, 106 Av. D
Smith Oliver, 45 James
Smith Sabin, 24 Peck slip
Smith Susan, 26 Monroe
Smith Thomas, 66 Oliver
Sniffen Frances, 126 Charles
Solomon Lewis, 250 William
Sommer Philip, 75 W. 20th
Southwell John, 71 Oliver
Speer Cornelia, 67 Norfolk
Spengler G. 575 Greenwich
Stadler H. 532 Pearl
Stearns Sarah, 496 Broadway
Stebbins C. S. 22 W. Broadway
Stebbins Sarah, 82 Canal
Stellwagen John, 24 Duane
Stephens W. 90 N. Moore
Stetson Susan, 17 Av. A

Stewart Joseph, 11 Elm *New York.*
Stocky Peter, 141 Cedar
Stone W. W. 90 Frankfort
Strange Jacob & Co. 99 James
Street William, 27 Cherry
Stripp John, 35 Rector
Stewart Sarah A. 364 Grand
Strans B. 85 & 87 Chatham
Stubenbord Jacob, 48 Beekman
Sutton ——, 49 Roosevelt
Swan Thomas, 266 W. 19th
Swan W. J. 368 Pearl
Sy Ruth L. 517 Broadway
Taggard John, 59 Monroe
Tappen ——, 339 6th
Taylor Ann, 22 Cherry
Taylor Bridget, 53 Catharine
Taylor James, 133 Liberty
Taylor Maria, 532 Broadway
Taylor Robert, 64 Vesey
Tecker Charles, 76 Greenwich
Territt James, 101½ Broad
Thomas Miss M. 481 Greenwich
Thompson Ann, 15 Madison
Thompson R. H. 42 Hudson
Tooker Mahala, 162 W. 17th
Toohill James, 33 Greenwich
Totten Eliza, 3 6th Av.
Townsend George, 109 Av. D.
Trignonan John, 112 Anthony
Tucker Margaret, 136 Mercer
Tutn Lewis, 563 Pearl
Turner J. 488 Pearl
Vail Jacob A. 296 Washington
Vancamp Elizh. 102 Cannon
Vanderpool Jacob, 482 Cherry
Vanhora John, 26 Bowery
Vannest Samuel, 270½ Bowery
Vantyne Ann, 476 Broadway
Vincent Samuel, 34 Bedford
Vitoh Mary A. C. 110 Greenwich
Vogler John G. 233 3d Av.
Voss Anna, 41 Cliff
Walker & Co. R. 135 Washington
Wallace William, 153 Cedar
Walters Henry, 150 Spring
Walty Nicholas, 52 Greenwich
Ward Martin, 176 Mulberry
Ware Edward, 16 Cherry
Warren Daniel, 619 Hudson
Waterson P. 352 Pearl
Watson & Magee, 60 Cherry
Way Benjamin, 366 Grand
Weaver Phœbe, 209 Thompson
Weeks Ann, 83 Beekman
Weeks Elizabeth, 158 Houston
Weise John, 101 Reade
Welch Edward, 14 Madison
Weldon James H. 235 Washington
Wemet Andrew, 204 Hester
West Frances, 508 Water
Westwood, J. 342 1st Av
Wetherill Jane E. 276 5th
White W. M. 2 West
Whitney Elizabeth, 197 Elm
Wilcox ——, 66 Eldridge
Wiles Lawrence, 88 James
Williams Charlotte, 108 Bowery
Williams William, 25 Chestnut
Wilson Deborah, 124 Columbia
Wilson James, 67 Fulton
Wilson Robert, 29 Washington
Wilson Sophia, 347 6th
Wine Julia E. 37 Bayard
Winchell William A. 125 4th Av
Winters John, 62 Roosevelt
Wirth John, 173 Houston
Wolf & Rischuiler, Wash'ton st.
Wood James B. 24 Bowery
Woods P. 73 Washington
Worth Solon, 376 Water
Wortman Rebecca, 182 Cherry
Wyatt David, 34 West Broadway
Yates John R. 144 Broad
Young Eliza, 215 Fulton

Boat Builders

Broome County.
Johnson J.   *Binghamton.*

Cayuga County.
Fish Charles & Co.   *Brutus.*
M'Donald H.   *Springport.*

Chautauque County.
Vail H., Maxville   *Chautauque.*

Chenango County.
Carter A.   *Greene.*

Erie County.
Graham Curtis   *Black Rock.*
Van Slyke C. A. Mechanic st.
        Buffalo.
Bixby Silas   *Clarence.*
Kibler Jacob   *Tonawanda.*

Jefferson County.
Britton John   *Cape Vincent.*

Kings County.
M'Coun Evert, 379 1st
        Williamsburgh.

Livingston County.
Martin J.   *Dansville*
Parker A.
Welch Henry H.
Thorp Andrew

Madison County.
Campbell A & Co. Chittenango
        Sullivan.

Monroe County.
Vinton E. Canal st.   *Rochester.*
Cram & Knapp, do
Benjamin Zina H. Park place
Hildreth J. 25 Mount Hope Av.
Barhydt W. Allen st. near Canal
Jones Seth C. Warehouse st.
Milner Joel P. Oak st.

Montgomery County.
Williams & Wemple *Canajoharie.*

New York County.
Baker J. 66 Robinson *New York.*
Brooks Nathan, 184 Christopher
Brush Henry S. 500 Water
Buckmaster John, 444 Water
Burr & Kassang, 300 Front
Crolius W.South cor.Montgomery
Delamontagnie Wm. 436 Water
Delamontagnie Wm. jr. 402 do
Downey J. 78 Montgomery
Donely P. 93 11th
Elmore William, 350 Front
Farr Eugene, 466 Water
Fish Robert, 404   do
Ingersoll C. L. 245½ South & 489
    Water
Letts John, 295 South
Munson George M. 293 West
Newman George C. 246 Front
Parsons & Saunders, South cor.
    Montgomery
Raymond Lewis, 122 Av. D
Rodman Wm. 480 Water
Ruck P. C. 49 Harrison
Stillman, Allen & Co. Francis's
    patent, foot 12th, E. R.
Sutton Albert B. 410 Water
Tobey John L. 309 West
Tollerton Robert V. 396 Water
Webb John B. 716   do
Weeks Richard P. 694   do
Wines Salem. 498 Water & 235
    Cherry

Niagara County.
Cady H. F. & Co.   *Lockport.*

Oneida County.
Swab D. Broad st.   *Utica.*

Baker C. New London   *Verona.*
Abel N.   do

Onondaga County.
Millener J. P. & G. W. Syracuse
        Salina.

Ontario County.
Hawthorn Wm. Geneva *Seneca.*

Orange County.
Smith S. B. Port Jervis *Deer Park.*
Marvis Thomas S.   *Newburgh.*
Corwin Silas   *New Windsor.*

Oswego County.
Baker James A. Dry Dock, betw.
    1st st. & Canal   *Oswego.*
Rogers & Dixon,   do
Miller Andrew, Floating Dock,
    Smith's Cove, foot of 1st
Colton Henry, foot of Front
Weeks Geo. S. foot of Main
Brown & Robinson, yard on River,
    above the Dam
Davis Thomas, Phœnix *Schroeppel.*

Queens County.
Smith Thomas, Raynor Town
        Hempstead.
Smith Richard,   do
Verity W., Roslyn *N. Hempstead.*

Rockland County.
James G. W., Nyack *Orangetown.*

Saratoga County.
Rogers Hervey H., Halfmoon
Hagaman C. C. Vischer's *Clifton Park.*
    Ferry
Vischer Garret,   do

Suffolk County.
Hart M. North Port *Huntington.*
Hart Prior

Ulster County.
M'Clansland J. Rondout *Kingston.*
Everson & Wilmot,   do
Warner & Phillips,   do
Lambert Thomas,   do
Snyder & Carroll,   do
Everson A.   do
Everson Morgan,   do
Williams & Hatheway, Rondout
Harnden G., Keyserike *Rochester.*
Hayes William, Port Benjamin
        Wawarsing.
Mills M.   do

Warren County.
Root David M.   *Queensbury*

Wayne County.
Lawrence Thomas W.   *Arcadia.*
Williams George   *Lyons.*
Robinson Philo   *Palmyra.*
Wade George W.

Yates County.
Harris Luther   *Benton.*
Sleeper H. P. Big Stream Point
        Starkey.

Bobbin and Spool Maker.

Albany County.
Savory Geo., Cohoes *Watervliet.*

Boiler Makers.—*(See Engines
and Boilers, also Machinists.)*

Birbeck George, jr. 221-3 West
        New York.

Cummings Daniel, 641 Hudson
        New York
Esler & Bunce, 25 Washington
        New York.
Griffin & Co. 192 Broadway
Pease & Murphy, 506 E. River
Prosser Thomas, 28 Platt
Stillman, Allen & Co. foot 12th, E.
    River

Belting Cloths.

New York County.
Bodmer Henry, jr. 7 William
        New York.
Livingston M. & W. 70 Broad
Platt, John R. 6 Spruce
Sheilds Geo. W. & Co. 70 Broad

Oneida County.
Hart & Munson, cor. Washington
    & Canal   *Utica.*

Oswego County.
Fitzhugh H. & Co. cor. 1st & 2d
        Oswego.

Rensselaer County
Crandall E. A. 282 River   *Troy.*

**Bonnet and Straw Goods
Makers.**

Albany County.
Gillmore L. 540 Broadway *Albany.*
Walker I. 536   do
Rawson E. B. 330   do

Columbia County.
Sur L.   *New Lebanon.*

Kings County.
Blake E. C. 82 Adams *Brooklyn.*
Cowan D. 90 Johnson
Simmons Joseph A. 125 Grand
        Williamsburgh.
Ashdown John, 154 Grand

Monroe County.
Wansley, Brothers, 55 Main
        Rochester.

Onondaga County.
Gilmore J. P. Genesee st. Syra-
    cuse   *Salina.*

Rensselaer County.
Strout E. B. & Co., Cannon Place
        Troy.
Ware Paul, 633 State

Bonnet Bleachers.

Oneida County.
Bradley D. 26 Hotel   *Utica.*

Rockland County.
Lyons J., Nyack   *Orangetown.*

Book Binders.

Albany County.
Van Benthuysen C. 407 Broadway
        Albany.
Harrison A. L. 3 Broadway
Seymour & Russ, 80½ State
Warner W. J. 7 N. Pearl

Broome County.
Grant William   *Binghamton.*

Chenango County.
Tompson & Pratt   *Norwich.*

Columbia County.

Elmer E. P. L. cor. Warren & 3d *Hudson.*

Duchess County.

Grubb J. 285½ Main *Poughkeepsie.*

Erie County.

Faxon J. 15 Webster's block, Main *Buffalo.*
Young C. E. 159   do
Peck Charles E. 161 do

Genesee County.

Kiesz G.   *Batavia.*

Greene County.

M'Farlane John   *Catskill.*

Jefferson County.

Knowlton & Rice   *Watertown.*

Kings County.

Barber W. S. 22 High *Brooklyn.*
Smith R. Harmer, 197 Fulton

Livingston County.

Bradley C. & Co.   *Dansville.*
Porter & Onterson

Monroe County.

Morse C. 20 Buffalo *Rochester.*
Marshall & Lacy, corner State &
    Buffalo
Drake Samuel, 12 Exchange
Morris Owen, under Museum,
    Exchange st.
Hawley N. G. 6 State
Morse Clarendon, 13 Front

New York County.

Alexander George W. 7 Spruce
    New York.
Anstice Henry, 27 Nassau
Avery George W. A. 105 & 106
    Merchants' Exchange
Ballou Leonard S. 41 Fulton
Berger Charles, 430 Pearl
Bithell James, 41 Ann
Bumstead Jacob, 55 Ann
Camp Ozias, 54 Gold
Cheasman Joseph B. 313 5th
Cills James H. 108 Beekman
Clark A. M. 56 Ann
Cheasman J. A. 1 Chatham Square
Colton & Jenkins, 142 & 144 Nas-
    sau
Cook & Somerville, 46 Ann
Eldridge E. L. 51 John
Elles Kelita S. 114 Nassau
Ellis Benjamin, 374 Pearl
Ellis John P. 102 Nassau
Everitt Geo. W. 105 & 106 Mer. Ex.
Fairclough & Hume, 194 Fulton
Faulkner Thomas W. 79 John
Felt David & Co. 174 Pearl
Fenwick Thomas J. 50 Ferry
Fry William H. 118 Fulton
Hoeffken & Nagel, 16 Dey
Hogg George, 54 Gold
Hutchinson David R. 216 Pearl
Ireland Henry, 120 Nassau
Johnson Robert, 111 Nassau
Jones W. L. 166 6th Av.
Keeler Samuel, 107 Fulton
Kimm Herman, 151 Fulton
Koethen J. L. 118 Fulton
Koch & Co. 160 William
Law George, 361 6th Av.
M'Leod Daniel, rear 50 Ann
M'Whood Edward, 142 Fulton
M'Grath Henry, 159 Pearl
Magrath & Brennan, 4 City Hall
    place
Mann George C. 151 Pearl
Matthews & Rider, 74 Fulton
Middlebrook Samuel, 122 Fulton

Miller J. B. 28 North William
    New York.
Morrell Arthur, 192 Fulton
Nelson Henry C. 18 Carmine
Nesbitt & Lewis, 108 Fulton
Owens Owen C. 169 Fulton
Parks John A. 25 Pine
Parks John B. 53 Fulton
Peacock Eber T. 298 Grand
Pfannmuller John, 5 Barclay
Randall Henry H. 113 Fulton
Rich & Loutrell, 61 William
Ront R. C. & Anthony, 8 Old slip
Sackmann J. H. & Brother, 63
    Vesey
Schmidt Julius, 78 Chatham
Shipman Asa L. 140 Fulton
Smith T. S. 7 Liberty
Spinning John H. 296 Broadway
Sprigman John. 86 Wall
Sibell & Mott, 1 Nassau
Taylor Edward G. 89 Nassau &
    128 Fulton
Thompson W. M. 169 William
Thinning J. H. 228 Broadway
Trow William, 51 Ann
Walker E. & Sons, 114 Fulton
Waters William, 55 Ann
Whitlock E. J. 58 Nassau
Winsor John, 22 Ann

Niagara County.

M'Coy Warner   *Lockport.*

Oneida County.

Merrell B. S. 98 Genesee   *Utica.*

Ontario County.

Underhill A.   *Canandaigua.*
Smith Wm. H., Geneva *Seneca.*
Derby, Wood & Co. do

Orange County.

Miller A. F.   *Newburgh.*

Herkimer County.

Adams F.   *Little Falls.*

Fulton County.

West A. Union Mills *Broadalbin.*

Orleans County.

Beebe A., Albion   *Barre.*

Queens County.

Bradlee Thomas   *Jamaica.*

Rensselaer County.

Hart & Jones, 225 River   *Troy.*
Fraser M. H. 216   do
Merriam, Moore & Co., 6 Cannon
    place

Schenectady County.

Bolles W. F. 81 State *Schenectady.*

Tompkins County.

Andrus, Gauntlett & Co. 69 Owego   *Ithaca.*

Washington County.

Strong M., Sandy Hill *Kingsbury.*

Bookbinders' Warehouses.

Abbot & Wilcomb, 295½ Pearl
    New York.
Cook James, 295½ Pearl
Griffon Hermon, 114 Nassau
Hoole John R. 124 Nassau
M'Ewin D. 155 Pearl
Seymour & Co. 97 John

Book Edge Gilders.

Heitkamp Charles, 107 Fulton
    New York.
Hoeffken & Nagel, 16 Dey
Shepperd John, 109 Nassau

Booksellers & Stationers,
(See Publishers, also Stationers.)

Albany County.

Tosoni Clement, 610 Broadway
    Albany.
Cook Peter, 464   do
Durrie Daniel S. 388   do
Harrison A. L. 3   do
Priest & Allendorph, 50 State
Hill N. 78   do
Pease E. H. & Co. 82   do
Little W. C. & Co. 51   do
Henry James, 67   do
Whitney & Bennett (Pap. Ware)
    59 State
Bender E. H. 75 State
Gould, Banks & Gould (Law
    Books) 104 State
Pierce J. M. 75 Washington
Debenpeck J. West Troy
    Watervliet.

Alleghany County.

Waggoner, Simeon & Co.
    Almond.
Thomas C. K. & C. W. *Angelica.*

Broome County.

Cook B. T. & L. *Binghamton.*
Everson T. & Co.
Pratt H. E.
Purdy S. J.

Cayuga County.

Gillman H. & Co. 65 Genesee
    Auburn.
Alden James M. 67 Genesee
Swisen J. C. 97   do
Derby, Miller & Co. 107 Genesee

Chautauque County.

Smith H. A. Jamestown *Ellicott.*
Post William & Co.
Parsons L.
Shaw W. D. Silver Creek
    Hanover.
Frisbee C., Fredonia *Pomfret.*
Johnson Dr.   do
Parsons Lorenzo *Westfield.*

Chemung County.

Hall F. *Elmira.*
Sickles & Preswick

Chenango County.

Saxe N. *Bainbridge.*
Babcock Judson *Greene.*
Thompson & Pratt *Norwich.*
Thorp C. A.
Chapman William E. *Oxford*

Clinton County.

Hasbrouck J. A., Keeseville
    Au Sable

Columbia County.

Lassell S. M. Chatham 4 Corners
    Chatham.
Elmer E. P. L. cor. Warren & 3d
    Hudson.
Carrique P. D. Warren st.
Winkoop P. S., 290 do
Sweet J. C. *Kinderhook*
Van Schaack P.
Smith F., Valatie

Delaware County.

Paine A. M. *Delhi.*
Howard C.

Reynolds G. M. *Franklin.*
Wright C. E., Deposit *Tompkins.*

Duchess County.

Roy J., Wappinger's Falls
    Fishkill.
Blackman W. B. *Fishkill.*
Sutherland W. W. Fishkill Landing
Nayell George, 276 Main
    Poughkeepsie.
Smith G. H. 305 Main
Wilson Wm. 295 do
Grubb J. 289½ do
Freeligh M. *Rhinebeck.*
Platt, Nelson & Co.

Erie County.

Phinney & Co. 186 Main *Buffalo.*
Danforth L. & Co. 230 do
Steele Oliver G. 206 do
Ott C. (Foreign Books) 198 Main
Fernald J. S. (Map & Chart, 12 Exchange
Sully James, (Methodist Books)
    203 Main
Schmidt Anthony, 409 Main
Derby G. H. & Co. 154 do
Butler T. & M. 159 do
Peck Charles E. 161 do
Hough E. Springville *Concord.*

Essex County.

Field Hiram, *Ticonderoga.*

Franklin County.

Heath F. T. *Malone.*
Seaver J. J.
Flanders F. D.

Genesee County.

Seaver Wm. & Son *Batavia.*
Kellows & Co.
Pixley & Bryant *Le Roy.*
Sampson R. L.
Stanley H. N.

Greene County.

Austin Charles *Catskill.*
Van Gorden James H.
Newton Gay *Coxsackie.*

Herkimer County.

Adams F. *Little Falls.*

Jefferson County.

Smith H. Sackett's Harbor
    Hounsfield.
Scribner Henry *Watertown.*
Knowlton, Rice & Co.
Sterling Geo.

Kings County.

Elliott & Co. 47 Atlantic *Brooklyn.*
Bennit Nostrand, 61 do
Wilder & Co. 151 do
Hayden G. L. 151 do
Black William, 57 do
Smith Thomas D. 202 Fulton
Nevin Michael, 176 do
Levin James, 252 do
Wilder A. M. 51 do
Nevin Anthony, 99 do
Storms & Phelps, 69½ do
Warner W., Washington cor. York
Smith R. Harmer, 197 Fulton
Rossell John, 174 York
Willis & Co. 125 Myrtle Av.
Doremus G. 162 do
Gander J. C. 89 Grand
    Williamsburgh.
Darbee Levi, 145 4th
Fowler William W. 280 Grand

Livingston County.

Niles Edward *Dansville.*

Porter & Outerson *Dansville.*
Sprague J. G.
Trembly J. R.
Shannon Geo. F.
Bradley C. & Co.
Bradley J. & L.
Turner L. & Co. *Geneseo.*
Beach & West
Godfrey Ira *Lima.*
Harding & Norton *Mount Morris.*
Whitney & Ladin
Camp James H. *Nunda.*
Swan & Ray

Madison County.

Mills, Crandall & Moseley
    Cazenovia.
Fay & Riddell *Hamilton.*
Young John, Canastota *Lenox.*

Monroe County.

Darrow Erastus, cor. Main & St. Paul *Rochester.*
Sage & Brother, 40 Buffalo
Gardner M. T. & Co. 69 Main
Boehnlein Geo. (German books)
    99% Main
Alling William, 10 & 12 Exchange
Fisher George W. 6 do
Hoyt David, 6 State
Morse Clarendon, 13 Front
Frye T. 40 Main, Brockport,
    Sweden.

Montgomery County.

Settle A. P. *Canajoharie.*
Bennett William H. Fort Plain
    Minden.

New York County.

Marked thus † are Law Booksellers only.
Adee D. 107 Fulton *New York.*
Adriance George W. 177 Bowery
Allen John, 139 Nassau
Appleton D. & Co. 200 Broadway
Axford John, 168 Bowery
Ayguesparse Adolphe. 90 Amity
Baker & Scribner, 36 Park row
†Banks, Gould & Co. 144 Nassau
Barnes A. S. & Co. 51 John
Bartholomew Edw. 56 Houston
Bartlett & Welford, 7 Astor House
Beach Brothers, cor. Nassau
Berard & Mondon, 315 Broadway
Berford & Co. 2 Astor House
Bidwell W. H. 120 Nassau
Black John. 113 Division
Blakley & Co. 3 Barclay
Blanchard Calvin. 86 Nassau
Blondel Charles 161 6th Av.
Blunt C. & G. 179 Water
Boyd James, 87 4th Av.
Bradburn John, 124 Fulton
Broadwell C. C. 190 4th Av.
Brain E. T. & Co. 16 John
Brittain Joseph, —— Merchants' Exchange
Brown Christian, 145 Hester
Brown William S. 296 Bowery
Buchannan James, 65% Chambers
Buckland & Sumner, 173 Broadway
Buckeley S. C. & Co. 3 Barclay
Bunce G. H. & S. A. 37 Chatham & 31 N. William
Burgess Wesley F. 22 Ann
Burnton John T. 241 Hudson
Burnton J. S. & R. 274 Bowery
Burnton J. W. & G. D. 49 6th Av.
Burnton & Brewer, 90 9th Av.
Burtis James A. 19 Peck slip
Burton George, 49 6th Av.
Butler H. V. & Co. 80 John
Cady & Burgess, 60 John
Canfield Alvah, 8th Av.
Carleton Frederick A. 435 Grand
Carlock William, 222 Division
Clark, Austin & Co. 206 Broadway

Carroll Edward, 72 6th Av.
    New York.
Carter R. & Brothers, 285 Broadway
Carville George, 84 Cedar
Chichester David, 6th Av.
Codd Thomas, 36 Ann
Coddington Robert. 366 Bowery
Colby Lewis, 122 Nassau
Collins & Brother, 254 Pearl
Colman Samuel, 55 William
Colman Wm. A. 304 Broadway
Cooledge Geo. F. & Brother, 323 Pearl
Cornwell William K. 91 Beaver
Crabtree John A. 143½ Nassau
Crane Stephen M. 374 Pearl
Crosby Orrin H. 37 William
Crowen T. J. 599 Broadway
Currier Nathaniel, 152 Nassau
Dana Daniel, 20 John
Day Robert, 237 Division
Dean William E. 12 Ann
De Lirac Gabriel, 418 Broadway
Dewitt & Davenport, 156 Nassau
Dexter Hamilton P. 153 8th Av.
Diossy John J. 1 Nassau
Disturnell John, 102 Broadway
Dodd M.W. Brick Church Chapel
Doggett John jr. 64 Liberty
Douglass Mary, 11 Spruce
Doyle, John, 146 Nassau
Dunigan E. & Brother, 151 Fulton
Dunn Hugh S. 135 6th Av.
Dunter H. P. 153 8th Av.
Dwight T. 252 Broadway
Elton Robert H. 179 William, 18 Division & 90 Nassau
Embree Lewis H. 134 Bowery
Eyre & Spottiswoode, 166 Pearl
Ezekiel Abraham, 330 Grand
Fanshaw Daniel, 75 Broadway
Fisher and Brothers, 74 Chatham
Fletcher Edward H. 141 Nassau
Fowler & Brother, 69 Division
Fowlers & Wells, 131 Nassau
Francis C. S. & Co. 252 Broadway
French Eli, 135 Nassau
French Samuel, 293 Broadway
Fry William H. 118 Fulton
Garrigue Rudolph, 2 Barclay
Gates, Stedman & Co. 116 Nassau
Graham William H. 151 Nassau
Graham G. C. & Co. 142 Fulton
Green & Spencer. 67 Bowery
Griffen Stephen. 134 6th Av.
Gloucester James. 38 West B'way
Gowan William, 178 Fulton
Hegue Samuel, 202 Division
Halsted Jacob R. 2 Wall
Harper & Brothers, 82 Cliff
Helmich & Co. 191 William
Holmes D. S. 12 Av. D
Huestis Charles F. 104 Nassau
Hueston Samuel, 139 Nassau
Huntington & Savage, 216 Pearl.
Hutchinson Enoch, 132 Nassau
Hyde William H. 135 Nassau
Ising Charles M. 248 8th Av.
Jackson J. M. 196 Houston
Jones William L. 152 6th Av.
Kavanagh Patrick, 253 Division
Kennedy John, 49 Mott
Kernot Henry, 633 Broadway
Kiernan Joseph, 311 Bowery
Kiggins & Kellogg, 88 John
King and Greeley, 102 Nassau
Kyle Thomas, 667 Hudson
Laidlaw Robert, 125 Fulton
Langley Henry G. 3 Astor House
Law George, 361 6th Av.
Lane & Scott, 138 Nassau
Leavitt & Co. 191 Broadway
Lebars Louis, 219 8th Av.
Levison John, 196 Chatham
Lewis Selinda, 184 6th Av.
Liddle John B. 44 Carmine
Lockwood J. L. & Co. 459 B'dway
Lockwood & Son, 411 do
Long H. & Brother, 43 Ann
Lovell William, 38 Hudson
Mahar Patrick, 1 6th

Maher Martin, 1 6th *New York.*
Manners Robert, 182½ Division
Marsh Richard, 416 Pearl
Martin Robert, 46 Ann
Martyn J. H. 143 Nassau
Maze Abraham, 237 Bleecker
M'Intire Wm. T. 101 9th Av.
Methodist Book Concern, 200 Mulberry
Miller Geo. & H. 645 Broadway
Moffet John, 103 Fulton
Monkfort J. 127 Grand
Montfort P. & D. 239 Canal
Murphy William H. 384 Pearl
Nafis & Cornish, 267   do
Neadle J. P. 96 Nassau
Newell Daniel, 126 do
Newman M. H. & Co. 199 Broad'y
Norton Chas. B. 71 Chambers
Nott William, 349 Hudson
Nugent Timothy, 116 Av. C
Nugent T. 171 7th
O'Ferrall James, 389 Hudson
Peacock E. T. 298 Grand
Perry John. 404 Broadway
Pratt, Woodford & Co. 159 Pearl
Post Sylvester S. 274 2d
Putnam George P. 155 Broadway
Radde William, 322 Broadway
Raynor Samuel, 76 Bowery
Redfield Justus S. 9 Clinton Hall & 127 Nassau
Redfield N. & Co. 481 Houston
Richard Frederick E. 80 8th Av.
Richard Matthew, 26 Av. A
Riker John C. 129 Fulton
Roberts Robert E. 263½ Grand
Rodriguez L. T. 331 Spring
Sadlier Dennis & J. 58 Gold
Saxton Charles M. 121 Fulton
Schroeder William. 159 3d
Schultz John H. & Co. 136 Nassau
Scott & Biggar, 104 Beekman
Scott Leonard & Co. 54 Gold
Scully Henry P. 51 Prince
Sears Robert, 128 Nassau
Sherwood J. M. 120 do
Simmons George W. 51 Liberty
Skinner Henry B. 106 Broadway
Skinner H. N. 249½ Greenwich
Slater John, 204 Chatham & 42 Division
Small Charles, 239 Pearl
Smith Thomas, 162 Nassau
Snell Isaac. 206 Greenwich
Spalding & Shepard, 199½ Broadway
St. John B. G. 140 Fulton
Stanford & Swords, 137 Broadway
Stedman & Co. 118 Nassau
Stegner John, 195 Division
Stringer & Townsend, 222 Broadway
Strong Thomas W. 98 Nassau
Tallis John & Frederick, 16 John
Taylor A. S. 297 3d Av.
Taylor William, 359 Broome
Taylor William H. 63 Lewis
Tiernan John, 116 Av. C
Tomkins James N. 37 3d Av.
Tripp Ervin H. 262 Greenwich
Trow John F. 49 Ann
Turner & Fisher, 76 Chatham
Turney G. W. & S. 75 do
Vale G. 3 Franklin square
Vanbeuren G. A. C. 221 Bleecker
Van Houten J. H. 391 Hudson
Virtue George. 26 John
†Voorhies John S. 20 Nassau
Walker Edward, 114 Fulton
Waterhouse & Co. 186 Greenwich
Watts Talbot, 102 Nassau
Welford J. G. 454 Grand
Wells J. C. 99 Nassau
Wells Richard. 527 Grand
Wesleyan Methodist Book Room, 5 Spruce
Westorman G. & B. Brothers, 651 Broadway
White Lucy L. 142 Grand
Wilcox Sullivan S. 143 Nassau
Wiley John, 161 Broadway

Wilson H. 521 Pearl   *New York.*
Wilson John, 186 W. 18th
Wilson Samuel D. 219½ Division
Wilson & Co. 15 Spruce
Wood Rich. & Geo. S. 261 Pearl
Wood S. & W. 261   do
Wrigley James, 394 Grand

Niagara County.

Byrne John D.   *Lewiston.*
Wright O. C.   *Lockport.*
Brown J. K.
Rogers Levi
Russell H. B.   *Niagara Falls.*
Spencer Oliver, Youngstown,   *Porter.*

Oneida County.

Grosvenor & Co. 49 Dominick   *Rome.*
M'Clure W. O. James st.
Savery U.
Tiffany I. 113 Genesee   *Utica.*
Tracy George. 58   do
Hawley & Fuller, 156 do
Paulsen Geo. O. Mechanics' Hall

Onondaga County.

Stoddard & Buck, Salina st. Syracuse   *Salina.*
Hall L. W.   *Syracuse.*
Wynkoop & Brother   do
Peck B. R. & Co. Genesee st. do
Saul George, (German books), Salina st. Syracuse

Ontario County.

Mattison & Sanford, *Canandaigua.*
Bemis George W.
Goodwin H. D.
Norton Samuel E.   *Phelps.*
Beardsley B. P.
Derby, Wood & Co. Geneva   *Seneca.*
Smith William H.   do
Holle R. F.   do

Orleans County.

Nicholson & Paine, Albion *Barre.*
Gilmore Aaron   do
Swan I. W., Medina   *Ridgeway.*

Oswego County.

Warner & Sims   *Mexico*
Pool John L. Commercial Bank Building, Bridge st.   *Oswego.*
Adriance Henry, 10 Phœnix block
Sloan James, Woodruff Block
Hill E. M., Pulaski   *Richland.*
Shumway O. O., Fulton   *Volney.*

Otsego County.

Phinney H. & E. Cooperstown,   *Otsego.*

Putnam County,

Watson G. Cold Spring   *Phillipstown.*

Rensselaer County.

Bliss P. 265 State, *Lansingburgh.*
Fish Walter, 332 State
Watson Robert, 186 River *Troy.*
Hart & Jones, 225   do
Young & Hartt, 216   do
Priest, Allendorph & Co. 286 River
Merriam, Moore & Co. 9 & 10 Cannon place

St. Lawrence County.

Pomeroy L. D., Ford st. Ogdensburgh   *Oswegatchie.*
Smith Justus   *Potsdam.*

Saratoga County.

Young T. G. Ballston Spa *Milton.*
Moore Albert A.   do

Berry M. M.   *Saratoga Springs*
Huling Beekman
Palmer A.   *Stillwater.*
Selley J. Schuylerville *Saratoga.*

Schenectady County.

Van Debogert G. Y. 99 State   *Schenectady.*
Bolles W. F. 81 State

Seneca County.

Munson H. M.   *Ovid.*
Clark John S.   *Seneca Falls.*
Osborne Joseph
Woodworth A. O.
Lundy Samuel D.   *Waterloo.*
M'Clintock Thomas

Steuben County.

Underhill R. L.   *Bath.*
Terbell William   *Painted Post.*
Graves J. B.

Suffolk County.

Wells Gurshom O.   *Riverhead.*

Tioga County.

Fay G. W. & Co.   *Owego*
Slosson F. & Co.

Tompkins County.

Andrus, Gauntlett & Co. 59 Owego   *Ithaca.*
Spencer D. D. S. & Co. 59 Owego

Ulster County.

Channing Thomas L.   *Kingston.*
Chipp Rodney A.
Winter A., Rondout

Orange County.

Carpenter S. G.   *Chester*
Vail Brothers   *Goshen*
Smith William
Banks H S. 61 Water   *Newburgh.*
Smith Daniel, 84 do
Wilson A. South Middleton   *Wallkill.*

Warren County.

Swan & Norris, Glen's Falls   *Queensburgh.*

Washington County.

Robinson R. C.   *Greenwich.*
Robinson P. C.
Howland, Harvey & Co. Sandy Hill   *Kingsbury.*
Hack John, North   *White Creek.*
Turner H. S.   *Whitehall.*

Wayne County.

Bristol & Mason, Newark *Arcadia.*
M'Carn James,   do
Van Buskirk J. T. Clyde   *Galen.*
Gallusha J. H.   *Lyons.*
Hopkins E.
Aldrich C.   *Palmyra.*
Scotten George

Westchester County.

Brewer James, Peekskill   *Courtlandt.*
Ganoung Leonard, Sing Sing   *Ossining*

Wyoming County.

Collier J. T. & Co.   *Attica.*
Dorrance Gardner
Page H. N.
Fuller E. L.   *Warsaw.*
Judd Charles J.

Yates County.

Bush E. N.   *Jerusalem.*

Bennett Henry B. Penn Yan *Milo.*
Cook & Miller,   · do
Warfield R. N. Rushville *Potter.*

Boot Crimpers.

Albany County.

Fitzsimmonds ——, 16 Quay
Albany.
Hodgeman F. A. West Troy
Watervliet.

New York County.

Bodmark Svante, 3 Duane
New York.
Bradley Frederick, 134½ 4th
Flamer Jacob F. 7 Jacob
Ford William, 23 Watts
Francis T. 12 Christopher
Henning Joseph H. 259 3d
Laurent Joseph, 206 William
Neuschwander John, 97 Chrystie
Roger August, 2 Jacob
Touseul John, 100 Reade

Rensselaer County.

Snyder Jacob, N. 2d st.   *Troy.*

Boot & Shoe Dealers. *(See also Boot and Shoe Manufacturers.) Marked thus* are Wholesale.*

Ramsey D. D. 547 Broadway
Albany.
Rafferty Mrs. C 696½ do
Hunt F. 662   do
Kelly P. 602   do
Young & Server. 520 do
Mead & Wait. 488 do
Wade & Carroll, 430 do
Trainor & Hill, 412 do
Snell James. 410   do
Dix Joshua Q. 404 do
Rankin & Miller, 392 do
Mitchell J. P. 390 do
Robinson & Dwight do
Wolverton G. A. & Co. 356 & 358
Broadway
Osborn J. 350 Broadway
Fitzsimmonds Thomas. 16 Quay
Hamilton A. 16 Little Basin
Coghlan J. 7 N. Lansing
Cullen P. 3   do
Clute F. R. 99 State
Duffy J. 172 Montgomery
Albert P. 58 Green
Doyle J. 152   S. Pearl
Porter D. 230   do
Johns T. 82   do
Cain William, 70 do
Dowsett I. 52   do
Burton H. 34   do
Lansing J. 14   do
Waterman R. 52   do
Trainor H. 63   do
Shloss A. 46 Green
Miller D. 222 Washington
Hewitt Thomas, 64 do
Bankin Wm. 39½ do
Tripp J. 57   do
Van Aernam A. West Troy
Watervliet.
Ayres F. S.   do
Galvin J.   do
Reardon Thomas do

Cayuga County.

Mitchell J. Port Byron *Mentz.*

Chautauque County.

Fenton & Baker, Jamestown
Ellicott.
Arnold & Hazard, do
Bliss W. G.   do
Green R., Fredonia *Pomfret.*
Shawls N.   do
Cole L. B.   do
Whitcomb & Starr, Fredonia

Chemung County.

Kelley W. D.   *Elmira.*
Hanford S. W. & H.
Mead Philip
Treadwell H. D.
M'Donald & Parkner
Robinson N.
Stills Isaac

Chenango County.

Rose N. P.   *Greene.*
Hughston & Randall *Norwich.*
Hammond J.
Peck A.
Cold F. B.   *Oxford.*
Northrop & Lord
Abels & Harrington, Pitcher Spa
Pitcher.
Knapp W. B.   *Sherburne.*

Columbia County.

King R. J. cor. Warren & Front
Hudson.
Surfleet William, Warren st.
Weinman H. 313   do
Elting A. V. V. 330 do
Shattuck S. 325 do
Bowman & Sharp, 316 do
Decker P.   do
Bogardus J. A.   do
Smith F., Valatie *Kinderhook.*

Delaware County.

England H.   *Delhi.*
Melgs J. P.
Bowen J. & Co. Deposit *Tompkins.*

Broome County.

Pratt William   *Binghamton.*
Fish & Squires
Harding C. E.
De Hart J.
Abbott W. & C.

Duchess County.

Thielman P. & Son, 292 Main
Poughkeepsie.
Haight Daniel. 280 Main
Hagadon John, 317½ do
Rase E. R.   309 do
Griffin R.   307 do
Hyde Liberty, 293 do

Erie County.

Inman H. 261 Main *Buffalo.*
Ramsdell O. P. & Co. 224 Main
Lewis John, 235   do
Schryver A. L. 207 do
Ramsdell C. 185   do
Williams O. H. P. 72 Lloyd
*Ramsdell Henry, 160 Main
*Randall Nelson, 152 do
Stow & Baldwin. 175 do
Volney & Randall, 74 do
Churchill P. 83   do
Jewett D. B. Springville *Concord.*

Genesee County.

Yates T.   *Batavia.*
Joslyn A.
Warren H. M.
Spencer & Merrill
Rupp M.
Phillips J. P.
Baker J.

Greene County.

Garrett Peter R.   *Coxsackie.*

Herkimer County.

Gray Geo. & Co. *Little Falls.*
Hall Wm. F.
Piper Luke F.

Jefferson County.

Griswold J.   *Adams.*

Bowker James A., Dexter
Brownville.
Kimball & Mann, do
Crook James,   do
Carter ——. Limerick
Luff & Redfield, Sackett's Harbor
Hounsfield.
Nevill & Yates   *Watertown.*
Bannister & Vincent
Fisk & Bates
Wood William
Todd Leonard
Kellogg & Rich. Carthage *Wilna.*
Buxton & Van Brocklin, do

Kings County.

Constant F. 41 Atlantic *Brooklyn.*
Hyde Zenas, 121 do
Bortine & Whitehouse, 123 Atlantic
Fowler T. H. 55½   do
Wheeler A. S. 70   do
Constant Peter, (ladies) 154 do
Kehlbeck ——. 164 do
Hoodlas S. R. 166 do
Creighton Thomas, Columbia st.
South Brooklyn
Irvine M. W. cor. Henry & Middagh
Jones C. H. 196 Fulton
Hallenbake J. A. (ladies shoes)
194½ Fulton
Whitehouse J. O. 166 & 168 Fulton
Moody Henry, 140 & 142
Mundell D. 116 Fulton *Brooklyn.*
Wheeler Andrew S. 220 Fulton
M'Mahon Philip. 234 do
Davis John, 96 Main
Lane William, 43 James
M'Clean P. 39   do
Leckey James, 37 do
Teare Daniel, 35 do
Cheap John, 59 Main
Burrell G. W. Adams cor. Tillary
Lush Carman, 268 Washington
Clark Levi G. 2 City Hall place
Waters J. 255 Fulton
Rigby Thomas, 131 Myrtle Av.
Mead Henry N. 135 do
Gilbert J., Myrtle Av. near Graham
Miller C., E. New York *Flatbush.*
Thurston Robert, 67 South 17th
Williamsburgh.
Anderson & Wells, 91 Grand
M'Neal S. 104   do
Savage Darius, 126 Grand
Gittens & Pillow, 130 Grand
Stephens D. K. 138 do

Lewis County.

Smith Rouseville   *Turin.*

Livingston County.

Wood D. J. & Co. *Dansville.*
Raynolds J. A.
Betts John
Snell Thomas
Grow J. D.   *Lima.*
Pratt Samuel W. Hemlock Lake
Livonia.
Stillwell C. H. Hemlock Lake
Archer Benjamin do
Woodford, Coy & Co.
Mount Morris.
Starkey J P. & Co.
Townsend C. & Van Horton
Brown Edgar M.   *Nunda.*
Wheeler & Chase

Madison County.

Comstock & Co.   *Hamilton.*

Monroe County.

Palmer J. B.   *Clarkson.*
Ostrander R. West Mendon
Mendon.
Locke William   do
Willard & Town, Churchville
Riga.

*Duffin James, 1½ South St. Paul
      Rochester.
Shale Geo. 10 do
Mallet S. E. 3 do
Stewart J. 69 East North st.
Alling S. Y. & L. H. 17 Main cor.
 of Water
Miller Henry, 92 Main
Kirley James, 24 do
Williamson W. 140 Buffalo
Grover E. H. 115 do
Diderick George, 100 do
Roades William. 92 do
Wood Louton, 84 do
Vanwinkle J. 16 do
Ireland John, 91 do
Watkins S. B. 87½ do
Lemon Stephen do
Burwell Alfred, 139½ do
Ray & Chittenden, 63 do
Alling John, 79 do
Coffrain E. S. 36 Exchange
Congdon J. E. 26 do
Henderson W. & G. 178 State
King R. Graham, 206 do
Gould George & Co. 16 do
Hatch J. W. & Co. 20 do
Sage & Pancost, 22 do
Hatch H. H. 32 Main st. Brockport
      Sweden.
Haight & Graves, 46 do
Wickes C. & Co. 23 do

New York County.

Agate William, 114 Bowery
      New York.
*Ayres H. L. & H. 256 Pearl
Baldwin C. H. 266 3d Av.
*Baldwin & Studwell, 262 Pearl
Barker J. Willard, 29 Walker
Bartlett N. M. 300 2d
Beach David, 322 & 340 Hudson
*Benedict & Bradley, 246 Pearl
*Benedict, Hall & Co. 255 Pearl
Bergen James, 277 Grand
Bertine P. 211 3d Av.
Bigelow & Gedney, 2 Bowery
Bishop Edward, 291 Grand
*Blanchard B. 269½ Pearl
*Bragg A. & Co. 269 Pearl
Bristoll W. B. & Co. 69 Catharine
Brooks Edwin A. 150 Fulton
*Brooks Lorin, 240 Broadway
Brown Wm. V. & Co. 162 Cherry
*Brown Wm. Smith, 26 Cortlandt
Brown S. K. 105 Bleecker
Bulkeley Stephen R. 179 8th Av.
*Burger Timothy H. 364 Pearl
Burkhard Joseph, 252 Houston
Burrell Samuel, 385 Greenwich
*Burt, Brothers and Co. 68 Broad
Byron Henry, 68 West Broadway
Cantrell Samuel, 336 Bowery
*Chamberlain Holbrook, 208 Pearl
Church A. B. 330 8th Av.
*Claflin Aaron, 252 Pearl
Clark Alexander, 138 Canal
Clercx Achille, 303 Broadway,
 French importer
*Corbett, O. G. 124 Water
Corney John, 8th Av.
Crombie —— 40 Av. C
Crosby Francis G. 40 E. Broadw'y
*Daniels S. & Co. 171 Pearl
Davidson & Dennison, 114 8th Av.
Davidson & Mallett, 462 Grand
Dean James L. 160 Canal
Delancy D. 6 Av. D
Deveau Peter B. 156 Chatham
*Deveau & Corbett, 130 Water
Devlin Arthur, 201 8th Av.
Dimm Henry, 374½ Grand
Dunham John, 162 Spring
Dunnington O. 278 3d Av.
Farguhue J. W. 155 Greenwich
Fawcett N.M. 203 3d Av.
Fawell H. 3 Cortlandt
*Fay & Stow, 272 Pearl
Fenton Thomas, 255 Hudson
Flint & Ely, 114 Canal
Fowler Duncan S. 454 Grand

Fowler John E. 202 Grand
      New York.
Fowler J. H. 308 2d
French George W. 18 Ann
*French James, 260 Pearl
*Frisbie Myron J. 248 Pearl
*Gale Andrew D. 225 Pearl
Gardner Henry, 18 Fulton
Garry James M. 564 Grand
*George & Burt, 144 Pearl
Gerry James H. 564 Grand
Graham John C. 91 Catharine
*Grannis & Stewart 96 Maid. Lane
Grill Daniel, 249 Houston
Groesback Nicholas, 227 Bleecker
Hallenbeck George W. 468 Grand
*Halsey, Utter & Co. 123 M'n L'n
Halsted J. 18 Carmine
Held John, 90 Chambers
*How C. W. & Co. 131 Maid. Lane
*Howard Charles H. 217 Pearl
*Howes R. W. & Co. 199 Water
Howser J. C. 96 Canal
Hutchinson O. 5 Fulton market
Hughes I. & Co. 170 Chatham
Hunt & Hunter, 279 Grand
*Ingersoll J. D. & Co. 222 Pearl
Jacobs & Kalische, Carmine st.
Jarvis Jeffrey, 109 Chatham
Jeffers William H. 467 Broadway
Jewell Hollis E. 49 Pearl
Johnson Henry F. 397 Hudson
Johnson Hiram, 246 Centre
Johnson John, 183 Greenwich
*Jones George, 178 Pearl
Jones Edward, 156 6th Av.
Jones Henry B. 14 Ann
Kaleski T. S. & J. 512 Greenwich
Kavanagh Thos. 201 3d Av.
Knox, Calhoun & M'Lintock, 224
 Canal & 177 8th Av.
Knower & Co. 304 9d
Kunz George, 231 Centre
Kuntz P. 308 9th
Langan Oliver, 104 Catharine
Lawless M. 75 3d Av.
Lazarus George. 299 Centre
Littell Andrew. 136 6th Av.
*Lovett & Southwick, 259 Pearl
Lyons Thomas, 274 Greenwich
M'Brien Edward, 136 Cherry
*M'Farland & Bragg, 172 Pearl
M'Farquhar Alex. 155 Greenwich
M'Feely Bernard, 144 Chatham
Maguire Bernard. 94 Catharine
Maguire P. H. & Co. 102 Catharine
*Marvin D. M. & Co. 42 Cortlandt
Matthews Henry, 243 Grand
*Meeker J. C. & Herbert, 94 Pearl
Millar Wm. 283 Greenwich
Miller Alvan, 211 8th Av.
Miller Joseph B. 134 Canal
Miller Robert & Co. 509 Greenwh
Mitchell William, 261 Hudson
Morehous D..& I. 185 Greenwich
Mulholland John, 310 8th Av.
Musliner Joseph, 570 Grand
*Newell W. M. & Co. 111 Pearl
Nicholson William N. 133 8th Av.
O'Connell B. 349 Houston
*Oatley N. K. 187 Pearl
Orr David, 326 Spring
Ostrander Hiram, 174 Canal
*Patten, Lane & Allen, 192 Pearl
Patterson W. G. 161 Greenwich
*Peirce Josiah, 121 Water
Perry William, 68 W. Broadway
Phillips Daniel B. 378 Pearl
Phillips & Clark, 158 Chatham
Porter A. E. 486 Hudson
Priest Francis, 2 Catharine slip
*Ransom J. H. & Co. 32 Cortlan
Reed Ferdinand, 18 Bowery
*Reed & Gay, 250 Pearl
Reynolds Lewis, 95 Houston
*Richards Wm. W. & Co. 212 Pearl
Riker Abraham, jr. 50 Catharine
Ringgold James, 225 Greenwich
Ringold J. P. 5 Carmine
Romaine W. S. 272 2d
Rogers Bradford, 414 Grand
Rogers Robert, 219 Hudson

Ross Anthony, 33 Frankfort
      New York.
Ross George H. 367 Houston
*St. John, Penney & Wells, 78
 Maiden Lane
Sammis Abel, 162 Grand
Sammis Daniel P. 484 Grand
Sammis Leander M. 188 Grand
Scribner Abraham S. 356 Grand
*Sears, Lyman & Co. 3 William
Sheldon W. 12 Carmine
Shuart Margaret. 178 8th Av.
Simpson C. 8th Av.
Smith Albert, 277 Pearl
Smith & Risley, 142 Chatham
Soffe Henry, 326 Bowery
Starling & Cushing, 133 Pearl &
 86 Beaver
*Stout & Ward, 253 Pearl
Stout James M. 100 6th Av.
Sutton Nathan A. 133 Chatham
Tate Isaac E. 427 Broadway
Thatcher John P. 283 Houston
Thompson E. & J. 8th Av.
*Tileston William M. 191 Pearl
Tilton Silas, 257 Greenwich
*Trask A. & A. G. & Co. 124 Maid-
 en Lane
Tuck Rufus P. 18 Carmine
Tuckworth John, 136 Spring
*Vose, Wood & Co. 131 Water
Walker James, 104 Canal
Walker John S. 419 Broadway
Walker Robert, 152 Canal
Wall Andrew, 552 Grand
Wardell Oliver T. 259 Bleecker
Warth John W. 50 Chatham
Waterbury & Sammis, 99, 101 &
 103 Catharine
Watkins & Carlock, 334 Hudson
Welch Lewis M. 309 Grand
*Wesson D. & A. 157 Pearl
Wiggins James, 212 Greenwich
Wilson Francis W. 126½ Canal
Williams John, 8th Av.
Withers Robert, 538 Grand
Wright William, 253 Greenwich
Young George, 124 Cherry
Young John, 49 Av. D.
Young William M. 18 Ann & 125
 Fulton

Niagara County.

Alden William *Lewiston.*
Wilson H. C. *Lockport.*
Sears Charles
Whitcher B. M.
Shepard Norman *Wilson.*
Vosburgh Abram

Oneida County.

Crossman J. *Annsville.*
Bacon H. *Camden.*
Dayton O.
Beitis R.
Edwards F. Dominick st. *Rome.*
Sheldon S. H. do
Graham John, James st.
Ohnmacht C. Canal st.
*Stevens & Whitmore, Dominick
Buell C., Waterville *Sangersfield.*
Moss E. do
Porter J. W. 145 Genesee *Utica.*
Henry J. 129 do
Callenen H. 129 do
Oley S. V. 109 Genesee
Laney J. 89 do
Vanderheyden J. 81 do
Hurley C. 75 do
Fay F. L. & Co. 44 do
Bronk J. H. 72 do
Graham John, 30 do
Nowland H. 132 do
Roberts H. H. 57 Hotel
Boulant M. V. 170 Genesee
Grumman Wm. 184 do.
Schneider H. 26 Seneca
Jones J. W. & Co. 6 Whitesboro
Thompson J. J. Fayette st.
Cantwell J. 3 Catharine

Thompson J. E.   *Whitestown.*
Tibbits W. K. Whitesboro
Sweatt C.   do

Onondaga County.

Phares J. Y.   *Geddes.*
Qua Charles A. & Co. Salina st.
Syracuse   *Salina.*
Stilwell R. & Sons, Salina st

Ontario County.

Childs H. H.   *Canandaigua.*
Lyon S.

Orange County.

Bartlett T. 64 Water   *Newburgh.*
Hayes Mrs. 102 do
M'Coun & Bradley, 14 Water
Wood M. H. 46   do
Hope S. W., South Middletown
          Wallkill.
Goodale A.   do
Houston & Wickham, do

Orleans County.

Chase G. & Co. Albion   *Barre.*
Phillips Daniel   do
Scovill & Huggins, do
Warner R.   do
Grover A. J.   do

Oswego County.

Betts Philander, 5 Empire block,
          1st st.   *Oswego.*
Green S.F. & Co. 2 Granite bl'k 1st
Lewis J. L. & Co. 1st st.
Murray & O'Brien, do
Skinner Edwin, 11 Phœnix bl'k 1st
Green S. F. & Co. Bridge st.
Bilkie Alexander, 1st st.
M'Lean James   do
Allyn & Fuller, Fulton   *Volney.*
Gasper & Griggs, do
Nettleton Edmond, do

Otsego County.

Fancher Selleck H.   *Unadilla.*

Queens County.

Roemer J.   *Flushing.*
Jackson Luther
Minnaugh James, Astoria *Newton.*
Powell S.   *Hempstead.*
Seabury H. P.
Daryea A.   *Jamaica.*

Rensselaer County.

Willett J. H. 296 State
          Lansingburgh.
Willette E. M. 4 Fake's Row
Eaton A. B. 268 State
Butterfield W. C. 126 River *Troy.*
*Tallmadge E. & Co. 189 do
Holmes T. W. 160   do
Cummings Franklin, 290 do
Faulkner Jonas, 236   do
Wood J. C. 1 Boardman's Build'gs
Melvin S. Francis, 4   do
Colburn Charles, 1 King   *Troy.*
Ransford & Meder, 224 River
Field F. 2 Cannon place
Hemstreet S. 52 Congress
Sutton James, 85   do

Richmond County

Crawford A. L. Port Richmond
          Northfield.

Rockland County.

Fox C. W., Piermont *Orangetown.*

St. Lawrence County.

Clark Jonathan E.   *Canton.*

Saratoga County.

Hawks Anthony, Ballston Spa
          Milton.

Schenectady County.

Wilber R. P. N.   *Duanesburgh.*
Brown J. 119 State *Schenectady.*
Wolf & De Forest, 115 & 59 State
Vedder M. 81 State
Ohlen George, 47 State
Ohlen G. 118   do
Houston W.   do
Gray R. 160   do
Fuller J. I. 6 Dock
Brown J.   do
Van Santvoord A. Ferry st.
Anderson G. 83   do

Seneca County.

Garrutt Jacob   *Fayette.*
Vreeland Jacob, Canoga
Cornell John I.   *Ovid.*
Kinkade Alexander
Ellis & Peck, Farmer
Galoup William, do
Mallory Lyman, do
Chapman John C.   *Seneca Falls.*
Seeley C. W.
Seeley W. H.   *Waterloo.*
Qua C. A.

Steuben County.

Stevens & Paxton   *Addison.*
Wornbough W. jr.

Suffolk County

Clark E. Greenport   *Southold.*
Clark James, do

Tioga County.

Hall & Chaffee   *Owego.*

Tompkins County.

Platts Heroy, cor. Aurora & Owe-
          go   *Ithaca.*
*Blue L. S.   51 Owego
Sidney E. 43   do
Moores J. 56   do
Hunt & Van Houton, 64 do
Warner Seth 95   do
Van Orman J. 34 Aurora
Guy George, 39   do
Benham S. 91   do
Richardson Wm. 119 Owego
Branch L. D. Trumansburgh
          Ulysses.

Ulster County.

*Shaw Prosper P.   *Kingston.*
Hendrix Wm. H.
Hasbrouk C. B.   *New Paltz.*

Warren County.

Dunning W., Glenn's Falls
          Queensbury.

Washington County.

Robertson J. L., North White
Creek   *White Creek.*

Westchester County.

Bird S. & Co. Tarrytown
          Greenburgh.
Armstrong, J. A.   do
Archer Henry, Hastings
Deall & Marshall, Portchester
          Rye.
Purdy I.   *White Plains.*

Wyoming County.

Loomis Harvey   *Attica.*
Adams A.   *Pike.*
Olin N. N.
Robinson W.
Truax John   *Warsaw.*
Bronson Isaac C.

Yates County.

Francisco M.   *Middlesex.*
Crane S. & J., Penn Yan   *Milo.*
Benham & Henry, do
Stanford D. C.   do
Mosher Wm.   do

Boot and Shoe Findings.
(See also *Boot and Shoe Dealers,*
    also *Leather Dealers.*)

Albany County.

Anable & Smith, 30 State *Albany.*
Guest & Laney, 43 Dean
Van Valkenbergh, Frost & De
    Ruyter, 18 Hudson
Gross Samuel. 34 Hudson
Hepinstall Geo. 25   do
Holt J. & Co. 48   do

Broome County.

Abbott & Son   *Binghamton.*

Erie County.

Wing H. & Co. 8 Exchange
          Buffalo.

Kings County.

Crook Thomas, 132 Atlantin
          Brooklyn.
Way B. 100 Grand *Williamsburgh.*

Oswego County.

Penwick M. & Co. Bridge st.
          Oswego.

Monroe County.

Alling S. Y. & L. H. 17 Main cor.
    Water   *Rochester.*
Congdon J. E. 26 Exchange
Hatch H. H. 32 Main, Brockport
          Sweden.

New York County.

Armstrong M. & Sons, 9 Ferry &
    64 Vesey   *New York.*
Bastow John. 494 Hudson
Beschormann Aug. H. 69½ Centre
Beschorrmann Fred C. 91 Bowery
Boyce Wm. 61 8th Avenue
Breff Jacob, 50 Cross
Brissel John, 149 W. Broadway
Buckley John, 68 Vesey and 202
    Pearl
Cary Clark W. 202 Pearl
Cauthers James, 286 2d
Clements Alex. M. 102 8th Av.
Coit Gabriel W. 50 Ferry
Emmens Henry, 41 W. Broadway
Everson G. F. & Co. 296 Pearl
Fischermann William. 15 Duane
Fleming J. 43 Christopher
Gallagher Jam. 37 W. Broadway
Gallagher Wm. jr. 40 Canal
Gillespie & Studwell, 298 Pearl
Godfroy Ed. & Sons, 299 Pearl
Gunning Edwin, 148 8th Av.
Hein Andrew, 505 Grand
Hein George, 186 Division
Hurley & Miles, 163 Division
Kaiser Jacob, 208 8th Av.
Kellogg C. H. & Co. 10 Ferry
Lillie Wm. 155 Bowery
M'Kenzie Wm. 507 Greenwich
M'Mullen D. 357 Bowery
Manwaring S. W. 497 Greenwich
Margraf Paulus, 192 William
Otto Charles C. 122 Mulberry
Perine Benjamin, jr. 119 Columbia
Purdy & Parker, 15½ Bowery
Rees Jens, 232 Houston
Reid James & Son, 189 Bowery
Richard George, 58 Reade
Royce W. M. 61 8th Av.
Smith Oliver B. 19 Jacob
Studwell Alexander, 304 Pearl
Tucker John B. 100 1st

Waterbury E. & Son, 307 Pearl
New York.
White John, 107 Division
Wilkie Warren S. 6 Ferry
Zimmerman A. 136 Laurens

Oneida County.

Loucks & Searls, 143 Genesee
Utica.
Gilbert E. M. 31 Genesee
Hubbell & Curran, 35 do

Rensselaer County.

Ross & Smith. 179 River Troy.
Van Allen B. 337 do

Boot and Shoe Manufac-
turers. (See also dealers; also,
shoemakers (Ladies.)

Albany County.

Brown S. 146 Columbia Albany.
Callahan P. 33 Quay
Cossin John, 719½ Broadway
Clow J 30 Orange
Conckling J. P. 22 Dean
Cook T. 162 S. Pearl
Dooley M. 203 Water
Dowsett T. C. 48 Washington
Dunham O. 56 Green
Fearey T. & J. 651 Broadway
Finn C. 508 do
Fox Luther O. 70 Green
Gett L. 10 Washington
Hallenbake G. 102½ Beaver
Harrison J. 127 Green
Reed Isaac M. 43½ Green
Herschberger N. 251 S. Pearl
Henson D. R. 166 Broadway
Hillman H. 24 Howard
Hoy P. 98 Beaver
Kain William, 79 Quay
Kennedy William, 13 Lawrence
Lant J. 39 Green
Leonard Thomas
Marsh S. 182 S. Pearl
Mead S. 51 Howard
Mills P. 97½ S. Pearl
Mould J. 9 Howard
Mulholland J. 102 Pier
Owens William, 327 State
Pike J. 2 N. Pearl
Pittinger A. 107 Lydius
Prest J. & D. 616 Broadway
Riley C. 40 Water
Rogers S. 247 S. Pearl
Sayle C. 68½ do
Scott J. 56 Lydius
Slawson S. 91 Green
Stone George C. 413 Broadway
Story R. 52½ Hamilton
Tracy A. 24 Quay
Trainor William, 33 Division
Treanor R. 10 Howard
Whitney J. 39 S. Pearl
Yates William, 51 Herkimer
Frink S. Reedsville Berne.
Canady J. do
Lanehart Wm., Dunnsville
Guilderland.
Vanderpool Charles do
Sterling —— Knowersville
Waggoner John, Centreville
Carhart ——,
Lake Morgan Knox.
Lake Benjamin
Alsey Michael
Gunsalus T., W. Troy Watervliet.
Howe A. do
Hoffman E. do.
Gunsalus George, do
Snider J. Westerlo.
Crandell J.

Alleghany County.

Barber G. P. Alfred.
Burdick R. F.
Richardson W. Almond.
Smith A C. & J. B.

Dunning Sutton Amity.
Mix Ehan
Bartlett Bela
Hunt, Swink & Co. Andover.
Green Lewis
Charles & Simons Angelica.
Helm Wm. B.
Hatch Silas G.
Alexander A. C. Belfast.
Cooper R.
Call V. H.
Ford & Roscoe
Seeley Hiram
Moore G. R.
Eldridge Milo Birdsall.
Daniels Lucius Bolivar.
Fitzgerald James E. Burns.
Fitzgerald Edwards
Fluent Nathan
Mosher William
Lewis Sheldon
Roup John. Whitney Valley
Hitchcock S. Caneadea.
Frisbee Hiram
Stevens William P. Cuba.
Roberts ——
Peckham C. Clarksville.
Weaver ——
King E. Friendship.
Sherwin Ethan
Sherwin A.
Hall J. A.
Coon A. A.
Hammond J.
Stevens William
Sisson D.
Merriman H.
Stillman M.
Crandell Ezra
Clark ——, Nile
Van Antwerp Amos, Grove Cen-
tre Granger.
Merritt C. Little Genesee
Genesee.
Nye & Butterfield Hume.
Nye & Corwin
Skiff & Marvin
Mait William B., Wiscoy
Tallman, Crandall & Co. Whites-
ville Independence.
Ingraham & Witter
Perry ——, Centre Independence
Housting Matthew, Black Creek
New Hudson.
Vanchoton James Ossian.
West Aaron
Congdon L. & L. Rushford.
Bell James R.
Green James
Dolan John
Adams Richard
Galt A. T. Scio.
Goddard John F. Wellsville
Chandler William West Almond.
Elliott I.
Maxon Moses Wirt.
Williams L. D.

Broome County.

Terwilliger A. Chenango Forks
Barker.
Herbage S. Binghamton.
Williams & Wood
Lloyd J. A.
Smith S.
White S. J. Susquehannah
Coleeville.
Ketcham J. & M.
Piersall D. W. Harpersville
Brown J. do
Brown E. M. Nineveh
Thompson A. Z. Lisle.
Niles S. Maine.
Seymour G. Whitney's Point
Triangle.
Sutherland A.
Sly George
Hodge F. Union.
Merserean J. P.
Norten W. A. Union Centre
Cummings J. D. do
Bescroft L. do

Stringham J. Windsor.
Smith George W.
Perkins H. & G.

Cattaraugus County.

Pratt Benjamin Ashford.
Folts Joseph J.
Thomas William B.
Gleason Eli Burton.
M'Lure E. R.
Pierce
Gleason Ransom
Benson J. L. Rutledge Conewango.
Newcomb Daniel
Hollister William
Babbit E. N. Ellicottville.
Woodruff & Harris
Williams R. S.
Brown A. R.
Grandy Farmersville.
Ferrington George
Baylett F.
St. John J. Franklinville.
Burlingame Ira
Fay Warren R.
M'Cluer James I.
Chandler A. B.
Ellis Richard Freedom.
Crawford William
Hilman Benjamin, Sandusky
Ellethorp Wm. T.
Ellethorp Chauncy
Armstrong J. M. Elton
Martin Samuel E.
Hancock Zina
Newcomb Luther Great Valley
Freeland Isaac
Hall E. Little Valley.
Childs D.
Fairbrother E.
Wooley D. W. C. Machias.
Truman E.
Velzy John, jr.
Stone S. B. Eddyville Mansfield.
Powers Isaac, do
Smith Daniel, do
Wright Eber New Albion.
Powell D. H.
Sissem J.
Morris C.
Worden W. S.
Hill A.
Hunt H. B. Otto.
Skeeles Luther
Andrews Willis, East Otto
Williams J. H. Perrysburgh.
Ward Reuben
Ward J.
Whiteley ——
Whitney ——
Hurd H. C.
Canfield L. S.
Weaver A.
Spaulding R. Randolph.
Wiggins J.
Reed B. F.
Gardiner D. P.
Hamilton N. T.
Reed T. T.
Billings N.
Tracy D. East Randolph
Brown A. do
Frary John, do
Green S. A. do
Jenkins E. do
Pitcher Wm. C. Rice.
Pierce B.
Fenton Erastus South Valley.
Thomas Geo, W. Yorkshire.
Wheeler Amasa

Cayuga County.

Tiffenny G. 59 Genesee Auburn.
Ross E. P. 91 do
Cook W. State st.
Duchars T. North st.
Stone H. do
Alexander A. do
Kine E. Weedsport Brutus.
Kinney D. do
Kinney A. S. do

Northrop & Appleby *Cato.*
Allen R. & Son *Ira.*
Marsh J. & Co. *Ledyard.*
Treadwell & Currie *Springport.*
Wyman William *Sterling.*
Vilas N.
Morse I. L. *Venice.*
Raymond D.
Conever G.

Chautauque County.

Mattison *Busti.*
Skinner and Hartwell *Charlotte.*
Hedges E. S.
Kirk H. & F.
Bennett James
Sherman B. B. Mayville
Chautauque.
Wolcben N. do
Walker H. S. do
Barnhart & Grover do
Carpenter E. do
Read L. H. *Cherry Creek.*
Bartlett Loomis
Spencer C. A.
Branch P. R.
Shedd S. K. *Ellery.*
Leach Winfield *Ellington.*
Rous Geo. W. *French Creek.*
Wilson Wm. S. Vermont *Gerry.*
Wilson N. J. do
Brown James, Irving *Hanover.*
Slocum J. do
Barnard B. Forestville
Gardner W. H. do
Farnham Wm. do
Barnes & Barnard, do
Slauson Samuel, Nashville
Gittings Samuel *Harmony.*
Hatlin William
Trask Geo. O.
Warden L. *Poland.*
Keyes Wm. D. & Son *Portland.*
Haight & Keyes, Salem cross roads
Bascum & Northum *Ripley.*
Pierce L.
Ecker & Johnson *Sheridan.*
Ecker Gilbert M. L. F.
Doty Philip
Shelly & Alden
Gifford Oliver P.
Osborn P. S. & H. B. *Sherman.*
Gilbert R. & J.
Graus J. *Villenova.*
Blackney ——
Harrington, Hale & Howell
Westfield.
Dick Morris
Howard B.
Ward Joseph
Booth Thomas

Chenango County.

Cannon C. C. & Co. *Bainbridge.*
Jacobs O.
Vanderburgh J. Bennettsville
Crego R. *Columbus.*
Jones L. P. *Coventry.*
Foot John
Ogden John & David *Guilford.*
Isbell Stephen
Sherwood John L.
Comstock A. *Linklaen.*
Smith L. J. *Macdonough.*
Brownell W. H. *New Berlin.*
Knapp Charles
Pope A.
Madison L., South New Berlin
Lyon S. *North Norwich.*
Hughston & Randall *Norwich.*
Hammond J.
Peck A.
Huddleston J. *Otselic.*
Hoadray J.
Smith Nelson *Oxford.*
Thurber C. P.
Walker Charles
Brown W. S. *Pharsalia.*
Frink R. B.
Frink H.
Hall B. P. *Pitcher.*
Hymes Heman

Randall Joseph *Pitcher.*
Chandler Walter
Ballard Dennis *Plymouth.*
Skinner William
Sipson Thomas, S. Plymouth
Lewis & Smith *Preston.*
Hall Samuel *Sherburne.*
Curtiss John & Son
Strant & Ertz
Read T. J. *Smithville.*
Whitmarsh Andrew
Van Alstyne C. *Smyrna.*
Mead G. C.

Clinton County.

Sanburn, Kingsland & Co. Keese-
ville *Au Sable.*
Shandrew F. E. Keeseville
Adams James, do
Menio —— *West Chazy.*
Brown J. *Mooers.*
Ayres Anson & Co. *Peru.*
Martin Samuel H.
Tonney Dennis *Saranac.*

Columbia County.

Ives H. Spencertown *Austerlitz.*
Starks E. do
Martin N. do
Vallee J. B. Canaan Four Corners
Canaan.
Clark H. S. *Chatham.*
Bates H. East Chatham
Clark B. V. Chatham Four Corners
Davis T. Malden Bridge
Jones L. do
Neefus R. H. Claverack
Van Deusen L. Smoky Hollow
Miller F. Churchtown
Vandebogart P. *Copake.*
Pulver J. I.
Wheeler C.
Edwards T.
Brusie J.
Horsradt J. A. *Gallatin.*
Snyder J. W.
Minkler & Conro *Ghent.*
Shultis J.
Granger S *Hillsdale.*
Latting R.
Lawton R. B. N., Front st. *Hudson.*
White C. & F. Warren st
Fellows B. do
Owens William, do
Kerz A. Columbia st.
Alger William, do
Heald H. Warren st.
Vanslyck J. J. Valatie *Kinderhook.*
Carroll A. do
Wells J. do
Bray J. jr. do
Bray J. do
Lillibridge B. L. do
Bachman P. I. *Livingston.*
Wagoner P. W.
Smith G. G.
Williams G. New Lebanon Centre
New Lebanon.

Cortland County.

Elder William *Cortland Village.*
Ballou Hosea
Campbell Densmore
Fisk William
Hitchcock Peter
Markham Chester *Preble.*
Out Matthias P.
Out Richard P.
Crofoot Franklin

Delaware County.

Gibbs J. *Andes.*
Roberts J. T.
Wager P. B. *Davenport.*
Dibble D. M.
Palmater B.
Wright S.
Willoby S.
Shaw G. M. *Delhi.*
Meigs J. P.
Cormaet & Heath

Hanford E. *Franklin.*
Judd E.
Bronson C
Beeser S.
Carrier E. K. *Hancock.*
Ingalsbe A. jr.
Wood C. Bloomville *Kortright.*
Bunker J. do
Jacobs J. M. *Meredith*
Knowles R. W.
Vandervoort C.
Stilson Wm. West Meredith
Norton T. H. Cloverville
Middletown.
Bowman J. do
Stevens A. *Stamford.*
Wood S.
Noble J., Hobart
Bradford W. H. Sidney Plains
Sidney.
Burrows H. 2d. Deposit *Tompkins.*
Edick J. E. do
Miller George, do
Benedict T. do
Burrows D. do
Whitman F. B. *Walton.*
Bunnell ——
Bery R. N.

Duchess County.

Platt H. *Amenia.*
Rose N.
Field J.
Ingham Wm. H., Union
Kinney H. W. *Beekman.*
Briggs G. C. *Clinton.*
Caryhard R.
Hermit A.
Ayers J. Clinton Hollow
Nelson J. H. do
Merritt H. *Dover.*
Baker N.
M'Coy William
Dutcher P.
Brown L.
Ervin & Austin *Fishkill.*
Allen W. H.
Lynn G., Matteawan
Forester H. L. do
Ahreet S. B. do
Smith R. W., Glenham
Carr E. A. do
Greenwood W. Wappinger's Falls
Cunningham J. H. do
Lucky C. (Ladies Shoes) do
Brower P. B. do do
Hadley J. F. do
Manning J. do
Cudner A. do
Norris H., Hughsonville
Miller A. do
Hasbrook F. J. do
Ackerson R. Fishkill Landing
Vanderwerker Wm. N. do
Connley D. C. do
Harrison M., Stormville
Brundge A. do
Hitchcock J. New Hackensack
Hinchman J. *Hyde Park*
Lansing J. F.
Dobbs B.
Miller J. K.
Thayer L.
Fribover J. *Milan.*
Ferow E., Rock City
Levings A. *Northeast.*
Bassett L.
Capror L.
Card W.
Husted P. W. *Pine Plains.*
Herman R.
Barnes W.
Du Bois P. F. *Pleasant Valley*
Van Ambergh J. D.
Gildersleeve W. Salt Point
Angevine V. do
Anthes & Candee, 274 Main
Poughkeepsie.
Cable John M 311 Main
Mark F. 273 do
Bower & Son, 209 do

Foley William, 361 Main
 Poughkeepsie.
Roan James, 396 do
Keech B. 29 do
Haubennestel L.
Dates T. Catharine st.
Dowd R. 9 Market
Eisel J. E. 4 Liberty
Rouch C. 138 Main
Vanderburgh R. 34 Washington
Remer V. New Hamburgh
Griffin C. jr. do
Shaver J. H. *Red Hook.*
Reed G.
Rynders J. *Rhinebeck.*
Barnes William
Sprague M. W.
Seeley W. Stanfordville *Stanford.*
Williams W. do
Rikert W. do
Clark I. do
Wing J. do
Crandall W. Attlebury
Colwell A. L.Verbank *Union Vale.*
Colwell D. E.
Pond N. A. *Washington.*
Haviland A.
Silvernail R.
Travis G. J.
Sanders A. Washington Hollow
Travers S. D. Hart's Village
Varney E. do
Doughty I., Lithgow
Doughty D., Mabbettsville

Erie County.

Davis Wm. & Co. *Alden.*
Brown Calvin
Powers ——
Hutchinson John, Williamsville
 Amherst.
Windnagle Michael, do
Houver John, do
Miller I. do
Bowen P. & J. Willink *Aurora.*
Ponds J. & J. do
Thompson Orrin do
Washburn John R. do
Phillips Seneca *Black Rock.*
Zimmer Gustavus do
Glazier Porter F. *Boston.*
Hill Alva.
Curran Wm.
Stanton James *Brandt.*
Albert J. 4 Commercial st.
 Buffalo.
Blanck F. C. 359 Main
Blum J. corner Commercial and
 Water
Braunlick ——, 318 Main
Cannon Patrick, 326 do
Cherer J. S. East Swan
Clor Michael, 17 Main
Costello T. P. (Ladies' Shoes) 1
 Swan
Cutting H. 75 Elliott
Denicombe I. 159 East Swan
Diebold A. 6 Commercial
Dietewig John. 367 Main
1 rost Thomas, 8 Water
Guck Thomas, 244 Main
Hanny J. State st.
Henning O. 2 Erie
Honk M. 207 Main
Hoss Geo. 18 do
Kline J. F. 8 do
Korn K., 2 Efner's Block, Com-
 mercial st.
Kranz J. M. Commercial st
Leibing C. 321 Main
Lewis John. 235 do
Lueders & Kiee. 22 do
Lynahon D. 22 Exchange
Mang Jacob, 332 Main
Marbus Henry F. cor. Main & Ex-
 change
Mitchell J. 3 Water
Pelman H. 5 Commercial
Reptie F. 191 East Swan
Schlink L. 408 Main
Schryver A. L. 207 do

Schumacher B. 6½ Commercial
 Buffalo.
Schumacher ——, Maiden Lane
Smith John M. 5 Commercial
Smith Peter. Water st.
Vaughan Otis, 161 Main
Waldroff E. Seneca st.
Walter F. Genesee House
Weber B. 2 East Swan
Wells J. 242 Main
Williams O. H. P. 72 Lloyd
Williams Wm. 55 do
Collins Otis *Cheektowaga.*
Crique Anthony
Barker & Rittersbaugh *Clarence.*
Long S. R.
Long H. C.
Graham Samuel
Metz Benjamin, Clarence Centre
Bickert John P.
Holt Arnold *Colden.*
Allen Alfred B. *Collins.*
M'Clure C. C. Springville *Concord.*
Watkins William, do
Tyler P. L. do
Pratt J. O. *Eden.*
Carpenter S.
Johnson E.
Brown Samuel
Eckett Jacob
Jones J. & O. East Evans *Evans.*
Black & Hammond
Weld S. *Hamburgh.*
Brindle Joseph, Water Valley
Buckmiller Martin, do
Morey Nathan, jr. *Holland.*
Rowley O. G.
Bruce Samuel *Lancaster.*
Miller John
Berstold George
Moore A. W.
Ammon A.
Serger F.
Johnson Jonathan
Neel Robert, Town Line
Jackson H. D., Akron *Newstead.*
Green F.
Jackson William
Goodspeed O. *Sardinia.*
Baily R. S.
Green O. J.
Candee Joseph
Hoyt A. C. *Tonawanda.*
M'Merrick Sylvester C.
Joselyn P. *Wales.*
Edmonds J. W.
Simons A.
Minton H. A.
Hall Ira
Barker G. South Wales

Essex County.

Brevoort Julius C. *Crown Point.*
Noble H. R. *Elizabethtown.*
La Motte & Turner
Noble R. & Sons *Essex.*
Holcomb M. S.
Patten James *Keene.*
Dickinson William H.
Sherman Elijah *Lewis.*
Smith Jacob *Minerva.*
Adams E. P.
Davis Amos, Moriah 4 corners
 Moriah.
Livermore Amos, do
M'Intire Peter, do
Smith Thomas, do
Harper William, do
Bartow Simon, do
Lane G. do
Sprague Ira, Port Henry
Reeve Appleton, do
M'Courts James, do
Lud David S. M. *Westport.*
Hoffnagle Edmund *Willsborough.*

Franklin County.

Wilcox Abel *Bangor.*
Haskell Ralph *Chateaugay.*
Gamble Thomas
Abbott George

Douglass Anson *Chateaugay.*
Patterson Levi
Popple Benjamin
Reilly Phillip
Scott Richard
Smith Jedediah
Cunningham Richard
Lincoln A. *Malone.*
Miller Enoch
Santon Thomas J.
Huntington D. N.
M'Kee William *Moira.*
Dreuson ——
Wilcox George, Brush's Mills

Fulton County.

Curtis S. E. *Broadalbin.*
Cornwell & Kelly
Eckenbrack Alex. *Ephratah.*
Bedford David D. *Johnstown.*
Philes Philip
Jones Harry C. Gloversville
Vrankin William V. do
Marlay James D.
Vail Buchanan & Co. Vail's Mills
 Mayfield.
Van Arnan Harmon, do
Van Arnam Hiram, do
Vandyke John, Mayfield Corners
Lefever & Van Valkenburgh,
 Northville *Northampton.*
Barker Levi, Northville
Dunning George *Perth.*

Genesee County.

Hoag Henry *Alabama.*
Brooks A. D.
Pierce L. H.
Taborn John
Cabot John *Oakfield.*
Roe Albert *Alexander.*
Geer William
Morse R.
Sweet J. B. *Bergen.*
Mullen Harvey
Beardsley ——
Thompson Stephen
Hill Peltire *Bethany.*
Chitenden B.
Ensign & Wentworth, East do
Perry R. do
Perry J. G. Linden
Bitter Enoch do
Cook W. K. *Byron.*
Montgomery Albert *Darien.*
Rogers & Lloyd
Chaplin Franklin, Darien Centre
Baldwin Ayres *Elba.*
Darling & Rimback *Le Roy.*
Foster & Allison
Veley James *Pavilion.*
Walt Hiram
Burnett Gilman
Donbed Warren
Wakeman Nathan *Pembroke.*
Kingdon Henry *Stafford.*
Delbridge William

Greene County.

Weldmar John *Athens.*
Van Loan Jacob
Pelton John
Allen A.
Lennon Charles, Acra *Cairo.*
Kneishken Stephen
Noble Walker
Porter Samuel
Plank Jacob M. Leeds *Catskill.*
Wardwell John, do
Mohaffy James *Catskill.*
Prindle P. J.
Hallated David
Comine Peter *Cossackie.*
Van Shaack John
Beatty Arthur
Laway Paul
Holton John
Folwer Willett
Wiand John *Durham.*
Spencer William L.
Kennedy Washington

Hart William   *Greenville.*
Hart John L.
Defrait Francis
Branton Ephraim   *Hunter.*
Baldwin Orrin   *Lexington.*
Rider Moses & John
Smith John
Price William, West Kill
Chase Austin, West Lexington
Norris ——
Schermerhorn J.N. *New Baltimore.*
Huyck John G.   *Prattsville.*
Laverack John
Graham G. W.   *Windham.*
Graham E.
Andrews Levi

Hamilton County.

Sturgis Aaron   *Lake Pleasant.*
Batchelor Benjamin
Wait Benjamin   *Wells.*

Herkimer County.

Warren P. H.   *Columbia.*
Stevens T. A.
Stevens Sylvenus
Willaber D. W.
Deavenport Benj.
Getman Timothy
Hartman T.
Mikle Luther
Morris Francis F.   *Frankfort.*
Beman Daniel
Richardson M.
Budlong Nelson
Lowell & Mosch, Mohawk
    German Flats.
Batchelder M.   *Herkimer.*
Petrie John
Bender Peter
Smith John
Wait L. D.   *Little Falls.*
Ramsey John
Chase M.
Tucker S.
Green Wm. H.   *Newport.*
Brown Jacob
Wood G. W.
Wood A. A. J.
Humphreyville David   *Norway.*
Tuttle Amos
Bassett Elisha   *Salisbury.*
Loyd D. W. C.
Smith S. Salisbury Centre
Burton L.   *Schuyler.*
Countryman G. D.   *Stark.*
Conklin A. T., Van Hornsville
Liver Robert   do
Gibson D. D. Starkville
Cook H. C.   do
Snyder J.   do
Dillenbeck J. L. do
Guiwits J.   do
Lewis John   *Warren.*
Wendell Jacob, Jordanville
Turner A.   do
Lewis John, Page's Corners
Hecox Andrew   do
Northaway Hervey   *Wilmurt.*
Chapman C.   *West Winfield.*
Preston L.
Bostwick & Hewes

Jefferson County.

Bliss S. & Co.   *Adams.*
M'Carty John
Worth William
Horth L. F.
Persons L.
Horth & Co.
Bundell O. W. & Co. Smithville
Suits Benj. Plessis   *Alexandria.*
Roof D.   do
Storm M. J. do
Van Dresser Chas. L. Alexandria Bay
Leonard Isaac, Alexandria Bay
Rugg S. & C.   *Antwerp.*
Burt B. Ox Bow
Gillett M. M. do

Bell George P.   *Brownville.*
Hunt James P.
Lawton Wm. H.   *Cape Vincent.*
Owen David
Powell F.
Briggs Edward
Briggs Daniel
Ackland Frederick
Whitcomb Almond
Muzzy G.   *Champion.*
Stark A. N.
Carter Ezra
Rose Jared
Gunn Willard
Phillips Hosea
Baldwin ——
Hawes C. L.   *Clayton.*
Flynn Thomas
Caswell P.
Vincent D. Depauville
Whittier & Ellsworth, do
Nobles F.   do
Morley H.   *Ellisburgh.*
Dunn J.
Albro L. H.
Sturdevant L. D. Woodville
Mead N. D.   do
Washburn J. Mannsville
Taylor N.   do
Perry H. Belleville
Bishop S. R. do
Seaton L. jr.   *Henderson.*
Kilby S. D.
Worthington & Auchard
Lane Charles, Sackett's Harbor
    Hounsfield.
Van Allen James, do
Patterson D.   do
Bingham Hiram, Evans' Mills
    Le Ray.
Skinner S. E.   do
Clement Jacob,   do
Allen G.   do
Breadwell Wm. Three Mile Bay
    Lyme.
Bazo & Putnam,   do
Snell & Tebo,   do
Yowan James,   do
Boll F.   do
Rector David, Millen's Bay
Richards Wm.   do
Richardson Daniel, Lafargeville
    Orleans.
Pollock Wm.   *Philadelphia.*
Kirkbride J.
Rogers O.
Nichols William
Keeler J.
Allen B.
Alford W. D.   *Rodman.*
Jones & Taft
Munger George, East Rodman
Beecher W., S. Rutland   *Rutland.*
Munger S.   do
Angell N   do
Flaherty J. O. Black River
Wolfe William,   do
Rawson Luther, Felt's Mills
Walradt A. M.   *Theresa.*
Spalsbury Richardson
Lull N. W.
Castler John S.
Twing Charles T.
Lewis Foster   *Watertown.*
Falibanks Samuel

Kings County.

Abercrombie G. Navy st. near Sands   *Brooklyn.*
Allen S. Myrtle Av. near Clanson
Atkins S. H. cor. Boerum & Pacific
Atkins W. 306 Atlantic
Baker John, 169 Myrtle Av.
Bennett Joseph, 104 Hudson Av.
Bennett W. J. & J. H. 96 Fulton
Bird Isaac, 67 Atlantic
Black James, 107 York
Booth T. 56 Myrtle Av.
Bostwick John, cor. Atlantic & Market
Boyle Daniel, 119 Front

Burns James, York st. near Washington   *Brooklyn.*
Burns J. 76 Tillary
Campbell Wm. 26 Main
Carbut J. 163½ Gold
Casay Patrick, 77 Hudson Av.
Cashon John. 34 Hicks
Chillcott John. 43 Fulton
Cochlan John. 26 Hudson Av.
Cox John. 103 Bridge
Crane T. Prospect near Fulton
Delignan Philip. 66½ Main
Dorohoe P. 277 Atlantic
Droscher L. Flushing Av.
Duffy & Ghallager, 13 Columbia
Dunn G. 70½ Bridge
Elias H. 40 Henry
Ellsworth J. W. 122 Johnson
Evans Evan. 3 Columbia
Fearey W. 126 Fulton
Fischer John, 12 Front
Fitzpatrick P. Franklin Av.
Force J. L. 93 High
Gaywood, G. C. 70 Nassau
Gillespie John. Columbia st.
Goodfried P. 36 Hudson Av.
Goodwin F. 56 Atlantic
Grebel John, 19 Hicks
Haas E. 51 Atlantic
Hampton Z. Smith st. near Sacket
Hand D. 141 York
Heathorn E. 323 Fulton
Herbert John. 53½ James
Herbert J. 69 Sands
Hicks H. A. 173 York
Hofman A. 37 Atlantic
Hollis Silas. Flushing Av.
Holly Joseph, Prince st.
Houlin J. Myrtle Av.
Huesman J. 107 High
Hughes H. cor. Smith & Atlantic
Hugly Frank. 5 Furman
Irvine M.W.cor.Henry & Middagh
Jones Thomas, 45 Stanton
Jordan J. 87 Prospect
Kavanoh C. 20 Columbia
Kennington F. 55 Main
Kienlu J. Prospect st.
Knapp E. P. & A. H. 63 Fulton
Knower Geo. S. 198 Fulton
Krehbiel J. 21 Myrtle Av.
Kruger J. 4 Boerum
Langhorst H. Flushing Av.
Lewis J. 5 Clinton
M'Allie John, 3 Linden row
M'Ginley John. 204 Atlantic
M'Guire Patrick, 103 Hudson Av.
M'Innery John. Columbia st.
Martin M. Water, near Jay
Oles Henry, Court st.
Oles H. 266 Adams
Ormend James, 34 Hudson Av.
Otto C. L. Boerum st.
Payne J. F. 50 Prince
Pelgrift J. 106 Gold
Pierson S. L. 242 Henry
Quinby D. F. Prince st.
Reid A. 182 Fulton
Roberts G. cor. Henry & Middagh
Robrechts C. 38 Hicks
Roe Walter. 230 Atlantic
Ryan P. 20 Columbia
Ryen P. 1 Howe's buildings, Water
Simms J. W. 169 Adams
Simmerman John, 69 Atlantic
Shields Patrick. 105 Atlantic
Smith Philip, 104 Washington
Stroffregan R. 99 Sands
Strohmaler J. 281 Adams
Todd James. 52 Hudson Av.
Tooker D. M. 161 Court
Tristam R. 155 Sands
Twaits Wm. 16 Hamilton Av.
Wainwright W. 214 Bridge
Ward W. 8 Baltic near Smith
Wellman William, 53 Atlantic.
Wilcox William H. 273 Fulton
Porter Thomas, Maspeth turnpike   *Bushwick.*
Davis H. Green Point
Cronk James, do
Ellsworth Isaac   *Flatbush.*

Halliley R. *Flatbush.*
Van Curen Cornelius, New Lots
Wendell C. East New York
Smith C. P. do
Hill T. do
Stryker J. *Gravesend.*
Emmons Peter V.
Wright S. *New Utrecht.*
Church James C. Fort Hamilton
Broaffe Simon, 275 South 4th
Wi iamsburgh.
Burr William H. 172 Grand
Butler J. 100 North 2d
Campbell James. 155 4th
Coen Thomas, 272 1st
Con ity T. 131 Grand
Contierce I. C. 183 Grand
Cullen P. 282 Grand
Churchin A. 1st cor North 10th
Durlington John J. South 7th
Dowling Dennis. 234 1st
Engle Henry. 243 Grand
Hall David. 282½ Grand
Hann P. 150 1st
Kelsey Edward. 127 Grand
Kraemer John. 228 1st
Ludlow John. South 4th
Monaghan Wil lam, 24½ North 3d
Mooney P. 247 1st
Moore T. 47 South 3d
Nichols R. 243 South 4th
Ochsner Karl, 292 South 1st
Peacock J. R. 436 Grand
Phillips Lambert A. 28 Grand
Ranch A. 197 South 3d
Roser Peter. 166 South 4th
Schneider Daniel. 222½ 2d
Smith Adam. 185 Grand
Smith C. L. 226 Grand
Smith John. 274 Grand
Smith J. Water
Stevens S. 160 Leonard
Stuart T. 223 1st
Warnes John. 225 2d
Wiggins D. H. 171 Grand
Wimmer J. 491 South 1st
Woodward W. A. 72 South 6th
Wright John, 232 Grand

Lewis County.

Baker L. *Denmark.*
Thrasher & Blinn
Cone T.
Vorse E.
Cottrell F. Copenhagen
Helgus Joshua, Brantingham
Greig.
Gillett A. *Lowville*
Griffiths D. *Martinsburgh.*
Martin J.
Fate A.
Merritt B., West Martinsburgh
Sullivan D. do
Litchfield Albert H. *Turin.*
Litchfield Luther
Thayer Enoch
Williams Thomas
Dewey Milton, Houseville
Johnson H. Constableville
West Turin.
Evans Peter do
Hinton L. do
Griffith — do
Jones J. Collinsville

Livingston County.

Gilbert Darius M. *Avon.*
Fayle Robert
Simonds Charles
Paige Abram, East Avon
Aull Robert *Caledonia.*
Tier William
Wilson Robert
Head John *Conesus.*
Dump B. F.
Sprague J. W. *Dansville.*
Niles E.
Shannon S.
Trembly J. R.
Londerboon J.
Wood D. J. & Co.

Snell Thomas *Dansville.*
Peck A. J.
Reynolds J. A.
Parker & Dick
Bates E.
Rudd John *Geneseo.*
Curry James
Smith Walter
Robinson Andrew G.
Suttim D. F. *Groveland.*
Benway Peter, East Groveland
Thompson William, do
Bush —. Cuylerville *Leicester.*
Arnold William G. *Lima.*
Mitchell J.
Pratt F. T. *Livonia.*
Dibble & Co.
Risden S.
Bennett S. N. Lakeville
Woodford Coy & Co.
Mount Morris.
Starkey J. P. & Co.
Gardner H. D. *Nunda.*
Phillips M.
Walker Conrad, Oakland *Portage.*
Spees Henry, Hunt's Hollow
Brown Asa F. Scottsburgh
Sparta.
Brown Solomon F. do
Woodford Chauncy, do
Whitehead Joseph C. *Springwater.*
Wilkins William, Dansville
West Sparta.
Parish —, Dansville
Harrington Ira *York.*
M'Farlin William
Weller E. Pifferdania
Sinclair —, do
Gilbert William, Fowlersville

Madison County.

Denison James *Brookfield*
Babcock Nathan
Clark & Gorton
Johnson Aaron
Keeler D. G. *Cazenovia.*
Hawley Francis
Greenland Joseph jr.
Shores E. F.
Gaskill J.
Richmond Wm. T. New Wood-
stock
Bentley & Shepard *De Ruyter.*
Benjamin Charles
Page John
Sherrill & Orton *Eaton.*
Williams H. F. & Co. Morrisville
Fowler & Williams, do
Sharp Richard, Leeville
Omans William, do
Weaver P. O. *Fenner.*
Ellis Asa *Georgetown.*
Bonny William P.
Hare William P.
Poole Thaxter *Hamilton.*
Curry E.
Atkins Charles
Plumbly C.
Rice W. M.
Town Elijah. Earlville
Swift & Co. Poolville
Clark George, Hubbard's Corners
Yale H. *Lenox.*
Johnson A. S.
Smith Asa. Oneida Depot
Beecher Hamilton, Canastota
Richardson J. D. do
Tryon W. & H. do
Gates George W. do
Bell Truman, do
Walrath J. L. Clockville
Slocum O. *Lebanon.*
Wadsworth A.
Mackley Robert *Madison.*
Dudley I. J.
Wright Jesse
Gilbert A.
Curtis S. Erieville *Nelson.*
Johnson C. S. do
Carpenter J. do
Stewart R. do

Smith Luther *Nelson.*
Truesdell David
Hall Abner, Peterboro *Smithfield.*
Hadden Hiram, do
Wilson J. M. *Stockbridge.*
Whedon Hiram
Walton Wm. E.
Strong Alvin 2d
Walrath J. J. Chittenango
Sullivan.
Vosburgh John, do
Walrath & Frederick, do
Colyer Jacob, do
Weaver & Doing, Perryville
Lower Peter R. Bridgeport
Sickler Z. do

Monroe County.

Withull J. *Brighton.*
Targeo A. South Chill *Chili.*
Fulton Robert. North Chili
Simonds Z. Clarkson Corners
Clarkson.
Smith J.. Jenkins Corners *Greece.*
Smith Joseph, do
Robins L. do
Chapin D., East Henrietta
Henrietta.
Chappell —, do
Wilson Henry. West do
Roswell A.P., E. Mendon *Mendon.*
Grosbeck H. do
Badger Smith, do
Corby —
Fox John H. West Mendon
Ball, Church & Co. Spencer's Ba-
sin *Ogden.*
Peck Horace M. *Parma.*
Winkoop John, Parma Centre
Scoville John D. *Penfield.*
Leona C. Fairport *Parrinton.*
Ely A. do
Brown Joseph, Bushnell's Basin
Cleaveland John *Pittsford.*
Shale G. 10 S. St. Paul *Rochester.*
Morrison J. 26 Andrews
Miller Henry, 92 Main
Roehrig Charles. 121 Buffalo
Williamson William, 140 do
Harris John. 130 do
Grover E. H. 116 do
Wood Luton, 84 do
Gray J. G. (Boots) 12½ do
Schribe P. do 6 Arcade
Cowles John. do 1 State
Baker A. & Co. 41 Main cor. Water
Watkins S. B. 97½ Main
Groh John, 103 do
Lemon Stephen, do
Burwell Alfred, 139½ do
Coffrain E. S. 36 Exchange
Turpin William, 70 do
Craddock J. 95 Sophia
Parry John. 106 S. do
Vick James, 186 State
Andrews R. cor. Waterloo & State
Fitzgibbon J. 97 Oak *Rochester.*
Post & Bunnell *Rush.*
Provost John
Goodenough Darwin, W. Rush
Davis W. Brockport *Sweden.*
Andrews Z., W. Webster *Webster*
Schermerhorn L. do
Clough John do
Brown W. Scottsville *Wheatland*
Hooper Francis

Montgomery County.

Bartlet Chandler *Amsterdam.*
Picket E. W.
Hewitt Thomas
Fulton A.
Van Deusen H. Hageman's Mills
Cuyler Henry do
Spore John, Cranesville
Morse Elisha F. do
Herring C. E. *Canajoharie.*
Winsman Henry
Keyser T. H.
Van Antwerp Wendell
Tiffany L. H., Ames *Canajoharie.*

Genini John, Ames *Canajoharie.*
Wendell Benjamin, Buel
Van Dusen. J. 4 cor's *Charleston.*
Taylor R. V. Minaville *Florida.*
Dean Daniel, Port Jackson
Hewitt J. do
Johnson D. do
Snyder John *Glenn.*
Crane L. B.
Rogers P. W.
Cole Enos, Fultonville
Combs Peter, do
Onderkirk Andrew. Smithtown
Johnson J. B., Fort Plain *Minden.*
Hadley Ira. do
Moxon William C. do
Hokirk Abraham do
Fisher John, . do
Lasher J., Fonda *Mohawk.*
Clark G. & H. do
Ansman J. C. do
Dillinback J. do
Van Deusen GHbert, do
Crotsenburg A. N. do
Shults Frederick do
Fritcher James do
Putnam J. M. . do
Veeder James do
Luthers George, Palatine Bridge
Palatine.
Showerman Joseph, Stone Arabia
Lasher Henry & U. do
Van Loon John, do
Saltsman David, do
Dillinback Levi, do
Shimael John, do
Paughburn Benjamin, do
Yates Elias *Root.*
Brougham John
Falensby Isaac
Lasher John *St. Johnsville.*
Hall Wilhem
Schram Levi
Egan J. H.

New York County.

Abraham Jacob, 185 Rivington
New York.
Abrams Isaac, 45 Goerck
Achtman Lorenz, 2 Av. C
Acton John W. 687 Broadway
Adler Benjamin, 279 Division
Adolphus D., W. 27th st.
Agate W. M. 114 Bowery
Albrecht Henry. 54 Sullivan
Albrecht, H. 179 4th
Albrecht Jacob, 108 1st
Albrecht Valentine, 189 Grand
Albus S. 6 John
Alden Charles, 277 Pearl
Aldis W. H. 8th Av.
Allon Hewlett, 215 Greenwich
Alloye Erath. 6¼ Cornelia
Alt Peter, 223 Varick
Althen Jacob, 272 Greenwich
American Company. 302 2d
Ament Anthony, 45 Frankfort
Anderson Patrick, 549 Greenwich
Andre Christopher, 39 Warren
Andrie Valentine. 600 4th
Anglin Thomas, 135 Monroe
Armitage Isaac, 26 Moore
Armstrong S. 3 Murray
Auffices Marcus. 439 Broome
Ayres William, 58 3d Av.
Ayres H. L. & A. 266 Pearl
Bachman G. 47 Hester
Backer Jacob, 32 6th Av.
Bad Jacob, 72 Grand
Baffun H. 44 Av. B
Baehle Clemens, 1 Bedford
Baker James, 76½ 9th Av.
Baker Michael. 662 Water
Baker Wm. 8th Av.
Baldwin Caleb H. 264 3d Av.
Baldwin George W. 237 Delancy
Baldwin and Studwell, 262 Pearl
Balke Henry, 27 Mulberry
Ball William, 67 Laurens
Ball William C. 57 Beekman
Balzer William, 21 Minetta Lane
Bane John, 564 Hudson

Bante H. 102 Bedford *New York.*
Barmore Christ. 242 E. 13th
Barmikel George, 70 Norfolk
Barros J. R. 17 8th Av.
Barry Owen, 50 Mulberry
Bartlett Nathan M. 300 9d
Basser James, 61 Church
Bassett Robert. 464 Washington
Batchelder Robert, 243 Canal
Batenberg William, 121 Lewis
Bau John, 660½ Pearl
Bauer George A. 219 Wooster
Bauer Valentine, 3 Gouverneur
Baanacher M. 24 College place
Baus Peter, 3 Chrystie
Beck Charles. 99 Cannon
Beck Frederick, 173 Broome
Becker Daniel, 480 Cherry
Becker Jacob, 32 6th Av.
Becker J. 164 3d
Beckmeier Henry. 78 Roosevelt
Beekman Lornhardt, 137 Pitt
Behen Thos. 207 Spring
Behm M. 654 Washington
Beisecker Charles. 153 Broome
Beker George F. 657 Water
Beker J. 20 3d Av.
Bell Johnston, 43 8th Av.
Benedict, Hall & Co. 255 Pearl
Benedict & Bradley, 246 Pearl
Benedum Jacob. 132 Lewis
Benner Henry, 71½ Wall
Beney J. 261 W. 23d
Benz George, 202 Greenwich
Benz Jacob, 838 Henry
Benz M. 72 Chrystie
Berendor H. 61 Stanton
Berl Charles. 604 Water
Bertine Daniel, 211 3d Av.
Beslin John, 13 Bayard
Besser J. 61 Church
Betts Curtis. 329 6th
Betts Nathaniel C. 174 8th Av.
Betz Conrad. 354 Madison
Beuermann Frederick, 70 Ridge
Beyerle F. 33 Av. B.
Beyhold J., W. 32d st.
Bidelman Henry. 91 Stanton
Bieber John, 69 Suffolk
Bigelow & Gedney, 2 Bowery
Biggam H. 160 Canal
Bill F. X. 151 Canal
Bineka Edward. 283 Walker
Bird Jacob, 8th Av.
Bishop A. 38 Thompson
Bishop E. 391 Grand
Bishop John C. 390 Bowery
Blanchard B. 268½ Pearl
Blaney Bernard, 216 Cherry
Blank George, 47 Oak
Blaze George W. 58 Fulton
Bloch Benjamin, 119 Elizabeth
Bloch Raphael, 128 Grand
Bloome Jacob, 27½ Morton
Bloom John & Jacob, 118 William
Bloszfeldt Charles, 147 Madison &
67 Broome
Blumenstiel Isaac, 480 Broadway
Bodenheimer David. 168 Leonard
Boehle Clemens, 1 Bedford
Boehm Matthias, 650 Washington
Boehrer John, 109 Thompson
Boettner C. 201 Fulton
Bogert Cornelius A. 474 Greenwh
Bohn D. 173 Canal
Bohn John, 309 Delancy
Bolger Henry, 96 9th
Bokelman John, 183 Av. B.
Bonenberger J. 93 Laurens
Boschert Xabia, 223 Walker
Bose Frederick, 211 Centre
Bosse Augustus, 55 Cherry
Bossuet Louis. 76 Bleecker
Borger H. 154 9th
Bounacher M. 16 College Place
Bouwman Bernardis, 502 Pearl
Boyce David M. 448 Houston
Boyce William, 275 2d
Boyd Daniel. 25 Columbia
Boyd James, 359½ 6th Av.
Boyd W. J., W. 24th st.
Brady Philip, 272 Mott

Bradly F. 134 4th
Brailing Henry, 116 Lewis
Brandan Jacob, 85 Allen
Brandstetter Jacob, 44½ Columbia
Branieff Daniel, 114 Church
Bransfield James, 364 Water
Bragg A. & Co. 269 Pearl
Brauer Conrad, 389 Broome
Brehm John, 296 Spring
Brehm Paul. 190 Spring
Bresland John, 55 Washington
Brewsett Ambrose, 189 Division
Brierley William, 192 Wooster
Brinckman Carston, 11 Moore
Bristol W. B & Co. 69 Catharine
Brindley Rinckles, 277 Pearl
Beining Michael, 257 Delancy
Broalbent James, 127 Perry
Brockhaws H. 8th Av.
Brook Lorin, 240 Broadway
Brom Jacob, 13 Delancy
Brophy Edward, 144 8th Av.
Brophy Thomas, 119 8th Av.
Brown James, 79 Av. B
Brown John, 152 Broad
Brown Patrick. 317½ Bowery
Brown William, 62 Wooster
Brown W. V. & Co. 162 Cherry
Broshatt Charles, 98 Willett
Bruck Jacob, 147 W. Broadway
Brudding John, 161 Bleecker
Brumm Adam, 454 Broadway
Brush Alfred. 343 Bleecker
Brush Valentine, 155 Houston
Buchanan John, 83 8th Av.
Buchet J. 239 3d
Bulman Thomas, 201 West
Burger Victor, 166 Church
Burger T H. 364 Pearl
Burkard Joseph, 107 Delancy
Burke John. 10 Pelham
Burke Bichard, 192 Varick
Burman Christopher, 149 Houston
Burns Patrick, 15 Amos
Burns Peter. 122 Ridge
Burr John, 31 Columbia
Burr S. 13 Av. C
Burrell Reuben, 329 Pearl
Burrell Geo. 383 Greenwich
Burrell Samuel, 385 Greenwich
Burrows Barry H. 7 John
Burt Brothers & Co. 68 Broad
Busch Gaspar, 156 Stanton
Butener Christian 201 Fulton
Butz Frederick, 297 Division
Byrne Edward, 30 Leonard
Byrnes Henry, 13 Wall
Byrnes P. 77 Stanton
Byron Henry, 66 W. Broadway
Cadwell William S. 910 Chatham
Cahill Michael, 413 Cherry
Cahill Sylvester, 367 Broadway
Camerden John. 190½ Division
Camp Michael, 134 Willett
Campbell Charles, 163 Thompson
Campbell Michael. 91½ Fulton
Campbell F. 62 W. Broadway
Canniff Jonas, 194 Delancy
Cannon Lawrence, 43 Orange
Cantrell S. 336 Bowery
Capent H. 131 Christopher
Carey Thomas, 260 10th
Carolan Michael, 871 Broadway
Carroll Edward, 18 Cortlandt
Carroll Philip, 240 8th Av.
Carter Isaac, 116 8th Av.
Casey Jeremiah, 26 Prince
Casey Laurence, 8 6th
Casey Patrick, 132 Av. C
Casey Michael, 58 W. Broadway
Cashel Thomas. 60 Spring
Cassin Martin, 77 Wall
Centlivre Henry, 17 Wall
Cheryinger J. 8 Albany
Chamberlain Holdroyk, 208 Pearl
Chrisholm Robert, 64 1st Av
Christ John, 177 Elm
Christman Jacob, 126 Willett
Christoph John O. 536 Broome
Chesterman Chas. 305 3d Av.
Claflin Aaron, 255 Pearl
Clark Alexander, 138 Canal

Clark Jeremiah, 117 Prince New York.
Clark John, 28 Mott
Clark Michael. 126 Division
Cherex ——, 303 Broadway
Clingit M. 148 Broome
Clos Peter. 35 West Broadway
Codey William, 35 Laurens
Coffee John, 298 Av. A.
Coffman & Thorburn, 14 Clarkson
Conn Lippman, 226 East Broadw.
Coile Charles, 96 Elizabeth
Colgan James, 150 Mott
Collens B., W. 27th st.
Cole D. M., W. 28th st.
Collins Patrick, 44 Hester
Collins William, 48 Downing
Colvin William, 929 Broadway
Columb T., W. 29th st
Combs Samuel B. 56 William
Conde Peter, 115 Goerck
Condra Jms. 12th bet. Avs. A & B
Conelly John, 15 Mulberry
Connor George, 157 Forsyth
Connor Thomas, 93 Sheriff
Conover John, 204 W. 18th
Conrad J. C. 9 Ann & 66 Market
Conroy John, 388 Hudson
Conway James, 500 Houston
Cosen P., W. 30th st.
Cook Samuel. 357 Madison
Cooney John R. 158 Av. B
Cooper John, rear 53 King
Cooper John, W. 19th st.
Copcutt Abel, 131 Christopher
Copping Charles, 53 Lispenard
Coppins Thomas. 43 Christopher
Corbett Otis G, 124 Water
Corbett S. 130   do
Corees Frederick, 202 William
Cordier Ferrol T. 49 Dey
Corey John. 171 Hester
Corishof Charles, 475 Cherry
Comon Lant, 248 Mott
Cornelison Michael, Sullivan st.
Costelle Michael, 18 Marion
Crawford Bernard, 382 Cherry
Crawford John, 45 Hamilton
Crawford John, 110 Madison
Creed T. 1. 6th
Crombie Hugh, 40 Av. C
Cromley James, 315 Bleecker
Crumley James, 315   do
Crook George H. 89 Cedar
Crowley Michael, 317 3d Av.
Cubberly David, 99 Fulton
Cullen Edward F. 159 Broadway
Culligan Felix, 203 Grand
Cunningham Matthew, 37 Grand
Cunningham G.
Curtin Jeremiah, 58 Robinson
Curtis M. O. 7 John
Dechermann Walter, 181 2d
Dehmer Henry, 35 M·Dougal
Dally P. 235 1st Av.
Dakin George, 200 Centre
Dakin John, 29 Elizabeth
Daly James, 195 Hester
Daly Patrick. 82 Fulton
Daly G. 35 Cherry
Damm Henry, 30 Broadway
Daniels S. & Co. 171 Pearl
Dare & Corrigal, 130 Beekman
Darragh C. 96 18th
Daus Adam, 184½ 7th
Daut John, 4 Sullivan
Davidson ——, 371 4th
Davis John H. 36 3d Av.
Davison James A. 199 William
Dayle C. 25 Amos
Dealing William, 245 Wooster
Dean Enoch, 227 Bowery
Dean J. L. 160 Canal
Dearr Clements, rear 155 8th Av.
Decker Phillips, 377 Broome
Degan G. Cornelia st.
Degray Young, 401 Houston
Delhi John, 48 Beekman
Deitsch & Co. 186 Broadway
Delancey David, 6 Av. D
De Lander William, 8 Henry
Delaney A. 347 Houston

Delb George, 18 Av. A New York.
Delense G., W. 29th st.
Dennis Henry, 114 Greene
Deppert J., W. 29th st.
Deppermann H. 321 Greenwich
Deschouse Augustus, 145 Mott
Detmus Aeit M. 42 Stanton
Devaney Patrick. 242 Cherry
Deveau & Corbett. 128 Water
Deveau P. B. 156 Chatham
Devlin Arthur, 201 9th Av.
Devlin Patrick, 173 Hester
Devoe Leonard, 4 Christopher
Dick John, 192 Nassau
Diefenbach I. A. 144 Essex
Diepold F. 352 Houston
Dimm Henry, 374½ Grand
Direck Jacob, 115 Anthony
Dischman Henry, 16 Walnut
Ditess Frederick F. 596 Broadway
Divine Thomas, 286 Water
Dobbs W. H. 29 4th
Dodd Francis, 285 Bowery
Dolan Charles, 174 W. Broadway
Dolan John, 120 W. 17th
Dollard Patrick R. 249 3d Av
Dollner Adam, 346 Greenwich
Donington Ogden, 276 3d Av
Donnelly Arthur, 374 Water
Donnelly Patrick, 93½ 11th
Donovan James, 146 Broadway
Dorald W. M., W. 28th st.
Dorsch Frederick, 72½ Delancy
Dose Philip, 235 3d
Dougherty D. 86 Murray
Dougherty William, 21 Rector
Dougless William, 18 Dover
Dowall B., W. 15th cor. 8th Av.
Dowd Dominick, 62 Mott
Down Mateas, 25 Cannen
Downey William, 2 Pine
Downhow Joseph, 218 12th
Downing James S. 76 8th Av
Downing Richard T. 156 do
Downing Thomas S. 205 do
Doyle Christopher M. 25 Amos
Doyle Michael, 30½ New
Drake ——, 204 Walker
Draper S. 136 4th
Dressler Hance N. 2 Park place
Dresslein Charles W. 249 Division
Driscoll G. 14 Cherry
Drude Christian, 116 Anthony
Duckworph J. 136 Clarke
Duk Christian, 174 Allen
Duffiand James, 245 Elizabeth
Duffy John, 67 Hester
Duggan Edward, 147 Division
Dunn John, 118 Broome
Dunham John, 152 Spring
Durnin Robert, 309 Mott
Duryea John A. 750 Washington
Dusel J. 145 Elm
Dusold George, 96 Rivington
Dusold Nicholas, 64 Orange
Dwyer John, 15 Oak
Earl Martin, 174 Christopher
Ebelher George, 111 Delancy
Eberle John, 111 7th Av.
Ebersold Philip J. 125 Delancy
Ecker Jacob, 546 Hudson
Eckhard Casper, 178 Spring
Eddy James W. 30 Houston
Edel Frederick, 65 Mercer
Edsall Peter, 64 King
Egan Stephen, 188 Mulberry
Ehrhart Daniel, 138 Allen
Eich Charles, 39 Madison
Eicke George, 82 Liberty
Eichhorn Adam, 244 E. 18th
Elsemann Maier, 64 Barclay
Eisenbeiss John G. 110 Suffolk
Elbert Henry, 15 1st Av.
Elbert M. 152 2d st.
Ellis Thomas, 81 Greenwich
Elkson A. 62 Washington place
Endres Michael, 93 Charlton
Engel Sebastien, 614 Greenwich
Engleman Frederick, 62 Reade
Ensch N. 611 4th
Epstein Simon, 73 Suffolk
Erath Henry, 77 Hamersley

Erath Joseph, 9 Bayard New York.
Ernest H. 186 3d
Ernest Henry. 206 3d
Eschatke S. 247 Centre
Ewald John, 160 Reade
Ewald Peter, 309 Broome
Ewald William, 160 Washington
Fadegan J. 119 West
Fagan ——, 105 6th Av
Fahrenholz Claus H. 239 Wash'ton
Faby John, 235 Walker
Fairweather Thos. 104 Mulberry
Fanning Michael, 2½ Maiden la.
Fanning Michael, 398 West
Farrell Hamilton. 3 Cortlandt
Fasig John. 113 Eldridge
Fawcett William, 203 3d Av.
Fay Michael, 109 Sheriff
Fay & Storr. 272 Pearl
Feeny John, 35 Oak
Fehrer Christopher, 258 Monroe
Fei John A. 214 Grand
Feldheim J. & S. 6½ & 23 4th Av.
Felt J. 118 Broome
Fennor John, 91 Leonard
Feely J. 317 8th st.
Fenner Joseph, 195 Church
Fenning Michael, 398 West
Ferris David, 1 Greenwich
Ferris Eugene, 44 Nassau
Fertig J. 201 Delancy
Fertig Peter. 211 Delancy
Fetigan John, 419 West
Fiege Augustus G. 81 Orange
Fiesel Joseph, 296½ 10th
Fink Joseph. 67 Lewis
Fischermann John, 1½ Ann
Fischermann Wm. 257 Broadway
Fitzgerald Francis. 94 Orange
Fitzgerald John, 5 Oak
Fitzgerald M. 22 W. Broadway
Fitzgerald Thomas, 89 Roosevelt
Fitzgerald C. S. 22 W. Broadway
Flannagan Jas. 497 Washington
Flashman Andrew, 22 Av. A
Fleming Michael, 51 Elizabeth
Fleury Victor, 9 Wall
Flynn Francis, 31 Prince
Flynn John, 16 Franklin
Fogel Daniel, 69 Warren
Foley James, 27 Roosevelt
Foley Jeremiah, 79 E. Broadway
Foote Andrew J. 112 Varick
Fowler D. S. 464 Grand
Fowler John, 186 do
Fowler John H. 306 2d
Fox Adam, 44 Allen
Fox Charles, 211½ Division
Fox H. 112 Houston
Fox John, 148 Houston
Francis A. 33 Cherry
Francis John. 274 3d Av.
Francisco David, 313 Delancy
Frank Ignate, 20 Av. B.
Frank Philip, 277 Stanton
Franke J. M. 377 1st Av.
Frankland R. 319 Water
Franks Charles, 1 Nassau
Franks James. 40 Whitehall
Frans Jacob, 41st st.
Freanor M. 22 Rector
Frederick Abraham J. 153 Perry
Frederick Nicholas, 126 Varick
French George, 4 Bleecker
French James, 250 Pearl
Freyfoole Jacob F. 42½ Norfolk
Frieary John, Av. B. bet. E. 19th & E. 14th
Friedrich Christian, 474 Hudson
Friederick N. 126 Varick
Frisbie M. J. 24 Pearl
Frische Charles, 21 Dey
Fritz Konrad, 9 Chambers
Frolich Tobias, 206 Rivington
Fuchs Henry, 112 Houston
Gaesenger Karl W. 79 Duane
Gafney Peter, 338 Monroe
Gaib Jacob, 466 12th
Gale A. D. 325 Pearl
Guiser G. 3 1st Av.
Galagher William, 40 Canal
Gallagher Jas. 37 W. Broadway

Gallagher Thomas, 216 Centre

New York.

Gallaway Tobias, 6 3d
Ganglofi A. 233 Av. 2
Ganton Julien, 89 Nassau
Gardiners Henry, 29 Fulton
Garthoffaer M., W. 29th st.
Garry James M. 664 Grand
Gast Andreas, 70 Vandam
Gavey James, 45 W. Broadway
Gay Jacob, 269 Bleecker
Geary John, 137 Orange
Gebauer Charles. 113 Essex
Gebhard August, 102 Cedar
Gebhardt Philip. 26 Hudson
Gehrels John A. 94 Duane
Gehring T. 38 Commerce
Geiger Francis. 254 William
Geis Nicholas, 19 Stone
Geist William, 16 6th Av.
George & Burt, 144 Pearl
Gerken Julius, 6 Stone
Gerst William, 102 Lewis
Gibbens Robert, 151 8th Av.
Giering Joseph. 179 Greenwich
Gildea John, 9 Bayard
Gilham John. 3 Vandam
Gilman Richard, 158 W. Broadway
Gilmartin John. 151 Forsyth
Gitsinger Francis, 716 Washingt'n
Glass John. 140 Perry
Glauber Abraham, 243 Bowery
Glaze G. W. 68 Fulton
Gleam George, 117 Clinton
Gledhill Henry, 550 Hudson
Gledhill W. 1 W. 11th
Gledhill Wright, 196 W. 11th
Gleeson Michael, 217 1st Av.
Glock A. 1 2d
Gloeck Philip. 22 Delancy
Glynn Michael, 199 Grand
Gobbel Mary, 137½ Sullivan
Gobel John, 114 Ridge
Goeckel J. 359 6th
Goehl Henry, 334 Madison
Goerg John, 78 Reade
Goetze Bernard, 10½ Thomas
Gohner Charles. 9 Elizabeth
Goiher Joseph, 361 6th
Golding James, 78 Centre
Goldschmid Jacob, 157½ Broome
Goldschmidt Frank, 161 Clinton
Goldstein Aaron. 142 Lewis
Goodman David, 382 Cherry
Goodman Henry. 118 Ludlow
Goos Adam, 43 West
Goos George, 104 Thompson
Gordon James, 464 3d Av.
Gordon H., W. 25th st.
Gorham J. 233 Broadway
Gos John, 56 Oliver
Gottfried Nicholas, 27½ Madison
Gow David, 480 Hudson
Graf George. 14 Norfolk
Graff Abraham, 119 Clinton
Graham J. C. 91 Catharine
Grannis & Stewart, 96 Maiden L.
Greb John, 141 Houston
Greene William, 83 Varick
Gregory John, 163 W. Broadway
Gressel Frederick, 145 Monroe
Griffin James B. 306 Grand
Griffith Charles B. 330 Bowery
Grill Adam, 27 Laurens
Grimm John. 720 Broadway
Grimm William, 31 Oak
Grimme Casper H. 70 Leonard
Grimme Edward, 22 Centre
Grimme Henry A. 558 Greenwich
Gross Henry, 126 Liberty
Gross Martin, 386 6th
Grosbeck Nicholas, 227 Bleecker
Grote Henry, 287 4th
Grubelsteins A. 265 25th
Grubener John, 238 Delancy
Grun John, 55 Mott
Guckler M. 228 3d
Gunn James, 23 Orange
Gutbrodt John, 193 Delancy
Gutman D. M. 380 Cherry
Guyer Frederick, 21 Thomas
Haas Francis, 20 Desbrosses

Habermann Andrew, 496 Houston

New York.

Hadley R. 132 Norfolk
Haely B. & J. 34 Ann
Hoffner Geo. P. 5 Greenwich Av.
Hagen Frederick, 112 Monroe
Hahn H. 7th Av.
Haisch Martin, 291 2d
Haldy Lewis. 14 Varick
Halifas C. 295 Houston
Hallenbeck G. W. Grand st.
Hollady James, 38 W. Broadway
Hallen James, 178 William
Halloday James. 64 Bayard
Hallory James, 142 Greenwich
Halsey, Utter & Co. 127 Maiden L.
Hamburger Herm. 255 Delancy
Hamilton David, 295 Madison
Hamilton Robert, 240 Walker
Hamman George, 423 Broadway
Hammel Thomas. 388½ Pearl
Hammel Bryan, 66 James
Hammer Charles, 230 Rivington
Hammill John, 177 Allen
Hanly David. 582 Water
Hanna William, 780 Washington
Hannan John, cor 9th Av.
Hannon John, 199 Bowery
Hansselt John G. 94 Franklin
Hapel M. 7th st.
Harburger Simon, 87 Columbia
Harer John, 572 4th
Harkins E. 48 Carmine
Harrison John. 114 Mulberry
Harrison Wm. 187 Chambers
Harsch Philip, 9 Vandewater
Hart Peter, 49 Mott
Hartenstein Harman. 80½ Cannon
Hartman Augustus, 113 Elm
Harvey Thomas, 51 Marion
Haupert F. 204 Cherry
Haston J. 61 Laight
Hautman Killeon, 211 Av. B
Hawkins Edward. 48 Carmine
Hawmil Thos. 387 Pearl
Hawthorn Thomas, 16 Stone
Hay Jacob A. 12 Beekman
Healy Sheffield. 39 Norfolk
Heil Jacob, 231 3d
Heilmann John G. 160½ W. 29th
Heimath George, 657 Greenwich
Heimerle Jacob, 123 Greenwich
Heinrich Christian, 43 Cannon
Heimroth Geo. 637 Greenwich
Heimroth J. Av. B bet. 12th & 13th
Heinemann Heindrick, 7 Trin. pl.
Hinemann Simon, 108 Spring
Heiner George, 118 Suffolk
Heinze Detrich, 239 W. 18th
Held John. 36 Wooster
Helferich C. N. 11 Clarke
Helfrich Wm. 167 Washington
Helmholz Christopher. 471 Pearl
Helmoth Simon, 55 Duane
Heneizite John, 164 16th
Henenlolher John, 75 Greenwich
Henn Peter, 19 Bayard
Henning J. & H. 257 3d
Hentz Alexander, 88 Lewis
Herber G. 309 8th
Herf John, 33 Vestry
Herhersch Robert, 168 Leonard
Herman William, 8 Thomas
Herold C. r. 264 2d
Herrlick Peter, 125 Suffolk
Herschberger Isaac, 45 Columbia
Hertel Henry, 39 Beekman
Hertling Henry, 33 Essex
Hertzler Joseph. 58 Broome
Herzog Philip. 165 Lewis
Hess Philip. 99 Pitt
Hessigmor P. 222 2d
Houman George, 170 Stanton
Heuman M. 212 Houston
Heunloller J. 75 Greenwich
Heupert Frederick. 204 Cherry
Higgins Henry, 166 11th
Higgins Jeremiah, 196 Greene
Higgins John. 284 Bleecker
Higgins Michael, 235 W. 17th
Hilbert Nathan, 551 Grand
Hill Archibald, 58 Watts

Hill Gottleib, 21 Thomas

New York.

Hill Hermann, 203 Church
Hill Justus. 21 Thomas
Hinser Nicholas, 611 4th
Hirschberger Ernst, 141 Pitt
Hirableber Julius. 162 Delancy
Hoehn William. 17 Duane
Hoffmann Aegidius, 17 Walnut
Hoffman George, 50 Attorney
Hoffman Henry, 18½ Whitehall
Hoffner G. P. 5 Factory
Hoffner Samuel. 1 Rivington
Hohl Michael, 93 Broad
Hollgatner G. 8th Av.
Hollorain James, 178 William
Human John. 260 Delancy
Honeywell John, 29 Bayard
Honnecker John, 17 Cannon
Honecker ———, 231 9d
Hoppel ———, 210 7th
Horbelt Martin, 25 Mulberry
Horman William, 81 12th
Horn Philip, 24 Reade
Hort William 190 8th Av.
Howard Charles H. 217 Pearl
Howlett Wm. 90 University place
Houser John C. 96 Canal
Houpt George, 42 Anthony
Hoyt Joseph W. 230 Bowery
Howes & Co. R. W. 129 Water
Huebner Jacob A. 179 William
Hueston Steph. 8 Gouverneur slip
Hughes John, 376 Water
Hughes John, 162 Lafayette place
Hughes & Co. Isaiah, 170 Chatham
Huhn John, 162 Waverley place
Hull Wm. H. 212 3d Av.
Humann Anthony, 21 Thomas
Humphreys Thomas. 200 Division
Hun Michael, 555 Pearl
Hunger John, 134½ Broome
Hunt Jacob, 388 Pearl
Hurly P. 143½ Greenwich
Huss V. 41st st.
Hutchinson James, 101 9th Av.
Hyde Benjamin, 50½ Fulton
Hyde William W. 276 Wash.
Hyland J. 176 7th
Ingersoll J. D. 222 Pearl
Inslee Samuel, 449 Hudson
Irwin Robert, 78 6th Av.
Jackson Dennis, rear 154 Orchard
Jacob Henry, 63 Attorney
Jacob Martin, 73 Market
Jacobus T. 143 Waverley place
Jaeger John, 38 Greenwich
Jaeger John C. 110 Cedar
Jeahrling L. 155 3d
Jarvis Jeffrey, 108 Chatham
Jetter Louis, 107 William
Jewell H. E. 49 Pearl
Jewell W. H. 420 West
Juckel Anthony, 44 1st Av.
Johnson A. S. 186 3d Av.
Johnson Henry J. 1 Murray
Johnson H. 245 Centre
Johnson John. 183 Greenwich
Jones N. jr. 242 Cherry
Jones George, 178 Pearl
Jones H. B. 14 Ann
Jones Edward. 156 6th Av.
Jones Peter, 100 Hester
Joyce David, 50 Spring
Juell Robert, jr. 84½ Bleecker
Jung C. H. 231 2d
Jung Frederic, 8th Av.
Jung Jacob, 299 Rivington
Kaery John, 15 Sullivan
Kahler Andrew, 604 Water
Kahn Isaac, 200 Delancy
Kaifer J. E. 12th st.
Kaiser John, 243 Stanton
Kalman B. 264 22d
Kallischkie & Jacobs, 512 Greenwich
Kaltenmarck Joseph, 126 Stanton
Karr John, 71 W. Broadway
Kass Antony, 28 Av. B
Katz Isaac, 259 Water & 234 Canal
Katzenberger Alex. 107 Columbia
Kavanagh Patrick, 67 Market

Kavanagh Thomas, 201 3d Av.
New York.
Kayser Theodore, 352 6th
Keane John S. 187 Chamber
Keane Thomas. 185 Bowery
Keary J. 15 Sullivan
Kearney Jas. 256 Broadway
Keegan Bernard. 134 Mott
Keeler Andrew. 21 Centre
Kealy F. S. 32 4th
Keers John, 829 Broadway
Keim Jacob. 109 Willet
Keiver Jacob. 496 12th
Keiser Paul. 119 Delancy
Keiz John. 130 Greenwich Av.
Kelly Archibald. 107 Amity
Kelly James, 63 West Broadway
Kelly Mury. 54 West Broadway
Kelly Peter, 226 Hudson
Kellner Louis, 66¼ Lewis
Kemner J. W. 31st cor. 7th Av.
Kennedy Roger, 196 Cherry
Kenney J. S. 69 Nassau
Kercher Jacob. 63½ Clinton
Kermode James. 102 Oliver
Kern William, 91 2d
Kornin James. 82 King
Kerr John. 71 W. Broadway
Kerr William, 142 Maiden lane
Kerrigan Thomas. 4 Cortlandt
Kersting John, 118 Elizabeth
Kiefner Andrew. 54 Attorney
Kiernan Joseph H. 67 W. 21st
Kiernan Patrick, 273 Madison
Kiesel Michael. 4 Walnut
Kitfner Christian. 46 Laurens
Kihm Jacob. 186 2d
Kimball & Beasley, 259 Broadway
King Charles, 85 Hamersley
King Michael, 450 Cherry
Kinney Henry, 182 W. 20th
Kinsalla Michael. 302 3d
Kinsalle Daniel, 43 Centre
Kipp John. 337 4th
Kirchers F. 8th Av.
Kirchers Frederick. 41 Cliff
Kircher John, 154 7th Av.
Kirchoff John. 131 Cedar
Kirwen Andrew. 46¼ Cortlandt
Kittler Charles, 70 Suffolk
Kitzer Jacob, 73 Cherry
Klaman John M. 354 Water
Klang & Vogt, 623 Washington
Klaphake Garitt, 76 Stanton
Kleiderer Jacob, 3 South William
Klein Philip. 58 Thompson
Kleiss John M. 130 Greenwich Av.
Klock P. 124
Kloepfer John, 223 Stanton
Klopfer Matteus, 92 W. 18th
Klopper J. 265 3d
Kluc P. 523 6th Av.
Knapp G. 7th Av
Knower G. S & Co. 304 2d
Knox William, 43 Hammond
Knox & Calhoun, 224 Canal
Koh Ehrhard. 65 Ann
Koch George. 8th Av.
Koch S. 367 Madison
Kocher John, 36 Broadway
Koedam Derrick, 88 Murray
Kohlhepp Sebastian, 37 Greenwich
Kolb Lewis, 86 Elm
Koob Philip, 67 Spring
Koon Valentine, 294 Greenwich
Koopmann Bernard, 22 Crosby
Koster Michael. 441 Greenwich
Kraft George. 17 Doyer
Kramer Peter. 80 Ridge
Krausz John, 65 Av. A
Kraux John, 7 Norfolk
Krapp John, 145 do
Krapp John M. 194 Rivington
Kreisenberg Henry, 3¼ Walnut
Kreiter Philip, 22 Sullivan
Kress Christian, 31 Ann
Kresy M., W. 30th st.
Kreutcher Christine, 38 Pearl
Krieff Frederick, 87 Laurens
Krug Adam, 405 Greenwich
Kruger C. 326 Houston
Krury A. 86 Elm

Küchen George, 4 Beaver
New York.
Kuentz ——. 221 Centre
Kuhlmann Henry. 1 Duane
Kuhn J. 191 Franklin
Kulman Bernard. 40 Monroe
Kunckel John M. 22 Peck slip
Kuntz Peter. 808 9th
Kunz Gaiser. 221 Walker
Kunz J. 55 Goerck
Kurfoszt Thomas. 142 Ludlow
Kurtz Frederick W. 110½ William
Kuster Frederick, 38 Thompson
Kydd William. 247 6th Av.
Laal J. 138 Houston
Labach Francis. 310 Rivington
Lahm F. 3 1st Av.
Lally Patrick, 8 Spring
Lamb Peter, 99 Chrystie
Lambart Frederick. 459 Broadway
Lambert Philip. 115½ Division
Lamm D. 24 Laurens
Lampard John G. 26 Hubert
Lane William. 9 Market
Lang John. 267 3d
Lang J. 21 Av. C.
Lang Peter. 156 Fulton
Lang William, 207 Centre
Largan Oliver. 104 Catharine
Langwasser Adam, 103 Broome
Lannon Charles, 35 Monroe
Larkin Daniel A. 89½ Forsyth
Larkin Michael C. 391 10th
Larkin M. C. 389 10th
Larkin & Mulcahy, 87 Forsyth
Lauer Peter, 87 William
Launy Bernard, 379 6th
Lauterbach Solon, 725 Broadway
& 307 Bowery
Lauterborn Peter, 185 Amos
Lavery Peter, 99 Oliver
Lawless Matthew. 76 3d Av.
Layman Thomas, 71 Anthony
Laying John. 30 Ann
Lazerus George, 239 Centre
Leamy David. 329 Pearl
Leamy Jeremiah, 194 8th Av.
Leamy Michael, 90 Broadway
Leavy Michael, 70 Willett
Lebrech Francis. 117 Ridge
Ledig George F. 23 Peck slip
Lee Richard. 19 Henry
Lefferts William H. 626 Hudson
Lehm Peter. 3 1st Av.
Leicht John M. 29 Broadway
Leifels Charles, 129 3d
Leight George L. 402 Water
Leight J. M. 222 Broadway
Lehing John B. rear 151 Forsyth
Lemlein Benjamin, 133 Spring
Leming Patrick, 578 Hudson
Lender M. 178 2d
Lennon James, 73 Nassau
Leonard Hugh, 1 White
Leonard Owen. 612 Water
Leonard Patrick. 210 Division
Leonhard Charles, 132 Forsyth
Leppert Charles, 470 Broome
Levy S. 186 2d
Lewenburger Jacob, 238 Stanton
Lewerth Peter, 46 Mercer
Lewis Joseph C. 19 4th Av.
Lienhardt Theodore, 108 Eldridge
Lilly Patrick. 100 Delancy
Limbeck Michael, 236 3d
Limmer Christian. 127 Ridge
Linden James. 52 Robinson
Linder Martin, 178 3d
Ling L. J. 153 3d
Linn J. & C. 522 Greenwich
Little Andrew. 186 6th Av.
Liuwig William. 140 Prince
Lloyd Robert. 8th Av.
Long Peter. 31 Cornelia
Lorimer Alexander. 23 4th Av.
Losch Albert. 109 Willett
Losch A. 146 3d
Lotalie John. 96 Reade
Loughry Mark, 198 William &
119 John
Louis M. 157 Broadway
Lout Philips, 78 Ludlow

Lovett & Southwick, 259 Pearl
New York.
Lustie I. 150 Broome
Lunny B. 379 6th
Ludwick William, Prince st.
Lutz Michael, 175 Elm
Lutzen Fred. 732 Washington
Lux Abraham. 403 West
Lux Henry, 212 Spring
Lyman, Sears & Co. 3 William
Lynch Hugh. 87 Centre
Lynch John, 26 Spruce
Lynch Michael, 194 Monroe
Lynch R. 200 Av. A
Lynn J. & C. 522 Greenwich
Lyons Thomas. 274 Greenwich
Lyons E. 121 Hammond
M'Alister Mary. 7 4th Av.
M'Bride Jms. 72 Greenwich Av.
M'Brien Arthur. 348 Hudson
M'Brien E. 136 Cherry
M'Callister M. 1 3d Av.
M'Carthy Michael. 33 Cedar
M'Canny ——, 475 Cherry
M'Collom James. 246 Mott
M'Comb William. 18 11th
M'Cool Barney, 60 W. Broadway
M'Cord William. 29 4th
M'Cormick John, 74 8th Av.
M'Cormick William. 69 Orange
M'Coy Alexander, 21 Oak
M'Coy John, 36 4th
M'Cue John. 20 do
M'Daniel Edward, 4 Orange
M'Dermott Hugh. 35 Centre
M'Dermott John, 66 Cherry
M'Dode J. 90 King
M'Donald John, 2 1st
M'Evoy Francis. 69 Factory
M'Farland & Brogg. 172 Pearl
M'Farquhar J. 155 Greenwich
M'Feely Bernard. 144 Chatham
M'Galliaudy Peter, 301 W. 19th
M'Geary James, 69 Maiden lane
M'Gillcuddy P. 55 Washington
M'Gill Philip. 402 8th
M'Ginlay Robert. 20 Oak
M'Ginlay R. 129 Cherry
M'Ginley Thomas. 33 Oak
M'Ginly Thomas, 210 E. 18th
M'Govern James, 97 W. Broadw
M'Guire Thomas, E. 17th bet. Av
A & 1st Av.
M'Guire Henry. 360 10th
M'Gunig R. Michael. 217 Centre
M'Grath Eugene. 437 Hudson
M'Grath John, 159 3d Av.
M'Hugh Patrick, 182 Mott
M'Intyre Hugh. 82 6th Av.
M'Kearning Phillip. 208 Centre
M'Keating Daniel, 260 Division
M'Kenna Michael, 90 do
M'Kenna Terence. 140 Laurens
M'Kernan J. 82 King
M'Kerracher W. G. 235¼ W. 16th
K'Kinzie Andrew. 64 7th Av.
M'Laughlin Daniel, 179 Hudson
M'Laughlin Daniel, 883 Broadw.
M'Laughlin John, 555 Greenwich
M'Laughlin John, 45 Broome
M'Linsock R. 172 Washington
M'Mahon James, 4 Bayard
M'Menomy George. 49 5th
M'Namara Patrick, 408 West
M'Namara Patrick, 383 Water
M'Sorley John, 99 W. Broadway
Maconbrey Robert. 124 6th Av.
Madden William, 107 Hudson
Mafart C. 350 6th
Maguire B. 94 Catharine
Maguire P. H. 102 do
Maguire Thomas, 23½ Centre
Mahon Constantine, 165 3d Av.
Maier Michael. 14 Ridge
Maier Xavier. 25th st.
Mainzer S. 43 Rose
Mairecolar Joseph, 130 Anthony
Major William. 49 Harrison
Mandelbaum Jacob, 47 Orange
Mang William, 14 Church
Manier C. 119 Christopher
Mann Christian F. 88 Hester

Maan Michael, 86 Vandam
　　　New York.
Manning Lawrence, 151 6th Av.
Mannies Mrs. 63 W. Broadway
Mannet M. 42 W. Broadway
Marion D. M. & Co. 212 Pearl
Marki Jacob, 558 Pearl
Marshall Samuel, 473 Washington
Marsters G. 5th Av. corner E. 21st
Marter Leonard, 12 Thames
Martin Dennis, 7 Franklin
Martin Frederick, 111 Wooster
Martin Hugh, 192 Broadway
Martin Jacob, 131 W. 20th
Martin John, 73 Ridge
Martin O. 654 Water
Martin Robert, 74 Nassau
Martin & Wilson, 24 Anthony
Marx Jacob, 105 Madison
Massman Abraham, 71 Cannon
Mastick Peter, 140 Hester
Mather Charles, 162 Division
Mathews John, 396 6th
Matt Aloese, 182 W. 18th
Matthews James, 182 Laurens
Mauer Joseph, 50 Dey
Maurer Frederick, 330 Houston
May John, 79 Ludlow
May Max, 2 Madison
Mayer David, 246 William
Mayer John, 80 Elizabeth
Mayer Raphael, 138 6th Av.
Mayer William, 25 Av. A.
Meeker & Herbert, 94 Pearl
Metr Henry, 4 Rose
Meisner Edward, 150 Broome
Melchior Kuhn, 431 Washington
Miller Jacob, 9th Av.
Meller William, 44 Roosevelt
Menkel John, 129 Varick
Mennon Lawrence, 151 6th Av.
Merkert Frederick, 385 Monroe
Merritt Charles L. 27 Forsyth
Merritt Ira, 158½ Bowery
Metz Morris, 252 Canal
Metiver Jaques, 21 Thomas
Meyer Claus, 80 9th Av.
Meyer Henry, 296 Greenwich
Meyer John, 50 Cross
Meyer John, 124 Broadway
Meyer Michael, 120 W. Broadway
Meygar ——, 70 17th st.
Michael Peter, 21 Le Roy
Michel George, 87 Cedar
Michels Joseph, 152½ Essex
Michelfelder, 239 3d
Middleton & Ryckman, 327 Broad-
　　　way
Mier C. 80½ 9th Av.
Miller & M'Clintock, 283 Green-
　　　wich
Miller Abraham, 285 W. 18th
Miller Abraham M. 211 8th Av.
Miller Charles, 7 Rector
Miller Charles A. 130 Forsyth
Miller Christian, 59 Vesey
Miller Christopher, 6th Av.
Miller Conrad, 43 Greenwich
Miller Francis, 123 Varick
Miller F. 317 West 17th
Miller George, 478 Greenwich
Miller Jacob, 9½ Albany
Miller Jacob, 568 Houston
Miller James, 2 Amos
Miller John, 159 Hammond
Miller John, 244 Division
Miller John, 400 Monroe
Miller John R. 191 6th Av.
Miller J. 176 7th
Miller Martin, 54 Pearl
Miller P. 7th Av.
Miller William, 283 Greenwich
Miller T. 139 3d
Miller & Jack, 509 Greenwich
Mitchell John, 17 Orchard
Mittnacht J. 204 Walker
Moench Peter, 450 Hudson
Moersch Peter, 161 Walker
Moeschen Christian, 91½ Duane
Moessan Jean, 216 William
Moll George, 34 Park Row
Mollstadter John, 117 Bowery

Mollstatter Lawrence, 20 Eldridge
　　　New York.
Monaghan John, 23 Crosby
Mondron Albert J. 183 Broadway
Monestier Adolphe, 21 Thomas
Monhouse I. & Son, 106 Greenwich
Monnie Cornelius, 118 Christopher
Moody John F. 318 Pearl
Mooney John, 94 Mott
Moore Adam, 79 Delancy
Moore J. 20 4th
Moran Alexander, 16 4th
Moran Francis, 73 Reade
Morgenthaler Jacob, 125 Elizabeth
Morrisey B. 599 Greenwich
Morrison John, 59 8th Av.
Morton William, 9th Av
Moses Philip, 71 Greene
Mostler John C. 93 Madison
Mowris Samuel, 600½ Grand
Moynihan T. 448 Washington
Moynihen S. 484 Houston
Muhlenbacher Wm. 188 Orchard
Muldoon Peter, 630 Hudson
Mulleder M. 469 Washington
Muller A. 284 18th
Muller Conrad, 43 Greenwich
Muller F. A. 11 Av. B.
Muller Francis, 317 W. 17th
Muller F. 64 W. Washington place
Muller George, 432 Water
Muller John, 441 Cherry
Muller John, 212 W. 16th
Muller John M. 102 7th Av.
Muller J. 24 Division
Muller Joseph, 125 Georck
Muller Michael, 469 Washington
Muller Phillip, 192 Varick
Muller P. 56 Av. B
Mulligan Bernard, 2 Dry Dock
Mulligan Owen, 80 King
Mulligan P. 381 3d Av.
Munns Henry, 93 Leonard
Murken Fred. 1 West Broadway
Murphy B. 5 Peck slip
Murphy Daniel, 168 Broadway
Murphy Hugh, 27 Morris
Murphy John, 198 W. 15th
Murphy John, Washington st.
Murphy John H. 688 Broome
Murphy Timothy, 285 3d Av.
Murphy William, 121 Roosevelt
Murray R. 165 16th
Murray William, 199 Cherry
Mustiner I. 570 Grand
Nacey Peter, 82 Delancy
Nan John, 61 Church
Nanz John, W. 26th st.
Neal Joseph, 14 Orchard
Nebauer John, 183 W. 19th
Negus Thomas, 171 Greenwich &
　　　174 Bowery
Neibert J. 439 Greenwich
Neligan Maurice, 110 Cedar
Nelson Allan B. 188½ W. 16th
Neuberger Emil, 27 Beekman
Neuhard Christian, 161 Clinton
Neumoller John, 71½ Cross
Neuschwander John, 97 Chrystie
Nevins Andrew, 653 Hudson
Newell W. M. & Co. 111 Pearl
Newman Ward, 371 Bowery
Nichols John G. 261 William
Nichols Harriet, 70 Chatham
Nightingale John, 215½ Division
Noble James, 114 Division
Noez Martin, 303 Houston
Nolan Thomas, 17 Orange
Nolz Martin, 303 Houston
Nolta William, 328 Stanton
Nolte John, E. 27th st.
Noonan Michael, 843 Broadway
Norkauer John, 115 Broome
Norwich Henry, 133 Av. C
Notte William, 328 Stanton
Nugent Michael, 74 King
Nutzel Andreas, 193 Suffolk
Oatley N. R. 187 Pearl
Oberlander Henry, 23 Prince &
　　　259 Broome
Oberlio Lawrence, 596 4th
O'Brien Christopher, 113 Orange

O'Brien John, 16 12th　*New York.*
O'Brien John, 80 Mott
O'Brien Joseph, 10 Marion
O'Brine Willem, 43 Centre
O'Connell Daniel, 360 Hudson
O'Connor John, 42 3d Av.
O'Dey James, 276 Water
O'Deay William, 41 Cherry
Odell Moses, 370 Bowery
O'Driscoll William, 12 Cherry
Odt George, 255 E. 13th
O'Geary Eugene, 56 Centre
O'Hanlon Flemming, 49 Prince
O'Keefe Timothy, 136 Orange
Old Adam, 791 4th
O'Meara James, 196½ Greenwich
O'Melia M. 105½ Hamersley
O'Neil Dennis, 40 Ann
O'Neill James, 221 Water
Oppenheimer E. 147 Attorney
O'Regan Daniel, 168½ William
Orr David, 326 Spring
Osborn Charles, 80 Broadway
O'Sullivan Patrick, 137 Walker
Ostrander H. 174 Canal
Owen William, 178 W. 17th
Pacolin Onesippe, 262 Broadway
Pahnlein George, 74 Thompson
Paine Charles W. 129 Fulton
Pane John, 564 Hudson
Pape Francis, 9 Clinton
Papp Frederick, 125 4th Av.
Parker George W. 1 Amity
Parker William, 127 4th Av.
Parnell Thomas, 52　do
Pasley George, 21 Oak
Patten, Lane & Allen, 192 Pearl
Patterson W. G. 161 Greenwich
Pattison John, 70½ Pike
Pendlebury Thomas, 21 9th Av
Peter Michael, 153 Franklin
Petrie John, 289 Pearl
Petterman J. D. 197 Broome
Pfeiffer Christoph, 108 Reade
Pfeiffer Frederick, 243 5th
Pfeifer John, 428 Monroe
Pfeifer William, 247 Broome
Pfester G. 437 4th
Philips & Clark, 158 Chatham
Phillips Daniel B. 378 Pearl
Pierpont W. N. 60 Greenwich
Piessnecker Fred. 359 Broome
Pietersen Peter, 86 Oliver
Pietsch William A. 25 Hester
Pigot John, 96 Orange
Pikel John, W. 21st cor. 9th Av.
Pinder William, 143 Chrystie
Pirro Peter, 4 Av. C
Plaatje Bartelt H. 18 Chambers
Pohnlein G. 74 Thompson
Pollion James, rear 90 Elizabeth
Porter Alexander E. 436 Hudson
Pors Nicholas, 296 Av. A.
Potter Henry, 47 Jay
Potts John A. 174 Orchard
Pow John, 560½ Pearl
Power James, 184 W. 18th
Presley George, 224 W. 16th
Preist F. 2 Catharine slip
Preist F. 115 Cherry
Prentice Elizabeth, 16th Av.
Prentis James, 199 9th Av.
Price John B. 277 6th Av.
Prinz Henry 3. 249 Stanton
Probst Gottlieb, 104 Ludlow
Prutting & Vogel, 693 Broadway
Purdy David H. 48 Walnut
Putzol M. 264 Stanton
Pye John, 212　do
Quarmby Joan, 88½ Hamersley
Quinzer Lawrence, 318 3d
Quick John R. 2 Wall
Quillen Joseph, 119 11th
Quinlan Patrick, 110 Roosevelt
Quinn Catharine, 51 Orange
Quinn Patrick, 10　do
Railly Francis, 72 E. 11th
Ramming Conrad, 307 Bleecker
Ranshlar Bernard, 172 Walker
Rapt Paul, 65 Forsyth
Rascol Augustin, 94 Reade
Rath A. E. 6½ Cornelia

Rath Daniel, 364 10th *New York.*
Raymond Frederick, 236 3d Av.
Raymond Simeon. 54 Rutgers
Rayner William E. 140 Centre
Ready John. 127 Nassau
Redler M. 73 13th W. Broadway
Reed David. 13 Chambers
Reed Ferd. 16 Bowery
Reed & Gay. 260 Pearl
Rees Lewis, 25 Sullivan
Rogan James, 193 Hester
Reich Samuel, 149 Chrystie
Reiching C.. W. 31st
Reigfei George, 29½ Cornelia
Reinhard Anthony, 31 Thompson
Reinkerner N. 280 2d
Reinwald Augus. & Co. 22 Spruce
Reilly James, 112 11th
Reilly John, 60 9th Av.
Reilly Thomas, 7 12th
Reinhard ——, 31 Thompson
Reisenacker Michael, 115 Willet
Reitenbach John, 337 Rivington
Remmy C. 317 5th
Retsch John, 323 Spring
Rettberg Charles, 18 Ludlow
Rettberg Christian, 17 Essex
Reutlinger Lipman, 207 Houston
Reynolds L. 332 Grand
Reynolds Matthew, 161 9th
Rhoades Richard, 192 Bowery
Rice John, 27 Murray
Richards Wm. W. & Co. 212 Pearl
Ridder Matthias. 73 W. 13th
Riede Jacob, 43 Sullivan
Riehl George, 139 Spring
Riegler G. 29½ Cornelia
Rieppl Margaret. 112 Bedford
Riggart Peter, 563 4th
Riker Abraham, 131 Division
Riker A. jr. 50 Catharine
Riley John C. 225 3d Av.
Riley P.. E. 24th st.
Ringgold James P. 5 Carmine
Ringhauser Henry, 335½ Bowery
Ringlebe John C. 212 Sullivan
Ringlebe J. Carmine st.
Ripp Anton. 237 W. 16th
Rippel J. 113 Bedford
Rittershoffer W. 34 Dey
Ritschy John Jacob, 14 6th Av.
Roach William. 135½ Liberty
Roberts W. 49 9th Av.
Robinson Joseph, 295 Canal
Rocco Sampson. 369 Bowery
Roche John, 6 Centre market pl
Roche John B. 60 Oliver
Roche P. 671½ Broadway
Roche William. 150 W. Broadway
Roe P. 137 Hammond
Roedel Edward, 208 Division
Roedel Henry, 208 Division
Roger Andrew, 104½ Orange
Rogers Amos S. 409 Broadway
Rogers Andrew B. 166 Barrow
Rogers Bradford, 414 Grand
Rogers James, 139 Greene
Rogers James E. 104 Broadway
Rogers Nathan A. 111 Nassau
Rogers R. cor. Hudson & Canal
Rogers Stephen N. 566 Houston
Rohn John, 431 Washington
Rohrig Justus, 3 Frankfort
Ronlands J. G. 292 6th Av.
Romain William H. 272 2d
Roos Henry, 591 Grand
Rosa Antony, 33 Frankfort
Rosenburg Joseph, 118 Rivington
Rosenfeld A. 157 Bowery
Rosentengel Fred. 26 S. William
Roshardt J. 115 Prince
Ross Edward, 148 Orchard
Ross G. H. 367 Houston
Rosswog John, 100 Beekman
Roth Valentine. 10 6th
Roth Vendel, 255 6th Av.
Rothhardt Jacob, 113 Prince
Rothfusz John. 123 Columbia
Roux Stephen, 94 Forsyth
Ruckert S. T. 559 4th
Ruf Frederick. 224 Rivington
Rufner John, 82 Eldridge

Rumsby George, 86 8th Av.
New York.
Rurnsey G. 188 8th Av.
Russell John J. 48 Vandam
Ruth Daniel. 364 10th
Ryan James, 277 Madison
Ryan Martin. 61 King
Ryckman Robert W. 117 B.way
Ryder Henry V. 110 Fulton
Ryder Uriah. 233 Broadway
Saelfeld Andrew, 165 Ludlow
Sackville John. 209 Bowery
Sagbold John C. 114 Charles
Salb F. 4 Crosby
St. John Rufus, 182 Christopher
Selley Francis, 11 Walnut
Salomon Francis, 65 4th Av.
Samek Samuel, 91½ Av. D
Sammis Abel, 150 Grand
Sammis Leander M. 188 Grand
Sammis D. P. 484 Grand
Sarles Hickson, 631 Broadway
Sathan ——, 199 William
Saul Augustus, 122 Clinton place
Saul A. 122 8th st.
Saunders Thomas, 26 John
Schachner George, 297 Division
Schade John, 96 Greenwich
Schaefer George, 6 John
Schaefer Lewis, 4 New
Schaeffer, C. W. 351 Broome
Schafer Geo. 226 Houston
Schafer John, 179 Hester
Schafer Nicholas, 197 Broome
Schaffer Charles, 59 Essex
Schaffer George, 1 Barclay
Schaffer J. 254 Houston
Schaffer John, 67 Laurens
Schaffner John, 576 Grand
Schaike Jacob, 240 W. 16th
Schambach H. 42 West
Schamberger Charles F., E. 25th
Schanzenbach Charles, 96 W. 20th
Scharf ——, 475 Cherry
Schazingen John, 8 Albany
Scheffmeyer ——, 141 Bowery
Scheffmeyer Michael, 59 Anthony
Scheideler William, 178 Prince
Schell Pol, 276 Spring
Scherer J 153 Franklin
Scherer Jacob, 176 Varick
Scheurmann C. 85 3d
Scheurmann Philip. 243 8th Av.
Scheurmann Philip, 77 3d
Schimel G., E. 28th st.
Schlauder Anthony, 199 2d
Schlegel George, 389 6th
Schleicher N. 125 3d
Schler Agust. 324 8th st.
Schloss L. 213 Houston
Schlund William, 726 Houston
Schmidlin Joseph. 46 Av. A
Schmidtlein John, 77 Greene
Schmidt John, 27 Chrystie
Schmidt John E. 136 Centre
Schneer Leopold, 268 Stanton
Schnees George, 235 Delancy &
28 Broome
Schneider John, 467 Greenwich
Schneider H. 11 Broome
Schneider Louis, 179 Prince
Schneider Matthias, 272 Spring
Schnurmann Henry, 196 Delancy
Schoberth Frederick, 194 Wooster
Schoeppler Michael, 79 James
Scholl John, 342 1st Av.
Scholl Philip, 187 11th
Schott Anthony, 700 Water
Schrack C. A. 6th Av.
Schrapper John, 106 Greene
Schreiber Henry, 68 Houston
Schreiber John, 44 Av. B
Schreiner Caspar, 155 Essex & 192
Clinton
Schrerber Martin, 246 6th
Schrieber Franz, 147 Lewis
Schroeder Ernest, 29 Perry
Schroff Gottlieb, 67 Mulberry
Schuart John, 79 Sullivan
Schumacher William, 106 Cherry
Schwartz Andrew, 17 Madison
Schwartz Peter, 116½ 3d Av.

Schweitzer Jacob, 11 Frankfort
New York.
Schwenk Frederic, 466 4th
Schweir Ernest. 22 6th Av.
Schwickert Anthony, 338 Mercer
Scollam Hugh, 30 Clark
Schranter F. E. 27th st.
Scribner Abraham S. 219 Bleecker
& 334 Grand
Scribner Sam. T. 3 Av. D.
Scullan H. 30 Clarke
Sebastian L. 267 W. 16th
Sechel Solomon, 29 Frankfort
Segar Henry, 73 Allen
Seigfried William, 33 Pitt
Seippel William, 125 Norfolk
Seith Michael, 92 Henry
Seleman Bernard, 57 Fulton
Senft Lawrence, 258 Walker
Senier James, 315 3d
Senpert M. 296 Greenwich
Sevestre Louis, 2 Eldridge
Shad John, 102 W. 17th
Shangambah Philip, 190 Duane
Shannahan M. 62 Montgomery
Shannon Hugh, 75 Orange
Shannon Philip, 94 James
Shannon Samuel, 145 Houston &
123 Av. D.
Shannon William, 24 James
Shaw Benjamin. 73 Canal
Shaw John, 370 Bleecker
Sheahan Daniel. 1 6th
Sheffmeyer George, 131 Bowery
Sherwood Andrew, 177 W. 17th
Sheumann Geo. 304 Spring
Sholl Daniel, 111 W. 17th
Shonwalter W. 50 Houston
Short Thomas, 162 W. Broadway
Shrack George A. 160 6th Av.
Shuart Isaac C. 126 8th Av.
Shuart John, 79 Sullivan
Shuhard George. 2 Crosby
Shutt Andrew, 29th West
Siebert Henry, 16 Cannon
Sievert Nicholas, 87 Charlton
Sipert Michael, 395½ Greenwich
Skeate George. 43 Beekman
Slater John. 241 W. 18th
Slattery Timothy, 187 Orange
Slider Henry, 64 Roosevelt
Smiley Charles, 369 Greenwich
Smith A. 277 Pearl
Smith A. 97 4th
Smith D. 36 9th Av.
Smith Charles H. 464 Washington
Smith George, 216 8th Av.
Smith H. 276 8th Av.
Smith Henry, 66 W. 17th
Smith Hugh. 222 W. 21st
Smith I. H. 376 Av. B.
Smith James, 392 Bleecker
Smith James, 313 1st Av.
Smith John, 212 Mott
Smith John, 10th Av.
Smith Nathaniel C. 174 8th Av.
Smith Nicholas. 412 Cherry
Smith William, 188 Bowery
Smith and Risley, 142 Chatham
Smullan Andrew, 284 Division
Sneider John, 96 Sheriff
Sleider P., W. 19th cor. 7th Av.
Snell William, 129 Henry
Soder William, 655 Washington
Soffe Henry, 326 Bowery
Sommer Louis, 105 Rivington
Souller Philip J. 11 5th
Southerland Charles R. 135 Charles
& 543 Hudson
Spaeth Josep., 73 Mulberry
Spear Albert I. 706 Greenwich
Specht Peter, 142 Elm
Spence Thomas, 573 Greenwich
Spanser John, 49½ Orange
Sperber John, 204 Rivington
Spillane James, 326 Pearl
Spor George, 34 James
Springsteen Abram. 232 Bleecker
Srutz Christopher, 141 Mulberry
Stain Isaac, 11 Hester
Stakem Peter, 107 19th
Stamp Peter C. 1 James slip

Stanford Thomas, 202 W. 21st
New York.
Stanley George, 29 Cornelia
Stanley William, 20 Walnut
Stansbury James F. 258 Canal
Stanf Sebastian, 247 2d
Stark Adam A. 323 Broome
Stark John L. 323 Broome
Stark Nicholas, 365 6th Av.
Starke F. 78 West Broadway
Starling & Cushing, 86 Beaver & 133 Pearl
Stauzenbach Eckhardt,194 W.16th
Stefan Herman, 230 Church
Stehl Bernard D. 616½ 4th
Steil John, 21 Mulberry
Stein Jacob, 85½ Pitt
Steindecker V. 281½ Broome
Steller John J. 43½ Allen
Stenir Francis. 38 Clinton
Stephens Bartholomew, 116 John
Stephens & Hughes, 170 Chatham
Stevens Pascal, 172 Hester
Stevenson John, 373 8th
Stewart William, 274 Canal
Stewrwald Peter. 176 3d Av.
Stiles Joseph, 154 Duane
Stillman James, 82 Allen
Stillman Thomas. 238 Greenwich
Stitt William J. 64 Av. C.
Stock M. 563 Grand
Stoller John J. 49½ Eldridge
Stout Joseph M. 100 6th Av.
Stout & Ward, 253 Pearl
Strass Charles, 186 Grand
Straub J. F. 282 E. 13th
Straub P. 7th Av.
Straus Bernard, 85½ Delancy
Stuart William, 46 Amity
Stulf Simon, 307½ & 318 West
Stumpf Mathes, 290 11th
Stupp Michael, 32 Vestry
Stupp Peter, 7th Av. cor. 18th
Sullivan D. 32 W. Broadway
Sullivan Timothy, 213 Canal
Susser Eugene, 175 Broadway
Sutton Thomas, 432 10th
Sutton N. A. 133 Chatham
Swain John, jr. 233 Broadway
Swaney Thomas, 246 8th Av.
Swany Andrew F. 57 Norfolk
Swartz Philip, 160 3d Av.
Sweeney Charles, 99 4th
Sweeney Patrick, 92 Cherry
Syers Joseph L. 675 4th
Taggart Edward. 217 Mott
Tallmage A. 675 4th
Tameier G. 84 Essex & 76 Hudson
Tanton J. H. 183 Varick & 693 Washington
Taylor Abner, 296 Greenwich
Taylor James, 44 Watts
Taylor Thomas, 133 Forsyth
Teare John, 439 Hudson
Tegen Michael. 23 Cornelia
Thalman Morris, 393 Broome
Thatcher John P. 233 Houston
Theilig Franz, 29½ Wooster
Theiss Henry, 39 Suffolk
Thiemann Wilhelm, 321 8th
Thomas Edward, 66 W. 13th
Thomas George, 201 Prince
Thomas J. C. 337 4th
Thorbun J., E. 27th st.
Tichner Marax, 46 Lewis
Tierman F., E. 22d st.
Tilton Silas, 257 Greenwich
Tilleston W. M. 119 Pearl
Tilley John, 294 Division
Tithorn John, 261 Rivington
Tittle Henry, 266 3d
Tobin William, 93½ James
Torny Dennis, 125½ Sheriff
Totman Aaron, 42 4th Av.
Townsend John R. 23 12th
Trapp Francis A. 32 Ann
Trapp Loui, 58 Walnut
Trask A. & A. G. 124 Maiden lane
Treanor Michael. 22 Rector
Trench E. 4 Bleecker
Trenor John. 646 Hudson
Tucker Charles E. 16½ Carmine

Tully Walter. 70 Bank *New York.*
Turkington Wm. 212 Church
Tyrall John, 20 Orange
Uckale Paul, 91 Henry
Ulrich George, 16 Dey
Ulshofer Johann, Av. A between 12th & E. 13th
Ulstch G. 112 Charles
Underhill Caleb. 145 Madison
Underhill Peter S. 52 Nassau
Van Duzer Henry R. 215 Mercer
Van Heynigen N. 158 Spring
Van Horn John, 33 3d Av.
Van Luzer Richard, 111 Stanton
Van Tobel H. 4th st.
Van Wagner John. 198 Greenwich
Vangan James, 343½ Water
Van Winkle A, 7 Christopher
Vaughan James, 343½ Water
Veld George, 70 W. 17th
Veigele C. bet. 16th & 17th
Veitenheimer Louis, 65 1st
Vetter C. 92 Norfolk
Vetter Peter. 90 Essex
Vetterley L., W. 30th
Venlquez J. 1 John
Vienot John P. 49 Anthony
Vieshon Francis J. 648 Greenwich
Vogel John, 117 Varick
Vogel Michael. 29 King
Vogt John. 4 Hammond
Voignier N. rear 53 Anthony
Voll M. 36 Bedford
Vose, Wood & Co. 131 Water
Wachter J. 147 Crosby
Wagner L. W. 31st
Wagner & Plock, 88 Broadway
Wehler M. 173 2d
Wuhler M. 166 do
Waldick William, 154 Prince
Waldmyer Martin, 671 Water
Walker Robert, 162 Canal
Walker & Wilson, 126½ do
Wall Andrew, 562 Grand
Wellaur John. 5 Pell
Wallhuiser Philip, 99 W. 18th
Walling Benjamin, 255 Spring
Walling John, 225½ Washington
Walling J., W. 29th
Walmood Philetus, 388 6th
Walter George, 119 Sheriff
Ward Henry. 62 Broadway
Wardell Richard. 615 Greenwich
Wardtz Henry, 80 Willet
Warth John W. 50 Catharine
Waterbury & Tammis, 99, 101 & 103 Catharine
Waters Michael, 62 Centre
Watkins John L. 114 Fulton
Watkins Osmer S. 7 Catharine
Warmuth B. 386 8th
Watkins & Carlock, 324 Hudson
Watson Patrick, 720 Washington
Watts Garrick, 200 E. 13th
Webber Alexander, 16½ Canal
Webber Jacob, 306 Spring
Webber Robert, 205 6th Av.
Weber Peter, 40th st. 9th Av.
Weckehle M. 385 6th Av.
Wedekind Augustus, 251 Walker
Wedekind Ernest, 105 Eldridge
Weed William, 86 Bowery
Weibel Joseph, 2 Pine
Weightman George, 166 Greene
Weil Simon, 165 2d
Weilhard John, 184 Church
Weiner Anthony, 1 Anthony
Weis George, 157 Broome
Weise John G. 101 Reade
Weiser T. 43 Centre
Weide Frederick, 255 Rivington
Welsh Michael. 154 W. 16th
Werner Adam, 155 Chrystie
Werner Caspar, 133 Cannon
Wessel Louis, 49 Hudson
Wesson D. & A. 157 Pearl
West John, 6 Mott
Westgate Isaac, 2 Rivington
Wetstein John, 17 Hudson
Wheeler Addison J. 22 Spruce
Wheeler William, 241 E. 11th
White Edward, 46 E. Broadway

White John, 16 Thompson
New York.
White Matthew, 42 Elm
White Maurice K. 613 Hudson
White William, 583 Greenwich
Whiting Perez S. 47 Canal
Whiting W. L. 436 Broadway
Whyte John, 13 3d Avenue
Wicht William, 376 Houston
Wiegand John C. L. 122 Eldridge
Wieman Henry, 13 Bedford
Wiesman John. 357 4th
Wigers John, 98 Wooster
Wiggins James, 212 Greenwich
Willuert Charles, 207 Broome
Will John, 8th Av.
Willan Robert, 400 Pearl
Wille Joseph, 218 5th
William Adam, 107 7th Av.
Williams John, 42 Nassau
Williams John, 8th Av.
Wilson J. 178 Houston
Wilson Matthew, 106 Roosevelt
Wimprass Abraham, 138 Norfolk
Windeler John H. 182 Division
Wineker N. N. 6th Av.
Wingal Christopher, 44 Spruce
Winter Louis, 110 Macdougal
Winter E J. 161 Broome
Winterfield Samuel, 17 Elizabeth
Withers R. 638 Grand
Wittenauer Louis, 15½ Thames
Wizendorf Henry, 6 Orange
Woest Frederick. 117 Charles
Wohlferdt August, 46 Grand
Wolf Henry, 40 Pell
Wolf Leonard, 42 Beekman
Wolf M. 295 Houston
Wolf Peter. 168 Delancy
Wolf T. 28 E. 10th
Wolf Valentine. 29 Ludlow
Wolff Jacob, 107 Essex
Woll John H. 7 Rutgers
Wolpert Martin, 161 Laurens
Woods John, 7 4th
Woods Patrick, 720 Washington
Woolmer Emanuel. 6 Pell
Worth J. 243 Delancy
Wrede A. 176 Varick
Wright William, 233 Greenwich
Wurster C. 6½ Greenwich Av.
Wikes George, 29½ Thompson
Xaverbill Francis, 151 Canal
Yates Henry, 179 12th
Youdale Jonathan, 21 Duane
Young Charles, 231½ 3d
Young G. 124 Cherry
Young J. 107 Houston & 49 Av. D
Young William M. 125 Fulton
Young William, 14½ Ann
Zabinski Adolphus, 144 Leonard
Zukschwest C. 100 Cherry
Zeller Hartman, 167 Forsyth
Zeller John, 204 William
Zimerman Carl, 209½ 1st Av.
Zimmerman Henry. 244 3d
Zimmerman Wm. 87½ Bowery & 243 Elizabeth
Zimmernauer L 70 Bayard
Zinzer H. L. 102½ Cherry

Niagara County.

Lichtenwalder Benjamin, Pekin
Cambria.
Pletcher John
Hagerty George,   do
Petts William   *Lewiston.*
Ridell George
Alden William
Barstow Moses, Pekin
Wilson H. C.   *Lockport.*
Sears Charles
Van Sickler Thomas
Glassford T. P. & G. W.
Whitcher B. H.
Whitting William
Paige Henry
Botsford Nathan
Ballou D. W.
Lewis D. G.   *Newfane.*
Prentice George

Whitney S., Olcott *Newfane.*
Lockwood William, Olcott
Hart B. H. *Pendleton.*
Millard Edw. Youngstown *Porter.*
Graves & Durfy, do
Graves David, do
Cleaveland —— *Royalton.*
Griswold G. & M. R. *Somerset.*
Nye Willard
Ducher Mathew P.
Shepard Norman *Wilson.*
Vosburg ——

Oneida County.

Roberts T. J. *Boonville.*
Halsted J. 181 Genesee *Utica.*
Needham W. M. 28 do
Gucker D., Varick st.
Enins J. 6 Main

Onondaga County.

Eaton S. *Lysander.*
Carpenter A. Baldwinsville
Allen & Baldwin, do
Stilwell & Son *Manlius.*
Tripp J. Bank Building, Syracuse
Salina.
Root A. Salina st., Syracuse
M'Dougal D. Genesee st. do
Bronson H. Water st. do
Wilson J., Warren st. do
Hancock Wm., do do
Murphy P. H. James st. do
Jordan Wm., Salina st. do
Tarke G. do do
Papple William, Park st. do
Kelly S. do
Hichcock O. *Skaneateles.*
Porter L.
Dyer Thomas

Ontario County.

Denton S. *Canandagua.*
Foster William K.
Lines S. V.
Green E. N.
Bradley Orrin L. *East Bloomfield.*
French & Judd
Lockwood Joseph *Gorham.*
Fisher Peter
Lackett Caleb, Larned's Corners
Hopewell.
Henry ——, Chapinsville
June. Joseph & Co. *Phelps.*
Hubble George
Carey Harvey
Ratcliff ——
Tallmadge J. Allen's Hill
Richmond.
Tungate Samuel, do
M'Michael Thomas, Honeoye
Moshier William, Geneva *Seneca.*
Savage & Ardell, do
Lunn Daniel L. do
Mitchell & Hayward, do
Coon & Turk, do
Cunningham ——, do
Gray Jo-hua, do
Mead ——, do
Crandall O. A. *South Bristol.*
Pitcher Henry
Turner W. J. *Victor.*
Beaver J. M.
Bushwell H. *West Bloomfield.*
Warren ——

Orange County.

Redker J. V. L. Salisbury Mills
Blooming Grove.
Finney John, Salisbury Mills
Foster J. L. *Chester.*
Tuthill S.
Foster E.
M'Coy R.
Rider William H. *Cornwall.*
Chatfield J. & N.
Hollett A. M.
Brundage F. (Ladies' shoes)
Avery Wm. Buttermilk Falls
Harris Edward, do
Highnoldt C. do

Terwilliger M. *Crawford.*
M'Cullough J. Port Ferris
Deer Park.
Birdsall N. do
Ridgway J. M. do
Kane A. *Goshen.*
Purdy B. S.
Smith Hiram
Redfield & Russell
Howell John
Pierson W. M.
Masters G. W. *Hamptonsburgh.*
Greeves A. Ridgebury *Minisink.*
M'Carter J. H. Slate Hill
Hartford J. F. Wells' Corners
Tapping F., Westown
Furgerson Wm. Unionville
Brown G. do
Jennings V. R. do
Utter John T. *Montgomery.*
Conklin Abram
Stevens W. S.
Peck Joseph
Odell John W. Walden
Clearwater N. T. do
Brooks O. T. *Monros.*
Drake G. Otisville *Mount Hope.*
Quackenboss D. P. do
Skinner E.
Van Sicklen T. 106 Water
Newburgh.
Morris Patrick, Water st.
Warren M. & J. W. 78 Water
Atwood William, 80 do
Rydel Michael, 90 do
Buchanan Isaac, 100 do
M'Coun & Bradley, 94 do
Anderson Joseph, Broadway
Pierce William, Colden st.
Leslie Daniel, Water st.
Mecklen Geo. 35 do
Wittencher Augustus, Front st.
Dennis Thomas, 2d st.
Barnett J. 3d st.
Hawthorn Samuel, *New Windsor.*
Taylor D. N. New Hampton
Wallkill.
Knibbs G. do
Ludlum W. T. South Middletown
Clark John, do
Gibbs M. H. do
Canfield J. G. do
Goodale A. do
Houston & Wickham, do
Smith B., Amity *Warwick.*
Stevens W. A. Edenville
Green J. New Milford
Demarest J. G. (Leather dealer)
Knapp J. Sugar Loaf
Jennings G. E. Florida
Lewis M. G. do
Stringham J. D. do

Orleans County.

Chase G. & Co. Albion *Barre.*
Hall Henry, do
Lafferty A. do
Martin B. G. Barre Centre
Dunham Mortimer, do
June John *Carlton.*
Rich Albert
June Benjamin
Fish Henry S. *Clarendon.*
Dutcher Platt
Bartlett R.
Collins S. *Gaines.*
Bidelman Wm. S.
Doll A. *Kendall.*
Bird A.
Huff Richard, Holley *Murray.*
Hurd Henry, do
Jenkins L. D. Hulburton
Downs David, Sandy Creek
Beers H. M., Medina *Ridgeway.*
Foster Wm. P. do
Ferguson I. & H. do
Gilbert T. do
Skinner I. do
Pratt C., Knowlesville
Hawley Gideon *Shelby.*
Allen W. P. Millville

Morehouse John *Yates.*
Eastman Benjamin
Ogden Edwin, Lyndonville
Coan Heman, do
Phillips Michael, do
Fuller Otis, do
Calkins ——, County Line

Oswego County.

Fuller Jesse *Albion.*
Pierce Horace
Whitney John
Carter J. & R., Carterville *Amboy.*
Pearson, Allen & Co.
Little Wm. *Constantia.*
Scott A.
Bentley J.
Champlin H.
Robbins E. P., Cleaveland
Robbins H. do
Dunn —— do
Watson & Co. Oswego Falls
Granby.
Bingham Philemon *Hannibal.*
M'Roy P.
Johnson P. *Hastings.*
Baxter E. W., Central Square
Pruden Joseph do
Ames & Mitchell *Mexico.*
Gregory & Merriam
Henry Chester
Gibbs Robert
Ames Harry, Colosse
Johnson Wm. do
Burghart David, Union Square
Halsey Wm., Prattville
Merriam S. G. *New Haven.*
Allen H. B.
Birch Hilan *Orwell.*
Pennick M. & Co. Bridge st.
Oswego.
Hunt Henry T. 1st st.
Foster Dennis, Seneca st.
Leverick J. B. 8 Phoenix Block
Warn John C. *Parish.*
Washburn Frank *Redfield.*
Salisbury D. C., Pulaski
Richland.
Keeney Chas.
Tucker & Keeney
De Corey Joseph
Wells Calvin
Allen Horace B., Phoenix
Schroeppel.
Hutchinson John do
Leslie Wm. do
Coburn N. Hinmansville
Clarkson Wm. do
Smith Charles, Gilbert's Mills
Whitmarsh Jacob *Scriba.*
Kinney Patrick
Selden J. & J. *Williamstown.*
Hall Joseph
Winfield Wm.
Cockran Samuel

Otsego County.

Soule B. St. John *Burlington.*
Park Avery
Chapin L. H., West Burlington
Wood Truman, Burlington Flatts
Lull & Son *Butternuts.*
Stevenson N.
Winney J. *Cherry Valley.*
Waldron S.
Howe O.
Maslin W.
Daly J. *Decatur.*
Tipple George
Kaple Chas.
Bilyea John *Edmeston.*
Bilyea Isaac
Joslyn Wm.
Simmons L. F.
Clarke John, West Edmeston
Nevins John *Exeter.*
White Freeland
Fisk Alanson, West Exeter
Palmer Ira, Schuyler's Lake
Atkinson George W. do
Cono S. B. *Hartwick.*

Benedict A.   *Laurens.*
Fuller B.
Hudson C.
Inglesby ——
Johnson James   *Middlefield.*
Warner Charles
Dusenbery Henry S.
Watson Nathan
Soules Selas A.
Bishop James
Face Henry
Hand Isaac
Bartlett A.   *Milford.*
Devoe J.
Thorn L. D.
Fitch H.   *New Lisbon.*
Cook J.
Hurd & Palmer
Duroe F.
Bonnett E. W.   *Oneonta.*
Pardee Henry S.
Brewer Jairus
Avery John
Dillingham John
Gorham Wm., West Oneonta
Green Clark,   do
Bush J. G., Cooperstown *Otsego.*
Bailey & Beadle do
Drake O.   do
Robinson H. M. do
Person E.   *Plainfield.*
M'Reynolds J.
Stricklin ——
Tracy ——
Hosford L. H.   *Richfield.*
Hitchcock J. B.   *Springfield.*
Hanford Wm. H.   *Unadilla*
Wood N.   *Westford.*
Childs Isaac S.   *Worcester.*
Peach B. F.
Wilsey Alonzo
Hanver Wm.
Oliver Henry
Snyder Martin, East Worcester
Stewart Samuel, do

Putnam County.

Knox Charles   *Carmel.*
Brown M.
Sheldon I.
Collins C. Farmer's Mills *Kent.*
M'Carter D.   *Patterson.*
Eastwood C.
Eastwood G.
M'Lean E. Cold Spring
    Phillipstown.
Conboy J.   do
Gardiner Wm. do
Costole J.   do
Frost J. W.   do
Barker J.   *Putnam Valley.*
Crosby S.   *Southeast.*
Northrop J.
Crosby S. S.

Queens County.

Wahmur Henry   *Flushing.*
Lelany M.
Wright P
Heaton J.
Kellam F.   *Hempstead.*
Van Nostrand William
Burtis Henry A.
Conklis Joseph, Rockaway
Beckhorn Joseph, Millburn
Cox Elbert, Raynor Town
Willet Samuel, Far Rockaway
Scott A.   do
Hulse & Snediker *Jamaica.*
Parshall & Oritman
Hoogland George
Amberman A
Leech O. P.
Fries J. Brushville
Everett P. Astoria   *Newtown.*
Casey L.   do
Stilwell J. M., Roslyn
    North Hempstead.
Wood John   *Oyster Bay.*
Stearnis Barn

Earl Henry   *Oyster Bay.*
Latting Joseph
Hawkhurst Edward
Thurston William
Thurston Samuel
Van Dam Scott
Farrington Samuel, Norwich
Layton A., Wolver Hollow
M'Queen A.   do
M'Kay & Johnson, Jericho
Tenbroeck G.   do
Townsend Walter, do
Thurston P.   do
Thurston N. & H. do

Rensselaer County.

Learned A. 213 State
    Lansingburgh.
Spicer J. 223 State
Johnston Geo. M. 209 State
Johnson James, 220 State
Willett J. H. 298 State
Peets Lewis, 197 Congress
Cobbett William, Ferry st.
Stiles S.   do
Wilbur K. & Co.   *Nassau*
Fisher H.   *Petersburgh.*
Gregory S. & E. M. *Sandlake.*
Bonham M. 40 2d   *Troy.*
Bonteeon P. 9 Congress
Bordelean C. 170 4th
Brown J. H 5 Grand Division
Brown & Prouty, 5 Boardman's
    Buildings
Bruce J. 2 Washington square
Bruce William, 3 Grand Division
Butterfield Wm. C. 126 River
Colburn J. 37 Federal
Cox Thomas, 69 Congress
Curtis J. Iron Works
Davis R. 3 Boardman's Buildings
Davis Robert, 351 River
Dolan J. 10 Congress
Dolan M. 11   do
Duffy S. 8   do
Eustace C. 288 River
Evans John, 134 4th
Felt G. K. near State Dam
Ferguson M. 9 N. 3d
Frink William P. 19½ Congress
Geer J. B. 21   do
Hagan ——, 288 River
Heudley Charles, 9 Boardman's
    Buildings
Hurlt A. Madison st.
Jones D. 310 River
Kirchner L. & L. 12 Congress
Lane John H. 363 River
Miller Wm. 56 Franklin st. Alley
Molley John, 159 4th
Packard C. D. 51 Congress
Parsons Francis, Ida Hill
Pike & Cornell, River st.
Prouty I. 46 Jacob
Rogers John, 139 Congress
Searles James, 124 Ferry
Seiler Joseph, 161 Congress
Spencer John, 113 River
Starks D. D. 86 Congress
Stow F. A. 345 River
Thomas J. P. South Troy
Tobin James, 396 River
Williams John L. 232 River
Wood B. 3 Franklin Square
Wood Edward T. 3 do

Richmond County.

Wilhelmi H. Tompkinsville
    Castleton.
Johnson J.   do
Jennings W.   do
Maines D. W. Factoryville
Wendling J. J. Richmond
    Northfield.
Rathgen J. Port Richmond
Riley T.   do
Lyons Robert, do
Hetherington W., Stapleton
    Southfield.
Temple R.   do

Rockland County.

Perry W. H. Nyack *Orangetown.*
Pitt A.   do
Leuttenberger J. do
Danforth Wm. Piermont

St. Lawrence County.

Denio H. F., Helena *Brasher.*
Elison William   *Canton.*
Turner D. Richville *De Kalb.*
Carlos J.   do
Titus James   *Edwards.*
Guiles Reuben, South Edwards
Gillet Jehiel   *Fowler.*
Sprague Chester F.
Rhodes C. A.   *Gouverneur.*
Smith B.
Smith W.
Goodrich T.
Giles, Powell & Co. *Hammond.*
Hicks Andrew & Co.
Rood Daniel B.
Rattigon James
Tennant James
Fell Chauncy B. W.
Cook & Bingham   *Herman.*
Drake Cyrus   *Hopkinton*
Knapp Willard
Goodnoe Nathaniel
Meacham Thomas
Sears James   *Lisbon.*
Shaw A.   *Louisville.*
Moore O.
M'Pherson B.
Stafford A.
Fairbanks C. P.
Dayton Edwin, Columbia *Madrid.*
Comstock E. L. do
Miller Alexander, Waddington
Dalton P.   do
Ferston Seth, do
Murray James   *Massena.*
Stone J. B.
Bush Parley
Cheeney Uriah
Vantine M. A.
Moore Orvis, Lewisville
Bancroft ——, do
Giffin John   *Morristown.*
Clute Richard
Phillips Henry
Bellinger Ira, Edwardsville
Stiles John,   do
Lamb Alvin   *Norfolk.*
Vilas Alden, Ford st. Ogdensburgh
    Oswegatchie.
Vilas Royale,   do
M'Naughton T. do
Rasey Alexander *Parishville.*
Davis D. H.
Burditt Amasa
Burnap Alvah
Lanphear, Sidney & Albert
    Pierpont.
Mosier Joseph H
Vroman Stewart   *Pitcairn.*
Lewis Daniel   *Potsdam.*
Hopkins Aaron
Perrin & Hosmer
Blaisdell Joshua (Ladies' Gaiters)
Johnstone Hiram
Johnstone John
Glines Benjamin, West Potsdam
Foote Elisha L. Crary's Mills
Copeland Le Roy, do
Whitmarsh E. F.   *Russell.*
Warner A.
Fogg N.
Taylor Orrin   *Stockholm.*
Sharp H.

Saratoga County.

Vaneps Alex. A.   *Carlton.*
Miller T.
Adams Peter
Hawley Henry T. (Ladies' Shoes)
Hanes Daniel, West Carlton
Monroe Wm. A.   *Corinth.*
Dewell A.
Allen D.

Reymond H.   *Corinth.*
Comstock G.
Hyer Alex. B.   *Edinburgh.*
Alverd Calvin
Kellogg E. P.   *Galway.*
M'Cloud
Bradock E.
Morehouse W.
Mosher J.
Olds Otis   *Greenfield.*
Kane Hugh
Mitchell William W.
Clark & Hewitt
Medberry Wm. A.
Wilson Thomas
Gifford John, Weed's Corners
Gilbert Platt C. South Greenfield
Cowles C.   *Halfmoon.*
Cowles B. C.
House Peter
Williams Moses, Ballston *Milton.*
Corey Alexander, do
Rice George   *Moreau.*
Rosell Peter
Stoddard John
Follick Jacob   *Saratoga.*
M'Crady G.
Northrup A.
M'Vity Thomas
M'Cliff Thomas
Scott H.
Sheopard John
Russell William
Robinson Edwin
Rice Ira S.   *Saratoga Springs.*
Walker A.
Clark John
Van Benschoten I.
Strebeck & O'Nell
Burhans H. W.
Wood Joseph   *Stillwater.*
Force John C
Bradt Daniel
Brown John   *Waterford.*
Waldorf M.
Green William   *Wilton.*
Gleason Amos

Schenectady County.

Wilber R. P. W.   *Dunnsburgh.*
Cousau J. 126 State   *Schenectady.*
Van Debogart J. 52 State
Van Debogart ——, 44 do
Springer A. P   do
Stenson J. 125 Union

Schoharie County.

Shafer Frederick   *Blenheim.*
Morehouse Munson
Slingerland T.   *Carlisle.*
Ostrum John H.
Swartbout James
Shoore J.
Hilsinger Jacob E.
Rich George
Phillips J.
Van Vant ——
Van Steenburgh John S. *Cobleskill.*
Abell Wm.   *Esperance.*
Dunning J. A.
M'Masters A., Sloansville
Burt W. Fultonham   *Fulton.*
Boice J.   do
Haynes P.   do
Burt C.   do
Adams George, West Fulton
Bickert ——, Breakabeen
Morse Jacob B.   *Gilboa.*
Brooks J.
Avery John   *Jefferson.*
Rockefeller George
Blodget John   *Middleburgh.*
Vandyke David
Hager David J.
Babcock A.   *Richmondville.*
Pullen Moses W.
Courtier J. W., Warnerville
Hale David   *Schoharie.*
Kniskern J. J.
Marsh Jacob
Fanning Horace

Cramer L.   *Schoharie.*
Hess A.
Hynds A., Hyndsville   *Seward.*
Fox Peter, Leesville   *Sharon.*
Haggert Tunis, Sharon Springs
Pains L., Sharon Centre
Hanson Peter, do
Vrooman N. do
Hartwell F.   *Summit.*
Baldwin G. G.
Loper C. D.
Martin A. Gallupville   *Wright.*
Livingston P. J. do

Seneca County.

Hecker Egidias   *Fayette.*
House John A.   *Romulus.*
House John
Chapman John C.   *Seneca Falls.*
Seeley C. W.
Burritt Stephen

Steuben County.

Rose John   *Bath.*
Smith Orrin
Secor W.
Hoyt S. P.   *Canisteo.*
Allen A. H.
Arnold James A.   *Cohocton.*
Shattuck Lucius
Wood Jacob
Cronk James A. North Cohocton
Spalding Chester   do
Cox George   *Erwin.*
Howell M. A.   *Hartsville.*
Scott W.   *Orange.*
Oviatt L.   *Painted Post.*
Fuller L. T.
Loch C.   *Woodhull.*
Herrick L.

Suffolk County.

Bellows & Gould, South Brookhaven   *Brookhaven.*
Holman Samuel, Port Jefferson
Conklin Lewis, do
Gildersleeve Ezra, Middle Island
Miller Enoch, Moriches
De Long J.   *Huntington.*
Mead Henry N.
Downs Isaac H.
Gildersleeve A. Cold Springs
Burr Townsend, do
Burr E. do
Fledham & Terry   *Riverhead.*
Conklyn Silas T.
Hubbs J. A.   *Smithtown.*
Lhommedieu David
Hildreth Joseph   *Southampton.*
Ellsworth Noah D.
Halsey Agee
Simons W. Smith   *Southold.*
Davis John
Corey Wm. H.
Fanning Phineas
Clark Silas, Mattituck

Sullivan County.

Cornwall D. Barryville   *Lumberland.*
Cummings J. do
Galloway G. Phillipsport   *Mamakating.*
Drake R. H. Bloomingburgh
Everett D. do
Talman J. Wartsboro
Larkin, J. do
Corwin L. do
Tuttle H. W. Burlingham
Atkins A. G. do
Black A. M. Monticello   *Thompson.*
Lyons & Burhans, do

Tioga County.

Clark J. D.   *Rickford.*
Donley & Ayres
Pope J. H.
Tyler Erastus

Atkins Willis   *Spencer*
Casey Daniel
Reynolds Gideon

Tompkins County.

Russell L. F. and Brother   *Enfield.*
Linnis S. Enfield Centre
Jones Niles, do
Hollister & Ferguson   *Newfield.*
Gilbert Lorenzo D.

Ulster County.

Hendrix W. H.   *Kingston.*
Dates Henry
Duffy James
Osterhout Jacob
Newburn Orin, Wall st.
Story A. J. do.
Near William
Green E.
Cashin Edward, Rondout
Thompson H. M. do
Wood & Cole, do
Charles David, High Falls
    Marbletown.
M'Guinnis H. Stone Bridge
Aldrich S.   *New Paltz.*
Corter J.   *Rosendale.*
Davis John W.   *Saugerties.*
Post Abram E.
M'Carthy John
Porter Joseph, Ulsterville
    Shawangunk.
Rogers Wm., Napanock
    Wawarsing.
Nutting ——, do.

Warren County.

Archibald S. R.   *Caldwell.*
Hawley Hiram
Chandler Shelden, Chestertown
    Chester.
Robertson & Palmer, do
Marshall W. do
Balcom Uriah,   *Hague.*
Gear M.
Holley Geo.   *Horicon.*
Lawrence A. M.
Salter Wm. Glenn's Falls
    Queensbury.
Schofield W. do
Danwick J. do
Benedick Ezra, do
Crandall J.   *Warrensburgh.*
Crandall Asa
Nutt Elijah
Pelchere P.

Washington County.

Demars Michael   *Argyle.*
Noland J.
Smith George, North Argyle
M'Millin Andrew, do
Matthew James B. do
M'Quera Daniel, South Argyle
Fitch S. S.   *Cambridge.*
Gow John
Archibald James
Green Samuel
Gillespie Thomas
Day Hiram
Odle John
Welch John
Connolly L. Cambridge Centre
Webb Abel, North Cambridge
Badger Samuel   *Easton.*
Buel Hiram
Taylor P. S. Union Village
Severn Jacob, North Easton
Weeks Giles, do
Perris Thomas N. South Easton
Kingsley Warren B. & Co.
    Fort Ann.
Smith A. F.
Swift Willis
Maxfield Orville
Brown Joseph
Crane Edwin   *Fort Edward.*
Miller John W.

Williams John   *Fort Edward.*
Vanderwarker James, Fort Miller
Johnson. Wells & Co.   *Greenwich.*
Johnson C. P.
Bryant Nahum
Johnson H. O.
Forbush George
Rice Alonzo, Centre Falls
Lewis Alanson. jr. Battenville
Hall William. East Greenwich
White Thomas. Lake
Hawkins William, do
Matthews S B.   do
Smith Archibald. Galesville
Scofield Lewis, North Greenwich
Bullink Samuel,   do
Wood W. S.   *Hampton.*
Waters Uriel
Willis Hiram
Wilson James M'C. West Hebron
                        Hebron.
Bump John H.   do
Wilbur Orrin H.   do
Pierce Hugh,   do
Crawford David,   do
Scott Benjamin,   do
Morehouse Daniel,   do
Smith Abram,   do
Carter ——,   do
Oatman John,   do
Morehouse David, East Hebron
Hand Josi. Sandy Hill *Kingsbury.*
Moss Ai,   do
Griffin Henry,   do
Murphy C. S.   do
Ferris John H.   do
Tarter Isaac,   do
Smith Abram,   do
Brierly James,   do
Ferris James,   do
Harding A. Adamsville
Mosher David   *White Creek.*
Buck D. M.
Crosbee John, Centre
Cookingham G. S., Buskirk's
 Bridge
Johnson W. W., N. White Creek
Chapin C.   *Whitehall.*
Griswold F. H.
Jillson S. F. & H. C.
Tierny J.

Wayne County.

Pennington J. W.   *Arcadia.*
Hoyt James
Rowland Edward
Shaver Jacob
Langworthy Robert
Delevine G. E. Newark
Martin A. S.   do
Patterson George, do
Harris John,   do
M'Gregor Peter,   do
Perry Samuel C. Clyde *Galen.*
Hayton David,   do
Rogers & Cosart   *Lyons.*
Rogers & Beadle
Marshall Stephen
Supple I. R.
Crout George
Boehmler & Francisco
Ripley H. Macedonville *Macedon.*
Brown & Bilbic   *Marion.*
Anderson E. M.   *Palmyra.*
Stead Thomas
Jessop G. G. & Co.
West David   *Rose.*
Riker Henry
Ogram John
Howland George
Lyman Levi A.
Wilson Jonathan
Shaver Henry   *Sodus.*
Okuffe William   *Williamson.*
Washburn L. D.
Pallister ——, Pultneyville
Merrill B. A.   *Wolcott.*

Westchester County.

Brindley William, (ladies shoes)
                        Bedford.

Brown A. Peekskill *Courtlandt*
Benedict John,   do
Raymond P. & Co. do
Bishop A. Tarrytown *Greenburgh.*
Newman Clarke, Cross Lines
                        Lewisborough.
Brown Harvey, (ladies shoes)
 Pleasantville *Mount Pleasant.*
See Abel, Pleasantville
Feed John,   do
Romer H.   do
See J. Israel,   do
Farrington T. do
Pelton H. F.   *Newcastle.*
Bath C.
Miller C. jr. Sing Sing *Osinsing.*
Clark John B.   do
Robinson Wm.   do
Ayles Stephen.   do
Murray Francis   *Poundridge.*
Slater Purdy, Portchester *Rye.*
Mack Charles   do
Baxter Stephen   *Westchester.*
Cox John
Nostrand A.   *West Farms.*
M'Gill William
Moore W. M.
Hopps Thomas   *White Plains.*
Matthias Henry
Riviere J. M.   *Yonkers.*

Wyoming County.

Parsons Wm. K.   *Bennington.*
Waiting John, Cowlesville
Lotson James,   do
Halsted & Matthews   *Castile.*
Burr T. J.
Hoagland P.
Connor M. O
Buck Phillip
Hitchcock O.   *China.*
Edwards B. F.
Brooks A.   *Eagle.*
Wratten & Shay, Eagle Village
M'Tigart ——, *Genesee Falls.*
Brown & Smith
Sarles Silas
Merwin James
Tower Asahel
Printis D. Wyoming *Middlebury.*
Ewell Columbus, do
Bezanson James, do
Gurnsey James,   do
Wait A.   do
M'Cabe William   *Orangeville.*
Chapin W. J. & Son   *Perry.*
Higgins E. & Co.
Ten Eyck J. W.
Barnes A. C.
Ball D. Perry Centre
Wiles ——, do
Heath S.   *Pike*
Withy J.
Griffith E.
Gardner Z. S.   *Sheldon.*
Emerick Frederick
Miller David, Strykersville
Raymond M. S. Varysburg
Bronson Isaac C.   *Warsaw.*
Truax John

Yates County.

Swarthout J. S.   *Barrington*
Condit J. D. & A. F.   *Benton*
Tozer ——, Belona
Pelton W. M. & C. A. Branchport
                        Jerusalem.
Paris James, Branchport
Taylor J. Middlesex
Francisco H. M. do
Crane S. & J. Penn Yan   *Milo.*
Howard J. B. Potter Centre *Potter.*
Windnagle J. E.
Stout James G.
Briggs N. William, Yatesville
Howell Yakely, Rushville
Hill H. P. V.   do
Swift James,   do
Tompkins D. & C. S. Dundee
                        Starkey.
Frazier Davis,   do
Embree S. F. Rock Stream

Botanic Medicines.

Columbia County.

Tilden & Co. (Manf'r.)
                New Lebanon.

Kings County.

Mortimer Thos. 3 York *Brooklyn.*
Hewett Wm. 70 High
Johnson Jacob P. 45 4th
                Williamsburgh.

New York County.

Atkinson Asher, 216 Greenwich
                New York.
Badger Alfred C. 59 Norfolk
Bellow Prosper, 150 E. Broadway
Belding C. T. 89 8th Av.
Blakesley A. W. 8th Av
Bolter R. M. 294 4th
Brouwer Abram, 3 Prince
Brown George, 74 Bowery
Cook. G. W. & Beakley Jacob,
 496 Broadway
Cregar Samuel, jr. 13 Bowery
Curtiss & Trall, 161 Greenwich &
 43 Bowery
Duffield Elizabeth, 466 Houston
Firth H. E. 266 Broome
Gibbs Desmond B. 204 Wooster
Gilbert & Warner, 107 John
Harseron James A. 58 Division &
 163 Stanton
Hubbs Mary F. 89½ Hester
Hunt J.D. 100 1st Av.
Hunt Stephanas, 232 Houston
Irish E. 5 3d Av.
Jimeson Cæsar, 42 Grand
Jones Ann L. 24 Greenwich Av.
Kirby S. R. 762 Broadway
Lapham P. 114 1st
Law & Boyd, 62 E. Broadway
Leathe Japtha, 502 Grand
M'Keag Robert, 347 Broome
Morris I. M. 119 Bowery
Newby Geo. 184 Canal
Peek William T. 98 John
Pollard Wm. 317 Broome
Pierson F. D. 184 12th
Shipley A. L. 175 Bowery
Sharp G. W. 175 Bowery
Stainburn J. W. 9½ Division
Stearns Chas. J. 119 Bowery
Stoddard Jeduthen, 143 3d Av.
Van Vleck I. H. 477 Greenwich
Vankleek Louisa M. 26 6th Av.
Vogel Charles F. 64 6th Av.
Wasson James W. 33 8th Av.
Wells Judge, 454 Hudson
Wick A. 8th Av.
Whipple David, 181 3d Av.
Winchester Hosea, 106 John
Wood John, 184 Canal
Wright Rufus, 64 E. Broadway

Wayne County.

Townsend Thomas   *Lyons*

Bottlers.

Early John, r. 41 Elizabeth
                New York.
Lethbridge G. P. 86 & 88 Fulton
M'Alpin Patrick, 92 Beekman
Nicholl Samuel, 64 Leonard
Oliver John, 138 Fulton
Pelletier Hippolyte, 134 Reade
Staff John J. 10 & 12 Ann

Bowling Saloons. (See also
                Porter Houses.)

Broome County.

Ball W. H.   *Binghamton.*
Graves V.

Erie County.

Cornish O. J. M., Long Wharf
    Buffalo.
Kenyon & Darling G. 12 Main

New York County.

Atwood Danus, 44 Vesey
    New York.
Buckley Wm. C. 263 Broadway
Burns A. C. 337 Broadway
Burns Stephen M. 360 Broadway
Coquell C. N. 51 Cherry
Dudley & Emmons, 177 Broadway
Dwyer John, 75 Robinson
Graves Charles B. 14 & 16 Vesey
Hamilton James, 54 E. Broadway
Hicks John, 200 South
Hooker & Odell, 304 Broadway
Horn James, 8 Ann & 149 Fulton
Kane P. 13 Park Row
Kimball Gard. W. 316 Broadway
Lockwood Timothy, 691 4th
Lourre G. H. 58 Cherry
M'Alpine, 332 Broadway
M'Kellan Henry, 233 Av. B
M'Monough James, 151 Chatham
M'Nally John, 202 Broadway
Mimne John M. 240½ Greenwich
Mitchell J. D. R. 138 Cherry
Newkirk James S. 332 Broadway
Plume Edward H. 27 James
Taylor Robert, 53 Bowery
Thorlev T. W. 102 Barclay

Niagara County.

Woodruff R. H. *Niagara Falls.*

Boxes.

Albany County.

Hantseh F. 62 Green *Albany.*
Tise J. P. 40 1st

Greene County.

Soper J. (Shaving box) *Ashland.*
Matthews J. do *Windham.*

Herkimer County.

Payne John M. (Cheese box manu-
  facturer) *Newport.*
Griswold G. F. do
Campbell John *Norway.*
Hurlburt Wm. H.
Bills Henry, Gravesville *Russia.*
Graves Henry
Frank James, jr. Cold Brook
Countryman Isaac *Stark*
Lyman F. Jordansville *Warren.*

Jefferson County.

Rice H. & R. (Starch & Cheese)
  Champion.

Kings County.

Newman Henry, (Packing boxes)
  Duffield st. *Brooklyn*
Westlake B. (Packing) 1st st. cor.
  8th *Williamsburgh.*

Lewis County.

Pinney Dunham, (Cheese) Lyonsdale *Greig*
Morgan Luther, (Cheese) *Turin.*

Madison County.

Babcock & Crandall, South Brook-
  field *Brookfield.*
Chandler O. *Cazenovia*
Payne Bradford *Georgetown.*
Staples E., Poolville *Hamilton.*

Monroe County.

Huntington A. B. (Band Boxes)
  4 N. St. Paul *Rochester.*

Oneida County.

Alder S. (Cheese) North *Western.*

Otsego County.

Rice T. W. (Cheese) *Middlefield*

Rensselaer County.

Cobby John, 7 Jacob *Troy.*

Saratoga County.

Bachellor S. & S. *Edinburgh.*

BOX, PACKING—MAKERS.

Bloomer Thomas, 33 S. William
  New York.
Coey William J. 46 Marion
Crouch William J. 167 Water
Dolohan John, 82 Pine
Dunn Edward, rear 698 Water &
  289 Pearl
Ernest Peter, 98 Norfolk
Green Alonzo, 347 Pearl
Gullich Adam, 79 Bowery
Harrott George, 292 W. 17th
Howland Pontus, 114 Troy
Links Jacob, rear 22 Laurens
Massonnat ——, 15 John
Miller Edward, 160 Malden Lane
Murphy Edward, 31 S. William
Nelson & Howard, 79 Pine
Pierson Israel, 6 Platt & 8 S. Wil-
  liam
Strights William C. 516 Water
Switzer Henry, 163 Water & 21
  Gold
Trotter Benjamin, 77 Wooster
Watkins Lewis, 167 Walker & 62
  Cliff
Watkis Charles L. 62 Cliff
Westlake Benjamin, 82 Pine
Williams George W. 98 Elm

Boys' Clothing. (*See also
  Tailors.*)

Brown J. 167½ Division *New York.*
Cornwell J. D. 92 Grand
Ellis & Isleton, 439 Broadway
Hyatt Sarah M. 4 Amos
Kavanagh John, 23 3d
Levy Lewis E. 152 Division
Myers Mary, 172 12th
Neldret Esther, 612½ 4th
Oliver Mrs. 231 6th Av.
Olssen Edward J. 74 Bowery &
  202 Fulton. *Brooklyn*
Smith & Michaels, 57 Fulton
Sutphen Elizabeth, 53 Av. D

Brad Makers.

Field Jude, cor. Av. C & 6th st.
  New York.

Branch Post Offices.

Broadway—J. C. Harriott, 422½
  Broadway *New York.*
Bleecker St. 212—Jas. A. Sparks
Chatham Square—Aaron Swarts,
  Chatham Sq. cor. E. Broadway
Union Square—844 Broadway

Brass Finishers. (*See also
  Founders—Brass.*)

Bard James M. 10 Canal
Bissicks & Barton, 109 Bowery
Brown & Carswell, 69 University
  place
Callen Wm. 268 Greenwich
Cribe Armand, 29 Spruce
Eddy George, 15 Dover
Eddy J. W. & G. M. 18 Platt
Gee George & Wm. 46 Eldridge

Heckman A. 63 Gold *New York*
Hidden Enoch, 661 Water
Johnson A. & H. 115 Charlton
Johnson John, 111 14th
Johnson William, 342 Water
Jones J. & H. rear 33 White
Kurst John, 254 Walker
Lawrence William B. 201 Front
  & 419 Cherry
McKinley Augustus C. 87 Centre
Martin Daniel, 11 Desbrosses
Martin Moses J. 84 Hester
Morgans Morgan, 91 Henry
Nichols C. L. & Co. rear 247 Grand
Nickinson & Gibbs, 247 Grand
Richards John B. 43 Eldridge
Schrader August, 19 Ann
Taylor & Jenkins, 829 Broadway

Brass Manufacturers. (*See
  also Founders—Brass.*)

Callen Wm. 268 Greenwich
Hiler Selah, 67 Bayard
Marks & Davol, 52 Broad—Agents
  for the Wolcottville Brass Co.
Mason, Mott & Farnham, 91 Jane
Smith & Jacobs, 67 & 69 Forsyth
  & 114 John
Walker Thos. & G. 44 W. 14th
West George, 2 Duane
Wetmore L. 15 Platt
Whittingham J. rear 90 Henry
Whittingham R. rear 98 Henry

Brass Washer & Smelter.

Kings County.

Coleman James, Lorimer near 1st
  Williamsburgh.

Brewers.

Albany County.

Kirk A. 904 Broadway *Albany.*
Tweedie & Darlington, 137 & 159
  Broadway
Eggleston & Putnam, 9 Dean
Brewer R. 28 Quay
Quin J. N., Ferry st.
Burt W. cor. Montgomery & Col-
  onie
Taylor & Sons, 83 Green
Boyd R. cor. Franklin & Arch
McCulloch, 30 Rensselaer
Chester J. & P. (Small Beer), 73 S.
  Pearl
Mansfield P. (Small Beer), 75 do
McKnight J. Canal & Hawk
Appleton & Welch, 317 Bowery
Dunlap R. & Sons, West Troy
  Watervliet.

Alleghany County.

Beers Thomas *Cuba.*

Broome County.

White S. & Son *Binghamton.*

Cayuga County.

Cornell & Co. Water st. *Auburn.*

Chautauque County.

Murray & Co. *Portland*

Chenango County.

White S. *New Berlin.*
White & Gardner *Norwich.*

Clinton County.

Sawyer Daniel, Keesville *Ausable.*

Columbia County.

Robinson George, 2d st. *Hudson*

Duchess County.

Vassar M. & Co.   *Poughkeepsie.*
Oharra L. (Lemon Beer)
                   Rhinebeck.

Erie County.

Argus John   *Black Rock.*
McLeish James, Buffalo Plains
Barr A.   do
Moffatt Wm. corner Mohawk &
  Morgan   *Buffalo.*
Moffatt James,   do

Genesee County.

Fish E. H.   *Batavia*

Jefferson County.

Heeth Elias   *Adams.*

Kings County.

Stacy George, Boerum near Ber-
  gen   *Brooklyn.*
Johnson John, Jay st. cor. York
Colman C. 114 Grand
                   Williamsburgh.

Livingston County.

Eschrich J.   *Dansville*
Houver J.
Kline Louis

Madison County.

Twist & Root   *Cazenovia.*

Monroe County.

Burtis & Co. Water st. *Rochester.*
Slater Wm. Alexander st.
Loupmair J. & Brothers, Water st.
Warren S. M. & Co.   do
Wilson William, Fish st.
Hyde M. A., Mumford *Wheatland.*

Montgomery County.

Bowell George S.   *Amsterdam.*
Smith J. C.   *Canajoharie.*

New York County.

Abbot D. jr. 103 Anthony *New York*
Adams Daniel, 138 Cedar
Barber Thomas, 120 Warren
Becher C. 38 Chatham
Beveridge J. & Co. 121 Warren
Bilsborow Robert, 180 Cherry
Burt Uri. 153 Greenwich—Brook-
  lyn agency, Main cor. Front
Chalmers & Sanderson, 25th st.
Dilge Joseph R. 231 3d st.
Earl & Watson, rear 254 W. 17th
Eggleston & Putnam, 267 Washt'n
Gelleg George. 156 3d
Gregory & Harmon. 6 Sheriff
Hazard Robinson. 35 Vesey
Jones David. 127 Broome
Kelly Thomas. 636 Washington
Kerr John & Co. 51 & 53 Leonard
Kinch William, 157 Sullivan
Kerchhoff Jacob. 96 W. 16th
Kirk Andrew & Co. 13 James
M'Lachlan A. 103 Greenwich Av.
Milbank C. & S. 58 Madison
Miles Wm. B. & A. 59 Chrystie
Miller Adam, 220 3d
Muhling Joseph, 41 Av. A
Nash. Beadleston & Co. 189 Amos
  & 59 Dey
Neu Charles, 123 Chrystie
Ormsby D. L. 255 W. 16th
Patterson Erastus, W.. 13th be-
  tween 9th & 10th Avs.
Pollock R. U. 114 Warren
Read & Brothers, 230 Washington
Schaefer F. & Max. 85 7th Av.
Sherwood Henry, 102 & 104 Duane
Simons George. 181 Broome
Solms Henry. 13 Clinton
Taylor J. & Sons, 342 Greenwich
Vassar M. & Co. 116 Warren

Wehn Doroghty, 169 Eldridge
                   New York.
Wehn Henry, 169 Eldridge
Wescott Samuel, 35 Vesey
Yager John, 281 E. 13th

Oneida County.

Thorn Stephen & Co. State st. near
  Court   *Utica.*
M'Quade & Pond, Jay st.

Onondaga County.

M'Ketchnie Robert, Water st. Syracuse   *Salina.*

Ontario County.

Gibson & Co.   *Phelps.*
Moore P., Geneva   *Seneca.*
Hutchinson & Morse

Orange County.

Beveridge J. Front st. *Newburgh.*

Oswego County.

Young & Co. 1st st.   *Oswego.*

Otsego County.

Spafford & Earnest, Cooperstown
                   Otsego.

Rensselaer County.

Nash, Beadleston & Co. 188 5th
                   Troy.
Reed & Brothers, cor. Ferry &
  Ship sts.
Cleary & Murphy, cor. Liberty &
  5th
Fitzpatrick & M'Intosh, South
De Freest & Potts, (root beer) 55½
  Congress

Schenectady County.

Peters A. Washington st.
                   Schenectady.
Lake D. & Son, (root beer) 77
  Union

Seneca County.

Sisson M.   *Seneca Falls.*

Tompkins County.

Huntington W. T.   *Ithaca.*
Hinds T. H.

Ulster County.

Von Beek Geo. F. South Rondout
                   Kingston.

Washington County.

Cook George   *Fort Edward.*

Brick Dealers.

Clark Daniel, 325½ West
                   New York.
Keylor James, 159 Monroe
Low Daniel. 20 Pine
Staten Island Brick and Granite
  Company. 74 Broadway
Woodbridge, 11 West & 34 Can-
  non

Albany County.

Nowlan J. 135, 137 139, 141 Grand
                   Albany.

Brick Makers.

Albany County.

Stanwix G. Beaver Creek
M'Evoy John. Schulyer Farm
Moore William,   do
Bassett Daniel E., cor. Hudson &
  Swan

Archer J. cor. Swan & Jay
                   Albany.
Leonard Solomon S. cor Hudson &
  Lark
Leonard J.   do
Van Ness Mrs. J. Lumber st.
White F. 49 Van Woert
Van Zandt & Brown, cor. Knox &
  Lydius
M'Duffie C. H. cor. Lydius &
  Snipe
Burhans & Goodrich. do
Geoghegan J. cor. Canal & Clark
Waggoner L. cor. Patroon & Lark
M'Cabe P. M. Patroon st.
Canady J. Reedsville   *Berne.*
Leabridge P.   *Coeymans.*
Harris S.
Sickler J.
Rogers F. West Troy Watervliet

Cattaraugus County.

Townsend B. C.   *Rice.*

Cayuga County.

Wright C.   *Moravia.*
Carr J. H.   *Springport.*

Clinton County.

Packard David   *Saranac.*

Delaware County.

Dean A. C. Deposit *Tompkins.*

Duchess County.

Vasser C.   *Poughkeepsie*
Martin C. G. Barrytown
                   Red Hook.

Erie County.

Barrows Th., Hydraulics *Buffalo.*
Stanford George,   do
Barker G. W. & Co. do
Reed Samuel, Son. do
White James,   do

Franklin County.

Wright Joseph, West Constable
                   Westville.

Greene County.

Parker James M.   *Cazsackie.*
Smith Isaac
Wolf Henry
Beatty William
Baker Ambrose
Puffer Amos
Miller John
Parker Madison
Wilson James
Van Bergen Peter
Steveson Patrick

Jefferson County.

Barnes Benjamin   *Theresa.*

Monroe County.

Buckland A.   *Brighton.*
Cobb & Baker
Wilson & Moon

Oneida County.

Garret J. P., S. Trenton *Trenton.*

Oswego County.

Osborn & Pierce & Co. ..*Hannibal.*

Putnam County.

Fisher P. & D., Cold Springs
                   Phillipstown.
Conkton H.   ·   do
Tenesdale D.   do

Queens County.

Peterson A.   *Jamaica.*

Rockland County.

Keisler B. *Haverstraw.*
Nickerson Z.
Henry J.
Waldron A.
Du Baun A.
Gardiner John
Mackey L. R.
Gardiner B. D.
Smith T. S.
Doyle Thomas
Sarvis I.
Gerow O. C.
Riley P.
Strang & Redner
Weed D.
Cosgrove B.
Elison L. T.
Smith & Simons
Briggs A.
Denton D.
Phillips & Fowler
Gillis S.
Milborne I.
Hubbard T.
Castle T. & T.
Lackford Thomas A., Caldwell's Landing

St. Lawrence County.

Shaw James *Morristown.*
Paige Smith, Ogdensburgh *Oswegatchie.*

Suffolk County.

Crassman A. B. Cold Springs *Huntington.*
Flint Orrin, Greenport *Southold.*
Robinson David, do

Sullivan County.

Hawkins S. R. Burlingham *Mamakating.*

Orange County.

Adams Nathaniel *Cornwall.*
Dunn P. *Goshen.*

Ulster County.

Maginnis John, Glasco *Saugerties.*
Hyser Edward, do
Hale Wm. C. do
Maginnis Wm. do
Overbah J. V. L. do
Delanoy D. do

Westchester County.

Lord Abram H. (stove lining) Peekskill *Courtlandt.*
Wood Samuel, Tarrytown, *Greenburg.*
Wood Wm. do
Frost J. W., Croton *Yorktown.*
Southard Thos. do
Frost Cyrus, do

Bristles.

Fischel F. S. & Von Stade. 44 Cliff *New York.*
Hilger & Co. 114 Water
Husemann & Co. 14 Platt
Livingston M. & W. 70 Broad
Mills Elisha, 138 Water

Britannia Ware Manufacturers.

Albany County.

Smith & Feltman, 23 Dean *Albany.*
Curtis D. 23 Church

Duchess County

Brown —— Mills st. *Poughkeepsie.*

Kings County.

Locke John D. Front st. near Pearl *Brooklyn.*
Pratt Geo. (Lamps) Jay near John

New York County.

Andrews J. D. 210 Water *New York.*
Benham & Whitney, 272½ Pearl
Capen & Molineux, rear 132½ William
Dixon James & Sons, 241 Pearl
Endicott & Sumner, 105 Elm & 195 William
Hague & Redfield, 17 Platt
Hart Lucius, 6 Burling slip
James M. E. & Co. 23 Cliff
Ketcham David, 77 Fulton
Ostrander & Norris, 234 3d
Smith Thomas, 77 Fulton
Sproat Josiah, 27 Fulton
Watkins I. T. 16 Catharine

Rensselaer County.

Prouty B. T. & Co. cor. Fulton & Mechanic sts. *Troy.*
Whitlock John H. 6 River
Pierce & King, (Importers) 235 River
Humiston Willis, 319 River

Brokers.

Albany County.

Lagrange G. 455 Broadway *Albany.*
Payne G. R. 438 do
Jackson J. 6 Douw's Building
Pitman R. H. 298½ Broadway
M'Canin & Comstock, 16 Exchange
Robbison S. 15 do
Groesbeck Brothers, 13 do
Evertson J. jr. 8 do
Benson G. & Co. 29 Maiden Lane
Hendrickson J. 38 State
Washburn & Co. 45 do
Clark & Jones, (Real Estate) 73 State
Hawley D. A. 23½ Hudson
Harvey J. 14 S. Pearl
Hurd J. N. M. 2½ Green
Fellows & Davis, 20 do
Lansing J. J. 5 James
Fitzpatrick A. F. (Real Estate) 38 Steuben
Noonan Thomas, (Real Estate) 38 Steuben
Fairlee S. (Real Estate) Dunnsville *Guilderland.*
Callender E., Cohoes *Watervliet.*

Cayuga County.

Tucker S. B. 117 Genesee *Auburn.*

Erie County.

Provost G. W., Huff's Hotel *Buffalo.*
Walsh John, 5 Commercial
Truscott George, 4 Exchange
Townsend & Co. 3 do
Goodenough R. A. 6 do
Gallup S. (Real Estate) Post Office
Meech A. B. do 223 Main
Salisbury G. H. do 246 do
Goodenough R. A. (Produce) 6 Exchange
Lawson & Foster (Produce) 3 Coburn Square
Manchester B. A. (R. E.) 6 Seneca
Maynard R. H. do 8 do
Le Gras E. do 6 do
Ganson Jas. M. 2 Spaulding's Ex.
Dole & Co. 194 Main
Jackson J. 2 do
Gridley F. 140 do
Horace Hills, cor. Main & Exch'ge
Palmer Alanson, 428 Main
Robinson & Co. 162 do
Baldwin Jas. J. 152 do

Kings County.

Cass Marcus M. 186 do *Buffalo.*
Hill J. T. Spaulding's Exchange
Eckley J. S. & Brothers, 12 Webster's Block

Kings County.

Beers E. 43 Fulton *Brooklyn.*
Lefferts R. & Co. 45 Fulton
Barnet George, (Exchange) 167 Grand *Williamsburgh.*

Monroe County.

Sikes R. 2 Minerva Block *Rochester.*
Watts James H. cor. Buffalo & Exchange sts.
Talman John T. cor. Buffalo & Exchange sts.
Munger Perley, (Real Estate,) 123 Buffalo
Pond Elias, (Land) 22 Buffalo
Wheeler & Ames, (Pawnbrokers) 15 Exchange
Ely Ebenezer, 44 Exchange
Ward L. A. (Ins.) 36 State

Madison County.

Barnes Ira G. *De Ruyter.*

New York County.

Brokers—Bill and Note.

Arcularius John P. 100 Wall *New York*
Beebe, Ludlow & Co. 49 Wall
De Becher. 27 Merchants Exch.
Comstock D. A. 44 William
Cook Frederick, 84 Wall
Edey Frere, 29 Merchants' Exch.
Geer Edward W. 4 Hanover
Gilman W. C. 18 Merch. Exch.
Hopper & Co. 101 Wall
Hotchkiss Jeremiah, 65 Wall
Humbert Aug. 19 Merch. Exch.
Kennedy T. & G. 108 South
L'Hommedieu J. H. 36 William
Ingles Moses, 60 Wall
Lake & Co. 44 William & 46 Exch.
M'Millan James, 38 Wall
Mills C. N. & Son, 2 Hanover
Mott Richard, 84 Wall
Mott William F. jr. 35 Wall
Pepcon, Hoffman & Tenbrook, 51 Wall
Richards Henry, 52 Wall
Robbins & Son, 52 Wall
Schack O. W. C. 69 Wall
Steele Jonathan D. 49 William
Tempest Thomas, 60 Wall
Thwing C. & E. W. 29 Wall
Titus Samuel, 35 Wall
Tompkins Ray, 35 Wall
Underwood J. A. & Son, 22 Merchants' Exchange
Warner Samuel B. 30 William
Warren & Rogers, 22 Hanover
Weeks E. C. 49 Wall
Whitmarsh & Andrews, 20 Mer. Exchange

Brokers—Cotton.

Adams & Lineau, 87 Wall *New York.*
Adams J. T. 89 Wall
Barnwall & Thomas, 74 Beaver
Cahoone, Kinney & Co. 153 Pearl
Earle, Dean & Co. 78 Wall
Gordon A. R. 89 Wall
Joyce & Murphy, 84 Old slip
Lentilhon E. 24 Exchange place
Maltbie, Munn & Co. 90 Wall
M'Bude W. 74 Wall
Merle, Bright & Co. 5 Hanover
Millett E. V. 74 Wall
Moorhead John, 28 Old slip
Nicholl & Co. 74 Wall
Stewart Thomas J. 86 Wall
Sus A. W. 87 Wall
Taber & Jenkins, 76 Wall

6

1

Talcott F. L. & Co. 91 Wall
    New York.
Truesdell Moore & Co. 91 Wall
Wasson & Jacobs, 141 Pearl
Wilson & Callet. 91 Beaver
Wotherspoon, Kingsford & Co. 81
  Beaver
Wright & Lewin, Post's Buildings
Wright W. P. Post's Buildings

BROKERS—CUSTOM HOUSE.

Bibby G. S. 25 Pine *New York.*
Campbell Thomas N. 25 Pine
Carter James C. 11 Nassau
Henry Peter S. 5 Nassau
Irwin Thomas, 14 Pine
Lyon David S. 1 Nassau
Lyon Edward, 1 Nassau
M'Donald Alexander. jr. 11 Nassau
Overton R. Carlton. 6 Wall
Pride George L. 3 Broad
Schuyler & Guiman, 5 Broad
Waring Thaddeus, 30 Wall
Wood & Niebuhr, 25 Pine

BROKERS—DRUG.

Babcock & Cox, 104 Wall
    New York.
Degen Charles R. 100 Wall
Divett K. F. 90 Wall
Gleim O. F. 43 New
Greene Charles A. 94 Wall
Greene John L. 94 Wall
Greene Randall H. 94 Wall
Harding Henry M. 93 Wall
Harvey William H. 60 John
Henschel & Hurter, 100 Wall
Jackson & Robins, 134 Water
Jauncey Edward N. 66 Front
Lamson G. W. & Co. 7 Fletcher
Lohman Isaac, 142 Front
Low S. Haskell, 8 Fletcher
Low Seth & Co. 8 Fletcher
Mabee & Co. 106 Wall
Mallerd Samuel, 166 Pearl
Newbould Edward, 88 Wall
Patterson E. C. & Co. 74 Wall
Porter Elijah, 8 Fletcher
Rolfe Daniel, 123 Water
Seymour, Davis & Co. 87 Wall
Seymour & Lefferts, 102 Wall
Southwick George W. 10 Old Slip
Sweetser E. Francis, 81 Pine
Sweetser Samuel, 82 Pine
Thompson Wm. R. 84 Maiden lane
Taft James H. 100 Wall

BROKERS—DRY GOODS.

Charles Robert, jr. 5 William
    New York.
Cleveland & Co. 34 Beaver
Davis D H. & Co. 72 Beaver
Davis & Kissam, 33 William
Dow Asa, 8 S. William
Robillard J. C. 86 Cedar

BROKERS—GENERAL.

Adams H. C. 41 Wall *New York.*
Adams P. C. 41 do Jauncey ct.
Bagert W. S. 50 Water
Bard & Son, 54 Wall
Barre J. P. 26 S. William
Bechet Claudius C. 36 Wall
Bierne John, 15 Washington
Brown H. 13 Front & 47 Wall
Chardon Anthony, 35 Wall
Davis D. H. (Silk) 72 Beaver
Deppermann & Alburtis, 96 Wall
Ford Gordon L. 7 Broad
Gleim O. F. 43 New
Gould Charles, 2 Hanover
Hobart H. C. 36 New
Hopper & Co. 101 Wall
Kurtheerdt Asher, 107 Water
Laudon Alexander H. 4 New
Lord William G. 35 Pearl

Rhodes Charles D. 68 Pine
    New York.
Seymour & Lefferts, 102 Wall
Simons A. E. 359 Pearl
Schenk S. C. 90 Nassau
Tracy George M. 2 Hanover
Van Nortwick W. B. 13 Front
Ward & Co. 54 Wall
Whitaker S. S. 36 Wall

BROKER—HAY.

Sturtevant D. & A. 130 Cedar
    New York.

BROKERS—HIDE.

Brown Wm. M. 5 Ferry *New York*
Terry Brothers, 50 do

BROKERS—INSURANCE.

Baldwin Sim. 70 Wall *New York.*
Bergen James, 37 do
Gilman William C. 19 Merchants'
  Exchange
James E. D. 60 Wall
Jones & Johnson, 90 Wall
Jones William E. 104 Wall
Lawson & Graham. 82 do
Molineux Wm. 5 Dey
Tooker, Smyth & Co. 57 South
Vanarnam Abraham, 8 do
Walker Samuel G. 121 Water

BROKERS—LOAN.

Conrey J. F. 60 Wall *New York.*
Smith Henry M. 65 do

BROKERS—MERCHANDISE.

Bradley & Co. 135 Water
    New York.
Burns David R. 129 Front
Butler Henry, 93 Wall
Forbes John E. 103 do
Gifford James N. 94 Wall
Leffreing C. R. 83 do
Manny Hesmann, 83 do
Patten W. D. 116 Water
Sawyer William B. 85 Wall
Scott & Bell, 91½ do
Smith & Rice, 122 Front
Turell Brothers, 92 Wall
Van Pelt Tunis, 117 Front
Walker William A. 132 South
Wilson J. 191 Bowery
White E. H. 103 Pearl
Wetherall Samuel, 164 Front

BROKERS—METAL.

Carter Henry, 42 Cliff *New York.*
Cass John C. 76 Wall
Caswell Nathan, 69 Wall
Fuller Joseph C. 230 West
Green Walter C. 97 Wall
Ingham T. 71 Wall
Sawyer William B. 85 Wall. (Also,
  hemp, bagging, linseed, &c.)
Smith Lewis F. P. 309 Water
Turell Brothers, 92 Wall
Williamson & Sawyer, 76 Wall

BROKER—OIL.

Johnson Franklin, 81 Water
    New York.

BROKERS—PRODUCE.

Bill Edward, 111 Broad, *New York.*
Cockcroft Jacob H. V. 33 Water
Croft & Rose (Naval Stores), 100
  Wall
Cronk Elisha P. 154 West
Darbefeuille Charles, 63 Wall

Deppermand & Alburtis (Naval
  Stores) 96 Wall *New York.*
Dewitt R. 126 Warren
Ducker Henry, 258 5th
Echarte F. 63 Wall
Edcy Henry, 113 Front
Fawcett Curtis, 13 Front
Fisher F. A. 28 Front
Forbes John E. 103 Wall
Hawkesworth James, 81 Wall
Hoyt William, 10 South
Kellogg Timothy, 40 South
Kemp Henry, 35 Pearl
Keith Charles, 85 Front
Lord William G. 35 Pearl
Manny Hermann, 85 Wall, (whale
  oil & bone, pot & pearl ashes,
  dye woods, &c.)
Marshall Francis D. 93 Wall
Matthews J. & Co. 93 Wall
Mills Levi A. 39 Water
Moulun, H. 60 Wall
Montgomery George, 128 Front
Moses David & Co. 114 Front
Parsons Solon, 154 West
Pidgeon Peter. 17 Water
Platt John, 25 Water
Pond, Gilman & Mack, 97 Wall
Powers C. 31 Coenties slip
Quackinbush A. 3 Broad
Randolph Joseph F. 57 Whitehall
Rea William, 60 Wall
Roberts, Brothers, 22 Exchange pl
Sawyer William B. 76 Wall
Skiddy Francis, 101 Wall
Smith J. Ogden, 63 Front
Spencer Jared W. 23 Water
Sperry Henry C. 8 South
Torrence Daniel,.93 Wall
White E. H. 103 Pearl
Willets Joseph, 35 Pearl
Williams Charles C. 21 South

BROKERS—REAL ESTATE.

Adams Hermann C. 23 & 25 Wall
    New York.
Beare Thomas M. 6 Wall
Blydenburgh R. P. 49 William
Broad Sanford S. 11 Wall
Burritt William J. 23 & 25 Wall
Carrol and Co. 68 Fulton
Chase A. H. 2 Wall
Cole & Chilton, 9 Wall
Dayton John A. 134 Water
Eaton D. C. 18 Wall
Fredericksaon C. W. 141 Pearl
Glentworth James B. 3 Broad
Hinman Samuel S. 3 do
Holden Oliver. 25 John
Holley Philologos, 10 Wall
Holly William C. 17 Nassau
Hoyt Charles, 68 Wall
James W. E. 23 & 25 Wall
Jenkins Edward, 3 Nassau
Johnson & Co. 170 Broadway
Keeler Walter. 3 Nassau
Leavenworth W. 5 do
Loomis Henry. 140 Broadway
Mattison Schuyler H. 3 Nassau
Nones A. B. 15 Wall
North American Land & Emigra-
  tion Co. 130 Broadway
Osgood George P. 6 Wall
Overton John B. 2 do
Peters Abel. S. 177 Reade
Pitkin John R. 68 Broadway
Quackinbush Andrew, 3 Broad
Sacchi G. A. 5 Broad
Seaman John F. 120 Water
Seely & Roberts, 140 Maiden lane
Sergeant Aaron & Son. 15 Wall
Smith Alonzo F. 10 Wall
Vail David L. 93 Wall
Vanderpoel A. B. 23 & 25 Wall
Wadsworth Charles, 9 Nassau

BROKERS—RICE.

Barrell George, 106 Wall
    New York
Talmage Daniel, 93 do

BROKER—SEGARS.

David Henry R. 93 Wall
New York.

BROKERS—SHIP.

Aitken Leverett H. 12 South
New York.
Baid & Hincker, 88 Wall
Bartlett Richard, 6 Jones' lane
Benson A. G. & A. W. 39 South
Cook & Smith, 110 Wall
Coit Gurdon S. 26 South
Duffy M. J. & Co. 23 Wall
Elwell John P. 57 South
Funck & Mincke, 93 Wall
Freeman M. M. & Co. 56 South
Holdrege Henry, jr. 93 Wall
Mailler & Lord, 108   do
Manning George, 90   do
Meincke A. F. 93   do
Platt Frederick L. 104   do
Place Nelson, 69 South & 100 Pine
Robertson David H. 88 Wall
Robinson S P. 59 West
Schwadt & Balcher, 105 & 107 Wall
Smith & Rice, 122 Front
Sutton Edward B. 84 Wall
Tooker, Smyth & Co. 57 South
Tuck Samuel B. & Son, 36 do
Underwood H. 111 Wall
Weisser William, 91 do
Willett John R. 114 do

BROKERS—STOCK & EXCHANGE.

Adams, M'Chesney & Co. 71 Wall
New York.
Allen M. 54 Merchant's Exchange
Allen William H. 60 Wall
Armour George A. 25 Pine
Ayres Thomas N. 64 Wall
Baker Moses, corner Chatham & Catharine
Bache G. P. 178 Greenwich
Bach & Pick, 174 Broadway
Bard Wm. & Son, 54 Wall
Barker Henry R. 62 Wall
Barrow James, jr. 1 Hanover
Baylis A. B. 1 Exchange place & 30 Merchants' Exchange
Belknap Edward, 62 Wall
Berend Bermann, 23 Wall
Betts J. E. & Co. 61 Wall
Biddle Edward R. 36 Wall
Bills O. A. Greenwich st.
Bladenburgh R. F. 47 William
Bleecker James W. 54 Wall
Bock William, 26 Wall
Borrowe William, 1 Hanover
Braisted Thos. H. 146 Chatham
Braisted W. C. 59 Bowery
Brandon J. 25 Merchants' Exch.
Braynard Thomas L. 81 Wall
Brown O. H. R. Merch. Exchange
Brown W H. 60 Merch. Exchange
Buck Charles, 60 Wall
Bucknor William F. 54 Wall
Bucknor William G. 54 Wall
Buckley & Deuel, 47 William
Burr Horace, 62 Wall
Burrill John E. 60 Wall
Carpender Charles P. 60 Wall
Carpender J. S. 68 Wall
Carpenter, Vandyke & Co. 29 Wall
Carpenter & Vermilye, 44 Wall
Case A. S. & Co. 163 Pearl
Chapman & Co. 61 Merch. Exch.
Christmas Charles, 60 Wall
Clark Allen, 78 Reade
Clark, Wm. 64 Chatham
Clark E. W. Dodge & Co. 54 Wall
Clarkson D. 32 Merch. Exchange
Claver James M. 16 Greenwich
Coit & Smith, 62 Wall
Coleman Thomas J. 63 Wall
Colegate Charles & Co. 67 Wall
Colvill Alfred, 2 Hanover
Comstock D. A. Jauncey court, 43 Wall
Conkling Enos S. 47 Wall

Cotte C. C. 122 Bowery *New York.*
Cox Wm. 69 Barclay
Currie Wm. & James, 45 Wall
Cutting Robert L. 31 Merch. Ex.
Darling S. A. 177 Greenwich
Decoppet L. & E. 60 Wall
De Launay, Iselin & Clark, 63 Wall
De Hervilly F. 3 Merch. Exch.
Draper & Glover, 54 Wall
Draz Francis, 85 Wall
Drew, Robinson & Co. 37 Wall
Dumazeaud & Lemoyne, 47 Wall
Dunning S. P. jr. 169 Greenwich
Dwight H. jr. 61 Wall
Dykers, Alstine & Co. 62 Wall
Ebbets John J. A. r. 35 Wall
Fay & Wilson, 74½ Wall
Felt & Co. 174 Pearl
Fendi Josephus G. 64 Wall
Ferris Andrew M. 35 Wall
Fisher & Denney, 8 Jauncey ct.
Foster A. S. 234 Pearl
Genin & Lockwood, 1 Hanover
Gifford Arthur N. 26 Merch. Ex.
Gilbert Cobb & Johnson, 52 Wall
Gilman Wm. C. 19 Merch. Ex.
Godard & St. John, 67 Wall
Goldschmidt John, 58 Wall
Goodliff James T. 25 Wall
Gourlie John H. 62 Wall
Graham Chas. 47 Wall
Grannies Charles B. 65 Wall
Greig A. M. 66 Wall
Green M. 190 Chatham
Groesbeck George, 68 Wall
Hamilton Jas. K. & Sons, 61 Wall
Harrison A. P. 60 Wall
Hart Emanuel B. 4½ Hanover
Hawes & Bills, 136½ Greenwich
Hays Dewitt C. 65 Wall
Hays Wm. H. & Co. 65 Wall
Hemphill Sam. 292 Greenwich
Henriques E. 71 Wall
Herolly T. D. 32 Wall
Hoguet A. 62 Wall
Holmes James E. 54 Wall
Hopkins & Sparks 1 Hanover
Hopkins & Weston, 53 Merch Ex.
Hough Joseph. 220 Broadway
Houghton Edward, 53 Wall
Houghton & Co 53 Wall
How Devid, 5 Wall
Hoyt & Hunt, 4 Hanover
Hunt James S. 4 Hanover
Huntington & Co. 27 Wall
Hyde N. 246 Greenwich
Jagger & Clark, 66 Wall
James Frederick P. 62 Wall
Jessup & Cole, 191 Greenwich
Johnson William, 190 Wall
Jones John, 150 Greenwich Av.
Ketcham T. & Co. 1 Hanover
Kettredge Hy. 268 Greenwich
Kouger & Tucker, 28 Wall
Lane Anthony, 49 Wall
Lee Leonard, 60 Merch. Ex.
Leroy Daniel, 69 Wall
Lewis Charles, 2 Pine
Lewis G. L. 39 Jauncey ct.
Little Jacob & Co. 44 Wall
Livingston Carrol, 67 Wall
Ludlow Thomas W. 52 Wall
M'Carty J. I. 38 Wall
M'Cormick ——, 81 Canal
M'Intyre Charles & Co. 35 Wall
M'Jimsey J. M. 58 Wall
M'Vickar Wm. H. 62 Merch Ex.
M'Kinstry Wm. 292 Greenwich
Marvin J. 45 Cortlandt
Mather Wm. 70 W. Broadway
Maxwell & Co 60 Wall
Mendel H. M. 186 Broadway
Miller Edmund H. 53 Wall
Miller & Hoffman, 51 Merch. Ex.
Monroe E S., Jauncey ct. 39 Wall
Morgan Henry T. 67 Wall
Morrison E. & Co. 47 Wall
Nathan Mendez, 60 Wall
Neilson Wm. H. 63 Wall
Niberson Wm. 22 Vesey
Nicholas A. 74 Wall
Nicholson Meadows T. 56 Wall

Norwood Andrew G. 51 Wall
New York.
Noyes Dan. L. 121 Bowery
O'Brien Wm. & John, 33 Wall
Odell L. 417 Broadway
Ogden H. 151 Fulton
Ogden Isaac G. 60 Wall
Ogden Thomas W. 62 Wall
Okell William & Co. 35 Wall
Olcott H. W. 54 Merchants' Ex.
Paine John, 51 Wall
Parker J. C. 46 Merchants' Ex.
Pepoon, Hoffman & Ten Brook, 51 Wall
Perego W. H. 157 W. Broadway
Pickersgill W. C. 49 Wall
Phaler James, 51 Wall
Platt Newton, 60 Wall
Plass M. 208 Broadway
Purdy Elijah, 22 Merchants' Ex.
Rankin John, 65 Wall
Rawdon, Groesbeck & Bridgham, 54 Wall
Ray James H. 54 Wall
Remington J. L. 169 Washington
Richards Henry, 52 Wall
Richards Timothy, 52 Wall
Robbins G. S. & Son, 52 Wall
Robinson Elisha D. — Hanover
Rogers J. W. 22 Merchants' Ex.
Rollins G. A. 35 Wall
Rudd & Wheeler, 38 Wall
Secchi G. A. 5 Broad
Sagory Charles, 4 Hanover
Sather & Church, 164 Nassau
Schell Frederick. 64 Wall
Schermerhorn John, 60 Wall
Schulz & Bleidorn, 76 Broad
Searls William & Co. 53 Wall
Sedgwick R. 62 Wall
Seymour William, jr. 65 Wall
Shipman Edward A. 60 Wall
Shipman William H. 64 Wall
Sloane Christian S. 23 Wall
Smith & Haus, 137 Chatham
Snelling Andrew S. 66 Wall
Spear Alvah & Son, 60 Wall
Stanley Daniel, 151 Leonard
St. John Ansel, 67 Wall
St. John L. 116 Chatham
Storey Stephen B. 262 Pearl
Sturges James H. 5 Bowery
Swam John L. 60 Wall
Swan J. S. 151 South
Sylvester S. J. 47 Wall
Tailer Edward N. 49 William
Tallmadge Benjamin H. 51 Wall
Taylor, Brothers, 76 Wall & 152 Pearl
Taylor E. N. 49 William
Tempest Thomas, 60 Wall
Thompson John, 64 Wall
Thorne T. W. jr. 64 Wall
Thorne William S. 58 Wall
Thwing C. & E. W. 29 Wall
Tice Jerome, 376 Hudson
Toland Blair M. 60 Wall
Toland Henry, 60 Wall
Tolerton H. F. 18 Fulton
Tompkins Ray, 36 Wall
Townsend R. T. 72 W. Broadway
Underwood J. A. & Son, 22 Merchants' Ex.
Van Rensselaer & Co. 54 Wall
Wadesworth Charles, 2 Nassau
Walker Alexander, 60 Wall
Walsh J. W. 30 Merchants' Ex.
Warner, Read & Lathrop, 40 Wall
Warner G. T. 316½ Broadway
Warrener & Co. 70 Wall
Warren John & Son, 65 Wall
Warrener & Co. 70 Wall
Waterhouse J. W. 146 Bowery
Weeks & Co. 56 Wall
Weeks, Kelley & Co. 42 Wall
Weston G. W. 86 Hanover
White F. & Co. 35   do
Wilcox Harvey R. 67 do
Williams Edward, 27 Merchants' Exchange
Williams B. T. 8   do.
Wilson James, 67 Vesey

Wilson D. 82 Wall *New York.*
Winter John G. Son & Co. 54 Wall
Wood Joshua B. Wall
Woods William, 180 Broadway
Wood B. 118 Canal

BROKERS—TEA.

Calwell W. H. 105 Front
   New York.
Cassidy James, 105 do
Leathem & Thompson, 96 Wall
Lester Gerard C. 13 Old Slip
Montgomery James, jr. 106 Front
Wardell Charles, 120 do
Wardell Henry B. 120 do

BROKERS—TOBACCO.

Agnew C. 116 Water *New York.*
Gentz John S. 87 Wall
Rader Maximilian, 93 do
Ruete Charles T. 79 do
Schwab A. F. 101 do

BROKERS—WINE.

Daly J. B. 106 Wall *New York*
Davis & Henriques, 99 Wall
Gifford James N. 94 do
Hayward H. S. 83 do
Monlun J. 60 do
Monlun Henry, 60 do
Scrymser J. & D. A. 113 do
Scrymser R. S. 113 do
Starin W. H. 109 do
Wyckoff J. N. & Son, 109 do

BROKERS—WOOD.

Barrell Geo. 105 Wall *New York.*
Thooft Bernard, 6 Broad

BROKERS—WOOL.

Greene John F. 156 Pearl & 79½
 Pine *New York.*
Pettibone Hiram A. 3 Broad
Ripley Joseph, 68 Pine
Smyth John W. 90 Wall
Terry, Brothers, 59 Ferry

Brokers.—(Continued.)

Oneida County.

Post N. J. (Exchange) 5 Genesee
   Utica.
Churchill V. H. & Co. 5 Exchange
 Buildings

Onondaga County.

Monroe A. Water st. Syracuse
   Salina
Tracy James G. Syracuse

Rensselaer County.

Deyoe George C. (Exchange) 294
 State *Lansingburgh.*
Warren Thomas E. 175 River
   Troy.
Adancourt Francis, (Exchange &
 Lottery) 190 River
Filkins A. G. (Stock & Exchange)
 228 River
Farwells L. (Exchange & Lottery)
 230 River
Corning James, (Stock & Exch.)
 228 River
Barney J. L. (Exchange) 212 River
Cornwell M. do 214 do
Niles ——, (Exchange & Lottery)
 230 River
Nichols John H. 3 1st

St. Lawrence County.

Judson David C. Water st. Ogdensburgh *Oswegatchie.*
Judson Daniel, Water st. Ogdensburgh

Bronzes.

Baack Edward, 81 Fulton
   New York.
Brandeis L. & Co. 11 Cedar
Moore Jonathan, 3 Dutch
Williams W. M. 136 Maiden lane

Broom Makers.

Albany County.

Tift J. *Coeymans.*
Clute John, Dunnsville
   Guilderland.

Genesee County.

Munger & Bardwell *Le Roy.*
Dickinson G.
Munson L.

Jefferson County.

Smith J. D. *Adams.*

Montgomery County.

Bronson George W. J.
   Amsterdam.
Craft A. P. Fonda *Mohawk.*
Bronson G. W. J. do

Oneida County.

Seaman J. S. 219 Genesee *Utica.*

Orange County.

Slingerland J., Wells Corners
   Minisink.

Schenectady County.

Toll C. H. *Glenville.*
Campfield G.
Sanders P.
Tull A. W.
Reese D. F.
Vedder H.
Elwood R.
Harwood & Wells (Agents for
 Shakers) *Niskayuna.*
Van Ness & Brothers *Rotterdam.*
Vedder I.

Schoharie County.

Kilmer Martin *Esperance.*
Kilmer J. *Schoharie.*

Washington County.

Tilton William *Greenwich.*

Brooms, Wholesale.

Eaton & Brothers, 78 Broad & 23
 Pearl *New York.*

Brush Manufacturers.

Albany County.

Armour J. B. 389 Broadway
   Albany.

Kings County.

Coombe John, 194 Pearl *Brooklyn.*
Steel William, (feather brushes)
 244 Adams
Fray Lucas, 230 Grand
   Williamsburgh.

Monroe County.

Patterson Thomas, cor. Main &
 Water *Rochester.*

Rensselaer County.

Ames J. 167 State *Lansingburgh*
Curren Thomas, River st.
Cross & Hoyt, Congress st. Alley
Gass Charles, do
Scott & M'Kinney, Alley bet. Con-
 gress & John
M'Murrey John G. cor. Richard
 & John
M'Murrey R. D. & D. 208 River
   Troy.

Seneca County.

Bruik George W. Farmer *Ovid.*

Saratoga County.

Holroyd Simeon *Waterford.*

Brushes and Bellows.

Allen & Son, 213 Washington
   New York.
Alcorn John, 51 Morton
Berrien Daniel, jr. & Co. 240 &
 357 Pearl
Berrien D. & Co. 226 Pearl
Betts Joseph E. 85 4th Av.
Blackett Wm. 225 3d Av. & 4th
 st. Bowery
Broker David, 8th Av.
Cassedy John, 65 Carmine
Carpenter H. 280 Washington
Dennis W. 192 & 194 Washington
Earl John, 112 Cannon
Flager Edward, 211 Water
Fenn N. 374 Bleecker
Fisher Abraham, jr. 12 Suffolk
Furnald Francis P. 180 Water
Goetzees M. 7th Av.
Graff John C. 187 W. 15th
Hoagland & Co. 199 Washington
Hopping & Meker, 95 Washing-
 ton
Lockwood C. cor. Water & Fulton
Laden & Son, 190 Washington
Loppell John K. 237 Pearl
M'Keachnie Allan, 385½ Grand
M'Murray John G. & Co. 278 Pearl
M'Murray R. D. & D. jr. 261 Pearl
M'Murray William, 214 Pearl
Mann Adam. 64 Essex
Mason Rush F. 306 Pearl
Middlemore Joseph, 112 Fulton
Moulin & Sylva. 444 & 446 Hudson
Mount R. E. & Son, 359 Pearl
Noe James H. 179 Greenwich
Noe Rowland J. 2 William
Parker Joseph N. 506 Pearl
Parshall James L. 33 Cherry
Peckham Emma, 5 Chambers
Philipoteaux G. 3 Maiden Lane
Parker I. N. 506 Pearl
Porter William C. 289 Hudson
Provost A. M. 203 Chrystie
Shaw E. D. 85 Catharine
Rung John A. 43 Av. B
Scanck Alfred, 86 Division
Sheehan William B. 295 Pearl
Slater William, 104 8th Av.
Smith Edmond L. 166 Water
Smith Himan, 247 Pearl
Smith Robert C. 294 do
Steele & Co. 305 do
Towner D. F. 296 do
Wallis Charles, 96 Gold
Wainwright Edwin, 218 Spring
West Joseph, 45 Fulton
White John F. 197 Greenwich
Winterble George, 90 Fulton

Otsego County.

Loomis Morgan *Worcester.*

Builders. (See also Architects; also Carpenters; also Masons.)

New York County.

Adams Samuel, 72 Irving place
Anderson Edmund, 67 Eldridge
   New York.

Anderson & Hawxhurst, 90 Leo-
nard *New York.*
Atkinson Samuel, 39 Attorney
Bailey S. B. 53 Greene
Baldwin Luther, 89 Delancy
Becker & Baker, 36 E. 19th
Beebe Robert, 577 4th
Beebe & Co. rear 129 Amity
Beekman J. S. 50 4th Av.
Bessey Samuel H. rear 66 1st
Betts James H. 81 Forsyth
Biglow & Ferries, 107 10th
Blackstone W. 132 Laurens
Bliss J. E. Av. 1 near 9th
Bogert & Frye, 150 Amos
Bowne Samuel C. 59 Elm
Brown J. M. 14 Elm
Brown William R. 44 Perry
Bunting John A. 22 E. Broadway
Butler & Lockwood. 92 E. 13th
Butler & Tracy, 27 Minetta lane
Cabrow Richard, jr. 102 24th
Carr P., E. 27th st.
Carr John, 116 Sullivan
Canfield Henry, 178 Laurens
Christie & Bogert, 135 Amos
Christy John W. rear 201 W. 15th
Clark James, rear 134 Laurens
Coffin J. & J. B. 345 4th
Conklin A. L. 802 Greenwich
Cooper J. M. 54 E. 13th
Corties I. B. 94 17th
Coultes John, 36 Rutgers
Cromwell Daniel, 123 Allen
Cumming & Pollock, 227 W. 19th
Davison Darius, 3 Nassau
De Camp Joseph, rear 37 1st Av.
Demarest & Onderdonk, 126 Amos
Devoe Daniel M. 178 Wooster
Dinaut Louis C. 88 Ann
Doremus J. R. 269 23d
Dubois James G. 22 Bethune
Duncomb Ashel S. 185 Elm
Edwards S. A. rear 30 Barclay
Eldridge Richard S. 157 Duane
Esler Henry, 246 Madison
Etchebry Louis, 108 Reade
Farley Wm. C. 232 10th
Feilding John W. 238 3d Av.
Fanbroock H. 102 Church
Finch George, 708 Broadway
Ford G. 7th Av.
Freeman E., W. 16th near 7th Av.
Freeman & Co. 50 Broadway
Gardiner T. 125 Rivington
Gardiner & Co. 105 Norfolk
Geer D. Thompson st.
Giles Gilbert, 26 Murray
Glascher & Romana. 149 Troy
Gottker J. H. cor. 5th st. & Av. B
Green John, 115 Walker
Hadden & Gedney, 135 Laurens
Haddock Thomas, 296 W. 19th
Hall Asbury F. 168 Allen
Hallock S. 84 Murray
Hatfield James, 166 Crosby
Hennessy Dennis, 168 Walker
Henry Robert, 178 Prince
Hibbets F. D.
Hicks & Sarine, rear 97 Forsyth
Hoe R. & J. 6 & 10 Liberty place
& Gansevoort,below Greenwich
Hunt Wm. S. 20th st.
Hutchings & Bleecker, 46 Ludlow
Johnson J. T. 70 7th
Johnson John W. 130 Clinton place
Johnston & Girahz, 287 12th
Jones David, 44 Eldridge
Kent Joseph, 168 Reade
Kerr H. 21 Dey
Keyser & Berrier, 192 4th
Kipp S. C. 33 4th Av.
Knapp D. H. 151 Orchard
La Forge Cornelius. 165 Barrow
Lampson D. C. 96 Chrystie
Lawall Jacob, 66 North Moore
Leaird Alexander, 201 5th
Lafurgy & Cousins, 100 2d
Lewis I. 23 Canal
Lockwood & Butler, 92 E. 13th
Lockwood & Palmatier, 49 1st
Losee Charles, 219 12th

Ludlam John, 11 Fell *New York.*
Ludlam John, 244 Madison
Mailler Wm. 196 Elm
Meeker & Angevine, 170 Mercer
Melville A., W. 29th st.
Miller Jeremiah. 60 Cliff
Mercereau John W. 53 Amos
Meyer J. S. 27th W. Broadway
Monilaws James, 3 Lafayette pl.
Morris T. cor. 1st Av. & 10th st.
Murphy D. 25th st.
Nestell J. J. 47 Eldridge
O'Connor Bartholomew, 242 9th
O'Connor & Hamill, 13 Reade
Overhiser A. 309 E. 9th
Packer John. 191 4th
Parker & Van Dolsen, 194 W. 20th
Paton Robert, 333 Hudson
Peck Charles, E. 22d near 2d Av.
Pendleson & Cocking, 64 Church
Pollard Otis, rear 142 Wooster
Powell T. W. & J. S. 203 7th
Price John J. T. 163 Orchard
Pugaley Robert. 90 6th Av.
Purss Joseph D. 103 W. Broadway
Reed & Taft, 62 White
Rogers E. F.. E. 27th st.
Rogers J. 123 12th
Richards John, E. 19th st.
Russell Hiram, 66 Attorney
Ryan James, 12 2d Av.
Sailsbury & Henry, 55 W. 13th
Sandford Charles, 20 Chambers
Schoonmaker Benj. J. 320 5th
Schoonmaker B. J. cor. 1st Av. &
7th
Schuyler John & Co. 75 8th Av.
Seal John S. 117 7th Av.
Shute T. W. Lafayette cor. Astor
place
Smith B. 219 8th Av.
Smith C. F. 130 Duane
Smith Ezra, rear 113 Greenwich
Smith George, 166 Prince
Smith Thomas, C. 89 Mer. Ex.
Smith James W. 307 West 21st
Smith Thomas, 89 Church
Smith W. H. 233 21st
Smith & Clark, 153 9th
Smith & Clayton, 243 5th
Sutton Silas, 14 6th
Snediker J. V. 2d Av. cor. 25th
Stansbury Edgar, 21½ Thames
Stephens James H. 784 Greenwich
Stuckey Alfred, 262 2d
Taylor & Little, 68 W. 13th
Tenbroeck H. 102 Church
Thomson John, 271 W. 19th
Thomson Wm. A. 444 Washington
Thomson & Son, 442 Washington
Tribit & Hardley, 161 Mercer
Tunison G. M. 129 16th
Urner J. R. 164 W. Broadway
Van Riper Anthony, 312 Broadway
Van Velsor & Gardiner, E. 9th st.
Volk H. 35 Horatio
Vorlies A. F., W. 26th st.
Vredenburgh Isaac, rear 11 Doyer
Webb George, 184 Wooster
Wells & Cochran, 76 Av. B.
Westervelt J. 2 Church & 199 Ful-
ton
Whip H. 743½ Greenwich
White Charles B. & Co. 567 4th
White John J. 55 Green
Whitlock & Harrington,138 Woos-
ter
Wight R. rear 141 Thompson
Williams Elias F. 73 Bowery
Williams Stephen H. 105 Bank
Winans Henry H. 54 Wooster
Winant & Degraw, 96 Cliff
Witherup & Armstrong. 50 Marion
Wright Charles B. 567 4th
Wright Richard, 141 Thompson
Wright William, 283 3d
Young George, 54 Houston

Builders' Materials.

Bullwinkle R. cor. 23d & 1st Av.
New York.

Byrne George C. 194 West
New York.
Chamberlin Enoch, 330 West
Denham Asahel A. foot W 20th
Gardiner T. 105 Norfolk.
Gay R. P. & Co. 209 Cherry
Hopper John M. rear 547 Broome
Hunt Woodward, 70 Willet
Loper & Davis, cor. 18th & Av. B.
Loveland & Berrian, 381 West
Nelson & Brown, 290 West
Schoonmaker Cyrus, 52 Lewis

Burr Blocks—Importers of.

Loughlin Martin, 8 Water
Livingston M. & W. 70 Broad
Norris Peter & Co. 45 Duane
Stacy James, 156 Allen
Tyack William, 66 Robinson

Burr Mill Manufacturers.

Cayuga County.

Warden E. A. Genesee st. *Auburn.*

Onondaga County.

Griffin R. *Salina*

Butchers and Meat Dealers.

Albany County.

Putnam & Shaw, Quay & Colum-
bia sts. *Albany.*
Clinton J. 175 Montgomery
Moore A. F. 175 do
Stillwell & Collins, 60 Green
Armstrong Wm. 165 & 165 S. Pearl
Russel & Vanguysland, 104 do
M'Quade J. 6 & 7 Centre Market
Castle William, 3 do
Van Meter A. 5 do
Bedell R. 4 do
Kirkpatrick E. 1 & 2 do
Snowden Chas. 9 & 10 do
Schwartz G. 11 do
Lindenstein Moses, 12 do
Eaton J. E. 13 do
Ostrander J. 14 do
Gibson Wm. H. 16 do
Lindsey William, 17 do
Frederick P. & J. 18 & 20 do
Sawyer A. 10 Centre Fish Market
Simmons E. 1 & 2 do do
Passengers A. 1 Cen. Veg. Mar.
Harper R. 2 & 3 do do
Saunders Z. M. 4 do do
Rull J. 6 do do
Cobb E. C. 7 do do
Brayton J. W. 5 do do
Bannin A. 8 do do
Dalton — 11 do do
Parker J. 9 do do
Palmer J. 13 do do
Mahan B. 14 do do
Beighton B. 15 do do
Chapman P. 16 do do
Hutson J. B. 17 do do
Gilchrist W. B. 18 do do
Roessle T. 19 & 20 do do
Bates C. 21 do do
Walch William, 9 Pine
Pattersby James, 19 Patroon
Veeder J. 15 Washington
Gibson Cornelius V., Bowery
Charles Thomas, 15 Canal
Harrison J. 59 Canal
Battersby J. 51 2d
M'Claskly J. 160 State
Perry Eli, 87 Washington
Bedwell J. West Troy *Watervliet.*
Troy J. do
Whipple M. do
Bedell & Co. do

Alleghany County.

Van Campen William *Almond.*
Corey J. 2d

Engle Matthias　　　　*Angelica.*
Booth Jacob
Reynolds Asa　　　　*Belfast.*
Fisk E. B., Wellsville　　*Scio.*

Broome County.

Burrows & Wilson　*Binghamton.*
West D. B.
Whitmore J. H.
Castle & Buckingham

Cattaraugus County.

Fuller A. M. D.　　　*Burton.*
Griffith Wm., Gowanda　*Persia.*
Roler J. P.　　do
Barrows E. B , East　*Randolph.*

Cayuga County.

Coonley & Willcox, Genesee st.
　　　　　　　　Auburn.
Patten J. E. State st.
Decker & Miller, North st.
Smith S. South st.
Fattz Wm., Weedsport　*Brutus.*

Chautauque County.

Ransom N. K. Jamestown *Ellicott.*
Jones Alexander,　do

Chenango County.

Willcox & Morris　　*Greene.*
Brown R. S.　　　*Oxford.*
M'Neil Charles A.

Columbia County.

Fowler A., Claverack
Dakin H. cor. Front & Warren
　　　　　　　　Hudson.
Root M. B. 314 Warren
Limbrick D. & Co.78 do
Remington J.　do
Hinman H. D.,Valatie *Kinderhook.*

Delaware County.

Uttenburgh J.　　*Davenport.*
Gregory G., Deposit　*Tompkins.*

Duchess County.

Beker A. Wapping Falls *Fishkill.*
Dean W. Hughsonville
Buckley Wm., Glenham
Washburn J. & J. C. Fishkill
　Landing
Parker T. E.　　*Hyde Park.*
Williams J. E.
Augevine Wm.　*Pine Plains.*
Bankerhorn & Turner
　　　　　　　Poughkeepsie.
Broas John (oysters, fruit, & fish)
Jillens James,　do.
Hoffman P. H. 239 Main
Peters I. F. 335　do
Wilsey T. B. 292　do
Pine & Spencer, 231 do
Sage P. W. L. 219　do
Simpson & Cary, Eastern Market
Taylor P. 433 Main
Pellon J. 123　do
Lasher S.　　　*Red Hook.*
Seymour R. T.　　*Rhinebeck.*
Pultz M.
Chamberlain H. Hart's Village
　　　　　　　Washington.

Erie County.

Zent P. Williamsville　*Amherst.*
Bodswell ——　*Black Rock.*
Hough Benjamin　　*Boston.*
Robbins Joseph, Springville
　　　　　　　Concord.
Heller Jacob　　　*Eden.*
Ferris and Straman　*Tonawanda.*
Hay William
Serles Samuel J.　　*Wales.*
Wilson J. (pork) 15 Exchange
　　　　　　　Buffalo.
Roberts T. Elk st.

Frign & Leclear, cor. Michigan &
　Seneca　　　　*Buffalo.*
Barnes Joshua, 201 Washington
Sheffier P. cor. Michigan & Batavia
Farthing J. cor. Main & Eagle
Bullymore T. 328 Main
Coats & Palmer, 25 Ohio
Vine Geo. 20 Terrace market
Cummins Henry, 18　do
Juden Frederick, 19　do
Burghart Peter, 11　do
Bailinger Wm. 9　do
Dickman Geo. 5 & 7　do
Laycock Thos. 1 & 9 do
Salisbury & Craig, 8　do
Farthing James, 6　do
Glass John, 2　　do
Leclear & Farthing, 4 do
Alberger Job, 1　do
Barnes John, 14　do
Burt Il B. 7　　do
Allberger F. A. 8 & 9 do
Dickey Anderson, 6　do
Lamb H. 3 & 4　　do
Boorom & Co. 2　do
Weppner J. 874 Main
Hoffer J. G. 394　do
Weppner A. 418　do
Bullymore R. 129 do

Genesee County.

Fowler R.　　　*Batavia.*
Winn R.
Ware W.
Buckley John　　*Le Roy.*
Clark and Reese

Greene County.

Kellogg & Wilson　*Catskill.*
Lovell James
Benjamin Joseph　*Prattsville.*

Herkimer County.

Lewis Henry　　*Herkimer.*
Welkler & Devendorf
Hammon W. & Son　*Little Falls.*
Clark John C.

Jefferson County.

Bliss & Gleason　　*Adams.*
Gillett Paul W.
Macomber & Alexander
　　　　　　　Brownville.

Kings County.

Abbott S. D. 50 Myrtle Av.
　　　　　　　Brooklyn.
Applegate D. P. Brooklyn Market
Baldwin T. H.　do
Bennett James, cor. South &
　Douglass, South
Bourdett S. S., Duffield st.
Brush Samuel, Market South
Bunford Edm Brooklyn Market
Burdett Stephen. 117 Hudson Av.
Byrne William, 154 Myrtle Av.
Carman James, 149　do
Carman Val. Brooklyn Market
Cornwall Lewis, 211 Adams
Charmau Edw. cor. Atlantic &
　Boerum
Colburt T. 314 Atlantic
Collet J. 162 York
Conklin Wm. N. 9 Hamilton Av.
Crummey John, Brooklyn Market
Crummey Owen,　do
Crummey H. Brooklyn Market
Crummey G. Flushing Av.
Crummey T. Brooklyn Market
Curry Michael, S. do
Davenport John, 114 Willoughby
Davenport R. S., Pearl cor. Con-
　cord
Dawson J. L. Brooklyn Market
Dowlan Patrick, Flushing Av.
Dickie Robert, 51 Tillary
Dougherty W. cor. Court & At-
　lantic
Dobson Thomas, 101 Fulton
Ellard J. cor. Columbia & Degraw

Elton T. 163 High
Fardington J. M. 79 Bridge
Fernald D., Tillary near Fulton
Floor William D. 153 Gold
Fitspatrick P., S. Brooklyn mkt.
Foster P. H. 3 Market
Gallagher Richard, Clinton near
　Congress
Hambler William, 25 Hicks
Harrison Robert F. T. Myrtle Av.
　cor. Adams
Haw R. South Brooklyn Market
Haynes Edward, Fulton st.
Holder John B. 138 York
Higbie & Lamberson, 163 Atlantic
Hopkins William G. Union st.
Cornwall Lewis, 211 Adams
Charman Edward, cor.
Kent Hamilton, 93 Orange
Kershaw John H. 145 Prospect
Kline L. W., Brooklyn Market
Kyker Timothy,　do
Leeson John, 114 Pearl
M'Clean J. cor Hicks & Atlantic
M'Kittrick E., Brooklyn Market
M'Kenney William,　do
M'Mahon Archibald,　do
Matthews J. Jay cor. High
Mee Chas. M. & Co. 229 Fulton
Meathe John, 114 Front
Morgan T. cor. Fulton & Court
Morris B. 102 Myrtle Av.
Morrell James R. 162 do
Martah James, 123 Smith
Nevin J. S. Brooklyn Market
O'Donnell John cor. Smith & Wy-
　koff
Orwald G. W. & A. F. 151 & 153
　Court
Peck Robert W.,Brooklyn Market
Quinn James,　do
Rogers J. 111 Atlantic
Ryder L. C. corner of Fulton &
　Middagh sts.
Ryder John S. 103 Atlantic
Schenck Daniel T. 85 Myrtle Av.
Shafor Mrs. Market st.
Simonson John R. 4 Linden Row
Simonson G. H. Brooklyn market
Stewart M. W. 173 Bridge
Stryker St. John, Brooklyn mkt.
Tilus James, Brooklyn　do
Truppal John,　do　do
Van Voorhis B. H. 1 Stanton st
Van Dine Peter J. Brooklyn mkt
Ward Benjamin, Myrtle Av.
Wooley Edward A. 184 High
Young & Co. S. Brooklyn market
Doane Winslow, Green Point
　　　　　　　Bushwick.
Ferguson James, 4th cor. 9. 7th
　　　　　　　Williamsburgh.
Gilchrist N. & J., S. 7th near 1st
Barckle Geo. 185 S. 4th
Sharr John, 281　do
Lapp Antro, 196 Ewing
Tice Aaron, 17 Grand
Quinlan J. & Co., 195 Grand
Cummings Geo. 288　do
Chapin K. 216　　do
Barnes George, 156　do
Warner Thomas, 220 1st
Wall Edward. 2d cor. N. 3d st.
Lathem Daniel, 266 1st
Smith Arnold, Union Av. corner
　Grand
Sache Adam, 110 Remsen
Barnes Geo. 145 4th

Lewis County.

Kent James　　　*Turin.*
Tolles H. Constableville
　　　　　　　West Turin.

Livingston County.

Davis ——　　　*Avon.*
Laidlaw Thomas　*Caledonia.*
Howarth & Roth　*Dansville.*
Doty & Kettle
Atwood W, B.
Hall R. J.　　　*Geneseo.*

Taylor ——, Moscow *Leicester.*
Gillett & Whipple *Lima.*
Terry Thomas, *Mount Morris.*
Parsons & Bowerman
Gould Levi *Nunda.*
Thayer & Chamberlin
Lent Henry, Oakland *Portage.*
Buckridge ——, Piffardania *York.*

Madison County.

Caswell & Hatch *Cazenovia.*
Wood D. Morrisville *Eaton.*
Curtis Joseph *Hamilton.*
French & Beaman, Chittenango
  Sullivan.

Montgomery County.

Morrel & Hoag *Canajoharie.*
Wetmore S. E.
Haggart Alex., Fonda *Mohawk.*

New York County.

Abelman Conrad, 110 Division
  New York.
Alden Joseph, 55 Fulton mkt
Allaire Anthony M. 462 Hudson
Allaire Charles, 7 Clinton mkt
Allaire Daniel D. 584 Hudson
Allaire Simeon, 301 Bleecker
Allard Nahum W. 154 Varick
Arthur Peter, cor. Av. C. & 2d
Andurless John. 246 Wash. mkt
Anderson John F. 3 Cath. mkt
Anderson Walter 5 Cath. mkt
Appleby James, 34 Cath. mkt
Anthony A. Washington mkt
Appleby John A. 42 Cath. mkt
Appleby Joseph C. & James, 25 &
  26 Catharine mkt
Aslacher Aaron, 43 Essex mkt
Asten Joseph C. 146 W. 16th
Atkins William D. 10 Union mkt
Baner ——, 15 Delancy
Bar Joseph, 226 Rivington
Barber Edward. 394 Pearl
Barker Usel B. 118 Greene
Barker Wm. L. 618 Broadway
Barker & Teller, cor 13th
Barmore Wm. 344 6th Av.
Barr Wm. H. 36 Clinton mkt
Barrett Patrick. 127 Mulberry
Bartine Thos. C. Washington st.
Basley Chas. J. 84 Thompson
Bathgate Geo. 353 4th Av.
Bauersachs J. M. 580½ Broome
Bazley Wm. 183 Church
Bazley & Bennett. 183 Church
Bear Joseph, 226 Rivington
Beasser John. 34 Spring
Bechstern Frederick, 9½ Hudson
Beebe J. W. 749 Greenwich
Beecher John D. 535 Broome
Beers W. P. 69 Orange
Behringer Jacob, 131 Hester
Bennett Geo. Av. A. cor. E. 13th
Bennett Wm. W. 10 Centre mkt
Bennett & Bazley, 183 Church
Bennie Aaron, 6 Clinton mkt
Bertholf John B. 45 Thompson
Broadway A. 107 Canal
Brown G. Clinton mkt
Brown Daniel H. 59 Cherry
Billigheimer Leopold, 90 Ridge
Bird Chas. N. 398 2d Av.
Bird Freeman B. 10 Wash. mkt
Birk Edward, 86 Washington
Bishop Wm. 219 2d
Black John P. 136 Hester
Black Thomas, 117 Anthony
Blair Edward, 835 Greenwich
Blair Wm. T. 53 Mott
Bloomfield George, 28 Av. C
Bloomfield George W. 30 Av. C
Borchers John W. 3 Wash. mkt
Borden Wm. D. 4 Centre mkt
Borshenger Joseph, 182 Houston
Bortzal Henry, 37 Goerck
Boutcher Robert. 82 Division
Bowrosan I. 191 Greenwich
Bowrosan Christian, 189 Greene

Bowens Wm. 350 3d Av.
  New York.
Boyce Jacob. 386 Houston
Brady John S. 20 Clinton mkt
Brady John W. 243 Walker
Brand Amos, 160 8th Av.
Brand Nathan, 218 Stanton
Brand John, 48 9th Av.
Brand John B. 8th Av.
Brandt & Liebman, 222 5th
Breikenidel Henry, 276 Mulberry
Brennan Patrick, 9 12th
Brewer Abm. 9 Clinton market
Brewer John. jr. 23 Essex do
Brickwell Peter, 101 4th
Brickwedell J. H. 71½ do
Briel Christian, 35 Delancy
Briel Daniel, 15 Essex market
Briggs Walter, 35 do
Bright Thomas, 390 Hudson
Broadway Alfred, 107 Canal
Broadway Edw. 69 University pl
Broadway T. E. 1 Clinton mkt.
Brogam Thomas, 691 Greenwich
Brogan J. 18 Hudson & 146 Centre
Brown Alex. 4 Washington mkt.
Brown Daniel, 59 Cherry
Bulger Patrick, 9 Fulton market
Burke Edward, 38 Washington
Burke John, 17 Washington mkt.
Bush David, 111 Monroe
Byrne Matthew, 34 Catharine mkt.
Byrnes John, 259 Mulberry
Calhoun Thos. Washington mkt.
Campbell Charles, 12 Essex mkt.
Campbell G. W. 52 Washington
  mkt.
Campf Fred. 73 Av. B
Captain Andrew, 26 W. Broadway
Carman Ebenezer L. & Co.18 & 19
  Centre market
Carman Samuel S. 17 Centre mkt.
Carnie William, 189 1st Av.
Carpenter Henry S. 37 Essex mkt.
Carpenter Stephen, 32 do.
Carstang W. 53 Washington mkt.
Case & Vandewater,886 Broadway
Casey Hugh, 93 W. 18th
Castel Wm. cor. 2d Av. & 2d
Ceraben Alex. 13 Mulberry
Chamberlain J. C. Wash'ton mkt.
Chappel John, 60 Fulton do
Chase G. H. 33 Washington do
Chase Mat. H. 33 do
Chivvis William, 84 Fulton mkt.
Churchill Reuben, 652 Greenwich
Clinch Joseph W. & Frederick, 25
  & 26 Centre market
Compton Wm. 15 Wash'ton mkt.
Concklin John R. 3 Clinton do
Conger D. T. 70 Houston
Conklin A. L. 902 Greenwich
Conklin Caleb, Washington mkt.
Conklin William, 143 Ludlow
Conway James, 46 Walnut
Coaway James, 19 Wash'ton mkt.
Conway John, 20 Catharine do
Conway Richard, 22 do
Cooper Charles, 29 Fulton mkt.
Cornell Henry, 71 Roosevelt
Cornell William H. 74 Roosevelt
  & 59 Fulton market
Costallo T. 12th bet. Avs. A & B
Costello Thomas, 310 1st Av.
Coughlin William, 117 Hudson
Coutman Abraham, 7 Bayard
Cox Leander M. 10 Clinton mkt.
Craft William, 164 Clinton
Crandell & Williams, 16 Washing-
  ton market
Crasto M. 122 W. Broadway
Crawbok James F. 617 4th
Crawbuck William,193 Greene
Crawford James, 323 3d Av.
Crisfield E. 65 Washington mkt.
Crist Christian, 219 W. 17th
Crommeline C. 24 Washington
  market
Crooks John, 20 Washington mkt.
Cross William H. 171 Stanton
Croxon Henry, 229 Thompson
Cruise James, 26 Catharine mkt.

Dakin Geo. H. Washington mkt.
  New York.
Daniel James, 477 Pearl
Danston Adam, 247 Stanton
Danzler Adam, 247 Stanton
Davison I. H. 76 9th Av.
Davidson Francois, 12 Clinton mkt.
Davis Thomas, 7th Av.
Dean John, 201 Stanton
Dean John E. 22 Centre market
Dean W. H. 54 Washington mkt.
Deforest Elias T. 61 Fulton mkt.
DeMott J. & Co. 27 Washington
  market
Dempsey Luke, 303 Mott
Devoe John 109 Ferry& 735 Green-
  wich
Devoe John, 6 Jefferson market
Devoe Moses, 10 Jefferson market
Devoe Thos. F. 8 Jefferson market
Devoe & Valentine, 688 Broadway
Dieffenbach Henry & Co. 29 Cen-
  tre market & 478 4th
Dill John, 568 4th
Dixon John, 56 9th Av.
Dodge Sewell V. 236 Bleecker, 14
  Av. B. & 36 Cornelia
Donovan John, 11 Tompkins mkt.
Dorst G. 7th Av.
Downing I. 138 4th
Downing J. 62 Thompson
Downing Jordan, 75 Grove
Downing Robert, 22 Prince
Driscoll Patrick, 97 Gold
Drumgold Henry, 197 6th Av.
Duchardt Herionmus, 193 8th Av
Duchardt Jacob, 161 8th Av.
Dunn S. 1 Washington
Duryea Levi, 22 Essex mkt. & 1st
  Av. between 3d & 4th
Eccleston Thomas, 24 Fulton mkt.
Eckstein Henry, 20 Wash. mkt.
Eckstein Peter. 270 Walker
Eddey Ellis D. 5 Clinton market
Eddey J. V. 16 & 18 Cath. mkt.
Eddey William, 263 3d Av.
Edwards & Burke, 12 Prince
Edwards Richard, 459 Grand
Eglinton Alfred, 36 1st Av.
Elahaty John, 227 Elizabeth
Elder Robert, 23 Fulton market
Emrick Philip. 33 Hester
Engert K. 173 3d
Evans & Berryman, Wash. mkt
Evans & William, Wash. mkt.
Farrington Joseph H. 68 James
Forris Lanning 141 W. Broadway
Ferris Philip, 197 Rivington
Fescher Carl. 3 North William
Finely John, 24 Scammell
Fink Arnest, Clinton mkt.
Fink Jacob H. 25 Clinton mkt.
Fink Lewis, 10th Av.
Fisher Albert, jr. 21 Fulton mkt.
Fisher & Lyon, 19 W'hington mkt
Flammers John G. 98 Mott
Flashman Charles, 144 Houston
Flemming Robert, 83 8th Av.
Flook Alfred. 616 & 838 Broadway
Flock John, 20 Washington mkt
Ford Henry, 276 Broome
Ford James. 237 W. 17th
Foster B. 87 Av. D
Foster Robert K. 246 3d Av,
Ford W. O. 8th Av.
Frankhauser & Kromel
Fraser Henry, 263 3d
Frazier Henry, 186 3d
Freeborn William, 34 9th Av.
Friedman Philip, 9 Essex market
Garrison & Beer, 12 8th Av.
Garside Joseph, 26½ James
Gells John, 208 Broome
Gerhedt John, 132 W. 17th
Gervaize & Ryer, Broadway, cor.
  E. 21st
Gillet, Jones & Burrett, 218 3d Av.
Gilder N. Clinton market
Glasham Geo. Washington mkt.
Glovor Thomas. 184 Prince
Glover Thos. & William, 4 Frank-
  lin market & 171 Forsyth

Glover William & Charles S. 36 Washington market *New York.*
Gock Frederick, 31 Eldridge
Godine Francis, 20 Fulton market
Goetchius George H. 50 Broome
Goodheart William, Washington
Goodman James; 27 Catharine mkt
Goodman James M. 147 Ludlow
Goodrich David. 548 Grand
Goring Jacob, 8th Av.
Gottlieb Link, 83 7th Av.
Graff John A. 2 Washington mkt
Graham Gilbert, 331 Bowery
Graham William, 359 Bowery
Granger B. 25 Washington market
Granger Francis B. 89 4th Av.
Grebe Henry H. 96 Hester
Green Henry, 208 Varick
Grieshaber Mattheus. 152 Broome
Grum Wm. B. 14 Washington mkt
Gugel Frederick, 71 Hester
Gumbereckl ——, 162 Walker
Gwyer Charles, 18 Fulton mkt
Gwyer C. 8 & 9 Washington mkt
Hagin Ed. Washington market
Haight Henry, 100 Av. C
Haight Philip R. 24 Essex market
Haight Silvanus, 23 Catharine mkt
Hall & Conklin, 67 8th Av.
Halstead W. H. 24 W'hington mkt
Halstead P. & Co. W'hington mkt
Hammell S. H. 30 W'hington mkt
Hanigan B. 19 Catharine market
Hannegan John & Co. 12 & 14 Catharine market
Hanshe Jacob, 13 Washington mkt
Hanshe John, 15 Jefferson market
Hanshe Wm. 16 Washington mkt
Harms Henry, 30 Thomas
Harpel G. W. 51 Washington mkt
Harpell John, 55 Washington mkt
Harpell G. M. 8 Washington mkt
Harris John, 40 & 48 Washington market
Harrold Christopher, 577½ 4th
Hart Samuel, 189 Forsyth & Washington market
Hartel J. W. 7th st. cor. 1st Av.
Hathaway Jabez, 42 Beekman
Hatzfeld William, 177 Division
Hauck John, 253 Rivington
Havemeyer Wm. F. 7th Av.
Hawkins James, 22 Clinton mkt
Hawkins Zopher, 81   do
Hawkins & Morgan, 833 Broadway
Haws George & Co. 27 Fulton mkt
Haynes S. Washington mkt
Hays William, 1 Centre mkt
Hayward William, 51 Fulton mkt
Hefert Michael, 9 Carmine
Heintz Charles, 222 Stanton
Held C. 8th Av.
Henning John F. 50 Fulton mkt
Henning Joseph L. 63 Fulton mkt
Hepburn William, 159 Division
Herald Robert, 98 Av. C.
Herbert Thomas, 100 Pitt
Herbert Thomas, 319 Rivington
Herid Robert, 96 Av. C.
Herman A. 239½ Division
Hernon James, 70 Mulberry
Herring Robert, 26 Av. D.
Hide Henry, 1 Gouverneur mkt
Hill John J. 83 Rivington
Hines William, 66 Wash. mkt
Hoffman Frederick, 167 2d
Hoffman Joseph, 241 3d
Holden H. N. 233 Wooster
Holden Horatio M. 43 Amity
Holden Samuel, Wash. mkt
Holdredge Charles W. 134 Hester
Houghkirk John H. 149 Lewis
Hopkins William H. 30 Essex mkt
Horgan James, 139 Walker
Horton James, 39 & 44 Cath. mkt
Hough James, 164 Varick
Houghtailin J. H. 7 Jefferson mkt
Hone C. A. 55 Gouverneur
Hove Jacob, 52 Broome
Howard Bethuel, 42 Wash. mkt
Howe James, 164 Varick
Hunt Richard, 5 & 7 Fulton mkt

Hurtrogg Fritz, 23½ Albany *New York.*
Hyatt Wm. Washington mkt
Hyatt William L. 165 Spring
Hyde Daniel S. 1 Jefferson mkt
Hyde Isaac V. 3   do
Hyde John W. 7 Washington mkt
Hyde Samuel, 9th Av.
Hyde Thomas, 2 8th Av.
Hyde William B. Clinton mkt
Ihlburg Philip, 134 Av. C.
Irving James, 22 Wash. mkt
Itschen Antony, 121 7th Av.
Jacacks Benj. 17 Wash. mkt
Jacacks George, 31 Wash. mkt
Jackson James D. 9 Wash. mkt
Jackson Wm. A. 17 Essex mkt
Jaques David, 12 Union mkt
Johnson James. 1 Fulton mkt
Jones Thomas E. 396 Greenwich
Jenkins Thomas L. 35 Fulton mkt
Jenkins Thomas M. 1st Av. bet. 3d & 4th
Jennings G. W. 21 Wash. mkt
Johnson Frederick, 15 Centre mkt
Johnson William. 3 Union mkt
Jolley Lewis, 336 3d Av.
Jones Thomas E. 396 Greenwich
Kainne Adam, 212 Broadway
Kankle Philip, 31 Av. A.
Keeler William, 136 Spring
Keeler Wm. 92 Wooster
Kehoe David. 2 Centre market
Keim Wm. 196 Rivington
Kals John, 147½ Washington
Kemphf Frederick, 73 Av. B
Kenkele Philip A. 140 Laurens
Kenkle Philip, 31 Av. B
Kent C. & C. 47 Fulton mkt
Kent James, 8 Tompkins market
Keyser E. Washington market
Keyser John, 43   do
Killm Hugh, 303 Bowery
Kine Adam, 212 Broome
Kinner John. 15 Clinton market
Kipp M. J. 32 Washington market
Knowles John G. 487 Pearl
Knubel Diedrick, 6 Carmine
Knubel H. 2   do
Kober George, 73 Delancy
Koebel & Harman, 239½ Division
Koblhep John, 217 2d
Kowl Chas. 298 Av. B
Kyser Henry, 30 Clinton market
Lalor Wm. 30 & 31 Centre market
Lang Jas. 7 Washington market
Larkin Jas. C. 27 Centre market
Latham H. 16 Washington market
Lender Dennis, 243 11th
Laundry Paul, 72 Av. D
Lauterbach Samuel, 253 Stanton
Laway John B. 62 Thompson
Lawrence D. 13 & 14 Centre mkt.
Lawrence Enoch 72 Av. D
Lawrence Wm. 45 Essex market
Leach J. L. 41 Washington mkt.
Legmann Fred. 222 5th
Leigh Wm. 97 9th Av.
Leroy M. 12th st. bet. Avs. A & B
Levinees Jos. 8 Washington mkt.
Lewis C. 7 Washington market
Lewis John, 6 Union market
Little Alex. 278 Delancy
Link G. 7th Av.
Logue John, 336 Henry
Long Samuel, 18 Clinton market
Lough Henry, 336 Henry
Loundry Paul, 72 Av. D
Lozier Charles, 9 Clinton market
Lozier Charles, 16   do
Lozier Washington, 11 do
Lowry Jas. 5 & 7 Centre market
Loyd John P. 125 Bank
Lunfelt C. 199 Delancy
M'Ardle Jos. 22 & 24 Centre mkt.
M'Aulay James, 834 Greenwich
M'Creery Wm. H. Clinton market
M'Cue Jas. 2 Washington market
M'Cullough D. 33 Washington do
M'Donald John, 209 Varick
M'Dougal Henry, 132 Norfolk
M'Intyre & Young, 66 3d Av.

M'Kee ——, 296 Stanton
New York
M'Kewon John, 30 6th Av.
M'Kinnin Robert, 1 Ridge
M'Lone & Crane, 9 Centre mkt.
M'Parlen James, Washington do
Manahan & Heaverty, 45 Elm
Manges Francis, 347 Pearl
Mangles Henry, 3 Fulton market
Manold A. 34 Av. near 34th
Manron Henry, 190 Hester
Marshall J. A. 29 Wash'ton mkt.
Martin Lawrence, 37 Clinton do
May Elliot, 87 Centre
M'Ilony Charles P. 94 4th
Menges Francis, 347 Pearl
Menges L. 39 Wooster
Merkle Robert, 7 Franklin mkt.
Merkle George, 2   do
Messerve J. F. 31 Catharine mkt
Messerve William, 11 do
Metchel Louis, 83½ Pitt
Meyer John, 6 4th Av.
Milleamann D. 269 Houston
Miller Ed. 10 outside Centre mkt
Milliman Theobald, 258 Houston
Mills Jacob, 7 Washington mkt.
Molter Jacob, 80 Av. B
Monagh John, 89 Bayard
Monaghan James, 148 Centre
Monaghan O. 33 Catharine mkt.
Montague Jas. 499 Houston
Montaigne John, 316 1st Av.
Montgomery Geo. 31 Fulton mkt.
Montross E. 81 Av. C
Mook James, 7 Centre market
Mook Thomas, 5   do
Mook William, 8   do
Mook William, jr. 12 do
Moore William, 47 Wash'ton mkt.
Morgan Charles. 120 Varick
Morgan James, 816 Broadway
Mosback Joseph, 196 Stanton
Moser A. 7th Av.
Mosher E. 356 Houston
Mounsey George, 42 W. 13th
Muirhead W. 562 Houston
Murphy Edward, 282 1st Av.
Murphy George, 221 E. 13th
Myers William, 56 Fulton mkt.
Nondaman Bernard, 86 Willet
Newby James L. 86½ Centre
Newsborn Thomas, 144 Ludlow
Nolan William, 194½ Varick
Norman John, 7 Franklin market
Nusbaum Frederick, 42 Essex do
Obendorser Isaac, 129 Ridge
Odell Adolphus L. 35 Clinton mkt.
Odell James, 25th st. 9th Av.
Odell William, 11 Essex market
Odell William H. 73 4th Av.
O'Kane John, 192 Av. B
Oliver L. 30 Washington market
Oliver Patrick, 110 11th
Oliver Peter, 454 12th
Olmstead Wm. F. Clinton mkt.
Omberson William, 172 William
Onderdonk & Sigison, 62 Centre
O'Neil Daniel, 24th st.
Orsten Jerry, 236 Spring
Owen Micah M. 16 Sullivan
Packer & Co. E. 238 Greene
Palmer James, 189 1st Av.
Palmer James, 57 Frankfort
Palmer John W. 97 Church
Palmer Joseph C. 48 Rutgers
Palmer Joshua H. 351 Bowery
Parr James, 230 W. 17th
Patterson B. W. Washington mkt
Patterson F. Clinton   do
Patterson J. M. 157 Av. C
Patterson Jacob M. Av. C cor. 10th
Patterson Samuel P. 73 Av. D
Paul Christian, 701 Greenwich
Pearsall Denton, 4 Fulton mkt
Pearsall Zophar, 6 Fulton mkt
Pesinger Jacob, 46 Essex mkt
Pendleton S. 30 & 32 Cath. mkt
Perick John, 186 Forsyth
Perin George E. 236 Greene
Peters Chas. Wash. mkt
Phelan Michael, 10 Cath. mkt

Phillips Ed. foot of Duane. N. R. &
28 Clinton mkt   *New York.*
Phillips John J. Wash. mkt
Phillips John. 11 Union mkt
Piercy S. 22 Wash. mkt
Pittman Wm. 8 Cath. mkt
Ponsford J. H 106 Greenwich Av.
Porter John. 8th Av.
Pool Wm. Wash. mkt
Footon Wm. 308 Clinton
Post John, 40 Fulton mkt
Powell Christian, 701 Greenwich
Powell & Kemp. 216 Stanton
Prendergast John, 594 Grand
Price Edward, 185 Perry
Quin Felix. 2 Union mkt
Raab George, 230 Walker
Raab Peter, 258 2d
Radcliff Wm. H. 1 Wash. mkt
Read G. 229 Houston
Reed David B. 6 Cath. mkt
Reed Horatio, 17 Bowery
Reed Jacob R. 2 & 4 Clinton mkt
Reed Wm. 97 9th Av.
Reed James, 229 Houston
Reeves C. H. Wash. mkt
Reeves James, 256 6th Av.
Reeves John, 672 Houston
Reid James, 22 & 23 Centre mkt
Reid Phillip, 20 & 21 Centre mkt
Reisst Frederick, 174 Av. A
Relilod Jos. 30 Av. B
Rengle David, 511 Grand
Revere Edward, 41 Wash. mkt
Rhoades Daniel, 35 Fulton mkt
Rhoades Thomas S. 37 Fulton mkt
Rhule Jacob F. 162 Av. B
Rice Bernard, 23 Clinton mkt
Richard John, 174 Hester
Ridsbock Jacob H. 274 Broome
Roberts John, jr. Wash. mkt
Robinson Chris. 1 Centre mkt
Rockefeler George, 126 Prince
Rockwood & Hoff, 17 & 18 Wash.
mkt
Romain Benj. Cath mkt
Romaine Ed. N. 2 Jefferson mkt
Romaine Nich. 7 Tompkins mkt
Romaine Philip W. 7 Cath. mkt
Roome Chas. E. 10 Clinton mkt
Rosendale Abram, 219 Rivington
Rosenbrook John H. 327 Av. B
Ruhle J. F. cor. Av. B. & 11th
Ryno Jediah. 28 Wash. mkt
Sailes Wm. S. 636 Hudson
Salmon J. M. 39 Elm
Salter Cornelius W. 507 Pearl
Samuel S. 208 Houston
St. John & Thompson, 73 Av. C
Schelm Lewis, 55 Av. B
Schlamp L. 56 Av. B
Schmid Jacob. 29 Av. B
Schmidt Charles, 119 Division
Schneider M. 172 3d
Shuster John G. 36 Grand
Scott John, 9 Cath. mkt
Scott John, 82 4th
Scott ——, 106 4th
Seaman Conklin, 81 Av. D.
Seaman Henry, 63 W. Broadway
Seaman Henry, 93 Walker
Seaman John L. 24 & 25 Centre
market
Searle William, 50 Carmine
Seely Lyman, 34 Clinton market
Soeyle Henry, 51 Av. A.
Senior George. 12 Essex market
Serle Wm. Bedford cor. Carmine
Seward Thomas, jr. 188 6th Av.
Stannon Joseph, 100 Mulberry
Sharp Alderman, 13 Clinton m'k't
Sherding C. 255 6th Av.
Sheriden John, 114 Anthony
Sherwood & Byron, 76 Spring
Shopp John, Washington market
Shopp Henry, Washington do
Shubert John, 193 Av. B
Shutz Charles, 134 Broome
Shumway James, 222 Church
Siagle Henry, 51 Av. A
Siemers C. R. 197 William
Silber Frederick M. 16 Jeff. mkt

Silberhorn Henry, 10 Washington
market   *New York.*
Silberhorn Henry, 94 Chrystie
Silberhorn William, 656 Wash'ton
Simoneon Carmon A. 56 Fulton
market
Simoeou James, 28 Centre market
Sims Samuel, 5 Jefferson market
Singer John, 76 West Broadway
Slater William. 308 Greenwich
Slote John, 52 Fulton market
Smith Alfred, 6 Wash'ton m'k't
Smith Charles, 119 Division
Smith George B. 183 Sullivan
Smith George B. 186 Prince
Smith Henry, 23 Washington m'k't
Smith Henry, 16 Fulton market
Smith Jacob O. 307 Broome
Smith John, 36 Elm
Smith John, 26 Walnut
Sneder Michael, 89 Av. B
Solomon James M. 39 Elm
Southwil John F. 295 Broome
Spadder John D. 45 Washington
market
Stamler Jacob A. 44 Fulton m'ket
Stang & Walters, 90 Av. B
Stanton Ponsford J. 54 Fulton do
Starr George, 4 Jefferson   do
Starr James H. 11 Washington do
Starr Thomas, 4 Washington do
Stavey Ernest B. 7th Av.
Stevens Henry, 21 Washington
market
Stevens Henry, 205 Wooster & 41
City Hall place
Stewart James L. 56 Washington
market
Stohr John, 92 Hudson
Storms Andrew, 2 Gouverneur
market
Storms & Romaine, 42 & 46 Catha-
rine market
Storms Stephen C. 2 Gouverneur
market
Strang John L. 9th Av.
Straus David, 195 Rivington
Strauss Bernhard, 113 Ridge
Strauss Julius, 17 Morris
Strouse P. 238 Houston
Sturges P. Washington market
Sturges Charles,   do
Summers Charles, 201 Stanten
Swanwen John, 101 Cross
Taffey George. 108 4th
Taylor William H. 79 Stanton
Teutner E. S. & Co. 149 7th
Thomas Wm. H. 73½ Av. C.
Thompson R. 10 Tompkins mkt
Thompson & Norvall, 683 Wash.
Thompson & Pratt, 586 Hudson
Thorn Leonard & Co. 5 Washing-
ton market
Tier David M. 24 Essex market
Tietgen Christian. 52 9th Av.
Tooley John, 175 Forsyth
Tracey John, 35 Moore
Underhill Elnathan, 22 Fulton mkt
Vail & Wyckoff, E. 18th cor. 1st
Av.
Vail William F. 101 Greenwich
Valentine Abrm. 11 Fulton mkt.
Valentine Benjamin, 46 do
Valentine G. 11 Washington do
Valentine J. S. 4 Washington pl.
Valentine Henry M. 184 Division
Valentine Isaac 17 Clinton mkt.
Valentine Isaac S 260 Wooster
Valentine James, 14 Clinton mkt.
Valentine John, 12 Fulton do
Valentine Saml. 1 Tompkins do
Valentine P. 50 Washington do
Valentine W. J.   do   do
Valentine Washington, 25 do
Valentine W. M.   do   do
Valleau Wm. 42 Perry & Clinton
market
Van Buren J. 49 Washington mkt.
Vanderbilt Clark, 99 Henry
Vanderoof Edw. L. 5 Washington
market
Vannorden B. S. 16 Centre mkt.

Van Wart & Cox, 9 & 11 Jefferson
market   *New York.*
Varian A. 4 Catharine market
Varian J. H. 2 Catharine do
Varian Jacob, cor. Av. B & 2d
Varian & Rollwagen, 12 15 & 17
Catharine market
Veldran Raymer S. 13 & 14 Wash-
ington market
Vogoil Orville N. 163 3d Av.
Vogel & Farrington, 14 Tompkins
market
Vogt Henry, 91 Hamersley & 344
Greenwich
Von Hagen Geo. & Co. 23 Albany
Wallace John P. 208 Delancy
Wallack Jos. 5 Washington mkt.
Walkington George, 38 Elm
Walther Louis. 126 Delancy
Ward Wm. 34 & 37 Washington
Warner Abraham, 3 Franklin mkt.
Warner Wm. F. 1 Catharine do
Warr Valentine, 196 W. Broadway
Waters James, 125 8th Av.
Watts William. 8 Franklin market
Way Thos. P. 21 Washington do
Webber James, 13 Tompkins do
Weeks Carlyle, 2 Fulton do
Weeks Philip, 38 Washington do
Welch Peter, 29 Prince
Wells Benjamin S. 9 Union market
Wells H. jr. 229 Church
Wells William, 1 Union market
Wesson P. C. 196 1st Av.
West John, 426 Cherry
Wheeler Andrew, 131 4th Av.
Wiess B. 256 5th
Williams Daniel, 5 Clinton market
Williams George, 96 Av. A
Williams Stephen, 57 Fulton mkt.
Williamson James, 71 4th
Willmot C. 8th Av.
Wilt Geo. A. 13 Washington mkt.
Wilt John B. 49 Fulton market
Wilt Jonathan, 14 2d Av. & 89
Washington market
Wilt & Martin, 29 Washington mkt.
Winship T. Grand st. cor. Monroe
Winslow George, 137 Av C
Wiseman Lawrence, 682 Houston
Wolf Martin, 52 Rivington
Wood Henry, 342 Greenwich
Wood ——, 55 Market
Woodcock J. G. 92 Fulton market
Woodcock W. P. 2 Tompkins do
Wooley Charles L. 56 Market
Wyckoff R. B. 325 1st Av.
Zanger & Berger, 38 Cath. mkt.
Zerber Alex. 13 Mulberry
Zimmer Michael, 17th Ward mkt.
Zimmer Michael, 2 Av. A
Zipp Jacob, 256 6th

Niagara County.

Wilson John, Pekin   *Cambria.*
Colburth Benjamin   *Lewiston.*
Doris Owen
Dean George
Goble Moses   *Lockport.*
M'Master   "
Carrman Luther
Tyson H.
Sutton Isaiah
Collett John
Crossett & Carey
Blain Thomas
Cannon G. & Son *Niagara Falls.*
Gates William   *Wilson.*

Oneida County.

Horton T.   *New Hartford.*
Morton O. M. James st.   *Rome.*
Brewer & Waters, Canal st.
Murdent J. 6 Water   *Utica*
Jones Evan, 186 Genesee
Mumford, M'Michael & Co. 50
Washington
Hallook N. 22 Liberty
Stevens G. Whitesboro st.
Salisbury Henry, Jay st.
Whiffen I. 39 John

Whiffen & Anderson, 14 Broad
Utica.
Hawthorn Wm. jr. 2 John
Broadway W. D. Clinton market
Crocker H.   do
Spencer A.   do
Harrington William,   do
Cowley Thomas,   do
Smith S. P. New London   *Verona.*
Newcomb B. & H. Durhamville
Fields N.   do

Onondaga County.

Davis C. Genesee st. Syracuse
Salina.
Bastable S.   do
Hunt & Drew,   do
Briggs C. 6 City-market, Syracuse
Evans A. M. 5   do
Lewis W. D. 2   do
Britton M. 1   do
Snow J. C. & H. Genesee st. do
Meldram J. James st.   do
Kimber Thomas, Salina st.   do
Duff A.   do
Duff William, Park st.   do
Webb H.   *Skaneateles.*

Ontario County.

Gooding A.   *Bristol.*
Scotten & Mason   *Canandaigua.*
Pierce Dwight
Peck Hiram & Co.   *Phelps.*
Shute M. H.
Yorke George, Geneva   *Seneca.*
Green James,   do
Dox & Nares,   do
Merrill George,   do
Wright William, do

Orange County.

Wells G.   *Chester.*
Clark C. 8   *Cornwall*
Buckley E. W. Port Jervis
Deer Park.
Lytle & Moore   *Goshen.*
Smith H.
Lytle W. C.
Wood L. C Slate Hill   *Minisinh.*
Senior George   *Montgomery.*
Gridley J. C. & C. H.
Evans C. 15 Water   *Newburgh.*
Smeed G. & J. 98 Water
Lile William, 15   do
Morris John R. Colden st.
Phillips Robert, 50 Water
Gorham W. H. 53   do
Dunnville B. 3d st.
Van Cleft H. So. Middletown
Wallkill

Orleans County.

Lewis, Blott & M'Nevin, Albion
Barre.
Flint Asher, Albion
Fuller E. Medina   *Ridgeway.*
Knapp Isaac, do
Allen J.   do
Foot Erwin, Knowlesville

Oswego County.

Austin & Co. Oswego Falls
Granby.
De Groat James, 1st st.   *Oswego.*
Willington Joseph C. Bridge st.
Oliver Robert,   do.
Robinson William, Water st.
Crampton & Buel,   do
Oliver R. Market Buildings, do
Willington Jos. C.   do
Dabney H. (vegetables) Bridge st.

Putnam County.

Washburn J.   *Carmel.*
Crosby E.
Haight F. J. & Co. Cold Spring
Phillipstown.
Truesdell A.   do

Queens County.

Rhodes & Cornwell   *Hempstead.*
Angevine & Snediker
Mott Robert, Far Rockaway
Creed Gilbert   *Jamaica.*

Rensselaer County.

Mercer & Higgins, 219½ State
Lansingbargh.
Brooks & Spotten, 223 State
Mercer Henry A. 295 State
Bartin Wm. R. 299   do   *Troy.*
Mann Wm. D. Fulton mkt
Belding W.   do
Lester A. & F.   do
Allen & M'Grath,   do
Smith George,   do
Sause & M'Grath   do
Alexander ——,   do
Gorman T. & J.   do
Wilkinson & Smith, 406 River
Roberts Peter, Hoosick st.
Funda John W. 102 Congress
Funda Peter, Wash. mkt
Funda James R.   do
Rorke John,   do
Spain & Funda   do
Peck C., Ida Hill
Holden B. South Troy
Clark Daniel, near State dam

Richmond County.

Morris J. E. Port Richmond
Northfield.

Rockland County.

Jones H., Nyack   *Orangetown.*
Doremus John, Piermont

St. Lawrence County.

Baker James   *Canton.*
Tilley John
Biskby Thos. cor. Isabella & Ford,
Ogdensburgh   *Oswegatchie.*
Coory Gilbert H.   *Potsdam*
Adams David A.

Saratoga County.

Cole James M. *Saratoga Springs.*
Bullard Augustus
Waldron A.   *Waterford.*
Ryan John

Schenectady County.

Hagadorne P. 143 State
Schenectady.
Steers D. 163 State
Van Brunt A. Canal st.
Haugh D.   do
Bradt D. C.   do
Lansing R. 36 Union

Schoharie County.

Morse & Richtmyer   *Gilboa.*

Seneca County.

Hayer J. C.   *Seneca Falls.*
Johnson & Roberts
Bisdee John   *Waterloo.*
Day Lyman H.

Steuben County.

Gould & Barney   *Bath.*
Buck G. W.
Waite & Keefer   *Erwin.*
Walt & Keefer   *Painted Post.*
Williams Wm.

Suffolk County.

Goldsmith Jeremiah,   *Southold.*
Thorn Wm. Greenport
Tuthill Timothy, Cutchogue

Tompkins County.

Stephens P. (Franklin mkt) Owego
st.   *Ithaca.*

M'Crea J. & T. (Bulls Head mkt.)
Aurora st.   *Ithaca.*

Ulster County.

Cropser Philip   *Kingston.*
Van Gaasbeek Edgar
Curven William
Johnson Thomas L.
Radcliff Hiram
Van Buren Henry
Ostrander W., Rondout
Brady John. jr.   *Saugerties.*
Dutcher & Gay, Ellenville
Wawarsing.

Washington County.

White & Stone   *Greenwich.*
Holbrook Peter, Sandy Hill
Kingsbury.
Carver S. & Son, Division st.
Whitehall.
Jillson S. T. Canal st.
Smith & Co. William st.

Wayne County.

Smith George   *Arcadia.*
Dexter John, Newark
Brown Nelson   do
Whitney James   do
Southard N. H.   *Lyons*
Palmeter & Agins
Denton J. W.
Parshall S. R.   *Ontario.*
Jarvis A.
Jarvis William P.

Westchester County.

Secor & Dorset. Peekskill
Courtlandt.
Gilchrist Harvey, Tarrytown
Greenburgh.
Lent David, Tarrytown
Tindall J. Sing Sing   *Osinsing.*
Montross C. A.
Brown Robert
Dalton Henry   *West Farms.*
Dalton Abram
Cooper Isaac
Cuthel John
Crisfield J.   *Yonkers.*

Wyoming County.

Wallbridge William   *Attica.*
Pollard S., Wyoming *Middlebury.*
Homan H. E.   *Perry.*
Taylor Henry

Yates County.

Cook ——   *Jerusalem.*
Wyman A. Penn Yan   *Milo.*
Chamberlain R.   do
Chidsey C.   do
Sherman Francis, do
Perry E.   *Potter.*
Twitchell M., Rushville
Dense E., Dundee   *Starkey.*
Sherman R. L. do

Butter Dealers. (See also
Cheesemongers, also Milk, Butter, &c., also Produce Dealers.)

Agnew Philip C. 4 Centre market
New York.
Allan & Rose, 296 Washington
Beattie Alexander H. 236   do
Babitt James, Centre mkt
Boyce John, 182 Greenwich
Carpenter D. P. 611 Greenwich
Clark & Judson, 183 Reade
Clearwater Rickeson, 183 Wash.
Emmons & Ford, 295 Washington
Enyard Isaac L. 228   do
Gustin G. W. & Co. 943   do
Harrison & Co. 144 West
Howell Caleb, 182 Washington
Mead N. Centre mkt
Morrison & Hyde, 298 Wash
Reed Silas, 216 Washington

Ronk Philip J. 204 Washington
New York.
Sexton & Cummins, 226 Fulton
Smith J. & N. 236 Fulton
Sturgis E. G. & Co. 276 3d
Turnbull A. & Co. 8 Centre mkt
Van Auken B. H. & Co. 184 Wash.
Van Norden James, 157 West
Wood Ira, 258½ Washington

Butter Ladles.

Otsego County.

Sadsit L. *Butternuts.*
Botsford G.

Butter Stamps.

Otsego County.

Seeley S. S. *Butternuts.*
Seeley Horatio
Seeley St. Paul

Buttons—Importers of.

Church Charles C. 189 Pearl
New York.
Chamberlin Jacob, 65 Liberty
Graves & Co. D. W. 77 William
Hayes Jonathan W. 61 William
Lombard & Buttrick, 57 Cedar
Marks & Davol, 52 Broad
Post & Knapp, 35 Nassau
Taylors & Richards, 45 Cedar
Watson Loring, 61 William

Button Makers.

Bagley Oliver B. 40 Maiden Lane
New York.
Broneman Samuel, 55 Ann
Dickinson Dexter, 187 Pearl
Doughty Samuel H. 60 John
Eaves Wm. rear 71 W. Broadway
Henry Alexander H. 102 Elm
Hopkins Enos, 97 Maiden Lane
Jauncey James W. 15 N. William
Kellogg Henry M. 54 Cedar
Lister Joseph, 106 10th Av.
Polm & Weaver, 229 10th Av.
Pomeroy Grove, 9 Cedar
Reeves William. 73 W. Broadway
Richards H. M. 157 Broadway
Robison & Co. 11 Cortlandt alley
Ross Daniel H. rear 83 Duane
Scovills & Co. 101 William
Stadermann John M. 130 Canal
Swartz Adam. 274 10th Av.
Welton J. C. & Co. 66 Cedar

Saratoga County.

Blake Robert, (Bone) *Waterford.*

Suffolk County.

Pratt Reuben, (Horn) *Riverhead.*

Westchester County.

Kiester H., Hastings *Greenburgh.*

Cabinet Makers. (*See also Furniture Warehouses.*)

Albany County.

Harris Edwin A. 533 Broadway
Albany.
Meads John, jr. 549 do
Shepard A. 605 do
Van Denbergh W. 664 do
Parsons H. 586 & 588 do
Arts John, 97 State
M'Chesney L. H. 106 & 110 State
M'Guire Thos. 116 do
Lynch P. 158 Green
Peters O. O. 16 Franklin

Martin A. J. 111 Arch *Albany.*
M'Kown A. F. 86 Pearl
Amsden J. B. 3 N. Pearl
Winne John, 15 do
Lock J. Chapel & Columbia
Smith Samuel D. *Coeymans.*
Lattee Jacob, Centreville
Guilderland.
Pangborn J. *New Scotland.*
Witbeck S.
Vanderlip E. (Coffins), West Troy
Watervliet.
Bland J. W.
Commary & Caulkins
Aikin J., Cohoes
Scott Lemuel do
Overbaugh & Davis

Alleghany County

Millard B. W. *Alfred.*
Hanney F. H. *Almond.*
Philbrick & Wright *Amity.*
Baker John L. *Andover.*
Brown Orlando *Angelica.*
Bumpus Wm. *Belfast.*
Hawley Daniel *Bolivar.*
Peabody Humphrey, Whitney's
Valley
Delano Nathan *Burns.*
Silsbee S. *Cuba.*
Robbins B. F. *Friendship.*
Makee J. M.
Green Amos & Matthew, Little
Genesee *Genesee*
Ladd & Mills *Hume.*
Stiles, Wildman & Co. Whitesville
Independence.
Merryfield H. & J. *Rushford.*
Davison J. E.
Curtis Lyman
Hatch N.
M'Call Milton
Haynes D. B. & J. A
Stanley —— *Sco.*
Coats W. H. Wellsville

Broome County.

Waters W. H. Chenango Forks
Barker.
Rennie A. *Binghamton.*
Wells Chester
Pratt Z.
Seymour A
Ronk J. C.
Mitchell J. *Lisle*
Balch & Scovill *Union.*
Nicholson J. *Windsor.*
Gurnsey H.

Cattaraugus County

Bass Horace *Ashford.*
Thomas Benjamin
Lampman Jacob & Stephen
Drake Isaac *Conewango.*
Harrison W. E. *Ellicottville*
Rowley E. R.
Matteson A. B.
Russell E. *Farmersville.*
Chappell Augustus *Franklinville.*
Cook S. N.
M'Cluer Porter
Foot P. P. *Freedom.*
Wheeler Isaac J. Sandusky
Keith J. & W. *New Albion.*
Hughson James R. *Otto.*
Miles Isaac L.
Goldthwait Moses, Gowanda
Persia.
Peacock Francis, do
Rollinson A. do
Peirce George I. *Randolph.*
Palmer W. L.
Calhoun Wm..
Frink E.
Latham C. H. & Co.
Hall A. East Randolph
Faulkner C. do
Holdrige E. do
Lee Henry
Davenport Calvin

Carter Miles *Yorkshire*
Merry Benjamin
Stringham Henry, Delavan

Cayuga County.

Richardson L. D. *Auburn*
Watson & Billey, Weedsport
Brutus.
Peat R. *Conquest.*
Remer S., Montezuma *Mentz.*

Chautanque County.

Marsh —— *Busti.*
Chamberlain M., Frewsburgh
Carroll.
Craw M. B. *Charlotte.*
Andrews A. J., Mayville
Chautauque.
Johnson H. N. do
Tracy A. do
Russell James, Dewittville
Utter James P. *Cherry Creek.*
Kilbourne William
Ford George, Jamestown *Ellicott.*
Breed William J. C. do
Rockwood Warren, do
Bartholomew & Dobbin *Ellington.*
Mack B., Irving *Hanover.*
Rice C. T. Silver Creek
Ellis T. G. Forestville
Johnson S. do
Manley Judson, Panama *Harmony.*
Morton —— *Mina.*
Woodford M. H. Fredonia *Pomfret.*
Strong ——, do
Hamilton A. L. do
Gifford W. Dunkirk
Lathrop L. L. Salem Cross roads
Portland.
Owen Ellis A. *Sherman.*
Baldwin B. *Villenova.*
Shaw John M. *Westfield.*
Shaw Thomas
Hall J.

Chenango County.

Fairchild Theodore *Bainbridge.*
French Nelson, Bennettsville
Olney J. *Columbus.*
Carrier C.
Barber J. S. *Coventry.*
Atherton & Barger *Greene.*
White D. *New Berlin*
Dye Thomas, South New Berlin
Simons William, do
Barber & Close *Norwich.*
Allen J. C.
Hitchcock J.
Bedient E. B.
Staunton N. D.
Fisher Charles *Oxford.*
Figary John E.
Frazier William
Gardner Daniel
Pettis Thomas
Hyde Charles P. *Pitcher.*
Havens John
Ruddoc Chester
Coy Tracy
Kenyon W. *Sherburne.*
Wilcox John *Smyrna.*

Clinton County.

Potter & Richardson, Keeseville
Au Sable.
Warner Edward *Beekmantown.*
Fonquett D. L. *Plattsburgh.*
Brown William

Columbia County.

Mayhew A. W. Spencertown
Austerlitz.
Holmes J. W., 4 cor. *Chatham.*
Ford J., East Chatham
Irish S. Malden Bridge
Bame C. Warren st. *Hudson.*
Wagoner A. do
Charlot J. H. do
Duxbury C. do

Bodurtha H. L.   *Hudson.*
Rockwell W. 228 Warren
Patton J., Valatie   *Kinderhook.*
Birckmayer P

Cortland County.

Punderford James   *Cincinnatus.*
Richards James
M'Farlan John   *Cortland Village.*
Huestis John H.   *Homer.*
Buckley John L.
Miller Franklin
Shirley Ezekiel
Pomeroy Austin L.   *Truxton.*
Pierce Hamlet F.   *Virgil.*
Ball S. G.
Lewis Joel

Delaware County.

Way J. M.   *Davenport.*
Edwards Charles   *Delhi.*
Coon & Wilcox
Judd A. B. & J.   *Franklin.*
Coleman C.
Lockwood H.   *Harpersfield.*
Strong E. P.
Brownell W. (cradle) Bloomville
                              Kortright.
Duren J. C.
Crane E.   *Meredith.*
Young T., Hobart   *Stamford.*
Hanford E. H. do
Freeman W. & W. G. Deposit
                              Tompkins.
Coon E. H.   do
Eells O. J.   *Walton.*

Duchess County

Merchant A.   *Amenia.*
Rosa J. H.
Lawrence & M'Alpine, Wapping-
    er's Falls   *Fishkill.*
Thorn B. Fishkill Landing
Chamberlain E. B.   *Pine Plains.*
Engleke H.
Mallory David S. 359 Main
                              Poughkeepsie.
Nelson & Hughson, 369 do
Weber D.
Woodruff C. H. 350 Main
Moon W. 150   do
Martin J. W.   *Red Hook.*
Barnes P.   *Rhinebeck.*
Cole G. W.
Carroll & Curtis
Wright A.   *Washington.*

Erie County.

Lord and Higgen   *Alden.*
Morrow Henry, William   *Aurora.*
Bowen Jason,   do
Adington Sam. H.   do
Johnson George   *Black Rock.*
Paine Simon   *Boston.*
Delong & Purington. 269 Main
Humberston John, 273   do
Forbes A. J. 3 W. Seneca
Stow George, 272 Main
Taunt Emory, 343   do
Cutler & Deforest, 233 do
Mead C R. 34 Exchange
White Isaac D. 201 Main
Bartel John P. 131 Genesee
Diebold S. cor. Pine & Batavia
Messenger Peter, Genesee st.
Atkins Joel (bedstead), 46 Clinton
Neiderlander J. & F. (chair) 311
    Main
Hersee & Timmerman. 307 Main
Staats P. 317   do
Croben Carl, 397   do
Kreft & Gray, 390   do
Christy Joseph, 384   do
Galligan William, 111 do
Cooley & Russell, 115 do
Jewett Charles   *Clarence.*
Shaffer Adam
Durboraw Thomas, Centre
Call Amos   *Collins.*

Gaylord Stephen B. Springville
                              Concord.
Barclay William   do
Ensign D. E. Water Valley
                              Hamburgh.
Guyer John   *Lancaster.*
Hoover William
Sleeper Frederick
Safford E. M. (bedsteads)
Osgood Ira, Akron   *Newstead.*
Maples & David, South   *Wales.*
Jones ———, Wales Centre

Essex County.

Marvin E. M. & Co. *Elizabethtown.*
Stanton John
Fanes A. F. Moriah 4 corners
                              Moriah.
Baker Dennis,   do
Allen C. C.   do
Beebe C. Schroon Lake *Schroon.*
Beach Horace   *Wilmington.*

Franklin County.

Wood Nelson   *Mauone.*
Schoolcraft P.
Hyde Samuel & John H.
Hutton George H.
Hastings Joel
Wood A. H.

Fulton County.

Gilbarne E.   *Broadalbin*
Derby George   *Ephratah.*
Clarke Samuel W.   *Johnstown.*
Whitney Ashael
Tar E. S. Gloversville
Wood E. Northville   *Northampton.*
Spalding E.

Genesee County.

Barnes W. G.   *Alabama.*
Joslyn B.   *Alexander.*
Kirkham C.   *Batavia.*
Buckston J. T.
Buckston C. T.
Griffith O.
Mott E.   *Bergen.*
Brown Lauren   *Bethany.*
Madison Samuel   *Darien.*
Hoyt ———
Parks Elisha   *Le Roy.*
Goodrich Asa
Burpee C. L.
Howard Henry   *Oakfield.*
Sanders Benjamin   *Pavilion.*

Greene County.

Hotchkiss Henry   *Cairo.*
Washburn Moses   *Catskill.*
Kortz James
Burchardt Edward H.   *Cassackis.*
Cowles David   *Durham.*
Pauley Jason, West Kill
                             Lexington.
Young Jacob B.   *Prattsville.*
Myers Jacob
Potter G. W.   *Windham.*

Herkimer County.

Kimpton William   *Fairfield.*
Shelden William I.   *Frankfort.*
Loomis Henry, (Turner)
Howell A. L. Mohawk
                          German Flats.
Roth George, Mohawk
Smith John M.   *Herkimer.*
Howell William, jr.
Hughs John E. (Turning shop)
                           Little Falls.
Young G. B. & Co.
Fisher James B.
Stevenson Gordon
Goldam K. G.
Porter Henry   *Newport.*
Barnes E. T.
Wright T. (Turner)
Du Bois David   *Newgoy.*

Fowler William H. Cold Brook
                              Russia.
Pratt Edwin,   *Salisbury*
Champion A. & W. Starkville
                              Stark.
Hyde J. E. Jordanville *Warren.*
Belshaw William, do
Fairchilds A. P. West Winfield
                              Winfield.

Jefferson County.

Bond & Stone   *Adams.*
Dunn John
Blasley R.
Bosworth Jabez, Adams Centre
Ball Warren. Plessis *Alexandria.*
Codman & Frisbie   *Brownsville.*
Darrows A., Dexter
Buckley James   *Cape Vincent.*
Pool C.
Babcock A. S.   *Champion.*
Woolson R. O.
Porter A. E. & D. C.   *Clayton.*
Stearns D. Mannsville *Ellisburgh.*
Bates M. W.   *Henderson.*
Harlow D. & Brother, Sackett's
    Harbor   *Hounsfield.*
Smith Asel, Sackett's Harbor
M'Lain Hector, Evan's Mills
                              Le Ray.
Barber William, Three Mile Bay
                              Lyme.
Clark William   *Philadelphia.*
Bates D. South Rutland   *Rutland.*
Dexter D. & S. Black River
Wilcox William S.   do
Allen John G.   *Theresa.*
Blood & Van Namel   *Watertown.*
Reed Abel & Brother
Edson Amos F., Carthage   *Wilna.*

Kings County.

Weeks Joseph S. corner Pacific &
    Columbia   *Brooklyn.*
Stephens B. 135 Atlantic
Martin John A. 117 do
Hartt S. R. 136   do
Riley Joseph, 36 Fulton
Brooks Thomas, 44 do
Rither & Christman, 46 Fulton
Hellmouth C. B. 52   do
Appleyard William, 54   do
Hafnagel John, 16 Hicks
Ferguson J. 76 & 78 Fulton
Barnett Alexander, 80 do
Laroes P. W. cor. Fulton & Mid-
    dagh
Thomas W. J. 81 Fulton
Heckel & Reynolds, Willoughby's
    Buildings near Tillary
Wolf Jacob, 200 Adams
Leequsne John F., Sanford cor.
    Willoughby Av.
Bucheenberger A., Myrtle Av
    cor. Steuben
Johnson A. I. Flushing Av. East
    Brooklyn
Hess John   *Flatbush.*
Kiefs J. East New York
Stevenson Obediah, 47 9th
                          Williamsburgh.
Baldwin John A. South 1st
Crawford Alexander A. 175 Grand
Schneeder G. J. 222 2d
Posthaner F. (Toilets) 222 2d
Hahn M. 192 Union Av.
Blum George, Powers st.

Lewis County.

Cunningham Foster L.   *Croghan.*
Chambers J. H.   *Denmark.*
Kellogg A. Copenhagen
Sonel D.   do
Tuttle M.   *Lowville.*
Hart Samuel C.   *Turin.*
Strickland Joseph
Strickland Albert
Barnes Judah, (chairs)
Cone & Clark, Constableville
                          West Turin.
Brinckerhoff Isaac, Collinsville

Livingston County.

Howell Abram A.   *Avon.*
Beecher Lewis W.
M'Crary David   *Caledonia.*
Parker & Jones   *Dansville.*
Attmeyer A. & Co
Cramner & Frear
Mitch George
Carter H. S.
Gardner Samuel   *Geneseo.*
Hunt Moses
Butterway A.
Gansevoorth John, Cuylerville
  Leicester.
Burpee ——   *Lima.*
Brown Alanson
Wadsworth Walter S. Hemlock
  Lake   *Livonia.*
Allsdorf & Lee, Hemlock Lake
Burpee E.   *Mount Morris.*
Ewing A. S.
Rider L. F. & Co.   *Nunda.*
Briggs J. W.
Werner John, Oakland *Portage.*
Grover David H. Springwater
Smith H. E., Fowlersville *York.*

Madison County.

Moon Wm. S.   *Brookfield.*
Stillman Ethan
Wells L. G.   *Cazenovia.*
Alden Samuel
Webber C. C.
Wood & Worth   *De Ruyter.*
Crumb J. H.
Wheeler & Parker   *Eaton.*
Allen J., Morrisville
Topliff E. C. do
Worlock Stephen   *Fenner.*
Stillman E.   *Hamilton.*
Wheeler & Parker
Rogers John, Earlville
M'Farland J. Oneida Depot *Lenox.*
Fleetwood N.   do
Sowter L. & F. Canastota
Gay Wm. L.   do
Hobart J. L.   do
Keeney Marvin, Clockville
Collister Lyman   *Madison.*
Klinck Geo., Peterboro *Smithfield.*
Worden Ira, Chittenango*Sullivan.*
Young Joseph,   do
Hyde E., Bridgeport

Monroe County.

Hanna D. T., West   *Mendon.*
Rich J. C.   *Penfield.*
Bell Wm. Curtis Block, Main st.
  Rochester.
Bloss, Tibbits & Co. 15 Water,
  wareroom 12 Front
Starr Frederick. 47 Main
Brown E. 81 State
Brewster & Fenn, 51 State
Leavensworth G., Lower Falls
Hayden James E. 14 Front
Graham & Myer, 90   do
Bloss, Tibbles & Co 12 do
Colver D. S. 84 Main, Brockport
  Sweden.
Smith J. Main st.   do
Beckwith Francis X. cor. Roches-
  ter st. & Main, Scottsville
  Wheatland.
M'Donald Isaac, do

Montgomery County.

Warren O. S.   *Amsterdam.*
Shuler Isaac C.
Hubbs Charles
Mason Horace & Co., Hagaman's
  Mills
Wentworth J. & C. *Canajoharie.*
Harris Jessie
Fannan C. H. Fultonville *Glenn.*
Hate George D., Smith Town
Writing David, Fort Plain *Minden.*
Charlesworth Morris,do
Foreman P. C., Fonda *Mohawk.*
Timmerman Charles, Fonda
Antis John C.   *Root.*

New York County.

Allen Robert, 268 Walker
  New York.
Allison Michael, 46 Vesey
Aschenbrenner George, 162 Elm
Axs Michael, 30 Clark
Baillie D & S. 137 Bowery
Baker William H. 164 3d Av.
Baltzer Frederick A. 107 Bleecker
Baldwin Edward, rear 59 Marion
Baldwin J. C. 137 Fulton
Baldwin James C. 183 Chatham
Bardhert George, 133 Norfolk
Darnes Benj. J. 279 Greenwich
Barnes M. H. 373 2d
Bauer Ernst, 163 W. 20th
Baudouhnes C. A. 335 Broadway
Beckwith Joseph P. 192 8th Av.
Belter John H. 372 Broadway
Bell Robert, 61 West Broadway
Bettryhimer Chs. 132 Rivington
Beverley Henry, 59 Gold
Biffar B. 4 Rivington
Bingham John W. 12 3d Av.
Bishop Dwight, 394 Hudson
Blanck Aaron P. 356 Hudson
Blanck Thomas J. 318 Hudson
Bogert Andrew W. 66 Bleecker
Bosch Bernard, 560 Broadway
Bouman James W., Oliver st.
Boyd George, 113 Wooster
Branch T. W. 113 Fulton & 34 Ann
Bridgeman Andrew, 196 6th Av.
Brown Francis, 110 Norfolk
Bruner Henry, 396 Hudson
Brymer William, 34 Great Jones
Buhler Christian, 161 Chatham
Bulyea Francis, 117 Essex
Burns & Trainque, 453 Broadway
Burke James W. 27th st.
Buttenheim Samuel, 479 Houston
Buxton John, jr. 181 Chatham
Campbell Solomon, 349 Bowery
Carter Nathaniel E. 74 Centre
Cash William, rear 36½ Orange
Cate Amass L. 24 Wooster & 101
  Canal
Chalmers William, 1st Av. c. 9th
Charles C. 544 Broadway
Chrilmers William, 1st Av.
Clark Stephen, 37 1st
Coles Joseph, 55 E. Broadway
Colsey Francis & Co. 349 G'wich
Connor James E. 139 W. 20th
Cookman Daniel, 44 Vestry
Corell Adam, rear 196 Amity
Corell Philip,   do
Curry James, 11 Doyer
Curry John, 70½ 3d Av.
Daly Timothy, 555 Broadway
Davies Richard, 46 9th Av.
Dawson G. W. 67 Chatham
Deahne J. F. 26 Broome
Deforeest John, 300 Broadway &
  27 Reade
Deming & Bulkley. 56 Beekman
Dennis Abram C. 37 Pitt
Denniston John A. 205 Fulton
Denniston R. 1 Laurens
Dessoir Julius, 499 Broadway
Donnelly William, 300 Mulberry
Drews Jacob, 65 Bayard
Dunn P. 54 W. 13th
Dwyar Edward, 113 W. Broadway
Earl Albert T. 6 Spring
Ebbinghousen G. & Co. 57 Suffolk
Edwards Edward, 54 Carmine
Edstrom E. 261 Bowery
Ellenu Fram 526 Broadway
Elliot William, 30 King
Ettling John, rear 78 Elizabeth
Eybsen Henry, 1 Norfolk
Fanning & Brother, 325 Pearl
Fanning S. 20 Catharine
Favor Z. C. 194 Fulton
Fisher John, 96 Sheriff
Fitzsimmons Francis, 199 Bowery
Flannagan James, 230 Centre
Foster Edward M. 9 Canal
Fowler Abraham. 19 Jefferson
Freese Henry, 42 Mott

(continued)

Friedsam Samuel, 209 Delancy
  New York.
Frost C. T. 706 Broadway
Frost Thomas, 543 Houston
Frost T. E. 28th st.
Frost William, 722 Broadway
Gable Conrad, 63 Av. B.
Ganglof Joseph, 168 Delancy
Garbrant & Leslie, 345 4th
Gardiner W. C. 69 Gold
Gates Asaph, 35 Av. D
Gee Richard, 328 Canal
Gormer Ludolph, 65 Beekman
Gibson Robert H. 456 Pearl
Glinsman & Iden. 57 Elm
Goetze Frederick A. 96 Houston
Gracey Henry J. rear 71 Laurens
Gray Robert, rear 16 Watts
Grill John, 3 Av. B
Grop Martin. 99 Delancy
Gullifer William, 106 Leroy
Guest John, 170 Franklin
Hahn John C. r. 541 Broome
Hanke Frederick. 205 Bowery
Hana L. 147 Essex
Harmel & Powers, 58 Mulberry
Hazlet James, 509 Hudson
Hazlet Wm. R. 115 Waverly Pl.
Heckel Christian, 105 Elm
Hellenbrand P. 683 4th
Heert Wm. r. 142 Wooster
Henderson Geo. 9th Av. bet. 16th
  & 17th
Hoiss Balthus, 251 Spring
Herman J. 99 Norfolk
Hess Antoine, 81 Ann
Hessel Francis, 908 6th Av.
Hewitt Francis, 592 Broadway
Hewitt & Morton, 598 Broadway
Hield Jacob, 50 Av. A
Higgins John, 176 Canal
Higgins John, 191 Mulberry
Hixon Joseph, 555 Broadway
Hobe Chas. F. 443 Broadway
Hoffman John, 21 Av. C
Hoffman J. G. & H. 64 Beekman
Hollenger Robert. 29 Carmine
Honey Hugh, r. 80½ Greene
Hoppel Fred. 371 & 373 Hudson
Horton Gilbert, 3 E. 13th
Hotalung Albert, 361 Hudson
Humphreys William S. 163 & 197
  Chatham
Hunt Samuel C. r. 96 Ludlow
Hutchings E. W. & Co. 475 Broad-
  way
Immich Henry, 4 Norfolk
Kassel Nicholas, r. 164 Eldridge
Kiefer Jacob, r. 108 Delancy
Kipp H. & Son, 10 E. Broadway
Kirill G. 407 Broome
Knapp L. E. 139 Chatham
Knipe William, 3 Delancy
Knipe William, 16 Pell
Koenig Jacob, 142 Ludlow
Kreig E. & Dohrsmann, 106 Nor-
  folk
Kracht George, r. 235 Bowery
Kruse Alexander r. 32 Chrystie
Honitzer S. 105 & 113 Elm
Ladarar Charles, 364 Hamersley
Lafetra Tylee W. 296 Hudson
Lamb Patrick, 15 Doyer
Lene John A. 23 Catharine
Lane S. A. 113½ Bowery
Laty Jacob, 261 Division
Lawrence Jer. & J. E. 20 Grand
Lee R. B. 228 Canal
Lee William, 16 Horatio
Leicht Conrad. 54 Reade
Lelck Martin, 113 Spring
Leighte Jacob, 261 Division
Leslie G. 345 4th
Lindeman Caspar, 127 Columbia
Litgow John, 135 6th Av.
Loeloff Theodore, r. 162 Elm
Lohman H. 30 Norfolk
Lowe Isaac N. 41 Howard
Loy P. & J. 371 Grand
Lyeman L. 63 Gold
M'Donnell H. W. 187 Mulberry
M'Farland Jas. 197 W. 20th

M'Graw Nicholas, r. 10 Rivington
　　　　　New York.
M'Graw N. 456 Broadway & 163 Bowery
M'Gregor Simon, 15 Doyer
M'Kennan John. 43 Hamersley
M'Keon & Cobb. 126 W. 19th
M'Laren William. 194 Greene
M'Menomy & Thompson, 151 Chatham
M'Namara Martin S. 230 Hudson
Maggs Joseph, 356 Bowery
Malaney James, 1 Bedford
Martin S. rear 38 E. Broadway
Martens C. 217 2d
Mark B. 167 Chrystie
Mason & Smith, 28 & 30 Attorney
Massie G. 127 Rivington
Maxwell Samuel, 66 University pl
Meeks J. & J. W. 16 Vesey
Mergraff Conrad, 14 Clinton
Messerschmidt G. rear 126 Amity
Meyer Louis, 222 William & 82 Frankfort
Miller Joseph, 234 5th
Miller Aaron, 209 Stanton
Miller James. 441 Broadway
Mitchell John, 538 Hudson
Mitchell John. 117 Charles
Moor Graft. 117 Pitt
Moore Jacob & D. 165 Christopher
Millenhagen J. 223 Greenwich
Monaghan & Gouldburn, 690 Broadway
Moran Daniel, rear 235 Bowery
Moses George. 70 E. 16th
Muchall Richard, 30 Clark
Muhlhauser J. 207 Houston
Munz Otto. 101 Delancy
Nation Robert, rear 87 Warren
Neller Martin, rear 39 Anthony
Nepper & Schmidt. 125 Canal
Neuberger Max. 177 8th Av.
Newhouse Benjamin, 275 Hudson
Newman J. 177 Laurens
Newmann William, 24 Wooster
Noble Robert, 423 Hudson
Norman Thomas, 25 Broome
Ogden M. H. 43 Elizabeth
Oldaker Alfred E. 360 Broome
O'Neil Charles, rear 107 King
Olsen Andrew J. 501 Broadway
Palm Eliza. 245 Broome
Palmer William, 70 E. Broadway
Pardoe Thomas, 31 Ridge
Parsons & Fisher, 97 4th & 109 M'Dougal
Parsons Henry, 552½ Broadway
Peckoner Joseph, rear 240 Water
Perry John, 124 Grand
Perkelos John, 57 Elm
Peter Adam, 231 Bowery
Phelps & Kingman, 118 & 120 Chatham & 442 Pearl
Phillips A. M. rear 109 Spring
Plate Adolp. L. 120 & 122 Wooster
Ponsot George, 342 Broadway
Powers John, rear 56 Mulberry
Prosser Humphrey, 36 Vandam
Pryer John, 293 East Broadway
Pulte & Hugle. 686 Broadway
Quincey George, 293 6th Av.
Rabson J. A. W . 30th st.
Raverty Daniel, 72 Bowery
Rawlings Alfred, 190 Henry
Reed Gustavus, 251 Bleecker
Riley John, 40 Hester
Riley Joseph, 47 Beekman
Robertson Wm. 4 Doyer
Robinain Henry, 149 Bowery
Robinson John, 71 Bayard
Robinson William J. 104 Madison
Rogers Ebenezer, 61 Downing
Roux Alexander, 479 Broadway
Ruez Adam, 262 Broome
Sauer Christian, 11) Pitt
Seyro John N. 78 Beekman
Schadle T. 44 4th Av.
Schelg Konrad, 74 5th
Schmidt Caspar J. 179 Chrystie
Schnars Adam, 200 2d
Schneider Charles, 70 Frankfort

Schott Ferdinand F. 222 12th
　　　　　New York.
Schultz Peter E. 5½ M'Dougal
Schultze Charles, 9 Elizabeth
Schwarz John, 63 Av. B.
Schwarzwaelder Christian, 9 East Broadway
Seebach George, 203 Stanton
Sellew T. G. 170 Fulton
Sevin & Brother, 51 Beekman
Sharp Wm. 61 Beekman & 66 Gold
Shey Conrad, 74 5th
Sieman H. rear 185 Bowery
Siller George, 15 Stanton
Simpson Wm. 591 Broadway
Slater Wm. 33 3d Av.
Sloan Charles S. 436 Pearl
Smith John, 105 Fulton
Smith John, 124 Eldridge
Smith George, 203 Wooster
Smith George, 374 Hudson
Snyder Henry, 225 Rivington
Sommer Phillip, 76 W. 13th
Sommer & Zeiglmairer, 452 Broome
Sommers Joseph, 34 Chrystie
Southack J. W. & C. 196 Broadway
Stappan Robb, rear 40 Pell
Stelle Jacob, 12 Columbia
Stevens Christian Y. rear 131½ Bowery
Stevens D. & A. 145 3d Av.
Stevenson Frederick. 291 Grand
Stoll Daniel, 261 Division
Swarts John, 214 Stanton
Swift A. W. 22 Rivington
Tallmann Tunis, 86 Hammond
Thaule & Bros, rear 100 Wooster
Theisz John, 581 4th
Thomas Ansel, 11 Clark
Thompson Isaac, 11 Mulberry
Thompson Jacob, 169 Church
Thompson W. S. 18 E. Broadway
Thompson Zachariah, 61 Greene
Tompkins William S. 69 Watts
Turner J. B. & Co. 71 Gold
Tully Patrick, 618 Greenwich
Van Nostrand Jacob, 3 Greene
Vincent Jos. & Co. 52½ Carmine
Vogel Ferdinand, 219 2d
Vowels George, 814 Broadway & 150 Laurens
Vrede Frederick A. 550 Broad'y
Wagner Anthony C. 94 Broadway
Walsh N. 8 6th Av.
Walter John A. 139 W. Broadway
Walters Michael, 445 Broadway
Waterbury Samuel. 60 Beekman
Watson James, 27 6th Av
Weber C. 207 Delancy
Webster John, 24 9th
Wedel Frederick, 130 Willet
Weil George P. 421 Broome
Weil H. & Brother, 138 Essex
Weisainger Frederick, 105 Elm
Wesensee Andrew, 382 Hudson
Westervelt James R. & Son, 279 Spring & 86 6th Av.
Wilford Edward, 910 Division
Williams Christ. C. 137 Fulton
Williams George W. 96 Elm
Williams John T. 739 Houston
Williams John, 559 Washington
Winson William, 227 Stanton
Wohlgemath F. 7 Chambers
Wright J. 9th Av. 23d st.
Young Robert, 128½ Grand
Zeller F. cor. Av A & 16th st.
Zerfass John, 232 Bowery

Niagara County.

Cook Lemuel　　　　*Lewiston.*
Northup C. E.　　　　*Lockport.*
Tucker W. C.
Murphy P.
Moore & Glass
Bennett B.
Church C. C.
Roahn George　　　*Newfane.*
Crossman E. D.　*Niagara Falls.*
Burdick ——
Cook Ira

Wright William　　　*Royalton.*
Sleeper James. Middleport
Nye Otis　　　　　*Somerset.*
Cresgh John G., Wilson
Bennett Thomas　　do

Oneida County.

Alcott C. Oriskany Falls *Augusta.*
Pease & Batchelder, do
Babcock J. L.　　　*Camden.*
Graves F.
Graves George
Stevens M. H.
Willard J. . Clinton　*Kirkland.*
Tibbets William H. Dominick st.
　　　　　　　　Rome.
Matteson J.　　　do
Buckingham E. D. Waterville
　　　　　　　Sangerfield.
Andrews A. Waterville
Peters & Co. Holland Patent
　　　　　　　　Trenton.
Fritz M. 177 Genesee st. *Utica.*
Space J. C. 24 Liberty
Perrine S. M. 69 Genesee
Kellogg S. 25 Liberty
Stuart J. 24 Liberty
Martin L. Varick st.
Jelliff F. G. Whitesboro
　　　　　　Whitestown.

Onondaga County.

Wells G. W. Baldwinsville
　　　　　　　Lysander.
Lynds & Co.　　　do
Ashley & Wilson, Salina st. Syracuse
Butler William & A. Syracuse *Salina.*
Rust C. & Son, Arcade do
Duell E. Warren st.　do
Hoytt C.　　　　*Tully.*

Ontario County.

Linnell H.　　*Canandaigua.*
Francis J. B.
Clark Edward
Plympton Henry *East Bloomfield.*
Millard Hiram　　*Gorham.*
Ketcham James　　*Phelps.*
Pierpont David, Allen's Hill
　　　　　　　Richmond.
Arnold C.. Honeoye
Beech E. Geneva　*Seneca.*
Hemiup Charles,　Geneva
Silsby, Buckley & Bennett, do
Viles William,　　do
Brown & Co.　*South Bristol.*
Slezer J. & D. E.　*Victor.*
Pilsbury A.　*West Bloomfield.*

Orange County.

Moore & Owens, Washingtonville
　　　　　Blooming Grove.
Smith I.　　　do
Colwell & Colefax　*Chester.*
Quick & Dutcher, Port Jervis
　　　　　　　Deer Park.
Wynans L.　　*Goshen.*
Owen S. R.
Hanford P. C. Unionville
　　　　　　Minisink.
Seares Henry　*Montgomery.*
Woolsey J. G., Walden
Jenkins J.　　　*Monroe.*
Edgar G. E. 17 Water *Newburgh.*
Scott Wm. Colden st.
Powell Thomas A. 22 Water
Schroden Henry F. Front st.
Preston A. South Middletown
　　　　　　　Wallkill.
Smith N. T.　　do
Vanduzer & Palser　*Warwick.*
Demerest & Vandervoort
Hoyt L., Florida

Orleans County.

Ledyard J. C. Albion　*Barre.*
Potter Russell, do
Strickland Mrs. do
Pullman A. H. & Brothers, do

Dunham John   *Carlton.*
Hall Moses
M'Allister T. G.   *Clarendon.*
Sherman ———   *Kendall.*
Porter S. M., Holley   *Murray.*
Blair & Brown, Medina *Ridgeway.*
Christie Henry, do
Comstock ———   *Shelby.*
Green A. C.   *Yates.*
Halsey Hiram, Lyndonville
Maxwell Hugh

Oswego County.

Stevens F. Cleaveland
       Constantia.
Hoyt Charles P. do
Davies John   *Hannibal.*
Lord W. R.   *Mexico.*
Le Roy Edward
Hale B. J.   *New Haven.*
Fitch H. P. Fitch's Corner
       Oswego.
Wright James M. 1st st.
Wood A. P. Ames' Buildings
Crysler H. W. Crocker's Build-
   ing, Bridge st.
Bickford James, do
Tibbits & Nichols, 1st st.
Goodwin Jas. Washington Mills,
   1st st.
Gurley Geo., Pulaski   *Richland.*
Mead & Cole, Fulton   *Volney.*

Otsego County.

Avery Amasa   *Burlington.*
Avery A.   *Butternuts.*
Harris L.
Brewer L.   *Cherry Valley.*
Day William H.   *Decatur.*
Becker Walter   *Edmeston.*
Hammond C.
Burdick Albert, W. Edmeston
Durfy J. Schuyler's Lake *Exeter.*
Ashcroft J.   *Hartwick.*
Strong C.   *Laurens.*
Murray Alexander   *Middlefield.*
Gould H.   *Milford.*
Wing ———   *New Lisbon.*
Cunningham Salmon & Son *Otsego.*
Leslie Richard A. Cooperstown
       Otsego.
Clark J.   *Plainfield.*
Kinney J.   *Richfield.*
Walker B.   *Springfield.*
Wilmot Daniel W.   *Unadilla.*
Draper & Chester   *Westford.*
Baker Sherman   *Worcester.*
Crandall Lewis R.

Putnam County.

Stowe Wm. D.   *Carmel.*
Clinton L.   *Patterson.*
Ketcham L. Cold Spring
       Phillipstown.
Nelson J. E.   do

Queens County.

Thum John G.   *Flushing.*
Raynor & Carman   *Hempstead.*
Carman Coles
Allen George   *Oyster Bay.*

Rensselaer County.

Hoag O.   *East Nassau.*
Brown M. T.   *Petersburgh.*
Adams W. L. 285 River   *Troy.*
Daniels A. C. 18 Congress
Taylor R. M. 45   do
Dunham David A. 56 do
Clapp Noah. 214 River
Green Robert, (Chairs & Furni-
   ture) 268 River
Ingram Aaron, 5 Grand Division

Richmond County.

Wilde John, Port Richmond
       Northfield.
Hageman A. Stapleton *Southfield.*
De Forrest J.   do

St. Lawrence County.

Smith Stephen   *Brasher*
Parkherst Gregory
Meredith Thomas G.   *Canton.*
Barrows Prosper
Lawrence Lorenzo
Conley Aaron
Giles A.   *Fowler.*
Vanderzee S. B.   *Gowerneur.*
King J.
Thayer T
Haskins Uri   *Hermon.*
Babcock Daniel K.
Whitney Edgar   *Lawrence.*
Hipburn Milo, Columbia *Madrid.*
Dearborn S. H. Waddington
Dezelleo John,   do
Richardson H. B. & Co. Columbia
Gage Samuel,   do
Stebbins Levi,   do
Tackrell John, Waddington
Buck Enos   *Massena.*
M'Allaster Benjamin *Morristown.*
Bisbee E. W.   *Norfolk.*
Munson H. S.
Guest George jr. Lake st. Ogdens-
   burgh   *Oswegatchie.*
Lewis & Rockland, Ogdensburgh
Chapman & Wright,   do
Hickok Myron B. Isabella st.
White & Carry,   do
Millard Henry.   do
Tupper Freeman   *Parishville.*
Copell William P.
Welch B. G.   *Pierpont.*
Carpenter William   *Potsdam.*
Batchelder Benjamin F.
Partridge Cyrus
Bailey Seymour
Barrows Aaron, Crary's Mills
Derby George H.   *Stockholm.*

Saratoga County.

Jones Hiram   *Carlton.*
Breck James B.
Taylor Charles O.   *Galway.*
Crittenden William
Glasser Joseph
Wing Charles B. Greenfield Centre
       Greenfield.
Newton R. B. *Saratoga Springs.*
Walker A.
Bradley D.
Chapin Joel
Evans William   *Stillwater.*

Schenectady County.

Brown A. E. 56 State *Schenectady.*
Winne Gerrit W. 35 Union

Schoharie County.

Baldwin John   *Blenheim.*
Kniskern John F.
Osterhout John H.   *Cobleskill.*
Dean Alexander   *Esperance.*
Buckingham J. Fultonham *Fulton.*
Wing George, Breaksbeen
Scofield James   *Gilboa.*
Street Warren P.
Bouck George   *Middleburgh.*
Bentley E. S.   *Richmondville.*
Rickett A.   *Schoharie.*
Ackerman A. (Chairmaker)
Sofford J. H. Hyndsville *Seward.*
Brown Amos, Gallupville
Baker Lyman   *Wright.*

Seneca County.

Pomroy Wm.   *Ovid.*
Bliss Edward
Allen Fayette, Farmer
Bergen Cornelius, do
Stewart & Larcum, do
Brim Gardner   *Seneca Falls.*
Hubbard H. W.
Morehouse A.
Sanderson James
Sairs Joseph   *Waterloo.*
Cook ———

Steuben County.

Downs A.   *Addison.*
Knight G. H.   *Bath.*
Slocum John
Conner Leonard   *Cohocton.*
Mallory & Lyon   *Painted Post.*
Egbert R. R.
Parcel John A.

Suffolk County.

Sammis Jessie   *Huntington.*
Conklin David, Babylon
Buckingham George *Riverhead.*
Wilson John   *Smithtown.*
Litchard Wm. & Co., Greenport
       Southold.

——— Sullivan County.

Preston J. V.   *Liberty.*
M'Williams J. S. Bloomingburgh
       Mamakating.
M'Williams R. J. Bloomingburgh
Drake John   do
Munce S. S., Burlingham
Jackson Cyrus B., Monticello
       Thompson.
Ballard L. A.   do
Mitchell William,   do

Tioga County.

Ogden J. B.   *Owego.*

Tompkins County.

Wortman John, Enfield Centre
       Enfield.
Cox Wesley   *Newfield.*
Hanurd Don C.

Ulster County.

Wells Daniel L.   *Kingston.*
Delamater Peter
Freer Josiah
King George, Milton *Marlborough.*
Coe L.   *New Paltz.*
Gleason George   *Saugerties.*
Du Bois P.
Brock & Tuttle, Napaneck
       Wawarsing.
Elting John H., Ellenville

Warren County.

Bebee Ira, Pottersville   *Chester.*
Harris N. Glenn's Falls
       Queensbury.
Cushing James, do
Grum Benjamin, do
Brock M.   do
Wilsey James   *Warrensburgh.*
Purnell John

Washington County.

Ashton Wm. S.   *Argyle.*
Ross James
Barton M. & R.   *Cambridge.*
Rogg Andrew
De Forest John   *Fort Edward.*
Booth George W.
Burnham W. E.   *Greenwich.*
Ashton John
Fenton C. & J.
Whitney Erastus, Centre Falls
Brown John, West   *Hebron.*
Nash H. B. Sandy Hill *Kingsbury.*
Woodworth H. P. do
Peireon H. B.   do
De Forest J. A.   do
Blashfield James   *Salem.*
Bowen David
Orcutt Mathew
Barton M. & R., North *White Creek.*
Richardson ———, Canal st.
       Whitehall.

Wayne County.

Granger James, Newark *Arcadia.*
M'Laughlin Michael
Munn Moses, Clyde   *Galen.*
Tipling & Cockshaw, Clyde

Frazier John _Lyons._
Turck A. F.
Boehmler ——
Hecox 8.
Bourne Richard _Marion._
Netterville J. W. _Ontario._
Jennee & Seeley
Prosens Anson _Sodus._
Jordan David _Williamson._
Church Hiram _Wolcott._
Colorford ——

Westchester County.

Ambler Wm. _Bedford._
Travis J. Peekskill _Courtlandt._
Dunning H. do
Vanderbelt J., Tarrytown
Greenburgh.
Wright Ambrose, (gothic furniture,) Hastings
Constant Lewis J. _New Rochelle._
Hageman & Doolittle, Sing Sing
Ossining.
Jennings Stephen, do
Pardoe Alfred, Portchester _Rye._
Byrne R. _White Plains._
Miller D.
Wheeler John _Yonkers._
Chiffa Francis F.

Wyoming County.

Shattuck Edward C. _Attica._
Sanburn D., Cowlesville
Bennington.
True J. W. _Castile._
Chapin E. _China._
Crosby A. G. Genesee Falls
Waldo Cecil, do
Davis Nathan, do
Barber Benj., Java Village _Java._
Rogers R. Wyoming _Middlebury._
Bartles Christopher, Wyoming
Horton A. 8. _Perry._
Hooper & Edgerly
Gordon D. P. & A. _Pike._
Eggleston W.
M'Cray ——, Varysburgh/_Sheldon._
Clark Elisha, do
La Ran N., Strykersville
Norris Wm. H. _Warsaw._
Galpin W. T.
Stedman L.
Miller John, Branchport
Jerusalem.

Yates County.

Brown Daniel _Middlesex._
Roat Joseph, Penn Yan _Milo._
Hopkins E. G. do
Curtis Samuel F. do
Holbrook Thos. do
Strobridge Charles, Potter Centre
Potter.
Warner Samuel. do
Everson Jacob, Rushville
Fowler Wm., Dundee _Starkey._
Andrews Allen
Redder C. 8.

Cameo Cutters.

Borrel Phillibert, 251 Broadway
New York.
Ellis & Wilson, 247 Broadway

Camphene, (_See also Lamp Stores._)

Erie County.

Wightman & Beckwith, 215 Main
Buffalo.

New York County.

Bush Wm. K. 336 Greenwich
New York.
Drew John, 24 Division
Engle James, 26 Burling Slip
Jackson Sidney L. 55 Greene
Jones Dan. L. 30 City Hall pl.
Lucas & Rogers, 2 6th

M'Cready Geo. W. 436 Broadway
& 6th Av. cor. 19th _New York._
Mings Peter. 103 Willet
Moore John K. 416 Cherry
Patterson Wm. T. 468 Hudson
Reilly Jas. Gansevoort cor. 9th
Av. & 156 6th Av.
Reilly John, 160 6th Av.
Reilly S. 185 Canal
Richmond C. H. 31 Chatham
Roth John, 23 Av. B
Schaffer John, 334 Houston
Tapscott James T. 86 South
Waterbury Joseph, 50 Av. D
Williams Wilmot, 138 Maid. Lane
Worth Peter, 85 Pitt

Orange County.

Nixon Edward, 2d st. _Newburgh._

Cane Makers.

Batley Joseph, 182 Broadway
New York.
Caulkins John S. 54 Nassau
Cox A. & Son, 16 Maiden Lane
Dillon Daniel, 39 Centre
Gilmour J. A. & J. 93 Chatham
Meyer & Popenhusen, 44 Cliff
Rohde Henry, 174 Broadway
Rose William E. 37 Reade
Schnei r Peter, 21 Maiden Lane
Walker Frederick, 26 N. William
Wolf Francis, 82 Fulton

Capstan and Windlass Manufacturers.

Deveau, Selick & Co. 720 4th
New York.

Capsules.

Planten Henry, 224 William
New York.

Cap Makers.

Abraham Morris, 465 Pearl
New York.
Aden & Brodek, 159 Pearl
Bunschuh John, 24 Av. B
Cohen H. & N. 35 Centre
Cohen Marcus, 141 Water
Cohen Philip, 256 Delancy
Colmin Joseph. 2 Cliff
Cristeller L. 111½ Division
Curtis & Weed, 156 Water
Cutbill H. 183 Maiden Lane
Denyer R. 64 Division
Eppstein E. & Brother, 31 Bowery
Erlanger Susmann. 128 Pitt
Feigl & Stein, 56 Chatham
Field Charles D. 37 Av. C. & 446
Grand
Fishblatt S. 109 John
Fox Charles, 102 Maiden Lane
Freystadt Jacob, 136 Water
Gies Anthony, 12 Rector
Guhrauer William, 260 Grand
Hart H. E. 137 William
Heimann Herman, 239 2d
Heyn F. 202 William
Hoveman Undone, 115 8th Av.
Jacobs Lewis 227 Canal
Kalish Philip, 316½ Grand
Kaplan Hyman, 6 Peck slip
Keefer John, 60 Anthony
King M. J. & M. A. & Co. 157 Water
Kohn Hezekiah, 23 Cedar
Krekel Frederick, 49 Av. B
Krekel John G. 49 Av. A
Loeberger Simon, 406 Grand
Levi Joseph, 2 William
Levi M. 141 Water
Levi Wm. 140 Water
Lewers Samuel, 118 John

Lippard Marih, 163 3d Av.
New York.
Manning & Faulkner, 145 Water
Marks I. & A. 97½ Bowery
Marks Isaac, 95 Bowery
Mawson Brothers, 161 Water
Mode Adolph, 31 Cedar
Mueller Louis, 29 Av. A.
Murray William, 125 Division
Naylor George, 139 Water
Newman Josman, 13 James
Oppenheimer Samuel, 18 Av. D.
Perron Charles, 160 3d
Peter John, 290 Broome
Phillips John D. & Co. 174 Water
Piering C. 160 3d
Pinner Samuel, 61 Bowery
Plaffmann Lawrence, 67 Av. A.
Raymond Charles P. 156 Pearl
Rascovar S. & Brother, 222 Will'm
Roll & Girbardt, 258 Wilham
Ross Bernard, 281 Spring
St. John, White & Williams, 146
Water
Salter Abraham, 246 Grand
Saltiel A. 27 Bowery & 264 Grand
Seger & West, 116 Maiden Lane
Silberman H. 120 Water
Smith W. Willard, 36 & 38 Cedar
& 54 William
Spiegelberg Isaac, 30 Spring
Thompson J. & Co. 109 Water
Treadwell George C. 172 Water
Tuska Philip H. 455 Pearl
Van Duzer W. A. 156 Broadway
Wiedennuf Conrad, 200 Houston
Weil Moses, 451 Grand
Witkowski B. & Co. 330 Bowery

Cap Front Makers.

Carlsbach & Jacob, 26 Cedar
New York.
Clark Isaac, 154 Water
Herz L. & Co. 173 Water
King Pineus, 2 Depeyster
Metz & Hoeter, 455 Pearl
Steinfield & Floersheim, 66 Fulton
Watson George, 156 Water

Cards (Machine) Manufacturers.

Cayuga County.

Sargent & Mortimer _Auburn._

Duchess County

Browning Wm. A. _Fishkill._

Rensselaer County.

Watson J. D. Hollow Road _Troy._

Card (Blank) Manufacturers.

Cook George, 65 Fulton _New York_
Field Cyrus W. & Co. 11 Cliff
Graf & Koverman, 26 Ann
Pike Horace B. 139 Nassau
Whittemore J. & Co. 192 Pearl

Cards, Playing & Visiting.

Cohen L. L 188 William _New York._

Car Manufacturers.

Albany County.

Gould James & Co. Hamilton st.
Albany.

Columbia County.

Waterman J. T. Water st. _Hudson_

Monroe County.

Reese, Ashley & Co. cor. West North st. & R. Road *Rochester.*

Oneida County.

Lyons D. A. 31 Bleeker *Utica.*

Rensselaer County.

Western R. R. Co. *Greenbush.*
Eaton, Gilbert & Co. cor. 6th & Albany *Troy.*

Tompkins County.

Conrad V. Aurora st. *Ithaca.*

Carpenters and Builders.
(See also Builders.)

Albany County.

Howard Matthew, 70½ Broadway *Albany.*

Wait C. B. 22 Orange
Beebe T. 123 Montgomery
Deforest B. S. & J. J. 31 Union
Austin & Clark, 52 & 54 Lydius
Conklin J. 70 Rensselaer
Halleck D. 79 Green
Johnston T. 77 Church
Watson S. 68 Westerlo
Cunningham I. 88 Bleeker
Boardman William, 46 Howard
Chadderdon A. M. 109 Beaver
Cameron William, 41 Grand
Allanson P. 1 Elm
Seymour L. 91 Grand
Ward J. C. & Son, 165 Lydius
Sexton & Poinier, 49 Franklin pl
Bancroft John, 3 James
Harrison Wm. H. 345 Washington
M'Entee J. 31 Canal
White Isaac, 62 Spring
Jones William, 88 Patroon
Kirtland & Thurber, 26 Wash.
Hotaling D. I. 95 Washington
Teel A. *Coeymans.*
Gibbons J. E.
Smith J., Dunnsville *Guilderland.*
Kaley John, do
Carhart ——, do
Kaley Henry, do
Moak John, do
Severson George, Knowersville
Relyea Peter, Centre
Nichols G. West Troy *Watervliet.*
Leonard E. do
Andrews N. do
Rogers & Robinson, W. Troy
Powell F. C. *Westerlo.*

Alleghany County.

Peirce Isa *Alfred.*
Potter B. F.
Vincent P. M.
Ellsworth John *Allen.*
St. John John
Knapp John F.
Sanborn Thomas
Frisby H. S. *Almond.*
Campbell M. M.
Stevens R. S.
Wheaton S. R. *Andover.*
Burr A. *Angelica.*
Spencer Smith
Barnum David
Spencer Charles
Brown Wm.
West James
Gastin E. W. *Belfast.*
Wilson M. C.
Knight A.
Gastin S.
Headley Joel *Birdsall.*
Dye L. I.
Dye Joseph
Davidson John J.
Kenyon George W. *Bolivar.*
Thomas Wm. *Burns.*
Augustine ——

Tilden E. *Burns.*
Clement Cyrus H. *Cascades.*
Easterbrook B. F. D.
Pettiplace Stephan
Richardson Andrew *Cuba.*
Richardson Andrew & Co.
Banks Burr
Jackson John W.
Cutter Stephen K.
Rutter Emerson
Savage Seth B.
Dunn B. C. *Friendship.*
Butterfield W. P.
Fairbanks M.
Applebee A.
Coon A. A.
Lord T. C.
Lord J.
Osterhoudt H.
Hageboom M.
Niver C.
Benson Wm. C. *Granger.*
Pennel James
Webstead John
Carman Samuel
Hatch Isaac, Short Tract
Pepper Thomas, do
Randolph G. Little Genesee *Genesee.*
Bass Joseph do
Partridge Elijah *Hume.*
Bliss J.
Davis N. G.
Wright Miles
Beardsley Augustus
Charles Jonathan *Rushford.*
Budd Byron, Wellsville *Scio.*
Carnell C. B. *West Almond.*
Boorn Calvin
Hoag Phillip *Wirt.*
Ryno John
Byrno Randolph

Broome County.

Whitbeck A. Chenango Forks *Barker.*
Henderson J. do
Jerome & Wells *Binghamton.*
Wilber Z.
Hill J.
Castle S.
Lewis John
Perkins A.
Aldrich S.
Harding A.
Harper G.
Ogden & Foote
Chafer J. A. Harpersville *Colesville.*
Draper L. H. do
Braman A. do
Adams James *Triangle.*
Balch J. B. *Union.*
Scovill D.
Belyea R.
Ufford C.
Andrus P.
Ward L. Union Centre
Thomas G. *Windsor.*
Gurnsey C.
Gurnsey R.
Sanford Lambert
Chapel J. C.
Smith S.

Cattaraugus County.

Gee Hiram *Ashford.*
Mason Charles, Rutledge *Connewango.*
Seager Orestus do
Seager Anson do
Brooklins Caleb do
Baldwin C. *Farmersville.*
Kingsbury Benjamin
Williams James
Crosby Alanson *Franklinville.*
Phillips O. W.
Gifford David
Crandall John *Freedom.*
Kingsbury Daniel, Sandusky
Tate Thomas, do

Jaquesh Alonzo E. Elton *Freedom.*
Owens Joseph F. do
Pixley Alonzo, do
Fisk Chester, do
Knight Daniel, do
Fisher Sawyer, do
Phelbreck Daniel, do
Adams E. *Great Valley.*
Bissell Thomas
Snyder George *Little Valley.*
Boutell Charles
Barton T. F.
Andrews Jasper *Machias.*
Bliton T. N.
Lafferty William R.
Joslyn James
Watson J. S.
Benton W. Eddyville *Mansfield.*
Bowen Moses, do
Bowen George, do
Myers Daniel, do
Harris Seth, do
Catrsel Jonathan *Otto.*
Cross Livingston
Eaton Isaac
Van Anstrand Jacob
Smith Solomon *Perrysburgh*
Johnson Jesse
Wright Z. L.
Hurd Garret
Lee Elon
Vanderhoof James
Sheldon James
Waters Jacob
Daily E. P. Gowanda *Persia.*
Forbush L. C. do
Hall Franslow, do
Knolls J. P. do
Potter Sylvanus, do
Potter William, do
Johnson Alfred, do
Van Ostrand J. G. do
Walden Myron, do
Wright Alfred *Portville.*
Percival James C.
Hopkins Harlow M.
Graves S. C. *Rice.*
Simmons A.
Guild H.
Braman N.
Morgan N.
Beebe Ira *South Valley.*
Cory John *Yorkshire.*
Cummings Abel
Langmaid William F. Delavan
Lovejoy C. do

Cayuga County.

Bodman A. L., (Bannister Fence,) Genesee st. *Auburn.*
Van Tuyl William, State st.
Manvord J. Water st.
Pomeroy & Wheeler, North st.
Brigham C. P. do
Everts William O. & Co. do
Turner E. W. Weedsport *Brutus.*
Smith E. do
Skelton S. D. do
Wilcox F. *Niles.*
Crowell J. D. *Victory.*

Chautauque County.

Woodard P. G. Mayville *Chautauque.*
Sheffield Judson *Cherry Creek.*
Newton Samuel
Carpenter W. C.
Crandall Samuel
Hyatt Smith William
Putnam Cornelius
Kilborn Hiram
Lyon Wilber *Clymer.*
Carroll Wm. Jamestown *Ellicott.*
Abbot Ezra, do
Coats Le Roy, do
Rous John Y. *French Creek.*
Reid James M.
Case Harvey
White La Fayette
Eddy Myron W. *Harmony.*
Jones J. Fredonia *Pomfret*

7

Quigby James — Portland.
Rice Andrew — Sheridan.
Warren Philander
Boshert Joseph
Boshert H.
Buck Ira D.
Green William — Sherman.
Johnson John
Gunnell George
Smith J.
Badger Elias — Westfield.
Abell Eber
Daniels Robert C.

Chemung County.

Mix Sylvester — Catharine.
Thompson N. N.
Thompson L. A.
Thompson P. M.
Rittenhouse William
Tallman H. C. — Elmira.
Conklin Ichabod
Webb A.
Salmon G. B.
Youngs & Reynolds
Stowell Abel
Bartholomew J.
Bell A. T.

Chenango County.

Beecher Daniel — Coventry.
Lewis Lemuel
Nash T. — Linklaen.
Hill & Thurber — New Berlin.
Chase H.
Thomas A. — Norwich.
Lewis E.
Morse H. L.
Wait D.
Randall W.
Smith J. M.
Miner S. W.
Childs E.
Abbott Aaron — Oxford.
Brown George F.
Bolles Elias
Dort Otis
Foot L. B.
Gilman William
Morehouse Squire R.
Potter Benjamin
Purdy Wilson
Perry John
Willoughby Ira
Young Freeborn
Willoughby Russell
Mirie James — Pitcher.
Warner Hiram
Kenyon Clark
Swain Oliver — Plymouth.
Merihew C. B.
Blodgett Thomas
Blodgett William
Glazier Franklin
Roland H. — Sherburne.
Jenkins J. S.
Burton George
Shaw K. S.
Ellsbury E.
Shelden S.
French H.
Dort E.

Clinton County.

Ferry & Son, Keeseville AuSable.
Mills, Brothers, do
Whitney Norman do
Day George — Plattsburgh.
Walker S.
Kean C.
Eagan William
Fitzgerald J.
Lafever J.
Fredo J.
O'Brien Patrick
Booth J.
Nutting V. P.
Clifford J.
Reynolds A.
Squires Josiah
Terbill Jonah

Markee Alexander — Plattsburgh.
Laraby J.
Lewiszell Z.
Pellaw Francis
Erno Seymour
Goodwin Lewis
Cavner John
Thomas Seth — Saranac.
Parsons Henry
Colburn Willard F.

Columbia County.

Sciam H. — Ancram.
Secor J.
Osborn L. — Austerlitz.
Mathers H. Spencertown
Spencer E. do
Bemus W. do
Allen C. W. do
Robinson A. — Chatham.
Lay O.
Booth J.
Lay J.
Vanalstine C.
Woodruff A.
Doty S.
Brown S.
Davis D.
Vosburgh B.
Miller S.
Smith J. E.
Strever L.
Thomas E. M.
Varley S. S.
Jones J. W.
Root A. — Claverack.
Shinkle C. F.
Murgittroid W. H.
Shaver P. Smoky Hollow
Anderson P. I. do
Burrows E. — Copake.
Strong P.
Bissell M.
Becker P. — Hillsdale.
Burdock R. L.
Andress H.
Vanderpool J.
Shufelt George
Althons J.
Crandall T. 1st st. — Hudson.
Macey R. G. & Co. 2d
King W. O. Union
Hoftaling C. J. Partition st.
Cheeny & Roberts, South Front st.
Calkins A. Union st.
Folger A. do
Smith G. Warren st.
Van Slyck, T. B. — Kinderhook.
Hoes & Crieley
Frentiss & Mesick
Merrill H. N. — New Lebanon.
Shumway W.
Sandford H.
Comstock A. P.
Bowman H.
Bowman E.
Sleighter H.

Cortland County.

Jacobs David — Preble.
Mitchell Stephen
Baldwin Silas
Hunter James
Vandenburgh Abraham

Delaware County.

Johnson C. & B. — Davenport.
Watress O. — Franklin.
Hawley C.
Maxwell S.
Goodrich J.
Kingsbury E. — Hancock.
Kingsbury G.
Colium E. Bloomville Kortright.
Brownell G. do
Lewis J. do
Gerow J. do
Wolf A. — Meredith.
Mitchell M.

Humastin G. — Meredith.
Burgen B. H.
Price N. B. — Middletown.
Bortle W. H. H
Price T.
Sanlord E. P. Clovesville
Tiler T. Hobart — Stamford
M'Gonald J. do
Grant J. F. do
Grant A. B. do
Scott Wm. do
Foster H. B., Deposit — Tompkins.
Freeman W. G. do
Ogden D. & E. do
Birch E. L. do
Hyde L. do
Fancher C. — Walton.
Niles H.
Hess M.
Cleaveland N.

Duchess County.

Tompkins S. H. — Ansenia.
Douglass J.
Douglass P.
Height D. — Clinton.
Rorack J.
Knapp Wm.
Barton A.
Carpenter J., Clinton Hollow
Palmer A. D. do
Boughton S. D. do
Chapman A. — Dover.
Jones T.
Lee W.
Ward E.
Bristol H.
Bristol A.
Ensign J.
Chapman L.
Thomas I.
Shiers J.
Hurd O.
Bowdish J.
Cook C. — Fishkill
Weeks S.
Barry C. F.
Gore G. H. Wappingers' Falls
Bishob D. do
Brewster Wm. H., Hughsonville
White S., Metteawan
Acker P. Fishkill Landing
Van Wagener W. A. do
Hopper A. do
Pollock B. F., New Hackensack
Finch & Van Dyck — Hyde Park
Banker Wm.
Way J. — Lagrange.
Neher P. L — Milan.
Copernall D.
Dedrick A.,
Corman J. — North East.
Tanner B.
Hutchinson H.
Covey A.
Chase L. A.
Culver W. A.
White C. — Pawling.
Herviland H.
Corbin A.
Corbin J.
Wilcox S.
Hoag T. — Pine Plains
Near J.
Newell ——
Cramer G. B. — Pleasant Valley.
Smith J. C.
Doughty D. H. ——
Armstrong Wm.
Lynch S.
Vale J.
Millord Robert — Poughkeepsie
Dudley H. H.
Lockwood J.
Vancleek B.
Williamson S.
Jones L. R.
Spade H cor. Church & Hamilton
Cannon A. 36 Hamilton
Potter F. A., Mill st.
Hevenor F. — Red Hook.
Shaver H.

M'Carty S.   *Rhinebeck.*
Curtis L.
Latson H.
Teal H.
Hannaburgh P
Fulton P.
Trouter J.   *Stanford.*
Rider E. G.
Davis H. S.
Barnard J. R., Stanfordville
Gregory B. Attlebury
Hall J.   *Unionvale.*
Hall A.
Dennis J. I.
Loveless A.   *Washington.*
M'Farland A.
Griffin J., Salt Point
Rust A.   do

Erie County.

Graham John M. Williamsville
     Amherst.
White Wm.   do
Green Gardiner,   do
Amalt John G.   do
Amalt Alex. G.   do
Cor William,   do
Neff Daniel,   do
White John. Willink   *Aurora.*
Eddy Nathan,   do
Payne Timothy,   do
Pratt B.   do
Pike Abner,   do
Hamilton Z. A.
Fullington & M'Martin *Black Rock.*
Stickney Orin
Foster K.   *Boston.*
Foster S.
Walker Stephen, cor. Erie & Terrace   *Buffalo.*
Roberts E. Miller st.
Ream V. 31 North Division
Colburn Israel B.   *Cheektowaga.*
Nano Michael
Jenkins Samuel
May Harvey
Hussey S.   *Collins.*
Danser Joshua   *Clarence.*
Sawtel Edmond
Bear Martin, Clarence Centre
Lake C. Springville   *Concord.*
Lincoln Thos.   do
Matthewson Geo. do
M'Millin Wm.   do
Maddison Fred.   do
Rockwood Valentine   *Eden.*
Rockwood Reuben
Redfield Wm. V.
Redfield R. M.
Johnson C.
Shattuck Moses
Claghorn J. M. East Evans *Evans*
Clark John   *Hamburgh.*
Morey Franklin   *Holland.*
Hunt David, 2d
Clark H.   *Lancaster.*
Buck Stephen
Judd Henry
Sleeper H.
Ely Joseph
Little Guy
Knight & Smith, Akron *Newstead.*
Loveless Alfred   *Wales.*
Cole Allen
Tallmann Wm.

Essex County.

Clarke C. M.   *Elizabethtown.*
Furman W. S.
Sheldon R.
Ladd Lewis
Felcher David   *Essex.*
Rowell N.
Davis B. R.
Green Wm.
Heald Noah   *Keene.*
Heald David
Sanders ——
Rixford Jordan   *Minerva.*
Doyne James T.

Havens Samuel T. Moriah 4 Corners   *Moriah.*
Edgerton E. S.   do
Edgerton James R.   do
Curtis Austin F.   do
Baker Dennis,   do
Baker E. D.   do
Putnam Madison,   do
Childs Gray,   do
Adams Cyrus B.   do
Dean Fordee,   do
Tart John,   do
Buck James,   do
Hendee Oliver,   do
Edgerton George,   do
Chilson ——,   do
Cheney Charles C. *Willsborough.*
Putnam D. P.

Franklin County.

Jackson Charles   *Bangor.*
Heath Daniel B.   *Chateaugay.*
Bullard Alonzo
Bridges Thomas
Mash Buel
Bowine O. F. N. C.   *Moira.*
Bowine Wm.
Johnson Charles & Sons, West Constable   *Westville.*
Waggoner Jason, W. Constable
Downs R. C.   do
Cushman Wm.   do

Fulton County.

Banker A.   *Ephratah.*
Caldwell James
Caldwell James, jr.
Beck Anthony
Morey A.
Mason John   *Johnstown.*
Thompson Nathaniel
Thyne Jno.
Younglove Jas.
Campbell Robert
Dunk John
Dye John K. Gloversville
Ackert James,   do
Long Adam,   do
Cross Luke M.   do
Peeck A. V. Vail's Mills *Mayfield.*
Wetherbee C.   do
Thorp Erastus   *Perth.*

Genesee County.

Rice A.   *Alabama.*
Peck W. J.
Jencks Wilber, Oakfield
Wright George,   do
Woodward Richard, do
Tisdall & Shaw   *Alexander.*
Dustin O.   *Batavia.*
Coleman J.
Palmer J.
Graham H.
Craig R. W.
Tuttle S.
Barner L.
Martin G. A.
Crampton J.   *Bergen*
Tone John
Lee Joseph
Moore James
Smith C. Stone Church
Ward Sherman,   do
Hall Chapin, North Bergen
Lucas John   *Bethany.*
Johnson R.
Stanley L.   *Le Roy.*
Field D. D.
Currier Asa
Wait Chester
Stewart John   *Pavilion.*
Snow David
Whitney Alvin

Greene County.

Howland Watson   *Athens.*
Wells James   *Cassackia.*
Lampman Nicholas T
Mackey Heary

Winans Williams H.   *Cassackia.*
Strong Charles   *Durham.*
Chittenden R. P.
Purdy Erastus S.   *Hunter*
De Bois Henry, East Kill
Faulkner Robert A.   *Lexington.*
Van Valkenburgh Abraham I.
Fellows Philip   *West Lexington.*
Lewis James   *Prattsville.*

Herkimer County.

Miller Christopher   *Columbia.*
Spohn Nicholas
Spohn Daniel
Spohn Levi
Haggerday & Sons
Petrie Henry
Petrie J. R.
Mitchen Nelson
Youngs Ward
Woolluber E. A.
Osterhout Joseph
Vanalstine A.
Achler Lavid
Wood M.
Chapel A.
Buell S. B.   *Fairfield.*
Cutler Warner   *Frankfort.*
Edick William
Johnson H.
Johnson J. W.
Dodge Gideon
Lee Alfred
Doriaty E. Frankfort Hill
Hall Anson   *Herkimer.*
Jones & Bell
Hall Alexander
Bowers Joseph
Bowers David
Chase William   *Little Falls*
Dorr & Coleman
Gildersleeve F. B.
Walton F. & Co.
Anderson S. H.
Levison Benjamin
Ransom M. M.
Cole James   *Newport*
Johnson Charles K.
Kelsey George
Fenner R.
Fenner E.
Quick W.
De Lano E.
Doty W. W.   *Norway.*
Wiggins Richard K.   *Ohio.*
Coppernott James M.
Coppernott William
Kilmer William H.
Tunnicliff W. Van Hornsville
     Stark.
Tunnicliffe T. T.   do
Fort & Gulwits   do
Archer Isaac, Starkville
Champion E.   do
Mosher J. Jordanville   *Warren.*
Barber A.   *West Winfield.*
Wicks C.

Jefferson County.

Bolton John, Alexandria Bay
     Alexandria.
Ellis A. P.   do
Northrop Jos.   do
Payne R. Ox Bow   *Antwerp.*
Crook Orwin   *Champion.*
Gunn Winthrop
Earl G.
Eddy Rufus
Smith S.   *Ellisburgh.*
Lewis J.
Wait Thomas F.   *Lorraine.*
Morrill Asa
M'Pherson P. S. Three Mile Bay
     Lyme.
Mosher C.   *Philadelphia.*
Spears John B.   *Rodman.*
Winslow Wm. N.
Green A. East Rodman
Wait D. C.   do
Beecher J. W. South Rutland
     Rutland.

Gypson Cyrus, Felt's Mills *Rutland.*
Seeber Henry   *Theresa.*
Seeber Daniel
Dresser Wm.
Myres Miles
Auborn Calvin   *Watertown.*

Kings County.

Barney J. B. 115 Myrtle Av.
          Brooklyn.
Baylis Thomas, 83 Washington
Booth B. H. 82 Lawrence
Booth S. 58 Myrtle Av.
Brown James S. 161 High
Burnett John O. 54 Poplar
Carman Joseph, Myrtle Av.
Chauncey D. & M. 12 & 14 Livingston
Colyer W. Myrtle Av.
Conner & Hedges, 138 Nassau
Cooper L. 76 Myrtle Av.
Dan Wm. L. 279 Adams
Dow Charles, Duffield st.
Edwards Joseph, Lafayette st.
Farrel Nathan, Livingston near Boerum
Funk John H. 271 Adams
Glover Frederick, 96 Washington
Graham S. cor. Myrtle Av. & Steuben
Gunliffe Henry, 113 Prospect
Haviland L. 142 Atlantic
Hunt Charles. Congress nr. Henry
Keely T. 89 Hudson Av.
Kerby James W. cor. Atlantic & Clinton
Kerr Robert, Furman near State
Ketcham C. J. 83 Adams
Latimer W. S. & Co. Columbia near State
Leonard Samuel, 143 State
Litchfield R. Schermerhorn near Court
M'Gee John, Atlantic Dock
M'Kee James, Atlantic st. Bedford
Morehouse C. Prospect near Hudson Av.
Morehouse S. Bond near Fulton
Murphy M. 19 Willow
Noe Wm. H. S., Schermerhorn nr. Nevens
O'Donnell J. Baltic near Smith
Opie Isaac, Bond near Fulton
Osman Samuel W. 61 Livingston
Pell Aaron, Flushing Av.
Phillips H.   do
Platt J. Schermerhorn nr. Boerum
Plumstead James M. 155 Atlantic
Queen Montgom. Pacific nr. Smith
Raymond Jas. Dean nr. Congress
Reeve T. 190 Livingston
Remsen & Abrams, Pearl near Front
Revere Isaac, Charles nr. Prospect
Rhodes N. B. 144 Concord
Roberts Henry, 105 Clark
Ross John, 190 High
Soaman Wm. Myrtle Av.
Sheldon R. A. 197 Atlantic
Simonson M., Adams cor. Nassan
Sipp Adrian I. 225 Atlantic
Sirey John, cor. Gold & Water
Spencer & Bonnett, Schermerhorn near Bond
Taylor T. 265 Washington
Thomas S. V. 34 Henry
Thomas Wm. H. 261 Gold
Van Riper & Allison, Columbia near Warren
Walters Samuel, 112 York
White John, 91 Willoughby
Whipple Richard, Strong Place near Degraw
White Charles, Schermerhorn near Nevins
White Geo. Amity near Henry
Wiggins & Taylor, Livingston nr Henry
Woodruff A. 31 Stanton
Dean John A. Green Point
          Bushwick.

Instone Thomas, Green Point
          Bushwick.
Free Samuel S.   do
Lane W. & J.   do
Hickey John   *Flatbush.*
Van Dytee A. J.
Young Edward
Stotoff A. C.
Phelps E. East New York
Ryder Lawrence   *Gravesend.*
Vorhees Stephen
Haviland William   *New Utrecht.*
Vorhees John I.
Kibby Geo. Fort Hamilton
Conover & Van Cleef, do
Stillwell Henry,   do
Williams S. F. 6th st.
          Williamsburgh.
Tilly S. 1st st.
Turton Thomas, 92 S. 8th
Scriner M. 177 Johnson
Huestis W. 166 S. 4th
Wilson James B. 151 1st
Price John J. S. 191 S. 2d
Gaylor Wm. H. 188 2d
Hoggett Wm. 73 Grand
Folk Abraham, 96 do
Ward Benjamin (ship) 97 Grand
Woglom Cornelius, 150 4th
Haight Wm. H. 96 S. 4th
Salter James, 3d st. near Grand
Golder Wm. N. 1st cor. 7th
Hopkins & Wright, do 9th
Brown John, N. 3d cor. 9th
Huestis J. Ainslie st. cor. 10th
Holmes Josiah, 132 N. 4th
Newry Samuel, 124 do
Barnes & Morrice, Lorimer st. nr. N. 2d
Rile Edward F. Devoe st.

Lewis County.

Rofinot Joseph   *Croghan.*
Zehr John
Appleton R.   *Denmark.*
Farwell S.
Chambers L.
Wood Harvey   *Diana.*
Becker Ephraim
Clarke Horace
Gould Jesse T. Brantingham
          Greig.
Perkins John, Brantingham
Gould Christopher, do
Perkins Aaron, do
Bush George   *Harrisburgh.*
Carter Charles & J.
Elmor Harvey
Humphrey M.
Snyder J.
Austin N.
Mead J.
Kisnor William
Conover J.   *Leeville.*
Moore M.
Emm Jasper J.   *Turin.*
Ragan Hanan
Kilham Charles D.
Dow Henry S.
Gillett Orris A.
Hubbard William
Hubbard William D.
Fisher Bradley
Drake Lorin
Allen David

Livingston County.

Riggs Merritt W.   *Avon.*
Dixon John
Rogers David S.
Stowell H. W.
Brown Harvey   *Caledonia.*
Place Robert
M'Naughton William
Nelson William
Gregg C. M.   *Conesus.*
Partridge David
Watson & Wheaton   *Dansville.*
Geiger John
Geiger Charles
Richie J.

Moore W. M.   *Dansville.*
Perham L. W.
Willey Anson
Deforest Benjamin
Van Vranken G.
Gross J. B.
Kromer L. Y.
Feustumacher Isaac
Feustumacher Horace
Feustumacher Calvin
Fetstumacher Henry
Feustumacher John
Haas John
Haas William
Stowell E.
M'Bride Hugh   *Genesee.*
Green & Dunn
Willard A.
Willard E.
Cooley G. N. Cuylerville
          Leicester.
Wright Ralph N. Cuylerville
Budrow ——, Moscow
Hyde E. & A.   *Lima.*
Atkins C. W.
Tyrrell John   *Livonia.*
Stillwell Bishop, Hemlock Lake
Fellows Ebenezer, do
Hamlin William H. *Mount Morris.*
Summers G. H.
Gale John P.
Carpenter S.
Howe A. B.
Gale P.
Baldwin Bagley & Co.   *Nunda.*
Russell C. F.
Spafford M. B.
Chase George
Van Winkle J.
Mosher Isaac, Hunt's Hollow
          Portage.
Dorris & Edwards   *York.*
Bigelow James, Fowlersville
Smith Anson, Greigsville

Madison County.

Gates Eli   *Brookfield.*
Gates Nathan
Denison H. H.
Dennison J. S.
Denison Horace
Green Allen
York Wheeler
Babcock Ezra
Babcock A. G.
Springstead J. C.   *Casenovia.*
Freborn S. E.
May Luke
Borden Thomas T.
Heath Thomas
Alden S. E.
Knight Ralph, New Woodstock
Savage Le Roy   do
Bly William H.   *De Ruyter.*
Babcock Loren
Hamilton M. M.
House Lorenzo   *Eaton.*
Walton Charles
Washburn Isaac
Cobb Nathan, Morrisville
Franklin ——, do
Hall F.
Lewis Isaac
Atkins Elijah, jr.   *Georgetown.*
Ray Ira
Atwood H. N.
Smith John   *Hamilton.*
Chappel Lewis
Beckwith S. M.
Gardner Charles
Peckham D. S., Cannstota *Lenox.*
Russell M. C.   do
Harlow Benj., Clockville
Everts W. A., Erieville *Nelson.*
Bump J., Peterboro *Smithfield.*
Bickford D.   do
Black Jared, do
Schuyler Jacob   *Sullivan.*
Hazeltine Ebenezer
Gale W. H. Chittenango
Porter M.   do

Davis Noble,Chittenango *Sullivan.*
Graves Hiram, do
Moyer John, do
Higley Harrison, Bridgeport

Monroe County.

Spencer Sylvester, North *Chili.*
Young Frederick, do
Stanton G. P.. Clarkson Corners *Clarkson.*

Hammon S. do
Hinkston Downs, do
Dwyer J. Jenkins' Corners *Greece.*
Phillips S. do
Smith R. do
Hyde Elisha, W. Mendon *Mendon.*
Willis & Delany do
Starr B. do
Gates Henry *Ogden.*
Talmadge A. Parma Corners *Parma.*

Brown J. W. do
Coffin George, do
Trimmer George, do
Stroup J. 87 S. St. Paul *Rochester.*
Fox Henry, 12 Water
Jones William, 12¼ Water
Boyce J. F. Achilles st.
Jones W. E. 1 North
Fox C. H. cor. North & Weld
Miles John, 4 Minerva
Murray C. 169 Mount Hope Av.
Mansfield Amos, 42 Monroe
Osborn Nehemiah, 132 Main
Fox Henry, 212 Buffalo
Jones John, Cherry st.
Damon D. F. Summit st.
Pavor William. School Alley
Taylor J. 250 State
Rice O. M. 199 State
Bell J. Front st.
Crittenden J. H. 11 Spring
Curtis W., Work st.
Atkinson C. Market st.
Atkinson George, 7 Market
Archer John, 78 Front
Coleman C. B. Ball's Buildings
Colman C. B. Ambrose st.
Parsons Lauren, 5 Kent
Pritchard J. W. 36 Hill

Montgomery County.

Campbell Charles *Amsterdam.*
Clark John M.
Young Wm. K.
Phillips Gortan
Fancher Thomas S.
Bradshaw James
Hagaman M. Hagaman's Mills
Tervilleger S. do
Hanson Abraham, Tribe's Hill
Davis & Casler *Canajoharie.*
Covenhoven J.
Snyder Nelson
Wiles Peter. Fultonville *Glen.*
Bell Richard, do
Cady H. C. Smith Town
Failing James, Fort Plain *Minden.*
Phillips George, do
Ehle James, do
Farnharson W. do
Phillips John, do
Failing Simeon, do
Hardendorf H. do
Hand Albert, do
Phillips Henry, do
Brower John J. Fonda *Mohawk.*
Sallsbury F. do
Cherry E. G, do
Markley D. do
Blanchard R. do
Briggs H. D. do
Ehle Daniel, do
Van Brocklyn J. do
Burch John do
Marselis L. Stone Arabia *Palatine.*
Eacker John, do
Lasher George J. do
Snell Peter, do
Walrath Silas, do
Dillinbech R. do

Van Wie Henry, Stone Arabia *Palatine.*
Showerman H. do
Vasman Charles, do
Kenyon M. D. L. Spraker's Basin *Root.*
Dillenbach James, do
Vrooman A. D.
Bander Elijah *St. Johnsville.*
Sitts Jacob

New York County.

Ackenback Thomas, 209 Greene *New York.*
Adams Aaron, 166 Allen
Adams George, rear 20 Chrystie
Adams Samuel, 72 Irving place
Aitkin John, 24 Hammond
Anderson Edm. rear 67 Eldridge
Anderson William, 285 Front
Anderson & Hawxhurst, 90 Leonard
Ayers Daniel, 177 Laurens
Ayre John E. 83 Wooster
Bailey Thomas, 13 Clark
Bailey S. B. 54 Greene
Balck Thomas, rear 147 Orchard
Baldwin Edward, 50 Marion
Baley ——, rear 55 Greene
Barber Thomas, 296 Mulberry
Beard William, 75 11th
Bearwald Louis, 70 Mott
Becker Garret, W. 19th bet. 5th & 6th Avs.
Bedell W. & C. 226 W. 18th
Bedford Donald, 97 Horatio
Beekman James S. 30 4th Av.
Beitel & Stoutenburgh,170 W. 13th
Bell Robert, 62 W. Broadway
Bennet Barnes, 41 Rutgers
Bennett John, 22 Water
Berne James, rear 117 Allen
Bessey S. H. rear 66 1st
Berrian Edward, 234 W. 19th
Betts James H. 31 Forsyth
Bigelow & Ferris, 107 E. 18th
Bird George W. 163¼ Madison
Bishop C. Jefferson
Blackstone W. rear 129 Laurens
Bliss J. E. 1st Av. bet. 8th & 9th
Bloomer Edgar, 65 Perry
Bloomer T. 33 & 40 S. William
Bloomfield Joseph, 56 Orchard
Board & Berry, 12 Frankfort
Bogart Timothy, 209¼ Wooster
Bogart D. B. 5th Av. cor. E. 19th
Bogart & Frye. 150 Amos
Boggs J. & J. Moore, 172 Chrystie
Bohonon Charles, 74 Broad
Bowne S. C. 89 Elm
Boyd Joseph L. 1 Congress
Books P. J. 61 Anthony
Brandeis Charles S. 566 4th
Brown J. C. 10 Dutch
Brown John, 23 Madison
Brown John M. rear 140 Elm
Brown Thomas, 114 do
Brown Thomas H. 54 19th
Brooker S. 22 Hester
Buchanan Edmund. 62 Laight
Burger Horton, 109 Forsyth
Burnett J. L. rear 218 3d Av.
Butler T. P. 199 Mercer
Butler & Lockwood, 92 E. 13th
Butler & Tracy, 27 Minetta lane
Buxton Thomas, B. 233 Division
Buxzee Isaac, 606 Greenwich
Call & Isaacs, 205 12th
Canham W. & Billin. 16 Clarkson
Carrick Thomas J. 7th Av.
Caulfield Henry, 178 Laurens
Chalmers & Moore, 68 Trinity pl.
Chesebro Albert, 22 Hudson
Christie & Bogart, 136 Amos
Christy & Demarest, Wyckoff al.
Churchwell C. N. 46 Eldridge
Clark George R. 137 Maiden lane
Clark James, 252 Delancy
Clayton William H. rear 15 Rose
Close William, 355 Washington & 13 Roosevelt

Cosy William J. 46 Marion *New York.*
Colver G. 515 Washington
Colver & Owens, 117 Troy
Conklin A. L. 302 Greenwich
Cooper James, 625 Hudson
Corlin E. 7th Av.
Coultas John, 36 Rutgers
Coulter William, 68 Beekman
Cox O. B. 29 Essex
Cox & Dalzell, 31 S. William
Craig Joseph T. 90 W. 19th
Cronin Patrick, rear 64 Roosevelt
Cronk John, East 19th bet. 5th Av. and Broadway
Crouch J. 120 Amity
Croxton John, 421 West
Cushier John H. 49 Sullivan
Davey Thomas, 29 Thompson
Davis John, rear 90 Vandam
De Camp Joseph, 37 1st Av.
De Lamater E. D. 181 9th
De Lamater John & Son, 10th Av. cor. W. 23d
Deanington Clement L. 400 Water
Dick Robert, 38 Rose
Dickeson James, 311 Av. 6th
Dinant L. C. 88 Ann
Dobbs H. & Son, 146 Perry & 39d
Dobson Thomas, 13 Morris
Dominick James, rear 5 Chrystie
Donaldson John, 431 Water
Donally James, 21 Av. B
Doran John, 4 Hall place
Doremus Peter C. 28 Charles
Doughty Cornelius D. 35 Cross
Downing John, 42 W. 11th
Dunbar Moses, 13 Eldridge
Dunham & Williams, 105 Bank
Dancomb Asahel S. rear 35 Orange
Dunn Edward, rear 289 Pearl
Duryea Jacob, rear 71 Watts
Dusenbury J. C. 28 Charles
Dyer Charles C. 510 Greenwich
Edwards T. 63 W. 13th
Elliott John, 240 W. 18th
Esler Henry, 254 Madison
Etter Samuel, 19 Front
Excell Robert, 3 1st Av.
Fanning Edgar T. rear 27 Chrystie
Farley William C. 234 10th
Farral John, 175 Grand
Fawpell Peter, 75 New
Felder J. W. 238 3d Av.
Ferguson James, W. 19th bet. 7th & 8th Avs.
Ferguson Thomas, 10 Oak
Finch G. 706 Broadway
Finley Geo. 170 W. 13th
Fisher William, 9 Elm
Flagg & Whitman, 21 Gold
Fletcher Joseph, 92 & 94 Essex
Fletcher & Hagadorn, 276 Front
Ford Ebenezer, 252 7th Av.
Foster, Lowerre & Hawley, 18 New
Fox William, 15th cor. 7th Av.
Gadvey Wm. H. & C. 11 Downing
Gale L. 337 Houston
Gardner Leonard, 35 Ludlow
Gardiner Thomas, 105 Norfolk
Geer Darius, 96 Thompson
Germond Wellington, 294 Henry
Giles Gilbert, 26 Murray
Gillman & Whitney, 124 Columbia
Gottker John H. 208 6th
Gouge Joseph, 5 Hudson
Gould Platt, 424 Cherry
Green Alonzo, rear 347 Pearl
Green George, 183 Eldridge
Grieves W. & L. Mabie, r. 8 C'r'stie
Grouch John, 120 Amity
Guggobz E. 142 Ludlow
Gulon Joseph, rear 57 Vesey
Hagart D. 20 W. 15th
Haig David, 100 Mercer
Hallock Samuel B. 144 W. 20th
Hallock Sylvanus, 22 Spruce
Halsey Samuel B. 216 Mercer
Halsey & Silver, 65 Columbia
Hand & Rogers, E. 23d bet. 3d & 4th Avs.

Harriot G. A. 292 W. 17th
New York.
Hardman Aaron, 142 Mulberry
Hardman T. R. 15 Trinity pl.
Harris John T. rear 87 Ann
Hatfield S. 166 Crosby
Haughwout Jacob, rear 16 Watts
Havemyer G. L. rear 191 W. 15th
Hawkins A. S. 130 Broome
Henderson ——, rear 17 W. 17th
Henderson George, 260 W. 17th
Hendrick G. W. 175 Elizabeth
Henry John T. 92 Reade
Henry M. M., W. 29th
Henry R. 58 E. 17th & 175 Prince
Heughan John, 69 Exchange alley
Hibbets P. D. 213 12th
Hicks & Sarine, 97 Forsyth
Hopper J. M. 547 Broome
Hooker Oliver, rear 15 Dutch
Horton Alexander H. 166 Reade
Horton Charles H. 17 Ann
Howell Albro, 95 Cliff
Howell Matthew, 27 Hester
Howes, Vanmater & Sylvs, 34 Gold
Howland Pontius, 114 Troy
Hoyt & Eakin, 26 Minetta Lane
Hunt William S. 213 W 20th
Hunt Woodward, 70 Willet
Huyck James, 127 Norfolk
Jacobi John, 464 Water
Jacobs David, 138 Wooster
Jarvis Jonathan, 8th st. near Lewis
Jennings Eli, 35 W. 13th
Johnston John, 87 Varick
Johnston & Giraty, 237 12th
Junk James, rear 480 Pearl
Kelly M. 12th st.
Kelly & Maher, 94 Fulton
Kerr H. rear 21 Dey
Keyser & Berrien, 192 4th
Kielley Matthew. 41 5th Av.
King Thomas H. 244 Front
Kipp Samuel C. 29 4th
Kipp & Polhamus, 815 Wash.
Knapp ——, rear 61 Mulberry
Knapp David H. 151 Orchard
Knapp J. R. 46½ Jay
Kysen John, 2 Norfolk
Latham Edward, rear 134 Chrystie
Latson Abraham, C. 92 E. 13th
Lawall Jacob, 66 North Moore
Leal David, 59 Gold & 77 Reade
Lefurgy & Cousins, 100 2d
Lewis Isaac, 23 Canal
Limouze A. rear 35½ Wooster
Little James, 157 Orchard
Locke John, 47 Ann
Lockwood William, 135 Crosby
Lockwood & Palmatier, 49 1st
Longstreet James, 14 Frankfort
Longstreet J. R., W. 19th cor 6th
Av.
Low Joseph, 7th Av. cor. W. 14th
Lowerre William W. 11 5th
Ludlam John, 244 Madison
Lynch John, rear 135 Walker
Lyon Abraham U. 29 Lewis
M'Afee & Bowden, 53 Ann
M'Clave John, W. 29th st.
M'Conaughy John, 89 Clinton
M'Cullough William, 239 12th
M'Faddn John C. rear 55 Madison
M'Ginnis Robert, 5 Depoyster
M'Grath T. 77 Hamersley
M'Gregor ——, 134 Crosby
M'Keon James, 136 W. 19th
M'Laughlan Arch. 634 Hudson
M'Leod David, 20 Bridge
M'Nulty Richard, 140 Suffolk
Macy Isaiah, E. 22d cor. 2d Av.
Martin Samuel, 47 Hamersley
Mathews Ananias, 127 Norfolk
Matthiessen Fred. 26 Chrystie
Megeough Patrick, 197 11th
Merrall Richard, 32 6th
Mersereau John W. 53 Amos
Miller Anthon, rear 46 Mulberry
Miller Edward, 160 Maiden lane
Miller Jeremiah, 60 Cliff
Miller William C. 1 St. John's lane
Mitchell Joseph, 75 5th

Monilaw James, 5 Lafayette place
New York.
Moore & Hamiltons, 340 6th
Moore James, 344 9th
Moore Robert, 7 Chestnut
More George F. 95 Gold
Morris William, 189 1st Av.
Mossman David, 90 Reade
Mount John, 282 9th
Munroe & Ferguson, 176 Chambers
Munson ——, 437 4th
Murray John, 4 Leroy
Murphy E. 31 S. William
Myers M. I. 135 M'Dougal
Nelson & Howard, 79 Pine
Nestell John J. 49 Eldridge
Newman Jesse, 177 Laurens
Nicholas Jacob J. 627 Hudson
Noyes H. 258 24th
Osborn William H. 183 Church
Overhiser Abraham, 277 9th
Owens J. W. 209 Greene
Paton Robert, 333 Hudson
Paulding George, 109 King
Paulscraft B. 7th Av.
Peck Zachary & I, 194 Av. B.
Peirce & Sturtevant, 75 10th
Pendleton & Cockin, 64 Church
Perkins & Ditz, 184 Ludlow
Perkins J. 21 Av. B
Perrenod H. R. 42 Dey
Pierson William S. 263 Grand
Polsom William, 172 Chrystie
Porteous R. 99 W. 19th
Potts John, 270 6th Av.
Powell G. W. & J. S. 203 7th
Prey Ephraim, 45 Charles
Prickitt William S. 708 Broadway
Prink William, 197 Wooster
Purdy Jonathan, 186 Eldridge
Reed Daniel V. 448 4th
Reed David, 438 4th
Reed Nathaniel, 5 Pitt
Reeve B. 433 Hudson
Roach John, 104 Madison
Roach John, 42 Anthony
Rogers I. 3 E. 13th
Rose Joseph F. 262 Water
Rudd & Aaird, W. 19th betw. 5th
& 6th Av.
Ryder George, 144 Henry
Salisbury James, 65 W. 13th
Sarles Jeremiah, 79 Forsyth
Savage P. R. & James F. 125 Pitt
Schoolmaker Cyrus, 59 Lewis
Schoonmaker Benjamin J. 74 7th
Schuyler & Gridley, 75 5th Av.
Scofield John L. 17 Suffolk
Searles & Williams, 57 White
Sexton William, 67 W. 14th
Shears William, 14 Roosevelt
Sherwood & Wyckoff, 149 Orchard
Shirlsoo James, 203 W. 20th
Shortill Edward, 13 Reade
Simmons Alpheus, 562 Hudson
Simpson & Pinckney, 23 New
Skippon John & Son, 71 Gold
Slingerland S. & J. 79 Perry
Sminck John, rear 67 Greene
Smith Daniel P. 10 Roosevelt
Smith George, 188 Spring
Smith James W. foot of W. 21st
Smith John N. 15 Laurens
Smith Leonard K. 80 Trinity place
Smith William H. 233 W. 21st
Smith & Clark, 183 9th
Spear Henry, 40 Greenwich Av.
Sprakar W. 117 13th
Sprague Wm. 30 Greenwich Av.
Stanley John W. 50 Gold
Stanley Thomas R. 48 Gold
Stapleton & Williams, r.70 Bayard
Stephens James, 62 W. 21st
Stephens J. W. 788 Greenwich
Stephens & Williams, 105 Bank
Stevens Isaac, rear 95 Forsyth
Stites George M. 54 Mercer
Storms Abraham, 86 Walker
Strachan John M. 475 Broome
Sutton Silas, 11 6th
Switzer Henry, 27 Platt, 21 Gold
& 163 Water

Taft R. 52 White   *New York.*
Taylor Abraham L. 371 9th
Tenbroeck Henry, 102 Church
Terhune Stephen G. 73 Sullivan
Terry Van Rensselaer R. 129
Warren
Thomas Wm. H. 25 Gold
Thompson J. 189 Church & 15Troy
Thompson W. A. 444 Washington
Tinkey Isaac. 100 King
Trimble J. M. 14 Theatre alley
Tucker Abner, rear 173 Forsyth
Tunison James F. 54 E. 13th
Tunison George M. 183 W. 16th
Turner & Hall, 29 South William
Uglow James, 429 6th Av.
Urner J. R. 16 York
Valentine Jacob H. 60 E. 16th
Van Colver Owen, rear 119 Troy
Van Nostrand H. 10½ Vandewater
Voorhies Robert C. 23 West
Vredenburgh Isaac, 11 Doyer
Vreeland William A. & Co. 14 &
16 South William
Wallgrove A. 9 Morton
Walker Hugh, 114 Elm
Welton Isaac, 127 Eldridge
Warner Jesse, 63 Thompson
Washburn William D. 3 New
Waterhouse J. 738 Washington
Watson James, 27 6th Av.
Weaver David, 11 Cortlandt alley
Webb John, 47 Allen
Webb & Comstock, 166 Franklin
Weed H. E. 36 University place
Weeks James L. 110 Henry
Wells & Cochran, 74 Av. B
Wells David, 94 W. 19th
Well Peter, rear 47 Vesey
Westervelt Jacob, 6 Church
Wheeler John, jr. 160 Barrow
Whip Henry, 743½ Greenwich
Whitaker William, rear 166 Mott
Whitney & Gilman, 124 Columbia
White & Landrine, 555 4th
Wight Richard, 141 Thompson
Williams Aldrich, 117 Essex
Williams Wm. S. rear 162 Elm
Wills John, 67 Reade
Wilson & Clayton, 15 Rose
Wilson Peter M. 117 Prince
Wilson & Strachan, rear 26 Trin-
ity place
Winslow Wm. rear 348 6th Av.
Witty John, Av. 7 nr. W. 20th
Wood George A. 54 E. 15th
Wood Richard, 117 E. 15th
Woodruff Cooper, 300 Mulberry
Yereyance R. & C. 73 Frankfort
Young D. F. 183 W. 20th
Young & Vreeland, 627 Hudson
Youngs George & W. 109 W. 21st
Zoffrien Edward, 29 Frankfort

Niagara County.

Strong Isaac L.   *Lewiston.*
Bacon Mortimer H.
Weston Wm.
Carpenter B. & J.   *Lockport.*
Vancleek J. E.
Moore Solomon B.
Mapes Isaac
Otis R. G.
Williams Walter
Hibbard Arthur L.
Tompkins Ira   *Newfane.*
Shaw & Vincent
Vandenburgh A. W. H.
Baldwin Wm. & Co.
Griffith Wm.   *Niagara Falls.*
Coursen Isaac F.
Hodgson & Robinson
Stevens Arnold, Youngstown
Porter.
Nesler N. D.   Jo
Olmsted Thomas   *Somerset.*
Read O. V.
Sciver Charles
Lamb ——
Ranson Alfred   *Wilson.*
Shelden Benjamin

Thompson John   *Wilson.*
Pettit Abram
Brown J. C.
Brown J. W.
Crampton F.
Little S. L.

Oneida County.

Clark H. Oriskany Falls
    Augusta.
King C., Stokes   *Lee.*
Dean B. C. Dominick st.   *Rome.*
Prince D. B.
Soper & Simmons
Case Wm. P. 40 Seneca st. *Utica.*
Kirtland H. 50 Liberty
Owens Benjamin, 24 Hotel
Millar Charles, 2 Division
Schwab J. Washington st.
Morgan G. S.   do
Scranton L.   do
Fuller J. S. Rome st.
Palmer ——, Fulton st.
Russ J. A. 29 1st
Francis & Bartlett, 44 John
Joslin J. S. 2 Jay
Wratten J., Steuben

Onondaga County.

Wise D. Baldwinsville *Lysander.*
Johnson Wm. Mulberry st. Syracuse   *Salina.*
Cole & Rhedigan, Washington st. Syracuse
Wells A. Water st. Syracuse
Billings J. James st. do
Brown H. K. Pearl st. do
Abel S.   do
Newton V., Wolf st. do

Ontario County.

Hoyt T. P.   *Bristol.*
Knapp D.
Thomas W., Bristol Centre
Kelsey Camp   *Canandaigua.*
Bunnell F.
Drew George
Neil Wm.
Cheney Darwin
Wells Jonathan K.
Church Ambrose
Jenkins B. F.   *East Bloomfield.*
Gleason Peter
Ellis W. H. Chapinsville
    Hopewell.
Edgarton Franklin   *Phelps.*
Walker Thos. C. Allen's Hill
    Richmond.
Hazlett John A. do.
Kipp N. N. Geneva *Seneca.*
Weight & Judd, do
Graves F.   do
Gaylord P.   do
Van Etton Joshua, do
Cool James,   do
Coddington Chas. do
Smith A.   do
Loveland A.   *Victor.*
Bassett J. M.

Orange County.

Hammond H. Port Jervis
    Deer Park.
Hammond Hosea, do
Coleman O. H. P. do
Smith R.   do
Gordon T.   do
Romine D.   do
Pritchard T. U.   *Goshen.*
Payne J.
Baldwin D.
Manning J H. Wells' Corners
    Minisink.
Axford C.   do
Benjamin J. Unionville
Carr R.   do
Wakeman W. B. Slate Hill
Wood Robert   *Montgomery.*
Desendorph Aaron *Newburgh.*
Hilton Wm.

Little Thomas   *Newburgh.*
Little Andrew
Hasmore Wm.
Walch Jonathan
Kimball Thomas
Burns G. South Middletown
    Wallkill.
Stewart J.   do
Moore J. K.   do
Van Horn R.   do
Horton O. H.   do
Elmore A. H. Amity *Warwick.*

Orleans County

Baker & Barlow, Albion *Barre.*
Harvey N. N.   do
Hopkins Sheldon, do
Hyde T. & Brother, do
Dye W. E.   *Carlton.*
Pitcher B. I.
St. John D. F.   *Clarendon.*
Winn James
Pike & Barnum   *Kendall.*
De Wolf J.
Amsden ——, Holley *Murray.*
Osman Stephen, do
Patterson James, do
Stedman ——, do
Prime C. C., Medina *Ridgeway.*
Alford B. H.   do
Hurd F.   do
Vankenseu W. do
Sawyer J. F., Knowlesville
Hicks M. S.   do
Prescott J.   do
Beecher Lyman   *Yates.*
Tuttle Jesse
Millis Walter
Barry Nathaniel
Hale Simeon, Lyndonville
Tall Nelson,   do
Blood Jackson, do

Oswego County.

Eanoz Jesse   *Albion.*
Frey Henry L.
Huntington S. B.
Ladden Amanzo
Patterson Wm. B.
Seamans William
Thayor Joseph
Pearse Joseph, Carterville *Amboy.*
Bliss D. J.   *Constantia.*
Dickie H.
Miles F.
Squiers A.
Russell L. S.
Ufford J.
Ward Samuel, Cleaveland
Potter Samuel, do
Groat James,   do
Harrington O.   do
Broadwell Henry, Oswego Falls
    Granby.
Broadwell Franklin, do
Smith Henry,   do
Fuller Joseph H. *Mexico.*
Aldrich Jefferson *Orwell.*
Cogswell George
Stowell Elom
Frenan Richard
Perkins R., Ames' Buildings, 1st st.
    Oswego.
Smith William C. do
Purmon Hyman F. do
Williams A. B.   do
Campbell J. H. cor. 1st & Mohawk
Taylor & Woodruff, do
Kneffin W. J. Crocker's Building, Bridge st.
Wilcox Heman, do Bridge st.
Anthony Edwin, do do
Stevens Zina D. Bates' Block, 2d story, 1st st.
Gillet E. L. cor. 1st & Schuyler
King Jesse, Wash. Mill, 1st st.
Chapin & Radcliff, do   do
Hoke George   *Parish.*
Rulison Marcus
Rulison Warren
Woodrough G. Pulaski *Richland.*

Woodrough S. Pulaski *Richland.*
Taylor James,   do
Watkins Philo B. do
Weed Albert H. do
Waters W. South Richland
Holmes Wm. Phœnix *Schroeppel.*
Wadkins Amasa, do
Knapp J.   do
Gates Perry,   do
Barnes Warren   *Scriba.*
Wareham Charles

Otsego County.

Howland H.   *Cherry Valley*
Metcalf H.
Bastian J.
Ackerman James P. *Edmeston.*
Curtis R. Alonzo *Exeter.*
Webster Wm. H.
Herkimer G. Schuyler's Lake
Snyder Albert do
Kenyon A.   *Laurens.*
Kenyon C.
Ward E.
Green Daniel M. *Middlefield.*
Fuller Wm. A.
Deyo Stephen
Howland Isaac
Thompson Henry P
Richmond Francis
Rice Thomas
Barney William
Brownfield P.   *Milford.*
Brock R. C.
Bundy H.   *New Lisbon.*
Watkins M.   *Oneonta.*
Derby F.
Chamberlin R   *Otego.*
Goodrich S. & F
Place G.
Loomis J
Rockwell A. S.
Church J.
Yoomans J.
Adams E.
Hawkins B.   *Pittsfield.*
Northrop, N. C.
Hawkins E.
Penney A.   *Plainfield.*
Collins H.
Thompson Wm. J. *Unadilla.*
Yeomans Solomon L.
Lobdell Richard *Worcester.*
Northrop E. D.
Griggs James
Wickham Jeremiah
Miller H. L. East Worcester
Davis John,   do
Schermerhorn N. & I., S. Worcester

Putnam County.

Frost Theodore   *Carmel.*
Kirk G.   *Kent.*
Kirk W.
Rundle E.
Jennings S.   *Patterson.*
Howe C. B.
Dean R.
Elwell O. Cold Spring
    Phillipstown.
Weeks W.   do
Butler J.   do
Purdy J. B.   do
Lovless H.   do
Lobdell W.   do
Winter T.   *Putnam Valley.*
Borger A.
Nicholson J.
Howse E. South East
Howse O.   do

Queens County.

Rider George, Rockville
Darling Thomas *Hempstead.*
Wells Obediah
Powell Sands
Hicks Stephen, Hicks' Neck
Smith Richard, Raynor Town
Higbie Stephen, Fosters' Meadow

Moody George, Foster's Meadow
     Hempstead.
Seaman David,   Far Rockaway
Hewlett Sylvanus,   do
Jones Aaron,   do
Skidmore Sylvester, do
Raynor H.   Greenwich
Rhodes Alexander, do
Smith Daniel   *Jamaica.*
Dean Henry, Brushville
Boerum Jacob, Centreville
Brinkerhoff H.
Morris S., Astoria   *Newtown.*
Wood Thomas, Roslyn
    North Hempstead.
Hegerman Daniel, Roslyn
Leek Conklin, Manhasset
Semmis Alfred   *Oyster Bay.*
Hamilton John
Prieor James
Millspaw E.
Kashouw Daniel
Underhill Samuel
Underhill Daniel
Underhill William
Hall Charles
Bell Henry, East Norwich
Snedicor Henry,   do
Horton W.   do
Weeks Jacob V. W., E. Norwich
Van Nostrand H. Wolver Hollow
Lewis Daniel,   Jericho
Hawxhurst Jacob, do

Rensselaer County.

Hayner A.   *Brunswick.*
Taylor H.
Miles T.   *Greenbush.*
Pierce A. State st. Alley
    Lansingburgh.
Nelson E. Congress st. Alley
Striker J. cor. John & North
Griswold D. S.   *Petersburgh.*
Allen J.
Ray James   *Pittstown.*
Mosher G. W.
Dutcher J.   *Sandlake.*
Sheperman L.   *Schodack.*
Brockway J.
Lee John
Brown H. W.   *Stephentown.*
Moore J.
Faye A.
Carrier J.
Fellows & Corpse, rear 14 River
    Troy.
Caswell Edw'd, 1 Franklin square
Cramer G. W: 10 Federal st.
Howes W. J., N.2d st. Alley
M'Donough Michael, do
Thayer H. 96 1st st.
Colegrove Samuel W. 196 2d
Ash John, 238 5th
Allard Horace, 36 & 38 Albany
Colegrove J. B. 17 Ferry
Peck John, rear 1 River
Fobes Z. E. River st. Alley
Hicks & Brower, Franklin Alley
Bowers & Salisbury, rear Board-
  man's Building
Henderson & Co. rear 105 5th
Knowles ——, 59 6th st. Alley
Otis C. rear Eaton & Gilbert's
  Coach Factory
Phillips Geo. 6th st. Alley
Cheney B. cor. 2d and Ida sts.
Rogers J. Ida Hill
Goewey William, Nail Works
Wells Z. 505 River

Richmond County.

Cane Lewis, Port Richmond
    Northfield.
Harloe William, Stapleton
    Southfield.
Wynant M., Rossville *Westfield.*

Rockland County.

Felter John E.   *Haverstraw.*
Costo S.
M'Kinsie J. R.

Demerest J. Piermont, *Orangetown*
Moison Edward, do
Tilt William,   do
Demerest A. B. Nyack
Bird Thomas,   do
Richard & Lyeth, do
Smith S. P.   do

St. Lawrence County.

Johnson Ethan   *Brasher.*
Bercks Asahel
Smith H. M.   *Canton.*
Kingsbury A.
Toby Thomas
Abernethey Cyrus
Washburn L. T.
Perry Abram
Tuttle Mills
Hutchinson F. J.
Packard Herman
Page Isaac C
Vanderzee D. Richville *De Kalb.*
Johnson C.   do
Wise D.   do
Hosmer Charles *South Edwards*
Nicol John   *Hammond.*
Nicol David
Shove Russell
Franklin David
Hubbard Jonathan
Schermerhorn Lanson
Rogers Robert
Rogers David
Gilmore William D.   *Hermon.*
Hamlin H. B.
Green William M.
Campbell Thomas
Tanner Lucius
Lorey Alvin
Howe Seymour   *Hopkinton.*
Armstrong James   *Lisbon.*
Dillingham Simeon
Dilling George A.
Stearns E. H.   *Louisville.*
Carpenter J.
Southworth L.
Bailey Ira
Stephens Richard
Lockwood W. Columbia *Madrid.*
Scott William, Waddington
Betheene Donald,   do
Braugh Oliver,   do
Danforth James,   *Massena.*
Gervin Lyman
Blackman Martin
Carpenter A. F.   *Morristown.*
Ward Israel
Scofield C. W.
Randall Silas
Coonradt P. A.
Hawkins Stephen
Lewis Leonard
Howard William
Scott Northrop
Collins Stephen
Vrooman Abraham
Petrie Jacob H.
Ryon Smith, Ogdensburgh
    Oswegatchie.
Ryon George,   do
Slocum Carlos,   do
Shepherd Timothy,do
Pearsons Urias, do
Stevens Guy C.   do
Hill James,   do
Bassett John,   do
Perry Stephen,   do
Buckman Seth C. do
Stevens Henry   *Parishville.*
Hicks John   *Pierpont.*
Dimick Joseph
Waller, Asahel & Judson
Streeter Almond   *Pitcairn.*
Watson James
Brockway J.
Wheeler Orson   *Potsdam.*
Stevens Jonathan
Wayne James K.
Patterson Porter
Clark David
Porter Orlin
Pixese Norris

Saratoga County.

Richey James   *Charlton.*
Heaton J. B.
Saunders E. B.
Anderson S. G.
Saunders Sherman
Smith David
Wilkie John, West Carlton
Sterling Peter,   do
Fowler William,   do
Parent John A.   do
Parent Joseph S. do
Higgins Solomon, Jonesville
    Clifton Park.
Higgins Platt, Jonesville
Smith Ezra, Graves' Corners
Lansing Jacob, Vischer Ferry
Comstock Wm. A.   *Corinth.*
Henry George
Barruss Calvin
Barruss Jesse
Carpenter E. W.
Burrows Hiram, Greenfield Centre
    Greenfield.
Mosher Cyrus
Carpenter Nathan M. N.
Rowland Lorenzo D.
Gibb David, do
Deuel Stephen
Darrow William C.
Knight S.   *Halfmoon.*
Corney G. Glenn's Falls *Moreau.*
Day P. E.   do
How T. C.
Wigg Peter
Austin G. A.   *Providence.*
Packar Benjamin
Cranson John
Cranson J. N.
Rowley William
Knickerbacker George
    Saratoga Springs.
Knickerbacker Henry
Hoyt Harmon
Hall Benjamin
Bacon Thayer
Huling E.
Darrow James
Huling N.
Langdon Joseph
Owen Hiram
Calkins J.
Patterson Robert
Patterson Hugh
Brown D.
Frasier John
Rodgers M. L.
Sherman Abraham   *Waterford.*
Rice Robert
Sherman Chauncy
Lawrence Samuel
Calkins Seth E.   *Wilton.*
Brackett William
Palmer Sidney
Godley William

Schenectady County.

Jones A. D.   *Duanesburgh.*
Wright E.
Broeffle William
Gray Jacob   *Glenville.*
Truax C.
Gifford Thomas   *Princetown.*
Wilkie T. & H. 10 Canal
    Schenectady.
Allen Lewis, Liberty

Schoharie County.

Morehouse A. C.   *Blenheim.*
Curtis Benjamin P.
Patchin John
Conchman John   *Broome.*
Wheaton Jacob   *Esperance.*
Soule William
Shaver Peter
Holmes A. C. Fultonham *Fulton.*
Stewart Robert, do
Becker ——, Breakabeen
Brower B.   do
Wilsey John P.   *Gilboa.*
Mudge David

Vausburgh Stephen *Middleburgh.*
Rockefeller Geo.
Bouck Alexander
Wooden John C. *Richmondville.*
Waldroff Jacob
Atkins J. E.
Shelden Norman
Shaver John F., Warnerville
Huddleston D. *Schoharia.*
Warner T., Hyndsville *Seward.*

Seneca County.

Kinne John H. *Ovid.*
Bennett Horace
Boughton Daniel
Bennett James
Brown Joseph I.
Fritts Thomas G. Farmer
Johnson Ira C. do
Wheating Lewis, do
Ford Elihu, do
Tindall Amos, do
Bergen Jacob, do
Parker Elias *Romulus.*
Parker Vincent
Townsley Amos

Steuben County.

Wood John *Cohocton.*
Warner Benjamin
Green Burrill
Hogersland John & Israel
Hartwell Aaron, North Cohocton

Suffolk County.

Randell Buel, Port Jefferson
Brookhaven.
Woodhull Brewster do
Roe Ebenezer, Patchogue
Smith M. do
Smith Nehemiah C. do
Price Charles do
Truell C. & Warren, do
Wells Manly *Riverhead.*
Corwin Henry W.
Jayne Peter *Smithtown.*
Homedieu Calvin L.
Newton Phillip A.
Fournier Peter *Southampton.*
Howell James
Foster Albert
Bishop Charles
Glover Daniel *Southold.*
Cleveland Joseph
Horton Jeremiah
Huntting Jonathan W.
Overton Francis
Bennett John
Prince Edward
Wells William
Horton George P.
Reeves Hubbard, Greenport
Beebe Henry. do
Beebe Theodore, do
Cleaves Orange, do
Wells Barnabas. Cutchogue
Gildersleeve Andrew, do
Corwin Barnabas, Mattituck

Sullivan County.

Gordon C. K., Big Eddy
Lumberland.
Hendricks A. do
Newkirk H. B. Wurtsboro
Mamakating.

Tioga County.

Cushman B. E. *Owego.*
Fox S.
Gorman J.
House E.
Hungerford C.
Mallett P.
Morse N.
Stroup U.
Sturges B. R.
Townsend A.
Tucker E.
Andrews Wm. *Richford.*

Gee John H. *Richford.*
Heath Seymour
Humphrey Erastus
Hutchinson John

Tompkins County.

Moore H. H., Prospect st. *Ithaca.*
Case Philip, Cayuga st.
Moore F. South Stone Bridge
Dutchers B. & J. do
Hyatt G. C. Green st.

Ulster County.

Shaw Wm. *Kingston.*
Phillips C. F.
Crook Peter
Schapmoes Wm.
Patterson A.
Chipp Henry
Davis J., Kyserike *Rochester.*
Booth R. *Rosendale.*
Brink Z. *Saugerties.*
Dodd Jerod
Webster Stephen
Van Vulkenburgh Lambert
Dewitt M. F.. Glasco
Burhans A. B.
Constant Gilbert, Port Ben

Warren County.

Collins Otis, Chestertown *Chester.*
Towsley Hiram, do
Lawrence Benjamin, do
Hotchkiss Nathan, do
Mowe Addison, do
Oakley A. J. *Hague*
Pratt C.
Russell Barnabas *Horicon.*
Hays T. D.
Darrow James
Mills Alonzo
Hodgson John, 2d *Johnsburgh.*
Smith Simon
Morehouse Miles
Freeman & Son *Queensbury.*
Root David M.
Tiffany A. C.
Darrow Henry *Warrensburgh.*

Washington County.

Lendrum Wm. *Argyle.*
Robertson Peter *Cambridge.*
Robertson James P.
Esman Lodowick
Robertson George
Jenkins John
Robertson George W.
Lourie James
Hall Benjamin, Cambridge Centre
Edie William, North Cambridge
Davis R., South Easton *Easton.*
Stanton Edward, do
Chapman Henry *Greenwich.*
Bradley Charles
Whipple James
Fisk Warren
Whipple Charles
Sherman Morgan L.
Daley N. *Hampton.*
Cook Asaph
Lyman E.
Copeland David, West Hebron
Hebron.
Reynolds Caleb, do
Fenton James, do
Patterson James, do
Copeland Robert, do
Streeter Denison, do
Copeland Levi, do
Brown John, East Hebron
Munson Wilson, do
Wheedon Newton, do
Carpenter A. C. Sandy Hill
Kingsbury.
Clarry Henry, do
Brown Calvin, do
Churchill Jacob, do
Miller John *Putnam.*
Miller Wm.

Darling George *Putnam.*
Darling Thomas
Bogg Peter
Archibald David F. *Salem.*
Peters James H.
Park Derastus
Qviatt D.
Russell Edwin *White Creek.*
Chase David
Jones Wm.
Day Oel, North White Creek
Rase John, do
Clark T. J. William st. *Whitehall.*
Wilson J. do
Wright C. W. Canal st.
Snow B.

Wayne County.

Lamoreaux Andrew *Arcadia*
Vandercook David
Brunk L. P. & C.
Wilson Robert, Newark
Wright Benj. do
Pickett John M. *Lyons.*
Bailey & Sherman
Pickett Charles
Welrath Henry
Remyon James
Freize Andrew
Ireland D.
Bailey S.
Crary S.
Pickett John
Bourne Richard *Marion.*
Smith Eli
Kenyon Friend
West Solomon
Hanna John *Ross.*
Ellsworth Wm.
Mason Harvey D.
Chaddock Wm., jr.
Feek Nicholas
Seabring John *Walworth.*
Hibbard Wm.
Cowell Samuel B.
Bolster Joseph
Barker S. S. *Williamson.*
Tuttle L. S.
Moody Cephas
White M. F.
Tinklepaugh ——, Pultneyville
Malcomb John, do

Westchester County.

Post J. L., Peekskill *Courtlandt.*
Fitch Jas. P. *West Farms.*
Carpenter Samuel
Harden Wm. H. *Yonkers.*
Haines F., Croton *Yorktown.*

Wyoming County.

Wilder William & Milton *Attica.*
Norton M.
Keith & Brower
Yeoman Vine *Bennington.*
Dunson John
Howes A. M.
Doolittle John, Cowlesville
Bancroft L. J. *Castile.*
Schofield H.
Martin Bela
Calkins Wm. H.
Quick M. S.
Wing A. C.
Bliss James, Genesee Falls
Bliss J. W. do
Holmes John T. do
Gibb Edward S. do
Olcott John do
Palmer J. Wyoming *Middlebury.*
Blackmer Wm. do
Caswell Peter do
Newcomb S.
Bosworth G. S. *Pike.*
Gregory A.
Hodge R.
Roberts J.
Everest J.
Ely Hugh
Hurd Chester *Warsaw.*

Barber William   *Warsaw.*
Barrows C.
Davidson A. G.
Davidson James I.

Yates County.

Syms John, Belona   *Benton.*
Farren A. C. do
Davis F. Branchport *Jerusalem.*
Terrence Solomon, do
Pratt Alexander M. *Middlesex.*
Adams L. L.
Warren I. A.
Collins N. B.
Smith James
Chaffer H.
Bush C. V. Penn Yan   *Milo.*
Southerland John, do
Gallaher James H. do
Siltor T. G.   *Potter.*
Silas Champlin
Schenck John J. Rushville
Stricker William do
Wilkin Leonard, Dundee *Starkey.*
Pierce H. W.   do
Kimball Stephen do

Carpet and Floor Cloth Dealers.

Albany County.

Corbiere Wm. A. 544 Broadway *Albany.*
Van Gaasbeek J. (wholesale) 24 Greene

Cayuga County.

Nye L. W. & Co. 79 Genesee *Auburn.*

Delaware County.

Shaw G. M.   *Delhi.*

Erie County.

M'Gregor R. & Co. (see advertisement—carpets) 198 Main*Buffalo.*
Cameron & M'Kay, 125 Main
Merrill & M'Ewen, 212 do

Kings County.

Stewart & Co. (wholesale) 162 Fulton *Brooklyn.*

Monroe County.

Brown & Williams, 52 Main *Rochester.*
Kidd Wm. cor. State st. & Mumford

New York County.

Aldrich & Sanfords, 440 Pearl *New York.*
Anderson H. 99 & 103 Bowery
Andrew John E. 198 Broadway
Bailey & Woolsey, 454 Pearl
Barker & Stewarts, 193 Greenw'h
Betts George W. 434 Pearl
Chalmers Alexander, 2 Cedar
Clinton Benjamin, 94 Bowery
Conkling J. & Co. 33 Cortlandt
Cook John, 41 Ann
Davenport S. W. 227 Greenwich
Dimick Jeremiah W. 452 Pearl
Earle Thomas, 201 Broadway
Emmerich & Vila, 60 Nassau
Ferris Thomas & Co. 450 Pearl
Gibbons Wm. 189 8th Av.
Gillespie James M. 111 Bowery
Gulon William H. 71 Division & 64 East Broadway
Hastings George & Co. 5 South William & 65 Stone
Higgins A. & E. S. & Co. 62 Broad
Hyatt J. 94 Bowery
Hyatt George E. L. 444 Pearl
Kelleher D. 450 Pearl
Lawrence Roderick, 49 Canal
Lewis W. 464 Pearl

Lounsbery Nehemiah, 254 Grand *New York.*
Lynes S. C. 70 Canal
M'Grorty James, 155 Chatham
M'Grorty Wm. 136 William
Martin Samuel, 186 Grand
Miller Frederick A. 60 Canal
Miller Hiram, 105 Bowery
Miller William, 201 Greenwich
Parker & Stewarts, 193 do
Perkins & Brother, 462 Pearl
Peterson & Humphrey, 432 Pearl
Phelps & Kingman, 118 & 120 Chatham & 442 Pearl
Sangar Rufus, 68 Cedar
Sloane William, 245 Broadway
Smith Shadrack, 482 Grand
Smith & Knupp, 254 Broadway
Smith & Lounsbery, 448 Pearl
Sparkman & Kelsey, 180 William
Sprague G. R. & Co. 66 Broad
Thompson & Co. 8 Spruce
Tinson R. N. & Co. 339 Broadway
Tobias Thomas, 560 Grand
Tracy Jared W. 328 Broadway
Underwood Benj. 100 William
Whinfield H. 71 Liberty
Wilson Clark C. 159 Chatham
Winn I. W. 452 Pearl
Young & Jayne, 460 Pearl

Oneida County.

Thomson Samuel & Son, Genesee st. *Utica.*
Vedder, Welbon, & Tyler, 78 Genesee

Onondaga County.

Dyer G. W. Salina st, Syracuse *Salina.*

Orange County.

Cushman Chas. U. 63 Water *Newburgh.*

Rensselaer County.

Lockwood & Orvis, (wholesale) 257 River *Troy.*
Marvins & Co. (wholesale) 259 River

Carpet Coverlid Maker.

Orange County.

Tatham Thomas *Middletown.*

Carpet Manufacturers.

Albany County.

Meech & Randall, (floor cloths) 7 Grand *Albany.*
Koonz Abram, 43 Grand
Russell E. & Son, (floor cloths) 32, 34 & 36 1st

Cayuga County.

Hunt A. H. 34 Genesee *Auburn.*
Hotchkiss & Smith, 34 Genesee

Columbia County.

Phillips J., Mellenville *Claverack.*

Duchess County.

Black R. 160 Main *Poughkeepsie*
Maldrum ——, 148 Main
Pelton C. M. Mill st.
Lorber A. (weaver) 151 Main

Montgomery County.

Green Wm. K. & Co. (Ingrain) *Amsterdam.*

Oneida County.

Butterfield ——, Durhamville *Verona.*

Rockland County.

Higgins E. & A. S. *Haverstraw.*
Wood J. Spring Valley *Orangetown.*

Westchester County.

Crowthec R. *West Farms.*
Smith J.
Mitchell I. W. & Co. *Yonkers.*

Carpet Shaking.

Brown Edwin T. 163 Mercer *New York.*
Elzie Arnold, rear 64 Mercer
Johnson Charles, 163 Mercer
Johnson T. rear 43 Sullivan

Carpet Weavers.

Cayuga County.

Green J. & W. 5 Genesee *Auburn.*

Columbia County.

Cole G. Warren st. *Hudson.*

Jefferson County.

Witt C. Felt's Mills *Rutland.*

Kings County.

M'Kernan T. 106 Fulton *Brooklyn.*
O'Hara J. 68 Main
Early James, 76 Main
Steel Joseph, 75 Main
Butler L. Hudson Av.
Kennedy Samuel, 36 Grand *Williamsburgh.*
Kennedy Samuel, 4th st.

Livingston County.

Campbell William *Caledonia.*
Findley ——

Madison County.

French B. *Cazenovia.*

Monroe County.

Taylor John, 1 Fish *Rochester.*
Dickson D. 283 State

Orange County.

Atkinson W. Water st. *Newburgh.*

Putnam County.

Grimes C. Cold Spring *Phillipstown.*

Rensselaer County.

Morrison James, 371 River *Troy.*
Cannon Ibri, 17 Jacob

Tompkins County.

Magilfry George *Enfield.*

Wyoming County.

Davidson J. J. *Warsaw.*

Yates County.

Wilson Wm. M. Rushville *Potter.*

Carpet Yarn Manufacturers.

Duchess County.

Whinfield Henry, Mill st. *Poughkeepsie.*

Orange County.

Harrison Joshua *Newburgh.*

Carriage Makers and Wheelwrights.

Albany County.

Trowbridge Charles, 707 Broadway   *Albany.*
M'Clelland William, 831 Broadway
Townsend E. 128 Church
Spring H. 74 Church
Chesebero & Elmendorf, 19 & 21 Church
Goold James & Co. cor. Division & Hamilton
Don P. C. 90 Green
Hawley A. & C. 54 Bleeker
Loyal Samuel H. 81 Hamilton
M'Donald Barney, 212 S. Pearl
Long & Silsby, 284, 286, 288 South Pearl
Dwyer William, 6 Grand
Taylor Thos. jr. 21½ Washington
Shnider P. 140 Lydius
Davidson R. 112 Patroon
Ball William, Reedsville   *Berne.*
Salt S.   *Bathlehem.*
De Groof O.
M'Donald H.   *Cosymans.*
Bailey John
Van Buren P.
Cook Charles
De Graaff Jacob   *Guilderland.*
Van Patten ——
Weaver F.
Chesebro W.
Champion B.   *Knox.*
Livingston Phillip, Dunnsville
Haire O. West Troy   *Watervliet.*
Witbeck & Jones
Waterman J.
Ward J. & Son   *Westerlo.*
Ward G.
Tompkins P.

Alleghany County.

Potter & Palmeter   *Alfred.*
Green Phillip
Hopkins E.   *Almond.*
Rawson S.
Comstock M. L.   *Andover.*
Duncan James   *Angelica.*
Ogden Samuel
Nichols Asa G.   *Belfast.*
Eagle William H.   *Burns.*
Jacobs Warren
Johnson W.   *Caneadea.*
Smith Amos R.
Bristol Izaiah
Allen Henry R.   *Cuba.*
Hickoox J.   *Friendship.*
Osterhoudt H.
Lamphear A.
Perkins Lionel   *Granger.*
Edwards J. & W. Little Genesee   *Genesee.*
Avery Nathan   *Hume.*
Mason Luther
Randall Ralph
Keeler Lewis B.
Burr, Partlow & Co. *Independence.*
Bradley Charles   *Rushford.*
Wier & Bixby
Wilber Thomas O.   *Scio.*
Runnels, Norman & Bro. Wellsville
Bronson Z. A. Wellsville
Lord Cornelius   *West Almond.*
Lord James
Brown David   *Wirt.*

Broome County.

Hopkins S. H. Chenango Forks   *Barker.*
Armstrong G.   *Binghamton,*
Loveland M.
Riley J.
Stockwell A. D.
Angell A. & J. C.
Campbell C.

Bishop J. F. Harpersville   *Colesville.*
Dort E.   do
Dort J. L.   do
Main G. Nineveh
Rood L. Centre Lisle   *Lisle.*
Gray W.   *Nanticoke.*
Sturtevant D. M. Whitney's Point   *Triangle.*
Chandler D. R.   *Union.*
Pitkin D.
Whittemore J. B.
Munson L.   *Windsor.*
Reed S.

Cattaraugus County.

Norton B.   *Ashford.*
Stimson Charles N.   *Burton.*
Campbell James
Robinson Elijah, Rutledge   *Conewango.*
Lattin L. B.   *Ellicotiville.*
Watkins C. L.   *Farmersville.*
Martindale W. B.
Graves Harvy   *Franklinville.*
Mason S. J.
Patterson James
Halenbeck Isaac, Sandusky   *Freedom.*
Ray George M. F.   *Great Valley.*
Norton William & Edwin D.
Pratt L. S.   *Little Valley.*
Menow Wm.   *Machias.*
Joslyn Alanson
Joslyn G. O.
Eddy W. H. Eddyville *Mansfield.*
Wiley Ephraim   *New Albion.*
Ballord Nathaniel   *Otto.*
Ferris S. H.
Smith Nathaniel, East Otto
Stilson Luther   *Perrysburgh.*
Stone Anson
Davis R. R.
Grannis David, Gowanda *Persia.*
Grannis Chauncey,   do
Foster Wm.   do
Hammond Wm.   do
Benoit X.   *Randolph.*
Hollister J.
Eddy I. B.
Champlin Jesse, East Randolph
Waterhouse James,   do
M'Cutcheon Andrew   *Yorkshire.*
Jackman Alonzo D.
Mason John, Delavan

Cayuga County.

Young T. V. Genesee st. *Auburn.*
Clapp J. & G. State st.
Applegate & Seymour, State st.
Magarr D. Water st.
Clapp A. North st.
Clark J. C.   *Aurelius.*
Wood R. A. Weedsport *Brutus.*
Storms J.   do
Cornell Wm.   *Cato.*
Olmsted C.
Everts ——   *Genoa.*
Bartlett A.   *Ira.*
Rich T.
Jones J. Montezuma   *Mentz.*
Martin E.   do
Dewitt & M'Mellen   *Owasco.*
Hoagden Charles   *Springport.*
Freeman D.   *Summerhill.*
Green J. W.   *Venice.*

Chautauque County.

Abbott & Co.   *Busti.*
Hascall ——
Osgood L.   *Carroll.*
Bartlett G. (Frewsburgh)
Carpenter Wm. A. *Charlotte.*
Arnold J.
Bernett R.
Wolebue J. Mayville *Chautauque.*
Millspaw S. E.   *Cherry Creek.*
Eddy W. A.
Thompson Abel
Pettis C.   *Clymer.*

Warner R. D. Jamestown *Ellicott.*
Burlin B.   do
Brown A. S.   *Ellington.*
Hale Vernon S.
Tuck James, Irving   *Hanover.*
Hull J. E.   do
Stebbins Chas. do
Waterhouse L. Nashville
Clark E. (Silver Creek)
Blanchard Wm.   *Harmony.*
Blanchard Chas.
Richards Peter
Thomas George
Mason & Dickinson, Fredonia   *Pomfret.*
Bissell O.   do
Camp & Cramer,   do
Bartholomew E. L.   *Portland.*
Fay & Peck
Hitchcock ——   *Ripley.*
Root ——
Crocker ——
Randall ——
Shelley H. A.   *Sheridan.*
Brown Aaron
Sperry Lewis   *Sherman,*
Wightman Ezra
Wilson G.   *Villenova.*
Macomber Thos. J.   *Westfield.*
Shepad Alvin
Crandall Wm.

Chemung County.

Paige Samuel   *Catharine.*
Brown Hiram
Hill W. M. & Co.   *Elmira.*
Tinbrook Peter B.

Chenango County.

Bixby J. J.   *Bainbridge.*
Main E. P.
Flagg J. C. South Bainbridge
Humphrey M., Bennettsville
Tuthill Sylvester   *Columbus.*
Hazen L. T.   *Coventry.*
Thayer Samuel
Parker Henry A.
Bristol O. G.
Green A. H. Genesee st. *Greene.*
Avery J. S.
Bilden Lorenzo M.   *Guilford.*
Laraway John D.
Paine Hiram, Guilford Centre
Jacobs H. E.   *New Berlin.*
Moshier W.
Owens A. & A. South New Berlin
Darr Thomas   do   do
Crandall S.   *North Norwich.*
Warner A. W.   *Norwich.*
Lettington Horace
Avery Roswell B.
Brown & Lee
Kenyon J.   *Otselic.*
Convers A.
Fish H.
Allen Joseph   *Oxford.*
Dudley Daniel
Knight Otis
Sperrin Thomas J.
Herrick B.   *Pharsalia.*
Morgan D. B.
Burnham Norman   *Pitcher.*
Anderson Orvin
Harrington J. H.
Nhare J. F.   *Plymouth.*
Fletcher J.   *Preston.*
Tuthill J.   *Sherburne.*
Burlingame A. J.
Carr H.
Mead G. C.   *Smyrna.*
James E. A.
Hart H.

Clinton County.

Kingeland & Isham, Keeseville   *Au Sable.*
Pierce A.   *Beekmantown.*
Cross Loyal
Howe ——, West Chazy   *Chazy*
Pratt ——   *Mooers.*
Armstrong ——

Mansfield A.   *Plattsburgh.*
Jackson D.
Harris & Brown   *Saranac.*

Columbia County.

Scism S.   *Ancram.*
Babcock E., Spencertown
    Austerlitz.
Walker I.   *Canaan.*
Benjamin W. H., Canaan Four
    Corners
Kinney S. & G.   do do
Hunt P.   *Chatham.*
Jenison J., Chatham Four Corners
Brown A. East Chatham
Branch A. North Chatham
Hermance P. V.   *Claverack.*
Decker Wm., Smoky Hollow
Shufelt ——, Mellenville
Loers P., Churchtown
Johns D. M.   *Copake.*
Sabins M.
Elliot W.
Boice A.
Spalding M.   *Gallatin.*
Smith W. H.
Snyder C.   *Ghent.*
Deming G.
Becker J.   *Greenport.*
Holden G. A.   *Hillsdale.*
Bushnell Geo. W.
Berger P. S., Union st.   *Hudson.*
De Lamater J. E, Public Sq.
French J. W., Columbia st.
Goff M.   do
Chamberlin & Waldo, Warren st.
Malh Wm. L. 4th st.
Sharp H.   *Kinderhook.*
Melins & Co.
Traver Wm. J. 4th st.
Messick M., Valatie
Fish H.   do
Miller J. P.   do
Niver N.   *Livingston.*
Smith J. P.
Mansfield L.
Shears H.
Petrie Nelson
Smith H. P.
Philkins E.   *New Lebanon.*
Haywood A.   *Stockport.*
Moore J. H.   *Stuyvesant.*
Drum R.
Allen J.   *Taghkanic.*
Roarbeck R.

Cortland County.

M'Lean John & Charles
    Cincinnatus.
Campbell Carter   *Cortlandville.*
Parker, William K.
Pencyer George, M'Grawville
Taintor Erving   *Harford.*
Hobert Amos   *Homer.*
Kingsbury Alfred
Crooker Geo. W.   *Marathon.*
Hamilton James   *Perble.*
Goddard Solomon   *Truxton.*
Jones William
Perkins Ebenezer   *Virgil.*
Bronson David
Holton Lester

Delaware County.

Shaver A. G.   *Andes.*
Connor B.
Rottermund H. H.
Taylor D.   *Davenport.*
Hoton T.
Andrews & Hollister   *Delhi.*
Churchill J.
Doan E.   *Franklin.*
Foote R.
Stone, Hubbell & Bunnell
M'Laughry L.   *Harpersfield.*
Jaquish E.   *Meredith.*
Dean J.
Sterry S. C.   *Stamford.*
Marshall W. H.
Mull H. & A., Hobart
Montgomery J. C. do

Demander G. Deposit   *Tompkins.*
Kingsley I. C.
Smith W. W.
Eells & Henford   *Walton.*

Duchess County.

Smith J. H.   *Amenia.*
Sterling William F.
Griffin C. N.
Smith J. M.
Wright W. H.   *Beekman.*
Boughton R. C.   *Clinton.*
Cornelius S.
Giddings J.   *Dover.*
Winniger N.
Dutcher A.
Burhams C.   *Fishkill.*
Vannosdal J. M.
Boyce J. H. Glenham
Sheever C. Wappinger's Falls
Van Voorhis H. Hughsonville
Ferdon J. A.   do
Van Vooris Wm. H.   do
Schouten S. Fishkill Landing
Jones George I. Fishkill Plains
Tille J.   *Hydepark.*
Nickerson T.
Williams William R.
Couse J.   *Milan.*
Eighmy G.
Dennis W. Jackson's Corner
Wyman H. Lafayette Corner
Cornell J. B. Rock City
Badgley J.   *Northeast.*
Fish A. J.
Sherman H.   *Pawling.*
Cole E.
Platt A.   *Pine Plains.*
Myers W.
Marsh J. C.   *Pleasant Valley.*
Mullen C.
Hervey John C. 126 Main
    Poughkeepsie.
Burhans P. 277   do
Ketcham I. 385   do
Frederick J. W. 421   do
Street Lewis F. 426 & 428 Main
Ellison John, 416   do
Holliday R. W. & Son, 18 Academy
Mosher G. 12 Washington
Heavnor J. W.   do
Lee D.   do
Low J. T.   *Red Hook.*
Hevenor P.
Thompson H.
Ostrom J. G.   *Rhinebeck.*
Schoonmaker J.
Hyslop J.
Danelson R.   *Stanford.*
Tripp S. G.
Manchester & Cane, Verbank
    Unionvale.
Price P. Verbank
Stearns L.   *Washington.*
Jones I. R.
Stearns N. Hart's Village
Knickerbocker A.   Washington
    Hollow
Thomas D. Washington Hollow
Hamelton E. C., Lithgow
Snyder F. Mabbettsville

Erie County.

Manard Nathan   *Alden.*
Seward M. L.
Fisher Joseph
Haskell W. Williamsville
    Amherst.
Klapp John,   do
Osmalt George,   do
Bennett W. N. Willink   *Aurora.*
Bass Milton,   do
Rouse D. A.   do
Adams Joel,   do.
Whitney W. W.   do
Jones Myron,   do
Justine Ashel   *Black Rock.*
Simons John   *Boston.*
Stanton J.   *Brandt.*
Sargeant & Hewson, 40 Exchange
    Buffalo.

Herrington A. K. Seneca Hydran-
    lics   *Buffalo.*
Chamberlain H. S. cor. Pearl &
    Mohawk
Williams Watkins, Main above
    Chippewa
Rice D. S. Terrace
Delbrich Peter cor. Lock & Erie
Aldrich Sidney   *Clarence.*
Garrett Rueben
Jofford S. T.
Ayres H. M.
Graubner William
Haynes William, Centre st.
Kerr & Kane   *Collins.*
Grannis G.
Cobleigh Joel, Springville
    Concord.
Watson Jacob   do
Harrington P. B.   do
Fay A.   do
Chapin Milton   *Eden.*
Long Abram
Kingsley W. East Evans   *Evans.*
Tiffany Edward, Water Valley
    Hamburgh.
Warner H. & Co. Hamburgh Centre
Halsey S. G.   *Lancaster.*
Burke George
Kurts & Zahm
Sleeper Ira
Draper S. C.
Grimes & Sloan
Wartman Samuel
Fish Rufus, Akron   *Newstead.*
Eckereon & Brown, Akron
Simon R.   *Sardinia.*
Nagle Jacob   *Tonawanda.*
Aylesworth John   *Wales.*
Adams ——

Essex County.

Branch L. B. Port Kent
    Chesterfield.
Adgate Asher,   do
Hoag N. P.   *Elizabethtown.*
Fletcher Adams   *Essex.*
Richardson John
Brown W. Whallonsburgh
Everest George, Moriah 4 corners
    Moriah.
Douglass Joseph,   do
Smith Ezra C.   do
Millar George, Port Henry
Lockwood L. C. Schroon River
    Schroon.
Oakley Daniel,   do
Smith Edmond J.   *Westport.*
Richardson John   *Willsborough.*
White William H.

Franklin County.

Holton Josiah J.   *Bangor.*
M'Donald Victor
Hull Truman C.   *Chateaugay.*
Allen John W.
Grumore Joseph
Brown Daniel   *Malone.*
Beardsley Charles and Brothers
Darling N.
Abbott Moses
Wetherell L.   *Moira.*
Bently A. Brush Mills
Johnson Charles & Son, West
    Constable   *Westville.*

Fulton County.

Sears Ira T.   *Broadalbin.*
Saunders Heary, Hooseville
Banker A.   *Ephratah.*
Ayersinger Phillip   *Johnstown.*
Comrie Alexander
Settle Hiram
Stewart Charles N.
Welch Geo. Gloversville
Peck Jesse, Vail's Mills   *Mayfield*
Smith A.   *Northampton.*
Hadley M.
Le Roy Jonas   *Perth*
Kittle H. J.   *Stratford.*

Genesee County.

Hatherway O. C.   *Alabama.*
Starkweather S.
Silloway H. Oakfield
Clark J.   *Batavia.*
Miller G. W.
Tyrrell & Wilson
Peck A.
Coles & Tear   *Bergen.*
M'Queen James
Campbell Alexander
Oliver & Bradley   *Bethany.*
Stebbins Lyman
Sebbins Edmond
Thomas N. G. East Bethany
Voorhees J. & G., Linden
Loomis E.   *Byron.*
Pendill F.
Stewart James S.   *Elba.*
Upham A. S.   *Le Roy.*
Brinsmade C. G.
Sanford & Pierce
Ladd Thomas C.
Tompkins Warren   *Pavilion.*
Dodge Harvey   *Pembroke.*
Tirrell Amos, Corfu
Butler John

Greene County.

Tuttle D. & Son   *Ashland.*
Miller Sidney   *Athens.*
Wells A. & E.   *Cairo.*
Boughton James, Acra
Conover M.   *Catskill.*
Comfort Joel D., Leeds
Burns Richard   *Coxsackie.*
Chezitree Egbert   *Durham.*
Simmons Daniel
Cook Ranson   *Greenville.*
Fordham Justin P.   *Hunter.*
Herrick James P.   *Lexington.*
Johnson E. East Lexington
Hunt George   *Prattsville.*
Decker Henry S.
Doty & Doty   *Windham.*
Cole Alonzo, Hensonville

Herkimer County.

Elwood Alonzo   *Columbia.*
Woodward William
Huston William
Overacker Peter
Sever S.   *Danube.*
Denman John
Mason W. C.   *Fairfield.*
Myers Jeremiah   *Frankfort.*
Thomas John
Bronson & Edwards, Mohawk
      German Flats.
Brown & Woodruff
Sherman Truman
Wetherstine John D.   *Herkimer.*
Devendorf John D.
Lake George
Burrill & Smith   *Little Falls.*
Stewart Daniel
Conine Peter
Voorhees B. P.   *Newport.*
Birst Hiram
Buell & Weeks
Elkins William H.
Crandall R. H.
Broughton S. R.
Lyman H. W. Jordanville *Warren.*
Bronson Job, Crane's Corners
Eggleston ——   *Winfield.*
Moore & Curtis, W. Winfield

Jefferson County.

Dodge G.   *Adams.*
Wright C.
Arms & Son, Adams Centre
Wright P. & Co.   do
Scott H. L., Plessis   *Alexandria.*
Townsend G. W. do
Fackney James, Ox Bow *Antwerp.*
Lord & Lewis   *Brownville.*
Lawton Oliver
Peck ——, Perch River
Hackett John   *Cape Vincent.*

Merriam R. T. & Z.   *Champion.*
Ayer A.   *Ellisburgh.*
Palmer G. W. '
Pollock J., Woodville
Hurd A. L., Belleville
Freeman J.   do
Overton Henry F.   *Henderson.*
Stever & Acker, Evans' Mills
      Le Ray.
Rawson Timothy,   do
Copeland Asa   *Lorraine.*
Lucas & Wood, Three Mile Bay
      Lyme.
Barber Marcus,   do
Baker G.   *Philadelphia.*
Houghton L.
Salr J.
Houghton A.
Spear & Tuttle.   *Rodman.*
Roberts Joshua, Felt's Mills
      Rutland.
Moak John   *Theresa.*
Tuttle & Scoville   *Watertown.*
Colwell James H.

Kings County.

Glam W. 19 Willow   *Brooklyn.*
Benton G. M. cor. Pacific & Willow
Latimer W. S. & Co. Columbia
   near State st.
Lewis Alexander, Doughty st.
   near Columbia
Cole Samuel, 19 Hicks
Walters J. & T. cor. Poplar &
   Henry
Fruin Wm. & Robert, cor. Hoyt &
   Warren
Farringhty P. cor. Hoyt & Baltic
Oliver J. B. cor. Fulton & Water
Learey E. D. Wash. near Front
Mortimer T. Water near Pearl
Cavill William, 115 Front
Jeffers William, Pearl st.
Herbert Joseph, 45 Prospect
Hughes J. York st. near Pearl
Scudder David, 9 Myrtle Av.
Ralph James, 30 Liberty
Seaman Lewis W. 52 Myrtle Av.
Wright Mott, Marshall st.
Kiernan Francis, 258 Plymouth
Ryerson Jerome, Hudson Av. near
   Concord
Duffy J. Gold st.
Downey John, Hudson Av.
Perine Wm. T. Fulton Av.
Edwards H. Myrtle Av. near
   Spencer
Jones Evan,   do   do
Platt Gilbert, Flushing Av. East
      Brooklyn.
Bond Lewis, Bedford Av. corner
   Flushing
Kelly James. Atlantic st. near
   Bedford Av.
Smith E. Bedford Av. near Atlan-
   tic Av.
Lodge J. Bushwick Av. *Bushwick.*
Vincent Martin, New Lots
      Flatbush.
Murphy T.
Stillnwerl J.
Van Mater C.   *Flatlands.*
Millspawn R.
Durven I. Flatland Neck
Skidmore Isaac, Canarsie
Ditmas Clinton   *Gravesend.*
Church James C. Fort Hamilton
      New Utrecht.
Thorne Duryea K. 237 & 239 1st
      Williamsburgh.
Ackerly Wm. 2d cor. N. 1st
Bryant George, N. 1st st. cor. 3d
Propeal John K. 349 3d
Waters Thomas, 3 N. 3d
Titus Charles, 2d st. near N. 4th
Dauber Frederick, Wither st.
Conselyea William, N. 2d st.
Stadtmuller Adam, 194 Wykoff

Lewis County.

Putnam R.   *Denmark.*

Clark Wm. Copenhagen *Denmark.*
Van Slyke J.   do
Potter H.   *Lowville.*
Scofield D.
Hasen H. West Martinsburgh
      Martinsburgh.
Sackett C. C.   *Turin.*
Williston Charles
Lyman Perley
Shaver Isaac, Houseville
Williams Henry, Constableville
      West Turin.

Livingston County.

Robinson W. S.   *Avon.*
Waldo Reuben
Thomas Matthew P. East Avon
Renwick Archibald   *Caledonia*
Teele Christopher
M'Naughton Wm.
Huffman Franklin   *Conesus.*
Lozier J. G. & Brothers *Dansville*
Welch & Carpenter
Brown & Harrison
Brown Aaron
Bennett J. T.
Haas & Dakin
Vaughn & Adams
Harrison & Porter
Shepard John
Griger C.
Teasdale & Robinson
Cole Charles   *Genesee.*
Barnes A. L.
Evert Nelson   *Groveland.*
Poland William
Watson Joseph
Van Tine & Bush, Cuylerville
      Leicester.
Van Ness George, jr.   *Livonia.*
Salsich Joseph
Roberts L. J. Hemlock Lake
Morton Robert,   do
Williams Marvin, Lakeville
Goodrich & Root   *Mount Morris.*
Conkey J.
Morse D.   *Nunda.*
Holmes David
Cain Henry, Oakland   *Portage.*
Nair Isaac, Hunt's Hollow
Palmer H.   do
M'Cabe ——   *Sparta.*
Hendershott H. & J. Scottsburgh
Jenks Hiram, Byersville
      West Sparta.
Foster John   *York.*
Wade A. D. Greigsville
West W. Fowlersville

Madison County.

Clark L. P.   *Brookfield.*
Holmes Seth
Fitch Julius O.
Babcock John, Leonardsville
Lamphire & Burdick,   do
Fitch & Brown, North Brookfield
Avery Joseph,   do
Reed L.   do
Hodge H. B.   *Cazenovia.*
Combs Charles E.
Fisher & Abbott
Rouse Brothers & Bump
Billings Fletcher
Lovejoy H.
Morse, Savage & Co. New Wood-
   stock
Cleveland S.   do
Stillman C. A. & Co. *De Ruyter.*
Maxson Le Ray
Fryer James F.   *Eaton.*
Booth A. A.
Patridge & White
Wales & Brigham, Morrisville
Bauder J. Pratt's Hollow
Atkins Elijah, jr.   *Georgetown.*
Abert George   *Hamilton.*
Reed Daniel, jr.
Monson & Pratt
Cushman A. Earlville
Gardner S. D Poolvill
Whitcomb M.   do

Reese R. J. Oneida Depot *Lenox.*
Nellis S. K. Canastota
Chapman Cyrus, do
Phillips Geo. W. Wampsville
Seeley Wm. Clockville
Armstrong Jaben *Lebanon.*
Slocum F.
Blakeslee K. *Madison.*
Manchester F. H. Solsville
Travis H. & C. Peterboro
Smithfield.
Nichols A. S., Chittenango
Sullivan.
Mathews Joseph L. do
Campbell James. Perryville
Wheat J. D. Bridgeport
Jepson Eli,   do

Monroe County.

Gorham E. L. *Brighton.*
Downs T.
Bailey James, North Chili *Chili.*
Price William, Clarkson Corner
Clarkson.
Hilton N.   do
Powell S.   do
Wisner P. S. Jenkins' Corner
Greece.
Martin J. East Henrietta
Henrietta.
Williams H., West do
Williams J.   do
Daggett A. K. East Mendon
Mendon.
Knapp O.   do
Palmer & Claffey, West Mendon
Rice George *Ogden.*
Efner J. V. Parma Corner *Parma.*
Veazie Chas. Parma Centre
Burns & Hopkins *Penfield.*
Kimble D.
Howard L. T. Fairport *Perrinton.*
Yonng R. R.   do
Buell O. Bushnell's Basin
Baker James, Churchville *Riga.*
Tupper Marshall   do
Cunningham J., Litchfield st.
Rochester.
Lane Gaines, 57 South St. Paul
Housam T. cor. Achilles & North
Corris & Stewart, 13 North
Walter Valtin,   do
Fluck G. 119 East North
Guy & Mahan, 147 Buffalo
Boorman R. cor. Buffalo & Trow-
bridge
Filon M. 125 Main
Cummington Thomas, 5 Spring
Williams James H. 79 Exchange
Hall J. W. 136 South Sophia
Bowman John, 135 do
Southwick J. M. 68 State
Morris W. S. Mill st.
Springstead H. S. 1 Smith
Heath A. & A. *Rush.*
Barnes Isaac, Clinton st. Brock-
port *Sweden.*
Greenough E.   do
Preston F. West Webster *Webster.*
Weller R.   do
Van Ness J.   do
Rafferty Patrick, Scottsville
Wheatland.
Brooks George,   do

Montgomery County.

Payne Wm. *Amsterdam.*
Young J. L.
Colebrook C.
Sparbeck Martin, Cranesville
Degraff A. J.   do
Peck ——, Hagaman's Mills
Van Allen H. *Canajoharie.*
Castler John H.
Joslyn John, Ames
Winne C. P. Buel
Snyder Isaac, do
Vougt D. *Charleston.*
Van Patten C. C. Minaville
Florida.
Hill S. M. Fort Jackson

O'Brien & Lingenfatter *Glen.*
Penire John
Stevens John, Fultonville
Kline Wm. W.   do
Mabee Peter, Smithtown
Prince John, Voorhees
Burke John D. Fort Plain *Minden.*
Bush A. & Kline A. P. do
Jeder & Kline, Fonda *Mohawk.*
Fisher C. E.   do
Godevin H.   do
Vosburg Levi, Palatine Bridge
Palatine.
Fuller Alva,   do
Lasher Jacob S., Stone Arabia
Wier S. Spraker's Basin *Root.*
Quackenbush D. do
Snell Jonas *St. Johnsville.*
Saltzman Wm.

New York County.

Allen Jos. 123 Grand *New York.*
Beardsley Charles, 32 Canal
Beatty C. & A. 57 3d Av.
Benson Wm. J. 83 18th
Brewster J. & Sons, 396 Broadway
Butler John P. 70 Prince
Butler John F. 102 Crosby
Dearman Wm. H. 162 Crosby
Donnell Robert, 166 Centre
Dubois Peter, 22 Amity
Dusenberry & Vanduser, 137
Chrystie
Elderd & Van Orden, 175 4th
Ellis Wm. 295 & 297 E. Broadway
Fancher George, 54 E. 13th
Flandrau Wm. 138 Elizabeth
Ford Isaac, 116 Elizabeth
Foster Henry, 263 Mercer
Gilbert Eli, 38 Canal
Godwin Joseph H. 114 Elizabeth
H ll William T. 105 Walker
Ham John C. jr. 360 Broadway
Kaufman William, 17 White
Lawrence & Collis, 12 Vesey & 6
Barclay
Lawrence Jacob, 274 Henry
Ludlum & Smith, E. 19th near 3d
Av. & 6th
Lyon A. & W. E. 8 Christopher
M'Cormick E. 11 Cortlandt alley
M'Kinstrey R. jr. 450 Broadway
M'Rea William, 88 Leonard
Marsh, Foster & Co. #03 Mercer
Martin William S. 106 10th Av.
Manee A. 136 East Broadway
Mead Joshua, 291 3d Av.
Miner & Stephens, 26 & 27 Canal
Mix Isaac jr. 440 Broadway
Motel Christopher, 442 Anthony
Murphy Martin, 113 Sheriff
Palmer David, 141 Sullivan
Reynolds Uel, 160 Suffolk
Russell R. M. 209 Sullivan
Seaman Thomas V. 136 Clinton pl.
Smithson Charles, 5 7th
Stivors William, 99 1st Av.
Sparling Thomas, 264 Elizabeth
Stephenson J., E. 27th
Stratton Exra M. 106 Elizabeth
Swenarton John, 295 Greene
Thompson Major, 27 Wooster
Tine Joseph, 119 Walker
Underhill George D. 197 Mercer
Voorhees John, 6 Lafayette place
Weir Abraham J. 266 Mott
Wilmot Alexander, 75 Allen
Williams, William 98 Elm
Wood, Tomlinson, & Co. 410
Broadway

Niagara County.

Cain John B. Pekin *Cambria.*
Platt J. & W. *Lewiston.*
Baright Allen *Lockport.*
Perigo J. H.
Howard & Fenn, *Newfane.*
Rice Joseph
Langdon & Cooley
Churchill Otis *Niagara Falls.*
Tibbetts A. C.

Wires Morris H. *Pendleton.*
Tryon & Denis, Youngstown
Porter
Phillips Henry
Lusk Silas, Reynale's Basin,
Royalton.
Briggs Hiram E. *Somerset.*
Bentley J. C. Tonawanda
Wheatfield.
Egleston G. B. *Wilson.*
Brown S. B.

Oneida County.

Tuttle W. *Boonville.*
Brown J. & Co. *Bridgewater.*
Waldron & Gaylord *Camden.*
Barber & Staples
Humeston E. F.
Eastman I. S. *Deerfield*
St. John William P.
Lewis R.
Baldwin E. S. *Florence.*
Haven Geo. Clinton *Kirkland.*
Sheldon J. & Co. West Branch
Lee.
Richardson J. P. *New Hartford.*
Eastman P. S.
Palmer E. A. Clayville *Paris.*
Peggs R. Dominick st. *Rome.*
Dill J. W.
Davis T. & Co. Holland Patent
Trenton
Jones J. Prospect
Thomas E. & Co. S. Trenton
Jones Thomas, 49 Whitesboro
Utica.
Lewis D. 6 Seneca
Hamlin W. D. Fayette st.
Seaton & Chapman, Whitesboro st.
Mather J. John st.
Lyons D. A. 36 Bleeker
Carpenter C. 27 John
Jones J. T. 7 Catherine
Judson A. *Vernon.*
Rose J., Hampton *Westmoreland.*
Hallenbeck D., Yorkville
Whitestown.
Wilson & Co. Whitesboro

Onondaga County.

Shaver J. *Cicero.*
Aylworth O. *Fabius.*
Case W. W. *Geddes.*
Patten J.
Houghton A., Cardiff *Lafayette.*
Peck & Avery *Lysander.*
Northrop T.
Cronkhite H. Baldwinsville
Lush W.   do
Chittenden S.   do
Wilder & Bennett *Marcellus.*
Ashby & Soules
Dewell & Hopkins *Manlius.*
Beach & Cable *Pompey.*
Roach & Wynekoop, Orange st.
Syracuse *Salina.*
Phelps R. R. (dealer) Genesee st.
Ames John,   do
Hoyt & Stevens, cor. Genesee st.
& Fayette
Luther & Fogarty, James st.
Griffith & Silver,   do
Clark & Hungerford, Park st.
Nott C. A.   do
Springer F. Salina st.
Warden L. S. *Skaneateles.*
Hall J.
Cately S. & Co. *Tully.*
Reed P *Van Buren.*

Ontario County.

Worden S. *Bristol.*
Hayes Mumford, East *Bloomfield*
Tozer John, Reed's Corners
Gorham
Parsons Daniel *Phelps*
Spencer Albert
Taylor ——
Nelson A.
Wright Charles

Shaw W. Allen's Hill *Richmond.*
Merrill Nelson, do
Batchellor J., Honeoye
Squires James H. Geneva *Seneca.*
Freehour Henry, do
Rose S. H. do
Brandage William, do
Allerton John, do
Ayres Bailey, West *Bloomfield.*
Webb John, do

Orange County.

Giles Daniel, Washingtonville
    Blooming Grove.
Still Henry, jr. do
Wyatt W., Craigville
Marvin B. *Chester.*
Brewster O. *Cornwall.*
Mekeel Thomas, Buttermilk Falls
Bodine F. M., *Crawford.*
Schoonmaker A.
Skinner N. Port Jervis *Deer Park.*
Ray W. V. *Goshen.*
Roe D.
Campbell J. A. Wells' Corners
    Minisink.
Conner H. do
Hart Wm. H., Westown
Hanford P. C. Unionville
Post & Bennett, do
Newton G., Ridgebury
Howell & Wood, Slate Hill
Brown & Whaly *Montgomery.*
Sears W.
Overhiser & Gillispie
Hatch E., Walden
Docker Jacob D
Boyce John *Monroe.*
Hanford J. M. *Mount Hope.*
Van Clark L., Otisville
Thorn S., Finchville
Swezey J. W.
M'Cullum S. T., Weston Av.
    Newburgh.
Powell J. W.
Donaldson Thomas, Front st.
Lature A. W. do
Case D. F. New Hampton *Wallkill.*
M'Ewen & M'Coy, do
Kain H. & Co. South Middletown
Houston James, do
Riker S., Amity *Warwick.*
Rose J. A. do
Dusenbury J., Edenville
Culver B. do
Harrison T., New Milford
Walsh T. E.
Conklin S. Sugar Loaf
Hunter J. do
Woodruff E., Florida
Many W. H. do

Orleans County.

Sears H. & I. U., Albion *Barre.*
Smith N. P. do
Sanderson Hiram, do
Childs Horatio *Carlton.*
M'Alister E. *Clarendon.*
Avery J. & C. *Kendall.*
Tillman J. & A. Medina *Ridgeway.*
Bideman Wm. do
Card A. do
Bennett & Davis, do
Trowbridge ——, Knowlesville
Topliff L. do
Belding A. do
Bailey J. *Shelby.*
Bartron I. C.
Mead John *Yates.*
Haines & Olds
Palmer B., Lyndonville
Fellows Wm. L. do
Mory David, do

Oswego County.

Stowoll William H. *Constantia.*
Perkins J.
Tarpenny D. Cleaveland
Hurst W. do
Hazen D. do

Rice Aaron & Co. Oswego Falls
    Granby.
Gardner S. H. & H. A. do
Byington Rufus & Co. *Hannibal.*
Perkins William
Harris J. Central Square *Hastings.*
Penfield A. & W. *Mexico.*
Huntington & Barnes
Elmer Edmund
Turner Cyrus
Lamb John S.
Barrus A., Colosse
Gray Peter, do
Head C. L. *New Haven.*
Tunis Clanson, Bridge st. *Oswego.*
Battis Andrew, do
Sheridan Patrick, do
Disbro & Denton, 2d st.
Gleason Benj. cor. 2d & Bridge
Weatherby Luther, do
Harter Isaac *Parish.*
Harmon Calvin C. Pulaski
    Richland.
Mathewson C. A. do
Thomas Luther B. do
Ingersoll R. L. do
Davids Charles, do
Dewey Samuel, South Richland
Cable Charles & Nelson, Phœnix
    Schroeppel.
Capron David, Phœnix
Wood L. Gilbert's Mills
Payne A. C. Hinmansville
Garrison John *Scriba.*

Otsego County.

Langdon S. West Burlington
    Burlington.
Thompson L. Burlington Green
Taylor T. Burlington Flats
Kynion J. P. *Butternuts.*
Ford E. J.
Cord Wm. P.
Fitzgerald Wm. *Cherry Valley.*
Striker J.
Peeso A.
Davis J. *Decatur.*
Wright Hanson
Lines & York *Edmeston.*
Maxon Ephraim, West Edmeston
Perry John
Phelps Henry, South Edmeston
Shepard E. M. *Exeter.*
Green Jason C. Schuyler's Lake
Welch Albert do
Morelette E. *Hartwick.*
Wilcox A. *Laurens.*
Barnard D.
Mosher H.
Hoag J.
Hopkins F.
Briggs Elihu C. *Middlefield.*
Brown Rensselaer
Rowland Joel
Jones Daniel C.
Velie John V. Middlefield Centre
Smith Lorenzo do
Barney D. *Milford.*
Cronkhite E.
Cronkhite Lewis
Seward C. B.
Pride F. *New Lisbon.*
Thurston J.
M'Call Horace *Oneonta.*
Bond ——
Birdsall Henry *Otego.*
Goldsmith Alfred
Smith Milo
Johnson A. D. *Plainfield.*
St. John C.
Griffith P. *Richfield.*
Clump L. R. *Springfield.*
Carroll M.
Johnson T.
Francis T.
Bragg Joel C. *Unadilla.*
Bragg & Padgett
Edson Willis F.
Hanford David
Padgett Lorenzo D.
Edson & Hanford

Platner S. *Westford.*
Salisbury D.
Wilson George *Worcester.*
Wright John
Robbins C. R.
Campaine Wm. East Worcester

Putnam County.

Post A. S. Farmers' Mills *Kent.*
Dubois J. P. Cold Spring
Tuthill J. H. do
Mekeel W. *Phillipstown.*
Mosier J. E.
Ager A. *Putnam Valley.*
Smith J.
Sillick J.
Cole —— *Southeast.*

Queens County.

Ellis S. *Flushing.*
Doty & Nostrand
Pine Samuel M. *Hempstead.*
Platt Eldrid
Wright William
Wright Israel
Hewlet Peter T. Rockaway
Wright James, do
Cornell Samuel, Millburn
Gildersleeve J. Raynortown
Rodes Andrew do
Pearsall Thomas, Far Rockaway
Smith William do
Smith Thomas, Merrick
Hendry James R. *Jamaica.*
Crossman S. B.
Reeve L. & Co.
Bennett B. East Jamaica
Denton William L. do
Brush William A. Brushville
Everett & Watts
Burrows John *Newtown.*
Proctor Abraham
Bayles Gustavus
Tifton E.
Morris C. R. Astoria
O'Brien Patrick
Prillon J. Lewis, Roslyn
    North Hempstead.
Lacy John D. Roslyn
Wright A. do
Cornell C. & Jas. Manhasset
Rapalyea Daniel, Cow Neck
Williams William H. Lakeville
Golden M. *Oyster Bay.*
Ludlam Samuel Y.
Platt William H. East Norwich
Hart Samuel, Jericho
Kirby James B. do
Coles J. & E.

Rensselaer County.

Backenstyre D. *Brunswick.*
Maxon P. *Grafton.*
Hyler Geo. W. *Greenbush.*
Clark H. B. *Hoosick.*
Burrall J.
Lottage Thomas
Woodard & Gorslin, River st.
    Lansingburgh.
Sterry S. Congress st. Alley
Bullis Wm. jr. East Nassau
    Nassau.
Goewey D. B. *Pittstown.*
Hunter G.
Bonesteel & Co. *Poestenkill.*
Martin J. *Sandlake.*
Hare J. *Schodack.*
Witbeck J.
Barnes P. *Stephentown.*
Ogden Joseph, 268 River *Troy.*
Derrick Ira, 364 do
Birge T. cor. Congress & 7th sts.
Ballou Smith, 7 Jacob
Boynton Warren, near Bridge
Ball & Hedenberg, 1 Hill
Middleton David, 195 4th
Lown & Bunker, 68 & 70 6th
Eaton, Gilbert & Co. cor. 6th &
    Albany
Hear John O. Adams near 2d

Wilkerson Peter, William near
  State   Troy.
Tripp W. G. 6th near Ferry
Fox I. F. 517 River

Richmond County.

Marsh Isaac, Richmond
                    Northfield.
Wandel John, Stapleton
                    Southfield.
Oakley J. Rossville   Westfield.

Rockland County.

Allison & Polhamus   Haverstraw.
Taylor A. Nyack   Orangetown.
Christie A. L. do
Johnson William, Piermont

St. Lawrence County.

Champlin Thomas   Canton.
Bunker A. Richville   De Kalb.
Curtis L.   Depeyster.
Brewster T.   Fowler.
Smith & Eaton   Gouverneur.
Wrythe ——
Smith T. & Co.
Nichols John   Hammond.
Nichols David
Eustis Tobias
Story Amos
Hasting Benjamin R.   Hermon.
Kellogg Chester
Weldon Ethan R.
Fordham Thomas S.
Lindsley Henry   Hopkinton.
White Nelson
Crook Samuel
Betts Reuben   Lawrence.
Dana Moody
Tayer Titus V.   Lisbon.
Norway William
Marshall Lorenzo
Harmon Horace   Louisville.
Harris J.
Read William, Columbia Madrid.
Dixon Ambrose, do
Lockwood William, do
Ford Robert, Waddington
Trusdell Lewis, do
Armstrong John, do
Martin Hiram   Massena.
Holliday M.
Voshburgh Abraham Morristown.
Giffin David
Stow G. W.
Cutting D. H.   Norfolk.
Clark Joseph
Allen George, Ogdensburgh
Perkins Cyrus, Isabella st. Og-
  densburgh   Oswegatchie.
Lamb Israel & Son, Isabella st.
  Ogdensburgh
Perkins Cyrus   Parishville.
Allen Sewall
Ansted Peter
Platt N. G.   Pitcairn.
Hyde Henry H.   Potsdam.
Simonds James L.
Fuller Stephen
Clapp Silas
Holcomb Hiram   Stockholm.
Rice Eber
Stearns R. F.

Saratoga County.

Knapp Benj. K.   Charlton.
Heston Russell
M'Cornie J. P. West Charlton
Dedrick Richard M. Clifton Park
Banker Edward, Jonesville
Pearse James V. Vischer's Ferry
Graves Samuel, Graves' Corners.
Bartlett Luke C.   Corinth.
Copfin Read   Edinburgh.
Seaver James
Allen Sylvester   Galway.
Allen John
Ward W.
Owen Matthew, Greenfield Cen-
  tre   Greenfield.

Young A. Greenfield Centre
                    Greenfield.
Wheeler Jos. 2d, Jamesville
M'Nutt B.
Barber Benj. J. West Greenfield
Gray ——, do
Barber Seth, do
Latham G. W. North Greenfield
Bartlett Joseph,
Rosekrans Benj.   Half Moon.
Thorp D.
Gould Joel   Malta.
Simpson John
Denton Lewis
Vincent Platt
Bix S .B. Glenn's Falls Moreau.
Hazzard W. R. do
Gamble Jas. do
Blake J. J.   Providence.
Bartlett Ira   Saratoga.
Shropard Barney
Howland Isaac
Esmond S.
Neher Edward
Fisher & Wiser Saratoga Springs.
Nelson Samuel
Vancuren Cornelius
Smith Gilbert B.   Stillwater.
Jones John   Waterford.
Steenbaugh Henry
Stanburg James
Martin Hiram   Wilton.
Potter Jonathan

Schenectady County.

Gray Jacob   Glenville.
Chasmer R.
Wright James, 9 Rotterdam
                    Schenectady.
Lyon C. 87 Union
Van Pelt I. Ferry st.
Seman B. Malden lane

Schoharie County.

Thomas Hiram   Blenheim.
Fero J.
Brown George   Carlisle.
M'Lein J. D.   Cobleskill.
Fero David
Simpkins   Esperance.
Quick D. C. Sloansville
Phelps G. do
Phelps David do
Clark Merit B. Fultonham Fulton.
Burget T. A. do
Dibble Isaac, Breakabeen
Loveland Freeman, West Fulton
Simmons W. H. do
Smith Amos   Middleburgh.
Wolford Henry ....
Wilber Abram
Vaughan Isaac   Richmondville.
Winters Wm.
Hallenbeck John
Crauts Henry
Winter William   Schoharie.
Clements Wm. Central Bridge
Rickett Peter A.
Rickett H.
Calkin James, Hyndsville Seward.
Brown A. Gardinerville
Brown Henry do
Wilsoy E. Gallupville   Wright.

Seneca County.

Piersons J. Canoga   Fayette.
Boardman Levi, do
Van Horn John   Lodi.
Thompson Henry   Ovid.
Queerin John
Clark John
Eyelenburgh ——, Farmer
Carman Caleb do
Smalley Joel   Romulus.
Venesce Isaac
King John G.
Yunt Wm.   Waterloo.

Steuben County.

Smith G. G. & W. E.   Addison.

Fox G. P.   Avoca.
Fletcher & M'Cain   Bath.
Graham M.
Barney N.
Smith N.   Cameron.
White J. E.   Canisteo.
Wood G. H.   Cohocton.
Conely M. T.
Nicholson W. O. North Cohocton
Sheffield John, do
Burrell Alonzo   Greenwood.
Batchelor Joseph
Smith D. A.   Hornellsville.
Smith C. F
Rogers C. G.
Graham R. H.   Howard.
Preston E.
Palmer Benjamin   Orange.
Edson Rufus   Prattsburgh.
Hayes S.
Simpson Chester   Pulteney.
Bradt & Bently   Reading.
Jones A.   Urbana.
Bell P.
M'Keagen Joseph
Myatt O.
Morrison H.   Woodhull.
Newell A.

Suffolk County.

Overton Alanson, Middle Island
                    Brookhaven.
Hudson Nathaniel, do
Skinner Wm., Patchogue
Miller Isaac L.   Huntington.
Sammis Frederick
Velsor Charles, Comac
Griffith James, Northport
Grossman Francis G. Babylon
Udall Jonas do
Pugsley John G.   Riverhead.
Smith Wm. F.   Smithtown.
Jaggar Henry   Southampton.
Payne Wm

Sullivan County.

Forbs E.   Liberty
Crane Joseph M. Bloomingburgh
                    Mamakating
Vankuren S. do
Newkirk A. W. Wurtsboro
Terwilliger S. S. Burlingham
Bowen D. do
Mapledoram John, Monticello
                    Thompson.
Smith Alex. do

Tioga County.

Robinson Calvin J.   Richford
Smith Julius C.

Tompkins County.

Williamson Nelson, Enfield Cen-
  tre   Enfield.
Miller Amos, do
Wilcox Henry do
Allen Wm.   Groton.
Smith Wm. S. & Co.   Hector.
Carr & Wyckoff, North Hector
Hoyt W. S. 98 Tioga st. Ithaca.
Curtis E. 51 do
Cowdry A. & S. 17 Aurora
Bower J. 156 Owego
Miller H. H.   Newfield.
Pierson T. H.
Everhard Wm.
Cuffruan D. P. Trumansburgh
                    Ulysses.
Crequa J. & A. do
Tinner W. do

Ulster County.

Peters Wm.   Kingston.
Perrine Abram J.
Wells G. & S.
Houghtaling T. L.
Merritt John T.
Dodge John, Rondout
Van Vleet Edward, High Falls
                    Marbletown.

Windfield John, Stone Ridge *Marbletown.*
Rosa Isaac, Stone Ridge
Davis James, do
Drake W. *New Palts.*
Whitmore J.
Low J. D.
Quick Wm. G.
Silkworth T. Libertyville
Krom Edgr. Kyserike *Rochester.*
Maines & Montross *Saugerties.*
Hansen J.
Smith Hiram
Cooper John
Simons A.
Thomas L. *Shandaken.*
Decker M. *Showangunk.*
Dill D
Dutcher & Cox, Ellenville *Wawarsing.*
Decker J. do

Washington County.

Lester John L. North *Argyle.*
Selfridge Oliver, do
Harshaw David, jr. do
Congdon William, South Argyle
Christie William, jr. do
Ackley Orrin *Cambridge.*
Selfridge Oliver
Robertson Thomas
Bishop William
Ketchum Wm. Cambridge Centre
Willis John. North Cambridge
Harrington David, North *Easton.*
Ward Edward
Briggs Cornelius
Miller & Skinner *Fort Ann.*
Mason Orville T.
Carter David P.
Pike & Hunter *Fort Edward.*
Pike Samuel, Fort Miller
Durkee William, do
Andrews, Moore & Co. *Greenwich.*
Adams Zacheus
Mayhew Peter
Weir Alonzo, Battenville
Clark J. B., Lake
Weaver Levi M., Lake
Sherman E. B., Galesville
Miller Joseph, do
Heath George, do
Clark R. H. *Hampton.*
Rogers Sidney T., West *Hebron.*
Moore Alexander. West Hebron
Williamson John C. do
Skinner A. A., Sandy Hill *Kingsbury.*
Miller J. A. do
Knapp R. do
Middleworth H. V. do
Mead M., Smith's Basin
Russell C. & C. *White Creek.*
Wait H. & Z. Centre White Creek
Jamison John, North do
Lovejoy H H.
Bristol A. G. William *st. Whitehall.*
Bristol J. C. do
Greenough J.

Wayne County.

Izzenbrager Henry *Arcadia.*
Briggs Joseph A. Newark
Riggs A. do
Tracy S. R. do
Trear John L. do
Seeley John, do
Grost Peter, do
M'Elwain James *Lyons.*
Cady & Stanton
Shaw E.
Paine Thomas, Alloway
Hinckley A. S., Macedonville *Macedon.*
Bull George F. *Marion.*
Myers —— *Ontario.*
Sherman & Crandall *Palmyra.*
Collins Chauncy B. *Rose.*
Thomas Wm. H.
Brown John R. *Sodus.*
Silvers John, Alton
Benjamin Elijah, South Sodus

Mason H. G. *Wolworth.*
Griffin —— *Williamson.*
Moody Sidney C.
Bowling John
Miller George W.
Johnson J. *Wolcott.*

Westchester County.

Jessup L., Peekskill *Courtlandt.*
Johnson Jas. do
Gallaudett Haywood,East *Chester.*
Bird Hiram, Tarrytown *Greenburgh.*
Connover Wm., Dobb's Ferry
Coles Adam *Mamaroneck.*
Lawrence J.
Ward Joseph, Pleasantville *Mount Pleasant.*
Baker Harvey *New Rochelle.*
Lecount William
Lefevre Prosper
Birdsall D. D. Sing Sing *Ossining.*
Buckhout Henry L. do
Dubois Charles S. do
Henman James *Pelham.*
Pugsley & Slater, Portchester *Rye.*
Webb H. do
Valentine Gideon *Westchester.*
St. John Wm. H. *West Farms.*
Frost & Ward
Doren Christ'r. V. *White Plains.*
Wallace Gilbert G.
Anderson Wm. H. *Yonkers.*
Warner & Majoy
Bashford James

Wyoming County.

Newton Levi *Attica.*
Rycord Charles
Howes R. & L. *Bennington.*
Miller Bruce, Cowlesville
Conklin Wm. H. *Castile.*
Knapp & Upham
Eastwood Isaac
Price Harvey *China.*
Perkins James
Clark Quartus *Eagle.*
Bristol & Humphrey *Genesee Falls.*
Miller George V.
Shaw Samuel
Bickford Thomas *Java.*
Cooper ——, Java Village
Stedman Reuben, Wyoming *Middlebury.*
Dalbeer Wm. & Son *Perry.*
Carr John
Newton H.
Williamson James
Blanchard S. G *Pike.*
Kendall A.
Willard A.
Hall Frederick *Sheldon.*
Pedingall —, Varysburgh
Buxton C. & T. *Warsaw.*
Ensign J.
Reddish H. J.

Yates County.

Darrin D. *Barrington.*
Fowlison E.
Ludlow Thomas, Bellona *Benton.*
Garrison S. do
Genning O., Italy Hollow *Italy.*
Lares ——, do
Van Loon ——, do
Bucklin A. G. *Middlesex.*
Miles P.
Rooney John *Milo.*
Brigden Timothy, Penn Yan
Wood & Bruen, do
Aplegate J. D. do
Cooley James. do
Townsend H. do
M'Connell Peter H. *Potter.*
Thomas A. 2d
Sayre John, Rushville
Whitney & Warren, Rushville
Gordon David, do
Shoemaker S., Dundee *Starkey.*
Hudson Samuel E. do
Hurd Artemus, Rock Stream

Carriage Trimmers.

Broome County.

Benedict Wm. S. *Binghamton.*

Columbia County.

Schemerhorn W. *Chatham.*
Spears Wm., Valatie. *Kinderhook.*

Delaware County.

Beekly W. R. *Stamford.*
Noble Wm. W., Hobart

Duchess County.

Burnett H. M. *Poughkeepsie.*

Erie County.

Bosche John, 4 Exchange pl. *Buffalo.*
Hanson A. 46 Erie

Genesee County.

Guison Jacob *Batavia.*

Herkimer County.

Baker C. W. *Newport.*
Campbell A. W.

Monroe County.

Wright R. B. *Penfield.*
Eves Henry M. 125 Main *Rhoste.*
Jeffreys C. B. 66 State
Laing T. T. 57 do

Carvers. (*Marked thus* are Ship Carpers.)

Duchess County.

Theal U. *Poughkeepsie.*

Kings County.

Buck George H. 62 Washington *Brooklyn.*

New York County.

*Anderson Jacob S. 226 South *New York.*
Aube Peter, 21 Spruce
Auld Wilberforce, 96 Walker
Banta John W. 380 Bleecker
Barry & Losee, 102 Elm
Beadle Edward, 44 Vestry
Bell Richard, 23 6th Av.
Browne John S. r. 157 Wooster
Chatsin Henry, 360 Broome
Coneley William S. 29 Chambers
*Cromwell John L. 222 South
Darlington & Jackson, 204 Centre
Davis James, 396 Washington
Docheslaw Joseph, 223 2d
*Dodge Charles, 253 South
Doran John B. 113 Elm
Doughty John H. 387 Grand
Eschenbach C. J. 116 Rivington
Fash William B. 64 W, 13th
Fisher Peter G. 174 Hester
Fox Herman, r. 139 Bowery
Harding John T. 95 Bowery
Harding Richard, 257 William
Harris Abraham, 193 Fulton
Hartung Abel, r. 42 Suffolk
Hartung Emil, 24 Wooster & r. 40 Suffolk
Heiss Dalthas, 251 Spring
Hern John J. 315 Broadway
Hoffmast Amel r. 121 Norfolk
Herrigan Robert, 46 Rose
Jenkins James H. 95 Bleecker
Ledille P. F. 92 Elm
Luff J. V. & G. W. 105 Elm
Marcellus John, 114 2d Av.
*Millard & Brooks, 290 South

8

Miller Edwin N. 179 Chrystie
    New York.
Miller George A. 205 Chrystie
Millikin Robert. 42 Beekman
Mitchell R. E. 25th st.
Mott De Witt C. 15 Bowery
Murphy & Gunning, r. 52 Mac-
    dougal
Floss Adam, 14 Spring
Reinbold A. 164 Broome
Roehore Frederick, 281 Grand
Sedilie Peter F. 93 Elm
Short William, 169 Fulton
Smith & Crane, 138 Wooster
Smith W. 28 Commerce
Stuart David. r. 97 Forsyth
*Weeden John, 275 South
Werner Ernest, 100 Attorney

Casks (Empty) Dealers in.

Bowden William, 557 4th
    New York.
Dawson Wm. & Son, 15 Mott
Galloway John A. 110 Warren
Platt Charles S. 54 Spring

Cement Dealers.

Beeman R. 120 Fulton *New York.*
Kenny James F. 243 Front
Kingston Lime & Cement Co. 409
    West & 271 Pearl
Lawrence John W. 142 Front
Nelson & Brown, 290 West
Ogden & Martin, 104 Wall
Woodward M. W. 142 Front

Cement Manufacturers.

Madison County.
Kennedy David   *Sullivan.*

Monroe County.
Ross B. & Co. 91 Main *Rochester.*

Schenectady County.
Van Ess J. D.   *Glenville.*

Ulster County.
Kingston Lime & Cement Co.
    Kingston.
Lafever Peter C. & Co.
Cement Mills, Eddyville
Depuy Jacob H. High Falls
    Marbletown.
Bruce Nathan,   do
Ogden & Martin,   do
Hasbrouck Isaac L., High Falls
Van Wagner A. & G. *Rosendale*
Budington E. W.
Booth Thomas   *Saugerties.*

Chain Cables.

Aymar Wm. & Co. 50 South
    New York.
Carnen P. C. 167 South
Merritt & Co. 58 South

Chair Manufacturers. (*See also Cabinet Makers.*)

Albany County.
Winne W. B. 83 State *Albany.*
Mosely H. T. 17 Church
Smith William, 21 Washington
*Palmer E. D. 81 State

Alleghany County.
Root S.   *Rushford.*
Hills Horace   *West Almond.*
Hills Almon
Hills Levi

Broome County.
Seymour A.   *Binghamton.*
Andrews G. W.   *Windsor.*

Cattaraugus County.
Butler Hiram   *Conewango.*
Latin & Lairy   *Ellicottville.*
Tingue Henry   *New Albion.*
Rogers T. L.   *Otto.*

Chautauque County.
Cook Elihu, Panama *Harmony.*
Neff ——, Fredonia *Pomfret.*
Lee & Crosby   *Portland.*
Cushing & Kellogg *Sherman.*
Smith James   *Villenova.*
Robinson Hiram   *Westfield.*
Timpson Hollis

Chenango County.
Bilden Z.   *Guilford.*
Washburn J. Y.   *Oxford.*

Clinton County.
Brooks ——   *Mooers.*

Delaware County.
Barnes L.   *Franklin.*

Duchess County.
Depew J. 351 Main *Poughkeepsie.*
Chichester S. & Co. Water st.
  ·South of Main
Strong, Lewis & Co. Upper Land-
    ing
Hamilton J. 356 Main

Erie County.
Upham L. (Cane Seat Chairs)
    Black Rock.
Neiderlander J. & F. 311 Main
    Buffalo.

Franklin County.
Whiting & Rickey Ft. *Covington.*

Fulton County.
Kingsley S. W.   *Broadalbin.*

Greene County.
Brady George C.   *Athens.*
Kortz James   *Catskill.*
Hitchcock Asa   *Durham.*
Ingersoll J. & Co.   *Hunter.*
Wheelock Bloomfield J.
Neal & Norcott
Bushnell & Inman, Bushnellsville
    Lexington.
Manfield Lewis   *Windham.*

Herkimer County.
Hastings Henry   *Frankfort.*
Crossman J. & Wm. W.
Barnes E. T.   *Newport.*
Clark John
Smith E.
Champion A. & W. Starkville
    Stark.
Lyman H. W. Jordanville *Warren.*

Jefferson County.
Daxter D. & S. Black River
    Rutland.
Warner S.   do
Brown J. H. Felt's Mills
Britton A. N.   *Theresa.*

Kings County.
Ferguson J. 76 & 78 Fulton
    Brooklyn.
Scott Henry, 2d cor. South 2d
    Williamsburgh.
Croak F. Grand cor. 3d
Moger A. F. Grand
Michaels F. H. 102 N. 3d

Velsor County.
Velsor George, 102 N 2d
    Williamsburgh.
Chamberlain Agust, 129 Leonard
Sultan K. (chairs & sofas) 92 School

Livingston County.
Burpee A. E.   *Dansville.*
Howland A. W.

Madison County.
Denison William R. *Brookfield.*
Clark R. L.
Marsh Joseph, Morrisville *Eaton.*
De Forest, A. B.   do
Moses Richard,   do
Gibbs William   *Fenner*
Willard Joshua   *Hamilton*
Keyes Lorenzo D.

Monroe County.
Cushing W. T. Jenkins' Corner
    Greece.
Gibson A. R.   *West Mendon.*
Graham D. Curtis' Block Main
    Rochester.
Cowles Norman,   do
Starr Frederick, 47 Main
Brewster & Feen, 61 State
Leavensworth G. Lower Falls
Hayden C. J. Front st.
Hayden James E. 14   do
Graham & Myer, 20   do
Bloss, Tibbles & Co. 19 do
Beckwith Francis X. cor. Roches-
    ter & Main, Scottsville
    Wheatland.

New York County.
Andrus R. C. Broadway
    New York.
Baldwin John A. 344 Greenwich
Barnes William, jr. 224   do
Barns Ambrose W. 114 Chatham
Bilyeu William, 296 Delancy
Blauvelt Herman, 40 Thompson
Blauvelt Richard D. 80 Bowery
Blanck A. P. 356 Hudson
Boyce J. & Son, 220 Greenwich
Bradley Joseph, 317 Pearl
Chafer Adam, 112 7th Av.
Chochard H. L. 529 6th Av.
Chainaw William, 9th Av.
Collins William R. 40 Pitt
Commerford & Redgate, 443
    Broadway & 270 Mott
Conklin H. 87 Bowery
Conklin Gilbert, 139 Elm
Cook A. 16 Bowery
Cooper James, 144 Stanton
Day Silas, 270½ Bowery
De Lamontanye J. 53 Bowery
Demerest C. W., 29th st.
Dorion Stephen H. 58 Gold
Dorr Henry, 123 W. 17th
Ey Joseph, 24 9th
Feltman Trucot, 18 Mulberry
Fenerich C. W. 28th st.
Forsyth John, 40 1st Av.
Gildersleeve Thos. J. 237 Delancy
Haller G. rear 431 Washington
Hamilton William, rear 37 Pitt
Hoffnar A., W. 32d st.
Ingersoll & Halsey, 71 Bowery
King M. W. & Son. 466 Broadway
King William G. 405 Grand
Klaus Adam, 165 Mulberry
Kleim George, 4 Forsyth
Laffetra S. W. & Son. 288 Hudson
Lange I. H. rear 124 Amity
Laycock James, 18 Pell
Leviness William, 81 Forsyth
M'Clain John, 155 Christopher
Macgar Frederick, 70 W. 17th
M'Glinchy James, 210 Mott
Martin Michael, 2½ Monroe
Margreff C. 74 Clinton
Mason Joel W. 377 Pearl & 13½
    Oliver
Meir L. 104 W. 17th
Moger Levi J. 163 E. 17th

Montaye Abraham B. 225 Houston
New York.
Murlett Samuel, 80 Thompson
Peek M., W. 32d st.
Pasco & Co. 53 Ann
Porter John, 180 Wooster
Porter Theodore, 26 Allen
Postherius John, 67 Elm
Ritter George, 185 Rivington
Salyers M. & E. 129 Amos
Sammis Stephen H. 55 Gold
Schiele Geo. rear 165 Mulberry
Schneider Henry, 225 Rivington
Smith G. & Co. 470 Grand
Smith Lewis, 247 Spring
Smith Robert J. 189 & 191 Allen
Steurer Jacob, 80 W. 19th
Thompson John, 191 Church
Tweed & Bonnell, 5 Cherry & 10 Ridge
Wallace & M'Keever, 480 Water
White Ebenezer B. 90 Ann
Whitlock & Harris, 166 Fulton
Wilding Edward, 61 Willet
Zeller F. rear 56 & 58 Attorney

Niagara County.

Brown & Parmelee   *Wilson.*

Oneida County.

Empey A.   *Florence.*
Burlingame, Willard & Co. Clinton   *Kirkland.*
Tibbits W. H. Dominick st. *Rome.*
Matteson J.   do
Kellogg S. 25 Liberty   *Utica.*

Ontario County.

Collins Albert, Honoye *Richmond.*
Heming Charles, Geneva *Seneca.*

Orange County.

Moore & Owens,Washingtonville
Blooming Grove.
Crissey C. M.   *Chester.*
Gardiner B.   *Goshen.*
Gardiner C.
Van Sickle William, Unionville
Minisink.
Titus R.   do
Bridley Joseph C.   *Montgomery.*
Warring A. Water st. *Newburgh.*
Kain John, Colden
Demarest John, South Middletown   *Wallkill.*
Truesdall J., Amity   *Warwick.*

Otsego County.

Ackerman Edwin R.   *Edmeston.*
Bently George W., West
Ellery & Holder, Cooperstown   *Otsego.*
Edwards E. Cooperstown

Queens County.

Eldend T. E.   *Flushing.*

Rensselaer County.

Birge & Brother, cor. River & Adams   *Troy.*
Barrenger A. P. 279 River
Marble E. T. 279   do
Parkin Nathan, near the bridge

St. Lawrence County.

Estabrook J. W.   *Canton.*
Estabrook E. W.
Barnes & Kilmer   *Gouverneur.*
Jenness & Rice   *Hermon.*
Clark Simeon T.
Crowley Martin P.   *Massena.*
Burney Thomas
Allen George, Main st. Ogdensburgh   *Oswegatchie.*
Rugg George   *Potsdam.*
Hitchcock Willard M.
Rugg George & Co.
Derby Jesse   *Stockholm.*

Saratoga County.

Parker Benj.   *Providence.*
Lyons Hiram
Bentley Henry
Wait Andrew
Allen Job
Tabor Horace
Emmons E.   *Saratoga Springs.*

Seneca County.

Bull James L.   *Waterloo.*

Suffolk County.

Smith Carman   *Huntington.*

Ulster County.

Brinkerhoff John W. *New Paltz.*
Pettitt G. Pine Hill *Shandaken.*

Warren County.

Wilmarth M. L. Glenn's Falls
Queensbury.

Washington County.

Fenton C. & J.   *Greenwich.*
Warren J. R. North *White Creek.*

Wayne County.

Hecox S.   *Lyons.*

Westchester County.

Keeler D. Peekskill *Courtlandt.*

Wyoming County.

Davis Anthony   *Genesee Falls.*
Putnam L. B.   *Warsaw.*
Bartlett Alanson

Yates County.

Curtis Samuel F. (dealer) Penn Yan   *Milo.*
Strobridge Lyman H. (dealer) Potter Centre   *Potter.*

Chair Seat Makers.

Abel J. 290 Broome   *New York.*
Blestine John, 276 Rivington
Buckhardt F. 196 W. 21st
Lally Thomas, rear 231 Bowery
Matthews George D. 40 Canal
Steuver J. 80 E. 19th
Wessensee Andrew, 6th Av.

Champagne.

Irroy B. & S. 49 Broadway
New York.

Chasers of Jewelry and Silverware.

Baskirk J. 5 Dey   *New York.*
Batchelor Nathaniel, 90 Cortlandt
Bridgwood Thos. H. rear 17 John
Brownell Benjamin B. 66 Ann
Froment Anre. 63 Ann
Jennings H. W. 63 Ann
Jones William, 96 Nassau
Marshall Jos. H. 189 Broadway
Randolph J. F. 161 Fulton
Shipper Nicholas L.296 Broadway
Smith Jonathan & Son, 102 Reads
Walker & Randolph, 161 Fulton

Cheesemongers — (See also *Butter Dealers,* also *Provision Dealers.*)

Allen Uriah, 8 Washington mkt.
New York.
Brown Turner, 231 Fulton
Burr W. H. & H. 194 Washington

Bushfield J. 20 Washington mkt.
New York.
Clearwater R. 183 Washington
Collins Wm. 11 Washington mkt.
Denslow John W. 14   do
Emery & Godley, 14 & 15 do
Flint & Co. 5   do
Fonda Alfred & Co. 12   do
Fraser Cornelius, 7   do
Grant Gilbert W. 134   do
Haskill Wm. 17   do
Hayes Wm. H. 30   do
Hopper Samuel H. 13 Clinton mkt.
Howell Caleb, 182 Washington
Hewison George, Clinton mkt.
Jackson & Nix, 9 Wash'ton mkt.
Keephart Wm. 7   do
Main R. & Son, 32   do
Martin Joseph D. 39 Clinton mkt.
Martin Stephen, 18   do
Powell S. W. & J. 203 7th
Purdy Gilbert R. 38 Clinton mkt.
Richmond Ira D. 7 & 9 Washington market
Robinson Alexander C. & Co. 35 Clinton market
Smith J. & N. 236 Fulton
Turnbull & Leckler, 190 G'wich
Van Aukan B. H. & Co. 196 Washington
Wells J. & Co. 10 Wash'ton mkt.
Woodward R. S. 16   do

Cheese Press Manufacturer.

Madison County.

Everts Warren A. Erieville
Nelson.

Chemical Works.

Clinton County.

Taite & Weed, (Naptha and Acetate of Lime)   *Plattsburgh.*

Kings County.

Phœnix Chemical Works, John D. Perrin, agent, St. Felix st.
Brooklyn.
Kuh L. & Westfalls, Franklin Av.
Union Chemical Co. Kent Av. nr. Division
Kalbfleisch Martin, Green Point
Bushwick.

Oswego County.

Thrall George S.   *Mexico.*

Chemists.

Antisell Thomas, 148 Grand
New York.
Ball S. X. 126 Nassau
Ballard O. M. 46 Cortlandt
Barling John, Jane near West
Beastall Wm. 90 Fulton
Boetler & Co. 192 E. Broadway
Breakall J. B. 9th Av. bet. 24th & 25th
Breakell Ralph B. 291 6th Av.
Chilton James R. 55 Warren
Congreve J. M. 7 Greenwich Av.
Currie John H. 53 Prince
Davidson Alan M. 229 Monroe
Dixon James, 41 Barclay
Doremus & Harris. 179 Broadway
Feuchtwanger Lewis, 80   do
Grant Robert, 316   do
Jackson & Johnson, 139 & 291 Front
Jeffries & White, 129 Water
Kent Edward N. 116 John
Landschuetz & Riesberg, 246 5th
Lyon Emanuel, 420 Broadway
Mallerd Samuel, 166 Pearl
Moser T. 110 Hester

N. Y. Chemical Manufac. Co. 4
Park place   *New York.*
Paulus Gustavus, 179 William
Pollock Julius, 351 6th
Poulin, Rogers & Keeney, 13 W.
Broadway
Riesberg & Landschuetz, 18th st.

China and India Goods—Importers of.

Dow George W. & Co., 7 Burling
Slip   *New York.*
Davis & Kissam, 23 William
Moses Isaac & Brothers, 64 Beaver
Munsell & Whittemore, 29 Pine
Sale William A. jr. 124 Water

China, Glass and Earthenware Dealers.

*Marked thus * are Wholesale.*

Albany County.

M'Intosh W. & E. (Importers) 416
& 418 Broadway   *Albany.*
Van Heusen & Charles (importers)
62 & 64 State
Gregory & Co. (importers) 51
State
Lee Thomas, 98 State

Cayuga County.

Mason Z. M. 82 Genesee *Auburn.*

Chemung County.

Richards H. H.   *Elmira.*
Elmore J. N.

Columbia County.

Gifford A. cor. Warren & Front
    Hudson.
Geze H. cor. Warren & 6th

Duchess County.

Ransom J. (importers) 330 Main
    Poughkeepsie.
Farrington G. W. 266 Main

Erie County.

Patterson John, 168 Main *Buffalo.*
*Glenny William H. 62 & 166
Main

Greene County.

Hyde Nelson   *Catskill.*
Fiero Joshua, jr.

Herkimer County.

Holmes J. W. & Co. *Little Falls.*

Jefferson County.

Story Frederick   *Watertown.*

Kings County.

Field Thomas F. 167 Atlantic
    Brooklyn.
Ovington & Brothers, 184 Fulton
Coope David, (importer) 91 do
Muchmore Joseph F. 37 Myrtle
Av.
Mallery Henry, 15 Myrtle Av.
Titus Ansel, 145 Fulton
Stevenson Charles, 269 Adams
Watson J. L. 95 Myrtle Av.
Colyer C. W. & Co. 141 do
Buel A. G. 27 S. 7th *Williamsburgh.*
Philpitt Geo. B. 99 Grand
Stott Alex. & Co. 99 do

Livingston County.

Chapin B. I.   *Dansville.*
Crane O. T.

Madison County.

Curtis & Dana   *Cazenovia.*

Monroe County.

Davis Charles, Spencer's Basin
    Ogden.
Peck George (importer) 11 Buffalo
    Rochester.
Brackett A. J. (import) 15 Buffalo
Banker T. W. 176 State
Cushman & Brown, 190 State
Thompson & Hurd

New York County.

American Pottery Manufacturing
Company, 9 Cedar *New York.*
Andrews Henry T. 70 Catharine
Arnold & Hawley, 101 Pearl
Ashton William, 344 6th
Austin Isaac V. 579 4th
Baul Matthew, 189 9th Av.
Baxter Mary, 140 Orchard
Bedell D. B. & A. K. 30 9th Av.
Beekman James, 41½ 3d Av.
Betson James, 49½ Prince
Beynes John, 562 Grand
Billsland Martha. 701 Broadway
Birdsall Helen, 22 Greenwich Av.
Boswell Henry W. 244 Bowery &
227 Grand
Brady Patrick, 46 Catharine
Brennan James, 16 Clinton mkt
Bueles Peter, 115 Division
Burlow R. 76 Pearl
Cain Peter, 424 Grand
Cauldwell Ebenezer, 427 Pearl
Cauldwell E. & Co. 77 Pearl
Chauncey Wm. & Co. 10 Old slip
Cheeseman O. 136 Pearl
Clapp & Co. 138 William
Coffey John, 31 Carmine
Collamore Davis, 447 Broadway
Connor Mrs. N. 8th Av.
Cook Thomas, 98 Canal
Coppell Sarah, 325 Bleecker
Corlies Henry P. & C. 186 Pearl
Cox Bridget, 136 Orange
Cranna George, 86 9th Av.
Cross Alex. 184 8th Av.
Dare & Webb, 77 Catharine
Decker Richard, 101 Broad
Dellinger James A. 237 Hudson
Dermut Theodore, 28½ Carmine
Devries Solomon T. 142 Grand
Donnelly Hugh, 131 Houston
Duff Mary W. 383½ Bowery
Durell Joseph G. 462 Pearl
Edeler Francis A. 367 Bowery
Evans Joseph D. 89 Pearl
Filley William, 11 Old slip
Fitzpatrick Æneas, 150 Houston
Francis William A. 76 Dey
French William Y. 553 Grand
Frere & Conklin, 78 Pearl
Gardner William, 258 Greenwich
Garry John, 156 Lewis
Gervie Hannah, 39 Spring
Good Jane M. 1 Av. D.
Griffen J. W 264 Bleecker
Griffin J. 54½ Carmine
Gunton Mary A. 166 6th Av.
Hadley Frederick, 209 Greenwich
Hadley Jacob, 250 Grand
Hadley John H. 190 Division
Hadley John S. 190 Division
Hadley Ritter, 164 Bowery
Hains Elijah, 92 Delancy
Hall Suren, 5th Av.
Haydock H. W. & Co. 71 John
Heath W. E. 918 Broadway
Hillier William, 50 Lewis
Hitton John, 187 Division
Hobby James R. 351 Grand
Hoffman Peter, 294 Houston
Hughes Edward, 195 6th Av.
Hughes Edward, 225 Broome
Hunt Frederick P. 256½ Canal
Innes E. S. & Co. 108 Water
Jackson William, 262 Canal
Jones John, 321 Bowery
Kelly Thomas, 148½ Hester

Lawn Rosanna, 341 E. 13
    New York.
Lee Charles, 232 Bleecker
Lee Patrick, 379 Cherry
Lovett James, 269 Bowery
Lowerre John M. 90 Pearl
Lutz Stephen, 292 Av. A.
M'Coy Patrick, 93 Av. D.
M'Dermot Theodore, 28½ Carmine
M'Kinley William, 147 3d Av.
M'Manus Daniel, 142 Orange
M'Sorley Thomas, 86 8th Av.
Macdonald Francis, 240 1st Av.
Marlor H. 60 4th Av. & 25 Division
Marshall T. W. 184 Spring
Mayer T. J. & Joseph, 69 Pearl
Miller Caleb, 48 Av. D.
Miller & Smith, 80½ Pearl
Miller & St. John, 48 Av. D.
Miles Charles, 260 9th Av.
Monahan Edward, 78 Catharine
Moran John, 284 2d
Murphy Thomas, 62 3d Av.
Nevey Josephine, 87 Goerck
Newsham W. 296 Broadway
Niffin Samuel, 41 Spring
Noonan Thomas, 262 Greenwich
O'Hara James, 391 Broome
Page Pelatiah P. 17 Catharine
Parker Gaius, 361 6th Av.
Paul Mathew, 189 8th Av.
Peirce and Wilson, 76 Pearl
Prime L. W. & Co. 22 Division
Puels Peter, 115 Division
Roberts Robert, 343 Grand
Rose George, 4 James slip
Roswell H. W. 244 Bowery
Roth John, 18 Av. A
Rowland William F. 500 Hudson
Satterlee Douglass R. 8 Cedar
Sears Hector, 225 Greenwich
Seymour J. & J. F. 63 Pearl
Stevenson Henry, 270 Pearl
Stiles Joseph, 22 W. Broadway
Stonebridge J. & W. 312 Spring &
98 Pearl
Stott Alexander, 505 Grand
Sutton & Baker, 22 Cedar
Taylor, Wright & Kemp, 62 Pearl
Thomas Levy, 109 Canal
Toelen Daniel, 417 Cherry
Trainer H. 69 1st
Tredwell S. L. 195 Pearl
Underhill Levi, 148 Greenwich Av.
Underhill Moses, 359 Hudson
Underhill & Lloyd, 65 Pearl
Van Buren D. 22 Greenwich Av.
Van Ordt Anthony, 15 7th Av.
Walton John B. 338 Spring
Wild J. 262 Canal
Willett G. & Son, 274 Pearl
Willetts S. & E. 113 Water
Williams James, 186 Pearl
Williams Peter, 96 Catharine
Woods John, 40 Catharine

Oneida County.

Butler W. C. 159 & 161 Genesee
    Utica.
Whiting J. 123   do

Onondaga County.

Pierce S. P. (importer) Salina st.
Syracuse   *Salina.*

Ontario County.

Lacy J. W. Geneva   *Seneca.*

Orange County.

Jennings N. (wholesale) *Goshen.*
Falls Hiram, 66 Water *Newburgh.*
Lockwood I. N. 7 do
Sweezy J. G. South Middletown
    Wallkill.

Oswego County.

Baker C. N. cor. 1st & Cayuga
    Oswego.
M'Cue James, 4 Phoenix block 1st
Mallen & James, 7 Eagle block do

Rensselaer County.

Aldrich A. W. 6 Fake's row
   Lansingburgh.
Slason A. (importers) 165 River
   Troy.
Pierce & King (importers & wholesale dealers), 235 River
Farris & Rockwell (importers), 263 River
Weed & Hamblin (importers), 345 River
Crane A. 52½ Congress

Schenectady County.

Ohlen Geo. 47 State, *Schenectady*
Davis J. H. 152 do

Ulster County.

Tappan G. Rudolph *Kingston.*

Washington County.

Adams J. P., Canal st. *Whitehall.*

Wyoming County.

Fuller E. L. *Warsaw.*

China, Glass and Earthen ware—Importers of.

Alcock Richard E. 42 Stone
   New York.
Arnold & Howley, 101 Pearl
Baker, Griffen & Co. 6 Liberty
Beach & Vandewater, 178 Washington
Barlow Richard, 78 Pearl
Cartlidge Charles & Co. 106 Water
Cheeseman Oscar, 136 Pearl & 102 Water
Collamore Ebenezer, 293 Broad'y
Curtis & Lumby, 2 Liberty
Dalesme A. & Co. 7 Pine
Dare & Webb, 77 Catharine
Davenport T. & J. S. 174 Wash'ton
Decker Richard, 101 Broad
Didier E. 43 John
Douglas Brothers, 73 Broad
Drummond J. P. 47 Maiden lane
Gill Theophilus A. 105 Liberty
Hammersley William S. & Co. 11 Old slip
Harris J. W. & T. 83 Water
Haviland D. G. & D. 47 John
Haviland R. F. 82 Maiden lane
Jackson Job, 113 Water
Jackson John C. 113 Water
Lawrence & Veltman, 47 Cortl'dt
Leigh Charles C. 230 Bleecker
• Mumford Benjamin A. 101 Pearl
Moore Daniel. 115 Maiden lane
Moore Thomas D. & Co. 89 Water
Ogsbury Francis W. 56 Cortlandt
Perier Alphonse, 287 Pearl
Quettier George, 119 Liberty
Sears Hector, 226 Greenwich
Seymour J. & J. F. 63 Pearl
Shaw James M. 70 Chatham
Skillin Simeon D. 101 Water
Stouvenel J. & Co. 737 Broadway, 3 John & 58 & 60 Vesey
Taylor, Wright & Kemp, 62 Pearl
Thomas Levi, 100 Canal
Thomson & Parish, 79 Pearl & 46 Stone
Tredwell S. L. 196 Pearl
Veghte & Bergh, 43 Water
Veltman Hiram & Co. 35 Cortla'dt
Weed William C. 59 Pearl
Wetmore R. C. & Co. 85 Water
Williams J. 186 Pearl
Willets Oliver & Son, 275 Pearl
Willetts S. & E. 113 Water
Winkley Henry, 101· Water
Wood Frederick, 43 Water
Woram Haughwout, 561 & 563 Broadway

China Painter.

Maddock & Leigh, rear 29 Spruce
   New York.

Chiropodists.

Berhard Madame, 425 Pearl
   New York.
Littlefield J. 41 Merchants' Ex.
Shiriakoff Stephen, 223 Broadway

Chocolate and Cocoa.

Corell John, 172 Forsyth
   New York.
Effray Felix, 457 Broadway
Goavert Joseph, 376 Pearl
Kitchins G. 90 Elizabeth
Mendes Eugene, 192 Fulton
Mitchell Michael, 154 Attorney
Poillon Peter, rear 90 Elizabeth
Rey John B. 102 Front

Chocolate and Cocoa Manufacturers.

Albany County.

Payne & M'Naughton, 7 Broadway
   Albany.

Duchess County.

Outwater Wm. B. *Hyde Park.*

Kings County.

Crommelin J. R. Lafayette st.
   Brooklyn.
Crommelin F. D. P. Hudson Av.

Chronometers.

Bliss & Creighton, 44 Fulton
   New York.
Blunt E. & G. W. 179 Water
Eggert D. & Son, 239 Pearl
Giroud Victor, 394 Broadway
Glover Henry, 119 Wall
Negus P. S. & Co. 84 Wall
Robjohn Thomas, 222 Water
Stewart Arthur, 68 Merchants' Exchange

Churn Manufacturer.

Monroe County.

Rich J. C. (patent) *Penfield.*

Cider and Vinegar.

Baker A. D. 6 South *New York.*
Bogart Isaac, 6 Front
Brown Leonard, 90 W. 2d
Crane Josiah & Son, 6 South
Edwards J. D. 102 Barclay
Edwards Moses C. 4 South
Jackson Nathan, 184 3d Av.
Osgood Samuel, 27th st. 1st Av.
Tucker Albert. 7 South
Voss John, E. 19th between Broadway & 5th Av.

Cigar Box Makers.

Kirby Caleb, rear 9 Franklin
   New York.
Klingdhoefer Conrad, 411 Monroe

Cigar Dealers.

Adams W. A. 334 Water *New York.*
Anderson J. & Co. 106 Broadway
Ashby Isaac, 50 8th Av.
Bacharach N. 592 Grand
Bear & Tanenbaum, 167 Av. D

Bedin Edward, 100 Nassau
   New York.
Bahrend Edward, 94 3d Av.
Blunck Charles, 278 8th Av.
Boves Jose M. 57 Pearl
Bower Morris, 4th Av.
Brettell Edward W. 216 Wooster
Brophy Timothy, 816 Hudson
Bruck Max, 118½ Norfolk
Bundy Abram, 275 Houston
Bunzl J. & Dormitzer. 176 Canal
Burr Catharine P. 212 Broadway
Burrucker Frederick, 178 Walker
Burrucker J. 178 Division
Burrucker John P. 113 Hester
Bushman John, 463 Greenwich
Carroll S. 226 12th
Centee Jonas, 12 West
Cohen Moses S. 26 New
Cook Charles J. 45 Canal
Cook George H. 391 Hudson
Cook John, 34½ Bowery
Connor Hugh, 254 Walker
Cornish John, 90 Av. D
Costa John B. 69 Barclay
Covington J. T. 262 3d Av.
Crepos Carlos R. 186 Chatham
Crossman Anthony, 303 Houston
Darling Jonathan C. 415½ Broad'y
Dermott Wm. 25th st. 9th Av.
Duntze & Dormitzer, 176 Canal
Duryee Daniel, 253 Water
Eckart Charles, 11½ Bowery
Eitel George M. 262 West
Ely Benjamin, 401 Greenwich
Erler Charles J. 221 Front
Ettinger Samuel, 81½ Bowery
Fatman Lewis & Co. 200 Front
Fick William, 214 Division
Fields Susan, 148 Centre
Fountain John M. 81 Av. B
Gilsey Peter. 120, 169, 559 Broadway, & 34½ Bowery
Ginoohio L. & Co. 491 Washington
Goldsmith J. 366 Houston
Gould John W. 107 Av. C
Gray William H. 28 Thomas
Haddock W. J. & R. 554 Hudson
Hamilton Harriet M. 556½ Pearl
Hanna Matthew, 271 6th Av.
Hart Henry B. 21 Old slip
Hefner John, 166 Stanton
Heilbut S. 87 Canal
Heins Margaret. 204 Cherry
Henriques David M. 2 Maiden lane
Hill William H. 266 Spring
Hinds Mark. 204½ Cherry
Hitzelberger Chris'tr. 315 Bowery
Hoffman & Schubart, 362 Division & 72½ Bowery
Joseph John, 7th Av.
Kagel Gotlieb, 203 Chatham
Kennagh Henry, 116 3d Av.
Kennedy William D. 226 Centre
Kenneth & Laverty, 108 Wall
Kirby Caleb, 121 Bowery
Klasset John, 9 Essex
Kuster Hermann. 20½ Stanton
Lalor Michael. 211 2d
Larkin Charles, 5 Av. A
Lepine Mitchell, 72 Division
Ledley James, 227 Delaney
Lichdenberg Benj. 189 Houston
Lichtenhein Simon A. 54 Bowery
Lockhart John. 166 3d Av.
M'Alpine David H. 86 Catharine •
M'Coy James, 102 Bowery
M'Donnell Margaret, 115 W. 21st
Mahler Gustavus, 365½ Bowery
Mally Godfred, 61 Anthony
Martin John, 50 8th Av.
Marcus Joseph, 358 Hudson & 184 Varick
Marcus & Goodman, 443 Hudson
Menike Julie, 47 Canal
Metzger Susman, 250 Division
Metzger M. 9 Peck Slip
Meyers H. 142 Division
Miller Xavier, 186 8th Av.
Miller David, 254 8th Av.
Molau Chas. A. 73 Wall
Morrell Alexander W. 294 10th

Morris Edwin, 305 Broadway
New York.
Murphy Patrick, 256 Grand
Myres Lewis, 559 Grand
Newcombe Jane, 145 Broadway
Newman D. 61 William
Nolan Geo. 296 Houston
Payne,Joseph R. 361 Pearl
Oldenbuttel Henry, 192½ William
Oliver Ebenezer, 106 Delancy
Olmstead Joseph, 575½ Grand
Rader Maximilian, 46 Chatham
Rahur Robert, 192 Division
Read William, 305 Spring
Reid John H. 165 Chatham
Reilly Isabella, 41 Av. D.
Riley Mrs. 31 Av. D.
Rippon Casimer, 130½ Bowery
Rodriguez L. T. 331 Spring
Rosenstein David, 302 Houston
Salinero Francis, 295½ Grand
Salinero John, 327 Spring
Salinger Isaac, 12 Ludlow
Schark Louis, 155½ Canal
Scars E. P. 38 W. Broadway
Shaffner Daniel, 64 Av. B
Shaphoff Charles E. 240 Division
Shollbut Simon. 87 Canal
Sheppard David 460 Hudson
Simmert August, 50 Hudson
Simonson A. 152 W. Broadway
Simonton Samuel, 60 Leonard
Skiffington Rebecca, 96 Centre
Smith Levi. 30 Houston
Snowhill Levi S. 6 Cortlandt
Snyder H. & W. J. 81 Beaver
Story Henry E. 263 Hudson
Straus Meyer, 289 Houston
Straus M. S. 92 Houston
Tanenbaum Isaac. 107 Avenue D
Taylor Geo. W. 339 Houston
Taylor Mary, 339 Houston
Telle Hamilton C. 347 6th Av.
Thornal J. & Co. 603 Broadway
Tilleson Hans S. 132 Cherry
Tillotson Elias, 71 Hester
Van Deuren Abraham S. W. 137½ Division
Vonsalzen Henry, 196 Division
Volger Charles H. 66 Av.D
Ward Caleb, 68 8th Av.
Warner Simon, 100 Stanton
Warsawer Simon, 135½ Canal
Wasserdiettinger Jacob, 9 Clinton
Wilson J. C. 223 Greenwich
Williams & Co. 52 Bowery
Winser Edward, 81 9th Av.
Wyre Andrew, 438½ Broadway
Yasinski Casmer W. 205 Spring

Cigar Importers.

Allnutt T. 464 Broadway
New York.
Angusto M. 111 Water
Austin C. E. 85 Wall
Bances Francisco J. 167 William
Beanville John P. 102 Front
Beers & Bogart, 177 South
Belmont Simon E. 246 Centre
Boutete Antoine, 14½ Carmine
Butler Francis, 205 Water
Bretzfeld G. 44 Division
Celcis Andres. 100 Nassau
De MaCarty G. 78 Broadway
Derby Aaron C. 105 Fulton & 66 Ann
De Ruga Manuel. 20 S. William
Faber G. W. 101 Front
Francia & Co. 83 Front
Gilsey P. 130 Broadway
Griffith Edward, 142 Front
Hanau Philip, 203 Bowery
Henriques A. 2 Maiden lane
Henriques David M. 608 Broadway
Hoffman & Schubart, 262 Division
Lemon William C. 4 Wall & 213 Duane
Lillie & Razines, 109 Water
Manzanedo Joe, 128 Front
Norales & Lunar, 118½ Nassau

Morris Edwin, 305½ Broadway
New York.
Rader Maximilian, 46 Chatham
Renaud & Francois, 21 Beaver
Ryder A. F. 67 Centre
Saddler James, 234 Broadway
Salisbury S. 171   do
Samanos Augustus A. 94 do
Satrustequi Patrick, 6 do
Seixas Benjamin M. 3 Maiden la.
Siergriest Joseph, 557 Broadway
Skiffington R. 96 Centre
Straus Myer. 92 Houston
Symington & Kelly, 111 Front
Taylor Moses & Co. 44 South
Thomas William H. 126 Front
Thornal J. & Co. 603 Broadway
Trujillo & Barreiras, 106 Wall
Tappert & Co. 243 Bowery
Williams M. A. & Co. 51 Bowery

Cigar Manufacturers.

Albany County.

Huschberg Henry,150 Washington
Albany.

Cayuga County.

Richardson J. B. 69 Genesee
Auburn.

Erie County.

Smith T.   *Black Rock.*

Cigar Makers.

Acorn Peter & J. 230 Canal
New York.
Adgne Samuel, 81½ Bowery
Adler Seigmund, 252 Delancy
Adrian Michael J. 300 Division
Akers Robert S. 57 Centre
Alberti Otto & Co. 369½ Pearl
Allnut Zuchariah, 464 Broadway
Altmayer Samson, 236 5th
Andres Andres, 166 Second
Appleby Leonard. 119 Water
Atkinson Thomas, 28 Columbia
Bacharsch Nathan, 593½ Grand
Baker Peter. 318½ Grand
Beach Joseph, 219 Greenwich
Bear Bernard, 284 Greenwich
Bechtold Simon, 115 Pitt
Bell D. 315 Bowery
Bellmont S. E. 246 Centre
Benjamin M. 205 Broome
Berger John, 448 Cherry
Biggs Edward, 87 Columbia
Block Isaac, 106 Suffolk
Bojanus Ernest. 129 3d
Boyd James. 547 Grand
Brand Joel, 333 Bowery
Brandt George F. 40 Beekman
Brettenbach Samuel, 249 Canal
Bretzfeld George, 44 Division
Briedgman Henry. jr. 39 8th Av.
Briggs E. 90 Houston
Brower A. J. 1 Odd Fellows' Hall, Centre st.
Bundy Abram
Burr Mrs. C. F. 212 Broadway
Burridge Thomas, 431 Water
Burracker John, 178 Division
Bushman J. D. 463 Greenwich
Butler Francis, 205 Water
Camer Andrew, 481 Houston
Cohn Meyer A. 192 Houston
Commerce Matheas, 145 G'wich
Cook Charles J. 45 Canal & rear 10 Crosby
Cornish J. 90 Av. D
Cornish Wm. E. 354 Bowery
Daly John T. 106 Wall
Davis David M. 298 Delancy
Dedley James, 227 Delancy
Detmer George, 326½ Bleecker
Dormitzer & Co. 76 Catharine

Doush Peter, 1 Walnut *New York*
Droll George, 552 4th
Drummond M. J. 234 Grand
Eisenman Joseph, 76 Ridge
Fatman Louis & Co. 200 Front
Ferreira Emanuel, 368 Cherry
Ferst Abraham & Son. 370½ Grand
Fetters Henry F. 65 Walnut
Fick David, 243½ Grand
Fick Wm. 214 Division
Fields S. 148 Centre
Fischel Albert, 154 Attorney
Fisher Julius, 157 Washington
Fisk Samuel, 90 Clinton
Fredericks Richard, 31 Av. C
French & Swartz, 260 South
Frenk Louisa, 388 Greenwich
Friedman E. 267 2d
Fritz Charles, 52 Av. A
Fountain J. M. 81 Av. B
Ganther Philip, 283 6th Av.
Gebman John, 126 Willet
Gent John U. 170 Walker
Gilsey P. 160 & 569 Broadway, also 34½ Bowery
Ginocchis & Co. 491 Washington
Godfrey Abram, 99 Reade
Goodman Aaron. 7 1st Av.
Gould John W. 107 Av. C
Grambes George, 168 Delancy
Grossman A. 303 Houston,
Hahn Abraham, 129½ Pitt
Hall Joseph, 80 Barclay
Hancock Hewlitt, 243 Greenwich
Hardy Charles, 117 Av. D
Harman Abram, 21 Av. C
Harman G. 190 Bowery
Hart Elias C. 133 9th Av.
Haslach P. 79 Thompson
Hazelbarth A. 496 Houston
Heiser Henry, 157 Bowery
Herman Abraham, 82 Ridge
Hertz John C. 310 Grand
Hempel Euger, 905½ Division
Hildebrandt Charles, 140 Lewis
Hill Wm. H. 265 Spring
Hinch & Schroder, 49 3d Av.
Hoffman Jacob, 116½ 7th Av.
Hoffman & Schubart, 262 Division & 72½ Bowery
Hollander Lewis, 44 Columbia
Hoole John, 79 Essex
Horvetz Raphael, 198 Delancy
Hull Henry, 133 Lewis
Hutmacher Jule, 168 Washington
Hyer Julius, 18 Av. D
Jarard Alfred, 305 Rivington
Jeckel Fred. W. 211 2d
Jerrard Allen, rear 145 Delancy
Kaylor Valentine. 104 7th Av
Kelley William, 86 Houston
Kip James, 21 Av. D.
Kleiner Nathan, 196 Pitt
Knappman Charles, 191 Cherry
Knauer A. 62 Av. A.
Kraus Aaron, 243 Broome
Kroeter Charles, 396½ Greenwich
Labl Laser, 55 Attorney
Lancraft Joseph, 55 Houston
Land Theodore, 393 Pearl
Larkin C. F. 6 Av. A.
Lear Herrman O. 360 Grand
Ledley James, 227 Delancy
Lehrberger Isaac, 208 Stanton
Lehrberger Samuel, 190 Columbia
Lepine Mitchell, 12 Division
Lewis Charles, 54 4th Av.
Lewis J. 97 Columbia
Lichtenhein David, 309 Division
Lichtenheis S. A. 54 Broadway
Lichtenstadter S. 206 Delancy
Lincke Alexander, 131 Reade
Luckey Samuel, 245 Bleecker
Ludwig Philip, 25 Av. C.
M'Alpin J. 96 Catharine
M'Coy Edward, 16 Canal
M'Coy E. & J. B. 102 Broadway
M'Entee Jas. 186 W. 18th
Macus Joseph, 164 Varick
Mahler G. 256½ Bowery
Mason John W. 31½ Carmine
Metzger M. 9 Peck slip

Metzger S. 250 Division
New York.
Meyer Christian F. 122 Prince
Meyer Frederick, 122 Prince
Meyer J. 18 Av. D.
Meyers Herse, 142 Division
Meyers Matthias. 62 Walnut
Miller Isaac, 70 Essex
Mitchell Peter, 410 Grand
Morrell A. W. 394 10th
Murphy Ann, 75 6th Av.
Myer Benjamin, 205 Broome
Niemann A. 8 Astor house
Olmstead J. 576½ Grand
Olmstead T. W. between 23d & 24th sts. 9th Av.
Orth Paul, 537½ Pearl
Ottes Joseph, 57 Ludlow
Pavie Edmund A. 107 Houston
Peters Charles, 101½ Pitt
Pforzheim Wolf, 209 Delancy
Phelen William W. 392 Pearl
Piats Adam, 47 Av. A.
Porras & Brook, 189 Houston
Print Samuel, 322 Bowery
Rader M. 45 Chatham
Rapp Goldsmith, 136 Houston
Read William, 305 Spring
Reid John H. 166 Chatham
Rezogatii Joseph, rear 144 Elm
Richards Robert G. 117 8th Av.
Riker Alfred, 3 Bedford
Rippon C. 130½ Bowery
Rodefeld Henry, 365 Madison
Rodregine Charles, 106 Chatham
Rodriguez L. I. 331 Spring
Rogers Charles, 151 Duane
Rohler Robert. 192 Division
Boome Edward, 134 Water
Rosenbaum & Bradig, 77 Centre
Roserfeld Louis, 196 Rivington
Rosenstein David, 302 Houston
Royce John E. 207 8th Av.
Ruhl Isaac G. 200 William
Sax John, 208 Rivington
Schaffner Daniel, 64 Av. C.
Shapnoff H. B. 240 Division
Schrader G. F. 64 Av. C.
Schreiber Christian, 139 Centre
Schondorf Charles, 235 Houston
Schulhoff A. 164 3d
Schwabbe Henry, 177 Bowery
Secor Huyler, 265½ 3d Av.
Shark Louis. 155½ Canal
Shea John, 324 Madison
Sheppard David H. 469 Hudson
Shoudarf Chas. 235 Houston
Shriver C. 139 Centre & 165 Spring
Silberstader W. 382 Grand
Smith Chas. K. jr. 1 Sheriff
Smith Walter T. 86 Mercer
Snyder J. J. 17 Laurens
Soneld Samuel, 609 Grand
Speaights C. 73 Bowery
Stahl Hugo, 199 Delancy
Staffer James, 70 Orchard
Steimke Diedrick H. 203½ Centre
Strauss M. S. 289 Houston
Tallman Ralph, 136 Houston
Terush Peter, 1 Walnut
Thompson Thomas, 220 5th
Tillesen Hans S. 20 4th Av.
Toupett Francis C. 240 Bowery
Trask William F. 162 3d Av.
Troll George, 552 4th
Van Pelt Jacob, 133 Orchard
Van Salzen Henry, 196 Division
Volz Adam, 41 Av. B.
Wade Mrs. J. 69 Division
Ward Caleb, 70 8th Av.
Warsawer L. 137 Canal
Wayne Thomas J. 19½ Chatham
Weber August, 156½ William
Werner Simon, 100 Stanton
Williams M. A. & Co. 51 Bowery
Willson Benj. C. 351 Broome
Wilson John C. 223 Greenwich
Writer W. 202 Broome
Zenke Adolph, 269½ Pearl
Zimmerman Fred. 70 Thompson
Zoeller F. A. 404 2d Av.

Orange County.

Mount Wm. Edenville *Warwick.*
Hoyt W. H.

Ulster County.

M'Clung Anthony *Kingston.*
Myyea Lorenzo *Saugerties.*

City Despatch Posts.

Boyd John T. 45 William
New York.
Figgins Daniel, 235 Grand & 142 Fulton
Swartz Aaron, 7 Chatham Square

Clergymen.

To denote the different denominations the following abbreviations will be used : (B) Baptist, (C) Congregationalist, (F B) Freewill Baptist, (Ch) Christian, (L) Lutheran, (M E) Methodist Episcopal, (M) Methodist, (D R) Dutch Reformed, (F) Friends, (E) Episcopal, (P) Presbyterian, (R C) Roman Catholic, (Ut) Unitarian, (Uv) Universalist.

Albany County.

Kennedy D. (D R) *Albany.*
Wyckof I. N. (D R)
Lindsey J. (M E)
Clarke J. (M E)
Hall B. M. (M E)
Fraser J. (M E)
Starks D. (M E)
Noble Edward (M E)
Sprague W. B. (P)
Campbell J. N. (P)
Campbell W. H. (D R)
Potter Horatio (E)
Kip W. I. (E)
Selkirk E. (E)
James W. (P)
Pohlman I. N. (L)
Demerest — (D R) *Reedsville*
Berne.
Curtis — (L) *do*
Sayre E. (M E)
Lansing J. A. (D R) *Bethlehem.*
Willis R. (D R)
Covel S. (M E)
Peltz Philip (D R) *Coeymans.*
Hoyt P. L. (M E)
Wright D. J. (M E)
Jolly H. A. (M E)
Crouuse A. (L) *Guilderlands.*
Petman —
Davis William (D R)
Jones D. A. (D R) *Knox.*
Chase John (M E)
Washburn Robert (P E)
Rensselaerville.
Witherspoon A. (M E)
Doe — (M E)
Haynes H. (B)
Cornell N. (B)
Drake I. (F)
Witherill M. (M E) *Waterviet.*
Gregory O. H. (D R) West Troy
Wycoff T. (D R) *do*
Burrows — (B) *do*
Yates James F. (M E) *do*
Houghtaling J. B. (M E) do
Pierson Thomas W. (M E) do
Leonard Jacob (M E) Cohoes
Stanton J. (P) *do*
Van Wreath B. (R C) *do*
Shackelford Jr W. (P) *do*

Alleghany County.

Hull N. V. (B) *Alfred.*
Wakeman J. (P) *Almond.*
Elliott Jesse (B)
Noel — (B) *Amity.*

Hammond — (P) *Amity.*
Burlingame — (M)
Rosin A. (C) *Andover.*
Hunt E. (M)
Hall N. E. (B) *Angelica.*
Brownell Veramis (M E)
Thibon Lewis (E)
Thomas B. (B) *Belfast.*
Russell Daniel (P)
Parker Schuyler (M E)
Brownell V. (M) *Birdsall.*
Cherryman Reuben (B) *Bolivar.*
Pratt E. B. (M E)
Anson Leonard (B) *Cuba.*
Smith — (B)
Spear Francis (B) *Clarkville.*
Backus William (P) *Friendship.*
Call O. B. (B)
Robbins B. F. (B)
M'Kinstry W. (M)
M'Creery Jos. jr. (M E)
Wellman A.
Holliday J.
Weeber W. M.
Haskell W. M. (M E) Short Tract
Granger.
Bigabee — (M)
Bailey James (F B) Little Genesee
Genesee.
Green Henry P. (F B) *do*
Van Antwerp (P) *Hume.*
Babcock — (B) Independence Centre
Independence.
Graham — (M) Whitesville
Chase John B. (B)
Parker — (M) Black Creek
New Hudson.
Emery — (P) *do*
Doolittle Miles (P) *Rushford.*
Harris E. L. (B)
M'Ewen John (M E)
Thomas E. (M E)
Hunt Benjamin (Uv)
Hammond Nathaniel (P) *Scio.*
Babcock Ronse (B)
Coldman M. (B) *West Almond.*
Cherryman — (T B) *Wirt.*

Broome County.

Powell O. S. (P) Chenango Forks
Barker.
Pitts L (M) *do*
Wilcox J. (M) *do*
Howrigan J. (R C) *Binghamton.*
Andrews Edward (E)
Palmer N. (E) Harpersville
Colesville.
Bourne C. C. (B) *do*
Huntington D. (E) *do*
Hoyt Wm. W. (P) Nineveh
Wood M. (P) *Conklin.*
Arnold C. C. (M)
French — (P) Centre Lisle
Lisle.
Boyce Wm. C. (P) *Maine.*
Gates Wm. (B)
Church J. (B)
Cole U. J. (B) Whitney's Point
Triangle.
Lewis J. N. (P) *do*
Wakeman M. M. (P) *Union.*
Silsby W. (M)
Pine N. (C) Union Centre
Boswell J. R. (M) do
Hills J. M. (B) *do*
Gilbert H. W. (P) *Windsor.*
Graigg A. (P)
Tryon T. D. (M)

Cattaraugus County.

Bruce N. F. (E) *Ellicottville.*
Morris Thomas (S)
Cowles S. (P)
Richmond C. M. (B)
Huft S. (M)
Foot John (P) *Franklinville.*
Bewis — (B)
Nobles — (M)
Phillips W. F. (B) *Freedom.*
Jenkins David (B)
Flynn Wm. H. (F B) *Elton.*

Lacky Benj. (M)   *Great Valley.*
Scofield Isaac (M E)   *Leon.*
Blackford Ira (M E)
Gowdy G. J. Eddysville *Mansfield.*
Davis Eber (M)   *New Albion.*
Hunt W. I. (C)   *Perrysburgh.*
Barnes N. H. (C)
Tackett I. H. (M E)
Allerson ——— (B)
Baker C. S. Gowanda   *Persia.*
Kent John F. do
Rice James H. do
Taylor E. (C)   *Randolph.*
Moore H. H. (M E)
Howard I. (B)
Plump H. U. (F B) East Randolph
Searl S. (M)   *Rice.*
Simmons A. (M)
Hall A. S.   *South Valley.*

Cayuga County.

Ayrault Walter (E)   *Auburn.*
Mills Henry (P)
Hickok L. F. (P)
Hopkins Samuel M. (P)
Smith J. F. (P)
Lathrop Leonard E. (P)
Nelson Henry A. (P)
Fearne W. H. (M)
Warner George W. P.   *Aurelius.*
White W. W. (M) Cayuga
Goodell William (P)
Pomeroy Medad (P)
Sawyer G.(M) Weedsport *Brutus.*
Avery Charles E. (P) do
Peck Whitman (P)   *Genoa.*
Franklin Wm. S. (P) 4 corners
Morgan John C. (P)   *Ira.*
Weaver L. G. (M)   *Ledyard.*
Hall H. C. (M)   *Mentz.*
Williams William (P)
Graves A. S. (M)   *Moravia.*
Conklin Luther (P)
Hamilton A. (M)   *Owasco.*
Baker Joseph D. (P)   *Scipio.*
Lamkin D. (M)
Anderson Charles   *Bennett.*
Barber Elihu (P)   *Springport.*
Johnson Charles (P) *Summer Hill.*
Everett Ebenezer (P)   *Victory.*

Chautauque County.

Broadhead R. J. (M)   *Busti.*
Pullock Wm. (Ch)
Kidder F. (B)
Colman E. (C)
Edson ——— (C)   *Carroll.*
Hibbard O. D. (C)
Sage J. H. (C)   *Charlotte.*
Leach ——— (M)
King ——— (M)
Burrill ——— (M)
Moran Robert S. (M E) Mayville
          Chautauque.
Hallock John K. (M E) Mayville
Illeloy ——— (B) do
Phelps H. (B) Dewittville
Willoughby B. C. (B)
          Cherry Creek.
Johnson O. B.
Street O. (C). Jamestown *Ellicott.*
Blim ——— (P) do
Gray A. W. (P) do
Norton N. (M E) do
Rathbun B. (B) do
Hequenborg C. L. (P) do
Todd Wm. (P) Ellington
Lighthall ——— (B) do
Peat John, (M E) do
Rowley F. S. V.   *French Creek.*
Haling Daniel
Rous James H.
Scott John, (M E) Vermont *Gerry.*
King David (M E)
Walth ———, Silver Creek
          Hanover.
Williams W. (B) Irving
Chapin J. E. (M E) Forestville
Churchill S. C. (M) do
Wood ——— (B) do
Bennett Jas. (B)

Sisson H. S.   *Harmony.*
Robinson John (M E) Panama
Burgess Alvan (M E) Ashville
Muse Eauntley (M E) do
M'Kinnie ——— (C) Fredonia
          Pomfret.
Griswold ——— (B) Fredonia
Tyler ——— (E) do
Thomas Sam. C. (M E) do
Stillman ———, (C) Dunkirk
Lane L. F. (P)   *Portland.*
Blynn Theodore (M E)
Lahatt Charles (B)
Roberts ——— (B)
Orton S. G. (P)   *Ripley.*
Uncles Joseph (M E)   *Sheridan.*
Henry John N. (M E)   *Villanova.*
Tinker Reuben P. (P)   *Westfield.*
Arey Chas. (E)
Whallon J. H. (M E)

Chemung County.

Hurd ———   *Big Flats.*
Saunders ———
Whiting Francis (P)
Nivens E.   *Catharine.*
Bull J. M. (M E)
Goodrich Chas. (P) Havana
Huggins Morrison (P) do
Bowne C. L. (M E)
Wilson Moses E. (E)
Hewitt ———   *Cayuta.*
M'Dowell O. (M E)
Wheeler C. (M E)   *Chemung.*
Shearer B. (M E) Salubria *Dis.*
Sheardown T. do
Hull Andrew (E)   *Elmira.*
Fowler P. H. (P)
Crow Moses (M E)
Bush Leverett (E)
Dickinson E. W.
Sheridan John
Pratt E. G. Horse Heads
Carr C. C. (P) do
Cranmer E. G.
Andrews Wm.   *Erin.*
Rumsey Earl
Goldsmith Benj. M. (P) *Southport.*
Colson Ebenezer (M E)
Shaw J. (M E) Millport *Veteran.*
Shaw ———, do

Chenango County.

Foote I. (E)   *Eainbridge.*
Davison J. (P)
Beecher ——— (M)
Virgil A. (B) South Bainbridge
Hobb ——— (Uv) do
Robinson ——— (B) Bennettsville
Hendricks —— (B) do
Tompkins W. (P)   *Columbus.*
Bartlett ——— (Uv)
Hoyt J. B. (P)   *Coventry.*
Thurston E. D. (M)
Parker Aaron (P)
Orten A. G. (P)   *Greene.*
Rogers F. (E)
Van Horn I. W. (B)
Porter G. P. (M)
Foot Israel (E)   *Guilford.*
Gay Albert (B)
White W. (M)
James Justus (P) Gailford Centre
Bennett ——— (B)   *Macdonough.*
Wright S. (P)   *New Berlin.*
Post G. F. (B)
Fox R. (M)
Whittingham R. (E)
Chamberlin ———, (B) South New
Berlin
Burritt C. D. (M)   *Norwich.*
Clark Daniel, jr. (P)
Stone M. (C B)
Goodale Samuel (E)
Turner H.   *Otselic.*
Lawton ———, (B)   *Pharsalia.*
Fairchild J. (B)
Lee H. W. (P)   *Pitcher.*
Crandall Nelson (B)
Peck L. H. (M)
Carver Shubael (P)

Davis ——— (M)   *Pitcher.*
Williams B. S.   *Plymouth.*
Beecher E. B.
Crandall J. M. South Plymouth
Tuthill A. C. (P)   *Sherburne.*
Fox J. W. (C)
Munford ——— (P)
Thurston D. W. (M)
Wilson W. D. (E)
Moore ———, (F B)
Rowland B. (F B)

Clinton County.

Mattocks John (P) Keeseville
          Au Sable.
Kingley W. (B) do
Grey W. P. (M E) do
Foster L. S. (W M) do
M'Donald M (R C) do
Luther Z. M. P. (P) *Beekmantown.*
Pegg John (M)
Brinkerhoff A. D. (C) *Champlain.*
Chamberlain ———, (M)
Lappett Joseph (R C)
Barnes ———, East Chazy *Chazy*
Taylor ——— do
Johnson ———, West Chazy
Blake ———, do
Seaton Charles   *Mooers.*
Plumbley J.

Columbia County.

Ham ——— (M)   *Ancram.*
Woodbridge T. (R)   *Austerlitz.*
Utley S. (C)
Scobey Zeph. D. (M E)   *Canaan.*
Betts ———, (P B)
Wicks J. (C) Canaan Four Corn.
Kerr Geo. (M E) do
Kent B. (P) Canaan Centre
Scarritt ———, (B) Flat Brook
Seymour T. (M E)   *Chatham.*
Pierce W. W. (M E)
Stover Samuel (M E)
Forter E. S. (D R) Chatham Four
Corners
Geralds Thomas (M E) New Con-
cord
Furgeson A. H. (M E)
Benjamin D. C. Chatham Centre
Boice J. C. (D R)   *Claverack.*
Himrod J. S. (D R)
Tiffany F. T. (E)
Dewey J. C. (L) Churchtown
Wackerhagan A. (L)   *Clermont.*
Murden B F. (D R)   *Copake*
Ham Jeremiah (M E)
Verder H. (R)   *Gallatin.*
Boyd ——— (D R)   *Germantown.*
Vandervoort J. C. (D R)   *Ghent.*
Gray J. (D R)
Lewis G. W. (L)
Markes D. L. (M E)   *Hillsdale.*
White H. (M)
Capron ———, (B)
Robinson ——— (B)
Landis R. W. (P)
Harling Henry (P)   *Hudson.*
Collins ——— (Uv)
Gasman J. (D R)
Suthill J. H. (E)
Coles Geo. (M E)
Church Leroy (C B)
Macy A. (F)
Van Zandt B. (D R)   *Kinderhook.*
Chase Hiram (M E)
Strobel ——— (L)
Niles H. (P)
Crispell C. E. (D R)   *Livingston.*
Palmer L. (B)
Stockwell G. S. (B)
          New Lebanon.
Churchill S (P)
Day ——— (C)
Dixon A. (M)
Jones Adam (M E)
Kendall E (M)
Churchill C. (P)
Browning Wm. G. (M E)
          Stockport.
Murden B. F. (D R)   *Taghkanic.*

Knapp S. M. (M E) West Taghkanic   *Taghkanic.*

Cortland County.

Stark J. T. (C B)   *Cincinnatus.*
Soule Justus (M)
Jewel Frederick S. (P)
Dunham H. R. (P) *Cortland Village.*
Simmons J. P. (B)
Perne W. H. (M)
Randolph W. B. (Uv)
Ward S. R. (C)
Fancher Ezra (P) M'Grawville
Darbey Chauncey (C B)   do
Bush E. (M)   do
Tillinghast W. (B)   *Freetown.*
Lord —— (P)   *Harford.*
Maryatt D. P. (B)
Brown Charles (Uv)
Lason John L (Ch)
Fessenden Thos. K. (P) *Homer.*
Havens H. (B)
Cobb Wm. (M)
Phelps Chas. E. (E)
Terry P. (P)   *Marathon.*
Ives Benoni I. (M E) *Preble.*
Harrington Moody (P)
Colwell A. (B)   *Scott.*
Dean Wm. (M)
Hull Varuam (7th day B)
Pease David (B)   *Solon.*
Warren Wm. (M)   *Taylor.*
Wire Augustus (M)
Benson Henry (M)
Reed E. D. (B)   *Truxton.*
Robinson S. N.
Thatcher Moses (P) *Virgil.*
Dewitt J. V. (B)
Hewett Jasper (M)

Delaware County.

Lang J. (P)   *Andes.*
Pierce J. W. (P)
Smith Wm. H. (M)
Graham J. (P)   *Bovina.*
Jones F. (P) Downsville *Colchester.*
Blake W. (M) do
Ostrander D. B. (M) Downsville
Ferguson S. D. (M) *Davenport.*
Pendle M. L. (M)
Waters G. (B)   *Delhi.*
Westcott E. (B)
Hervy F. B. (Scotch P)
Carter Thomas (M E)
Grant D. (Ch)
White S. J. (P)   *Franklin.*
Ingersoll J. F. (P)
Kerr G. (D R)
Morse C. (B)
Bourne C. (B)
Chatterton J. C. (M E)
Smith J. W. (M E)
Frasier —— (P)   *Hamden.*
Burr B. L. (M) Hancock
Hall D. B. (P)   *Harpersfield.*
Hayes G. (Ch)
Gibson J. D. (P) South *Kortright.*
Hill E. A. (M) Bloomville
Irving —— (P)
Wells J. (M E)
M'Auley Wm. (P)
Chapman C. (P)   *Meredith.*
Powers I. (B)
Green D. (F B)
Smith J. (B)
Kerr R. (M E) Margaretville
          Middletown.
Stout E. S. (M E) do
Akerly A. (M E) do
Trotter A. (P)   *Roxbury.*
Cornell J. D. (P) *Stamford.*
Wells J. (M) Hobart
Curtiss W. A. (E) Hobart
Fish J. B., Sidney Plains *Sidney.*
Allen A. P. (P) Deposit *Tompkins.*
Richmond J. L. (B) do
Stevens S. G. (M E) do
Matthews O. P.(M E) Cannonsville
Pattengill I. S. (P) *Walton.*
Brown J. C. (E)
Seymore S. (B)
Gibson David (M E)

Duchess County.

Friselle A. C. (P)   *Amenia.*
Barber H. (C)
Lent M. R. (M)
King Lucius H. (M E)
Turner D. B. (M) *Beekman.*
Foss J. (B)   *Dover.*
Kipp F. M. (D R) *Fishkill.*
Clark J. F. (P)
Crusa C. F. (E)
Stebbins S. J. (M E)
Lester J. (M) Wappingers' Falls
Andrews G. B. (E) do
Reed N. A. (B)   do
M'Gregor E. R. (P) do
Van Dusen M. (M) do
Scallon T. L. (R C) do
Price E. (P) Hughsonville
Williams Fenwick (P) do
Miller W. A. (D R) Glenham
Donally Francis (M E) do
Davy J. T. M. (P) Matteawan
Robertson J. J. (E) do
Miller —— (M)   do
Genung B. M. (M E) do
Van Deusen M. (M E) W. Fishkill
Harkness J. (P) Fishkill Landing
Heyer Wm. S. (D R) do
Polhemus A. (D R) Hopewell
Warren J. (B) Fishkill Plains
Vanclief R. W. (D R) New Hack-
    ensack
Sherwood R. (E) *Hyde Park.*
Ten Eyck Wm. H. (D R)
Ostrander Wm. (M)
Mandeville —— (P) *Lagrange.*
Warren J. (B)
Spoor J. (Ch) Milanville *Milan.*
Gros H. L. (B) *North East.*
Dickerson J. L. (M)
Sayers Wm. N. (P) *Pine Plains.*
Ellis Thomas (M E)
Russell A. A. (B)
Wile B. F. (P) *Pleasant Valley.*
Andrews L. B. (M)
Davis S. (E)
Ambler E. C. (B)
Farrington T. (P)
Turner D. B. (M E) *Poughkeepsie.*
Waldo L. F. (C) 43 Garden
Ludlow H. G. (P) 96 Cannon
Mann A. M. (D R) 216 Main
Vincent L. M. (M) 30 Washington
Jewett Wm. (M E)
Kettell George F. (M E)
Richardson M. (M E) Mansion sq.
Thomas Wm. B. (E) 61 Market
Buel S. (E) 60 Washington
Traver A. D. (E) 86 Catherine
Smith J. H. (B) 290 Mill
Fay E. (B) 3 Union
Williams F.T. (P) New Hamburgh
Shaver C. (D R) *Red Hook.*
Shaffer J. N. (M)
Hoff B. (D R)   *Rhinebeck.*
Smith C. A. (L)
Bradley T. (B)
Peck L. W. (M)
Wing J. (P) Stanfordville *Stanford.*
Burch L. (B)   do
Roberts P. (Ch) do
Ambler S. (B)   do
Rider J. (M)   do
Hall J. F. (P)   do
Deual A. (P)
Johnson A. (B) Attlebury
Adams ——, (M) Verbank
          Union Vale.
Wheaton H. (E) Lithgow
          Washington.

Erie County.

Remington —— (P)   *Alden.*
Branch —— (B)   *Amherst.*
Bush Wm. (M) Spring Brook
          Aurora.
Scutt Milo, (M) Willink
Gail S. (B)   do
Saxe J. B. (Uv) do
Sanford ——, (P) Griffin's Mills

Dunbar James, (P) Willink *Aurora.*
Going Eliab, (B) do
Heacock Jos. S. (P) *Black Rock.*
Sax J. B. (Uv)   *Boston.*
Turnocker George (F B)
Shelton Wm. (E) *Buffalo.*
Ingersoll Edward (E)
Schuyler Montgomery (E)
Thompson M. L. R. P. (E)
Burtis Arthur (P)
Heacock G. W. (P)
Lord John C. (P)
Carlton Thomas (M E)
Seager S. (M E)
Burch Charles (M E)
Fuller James M. (M E)
Hotchkiss V. R. (B)
Sheldon C. F. (B)
Von Puttkammer Alex. (B)
Hosmer George W. (Ut)
Smith S. R. (Uv)
Everett L. S. (Uv)
Guth F. (R C)
Schmidt Anthony (R C)
O'Reilly Bernard (R C)
Soldan C. F. (Ev)
Caraher Bernard (R C)
Guenther F. H. (L)
Grabau A. (German)
Burger Morritz (German)
Jahnke F. (German)
Giustiani —— (German)
Timmerman John *Clarence.*
True M. B.
Kuchler M.
Fillmore G.
Danforth Francis (P)
Crocker —— (P)   *Colden.*
Mills F. (B) Springville *Concord.*
Eddy Hiram, (P) do
George Isaac, (Uv) do
Mason —— (M)   *Eden.*
Miller —— (M)
Avery —— (P)
Fuller —— (B)
Scott ——, (P) East Evans
          Evans.
Taylor ——, (P) do
Sawyer ——, (B) Water Valley
          Hamburgh.
Ensign Asher (F B)
Rogers Aaron (Uv) *Holland.*
Caldwell Abel (P)
Munger Hervy (B) *Tonawanda.*
Vincent Joshua (B)
Hinds E. (M)   *Wales.*
Hudson Clark (M)

Essex County.

Miller A. Port Kent *Chesterfield.*
Herrick Step. L. (C) *Crown Point.*
Stevens Chauncy C. (C)
Perry Charles (B)
Taylor R. M. (M E)
Hurlburt E. (B) *Elizabethtown.*
Champlin Albert (M)
Hall Aaron (M E)
Fradenburgh S. (M E) *Essex.*
Sawyer Sawyer (B) *Jay.*
Hager C. L. (M E)
Brownson —— (P) Upper Jay
Miller J. (P) Ausable Forks
Lambert George (W M) *Keene.*
Comstock Cyrus *Lewis.*
Bush Wm. S. *Minerva.*
Foster W. W. (M E) Moriah &
   Corners   *Moriah.*
Rawson C. M.   do
Stowell S. H.   do
Hewes S. (M E) *Schroon.*
Eastman —— (C) *Ticonderoga.*
Morley —— (B)
Townsend G. H. (M E)
Pomeroy B. (M E) *Westport.*
Fredenburgh —— (M E)
          Willsborough.
Manly Ira (P)
M'Collum Jacob (B)
Newhall Ebenezer (C)
Shedd Marshall (C)
Eames J. (M E) *Wilmington.*

Franklin County.

Williams Stephen H. (C) *Bangor.*
Stratton R. (M E)
King R. E. (M E) *Bombay.*
Millar A. M. (M E) *Burke.*
Miller Andrew (P) *Chateaugay.*
Clark Alonzo A (M E)
Stwater H. S. (E)
Marvin Benjamin (P) *Constable.*
Gillette C. (P) *Fort Covington.*
Gillette M. D. (M E)
Long William *Malone.*
Smith E. (M E)
Babcock O. W.
Woodruff Silas (P)
Holbrook E. A.
Paddock Stephen
M'Cabe B.
Reed F. B. (P) *Moira.*
Swatter R. (M)
Pierce J (B)
Miller Allen (M E) *Westville.*

Fulton County.

Montieth Wm. J. (P) *Broadalbin.*
Smith William (E B)
Hurd W. F. (M E) *Johnstown.*
Barber C. (M E) Gloversville
Stevens D. (M E) do
Wood J. (P) Mayfield Corners *Mayfield.*
Lyon David *Northampton.*
Pomeroy C. (M E)
Richards A.
Heywood Leonard, Crosby Creek
Graham J. M. (P) *Perth.*
Bloodgood A. (P)

Genesee County.

Worcester A. (M E) *Alabama.*
Kidder —— (P) *Alexander.*
Nichols David (M)
Goff —— (Uv)
Bolls J. A. (E) *Batavia.*
Sunderland B. (P)
Stimpson S. M. (B)
Steele Allen (M)
Houghton D. C. (M)
Cheeseman J. K. (M)
Short —— (P) *Bergen.*
Wood Joseph (P) Stone Church
Clute ——, (P) North Bergen
Lane George W. (P) *Bethany.*
Hager Jacob (M E)
Leavensworth Hobart (B)
Hart Jacob (P) East Bethany
Preston J. B. (P) *Byron.*
Hood H. (M)
Smith —— (P) *Darien.*
Vaughan John W. (M E)
Corbin —— (B)
Corwin G. S. (P) *Elba.*
Seagert M. (M E)
Wait R. L. (M E) *Le Roy.*
Chipman T. R. (E)
Barrell A. C. (B)
Cook Stephen (C)
Lanning G. (M E) North Le Roy
Fancher Bela (P) *Oakfield.*
Ewell H. B. (B) *Pavilion.*
Hart J. B. (P)
Tuttle W. S. (M)
Fisk N. (Uv)
Woodruff ——, (B) *Pembroke.*
Chichester D. (P)
Ward —— (E) *Stafford.*
Jenkins J. B. (M E)

Greene County.

Stoughton Norman H. (E) *Athens.*
Hazer Henry (B)
Mire Walter (L)
Betts William R. S. (D R) Leeds *Catskill.*
Smith William C. (M E)
Still John K. (M E)
Judd Gideon N. (P.)
Murdock David (B)
Noble Louis L. (E)
Searle Jeremiah (D R) *Coxsackie.*

Dorman J. C. *Coxsackie.*
Barrows L. A. (E) *Durham.*
Smith Marcus (P)
Fitch Silas (M E)
Rogers Aaron (do)
Hopper Edward, (P) *Greenville.*
Cran Lyman (M)
Lord Mr. (B)
Chatterton James (M)
Osboon Henry (P) *Hunter.*
Mitchell —— (M)
Peck ——, (M) East Kill *Lexington.*
Gould William F. (M E)
Pettit Hezikiah (B)
Buck J. Judson (P) E. Lexington
Mitchell Wm. D. do
Peltz Philip (D R) *New Baltimore.*
Wykoff Abraham V. (D R) *Prattville.*
Lee Addi (M E)
Curtiss Marcus M. (M E)
Van Dycke L. B. (P) *Windham.*
Bancroft George C. (M E)

Hamilton County.

Rutherford —— *Wells.*
Pecket Samuel
Neally Elder

Herkimer County.

Brown M. C. (B) *Columbia.*
Adams A. (M) *Fairfield.*
Applegate —— (E)
Penfield Jesse (M) *Frankfort.*
Henry George W. (M)
Seeley A. (D R)
Fowler R. G. (B)
Lee Stephen (M) Frankfort Centre
Dedrick Peter, (M) West Frankfort
Casler L. (B) Mohawk *German Flats.*
Stark J. L. (D R) do
Fish ——, Ilion
Murphy James (D R) *Herkimer.*
Downing J. E. (M)
Barry —— (B) *Little Falls.*
Livermore E. (E)
Orvis S. (M)
M'Miniman —— (R C)
Francisco C. (L) *Litchfield.*
Ritchie George G. (B)
Hyde George C. (C) *Newport.*
Slee John (M E)
Brown William (B)
Whippill Eleazer (M E)
Whitcomb T. F. (Uv)
Prestcott F. W. (B) *Norway.*
Slee —— (M)
Pratt Rufus (P) *Russia.*
M'Coon Daniel, (B) Poland
Cass Milo G. (P) *Salisbury.*
Robinson J. S. Van Hornsville *Stark.*
Smith R. (L) Starkville
Smith —— (B)
Ferguson Nelson, (B) Jordanville *Warren.*
Jerome William, (M) Jordanville
Thurston Thomas W. (M) *Wilmurt.*
Pratt P. S. *Winfield.*
Lawton I. D. (B) West Winfield
Tremain —— (M) do
Arnold —— (M) do

Jefferson County.

Bingham J. S. (M) *Adams.*
Waker D. (M)
Clark C. E (B)
Hartshorn C. (B)
Whipple H. B. (E)
Bright —— (B) Adams Centre
Langworthy G. M. (S D B) Adams Centre
Shepard Lewis M. (P) *Smithville.*
Tripp W. (M E) do
Zimmerman Josiah (M E) *Alexandria.*

Hill Wm. H. (E) *Brownville.*
Wood Samuel H. (P)
Hill Wm. H. (E)
Atkins L. L. (M E)
Redhead R. (M E) Pillar Point
Skinner ——, (Uv) Dexter
Norton S. H. (E) *Cape Vincent*
Jackson D. (P)
Reed E. (B) *Champion.*
Folsom George (P)
Pennock Wilson (M)
Davis —— (B)
Benedict T. N. (C)
Blunt E. (B) *Clayton.*
Dagan J. F. (M E)
Brown B. G. (M) Depauville
Baker G. do
Griffiths A. (B) do
Peck N. R. (M) *Ellisburgh*
Rice L. (Uv)
Hibbard F. (P) Woodville
Burchard J. D. (C) do
Burchard J. (P) Belleville
Bishop J. F. (B) do
Leet C. W. (M) do
Brown L. (M) *Henderson.*
Johnson J. R. (B)
Townshend E. G. (P) Sackett's Harbor *Hounsfield.*
Stearns R. D. (E) Sackett's Harbor
Barber R. N. (M) do
Lamb J. H. (M E) Evans' Mills *Le Ray.*
Rosseel J. A. (B) do
Freeman Joshua (B) *Lorraine.*
Wilcox Lumond (P)
Rice L. (B) Three Mile Bay *Lyme.*
Cokine John B. (M E) do
Canfield J. (P) Chaumont
Wightman A. O. (C) Lafargeville *Orleans.*
Sawyer E. (B) do
Loomis S. B. (W M) Watertown *Pamelia.*
Woodruff H. (M E) Pamelia Corners
Dutton N. (C) *Philadelphia.*
Sleeper Thomas D. (M E)
Spear N. (C) *Rodman.*
Loverys J. (M E)
Doane H. (C)
Tilden H. O. (M) Black River *Rutland.*
Peck John (B) do
Lewis John R. (M) *Theresa.*
Fiske —— (E)
Hurd —— (P)
Chittenden Wm. E. (P)
Norton Levi W. (E) *Watertown.*
Snydier Peter (P)
Brayton Isaac (P)
Nash J. A. (B)
Arnold Ebenezer (M E)
Gary George (M E)
Stewart John H. (Uv)
M'Farland F. P. (R C)
Lyon Moses (M E) Carthage *Wilna.*
Powers John M. (R C) do
Davis Sylvester (B) do
Corbin Ira H. (M E) Natural Bridge
Rodgers ——, (P) do

Kings County.

Garlish H. (L) Court st. South Brooklyn *Brooklyn.*
Smith Wm. W. (M) 114 Navy
Fish J. F. (E)
Stone John S. (E)
Lewis Wm. H. (E)
Vinton Francis (E)
Cutler Benjamin C. (E)
Johnson S. R. (E)
Diller J. W. (E)
Spooner J. A. (E)
Johnson Evan M. (E)
Bacon D. W. (R C) 82 York
Maguire Hugh (R C) Kent Av.
M'Donough James (R C) Jay st.
Schneller J. A. (R C) 74 Warren
Hodge J. L. (B) 219 Washington

Taylor E. E. L. (B) 102 Joralemon
    Brooklyn.
Haynes Ames, (B) Franklin near
    Park Av. East
Dwight M.W. (D R) Joralemon st.
M'Laren Malcom, (D R) 82 State
Oakey P. D. (D R) Smith st.
Woodbridge S. M. (D R) 3d Av.
Elmendorf A. (D R) Bedford st.
    Gowanus
Cox Samuel H. (P) Oxford st.
Jacobus M. W. (P) 51 Remsen
Spencer I. S. (P) 104 Pineapple
Lewis Wm. B. (P) 48 Willow
Noyes Daniel P. (P)
Lock Nathaniel C. (P) Court st
Spear Samuel T. (P) 3 Warren
Storrs R. S. jr. (C) 35 Livingston
Beecher Henry W. (C) 18 Willow
Sprague I. N. (C) 240 Bridge
Green J. C. (C)
Lansing D. C. (C)
Farley Fred. A. (Ut) 70 Pacific
Thayer T. B. (Uv) 9 Willoughby
Burnett William. (M) 145 High
Alburtus John, 205 Henry
Bangs Nathan, 19 High
Norris William H. (M E)
Hoyt William C. (M E)
Curry D. (M E)
Law Joseph (M E)
Stopford William K. (M E)
Seney R. (M E)
Latham H. D. (M E)
Gothard W. (M E) East Brooklyn
Clark Laban, (M E) Green Point
    Bushwick.
Clark S. H. (M E) Green Point
Birch James, (M E) do
Strong T. M. (D R) *Flatbush.*
Newman W. H. (E) do
Woodruff George W. (M E) do
Schoonmaker M. V. (D R) East
    New York
Baldwin John A. (D R) *Flatlands.*
Labaugh A. (D R) *Gravesend.*
Labaugh I. P. (E)
Currie R. O. (D R) *New Utrecht.*
Scofield T. (E)
Boughton J. D. (M E)
Reynolds Charles (E) 60 South 8th
    Williamsburgh.
Jocelyn S. S. (C) 164 South 3d
Mason A. P. (B) 72 South 4th
M'Lane J. W. (P) 120 4th
Fash G. W. (E) Meserole st.
Raffeiner John (R C) 193 Montrose
    Av.
Hudson Joshua, (M) 513 Grand
Stevenson P. E. (P) 92 South 3d
Van Doren W. H. (D R) 51 South
    3d
Matthias John J. (M E) cor. Grand
    & Ewing
Collins William F. (M E) do
Meredith Samuel, (M E) do
Janes E. L. (M E) do
Haskins S. M. (E) 91 South 5th
Malone Sylvester, (R C) Water st.
    near North 3d
Lyon Henry, (Uv) 67 South 4th

Lewis County.

Smith A. M (M E) Copenhagen
    Denmark.
Brown T. D. (M E) do
Cone R. J. (C) do
Palmer Harvey *Diana.*
Cronk Jarvis
Cleaveland Waitstill, Brantling-
    ham *Greig.*
Sears David T. Port Leyden
Hart S. *Harrisburgh.*
Bailey Charles
Holcomb C. (C) *Leyden.*
Hubbard Levi
Havens Elder
Stebbins L. D. (M E) *Lowville.*
Tyler George P. (P)
Renouf Edward A. (E)
Wright B. S. (M E) *Martinsburg.*
Yale Calvin (P)

Morris H. W. (P) *Martinsburgh.*
Lathrop O. C (M E) *New Bremen.*
Dunn David *Osceola.*
Hurd Nathaniel (C) *Turin.*
Wightman Abel S. (M E)
Streeter Randolph (B)
Pritchard David E. (Welch)
Jones John R. (M) Constableville
    West Turin.
Sullivan O. (R C)
Kopp M. (R C)
Chapin A. L. (P)

Livingston County.

Eastman Geo. B. (E) *Avon.*
Cochran Wesley (M E)
Walworth E. B. (P) E. Avon
Curtiss W. B. do
Pierpont H. B. (P) W. Avon
Denoon Alex. (P) *Caledonia.*
M'Luren D. C. (P)
Brewster Loring (P) *Conesus.*
Sandford Hiram (M E)
Eggers Harmon (D R) *Dansville.*
Howard R. (E)
Heckenburg C. L. (P)
Curry W. F. (P)
Selmser John (L)
Raines John, jr. (M E)
Parker Robert (M E)
Ferris D. (M E)
O'Flaherty M. (R C)
Ward H. G. (P) *Geneseo.*
Ward F. D. W. (P)
Judd Salmon (M)
Bakewell Wm. J. (E)
Van Lew John (P) *Groveland.*
Scouler J. B. (P) Cuylerville
    Leicester.
Leonard —— (P) Moscow
Spoors ——, (B) do
Barnard John (P) *Lima.*
Copeland John (M)
Dutton Chas. E. (Uv)
Hibbard F. G. (M)
Riley Benj. G. (P) *Livonia.*
Hough J. S. (P)
Olney ——, (B) S. Livonia
Polter S. L. (B) Lakeville
Dodge Jonas (M E) do
Roberts Orren (Uv) do
Van Rensselaer M. (E)
    Mount Morris.
Burney G. W. (M)
Parker John (M E)
Bulkley C. H. A. (P)
Bacon C. (B)
Lusk Wm. (P) *Nunda.*
Cola J. D. (B)
Baker S. S. (M E)
Waldo G. P. (E)
Kelsey A. (Uv)
Kay H. (P) Oakland *Portage.*
Sabins Rufus, (B) Hunt's Hollow
Griswold Asa, (E) do
Edson J. S. (M E) do
Baker —— (M) do
Halsted ——, (B) Scottsburgh
    Sparta.
Kellogg Levi (F B) do
Hunter Wm. (P) *Springwater.*
Wilson James (M E)
Herring John (A. R. P) *York.*
Bowden ——, (C)
Bambridge (P)
Sprague D. Piffardania

Madison County.

Bailey Eli S. *Brookfield.*
Ainsworth Spencer C.
Maxson Wm. Leonardsville
Crandall Sam. South Brookfield
Ferguson ——, North Brookfield
Clark W—. (B) *Cazenovia.*
Holmes —— M. (M)
Johnson J. R. (C)
Cox S. H. (E)
Hell J. H. (M) New Woodstock
Fisher Thomas (B) *De Ruyter.*
Butcher —— (M)
Irish J. R. (Seventh Day B)

M'Downald —— (P) *Eaton.*
Putnam Daniel (B)
Teeple J. J. (B) Morrisville
Hammond H. L. (P) do
Blakeslee Chas. (M) do
Eddy ——, (Uv) do
Gaylord (P) *Georgetown.*
Pearsons (C B)
Kern (M)
Smith Giles M. (P)
Haskell (C)
Richards Wm. M. (P) *Hamilton.*
Crocker Amos, jr. (P)
Andrews Edward (M)
Millett Daniel (E)
Scofield A. (Free Church)
Higgins F. D. (M) Earlville
Crocker Amos (P) Poolville
Starr A. (M) E. Hamilton
Potter J. (Uv) Hubbard's Corners
Nichols James, (P) Oneida Depot
    Lenox.
Huntley L. J. (B) do
Drake F. T. (D R) Canastota
Stickney W. (Free Church) do
Newman (M) Canastota
Cooder Wm. H. Wampsville
Spaulding S. (B) Clockville
Bridge Geo. (B) do
Newman J. P. (M)
Palmer Nelson (B) *Madison.*
Platt M. S. (P)
Davis L. D. (M)
Queal R. (Uv) Erieville *Nelson.*
Garnett H. H. (Free Church) Pe-
    terboro *Smithfield.*
Hall George (P) Peterboro
Haywood S. S. (B) do
Stow T. (Free Church) do
Parks Isaac (M) *Stockbridge.*
Copeland J. (M)
Ranney E. (B)
Jackson D. S. (B)
Abel James (D R) Chittenango
    Sullivan.
Swan L. E. (C B) do
Colgrove Geo. (M E) do
Shute Henry (B) Bridgeport

Monroe County.

Gray B. B. (C) *Brighton.*
Bowen J. W. (B) North Chili.
Fenner James (Cong.) do
Abel Asa, (M E) do
Short H N. (P) do
Balentine William (P) do
Goodman R. S (P) Clarkson Corner
Somerville —— (Ut) *Greece.*
Holliday —— (Ut.) Jenkins'
    Corner
Kittredge Charles, (P) do
Gilbert O. (C) do
Gilbert S. (B) do
Robinson J. R. (M E) E. Henrietta
Stearter H. (P) do
Fuller Timothy (B) West Henrietta
Hill R. W. (P) East Mendon.
Parish R. W. (B) do
M'Mahon J. (M E) West Mendon
Fay E. (C) do
Eaton —— (E) do
Beardsley O. C. (P) do
Stiles L. (M E) Spencers' Basin
    Ogden.
Brown J. (M E) Parma Corner
    Parma.
Parsons John, (B) do
Buck Wm. (M E) Parma Centre
Fariman G. (P) do
Dick R. (F B) do
Theal Thomas (B) do
Woodward Jonas (B) *Penfield.*
Parker T. (F B)
Bellamy Thomas (P)
Hudson T. B. (M E)
Billington L. W. (P) Fairport
    Perrinton.
Straight F. W. (F B) do
Smith H. (Uv.) do
Deering A. (F B) Bushnell's Basin
Richardson John B. (C) *Pittsford.*

Maxwell J. E. (B)   *Pittsford.*
Buck Z. J. (M E)
Miles S. (Uv)
Brooks ——— (P)   *Riga.*
Montgomery G. W. (Uv.)
                        Rochester.
Davis ——— (B)
Lee H. St. Luke's Church (E)
Van Ingen John, Grace do (E)
Hall A. G. (Pres.)
Buck D. D. (M E)
Deforest Charles, (C)
Alexander R. (R C)
Shaw James B. (P)
Gulick J. G. (M E)
Peck Henry (C)
O'Reilly William (R C)
Fitzpatrick John P. (R C)
Cooper Charles D. (E)
Hickock Milo J. (P)
M'Alvaine J. H. (P)
Schneider Leonard S. (R C)
Stanwood H. (B)   *Rush.*
Hibbard F. G. (M E)
Chandler Chas. N. (B) Brock-
port   *Sweden.*
Smith H. R. (M E)
Cowles A. C. (P)
Rollins D. M. L. (F B)
Mann ——— (B)   *Webster.*
Mandeville John, (M E)
Buttolph Milton, (C) Scottsville
                        Wheatland.
Terry George W. (M E)
O'Connor Edward, (R C)
Doolittle Henry L. (P)

Montgomery County.

Goodale M. S. (P)   *Amsterdam.*
Harris J. M. (B)
Chip W. M. (M E)
Wade A.
Franklin M. (E)
Atwater E. P. (P) Tribes Hill
Sholl William N. (Eng. E. L.)
                        Canajoharie.
DeWett John (D R)
Rumpff Adolph (German L)
Leonard C. H. (M E)   do
Nicholls Asahel, (F B) Ames
Hervey ——— (M)
Stevenson James, (D R) Minaville
                        Florida.
Warner Horace (M E)
Poulisen C. Z. (D R)   *Glen.*
Roof G. L. (P)
Hurd W. F. (M E)   *Johnstown.*
Van Alstine N.   *Minden.*
Diefendorf Benjamin L
Eisenlord J.
M'Lane Charles G. (R D) Fort
Plain
Isball Bishop, (M E)   do
Fenton Asa F.   do
Starks J. L. (D R)   *Mohawk.*
Simmons G. C. (M) Fonda
Van Olinda D. (D R)   do
Jukes C. (D R) Stone Arabia
                        Palatine.
Rumpf A. (L)   do
Squires O. J.   *Root.*
Carle J. H.
Knieskern ——— (D R)
                        St. Johnsville.

New York.

BAPTIST MINISTERS.

Armitage Thomas, 152 Clinton,
(Norfolk) Norfolk cor. Broome
Baker Luke, 55 Franklin, (Church
of Christ) 138 Laurens
Bellamy David, 84 4th Av. (Hope
Chapel) 718 Broadway
Bigelow John R. 62 1st, (Zion)
486 Pearl
Brown Thomas B. 80 E. 16th (7th
Day) 11th, between Bowery &
3d Av.
Corey S. A. E. 24th, near 4th Av.
(19th st.) 12th near 3d Av.

Clapp William S. 203 Monroe,
(Olive Branch) 328 Cherry
                        New York.
Cone S. H. 394 Broome, (First)
Broome cor. Elizabeth
Davis Charles L. 103 Goerck,
(Baptist Welsh), 141 Chrystie
Dowling John, 35 Bedford, (Be-
rean) Dowling, cor. Bedford
Dunbar Duncan, 46 W. Washing-
ton pl. (Beriah) Macdougal
opposite Vandam
Eddy H. J. Henry, cor. Clinton,
(Cannon st.) Cannon n. Broome
Everts W. W. 191 Hudson, (Laight
st.) Laight cor. Varick
Judd Orin, 59 E. 16th (Union) 4th
Av. bet. 22d & 23d
Lathrop Edward, 143 10th, (Taber-
nacle) Mulberry near Chatham
Marsh L. G. 21 Av. A (Ebenezer)
19 Av. A
Raymond J. T. 79 Mercer, (Aby-
sinian) 44 Anthony
Remington S. 186 Chrystie, (Stan-
ton) Stanton near Forsyth
Seiley J T. 207 9th, (5th st) 322
6th
Spencer W. H. 43d bet. 8th & 9th
Avs. (Bloomingdale) 43d st.
Stewart I. R. 177 Cherry, (Mari-
ners' 1st) Cherry between Pike
& Rutgers
Sommers C. G. 82 Madison, (South)
450 Broadway
Taggart J. W. 206 W. 22d (16th)
W. 16th near 8th Av.
Wheat A. C. 134 Christopher,
(North) Bedford corner do
Williams W. R. 27 Grove. (Amity
st.) Amity corner Wooster

CONGREGATIONALISTS.

Cheever G. B. 21 E. 15th, (Church
of the Puritans) Broadway cor.
15th
Cheever Henry T. 17 Eldridge,
(First Free) Chrystie near De-
lancy
Cochran Samuel D. (Free Congre-
gational) 151 Sullivan
Crocker A. B. 169 E. Broadway
(Eastern) Madison & Gouver-
neur
Harrison Joseph, 44 Thompson,
(Providence Chapel) 44 do
Patton William, (Hammond) cor.
Factory
Ray Charles B. 152 Orange,
(Bethesda) 561 Broadway
Schimerhorn William, (Fourth
Cong.) 104 W. 16th
Thompson Joseph P. 57 North
Moore, (Tabernacle) 240 B.way
Zender J. D. L. 173 Av. B (French
Cong.) Fulton near William

DUTCH REFORMED.

Busche F. 36 Chrystie, (German
Reformed) 21 Forsyth
Cornell F. F 209 5th (Manhattan)
Av. B corner 5th
Ebaugh John S. 149 4th Av. (17th)
W. 17th near 6th Av.
Ferris Isaac, 109 E. Broadway,
(Market st.) cor. Henry
Fisher G. H. 196 M'Dougal,
(Broome st.) cor. Greene
Guldin J. C. 122 Rivington, (Ger-
man Evangelical) Houston
Hardenbergh J. B. 329 Greenwich
(Franklin st.) near Church
Hutton M. S. 106 9th, (Dutch)
Wooster, cor. Washington pl.
Knox John, 396 4th (Collegiate)
Lafayette pl. cor. 4th
Lord Jeremiah, (Harlem)
Macauley I. M. 56 Amity, (South)
5th Av. cor. 21st
Marsellus N. I. 45 Hammond,
(Bleecker st.) cor. Amos

Van Aiken Enoch, 13 Grand
(Bloomingdale)   *New York.*
Van Nest A. E. Broadway, 2d
house above 20th (21st st.) near
6th Av.
Whitehead C. (Greene st.) corner
Houston

JEWISH SYNAGOGUES.

Cohen S. M. 437 Grand (Temple
of the Emanuel) 56 Chrystie
Danziger Marks, 124 Attorney
(Shaary Shomaim) 122 Attorney
Hecht Jonas, 126 Broome, (Anshi
Chesed) 38 Henry
Isaacs S. M. 669 Houston (Shaary
Tephila,) 112 Wooster
Heitner Lehman, at the Church
(Rodolph Sholom) 166 Attorney
Leo Ansel, 134 Elm, (Bnai Jeo-
humn) 119 Elm
Lyons J. J. 56 Crosby, (Sheareth
Israel) 60 Crosby
Noot Simon O. 154 Pearl, (Bnai
Israel) 159 Pearl
Salinger J. at the Church, (Beth
Israel) Centre between Pearl &
Duane

LUTHERAN.

Boehn Theodore, 170 2d, (Evan-
gelical) 127 Columbia
Geissenhainer F. W. 76 E. 14th,
(Lutheran) 6th Av. cor. 15th.
Held A. H. M. 198 Allen, (St.
Mark's) 6th bet. Avs. 1 & 2
Martin Charles, 413 Broome, (St.
James) Mulberry near Grand
Stohlman C. F. E. 16 Bayard, (St.
Matthew's) 79 Walker

METHODIST EPISCOPAL.

Ammerman O. V. 176 Duane, (Du-
ane st.) 180 Duane
Bainbridge Thomas, (41st st.)
near 8th Av.
Barney Isaac, W. 25th, bet. 7th &
8th Avs. (African Union) 15th
near 7th Av.
Buck Valentine, 76 Frankfort,
(John st.) John st.
Chamberlain Parmele, 280 2d,
(2d st.) 276 2d
Clark Davis W. 454 Greenwich,
(Vestry st.) near   do
Crawford John, 63 Madison. (Mad-
ison) Madison cor. Catharine
Crawford M. D. C. 313 9th (9th st.)
Av. B cor 9th
Doering C. H. 19 Av. C, (German
Mission) 2d bet. Avs. B & C
Ferris Isaac, 218 Sullivan, (Sulli-
van st.) 214 Sullivan
Field Julius, 127 Norfolk, (As-
bury) Norfolk bet. Rivington &
Stanton
Griswold E. E. 302 Mulberry,
(Mulberry st.) Mulberry near
Bleecker
Hall Eli M. Brooklyn, (1st Af-
rican) 227 2d
Haven Erastus O. 251 W. 24th,
(Chelsea) 20th bet. 8th & 9th
Avs.
Hedstrom O. G. 4 Carlisle, (North
River Floating Bethel) foot
Rector
Macomber J. W. near Church,
(15th st. Home Mission) near
3d Av.
Meed Nathaniel, 14 7th, (7th st.)
near 2d Av.
Osborn A. M. 192 18th, (18th st.)
18th near 8th Av.
Putney C., Harlem, (Harlem) Har-
lem
Ross Peter (Zion) 158 Church
Sillick Bradley, Yorkville, (York-
ville) Yorkville
Sillick John A. 339 Cherry, (Mar-
iners') Cherry near Clinton

Smith Daniel, 57 Green, (Green st.) 61 Green *New York.*
Smith John G 5 Willett, (Willett st.) Willett near Grand
Stillwell Wm. M. 112 Chrystie, (Savior's) 42 1st
Stocking Davis, Jane st. (Jane st.) Jane st. bet. 8th & Greenwich Avs.
Stratton John B. bet. 2d & 3d Avs. (27th st.) bet. 2d & 3d Avs.
Swartz Wm. Bloomingdale, (German Home Mission) Bloomingdale
Van Deuzen S. 47 Morton, (Bedford st.) cor. Morton
Wood J. W. B. 19 Forsyth, (Forsyth st.) 12 Forsyth

METHODIST PROTESTANT.

Covell James, 129 Wooster, (Protestant Methodist) Convention Hall, 115 Wooster
Johnson Wm. H. 111 Suffolk, (Attorney st.) 91 Attorney
Rowlands William, 195 Orchard, (Methodist Calvinistic) (Welch) 73 Allen

PROTESTANT EPISCOPAL.

Abercrombie R. M. 10th Av. N. 155th, (St. Andrew's). Harlem
Anthony Henry, 156 2d Av. (St. Mark's) Stuyvesant nr. 2d Av.
Balch L. P. W. 96 2d Av. (St. Bartholomew's) Lafayette place cor. Great Jones
Bedell G. T. 10th cor. 5th Av. (Ascension) 5th Av. cor. 10th
Berrian Wm. 50 Varick, (Trinity) Broadway cor. Rector
Clapp Caleb, 6th n Av. C, (Nativity) 6th n Av. C
Cook Thomas, 276 Houston, (St. Simon's) (German Mission) 188 Houston
Cox Richard, 142 Mercer, (Zion) 26 Mott
Crummell Alexander, 13th st. John's Lane, (Church of the Messiah) (Colored) 473 Houston
Duffee Cornelius R. 64 Lexington Av.
Eigenbrodt Wm. E. 53 Amity, (All Saints) 286 Henry
Evans Benjamin, 172 Broome, (Holy Evangelists) 15 Vandewater
Forbes John M. 477 Hudson, (St. Luke's) Hudson near Barrow
Halsey ——, (Christ Church) 81 Anthony
Hart A. B. 5 Mercer, (Church of the Advent) 9th Av. bet. 41st & 42d
Harwood Edwin, 5th Av. n.179th, (St. James') Hamilton square
Hawks Fran. L. 16 11th, (Church of the Mediator) University
Henry C. S. 146 Macdougal, (St. Clement's) 110 Amity
Howland R. S. 9th Av. near W. 23d, (Church of the Holy Apostles) 9th Av. cor. W. 28th
Hoyt Ralph, 117 Madison, (Good Shepherd) Market cor. Monroe
Johnson D. V. M. (Floating Church) for Seamen, foot of Dey
Jones Lot, 77 2d Av. (Epiphany) 130 Stanton
Leonard A. S. (Emanuel) Thompson cor. Prince
Millett James, (Church of the Holy Martyrs) Ludlow near Grand
Muhlenberg W. A. 110 W. 20th (Church of the Holy Communion) 20th cor. 6th Av.
Onderdonk B. T. 106 Franklin
Pardee Isaac, 13th st. Mark's place (Redemption) 11th st. nr. 3d Av.

Parker B. C. 114 E. Broadway (Church of our Saviour) Floating Church for Seamen. foot of Pike *New York.*
Pond Jesse, 50 4th (St. Matthews) Christopher near Bleecker
Price Joseph H. 62 2d Av. (St. Stephens) Chrystie cor. Broome
Richmond Wm., Bloomingdale (St. Michael's) Bloomingdale
Richmond William, Bloomingdale (St. Mary's) Manhattanville
Schroeder J. F. 3d st. Clements pl. (Church of the Crucifixion) University place
Seabury Samuel, 125 W. 13th (Annunciation) W. 14th between 6th & 7th Avs.
Shimeall R. C. 16 10th (St. Jude's) 25 6th Av.
Southard S. L. door next to Church (Calvary Church) 4th Av. bet. 21st & 22d
Taylor Thomas H. door next to church (Grace) Broadway cor. 10th
Tyng S.H. 66 E. 16th (St.George's) 36 Beekman cor. Cliff, & Stuyvesant square
Verren Antoine. 99 Franklin (Du Saint Esprit) (French) Franklin cor. Church
Whitehouse H. J. 120 11th (St. Thomas) 615 Broadway
Williamson C. H. 68 Duane (Du Saint Sauveur) (French) Franklin cor. Church

NEW JERUSALEM.

Bush George, 16 Howard (New Jerusalem)Broadway cor. Leonard
Wilks Thomas, 6 Jane (New Jerusalem Second Society,) New York University

PRESBYTERIAN.

Adams Wm. 601 Houston (Central) 406 Broome
Alexander J. W., Beach cor. Varick (Duane) Duane cor. Church
Bannard Wm., E. 29th bet. 5th Av. & Lexington Av. (Madison Avenue) bet. 5th Av. & University place
Burchard S. D. 113 W. 13th (13th st.) 117 W. 13th
Butts Joshua, E. 87th near 3d Av. (1st) (Yorkville) E. 87th near 3d Av.
Campbell A. E. 24 M'Dougal (Spring) 250 Spring near Varick
Carpenter H. S. 64 Varick (Canal) 82 Canal cor. Greene
Dickenson R. S. S. 103 Prince (Houston) Houston cor. Thompson
Gillet Ezra H. Harlem (Harlem) 127th near 3d Av.
Hatfield Edwin F. 251 Madison (7th st.) Broome cor. Ridge
Knox James, 22d near 4th Av. (Tenth) 3d Av. cor. 21d
Kreves M. 141 Henry, (Rutgers) Rutgers cor. Henry
Lillie John, 82 6th, (Stanton) cor. Forsyth
Lowrie J. C. next door to church (Forty-second street) 8th Av. cor. 42d
M'Elory J. 427 Broome, (Scotch) Grand cor. Crosby
Mason Erskine, 261 Greene, (Bleecker street) Bleecker opposite Crosby
Noble Mason, 97 Av. B (Eleventh) Av. C cor. 4th
Ostrum Jas. I. 181 W. 21st, (Eighth Avenue) W. 20th near 7th Av.
Pennington J. W. C 26 W.Broad'y, (First) (colored) Marion corner Prince

Phillips Wm. W. 62 Hammond, (First) 6th Av. cor. 11th *New York.*
Potts George, 27 5th Av. (Tenth street) University pl. cor. 10th
Rosevelt ——, 216 W. 22d, (North) W. 22d bet. 8th & 9th Avs.
Skinner Thomas, 18 Grove, (Carmine) Carmine opposite Varick
Smith A. D. 120 2d, (Brainard) 91 Rivington
Smith Edward D., W. 20th near 9th Av. (Chelsea) W. 22d near 9th Av.
Snodgrass Wm. D. 766 Broadway, (Fifteenth street) between 3d Av. & Irving place
Spring Gardiner, 3 Bond, (Brick) Beekman cor. Nassau
Stiles J. C. 26 Amity place, (Mercer) Mercer nr. Waverly place

PRESBYTERIAN ASSOCIATE.

Blair Hugh H. 36 Perry, (Third) 41 Charles
Clements Alexander, 237 24th (Fourth) 253 W. 24th n. 9th Av.
Stark Andr'w, 110 Sullivan, (First) Grand cor. Mercer
Waddle David, near Church, (Second) Forsyth cor. Houston

PRESBYTERIAN ASSOCIATE REFORMED.

M'Laren Wm. 90 Watts, (Fourth) Franklin opposite Varick
Wright A. H. 800 Greenwich, (Fifth) Jane near Abington

PRESBYTERIAN REFORMED.

Chrystie James, in New Jersey, (First) 101 Sullivan
Little John, (Third) Waverly pl. cor. Grove
M'Leod John N. 87 W. 20th, (Reformed Presbyterian) 12th W. of 6th Av.
Stevenson Andrew, 99 Troy, (Second) 11th bet. 6th & 7th Av.

PRIMITIVE CHRISTIANS.

Barr Oliver, 61 Pitt, (Suffolk st. Christian Church) bet. Delancy & Rivington
Hogg Thomas, (Primitive Christians' Congregation) 639 B'dw'y

ROMAN CATHOLIC.

Buchmezer Ambrose, 135 2d, (St. Nicholas) German, 2d n. Av, A
Cummisky James, at Church, (St. Columbas) 25th n. 8th Av.
Curran Michael, near church, (St. John Evangelist) near Deaf and Dumb Asylum
Hughes J. 263 Mulberry, (St. Patrick's Cathedral) Mott c. Prince
Kein Richard, 357 10th, (St. Bridget's) 8th near Av. B
Lafant Arnet, 26 Canal, (St. Vincent de Paul) (French) 26 Canal
Lutz Joseph, (St. John Baptist) (German) 30th bet. 7 & 8th Av.
M'Carran Michael, 67 6th Av. (St. Joseph) 6th Av. cor. Barrow
M'Closky George, 44 2d Avenue, (Church of the Nativity) 2d Av. bet. 2d & 3d
M'Kenna Patrick, 23 Oliver, (St. James') 32 James
Maginnis John, 13 City Hall pl. (St. Andrew's) Duane cor. City Hall place
Pise Charles C. 15 Barclay, (St. Peter's) Barclay cor. Church
Rumpler Gabriel, at Church, (Church of the Most Holy Redeemer) (German) 153 3d
Starr Wm. 11 Ridge, (St. Mary's) Grand cor. Ridge

Varella F. 23 Reade, (Transfiguration) 45 Chambers New York.
Welsh John, near church, (St. Paul's) Harlem

UNITARIAN.

Bellows H. W., E. 20th nr. Broadway, (Church of the Divine Unity) 548 Broadway
Osgood ——, (Church of the Messiah) 728 Broadway

UNIVERSALIST.

Balch Wm. S. 728° Greenwich, (Third) 208 Bleecker c. Downing
Chapin E. H. 13 Murray, (Fourth) Murray cor. Church
Fay C. H. 169 Rivington, (Second) 85 Orchard

WESLEYAN METHODIST.

Harris Dennis, 33 Vandam, (Wesleyan Methodist) 95 King
Lee Luther, 80 3d, (Wesleyan Methodist) 4th st.

MISCELLANEOUS.

Bigler David, 522 Houston, (United Brethren, (Moravian) Houston cor. Mott
Chase H. 59 Market, (Mariners) 73 Roosevelt
Snow S. S. (Second Advent) 67 Crosby
Westervelt Samuel, 52 Charles, (True Dutch Reformed) King n. M'Dougal

Niagara County.

Kendall W. C. (M E)   Cambria.
Rogers ——, (M E) Pekin
Halsey Herman (P)   do
Fearsall Joseph (M E) do
Galusha E. (B)   Hartland.
Treadway Amos C. (E) Lewiston.
Aller S. N. (P)
Dewey Wm. (P) Pekin
Wisner W. C. (P)   Lockport.
Gilman E. W. (C)
Platt C. H. (P)
Winchell R. (B)
Lape Thomas (L)
Cook —— (Uv)
Slaughter Wm. B. (M E)
Mason S. R. (B)
M'Mullen C. D. (R C)
Scott E. J. (B)   Newfane.
Callahan Henry (P) Niagara Falls.
Munger Harvey (B)
Hurd Zenas (M E)
Reed Sylvanus (E)
Vincent J. (B)   Pendleton.
Hurlburt R. L. (P) Youngstown
    Porter.
Smith Sumner C. (M E) do
Sawyer William (B)
Browning C. (B)   Royalton.
Woodward Charles M. (M E)
Closs Reuben H. (P) Middleport
Noble John, (E)   do
Luce Alfred W. (M E)   do
Walker G. C. (B)   Somerset.
Stratton E. H. (P)
Payne Thomas (P)
Gridley J. S. (M)
Pettit H. (B) West Somerset
Bowman J. M. (M E) Tonawanda
    Wheatfield.
Root Nathaniel, Tonawanda
Warren A. (B)   do
Benedict Elisha B. (P)   Wilson.
Morrison J. H. (B)
Lawton Daniel B. (M)

Oneida County.

Carr J. J. (Ch)   Annsville.
Brown —— (B)
Van Valkenburgh —— (P)
Holmes Wm. E. (P) Taberg

Rogers Lucius C. (M E)   Augusta.
Hamilton H. S. (P) Oriskany Falls
Dewey Sanger (M E)   do
Bartholomew O. (P)   do
Williams —— (B)   do
Ferguson David (M E)   Boonville.
Jones J. W. (M E)
Renouf Edward A. (E)
Smith D. (B)   Bridgewater.
Brace S. W. (C)
Graves C. (B)
Benedict Thomas N. (E)
Kirk R. R. (C)   Camden.
Smith A. P. (E)
Stanton F. H. (M E)
Sims J. N. (W M)
Skinner A. (Uv)   Deerfield.
Potter R.   Florence.
Fuller B.
Gardner R.
Mason Darius (M E)   Floyd.
Raymond S. W. (C)   Kirkland.
Sawyer Thomas J. (Uv) Clinton
Cook R. (M E)   do
Vermilye R. G. (C)   do
Barton John (P)   do
Boyd J. R. (C)   do
Strong Salmon (P)   do
Paddock B. G. (M E)   do
Chichester D. (M E)   Lee.
Hays —— (M E)
Hethaway —— (Uv)
Hawkins Franklin (M E)   Marcy.
Lathrop S. G. (M E) Deansville
    Marshall.
M'Kown A.L. (M E)   NewHartford.
Paddock Wm. H. (E)
Payson Elliott H. (P)
Mills Abiram (C)
Baker Wm. (E) Paris Hill   Paris.
Cordell J. G. (C)   do
Waugh John. (P) Sauquoit
Comfort S. (M E)   do
Rowe H. F. (M E)   do
Roberts M. (C)   Remsen.
Knox Wm. E. (P)   Rome.
Vogel H. C. (B)
Beecham Wm. (R C)
Erwin J. (M E)
Gregory A. (E)
Jones Thomas R. (Welch Ch)
Gridley A. D. (P) Waterville
    Sangersfield.
Butts D. B. (C)
Benedict ——, (E) Waterville
Hayhurst —— (B)   do
Buckingham J. (Ut) Trenton Village
    Trenton.
Davis J. W. (P) Trenton Village
Pierce ——, (Ut) Trenton Falls
Beardsley Northrop, (E) Holland Patent
Wyatt Wm. (M E)   Utica.
Foster Isaac (M E)
Burgess Nathan B. (E)
Leeds George (E)
Perry Marcus A. (E)
Prosi Pierre A. (E)
Wetmore Oliver (P)
Goodrich Chauncey E. (P)
Spencer Theodore (P)
Thacher Washington (P)
Brace Samuel W. (P)
Spencer William H. (P)
Stryker Isaac P. (P)   Vernon.
Brainerd Israel (P)
Burchard Eli (P)
Rockwell T. B. (M E)
Dunham M. (M E) Vernon Centre
Phinney S. C. (M E)   do
Avery R. A. (C)   do
Matchin Chas. (P) Oneida Castle
Brown E. C. (M E)   Verona.
Butler Chas. F. (P.)
Hawkins W. (M E) M'Connellsville
    Vienna.
Corliss —— (P) Westernville
    Western.
Spencer F. A. (P) Hampton
    Westmoreland.
Mattison A. F. (M E) Hampton
Spalding Erastus   do

Round N. (M E)   Whitestown
Long W. R. (P) Whitesboro
Matson Wm. A. (E)   do
Camp Phineas (P)   do
Green Beriah (C)   do
Whicher B. W. (E)   do
Fullonton J. (F B)   do
Pritchett E. C. (P) Oriskany
Graves N. D. (P) New York Mills

Onondaga County.

Hoag E. (M E)   Camillus.
Kingsley David H. (P)
Williams Wm. W. (P)
Baldwin Truman (P)   Cicero.
Park J. M. (M E)   Clay.
Otis Ashbel (P)   De Witt.
Mattoon Chas. N. (P)   Elbridge.
Hasford ——. (P) Jordan
Austin C. H. (M E)   do
Rice Spencer M. (E) do
Bebee ——, (B)   do
Barnes Z. (M E)   do
Hough James J. (P)   do
Whedon D. A. (M E)   Fabius.
Waldo Daniel (P)   Geddes.
Paddock Z. D. (M E) Cardiff
    La Fayette.
Delevan Geo. E. (P)
Beach Edward C. (P)   Lysander.
Houghton R. (M E)
Alden B. (M E) Baldwinsville
Walker Townsend (P) do
Bishop Theodore M. (E) do
Gay John L. (E)   Manlius.
Hastings P. C. (P)
Robbins A. (M E) N. Manlius
Parker D. D. (M E)   do
Cleaveland R. F. (P) Fayetteville
Knox L. L. (M E)   do
Bowdich L. (M E)   do
Pise David, jr. (P)   do
Wright ——, (B)   do
Strong Wm. L. (P)   do
Hyde Orin (P)   do
Parsons L. (P)   Marcellus.
Thompkins J. (P)
Everdell R. (M E)
Fancher D. (M E)   Onondaga.
Collins Wm. W. (P)
Pomeroy Thaddeus, (P)
Clark Clinton, (P)
Strong A. K. (C)   Otisco.
Cross A. (M E)
Lewis Clement, (P)
Strong Addison K. (P)
Hastings S. P. M. (P)   Pompey.
Smith James C. (P)
Phillips B. (M E)   Salina.
Castleton Thomas, (P)
Adams John W. (P) Syracuse
Myers Joseph (P)   do
Hulin Geo. H. (P)   do
Lathrop Alfred C. (P)   do
Newell Wm. W. (P)   do
Lee Chas. G. (P)
Gregory Henry (E)   do
Chapin H. E. (M E)   do
Dunning C. L. (M E)   do
Ashley Wm. B. (E)   do
May Saml. J. (Uv)
Allen E. W. R. (M E) Liverpool
Sherwood Elisha B. (P)   do
Seymour Chas. (E)   .Skaneateles.
Bush S. W. (P)
Hartwell J. (M E)
Andrews B. (B)   Spafford.
Dean W. (M E)
Darling J. W. (F B)
Atwell I. (M E)   Tully.
Brown ——, (B) Vesper
Goope J. W. (M E)   Van Buren.

Ontario County.

Ewer Seth, (B)   Bristol.
Dutton M. (Uv)
Reed A. (M) Bristol Centre
Robinson M.   Canadice.
Daggett O. E. (P)   Canandaigua.
Whitney Leonard (Free Church)
Arnold J. T. (M)
Beach B. B. (E)

Kendall H. (C) *East Bloomfield.*
Davis M. (E)
Hammond J. (D R) *Gorham.*
Durham —— (P) Larned Corners
Flagler Isaac (P *Hopewell.*
Durham Jas. (M E)
Burch R. (M E)
Wiggins M. (B) *Manchester.*
Watts J. (M E) Port Gibson
Parker Robert (M E) *Naples.*
Manderville —— (M E) *Phelps.*
Lloyd —— (P)
Wheeler Eli, (E) Vienna
Norton George H. (E) *Richmond.*
Eaton J. T. (E) Allen's Hill
Day W. (P) Richmond Mills
Billington C. W. (P) do
Robinson ——, (M) Honeoye
Bulkley ——, (C) Geneva *Seneca.*
De Lancey W. H. (E) do
Dennis John, (M E) do
Hogarth Wm. (P) do
Bissel W. H. A. (E) do
Haskell ——, (B) do
Tarrington ——, (P) do
Abeel G. (D R) do
Dwight Henry, (P) do
Moser John R. (P) do
Powell —— (C) *Victor.*
Wood E. (M E)
Hogeboom Robert (M E)
Johnson —— (Uv)
Fisher —— (C) *West Bloomfield.*
Brown Silas C. (C)
Willard David (Ch)

Orange County.

Lewis J. N. (P) Salisbury Mills
Blooming Grove.
Dean Artemas, (P) do
Wood James W. (P) *Chester.*
Robinson Phineas (P)
Silliman Jonathan (P) *Cornwall.*
Wilkins William (M)
Hamilton Charles (M)
Crane Daniel, (P) Canterbury
Cruickshank ——, (D R) do
Potter T. (M) Buttermilk Falls
Gibson John B. (E) do
Mesiter U. (M) do
Green Abijah. (P) do
Sprole W. T. (P) West Point
Leggett John (P) *Crawford.*
Van Wyck G. (P) Port Jervis
Deer Park.
Leach R. (B) do
Cushing J. (E.) *Goshen.*
Lounsbury Wm, (M E)
Snodgrass William (P)
Ward S. (R C)
Ferris Ira, (M E) Sugar Loaf
Kimball J. *Hamptonburgh.*
Johnston —— (P)
Wallace R.
Herr —— (M) *Minisink.*
Burrows William (M)
Wilson T. (P) Well's Corners
Seward A. (P) Ridgebury
Bull R. (P) Westown
Judd Gideon N. (P) *Montgomery.*
Humphreys H. (M E)
Lee Robert P. (D R)
Hart W. H. (E) Walden
Schoonmaker (D R) do
Ten Eyck J. B. (D R)
Freeland —— (P) *Monroe.*
Fields A. C. (M E)
Dikeman J. B. (M E)
M'Cabe B. G. (M) Monroe Works
Ball Hosea (P) do
Loomis F. (M) *Mount Hope.*
Edgar E. B. (P)
Batey J. (C)
Van Zant A. B. (D R) *Newburgh.*
Johnson J. (P)
M'Connell J. (P)
Calder J. L. (M E)
Scott D. (B)
Brown John (E)
Duffy —— (R C)
M'Carty —— (P)

Gray John (P) *Newburgh.*
Armstrong Robert G. (P)
Bloomer R. H.(M E) N. Newburgh
Carpenter Chas. W. (M E) do
Prime R. (P) Scotchtown *Wallkill.*
Lookwood L. C. (C) South Mid-
dletown
Wood D. P. (T) do
Worthington Albert, (P) do
Bebee G. (B) do
Timlow G. W. (E) do
Barritt ——, (B) do
Roamer ——, (E) do
Hartwell P. P. (B) *Warwick.*
Vanderveer F. F. (D R)
Vanderveer F. H. (D R)
Hartwell P. (B)
Seeley H. C. (P) Amity
Timlow Wm. (P) do
Carrier ——, (M) Edenville
Waters T. (M) New Milford
Cummings C. (P) Florida
Pierson George, (P) do
Westcott W. A. (P) do

Orleans County.

M'Harg Wm. N. (P) Albion *Barre.*
Ilsley Silas, (P) do
Wilber A. D. (M E) do
Kidder P. P. (E) do
Gaston A. H. (P) Barre Centre
Mosher Wm. (B) *Carlton.*
Blood H. (B)
Conable F. W. (M E) W. Carlton
Fish H. S. (Ch) *Clarendon.*
Bennett A. (F B)
Mudge W. (B) *Kendall.*
Bridgeman Geo. (E)
Brooks Roswell (P)
Lancton J. B. (M E)
Bailey —— (B) *Murray.*
Hand Amos (M)
Paine —— (M)
Abell Asa (M E)
Derr John F. (M E)
Copeland J. (P) Holley
Clark —— (B)
Brown P. E. (M E) Medina
Ridgeway.
Church S. C. (M) do
Furman C. E. (P) do
Reid —— (B) do
Pertington J. (P) Knowlesville
Ripley A. P. (M E) do
Smith T. J.(Uv) Ridgeway Corners
Childs J. D. (Ch) *Shelby.*
Baker S. H. (M E) Millville
Kellogg E. W. (P) do
Haines R. (P)
Phileo N. (B) *Yates.*
Smith Russell T. (B) Lyndonville
Chamberlain Israel (M) do
Ferguson W. M. (M) do
Hill —— (P) do

Oswego County.

Wilson James B. (P) Sand Banks
Albion.
Sherwood Norman B. (P) *Amboy.*
Smith D. B. (M E) Cleaveland
Constantia.
Porter Geo. S. (E) West Granby
Granby.
Hough James (B) *Hannibal.*
Hubbard John N. (P)
Braman Thomas (M)
Squires O. (M E)
Woodin P. (B) Central Square
Hastings.
Morse W. (M E) do
Turney J. (M E) do
Weed T. A. (P) *Mexico.*
Stanley Henry (E)
M'Faland David (B)
Whitcomb Lewis (M E)
Castle Allen (M E)
Newell ——, (B) Colosse
Scovill Ezra, (P) Prattville
Robinson R. (P) *New Haven.*
Judson A. (P) *Oswego.*
Butterfield Isaac (B)

Phelps A. (M E) *Oswego.*
Kinney John (R C)
De Zeng Edward (E)
Phelps A. P. (M E)
Condit R. W. (P)
Davenport John S. (E)
Hapgood Geo. G. (M E)
Stevens Henry E. (M E)
Foltior Julius S. (R C)
Judson Aaron (P)
Kinsley H. (M E) *Palermo.*
Tuller A. (M E)
Aldridge Asahel (M E) *Redfield.*
Cole O. C. (M) Pulaski *Richland.*
Crane W. I. (B) do
Salmon Thomas, (P) do
Stanley —— (E)
Roney D. W. (M E) *Schroeppel.*
Smith O. W. (F B) Phœnix
Hanson Luther, (F B) do
Redfield H. S. (P) do
Kinsley ——, (M) Gilbert's Mills
Dady Lemuel, (P) Fulton *Volney.*
Townsend T. A. (P) do
Bishop T. M. (E) do
Hewett J.T. (M E) do
Arnold J. (M E) *Williamstown.*
Jones Philip (M E)
Graves Frederick (P)

Otsego County.

Barrett C. G. (B) West Burlington
Burlington.
Beach A. B. (E) *Butternuts.*
Marcy D. S. (Uv)
Baldwin Ely (B)
Burnside Wm. (B)
Anderson L. C. (M E) Gilbertsville
Bradford Thomas T. (P)
Ransom J. (E) *Cherry Valley.*
Searles J. M. (M E)
Parsons Geo. (M E) *Decatur.*
Beebe R. O.
Palmer James S. (Uv.) *Edmeston.*
Southworth Reuben (M E)
Wells Justus (B)
Blodgett L. P. (P) *Exeter.*
Southworth W. (M E)
Preston —— (B)
Bixby William (M E) *Hartwick.*
Pixley —— (B)
Wales E. V. (P) *Laurens.*
Pattengill L. (B)
Elliott G. C. (M)
Elliott D. T. (M E) *Middlefield.*
Parmelee Alvan (P)
Phillips J. W. (P) *Milford.*
Wright John T. (M E)
Howe George W. (B)
Gregory P. S. (B) *New Lisbon.*
Fitch H. (B)
Riggs Zenas (P)
Denison E. (M E) *Oneonta.*
Wells A. R. (M E) *Otego.*
Spencer Ellphalet M. (P)
North E. L. (M E) *Otsego.*
Marvin M.
M'Harg Chas. K. (P) Cooperstown
Battin S. H. (E)
Bristol D. W. (M E)
Gates G. W. (B)
Ketcham —— (P) *Pittsfield.*
Jervis T. B. (P) *Richfield.*
Appleton —— (E)
Tracy Solomon J. (P) Springfield.
Wilder —— (B)
Robinson —— (P)
Halstead H. (M E)
Daniels A. E.
Adams Norman R. (E) *Unadilla.*
Hawes Josiah (P)
LaGrange John (B)
Wadsworth Charles (P) *Westford.*
Spafford E. (B)
Queal A. (M E)
M'Donald W. C. (M E)

Putnam County.

Livingston Henry G. (P) *Carmel.*
Ely Samuel
Keyes Charles B. (B)

Lent A. (B)   *Patterson.*
Benedict E. P. (P)
Griffin M. (B)   *Phillipstown.*
Van Buren B. (P) Cold Spring
Silleck A. F. (M)   do
Vellanis J. R. (C)   do
Jones A. (B)   do
Shaw W. B. (E)   do
M'Leod E. (P)   *Southeast.*

Queens County.

Golden H. (P)   *Flushing.*
Gordon William R. (D R)
Merwin J. B. (M E)
Holmes David (M)   *Hempstead.*
Rushmore Lorenzo D. (M)
Collins William F.
Herriman —— (E)
Shields —— (P)
Dixon William (M E)
Young Timothy C. (M E) Rockaway
Bruce V. (E) Near Rockaway
Schoonmaker Jacob (R D)
                         Jamaica.
Johnson William L. (E)
Osborn D. (M E)
M'Donald James M. (P)
Goldsmith John (P) Newtown
Garretson G. I. (D R)   do
Shelton M. (E)   do
White N. (M E)   do
Bishop A. H. (R D) Astoria
Clark F. J. (P)   do
Taylor George (M E)   do
Curran M. (R C)   do
Bates E. O. (M E) Roslyn
                     North Hempstead.
Schoonmaker R. (D R) Munhasset
Earl M. (B)   *Oyster Bay.*
Bailey Winthrop (E)
Smith N. E. (D R) Wolver Hollow
Douglass Stephen (E) Jericho
Thompson —— (M E)   do

Rensselaer County.

Devol C. (M E)   *Brunswick.*
Ludlum M.(M E)   *Greenbush.*
Fisher Samuel (P)
Fisher Josiah
Stinson E. P. (D R)
Seage J. (M E)   *Hoosick.*
Beeman J.
Gordon Thomas (P) Hoosick Falls
Twing E. T. (E)   *Lansingburgh.*
Huwes C. W. (B)
Parks S. (M E)
Spicer T. (M E)
Reed V. D. (P)
Farley Anthony (R C)
Brooks A. L. (P)
Potter L. (M E)   *Nassau.*
Hurlburt J. (P)
Holmes Edwin (D R)
White A. W. (M E)   *Petersburg.*
Sanford L. A. (M E)   *Pittstown.*
Smith P. H. (M E)
Fuller C. (M E)
Barbour Philander, (P) North Pittstown
Graves J. (M E)   *Sandlake.*
Chamberlin C. (M E)
Hubbard C. (P)
Fonda J. D. (D R)   *Schaghticoke.*
Noble Jonathan H. (P)
Bailey Wm. (D R)   *Schodack.*
Smith John (P)   *Stephentown.*
Tucker John (E) 30 2d   *Troy.*
Noyes R. (M) 5th st. alley
Baldwin G. C. (B) 101 1st
Van Kleeck R. B. (E) 102 4th
Warren ——, (B) cor. 7th st. & Grand
Shepherd S. (P) 7th st.
Wadsworth C. (P) cor. 8th st. & Jacob
O'Reiley Peter (R C) 180 North
Miller Wm. A. (M E)
Corry John (R C) 190 N. 2d
Lewis Z. N. (M)
Haydn Gardiner (P)

Garnet Henry H. (P)   *Troy.*
Waldo J. C. (Uv) 13 6th
Corliss C. T. (Uv) 75 N. 3d
Bullions P. (P) 29 7th
Stow I. (M) Ida Hill
Phillips Z. (M E)
Lewis Z. N. (M E)
Farr A. A. (M E)
Havermans Peter (R C) 196 3d
Beman N. S. S. (P)
Pierpont John (Ut) 132 1st
Lounsberry Edw'd (E) 19 Liberty

Richmond County.

Thompson Wm. (C) Tompkinsville
                     Castleton.
Moore D. (E) Richmond *Northfield.*
Brownley Jas. (P) Port Richmond
Gilmore G. (M E)   do
Osborn T. (M E) Rossville
                     Westfield.
Lefevre J. W. (M E) do
Taylor ——, (P E)   do
Pike ——, (B)   do

Rockland County.

Quick P. J. (D R)   *Clarkstown.*
M'Keon F. (R C)   *Haverstraw.*
Evans John (M)
Freeman A. S. (P)
Winans Rodney (M)
Willard L. (P)
Hageman C. S. (D R) Nyack
                        Orangetown.
Kittle A. (D R) Nyack
Davidson I. S. (P) do
Hitchens G. (M) do
Cole I. D. (D R) Tappan
Boyd J. N. (P) Spring Valley
Isham Charles (M E) Middletown
Lord Daniel (D R) Piermont
Laushead S. D. (M E)   *Ramapo.*
Allen P. (D R)

St. Lawrence County.

Hunt W. W. (M E)   *Brasher.*
Jones Charles (P) Brasher Falls
Montague P. (C) South   *Canton.*
Pettibone Roswell (P)
Johnson Hiram S. (P)
Wilber ——, (B)
Wells M. A. (E)
Goodrich ——, (Ut)
Nichols W. A. (M E)
Vandercook J. C. (M E) S. Canton
Crowley P. M. (M E)   *De Kalb.*
Cross G. (C) Richville
Parsons B. B. (C)   *De Peyster.*
White L. D. (M E)
Jones Reuben (B)   *Edwards.*
Banister Isaac, (Ch) S. Edwards
Pierce ——, (M)   *Fowler.*
Slater L. (M E)   *Gouverneur.*
Beckwith Baruch B. (P)
Ferguson L. D. (M E)   *Hammond.*
Brown J. N. (M E)
M'Gregor R. M. (P)
Batchelder ——, (P)   *Hermon.*
Wilder ——, (B)
Moore Wm. D. (M)
Crowley ——, (M)
Wood Enos (P)   *Hopkinton.*
Jones E. W. (M E)
Cutter B. B. (C)   *Lawrence.*
M'Cauley James   *Lisbon.*
Eastman Morgan (C)
Pease Ebenezer (M E)
Midleton John
Miller Levi   *Louisville.*
Clark J. (M)
Parsons Benj. (P) Columbia
Wood S. M. (C)   *Madrid,*
Alden
Bailey ——, (C)
Halsey Chas. F. (P) Waddington
Hanson J. (E)   do
Pease Samuel (M E)   do
Phalan P. (R C)   do
Benedict ——, (C)   *Massena.*
Jones Wm. (M E)

Goodspeed Elias (B)   *Massena.*
Miller Levi, (E) Lewisville
Roberts E. J. (E)   *Morristown.*
Brown J. (M)
Young Samuel (P)
Kinney G. W.   *Norfolk.*
Rowley G. B. (P) Raymondville
Blackman A. (M E)   do
Savage John A. (P) Ogdensburgh
                        Oswegatchie.
Williams Sol. (P) Ogdensburgh
Peters Hewlet R. (E)   do
Webb J. N. (B)   do
Shepard Hiram, (M E)   do
Howard Joel M. (B)   do
M'Kay James, (R C)   do
Burnap Bliss, (C)   *Parishville.*
Moxley O. W. (B)
Brand G. (B)
Warner H. A. (M E)
Livingston Joseph A. (M E)
Montague Philetas (C)   *Pierpont.*
Whitfield —— (B)
Smead Elijah (M E)
Crary Nathan (P M)
Bowles Charles (P)   *Pitcairn.*
Plumb Elisha W. (P)   *Potsdam.*
Gorrie Peter D. (M E)
Hunt Isaac L.
Hubbard Isaac G.
Wallace Jonathan
Douglass Jonathan
Andrews Wm. W.
Ide John
Brainard Asa (P)
Plank G. W. (M E)   *Rossie.*
Kinney Silas C. (M E)   *Russell.*
Pettibone P. C. (C)   *Stockholm.*
Nichols Lucius (P)
Taylor E. D. (C)
Bigelow A. F. (M E)
Newton O. (M E)

Saratoga County.

Clamy John   *Charlton.*
Steel R. H.
Poor D. (M E)
Williams H. (M E)
Johnson Andrew, West Charlton
Randall Moses (B)   *Corinth.*
Rogers John B. (M E)
Brown M. (M E)
Voorhies J. N. (D R)   *Day.*
Carr Wm. H. (P)   *Edinburgh.*
Barnum P. J. (P)
Corey Daniel (B)
Lane —— (P)   *Galway.*
Myers —— (B)
Garnell —— (B)
Barber —— (B)
Harris J. (M E)
Mosher —— (Ch)
Rider ——
Atwell Paul P. (M E) Greenfield Centre
                        Greenfield.
Bogart —— (B) Jonesville
Day —— (B) North Greenfield
Benedict T. (M E) Jonesville
Kelley R. (M E)
Keach J. (B)   *Halfmoon.*
Tripp —— (B)
Ensign D. (M E)
Frazer W. N. (M E)
Burnham J. D. (M E)
Starks H. L. (M E)   *Malta.*
Fox Norman (B) Ballston *Milton.*
Griffin Richard, (M E) do
Geer Jarvis G. (E)   do
Wickes Thomas S. (P) do
Treadwell C. W. (P)   *Moreau.*
Freeman E. (B)
Washburn Robert, Gansevoort
                     Northumberland.
Slawson H. (D R) Gansevoort
Birkley John,   do
Dubois John, (D R)   do
Germond Peter D. (M E)
                        Providence.
Speer R. (M E)
Negus Elder (B)
Haight —— (Ch)

Emerson Oliver, (M E) Schuyler-
ville *Saratoga.*
Stiles Stephen (M E)
Chester C. H. (D R)
Kingsbury A. (B)
Saratoga Springs.
Chester A. T. (P)
Foot O. (M E)
Poor J. (M E)
Brown J. E. (M E)
Welldoller P. E. (E)
Weaver P. (M)
Ermond D. (M)
Clay James (M)
Spear R. H. (M)
Daly T. (R C)
Wescott Israel (B) *Stillwater.*
Seelye E. G. (P)
Fairbairn —— (E)
Connor J. (M E)
Coleman S. (M E) Mechanicsville
Dickson M. (D R) *Waterford.*
Bullions A. (P)
Edwards Edward E. (E)
Baker G. W. (B)
Quinlan J. (M E)
Ford Abel (M E) *Wilton.*
Divine Ransom (B)

Schenectady County.

Earl Joseph (B) *Duanesburgh.*
Aspenwall J. A. (Ut)
Wiley A. G. (C)
Metcalf K. (E)
Donald J. (D R)
Ingalls Wilson (D R) *Glenville.*
Bowen —— (B)
Kelly —— (M E)
Poor —— (M E)
Raymond H. A. (D R) *Niskayuna.*
Rosencrans Joseph (D R)
Princetown.
Nott John (D R) *Rotterdam.*
Mead C. S. (D R)
Van Vechten J. (D R)
Schenectady.
Backus J. C. (P)
Steele A. (M E)
Lindley J. (M E)
Day H. G. (B)
Graw J. (D R)

Schoharie County.

Clark William (P) *Carlisle.*
Squire J. (M E) *Cobleskill.*
Tiffany W. H. (M E)
Spaulding C. (D R)
Dixon William E. (P) *Esperance.*
Giddings C. E. (M E)
Squires O. J. (M E)
Broyse Frederick, Fultonham
Fulton.
Morey Stephen, West Fulton
Jones L. do
Scott Russell R. (M E) *Gilboa.*
Van Gaasbeek De Witt C. (M E)
Salisbury William (P) *Jefferson.*
Couchman M. (M E)
Mitchell W. B. (M E)
West Jacob (D R) *Middleburgh.*
Belknap J. W. (M E)
Sternburgh ——, (L)
Russell D.
Deifendorf Benjamin (L)
Richmondville.
Covey —— (B)
France —— (M) Warnerville
Cook —— (Ch) do
Wells R. (D R) *Schoharie.*
Gregg M. B. (M E)
Keyser ——
Fulton John (B) Leesville
Sharon.
Kling Marcus (L) Argusville
Bogardus N. (D R) do
Eckle ——, Sharon Centre
Covey Walter *Summit.*
Mitchell William B.
Lamont Hiram (M E)
Ferguson S. D. (M D)
Scott R. S.

Hammond E. S. (D R) Gallupville
Wright.
Gregg M. B. Gallupville

Seneca County.

Bassler Benjamin, (D R) Farmers-
ville *Covert.*
Señer James (L) *Fayette.*
Gross J. B.
Willis Ditrick
Tinkham Joseph K (M E) Ca-
noga
Wheeler Martin (M E) *Junius.*
Harris Hiram (P)
Lounsbury Thomas (P) *Ovid.*
Smith Mation M (P)
Townsend E. G. (M E)
Bassler Benjamin B. (D R) Farmer
M'Carthy William (B)
Lord Edward I. (P) *Romulus.*
Barton Morris (P)
Bradford Benjamin F. (W M)
Seneca Falls.
Burnham G. W. (Advent)
Douglass Malcolm (E)
Hoff M. (B)
Harrington Ransley (M E)
M'Call Alexander (P)
Bogue Horace P. (P)
Compton J. M. (D R) *Tyre.*
Gridley Samuel H. (P) *Waterloo.*
Macurdy David H. (E)
George Augustus C. (M E)
Hough —— (B)
Chapin Ephraim (P)

Steuben County.

Parmelee Anson H. (P) *Addison.*
Ashworth Joseph (M E)
Clarke D. (M E)
Spencer —— *Avoca.*
Bradley William (M E)
Brown J. J. (M E)
Tuttle J. K. (M E) *Bath.*
Miller L. M. (P)
Hood George (P)
Tappan ——
Corson Levi H. (E)
Hamilton Lewis (P) *Campbell.*
Smith C. G. (B) *Cohocton.*
Spinks John (M E)
Adams Asa (P)
Havens Elijah (W) North Cohoc-
ton
Strough Joseph (P) South Dans-
ville *Dansville.*
Cogswell J. M. *Hornby.*
Gray John (P)
Pattengeil Horatio *Hornellsville.*
Gould Carlos (M E)
Doolittle S. (M E)
Lilly Foster (P)
Rose Levi (P) *Howard.*
Chambers Richard
Kinney M. C. *Jasper.*
Everest Geo. T. (P)
M'Kenney I. J. B. (M E)
Hanover Daniel *Lindley.*
Davidson C. R. (M E) *Orange.*
Rogers Lewis L. (M E)
Abbey David (P) Mead's Creek
Fellows Nathan *Painted Post.*
Towsey Thomas (M E)
Gilbert John D. (E)
Brooks A. L.
Skinner G. M. (E) Corning
Seaver H. N. (M E) do
Hotchkin James H. (P)
Prattsburgh.
Pennington W.
Smith B. C. (P)
Hall James (M E)
White Samuel (P) *Pultney.*
Donelson Charles *Reading.*
Hurd Bryant
Brown J. J. *Thurston.*
Bowlette James (P) *Tyrone.*
Nichols Samuel (M E)
Russell Benj. (P)
Wilson R. E. (P) *Urbana.*
Sesek R. M. (M E)

Jones Alva R (M E) *Urbana.*
Russ L. W. (E) *Wayland.*
Bronson J. *Wayne.*
Bronson E.

Suffolk County.

Harries Thomas (C) Miller's Place
Brookhaven.
Hunt E. (C) Patchogue
Thomas J. H. (C) do
Osborn T. G. (M E) Patchogue
Evans James S. (P) Middle Island
Carpenter Wm. (M E) do
Parsons H. M. (P) Moriches
Owen Thomas (P) do
Hawkins Nathaniel (C) Fireplace
Tomlinson George, Bellport
Osborne Gilbert (M E) Patchogue
Shelton F. W. (E) *Huntington.*
Hollis Geo. (M E)
M'Dougal J. (P)
Earl S. H. (B)
Hatfield H. (M E) South Hunting-
ton
Platt Ebenezer (P) Northport
Jaggor E. (M E) do
Vail Edward G. (M E) Babylon
Corr James W. (E) *Islip.*
Krowles C. J. (C) *Riverhead.*
Sizer F. W. (M E)
Carll M. M. (Swedenborgian)
Downes Azel, (C) Baiting Hollow
Hallock L. (C) Wading River
Turner Geo. (C) Aquebogue
Edwards J. C. (P) *Smithtown.*
Hebbard E. S. (M E)
Wilson Hugh N. (P) *Southampton.*
Weed Levi S. (M E)
Smith E. F. (M E) Westhampton
Francis A. S. (M E) Sag Harbor
Seaman S. A. (M E) Bridgehamp-
ton
Wiswell George F. (P) *Southold.*
Huntting Jonathan (P)
Huntting Wm. (P)
Clark Henry, (P) Orient
Beers Daniel, (P) do
Hill F. C. (M E) do
Blakeman P. (C) do
Woodbridge John, (P) Greenport
Swallow ——, (C) do
Ackley Alvan, (B) do
Darrow George, (B) do
Mead A. H. (M E) do
Youngs Ezra, (P) Cutchogue
Lawrence Amos E. (P) do
Frost J. H. (M E) do

Sullivan County.

Romer James H. (M E) *Bethel.*
Bangs Nathan H. (M E) *Callikoon*
Duryea Isaac (P) *Fallsburgh.*
Petrie James (P) *Liberty.*
Davy —— (M)
Murphy —— (B)
Kyte Felix (C) *Lumberland.*
Bellows A. H. (M) Berryville
Mills S. W. (D R) Bloomingburgh
Mamakating.
Isham Chas. (M) Bloomingburgh
Reed John (Seceder) do
Vail Adee, (M E) Wurtsboro
Hillman Alex. C. (D R) do
Hammond H. (P) *Neversink.*
Day B. (M E) *Rockland.*
Winner J. O. (M E)
Larcom Thomas, (P) Beaverkill
Whiston O. (U) Monticello
Thompson.
Adams James, (P) do
Bloomer Wm. (M) do
Fowler E. K. (E) do

Tioga County.

Torrey O. L. (M E) *Barton.*
Coryell V. M. (M E)
Stowell —— (B)
Worden P. S. (M E) *Berkshire.*
Conklin O. P. (P)
Benedict Edwin (P) *Candor.*

Bailey John, (E)   *Candor.*
Round W. (M E)
Ford Marcus, (P) Newark Valley
                            Newark.
Shumway Geo. R. H. (P)
Fivah Mark, (M) Newark Valley
Colburn Hanford, (M E) do
Snyder John M. (M)   do
Jewell Joel, (P) West Newark
Davidson J. W. (M E)   *Nichols.*
Wells J. (M E)
Hay Philip C. (P)   *Owego.*
Wilcox S. C. (C)
Watson Geo. (E)
Dana A. J. (M E)
Pratt J. H. (B)
Gilbride M. (R C)
Willson Geo. (Wes)
Whitham J. (M E) Flemingville
Morse David J. (P)   *Richford.*
Elwell R. (M E)   *Spencer.*
Cushman M. R. (P)
Congell V. M. (M E)   *Tioga.*
Ripley —— (B)
M'Cullough Sam. J. (P)

Tompkins County.

Parker Samuel (P)   *Caroline.*
Young E. A. (M E) Slaterville
Grimes J. M. (M E) Speedsville
Voorhies Stephen (P)   *Danby.*
Ellis B. (M E) North Danby
Owen E. (M E) South Danby
Spaulding G. (P) Varna   *Dryden.*
Hesler O. (M E)   do
Miller W. H. (M E) do
Jewell Moses (P)   *Enfield.*
Pindar Wm. E. (M E)
Wood A. (M E)   *Groton.*
Brown S. H. (M E)
Kinney P. R. (P) West Groton
Sackett H. A. (P) Groton Hollow
Platt Adams W. (P)   *Hector.*
M'Etheny T. M. (M E)
Stilwell R. L. (M E)
Scofield S. R. (P) Mecklenburgh
Chubbuck A. E. (M E)   do
Wisner Wm. (P)   *Ithaca.*
Henry James V. (D R)
Reed F. (M E)
Walker Wm. S. (E)
Glanville A. (B)
Crocker Geo. (B)
Griswold Levi, (P) Ludlowville
                            Lansing.
Benjamin A. (M E) N. Lansing
Mercereau Lawrence (P) *Newfield.*
Minier S. (M E)
Root D. M. (B)
Porter Samuel (P)   *Ulysses.*
Hudson Elisha (M E)
Hamilton D. H. (P) Trumansburgh
Clapp Ralph, (M E)   do
Harris H. (M E) Jacksonville

Ulster County.

Hermance John P. (M E) *Esopus.*
Fort Abraham (D R)
Cruickshank J. C. (D R)   *Hurley.*
Sanford P. P. (M E)   *Kingston.*
Hoes J. C. F. (D R)
Shook C. (B)
Phillips Benj. T. (P) Rondout
Pelton C. F. (M E)   do
Nichols W. S. (B)   do
Quinn Wm. (R C)   do
Siebke C. H. (P)   do
Van Dyck C. L. (D R) Stone Ridge
                            Marbletown.
Smith Wm. H. (M E) Stone Ridge
Hawkshurst R. (M)   do
Hall R. (P) Milton   *Marlborough.*
Oldria E. (M E) do
Hukley —— (E)
Stilt C. H. (D R)   *New Paltz.*
Washburn J. C. (M E)
Brush Wm. (D R) Tuthill
Schenck M. L. (D R)   *Plattekill.*
Lakin A. S. (M E)
Wycoff C. (D R) Accord *Rochester.*
Strong T. C. (D R)   *Rosendale.*
Benedict Nathan D. (B)

Hulbert V. M. (D R)   *Saugerties.*
Van Doran —— (D R)
Ostrander Henry (D R)
Van Santvoord C. (D R)
Schenck M. S. (D R)
Nichols R (E)
Crandall B. C. (B)
Cornell R. (L)
Gillegan ——   (R C)
Gray H. (M)
Oakley P. C. (M E)
Alliger J. B. (D R) Bruynswick
                            Shawangunk.
Demarest J. T (D R) Ulsterville
Quakenboss D. M. (D R) Napanock
                            Wawarsing.
Buck H. (M E) Napanock
Ayers —— (D R) Ellenville
Newman Thomas (M E) do
Rice Nathan (M E)   *Woodstock.*
Gulick A. (D R)

Warren County.

Clapp R. C. Chestertown *Chester.*
Baldwin J. (B)   do
Coe Benjamin, (M) do
Townsend (M)   *Hague.*
Cobb D. A. (B)   *Hericon.*
Smith Caleb (B)
Graves Oliver (B)
Burage Lathrop (E)
Smith W. J. (M)
Burnham B. S.   *Johnsburgh.*
Davison William H.
Turner Edward
Harrington Gamaliel W.
Millin Elder
Smith David
Sherwood Lorenzo D.   *Luzerne.*
Abbott John W.
Fennel A. J. (P) Glenn's Falls
                            Queensbury.
Walker J. F. (M E) Glenn's Falls
Little R. M. (M)   do
Baker J. (Uv)   do
Reynolds ——, (B)   do
Smith C. (P)   *Warrensburgh.*
Clements —— (M)

Washington County.

Osborn Amos (M E)   *Argyle.*
Newton E. H.   *Cambridge.*
Bullions Alexander
Bullions David G.
M'Laury Thomas C.
Lusk H. K.
Brownell E.
Morris Wm., Buskirk's Bridge
Harwood John (M E)   *Easton.*
Watts Parmenas (M E)
Shurtliff Asaph (M E)
Brown William (P)
Meeker H. (M E)   *Fort Ann.*
Fisher Geo. (B)
Burrows J. F. (M E)
Bostwick J. (E)   *Fort Edward.*
Meeker —— (M)
Moore —— (B)
Hubbard J. B. (P)   *Granville.*
Gilbert C. C. (M E)
Gardner S. (M E)
Doolittle C. (P) North Granville
Mason J. O. (B)   *Greenwich.*
Marvin U. (D R)
Stillman S. L. (M E)
Grenell J. B. (C)
Wright Stephen, (B) Lake
Mason Jerome, (B) Galesville
Bingham Moore   *Hampton.*
Rose A. C. (M E)
Shand A. West Hebron   *Hebron.*
Shiland A.   do
Laing Thomas, North Hebron
Weit Archibald,   do
Pratt R. East Hebron
Fitcher J. H. (D R)   *Jackson.*
Crumb —— (B)   *Kingsbury.*
Tayler G. P. (P) Sandy Hill
Miner Sherman (M) do
Peck G. (B)   do
Bostwick S. B. (E) do
Murphy John, (R C) do

Law Isaac   *Putnam.*
Lambert A. B. (P)   *Salem.*
Hitchcock P. M. (M E)
French ——
Frillman J. O. North White Creek
                            White Creek.
Harrower P. P.   do
M'Lowry T. C.   do
Browne ——   do
Amer Wm. (M E)   *Whitehall.*
Cannon J. (B)
Grant Wm. (Bethel)
Kellogg Lewis (P)
Sleight J. N. (E)
Olivett O. (R C)

Wayne County.

Shumway G. W. R. H. (P)
                            Arcadia.
Chase (M)
Tomlinson D. C. (Uv)
Moore J. G. (B)   *Butler.*
Reynolds R. (M E)
Vrooman J. B. (B) Clyde   *Galen.*
Acly Chas. G. (E) do
Kellogg I. H. (M E) do
Ward John, (P)   do
Dunning Richard (P)   *Huron.*
Hawley Charles, (P) Lyons
Wardwell T. F. (E) do
Goodwin W. H. (M E) do
Webb W. R. (B)   do
Denler Phillip,   do
Mentz ——, (M)   do
Ingraham Ira (P)   do
Wood E. G. (B)   *Macedon.*
Calloway Edgar (Ch)   *Marion.*
Mann Royal (P)
Hamilton —— (C)
Forbes M. (B)
Stanton —— (Ch)
Manley Lyman (P)   *Ontario.*
Draper A. F. (B)
Hekok —— (M)   *Palmyra.*
Harrington D. (B)
Clark John W. (E)
Eaton Horace (P)
Platt E. A. (P) East Palmyra
Watts ——, (M)   do
Peck Wm. (M E)   *Rose.*
Wickson George (P)
Wilkins Andrew (B)
Kittredge Hosea (P)   *Sodus.*
Jones A. N. (B)
Powers H. (B)
Robinson John (M E)
Caine John (M E)
Maine E. F. (B)   *Walworth.*
Wade Isaac M. (B)   *Williamson.*
Wright Thomas (P)   *Wolcott.*
Chapin A. (M E)
Wadhams A. (B)
Knight R. W. (D R)

Westchester County.

Elliott Joseph (M E)   *Bedford.*
Ingliss David (P)
Gifford M. (B)
Partridge A. H. (E)
Clark L. (M E) Mechanicsville
Osborn Elbert (M E)   *Courtlandt.*
Mulnix Amos N. (M E)
Knapp George W. (M E)
Gordin George S. (M E) Peekskill
Westbrook C. (D R)   do
Holliday D. M. (P)   do
M'Kee William, (P)   do
Chalker R. A. (M E)   do
Griswold M. (P M)   do
Lee & Maddach, (W M)   do
Underwood ——, (B M)   do
Duncan —— (E)   *East Chester.*
Henson J. (M E)
Keys C. C. (M E) Tarrytown
                            Greenburgh.
Underhill C. H. (B) do
Wilson J. (D R)   do
Creighton Wm. (E) do
Campbell J. (M E) do
Myer Wm. (E) Dobb's Ferry

Kellogg S. (P)Dobb's Ferry Greenburgh.
Bullard Enos, (B) Cross Lines Lewisboro.
Frame J. (P) do
Ward John (E) Mamaroneck.
Osborn E. (M.) Pleasantville Mount Pleasant.
Luckey John (M) New Castle.
Sing Charles B. (M)
Coit Thomas W. (E)
Nichols Jarvis Z. (M E)
Devinne D. (M E) New Rochelle.
Sing C. B. (M E)
Harris R. W. (E) Mile Square North Castle.
Beach J. B. (M E) Sing Sing Ossining.
Lundy —— (P) do
Halsey —— (E) do
Wheelock A. (B) do
Acker J. (R C) do
Brewer W.W. (M E) Pound Ridge.
Bryan E. D. (P) Portchester Rye.
Bull Edward, (E) do
Riley John (R C) do
M'Laughlin M. (P) Somerstown Village Somers.
Partridge A. H. (E) do
Jackson M. (E) Westchester.
Carter A. B. (E) West Farms.
Van Amburgh M. (P)
Platt E. (P)
Simonson J. (D R)
Rodman Jno. (E)
Harris R. W. (E) White Plains.
Schenck S. (P)
Brown Paul R. (M E)
Ferry S. C. (M E) Yonkers.
Demond Isaac S. (D R)
Storrs H. L. (B)
Miller D. H. (B)
Croft J. (M E) Croton Yorktown.

Wyoming County.

Morgan Charles (P) Attica.
Parsons D. F. (M E)
Chichester Isaac (P) Bennington.
Smith E. (B)
Richardson R. (F B) Cowlesville
Reed James (B) Castile.
Toof E. M. (P)
Kingsley J. C. (M E)
Stanton John (M)
Keep E. W. (B) China.
Clark E. W. (B)
Hines Gustavus (M E) Covington.
Allen John B. (P)
Niles S. (F B) Eagle.
Rykert G. (Uv.)
Ballou J. M. (P) Gainesville.
Cooley Wm. (M) Genesee Falls.
Huntley David (B)
Holmes D. N. (M E) Java.
Twichell P. Wyoming
Olney —— (B) Middlebury.
Blackmer —— (F B)
Williams —— do
Osgood —— do
Benedict G. (M E)
Morey ——
Platt W. K. (M E) Orangeville.
Page Joseph R. (C) Perry.
Brooks W. R. (B)
Burlingham C. D. (M E)
Brown J. S. (U)
Page Joseph (P)
Hodgeman T. H. (P) Perry Centre
Lord C. B. (C) Pike.
Smith H. (B)
Roberts B. T. (M E)
Ely Hugh (M)
Bronson S. H. (M)
Abbe C. M. F. (F B) Varysburg Sheldon.
Ward C. (P) Strykersville
Ward Nathaniel, (B) do
Young A. T. (P) Warsaw.
Barrett A. C. (B)
Kidder C. (C)

Nettleton K. D. (M E) Warsaw.
Meacham Thos. (E) Weathersfield.

Yates County.

Sunderland D. (B) Barrington.
Olney ——
Congdon Sylvester L. (M E)
Sutherland A. (M) Benton.
Litchfield —— (B) Benton Centre
Plumley A. (M) Belona
Eddy Alfred (P)
Frazer William (P) Branchport
Davis C. S. (M E) Jerusalem.
Mosiers —— (B)
Cobb Arding (F B) Middlesex.
Parks —— (B)
Parker Samuel (M)
Tower Philo (M E)
Hawley Silas, (C) Penn Yan Milo.
Robinson W. W. (P) do
Wright A. (M E) do
Smith ——, (B) do
Stryker P. M. (E) do
Douglass D. (W M) do
Chase A. (M) do
Adams Samuel C. (M) Milo Centre
Johnson Leander, Potter Centre Potter.
Benson J. (M E) do
Tooker M. (M) Rushville
Gibson M. (P) do
Hancock R. T. (M E) Starkey.
Shedd P. (B) Dundee
Frazer O. (P) do
Smith John (P) do
Stacy T. (M E) do
Ward C. G., (Ch) do
Pratt Ethan, (P) Rock Stream

Clerical Robe Maker.

Newport Elizabeth, 7 Amity New York.

Clock Dealers.

Kings County.

Dougher P. 27 Atlantic Brooklyn.
Pettibone L. W. (manu.) 71 Bridge
Hunt John, 124 Grand Williamsburgh.

Monroe County.

Cook & Stillwell, cor. Buffalo & Exchange Rochester.
Watts Charles, 72 Buffalo, do
Brinsmaid H. 5 State

New York County.

Andrews Franklin C. 3 Cortlandt New York.
Bemsel Peter C. rear 101 Reade
Blakeslee R. jr. 54 John
Bogart Robert, 339 Hudson
Bohringer Joseph, 138 Houston
Brewster & Ingraham, 44 Cortlandt
Brown J. C. 46 do
Bryant Ezekiel D. 43 Duane
Bunker Thomas G. 272 5th
Burns S. D. 436 Pearl
Cables Stephen, 412 Grand
Chase Geo. W. 4 3d Av.
Clarke, Gilbert & Co. 46 Cortlandt
Collins William, 105 Fulton
Conant W. S. 177 Pearl
Dunn Wilson, 244 5th
Forback Joseph, 122 Willet
Graham David, 41 Norfolk
Guy P. Adolphe, 158 3d Av.
Ives Enos, 105 Fulton
Johnson Wm. S. 20 Cortlandt

Lomes John, 229 2d Av. New York
Riesler E. 223½ Division
Pond & Johnson, 46 Cortlandt
Rockwell Henry, 167 Pearl
Rodgers James, 257 & 410½ Broadway
Schlaefer Carl, 25 Av. A
Shrive Samuel, 2d Av.
Smith John, 105 Fulton
Smith Ransom, 7½ Bowery
Smith & Taylor, 105 John
Sperry C.S. 167 Pearl
Sperry Timothy S. 223 Hudson
Sperry Wm. S. 535 Broadway
Sperry & Shaw, 293 Pearl & 18 Maiden lane
Wangler Joseph, 273 3d Av.
Wheeler Wendell, 354 Houston

Rensselaer County.

King Reuben, (manuf.) 305 State Lansingburgh.

Clothes Renovators.

Monroe County.

M'Callum Peter, 88 North St. Paul's Rochester.
Paul Robert, 50 Exchange

New York County.

Collins Jeremiah, 109 Spring New York.
Cook James, 52 Fulton
Cox Abraham, 40½ Beekman
Davis Edward, 221 2d
Henry Joseph, 19 Duane
Hopper David, 456 Broadway & 161 Bleecker
Jacob L. 227 Canal
Shorter John, 8 Reade
Smith William, 78 Fulton
Weddington Thomas, 16 Church

Rensselaer County.

Smothers John, 10 1st Troy.

Clothiers and Ready-made Clothing. Marked thus * are wholesale. (See also Tailors.)

Albany County.

Bulger Richard, 1 & 2 Exchange Albany.
Davis R. C. 2 do
Parker W. W. 495 Broadway
Cooney M. cor. Maiden lane & Broadway
Kirk Abram, 497 Broadway
Pohlman Charles, 622 do
Lawton Anthony, 434 do
Allen H. W. 426 do
Shepard J. G. 431 do
Dix Perry, 421 do
Hermance J. 417 do
Dorr E. 415 do
Street Richard, 409 do
Murry Hugh, 401 do
Rooney M. 399 do
Cook Thomas. jr. 395 do
Derby L. L. 373 do
White J. 323 do
Neving J. & S. 329 do
Donald J. 1 Sta e
Higgins T. 21 Lawrence
Matimore F. 23 do
Park Wm. 18 Little Basin
Sullivan T. 13 do
Lynch O. 10 do
M'Cotter —— 9 do
Lynch J. 10 N. Lansing
Tuey T. 2 do
Welsh P. 7 do
Swift H. 55 Quay
Baird J. 171 S. Pearl
Schur J. 165 do
Harman S. 54 do

Shirley E. 41½ S. Pearl   *Albany.*
Wyman Mrs. H. 38 Green
Baker T. S. 518 Broadway
Lansing K. V. R. 454 do
Potter, Waterman & Co.   West
  Troy   *Watervliet.*
Sutherland D. P. West Troy
Leog & Colen,   do
Agan Keran,   do
O'Conner Thomas,   do
Isaacs L.   do
Butts H. L. & Co. Cohoes

Alleghany County.
Searle D. H.   *Rushford.*

Broome County.
Doubleday J. H.   *Binghamton.*
Meyer & Levi
Noland W. H.

Cattaraugus County.
Reid Wm.   *Randolph.*

Cayuga County.
Griswold F. L. & Co. 89 Genesee
              Auburn.

Chautauque County.
Butler & Westcott, Jamestown
              Ellicott.
Mason B. B.   do
Coddington D. Irving   *Hanover.*
Sexton A. Forestville
Frisbee M. Fredonia   *Pomfret.*
Ogle William   *Westfield.*

Chemung County.
Alexander S. S.   *Elmira.*
Davis L. & Brother
Holland David
Steele F. C.
Kane John A.
Butler & Doblin
Fish Charles
Snell James H.
Cole J. M., Millport   *Veteran.*

Chenango County.
Dinner & Bradley   *Greene.*
Beardsley C.   *New Berlin.*
Mann & Cook   *Norwich.*
Duryea J. K.
Curtiss & Allendorf
Sherwood N.
Conway Thomas

Clinton County.
Whitney W. Keeseville   *Au Sable.*
Hartwell A.   *Plattsburgh.*
White John

Columbia County.
Sylvester Mitchell, Warren st.
              Hudson.
Baker A. W. Warren st.
Silberston M.   do
Benton R.   do
Sylvester Marks, 310 Warren
Smith F., Valatie   *Kinderhook.*

Delaware County.
Kennedy G. D.   *Delhi.*
Sawyer & Co.
Blum L. Deposit   *Tompkins.*

Duchess County.
Northrop D. B.   *Fishkill.*
Wise M. 206 Main   *Poughkeepsie.*
Anhalt Jacob, 282 Main
Bahret J. 280 Main
Slee J. 272 Main
Rosenbaum P. & J. Main st.
Harrison C. B. 285½ Main
Ayhault Jacob, 283½ Main
Marvis Aaron 283 Main
Baker J. 229 Main

Wood H. 12 Market   *Poughkeepsie.*
Peters Wm. H.   *Rhinebeck.*

Erie County.
Lesler & Joseph, 2 Stowe's block
  also 120 Main st.   *Buffalo.*
Murphy John B. 24 Commercial
Hyman S. 9 Commercial
Jacob M. Commercial st.
Wust Frederic,   do
Diebold A. 6   do
Alexander Julius, do
Strass A. & G.E. 3½ do
Dubeld S.   do
Werle A.   do
Lenhart J.   do
Stambach H. G. 2   do
Chandler Andrew, 2 Water
Rohr John, 1 Efner's block, Com-
  mercial st.
Schulze J. P. 18 Main
Robert P. Erie block, Commercial
Wormwood Charles, cor.Commer-
  cial & Water
Heideback George, 20 Main
Cuttner & Dobbin, 104 Main
Rowan Martin, 100   do
Grunwald A. 99   do
Noah M. W. 96   do
Levy A. L. 94   do
Smith E. W. 88   do
Lyon James S. 5 Spaulding's Ex.
Lessler & Joseph, 120 & 92 Main
Gitzky J. M. 75 Main
Stambach & Brother, 1 Main
Mahon Walter, 12 Main
Carland Wm. Gothic Hall, Main
Moltz Mark, 157 Main
Jewett D. B. Springville   *Concord.*
Wilson Wm. H.   *Lancaster.*

Franklin County.
Wiggins & Weaver   *Malone.*
Fisk J. D.
Lindsay A.
Wilcox H.

Greene County.
Hood John   *Catskill.*

Herkimer County.
Tryon Norman   *Little Falls.*

Jefferson County.
Morse Chauncy, Evans' Mills
              Le Ray.
Clark James M.   *Watertown.*
Streeter Nelson W.
Horr Peter
Hays Lawrence
Holcomb Orlin H. Carthage
              Wilna.
Parker & Hooker   do

Kings County.
Mortimar James, 82 Fulton
              Brooklyn.
Olssen Edward J. (Boys) 202
  Fulton
Stillwell Samuel, 134 Fulton
Bennett Andrew M. 102 do
Brien Thomas, 110   do
Roose Frederick, 51 James
Quin P. 76 Main
Bryan Joseph, 87 do
Mortimer John, 85 do
M'Grath B. 57 do
Julian William, Flushing Av. near
  Graham st. East Brooklyn
Farquharson Miss E. 169 Grand
              Williamsburgh.
Steckemesser William, 316 Grand
Balton Mrs. E. 248   do

Livingston County.
Brockway S.   *Dansville.*
Palmer E. S.
Leach & Mercer   *Geneseo.*

Howes William   *Geneseo.*
Patterson R. W.
Skellings H.   *Mount Morris.*
Samuel I. S.
Brown Edgar M.   *Nunda.*
Grover Silas

Madison County.
Case & Thomas   *Hamilton.*

Monroe County.
Madden G.A. 29 Buffalo *Rochester.*
Hawksworth J. 118 Buffalo
Seligman M. 36   do
Greentree & Willie, 34 do
James & Warren, 32   do
Burke P. Y. 26   do
Seligman M. 2   do
Bower J. 9 Main
Sanderson J. 8 Main st. Bridge
Bower S. 2   do
Cox James, 2   do
Hoyt Hiram, 1   do
Robinson J. A. 6 Bridge
Hoyt J. F. & U. G. 4 Main
Shelton ——, 10   do
Way A. C. & Sons, 3 Bridge
Katz J. & Brother, 11 Main
Shields & Preston, 12   do
Owen Orange, 13   do
Wolf & Buchanan, 15   do
Callender S. S. 23 Exchange
Bigelow Abner J. 17   do
Wilkin Geo. A. 16   do
Hyde O. A. 10 State
Samuel J. S. 3 Front
Rockwell M., 5 Front (Boys)
Greentree E., 9 do
Henry John, 68 Buffalo
Scott Lloyd, 48 Exchange

Montgomery County.
Hawley & Smith   *Canajoharie.*
Lawyer Lewis F.

New York County.
Abbatt Wm. D. & Co. 295½ Pearl
              New York.
Adler F. & Co. 222 Bowery
Anhalt Jacob, 26   do
Armstrong Robert, 369 6th Av.
Atkinson A. S. 128 Beekman
Autlers Henry, 313 Houston
Bach Jacob L. 146 William
Baker Hyman, 9 Orange
*Baldwin, Starr & Co. 8 & 10 Cedar
Barnard Israel, 76 Catharine
Barnet H. 84   do
Barnum P. C. & Co. 194 Chatham
Beers J. H. 174 & 176   do
Bellamy J. 3 Park row
Bennett Morris J. 35½ Chatham
  & 27½ North William
Berliner Charles, 62 Orange
Biggy Edward, 174 Varick
Bloomer & Holmes, 35 Nassau
Booth J. C. & Co. 27 Cortlandt
Boughton & Knapp. 33 Maiden lane
Bouton Ebenezer, 28 Bowery
Boyce & Co. 15 Peck slip
Blackwell John P. 179 Broadway
Bradford Andrew, 35 Oak
Brady, Anderson & Co. 86 Liberty
Bramley Charles, 329 Delancy
Brett Sylvester, 25 Chatham
Britton & Parselles, 256 Bleecker
*Brooks H. & D. H. & Co. 116 &
  116 Cherry
Broron & Son, 114 Catharine
Brown J. W. 12 Cherry
Brown Andrew & Son, 114 Cherry
Brown Eugene, 56 Bowery
Brown James M. 86 Cherry
*Brown Lewis B. 179 Pearl
Browne & Purdy, 200 Chatham
Buckley & M'Kinley, 108 Houston
Bush D. & Co. 256 William
Campbell J. 311 Water
Cardoze Henry, 13 Chatham & 164
  Nassau

Calrow Richard, 590 Houston
New York.
Chadeayne Andrew. 80½ Bowery
Chanfrau Peter F. 136 Beekman
Chichester Aaron, 98 Bowery
Chichester & Co. 235 Greenwich
Church Charles M. 78 Chatham
Clark Thomas H. 106½ Bowery
Close Aaron, 187 Greenwich
Close J. B. & Co. 12 Bowery
Cogswell H. 150 8th Av.
Cogswell Jacob, 133½ Chatham
Cohan Charles, 117   do
Cohen Charles, 96 Catharine
Cohen Levin. 22 Catharine slip
Colahan & Fox, 128 West
Coleman H. 495 & 497 Washington
Coleman Timothy. 76 South
Colligan Patrick, 323½ West
*Conant F. J. & Bolles, 160 Broad'y
Conklin John W. 155 8th Av.
Conklin Wm H. 369 Hudson
Conklin Wm. L. 8 Bowery
Costello J. 43 West
Costelloe Mrs. 249 West
Coyle Henry, 60 Orange
Craft John, 321 Water
Craigie J 136 Nassau
Crans Weller, 4 Fulton
Creighton John. 361 Hudson
Cromwell Israel A. 123 Chatham
Crothers John, 282 Water
Culbert Alex. C. 282 do
Davenport & Gardner, 47 Broad'y
Davis Charles, 7 City Hall square
    & 129 Chatham
Davis E. & J. 180 Chatham
Dawson Margaret, 128½ Division
Deeley Edward, 75 & 89 Chatham
*Degroot William H. 84 & 86 Fulton, 47 & 49 Gold
*De Groot E. & Co. 142 Fulton
*Devlin D. & J. 33 & 35 John
Dickinson John B. 79 Cherry
Dittenoepher Ephraim,85 Chatham
Dittenhoeffer & Wolf, 352 Water
Dittenhoeffer B. 78 Bowery
Doblin Adolphus, 112 William
Dockstader Barnet, 96 8th Av.
Dolsen William, 14 Bowery
Donovan Wm. 2¹ West
Donnelly Peter, 89 Wall
Donnelly P. 116 Water
Dowe John I. 500½ Grand
Doyle Michael, 399 10th
*Draper & Eldridge,20 Maiden lane
Duvall William, 106 Fulton & 59
    Cherry
Emery & Coleman, 263 Pearl & 40
    Fulton
Emmons & Jones, 11 Peck slip
Esler Edward, 291 8th Av.
*Evans Edward, 70 Fulton
Felleman Israel, 17 Chatham
Felleman L. M. & Co. 15 & 71
    Chatham
Ferdinand J. 225 Fulton
Fitzgerald Edward, 81 William
Fitzgerald G. 1 Av. D
Fitzpatrick John, 154 8th Av.
Finch Amos, 306 & 187 Greenwich
Fox George P. 65 Chambers
Fox Samuel, 29 Chatham
Frank Philip W. 372 Water
Frank Wolf K. 100 Cherry
Frey, Sands & Co. 187½ Greenwich
Frisby Edward, 31 South
Gans Samuel M. 113 Roosevelt
*Garnsey Albert, 18 Maiden lane
Garthwaite & Darcy, 123 Maiden
    Lane
Gavitt A. T. 237 Greenwich
Germond, Freeman & Bradford.
    62 John
Ghuske Max, 331 Water
Gilbons J. 418 West
Gillespie Isaac H. 163 Cherry
Gloyne Samuel, 43 Roosevelt
Golit Simon, 68 Orange
Graham Robert, 72 Thompson
Green George T. 110 Chatham

Gregory J. W. 245 Grand
New York.
Griswold E. W. 221 Greenwich
Gross C. 162½ Bowery
Grower John, 480 Greenwich
Gutierrez Alonzo, 345 Water
*Hadden, Taylor & Co. 69 John
Haight Elisha. 82 Bowery
Haight C. G. 334½ Grand
Haight J. 114 Bowery
*Hall Andrew, 84 & 86 Vesey
*Hall Charles. 80 Vesey
Hamilton R. H. 302 West
Hanly W. 211 West
Hanna John A. 495 Washington
Hara I. K. 49 John
Harbutt & Cooper, 118½ & 272½
    Bowery
Harly N. 264 West
Harris Henry, 4 Orange
Harris John, 68½ Bowery
Harris Joseph, 2 Catharine slip
Harris J. 19 West
Harris Marcus E. & Co. 121 Chatham
Harris Morris, 145 Greenwich
Harris J. & Bros, 186 Chatham
Hart Nathan 8. 127 Chatham
Hatfield Sampson, 164 Broadway
Hays John, 363 Hudson
Hallman E. 197 Houston
Hennel Frederick, 454 Pearl
Henry John & Co. 49 John
Herwick C. 122 Canal
Hewit & Coulson, 148 William
Hewlett Leonard, 200 West
Hilt Wm. 267 Water
*Hirshfield & Barnett. 137 William
Hoffman S. N. A. & 396 Water
Hogan Pat'k. 39 South & 12 West
Holland M. 249 West
Horton & Barnum, 206 Chatham
Hoyt George A. 22 Bowery
Husted L. V. 217 Greenwich
Hutchins Francis W. 165 William
Hyde George A. 106 Fulton
*Ingraham H. K. 81 Cedar
Isaacs John. 147 Washington
Isaacson Asley, 98 Orange
Isaacson Elias. 85 Chatham
Jacobs Aaron B. 19 Chatham
Jacobs William H. 3 Maiden Lane
*Jennings A. G. 63 Liberty
Jacobe Jacob, 238 Bowery
Jeffries George C, 106 Bowery
Joseph M. 25 2d
Kaiser John, 60 Av. B
Kerrigan M. 8 Walnut
Kerwin Thomas, 133 3d
*Kirby I. F. & Co. 45 Cedar
Koffman Sam. & A. 396 Water
Leaby Tobias, 152 Division
Leon Abraham, 95 Chatham
Leon Isaac A. 97 Chatham
Lepine James, 63 Chambers
Levi Judah, 285 Water
Levi Julius, 2 Orange
Levie George. 136 Nassau
Levy Abraham, 29 & 11½ Chatham
Levy Arthur L. 75 William
Levy Emanuel, 107 Chatham
Levy Isaac & Co. 64 Bowery & 57
    Chatham
*Levy Joseph & Co. 57 Chatham
Levy J. & Co. 398 10th
*Lewis John W. & Co. 202 Pearl,
    113 Maiden Lane, 251 Water &
    20 Peck slip
*Lewis & Hanford, 252,254, 256, &
    258 Pearl
Lesoman S. 170½ Bowery
*Lithauer J. & L. 191 William
Livingston Solomon, 46 Houston
Livermore I. 263 Second
Londner Meyer, 88 Bowery
*Longstreet C. T. 64 Nassau
Lundner H. 11 & 17½ Chatham
Lyon David M. 229 Water
M'Caffray Arthur, 30 Catharine
M'Caffray Hugh, 78 Catharine
M'Carthy T. 388 West
M'Cay & Co. R. 184½ Bowery

M'Cormick James, 68 Orange
New York.
M'Cormick John, 76 Orange
M'Cormick James, 78 Orange
M'Cully Joseph P. 97 8th Av. ,
M'Evoy & Sons, 382 Grand
*M'Orath & Thorn, 123 William
M'Leod R. 1 Cortlandt
M'Ilhargy Chas. 530 Greenwich
M'Caa Alexander, 70 Orange
Mann & M'Kimm, 17 Carmine
M'Lellan John, 154 Cherry
M'Niff John, 106 8th Av.
Magill J. 358 Grand
Mangin Wm. 80 Orange
Mariners' Family Industrial Society, 324 Pearl
Marks Nathaniel, 109 Chatham
Markley & Trego, 196 Greenwich
Martin John T. 89 Nassau
*Matthiesen Wm. 36 Platt
Maxwell & Sickles. 110 Chatham
Maxwell Wm. A. 128 Chatham
*Mead, Close & Co. 78 Cherry
Mead & Goodwin, 1 South
*Mead H. C. & Co. 3 James slip
*Mead W. A. & Co. 80 Cherry
*Merritt Jos. G. 18 Catharine slip
Meyer Nathan, 21 Carmine
*Michael J. 63 William
Moesbyll P. A. 130 Cherry
Moore John A. 109 8th Av.
Moore Samuel W. 662 W.
Moral David, 131 8th Av.
Morony James, 11 Orange
*Morrison & Levy, 134 William
Moss B. A. 915 Washington
*Moss, Fridenberg & Co. 69 William
Mullen A. 15 Peck slip
Murray James, 90½ Hamersley
Murray John, 19½ Carmine
Murray Stephen S. 63 Cortlandt
Newman I. 79 Greenwich Av.
Newman Julius J. 111 Chatham
Newmark Simon, 13 James slip
Ohly John, 580 Houston
Olssen E. J. 74 Bowery
Olsted Lawrence, 13 Carlisle
O'Neil & Brothers, 375 Cherry
*Paret John, 76 John
Paterson Robert, 114½ Bowery
Payntar J. G. & Co. 203 Greehwich
Peck George A. 328 Water
Pettet William, 152 Chatham
*Pfeiffer & Frankenheimer, 13
    William
Phillips Lewis, 311 Water, & 56
    Orange
Pierson J. S. & Co. 13 Cedar
Pike David, 100 Orange
Pinner S. 288 Grand
Pinner B. 290½ Grand
Pinkney J. L. 214½ Bowery
Plato & Cohen. 244 Canal
Potter E. A. 91½ Canal
Potter Joseph, 156 Canal
Post B. J. 111 9th Av.
Post A. J. 86 9th Av.
Prescoe John. 87 Orange
Purdy Richard F. 200 Chatham
Rae & Scofield, 24 Bowery
Reynolds Benjamin, 90 South
Reynolds J. 214½ West
Reynolds Morris, 90 South
Rhodes S. 29½ Chatham
Rhodes Zachariah M. 21, 26½ &
    31 Chatham
Rice Simeon, 139 Pitt
Rich Michael, 210 Chatham
Rich & Brothers, 130 Chatham, &
    18 Bowery
Richards Brothers, 26½ Chatham
Rode Zachariah, 82 Chatham
Rose Wm. 137 Washington
Rosenfeld Samson, 32 4th Av.
Ross & Leitch, 115 & 117 William
Ryan Daniel, 55½ Chatham
Salomon Harris, 52½ Bowery
Samuels S. 127 Chatham
Samuels Lesser, 91 Chatham
Schneider H. 199½ Division

Schnell F. 160 Bowery *New York.*
Schentley H. 296 Bleecker
Scott John D. 33 Nassau
Seidner Mark, 34 Rector
Seligman B. 121 & 123 Chatham
*Seligman & Samuel, 19 Cedar
*Shepard James, 38 Maiden Lane
Sink Lewis. 103 Chatham
Skidmore Stephen H. 149 Spring
Slovin M. 26 West
Smith Daniel P. 102 & 122 Fulton
Smith R. 231 Greenwich
Smurray S. 171 Washington
Sondheim L. & B. 26 N. William
Sperling John G. 2½ Bowery
Stamper I. & Brother. 4 Bowery
Steinhardt Selig, 6 & 14 Catharine
    slip
Steinhardt ——, 176 Bowery
Stewart T. G. & Son, 26 Liberty
Stiles A. & Co. 58 Bowery
*Stillwell & Montross. 112 Fulton
Stokler James, 196 West
Swift J. W. 270 Canal
Teittenhoefer A. 105 Chatham
Thompson Richard, 113 Prince
*Thompson & Nixon, 87 Cedar
Tickner Solomon, 26 Orange
Tittenhoefer Bernard. 78 Bowery
Tobias David, 544 Grand
Tooker Abner. 159 Greenwich
Torrens Samuel, 375 Hudson
Traynor John L. 61 Cortlandt
*Trowbridge, Dwight & Co. 118
    Pearl
*Tulene, Baldwin & Co. 66 Nassau
Tusch Jacob, 64 9th Av.
*Vanderbilt Jacob, 36 Maiden L.
Vanderbilt W. S. 418 Broadway
*Van Deventer J. & W. 57 Maiden
    Lane
Van Saun Abraham, 301 Hudson
Vernol J. A. & L. & Brothers, 69
    Chatham
Waitzfelder Morris, 79 Chatham
*Wanzer, Minor & Co. 126 Pearl
Ward Michael. 21 Madison
Ware John P. 68 & 192 Chatham
Watson Alexander, 90 Bowery
Watson William H. 90 Bowery
Webster Simon, 6 Orange
Weil B. 180 Houston
Weinstein A. 153 Houston
Weyman & Co. E. H. 29 Maiden L.
White H. 145 Greenwich
Williams Wm. B. 268 8th Av.
Wilson Joseph, 125 Division
Witherspoon James, 131 Wooster
Wolbach Simon. 203 Houston
Wood A. L. & W. S. 110 Bowery
    & 109 Houston
Wolfenstein J. & Brothers, 182 &
    186 Chatham
Wolf Joseph, 352 Water
Yates John R. 144 Broad
Youngs Sidney B. 144 Canal
Zig Lewis, 87½ Chatham

Niagara County.

Ballard & Thompson   *Lockport.*
Scribner James
Moses Marcus
Place George S.
Howe I. S.
Thompson James E.

- Oneida County.

Kingsbury T. L. Dominick st.
    Rome.
Stoker J.   do
Orr William, James st.
Kingsley T. L. Waterville
    Sangersfield.
Bailey Wm. L. 50 Genesee *Utica.*
Andross Wm. A. 40 do
Kaliski S. 27   do
Kingsley T. L. 32   do
Staring E. 62   do
Rice J. B. & Co. 66 do

Yates R. V. 94 Genesee st. *Utica.*
Roberts Thomas D. 118 do

Onondaga County.

Isaacs A. Genesee st, Syracuse
    Salina.
Felleman I. Genesee st. Syracuse
Groff J. Water st.
Longstreet & Ballard, Water st.
Yates C. A. Salina st.
Titsworth R.   do
Yates J. Clinton Square
Levy J.   do
Brown G. S.   do
Selant G. Salina st.

Ontario County.

Mitchell Isaac W. *East Bloomfield.*
Willie & Fink, Geneva   *Seneca.*
Woodruff S. R.   do
Judson & Savage do
Arnold W. W.   *Victor.*

Orange County.

Smith I.   *Chester.*
Ackerman J. B.   *Goshen.*
Benjamin I. 83 & 71 Water
    Newburgh.
Nelson Henry, 81   do
Japha E. & Co. 85   do
Stranahan James, 104 do
Mish Charles, 29   do
Francks & Hirschbery, 23 Water
Sterling A. & R. 3d st.
Gale B. C. South Middletown
    Wallkill.
Bromley A. A.   do
Pierson J. P.   *Warwick.*

Orleans County.

Smith Charles, Albion   *Barre.*
Phillips E.   do
Harrington C. A. & Co. do
Hopkins M. P. Medina *Ridgeway.*
Pike A.   do

Oswego County.

Kiety & Butler   *Mexico.*
Jacob A. B. Seneca st.   *Oswego.*
Temple John F. do cor. 1st
Williams W. A. 6 Phœnix Block
    1st st.
Goulding & Klock, 1st st.
Buckhart William B. do
Issacson Benjamin, cor. Bridge &
    Water
Hanna A. Fulton   *Volney.*

Putnam County.

Cornwall J. Cold Spring
    Phillipstown.

Rensselaer County.

M'Auley George, 290 State
    Lansingburgh.
Twining A. C. 10 Fake's Row
Bendon Eugene, Water st.   *Troy.*
Higgins Patrick,   do
Develin Charles, 125 River
Aaron & Louis. 125   do
Graham George, 127 do
Strahan Robert. 129   do
Sipperly Levi. 150   do
Sipperly David N. 152 do
Wilkinson Geo. P. 154 do
Randall & Wilkinson, 156½ River
Myers A. 188   do
Randall & Wilkinson, 196   do
Mattice J. C. 210   do
Wilkinson J. B. 222   do
Bundy E. S. 250   do
Agan K. 274   do
Van Valkenburgh L. & Co. 304 do
Bennett Lyman, 308   do
Van Horn E. 49 Congress
Syrs & Levy, 66   do

Rockland County.

Marks A. & Son   *Haverstraw.*

Gordan W.   *Haverstraw.*
Harris John A.

St. Lawrence County.

Thatcher & Storrs   *Stanton.*
Healy R.   *Herman.*
Pope T. Popes' Mills   *Macomb.*
Skinner Thomas D. Ford st. Og-
    densburgh   *Oswegatchie.*
Wiggins George W.   *Potsdam.*
Weaver Frederick M.

Saratoga County.

Shehan & Moriarty
    Saratoga Springs.
Chubb S. M.
Shofield & Hall
Lane William H.

Schenectady County.

Thompson & Ely, 111 State
    Schenectady.
Van Vranken William, 83 do
Davis D. G.   do 114   do
Ellis & M'Allister, do 138   do
Fuller J. I, 6 Dock

Steuben County.

Alexander S. & J.   *Addison.*
Melong & Quackenbush   *Bath.*
Fox A.
Young F. E.   *Erwin.*
Farr John   *Orange.*
Thompson G. & Co. *Painted Post.*
Lachmeinsky Newman
Goldstein H.
Howell C. G.

Sullivan County.

Murray & Lenham, Big Eddy
    Lumberland.

Tioga County.

Leonard ——   *Owego.*
Skinner W. H.
Rode S.

Ulster County.

Bellamy William   *Kingston.*
Anhalt Jacob
Magnus Morris
Bernstier Isaac
Morgenstern Samuel
Jacobs Michael, Rondout
Dougherty Michael, do
Jacobs A. B.   do
Sims William   do
Malou P. Eddyville
Cohen Albert   *Saugerties.*
Stern Marx
Samuels N., Napanock
    Wawarsing.

Washington County.

Wheelock S. B.   *Greenwich.*
Levi Jacob
Bryant Nahum
Allen W. C
Hall A.

Wayne County.

Lewis & Herrick   *Lyons.*
Klink S. H.
Althen P. G.
Horton H. M.   *Ontario.*
Williamson John   *Palmyra.*
Crandall ——
Butler B.
Huyck Peter P.

Westchester County.

Tier H. D. P Peekskill *Courtlandt.*
Hall N.   do
Wright J. S.   do
Linbarga John, do
Yoe Clement, Sing Sing *Ossining.*

Wyoming County.

Gladding & Co .... Attica.
Clark 8. F. .... Perry.
Runyon H.
Comstock, Andrews & Co.
.... Warsaw.

Yates County.

Cooley G. Penn Yan .... Milo.
Sprague & Earl, ... do
Gillett & Whitehouse, do
Stewart & Tuncliff, ... do
Pratt Robert, ... do
Benham S. S., Dundee .... Starkey.

Clothing (Ladies') second hand.

Cohan Hannah, 119 Chatham
.... New York.
Cox Charlotte, 65½ Chatham
Felleman Moses, 65 .... do
Pike Daniel, 81 .... do
Pike Emanuel, 113 .... do
Pike Rachel, 132 Walker
Rogers Reuben P. 191 Chatham
West Catharine, 88 .... do

Clothing (Gentlemens') second hand.

Bennett Anna, 94 James
Boyd James, 87 4th Av.
Cavuny T. 489½ Pearl
Crulay Thomas, 215 Centre
Goldsmith Jacob, 131 Washington
Grangat Peter, 124 Delancy
Levie George, 136 Nassau
M'Caffery H. 80 Catharine
M'Caffery A. 39 .... do
M'Intyre John, 104 Orange
Matthews Thomas, 18 Centre
Quig J. 128 Division
Wilkinson Joseph, 145 Orange
Wolf Moses D. 108 .... do

Cloths, Cassimeres & Vestings—(See also Importers General.)

Babcock, Gould & Co. 49 Nassau
.... New York.
Baldwin Caleb & Co. 55 Cedar
Barnes & Thayer, 44 Maiden lane
Bassett & Aborn, 13 Pine
Benjamin Wm. M. 81 Maiden lane
Biarnois Freres, 72 Maiden lane
Blackwell, Whittemore & Carhart. 77 William & 16 Liberty
Blauvelt David, 521 Greenwich
Bottomley John, 112 Pearl
Buckingham, Ward & Co. 96 William
Bramhall, Abernethy & Collins, 47 & 49 Liberty
Buckley James, jr. 77 Pine
Buckley W. 43 Pine
Burk James, jr. 46 Maiden lane
Chichester & Heath, 12 Maiden lane
Church Chas. M. 78 Chatham
Clark & West, 158 Broadway
Clifford ——, 100 William
Cook Wm. P. & Co. 104 William
Crane & Nitchie, 52 Maiden lane
Creed, Bockee & Co. 62 Maiden lane
Cromwell, Haight & Co. 68 Maiden lane & 11 Liberty
Delius Chas. A. 9 S. William
Delius Daniel A. 20 William
De Ronge & Moran, 50 Broad
Dunderdale F. 32 Maiden lane
Dunderdale Joseph. 47 Nassau
Earle John E. 99 William
Fleet Oliver S. 58 Maiden lane
Gauley J. A. & Co. 42 Maiden lane

Godfrey & Mead, 7 Cedar
.... New York.
Graef Arnold, 74 Beaver
Gregory & Foote, 39 John
Groeschke C. A. & Co. 66 Beaver
Grosmann Brothers, 52 Broad
Habirshaw Wm. 37 John
Halsted S. & S. 41 John
Harmann Isaac & Co. 91 Cedar
Hart W. & J. 232 Bowery
Holcomb, Vancleef & Kain, 7 Nassau
Hook & Townsend, 79 Maiden lane
Hunt Thomas & Co. 92 William
Hunt W. G. & Co. 80½ William
Jones F. M. & Co. 64 Liberty
Knoepfel W. H. & Co. 97 William
Kroger Bernard, 110 Pearl
Lachaise & Fauche, 43 Broad
Lester Andrew & Co. 19 William
Lewis, Fairman & Co. 69 Liberty
Lockwood W. 229 Greenwich
Loeschigk, Wessendonck & Co. 40 & 42 Broad
Lowrys & Woods, 69 Liberty
Lummis W. M. & Co. 73 William
Lydecker John R. 515 Greenwich
M'Cord George, 9 Cedar
Marie Camille, 67 Liberty
Montgomery John B. 1 Cedar
Morris L. B. & O. H. Wilson, 120 Chatham
Mortimers & Gawtry, 21 John
Moss, Fridenberg & Co. 69 William
North Alfred, 62 Liberty
Opdyke Geo. & Co. 55 Liberty
Pattison Thomas, 1 Bowery
Peck, Covert & Co. 78 William
Peyret A. 62 John, and dealer in Platina plate and wire
Pinkney James W. 55 William
Raynolds Alfred L. 41 Pine
Robins John, 426 Pearl
Rockwell David & Co. 464 Pearl
Schulting Herman, 157 William
Scott & Clark, 525 Greenwich
Spaulding, Thomas & Vail, 41 John
Spies, Christ & Co. 55 Beaver & 20 Exchange place
Sykes John, 77 Pine
Tanner & Burtis, 20 Liberty
Thayer Isaac T. 44 Maiden lane
Tilton, White & Hewlett, 34 Lib'ty
Trowbridge Henry & Co. 76 John
Van Wagenen & Yeoman. 90 W'm
White, Griffith & White. 61 Cedar
Winston F. S. & Co. 100 Broadway
Woodhead J. & T. 58 John
Wright A. 238 Bowery
*Zabriskie A. C. & Co. 519 Green'h

Clover Mills.

Herkimer County.

Countryman I. .... Stark.
Van Horn C. T. E., Van Hornsville

Orange County.

Demerest D. D. New Milford
.... Warwick.
Racine J., Racineville

Otsego County.

Coffin Peleg .... Middlefield.

Saratoga County.

Bennett J., Portville .... Moreau.

Coach Laces & Trimmings.

Delapierre B. 25 Howard
.... New York.
Jube J. P. 83 Bowery
Magnus James S. 141½ Fulton
Partington T. 11 Cortlandt alley

Sebrett Lewis, 105 Walker
.... New York.
Wilmot Alexander, 75 Allen

Coach Lace Manufacturers.

Ontario County.

Pitts J. G., Geneva .... Seneca.

Rensselaer County.

Connelly John, 329 River .... Troy.

Wayne County.

Torry & Saxton, Clyde .... Galen.

Coach Smiths.

Manee Abraham, 126 E. Broadway
.... New York.
Sutton Isaac, 74 Allen
Williams William, 105 Walker

Coal and Wood Dealers.

Albany County.

Wilbur & Townsend, 173 & 175 Broadway .... Albany.
Luther Geo. W. (wood) 26 Quay
Taylor I. (coal) 166 Broadway
Judson I. E. (wood) 19 Orange
Belknap, M'Kercher & Campbell, (coal) cor. Spencer & Montg'y
Mead Oliver, (wood) 101 Montg'y
M'Auley M., Dallius cor. Arch
Schuyler I. 87 Basset
Strevel H. (wood) 113 S. Pearl
Curran H. D. & Co. (coal) 29 Columbia
White J. G. (coal) cor. Hudson & Eagle
Hogan T. 168 Lydius
Nowlan J. 178 .... do
Groesbeck J. 45 Columbia
Strevel Wm. (wood) 46 Swan
Ives C. P., West Troy .... Watervliet.

Columbia County.

M'Arthur C. & Son, Water st.
.... Hudson.
Rogers I. & Co. North Front st.
Platt I. cor. State st. & Front
Livingston H. .... Livingston.

Duchess County.

Brett F. Fishkill Landing .... Fishkill.
Devor C. C. .... Hyde Park.
Howland C. J.
Parker J. G. 299 Main .... Poughkeepsie.
Hill N. & Son, 14 Academy
Foster D. C. & Co. Main st. Land'g
Reynolds L. & Son, ... do
Millard & Mills, New Hamburgh
Hull W. .... do
Martin A., Barrytown .... Red Hook.

Essex County.

Rand A. A. .... Willsborough.

Kings County.

Aanett James (coal) 7 Water
.... Brooklyn.
Arcularius F. I. cor. Columbia & Pacific
Baldwin & Jackson, Myrtle Av.
Bates & Berry, (coal) Flushing Av. cor. Kent
Bickers Walter, (coal) cor. Atlantic & Furman
Conklin Erastus A. (wood) cor. Atlantic & Smith & 60 Myrtle Av.
Craven T. & Co. (coal) cor. Atlantic & Columbia
Davis Edmond, (wood & charcoal) 177 Atlantic
Downer A. J. Atlantic Dock
Duck James. (coal) Plymouth nr. Catharine Ferry

Duryee E. N. (wood) 54 Myrtle Av. *Brooklyn.*

Endicott J. & Co. (coal) cor. State & Furman

Everett, Thompson & Co. (coal) Columbia near Fulton

Kelsey W. & C. (coal) 12 Atlantic

M'Namee John, (coal) Hudson Av.

Muchmore & Day, (coal) 87 Myrtle Av.

Muchmore D. M. & Co. (wood) cor. Atlantic & Boerum

Muchmore J. (wood) Washington st.

Muchmore L. M. (coal) cor. Court & Pacific

Pettit & Shotwell, (wood) cor. Atlantic & Furman

Rogers C. (wood) Plymouth foot Washington

Rogers J. & Son, (coal) cor. Adams & Water

Simmons I. (wood) Baltic near Court

Spence Wm. (coal) Plymouth nr. Bridge

Suydam. Johnson & Delicker, (coal) Furman near State

Thurston G. H. (coal) 363 Atlantic & 57 Court

Van Brunt N. R. (coal) 83 Myrtle & cor. Pearl & Plymouth

Yates James G. (coal) Bridge cor. Front & Prospect cor. Pearl

Messerole A. (coal) Green Point *Bushwick.*

Place Charles, (wood) 1st st. *Williamsburgh.*

Truslow Wm. & Brothers, (coal) 111 1st

Winterton Wm. (coal) 127 1st st.

Aldworth Henry & Son, 5 Grand

Tuttle S. (coal) foot of do

Byard & Hugh (wood) 241 1st

Garwin Geo. (coal) 11 N. 2d

Livingston County.

Howe Abiram (coal & lime) *Dansville.*

Madison County.

Nellis S. K. Canastota *Lenox.*

Monroe County.

Wright G. & H. S., S. St. Paul st. *Rochester.*

Rochester N. T. & Co. 69 Exchange

Hannah R. D. 163 Buffalo

New York County.

Abbott T. B. & A. B. 833 Greenwich *New York.*

Ambler Charles A. 199 Bowery & 88 Clinton

Andreas & Son, 69 Greenwich Av.

Ashfield Alfred, 441 Grand

Bailey Robert, 377 Water & 13 & 15 Batavia

Baker Cornelius & Son, iron stores Washington cor. Murray, 61 Leonard & 13th cor. Hudson

Bass & Morrow, 34 & 36 Washington

Beldon Wm. A. 674 4th

Belloni Louis J. 809 Broadway & 73 Wooster

Benjamin Everard, 205 Franklin

Bicknell Joseph I. W. 15th near 9th Av.

Blackwell Charles D. 9 Hester

Boureau Henry, 36 Water

Brenan & Willee, 59 Cross

Bridge E. T. 16 Wall

Brigham Thos. J. 140 Waverly pl.

Brown John, 299 Rivington

Brown G. B. 395 9th & 7 Hall pl.

Buckman Mahlon, 626 Greenwich & 41 Washington

Cany Edward, 177 Wooster & 882 Broadway

Carhart J. S. 305 W. 16th *New York.*

Carman Wm. S. Harlem

Chichester John B. 211 Greene

Clark Stewart E. 227 Thompson & 228 Sullivan

Clinton Peter, 572 Greenwich

Coleman David, 215 W. 18th

Conklin G. F. 288 3d Av.

Connolly P. 711 Washington

Corwin Elisha, 189 Greene

Costar Henry R. & Co. 142 Elizabeth

Coster & Powell, Stuyvesant cor. 9th & 350 8th Av.

Dauphin & Susquehanna Coal Co. 54 Wall

Delaware & Hudson Canal Co. 31 Wall, West cor. Beach, Gouverneur cor. Front & 572 G'wich

Dengeldier J. B. & Co. 92 24th

Dickerson Thos. Stokes, 105 & 107 Anthony

Dickinson James, 17 Essex

Dick & Merrith, 197 Bowery

Dodge's William Sons, 89 Gold & 82 Wall

Dolan Thomas, 263 13th

Dolan Patrick, 208 Mulberry

Dusenberry & Miller, 68 Wooster

Egan William, 512 Greenwich

Ferguson George, 28 Oak

Felter James I. 166 Chrystie

Fitch Thomas, 20 6th & 350 6th

Fitzdule J. & Co. 414 Water

French D. 22 4th & 579 Hudson

Fuller ———, 620 Houston

Gantz John I. 250 Cherry

Guest Francis B. 8th Av. cor. 40th

Harris J. D. & Co. 490 Water & Delancy, cor. Goerck

Haven C. C. 8 Pine

Heckscher Charles A. 44 South

Henderson & Martin, 438 Washington

Hutchinson Benjamin, 23 Walnut

Jackson Lewis E. 272 3d Av.

Jenkins C. E., Harlem

Johnson John, do

Kearney J. 8th Av W. 29th

Kerrigan Patrick, 504 Washington

Kirk E. 85 Liberty

Lowther Charles, 95 6th Av. & 402 Washington

Lowther Thomas D. 229 Thompson & 402 Washington

M'Govern Hugh, 754 Washington

M'Kennoy Paul, W. 23d st.

Maass Herman, 32 1st Av.

Maher Thomas, 632 Washington

Martin Richard, 438 Washington

Martin William. 60 Cherry

Maryland Mining Co. 71 Merchants' Exchange

Mesler William, 77 King

Mills & Secord, 23 Tompkins

Moore James, 219 Delancy

Nevin George P. 78 Thompson

Newcomb John, 163 Orchard & 249 & 347 3d

Nexsen Elias W. 36 & 38 Cherry

Norris John D. 461 Washington

O'Connor M. 333 Rivington

Oliver J. R. 377 Water

Olwine Jacob K. 377 Water

Ostrom J. P. 19th Av. and 26th st.

Ostrom Shephard, 145 Christopher

Patterson Robert 64 W. 21st

Pelroy Henry, 95 Eldridge

People's Line. 132 Washington

Pennsylvania Coal Co. 31 Wall

Phillips & Oakley. 62 W. 13th

Popham William H. 696 Broadway and 190 Amos

Pratt Isaac L. 31 Wall

Price Walter W. 3 Broad & 624 Washington

Queripel Henry, 19 Forsyth & 169 Greene

Queripel Samuel P. 17 Anthony

Quin John, 24 Hamilton

Raap John H. 367 Rivington

Randolph Stuart F. & Co. 74 Wall, 287 East Broadway 134 4th Av. & 250 Cherry *New York.*

Rawdon F. 71 Merchants' Exch.

Reeve Samuel B. 506 West, 95 Murray & 7 Canal

Reeves & Co. 142 Jane

Reid John, 54 Attorney

Ridabock & Schmelzel, 211 Grand and 6 Spring

Ritch & Mead, 160 Water

Robinson Henry, 570 Water

Silleck Henry G. 7th Av. bet. 18th & 19th st.

Simpson Joseph P. 76 & 78 Thompson 9 Christopher

Skidmore R. & B. 250 Washington

Southart & Kissam, 270 W'hington

Spencer Wm. 92 Crosby & Grand cor.Chrystie

Starbuck M. 69 Nassau

Sykes Lorenzo A. 588 Gre enwich

Taylor John, W. 22d cor. enwich 8th Av.

Taylor Richard, E. 22d cor. 3d Av.

Terbell Jeremiah, 519 Hudson

Thompson S. & Nephew, 275 Pearl 43 Gold, 69 University place, 485 Water & Rivington c. Suffolk.

Tisdale James, 141 Cherry & 414 Water

Truslow & Brothers, 126 Grand & 200 Cherry & Williamsburgh

Tuthill James M. 322 Cherry

Wagstaff ——— 331 Delancy

Waker Samuel, W. 24th st.

Wallace James, 191 W. 13th

Ward Sylvanus S. 411 W'hington

Warner George, 670 Houston

Washington Coal Co. 67 Wall

Week Jacob, 15 Hamersley

Weeks Jacob, jr. 313 Bowery & 1 Bedford

Weldon Asa W. 40 South

West Nicholas W. 134 Washington & 300 Henry

Whittemore Albert O. 441 Grand

Willey J. 506 West

Williams J. & M. 616 Greenwich

Winterton William, 91 Wall & 305 Henry

Wood Nathaniel E. 69 8th Av. & 680 Houston

Wood & Mabbett, 192 Chambers & 288 Washington

Worth J. L. & F. W. 24 Broadway & 4th cor. Thompson

Wright & White, 184 Monroe

Young Charles L. & Co. 30th cor. 3d Av. & 195 Stanton

Oneida County.

Bushnell & Meeker (coal) cor. of Pine & Canal *Utica.*

Bailey John, Cornelia st.

M'Quade & Clark, Jay st.

Walcott Benjamin S. *Whitestown.*

Orange County.

Farnham W. H. Port Jervis *Deer Park.*

Conklin John, Port Jervis

Oswego County.

Paddock Henry, (coal) Front st. *Oswego.*

Queens County.

Peck & Fairweather *Flushing.*

Peck Isaac & Sons

Hamilton Charles, (coal)

Edwards A. B. Raynor Town *Hempstead.*

Covert & Green (coal) *Newtown.*

Mills & Blackwell, Astoria

Carrington James W. do

Mills Edward, do

Rensselaer County.

Judson D. River st. *Lansingburgh.*

Stackpole & Watkyns, Front st.
Troy.
Noyes & Son, (coal) cor. River &
Ferry sts.
Arnold O. A. 401 River
Mallory E. L. Mechanic st.

Richmond County.

Marfleet D. Tompkinsville
Castleton.
Bodine William & Brother
Christopher Richard, Port Rich-
mond *Northfield.*

Rockland County.

Smith D. D. & T. Nyack
Orangetown.

Saratoga County.

Smith D. G. *Waterford.*
Hardick & Brieze

Schenectady County.

Rosa A. *Schenectady.*

Ulster County.

Styles John P. *Saugerties.*

Westchester County.

Smith S. W. (coal) Sing Sing
Ossining.
Lyon William, (coal) Portchester
Peck James H. (coal) do *Rye.*
Arnoe M. (coal) *Westchester.*

**Coffee (and Corn Mill) Ma-
nufacturer.**

Duchess County.

Swift B. Hart'sVillage *Washington.*

**Coffee and Spice Manufac-
turers.**

Albany County.

Thomas John, jr. 10 Exchange
Albany.
Chase L. A. & Co. 9 Exchange
Kinney & Schiffer, 24 James
Copp & Van Alstyne, 47 Wash-
ington

Erie County.

Bradford J. L. & Co. 253 Main
Buffalo.

Kings County.

Waring William & Co. 48 Fulton
Brooklyn.
Duffy James, Jay cor. Chapel
Wade J. M. 166 S. 4th
Williamsburgh.
Withington, Wilde & Welch, Ains-
lie cor. 9th

Monroe County.

Van Zandt J. J. cor. Race & Aqueduct sts. *Rochester.*

Oneida County.

Griffiths J. 23 Liberty *Utica.*

Onondaga County.

Booth George H., Salina st. Syracuse *Salina.*

Rensselaer County.

Oakes James, 11 N. 3d *Troy.*
Bogardus J. M. & Co. n. the Bridge
Childs Austin, 5 4th

Coffee, Essence of.

Szadecsky, E. L. 93 Murray
New York.

Coffee Houses. (*See also Eating Houses.*)

Blin S. 7 Warren *New York.*
Bone Francis, 17 Ann
Boulard Adolph, 83 Duane
Brown George, 71 Pearl
Brown J. P. 86 & 88 Maiden Lane
Ehrmann Earnest, 204 William
Exertier Charles. 220 William
Fassert & Schmidt, 17 N. William
Fink Maria, 5 Merchants' Exch,
Foss Henry, — Essex market
Fossett James, 11 Pine
Hartung William. 193 William
Jacobs Jane, 28 Clinton market
Kochenrath Charles, 218 William
Marshall Samuel. 2½ Bowery
Myers Mary, 27 Clinton market
O'Connor Daniel. 474 Pearl
Nelson Gustaf & Lovgreen, 40
Clinton market
Palmo Ferdinand, 307 Broadway
Reed Lydia, Essex market
Taylor John, 243 Centre

Coffee, Importers of.

Aymar & Co. 34 South *New York.*
Blair H. B. 217 Fulton
Bieidorn Henry. 76 Broad
Delafield H. & Wm. 79 Front
Des Arts & Heuser, 78 Water
Harmony's P. Nephews & Co. 63½
Broadway
Howland & Aspinwall, 54 & 55
South
Mason & Thompson, 33 Pearl
Sale William A. jr. 124 Water
Taylor Moses & Co. 44 South
Thurston F. G. & Co. 49 South

**Coffee Roasters and Spice
Factors.**

Barker Daniel, 347 Water
New York.
Beard & Cummings, 281 Front
Beecher & Nelson, 196 West, 205
W. 17th & 143 8th Av.
Blair Peter. 217 Fulton
Bohde Charles, 20 2d Av.
Brimlow William, 16 James slip
Brundage Ebenezer, 16½ Essex
Cairns & Oakley, 236 Front & 264
W. 19th
Chasmar C. & E. 334 3d
Chasmar Henry, 87 Eldridge
Clarke & Brown, 86 & 88 Maiden
lane & 15 Cedar
Cooper Sidney A. 296 Mulberry
Gilbert Colgate, 93 Fulton
Gillies Wright, 236 Washington
Heins & Kinsey, 212 West
Halloran Richard. 458 Water
Hicks William H. 180 Cedar
Isham Henry R. & J. G. 71 Fulton
& 103 Front
Kitchen George, 7 Dutch
Liscomb H. P. 62 Barclay
Loughlin Thomas, rear 29 Hester
Lupton Henry, 3 Suffolk
Maher Richard, 31 Attorney
Moller & Sand, 23 New
Munnie Martha, 165 W. 14th
Neil J. 62 Beach & 280 W'hington
Parker Edward, 92 Murray
Rowley L. 121 West
Williamson, Mann & Co. 94 Front
Withington, Wilde & Welch, 7
Dutch
Wreden Christopher, 86 Elizabeth

Coffin Warehouses.

Kings County.

Verback Samuel, 22 Henry
Brooklyn.

Harper James, Court st. South
Brooklyn *Brooklyn.*
Miller Joseph, 13 Clinton
Ketcham A. T. 9 Clinton
Burrell S. N. cor. Court & Mon-
tague
Gillen James, Nassau cor. Adams
Parsons N. A. & Myrtle Av.
Baisly John, 309 Fulton
Harper J. 166 York
Cornwell S. H. 98 Myrtle Av.
Bourdett Edward, 300 Hudson Av.
M'Cadden Henry, 14 Grand
Williamsburgh.
Snyder John, 344 Grand
Freestone W. 167 Union Av.

Monroe County.

Child J. *Pittsford.*
Thompson H.
Brown Edwin. 80 Main *Rochester.*
Allen D. W. 119 Buffalo
Moran John, 71 State
Brown E. 81 State

Rensselaer County.

Seelye S. 241 State
Lansingburgh.
Clark C. A. 296 State
Burns John, N. 2d st. Alley *Troy*
Lovett E. 42 5th
Golden G. D. cor. State & 5th

Comb Manufacturers.

Albany County.

Forth F. 178 Washington *Albany*

Duchess County.

Sweet, Nichols & Shields. Wappinger's Falls *Fishkill.*
Sedgwick & Co. (card comb) Mill
st. *Poughkeepsie.*

Erie County.

Graf Alexander, 82 Main *Buffalo*

Greene County.

Matthews J. F. & E. (wood)
Windham.
Cowles & Rowley (wood)

Kings County.

Newell Daniel, 59 Tillary
Brooklyn.
Vanderhooff & Co. 137½ Tillary
Tyler J. & Mosier, 1st st.
Williamsburgh.
Jordan David C. Leonard st.

Rensselaer County.

Wheeler W. & Co. (curry comb)
Ida Hill *Troy.*

Comb Warehouses.

Arnold & Southworth, 169 Pearl
New York.
Bartlett A. L. 29 Cedar
Brown & Tasker. 111 William
Eberens Morits, 50 Attorney
Fenn John, 45 Ann
Fraser Jesse, 58 Nassau
French John, 312 Spring
Jordon David C. 85 Fulton
Mandeville Wm. A.C. 59 Marion
Moulton Albert, 10½ Division & r.
4 Doyer
Palmer Thomas, 83 Duane
Peck A. T. 144 Pearl
Post & Knapp, 35 Nassau
Quimby Zebedee M. 303½ Broad-
way
Rall & Palmer, r. 118 Eldridge
Tasker & Carton, 2 Cedar

Commissioners of Deeds.

Amerman Abraham B. 20 Chambers　　　*New York.*
Amerman Jacob K. 52 John
Andrews Robert W. 74 Wall
Austin Wm. 79 Nassau
Baldwin James M. 20 Nassau
Beebe Jeremiah S. 5 Hanover
Belknap D. P. 64 John & 190 East Broadway
Benedict Charles L. 70 Wall
Betts Wm. C. 51 William
Bissell John, 11 Wall
Bogert Cornelius, 192 Broadway
Brewster Mason S. 75 & 77 Nassau
Buckley T. C. T. 79 Nassau
Burdett Charles, 5 City Hall
Bushnell Charles I. 65 Wall
Callicot T. Carey 45 William
Campbell Robert B. 72 Wall
Carpenter George, 13 Chambers
Chapman Lebbeus, jr. 38 Wall
Coe Frederick A. 52 John
Comstock Nathan, jr. 9 Chambers
Crolius Clarkson, 74 Ludlow
Cruger Henry D. 55 Broadway
Cushman J. Newland, 73 Nassau
De Forest Henry G. 58 Wall
De Witt Cornelius J. 88 Nassau
Dodge William, 72 Wall
Doherty John, 23 and 25 Wall
Dresser Horace, 79 Nassau
Dustin D. H. 41 Wall
Edwards John A. 74 Broadway
Edwards Walter, 64 Wall
Embree Robert C 76 Nassau
Everett Nicholas C. 117 White
Fleetwood S. H. 20 Nassau
Ford Gordon L. 7 Broad
Gamble B. F. 30 2d Av.
Gardiner A. S. 54 Wall
Genet Henry W. 35 Wall
Gerard James U. jr. 79 Nassau
Graham Dewitt C. 20 Beekman
Gray Epenetus C. 64 John & 136 2d
Hale James W. 108 West 13th
Halstead J. O. 83 2d Av. & 18 Wall
Harned William H. 15 Centre
Harrison Thomas, 44 Wall
Hobart Dayton. 11 Wall
Hoppin William J. 64 Wall
Hoxie Nathaniel B. 27 Beekman
Hudson George, 87 Wall
Hudson W. W. 20 Nassau
Hughson Frederick. 87 Wall
Hurry Edmund, 613 Hudson
Hyatt James P. 61 Wall
Hyslop Thomas, 17 Wall
Jacques Eden S. 127 Fulton & 310 West 22d
Knox J. M. 20 Nassau
Ketchum Edgar, 69 Nassau
King Frederick W 65 Wall
Lawrence J. C. 65 Wall
Leaman D. 345 Bowery
Lee F. R. 245 Bowery
Leyne Maurice, 12 Wall
Luckey Freeborn G. 75 & 77 Nassau
Lynch James, 25 Nassau
Marvin Dan, 90 Nassau
Maclay Moses B. 9 Nassau
Mason John M. 20 Nassau
Maxwell Wm. H. 68 Broadway
M'Kinstry Charles, 4 New
Meeks William H. 50 Wall
Miller Nehemiah, 170 Broadway
Milspaugh Philip, 28 Beekman & 171 Spring
Morange H. H. 3 Nassau
Morris Wm L. 6 Broad
Nelson & Newton. 61 Wall
Nones Joseph B. 98 Broadway
Osborn Charles F. 147 Mulberry
Phelps James L. jr. 52 John
Porter Edmund J. 5 City Hall pl
Rogers E. N. 187 Fulton
Romaine Worthington. 20 Nassau
Romeyn Theodore, 4 New
Rowland Wm. S. 28 Beekman

Ruggles P. T. 20 Nassau
　　　　　　　　New York.
Sealey Benjamin T. 34 Liberty
Seamen David, 105 Fulton
Sherman F. H. 12 Wall
Smith Charles Henry, 38 Wall
Smith Russell, 54 Wall
Smith Thomas J. jr. 76 Wall
Smith William E. jr. 111 Charles
Sommers Thomas S. 71 Cedar
Sparks William H. 6 Wall
Spear Charles, 60 Wall
Stafford Wm. R. 71 Wall
Stogdill Wm. H. 80 Nassau
Strebeigh Robert M. 154 Nassau
Striker George H. 70 Wall
Strong Joseph, 58 Wall
Taylor D. B. 142 Nassau
Terry Edmund, 44 Wall
Tillon F. 1 Nassau
Townsend John J. 69 Wall
Upton F. H. 72 Wall
Vanvoorhis Corn's W. 80 Nassau
Waire & Delany, 69 Nassau
Waterman Thomas W. 3 Nassau
Waters George G. 74 Broadway
Watson Alexander, 75 & 77 Nassau
Weeks John A. 58 Wall
West Edward C. 35 Wall
Wheeler C. B. 15 Wall
Wheeler David E. 62 Wall
White J. E. 11 Nassau
White J. W. 11 Nassau
White John H. 74 Wall
Whitehead Jno. 4 Merchants' Ex.
Wight Amherst, 93 West 15th
Williams James, 6 Trinity place
Woodruff & Goodman, 106 Broad'y
Young Francis G. 66 Wall

Confectioners.

Albany County.

Anderson Miss Grace, 570 Broadway　　　*Albany.*
Flaherty William, 205 do
May E. 5 N. Lansing
Anderson G. 81 State
Briars J. 121 do
Clarkson M. 98 do
Gock D. 62½ Greene
Campbell ———, 89 Greene
Winne M. L. 100 S. Pearl
Denniston William, 22 do
Taylor Mrs. R.
Wait & Vernam, 176 N. Pearl
Clapp A. C. 11 Wilson
Smith D. 40 Washington
Mosier G. H. 78 do
Briars Benj. 456 & 458 Broadway
Frost S. Cohoes　　　*Watervliet.*

Broome County.

Tickaner Henry　　　*Binghamton.*

Columbia County.

Weaver J. Warren st.　　　*Hudson.*
Paul C. 96 do

Duchess County.

Tooley A. Wappingers' Falls　　　*Fishkill.*
Frost S. 327 Main　　　*Poughkeepsie.*
Cambot A. 261 do
Lobdell S. 23 Market
Smith James & Son, 7 Market st.
Holdroid G. Mill st.
Clarck P. H. do
Bell S.　　　*Rhinebeck.*

Erie County.

Vancluck William H. 284 Main　　　*Buffalo.*
Adams James T. 308 do
M'Arthur A. & J. 240 do
Hoth James, 1 Birkhead Building, Commercial st.
Smith N. H. 7 Main
Benson & Co. 138 do

Fulton County.

Mowras Henry　　　*Johnstown.*

Kings County.

Terrain J. B. 269 Smith　　　*Brooklyn.*
Woodruff Mrs. E. 70 Bridge
Rafford Miss S. 57 Sands
Barrows S. W. & W. 209 Fulton
Vail William, 152 Myrtle Av.
Beardall Mrs. C. 16　　　do
Elliott John, 132 1st
　　　　　　　　Williamsburgh.
Howe John, 141 4th
Spangerbergh Edw. 167 Grand

Monroe County

O'Brien M. 82 Buffalo　　　*Rochester.*
Bond J. 74　　　do
Polly George, 61 Main
Winslow John, 71 do
Mahlerwein Philip, 95 Main
Monnolly James, 24 Glasgow
Laidler William, 79 State

New York County.

Abbott S. 683 Grand　　　*New York.*
Agnew Maria. 5 Allen
Allen Russel W. 243 Greenwich
Arend George, 268 Dowery
Armstrong Mary, 212 Elm
Austin Jacob, 461 Hudson
Bateson Christ. R. 362 Broome
Banning Alpheus, 115 Spring
Barguet Jos. H. 246½ Greenwich
Barlow W. H. 115 Av. C.
Barnes Mary, 75 Sullivan
Barns John C. 359 Grand
Barter Catherine, 71 Hamersley
Bartow Louisa, 115 Av. C
Baxter Joseph W. 301 4th
Beaudoin Henry, 119 Elm
Buchle Nicholas, rear 7 Walnut
Becker Catherine, 815 Broadway
Belknap Dayton C. 360 Grand
Berland Adolphe, 115 Franklin
Beyer George H. 261 6th Av.
Birge W. 277 Bleecker
Black Eliza, 41 Av. D
Black John, 182½ Bowery
Biancard Lewis. 80 Prince
Bogart Lydia. 36 1st
Bogart J. Z. 217 Spring
Bond Henry, 148 W. Broadway
Borchars Magdalen, 98½ Fulton
Borsjers Job. 16 Clarkson
Borstell J. 239 Bowery
Boyd Thomas. 99 8th Av.
Boyle Grace. 199 11th
Braden John, 75 Canal
Brigg Moses A. 29 Av. A
Brinkman Jane, 238 Canal
Brower J. 253½ Division
Brower Ann, 470 4th
Brummel Adonijah, 408½ Grand
Brummel William, 76 3d Av.
Bullinger Ensey. 146 Spring
Bunny C. 71½ 13th
Burns Mary, 10th Av. 19th st.
Bupignac S. H. 444 Broadway
Buxton Thomas B. 233 Division
Cain Theodore, 233 Hudson
Carberry Bernard. 499 Pearl
Carr James, 293 1st Av.
Carroll Jane, 44 Marion
Carter Julia, 343 Canal
Cawley John, 19 Elm
Cavanagh H. 210 3d Av.
Chandler Eleanor. 117 Elm
Christman Chas. G. 406 Pearl
Clark William, 403 Cherry
Clarke E. 239 1st Av.
Clarke Timothy. 81 4th
Clary Joseph, 188 Amos
Clear John, 64½ Sullivan
Cline Mary, 172 Stanton
Coffin Edward. 91 7th Av.
Colony & Ingalls, 89½ Canal
Condy Alexander, 6 Thomas

Conelly Patrick, 630 Hudson *New York.*
Conly Thomas, 32 Av. A
Cornell James, 193 Canal
Corr Patrick, 195 11th
Corson John, 80 Oliver
Costa J. B. 69 Barclay
Costello Catharine, 234 Thompson
Cotte Peter. 19 W. Broadway
Craig James, 482 Houston & 127 3d Av.
Creighton James, 316 Hudson
Cruise Peter, 19 Walnut
Culver Sarah. 424 Greenwich
Cunnington S. 101 do
Currier J. A. 191 do
Cuthbert Joseph P. 231½ Division
Dashear Peter, 476 Hudson
Dasher J. 8th Av. 27th st.
Dartvis P. B. 200 Church
Dean Henry, 741 Broadway
Deun Jeremiah. 217 Spring
Dean Susan P. 179 6th Av.
Dearborn Henry, 92 Division
Detiot George X. 241 Canal
Desher Peter, 476 Hudson
De Toure Henry, 346 1st Av.
Dias Samuel, 88 Mott
Dodworth Elizabeth, 493 Broadwy
Doggett Mathilda, 390 5th
Donald Elizabeth. 40 Wooster
Donelly Sarah, 366 Water
Donzelmaan John F. 68 Division
Drober John, 38 Division
Dufaugeray Mrs. 517 Greenwich
Earle J. 79½ Bowery
Ebling Joseph E. 200 Bowery
Edwards Emma. 27½ Howard
Effray Felix, 457 Broadway
Eggers Lewis, 190 Division
Erdenbrecker L. & Brothers, 17 Av. C.
Ernst Frederick, 151 Houston
Evans Edward A. 123 Lewis
Evans Mary, 70 Catharine
Eyyers Lewis, 190 Division
Farall John, 175 Grand
Farrell Elizabeth, 496 Greenwich
Faulkner Henry, 192½ Greene
Felt George W. 146 Orchard
Ferris Owen, 3 6th Av.
Ficke Frederick, 39½ Frankfort
Fielding Patrick, 484 Houston
Finley D. 26 Thompson
Fistie Henry N. 40 Chatham
Fitzgerald Margaret, 230 Division
Fitzgerald Thomas, 232 Division
Firth John, 166 W. 20th
Fletcher Wm. 111 W. Broadway
Flynn Ann, 59 Grand
Flynn Margaret, 122 Mott
Foley Catharine, 153 Orange
Foreman J. P. 281 Spring
Foss Nicholas, 169 Leonard
Fox Henry F. 181 Spring
Fradenburgh G. 130 13th
Frazee Susan M. 87 Bleecker
Frazer Matthew, 183 11th
Frisch Henry, 49 Cortlandt
Gafney James, 96 Ridge
Gale L. 337 Houston
Gallagher M. 29½ Frankfort
Garbett Zachariah, 5 Amos
Gardner Frederick, 134 9th Av.
Geer Samuel W. 189 W. 20th
Geronimo G. 99 4th Av.
Gibson John, 73 6th Av.
Giraud F. V. & Son, 76 8th Av.
Goldan M. 224 W. 17th
Gorman Catharine, 55 Laurens
Grady Michael, 63 Church
Greenfield & Co. 102 8th Av.
Grube John, 38 Division
Guerin Francois, 120 Broadway
Gundersheimer Henry, 609 4th
Hachmann Johann H. 121 Orange
Haddock James, 558 Hudson
Hall William L. 184 Chatham
Halifas Christian, 295 Houston .
Hallock Edward, 73 Chatham
Harrison Mrs. 211 Rivington
Harris Sarah, 13 8th Av.

Hart Mary, 420 Cherry *New York.*
Hart Thomas, 93 Oliver
Hassenau John. 63 1st
Healay Michael, 75 19th
Heart Owen, 171 Mulberry
Heath T. & W. H. 62 Warren
Helferich Charles N. 7 Clark
Helliker Mary A. 108 G'wich Av.
Henry John G. 249 Grand
Hess W. 186 6th Av.
Heth Franklin, 451 Hudson
Higgins Mrs. 91 3d Av.
Higham James. 34 Av. C
Hill Amanda, 114½ Bleecker
Hillanbland Peter, 683 4th
Hillbrand John. 247 Houston
Hill Joseph, 25 Rector
Hines Cleus, 299 Madison
Hines Sarah, 207 Canal
Hodgkins T. G. 148 Greenwich
Holand Martin, 54 Columbia
Hollings H. 115 1st
Hood Wm. 68 Stanton
Hunt C. 416 3d Av.
Hunt Henry, 218 Bleecker
Huttemeir Hermann, 108 Division
Hynds Lucy, 63 do
Jackson Mary, 174 6th Av.
Jacquin J. L. 23 8th Av.
Jenkins J. & H. 201 W. 20th
Jeroneiman George, 99 4th Av.
Jervis Mrs. W. 366 Broadway
Jester Frances J. 381 Pearl
Johnson Cornelius, 128 Wooster
Jones W. J. 309 3d Av.
Kearns Philip, 349 Houston
Kemp Barnhart, 383 Greenwich
Kingsland Eliza, 144 Suffolk
Kinnersley Henry, 220½ Broome
Kipp James I. 68 Av. D
Lakener F. 145 Spring
Lammerman John, 150 Chrystie
Lang Eliza, 207 Centre
Latham Samuel C. 146 Varick
Lawrence Sarah, 20 Crosby
Le Comte Nicholas, 234 G'wich
Le Comte Vincent, 290 do
Lee William, 522 Pearl
Lefurge Catharine, 208 Canal
Leggett R. 403 Pearl
Lelong Joseph, 67 9th Av.
Lemmerman John, 150 Christopher
Lenderys Michael, 67 Bayard
Leonard Thos. 118 W. 21st
Levon Joseph, 109 Broome
Lewis Albert, 342 9th
Libenbeck Charles, 1043½ Ludlow
Lilly John. 46 Division
Linsey B. 77 Broome
Lock David Godwin, 35½ Carmine
Lockhart Eliz. 935 Broadway
Lonnas August, 223 Division
Loughran Thomas, 78 Centre
Lynch Johannah, 404½ Grand
Lynch John. 361 do
Lyons Wm. S. 176 6th Av.
M'Alany Francis. 69 Marion
M'Ardle John, 277 Hudson
M'Cadden James, 350 Hudson
M'Cochray Sarah, 1 Factory
M'Cune Charlotte, 15 Bedford
M'Evoy Elizabeth, 495 Greenwich
M'Elroy James, 140 Grand
M'Ewen John F. E. 16th c. 3d Av.
M'Gill Edward, 465 Greenwich
M'Kibb James, 232½ Division
M'Lellan Mary Ann, 224 Sullivan
Maguire Mary, 311 1st Av.
Maillard Henry & Co. 401 Broadway
Mann Albert, 128 Grand
Markert Andreas, 300 Broadway
Marler Elizabeth. 234 8th Av.
Marshall & Clark, 631 Broadway
Martin John, 267 Hudson
Mason Henry, 395 Monroe
May Henry, 191 Rivington
Meisterlin Henry, 238 Division
Meyer Charles, 398 Grand
Meyer John G. 211 Madison
Moffat John J. 679 Broadway

Mollenhagen J. 223 Greenwich *New York.*
Molloy Bridget, 239 Division
Moorhead R. 35½ Carmine
Monson Esther M. 15 Bowery
Morehead Wm. 126½ Greenwich Av.
Morrell Alexander W. 394 10th
Morrell Willett, 630 Water
Morris Samuel W. 140 Lewis
Mount David C. 182 Essex
Mulgrew Neil, 50½ 6th Av.
Mullalley Cath. 245 Rivington
Mustica Jos. & Co. 450 Pearl
Myers Wm. 9th Av. b. 25th & 26th
Nelson Wm. 79½ Bowery
Norris C. 115 Hudson
Norris Wm. C. 73½ Canal
Nuskey J. H. 225 W. 17th
O'Driscoll Florence. 89 Oliver
O'Neill John F. 304 Grand
Orford Samuel, 107 Orange
Osmers Richard, 9 6th Av.
Oystermin Isaac, 1½ Howard
Parsons Joseph, 45 Av. D
Parker Hugh, 9th Av.
Patten Patrick, Centre cor. Reade
Patterson Hiram D. 71 Cannon
Paul Thomas, 445 Greenwich
Percival George F. 22 Madison
Percy John, 187 Hester
Petelers Alois, 252 4th Av.
Peverelly Anthony, 287 Bleecker
Pickering Hannah E. 312 Grand
Pinsent John, 350½ Bowery
Plammy Jas. 62 W. Broadway
Pool Samuel, 362 Madison
Pope Joseph, 51½ Bowery
Preudhomme Eugene Theodore, 76½ Bleecker
Pussedu P. 153 Fulton
Quick Peter, 157 W. Broadway
Quinion Joseph, 145½ Walker
Quinn James A. 243 Bleecker
Ralph Ellers, 50 W. Broadway
Rauch Geo. 470½ Broome
Raynor Nathan W. 500 Grand
Rector Jacob J. 82 Bleecker
Reinecke Chas. 286 Houston
Rey John B. 102 Front
Reynolds Charles, 418 Hudson
Riesby Charles, 43 Walnut
Rinemer George, 287 Madison
Robertson Wm. 161 3d Av.
Roche Francis. 89 Roosevelt]
Rogers A Y. 651 Washington
Rolet F. 58 Carmine
Roper John, 434 12th
Rosenblatt B. 166 2d
Roworth Samuel W. 45 Division
Russell James, 42 Hubert
Ryder Wm. 180½ Division
Schwartz Charles, 50 Chrystie
Schroder I. 6 Hoboken
Scriber Sarah, 207 Canal
Serre Peter, 294 Bowery
Service Thomas, 406 10th
Shannon Mary, 73 Bowery
Sheriden P. 111 Broome
Singleton Ann, 256 8th Av.
Silva Elizabeth, 26 James
Skinner Henry, 78 Reade
Smith David. 599½ Greenwich
Smith Jane, 96 James
Smith John, 26½ Carmine
Smith Julia, 319½ Church
Smith Michael, 372½ 10th
Smith Wm. 180 Division
Spear Wm. C. 159 Duane
Speckler B. 619 Hudson
Spotten Thomas, 118 Bowery
Summers Wm. 530 Grand
Staniford Wm. 355 3d Av.
Stebbins Wm. 304 Houston
Stephens John, 320 Greenwich
Stevens Mary, 191 Canal
Stewart & Bussing, 418 Pearl
Stiles L. C. 88 Av. D
Stillbogen Henry, 49 Leonard
Stoddard Jadethan, 143 3d Av.
Stold Conrad, 322 Monroe
Stonehouse Alex. 81 Crosby

Stookey Isaac, 330 Grand
New York.
Strath Wm. 105 Hamersley
Struelens Nazairs. 81 Duane
Stuart R. L. & A. 285 Greenwich
Sweeny Theodosia, 84 Bowery
Taber James. 295 Bleecker
Talmadge Harvey E. 607 4th
Tappan Mott, 57 Houston
Taylor John. 337 Broadway
Taylor Martha, 135 Elizabeth
Theis Matthew, 47 Av. B
Thickbroom Jabez, 240 Division
Thomas Frederick, 214 Houston
Thompson James, 235 Broadway
Tibbetts Geo. W. 191 Cherry
Tice Mathew, 47 Av. B
Vanderbelt E. & J 345 Broome
Vanitestine Ann, 113 Lewis
Van Buren J. 36 M'Dougal
Vicker J. 56 3d Av.
Villersdorff J. 371 Pearl
Vogt Henry, 377 Hudson
Wegemann & Zennegg, 71 Duane
Wagener J. H. 230 E. 25th
Wagner Daniel B. 760 Broadway
Wahman Fred. 77 Av. B
Wainright Peter, 432 Cherry
Wallace John, 222 Bowery
Walters John, 133 W. 20th
Walton John, 121 Division
Washburn L. 18 8th Av.
Wasson D. 33 8th Av.
Waters Mary, 42 Cross
Watson Thomas, 568 Grand
Weldon Anne, 64 4th Av.
Weller & Son, 713 Broadway
Weston John H. 355 Hudson
Weston George, 354 Hudson
Wetmore E. 304 Grand
Wheeler Charles E. 367 6th Av.
Whitmore Euphemy, 322½ Grand
White John, 19 Catharine
Wicks Margaret, 161 Walker
Widger Hester, 265 Bleecker
Wild Horatio N. 451 Broadway
Wiley John, 18 Greenwich Av.
Wiley Mike, 197 W. 17th
Williams C. 515 Hudson
Willersdorff Israel, 371 Pearl
Willford Rachel, 1 Christopher
Willis Asa, 125 Cedar
Wilsey Mary, 32 Division
Wilson Peter, 77 W. 17th
Wintermute Joseph, 62 Carmine
Wolff Harris, 5 Roosevelt
Wood Geo. A. 199 3d Av.
Wragg Wm. 146 8th Av.
Wyatt Edmond, 281 Hudson

Oneida County.
Elmer L. E. & C. W. Dominick st.
Rome.
Cavanaugh G. 202 Genesee *Utica.*
Hackett Wm. 126 Genesee
Hackett C. 180   do
Pomeroy & Crippen, 22 & 24 Fayette
Wilkins L. 23 & 25 Bleecker

Onondaga County.
Ragg Wm. Arcade Building, Syracuse
Salina.
Ormsbee L. J. James st. Syracuse
Thurber P. & Co. do   do
Eddy H. T. Pearl st.   do

Ontario County.
Page J. M., Geneva   *Seneca.*
Carroll Francis, do

Orange County.
Gardiner Lewis W. 105 Water
Newburgh.
Winslow T. Middletown *Wallkill.*

Queens County.
Wood Albert   *Hempstead.*

Rensselaer County.
Mills Thomas, 316 State
Lansingburgh.
Taylor John W. 148 2d *Troy.*
Smith N. 54½ Congress
Martling J. O. 78 do
Newcomb Abraham, 172 River

Saratoga County.
Howland E.   *Waterford.*

Tompkins County.
Morehouse Geo. & Co. 50 Aurora
Ithaca.

Ulster County.
Fredenburgh ——,   *Kingston.*
Van Schaick Gell, Ellenville
Wawarsing.

Wayne County.
Hewlett Wm.   *Lyons.*

Westchester County.
Wood Samuel S. Peekskill
Courtlandt.
Polhill James   do

Consuls, Foreign.

Austria, August Belmont. 67 Wall
New York.
Baden, John W. Schmidt, 56 New
Bavaria, Geo. H. Siemon. 114 Pearl
Belgium, Auguste Moschet ; v.
con. Hypolite Mali. 27 Beaver
Brazil, Luiz H. F. Deaguiar, con.
gen. ; Louis F. Desganiere v.
con. 34 Platt
Bremen, Hermann Oelrichs, 37
New
Buenos Ayres, Livingston Schuyler, 24 Beaver
Chili, Franklin H. Delano, 78 South
Denmark, Meincke A. F. 93 Wall
France, Auguste Simounet, 72
Greenwich. Louis Borg, v. con.
Frankfort, Frederick Wissman,
20 S. William
Great Britain, Anthony Barclay,
58 Barclay, Robert Bunch v. con.
Greece, Eugene Dutilh, 23 S. William
Hamburgh, Theodore Des Arts,
78 Water
Hanover. Louis M. Meyer, 34 New,
v. con. Edward Stucken
Hesse Darmstadt, Anthony Bollerman, 156 Broadway
Hessian. Conrad W. Faber. 40 New
Lubec, George W. Kruger, 73 New
Mecklenburg, Charles A. Heckscher, 44 South
Mexico. William George Stewart,
74 Broadway
Montevideo. John L. Darby, 145
Front, G. F. Darby v. con. 69 Wall
Naples, Sebastiano Dacorsi, 71
Broad
Nassau, Wm. A. Kobbe, 17 William
Netherlands, John C. Zimmerman,
21 Exchange place
New Grenada, Gregorio Dominguez, 30 Coenties slip
Norway. C. Edw. Habicht, 94 Wall
Peru, Thomas Galwey, 46 Water
Portugal, C. H. S. Desganiere, 62
Water
Prussia. John W. Schmidt, 56 New
Roman States, L. B. Binsse, v. con.
83 William
Russia, Alexis Eustaphieve, 107
10th, George E. Kunhart, v. con.
69 West
Sardinia, Sebastiano Dacorsi, 71
Broad
Saxe Gotha and Altenburg, Carl
Hiprichs, 114 Pearl
Saxony, John W. Schmidt, 56 New

Saxe Weimar, Edward Stucken,
34 New   *New York.*
Sicilies, Rocco Martuscelli, 71
Broad
Spain, Francisco Stoughton, 115
Leonard
Sweden, C. Edward Habicht, 94
Wall
Switzerland, Louis P. De Luze, 43
New
Tuscany, William H. Aspinwall,
55 South
Venezuela, Williams P. 51 Greenwich
Wurtemburg, Leopold Bierwirth,
40 New

Cooks, Public.

Emmons, James, 66¼ Mercer
New York
Figaro Augustus, 43 Thompson
Gassin Henry, 109 Leonard
Jauvin P. 41 Frankfort
Tyson William A. 81 Thompson
Williams Peter, 27¼ Sullivan

Coopers.

Albany County.
Thomas John, 26 Dean *Albany.*
Traverse J. Montgomery st.
Pennie John & J. C. 63 Jackson
Hawe Matthew, 55 Dean & 63
Liberty
Powers F., Trotter's alley
Hawes Wm. 74 Quay
Hawes M. 63 Liberty
Finney F. C. 29 Rensselaer
Parr H. 96 Franklin
Golden Thomas, 105 Washington
Mersellus   *Guilderland.*
Chichester & Fellows, West Troy
Steam Cooperage *Waterviiet.*

Alleghany County.
Wardner F.   *Almond.*
Young D.   *Andover.*
Pratt Charles   *Angelica.*
Portio Horatio
Lesner Levi   *Bolivar.*
Paine Ebenezer, Whitney Valley
Burns.
Johnson Henry   *Cancadea.*
Slayton Joseph B.   *Clarkville.*
Foster H. C.   *Friendship*
Hunting A. M.
Gordon Joseph
Reynolds Aziza   *Granger*
Reynolds Richard
Botsford John H.
Benson Martin
White Asa N.
Reynolds Geo. A., Short Tract
Scott Elijah   *Hume*
Hildrith Samuel
Caner Henry
Cutter Wm. Whitesville
Independence.
Mallory Sylvester *New Hudson*
White Charles   *Rushford.*
Smith
Weed Wm. Wellsville   *Scio.*
Foster E.   do
Alton George, W Almond *Almond.*
Babcock Ira   *Wirt.*

Broome County.
Meloy H., Chenango Forks *Barker*
Boughton E.   *Binghamton.*
Servier R.
Tice J., Nineveh   *Colesville.*
Crittenden G. C.   *Maine.*

Cattaraugus County.
M'Kay Hiram   *Burton.*
Phillips Sawyer
Kidder John M.   *Franklinville.*
Osborne R., Sandusky *Freedom.*

Gross B. *New Albion.*
Lane Andrew
Brown Franklin, East Otto *Otto.*
Weed O., E. Randolph *Randolph.*
Blood Samuel *Yorkshire.*

Cayuga County.
Fanning C., State st. *Auburn.*

Chautauque County.
Wood D., Mayville *Chautauque.*
Scofield ——, De Wittville
Matteson A. *Cherry Creek.*
Wilcox E. W.
Hinche S. N.
Winson C. *Ellery.*
Mitchell Thomas, Jamestown
Ellicott.
Curtis Hiram, do
Fuller William *Ellington.*
Matthew White *French Creek.*
Rous Abial
Morgan Ezra
Carpenter John *Harmony.*
Mattson John, Blockville
Scott John W. *Sheridan.*
Merrill R. G. *Sherman.*

Chemung County.
Beardsley Cyrus *Catharine.*

Chenango County.
Bennett R., Bennettsville
Bainbridge.
Cook S.
Watters William *Greene.*
Babcock C. *New Berlin.*
Medbury A.
Scott A. C. *Norwich.*
Peacock D.
Millard Stephen H. *Oxford.*
Swain O. *Plymouth.*
Meadbury George *Sherburne.*
Pope S. *Smyrna.*

Columbia County.
Moore Wm. Water st. *Hudson.*
Hamblin J.
Crissey J. Public Square
Thompson L. do

Cortland County.
Sloan James *Preble.*

Delaware County.
Bisbee S. & C. *Delhi.*
Brownville J. W. Bloomville
Korbright.
Gough H. *Meredith.*

Duchess County.
Baylis E. *Hyde Park.*
Fowler J.
Sleight J. E.
Ferow J. Rock City *Milan.*
Stanton Isaac, (Buckets & Churns)
906 Main *Poughkeepsie.*
Crawford I. 396 Main
Burns John, 195 do
Osborn T. R.
Osborn R. C.
Barringer J. *Red Hook.*
Paulding William *Rhinebeck.*
Jennings O.
Row N. C.

Erie County.
Baker J., Williamsville *Amherst.*
Driesbach J. do
Shisler Joseph. do
Elliott G. W. do
Stillwell George, do
Windnagle J. do
Calkins Jonas, Willink *Aurora.*
Lyons Stephen W. *Black Rock.*
Manning S. P.
Penhallow Thomas *Boston.*

Penhallow Thomas, jr. *Boston.*
Stedson James *Brandt.*
Wilson L. Miller st. *Buffalo.*
Campbell John B. *Cheektowaga.*
Campbell Henry
Rissen John
Rice —— *Collins.*
Childs Lewis, Springville *Concord.*

Fulton County.
Carmichel Peter *Johnstown.*
Weber John

Genesee County.1
York Z. *Batavia.*
Wilcox Harmon *Bergen.*
Crosby John
Allen I. East Bethany *Bethany.*
Simons Darwin C. *Le Roy.*
Anderson Daniel
Powers Edwards, East Pembroke
Pembroke.

Greene County.
Smith Nehemiah, Leeds *Catskill.*
Sears John *Durham.*
Booth Daniel
Eastland George *Greenville.*
Beardsley William *Lexington.*
Hogboom Cornelius
Hogboom Jacob
Scanling Robert *Prattsville.*
Jones Daniel L. Union Society
Windham.

Herkimer County.
Winser Smith *Fairfield.*
Stevens Hiram
Green John
Durst Eli *Frankfort.*
Miller W. Mohawk *German Flats.*
Foster S. *Manheim.*
Hawkins Henry *Newport.*
Raynolds S. J.
Crumbye Minor *Norway.*
Champion A. & W. Starkville
Stark.
Pelt Joseph *Warren.*

Jefferson County
Truesdail L. P. *Adams.*
Merrill S.
Lines John *Cape Vincent.*
Rary J. *Ellisburgh.*
Kirkland E. & W. D. Belleville
Church John, Mannsville
Smith Amos, Evans' Mills *Le Roy.*
Griswold N. W. do
Hastings L. do
Pierce Joseph, do
Ellis Z. Three Mile Bay *Lyme.*
Pitcher E. *Philadelphia.*
Lawrence Wm. *Rodman.*
Boynton G. East Rodman
Doud H. D., So. Rutland *Rutland.*
Doud G. do
Doud S. do
Clark E. C. Felt's Mills
Chittenden A., Carthage *Wilna.*
O'Harra B.

Kings County.
Robbins J. N. 120 Furman st.
Brooklyn.
Lyon & Haff, Pierpont's Dock
M'Donald Wm. 88 Furman
Morris Wm. Furman st. near Fulton ferry
Hurdon Eugene, cor. Water st. & Dock
Brower Samuel C. cor. Front & Adams
M'Laughlin P. John st. near Jay
Riordan M. 80 Pearl st.
Rome Geo., Adams st. cor. Myrtle Av.
Marrin Wm., John st. nr. Hudson Av.

Hutchins Jno. 3 Wesley pl., South 2d st. *Williamsburgh.*
Affleck James, 18 North 3d
Sawyer George B. cor. 5th & 2d

Lewis County.
Kidney O. *Denmark.*
Watson D.
Hurlburt T.
Hart S. *Harrisburgh.*
Bailey D.
Williams S. *Lowville.*
Wood A., West *Martinsburgh.*
Holcomb Lester *Turin.*
Holcomb Anson
Strickland Simeon S.
Strickland Henry
Miller John, Houseville
Dow & Eames, Constableville, *West Turin.*

Livingston County.
White William *Caledonia.*
Moore G. B. *Conesus.*
Chapin J.
Ingalls John
Burgess Benjamin
Wilklow Peter *Dansville.*
Eschrish John
Sterling D. G.
Day R. G.
Hendiker S.
Van Riper John *Genesee.*
Sage Edwin
Wright Thomas *Lima.*
Hudson F. Hemlock Lake *Livonia.*
Lindsley Heman
Griswold B.
Holmes C. *Mount Morris.*
Andrus John L. Oakland *Portage.*
Patterson Charles, do
Doane & Westcott, Hunt's Hollow
Tingley J. & O. do
Persel E. *Springwater.*
Toles ——, West Sparta *Sparta.*
Canahan S. *York.*
Cannahan E.
Warner D. L. Greigsville

Madison County.
Clark & Crandall *Brookfield.*
Clark James
Crandall John A. So. Brookfield
Babcock H. do
Loomis L. *Cazenovia.*
Rouse James
Beckwith R.
Beckwith J.
Johnson David
Parsons E. L.
Gunn Wm. E. New Woodstock
Ellis H. do
Merriam Jas. Morrisville *Eaton.*
Thurston C. & A. *Hamilton.*
Wood A. Hubbard's Corners
Burdick Henry, Canastota *Lenox.*
Collar E. do

Monroe County.
Benton Elihu, North Chill *Chili.*
Pease A. S. Jenkin's Corner *Greece.*
Angevine Wm. P. West Mendon
Mendon.
Gallentine H. do
Ladell O.W. Parma Centre *Parma.*
Tibbetts Stephen *Pittsford.*
Stickland E.
Patterson Wm. Clay st. *Rochester.*
Knowles John, do
Wood John, High st.
Dinsmore & Dalton, 7 High
Hilton J. Lyell st.
Campbell John, Lyell st.
Price Thomas, White st.
Campbell James, Smith st.
M'Elvy J. do
Foulds Andrew, Jay st.
Hanvey Thomas, Oak st. nr. Canal
More Ephraim, cor. Larrimer & West st.

Helden J. cor. Lyell & Mayne st. *Rochester.*
Monhagan David. Lyell st.
Murray Robert, Mayne st.
Hanvey Walter, do
Manrer Jacob & John, Tonawan-
da st.
Stout William, Grape st.
Stout Robert, Romeyn st.
Freeman O. D. near steamboat
landing
Beard Isaac *Rush.*
Gallentine J.
Edson Freeman M. Scottsville
Wheatland.
Hyde Harvey do
M'Phillips John do
Garbutt P. do

Montgomery County.

Fox Theodore *Amsterdam.*
Smith John
Heath D. N.
Abrahams J. *Canajoharie.*
Strossman William
Norton James M., Buel
Alpaugh Philip do
Hughes W. E. Fonda *Mohawk.*
Hart C. N. & Co. do

New York County.

Adema Francis, 106 Beekman
New York.
Aikman Hugh, 89 Pine
Allen John, 14 S. William
Asten William, 42 Water
Bailey Edward. 203 Amos
Bailey H. C. 163 Christopher
Bailey York. rear 107 Canal
Baker Daniel, 276 Front
Bartholemew John, r. 11 Forsyth
Beam John & Gilbert. 130 Broad
Bearns Henry M. 31 Old slip
Bensel J. McJ. 4 Depeyster
Behsell William P. 476 Broome
Betts George, 11½ James slip &
182 Madison
Betts James W. 11½ James slip
Bonsall Robert. 18 Burling slip
Briggs Aaron T. 245 Cherry
Burdett R. 120 William
Carter Charles, 94 & 96 Goerck
Chapin Isaac F. 32 Old Slip
Chase Jesse, 1 Coenties slip
Clancy Michael, 37 Pitt
Coburn John, 118 Broadway
Coleman James, 20 Fletcher
Coleman John, 26 Platt
Colgan Owen, 135 Charlton
Connolly M. & J. W. 22d corner
7th Av.
Cook Thomas M. 168 Washington
Coon Nelson, 19 Burling slip
Cornish John, 63 Washington
Cosgrove James, 10 Burling slip
Cyingar G. 173 Broome
Dandridge James, 7 Anthony
Dawson William & Sons, 15 Mott
Decker James P. 142 Liberty
Donhand Francis, 66 Front
Dubourdieu & Dunphy, 26 New
Dufau John, 29 S. William
Dufau John B. 13 Stone
Duffy Bernard, 9 Fletcher
Eigenger George, 173 Broome
Flandreau Elijah, 4 Coenties slip
Folger Robert J. 186½ South
Foust John. 19 Pitt
Gardiner John, 148 Forsyth
Gardiner Henry, 790 Greenwich
Geraghty James, 70 Liberty
Giraud F. & J. 29 Depeyster
Graff Henry, 23 Beaver
Griffin John A. 175 Reade
Hadley Daniel, 205 Amos
Harris George W. 716 Water
Hill Rowland, 227 Washington
Hinson James, 8 Water
Hoffmeister J. 98 Wall
Hopkins Edwin A. 152 3d
Hui George, 8th Av.
Jaurey Charles, 45 Pearl

Johnston Wm. 46 Eldridge
New York.
Kelly O. J. 41 West
Keys D. & Sons, 91 Suffolk
Klein Frank A. 181 W. 19th
Kneisle Andre, 38 W. Broadway
Knox A. & R., E. 27th st.
Lacey & Edwards, 96 Wall
Lynch Alexander, 167 Mulberry
M'Ewen & Thompson, 55 Goerck
M'Laughlin & Wiley, 23 Old Slip
& 3 Temple
M'Mahon Michael, 269 South
Mahany John, 98 Oliver
Maher Daniel, 167 Maiden lane
Mallett Peter, 29 Lewis
Maxwell P. 22 West
Mead G. B. & H. R. 97 Pine
Merrick Patrick, 75 New
Montaye John, 186 Hester
Moore Michael S. 24 Moore
Morgan W. & Davis, 660 Water
Mueller Conrad, 96 W. 20th
Murray James, rear 58 Chrystie
Nelson & Howard, 79 Pine
O'Brien Francis, 66 Broad & 121
Beekman
O'Donnell Hugh, 18 Canal
O'Grady Thos. 7th Av.
Owen Edward, 182 Chrystie
Pents D. C. & Son, 2 Gouverneur's
lane
Pentz George W. 51 South
Perry Munally, 28 do
Philliss & Harvey, 34 Stone
Platt Ellison, r. 56 & 58 Attorney
Price Charles, 23 Cedar
Reed John F. 142 Bond
Robinson H. H. 15 Burling slip
Shay & Adair, 87 Pine
Shields David, 44 Malden lane
Shortland Thomas. 50 West
Siedler John, 84 Walnut
Sillier F. 126 W. 19th
Speir John, 7 Depeyster
Spencer William, 13 New
Strang & Bogert, 140 Broad
Strong Henry E. 372 Bleecker
Stutt John, 60 5th
Taggart Michael, 42 Nassau
Tsiman Wm. G. & Co. 18 Fletcher
Terheun & Martin, 26 Water
Tracy Patrick, 109 Sheriff
Van Cott J. 37 Essex
Vanhouten Gilliam, 95 Cliff
Van Riper & Sands, 59 1st
Van Tassell B. A. 7 Weehawken
Waydell John, 36 Dover
Wanzer C. & J. D. 357 6th
Weeks John, 624 Water
Weis Stephen, 248 E. 13th
Wentworth Josi. W. 147 Chrystie
Whipple Wm. 2 Coenties slip &
65 Sheriff
White Stephen, 248 13th
Wiley & Hopper, 21 Old slip
Wilson Thomas, 9 Thames
Winslow John C. 244 Front
Youle Adam W. 614 Water
Young & Moore, 136 Broad

Niagara County.

Keyes O. Pekin *Cambria.*
Simons —, do
Woodruff Theophilus *Newfane.*
Ditner Theodore
Forsyth John
Stahl E. W.
Wood Silas
Holden Jos. Youngstown *Porter.*
M'Arthur John, do
Trumble M. do
Hoyt Isaac *Royalton.*
Lee Robert *Somerset.*
Burgess Pliny A.
Shipman Clark *Wilson.*
Dennison Joseph

Oneida County.

Brown & Wright, Oriskany Falls
Augusta.

Cowles S. H. James st. *Rome.*
Welsh William, Rome st. *Utica.*
M'Donough J. Catharine st.
Child Erastus, Whitesboro
Whitestown.

Onondaga County.

Williams W. R. Park st. Syracuse
Salina.
Burrett S. Wolf st.
Kinney S. do

Ontario County.

Smith H. *Bristol.*
Groff J.
Hathaway C.
Beech L. Bristol Centre
Shepard Samuel *Canandaigua.*
Leston Silas E. *East Bloomfield.*
Dibble Spencer
Shoemaker Nicholas *Hopewell.*
Witt George, Larneds' Corners
Perhannes J. do
Brufield L. *Manchester.*
Crum Abraham *Phelps.*
M'Mellen ——
Booth Cyrus & Co. Honeoye
Richmond.
Davidson M. Richmond Mills
Hill James, Geneva *Seneca.*
Hill C. D. do
Conner James *South Bristol.*
Wilder W. W.
Allen Miles
Salter S. O. *Victor.*
M'Lane J. & G.
Lee Charles *West Bloomfield.*
West M.

Orange County.

Bigsby D. S. *Chester.*
Colwell James *Crawford.*
M'Nab J., Ridgebury *Minisink.*
Tryan S., Wells' Corners
Harding B. N. Otisville
Mount Hope.
Gearns G. Water st. *Newburgh.*
Collie Wm. South Middletown
Wallkill.
Cofkendell Z. G. Amity *Warwick.*
Jackson J. do
Lesler G. Florida

Orleans County.

Young David, Albion *Barre.*
Clough George *Kendall.*
Smith N. P. Knowlesville
Ridgeway.
Spencer S. M. Oak Orchard
Grant L. A. G. B. *Shelby.*
Beach F. D. Lyndonville *Yates.*
Shepherd O. do
Austin Harrison, County Line

Oswego County.

Purdy William *Albion.*
Sperry Anson *Constantia.*
Marsh W.
Dickie William
Horton J. H. *Hannibal.*
Demott Charles
Fitzhugh H. & Co. cor. 10th &
Utica sts. *Oswego.*
Mathews H. cor. Mohawk & 11th
Pardee W. J. 10th near Syracuse
Av.
Rice John P. Phoenix *Schroeppel.*
Goold John do
Brockway D. Gilberts' Mills
Quance Henry *Scriba.*
Humphrey & Dodge *Williamstown.*

Otsego County.

Stephens Lyman *Edmeston.*
Talcott Albert
Pope J. H. *Middlefield.*
Norton Joel
Pathee Caleb *Oneonta.*
Browne Jacob

Scofield William H. *Oneonta.*
Barnes John
Barnes Harvey
Ingles John
Patterson William
Yarn Ira
Mickel William
Canfield David
Carnathan John *Worcester.*

Queens County.

M'Kay James, Cow Neck
 North Hempstead.
Wilson Henry *Oyster Bay.*
Shragur George

Rensselaer County.

Ives C. P. 341 State *Lansingburgh.*
Rogers David M. r. 201½ John c.
 Grove
Smith Jas. John st. Alley
Tallman J. Pitt st.
Francher David, Pitt st.
Allen Richard, 448 River *Troy.*
Downing M. r. 132 River
Harvey Henry, r. 165 4th
Bentley John, 193 4th
Sanders Daniel, 470 River

St. Lawrence County.

Blanchard Wm. *Canton.*
Thompson & Co. Richville
 De Kalb.
Sterling & Cone *Gouverneur.*
Smith Isaac E. & Co. *Hammond.*
Colborn Thomas, Waddington
 Madrid.
Page George *Morristown.*
Halsey Balseyman, (stave maker)
 River st. Ogdensburgh
 Oswegatchie.
Chattersen Hiram & Jas. Main st.
 Ogdensburgh
Laughlin & Foster *Pierpont.*
Heaton Lorenzo D. *Potsdam.*
Wise Samuel

Saratoga County.

Batt John *Carlton.*
Smith Andrew
Genner N. B.
Murry C. B. (churn maker)
Chapman P. (tubs) *Providence.*
Barker Edward (pails)
Barker A. (tubs)
Rugg Orvin *Saratoga Springs*
Driscoll John *Waterford.*
Murry Daniel
Picket Ezra
Sheriden Thomas
Hanley Thomas

Schenectady County.

Granger J. Church st. *Schenectady.*

Schoharie County.

Knickerbocker Thomas *Blenheim.*
Shafer Lewis
Granby Wm. M.
Partridge N. Sloansville
 Esperance.
Boke W. Fultonham *Fulton.*
Bosman C.
Burt C. B.
Burt Peter A.
Decker John
Decker Reuben
Robinson Samuel *Jefferson.*
Brady Peter

Seneca County.

Proudfoot James *Seneca Falls.*
Southwell Asa B.
Hill Lemuel J.
Bostwick Daniel W. *Waterloo.*

Steuben County.

Davis James *Cohocton.*

Havens Wm. *Cohocton.*
Havens Joseph, North Cohocton

Sullivan County.

Kerr James, Bloomingburgh
 Mamakating.
Mahr P., Monticello *Thompson.*

Tioga County.

Robinson S. S. *Richford.*

Ulster County.

Perkins H. J. *Lloyd.*
Buckout T. G. Louisburgh
Weddle Wm. do
Merritt John, do
Buckoult D., New Paltz Landing
 New Paltz.
Du Bois Wm. B. (paint kegs)
 Saugerties.
Hanna David (kegs)
Coleman & Co. *Woodstock.*

Warren County.

Brooks Elnathan *Hague*
Vaughn E. S., Glenn's Falls
 Queensbury.

Washington County.

Howland & Hastings *Argyle.*
Shiland Oliver, North Argyle
Stephens John *Cambridge.*
Dunehue John
Archer J. W.
Stephens J. G.
Henmerson Nathan, South Easton.
 Easton.
Russell Jehiel *Greenwich.*
Montgomery Robert. Centre Falls
Stoddard John, North Greenwich
Clements Daniel, West Hebron
 Hebron.
Winn Eliphas, do
Winn Joseph, do
Winn Osborn, do
Brown Jonathan, do
Munson William, do
Thompson Joseph *Putnam.*
Spaulding Peter
Spaulding Samuel

Wayne County.

Thesler William *Lyons.*
Hudson Charles A. East *Palmyra.*
Feller & Co. do
Nichols John *Ross.*
Chustler Adam

Westchester County.

George Samuel W., Peekskill
 Courtlandt.
Robertson Henry, Sing Sing
 Ossining.

Wyoming County.

Sargent H. W., Cowlesville
 Bennington.
Smith George *Castile.*
Kellogg E.
Wildman Joseph
Havene E., Wyoming *Middlebury.*
Loomis W. *Pike.*
Flint C., East Pike
Smith & Clark, East Kay
Tuttle R. *Sheldon.*
Adams Charles

Yates County.

Coffin Wm., Belona *Benton.*
Loomis O. G. *Middlesex.*
Clark Stillman
Fargo R. R., Penn Yan *Milo.*
Bennett A. do
Andres Stephen *Potter.*
Torey H., Rushville
Pfaat Peter. Potter Centre
Andres S. F. do

Layams Jacob, Potter Centre
 Potter.
Barber C. do
Smith Conrad, do
Householder M. do
Bellows Chas., Dundee *Starkey.*
Shannon R. L. do

Coppersmiths. (*See also Tin and Sheet-iron Workers.*)

Benson John, 25 Old Slip
 New York.
Blackhall Edward, 14 Orange
Brooks & Cummings, 123 Av. D
Burkhard Peter. 61 Vesey
Clark John, 168 Division
Cunningham William & Sons, 431
 Greenwich
Dunn Joan, 20 Burling slip
Dusenbury Thomas, 265 Water
Farr & Briggs, 217 Franklin & 30
 Rector
Gowers & Casey, 220 West
Graves Wm. H. 276½ Water
Hannah & Launey, 294 do
Haser John, 15 Frankfort
Haynen Charles W. 244 Water
Knox Edward, 215 Fulton
Labussiere Stephen, 57½ Vesey
Launy O. 294 Water
Lawrence Wm. B. 419 Cherry
Lightbody Collin, 152 Front
Lightbody James, 85 Market
Lynch & Benson, 122 Warren
M'Intosh Robt. 30 North William
Micholup Jacob, 243 Bowery
Miller A. 70 Av. D
Mills Abner, 52 Av. D
Neumann Jacob, 15 Dover
Newman James, 260 Bowery
Primout Petar, 98 Reade
Stillman, Allen & Co. foot of 12th
 E. R.
Stump & Jenkins, 219 West
Sweet Ezra B. 133 Canal
Williamson Hugh, 3 M'Dougal
Wright John, 158 Cherry
Youngman Frederick, 5 James

Copyists.

Ashwin William M. 30 Wall
 New York.
Barton Joseph, 11 Wall
Brooks C. 75 Nassau
Eytinge S. D. & Co. 1 Crosby
Ferris Charles, 20 Nassau
Morson Charles T. 65 Wall
Peile Thomas, 8 City Hall place
Smith George, 11 Wall
West Thomas G. 51 Liberty
Wilson Wm. M. 68 Nassau

Cordage, Rope and Twine Dealers.

Bonnar James S. 86 John
 New York.
Buchanan O. S. 179 Water
Cebra & Cuming, 106 Pearl
M'Arthur Joseph, 20 Cedar
Merritt & Co. 58 South
Tucker, Cooper & Co. 70 South
Wall, Richardson & Engle, 290
 Front

Cordage, Rope and Twine Manufacturers.

Albany County.

Newbury George D., West Troy
 Watervliet.
Kellogg & Co. West Troy

Duchess County.

Fanning W. A. & Co. 159 Main
 Poughkeepsie.

New York County.

Aymar William & Co. 50 South
New York.

Bayles N. H. 196 South
Coles & Thorn, 91 West
Dunn John, 8 Liberty
Hicks James M. 68 South
Lawson,Clucas & Leeds,126 Water
Leach Adam C. 180 Ludlow & 171
Essex
Stewart Duncan. 36 W. 20th
Thursby John, 242 Front

Oneida County.

Davis R.   New Hartford.

Queens County.

March John   Newtown.

Rockland County.

Sloat J. & Co.   Ramapo.

Suffolk County.

Roe John. Patchogue Brookhaven.
Woodhul Brewster

Wayne County.

Pooley & Butterfield   Palmyra.

Westchester County.

York John   West Farms.

Cards, Fringes, Tassels, Gimps, &c.

Baker F. 68 Duane   New York.
Benjamin W. jr. & Co. 31 Broad
Booth D. A. 100 William
Broneman Samuel, 55 Ann
Corrigan T. & Brother. 404 Grand
Crosley Chas. Wm. 589½ Broad-
way & 170 Mercer
Delapierre B. 476½ Broadway
Dale T. 43 Maiden lane
Duncan James, 487 Greenwich
Faxon Thomas C. 24 John
Flack George, 434 Hudson
Foot T. C. & D. D. 100 William
Friend Harman, 140 Water
Garelly J. G. 90 William
Gurney H. G. 8 Liberty
Hagan Patrick, 272½ Broadway
Heylin Wm., W. 24th st.
Jaeger, Scheuch & Kimm, 38 John
Kastor Abraham, 391 Broadway
Kohlsaat Brothers, 413 Broadway
& 48 John
Lawrence Brothers, 50 John
Lazarus J. L. 156 Broadway
Leuthold Charles, 29 Spruce
Lowitz, Becker & Cludius, 59 John
Magnu James S. 104 Fulton
Maynard Rosina, 451 Pearl
M'Rae John, 117 Canal
Millward Jas. 67 Maiden lane
Purdie Alex. 46 Beekman
Staderman J. M. 39 Norfolk
Van Blankensteyn & Heinemann,
103 William
Wagner George & Co. 42 John
Williams Brothers, 90 Fulton &
52 John
Yates Benj. S. 73 Bleecker
Zahn W. H. 56 John

Corks—Importer of.

King Wm. 192 Water New York.

Cork Cutters.

Bennet G. 24 Catharine New York.
Hafferty Brothers & Co. 194 Water
Lowerre James, 163 Water
Payne John, 51 Fulton
Sparkman & Truslow, 154 Water

Corset Makers.

Bishop M. 108 Hudson New York.
Bowles James, 455½ Broadway
Braisted Jane, 337 Bleecker
Brown Eliza C. 223 Hudson
Conroy Wm. 469 Pearl
Dewland Geo. F. 218 Greenwich
Farrow Madame, 491 Broadway
Fleckner E. R. 329 Bleecker
Gilbert Anne, 203 Division
Graham Hannah E. 225½ Division
Hall Margaret Ann, 178 Mulberry
Hayward Mery A. 167 6th Av
Hewitt Marion, 382 Broadway
Hume Mary, 160 6th Av.
Lambert Eury, 420 Broadway
Linacre Catharine, 4 Marion
Love Agnes, 243 Hudson
Matin Elise, 3 Amity
Pattillow F. 237 Bleecker
Feddie Margaret, 263 Grand
Frendergrast Wm. 55 Canal
Prospers Madame. 367 Broadway
Sherman Ann, 425 Broadway
Simms Wm. 232 2d
Taylor Francis, 270 8th Av.
Tierney & Hall, 321 Greenwich
Todd Rosanna, 99 4th Av.
Van Nostrand Mary, 3 Green
Wheeler Bethuel C. 327 Bleecker
Willington Ann, 28 Walker
Woodward N. & Co. 311½ B'way
Wright Elizabeth S. 168 Bowery

Costumers.

Allen Andrew J. 280 Broadway
New York.
Dejonge Julius, 66 Warren
La Fata F. 451 Pearl
La Fata Frances, 422 Broadway
Taylor John Geo. 56 Prince
Taylor M. 172 W. Broadway
Walker Robert S. 164 Walker
Wallace Mary Ann, 27½ Chrystie
Williams Richard W. 366 Broome

Cotton Ball Cord Manufacturers.

Boggs Wm. 406½ Broadway
New York.
Duncan James, 487 Greenwich
Martin Thomas, 22 Hamersley

Cotton Batting Manufacturers.

Albany County.

M'Vee H. Cohoes   Wateroliet.
Scovill & Gilmore
Coyle N.

Orange County.

Burns J.   Newburgh.

Cotton Goods Manufacturers.

Albany County.

Chadwick William N., Cohoes
Wateroliet.

Cayuga County.

Moravia Cotton Factory, A. Cady,
Agent   Moravia.

Duchess County.

Taylor & Forbes, 21 Market
Poughkeepsie.
Clark A. Stamfordville Stamford.

Chenango County.

Farmers & Mechanics Manufacturing Company   New Berlin.

Franklin County.

Magill Hugh & Co.   Malone.

Greene County.

Morse Burton G.   Prattsville.

Herkimer County.

Kenyon V. S.   Newport.
Waterman H.
Potter & Arnold, Poland Russia.

Jefferson County.

M'Collom Hiram, Carthage
Wilna.

Kings County.

Wood Joseph, Bedford Av. cor. of
Flushing Av. East Brooklyn
Brooklyn.

New York County.

Adams William, 36 Cedar & 28
Perry   New York.
Brett Theodore F. 108 Maiden lane
Farr I. & G. 220 Fulton
Gwynne Thomas, 26 Cedar
Haggerty William C. 77 Pine
Halliday David, 103 Maiden lane
M'Intosh Thomas, 156 Pearl
Martin Robert, 100 Troy
Ross George, 103 Maiden lane
Souter Conrad, 242 5th
Schellpot David, 242 5th

Niagara County.

Niagara Manufacturing Co. Vail,
Mitchell & Co. Proprietors

Oneida County.

Bradish & Draper, (Sheetings)
Stittsville   Trenton.

Onondaga County.

May F.   Manlius.
Remington E.

Orange County.

Burns J.   Newburgh.

Otsego County

Chadwick J.   Burlington.
Union Cotton Co.   Hartwick.
Clinton & Morehouse
Laurens Cotton Co. (Sheetings)
A. J. Chapman, Agent Laurens.
Hope Factory (Sheetings) Otsego.
Oaksville Cotton Manufactory,
Oaksville
Arkwright Manufacturing Co.
(Printing Goods)   Pittsfield.

Rensselaer County.

Tremont Manufacturing Co. (Cottons) H. Patterson, Agent
Hoosick.
Caledonia Cotton Manufactory, A.
Russell, Agent
Turner James, (Satinet Warps &
Wadding)   East Nassau.
Briggs Amos & Co. Schaghticoke
Smith, Wheeler & Platt (Wadding)
Stephentown.

Saratoga County.

Wheeler Calvin, Ballston Spa
Milton.
Cook Ziba M. (Printing Cloths)
Cook Samuel H.   do
Cook James M.   do

Schoharie County

Colba, Reed & Co.   Gilboa

Washington County.

Butterworth J. B. Battenville
Greenwich.

Cotton (Damaged) Dealers in.

Field, Cyrus W. & Co. 11 Cliff
New York.

Cotton Mender.

Carroll Peter, 95 Pine *New York.*

Cotton Merchants.

Brett James, 3 Jones lane
New York.
Bronson Silas, 118 Pearl
Coit Henry, 43 South
DuBerceau E. & L. Bouquet, 28 Old slip
Butterworth John F. 87 Merch. Exchange
Goldthwait F. 108 South
Hills H. W. & S. 3 Hanover
Kennedy T. & J. 108 South
Leverich Henry S. 29 Burling slip
Lorat L. 68 Wall
Lucey Robert V. 95 Pine
Mann F. 156 Pearl
Mills Drake, 151 Front
Moore William S. 295 Water
Murphy Cornelius, 110 South
Parmalee A. O. 118 Pearl
Stone J. & S. 118 Pearl
Sus A. W. 97 Wall

Cotton Presses.

Bullock Smith W. 37 S. William
New York.
Dillon Robert, 28 & 30 Burling slip
Starr, Minturn & Co. 25 Peck slip
Teddeman P. H. 22 West
Van Vliet Henry H. 33 West

Cradles (Grain)—Manufacturers.

Duchess County.

Balis A. P. *Amenia.*
Bird H.
Morgan W.
Muller R. Stanfordville *Stanford.*

Genesee County.

Naramor H. *Batavia.*

Herkimer County.

Hager Edwin L. *Frankfort.*

Livingston County.

Rose Charles *Caledonia.*
Hatch Henry G.
Chadwick Joseph *South Avon.*

Monroe County.

King & Hitchcock, Spencer's Basin *Ogden.*
Crossman, Eaton & Co. Curtis' Block, Main st *Rochester.*

Niagara County.

Petit Reuben *Somerset.*

Ontario County.

Gould & Weaver *Phelps.*

Otsego County.

Follett J., Schenevas *Maryland.*

Rensselaer County.

Grant I. T. & Co. *Schaghticoke.*
Bryan H. C. & Son

St. Lawrence County.

Flanders David *Parishville.*
10

Yates County.

Williams & Son, Penn Yan *Milo.*

Cutlers.

Monroe County.

Clifton Henry, 1 Buffalo *Rochester.*
Sanborn & Stratton, 6 South
Buffham R. D. 116 Main
Kedzie J. & Co. 11 State
Crane John, 30 Ferry

New York County.

Alviset A. 556 Pearl *New York.*
Brombacher Jacob, 108½ Cherry & rear 36 Cherry
Clark George, rear 78 Grand
Fisher William, 435 Washington
Grossbarth Philip, 51 Hudson
Hall & Moses, 238 Pearl
Heinsch Rochus, 91 Nassau
Herbert Conrad, 83 Av. A.
Ibbotson Brothers & Co. 218 Pearl
Jackson, Smith & Co. 81 John
Klauberg Carl, 195 William & 12 Spruce
Klauberg Carl, jr. 76 Chatham
Moeller & Kaemmerer, 300 Division
Moen A. R. 128 Water
Nixon John C. & Son, 44 Chatham
Reinbold Andrew, 164 Broome
Saphar George, 199 W. 16th
Schaub Frederick & Co. 106 Elm
Taylor Peter G 214 Pearl
Turner Thomas & Co. 60 Broad
Vincent John, 96 Ridge
Waite John, 106 Elm
Waterville Manufacturing Co. 86 William
Wild William, 160 Division & 40 Eldridge
Zindell Henry, 546 Pearl

Oneida County.

Shepard George, Mechanics' Hall *Utica*

Onondaga County.

Pearson J. Clinton square, Syracuse *Salina.*

Daguerrian Artists.

Albany County.

M'Bride H. Exchange *Albany.*
Meade & Brothers, do
Dewell T. do
Sisson J. S. 496 Broadway
Churchill Renselaer, 55 State

Broome County.

Coburn A. *Binghamton.*
Holden C. *Maine.*

Cayuga County.

Stone J. F. 99 Genesee *Auburn.*
Senter & Sherwood, 111 do

Chautauque County.

Gray John C. Jamestown *Ellicott.*
Ward Sylvanus *Westfield.*

Chenango County.

Orten J. G. & C. *Greene.*
Brenman J. *Norwich.*
Marquis J. B. *Oxford.*

Columbia County.

Surck J. 233 Warren *Hudson.*
Spencer W. H. do
Walker L. E. *Kinderhook.*

Duchess County.

Hine L. (travelling artist) *Hydepk.*
Brant J. D.
Briggs Mrs. 294 Main
Poughkeepsie.
Webster J. B. 254 do
Walker S. L. 14 Garden

Erie County.

M'Donnell & Co. (see advertisement.) 192 Main *Buffalo.*
Evans O. B. (see advertisement,) 230 Main
Stevens Mrs. Lewis, cor. Main & Erie
Benton R. O. 268½ Main
Bean A. 290½ do
Mead Mrs. C. 156 do

Genesee County.

Carpenter J. E. *Le Roy.*

Greene County.

Parker William H. *Durham.*
Hill Levi L. West Kill *Lexington.*

Kings County.

Franklin William Henry, 166 & 168 Fulton *Brooklyn.*
Leathers James B. 164 Fulton
Stanbury J. B. 43 do
Crowell S. 63 do
Adams Thomas, 101 do
Atkins Joseph, 219 do

Livingston County.

Duncklebury William *Dansville.*
Hoes James H.
Raymond J. F. *Lima.*
Batten W. B. *Nunda.*

Madison County.

Fairchild Abel *De Ruyter.*

Monroe County.

Sheldon H. T. 26 St. Paul *Rochester.*
Marsh E. K. 16 Buffalo
Faulkner L K. 13 Arcade Exch.
Mercer & Co. c. Main & St. Paul

Montgomery County.

Dastie A. P. *Amsterdam.*

New York County.

Allen ——, 204 Chatham
New York.
Armstrong J. S. 315 Broadway
Babb William G. 219 Greenwich
Barcalow Richard. 80 Bowery
Barnes James T. 170 Broadway
Barton Samuel K. 74 Chambers
Beals Albert A. 156 Broadway
Beals Henry S. 183 do
Bogardus Abrm. 217 Greenwich
Bogert William, 345 Bleecker
Brady Matthew B. 205 & 207 Broadway
Burgess N. G. 187 Broadway
Butler William H. 251 do
Clarke Ephraim M. 226 Bleecker
Cohen James, 54 Canal
Davis J. D. 47 Chatham
Dowd Albert, 233 Broadway
Durang William H. 303 do
Eddy Lewis, 189 7th
Fowler William H. 257 Broadway
Gardner John B. 298 do
Gurney Jeremiah, 189 do
Haas Philip, 289 do
Haddington Lewis L. 130 do
Hanson Peter, 189 Bowery
Harris Hiram V. 233 Broadway
Harrison & Holmes, 289 do
Hay J. R. 237 Bowery

Henderson John, 92 Bowery *New York.*
Helmes John C. 111   do
Holbrook Eber C. 166 Fulton
Horsley P. N. 106 & 130 Broadway
Howard L. Norman, 492 Grand
Hughes Frederick N. 88 8th Av.
Humphrey O. A. 94 Canal
Insley Henry E. 122 Broadway
Jaquith Nathaniel C. 98   do
Jenkins S. 290   do
Kearsing G. T. & W. F. 177 do
King William H. 37 Chatham
Knapp William R. 103 Bowery
Langenheim & Beckers, 201 Broadway
Lawrence M. M. 203 Broadway
Lewis & James, 9 Bowery
Lewis W. & W. H. 142 Chatham
Maitland R. E. 74 Canal
Mayers John S. 82 Canal
Montalvo Ramon, 323 Broadway
Morand Augustus, 132 Chatham
Peters Otis T. 411 Broadway
Plumbe —— 251   do
Rabb Wm. G. 219 Greenwich
Rice Samuel N. 194 Canal
Schie Louis, 119 Elizabeth
Shaw E. 359 Broadway
Smith Samuel, 276 8th Av.
Stanley & Lansing, 323 Broadway
Thompson E. C. 214   do
Thompson Josiah W. 315 do
Walsh Thomas S. 61 W. Washington place
Washburn W. W. 252 Broadway
West Aaron L. 179   do
Weston James P. 192   do
White Edward, 247   do
Woodbridge J. J. 90 Chatham

Niagara County.

Scovill T. P   *Lewiston.*
Burtis R. B.   *Lockport.*
Bruce N. W.
Derry H. E.   *Niagara Falls.*

Oneida County.

Hovey J. S. Dominick st. *Rome.*
Dunning U. 59 Genesee *Utica.*
Johnson D. B. 94   do
Clark F. J. & Brother, 128 do
Davie D. D. T. Devereux Block

Onondaga County.

Clark J. M. & Brothers, Genesee st. Syracuse   *Salina.*
Green & Benedict   do

Ontario County.

Finley Marshall   *Canandaigua.*
Sinsabaugh ——, Geneva *Seneca.*
Smith & Co   do

Orange County

Owen N.   *Goshen.*
Walker & Horton, Washington Hall   *Newburgh.*
Easterly Daniel, 66 Water
Gunn Mrs. E. 41   do

Orleans County.

Harvey Geo. M. Albion   *Barre.*

Oswego County.

Nichols A. C. Bates' Block *Oswego.*
Gray & Kennedy, 1st st.

Otsego County.

Squiers G. W. Cooperstown *Otsego.*

Putnam County.

Rees A. Cold Spring *Phillipstown.*

Queens County.

Conklin N. W.   *Jamaica.*

Rensselaer County.

Pardee Phinehas, 2 Fake's Row *Lansingburgh.*
Baldwin S. C. 216 River *Troy.*
Tomlinson William A. Boardman Buildings
Wyatt D. W. 54 Congress

Saratoga County.

Waterberry P. R. *Saratoga Springs.*
Stevens & M'Kernon
King Minor   *Waterford.*

Schoharie County.

Nellis Jacob   *Schoharie.*

Tioga County.

Gibson E. G.   *Owego.*

Tompkins County.

Lawler & Clark, 37 Owego *Ithaca.*
Bartholomew Prof. 28 Aurora
Lathrop M. S. 92 Owego

Ulster County.

Osterhout Jeremiah *Saugerties.*

Warren County.

Nims Wm. Glenn's Falls *Queensbury.*

Wayne County.

Brown D. W.   *Arcadia.*
Allen A.   *Lyons.*
Goddard ——
Worth ——
Wright E. R.   *Marion.*
Williams F. P.   *Palmyra.*
Robinson Thomas

Westchester County.

Armstrong Miss, Peekskill *Courtlandt.*

Wyoming County.

Culver William   *Attica.*

Yates County.

M'Allister W. D. Penn Yan *Milo.*
Tinsley Wm.   do

Daguerreotype Apparatus.

Anthony Edward, National Daguerrean Depot, importer and manufacturer, cases, plates, chemicals, &c. &c., of the best quality, 205 Broadway *New York.*
Harrison C. C. 85 Duane
Kent Edward N. 116 John
Langenheim & Beckers, 201 Broadway, Agents for Voigtlander's apparatus
Lewis W. & W. H. 142 Chatham
Scovill J. M. L. & W. H. 101 William
Forster Thomas, 46 Vesey

Dentists.

Albany County.

Austin I. C. 583 Broadway *Albany.*
Newcomb D. 587   do
Monroe J. 74 Green
Douglass G. 77 Lydius
Russell J. 75 Ferry
Van Namee S. 111 South Pearl
Van Varnum H. West Troy *Watervliet*

Alleghany County.

Fuller ——   *Cuba.*
Bailey James, Little Genesee *Genesee.*

Broome County.

Smith M. P.   *Binghamton.*
Robie J. C.
Allaben W. N.   *Colerville.*

Cayuga County

Matson L. 75 Genesee st. *Auburn.*
Rathburn E. 101   do
Hamilton J. P 109   do
Smith S. N. 116   do
Ball S. William st.

Chautauque County.

Harrison J. Jamestown *Ellicott.*
Johnson E. Fredonia *Pomfret.*
Cherry A. E.
Fellows E. W.   *Westfield.*

Chenango County.

Hodge Richard   *Greene.*
Avery T. H.   *New Berlin.*
Parmalee E. H.   *Norwich.*
Burlingame D. C.
Eccleston Charles H.   *Oxford.*
Packer W. W.
Monroe Henry
Smith D.   *Sherburne.*

Columbia County.

Crossman E. 302 Warren st. *Hudson.*
Vanvleck H. H. & W. B. 290 Warren
Flagler L. B.   *Kinderhook.*
Merwin D. E. Valatie

Cortland County.

Gleason Levi   *Cortland Village.*

Delaware County.

Brown T. W.   *Delhi,*
Peabody D.
Merwin J. I.
Merwin P. B.
Williams L.
White T. A.   *Franklin.*
Everett C. W.
Park William, Deposit *Tompkins.*

Duchess County.

Blackman W. B.   *Fishkill.*
Mapes S. Fishkill Landing
Betts C. S.   *Pine Plains.*
Palmer W. A. 288 Main st. *Poughkeepsie*
Fonda A. 264 Main
Roberts C. H. & W. B. 254 Main
Simpson F. H. cor. Main & Market
Cross W.   *Rhinebeck.*

Erie County.

Quinlan John D. 2 South Division *Buffalo.*
Lewis J. 280 Main
Hayes George, 1 South Division
Harvey Charles W. 2 Division
Hayes & Bristol, cor. Main & South Division
Brown B. S. 211 Main
Reynolds H. H. 235 Main
Oliver Frederick. 157½ Main
Nash Wm. Springville *Concord.*
Carle Fullerton   *Eden.*
Knott S. E. S. H.   *Hamburgh.*

Essex County.

Hale Heman   *Essex.*

Franklin County.

Holbrook E. A.   *Malone.*
Nichols S. S.
Dunton Augustus T.

Fulton Cou.

Bronson ———, Northville
Northampton

Genesee County.

Dodge E. S. *Batavia.*
Stevens N.
Ganson H.
Barber John G. *Le Roy.*

Greene County

Smith Marcus W. *Durham.*
Fryer Frederick M. *Prattsville.*

Herkimer County.

Frankl'n B. W. *Little Falls.*
Ostrander J.
Kellogg J. C.
Perkins J. A. *Newport.*

Jefferson County.

Coe H. A. *Theresa.*
Wells & Robinson *Watertown.*
Dunning Uri
Bates James K.

Kings County.

Stratton H. N. 139 Atlantic
Brooklyn.
Miller J. E. 50 Pacific
Bridges S. W. 86.Fulton
Stillwell Charles H. 73 Henry
Bridges M. K. 109 Henry
Skinner S. cor. Henry & Montague
Lyman B. S. 109 Clinton
Vose John G. H. 232 Fulton
Brockway & Sons, 268 do
Dillingham W. S. 113 do
Northall & Holmes. 261 Wash.
Wood George. 9 Tillary
Rushmore E. C. South 7th st.
Williamsburgh.
Griswold A. H. 97 4th
Skinner John, 128 4th

Livingston County.

Farley & Bristol *Dansville.*
Smith Silas *Geneseo:*
Grant H. C. *Lima.*
Chittenden Nelson *Nundu.*
Coe W. L. Scottsburgh *Sparta.*

Madison County.

Dwinelle Wm. H. *Cazenovia.*
Allen J. L.
Rice J. W. T.
Fairchild Abel *De Ruyter.*
Holmes A. M. Morrisville *Eaton.*
Littlejohn N. M. *Hamilton.*
Hunt Nelson
Clark J. C. Chittenango *Sullivan.*

Monroe County.

Perkins A. J. 23 North *Rochester.*
Clark A. 42 Monroe
Duncombe C. H. 5 William
Haines D. cor. Buffalo & Exchange
Wanzer H. C. 16 Buffalo
Faulkner L. K. 13 Arcade Exch.
Wright & Proctor, 4 do
Naramore J. 2 Reynolds' Arcade.
Mills C cor. Buffalo & State
Beers & Morgan, Emporium block
cor. North St. Paul & Main
Gillett W. B. 47 Main
Fenn & Smith, cor. Troup & Livingston Place
Allen N. 109 State
Mix E. H. cor. Main & Clinton st.
Brockport *Sweden.*

Montgomery County.

Duel J. G. *Amsterdam.*
Foote & Brownell *Canajoharie.*
Kellogg D. S. Fort Plain *Minden.*

New York County.

Abel P. H. 27 Wooster *New York*
Alcook James, 78 Chambers
Alker Adolphus L. 341 4th
Allen Charles C 28 Warren
Allen James, 355 Broome
Ambler J. Gardiner, 26 Park place
Arnold William, 5 Warren
Ayres James B. 195 Fulton
Baker Charles O. 605 Broadway
Baker Elijah, 100 Chambers
Barbour James G. 7 6th Av.
Barlow Edward, 471 Hudson
Baure P. T. 203 Bleecker
Beardsley Myron, 50 W. 13th
Beardsley W. 157 W. 13th
Benne David F. 203 Bleecker
Bennett William C. 211 Bleecker
Berhard Lyon. 425 Pearl
Blaisdell John H. 341 Broadway
Blake Elihu, 15 Park place
Blankman H. G. 115 Chambers
Brigham H. A. 351 4th Av.
Brodhead Levi R. 459 Broadway
Bronson William H. 45 E. 13th
Brown A. W. 12 Park place
Brown C. D. & J. 469 Broadway
Bryant William J. 30 Factory
Burdell Galen, 362 Broadway
Burdell Harvey, 362 do
Burdell John, 3 4th Av.
Burras Thomas H. 1 Oliver
Buskey Joshua, 27 Murray
Caudee John G. 20 Park place
Carman Abraham V. 17 6th Av.
Carroll James, 77 Bowery
Castle Alexander C. 518 Broadw'y
Chase Frederick P. 87 Bleecker
Clarke Frederick A. 218 9th
Clay George, 94 Grand
Clowes G. 377 Hudson
Clowes Joseph W. 397 Hudson
Covell Lemuel, 208 Bowery
Crane J. W. 11 Le Roy place
Crowell J. M. 684 Broadway
Dodge J. Smith, 13 Bond
Dodge Nehemiah, 634 Broadway
Dodge W. & J. L. 634 do
Dunning Edwin J. 1 Bond
Dutcher Benjamin C. 135 Grand
Forbes Wm. G. 22 North Moore
Foster Joseph H. 14 Warren
Foster & Co. 367 Broadway
Fowler James, 362 do
Francis J. W. 1 Bond
Gilbert John, 196 W. 18th
Glenny George, 430 Broome
Grandin William E. 62 White
Gregory Lewis H. 333 Broome
Gunning J. B. 53 Bond
Harris Michael, 250 Hudson
Hassell Samuel, 377 4th
Hawes George E. 8 Park place
Helnis Francis J. 644 Greenwich
Herriot J. Groshen, 268 Spring
Hinton John H. 194 8th Av.
Holmes William H. 276 Grand
Holt W. G. 491 Broadway
Houpt Thomas J. 303 Broadway
Houston Patrick. 2 Park place
Howe Bezaleel, 379 Broome
Howe John M. 227 Grand
Howe Samuel, 117 Spring
Ing Edward, 19 Murray
Jarvis I. 452 Grand
Jennings Thomas, jr. 189 Church
Johnson A. 35 Bond
Johnson William E. 245 Henry
Jones Arthur W. 7 Bleecker
Joseph Diones, 158 Washington
Judson Stites W. 165 E. Broadway
Knapp A. 89 Av. C.
Kimball Horace, 522 Broadway
Lane James A. 86 4th Av.
Levett Morris, 698 Broadway
Lord Benjamin, 292 4th
Lounsberry Silas, 69 Chambers
Lovejoy John, 638 Broadway
Lozier Edward W. 292 Spring
Main Stephen A. 289 Bowery
Manson Thomas, 20 6th Av.

Middleton Wm. B. 67 Chambers
New York.
Miller Amos, 21 Greene
Miller Charles, 157 Grand
Miller D. 157 Grand
Mitchell Henry, 108 Bowery
M'Ilroy Archibald. 69 W. 14th
Morris Frederick W. 198 Fulton
Morris & O'Connor, 198 Fulton
Oakley Andrew O. 10 Delancy
O'Connor Henry C. 198 Fulton
Osborn Matthias T. 551 Broome
Paige David S. 11 Hoboken
Paine Thomas, 472¼ Broadway
Parkhurst William H. 97 Fulton
Parmly David R. 11 Park pl.
Parmly Eleazar, 1 Bond
Parmly Jehial, 3 Bond
Parmel & Dunning, 1 Bond
Parsons Wm. E. 36 Christopher
Peck Charles A. 382 Grand
Place Charles, 9 Allen
Pratt Linus, 129 E. Broadway
Preterre Eugene. 169 Bowery
Ransom Albert, 5 Chambers
Rich John B. 333 4th
Riggs Alfred, 313 4th
Robins John C. 50 E. Broadway
Ross Samuel, 38 Barclay
Root E. D. 373 Broadway
Rowell Charles S. 11 Chambers &
365 Broome
Rowell Warren, 149 Madison
Schaffer George F. 75 Warren
Schapp Richard, 216 Bowery
Sheridan Dr. 141 Houston
Sherwood Valentine, 271 Bowery
Schoonmaker Henry E. 586 Houston
Smillie George, 91 Chambers
Spoonar S. 106 Liberty
Stacey Henry C. 61 Franklin
Stanfield Otis, 467 Broadway
Steck Frank, 297¼ Broadway
Stinebergh David, 262 Grand
Stockton S. W. 258 Broadway
Straight Chester L. 139 Grand
Stratton James T. 229 Grand
Thomas Porter, 405 Broome
Thompson Leander, 112 Canal
Tierney George B. 451 Broome
Trendelenburg T. E. 60 Lispenard
Trenor James, 60 Warren
Trenor ———, 1 University pl.
Vail Addison, 373 Broadway
Van Praag Aaron, 383 Broadway
Van Zandt John W. 108 Bowery
Wait Thomas G. 209 Bleecker
Wekes John F. 35 Thompson
Ward M. & Co. 83 Maiden Lane
Ware Jonathan S. 29 Bond
Westlake Albert, 8 Park pl.
Whiting Seymour, 50 E. Broadway
Wilbor Wm. H. 108 Grand
Wilson Alfred, 59 E. 14th
Woofendale Isaac, 27 W. Washington pl.

Niagara County.

Bristol & Walter *Lockport.*
Chase S. L.
May & Holmes
Gaskill

Oneida County.

Van Valkenburgh A. T. *Camden.*
Noble W. H. Clinton. *Kirkland.*
Priest A. N. Clayville *Paris.*
Perkins & Allpart, Dominick st
Rome.
Cowles & Driggs, do
Harris G. W., Waterville
Sangerfield.
Coggeshall Jas. S. do
Duman E. 42 Genesee *Utica.*
Foster G. A. 104 Genesee
Colling A. H. 4 Broad
Ellis J. W., Hampton,
Westmoreland.
White H. R., Whitesboro
Whitestown.

Onondaga County.

Wescott A. Salina st. Syracuse
Salina.
Campbell C. F. Salina st. Syracuse
Chandler J. & Son, Genesee st.
Glynn G. do
Smith A. F. Water st.

Ontario County.

Wilson E. F. *East Bloomfield.*
Crane D. O. Geneva *Seneca.*
Newell L. do
Smith J. do
Griffing I. H. do

Orange County.

Davis I. L. *Chester.*
Howell Geo. *Goshen.*
Fine J. M.
Royce W. A. 85 Water
Newburgh.
Grant C. W. 43 Water
Gunn Enos, 71 Water
Dayton S. South Middletown
Wallkill.
Hoyt W. H. *Warwick.*

Orleans County.

Gates S., Albion *Barre.*
Briggs S. B., Albion
Blakesly J. M., Medina *Ridgeway.*

Oswego County.

Allen Warren *Mexico.*
Lenox Samuel, Lawrence Build-
ings, Bridge st. *Oswego.*
Vandenburgh D. 5 Eagle Block,
1st st.
Goldey D. S. 10 Phœnix Block,
1st st.
Fitch C. P., Fulton *Volney.*

Otsego County.

Blackwell E. Burlington Flats
Burlington.
Byron E. P. Cooperstown *Otsego.*
Peak G. M. do

Putnam County.

Davis G. R. Cold Spring
Phillipstown.

Queens County

Hall H. D. Hempstead Branch
North Hempstead.

Rensselaer County.

Dunham S. J. Hathaway's Row
Lansingburgh.
Welch S. P. 233 State
Honsinger E. 204 River *Troy.*
Jeffers G. A. cor. River & 1st
Arnold H. B. 11 1st
Hogan ——, 45 3d
Paine H. J. 8 2d
Ross ——, 14 3d
Young O. R. 6 3d
Young H. H. 104 3d
Buswell ——, 133 3d
Washburn J. S. 11 4th
Rainey J. H. 47 5th
Nelson T. 113 5th
Wheeler L. C. 6 Albany

Richmond County.

Gale A. G. S. Tompkinsville
Castleton.

St. Lawrence County.

Waid D. *Gouverneur.*
Blodgett S. S. Ogdensburgh
Oswegatchie.
Austin John, do
Nichols John R. *Potsdam.*

Saratoga County.

M'Allister J. M. *Saratoga Springs.*

Loomis R. *Saratoga Springs.*
Carpenter Charles
Warren G. W.
Brockway J. & Son *Waterford.*

Schenectady County.

Lacy J. 100 State *Schenectady.*
Bradt F. J. 115 State
Burham S. B. 41 State

Schoharie County.

Nellis Jacob *Schoharie.*

Seneca County.

Reynolds Robert R. *Ovid.*

Steuben County.

Lawrence J. W. *Bath.*
Dart Allen

Suffolk County.

Sutton Lyman B. Port Jefferson
Brookhaven.
Conkling Nathaniel, Patchogue
Arthur Franklin O. *Smithtown.*

Tioga County.

Lefler B. C. *Owego.*
Fisher G. L.

Tompkins County.

Mattison A. 90 Owego *Ithaca.*
Miles C. S. 8 Seneca

Ulster County.

Finch Wm. B. Main st. *Kingston.*
Thompson W. W.
Lathrop H. B. *Saugerties.*
Wilson Dr. Galesville
Shawangunk.

Warren County.

Cadwell E. C. Glenn's Falls
Queensbury.

Washington County.

Crosby J. B. *Greenwich.*
Brockway W. W. North White
Creek *White Creek.*

Wayne County.

Hooker C., Newark *Arcadia.*
Peck Arvine, Clyde *Galen.*
Sylvester E., Ware *Lyons.*
Wright C. R. *Marion.*
North H. M. *Palmyra.*
Perkins & Johnson
Belden R. *Sodus.*

Westchester County.

Fuller E. D., Sing Sing *Ossining.*
White N. P. *Yonkers.*

Wyoming County.

Collier John T. *Attica.*
Scrotom H. M. *Perry.*
Collins & Hutchinson *Pike.*
Walker E. *Warsaw.*

Yates County.

Elmendorf Joseph, Penn Yan *Milo.*
Harkness James, Rushville *Potter.*
Sleeper H., Dundee *Starkey.*

Designers.

Kings County.

Sickels Gerard, rear 99 Washington *Brooklyn.*

New York County.

Chapin J. R. 75 Nassau *New York.*

Designers—Calico.

Junker Charles, 164 3d *New York.*
Robley J. 17 Post's Buildings

Diamond (Glaziers) Makers.

Dickinson John, 22 John *New York.*
Shaw Joshua, 142 Nassau

Dispensaries.

Eastern, 74 Ludlow *New York*
Homœopathic, 57 Broad
New York City, 113 White
Northern, Waverly place corner
Christopher

Distillers.

Albany County.

Classen H. & Son, 840 Broadway
Albany.

Broome County.

Baker D. & W. *Colesville.*
Townsend H. *Kent.*

Cayuga County.

Carpenter J. H. *Niles.*

Chautauque County.

Smith R. B., Smith's Mills *Hanover.*

Duchess County.

Fletcher R. N. *Unionvale.*

Erie County.

Thornton James *Black Rock.*
Clark & Williams, (rectifying) 8
Ohio *Buffalo.*

Greene County.

Hardy, Rundle & Co. *Greenville.*

Herkimer County.

Mason Daniel *Frankfort.*
Degrist James O. *Little Falls.*
Smith N. *Newport.*
Morss N., West Winfield *Winfield*

Jefferson County.

Angell William H. *Pamelia.*
Hungerford Orville *Watertown.*

Kings County.

Sneden, Schenck & Co. cor. Fur-
man & Joralemon *Brooklyn.*
Young Wm. (cordials) 116 Hud-
son Av.
Manley & Embury, Tillary cor.
Gold
Wilson Charles, Flushing Av. cor.
Skillman
Engle James, 1st st. *Williamsburgh.*
Ely N. C. & Co. cor. 1st & N. 4th
Cogswell, Crane & Co. do

Madison County.

Morse Ellis *Eaton.*
Bicknell & Norton, Morrisville
Hubbard Harvey, East *Hamilton.*
Edgarton J. S., Bouckville
Madison.
Hill John, Perryville *Sullivan.*
French & Walrath, Chittenango

Monroe County.

Walcott A. F. & G. P. Clarissa st
Rochester.
Conkey J. & E. Steamboat Land-
ing

Montgomery County.

Wells J. J., Minaville *Florida.*

New York County.

Distillers—Cordials.

Andrews George, 165 Av. C
 New York.
Church Charles, 527 Hudson
Dunn William, 127 Roosevelt
Goodnow Lewis P. 199 Chambers
Gordon Philp, 55 Vesey
Hoffman Charles & Co. 255 3d Av.
Hughes Patrick, 88 Cherry
Hutchings Thomas G. 104 Barclay
Jarvis Zophar R. 218 Bowery
Knapp Cyrus & Co. 256 Washington
Lowerre, Troutman & Co. 80 Duane
M'Cormick Patrick, E. 22d b. 2d & 3d Avs.
Mogenier John J. 96 Warren
Newell Garry T. 197 6th Av.
Oaks William, 10 Mulberry
Pray Henry, 303 West
Roy John B. 102 Front
Riley Patrick, 148 2d
Wade John, 575 Grand

Distillers—Grain.

Bertram J. A. & Lehritter, 73 Bayard
 New York.
Gallagher Patrick, 360 1st Av.
Manley & Embury. 50 South
Parks & Jackson, 86 7th Av.

Distiller—Molasses.

Havens Henry & Son, 164 Front & 120 Elm
 New York.

Distillers and Rectifiers of Spirits.

Allen Matthew. 312 W. 17th
 New York.
Bachis, Sons & Co. 101 Wall
Blodgett George B. 447 Water
Bohne Charles W. 29 James
Bryan & Fagan, 260 5th
Cogswell, Crane & Co. 104 Wall & 116 Front
Dayton & Sprague, 107 Front & 71 & 73 Robinson
D'Homergue John, 140 W. 17th
Duke William S. 119 Front & 64 Clinton
Ely Nathan & Co. 140 Front
Havens H. & Son, 164 Front
Hopke Matthias M. 207 Greene
Hood Andrew & Hayward, Chrystie cor. Delancy
Johnson Wm. M. & Sons, 266 West 16th
Johnson H. & Co. 445 Water
Johnsons & Lazarus, 242, 244 & 246 Washington
Kelly John J. 69 & 61 Lewis
Manly & Embury, 50 South
Minturn W. H. 120 Water
Mullen & M'Guire, 132 Elizabeth
O'Donnell & Geraghty, 101 & 103 W. 18th
Pirnie P. B. & H. 24 Orange
Reilly John M. & Co. 172 South
Rogers & Crane, 123, 332 & 325 Front
Schilling Andrew, 158 3d
Scribner & Coolidge, 134 Front & 105 Columbia
Sneden, Schenck & Co. 176 Front
Snediker William. 113 Troy
Stanton Jonathan H. 323 Front
Thompson & Co. 119 Front & 56 Cherry
White Campbell P. 56 Broad

Distillers—Syrups.

Cott Peter, 19 W. Broadway
 New York.

Dimond Patrick, 47 Centre
 New York.
Lowerre, Troutman & Co. 80 Duane

Distillers—Turpentine.

Cronkright James, 148 Maid. Lane
Pugh Thomas & Co. 55 Greene
Tapscott James T. 86 South

Distillers—Continued.

Oneida County.

Brown & Wright, Oriskany Falls
 Augusta.
Capron E., Delta *Lee.*
Tower D. & J., Waterville
 Sangersfield.

Onondaga County.

Kellogg Daniel, Jordan *Elbridge.*
Graves Wm. T & Co. do
Norton Coon & Co. Marcellus Falls *Marcellus.*

Ontario County.

Beardsley, Gilbert & Co. *Phelps.*
Owen Lyman, Richmond Mills
 Richmond.

Orange County.

Hulse William *Blooming Grove.*
Royce T. C. & Brother *Cornwall.*
Hiland Maltery
Bull D. F. Bullville *Crawford.*
Carpenter D. *Goshen.*
Demerest D. D. New Milford
 Warwick.

Orleans County.

Spencer S. M., Oak Orchard
 Ridgeway.

Oswego County.

Knowlton Dean O. Pulaski
 Richland.

Otsego County.

Brooks William *Middlefield.*
Pierce Levi H.
Ely & Murray
White H. *New Lisbon.*
Shepherd Isaac *Oneonta.*

Rensselaer County.

Ingram H. & Co. 171 River *Troy.*
Inghram William & H. cor. Washington & 4th

St. Lawrence County.

Averell James G. Water st. Ogdensburgh *Oswegatchie.*
Parish George *Parishville.*

Seneca County.

Shoemaker John *Seneca Falls.*
Fetzinger Thomas & Co. *Waterloo.*
Howe Thomas & Co.

Steuben County.

Blank J. & Co. *Bath.*
Dodge Erastus *Painted Post.*

Sullivan County.

Hawkins S. R., Burlingham
 Mamakating.

Tompkins County.

Houtz John H. & Co. *Dryden.*

Wayne County.

Kelley Patrick, East Palmyra
 Palmyra.

Yates County.

Andrews & Briggs, Dundee
 Starkey.

Dock Builders.

Kings County.

Lake William & Brothers, Water st. near N. 2d *Williamsburgh.*

New York County.

Corwin Edward C. 104 Barclay
 New York.
Gilbert John S. & Z. Secor, 118 Broadway
Sherman & Kuyler, 211 9th st.
Spies Francis. 50 South

Docks.

Atlantic, 74 Broadway *New York.*
Balance, 241½ South
Dry Dock, foot 10th E. R.
Screw Dock, 232 South
Sectional, 254 South

Dog Power Manufacturer.

Dutchess County.

Cudner P. & Co. *Hyde Park.*

Door, Sash & Blind Makers.

Albany County.

Easterly T. 15 S. Pearl *Albany.*
Fowler Gilbert C. 96 Herkimer
Vanderzee J. 203 Hamilton
Rogers & Robinson, West Troy
 Watervliet.

Alleghany County.

Burdick Wm. S. *Alfred.*
Stillman Ford *Almond.*
Wheaton S. S. *Andover.*
Sanford Joseph *Angelica.*
Spencer Smith
Knowlton & Satterly *Belfast.*
Barnes Elias *Bolivar.*
Mitchell R. W. *Rushford.*
Peterson Wm.
Babcock Rouse *Scio.*
Babcock Lorenzo, Wellsville

Broome County.

March & Harding *Binghamton.*
Bennett E. C.

Cattaraugus County.

Beecher Moses *Ellicottville.*

Cayuga County.

Slover I. Genesee st. *Auburn*
Putnam & Stuart, North st.
Putnam E. F. *Locke*

Chautauque County.

Partridge & Co. Jamestown
 Ellicott.
Scott & Barrows, do
Green —, Forestville *Hanover.*
Buck O. A. & Brothers, Fredonia
 Pomfret.
Woodford M. H. Fredonia

Chemung County.

Booth & Aspinwall *Elmira.*

Chenango County.

Fairchild & White *Bainbridge.*
Fairchild & Long, S. Bainbridge
Kenyon W. *Sherburne.*

Clinton County.

Hoag David, Keeseville *Au Sable.*

Cortland County.

Bliss L. & Co.   *Truxton.*

Delaware County.

Lockwood L.   *Stamford.*
Grant A. B. Hobart
Scott Wm.   do

Duchess County.

Woodruff F. 401½ Main
          Poughkeepsie.
Griffing O. A. 398 Main
Bradley W. E. Upper Landing
Thompson Wm. T. Mill st.
Armstrong C. & Co. 127 Main
Morse C. B.   *Rhinebeck.*
Gemond R. M. Verbank *Unionvale.*

Erie County.

Husted Sangster & Co. Seneca
     near Michigan   *Buffalo.*
Boynton P. N. 69 & 71 Ellicott
Thayer & Brother, cor. Oak &
     Clinton
Hastings Thomas B. Mechanics st.

Genesee County.

Rogers Nathaniel   *Stafford.*

Jefferson County.

Rounds C. H. Dexter *Brownville.*
Starks A. D. Black River
          Rutland.
Marble George W.   *Theresa.*
Hubbard Chas. E.   *Watertown.*
Stevens Hiram
Reed Abel & Brother

Kings County.

Cox P. R. Columbia near Warren
          Brooklyn.
Woodworth G. H., Smith near
     Pacific
Walls G. R. cor Livingston & Bo-
     erum
White & Kirk, cor. Livingston &
     Bond
Moore L. 40, 42 & 44 Water
Abrams Jos. Pearl st. nr. Front
Fithian & Joy, Bridge st. near
     Fulton
Van Heusen G. K. 71 Bridge
Langdon Calvin M. 174 Gold
Nevins Isaac W., Duffield near
     Johnson
Nevins & Gardiner, 135 Carll
Caldwell Stephen, Duffield st.
Brookes John, Remsen Farm near
     Clove Road
Cross M. & Co. Cross Dock, Kent
     Av.
Fenton H. B. Green Point
          Bushwick.
Homan & Milnes, 150 4th
          Williamsburgh.
Dikeman Robert, 153 Grand
Hawkins A. 126   do
Driggs Ensine, N. 2d cor. 5th
Wooley & Butler, 10th st. n. Grand
Atmore Isaac, foot of N. 3d
Riker Henry, N. 6th cor. 3d
Tucker Wm. 438 Grand

Lewis County.

Gould G. H. Constableville
          West Turin.

Livingston County.

Bouton J.   *Dansville.*
Chamberlin E. S. *Mount Morris.*
Tyler Harvey S. *Springwater.*

Madison County.

Van Driesen & Bliss *Cazenovia.*

Monroe County.

Robins Johnson J. Phœnix Build-
     ings   *Rochester.*
Coleman Alex. Phœnix Buildings,
     Aqueduct st.
Higgins P. 212 State
Spencer A. K. 6 Selye Buildings
Van Vlack T. W.   do
Peelor H. Brown's Race
Pritchard J. W. 86 Hill

Montgomery County.

Kellogg & Andrews *Charleston.*

New York County.

Anner J. H & P. A. 627 Hudson
          New York.
Anner Peter A. 40 4th
Badeau Harrison N. 172 Chrystie
Bailey Charles, 7 Stanton
Bannan Thomas, 32 Columbia
Bausher Henry, 7 & 17 Suffolk
Bayles John C. 21½ Catharine
Bell Robert. 147 Orchard
Berry Martin R. 1 St. John's lane
Bogart Wm. M. 185 Prince
Brush E. B. 310 E. 25th
Clark Jacob D. 212 Houston
Coady Abm. 146 W. 17th
Coles Cornelius, 113 Canal
Decker Thos. rear 16 Watts & 290
     Hudson
Delamater Edward D. 181 9th
Dixon John D. 105 W. Broadway
Driggs John F. 194 Amity
Driggs S. B., E. 23th st.
Falconer E. 216 W. 21st
Fenwick Wm. 12th bet. Avs. B
     & C
Fisher Thos. J. 34 W. 13th
Flanigan L. 9th Av. near 37th
Fraser J. H. 16 W. Broadway
Geffry John E. 144 W. 20th
Gatty George, 293 Hudson
Giles Gilbert. 26 Murray
Gowdey James, 95 W. 24th
Greves Rich. & C. W. 59 Mangin
Hallsted Benjamin, 45 Beekman
Halsey Lawrence W. 229 W. 17th
Hardenbergh H. V. & D. W. 135
     Amos
Henton Jonathan. 270 5th
Holmes John F. 89 Delancy
Horn Albert. 117 W. 19th
Hunt J. I. 132 Laurens
Hunt Richard G. 147 Av. C
Jacobus David, rear 138 Wooster
Kane Matthew, 197 W. 13th
Lodewick John, 207 Wooster
M'Kenzie Daniel. 146 W. 17th
Mandeville S. 13 Stanton
Martin Lemuel. 140 3d Av.
Moore Henry, 829 Broome
Newton Jonah, 270 4th
Nostrand J. 262 W. 24th
Osborn J. 507 Grand & 86 Broome
Plum Nath. D. 168 Chambers
Price Abel, 5 Spring
Purdy Hiram, rear 79 Elizabeth
Quick James R. 127 Norfolk
Read D., W. 28th st.
Robertson Henry F. 961 9th
Roome Peter. rear 69 Laurens
Shields Edward N. 228 W. 18th
Smack E. & S. K. 19th st. n. 1st Av.
Smith Edwin, 216 W. 21st
Springsteen H. & C. 895 G'wich
Stubbs Samuel N 73 E. 13th
Taylor Henry, 42 Av. D
Terhune Thomas. 27 2d
Toung M. 541 Water
Voorhes E. M. rear 161 Bleecker
Welch J. & J. D. 65 Hester
Wight Richard H. 94 Thompson
Wilhelm & Laing. 210 Grand
Willard & Co. 158 Stanton
Wood Richard G. 126 W. 19th

Niagara County.

Root G. D.   *Lockport.*

M'Cullor & Nickerson,
          Niagara Falls.
Fosgett H. Youngstown *Porter.*

Oneida County.

Clark H. Oriskany Falls, *Augusta.*
Hammond & Allen,   *Camden.*
Simmons, Evans & Co. James st.
          Rome.
Kingsbury Wm. 36 Seneca *Utica.*
Read D. Washington st,
Huntington H. L. Fulton st.

Onondaga County.

Gable M., Baldwinsville *Lysander*
Kingsley L. Water st., Syracuse
          Salina.
Robertson J. R. Lock st.

Ontario County.

Harris & Co. Chapinsville
          Hopewell.
Edgerton, Franklin & Co. *Phelps.*
Earle Eli P. Geneva   *Seneca.*
Flowers D.   do
Wilson S.   do
Monroe T.   do

Orange County.

Merritt C.   *Cornwall*
Turner J. & A. Fort Jervis
          Deer Park.
Wood W. H. Slate Hill *Minisink.*
Goldsmith E. H. Colden st.
          Newburgh.
Frost C. South Middletown
          Wallkill.
Bugsby C. T.   do
Smith John D.   do

Orleans County.

Andrews George, Knowlesville
          Ridgeway

Oswego County.

Ogden J. & Co. Oswego Falls
          Granby.
Burr & Gilmore, Crocker's Build-
     ings, Bridge st.   *Oswego.*
Nipincot & Newbury, Washington
     Mills, 1st st.
Bennett & Maltby, Pulaski
          Richland.
Wright Joshua B.   do

Otsego County.

Bookman Erastus D. *Edmeston.*

Queens County.

Vermilyea N. D.   *Hempstead.*
Brickerhoff H.   *Jamaica.*
Millington M. V. Hempstead
     Branch   *North Hempstead.*

Rensselaer County.

Ingraham R. 483 River *Troy.*
Winnea E. 4 Federal
Hyde J. R. cor. Mechanic &
     Grand Division
Neer & Seaver, 466 River

Richmond County.

Taylor A., Stapleton *Southfield.*

Rockland County.

Gurnee S. Spring Valley
          Orangetown.

St. Lawrence County.

Smith Sidney   *Canton.*
Burdick S., Waddington *Madrid.*
Cook E. Lake st. Ogdensburgh
          Oswegatchie.
Guest G. 2d,   do
Dimick Lyman & Erastus *Pierpont.*

Hand Orra *Potsdam.*
Rich W. West Potsdam

Saratoga County.

Trumbull James & Co. Glenn's
Falls *Moreau.*
Cornell H. R. & Co. *Stillwater.*

Seneca County.

Powell & Jones *Seneca Falls.*
Westcott H. P.

Suffolk County.

Skidmore Luther *Riverhead*
Corwin & King, Greenport
Southold.

Sullivan County.

Allen T., Monticello *Thompson.*

Ulster County.

Fredenburgh Wm. *Kingston.*
Burhans D. *Saugerties.*
Carpenter B., Ellenville
Wawarsing.

Washington County.

Phillips & Deanis, Galesville
Greenwich.
Andrews J. & L. Sandy Hill
Kingsbury.
Robertson Wm. H. *Putnam.*

Westchester County.

Clark L. M. Tarrytown *Greenburgh.*
Hopkins John C. *New Rochelle.*
Hagerman & Doolittle, Sing Sing
Ossining.
Foster D. J. Sing Sing
Paten J. *Yonkers.*

Wyoming County.

Dewey H. *Castile.*
Abbot Joshua *Genesee Falls.*

Yates County.

Bush C. V. Penn Yan *Milo.*
Beekman B. B. Dundee *Starkey.*

Draughtsmen.

Bailey J. H. 23 Chambers
New York.
Chapin John R. 75 & 77 Nassau
Haight A. R. 126 Fulton
Sherman William, 25 Renwick
Sickels Gerard, rear 274 Pearl
Thomas William. 135 E. 30th
Wade William, 236 Broadway
Wallin Samuel, 299 do

Druggists.

Albany County.

Briggs R. B. 4 Exchange *Albany.*
Burton Benjamin. 1 Delavan House
Huyck A. 497 Broadway
Keyser Wm. H. 635 do
Pierce W. H. 566 do
Frothingham C. 440 do
Vandenbergh A. F. do
Wharton W. A. 381 & 383 do
Dean G. F. 293 do
Pulling H. P. 70 State
M'Clure & Co. 74 do
Dexter Geo. 77 do
Rossman J. B. 70 Lydius
Springstead & Bullock, 88 S. Pearl
Merrill L. A. 33 S. Pearl
Burrows & Nellegar, 43½ S. Pearl
Perkins & Gardiner. 34 Beaver
Ford & Grant (wholesale) 32 & 34
Washington
Tucker W. West Troy *Watervliet.*

Burrows & Van Alstyne, W. Troy
Watervliet.
Liney J. do
Brooks P. P. Cohoes
Wood W. D. do
Terry I. do

Alleghany County.

Dwight A. L. *Almond.*
Charles R. *Angelica.*
Thomas C. K. & G. W.
Palmer Enos *Cuba.*
Barney Anthony *Independence.*
Horton Jonathan, Whitesville
Thorp John H. do
M'Call & Bartlett *Rushford.*

Broome County.

Smith & Eldridge *Binghamton.*
Trivet R. C. (wholesale)
Stowe J. Harpersville *Colesville.*
Robbins E. jr. *Union.*

Cattaraugus County.

Barson, Graves & Co.
Franklinville.

Cayuga County.

Vananden H. G. 5 Genesee *Auburn.*
Steel R. 61 do
Hunt Thomas M. 71 do
Tuttle C. N. (patent) 101 do
Fowler H. G. 117 do

Chautauque County.

Henderson W. W. Charlotte
Post W. & Co. Jamestown *Ellicott.*
Parsons L. do
Shaw W. D. Silver Creek
Hanover.
Sexton A. Forestville
Clark ——, Fredonia *Pomfret.*
Burrett C. do
Bess C. Dunkirk
Babcock Henry M. *Westfield.*
Parsons Lorenzo

Chemung County.

Elliott H. W. *Elmira.*
Beadle Tracy
Ogden W.
Payne B.
Seaman Horace, Millport *Veteran.*

Chenango County.

Akley A. M. *Bainbridge.*
Adams A. D. *Greene.*
Mitchell H. & Son *Norwich.*
Harris H.
Sands & Co. *Oxford.*
Packer W. W.
Clark E. & Lyons *Pitcher.*
Park Nehemiah
Cushman & Smith *Sherburne.*
Buckingham A.

Clinton County.

Hasbrook J. A. Keeseville
Au Sable.
Pollard Ablatha, do
Mooers Wm. *Plattsburgh.*
Moore & Stoddard

Columbia County.

Read E. Spencertown *Austerlitz.*
Lasell S. M. Chatham 4 corners
Barrenger H. J. Warren st.
Hudson.
Storrs W. & G. do
Punderson & Ham do
Rossman & M'Kinstry, 395 Warren
White H. R. Warren st.
Flagler L. B. *Kinderhook.*
Abbott & Van Slyck, Valatie
Tilden & Co. (steam drug mill)
New Lebanon.

Cortland County.

Bradford Daniel *Cortland Village.*
Thayer W. S.
Kinner & M'Graw

Delaware County.

Steele E. *Delhi.*
Fitch A.
Howard C.
Dales & Butts, (Patent) Bloomville
Kortright.
Williams & Briggs, Deposit
Tompkins.
Bowman I. B.

Duchess County.

Roy J. Wappinger's Falls *Fishkill.*
Van Wyck & Carey
Mapes J. D. & S. Fishkill Landing
M'Keen L. do
Williams A. T. *Hyde Park.*
Bostwick R. W. & S. Pine Plains.
Van Voorhis & Trowbridge, 319
Main *Poughkeepsie.*
Dame M. 267 Main
Trivett E. 286 Main
Bockee Jacob, 297 Main
Vanvalkenburgh & Coffin (whole-
sale) 249 Main
Smith M. 217 Main
Righter Peter, 375 Main
Barnes & Deyo, 137 Main
Freligh M. *Rhinebeck.*
Platt, Nelson & Co.

Erie County.

Kezeler W. H. 1 Stow block,
Commercial st. *Buffalo.*
Champlin O. H. P. 251 Main
King Wm. 249 do
Coleman Charles, 268 do
Matthews A. I. 221 do
Clark Oliver P. 290 do
Coleman John H. 220 do
Jackson & Farr, 396 do
Chambers & Co. 10 Terrace
Herbolsheimer & Wehner, 347
Main
Hauenstein John, 359 Main
Davis E. H. Long Wharf
Ralston A. & Co. 148 Main
Smith Wm. (wholesale) 142 Main
Hollister R. 177 & 179 Main
Carlisle John. 38 do
Parker R. 136 do
Reynolds A. 155 do
Guenther & Stevens, 163 Main
Bristol C. C. 225 Main
Baker Wm. W. *Colden.*

Essex County.

Perry Abijah *Elizabethtown.*
Smith Charles D. *Ticonderoga.*

Franklin County.

Congdon Job *Fort Covington.*
Heath F. T. *Malone.*
Pangbora I. W.
Amsden L.

Fulton County.

Clark Roswell *Broadalbin.*
Haring George M. *Johnstown.*
Smith Dudley P.
Smith Daniel

Genesee County.

Wilcox J. B. *Alabama.*
Montgomery Harvey *Alexander.*
Seaver Wm. & Son *Batavia.*
Fellows & Co.
Pixley & Bryant *Le Roy.*
Stanley H. A.
Barber John G.
Haynes —— *Stafford.*

Greene County.

Wey Wm. H. *Catskill.*
Moses Hiram R. *Prattsville.*

Herkimer County.

Morey Lawrence L. Mohawk
     German Flats.
Woodworth W. W. & E. M. Mohawk
Hoffman James *Herkimer.*
Hunt Charles P. *Little Falls.*
Wheeler James
Phillie B.   *Newport.*

Jefferson County.

Merriam S. A.   *Adams.*
Sherman R. R. *Antwerp.*
Brockway Henry *Brownville.*
Ayers Jesse
Massey Wm. P.
Wells Wm. *Cape Vincent.*
Camp Geo. & Son, Sackett's Harbor   *Hounsfield.*
Kimball D. S. Sackett's Harbor
Stockwell E. S. *Theresa.*
Clark Silas *Watertown.*
Scribner Henry
Smith John
Camp Talcott H.
Hoyt & Gregory

Kings County.

Quirk F. T. & Co. cor. Atlantic &
Columbia *Brooklyn.*
Alvord Charles, 43 Atlantic
Blagrove Wm. P. 115 do
Ayres Gabriel D. cor. Atlantic &
Henry
Leeds Stephen P. cor. Court &
Atlantic
Hibbard J. B. 64 Atlantic
Bassett F. 156 do
Taylor Wm. H. cor. Columbia &
Degraw
Hotchkiss Alvah, 7 Union
Wright C. M. cor. Columbia &
Sacket
Smith Chas. C. cor. Dean & Smith
Nichols Wm. 130 Court
Mead Paul, cor. Smith & Baltic
Corbett M. do & Warren
Davis R. J. cor. Clinton & Fulton
Lambert P. S. Fulton st.
Bailey W. (wholesale) 205 Fulton
Goldsmith J. A. 174 Fulton
Wilson George, 158 do
Stahl H. 246 do
Smith James W. Court st. cor.
Montague
Howard John G. 49 Fulton
Rice J. & Son, 27 James
Marschalk Wm. H. 73 Main
Thornton J. W. 114 York
Stevens E. W. 77 Sands
Price S. T. B. 106 High
Osborn Samuel J. 196 High
O'Reilly Francis, 212 Bridge
M'Allister Thomas, 216 do
Ely W. A. 31 Myrtle Av.
Skerritt C. 251 Fulton
Blagrove C. J. 86 Myrtle Av.
Prince Christo., Fulton cor. Pearl
Mountain G. F. Fulton cor. Adams
Theall Elisha, 50 Hudson Av.
Smith D. E. 140 York
Bellingham John, Prospect cor.
Gold
Pierce John, 101 Myrtle Av.
Van Beuren C. 121 do
Palmer R. H. 159 do
Parker H. 152 do
Manley G. V., Navy st.
Evans M. Myrtle Av. cor. Clauson Av.
Squire O. Myrtle Av. nr. Graham
Rotten Edward & Co. 21 S. 7th
    Williamsburgh.
Miller Charles, 55 4th
Thompson Wm 235 S. 4th
Brown E. J. 229 S. 3d
Atwater William, 149 4th
Hebberling G. 313 Grand
Newman James, 304 do
Butler J. V. B. 170 do
Nowill James D. 25 do

Boswell H. C. & Co. 118½ Grand
    Williamsburgh.
Jacobson L. C. 227 1st
Miller Charles, 470 Grand
Buchholz C. G. jr. Graham Av.
cor. Remsen st

Lewis County.

Doig J.   *Lowville.*
Peden J. & H. H. *Martinsburgh.*
Chase William
Runge R., Constableville
    West Turin.

Livingston County.

Campbell Duncan *Caledonia.*
Niles Edward *Dansville.*
Doty & Farnam
Wetmore C. G. & Co.
Shannon George F.
Walker W. R. *Geneseo.*
Metcalf E. P. & C.
Pelton Jonathan G., Cuylersville
    Leicester.
Dayton D. D. *Lima.*
Thompson Harry *Livonia.*
Whitney & Laflin *Mount Morris.*
Stanley & Amos
Camp James H. *Nunda.*
Swain & Ray

Madison County.

Coburn L. D. *Cazenovia.*
Fairchild John
Potter O. C.
Foord Alvin
Whitford & Randall *De Ruyter.*
Kingman L. M., Morrisville *Eaton.*
Foote John J. *Hamilton.*
Hartshorn & Maydole
Lamb D. Oneida Depot *Lenox.*
Stoddard & Co.
Young John, Canastota
Fuller Saml. Chittenango *Sullivan.*
Teller I. T. do
Arndt P. S. do

Monroe County.

Van Buren B., Fairport *Perrinton.*
Church Peter, Churchville *Riga.*
Thayer P. P. 94 Buffalo *Rochester.*
Swan L. B. 19 Buffalo
Pitkin William, 14 Buffalo
Winslow & Young, 51 Main
Worden C. 89 Main
Wade H. D. cor. Main & St. Paul
Post & Willis; 4 Exchange
Adams & Conklin, 14 do
Hawks J. & T. 32 do
Kershaw Seth, 182 State
Frye T. 40 Main, Brockport
    Sweden.
Chappell E. T. & G. 46 Main do

Montgomery County.

Settle A P. *Canajoharie.*
Wetmore A. & Co.
Stevens John H. Fultonville *Glen.*
Ferguson John P. Fort Plain
    Minden.
Babcock John H. do
Fritcher Peter, Fonda *Mohawk.*

New York County.

DRUGGISTS, WHOLESALE.

Anderson & Maclay, 199 Water
    New York.
Boyd & Paul, 40 Cortlandt
Boyer & Holton, 122 Water
Burger William, 34 Cortlandt
Bush Henry V. 319 Greenwich
Bush & Clickener, 81 Barclay
Carle John & Co. 153 Water
Carnes & Haskell, 89 Maiden lane,
Importers of Foreign Drugs
Chapman H. T. 77 Fulton
Clark & M'Connin, 6 Fletcher

Comstock & Co. 57 John
    New York.
Cumming Thos. W. 178 G.wich
Elsworth William H. 100 Murray
Fahnestock B. A. & Co. 49 John
Frothingham & Beckwith, 149
Cedar
Graham & Co. 10 Old slip
Greenleaf & Kinsley, 45 Cortlandt
Haskell & Merrick, 10 Gold
Haviland R. B. & Co. 177 B.way
Haviland, Keese & Co. 80 Maiden
lane
Haydock, Corlies & Clay, 218
Pearl
Hibbard Timothy R. 96 John
Hill Alfred, 208 Greenwich
Horsey Joseph, 84 Maiden lane
Hooper T. 169 Pearl
Hurd Augustus, 54 Cortlandt
Ingersoll & Brother, 230 Pearl
Jauncey William H. 273 Front
Jenkins J. W. & Co. 242 Pearl
Lamson Geo. W. & Co. 7 Fletcher
Lanman David T. 69 Water
Lapping, Low & Co. 214 Pearl
Law & Boyd, Dealers in Botanic
Medicines, 62 East Broadway
Laurence George N. 121 Maiden
lane
Leeds & Hazard, 121 Maiden lane
Lewis & Price, 55 Pearl, paints,
oils, glass, &c.
Marsh & Northrop, 69 Pearl, dye
stuffs, paints, oils. glass, &c.
Minor Cyrus S. & Co. 296 Pearl
Minor Israel & Co. 214 Fulton
Moore & Taylor, 81 Maiden lane
Morrison John G. 188 Greenwich
Moss Reuben E. 542 Grand
Nordquist C. J. & Co. 390 Broome
Norton. Babcock & Wool, 139
Maiden lane
Osgood & Jennings, 186 Pearl
Olcott M'Kesson & Co. 127 Maiden
lane
Penfold J. & W. & Co. 4 Fletcher
Phillips C. H. 145 Greenwich
Pou & Palanca, 96 John
Quackinbush Benj. 709 G.wich
Rust & Houghton, 83 John
Sanborn Luke H. 96 Wall
Schieffelin H. M. & Fowler, 142 &
145 Front
Schieffelin Phillip & Co. 167 Water
Schieffelin Brothers & Co. Importers of Drugs, 104 & 106 John &
11 Platt
Sherwood & Coffin, 64 Pearl
Smith, Stratton & Wood, 141 Maiden lane & 21 Fletcher
Sweetser E. F. 81 Pine
Sweetser & Hall, 82 Pine
Taft James H. 100 Wall
Thayer William W. 319 Pearl
Townsend Walter B. & Co. 226
Pearl
Thomas & Maxwell. 86 William
Trippe Joseph E. 123 Maiden lane
Trippe J. & J. F. 90 & 92 do
Underhill William, jr. 182 Water
Ward M. & Co. 83 Maiden lane
Wheeler & Hart, 112 Cherry

DRUGS, IMPORTERS OF.

Boving & Witte, 94 John
Breithaupt P. A. & Chun, 25
Beaver
Chapman Henry T. 77 Fulton
Des Arts & Heuser, 78 Water
Fiedler Ernest. 32 Broadway
Field Cyrus W. & Co. 11 Cliff
Horsey Joseph, 84 Maiden Lane
Koop Fischer & Co. 54 New
Leberthon John L. 43 New
Lee James & Co. 36 New
Loeschigk, Wesendonck & Co. 40
Broad
Manzanedo Jose, 123 Front
Michel John, 43 New
Moore & Taylor, 81 Maiden Lane

Phelps George D. & Co. 46 Cliff
New York.
Rilliet Henri, 66 Broad
Routh H. L. & Sons, 69 New
Sale Wm. A. jr. 124 Water
Sands A. B. & D. 141 William cor.
Fulton
Schiefelin Philip & Co. 107 Water
Schneider C. H. 32 Platt
Thomas & Maxwell, 86 William
Tripler Archibald B. 26 S. William
Ward M. & Co. 63 Maiden Lane
Wichelhausen, Sechnagel &
Schwab, 165 Water

DRUGGISTS—RETAIL.

Abel Charles D. 1 Hammond
New York.
Abell Thomas M. 47 Cherry
Adamson & Oliff, 6 Bowery & 699
Broadway
Andrews Jarvis M. 46 Pearl
Anistaki John, 104 Cherry
Ashmead Chilion, jr. 562 Grand
Bangs Franklin H. 472 Greenwich
Banks Abraham, 58 Chatham
Bassett John W. 644 Broadway
Belding Charles S. 99 8th Av.
Belknap Daniel D. 102 Av. C
Bell Wilson F. 1 Christopher
Billings George. 82 Av. C
Boetler & Co. 182 E. Broadway
Bower R. S. 433 Broadway
Bowron & Co. 10th cor. 1st Av.
Boyd Alexander P. 190 Hester
Brandis Herman M. 66 Av. B
Breakell T. 9th Av. W. 28th
Bredel Peter, 515 Pearl
Brigeam & Miller, 17 & 109 Av. D
Brown A. 88 8th Av.
Brouwer Abraham, 3 Prince
Bruckman Philip, 306 Houston
Bryant Geo. N. W. 715 Broadway
Bryen & Harris, 423 Greenwich
Burnett John M. 324 Broome
Busteed George W. 331 & 455 3d
Av.
Byrne H. F. 76 James
Carpentier R. S. 3 Mulberry
Cecil William, Yorkville
Chabert Julian X. 443 Grand
Chapin Reuben S. 186 Stanton
Chichester Edward L. 293 Madison
Chilton Howard. 290 4th
Chilton Washington, 756 Broadway
Clapp Otis W. 819 Broadway
Clapp ——. 168 Division
Clark Augustus G. 19 Sullivan
Clarkson Fred. 119 Rivington
Clay A. 42 Bank
Clay Daniel. 130 Franklin
Cleaveland Elisha W. 144 Spring
Cochran James, 150 Division
Coddington J. & I. 303 Hudson &
715 Broadway
Coggeshall George D. 421 Pearl
Colby George. 351 Pearl
Cole David Z. 77 9th Av.
Conway E. 397 Pearl
Cooke Ebenezer. 306 Grand
Cook Miles L. 189 6th Av.
Coon John V. 85½ Bowery
Covel James. 141 Wooster
Cox Charles B. 10 8th Av.
Crandall Harlan H. 212 6th Av.
Crumbie James. 363 Bowery
Crumbie Wm. D. 286 Bowery
Cumming T. W. 178 Greenwich
Curtis & Trall, 161 Greenwich
Davidson Allen M. 49 Gouverneur
Davis John J. 332½ Grand
Dawson J. 272 Division
Day Francis W. 130 8th Av.
Dayton T. Steel, 819 Pearl
Dean Benjamin, 29 Spring
De Forrest Theodore R. 42 Greenwich
De Grandval Elias L. & Co. 32
Walker
Delaverne G. W. 138 6th Av.

Delluc & Co. 581 Broadway, 2 Park
Row & 250 4th Av. New York.
Deromas Pierre, 59 Chatham
Dewer J. 104 Chambers
Dodd David. 47 Rutgers
Dodd John B. 771 Broadway
Dodge Edmund. 88 8th Av.
Douglass Robert, 423 Greenwich
Downing Thomas K. 54 Market
Drinker J. D. 554 Greenwich
Drummond Samuel. 52 Reade
Dugliss Daniel H. 241 Division
Dunlop Robert, 979 Houston
Dupuy Eugene, 609 Broadway
Eager W. B. 95 Hudson
Edwards Frank S. 907 Broadway
Elliott James W. 7th Av. bet. 19th
& 20th & 8th Av. cor. 41st
Ellecott J. P. 2d Av. cor. E. 27th
Ely & Clarke, 379 Greenwich
Fay Charles P. 165 Chambers
Flannery John, 469 Pearl
Forbes Wm. 505 Pearl
Forest S. R. 42 Greenwich
Forman Wm. H. & Co. 374 Grand
Fortenbach Wm. 14 Hudson
Foss George, 58 Chatham
Francis Ephraim B. 317 Rivington
Frederick M. B. 9 Chambers
Freeman Wm. B. 50 3d Av.
Frey John, 169 Bleecker
Gahaudan Arthur W. 51 6th Av.
Gabaudan & Condie, 156 8th Av.
Goble Albert W. 111 Houston
Gaffreau G. A. 77 E. Broadway
Gerber Frederick, 110 Hester
Gibbs Isaac H. 202 Delancy
Gilchrist W. 211 Elm
Goodrich Darius N. 299 Av. A
Gough A. H. & Co. 123 Fulton
Gray Edward, 26 Madison
Green Thomas T. 399 Broadway
Greene Job W. 11½   do
Greenly Philo P. 186 Grand
Griffiths J. M. 148 Delancy
Guion Edward M. 127 Bowery
Hall William H. 624 Hudson & 31
Bleecker
Halland & Genin, 107 Christopher
Hallock James C. 187 Spring
Halsey William S. 554 Pearl
Hamilton Wm. D. 9th Av. 21st
Hanks Azrel, jr. 150 Prince
Hanna Henry N. 143 Hester
Hardy Thomas, 9th Av. n. 28th
Harlow John M. 74 Stanton
Hasse Lewis H. 42 Av. A
Hedges & Fisher, 488 Hudson
Hendrickson Thomas, 65 Ann
Hinton John, 194 8th Av.
Hogeboom P. 79 Greenwich Av.
Holmes & Co. 696 Broadway
Hunt Antonia J. H. 260½ Bowery
Hunter Galen, 104 6th Av.
Hunter James, 369 Broome
Huntington Joseph C. 277 3d Av.
Husband Richard J. 107 9th Av. &
40th, bet. Broadway & 7th Av.
Hutchings C. S. 144 W. Broadway
Jackson Frederick. 120 Cherry
Janson John, 196 Grand
Jarvis Aaron, 218 Bowery
Jeffres Wm. F. 112 Thompson
Jennings Charles H. 406 Grand
Jennings & Lane, 8th Av.
Johnson W. J. 42 Bank
Jerome & Co. 21 Spruce
Jones Hiram. 30 Orange
Jones John. 792 Houston
Julian Michael P. 443 Grand
Kiersted Christopher, 144 9th Av.
Kiersted Henry T. 529 Broadway
Kipp John G. Yorkville
Kruger I. 145 Greenwich
Kirst G. 181 Canal
Knapp Gilbert P. 862 Hudson
Laurence Chas. N. 163 Rivington
Langley E. O. 433 Broadway
Large E. 88 9th Av.
Leavitt Eli, 214 Division
Ledeboer B. 127 Christopher
Leggett Joseph, 120 Av. C

Lewis James S. 527 Greenwich
New York.
Lindsay G. 83½ 6th Av.
Lobstein Eliza, 175 2d
Loines Wm. H. 296 & 298 Hudson
Lyme James, 461 Broadway
Lyon Eliphalet. 472 Grand
M'Alister J. & Co. 127 Chambers
M'Closky D. W. C. 515 Broome
M'Kenzie Thos. 47 Cherry
M'Intyre Ewen, 872 Broadway
M'Leod Alex. 403 Hudson
Mann Ferdinand, 92 9th Av.
Mann Wm. B. 278 Broadway
Marsh Alfred, 207 Varick
Marsh Charles. 208 Cherry
Marvin David. 34 Rector
Mathison R. 298 8th Av.
Maunder Wm. 47 Hudson
Megivney James. 279 Houston
Meakim J. & A. 511 Broadway
Mercereau T. W. V. P. 856 B'way
Merkle P. 43 Av. B & 393 Grand
Metz Hermann. 7 Av. B
Milhau John, 183 Broadway
Miller John, 279 1st Av.
Miller & Van Antwerp, 753 Greenwich
Mills & Sleight, 44 James
Milnor Wm. H. 905 3d Av.
Molwitz & Schultz, 609 4th
Moran James, 292 Division
Morello & Robbins, 595 Pearl
Mortamore Lewis, 196 William
Morton Henry, 149 Elm
Morton George, 153 Grand
Moser Theo. 110 Hester
Moss R. E. 542 Grand
Mott ——, 169 Bleecker
Murphy Wm. 9 Av. C
Neergaard Wm. 523 Pearl
Newman Geo. A. 172 Cherry
Nichtern Ponce M. 134 Liberty
Nietsch Adolphus & Moneypenny, 185 Canal
Nordquist C. I. 390 Broome
O'Brine J. 30 3d Av.
O'Neal Michael, 511 Pearl
Overton Wm. P. 105 Av. B
Passmore Edward, 36 Catharine &
610 Grand
Parsons Geo. F. A. 71 Canal
Paulsen Louis, 209 Stanton
Paulus Gustavus, 179 William
Payfer F. X. 532 1st Av.
Payton Edmund H. 656 Greenwich
& 79 8th Av.
Payton Josiah, 104 Chambers
Perry Robert, 400 10th
Pendlebury J. 7th Av.
Phillips Chas. H. 148 Greenwich
Preterre Peter, 515 Pearl
Price P. 130 Fulton
Price & Butler, 349 Cherry
Pridham H. C. 4th Av.
Priest Abel, 240 8th Av.
Pujos Henry, 30 2d Av.
Quackenbush B. 709 Greenwich
Ring Chas. H. 192 Broadway
Riker & Berrian, 353 5th Av.
Ritter Thomas, 104 Cherry
Rodgers A. 73 W. Broadway
Rogers & Co. 551 Broadway
Rogers Arthur, 202 Spring
Rollins Aaron B. 60 Av. C
Rosenmuller Lewis A. 172 8th Av
Rosine Pehr O. 242 Stanton
Ross John H. 63 Roosevelt
Roskopf Philip, 123 Cedar
Runge Fred. R. 110 Hester
Rushton, Clark & Co. 110 & 273
Broadway & 10 Astor House
Sandham G. A. jr. 9th Av. 38th st.
Sanders Henry L. 325 Bowery
Sands Edward H. 71 James
Sands Robert A. 188 Bowery
Sargent D. 19 3d Av.
Sauer John, 49 Av. A
Schiefelin John L. 126 Canal
Segar Simeon, 60 Walnut
Sheppard Henry, 190 Av. B
Sherwood & Wear, 93½ Chatham

Shipaley Alfred L. 175 Bowery
New York.
Smith Benj. R. 381 Monroe
Smith Christian, 371 Greenwich
Smith J. M. C. 57 W. Broadway
Smith John S. 488 Broadway
Smith Willis P. 117 7th Av.
Stelle Nelson, 158 Grand
Stewart Walter L. 30 N William
Stout Thomas J. 515 Broome
Styles Henry. 2 9th Av.
Sutton Theophilus E. 331 3d Av.
Sweeney Francis, 51 3d Av.
Tackaberry John T. 63 Bowery
Talman Dowe D. 641 Hudson
Tarrant James, 266 Greenwich
Taylor Arthur. 81 Houston
Taylor Samuel. 267 Bleecker
Thorne James G. 584 Grand
Thorp Henry C. 48 8th Av.
Thurmon W. M. 161 Canal
Traphagen Geo. H. 380 Pearl
Trimmer Henry. 27 Whitehall
Troutman J. W. 305 Stanton
Tucker Daniel B. 394 Grand
Tully Marcus C. 146 Broome
Uhl David. 51 Mercer
Van Arsdale Henry, 121 Hester
Van Buren John C. M. 224 8th Av.
Van Lier Martinus A. 129 Greenwich & 128 Washington
Vanzandt Peter, 84 9th Av. & 255 W. 19th
Vogeley Frederick G. L. 282 2d
Vondersmith E. W. 162½ Bowery
Waite Geo. S. 14 1st Av.
Walters Wm. A. 111 Houston & 50 Suffolk
Walldorff H 317½ Bowery
Warner E. B. 206 Bleecker
Watson J. 267 Bleecker
Watts J. H. 21 6th Av.
Weaver James, 186 Church
Weir James, 266 Grand
Weismann & Cassebeer, 257 Broome & 386 Broadway
Wells Fred. C. 237 8th Av.
Wheeler & Hart. 112 Cherry
Whitaker Samuel P. 190 3d Av.
White Alfred W. 2 1st Av.
White P. A. & Co. 47 Frankfort
Wilson Henry, 576 Hudson
Winship A. L. 196 Canal
Winzer Ernest, 85 Division
Witherell John, 72 Oliver
Wood W. G Harlem
Wright J. K. 383 3d Av.
Wyatt Walter H. 18 Bayard
Wynans Henry D. 268 Rivington

Niagara County.

Thomas Ambrose   Lewiston.
Curtis J. H.   Lockport.
Morse & Lull
Murray Heary
Rolston Linsley
Conger G.   Niagara Falls.
Wright O. P.   Wilson.
Crosby J. W.

Oneida County.

Lewis J. M.   Boonville.
Barrows C., Clinton   Kirkland.
Lighbody J.   New Hartford.
Bissell & Co. (wholesale) Dominick st.   Rome.
Dudley & Hill, Dominick st.
Marchisi J. B. 167 Genesee Utica.
Kellogg G. A. 141   do
Foster & Dickinson, 117 do
Hitchcock A. 45   do
Warner J. E. & Co. 22 & 24 Genesee
Greenman & Smith, 112   do
Butler T. K. & Co. 114 do
Mortley A. B. 188   do
Brook & Pierce, 10 Fayette
Cass O. D. Columbia st.
Turner J.   Vernon.
Carter S.
Brown P. Hampton Westmoreland.

Onondaga County.

Richards W., Jordan   Elbridge.
Tucker C. H. & Brother. Jordan
Greenman S. H.   Marcellus.
Foot D. Y. Salina st. Syracuse
Salina.
Livingston & Mitchell, (wholesale)   Salina st. Syracuse
Homchett M. W.   do   do
Moore D. A. Water st.   do
Dillage Brothers. do   do
Lampman & Williams, do   do
Dana J. D. & Co. 7 N. side Canal
Syracuse
Schoonmaker H. Genesee st. do
Brace D. Canal st.   do
Beer William, Salina st. do
Snook J. jr.   Skaneateles.

Ontario County.

Chipman & Remington
Canandaigua.
Cheney & Sons
Sanders C. C
Elmore J., Geneva   Seneca.
Platt A. D. do
Kelly L. & Co. Geneva
Parmelee H.   do

Orange County.

Carpenter J. G.   Chester.
Reeve & Horton   Goshen.
Elliott Henry W.
Eager George   Montgomery.
M'Cormick W. J.   Monroe.
Cooke & Harris, Otisville
Mount Hope.
Terry W. C.
Edmondson D. C. 91 Water
Newburgh.
Fowler J. V. B. (paints and oils) 93 Water
Barclay Alexander, 90 Water
Gorham John R. 40 Water
Peck E. Colden st.
Van Nort John F. 34 Water
Lewis O. New Hampton Wallkill.
Starr J. L. South Middletown
King J. T.   do

Orleans County.

Nicholson & Paine, Albion Barre.
Fanning Thomas C. do
Gilmore Aaron,   do
Swan Isaac W. Medina Ridgeway.
Vibbard Smith   do
Grover L. C. Knowlesville
Cheeseman E.   do

Oswego County.

Warner & Sims   Mexico.
Colwell Justin B., Granite Block, cor. 1st & Bridge   Oswego.
Moore & Smith, Bridge st.
Dillworth George, Granite block, Bridge st.
Canfield Calvert, 12 Phoenix block, 1st st.
Mead C. M. Woodruff's blk 1st st
Bickford J. jr. cor. 1st & Bridge
Jones & M'Carty, Pulaski Richland.
Angell & Seeley,   do
Doane Ira,   do
Rice John P., Phoenix Schroeppel.
Shaw William B., Fulton Volney.

Otsego County.

Hitchcock George   Butternuts.
Wing Walter
Johnson P. E. Cooperstown Otsego.
Comstock & Co. do

Putnam County.

Watson G. Cold Spring
Phillipstown.
Roese A.   do

Queens County.

Snediker M.   Hempstead.

Smith John W.   Hempstead.
Bushmore B. F.

Rensselaer County.

Parmelee & Cory, 338 State
Lansingburgh.
Walsh Heber, 292 State
Montgomery W. 250 State
Thompson J. L. & Co. 161 River
Troy.
Robinson & Griswold, 201 River
Baum & Hawley, 219   do
Wickes S. (wholesale) 227 &o
Dater & Brother, 245   do
Waters & Von Schaick, (wholesale) 271 River
Prescott John F. 234 River
Heinstreet & Andres. 240 River
Halsted & Young, 320 do
Orvis P. D. & Co. 305 do
Heimstreet C. 10 State
Rowells R. H. 48 Congress
Thorburn Adam. 50 Congress
Bordeaux & Stoddard, (wholesale) 55 Congress
Rowell S. 76 Congress

Richmond County.

Wardle H. Tompkinsville
Castleton
Gale A. G. S. Port Richmond
Northfield.
Feeny Jos., Stapleton, Southfield.

Rockland County.

Blauvelt Saml. C.   Haverstraw.

St. Lawrence County.

Huntington Franklin   Canton.
Brown Amasa & Co.
Smith H. D.   Gouverneur.
Manley A. S. & Co.   Hermon.
Ross & Manley, Columbia
Madrid.
Bacon Amos, Water st. Ogdenburgh   Oswegatchie.
Sprague J. & Co. Ford st.
Hare H. R.   do
Humphrey H. S.   do

Saratoga County.

Olcott L. B. & Co. Ballston
Milton.
Westcott J. H.   do
Curtis H. L.   do
Vandercook C. Schuylerville
Saratoga.
Fish George H. Saratoga Springs.
Huling E. J.
Hill F. T.
Mitchell & Poor
Waldron Wm. A.   Waterford.
Higgins John

Schenectady County

Snell D. H. 193 State Schenectady.
Truax A. 117   do
Constable D. C. 63 do
Fuller R. 130   do

Schoharie County.

Messenger Storrs   Esperance.
Howe John, Warnerville
Richmondville.
Throop O. B.   Schoharie.

Seneca County.

Manson H. M.   Ovid.
Osborne Joseph   Seneca Falls.
Clark John S.
Woodworth A. O.
M'Clintock Thomas   Waterloo.
Lundy Samuel D.

Steuben County.

Beach Wm.   Addison.

Hess A.   *Bath.*
Seaver Hawley   *Erwin.*
Barnes H. R.   *Orange.*
Terbell Wm.   *Painted Post.*
Graves J. B.

Suffolk County.

Preston Sheldon C. Greenport
         Southold.
Corwin G. H. & Co. do

Sullivan County.

Piercy L. W., Monticello
         Thompson.

Tioga County.

Pinney J. L. & Son   *Owego.*
Fay George W. & Co.

Tompkins County.

Schuyler P. C. 106 Owego *Ithaca.*
Schuyler G. W. 42   do
Curran O. B. 36   do
Halsey B. S. 92   do
Tompkins R. C. Trumansburgh
         Ulysses.
Atwater R. & W. G.

Ulster County.

Clay C. S. cor. N. Front & Wall
         Kingston.
Myer Jesse
Parsell John L.
Knapp & Co. Rondout
Van Dusen G. N. do
Jones D. New Paltz Landing
         Lloyd.
Corbin Albert, Ellenville
         Wawarsing.

Warren County.

Sheldon N. E. Glenn's Falls
         Queensbury.
Peck Charles,   do
Clark & M'Niel,   do
Peck B.   do
Peck William,   do

Washington County.

Barker Perry C.   *Greenwich.*
Brown J. H. Sandy Hill
         Kingsbury.
Monroe N. Chapin's Block
         Whitehall.
Turner A. S. Canal st.
Wright D. S.   do

Westchester County.

Ruby Geo. W. Peekskill
         Courtlandt.
Fountain Cyrus H. do
Brewer James.   do
Bailey I. Tarrytown *Greenburgh.*
Welling S.   *New Rochelle.*
Carpenter J. Sing Sing *Ossining.*
Jones Burhiss,   do
Levi Abm. G. Portchester   *Rye.*
Ward Samuel   *West Farms.*
Thomas Frederick
Guion Elijah   *White Plains.*
Howland John H.   *Yonkers.*

Wyoming County.

Collier J. T. & Co.   *Attica.*
Dorrance Gardner
Mitchell David   *Perry.*
Lloyd J. W.   *Pike.*
Potter L. Varysburg   *Sheldon.*
Lansing E. H.   *Warsaw.*
Frank Augustus

Yates County.

Rush E. N.   *Jerusalem.*
Huntington E. H. Penn Yan *Milo.*
Lapham J. H.   do
Wells Geo. D.   do
Otis Abijah, Rushville   *Potter.*

Warfield R. N. Rushville   *Potter.*
Murdock L. C. Dundee   *Starkey.*

Druggists—Glass Ware.

New York County.

Newcomb Hervey C. 142 Front
         New York.
Rorks James, 102 John
Ross Andrew, 124 Maiden lane
Schieffelin H. M. & Fowler, 142 &
   144 Front

Drum Manufacturer.

Albany County.

Killman G. 119 Orange   *Albany.*

Dry Docks.

Albany County.

Barnard J. M. West Troy
         Watervliet.
Wheeler William

Greene County.

Hadden Cornelius   *Athens.*
Baldwin Jedediah *New Baltimore.*
Baldwin Henry

Rockland County.

Palmer & Snediker   *Haverstraw.*

Dry Goods.

Albany County.

Arrowsmith J. W. 234 S. Pearl
         Albany.
Bailey & Ostrom, 73 Washington
Blainer H. & Co. 348 Broadway
Bleecker Geo. M. (importer) 406
   Broadway
Boyd S. V. 390 & 428 Broadway
Brown W. G. 490   do
Burton S. P. 198 & 200   do
Cassidy Wm. W. cor. Swan &
   Lumber
Cone J. & J. I. 72 S. Pearl
Crapo S. 56 State
Duffy Miss, 498 Broadway
Ederer A. 43 S. Pearl
Ehrich J. 2   do
Fryer & M'Michael, (wholesale)
   226 Broadway
Gay & Mygatt, 436 Broadway
Harley Edward, 815   do
Hendrickson Mrs. A. 92 S. Pearl
Holmes H. B. 16   do
Howe Silas B. 481 & 483 B'dway
Humphrey J. J. (wholesale) 56
   State
King Rufus H. & Co. (wholesale)
   49 State
Lehrberg & Sederen (wholesale)
   380 Broadway
Levey, Hiller & Co. 52 S. Pearl
Luke S. & H. 8   do
M'Elroy James, 636 Broadway
M'Elroy Wm. 645 & 647   do
Mabbitt J. G. 384   do
Mesick H. T. 340   do
Minster S. (wholesale) 24 S. Pearl
Nowwitter J. 40   do
Peck C. A. & Co. 61 Washington
Perry N. W. 594 & 596 Broadway
Post S. A. (importer) 478   do
Redstone I. 82½ S. Pearl
Samson A. 209 & 211 do
Sheldons & Wood (importers), 467
   & 469 Broadway
Sheline A. 43 S. Pearl
Slosh Moses, 346 Broadway
Smith, Carey & Moseley (whole-
   sale) 477 & 479 Broadway
Spellman B. R. & R. L. 494 B'way

Sporborg J. 36½ S. Pearl *Albany.*
Stearns J. G. 538 Broadway
Stern Isaac, 38 S. Pearl
Stillwell W. B. 90 State
Strong A. M. & W. N. (importers)
   n. Farmers' & Mechanics' Bank
   Broadway
Taylor & De Forest, 422 B'dway
Tripp J. (wholesale) 41 W'hington
Van Allen C. 30 S. Pearl
Van Gaasbeck & Emerson, 482
   Broadway
Van Zandt & Brown, 788 & 790
   Broadway
Waterbury R. P. & Co. 595 B'way
Waterman J. & S. 13 Washington
Watson C. & W. H. 68 State
Wheeler T. V. L. 581 Broadway
White G. (importer) 554   do
Wilder N. H. 37 Washington
Wiles L. 68 State
Wiles R. P. & T. H. (wholesale)
   32 S. Pearl
Woodburn & Dey Ermand, (whole-
   sale) 35 & 37 State
Potters, Waterman & Co. West
   Troy   *Watervliet.*
Lobdell J. D. West Troy
Lobdell A. S. & Brother W. Troy
Goldsmith L. Cohoes
Jones H. & S.   do
M'Entee P.   do

Broome County.

Burchard D. S.   *Binghamton.*
Wickham & Bennett

Cayuga County.

Hall C. & Co. 32 Genesee *Auburn.*
Hollister A. W. & Co. 63 Genesee
Waldo E. H. 75   do
Woodruff H. 77   do
Rathburn & Clary, 81   do
Pratt & Fay, 83   do
Svison E. 87   do
Goss, Satwell & Co. 102   do
Stow & Camp, 94   do
Bartlett & Holmes, 78   do
Pomeroy H. B. 49   do
Henderson & Co. Weedsport
         Brutus.
Ives N.   do
Ingraham, Havens & Co. do
Durkey & Wilson   do
Baylies A. & Co.   do

Clinton County.

Vilas & Crosby (wholesale)
         Plattsburgh.
Hewett Stoddard & Co (whole-
   sale)
Hartwell A.
Sawyer P

Columbia County.

Hubbell L. cor. Front & Union
         Hudson.
Macy A. C. 159 Warren
Dean S. 289   do
Hoffman, Van Deusen & Co. 299 do
Ehrich J. & J. 299 Warren
Guernsey & Terry, 311 Warren
Jordan E. cor. Warren & 6th
Plank P. 319 Warren
Andrus J.
Skinner H P. & Son, 150 Warren
Evans R. W., Warren st.
Sprague S. cor. Warren & 2d

Duchess County.

Langstadter J. & S., Wappinger's
   Falls   *Fishkill.*
Lillie I. W. 328 Main *Poughkeepsie.*
Cornwall Wm. & Son, 326 Main
Adriance & Morgan, 324   do
Bowne J. & Co. 318   do
Gosline J. (wholesale) 316   do
Wright Joseph, 314   do

Vankleek George M. 312 Main
Poughkeepsie.
Heath, Caldwell & Crosby, (wholesale) 310 Main
White Wm. W. & Son, 208 Main
Rothchild & Bernheimer, 300 do
Vankleek George & Co. 296 Main
Jewitt & Wood, 294   do
Miller J. W. (wholesale) 292 do
Adler & Herman. 290   do
Beach Edward, 262   do
Finlay N. M. 256   do
Slee Robert, 254   do
Trowbridge & Wilkinson. 321 do

Erie County.

Craig James D. 286 Main *Buffalo.*
Goodrich G. H. & Co. 274 Main
Dahlman L. & Co. 276   do
White George, 288   do
Horwitz G. 282   do
Gilbert William A. 270   do
Morrow Thomas, 222   do
James William L. 236   do
Sherman Richard R. 214   do
Millard H. 212   do
Murray John & Co. 210   do
Perkins T. G. 204   do
Murrays & Cumming, 192   do
Titus & Miller, 184   do
Morse David R. 190   do
Bishop W. B. 208   do
Compton M. 218   do
Georger F. A. 406   do
MacGregor R. & Co. (see advertisement) 198 Main
Koons Jacob H. 407 Main
Handel Francis J. 405 do
Hollister James, (wholesale) 178 Main
Fitch B. & Co. (wholesale) 172 Main
Allen & Carpenter, (commission) 152 Main
Fitch & Bennett, 144 Main
Stone T. H. (wholesale) 140 Main
Townsend & Whitcomb, (wholesale) 138 Main
Fitch, Holbrook & Dee, (wholesale) 136 Main

Genesee County.

Comstock A. O.   *Le Roy.*
Murphy A. B.
Browning, Kelsey & Tompkins

Greene County.

Remsen John A.   *Catskill.*
Hyde Nelson
Messick Peter
Fiero Joshua, jr.
Lusk Jason   *Coxsackie.*
Lasher & Myer
Vandenburgh & Stoutenburgh

Herkimer County.

Butrill J. G.   *Herkimer.*
Burck Thomas   *Little Falls.*
Buell & Fuller
Herkimer Warren
Reed P. & E.
Foote S. N.
Altamyer A. & Brother
Pratt & Co.
Richmonds S. M. & A.
M'Key Edward

Kings County.

Adams J. J. 171 Fulton *Brooklyn.*
Arnold A. F. 137 Myrtle Av.
Arnold A. F. 98 Main
Birdsall M. 332 Fulton
Bradley J. P. 192 Fulton
Cathcart & Swan, 101 do
Crawford J. P. 265   do
Delano & Son, 196   do
Desendorf Henry C. 141 Concord
Dougherty Mrs. M. 133 Court
Gallagher John, 87 Hudson Av.

Gilbert R. 121 Prospect *Brooklyn.*
Griffing B. 156 Atlantic
Haley E. L. 161 Fulton
Havers J. 80 Main
Handley D. 257 Smith
Hinman R. B. 14 Fulton
Hobbs T. M. 143   do
Holt B. 109   do
Horton & Son. 186   do
Hubbard James, 97 & 99 Main
Hughes H. G. 165 Fulton
Jackson R. 285 Hudson Av.
Johns James F., Myrtle Av.
Journeay & Burnham, 123 Atlantic
Lawrence W. G. 266 Fulton
Lewis Elijah. 154   do
Lewis & Williams, 200   do
Lewis E. jr. 163   do
Lockwood E. C. 129 Myrtle Av.
Losier George, 231   do
May Jacob J., Smith cor. Wykoff
Morgan & M'Corkle, 111 Fulton
Newman T. A. 92 Main
Odell J. 48 Hudson Av.
Petit Robert, 147 Fulton
Phillips Wm. 130 Bridge
Ross John, 56 Hudson Av.
Rossiter & Armstrong, 105 Fulton
Staples R. M. 53 Atlantic
Stevenson H. 244 Fulton
Tooker John A. 197 Myrtle Av.
Tyler Mrs. E. 132 Gold
Underhill H. S. 150 Fulton
Van Doren Charles W. 264 Fulton
Webster H. D. 238 Fulton
Welch Elizabeth, 42 Hudson Av.
Wheelhouse James V 257 Fulton
Wilber B. S. 271 Fulton
Young E. 77 Bridge
Billings Edwin, 23 South 7th
Williamsburgh.
Witt Henry, 59 4th
Bigerman John, 132 Ewing
Nichols W. V. 91 4th
Maguire Miss A. E. 117 Grand
Smith Andrew T. 229   do
Howell Joseph R. 244   do
Sharpe John, 72   do
Dunn Wm. O. 94   do
Hamilton J. 144   do
Ufford L. W. Grand st. cor. 2d
Miller John C. 251 2d
Scharschug & Burhe, 342 Grand
Lawrence W. 141 Ewing

Monroe County.

Kendricks C. & Son, 21 Buffalo
Rochester.
Stringer George. 116 Buffalo
Chapman Timothy 24   do
Cruden & Brennan, 16   do
Altman & Stetthelmer, 57 Main
Greenough W. H. 49   do
Newcomb Loder, & Co. 63 do
Gifford M. 40 State
Altman Jacob, 24 State
M'Knight & Pardee, 42 State
True C. F. 52 State
Barber, Bullard & Co. 42 State

New York County.

DRY GOODS—COMMISSION MERCHANTS. *(See also Merchants—Commission.)*

Anderson & Starr, 9 Broad
New York.
Arnold D. H. & Co. 60 Pine
Arnold Edward H. 34 Beaver
Atwater, Gould & Co. 24 Broad
Auchincloss Hugh & Sons, 49 Beaver
Babcock Benjamin, 42 Beaver
Barrows & Pitcher. 38 Pine
Beals, Bush & Co. 32 Broad
Bird George, 26 & 28 Broad
Bock, Swan & Inglis, 51 Pine
Bogert E. & Co. 43 New
Brigham D. & Co. 33 Broad
Brown & Dimock, 70 Beaver

Bullocke John, & Henry Bragg, jr.
38 Pine   *New York.*
Burnham Gordon, 41 Liberty
Carville Charles, 17 Broad
Coffin, Bradley & Co. 44 Ex. place
Cottenet F. & Co. 48 Broad
Crafts & Stell, Manchester, England & 27 Pine
Crocker Stephen, 51 Broad
Curtis L. & B. & Co. 39 Broad
Dale & Wright, 42 Ex. place
Davis Lockwood & Co. 8 South William
Fearing & Hall, 55 Ex. place
Gihon John & Co. 62 & 64 Pine
Graves E. & R. R. 74 Pine
Harris Caleb S. 46 Ex. place
Hooman Clement, 43 New
Hoyt & Tillinghast, 46 & 49 Pine
Huntington F. A. & Son. 66 Cedar
Hutchinson & Tiffany, 50 Ex. pl.
Johnston, Brother & Townsend, 39 Pine
Keeler Amos, 28 Ex. place
Kellogg Ralph, 8 South William
Le Baron C. B. 55 Pine
Langley Wm. C. & Co. 25 Broad
Lawrence. Trimble & Co. 35 Broad
Lefferts James & Co. 29 Broad
Lord & Snelling, 42 Exchange
M'Call & Strong, 35 William
Mabee & Waterbury, 31 Pine
Macgregor, Timpson & Co. 47 Broad
M'Curdy, Aldrich & Spencer, 30 Broad
Mease Charles B. 8 South William
Nesmith & Co. 50 & 52 Pine
Nevins & Co. 16 Broad
Newton James W. 24 Pine
Putnam T. & Co. 68 Pine
Raymond Albert R. 2 Pine
Richards, Blake & Co. 96 Broad
Richards & Cronkhite, 54 & 56 Exchange place
Richardson, Watson & Co. 41 & 43 Exchange place
Roberts E. G. 70 Pine
Sands, Fuller & Co. 59 Pine
Seaver & Dunbar, 31 Broad
Shepard & Howe, 38 Exchange pl.
Shepard, Wright & Ripley, 37 Pine
Skinner Francis & Co. 39 Broad
Spring Marcus & Co. 51 Ex. place
Snow Robert H. 51 Broad
Stanton, Barnes & Hamilton, 21 Broad
Stanton, Knapp & Woodruff, 43 & 45 Broad
Stebbins R. & D. M. & Co. 59 Broadway
Stevens Henry, 46 Exchange pl.
Stone & Co. 48 Exchange place
Thomas Brothers, 43 Ex. place
Torry Joseph. 40 Pine
Townsend Daniel Y. 54 Cedar
Tucker, Thatcher & Co. 15 Broad
Vandervoort P. H. & Co. 20 Broad
Waldo C. & F. 32 Pine
Waldo Horace, 27 & 29 Pine
Wells, Brothers, 19 Broad
White William, 233 Pearl
Wight, Sturgis & Shaw, 54 Pine
Wilbur Marcus, 3 Pine
Willard & Wood, 40 & 42 Broad
Wolcott & Slade, 13 Broad
Wood, Merritt & Co. 26 Pine

DRY GOODS—DOMESTIC. *(See also Yarns, Batts, Wicks, &c.)*

Barrows & Pitcher, 38 Pine
New York.
Beach H. C. 72 Pine
Bellman Vincent, 72 Liberty
Brett T. F. 103 Maiden Lane
Canfield Mandlebert, 12 Cortlandt
Dawley & Furman, 24 Liberty
Dudley J. G. & Co. 102 Pearl
Guest William A. 61 Liberty

Hart, Morehouse & Merrit, 40 Pine New York.
Laughlin, & Avery, 22 Liberty
Lockwood John. 58 Liberty
Mix Charles, 4 Pine
Powers George W. 18 & 20 Cedar
Ross George, 103 Maiden Lane
Spear, Ripley & Co. 66 Liberty
Starr & Babcock, 76 Cedar
Tarbox George W. 8 Pine
Thomas Archibald A. 4 Pine
Underhill Lancaster, 52 Cedar
Winthrop Thomas C. 18 Pine
Waterbury Charles A. & Co. 106 Broadway
Wood John, 166 Pearl

DRY GOODS—IMPORTERS OF.

(See also Silks & Fancy Dry Goods, also Importers General, also Dry Goods Jobbers.)

Allen, Hazen & Co. 52 Exchange pl. New York.
Arnold A. & Co. 50 Canal & 49 Howard
Arnold & Southworth, 19 Cortlandt
Artois & Dennison, 35 Liberty
Ashton & Gillilan, 47 Exchange pl.
Afterbury Lewis, jr. & Co. 63 Pine
Badnall Brothers, 82 Beaver
Baldwins, Dibbles & Work, 127 Broadway
Ballin & Sander, 15 William
Beach, Clarke & Co. 15 Cortlandt
Becar & Benjamin, 104 Pearl
Behrend G. 1 Cedar
Benjamin W. jr. & Co. 31 Broad
Benkard & Hutton, 53 Beaver
Bennett H. C. 138 William
Boker John G. & E. 4 William
Born & Schuchardt, 50 Exchange pl.
Boiceau & Busch, 123 Pearl
Bottomly John, 112 Pearl
Bouck Christian W. & Brother, 61 Cedar
Bourry d'Ivernois & Co. 127 Pearl & 80 Beaver
Bowie J. S. & L. 85 Beaver
Brennan John, 87 Beaver
Brown A. Speirs, 58 Pine
Bulkley & Co. 69 Pine
Butterfield Brothers, 38 Broad
Cameron & Brand, 42 & 44 Pine
Chase & Walker, 52 Exchange pl.
Clapp & Kent, 126 Broadway, & 87 Cedar
Clark, Work & M'Lean, 128 Pearl
Clark & West, 158 Broadway
Conkling Jonas & Co. 150 Pearl
Connah Joseph, 46 Beaver
Crook Richard L. 22 Pine
Curtis L. & B. & Co. 39 Broad
Cushman & Co. 6 Cortlandt
Dambmann Charles F. 62 Beaver & 109½ Pearl
Daniels, Brothers & Co. 96 Beaver
Davis E. M. & Co. 16 Exchange pl. & 69 Beaver
De Ronge & Moran, 50 Broad
Dickerson, Churchill & Co. 140 Pearl and 106 Water
Engler Charles, 13 S. William
English George B. 22 Exchange pl.
Ernenputsch John C. 1 Pine
Escher & Rusch, 50 Beaver
Eytinge S. 4 S. William
Fanfernet & Duluc, 19 S. William
Fraser & Greenhill, 36 Pine
Gignoux Claudius & Co. 11 William
Goldschmidt Ludwig & Co. 64 Broad
Grant & Barton, 125 William
Graydon, Swanwick & Co. 59 Pine
Greenways & Hudson, 115 Pearl
Hadden David & Sons, 61 Pine

Hamilton & Freeman, 6 S. William New York.
Hardt & Co. 22 William
Hastings G. & Co. 5 S. William
Harrison Thomas E. & Co. 39 Beaver
Hall Bros. 43 Beaver
Hennequin, Henry & Co. 20 William
Henrys, Smith & Townsend, 109 Pearl and 66 Beaver
Hessenberg G. & Co. 3 William
Hiltman John L. 142 Bowery
Holmes S. & L. 22 John
Hoose & Victor, 89 Pearl
Hunt, Brothers & Co. 18 Exch. pl. & 67 Beaver
Hutchison William R., r. 35 Wall
Inglis William & Co. 56 Pine
Jones S. T. & Co. 49 Exchange pl.
Jung & Behrmann, 21 S. William
Kaupe E. & Cummings, 74 Beaver
Keeley James, 12 Pine. Linen and Cotton Threads, Bindings, &c.
Keen James, 12 Platt
Kessler & Co. 42 Exchange place
Kohnstain Salomon. 1 William
Kumpan Ignatius, 42 Nassau
Lachaise & Fauche, 43 Broad
Lane, Lamson & Co. 36 Exch. pl.
Lane & Guilde, 43 William
Lehmaier Brothers, 5 William
Lipmann Adolph, 89 Beaver, Importer of Belgian Cloths
Lissak A. H. & Co. 22 Liberty
Little, Alden & Co. 29 Broad
Loeschigk, Wessendonck & Co. 40 Broad
Lord & Taylor, 99 Maiden lane & 61 & 63 Catharine
Lottimer & Large, 61 Broad
Lummis William M. & Co. 73 William
M'Clune Thomas & Co. 49 Broad
M'Farlane Andrew, 14 Cedar
Mali H. W. T. & H. 27 Beaver
Marsh, Fisher & Booth, 53 Pine
Merritt, Ely & Co. 50 & 52 William
Mills & Co. 6 Cortlandt
Mitchell, Andrew & Co. 65 Pine
Moore C. W. & J. T. & Co. 71 Broadway
Moran & Iselin, 47 Broad
Morlot Charles, 40 Beaver
Muller Peter D. 33 Broad
Murray Donald, 43 Pine
Nathan James, 99 Pearl
Napier John, 31 Pine
Nevins & Co. 18 Broad
Newell Zenas, 89 William
Norris Henry & So. 34 Pine
Noveli P. 74 Pine
Oakey Daniel & Co. 26 Beaver
Odell & Haslehurst, 4 William
Owen James, 185 Pearl
Paton & Co. 28 John
Paton & Stewart, 67 Pine
Pettison Godfrey & Co. 43 & 45 Broad
Petrie J. & A. 27 William
Redmond William, 30 Pine
Reimer & Mecke, 41 William
Reiss, Brothers & Co. 62 Exch. pl.
Renard & Co. 116 Pearl
Riggs, Babcock & Co. 23 William
Robinson John & Co. 87 Beaver
Rodgers, Catlin & Co. 118 Pearl
Rokenbaugh, Conner & Dater, 57 Maiden lane
Rose & Graham, 5 Nassau
Rolker A. & Mollmann, 96 Pearl
Scheitlin A. & E. 113 Pearl
Schlesinger & Schlieper,27 Beaver
Schuchardt & Gebbard, 21 Nassau
Schulten J. W. & Hurd, 34 Broad
Schwendler Frederick,22 William
Siegman Brothers, 41 Pine
Seligman J. & Brothers, 46 Pine
Smith, Thurgar & Co. 64 & 66 Pine
Smith & Lawrence, 68 Beaver
Speyer Phillip & Co. 51 Broad
Spies, Christ & Co. 65 Beaver

Stone & Starr, 31 Pine New York.
Strang, Adriance & Co. 2 Maiden lane
Stewart I. J. & Co. 50 William
Syz, Irminger & Co. 48 Beaver
Tauber John A. 102 Pearl
Thirion, Maillard & Co. 44 Broad
Thompson, Quick & M'Intosh, 45 Exchange place
Tooker, Mead & Co. 35 Pine
Tousend C. A. & Co. 5 William
Tracy, Irwin & Co. 10 Maiden la.
Tryon Francis, 19 John
Tryon Joseph, 66 Broad
Victor Frederick & Achelis, 9 S. William
Vombaur H. O. 65 Broad
Von Sebt William & Co. 122 Pearl
Walker & Brother, 73 Pine
Wallerstein David, 42 William
Warburg Edward, 55 Broad
Watson Andrew H. 98 Maiden la
Watt & Sherman. 40 Exch. place
Wennberg John F. 17 Nassau
Wiencke Edward, 34 Pine
Whitewright Wm. 98 Maiden la.
Whitewright William, jr. & Co. 45 Exchange place
Whitthaus R. A. & G. H. 51 Exch. place
Woodbury, Hope & Co. 124 Pearl & 68 Water
Woodhead J. & T. 55 John
Wrigley Joseph. 73 Pine
Zollikoffer & Wetter, 11 S. William & 69 Stone

DRY GOODS, JOBBERS. (See also Dry Goods, Importers of.)

Andrew Lester & Co. 19 William
Anthony C. L. & Co. 74½ Pine
Arnold A. & Co. 50 Canal & 49 Howard
Arnold & Southworth, 19 Cortlandt
Avery, Hilliard & Co. 123 Pearl & 76 Beaver
Baldwin, Dibblee & Work, 127 Broadway
Banks George, 25 Catharine
Barker James W. & Co. 71 & 73 Catharine
Barnes H. W. 64 Liberty
Barnes & Pharo, 30 & 32 Liberty
Bassett & Aborn, 11 Nassau & 31 Pine
Bates Thomas, 10 Cedar
Baleys & Wright, 26 Cedar
Beach, Clarke & Co. 15 Cortlandt
Beach Theodore, 181 Greenwich
Bebb & Graham, 165 Pearl
Beckley S. M. & Co. 142 Broadw.
Bennett H. C. 138 William
Beirne & Burnside, 10 Pine
Bernhard Isidor. 59 William
Bernheimers, Newhouse & Co. 27 William
Bierhoff Louis, 20 Grand
Bigley John E. 60 Cedar
Blackford Edward, 409 Pearl
Bolles E. L. 50 Beaver
Booth & Tuttle, 62 Cedar
Bradner & Co. 9 Nassau
Brady Thomas, 114 Pearl
Bragg, Whittemore & Massey, 46 Cedar
Bramhall & Hastings, 57 Liberty
Brown A. & G & H. 8 Cortlandt
Brown & Dimock, 70 Beaver
Browning B. F. 31 Liberty
Browning & Hull, 7 Pine
Bruce J. & R. & Co. 175 Pearl
Bulkley & Claflin, 68 Cedar & 18 & 20 Pine
Carlisle & Stedman, 165 Pearl
Carolan Dennis, 7 William
Carrington & Orvis, 12 Cedar
Chandler, Starr & Co. 3 Pine
Chambers & Heiser, 43 Liberty
Chamberlain & Bancroft, 36 Broadway

Chandler Joseph, 27 William
New York.
Chapin & Bennett, 37 Liberty
Cheesebrough, Stearns & Co. 37 Nassau & 56 Liberty
Chittenden, Bliss & Co. 73 Broadway
Clapp & Kent, 128 Broadway
Cock E. & W. & Co. 33 Liberty
Colgate, Abbe & Co. 43 John
Compton & Turner, 35 Nassau
Conklin & Co. 33 Cortlandt
Converse, Todd & Graydon, 53 Liberty
Corlies George W. 283 Pearl
Crane & Co. 29 William
Cromwell Wm. & Co. 75 William
Cummins, Collins & Seaman, 11 William
Cushman & Co. 6 Cortlandt
Cutler John, 48 Beaver
Cutter C. N. 23 & 24 Nassau
Dart R. & N. 123 Maiden lane
Dibblee, Richardson & Co. 108 Water
Dibble William, 78 Cedar
Dittenhoeffer Isaac, 44 Beaver
Donnelly T. & N. 7 S. William & 63 Stone
Doremus & Nixon, 54 Liberty & 39 Nassau
Draper, Aldrich & Co. 67 Liberty
Duyckinck & Howell. 62 Cedar
Eakin, Robertson & Co., 111 Wm.
Earle John E. 99 William
Eno, Mahony & Co. 74 Broadway & 11 New
Eversten B. & Co. 3 Cedar
Falconer John & Co. 64 Cedar & 22 Pine.
Ferris N. & Co. 28 Liberty
Field & Beardslee, 41 Pine
Field, Merritt & Co. 131 William
Fisher Isaac F. 444 Grand
Ford Benjamin F. 74½ Pine
Forest & Smith, 53 Cedar
Foster & Polhamus, 12 Cedar
Freeland, Stuart & Co. 59 Broad'y
Frink Samuel E. 66 Cedar
Frost Samuel, 62   do
Fuller & Hertzel, 17 do
Gilbert, Prentiss & Tuttle, 56 John
Goldsmith, Haber & Co. 134 Wm.
Gray John A. C. & Co. 59 Cedar
Greenways & Hudson, 115 Pearl
Halsted, Haines & Co. 31 Nassau
Halsted & Brokaw, 23 William
Hamlin, Sloan & Squires, 48 Cedar
Harman I. & Co. 21 Cedar
Hastie W. S. 36 Broadway
Heidelbuck, Seasongood & Co. 34 Beaver
Hellman & Stadeker, 6 S. William
Henrys, Smith & Townsend, 133 Broadway, cor Cedar
Holmes & Babcock, 74½ Pine
Hopkins, Allen & Co. 129 Broadw.
Hosmer & Hubbard, 45 Liberty
Hoxie & Willcox, 10 Pine
Humphrey & Merrill, 74½ Pine
Hurlbut, Sweetser & Co. 29 Libt'y
Ingersoll D. W. & Co. 12 Pine
Jackson & Underhill, 22 Cedar
Jakobi A. & Co. 8 Pine
Jowett Isaac T. 68 Beaver
Jennings G. & Co. 156½ William
Journeay A. jr & Co. 14 Maiden lane
Keeler R. 28 Exchange place
Kellogg S. T. 52 Beaver
Kirby L. & V. 67 Cedar
Kitchen, Montross & Wilcox, 9 Pine
Lane R. & A. 11 Maiden lane
Lane. Brothers, 18 Cedar
Lane & Guild, 48 William
Lathrop F. S. & D. & Co. 59 John & 115 & 117 William
Lathrop & Leddington, 16 Cortlandt
Lawrence S. & T. 77 Cedar
Leddy & Sheridan, 195 Greenwich
Lee & Case, 68 B'dway & 15 New

Lee, Fenton & Phelps, 22 Cortlandt
New York.
Lester David, 13 Cedar
Loder Noah, 35 Liberty
Loomis, Judson & Co. 57 Cedar
Lord & Taylor, 61 & 63 Catharine & 99 Maiden lane
Lord, Warren, Salter & Co. 44 & 46 Broad
Lyman, Converse & Pomeroy, 50 Liberty
M'Dougall & Rushmore, 84 Cedar
M'Harg & Richardson, 65 Liberty
M'Kenzie Alexander. 85 Beaver
M'Kenzie, Cadow & Co. 34 Beaver
M'Menomy John, 132 Bowery
M'Neil, Fitch & Jerome, 89 Lib'ty
M'Williams & Gregory, 22   do
Mack A. & L. 30 Cedar
Malcolm & Gaul, 62 Liberty
Malezieux Gourd Freres & Co. 109 Pearl and 60 Beaver
Maltby E. & Son, 27 William
Manning & Leavitt, 160 Broadway
Marsh & Frear, 66 Nassau
Martin & Osgood, 15 William
Marshall & James, 162 Pearl
Merrill, Deuel & Co. 5 Pine
Miller & Chamberlain, 36 B'dway
Moore L. H. 45 Beaver
Morgan, M'Clung & Co. 62 Beaver
Morley. Hyde & Co. 99 Pearl
Mygatt & Conkling, 190 Pearl
Newell Zenas, 39 William
Nixon M. A. 103 William
North Alfred, 63 Liberty
Oakley D. W. 100 Maiden lane
Odell Thomas B. 52 Cedar
Otis, Johnes & Co. 55 Cedar
Parsons & Lawrence, 10 Pine
Peck & Bloodgood, 41 Liberty
Peck, Bradford & Richmond, 76 Cedar
Perkins, Warren & Co. 39 Broad'y
Perkins, Brooks & White. 89 W'tr
Petits. Banister & Harris, 23 Nassau
Pierce & Hall, 42 Beaver .
Pomeroy & Durkee, 34 Beaver
Pomeroy & Leonard, 24 Liberty
Pratt Charles G. 28 Cedar
Pritchard William H. 54 Beaver
Quick John S. 17 Cedar
Reid John & Co. 10 Pine
Roberts & Rees, 162 Chatham
Robertson, Brother & Co. 14 Wall
Robinson Wm. R. & Co. 6½ Pine
Rodgers, Catlin & Co. 118 Pearl
Rosenbaum M. & Co. 16 Cedar
Rust & Wyles, 88 Cedar
Sanderson & Griggs, 86 Cedar
Seaman William, 76 Pine
Seaman & Peck, 122 Broadway
Seixas Jacob L. 16 Exchange pl.
Scott & Clark, 529 Greenwich
Shelden H. & Co. 124 Broadway
Skidmore & Co. 58 Cedar
Smith, Congdon & Strong, 144 B'dy
Smith Ira, jr. & Co. 104 Pearl & 7 Old slip
Staats Abraham L. 37 Catharine
Stagg John P. & Co. 182 Pearl
Starr Chandler & Co. 3 Pine
Stern Emanuel A. 46 Beaver
Steward John. jr. & Co. 97 Pearl
Stewart A. T. & Co. 282, 284 & 286 Broadway
Stone & Starr, 31 Pine
Struthers & Vail, 34 Pine
Sutphen Ten Eyck, 1 Pine
Sutro Charles, Beaver st. .
Taylor & Hogg, 60 Liberty
Tefft E. T. & Co. 36   do
Terbell, Jennings & Co. 53 Cedar
Tilton, White & Hewlett. 34 Lib'y
Townsend C. A. & Co. 5 William
Townsends & Milliken, 33 Nassau
Tuttle Albert S. 9 Pine
Tweedy, Moulton & Plimpton. 47 Broadway & 75 Trinity place
Underhill Abraham S. & Co. 19 Cedar
Underhill George & Co. 81 Cedar

Van Buren & Churchill, 29 Nassau
New York.
Van Dusen, Jagger & Co. 39 Lib'y
Vincent, Beekman & Titus, 61 do
Wallis & La Tourrette, 6 Cedar
Walter Moses D. 72 Beaver
Walter I. D. & Co. 40 Beaver
Ward, Burdett & Parkhurst, 28 Pine
Waring W. F. & S. 14 Cedar
Warner & Loup, 107 Pearl & 80 Beaver
Waterbury C. A. & Co. 105 Broadway
Weed, Masters & Co. 18 Wall
Wheelock & Scott, 60 William
White, Bernos & Co. 201 Pearl & 105 Maiden lane
Wickham & Hutchinson, 164 Pearl
Wiley L. M. & Co. 162 Broadway
Willes & Baldwin, 24 Pine
Williams, Bradford & Co. 14 Cortlandt
Williams & Bruce, 49 Cedar
Williams, Murfey & Benedict, 79 Cedar
Wilson L. O. & Co. 13 Dey & 12 Cortlandt
Woodward Arnold, 40 Cedar
Woodward, Mount & Co. 26 Liberty
Wright & Groesbeck, 22 Cedar

LINEN--IMPORTERS OF.

Becar & Benjamin, 104 Pearl
New York
Bullocks J. & H. Bragg, jr. 38 Pine
Conner ———, 98 Maiden lane
Harden George, 66 Pine
Nicholson John, 50 Pine
Smith Egbert B. 58 Pine
Stewart Robert & Son, 74 Pine

DRY GOODS—PRINT WAREHOUSES

Garner & Co. 33 Pine *New York*
Lee & Brewster, 44 Cedar
Lee, Judson & Co. 56 Cedar & 30 Pine

DRY GOODS—REFINISHERS, PACKERS AND PRESSERS.

Bullock John, 87 South William
New York.
Dennis & Barber, 116 Maiden lane
Doughty Samuel H. 60 John
Klinkenberg ———, 781 Washington
M'Auslan Thomas, 221 Pearl
M'Kinnon Donald. 66 Broad
Migeon Henry & Co. 341 West
Ruger G. O. 73 Greenwich
Salisbury John L. 53 Liberty
Wilkie John, 86 Cliff
Wright G. W. 29 Gold
Wright John, 221 Pearl

DRY GOODS—RETAILERS.

Abel S. C. 15 Catharine
New York.
Abrahams Judah, 250 Houston
Addoms John, 275 Broadway
Ahles & Suttler. 345 Broadway
Aitkin Walter, 505 Greenwich
Alexander James, 164 Canal
Alexander Mandel, 255 5th
Altmayer A. & Brother, 51 Av. D
Andrews B. & Co. 314 2d
Andrews James E. 460 Grand
Andrews S. W. 298 2d
Armstrong & Co. 225 Greenwich
Armstrong James, 258 3d Av.
Arnold A. & Co. 50 Canal & 49 Howard
Arnold Henry, 1½ Av. D
Atwill John, 191 Hudson
Babor Alfred, 157 William
Bachman Philip L. 387 Monroe
Banks George, 25 Catharine
Banta James A. 320 Bleecker
Barker J. W. & Co. 71 & 73 Catharine

Barker Stephen, 281 Grand
New York.
Bauckman ——, 97 Sheriff
Baum Simon, 129 Clinton
Beach J. S. 243 Greenwich
Bear Isaac, 105 Av. D
Beck Jas. & Co. 355 Broadway
Beekman & Cutter, 66 Canal
Bennett Anna, 301 Houston
Bergstolen Lewis, 61 Av. B
Berk A. 138 Walker
Bernhard B. 297 Bowery
Bernhard & Rosenberg, 281 Houston
Bernkopf Marx, 72 Cannon
Bettman Judah, 49 Lewis
Birdsall James H. 647 Broadway
Bishop John, 443 Pearl
Black A. D. 313½ 8th Av.
Blauvelt D. T. 521 Greenwich
Bleakie R. H. 257 6th Av.
Bodine G. M. 323 Grand
Boggs Wm. W. 68 Hudson
Bond Wynter S. 106 6th Av.
Bradley Wm. 266 3d Av.
Brennan, M'Bernay & Co. 315½ Grand
Brinck & Russell, 68 Canal
Brookheim Jacob, 24 Av. C
Brown Richard, 645½ Broadway
Buckman Solomon, 97 Sheriff
Burdett Geo. C. 136 Walker
Butts Charles, 249 Greenwich
Byrne Brothers, 169 Grand
Campbell James, 603 Pearl
Campbell & Wright, 190 Hudson
Campion David P. 305 Grand
Carolin D. 66 Prince & 7 William
Casey James, 109 Roosevelt
Childs Evander, 272 Canal
Childs & Ramsey, 416 Grand
Clarke John, 334 8th Av
Clark Hosea F. 167 Greenwich
Cohen Michael, 383½ Grand
Cohn Leopold, 236 Houston
Cole Phino, 689 Broadway
Conlan Samuel, 60 Centre
Connor Daniel, 160 3d Av.
Content Simon, 335 Grand
Cooper Samuel, 322 Bowery
Cornell Albert & Amerman, 503 Greenwich
Corrigan & Brother, 404 Grand
Cowperthwait Geo. E. 295 2d & 135 Houston
Cox Samuel H. 19 Greenwich Av.
Crocheron David, 200 Greenwich
Crocheron James M. 234 Bowery
Cropsey Andrew, 94 Canal
Cropsey James, 124 Canal
Cropsey Jasper F. 83 Canal
Crown S. 20 Division
Cushing D. S. & Co. 181 Greenw'h
Cushing Josiah D. & Co. 241 do
Daly Mathew, 345 Grand
Danaher P. H. 426 Grand
Davis Alfred, 66 Av. D.
Davis B. 50 Roosevelt
Davis Robert E. 147 6th Av.
Dayton W. P. 641 Broadway
Dean Seth, 231 8th Av.
Debevoise Michael C. 35 Catharine
Decker J. H. 512 Grand
Demorest Wm. J. 209 & 211 Varick
Devine Joseph M. 30 Thompson
Dickson Thomas, 8 3d Av.
Dispecker Moses, 218½ Bowery
Dobson Wm. 153 Greenwich
Dolin Richard, 365 Pearl
Donnelly N. S. & Co. 397 Grand
Dow Maria, 175 6th Av.
Duffy J. A. & Co. 520 Grand
Ehrenreick Jacob, 174 Houston
Eichtershaimer A. 238 Cherry
Ellecott P. J. 32 Av.
Elabergh Isaac, 68 Suffolk
Ely Benjamin, 401 Hudson
Emden J. 52 Av. C
Emden Joseph, 121 Sheriff
Enehrenreich Jacob, 147 Houston
Epstein & Bloch, 165 Broome
Evans John, 417 3d Av.

Fanning Edward, 226 Bowery
New York.
Fanpecker W. 313 Bleecker
Farvy John, Yorkville
Farvey Michael, do
Feist Jacob, 29 Av. A
Ferguson Charles, 143 West Bdy.
Ferguson Isaac, 149 Varick
Finch Ezekiel K. 31 Catharine
Fisher J. F. 444 Grand
Forrester Hiram M. & George, 242 Bowery
Fountain G. P. 663 Broadway
Frank & Straus, 312 Bowery
Frink Baruch H. 23 Av. D
Gansline Henry, 309 Houston
Gaylord Elizabeth, 298 Spring
Gaylor Charles, Yorkville
Geer G. Warren, 84 6th Av.
Gerstle Joseph, 211 Stanton
Gilley F. W. & W. F. & Co. 126 Bowery
Godwin Hannah M. 79 Av. C
Goldfield Nathan, 270 2d
Goldman John, 12 Av. B
Goldstein Henry, 66 Essex
Goldwogel Meyer, 77 Ludlow
Gough Henry G. 351 6th Av.
Grandy & Schuyler, 310 & 312 2d
Greenberg & Co. 240 Greenwich
Grossmayer Henry, 290 2d
Gunst Abraham, 278 Bowery
Haddock & Wright, 309 Grand
Haggerty & Beagh, 181 Greenw'h
Haight James P. 635 Grand
Haight & Prime, 518 Grand
Hall Alonzo B. 171 8th Av.
Hall & Andrews, 2d cor. Av. D
Hall Harrison, 29 Catharine
Hall Herbert & Co. 15 Carmine
Hamburghor B. M. 3½ Av. B.
Handley Wm. 311 West
Hannan James, 195 3d Av.
Harned Wm. 32 8th Av.
Hart Wm. & Joseph, 232 Bowery
Hatter Robert, 85½ Willet
Hawkins Willet N. 53 Catharine
Haydock James, 310 Spring
Hearn Brothers, 425 Broadway
Heath James, 150 6th Av.
Healey J. J. 169 Greenwich
Heidenheim Abhm. 43 Columbia
Heller William, 197 Division
Herdt John. 353 Houston
Herman Abraham S. 313 Division
Herman Joseph, 269 Division
Heyman E. 31 Av. C.
Heymonn Morris, 275 Bleecker
Higbie J. S. 146 Greenwich
Hilborn David, 164 Lewis
Hildburghauser H. 448 Grand
Hiltman J. L. 442 Bowery
Hitchcock & Leadbeater, 347 Broadway
Holmes & Coy, 395 Broadway
Hook Charles G. 380 Bowery
Huey Marshall M. 13½ Carmine
Hughes Thomas, 294 Grand
Huston Mrs. 56 Av. C
Huthler & Brandes. 266 William
Hutton John, 84 Hudson
Isaacs John, 147 Washington
Isenbeck Philip, 287 Houston
Jackson Anthony, 302 Broome
Jenkins John, 11 3d Av.
Johnson Robert, 279 3d Av.
Jones Morris, 240 Bowery
Jones Owen, 169 8th Av.
Journeay ——, 81 Catharine
Kahn Isaac, 379 Grand
Kaiser David, 162 2d
Katzenstein Israel. 150 Canal
Kavanagh Mary, 509 Pearl
Kean Martin, 91½ 11th
Keller Wm. 493 Greenwich
Kelly Hugh & Co. 138 Bowery
Ketcham E. C. 158 Division
Kiggin Bernard, 27 Prince
Killeen George, 91 8th Av.
King Patrick, 345 Pearl
Kingham George, 378 Cherry
Kinzey Owen, 187 8th Av

Knowles William, 40 8th Av.
New York.
Koch Isaac, 452 Grand
Kratzenburge Steven, 74 Amity
Kutz Seligman, 164 Essex
Laderer Leopold, 421 Grand
Laderer Michael, 272 Houston
Laderer Wolf, 88 Av. B
Laderer Wm. 162 3d
Lambert J. & Co. 523 Greenwich
Lang Jacob, 177 6th Av.
Landler S. 42 Av. C
Lane John S. 23 Catharine
Lane & Porter, 65 Catharine
Langstadter J. & B. 193½ Division
Lansburgh S. & Co. 11 Carmine
Lappen John, 162½ 3d Av.
Latham Mrs. 140 Walker
Lasher W. 8th Av
Laube Jacob, 17 Rector
Lavenwood E. 263 3d
Lawrence Wm. E. 280 Beekman
Le Boutillier Brothers, 58 Canal
Leddy & Sheriden, 195 Greenwich
Leggat William, 74 Hudson
Leszyrisky H. S. & L. 8th Av.
Lindley & Curtiss, 179 Greenwich
Livingston Simeon, 13 Carmine
Lockwood W. 229 Greenwich
Lord John A. 133 Spring
Lord & Taylor, 61 & 63 Catharine & 99 Maiden lane
Losee Lewis, 311 Grand
Lucas Archibald, 276 Bleecker
Ludlum Nich. S. 283 Greenwich
Lydecker J. R. 515   do
Lyon Albert, 270 Bleecker
Lyon Peter P. 140 Canal
M'Cabe Daniel, 117 Av. C
M'Donald Mary, 360 Bowery
M'Gowan F. 9th Av. & 37th
M'Farlane John, 302 Spring
M'Govern Mrs. 134 Division
M'Kinlay William, 463 Pearl
M'Sorley James. 347 Houston
Mabbett James & Son, 219 Greenwich & 71 Barclay
Maloy John, Horatio cor. West
Mann Simon, 249 Centre
Mann R. J. Harlem
Marcher James, 911 Broadway
Marx John, 128 Delancy
Mason Charles, 103 Houston
Mather James M. 294 2d
Mathews William, 60 Catharine
Michaelbacher A. 161 Houston
Miller Thomas, 15 Greenwich Av.
Mendelbaum David. 61 Norfolk
Mingesheimer & Hahn, 227 Delancy
Meehen Henry, 280 West
Merchant Charles C. 291 Broadw.
Merrill Joseph, 129 8th Av.
Meyer Jacob, 516 Pearl
Meyer A. S. 346½ Bowery
Michelbacher A. 161 Houston
Montgomery C. J. 412 Pearl
Mooney Arthur, 185 Grand
Moore, Charles & Co. 446 Grand
Moore John N. 254 Bleecker
Moore Wm. 10 Greenwich Av.
Morris S. B. & Co. 102 6th Av.
Morris & Wilson. 130 Chatham
Morris & Bremner, 434 Grand
Moses Henry, 191 Houston
Mowbray Oliver, 142 Canal
Muir Thomas, 493 Greenwich
Mulligan & M'Mullens, 157 6th Av.
Murphy John, 143½ Greenwich
Myers Michael, 485 Broadway
Nelson Andrew, 285 3v. Av.
Nowberger L. & F. 276½ Bowery
Nicholson Ann E. 212½ Bowery
North Brothers. 18 S. William
Nuspam C. 187 Rivington
O'Conner G. 64 Montgomery
Offner Henry, 304 Rivington
O'Havan William, 364 Cherry
O'Farrell H. 9th Av. 36th st.
O'Neil Mary, 191 Grand
O'Neil Patrick, 519 Pearl

Oettinger & Goldstein, 297 Houston *New York.*
Oppenheim Isaac, 75 Av. B
Osderweis Morris, 222 Rivington
Park Timothy, 364 Bleecker
Patten James, 267 Greenwich
Parker Leonard K. 98 9th Av.
Parmer W. A. 302 2d
Pattison Thomas, 1 Bowery
Phipps J. L. 453 Greenwich
Pfeiffer J. M. 56 Av. C
Poillon C. & A. C. 57 Catharine
Porter Thomas, 234 3d Av.
Post Bartholomew, 84 Av. C
Post & Young, 195 Spring
Plato David & Cohen, 344 Canal
Prall Wolf, 136 Av. C.
Quin James, 372 3d Av.
Quigley James. 178 3d Av.
Rea Robert, 251 Centre
Raleigh P. & Co. 316 8th Av.
Ramsey Matthew R. 416 Grand
Rathbone M. 44 Pearl
Remsen Daniel D. 271 Grand
Reynolds John, 214½ West
Roberts S. D. 163 Greenwich
Roberts David. 395 6th Ad.
Roberts & Rees, 162 Chatham
Roberts & Williams, 62 9th Av.
Robins John. 426 & 428 Pearl
Rogers & Co. 551 Broadway
Rogers R. & W. 436 Grand
Rohr John G. 260 Canal
Rosenberger Moses. 135 Pitt
Rosendale Aaron. 197½ Division
Rossman Henry, 163 Houston
Rossman Simon, 165 do
Rothschild Samuel, 419 Grand
Rumnay T. W. 242 Bleecker
Sackett Jeremiah L. 339 do
Saunders James R. 43 3d Av.
Seaman Abraham, 246 Stanton
Seaman T. & Son. 8th Av.
Seaman & Muir, 321 Broadway
Schoutz Louis, 43 Av. D
Seagrist F. 8th Av.
Self Edward, 188 Varick
Schutz Marx, 257 Houston
Schutz Mayer, 221 Houston
Schwab & Minzesheimer, 347 Grand
Schwarz Abraham, 244 2d
Scott & Clark, 225 Greenwich
Scott James J. 136 Canal
Scott William, 118 Hudson
Scudder Alanson H. 282 Bleecker
Sherwood & Chapman, 197 Spring
Shiels & Weddell, 392 Bowery
Shirley D. 183 6th Av.
Schloss & Heilbroner. 47 Norfolk
Sholle Brother, 223 Division
Simmons Henry, 100 Hudson
Simpson Mrs. 212 Bowery
Sloan & Co. 501 Greenwich
Smyth Bernard, 506 Grand
Smith John, 8th Av.
Solliger Leopold, 192 2d
Spaulding & Williams, 167 6th Av.
Staats Abraham L. 37 Catharine
Stein Charles, 200 Rivington
Stern David G. 172 Bowery
Stern & Erdman, 212 Houston
Stern Simon, 194 2d
Stern & Tichner, 364 Grand
Stevenson Joseph, Harlem
Stewart George, 379 Broadway
Straus Jonas & Brother, 203½ Division
Stratford James, 8th Av.
Strausz Henry, 162 3d
Suydam & Haff, 492 Grand
Taggart William, 50 Greenwich
Tate Thomas, 86 Canal
Tate William, 157 8th Av.
Taylor William P. 59 Catharine
Taylor & Armstrong, 213 G.wich
Teague Edward, 204 8th Av.
Teller William, 493 Greenwich
Terbell, Jennings & Co. 24 Cortlandt
Thompson Thos. J. 272½ Bleecker
Towle Thomas, 193 Spring

Towle S. & M. E. 261 Grand *New York.*
Townsend James H. & Co. 707 Greenwich & 92 9th Av.
Triglar John, 357 3d Av.
Traynor John L. 61 Cortlandt
Ubsdell & Peirson, 64 Canal & 51 Howard
Vanbecker Walruf, 318 Bleecker
Van Buskirk R. & G. 686 Wash'ton
Vandycke Peter, 71 8th Av.
Van Saun Henry, 313 Hudson
Walder M. 28 Av. A
Waldheimer J. 199 Houston
Walker Adam, 333 Grand
Waller I. W. 204 Houston
Wandell Benjamin C. & Co. 92 9th Av.
Warner Samuel, 83 Houston
Waters Catharine, 291 Wooster
Weichselbaum Charles, 250 Houston
Webb William, Harlem
White John, 278 Bleecker
Whitely George, 275 6th Av.
Wightman Jasper, 200 3d Av.
Wildey C. & A. 279 Greenwich
Wiley L. M. & Co. 194 Broadway
Williams, Bradford & Co. 14 Cortlandt
Williams Ebenezer L. 83 Cath'rine
Williams G. B. & Co. 141 Spring
Williams & Gibson, 245 Greenwich & 141 Spring
Woods John, 445 Pearl
Wormser Simon, 384 Cherry
Wright Adam, 238 Bowery
Wyman Rodolf, 9 Av. B
Young Abraham, 196 Delancy
Young T. S. 291 Grand
Zabriskie & Van Riper, 519 Greenwich

DRY GOODS—RUSSIA GOODS—IMPORTERS OF.

Davis & Kissam, 32 William
Dow George W. & Co. 7 Burling slip
Manwaring David W. 245½ Front
Peck H. N. & Co. 130 Front

DRY GOODS—WOOLENS—IMPORTERS OF.

Balmforth Christopher, 77 Pine
Boker John G. & E. 4 William
Bottomley John, 112 Pearl
Buckley James, jr. 77 Pine
Buckley Amon, 42 Pine
Dambmann C. F. 62 Beaver & 109½ Pearl
Emerie Joseph. 22 Exch. place
Graef Arnold, 74 Beaver
Groeschke C. A. & Co. 66 Beaver
Hudson Joseph, 72 Pine
Ives G. R. 66 Pine
Kroger Bernard, 110 Pearl
Kumpan Ignatius, 42 Nassau
Lowrys & Woods. 60 Liberty
Luhning John & Co. 84 Beaver
Mali H. W. T. & H. 27 Beaver
Marie C. 67 Liberty
Outram John, 41 S. William
Robinson John & Co. 37 Beaver
Ross Robert S. 20 Liberty
Schenck Oscar & Co. 132 Water
Seigman Brothers, 41 Pine
Shaw George, 40 Stone
Sykes John, 77 Pine
Whitaker John, 41 S. William
Winterbottom Thomas, 41 S. William
Wrigley J. 78 Pine

Oneida County.

Hovey George, *Camden.*
Sigman S.
Lehmair Benj., Dominick st. *Rome.*
Phelps S. do
Stimson N. James st.
Dutton James, 91 Genesee *Utica.*

Bronner M. & Sons, 52 Genesee *Utica.*
Gaston S. B. 54 do
Kellogg F. V. & C. C. 56 do
Abbott Brothers, 66 do
Thomson S. & Son, 74 do
Wells A. L. & Co. 76 do
Vedder, Welbon & Tyler, 78 do
Bailey Lewis, 80 Genesee
Wells J. B. 88 do
Swartwout & Golden, 90 do
Mills S. D. 100 do
Stacy & Walker, 104 do
Camp Harry, 106 do
Bidwell J. 106 do
Doolittle & Norris, 110 do
Gaffney O. & M. 136 & 138 do
Harrison & Hale, 140 do
Gaffney P. 144 do
Kern Aaron, 58 Hotel
James T. B. & Co. 54 Hotel
Hershfield L. & A. 168 Genesee
Silberberg M. 101 Fayette
Maltby N., Vernon Centre *Vernon.*
Bradley H., Whitesboro *Whitestown.*
Smith Apollos, do

Onondaga County.

Bigelow O., Baldwinsville *Lysander.*
Fryer J. & Co. do
Sharp P. J. & Co. do
Allen & Case, do
Williams — do
Ball S. R. *Marcellus.*
Moses C. & Son
Case N. G.
Dalliba S.
Cadwell & Raynor, Salina st. Syracuse *Salina.*
Whitlock J. H., Globe Buildings, Syracuse
Cameron & M'Donald, 3 do
Woodward A. do
Butler A. T. Genesee st.
Brothwell W. C. do
Rothschild & Rosenback, Genesee st. Syracuse
Abbotts H. G. & W. E. (wholesale) Genesee st
Spencer, De Wolf & Slasson, Genesee st.
Davis James S. & Co. 6 Genesee
Bronner & Kraft, Genesee st.
Cane M. do
Prendergrast E. R. Water st.
Kellogg, Griswold & Co. do
Lynch & Co. Salina st.
Titus Silas, (wholesale) Salina st.
Gage I. L. do
M'Carthy D. (wholesale) do
Pardee C. *Skaneateles.*
Burnett C. jr.
Bean H. L.
Burnett S.

Ontario County.

Sims & Wheat, Geneva *Seneca.*
Lawrence R. H. do
Smith & Hogart, do
Cobb & Smith, do
Lehmair L. & M. do
Britton P. A. do
Wheeler J. J. do
Seeley H. H. & G. C., Geneva

Orange County.

Hasbrouck C. H. 51 Water *Newburgh.*
Chandler A. K. 76 Water
Clark H. F. & Co. 74 do
Masters J. C. (wholesale) 87 Water
Miller James W. 25 Water

Oswego County.

Malcolm Wm. S. 1st st. *Oswego.*
Coplin L. 1st st.
Abby D. C., Bates' Block, 1st st.

Bronner, Kraft & Exstain, 2 Eagle
  Block, 1st st. *Oswego.*
Eagle & Stone, 3 Eagle Block
Hart J. M. & Co. 5 do
Wells Stanton B. 6 do
Newkirk Warden, 1st st.
Herrick Dwight, 14 Phœnix Block
Burt E. Park, 1st st.
Robins Nathan, do

Queens County.

Rushmore L. D. *Hempstead.*

Rensselaer County.

Falton B. O. 227 State
  Lansingburgh.
Chichester E. 229 State
Heimstreet S. 243 do
M'Auley George. 230 do
Bull Stephen C. & Co. 291 State
Younglove A. S. & M. 266 do
Walbridge Henry T. 260 do
Hitchcock Charles, 256 do
Day H. W. 246 do
Chichester Wm. S. 244 do
Wheaton J. S. 242 do
Van Schoonhoven & Proudfit. (im-
  porters) 163 River *Troy.*
Clark & Brother, 156 River
Wells George, 162 do
Reed & Sill, 176 do
M'Lachlin W. A. 178 do
Lee William, 182 do
Southwicks & Forbes, 211 & 213
  River
Danchy G. & C. (wholesale) 255
  River
Lockwoods & Orvis, (wholesale)
  257 River
Marvins & Co. (wholesale) 259 R'r
Quackenbush G. V, S. 202 River
  & 9 State
Buell James. 218 River
Brewster A. 244 do
Canivan Thomas, 302½ River
Gunnison & Stewart, 304 do
Roth John, 306 do
Mosher H. 303 River
Flagg J. 7 Boardman buildings
Alden J. J. 3 Cannon place
M'Govern James, 41½ Congress
Fry W. B. (wholesale) 50 do
Bristol George, 52 do
Brown Mrs. 85½ do
Montague O. 41 Ferry

Rockland County.

Blauvelt Mrs. S. D. Nyack
  Orangetown.
Demarest A. B. Nyack

St. Lawrence County.

Forbes A. D. Ford st. Ogdensburgh
  Oswegatchie.
Guest J. H. (wholesale) Ford st.
  Ogdensburgh
Bronner & Craft, Ford st. Ogdens-
  burgh

Saratoga County.

Hill Chauncey, Ballston Spa
  Milton.

Schenectady County.

Matthews A. & Son, 121 State
  Schenectady.
M'Camus W. & Co. 113 State
M'Donald D. 107 do
Ostrom & Anderson, 105 do
Brown & Lee, 103 do
Matthews J. & Son. 97 do
Campbell J. & W. H. 93 do
Barringer Wm. & Co. 79 do
Ohlen J. & Co. (wholesale) 73
  State
Furman R. 65 State
Vedder Stephen Y. 61 State
Potter C. S. 43 do
Groot C. S. & Co. 37 do
Candee Wm. L. 33 do

Ulster County

Tappan H. J. *Kingston.*
Soper D. Leroy
Liddle William
Perkins & Putnam
Hoyt Wm. & Co. Rondout
Sims William, do

Westchester County.

Odell J. S. Peekskill *Courtlandt.*
Smith F. O. do
Mildedeberger Minard. Tarrytown
  Greenburgh.
Marshall & Stevens, Sing Sing
  Ossining.
M'Cord & Smith, Sing Sing
Van Zandt & Stevens, do
Kelly S. W., Portchester *Rye.*
Boyce E. F. do
Peck Henry A. do

Dry Goods, Groceries and Variety.

Albany County.

Van Aernam T. B. 244 Washington
  Albany.
Erwin W. H. 238 Washington
Hazeltine S. 30 do
King Samuel W. 52 2d
Zeh David, 40 Hawk
Warner A. *Berne.*
Tyler D. E.
Patten J. & Co.
Settle J.
Benedict Zadock
Settle E.
Deitz J. A. & Brother
Conger A.
Dyer B. & Sons
Miller E.
Lawrence R.
Kimmey R. & J. *Bethlehem.*
Johnson N. H. *Coeymans.*
Lawton, Willis & Colvin
Sheirs John B.
Sarles W.
Dawson William
Briggs A. N.
Dorman George W.
Hull William B.
Irwin H. *Guilderland.*
Hallenbake G. Y.
Quackenbush J. I. Knowersville
Batterman G. C. & J. M. do
Beebe H. T. Dunnsville
Brummaghim H. do
Burckley & Johnson *Knox.*
Allen A.
Lee Benjamin
Young B. *New Scotland.*
Huick P. L.
Gardiner M.
Van Wie Isaac, Clarksville
De Long W. do
Mann A. do
Frisbee F. *Rensselaerville.*
Cook Chester
Huyck & Dwight
Dwight A.
Milford R. L. & Co.
Frisbee M.
Hunt Oliver
Smith H.
Potter W.
Moore R. C. H.
Bellamy George
Laraway George
Devereaux & Kenyon
Smith H. C.
Upham J. M.
Morris L. *Watervliet.*
Wigney A. W. West Troy
Fitzgerald P. do
Teal Philip. do
Palmer & Thornton, do
Bennett Wm. C. do
Chollar, Sage & Dunham, W.Troy
Worthington L. P. West Troy
Bacheldor C.
Disabell F. do

Farman F. W., Cohoes *Watervliet.*
Simmons D. do
Vanloon & Waterman, Cohoes
Heimstreet J. do
Buss R. do
Marrin J. J. do
Pattershall D. E. *Westerlo.*
Green J.
Lawrence & Disbrow
Robbins H. E. & Brother
Saxon Thomas
Lay & Pinney

Alleghany County.

Green Luke & Co *Alfred.*
Fenner Isaac
Green Gideon
Brundage Morris
Waldorf George, Phillip's Creek
Fish J. C. *Allen.*
Smith A. C. & I. B. *Almond.*
Angell Jesse
Rawson Isaac
Major M. L.
Crandall Henry W.
Cutler Ira
Ewers E. W.
Parker A. E. & Son *Amity.*
Waldorff George
Stewart J.
Hunt, Swink & Co. *Andover.*
Russell S. & Co.
Kruson & Porter
Hale D. J.
Sherman B. *Angelica.*
Stanton E. & Co.
Dautremont C.
Davis & Charles
Lockhart J. & A.
Stanley N. & S.
Aldrich V.
Renwick Albert *Belfast.*
Chamberlain, Hughes & Co
Cuyler W. T.
Tucker A.
Benjamin G.
Wilvliet Alfred G.
Fisk H. T. *Birdsall.*
Thomas Stephen *Bolivar.*
Hoyt Nelson
Jones Charles D. *Burns.*
Pickett Benj. Whitney's Valley
Pratt & Havens, do
Dake John E. *Canaseda.*
Nicholson A. S.
Spencer W.
Oakes Thaddeus
Hervy H. W.
Rounsville J. P.
Fay Sylvester. Clarksville
Murray Joseph P. do
Willard & Co. *Cuba.*
Guilford S. & W.
Lee & Rand
Stevens & Wheeler
Butts Lucian
Palmer Joseph
Wellman A. *Friendship.*
Colwell W.
Hartshorn P.
Whitewood L.
Scott R. & Co.
Stowell F. L. & Co.
Atwood F. B. & F. D. *Granger.*
Kinney, Townsend & Co. Grove
  Centre
Hyrault, Van Ryper & Son, Short
  Tract
Ennis Matthew S. & Co. Little
  Genesee.
Skiff Wm. R. & E. *Hume.*
Emerson Wm. N.
Sweet George H.
Skiff & Moore
Gillispin J. C., Wiscoy
Fink E. H. do
Smith Charles W., Wiscoy
Huntley Hiram do
Green J. W. & Son *Independence.*
White C. D. C. & Co. *Whites-*
  ville
Haskins, Tollman & Co. do

11

Wood A. & B. F. & Co. Spring Mills   Independence.
Huntington E. Spring Mills
Robbins J. & Co.   do
Card & Crittenden, Centre Independence
M'Graw John & Co. New Hudson.
Jameson Hugh D. Black Creek
Spalding Isaac C.   do
Lemon & Smith   Ossian.
Jewett F.
M'Call Nelson   Rushford.
Higgins, O. T. & Co.
George H. & Co.
Boardman Henry
Colby A. W.
White Washington
Swift Tourman
Gordon J. & L.
Carl Wm.   Scio.
Farnum C. L., Wellsville
Mott Samuel   do
Gordon Wm. H.   do
Prentiss James G.   West Almond.
Russell & Morris   Wirt.
Miner A. W.

Broome County.

Knapp A., Chenango Forks Barker.
Lowell D.   do
Root G. W.   do
Meloy F. W.   do
Hagaman M. & J.   do
Rogers J. B.   do
Boyd & Crosby   Binghamton.
Lewis F. S. & Co.
Green & Eldridge
Ford R. A. & Co.
Tompkins F. W.
Congdon & Merrill
Hall S. H. P.
Lathrop F. B.
Packard C. J.
Hall G. C.
Cary S. F. & Co.
Stowers U. M.
Sisson B. F.
Vanagne C.   Chenango.
Kattel A. E.
Northrup & Olendorph Colesville.
Patrick & Blakely
Ketcham E. Harpersville
Olendorph H. A.   do
Edgerton & Bush, Nineveh
Corbett I. Corbettsville   Conklin.
Johnson C. & Co.   Lisle
Stoddard G. W. & W. H.
Dixon A. Centre Lisle
Lines & Crane, Union Village
Gleason M. Centre Lisle
Kingsley & Austin, Upper Lisle
Campbell & Church,   do
Cushman U.   do
Lincoln Wm.   Maine.
Pollard & Chollar
Clark A. H.
Whitney & Blakely   Triangle.
Jackson W.
Bloomer J. F.   Union.
Badger & Twining
Balyea & Wheeler
Edwards Charles
Benedict M. M.
Robbins E. jr.
Keeler C. E.
Green H. H.   Windsor.
Bronson & Judd
Whitmore, Dusenbury & Co.
Belden James R.

Cattaraugus County.

King & Wilson   Ashford.
Butterworth, Fox & Co.   Burton.
Bascom G.
Willard E.
Smith & Johnson
Hunt A. O.   Carrollton.
Wainer Daniel
Fuller Howard, Ten Mile Spring   Cold Spring.
Colvill, Hopkins & Co. do

Barlow Foster D. Ten Mile Spring   Cold Spring.
Carr Stephen & Co.   do
Grant Henry D.   Conewango.
Barlow Foster D.
Hell Amos
Aldrich Frederick
Colman & Beecher   Ellicottville.
Colman E. S. & L. L.
Skinner P. V.
M'Coy S.
Phelps J. W.
Hull C. C.
Cummins J. T. & Co.   Farmersville.
Cross Luther
Salisbury Reuben R. & Co.   Frankinville.
Adams & Woodruff
Salisbury L. & Co.
Gilbert T.
Howard Talcott   Freedom.
Holmes E. & M., Sandusky
Jameson Reuben M. do
Beebe Darius,   do
Reckard Ziba C., Elton
Cross Wm.   Great Valley.
Ellsworth Eli
Nelson Wm. J.
Howe H.   Little Valley.
Twomley & Winslow   Machias.
Salisbury J. R. & Co.
Whitcher R. L.
Pollard J. R.
Wright J. H.
Eddy H. W. Eddyville Mansfield.
Whitcomb J.   New Albion.
Waters & Allen
Stevens G. F.   Olean.
Allen C. B. & W. D.   Otto.
Darling John P.
Elliott Wm. F. & Co.
Laing John. East Otto
Cooper & Hunt   Perrysburgh.
Clark Luther, Versailles
Beals Timothy,   do
Brown & Brother, do
Brown David, Gowanda   Persia.
Chaffee A. D.   do
Chaffee A. W. W. do
Chaffee J. H.   do
Ferris William,   do
Gardner L. M.   do
Hooker H. N.   do
Henry E. W.   do
Jay J. M.   do
Jenks L. S.   do
Orr Leander,   do
Perry B. F.   do
Springer S. C.   do
Sellew A. R.   do
Spencer F. F.   do
Welch Porter,   do
Milbor J. B.   do
Warner Zimri,   do
Webster Gideon,   do
Vosburgh Wm.   do
Dusenbury, Wheeler, Gregory & Co.   Portville.
Wright C. & Co.
Camp Wm. H   Randolph.
Migbelles Florentine F.
Johnson & Leach
Crowley R. & Co.
Garfield Eliakim
Sheldon & Bennett
Nutting & Doud, E. Randolph
Merrick, Nutting & Son
Hall Amos
Chamberlain Benjamin
Waring James   Rice.
Converse John   South Valley.
Lincoln Solomon   Yorkshire.
Marsh H. L. & G. O.
Cobb Lucius
Marsh Elliott L.
Bailey George W., Delavan

Cayuga County.

Muir Wm. Genesee st.   Auburn.
Jenkins R. & J. L. 66 Genesee

Beardsley S. 74 Genesee   Auburn.
Knight H. L. & Co. 69 Genesee
M'Intosh J.   Aurelius.
Thompson J. A.
Fitch S. & Brother
Kinney A. S. Weedsport   Brutus.
Ingraham W. S.   Cato.
West A.
Hickock J. & C.
Thornton F. E. & Brother Fleming.
Brownell R. M.   Genoa.
Farrow H. & Avery
Avery E.
Adams D. & Sons
Seymour L.
Titus Wm.   Ira.
Stewart Wm. R. & Surdam
Howe O.   Ledyard.
Morton H. & G. P.
Dougherty J. & Hulbert
Avery A.
Calvert Wm. M.   Locke.
Murphy M. D.
Bell Samuel, Montezuma   Mentz.
Lathrop Wm.   do
Foster J. & Son, Troopville
Seymour J. H. Port Byron
Clapp B. B.   do
Hamilton C. H.   do
Aikin D.   do
Hatfield S. A.   do
Ross Z.   do
Smith T. W. & J. T. do
Gordon & Cady,   do
Russell, Sitzer & Co. do
Cady A.   Moravia.
Porter S.
Jewett & Wood
Dibble O.
Slade Wm.   Niles.
Weeks & Westfall
Carman C. & Brother
Cuykall & Thompkins   Owasco.
Dunning Wm. H.
Vanschaick P. H.   Sempronius.
Beardsley J. E.   Scipio.
Howland S.
Watkins G. L.
King & Warner
Thomas A. & Son
Haskins L. & Capen   Springport.
Mersereau D.
Yawger J. P.
Smith & Cozzens
Griffin J.
Bennett Wm.
Everett & Co.
Chase Wm. H.
Barton & Eldridge
Simons & Brother
Hunter J. P.   Sterling.
Longley L.
Longley W. F.
Baker H.   Summerhill.
Brownell H. N.   Venice.
Bennett Wm. D.
Sprague Wm.
Doughty & Mosher
Underhill A.
Hager & Knapp   Victory.
Sayre W.
Conger & Hawley

Chautauque County.

Clark V.   Busti.
Cary S. F.
Brown L. B.   Carroll.
Fenton W. H. H. Frewsburgh
Badlong G. P.   do
Gould & Bartlett,   do
Read A.   do
Langworthy A   Charlotte.
Dewy P.
Brown E. T. & Co.
Burrows J. B. Mayville   Chautauque.
Whallon S. S.   do
Crafts W. W.   do
Hawkins W. W.   do
Stedman & Son,   do
Peacock Wm.   do

Green J. O. & T. & Co. Mayville
 Chautauque.
Smith J. M. do
Scofield Wm. & Co. Do Wittville
Russell John, do
Morse Asa, do
Thomas N. S. *Cherry Creek.*
Carr & Wheeler
Williams J. W. *Clymer.*
Steward & Terry
Voroe & Shedd *Ellery..*
Barrett W. E. Jamestown *Ellicott*
Keeler & Parks, do
Wilcox & Brother, do
Green J. H. & S. C. do
Grant & Forbes, do
Lowry & Co. do
Kent Alonzo, do
Butler Charles, do
Allen & Marris, do
Crosby Samuel, do
Hatch Mason D. *Ellington.*
Phipany George J.
Farmer John F.
Jones W. H. *French Creek.*
Palmer S. E. Vermont *Gerry.*
Newton H. J., Irving *Hanover.*
Sackett J. do
Kent J. P. do
Frenell James, do
Camp Albert H. Forestville
Colvill & Hopkins, do
Morrison O. do
Churchill J. C. do
Cary V. R. Nashville
Carter J. & Co. do
Smith P. B. & Co. Smith's Mills
Swift & Shaw, Silver Creek
Lee, Snow & Co. do
Farnham H. W. do
Lockwood C. do
Dow A. & Co. do
Bly & Welch *Harmony.*
Kent & Wygant
Stewart John, Panama
Hoyt Joseph. do
Hoyt & Davis, do
Farrand Alonzo, do
Ralph J. *Mina.*
Robinson J.
White S. & Son, Fredonia *Pomfret.*
Walker & Taylor, do
Lewis C. M. do
Grant, Forbes & Co. do
Barrett & Hutchenson do
Pemberton H. do
Risley L. G. do
Frazier & Store, do
Dudley & Co. do
Perkins & Webster, do
Hilton & Lampson, do
Douglass D. W. do
Graham W. M. C. do
Butler & Kingsley, do
Bradley & Shaw, Dunkirk
O'Neal William, do
Riley, Benton & Co. *Portland.*
Abrams A.
Morrison R. S. & Co. Salem Cross
 Roads
Thompson & Wells, do
Minton, Haight & Co. do
Bell William *Ripley.*
Ecker John J. *Sheridan.*
Miller & Hawley *Sherman.*
Ranson Henry
Green J. & O. & Co.
Hopkins G. *Villenova.*
Mark, James & Son
Cox & Warner
Knight & Miner *Westfield.*
Babcock Jared R.
Johnson & Brothers
Couch Addison P.
Babcock Henry M.
Kinnan T. & J. H.
Morse William R.
Buck & Minton
Waters, Franklin & Co.

Chemung County.

Gibson Samuel C. *Big Flats.*

Tuttle L. A. & Co. *Big Flats.*
Vedder Horace
Campbell John & A. G. & Co.
 Catharine.
Thompson & Hezen
Goodwin E. H. *Havanna*
Haight George, do
Eastman R. R. do
Tracy D. do
Kellinger Wm. S. do
Vaughn —— do
Jackson G. W. & H. B. do
Decker S. C. do
Broederick & Campbell, do
Hitchcock G. V. do
Thomas E. H. do
Purdy Guy *Cayuta.*
Wood L. & J.
Drake & Blake
Cowell Matthew *Chemung.*
Ramsdell Lyman
Tiece Jacob
Abbey F. H. & Co. Salubria *Diz.*
Guinnip A. M. do
Robins A. do
Congdon & Mills, do
Deming C. W. do
Hillerman H. M. do
Chapman & Co. do
Bellamy A. do
Ward W. do
Herring Wm. H. do
Evans & Graham, do
Watson & Julet, Beaver Dams
Skinner E. L. *Elmira.*
Tuthill D. H.
Jones J. R.
Stobo John
Hill J. & H.
Covell R. & E.
Elmore J. N.
Hart & Bulmer,
Wells J. C.
Little Baldwin,
Hamlin & Rice
Hallock & Thompson,
Newcomb, Loder & Co.
Holmes E. F.
Colden C. & Brother
Wintermate Isaac, Horse Heads
Bennett George, do
Wintermate & Underhill, do
Bryant ——, do
Walker T. S. *Southport.*
Tracy & Lockwood
Mosher J. B. Millport *Veteran.*
Stoll J. C. do
Babcock & Frost, do
Tompkins Hiram, do
Seaman H. do
Botsford A. do

Chenango County.

Newell Dexter *Bainbridge.*
M'Cullom & Co.
Betts P. J.
Bishop Elisha
Owens A. G.
Jackson M. & Co. So. Bainbridge
Shutts J. & Co. do
Bennett I., Bennettsville
Van Horn David, do
Storrs H. E. *Columbus.*
Church, Eggleston & Co. *Coventry.*
Phillips G. D. & Sons
Barnes F. S. & Co. Livermore's
 Corners *German.*
Birdsall, Nichols & Lyon, Ex-
 change square *Greene.*
Binghand & Maynard
King & Hitchcock
Lewis, Gilman & Co.
Cushman U. & Son
Rathbone & Thurber
Barnard C. E. & Son
Julian F. Exchange Building
Sherwood I. H. do
Squiers Charles, do
Beebee Daniel *Guilford.*
Hull John, jr.
Baldwin W. Guilford Centre

Hill J. P. *Macdonough.*
Hill T.
Williams G. W. *New Berlin.*
Carr R. D.
Brown William T.
Knapp T. S.
Welch & White
Medbury Charles
Wood E. jr. South New Berlin
Crandall N. & T. do
Matthewson J. E. do
Miller T. *North Norwich.*
Murray & Kinyon *Norwich.*
Slater B.
Wood & Sanford
Wheeler Chauncey G.
Milner & Babcock
Brooks L. & Son
Bedford D. E. S. & D.,
Steere & Holmes
Kershaw James
Frink Benjamin
Johnson R. J. & Co.
Van Size E. H.
Bowen & Waldron *Otselic.*
Parker A.
Baldwin Rufus *Oxford.*
Bacon & Tracy
Chapman & Thorp
Locke C. F. T.
Locke J. V. W.
M'Neil & Sheldon
Mygatt & Miller
Newkirk T. G.
Perkins Erastus
Tuttle Cyrus
Tuttle Arad
Clark E. & Son
Allen & Brown *Pharsalia.*
Fairchild & Forbes *Pitcher.*
Bowen W. & J.
Blackman & Smith
Parco Z.
Taylor W. & Co. Pitcher Spa
Sibley J. *Plymouth.*
Ludington James S.
Slater B. South Plymouth
Smith & Brownell *Sherburne.*
Gorrett & Pratt
Upham A. G. & E. G.
Cooke & Elabre
Cole L. C.
Shaw & Knapp
Cushman & Smith
Read Horace S. *Smithville.*
Tarbell Seymour
Ransom J. V. *Smyrna.*
Kinyon G. J. & Son
Strew John
Shepard Trowbridge
Isbell Elmour

Clinton County.

Kingsland & Co. Keeseville
 Au Sable.
Gerfield E. H. & Co. do
Green & Powers, do
Tabor William, do
Spencer & Adgate, do
Hoffnagle M. L. do
Hoffman J. do
Matthews H. & H. O. do
M'Guier J. do
Boynton B. B. do
Taggard J. W. do
Dickinson James *Beekmantown.*
Simonds B. J.
Rogers J. A. J. *Black Brook.*
Farrington J. R.
M'Gregor John
Duncan John T.
Nye F. & B. *Champlain.*
Whiteside Thomas J. & Sons
Doolittle L.
Bigelow John
Underhill William B.
Savage J. & H. D.
Moon D. D. S.
Stowe E. G.
Moon Pliny
Moore N. C.

Fuller H. H. — *Champlain.*
Moore W.
Perry L.
Webb & Cook
Gates E. M.
Leonard A. & B.
Slingsby Thomas & Co.
Cooper E.
Catlin J. & Co.
North N. — *Chazy.*
Grant D.
Morton M. M.
Stiles Medding, West Chazy
Lawrence P. — do
Medding & Son, — do
M'Coy John — *Clinton.*
Marshall & Co. — *Ellenburgh.*
Hovens J. W. & Co.
Ransom, Fisher & Co.
Fitch J. J. & Co. — *Mooers.*
Knapp A.
Shedden S. S.
Douglass ——
Finny John
Stearns & Beckwith — *Peru.*
Day & M'Intyre
Elmore F.
Channel L. L.
Ayres T. I.
Barker J. H. & Co.
Barton C. D.
Marshall Paul — *Plattsburgh.*
Moore C C.
Myers L.
Douglass Wm.
Bailey James
Bromley John H.
Goldsmith Thomas
Cottrill R.
Cady Charles
Marshall Levi
Ricord Joseph
Conway Terrence
Palmer William & Sons
Webster George W.
M'Murray F.
Morgan Wm. & Son
Platt M. K.
Hedge Wm. H.
Buck & Benedict
Sprague & Averill
Kimball Ebenezer — *Saranac.*

Columbia County.

Pomeroy L. & Sons — *Ancram.*
Wilber A.
Rockefeller J. A.
Tyler A. B. — *Austerlitz.*
Bell A.
Read E., Spencertown
Dickerman S. C. do
Clark J. E. — do
Brown H. H. — *Canaan.*
Frisby S.
Wait D. P. & J. A., Canaan Four Corners
Cornwall A. D. — do do
Woodworth W. S., Flat Brook
Daly S. — *Chatham.*
Harder P
Ray D.
Cady S. S.
Wood J. & Son
Van Valkenburgh L. Malden Bridge
Palmer G. W. — do
Cornwall George G. — do
Huested S. R. — do
Cobrun E. L. Chatham Four Corners
Crandall S. — do
Mesick & Shufelt, — do
Van Alstine Wm. L. — do
King C. A., Chatham Centre
Vadder H. — do
Edwards U. Flat Brook
Palmer O., East Chatham
Flint J. D. — do
Carr Wm., North Chatham
Lasher J. & Co., . — do
Michael A. — *Claverack.*

Shoemaker J. V. — *Claverack.*
Van Wyck S. M.
Miller W. J.
Ham & Shelden, Hoffman's Gate
Daniels A. C, Mellenville
Sheldon A., Churchtown
Finger G. — *Clermont.*
Elkenburgh J.
Leroy Levi
Van Benschoten Wm. M. — *Copake.*
Coons Wm. W.
Copake Iron Works
Reynolds E. & J. D.
Weaver P. A. — *Gallatin.*
Rockefeller J. A.
Chadwick W. H., Gallatinaville
Snyder L. Jackson Corner
Lawrence H. — *Germantown.*
Sturgess J.
Rockefeller P.
Waltermire J. D. — *Ghent.*
Bartlett R. H. — *Hillsdale.*
Pixley M.
Dimmick & Bulkley
Murray Henry W.
Williams Peter C.
Snyder John T.
Tyler Major M.
Tracy Eleazer
Allen O. H. Front st. — *Hudson.*
Wells George — *Kinderhook.*
Parsons A.
Benjamin E. D.
Sweet J. C.
Benoyar H. M., Valatie
Penoyar R. S. — do
Leonard M. — do
Link & Co. — do
Carpenter E. O. & Co. do
Miller J. & P. P. — do
Vosburgh E. — do
Wagoner J. M. & J. — do
Lederer M. — do
Bogardus J. & Co. — *Livingston.*
Baker H.
Hollenbeck J.
Pierce J. & Co.
Du Bois H. A.
Barringer R.
Le Sur J. — *New Lebanon.*
Davis K. M. & Sons, New Britain
Everett F. W. New Lebanon Springs
Tilden & Co — dc
Pierce P. G. — do
Nichols N. — do
Lewis & Lester, Moffatt's Store
Vosburgh M. — *Stockport.*
Chittenden G. & Brothers
Houghtaling & Co. — *Stuyvesant.*
Van Allen A. A. & Co.
Mandville William G.
Whitbeck C. — *Tughkanic.*

Cortland County.

Kingman Oliver — *Cincinnatus.*
Kingman Charles
Kingman J. & J.
Bean Jeremiah
Schermerhorn D. *Cortland Village.*
Barnard William O.
Ballard & Webb
Dickson Andrew
Sturtevant & Doud
M'Graw P. H. & Co. M'Grawville
— *Cortlandville.*
M'Graw & Green, M'Grawville
Kinney & Holmes, — do
Isaacs George — *Freetown.*
Dewey & Seber, Freetown Corners
Pierce Samuel B. — do
Hart Samuel — *Harford.*
Stevens Riley
Barber Jedediah — *Homer.*
Sherman William & Son
Sherman John
Thomas E. F.
Westcott C. & Co.
Phillips E. F.
Cushing James E. Little York

Griffith A. East Homer — *Homer.*
Hunt Asa — *Lapeer.*
Carley Alanson & Son — *Marathon.*
Roe John M.
Roe & Rogers
Frost & Ward — *Preble.*
Whiting A. L. — *Scott.*
Bierce & Kinney
Emerson Samuel — *Solon.*
Rockwell Darius — *Taylor.*
Miller Edward — *Truxton.*
Babcock Asa
M'Kay Hiram C.
Hicok James C.
Pierce & Coats
Patrick Halsey, Cuyler
Davison ——, — do
Snyder William — *Virgil.*
Snyder William & Co.
Grow & Squires
Messenger Hiram J. East Virgil
Bean Chauncey — *Willett.*
Dyer John S.

Delaware County.

Hawver A. — *Andes.*
Emory John
Morse R.
Shaver D. B.
Ballantine D.
Murry R. — *Bovina.*
Byrutha J.
Archibald William
Elwood H. Downsville — *Colchester.*
Radeker B. — do
Shaver P. Pepacton
Hunter A. do
Payne George C. — *Davenport.*
Stimpson D. & Co.
Woodrich Z. E.
Fero E. B. West Davenport
Gould J. H. — *Delhi.*
Pardee D. H.
Blanchard & Woodruff
Ramsay W. F.
Millard R. & Co.
Goodman N. W.
Marvine C.
Gilbert G.
Lovell H. O.
Sheldon C. B.
Elwood J.
Douglass A. jr. — *Franklin.*
Watrous W.
Noble W. & C.
Mitchell D.
Grant A. H.
Holmes I.
Gates A. J. — East Croton
Treadwell A. T. & Co. do
Treadwell C. H. & Co. do
Titus & Shaw — *Hamden.*
Chase A. B.
St. John C.
Griswold E. & Co.
Wheeler M. — *Hancock.*
Frisbie H.
Rieve W. & Co.
Richards & Williams
Lakin S. S.
Lewis H.
Twaddle J. M.
Peck & Harper — *Harpersfield.*
Gibbs R. B.
Hamilton & M'Murdy
Andrews A. — *Kortright.*
Keeler B. North Kortright
Bushnell & Son, Bloomville
Teyrell J. H. & Co. — *Meredith.*
Douglass Edward
M'Murry J.
Stilson N. West Meredith
Stilson A. — do
Elmendorph, Chamberlain & Co.
Margaretsville — *Middletown.*
Sands R. do
Angle F. Clovesville
Humphrey R. do
Griffin Asa, do
Griffin M. do
Vandemark J. do

Dimmick N. Arkville *Middletown.*
Beater & Mead *Roxbury.*
Burham A. H. & Co.
Bidwell T. C. & Co.
Keator S.
Moore & Howell, Mooresville —
Roxbury.
Babcock & Co. do
Griffin C. *Stanford.*
Judson S.
Cowles J. F. & Co
Bush J. Hobart
Babcock B. V. do
Moore & Foot, do
Griffin O. & B. do
Kilpatrick & Griffin, Hobart
Hanford J. W. & Co. do
Perkins and Grant, do
Rogers & Fish, Sidney Plains.
Sidney.
Merritt E. Deposit *Tompkins*
Dean A. C. do
Devereux, Clark & Co. Deposit
Ford W. L. do
Wheeler W. & Finch do
Hadley B. E. do
Hulse M. R. do
Church & Birge, do
Powell T. M. do
Cable A. M. do
Fitch N. *Walton.*
Gay D. H.
Coleman J. S.
St. John A. F.
Fancher & Leely

Duchess County.

Reed C. & N. *Amenia.*
Conklin D. G.
Hunt J. L.
Nase W. H. South Amenia
Andrews M. do
Hitchcock & Winchester,
Wattles C. do
Price & Meddaugh, do
Hunt J. D. Leedsville
Bostwick Wm. H., City
Peters J. *Beekman.*
Vanderbargh J.
Holmes W. A.
Holmes J. S.
Peters C.
Rogers S. B. Poughquake
Upton P. C. *Clinton.*
Westfall A. R.
Armstrong G. H. Clinton Hollow
Combs M. H. do
Shults D. H. Shultzville
Dutcher L. S. & Co. *Dover.*
Wheeler S. South Dover
Chapman & Ross, do
Somers & Chapman, do
Titus S. do
Vincent J. Chestnut Ridge
Huestid I. N. & E. H. Dover Plains
Mabbett J. R. do
De Forest J. G. do
Van Wyck & Carey *Fishkill.*
Northrop D. B.
Bowne F. H.
Jones J.
Hayt T. A.
Sweet E. D. & Co. Wappinger's
Falls
Townsend C. A. do
Whelley T. do
Crilly J. do
Brown T. do
King W. G. do
Myer W. D. Hughsonville
Van Kleeck E. do
Hoyt T. A. Glenham
Wescott G. W. do
Burroughs T. Low Point
Davis D. Matteawan
Hubbell J. L. do
Cooks A. M. Fishkill Landing
Teller W. do
Pugsley C. B. do
Kelley & Seaman, Stormville

Hopewell W. M., Hopewell
Fishkill.
Vanbeamer D. Fishkill Plains
Vanwyck R. S. do
Collins D. *Hyde Park.*
Gillender J.
Travis O.
Doty O. W.
Brown & Mosher
Smith J. G. *Lagrange.*
Vandwyck R. S.
Billings J.
Brooks V. Arthersburgh
Snyder L. Jackson's Corner
Milan.
Buckuam K. K. Milanville
Knickerbocker J. Lafayette Cor-
ners
Killmore H. do
Shook & Travers, Rock City
Schultz J. G. do
Hurd W. T. *Pawling.*
Craft J.
Thayer J. P.
Stark J. W. & T. W.
Stark & Wooding
Howard T. Campbellville
Dixbury G. H. *Pine Plains.*
Hedges & Davis
Bostwick R. W. & Son
Wiserodt & Hoffman
Pulver W. W. & S., Pulver's Cor-
ners
Holmes J. O. *Pleasant Valley.*
Collins & Wiggins
Duncan J. B
Dudley F.
Pearsall G. T. Salt Point
Vanderburgh R. D. C.
Graham A. J. New Hamburgh
Poughkeepsie.
Mills S. H. f do
Ward, Wells & Co. do
Travis E. Rochdale
Elmore A. *Red Hook.*
Kemball E.
Masseneau R. C.
Martin J.
Schultz, Dedrick & Co.
Cuck D. Upper Red Hook
Elting Wm. do
Lasher P. H. Tivoli
Martin R. G. Barrytown
Piatt & Reed *Rhinebeck.*
Cowles W. S.
Jennings J. F.
Soper D. L.
Denny M. S.
Welch S.
Bayly J. A.
Pink G.
Stewart & Miller *Stanford.*
Halstead N. & Co.
Congdon R. D.
Thorn L.
Davis C. F. Attlebury
Duncan O. *Union Vale.*
Fletcher R. N.
Vincent D. D.
Davis A. D., Verbank
Frost W. *Washington.*
Sharpsteen Wm.
Simmons J. S. Washington Hollow
Coffin & Ketcham, Salt Point
Height H. C. Hart's Village
Sherman I. G. Mabbettsville
Holbroock N. Lithgow
Lacy J. J. & J. T., Lettlevest

Erie County.

Butler Samuel M. *Alden.*
Spencer, Stone & Co.
Ward Samuel & Co.
Peck B. F. Alden Centre
Miller B. Williamsville *Amherst.*
M'Neil John & Co. do
Herr E. & H. do
Moulton Arthur H. do
Egert Christian, do
Snyder Michael, do
Willhelm John, do

Card Nathan, Willink *Aurora.*
Peno Henry Z. do
Keyser, Henry, do
Waldo S. & Co. do
Holmes Stephen, do
Palmer G. H. & Co. West Falls
Holmes Allen, do
Baker Reuben, do
Baker & Brewer, Griffin Mill
Thompson Harry *Black Rock.*
Thornton Henry
Manly Seth F.
Bennett Henry A.
Churchill John *Boston.*
Cary Asa
Adams Mortimer
Lawrence J.
Cooke E. North Boston
Brown a. & L. *Brandt.*
Kirby Charles
Haberstro Jos. 401 Main *Buffalo.*
Krettner J. 382 do
Samson J. 368 do
Dingers Mary F. 356 do
Smith P. A. 399 do
Edwards L. E. 68 Lloyd
Beyer Jacob, 117 Genesee
Bidwell & Co. 2 Webster's Block
Warren O. & Co. *Clarence.*
Baily J. B.
Miller David
Kreighloh John, Clarence Centre
Vantine David do
Metz Andrew do
Maltby Benjamin *Colden.*
Kerr & Kane *Collins.*
Sherman & Godfrey
Sherman Benj. W.
White & Kerby
Smith Cornelius, Collins Centre
Collins.
Spencer, Richmond & Co. Spring-
ville *Concord.*
Eaton & Blake, Springville
Nash Daniel, do
Leach George, do
Pratt Lyman *Eden.*
Webster & Sweet
Skanlin Morris
Webster Joseph
Tift George
Trask ——, East Evans *Evans.*
Holt ——, do
Clark John *Hamburgh.*
Lockwood Tim. Water Valley
Rathborn & Parks, do
Riley Philip D. *Holland.*
Dickerman M. L. & Co.
Paul David
Bruce W. W. & Co. *Lancaster.*
Carpenter Thurston
Kircholtes Frederick
Kieffer Peter
Neal Robert, Town Line
Hooker Andrew *Newstead.*
Adams, Knight & Co. Akron
Rich C. B. do
Wainwright J. & Co. do
M'Neal J. W. & Co. do
Jackson & Osborn, do
Hastings S. P. *Sardinia.*
Baily R. S.
Vandervoort J. D. *Tonawanda.*
Walker & Striker
Therron & Patterson
Vanbrunt Jacob
Hunt A. D.
Johnson Seldon
Bush & Fanning
Kibler Jacob
Patch O. & T. *Wales.*
Fuller Turner, Wales Centre
Stevens A. do
Warner D. S. South Wales

Essex County.

Hammond A. Co. *Crown Point.*
Penfield, Harwood & Co.
Haile C. & H.
Fuller William
Brown George

Russell Samuel   *Crown Point.*
Dike & Rider
Whallon & Judd   *Elizabethtown.*
Root & Brainard
Noble H. R.
Meigs Guy
Whitcomb P. S. & Co.
Ross H. H.   *Essex.*
Noble R. & Sons
Lyon W. G.
Gifford C. M.
Clemons Noble
Gould John
Ross, Low & Gould
Whallon & Van Vleck   Whellons-
   burgh
Blish & Buttrick   *Jay.*
Newell Hiram
Newell Lucius
Parmort James H. & Co.
Downer John B. Upper Jay
Jaques Truman, Ausable Forks
Rogers J. & J. & Co.   do
Fales Justus G.   do
Gilbert & Griswold,   do
Burt P. K. & Co.   do
Dickinson G. C.   do
Brewster Ormel   do
Merritt & Mihill   *Keene.*
Partridge Stephen
Wilder Amherst H.   *Lewis.*
Smith & Blood
Merriam William S.
Evans W. & R.   *Minerva.*
Conory Solomon
Titus Russell L. Moriah Four
   Corners   *Moriah.*
Stone N. S. Moriah Four Corners
Stone Hiram,   do
Sherman George,   do
Miller Charles,   do
Sherman Kinsley,   do
Richmond Otis T.   do
Hall Eliphalet,   do
Lee John A.   do
Wheelock H. S. Port Henry
Fort L. A.   do
Collins Ebenezer,   do
Whalon Reuben,   do
Shepherd D. C.   do
Whitaker Silas H.   do
Imus Tabor C.   *North Hudson.*
Adirondac Iron Works, Adirondac
   Newcomb.
Leland James M. Schroon River
   Schroon.
Ireland Wm. Schroon Lake
Hull Lorenzo,   do
Bugbee & Weed   *Ticonderoga.*
Wilson & Calkins
Weed & Tredway
Sunderlin W.
Moses Alonzo
Cutting Franklin H.   *Westport.*
Low John H.
Page Freeborn H.
Pierce H. & J.
Eddy James W.
Richards William
Richards Cyrus W.
Ludd David S. N.
Allen D. L.
Delano J. R. Wadham's Mills
Delano & Merriam,   do
Wadham Wm. L.   do
Braman David,   do
Forbes Albert G.   *Willsborough.*
Jones D. H.
Ross Henry H. 2d
Sheldon Charles
Weldin Abram
Lansing Wendall   *Wilmington.*

Franklin County.

Dickinson J. & Sons   *Bangor.*
Bentley H.
Drake James C.
Datterson D.
Stevens G. & H. D. North Bangor
Mills F. J.   *Bombay.*
Mills & Fulton

Ware J.   *Bombay.*
Reynolds Benjamin & Co.
Robinson & Russell
Reynolds Gates
Goodspeed J. L.   *Burke.*
Mitchell & Bush
Meigs D. C.
Smith Giles
Wead S. M.   *Chateaugay.*
Meigs E. L.
Smith H. B. & Co.
Roberts Theodore
Roberts Alanson
Leary Michael
Roberts George W. & Co.
Gillett S. W.   *Constable.*
Bickford H. N.   *Dickinson.*
Hoyle William   *Fort Covington.*
Manning & Tuthill
Mears & Mears
Marsh Charles
Norton G. F.
Stiles E. & Son
Martin H.   *Harrietstown.*
Martin W. F.
Goldsmith ——
Lewis & Andrus   *Malone.*
Meigs Moses & Co.
Clark S. S.
Clark B. S. W. & Co.
Knapp W.
Daggett & Blaisdell
Morse N.
Fisk J. D.
King W W.
Parmelee & Carpenter
Stevens D. H. & B.   *Moira.*
Lawrence D. W. & Co.
Button H. G. & Son, W. Constable
   Westville.
Cushman A. W. West Constable

Fulton County.

Richards O., Bleecker Falls
   Bleecker.
Mills & Rowley   *Broadalbin.*
Blair Joseph
Capron & Hawley
Burr A. & C. H.
Conda Wm., Union Mills
Stairs John, Hill's Corners
Mann & Hayes, Hoosville
Vanvort James G.   *Ephratah.*
Nellis Avon
Getman Rensselaer
Getman Chauncey
Davis M. O. & Sons   *Garoga.*
Smith & Dewey   *Johnstown.*
Matthews Henry B.
Heagle & Briggs
Miller Timothy W.
Getman Daniel
Edwards Daniel
Anderson Archibald
Burton & Wells
M'Laren & Dorn
M'Kinley Peter J.
Churchill H. & A. C., Gloversville
Burton E. L. & E. C.   do
Wooster & Street, Kingsboro
Potter Lucius F.   do
Simmons Marsellis, Vail's Mills
   Mayfield.
Major Joseph A., Vail's Mills
Brown John, Mayfield Corners
Getman David,   do
Fay W. O.   *Northampton.*
Smith F. & H. D.
Wood A.
Lefever & Van Valkenburgh,
   Northville
Spire Joseph F., Northville
Smith Benj.   do
Barker Fayette,   do
Cook Seth, Osborn's Bridge
Burr Geo. W.   *Oppenheim.*
Swartwout John
Benedict J. M.   *Perth.*
Davis James
Hays & Mann
Bartlett A. & Co.   *Stratford.*

Genesee County.

Williams R. B. & Co.   *Alabama.*
Strickland B. & Co. Oakfield
Moulton & Dirstine   *Alexander.*
Blodgett Heman
Marsh ——
Foote John   *Batavia.*
Wells Wm. H. & Son
Smith A.
Ley G. A.
Smith Nathan T.
Thorn & Holden
Hubbard E. F.   *Bergen.*
Fay Edward
Bushnell ——, North Bergen
Merrill ——   do
Doolittle J. D., West Bergen
Kendall Charles   *Bethany.*
Worthington Daniel L., East
   Bethany
Prindle Daniel R., East Bethany
Hall Charles B.   *Byron.*
Seaver J. W.
Mitchell James R.
Bean & Boynton, South Byron
Beecher J.   do
Biddle & Chapin   *Darien.*
M'Intyre & Madison
Harlow Augustus, Darien Centre
Jones Phillip F.   do
Stone A.   do
Harlow A. & Son,   do
Saunders Elisha C.   do
Raymond Wm. C. & Co.   *Elba.*
Dickey Gilman
Greenandyke R. A.   *Le Roy.*
Morgan & Jackson
Pratt Adam
Burton March & Co.   *Oakfield.*
Gibson James
Sprague W. M.   *Pavilion.*
Lauderdale J. & Co.
Cook C. W.   *Pembroke.*
Wright G. W. & Co. E. Pembroke
Porter H. F. & Co. Corfu
Darrow A. M.   do
March Samuel   *Stafford.*
English Charles

Greene County.

Strong D. B.   *Ashland*
Tuttle Albert
Tuttle D. & Son
Orson Jonas   *Athens.*
Bennett John
Van Loon Casper
Evarts George M.
Coffin John B.
Nicholas Sylvester
Foster James G.
Lyons James M.   *Cairo.*
Stephens Philander
Noble & Webster
Stevens Ezra M.
Cornwall Eliza
Osborn John R.
Jason Stevens
Thomas John, Acra
Gilbert Ebenezer   *Catskill.*
Ruland Barnet
Francis Samuel
Prindle Ezra J.
Greene Jacob R.
Pinckney & Korts
Coonwall Charles
Harris Samuel, Leeds
Whittlesey ——,   do
Miller B.   do
Bessack Wm. J.   *Coxsackie.*
Gay Thomas W.
Adams & Farmer
Stouterburgh Walton S.
Hubbell & Gay
Fitchett Peter
Raymond George
Reed G. & A.
Heermance W. V. B. & H.
Smith & Hamilton
Lampman Obadiah
Peck Henry J.   *Durham.*
Cleaveland Lyman E.

Pierce Amos *Durham.*
Tripp Alfred
Marks & Bradley
Cowles James H.
Dodge Andrew *Greenville.*
Ecklen James
Williamson John G.
Butler Aaron
Bentley Alexander N.
Wackerhager Edward
Stevens ——
Ramsdell Nehemiah
Hurtt James S.
Edwards W. H. *Hunter.*
Lockwood & Beachies
Kerr Robert R.
Kreisted J. H. & Co. East Kill
O'Hara B. & S. *Lexington.*
Haicott George W.
Hare Revilo, West Kill
Bushnell J. D. & E. P. & Co. West
   Kill
Bushnell & Inman, Bushnellsville
Chase West, East Lexington
Pratt D. & Co do
Peck & Hitchcock, do
Burtzol Francis, do
Sherman Joseph *New Baltimore.*
Haight Leonard
Raymond John
Hinman William
Allen Andrew
Humphrey Alvord T. *Prattsville.*
Monfort William
Gleason Lafayette
Fean Frederick A.
Cowles D. P.
Pitcher Dorlan
Meilgan ——
Robertson Elbert *Windham.*
Matthews & Haint
Potter & Phelps
Peck Erastus T. Big Hollow
Lake & Winters, Hensonsville
Bailey & Dedrich, do
Distin William S. do

Hamilton County.

Burritt Nelson B. *Lake Pleasant.*
Call Samuel
Burnett Franklin
Peck Richard
Weld William R.

Herkimer County.

Bernard Cyrus *Columbia.*
Lake Isaac
Plunk John P.
Kritzinger William *Danube.*
Simms & Moore
Green Z. & Co.
Kenyon V. S. *Fairfield.*
Buell & Mather
Gage A. S.
Stevens W. R. *Frankfort.*
Burton Dexter
Devendorf Chauncey
Dygert William
Stillwell & Marshall, Mohawk
   German Flats.
Smith S. C. & W. B. Mohawk
Devendorf Cornelius, do
Clark & Brim, do
Brown John F. do
Remington & Morgan, Ilion
Reese F. do
Dygert & Morgan, do
Rasbaen M. W. *Herkimer.*
Caswell Warren, jr.
Caswell Edwin
Bellinger & Morgan
Rusback & Quackenbush
Smith Nicholas
Beardslee & Hinds *Little Falls.*
Feeter James & Geo. A.
Bucklin James H.
Jones Henry B.
Sabin Daniel
Saunders J. G.
Gay & Snell
Lewis J.

Green George *Little Falls.*
Day A. *Litchfield.*
Hosford Mathew, Cedarville
Carryll & Cook *Manheim.*
Seely ——
Plants P. B. & Co. *Newport.*
Buckley & Wilson
Willard G. N.
Cady F. D.
Burlingame H. G.
Chasel Y. E.
Stebbens & Ives *Norway.*
Rust A.
Abub Albert *Ohio.*
Stanton F. & H. *Russia.*
Johnson Charles
Fellows Joel, Poland
Barker James, Cold Brook
Bounes Samuel, Postville
Carryl & Cook *Salisbury.*
Ives F. & Co.
Hopson James, Salisbury Centre
Pitt John C. do
Budlong Samuel *Schuyler.*
Gordon Ira
Hough Newton
Phillips Nelson S. Van Hornsville
   Stark.
Van Horn & Shumway, do
New Hope Manuf. Co. do
Hall John B. Starkville
Wightman C. D. & O. E. Jordan-
   ville *Warren.*
Hyde P. P. Jordanville
Kinne William, do
Crouse William, do
Porter & Cumming *Winfield.*
Catlin O.
Thomas L. G. & Co., W. Winfield
Foster N. do
Cameron W. do

Jefferson County.

Eddy, Whipple & Johnson *Adams.*
Salisbury & Bond
Whipple John H.
Smith & Bellden
Salisbury O. S. Smithville
M'Geagor M. do
Bliss & Gibbs, Adams Centre
Davis John, do
Davis Joseph, do
Harris & Loveland, do
Butterfield & White, Redwood
   Alexandria.
Dezeng & Co. Redwood
Suits & Hosford. Picasis
Corliss & George, do
Fuller & Thompson, Alexandria
   Bay
Walton & Co. Alexandria Bay
Corlis Lyman, do
Chapin A. *Antwerp.*
Fowle L. N.
Ellis J. P.
Bailey A. I. & Co.
Green J. N. & Co.
Payne & Freeman. Ox Bow
Cooper N. J. & E. F. do
Stevens O. *Brownville.*
Cathcard William A.
Bell George P.
Ontario Cotton Mills
Avery Charles B. Perch River
Wilson A. do
Smith ——, do
Bell James & Co. Dexter
Norton, M'Gunn & Beally, do
Ackley & Lawton, do
Tesher & Stobbins, do
Smith Levi, Limerick
Starkey C. P. *Cape Vincent*
Crevelln W. J. & Co
Bartlett R. C.
Harris W. W.
Harris Zebulon
Frary Russell
Cross & Hinckley
M'Niel & Spencer *Champion.*
Spencer A. H. & G. M.
Angel B. G. & Co. *Clayton.*

Rice L. J. & Co. *Clayton.*
Eggleston & Hale
Barker A. F.
Reade Thomas M.
Eddy A. L.
Ingles & Huntingdon, Depauville
Johnson S. P. do
Searles & Co. *Ellisburgh.*
Fisk A. T. & Co.
Waite & Hopkinson
Dickinson & Bigelow, Belleville
Bennington L. A. do
Durfee & Co. do
Grennell G. G. do
Sheffield & Co. Mannsville
Wardwell & Steele, do
Earl & Wilder, do
Wolley & Chapman *Henderson.*
Green Henry, jr.
Burnham Edwin
Sacket G. A. & Co. Sackett's Har-
   bor *Hounsfield.*
Buck Robert, Sackett's Harbor
Robbins R. E. do
Guiteau A. B. do
Day L. W. do
Gladwin G. & Co. do
M'Niel & Spencer, Great Bend
   Le Ray.
Potter Cicero, do
Cook A. M. Evans' Mills
Douglass & Palmer, do
Comstock W. G. do
Bingham Hiram, do
Brown Moses *Lorraine.*
Jones J. Miller's Bay *Lyme.*
Lamphere & Lyons, Three Mile
   Bay
Schuyler D. J. do
Day & Carlisle, do
Parker G. do
Wilcox and Son, do
Coy F. S. do
Smith & Inman, do
Hamblen A. C. do
Vincent W. do
Bushnell & Lamson, Lafargeville
   Orleans.
Dewey D J. do
Harger ——, Pamelia 4 corners
   Pamelia.
Pollock Pitcher *Philadelphia.*
Hatch S.
Weaver R.
Van Valkenburgh M.
Woodward C. D.
Sterling J.
Seaman A.
Strong Wm.
Hunt & West *Rodman.*
Handford W. R.
Moffatt Wm. H.
Wait T. & Co. East Rodman
Oaks Oscar S. South Rutland
   Rutland
Jones Wm. do
Hazelton Geo. W. Black River
Wheelock O. & Son, Felt's Mills
Howard J. R. do
Felt O. A. & S. do
Bennington & Atwell *Theresa*
Bullard & Walradt
Banney & George
Richardson Daniel W. *Watertown.*
Welch Abram
Wuckley A. J.
Vaughn Ray G.
Seligman J. & H.
Keeler & Fuller
Utley Albert M.
Lee & Hunt
Herrick William W.
Banister & Vincent
Campbell & Brayton
Utley Orrin C.
Upham & Sawyer
Hungerford Richard
Ely Adriel
Hawks William K.
Peck A. J.
Davis Joseph, Burrville
Collom Hiram, Carthage *Wilna.*

Fox Noah, Cartnage   *Wilna.*
Spencer Ambrose H. do
Kilburn Jared A.   do
Morrow James H.   do
West & Peck,   do
Johnson John B.   do
Ellis Archellus. Natural Bridge
Pool Abram,   do
Sanders Edson,   do

Kings County.

Provost Peter C. Green Point
                            Bushwick.
Denyson Isaac   *Flatbush.*
Lott Englebert
Schoonmaker Richard L.
Eldred A. East New York
Ackley N.   do
Smith Joseph,   do
Hendrickson John,   *Flatlands.*
Read Wilson
Lott John, Flatland Neck
Donly Bernadus   *Gravesend.*
Schoonmaker Martin
Wright Steadman   *New Utrecht.*
Cropsey Wm. W

Lewis County.

Rivet Joseph   *Croghan.*
Bardwell S. T.   *Denmark.*
Buck A.
Hurlburt E.
Van Vechten G. T.
Potter H. D. Copenhagen
Angle & Barker, do
Snell F. A.   do
Stephens A.   do
Ward E. & Co.   do
Farago Charles L.   *Diana.*
Williams & Lindsley, Branting-
    ham   *Greig.*
Edgebert F.   *Harrisburgh.*
Johnson E. R.   *Leyden.*
Foster Hiram
Howard & Williams
Wells George
Vrooman G.   *Lowville.*
Leonard C. P.
Leonard C. P. & Co.
Brown J.
Fowler & Mills
Lewis J. C.
Northrup F. W.
Doig A. W.
Benedict J.
Mappa J. & Co.   *Martinsburgh.*
King Wm.
Sheldon J. H.
Smith M.
Easton & Co. West Martinsburgh
Curtis C.   do
Leonard V. R.   do
Dagan Albert G.   *Turin.*
Thayer Harrison J.
Humason James J.
White Albert A.
Wilcox Jefferson
Foster Walter B.
Ragan Henry
Goff Selden, Houseville
Miller & Duff, Constableville
                       West Turin.
Goff & Miller,   do
Coyl P. C.   do
Pratt J. A., Collinsville
Thompson S. C. do

Livingston County.

Hawley W. C.   *Avon.*
Firman David
Sabin John
Chandler W. H. & L.
St. John Charles R., East Avon
Chadwick Josiah, South Avon
Brown & Burgess   *Caledonia.*
M'Donald Benjamin S.
Rockafellow Kingsbury, *Conesus.*
Ripley O.
Faulkner R. S.   *Dansville.*
Britton & Co.

M'Cartney D.   *Dansville.*
Bradner & Welch
M'Cartney & Edwards
Bryant & Co.
Hyland George
Brown & Welch
Barrett S. L.
Smith S. W.
Lord H. S. & J.
Brace E. B. & Son
Hess J. & H. H.
Matson N.
Brown M.
Beach J. T.
Newton Isaac   *Genesee.*
Walker William
Noyes R. G.
Turner L. & Co.
Metcalf E. P. & C.
Vance Charles R.
Cone & Birge
Aten John   *Groveland.*
Childs Oliver, Cuylerville
                       Leicester.
Bronson E. V.   do
Forbes & Noble, Moscow
Jones & Tilton,   do
Thompson Theodore, do
Carter & Parmelee   *Lima.*
Godfrey Ira
Clark & Draper
Pierce Charles P.   *Livonia.*
Palmer & Clark
Barnes M. S. & Co.
Bradner & Carroll, Hemlock Lake
Hill & Lemon,   do
Clark & Marks,   do
Stephens Elijah & E. R. do
Dixson R. & C. W.   do
Hastings Alonzo, South Livonia
Wells J. H.. Lakeville
Sleeper & Bingham *Mount Morris.*
Hinman Wheeler M.
Conkey R. R.
Ridsdale & Bailey
Miller David
Warner & Goodale
Richmond B. P.   *Nunda.*
Warner L. B.
Grover Silas
Whitcomb W.
Richardson J.
Houghton, Barrett & Co.
Coe & Crary
Fitch J. & G., Oakland *Portage.*
French S. W. & Co. Hunt's Hollow
Bradner L. & Co. Scottsburgh
                       Sparta.
Coller C. A.   do
Dyer Daniel E.   *Springwater.*
Clark & Bradner
Grove Harvey T.
Spinning William, Kyserville
                       West Sparta.
Passage Andrew, Byersville
Stower Samuel,   do
M'Donald David   *York.*
M'Pherson James
Dean & Beach
Casey & Grant, Fowlersville
Fraser William,   do
Dickey & Lawson, Graigsville
Jones J.   do
M'Pherson D. & Brothers, Piffar-
    dania

Madison County.

Bailey & Babcock   *Brookfield.*
Clark Maxon. jr.
Brownell Nathan
Crandall Thomas A.
Brand W. & N. V., Leonardsville
Crumb A. K.   do
Clark D., South Brookfield
Livern & Beebe, North Brookfield
Marsh Isaac,   do
Clark & Hobbie   *Cazenovia.*
Clark & Dunning
Ham & Gridley
Woodward Jonathan
Hough & Groff

Pulford, Sweetlands & Co.
                       Cazenovia.
Litchfield & Guitean
Lathrop Philetus, New Woodstock
Avery T. M.
Birdsell & Merchant   *De Ruyter.*
Rider J. R.
Jencks E. D.
Sutton George W.
Coleman N. T. & H.
Elmore J. N.
Walker S. G.
Coon J. A. & Co.
Butler & Burt   *Eaton.*
Coman Ellis
Felton David
Townsend Edward
Tillinghast C., Morrisville
Kingman L. M.   do
Lewis R. M. & H. do
Cloyes Hiram D.   do
Ayer & Phelps,   do
Barnett E. B.   do
Cleveland T. L.   do
Shepard Wm. J.   do
Chamberlin & Peet, Pratt's Hollow
Smith A. Y., Leeville
Darrow J. E.   do
Ferguson O. K.   *Georgetown.*
Clarke & Hobbie
Howe O. B. & Co   *Hamilton.*
Barker E. R. & Co.
Pierce & Cobb
Pearl E. & Co.
Mott Thomas S.
Rhodes & Slocum
Osgood & Whitman
Kershaw & Hyde, Earlville
Leavenworth E. W.
Peck Nathan, Poolville
Nash C. R. & Co. Hubbard's Cor's
Goodwin S. H. & Co. Oneida Depot
                       Lenox.
Rivenburgh & Thompson, do
Palmer P.   do
Davis D.   do
Hibbard T. M. & Co.   do
Soper & Tryon,   do
Crouse J. & D. Canastota
Wilson & Howell, do
Fiske & Messenger, do
Curtis F. B. & Co. do
Reese & Davis,   do
Smith & Gaul, Wampsville
Hill A.   do
Kirkland George T. Oneida Valley
Cady N. S. & D. Clockville
Hoppin C.   *Lebanon.*
Howard A. & Co.   *Madison.*
Root & Lewis
Lucas & Co.
Kershaw M. Solsville
Jackson Amasa, Erieville *Nelson.*
Donaldson John
Curtis J. G. Peterboro *Smithfield.*
Barnett James, do
Adkins C. A. & Co.   *Stockbridge.*
Wood David
Lewis Zachariah
Whedon Hiram
Abercrombie Wm. T.   *Sullivan.*
Goff L. Perryville
Marsh Spencer, Bridgeport
French A. J. & R. B. Chittenango
Sims & Bates,   do
Crouse James,   do
Jenkins & Harrington, do
Walrath James,   do
Beebe Lewis & Co. do

Monroe County.

Harmon & Mudge, South Chili
                       Chili.
Andrews Orson, Clarkson Corners
                       Clarkson.
Raymond Alonzo, Jenkins' Corner
                       Greece.
Raymond & Davis, do
Wilder A.   do
Phelps Alfred,   do
Walker E.   do
Holding D.   do

Jones J. B. East Henrietta
            Henrietta.
Wheeler B. West Henrietta
Holden T. H. East Mendon *Mendon.*
Sherwood A. do
Briggs R. Mendon Centre
Allen & Dixon, West Mendon
Ball Church & Co. Spencer's Basin
Morse & Brown, Parma Corners
            Parma.
Raymond A. B. Parma Centre
Hadley N. G. do
Lewis D. E. *Penfield.*
Corning & Chadwick, Fairport
            Perrinton.
Dickinson T. W. Fairport
Jameson, Willard & Co. Church-
ville *Riga.*
Smith Phineas A. 181 Buffalo st.
            Rochester.
King R. Graham, 206 State
Crosby & Danchy *Rush.*
Arnold E.
Hart H. B.
Seely J. A. 18 Main st. Brockport
            Sweden.
Hale & Whitteman, 20 Main
Whitney E. & Co. Main st.
Goold, Ganson & Co. 52 Main
Norton D. S. Main st.
Corning Wm. & Co. *Webster.*
Stearns N. & Co.
Andrews L. C. Scottsville
            Wheatland.
Edson F. M. do
Carpenter Ira, do
Hanford Wm. H. do
Garbutt J. W. Garbuttsville
Garbutt Philip, Mumford
Comstock A. O. & Co. do

Montgomery County.

Miller Cornelius *Amsterdam.*
Stewart John & Co.
Barnum E. H.
Dean Jehiel
Stewart Thomas
Bell James
Bell Harvey
Sturtevant Joseph W.
Warwick George
Green Wm. R. & Co.
Marselis A. Hagaman's Mills
Crane Abraham, Cranesville
Hull A. W. Tribe's Hill
Smith & Co. *Canajoharie.*
Betticher F. D.
Adams Wm.
French W. & Co.
Kittle George W.
Mumford T.
Reed Joshua
Richards T. M.
M'Master & Griffin
Bragdon & Wilson
Ehle Charles
Snell & Berry
Robinson C. G. Ames
Burrell M. do
Hamilton Samuel C., Buel
Brumley E. H. *Charleston.*
Davis A. J.
Eddy M. F.
Bowman J. J. Burtonville
Scott D. M. do
Frost J. S. Charleston Four Cor-
ners *Charleston.*
Carle H. do
Jackson William *Florida.*
Livingston Charles, Minaville
Cady J. & D. do
Witt William H. do
Newkirk Francis, Port Jackson
Schuyler J. J. & Co. do
Kline A. W. do
Able A. J. *Glen.*
Vischer & Van Denbergh
Brumley Oscar
Bigsby & Arganign, Fultonville
Mann James R. & W. A. do
Voorheese & Able, do

Stivin & Freeman, Fultonville
            Glen.
Van Alstine John A. Smith Town
Putnam Peter, do
Stillwell Elias, Fort Plain *Minden.*
Beekman D. do
Walrath Alfred, do
Reed Warren, do
Tingue Alexander, do
Haslet Peter, d)
Kooller Solomon. do
Tingue & Wagner, do
Life, Joel & Rufus, do
Shearer & Only do
Davis M. O. & Son, Fonda
            Mohawk.
Gates Perry, do
Fonda D. H. do
Fisher & Dochstader, do
Kline James W. do
Baker William, Palatine Bridge
            Palatine.
M'Master & Guffin. do
Jukes Thomas, Stone Arabia
Bowdish John *Root.*
Hoag Stephen
Vrooman Barney
Lyker C. H.
Hoag Ira
Barns John, jun. Flat Creek
Spraker D. Sprakers' Basin *Root.*
Cohen Aaron, do
Haight S. R. *St. Johnsville.*
Adams George H.
M'Alister Charles
Wilsey R. C. & Co.
Butler W. J. & Co.

New York County.

Dodge John P. Harlem

Niagara County.

Schmeck Samuel & Co. Pekin
            Cambria.
Pells William H. *Hartland.*
Jamieson A. J.
Campbell Angus *Lewiston.*
Hotchkiss William
Whitman John L.
Hotchkiss & Scovill
Bairato A. S. & Co.
Cornell Nelson
Kelsey & Loucks, Pekin
Marks S. H. *Lockport.*
Nelson & Vampton
Dole & Shepherd
Dunlap W. J.
Keep W. & Co.
Davis G. W.
Shaeffer J.
Wilkinson & Chryslen
Shoemaker George
Elliott & Pearson
Thayer J.
Metz H.
Plate James
Lilienthat & Nettre
Vail, Mitchell & Co.
Storrs O. & Co.
Eshbaugh Henry *Newfane.*
Olcott D. T.
Hawley P. D.
Cooper J. D. Olcott
Wright & Outwater
Woodruff R. H. *Niagara Falls.*
Callahan J. G.
Walsh M.
Lewis William R. *Pendleton.*
Belenger Simon
Simons Austin
Doll & Emerson, Youngstown
            Porter.
Davis J. & Co.
Holland Robert
Hotchkiss George C.
Marshall James
Lane Alexander
Clark E. M. & Co *Royalton.*
Duulap Thomas, Middleport
Craig John, do
Baker Alden S. do

Calwell & Sleeper, Gossport
            Royalton.
Herrington ———, Orange Port
Pratt Francis O. *Somerset.*
Matthewas James
Taylor Christopher L.
Wilson Luther
Baldy J. B. & L. B.

Oneida County.

Jarvis & Seaton *Annsville.*
Larabee J.
Kenyon & Church, Oriskany Falls
            Augusta
Buckingham D. P. Oriskany Falls
Hungerford & Wright, do
Hawley H. do
Knox J. J. do
Bamber A. & T. *Boonville.*
Cross & Treat
Warner & Wait
Bamber R.
Tinsley J.
Douglass & Owens
White L. Alder Creek
Churchill J. do
Manning D. *Bridgewater*
De Wolf S.
Blivin A. & Sons
Babcock P.
Osborn E. P. *Camden.*
Trowbridge A.
Tracy J. H.
Spencer T.
Hinckley A. H.
Fifield F. & Co.
Curtis A.
Miner Brothers
Barnes A. W.
Morgan J. E. & T. E. *Deerfield.*
Leland J. D. & Co.
Davis J. H. North Gage
Dorrence D. G. & Co. *Florence.*
Davis L. S. & Co.
Cowles Junius A.
Wilcox & Empey, East Florence
Hale & Clark *Floyd.*
Mills R., Franklin *Kirkland.*
Parmelee & Co. do
Kinney O. B. Clinton
Cook J. L. & J. S. do
Hart C. E. Manchester
Pixley & Wetmore
Fake P. & Son, Clinton
Butler B. do
Stokes C. *Lee.*
Kenyon O.
Cornish A.
Taft V.
Walworth E. Delta
Elmer E. do
Elmer, Phillips & Co. do
M'Gregory H., Stokes
Mitchell & Co. West Branch
Hanchett J. Deansville *Marshall.*
Barker G. W. do
Baxter E.
Lyon S. *New Hartford.*
Butler Francis
Carpenter J.
Grannis F. W.
Savage F. S. Sauquoit *Paris.*
Davis J. L. do
Everett E. do
Budlong C. A. & Co. Cassville
Lord & Mott, Clayville
Owen & Jones *Remsen.*
Ray E. & Co.
Howe & Co.
White William
Billings & Owens
Roberts ———
Mudge, Langford & Co. Dominick
st. *Rome.*
Hill Brothers, do
Armstrong J. & E. B. & Co.
            James st.
Hayden H. & Co. James st.
Northrop & Ethridge, Parker's
Building
Cady D. & Co. Dominick st.
Parker & Mudge, do

Tower H. D. & Son, Waterville
 Sangersfield
Putnam & Damon, do
Stafford J. W. & W. B. do
Clark & Newell, do
Candee & Osborn, do
Mott G. & H. do
Roberts M. Steuben.
Greenfield J.
Billings & Co. Holland Patent
 Trenton.
Fox C. F. do
Candy & Meigs, do
Wells R. do
Tyler C. Stittsville
Douglass T. J. & Co. Trenton Village
How & Billings, do
Watkins G. W. Prospect
Watkins C. do
Johnson G. B. & J. do
Rowley & Currey, South Trenton
Watkins C. Varick st. Utica.
Case's S. Sons Vernon.
Ingersoll & Bell
Nye & Fuller
Foot & Pitcher, Vernon Centre
Williams J. L. do
Welton Thomas J. do
Leet H. do
Maltby N. Verona.
Leet H. N.
Rathbun A. New London
Williams C. do
Rathbun S. Rathbunsville
Crous & Clement, Durhamville
Fox & Gregory. do
M'Cune F. S. M'Connellsville
 Vienna.
Wood Charles, do
Wilcox T. A. do
Kerr Mrs. A. do
Conant A. North Bay
Brayton H. M. & G. Westernville
 Western.
Brayton & Ely, do
Jones G. W. do
Greenfield M. do
Brill D. & Son. North Western
Nolton T. Lowell Westmoreland.
Kellogg & Brother, Hampton
Brown & Brother, do
Peck T. B. do
Gross & Jenkins Whitestown.
Balis George
Steadman William, Whitesboro
Bradley H. do
Griswold & Co. do
Smith A. do
Montgomery A. & Co. do
Symonds F. do
Brown H. do
Balis D. G. Oriskany
Lovell & Boddy, do
Blanchard E. F. do
Hoag N. H. New York Mills
Hoag S. do
Wood W. W. do
M'Collum J. do
Swartwout, Golden & Higgins do

Onondaga County.

Car J. & Son Cicero.
Cushion S.
Warren S.
Markham & Bennett, Brewerton
Cushion A. do
Green & Loomis Clay.
Powell O.
Freeman J., Euclid
King J. & A. De Witt.
Wood A. & Co. Elbridge.
Sherwood & Co.
Daggett H. B. & Co. Jordan
Dales J. do
Moulton H. C. do
Graves C. G. do
Thomas W. R. & Co. do
Hall H., Peru
Corbin S. H. Fabius.
Litchfield & Bacon

Pope O. & Co. Fabius.
Paige & Hubbell Geddes.
Vrooman E.
Spaulding & Stewart
Price M. F. La Fayette.
Davison A. Cardiff
Gilbert ——, do
Spencer J. do
Betts C. Lysander.
May E. Manlius.
Remington H
Smith C.
Gage H. H
Rhodes E.
Mahee J.
Beard B. C. & H. Fayetteville
Cronse Brothers & Co. do
Blanchard & Jewett, do
Seymour, Pratt & Co. do
M'Viccar & Co. do
Easton Charles D. Onondaga.
Bosworth H. S., South Onondaga
Gilbert S. do
Patterson A. Onondaga Hollow
Smith W. G. Otisco.
Searl A.
Adams A., Amber
Beard H. L. Pompey.
Bartlett A. jr.
Southward D. G. Pompey Centre
Taylor J. M., Delphi
Bates I. do
Dana M Water st. Syracuse
 Salina.
Childs N. M. Salina st. Syracuse
Freeman A. Exchange st. do
Lynch J. & Sons, do do
M'Carthy J. Park Av.
Avery F. S.
Corbin Z.
Corbin J.
Jaqueth S.
Hicks J. F.
Gleason L.
Allis C. W. & Co. Skaneateles.
Brinkerhoff A.
Roundy & Hurlbut Spafford.
Woodward J.
Anderson Thomas B., Borodino
Legg W do
Trowbridge & Arnold Tully.
Gillett O. A.
Hall J. B.
King H. F. & A. & L.
Earle & Clark, Vesper
Patten William, do
Glass J. J. Van Buren.
Larkin J.

Ontario County.

Francis S. Bristol.
Andrews N. C.
Case Oliver, Bristol Centre
Cook C. J. do
Branard L. J. do
Secom Canadice.
Spring Daniel Canandaigua.
Mosher C. & J.
Hart & Murray
Daniels Albert
Stannard Andrew J.
Bettman & Co.
Gorham N.
Field & Graves
Hyde Evander
Webster & Morgan
Ballentine & Duncan
Richardson & King
Smith Seneca
M'Ketchnie J. & A.
Mitchell J. W. East Bloomfield.
Porter & Hough
Yamens M. Manchester.
Cole N. K.
Wells ——, Port Gibson
Beardsley E. & Co. Phelps.
Swift George & Co.
Ford O. B.
Redfield L.
Harton C.
Bentley Perry, Allen's Hill
 Richmond.

Gilbert Edwin, Honeoye
 Richmond.
Gregory M. M. do
Pierce Evelyn, do
Pierpont D. A. & O. E. Honeoye
Teal J. C. P. & Co. Geneva Seneca.
Becker V. do
Backenstoe John, do
Hemieup & Cone, do
Morris C. L. do
Stevens J. V. B. Seneca Castle
Runyon & Holly, do
Cook Moses, do
Devaraux H. do
Wilcox & Brace So th Bristol.
Dunton W. J.
Dickinson A. P. Victor.
Simons & Lewis
Peck Solon West Bloomfield.
Peck & Leach

Orange County.

Van Allen R. & Co. Salisbury
 Mills Blooming Grove.
Walsh M. Salisbury Mills
Hunter Wm. B. Craigville
Jaques John, Washingtonville
Warner Robert S. do
Moffat Charles E. do
Tuthill. Seely & Johnson Chester.
Barnes N.
Smith I.
Yelverton & Thompson
Masterton William
Cocks W. & C. Cornwall.
Lewis James
Clarke Nathan
Barrett James M.
Chadrayne Henry F
Nelson C. Buttermilk Falls
Berard & Mearns, do
Denton James, do
Dewitt J. Port Butler West Point
Taylor O. & Co. Crawford.
Smith & Hornbeck
Morrison John
Durkey D. G.
Wallace Wm. W. Bullville
Noble Wm. C. Hopewell
Marvin F., Port Jervis Deer Park.
Wilkins W. do
Cuddeback & Wheat, Port Jervis
Mondon N. L. & Brother, do
Van Fleet & Godfrey, do
Hilferty D. do
Bennett William H. do
Conklin J. do
Farnum H. H. do
Reeve C. W. Goshen.
Jennings N.
Newman H. C.
Sayer William M.
Popino L. W.
Crane & Wallace
Wallace H.
Brown Henry Hamptonburgh.
Faulkner Samuel
Everett J. Minisink.
Brown O. J.
Webb E. A. Ridgbury
Gregory E. Howell's Depot
Horton A. J. do
Winfield M., Well's Corners
Pauley T. do
Hatch William, Westown
Smith L. L. Unionville
Adams & Pierson, do
Chermar & Coleman Montgomery.
Neil Henry V.
Bookstaver A.
Sears James W.
Fuguett John B.
Hill Marcus K. Walden
Knapp E. W. do
Weller George, do
Neafie Henry F. do
Burtholf J. H. Monroe.
Knight C. B.
Seaman William
Tenbrycke M. F. Monroe Works
M'Farlan H. do

Turner P. Turner's Depot *Monroe.*
Dodge, Mullock & Co. Otisville
Corwin G. L. *Mount Hope.*
Jackson A. W.
Seybolt & Co. Otisville
Jessup T. & Co. 67 Water *Newburgh.*
Cornwell G. & Son. 69 Water
Gerow L. & Co. 101 Water
Carver Daniel, 101 Water
Colvill William, 112 Water
Jamison John. 56 Water
Reeve & Smith, 68 Water
Wood Isaac. jr. 70 Water
Haight Stephen, 74 Water
Smith & Booth, 82 Water
Masters John C. 87 Water
Parmelee & Robinson, 96 Water
Bebee William H.
Halsted Charles, jr. 26 Water
Carpenter J. *New Windsor.*
Tyler & Stanbrough
Vail John D.
Bradner J. S. Scotchtown *Wallkill.*
Phillips H. New Hampton
Gardiner S. F. & Co. do
Tyler L. H. do
Denton T. J. & G. W. do
Carpenter J. A. do
Payne J. do
Shaw & Hanford, S. Middletown
Little & Evans, do
Hoyt J. W. do
Vail L. do
Denton & Murry do
Van Duzer V. *Warwick.*
M'Ewen M.
Cowdry J.
Roe J.
Vail R. C. *Amity*
M'Daniel G. W. do
Hoyt Isaac. do
Carpenter J. do
Roe G. W. Edenville
Gale T. New Milford
Demarest & Vandervoort
Halleck D. & W. Sugar Loaf
Aspell A. V. Florida
Smith Z. W. & C. do
Vail W. L. do
Aspell C. J. & Co. do

Orleans County.

Swan & Cornwall, Albion *Barre.*
Sipes George, do
Sickels G. H. & Co. do
Palmer & Beckwith, do
Thompson A. J. do
Fanning T. C. do
Hazen James, do
Berry C. R. do
Joslyn & Abeel, do
Potter C. S. do
Baker Hiram, do
Springsteen F. E. do
Harrington C. A. & Co. do
Herrick & Crane, Barre Centre
Matison Benjamin, do
Garbutt E. H. *Carlton.*
Cochrane & Bentley
Sherwood T *Clarendon.*
Copeland B. & G. M.
Tenny Ansel *Gaines.*
Stone Alanson
Danolds C. A. & D. H. Eagle Harbor
Peet, De Groff & Co. *Kendall.*
Aplain N.
Webster S. & E. K. Kendall Mills
Frisbey Hiram S. Holley *Murray.*
Buell Hiram A. & Co. Holley
Roblee Morgan J. do
Reid & Hine, Hulburton
Hines Joel, Hinesburgh
St. Clair ——, Sandy Creek
Hopkins M. P. Medina *Ridgeway.*
Baker William P. & D. Medina
Burrows I. K. do
Dunlap & Newull, do
Craig Joseph, do

Fairman Bottsford, Medina *Ridgeway.*
Wilcox T. S. do
Milies F. M'Martin, Knowlesville
Davis Oliver, do
Bolk & Perkins, do
Kirkham T. do
Pell Wm. H. Ridgeway Corners
Castle R. S. & Co. *Shelby.*
Rockwell, Colt & Co. *Yates.*
Mead John
Saxe Peter
Babcock & Parmelee, Lyndonville
Bowen S. C. & Co.

Oswego County.

Boom John *Albion.*
Comstock Samuel A.
Gibson James T.
Stillwell Geo. W.
Coats W. Amboy Centre *Amboy.*
Carter J. & R. Carterville
Miller Robert, West Amboy
Mooar Jason *Constantia.*
Perkins C. A.
Winchester R.
King Wm. H.
Fanner & Brown, Cleaveland
Aspell J. do
Potter A. do
Marble Cyrus, do
Peabody D. do
Willard J. E. & Co. Oswego Falls *Granby.*
Dodge Alanson, Oswego Falls
Mann John, do
Brewster S. W. *Hannibal.*
Bent S.
Brackett & Hewlett, Hannibal Centre
Devendorff L. F. *Hastings.*
Whitman J.
Conde Henry S. Central Square
Dodge P. S. do
Lewis B. G. do
Adams C. W. do
Baum L. S. do
Parkhurst J. do
Waterbury P. do
Newell M. *Mexico.*
Burrough J. M. & Co.
Stowe S. H. & B. S.
Peck & Conklin
Webb Henry
Whitney & Forsyth
Butler R. A.
Markham & Webb, Colosse
Whitney O. H. do
Andros Chester, Union Square
Merriam S. G. *New Haven.*
Allen S. O.
Strong Nathan *Orwell.*
Olmstead O. B.
Andrews Allen, 1st st. *Oswego.*
Reed Walter do
Beattie J. & N. do
Moore & Smith, Bridge st.
Allen S. O & Co. Hart's Build'gs, Bridge st.
Sacket Lewis, 7 Eagle Block
Mack & Co. 3 Central Bl'k, 1st st.
Wallace E. L. Jennings Corner *Palermo.*
Jennings David, jr. do
Place M., Vermillion
Ford & Allen *Parish.*
Russell Morton
Dimmock Daniel *Redfield.*
Jones & M'Carty, Pulaski *Richland.*
Angell & Seeley, do
Wright & Crawford, do
Bond G. W. & Co. do
Sikes & Goodwin, do
Clark James A. do
Wardwell N. M. do
M'Chesney Jas. A. Port Ontario
Dewey Samuel, South Richland
Rice John P., Phœnix *Schroeppel.*
Putnam Wm. R. do
Sweet A. R. & Co. Phœnix
Hale Marshall do

Humphrey & Hanchett, Phœnix *Schroeppel.*
Savage, Titus & Co. do
Murphy Stephen, Gilbert's Mills
Hale M. & Co. Hinmansville
Perine & Betts. do
Stone H. & F. S. *Scriba.*
Jerrett Eben
Phillips & Schenck, Fulton *Volney.*
Phillips & Lusk, do
Parsons J. R. do
Comstock Charles, do
Marsh A. &. Co. do
Moore N. F. do
Fullerton R. & Co. do
Case J. & S. F. do
Tucker Charles P. do
Clough Hamilton, do
Tucker & Knox, do
Gardiner De Witt, do
Tucker Almon, do
Kenyon G. P. do
Tucker J. C. & S. N. do
Wood & Spicer, do
Griswold Samuel, Hull's Corners
Godfrey Wm. J. *Williamstown.*
Herding William
Burdick Austin
Freeman M. H.
Humphrey & Dodge

Otsego County.

Peck & Brothers *Burlington.*
Moss T. West Burlington
Hemenway & Smith, West Burlington
Simmons George, do do
Arnold A. E. do do
Lawrence George R. Burlington Flats
Park A., Burlington Green
Russell Dorr, do
Lull & Gilbert *Butternuts.*
Moore & Perry
Browne & Co.
Wilkins S. *Cherry Valley.*
Duffin Wm. W.
Robinson L.
Lewis M.
Laue & Dickinson
North & Brown
Platner W.
Allen G.
Hall G. & W.
Giles & Co.
Lansing J. E. *Decatur.*
Caryl Leonard
Storrs John
Chamberlain E. *Edmeston.*
Waldo E. & Son
Smith M., South Edmeston
Spurr Daniel H. & Co. do
Sheldon, Hazard & Co. West Edmeston
Arnold Otis B. & Co. do
Jones Wm. P. *Exeter.*
Harp & Brooks, Schuyler's Lake
Matteson H. A., West Exeter
Huntley E. do
Newton & Chapel *Hartwick.*
Harrington C. L.
Bissell F. H.
Wilcox Thomas
Comstock Wm. *Laurens.*
Strong & Dean
Fields Wm. P.
Steere E. B.
Knight C. W.
Carpenter N. O. *Maryland.*
Chase Geo. W.
Thompson John T.
Slingerland, Cass & Co. Schenevas
Brown Amos H. do
Flint Amos, do
Gilbert L. M. & B. M. *Middlefield.*
Parshall & Slawson
North & Brown
Briggs George L.
Fowler George R.
Eston Stephen *Milford.*
Spofford & Winsor

King H. *Milford.*
Winsor D.
Steere A. C. & Co.
Moore & Perry
Peck George I. *New Lisbon.*
Stetson John S.
Harrington D.
Dickerman J.
Ford E. R. & Son *Oneonta.*
Brown E. S. & Co.
Shepherd & Osborne
Huntington S. & C. P.
Yager D. I. & Co.
Smith M. F.
Smith & Broadfoot *Otego.*
Follett S. R. & Co.
Austin C. R.
Hunt H.
Cole & Olmstead
North C. *Otsego.*
Johnson W. P.
Story J. H. Cooperstown
Ernst G. W. do
Leek Thomas B. do
Cockett J.
Nellis J. H.
Childs C. *Oaksville.*
Spafford J. C. *Pittsfield.*
Arkwright M. & Co.
Babcock Henry H. *Plainfield.*
Brewer P.
Lewis R.
Osborne S. *Richfield.*
Hosford M. K.
Elwood A. R.
Babcock O.
Vaughan J. D.
Bigelow Wm. L. *Springfield.*
Gray & Davy
Dutcher D.
Smith P.
Hayes Clark I. *Unadilla.*
North Samuel
Packard Edward M.
Watson Arnold B.
Watson & Hays
White F. A. & C. J.
Williams A. D. & Co.
Sterling Isaac, Unadilla Centre
Searls & Sterling, do
Searls Fitch, do
Griggs John R. *Westford.*
Rosobome & Jackson
Bigelow & Wright *Worcester.*
Cook John & Wm.
Lamoure Isaac
Caryl Leonard
Clark Almon B.
Chamberlain John B.
Hayden J. L. East Worcester
Bigelow E. B. & Son, do
Thurber E. R. & D. W. do
Becker A. South Worcester
Gott & Burroughs, E. Worcester
Caryl & Hayden, do

Putnam County.

Cole M. J. *Carmel.*
Clausen & Hazen
Ladington G. *Kent.*
Boyd B.
Smalley J.
Townsend H. Farmer's Mills
Smith & Townsend, do
Doughty G. W. do
Hoyt J. C. *Patterson.*
Cowles & Son
Cowles & Patrick
Banks N. O.
Rogers J. T.
Hayt H. & R. S.
Crosby H.
Dikeman J. W. Towner's Corner
Goodsell C. R. Cold Spring
Phillipstown.
Woods W. do
Nelson & Couch, do
Wells W. H. do
Southard J. G. do
Ladue A. H. do
Baxter E. C. do

Ferris & Sears, Cold Spring
Phillipstown.
Wright & Riggs, do
Deavenport W. & Son, Cold Spring
Mangan S. S. do
Brinkerhoff B. H. do
Goodsell & Nelson, do
Croft M. *Putnam Valley.*
Tompkins A.
Perry W.
Tompkins J.
Roberts J. B. & Co. *Southeast.*
Brush F.
Read D. & Co
Foster E.
Crane J. L. & Co.
Denton S.

Queens County.

Smith A. C. *Flushing.*
Griffin & Peck
Leonard William
Clement & Bloodgood
Lowerel J. M.
Lowerel Samuel G.
Peck & Fairweather
Peck Isaac & Son
Snediker S. C. & J. & Co.
Hempstead.
Stevens J. H.
Weeks, Pine & Co.
Smith M. Rockville
Pearsall Wright, Rockaway
Denton Oliver S. do
Pettit Robert, do
Tappen George, Millburn
Andrews Thomas, Far Rockaway
Hewlett N. Near Rockaway
Raynor Benj. R. Raynor Town
Charlick Willett, do
Smith Willett. do
Smith Julius, Merrick
Johnson Martin J. & Co. *Jamaica.*
Brush Richard
Thraner & Smith
Rider James & Co.
Woolley S. T. & Brother
Mills & Anthony
Skidmore & Jaggar
Rhodes R. P. East Jamaica
Brush Thomas, Brushville
Bergen Jacob L. do
Nostrand J. W. Forster's Meadow
Lawrence & Bush *Newtown.*
Van Alst John I.
Moore C. L.
Schenck John R. Roslyn
North Hempstead.
Bogart Daniel, jr. Roslyn
Valentine Wm. M. do
Kirby Jacob M. do
Kirby Caleb, do
Willis Wm. H. do
Mitchel Wm. A., Manhasset
Baxter Israel H. Cow Neck
Havens John K. Great Neck
Pool Samuel H. Lakeville
Duryea Hewlett, do
Lewis Elias, jr. Westbury
Hendrickson & Fleet, Hempstead
Branch
Titus & Chapman, Cow Neck
Sammis & White *Oyster Bay.*
Ludlam James M.
Parish Richard L.
Vernon C. & J. East Norwich
Albion Jacob, Jericho
Carll Joel, do
Weeks Wm. M. & W. do
Frost & Mount, do
Coles Isaac, do
Craft Peter, do

Rensselaer County.

Whitford J. & Co. *Berlin.*
Dennison D. E. & Co.
Culver J. A.
Albertson P. *Grafton.*
Tilley John
Scriven C. W.
Lansing William *Greenbush.*
Brown ——

Gaines William *Greenbush.*
Warner E.
Dearestyne & Brothers
Parsons H. K. & Co. *Hoosick.*
Thayer A. & Son
Powell William
Fisk R. & Son
Russell A. & Co
Hewks H
Rayner William C.
Armstrong J.
Jaques E. *Nassau.*
Van Valkenburgh Smith
Watkins L. S.
Tifft & Thomson
Tifft J.
Wilbur K. & Co.
Davis K. M. East Nassau
Lewis & Lester, do
Norton G. W. do
Hemenway & Son, East Nassau
Ambler S. do
Scrivens & Co. *Petersburgh.*
Reynolds, Phillips & Co.
Eldred P. W.
Brimmer G.
Carpenter G. W. *Pittstown*
Miller G.
Jenkins C.
Tyler M. R.
Miller J. F.
Perry T.
Barry C. H.
Chapman ——
Reed D. *Poestenkill.*
Gregory J. E.
Hymes E. S.
Barber G.
Harrington G.
Fox A. R. S. H. *Sandlake.*
Tourtellott Wm. C.
Page P.
Arnold & Wight
Shipley H., West Sandlake
Snyder Wm. H. do
Lown L. M. do
Boyce J. do
Briggs Amos & Co. *Schaghticoke.*
Smith E.
Briggs N.
Baker C.
Smith J. D. *Schodack.*
Hogeboom & Schermerhorn
Seaman N.
Van Hoozen J.
Loster N.
Brown R. A. *Stephentown.*
Wheeler C. H.
Sweet & Reynolds
Cane William R.
Latham J.
Coleman I. B.
Carpenter A.
Clements S. G. 62 Congress *Troy.*
Grant & Bulson, 53 do
Lamb & Start, 71 do
Harris Edmond S. 68 do
Mellery P. S. & A. 70 do
Barnhart H. 76 do
Allen Daricus, 80 do
Felton & Briggs, 82 do
Main James T. 104 do
Hicks & Mattison. 86 do
Powers L. & J. 89½ do
Marston & Stone, 95 do
Graham Charles, 162 3d
Thalimer Peter, (nail factory)
Main J. T. do

Richmond County.

Delvin T., Tompkinsville
Castleton.
Wandel Walter I. do
Thompson J. C. do
Degroot Jacob, Factoryville
Snedeker J. W. do
Townley J. do
Thompson E., New Brighton
Johnson J., Richmond *Northfield.*
Stevens S. D. do
Cole G. A., Rossville *Westfield.*
Cole Henry, do

Seguine H. Rossville   *Westfield*
La Forge H.   do
La Forge S. J. do

Rockland County.

Tompkins C. & Co. *Haverstraw.*
Marks E. & A.
Denoyelles & Gurnee
Marks A. & Co.
Sherwood George
Gerow O. C.
Knapp S.
Knight Wm. M. & H.
Foster Thomas
Blauvelt John G., Piermont
      Orangetown.
Taulman P. H., Piermont
Ackerson D. F., Nyack
Perry & Clark,   do
Smith D. D. & T.   do
Clark Daniel M.   do
Applebay E.   do
Demarest D. D.   do
Hoffman M.   do
Servant J., Piermont
Blauvelt J. I., Tappan Village
Requa James H.   do
Devor William,   do
De Clark David, Nanuet
Demerest D. P.   do
Dederer J., Blanveltville
De Baun G., Spring Valley
De Baun J. I.   do
Wood J.   do
Tallman P. D.   *Ramapo.*
Tallman Tunis I.
Gurnee J.
Secor John I.
Johnson A., Munsey
Cassedy A.   do
Ten Eyck J. W., Suffren Depot
Sloat J. & Co., Sloatsburgh

St. Lawrence County.

Morse Harvey D. & Co. *Brasher.*
Agerton Orvis D. & Co.
Hulbert Calvin T.
Taylor Henry & Co.
Cruser Jonas
Alexander & Skinner
Nevin David
Goff Ephraim C.   *Canton.*
Barnes John L.
Miner & Wood
Cooke Christopher
Mack & Robinson
Gibson Philo
Caldwell Theodore
Rich M., Richville   *De Kalb.*
Barber M. do
Barber & Chandler   *Depeyster.*
Pickett J. B.   *Edwards.*
Martin William
Shaw E., South Edwards
Abbott E. W.   *Fowler.*
Fuller & Peck
Sheldon & Co
Sterling & Co.   *Gouverneur.*
Egert A. S. & C. P.
Bond William
Barnes E. S.
Morse Abel P   *Hammond.*
Rood Daniel B.
Consall James H.
Smith, Griffin & Co.
Cain John P.
Childs Mark A.
Maddock & Learned   *Hermon.*
Cook & Bingham
Manley A. S. & Co.
Culver Z. & Son   *Hopkinton.*
Kellogg & Wright
Chittenden C. S. & A. H.
Carpenter & Blish   *Lawrence.*
Sanders & Barnard
Whiting & Mead
Hulburd & Underhill
Newland Jacob
Barnard William
Lavery Levi
Lawrence N. D. Nicholville
Day Lyman,   do

Wilson Benjamin F   *Lisbon.*
Moore N. D.   *Louisville.*
M'Mailin ——
Britton D.
Cooper A. B.   *Macomb.*
Covel Russell
Goss Austin J., Columbia *Madrid.*
Goss Alfred,   do
Dart Henry,   do
Feller John A.   do
Cogswell J.   do
Rutherford T. & Sons, do
Dodds George, Waddington
Redington James,   do
Orvis David A.   do
Rutherford Thomas,   do
Harper & Dezelle,   do
M'Martin A.   do
Phillips A. B.   *Massena.*
Ransom & Clark
Hawkins H. Massena Point
Mears A. Racket River
Allen & Balch, Massena Springs
Moore N. D. Lewisville
M'Martin ——, do
Chapman G. A. & Co. *Morristown.*
Ford C.
Hindmarsh P. W. & Co.
Canfield S.
Hitchins Leonard
Brewer John, Edwardsville
Bradley H. & Co.   *Norfolk.*
Sackrider Norman
Dimmick Charles
Hall G. J.
Putnam Daniel C.
Sackrider E. W.
Sackrider Christian
Dix Samuel, Ford st. Ogdensburgh
      Oswegatchie.
Jones & Wells, Ford st.
Angel William H. Water st.
Burns R. M. Ford st.
Cadier A. G.   do
Seymour George & Sons, do
Hobert S.   do
Allen E. B. & Sons, Water st.
Brooks E. D.   *Parishville.*
Oliver S. P.
Smith A. S.
Flower & Gilbert
Kilsey C. & Co.
Welch Martin   *Pierpont.*
Welch Russell
Paul E. R.   *Pitcairn.*
Cox Charles,   *Potsdam.*
Goulding William M.
Leet Charles W.
Goulding & Leet
Clark Theodore
Clark Henry J.
Clark J. & Son
Sanford Wm. A.
Clark Samuel P.
Munson Royal H.
Smith Abiel M.
Peck Hiram H.
Peck Comer H.
Peck & Brother
Larned William Z.
Larned Charles R.
Larned & Co.
Partridge Samuel H.
Redway Harvey N.
Partridge & Redway
Barroughs John & Calvin
Moorel Truman, W. Potsdam
Bentley Franklin
Moore & Bentley
Hemingway O. & A.
Skeels Albert M.
Hunt Truman, Crary's Mills
Goodrich J.   *Russell.*
Halsted R. H.
Dustin D.   *Stockholm.*
Ashley R.
Holmes Curtis
Hurlburd H. & Co.
Chapman D. & Co.

Saratoga County.

Belding Hiram   *Charlton.*

Sweetman J. A.   *Charlton.*
Callaghan M. B.
Waldraf John B.   *Clifton Park.*
Beal George W.
Sherwood Harvey
Rogers Harvey H. Halfmoon
Mitchell Smith L. Jonesville
Cole Nelson, Rexford Flats
Hegeman C. C. Vischers' Ferry
Chadsey ——,   do
Visches Garrett,   do
Mallory Zina   *Corinth.*
Davis Joseph
Houghton T. J. & Co.
Martin M. A. & Co.
Sims Benj. F.
Barker John   *Edinburgh.*
Snedicar Christopher
Vanderburgh Abram
Thompson & Davis   *Galway.*
Foster H. C. & Co.
Freeman & Blanchard
Masters M.
Bidwell Reuben
Major James
Muin & M'Kindley
Gearn William, Greenfield Centre
      Greenfield.
Weeden R. C. & J.
Dake Calvin W. West Greenfield
Young Sydney, do.
Freeman Hiram S. Jamesville
Angell E. Porters' Corners
Eddy & Scott, Weeds' do
Rockwell J.   *Hadley.*
Rockwell E. L.
Kenyon George
Wait David & Co.
Conklin Gordon
Noxon A. & Wiley   *Halfmoon.*
Noxon James
Philo N. G.
Burtis R. & Co.
Wakeman & Wait, Ballston Spa
      Milton.
Booth Wheeler K. Ballston Spa
Lee & Mann,   do
Bristol L. W.   do
Bushnell & Slocum   do
Town A. & N. F.   do
Garrett A. D. W.   do
Clapp R. P. & Co.   do
Mann A. A.   do
Sprise Robt. West Milton
Young Noah S. do
Chapman & Johnson, Ballston
Van Ostrand H.   do
Hopkins & Dix, Glenn's Falls
      Moreau.
Hopkins H. K. Glenn's Falls
Wilcox T. Portville
Harriss John, Gansevoort
      Northumberland.
Balou S. S.   *Providence.*
Richardson P. Schuylerville
      Saratoga.
Cramer James P.   do
Dillingham S. H. & T. N. Schuy-
      lerville
Losee H.   do
Mott C. F.   do
Vandercook O.   do
Lockwood E. Victory
Wood & Vail, do
Chapman E. & Son, Victory
Reed C. J.
Fields G. M.
Wright C. J.
Dean William
Reynolds Amos
Brashier John S.
Westcott Jas. H. Saratoga Springs.
Alger & Snyder
Brown C. N.
Burlingame C. W.
Root T.
Coleman Nathan
Comstock Wm. P.
Fonda Wm. A.
Fonda Ferdinand
Bushnell & Wood
Nehex P. M.   *Stillwater.*

Eddy Samuel G.   *Stillwater.*
Bloomendale Cornelius, jr.
Bradt Daniel. jr.
Albro John A.
Munger Morgan
Dinscom Edward. Bemus Heights
Scott William & Co.   *Waterford.*
Waterman S. S.
Brewster Abram L.
Ten Broeck H. H.
Comstock T. F.   *Wilton.*
Perry Cyrus
Barrows Amos

Schenectady County.

O'Neil James   *Duanesburgh.*
Wood B. F.
Braman & Crawford
Quackenbush J.
Sheldon B.
Hoag & Briggs
Donnan J.
Campfield G.   *Glenville.*
Howe, Cundy & Co.
Reese D. F.
Cundy P.
Van Patten A. C.
Van Horenburgh A.   *Niskayuna.*
Miller J. P.
Barringer D & Co. 51 State
   Schenectady.

Schoharie County.

Martin George W.   *Blenheim.*
Pierce Hiram
Vroman Chauncy
Matice Henry   *Broome.*
Lay & Hess
Haven Henry
Cherritree George
Wiley M.
Laraway George H.
France J. & Z.   *Cobleskill.*
Swart & Ferguson
Stryker Dewitt C.   *Conesville.*
Boughton Mathew R.
Turnbull James   *Esperance.*
Sprague William
Topping Robert M.
Ball Abram P.
Isham A. H.
Larkin J, Sloansville
Topping G.
Reed John & Co.   *Gilboa.*
Reed Luman & Co.
Mackey Daniel & Co.
Grant & Co.
Matice Adam P.   *Jefferson.*
Watson Hezekiah & Son
Bellinger & Ferguson
Stanton Geo. S. & Co. *Middleburgh.*
Jones Augustus
Bellenger Peter J.
Becker David
Matson H. & C.
Manning Charles & Co.
Vroman James D.
Wells John D.
Lewis Sylvester   *Richmondville.*
Dickinson Silas
Warner Peter H.
Garrison Andrew
Legur & Mann, Warnerville
Warner Hammond do
Westcott Sylvester do
Carl G. & J.   *Schoharie.*
Osterhout Peter
Lintner A. J.
Clark & Weatherwax
Roberts J. W.
Orcutt & France
Vroman D.
Snyder P.
Williams O. H. Central Bridge
Hilton Phillip, Hyndsville *Seward.*
Hynds G. O. do
Hynds Andrew, do
Johnson & Merrill, do
Deifendorf Jacob, do
Gardiner D. B., Gardinersville

Beekman H.   *Sharon.*
Brown K. W.
Snyder James, Argusville
Snyder & Fox. Sharon Centre
W. N. Becker. Sharon Springs
Denoyella M. N. do
Judd W. L., Leesville
Beekman Cor. Gardinersville
Fort Dewitt C.   *Summit.*
Van Buren John B.
Hartwell & Courtier
Rider D. L. & M.
Ostrum & Voaghan
Lake & Gourtier
Harder M.
Oliver A.
Dominick W. Gallupville *Wright*
Whipple & Gordon, do
Schoolcraft Isaac, do
Lawrence Morgan, do

Seneca County.

Pratt J. R.   *Covert.*
Beary Wm.   *Fayette.*
Goodyear Lewis
Haskins Henry, Canoga
M-Intyre & Kize, do
M-Duffee James, Romulus
Watkins Seth, Waterloo
Fatzinger Samuel, do
Mickly Edmund, do
Woodworth Augustus   *Lodi.*
Mott John D.
Ellison Michael B.
Miller Y. W.
Miller Gilbert T., Townsendville
Ganong Gilbert, do
Ferguson & Sprague   *Ovid.*
Gray Wilson
Cowles Henry D.
Covert & Baldwin
Bailey & Young
Sandford Halsey
Reed Warren
Hinman L... Farmer
Wright J. C. do
Munday H. S. do
Chester E. do
Wintersteen J. D. de
Steele R. R.   *Romulus.*
M'Duffie James
Chapman John C. *Seneca Falls.*
Ditmars A. W. & J. V.
Gay John S.
Gould S. S.
Hoskins C. L.
Partridge E.
Pollard Henry
Woodworth A O.
Fatzinger S. & J.   *Waterloo.*
Fatzinger Thomas & Co.
Magu Wm.
Inslee & Morgan
Gay & Noyes
Watkins J. & Son
Swift Moses H.
Warner Henry
Merrill C. & Co.
Ridgeway A. B.
Wordworth & Lisk
Morgan & Slawson

Steuben County.

Gillett C. E.   *Addison.*
Smith Wm. R.
M'Kay & Taggart
Jones H. R.
Warnbough W. jr.
Price & Coburn
Blakeslee & Smith   *Avoca.*
Wilk B.   *Bath.*
Fier & Carter
Dudley J. Q. & J. K.
Whiting & Co.
Ellis & Howell
Whitney L. C.
Rogers R. C.
Robie & Hunter
Fenne H. M.
Church R. N.
Cook H. H.

Axtell H. S.   *Bradford.*
Merriman, Monson & Co.
Mitchell & Co.
Hubbard D. S. & Co.   *Cameron.*
Smith & Fitch   *Canisteo.*
Taylor N. C.
Rathbone W. R.
Gilbert Wm. D.   *Caton.*
Blood & Halsey   *Cohocton.*
Hall & Chase
Hendryx Thomas
Eldred W. M.
Gilbert Wm. A. North Cohocton
Grover H. A. do
Rogers W. C.   *Dansville.*
Brooks H. S.   *Erwin.*
Brooks W. A.
Smith R. O. & Co
Badger L. W.
Potter H.
Smith D. A. & Co.
Olen Samuel   *Greenwood.*
Stevens & Co.
Davis John & Co.
Mix Emmit
M'Clay Wm.
Slauson D. D.   *Hornby.*
Smith A. L.   *Hornellsville.*
Tattishall R.
Wilson & Landers
Adait Martin
Alley J. & G.
Lawrence Grover H.
M'Connell & Olmstead   *Howard.*
Stebbens & Smith
Soule Richard
M'Neil F. S.   *Jasper.*
Sampson H. C.
Middlebrook, Morgan & Moore
   Lindley.
Harrows B.
Newcomb A. S.   *Orange.*
Bennett L. B.
Webber George
Webber Lorenzo
Nichols Wm.
Mallory W. M.   *Painted Post*
Bostwick, Field & Otis
Arnold W I.
Hoyt S. T. & Co.
Phelps Thomas H. G.
Robinson R. E.
Bertholf & Laud
Williams G. D.
Wolcott & Decost
Bulkley Andrew
Smith Bishop   *Prattsburgh.*
Boyd & Goodrich
Hayes & Ainsworth
Vantyle Thomas
Bass Andrew   *Pulney.*
Smith & Holden
Gulick E. & Co.
Conklin Isaac & Co.   *Reading.*
Griggs Saml & Son *Troupsburgh.*
Murdock James B.
Fenton Ebenezer
Bowen Lewis E., West
Livingston & Compton   *Tyrone.*
Weaver & Co.
Weller Charles
Bradford Clark
Jackson & Co.
Hastings W. & L. D.   *Urbana.*
Rose Delos
Randall John
Adsitt & Davis
Chapman Richard L
Wheeler O.
Mitchell John B.   *Wayne.*
M'Nulty & Hancock
Eveland J.
Grover L. C.   *Wayland.*
Bronson James
Mitchell & Co.   *Wheeler.*
Rockwell C. & G.   *Woodhull.*
Warner & Arnold
Lattimore S. V.
Leach J. C.

Suffolk County.

Smith Jonas, South   *Brookhaven.*

Oakes Edward, South *Brookhaven.*
Gould Isaac N. do
Mills & Davis, do
Hallock Chas. D. do
Mount John S. Setauket
Jayne Carlton, do
Rich Thomas J. Port Jefferson
Hulse Lewis, do
Tucker Thomas, do
Darling Charles W. do
Hutchinson John, Mount Sinai
Davis Timothy, do
Hutchinson & Benjamin, Middle Island
Rich George, do
Terry Isaac, Yaphank
Mills & Overton, do
Wilbur J. Manorville
Robinson P. S , Morich*s
Robinson Rogers, do
Osborne Jacob, do
Howell William, do
Clark William, do
Fanning James M. do
Ellotson Thomas, Fireplace
Raynor & Co. Bellport
Roe William, Patchogue
Woodhull Brewster, do
Howell Walter, do
Deery Thomas, do
Douglass & Son do
Havens John, do
Conklin Warren S. do
Howell & Havens, do
Roe John & W. do
Parsons Thomas F. *East Hampton.*
Hunting James M. & Brother
Conklin Stephen P.
Hand Nathaniel, Amagansett
Parsons David D., Springs
Conklin E. T. & Co. *Huntington.*
Woodhull & Skidmore
Scudder G. A. & Co.
Smith Henry S.
Lewis J. S. & H. S.
Walters James, Comac
Whitman Z. D. do
Higbee & Smith, Northport
Bunce S. E. do
Kellogg F. do
Scudder J. do
Farmingville & Ketcham, Farmingville
Willetts Charles, Babylon
Robinson W. & J. do
Seaman L. do
Smith & Bunce, do
Robbins W. W. & L. do
Reed James, do
Porter J. H. Amityville
Williams N. do
Cornelius Gordon, do
Morris James T. do
Tooker Wm. A. Cold Springs
Sprague Valentine *Islip.*
Carll James H.
Jendder Wilmott
Clock Seth R.
Robbins William
Foster Herman D. *Riverhead.*
Vail David F.
Corwin & Davis
Terry & Wells
Wells & Griffing
Vail John R.
Wells Benjamin F. Upper Aquebogue
Wheeler Lyman B. *Smithtown.*
Mills Jesse
Blydenburgh Richard
Huntting John S.
Olmsted Francis
Darling Washington
Hildreth Lewis *Southampton.*
Foster J. & Co.
Rhodes Robert R.
Howell Frederick
Rogers John
Herrick Austin
French William C.
Parsons Charles
Squires Alvin, Good Ground

Wells Wm. H. *Southold.*
Terry Frederick K.
Goodliff Allan A.
Case Hutchinson H., E.Cutchogue
Case B. F. do
Webb Daniel, Cutchogue
Webb Benjamin, do
Goldsmith & Tuthill, do
Betts William, do
Horton J. F., Mattituck
Wiggins D. B. & C. Greenport
Tuthill Schuyler B. do
Havens Walter, do
Corwin & Lyon, do
Wells & Carpenter, do
Clark James, do
Brown Theodore M.. Orient
Gillett L. Wellington, do
Champlin & Young, do
Holmes Marvin. do

Sullivan County.

Ross C. B. *Bethel.*
Ross J. P.
Linson W. V. K. White Lake
Kiersted W. & Co. Mongaup Valley
Ray Miles *Fallsburgh.*
Palin Edward & Co.
Ludington H. R.
Andrews S. Sandburgh
Smith Stephen. do
Morse Medad T. & Co. Woodburne
Wood & Dean, Hasbrouck
Divine J. H. do
Norris Stiles T. L. *Forestburgh.*
Wales & Forbes *Liberty.*
Clements & Fulton
Garrett Levi
Watkins & Kilburne
Gildersleeve & Co.
Horton & Co.
Rickey, Stevens & Co
Bush James F. Parksville
Young E. & Co. do
Stevens W. H. & D. L., Stevensville
Fuller & Young, Barryville
Lumberland.
Brown J. H. do
Thomas & Gardiner, do
Woodard C. S. Beaver Brook
Murry & Leinham, Big Eddy
Hughes J.J. do
Cudney D. *Mamakating.*
Budd J. & Son, Phillipsport
Langdon L. S. do
Phillips W. L do
Tice & Martin, do
Shults J. S. do
Decker Lucas, Bloomingsburgh
Wood Cornelius, do
Wakeman D. D. do
M'Cullough Wm. Wurtsboro
Morris & Lefever, do
Bull S. M. do
Henderson Smith, do
Bennett Eli, do
Hamilton George, Burlingham
M'Elhone James, do
Cooke & Bushnell *Neversink.*
Hammond & Wells
Johnson J. J. & Son
Northrop G. W.
Heaton H.
Clark N. C. & Co.
Hensie John
Babcock A. E.
Reynolds J.
Kimble M.
Fitch ——
Towner R. B., Monticello
Thompson.
Cady & Russell, Monticello
St. John F. M. do
Foster James H. do
Bushnell M. L. & Co. do
Deniston Eli, do
Dewey Charles A. do
Fortman Thomas, do
Howell H. W., Bridgeville

Tioga County.

Mills S. *Barton.*
Bensley D.
Hallenbeck G.
Conklin G.
Barker J.
Brooks T. I.
Fordham & Perkins
Fairchild & Co.
Shepherd Isaac
Wells & Harris
Park George
Johnson C. P *Berkshire.*
Gould & Williams
Barnagar S. *Candor.*
Sackett J. J.
White M. L.
Lincoln O. & Son, Newark Valley
Newark.
Byington L. Newark Valley
Noble W. T. do
Heaton A. C do
Hunt D. W. East Newark
Barstow G. H. *Nichols.*
Barstow O. A.
Wilson & Kirby
Goodrich B. G. & Co. *Owego.*
Bacon G.
Bell & Co.
Truman E. D. & S. S.
Ranson C. & F.
Truman L. & Brother
Ely William A.
Hubbard W. N. & Co.
Ely James
Truman, Stone & Co.
Nichols T. M.
Cameron R.
Brown R. & F.
Hyde A. T.
Matson N.
Hurlbut E. B.
Dean & Perkins
Thomas A. R. & Co.
Wheeler L.
Cameron John
Storrs A. P.
Slosson F. & Co.
Greenleaf & Hewett
Steele R.
M'Neil R. C.
Rich, Pierson & Co. *Richford.*
Griffin Simeon R.
Miller & Hall *Spencer.*
Nicholls & Hall
Post W. & T. L.
Fisher S. & G.
Emmons L.
Gasey A. T.
Light G. L. & Co. *Tioga.*
Hoyt J. S.
Mitchell ——
Ransom C.

Tompkins County.

Bush Isaac L. *Caroline.*
Preston L.
Thomas Walter J.
Hollister Noah *Danby.*
Clark William
Bushnell A. L. *Dryden.*
Fitts & Sears
Dwight & Ferguson
Houtz John H. & Co.
Bement, Reynolds & Co. *Groton.*
Clark & Son
Trumbull N.
Marsh D. B.
Kirtland John *Hector.*
Baker E. & Co. Burdett
Ingersoll A. H. do
Bodle & Earles, Mecklenburg
Treman Madison, do
Potter John, Waterburg
M'Sallen John, Searsburg
Smead L., Logan
Baker E. & Co., North Hector
Squires & Wilcox, do
Whiteman G., Reynoldsville
Tracy Nathaniel, Cayutaville

Culver L. H. (wholesale) 45, 47, 49 Owego *Ithaca.*
Quigg J. & W. 30 Owego
Seaman & Snyder, 32 Owego
Hinckley C. W. & Co. 34 Owego
Winton S. H. 48 Owego
Lycan & Hance, 50 do
Hopkins & Co. 52 do
Finch & Stowell, 62 do
Corwin J. C. 55 do
Wood D. T. 51 do
Herrick N G. 144 do
Hibbard H. F. 110 do
Wilgus H. 111 do
Greenley F. T. & Co. 94 Owego
Terry J. B. 92 do
Kendall John, 91 do
Curtis E. F. 93 do
Harris S. 60 do
Hannemore H. H. 63 do
M'Lane W. G. 33 do
Whiton J. S. 115 do
Atwater E. A. 35 do
Townsend J. 11 Aurora
Gultner G. & A. 12 do
Roe D. 15 do
Tichenor J. 32 do
M'Lure G. 29 do
Kellogg H. 50 do
Gould & Co. 27 do
Taber W. C., Inlet
Burr H. F. & Co. *Lansing.*
Davis Charles
Dudley Percival S. *Newfield.*
Lanning Charles W.
Anderson James H.
Ramsey David
Everhance George
Camp & Stone, Trumansburgh *Ulysses.*

Dumond & Co. do
M'Lallen & Hester, do
Allen Benjamin, do
Clock & Crequi, do
Jamison Daniel, do
Teed Wm. H. do
Tompkins R. C. do
Atwater R. & W. G. do

Ulster County.

Bushnell C. West Hurley *Hurley.*
Voorhees, Van Anden & Masten *Kingston.*
Burhans C. & J. S.
Dubois Elijah
Shaffer Charles W.
Dillon Jacob W.
Kerr Wm. & Sons
Mulks Moses
Keator H. & Co.
Eckert & Van Vleet
Reynolds Williams
Wheeler E. & Co.
Schoonmaker L. & A.
O'Neil Edward
Liddle William
Bringham E. M. & Co.
Disbrow D. A.
Beatty William
Booth & Smith, Wilbur
Hyde C. W., Rondout
Mellon Sarah, do
Moore William C. do
Marner S. H. do
Hanraty Francis, do
Meloy James, do
Livingston & Leroy, Rondout
Shufelt Alexander W. do
North George, do
Sudam Edmond, do
Cornell T. W., Eddyville
Requa W. H. & S. do
Husted & Low, do
Terwilliger James D. *Lloyd.*
Perkin H. J., Landing
Barrett A. J. New Paltz Landing
Hardenburgh J. do
Du Bois J. C. do
Elmore R. F. do
Van Buren Cornelius. *Marbletown.*
Ostrander Thomas

Grey H. F. High Falls *Marbletown.*
Story, King & Co. do
Clearwater & Schoonmaker, High Falls
Stillwell & Bloom, Stone Ridge
Abeel Hector. do
Lounsbury John, do
Hasbrook M. & Co. do
Vandermark Jacob, do
Gillis J. H., Milton *Marlborough.*
Townsend J. P. do
Pratt L. do
Lewis D. do
Fletcher M. J.
Carpenter J.
M'Elrath William
Spence R.
Barnes & De Garmo *'New Paltz.*
Elting E. S.
Schoonmaker I. & J. L. Libertyville
Sammons H. D., Tuthill
Turner B. jr. *Olive.*
Bartlett H. B.
Tappan J. J.
Vangaasbeek J. H. J. Shokan
Constable Moses, Modena *Plattekill.*
Ruggles ---- do
Hornbeck J. Kyserike *Rochester.*
Decker A. H. do
Hasbrouck E. do
Depuy R. W. & Sons, Accord
Decker M. do
Davis Jacob, do
Deyo C. I. Pine Bush
Lafever P. C. *Rosendale.*
Du Bois S. L.
Snyder W. H. jr.
Budington C. W.
Butzel John L. *Saugerties.*
Stranahan D. G.
M'Carthy Edmond J.
Russell D. M. & P.
Gay J. E. & W. A.
Woodruff Elias
Hommell S. S.
Gillespie P. M.
Bartel & Benwick
Burhans Cyrus & Co.
Schoonmaker Peter D.
Miller John F. & Co.
O'Farrell Margaret
Van Buskirk William
Biglow E. D. & Co. *Bristol*
Adams Wm. do
Isham C. & G. do
Trumbour William H. do
Woodward ---- do
Martin H. D. Glasco
Turck Abram, do
Kellogg N. & Co. do
Newkirk & Simpson *Shandaken.*
Isham Sherrell & Co.
Guigo C. Pine Hill
Smith I. Smithville
Bruyn E. & J. *Shawangunk.*
Robinson R.
Crist S. & Co. Ulsterville
Belyea B. B. do
Jackson & Lang, Bruynswick
Broadhead, Deyo & Brother, do
Vernoy A. Bruynswick
Kelley Felix *Wawarsing.*
Hungerford Abel
Cutter Samuel W.
Perkins N. S.
Benedict J. & Co.
Whitaker & Wilkinson, Middleport
Decker Cornelius, do
Vermoy M. do
Lawrence L. Port Benjamin
Coutant A. G. do
Ellenville Glass Co. Ellenville
Sheldèn & Mastin, do
Van Benschoten C. do
Pomeroy & Newkirk, Southwick
Sanford James M. Ellenville
Bloomer J. L. & Son, do
Westcott James, do
Sinsabaugh & Hanford, do
Tuttle, Broadhead & Co. do

M'Creary & Webb, Napanock *Wawarsing.*
Hornbeck J. M. do
Bauge & Co. do
De Forest A. *Woodstock.*
Baker C.

Warren County.

Cameron William J. *Athol.*
Aldrich David
Johnson Sanford
Fuller James
Davis W.
Bacon & Peck *Caldwell.*
Wood Hiram
Fuller R. P. & S. Chestertown *Chester.*
Robertson, Faxon & Co. do
Leggett & Arnold do
Smith E. B. & E. H. do
Young William, do
Starback & Mead, do
Collier Joshua, Potterville
Codman William, do
Bevins Alva *Hague.*
Smith Richard P. *Herioon.*
Smith Joseph A.
Osborn Charles & Co.
Barnes L. B. *Johnsburgh.*
Gilchrist Spencer
Noble David, 2d
Roblee Norman
Ordiway Jones
Noble John, 2d
Armstrong Adam
Dayton Silas *Luzerne.*
Stewart I. D.
Wells W. H.
Wells Reuben
Ferguson Henry, Glenns' Falls *Queensbury.*
Morgan & Lapham, Glenns' Falls
Shattock & Foster, do
Locke William R. do
Mott Z W. do
Hawley & Goodrich, do
Cheney Arms & Co. do
Wing Henry, do
Verney & Potter, do
Rockwell Charles, do
Cronkhite Orville, do
Sherman Augustus, do
Ranger Samuel, do
Hurley James, do
Cowles Daniel H. & Co. do
Vaughn E. S. do
Coffin Martin do
Seeley L. C. P. do
Russell & Griffin *Warrensburgh.*
Bishop J. W.
Warren N. J.
Burhans & Gray

Washington County.

Doud Edward *Argyle.*
Rouse John C.
Stewart James
Stiles Ransom
Rouse William H.
Clark John, North Argyle
Stevenson & Stewart, do
Shannon James, do
M'Call Aaron, South Argyle
Stewart Samuel, jr. do
Levingston & Co. *Cambridge.*
Coulter & M'Clellan
Robertson & Co.
M'Clellan Clark
Wells Leod
Ingraham & Co. Cambridge Centre
Brownell E. North Cambridge
Houghton Andrew, Buskirk's Bridge
Pratt Jesse
Mowry & Co. *Easton.*
Eddy & Co.
Barker Aaron
Crandell Holder
Mosher Eugene
Hoag Jonathan

Toby & Crandall, N. Easton *Easton.*
Potter Sanford R. do
Worth Alfred, do
Beadle & Baker, S. Easton
Gale Frederick A. Galesville
Robertson Joel, do
Hillebert John *Fort Ann.*
Bacon Joseph
Clements George
Clements Isaac
Miller & Skinner
Corning J. & S.
Baker I. V.
Thorn Charles
Cheeseman & Hodgeman *Fort Edward.*
Nash Edwin B.
Bassett F. M., Fort Miller
Bassett & Nichols, do
Bragg & Guy, do
Andrews, Selleck & Andrews *Greenwich.*
Southworth Joseph
Patteys & Bratt
Whipple Henry
M'Neil & Tobey
Barnard J. & Son
Joyner Luman
Keith William J., Centre Falls
White W. W., Battenville
M'Lean A. M. & D. W. do
Hicks Asa, do
Beebe & Stone, East Greenwich
Jacobie William. do
Matthews Abram, jr. Lake
Stewart Walter G. do
Matthews Sidney, do
Jones C. D., Galesville
Reid William, North Greenwich
Adams H. M. *Hampton.*
Shaw J. C.
Bocks William J. West Hebron *Hebron.*
M'Clellan James R. & Co. do
Woodward & Co. do
Bull Henry, North Hebron
Munson Asa E. East do
Frazier John, do
Durkee L. S. *Kingsbury.*
Dewey Allen, Sandy Hill
Kenyon & Culver, do
Wing & Clark, do
Cronkhite & Rice, do
Cronkhite M. & L. · do
Cronkhite Wm. W. do
Harvey J. W. Patten's Mills
Smith Ezekiel, Smith's Basin
Easton George *Putnam.*
Burnett James
Gourlie Alexander C.
Freeman Marvin *Salem.*
Atwood & Clemlem
Robertson Abner C.
King & Gould
Valentine & Lawrence
Hastings Elijah
Sisson D. P. *White Creek.*
Niles & Houghton
Pratt W. S. White Creek Centre
Wells L. North do
Robertson Wm. P. do
Walkley B. W. do
Crocker & Staples do
Bascom & Gaylord, Canal st. *Whitehall.*
Burdett G. C. Canal st.
Allen Mrs. C. do
Day Orrin do
Griswold A. H. do
Martin A. & Co. · do
Morris M. J. & Co. do
M'Ghee J. & W. F. do
Jillson N. T. . do
Parke J. H. H. Park Place
Russigdel D. M. Chapins' Block
Caldwell & Co., Phœnix Place
Kirtland John, do
Griswold J. C. William st.

Wayne County.

Crosby James S. *Arcadia.*

12

Owen Jesse *Arcadia.*
Adams & Winfield
Blackmer & Jackson, Newark
Torrey R. S. do
Stone R. do
Blackmer H. & O. do
Ford & Grant, do
Allerton Taber & Co do
Owen & Winegar, Fairville
Conger & Hawley, Westbury *Butler.*
Bacon & Ingersoll, do
Graves Henry K. South Butler
Bellamy Frederick, Clyde *Galen.*
Miller Cornelius, do
Miller Isaac, do
Pardee & Elliott, do
Chapman Fredus, do
Stokes James H. do
Hovey Hiram, · do
Frisbie & Nichols, do
Olmsted M. do
Griswold Wm. H. Lock Berlin
Blackmer E. *Huron.*
Rice O. *Lyons.*
Knowles J. & Brothers
Dewey & Wells
Tredway A.
Demon J. M.
Mirrick, Carmel & Co
King H. & D. W.
Thurston E. G.
Watrous D.
Dean George C.
Cramer G. W.
Adams J. John & Son
White E. N.
Hawkins William, Macedonville *Macedon.*
Purdy & Willits
Purdy Alexander
Davis W. D. *Marion.*
Rich Marvin
Pond J. N.
Haskins J. G. L.
Patterson Joseph *Ontario.*
Horton H. W.
Tucker Wm. S. *Palmyra.*
Davis S. S. & Co.
Rogers C. H. & Co
Lovett & Scotten
Pardee R. G.
Pardee & Higby
Aldrich David S.
Elmendorf A.
Clark & Winchester
Ritter M.
Thomas E. N. *Rose.*
Wright Charles S.
White John *Sodus.*
Rogers J. C.
Dunning Lewis & Co.
Demmon J. M.
Lapham Nelson, Joy
Taylor A. Sodus Centre
Warren Samuel, South Sodus
Warren A. P. & G. D. do
Forbes Thomas, Alton
Leonard Oliver, do
Fish P. do
Mockridge William, Sodus Point
Billings & Coggwell *Walworth.*
Richmond & Jackson
Lusk J. D.
Miller Harvey D. West Walworth
Stoutenburg Wm. J. *Williamson.*
Pardee & Camp
Phelps George D. Pultneyville
Reynolds John, do
Todd B. & Son, do
Hawks Albert *Wolcott.*
Underhill & Hendrick
Foote ——
Arne George
Armstrong Thomas, jr.
Underhill David
Preston & Howland, Red Creek

Westchester County.

Bates Nehemiah S. & Son *Bedford.*
Miller George W.
Purdy Ebenezer J.

Huested Wm. W. *Bedford.*
Smith Samuel S.
Gardner, Rogers & Co.
Orton & Seaman, Mechanicsville
Whittock John B. & Son, do
Smith N. Y. & Son, do
Frost Niles, Peekskill *Courtlandt.*
Taught F. S C. do
Smith James L. do
Russell Wm. H. do
Hubbell & Mead, do
Royce & Clark, · do
Hopkins E. do
Depew Henry W. & Co. Peekskill
Mead John, do
Lyons William H. do
Denike Jacob, do
Tompkins Griffin H. do.
Briggs J. & E. do
Denike William do
Guyer C. H. do
Valentine Fisher F. *East Chester.*
Drake Susan
Burtiss Wesley
Underhill A. U.
Bertine Samuel
Taylor John C. Underhill Roads
Chapman John, Tarrytown *Greenburgh.*
Haight Henry L. Tarrytown
See Sames S. do
Fowler J. Q. do
Brown George R. do
Odell J. & N. H. do
Dean Thomas, do
Clark A. R. do
Taferge Isaac, Hastings
Schlosser J. M. do
Smith T. do
Lent Mrs. Henry do
Odell Wm. & Isaac, Dobb's Ferry
Waldo E. W. do
Sidd & Turk *Lewisborough.*
Newman Clark, Cross Lines
Hunt William, do
Crissie J. Lower Salem
Dickensen Wm. H. Dick Corner
Hatcher & Hawley, South Salem
Marshall John G. *Mamaroneck.*
Purdy Joshua
Britt Gilbert
Banks & Clark, Pleasantville *Mount Pleasant.*
Montross Robert, Pleasantville
Farrington Townsend, do
Lane W. H. *New Castle.*
Browner & Fish
Merritt & Potter
Pine John *New Rochelle.*
Underhill Samuel
Underhill George
Bardeau A.
Secor Franklin B.
Bolton John
Barton & Lecount
Townsend & Kinch, Mile Square *North Castle.*
Smith Samuel P. Mile Square
Sutton G. do
Stevens Clark *North Salem.*
Van Schoit Alva
Bailey George, East Salem
Howe E.
Chase & Cole, Croton Falls
Williams & Owen, do
Turk & Jones, do
Quimby R. Sing Sing *Ossining.*
Griffin Squire, do
Nichols S. C. do
Knox C. H. do
Benedict Ezra R. do
Pell Stephen S. *Pelham.*
Horton Francis, City Island
Lockwood William *Poundridge.*
Lockwood Alsop H.
Smith William *Rye.*
Strong Daniel
Gedney John B. Milton
Lyon Wm. Portchester
Mosier Samuel & William, do
Bailey H. Somerstown Village *Somers.*

Turk O. W. & W., Somerstown Village *Somers.*
Adee Jas. & John T. *Westchester.*
Brown Sidney B. & Son
Arnoe M.
Benson John
Parson Robert
Walton C. *West Farms.*
Smith Ralph H.
Mapes Daniel
Cooper John
Golden Isaiah
Miller Elijah
Ure Henry
Shaw William
Purdy Hart *White Plains.*
Palmer Robert
Flanderows John
Bashford E. A. *Yonkers.*
Farrington T. O.
Waring J. & E.
Rose L. P.
Lawrence S G.
Crisfield J.
Warner & Briggs
Barritt S. G. Hart's Corners
Frost Cyrus, Croton *Yorktown.*
Cox David, do
Travis Samuel, do

Wyoming County.

Putnam John S. *Attica.*
Doty L.
Walcott & Wright
West G. N.
Wyman & Bigelow
Goodwin W. B.
Gladding H. D. & Co.
Wilber & Bates
Hoskins G. G. *Bennington.*
Rowley H. K.
Bass S. B., Cowlesville
Folsom B. R. & Co. do
Halsted & Matthews *Castile.*
Pierce & Sherman
Higgins G. H.
Burr T. J.
Smith J. W. *China.*
Swift James C.
Smith & Martin *Covington.*
Gordon James, Peoria
Frazier John D. do
Morgan E. C., La Grange
Scott & Cole *Eagle.*
Ayett Wm. S.
Pratt Ira F. *Gainesville.*
Truesdell Levi *Genesee Falls.*
Green Horace
Platt Nathan
Forsyth George
Flint Robert
Currier Joseph *Java.*
Currier N. P., East Java
King & Richards, Java Village
Umphrey Nelson J. do
Bronson James, North Java
Potter Philo, do
Ferris James C., Wyoming *Middlebury.*
Caswell & Wells, do
Murray Edward I. do
Collar & Stevens, do
Gould J. H. do
Richards Daniel *Orangeville.*
Norton & Co. Johnsburgh
Bailey John B. *Perry.*
Merrill S. W. & Sons
Page H. N.
Barton H. W.
Smith R. H.
Clark S. P.
Lathrop Jason, Perry Centre
Purdy & Benedict, do
Ayrault L. *Pike.*
Sherrill A. P.
Gillespie J. C.
Platt J. L. & Co.
Gould R. & Co.
Renwick J.
Robinson R.
Fuller & Kelly

Smith & Wheeler, East Pike *Pike.*
Harney N. A. do
Umphrey & Martindale *Sheldon.*
Ainsworth W. H., Varysburgh
Burrett George, Strykersville
Webster E. do
Darling & Breck *Warsaw.*
Comstock, Andrews & Co.
Gould Roswell
Frank Augustus, jr.
Fargo F. F. & Co.
Frank A.
Choate A.

Yates County.

Holmes Horace & Co. *Barrington.*
Bogert & Simmons *Benton.*
Haight A.
Harris & Miller
Gage & Wolcott, Benton Centre
Cole & Savage, do
Coddington Benjamin, Belona
Kelsey Charles R. do
Scott Wm., Italy Hollow *Italy.*
Barber George, do
Wells R., Italy Hill
Shaddock ——, do
Dorman Joel, Branchport *Jerusalem.*
Ellsworth Jas. & Co. do
Weaver M. H. & L. S. do
Van Ander L. & Co. *Middlesex.*
Baker G. & Son *Mile.*
Raplee Miles G.
Shepard & Ford, Penn Yan
Hamlin Myron, do
Jones E. B. do
Rose D. do
Benham James & Co. do
Streeter & Green, do
Steel George & Co. do
Shelden Eli, do
Ellsworth & Brien, do
Sharp & Ketcham, do
Hancock & M'Nulty, do
Hsgen A. F. do
Stewart & Tuncliff, do
Hunt & Eastman, Milo Centre
Hollowell G. H. do
Turner James W. *Potter.*
Wiswell L. C. & Co. Rushville
Caswell & Case, do
Wiswell John & Co. do
Tyler Benjamin, do
Soper H. *Starkey.*
Andrews ——
Oldfield D., Dundee
Hamlin Wm. B. & Co. Dundee
Raplee J. T. do
Newcomb H. B. do
Eaton, Spicer & Co. do
Murdock N. F. do
Hollister & Sutfin, do
Tuttle Charles, do
Barnes & Shark, do
Newcomb H. A., Rock Stream
Morris J. T. & Co. Big Stream Point

Duck, (Sail) Dealers in.

Bulkley G. 88 South *New York.*
Ellsworth 195 West
Fardon Abrm. & Sons, 87 South
Flanders Benjamin, 88 do
Fox & Polhemus, 59 Broad
Maull Raymond T. 114 Wall
Peck H. N. & Co. 130 Front
Raritan Duck Co. 38 Broadway
Taylor & Merrill, 36 Burling slip

Dundee Goods.

Cameron & Brand, 42 & 44 Pine *New York.*
Fraser & Greenhill, 36 Pine
Tooker, Mead & Co. 35 Pine

Dyers.

Albany County.

Niblock J. 43 Hudson *Albany.*

Laycock C. 17 Norton *Albany.*
Giffen William, 20 do
Condon J. 36 Orange

Cayuga County.

M'Kibbin P. Genesee st. *Auburn.*
Smith O. do

Columbia County.

Castle C. Spencertown *Austerlitz.*
Myers C. Diamond st. *Hudson.*

Erie County.

Strup Theobald, 419 Main *Buffalo.*
Chester J. 337 Washington

Greene County.

Hood John *Catskill.*

Jefferson County.

Witt Charles, Felts' Mills *Rutland.*

Kings County.

Champlain F. 50 Fulton *Brooklyn.*
Cormier A. 195 do
Trew G. 125 Prospect

Livingston County.

Crossen William M. Hemlock Lake *Livonia.*

Madison County.

French B. (fancy dyer) *Cazenovia.*

Monroe County.

Bishop John H. 77 Exchange *Rochester.*
Loary D. foot of Furnace st.

New York County.

Adam & Wilmin, 88 Reade *New York.*
Banfield Frederick, 301 Bowery
Berger, Aime & Co. 186 W. 20th
Booth James W. 85 Bedford
Callahan William D. 239 Bleecker
Carter Samuel, 152 Wooster
Clement J. 133 Division
Clymer William, 276 Walker
Cormier Ambrose, 197 Walker & 89 Canal
Court & Deschaux, 579 Greenwich
Daniels F. 618 Greenwich
Denis & Co. 377 Grand, 140 Greenwich Av. & 365 Bowery
Dennis Oliver, E. 26th
Dennis & Barber, 116 Maiden Lane & 140 Greenwich Av.
Donaldson Jane, 17 Spring
Gandler Valentine, 237 3d
Garnet George, 148 Franklin
Guerrier Hues, 29 Dey
Haasser J. 210 Houston
Hare Catharine, 12 Henry
Harrison Thomas & Co. 47 1st. Av.
Haydon William L. 9th Av.
Hesse Victor, 35 Sullivan
Jolly Charles, 564 Broadway
Kachant Charles, 210 Houston
Lafferty E. 263 Rivington
Lamy H. 5 Barclay & 253 Bl'cker & 9th Av. bet. 24th & 25th
M'Cann George, 1 Chatham sq.
Marwedel Ferdinand, 524 Grand
M'Coy John, 275 Greenwich
Martin Robert, 100 Troy
Michaell Julius, 217 Houston
Moneypenny John, 163 Canal
Moneypenny Anne, 153 do
Napier Alexander, 143½ Bowery
New York Dying & Printing Establishment, 45 John
O'Neil John, rear 286 W. 17th
Percival Pearce, 257 Bleecker
Prince Bernard, 23 Frankfort

Probst Peter, 1 11th   *New York.*
Redman, Schofield & Whitbread
  Dyers & Refinishers of Cotton,
  Woolen, & Silk goods. Kennedy & Gelston agents, 5½ Pine
Rennie James. 16 Cedar
Short John, 245 Grand
Smith Thomas, 70 Allen
Smith William, 173 2d
Soris & Co. 269 Grand, 289 Bleecker, 2 Astor place, 256 Greenwich 293 2d, 248 8th Av. 189 Fulton, 30 John & 484 Pearl
Valentine E. rear 170 W. 2d
Westbrook Samuel, 111 8th Av.
Walters Andrew, 78 Grand

Onondaga County.

Entwistle W. Salina st. Syracuse
    Salina.

Rensselaer County.

Warrick J. & Shacklady C. W. 435 River   *Troy.*
Hall A. cor. River & Jay

Richmond County.

New York Co. Factoryville
    Castleton.
Crabtree & Wilkinson, do

Rockland County.

M'Questian & Co. (Print)
    Haverstraw.

Schenectady County.

Venables T. 80 State *Schenectady.*

Wyoming County.

Davidson J. J.   *Warsaw.*

Dye Stuffs, Dye Woods, Chemicals.

Blanco B. 87 Front   *New York.*
Des Arts & Hueser, 78 Water
Halsey, William & Co. 182 Water
Ingersoll & Brothers, 230 Pearl
Koop, Fischer & Co. 54 New
Lee James & Co. 36 New
Milhau John, 183 Broadway
Morgan James L. 47 Fulton
Partridge Wm. & Son, 27 Cliff
Pentz & Co. 55 Water
Russell & Styles, 135 Water
Sale Wm. A. jr. 124 Water
Sandford H. J. 159 Maiden Lane

Dye Wood Manufacturers.

Albany County.

Rathburn J.   *Bethlehem.*

Duchess County.

Hughson W. & T. L. Wappinger's Falls   *Fishkill.*
Gifford, Sherman & Innis
    Poughkeepsie.

Kings County.

Partridge Alfred   *Gravesend.*

Ulster County.

Winchester A.   *Kingston.*

Westchester County.

Sandford John & Henry, (extract of logwood) Portchester   *Rye.*
Russell Geo. (extract of logwood)
    Yonkers.

Eating Houses.

Alhambra, 156 Water, W. Dillon
  Proprietor   *New York.*

Allen H. C. 15 Wall   *New York.*
Amerman Cornelius, 341 Spring
Annin Alexander, 372 Pearl
Baldwin & Bovee, 21 Bowery
Bamford Jno. 7th Av. cor. W. 21st
Barney S. W. & J. J. 106 Church
Barnwell Patrick. 228 Broadway
Barnswell T. 336 3d
Bassett N. 229 Washington
Betts D. F. 47 Ann
Beebe R. W. 21 Bowery
Besson Jeremiah, 130 Canal
Blake Asa, 64 Whitehall
Bonnard J. B. 16 Nassau
Brothers Perkins, 230 Centre
Brower John, 407 West
Brown Benj. 71 Pearl
Brown Isaiah S. 131 Water
Brown Seely, 51 Nassau
Brown Geo. W. 123 & 125 Water
Brundage Nich. L. 137 Chatham
Budd Wade H. 337 Spring
Buermeyer Ernest, 101 Broad
Burguet Henry, 76 Centre
Butler Isaac, 1 Bowery
Carlisle Joseph, 480 Broome
Carter J. M. 61 Elm
Catlin David, 213 West
Chamberlain Benj. 310 Pearl
Cisco Abraham, 16 8th Av.
Clark Andrew, 177 West
Clark Arthur, 18 Bowery
Clark & Brown, 15 Cedar
Cline S. B. 68 Watt
Cole Dan., 1 Division
Collins Peter, 333 Water
Coon & Hahn, Rotunda Merch. ex.
Copelwann Otto, 10 West
Cosby Mills, 30 Old slip
Creedion Patrick, 48 Canal
Crook S. H. & C. K. 27 Fulton
Crook S. J. H. & B. E. Cook, 19
  Fulton mkt.
Damm & Francin, 15 Nassau
Dean T. 41 Canal
Delano Albe. 141 Water
Delano Albert, 1 Depeyster
Delmonico P. A. & L. 2 S. William
Dietterlen & Co. 89 Canal
Dickson S. S. 80 Broadway
Douglass Hez. C. Post's Buildings
Downing Thomas, 35 Broad
Dunham E. W. 1 Nassau
Earl Charles, 4 Battery pl.
Eldredge Horace N. 103 Nassau
Ellis J. 141 Water
Ferguson James, 395 Broome
Ferris Ebenezer G. 62 Chatham
Fink Maria, 35 Merch. Ex.
Fisch J. 74 Greenwich
Fitch David H. 60 Nassau
Fitzgerald James M. 534 Pearl
Fitzgerald John, 41 Elm
Fitzsimmons James, 31 Peck slip
Forbes A. B. 302 3d Av.
Foster & St. John, 84 Nassau
Fusset M. J. 11 Pine
French R. 170 Nassau
Gaffney James, 355 Spring
Gage Samuel, jr. 39½ South
Gamble James S. 1 Dey
Gardner Henry, 424 West
Gast Xavier, 80 Ann
Genteer Andrew. 108 Chatham
Gilbert Richard L. 30 Ann
Goodnough F. 28 Park Row
Gould David H. 10 Fulton
Greely Joseph M. 114 6th Av.
Greene Wm. C. 12 Beekman
Gruber Peter, 137 Av. D
Gunter Harmon H. 147 Fulton
Harrison John, 12 Wash'ton mkt.
Hartnett John B. 5 Catharine slip
Henderson J. W. 10 Wash't'n mkt.
Hoagland J. H. 6 West
Hollister D. M. 32 Bowery
Hook Benjamin, 12 South
Howard & Brown, 168 Nassau
Hull Wm. 12 Catharine slip
Hyatt John, 6   do
Jackson & St. John, 17 & 19 do
Jenkinson D, 12 Washington mkt

Jesup B. 39 William   *New York.*
Jewell Wm. H. 420 West
Johnson Edmond E. 31 Canal
Johnson & Rogers, 144 Fulton
Johnson Wm. 213 West
Keller Peter, 63 Av. C
Kellogg George W. & Co. 8 Fulton market
Kelly S. 11 Washington market
Kidder Samuel, 117 Av. D
Kirk Thomas, 395 Bowery
Latham Abm. M. 616 Water
Ledwith Michael, 65 G'wich Av.
Lessel James W. 5 Chatham sq.
Levere G. W. 88 W. Broadway
Lockwood Julia, 4 Jefferson mkt.
Lovejoy C. M. 143 Mercer
Luscomb Henry, 215 Washington
M'Carthy Charles, 94 Greenwich
M'Donough John, 15 Beaver
M'Queen John, 592 Grand
Marshall W. K. 2½ Bowery
Marsh Moses, 23 West
Mattern Peter, 122 Houston
Mattern W. 127 West
Mead Ardon, 381 10th
Mead Jesse H. 76 Cherry
Mercer Edwin J. 107 Nassau
Merritt Andrew, 173 William
Meschutt P. F. & D. C. 49 Bowery
Mills Lorenzo, 357 4th Av.
Mitchell John, 57 West
Moore John, 85 Nassau
Monahan Patrick, 17 Washington
Morton Peter, 122 Houston
Mudget Samuel, 166 Washington
Munson Stephen, 12 & 13 Fulton market
Murphy Thomas, 115 Cherry
Newman John, 29 Peck slip
Nott Hiram, 89 Nassau
Oates & Co. cor. Lispenard & Broadway
Paaschen Hammond, 222 Centre
Palmo F. 307 Broadway
Palmer William, 141 Av. C
Parker Charles, 20 Dey
Pearsall David, 2, 3, & 4 Fulton market
Perkins Brothers, 231 Centre
Pettit & Crook, 91 Wall
Plet Sarah, 35 Anthony
Pontin Paul & Anthony Doser, 296 2d
Potter N. 111 Nassau
Quinn Catharine, 10 Battery place
Rau Adolphus, 60 Broadway
Rea Isaac, 30 Bowery
Reed Louis D. 6 Battery place
Ridabock Charles, 68 Wall
Rieckerts George, 118 Chatham
Robinson Adolph, 56 West
Roome N., W. 29th st.
Rost Jane, 130 & 132 Beekman
Rowe James G. 18½ West
Rowe William, 96 Vesey
Rowe & Waldrom, 100 do
Rowland Treadwell, 349 Spring
Rushton W. G. Merchants' Ex.
Savery John S. 16 Fulton market
Schaffner Michael, 366 Pearl
Scherer Mary, 231 Grand
Schnackenberg C. 300 3d Av.
Scott & M'Laughlin, 179 Broadway
Seymour James. 37 West
Seymour Wm. 39 Cedar
Shay William E. 47 Ann
Sisco N. 16 6th Av.
Slade G. 14 Washington market
Slocum Wm. 196 South
Smith Chatfield H. 393 Bowery
Smith Eunice, 307 West
Spencer Martin W. 17 Wall
Steele P. R. 223 Broadway
Stoltz & Berry, 6 Broad
Sweeny Daniel, 66 Chatham
Sweet Abm. M. 8 Fulton
Taylor Brothers, 161 Pearl
Ten Eyck & Smith, 56 Canal
Thompson & Swift, 23 & 25 Pine
Tucker Elihu L. 145½ & 147 Bowery

Vandyke & Brinley, 23 & 25 Catharine slip
Varndell Wm. 145 Bowery
Versfelts Edward, 473 Pearl
Walker & Shurragar, 39 William
Walley Jacob, 60 W. Broadway
Ward Joseph, 190½ South
Watson James, 18 Fulton market
Way Frederick H. 203 Wash'ton
Webb Henry, 54 W. Broadway
Wedekind H. 60 Beaver
Wentworth S. Wm. 113 John
White William, 2 West
White William, 116 Houston
Whittemore Ira, 142½ West
Willis Thomas, 48 Gold
Wilson J. 58 Beekman
Windust Edward, 11 Park row & 11 Ann
Wyeth Edward. 604 Grand
Youngs Edmund, 123 Beekman

Edge Tool Makers. (See also Axes, also Cutlery, &c.)

Alleghany County.

Spear Roswell   *Friendship.*
Wakeman A.   *Hume.*

Cattaraugus County.

Patterson James   *Franklinville.*

Cayuga County.

Wadsworth D.   *Aurelius.*

Chautauque County.

Waters Franklin & Co. *Westfield.*

Chemung County.

Eaton C. B.   *Elmira.*

Chenango County.

Maydole David   *Norwich.*
Balcom George   *Oxford.*
Sanford Beardsley   *Pitcher.*
Leonard Rufus   *Smyrna.*

Cortland County.

Babcock Porter   *Marathon.*
Williams Eleazer

Duchess County.

Bedell T. Clinton Hollow *Clinton.*
Albertson A.   *Hydepark.*
Hevenor B. D.   *Rhinebeck.*
Rodgers S.   *Stanford.*

Erie County.

Avery Amos, East Evans *Evans.*

Jefferson County.

Ryther P. H.   *Theresa.*
Ransom & Lord   *Watertown.*
Hadcock Solomon
Skinner A. R.

Kings County.

Green A. D. (Plane Irons) 177 1st *Williamsburgh.*

Madison County.

Parker Josiah   *Fenner.*
Holmes Daniel   *Stockbridge.*

Monroe County.

Baker B. West Mendon *Mendon.*
Bryan W. W. 6 S. St. Paul *Rochester.*
Barton D. R. 3 Buffalo
Brayer & Martin, Madison st.

New York County.

Balcher Brothers, 221 Pearl st.

Berry John C. 33 Attorney *New York.*
Burdett J. A. 176 Chambers
Clarkson William, 40 Eldridge
Collins H. (axes) 46 Broad
Collins & Co. (axes) 283 Pearl
Fish O. F. 146 Bowery
Hamilton John P. (axes) 1 Beaver
Harvey Geo. (bits) 89 Elizabeth
Horton William, 191 Lewis
Leverett John, (axes) 46 Broad
Mason & Demming. 33 Columbia
Marby Luke, 54 Centre
Price John, (axes) 40 Eldridge
Proctor Geo. W. 70½ Bowery & 44 Elizabeth
Sheffield James M. 141 Av. C
Simmons D. & Co. (axes) 13 Gold
Standish Miles. 89 Perry
Vetter Francis, 38 Clinton
Watts Lewis H. 85 Av. D

Niagara County.

Tivy Alfred   *Lewiston.*
Helmes John   *Lockport.*

Oneida County.

Cruikshank D.   *Deerfield.*
Faber C. L. Franklin   *Kirkland.*
Millard S. A. Clayville *Paris.*
Purdy S. James st.   *Rome.*
Windsor A. Packet Dock *Utica.*

Onondaga County.

Squiers A.   *Tully.*

Oswego County.

Barker Ebenezer   *Albion.*
Wells C. R.   *New Haven.*
Davis & Gage, 1st st. *Oswego.*
Dale Geo. Pulaski   *Richland.*
Rust & Van Waggoner, Fulton *Volney.*
Worlock John   do

Otsego County.

Parker & Randall   *Edmeston.*

St. Lawrence County.

Hill & Rhodes   *Gouverneur.*

Washington County.

Orven Jacob, Galesville *Greenwich.*
Hand E. F.   *White Creek.*

Egg Dealers, (Wholesale.)

Mabbett & Thurston, 19 Greenwich *New York.*
Young A. 184 Washington

Egg Powder.

Chamberlain William, 58 Chatham *New York.*

Electricians.

Everett Jesse, 17 Park Place *New York.*
Humbert Wm. H. 542 Broadway
Smith S. B. 293 Broadway

Emblems for Societies.

Doughty John H. 387 Grand *New York.*

Embroiderers.

Kings County.

Street C. 187 Fulton   *Brooklyn.*
Lander A. J. 211   do

New York County.

Cannata ——, 496 Broadway *New York.*
Massonat M. 28 White

Enamelled Works.

Bishop Edwin, 7 Dey   *New York.*
Marshall Alexander. 409 Cherry
Murphy J. G. 57 White
Poret ——, 22´   do

Engine Builders, Steam & Fire. (See also Founders; also Machinists.)

Albany County.

Vattel M. 4 Orange   *Albany.*
Stark & Pruyn, 52 and 54 Liberty
Haight James O. 11 Church

Kings County.

Berdon & Co. 102 Front. *Brooklyn.*

Monroe County.

Rochester Furnace and Steam Engine Works, cor. State & Mumford *Rochester.*
Kidd William, Brown's Race

New York County.

Birkbeck Geo. jr. 221 & 223 West *New York.*
Dunham H. R. & Co., 96 North Moore, and foot 33d st. N. R.
Esler & Prince, 17 West
Farnam G. B. (Fire) 31 Fulton
Glass John. 106 Goerck
Mattewan Company, 66 Beaver
Milligan Wm. E. 115 Warren
Morris Peter & Co. 45 Duane
Pease, Murphy & Co. 506 Cherry
Secor T. F. & Co. 413 9th
Smith James, (Fire engine) 71 West Broadway
Stillman, Allen & Co. foot 12th st. E. R.
Van Ness Abraham, (Fire engine) 151 Essex

Oneida County.

Higham & Co. cor. Whitesboro & Fayette sts. *Utica.*

Onondaga County.

Griffin R. Salina st. Syracuse *Salina.*

Rensselaer County.

Mann C. F., Fulton Works *Troy.*

Saratoga County.

Button Lysander   *Waterford.*

Engine Turners.

Banderet Cæsar, 42 Ann *New York.*
Barbier Eloy, 71 Nassau
Bon Charles, 65 Ann
Mason Daniel, 4 Liberty place

Engineers—Civil.

Chenango County.

M'Call E. B.   *Oxford.*

Erie County.

Wallace Wm. 190 Main   *Buffalo.*

Kings County.

Beers S. A. 157 Adams *Brooklyn.*
Graves Roswell, 207 Fulton
Murphy F. D. 191 3d *Williamsburgh.*

Monroe County.

Pomeroy H. 55 State *Rochester.*

New York County.

Campbell Ethan, 289 Broadway
    New York.
Clarke John T. 54 Wall
Cochrane James, 6 10th
Coffee Joseph E. 235 West
Gardiner Perry G. 10 Wall
Gwynne J. S. 33 West
Hunt W. G. 54 Wall
Hyde J. B. 54 Wall
Jervis John B. 54 Wall
Keller Charles M. 47 Wall
Kingsley & Pirsson, 5 Wall
Linsay Wm. H. 299½ Broadway
Matthews Samuel, 7 Av. D.
Pirsson Joseph P. 5 Wall
Savery A. & Co. 16 Wall
Schuyler R. & G. L. 2 Hanover
Serrell Wm. 289 Broadway
Turner Duncan, 87 Warren

Oneida County.

Van Vlack H., James st. *Rome.*

Oswego County.

M'Nair John, 1st st. *Oswego.*

Warren County.

Fairbanks Rufus, Glenn's Falls
    Queensbury.

Engineers' Drawing Paper.

Durand, Baldwin & Co. 40 Wall
    New York.

Engravers.

Albany County.

Gavit & Duthie, (Bank Notes) Exchange *Albany.*
Forbes E. (wood) Exchange
Carson R. (wood) do
Pease R. H. (wood) Broadway
Rawdon, Wright & Hatch, (Bank Note) 80½ State

Columbia County.

Spencer W. H. Warren st. *Hudson.*

Duchess County.

Power H. R. 299 Main *Poughkeepsie.*

Erie County.

Wightman E. 156 Main *Buffalo.*
Butler F. P. 17 Spaulding Exchange

Fulton County.

Balch Vestus *Johnstown.*

New York County.

Engravers—Bank Note.
Danforth & Hufty, 1 Wall
Durand, Baldwin & Co. 40 Wall
Harris B. 58 Nassau
Rawdon, Wright, Hatch & Edson, 48 Merchants' Exchange
Toppan, Carpenter & Co. 29 Wall
Wellstood, Benson & Hanks, 52 Merchants' Exchange

Engravers—Cameo.
Ellis S. 247 Broadway
Barrel P. 251 do

Engravers—Card.
Archer John, 96 Broadway
Clark James, 122 Fulton
Cochrane Wm. J. 72 Lispenard

Corbett George, 247 Broadway
    New York.
Delnoce Lewis. 96 Fulton
Demarest Abraham, 2 Pine
Folger William B. 118 John
Gimbrede Joseph N. 4 John
Halbert Augustus, 96 Fulton
Harrison David R. 71 Nassau
Heath William H. 142 Fulton
Jervis William, 366 Broadway
Lander John, 2 John
M'Lees A. & J. 68 Chambers (Irving House) & 170 Broadway
Marsh William R. 1 Cortlandt
Smith William D. 1 Ann
Starr Lemuel W. 177 William
Stout William C. 247 Broadway
Stout & Hyatt, 2 Maiden Lane
Strong Thomas W. 1 Marion
Warner Alfred, 3 Wall
Whaites E. P. 1 Cortlandt

Engravers and Dye Sinkers.
Alderton Wm. 295 Pearl
Ball & May, 96 Fulton
Brady James, 98 Nassau
Bridgens William H. 180 William
Denyer Robert J. 64 Division
Feely John, 15 N. William
Goll Frederick, 78 Fulton
Hoole Edmund, 175 William
Lawton Rich. C. 156 N. William
Lovett Thomas, rear 7 Dey
Moore John, 92 Merchants' Exch.
Simps J. C. rear 75 & 77 Nassau
Smith Frederick B. 122 Fulton
Turpin James, 6 Liberty place
Wahlmann Frederick, 175 Duane
Ziegler G. F. 338 Broadway

Engravers—General.
Archer John, 96 Broadway
Ashton W. H. 91 Cliff
Bailey William A. 299 Bowery
Blake William W. 309 Greenwich
Bolen John G. 104 Broadway
Bowley Charles, 556 Broadway
Buskirk J. 5 Dey
Clausen James M. 1 Murray
Collins John H. 151 Fulton
Combs & Anderton, 209 Grand
Cornell & Hyde, ¼ Warren
Craven John D. 177 Broadway
David S. S. 607 do
Dangerfield D. Alexander 2 Wall
Dempsey J. 252 Broadway
Dick Archibald L. 66 Fulton
Doney Thomas, 251 Broadway
Doty & Bergen, 120 William
Dugan John. 123 Fulton
Dugan A. 153 6th Av.
Dunnel Wm. N. 151 & 155 Fulton
Durand William, 42 Ann
Emmet John M. 173 Varick
Esler & Bunce, 26 Washington
Everdell Charles, 696 Broadway
Everdell J. 2 Wall & 302 B'dway
Everdell Wm. & Son, 104 Fulton
Ewbank James S. 700 Broadway
Fagan Edmund W. 333 Broadway
Feeley John, 15 N. William
Gallagher C. F. 4 Liberty place
Glegler George F. 338 Broadway
Gihon Thomas, 8 City Hall place
Gray W. T. 5 Dey
Halbert Augustus, 96 Fulton
Halpin Frederick, 34 Liberty
Harris Belinda, 58 Nassau
Harrison Charles, 25 John
Hicks Charles C. 11 Madison
Hoeh George. 75 W. Broadway
Hoole J. R. 124 Nassau
Horton John S. 60 do
Hunt Samuel V. 42 John
Hyatt Augustus, 260 Broadway
Ives J. S. 25 John
Jervis William, 366 Broadway
Jones James P. 48 Nassau
Jones A. 34 Liberty
Kelly J 141 Fulto
Lowe A. 150 do

M'Lees A. & J. 60 Chambers & 170
    Broadway *New York.*
Marchand Julius, 71 Nassau
Marsh William R. 1 Cortlandt
Moore William, 42 Ann
Narine & Co. 21 Wall
Neale Thomas, 67 Bowery
Newman A. C. 298 do
Okie G. W. 107 Canal
Ormsby W. L. 116 Fulton
Ourdan Joseph, 47 Gold
Packard Rawson, 47 do
Paradise John W. 4 New
Pittes Thomas, 296 Pearl
Pollock Thomas, 76 Nassau
Pretlove David, 24 Thames
Prudhomme J. F. 348 Broadway
Remmey Charles H. 210 Chatham
Rice & Buttre, 61 Fulton
Ritchie A. H. 23 Chambers
Roberts Robert, 562 Broadway
Schultheis Christian, 39 Ann
Shipper N. L. 178 6th Av.
Simpson Joseph, 60 Fulton
Stout & Hyatt, 2 Maiden lane
Summerville S. 193 Greenwich
Tompson William, 169 William
Vasseur Hermann, 92 Fulton
Walker C. W. 161 Fulton
Wallin Samuel, 289 Broadway
Waters John P. rear 22 Dey
White & Randolph, 161 Fulton
White Edward, 22 John
Ziegler G. F. 338 Broadway

Engravers—Historical, Portrait & Landscape.
Barnard William S. 19 Beekman
Burt Charles, 66 Fulton
Corbett George, 247 Broadway
Halpin Frederick, 34 Liberty
Jackman William G. 262 B'dway
Jones Alfred. 34 Liberty
Jones Fitz Edwin, 143 Forsyth
M'Rea John C. 6 City Hall place
Nichols F. B. rear 75 & 77 Nassau
Ormsby Waterman L. 116 Fulton
Prud'homme John F. E. 346
    Broadway
Rice & Buttre, 61 Fulton
Ritchie Alex. H. 23 Chambers
Shepherd Geo. M. 152 William
Smith Wm. D. 2 Ann
Wellstood Wm. rear 75 Nassau

Engravers—Map and Chart.
Atwood John M. 19 Beekman
Copley Charles, 16 Burling slip
Ensign & Thayer, 50 Ann
Sherman & Smith, 135 Broadway
Smith S. 135 Broadway

Engravers—Music.
Ackerman S. 89 Nassau
Quidor Geo. W. 333 Broadway
Roshore J. T. B. 20 Cortlandt

Engravers—Seal.
Brown Thomas, 251 Broadway
Francis Arthur W. 38 Reade
Lovett John D. 1 Cortland
Lovett Robert, 5 Dey
M'Lees A. & J. 69 Chambers & 170
    Broadway
Stout & Hyatt, 2 Maiden lane

Engravers—Stencil.
Newton M. 199 Water
Pittis Thomas, 296 Pearl
Simpson Joseph, 98½ Fulton

Engravers—Wood.
Avery Samuel P. 129 Fulton
Badeau J. F. 102 Nassau
Baker Samuel F. 140 do
Beadle Edward N. 289 Broadway
Bobbett & Edmonds, 90 Nassau
Bookhout Edward, 118 do
Bridges Wellington E. 140 do

Butler Warren C. 1 Spruce
　　　　　　　New York.
Cammeyer Dewit C. 59 Fulton
Caughey John, 136 Nassau
Charles Maurice. 142 Fulton
Childs Benj. F. 64 John
Cochran Wm. J. 72 Lispenard
Dunnell Wm. N. 141 Fulton
Durand Elias W. 42 Ann
Elton R. H. 175 William
Ende Louis, 64 John
Fay & Gulick, 80 Nassau
Felter John D 140 do
Haight A. R. 128 Fulton
Herrick Henry W. 64 John
Herrick William F. 64 do
Hillyard Henry. 66 Fulton
Horton Tudor, 50 Nassau
Howland Joseph T. 69 do
Howland Wm. 69　　do
Jocelyn A. H. 64 John
Kinnersley Augustus, 64 John
Kinnersley Henry, 64　do
Leslie & Traver, 98 Broadway
Loomis Pascal, 64 John
Lossing & Barritt, 71 Nassau
Major Richard, 117 Fulton
Minton J. 64 John
Neville Edgar, 122½ Fulton
Norman Wm. T. rear 61 Ann
O'Brien Robert, 64 John
Orr W. & Brother, 75 & 77 Nassau
Richardson J. W. 47 Gold
Richardson James H. 90 Fulton
Riches William, 31 Renwick
Roberts William, 13 Chambers
Smith D. T. 89 Nassau
Stafford John W. 64 John
Strong Thos. W. 98 Nassau
Tramper & Co. 168 William
Whitney E. J. 194 Nassau

Engravers—Xylographic.

Brownson William M. 56 Gold
Crump Samuel, 60 Nassau
Felt David & Co. 191 Pearl
Narine & Co. 21 Wall

Engravers.—Continued.

Oneida County.

Creen W. H. (wood) Devereaux
　Block　　　　　　*Utica.*

Onondaga County.

Chase B. Salina st. Syracuse
　　　　　　　　Salina.

Orange County.

Pierce Hart L.　　*Newburgh.*

Rensselaer County.

King Myron, 6 State　*Troy.*

Engravings and Prints.

New York County.

Audubon V. G. 43 Beaver
　　　　　　　New York.
Biggar James B. 69 Canal
Colman Wm. A. 204 Broadway
Currier Nathaniel. 154 Nassau
Goupil, Vibert & Co. 289 Broadway
Kellogg & Comstock, 150 Fulton
Neale John. 56 Carmine
Powell Sydney T. 251 Broadway
Risso & Leefe, 18 Cortlandt

Exchange Offices.

Ashley Martin, 268 Greenwich &
　196 Chambers　　*New York.*
Axell Harry. 96 James
Bache George P. 178 Greenwich
Bache & Peck, 174 Broadway
Baker John H. 549 Grand
Baker Samuel T. 212 Broadway
Barker John S. 80 Barclay
Barnet George, 134 Houston

Barringer Paul, 92 Elizabeth
　　　　　　　New York.
Bauer A. 192 Division
Beirne John, 15 Washington
Bignall Daniel, 132 Clinton place
Bills O. A. 11 West & 136 Greenwich
Blackall Wm. 3 Mulberry
Blauvelt James M. 160 Greenwich
Bonsall R. W. 212½ & 234 Hudson
Braisted Thos. H. 6 Division & 146
　Chatham
Brown Samuel. 98 Church
Brown John, 290 Mott
Brown.John, 642½ Greenwich
Bross Gary, 647 Church
Bull A. 11 Broadway
Carter Wm. 131 Walker
Ceragioli Charles, 25 Spruce
Chase Dexter. 66 Mercer
Clark Abner W. 144 Division
Clark Alex. 69 Cedar
Clarke A. 78 Reade & 87½ Cedar
Clark Joseph, 338 Hudson
Clark L. M. 389½ Pearl
Clark Wm. 64 Chatham
Clauson Wm. 78 Ridge
Clement A. G. 34 Fulton
Clements & Canfield, 23 Old Slip
Clover J. M. 160 Greenwich
Clute J. L. 39 Sheriff
Cohen A 172 W. Broadway
Cotte J. B. 138 Bowery
Cousens Job. 34 Park Row
Crawford Wm. 50 Thompson
Creamer H. C. 56 Essex
Crombie James A. 21 Ann
Cummings M. 173½ Mulberry
Curry James, 45 Canal
Curtis John, 455 Houston
Darling S. A. 177 Greenwich
Desendorf James, 307 Greenwich
Dominick Francis N. 258 Bowery
Dunning Smith, 169 Greenwich
Evans Thomas, 1 Murray
Farrow Wm. 366 Grand
Finley Andrew, 36 Fulton
Foster & Gregory, 166 Greenwich
Foster Amasa S. 234 Pearl
Frink John, 47 Church
Frink & Mills, 99 W. Broadway
Gage George, 181 Broadway
Garwood Phas, 51 Cortlandt
Gathawy E. J. 12 Av A
Gibson John D. 144 Varick
Gleeson Geo. 350 6th Av.
Glover J. M. 160 Greenwich
Gourlay John F. 131½ Orange
Gregory & Foster, 166 Greenwich
Griffith Enoch, 86½ Hamersley
Halley Walter, 34 6th Av.
Hays John, 50 Thompson
Hemphill Samuel. 292 Greenwich
Henry John S. 150 Duane
Henry J. O. 196 Broadway
Henry M. 130 Greenwich Av.
Herring John, 3 4th Av.
Hetterich John, 32 Bowery
Hhritner Daniel. 92 Sheriff
Hough Joseph, 220 Broadway
Holley B. M. 252 6th Av.
Holland E. 67 9th Av.
Howel ——. 156 Suffolk
Hyde Edwin N. 246 Greenwich
Jackson D. 30 W. Broadway
Jennings Wm. 37 8th Av.
Jessup & Cole, 191 Greenwich
Johnson Charles, 23 Laurens
Johnson Hiram. 102 Barclay
Johnson Samuel, 56 Pearl
Johnson Wm. 65 Charlton
Jones John, 72 W. Broadway
Jones Samuel. 72 W. Broadway
Jones Wm. 11 Broadway & 108
　Church
Kaminski Alexander, 39 Suffolk
Kay George, 196 Houston
Keaye Geo. 161½ 3d & 5 Av. D
Keeler Thaddeus. 3 Crosby
Kemp Jeremiah G. 11 Clark
Kent Wm. 176½ Mulberry
Lappin Edward, 60 Elizabeth

Lawrence James, 125 Duane & 42
　W. Broadway　　*New York.*
Lee George, 240 Division
Leland Lemuel, 56 Pearl
Ludlum David, 40 Sheriff
Lyons Matthew, 2½ Roosevelt
M'Brien Charles, 116 Chatham
M'Cauley Wm. 54 Chatham & 59
　E. Broadway
M'Kee John, 84 9th Av.
M'Mannis Patrick H. 19½ Grand
M'Manus Charles, 190 Chatham
Mackay Wm 29½ Park Row
Mather Wm. 70 W. Broadway
Matthews Wm. 70 W. Broadway
Mead James, 5 Bayard
Mead John W. 197 Varick
Mendell Henry, 184 Broadway
Miller James A. 96 Elizabeth
Miller Wm. S. 24 W. Broadway
Morford & Vermilye, Greenwich
　cor. Dey
Morrison William J. 224 6th
Morton George W. 333 Houston
Mott Samuel G. 257 Centre
Murray W. G. & Co. 146 Fulton
Nathan Benjamin, 34 Elizabeth &
　87 4th Av.
Odell Lawrence, 417 Broadway
Oxx William, 69 Barclay
Parks Lemuel W. 79½ Chambers
Perkes Smith A. Park row
Payson Stephen, 66 Fulton
Pearl Joseph, 32 Laurens
Petit ——, 334 Houston
Petty Ezekiel, 534½ Grand
Phelan John G. 96 Cross
Plass Jehoiakim N. 184 Broadway
Plass N. & C. T. Barnard, 208
　Broadway
Price John, 140 Anthony
Reed David L. 238 Grand
Reilley Joseph, 92 Goerck
Riley Edmund, 198 Franklin
Robinson Samuel W. 410½ Grand
Roe Walter A. 652 Hudson
Rowe Samuel, 26 Crosby
Russel James, 12 Av. A
Samuels E. 569 Pearl
Samuel Daniel, 58 Cherry
Sather & Church, 164 Nassau
Seaman William, 299 Houston
Sebert John, 147 Church
Secor John M. 417 Broadway
Seixas Gershom I. 496½ Houston
　& 126 Beekman
Seixas H. M. 496 Houston
Shearon John, 34 Old slip
Simmons John, 216½ Canal
Simmons J. E. H. 24 Crosby
Simons Ebenezer A. 559 Pearl
Simonson Daniel, 155 Orange
Smith C. H. 267 Center
Smith James. 126 Duane
Smith John, 157 W. Broadway
Smith Moses, 122 Cherry
Smith Peter, 59 Anthony
Smith & Hews, 137 Chatham
Squire & Noyes, 191½ Bowery
Stanley D. 159 Church
Stetson Decatur, 88 Sullivan
Stetson John, 68 Thompson
Stetson Leander, 532½ Broome
Stewart James I. 170 Greenwich
Stewart Sarah, 86 Anthony
Stephens Asa, jr. 405 Hudson
Story S. 262 Pearl
Stuart Edwin A. 77½ Broome
Sturges James H. 5 Bowery
Suvear Joseph, 194 Houston
Thompson Thomas, 8 Mulberry
Tice J. 376 Hudson
Tolerton John G. 320 Grand
Tooker Edw. W. 268 Greenwich
Townsend James, 54 W. Broadway
Tripp Edward A. 242 7th
Troup & Reed, 684 Houston
Tuohill John, 42 Water
Vanderbilt Aaron J. 81 Canal
Vanduzer S. & W. A. 170 Greenwich

Warner George T. 316½ Broadway & 23 Elm *New York.*
Warren John, 86 W. Broadway
Waterhouse John H. 146 Bowery
Watson James, 109 Pitt
Webster D. P. 7 Ann & 126 Broad
Webster S. T. 172 W. Broadway
White F. & Co. 35 Wall
White Mason, 5 Battery place
Whitmore John H. 4 Thomas
Wilkinson John, 215 Centre
Williams James, 81 Canal
Williamson Arthur, 77 Centre
Wood Benjamin, 48 Canal
Wood George, 155 Walker
Woods William, 180 Broadway & 225 Centre
Woodruff C. B. 3 Greenwich
Wright John C. 111 7th Av.

Expresses.

Adams & Co., 16 *Wall street.*—Boston, Mass.; Worcester, Mass.; Norwich. Conn.; New London, Conn.; New Haven, Conn.; Hartford. Conn.; Trenton. N. J.; Philadelphia. Pa. ; Wilmington. Del.; Lancaster, Pa.; Harrisburgh, Pa.; Carlisle, Pa.; Chambersburgh, Pa.; Lewiston. Pa.; Baltimore, Md.; Washington. D. C.; Norfolk, Va.; Fredericksburgh. Va.; Richmond, Va.; Petersburgh, Va.; Cumberland, Md ; Pittsburgh, Pa.; Wheeling. Va.; Cincinnati, Ohio ; Louisville, Ky.; St. Louis. Mo.; New Orleans. La.
Butterfield, Wasson & Co., 88 *Broadway, cor. Wall.*—Runs to Albany and Buffalo, and the intermediate stations on the Railroad between.
Evins & Co., 16 *Wall st.*—Providence, Newport, Fall River. Taunton. New Bedford. Nantucket.
Harnden's, 6 *Wall st.*—Boston, Providence, Philadelphia, New Haven, Hartford, Springfield, and Foreign.
Kingsley & Co, Broadway. cor. Wall.—Boston, Fall River, Newport, Providence, Phila'phia, Wilmington. Del.; Lancaster. Penn.; Harrisburgh, Penn.; Carlisle, Pa.; Chambersburgh, Penn.; Lewiston, Penn.; Baltimore. Md.; Washington, D. C.; Norfolk, Va.; Richmond. Va.; Cumberland, Md.; Pittsburgh. Penn.; Wheeling, Va.; Cincinnati. Ohio ; Louisville, Ky. St. Louis; New Orleans.
Livingston & Co. 6 *Wall st.*—Philadelphia, Baltimore, Washington. Pittsburgh. and South.
Livingston & Furgo.—159 *Main st. Buffalo.*—Run in connection with Wells & Co., and Butterfield. Wasson & Co.—Erie, Cleveland, Sandusky, Columbus, Cincinnati, Louisville, St. Louis, Chicago, Milwaukee, Detroit, and South & West.
Livingston, Wells & Co. 10 *Wall st.*—Paris, Havre, Bordeaux, Liverpool, London, Southampton, Glasgow, Bremen, and the principal places in Great Britain and Germany.
Lount & Co. 88 *Broadway, cor. Wall.*—San Francisco. Sacramento city. Stockton, and all parts of the mines.
Pullen & Co. 10 *Wall st* —Troy, Ballston. Saratoga, and Whitehall. In connection with Wells & Co.
Rice & Peck, 1 *Nassau street.*—Corning. Elmira, Factoryville, Towanda, Owego, Binghamton, Great Bend, Deposit, Hancock, Collikoon, Big Eddy, Honesdale, Port Jervia.

Smead's Canada Express, 159 Main st. Buffalo.
Virgil & Rice, 10 *Wall street.*—Northern, and Canada East, Troy, Ballston, Saratoga and Whitehall, Burlington. Plattsburgh, Champlain, St. Johns, Montreal.
Wells & Co. 10 *Wall st.*—Albany to Buffalo, and intermediate stations, Erie, Ashtabula, Painesville, Cleveland, Sandusky, Toledo, Monroe, Detroit, Ann Arbor, Jackson, Marshall, Battle Creek, Kalamazoo, Paw Paw, Niles, New Buffalo, Chicago, Little Fort, Racine, Southport, Milwaukee, Tiffen, Kenston, Bellefontaine, Urbana, Springfield, Columbus, Xenis, Cincinnati.

Extension Table Makers.

Hobe Charles F. 443 Broadway
New York.
Nash & Son, 61 Mangin

Fancy Goods Dealers. (*See also Watches and Jewelry ; also Toys ; also Millinery; also Silks and Fancy Dry Goods.*)

Broome County.

Cook B. T. & L. *Binghamton.*
Noland W. H.
Harrington D. & C.

Cayuga County.

Lester & Bradley, 80 Genesee
Auburn.

Columbia County.

Colbrook Mrs., Warren st. *Hudson.*
Newbury Hannah, Warren st.

Duchess County.

Berry W. 329 Main *Poughkeepsie.*
Palmateer P.
Haight H. 233 Main
Danvers Mary, 15 Market
Ketcham I. 8 do
Drake Mrs. 138½ Main

Erie County.

Walker John, 430 Main *Buffalo.*
Cameron & Fuller, (importers) 3 Commercial
Hollidge E. (wholesale) 228 Main
Heermann F. (importer) 278 do
Barnum S. O. (variety) 215 Main
Blancan Peter. 229 do
Flersheim & Brother, 93 do
Bryant Warren. 145 do
Bristol C. C. 225 do

Kings County.

Goole G. 131½ Atlantic *Brooklyn.*
Hulse Chas. W. 139 do
Knocke L. 147 do
Vanderhooven G. W. 213 Atlantic
Vaughan Miss J. 55 do
Walter F. 57½ do
Ferrally C. 60 do
Pitcher E. 153 Court
Marshall Jas., cor. Smith & War'n
Riecks C. W 180 Fulton
Wyvill A., Middagh near Fulton
Harvey T. R. 224 Fulton
Stewart Mrs. M. H. 101 Fulton
Hickman Mrs. A. 101 do
Brewster Elisha, 92 Main
Pitt Mrs. C. 75 Sands
Waterman Mrs. M. J. 75 Prospect
Leonard Mrs. J. Nassau cor. Jay
Richards R. (importer) 41 Myrtle Av.
Smith John M. (laces) 275 Fulton
Van Cleef John, 259 do

Van Riper Mrs. Esther, 259 Fulton
Brooklyn.
Atkins Mrs. E. 219 Fulton
Woods Thomas, 209 do
Harvey J. 199½ do
Voris V. 193 do
Purchase Miss E. 191 do
Querrean Mrs. C. 187 do
Bradbrook Miss S. 201 do
Wheeler Horatio, 193 do
Coggeshall Mrs. L. B. 189 do
Conklin Mrs. Mary, 82 Myrtle Av.
Banker Miss A. 97 do
Smith E. W. 142 do
Miller John, 155 do
Bradley C. 155 do
Moran Joseph, 148 do
Lucky J. R. 140 do
Smith Miss S. 42 South 7th
Williamsburgh.
Saunders Thomas, 53 S. 7th
Kemp Miss C. & Pearson, 82 S. 4th
Willetts Miss H. A. 93 4th
Hatkins Mrs. J. 121½ Grand
Hineson J. 123 do
Ryan Thomas, 159 do
Houpt F. E. 185 do
Swanton George, 312 do
Phillips Mrs. H. M. 256 do
Myers Mrs. A. 216½ do
Guns Mrs. M. 208 do
Gildersleeve R. O. 180 do
Cotsy Mrs. C. M. 152½ do
Sidell Wm. 30 do
Shuttleworth James, 74 do
Gill John, 148 do
Klaen Mrs. Kosper, (military) 149 Ewing

Monroe County.

Scranton Henry, 52 Buffalo
Rochester.
Conolly James, 36 Buffalo
Stanton & Brother, 8 Exchange
Gormly S. 54 State
Allen H. (bazaar) 27 Buffalo

New York County.

FANCY GOODS—IMPORTERS OF.

(*See also Importers General, also Dry Goods Importers, also Silks and Fancy Dry Goods.*)

Ahrenfeldt Charles, 25 Liberty & 56 Maiden lane *New York.*
Allcock & Allen, 341 Broadway
Althof & Ahlborn, 59 Maiden lane
Arnold, Southworth & Co. 169 P'rl
Bache Semon & Co. 21 Cedar
Baker A. 102 William
Bayleys & Wright, 26 Cedar
Berly Frederick. 15 John
Bernheimer & Hausmann, 38 B've
Bevier J. L. 72 Liberty
Binsse Louis E. 83 William
Bishop Victor, 23 Maiden lane
Bougera Elie, 80 John
Bridgman & Day, 189 Pearl
Brown Moses P. 17 Cedar
Butler Edwin J. 193 Pearl
Calhoun & Vanderburgh, 135 Pearl & 88 Beaver
Carleton & Frothingham, 127 & 129 William
Carter, Halsey & Baldwin, 160 Pearl
Cary William H. & Co, 243 & 345 Pearl
Chandler Job & Foster, 61 Maiden Lane
Church Chas. C. 189 Pearl
Churchill & Kittal, 76 Maid Lane
Colvill & Fleming, 71 Maid. Lane
Cook, Levi & Co. 71 Broadway
Cooke Lyman & Co. 87 Pearl
Cromwell W. A. 24 Cedar
Defiganiere Louis F. 34 Platt
Deraismes J. & Co. 83 William
Deraismes & Dumoulin, 73 Maid. Lane
Descombes L. J. 156 Broadway

Draper & Rowland. 5 Maid. Lane
New York.
Duhain L. 25 John
Engler Charles. 13 South William
Erhard & Sons, 161 William
Fahreguettes Efils & Morra, 73 William
Fellows, Wadsworth & Co. 17 Maiden Lane
Forbes James H. 45 Cortlandt
Gerson S. & Co. 52 Maid. Lane
Gerstle Henry, 3 Cedar
Goddard Joseph W. 95 William
Grassie & Coffin, 45 Maid. Lane
Groesbeck & Co. 30 Maiden Lane
Grosheim C. F. 12 Gold
Hen Edward. 23 Liberty
Herzberg Julius, 116 William
Hine Charles D. 89 William
Hinrichs C. F. A. 150 Broadway
Hulberton J. W. 75 Maiden Lane
Houdbert-Boucher Josephine, 22 Warren
Kellogg & Houghton, 152 Broadway 233 Pearl & 27 S. William
Kipling Richard, 32 Maid. Lane
Klett Charles, 16 Platt
Knight Daniel M. 23 Cedar
Laumonier Joshua, 46 Maid. Lane
Le Gal, Bouland & Co. 96 William
Legoux & Pardessus, 55 Maid. L.
Levy Mark & Brothers, 49 Maiden Lane
Lilliendahl C. D. W. 133 William
Lowitz, Becker & Cludius, 66 John
Lyon William H. & Co. 79 Cedar
M'Kewan John, 47 Fulton
Marvin A. B. & Co. 93 William
Murray Peter, 35 Maid. Lane
Nagle & Co. 110½ William
Pardow J. 95 Maiden Lane
Pascal & Haran, 130 Canal
Pasquier & De Lussan, 47 Nassau
Pike & Ladd, 89 Nassau
Plunkett A. & W. H. Coles, 104 William
Ramee & Matthiesson. 105 William
Renard & Co. 116 Pearl
Rice & Smith, 727 Broadway
Riesheim & Berlyn, 61 William
Rosenfield Louis & Brothers, 28 Cedar
Rosenthal Joseph & Brother, 25 Cedar
Sebastian Christian, 207 Walker
Sheehan & Duggan, 97 Maid. Lane
Sill & Thompson, 23 Maid. Lane
Sittenfeld Ferdinand, 45 Delancy
Smith C. P. 71 Liberty
Sondheim H. & Co. 5 Cedar
Spelman, Fraser & Co. 83 Cedar
Talmadge & Burch, 151 Broadw'y
Tauber John A. 102 Pearl
Taylor P. G. & Co. 214 Pearl
Tetercl & Blain, 124 Pearl
Von Keller Hermann, 99 & 101 William
Ward, Dickson & Co 41 Maid. Lane
Ward, Peck & Co. 102 & 104 Maid. Lane
Webb & Raymond, 53 Liberty
Wedeles & Meyer. 53 Cedar
Weibe J. A. 86 William
Woodworth F. A. 325 Broadway

FANCY GOODS—RETAIL.

Abeel Catharine, 313½ & 377½ Grand
Adams W. 198 Chatham
Adelsdorfer & Neustadter, 415½ Grand
Albro Wm. 455 Hudson
Alexander E. & Son, 38 Bowery
Allcock & Allen, 341 Broadway
Althof Louis, 567 Broadway
Anderson Ebenezer, 216 Canal
Appleton A. 292 Bowery
Artault Francois A. 539 B'dway
Ashton Mary, 344 6th
Atkinson Amelia A. 379 Hudson
Aymar William, 214 Spring

Bamberger Louis, 46 8th Av.
New York.
Barr Gerrit, 119 Troy
Barton J. 78 W. Broadway
Bateson C. R. 262 Broome
Behrend S. N. 5 1st Av.
Bell Charles, 326½ Bowery
Bernhard Isidor, 100 Bowery & 59 William
Bettman A. M. 490 Grand
Blair David, 281 Greenwich
Blum Catharine, 854 Broadway
Boddy George. 64 Catharine
Bothwell David, 343 1st Av.
Boyce M. 297 Hudson
Boyd Henry, 25 8th Av.
Bradley E. 204 Spring
Bradley William, 266 3d Av.
Brady P. 471 6th Av.
Briggs James H. 210 Spring
Bromley John, 296 Grand
Brown Philip, 198 Spring
Brown Wm. 265 3d Av.
Brown & Seidner, 34 Rector
Browne Maurice F. 105 8th Av.
Browne Robert W. 386 Bowery
Browne Wm. H. 223 Hudson
Brownlee Matilda, 126 Allen
Burrell & Taylor, 289 Grand
Bursey Mary, 49 Mulberry
Busteed Anna, 164 Walker
Campbell James, 32½ Chatham
Carnet George, 28 Rector
Carroll Edward, 72 6th Av.
Cerf & Stern, 20½ Bowery
Chailly A. 166½ Bowery
Chapman Robert, 246 Bleecker
Chesterman C. 304 3d Av.
Childs E. 272 Canal
Chubb Elizabeth, 106 Hudson
Clare John, 54 Sullivan
Clarke Elizabeth, 547 Broadway
Cochran Isabella, 99 9th Av.
Cohen J. & Son, 36 Grand
Coleman Josephus, 45½ Carmine
Collier Thomas, 262 Bleecker
Combs Elias, 268 Grand
Conacher John, 229 6th Av.
Conklin Eleazer M. 237 Sullivan
Conklin Margaret, 89 Division
Conley S. 430 Hudson
Cook John, 80 Canal
Cooke M. L. 422½ Grand
Cooper Ann, 57 W. Broadway
Cope . 50 Av. D
Corwith David H. 99½ Catharine
Covel, Ely & Covel, 218½ 6th Av.
Cox Carson A. 93½ Canal
Crandal Jesse, 29 Hudson
Cropsey Andrew, 94 Canal
Crown S. 20 Division
Culver Samuel. 434 Greenwich
Dannenbaum & Woolbach, 339 Grand
Davis Francis, 397 Grand
Davis James S. 300 Bleecker
Davis Thomas, 598 Grand
Dayton William P. 641½ B'dway
Deferee William H. 368 Hudson
Demarest Henry, 607 Broadway
Dewland Geo. 216 Greenwich
Demarest Henry & Co. 305 Hudson
Derr R. A. 390 6th Av.
Doran James, 194 Canal
Doran Ann, 110 3d Av.
Doubet A. 565 Broadway
Dreyfus Benedict, 467 Pearl
Drysdale Isabella. 46 4th Av.
Drysdale M. 117 Varick
Dugard Jose, 179 9th Av.
Dwyer Mary Ann, 436 G'wich
Earle M. 28 8th Av.
Earle Wm H. 40 4th Av.
Ehrenstrasser B. 96 Rivington
Elbrechter Philip, 180 Canal
Elbreich S. 238 3d
Elder Elizabeth, 527 Pearl
Elston David, 292 Hudson
Ely Caroline, 260 Spring
Erskine John, 212 8th Av.
Evans Thomas, 67 Catharine
Eveleigh Sarah, 148 Spring

Ezekiel Abm. 366 Grand
New York.
Fanning Edward. 226 Bowery
Fanning Sidney, 272 Bleecker
Farrar Wm. H. 343 6th Av.
Ferguson John S. 250 Bowery
Finkelmeier John P. 395 Grand
Fishel J. 271 Spring
Fisher Thomas C. 105 Bleecker
Fitzgerald Morris. 214 Rivington
Fletcher John, 333 Broadway
Flurey Mary, 243 Division
Flynn Thomas. 32 2d
Foley Ellen, 12th st.
Forbes Susan H. 345 Bleecker
Foulds Robert. 172 Chatham
Fowler Elizabeth. 202 Grand
Frank & Straus. 312 Bowery
Fraser Robert, 233 Broadway
Frazer William. 368 Bowery,
Freedman S. 180½   do
Frumber Fred. 139 Wooster
Fuller Elizabeth. 139 Hammond
Geoghegan Thomas, 86 4th
Gerling F. 273 Greenwich
Giffing Wm. H. 3 Greenwich Av
Girvan Thomas, 286 Bleecker
Glassford James, 679 Broadway
Glassford Robert W. 322 Bleecker
Goodkind Wm. 299 Grand
Gros M. & Son, 272 Greenwich
Gunzenhauser Lewis H. 326 Bleecker
Hall Thomas, 133 Spring
Hamilton Robert, 6 Battery place
Hancock Wm. 208 3d Av.
Hanneman Leopold, 137½ Washington
Hannah Ellen, 122 G'wich Av.
Hanrahan Ann, 143 Walker
Hardy Alex. 529 Greenwich
Hart J. jr. 262 Bowery
Harvey Charles, 304 do
Hayes Catharine, 85 Catharine
Healy Daniel, 88½   do
Healy E. 156½ Greenwich
Hector Mary, 234½ Bleecker
Heintzer W. 569 Broadway
Heller Jonas, 381 Grand
Herdman A. & M. 30 Division
Hermann S. 615 Greenwich
Hetfield F. O. 449½ Hudson
Heyman Ezekiel, 268 Bowery
Heyn Ernest, 437½ Broadway
Higbee J. S. 105 Greenwich
Hildreth Lotin, 262 3d Av.
Hope Cornelius L. 376½ Bowery
Hope Margaret, 91 Hudson
Howard John B. 269 & 280 Broadway
Howe H. 31 M'Dougal
Howe Wm. P. 281 1st Av.
Hawkins W. 388 3d Av.
Hugh & Co. 486 Pearl
Hughes Elizabeth, 121 Troy
Hughes James N. 341 6th Av.
Hull W. 9th Av. near 26th
Hutchings Samuel L. 60 M'Dougal
Hutchinson Jane, 340½ Bleecker
Israel Jacob, 7 Battery place
Jackson Lewis E. 270 3d Av.
Jackson Mary A. 204 Division
Jacobus Janette, 433 Pearl
James Rachel. 112 Canal
Jarvis Jeanette. 737 Broadway
Jeens William M. 239 Bleecker
Jewesson Jeremiah J. 211 Division
Johnson John, W. 21st cor. 9th Av.
Jones & Linthwaite, 378 Bowery
Johnson E. 30 Hudson
Kavanagh M. 509 Pearl
Kastor Abraham, 391 Broadway
Katzenstein Israel, 150 Canal
Kelly M. 84 7th Av.
Kelly P. jr. 641 Hudson
Kellock J. 357 Hudson
Keeler Smith, 526 Pearl
Kempton Ann, 5 Lewis
Ketcham Azariah C. 166 Division
Koohler Mary, 5 4th Av.
Kuh Jacob & Bush, 176 Canal
Kulenkampff Herman,167 Chath'm

Ladies Depository, 850 Broadway New York.
Lang Henry, 201 6th Av.
Langdon Edmond G. 86 Hudson
Langstaedter Jacob & B. 193½ Division
Langsing J. 329 Broadway
Lauber Barnet, 257 Hudson
Leeper C. 172½ Bowery
Lebars & Co. 219 8th Av.
Lengfeld J. & Brothers, 260½ Bowery
Leonard Robert, 221 Hudson
Leopold Laderer, 421 Grand
Lichtenberg, Myer & Co. 264 Bowery
Lichtenstein M. H. 92 Bowery
Lincoln Abby, 235 3d Av.
Lindley & Mundy, 250 Bleecker
Lindsey Mrs. 541 Greenwich
Little Andrew, 331 Hudson
Lock George, 315 5th
Lockhart Thomas, 158 6th Av.
Logemann William, 7 Chambers
Lonergan Eliza T. 350 Bowery
Long Eliza. 46½ 6th Av.
Loupie Jacob, 13 Rector
Lyon Phoebe, 83 4th
M'Cormick Julia, 67 4th Av.
M'Court Catherine, 117 Hammond
M'Cullough Isabella, 23 Morris
M'Dougall M. 294 8th Av.
M'Gee Amos H. 60½ Division
M'Glinch E. 463 Greenwich
M'Govern James C. 134 Division
M'Govern Thomas, 134 Division
M'Intyre Mary, 234 3d Av.
M'Kane G. 4 Av. B
M'Quoid William, 235 8th Av.
M'Williams Thos. 733 Wash'ton
Maverick M. 48½ Carmine
M'Kenzie E. 61 Division
Malherbe Armand, 463 Broadway
Mansfield J. 92 Canal
Many Thomas, 497 Pearl
Manning Catherine, 497 Pearl
Marcellus Helen M. 793 G.wich
Marsden John, 20 Clinton slip
Masterson John H. 47 Av. D
Mead Jane E. 488 Grand
Merrit A. 87 9th Av.
Merryman D. 459 Hudson
Miller Mary, 45 Av. B
Millard E. 186 6th Av.
Montgomery Hugh, 486 Pearl
Mood Peter. 74 Hudson
Moody Samuel, 183 9th Av.
Moore Ambrose, 292 Grand
Moore Elizabeth, 52 6th Av.
Moore James H. 120 6th Av.
Moore & Lion, 96 Canal and 92 Bowery
Morunge Henry, 88 Chatham
Morgan Barnum, 514 Hudson
Morgan David, 104 Division
Morrison J. M. 251 Grand
Morris Hetty & E. 232 Bleecker
Morissy Rosanna, 80½ King
Morton & Murray, 469 Broadway
Morton T. & Brother, 63 Elizabeth
Mullens P. 157½ Greenwich
Murphy John, 11½ Washington
Neaumann Jachiel, 478 Hudson
Nesbitt Alexander, 177 3d Av.
Newburger Wm. 42½ Columbia
Newram George, 389 Greenwich
Norris Catherine, 115 Hudson
Oakley & Chassell. 16 Cortlandt
O'Keeffe Ellen, 616½ 4th
O'Keefe J. K. 15 3d Av.
Olsted Lawrence, 13 Carlisle
O'Meara J. 261 Greenwich
O'Meara Jeremiah 8. 148 Canal
O'Neall P. 519 Pearl
O'Neil Miss, 181 Grand
Osborn Eliza. 514 Grand
Pack M. 307 3d Av.
Palmer James. 63 Av. D.
Parker E. 252 3d Av.
Parker James, 203 Spring
Parkson John. 234 Greenwich
Parkinson Edward, 122 10th

Pascal & Horan, 130 Canal New York.
Passenbronder Eliz. 268 Bleecker
Paterson James, 192 Canal
Patten W. B. & J. 263 Greenwich
Patterson James A. 203 6th Av.
Patterson Joseph, 556 Hudson
Paul Thomas. 455 Greenwich
Pearson Charles B. 273 Grand
Peck Isaac L. 130 Division
Pelton Mrs. 432 Greenwich
Peyser F. M. & Co. 363 Broadway
Plain Frances B. 58 Carmine
Popper S. & D. 367 Grand
Post Mrs. B. cor. Av. C. & 6th
Powell M. 87 8th Av.
Power Margaret, 552 Grand
Proctor H. 302 Bowery
Quigg Edward. 128 Division
Quimby Zebedee, 303½ Broadway
Quin M. 401 3d Av.
Quinlan & Brother, 5 Cedar
Rafferty Rosanna, 593 Broadway
Rague R. K. Ann, 114 Av. C.
Reed E. 26 Spring
Reed Lewis. 340 6th Av.
Ress H. 353 10th
Regue James, 114 Av. C.
Renans Caroline, 161 Division
Reynolds Anne, 126 W. 21st
Rice Ann Eliza, 156 Spring
Rice Henry, 76 Canal
Richardson Ann, 167 6th Av.
Riddock Joseph. 2 Stuyvesant
Riggs Daniel, 207 3d Av.
Rikeman Ann A. 4 5th
Rintskopf Barnard W. 417½ Grand
Robinson Jane, 329 6th
Rosa William, 137 Washington
Rosenblatt Asher, 108 Canal
Rosenblatt George. 458 Grand
Rosenblatt Sigmond S. 486 Grand
Rosenfeld M. H. 240 Bleecker
Rosenheim & Brother, 381½ Grand
Rothschild Benjamin, 300 2d
Rourke Patrick, 249 Greenwich
Runney T. W. 242½ Bleecker
Samuels J. 277 Greenwich
Saunders A. & S. 287 Broadway
Scanlan Johanna. 485 Greenwich
Schmitt B. L. 54½ Bowery
Schwab Lewis, 43 Av. D
Schwab Levi. 417 Grand
Sedgwick Roderick, jr. 144 Canal
Selzas Samuel, 23 Clinton market
Seely H. 177 Greenwich
Sell & Hammond, 29 Cedar
Sewell Thomas, 516 Grand
Shanks Sarah, 114 Bleecker
Shaw Otho, 238 8th Av.
Shaw E. 291 2d
Shotwell John, 32 College place
Sigmond Lantar, 42 Av. C
Silverman Jacob, 382 Grand
Silverman Solomon, 32½ Division
Simon George, 202 Av. B
Simmons Louis. 198 Bowery
Sinclair Wm. T. 56½ Canal
Skelly Mrs. 143 Greenwich
Slade Edmund, 34 1st
Sloan Margaret, 568½ Grand
Smith James Y. 207 6th Av.
Smith Jane, 38 Lewis
Smith W. 54 3d
Smith Edward, 407 Greenwich
Smith Maria, 70 West Broadway
Snell Susan A. 7th Av. between 19th & 20th
Sondheim Lewis, 184 Bowery
Sondheim Simon. 225 Hudson
Speyer David, 154 Canal
Staunton J. 377 Broadway
Straus & Bros J. 202½ Division
Stannage L. 339 6th Av.
Stein Charles, 200 Rivington
Steinbrenner Fred. 96½ Bowery
Stern M. 369 Grand
Stewart Robert, 271 Greenwich
Stephenson Margaret, 142 Walker
Stevens John, 311 Hudson
Stewart Sarah E. 193 6th Av.
Stivers D. A. 356 3d Av.

Stone Margaret, 443 & 425 Pearl New York.
Stoney Henry, 44 6th Av.
Stonier & Co. 382 Bowery
Storm Keziah, 209 3d Av.
Storms William P. 230 Bleecker
Strauss Simon. 253 Hudson
Stump Jane, 217 Canal
Sullivan Patrick, 56 Walnut
Sunter Emily, 291 Bleecker
Sutton M. R. 220 Division
Sweeney Charlotte, 75 West Bdy.
Swift Anne, 250 Canal
Taft Henry, 155 Madison
Taylor B. F. 444 Cherry
Taylor Mary, 91 9th Av.
Taylor Richard, 547 Hudson
Teller Rebecca. 171 3d Av.
Telfer David. 640 Hudson
Thompson James, 58 Catharine
Thorndon Mary, 67 King
Thorn L. 57 8th Av.
Tiffany, Young & Ellis, 271 Bdy.
Tillman Abbe, 1 6th Av
Toal Charles, 90 Catharine
Towers Alfred, 58 3d Av.
Trimble James L. 206 Canal
Tripler John H. 396 Grand
Tubbs Ann, 122 4th Av.
Turner Miss 35 6th Av.
Turnbull W. C. 254 Bowery
Tuttle George W. 311 Broadway
Ulman Julius, 78 Bowery
Ulmann John, 223 Greenwich
Umber Mrs. 431 Grand
Van Tuyl A. P. 341 Grand
Vignot Amedee, 206½ Canal
Vance T. 241 Grand
Voeltzel William, 107 6th Av.
Volkers Peter, 138 Division
Wahlms Haman, 180 Essex
Walsh Mary E. 53 Houston
Walton Ruth & Harriet Withers, 536 Grand
Warenstadt Janette, 37 Carmine
Ward Mary, 132 Sullivan
Ward William W. 152 Prince
Watkins George, 338 Bowery
Watson Richard, 150½ E. B'dway
Watts Talbot, 7 Bowery
Weimer Jacob, 386 Pearl
Welden R. 203 3d Av.
Wertheim Isaac, 447 Pearl
Wetherald Mary A. 441 Pearl
White Michael, 116 Division
Wickes Jonathan O. 204½ Sullivan
Wilhelms Daniel, 491 Broadway
Willetts Charles W. 98 Stanton
Williams Ellen, 322 Division
Winterton & Kirby, 739 B'dway
Wiskeman Margaret, 571 B'dway
Woodburn Mrs. 668 Greenwich
Woodworth F. A. 325 B'dway
Wopschal Amelia, 26½ Leonard
Wright David B. 122 6th Av.
Young Rebecca, 365 Broadway
Young R. R. 435 Pearl

FANCY GOODS, WHOLESALE.
Amburger & Stevens, 89 William
Bishop Nathaniel C. 15 John
Bouck Christian W. & Brother, 61 Cedar
Brown & Tasker. 61 John
Brunswick Hyman, 145½ Hester
Chassell John, 16 Cortlandt
Conant William S. 177 Pearl
Crocker & Washburn, 58 John
Dupre Joseph & Co. 106 William
Egar Albert E. 31 Cedar
Elmore Wm. H. & Co. 33 Cedar
Feist George, 26 Cedar
Gill Thomas, 217 Pearl
Goddard & Burchard, 29 Nassau
Goll J. Emile, 119 Pearl
Gross Garelly, Julius & Co. 90 William
Harrop John, 45 Duane
Hart Hyman E. 78 John
Hays J. W. 11 William
Henry Henry S. 150 Water

Hinrichs C. F. A. 150 Broadway
    New York.
Houghton & Arnold, 2 Pine
Hyde D. C. & Co. 1 Hanover sq.
Keelar & Fuller, 53 Nassau
Knight D. M. 23 Cedar
Lliendahl C. D. W. 133 William
Link J. & R. 181 Broadway
Low Emory, 214 Pearl
Mairs James & Co. 177 Pearl
Matthews & Hunt. 168 Pearl
Miller William J. 9 Maiden lane
Moore, Hudson & Foster, 3 Dutch
Oakley & Chassell, 16 Cortlandt
Penninam, Baxter & Faxon, 62
    William
Post & Knapp, 35 Nassau
Purdy & Robbins, 34 Maiden lane
Prestele Joseph. 103½ Bowery
Quinlan & Brother, 5 Cedar
Ramsay A. J. 25 Maiden lane
Rhodes Charles D. 73 Pine
Robinson Henry, 70 William
Satterlee D. R. 8 Cedar
Siegert John H. & Co. 29 Cedar
Sluyter W. R. & Co. 42   do
Spelman, Fraser & Co. 83   do
Stern Myer, 369 Grand
Stewart John, 31 Cedar
Swift Edward, 16 Chestnut
Thayer Erastus D. 93 Maiden lane
Toal Charles, 90 Catharine
Van Blankensteyn & Heinemann,
    103 William
Van Eps George K. 64 Cedar
Van Valkenburg Aaron, 187 Pearl
Ward Peck & Co. 102 Maiden lane
Watson Loring, 61 William
Weed William H. & Co. 195 Pearl
Williams Luther & Co. 84 William

Fancy Goods—Continued.

Oneida County.

Barnum E. S. & Son, (importers)
    71 Genesee   *Utica.*
Roth N. 42 Genesee
Murdock & Collins, 46 Genesee
Bailey & Brothers, 122   do
Wing S. 196   do
James T. B. & Co. 54 Hotel
Mode A. 172 Genesee

Oswego County.

Waters James, (Oswego Bazaar)
    5 Phœnix Block, 1st st. *Oswego.*

Putnam County.

Jones Mrs. Cold Spring
    Phillipstown.
Rudolph Mrs. do

Queens County.

Parsels Miss M.   *Jamaica.*
Bell Adelia
King Mrs. S.

Rensselaer County.

Bardwell R. D. 166 River   *Troy.*
Kenyon —, (fancy bazaar) 180
    River
Allan A. R. 214 River
Harris & Wilcox, 226 River
Goldsmith T. 2 Boardman's B'gs
Vail Milsa. 316 River
Benedict H. S. 2 King
Griffiths Theophilus, 3 Franklin sq

Schenectady County.

Xavier J. 112 State   *Schenectady.*
Abbott J. & J. C. 109 State

Tompkins County.

Avery & Woodworth, 90 Owego
    Ithaca.

Wayne County.

Simon Wm. H.   *Lyons.*

Westchester County.

Taylor G. W., Peekskill *Courtland*

Wyoming County.

Carpenter & Steele   *Warsaw.*

Fanning-Mill Manufacturers.

Chautauque County.

Johnson Daniel, Irving *Hanover.*
Hall & Brown,   do
Hazleltine —,   do
Burr Jabez   *Sheridan.*

Chenango County.

Griswold C. W., South *Bainbridge.*
Anderson P.   *Sherburne.*

Clinton County.

Shinville Benj. T.   *Plattsburgh.*

Columbia County.

Kaiser J.   *Hudson.*

Erie County.

Davis Otis   *Brandt.*

Lewis County.

Krake J., Copenhagen *Denmark.*

Montgomery County.

Smith Doddridge   *Amsterdam.*
Fancher & Bell

Onondaga County.

Henderson William   *Otisco.*
Clark P., Amber

Rensselaer County.

Grant I. T. & Co.   *Schaghticoke.*
Bryan H. C. & Son

St. Lawrence County.

Kastmer John & Co.   *Hammond.*
Mills Wm. F.   *Potsdam.*

Schoharie County.

Shinville Peter D.   *Esperance.*

Ulster County.

Peters James   *Kingston.*
Marquart S. M.

Washington County.

Grace Morrel   *Fort Edward.*
M'Grange T., North *White Creek.*

Wayne County.

Gilbert John   *Lyons.*
Reynolds William
Runyon James
Putney H. W.

Fashions—Reporters of.

Oliver Thomas, 157 Broadway
    New York.
Scott Genio C. 146 Broadway
Wheeler A. 4 Cortlandt
Williams P. P. 170 Broadway

Faucet Makers (Brass.)

Fenn G. & Co. 39 Spruce
    New York.
Metcalf Albert W. 53 & 65 Centre
Payne & Smith, rear 392 Broadway

Feather Dealers—Bed.

Brainard I. 171 Chatham
    New York.

Farmer George, 3 Pine *New York.*
Forster James, 22 Fulton
Hall Moses C. 159 Chatham
Marten M. 99 W. Broadway
Mellen A. & Co. 168½ Chatham
Parker & Ritter, 168 Greenwich
Pomroy H. 303 Division
Willard Martin, 150 Chatham

Feathers, Military & Fancy Manufacturers.

Chagot Theodore, 390½ Broadway
    New York.
Lemerciér Gaston, 172 William

Feed Dealers.

Albany County.

Bement C. N. 9 Hudson   *Albany*
Cumming J. 187 Bowery

Kings County.

Halberton ,W. S. Court st. near
    Fulton   *Brooklyn.*
Silliman G. 100 Gold
Cox & Truslow, 144 4th
    Williamsburgh.
Sharpe John L. 7 Grand

New York County.

Ackermann & Hallenback, 218
    Duane   *New York.*
Aims Wm. F. 118 E. 13th
Allen & Moore, 194 10th Av.
Amory James, 44 Mott
Anderson John B. 1 Horatio
Baldwin James A., Harlem
Bants Albert, 84 Greenwich Av.
Baxter Samuel, 57 Elm
Becker Henry I. 203 West
Berger Abram S. 36 Av. C.
Bergen Isaac H. 204 Mott
Bloom Edward N. 348 3d Av.
Byrne George C. 194 West
Butler J. & Co. 660 Washington
Butler J. 181 Christopher
Carpenter D. L. & J. G. 237 Bowery
Carpenter R. 145 10th
Cooper Thomas G. 38 Greene
Dell William, 275 W. 17th
Debaun Jacob, 245 Spring
Devoy John M. 80 Suffolk
Eden Henry, 225 8th Av.
Eden John, 182 W. 20th
Ewing Wm. 756 Washington
Fowler Henry & Co. 3 Peck slip
Frazee & Pine, 235 Front
Gallagher John M. 607 Grand
Gardner Champlin, 82 Market
Gay Robert P. & Co. 269 and 271
    Cherry
Gilman & Conover, 97 Laurens
Griffin Patrick, 589 Greenwich
Halsey Isaac. 21 Walnut
Halsey Stephen R. & Co. 23 Pitt
Haviland J. G. 660 Washington
Haviland Samuel C. 75 Rutgers
Harriott W. & J. 164 Charles
Hilpon Peter, 182 Christopher
Holcomb & Bergen, 89 West
Hustel Samuel M. 98 7th Av.
Hyatt Edgar, 333 3d Av.
Jimmerson Robert J. 58 Forsyth
Kent Henry, 98 Goerck
Kelly —, Yorkville
Kester George, 299 6th
Ketcham Henry S. 100 Norfolk
Kirby & Robbins, 330 Delancy
Ladue Nathan W. 18 4th
Lane David, 143 10th
Lane P. H. & W. 399 West
Lee James, 282 Av. A.
Levingss & See, 145 Sullivan
Livingston Thomas, 198 Mercer
Lynch & Davett, 196 West
Mace William H. 135 Forsyth

Martine Archer, 402 West
New York.
Martine Archer C. 254 6th Av.
Mooney Nicholas, 123 Mott
Moore & Halman, 373 3d Av.
Moore Joshua, 342 Monroe
Mount John W. & Co. 161 West
Murphy Hugh. 448 Houston
Nostrand T. 3 Peck slip
Orr John, 37½ Clinton
Patton Robert R. 12 Broadway
Phillips & Sheddon, 306 West and 192 W. 16th
Pine Gilbert J. 89 Av. D.
Ploger & Co. 69 11th
Powell Oliver S. 191 Delancy
Randolph & Shotwell, 173 Christopher
Rogers Robert, 44 Wooster
Rowan J. C. 29 Moore
Sarles Ward, 127 W. 20th
Schrodler Henry, 169 19th
Shapter John. 118 Pitt
Sherwood Charles, 174 4th
Shipman William M. 214 Delancy
Sideeher & Gordon, 74 Pearl
Sainey J. S. 248 Houston
Smith Charles, 235 1st Av.
Smith Woodhull. 70 Sheriff
Spear Charles, 22 Albany
Spence James, 2 Horatio
Spinning Aaron, 190 Elizabeth
Spinnings Benj. F. 20 6th
Taylor John, 314 1st Av
Thoonal W. 10th Av. cor. 26th
Tooker Jesse; 132 Suffolk
Tucker Melvin L. 50 & 52 Watts
Valentine George, 347 Cherry
Van Loan Isaac N. 103 Sheriff
Wallaben A. & Co. 35 Hamersley
Ward Theodore, 562 Broome
Willis Daniel, 68 King
Willets Andrew & Co. 86 Market slip
Witpen John. 197 9th
Wood Jonas. 100 Thompson
Wood & Cannon, 205 Chambers

Fence, Railing, Shutters, &c. Makers, (Iron.)

Albany County.

Covert H. W. Steuben cor. Water
Albany.
Carlos J. D. 18 William

Duchess County

Arnold B. & Son, 173 Main
Poughkeepsia.

Erie County.

Larkin Levi H. 13 Clinton Buffalo.
Eddy Robert M. Terrace n. Erie

Herkimer County.

Van Steinburgh Jonas Newport.

Kings County.

Carhart Isaac, 291 Adams
Brooklyn.
Stillwell G. W. Court n. Dean
Teale John P. 230 Grand
Williamsburgh.

New York County.

Alexander Wm. 98 Grand
New York.
Althause S. B. & Co. 20 Mercer & 443 Broadway
Archer & Vanderbeek, 250 18th
Badger Daniel D. & Co. 44 & 46 Duane
Barnes R. & Co. 161 Suffolk
Carnley Thomas & Turpin, 215 Grand
Chambers & Wickersham, 61 Lewis

Cornell J. B. & W. W. & Co. 141 & 143 Centre New York.
Darling & Brothers, 94 10th
Freeman James C. 106 11th
Greenin John S. 764 Greenwich
Groy J. N. 45 Greene
Harnod & Rothery, 19 E. 26th
Herring Silas C. 137 & 139 Water
Howell Matthias, 159 Hammond
Jackson George R. & Co. Excelsior Iron Works, 199 Centre
Moore Rinhard, 235 W. 16th
Reissennreber F. 1 Cortlandt
Requa Austin & Co. 221 Canal
Robertson John C. 60 Rivington
Smalley Joseph, 141 Stanton
Waite R. T. 69 Bank

Tompkins County.

Page L. E. (patent) Trumansburgh Ulysses.

Felt Manufacturers.

Cuthbert Thomas, 52 Beaver
New York.

File Makers and Cutters.

Kings County.

Pierson George, Boerum near Pacifin Brooklyn.

Monroe County.

Jones J. H. Curtis Block, Main st.
Rochester.

New York County.

Burr Walter, 48 Columbia.
New York.
Curtis John W. 50 Harrison
Dougherty, Birks & Farmer, 97 Mangin near Stanton
Evans, Davis & Co. 212 Pearl
Godby Thomas, 102 Goerck
Hoe R. & Co. 29 & 31 Gold and Broome cor. Sheriff
Harner James, 22 Cliff
M'Clain Orlando D. 167 Spring
Willmott Sam. D. 8 Liberty
Worrall & Co. 96 & 98 Elm & 67 Duane

Oneida County.

White & Adey, Fulton st. Utica.

Rensselaer County.

Fox R. G. Ida Hill Troy.

Rockland County.

Slynn J. Spring Valley
Orangetown.
Evans, Davis & Co. Ramapo.

Westchester County.

Russell John, Sing Sing Ossining.

Filter Makers.

Gibson Walter M. 349 Broadway & 66 Frankfort New York.
Jennison Wm. H. 132 Mercer
Latting Waring, 278 Broadway
Sweet Wm. 224 Canal

Fire Brick.

New York County.

Decasse Jules, 32 West & 54 Cannon New York.
Kemble Wm. 79 West
Kreischer B. 58 Goerck
Nelson & Brown, 288 West

Radford Henry & Co. 202 West
New York.
Thompson S. & Nephew, 275 Pearl

Oneida County.

White & Sons, Whitesboro st.
Utica.

Rensselaer County.

Hudson & Co., South Troy Troy.

Fire Works.

Purdy & Robbins, 34 Maiden lane
New York.
Reynolds & Brothers, 85 Liberty & 11 Nassau
Vultee P. L. 116 Chatham

Fishing Tackle.

Brown John J. & Co. 103 Fulton
New York.
Conroy J. & J. C. 52 Fulton
Crook Jabez B. 50 Fulton
Fizmegan Thomas, 96 Madison
Fitzsimmons S. rear 150 Wooster
Karr George, 194½ Grand
Simpson Paul J. 18 Spruce
Welch Benj. D. 83 Cherry

Fishmongers.

Albany County.

Chapman I. A. 3 & 5 State Albany.
Cushman & Co. 20 & 22 State
Parkor J. North Market
Sanders J. B. & Co. 72 Quay

Greene County.

Goetschius John Catskill.

Kings County.

Rogers J. 111 Atlantic Brooklyn.
Applegate L. & E. 163 Myrtle Av.
Juggins John H.   do
Robertson Alexander, Market
Mott Wm.   do
Brewster B. A.   do
Bedell Daniel,   do
Potter Joseph,   do
Mott & Crosby,   do
M'Laughlin L.   do
Powell Isaac, 4th st. cor. South 7th Williamsburgh.
Davis Henry, 27 Grand
Oyston James, 156 do

New York County.

Avery L. & I. Clinton Market
New York.
Baker Elisha, 1 Fulton
Banker J. & Son, 108 Washington market
Birdsall S. C. cor. Av. B & 11th st.
Bisbee Cyrus, 13 Catharine mkt.
Brady Geo. W. 9 Centre market
Braisted G. D. 1 Jefferson market
Brown & Gray, 16 & 20 Washington market
Brown Jos. 9 Washington market
Brown L. 23 Catharine market
Chappell S. & Co. 12 & 14 Washington market
Christian R. O. Clinton market
Cochran Philip, 1 Centre market
Cole & Teller, 10 & 12 Fulton mkt.
Conely John. 7 Centre market
Crocker David, 3 Fulton market
Crocker I. 15 Catharine market
Davidson & Speer, 196 Clinton
Davy Chas. S. 3 Clinton market
Delancey Abraham, 29 Goerck
Delancey David, 237 7th
Delancey John, 181½ Clinton
Dennett A. 24 Washington market

Dennisson J. 1 Gouverneur mkt.
New York.
Dickson M. 107 Washington mkt.
Downey J. Centre Market
Doxey Abram. 1 Essex
Edmonds Wm. 97 Hester
Edwards Isaac S. 12 Essex market
Eldredge R. N. & Co. 6 Washington market
Ellsworth N. S. 25 Centre market
Everts S. P. (see advertisement), 248 Fulton
Field John, 96 Av. C
Foskett Ezra, 133½ Orchard
Garthwaite & Clayton, 11 Essex m.
Gilbert H. S. 17 & 19 Catharine m.
Gordon & Shadbolt, 10 Catharine market
Green D. M. 35 Washington mkt.
Green & Guire, Washington mkt.
Greenley Wm. A. 3 1st
Gross S. A. 2 Centre market
Gayre J. B. & Son, 7 Washington market
Hadley R. & C. 1 Clinton market
Hall Peter, 11 Franklin market
Harris Cilas, 2 Clinton market
Hawks J. W. Washington market
Haywood William, 28 Forsyth
Hewitt Wm. 2 Fulton market
Hewitt & Stuart, 324 Houston
Hiscox J. S. 36 Washington mkt.
Hiscox J. D. 19 Washington mkt.
Jarvis William, Tompkins market
Johnson Leonard L. 111 Broad
Johnson William, 13 Centre mkt
King Alvah M. & Co. 11 Washington market
Kingsland Cornell & Avery North, 2 Clinton market
Kittredge W. H. Clinton market
Laurence & Vanderwort, 72 Av. D
Loper & Griffin, 30 Fulton market
Lumbreyer John, 3 Essex market
Lumbreyer Phillip, 1 Essex mkt
Macfarland Benj. 76 W. B.way
M'Aviney Cormick. 1 Centre mkt
M'Farland Sidney, 162 Laurens
M'Kreokan John. 4 Jefferson mkt
Manterstock William, 1 Clinton market
Manwaring Daniel, 15 Fulton mkt
Manwaring Myer, 7 Catharine market
Manwaring Rodney, 11 Catharine market
Marsh David, 37 Washington mkt
Mastin Jesse W. 2 Catharine mkt
Matthews Townsend, 32 Fulton
Maynard Samuel, 22 Catharine market
Middleton & Tuthill, 21 Fulton do
Middleton William H. 14 Fulton do
Miller Peter H. 11 Centre market
Mitchel D. W. Washington mkt
Morell Alex. W. Av. C near 10th
Morse Daniel, 599 Grand
Mosshette Steph. 15 Washington market
Mott Isaac, 9 Catharine market
Mott Isaac, 472 Cherry
Mott N. 122 West Broadway
Mott Selah. 386 Houston
Nelson, Wells & Co. 81 Dey
Odell Reuben, 75 Ridge
Owens Edward, 13 Centre market
Parker Zebediah, 4 Catharine mkt
Pearsall David, foot Duane
Penniman Benjamin S. & Co. 3 Washington market
Racey Joseph H. jr. 8 Centre mkt
Racket Jeremiah, 35 Fulton mkt
Rathbun N. Washington market
Reminger John, 543 Grand
Richardson James J. 19 Centre m.
Rogers G. & Co. 13 Fulton mkt
Rogers M. & Co. 27 Fulton mkt
Shadwick William, Catharine do
Smart Jas. 30 & 32 Washington do
Smith John, 5 Essex market
Sparks Joseph, 31 Av. B

Stewart John R. 324 Houston
New York.
Story William, 116 Greene
Tinker Allen. 2 Catharine market
Tinker William, 24 Catharine mkt
Tuttle John B. 258 Wooster
Van Blarken Samuel, 586 Hudson
Vanderwort H. 72 Av. D
Vanduzer & Smith, 7 Essex mkt
Van Nostrand John. 15 Centre do
Waring, Comstock & Co. 14 & 16 Catharine market
Watson William B. Tompkins mkt
Wayte Edwin, 236 Greene
Wells Wait, 28 Washington mkt
Whitten George. 3 Jefferson mkt
Wood Thomas, 1 & 2 Centre mkt
Woolsey Eli, Washington market

Queens County.

Southard Hewlett, Raynor Town
Hempstead.
Herbit Edward, Raynor Town
Smith Henry,   do
Raynor Samuel,   do
Loosel Leonard,   do

Rensselaer County.

Wilson & Wilkes, under Washington market   *Troy.*

Tompkins County.

M'Kay A. M. Tioga st.   *Ithaca.*

Washington County.

Gibbs D. J. Phœnix Place
Whitehall.

Fish, Salt—Dealers in.

Birdsall B. 477 Broome *New York.*
Browne & Watson, 165 West
Chadwick Robert, 8 Catharine m
Demarest Peter P. 7 South
Gibbons John, Washington mkt
Lewis, Burch & Brown, 42 Front
Prandy Thomas. 257 Front
Sparks Joseph, 1 Av. B
Smith & Bertine, 100 Murray
Wells Nelson & Co. 81 Dey
Wilcox J. & Co. 8 Washington m.
Woodruff A. & Robinson, 14 Coenties slip & 44 Front
Woodward & Cromwell, 41 Front

Flag Makers.

Mills Francis, 38 Barclay
New York.
Newell Susan, 166 William
Pierson Catharine, 26 Stone
Wilson Mary, 2 Trinity place

Flax Dealers.

New York County.

Macgregor & Morris, 10 Broadway
New York.
Wall, Richardson & Engle, 220 Front

Rensselaer County.

Smith, Dove & Co. 167 River
Troy.

Washington County.

Darrow Hiram   *Cambridge.*
Smith J. & B.   *White Creek.*

Flax Mills.

Lewis County.

Johnson Timothy B.   *Turin.*

Washington County.

King Hiram   *Cambridge.*
Brownell M Buskirk's Bridge
Wright B. North Cambridge

Wyoming County.

Windsor A   *Pike.*

Flour Dealers.

(See also Feed, also Grain, also Merchants' Produce Commission, also Produce Dealers, also Merchants Commission, also Merchants Forwarding and Commission.)

Albany County.

Crook & Palmer, 9 State *Albany.*
Cary Samuel, 13   do
Peck & Joy, 8   do
Lathrop, Durant & Co. 35 Quay
Knapp H. 27 Quay
Aiken E. C. 73 do
Hall S. 117 Pier
Craft B. F. 115 do
Goddard C. W. 98 do
Fish S. M. & Co. 84, 85, & 86 Pier
James Thomas, 49 Quay
Grant & Sayles, 61   do
Artcher & Lyman, 63 do
Chapman W. & Son, 81 do
Wing & Byrne, 90   do
Rankin S. 108 S. Pearl
Hewett H. B. & Co. 111 Pier

Broome County.

Ishbell & Way   *Binghamton.*

Cayuga County.

Hutchins C. A. South st. *Auburn.*

Chautauque County.

Frew H. A. Frewsburgh *Carroll.*

Columbia County.

M'Arthur C. Water st.   *Hudson.*
Harden G. Franklin square

Erie County.

Needham C. H. cor. Washington & Ohio   *Buffalo.*
Mesmer Michael, 272 Main
Rathborne R. W. 39 Seneca
Tifft George W.
Butler E. T. & Co. on Ship Canal
Burkle & Pease, cor. Canal & Lloyd

Kings County.

Pettit & Shotwell, cor. Atlantic & Furman   *Brooklyn.*
Coit & Brother, 169 Atlantic
Brush & Van Wyck. 14 do
Frost Isaac, (wholesale) 21 Fulton
Dargen Peter,   do   31 do
Catlin L. 37   do
Vandevoort & Co. 203 Pearl cor. Tillary
White S. Atlantic st. Bedford
Cox & Truslow, (wholesale) 144 4th   *Williamsburgh.*

Madison County.

Sears S. G.   *De Ruyter.*
Rogers & Firman   *Hamilton.*

Monroe County.

Patton H. 13 St. Paul *Rochester.*
Stebbins & Killick, cor. S. St. Paul & Ely
Johnson Samuel D. 20 S. St. Paul
Richmond George, Curtis Block, Main st.
Parsons James, Water st.

Adamson John, 26 Main *Rochester.*
Garrison Jacob S. 223 Buffalo
Jenks Cyrus, 124   do
Lane C. 112   do
M'Killip S. 106 & 108   dc
Richards N. S. 85 Main
Killick W. 115   do
Dopkins N. W. 131½ do
Mumford E. P. 139   do
Coleman Samuel B. cor. Sophia & Adams
M'Millen J. 246 State
Hall J O. 201   do
Smith & Hamilton, 6 Work
Eastwood Joseph, Front st.
Parsons S. & Co. 18 do

Montgomery County.

Abrahams & Almy   *Canajoharie.*
Diefendorf John I. Fort Plain
             Minden.

New York County.

Ackerman Bernard, 95 Barclay
            New York.
Allan & Whittlesey, 21 South
Angevine D. & L. 218 Washington
Armour Paul. 93 Wall
Arrosmith & Wheeler. 125 Broad
Banks Theodore, 241 Front
Barratt A. & Co. 47   do
Beals H C. 22 South
Bogert Benj. C. 102 Barclay
Bradner, Bell & Co. 74 Cortlandt
Brett Theodorus. 147 Cedar
Brinkerhoff Jacob, 126 Warren
Buckley John L. & Co. 31 Front
Buxton Vanderbilt L. 142 West
Camp & Wells, 119 Broad
Carpenter D. L. & J. G. 329 Bowery
Carpenter & Birdsall, 152 West
Clark Alfred H. 161   do
Clark & Knox, 126 Warren
Cleland James, 180 South
Coles & Dakin. 154 West
Cox & Truslow, 120 Broad
Cromwell & Birdsall. 209 Front
Davis A. B. & S. 186 South
Demarest & Hoyt. 122 West, also dealers in grass seeds
Dunham Edward & Son. 5 South
Fenby Andrew H. 33 Front
Ferris Horatio N. 125 West
Fish & Co. 11 South
Ford & Raynolds. 90 Cortlandt
Frazee & Fine. 235 Front
Frost I. T. & J. G. 232 & 234 Front
Gay R. P. & Co. 269 & 271 Cherry
Hance & Reeve. 9 James' slip
Haring J. S. & Co. 35 Peck slip
Harriot W. & J. B. 124 & 126 Charles
Hecker & Brother, 201 Cherry
Herrick E. W. 23 South
Herrick John B. 11 Coenties slip
Herrick & Van Boskerck, 121 Broad
Hill, Grosbeck & Co. 45 Pearl & 32 Bridge
Holcomb Charles M. 268 Front
Holcomb Elisha E. 17 James' slip
Holcomb & Bergen. 89 West
Holt Philetus H. 230 Front
Hoogland Andrew, 215 Front
Johnston William, 328 Hudson
Jones, Birdsall & Rowland, 243 Front
Kanenbley Frederick, 129 West
Lane & Mangam, 90 Broad
Leland, Adams & Co. 18 South
Lewis S. W. 24 South
Littell Elias B. & Co. 10 James' sl.
Luers & Jurgens, 94 Barclay
Lynch & Davett. 196 West
Meserole A. & J. V. 12 Coenties sl.
Mettler S. 92 West
Morgan M. C. & Co. 66 Dey
Mount D. H. & Co. 394 West
Neefus Peter, 213 Front
Norton John W. 23 South

Oakley W. & G. & Co. 105 West
            New York.
Patton R. R. 12 Broadway
Phillips & Sheddon. 306 West
Powell M. M. 123 Broad
Randolph & Shotwell, 173 Christopher
Randolph & Tucker, 53 Whitehall
Reynolds Richard M. 247 Front
Romer John, 171 West
Southmayd Lewis O. 90 West
Spencer Christopher V. 9 South
Sperry H. C. 8 South
Stryker Cornelius C. 219 Front
Suydam, Sage & Co. 2 & 3 South
Terhune Martin, 201 Chambers
Timpson T. S. 21 Coenties slip
Vail Joseph W. & Co. 32 Pearl
Valentine Step. & Son, 160 Cherry
Waring Hiram & Co. 121 West
Weeks & Douglass, 16 South & 127 Broad
Wolfe Nathan H. 17 South
Woodward J. C. 17 Water
Wood & Cannon. 205 Chambers
Wright John B. & Co. 9 South
Wright & Losee, 18 Front

Oneida County.

Barnes & Hinman, 2 Main   *Utica.*
Dows & Kissman, cor. Seneca & Canal
Ray E. C. cor. Hotel & Canal
Wilcox W. C. 19 Liberty
Thurber I. 27   do
Livingston V. V. 12 Catharine

Onondaga County.

Woodruff & Barker, Water st. Syracuse   *Salina.*

Oswego County.

Wyles William, cor. 1st & Cayuga
            Oswego.
Carrington & Pardee, foot of 1st

Rensselaer County.

Lawrence John J. Agent 296 State
           Lansingburgh.
Howland, Bills & Thayer, 148 River   *Troy.*
Sage William F. & Co. 143 River
Moore & Tibbitts, 145   do
Walker J. K. 149   do
Willard John N. 147   do
Boughton Josiah, 389   do

Rockland County.

Miller S., Piermont   *Orangetown.*

Schenectady County.

Maxon G. G. 11 & 13 Canal
           Schenectady.
Draper John, 9 Canal

Ulster County.

Taylor James A. & Co. Rondout
            Kingston.

Washington County.

Taylor G. H.   *Fort Edward.*

Flouring and Grist Mills.

Albany County.

Shephard & Vanzandt   *Albany.*
Shepherd A. D. & Co. 106½ Pier
Tivoli R. Road Mills, Van Rensselaer Creek
Smith, Patten & Co. Fort Orange Mills
Lobdell L., Reedsville   *Berne.*
Tyler O.   do
Settle E.   do
Rathbone J.   *Bethlehem.*
Briggs Wm. S.   *Coeymans.*

Ten Eyck B. & A.   *Coeymans.*
Kimmey Phillip
Batterman John M.   *Guilderland.*
M'Donald Erastus
Lagrange Anthony   *New Scotland.*
Bennett R.
Slingerland T.
Conklin G.   *Rensselaerville.*
Copley C.   *Watervliet.*
Howland, Bills & Thayer, West Troy
Rarhard J. M. West Troy
Verplank C. J. D.   *Westerlo.*
Lobdell I.
Morse A.

Alleghany County.

Wilson James S.   *Amity.*
Burrell George P.
Hall & Bundy   *Andover.*
Morse A.   *Angelica.*
Brown D. & Son
Smith J. Whitney Valley   *Burns.*
Whitney Erastus
Kirkpatrick Wm. A.   *Cuba.*
Powers John
Mix Irn   *Friendship.*
Stowell I.
Miner J. N
Merriman L.
Ferris A. S.
Townsend S.
Van Nostrand L. Short Tract
           Granger.
Paul John   *Hume.*
Stone Hiram, Wiscoy
Gordon & Co.   *Rushford.*
Grimard Gustavus
Root & Miner   *Wirt.*

Broome County.

Rogers & Co. Chenango Forks
           Barker.
Lewis H   *Binghamton.*
Weed W. S.
Barnes A.   *Colesville.*
Harper Judge
Barnos J. A. Harpersville
Harpers Robert,   do
Potter T.   *Conklin.*
Corbett S., Corbettsville
Adams & Randall   *Lisle.*
Butler & Lincoln   *Maine.*
Mersereau I. P. D.   *Union.*
La Grange J. Nanticook Mills
Dusenbury & Barnum   *Windsor.*
Hotchkiss & Co.
Doolittle & Co.
Buel G.
Doolittle G.

Cattaraugus County.

King. Rockwell & Co.   *Ashford.*
Scovy Alexander
Carpenter A. R.
Thorp & Farloy, Seeleysburgh
           Conewango.
Crumb & Clark, Clear Creek
Gardner & Shankland *Ellicottville.*
Weed William F.   *Franklinville.*
Kendall James   *Freedom.*
Pinney & Holmes, Sandusky
Ellis John   *Great Valley.*
Tullett & Colgrove   *Machias.*
Allen F.   *New Albion.*
Jacket William   *Otto.*
St. John Selleck
Thompson——, East Otto
Larkins Nathan,   do
Howe Zimri, Gowanda   *Persia.*
Howe Rollin.   do
Howe Milbar,   do
Stewart Charles.   do
Dusenbury, Wheeler, Gregory & Co.   *Portville.*
Helmes C. C.   *East Randolph.*
Townsly Charles   *Rice.*
Runb John
Brow Norman   *South Valley.*
Parker Franklin   *Yorkshire.*
Woods David H.

Cayuga County.

Hills W. & Co. Genesee st. *Auburn.*
Beardsley S. 74 Genesee
Allen E. jr.   *Aurelius.*
Williams J., Weedsport   *Brutus.*
Healy & Cramer, do
Smith R.   *Ledyard.*
Squires Wm. H.
Bostwick H.   *Locke.*
Parsons A. C.
Gray J. S. Troopsville   *Mentz.*
King & Wood   *Moravia.*
Keeler William
Loomis Thomas
Fell M.   *Scipio.*
Howland C. W.   *Springport.*
Yeuger P.
Thompson Thomas
Kevil William   *Sterling.*
Tilford G. S.
Conger J.
Murdock L.   *Venice.*
Pierce N.   *Victory.*

Chautauque County.

Brown & Allen   *Charlotte.*
Carting & Peck
Crafts, Whiteside & Co. Mayville
                                 Chautauque.
Kent Joseph   *Cherry Creek.*
Pier & Griffith, Jamestown N.*Ellicott.*
Edgerton Edward,   do
Chandler Seth W.   *Ellington.*
Wheeler Henry
Haynes Austin D. *French Creek.*
Drury E., Forestville   *Hanover.*
Peterman A.   do
Smith R. B. & Co. Smith's Mills
Norton Sereno   *Harmony.*
Whipple Alfred, Panama
Carpenter Israel, Blackville
Tift ——, Fredonia   *Pomfret.*
Morton & Colburn, do
Jewett G. R. & Co.   *Portland.*
Wells, Churchill & Co. Salem
  cross roads
Kip & Miller   *Sherman.*
Hall George   *Westfield.*
Dewey R.
Walker John R.

Chemung County.

Catlin P.   *Catharine.*
Gull Ira   *Elmira.*
Arnot Stephen
Ely J. C.
Arnot John, Millport   *Veteran.*
Grandall Henry, do

Chenango County.

Cowen John & Sons   *Greene.*
Haynes, Delevan & Muckart
                                 Guilford.
Pulford & Pool   *Lincklaen.*
Root R.   *Macdonough.*
Beardsley J.   *New Berlin.*
Goodsell O. C.
Fox C.   *North Norwich.*
Miller T.
Guernsey Wm. G.   *Norwich.*
Brown E. D.   *Otselic.*
Lewis Clark, jr.   *Oxford.*
Lord R. & D.   *Pharsalia.*
Blackman Roswell & Co. *Pitcher.*
Allen E. B.
Frink Coddington   *Plymouth.*
Greene N. F.   *Sherburne.*
Curtiss John
Kershaw John
Furman W.
Birch L. D.
Munson A.   *Smyrna.*
Scarritt J.

Clinton County.

Kingsland, Green & Co. Keeseville
                                 Au Sable.
Keese & Tomlinson
Blaney ——, East Chazy   *Chazy.*
Orms J., West Chazy

Shedden B.   *Mooers.*
Messenger ——
Hewitt N. G.   *Peru.*
Lapham N.

Columbia County.

Van Deusen R.   *Ancram.*
Whiting & Co.   *Canaan.*
Stewart S. W.   *Chatham.*
Tompkins S., Chatham 4 Corners
Coon C., North Chatham
Lawton J., East do
Miller W. J.   *Claverack.*
Bashford B., Smoky Hollow
Weaver P.   *Gallatin.*
Wheeler P. A.
Gilbert L.   *Ghent.*
Wheeler Richard A.   *Hillsdale.*
Loop Phyler A. & Havilla
Bailey William
Williams Sylvester
Lathrop G. M. & Co. (Kinderhook
  Steam Mill)   *Kinderhook.*
Wild N., Valatie
Herrmance H.   *Livingston.*
Pierce J. & Co.
Adams Wm. H.   *New Lebanon.*
Hoag & Pulver
Brown & Miller   *Stockport.*
Huber & Morey   *Stuyvesant.*

Cortland County.

Cole George L.   *Cincinnatus.*
Mudge Abram, *Cortland Village.*
Riggs Lewis
Austin Asa. M'Grawville
M'Graw Hiram, do
Gray Henry   *Harford.*
Smith Noah R.   *Homer.*
Riggs Lewis
Carpenter Eli, East Homer
Summer Samuel, do
Cushing James E. Little York
Adams Benjamin   *Marathon.*
Philley Uriah   *Preble.*
Babcock R. P.   *Scott.*
Grout S. N.
Pond George   *Truxton.*
Crain Almiron W.
Ellis Elihu
Byram Josephus   *Virgil.*
Hart William
Adams Stephen   *Willett.*

Delaware County.

Wilson C.   *Colchester.*
Downs G. W. Downsville
Cowley Ledyer   *Davenport.*
Cleaveland William ——
Edgarton & Burdick   *Franklin.*
Hymes & Co.
Tompkins J.   *Harpersfield.*
Gibbs B. F.
Fox A. R.   *Meredith.*
Carpenter A. & J. Margarettsville
                                 Middletown.
Becker C. & Co. Hobart *Stamford.*
Gregory U. Deposit   *Tompkins.*
Sillaman A.   *Walton.*
Townsand ——

Duchess County.

Husted E.   *Amenia.*
Peters T.   *Beekman.*
Peters C.
Manchester H.
Marquart D. G. Clinton Hollow
                                 Clinton.
Leroy S. & A.   do
Shultz D. H. Shultzville
Ketcham J. M. Dover Plains *Dover.*
Shelden E.   do
Preston E.   do
Hughson W. & T. L. Franklindale
  Flouring Mill, Wappinger's Falls
                                 Fishkill.
Walsh William H. Matteawan
Tioronda Flouring Mills
                                 Burnsville.
Van Vorn S. A. Hopewell

Dunham E.   *Hydepark.*
Allen I.
Codwis N.   *Lagrange.*
Furgison B.
Schultz D. Rock City   *Milan.*
Benedict B.   *Northeast.*
Carrman P.
Potter & Gear
Carman R.   *Pine Plains.*
Thomas R. & H.
Hoffman A.
Bentley H.
Henry J.   *Pleasant Valley*
Ward J. O.
Lamoree J. V. Salt Point
Lent D. B. cor. Smith & Clinton
                                 Poughkeepsie.
Fraleigh J. P.   *Red Hook.*
Shultz B. D.
Fritz P.
M'Carty S.   *Rhinebeck.*
Wing J. Stanfordville   *Stamford.*
Wilbur Z.   do
Thompson E. P. Stanfordville
Brownell J.   *Union Vale.*
Leroy J. Verbank
Thorn & Dorland   *Washington.*
Duel I.
Coffin —— Salt Point
Tompkins ——, Hart's Village

Erie County.

Witmire & Rutt, Williamsville
                                 Amherst.
Frick Christian Z.   do
Getz Joseph,   do
Lintz & Foglesongerd, do
Foglesonger & Eggert, do
Jones Joseph, West Falls *Aurora.*
Gales Lockwood, Griffin's Mills
Burkle & Pease   *Black Rock.*
Burnham Milo
Tift Geo. W.
Howell Stephen W.
Reed & Thompson
Penfeld & Moore
Paine Simon   *Boston.*
Abbott Chauncey
Cooper W. W. North Boston
Tift Geo. W.   *Buffalo.*
Butler E. T. & Co. on Ship Canal
Burkle & Pease, c. Canal & Lloyd
Shope & Strickland   *Clarence.*
Brown R. Clarence Centre
Buffum Albert   *Colden.*
Plumb Ralph   *Collins.*
Lawton Geo.
Badgley Morgan, Springville
                                 Concord.
Cook A. W.
Berland John, East Evans *Evans.*
Earl J. & W.   do
Long Isaac, Water Valley
                                 Hamburgh.
M'Clure Heman, do
Orr Alvin   *Holland.*
M'Lean John   *Lancaster.*
Bowman Eli H.
Vogdis C. Akron   *Newstead.*
Loveland W.   *Sardinia.*
Willis Grovener   *Wales*
M'Coon ——, South Wales
Pollard Benj. Wales Centre

Essex County.

Whitcomb P. S. & Co.
                                 Elizabethtown.
Rice G. W. & L.
Palmer H. & Son   *Essex.*
Cady Louis, Whallonsburg
Lamb ——   *Keene.*
Barnes T. S.   *Minerva.*
Wheelock Hubbard S., Moriah
  Four Corners   *Moriah.*
Collins Ebenezer, Moriah Four
  Corners
Whalon Reuben   do
Little Nelson, Schroon River
                                 Schroon.
Wyman Alonzo   do
Ross Henry H. 2d   *Willsborough.*

Franklin County.

Porter Henry R. *Bangor.*
Bacon Charles
Dickinson J. & Sons
Douglass Calvin *Chateaugay.*
Church Samuel
Horton Hiram *Malone.*
Whipple H. W.

Fulton County.

Chase Benj. *Broadalbin.*
Edwards John *Ephratah.*
M'Learen Duncan *Johnstown.*
Wells John E.
Vail Buchanan C. Co. Vail Mills
Stanly Thos. Mayfield Corner
Lefever C. Van Valkenburgh, Northville
Slocum Reuben *Northampton.*
Hyatt John S. *Stratford.*

Genesee County.

Rix & Mooses *Alexander.*
Sharrick A. M. *Batavia.*
Bergen Rail Road Co. *Bergen.*
Brown Daniel *Bethany.*
Wood Erastus, East Bethany
Barrows & Hooper, Linden
Terry Zeno *Byron.*
Smith Hiram *Elba.*
Lathrop Joshua *Le Roy.*
Tomlinson John
Haskins S
Lampson M. P.
Olmsted O. *Oakfield.*
Nobles Calvin
Bailey —— *Pavilion.*
Fisher Robert *Stafford.*
Godfrey & Hall

Greene County.

Strong D. B. *Ashland.*
Harris Samuel, Leeds *Catskill.*
Jennings Ebenezer *Greenville.*
Sherrill & Shaw
Jones Benjamin *Hunter.*
Smith James *Lexington.*
Bushnell A. Westkill
Bailey & Diedrich, Hensonsville *Windham.*

Hamilton County.

Chamberlain Wm. *Wells.*

Herkimer County.

Ayres O. P. & Co. *Columbia.*
Hutson Samuel & Co.
Orendorff Wm. F.
Haupt Samuel *Danube.*
Davis Cornelius
Phillips Wm. *Fairfield.*
Mason Daniel *Frankfort.*
Bridenbecker J.
Payne C. Payne's Hollow *German Flats.*
Bellenger F. P. *Herkimer.*
Drake M. *Little Falls.*
Morgan J.
Inghan Harvey *Manheim.*
Waterman H. *Newport.*
Plants P. B. & Co.
Holt Abbot, Gravesville *Russia.*
Cheever E. P. Poland
Fenner Alex. Cold Brook
Elwell ——, Postville
Darling Edgar, Salisbury Centre *Salisbury.*
Hyatt John S. do
Sweet V. *Schuyler.*
Van Horn D. Van Hornsville *Stark.*
Van Horn & Fox, do
Hall & Haskins, Starkville
Weatherbee Alvin, Page's Corner *Warren.*
Carver & Walker, West Winfield *Winfield.*
Hull & Guild, do
Rider A. do

Jefferson County.

Woodard S. & D. *Adams.*
Butterfield & White, Redwood *Alexandria.*
Clark Jason, Plessis
Brown & Kirby *Brownville.*
Knapp & Harris
Bradley John, Dexter
Clark C. E. *Champion.*
Fasker ——
Colburn Otis L.
Johnson S. P. Depauville *Clayton.*
Millard H. *Ellisburgh.*
Cook S. Woodville
Reed H. L. *Henderson.*
Clarke C. E. Great Bend *Le Ray.*
Graves Samuel, Evans' Mills
Brown Parley *Lorraine.*
Lamon Gilbert
Gopely A. Three Mile Bay *Lyme.*
Dubois W. Lafargeville *Orleans.*
Angell Wm. H. *Pamelia.*
Corey Benjamin
Frazier G. *Philadelphia.*
Wadsworth N. South Rutland *Rutland.*
Poore & Co. Black River
Felt O. A. & S. Felt's Mills
Ranney Anson *Theresa.*
Ashley S. H.
Baker Thomas & Son *Watertown.*
Kimball & Sasher
Howk Peter S.
Moulton & Symonds
Marrill Hiram
Guyott Bazille, Carthage *Wilna.*
Kimball J. do
Christian Wm. Natural Bridge

Kings County.

Howe Calvin J. corner Fulton & Furman *Brooklyn.*
Laidlaw & Blatchford (Union Flour Mills) foot Bridge st.

Lewis County.

Prame Martin *Croghan.*
Howard D. S. Lyonsdale *Greig.*
Hart Sylvester *Turin.*
Dewey Cadwell
M'Carty Timothy
House Leonard, Houseville
Jones Evan, Constableville *West Turin.*

Livingston County.

Williams R. S. & Co. *Avon.*
Morton J. & C.
Wadsworth Wm. W.
Hawley & Fuller, South Avon
M'Kay John *Caledonia.*
Rockafellow G. *Conesus.*
Williams :. C. & Co. *Dansville.*
Porter M. & Son
M'Whorter J.
Chapin B. S. & Co.
Stanley E. L. & Co.
Bradshaw B. F.
North H. P. *Geneseo.*
Cuyler Wm. T. Cuylerville *Leicester.*
Phelps Dennis, Moscow
Gilbert Wm. S. Hemlock Lake *Livonia.*
Dixon Amos, do
Olmstead L. F. Lakeville
Totten Geo. W. J. *Mount Morris.*
Cook & Billenger
Swain S. & Sons *Nunda.*
Van Kleek B.
Messenger O. F., Oakland *Portage.*
Hunt Horace, Hunt's Hollow
Vice Thomas C. Scottsburgh *Sparta.*
Cummins Moses A. *Springwater.*
Fowler Thomas
M'Cortney James F. & Co *West Sparta.*
Brown Geo. W. *York.*
Bailey E. C.

Madison County.

Babcock P. *Brookfield.*
White D. D.
Hoxie L. & T. Leonardsville
Babcock Elisha, South Brookfield
Snow S. & Son *Cazenovia.*
Burton Wm. & Son
Atkinson Wm.
Pierce Nathan, New Woodstock
Benjamin Patrick *De Ruyter.*
Tracy T.
Vail Jonathan
Morse Ellis *Eaton.*
Reeder Wm. Morrisville
Lobdell Lewis *Fenner.*
Isbell E. *Georgetown.*
Felt Wm. Earlville *Hamilton.*
Thompson Amos, East Hamilton
Dunbar David, Hubbard's Corners
Smith John. Oneida Depot *Lenox.*
Fox Albert, Oneida Valley
M'Cagg Matthew, Clockville
Armstrong Jaben *Lebanon.*
Cleveland Erastus *Madison.*
Hicks F.
Poole Oliver, Erieville *Nelson.*
Meredith Thomas
Gilbert Titus, Peterboro *Smithfield.*
Downer E. Siloam
Parmelee John H. *Stockbridge.*
Merrill & Dexter
Parker & Burroughs
Paddock S. D. *Sullivan.*
Parsons Reubin, Chittenango
Lobdell Lewis, Perryville
Sayles Oney, Bridgeport

Monroe County.

Harmon A. & E. South Chili *Chili.*
Wilson & Barnett, East Mendon *Mendon.*
Hanford W. jr. West Mendon
Finch Hiram do
Wright Henry, Parma Corner *Parma.*
Cook Samuel, do
Davis Horatio, Parma Centre
Rowe J. B. *Penfield.*
Miller S.
Weaver J.
Lincoln A. *Perrinton.*
Richardson R. *Pittsford.*
James & Randall, Churchville *Riga.*
Ely Samuel P. St. Paul st. *Rochester.*
Burbank G. W. Crescent Mills, Water st.
Hill Charles J. Williston Mills, Water st.
Prindle W. C. & Co. Water st.
Parsons James, do
Snow Jerome, 5 Buffalo
Beach & Aynault, City Mills, Aqueduct st.
Williams S. P. Aqueduct st.
Beach E. S. Aqueduct Mills
Kempshall Thomas, Aqueduct st.
Livingston James K. 7 Buffalo.
Holmes & Fish, 83 Exchange
Holmes & Fish, Granite Mills, State st.
Chapell J. corner Fitzhugh & Canal st.
Bradfield J. & Co. Clinton Mills, Brown's Race
Smith Horace P. W'hington Mills, Brown's Race
Seward Moses B. Shawmut Mills, Brown's Race
Putnam Joseph & Co. Boston Mills, Brown's Race
Stone J. C. Rough & Ready Mills, Brown's Race
Williams John & Co. Whitney Mills, Brown's Race
Jennings A. *Rush.*
Winens Theodore, West Rush
Smith H. *Wheatland.*

Edson F. M. Scottsville *Wheatland.*
Carpenter Ira,   do
Smith Hiram,   do
Harman H. & R., do
Scofield & Shadboldt, do
Garbutt Philip, Mumford

Montgomery County.

Conner Gilbert, Hagaman's Mills, *Amsterdam.*
Candee Wm. L.   do
Zeeley & Murrill   *Canajoharie.*
Wiles John I.   •
Bingham Ames F. Ames
Burton J. Burtonville   *Charleston.*
De Graff Isaac, Minaville *Florida.*
Wells J. J.   do
Sweet Samuel, Port Jackson
Falkner Joel   *Glen.*
Wagner P. J., Fort Plain *Minden.*
Hart C. N. & Co. Fonda *Mohawk.*
Jones Abijah,   do
Crouse R., Stone Arabia *Palatine.*
Conover John W.   *Root.*
Brown Henry L.
Barns Hiram
Butler J. & Co.   *St. Johnsville.*
Elwell J. F.

New York County.

Hecker & Brother, 199, 201 & 203
Cherry   *New York.*
Kelsey & Son, 270 5th

Niagara County.

Lapp J. B., Pekin   *Lewiston.*
Douglas & Jackson   *Lockport.*
Spalding L. A.
Harwood H. M.
Van Horn J.   *Newfane.*
Stahl Enoch & W.
Tompkins Ira
Olmsted Silas & Co. *Niagara Falls.*
Porter Peter B.
Davis N. R. & Co. Youngstown   *Porter.*
Peckham & Pratt   *Somerset.*
Wilson Luther   *Wilson.*

Oneida County.

Allen B., Oriskany Falls *Augusta.*
Couch Geo. W. do
Hawkins S.   *Boonville.*
Curtis L.   *Camden.*
Graves W. W.   *Florence.*
Tower J. H., Clinton *Kirkland.*
Walworth E., Delta   *Lee.*
Scothan P.   do
Kellogg F.   *New Hartford.*
Gilbert H , Sauquoit   *Paris.*
Wooster D., Trenton Village   *Trenton.*
Morgan W., Trenton Falls
Murdock E., Fulton st.   *Utica.*
Hopkins C. H. cor. Main & Bridge
Rathbun S. Rathbunsville *Verona.*
Macomber P., North   *Western.*
Dexter S. N., Oriskany *Whitestown.*
Colman A. H., Walesville

Ontario County.

Dixon Amos   *Canadice.*
Shepard M. & L., East *Bloomfield.*
England John, East Bloomfield
Harwood Oliver, Bushville   *Gorham.*
Sterry & Munson   *Hopewell.*
Garlinghouse L. B.
Livingston ——   *Manchester.*
Dewey E. B., Manchester Centre
Pinkney T. A. & Co.   *Phelps.*
Prescott J. H.
Parsons J. & Co.
Keller John
Ranney Thomas
Finch Hiram, Richmond Mills   *Richmond.*
Johnson J. R., Geneva   *Seneca.*
Ride John,   do
Lee D. W.   do

Reed W., Seneca Castle   *Seneca.*
Van Ostrand John, Flint Creek
Osborne & Dwey   *Victor.*
Hamilton John
Cutting M.
Mills R. R.
Peck Solon,   *West Bloomfield.*
Wight & Hopkins

Onondaga County.

Richardson G. & W. M. Jamesville *De Witt.*
Kellogg Daniel Jordan *Elbridge.*
Daniels & Boardman, Jordan
Smith D.   *Fabius.*
Parker S. C., Baldwinsville   *Lysander.*
Johnson J.   do
Williams J.   do
Reiley & Wood, Fayetteville   *Manlius.*
Talbott E.   *Marcellus.*
Mills C., Marietta
Tinkham A. & Co. Marcellus Falls
Crosby, Estis & Co. South Onondaga   *Onondaga.*
De Mantfredy A., South Onondaga
Sloan D. W., Watervale *Pompey.*
Woodruff & Barker, Water st. Syracuse   *Salina.*
Coon H. J. Genesee st.
Legg, Hawley, Leach & Co.   *Skaneateles.*

Orange County.

Moffat H.   *Chester.*
Townsend Wm. H.   *Cornwall.*
Sloat A.   *Crawford.*
Furnham ——, Port Jervis   *Deer Park.*
Bennett James,   do
Brown H.   *Hamptonburgh.*
Evans Wm., Westown *Minisink.*
Racine J., Well's Corner
Manning Hiram, do
Thompkins L.   do
Kimball G., Unionville
Squires W. E.   *Montgomery.*
Millspaugh C.
Mead & Brown
Ambler J. W. & Co. Walden
Jenkins T.   *Monroe.*
Turner P., Turner's Depot
Little & Ketcham   *Mount Hope.*
Bebee Wm. H.   *Newburgh.*
Roe William J.
Wyant ——
Ambler & Co.
Clark J., Middlehope
Morton Charles   *New Windsor.*
Phillips G., Newhampton *Wallkill.*
Little H., South Middletown
Demerest & Lazer, New Milford   *Warwick.*

Orleans County.

Ward & Wilson, Albion   *Barre.*
Beach & Collins   *Carlton.*
Sturges M. D.   *Clarendon.*
Beach & Collins, Eagle Harbor   *Gaines.*
Webster S. & E. K., Kendall Mills   *Kendall.*
Balcomb Abner   *Murray.*
Southworth Augustus, Holley
Gibson Waters. Sandy Creek
Safford & Lowber, Medina   *Ridgeway.*
Stanford & Wells,   do
Nathgate S.   do
Spencer S. M. Oak Orchard
Grant L. A. G. B.   *Shelby.*
Gould H. O.   *Yates.*
Parsons Joel C.
Gould & Chamberlain, Lyndonville

Oswego County.

Anderson ——   *Albion.*
Barnes Wilbert
Carter J. & R. Carterville   *Amboy.*

Robbins James, West Amboy   *Amboy.*
Parker James, Oswego Falls   *Granby.*
Henderson James, Hannibal Center   *Hannibal.*
Skinner James
Goit David   *Mexico.*
Snell & Beebe
Nichols Hezekiah   *New Haven.*
Chapman Richard
Pratt Daniel. Orwell   *Orwell.*
Salisbury John
Fitzhugh H. & Co. Lake Ontario Mills, 1st st.   *Oswego.*
Wyman Truman, (Eagle Mills) 1st st.
Penfield, Lyon & Co. (Washington Mills) 1st st.
Keeler Mason S. Ames' Buildings
Doolittle & Mollison, (Empire Mills) 1st st.
Mathews Henry (Express Mills)
Pardee Wm. J. (Congress & Quaker Mills) 1st st.
Cochran, Lyon & Co. (Skenandoah Mills)
Merrick & Davis, (Seneca Mills) between Canal & River
Burckle & Co. (Ontario Mills) Varick's Canal
Ransom & Seely, (Atlas Mills) Varick's Canal
Hatch, Stevens & Co. (Star Mills) Varick's Canal
Bond & Uhlhorns, Varick's Canal
Wright Henry C. (Crescent Mills) Varick's Canal
Beardsley & Bunker, (Premium Mills) Varick's Canal
Bogart & Smith, do
Lewis & Beardsley, (Exchange Mills) Big Dam, 1st st.
Campbell J. Vermillion *Palermo.*
Becker & Allen   *Parish.*
Alden E.   *Redfield.*
Porter & Fuller, Pulaski   *Richland.*
Sykes & Southworth, do
Knowlton Dean O.   do
Gillespie Henry,   do
Holmes J. South Richland
Breed & Conger, Phenix   *Schroeppel.*
Gilbert Hiram (Gilbert's Mills)
Waugh John P.   *Scriba.*
Nelson Willie S., Fulton *Volney.*
Pond H. P.   do
Clark H.   do
Clark F. W.   do
Chesbro & Cone, do
Lyon Joseph B.   do
Cromwell Jacob   *Williamstown.*

Otsego County.

Park Dow A.   *Burlington.*
Kenyon T. West Burlington
Hawkins V. R. Burlington Flats
Stickney Wm.   *Edmeston.*
Beardsley Abijah, S. Edmeston
Bissell & Daly   *Hartwick.*
Crafts E.   *Laurens.*
Harrison Wm
Sweet J.
Doolittle J.   *Milford.*
Elwell L.
Goodyear J.
Lull R.   *New Lisbon.*
Scott W.
White H.
Goodyear J.   *Oneonta*
Sleeper Ephraim, West Oneonta
Rockwell & Hunt   *Otego.*
Phillips John
Johnson W. P.   *Otsego.*
Gregory Stephen, Cooperstown
Wilbur & Co.   *Plainfield.*
Weidman & Laraway   *Unadilla.*
uy G.   *Westford.*
Jennings Anthony   *Worcester*
Caryl John

Shearer Andrew — *Worcester.*
Champou John, East Worcester

Putnam County.

Haines D. C. & Co. Farmers Mills — *Kent.*
Hayt H. — *Patterson.*
Dean G. T.
Heviland B.
Duell J.
Knapp F. — *Phillipstown.*
Warren J.
Meksel W.
Fost J. — *Putnam Valley.*
Winter T.
Foster E. — *Southeast.*
Doane —
Knapp —

Queens County.

Hamilton Charles — *Flushing.*
Nichols Gideon S. — *Hempstead.*
Pehl V. M.
Mott Isaac D.
Cornell Leonard
Smith Parmenas, Rockville
Davidson Alexander. do
Smith Oliver. Millburn
Rayner Daniel, Rayner Town
Conarles John, — *Jamaica.*
Simonson Daniel H., Forsters' Meadow
Johnson & Higbee. Springfield
Kicks Joseph, Roslyn — *North Hempstead.*
Lyston Charles, Roslyn
Reynolds J. Cow Neck
Cook Henry, do
Harrold William, Jericho — *Oyster Bay.*

Rensselaer County.

Cropsey A. — *Brunswick.*
Raymond J. — *Greenbush.*
Warner M.
Coss —
Pulver William, East Nassau — *Nassau.*
Wood N. D. do — *Schodack.*
Downer R. & J. — *Schodack.*
Vail, Hayner & Fellows, 151 & 153 River — *Troy.*
Danker Jacob, Hollow Road
Herrington Horace, Nail Factory
Boutwell O. River near State Dam
Hooker J. H. near State Dam

Richmond County

Mallet Thomas. Rossville — *Westfield.*

Rockland County.

Goetcheus A — *Haverstraw.*
Knapp S.
Thiell J. B.
Eckerson J. Spring Valley — *Orangetown.*
Stilwell J.

St. Lawrence County.

Hubbard Ebenezer S. — *Brasher.*
Nevin Benjamin, Helena
Gibson Philo — *Canton.*
M'Arthur Orange
Buttolph Ira
White R. Richville — *De Kalb.*
Rushton Henry — *Edwards.*
Thomas A. South Edwards
Brown A. J. — *Fine.*
Sheldon & Co. — *Fowler.*
Hall, Henry H. & Co.
Houck Harmon
Fosgate J. — *Gouverneur.*
Sherwin Isaac C. — *Hermon.*
Stokes J. L.
Hopkins Isaac R. — *Hopkinton.*
Gibson Timothy, Nicholville — *Lawrence.*
Van Rensselaer Henry — *Lisbon.*

Redington George — *Louisville.*
Pope Timothy, Pope's Mills — *Macomb.*
Horton John, Columbia — *Madrid.*
Howland & Aspinwall, Waddington
Ogden ——, do
Montgomery A. T do
Haskell Lemuel — *Massena*
Orvis U. H.
Redington George, Lewisville
Sackrider N. — *Norfolk.*
Hall G. J. Raymondsville
Haskell Henry T. Ogdensburgh — *Oswegatchie.*
Averill & Judson
Turnep William
Parish George — *Parishville.*
Cox Gardiner — *Pierpont.*
Hicks O.
Clarkson Levinas — *Potsdam.*
Bailey Alexander, West Potsdam
Crary Edward, Crary's Mills
Rose William B. — *Russell.*
Gibson Warren — *Stockholm.*
Nichols & Davis

Saratoga County.

Marvin James & John — *Charlton.*
Conner Gilbert M.
Vischer Garrett, Vischer Ferry — *Clifton Park.*
Edwards E. — *Corinth.*
Mallory Zina
Beecher Ely — *Edinburgh.*
M'Kindly William — *Galway.*
Mann —
Foster H. C.
Frulk & Myers
Usher John — *Halfmoon.*
Ashman James, Meltaville — *Malta.*
Arnold Simeon, do
Rowland Hiram, — *Milton.*
Larkin Nelson, W. Milton
Taylor Wm. C. Milton Centre
Ashman James, Ballston Spa
Sill E. & Gurdon — *Moreau.*
Cronkhite George, Glenn's Falls
Hagerdorn Jonathan — *Providence.*
Westcott & Co.
Coffin Leathan
Cramer G. Schuylerville
Rogers H. Victory — *Saratoga.*
Granger S. do
Carrigan J. & J. *Saratoga Springs.*
Tearse Archibald — *Stillwater.*
King Horace — *Wilton.*

Schenectady County.

Curtis H. P. — *Glenville.*
Settle Paul — *Rotterdam.*
Kilghorn William, (City Mill) 27 Water — *Schenectady.*

Schoharie County.

Baird Joseph — *Blenheim.*
Hawyer Henry — *Broome.*
Goodyear George — *Cobleskill.*
Gale S. S.
Barwer D. J.
Richtmyer B. H — *Conesville.*
Foster S. Sloansville — *Esperance.*
Murphy P. & P. Fultonham — *Fulton.*
Berg Philip, Breakabeen
Haynes A. West Fulton
Reed John & Co. — *Gilboa.*
Mahan William
Rockaway Jessee — *Jefferson.*
Hickook David
Manning George — *Middleburgh.*
Boret Peter, jr.
Sabins James M.
Mann David — *Richmondville.*
Shaver Adam H. Warnerville
Westover John
Griggs J. P. — *Schoharie.*
Westerhouse Geo. Central Bridge
Utman C. — *Seward.*
Miller & Warner, Hyndsville

Adams J. — *Summit.*
Shafer John
Sporbeck George W.
Adams Wm. H.
Becker Wm. Gallupville — *Wright.*

Seneca County.

Mandival Elijah, Canoga — *Fayette.*
Ingersoll M. H. — *Lodi.*
Wyckof & Evans
Ingersoll C. M.
Mosher —
Wheeler, Bennett & Co — *Ovid.*
Vail Benjamin A. Farmer
Chamberlin J. F. — *Seneca Falls.*
Downs & Carey
Dey Samuel & Co.
Hall Hans & Co.
Fitch & Leach
Oatman W. G.
Wier H. S.
Kendig D. S. — *Waterloo.*
Marker Jacob
Wilson Joel
Wood Wm. W.

Steuben County.

Kinson C. W. I. — *Avoca.*
Burnham G W.
Squier S. W.
Cook C. — *Bath.*
Beckwith Amasa
Hallock B.
Monson Merriman & Co. — *Bradford.*
Hubbard Daniel — *Cameron.*
Rowley John P. — *Canisteo.*
Stevens C. H. & O.
Breese A. B. — *Catoi.*
Chase N. B. — *Cohocton.*
Pierce J. W.
Kendall T. — *Dansville.*
Erwin S. H. — *Erwin.*
Stevens Alexander H. — *Greenwood.*
Burndrage John
Mix & Co.
Davis Evan — *Hornellsville.*
Stevens E. G.
Morey & Shull
Miller & Graves — *Howard.*
Goff William
Johnson Nelson — *Jasper.*
Ryors J. W. — *Lindley.*
Babbitt J. F. & Co. — *Orange.*
Hammond & Johnson — *Painted Post.*
Hathaway George W.
Hopkins Henry — *Prattsburgh.*
Reynolds Harry B. — *Troupsburgh.*
Murdock James B.
Sunderlin Eli — *Tyrone.*
Weller Charles
Force Lyman & Co.
Baker Mrs. C — *Urbana.*
Mitchell & Mills
Patchin Warren — *Wayland.*
Hedges Isaac — *Woodhull.*
Warnbough William

Suffolk County.

Jayne Edmund, Patchogue — *Brookhaven.*
Saxton Richard, do
Oally Nathaniel, Babylon — *Huntington.*
Carll Elbert, do
Swearey I. — *Riverhead.*
Jaggon & Luce
Albertson Richard
Blydenburgh Isaac — *Smithtown.*
Phillips George S.
Horton Daniel
Dunkall Augustus — *Southold.*
Youngs Hampton
Appleby J.
Vail Daniel, Greenport
Tuthill Lewis, do
Lerzy Walter, Mattituck

Sullivan County.

Gardiner Thomas & Calkins, Barryville — *Lumberland.*

Gumar P. *Mamakating.*
Mills Horace, Bloomingburgh
Hart George, Burlingham
Reynolds J. *Rockland.*

Tompkins County.

Roe David C. *Caroline.*
Mott William. 2d
Beers Isaac M. *Danby.*
Fitts & Sears *Dryden.*
Houtz John H. & Co.
Tremens Jared *Enfield.*
Demsion J. M. *Groton.*
Walpole M. F.
Miller Charles, Burdett *Hector.*
Hubbell ——
Treman Calvin, Mecklenburg
Knight John, North Hector
Halsey R. & W. head of Oswego st. *Ithaca.*
Williams T. S. & Co. Cascadilla Mills, 2 Linn st.
Myers Andrew *Lansing.*
Robinson Charles *Newfield.*
Dean John
Blakesley H. D.
Everhard Peter
Dean Samuel G
Terry James, Trumansburgh *Ulysses.*
Treman Jonathan, do
Colgrove A. C. do

Tioga County.

Lincoln Otis, Newark Valley *Newark.*
Nichols T. M. *Owego.*
Call J. P.
Leach S.
Pearsall W. S.

Ulster County.

Depuy Jacob H., High Falls *Marbletown.*
Hasbrouck Joseph O., Tuthill *New Paltz.*
Moore H. M., Libortyville
Broadhead Richard, Accord *Rochester.*
Pruyn I. D. do
Hornbeck Benj. C. *Wawarsing.*
Cathkamire Henry, Napanoch
Bange & Co. do

Warren County.

Pendell E. *Athol.*
Fuller James
Crandall Peter *Caldwell.*
Smith Thomas *Hague.*
Dunn John D. *Johnsburgh.*
Graves Horatio
Conkhite George, Glenn's Falls *Queensbury.*
Burhans & Gray *Warrensburgh.*

Washington County.

Reid John *Argyle.*
Jackson James *Cambridge.*
Barker Benajah *Easton.*
Gele Frederick A., Galesville
Hodgeman F. D. *Fort Edward.*
Velie L. S., Fort Miller
Thompson James *Fort Ann.*
Baker William
Mowry Wm. & Co. *Greenwich.*
Burdick Matthew, Centre Falls
M'Neil William, East Greenwich
Norcross F., Lake
Gamble R. G., Galesville
Allen Nathan *Hampton.*
Moore John, Sandy Hill *Kingsbury.*
Weeks Henry, do
Palmer ——, Patten's Mills
Goodrich Gustavus A. *Putnam.*
Bennett Julius *White Creek.*
Baldwin L. *Whitehall.*

Wayne County.

Rice R. *Arcadia.*

Morley & Hyde *Arcadia.*
Hill Charles B.
Chapman & Redfield, Clyde *Galen.*
Briggs & Miller, do
Leighton Nathan *Huron.*
Leach M. S. & H. J. *Lyons.*
Merrick Ira
Ennis R., Alloway
Young & Moore, Alloway
Willits & Co. Macedonville *Macedon.*
Wilkerson & Brother, do
Smith A. C. do
Young & Healer *Marion.*
Boyce Peter *Palmyra.*
Jossup G. G.
Palmer Phillip
Seaman L. L.
Moore & Sherman, East Palmyra
Harrison G. O. do
Young Henry *Rose.*
Swails Wm. Sodus Point *Sodus.*
Wright James *Wolcott.*
Pierce Nathan

Westchester County.

Swaine James P. *East Chester.*
Core Francis, Tarrytown *Greenburgh.*
Cox Wm. *New Castle.*
Lee Thomas R., Croton Falls *North Salem.*
Washburn Oliver, Sing Sing *Ossining.*
Raymond & Schuyler *West Farms.*

Wyoming County.

Folsom Benj. R. *Attica.*
Yeoman Chas. Cowlesville *Bennington.*
Priestly ——, do
Price E. T. *Castile.*
Parshall Amzi
Jackson Asahel *China.*
Sprague James *Covington.*
Sprague P. C.
Whaley M. *Eagle.*
Blodgett Lewis *Grimesville.*
Williams George *Genesee Falls.*
Torrey A. & Sons, (Wyoming) *Middlebury.*
Richards Peter, Johnsburgh *Orangeville.*
Bailey C. P. & Co. *Perry.*
Severance N.
Smith R. H.
Davis G. P. & Co.
Norton H. N. *Pike.*
Mills M. H.
Wilder & Hodge, East Koy
Raymond B. N. Varysburgh *Sheldon.*
Frank Augustus, Strykersville
Clark John F. *Warsaw.*
Bronson & Whitcher

Yates County.

Booth S. *Jerusalem.*
Ritley Peter H., Branchport
Casner & Scheets, Penn Yan *Milo.*
Gillett E. M. & Co. do
Strobridge Sandford, Potter Centre *Potter.*
Townsend L. G., Dundee *Starkey.*
Dunn H. S.
Mertin C.

Fly Net Manufacturer.

Havemeyer Charles H. 104 John *New York.*

Forges—Portable.

New York County.

Flagler Edward, 211 Water *New York.*

Westchester County.

Flagler Edward, (manufacturer) Peekskill *Cortlandt.*
Gilbert W. T. & Co. (manufact'r.)

Fork Manufacturers.

Albany County.

Engle H., Reedsville *Berne.*

Chautauque County.

Waters, Franklin & Co. *Westfield.*

Chenango County.

Sanford G. *Macdonough.*

Madison County.

Hills & Denison, (hay forks) *Brookfield.*
Brand N. & Co. Leonardsville

Montgomery County.

Case, Pardee & Co. *Amsterdam.*

Oneida County.

Bagg G. W. & Co. Cassville *Paris.*

Orange County.

De Puy & Schoonmaker *Middletown.*

Otsego County.

Warren J. V. *New Lisbon.*
Brand N. & Co. *Plainfield.*

Rensselaer County.

Trull John M. *Troy.*

St. Lawrence County.

Taylor, Hubbard & Co. *Brasher.*
Buttolph, Sprague & Co. *Stockholm.*

Founders.

BRASS AND BELL.

(See also Brass Manufacturers; also Brass Finishers.)

Albany County.

Lamb P. W. 57 & 59 Liberty *Albany.*
Cuyler E. 56 Green
Maxwell J. 94 South Pearl
Orr William 54 Beaver
M'Elroy Wm. 63 do
Meneely A. West Troy *Watervliet.*

Duchess County.

Pearl C. 425 Main *Poughkeepsie.*
West William B. 364 Main

Erie County.

Good A. 21 Ohio *Buffalo.*
Calligon & Brothers, Lloyd st.

Greene County.

Brown Robert *Cazsackie.*

Kings County.

Rich & Co. 11 Water *Brooklyn.*
Benson John, 58 Water
Benson Wm. J. & Co. Water near Washington
Lee Benjamin, Flushing Av. near Classon Av.
Tuttle & Cowley, 105 1st *Williamsburgh.*
Lawrence George, 172 4th

Madison County.

Walrath D. Chittenango *Sullivan.*

Monroe County.

Dickinson H. W. 1 Buffalo
Rochester.
Cole Darius, 73 State
Wray Henry, 66 State

New York County.

Bard Jas M. 12 Canal *New York.*
Benson John, 25 Old slip
Bissicks & Barton, 109 Bowery
Broad J. H. 618 4th
Brown Henry, 56 & 58 Cannon
Brown Edgar M. 636 Water & 339 Cherry
Buckley Wm. 114 & 116 Cannon
De Coudres L. & Son, 18 Corlears
Dod & Van Horn, 107 Lewis
Dunphy Richard, 33 Desbrosses
Engen John, rear 34 Bank
Gerow & M'Creary, 335 Stanton
Graves John T. 48 Duane
Hare James, 370 Washington
Henderson Robert, r. 149 Spring
Hidden Enoch, 12th cor. Av. C
Hovenden R. & J. B. 178 Prince, (copper brand makers)
Ives Alfred & Co. 497 Cherry
Rawrence Wm. R. 401 Front & 419 Cherry
Lynch James, 48 Duane
M'Keena James, 20 Spruce
M'Kinley Augustus C. 87 Centre
Martin M. J. 84 Hester
Moffet James G. 191 Prince
Morgans M. jr. 91 Henry
Offorman John C. 47 Eldridge
Pollock G. & Co. 23 Centre
Riley John, 93 Reade
Soffe Henry. 103 Elm
Stillman, Allen & Co. ft. 19th E. R.
Sullivan Michael, 32 5th
Timpson C. B. & Co. 126 Cherry
Vanhorn & Dod, 101 Lewis
Wallace Wm. 5 Sullivan
Wallace & Bruns, rear 45 Rose
Welch R. H. rear 151 Essex
Whittaker Thomas, 92 Reade
Whittingham R. rear 96 Henry

Oneida County.

Price & Dana, 92 Genesee *Utica.*

Onondaga County.

Brower L. M. Genesee st. Syracuse *Salina.*
Brower A. G. Clinton st.

Orange County.

Stanton, Clark & Co. Front st.
Newburgh.

Rensselaer County.

Howard E. S. & Son, 25 N. 2d
Troy.
Mann Chas. F. Fulton Works

Ulster County.

Gallagher & Rashmore *Kingston.*

FOUNDERS FACING DUST.

Robertson Geo. O. 303 W. 27th
New York.

FOUNDERS IRON—(See also Iron Merchants, also Fences Iron, Railing, &c. also Safes.

Albany County.

Voss & Co. South Broadway & 12 & 14 Maiden lane *Albany.*
Thomas C. Collins, cor. S. Lansing & Quay
Potts J. C. cor. Hamilton & Grand
Townsend F. & Co. cor. Hawk & Elk
Jagger, Treadwell & Perry, 110 Beaver
Lamb P. W. 57 & 59 Liberty

Cobb Wm. 192 Washington
Sarles W. *Coeymans.*
West Troy Foundry, Chollar, Sage & Dunham, West Troy
Watervliet.
Cohoes Iron Foundry, Cohoes
Ogden & Co. do

Alleghany County.

Neal D. S. *Angelica.*
Sherman D. *Belfast.*
Graves Wm. & L. *Cuba.*
Dodge Mills & D. Wiscoy Hume
Graves & Allen, Whitesville
Independence.
Hammond & Stone *Rushford.*
White Samuel

Broome County.

Overhiser B. H. *Binghamton.*
Hotchkiss G. *Windsor.*

Cattaraugus County.

Beecher Moses *Ellicottville.*
M'Lure James *Franklinville.*
Nutting & M'Callister, East Randolph *Randolph.*
Rice Edwin *Yorkshire.*

Cayuga County.

Rockwell D. *Cato.*

Chautauque County.

Look S. B. Mayville *Chautauqua.*
Tew & James, Jamestown
Ellicott.
Williams D. S. do
Clark Cephas, do
Lincoln Cyrus, do
Hickey Lyman, do
Barker & Co. Silver Creek
Hanover.
Dickinson S. H. & Son, Fredonia
Pomfret.
Lester & Redington, Fredonia

Chenango County.

Darby & Lyon *Greene.*
Weller H. & Son *Norwich.*
Wilcox E. P. *Oxford.*
Birch L. D. *Sherburne.*
Sabin A.

Chemung County.

Phillips & Wheeler *Elmira.*
Leach, Potter & Covell
Sampson J. C.

Clinton County.

Goulding, Green & Conse, Keeseville *Au Sable.*
Moore N. *Champlain.*
Finley & Smith
Davis & Weaver *Peru.*
Barton C. D
Smith, Bonner & Co. *Plattsburgh.*
Hobart & Weston

Columbia County.

Bemus M. Spencertown *Austerlitz.*
Hulburt P. *Chatham.*
Page J. Chatham Four Corners
Spalding M. Gallatin Furnace
Gallatin.
Burton George *Hillsdale.*
Gifford E. Hudson Furnace
Hudson.
Reynolds R. (Valatie Furnace)
Valatie *Kinderhook.*
Hanna & Carpenter, Valatie

Cortland County.

Freer A. & S. D. *Cortlandville.*
Sanders Jacob *Homer.*

Duchess County.

Dutcher L. S. & Co. *Dover.*

White Wm. A. *Dover*
Adriance & Rose, Wappinger's Falls *Fishkill.*
Barhyte D. R. Fishkill Landing
Adriance, Coller & Barnes, 494 Main *Poughkeepsie.*
Arnold Benj. & Son, 374 Main

Erie County.

Frick J. & J. Williamsville
Amherst.
Waldo S. & Co. (ploughs) Willink
Aurora.
Wilkinson & Co. 64 Main *Buffalo*
Jowett & Root, 31 Main
Dudley Thos. J. 98 Main
Larkin L. H. 13 Clinton
Slur & Tucker *Collins.*
Broomfield David, Springville
Concord.
Barton Jesse, Water Valley
Hamburgh.
Dunham, Knight & Co. Akron
Newstead.

Essex County.

Porter John *Ticonderoga.*

Franklin County.

Meigs & Wead *Malone.*
Moses O. & Son
Keeler A. S.

Fulton County.

Cleaveland, Northrup & Cleaveland *Broadalbin.*
Moore D. Northville *Northampton.*

Genesee County.

Hurlbert T. *Batavia.*
Smith J. R.
Smith & Bosworth, Linden
Bethany.
Bacon, Mitchell & Co. *Le Roy.*
Coman & Webb
Thatcher Lucius *Pembroke.*
Lay, Ganson & Co. *Stafford.*

Greene County.

Fowks Wm. Leeds *Catskill.*
Brown Robert *Coxsackie.*

Herkimer County.

Johnson C., Mohawk
German Flats.
Heath Henry M. *Little Falls.*
Brady & Cunningham
Petrie D. & J.
Stansel Oliver, Van Hornsville
Stark.
Remington & Harrington, Mohawk
German Flats.

Jefferson County.

Rogers C. W. *Adams.*
Saunders M.
Lord Wm. & Son *Brownville.*
Skinner & Brothers
Forsyth James *Cape Vincent.*
Burton W. R. *Clayton.*
Beebe I. *Ellisburgh.*
Jones Francis H. *Henderson.*
M'Kee & Hammond, Sackett's Harbor *Hounsfield.*
Woodruff Horace W. *Pamelia.*
Sterling J. *Philadelphia.*
Wilson & Chadwick *Theresa.*
Smith Wm. *Watertown.*

Kings County.

Stillwell G. W. Court st. nr. Dean
Brooklyn.
Borbeck Alex. & Son, Water st. near Fulton
Taylor William, (Columbia Iron Foundry) Adams st. nr. Water

Wood Lofters, 109 1st
Williamsburgh.
Strickland & Brown, 86 Grand
Ritchie James, 8th st. near do
Terry T. H. Power st. nr. Union
Av.

Lewis County.

Hanson & Co.   *Denmark.*

Livingston County.

Teele Christopher   *Caledonia.*
Elyea C.
Smith Duncan
M'Kay Geo. R.
Sweet, Whitaker & Co. *Dansville.*
Gilman F. & M.
Curtiss Wm.
Lochlin N.
Clement & Hadnutt   *Geneseo.*
Tukebury & Sons, Cuylerville
Leicester.
Forbes & Clute,   de
Spencer Samuel   *Lima.*
Vary Wm. & Brother
Brown H. C.   *Mount Morris.*
Bell Alfred   *Nunda.*
Martin Samuel C. Oakland
Portage.
Marshall Chas. S. Scottsburgh
Sparta.

Madison County.

Green Robert   *Brookfield.*
Shapley M. W. & J. *Cazenovia.*
Chubbuck & Beckus
Ayres & Arnold   *De Ruyter.*
Cross J. & Son, Morrisville
Eaton.
Wheaton, Kasson & Burt, Oneida
Depot   *Lenox.*
Walrath Daniel, Chittenango
Sullivan.
Kellogg & Webber, do

Monroe County.

Martin D. M. (plough cast) Jen-
kins' Corner   *Greece.*
Williams J., W. Henrietta
Henrietta.
Smith Z. (stoves) W. Mendon
Mendon.
Yorks E. L. do   do
Hebbard Sterling A. Churchville
Riga.
Cherry Wm. H. 70 S. St. Paul,
Rochester
Carpenter & Co. 14 Water
Bull D. R. 14 Court
French John M. 87 Exchange
Jones S. C. & E., Brown's Race,
foot of Furnace
Bristol A. G. Trowbridge st.
Fitch, Bang & Co. Brockport
Sweden.
Tarbox H. Scottsville
Wheatland.
Frexier James, Mumford
Blair James,   do

Montgomery County.

Potter & M'Elwans   *Amsterdam.*
Shires Robert
Chase Welcome U. & Cyrus B.
Ehle Charles   *Canajoharie.*
Failing & Barber, Fort Plain
Minden.
Van Alstine A. A.   do
Johnson & Dubois, Palatine Bridge
Palatine.

New York County.

Allaire James P. 486 Cherry
New York.
Beebe J. & Co. 190 Fulton
Bent & Randall, 406 Cherry
Birkbeck George, jr. 232 West
Boyle & Coleman, 304 Broome
Brady A. & G. W. 30 Greene

Braid & Harpers, 72 Lewis
New York.
Browning Wm. 96 North Moore
Columbian Foundry, 43, 45 & 47
Duane
Colwell Lewis, 72 Charles
Copeland C. W. 464 Cherry
Dale J. D. & Co. W. 26th
Danverse, Dally & Co. 1st Av. bet.
25th & 26th
Davis Charles, 223 Elizabeth
Davis Stephen A. 94 Clinton
Dranfield Geo. 424 Broadway
Dunham H. R. & Co. 96 North
Moore
Farrell Edward, rear 274 Water
Force D. C. 79 Goerck
Hare & Pugh, foot W. 13th
Hay Andrew, 135 & 137 Thompson
Herring S. C. 742 Greenwich
Hoe R. & Co. 29 & 31 Gold &
Broome cor. Sheriff
Hogg & Delamater, 260 West
Holloway J. Yorkville
Jackson James L. 315 Stanton
Janes, Beebe & Co. Reade near
Centre & 190 Fulton
M'Ilvaine B. R. 464 Cherry
M'Kinley & Smith, 31 3d Av.
Mayher John & Co. 502 Water
Miller Wm. L. 40 Eldridge
Milligan W. E. 115 Warren
Morgan Geo. 258 & 260 3d
Morris Peter & Co. 45 Duane
Mott & Ayres, W. 20th st.
Mott Jordan L. 264 Water
O'Donnell John, 269 Stanton
Pearson Thomas, 91 Elizabeth
Pease & Murphy, 506 Cherry
Peck W. B. & Co. 740 Greenwich
Pratt & Briggs, 60 & 62 Attorney
Richards T. B. & J. 143 Perry
Rodman & Co. 230 West & 370
Washington
Secor Theodosius F. & Co. foot
9th E. R.
Small W., West st. cor. Beach
Snediker F. A. 123 Clinton
Staats B. E. 223 Pearl
Stillman, Allen & Co. ft. 12th E.R.
Terry Thomas, 46 Cannon
Tupper C. H. 88 Av. C
Warts H. A. 24th st.
Waterman H. 239 Cherry
Webb Philander, 59 & 61 Goerck
West st. Foundry, Wilson Small,
West st. cor. Beach
Worrall & Co. 24 Elm & 67 Du-
ane

Niagara County.

Pound A.   *Lockport.*
Gevaner S. & E.
Moore John (ploughs) *Newfane.*
Doty, Ford & Co. *Niagara Falls.*
Griswold G. & M. R.   *Somerset.*
Hemmingway H. N. & S. F.
Wilson.

Oneida County.

Wood & Phelps   *Camden.*
Rogers, Spencer & Co. (Willow
Vale Works) Washington Mills
New Hartford.
Price & Dans, 92 Genesee *Utica.*
Hart & Dagwell, Cordelia corner
Canal
Bailey, Wheeler & Co. (Eagle
Furnace) Columbia st.
Peckham J. S. & M. (hollow ware,
16, 18 & 20 Catharine
Terwilliger F. & Co. Whitesboro
Whitestown.

Ontario County.

Keller Jacob S.   *Canandaigua.*
Lampert J. & N. P.
Granger Albert
Stiles R. C. & Co. *East Bloomfield.*
Brown & Osband, Richmond
Mills.   *Richmond.*

Johnson John R. Geneva *Seneca.*
Burrell E. J.   do
Tetus & Carpenter   *Flint.*

Orange County.

Fitzgerald W.   *Chester.*
Southfield Iron Furnace *Monroe.*
Townsend's W. H. & P. (Monroe
Works)
Speir & Wilson, Western Av.
Newburgh.
Corwin, Halsey & Co. West. Av.
Stanton, Clark & Co. Front st.
Wheeler & Co. South Middletown
Wallkill.

Orleans County.

King S. L. & Co. Albion   *Barre.*
Miller A.   *Clarendon.*
Bellows ―――, Holley *Murray.*
Bathgate G. Medina *Ridgeway.*
Clenant J. & J. do
Morse Lucius, Knowlesville
Sinclair Heman, Lyndonville
Yates.

Oswego County.

Beebe & Son   *Marks.*
Talcott D. & Son, 1st st *Oswego.*
Carrier C. & Co. 2d cor. Bridge
Snow & Dodge, Pulaski *Richland.*
Dewey Samuel, South Richland
Sisson Wm. Fulton   *Volney.*
Dutton John E. do

Otsego County.

Rice T. T.   *Butternuts.*
Baker H.   *Oneonta.*
Baker Harvey
Hodge & Jenks
Culver F. & Co.
Shipman O. N.   *Springfield.*
Hubbell Hiram

Putnam County.

West Point Foundry *Gouverneur.*
Kemble ―― Cold Spring
Phillipstown.

Rensselaer County.

White & Wood   *Hoosick.*
Thatcher & Hutchins, State st.
Lansingburgh.
Dorval Edward, State st. Alley
Cronk J. & Son, Congress st. Al'y
Smith Thomas   *Nassau.*
Starbuck N. B. 312 River *Troy.*
Pease, Keaney & Co. 2d cor. John
Eddy Chas. (Phœnix Foundry)
509 River
Noyes & Hatton, (hollow ware)
Morrison & Tibbitts, (Green Island
Furnace) warehouse 259 River
Dunham A. T. & Co. 261 River
Anthony David & Co. (Washing-
ton Foundry) store 294 River

Richmond County.

Bush Richard, Rossville *Westfield.*

Rockland County.

Beebe Henry   *Haverstraw.*
Archer J. & E. W. Piermont
Orangetown.

St. Lawrence County.

Cruser Jonas .   *Brasher.*
Alexander & Skinner
Fuller & Peck   *Fowler.*
Shelden & Co.
Fox & Rich   *Gouverneur.*
Melott John & Newell, Columbia
Madrid.
Loomis & Wright, Waddington
Wickins John,   do
Sackrider Norman .   *Norfolk.*

Chauncy A. & Co. Ogdensburgh
Oswegatchie.
Alden A. E. & W. C. Ogdensb'gh　*Potsdam.*
Knowles & Watkins
Burr J.　*Russell.*

Saratoga County.

Vail & House　*Halfmoon.*
Hopkins & Dix, Glenn's Falls
Moreau.
Cramer James P.　*Saratoga.*
Perry Wm. & Co.
Saratoga Springs.

Schoharie County.

Gardner Jacob J.　*Esperance.*
Waldron John, Breakabeen
Fulton.
Chichester David E.　*Gilboa.*
Whiting Chas.
Gilbert & Tippits　*Middleburgh.*
Wells & Gilbert
Wood & Tabor　*Richmondville.*
Van Scoyck ——　*Seward.*

Seneca County.

Ely W. H. & Co. (Eagle Furnace)
Ovid.
Pixney & Clapp, Farmer
Downs, Mynderse & Co.
Seneca Falls.
Clary G. H. M.
Purdy John　*Waterloo.*
Newcomb & Richardson

Steuben County.

Horn Lewis L.　*Addison.*
Biles & Roble　*Bath.*
Erwin & Bennett　*Erwin.*
Brooks & Co.
Payne D. W. & Co.　*Painted Post.*
Williams & Noble　*Prattsburgh.*
Benham Moses　*Reading.*
Keeler J. H.　*Urbana.*
Mitchell John B.　*Wayne.*
Warner S.　*Woodhull.*

Sullivan County.

Wheeler & Fairchild, Monticello
Thompson.

Tioga County.

Springsted ——, (Novelty Works)
Owego.
Camp H. (Owego Furnace)

Tompkins County.

Scovill H., Burdett　*Hector.*
Tremans & Brothers, Factory Hill
Ithaca.
Conrad V. (Franklin Furnace)
Aurora st.
Crequa John & Co. Trumansburgh
Ulysses.
Spink & Co. Trumansburgh

Ulster County.

Gallagher & Rushmore *Kingston.*
Baldwin J. W. & Co.
Maines & Montross　*Saugerties.*
Bloomer J. L. & Sons, Ellenville
Wawarsing.

Warren County.

Stevens W. S.　*Luzerne.*
Hitchcock Dwight
Phœnix Furnace, Glenn's Falls
Queensbury.
Hopkins & Dix, Glenn's Falls

Washington County.

Eddy & Co.　*Easton.*
Woodruff E. & Co.　*Fort Ann.*
Kingsley Caleb
Kingsley & Everest

Northrup N. C. & Son, Sandy Hill
Kingsbury.
Holbrook Lyman, Sandy Hill
Griffith Samuel P.　do
Warner S. W., North *White Creek.*
Nise D. P. & L., William st.
Whitehall.
Merrill C. L. & Co. William st.

Wayne County.

Taft Newell　*Lyons.*
Barber G. S
Pond J. N.　*Marion.*
Atwater Benjamin
Wilcox Orrin
Holmes Myron　*Sodus.*
Cook E. B. Sodus Point
Leavenworth, Hendrick & Co.
Wolcott.

Westchester County.

Van Wait & Wildey, Tarrytown
Greenburgh.
Fowler, Horton & Co. Sing Sing
Ossining.
Vredenburgh W. D. & F. Sing Sing
Abendroth & Brothers, Portchester
Rye.
Mott Jordan L.　*West Farms.*

Wyoming County.

Chapman J.　*Attica.*
Goff & Daggett, Cowlesville
Bennington.
Belden & Scott　*Castile.*
Hicks E. & Co.　*Perry.*
Bachelder Thomas
Comstock, Andrews & Co.
Warsaw.

Yates County.

Jones E. B. Penn Yan　*Milo.*
Cooley James, do
Stebbins F. A. do
Blodgett ——　*Potter.*
Ferris R., Dundee　*Starkey.*
Byington B.　do

FOUNDERS—STEREOTYPE.

Albany County.

Stevens E. J. 75 State　*Albany.*
Van Benthuysen C. 407 Broadway

New York County.

Baner & Palmer, 201 William
New York.
Benedict S. W. 16 Spruce
Davison Clement, 33 Gold
Dill Vincent, 21 and 23 Ann
Dill Vincent L. 198 Fulton
Hobbs William, rear 61 Ann
Jones J. P. & Co. 163 William
M'Nichol John, 11 Spruce
Savage Charles C. 13 Chambers
Seward Thos. 71 Greenwich Av.
Smith T. B. 216 William
Trow John F. 49 & 51 Ann
Turney & Lockwood, 16 Spruce
Valentine Richard C. 45 Gold

FOUNDERS—TYPE.

Erie County.

Lyman Nathan R.　*Buffalo.*

New York County.

Bray & Walker, 59 Ann *New York.*
Bruce George & Co. 13 Chambers
Conner James & Son, 25 Ann
Duryee George W. 9 Spruce
Green Hannibal H. 10 Reade
Hagar William, 23 Gold
South Charles J. 266 William
Wells & Webb, 18 Dutch
Whiting Charles, 93 Ann
White John T. 53 Cliff

FOUNDERS—ZINC.

Erhard & Sons, 216 William
New York.

Frames, Looking-Glass & Pictures.

Albany County.

Annesley Lawson, 517 Broadway
Albany.

Alleghany County.

Mallory George　*Andover.*

Columbia County.

Kimball J. W. Warren st. *Hudson.*

Duchess County.

M'Kean R. S. 3 Garden
Poughkeepsie.

Erie County.

Brown C. W. & Co. 167 Main
Buffalo.
Deuther Geo. A. 275　do
Waldron E. G. 127　do

Kings County.

Dougher P. 27 Atlantic *Brooklyn.*
Kidder Stephen, 117 do
Knight R. 27 Fulton
Kidder John & Son, Bedford
Bennett Charles, 33 Grand
Williamsburgh.

Monroe County.

Schutt Joseph, Curtis' Block, Main
Rochester.
Elder Adam, 4 Arcade
Thompson John, 35 State

New York County.

Baker & Douglass, 6th Av. cor. 4th
New York.
Barter Thomas, rear 296 Mulberry
Bell R. V. 33 6th Av.
Bishop James, 26 Frankfort
Boasburg & Rossicke, 21 Spruce
Byckenberg F. A. 238 William
Conlor & Widzer, 66 Centre
Craig John, rear 87 Eldridge
Davis Amos, rear 9 Orange
Del Vecchio J. R. 495 Broadway
Dersch John H. 87 Elizabeth
Dexter Elias, 216 Bleecker
Dexter George W. 120 Grand
Deglis Hosea, 11 Park row
Harrington Coleman, 19 Henry
Hathaway W. N. 79 Forsyth
Heins John J. 315 Broadway
Hendles Thomas T. 67 White
Hooper & Brother, 106 Fulton
Hudson & Smith, 42 Ann & 129
Fulton
Hurley Cornelius, 67 Forsyth
Jenkins J. H. 85 Bleecker
Johnson W. N. 304 Bowery
Kenedy F. 373　do
Lane W. 196 6th Av.
Lewis Robert, 209 Fulton
M'Feake & Wilmurt, 718 Bowery
M'Quillon Barnard, 44 Catharine
Marcher James, 591 Broadway
Mead Wm. 112 Bowery
Menger Louis R. 59 Beekman
Merrian Benj. W. 130 Chatham
Miller W. 364 Houston
Munts & Jebel, 78½ Norfolk
Nagle Nicholas, 85 Essex
Oestereicher F. 132 Houston
Searles & Williams, 57 White
Sigler H. V. 50 Crosby
Sigler Samuel J. 67 & 69 Forsyth
& 46 Gold
Silva John J. rear 119 Walker
Smith George, rear 104 Norfolk

Spender A. H. 71 Av. B. *New York.*
Slodder W. K. rear 7 Orange
Tabel & Mino, 78½ Norfolk
Tinker Lewis J. 198 Canal
Townley J. H. 57 Frankfort
Tracey & Newkirk, 124 Grand
Underwood Sarah, 186 Fulton
Waller & Kreps, 13 Spruce
Walsh William, rear 31 Attorney
Weiser Thomas B. A. 42 Centre
Weston John L. 595 Broadway
Wood Jesse C. 46 Av. D

Oneida County.
Forster & Burnham, 52 Hotel *Utica.*

Rensselaer County
Smyth Joseph, 21 Congress *Troy.*

Westchester County.
Ramseyer Christian, Dobbs' Ferry *Greenburgh.*

Freighters. (See also Agents Freight, also Merchants Forwarding.)

Columbia County.
Hallenbeck W. H. & H. *Hudson.*
Best C.
Coffin. Holmes & Co. Water st.
Livingston H. *Livingston.*
Davis Alexander *Stuyvesant.*
Wendover & Sargent

Delaware County.
Dill & Hulce, Deposit *Tompkins.*
Wheeler & Co. do
Ford Wm. L. & Co. do

Duchess County.
Adriance, Hopkins & Co., Low Point *Fishkill.*
Rankin James M. Fishkill Landing

Greene County.
Hunt & Nelson *Coxsackie.*
Reed G. & A.
Barker & W. & W. D. Kirtland
Sherman Edward *New Baltimore.*
Southwick William
Reynolds Jacob

Orange County.
Clark N. T. *Cornwall.*
Gregory E. Howell's Depot *Minisink.*
Dill, Dodge & Co. Otisville *Mount Hope.*
Caldwell Seybolt & Co. Otisville
Powell, Ramsdell & Co. *Newburgh.*
Carpenter B. & Co. Front st.
Crawford Mailler & Co. do
Wardrop, Smith & Co. do
Carpenter J. *New Windsor.*
Denton T. J. & G. W. New Hampton *Wallkill.*
Gardiner S. F. New Hampton
Denton & Murry, South Middletown

Putnam County.
Wright G. Cold Spring *Phillipstown.*
Colwell D. do
Warren H. do
Cronk W. do
Brewster C. do

Suffolk County.
Tuthill, Ellsworth N., Greenport *Southold.*
Tuthill Silas, Cutchogue
Goldsmith Daniel, do

Rackett John, Orient *Southold.*
Rackett Sherry, do
Rackett Sidney, do

Ulster County.
Fitch E. & Co. *Kingston.*
Scott Thomas, Wilber
Cornell T. & Co. Rondout
Cornell T. W. & Co. Eddyville
Cox Isaac, do
Elting A. & Son, New Paltz Landing *Lloyd.*
Sears S. Milton *Marlborough.*
Field John *Saugerties.*
Kellogg & Co. Glasco
Fitch & Co. do
Delanoy Daniel, do
Overbah J. V. L. do
Brundage Jonathan, *Wawarsing.*
Ludlum James, Napanock
Tuttle Broadhead & Co. Ellenville

Wayne County.
Blackmer A. T. *Arcadia.*
Grant & Co.
Blackmer E.
Stone R.

Fruit and Confectionery.

Albany County.
Starr A. G. S. 666½ Broadway *Albany.*
Reid John, 582 Broadway
Parker Joseph, 604 do
Cowell & Higby, 77 State
Byrnes J. 4 S. Pearl
Corriston J. 126 Washington
Avery & Co. 351 & 353 Broadway
Marcellos C. (Fruit) 126 State

Erie County.
Courtier R. & Co. (Foreign and Domestic Fruit) 8 Packet Dock *Buffalo.*

Kings County.
Thompson J. & A. 20 Clinton *Brooklyn.*
Rhony Mrs. P. 260 Fulton
Smith William, 19 do
Davis T. 75 do
Huttinware F. 90½ Main do
Brown L. 96 do
Johnson H. W. 159 Pearl
Chapman E. G. 11 High
Handley Benjamin, 269 Fulton
Woodhouse Mrs. E. 223 do
Wakelins Mrs. A. 217 do
Stales J. 105 do
Molow M. 195 do
Hayes Mrs. M. 175 do
Pendrell William, 319 do
Barnett A. 331 do
Ostrander L. C. 3 Hudson Av.
Lewis Henry, 25 do
Woodbury S. A. 173 Myrtle Av.
Bensie Alexander, 19 Atlantic st.
Alford Mary Ann, 43 do
Drew Walter, 55 do
Hartshorn Charles, 119 do
Lawless John, 210 do
Murphy James, 8 Hicks
Ordan Joseph, 47 S. 7th *Williamsburgh.*
Neher Frederick. 136 4th
Piper Mrs. J. 131½ Grand
Coyle Henry, 169 do
Gibbons John, 310 do
Wood Daniel, 268 do
Patterson Miss R. 189½ do
Baker Daniel, 54 do
Ales N. 76 do

Monroe County.
O'Brien Bartholomew, cor. Main & St. Paul *Rochester.*

Hastings S. & Co. cor. Buffalo & Front *Rochester.*
Lawrence F. S. 37 Exchange
Johnson William, 18½ do
Lawrence W. T. & F. S. 20 Ex.
Orchard & Son, 1 Waverly Block, State st.
Crerar Thomas, 75 State

Oneida County.
Hamell H. 14 Genesee *Utica.*
Richmond I. H. 10 Liberty
Battey P. 6 Bleecker

Onondaga County.
Ford E. Genesee st. Syracuse *Salina.*
Tackney J. Water st. do

Orange County.
Stanbrough L. H. *Newburgh.*

Rensselaer County.
Connel James, 278 River *Troy.*
Miller L. 278 do
Eustace C. 366 do
Whalin Martin, 390 do
Leonard Thomas, 126 North 2d
Havey Mrs. 147 do
Moore Mrs. 45 Jacob
Martling E. 337½ River
Sinsabough George W. 42 1st
Vinton Charles, 4 Cannon place
Oetranders Mrs. S. 21 Congress

Saratoga County.
Wager John H. *Saratoga Springs.*
Mitchell C. P.

Ulster County.
Hamblin W. H. *Kingston.*
Tappan T.
Van Schaick G. M., Ellenville *Wawarsing.*
Gerard John, Ellenville

Warren County.
Bennett C. R., Glenn's Falls *Queensbury.*

Westchester County.
Forkill James, Tarrytown *Greenburgh.*
Foster A. do
Foster H. do
Revere C. do
Disbrow J. P. *New Rochelle.*
Arnoe Frederick
Delanoy Ebenezer, Sing Sing *Ossining.*
M'Neil Robert, Portchester *Rye.*
Brown William *Yonkers.*

Fruit—Foreign and Domestic.

Columbia County.
Wilson H., Front st. *Hudson.*

Kings County.
Bogert L. Abraham, 15 Atlantic *Brooklyn.*
Wright H. P. & Co. 17 Atlantic
Worthington & Thompson, 107 do
Prince J. W. & Co. 66 Atlantic
Keenan D. Jr. 47 Fulton
Harrison John, 75 do
Bissell W. L. cor. Fulton & Middagh
Moof Mrs. C., Market
Burkaloo Mrs. E. do
Furlong Mrs. do
Shafer Mrs. do
Patten Mrs. N. do
Martin Mrs. do
Kelly William, do

Hawkins Mrs. R. Market *Brooklyn.*
Williams Mrs.   do
Sutton Mrs.   do
Slone Mrs.   do
Williams Miss E.   .do
Carman Mrs.   do
Cunningham Mrs. do
Watson Mrs. S. A., South
M'Ardel Mrs. E.   do
Morris Edward Y. 82 Grand
Williamsburgh.

New York County.

FRUIT—WHOLESALE.

Allen & Poillon, 58 Front
New York.
Archdeacon Peter, jr. 77 Wall
Backhouse & Cone, 16 Fulton
Badeau & Lockwood, 209 Washt'n
Baker Abel, 227 Fulton
Balen P. & Co. 186 Front
Beecher, Draper & Devlin, 95 Wall
Bennett Martin, 196 Front
Bowne & Watson, 165 West
Bush Wm. K. 195½ Greenwich
Carland E. 11 James slip
Cropsey & Gilmartine, 158 Front
Dawson Wm. H. & Co. 119 do
Drake Edmund, 245 Fulton
Gendar Robert, 24   do
Gilmartin D. & Co. 196 Front
Hankins Charles M. 69 Dey
Hardtwig Wm. E. 209½ Division
Hovey Roswell, 100 Barclay
Howes, Godfrey & Co. 96 South
Ivelin Hyacinth & Son, 221 Fulton
Johnson L. L. 111 Broad
Kellogg E. Bruyn, 96 Barclay
Kieran James, 192 Washington
Lewis, Burch & Brown, 49 Front
Main Wm. S. 67 Dey
Meacham & Stow, 92 South
Miller & Parsons, 181 Washington
Niles A. F. 149 Fulton
Niles John & Co. 254 Washington
Pendleton Otis & Co. 21 Fulton
Pierce John S. 192 Wall
Provost Daniel R. 79 Dey
Rich & Knowlton, 172 Front
Ross & Thomas, 210 Washington
Smith & Thompson, 59 Vesey
Thomas & Haley, 213 Washington
Thompson & Litchfild, 11 Washington market
Tyson & Van Alst, 20 Fulton
Van Buren John, 81 Vesey
Ward Willett C. 105 Front
Woodward & Cromwell, 41 Front

FRUIT—RETAIL.

Acker Henry C. & Co. 94 Wall
New York.
Allen John, 389 Hudson
Ametrano A. jr. 6 Fulton market
Archdeacon F. jr. 419 Broadway
Bates Albert, 615 Greeawich
Bateson C. R. Park Row cor. Ann
Broas John H. & Co. 196 West
Brower C. L. 489 Hudson
Brower Ann, 456 4th
Brown & Johnson, 8 Wash. mkt
Burke Martin, 153 Greenwich
Burrill S. 42 Division
Cassidy Cornelius, Centre mkt
Chambers William, 331 Bowery
Chitty Charles W. 370 Canal
Clary J. 186 Ames
Coghlan William, 82 Ridge
Curran Thomas, 8 Franklin square
Cumington Sam. 101 Greenwich
Denzi Louis, White cor. Broadway
Downs Mary, 106 Pitt
Dugan Maria, 35 West Broadway
Dupignac B. H. 444 Broadway
Dupigaac G. W. 466 Broadway
Falcon M. 61 Vandam
Fisher & Marston, 2 Wash. mkt
Flock Stephen, Centre mkt
Frost Horton, 135 West
Garnes & Son, Centre mkt

Gillies Hannah, 5 Gouverneur mkt
New York.
Habich & Heylegist, 47 Canal
Hartshorn Elizabeth & Dyckman, 1 Clinton mkt
Hearty Patrick, 205 Bowery
Hope M. 91½ Hudson
Hollis John, 79 6th Av.
Hyams Jacob, 46 Division
Johnson Leonard L. 118 Broad
Kelly Patrick, 8 Battery place
Koser Lewis, 26 Malden Lane
Lynch Dominick, 348 Hudson
M'Cabe Patrick, 74 Division
M'Carty Lewis, 1 Wash. mkt
Magins W. 316 Spring
Masoner John, 29 Av. B.
Mayock Dominick, 161 Duane
Meacham & Stow, 92 South
Moore T. 71 Greenwich Av.
Monehan O. Centre mkt
Nash Ann, 182 2d
Nugent William, Centre mkt
Parker John B. 31 Clinton mkt
Pierce John S. 102 Wall
Piercy Margaret, 188 Division
Plemey James, 62 West Broadway
Ryder William, 180½ Division
Roy Richard, 2 Cortlandt
Sands Charles, 1 Pike
Sand S. F. Centre mkt
Smith Harry, 169 Chrystie
Smith William, 126 Broadway
Switzer Martin, 180 William
Van Buren John, 81 Vesey
Wade James, 62 Division
Walsh John A. 69 Cortlandt
Washburn Ledroit, 18 6th Av.
Waters Michael, 5th cor. Av. A.
Williams Benjamin, 81 Av. D.
Williams & Boyer, 181 West Broadway

Rockland County.

Redding B., Nyack *Orangetown.*

Steuben County.

Davis James C. *Painted Post.*

Washington County.

Tohlman D., Chapin's block
Whitehall.

Fuel Saving Apparatus.

D. Griffin & Co. 192 Broadway
New York.

Fur Dealers and Furriers.
(See also Hats & Caps. Marked thus * are wholesale.)

Kings County.

Donovan Geo. 183 Pearl *Brooklyn.*
Finn William, 192 Pearl
Cochran John W. cor. Willoughby and Raymond
Williams & Chesbro, Nostrand Av. near Myrtle Av.
West Elisha, 196 Grand
Williamsburgh.

New York County.

*American Fur Company.73 Broad
New York.
Bates Martin. 178½ Water
*Bechtel & Dreyer, 31 Beaver
*Bennett Frank. 19 John
*Boughton & Parker, 178 Water
*Burghardt John S. 227½ Cherry
*Campbell W. S. 138 Water
*Centre A. H. & Son, 185 Water
*Chouteau Peter, jr.& Co. 40 Broadway
*Crooks Ramsay, 73 Broad
*Dodd Freeman, 159 Water
Dubac Paschal, 515½ Greenwich

Felsenheld Wolf, 127 Delancy
New York
*Finn Archibald T. 171 Water
*Fosdick Wm. R. 1 Beaver
*Frantzee F. W. 44 Cortlandt
*Gault & Ballard, 120 Maiden lane
*Gunther C. G. & Sons, 48½ Maid. lane
Halpen & Arons, 172 Water
*Hazlett James, 7 Burling slip
*Hirschfield & Lomer, 146 Water
Hoguet Joseph, 10 John & 642 Broadway
*Huster Henry, 40 Maid. lane
*King Charles & Co. 133 Water
*King M. J. & M. A. & Co. 157 Water
King & Samuels, 173 Water
Landry Francis, 663 Broadway
*Lang Leopold, 36 Maid. lane
*Lasak F. W. 19 John
*Leeds & Robbins, 144 Water
*Leonard Willard, 173 Water
*Levi Philip, 140 Pearl
*Lord John C. 164 Water
M'Collum John, 164 Canal
Marckwald M. B. 159 Water
*Mawson Brothers, 161 Water
*Moser Wm. 43 Maid. lane
Muller A. H. 140 Maid. lane
*Oppenheim J. M. & Co. 177 Water
Pettenger F. 246 3d
*Phillips Alexander, 83 Maid. lane
*Phillipe John D. & Co. 174 Water
*Phillips Samuel, 163 Water
*Prentice J. H. & Co. 166 Water
*Prince Henry, 224 Bleecker
*Randall John. 176 Water
*Rataux & Guille, 39 Maid. lane
*Raymond Henry, 8 Burling slip
*Raymond L. Ward, 173 Water
*Raymond Jas. H. 8 Burling slip
*Reboul & Whittemore, 171 Water
*Ryder E. T. & S. 194 Water
Saroni & Archer, 161 Water
Stief Frederick H. 34 Bowery
*Treadwell George C. & Co. 172 Water
*Vantine Charles, 150 Water
*Wendel John D. 11 Gold
*White W. A. & A. M. 175 Water
*White Eli & Sons, 166 Water
*White Lewis J. 171 Water
Whiteman Niklas, 13th bet. Avs. B & C
*Williams Ransom G. & Co. 94 Pearl
*Zugalla Charles H. 12 Maid. lane

Furnaces, Hot Air.

Barrow E. 118 Beekman
New York.
Bosworth D. 86 Cliff
Bull James H. 125 Eldridge
Cook William G. 169 Fulton
Culver & Co. 52 Cliff
Hitchings Anthony E. 141 10th
Janes, Beebe & Co. 120 Fulton & Reade cor. Centre
Kreemer J. B. 811 Broadway
Trowbridge F. H. 210 Water
Tuttle & Bailey, 210 Water
Walker George, 292 & 296 Broadway
Wilson Carrington, 329 8th Av.
Wright Albert H. 265 Cherry

Furnaces, Portable.

Barron, Brothers, 252 Broadway,
(see advertisement) *New York.*
Gree, Quenzer & Christian, 69 Av. C.

Furniture Dealers.

Albany County.

Howe D. & R. L. 93 State *Albany.*

Long Wm. 191 Green　Albany.
Peters G. O. 16 Franklin
Martin A. J. 11 Arch
M'Kown A. F. 66 S. Pearl
Merrifield & Wooster, 49 S. Pearl

Broome County.

Andrews U. T.　Binghamton

Cayuga County.

Parsons, Hewson & Co. Genesee
st.　Auburn.

Chemung County.

Nye J. A.　Elmira.
Robinson J. M
Vaile B.

Chenango County.

Hoyt C. & Son, Canal square
Greene.

Columbia County

Chrysler M. H. & Co. 264 Warren
Hudson.

Jefferson County.

White Fred.　Watertown.
Blood & Van Namee
Gallagher R. Carthage　Wilna.
Jones Lewis,　do

Kings County.

Revell F. H. 25 Atlantic Brooklyn
Weeks Joseph S. 45 Atlantic
Stephens B. 126 Atlantic
Blackwell John, 52 Atlantic
Whitney B. S. 114 Court
Radford H. 66 Fulton
Agar Wm. 152 Fulton
Drew Mrs. Elizabeth, 130 Fulton
Werner J. J. 25 Fulton
Moriarty D. 47 James
Abbott B. B. cor. York & James
Foley J. 66 Hudson Av.
Baldwin John, 87 Grand
Williamsburgh.
Walters James D. 148 4th

Monroe County.

Hayden C. H. 6 Front　Rochester.
Scott Lloyd, 48 Exchange
Packard S. H. 29 State
Hayden C. J. 56 Front

New York County.

FURNITURE DEALERS (NEW).

Ash John, 191 Chatham New York.
Baldwin Danforth, 195 Chatham
Baldwin J. C. 183 Chatham
Barnes Moses H. 273 2d
Bohlm L. 245 Broome
Brainard Isaiah, 171 Chatham
Branch Wm. L. 48 Broadway
Bradley J. 317 Pearl
Bruner & Moore, 174 Fulton
Buhler Christian, 161 Chatham
Buhler M. 15 E. Broadway
Buxton John, jr. 181 Chatham
Byrne James, rear 84 Essex
Clark Jothum, 46 Broadway
Clanghley & Co. 282 Bowery &
60 1st
Conklin Henry, 87 Bowery
Cook Amzi, 66 Broad & 15 Bowery
Cooke James H. 92 Broadway
Cowperthwait S. N. 14 E. Br'dway
De Witt Josiah H. 192 6th Av.
Edstrom Edwin, 261 Bowery
Fanning Solomon, 20 Catharine
Freeze Henry, 44 Mott
Frost Wm. 732 Broadway
Gardiner Wm. C. 69 Gold
Gentil Thomas, 264 Canal
Georgi C. L. 171 & 172 Fulton
Gorman H. 126 Greenwich Av.
Gorth Peter, 62 Av. B

Graham Jos. 68 Mulberry
New York.
Hanley Philip, 199 Chatham
Henderson Emma, 260 W. 17th
Herkner Henry, 170 Fulton
Humphreys Wm. 43 Chambers
Humphreys Wm. S. 163 Chatham
Johnson & Sloan, 458 Pearl
Jutten Benj. 310 Hudson
Kemp Rufus C. 350 Broadway
Kirkbright David, 190 W. 18th
Knipe Wm. 19 Pell
Lane Stephen, 113½ Bowery
Lee D. & W. H. 166 Fulton
Logan John, 28 3d Av.
Lowe Isaac N. 41 Howard
M'Nulty Thomas, 86 E. Broadway
Morrell Tunis, 218 Broadway
O'Grady & Cassin, 13 E. Br'dway
Reeve B. 423 Hudson
Reid Gustavus, 251 Bleecker
Ringuet & Marcotte, 477 Br'dway
Robenson Jas. 71 Bayard
Robertson Wm. 4 Doyer
Silvey Mary Ann, 193 Chatham
Sloan C. S. 436 Pearl
Smith George, 374 Hudson
Smith Gilbert, 470 Grand
Sneden George, 263 Bowery
Stevens Andrew, 57 6th Av.
Stewart E. 905 Canal
Theal Joseph, 116 E. Broadway
Thompson Isaac, 11 Mulberry
Wilkinson R. 295 17th
Westervelt Jasper C. & Son, 9
6th Av.
Woodruff Abiel C. 178½ Broad-
way

FURNITURE DEALERS — SECOND HAND.

Andrews Henry T. 53 Oak
New York.
Barr James, 150 Orange
Brady Michael, 208 Mott
Brisben Thos. 129 Division
Brown John T. 9 Spruce
Caveny Thomas, 489 Pearl
Davis Thomas, 52 & 54 Ann
Duffy John, 12th st. near 9th Av.
Evers Patrick, 58 Orange
Flight Wm. 113 Av. C
Gates Asa, 35 Av. D
Gentil Thomas, 254 Canal
Gloucester E. 40 W. Broadway
Holmes David, 231 Broome
Jones Isaac F. 56 Ann
Jutton Benj. 310 Hudson
Kerley James, 127 Canal
King Richard, 44 Centre
Lazarus Henry B. 611 Pearl
Lloyd Samuel, 102 Thompson
M'Divitt James, 44 E. Broadway
M'Glone James, 4 Bayard
Marley Daniel, 55 & 57 Ann
Martin Patrick, 215 Centre
Mehan Elizabeth, 136 Division
Mellor Eliza, 129 Sullivan
Morgan James, 165 Prince
Moore John, 237 Centre
Murray Jeremiah, 46 Av. F
Pickering Edward, 196 Division
Rafferty Martin, 2 James
Roach Thomas, 57 Centre
Rogers Reu. F. 99 & 101 Chatham
Salt Wm. 60 W. Washington pl.
Simms Wm. 188 W. 16th
Slevin John, 219 Centre
Storey Joseph, 208 Spring
Tuzer Edward, 252 Canal
Williams John, 29 Hancock

Oneida County

Foster & Burnham, 59 Hotel
Utica.

Orange County.

Cushman Chas. U. 63 Water
Newburgh.

Oswego County.

Wright James M. 1st st.　Oswego.
Bickford James,　do
Phillips & Schenck, Fulton
Volney.

Rensselaer County.

Lavender John B. 219 State
Lansingburgh.
Seelye Seth, 241 State
Clark C. A. 296　do
Bradshaw J. 272 do
Chapman D. W. 30 Ferry　Troy
Daniels A. C. 16 Congress
Adams A. A. 338 River
Vanderheyden Jacob, 180 River
Adams W. L. 385　do
Perkins Wm. 317　do

Saratoga County.

Lane H. S. & Co.　Waterford.
Potter C.

Tompkins County.

Denming F. 79 Owego　Ithaca.
Whiton George, 11 Aurora
Leonard H. 122 Owego
Benham W. U. Aurora st.
Shirley & Credit,　do

Yates County.

Crane Cyrus, (chairs) Branchport
Jerusalem.

Washington County.

M'Fadden George S.　Argyle.
Bennett J. William st.　Whitehall.
Chapman J. C. & T. D. do
Hall J. K.

Gardens, Public.

New York County.

Atlantic, Wm. Allison, 9 B'dway
New York
Castle, Battery
Hunt & Husted, 100 Av. B
Niblo's, John Niblo, 587 B'dway
Towney J. cor. Av. B. & 7th st.
Vauxhall, Bradford Jones, 2 4th Av.

Gas-Fixture Manufacturers.

Albany County,

Munsig Wm. 628 Broadway
Albany.

Erie County.

Hamton T. S. cor. Pearl & Seneca
Buffalo.

Kings County.

Guild C. M. 46 Fulton　Brooklyn.
Coope David, 91 do

Monroe County.

White & Morrille, 21 Front
Rochester

New York County.

Alcock & Allen, 341 Broadway
New York.
Brown & Carswell, 69 University
place
Bray George, 116 3d Av.
Cox J. & I. 15 Maiden lane
Dietz Brothers & Co. 137½ Wil-
liam
Dipple & Pickard, 90 Leonard
Donaldson J. & T. 85　do
Down Samuel, foot of West 23d
Finch & Carter, 37 Bowery

Sea Co. New York Solar, 130 Broadway *New York.*
Johnston & Brothers, rear 111 E. 15th
M'Kewen & Wills, 10 4th Av.
Mitchell Vulcram, 132 Mercer

Onondaga County.

Dareott George, jr. Genesee st. Syracuse *Salina.*
Ward J. B. do

Rensselaer County.

Pierce & King (gas, steam & water) $25 River *Troy.*

Gaugers.

New York County.

Blackwell Edward U. 136 Maiden lane *New York.*
Blackwell Jacob, 136 Maiden lane
Boyd Andrew A. 85 Front
Bradley Edward W. jr. 216 Wall
Chivvis Peter, 40 South
Donnovan Thomas W. 26 South
Ellison Richard, 149 Front
Houghton T. L. 116 South
Ide Willard. 97 Wall
Nicholls Henry L. 59 South
Oram James D. 186 Front
Radcliff Charles, 59 West
Smith & Chichester, 111 Wall
Van Boskerck Ab., 126 Broad
Vosburg John S. 53 West
Walker & Pyatt, 6 Front
Welling Charles H. 93 Pine

Gents' Furnishing Stores.

(See also Clothiers and Ready-made Clothing, and also Linen ready made.)

New York County.

Agate Joseph, 237 Broadway *New York.*
Bennett Wm. 86 Chatham
Booth J. C. & Co. 27 Cortlandt
Canfield David W. 2½ Maiden lane
Chapman Horace H. 1 do
Chapman John, 80 Chatham
Cooks John, 64 do
Davis John, 96 do
Driow E. 150 Greenwich
Davies Jones & Co. 106 William
Emmons G. T. 110½ Bowery
Furman Saml. H. 25 Cortlandt
Germond, Freeman & Bradford, 62 John
Harris James, 313 Broadway
Haslett J. C. 5 Chatham
Hatch C. B. & Co. 97 William
Hatch William B. 722 Broadway
Herrick & Scudder, 95 William
Holl William P. 69 Nassau
Hulse Amos, 60 Bowery
Hulse Joseph C. 28 N. William
Hutschler & Brandes, 22½ Chatham
Koopman P. 96 Chatham
Kowing F. 266 Bowery
Levy B. 33 do
M'Kinley Edward, 1 Park row
M'Kinley William, 100 Chatham
M'Gill J. 90 Chatham
Morgan D. 184 Division
Macgregor J. C. 207 Broadway
Perego Ira, 74 Maiden lane
Petrie William W. 153 Broadway & 46 Chatham
Raymond Asahel, 53 Chatham
Reed Harman, 95 Liberty
Sanxay Joseph F. 146 William
Scott John P. 157 Fulton
Shardlow Wm. L. 266 Broadway
Shephard William H. 236 do
Sillecks & Co. 66 Fulton

Stone & Greocen, 197 William & 65 John *New York.*
Sturges Samuel B. 76½ Chatham
Sturges William. 96½ do
Torrens S. 373 Hudson
Tracy George M. 84 William
Trowbridge G. A. & Co. 70 do
Underhill Mrs. L. 79 Canal
Vanhouten Rebecca, 95 Nassau
Vonhutschler Caroline, 90 Bowery
Welsh T. & C. 436 Broadway
Wakeman W. & W. 76 Maiden L.
Washburn & Seymour, Nassau cor. John
Waterbury G. G. 256 Broadway
Willis & Saxon, 175 do
Woolsey William, 49 William

Gliders. *(See also Carvers.)*

Coneley William S. 29 Chambers *New York.*
Conner & Winser, 156 Centre
De Rogy S. & Co. 238 Broadway
Egan David D. 172 Canal
Flavell M. 281 Grand
Knight John. 57.White
Hines John J. 315 Broadway
Paret W. L. 347 4th st.
Scardefield George, 41 Howard
Shepperd J. P. 167 Nassau
Shaw George, 25 Platt
Short William, 160 Fulton
Tracy & Newkerk, 124 Grand
Underwood S. 166 do
Wilmurt Thomas A. 96 Walker

Glass Cutters.

Decker Thomas, 220 Hudson *New York.*
Hartshorne & Devoe, 44 Eldridge
Levy John, 174 Rivington
Madden Philip. 87 Eldridge
Neeves & Wallis, 89 Elizabeth
Neeves James, rear 87 Elizabeth
Roe & Camblen, rear 59 Ann
Stouvenel J. & Co. 58 & 60 Vesey, 737 Broadway, & 3 John
Taylor Isaac, 61 Elizabeth
Turner & Lane, 43 & 45 Duane

Glass, Importers of Looking Plate.

Bache Semon & Co. 21 Cedar *New York.*
Bendit Adolphe, 1 Cedar
Dolan J. T. & Son, 262 Pearl
Douglas Brothers, 73 Broad
Geisse William & Sons, 11 Gold
Hensken & Unkhart, 17 & William
Muller Charles, 20 Platt
Noel & De Courcy, 42 Broadway & 49 New
Platt Isaac L. 5 Spruce
Rolker A. & Mollmann, 96 Pearl
Roosevelt & Son, 94 Maiden lane
Wallace Kreps, 13 Spruce

Glasses—Looking.

Albany County.

Burton J. & Co. 3 Green *Albany.*
Riley George, 1 do

Erie County.

Deuther Geo. A. 265 Main *Buffalo.*
Brown C. W. & Co. do
Waldron E. G. 127 do

Kings County.

Frothingham Jas. 141 Fulton *Brooklyn.*

New York County.

Baker J. T. 186 11th *New York.*

Cammeyer Augustus F. 49 Fulton *New York.*
Collins Henry. 297 Pearl
Del Vecchio J. R. 493 Broadway
Dexter Elias, 216 Bleecker
Dugliss Hosea, 24 North William & 11 Park row
Egan David D. 172 Canal
Hinds J. Scott's alley, n. Franklin
Hooper & Brother, 106 Fulton & 253 Pearl
Hudson & Smith, 119 Fulton
Johnson Wm. N. 204 Bowery
Kennedy Thomas, 273½ Bowery
Kingsland Richard, 28 Cortlandt
Kingsland R. 2 Liberty
Koelble Joseph, 161 3d
Lane Wallace, 198 6th Av.
Lewis Robert, 209 Fulton
Lyon E. W. 182 Chatham
M'Quillin B. 274 6th
Mackenzie John, 462 Grand
Marshall Matthew, 507 Broadway & 53 Mercer
Mead Wm. 113 Bowery
Merriam Benj. W. 130 Chatham
Oestereicher Fred. 132 Houston
Pollen & Colgate, 287 Pearl
Remy Peter, 21 New
Smith James. 148 Chatham
Smith Wm. 291 Hudson
Tinker L. G. 198 Canal
Von Held J. 566 4th
Waller & Kreps, 13 Spruce
Werton John L. 595 Broadway
Williams J. H. & Son, 315 Pearl
Williams B. 353 6th
Williams & Stevens, 353 Br'dway
Wilmist T. A. 96 Walker

Onondaga County.

Simmons A. Baldwinsville *Lysander.*

Glass Manufacturers.

Clinton County.

Lane Matthew & Co. Bedford *Saranac.*

Erie County.

Reed, Allen, Cox & Co. *Lancaster.*

Jefferson County.

Dezeng & Co. (Window Glass) Redwood *Alexandria.*

Kings County.

Brooklyn Flint Glass Co. George M. Wheaton, Agent, 65 Atlantic *Brooklyn.*
Phenix Glass Works, R. B. Clark, Sec. John st. near Hudson Av.
Berger & Walter, (Flint Glass), 90 Ewing *Williamsburgh.*

Niagara County.

Hildreth & Co. *Lockport.*

New York County.

Averill Elisha, 142 Front, Agent for Phenix Glass Co. *New York.*
Berger Walter, 39 Maiden lane
Brooklyn Flint Glass Co. 39 South William
Forman W. G. 29 South William
Gill T. A. 105 Liberty
Lyman G. Dummer & Co. 25 Cliff
New England Glass Co. Thos. D. Moore & Co. 87 & 89 Water
Newsham Wm. 298 Broadway
Pollen & Colgate, 287 Pearl
Williams & Stevens, 353 Br'dway
Rorke James, 102 John
Slane & Burrell, Agents for American Flint Glass Works, 6 Platt
Sutton & Baker, 23 Cedar

Oneida County.

Howe, Scofield & Co. Dunbarton
Factory   *Verona.*
Fox & Gregory, Durhamville

Oswego County.

Landgraff A. & Son, Cleaveland
          Constantia.

Rensselaer County.

Fox A. R. & S. H. (Window)
          Sandlake.

Saratoga County.

Granger James & Co. Mt. Pleasant   *Greenfield.*

Wayne County.

Stokes & Ely, Clyde   *Galen.*

Glass Platers.

New York County.

Hinds Joseph, Scott's Alley, near
Franklin   *New York.*
Marshall Mathew, rear 53 Mercer
& 507 Broadway
Remy Peter, 21 New

Glass Stainers & Enamel-
lers.

Adams Samuel M. 216 6th Av.
          New York.
Cares Robert, 5 Spruce
Falconer Hugh M. 67 E. 14th
Gibson Wm. 77 White
Hanington Wm. J. 364 Broadway
Morgan George, 542 Broadway
Reed George. 94 Av. C
Roe & Camblin, 59 Ann
West James, 490 Broadway
West Joseph B. 95 4th Av.

Glass—Window. (See also
Oil, Paints & Glass.)

Burlage R. W. 52 New *New York.*
Clark & M'Connin, 6 Fletcher
Heroy Jas. H. 42 Cliff
Morgan, Walker & Smith, 48 Cliff
Noel & De Courcy, 42 Broadway
& 49 New
Rolker A. & Mollmann. 96 Pearl
Schanck, Downing & Co. 108 Ful-
ton
Sutton & Baker, 23 Cedar
Warrington & Richards, 33 Bur-
ling slip, Ag'ts of Batsto Factory

Glaziers. (See also Sash &
Blind Makers—also Painters &
Glaviers.)

Benedikt Abraham, 210 Stanton
          New York.
Beandt B. 187 7th
Craig I. cor. 4th st. & Broadway
Fisher L. 246 2d
Forster T. V. 24 Church
Gains Albert, 94 Norfolk
Kane M. 192 W. 13th
Litton E. 207 Church
Philip Levy, 257 Delancy
Robertson H. P. 261 8th
Rooney P. 332 2d Av.
Stukey & Keaf, 98 Av. C
Shaw J. 142 Nassau
Stamford T. 75 10th
Stransky Solomon, 186 Delancy
Terhune T. 27 2d

Globe Manufacturers.

Albany County.

Standish Z. 291 Washington
          Albany.

Monroe County.

Horton T. S. & Co.   (Cornell's
Globes)   *Rochester.*

New York County.

Vale Gilbert, 3 Franklin Square
          New York.

Glove and Mitten Makers.

Fulton County.

Back Christian   *Johnstown.*
Becker John
Bertrand Eugene & Brothers
Cuyler David H.
Gilbert Marcellus
Hill Samuel W.
M'Laren & Dorn
M'Marten James J.
Richetts Jonathan
Van Voast A. S.
Allen William C. Gloversville
Ballentine Robert,   do
Belden N. & M. C.   do
Burr F. & D.   do
Burr Horatio L.   do
Burr James H.   do
Case James S.   do
Case Urial,   do
Case Z. & W.   do
Cheadle Augustus,   do
Fairbanks Miles,   do
Frank Dennis,   do
Haggart Daniel,   do
Haggart Sherwood,   do
Hayes Newton F.   do
Hosman Alanson,   do
Judson Alanson,   do
Kasson Austin,   do
Kenyon Wanton,   do
Kenyon William,   do
Leonard Daniel,   do
Leonard Edward,   do
M'Nab John,   do
Mills Charles,   do
Mills D. C. & S. S.   do
Parsons H. C.   do
Place Israel,   do
Place Urial M.   do
Richardson Samuel,   do
Russell Nathan C.   do
Smith H. S.   do
Spalding David,   do
Stanley Ashael B.   do
Sunderlin Charles,   do
Tarr Daniel S.   do
Ward Elias G.   do
Washburn & Knowles,   do
Welch Nathaniel W.   do
Welch T. & G.   do
Window Charles,   do
Baird Stephen, Kingsboro
Brown David N.   do
Case Darius,   do
Clark Darius,   do
Hancock Samuel,   do
Hancock Willard J.   do
Lee Ira   do
Leonard Clinton,   do
Leonard Hiram,   do
Leonard Josiah C.   do
Parsons Hiram A.   do
Phelps Gilbert,   do
Phelps Joel,   do
Phelps Roswell,   do
Fruith Humphrey,   do
Rose Willard,   do
Shutts Silas,   do
Smith Denton,   do
Smith De Witt,   do
Smith James,   do
Steele Joseph,   do
Stewart Duncan,   do
Thomas Elliott,   do
Thomas James W.   do
Van Nattie James,   do
Ward William,   do
Wooster Jonathan,   do
Wilkins John,   *Mayfield.*

Becker Henry   *Mayfield.*
M'Ewen James
Wilcox Willard
Carnduff William   *Perth.*
Smith B.
Calderwood Andrew

Monroe County.

Strong Myron, 17 State *Rochester*

New York County.

Baker William, 299 Broadway
          New York.
Elterich John, 144 Mott
Field Charles, 404 Broadway
Hawkins & Pullman. 361 Pearl
Haynes Thomas, 379½ Pearl
Kindon Henry, 296 Pearl
Mullins Dennis, 329 Pearl
Peacock William, 133 Beekman
Rogers Thomas, 69 Ann

Tioga County.

Lincoln O. & Son, (buckskin) Newark Valley   *Newark.*

Washington County.

Taber S. & William H.
          White Creek.

St. Lawrence County.

Hill Chs. Ford st. Ogdensburgh
          Oswegatchie.

Gloves—Importers of. (See
also Hosiery and Gloves.)

Beer Cerf & May, 41 Beaver
          New York.
Brown R. W. 386 Bowery
Brue Eugene, 1 Hanover sq.
Driver Eugene, 150 Greenwich
Fanfernot & Dulac, 18 S. William
Frazer William, 366 Bowery
Hall Brothers & Co. 43 Beaver
Wahlen & Schmidt, 58 Cedar
Williams E. L. 83 Catharine

Glue Manufacturers.

Albany County.

Conolson Thomas, jr. 510 Bowery
          Albany.

Erie County.

Evans Richard   *Buffalo.*

Kings County.

Cooper Peter   *Bushwick.*

New York County.

Baxter C. H. & Co. 143 Maiden
lane   *New York.*
Bodine, Baeder & Co. 235 Pearl
Cooper Peter, 17 Burling slip
Cumming Charles, 2 Platt
Gerker Henry, 174 Fulton
Hart George, 140 Maiden lane
Richards Stephen, 63½ Gold
Salter A. & Co. 100 John
Whitmore G. (Dealers) 148 Fulton

Goatskins—Importers of.

Sale William A. jr. 124 Water
          New York.

Gold and Silver Refiners.

Barnard A. 2 Wall, & 184 Laurens
          New York.
Billing Michael, 115 Sheriff
Dovenor William, 361 W. 16th

Kemp W. H. 96 Canal *New York.*
Platt & Brother, 4 Liberty place
Prime, Roshore & Co 177 Broadway
Savage Charles, rear 156 William
Solomon, Morris & Co. 45 Ann
Warwick John, rear 17 John
Waters John, rear 93 Dey
Walker D. 198 Fulton

Gold and Silver Watch Cases.

Clark & Andrus, 47 Dey
New York.
Catlin F. 16 W. Broadway

Gold Beaters.

Albany County.

Barrett Wm. (Dentists' articles) 49 Hudson *Albany.*

Erie County.

Cottier Robert, (Dentists' gold & Tin Foil. See Advertisement.) 186 Main *Buffalo.*

New York County.

Ashmead & Hurlbutt, (Dentists' Gold Foil) 258 Bdy. *New York.*
Cooke & Harris, rear 85 Cedar
Dean John, 86 Chatham
Freeman James, 72 West Broad'y
Gordon J. 122 William
Griffin Charles, 374 Pearl
Haddon William, 86 Chatham
Harris James, 95 Elm
Hatt Joseph, 177 William
Jenkins Frederick, 339 Bowery
Jordan Conrad, 122 William
Kearsing George & Co. 49 Lispenard
Kemp Wm. H. 95 Canal
Mitchell Thomas, 409 Hudson
Mott Joseph, 39 Elizabeth
Ruggles Robert B. 28 Dey
Shaw John, 56 Willet
Snedecor G. 28 Rivington
Thomas Thomas, 91 Cliff
Walker David, rear 198 Fulton
Waugh James L. 112 Franklin
Williams William J. 368 Broome

Gold Pen Manufacturers.

Erie County.

Brown Samuel, 146 Main *Buffalo.*

New York County.

Andrews Francis L. 42 Nassau
New York.
Bagley A. G. & Co. 189 Broad'y
Bard & Brothers, 101 William
Beers & Clark, 25 John
Berrian A. J. & Co. rear 75 & 77 Nassau
Blakeney Thos. & Co. 44 Nassau
Blancney Wm. E. 44 Nassau
Greaton John W. 71 Cedar
Lovajoy Daniel, rear 15 Watts
Magee, Hulse & Blonder, r. 7 Dey
M'Pherson John B. 5 Dey
Mier P. 138 William
Munson Benjamin, 122 Fulton
Savage John Y. 99 Fulton
Smith G. & E. M. & Co. 16 & 18 Maiden lane
Spencer & Rendel, 170 Broadway
Van Brunt T. H. 5 Dey
Wilmarth, Brother & Co. 1 Cortlandt

Gold Washer Manufacturer.

Simonson Charles M. 102 Broad'y
New York.

Grain Dealers. (*See also Merchants' Commission—also Produce Dealers—also Flour Dealers— also Feed.*)

Albany County.

Hallenbeck M. I. 7 Hudson *Albany.*
Tweedle & Darlington, 86 Quay
Hilton J. cor. Quay & Herkimer

Cayuga County.

M'Quegg & Daniels, Port Byron
Mont'r.

New York County.

Benton John B. 89 West
New York.
Conover Daniel D. 88 West
Crane Elijah, 105 West
Farrand Joseph S. 134 Cedar
Holcomb & Bergen, 89 West
Manning Stille, 99 West
Mettler Samuel, 92 West
Speer Charles, 22 Albany
Vanderbelt Jacob, 90 West
Vansyckel E. & Co. 88 West
Young & Bonnell, 92 West

Saratoga County.

Enos S. B. & Co. *Waterford.*
Stewart George H. & Co.
House John
Bennett & Cropsey
Scott William
Waterman S. S.

Ulster County.

Anderson Chas. (feed) *Kingston.*

Grain Elevators. (*See also Storage—also Merchants Commission.*)

Erie County.

Pratt L. H. & Co. *Buffalo.*
Rogers Geo. W. cor. Michigan & Ohio
Hollister John, 28 Central Wharf
Smith Brothers, Creek & Skinner's slip

Oswego County.

Platt James, foot of 1st st. *Oswego.*
Bond & Uhlhorns, 1st cor. Seneca
Carrington & Pardee, foot of 1st

Grates & Fenders.
(*See also Founders—also Fence & Railings—also Stoves.*)

Albany County.

Henderson & Weller, 564 Broadway *Albany.*

New York County.

Carson & Smith, 110 E. 14th
New York.
Conover & Wooley, 108 Canal
Cornell J. B. & W. W. & Co. 141 & 143 Centre
Gilhooly John, 118 Nassau
Gilhooly Michael J. 78 Nassau
Goadby Thomas, 213 Grand
Hampton Adam, 80 Gold
Hicinbotham William, 241 & 267 Broadway
Jackson Geo. R. & Co. 199 Centre
Jackson W. & N. 238 Front
Kenzie Thomas, 35 5th Av.
Moore Richard, 235 W. 16th
Putnam Stephen, 69 4th Av.
Stoveken & Cox, 10 Barclay

Onondaga County.

Moshall J. H. Warren st. Syracuse *Salina.*

Grate Setters. (*See also Masons.*)

Baines James, 39 Ann *New York.*
Donovan Daniel, 12 Carlisle
Early Henry, 207 Grand
Fitzpatrick Chas. 112½ Bleecker
Fletcher Patrick, 19 Oak
Kelly J. 140 Elizabeth
Kinsey James, 57 Great Jones
King J. D. 74 Eldridge
Quinn Edward, 42 Nassau
Lecount Joseph, 122 E. Broadway
Van Note Wm. & H. 41 Greene

Grind Stone & Plaster Dealers.

Albany County.

Davis N. 77 Quay *Albany.*

New York County.

Civill Anthony, 190 West
New York.
Keylor Wm. 49 Grand
Noyes Samuel & Son, 1 South & 47 Washington
Randolph Geo. F. 39 Washington
Randolph Obadiah W. F. 67 Whitehall
Soule, Whitney & Co, 81 & 82 West
Wilmott Samuel D. 8 Liberty
Wood Moses Q. 260 & 265 Front

Groceries & Provisions— Retail.

Albany County.

Albert J. 220 Washington *Albany.*
Armatage W. M. 58 Canal
Ballie C. 66 John
Bammall G. G. 60 Beaver
Barry T. 182 Green
Bender Wm. 429 Lydius
Bergam Charles, 28 Quay
Birch G. A. 45 Washington
Blako O. 15 Columbia
Blair J. T. & Co. 51 Chapel
Blanchard E. 77 Church
Blank T. 121 Church
Bortle R. 272 Broadway
Bowles & Co. 82 Quay
Brooks J. 79 Greene
Brower A. B. 194 Broadway
Brown D. 26 Lawrence
Brown M. 17 Canal
Brumaghia & Van Alstine, 68 Washington
Buckley E. 69 Rennselaer
Bulger J. 26 Quay
Burbank J. 171 Church
Burns Michael, 214 Broadway
Burton S. P. 196 & 200 Broadway
Buss C., Green cor. Herkimer
Bygate R. 373 Lydius
Cameron D. Hamilton cor. Eagle
Campbell Geo. 643 Broadway
Campbell J. W. 9 Ferry
Carhart W. 257 State
Carmedy P. 95 Franklin
Carroll William, 82 Water
Castigan John, 106 & 108 Orange
Chamberlin N. W. 860 Broadway
Cherry C. 89 Canal
Clark L. Maiden Lane & Lodge
Clark John A. 510 Broadway
Clark M. Lodge cor. Pine
Cohen & Rothschilds, 133 S. Pearl
Connon J. 42 Union
De Forest C. A. 76 Green
De Forest Z. M. P. 206 Water
Dermody H. 16 Van Schaick
Drogan C. 3 Morton
Dundan J. 36 Division
Dunn P. 322 State
Dygert E. 223 Hamilton
Eaton S. S. 82 Washington
Eagan J. 99 Canal

Eggleston J. M. 22 Quay　*Albany.*
Elder G. 11 Chapel
Evers J. 11 Van Schaick
Ewing P. H. 24 Daniel
Falke Henry, 844 Broadway
Fauth J. 27 Alexander
Fazukerly W. 170 Jefferson
Feilly F. 133 Church
Fennett D. 30 Canal
Finch O. 35 South Pearl
Fisher J. D. 45 Lerk
Fitzsimmons & Smith, 15 Quay
Flaherty P. O. 160 South Pearl
Flannigan John, 175 Green
Flood Mrs. 46 Water
Fortune E. 326 Lydius
Fox P. 70 Arch
Frederick I. C. 80 Washington
Friger John, 778 Broadway
Gates O. T. Park State st.
Gavitt D. L. 160 Washington
Gibson W. 160 Broadway
Goffe H. 27 Van Schaick
Goffe Wm. B. & John, 84 N. Pearl
Gram A. 67 Broadway
Grattan F. 326 Bowery
Greenwood W. S. & C. C. 598 &
　600 Broadway
Grey J. 17 South Pearl
Griffin R. N. 201 Broadway
Hamilton J. 14 Columbia
Harrison J. 71 Canal
Harrogan J. 22 Canal
Hart J. 48 2d
Hart O. 67 Church
Harvey L. Z. 1 South Pearl
Haswell & Ranson, 138 Green
Hawkins Henry, 59 Beaver
Hayes M. 199 Green
Heffernan J. 194 South Pearl
Hennessy T. 16 Van Zaat
Higgins B. 29 Van Woert
Hill G. 43 Canal
Hill George, 62 & 72 Pier
Hill H. 45 Pier
Hill Henry A. 135 Orange
Hilton S. V. A. 837 Broadway
Hogeboom E. & J. 149 Broadway
Holden H. 175 Montgomery
Holler J. 180 Bowery
Houll Oliver. 3d & Swan
Huber J. 911 Bowery
Hurst Wm. & C. 22 South Pearl
Isdell W. 126 Lydius
Jaynt J. 140 South Pearl
Jones John, 675 Broadway
Jordan Mathew, 555 Broadway
Kaernan Wm. 222 Eagle
Kearney T.
Keelin J. 50 Arch
Kelly P. 106 Broad
Kelly T. 40 Montgomery
Kennedy D. 51 1st
Kennedy Phillip, 56 Union
Kernan Thomas, 100 Canal
Kerr W. & J. 18 South Pearl
Kitton P. 136 Broadway
Kirkpatrick Mrs. 15 South Pearl
Kirkpatrick P. 237 Bowery
Kinney J. 132 Arch
Kinney J. S. 74 Pier
Lamb P. 68 Lydius
Lamour T. & O. 29 Washington
Lathrop D. 59 Washington
Lawlor F. 261 State
Lawrence A. L. 114 Pier
Lightbody Andrew, 67 Church
Leonard T. 76 Franklin
Loomis S. A. 86 South Pearl
Lord John & Son, 29 Washington
Lynch B. 203 Green
Lyons Charles, 14 Quay
Lyons J. W. 42 Canal
M'Bride J. & W. 262 Washington
M'Cabe I. 24 Van Woert
M'Caughan John, 193 Broadway
M'Claffy ——, 47 Lumber
M'Cole J. & Co. 9 Plain
M'Entee J. 169 Green
M'Evay J. 179 Green
M'Govern J. 49 Arch
M'Lelland ——, 180 Montgomery

M'Man F. 86 North Ferry　*Albany.*
M'Nulty C. 150 South Pearl
M'Shane F. 786 Broadway
Maloy W. Maiden Lane & Lodge
Malvine J. 76 Beaver
Martin J. 3d & Swan
Matthews A. 56 Lawrence
Mead T. 9 North Ferry
Merrifield W. 207 Lydius
Miles J. 110 Arch
Miller Chas. 796 Broadway
Miller Nathaniel, 599 Broadway
Mix H. & S. 286 South Pearl
Moakler M. 19 Canal
Monohan J. 11 Lawrence
Moore J. 58 Green
Morrow James, 184 Broadway
Mount D. 315 State
Mulligan P. 186 Swan
Mullvine J. 78 Beaver
Murphy J. 201 Hamilton
Murphy J. 107 Beaver
Murphy P. c. Schuyler & Franklin
Murphy P. 184 South Pearl
Murphy R. 169½　do
Murray John, 8 Columbia
Neff Wm. 1 Daniel
Neagle T. 158 State
Nessle W. & I. P. 566 and 568
　Broadway
O'Brian Mrs. S. 101 Beaver
O'Connell Richard, 8 Clinton
O'Connor J. 37 Division
Ohill John, 180 Broadway
O'Neill —— 5 Little Basin
O'Priest C. 2 Columbia
Osborne & Hadley, 91 S. Pearl
Osborn W. L. 310 South Pearl
Peck R. W. 40 Washington
Pemberton E. & J. 65 N. Pearl
Pester Wm. 312 State
Power Daniel, 142 Broadway
Putnam & Shaw, 1 Columbia
Quin Mrs. M. 165 Broadway
Raferty Mrs. C. 700 Broadway
Raferty Mrs. T. 13 Quay
Ramsey James, 617 Broadway
Riley C. 53 Canal
Riley E. 52 2d
Riley O. 22 Van Woert
Roe M. 56 Lawrence
Russell J. 150 Washington
Ryan E. 55 Lawrence
Ryan P. 138 Jefferson
Sayles James, 110 Water
Scanlan D. 13 Quay
Schuyler C & Co. 670 Broadway
Schworer J. 200 Washington
Schwartz S. 46 Green
Scott Wm. B. 49 2d
Servis Wm. 334 Lydius
Shaver J. 90 Washington
Shields H. 345 State
Shorkey J. 59 Lawrence
Shouts J. A. 210 Water
Sicales J. A. 76 S. Pearl
Simpson J. 234 S. Pearl
Simons John, 780 Broadway
Simons N. E. 87 Lydius
Slaver M. 79 Broadway
Slack G. 376 Lydius
Smith B. 16 2d
Smith B. 366 Pearl
Smith D. 8 S. Pearl
Smith Mrs. M. 177 Broad
Smith & Packard, 45 Green
Smith R. 72 Washington
Speare E. 12 Little Basin
Spencer F. 190 Bowery
Stein M. 68 Westerlo
Sutliff T. M. 747 Broadway
Swarts A. 128 Arch
Tackers J. 239 S. Pearl
Tallman D. 5 N. Lansing
Taylor J. 122 Greene
Thompson ——, 99 Church
Triger C. 260 Bowery
Van Buren S. G. 102 Beaver
Vanderlip D. R. 279 State
Vanderlip E. jr. 21 Green
Van Valkenburgh Wm. & Little
　Basin

Vanzant G. D. 646 Broadway
　　　　　　　　　　Albany.
Veeder & Bates, 114 S. Pearl
Waddell J. W. 192 N. Pearl
Waddell S. 95　　do
Wall J. 160 Green
Walls P. 138 Swan
Wallace C. 108 Orange
Wallace Matthew. 713 Broadway
Waugh George, 342 Bowery
Weeks & Belyea, 79 Pier
Welch James, 649 Broadway
Welsh P. cor.Mulberry & Franklin
White J. F. 190 Water
White J. 50 Van Schaick
Wilbur R. 56 Lydius
Wilkinson A. 45 Grand
Wilkins H. 177 Montgomery
Williams J. H. 9 N. Pearl
Williams Wm. C. 289 Washington
Winne Jacob L. 734 Broadway
Winters Wm. P. & S. Pearl
Wood J. S. 41　　do
Wormer Peter, 287 Washington
Wright Henry, 163 Broadway
Young George, 17½ S. Pearl
Young S. & P. 666 Broadway
Young S. & Co. cor. Lydius &
　Grand
Keffer Peter　　*Cosymans.*
Keller John
Lawton Wm. O.
Ellis David　　*Watervliet.*
Thorn F.
Wheeler Wm.
Bratt William, Cohoes
Caw & Quackenbush, Cohoes
Hollister W. H. & Co.　do
Lansing W. H.　　do
Livingston C. S.　　do
Snider H. H.　　do
Stevens William,　do
Vanderworken J. B.　do
Barry Thomas, West Troy
Bedell J. C.　　do
Bestie J. C.　　do
Brady J.　　do
Burnside R.　　do
Carr D.　　do
Collins L. D. & Co.　do
Collopy William,　do
Crowner & Waterman, West Troy
Crummy J.　　do
Davis H.　　do
De Graff A.　　do
Duncan C. C.　　do
Evans M.　　do
Fox J.　　do
Gage D. C.　　do
Gardiner L. & Co.　do
Gearn P.　　do
Gleason William,　do
Greeman S. & Co.　do
Gunnison & Co　　do
Hutchinsen C.　　do
Keenan P.　　do
Kimberly & Cole,　do
Learned George,　do
M'Cormick T.　　do
M'Donald & Van Olinda,　do
Magyre P.　　do
Mattoon R.　　do
Montgomery G. K.　do
O'Conner P.　　do
Potter, Carey & Co.　do
Potter J.　　do
Powell E. H.　　do
Quinn John,　　do
Richardson A. & T.　do
Rogers P.　　do
Rose C. B. & Co.　do
Scovill & Hart,　　do
Stewart J. H.　　do
Sweet & Benjamin,　do
Tinney Benjamin,　do
Welch K.　　do
Wilbur & Hollister,　do
Gould David　　*Western.*
Showres William

Alleghany County.
Dart J.　　*Amity.*

Finn P. T. *Amity.*
Arnold J. C. *Angelica.*
Royce T.
Hull H. E.
Knapp & Smead *Belfast.*
Woods James M.
Smith T. *Caneadea.*
Fay Lambert *Clarksville.*
Smith & Parks *Ceba.*
Merritt B.
Swift & Sibley
Smith C. H. & Co. Little Genesee *Genesee.*
Nichols Solon *Rushford.*
Bidwell H.
Woodworth William
Perry N. *Scio.*
Armstrong Wm. E.
Clark John B., Wellsville

Broome County.

Root W. R., Chenango Forks *Barker.*
Green E. do
Comstock W. do
Abbott & Son *Binghamton*
Bexford L. M.
Harvey L.
Briett & Deming
Hasson Wm.
Cone O.
Cotten C. B.
Smith L. L.
Brown D. M.
Bigler P.
Ballis S.
Abbott W. & C.
Saunders L.
Smith K.
Ross E.
Stowe J., Harpersville *Colesville.*
Van Buren & Conklin *Conklin.*
Fanning Asa *Union.*
Norton W. A., Union Centre
Carter H. W. *Windsor.*

Cattaraugus County.

Thomas H. B. *Ashford.*
Clark Alfred *Burton.*
Rosey H. & Co. *Ellicottville.*
Ingalls H.
Brooks C. & M.
Bares & Graves *Franklinville.*
Sturgis Albert
Holmes J.
Rose C. A. *Otto.*
Griffith Philander, East Otto
Fitch Charles L. *Randolph.*
Woodruff Austin

Cayuga County.

Rising J. 3 Genesee *Auburn.*
Wilson H. 1 do
Brown J. 13 do
Wetherby D. 70 Genesee
Groat A. C. & E. H. 96 Genesee
Hudson & Wilbur, 99 do
Monger A. C. 109 do
Clark & Sittser, 113 do
Quick & Hall, 1 Exchange Block
Groot S. Y. & A. C. 119 Genesee
Hinman L., State st.
Cheppel & Swift, State st.
Wakeman Wm., North st.
Clark Wm. do
Reed S. W. do
Dady J. do
Purdy J. do
Williams L., South st.
Reid J., State st.
Havens W. E., Weedsport *Brutus.*
Ryant H. do
Bostodae L., Montezuma *Mentz.*
Britt & Hurd, do
Ross & Patrick, do
White E., Port Byron
Babcock M. V. *Springport.*

Chautauque County.

Bush S. *Busti.*

Gifford William, Mayville
 Chautauque.
White R. T.
Chase Seth S. *Cherry Creek.*
Jones Albert, Jamestown *Ellicott.*
Burrows James, do
Curtis Hiram W.
Durkee Orlando *French Creek*
Crosby E. C. *Poland.*
Barton & Palmer, Fredonia
 Pomfret.
Burrett C. do
Tift do
Van Kleek ——, do
Smithers ——, do
Thorp John *Sherman.*
Manaison John
Hines Roselle *Westfield*
Cady William
Nicholson Alphonso
Hamilton Stephen J.
Jones Caleb
Chatsey Freeman
Ogle William

Chemung County.

Howard & Patchin, Havana
 Catharine.
Goodwin & Holman
Taylor ——
Webber ——
Anthony Jacob, Salubria *Dix.*
Atwood H. do
Hennessy J. *Elmira.*
Thompson J. C.
Rogers S.
Luce S. S. & Co.
Holden Fox
Sturges W.
Lyon Z. M.
Jones E. 2d
Redington J.
Keyes S.
Hall S.
Cherry W.
Shackelton B. D.
Kelly & Dumars
Daniels R.
Hill E. & Son
Tillottson & Sayre
Colton E. V.
Cook Miles
Sharpstine & Sayre
July G. W. Horse Heads
Carpenter W. T. do
Lyon —— do

Chenango County.

Piersall D. *Bainbridge.*
Ransford E. V.
Angell Dexter *New Berlin.*
Hancox Nathan
Steere Samuel
Randell N. S. *North Norwich.*
Gordon Richard
Smith & Sheehy *Norwich.*
Sturges J. O.
Rogers D.
Walt William C.
Noyes & Houk
Moore Joseph H.
Ray A. M. *Otselic.*
House H.
Fisk Seth H. *Oxford.*
Root Joshua
Smith & Wilcox
King Thomas
Baker W. *Pharsalia.*
Whitford & Fuller *Sherburne.*
Poltney H A.
King R. E.
Reynolds John
Baker A.
Leonard J. B. *Smyrna.*

Clinton County.

Reynolds J. W. Keeseville
 au Sable.
Jones H. do
Fitzpatrick M.

Patterson Charles *Black Brook.*
Moore H. B. *Champlain.*
Stalle William H.
Webster Benjamin
Wildow B.
Feselle Fabien
Fadden Joseph
Paine ——, West Chazy *Chazy.*
Parsons & White *Plattsburgh*
La Force Joseph
Senecal ——
Borde Andrew
Bromley John
Young Bernard
Conway T.
Hoag David
Davis Francis
Gordon George
Demara John
Gero J.
O'Brien Patrick, Cadyville
Gordon John, Elsenow Forge
Buck H. A. *Saranac.*
Roland William, Redford

Columbia County.

Stanard E. W. *Claverack.*
Miller L. Smoky Hollow
Brusie N. *Copake.*
Baker A. M. & Co. Warren st.
 Hudson.
Best H. & W. Public Square
Bogardus, Groat & Co. 330 Warren
Carpenter A. Franklin Square
Carpenter George W. do
Carpenter J. cor. Union & Front
Clawson J. Columbia st.
Crapser J. Warren st.
Davis J. do
Farry J. do
Forshew G. do
Friss John, cor. 8th & Warren
Gaul J. H. Columbia st.
Gaul J. R. do
Ham H. Warren
Harden G. Front cor. Franklin sq.
Holenbeck W. H. Public Square
House H. 323 Warren
Hubbel George C. cor. Water &
 Ferry
Lilly F. H. Warren st.
M'Arthur C. Water st.
Mallery J. E. 233 Warren
Meech A. North Front
Moore J. D. cor Warren & 7th
Morrison C. V. H. cor. Warren &
 3d
Morrison H. Warren st.
Nickerbocker W. P. & H. N. do
Poultney & Morris, cor. Warren
 & Front
Rogers H. W. Columbia st.
Rorabeck E. A. East Public Sq.
Rowley & Miller, Public Square
Rowley Wm. A. & Co. Warren st.
Sharp W. H. 289 do
Slocum J. 161 do
Spaulding N. A. cor. Warren &
 4th
Stever & Elmendorf, Warren st.
Van Deusen H. B. 262 do
Waterman S. S do
White J. corner Warren & 7th
Williams J. L. Warren st.
Griffin E. L. Valatie *Kinderhook.*
Burton G. W. do
Mesick J. M. do
Pulver P. W. do
Clapp J. do
Gressor T. do
Van Alen I. P. & Co. Valatie
Ray G. do
Race R. H. do
Dedrick M. C. do
Oakley T. & W. *Stockport.*
Van Fenoy William
Brown & Miller
Clapp H. *Stuyvesant.*

Cortland County.

Gillett Homer *Cortland Village.*

Copeland G. N. *Cortland Village.*
Randall A. H.
Barnum ——
Durkee Albert *Homer.*
Smith Wm. R.
Roberts Benj.
Thayer Wm. *Marathon.*
Van Volen Stephen *Preble.*

Delaware County.

Clinton George N. *Andes.*
Williams J. Downsville
 Colchester.
Fitch C. & A. J. *Delhi.*
Wilson F. *Hamden.*
M'Nett T. A. North Kortright
 Kortright.
Lewis M. Bloomville
Wood S. do
Thorp D. M., Hobart *Stamford.*
Bixby J. H. Deposit *Tompkins.*
Bixby H. & Co. do

Duchess County.

Jackson A. Hughsonville
 Fishkill.
Thorne J. T. Glenham
Jaycox D. S. Matteawan
Underhill S. do
Cromwell & Vanvliet, Fishkill
  Landing
Knox W. H. do
Ely I. *Hyde Park.*
Metcalf T. jr.
Pells L. L.
Smith W. W. *Pine Plains.*
Chamberlain E. B.
Terrill J. *Pleasant Valley.*
Annin Wm. 25 Market
 Poughkeepsie.
Baker A. Bridge st.
Baker Henry, 434 Main
Banker J. 348 do
Bennett P. W. 395 do
Blanchard J. 239 do
Bloomfield D. C. cor. Water &
  Union
Brooks J. 136 Main
Brooks T. 119 do
Carson G. 406 do
Clark Geo. 269 do
Clegg T. cor. Main & Clover
Colwell C. 342 Main
Davis A. A. 29 Washington
Degroff Robert, 338 Main
Frisbie P. 278 do
Gifford J. W. & J. 19 Mill
Gilkinson T. 396 Main
Griffin I. 436 do
Hagadon C. D. 315 do
Hopkins E. G. & L. J. 331 do Main
Hopkins Mrs. Phœbe, 109 Cannon
Hunter E. 133 Main
Johnson J. 335 do
Krieger D. 138 do
Kelly M. jr. cor. Morrison &
  Bridge
Leopard F. 139 Mill
M'Lean A. J. 31 Market
M'Lean John, 241 Main
M'Lean & Mory, cor. Main &
  Washington
Mavret Peter M. 96 Market
Mills J. H. 271 Main
Moore Wm. 365 do
Morgan Caleb & Son, 345 Main
Myers H. D. 271 do
Nelson Admiral, 75 Union
Perry Thos. M. Hunt's Landing
Platte T. cor. Hamilton & Main
Rappelyea, J. jr. 95 do
Sherman I. W. 141 Mill
Smith Abraham, 344 Main
Smith M. 217 do
Taylor R. 261 do
Trowbridge & Wilkinson, 321 do
Vincent J. C. 261 Main
Wheeler W. H. 331 do
M'Clusky M. do
Bates W. *Rhinebeck.*
Ohara L.

Williams Wm. *Rhinebeck.*
Noxon T. C.
Jennings & Greet
Marquet L.

Erie County.

Hinkley Geo. Williamsville
 Amherst.
Koch John, do
Kieffer Jacob, do
Irr Michael, do
Baumgardiner Philip, do
Rappelyea David, do
Beeres Alfred, do
Witmire Christian, do
Pratt Wm. S. Willink *Aurora*
Crowder Jacob *Black Rock.*
Scally John
Dugan Michael
Hibberd Daniel
Bellinger John
Klepper George
Libley C.
Argus John
Adams Hiram, 37 East Seneca
 Buffalo.
Allen J. 49 Ohio
Almendinger C. F. 415 Main
Aulet James, S. Division
Barnum Austin, 7 Exchange
Basso P. 409 East Seneca
Baum C. 3 Water
Beard D. C. 103 & 105 Main
Beiler Geo. cor. Commercial &
  Water
Beiler M. cor. Lloyd & Water
Bergtold J. 386 Main
Beyer P. cor. Main & Chippewa
Beyer & Urban, (variety) cor.
  Oak & Genesee
Black G. 366 Main
Bleiler Kasper, cor. Lloyd &
  Prime
Bond E. T. 11 East Seneca
Bond R. D. 7 do
Brayman H. 138 do
Brenckle Leopold, Exchange st.
Brown Israel, c. Chicago & Swan
Brown John, 167 East Seneca
Brun O'Brien, 47 do
Burg Michael, 350 Main
Callender S. N. 229 Main
Card Wm. 75 Elliott
Cartright E. 52 East Eagle
Carey & Brown, 41 East Seneca
Chandler D. O. 30 do
Chapin Hollis, 42 do
Churchill & Parker, cor. Court &
  Main
Clark James, 29 Ohio
Clark W. H. 9 Ohio Buildings
Colston John, 4 Terrace
Cook John, 209 Genesee
Coventry Robert, 28 Terrace
Cross Daniel, 47 Ohio
Currie Wm. & Co. 9 Birkehead,
  Block Commercial
Danner M. cor. Batavia & Cedar
Demicke Frederick, Exchange st.
Demuth M. 184 S. Division
Denny Jacob, Court st.
Diebold Sebastian, cor. Batavia &
  Pine
Dolen James, 164 East Seneca
Dolen Thomas, 7 Terrace
Doll M. 71 Genesee
Dost Jacob, 367 Main
Duggan Patrick, 302 East Seneca
Dunn Wm. 161 East Swan
Durick J. R. 247 Main
Elerhart Christian, cor. Court &
  Main
Emery D. F. 360 Main
Eva Adam, Exchange st.
Fisher G. cor. Michigan & Gen-
  esee
Fleming John, Long Wharf
Foley B. Perry st.
Fonchron J. & J. 61 Genesee
Fougeron & Brothers, Niagara &
  Mohawk

Gage Geo. 5 E. Seneca *Buffalo.*
Gerhart J. P. 10 W. Genesee
Gilmore E. Norton st.
Gilmore W. do
Graesser V. Genesee st.
Graetz G. M. 375 Main
Griffith John, 294 do
Hamlen & Webster. 1 E. Exchange
Hammond W. S. 144 S. Division
Hanstelle Matthias, 133 Genesee
Harmon J. & Co. 29 Main
Hartman J. Genesee st.
Hastings E. 257 Main
Hellriecel, cor. Elm & Genesee st.
Hendrick H. Terrace
Hills W. H. 66 Eagle
Huff Oliver W. 19 Exchange
Huuner John. E. Seneca
Jackson J. 3 Main
James Nelson, 290 E. Seneca
Johnson Daniel, 104 Ohio
Johnson Henry W. 1 Eagle
Josselyn Alanson. 9 do
Kendall L. F. 402 Main
Kennedy Thos. 26 Commercial
Kensman Henry, Washington st.
Kimball L. 430 Main
Kinsey S. 360 Main
La Fort B. Batavia st.
Lameon W. 51 Ohio
Lattau Michael, Rock st.
Lee R. H. 279 Main
Lee T. R. Ohio st.
Levake Thomas, cor. Michigan &
  Seneca
Lewis Jared, 265 Main
Lewis Samuel, 3 U. S. Hotel block
Lickel A. Hydraulics
Lux Nicholas, cor. Dock & Water
Lynch P. 166 E. Seneca
M'Allester A. W. 7 E. Seneca
M'Carthy ——, Ohio st.
M'Cleavy Richard, 9 Water
M'Cullough ——, 182 S. Division
M'Gowan Andrew, 42 N. Division
M'Lean John, Rock st.
Martin & Husson, 366 Main
Melancon J. P. Exchange
Memno Geo. Lock st.
Merritt Jesse, cor. S. Division &
  Chestnut
Messenger Geo. cor. Genesee &
  Elm
Meyer A. cor. Batavia & Walnut
Michael Nicholas, 41 N. Division
Miller A. D. A. 30 Clinton
Morse Joel, 39 Ohio
Mosier & Yale, 241 Maine
Noyes & Co. 288 Main
Oneil Wm. 189 S. Division
Ottenot Nicholas, 370 Main
Palmer H. D. 26 Ohio
Parker A. 18 E. Seneca
Paul M. 35 Genesee
Peabody J. M. 155 E. Seneca
Persch H. C. Terrace
Peters T. C. & Brother, cor. Ex-
  change & Washington
Pfeffen & Hares, 18 & 20 E. Seneca
Pfeifer P. 348 Main
Phillips G. Michigan cor. William
Pierce Hiram W. 2 Pearl
Pinner M. (fancy groceries) 284
  Main
Plynchon L. K. 22 E. Seneca
Prothais John, 6 Main
Rathburn & Emerson, 45 E. Seneca
Ream Geo. Rock st.
Rectenwalt F. cor. Batavia & Pine
Reed & Co. 10 Batavia
Rice Edward, 76 Main
Ripont J. 81 Batavia
Rose E. 340 Main
Rudoff Brothers, 426 Main
Sadway John J. 412 do
Scantz J. G. Batavia st.
Schenck Joseph, Hydraulics
Scheu Solomon, Rock cor. State
Schiefs C. 41 Genesee
Schmidt J. G. 88 do
Schranch Michael, Water st.
Schrodt J. 12 do

Schuster F. 56 Clinton *Buffalo.*
Schweigle Peter, 379 Main
Sexton Jason, 222 do
Shilling Wm. 22 Eagle
Shoemaker Joseph H., N. Division
 & Elm
Shusler G. 287 Main
Sidway J. 372 do
Sinset Adolph, 51 Genesee
Sirret E. cor. Batavia & Michigan
Sloan Brothers, cor. Exchange &
 Washington
Smith E. C. 193 E. Swan
Spencer A. B. 1 Packet Dock
Spengler M. Genesee st.
Stiner J cor. Batavia & Elm
Stockbridge I. M. 97 E. Seneca
Tatu P. C. 47 Genesee
Taylor R. M. 227 & 359 Main
Taylor R. M. & Co. 309 do
Taylor & Whitney, 576 do
Tiphaine Victor (fancy) 187 do
Tripp A. F. & Co. 41 Ohio
Trobridge B. H. 386 Main
Twichell A. 106 do
Urban G. & H. 83 Genesee
Voltz Geo. 392 Main
Ward Wm. Rock st.
Warner A. B. & Co. 22 E. Seneca
Webster & Scott, 9 E. Seneca
Wechler Joseph, 391 Main
Weimer J. A. cor. Batavia & Mi-
 chigan
Welsh & Latts, near cor. Niagara
 & Mohawk
White C. B. 22 Exchange
White P. A. 299 E. Swan
Wilber L. D. Terrace
Wilbert & Clark. 25 Main
Williams & Clark, 95 E. Seneca
Wilson Jefferson, 300 do
Wirt Hiram, 342 Main
Wolf J. J. 234 do
Woodle D. 7 Commercial
Woodruff W. cor. Washington &
 Seneca
Woodward A. T. 190 E. Seneca
Goddard E. & N. A. Springville
     Concord.
Mills Godfrey *Eden.*
Casper John
Johnson J. East Evans *Evans.*
Havens J. W. *Lancaster.*
Gardiner Joseph
Grant Joseph
Seuffer John
Hansel Michael
Kuhn F.
Porcher Phillip
Draper Anson *Newstead.*
Hooker Andrew, Akron
French H. Wales Centre *Wales.*
Clark Heman

Essex County.

Colvin S. Port Kent *Chesterfield.*
Boardman E. do
Williams Edm. C. *Elizabethtown.*
Hendee Ephraim P. Moriah 4 cor-
 ners *Moriah.*
Cook David, Moriah 4 corners
Edgerton D. C. do
Loveless Charles, do
Barton Nelson, do
Swinton James M. do
Fenagon James, Port Henry
Douglass John C. do
O'Brien James, do
Baker Milot *St. Armand.*
Marshall & Quinn *Ticonderoga.*
Walcott L. R.
Hyde R. C.
Baldwin B. H.
Bryan R.

Franklin County.

Leary Michael *Chateaugay.*
Mahony James
Burke Thomas
Hilliker H. W.
Green & Beman *Malone.*

Lathrop L. C. *Malone.*
Field & Berry

Fulton County.

Cook J. F. *Broadalbin.*
Clark Roswell
Eckenbrock Alex. *Ephratah.*
Steward Daniel *Johnstown.*
Haring Ambrose S.
Haring James H.
Tiffany Asa S.
Ripton Thomas
Gilchrist Peter
Fraser James G.
Mason F.
Balantine James
Wiley Isaac
Dun James
Cumrie William
Leonard Austin, Gloversville
Gordon Alexander B. do
Berry Hiram *Mayfield.*
Willard Reuben, Northville
    Northampton.
Parker W. C. Cranberry Creek

Genesee County.

Russ J. *Alabama.*
Geer William *Alexander.*
Beech L.
Manville B. F.
Russell C. A. *Batavia.*
Wilson John
Kenyon John
M'Cullunt J. C.
Eager J. & R.
Wilson & Austen
Wilson S. A.
Knowles G.
Fisher William *Bergen.*
Beardsley J. B.
Granger F.
Richards Walter, Linden *Bethany.*
Hewes Jacob *Le Roy.*
Chamberlain & Starr
Gray Elijah
Colony —— *Oakfield.*

Greene County.

Van Loane Henry *Athens.*
Howland Nathaniel
Haviland James T.
Howland Darius
Mayo George *Cairo.*
Hine Harlow
Wickes George
Telfair William, Acra
Johnson Asa do
Simmons Peter *Catskill.*
Grant Alexander J.
Foote Alfred
Bulkley Terzean
Edwards John
Scott William
Friar Hiram
Saxe Paul S.
Abeel John J.
Wilcox J.
Page W. & Co.
Steward Hector L.
Mosier Samuel
Du Bois Samuel
Vanderburgh William *Coxsackie*
Green Joel
Sager James H.
Bogardus Peter J.
Smith Moses
Newton Gay
Mackey John C.
Baker Ambrose
Beers Silas *Prattsville.*
Sikes Harvey
Carl Jasper
Hunt Charles R. *Windham.*

Hamilton County.

Abraham D. R. *Wells.*

Herkimer County.

Sholl I. *Danube.*

Van Alstine D. *Danube.*
Owens A.
Reed T.
Davis & Smith
Rofikrants A. G.
Maxfield D.
Phillips & Ford *Fairfield.*
Franklin S. C.
Hegeman Cornelius *Frankfort.*
Folts & Fox
Graves W. & C.
Heald John W. D.
Crosby John B.
Elwood & Folts
Dygert R. N.
Bridenbecker Wm. & J. W. (Pro-
 duce)
Hulse J. M. (Produce)
Austin George, West Frankfort
Colvin E. B. do
Davis John, jr. do
Bettinger Jacob, do
Lincoln Samuel, do
Morris John, (Produce) do
Mory Lawrence L. Mohawk
    German Flats.
Woodworth W. W. & E. M. Mo-
 hawk
Shoemaker & Ethridge, Mohawk
Grants Marks H. do
Spinner Christian F. *Herkimer.*
Hayck Hervy
Putnam William
Hoffman James
Spinner Charles
Staring & Van Slyke *Little Falls.*
Van Alstine James
Collins D. C.
Green L.
Willcox ——
Lewis Charles
Carroll Lewis
Casler Levi
Peak ——
Werry H.
Platner George H.
Walrad A. *Manheim.*
Snell A.
Ransom Daniel
Bagg D. *Newport.*
Christman J.
Sykes Francis
Brown Jacob
Owens David
Howe Joseph
Phillio D. B.
Buckley Wm. S.
Corss Isaac *Norway.*
Lathrop A. Van Hornsville *Stark.*
Tunnicleff T. do
Tunnicles Wm. *Warren.*
Lewis John, Page's Corners

Jefferson County.

Dolinger John, Redwood
    Alexandria.
Corlis Franklin, Plessis
Millard J. Y.
Thompson Arthur, Alexandria
 Bay
Earl O. R. *Brownville.*
Treman Abner
Brookway Henry
Materson P., Dexter
Miller John S. do
Rockwood G do
Avery Chas. B. Perch River
Gaudie J. T. *Cape Vincent.*
Ainsworth R
Haboy C.
Wait J. T. *Champion.*
Fowler & Eggleston *Clayton.*
Bedell C. P., Depauville
Felloe Abel S. do
Hall F. Sackett's Harbor
    Hounsfield.
Bacon N. E. do
Millington D. do
Luff & Redfield do
Hungerford Edward, Evan's Mills
    Le Ray.

Robbins Solomon, Watertown
     Pamelia.
Parker F. & G. *Theresa.*
Kelsey Jesse
Stockwell E. S.
Porter Robert *Watertown.*
Burt Franklin N.
Witgastein Solomon
Clark Silas
Baker & Woodruff
Butterfield Uri
Porter George
Woodruff & Andrus
Wilson Clark
Mundy Pierson
Hayes L.
Phillips Richard
Woodruff Gilbert
Gifford & Reed
Hersey Joseph
Hoy & Gregory
Rice Reuben & Son, Carthage
     Wilna.
Morse Samuel do
Warren Orson H. do

Kings County.

Allas John, 237 Adams *Brooklyn.*
Allen Wm. H. 209 Atlantic
Amermann N. 40 Carlton Av.
Anderson B. 155 Jay
Atkinson James, 330 Atlantic
Atterbury & Haskins, 14 Tillary
Auld & Kindall 10 Hamilton
Baker J. M. & Co. Pearl cor. Willoughby
Baker M. J. Union Av. cor. Columbia
Baldwin Louis N. Myrtle Av. cor. Gold
Baldwin & Burtis, 127 High
Barnes George, 99 Bridge
Beach Lewis, Pearl c. Myrtle Av.
Bedell Robert, 26 Tillary
Beers John H. 71 High
Behm John, 29 Johnson
Benjamin J. H. 155 Nassau
Bigelow J. B. 56 Hicks
Blake John, 59 Concord
Boxls Henry, 120 Sands
Braham James, 40 Hudson Av.
Bramgan Patrick. Prince cor. Tillary
Briody Patrick, Main cor. Front
Brower Mrs. M. F. 149 Gold
Brush J. 270 Atlantic
Buger Wm. Myrtle Av. cor. Nostrand
Bullwinkle John, Myrtle Av. cor. Classon Av.
Bullwinkle John & Co. 153 Myrtle Av
Burdge U. D. 11 Clinton
Byrne J. 28 Columbia
Cadmus Richard, 60 Main
Campbell Isaac, 75 Bridge
Campbell Thos. Front cor. Washington
Carbery B. Hudson Av. c. Tillary
Carney John, Adams cor. York
Carpenter Chas. & Andrews, 77 Main
Carroll M. 172 Prospect
Carrol Patrick, 5 Hudson Av.
Chamberlain James, Flushing Av. cor. Classon
Chapman Nath. Court c. Atlantic
Chapney S. T. 76 Henry
Chatelle F. 213 Lafayette Av.
Childs G. C. 243 Bridge
Childs G. C. 69 Nassau
Clayton Joel, 26 Hudson Av.
Clayton J. C. 161 Johnson
Collins Thos. Hudson Av. c. Marshall
Colyer & Powell, Flushing Av. c. Kent
Connolly Wm. H. Hamilton Av. cor. Carmel
Conklin J. W. 171 Prospect
Conway Mrs. E. Hudson Av. cor. Front

Cook M. 114 Bridge *Brooklyn.*
Cook & Duval, Dean n. Boerum
Corlay Patrick, 243 Marshall
Cornell Wm. H. 190 Fulton
Cosby John, Hicks cor. Cole
Crisp John, 1 Henry
Cullan John, 12 Hudson Av.
Davis B. W. 58 Fulton
Davis S. S. 1 Atlantic
Davis Wm. 149 Hudson Av.
Davis & Flits, Columbia c. State
Dawson T. 31 State
Delaney Jno. Columbia cor. Union
Dennis Chas. 94 Fulton
Dermott Peter, 283 Hudson
Dix E. H. & Co. Court c. Sackett
Dolben John, Pacific cor. Willow
Dolscheid Wm. 40 Carlton Av.
Dosher Henry, Jay cor. Prospect
Dougherty Cornelius, Water cor. Hudson Av.
Dougherty Daniel, Smith c. Dean
Dougherty H. Jay cor. Water
Dougherty James, Jay cor. Water
Dougherty N. Columbia c. Warren
Dougherty Wm. Jay n. Water
Driscoll Simon, 89 Hudson Av.
Dubber P. 42 Hicks
Duval & Cook, Dean n. Boerum
Eames Luther. 88 Hicks
Early Patrick, 25 Columbia
Eckhert Henry, 89 Prospect
Evans Richard, 132 Myrtle Av.
Farren D. Furman cor. Joralemon
Ferris John W. Myrtle Av.
Fils & Davis, Columbia cor. State
Fitzsmons Thos. Myrtle Av. cor. Skellman
Flanders J. 16 Court
Fogts G. 95 Bridge
Food M. cor. Columbia & Baltic
Foot Isaac S. 88 Washington
Foot P. F. Myrtle Av. cor. Adams
Ford John, 147 Tillary
Foster A. J. Navy cor. Lafayette
Foster L. H. 115 Willoughby
Frick H. & Co. 245 Hudson Av.
Frost Isaac, 158 Johnson
Frost James & Sons, 83 Concord
Gagnon Eusebe, 166 Gold
Gardner David B. 97 & 99 Gold
Genning James O. Hudson Av. c. Lafayette
Gettins A. Jay cor. Water
Gillen John, Lawrence c. Tillary
Graham John, 20 Hudson Av.
Green M. 129 Tillary
Gunther F. W. 120 Hudson Av.
Haas Carlton, 61 Tillary
Hade George, Water cor. Jay
Hall Isaac, Baltic st.
Hall James B. Atlantic cor. Bond
Halliard John, Front cor. Adams
Halpine Richard, John cor. Gold
Harris H. & Co. 106 Hudson Av.
Hatfield F. D. Myrtle Av. corner Frankfort
Havens J. C. 117 Sands
Henry J. Henry cor. Orange
Herbert & Case, 109 High
Hicks N. W. Pearl cor. York
Hinck Lawrence, 131 Tillary
Hinck L., Hoyt cor. Livingston
Holden C. B. Bedford cor. Atlantic
Hollister Nathan, 71 Atlantic
Holling John, Hamilton Av.
Hollman Herman, 207 Lafayette
Holmes Chas. 206 Gold
Horton C. C. Columbia c. Sackett
Howell James, 29 Hudson Av.
Hudson Thos. D. Flushing Av.
Hunt J. W. jr. 101 Prospect
Jenkins J. Navy st.
Johns S. C. Smith c. Baltic
Johnson Wm. Columbia c. Union
Johnston J. J. State c. Furman
Kayser F. 151 Myrtle Av.
Keeler Charles B. 83 Fulton
Kelly John, 19 Columbia
Kelly S. 44 Main
Kemp William, 89 Main

Kirkman H c. Atlantic & Boerum
     Brooklyn.
Klindrer C. 19 Columbia
Knowland Mrs. E. 200 Bridge
Kolyert ——, 144 York
La Blanc A. C. 186 Nassau
Lane T. cor. Atlantic & Willow
Landers Joseph F. 129 Atlantic
Layer C. A. Tillary st.
Lering J. S. cor. Bond & Schemerhorn
Leverich L. S. 4 York
Lippin John, 156 York
Loane & Leach, 96 Bridge
Lockwood & Co. 158 Sands
Longbotham & Caldwell, 72 Hicks
Losey D. cor. Douglass & Smith
Lynch Thos. cor. John & Jay
Lynch Wm. 174 Hudson
Lynde J. H. 102 Gold
Lyon J. cor. Hicks & Sackett
Mackay Patrick. 16 Atlantic
M'Allister A. Nassau cor. Gold
M'Cabe Hugh, cor. Front & Jay
M'Carty J. Tillary cor. Prince
M'Carty Timothy, Tillary st.
M'Carty T. cor. Bond & State
M'Cay C. cor. Dock & Water
M'Comb J. cor. Columbia & Degraw
M'Cormick J. 156 Johnson
M'Dade John, 55 Hudson
M'Donald B. Myrtle Av.
M'Entee Owen, 65 Hudson
M'Glinn T. Court cor. Amity
M'Kinney James, 37 Amity
M'Lane D. Amity st.
M'Laughlin E. Little cor. Plymouth
M'Laughlin Mrs. M. 23 Columbia
M'Laughlin W. Tillary n. Hudson
M'Quades S. Columbia st.
Maher P. cor. Columbia & Dougherty
Meigrot L. Adams cor. Plymouth
Maloy G. cor. Baltic & Hoyt
Manning A. 95 Orange
Many Richard, 79 Tillary
Markey A. cor. Pearl & Plymouth
Markey ——, cor. Front & Main
Marmick J. Marshall cor. Little
Mathews Wm. cor. Pearl & John
Meeker Wm. J. 333 Fulton
Mehrtens W. Water near Fulton
Meislahn & Kelting, 19 Concord
Mekelvy C. & S. cor. Smith and Wyckoff
Metcalf W. cor. Clinton & Warren
Meyer Claus, Fulton near Gold
Meyer L. foot of Hamilton Av.
Milford W. 3 Market
Milgate M. 179 Myrtle Av.
Millard John, 105 Concord
Millburn J. cor. Boerum & Pacific
Miller D. W. cor. Smith & Butler
Moffatt R. Jay cor. Concord
Moore James, 69 Tillary
Moran Thomas, Myrtle Av.
Morril E. B. 156 Fulton
Morris John, 134 Henry
Morrison E. L. cor. Fulton and Hudson
Mulligan S. 74 Atlantic
Mulway M. 26 Columbia
Murphy P. Myrtle Av. c. Franklin
Murray J. cor. Pacific & Willow
Neville John. Carrol st.
Niebuhr H. Myrtle Av. c. Steuben
Oakley Henry, 206 Adams
O'Brian P. Amity op. Willow
O'Brian Thomas, 44 Hudson Av.
O'Connell James. 91 York
O'Donnell A. 63 Sands
O'Donnell C. Bond cor. Douglass
Oliver Frederick, 151 High
Orth & Buttz, cor. Myrtle Av. & Willoughby
Parsons ——, Court cor. Warren
Peitts Samuel, 33 Amity
Pettit Stephen, 29 Hicks
Pettit T. Division st. cor. Wallabout road

Phineas Baldwin & Co. Myrtle Av. cor. Adams　*Brooklyn.*
Plent Wm. Columbia st.
Plunkett John. 50 Little
Powell L. B. Myrtle Av. cor. Lawrence
Purgold G. F. cor. Everett and Dougherty
Purgold & Albrecht, 101 York
Quaid J. cor. Milton & Bergen
Randolph J. D. F. 187 Gold
Raynor Wm. 42 Henry
Reeds John, 54 Stanton
Reese & Davis, 139 Jay
Relly J. Flushing cor. Bedford
Remer Henry, 166 Hudson Av.
Richardson M. 23 Hicks
Richmond Warren, 197 Fulton
Riddon B. 37 Main
Rieds Henry, cor. Smith & Dean
Robbins M. R. cor. Kent st. and Myrtle Av.
Romay Patrick, 209 Myrtle Av.
Sargent J. cor. Smith & Wyckoff
Schneider Martin, 143 Concord
Scranton & Co. cor. Atlantic and Henry
Segelkin H. cor. Smith & Degraw
Segelkin H. Bond st.
Seller Mrs. D. G. Hudson Av. cor. Tillary
Selleck J. & Co. 152 Prospect
Sencerbox & Co. cor. Columbia & Prospect
Shaeffer Lewis, cor. Boerum & Livingston
Sheridan N. 77 Tillary
Shields J. Plymouth cor. Little
Silver Chas. A. 269 Washington
Simpson James S. cor. Irving & Columbia
Sirey Mrs. York cor. Pearl
Smith A. 173 Johnson
Smith B. F. 25 James
Smith Israel, Myrtle Av-
Smith J. M. 5 Linden row
Smith Peter, Columbia st.
Smith & Torney, 107 Gold
Sniffen Caleb, 76 Bridge
Spratt S. W. 31 Hudson
Steen Christopher, Clove road
Steenwerth Margaret, Bedford st.
Stewart J. O. Clove road
Stillwell G. 277 Fulton
Story Rowland, 122 Fulton
Stunworth Chas. 137 Prospect
Sutton Stephen, 71 Fulton
Sutton & Young, 77 Fulton
Taylor J. cor. Main & Front
Tienckin D. Bridge cor. Tillary
Tienckin Henry, cor Myrtle Av. & Bridge
Tisner James, cor. Washington & York
Thompson J. John cor. Little
Treisner & Scheitzger, Washington cor. Prospect
Vandervoort & Co. 28 Pearl
Van Nostrand Aaron, Atlantic cor. Franklin
Von Glahn Henry, 91 Adams
Walker J. 1 Bergen
Walker Thomas, 109 Front
Ward B., Bow cor. Atlantic
Wardensbury John L. Myrtle Av. cor. Kent
Warren William, 26 Chapel
Weeks Willett, Myrtle cor. Hudson Av.
Wells J. N. 250 Gold
Welsh John J. 271 Bridge
Wheelin John, 235 Hudson Av.
White S. Atlantic cor. Bedford
Williams J. Smith cor. Baltic
Williams C. F. 81 Johnson
Williamson Wm. J. 182 Bridge
Worthington & Thompson, 107 Atlantic
Wright H. P. & Co. 17 Atlantic
Beals R. & H. Bushwick cor.　*Bushwick.*
Prevost John C., Green Point

Tiebout & Harris, Green Point　*Bushwick.*
Meserole W. M. & A. do
Ruland Charles　do
Lemington John, New Lots　*Flatbush.*
Lohman John, East New York
Reed Philip,　do
Romane B.　do
Durland Wm., Canorsie *Flatlands.*
Skidmore Isaac, do
Anderson Joseph, 140 S. 2d　*Williamsburgh.*
Anderson Joseph, 29 N. 2d
Bain James, 75 N. 4th
Baker Geo. W. 184 Grand
Bates Wm. E. 41 S. 7th
Battermall H. N. 6th st. cor. 7th
Becker Henry, S. 6th
Bedell & Burtis, 33½ Grand
Bedell G. C. & E. Bushwick Av.
Bell Thos. 224 Grand
Bennett Jacob, Bushwick Av.
Betton Chas. 143 Ewing
Blomker Henry
Brissenden J. H. Varet st.
Calhoun Jas. 2d st. cor. N. 5th
Carpenter & Brother, 182 Grand
Carey Martin, 76 N. 4th
Cassidy John, 27 S. 2d
Conselyes Jos. jr. Grand st. cor. Bushwick Av.
Conselyes Wm. Wither st.
Cooper J. W. 1st st. co. N. 3d
Cooper J. F. 286 Grand
Cornell T. W. 186 S. 3d
Cosgrove J. 6 N. 2d
Coyle Chas. North 6th st. near 2d
Cullivan P. 27 Remsen
Daniels Mrs. F. 2d st. cor. S. 6th
Davis & Scott, 406 Grand
Dewing Wm. G. 155 4th
Dickinson S. S. 174 Grand
Dillingham J. South 6th st.
Droll F. E. 31 Grand
Eiseman P. Ewing st.
Ewen S. F. 24 N. 4th
Falvey Daniel, 62 Grand
Foleh Thomas, 84 Grand
Ferry Edwin, 101 S. 3d
Fitzgerald M. 1st st. cor. N. 10th
Flaherty P. 1st st. cor. N. 7th
Fogerity John, 1 N. 8th
Furl Samuel, 1st st. cor. N. 9th
Gallaudet James, 106 Grand
Gilbert Mrs. N. 8th 6th st. cor. 3d
Gorman John. 296 S. 4th
Gorwin Miss A. 244 S. 4th
Healy John, 25 S. 2d
Heins J. H. North 6th st. cor. 3d
Hulse & Bennett. Bushwick Av.
Hulsebarry Henry, 93 N. 4th
Jack James, 1st st. cor. Lorimer
Jackson John, N. 3d
Lenon Arthur, 20 N. 2d
Lockwood Alex. 210 S. 4th
Loughran J. South 7th st.
Loverty James, 200 1st
M'Guire John, 110 4th
M'Millan Daniel, 262 2d
Mangles Henry. 250 S. 3d
Manjer Chas. 465 Grand
Marston L. 369 Grand
Manler Wm. Boerum st. corner Leonard
Mears John, Montrose Av.
Meyer H. Union Av. cor. N. 2d
Moore Alex. 206 1st
Morrell & Rumple, 59 S. 2d
Morris James, 202 1st
Murphy Edward, 39 2d
Myer Henry, S. 8th st. cor. 4th
Myers H. 127 S. 1st
O'Brien M. 278 Grand
O'Brien Wm. 321 Grand
O'Grady James, 2d st. cor. North
Oltman Henry, Graham Av.
Organ M. South 1st
Parkhurst & Adams, 169 S. 2d
Phillips Mrs. Susan, 33 3d
Phillips B. C. 4th st. cor. N. 1st
Pirrie Wm. 1st st. cor. N. 9th

Rankin Henry, 287 S. 4th　*Williamsburgh.*
Reilly Daniel, 99 2d
Reinhard H. 116 N. 4th
Richardson E. A. H. 43 Remsen
Scultz Jas. B. 244 Grand
Shea Thos. 13 Grand
Short Patrick, 239 2d
Shreves Mrs. Sarah, 264 S. 4th
Smalley S. 153 Grand
Smith D.
Smith Edmund, 240 1st
Smith Giles, 96 N. 2d
Smith Henry A. North 2d st.
Smith I. F. 10 Grand
Smith John, 148 1st
Smith James, 270 1st
Smith Wm. 267 S. 4th
Smith W. H. 37 S. 7th
Sparling G. 187 S. 4th
Sparrow George, 150 S. 4th
Struse D. 12 Grand
Sweeny Dennis, 46 10th
Swift Francis, 515 N. 2d
Tangtat John. 1st st. cor. N. 2d;
Timmes John, Ewing st.
Tonges Chas. H. 16 S. 7th
Videto Jacob, 94 4th
Vollkommer Jos. 131 Ewing
Von Oren J. 104 4th
Walters J. H. 266 Grand
Wessel & Immen, 106 S. 2d
White A. 3. 109 S. 2d
Wilson John H. 142 4th
Winters John, 45 S. 4th
Wintjen J. & Co. Union Av. cor. 2d st.
Wreden C. 85 N. 3d
Zimmer Henry, Ewing st. corner Montrose Av.
Zimmer Jacob, 106 Remsen

Lewis County.

Hammond H.	*Denmark.*
Cook S. D.	*Lowville.*
Jones E.	*Martinsburgh.*
Kilham S. E.	*Turin.*
Litchfield Lyman N.	
Hoskins G. P. Constableville	
	West Turin.

Livingston County.

Hassenger Chas.	*Avon.*
Palmer Gilbert, East Avon	
Ferguson Alex.	*Caledonia.*
Fulton C.	
Taft J. Y. & M.	*Dansville.*
Halstead M.	
Payne E. E.	
Stacey O. D. & H.	
Wetmore C. G. & Co.	
Reese Wm.	
Segler Chas.	
Curtiss William	
Syke, Folgelle & Co.	
Clark Wm. C.	
Owen Lyman	
Brown Wm.	
Smith D. R.	
Reese W. F.	
Draper & Doty	
Jones H. & Sons	
Brown & Williams	
Edwards A. C.	
Crank J. D.	*Geneseo.*
Tomlinson R. & J.	
Wilson Samuel J.	
Wilson J. W.	
Greenfield & Morgan, Cuylerville	*Leicester.*
Atherton Oliver, Moscow	
Stevens A. L.	*Lima.*
Gragg & Co. Hemlock Lake	
	Lincoln.
Totten & Hill	*Mt. Morris.*
Phelps Lester	
Bacon James B.	
Edgecomb A. P.	
Mordaff A. D.	
Ketchum C. L.	
Swan S. jr. & Co.	*Nunda.*

14

Wheeler & Chase   *Nunda.*
Gillett L.
Carter Peter
Van Riper G. J. & C. Oakland
     Portage.
Tadder Hiram, Oakland
Brown John   *Springwater.*
Fraser James   *York.*
Skelley Alex.

Madison County.

Gorton Benjamin   *Brookfield.*
Main J. C.
Alby Laban, North Brookfield
Cheesman & Bissell   *Cazenovia.*
Bishop Thomas
Hart A. & Son   *De Ruyter.*
Sears S. G.
Allen Henry   *Eaton.*
Blynn Edward
Boothe Levi, Morrisville
Stone T. K.   do
Anderson John, Leeville
Foote John J.   *Hamilton.*
Hartshorn & Maydole
Burns G. F.
Thetge Benjamin, Earlville
Stewart R. J., Oneida Depot *Lenox.*
Morse L.   do
Brooks L.   do
Fay Nahum, Canastota
Watkins C. W.   do
Conley John,   do
Gey Wm. L.   do
Peckham D. S.   do
Colton F. A.   do
Colton C. L.   do
Cook Timothy,   do
Stewart J. J. & A. Wampsville
Wadsworth J. Erieville   *Nelson.*
Griffith David,   do
Eastman N., Peterboro *Smithfield.*
Hale E. G., Siloam
Koons P. I.   *Sullivan.*
Clark George
Murray & Ives
Childs James H.
Clark Martin
Campbell A. & Co. Chittenango
Pennock & Burns,   do
De Witt Wm.   do
Adams Benj., Bridgeport

Monroe County.

Fulton Robert, North Chili *Chili.*
Palmer J. B., Clarkson Corners
     Clarkson.
Avery A.   *Greece.*
Hovey H., Jenkins' Corners
Ogden M., West Mendon *Mendon.*
Cutler C. F.   do
Fox J.   do
Davis Charles, Spencer's Basin
     Ogden.
Pickett J.   *Penfield.*
Starling R.
Chartre H.
Van Buren B., Fairport *Perrinton.*
Hunt S. R., Bushnell's Basin
Chambers J.   *Pittsford.*
Ecler William
Parker Thomas S.
Brown John
Church Peter, Churchville *Riga.*
Adams Walter E. 5 Monroe
     Rochester.
Adams & Conklin, 14 Exchange
Alexander J. & A. S. 129 Main
Annet & Haslip, 39 Adams
Armstrong John, 318 Main
Archbold James A. 19 Buffalo
Avery George A. 19   do
Bacon William, 117 S. Sophia
Baller Jacob, cor. E. & W. North
Bardwell Edward, 133 Main
Beatty M. 31 Front
Bell & Goodman, 19 Buffalo
Benedict I. L. 189 State
Billings & Gilbert, 87 Main
Boughton E. S. 220 Buffalo

Bostwick L. 6 Front   *Rochester.*
Braman David M. 172 Buffalo
Breck M. B. & Co. 67 Main
Brewster S. L. & J. H. 16 South St.
   Paul & 70 Main
Brown John N. 100 S. St. Paul
Braithwaite F. 172 State
Bullock Wm. 29 Front
Canley D. H. & Brother, 23 Front
Carll John, 191 Buffalo
Cavenaugh Matthew, 14 & 16
   Sheldon's Dock
Christy Robert, 102 S. Sophia
Cline & Raymond, 135 Main
Cockrane J. 28 Main
Cole C. 69 Adams
Coleman S. B. cor. Sophia & Adams
Collen Patrick. 142 State
Conars Christopher, 113 S. Sophia
Conkey J. & E. 70 Main
Cook I. D. cor. Andrews & Clinton
Cootworth R. cor. Spring & Ex-
   change
Crombie John, 9 Buffalo
Cummings Wm. 124 do
Cushman & Brown, 190 State
Cusgrove Felix. 6 Lyell
Daily William, 110 Main
Davis J. 271 State
Dougherty James, 17 S. St. Paul
Doyle Edward, 30 Front
Drum O D. Rochester Block
Duffy E. 244 State
Eagan J. Front st.
Eichmen Isaac, 43 North
Eldredge Asahel, 214 Buffalo
Eno Anthony, 17 Monroe
Falconer Alexander, 177 Buffalo
Fay H. F. 65 Main
Fitzgerald William, 25 St. Paul
Flanders B. 117 Main
Ford E. Market
Fruin R. C. 69 S. St. Paul
Gardiner N. H. 81 Exchange
Gibson B. 192 State
Goodman James, 71 S. St. Paul
Gorman Mathew, 14 Buffalo
Grant A. & Co. 43 Exchange
Griswold A. & Co. 56 State
Harris F. A. cor. Monroe & Union
Harn John, 98 Main
Hickock B. E. Exchange
Higgins William, 214 State
Hilton J. Frankfort st.
Hildreth J. 35 Mount Hope Av.
Houghton T. B. 68 Main
Hubbell & Vose, cor. North &
   Delavan
Hughes William, 200 Main
Hughes Thomas, cor. Oak & Jay
Judson Henry, 94 S. Sophia
Karing William, Clinton st.
King R. cor. Buffalo & N. Sophia
Kingsley Seth, 233 Main
Kingsley James, 62 North
Kilgour George, 12 Monroe
Kinseller Michael, 26 Front
Kidd J. M. 189 State
Laurence J. S. 27 Exchange
Levy H. 57 N. Clinton
Logan Michael, 170 State
Lunt & Crawford, 248 do
Lyons D. J. c. Prospect & Adams
Lyndon F. cor. High & Adams
M'Creedin John, 117 Buffalo
M'Donald John, 174 State
M'Donall M. 114 E. North
M'Dougall A. 3 Monroe
Mackenzie A. F., Mount Hope Av.
Madden M. 100 N. St. Paul
Managhan Hugh, 192 State
Meyer J. Sebastian. 101 Main
Minniss M. 34 Brown
Monaghan Michael, 26 St. Paul
Montgomery Andrew, cor. Mon-
   roe & Union
Mudgett William, jr. 69 Buffalo
Neil James, 119 S. Sophia
Newton F. A. 120 Main
O'Neil William, jr. 88 St. Paul
Orchard R. P. 2 Waverly place
Osborn N. P. 11 S. St. Paul

Parker John, G. 49 Main
     Rochester.
Parkhurst H. & J. Weighlock
Paddock H. G. cor. Alexander &
   Cayuga
Perkins J. H. 22 Hunter
Quigly T. 53 Prospect
Reilly John, 151 Main
Rigney John, 12 St. Paul
Rigney Owen, 184 State
Rogers Marvin, 91 Spring
Rnney Patrick, 111 Buffalo
Rosecrants M. 137   do
Rupp B. cor. Atwater & Clinton
Russell William G. 55 St. Paul
   cor. Court
Sach George, 75 North
Scrafield Robert, 208 Main
Semple Andrew, 43 Front
Schlitger George, 22 St. Paul
Sheridan John, 36 Front
Sheridan Peter, 107 Buffalo
Sheldon O. L. & Co. 8   do
Simmons E. R. & S. 116 Main
Sheridan Peter E. 105 Buffalo
Smith & Gould. 211   do
Smith Abba, 193   do
Smith C. D. & Brother, 15 S. St.
   Paul
Speed David, 1 Park place
Stewart J. cor. North & Bowery
Stimpson W. B. 89 N. St. Paul
Sweet C. H. 123 Buffalo
Sylee John B. 94 Brown
Thompson I. H. cor. State & Jay
Townsend N. cor. Buffalo & Eli-
   zabeth
Tracy John, 74 N. St. Paul
Wadsworth W. cor. Spring & Fitz-
   hugh
Washburn T. S. cor. Franklin &
   Andrew
Watters D. 5 Market
Weepey Abraham, 123 Main
Weldin George, Buffalo st.
Wigney W. B. cor. Dean & Jones
Wilson Robert, 112 E. North
Wilson Richard, Buffalo st.
Witherspoon I. F. 67   do
Wheeler W. Mayne st.
Whittlesey F. C. 76 Buffalo
Wright Thomas, 193   do
Worden J. 89 Main
Young Henry, 22 Spring
Davis Isaac, Brockport   *Sweden.*
Carter A. A. Canal st. do
Carnes T. & Co. do   do
Olds E. D.   do   do
Davis H. C. & Co. 12 Main
Spaulding S. 16   do
Wright J. H. 28   do
Harrison J.   do
Seeley W. B. 19   do
Kingsbury S. & Co. 5 do
Skidman W. E. 1   do
Marlette R.   *Webster.*
Bristol G. T. Scottsville
     Wheatland.
Lewis David B.   do
Phelps J. Mumford

Montgomery County.

M'Donald & M'Clumpha
     Amsterdam.
Paige Freeman
Morris Abraham V.
Powell Hosea
Candee D. P. Hagaman's Mills
Thatcher Andrew, Cranesville
Crane Abraham R.   do
Brown Constant   *Canajoharie.*
Easton James S.
Van Alstine J. T.
Ross Adams
Germain L. S.
Gordinier Cornelius
Watts R. W.
Winsman R.
Marshell L., Buel
M'Clary Wm. Port Jackson
     Florida

Newkirk Francis, Port Jackson
Florida.

Ide Reuben I.   do
Livermore Emory,   do
Pettingel Wm.   do
Young Charles,   do
Francisco Voorhees, Fort Hunter
Fisher James & John,   do
French Benj. C. Phillip's Locks
Wemple & Brother,   do
Sanda David,   do
Phillips Dana,   do
Scriss & Livermore,   do
Austin Orestus O. Fort Plain
Minden.

Westle Jonas,   do
Norton Solomon,   do
Gamet Aaron,   do
Clark, Newkirk & Wood, do
Bennett Wm. H.   do
Aplin James,   do
Haggart John B., Fonda *Mohawk.*
Warlord Jewell, Sprakers' Basin
Root.

Spraker George
Failing Jacob   *St. Johnsville.*

New York County.

Abel Thomas, 241 8th Av.
New York.
Ackerman & Co. 789 Greenwich
Ackerman John P. 186 Spring
Ackerman & Deyo, 206 Allen
Ackerman & Smith, 260½ Division
Ackerson Abraham, 150 W. 20th
Ackland —— 160 Grand
Adams Adolph, 19 Ann
Adams E. K. & J. 700½ Greenwich & 293 W. 18th
Adicks Henry & Co. 97 Duane
Agas Lewis, 77 Centre
Agne Henry & Co. cor. Av. A & 12th
Agnus Henry, 26 Av. B
Agnew William H. 230 Delancy
Afferman H. 186 3d Av.
Agabo F. 383 Cherry
Aguire & Galway, 44 Water
Ahler Herman, 77 6th Av.
Ahmuty Arthur. 176 W. 18th
Ahrens A. & F. 390 3d Av.
Ahrens Frederick, 161 Hester and 475 Washington
Ahrens George G. 180 William & 96 Spruce
Ahrvas P. & Co. 519 Pearl
Albert Henry, 173 Av. A
Albert Peter. 194 Houston
Albers Claus. 60 Market
Albers George, 635 Houston
Albrecht Peter, 194 Houston
Albro Albert T. 379 Bowery
Albro Benjamin & Co. 106 Division & 256 Grand
Albro Richard, 152 Norfolk
Albro Stephen V. 328 Bowery
Albro William H. 253 Bowery
Alexander A. 663 Houston
Alfka John, 104 Grand
Allen A. & Co. 299 8th Av.
Allen J. B. & Co. 30 8th Av.
Allen John, 110 Vesey
Allen J. B. & Co. 22 8th Av.
Allen William, 375 3d Av.
Allers John A. 19 Counties slip
Allison John, 229 6th Av.
Allison Thomas H. 523 Grand
Allstadt J. C. 41 Greenwich
Allsted Henry, 41 Greenwich
Alsgood Peter, 344 Hudson
Anderson Jane. 47 Spring
Anderson Jonathan, 38 E. B'way
Anderson C. V. & J. 71 Mulberry
Anderson Thomas, 126 Broome
Andrews Thomas, 61 Fulton
Anton & Pohlman, 14 Thomas
Anthony Michael, 506½ Greenwich
Aufenanger Anth. 615 Washington
Apgar Levi & Co. 180 Washington

Arbogast Philip, 237 Houston
New York.
Archer Benjamin. 567 Houston
Archer William, 162 8th Av.
Arcularius, Bonnett & Co. 200 Front
Armstrong Thomas, 166 Cedar
Arppen H. 8 South
Aschoff Jacob, 52 Amos
Asher Henry, 102 John
Ashley & Fish, 105 South
Atcher Bridget. 47 Ludlow
Atkinson Edward, 153 Leonard
Auer John, 250 6th
Aufderhaide John G. & Co. 20 Reade & 94 Walker
Aufenanger A. 615 Washington
Aufenanger Henry, 563 Broome
Augustus C. 11 Centre market pl.
Augustus Charles, 77 Cherry
Ausderoh Hammond. 197 3d Av.
Austerich J. H. 122 3d Av.
Avery John W. 349 Water
Ayres Louis, 63 Duane
Ayres & Tunis, 176 Washington
Babbage C. 166 South
Babbidge Calvin, 166 South
Badeau Henry, 901 Broadway
Badeker A. West 29th st.
Badgers H. 191 South
Bailey Charles D. 27 Division
Bailey Elbert, 196 Elm
Baisley Henry W. 37 1st Av.
Baker Edmund S. 163 Rivington
Baker Hobart M. 196 Mott
Baker N. 168 3d.
Baker Samuel O. 189 Grand
Baldwin Aaron, 214 3d Av.
Balken J. 36 Mercer & 136 Stanton
Ball James R. 229 Bleecker
Ballagh W. & Robert, 1 Chambers
Ballwinckel J. H. 46 Sullivan
Baltzar George, 86 Broome
Bamberger Henry, 126 Ridge
Bamman J. & Co. 211 Duane
Bamman J. 326 6th
Bammann John, 247 Elizabeth & 309 Rivington
Bancroft Willis S. 59 M'Dougal
Baner N. 167 3d
Bannan Owen, 262 W. 17th
Bankin C. 110 William
Bankin S. & Co. 79 John
Barber S. & Co. 79 Water
Barclay Samuel, 103 7th Av.
Barden Ann, 143 W. 15th
Bardon L. 25th st.
Bargar John, 445 Cherry
Barklage John H. 51 Mulberry
Barkley James, 360 3d & 16 Av. C
Barkley John F. 273 8th Av.
Barkley J. cor. 3d & Av. C
Barner C. J. 186 West
Barnwell Moses, 69 W. Broadway
Barr John, 38 Essex
Barrenpohl John, 300 Pearl
Barrett Edward, 247 W. 16th
Barrett John, 22 James
Barstow & Co. 133 Front
Barton James, 68 Bedford
Batterson John, 26th st.
Bauman Francis, 28 Cross
Baumann Henry, 67 Cross
Baurman John G. 170 Essex
Beam & Westervelt, 153 Spring
Bearros & Fisher, 245 W'hington
Beatty W. C. 621 Hudson
Becker Adolph. E. 168 W'hington
Becker John, 562 4th
Becker William, 212 Mulberry
Becker Nicholas, 91 Av. A
Becker & LaStitute, 168 W'hington
Beckermann John A. 1 Pitt
Beckermann Thos. C. 297 11th
Bedford T. 653 Greenwich
Beecher Nelson H. 143 8th Av.
Beeker John, 562 4th
Behan John & Co. 268 Stanton
Behan James, 20 Cherry
Behrman John, 69 Av. B
Behrmann Henry, 218 Wooster
Bell George & Co. 597 South

Bell Joseph M. 50 Hester
New York.
Belknap & Haviland, 252 Washington
Bellmer C. & Co. 386 Hudson
Bemmann John, cor. Av. C & 6th
Bemmer John, 85 Av. C
Bender George. 232 3d
Benedict William, 104 Madison & 22 Roosevelt
Benken Christian, 504 Pearl
Benken Harman, 562½ Pearl
Benken William, 16 Dey
Benman O. 262 W. 17th
Bennett Tunis & Palmer, 17 Grand
Benning J E. 228 Walker
Benson C. S. 217 Bleecker
Benson & Young, 46 Amos
Berne Thomas, 175 11th
Berrian H. P. cor. 27th & 2d Av.
Berrian William D. 9 1st Av.
Berry David, 258 Cherry
Berschman H. 11 Vandewater
Besges J. 443 Cherry
Besson & King, 309 4th
Berry & Palmer, 93 West
Bessan & Bramer, 151 West
Betters John, 212 Cherry
Betjeman C. & Co. 150 3d Av.
Betjeman Henry, 16 Anthony
Betjeman N. 127 W. Broadway
Betjemann C. 64 W.   do
Betjemann Luder & Co. 151 6th Av. & 16 W. 14th
Betteyman W. 137 W. Broadway
Bottyman John, 649 Hudson
Bickerman J. A. 296 Division
Bickman H. 460 Greenwich
Bigley Cornelius, 38 Whitehall
Billings H. S. 163 Greenwich
Bingham L. A. Yorkville
Bininger A. & Co. 141 Broadway
Birdsall Benjamin, 477 Broome
Birdsall Samuel. 299 Spring
Birdsall & Russell, 225 Houston
Bisschoff H. H. 386 Washington
Bittel Jacob. 142 3d
Bitter John W. 29th cor. 8th Av
Blackall Edward, 14 Orange
Blackwood James, 63 8th Av.
Blaire C. 399 Monroe
Blair Edward, 399 do
Blake John, 218 Elizabeth
Blake Patrick, 319 9th
Blake Thomas, 236 Mulberry
Blendermann L. 55 Tompkins
Bloome Henry, 437 Cherry
Bloomer & Fox, 631 Washington
Blomker Henry, 279 Walker
Blume Louis, 126 Laurens
Bockhorn John W. 55 Wooster & 483 Broome
Bode John H. 69 Grand
Bode John L. 40 Beekman
Bodenstab & Miller, 212 Delancy
Bode John, 2 Bayard
Bode John H. 39 Wooster
Bode John L. 40 Beekman
Bogart Andrew, 162 E. Broadway
Bogart Augustus L. 60 Forsyth
Bogart P. L. 162 E. Broadway
Bohan James, 246 Mulberry
Bohde Charles, 18 3d Av.
Bohlam ——, 37 Spring
Bohlken Henrich, 40 Trinity
Bohlen Hermann, 15 Prince
Boken John D. 353 Broome
Bohne J. H. & Co. 453 Greenwich
Bohlen Anthony, 513 Pearl
Bohman D. 814 Washington
Bolon Dedrick, 16 Reade
Bolting F. 366 Washington
Boltmon Henry, 175 8th Av.
Boken John D. 353 Broome
Bonesteel & Wheeler, 32 Bedford
Borchers Carl M. 60 Nassau
Borchers H. & Co. 110 Washington
Borchers S. 65 Anthony
Borchers T. 45 Church
Borger John J. 86 James
Bormann Hermann. 153 Chrystie
Bosch John H. 11 Franklin

Boschen John H. & Co. 321 Rivington & 113 Broome *New York.*
Boschen H. 41st st
Boschert Charles F. 204 Av. B
Boscker H. 26 W. Broadway
Bosing Dedrich, 16 Elm
Bostwick & Masterson, 57 Water
Bouer Anthony, 287 Stanton
Bouers T. & Co. 169 Lewis
Bovers Frederick & E. 708 4th
Bowden Andrew, 89 Hudson
Bowen Francis, 336 Houston
Bowron & Young, 46 Amos
Boyd Andrew C. 19 Washington
Boyd Michael, 7 Orange
Boylan James. 156 W. 16th
Boyle E. I. 106 Essex
Boyle M. 361 4th
Bracher Christopher, 40 Stanton
Brachen Edward, 346 12th
Bradley George, 40 Av. A
Bradley James, 195 Mott
Bradley Michael, 377 8th
Bradley Wm. C. 254 Broome
Brady Charles, 11 Whitehall
Brady James, 597 Grand
Brady John, 199 Madison
Brady John, 425 Grand
Brady Margaret, 36 & 40 Frankfort
Brady Patrick, 134 W. 20th
Brady Patrick S. 399 Grand
Breggemann A. L. 34 Reade
Branson Louis, 26 Troy
Brand Christian, 253 6th Av.
Brand Claus, 262 Rivington
Brand John, 241 Washington
Brautigam John, 477 Canal
Breckevadel J. A. 236 Church
Breaden F. 100 Anthony
Breman George V. 147 Delancy
Brett James T. 62 North Moore
Brewer Ernst, 211 Duane
Bricks Daniel, 96 Sheriff
Brickwedel Chas. 166 W. Broad'y
Brickwedel H. & Co. 121 Washington & 239 William
Brickwedel Martin H. 36 Wooster
Brickwedel John A. 226 Church
Brien E. O. 156 13th
Briggs Isaac V. 18 Hester
Briggs Wm. E. 62 Division
Brinckmann Diedrick, 406 West & 64 Orange
Bris Frederick, 96 Willet
Brissell Ann M. 95 Av. A
Brittan John, 5 Hoboken
Britton David, 217 Greene
Broadhead, Storm & Co. 169 Washington
Brock Robert, 125 Hammond
Brogan Edward, 147 Anthony
Brolay Wm., W. 27th st.
Brommer John, 109 Stanton
Brononsky John, 427 6th Av.
Brons John H. 37 James
Brooks Peter & Co. 116 6th Av.
Brooks Wm. S. 509 Grand
Brophy Mary, 62 Cannon
Brower Gerrit, 77 Av. D
Brower Isaac D. 121 Spring
Brown Geo. & Co. 586 Hudson
Brown Henry, 77 Sullivan & 246 William
Brown J. F. 5 6th Av.
Brown J. H. 306 Greenwich
Brown John, 15 Hester
Brown John J. 38 Anthony
Brown Martin, 46 W. Broadway
Brown Montague G. 290 5th
Brown Peter, 491 Pearl
Brown Richard, 34 Pitt
Brown Samuel, 455 Greenwich
Brown William, 97 Perry
Brown W. A. & Co. 12 James slip
Brown Wm. J. 447 Hudson
Browning Aaron, 52 Perry
Browning A. & Co. 89 4th
Browning Henry. 26 Orange
Browning John F. 89 4th
Bruckmann Caspar & Co. 301 Av. A
Brukas James, 430 Monroe

Brunee Claus, 93 Bedford *New York.*
Brunjes John F. 153 Washington
Brunjes Peter, 251 South
Brunie C. 93 Bedford
Brunis Dedrich, 288 Av. A
Brunjes Deiderick, cor. Av. B & 2d st
Brunjes Hanre, 290 Av. A
Brunjes Hermann H. 322 Grand
Bruns Christian, 34 Grand
Bruns John C. & Henry, 192 Duane
Bruns Wm. D. 166 William
Brush H. J. 152 13th
Brush C. J. 282 Greenwich
Bryan James, 187 3d
Buckman & Smith, 123 Av. C
Budelman Henry, 145 Broome
Budke George, 417 West
Budke Henry, 367 6th Av.
Bueck Augustus & Co. cor. Broadway & 12th
Buffom Solon, 71 Ludlow
Buffum S. & Co. Av. B. cor. 8th
Buhner Joseph, 236 Rivington
Buhsea Diedrick, 23 South
Buhsen N. 41 & 42 West
Bulkley & Lockwood, 110 Wall
Bulling Bennett, 102 Cedar
Bulling J. D. 38 Washington
Bullancamp W. cor. Av. A & 13th
Bullwinckel John H. 46 Sullivan
Bullwinkel Claus, 40 Trinity pl.
Bullwinkel Henry, 328 8th
Bullwinkel M. 187 Varick
Bullwinkle Charles, 93 Av. A
Bultmann Diedrick, 35 Grand
Bunce John W. 117 Monroe
Bungar John H. 141 Duane
Bungers Lewis, 41 Chrystie & 209 Walker
Bunges T. 138 Liberty
Bunker & Co. 187 Broadway
Burdorf Herman, 254 Stanton
Burgher, Hurlbut & Co. 39 Water
Burke Dennis, 97 1st
Burke John, 349 Madison
Burke Mary, 76 Orange
Burke Michael, 48½ Mulberry
Burkehatter S. 2 Church & 191 Fulton
Burnholst L. 299 1st Av.
Burniston Wm. C. 232 12th
Burns John, 306 Greenwich
Burns Michael, 184 Av. A
Burns Peter, 33 Washington
Burns Robert, 234 West 17th
Burns W. D. cor. 20th & 1st Av.
Burroughs John, 1 Thomas
Burton Charles S. 240 Canal
Busch Claus, 282 Greenwich, 1 Jane & 108 Thompson
Busch Peter W. 201 Lewis
Buschman Albert. 814 Washington
Buschmann Deiderich, 771 Wash.
Buseng Frederick, 366 Wash.
Bush Henry J. 152 West 13th
Bushing Clouse D. 596 Water
Bush F. W. & Co. 399 6th
Bush W. K. 197 Greenwich
Bushen D. 23 South
Busing D. 62 Duane
Busing T. 356 Washington
Buske H. P. 904 Front
Bussing F. 366 Washington
Butler Edward, 34 Henry
Butler Harris, 161 11th
Butler James, 23 Madison
Butler R. E. 628 Water
Bullar Sarah, 628 Water
Butt C. & Co. 411 Broome & 62 Elm
Butt George, 84 Roosevelt
Butt John, 118 10th Av.
Buttle H. & Son, 126 Spring
Buttle Stephen S. 196 Spring
Butts Daniel R. 202 Stanton
Buxton Charles C. 330 Bleecker
Byarnes T. 176 1st
Byrne I. L. 19 Washington
Byrne H. 111 Washington
Cahrs Diederick, 19 Bayard
Cairns David, 96 8th Av.

Calhoun John, 241 Water *New York.*
Callaghan Daniel, 264 Canal
Cameron John, 177 Spring
Calvelage B. 53 Cliff & 59 Beekman
Campbell Chs. 3 Centre mkt. pl.
Campbell E. West 26th st.
Campbell John, 57 Elizabeth
Campbell Solomon. 353 Bowery
Campbell Patrick, 43 Orange
Cane Henry, 213 Hester
Cannye Augustus, 34 White
Cappelman Carsten, 67 Hudson
Cappleman Eymer, 766 Green'ich
Carew William H. 19 Bowery
Carey Hugh. 61 Stanton
Carey Lorenzo, 490 Pearl
Carlough H. 703 Washington
Carolus J. T. W. 231 Monroe
Carney Michael, 66 West 22d
Carney Patrick, 222 12th
Carney William & Co. 139 Stanton
Carinan C. & R. Harlem
Carolus William, 231 Monroe
Carpenter C. M. & Co. 469 Pearl
Carpenter H. & W. 93 Houston
Carr Charles, 15 Thames
Carr John, 196 Av. B & 11th st.
Carr Patrick, 390 6th
Carroll W. 402 10th
Carroll Peter, 60 Watts
Carson Joseph, 323 Rivington
Carter George, 267 Stanton
Caruana Stephen B. 59 10th Av
Cary Lorenzo, 490 Pearl
Casey John & Co. 456 12th
Casey M. L. West 28th st.
Casey & Flanagan, 497 Houston
Casey Patrick, 256 Mott
Cash Thomas, 473 6th Av.
Casseboom & Cage, 85 West
Cassedy Margaret, 278 W. 17th
Cassidy Hugh, 62 Willet
Cassidy James, 32 Orange
Cassin Thomas, 59 Orchard
Castree John, 191 Hudson
Caswell J. & Co. 87 Front
Cathmin John & Co. 23 Roosevelt
Cavenagh Dennis, 5 Oak
Cavanagh Edward, 253 Mott
Cavenagh Francis, 24 Mulberry
Cavenagh James, 597 Greenwich
Cavins D. 96 8th Av.
Chambers John, 34 Rutgers
Chambers William, Av. D & 8th st.
Cheesebrough Hallam, 29 Old slip
Christman B. 124 Willet
Clancy Terence, 21 Pell
Clanney James, 106 South
Clanssor John, 110 Church
Clark Ann, 119 Willet
Clark Ebenezer, 622 Water
Clark Henry, 102 Anthony
Clark James, 305 Washington
Clark Thomas, 119 Willet
Clark & Doremus, 74 9th Av.
Claughley Reuben, 329 3d Av.
Clausen Henry, 305 Broome, & 204 Spring
Clausen C. 67 West Broadway
Clausen Henry, 198 Elm & 869 Broome
Claussen H. 111 Forsyth
Claussen John, 160 Church
Claussen Reddi & Co. 8 Front
Claussen & Witle, 137 Liberty
Classon H. 119 West Broadway
Clats John, 232 Delancy
Clousen Henry, 119 W. Broadway
Clousen Clous, 67 W. Broadway
Clute John, 99 Chrystie
Cobb Ebenezer H. 430 Broadway
Cocks Samuel, 18 Grove
Cooks John D. 192 South
Coddington Charles, 111 South
Coffay J. 158 Maiden lane
Cogan Philip, 342 6th
Colehan Ann, 94 Mott
Collins Charles, 5 Cherry
Collins Joseph, 46 Trinity
Collins Michael, 217 Church

Collins Michael, 222 Church
New York.
Collins Margaret, 3 Cherry
Colony & Ingalls, 89½ Canal
Cole Dor, 49 Greenwich
Colton Clinton, 2 Washington sq.
Conway James, 206 West
Convoy Thomas, 89 Mulberry
Condon Michael T. 241 Centre
Conelly Mary, 79 Mulberry
Conklin George Y. 71 Essex
Conlan Matthew, 61 Cross
Conoughty Hugh, 476 Cherry
Conroy Michael, 34 Frankfort
Conroy Owen, 208 Varick
Conway James, 206 West
Conway John, 45 Henry
Conway M., W. 28th st.
Cook —— 360 Houston
Cook Frederick, 241 Greenwich
Cook D. 231 1st Av.
Cook D. 361 12th
Cook G. 81 Av. C
Cook Henry & Co. 651 Hudson
Cook James H. 100 Broome
Cook Martin, 58 Oliver
Cook John, 765 Broadway
Cook John F. 75 5th Av.
Cook & Knomer, 49 Av. C
Cook William E. 672 & 674 Houston
Conner O., W. 28th st.
Cook & Fink, 221 1st Av.
Coop Froderick, 269 Rivington
Coop & Kirmer, 622 4th
Cooper D. R. 563 Washington
Cooper J. L. & Co. 16 Dey
Cooper Thomas T. 90 Grand
Copperman C. 67 Hudson
Cordes Carsten, 154 William
Cordis C. 264 13th
Cordts Henry I. 16 Orange
Cordts J. H. & Co. 334 6th
Cordtsholm & Co. 131 White
Coreau T. 92 Ridge
Corley Chas. G. 301 Greenwich
Corr Patrick, 230 8th
Corregan, Morton & Co. 236 13th
Corse C. 34 4th
Corse Henry, 718 Washington
Corven Philip J. 50 Elm
Corwin Oliver & Co. 208 Front
Corwin Wm. S. 639 Broadway
Corwin & Morgan, 257 Washington
Costelloe James, 122 E. 20th
Coth Henry H. 179 Delancy
Cotter Patrick, 247½ Division
Coudon M. T. 241 Centre
Coughlin Maurice, 6 Marion
Coughlin Richard, 73 Cherry
Coutant Peter, 16 3d Av.
Cox T. J. & E. cor. 29th & 4th Av.
Cox James, 60 Henry
Craavy Julia, 109 Av. C
Crick George, 194 Av. D
Cramer P. Fisher, 47 Vandam
Cramsey James, 111 Varick
Crane Charles, 734 Washington
Cratzenburg S. 94 Amity
Craven Christopher, 48 Mott
Crawford Joseph, 209 Henry
Crea Christopher, 24 Roosevelt & 46 Mott
Crean Patrick, 96 Broome
Creed James, 51 Anthony
Crilley John, 235 11th
Crockeron N. 8 West
Crosby Charles, 77½ Orange
Crowe Charles, 7 Pearl
Crowe Patrick, 48 Frankfort
Crown Anthony, 150 Anthony
Crum Henry, 172 Varick
Crumbeck John L. 304 Water
Crussman Hermana, 355 Grand
Culse Christopher, 47 Troy
Cummings James, 250 2d
Cummings Jeremiah, 446 Cherry
Cummins John, 43 Spring
Cunningham James, jr. 91 4th Av.
Cunningham John, 66 Broome
Cunningham Thomas, 217 Delancy

Curdts Carsten, 264 E. 12th
New York.
Curdts John H. 183 Lewis
Curtane David, 8 Mulberry
Curtis Robert, 29 Whitehall
Curtiss Charles, 67 Av. D
Dahl Herman, 263 E. 21st
Daly Maurice, 391 3d Av.
Daly Patrick, 37 Cross
Daniels James C. 34 Moore
Dannerman John. 208 Grand
Darcy James, 60 Pitt
Daser Henry, 49 Greenwich
Dasdome Mary, 278 Water
Davenport & Newton, 155 Av. C
Devine Martin, 56 Crosby
Dayton William, 16 King
Deckart Anthony, 44 Broome
Deckelmann J. Av. A cor. E. 17th
Deckelmann Wm. 169 3d
Decker Henry, 67 Av. C
Decker Henry, 8 Marion
Decker Henry, 170 Amos
Decker Henry, 86 Bleecker
Decker I. C. cor. 2d Av. & 26th st.
Decker J. H. 7th Av. cor. W. 20th
Decker J. H. 33 W. Broadway
Decker John F. 9 Pell
Decker Reimelt, 658 Houston
Deeds & Linneman. 194 Walker
Deffea Philip, 233 3d
Degrauw Walter N. 1 Fulton mkt.
Deich Hormann, 22 Orange
Deickman Henry, cor. Greenwich & Canal
De Languillette E. H. 85 Delancy
Delano Christopher, 56 Charlton
Demaray David, 150 West
Deming & Tufts, 67 3d Av.
Demott Henry, 471 Houston
Dempsey Dennis, 36 Scammel
Denney Wm. H. 118 Av. C
Dermott John, 490 Greenwich
Descha John, 53 Anthony
Dessoye Geo. & Co. 15 Anthony
Deuzer Valtine, 570 4th
Devhor H. 51 West
Deverman John H. 249 Stanton
Devine Martin, 56 Crosby
Devine James, 62 Roosevelt
Deyo A. 272 Houston
Dick D. H. cor. 6th Av. & 12th st.
Dick James, 171 6th Av.
Dick John, 268 Water
Dick Wm. 36 Reade
Diederich John, 35 Marion
Diekman Jerry, 667 Water
Dierck John F. 455 Pearl
Diersen Hermann, 216 3d Av.
Diericks F. F. 537 Pearl
Dieck J. W. 268 Water
Dikman J. 196 Broome
Dikeman Henry, 162 Elm
Dines George, 51 Ludlow
Doencher Henry, 8 Dowaing
Dogherty Patrick, 70 Cherry
Doam Jacob, 45 Orange
Dohrman John, 22 Old slip
Dohrman Augustus F. 76 Bayard
Dohrman Henry, 91 Greenwich
Dohrman Henry & Co. 112 Centre
Dohrmann H. & Co. 96 Cherry
Dolbeer Stephen, 47 Bayard
Donahoo James, 79 Mott
Donegan Daniel, 328 8th
Donely A. 44 Laurens
Donlin Michael, 84 Hamersley
Donnelly Edward L. 143 Broome
Donnell J. O. 38 Laurens
Donovan Henry, 337 3d Av.
Donovan James, 57 Montgomery
Donzeeman John F. 23 Dey
Doolan Edward, 96 Suffolk
Dooley John, 221½ Elizabeth
Dopman J. 194 Greenwich Av.
Dorcher Carsten, 235 Water
Doremus Henry S. 186 W. 19
Doren ——, 105 Hester
Dorgan John, 7 Columbia
Dorscher & Borschers, 147 Church & 37 Anthony
Dorset Joseph I. 605½ Water

Doscher Fred. & Co. 211 Sullivan
New York.
Doscher T. cor. Av. C & 12th
Doscher Carstein, 395 Water
Doscher Chas. H. 216 5th
Doscher Claus, 139 Monroe & 22 Rutgers
Doscher F. & Co. 226 2d
Doscher Henry, 49 Greenwich
Doscher H. & Co. 62 Forsyth
Doscher John, 206 Elm
Doscher Marten, 592 Grand
Doscher Martin, 245 W. 17th
Doscher Reinhold. 82 Reade
Dosher Fabeau, 236 2d
Dost Albert, 61 Nassau
Dougherty John, 6 Jacob
Douglass Patrick. 75 Willett
Doussher John, 11 Howard
Dowd James, 188 Laurens
Dowdall Thos. 148 W. 17th
Dowd Richard. W. 28th st.
Dowling Patrick. 189 Av. C
Downey Michael. 111 Mulberry
Dreseng Henry, 290 Grand
Dreyer E. & Co. 109 6th Av.
Driggs Chester, 681 Broadway
Drippe G. H. & Co. 189 Cherry
Driver John, 114 Lewis
Drodge Wm. 53 Av. B
Droge Claus & Co. 204 William
Droge Henry, 95 Christopher
Drogo John, 196 Division
Droge John, 3 Cortlandt
Droge Wm. 575 4th
Drummond John J. 40 Greenwich
Du Bois Eben S. 13 Greenwich Av.
Drucker Henry, 213 Delancy & 9 Pell
Ducker Melchior, 596 Houston
Ducker J. 34 Ann & 105 Nassau
Duffy James, 18 Hester
Dulishanty John, 395 West
Dulsco Martin, 720 Washington
Ducan John & Son, 407 Broadway
Dunn Henry, 50 1st Av.
Dunn John, 97 18th
Dunn Michael, 269 6th Av.
Dunner John & Co. 23 4th
Dunn Robert, 67 Lexington Av.
Duschar Fred. cor. 12th & Av. C
Dusenberry Chas. 33 Christopher
Dyer Peter, 29 Pitt
Dykes Francis, 286 Hudson
Eadie James, 556 Greenwich
Eagats Fred. 388 Cherry
Ealert Christian, 26 Howard
Early Mrs. 31 Vesey
Eate John. 64 Greenwich Av.
Ebbets Richard, 270 Spring
Ebbitt Humphrey, 61 Watts
Eckart Chas. 23 Pitt
Eckers Louis, 83 Duane
Eckhoff Fred. 110 Church
Eden Henry, 269 8th Av.
Eden John, 185 W. 20th
Eden John, 196 6th Av.
Edgar B. W. & F. 24th st
Edgar James, 389 Bowery
Edgar James M. 100 9th Av.
Egan John, 535 Washington
Egan Patrick, 95 Washington
Egbers John G. & Co. 140 4th
Egbers John G. 817 Broadway
Eggers Lewis, 470 Water
Eggers Luhr, 550 Hudson
Eggers Lewis, 83 Duane
Ehni John A. 164 2d
Ehrichs John, 6 Washington
Ehrichs John H. 52 Centre
Ehrichs John, 33 Washington
Ehrichs & Co. 469 Broome
Ehrings John, 8 Franklin
Eickhoff F. 100 Church
Eicks & Miller, 686 Washington
Eilert Christopher, 1 Crosby
Elmers Frederick, 220 Water
Edicker John, 32 Attorney
Einsel Valentine, 22 Laurens
Elfers Henry, 79 W. 18th
Ellenwood William, 111 Orange
Ellers John H. 65 Av. C.

Elliott Robert, 698 4th *New York*
Ellimers T. & Co. 288 Madison
Ellis Herman. 45 Mott
Ellis John, 360 Cherry
Ellmers Fredk. & Co 280 Madison
Elsey James, 257 Bowery
Ely & Shafton, cor. Forsyth & Broome
Emens Isaac. 466 Hudson
Emmer J. 389 5th Av.
Engeman Bernard. 99 Broome
Engle Carsten, 249 Bleecker
Entamin Frederick, 92 Av. D.
Epstien Henry, 52 Carmine
Eslman Alex. 616 Washington
Ergatt Jacob, 282 2d
Erich John, 410 10th
Erich J. H. & Co. 512 Pearl
Evans David, 28 Sullivan
Evans Hugh. 310 Stanton
Evans William, 98 Carlton
Evans William & Co. 278 Water
Evarts & Hays. 221 E. Broadway
Everett & Birdsall, 255 Houston
Evers John. 71 4th st.
Eversley Christian, 25 Horatio
Eversly Charles, 115 Rivington
Fadden C. & Co. 36 & 84 Henry
Fangmeyer Henry, 93 Varick
Parally Edw. 299 Washington
Farral P. 100 11th
Farrell Christopher, 23 Oak
Farren Matthew, 112 10th Av.
Faulkner Jacob, 249 Henry
Fealy M. E. 24th st
Fearon Hamilton, 53 Mulberry
Fecken John, 260 Mott
Fedden Christopher, 84 Henry
Fedden C. & Co. 36 Henry
Fegebank Henry, 56 Irving pl.
Feeks Abijah S. 280 Walker
Feeks Stephen H. 166 Delancy
Feis F. 34 Madison & 43 James
Feiss Henry, Walnut cor. Water
Feiss H. 690 Water
Feis John, 64 Walnut
Felsh Charles, 60 South'
Feldhusen Harman, 56 M'Dougal
Feldmann Harman H. 3 Cortlandt
Fether H. D. 596 Broadway
Fenker Henry, 9 Jacob
Fennemann Jacob, 42 Monroe & 49 Hamilton
Fennimann John, 24 Barclay
Ferddermann Wm.W. 130 Wooster
Ferguson James, 121 19th
Ferns Hamilton. 53 Mulberry
Ficker M. 247 Bowery
Ficker L. 108 Clinton
Fiel John, 94 Mulberry
Field & Jan s, 160 Cherry
Fiold Rodman E. 86 3d Av.
Fiecke Henry, 76 Hamersley
Ficken Martin. 247 Bowery
Fikin Lewis, 108 Clinton
Finagan Catharine, 356 Broome
Finan Michael, 61 Orange
Finck Christopher. 24 Jacob
Finck Conrad, 151 Broadway
Finck Jacob, 161 4th, 13 Jersey & 276 Mulberry
Finck Jacob, 176 2d
Finck Otto, 187 Wm. & 21 Spruce
Finck Peter, 21 Sullivan
Finck P. & Co. 7 Desbrosses
Fincken Louis, 254 Front
Finity M. 83 Washington
Fink D. 312 3d Av.
Fink Diederick, 364 Hudson
Fink George, 17 Elm
Fink Jacob, 101 4th
Fink Jacob, 176 2d
Fink Jacob & Co. 147 7th
Fink Lewis, 536 Pearl & 254 Front
Fiak Martin, 261 Spring
Fink O. 157 William
Fink & Cook, 163 Av. B.
Finnegan F. West 29th st.
Finlgan C. 356 Broome
Finigen F. 67 Ridge
Finnigan Patrick, 57 Ridge
Firgin Henry, 46 Orange

Fisher Elijah, 195 Greene *New York.*
Fisher John, 570 Greenwich
Fisher John D. & Co. 63 Bedford
Fisher Richard, 213 Bowery
Fisteng Harmon, 177 Elm
Fitschen John H. 14 Mercer
Fitzgerald James, 175 Av. B
Fitzgerald Thomas, 45 Frankfort
Fitzpatrick N. 24 Roosevelt
Fitzpatrick Peter, 20 Rivington
Fitzpatrick William, 74 Spring
Fitzsimmons William, 380 Wash.
Flaacke Henry, 299 West 19th & 145 Cedar
Flaacke Henry, 150 Washington
Flaacke John F. 148 Washington
Flanagan James, West 21st cor. 9th Av.
Flanagan M. cor. 6th & Lewis
Flaten & Co. 565 Houston
Fletcher Robert, 415 Cherry
Flink Jacob, 257 3d Av.
Flood James, 346 6th
Flood M. 195 Varick
Floyd William. 4 Goerok
Flynn M. West 26th st.
Flynn Thomas, 65 Mott
Fogal George, 240 West 16th
Foggin & Utter, 94 Av. D.
Foley Patrick, 732 Washington
Follinar Claus, 7th Av. cor W. 30th
Foost A. 146 Greenwich
Foote Edward Y. 104 South
Ford Dennis, 506 Greenwich
Ford Henry & Co. 160 Broome
Forhan M. 59 Greenwich
Foster Wm. R. 174 Division
Fort Henry, 290 Broome
Fowler Eliza, 53 Delancy
Fowler J. O. 260 Greenwich
Fowler & Kniffen, 428 Greenwich
Fowler & Odell, 589 Grand
Foy Edward, 61 Orange
Francke William, 104 Cedar
Fraser John F. 176 W. 17th
Frazer Robert, 287 do
Freese Harman, 11 Duane
Freese J. 13 W. Broadway
Freudenburg Charles, 136 Church
Freudenthal C. 2 Thomas
Freudenthal G. 136 W. Broadway
Freudenthal John D. 39 Green'h
Frericks Henry, 96 Broad
Frese John H. 112 Reade
Frieke W. D. cor. 24th & 2d Av.
Frost Charles H. 45 Norfolk
Frymuth Wm. H. 101 W. 17th
Furlong M. 399 6th
Gafney Bernard, 284 1st Av. & 25 Prince
Gafney M. 294 1st Av. cor. 12th
Gafney Mrs. Ann. 194 Houston
Gafney Owen, 194 Houston
Gale Daniel, 190 1st & 341 Houston
Gallagher Michael, 343 6th Av.
Gellier Wm. 19th bet. Avs. A & B
Gellen Edward, 49 Elizabeth
Gandy —— 222 Mulberry
Gandy & Wells, 456 West
Ganoug & Smith, 9th Av.
Garding H. 2.Forsyth
Garger John B. 92 Varick
Garms Christopher, 21 Mott
Garms Claus, 156 Houston
Garms Peter, 2 Clarkson
Garnsey John C. 396 10th
Garrison E. M. 719 Washington
Garrison A. & C. 147 Allen
Gartelmann John, 66 Bedford
Garvey W. M. 43 Cherry
Gasper Brothers, 62 Water
Gassner & Young, 182 Chatham
Gatz F. A. 383 Cherry
Gaynor Hugh, 387 Hudson
Gaynor John, 654 Grand
Gedney W. T. & G. W. 121 Canal & 174 W. Broadway
Geerken John, 274 Water
Geery Wm. 196 3d Av.
Geery I. & W. 142 Walker & 719 Broadway

Geiger Martin, 160 Hester *New York.*
George Theodore, 195 Delancy
Geraghty Patrick, 600 Pearl
Gerdem L. 125 1st
Gerding Henry, 84 Division
Gerhold Martin. 306 Greenwich
Gerken H. 410 3d Av.
Gerken George, 200 Stanton
Gerken Henry, 305 Grand
Gerken Herman, 113 Mercer
Gerken Herman, 109 Prince
Gerken John, 23 Av. A
Gibbous John, 112 12th
Gibney P. 266 13th
Gielger A. 531 6th Av.
Giesker Frederick, 110 Reade
Giesson George C. 77 Bowery
Gilchrest John W. 402 Broome
Gilchrest John, 230 Mulberry
Gilmartin Daniel, 489 Pearl
Gillespie C. 39th st.
Gilling Frederick, 193 Barrow
Gillin Anthony, 93 Mulberry
Gillis Isaac, 61 Delancy
Gillis Samuel, 44 Houston
Girhardt Balthasar, 113 Delancy
Glander Henry, 125 Columbia
Ghlan C. Vohn, 36 4th
Glander Henry A. corner Av. A & 7th
Gleeson James, 115 Orange
Gleeson Wilson, 55 Mulberry
Glensman H. 26 Forsyth
Glimm Christian. 16 Hamersley
Glimm John H. 131 Washington
Glinsman Henry, 220 Walker
Goeheln Anthony, 74 Chrystie
Goetz J. 250 5th
Gohde, Coad & Frederick & Co. 217 Division
Goold A. A. 187 Bowery
Goodwin & Marriott, 101 Madison
Gorger John B. 93 Varick
Gorman Ann, 256 Mulberry
Gorman J. 283 W. 16th
Gorman Timothy, 107 Cherry
Gotebead J. 47 Carmine
Gotmiller C. 2 Elm
Gottyen F. 380 Washington
Grady O. Yorkville
Graf John, 215 3d
Grafelman Martin, 56 Sheriff
Grafelman Thomas, 148 Lewis
Graham Duncan, 190 Washington
Graham James, 234 W. 16th
Graham Joseph, 53 Mulberry
Graham Margaret, 61 7th
Graham Robert, 499 6th Av.
Green Charles E. 71 Houston
Green Geo. W. & Co. 4 3d Av.
Green Jeremiah, 620 4th cor. 7th
Green John, 32 Gouverneur
Green John, 76 Nassau
Green J. B. 37 Pike
Green William F. 145 Madison
Greenwood H. B. Broadway cor. Broome
Gregory Francis, 316 Monroe
Grier Andrew, 30 Bleecker
Grieve John, 76 Nassau
Griffin John L. 191 Division
Griffith Richard, 262 W. 17th
Griffiths Hugh, 77 Av. C.
Grogan Lawrence, 148 Leonard
Groex William, 160 Walker
Groteclose John, 45 King
Groth Henry, 246 Walker
Grotheer Harman, 266 Delancy
Grothy John, 42 Stanton
Grupe Carston, 228 Greenwich
Guiger —— Yorkville
Gullok John, 73 King
Gustin G. W. & Co. 243 Wash.
Haaseman Benjamin, 67 Mott
Habener Frederick, 236 Stanton
Hack William, 26 Clarke
Haoken Carsten, 93 John
Haddon John, 148 3d Av.
Hadwick John, 210 South
Hagan Thomas J. 347 3d Av.
Hagemeyer Frederick W. 7 Mosse

Hahn Christopher, 241 West 17th New York.
Hahn Frederick, 6th Av. c. 4th st.
Hahn Geo. R. 6 Downing
Haha Henry, 182 Spring
Hahn Henry, 41 Mulberry
Hahn John H. 40 W. 13th
Hahne H. 255 Stanton & 40 E. 13th
Haight H. & J. 171 2d
Haines John, 292 Madison
Hall Henry & Co. 84 Elm
Hall George & Co. 31 John
Hallet A. F. 504½ Grand
Hallett Samuel J. 312½ Grand and 424 Hudson
Halliday John, 63 Greenwich Av.
Halmke B. 141 Greenwich
Haipaus F. 1st Av. & 24th st.
Halsey L. T. 14 Dey
Halst John, 100 Cherry
Halstead John, 20 Carmine
Hamann J. H. 400 2d Av.
Hamilla John, 669 4th
Hamilton J. H. 230 18th
Hamilton Joseph F. 62 Roosevelt
Hamilton Robert, 74 W. 19th
Hamilton Robert H. 202 West
Hammond J. H. 21st st. c. 1st Av.
Hancon G. 96 John
Hanas H. & Co. 246 3d Av.
Hand George, 480 Houston
Handley William, 104 Cliff
Hisfeld Christian, 64 Grand
Henken Carson, 83 W. Broadway
Hankins Dedrick, 252 3d
Hanley William, 104 Cliff
Hanmer & Horton, 64 Division
Hanratty John, 264 7th
Happel Balthaser, 583 4th
Hardman John, 123 Willet
Hardtwigg W. E. 209½ Division
Harges Albert, 224 Broome
Harkins Bartholomew, 110 W.17th
Harms Alexander, 136 Forsyth & 12 Spring
Harms Henry, 218 Centre and Anthony cor. Centre, 168½ Stanton, 81 W. Broadway, and Varick cor. Franklin
Harneit Frederick, 197 Mulberry
Harnett John, 15 City Hall place
Harpen ———. 6 South
Harris James, 197 Washington
Harris & Moore, 29th st.
Harles A. 326 Broome
Harrison John, 922 Mott
Harmann Adam, 102 W. 20th
Hartman J. 123 Willet
Hart John, 216 11th
Hart Thomas S. 15 Elm
Hasbrook Benjamin, 560 Broome
Hasencamp & Co. 317 Greenwich
Hasenbalg Charles, 37 Thompson
Hashagen John C. 535 Greenwich
Hashagen John C. 186 Prince
Hashagen John C. 4 6th Av.
Hashmag an H. 508 Houston
Haslett William H. 183 13th
Hassenbrook H. 74 Av. B.
Hasselbrock C. 74 Av. B.
Hatfield Jesse, 31 Norfolk
Haughwout Simon, 66 Av. D.
Havens H. P. & Son, 434 Water
Haviland S. & Son, 139 Division
Hawkins Charles F. 46 Rivington
Hawks Ianess, 92 Oliver
Hawxhurst Charles, 106 Hammond
Haydock W. H. 191 Division
Hayne John, 278 Madison
Hays S. 76 Henry
Healey Edward, 159 Bowery
Healy Michael, 364 1st Av.
Healy Michael, 2 James
Healy Patrick, 83 Forsyth
Healy Richard, 173 Forsyth
Hearney John, 6 Goerck
Hecker John, 921 Broadway
Hecket John, 16 Marion
Hessemann J. H. & B. 47 Broome
Heins Claus, 17 Bayard
Hein Frederick W. 656 Water
Hein Philip, 16 5th

Hein E. & Co. 77 6th Av. New York.
Hein T. W. & Co. 656 Water
Heise Ephraim, 76 3d
Heinsman Henry, 267 William
Helmke John H. 291 Centre
Heinrichs Augustus, 179 Houston
Heins Claus, 139 Fulton
Heinsohn J. C. & Co. 38 2d
Heinsohn C. H. Walnut c. Cherry
Heisohn Carsten H. 442 Cherry
Heiss T. 332 Water
Helmke Behrend, 141 Greenwich
Helmke Henry, 197 Washington
Helmke John, 13 Clark
Hemingway Jacob M. 92 Ridge
Heneken Henry, Water c. Moore
Henken & Co. 83 W. Broadway
Henken Allrick, 10 Howard, 283 Water & 10 Dover
Henley Thomas, 61 4th Av.
Henry Nicholas, 551 4th
Henry Samuel, 117 South
Herbert John, 102 Pitt
Herman'A. 164 20th
Hermann H. 128 Av. C
Hermann F. & Co. 409 Broome
Herring Silas C. 742 Greenwich
Hesslein J. 290 E. 25th
Hesse Bernard, 13 Orange
Hessen John C. 167 7th
Heyn F. 36 6th Av.
Hicks Harris, 161 11th
Higbie ———, 180 1st Av.
Higgins L. & J. 48 6th Av.
Hihan Henry. 41 Mulberry
Hillebrandt Claus, 143 Fulton
Hilman John F. 347 Greenwich
Hilmcke C. 23 Bedford
Hilpert Peter, 639 Greenwich
Hilton John, 187 Division
Hinck Areud, 28 Duane
Hinck Peter W. 14 Church
Hines E. 19th Av. c. 31st
Hingston Edward, 107 Bayard
Hinnaus, H. Av. B c. 31st
Hinnou P. 92 Broad
Hinou John H. 195 Av. B
Hins Charles, 17 Bayard
Hinsch Gustava A. 207 3d
Hipper ———, 86 3d Av.
Hobby Joseph H. 155 South
Hoe K. 699 Washington
Hoest J. & T. & Co. 121 Roosevelt
Hoest John & Co. 106 Av. D
Hoest Peter, 121 Roosevelt & 151 South
Hoeilmein John, 237 11th
Hoff Peter C. 263 Delancy
Hoffman Chas. F. 355 4th Av.
Hoffman Nicholas, 530 Grand
Hoffman, Bailey & Co. 62 Water
Hogen Michael, 360 9th
Hogan Patrick, 37 Vesey
Hogan Patrick, 12½ Washington
Hogans William, 66 Walnut
Hohman Lewis, 27 Av. A
Hohn John G. 82 Orange
Holdga H. 97 Gold
Holers Christopher C. 10 Stone
Holland Marcus, 231 Warren
Hollig John, 159 Greenwich
Hollings John, 783 Washington
Hollings John F. C. 290 West
Hollings Martin, 97 W. Broadway
Holling John, 161 Greenwich
Hollmann H. & Co. 36th st.
Hollmann G. 237 11th
Hollmann H. & Co. 512 Pearl
Hollsberg H. C. & Co. 94 Pearl
Holsberg John H. 47 Laight
Holst John H. 84 Oliver
Holstein Henry, 165 Stanton
Holstein F. & Co. 55 4th
Holstein John H. 131 Delancy
Holsten Frederick, 37 4th
Holsten Hermen, 64 Houston
Holston John & Co. 215 Rivington
Holt Daniel, 40 Market
Holtje Hermann, 66 Exchange pl.
Holton Gustavus, 699 Greenwich
Holsderber John, 123 W. 18th

Hope Thomas & Co. 123 Chambers New York.
Hope A. S. & Co. 139 Greenwich
Hopke Eide F. 96 Cedar
Hopkins & Ward, 215 West
Hoppel Benjamin, 583 4th
Hoppen Daniel & Co. 23 Charles
Horsbery Carsten, 34 Whitehall
Horsman John, 77 Sullivan
Hotchkiss Fenner & Co. 81 Water
Hotten Henry, 106 7th Av.
Howe John, 130 Ludlow
Howe Thomas, 260 11th
Howe Wm. 35 Columbia
Howell B. H. 227 Front
Howenstine Wm. B. 442 Greenwich
Hoy Thomas, 23 Mulberry
Hoyt Walter, 242 2d
Hubbs ———, 86 Clinton
Hubener F. 7th Av. c. 2d
Huchting Carson, 397 Washington
Hucker Jacob, 37 Delancy
Hughes John, 396 Av. A.
Hulle Jno. D. & Co. 8th Av. c. 20th
Halle John L. 398 West
Hullings J. 783 Washington
Hulsberg Henry, 93 Oliver
Hulsberg F. 177 Church
Hulseberg Hen. & Co. 378 Water
Hulsekemper Ariel, 163 Rivington
Halsekemper Wm. 25 Crosby
Huner John, 103 Stanton & 242 Division
Huner F. & Co. 243 Division
Hunen & Eggins, W. 21st c. 7th Av.
Hunt John E. 177 Henry
Hunt Henry, E. 23d c. 2d Av.
Hunt Nehemiah, Amity cor. Sullivan
Hunt & Heron, 751 Greenwich
Hunt & Smith, 198 South
Hunter J. 409 Greenwich
Hunter Jacob, 264 3d Av.
Hunter George J. 292 Water
Hurson Myles, 109 7th Av.
Husemeyer Henry, 34 Jay
Hustace Elijah, 204 South
Hutchings John, 148 Delancy
Hutchings John, 35 Forsyth
Hynes Peter, 16 Prince
Immen John, 190 Stanton
Immen Lewis, 89 Bedford
Inbusch Brothers, 112 Greenwich
Inteman F. 92 Av. D
Iooat Henry, 133 Greenwich
Irvine George, 296 Washington
Irwin Hugh, 310 Stanton
Irwin Robert, 239 do
Jackson William H. 357 6th Av.
Jacobs Henry, 91 Stanton
Jagels J. 63 Canal & 235 Church
Jager Hermann, 517 Water & 297 Cherry
Jenkins John J. 64 Spring
Jewel Aaron C. 332 West
Johnson John, 192 Cherry
Johnson Samuel S. 136 Forsyth
Johnson William, 77 Orchard
Johnson William. 162 6th Av.
Jones Lawson, 13 Marion
Jones Thomas, 194 Greene
Jones W. W. 171 Front
Jones & Co. 246 Delancy
Jonns Dedrick, Av. A cor. 13th
Joost A. 145 G'nwich & 61 Nassau
Joost H. 131 Greenwich
Joost Tonjes. 343 Monroe
Jordon Charles, 125 1st & 315 Houston
Jouy Louis, 52 Reade
Judge John, W. 29th st.
Juhring John C. 269 6th Av.
Jurgens C. 58 Anthony
Jurgens Henry, 144 Sullivan & 69 Greenwich
Jurgens Nicholas & Co. 84 King
Jurgins John R. 176 Hester
Kackisen John, 45 Av. A
Kahler H. & Co. 40th st.
Kahrs T. & H. 393 3d Av.

Kaht C. 15 Thames   *New York.*
Kalveriage Bernard, 69 Beekman & 53 Cliff
Kane Henry, 215 Hester
Kanenbley A. & Co. 374 Monroe
Kannebly E., W. 10th st.
Karr Anthony, 73 Mott
Karr & Mount, 397 Broome
Karsh M. 153 Broome
Karst G. H. 18 Elm
Karstens G. H. 61 Duane
Karts Joseph, 90 Willet
Kassen H. 393 4th
Kossenbrock Henry, 99 Cherry
Kassinbrock John H. 87 Oliver
Kastens G. A. 40 Washington
Kattenhorn George, 231 Rivington
Kattenhorn Herman, 16 2d Av.
Kattenhorn John, 129 Reade
Kattenstroth Henry, 110 Fulton
Kaufman Jacob, 101 Pitt
Kavanagh John, 359 12th
Kealey John, 185 E. 17th
Kean John, 651 Greenwich
Kean Patrick, 93 11th
Keating Henry, 504 Greenwich
Keating John D. 21 Peck slip
Keating Thomas, 229 Stanton
Keefe D. O. 485 Washington
Keegan Daniel, 91¼ Orange
Keeler Samuel, 74 Horatio
Keeler T. 323 Greenwich
Keeler M. C. 310 9th
Kegley David, 442 Greenwich
Kehoe Matthew, 701 Washington
Keilty James, 454 Washington
Keiners Robert, 42 Clinton
Keller Henry, 310 9th
Keller John N. & Co. 150 9th
Kellers John F. 172 4th
Kellstadt John M. 81 Pitt
Kelley James, 90 19th
Kelley Michael, 195 Av. A.
Kelly Anthony, 27 Roosevelt
Kelly John, 101 Thompson
Kelly J., W. 27th st.
Kelly Mary, 33 Frankfort
Kelly Mary, 82 Oliver
Kelly Michael, 423 3d Av.
Kelly Michael, 497 Houston
Kelly Michael, 349 Water
Kelly Thomas, 241 Mulberry
Kelly Jane, 228 E. 13th
Kelly William, 195 Mulberry
Kelly Wm. 12th bet. Avs. A & B
Kelly & Meeks, 344 3d Av.
Kemp A. 116 Wall
Kemp Peter, 342 Houston
Kempers Huls, 123 Grand
Kennabley Henry, 319 Stanton
Kennably Harman. 344 Madison
Kenyon Samuel B., Harlem
Kennaday Daniel, 356 4th Av.
Kenny Owen, 37th st.
Keough Edward, 21 Monroe
Kerly Philip, 300 1st Av.
Kerley Bernard, 300 1st Av.
Kern Mary, 265 Bowery
Kernan E. 629 4th
Kerr Henry A. 746 Broadway
Kerrigan James, 112 Mott
Kerting H. 504 Greenwich
Kervan Elizabeth, 629 4th
Kester George, 86 Av. B
Kester G. & H. 532 Broome
Ketcham Abel, 94 Hester
Kielly Michael, 9 Greenwich Av.
Kerry Rufus & Co. cor. Chamber & Washington
Kenney A. cor. 1st Av. & 26th
Kenney Patrick, 99 Church
King Augustus, 193   do
King John, 643 Washington
King S. & Co. 147 Charles
Kinm H. A., Harlem
Kirby John, 543 Washington
Kirtland A. 205 South
Klemen Henry, 265 Bleecker
Kleuck Christo F. 269 Madison
Klanck Martin W. 365 Monroe
Klim Deiderick, 104 Stanton
Klikner Henry, 90 Reade & 3 Mott

Klomburg Henry, 16 Hammond   *New York.*
Klomburgh John H. 31st st.
Kloppenburg H. 760 Greenwich
Knspheide Henry, 231 W. 21st
Knapp Reuben & Co. 641 Houston
Knapp J. & Son, 101 West
Knebel Henry, 460 4th
Knibel Henry, 139 Reade
Knolton D. 63 2d Av.
Knostman William, 26 Ann
Knowlton Dyer, 52 2d Av.
Knox Andrew, 12th cor. 7th Av.
Knubell Diederich, 10 Carmine
Knubel Herman, 122 6th Av.
Kiernan John, 53 Allen
Killeg Patrick, 213 W. 16th
Kinley John, 244 Cherry
King James W. 309 4th
King John, 59 W. Broadway
King William, 106 Mulberry
Kinney Owen, 122 Anthony
Kipp William, 57 Stanton
Kirby John F. 543 Washington
Klinker Henry, 8 Mott
Kirch Michael, 151 Broome
Klopenburg H. 760 Greenwich
Knoetmann William, 26 Ann
Knapp R. & Co. 641 Houston
Koade Lodewig, 40 Mott
Kobbe Benjamin, 213 Wooster
Kohler Otto, 227 Broome
Kohne C. 187 Mott
Kock L. E. 36 Houston
Koche L. E. 105 Henry
Koppenburg H. 109 Hammond
Kolb Henry, 55 6th Av.
Kolb Jacob F. 13 Hammond
Kooner E. C. & Co. 49 W. Br'dway
Koop C. & H. 18 6th Av.
Korf H. 69 Oliver
Korff John D. 248 Greenwich
Kornahrens J. 219 Spring
Kornahrens Henry & Co. W. 31st cor. 7th Av.
Kornahrens Hermans, 272 Grand
Korner E. C. 49 W. Broadway
Koster Henry, 330 3d
Kothe Henry, 56 6th Av.
Krack George R. 101 Av. C
Krack Henning D. 77 Prince
Krack A. T. & C. H. Cordes, cor. Av. D & 9th st.
Kreuter John H. 96 Rivington
Kriete Geo. H. 25 Stanton
Krey John & Co. 79 Mercer
Kröger Ernest H. 304 Delancy
Krone Christian A. 32 Broome & 66 Houston
Kroos Benj. 116 Anthony
Kroos C. 7th Av. cor. W. 19th
Krooez Carsten, 171 Varick
Kroppenberg Gottlieb, 263 Water
Krumbeck John L. 304 Water
Krunfus Henry, 227 Walker
Kruse Matthias, 543 Grand
Kruse Thomas, 390 Rivington
Kuhlmann Chas. 667 Greenwich
Kuhlmans Wm. 116 Delancy
Kutyemeyer Henry, 372 Broome
Kyle Thomas, 328 West
Ladd Jas. 196 1st Av.
Laforge Jacob, 18 Broome
Lages Franz H. 31 Old slip
Lahr Adam, 214 3d
Lahr Henry, 12th bet. Avs. A & B
Lahr John, 400 Cherry
Laing Hugh, 97 Washington
Lamb Thomas, W. 26th st.
Lamm Daniel, 24 Laurens
Lampe John H. 364 Water
Landwar John, 17 Roosevelt
Lane Geo. A. 246 3d
Lane Maltby G. 149 10th
Langhaar Henry, 204 Chrystie
Langan John, 608 Washington
Lankanau John S. 233 Bowery
Lannamann & Doede, 126 Walker
Larney Patrick, 69 Cherry
Lasses Lane, 130 Cherry
Laurie John, 13 Leonard
Lauer G. 243 6th

Lawler Jas. 496 Greenwich   *New York.*
Lawrence Farlay, 236½ Elizabeth
Leahy Patrick, 234 12th
Lear Adam, 214 3d
Leavenworth M. 52 Av. A
Leavens & Babcock, 34th st.
Lee Thomas, 12 Broome
Lee James, 500 Greenwich
Lechterecker Henry, 34 Av. B
Leckey Francis, 166 Elizabeth & 132 Chrystie
Lee & Platt. cor. Pitt & Broome
Leggers Lewis, 670 Water
Leggett A. 10 & 11 Fulton market
Leggett W. E. 14 & 15   do
Lehey P. 234 12th
Lein Louis, 29 Av. A
Lein J. L. 339   do
Leinninger John, 112 Clinton pl.
Leak J. H. 315 Broadway
Lennox John, 7 2d Av.
Lent Isaac L. 296 Spring
Leohman Wm. 105 Crosby
Leonard Dominick, 123 Mott
Leonard Thomas, 390 5th
Leonard Thomas, 231 1st Av
Leopold Martin. 20 Bayard
Lesers Louis, 130 Cherry
Leurssen G. 794 Greenwich
Leviness Amos, 157 Spring
Leviness Gilbert U. 88 W. 20th
Levi, Apgar & Co. 180 Washington & 44 Cherry
Lewis Enoch, cor. Av. D. & 3d st.
Lewis John, 185 Lewis
Lewis William, 96 Monroe
Lewis & Woodruff, 96 Houston
Lindeman Wm., W. 25th st.
Lindemann John G., W. 29th st.
Lindemann & Sums, 68 Barclay
Linnemann Frederick, 35 Murray
Linnemann Gerard, 33 Lispenard
Linnemann Henry, 161 Church
Linnemann Frank, 194   do
Linnemann C. 225   do
Lintz W. 165 Maiden lane
Litjen Frederick, Amity c. Greene
Littell Thomas F. 203 Church
Little William B. 606 4th
Lockwood Samuel, 250 9th Av.
Lockwood, Hanford & Co. 51 Roosevelt
Logan G. 69 South
Lohman Henry, 3 Anthony
Lohden Henry, 111 Perry
Lohden Hermann, 785 Greenwich
Lohden H. 125 Broome
Lohman E. D. 262 Walker
Lohmann Henry, 239 Stanton
Lohmann Henry, 291 Front
Lohmann William, 105 Crosby
Lohmeyer Henry, 3 Anthony
Lohmeyer Herman. 24 Reade
Lehsen Lohder, 303 Centre
Lohsen H. 40 Av. A
Loose Henry D. 121 Av. C.
Louch P. & Son, 191 E. 16th
Louer George, 243 5th
Loughrin Miles, 94 W. 18th
Louis Benn, 33 W. Broadway
Lord Bowen G. 191 8th Av.
Lord T. W. & Co. 119 Bleecker
Lord S. & R. 169 Front
Lotz John G. 190 6th Av.
Love Joseph, 163 W. 15th
Lowe Frederick. 290 Broome
Lowery J. & L. 121 Front
Lowry ——, Yorkville
Lucas James, 192 W. 16th
Ludlam S. 263 Greenwich
Ludvick Samuel, 215 Broome
Ludwick S. 206   do
Luerssen Gerhard, 794 Greenwich
Luhring John F. 78 Roosevelt
Luhrs A. & N. 15 Dry Dock
Luhrs Benjamin, 22 Thomas
Luhrs Henry, 76 6th Av.
Luhrs John, cor. 5th & Lewis
Luke Mary, 642 Greenwich
Luke John H. 52 Elm & 315 Broadway

Luke J. H. 115 Anthony *New York*
Lullmann John, 573 Greenwich
Lullmen John, 77 6th Av.
Luse Henry D. & Co. 121 Av. C
Lussen O. 26 Hudson
Lussford Garret, 794 Greenwich
Luther & Hampton, 85 Canal
Lyman E. & Co. 66 Front
Lynch Wm. 584 Washington
Lynch Alexander, 167 Mulberry
Lynch James, 105 Cherry
Lynch Peter, 41 Vesey
Lynch R. A. 314 9th
Lynch Wm. 518 Pearl
Lynch & M'Kenna, 32 Centre
Lyon & Johnson, 56 4th Av.
Lyons Michael, 117 Mulberry
Lyons Michael, 233 Elizabeth
M'Aleer Patrick. 59 Roosevelt
M'Alarney Bernard, 66 Ridge
M'Anolly E. & A. E. 26th st.
M'Ardie James, 81 Ludlow
M'Ardie John, 430 Cherry
M'Auley Patrick, 83 Mulberry
M'Bride Hugh, 49 Orange
M'Bride Matthew, 221 Thompson
M'Bride Owen, Av. A. c. E. 15th
M'Cabe M. 709 4th
M'Cabe Michael, 94 Centre
M'Cabe Thomas,-36 Sheriff
M'Cafferey Bernard, 234 Elizab'th
M'Caffrey J. 1 Dominick
M'Caffrey Michael. 378 6th
M'Cahill Edward. 266 11th
M'Calvy H. 446 Cherry
M'Canlees ——, 555 6th Av.
M'Cann Michael, 130 W. 16th
M'Cartin Denis, 14 Pelham
M'Carty Richard, 26 Trinity pl.
M'Cawley James, 39 Washington
M'Cay George, 4 Washington
M'Chain John & Co. 52 Marion
M'Clain John, 374 10th
M'Clelland Thomas, 307 8th
M'Clennon Jervis, 81 Tompkins
M'Collum Patrick, 106 11th
M'Connellogue Chas. 343 Madison
M'Cord Albert, 69 Delancy
M'Corley J. 39 Washington
M'Couch Michael, 270 E. 13th
M'Crann Francis, 92 Mulberry
M'Crossin Dominick, 561 4th
M'Cullum ——, 106 11th
M'Dermott James, 183 Ludlow
M'Dermott John, 490 Greenwich
M'Devit James, 127 Cherry
M'Donald J. H. 19 Lewis
M'Donald Wm. 72 W. 17th
M'Donugh B. 533 Washington
M'Donell J. 31 Broome
M'Donnell Michael, 90 Orange
M'Dougall Charles, 148 Stanton
M'Dougall Alexander, 34 Old slip
M'Elroy John, 336 Madison
M'Elroy E. L. & Co. 206 Grand
M'Entaa Thomas, 242 Mulberry
M'Entee James, 143 Av. C
M'Farland A. 4th Av. c. 12th
M'Farland Alex. 116 4th Av.
M'Geeh John, 179 Bowery
M'Geffey M. 378 6th
M'Geffry James, 21 Clark
M'Gann John, 49 Marion
M'Garr Samuel, 62 Av. B
M'Garvey William, 197 Rose
M'Ginn F. 200 Av. A
M'Girr Samuel, 89 Av. B
M'Giveney F. 26th c. 2d Av.
M'Gonegal John & Co. 190 Varick
M'Govern John, 272 Walker
M'Gowan Michael, 63 Mott
M'Gowen Samuel, 87 9th Av.
M'Gran Catharine, 232 Varick
M'Grath E. 63 Anthony
M'Grath Edward, 144 Church
M'Grath Thomas, 71 Orange
M'Grath John, Harlem
M'Guire Charles, 291 Greenwich
M'Guire John, 221 W. 16th
M'Guire Patrick, 249 Mott
M'Guire Wm. 283 Spring .
M'Guire T., Harlem

M'Kay Michael, 26 Christopher
New York.
M'Kee Joseph, 292 Broome
M'Keever Bernard, 1 Gansevoort
M'Keever Patrick, 48 Chrystie
M'Keever Wm. 19 James
M'Kenna Francis, 87 Orange
M'Kenna James, 396 Cherry
M'Kenna Thomas. 23 Monroe
M'Keown Alex. 379 Washington
M'Keon Matthew, 56 Spring
M'Koon Michael, 299 Bleecker
M'Keon Thomas. 87 Catharine
M'Kiernan Dennis, 245 3d
M'Kigney Samuel, 32 Marion
M'Kimmin John, 112 Church
M'Kinley Thomas J. 32 Vandam
M'Kinney David, 121 Cherry
M'Kinsby, A. 27th st.
M'Kown Arthur, 185 Av. C
M'Laughlin Charles, 98 Mulberry
M'Laughlin James, 19 Oak
M'Lean John, 374 10th
M'Lean T. 155 Maiden Lane
M'Loghlin Alice, 41 Cross
M'Mahon F. 336 3d Av.
M'Manus Patrick. 76 Pearl
M'Michael John, 40 South
M'Minegar S. 60 Lewis
M'Monigal Charles, 187 Monroe
M'Monigal John, 245 9th Av.
M'Mullin James, 239 W. 16th
M'Munigle Samuel, 60 Lewis
M'Nally Peter, 6 Columbia
M'Nally Michael, 264 11th
M'Naughton A. P. 323 Madison
M'Neil Andrew, 76 King
M'Nulty Charles, 113 Monroe
M'Nulty John, 81 Mulberry
M'Perk Henry, 385 6th
M'Quade J. 780 Washington
M'Quaid Patrick, 312 1st Av.
M'Vitties William H 179 Av. A.
M'Whorter Alexander, 61 Warren
Maas Herman, 30 1st Av.
Maas Philip, 293 E. 22d
Maass H. 26 1st Av.
Macy & Jenkins, 146 Fulton
Mace Lewis, 284 Av. A.
Maguire Barney, 231 W. 16th
Maguire Charles, 168 Front
Maguire Patrick, 352 Greenwich
Madden James, 82 University pl.
Mahlman & Blohm, 113 Spring
Mahlstat F. & G. Teuben, 174 Walker
Mahnken Cord, 223 Grand
Mahnken H. 237 Washington
Maier Martin, 369 Pearl
Main R. P. 96 Pearl
Makar P. West 26th st.
Malony P. 61 Washington
Mangels A. N. 391 6th Av.
Mangels John, 186 Hester
Mangels John, 711 4th
Mangels Henry, 18 6th Av.
Mangels Henry C. 175 Hester
Mangels William J. 40 Roosevelt and 534 4th
Mangel W. & J. 53 Av. A.
Mangels & Wilkens, 66 Roosevelt
Mangel J. T. W. 71 Chrystie
Manke A. 21st st. cor 2d Av.
Manke Henry, 8 Av. C.
Manshed H. 47 West
Mansher Herman, 229 Delancy
Mapes William H. 210 8th Av
Mapes James, Harlem
Marratt & Goodwin, 101 Madison
March John, 95 Cherry
Marin ——, 385 1st Av.
Markey James F. 477 Pearl
Marten John, 17 Elm
Martenhoff John H. 77 Bayard
Marten Carsten, 370 Broome
Martens John, 26 City Hall place
Martens John, 59 Duane
Martens H. & Co. 92 Broome
Martin Carsen, 162 Broome
Martin Henry, 69 Thompson
Martin Hugh, 1 Hudson
Martin R. 62 Hester

Martin Thomas, 74 Orange
New York.
Martin Thos. N. 228 W. 16th
Martine John. 4 5th
Martine S. D. 539 Greenwich
Martins H. & Co. 92 Broome
Maschmeyer Fred. W. 20 Perry
Martendorph John, 74 Crosby
Mason Nehemiah, 104 South
Masterson Andrew, 373 Cherry
Masterson A. 67 Gouverneur
Matthews A. West 25th st.
Matthew Alex. 264 Greenwich
Mattfield Henry, 162 Mulberry
May Michael, 197 Elm
Mayer Jacob, 117 Sheriff
Mayer John, 122 Washington
Maxwell Alex. 642 Greenwich
Maxwell C. 134 Greenwich Av.
Mead John B. 22 Jones
Mechanics' Grocery Association, 226 7th
Mechendorf H. D. 182 Grand
Medad, Platt & Co. 184 South
Medon Peter, 6 Mulberry
Meeham Patrick, 62 Prince
Meehan James, 322 12th
Meehan James. 47 Hester
Meehan John, 223 E. 13th
Meeker Francis, 226 3d
Mehl George, 189 Av. B.
Mehrtens Henry, 352 Cherry
Mehrtens John, 196 Broome
Meier Jotat, 323 Broome
Meigs & Wheeler, 167 South
Meislahn Albert, 14 Trinity place
Meislahn Albert & Co. 78 Fulton
Melley W. & C. 18 James
Mensher H. 47 West
Merriman John, 142 Prince
Merritt C. S. & Co. 188 Spring
Merritt J. M. 21 Greenwich Av.
Monken H. 237 Washington
Merchant George W. 47 Leonard
Meschendorf H. D. 152 Elm
Meschendorf Johann G. 74 Crosby
Metscher Michael, 72 Orange
Meyer Christi, 291 Madison
Meyer Christopher, 125 Walker
Meyer Cord, 83 Delancy
Meyer Diedrich, 19 Orange
Meyer Ferdinand, 62 Elizabeth
Meyer H. J. cor. West & Rector
Meyer Harman, 31 Christopher
Meyer Harmen, 45 Anthony
Meyer Henry, 81 Hudson & 54 Frankfort
Meyer Henry, 134 Elizabeth
Meyer Herman, 154 Washington
Meyer Holtz, 57 West & 41 Greenwich
Meyer John D. 204 Division
Meyer John D. 160 & 260 South
Meyer John D. & Co. 246 3d Av.
Meyer John F. 636 Hudson
Meyer J. F. 562 Hudson
Meyer John H. cor. 10th & Av. C
Meyer Louis, 26 Essex
Meyers Jacob, 15 Pell
Meyerholtz H. 57 West & 41 Greenwich
Michaelsen Daniel, 61 Oliver
Michan Neil, 151 East 16th
Michel John, 381 Bowery
Micus Andrew, 34 Hester
Middendorf J. C. 195 9th Av.
Miller Charles H. & Co. 123 Av. C
Miller C. 189 Varick
Miller Claus, 22 Bedford
Miller Cord, 160½ 3d Av. & 14 Minetta lane
Miller Franz H. 93 Greenwich Av.
Miller Henry, 65 Av. A
Miller Henry, 248 Walker
Miller Henry, 323 Broome
Miller Herman, 153 Suffolk
Miller H. & Co. cor. 24th & 3d Av.
Miller John, 17 North Moore
Miller John & Co. 117 Bleecker
Miller John F. D. 100 Roosevelt & 73 Nassau
Miller John N. 60 Thompson

Miller Joseph, 25 Goerok
New York.
Miller Martin, 85 Liberty
Miller T. H. 2 Bank
Miller William, 59 Market
Miller ———, Yorkville
Miller & Co. cor. Horatio & 4th
Miller & Co. 313 Pearl
Miller & Eicks, 685 Washington
Miller Wm. & Co. 89 Bleecker & 132 Rivington
Mills C. H. & Co. 122 Av. C
Mills Joseph, 445 12th
Minerly Harvy F. 101 8th Av.
Minck Henry, 59 Mulberry
Mitchell John. 381 Bowery
Moein John, 310 Mott
Mollenhauer John, East 18th cor. 3d Av.
Moller Michael. 153 Varick
Mollman John, 7 Desbrosses
Monaghan Hugh, 19 Cherry
Monahan William. 13 Washington
Mone Dennis, 88 Ridge
Monholland Patrick, 279 Madison
Monighoff William, 209 Mercer
Montross Enos, 61 Av. C
Moody W. P. 141 Bowery
Moody Winfield S. 75 Bowery
Moore Alonzo, 176 Delancy
Moore Dennis, 88 Ridge
Moore H. 154 W. Broadway
Moore James, 336 Water
Moore Joshua, 341 Monroe
Moore Peter, 217 2d
Moore Sampson, 56 W. Broadway
Moorhead James, 163 Grand
Moorhouse Stephen, 80 Varick
Moran John, 155 3d Av.
Morehouse Albert, 168½ Cherry
Morgan H. R. 174 Front
Morris Edward, 148 6th Av
Morris E. 135 11th
Morris S. 336 3d Av.
Morris Thomas, 571 Greenwich
Morris & Fowler, 69 University pl.
Morrisay Dennis, 19 Madison
Morse John, 95 Cherry
Morton & Corrigan, 236 E. 13th
Mosher Isaac, 30 Sullivan
Moss John, 25 Leonard
Mott John G. & Son. 122 Beekman
Mott R. & C. 211 Walker
Mowbray John, 44 Fulton
Muhle John L. 243 Canal
Muhlenbrink John, 13 Spring
Muhler Henry, 71 Grand
Muhler H. & Co. 80 Wooster
Muldowney R. 24 Morris
Mulholland Chas. 233½ Division
Mullaly Patrick, 181 Broome
Muller D. 78 Nassau
Muller Henry, 80 9th Av.
Muller John, 203 Centre
Muller John F. D. 46 Cherry
Muller L. T. 69 6th
Muller Martin, 85 Liberty
Mulligan Thomas, 196 Leonard
Mullily P. 181 Broome
Mulrooney Richard, 20 Mulberry
Mulvany E. cor. 24th st. & 2d Av.
Mulvey Michael, 76 Mulberry
Murphy Bernard, 43 Jay
Murphy John, 89 Cherry
Murphy John, 133 Orange
Murphy Patrick, 24 Roosevelt
Murphy P. 461 12th
Murphy Thomas H. 15 Elizabeth
Murray James, 258 Mott
Murray John, 57 Crosby
Murray Patrick. 56 Washington
Murray Robert L. 377 Pearl
Murray Thomas D. 309 Delancy
Myer George, 342 Front
Myer J. D. 260 South
Myer J. 122 Washington
Myer M. 31 Christopher
Myer Wm. 369 Pearl
Myers Catharine, 13 Perry
Myers H. 154 Washington
Myers Jacob, 15 Pell
Myers John T. 49 Hester

Myers Louis & Co. 110 White
New York.
Myrick & Hyde, 119 Christopher
Namenkamp C. 197 1st Av.
Nanry Charles M. 86 & 86 Pine
Nealis William, 21 Orange
Nebs John, 26 Hamilton
Neidhart Augustus, 103 4th
Neidhart N. 54 Charles
Neilly Randall, 388 Broome
Nelson James, 377 Greenwich
Nestell Adam, 148 Broad
Nettles Ann, 66 E. Broadway
Newcity Louis P. 171 Attorney
Newman David, 81 Broad
Newton Nelson, 299 Hudson
Nicholas John, 190 2d
Nicholas F. L. 37 Greenwich Av.
Nichols P. 530 Broome
Nichols & Beam, 100 West
Nichols John R. 112 South
Nicholson Jas. W. 36th st.
Nicolas, Peters & Co. 4 9th Av.
Niemann Henry & Co. 341 Pearl & 17 Cherry
Nieman H. W. & Co. 191 Prince
Nieman R. 17 Cherry
Nieschlag Louis, 112 Centre
Nietsch C. F. 223 Broome
Nolan John, 485 Pearl
Nolan Wm. 466 Greenwich
Noll Conrad, 84 Pitt
Noltee Henry, 46 Gold
Nolten D. 53 2d Av.
Noman Delderick, 262 Walker
Noonan Chas. 109 Av. D
Noonan Daniel, 92 Greenwich
Noonan Nicholas, 255 7th
Nott Wm. 178 William
Noxon Owen, 256 Division
Nugent Thomas, 102 Cherry
Numenkamp C. L. 197 1st Av. & 179 Av. A
Nunnenkamp C. L. & Co. 158 11th
Oakley Wilmot, 355 Pearl
Oakley & Rapelye, 549 Hudson
O'Brian Lewis, 100 Columbia
O'Brien Anne, 156 W. 13th
O'Brien Daniel, 44 Gold
O'Brien John, 18 Oak
O'Brien Michael, 88 W. 18th
O'Brien T. H. 37 Burling slip
Obrock Christian F. 36 Warren & 68 Church
Obrock John H. 222 Grand
O'Conel Michael, 18 Anthony
O'Connor Denis, 360 10th
O'Connor John, 10 Caroline
O'Connor Peter, 33 Cross
O'Donnell Jas. 90 Gold
O'Donnell John, 21 Cherry
O'Donnell Sarah, 38 Laurens
Oeters J. & M. 202 Stanton
Oeters Martin H. 293 Stanton
Offermann Claus H. 30 Howard & 46 Canal
Offermann H. & Co. 317 1st Av. & 74 E. 17th
O'Gara John, 13 Mott
O'Grady James, 338 Water
Ohair James, 313 Bleecker
Ohineyer H. L. 84 Reade
O'Keefe D. 485 Washington
Olandt Claus, 29 11th
Oldenberg Wm. 171 Lewis
Olmsteed Chas. 300 Washington
Olwell James & M. 188 6th Av.
Olwell John, 30 Roosevelt
O'Meare Ann. 26 Oak
O'Neal Bernard, 12 Mulberry
O'Neil John, 64 Mulberry
O'Neil & Brothers, 59 Washington
O'Neil Patrick, 257 E. 18th
O'Neill John, 101 10th Av.
O'Neill Sarah, 1 Dry Dock
O'Neill Patrick, 299 6th
O'Reilly Hugh, 6 Batavia
O'Rielay Bernard, 109 Orange
O'Rourke Michael, 43 Watts
Ort H. & Co. 112 Reade
Orth Jacob, 574 Grand
Ortland John W. 127 Prince

Ortland J. & W. 131 Wooster
New York.
Oshos Wm. 433 10th
Osmers Johann, 117 Greene
Osmurs John, 110 Prince
Osterholt Ehler, 96 Washington & 28 3d Av.
Osterholt Elliot & Co. 542 Broome
Ostermeyer Fred. 415 West
Oston John, 432 Water
O'Sullivan Ann, 31 Cross
O'Sullivan Timothy, 119 Mulberry
Oth Jacob, 574 Grand
O'Toole Michael, 29 Pearl
Ottan Henry, 98 Broad
Otten Christopher, 42 Sheriff
Otten Cord, 180 Broome
Otten Frederick, 124 Division
Otten H. 63 Walnut
Otten H. 669 Water
Otten John, 12 Christopher
Otten John, 139 M'Dougal
Otten John, 114 Broome
Otten Luder, 87 James & 250 Rivington
Otten Luke, 229 William
Otten & Martens, 114 Willet
Ottens Hannah, 71 Delancy
Otter Harman, 71 Lewis
Otto Henry, 231 Madison
Oukemp Chas. 161 Rivington
Owen John D. 106 Charlton
Owens Philemon S. 190 6th Av.
Packard Abiel, 39 Bank
Packard A. R. 41 do
Packard I. H. 49 Broome
Pelas Joseph, 717 Greenwich
Palmer Stephen, 387½ Grand
Pape Carsten, 4 Monroe
Pape Claus, 210 Church
Park J. 231 9th
Park John, 1st Av. bet. E. 19th & E. 20th
Park & Reynolds, 7 1st Av.
Park & Tilford, 112 6th Av.
Parker Asa, 342 Broome
Parker James, Harlem
Parker W. 15 South
Parker Wallis, 53 Cherry
Parker Wm. & Son, 16 South
Partridge Josiah, 234 Wooster
Patrick Robert M. 410 Pearl
Pauls Henrick, 77 Reade
Peacocke James, 38 James
Peal Christopher, 245 Houston
Pearsall Wm. 273 Water
Pell John, 126 8th Av.
Pender George, 222 3d
Perine Thomas D. & Brother, 105 Canal
Perkins & Co. 113 Bowery
Perkins Erastus G. 113 do
Perkins Jacob S. 207 Fulton
Perrine Wm. 105 Canal
Perry Patrick, 20 James
Pershall D. T. 211 Broome
Peters Carsten, 93 Market
Phalen John, 80 Cherry
Phaley T. 169 Broome
Phelan James, 106 Stanton
Phelan Joseph, 102 Norfolk
Phelem Thomas, 363 Cherry
Phillips John, E. 37th st.
Pick Philip, 168 Madison
Pickfords John, 90 Lewis
Piemann Diedrich, 114 Monroe
Pieper H. 73 James & 69 Oliver
Pieper & Julius, 60 Bayard
Pierce James, 185 Bleecker
Pitman W. E. & T. B. 206 Hudson
Pitts J. & F. 51 Grand
Platt J. A. 126 Willet
Ploger Ernest, 69 & 107 3d Av.
Pomeroy I. 19 Goerck
Ploger & Co. cor. 3d Av. & 11th
Poggensell Edward H. 236 Washington & 268 Greenwich
Pollen J. H. 63 Water
Plume & Lamont, 68 Water
Pope Henry C. 78 Hester
Pohlker Henry, 94 Cherry

Pohlmann A. 14 W. Broadway
New York.
Polhemus Abram, 361 Bowery
Pollock David, 42 Spruce
Pollock E. 107 Greenwich Av.
Pollock Joseph, 115 12th
Pomeroy John B. 19 Goerck
Pope Aaron, 8th Av. cor. 29th
Pope Charles, 362 3d Av.
Pope Henry C. 114 Broome
Pope C. 210 Church
Pope Henry, 209 Broome
Pope John W. 130 6th Av.
Pope Peter W., W. 27th st.
Pope & Schriefer, 94 7th Av.
Pope Henry C. cor. 21st & 1st Av.
Porshenger Joseph, 183 Houston
Porter Robert, 534 & 536 Pearl
Porsman Henry, 300 8th Av.
Postels John, 127 Elm
Pottebaum C. H. 258 Broome
Potter Robert W. 62 Walnut
Powers Nelson H. 321 Hudson
Power J. 156 Maiden lane
Prangen Nicholas, 89 11th
Prechot Henry, 300 8th Av.
Prehet H. 87 Crosby
Prentice William R. 148 Prince
Prichard & Wing, foot Montgomery
Price & Mitchell, 75 Catharine
Friggs John & Co. 531 Greenwich
Primrose Robert, 676 Water
Prior Horace, 306 Spring
Prusch Carsten, 126 Walker
Puckhafar Charles, 151 Broadway
Puckhafar John, 385 Broome
Pulins Samuel R. 322 Hudson
Pulschen Harman. 192 Church
Pulschen Henry, 19 Anthony
Pulschen John C. 47 Vesey
Palte John C. 281 Mulberry
Pundt Martin, 18 Orange
Pundt & Miller, 198 Hester
Purcell John, 114 W. 19th
Pusing Demar, 16 Elm
Purdy Joel B. 175 Church
Py Conrad, 232 Delancy
Quackenbush C. 160 Hammond
Quackenbush John J. 90 Vesey
Quackenbush & Carlough, 7 Washington
Quade Ludwig, 40 Mott
Quin William, 262 Mott
Quin Michael & Henry, 18 Desbrosses
Quinby Brothers, 278 Walker
Quinlisk James, 130 Av. C
Quinlan E. West 27th st.
Quinn John, 73 Cannon
Quinn John, 70 West 18th
Raab John, 154 3d
Rache J. H. 1 Hester
Radars Henry, 378 Greenwich
Rader Frederick, 501 Broome
Radford Thomas, 652 Greenwich
Radford Lewis, 206 Varick
Raker S. cor. 1st and Bowery
Rampe Francis, 70 Delancy
Ranges J. & Co. 387 6th Av.
Rankin Henry, 64 Hester
Rankin J. A. & Co. 618 Broome
Rapelye James R. 9 Catherine sl.
Rapp John H. 66 Av. C.
Rapp John, 154 3d
Rapp John, 187 3d
Rascoe Ann M. 287 2d
Ray Robert, 192½ Greene
Raynor John, Harlem
Read Robert, 290 Washington
Read Jesse, 59 Cortlandt
Reata Christian, 124 Willet
Redefeldt T. 194 Bank
Redmond James, 479 Greenwich
Recka Herman, 87 John
Reed James, 353 Bowery
Reed Robert, 230 Washington
Reed Isaac H. 17 South
Reed L. F. 562 Washington
Rees Lewis, 26 Sullivan
Reese John D. & Co. 61 Gold
Reichert Matthews, 169 2d

Reilly John, 230 W. 16th
New York.
Reilly Mary, 20 Clark
Reilly P. 24 Madison
Reilly Terence, 229 11th
Reilly Thomas, 39 W. 13th
Reimers Chas. 67 Mott
Reiners R. & H. 146 Rivington
Reiners John, 496 6th Av.
Reiners R. 42 Clinton
Reinhard Christ. 119 Delancy
Renney N. & H. M. 167 Orchard
Rerberding John H. 56 Cross
Reetberg Henry, 175 Hester & 154 Stanton
Rettemer Peter, 166 Monroe
Reuman C. H. 255 Washington
Reumann Henri, 94 Murray
Revels F. Walnut cor. Front
Revill Stephen, 130 Houston
Reyels Frederick, 76 Walnut
Reynolds John, 35 Prince
Reynolds Hugh, 97 Orange
Reynolds James, 186 Chrystie
Reynolds Mike, 54 Av. D.
Reynolds John, 279 10th
Reynolds M. 313 6th
Reynolds Robert, 316 Mott
Reynolds William, 159 Houston
Rice John, 22 Av. A.
Rich J. R. 423 Hudson
Richers Harman, 87 John
Richies Harman, 42 Roosevelt
Richters John & Co. 24 West
Richter John A. 873 Grand
Riechers Harman, 42 Roosevelt
Rieck Ahrent H. 8 Murray
Riely James, 599 Water
Rienges John, 237 6th Av.
Rigelman John, 185 3d
Riker Helena J. 305 Bowery
Riley John, 192 East 23d
Riley H. 599 Water
Riley Patrick, 24 Madison
Rinken Charles, 167 Elizabeth
Rintelen Adam C. 40 Hamersley
Rippe George H. D. 189 Cherry
Ripper John, 56 Frankfort
Risner & Phillips, 64 Water
Ritter John, 264 18th
Roberts George, 90 Crosby
Roberts Henry M. & Co. 123 Bowery
Robertson C. 271¼ Division
Robinson John, 87 Bedford
Roche John, 46 Whitehall
Rodefeldt Frederick, 731 Washington
Rodenburg J. & Co. 2 Crosby
Roe E. W. 281 Bleecker
Rogan Henry, 200 Broadway
Rogan John C. 21 Thames
Rogers G. & T. Harlem
Rogers Theodore, 202 W. 17th
Rohan & Gaffney, 45 9th Av.
Romer W. J. 179 South
Ronner John, 86 Elm
Rooney James & Co. 43 Spring
Roost A. 146 Greenwich
Roseman Henry, 69 Hester
Rosenbaum John H. 33 Cherry
Rosenbaum Samuel, 383 3d
Rosentreter Otto F. 11 James
Rosentreter Peter, 1 Carmine
Roswell Skeel & Co. 119 West
Roth M. 156 2d
Rothert John M. 292 Pearl
Rothert William, 271 Washington
Rottger Joseph, 106 Cedar
Rottger Henry, 318 6th Av.
Rottman J. 44 Hester
Rourke Thomas, 210 Elizabeth
Rourke M. P. 43 Watt
Rover Frederick, 171 Broome
Rowald Charles, 5 Front
Rowland Davis, 235 8th Av.
Rowe Matthew, 12 Mott
Roy Patrick, 236 Madison
Ruddan Michael, 105 Thompson
Ruders Frederick, 301 Broome
Rugan Henry. 200 Spring
Rupper Francis, 224 3d

Runge August, E. 19th cor. Av. A
New York.
Rush Luther, 144 8th Av.
Russell & Copland, 56 South
Rust Andrew, 376 5th Av
Rust Tuder, 144 8th Av.
Rutzler J. 104 Ludlow
Rutzier John, 101 Delancy
Ryan Francis, 30 Madison
Ryan Daniel, 106 Cedar
Ryan George, 183 Av. C.
Ryan John, 479 Pearl
Sagehorn C. 226 Greenwich
Sageman John W. & Co. 30 Barclay
Sallas Henry, 540 Grand
Samson Moses, 262 3d Av.
Sanderson T. R. cor. 3d Av. & 7th
Sanford Peleg B. 392 Houston
Sanford William H. 411 Cherry
Sanford, Nicoll & Co. 150 Rivington
Sasey John, 285 Elizabeth
Sarles Ward, 127 W. 20th
Sanneborn S. cor. Bowery & 2d
Saul George, 48 Lewis
Saunders & Co. 4 Manhattan pl.
Saxton John, 164 Maiden lane
Saxton James, 87 W. 19th
Sayer J. H. 6 Broome
Schade John, 326 1st cor. E. 18th
Schaffer Nicholas. 299 Houston
Schaffner Frederick, 264 Delancy
Schaffner L. 243 Broome
Scheeper John, 16 Minetta lane
Scheper Frederick & Co. 10 Orange
Scherf Frederick, 313 3d Av.
Schersten Peter, 87 Grand
Scheu Philip, 109 11th
Schenck Peter, 20 Rutgers
Schierenbeck Ahrend, 59 Peck sl.
Schilling I. H. & Co. 40 Laurens
Schattlen T. N. 294 Walker
Schloendorff Geo. 102 Cliff
Schloendorff G. 77 Frankfort
Schlondorff Sims, 161 Cherry
Schloo Chas. 1 Duane
Schluer & Co. 167 Mott
Schmale Fred. 365 Greenwich
Schmale Henry, 73 Hudson
Schmultz J. 29 Walnut
Schmadeke A. 68 Mulberry
Schmedes Diederich, 123 Delancy
Schmidt Herman, 9 Frankfort
Schmonsees David, 14 Prince
Schnell F. 8 Hague
Schnicing Henry, 165 Greenwich
Schnirring H. 166 Greenwich & 16 Downing
Schnitker Henry, 990 Broadway
Schrader C. & F. 921 Broadway
Schrieber Christian, 322 Stanton
Schrieber John, 230 Stanton
Schriefer Reinhard B. 63 Nassau
Schriffir Henry, 69 3d Av.
Schriever C. & Co. 98 Hudson
Schroder John, 186 6th Av.
Schroder Christian, 201 W. 21st
Schroder D. 142 W. 16th
Schroder Henry, 367 Pearl
Schroder Henry, 10th cor. 3d Av.
Schroder John H. 126 W. 20th
Schroeder John, 682 Greenwich
Schropfer Valentine, 121 Ridge
Schottler John N. 294 Walker
Schulken & Lane, 312 Pearl
Schullern Andrew, 119 Av. D
Schults Amos, 269 Spring
Schultz John, 100 Broad
Schweblus Jacob, 274 Houston
Schwamedehl J. 177 11th
Schultz F. 61 West
Schwanwedel John, 26 Mulberry
Schwarte John H. 64 Beekman
Schwarte G. H. 17 Rose
Scott Jas. 186 South
Scott John S. 76 Nassau
Scott Nicholas, 186 Forsyth
Scott S. & Son. 818 Broadway
Scroder John, 202 6th Av.
Scroder John, 44 Laurens

Scully Patrick, 360 Madison
              New York.
Sealen Fred. 405 West
Sears Henry, 10th Av.
Seaman Samuel, 194 Varick
Seaman Samuel C. 52 Division
Seebeck John C. 488 Houston
Seebeck Henry, 179 Av. A
Seeber H. cor. 25th & 1st Av.
Seedorf H. 720 Washington
Seedorff Engelke, 458 Broome &
  53 Greene
Seedorff John D. 478 Water
Seedorf I. 100 1st
See & Platt, cor. Pitt & Broome
Seffke Frederick, 62 James
Segelken Claus, 86 3d Av.
Segelken Fred. 115 Rivington
Segelken C. 86 3d Av.
Seickman D. 24 Crosby
Seimes Louis, 68 Barclay
Semcken Henry, 486 Cherry
Sembroad Fred 46 Av. A
Sengstacken Henry, 118 Orange
Sexton Michael, 51 Mulberry
Shaffer Nichols, 299 Houston
Shalthoff G. F. 103 Av. C
Shane Patrick, 146 Anthony
Shanley Patrick, 116 Mulberry
Shannon Samuel, 282 Stanton
Shapter John S. 220 Stanton
Shaver Philip C. 47 Mangin
Shay Michael, 35½ Washington
Shea Edward, 49 Cherry
Shechuns J. & Co. 224 12th
Shee Wm. 422 16th
Shealds W. 49 Christopher
Sheridan A. 225 W. 21st
Sheridan J. & Co. 86 Broome
Sheridan Patrick, 194 Broome
Sheridan Wm. 95 James
Sheriden Philip, 367 1st Av.
Sherlock Edward, 90 Centre
Sherman Gardner & John, 97
  Catharine
Sherrill Rush, 518 Hudson
Shevelin C. 73 Goerck
Shiels William, 49 Christopher
Shipman William M. 214 Delaney
Shmults John, 394 Monroe
Shoemaker Dederick, 191 Hester
Shoemaker Frederick, 127 Mott
Shreswar Martin, 307 West 17th
Shroeder J. 80 13th
Shroeder & Co. 60 Washington
Shults Francis, 378 Water
Shulhaper & Co. 245 Houston
Shultz Peter J. 650 Washington
Shumway Jane, 3 Carmine
Shutzer Samuel, 68 Av. A
Sibberns Augustus, 346 3d Av.
Siebein John L. 1 Whitehall
Sieckmann Diedrick. 149 Church
Siefke Herman, 81 W. Broadway
Siekmann Diedrick. 67 Roosevelt
Sielken John, 127 Spring
Sifke H. 62 James
Siedenburg J. C. 7th Av.
Silva J. B. 67 Market
Silvester John, 19 Rivington
Simkins Thos. West 25th st.
Simmons & Norton, 3d Av.cor. 27th
Simon Ernst, 197 Delancy
Skellenger Benjamin, 208 W. 17th
Sletrieders T. W. 151 Christopher
Small John, 514 Greenwich
Smalley David, 35 Rivington
Smalley Enos B. 21 Stanton
Smecken H. 486 Cherry
Smith Abel S. 292 Bowery
Smith Albert W. 562 Broome
Smith Atchison P. 162 4th
Smith B. & H. cor Greenwich Av.
  & 11th
Smith & Barker, 124 Warren
Smith Bernard, 514 Water
Smith Bernard, 221 West 17th
Smith Carll, 251 Rivington
Smith David, 599 Greenwich
Smith Edwin, 40 Peck Slip
Smith Isaac H. 36 Peck Slip
Smith I. W. 170 Front

Smith Jefferson, 30 Hudson
            New York.
Smith James, 56 Sullivan
Smith Jacob, Harlem
Smith John, 148 Orange
Smith John H. 439 Greenwich
Smith John M. & Co. 59 Henry & 29
  Front
Smith Joseph, 533 Broome
Smith J. J. 101 Av. C
Smith J. 163 Duane
Smith Patrick, 8 Pitt
Smith Philip, 130 Av. C.
Smith Philip, 410 Cherry
Smith Samuel, 480 Pearl
Smith Samuel, 247 Bleecker
Smith Thomas, 481 Pearl
Smith Walter, 254 Houston
Smith William, 714 Greenwich
Smith William E. 613 Water
Smullen J. 367 1st Av.
Snedikor Henry, 141 Waverly pl.
Snowdon Wm. 38 Lewis
Snyder George, 13th st. cor. Av. B
Snyder Samuel, 89 Chambers
Sonneborn Frederick, 323 Bowery
Souza Moses, 248 Washington
Souza T. 347 Hudson
Soule G. W. 50 Water
Spafford W. A. & J. B. 342 West
Spalthoff Gerry F. 103 Av. C
Spangenberg Henry, 40 Av. D
Sparks Alexander F. 264 Madison
Sparks Samuel, 286 William
Sparks Samuel, jr. cor. 1st Av. &
  7th
Sparks Sylvester, 340 6th Av.
Sparks William E. 13 1st Av.
Sparrow W. B. 176½ South
Spaulding Abel, 113 9th Av.
Spence Jas. 137 Greenwich Av.
Spengenberg H. 40 Av. D
Spervealage J. H. & Co. 85 Mott
Spiker Wm. 19 Mulberry
Spilker Henry, 103 Cedar
Spink John, 535 6th Av.
Staats Jacob, 52 Av. A
Stadefoldt F. 401 Pearl
Stadlmair Nicholas, 177 7th
Stagg B. & Co. 187 Washington
Stagman Conrad, 221 3d Av.
Stainford Daniel T. 64 2d Av.
Staples John, 182 Bowery
Stark John, 400 6th
Starkweather H. 63 Water
Steemann Henry, 1 Walnut
Steggmann Conrad, 221 3d Av. &
  E. 25th cor. 2d Av.
Stegman Henry, 769 Washington
Stell Deiderick, 354 6th
Steil D. & W. 343 3d
Steiman H. & Co. cor. Henry and
  Walnut
Stein Frederick, 17 M'Dougal
Steir William, 343 3d
Stelling Claus, 390 Houston
Stelzriede F. W. 649 Washington
Stemmermann Claus, 354 6th Av.
Stenson Robert, 307 Mott
Stephan G. S. 53 West
Stephens Philip, 137 Elm
Stertefeldt Frederick, 111 Elm
Steuber F. 100 Elm
Steurd Samuel, 385 Monroe
Steurer Catherine, 80 W. 19th
Stevens Augustus, 431 West
Stevens Curd, 14 Stone
Stewart Robert, 48 Watts
Stewart Thomas, 240 Houston
Sthmale Thomas, 72 Hudson
Sthruse Hen, 295 9th
Stiles John, 15 Moore
Stold F. & Co. 351 Cherry
Stollmeyer Francis, 64 Division
Stollmeyer Francis, 306 Spring
Stone & Co. 382 Pearl
Stonemeyer H. & Forst A. 142
  William
Stopenhagen Ernst C. 17 Broome
Stopenhagen John, 73 James
Storr George, 196 Rivington
Story William, 396 Pearl

Strehr Otto, 55 4th   *New York.*
Strauss Gubst H. 151 Chrystie
Streuben F. & Co. 48 Mulberry
Stroeleen John, 73   do
Strohmewer Fred'k. 179 Rivington
Struess Henry, 30 Mulberry
Struss William, 207 Hester
Stucke Henry, 339 Monroe
Stucke Hermann, 4 Madison
Stuhke H. 4   do
Stuke & Tietjan, 337 6th Av.
Stumpf Charles, 55 Broome
Sturcke C. 379 Water & 97 Oliver
Sturcke & Bornman, 110 South
Stürs Henry, 416 10th
Suche I. H. 563 Pearl
Suckman D. 144 Church
Sullivan Jeremiah, 189 Monroe
Sullivan J., W. 25th st.
Sullivan Patrick, 390 Pearl
Sullman John, 573 Greenwich
Suydam Israel, 76 Cliff
Swemdale John. 177 11th
Swanton John, 62 Montgomery
Swezey S. & Roe, 268 Division
Swoll Francis, 32 Oliver
Sylvester J. 177 Chrystie
Tacke Christopher, 14 Leonard
Taffe James, W. 18th cor. 7th Av.
Tangeman H. 450 Water
Tape Chas. 167 Stanton
Tape William, 264 Walker
Taske Mrs. 15 West
Taylor Isaac C. 3 Av. D
Taylor Joseph, 44 Attorney
Taylor Moses B. 96 Elm
Taylor Valentine, 195 W. 16th
Taylor & Warren, 87 Pike slip
Tate George, 19 Av. A
Tebe Herman, 164 Leonard
Teinkin John F. 294 11th
Teitjein Henry, 489 Washington
Tennis Jergin & Co., 513 Houston
Tensor V. 570 4th
Tepe Barney, 430 Monroe
Terrill Mary. 115 E. 16th
Terry Z. & G. 167 Church
Teuben George, 162 Orange
Teuben & Mahstadt, 174 Walker
Teves Christian, 690 Water
Teves John H. 374 Cherry
Teyn Andrew, 94 Oliver
Teyn Fred. 380 Water
Thagan James, 17 City Hall pl.
Thall L. 246 2d
Thalman F. & Co. 145 Prince
Theal Joseph, Yorkville
Theurner Chas. 27 Av. C
Thieleng Wm. C. & Co. 14 Ha-
  mersley
Thies & Co. 301 2d Av.
Thies Wm. 557 Greenwich
Thielemann Fred. 246 Hudson
Thistle John, 77 Av. C
Thomas John, 169 Allen
Thompson & Co. 89 Catharine
Thompson Robert, 86 W. 20th
Thompson Thomas, 266 Spring
Thorp George, 218 Division
Thumann John H. 616 Greenwich
Thurner Chas. 27 Av. C
Tice George, 206 Division
Tief Ann, 106 Madison
Tiemeyer G. H. 345 3d Av.
Tiemeyer Gerad, 101 Reade, &
  E. 20th
Tiencken Sebs, 404 West
Tiencker Henry, 95 Hester
Tienken H. 41 Allen
Tienke John D. 233 8th Av
Tietjen B. 142 Madison
Tietjen Heinrick, 43 Whitehall &
  5th Av. cor. 21st
Tietjen Henry, 30 Spruce
Tietjen John H. & Co. 232 W. 16th
Tietyen Bernard, 143 Madison
Tighe Patrick, 62 Cherry
Tighe Richard, 68   do
Tigh Michael, 264 Stanton
Tilford James A. 1 3d Av.
Tilton Jacob, 96 Vesey
Timerman Henry, 239 Wash'ton

Tinkn John, 105 Henry *New York.*
Tobin Michael, 16 Madison
Tobin Robert, 17 W. 18th
Toles & Chittenden, 234 Henry
Tompkins Elijah G. 66 Carmine
Tompkins Thomas, jr. 117 Greenwich Av.
Toneke Ortges, 25 Cherry
Tonjes Joost, 342 Monroe
Tooker Jesse, 153 Stanton
Topham & Stebbins, 25 Coenties slip
Town T. Av. A cor. 18th
Torrick Ortges, 25 Cherry
Towers Thomas, 408 3d Av.
Townsend Samuel S. 128 3d Av.
Tracey Dennis, W. 29th
Tracy Daniel, 44 9th Av.
Tracy Keran, 147 W. 15th
Travers John, 235 E. 13th
Treadwell E. 4 Broad
Trow William H. 127 Crosby & 73 Beekman
Truesdell Arnold F. 100 8th Av.
Tyson William, 46 West
Turner George, 513 Houston
Tully John, 37 Washington
Underhill Adna H. 681 Houston
Usher John C. W. 98th st
Usse August & Co. 305 Stanton
Utler Abram, 94 Av. D.
Van Axt Henry, 329 Bleecker
Van Axte Henry, 289 do
Van Benschotten J. 161 Broadway
Vanbergen John, 112 Walker
Van Bergin Nicholas, 35 2d Av.
Van Beuren S. 700 Greenwich
Van de Wielf John B. 123 do
Van Dohlen F. & Co. 425 do
Vanduzer James, 148 Rivington
Van Hoesen P. D. 719 Greenwich
Vanhorn Cornelius, 146 Leonard
Van Nest P. & Co., 73 Front
Van Ningen A. jr. 113 Canal
Van Lee H. 434 10th
Van —, 502 Hudson
Vannext Henry, 323 Bleecker
Vanraden —, 153 Washington
Venstaden John H. 93 7th Av.
Vanston James, 640 Greenwich
Van Valer Cornelius, 93 Hester
Van Voorlish J. A. & Co. 30 Barclay
Vanvorst Thomas, 88 2d Av.
Van Voorst —, cor. 6th & 6th Av
Vanwart Lawrence M. 114 Amity
Vehelage J. 363 Greenwich
Vegan Henry, 193 Houston
Vehelage Hermann, 191 Franklin
Vehelace T. H. 319 Washington
Veesing Enoch, 36 Av. B.
Vetter John, 121 Pell
Vitte Edward E. cor. 3d & Av. D
Vogelsang F. & Co. 397 Monroe
Vogilsang & Co. 99½ Washington
Vogts —, 19 Mulberry
Vohnglahn J. & Co. 43 Crosby
Volgers Richard, 341½ Madison
Volgers & Ahrens, 13 Walnut
Vollers Andrew, 867 Broadway
Vollmer P. 8 Av. B
Von Dohlen Allerich, 85 9th Av.
Von Dohlen H. 36 Sullivan
Von Dohlen Claus, 36 Spruce
Von Dohlen Frits & Co. 99 9th Av.
Von Dohlen F. & Co. 425 Greenwich
Von Glahn Christopher, jr. 46 Troy
Von Glahn Christoph, 33 9th Av.
Von Glahn J. 43 Crosby
Von Glehn Hilbrand, 65 Orange
Von Holt George, 66 Hudson
Von Holt George, 90 Beekman
Von Lehe H. 416 10th
Vonohlen Henry, 129 Christopher
Vortman & Co. cor. 4th & Av. A
Vornholt George, 90 Beekman
Vortman C. 54 Av. A cor. 4th
Voss Adam H. 142 William
Voss Christopher, 171 Prince
Voss A. H. 96½ Fulton
Voss John, 45 Oliver

Voss John H. & Co. 19 Pell *New York.*
Vreeland R. T. 618 Greenwich
Vullmer Howell, 8 Av. B.
Wade Patrick, 57 Orange
Weesea Adam, 95 Gold
Wagers John. 299 1st Av
Wagner H. 79 E 18th
Walt William S. 301 E. Broadway & 284 Henry
Wakinslaw J. 34 Division
Walker Catharine, 14 Marion
Walker Elliot, 33 Downing
Wallace D. 58 Elm
Wallace John. 173½ Division
Wallace Martin B. 153 4th
Wallace Samuel, 307 Mott
Wallage J. 28th st. 10th Av.
Wallman F. 19 Trinity place
Walsh Martin, 114 Mulberry
Ward Daniel, 34 Elizabeth
Ward James, 191 11th
Ward Philip, W. 25th st.
Ward William, 281 3d
Wardell Christopher, 46 Madison
Ware Edward, 16 Cherry
Warner Allen C. 96 Grove
Wassem George, 216 Varick
Waterhouse Robert, 195 Broome
Waters Rodman, 187 1st Av.
Wathan Edward, 79 3d
Watson William, 196 E. 13th
Wawne Richard, 539 Broome
Wawne Thomas, 525 6th Av.
Webb J., W. 27th st.
Weber George, 23 Broome
Weed Patrick, 57 Orange
Wedemeier John. 96 Leonard
Weeden Christopher, 228 Cherry
Weegen Henry, 171 Walker
Weegen G. 206 Hester
Weeks & Carpenter, 71 Centre
Weeyen Gilbert, 206 Hester
Wegener Charles, 116 Broome
Wegener C. 116 Willet
Wehmann Gottlieb E. 14 Elm
Wehmann Hinrich, 342 Madison
Welch Edward P. 189 3d Av.
Weld A. 76 South
Wellbrock F.335 Rivington
Welsh John, 56 James
Welsh Mary, 59 Oak
Wendelcke Henry, 86½ Stanton
Wendleng George, 279 do
Wernsing H. 487 Pearl
Wernsing Herman, 40 City Hall pl.
Wersbe Frederick, 86 10th Av.
Wersebe D. H. 76 Av. D
Wersebe Justus, 440 Cherry
Wessell Frederick, 143 Spring
Wessell Frederick, 151 Division
Wessell Henry, 121 Stanton
Wessell John, 26 Spring
Westervelt Christ. Z. 265 6th Av.
Westfall J. & D. 194 South
Wetpons John, 439 Cherry
Wetteran Daniel, 49 Rivington
Wettereau John P. 75 Forsyth
Wettig William, 6 N. William & 209 William
Wetson Henry, 115 E. 13th
Wetyen Henry, 109 3d Av.
Wetyien John H. 230 6th Av.
Weyman Henry, 170 3d Av.
Wheeler E. P. & Co. 121 E. B'way
White B. & Co. 26 Charles
White F. & Co. 71 Duane
White Joseph, 213 10th Av.
White Robert, 60 Hester
White Thomas, 136 White
Whitney & Merrill 4 6th
Whitemore Jas. O. 260 Broome
Whitley Olive, 18 Greenwich Av.
Wiohel Henry, 74 Hamersley
Wicht Frederick, 163 Church
Wicht Frederick & Co. 71 Duane & 65 Leonard
Wiegers John, 299 1st Av.
Wiemann Chris. 29 Tompkins
Wieneken Henry, 2 Elizabeth
Wiese Charles & Co. 374 Monroe
Wiese F. 127 Columbia

Wilbrook C. 16 Broome *New York.*
Wilkins Henry, 46 Canal
Wilkins. Furss & Co. 475 Broome
Wilkins Theodore, 84 West
Will George, 12th c. Av. B
Willert John, 216 Rivington
Willetts S. East bet. Delancy & Rivington
Williams Abraham, 250 6th Av.
Williams George H. 375 6th Av
Williams John M. 617 Greenwich
Williams Matthias, 126 Leroy
Williams & Boyer, 161 W. Broadway
Williamson John. 531 Broome
Williamson John, 118 Norfolk
Wilmot O. 354 Pearl
Wilshusen Diedrick. 105 Broad
Wilson Andrew, 79 W. 17th
Wilson Edward B. 1 M'Dougall
Wilson Henry, 208 Cherry
Wilson Thomas P. 205 William
Wilson Zelotes, 264 8th Av.
Wilson & Hunt. 130 West
Willis J. & Co. 414 Greenwich
Winant & Sephton, 38 Av. D
Winckiemann C. F. N. 92 Mott
Winkelmann E. 213 W. 16th
Winkelman D. 318 9th
Windeler Charles, 16 Av. D
Winna Roger, 34 Orange
Winter J. 166 Forsyth
Winters J. 39 Ann & 142 Fulton
Wintjen Claus, 162½ Greenwich
Wintjen Henry, 43 Whitehall
Wintyen Claus, 125 Liberty
Wintzon Louis. 8 Oak
Wippenhorst Wm. 320 Delancy
Wisa C. 374 Monroe
Wittemore J. O. 360 Broome
Witpen John, 439 Cherry
Witpens John, 141 Av. C
Witschan John G. 239 3d Av.,
Witschen Claus, 327 4th
Witschen John, 239 3d Av.
Witte Erich. 69 4th
Witte Frederick, 198 Monroe
Witte Peter, 141 Walker
Witte & Clausen, 156 Washington
Witter E. 69 4th
Witter Henry, 194 Hester
Witty Ehri, 47 Hammond
Wohlars Herman, 23 Grand
Wohicken Lewer, 288 Rivington
Wohlers Diedrich, 584 Wash'gton
Wohltmann Chris. 549 Houston
Wolf H. 205 Houston
Wolfe William, 92 Cherry
Wolfer & Hein, 34 Av. B
Wolters Ernest, 405 Hudson
Worft J. 108 Av. D
Wood Henry, 64 Cannon
Wood James L. 37 Frankfort
Wood John, 66 7th Av.
Wood William V. 56 Av. C
Wood Ransom E. 70 Water
Wood & Hart, 246 Front
Woodward & Parse, 304 5th
Woodhull & Co. 397 Front
Woolay James, 220 5th
Working Man's Union Protective, store 455 Hudson
Wooster Benjamin, 227 Houston
Wreden Christopher, 238 Cherry & 196 Rivington
Wrieden John, 424 Washington
Wright Chas. S. 169 4th
Wright Giles, 116 South
Wright John B. 34 Elizabeth
Wubenhorst Conrad. 170 6th Av. & 21 Ann
Wucherman Ida, 290 Division
Wursebe Justus, 440 Cherry
Yale V. J. 6 Union pl.
Yoost Albert, 145 Greenwich
Young Claus, 140 Perry
Young Frederick, 122 Mott
Young Jacob, 29 M'Dougal
Young John, 117 Willet
Zeiter Jacob, 96 Pitt & Av. A. cr 16th
Zeveck Henry, 122 Delancy

Keller Theodore, 40 Av. A
New York.
Zomus D. Av. A. c. 12th

Niagara County.
Corbett George, Pekin, Cambria.
Carr John, do
Fairman C. G, Lewiston.
Adams E. A.
Simpson James
Kelly M.
Ballou & White Lockport.
Caldicott J. B.
M'Grath M.
Daveraux & Palmer
Ringueberger J. & N. S.
Rogers S.
Bond Robert
Caswell L. R.
Colley William
Cram H. H.
Belden R. C.
Alexander John
Paine D.
Watson William
Tucker D. G
Riggs ----
Strong Charles
Sterling J. B.
Moyer E. N.
M'Kim Daniel
Van Denler ----
Williams & Van Dorn
Pettibone S.
Cross S S.
Whrehim S.
Whitmore W. W.
Greenman P.
Baldwin A.
Wilcox & Gould Niagara Falls
Curtis A. H.
Masonel J. A.
Garret Thomas
Cannon John
Kelsey George Pendleton.
Bolard Jacob
Conner D. Youngstown, Porter.
Lane J. P. Middleport, Royalton.
Kayner George, Orangeport
Sweeney & Kent, Tonawanda
Wheatfield.
Sweeney William, do

Oneida County.
Palmer S. Oriskany Falls Augusta.
Cox D. P. & Co. Camden.
Rowe A. North Gage Deerfield.
Northrop & Field, Deansville
Marshall.
Scofil J. Dominick st. Rome.
Roberts G. G. do
Shepard D. C. James st.
Hager D. & J.F. do
Dickinson Jacob, Canal st.
M'Clusky S. do
Beecham J. James st.
Miller J do
Jacobs J. do
Scofil & Dunning, Canal st
Elmer L. E. & C. W. Dominick st.
Ranyan J. James st.
Williams W. do
Merrill, Hayden & Co. James st.
Dugan & Willis, do
Agne P. Whitesboro st. Utica.
Allen I. C. 108 Fayette
Bailey L. Whitesboro st.
Barber D. 104 Fayette
Barnes A. A. John st.
Baxter & Hull, 8 Liberty
Bowman F. F. 12 Genesee
Brennan M. 31 Bleeker
Bristol Wm. 106 Genesee
Budlong L. 11 do
Bullock B. F. 26 Charlotte
Cadwell E. 96 Liberty
Comstock S. 14 & 16 Genesee
Cooley W. Steuben st.
Crandall H. 22 Bleeker
Day J. 17 Carhamm

Devine A. Whitesboro st. Utica.
Dixon Mrs. E. 5 do
Dobson C. L. 164 Genesee
Donaldson D. 21 & 22 Bleeker
Gardner A. 16 Bleeker
Green William, Montgomery st.
Green W. H. 2 Whitesboro
Grove G. W. & Co. West st,
Hackett John, 176 Genesee
Hahn J. M. Whitesboro st.
Haigh J. do
Henery William, 203 Genesee
Hitchcock A. 45 do
Jones D. B. & Co. 18 do
Jones R. & Son, 93 do
Kellogg G. A. 141 do
Lewis J. Columbia st.
Long O. F. & W. W. Columbia st.
M'Avoy A. Broad st.
M'Cann H. 11 Catharine
M'Quade J. 12 do
Masseth J. Whitesboro st.
Mather A. D. 163 Genesee
Meegen P. 26 John
Miller N. 84 Liberty
Morgan D. 4 do
Mumford, M'Michael & Co. 50 Washington
Owens Thomas, 72 Broad
Parker J. 165 Genesee
Parker W. B. 4 Whitesboro
Parker T. 14 Liberty
Perkins David, 29 Genesee
Perkins T. P. 11 Whitesboro
Pomroy & Crippen, 22 & 24 Fayette
Regan Thomas, 83 Bleeker
Roberts E. Whitesboro st.
Rose A. 41 Genesee
Rose E. 23 Main
Rouck Charles, Whitesboro st.
Schneider G. H. do
Shadrack D. 71 Bleeker
Smith T. Packet Dock
Spanton J. 13 Carnahan
Sullivan L. 25 Main
Thomas D. 2 Seneca
Moble M. 90 Bleeker
Tuthill H. 19 do
Tyrill H. 86 Liberty
Van Sise T. 12 do
Vaughn Thomas, 8 John
Vedder F. 212 Genesee
Warren R. E. 20 Genesee
White Thomas, 16 Liberty
White R. Whitesboro st.
Whalen M. 4 Main
Whitman H. 32 John
Witbeck W. W. 72 John
Wright J. W. 102 Fayette
Turner J. Vernon.
Carter S.
Dickinson A.
Smith S. P. New London Verona.
Williams B. do
Davis ---- do
Hagar & Brother, do
Tubbs J. Higginville
Frazee C. Durhamville
Newcomb B. & H. do
Fields N. do

Onondaga County.
Barker O. Geddes.
Lake H. & Co
Gillson L. Marcellus.
Herring A. Marcellus Falls
Ashby & Olmstead, Water st. Syracuse
Salina
Bartlett A. Genesee st
Barquet S. Water st.
Beadt J. F. Genesee st.
Bennett & Bolton, Warren st.
Bickford D. B. Genesee st.
Blair Wm. K. James st.
Brown M. Water st.
Buff L. Salina st.
Cadwell S. W. James st.
Castle & Johnson, do
Church T. Genesee st.
Cling A. Salina st.
Coles Elijah, Clinton square

Crippen A. Park st. Syracuse.
Dallman W. & H. Salina st.
Dallman Wm. Exchange st.
Dooy D. do
Dumford H. W. Genesee st,
Farnsworth J. Water st.
Fesenmeyer A. Salina st.
Garde J. do
Garson I. Canal st.
Hall J. C. Genesee st.
Hayden J. & Co. James st
Jaycox J. M. do
James V. C. Water st.
Ketcham ----, Warren st.
Kingsley H. & Co. James st.
Koehnlein J. C. Salina st.
Lathrop R. C. Warren st.
Lathrop David L. Granger Block
Listen A. Salina st.
Litchfield E. W. & Co. Salina st.
M'Arthur J. Clinton square
M'Gork J. James st.
M'Gurk A. Pearl st.
M'Gurk C. Salina st.
M'Gurk P. do
Mathews E. S. Wolf st
Mason A. Free st.
Misser M. Lock st.
Norton & Earl, Salina st.
Phinney M. Genesee st.
Pierson C. Salina st.
Plowsight J. Genesee st.
Raymond J. Salina st.
Rhyme F. Clinton square
Sabin John S. James st.
Seifker J. H. Salina st.
Shirley C. Arcade Building
Slavin H. W. Genesee st.
Sulivan M. Canal st.
Sumner C. S. Warren st.
Sumner Increase, Genesee st.
Town E. & Co. 6 Townsend's block
Waggoner G. H. & P. Salina st.
White A. Genesee st.
Willard J. L. 4 Williams' block
Wood N. Exchange st.
Yorkey J. Salina st.

Ontario County.
Corson J. & Son Canandaigua.
Benham & Dailey
Smith O. H. & O. M.
Lincoln Anson S.
Tracy J.
Steward Austin
Sersanet Marcus Phelps.
Cherrock W.
Edmonston O.
Norton Samuel E
Beardsley B. P.
Williams David, Allen's Hill
Richmond.
Teal H. N., Geneva Seneca.
Hudson Wm. do
Chapin Daniel, do
Bradt A. H. do
Dillon F. do
Knight R. do
Whitwell Jas. do
Elmore & Mack, Geneva
Tamlingson N. do
Sillivan Michael, do
York George, do
Bradley P. do
Green D. do
M'Donah ----, do
Baxter Thomas, do
Prescott ---- do
Yeomans Caleb, do
Lowthorp S. do
Nevins F. do
Taylor D. O. do
Bray Michael, do
Dorsey Upton, do
Lambert T. R. do

Orange County.
Kershaw W. L., Washingtonville
Blooming Grove.
Wood J. D. Chester.
Hoyt G. L.

Foster D. B. *Chester.*
Veil S. R. do
Jackson T. J. do
Welling Wm. do
Purdy Samuel H. *Cornwall.*
Mahedy P., Buttermilk Falls
Corwin J. E., Port Jervis
Deer Park.
M'Vey T. K. do
Smith A. T. do *Goshen.*
Sears E.
Payne A.
M'Niece Wm.
Clark J.
Connoley C.
Kitchell S. B.
Crane John
Beadle Wm. W.
Clark B. M.
Doty C., Westown *Minisink.*
Moore & M'Nish, Slate Hill
Senior George *Montgomery.*
Brooks O. Y. *Monroe.*
Ray Wm. Otisville *Mount Hope.*
Broadwell & Thompson, Otisville
Austin ——, 36 Water *Newburgh.*
Barnes Charles, Liberty st.
Birdsall & Ostrum, do
Carr Austin, Colden st.
Clinagston John, 58 Water
Colden C R. & A. 36 do
Colyer D. K. Liberty st.
Comstock Anson, Colden st.
Coyles James, 3d st.
Donday Wm. H. Liberty st.
Duke Matthew, 3d st.
Eager Wm. 4 Water
Edwards L. W. & Co. 97 Water
Farnham John & Co. 78 do
Fitchey John, Colden st.
Gammell Mrs., Broadway
Henrati P. Liberty st.
Jameson J. B. Front st.
Jones Seth, Front st.
Lawson R. & Co. 42 Water
Lendrum A. 41 do
Lendrum & Perry, Broadway
Lendrum George, 31 Water
Lilburn B., Front cor. 1st
Little & Wilseman, Front st.
M'Cartney A. Colden st.
M'Clughan Joseph, do
M'Crosky John, Broadway
M'Donald John, 32 Water
M'Lean Cornelius, 3d
Marsh & Toleman, Western Av.
Moores Nathaniel, 19 Water
Noe Albert, 99 do
Oakley Samuel, 121 do
Polhamus John, 75 do
Purdy Henry L. 114 do
Quaid John, 117 do
Richmond T. cor. 1st & Water
Ringland John, Western Av.
Ryan Thomas, do
Sanxay J. H. H. 58 Water
Sims Matthew, Broadway
Stevens W. J. Colden st.
Tompkins & Scofield, Broadway
Van Nort B. W., Front st.
Waters John H. 30 Water
Welling Frederick, 45 do
Wilson & Taggart, 115 do
Wright W. Colden st.
Shoms Hiram *New Windsor.*
Phillips & Puff, New Hampton
Wallkill.
Swaim A. South Middletown
Mapes Z. G. do
Conklin S. S. do
Hulse G. & H. do
Little J. jr. do
Kellogg Z. do
Broadwell & Thompson, do
Sproat M. L. do
Dunn R. Edenville *Warwick.*
Travis T. New Milford
Demarest F. W. do
Irwin W. D. do
Randolph J. F. do
Winfield C. G. do

Orleans County.

M'Connell S. Albion *Barre.*
Brink Henry, do
Joslyn & Abiel, do
Harrington W. J. do
Woolford H. C. do
Hunter C. do
Geer William, do
Hooker P. do
Woolford & Wall, do
Miller James, Holley *Murray.*
Smith I. C. do
Russell ——, do
Brown & St. John, Hulburton
Allison ——, Hinesburgh
Ives A. M. & Bush, Medina
Ridgeway.
Fuller E. Medina
Britt O. E. & L. do
Whalen & Parker, do
Harker H. do
Parker C. C. do
Thompson ——, Knowlesville
Fuller William, do *Shelby.*
Lawrence ——
Bentley Elijah
Seeley ——, Shelby Basin
Wilkeson —— do
Perkins M. S. Lyndonville *Yates.*
Ingle I. L. do

Oswego County.

Gurley Ashur *Albion.*
Noble & Pierce, Central Square
Hastings.
Lawrence & Ford *Mexico.*
Stacy J. M.
Campbell George A.
Doolittle Solomon
Loomis L. D. Texas
Thomas M. B. Orwell
Allen A. F. & D. cor. 1st & Cayuga
Oswego.
Baker Charles N. cor. 1st & Cayuga
Black Mrs. cor. Water & Seneca
Blackwood Peter, 1st st.
Blackwood William, Water st.
Briggs J. D. 1st st.
Burnam Caleb, cor. Water & Seneca
Campbell & Spencer, Water st.
Carlton Martin, Canal
Cary Horatio J. 1 Granite Block
Clark Sidney, 1st st.
Curry Samuel, Curry's Block
Davis David, 1st st.
Dillworth George, Granite Block
Donnelly Michael, Bridge st.
Dunn Cornelius, cor. Bridge & 1st
Gilbert Nirum, Water st.
Hickey Mrs. H. P. corner Bridge & 2d
Johnson Abel D. 1st st.
Jordan Cyrus, Water st.
Kelley J. F. 1st st.
Kerr Angus, 1st st.
Kishner John, cor. 1st & Seneca
Klock Jeremiah, 1st st.
Lake John L. Canal
Lockhart James, 1st
Luce Stephen, do
Lyon Thomas, do
Mack E.H. & S. J. do
M'Avoy Peter, do
M'Cue James, Phœnix Block
M'Vanna Thomas, 1st st.
Martin Joseph, do
Osborn C. N. cor. 1st & Seneca
Peck John, F. M. 1st
Pond Daniel, do
Rossitter Edwin W. (Agent for China Tea Co., cor. 1st & Seneca
Ruggles Van Rensselaer P. 1st
Sellus Henry, cor. Van Buren & 1st
Stevenson Edward, 1st st.
Swart Abram, cor. 1st & Cayuga
Valto Gay Tano, Bridge st.
Wale Philip, Bridge st.
White Walter W. 1st st.
Wyles William, cor. 1st & Cayuga

Doane Ira, Pulaski *Richland*
Bumpus T. J. do
Cross H. W. & Son, Pulaski
Mayhew William, do
Stearns Lawrence N. do
Page William, Port Ontario
Bigsby H. Phœnix *Schroeppel.*
Rice J. E. do
Franklin R. do
Fralick J. do
Diefendorf Augustus, do
Thompson George, do
Stewart H. *Hinmansville*
Hutchinson John C. & Co. do
Chapman C. do
Woolson E. *Scriba.*
Hull & Holden, Fulton *Volney.*
Clark Charles E. do
Slocum C. C. & Co. do
Sabins Nelson, do

Otsego County.

Light I. West Burlington
Burlington.
Austick John, Schuyler's Lake
Exeter.
Cone S. B. *Hartwick.*
Brown A. S. *Milford.*
Peters Isaac H. *Oneonta.*
Chamberlin Moses W.
Dodge L. C. *Otego.*
Davis Robert, Cooperstown *Otsego.*
Doubleday Seth & Son, do
Robinson A. do
Barker M. *Plainfield.*
Weidman Peter *Unadilla.*

Putnam County.

Purdy H. R. Cold Spring
Phillipstown.
M'Carty H. Breakneck, Cold Spring
Smith & Carris, do
Kirley R. do
Kaphman A. do

Queens County.

Buckles W. T. *Flushing.*
Eutank James & Son
Wood Valentine *Hempstead.*
Clows Thomas H.
Simonsen A.
Cornwell Henry C.
Seabury R. S.
Smith P. Rockville
Pearsall David, Rockaway
Abrams Whitehead, do
Keller Matthew, Christian Hook
Pettit Joel. do
Baldwin Thomas, Millburn
Hedgeman John, do
Lott John I. do
Treadwell Timothy, do
Hedgeman John, do
Lott John I. Hick's Neck
Hendrickson & Simonson, Foster's Meadows
Pine Reuben, Trimming Square
Caffrey Wm. Far Rockaway
Farrell Patrick, do
Baldwin Wm. Merrick
Moore Cornelius, do
Smith Elijah A. do
Kendry James *Jamaica.*
Snodiker Daniel
Durland Wm. Springfield
Amberman N. do
Bailey Ephraim, do
Johnson James *Newtown.*
Scergel J. H. Astoria
Townsend W. J. do
Crissey E. A. do
Blackwell H. F. do
Mills Edwin, do
Titus & Chapman, Manhasset
North Hempstead
Duryea H. E. *Oyster Bay*

Rensselaer County.

Miller M. *Greenbush.*

Morris A.   *Greenbush.*
Simmons F. B.
Folwer & Traver
Heydon E. B.
Mosher J.   *Hoosick.*
Carter F.
Gilmore Wm. 150 State
                         Lansingburgh.
Trazer I. G. 155 State
Hawkins J. 164   do
Fisher R. 172   do
M'Kelsey David, 186 do
Brust David, 218   do
M'Kee P. 231   do
M'Donald R. L. 240 do
Dyer M. C. 245   do
Gaston C. L. 257   do
Osborn Stephen, 293 do
Groesbeck A. & Co. 297 do
Barton Wm. R. 299   do
Nelson R. A. 317   do
Striker J. 327   do
Van Deecarr A. 325   do
Cottrell C. 341   do
Corwell G. W. 324   do
Rice Charles, 302   do
Wing Lansing, 300   do
Van Buskirk & Pickets, 296 do
Follett R. F. & Co. 296 do
Cross & Hoyt. Congress st. Alley
Flack D. H. 290 State
Purcey G. W. & A. J. 6 Fakes' Row
Jewett & Knickerbocker, 232State
Dummer John, 234 State
Nichols G. 226   do
Thompson R.   *Schaghticoke.*
Clegg Wm.
Gage & Smith   *Schodack.*
Adams D. 356 River   *Troy.*
Adams Henry, 158 4th
Armes W. 439 River
Adait A. M. 1 & 2 do
Barry Chas. H. 26 6th
Barringer M. 79 Congress
Berton James, 28 Division
Bendon Eugene, Water st.
Benson Russell F. 91 River
Bigelow Martin, 74 Congress
Bosworth S. & Son, 12½ River
Bosworth R. & J. V. 250 do
Bowman Chas. 460   do
Brackett Wm. F. 144 2d
Brewster V. 98 Congress
Brownson Nathan, 324 River
Burke James, 218 4th
Bunsted Wm. 185 2d
Casey Mrs. 158 5th
Calley W. D. Ida Hill
Chamberlin Philo, 65 Congress
Clancy Wm. cor. Hill & Washington
Claroy Mrs. R. 197 4th
Clum J. H. 52 6th
Churchill & Thompson, 289 River
Clapp & Nelson, Front st.
Chamberlin O. 46 N. 3d
Christian Joseph A. 80½ 2d
Cole & Dutton, 26 Ferry
Collins Mrs. C. 145 Congress
Conloy M. 173   do
Cross & Houghton, 425 River
Curtis Henry, 414   do
Curson Andrew, 272 N. 2d
Dakin James F. cor. Front & Congress
Davis Henry, 87 Congress
Devens Samuel, Front st.
Dexter U. 54 Congress
Donaldson O. 37 Grand Division
Dowell R. D. M. 167 4th c. Ferry
Duffy Catharine, 190 4th
Dunn Patrick, 222 River
Dunivan Thomas, 111 2d
Eddy Wm. 48 N. 3d
Egerton L. Congress st.
Ellis Thomas, 21 Hutton
Emerson John, Ida Hill
Fales C. & F. A. 90 Congress
Farrell John, 15 Federal
File John H. cor. Rensselaer & River

Gials Gilbert R.   *Troy.*
Gilliland Wm. 280 River
Glennon Dennis, cor. N. 3d & Hutton
Golden M. 196 Congress
Goodell E. 103 N. 3d
Gould Robert, 76 Federal
Greenwood Wm. A. 2 N. 4th
Haffnan Christopher, 177 6th
Heath Daniel, Hoosick st.
Henry Wm. 26 Division
Hendry Robert, 219 4th
Higgins Patrick, Front st.
Hogan M. 217 4th
Hogan Mrs. M. 170 5th
Honregan Thomas, South st.
Hughes & Crandall, 51 Congress
Huntington M. L. & Sons, Fulton market
Ingram I. M. 2 N. 2d
Isaac T. Hollow Road
Jordan Peter, 161 3d
Jordan J. 174 4th
Kelley Mrs. 34 Hutton
Keeff John, 209 4th
Knowlton Mrs. A. 177 4th
Kiffle Mrs. Front st.
Leo John, 187 4th
Linsey A. 1 N. 3d
Liney R. 119 2d
Leonard J. 128½ 2d
Lord, Morrison & Co. 371 River
Lockwood Saml. G. River st. near State Dam
Lown Jacob,   do
Lovejoy I. Washington market
M'Elwee Robert, 171 Congress
M'Gehan John, 8 Hutton
M'Keon Patrick, 251 4th
Mains Wallace, Troy Iron Works
Manahan Patrick, cor. Hill & Washington
Morris John, jr. North Troy
Morrison & Lord, cor. N. 3d & Federal
Morrison James, jr. 359 River
Mosher Zabad, 262 N. 2d
Murphy P. 150 5th
Murphy B. 137 Congress
Nolen Peter, South Troy
Oakes James, 11 3d
O'Neal Thomas, 95 Jacob
Parkhurst I. 107 3d
Perry A. S. & Co. 202 River
Phillips T. N. & B. F. 76½ Congress
Pillsworth Edward, 186 5th
Powell V. R. 20 7th
Prince & Pulbert, cor. State & Front
Purcell Ann, 136 2d
Rellay John L. 92 River
Riordan John, 194 4th
Roberts J. H. & Co. Hoosick st.
Rounalds Barney, 191 4th
Rousbrank M. 17 State
Ryan F. 140 6th
Ryan Dennis, 199 4th
Ryan Wm. 10 7th
Sege Russell, 130 River
Sage Henry R. 406 do
Sheridan John, 1 do
Sears H. H. 198   do
Shanly Wm. 172 5th
Shaughnansey Mrs. 133 3d
Simmons Wm. A. 23 Federal
Simmons J. F. 83 Congress
Sherman Wm. C. 203 do
Smith J. 187   do
Stearns S. K. 54   do
Stone Thomas, 151 do
Stone J. 215   do
Stone Mrs. 23 7th
Stickney Thomas, 462 River
Sullivan James O. 157 Front South
Tedford Wm. 96 Congress
Towle John, South Troy
Truworthy Wm. F. 11 Hoosick
Turner J. W. 149 5th
Vanderheyden R. cor. Front & Division
Vanderwerken J. 54 Congress
Van Tuyl A. 359 River

Werner Wm. H. cor. 5th & State
                              Troy.
Warner Ebenezer, 21 7th
Walton W. 10 N. 2d
Ward Mrs. 109 2d
Waterbury S. C. 101 2d
Welch Mrs. 298 4th
Whyland J. L. 81 Congress
Wilber Curtis, 200 4th
Wilcox A. 4th st.
Wood Ephraim, 328 River
Wright & Britton, 2 Franklin sq

Richmond County.

Braniff T. Tompkinsville
                         Castleton.
Carroll J. S. New Brighton
Burger James G. Port Richmond
                         Northfield.
Stafford James,   do
Ludlow & Co. Stapleton *Southfield.*
Colton John,   do
Mullan James,   do

Rockland County.

Benson George   *Haverstraw.*
Smith Benjamin
De Baun Samuel
Van Houton Ralph
Moores J. T.
Kiles D. S.
Gurnie E.
Hagan A. J. Piermont
                         Orangetown.
Earle E. I.   do
Blanch T. 3d   do
Tallman T. S. Nyack
White John,   do
Lusk Wm. P. Piermont
Fox C. W.   do
Merritt James F. do

St. Lawrence County.

Nash Alfred   *Brasha.*
Jones ——
Chandler ——
Post E. E. & H. A.   *Canton.*
Brown Amasa O & Co.
Smith H. M.
Wright Jared S.
Thrull B.   *Gouverneur.*
Goodrich W. & Co.
Consall James H.   *Hammond.*
Hatch John   *Harmon.*
Wheeler Isaac
Ross & Manley, Columbia *Madrid.*
Tupper & Campbell, do
Westcott P. S.   do
Knowlan Thomas, Waddington
Anderson A. A.   *Massena.*
Davis ——, Massena Springs
Floyd G. W.   *Norfolk.*
Waterman C. E. & C. Ogdensburgh *Oswegatchie.*
Dillon P. W. Lake & River st.
Lyon George,   do
Adams Amos, Lake st.
Woolley Joel M. Ford st.
Woolley J. L.   do
Ornell J. N. cor. Ford & Isabella
Bacon Thomas   do
M'Nulty James, Water st.
Platt M. S.   do
Baldwin Luke   do
Huntingdon C. R. & O. do
Kellogg Horace, Ford st
Atchison Thomas   do
Cummings Wm.   do
Bliss H. C.   do
Dennis Eli   do
Burn John   do
Bayargeon Joseph,   do
Perkins Joseph,   do
Jackson M. F.   do
Woolley Joel M.   do
Spaulding M. W. Isabella st.
Clark Nathan   *Potsdam.*
Traver Perry
Fling Henry S.
Dustin Delos

Saratoga County.

Ellis Elijah   *Corinth.*
Kellogg E. P.   *Galway.*
Ogden Ira. Ballston Spa   *Milton.*
Green & Thompson, Glenn's Falls
     Moreau.
Wheeler A. Portville
Hamilton J.
M'Lean James, Gansevoort
     Northumberland.
Reymond Edward, Gansevoort
Wilson Ephraim,   do
Peder A.   *Providence.*
Pecker Wm. Schuylerville
     Saratoga.
Ensign Seymour,   do
Carrington Robert, do
Cox Wm.   do
Lord H. Victory
Wheldon Wm. H. Victory
Brisbin Joseph *Saratoga Springs.*
Paterson A.
Rockwell C. A.
Cogan P.
Martin R. H.
Fonda H.
M'Donnell & Bennett
Dake C. W.
Flanagan S.
Martin & Patrick
Hall & Carpenter
Benedict H.
Perry Wm.
Doughty S. A. & Co.   *Stillwater.*
Smith Jas. W.
Nelson C. C.
Scofield Joseph, Bemus Heights
Lang W. R.   *Waterford.*
Sheriden Thos.
Cook P.
Conaughty John
Brewster Courtland
Grigg David

Schenectady County.

Anderson J. 179 State
     Schenectady.
Barhydt A. V. S. 24 Ferry
Barhydt C. W. & G. S. 140 State
Bensen R. V. 110 Union
Blake P. Maiden lane
Cain Isaac, 13 Rotterdam
Carpenter Coles, 157 State
Champion H. 127 Union
Chrisler Wm. 9 Rotterdam
Clute C. B. State st.
Clute G. M. 109 State
Clute John F. 124 State
Combs Thos. 81 State
Cunningham R. K. 125 Union
Elder W. & J. 38 State
Eldred E. 163 State
Erkson J. 142 State
Felthousen J. D. 141 State
Freeman J. Y. 90 State
Fullogar J. 36 Union
Gifford & Co. 26 State
Hill S. P. 37 Union
Hotaling & Kilmartin, 9 Water
Houlahan Wm. Dock st.
Jones Eli, 1 State
M'Clelland J. 187 State
M'Kenney J. C. 10 Washington
M'Sherry J. Canal st.
Millard & Crane, 164 State
Miller J. 193 State
Miller ——, 2 State
Pickett J. 76 Union
Powell D. L. 63 Union
Prout J. A. Dock st.
Sales B.
Schermerhorn H. 27 State
Schermerhorn W. B. & Son, 155
     State
Smith T. L. 1 & 2 Dock
Strong M. 4 Dock
Truax I. I. 55 State
Van Buren F. cor. White & State
Van Inger H. S. 17 Canal
Vedder J. 65 Ferry
Walker James, 104 & 106 State

Waltermire J. M. White st.
     Schenectady.
Weed E. State st.
Weed H. 124 Union

Schoharie County.

Russell John   *Broome.*
Van Leuven Geo. M.   *Conesville.*
Bogardus Jas.   *Gilboa.*
Danforth David B.   *Middleburgh.*
Carpenter & Vroman

Seneca County.

Buchanan Chas.   *Fayette.*
Tuttle Horace   *Ovid.*
Dunnett & Chapman
Almy Jas. O. Farmer
Wintersteen Daniel S. Farmer
Buckley D.   *Seneca Falls.*
Chapman J. C. & Co.
Chapman T. N.
Gibbs A. S.
Hill L. J.
Pixley Chas.
Pollard Wm. P.
Smith Jacob
Stockman J. L.
Mordon C. H. & I.
Twist Chas.
Woodworth A. O.
Denel Joshua T.   *Waterloo.*
Kendig D. S.
Millikin J. & Co.
Wilson Joel

Steuben County.

Sleeper H. & Co.   *Addison*
Jones & Brown
Smith M. & Son
Bostwick & Chandler
Rose H. S.   *Avoca.*
Disbrow & Co.   *Bath.*
Thompson I. H.
Hadley S.
Williams D.
Brown A. E.
Hendrick T.   *Cohocton.*
Eldird W. M.
Mixon John
Stanton George   *Erwin.*
Seeley H.
Carpenter & Wells
King Andrew   *Greenwood.*
Scott & Striker
Lawrence H.   *Hornellsville.*
Neeley J. D.   *Howard.*
Moore Dennis
Hubble R. G.   *Orange.*
Ruscoe P.
Goodrich D. W.
Herring C.
Davenport Lewis   *Painted Post.*
Abbott Hiram
Pace M. J.
Murrey John & Co.
Page A.
Benjamin D.
Davis Jas. C.
Hollenbeck Jacob
Robinson R. E.
Buckley Andrew
Neff Henry   *Prattsburgh.*
Seeley Reuben
Newman A.
Harris N.   *Reading.*
Watrous Samuel   *Tyrone.*
Woody Augustus   *Urbana.*
Randall John W.
Kellogg J. M.
Gardiner A. D.   *Woodhull.*

Suffolk County.

Hicks J. A. & C. T.   *Huntington.*
Shepard George H.
Doty B. B. Cold Springs
Sammis W. G. do
Merrills Charles   *Southold.*
Cochran Wm. D.
Lewis John, Greenport
Beckwith J. S.   do

Jennings Jonathan, Greenport
     Southold.
Chapman J. C.   do
Webb David,   do

Sullivan County.

Green E. A. & G. R. Big Eddy
     Lumberland.

Tioga County.

Chatfield T. J.   *Owego.*
Patch T. P.
Kingman & Co
Teed T. G.
Clark Wm.   *Spencer.*

Tompkins County.

Dennis Elihu, Enfield Centre
     Enfield.

Ulster County.

Russell James   *Kingston.*
Mastin C. jr.
Kraft John
Davison Peter
Chipp Warren
Van Gaasbeck Edgar
Fish Daniel
Davison William
Ewen George W.
Radcliff Hiram
Montgomery William
Acker F.
Samuels John,   *Rondout*
Anderson Roamer & Co. do
Acley & Norris.   do
Deyo Richard,   do
Anderson Charles,   do
Barrenbrook G.   do
More Wm. C.   do
Knapp & Co.   do
Eaton Abel,   do
O'Riley A.   do
O'Riley Charles.   do
O'Riley John,   do
O'Riley Terrance,   do
Kraft John, Wilber
Dimond George, Eddyville
Brannagan P.   do
O'Riley & Welch,   do
Secor Alexander,   do
Van Wagner Wm.   do
Elton Peter R. High Falls
     Marbletown.
Green John,   do
Auchmoody James   *Rosendale.*
Webster Orange   *Saugerties.*
Raymond W. H.
Finger Henry L.
Shaffer Stephen N.
Canfields ——, Bristol
Kerr Morgan   *Wawarsing.*
Dutcher & Gay, Ellenville

Warren County.

Marshall William, Chestertown
     Chester.
Rockwell E. L.   *Luzerne.*
Aldrich Hugh
Stewart Daniel
Brown Clark I. Glenn's Falls
     Queensbury.
Knapp Reuben,   do
Johnson F. A.   do
Burper Mason L.   do
Pike & Fairbanks, do
Jubert & Bursack, do
Dougherty John,   do
Peck William,   do
Tillotson John,   do
Baker Alanson,   do
Peck Charles,   do
Clark & M'Niel,   do
Malory Darling,   do
Goodspeed S.   do
Brown C. J.   do
Farlin F. A.   *Warrensburgh.*

Washington County.

Maddon Boyd   *Argyle.*

15

Mack Charles, North Argyle
    Argyle.
Bain Alexander, South Argyle
Ransom Darwin   *Fort Ann.*
Clark N. M.
Harvey George
M'Clure Thomas
Pattison Israel
Parish William
Salmonds Philander
Stevens William
Vaughn Wm. M.   *Fort Edward.*
Buck Philander
Reeves John M.
Ackerman Charles. Fort Miller
Calkins Jas. Fort Edward Centre
Bosworth Wm.   *Greenwich.*
Moore C. H.
Murch Rectus
Gunu C. J.
Jones J.
Boon Martin, Lake
M'Clellan John R. West Hebron
    Hebron.
Crawford Andrew T. do
Hathaway Peter,   do
Doubleday H. M. *Kingsbury.*
White Charles, Sandy Hill
Vaughn A. W.   do
Weeks R. C.   do
Black J. C. Chapin's Block
    Whitehall.
Bartlett E. Phœnix place
Dwight & Brown, Canal st.
Billett James, Exchange
Greene Simon, Chapin's Block
Johnson R. C. Canal st.
Jillson Cyrus, do
Nichols C. D.   do
Ostheim M. Phœnix place
Patterson William
White A. G. Canal st.
Warren F.   do
Renois Antoine, do
Polly J. & Son, William st.

Wayne County.

Bennett James   *Arcadia.*
Harrison Sidney
Davis George
Devinna R.
Phillips J.
Adams & Winfield
Decker J.
Hill Charles B. Newark
Goodchild Henry, Clyde *Galen.*
Wood R.   do
Humphrey ——, do
Sloan Wm. O. do
Congdon Joseph, do
Griswold Wm. Lock Berlin
Griswold J. H. do
Roeaback & Dunn *Lyons.*
Knowles & Brothers
Rushford S.
Bartlett C.
Palmeter C. D.
King H. & D. W.
White E. W.
Cramer & Holliday
Holliday C. J.
Price E. B.
Corning J W. *Palmyra.*
Drake William
Tubbs D.
Everson William E.
Sexton S.   *Sodus.*

Westchester County.

Smith Holly   *Bedford.*
Curry C. Peekskill *Courtlandt.*
Coles Nathan W. do
Decatur & Clinton, do
Briggs T.   do
Griffin A. N.   do
Howland G. M. do
Bird Samuel, do
Denike H. F.   do
Tompkins A.   do
Lent & M'Chaim, do
Hunt Theodorus *East Chester.*

Shute Gilbert   *East Chester.*
Shute Benjamin
Cole James, Hunt's Bridge
Sheriden Patrick, Tarrytown
    Greenburgh.
Lockwood Henry, Dobb's Ferry
Fredericks C *New Rochelle.*
Kissam Joseph M.
Stewart Warren A.
Cashmie Timothy
Smith Hugh
Fisher & Acker, Sing Sing
    Ossining.
Smith Jonas C. do
Mangam Daniel D. do
Lynch Charles, do
Ludlam David S. do
Buckhout Alfred, do
Jones & Burbiss, do
Vanhorn B.   do
Wilson Edward, do
Sherwood George, do
Vanaiclin Silv. Portchester *Rye.*
Bird James, do
Provost William, do
Haviland James, do
Horton William, do
Merritt Clark S. do
Parker James *West Farms.*
Tier D.
Johnson William
Smith Henry
Green Jacob
Wells James
Miggens John
Horton E. *White Plains.*
Chambers Samuel W. *Yonkers.*
Lent & Co.
Morgan P. N. Tuckahoe
Barker Isaac, Harts' Corners

Wyoming County.

Ellis O. R.   *Attica.*
Buck & Vincent
Goodrich & Kingsbury
Nichols Gail, Cowlesville
    Bennington.
Upham Samuel *China.*
Church Lyman *Genesee Falls.*
Brigham Lyman
Reynolds George
Keith D. & W. R. Wyoming
    Middlebury.
Hill & Calkins *Perry.*
Huntington E.
Steele Charles *Pike.*
Lloyd J. W.
Straup Nicholas *Sheldon.*
Deslinger Peter
Bankman Augustus
Cling Nicholas
Kenster John. Strykersville
Warren & Bates *Warsaw.*
Wilkin Leonard
Potter & Carr
Otis Matson
Otis Orrin

Yates County.

Holden William   *Benton.*
Brazee M.
Collins Stephen *Middlesex.*
Shelden E. Penn Yan *Milo.*
Tuell & Watson, do
Nichols ——, do
Aldrich John, Rushville *Potter.*
Spicer James, Dundee *Starkey.*

Grocers—Wholesale. (*See
also Grocers. also Merchants Produce Commission, also Produce
Dealers, also Merchants Commission.*)

Albany County.

Neef & Fort, 685 Broadway
    Albany.
Mitchell William, 366 do
Wadley M. S. & Co. 347 & 349 do

Wait & Vernam, 359 & 361 B'dway
    Albany.
Crapo William & Co. 17 State
Hinsworth & Northrup, 15 do
Davis William. 11   do
Wilson & Grimwood, 7 do
Stanton G. W. jr. 3 do
Weidman & Shell, 10 do
Cook & Wing, 12   do
Batcheldor G. & E. C. 18 do
Wilson Monteath & Co. 48 Quay
Bulkley & Crapo, 50 do
Cook Asher, 47   do
Esmay Isaac, 28 Dean
Monteath & Co. 34 do
Maher J. 52½ State
Merrin G. 7½ Hudson
Bulger E. 56 Quay
Hendrickson M. & J. cor. Hudson
  & Quay
Schoolcraft, Raymond & Co. 14 &
  16 Hudson
Sayles J. & G. M. 52 Quay
Tarbell George S. 65 do
Moore S. B. 4 Division
Cowell & Flaherty, 116 & 117
  Quay

Clinton County.

Nichols & Lynde *Plattsburgh*

Columbia County.

Hubbell George C. cor. Water &
  Ferry   *Hudson.*

Erie County.

Barber A. T. 3 Packet Dock
    Buffalo.
Jamieson John, 4 Birkhead Build-
  ing, Commercial st.
Tyler A. 11 Exchange
Catlin Ira & Brother, 4 Packet
  Dock
Cowing H. O. & Co. Prime &
  Dock sts.
Prothais John, 6 Main
Clark & Collins, Buffalo Ware-
  house
Peck William, 8 Ohio Buildings &
  Dock
Brayman L. H. 45 Ohio
Moore George A. & Co. 42 Main
Williams John W. 180 do
Diebold Jacob, 176 do
Smith William, 142 Main
Hager Henry & Co. 62 do
Flagg Samuel D. 58 do
Fiske William, 48 do
Yaw Ambrose P. 44 do
Moore G. A. & Co. 42 do
Peter J. F. 34   do
Leichtenstien P. 32 do
Taylor & Haight, 30 do
Miller A. D. A. 28 do
Beers & Kip   do
Havens E. S. & Co. 19 Main
Smith L. D. & Co. 11 Websters'
  Block, Main
Guenther & Stevens, 163 Main
Jewett & Johnson, 33 do
Gregory & Huntley, 1 Websters'
  Block
Bennett & Scott, 5   do
Milliken C. A. 58 Main

Greene County.

Edwards John   *Catskill*

Kings County.

Cornell & Mead, 2 Atlantic
    Brooklyn.
Jones Samuel S. 28 Fulton
Rhodes Wm. & Co. 34 Fulton
Whitney J. C. & D. D. 20 Fulton
Potter J. & Co. 23 Hicks
Valentine, Bergen & Co. 29 Fulton
Suydam J. S. 33 Fulton
Gerald Thomas J. 7 Front
Allen & Co. 270 Washington

Monroe County.

Brewster S. L. & J. R. 16 S. St. Paul & 72 Main *Rochester.*
Rigney John, 12 S. St. Paul
Houghton T. B. 68 Main
Parker John G. 43 Main
Smith & Perkins, 29 Exchange

New York County.

Abbey & Freeman, 61 Front *New York.*
Ackerson A. 150 20th
Adams & Cushman, 75 Front
Addicks J. D. 68 Nassau
Ahren G. G. 180 William
Alger & Brother, 85 Dey
Allen John, 110 Vesey
Allen & Rogers, 226 Front
Arcularius, Bennett & Co. 202 Front
Arcularius P. G. & Philip I. Roome, 115 West
Arens Otto, 513 Pearl
Ashbey & Fish. 105 South
Atwater, Mulford & Co. 135 Front
Avery Frederick, 71 & 73 Water
Ayres & Tunis, 175 Washington
Babcock & Co. 55 & 57 Water
Baker & Scudder, 71 Dey
Balen & Co. 186 Front
Barber S. & Co. 79 Water
Barnes & Mackey, 194 Greenwich
Barnet & Bidleman, 64 Dey
Barstow Samuel, 133 Front
Bartlett, Perry & Co. 4 Front
Bass, Clark & Dibble, 106 West & 145 Liberty
Beach, Case, & Co. 58 Cortlandt
Besle, Melick & Dewitt, 110 Broad
Bearns James S. 265 Washington
Beatty J. & Co. 174 Greenwich
Belknap & Haviland, 252 Wash'n
Bell George & Co. 107 South
Bearns J. S. 265 Washington
Benson Charles S. 217 Bleecker
Berry & Palmer, 93 West
Besson John, 184 West
Besson & Brouwer, 151 West
Bininger & Cozzens, 56 Vesey
Bird William E. 214 Front
Blydenburgh & Co. 3 Coenties sl.
Blossom Henry E. 182 Front
Bodine John, 77 Dey
Bonnett A. & Co. 202 Front
Bostwick & Masterton, 57 Water
Boyce John, 182 Greenwich
Brainerd George W. 103 Murray
Brodhead, Storm & Co. 68 Cortlandt
Brush Jesse, 17 Front
Brush Platt, (see advertisement) 160 West
Bunn & Herder, 90 Murray
Burdick & Martin, 236 Front
Burger, Hurlbut & Co. 89 Water
Burkhalter C. & Co. 221 Fulton
Burkhalter Stephen, 191 Fulton
Bushe Henry P. 204 Front
Cain J. H. & Co. 234 Fulton
Canran, Hopkins & Co. 60 Front
Carew W. H. 19 Bowery
Carland Edward, 11 James' slip
Carpenter C. M. & Co. 458 Pearl
Caswell John & Co. 87 Front
Chenery & Johnson, 28½ Front
Cocks John D. 192 South
Coles Henry, 229 Fulton
Collins A. T. & J. W. 22 Coenties slip
Colton Clinton, 2 Washington
Coman, Hopkins & Co. 60 Front
Concklin & Bailey, 96 Barclay
Concklin & Moore, 155 West
Conklin & Smith, 141 Front
Conley & Kirk, 233 Front
Conover & Labagh, 56 Front
Cooper Thomas P. 182 South
Cooper, Storm & Smith, 15 Coenties slip
Corwin Oliver & Co. 203 Front
Corwin & Morgan, 257 Washing.

Coursen Geo. H. 76 Cortlandt *New York.*
Cowenhoven & Decker, 55 Whitehall
Craig & Lane, 190 Front
Crane & Russell, 41 Water
Crissey & Haviland, 90 Dey
Crooke, Fowks & Co. 104 West
Crooker & Rogers, 182 South
Dater, Miller & Co. 161 Front
Davis James, 2 Coenties slip
Demaray David, 150 West
Demarest, Vreeland & Joralemon, 76 Vesey
Denison C. & L. & Co. 84 Dey, 126 West & 262 Fulton
Denton, Smith & Co. 47 Front
Devoe Isaac H. 50 Water
Dole & Co. 62 Front
Donohue J. H. 239 Front
Dow, Wilson & Herriman, 53 Front
Duckworth & Haviland, 220 Wash.
Duckworth M. H. 61 Dey
Earle & Porter, 95 & 97 Front
Elder & Painter, 75 Dey
Elmore & Zabriskie, 108 Murray
Elliot Volney, 201 Washington
Emanuel Thomas M. 146 Front
Evans Ira P. 96 Front
Evans & Carman, 83 Water
Faile E. G. & Co. 191 Front
Ferguson & Sherman, 6 Water
Fiske & Wooster, 48 Water
Flateau & Co. 191 Front
Foote & Bush, 204 Front
Foster H. & Co. 114 Wall
Foster Wm. R. 174 Division
Fowler & Odell, 76 Vesey
Franklin Mullard, 127 West
Fuller, Waller & Co. 143 West
Gasper Brothers, 52 Water
Giraud Andrew F. 161 West
Goolda A. 187 Bowery
Graves Jared W. 120 West
Greenwood Benj. & Co. 62 Dey
Gross & March, 65 Front
Gulick & Holmes, 162 West
Hall Wm. & John T. 51 Cortlandt
Halsey Lewis T. & Co. 74 Dey
Hamilton & Dater, 180 West
Hamilton & Herriman, 57 Front
Harper & Co. 92 Front
Harrison James, 197 Washington
Hart J. Moses, 54 John
Hasbrouck John L. 104 Murray
Hawkins & Stewart, 102 Murray
Herbert, Olmstead & Co. 72 Front
Hoffman, Bailey, & Co. 62 Water
Hope A S. & Co. 189 Greenwich
Hopkins & Ward, 215 West
Hoppock M. A & Co. 230 Fulton
Hoppock & Greenwood, 238 Washington
Hotchkiss, Fenner & Co. 81 Water
Howell B. H. & Co. 227 Front
Hoyt James M. & Sons, 176 Washington
Hubbard A. & J. W. & Co. 37 Peck slip
Hunt Wilson J. 190 West
Hunter John B. 177 Henry
Hustace John, 239 Fulton
Hyde Samuel L. 41 Water
Ireland's Joseph Sons, 82 Dey
Jessup & Fox, 178 South
Johnson Leonard L. 111 Broad
Kattenhorn & Romaine, 264 Washington
Kent, Poag & Co. 1 Front
Ketchum & Perry, 84 Front
Kinnan Peter, 92 Broad
Kirtland Gilbert A. 205 South
Knapp J. L. & Son, 101 West
Krider & Mallet, 76 Grand
Leggett Abraham, 205 Front
Lethbridge Robert & Co. 86 South
Lintz William, 165 Maiden lane
Lippincotts & Raynolds, 68 Front
Lord S. & R. 169 Front
Lovell Joseph, 49 Water
Lowrey J. & A. 121 Front
Ludlam W. & A. B. 124 Beekman

Lyman E. & S. 166 Front *New York.*
Lynch William, 513 Pearl
McGeah J. 119 Bowery
McGuire Charles, 168 Front
McLean Thomas M. 165 Maiden la
Macy & Jenkins, 146 Fulton
Mallory William. 181 South
Manners David S. 225 Fulton
Marsh T W. & A. 153 West
Martens & Witschief, 92 Barclay
Martin C. S. 63 Front
Martin P. & W. 59 Cortlandt
Martin William A. 69 do
Mead & Belcher, 55 do
Mead Ralph & Co. 13 Coenties sl.
Mead, Rogers & Co. 61 Water
Meads & Co. 47 Water
Mettler Wilson, 63 Dey
Millard Franklin, 127 & 128 West
Mills James M. 218 Front
Mills & Thompson. 51 Cortlandt
Morgan Henry R. 174 Front
Moore John J. & Co. 216 Front
More David L. & George O. 267 Washington
Moreau & Parker, 91 Barclay
Morrell Thomas, 290 Front
Moser & Woolsey. 242 Front
Nichols & Beam, 100 West
Nicoll S. T. & Co. 67 and 69 Front
Nostrand & Carman, 179 West
O'Donohue John, 239 Front
Olmstead Harrison, 15 James sl.
Olwell J. & M. 179 West
Onderdonk & Mercer, 59 Water
Osborn Abner, 186 Greenwich
Otis & Woodward, 78 Front
Park Charles F. & Co. 117 West
Park Rufus, 67 Dey
Parker W. 15 South
Penfold & Schuyler, 178 Front
Pepoon & Olcott, 71 and 73 Front
Perry Sam'l, 3 Front and 28 Moore
Platt Medad & Co. 184 South
Plume & Lamont, 70 & 72 Water
Post J. A. 76 Cortlandt
Pritchard, Wing & Co. South cor. Montgomery
Quackenbush & Bamber, 172 West
Quackenbush J. J. 90 Vesey
Radford Henry & Co. 202 West
Rathbone Henry, 33 Water
Rickman Garrett W. 41 Water
Richter J. 24 West
Roberts, Spencer & Co. 106 Front
Romer, William J. 179 South
Rowe, Woodruff & Carter, 178 Washington
Rowland James, 78 Cortlandt
Ranyon M. T. 291 South
Russell Crane, 41 Water
Russell & Copland, 56 South
Ryckman Garrett W. jr. 41 Water
Sackett, Belcher & Co. 58 Pearl
Sagehorn & Kornahrens, 240 Washington
Schiffer Sam. & Brother, 184 Front
Schnibbe J. C. 31 John
Scott James, 18 James slip
Scott & Abbatt, 29 Burling sl.
Scribner & Coolidge, 134 Front and 118 Sheriff
Scrymser William & John, 126 Front
Sherman & Collins, 51 Front
Sherwood Nelson, 466 Pearl
Shotwell & Doscher, 224 Wash.
Skeel Roswell & Co. 119 West
Smith Denton & Co. 47 Front
Smith Edwin, 40 Peck sl.
Smith John W. & Co. 170 Front
Smith Samuel G. 14 Fulton
Smith & Barker, 134 Warren
Snyder E. & J. A. 13 S. William
Soule George W. 50 Water
Southworth & Litchfield, 5 Coenties slip
Sparrow William B. 176½ South
Stanton & Jarvis, 51 Front

Starkweather Henry, 62 Water
              New York.
Stewart & Coffin, 157 South
Stillwell, Brown & Co. 72 Cortlandt
Story Rufus, 7 & 9 Front
Sturges, Bennet & Co. 123, 125, 127 Front
Suydam Henry, sen. 43 Front
Suydam, Reed & Co. 107 & 106 West
Swezey Noah T. 176 South
Swift & Weldron, 100 Front
Taylor Benjamin S. 80 Vesey
Taylor & Ritch. 135 Front
Taylor & Warren, 87 Pike slip
Teal Lewis, 171 West
Terrett Gilbert R. 171 Front
Terrett H. B. 261   do
Titus & Barnes, 64   do
Underdonk & Mercer, 59 Water
Underhill G. M. K. 195 South
Underhill & Bool, 181 South
Valentine A. G. & Bartholomew, 168 Front
Van Cleef Isaac, 15 Burling slip
Van Kleeck W. H. & Co. 159 West
Van Nest Peter & Co. 173 Front
Van Nostrand J. & H. 115 West
Van Schaick & Place, 101 Murray
Wagstaff & Goff, 70 Cortlandt
Wardwell, Knowlton & Co. 96 Front
Waring and Webster, 191 and 192 West
Warren & Co. 54 Front
Weeks & Carpenter, 71 Centre
Weld Addison, 76 South
Wells & Van Benschoten, 62 Cortlandt
Wetmore O. & A. 99 Front
Wheeler Ezra & Co. 89 Front
White Thomas B. & Co. 15 Water and 6 Bridge
Whitlock B. M. & Co. 84 Front
Whitlock J. W. & Co. 122 do
Williams C. P. & E. 192   do
Williams R. S. & Co. 92 South
Williamson & Vail, 164 West
Wilson & Cobb, 62 Front
Wilson & Fyfe, 6 Old slip
Winans & Jones, 79 Front
Wisner & Bunker, 11 Old slip
Wisner & Phillips, 64 Water
Wood Ransom E. 70 & 72 Water
Wood & Grant, 90 Front
Wood & Hartt, 246   do
Woodhull & Co. 207 do
Worthington & Shufeldt, 105 Murray
Wray Stephen, 167 West
Wright C. & F. 222 Washington
Wyckoff Henry S. 43 Front
Wyckoff Samuel S. 102 Vesey
Wygant Edwin, 68 Dey
Yelvertons & Fellows, 60 Water
Evelin R. & Son, 231 Fulton
Youngs & Howell, 167 Front

Oneida County.

Jones T. E. & Co. 129 Genesee
              Utica.
Foster & Dickinson, 117 Genesee
Butler T. K. & Co. 114 Genesee
Hall & Whitaker, 160 Genesee
Jones J. O. 14 Fayette
Ray E. C. cor. Hotel & Canal sts.
Swift Wm. P. cor. Liberty & Hotel sts.
Bows & Kissam, cor. Seneca & Canal sts.
Wicker J. C. cor. Liberty & Hotel sts.

Onondaga County.

Livingston & Mitchell, Malcolm's
   Block, Syracuse   *Salina.*
Allen H. Water & Warren sts.
Cobb Alfred, 2 Williams' Block
Green V. Water st.

Orange County.

Whitney D. B. Port Jervis
           Deer Park.
Smith T. A.   do
Powell, Ramsdell & Co. *Newburgh.*
Carpenter B. & Co.
Crawford, Mailler & Co.

Oswego County.

Whitney & Tower, Bates' Block,
   1st st.   *Oswego.*
Biddlecomb & Ayres, Water st.

Rensselaer County.

Lambert Thomas A. 362 State
         Lansingburgh.
Russell C. H. 141 River   *Troy.*
Bates & Griffin, 171 River
Hillman Jos. 173 River
Doughty S. G. & Co. 166 River
Hunter & Graves, 183 River
Nazro John P. 217 River
Wooster G. L. 229 River
Smith & Wood, 237 River
Scott & Lemon, 241 River
Haight & Gillespie, 269 River
Armstrong & Squires, 277 River
Dauchy & Flood, 293 River
Briggs Wm. 406 River
Marshall A. 423 River
Dodge & Van Ostrand, 291 River
Dater & Carr, 299 River
Arnold Jas. 301 River
Ten Broeck & Steenbargh, 303 do
Battershall & Weed
Britton & Webb, 325 River
Hakes & M'Doual, 327 River
Smith & Safford, 343 River
Loveland & Swartwout, 347 River
Weed & Thurman, 349 River
Vanderwerken J. & Son, 279 River

St. Lawrence County.

Wheelock Ira, Water st. Ogdens-
   burgh   *Oswegatchie.*
Stilwell Smith, Ogdensburgh
Robbins & Lankton, do
Averill James G.   do

Schenectady County.

Carley G. Q. State st. *Schenectady.*

Ulster County.

Anderson, Romar & Co. Rondout
            Kingston.
Schoonmaker & Eaton, Rondout

Guano.

Harmony's P. Nephews & Co. 63½
   Broadway   *New York.*
Kentish & Co. 40 Peck slip

Gun, Pistol & Rifle Manufacturers. (*See also Gunsmiths.*)

Albany County.

Beebe Geo. 6½ S. Pearl *Albany.*
Churchill O. 26 Green

Erie County.

Smith P. 6 Birkhead Building
            Buffalo.

Greene County.

Solley J. F.   *Catskill.*

Herkimer County.

Remington E. (Gun Barrels), Il-
   lon   *German Flats.*

Monroe County.

Passage Christoph. Stone's Block
   cor. Main & Saint Paul st.
            Rochester.

Billinghurst Wm., Curtis' Block
   Main st.   *Rochester*
Moore Wm. H. 6 S. St. Paul
Child J. C .17 Buffalo
Miller John, 42 Main

New York County.

Blunt & Syms, 44 Chatham & 177
   Broadway (see advertisement)
            New York.
Bolen John G. 104 Broadway
Fish Daniel, rear 374 Pearl
Huson Wm. 570½ Grand
Muller I. F. & H. Gonzalez, 41 Cross
Reynolds Francis, 49 Chatham

Onondaga County.

Rector J. H. Water st. Syracuse
            Salina.
Robinson J. O. Syracuse

Guns & Pistols—Importers of.

New York County.

Barnes C. L. & Onion, 99 Maiden
   lane   *New York.*
Blunt & Syms, 44 Chatham & 177 Broadway
Cooper Henry T. 179 Broadway
Cooper Joseph, 233 Broadway
Huesmann & Co. 14 Platt
Joseph B. & Hart, 74 Maiden lane
Keutgen Chas. 82 John
Lampe J. H. 10 James slip
Lamerche E. & H. 100 Pearl
Moore & Baker, 204 Broadway
Mullins John, 140 Nassau
Petrie W. W. 46 Chatham
Struller Louis, 28 Platt
Spies A. W. & Co. 91 Maiden lane
Von Keller, 90 William
Waller Fred. 26 Broadway
Wolfe & Gillespie, 192 Pearl
Young, Redfield & Leavitt, 19 Maiden lane

Gunsmiths. (*See also Guns & Pistols Manufacturers.*)

Albany County.

Scott W. J. & R. H. 9 Beaver
            Albany.
Van Volkenburgh, 11 Beaver

Alleghany County.

Henderson D.   *Andover.*
Eldridge & Schenck *Angelica.*
Benson Isaac   *Hume.*

Broome County.

Bartlett J. & R. *Binghamton*

Cattaraugus County.

Blackman George *Ellicottville.*
Goodell Absalom   *Olean.*

Cayuga County.

M'Clallan H., North st. *Auburn.*

Chautauque County.

Russell N., Mayville *Chautauque.*

Chemung County.

De Witt W. P.   *Elmira.*

Chenango County.

Church Wm. H.   *Norwich.*

Columbia County.

Steens A. C. 283 Warren *Hudson.*

Cortland County.

Slocumb Hardin   *Homer.*

Duchess County.

Berry W. 229 Main *Poughkeepsie.*

Erie County.

German C. 74 Main *Buffalo.*
Bangasser & Lobert, 92 Main
Crandall Geo. E., Springville
Concord.

Essex County.

Stone J. *Elizabethtown.*
Stearling Calvin, Moriah Four
Corners *Moriah.*

Franklin County.

Dickinson J. & Sons *Bangor.*

Genesee County.

Clark L. *Alabama.*
Vosburgh S.
Joslyn I. M. *Batavia.*

Herkimer County.

Devendorf Lewis *Litchfield*

Jefferson County.

Skinner A. R. *Watertown.*
Robinson L.

Kings County.

Coles John K. 50 Fulton *Brooklyn.*
Dinnen John, 107 Hudson Av.
Thatcher Joseph, Flushing Av.

Livingston County.

Brown George A. *Dansville.*
Weeks D.
Roberts Geo., Fowlersville *York.*

Madison County.

Hatch John *Cazenovia.*
Robinson Luther, Chittenango
Sullivan.

Montgomery County.

Parker Wm. *Amsterdam.*
Buddle John *Canajoharie.*

New York County.

Barr William, 105 Beekman
New York.
Bertholf James, 78 Barclay
Bolen J. G. 104 Broadway
Blakely John, 44 Sheriff
Fish D. 374 Pearl
Fisher John, 40 Chatham
Godfrey James, 91 Market
Hall John, rear 91 Fulton
Hasselmeyer Chas. 120 Delancy
Hopkins Reuben, 80 Catharine
Huson William, 570½ Grand
Illingworth Thomas, 356 Houston
Latham James, 399 3d Av.
Leach John, 89 Elizabeth
Leete William B. 96 Perry
M'Larty William, 109 Cherry
Macfarlane Andrew, 5 Dey
Marsten Robert, 211 Fulton
Morgan William, 73 Reade
Reynolds F. 48 Chatham
Rose Joseph, 60 Catharine
Simpson M. E. 18 Spruce
Simpson Paul J. 16 do
Sprague & Marston, 794 Wash'ton
Zettler John, 71 Allen

Niagara County.

Cook E. W. *Lockport.*

Oneida County.

James M. 4 Bleeker *Utica.*
Abby G. T. 9 Catharine
Adams & M'Coy, 4 John

Ontario County.

Miller Cyrus, Honeoye *Richmond.*
Gardiner C. L. Geneva *Seneca.*
Gardiner Wm. do

Orange County.

Amory S. B. *Goshen.*
Lane A. *Mount Hope.*
Dotzert C. *Newburgh.*

Orleans County.

Abby R. Albion *Barre.*

Oswego County.

Courtney Wm. T. 4 Office Row,
Bridge st. *Oswego.*

Otsego County.

Hawks C. Schuyler's Lake *Exeter.*
Taylor Robert W. *Middlefield.*

Queens County.

Kellum E. *Hempstead.*

Rensselaer County.

Caswell J. M. jr. 161 State
Lansingburgh.
Cushing A. D. 25 2d *Troy.*
Lewis Nelson, 60 Congress

Schenectady County.

Waggoner P. jr. 139 State
Schenectady.

Steuben County.

Voorhees J. *Avoca.*

Suffolk County.

Terry Isaac *Riverhead.*

Sullivan County.

Bowers J. W. Barryville
Lumberland.

Tompkins County.

Coon L. & Sons, 37 Aurora *Ithaca.*
Briggs J. 51 Aurora

Ulster County.

Berry Gilbert *Kingston.*
Vignes John

Warren County.

Buswell James, Glenn's Falls
Queensbury.
Buswell Martin, do

Washington County.

Prentiss Mas. North *White Creek.*
Selden A. William st. *Whitehall.*

Wayne County.

Bennett O. *Lyons.*

Westchester County.

Gregory J. Peekskill *Courtlandt.*

Yates County.

Gilbert & Bales, Penn Yan *Milo.*

Gutta Percha Goods.

Kings County.

American Gutta Percha Co., Armstrong S. T. & F. W. Prop., 40,
42 and 44 Water *Brooklyn.*

New York County.

American Gutta Percha Company,
Samuel T. Armstrong, 120 Ful-
ton *New York.*
Day Horace H. 23 Cortlandt

Gymnasiums.

Fuller William, 16 Cortlandt
New York.
Mourguin P. 598 Broadway
Ottington Charles F. 15 Canal
Rich John B. 109 Crosby
Walker John B. 421 Broadway

Hair Cloths.

Orange County.

Steritt —— *Newburgh.*

Hair Dressers.

Albany County.

Van Vranken David, 805 Broad-
way *Albany.*
Crosby John, 2 & 3 Stanwix Hall
Building
Simmons Jacob, 27 Maiden Lane
Winters J. 3 Delavan House
Pope Thos. 100 State
Crannell M. 136 State
Van Vranken F. 61 Dean
Bendall H. 32 Hudson
Levy D. 170 S. Pearl
Johnson IL. 107 S. Pearl
Morgan E. 80 S. Pearl
Garrison T. 29 S. Pearl
Norris J. 12 S. Pearl
Gibson S. 6 Beaver
Weymouth A. 5½ Beaver
Dioll J. K. 23 Daniel
Tonk George, 334 Washington
Van Epps Francis, Congress Hall
Morris H. B. 70 Washington
Gordon G. W. West Troy
Watervliet.
Parker A. do
Rouse Wm. do
Selden C. F. do
Phelps A. L., Cohoes

Broome County.

Noland H. *Binghamton.*
Coats, Barker & Co.
Barrett S.

Cayuga County.

Miller J. Genesee st. *Auburn.*
Swarts George. do
Laughlin Wm. 127 Genesee
Quincy J. W. 129 do
Freeman M. L. do

Chautauque County.

Davis H., Fredonia *Pomfret.*

Columbia County.

Rexford A. Warren st. *Hudson.*
Malcher J. do
Deyo G. do
Atwater R. do
Deyo J. do
Fell B. Diamond c. 7th
Mower Wm. Warren c. 5th
Smith A., Valatie *Kinderhook.*

Delaware County.

Jones W. H., Deposit *Tompkins*

Duchess County.

Vermony C. E. under East House
Poughkeepsie.
Williams H. basement of Pough-
keepsie Hotel
Gillias J. 137 Main
M'Lane Wm. 26 Market
Renworthy R. 13 Market
Boston U. 12 Garden
Elmendorf N. B. *Rhinebeck.*

Erie County.

Lott Urias, 2 Pearl *Buffalo*

Thomas H. K. Pearl c. Terrace
Buffalo.
Neidhart Jacob, Merchants' Hotel
Krouss W. E. do
Gardner Luchas, Main c. Exch'ge
Jackson Henry, 1 Main
Cook Edward, 9 Exchange
Mitchell John, 5 Terrace
Harvey Samuel, 23 Lloyd
Adams Jas. 312 Main
Basty & Colt. 204 Main
Sage John, 310 Main
Qualls W. M'Carthur's Garden
Sands C. T. 226 Main
Simpson John, 205 Main
Francis Isaac, Commercial Hotel
Block
Davidson D. N., Phelps House
Henry James, Western Hotel
Brown Joseph. Exchange st.
Burford Geo. 9 Main
Lansing Peter, 81 Main
Jackson H. 141 Main
Berthand Chas. 147 Main

Genesee County.

Leonard J. *Batavia.*
Leonard D.
Wood Sampson *Le Roy.*

Greene County.

Johnson Cæsar *Catskill.*
Cross Martin
Fryer Jacob *Prattsville.*

Kings County.

Flood A. 27½ Atlantic *Brooklyn.*
Brown A. 111 Atlantic
Merle John, 68 Atlantic
Lewis S. H. 4 Hamilton Av.
Barton F. 8 Hicks
Pelletrean John, 4 Henry
Kever Alexander. 91 Cranberry
Cornailus Joseph J. 126 Fulton
Hintewender J. A. Montague Hall
Haight R. 348 Fulton
Carnes P. 61 Fulton
Tresher Philip, 79 Fulton
Jordan James, Mechanics Exc'ge
Front st.
Birdsall J. A. 1 York
Brasso C. 48 Main
Sloper J. C. 83 York
Clandel A. 57 Sands
Striker Henry, 115 Concord
Stokes James, 232 Fulton
M'Cloud Wm. 313 do
Doubleday Henry. 75 Hudson Av.
Briggs Mortimer N. 103 Bridge
Head Henry, 100 Myrtle Av.
Stewart William, 54 Prince
Aeschelman George, Flushing
Av. near Classon
Telford John E. 68 South 7th
Williamsburgh.
Snyder Thomas, 45 South 7th
O'Nell Terrens. 204 1st
Rose George F. 105 Grand
Vessey William, 112 Grand
Curchin W. T. 1st st.
Orange William, 234 1st

Livingston County.

Hamilton D. *Dansville.*
Pease E. C.
Schermerhorn James
Titball H. H.
Imray Robert *Geneseo.*
Schermehorn J.
Thompson Robert, Cuylerville
Leicester.
Challis Wm. Hemlock Lake
Livonia.
Johnson J. W. *Mount Morris.*
Parker Wm. H.
Bard Nicol *Nunda.*

Madison County.

Osborn T. E. *Cazenovia.*
Chavous & Randolph *Hamilton.*

Monroe County.

Allen Richard A. 10 Canal Dock
Rochester.
Sears Francis, 4 S. St. Paul
Ernisse A. Ontario st.
Renner Martin. Clinton st.
Crowley Bartholomew. 46 Main
Brown James, 68½ Buffalo
Francis Ralph. Eagle Block
Haight William, cor. State & Buffalo
Stanley J. & Co. 9 Arcade
Sage John D. 3 Arcade
Morris J. P. 75 Main
Moor J. 99½ Main
Ray D. H. 133 Main
Morton Jones H. 14½ Exchange
Pope Arthur. 94½ State
Montgomery Robert, 193 State
Patterson D. Waverly Place
Gell J. H. 33 Hill
Barrier A. J. 6 Main st. Brockport
Sweden.

Montgomery County.

Wood J. *Canajoharie.*
Hayner C. L.
Lansing Moses, Fort Plain
Minden.
Gibson Sewel, Fonda *Mohawk.*
Adams Joseph, do

New York County.

Aarons Catherine, 196 Cherry
New York.
Anthes Peter. 268 3d
Anthony John P. 13 Duane
Arnold P. 9 4th Av.
Badenkop James F. 233 Broome
Bailey Linn, 9 Morris
Baker Stephen J. 29 Park row
Ball William S. 64 9th
Barthe Charles, 73 Orange
Bastien John, 6 Albany
Bell H. 108 Centre
Benben Samuel, 138 Monroe
Bennett Jacob, 473 Grand
Bennett Joseph R. 199 Wash'ton
Benson John. 393 Water
Bentz John G. 9 Carlisle
Berbice Joseph. 7th Av
Bergold N. 109 Suffolk
Bernard J. T. 41 Cortlandt
Bess P. E. 6 Albany
Bessant Charles W. 87 Mer. Exch.
Bishop Henry, 90 Houston
Bitter Louis, 16 Catharine slip
Blair Lewis. 156 Fulton
Blanc Joseph H. C. 218 9th Av.
Blehel Charles, 65 Beekman
Bock Frederick, 27 Thompson
Bock Joseph, 1 Tryon row
Boerckel Jacob. 168 2d Av.
Bollet Gottlob, 50 Delancy
Bord George F. 73 Mulberry
Boucsem A. 8th Av.
Bourgard Philip, 5 Frankfort
Bowen William, 546 Grand
Boves J. W. 57 Pearl
Bower W. C. 51 Pearl
Boyd Alexander, 86 W. Broadway
Boyer Alexander, 558 Pearl
Boyle C. 87 Cherry
Boyle Patrick. 86 Cherry
Brackmann Bernard. 9 4th Av.
Brandly Vincent, 2 Thompson
Brooks William, 1 Doyer
Brown H. M. 15 8th Av.
Bruce William H. 27 Beekman
Bunce Charles F. 441 Hudson
Burton Ezra T. & Gifford, 503
Grand
Buxton & Franklin, 97 Nassau
Cabrera Bennett. 99 Roosevelt
Caldwell Mrs. 651 Hudson
Cambell John, 548 Hudson
Campbell James, 75 James
Campbell James, 326 Bleecker
Caprico & Contrelll, 2 Beekman
Carman James W. 180 Varick
Carl George, 33 Av. A

Carnet G. 26 Rector *New York*
Catling George, 70 Bowery
Cavanna Augustus, 63 Broadway
Cazaux John, 59 Suffolk
Chamberlain Elizabeth, 73 Chambers
Chappel William, 221 Centre
Chase George W. 4 3d Av.
Chatman Alfred F. 2 Franklin sq.
Chatters George, 34 N. William
Christopher & Butler, 5 Roosevelt
Churcher George. 593 Grand
Cinser Benj. 81½ 9th Av.
Ciprico George, 10 Frankfort
Clirehugh Wm. S. 179 Broadway
Coggar Lorenzo C. 22 Marion
Colby John, 93 8th Av.
Colby Wm. 238 W. 16th
Coleman John P. 253 3d Av.
Coon John. 3 Bedford
Correo John, 187 Broadway
Correo Vito. 26 Dey
Corbyn Sylvester E. 262 Walker
Courtois Guler, 359 Broadway
Central Joseph, 2 Beekman
Covana A. 87 Broadway
Covin J. 1 Bedford
Cristadoro Joseph, 6 Astor house
Cross Wm. H. 205 Duane
Crossman Samuel E. 62 Cortlandt
Cue P. 178 Christopher
Cunningham Ellen, 30 Rector &
23 Morris
Curren Peter. 342 Broome
Curry David T. 147 Church
Davidson John W. 161 Hammond
Dehart Gilbert, 135 W. Broadway
Delsart Louis, 93 King
Dennis Amity, 4 Amity
Depark Antonio. 6 4th Av.
Dibblee Wm. 263 Broadway
Diddell Mason, 4 Coenties slip
Diddell Robert. 5 Cortlandt
Diepfenbach G. 107½ Av. D
Dillmeir Michael. 17 1st Av.
Dobins Samuel, 9½ G'wich Av.
Dorson Wm. 140 Center
Dresher Charles, 200 Canal
Dresher Jacob, 241 Division
Dustin Geo. W. 134 Beekman
Dubois Wm. H. 92 King
Durkin Abram L. 153 Hester
Edmondson Richard, 210 Grand
Edwards Austin A. 100 Houston
Ehlers G. 7th Av.
Ehrens Catharine, 196 Cherry
Eicke Henry C. 138 Liberty
Ellers George, 110 7th Av.
Farr William, 105½ Broad
Fairgrieve Wm. 122 Roosevelt
Ferrari G. 4 Vesey
Finkenauer Philip, 266 Division
Finley Andrew, 38 Fulton
Forester Frank, 86½ Broome
Force Hiram, 4 Stuyvesant
Frey Anthony, 71 Willet
Frieke Charles, 67 Chambers
Fritz Jacob, 47½ Whitehall
Futterer Cassimer, 97 7th Av.
Gage Moses, 271 Bleecker
Gardener John, 117 E. 16th
Gardner Edward, 139 Hammond
Gardner Robert G. 1 Barclay
Gering Christian F. 174 Cherry
Gelabert William, 57 Pearl
George Frederick S. 286 Houston
Gessner Wm. C. 3d Av.
Gibbons Frederick, 92 B'dway
Gibbs Elizabeth, 153 Elm
Gibson James, 367½ Bowery
Giffin Azariah, 1 Barclay
Giffin James, 30 Broadway
Gilbert Lawrence, 8½ Division
Gilland David, 171 do
Gilliland D. 296 do
Godby Ann. 259 Greenwich
Godfrey Sebastian, 81 Delancy
Gogelun Matthew, 22 Broome
Gossenberger William, 26 Vesey
Gottlieb Frederick W. 402 B'way
Graf Philip, 130½ Greenwich Av.
Grandjean Agias, 70½ Essex

Grant James, 4 Ann   *New York.*
Grasmuck F. 59 Montgomery
Green Henry S. 13 Bayard
Griffin John. 102 Greenwich
Guignon Peter, 240   do
Hagerman J. L. 842 Broadway
Haley George B. 119 Lewis
Hall Henry P. 204 Chambers
Hardt Philip, 309½ 6th Av.
Harvey James, 61 Broadway
Herold A. 158 16th
Hauencheid Joseph, 87 Division
Haugh H. 22 Morris
Haybgin J. 195 1st Av.
Hazzard William A. 456½ B'way
Heck William, 36 Old slip
Heitz John F. 22 Rector
Heller Charles, 297 Mott
Hempel Michael. 6 Oak
Hengstler V. 169 Christopher
Hentshel Frederick, 11 West
Herger Louis, 219 Grand
Hering Philip, 228 Stanton
Heritau Jules, 76 Reade
Herold August, 158 W. 16th
Heshburg Theodore, 7 Av. C
Heybyrne John. 211 1st Av.
Hill William. 13 Nassau
Hodes Joseph, 249 Delancy
Hoffman George, 486 Greenwich
Holloway William, 587 Grand
Hooker & Bassford, 170 Varick
Hopp John, Av. A bet. 12th & 13th
Hopp Magnus, 170 Delancy
Horn George, 67 Ludlow
Hubbard Isaac G. 189 3d Av.
Hushstand Michael, 52 Walnut
Innis W. C. 45 Canal
Jacobs Matthias, 259 6th Av.
Jacobs Wesley B. 162 Grand
Jackson H. 377 6th Av.
Jackson James, 125 Duane
Jackson Thomas D. 256 Greenw'h
Jackson Wm. H. 696 Broadway
Jaclard Sebastien, 1 Ann
Jaiger T. H. 209 6th Av.
Jardine Faustino, 32½ Carmine
Jey Henry. 317 Bleecker
Jefferson Stephen R. 38 Pike
Jessel Gotthold, 6 Franklin
Jetter Jacob, 16½ Canal
Johnson John D. 13 Beekman
Johnson K. W. 140 Spring
Kallman J. F. 253 3d Av.
Kassenbreck Christopher, 71 Jas.
Keller Adam, 93 Sheriff
Kelly Alexander, 188 12th
Kelley G. 371 3d Av.
Kennel Jonathan. 69 Vesey
Kidwell T. 13½ Catharine
King W. H. 19 Duane
Kinkele Charles, 97 Leonard
Klingler John L. 46 Bayard
Krahle Frederick, 43 Cross
Kreltting Matthew, 507 Pearl
Lambert Alexander, 145 Canal
Laniger Conrad, 177 3d
Lascala James, 303 Broadway
Lauck John, 13 Bridge
Laughlin Daniel. 57 Mulberry
Leon A. 107 Chrystie
Leon Ezekiel, 35 6th Av.
Leon Jacob, 129 Forsyth
Leroy Jean, 9 Centre market pl.
Leroy Louis, 189 Hester
Lewis Daniel. 169 & 176 Broad'y
Lewis William. 138 Beekman
Lewis W. H. 626 Water
Lias D. 15 John
Lisgrau George, 128 Ridge
Lo Piccolo Joseph, 2 Park Place
Long S. A. 168 8th Av.
Louis William H. 626 Water
Lowe Samuel, 40 Vandam
Lowe William. 430 Greenwich
Luhn Casper, 241 2d
Lurch Edward, 137 Bowery
Lutz Clement, 2 Ludlow
Lynch B. 52 Dominick
Lyons Charles H. 316 Pearl
Macarthur J. 99 Fulton
Malquit Louis A. 13½ Chambers

Mancini Guido, 155 Broadway   *New York.*
Maniort John, 90 Broadway
Mason John A. 26 Fulton
Mason Joseph P. 201½ Bowery
Mathews Frederick, 163 Lewis
Mayer & Giess. 9th Av.
Mayer J. 905 4th st.
Mazza S. 721 Broadway
M'Gregor Thos. B. 164 Hammond
M'Kay Duncan, 399 Pearl
Medhurst & Heard, 27 Maid. lane
Menges Louis, 22 Desbrosses
Meneth Leonard, 243 2d
Michaelis William. 1 Albany
Miller Lewis, 295 Bowery
Miller Thomas. 80 Bleecker
Miller William, 95 West Broad'y
Mistler Martin, 195 Walker
Mitchell James. 143 Spring
Mohn David, 578½ Grand
Montcalm W. 9th Av.
Morell Frederick. 306 Houston
Morgan James, 470 Hudson
Motte Augustus, 299 Broadway
Munter John A. 195 William
Myers C. D. 22 2d Av.
Myers Francis, 18 W. Broadway
Napoleon John, 259 Centre
Nelson Gilbert, 27 Cherry
Newman T. 107½ Av. D.
Nicholls W. H. 132 Clinton place
Norahausser J. 130 Delancy
Nyes Barney, 52 Dominick
Ott M. 71 17th
Pankey Edward, 5 Battery place
Parker Thomas, 120 Beekman
Parker Wm. J. 349½ Broadway
Paul William, 84 Pearl
Peach Emanuel C. 14 Centre
Pearce Isaac, 19 Stanton
Pease William, 512 Hudson
Phelon Edwin, 197 Broadway
Phillip William, 181 Varick
Piazza Christian, 9 Amos
Pilling John, 194 Prince
Pinheiros Joaquim J. 2½ Stanton
Pleat Anasthaus, 3 Orange
Plet Cherry L. 582 Houston
Potter Frederick A. 2 Hanover
Potter John A. 98 Beekman
Poyer A. L. 23 College place
Pozzoni Joseph A. 566 Broadway
Pucenberger Jacob, 71½ Allen
Ransing William M. 334 9th
Rau George A. 22 Broome
Resield Charles, 76 Roosevelt
Reif George, 152 2d
Reinmund Julius, 171 Attorney
Revel Balthaser, 5 Walnut
Rhoades ——. 38 Wooster
Ridgway Charles, 77 Chambers
Reister William, 70½ Mulberry
Robinson John N. 26 Carmine
Roder John, 161 Av. C
Roe R. 186 Spring
Rost Philip, 277½ Houston
Roszler Valentine, 200 Rivington
Roth Charles, 341 Madison
Rowe Richard, 186 Spring
Runge Alexander, 275 Bowery
Sebzor Jacob, 41 Av. B
Scherzer George, 598 Grand
Schmidt Henry, 205 8th Av.
Schoning George, 62 8th Av.
Schreiber Christian, 338 3d
Schreel H. 379 Cherry
Schroeden Adam, 184 Rivington
Schwartz Henry, 5 James' slip
Sechel Max, 29 Frankfort
Sharileau Francois. 367½ G'wich
Sharrot Richard, 325 Spring
Shaves John, 63 Oliver
Shellds O. 679 4th
Sherwood Jeremiah, 209 Amos
Sherwood John J. 107 Hudson
Sherwood Thomas. 155 Canal
Shrill Henry, 273 Cherry
Silva Francis J. 123 E. Broadway
Sleeper Gardner, 3 James
Slocum J. 5 Henry
Sloper John, 5 Henry

Smith Benjamin W. 127 Fulton   *New York.*
Smith Charles H. 110 Houston
Smith George L. 33 Av. D.
Smith Valentine, 104 Bayard
Schoning G. 82 8th Av.
Southward Charles F. 55 Madison
Staebler John, 86 Lewis
Stark George. 413 Greenwich
Stark Michael, 413   do
Stewart C. J. 706½ Broadway
Stoll Joseph, 203 Mott
Stupp Anthony, 323 Spring
Sutton John, 432 10th
Swan Thomas, 195 Hester
Swarts Adam, 104 Pitt
Tessler Peter, 459 Broadway
Tetter T. 16 Canal
Thatford Gilbert S. 38½ Ludlow
Thatford Joseph, 402 Grand
Thompson James. 39 Leonard
Thompson John, 3 Roosevelt
Tinsdale E. East 27th st.
Toellner Gustavus. 564 Pearl
Tollbert William. 469 Houston
Torrens Joseph, 57 Cherry
Van Norden C. P. 160 Varick
Van Pelt William, 41 Howard
Vatet Eugene, 189 Broadway
Vendoff J. 7th Av.
Vidal T. C. B. 110 West
Vidal Ulysses B. 95 Gold
Vito Carrao, 26 Dey
Wade George, 116 Water
Waerecy Ferdinand, 57 Av. C.
Wainwright Thomas H. 233 Grand
Waldron N. A. 141 W. Broadway
Walker William, 156 Cherry
Washington & Peters, 8 Division
Wastlich John A. 36½ Bayard
Weekes J. 162 Greenwich
Weekes Uriah R. 102 North Moore
Weglehner John, 74 Spring
Welmer William, 164 7th
Wicks U. R. 105 North Moore
Williams Foster B. 143 Hester
Willick Francis, 92 Goerck
Wiles F. 57 Av. C.
Windorf Jacob, 116 7th Av.
Wittmer August, 111 Delancy
Wright William, 104 Barclay
Yates Thomas S. 1 6th
Zoeller Philip, 50 Delancy

Niagara County.

Slaughter J.   *Niagara Falls.*

Oneida County.

Pollard W. H. James st.   *Rome.*
Thompson S. B.   do
Johnson Wm.   do
Gilbert A. Dominick st.
Dufranolt H. 171 Genesee   *Utica.*
Batchelor D. Exchange Buildings
Batchelor J. F. 68 Genesee
Lippins F. C. 122 Genesee
Smith & Johnson, 198 Genesee
Freeman Wm. 2 Bleeker
Brown Geo. L. 3 Main

Onondaga County.

Foster J. Salina st. Syracuse
    Salina.
Smith C.   do   do
Paine R. Syracuse House, Sy'cuse
Chase & Bessin, Warren st.   do
Paline R. Genesee st.   do
Smith Wm. B. Salina st.   do
Jackson F. Clinton sq.   do
Hedgeudes G. S. Salina st.   do
Lewis Horace,   do   do

Ontario County.

Johnson Henry   *Canandaigua.*
Kelly James
Haley A.
Duffin J. W., Geneva   *Seneca.*
Wellington John
Beebe A. J

Orange County.

Reynolds A.   *Goshen.*
Kidd A.
Franklin L. P. 2d st.   *Newburgh.*
Wood Stephen
Wood G. M. South Middletown
             Wallkill.

Orleans County.

White Riley, Albion   *Barre.*
Riley Wm.   do

Oswego County.

Payne E.   *Oswego.*
Grant Tudor E. 1st st.

Putnam County.

Douttell G. Cold Spring
             Phillipstown.

Queens County.

Garasemof D. F.   *Jamaica.*

Rensselaer County.

Frost W. 271 State *Lansingburgh*
Wicks James. 2 Fake's Row
Baltimore James, Front c. State
             Troy.
Wolf Charles, 126 River
Addison Thos. 150   do
Rich Wm. 226   do
Jackson Wm. 314   do
Bonn & Cunthier, 328 River
Roth Thomas. 323 River
Baltimore Wm. S. 9 1st
Jones Wm. 136 2d
Parker Albert. 1 Albany
Fletcher Thomas. 51 Congress
Hector Thomas, 67   do
Fletcher B. 73   do

Rockland County.

Buck B., Piermont   *Orangetown.*
Hart H.   do

St. Lawrence County.

Danton O. W. Ogdensburgh
           Oswegatchie.
Nash John   do

Saratoga County.

Curtis W.   *Waterford.*
Wort Geo.

Schenectady County.

Garlock A. G. 133 State
          Schenectady.
Dana F. 147 State
Wandell R. 171 State
Latour F. 138 State
Thompson F. 3 Dock

Seneca County.

James T.   *Seneca Falls.*
Wright Joshua

Tompkins County.

Moore & Lewis, 72½ Owego
          Ithaca.
Thomas T. H. 37 Owego
Sager S. A. Aurora st.
Johnson J.   do

Ulster County.

Rosakrans Henry C.   *Kingston.*
Hammersmith J., Rondout

Washington County.

Van Vrank Daniel   *Cambridge.*
Lusee James, Sandy Hill
          Kingsbury.

Wayne County.

Holley A.   *Arcadia.*
Duffin Wm., Newark
Atkins J. C., Clyde   *Galen.*

Thompson George   *Lyons.*
Norris Benjamin
Lloyd L.   *Palmyra.*

Westchester County.

Quinn Jas. Peekskill *Courtlandt.*
Green Hawley, do
Foster H. Tarrytown *Greenburgh.*
Treulieb H. Sing Sing *Ossining.*
Driggs H.   do
Campbell J. B. Portchester *Rye.*
Jacobus John   *Yonkers.*

Yates County.

Fowler Lyman, (Penn Yan) *Milo.*
Gasner H. H.   do
Monroe Wm. H. Dundee *Starkey.*

Hair Dressers' Articles—Importer of.

Defiganiare Louis F. 24 Platt
          New York.

Hair (Human)—Importers of.

Jaclard S. 1 Ann   *New York.*
Lias D. 15 John

Hair Seating & Curled Hair.

Kings County.

Hodgkins A. 30 S. 7th
          Williamsburgh.

New York County.

Attwater E. M. 32 Cliff *New York.*
Beiser Andrew, 145 Fulton
Bodine, Beder & Co. 235 Pearl
Burkhard F. 196 W. 21st
Cumming Chas. 2 Platt
Devling Francis, 175 W. 19th
Dixon & Taylor, 119 W. 17th
Gerker Henry. 174 Fulton
Horau Denis, 72 Bowery
Johnson Geo. 165 William & 246
   6th Av.
Martin Henry, 437 Broadway
Metz Julius, jr. 32 Cliff
Towner 'Renhen H. 306 Pearl &
   313 Rivington
U. S. Hair Manufacturing Co. 306
   Pearl & 303 Madison
Wilkins Wm. 10 E. Broadway

Rensselaer County.

Edge Ruth, Hoosick st.   *Troy.*

Hair Workers.

Albany County.

Stiles Miss M. (dealer) 23 Hudson
          Albany.
Bendall H. 32 Hudson

Duchess County.

Gray J. 290 Main   *Poughkeepsie.*

Kings County.

Bourdett Mrs. Eliza, 218 Fulton
          Brooklyn.

Monroe County.

Brown Jas. 68½ Buffalo *Rochester.*
Robinson J. 19 Exchange
Sears C. 62 State
Crane J. M. & Co. 56 State

New York County.

Chatman A. F. 2 Pearl *New York.*
Chubb Mary Ann, 5 Chambers
Davy Bertha E. 10 Division
Godby Ann, 259 Greenwich

Gracemann & Mackie. 311½ B'way
          New York
Jackson M. A. 295 Division
La Rue Mary, 168 Canal
Lias D. 15 John
Link J. & R. 181 Broadway
M'Kay Duncan, 399 Pearl
Malquit Louis A. 13½ Chambers
Martelle & Co. 37 Maiden lane
Martin Henry, 427 Broadway
May Edward, 207 Spring
May Isadore, 302 Houston
Peckham & Co. 5 Chambers
Ramsay M. 261½ Bleecker
Raphael Isidore, 405 Pearl
Robertson Wm. 48 Division
Rowan E. S. 299½ Broadway
Schmitt Henry, 195 Walker
Schultz Ann L. 122 Canal

Oneida County.

Dufraineit H. 171 Genesee   *Utica.*

Rensselaer County.

Wyatt J. 21 Congress   *Troy.*

Hame Makers.

Chautauque County.

King Aaron N.   *Harmony.*

Chenango County.

Blackman R. & Co.   *Pitcher*
Eldridge Edson

Duchess County.

Bickner E.   *Fishkill.*

Livingston County.

Hall & Summers   *Mount Morris*

New York County.

Lawson J. 35 Willett   *New York.*

Hammer Manufacturers—
(See also Founders, also Edge Tool Makers, also Blacksmiths.)

Otsego County.

Chatfield & Steere   *Laurens*
Warren J. V.   *New Lisbon.*

Hardware.

Albany County

Corning Erastus & Co. (Importer)
  151 & 153 Broadway   *Albany.*
Steele Korwell, 420 Broadway
Wright N. & Co. 414 Broadway
Fry D. (importer) 40 State
Davidson & Viele, (importers) 46
  State
Warren & Steele, (importers) 66
  State
Pruyn & Vosburgh, (Importers)
  39 State
Humphrey & Co. (Importers) 41
  & 43 State
Humphrey & Lansing, (Importers)
  63 State
Miles N. E. 94 State
Jorden C. 21 Washington
Lamour T. & G. 39 Washington
Brown Wm. (Harness & Coach
  Trimming Manuf.) 13 Church
Whitbeck F. M. West Troy
          Watervliet.
Lobdell A. S. & Brother, W. Troy
Van Gantvard J. Cohoes

Alleghany County.

Crandall D.   *Almond.*
Dodd J. & Co.
Smith E. L.   *Angelica.*

Rice Avery, Whitesville
     Independence.
Lathrop Isaiah *Rushford.*

Broome County.

Sampson J. E. *Binghamton.*
Gregory G. W.

Cayuga County.

Watrous & Osborne, 73 Genesee
     Auburn.
Chote J. & Sons, 92 do
Hayden, Holmes & Co. (manufacturers) 6 & 7 Genesee
Terrell I. F. 64 do
Horton Stearns & Co. 85 do
Avery A.   *Genoa.*

Chautauque County.

Gibbs O. H. Mayville *Chautauque.*
Few & Jones, Jamestown *Ellicott.*
Williams B. E. do
Balding J. & Co. *Ellington.*
Hart & Lester, Fredonia *Pomfret.*
Harrington & Finney *Westfield.*

Chemung County.

Hinman G. T. Havana *Catharine.*
Keyser Peter, do
Watrous Riggs *Elmira.*
Scribner & Sampson

Chenango County.

Clark E. & Lyons *Pitcher.*
Park Nehemiah

Clinton County.

Fitch & Cook, (wholesale)
     Plattsburgh.

Columbia County.

M'Arthur C. Water st. *Hudson.*
Seymour George E. 309 Warren
Besaac H. W. 329 do
M'Kinstry R. do
Platt I. do
Bain P. W. Valatie *Kinderhook.*
Whiting C. jr. do

Delaware County.

Shaver & M'Nair *Andes.*
Hathaway N. *Delhi.*
Griswold & Wright
Perry & Howe

Duchess County.

Dean & Harton *Fishkill.*
Sweet E. D. & Co. Wappingers'
 Falls
Tallmadge William H. (wholesale) 260 Main *Poughkeepsie.*
Hannah George, 258 Main
Storm & Uhl, 279 do
Pearl Charles, 425 do
Judson N. W. H. *Rhinebeck.*

Erie County.

Pratt & Co. (importers) 222 Main
     Buffalo.
Pratt & Letchworth, (manufacturers) 165 Main
Folger Edward, (importer) 192
 Main
Miller John, 397 Main
Wackerman T. M. 23 Genesee
Newbould J. A. & F. W. 23 Main
Vollmer C. 381 do
Stucki John, 344 do
Jewett & Brother, 217 do
Patterson John, 270 do
Horton & Crane, 68 do
Shepard S. & Co. 56 do
Parmelee & Hadley, 119 do
Peugeot & Brother, 121 do
Dudley S. & Sons, 4 Websters'
 Block
Thomson Brothers, 9 do

Fulton County.

Livingston Daniel C. *Johnstown.*
M'Kie Peter

Genesee County.

Belden Otis & Co. *Batavia.*
Haney R.

Greene County.

Sauve Francis *Catskill.*
Cooke Frederick
Powers John
Mann John
Gardiner Edwin L. *Coxsackie.*
Kimball Elias W. *Prattsville.*

Herkimer County.

Ashley George *Little Falls.*

Jefferson County.

Blackstone & Wright *Adams.*
Harmon Samuel
Lord William & Son, *Brownville.*
Canfield T. Seckett's Harbor
     Hounsfield.
Wright Cyrenus H. *Watertown.*
Van Buren J. S.
Cooper & Woodruff
Otis David D.
Stanley Hopkins

Kings County.

Dwenger G. H. cor. Atlantic &
 Henry   *Brooklyn.*
Bayliss D. B. 134 Atlantic
Leech B. C. 160 do
Damerel George, Pacific near
 Boerum
Dikeman Henry, 70 Fulton
Young & Palmer, 236 Fulton
M'Donnal P. 64 Front
White & Burrell, 253 Fulton
White & Knapp, 155 do
Backus E. 134 Myrtle Av.
M'Carnan Peter, do
Tucker F. D. 11 & 13 S. 7th
    Williamsburgh.
Anderson Joseph, 263 S. 4th
Morrell F. V. & T. I. 115 Grand
Brown David H. 223 do
Morrell & Brother, 238 1st.

Livingston County.

Brown & Grant *Dansville.*
Reynale Geo. P. & Brother
Wood G. G.
Gilman F. & M.
Parker A.
North H. F. *Genesee.*
Buell Mortimer
Spencer Samuel *Lima.*
Hall & Summers *Mount Morris.*
King G. W. *Nunda.*
Davis F.

Madison County.

Ayres & Arnold *De Ruyter.*
Foot E. W. *Hamilton.*

Monroe County.

Amsden A. K. 6 S. St. Paul
     Rochester.
Sanborn & Stratton, 6 S. St. Paul
Bryon W. W. (mechanic's tools) 6
 S. St. Paul
Miller Alexander, 30 Main
Smith, Badger & Co. (building and
 house furnishing hardware,) 3
 Buffalo
Child J. C. 17 Buffalo
Belden Ira & Co. corner Buffalo &
 Exchange
Avery & Burke, 4 & 6 Buffalo
French John M. & Co. (hollow
 ware) 49 Exchange
Cheney J. M. 24 Exchange
King R. Graham. 206 State

Fassett M. R. (saddlery hardware)
 4 S. St. Paul
Banker & Varney, (saddlery hardware) 20 Buffalo
Lathrop W. E. (saddlery hardware) 5 Exchange
Peck C. & S. 3 Main, Brockport
     Sweden.
Hanford Wm. H., Scottsville
     Wheatland.

Montgomery County.

Williams Henry E., Fort Plain
     Minden.

New York County.

HARDWARE—CABINET MAKERS'.

Best Richard & Co. 274 Pearl
     New York.
Leech George, 225 Pearl
Smith Joseph L. 24 No. William
Thorp A. & H. S. & Co. 163 William
Toler John, 274 Pearl

HARDWARE—DOMESTIC COMMISSION MERCHANTS.

Adams Joseph H. 227 Pearl
     New York.
Alford & Dash, 5 Platt
Blackwells & Burr, 87 Water
Blivins & Mead, 9 Platt
Clark & Wilson, 13 Cliff
Collins & Co. 263 Pearl
Cox H. Henshaw, 4 & 6 Pearl
Cromwell Henry, (see advertisement) 79 Barclay
Daniels John, 230 Pearl
Leverett Josiah S. 46 Broad
Pettibone & Clark, 19 Platt
Pike David B. 7 Platt
Richards & Fleury, 21 Platt
Russell & Erwin, 92 John
Russell J. & Co. 3 Cliff
Thomas & Franklin, 89 Water
Upham Joseph, 12 Platt
Weed J. M. 179 Pearl
Willmott Samuel D. 6 Liberty
Wilson D. M. & Co. 78 & 80 Broad

HARDWARE—FANCY.

Chevalier J. D. 187 Broadway
     New York.
Hamilton Francis, 132 Division
Miller William J. 9 Maiden lane
Smith Wm. H. & Co. 4 do
Strong Wm. B. 140 Division
Tomes Francis & Sons, 6 Maiden
 lane
Wallace William. 385 Bowery
Warren Thomas, 48 Maiden lane

HARDWARE AND CUTLERY—
IMPORTERS OF.

Alexander R. H. & Co. 86 John
     New York.
Barton, Brothers, 18 Cliff
Beaham & Whitney, 272½ Pearl
Belknap Augustus, 50 Cortlandt
Benedict & Rockwell, 81 Pearl
Bishop Thomas E. 89 Maiden lane
Blacket W. 364 Bowery
Boker Hermann, 50 Cliff
Boyd J. M. 95 Maiden lane
Boyd & Wilkins, 38 Cortlandt
Bryce William & Co. 228 Pearl
Butcher W. & S. 4 Platt
Canning Edward, 60 Broad
Chaace Wm. Son & Co. 42 Cliff
Childs E. 50 Division
Clarkson Wm. 9th Av.
Congreve Chas. 58 Maiden lane
Cornell, Brothers, 26 Cortlandt
Cornell, Willis & Co. 36 do
Corning E. 132 Pearl
Crolius Edward, 26 Fulton
Delevan D. E. 489 Broadway
Dennistoun & Disbrow, 85 Pearl
Dixon C. P. 4 Cedar
Duryee P. 201 Greenwich

Elliman, Brothers, 211 Pearl
New York.
Ermenputsch John C. 1 Pine
Farmer J. W. 248 Broome
Field F. E. & A. 13 Platt
Gascoigne & Pomeroy, 15 Gold
Greaves W. & Son, 241 Pearl
Halsted A. L. & Son, 259 do
Halsteds & Dash. 54 Broad
Hanford A. G. 256 Cherry
Harrison E. 233 Pearl
Heyer Edward P. 85 Maiden lane
Hilger & Co. 19 Platt
Hill Richard & Co. 83 John
Hill Thomas. 48 Cliff
Hill, Brothers & Co. 48 Cliff
Hobson J. C. 214 Pearl
Hunt I. L. & N. S. 215 Pearl
Hyslop & Brother. 220 Pearl
Ibbotson & Horner, 22 Cliff
Ibbotson, Brothers & Co. 217 Pearl
Ibbotson, Peace & Co. 221 Pearl
Ingoldsby & Halstead, 119 Maiden lane
Irving & Van Wart, 12 Platt
Jackson, Smith & Co. 81 John
Jacot Edward H. 15 Platt
James N. E. & Co. 23 Cliff
Jellinghaus & Co. 55 Broad
Jennings J. E. 154 Maiden lane
Kay Edward, 100 William
Keutgen Charles, 82 John
Lagrave Alfred F. 210 Greenwich
Langdon & Bullus, 71 Broad
Leon H. 45 Maiden lane
Lavingston W. H. 103 Pearl
Little Charles S. 33 Fulton
Lowerre S. 307 Spring
Luyster P. H. 296 Bowery
Marshall Edward, 77 John
Marshes & Shepherd, 212 Pearl
M'Clain O. 167 Spring
Meyer Theodore A. 59 William
Mottram Thomas & Sons, 104 John
Moulson Brothers, 6 Pearl
Neustadt & Barnett, 42 Maiden la
Newbold John A. 55 John
Newbould & Russell, 140 Fulton
Nitchie John E. 13 Gold
Oakly & Fox, 30 Cortlandt
Osborne & Swan. 31 Fulton
Patrick Richard & Co. 241 Pearl
Patterson Henry A. & Co. 27 Bowery
Pickering W. S. 22 Cliff
Pedrouceti John, 213 Division
Reid & Sprague, 93 Pearl
Reynolds & Grose, 17 Platt
Richards Henry B. 93 Maiden la.
Robbins Elisha, 142 Pearl, and 108 Water
Robins Chauncey, 83 John
Rolker A. & Mollmann, 96 Pearl
Roosevelt Samuel, 3 Platt
Roosevelt & Son. 94 Maiden lane
Russell G. 82 9th Av.
Sackett, Lynes & Co. 83 Pearl and 60 Stone
Savage Thomas, 13 Gold
Scheidt G. Ald. 9 South William
Scholefield Joshua & Sons, 211 Pearl
Seymour W. N. & Co. 4 Chatham square
Seymour & Co. 6 Catharine
Sheldon Smith & Co. 271 Pearl
Stanley A. 41 Bowery
Stenton William & Son, 90 Cliff
Sumner ——, 251 Greenwich
Swords George H. 116 Broadway
Tarratt Joseph & Sons, 241 Pearl
Taylor F. G. & Co. 214 Pearl
Thomas & Co. 67 Broad
Thomas & Franklin, 89 Water
Tillotson Thomas, 77 John
Tousley C. 266 Bleecker
Townsend, Sayre & Clark, 60 Broad
Van Antwerp, Hubbell & Co. 87 Pearl
Vorwerck Charles W. 7 Platt
Walscheid William, 65 Broad

Walsh, Mallory & Co. 211 Pearl
New York.
Way & Sherman, 221 Pearl
Weed J. M. 179 Pearl
Wellington F. E. 82 John
Wilson J. 216½ Bowery
Whyte John, 333 Pearl
Widdifield & Cohu, 23 Liberty
Willets & Co. 303 Pearl & 64 Cliff
Willson E. & R. M. 126 Bowery
Wilson D. M. 78 & 90 Broad
Windle James B. & Co. 56 Maiden lane
Wolfe & Bishop, 87 Maiden lane
Wolfe & Gillespie. 193 Pearl
Woodcock William N. 212 Pearl
Wright & Smith, 249 Pearl
Wyckoff Jacob V. D. 182 B'way

PIANO FORTE HARDWARE.

Gill John, E. 26th 3d Av.
Thorp A. & H. S. & Co. 280 Pearl
Wake William, 10 Reade

SADDLERY HARDWARE.

Barrett William, 89 Reade
Buck W. J. & John Blunt, 209 Pearl
Clark C. 65½ Bowery
Donaldson & Breakey, 203 Bowery
Garthwaite William. 191 Bowery
Harmer, Hays & Co. 273 Pearl
Hayden P. & T. 219 Pearl
Jones & Bouton, 57 Bowery
Jube John P. 83 Bowery
Luqueer J. A. & R. S. 105 Pearl
Smith Sheldon & Co. 271 Pearl
Tovt John W. 110 Pearl
Van Nest Abraham R. 222 Pearl
Vannest John, 114 Pearl
Wade, Morrison & Co. 178 Pearl
Wilson J. 105 Bowery
Welles J. 398 Pearl

HARDWARE AND CUTLERY— RETAIL.

Abrams & Johnson, 443 Broadway
Baldwin & Many, 34 John
Barry John, 76 Catharine
Berrian J. & C. 601 Broadway
Blackett John, 646 Broadway
Blackett John, 78 Houston
Blackett William, 225 3d Av. & 364 Bowery
Boyd Nathaniel I. 522 Grand
Braudiaud Gaspart, 271 3d Av.
Brooker Stephen, 248 Division
Brower John I. 238 Water
Childs H. 50 Division
Clark W. 191 Bowery
Clarke & Cocks, 191½ Bowery
Conover Stephen, 296 Broadway
Conway George F. 919   do
Cox J. & J. 15 Maiden lane
Cranwell H. 79 Barclay
Cunningham Walter S. 9 Carmine
Delavan Daniel E. 489 Broadway
De Mott William J. 78 Houston
Devoy Michael, 55 Av. D
Dixon Hiram W. 355 6th Av.
Duryee Peter, 201 Greenwich
Elting William P. 438 Hudson
Fendall & Donnel, 160 6th Av.
Fish Charles F. 146 Bowery
Gilmer W. 8th Av.
Graham James L. 99 Canal
Guion George W. 174 West
Hamilton John P. 186 8th Av.
Hamilton William A. 132 Division
Hanford Albert G. 256 Cherry
Hanford Cyrus. 256   do
Herder Abraham, 62 South
Heynes A. 334 Henry
Hine Charles S. 15 Bowery
Hull & M'Mullin, 62 Vesey
Hutchinson Stephen, 362 Grand
Hynes Abraham, 334 Henry
Ives E. 105 Fulton
Jennings J. E. 154 Maiden lane
Kelly Joel, 1 Av. C

Kenyon J. S. Harlem　*New York.*
Kissam J. A. 67 Fulton
La Grane J. J. 205 Greenwich
Lee Frederick R. 245 Bowery
Levi John. 74 Vesey
Lowerre Seaman, 309 Spring
Luyster Peter I 298 Bowery
Many Vincent W. 501 Hudson
Marshes & Shepherd. 212 Pearl
Martin A. A. & Co. 269 Greenwich
Martin & Vosburgh. 127 8th Av.
M'Ceddin Barney, 181 Prince
M'Clain Orlando D. 167 Spring
M'Clusky Henry, 45 Orange
M'Intire Charles H. 304 Hudson
M'Intire William N. 80 6th Av.
Mean Anthony, 199 W. 17th
Merrill Charles, 556 Grand
Monda Francis, 42 Centre
Morris Edward M. 48 Catharine
Patterson H. A. & Co. 27 Bowery
Pedroncelli John, 213½ Division
Peterson R. E. & W. T. 144 Bowery
Phillips George, 415 Hudson
Pratt, Rokes, Webb, & Co. 126 Water
Post J. R. 586 Hudson
Quimby George, 132 6th Av.
Reiner Augustus, jr. 217 8th Av.
Richardson B. 8th Av.
Rigby John H. 60 Chatham
Robinson H. 149 Bowery
Russell George, 82 9th Av.
Sapher George, 199 W. 16th
Searle A. 18 Horatio
Seymour W. N. & Co. 4 Chatham square
Skillman A. B. 271 Greenwich
Slavin Charles, 40 South
Smith Elias L. 490 Grand
Stansberry C. 330 8th Av.
Stansbury David W. 152 8th Av.
Stead Robert, 66 3d Av.
Stoker John, 61 9th Av.
Stratton E. 403 3d Av.
Sullivan John W. & C. 74 6th Av.
Tibbetts I. M. 112 Beekman
Tice Alfred E. 46 Av. A
Timpson C. B. & Co. 126 Cherry
Tomas T. & Son, 63 Nassau
Tousley Charles, 266 Bleecker
Tucker John, 649 Broadway
Underhill J. 363 Grand
Usher John, 146 Greenwich Av.
Van Evans H. 222 Greenwich
Van Vechten R. 96 Division
Wallace Wm. 385 Bowery
Way & Sherman, 221 Pearl
White J. & Son, 81 Montgomery
Willson E. & R. M. 136 Bowery
Willson John, 216 Bowery
Wood Abraham, 392 Grand
Wood T. J. 42 Chatham
Wray Christopher, 36 Chatham
Wright Daniel D. 86 Houston
Zendell H. 546 Pearl

HARDWARE AND CUTLERY— WHOLESALE.

Ashton, Jackson & Co. 213 Pearl
Askham John, 115 John
Barton Brothers, 18 Cliff
Bayard & Wilkins, 112 Pearl
Bleecker & Bogart. 36 Cortlandt
Bliss Theodore E. 4 Platt
Boyd James M. 96 Maiden lane
Boyd & Wilkins, 112 Pearl
Brower John I. 238 Water
Butcher W. & S. 4 Platt
Carter Edward & Co. 213 Pearl
Churchill & Wetmore, 1 Platt
Clark P. B. & Co. 13   do
Cocker Samuel & Son, 6   do
Conant C. B. Ellis & Co. 217 Pearl
Corning E. 98 Water
Cox & Marshall, 4 Gold
Cromwell Henry, 79 Barclay
Danforth Jonathan, 2 Platt
Dwight, French & Co. 4 Gold
Harrison Elihu, 232 Pearl
Hendricks Uris, 33 S. William
Hopkins H. & J. 93 Barclay

Humphrey & Lansing, 50 Cortlandt
New York.
Hunt Edwin, 20 Platt
Hyslop & Brother, 210 Pearl
Ingoldsby & Halsted, 119 Maiden
lane
Lagrave A. F. 210 Greenwich
Lagrave John J. 205 Greenwich
Livingston William H. 103 Pearl
Long & Davenport, 10 Platt
Marshall L. & Co. 4 Gold
M'Clain Orlando D. 167 Spring
Moen Augustus R. 128 Water
Muller Charles, 30 Platt
Norton, Winslow & Co. 49 Broad'y
Oakley & Fox, 30 Cortlandt
Onderdonk J. Remsen, 100 Pearl
Parker William, 18 Platt
Parker Brothers, 3 Platt
Patrick Richard & Co. 241 Pearl
Quincy & Delapierre, 81 John
Reid & Sprague, 93 Pearl
Rowe John. 6 Platt
Russell John & Co. 13 Cliff
Sheehan & Duggan, 97 Maid. lane
Slark, Day, Stauffer & Co. 203 P'rl.
Smith Jacob, 95 Maiden lane
Smith, Torrey & Co. 50 Maid. lane
& 33 Liberty
Spear & Jackson, 104 John
Spies A. W. & Co. 91 Maiden lane
Tracy, Allen & Co. 116 Pearl
Tyson I. F. 4 Cedar
Underdonk J. R. 100 Pearl
Van Wagenen & Tucker, 172
Greenwich
Weed J. & M. 179 Pearl
Wetmore & Co. 81 Vesey & 205
Washington
Woodward & Connor, 205 Pearl
Wright & Smith, 249 Pearl

Niagara County.

Keep C. & Co.   *Lockport.*
Mack & Flagler
Flagler H. & Co.
Bellap J. T.
Pound Alexander
Fassett & Parsons *Niagara Falls.*

Oneida County.

Emerson H. Dominick st.   *Rome.*
Ralph Wm Holland Patent
Trenton.
Aylsworth Sylvester, 158 Genesee
Utica.
Foster & Co. 125 Genesee.
Sanger & Benedict, 125 Genesee
Sayre James & Son, (importers)
119 & 121 Genesee
Wood T. H. & G. W. 49 & 51 Gen-
esee
O'Neil Owen, 84 Genesee
Dana, Son & Co. (importers and
manufacturers) 92 Genesee
Sanders H. (carriage trimmings)
Franklin square

Onondaga County.

Bigelow O. Baldwinsville
Lysander.
Wheaton H. & C. A. (wholesale)
Salina & Water sts. Syracuse
Salina.
Sherman E. H. & J. A. Salina st.
Matthews J. P.   do
Forbes, Wright & Co. Water st.
Rope Charles & Co. (wholesale) 5
Townsend Block
Geer D. S. & S. F. Salina st.
Pearson H. (Tolls) Clinton square

Ontario County.

Clark M. & Co.   *Canandaigua.*
Parrish & Pierson
Waterman A. B.   *Phelps.*
Tillman John, Geneva   *Seneca.*
Proughty John S. do
Ackley C. B. & Co. do
Snyder R. .. do
Dickinson A. P.   *Victor.*

Orange County.

Beattie I. O. Port Jervis
Deer Park.
Merian & Smith   *Goshen.*
Brown Jas. S. 57 Water *Newburgh.*
Hathaway O. S. 54 do
Lawson J K. 62   do
Wier Edward, 88 do
Grummun J. B. (coach & saddle-
ry) 8 Water
Beattie J. O. South Middletown
Wallkill.

Orleans County.

Morehouse & Royce, Albion
Barre.
Hollenbake & Wood,   do
Jennings J., Medina   *Ridgeway.*

Oswego County.

Worster Alvah   *Hannibal.*
Clark Sidney, 1st st.   *Oswego.*
Cooper & Cornwall. 1st st.
Wheeler & Merriam, 5 Empire
Block, 1st st.
Merriam Isaac L. 3 Granite blk,
1st st.
Green John R. jr. Bridge st.
Cooley & Crane, 9 Phœnix blk
Merriam Aaron B. 1st st.
Briggs J. D. 1st st.
Rathburn & Co. Telegraph blk,
1st st.
Meacham & Norton, Pulaski
Richland.
Schryver J. C., Fulton   *Volney.*
Clark Eli, jr.   do
Wolcott J. J. & Co. Fulton

Otsego County.

Corey E. & H., Cooperstown
Otsego.
Doubleday Seth & Son, do
Stillman & Wood,   do

Putnam County.

Pelton H. & E. A., Cold Spring
Phillipstown.

Rensselaer County.

Warren & Mairs, 289 State
Lansingburgh.
Bornham J. 314 State
Fort G. 258 State
Thompson E. & Gale & Co. 169
River   *Troy.*
Ackley P. (hollow ware) 177
River
Heartt & Co. (importers) 181 do
Tator H. & Co. 193 River
Kellogg & Co. (importers) 215
River
Green & Cramer, (importers) 231
& 233 River
Warrens, Hart & Lesley, (import-
ers) 241 & 243 River
Mann & Kendrick, (importers) 341
River
Hubbell N. (importer) 309 River
Ross & Smith, (carriage trim-
mings) 179 River
Drake F. (carriage trimmings) 394
River

Rockland County.

Lane W. R.   *Haverstraw.*

St. Lawrence County.

Clark Jonathan E.   *Canton.*
Chaney A. & Co. Ogdensburgh
Oswegatchie.
Dix Samuel,   do
Pitkin N. S.   do

Saratoga County.

Harris Wm. Ballston Spa *Milton.*
Harris Arnold, do

Thomas George R. Ballston Spa
Milton.
Smith D. G.   *Waterford.*

Schenectady County.

Van Vorst Abm. A. 57 State
Schenectady.
Walker James, jr. 102 State
Yates J. I. 145 State

Seneca County.

Ferguson & Howell   *Ovid.*
Partridge E.   *Seneca Falls.*
Pontius & Barton
Bilsby & Keeler
Gray & Noyes   *Waterloo.*
Taylor E.
Young B. & Co.

Steuben County.

Church S. V. & E. F.   *Bath.*
Alley J. & G.   *Hornellsville.*
Compton & Walker *Painted Post.*
Selover & Wilson   *Prattsburgh.*

Tioga County.

Woodford R. & Co.   *Owego.*
Gregory & Co.

Tompkins County.

Pelton E. G. 46 Owego   *Ithaca.*
Conrad V. 108   do
Peckham J. S. & M. 56 Owego
Treman & Brothers, (wholesale)
107 Owego
Whitmore Geo. 103 Owego
Godley Wm. G. Trumansburgh
Ulysses.

Ulster County.

Sharp & Sahler   *Kingston.*
Styles John P.   *Saugerties.*

Warren County.

Cronkhite Orvill, Glenn's Falls
Queensbury.
Rockwell Charles, do

Washington County.

Anthony Elijah S. North Easton
Easton.
Adams J. P. Canal st.   *Whitehall.*

Wayne County.

Cressy A. F., Newark   *Arcadia.*
Sayles S. J., Clyde   *Galen.*
Fish Abel,   do
Perkins Rush, do
Butterfield & Walker   *Palmyra.*
Bowman Wm. H.
Wilder E. C. & Co.

Westchester County.

Field Charles W., Portchester *Rye.*
Daggett J.   do
Peck & Bush,   do

Wyoming County.

Gould J. H.   *Attica.*
Clark E. P.   *Perry.*
Windsor S.   *Pike.*

Yates County.

Morgan J. D., Penn Yan   *Milo.*
Brace & Hart, do
Murdock R. H., Rushville *Potter.*

Harness, Saddle and Trunk
Makers. *(See also Trunks.)*

Albany County.

Bell J. N. 473 Broadway *Albany*
M'Chesney C. B. 545 Broadway
Clendening Wm. 607   do
Edwards Charles I. 637 do

Lloyd & M'Micken, 344 Broadway
Albany.
Smith William. 311 do
Slason Edward B. 375 do
Whitney C. 6 No. Lansing
Whitney J. 12 Little Basin
Loughlen J. O. 155 Montgomery
Van Vleck Wm. 75 South Pearl
Palmer J. W. 85 Washington
Traver George, 24 do
Wagner C. *Bethlehem.*
Batchelder D. *Coeymans.*
Ward Henry, Guilderland Centre
Guilderland.
Yearsley H. West Troy *Watervliet.*
Prendle George *Westerlo.*

Alleghany County.

Ellis *Alfred.*
Lockwood J. *Almond.*
Curtis C.
Page & Huntley *Amity.*
Goodwin John M. *Andover.*
Ross A. *Angelica.*
Hills Reuben
Bullard J. J.
Seeley Gilbert *Belfast.*
Carter J.
Emory A
Carter E.
Stevens Wm. D. *Cuba.*
Eaton George
Alger J. *Friendship.*
Stowell L. 2d
Mill J. S.
Stillman M.
Sweet S. N. *Hume.*
Sweet D. W.
Ladd James,
Harrigan D. B. Whitesville
Independence.
Howe & Green *Rushford.*
Bell Joseph
Cole M. G. *Scio.*
Clark John B. Wellsville
Lattimer L. *Wirt.*

Broome County.

Tuttle & Scott, Chenango Forks
Barker.
Porter J. E. *Binghamton.*
Smith J. H.
Fancher & Hollister
Finch E.
Lawton C. C. Nineveh *Colesville.*
Thompson J. Harpersville
Stoddard G. S. *Lisle.*
Balch & Scovil *Union.*
Watson S. *Windsor.*

Cattaraugus County.

Bond O. *Franklinville.*
Guyle S., Sandusky *Freedom.*
Hoskins L. S. *Machias.*
Ballard Garriettson *Otto.*
Hall George, East Otto
Allen Orlanda, Gowanda *Persia.*
Bugbee Norman, do
Murphy W. H. do
Palmer Hiram, do
Perry Darwin, do
Kerr William, do
Knight Day *Randolph.*
Thomas James H.
Frisby L. G. East Randolph
Briggs Marvin, do
Barnes James R. *Yorkshire.*
Green George W.

Cayuga County.

Manley O. Genesee st. *Auburn.*
Shelden B. 55 Genesee
Sydam A. V. M. 86 Genesee
Spars W. V. Weedsport *Brutus.*
Rude J. do
Short —— *Genoa.*
Himrod L. *Ledyard.*
Hart G. Moravia
Boyles L. D. *Niles.*
Treadwell & Currier *Springport*

Chautauque County.

Spencer H. Mayville *Chautauque.*
Houston Warren *Cherry Creek.*
Sherman J. P. Jamestown *Ellicott.*
Sherman Silas, do
Hicks John, Irving *Hanover.*
Ballard ——, Silver Creek
Sackett E. D. Forestville
Lone G. W. do
Markham A. Nashville
Monger J. Fredonia *Pomfret.*
Stanley & Andrews, Fredonia
Smith H. F. Fredonia
Dorn J. Salem Cross Roads
Portland.
Russell E. *Ripley.*
Osborn & Briggs *Sherman.*
Brown —— *Villenova.*
Phelps Lorenzo F. *Westfield.*
Ramsey A. Z.

Chenango County.

Scott T. *Bainbridge.*
Stockwell L.
Steadman W. A.
Moffatt J. South Bainbridge
Perkins Joseph *Columbus.*
Green & Treadway *Coventry.*
Lewis C.
Weeden & Walker *Greene.*
Cohoon W. R.
Comstock Cyrus *Guilford.*
Smith William *Macdonough.*
Smyth W. *New Berlin.*
Potter J. South New Berlin
Alesworth M. do
Weeden & Knott *Norwich.*
Randall P. A.
Clark E. *Otselic.*
Knapp L. H. *Oxford.*
Watson A.
Woodlay T. T.
Fox Hubbard *Pitcher.*
Newire G. W *Plymouth.*
Brasee D. *Sherburne.*
Ringe W. O.

Clinton County.

Robinson ——, W. Chazy *Chazy.*
Percy John *Plattsburgh.*

Columbia County.

Ogden N. Spencertown *Austerlitz.*
Crego J. Canaan Four Corners
Canaan.
Pitts J. W. Malden Bridge
Chatham.
Fogarty J. Chatham Four Corners
Barker J. L. North Chatham
Stow D. B. *Claverack.*
Drury H. *Hills tale.*
Rorahack U. Warren st. *Hudson.*
Avery L. Columbia st.
Rossman S. Warren st.
Shaw S. H. 308 Warren
Tarry E. C. Warren st.
Frink J. C. Valatie *Kinderhook.*
Spears S. jr.
Bullis G. S.
Canfield P.
Vaetten H. S. *Livingston.*
Finch E. G. *New Lebanon.*

Cortland County.

Short J. *Cincinnatus.*
Higgins Charles
Brewer Henry, *Cortland Village.*
Peck N. B.
Wheadon Chas. H. *Homer.*
Short Hammond
Clark Caleb
Lund Alfred
Richardson Franklin *Marathon.*
Utley Isaac
Out John J. *Preble.*
Herrick Hiram W. *Scott.*
Pierce Albert *Truxton.*
Hibbard Ashley M.
Hulbert Jerome *Virgil.*

Delaware County.

Farnhan C. W *Andes.*
Miller T. *Davenport.*
England R *Delhi*
Fook & Elwood
Guild L. P. *Franklin.*
Bennett G. W
Jennings E.
Bartlett E. F.
Hill W. Bloomville *Kortright.*
Noble Wm. W. Hobart *Stamford.*
West H. Deposit *Tompkins.*
Dann G. W. do
Guild E. *Walton.*

Duchess County.

Hiscock J. *Amenia.*
Benjamin C. J. *Beekman.*
Weed E. *Clinton.*
Hungerford A. G. *Dover.*
Power H. *Fishkill.*
Wiley A. G. Hughsonville
Edmonds J. Fishkill Landing
Powell I. S. do
Phillips J. W. do
Westall G. *Hyde Park.*
White R. Lafayette Corner *Milan.*
Woodin E. *Pine Plains.*
Vanderburgh D. H. *Pleasant Valley.*
Seaman E. C.
Pettit H. 323 Main *Poughkeepsie.*
Bogardus James W. 303 Main
Carman C. 273 do
Barritt A. S. 237 do
Bogardus Stephen H. 234 do
Hermance E. Upper *Red Hook.*
Knickerbocker E.
Hendrick E.
Drury A. *Rhinebeck.*
Powers G. Stanfordville *Stanford.*
Shaffer N. L. do
Monfort A. *Washington.*
Warner D. Mabbettsville
Herviland N. H. do

Erie County.

Jacobs L. P. *Alden.*
Lehn John. Williamsville *Amherst.*
Barnard O. T. H. do
Walker Elihu, Williuk *Aurora.*
Hind Thomas, do
Meiser *Black Rock.*
Blakely Buel *Boston.*
Holsler G. 403 Main *Buffalo.*
Kobb Geo. & Co. 155 do
Georger Lewis cor. Ohio & Elk st.
Manning A. 3 East Seneca
Carpenter John H. 277 Main
Bohner A. 334 do
Cooke & Lytle, 10 Exchange
Kobb G. M. & Co. 117 Main
Cooper N. & Co. 123 do
West John *Clarence.*
Persall H.
Jobes Hiram *Collins.*
Wadsworth Henry, Springville
Concord.
Chase & Hayes, do
Wilcox David *Eden.*
Rotsted ——, Water Valley
Hamburgh.
Gerber A. W. *Holland.*
Harrison Thomas, Akron *Newsteas*
Hubbard F. *Sardinia.*
Sager John *Tonawanda.*
Clift —— *Wales.*

Essex County.

Noble H. R. *Elizabethtown.*
La Motté & Turner
Noble R. & Sons *Essex.*
Conger A. L.
Foster Hiram, Moriah Four Cor-
ners *Moriah.*
Foster Levi, do
Blem Geo. H. Port Henry

Franklin County.

Lincoln A. M.   *Fort Covington.*
Lathrop G. D.   *Malone.*
Ferguson A. W.
Clark Salmon

Fulton County.

Hart Robert   *Johnstown.*
Miller Jacob P.
Leach Joseph
Jeffers James H. Kingsboro
Oakley & Ridley, Northville
        Northampton.
Pease Geo.
Paul John O.   *Perth.*

Genesee County.

Gilbert David   *Alabama.*
Allen ————
Stoughton James   *Alexander.*
Manley Wm.   *Batavia.*
Ensign A. J.
Cart J. T
Tower J. M.   *Bergen.*
King Wm.
Bourn V.   *Darien.*
Newman Jacob   *Le Roy.*
Clark Theodore P.
Ingalsbe Silas & Son,   *Oakfield.*
Gilmore Wm.   *Pavilion.*
Gibbs H. East Pembroke *Pembroke.*
Dodge A. C.   *Stafford.*
Remington J.

Greene County.

Paulsen Lawrence   *Athens.*
Cure John   *Cutskill.*
Rowley & Coffin
Pierce Wm. E.
Bailey Wm. E.   *Coxsackie.*
Vandenburgh Matthias
Howe Robert   *Durham.*
Jones Richard H.   *Greenville.*
Weeden Peleg   *Prattsville.*
Steadman Chas.   *Windham.*

Herkimer County.

Huntly Lyman   *Columbia.*
Golder Benj.
Willoughby Wm.   *Fairfield.*
Putnam Jacob S.   *Frankfort.*
Casparos Daniel
Waffle John A. Mohawk
        German Flats.
Knight H. H.   do
Suiter James A.   *Herkimer.*
Carver Geo.   *Little Falls.*
Boorman Wm.
Sellman Joseph
Hosford Lorenzo, Cedarville
        Litchfield.
Ross S. A. M.
Thurston Elisha   *Newport.*
Spencer Orvin
Cole John   *Salisbury.*
Wiggins John, Salisbury Centre
Petris Wm. H. Starkville   *Stark.*
Babcock L. West Winfield
        Winfield.

Jefferson County.

Griswold J.   *Adams.*
Wilson H.
Sargent R. T. Plessis *Alexandria.*
Hamlin Wm.
Gill L.   *Antwerp.*
Hunt Jas. I.   *Brownville.*
Hunter Thomas, Dexter
Fox Geo.   do
Bates A. S.   *Champion.*
Benjamin S. S. & V. A. *Clayton.*
Albro W. T.   *Ellisburgh.*
Salisbury W. Belleville
Irwin W. H. & Co.   *Henderson.*
Lawrence Wm. L. Sackett's Harbor   *Hounsfield.*
Weaver R. Evans' Mills *Le Ray.*
Mason O. D.   do
Delano E. Three Mile Bay *Lyme.*

Bailey H. Lafargeville   *Orleans.*
Fuller A.   *Philadelphia.*
Moffatt C. D.   *Rodman.*
Roberts Wm. South Rutland
        Rutland.
Pickett L. C.
Veber Chandler C. Felt's Mills
Simmonds James   *Theresa.*
Richardson Alvah
Ogsburg Moses
Lewis Foster   *Watertown.*
Fairbanks Samuel
Hodgkins J. B. & B. F.

Kings County.

Fitzharris Thomas, 49 Atlantic
        Brooklyn
O'Neill Moses, 97 Atlantic
O'Donnell M. Columbia st.
Story R. R. 25 Fulton
Moore James L. 35 Fulton
M'Cartie J. H. 89 Fulton
Schreiber J. H. cor. Fulton & Main
Williamson L. 7 Water
Baxter John, 116 High
Knee Isaac, 17 Myrtle Av.
Lemnon John, 63 Hudson Av.
Fitkin Thomas, 176 Myrtle Av.
Edwards Thomas, 209 Myrtle Av.
Brown J. Myrtle Av. nr. Franklin
Jedica Henry, Flushing Av. near
    Graham st.
Forman T. Flushing Av. near
    Franklin st.
Church James C. Fort Hamilton
        New Utrecht.
Post S. L. 216 1st *Williamsburgh.*
Hofundill Wm. 7 Grand
Walter Geo. 276 1st
Dallawan John, 342 Grand

Lewis County.

Cooney O. W.   *Denmark.*
Merrill L., Copenhagen
Arthur I.   *Lowville.*
Forward & Virscher
Kilham P.   *Martinsburgh.*
Goady H., West Martinsburgh
Sackett E. E.   *Turin.*
Taylor James, Constableville
        West Turin.

Livingston County.

Hall John F.   *Avon.*
Palmer G. T. East Avon
Ayres Horatio N.   *Caledonia.*
Campbell Colin
Clark D.   *Conesus.*
Hall, Ingersoll & Co. *Dansville.*
Goodnow Charles
Wood G. G.
Drake J. W.
Hall Jacob B.   *Geneseo.*
Vanderbilt John
Rector M. H.
Burchard ——, Moscow *Leicester.*
Lindsley F.   *Lima.*
Thurston Henry D.   *Livonia.*
Archer Benj., Hemlock Lake
Heath Andrew J., Lakeville
Marsh John   *Mount Morris.*
Bourne B. F.
Cheynoweth T.   *Nunda.*
Ross J.
Whitehead Lewis, jr. Oakland
        Portage.
Coller C. A., Scottsburgh *Sparta.*
Bullard & May   *Springwater.*
Martindale A. S.   *York.*

Madison County.

Murphy & Bates   *Brookfield.*
Thomas S. & Son   *Cazenovia.*
Garratt G. H. & A. A.
Moore Jonah
Trimbock Isaac
Knickerbocker J. H., New Woodstock
Perry & Wallace   *De Ruyter.*
House L. H.

Stillman B. G.   *De Ruyter.*
Dennison Hatch   *Eaton*
Griswold George
Gilman Charles, Morrisville
Warmuth Benjamin   *Fenner.*
Warmuth Isaac
Stevens Chauncey   *Hamilton.*
Weaver E. H.
Wickwire Willard
Buel Eli, jr.
Stoddard H. D., Earlville
Pierce Leonard,   do
Fish A., Oneida Depot   *Lenox.*
Collins H. L., Canastota
Green Dorastus,   do
Hicks Lyman, Clockville
Burton J. E.   *Madison.*
Leonard Otis
Whitnell H. D., Erieville *Nelson.*
Ostrander & Austin, Peterboro
        Smithfield.
Brooks John H.   *Stockbridge.*
Eaton Andrew
Suits & Gaskell, Chittenango
        Sullivan.
Whitney Norman,   do
Hatch ——, Perryville
Slocum Geo. W., Bridgeport

Monroe County.

Hawkins James, North   *Chili.*
Bradley John, Honeoye Falls
        Mendon.
M'Bride G. B., West Mendon
Ball, Church & Co. Spencer's Basin   *Ogden.*
Riker J. M., Parma Corners *Parma*
Pigeon A. G.   *Penfield.*
Wright R. B.
Hine D., Fairport   *Perrinton*
Carter J., Bushnell's Basin
Ellsmore Thomas   *Pittsford.*
Russell Erastus
Daily Daniel, Churchville   *Riga.*
Willard & Town, do
Church J. W. 96 Buffalo *Rochester.*
Fassett M. R. 4 S. St. Paul
Lane J. H., Curtis' Block, Main st.
Gordon L. J. 92 Main
Lovecraft George, 90 Buffalo
Cook Elihu, 17 Exchange
Jewell William, 62 State
Pritchard A. R. 19   do
Jennings G. S. 2 Market
Havens A. A.   *Rush.*
Benson J. 26 Main, Brockport
        Sweden.
Dunning Richard, West *Webster.*
Severanbe S. O., Scottsville
        Wheatland.
Hooper Francis,   do
White E. & C. F.   do

Montgomery County.

Steve Cornelius   *Amsterdam.*
Close John
Manning Edward J. *Canajoharie.*
Warnek T. D.
Condon Wm. D. M. Burtonville
        Charleston.
Close Thompson, Minaville
        Florida.
Stewart H. Port Jackson
Vanderkirk Abraham   *Glen.*
Simpson George, Fultonville
Smith G. Smith Town
Warner G. Fort Plain   *Minden.*
Averell Wm. do
Lingunfelter J. L. Fonda *Mohawk.*
Putnam Fisher,   do
Vosburgh Jacob & Samuel, Stone Arabia   *Palatine.*
Almy Henry P.   *Root.*
Wier J. G. Spraker's Basin
Fox Elisha & Co.   *St. Johnsville.*

New York County.

SADDLE AND HARNESS MAKERS—
WHOLESALE.

Buck & Blunt, 209 Pearl *New York*

Harral, Sproulls & Co. 119 and 121 William   *New York.*
Jacobus, Condict & Co. 82 Maiden lane
Jamison Joseph, 8 Old slip
M'Kensie Richard, 72 Broadway
Smith T. & Co. 101 Maiden lane
Smith, Wright & Co. 129 Maiden lane
Trainor Patrick, 189 Broadway
Wade, Morrison & Co. 178 Pearl
Walsh Michael R. rear 224 Grand

Saddle and Harness Makers—Retail.

Abbott Walter S. 273 Bowery
Baldwin John, 110 16th
Beekman, Gerard & Benjamin, 13 Bowery
Bennett T. W. 145 3d Av.
Biesel Charles, 110 7th Av.
Bonner Marcus D. 300 E. B'dway
Borst Valentine, 140 W. B'dway
Bull John B. & James, 205 B'way
Butterfass Christian, 866   do
Callan John B. 219 Bowery
Campbell David, 8 4th Av.
Clark Cornelius, 65½ Bowery
Connell Richard, 11 E. 13th
Conway M. 10th Av. 28th st.
Cortelyou Ferdinand 8. 933 B'way
Coxhead Charles S. 702   do
Craddock J. F. 9th Av. 26th st.
Craven James, 32 Canal
Crawley Patrick. 37 Av. C.
Curr James, 296 Hudson
Davidson Robert, 863 Grand
Devoe John C. 350 Houston
Donaldson Joseph, 4 Rutgers
Donaldson & Breakey, 203 Bowery
Doyle Patrick, 157 E. Broadway
Dunn Randolph, 75 Allen
Edwards George, 206 F. 13th
Fisk Azariah, 272 Henry
Flannagan Francis, 45 Elm
Francis Charles, 39 Bowery
Fry Bernhard, 131 Pitt
Gibson Wood, 160 Fulton
Gilmore John, 92 6th Av.
Gohringer Wm. 655 Washington
Hayden P. & T. 219 Pearl
Hendricks Francis N. 306 Hudson
Heinig G. 9th Av. 35th st.
Hintchman D. B. & Co. 191 Bowery
Kaus John P. 293 W. 16th
Keily William & Son, 552 B'dway
Kellock George & Son, 454   do
Kelly William, 237 Canal
Kennedy John, 116 Duane
Kern Leopold, 373 6th Av.
Klee Sebastian, 56 Av. B.
Klein Conrad, 258 2d
Leo Thomas, 131 Grand
Littell John, 30 6th Av.
Longo Peter E. 103 Columbia
M'Cinne Robert, 120 8th Av.
M'Connell Joseph, 162 Houston
M'Guire John, 18 Jay
M'Guire P., W. 16th near 8th Av.
M'Kinsey R. 9th Av. 24th st
Macdonald Geo. 390 3d Av.
Macdonald & Lowry, 836 B'dway
Martin Patrick, 126 Liberty
Morrow William, 206 8th Av.
Motz Hans, 9 Av. B.
Murray Alexander, 41 Willet
Noble & Ray, 74 Bleecker
Playfoot David R. 124 Columbia
Pynn Simon J. 250 3d Av.
Rankine Henry, 242 8th Av.
Reilly John, 73 9th Av.
Rowan William C. 368 6th Av.
Ryer John B. 612 Broadway
Ryerson Geo. B. 279 Bowery
Savage M. 375 6th Av.
Segee Boltis M. 843 Broadway
Shaw John, 1 6th
Sheffler Joseph, 25 Av. A
Sniffen Francis A. 589 Hudson
Spicer George S. 6 Amos
Stalzer Frederick, 78 9th Av.

Stillings Isaac, 217 Canal   *New York.*
Stevens F. 260 W. 24th
Storms Christian 8. 53 Fulton
Tate John, 610 Hudson
Thompson James J. 87 Houston
Tompkins Samuel E. 118 Fulton
Trainor Patrick, 189 Broadway
Trainor Thomas, 5 W. Broadway
Treacy Thomas. 55½ Hamersley
Vanemburg Henry, 129 Duane
Wagenan Gustav, 8th Av.
Walke Thomas, 64 Broadway
Waters Charles, 692   do
Warden Benjamin, 59 3d Av.
Wells James, 396 Pearl
West Henry P. 159 Grand
Wilson John, 133 Bowery
Wilson John, 341 Pearl

Niagara County.

Heaton Samuel   *Lewiston.*
Dutcher J. M. Pekin
Foot Elijah,   do
Lewis A. B.   *Newfane.*
Sturdy William , *Niagara Falls.*
Evans William F.
Beals L. C. Youngstown   *Porter.*
Owens ———,   do
Shoemaker Jacob   *Royalton.*
Mason J. D. Reynale's Basin
Sherwood William M.   *Somerset.*
Hinman Jackson T.
Barton Samuel V. Wilson

Oneida County.

Collins L.   *Camden.*
Crouch 8.
Marr C. Clinton   *Kirkland.*
Buckley C. P. Deansville
          Marshall.
Keith Charles, James st.   *Rome.*
Merrill James,   do
Gotier L. 8.   do
Wolcott & Holtby,   do
Lumbard & Lund, Waterville
          Sangersfield.
Hotchkin M. C.   do
Hamilton M. F. Stittsville *Trenton.*
Lines M. H. 55 Genesee   *Utica.*
Darrow E. R. 41 do
Cherry M. 39   do
Shelden E. 9 Fayette
Kellott P. 4   do
Miller William G. 4 John
Knot J. M. 2   do
Dickinson J. F. Whitesboro
          Whitestown.

Onondaga County.

Allen G. A.   *Lysander.*
Allen & Baldwin, Baldwinsville
Robinson E. M.   do
Huntington C.   do
Dorchester E.   *Marcellus.*
Jones A.   *Pompey.*
Chase J. B. & Co. Salina st. 3yr. cuse   *Salina.*
Moyer J. Warren st.
Norgrove R. T. Water st.
Huntington S. T. Genesee st.
Vanalstine G. G. Warren st.
Johnson & Barnum, Salina st.
Scott & Satterly,   do
Sabin J.   do
Field & Kellogg   *Skaneateles.*
Smith A.   *Tully.*

Ontario County.

Hicks P. F.   *Bristol.*
Blank B. Bristol Centre
Herbert A. C.   *Canandaigua.*
Coy Charles
French & Judd   *East Bloomfield.*
Hardware & Stoves
Bradley William
Hill Thomas   *Manchester.*
White E.
Bursevill George   *Phelps.*
Shute M.

Douglass George, Honeoye
          Richmond.
Shaw Eli A. Allen's Hill
Watson Wm. Geneva   *Seneca.*
Pitts J. G.   do
Wentz William,   do
Reed Rodman,   do
Young M. C.   do
Page G. B.   do
Salisbury Thomas   *South Bristol.*
Peet A. L.   *Victor.*
Jacobs 8.
Ford A. C.
Wells Homer   *West Bloomfield.*
Parmelee B.

Orange County.

Coleman S. G. Washingtonville
          Blooming Grove.
Breed H. F. & W. H. Washingtonville
Olmsted E. A.   *Chester.*
Hurd C. R.
Wellington Peter
Hoyt J. L. Port Jervis *Deer Park.*
Coskey J. S.   do
Kinsey William   *Goshen.*
Bull W. Y.
Ludlum H. D.
Du Bois D. C. Well's Corners
          Minisink.
Du Bois J. E. Westown
Elmer H. D. Unionville
Millspaugh J. J.   *Montgomery.*
Goldsmith T.
Gregory J. S.   *Monroe.*
Jackson T. A.
Perritt H. D. Otisville
          Mount Hope.
Wheat S. K.   do
Anderson W. 89 Water *Newburgh.*
Peck Jonathan C. 62 do
Buckingham B. F. 1 do
Wiltsie John R. 44   do
Hatfield A. J. New Hampton
          Wallkill.
Mather T. D.   do
Stewart Wm. South Middletow
Cox J. B. & H. A.   do
Gulick F. Amity   *Warwick.*
Welling H. D. New Milford
White W. W.   do
Coleman B. F. Florida
King T.   do
Wheeler H. C.   do

Orleans County.

Hotchkins G. W. Albion   *Barre.*
Rich 8. B.   do
Wyman S. K. Barre Centre
Gates Wm. M.   do
Kellogg D.   *Clarendon.*
Hopkins Boyd, Kendall Mills
          Kendall.
Morse T.   do
Hurd P., Holley   *Murray.*
Cothrane John, Knowlesville
          Ridgeway.
Smith & Hill,   do
Livingspar ———   *Shelby.*
Foster Hiram, Lyndonville *Yates.*
Joy Sumner,   do

Oswego County.

Graves ———   *Albion.*
Copelin G. M   *Constantia.*
Duncan 8. P.
Worster Alvah   *Hannibal.*
Scott Reuben, Hannibal Centre
Woodin L. P. Central Square
          Hastings.
Clark W. T. Central Square
Pruyn M. W.   *Mexico.*
Campbell George A.
Hotchkiss Rufus
Slack Horace Prattville
Ransom H. F.   *New Haven.*
Slater Alvin D. Granite Block, 2d story, Bridge st.   *Oswego.*
Putney A. & Co. Office Row

Metcalf Daniel, 1st st.   *Oswego.*
Gordon Daniel D. do
Sessions Thomas B. do
Edick Daniel   *Parish.*
Tucker Sidney M. Pulaski
   Richland.
Burton Asa, Pulaski
Cutting N., Phœnix *Schroeppel.*
Dean Charles A., Fulton *Volney.*
Fuller Philander S. do

Otsego County.

Fitch O. L. H. West Burlington
   Burlington.
Stevens R. Burlington Green
Weeden S. G.   *Butternuts.*
Baker A.   *Cherry Valley.*
Baker D.
Biddle ——
Sheldon G.   *Exeter.*
Smith H.   *Hartwick.*
Wakefield B. F.   *Laurens.*
Comstock A.
Wellmer George
M'Combor Edgar   *Middlefield.*
Wickham L. B.
Allen C.   *Milford.*
Wright Worthington *Oneonta.*
Reynolds John
Shaver Edward B.
Coburn Levi   *Otego.*
Story George, Cooperstown
   Otsego.
Kipp B. F.   do
Stillman R.   *Plainfield.*
Tracy H.   *Springfield.*
Conklin D.
Carpenter Chester   *Unadilla.*
Herdman John   *Westford.*
Cooley James B.   *Worcester.*
Bennett Rufus M.

Putnam County.

Smith Jo.   *Carmel.*
Hazellton W. W. Farmers' Mills
   Kent.
Clinton & Hoyt   *Patterson.*
Fletcher & Hoyt
Howell J. N. Cold Spring
   Phillipstown.
Haight Wm. H.

Queens County.

Cornell Richard   *Flushing.*
Coon M.   *Hempstead.*
Weeks J.
Pine Oliver
Smith James, Far Rockaway
Baylis John   *Jamaica.*
Everett James
Rapalje D. I.   *Newtown.*
Ketcham C. Jericho *Oyster Bay.*

Rensselaer County.

Wells & Wilcox   *Berlin.*
Smith E. R. 259 State
   Lansingburgh.
Crabb Samuel, 277½ State
Green & Hait, 8 Fake's Row
Williams John & Co. 212 River
   Troy.
Townsend John B. 222 do
Thomas Job & Co. 262 do
M'Laughlin John F. 256 do
Powell E. 381 do
Dunn John W. 1 Federal
Conway P. B. 193 4th
Sickels D. W. 2 Franklin square
Burton Z. 39 Congress
Jones Wm. B. 101 do
Godson Thomas, 17 Ferry

Richmond County.

Ludlow E. A. Stapleton *Southfield.*

Rockland County.

Johnson Wm.   *Haverstraw.*
Coe S.

Wandle A. B. Piermont
   Orangetown.
Youmans J. Nyack

St. Lawrence County.

Bridge Robert C.   *Canton.*
Van Allen Orren
Symonds Joseph
Bowtell H. S. Richville *De Kalb.*
Grout W.   *Gouverneur.*
Sprague H. B.
Waldo Orange G. *Hammond.*
Rood Daniel B.
Barber Charles W. *Hermon.*
Farrington Joseph *Lawrence.*
Dayton Edwin, Columbia *Madrid.*
Jackson John F. do
Clark A. Waddington
M'Phee John   *Massena.*
Glynn James   *Morristown.*
Foster George M. Ford st. Ogdens-
  burgh   *Oswegatchie.*
Tobin Moses, Ogdensburgh
Leslie S. E.   *Parishville.*
Hopkins Aaron T. *Potsdam.*
Olmsted Edwin S

Saratoga County.

Luther John, Ballston Spa *Milton.*
Benedict C.   do
Thompson Peter, do
Rich C. F.   *Saratoga.*
M'Naughton M.
Johnson George
Meader J.
Thompson & Hartwell
   Saratoga Springs.
Dewey Daniel   *Stillwater.*
Johnson Charles *Waterford.*
Green William   *Wilton.*

Schenectady County.

Van Patten & Van Debogart, 128
  State   *Schenectady.*
Benedict A. 88 State
Lyon J. D. 54 do
Greenough D. F. 145 State
Lyon B. F. & J. H. 151 do
Dorn R. C. Dock st.

Schoharie County.

M'Carty George   *Esperance.*
Shout J. Sloansville
Frisbie D. K. Fultonham *Fulton.*
Pindle L. L.   *Gilboa.*
Bogardus G.
Shout George F. *Middleburgh.*
Doney William
Orr John W.   *Richmondville.*
Bunneson James
Dibble Lewis N.
Crawford E. H.   *Seoharie.*
Sweet S. P.
M'Intosh R. T. Gallupville
   Wright.

Seneca County.

Frantz Lewis S.   *Fayette.*
Roning Eli, Waterloo
Sackett J. W.   *Lodi.*
Weaver Henry   *Ovid.*
Bliss John B.
Van Court Thomas
Collins M. M. Farmer
Chandler C. S. do
Coleman J. M. *Seneca Falls.*
Carson J. P.
Dickerson J. W.
Lane John
Watkins William *Waterloo.*
Ackerman J. H.

Steuben County.

Coburn & Curtis   *Addison.*
Cook Knapp
Benton N.   *Bath.*
Falkner R.
Phelps W. J.
Able J.

Myers T. K.   *Cohocton.*
Rosenkrans C. J.
Wagman W.   *Dansville.*
Bullard D.   *Hornellsville.*
Benton L. D.
Ferrinbough John *Painted Post*
Hood U. D.
Snooks J. K.

Suffolk County.

Hawkins Samuel C. Patchogue
   Brookhaven.
Sutton James A. Cold Spring
   Huntington.
Tuthill J. Greenport *Southold.*

Sullivan County.

Crawford John D. Bloomingburgh
   Mamakating
Lefever M., Wurtsboro
Stringham W. H. do

Tioga County.

Barnes G. W.   *Richford*

Tompkins County.

Marshall Moses, Enfield Centre
   Enfield.
Brown J. M.   do
Smith Wm. S. & Co. *Hector*
Frost Geo. P. 23 Aurora *Ithaca.*
Benjamin S. 16 do
Heggie J. M. 37 Owego
Millspaugh S. 91 do
Stannard A. A. 69 do
Buskirk Phineas *Newfield*
Tracy Daniel L.
Anderson James H.

Ulster County.

Nichols Alonzo   *Kingston.*
Nichols A. G.
Johnson Daniel
Hasbrouck Daniel
Bogart Peter
Abbey G. C. Rondout
Abbey Stephen, do
Marshall Henry A. Eddyville
De Lamater Wm. High Falls
   Marbletown.
De Lamater R. Stone Ridge
Bruyn Z. & N.   *New Paltz.*
Vanderburgh Roberts *Saugerties.*
Barnes G. W. Napanock
   Wawarsing.
Campbell Jesse B. Ellenville

Warren County.

Albro N. Chestertown *Chester.*
Scofield William
Benedict S. Glenn's Falls
   Queensbury.
Landon John L. *Warrensburg.*

Washington County.

Hall James M.   *Argyle.*
M'Geoch Wm. North Argyle
Robertson William *Cambridge.*
Robertson & Johnson
Benson David S.   *Easton.*
Barr James, North Easton
Kingsley Warren *Fort Ann.*
Root Asa & Sons
Mitchell J. D.
Crawford John S. *Fort Edward.*
Curtis Seymour, Union *Greenwich.*
Meader G. W. do
Derby W. H.   *Hampton.*
M'Clellan R. West Hebron *Hebron*
Ingalls David do
Crawford A. T. do
Moss James M. Sandy Hill
   Kingsbury
Dickey O. H. do
Hallady —— do
Robinson B. F.   *Salem*
Robertson Alexander
Fisk Thomas B.

Briggs G. W. *White Creek*
Johnson John, N. White Creek
Porter R. do
Pierce Nathan, Canal st.
Whitehall.
Starr H. G. do
Penfield D. William st.

Wayne County.

Carman J. *Arcadia.*
Pennington J. W.
Ashley Edward
Schermerhorn Francis
Standbrough James, Newark
Terry & Saxton, Clyde *Galen.*
Foster D. *Lyons.*
Turbush M,
Miller F. D.
Rempsen & Swift, (Harness Pad)
Stacy O. M.
Finch & Thomas
Rathbone ——, Macedonville
Macedon.
Barnes Alonzo *Marion.*
Buckley L. G. *Palmyra.*
Sherman O. *Rose.*
Pfeffer —— *Sodus.*
Esbenship Andrew, Alton
Thompson Charles *Walworth.*
Wade C. B. *Williamson.*
Auchampack H.
Tarzaleai Martin *Wolcott.*

Westchester County.

Ambler Benj. *Bedford.*
Hurd Samuel W., Peekskill
Courtlandt.
Sullivan John
Jones A., Tarrytown *Greenburgh.*
Voris Zechariah *Mamaroneck.*
Baker Harvey *New Rochelle.*
Carpenter Stephen
Savey Sanford, Sing Sing
Osinsing.
Carpenter James, do
Morgan M. W., Portchester *Rye.*
Sniffen Edward do
Baxter Marvin S. *Westchester.*
Sleath Edward *White Plains.*
Banta John
Stone Wm. A *Yonkers.*

Wyoming County.

Walcott & Wright *Attica.*
Loomis Timothy
Vincent Amos, Cowlesville
Bennington.
Braiden Geo. E. *Castile.*
Shedd Daniel *China.*
Bond Levi *Genesee Falls.*
Umphrey Nelson *Java.*
Gould J. H., Wyoming
Middlebury.
Smith Jonathan S.
Gould J. H.
Kelly P. *Perry.*
Bullard N. & F.
Silver W., Perry Centre
Crittenden E. D. *Pike.*
Adams R.
Bullard F. O. *Warsaw.*
Johnson G. B.
Sherman E.

Yates County.

Randall C. H., Benton Centre
Benton
Eldridge H. do
Bridgeman A., Penn Yan *Milo.*
Morris J. F. do
Babcock J C. do
Casey Thos. G. *Potter.*
Sturtevant Josiah, Rushville
Henry Card, do
Murdock Martin, Dundee
Starkey.
Layton G. A. Jo
Hunt Wm. Rock Stream

Hat and Cap Trimmings.

Aller A. 158 Water *New York.*
Bates M. jr. 180 do
Carlebach & Jacob, 26 Cedar
Clark Isaac, 154 Water
Friend H. 140 do
Haight, Halsey & Co. 170 Water
Harris S. & B. 118 Maiden lane
Heath John, 169 Water
Kaupe E. & Cummings, 74 Beaver
King Leopold & Co. 173 Water
King P. 139 Water
Lemasson Auguste, 25 Gold
Maynard Frederick, 30 Cliff
Phillips John D. & Co. 174 Water
Sylvester W. F. 37 James
Taylor Nazareth B. 159 Water
Tucker James W. 171 do
Watson G. 165 & 167 do
West & Caldwell, 116 Maiden lane
White W. A. & A. M. 176 Water

Hat Block Makers.

Aikman R. & Son, 44 Rose
New York.
Beadman J. 192 Spring
Harsin G. 18 Fletcher
Oakley Daniel, 57 Bayard
Tood A. 36 Amos
Westfen J. B. 41 Mott

Hat Body (See also Hats, Caps and Furs) Manufacturers and Pressers.

Beadman J. 89 Sullivan *New York.*
Betts S. S. 410 Pearl
Stewart J. 266 Spring
St. John, Burr & Taylor, 148 Water
Willson J. (straw) 144 Greenwich Av.

Putnam County.

Foster E *Southeast.*

Hats, Caps and Furs.

Albany County.

Treadwell George C. & Co. 449 Broadway *Albany.*
Kelly James, 499 Broadway
Butters Silas, 485 do
Boyd Thomas, 537 do
Frothingham W. 444 do
Mayell A. & Co. 426 do
Van Namee James & Co. 402 Bd'y
Herrick E. S. 400 Broadway
Boughton D. 411 do
Hussey N. 387 do
Cotrell J. G. 48 State
Dickson Hugh, 54 State
Stores A. 80 do
Milwain J. 84 do
Tobin J. 60 Quay
Riley Michael, 74 Quay
Dunn J. 164 South Pearl
Robbins J. S. 35½ do
Hill T. H., West Troy *Waterobet.*
Kirnan ——, Cohoes

Alleghany County.

Richardson Erastus *Cuba.*
Leonard ——
Fuller S. W. *Rushford.*

Broome County.

Merrill & Root *Binghamton.*
Washburn M. D. & Co.
Dickenson G. *Windsor.*

Cattaraugus County.

Morrow John *Ellicottville.*
Seneare G. W.
Seneare & Hall *Randolph.*

Cayuga County.

Keyes L. V 47 Genesee *Auburn.*
Carpenter C. & H. 101 do
Henderson M., Weedsport *Brutus.*

Chautauque County.

Perkins S., Jamestown *Elliott.*
Whittaker W. H. do
Elmer Freeman, do
Woodard ——, Fredonia *Pomfret.*
Stevens P. H. do
Rockwell Daniel *Westfield.*

Chemung County.

Gardner N. W. *Elmira.*

Chenango County.

Haight D. *New Berlin.*
Carter John W. *Greene.*
Berry A. *Norwich.*
Griffing David
Brown Cyrus M. *Oxford.*
Northrop & Lord
Weaver C. B. *Sherburne.*
Hartwell B. *Smyrna.*

Clinton County.

Burroughs James M. *Champlain.*
Cooley Levi *Plattsburgh.*

Columbia County.

Lasell S. M., Chatham Four Corners *Chatham.*
Benedict W., Warren st. *Hudson*
Benedict H. do
Best R. E. 328 do
Brown Wm. 312 do
Tompkins R. H. 304 Warren
Tompkins C. 90 do
Beale J. R. *Kinderhook*
Kemper F.
Van Alen E., Valatie

Cortland County.

Rose John *Cortland Village.*
Kinney & M'Graw, M'Grawville
Hart Philip *Marathon.*

Delaware County.

Shaw G. M. *Delhi.*
Thurber A. J. (hats)
Northaway D. *Franklin.*
Stowe J. H., Deposit *Tompkins.*

Duchess County.

Butler C. D. *Beekman.*
Hurd R. B., Fishkill Landing
Fishkill.
Phillips Thos. R. 336 Main *Poughkeepsie.*
Freer James, 298 Main
Dean A. H. 284 do
Derrow S. R. 278 do
Vankleeck A. 266 do
Peters W. H. *Rhinebeck.*
Reed E.

Erie County.

Moore William *Black Rock.*
Ketchum & Comstock, 262 Main *Buffalo*
Meig J. 25 Genese
Cussack Martin, cor. Ohio and Indiana st.
Hall A. A. 156 Main
Bassett Thomas, 184 do
Phillips S. 34 do
Ransom A. R. 16 Webster's Block
Weber J. J. 151 Main
Bassett Gustavus, 161 Main
Robertson G. W. 171 do
Tweedy & Smith, 173 do
Stillman Horace. 169 do
Schenck Jacob S. 118 do
Smith Henry, cor. Commercial and Water st.

Essex County.

Field Hiram   *Ticonderoga.*

Genesee County.

M'Cormick F. & E. M.   *Batavia.*
Warner P.
Lord O. W.
Stanley John H.   *Le Roy.*
Ballan James

Greene County.

Strong & Ruggles   *Ashland.*
Wilcox H. R.
Olmstead Henry F.   *Catskill.*
Bosworth S. & Son
Coonwall Solomon
Taylor Elnathan H.   *Cossackie.*
Bennett William
Mann & Moorhouse   *Prattsville.*

Herkimer County.

Rand A. Mohawk   *German Flats.*
Bloomfield U.   *Herkimer.*
Usher William, Little Falls
Cook & Petrie,   do

Jefferson County.

Bassett & Co.   *Adams.*
Sigman Henry   *Watertown.*
Remington A. D.
Tubbs Alanson
Hammond Erwin A. Carthage
           Wilna.

Kings County.

Phillips John, 51 Atlantic *Brooklyn.*
Boss M. 59   do
Sheldon Julius, (caps) Everett st.
   near Fulton
Smith C. 192   Fulton
Peck Wm. H. 114   do
Peck James W. 98 do
Cristal Charles, 62 do
Fountain John A. 89 Fulton
M'Namara Michael, 74 & 76 Main
Young Jacob, Flushing Av.
Murray John, 79 Main
Connor Dennis, 55 do
Frost & Taylor, Flushing Av.
Biglow F. H. 199 Fulton
Steinburg L. 69 Hudson Av.
Helford James, 140½ Grand
          Williamsburgh.
Nefkoske A. 225 1st
Young John, 255½ Grand
Lewis Samuel, 178   do
Warner Geo. P. 34   do

Livingston County.

Henning C. D. & Co.   *Dansville.*
Hyland Geo.
Ming John & Co.
Perkins E. H.   *Genesee.*
Hill H. F.
Taggert A. Hemlock Lake
          Livonia.
Barney G. W.   *Mount Morris.*
Brown Edgar M.   *Nunda.*
White J.

Madison County.

Hawley Francis   *Oxmovia.*
Nickerson James
Spear Geo. W. & Co.   *De Ruyter.*
Comstock & Co.   *Hamilton.*
Gove & Bacon
Van Hooser A. D. Canastota *Lenox.*

Monroe County.

Ball Church & Co Spencer's Basin
          Ogden.
Holman Wm. T. 1 Main *Rochester.*
Meng John & Brother, 83 Main &
   15 State
Russell F. F. 77 Main
Clark & Gilman 93 State
Haywood & Son, 21 do

Taylor J. 76 Buffalo   *Rochester.*
Phillips O. 30 Arcade
Cornwall A. 22   do
Fonda J. 9 State
Harrison J. Main st. Brockport
          Sweden.

Montgomery County.

Hawley & Smith   *Canajoharie.*
Lawyer Lewis F.
Hazlet Wm. A. Fort Plain
          Minden.
Tappin P. S., Fonda   *Mohawk.*

New York County.

HATS & CAPS—RETAIL.

Alden Jacob M. 111 West
          New York.
Allen R. W. 16 Bowery
Alvord Geo. B. 168 Broadway &
   208 Chatham
Alvord & Bancker, 178 Broadway
   & 16 Bowery
Amidon Francis H. 301 Broadway
Archer Isaac H. & Brother, 260
   Greenwich
Atkins Chas. H. 200 Greenwich
Avery C. A. & Co. 120 Maid. lane
Ayers Reuben, 290 Bleecker
Backers, Osborn & Co. 13 Maiden
   lane
Bage R. 126 Malden lane
Banks Wm. 106 Canal
Banta Wm. 110 Canal
Baulch Wm. 35 Chatham, & 29
   N. William
Beach J. S. 243 Greenwich
Beatty C. 100 Bowery
Beaudin Dominic, 299 Broadway
Becket John. 287 Spring
Beebe Wm. H. & Co. 156 Br'dway
Belden D. W. 161 Water
Belzer John. 306 Grand
Bilderse J. 108½ Bowery
Bird Matthew, 134 Pine
Bogart Anderson, 90 Bowery
Brennen James H. 7 Av. D
Brewster Joseph B. 120 Bowery
Brown Geo. P. H. 168 Canal
Brown Wm. 126 Chatham
Bryant Martin L. 418 Grand
Bunce Hezekiah, 290 Bowery
Calleo J. 43 West
Clark Chas S. 270½ Broadway
Clark Geo. W. 245 Grand
Closkey J. M. 158 West
Coghlan John, 185 Pearl
Colahan John H. 128 West
Colahine Patrick, 149 West
Coleman Simon P. 109 Nassau
Conly Edward B. 23 Chambers
Cookley T. 269 Water
Costar James, 43 West
Coughlan John, 176 West
Cronk Samuel W. 251 Bleecker
Degan Francis, 9 Gold
Dellegan Wm. E. 234 Bleecker
Dobbins R. 9¼ Greenwich Av.
Donnelly Patrick. 56 Catharine
Duffy James, 403 West
Dullihantie John, 395 West
Dullihanty Michael, 186 West
Dunham Mehlon S. 300 Grand
Dupre François, 283 Canal
Dupree F. 37 Bowery
Eppsteen E. 21 Bowery
Espensch-id Nicholas, 107 Nassau
Fehsenheld W. 127 Delancy
Ferguson J. S. 250 Bowery
Field C. D. 57 Av. D
Finnegan Thomas, 154 Wash'ton
Fitzgibbou Patrick T. 26 Cath.
Fleming Wm. E. 49 Chatham
Foster Wm. B. 178 Chatham
Fowler Seaman, 280 Grand
Francke John, 91 Hudson
Franklin & Wolf, 244 Canal
Freeman Alpheus, 150 Bowery
Freystadt J. 136 Water
Genin John N. 214 Broadway

Green J. A. C. 24th st.   *New York.*
Hayward John. 276 Grand
Haley John, 235 Hudson
Haly Nicholas, 264 West
Hanly Dennis. 199 South
Harris T. J. 332 Bowery
Harrison Henry, 71¼ Canal
Heely Martin, 190 West
Hickok G. A. & Co. 31 Nassau
Hickok & Starr, 32 Cortlandt
Hill Ralph, 148 Nassau
Hobby E. 500 Grand
Hoffman A 415 8th Av.
Hogan Patrick, 12 West
Hunt Owen W. 56 Ann
Johnson Skidmore W. 545 Hudson
Kalish P. 376½ Grand
Karins Patrick, 96 Catharine
Keefe Thomas, 51 Chatham, 50 &
   282½ Bowery
Kellogg Joseph W. 128 Canal
Kelly & Co. 107 West
Kena F. 98 Catharine
Knox Charles, 128 Fulton
Koning Joseph, 65½ Chatham
Krekel J. G. 45 Av. A
Landa M. 157 Greenwich
Lawson & Sherman, 7 Bowery
Leary & Co. 3, 4 & 5 Astor House
Lester Joseph W. 186 Chatham
Lewock & Cahn, 283 Grand
M'Carty John T. H, 105 South
M'Inerhany Timothy, 167 Wash-
   ington
M'Intyre Rufus K. 99 Houston
M'Mannus John, 9 Bowery
Manhattan Hat & Cap Co. 478
   Grand
Maguire D. 154 Bowery
Markham John, 204 West
Markham Francis, 213 West
Markham Patrick, 263 West
Marks A. 97½ Bowery
Marks Henry, 93½ Bowery
Marony M. 122 West
Martin Lawrence Y. 227 8th Av.
Mason C. 403 Pearl
Mealio Lewis, 416 Broadway
Meany John, 146 West
Mcnay John, 53½ West
Mespan A. 280 West
Meyer Goldstein & Brother, 312
   8th Av.
Miden A. 301 Broadway
Monarque Jerem. H. 223 Bowery
Moral D. 181 8th Av.
Moreau & Leclere, 13 Av. D
Morony Michael, 122 West
Morris A. 61 Bowery
Mullan Edward, 86 6th Av.
Murch Charles G. 233 3d Av.
Murray John, 106 Catharine
New Hat Co. 148 Nassau
Nichols & Co. 240 Broadway
Obermeyer Charles, 242 3d
C'Donnell Patrick. rear 25 Cherry
O'Donoghue Timothy, 141 West
Peck George, 121 Water
Peck John B. 504 Grand
Phillips Edward, 236½ Bleecker
Phillips J. D. & Co. 174 Water
Price l. & Co. 110 Fulton
Rafferty & Leask, 123 Chatham
Rathbone D. L. 49½ Cortlandt
Reiter H. W. 54 Ann
Reynolds James, 268 Broome
Roberts W. H. & J. 205 Pearl
Rockwell & Barrows, 91 Cortlandt
Ryder E. T. & S. 194 Water
St. John Matthew C. 118 Broadway
Seronie & Archer, 151 Water
Scheidel Francis, 30 Av. B
Secor Oliver, 367 Hudson
Seymour Sylvester, 354 Pearl
Shannon John, 445 Hudson
Sillcock Peter M. 186 Canal
Simpson William, 139 8th Av.
Skinner Nelson, 108 8th Av.
Solomon S. 227 8th Av.
Spiegellery G. 203 Spring
Smith Peter T. 354 Pearl
Smith & Bonds, 32 Allen

16

Stephens Cornelius, 168 Canal
New York.
Teller John, 62 Bowery
Thompson Aaron Q. & Brother,
170 Broadway
Thompson Charles, 363 Bowery
Thompson James, 183 6th Av.
Tice Henry S. 9 Bowery
Tobin George, 93 Catharine
Todd Ira, 182 Broadway
Tombs John, 91 Canal
Treadwell G. C. & Co. 172 Water
Van Tassell T. 214 Greenwich
Warnock R. & J. 303 Broadway
Watson & Co. 154 Chatham
White Geo. W. 228 Greenwich
White & Williams, 148 Water
Wilde William, 74 Vesey
Willmarth P. C. 16 Bowery
Winter Louis, 58 Av. B
Winterton Charles H. 180 Canal
Wood James S. 51 Canal
Wooding James, 329 Hudson
Worth S. H. 89 Fulton
Yenni F. 309 Broadway
Young Charles, 280½ Bowery

HATS AND CAPS—WHOLESALE.
Alden J. M. 111 West
Archer Thomas, 147 Orchard
Avery C. A. & Co. 146 Water
Backus, Osborne & Co. 13 Maiden
Lane
Bage Robert, 126 Maiden Lane
Barton Allen, 151 Water
Beebe W. H. & Co. 156 Broadway
Belden D. W. 181 Water
Bostwick, Kent & Atwood, 184
Pearl
Boughton & Parker, 178 Water
Bragraw Louis S. 131 William
Breck Charles, 265 Pearl
Brewster Joseph, 176 Water
Bridge E. & Co. 117 Pearl
Campbell & Gray, 93 William
Cole Isaac P. 141 W. 19th
Comstock Andrew, 162 Water
Condit Israel D. 169 Water
Dorlon Joseph, 122 Water
Finchley C. J. B 76 Maiden Lane
Frost Henry, 227 Pearl
Gibb Charles M. 83 Pine
Gilbert, Camp & Co. 143 Water
Hall Asa & Son, r. 92 W. 17th
Heath John, 169 Water
Holdsworth & Co. 74 Fulton
Hudson George, 278 Rivington
Jacobs Samuel J. 145 Water
Keeler John, 121 Water
Levi Morris, 121 Water
Levi Philip, 140 Water
Lynes S. 62 Liberty
Maltby & Stare, 147 Water
Newton T. C. 33 Gansevoort
New York Hat Co. 16 Bowery
North River Hat Co. 214 Green'h
Peck George, 121 Water
Post C. H. & D. B. 142 Water
Rafferty & Leask, 7 Cedar
Rankin, Duryea & Co. 131 William
Roberts W. H. & J. 205 Pearl
Ryder E. T. & S. 194 Water
St. John, White & Williams, 148
Water
Sands & Raymond, 141 Water
Saroni & Archer, 151 Water
Schumann & Silberman, 190 Water
Seger & West, 116 Maiden Lane
Shipman Caleb H. & Co. 130 Maiden Lane
Smith Charles, 150 Water
Swift, Hurlbut & Co. 207 Pearl
Taylor A. & S. 126 Pearl
Taylor Hugh, rear 68 Beekman
Tredwell Edw. L. 25 Maiden Lane
Van Namee J. & Co. 166 Water
Van Winkle N. H. r. 199 W. 15th
Watson Chas. 169 Water
White J. P. 31 Pearl
Williams Ransom G. & Co. 84 Pearl
Williams & Cunningham, 194 do

Wright James C. 190 Maiden Lane
New York.
Wright Peter, rear 70 Beekman

Niagara County.
Bowne W.   Lockport.
Birdsall Horace
Cushing C.

Oneida County.
Barnard George, James st. Rome.
White J. & Co. Dominick st.
Bigelow & Church, Waterville
Sangerfield.
Sattlel A. Waterville
Stocking S. 34 Genesee   Utica.
Barnum Chas. 36 do
Wescott George, (wholesale) 48
Genesee
Williams & Kellogg, 62 Genesee
Latimore J. 60   do
Button I. A. 98   do
White & Mortley, 120   do
Brentnall P.   do

Onondaga County.
Herrick William, Baldwinsville
Lysander.
Hodge & Stevens, Salina st. Syracuse
Salina.
Wicks E. B. (wholesale) Syracuse
M'Clelland R. Water st.   do
Boyd Thomas, Clinton square do
Tuttle Chauncy, Genesee st.
Weaver S. G. & Co. do
Francis G.   Skaneateles.

Ontario County.
Bull George   Canandaigua.
Palmer J. M.
Williams Lyman   Phelps.
Wight & Clark, Geneva   Seneca.
Holmyshead T.   do
Perkins William, do
Seymour R.   Victor.

Orange County.
Birdsall N. Port Jervis Deer Park.
Vail Brothers   Goshen.
Vail A. E.
Senior T. H.   Montgomery.
Munson Willett L. 80 Water
Newburgh.
Warren M. & J. W. 78 Water
M'Coun & Bradley, 94   do
Harris John, jr. 87   do
Lawson W. C. 48   do
Brownly A. A. South Middletown
Wallkill.
Clark M. L.   do

Orleans County.
Miller H. & Co. Albion   Barre.
Parker C. Medina   Ridgeway.
Pike A.

Oswego County.
Betts Philander, 5 Empire Block,
1st st.   Oswego.
Phillips F., Lawrence Building,
Bridge st.
Willis Henry M. 1st st.
Buckhart Abraham, 1st st.
Stevens A. H. Pulaski   Richland.
Highriter J. C. Fulton   Volney.

Otsego County.
Stewart Levi   Milford.
Worthington J. R. Cooperstown
Otsego.
Hollister H.   do
Burker M.   Plainfield.
Hayes Charles   Unadilla.
Sherman Dwight

Queens County.
Crossman Charles   Hempstead.
Hatch William B.   Jamaica.

Rensselaer County.
Nobles S. C. 9 Fake's Row
Lansingburgh.
Lamott A. 270 State
Rousseau John, 238 State
Hatch Benjamin, 156 River Troy.
Force William, 184 do
Ellis David & Son, 196 do
Buckingham J. C. 206 do
Cook John, 212½   do
Rousseau & Boughton, 238 & 316
River
Leggett & Russell, 243 River
Barrenger A. P. 262   do
Darrows James H. 366   do
Hyman John, 296   do
Seiler Anthony, 56 Congress
Fry George, 68   do

Richmond County,
Classen J. Port Richmond
Northfield.
Lee, Morris & Co. Stapleton
Southfield.

Rockland County,
Mead E.   Haverstraw.

St. Lawrence County.
Smith J. & S.   Canton.
Goodrich & Co.   Gouverneur.
Montgomery William   Lisbon.
Benedict E. W. Ford st. Ogdensburgh
Atchinson Robert, Ogdensburgh Oswegatchie.

Saratoga County.
M'Kiterick B. Ballston Spa Milton
Parent Arthur,   do
Vibbard L. J. Saratoga Springs
Barrett A. K.

Schenectady County.
Lee D. M. 57 State   Schenectady
Van Horn J. E. 125 State
Benedict E. 85   do
Clute & Feller, 90 do

Schoharie County.
Cotrell J. G.   Esperance.
Lasell Chester   Schoharie.
Betts S. & L.   Seward.

Seneca County.
Kinyon C.   Seneca Falls.

Seneca County.
Stratton G.   Addison.
Vanderhoven J.   Bath.
M'Cauley J.
Keeler John   Painted Post.
Oviatt I.

Suffolk County.
M'Donald Alexander   Riverhead
Wiggins D. Greenport   Southold

Tioga County.
Smith S. L.   Owego
Raynaford F

Tompkins County.
Tichenor J. S. & Co. (wholesale)
44 & 58 Owego   Ithaca
Seymour J. W. 36½ Owego
Culver W. M. & M. 109 Owego
Branch L. D. Trumansburgh
Ulysses.

Ulster County.
Warren N. E.   Kingston.
Wilson Jonathan D.
Hopkins W. G.   Saugerties
Paynton A. Ellenville
Wawarsing.

Washington County.

Bennett Hazen W. *Fort Edward.*
Bassett Pardon *Greenwich.*
Miller David
Persons B. Sandy Hill *Kingsbury.*
M'Farlane M. *Salem.*
Allen John *White Creek.*
M'Nitt B. F. North White Creek
Andrews C. W. Canal st.
Whitehall.

Buel J. T. Canal st.

Wayne County

Scott Jacob, Clyde *Galen.*
Dickenson R. G. D. *Lyons.*
Hooper F. S.
Sanford & Birdsall *Palmyra.*

Westchester County.

Tucker Daniel, Mechanicsville
Bedford.
Sanders Jas. P. Peekakill
Courtlandt.
Lane E. M. do
Mann E. Tarrytown *Greenburgh.*
Tompkins G R. *New Castle.*
Coddington W. & J. M. Sing Sing
Ossining.
Hinman H. D. Portchester *Rye.*
Hinman & Deall, do
Waring William C. & Co. (Hat
Bodies) *Yonkers.*
Keeler E. B. & Co. (Hat Bodies)
Waring John T. do

Wyoming County.

Howard Anson *Castile.*
Mordoff —— *Perry.*
Root B. *Pike.*
Voorhees Wm. *Warsaw.*

Yates County.

Seymour W. H. & Co. (Penn Yan)
Milo.
Wheeler E. N. do
Thorp Geo. Rushville *Potter.*

Hat Case Maker.

Cantel Lazare, 15 W. Broadway
New York.

Hatters' Plush.

Aller Amos, 156 Water *New York.*
Bates Martin, jr. 178½ Water
Davenport Silas, 184 Water
Hirschfield & Lomer, 146 Water
Lord John C. 164 Water
Randall John, 176 Water
Sullivan Chas, 272 Water
Watson Chas. 169 Water

Hats—Straw.

Kings County.

Dunsmore Andrew, 121 Fulton
Brooklyn.
King Samuel, 96 Grand
Williamsburgh.
Beatty John P. North 1st st.
Roberts Edwin, 84 Union Av.

Monroe County.

Taylor J. (Palmleaf) 78 Buffalo
Rochester.

New York County.

Wilson E. 78 8th Av. *New York.*
Wright James, 12 Carmine
Wright Misses, 6 Carmine
Young Thos. 90 Bowery

Hat—Straw Dressers.

Beadman J. 192 Spring *New York.*

Beadman John, 89 Sullivan
New York.
Beckwith John, 287 Spring
Bedington George, 233 Grand
Berry Chas. H. 77 Chatham & 17
N. William
Betts Samuel S. 410 Pearl
Binns Nathaniel, 327 Hudson
Bown Fred. A. 183 Division
Burr Theodore, 173 Chatham
Clement John, 183 Division
Dudley Wm. 179 W. 20th
Fisher Nathan A. rear 3 Allen
Gahan Mary, rear 49 Dominick
Gillies Wm. 18½ Carmine
Githens Thomas, 38 Vestry
Golden Wm. 1½ Catharine
Goodrich Thos. S. 151½ Varick
Haywood Ebenezer, 270 William
Lidabeck Geo. 186 Houston
Mason C. 1 Division & 402 Pearl
Millson Jos. 144 Greenwich Av.
Pearson Margaret & C. 115 Hester
Pillow Wm. H. 1 Chrystie
Price Samuel, 262 William
Quin Joseph, 173 9th Av.
Robbins Orson, 191 E. Broadway
Robertson Robert, 141 Franklin
Rorke Mary A. 153½ Division
Sewall Thomas, 516 Grand
Stewart Jas. O. 271 William
Stewart John, 266 Spring
Todd Jas. 90 W. 16th
Whiteford Daniel, 80 Mulberry
Wilson Carington, 229 6th Av.
Winfield N., W. 19th cor. 8th Av.
Wootton Chas. L. 235 Division

Hat—Straw Manufacturers. *(See also Milliners.)*

Alden & Aldrich, 82 Beaver
New York.
Baker Calvin, 113½ Division
Barrett John G. 31 Essex
Barton Ann, 115 Canal
Beatt; Clement, 100 Bowery
Becket John, 287 Spring
Berry Charles H. 17 N. William
Binns Nathaniel, 327 Hudson
Binns Isaac, 309 Hudson
Blake Austin, 235 Bowery
Blake Hull, 235 3d Av.
Bracher T. 2 5th st.
Church William. 225 Hudson
Dewing Clark, 94 Houston
Dryden George, 63 Canal
Edmonson John, 224½ Bowery
Harrison Mrs. 69½ Division
Hedges Mrs. W. 297 Hudson
Hodges & Hersey, 34 Beaver
Jones William E. 180 3d Av.
Kendall Susanna, 136 Bowery
Kidd W. A. 21½ Carmine
Leland & Mellen, 171 Pearl & 121
Charlton
Maguire Dominick, 154 Bowery
Mein Robert, 184 Walker
Motley J. M. 146 Pearl
Noe Charles L. 23 Delancy
Palmer C. 501 Pearl
Quin Henry H. 404 Bowery
Read George W. & Jehial, 49
Cedar
Rothschild S. 270½ 2d
Sammis John, 61 Elizabeth
Sandford & Lamarr, 209 Bowery
Shafer & Nichols, 296 Bleecker
Simons C. H. 372 Bowery
Simmons Joseph A. 179 Bowery
Smith Hannah N. 112 W. B.way
Smith W. Willard, 36 & 38 Cedar
Smith H. W. 179 Church
Service William, 289 6th Av.
Stewart John, 266 Spring
Teasdale William C. 298 9d st.
Thomas Anne, 163 6th Av.
Underwood Wm. jr. 110 Hudson
Vanduser William A. 156 B.way
Walmsley Edward, 14 Catharine,
and 17 East Broadway

Walmsley R. J. 21 Catharine
New York.
White John, 62 Beach
Young Thomas, 98 Bowery

Richmond County.

Neron E. Tompkinsville
Castleton.

Hay Dealers. *(See also Feed.)*

Albany County.

Hilton J. cor. Quay and Hamilton
sts. *Albany.*
Brown J. C. (Presser) 127 Hudson
Hallonbeck J. M. 80 Eagle
Kinney R. & J. (Pressers)
Bethlehem.

Columbia County.

Harden G. Franklin Square
Hudson

Kings County.

Muchmore D. M. & Co. 12 Atlantic
Brooklyn.
Silliman G. 100 Gold
Hammond George, Concord cor.
Navy

Hemp—Importers of.

Tucker, Cooper & Co. 70 South
New York.

Hemp—Dealers in.

Macgregor & Morris, 10 Broadway
New York.
Wall, Richardson & Engle, 220
Front

Hide and Leather Dealers.
*(See also Leather Dealers, also
Hide and Leather Importers.)*

Kings County.

Hornby Frederick, 189 Hudson
Av. *Brooklyn.*

New York County.

Andrews Loring, 76 Gold
New York.
Armstrong M. & Sons, 9 Ferry &
64 Vesey
Auble Nathan & Co. 56 Cliff
Bunge Henry, 4 Ferry
Beatti & Sears, 76 5th
Beschormann Frederick C. 91
Bowery
Brahe A. H. & Co. 27 Ferry
Brooks J. & G. 19 Ferry
Brown Elijah T. 2 Ferry
Bulkley & Brooks, 48 Ferry
Bullard & Co. 14 Ferry
Butchers' Hide Association, 96 1st
Av.
Corse & Co. 18 Ferry
Cheshire George, 369 Houston
Columb Thomas, 232 do
Cox Henry R. 40 Bethune
Crawford Moses A. 7 Ferry
Cromwell Thomas, 46 do
Ely Epaphras C. 31 do
Field Josiah, 179 Elizabeth
Fraser Thomas, 38 Ferry
Gilman Nath. & Sons, 72 Gold
Griffin Charles H. 5 1st
Henning Henry, 22 Av. C
Hopkins Gerard, 52 Ferry
Hunn John & Co. 40 Bethune &
471 West
Hurley & Miles, 103 Division
Hoople William H. 33 Ferry
Hornby John, 9th Av.

Hoyt W. & O. 17 Ferry *New York.*
Hyde & Everitt. 22 Ferry
Knapp G. Lee & Palen. 10 Jacob
Kumbell William, 33 Ferry
Labaw Jonathan, 1 Jacob
Lapham Anson, 29 Ferry
Laurent Joseph, 208 William
Leupp Charles M. & Co. 20 Ferry
Manwaring S. W. 497 Greenwich
Marsh Benjamin, 16 Jacob
Mattison A. & J. 11 Ferry
Mattison & Ely, 23 Spruce
Melvin & Knapp, 4 Ferry
Miles & Gilman, 35 Spruce
Miller William P. 86 Gold
Palen George, 87 do
Rockwell J. S. 47 Ferry
Roes & Weed, 49 do
Schollenberger F. 353½ Houston
Scott Thomas & Son, 3 Jacob
Sherwood William, 23 Ferry
Smith James R. 25 do
Snull Thomas, 5 do
Stout T. & R. 51 do
Thorne, Watson, Corse & Co. 18 Ferry
Tucker F. B. 100 1st
Van Woert John V. 36 Ferry
Westervelt John, 46 Ferry
Young & Schultz, 37 do
Zimmerman Adam, 139 Laurens

Hides and Leathers.—Importers of.

(Marked thus[*] import Hides only.)

(See also Importers General, also Merchants Shipping and Importing.)

[*]Alsop & Chauncey, 43 South
Armstrong M. & Sons, 9 Perry & 64 Vesey
[*]Aymar & Co. 34 South
[*]Deforest W. W. & Co. 72 South
Dussol John, 24 Frankfort
[*]Harmony's F. Nephews & Co. 63½ Broadway
Mleg's Brothers, 3 Ferry
Moulis John, 26 Reade
Ratanx & Guille, 39 Maiden lane
Rockwell James S. 47 Ferry
[*]Sale William A. jr. 124 Water

Hinge Manufacturers.

Albany County.

Roy & Co. West Troy *Watervlict.*

Kings County.

Ransch A. & Betts, Duffield st.
Brooklyn.

New York County.

Prentice W. B. 34 Av. C.
New York.

Rensselaer County.

Kenny ——, near State Dam
Troy.

Hoe Manufacturers.

Chautauque County.

Waters, Franklin & Co. *Westfield.*

Chenango County.

Leonard Rufus *Smyrna.*

Oneida County.

Wilber & Co. Deansville *Marshall.*

Otsego County.

Stillman A. & Co. *Plainfield.*
Brown, Babcock & Coates

Rensselaer County.

Trull John M. *Troy.*

St. Lawrence County.

Taylor, Hubbard & Co. *Brasher.*
Buttolph, Sprague & Co. *Stockholm.*

Wyoming County.

Farwell George *Warsaw.*

Heist Wheel Maker.

Thomas Edward, 32 Spruce
New York.

Hoisting Machines.

Hogan Edward, 133 Laurens
New York.
Mahoney Daniel, 86 Walker

Homœopathic Medicines.

Dawley William, 159 Church
New York.
Dunnell H. G. 53 Broome
Freeman A. 298 E. Broadway
Mairs J. 462 Broome
Radde William, 322 Broadway
Smith J. T. S. 488 do
Washington John, 164 do

Hop Dealers.

Albany County.

Tweedie & Darlington, 86 Quay
Albany.

New York County.

Ryckman G. W. 60 Pearl
New York.

Hose Makers, (Leather.)

Albany County.

Slason Edward B. 375 Broadway
Albany.

Monroe County.

Jennings G. S. 2 Market *Rochester.*

New York County.

Bowie John H. & Co. 30 Ferry
New York.
Ludlum Jesse H. 46 Greene
Page & Maurice, 96 Walker
Rever Michael, 78 W. 13th
Wines Alexander, 229 West

Hosiery and Gloves.

Albany County.

Wiley Mrs. J. 42 South Pearl
Albany.

Kings County.

Brown Wm. 190 Fulton *Brooklyn.*
Bowman M. 138 do
Cottrell J. C. (importer) 222 Fulton
Mooney James, 94 Main
Garner M. 90½ Tillary
Savage W. L. 269½ Fulton
Couner Thomas, 219½ do
Bailey James, 157 do
Griswold James T. 25 S. 7th
Williamsburgh.

New York County
HOSIERY AND GLOVES—IMPORTERS OF.

Acker & Harris, 64 Cedar
New York.

Allen, Hazen & Co. 62 Exch. pl.
New York.
Arnold A. & Co. 62 Canal
Church & Swan, 149 Broadway
Hall, Brothers, 43 Beaver
Hard N. G. 214 Bowery
Hoose & Victor, 89 Pearl
Hughes, Ward & Co. 34 Broad
Keeley James, 12 Pine
Lockhart & Gibeon, 74 William
Mathews Robert F. 73 Cedar
Micholl Morland, 255 Broadway
Newsam Geo. 389 Greenwich
Paulson Charles, 54 Broad
Rumsey John W. & Co. 27 Cedar
Scheitlin A. & E. 113 Pearl
Stewart John, 31 Cedar
Stilley J. I. 502½ Houston

HOSIERY AND GLOVES—RETAIL.

Baker Wm. 299 Broadway
New York.
Baller Geo. 315 Grand
Barr A. 42 8th Av.
Battin Joseph H. 275 Greenwich
Bell Frederick, 194 Bowery
Bennett Wm. 84 Chatham
Brown Thomas H. 490 Grand
Bruns W. H. 326 do
Callis Thomas, 63½ Bowery
Church & Swan, 149 Broadway
Conacher John, 85 9th Av. & 239 8th Av.
Cook Edmond F. 45 3d Av.
Douglass Henry, 334 Bowery
Doyle Luke, 39 Catharine
Firdeser W. 149 Greenwich
Foggan John & Crooker, 162 Canal
Gardner Geo. 344½ Bowery
Hackett John, 31 Av. D
Harvey Charles, 304 Bowery
Hawkins S. D. 227 Grand
Healy David, 88 Catharine
Healy E. 167½ Greenwich
Healy John J. 169 do
Hedges W. 297½ Hudson
Henderson Catherine, 70 Catharine
Herrick & Scudder, 96 William
Hughes J. 325 Hudson
Hughes Thomas, 297½ Pearl
Jones M. 340 Bowery
Kellogg J. W. 128 Canal
Lawrie Alexander, 407 Broome
Leary John, 248 Bowery
Leopold D. 10½ Carmine
Levy Marcus H. 77 Chatham
Little Andrew, jr. 265 Greenwich
M'Cormick Michael, 265½ Grand & 19 Catharine
Macgregor James C. 207 Broad'y
M'Keanon Wm. 151 Greenwich
M'Lauglin Thos. 255½ do
Moore James W. 292 Bleecker
Morris J. & C. E. 234 do
Morton J. 119 Canal
Mullen W. 167½ Greenwich
Mullins D. 329 Pearl
Neale Charles, 23 Cannon
Nesbitt Alexander, 177 3d Av.
Newburger Levi & Emanuel, 276½ Bowery
O'Meara C. 261 Greenwich
Parish James, 76 Canal
Patton James, 267 Greenwich
Pattinson J. T. 507 Broadway
Paune E. H. 405 Bowery
Procter Wm. 302 Bowery
Racerk P. 249 Greenwich
Rankin & Ray, 104 do
Reides Mary, 360 Pearl
Richardson Mrs. 265 Hudson
Robinson Mrs. 356 Pearl
Roe T. 209 8th Av.
Russell Robert, 22 Carmine
Skelly Mrs. 141 Greenwich
Smith John J. 275 Grand
Spyer David, 154 Canal
Spyer Elias, 51 Catharine
Stoddard W., 264 Grand
Tauber B. 257 Hudson
Tobin G. 93 Catharine

Troy H. 384 Bowery *New York.*
Underhill Gilbert A. 59 Catharine
Veneables Richard, 132 Canal
Volger E. C. F. 147 Greenwich
Warner William, 344 Bleecker
White Wm. 90 Canal
Williams J. G. 47 Catharine

HOSIERY AND GLOVES—WHOLE-
SALE.

Brown Joshua W. 111 William
Brown Thomas H. 33 Cedar
Carpenter & Mackin, 17 Cortlandt
Davie James S. 96 Maiden lane
De Gray James, 41 John
Ely Giles S. 7 Cedar
Gilligan J. 895 Grand
Hancock John, 34 Cedar
Healy David, 86 Catharine
Herrick & Scudder, 95 William
Hinchman & Newton. 35 Cedar
Mathews Robert F. 71   do
Rogers T. 69 Ann
Tuggen & Crocker, 162 Canal
Wheeler John, jr. 57 William

Hotel Annunciator.

Jackson T. D. & Co. (see advertisement.) 122½ William
New York.

House Furnishing Ware-
houses. (See also Upholsterers.)

Kings County.

Gillespie E. R. 89 Atlantic
Brooklyn.
Bunce John, 92 Fulton
M'Auley J. H. 250 do
Rusher Joseph, 79 do
Andrews J. D. 84 Myrtle Av.
Watson J. L. 96   do
Furman H. 162   do

New York County.

Baldwin James C. 188 Chatham
New York.
Bandouine C. A. 355 Broadway
Barry John, 86 Catharine
Branigan F. 150 W. Broadway
Cate Amasa L. 103 Canal
Chenoweth John, 560 Hudson
Conklin Henry, 67 Bowery
Corning William B. 101 Hudson
Dawson George W. 67 Chatham
Denniston Robert, 1½ Laurens
Divine James, 90 W. Broadway
Fleming J. M. & Co. 316 Broadway
Flemming John, 26 Catharine
Graff & Son, 142 8th Av.
Hink William, 84 3d Av.
Hull M. C. 311   do
Hollis David, 66½ Vesey
Johnston Robert T. 38 Catharine
Jones Thomas, 314 Spring
Kenyon William F. 38 Catharine
Landgraf Charles J. 199 Mercer
Lorton G. J. 176 W. Broadway
Morris Edward M. 48 Catharine
Moylan James, 162 W. Broadway
Newhouse Benjamin, 368 do
Pearson Marmaduke, 363 6th Av.
Peterson R. E. & W. T. 144 Bow-
ery
Rosenbaum Magnus, 183 Spring
Scanlan Hugh, 215 Canal
Silvey Mary A. 192 Chatham
Simpson C. P. 79 Greenwich
Smith, Torrey & Co. 50 Maiden l.
Snedon George W. 263 Bowery
Spender Alfred H. 74 Av. B
Strong William B. 140 Division
Turner James B. & Co. 71 Gold
Wallace William, 265 Bowery
Watkins James Y. 16 Catharine
Webster John, 136 6th

Westcott R. W. 57 Greenwich Av.
New York.
Windle J. B. & Co. 56 Maiden lane.

Hydrant Manufacturer.

Bartholomew Fred. 82 Marion
New York.

Ice Dealers.

Kings County.

Andrews W. M. Agt. for Chrystal
Lake Ice Co. Baxter's & Law-
rence's Dock   *Brooklyn.*
Polhemus A. & G. 100 1st
Williamsburgh.

New York County.

Ascough John D. & Co. 190 West
New York.
Andrews H. B. & Co. 205 South
Bonesteel Robert G. 27 Com-
merce
Brown, Dennett & Brown, 106
North Moore
Derickson & Ackerman, 157
Charles
Fitch W. J. 396 Pearl
Gasque P. P. jr. 114 Christopher
Harris & Nicholls, 4 Vestry
Huyler & Wood, 30 Hammond
Keyser Ernest, jr. Av. 3 cor. 33
Knickerbocker Co. 190 Duane
Turnbull & Ackerson, 43 Harri-
son and 167 Bleecker
Winch Minot F. 157 Charles
Wood & Huyler, 30 Hammond
Wortendyke Cornelius R. & Co.
586 Greenwich & 187 Bleecker
Wortendyke & Hopper, 273 17th

Importers—General.

Bechel & Shomberg, 90 Front
New York.
Cocker James & Co. 83 John
Dowlan & Son, J. T. 283 Pearl
Dow George W. & Co. 7 Burling
slip
Emmerich & Vila, 80 Nassau
Faber Gustavus Wm. 101 Front
Fiedler Ernest, 22 Broadway
Fontaine Aine, 43 New
Francia & Co. 83 Front
Gill Thomas, 217 Pearl
Hasluck R. jr. 69 Pine
Hasluck & Co. 69 Pine
Hunt Brothers & Co. 56 Cedar
Lazarus Alexander & Co. 213
Water
Matthews J. & Co. 95 Wall
Meyer Meyer H. 139 Front
Morewood George B. & Co. 14
Beaver
Osborne John & Robt. 111 Wall
Victor & Achelis, 9 South William

India Rubber Goods.

Albany County.

M'Mullen James, 396 Broadway
Albany.

Erie County.

Strong Samuel, 46 Main *Buffalo.*

New York County.

Brooks S. 138 Fulton *New York.*
Church, Ellis & Tompkins, 30 John
Davenport Henry, 57 Fulton
Day Horace H. 23 Cortlandt
Dunham H. B. 67 Maiden lane
Fuller W. C. & Co. 38 Broadway
Goodyear H. B. 59 Maiden lane
Greacen John, jr. 96 Broadway
Hodgman D. 27 Maiden lane, man-
ufactory 25th st.

Knevitt G. M. (Rail Road Springs)
89 Broadway *New York.*
Newark India Rubber Manufac-
turing Co. 59 Maiden lane
Ray F. M. 96 Broadway
Seeley Samuel J. 11 Park row
Smith Martin M. 59 Maiden lane
Tryon Daniel, 277 Pearl
Union India Rubber Co. 19 Nassau
Ward Wm. 159 Broadway

Rensselaer County.

Hoyt A. (India Rubber Cloth)
Hollow Road   *Troy.*

Tompkins County.

Blue L. S. 51 Owego *Ithaca.*

India Rubber Shoes.

Atkinson Francis, 60 E. Br'dway
New York.
Breck Chas. E. 255 Pearl
Brooden & Bertha, 245 Pearl & 39
Cliff
Corsen Tunis, 326 Cherry
Frisbie J. M. (wholesale) 248 Pearl
(see advertisement)
Howes R. W. 129 Water
Tryson Daniel, 277 Pearl

Indigo—Importers of.

Aymar & Co. 34 South *New York.*
Blanco B. 87 Front
Cotheal & Co. 49 Water

Ink Manufacturers—Writ-
ing.

Albany County.

Starr A. G. S. 665½ Broadway
Albany.
Rosekrans & Ovens, 43 Dean

Erie County.

Prescott Wm. C. 6 Pearl *Buffalo.*

New York County.

Beastall Wm. 90 Fulton *New York.*
Blake Bele S. & Jackson, 118 John
Davids & Black, 112 John
Francis & Loutrel, 77 Maiden lane
Fraser & Everitt, 36 Gold
Hambridge Geo. 60 Clarkson
Jackson John I. 214 Centre
Knapp Henry, 199 4th Av.
Mooney & Parmenter, 76 Division
North Wm. 124 Willet
Ross Wm. P. M. 11 Spruce

Rensselaer County.

Burr O. Hollow Road *Troy.*

Saratoga County.

Eddy Geo. W. *Waterford.*

Ink Manufacturers—Print-
ing.

Monroe County.

Gregory & Co. (Phœnix Building) *Rochester.*

New York County.

Lagrange & Lingg, 71 Beach
New York.
Lightbody John G. 38 Rose
M'Creary John D. 321 & 323 Stan-
ton. Depot 3 Spruce
Mather George, 89 Beekman & 294
Front
Frout Wm. F. rear 65 Spring

Rensselaer County.
Burt O. Hollow Road   Troy.

Ink Stand & Sand Box Manufacturer.

Otsego County.
Holcomb G. & E.   Butternuts.

Inspectors.

New York County.

INSPECTORS—BEEF AND PORK.

Gardiner Thomas, 314 West
    New York.
Gardner Thomas, 529 W'hington
Getty Robert F. 357 West
Lewis John W. 313   do
Lippett Joseph F. 375 do
Seguine Columbus, 312 do
Seguine & Thompson, 516 Washington
Waters Martin, 550 Washington

INSPECTORS—CUSTOM HOUSE.

Roosevelt Jacob, 39 Pearl

INSPECTORS—DOMESTIC LIQUORS.

Bradley Edward W. 116 Wall
Vanborskerck A. 126 Broad
Walker & Pyatt, 6 Front
Wright Joseph W. 29 Moore

INSPECTORS—FLOUR.

Chamberlin Peter T. 133 Allen & 16 South
Hadden Thomas, 16 South
Tappan Christian P. 16 do

INSPECTORS—LUMBER.

Abbott Samuel B. 356 Cherry
Ackermann S. 18 Minetta lane
Barnes William H. 61 South
Bayles Daniel S. 33 Sheriff
Bennett Phillip, 324 Cherry
Burton T. 168 Christopher
Button John, 10 Stuyvesant
Constantine Thomas, 11 Tompkins
Davis John S. 708 Washington
Hicks Smith, 117 Cannon
Howell W. M. 275 Cherry
Kinny John, 370 Canal
Morris John I. 342 West
Sheffield Dudley, 304 5th
Tice Peter, 256 Cherry
Valentine Abraham M. 90 Av. B.
Young James D. 63 Whitehall

INSPECTORS—POT AND PEARL ASHES.

Cassidy, Palmer & Co. 49 West

INSPECTORS—TOBACCO.

Pearce & Jarvis, South c. Clinton

Intelligence Offices.

Bell Philip A. 99 Leonard
    New York.
Birdsall James, 422½ Broadway
Bookham Charles, 380   do
Briant Daniel S. 106 Chambers
Buckley John, 118 Nassau
Clark Charles, 95 Duane
Earickson Charles C. Agent, 360 Broadway
Employment Society's Repository, 2 Amity
Ferre Solomon, 314 Broadway
Green Matilda C. 332   do
Henderson Wm. 75 & 77 Nassau
Mason Clark, 424 Broadway & 139 Bowery
Saunders, Thorndike P. 478 B'way

Scudder John S. 70 Lispenard
    New York.
Servants' Agency, 360 Broadway
Stiner Morris, 222 Bowery
Thomas David, 7 Broad
Watts Isaiah, 240 Grand

Instruments.

MATHEMATICAL.

Albany County.
Meneely A. West Troy
    Watervliet.

Herkimer County.
Avery W. Salisbury Centre
    Salisbury.

New York County.
Brown Edmond & Son, 27 Fulton
    New York.
Davis William C. 115 John
Fehrens & Albrecht, 258 Stanton
Green James, 175 Broadway
Gregg & Rupp, 190 Water
King John, 90 South
King F. W. & R. 136 Nassau
Kutz Erastmus A. 180 Water
Megary Alexander, 190 Water
Merrill Robert, 149 Maiden lane
Pike Benjamin, jr., 294 Broadway
Prentice James, 183   do
Sawyer & Hobby, 156 Water
Shaw Robert L. 222   do

NAUTICAL.

Blunt E. & G. W. 179 Water
    New York.
Forster John, 222 Water
King John, 90 South
Pike Benjamin & Son, 166 Broadway

Onondaga County.
Chadloura John, Washington st.
Syracuse   Salina.

Rensselaer County.
Phelps & Gurley, 319 River Troy.

OPTICAL.

Madison County.
Spencer H. & C. A. Canastota
    Lenox.

New York County.
Oakes John, 140 Maiden lane
    New York.
Emmerich & Vila, 80 Nassau

PHILOSOPHICAL.

Columbia County.
Kendall E. (Thermometers and Barometers,) New Lebanon Springs   New Lebanon.
Kendall Brothers,   do   do

New York County.
Gender W. T. & T. V. 214 Greenwich   New York.
Green James. 175 Broadway
King John, 90 South
Large J. T. 118 John
Negretti O. 90 Fulton
Pike Benjamin, 294 Broadway
Prentice James, 183   do
Taglialue & Ronketti, 296 Pearl

Oneida County.
James M. (Telescopes) 4 Bleecker
    Utica.

Onondaga County.
Chadloura John, Washington st.
Syracuse   Salina.

Rensselaer County.
Phelps & Gurley, 319 River Troy.

Tompkins County.
Place D. (Telegraphic) 70 Owego
    Ithaca.

SURGICAL.

Albany County.
Owens E. 26 Beaver   Albany.

Erie County.
Sieffert John C. 5 East Swan
    Buffalo.

Kings County.
Allen Charles B. Sands st.
    Brooklyn.

Monroe County.
Clifton Henry, 1 Buffalo
    Rochester.

Iron and Steel Dealers. (See also Iron Manufacturers, also Iron Founders, also Hardware, also Steel Manufacturers and Dealers.)

Columbia County.
Seymour George E. 209 Warren
    Hudson.

Duchess County.
Trowbridge & Wilkinson, 331 Main   Poughkeepsie.
Degarmo E. & W. 430 Main
Allen J. H. & Co. 346   do

Erie County.
Thomson, Brothers, 9 Webster's Block   Buffalo.
Wilson G. B. (Pig Iron) Ohio st.

Essex County.
Cutting Franklin H.   Westport.
Allen D. L

Monroe County.
Hendricks C. & Son. 21 Buffalo st.
    Rochester.
Elliott & Fitch, 23 Buffalo
Rochester N. T. & Co. (Pig Iron) 69 Exchange st.

New York County.
Abeel John H. & Co. 368 Water & 190 South   New York.
Acosta John, 76 Broad
Alexander J. 94 Broad
Bech E. & Kunhardt. 69 West
Bent Bartlett, 54 Cliff
Bluecker & Oothout, 2 & 5 Cliff
Boorman, Johnston & Co 119 Greenwich
Breese & Elliott, 245 Water
Bruce J. M. & Sons, 192 Water
Cedwise Charles F. 210 South
Coalbrookdale Co. 26 Cliff
Congdon Charles, 26 Cliff
Cooper & Hewitt, 17 Burling slip (railroad iron)
Davenport & Slipper, 212 Water
Egleston & Battell, 166 South
Fuller Dudley B. & Co. 139 Greenwich
Gallaway Daniel A. 27 Old slip
Gilbert Charles T. 64 South
Habicht C. E. 94 Wall
Holdane & Feddeman, 52 West
Hopkins H. & J. 68 Barclay

Kemble William, 79 West
    New York.
Littlejohn D. & Co. 43 New
Mackie John F. & Co. 85 Broad
Moore John A. 77 Water
Murdock U. A. 51 New
Nichols Henry G. 79 Water
Nichols Robert. 79 Water
Olney J. N. 52 West & 255 South
Pearsall William, jr. 217 Pearl
Peck E. & Son, 27 Cliff
Pettee & Mann, 229 South
Pierson & Co. 113 Broad & 30 Front
Quincy & Delapiere, 81 John
Richmond William, 457 Hudson
Saltus & Co. 32 South
Sampson & Baldwin, 131 Green'h
Sheilds George W. & Co. 70 Broad
Smith Daniel E. 399 Water
Thomas & Co. 67 Broad
Thompson Samuel & Nephew, 275
    Pearl
Tisdale Sam. T. & Co. 218 Water
Tisdale & Borden, 70 & 71 West
    & 106 Washington
Trimble Merritt, 84 Broad
Tuckerman Joseph. 69 West
Tuckerman Lucius, 69 West
Westlake John & D. 230 South
Westlake & Coger, 233 South
Wetmore D. W. 218 Water
Wetmore & Co. 61 Vesey
Wilson D. M. & Co. 78 & 80 Broad
Wood Augustus B. 27 West

Oneida County.

Wood T. H. & G. W. 49 & 51 Ge-
    nesee   *Utica.*
Bushnell & Meeker, Pine c. Canal

Rensselaer County.

Prouty B. T. & Co. cor. Fulton &
    Mechanic sts.   *Troy.*
Noyes & Son, (pig iron) River c.
    Ferry
Tator H. & Co. 193 River
Kellogg & Co. (importers) 215
    River
Green & Cramer, (importers) 231
    & 233 River
Warrens, Hart & Lesley, (import-
    ers) 241 & 243 River
Scott & Lemon, (bar & bloom) 251
    River
Geer Gilbert, (pig iron) whole-
    sale, 299 River
Mallary & Ingalls, (pig iron)

St. Lawrence County.

Miller Wm.   *Morristown.*

Washington County.

Doubleday Danvers, Sandy Hill
    Kingsbury.

Iron Manufacturers.

Chenango County.

Burgess M.   *Bainbridge.*
Muckart N. R. & Co. *Guilford.*
Haight B. J.   *New Berlin.*

Clinton County.

Kingsland E. & J. D. & Co. (rolled
    iron, 200 hands) Keeseville
    Au Sable.
Rogers J. A. J.   *Black Brook.*
Duncan John T.
Jackson, Morgan & Co. (bloom
    iron)   *Saranac.*
Parsons G. & G. H. (bloom iron)
Spaulding Jeremiah & Son, (bloom
    iron)
Bailey H. & Co. (bloom iron)
Platt & Boynton, (bloom & finish-
    ed iron)

Columbia County.

Pomeroy L. & Sons (bar iron, 150
    tons annually)   *Ancram.*
Hudson Iron Works, Alex. C.
    Mitchell President, C. C. Alger,
    Agent—Capital $175,000—1750
    shares—Manufacture pig iron
    Hudson.

Delaware County.

Smith & Griswold   *Delhi.*
Raymond F. W. & Co. *Franklin.*
Thompson & Bassett
Ellis H., Clovesville *Middletown.*
Moore & Foote, Hobart *Stamford.*
Lennon N., Deposit *Tompkins.*

Broome County.

Corbett & Co. Corbettsville
    Conklin.
Butts R.   *Windsor.*

Duchess County.

Webb, Reed & Co. (Amenia Fur-
    nace, Wassaic pig iron) *Amenia.*
Beekman Iron Furnace, A. Ster-
    ling & Co. Owners, H. D. Ster-
    ling Agent—pig iron, 1500 tons
    annually   *Beekman.*
Fishkill Iron Furnace, C. V. V.
    Caswell—pig iron, 1500 tons an-
    nually, Hopewell   *Fishkill.*
Duchess County Iron Co. Alger,
    Perry & Wells, (pig iron) Spen-
    cer Corner   *Northeast.*
Marquet L. M.   *Rhinebeck.*
Tripp G., Stanfordville *Stanford.*

Erie County.

Grubiel, Burnett & Co. Williams-
    ville   *Amherst.*
Buffalo Iron Works, (wrought and
    nails) Benj. Hayden Agent
    Black Rock.
Baylis T. (wrought iron)

Essex County.

Crown Point Iron Co. (pig iron)
    Capital $40,000 *Crown Point.*
Penfield, Harwood & Co. (bar iron)
Whallon & Judd (bloom and bar
    iron—70 men, manufacture 1000
    tons per annum) *Elizabethtown.*
Noble H. R. (bloom and bar)
Whitcomb P. S. & Co. (bloom and
    bar—500 tons per an. 35 men)
Split Rock Forge, (bar and bloom)
Meigs Guy (bar and bloom)
Whallon James S., Whallonsburg
    Essex.
Purmert Jas. H. & Co.   *Jay.*
Downer John B.
Hall Monroe
Burt G. M. & B. V. & Co., Ausable
    Forks
Toby Jesse, jr. Upper Jay
Merritt James L.   *Keene.*
Merritt Samuel
Holt Harvey
Wilder Amherst H.   *Lewis.*
Merriam William S.
Wilder Alanson
Colburn D. K. Moriah 4 Corners
    Moriah.
Hull E.   do
Ferry John M. Port Henry
Goff George W.   do
Adirondac Iron Works (bar & pig)
    Adirondac   *Newcomb.*
Imus Tabor C.   *North Hudson.*
Forbes E. M. Schroon River
    Schroon.
Jackson F. H. (pig iron, 2000 tons
    per annum)   *Westport.*
Edwards Lazarus *Willsborough.*
Forbes Albert G.
Ross Henry H. &c
Hinds William   *Wilmington.*
Bell & Mihills
M'Leod Thomas J.

Franklin County.

Young H., W. Constable *Westville.*
Mann S.   do

Greene County.

Smith & Buell, (Malleable iron)
    Oakhill   *Durham.*

Jefferson County.

Stirling James   *Antwerp.*
Antwerp Co'y, Carthage *Wilna.*
Hodgkins J. P. & E. do
Hodgkins William, do
Crowner Joseph,   do
M'Collon Hiram,   do

Kings County.

Vulcan Iron Works, Water cor.
    Jay, Wm. Arthur, Agt. *Brooklyn.*

Montgomery County.

Wemple & Yates, Fultonville
    Glen.

New York County.

Brady A. & G. W. 29 Greene
    New York.
Collins John, 473 Broome and 41
    Wooster
Crookes Septimus, agent Coal-
    brookdale Co. 28 Cliff
Freeman F. 551 6th Av
Hall S. 129 Amos
M'Farlin Henry, 75 Broad
Mackie J. F. & Co. 85 & 87 Broad
M'Kinley R. & V. Smith, 31 2d Av.
Miller William L. 40 Aldridge
New Jersey Iron Co. 87 Broad
Townsend, Westervelt & Wright,
    590 and 592 Water, and 265 and
    267 Cherry
Tupper Charles H. 268 11th bet.
    Av. C. and Dry Dock
Tyrell Peter, 59 West

Oneida County.

Armstrong & Co. Taberg Furnace
    Taberg   *Annsville.*

Oswego County.

Constantia Iron Co. (pig iron)
    Constantia.

Otsego County.

Green Nelson   *Edmeston.*
Coon John, West Edmeston
Comstock William   *Laurens.*

Rensselaer County.

Albany Iron Works, Erastus
    Corning & J. F. Winslow, Pro-
    prietors   *Troy*

Richmond County.

Hunt N. (malleable iron) Staple-
    ton   *Southfield.*

Rockland County

Perkins E. & Son *Haverstraw.*
Ramapo Manufacturing Co.
    Ramapo.
Suffern J., Suffern

St. Lawrence County.

Freeman L. & E.   *Edwards.*
Fuller & Peck   *Fowler.*

Ulster County.

Bange & Co. Napanock
    Wawarsing.
Mains & Montross   *Saugerties.*

Washington County.

Kingsley & Everest *Fort Ann.*
Kingsley Caleb

Wayne County.

Davis, Willard & Co. (pig iron)
    Ontario.
Titus Lucius B. & Co   do
Leavenworth Hendrick & Co.
    Wolcott.

Iron Pipe Manufacturers.

Ball J. & Co. Centre cor. Reade
    New York.
Brick Joseph W. (Executors of)
    26 Centre
Norris, Gregg & Norris, 62 & 64
    Gold
Prosser Thomas, 28 Platt
Walworth, Nason & Guild, 79 John
Warrington & Richards, 29 Burling slip, agents of Batsto's furnaces
Wright Albert H. 256 Cherry

Iron (Scrap.)

Andrews William D. 456 Water
    New York.
Bacon John & Son, 413 Water
Dilworth James, 14 Goerok
Hazell Peter, 377 10th
Mackie John, 43 South
M'Bride Patrick, 217 Stanton
M'Cabe Patrick. 70 Pike
Murray John. 172 11th
Richmond Wiliam, 467 Hudson
Rogers William, 240 Stanton
Smith Lewis E. P. 309 Water
Westlaker I. D. 280 South
Woodhouse James 8. 419 Water

Ivory Black Manufacturers.

Kings County.

Adair Henry, Little Dock st.
    Brooklyn.
Mollir C. & G. Wither st.
    Williamsburgh.

Westchester County.

Shackler Morris, Hastings
    Greenburgh.

Ivory Workers.

Ball Thomas W. 12 Spruce
    New York.
Fenn John, 45 Ann
Ford F. J. 96 Fulton
Grote F. 78   do
Helmuth John G. 24 Reade
Phyfe John, rear 19 Murray
Reinhardt Nicolaus, 77 Duane
Shardlon Samuel, 118 Fulton
Valentine Daniel, 963 Houston
Vandanburg T. D. 92 Fulton

Japanned Ware. (See also Copper and Sheet Iron Works.)

New York County.

Carter Edward & Co. 30 Old slip
    New York.
Hague & Redfield, 17 Platt
Looke John D. 192 Water
Muller Nicholas, 299½ Bleecker
Rusher J. B. & G. 22 Old slip
Smith S. & Brother, 77 Fulton
Sprout Josiah, 27   do

Putnam County.

Felton A. A. & E. A., Cold Spring
    Phillipstown.

Japanners.

Backus G. A. 44 Fulton

Cook John, 44 Fulton   New York.
Dunn J. 135 Canal
Kane George, 374 Pearl
M'Gill Charles, rear 371 Pearl
Minard John, 295   do
Parshall James L. 33 Cherry
Smith John, 117 Beekman
Smithson Henry, rear 91 Fulton
Steel & Co. 306 Pearl
Wildes Thomas & Co. 30 Old slip

Javelle Water.

Goupil Frances, 39 Thomas
    New York.

Jewellers.

(See also Pencil Case Makers—also Silversmiths—also Watchmakers—also Watches and Jewelry—also Watch Jewellers.)

Albany County.

Burgess L. G. 10 Plain   Albany.
Reily J. H. 6 Beaver

Erie County.

Burdett H. 156 Main   Buffalo.
Stephenson Y. & Co. 200 Main

Kings County.

Cobb Livingston, Liberty st. cor.
    Sprague place   Brooklyn.
Chase John D. 203 Fulton

Monroe County.

Larson E. 12 Arcade   Rochester.
Steen H. S. 5 State
Tozer J. F. 5   do

New York County.

Ackerman Abraham, 144 Reade
    New York.
Alexander Isaac & Co. 12 Fulton
    & 422 Grand
Allan Alexander, 276 Bowery &
    111 Division
Anrich Louis. 72 Chatham
Arrowsmith & Rait, rear 7 Dey
Arthur, Jahns & Co. 15 Beekman
Austin Lavinus, 247 Broadway
Ayres Eleazer, 96 Nassau
Badger Geo. J. 376 Grand
Bailey E. B. 16 Cortlandt
Baldwin & Co. 170 Broadway
Baldwin & Sexton, 146 Reade
Beach D. 5 Wall
Bebee Wm. 102 Reade
Berenbrolek Fred. 17 John
Billing M. 312 Rivington
Bloomer Chas. 542 Hudson
Bowden & Merritt, 5 Dey
Brainerd, Jaffroy & Babcock, 10
    Cortlandt
Bridge Daniel, 4 Liberty place
Browne, Clarke & Co. 15 Beekman
Buckenham Geo. rear 16 Dey
Burr & Stevens, 215 Broadway
Butler Thos. 146 & 139 West
Carter & Pierson, 11 Maiden lane
Chamberlain M. jr. 63 & 65 Ann
Chamberlain S. W. rear 61 Ann
Chattelier, Downinge & Co. 73
    Nassau
Clapp Benj. W. rear 75 John
Clarke Henry, 102 Reade
Clark & Rogers, 65 Ann
Clarke Richard J. 189 Broadway
Clayton Edwin B. 284 Grand
Collins & Young, 1 Cortlandt
Colton D. A. & Co. 9 Maiden lane
Corbitt Alex. 137 Division
Davis Jacob, 270 Bowery
Deguerre Joseph, 30 Reade

Demarest W. H.'s Dey   New York.
Dominick Edwin H. 294 Grand
Downing & Baldwin, 145 Reade
Downing & Hoyt, 4 Cortlandt
Dubosq H. & W. & Co. 170 B'way
Durand Boltez M. 6 Madison
Earle Wm. H. 6 Liberty place
Edouards Ches. 206 William
Edwards Jas. A. rear 9 Elizabeth
Elkins J. & R. 60 Reade
Falkenaw Adelbert. 91½ Division
Farquhar Jas. 81½ 8th Av.
Faulkner J. W. 359 Broadway
Franklin H. 100 Chatham
Freeman N. A. 289 Broadway
Froment & Williams, r. 9 Elizab'h
Gandar W. T. 214 Greenwich
Ginocchio John B. 118 Canal
Goldsmith Mayar, 276½ Grand
Greene J. W. 64 Maiden Lane
Grinnell & Salisbury, 23 do
Gunzenhauser Antoin, 99 Reade
Haack Peter J. 110 W. Broadway
Hall Russell, 114½ Allen
Holmes Adrian B. 106 Hudson
Horn George, 6 Centre
Howard Patrick. 36 Maiden Lane
Hoyt Seymour, 256 Pearl
Huntington David, 199 Greenwich
Ideson Allison B. 15 Leonard
Jacobs Angel, 100 Chatham
Jacobs Lionel, 204 Canal
Katen A. J. rear 183 Broadway
Kayser Henry, 407 Grand
Kayser John C. 160 Pearl
Kelley George, 24½ Water
Kelly & Goodwin, 247 Grand and
    22 Maiden Lane
King Walter, 111 Division
Labagh Jacob, rear 83 Duane
Ladd George, 441 Broadway
Landon John E. 247 Hudson
Lang Daniel, 391 Pearl
Maery John, 349 Pearl
Marshall J. H. 189 Broadway
Megie Benj. G. rear 61 Ann
Melville & Co. 17 Maiden Lane
Moeligh Louis, 196 Canal
Moir J. & W. 315 Hudson
Montag Julius F. 325 Broadway
Morse & Andrews, rear 5 Dey
Mott J. C. & Co. rear 60 Reade
Oertle Francis, 161 Division
Osborn & Sears, 150 Reade, Office
    6 Dey
Ott Balthasar, 108 Roosevelt
Palmer & Newcomb, 30 Cortlandt
Palmer, Richardson & Co. 22 Maiden Lane
Peckham & Rumrill, 17 John
Pfeiffer & Francke, rear 36 Cortlandt
Pithon Antoine, 90 Nassau
Price R. 63 Ann
Rait Robert, 261 Broadway
Randel Geo. W. 172 Broadway
Randel & Baremore, 4 Liberty pl.
Richards H. M. 137 Broadway
Richards Ira & Co. 157 Broadway
Richardson & Miller, 22 Maiden Lane
Ripling R. 32 Maiden Lane
Rivinius & Klinger, rear 16 Dey
Rogers James, 399 Hudson
Roso William E. 37 Reade
Sackett, Daries & Cotter, 170
    Broadway
Salisbury & Co. 171 Broadway
Saffen & Stites, rear 63 Ann
Schubbehar R. A. 251 Hudson
Schelpf Philip, 22½ Ann
Schlaefer Carl, 59 Av. A
Schlossheimer Falk, 166 Cherry
Sewall J. N. 17 Maiden Lane
Shannon John S. 254 Greenwich
Simons John R. 86 Ann
Slack & Brother, 44 Maiden Lane
Stebbins W. & Co. 264 Broadway
Stone Chauncey C. 188 Canal
Straede Charles, 314 Grand
Stewart Charles, 13 John and 328
    Broadway

Stewart Henry, 449 Broadway
     New York.
Surname John B. 216 William
Tenney Daniel I. 251 Broadway
Thomas R. F. 276 Bowery
Tiffany, Young & Ellis, 271 B.way
Tifft & Whiting, 175 Broadway
Turney Hugh. 4 Liberty place
Vanderveer C. 55 W. Broadway
Weed H. B. 169 Spring
Wery Frederick, 76 Reade
Wettergreen Frederick, 14 John
Williams Alfred, rear 83 Duane
Winstanley H. R. 115 Roosevelt
Young Walter, 209 Grand

Jewelry and Miniature Cases.

Monroe County.

Thompson H. A. Main cor. St. Paul
     Rochester.

New York County.

Braillard F. 33 Dey *New York.*
Hartnett C. & J. 2 Cortlandt
Lepine Louis, 19½ Duane
Perenod H. R. 42 Dey

Oneida County.

Fisk Isaac, 3 and 5 Liberty *Utica.*

Rensselaer County.

Blake J. 1 1st   *Troy.*
Seamans J. M. 3d cor. River

Junk Dealers.

Albany County.

Welch H. 198 S. Pearl *Albany.*

Kings County.

Duffy James, Henderson Av.
     Brooklyn.
Hawley Thomas, Union Av.
     Williamsburgh.

New York County.

Anderson Charles M. 431 Water
     New York.
Autrup Swane, 86 Pine
Baldwin P. 36 Rector
Bennet Humphrey, 176 Stanton
Bleifuhs Francis, 228 2d
Boylan Lawrence, 238 W. 16th
Boyle James, 90 Sheriff
Brudon Augustus, 222 3d
Brown Wm. B. 462 Washington
Bubser Mary, 187 Ludlow
Bucanan C. L. 16 Burling sl.
Buchanan C. S. 179 Water
Burrows John, 81 W. 17th
Cain B. 428 Cherry
Callahan Patrick, 697 Greenwich
Carroll Catharine, 259 Stanton
Carroll Patrick, 106 Willet
Cassady Dennis, 140 Varick
Cavanagh Patrick, 30 Rector
Christal Michael, 170 South
Cline Michael, 13 Carlisle
Collins Miles, 8th Av.
Cook William, 41 Ann
Cooney Pat'k, 10 Gouverneur sl.
Cosgrove Terrence, 196 Mott
Coyle Dennis, 89 Goerck
Crosby Anthony, 69 Orange
Crowson —— 77 Orange
Culhane Patrick, 466 Water
Delaney John, 90 Hamersley
Dilworth James, 14 Goerck
Donnelly James, 42 Delancy
Donovan Timothy, 33 Moore
Doyle Redmond, 53 Madison
Draddy Patrick, 155 South
Duffy Bernard, 8½ Gouverneur
Duffy Pierce, 117 12th
Dunn John, 50 West

Early Hugh, 71 Thompson
     New York.
Egan Keiran, 19 Burling sl.
Fagin Peter, 211 Av. A
Farrell Wm. 236 Division
Field C. W. & Co. 94 Beekman
Finigan John. 428 Cherry
Fitzsimon John, 110 Goerck
Fitzsimmons Thomas, 24 Broome
Gallowin John. 101 Gold
Galloghor Bridget, 131 Walker
Gallagher John. 55½ Orange
Gallagher Patrick. 94 Mulberry
Ganter John, 224 Delancy
Gavagan Edward, 9 Hoboken
Giles John. 91 Orange
Gillin G. 492 Greenwich
Gillon Wm. 42 W. Broadway
Glinnen Michael, 174 South
Goggin Thomas, 117 W. Br'dway
Goggins Michael, 44 W. Br'dway
Gormly Patrick, 149 Pearl
Green Daniel, 54 Cherry
Harkins Charles, 84 Cross
Hartnedy Cornelius, 272 South
Hendrickson Peter, 59 Willet
Holly Mary, 115 King
Kain Bernard, 428½ Cherry
Kating Thomas, 105 Broad
Kavanagh Daniel, 4 Madison
Keene Owen, 102 Norfolk
Kelly Patrick, 292 6th
Kenna Michael, 38 9th Av.
Lyons John, 34 Laurens
M'Cabe John, 57 Sheriff
M'Carthy Edward. 52 Thompson
M'Fee John, 68 Hamersley
M'Geough John, 241 Stanton
M'Gunnigal James, 151 Orange
M'Hugh Mary, 190 West 16th
M'Intyre Robert, 186 West 16th
M'Kee Bernard, 357 Cherry
M'Kenna James, 398 Cherry
M'Kenna Thomas, 19 Carlisle
M'Knight Francis, 235 Stanton
M'Laughlin Patrick, 135 Walker
M'Mahon M. 230 13th
M'Manus Elizabeth, 65 Orchard
M'Manus Owen, 47 Laurens
M'Parlan William, 152 Walker
M'Sweeny John, 120 Roosevelt
Madgan Michael. 673 Washington
Maguire James, 398 Cherry
Manning John, 97 Greenwich Av.
Martin Daniel, 17 Orange & 62 Hester
Mattalier John, 60 Spring
Melvill Alex. 687 Washington
Miles William, 68½ Hamersley
Mooney Patrick, 68 West 14th
Moss Edward, 54 Walnut
Moss Thomas, 39 & 63 Orange
Moylan J. 162 West Broadway
Munger Henry, 133 Pitt
Murphy Dennis, 360 South
Murphy Patrick, 8 Walnut
Norton Thomas, 195 Hester
O'Connor James, 290 Front
O'Connor Michael, 25 Morris
O'Dwire William, 700 Water
Pfaff John H. 6th Av.
Quilen Bernard, 21 Oak
Raundtree R. 156 Christopher
Redmond John, 66 7th Av.
Regan Mary, 125 Roosevelt
Riordin David, 68 Centre
Rogers William, 240 Stanton
Bowantry Michael. 156 Christ'r
Rush Daniel, 340 3d
Russell Hugh, 119 Ridge
Sammis Israel, 208 West 21st
Shanny James, 51 Harrison
Slavin Michael, 26 West
Smith Ann, 29 Av. C.
Smith John, 189 South
Smith Michael, 175 West 14th
Stoker J. Jr. & Co. 64 9th Av.
Sweeny Edward, 167 Broome
Sweeny John, 76 Orange
Sweet James, 227 West
Thompson James, 94 9th Av.
Watts Janett, 102 West 16th.

Welsh John, 71 West Broadway
     New York.
White P. 41 Peck Slip

Oneida County.

Potter D. 17 Bleeker *Utica.*

Rensselaer County.

Powers Jonathan, 6 Federal *Troy.*
Young Wm. 142 4th
Hall Charles J. 19 Division
Prouty Benjamin

Kaleidoscope Maker.

Behrend Samuel N. 5 1st Av.
     New York

Kit Cutters.

Adam M. 86 Reade *New York.*
Kraft Franz. 171 Delancy
Kretschmar Edward, jr. 539 Pearl
Morg Christian, 21 Mott

Knitting Factory.

Egleris & Bailey, Cohoes
     Watervliet.

Knob manufacturers. (See also Locks—also Turners.)

Albany County.

Pond J. M. 11 Church *Albany.*
Argillo Works, (also locks and latches)

Oneida County

M'Lean S. Whitesboro st. *Utica.*

Saratoga County.

Harrison John *Stillwater*

Laces and Embroideries—Importers of.

Armstrong & Martin, 30 Pine
     New York.
Boscher Alexander, 9 Cedar
Bruner William, 1 South William
Chancerel Anne, 25 Park pl.
Cochran S. & Co. 143 Pearl
Cochranes A. & Co. 81 William
Crane & Thomson, 53 John
Dettlebach M. & Co. 54 Beaver
Eastman, Sheldon & Townsend, 42 Cedar
Farrell Thomas & Co. 14 John
Fishers & Robinson, 131 Pearl
Griffin & Pullman, 98 William
Hall Bros. 43 Beaver
Higgins J. & Co. 89 William
Hill Brothers, 49 John
Hughes, Ward & Co. 24 Broad
Jaffray & Sons, 73 Broadway
Joly Freres, 44 Beaver
Lowndes Thomas, 18 William
Pearce George & Co. 19 Broad
Phillips Henry, 57 William
Phillips & Sons, 76 William
Roberts Peter. 373 Broadway
Robinson Henry, 70 William
Rogers & Walker, 105 William
Scott Charles, 87 Beaver
Schroden & Surtyer, 72 William
Sharp James R. 86 Cedar
Shepherd Thomas, 371 Broadway
Strahlheims S. & Co. 78 William
Wetherald & Young. 57 William
Wilson R. & G. 20 Liberty
Wyeth Rogers & Co. 128 Pearl
Uhlfelder E. 56 Canal

Laces and Embroideries—Retail. *(See also Dry Goods, also Millinery.)*

Albany County.

Hindman A. G. 534 Broadway *Albany.*

Leash John, 522 do
Barclay H. M. 512 do

New York County.

Aitken & Miller, 423 Broadway *New York.*
Appleton Ann, 292 Bowery
Bernhard Benjamin, 297 Grand
Bradbrook J. C. 297 Broadway
Cook John, 80 Canal
Corwith David H. 29½ Catharine
Crown Anthony, 20 Division
Desfourneaux & Exertier, 459 Broadway
Dover James. 149 Canal
Drummond M. J. 331 Grand
Ely Benjamin, 401 Hudson
Evans Robert M. 82 Canal
Evans Thomas. 67 Catharine
Evans Thomas R. 202 Bowery
Falconer William, 653 Broadway
Farrell J. & T. & Co. 557 do
Fraser Robert, 283 do
Freedman Solomon, 180½ Bowery
Gilligan John. 325 Grand
Godefroy F. 349 Broadway
Goodkind William, 299 Grand
Griffin & Pullman, 88 William
Hanrahan A. 142 Walker
Harrison C. 639 Broadway
Hays Mrs. 85 Catharine
Heath L. C. 319 Grand
Heineman & Rosenbaum, 313 do
Henderson Thomas, 174 Bowery
Heyman Ezekiel, 258 do
Higgins John, 89 William
James M. & J. 112 Canal
Jones Morris, 240 Bowery
Jones Robert S. 278 do
Kingsler H. 129 Broadway
Kirkland James, 96 Amos
Leeper Christopher, 172½ Bowery
Mansfield John, 92 Canal
Massonat Margaret, 28 White
Meara C. J. 303½ Greenwich
Morgan John W. 154 Fulton
Mount Elizabeth, 42 Catharine
Newman Edward H. 331½ B'way
O'Meara James, jr. 148 Canal & 263 Greenwich
Peck I. L. 120 Division
Phillips Albert, 311½ Grand
Rafferty R. 593 Broadway
Rannell & Downer, 44 Beaver
Roberts Peter, 573 Broadway
Robinson William, 287 Grand
Scanlan J. 485 Greenwich
Schwab & Minsesheimer, 247 Grand
Scott Charles, 67 Beaver
Scott William & Co 509 B'dway
Shancks Sarah, 114 Bleecker
Shepherd Thomas, 371 Broadway
Simmons L. 196 Bowery
Simpson S. 212 do
Son Isaac. 41 Catharine
Stonier Thomas M. 362 Bowery
Tallman Sophia, 226½ Bowery
Thomson John, 53 Division
Trimble J. N. 206 Canal
Uhlfelder John, 56 do
Vance Thomas, 225 Grand
Van Tuyl Andrew P. 341 Grand
Warner William H. 405 B'dway
Waterkeyn Joseph, 373 Bowery
Williams J. G. 47 Catharine
Wilson W. D. 71 William
Keeng R. R. 565 Broadway

LACES AND EMBROIDERIES—WHOLESALE.

Bannard J. W. & Co. 93 William
Butterly & Devin, 66 do

Cochran & Co. 142 Pearl *New York.*
Crans & Thomson. 59 John
Dietz Morris, 418 Broadway
Farrell T. & Co. 14 John
Freres Gilbert, 43 do
Green Richard S. 110 William
Hill Brothers, 49 John
Love Robert, rear 22 W. 17th
M'Arthur Wm. & Co. 72 William
Scanlan J. 485 Greenwich
Thomas James, 96 Cedar

Ladder Makers. *(See also Carpenters.)*

New York County.

Gallager Daniel, 81 1st Av. *New York.*

Sweet M. 72 5th

Oswego County.

Hyde Charles, Bride st. *Oswego.*

Lamps, Chandeliers, and Burning Fluid, &c. *(See also Camphene.)*

Albany County.

Thorn S. T. *Albany.*
Wright & Co. (Coach Lamp) 95 Green

New York County.

Baldwin Charles A. 59½ Bowery *New York.*
Boireau Alphonse, 145 Fulton
Boswell H. W. 244 Bowery
Brown John A. 420 Pearl
Carpenter Higbie, 369 Grand
Carter William, 559 Pearl
Clime Frederick, 7th Av.
Cox J. & I. 15 Maiden lane
Dardonville H——, 445 Broadway
Dietz, Brother & Co. 13 John, and 134 William
Drew John, 241 Division
Ducreux Claude, 364 Broadway
Edwards George, 116 Nassau
Endicott & Sumner, 106 Elm and 195 William
Fay J. O. 136 Fulton. (See Advertisement)
Fuller Charles, 273 Greenwich
Gardner George W. 18 3d Av.
Gosselin Edward, 80 Pine
Gruet Frederick T. R. 41 3d Av.
Halstead Charles J. 46 Broome
Hull & Jackson, 96 Wooster
Jones Edward, 252 Division
Jacob R. 236 Greenwich
Lloyd Edward, 79 John
Lorton George J. 156 W. B.way
Lorcenstein & Leroy, 269 B.way
Lucas & Rogers, 2 5th st.
Lutz John, 129 Willet
M'Cready George W. 169 6th Av. and 495 Broadway
M'Donald Peter Mrs. 159 Duane
M'Namara Henry, 390 Mott
Michell B. 8 Catharine, & 5 Chatham square
Mitchell & Kitchen, 4 Cortlandt & 132 Mercer
Moffett James G. 121 Prince, and 156 Fulton
Moore E. 172 Monroe
Moore K. 416 Cherry
Moran John, 294 2d
Morgan Asher R. 152 William
Morgan John W. 154 Fulton
Muller Nicholas, 2½½ Bleecker
Overton R. Carlton, 12 Allen
Philipe Joseph J. 139½ Bowery
Reilly Patrick H. 218 Canal
Reichmann Charles H. 31 Bowery
Reily D. H. 218 Canal
Reily J. 494 Grand
Reilly James, 156 9th Av.

Reilly John, 49 Carmine *New York.*
Reilly Solomon, 135 Canal
Rimmington George, 36 Cherry
Sanders & Brother, 1 Chatham sq.
Shute Peter, 166 & 376 3d Av.
Smith William H. 261 Grand
Starr Charles, jr. & Co. 117 Fulton & 48 Duane
Starr W. H. & Fellows, 67 Beekman
Stouvenel J. & Co. 3 John & 737 Broadway
Teets Philip, 296 Greenwich
Tyson Arthur B. 364 Broome
Wellings John T. 108½ Goerck
Woram & Haughwout, 561 & 563 Broadway

Lamp Wick Makers. *(See also Batting and Wicking.)*

New York Manufacturing Company, 6 Broadway *New York.*
Scott John, 22 Spruce

Lantern Manufacturers.

Edwards George, 116 Nassau *New York.*
Miller B. D. 209 Water
Porter William, 258 Water
Whipple Peter E. 52 Av. C

Lapidaries.

Albert Charles, 181 Broadway *New York.*
Chinery William, 22 Spruce
Mason J. C. & W. 156 Fulton
Royle & Baptiste, 25 John

Last and Tree Manufacturers.

Chenango County.

Adams John, *Oxford.*

Columbia County.

Woolley S. F. Public square *Hudson.*

Erie County.

Wing H. & Co. 8 Exchange Buffalo, also at Niagara Falls. (See Advertisement.)

Monroe County.

Curtis H. N. Main st. *Rochester.*
Shepherd & Markham, Globe building, Main

Montgomery County.

Marselis V. *Amsterdam.*

New York County.

Adams Jonathan, 22 Jacob *New York.*
Anchor Robert, 276 Hudson
Bradley F. 134 4th
Colladay Chas. H. & Co. 22 Ferry
Everson & Jonson, 15 Jacob
Harley & Miles, 106 Division
Kocher J. 36 Broadway
Kennedy Edward, 9 Jacob
Lindsley Lewis M. 10 Ferry
M'Kenzie William, 177 West 14th
Minor Henry C. 15 Jacob
Ruland William, 13 Jacob
Wilkey Warren S. 8 Ferry
Wing George F. 53 Frankfort
Wright ——, 301 Houston

Oneida County.

Loucks & Searls, 143 Genesee *Utica.*

Jones E. 27 Genesee

Onondaga County.

Bolins E. Water st. Syracuse
Salina.

Oswego County.

Hallowell Thos. C. Crocker's
building, Bridge st. *Oswego.*

St. Lawrence County.

Isham Nathan *Canton.*
Isham William

Laundries.

New York County.

Beman Elitha G. 133 Nassau
New York.
Ruys Cornelius, 103 Av. B
Underwood Joshua, 116 West 16th

Lead (Black) Manufacturer.

Warren County.

Kelly James F. Glenn's Falls
Queensbury.

Lead Mines.

Columbia County.

M'Intire H. (Proprietor) *Ancram.*

Lead—Pig and Bar.

Hart Lucius, 6 Burling slip
New York.
M'Cullough James, 159 Front
Rogers Charles H. & Co. 107 South
Spring Valley Shot and Lead Manufacturing Co. James M'Cullough President, 159 Front
Wildes Thomas, 30 Old slip

Lead Pipe. (*See also Gas Fixtures, also Plumbers.*)

Chautauque County.

Judd Z. Fredonia *Pomfret.*

Chemango County.

Munroe, Packer & Co. (Hydraulic
Rams) *Oxford.*

Kings County.

Cornell Samuel G. 21 James
Brooklyn.

New York County.

Burns John, 46 Av. C *New York.*
Le Roy Thomas Otis & Co. 261 &
263 Water
Tatham & Bro. 247 & 249 Water

Otsego County.

Thayer C. Cooperstown *Otsego.*

Lead—Sheet.

Cornell Samuel G. 175 Front
New York.

Lead Pencils—Importers of.

Hart Moses, 561 Grand *New York.*
Hynes Abraham, 234 Henry
Lemean M. L. 414 Pearl

Leather Dealers. (*See also
Boot and Shoe Dealers, also
Tanners, also Hides, also
Boot & Shoe Findings.*)

Albany County.

Humphrey Friend, (Hides) 16 State
Albany.
Forsyth & Robbison, (Hides) 6
State
Conkling J. P. 22 Dean
Van Valkenbergh, Frost & De-
Ruyter, 16 Hudson
Gross Samuel, 34 Hudson
Hepinstall Geo. 25 do
Holt J. & Co. 48 do

Chautauque County.

Green R. Fredonia *Pomfret.*
Whitcomb & Star, Fredonia

Columbia County.

Anable G. H. Franklin sq. *Hudson.*
Reynolds A. Pub. sq.
Anable J. S. do
Herrick C. L. *Kinderhook.*

Duchess County.

Southwick Richard E. 266 Main
Poughkeepsie.
Degarmo E. & W. 430 Main
Southwick Edward C. 370 do
Boyd David, 360 do

Erie County.

Schottkopf T. F. 360 Main *Buffalo.*
Hutchinson John M. Cone & Pearl
Bull I. & Co. Lloyd st.
Rumsey Fayette, 15 Webster's
block
Bush & Howard, 131 Main
Jones Hiram R. 6 Webster's block,
Main st.
Matthewson, Newell & Co. 6
Webster's block
Case N. & Co. 14 Exchange
Rumsey Aaron & Co. 4 Exchange
M'Ewen Stephen, Springville
Concord.

Herkimer County.

Johnson C., Mohawk
German Flats.
Buchanan R. & Co. Mohawk

Jefferson County.

Griswold J. *Adams.*
Fisk & Bates *Watertown.*

Kings County.

Davidson Alexander, 90 Middagh
Brooklyn.
Mills N. & Co. 43 Fulton
Samuel Charles, 235 Adams
M'Carnan Peter, Myrtle Av.
Anderson & Wells, 91 Grand
Williamsburgh.
Dunham M. 176 Grand

Lewis County.

Smith Rouseville *Turin.*

Livingston County.

Pratt Geo. & Geo. F. *Livonia.*
Pratt Samuel W. Hemlock Lake
Stillwell C. H. do

Madison County.

Allen R. & Son *Cazenovia.*

Monroe County.

Alling S. Y. & L. A. 17 Main
Rochester.
Keeler Rufus, 2 Water
Noonan Jerem. (morocco) Globe
Building, Water st.

Graves D. & L. Water st.
Rochester.
Kirley James, 24 Main
Sage & Pancost, 22 State
Churchill L. & H. 2 Hill
Haight & Graves, 46 Main, Brock-
port *Sweden.*
Wickes C. & Co. 22 Main

New York County.

Armstrong M. & Sons, 9 Ferry &
64 Vesey *New York.*
Brooks James & George, 19 Ferry
Cormier Emili L. 155 Greenwich
Crawford M. A. 7 Ferry
Evans George, 55 Frankfort
Gorum G. W. 154 Water
Knaufft Ferdinand, 83 Gold
Lillie William, 165 Bowery
Lottin John, 56 Frankfort
M'Mullen David, 357 Bowery
Marshman Benj. 30 Spruce
Miller Wm. F. & Co. 86 Gold
Neidhardt Charles. 51 Frankfort
Palen George, 87 Gold
Perine Benj. jr. 119 Columbia
Pinkham J. & Co. 27 Spruce
Radley Enos, 125 Sheriff
Tilley John & Son, 33 Suffolk
Tremper Harman, 471 Grand
Wilde & Wright, 20 Jacob
Wilkey Warren, 8 Ferry

Oneida County.

Edwards F. Dominick st. *Rome.*
Stevens & Whitmore, (wholesale)
Dominick st.
Vedder J. F. J. 43 Genesee *Utica.*
Hubbell & Curran, 35 Genesee
Gilbert E. M. 31 Genesee

Onondaga County.

Van Buren & Clary, Water st. Syracuse *Salina.*

Ontario County.

Cunningham & Johnson, Geneva
Seneca.

Orange County.

Hathaway O. S. 57 Water
Newburgh.
Farnum & Jenning, 62 Water
Houston & Wickham, Middletown
Wallkill.
Hope S. W. do

Oswego County.

Cramp James, 1st st. *Oswego.*
Nettleton Edward, Fulton *Volney*

Otsego County.

Fancher Selleck H. *Unadilla.*

Rensselaer County.

Morey John, State st.
Lansingburgh.
Ross & Smith, 179 River *Troy.*
Richards C. L. 249½ River
Plum David B. 257 do
Van Allen S. 237 do
M'Vity Thomas & Co. 5 Franklin
square
Haight I. & L. 74 Congress

Saratoga County.

Powell & Powers *Waterford.*
Morgan Thos. C.

Schenectady County.

Foster J. G. 109 State
Schenectady.

Tompkins County.

Stoddard S. & E. Owego c. Aurora
Ithaca.
Leslie & Covert, 31 Aurora
Esty J. & Son. 39 Tioga

Ulster County.

Abbey Stephen, Rondout
                Kingston.

Westchester County.

Brown James & Co. (wholesale)
  Peekskill   *Courtlandt.*

Leather (Patent) Manufacturers.

Simpson W. H. foot of Clinton Av.
                Brooklyn.

Leeches.

Cleu J. F. 7 John   *New York.*
Witte G. A. & H. 26 John

Leechers and Cuppers.

Austin Jacob M. 264 Broome
              New York.
Capell Amelia, 28 Chrystie
Cornwell Jeremiah, 279 Delancy
Hamilton Elizabeth, rear 49 Mott
Lane Mary, 176 Varick
Lynch Sophia A. 460 Grand

Letter Files.

Smith & Buttles, 140 Fulton
              New York.

Life Preservers.

Henike John F. 10 Ann *New York.*

Lighters.

Kings County.

Durkee H. H. Commercial Wharf
              Brooklyn.
Truppal M. Furman near Fulton

New York County.

Beardsley Chas. S. 12 South
              New York.
Boyer & Co. 21 Coenties slip
Crandall & Whiting, 23 do
Lyon & Hent, 100 Wall
Rodman John, 120 Wall
Sands Hart, 66 South

Lime Dealers. (*See also Builders' Materials ; also Cement.*)

Essex County.

Frisby Guy   *Willsborough.*
Rigly Levi, jr. (brick)

Jefferson County.

Cook A. (white lime)   *Theresa.*

Kings County.

Ostrom A. P. (lime and brick) foot
  of Pacific st.   *Brooklyn.*
Voorhis W. & P. foot of Amity
Bell J. (manufacturer) do
Van Wagner D. H. (cement) foot
  of Adams st.
Haverstock & Johnson, (brick)
  John st. bet. Jay and Bridge
Johnson J. jr. Kent Av. n. Flush-
  ing Av.
Valentine J. C. (brick) Green
  Point   *Bushwick.*
Trafford A. (brick) 1st st.
         Williamsburgh.
Keith Edwin S. (brick) 245 1st
Dayvear T. A. 3d c. North, (shell
  lime manufacturer)

Willett Thomas, (brick) 127 1st
        Williamsburgh.
Potter H. P. 5th near North (shell)

New York County.

Briggs J. N. 217 West *New York.*
Bullwinkle Richard, Rivington
  cor. East
Byne George C. 194 West
Candee, Arnold & Co. foot of E.
  25th
Chamberlin Enoch, 330 West
Cool & Brother. 265 West
Croton & Sparta Co. West corner
  Bethune
Cumming John P. & Thomas, 229
  10th Av.
Donnell E. 500 West & 101 Morton
Denman A. A. foot of 20th st.
Doke D. & I. foot of W. 28th st.
Fryer Isaac, 412 West
Fryer John, 412 West
Gould & Conover, 41 Tompkins
Hoagland John E. 470 West cor.
  Bethune
Keeler David B. 245 South
Keeler & Ostrom, 480 Water
Kenny James F. 343 Front
Kingston Lime & Cement Co. 412
  West and 271 Pearl
Knapp Henry B. 21 Av. B
Knapp ———, 2d st.
Loper & Davis, E. 18th cor. Av. B
Loveland & Berrien. 381 West
Montgomery H. V. 267 E. 18th
Nelson & Brown, 290 West
Roberts Chas. & R. S. 250 South
Roberts & Benjamin, 269 E. 21st
Robinson & Bullwinkle, 23d cor.
  1st Av.
Trafford Abraham, Tompkins cor.
  Delancy

Linen Ready-made—Retail. (*See also Gentlemen's Furnishing Stores.*)

Agate Joseph, 237 Broadway
             New York.
Beman Elitha C. I Astor House &
  134 Nassau
Bennett William, 84 Chatham
Blake Wm. W. 369 Greenwich
Bradbrook G. A. 297 Broadway
Brenna Madame, 40 Reade
Bruns William H. 326 Grand
Chapman John, 80 Chatham
Charpentier ———, 82 Broadway
Cleaveland Mary, 603 Broadway
Cook John, 84 Chatham
Davis John, 96 Chatham and 91
  William
Duncan Margaret, 33 Av. C
Duncomb David S. 28 Liberty
Emmons George F. 110½ Bowery
Evrard James, 192 Grand
Fanshaw Charles, 181 3d Av.
Ferguson J. B. 40 Carmine
Fitzsimmons B. 195 Av. A
Glassford James, 679 Broadway
Harris J. 313 Broadway
Haslett John C. 5 City Hall sq.
House, Brothers, 34 N. William
Hulse Amos, 60 Bowery
Hulse Josh. C. 28 N. William
Hutschler Caroline, 90 Bowery
Hutschler Jacob V. 93½ Chatham
Jones Mary Ann, 98 Cannon
Jubin Mary, 43 Beekman
Kearney Mrs. 564 Broadway
Kline Nicholas, 543 Pearl
Koopman Peter, 96 Chatham
Kowing Francis, 286 Bowery
Leighton Charles, 10 Park pl.
Levy Barnett, 83 Chatham
M'Gill James, 90 Chatham
M'Kinley Edward, 1 Park Row
M'Neill Eliza A. 72 Bowery
M'Menomy J. 132 Bowery
Mariners Family Industrial So-
  ciety, 322 Pearl
Marshalls ———, 90 Chatham

Miller Phœbe, 268½ Bowery
             New York.
Morgan David, 164 Division
Palmer & Farr, 459 Broadway
Parker William, 178 Canal
Parsells James C. 69 Chambers
Phelps Jane M. 200 Grand
Quigg Edward, 128 Division
Roe Townsend V. 209 8th Av.
Sanger ———, 89 Bowery
Schaffer Theresa, 85 Houston
Schwerin M. 75 William
Scott John F. 157 Fulton
Shannon Eliod, 492 Pearl
Shardlow Wm. L. 266 Broadway
Shepard William H. 256 do
Simpson Samuel S. 212 Bowery
Sims Jane, 339 Bleecker
Steiner Samuel, 96 Suffolk
Sturges Samuel B. 76½ Chatham
Sturges William, 96½ do
Torrens Samuel, 375 Hudson
Tripler John H. 396 Grand
Troy Henry, 384 Bowery
Underhill Louisa, 384 Bowery
Van Houton Rebecca, 85 Nassau
Ware Edwin A. 262 Grand
Waterbury G. G. 259 Broadway

Linen.—Ready-made.—Wholesale.

(*See also Gentlemen's Furnishing Stores.*)

Aronson H. 70 William
Brandes Carl, 93½ Chatham
Chapman H. H. 1 Maiden Lane
Davis John, 91 William
Ferguson Joel B. 40 Carmine
Ferris & Penfield, 55 William
Furman S. H. 25 Cortlandt
Guion Henry C. 191 Fulton
Harding C. L. 26 College place
Herrick & Scudder, 95 William
Judson D. & L. N. 36 Platt
Lewis P. & H. 85 William
M'Kinley William, 106 Chatham
Morison T. A. 185 William
Parker William, 192 Canal
Schwerins M. 75 William
Stone & Greacen, 107 William
Vultee Gertrude, 114 Chatham
Wakeman W. & W. 76 Maiden l.
Wilson Morris, 83 William
Woolf Morris, 61 Maiden lane
Woolsey John, 34 Platt

Liniment Manufacturers.

Stanton & Arthur, (Hunt's Lini-
  ment) Sing Sing *Ossining.*
Kellinger Dewitt C. (Kellinger's
  Liniment   *Yonkers.*

Liquorice Refiner.

Kings County.

Smith Abel, Lorimer cor. North
             Brooklyn.

Lithographers.

New York County.

Akerman J. 130 Fulton *New York.*
Bonap Thomas, 124 Nassau
Brown E. jr. 142 Fulton
Buchanan & Co. 198 Fulton
Burton C. W. 392 Broadway
Butler Benj. F. 90 Fulton
Copley Chas. 19 Burling slip
Currier Chas. 33 Spruce
Currier N. Nassau & Spruce
Dalley Henry, 56 Chatham
Davignon & Hoffman, 332 B'dway
Endicott Wm. & Co. 59 Beekman
Grosvenor Seth, 132 Broadway

Hayward George, 206 Pearl
New York.
Henneberger Martin, 199 Division
Jones Edward, 90 Nassau
Major J. & D. 49 Wall
Meyer F. & Korff. 7 Spruce
Melogan Alex. 36 Maiden lane
Michelin Francis, 111 Nassau
Miller Peter, 102 Broadway
Miller & Boyle, 102 Broadway
Nagel & Weingartner, 74 Fulton
Palmer T. & Co. 98 Nassau
Probst John. 129 Fulton
Raab Francis, 88 Nassau
Raynor R. J. 252 Broadway
Robinson Henry B. 31 Park Row
Risso & Leefe, 18 Cortlandt
Ross Wm. W. 19 Wall
Sarony & Major, 117 Fulton
Serrel & Perkins, 75 & 77 Nassau
Serrell H. R. 262 8th Av.
Snyder Geo. 138 William
Trembly R. 70 Beekman
Vinten Charles, 96 Nassau
Willis Wm. R. 96 Nassau
Wood Thomas, 117 John

Lithographic Goods.

Funke Herman, 50 Cliff New York.

Livery Stables.

Albany County.

Yates H. & H. 56 Montgomery
Albany.
Chamberlin J. H. 672 Broadway
Conklin C. 104 Church
Dexter C. Liberty & Hamilton sts.
Wallace A. F. 41 Division
Davids Isaac, 42 Division
Huddleston J. H. 19 Church
Brasure J. W. 103 Lydius
Harris O. & Son, 43 & 45 James
Slawson W. F. 17 Maiden lane
Kelso J. 48 Spring
Spencer H. West Troy Watervliet.
Woodbeck M.   do
Scovill & Hart,   do
Kelly P.   do
Morrison & Greenman, do
Miller G. W. Cohoes

Alleghany County.

Howell Geo.   Almond.
Jones & Smith
Hartshorn F. M.   Angelica.
Hastings Warner   Cuba.
Walker Jabez F.   Rushford.
M'Call & Cady

Broome County.

Willard O. H. Chenango Forks
Barker.
Denison B. A.   Binghamton.
Morgan F. A. & Co.

Cayuga County.

Carpenter L. E. & W. H. State st.
Auburn.
Austin S. S. Garden st.
Bennett H. V. Weedsport Brutus.

Chautauque County.

Bond Wm. D. Mayville
Chautauque.
Eddy & Forbes, Jamestown
Ellicott.
Kennedy Chas.   do
Barber B. B.   Westfield.
Stevens Chauncey

Chenango County.

Rider Geo. L.   Norwich.
Mabie John M.
Willcox E. H.
Clarke Peter W.   Oxford.

Hervey U.   Sherburne.
Hoyt H. B.

Columbia County

Cox W. & Co. Warren st. Hudson.
Bruce J. 5th st.
Miller C. H. (National Hotel)

Cortland County.

Merrick & Randall
Cortland Village.

Delaware County.

Dean J. P. Deposit   Tompkins.

Duchess County.

Ransom B. E.   Amenia.
Baxter N.   Fishkill.
Light W.
Myers H. C.   Pine Plains.
Pollock F. 283 Main Poughkeepsie.
Boice B. D. 3 Catharine
Butler I. 36 Market
Lewis A. B. 6 Washington
Pultz E.   Rhinebeck.

Erie County.

Lightfall Henry, Williamsville
Amherst.
Miller J. S. Washington Buffalo.
Miller C. (Western Hotel Block)
Stevenson Brothers, 301 Main
Harris J. Perry st.
Metzger G. Washington st. n. P. O.
Burton Lauren, Pearl st.
Mount Geo. 28 Pearl
Heath T. Springville   Concord.
Bush & Fanning   Tonawanda.
Theron & Patterson

Genesee County.

Ferren & M'Cormick   Batavia.
Beech Henry
White N. A.   Bergen.
Pitman & Wilcox
Harris D. P.   Le Roy.
Arnold T. H.

Greene County.

Beach George L.   Catskill.
Steward Austen   Coxsackie.

Herkimer County.

Spencer Philander   Frankfort.
Smith N. F.   Herkimer.
Spencer Philander
Richmond A.   Little Falls.
Howe Joseph   Newport.

Kings County.

Sabin C. G. cor. Pacific & Colum-
bia sts.   Brooklyn.
Murray P. 19 Columbia
Wade Wm. W. State cor. Hicks
Hinchy John, Columbia nr. State
Carll Conklin, 23 Fulton
Olivmore & Jarvis, 277 Hicks
Powell Wait, 37 Henry
Hendrickson P. 12 College place
Tigney W. Love lane nr. Hicks
Robertson Wm. Henry st.
Carberry C. Schermerhorn st.
Scudder J. P. 4 & 6 Water
Snedeker E. V. W. 74 do
Arthur John, Washington st. near
Tillary
Morris James, Liberty st.
M'Carty Edward, Navy st.
Nevalle Edward, South 7th cor.
1st   Williamsburgh.
Coleman C. 99 Grand
Ackarly Wm. Water st. nr. Grand

Livingston County.

Warren & Mumford   Dansville.
Henry & Titsworth
Chamberlin C. J. & R.

Chadwick N.   Dansville.
M'Master J. D.   Geneseo
Wilcox & Gragg
Bissell George
Yerks A.   Lima.
Garlinghouse L.   Mount Morris.
Grover Hiram C.   Nunda.

Madison County.

Eggleston L. A.   Cazenovia.
Stiles L. H & Co.
Maxson & Burdick   De Ruyter.
Wallace John P.
Benjamin Wm. C.   Eaton.
Grove James   Hamilton.
James Coles
Allen J. W. Oneida Depot Lenox.
White E. R. Canastota
Montroes John,   Jo
Frederick & Bressean, Chittenan-
go   Sullivan.

Monroe County.

Staring R.   Penfield.
Morgan H. W. Fairport Perinton.
Wood D.   Pittsford.
Shaw H. N. 90 Main cor. of Stone
Rochester.
Fish James E. 3 Minerva
M'Farlin B. 100 Main
Baker B. M. 36 Fitzhugh
Charles Stephen, 4 Spring
Walbridge D. T. 76 State
Walbridge G. W. 57 do
Shaw J. W. 69   do
Brown E. 85   do
Hall J. O. 201   do
Davis W. & W. Frankfort alley
Brainard & Cary, Brockport
Sweden.
Jones R. D. Main st,   do

Montgomery County.

Deforest David   Amsterdam.
Keasted William
Smith George   Canajoharie.
Harris M. L.
Morgan G. W. Fonda   Mohawk.

New York County.

Abbott W. S. 366 Broadway
New York.
Austin John J. 37 2d
Banfield Frederick, 21 3d
Barker Patrick, 121 Amity
Barr Thomas J. 51 Franklin
Barratt Richard, 164 Crosby
Bartine Cornelius S. 34 Canal
Beach & Phillips, 14 & 16 Murray
Beebe Reuben W. 21 Bowery
Bellows Frederick, 275 Spring
Bemis Thomas H. 286 E. B'dway
Bemroes & Scaioh, 36 Cliff
Bertrand Charles, 10 Suffolk
Bidleman & Arndt, 164 W'hington
Black Thomas, 95 Great Jones
Bogardus Richard, 525 Hudson
Booth Charles L. 145 10th & 176
Crosby
Bowden Thomas, 50 Bayard
Bradley Catherine, 122 Duane
Bradley James, 3 Greenwich
Broderick James, 187 9th
Brower Abraham & Co. 660 & 661.
Broadway
Brown Alonzo, 103 Liberty
Brown Edward, 9 1st
Brown James R. 102 Mercer
Brown Moses C. 24th st. n. 2d Av.
Brown Thomas, 2 Cortlandt alley
Branell Wm. 34 Canal
Burbank Paul D. 62 E. 14
Burke John, 205 Greene
Butler John P. 70½ Prince
Carland & Bedell, 142 Hester
Cavin John, 140 Liberty
Chamberlin A. S., E. 24th st.
Chichester E. 24 & 26 Cherry
Clancy Terence, 21 Pell
Cleary Philip, 161 9th

Cleaver Henry, 16 Pearl
             New York.
Coddington James, 67 Watts
Cole Isaac K. 50 Water
Collyer Henry W. 150 Attorney
Confrey Joseph, rear 18 Mulberry
Conklin & Colyer, 96 Houston
Cooper John, 121 6th Av.
Cooper George H. 100 Norfolk
Cooper W. & Co. 103 Charles
Cornwell Jonathan J. 46 Greene
Cowan William, 94 & 96 Mercer
Cowscell William, 130 Chrystie
Deal Jacob, 187 Essex
Dilks Thomas H. 169 Mercer
Dimond N. 9 Beaver & 63 New
Douglass H. 66 Grand
Duffy Peter, 89 Leonard
Duncan & Douglass, rear 66 Grand
Edsall C. 29 Anthony
Eldred Henry, 121 Grand
Ellis John, 192 Eldridge
Ervin Wm. 338 Madison
Flinn Morris, 77 Trinity place
Floyd Charles A. 102 Laurens
Foley J. B. & T. H. 299 Mott
Gallagher Charles, 34 Spruce
Gatfield John H. 31 Crosby
George Nathaniel, 48 Laurens
Gidney George, 84 2d Av.
Gillespie & Turnure, 127 & 161 E.
   Broadway
Girdler Thomas, 250 Wooster & 3
   University place
Gordon John, Cortlandt alley
Gray Samuel S. 23 & 25 Houston
Haight T. D. 79   do
Hamilton James, 26 Pell
Harrison & Van Ranst, 103 Hester
Harrison & Fleet, 19 & 21 Roose-
   velt & 44 Hamilton
Hathorne George C. jr. 42 E. 12th
Hawkes Edward, 1 & 3 Murray
Hegeman Jacob, 294 E. Broadway
Hendrickson John B. 77 Houston
Hughes James, rear 166 Mulberry
Hurson John, 177 12th
Irwin William, 456 Grand
Jackson Nathaniel, 684 Broadway
Jarvis David S. 851   do
Johnson Frederick, 12 Whitehall
Johnson W. & D. 102 Bedford
Johnson Jacob, Lexington Av.
   cor. 24th
Kenna Edward, 251 Washington
Kerr Thomas, 62 Monroe
Kerr W. H. 156 Crosby
Klein Joseph, 203 3d
Lamb Chester, William c. Frank-
   fort
Lawrence James, 111 W. 24th
Lewis Charles, 130 Thompson
Lewis Platt, 172 Eldridge
Ludlam George T. 16 4th Av.
Lynch Charles, 74 Trinity place
Lynch John, 66 Mercer
M'Canly D. E. 24th near 3d Av.
M'Carthy & Barret, 102 Crosby
M'Coneghty John, 60 Franklin
M'Dermott Patrick, 228 Sullivan
M'Dole George, 23 Greenwich
M'Dowell John G. & Bradley, 3
   Greenwich
M'Guire James, 134 M'Dougal
M'Manus Patrick, 47 Mulberry
Madden Patrick, 194 Duane
Maguire James, 134 M'Dougal
Martin William, E. 24th st.
Marvin Joseph C. 6 Howard
Miles William H. 54 Lafayette pl.
Nodine Frederick J. 158 Amos
Norris Thomas, 110 9th
O'Brien Morgan, 9 & 11 6th
Olvaney James, 2 Montgomery
O'Neill James, 64 University pl.
Peters Valentine H. 73 W. 24th
Philbin Martin, 118 Clinton place
Place & Chichester, 96 Cherry
Pope Charles jr. 33 North Moore
Powell Albert, 665 Houston
Powell Moses, 665 Houston
Quarry James, 20 Amity

Quin Hugh, 65 Reade *New York.*
Reed Willard S. & Trusdill, 174
   Mercer
Rollins William, 18½ Jay
Renville Thomas, 32 Carmine
Reynolds John N. 160 Suffolk
Reynolds Robert, 180 Eldridge
Richardson Edwin, rear 358
   Broadway
Richey Robert, 163 Washington
Roe Frederick, 6 University place
   & 114 Clinton place
Rooney Patrick, 12 Lafayette pl.
Rourke Edward, 25 Amity place
Ryder William, 96 Laurens
Ryerson & Howard, 842 Broadway
Ryerson & Willets, 146 4th Av.
Seech & Benroes, 56 Cliff
Shelden A. M. Harlem
Simonson William, 24th near 3d
   Av.
Smith Edward, 137 W. Broadway
Smith Jacob M. & John H. 29 Jef-
   ferson
Smith Jesse, 29 Jefferson
Spicer & M'Mann, 508 Broadway
Taylor Thomas W. 52 Watts
Thurston & Townsend, 72 Reade
Townsend Wm. 228 W. 21st
Tyson Wm. & Co. 224 Henry
Underhill Monmouth H. 4 Riving-
   ton
Van Deusen Robert R. 73 Prince
Vanhorn David, 169 Suffolk
Valentine & Cocks, 75 Allen
Van Voris Lewis, 51 Christopher
Van Voris Nathaniel, 51   do
Vogell Jacob, 25 1st Av.
Walsh John, 12 Murray
Walters Henry, 229 Mercer
Weir George R. 124 Clinton place
Williams Robert L. 18 W. 13th
Wilkins W. H., E. 24th st.
Wilmot James, 48 Essex

Niagara County.

Cornell N.   *Lewiston.*
Beardsley J. T.
Pease & Halladay   *Lockport.*
Williams M. B.
Baright Allen
Steel Enos
Hamlin George E. & Co.
           Niagara Falls.

Oneida County.

Houk, Hollister & Co. James st.
           Rome.
Bates J. W. 191 Genesee *Utica.*
Bates & Co. 95 Hotel
Pearson G. 29 Fayette
Mapes J. H. & J. C. Varick st.
Lumbard H. Catherine st.
Clark J. A. cor. John & Broad
Hawley Wm. H. 8 Broad
Hawley B. 7 John
Hawkins M. H. 13 Broad

Ontario County.

Benham & Dailey   *Canandaigua.*
Anderson D. & J.
Blood & Maxwell
Taylor Allen   *East Bloomfield.*
Ingersoll Edwin E.   *Phelps.*
Dey Mrs. M. M. Geneva *Seneca.*
Brown Richard,   do
Bartlett Buell H. do
Lewis Joseph,   do
Pierce William L. do
Morgan Nathan   *Victor.*

Onondaga County.

Baker C. Salina st. Syracuse
           Salina.
Patterson & Corning, Syracuse
Keeler T. J. & C. S. Fayette st.
Clark G. W. Warren st.
Cleaveland G.   do
Downs & Hatch, Water st.
Kain M. Canal st.

Orange County.

Welling & Wood   *Chester.*
Van Nort J. S.   *Goshen.*
Makinson J. M. Colden st.
           Newburgh.
Felter Samuel W. 3d st.
Whited John, Front st.
Jacks James,   do
Hines & Seeley, South Middletown
           Wallkill.

Orleans County.

Clark Ira, Albion   *Barre.*
Platt E   do
Hopkins H. do
Britt V., Medina   *Ridgeway.*

Oswego County.

Martin & Hewett   *Mexico.*
Knox David H. 1st st. *Oswego.*
Hawkins & Pierce, 1st st.
Briggs Rufus,   do
Hawkins R. & Co. do
Peck Barney, Pulaski *Richland.*
Alvord Seth W., Phœnix
           Schroeppel.

Otsego County.

Lewis William, Cooperstown
           Otsego.
Willoughby Z.   do

Queens County.

Sammis W.   *Flushing.*
Blake Ira
Howe A., Astoria   *Newtown.*

Rensselaer County.

Davis Clark, Richard st.
           Lansingburgh.
Ganley D. 281 River   *Troy.*
Beach E. D. 3 1st
M'Keon Patrick, 201 4th
Crowley F. & T. 12 State
Filkins C. B. 34   do
Carle John, 48   do
Hyde Robert, 87 Congress
Wallace C. 41 Ferry
Granger H. W. 8 do

St. Lawrence County.

Carr D. D. T. cor. Lake & Main,
   Ogdensburgh   *Oswegatchie.*
Clark John W.   *Potsdam.*

Saratoga County.

Snyder Philip *Saratoga Springs.*
Knickerbocker John
Dexter Stephen
Munger Morgan   *Stillwater.*
Carrier R.   *Waterford.*
Bedell J.
Palmer P. S.

Schenectady County.

Dodge L. 164 State *Schenectady.*
Schermerhorn J. 27 State

Seneca County.

Schooley Wm. J.   *Ovid.*
Gifford W. C. *Seneca Falls.*
Johnson B. G.
Milk George
Shoemaker H.
Fires & Hulbert   *Waterloo.*
Laing John

Tompkins County.

Newman L. & Co. 21 Tioga *Ithaca.*
Babcock, Cowles & Mott, 119
   Owego
M'Whorten & Wilcox, 19 Owego

Ulster County.

Davis Joseph F., Rondout *Kingston*

Warren County.

Carpenter C., Glenn's Falls
　　　　　　　　Queensbury.
Higbee R. W.　　do

Washington County.

Starkey & Babcock　*Greenwich.*
Langworthy & Cornell
Middleworth H. V., Sandy Hill
　　　　　　　　Kingsbury.

Wayne County.

Rowland Henry　　*Arcadia.*
Paine Wm., Newark
Kenyon Weller
Lyon ——, Clyde　*Galen.*
Bennett John　　*Lyons.*
Warren H.
Barnum O.
Pattee Alden　　*Marion.*
Martin A.　　　*Palmyra.*
Rogers Charles
Thompson & Gates

Westchester County.

Fitchet Charles H., Peekskill
　　　　　　　　Courtlandt.
Milletts Samuel, Peekskill
Sullivan John,　do
Urmy Jackson, Sing Sing *Ossining.*
Birdsall Joseph,　do
Deforest Hiram　*White Plains.*

Wyoming County.

Ashley & Robinson　*Attica.*
Walker A. B.　　*Perry.*
Hopson A.　　　*Pike.*
M'Elwain J. A.　*Warsaw.*

Yates County.

Thompson Nelson, Penn Yan *Milo.*
Tuel A. & A.　do
Rolph Wm., Rushville　*Potter.*
Stoll C., Dundee　*Starkey.*
Harpending A., Dundee

Lock Manufacturers. (See also *Locksmiths.*)

Albany County.

Argillo Works (Knobs & Latches)
　　　　　　　　Albany.

Fulton County.

Hill Geo.　　　*Johnstown.*

Herkimer County.

Yale Lewis (Bank Lock) *Newport.*

Kings County.

Crooker Zenas & Sons, Brooklyn
Lock Co. 156 Atlantic *Brooklyn.*
Du Bois N. G. Concord c. Liberty

New York County.

Austen W. O. 59 Marion *New York.*
Broad John H. 518 4th
Carpender & Fye, 424 Broadway
Clark Walter, 145 Centre
Day & Newell, 589 Broadway
Derby Geo. 259 Water
Drungold B. 249 8th Av.
Dunn John, 186 2d
Ferguson R. Av. A bet. 12th & 13th
Garret Geo. 6 3d
Griffin Edwin, 205 Chrystie
Hamel & Arens, 4 Forsyth
Hossley Robert, 81 Perry
Hayes Matthew, 182 Division
Mackrell & Richardson, 292 Houston
M'Craken Francis, 266 Spring
M'Sorley Hugh, 713 Washington
Manix J. & J. 170 Reade
Russel Theophilus, 103 Walker

Russell & Erwin, 92 John
　　　　　　　　New York.
Sinclair Wm. C. 204 Bleecker
Sparks Wm. H. jr. 31 Allen
Tappan & Haggart, 57½ Bowery
Upton Francis R. 72 Wall
Vanbenthuysen I. E. 80 Av. C
Vannostrand Wm. B. & Co. 36 Jay
Venten David, 56 Jane

Oneida County.

Price & Dana, 92 Genesee　*Utica.*
Higgs & Potter, 13 Bleecker

Onondaga County.

Geer D. S. & S. P. Salina st. Syracuse　　　　　　*Salina.*

Queens County.

Lawrence A.　　*Flushing.*
Searing Seaman G.　*Jamaica.*

Rensselaer County.

Lillie Louis, (Bank Lock) cor. 2d & Ida sts.　　　*Troy.*

Westchester County.

Rikeman & Seymour, Peekskill
　　　　　　　　Courtlandt.
Drumgold John, Portchester *Rye.*

Locksmiths & Bellhangers.
—(See also *Lock Manufacturers.*)

Albany County.

Woolensack J. 6 Liberty *Albany.*
Love A. 86 Green
Blackall J. & W. Hamilton st.

Duchess County.

West Wm. B. 364 Main
　　　　　　　Poughkeepsie.

Erie County.

Bristol E. 19 East Swan *Buffalo.*
Lane Wm. Elk st.
Taylor D. East Swan near Main

Kings County.

Brown Jas. 55 Atlantic *Brooklyn.*
Beckett H. Orange st. near Henry
Phillips P. Pearl st. near Concord
Dalton Wm. 255 Adams
Dinnen John, 107 Hudson Av.
Thomas T. Myrtle Av.
Millwood Jas. 65 South 7th
　　　　　　　Williamsburgh.
Hancock R. 294 South 4th
Strickland & Brown, 33 Grand
M'Gaviston H. 169 4th
Fletcher Joseph, 173 4th

Livingston County.

Swingle Geo.　　*Dansville.*
Brown Stephen

Monroe County.

Sherlock & Co. (Curtis' Block)
Main st.　　　*Rochester.*
Wray Wm. 66 State
Bruce Alex. 29 Front

New York County.

Bannan Chas. 32 Columbia
　　　　　　　New York.
Berbeck Christopher, 115 Broome
Biehn John, W. 30th st.
Blackett John, 93 Houston
Blakely John, 44 Sheriff
Blakely Jos. & Sons, 555 Hudson
Bleackley John, 44 Sheriff
Bohannan Wm. W. 617 Hudson
Brettell Edward, 196 Wooster
Broad J. H. 518 4th
Brown Ralph, 211 Greene & 597 Broadway

Buckley Edward, 12 James
　　　　　　　New York.
Canney Jas. 485 Broome
Carroll Edward, 82 Pitt
Claude Nicholas, 42 Church
Colton Patrick S. 199 Bowery
Cory Chas. 302 Division
Cross Thomas, 221 Water
Daniels Wm. 149 Chrystie
Deacon Thomas, 4 Clarkson
Derby Geo. 259 Broadway
Devins Wm. 135 Greenwich
Devoe Henry F. 330 West
Diehl Philip, 504 Pearl
Duncan & West, 55 Dey
Ellin Sidney, rear 67 W. 22d
Ellin T. S. 163 Varick
Ewing Geo. 438 Grand
Ferguson Jesse, 22 College place
Ferguson R. Av. A bet. 12th & 13th
Fletcher Job, 123 Av. D
Foley Patrick, 8 3d Av.
Fowkes T. 24½ Carmine
Gallagher Michael, 178 6th Av.
Garrets Geo. 6 3d
Garvey John, 298 Bowery
Geushelmer Henry, r. 316 Grand
Gilley John, 374 Broome
Grunin John S. 754 Greenwich
Hasselmeyer Chas. 130 Delancy
Hayden l. 13 Thames
Hayden Patrick, 124 Walker
Hayes Matthew, 202 Division
Helsser Jacob, 207 W. 17th
Hetherington J. 503 Houston
Hill Joseph, 7 3d
Hitz Jas. rear 879 Broadway
Hoban John, 187 W. 21st
Hodgkins John, 58 Cross
Howarth J. 178 W. 20th
Holmes David, 231 Broome
Jacobus Jas. G. 217 Church
Jackson E. B. & Co. 133½ William
Jones John, 134 Orange
Kedney Jas. 193 11th
Kelley Philip, 50 Dey
Kennedy John, 31 S. William
Kleyer Louis, Harlem
Knox Joseph, 602 Grand
Lausser Gotlieb F. rear 92 Essex
Ludlow R. 713 Washington
M'Gregor Hayman, 179 Chrystie
Mouda F. 42 Centre
M'Dowell J. T. 166 Division
M'Neal Hugh, 26 Centre
Mason & Claude, 44 Anthony
Manix John, 170 Reade
Price John, 88 Laurens
Price Wm. 124 Greenwich Av
Pulley Henry, 30 West Broadway
Pye Wm. M. 43 Cannon
Requa A. & Co. Watts cor. Canal
Sanders Jaques, 24 W. Broadway
Schmaelxle Carl, 123 Division
Schuman Gottlieb, 12 Clinton
Schwingrouber L. 94 Reade
Shaw R. 35 John
Sheen Hugh, 551 Greenwich
Smith Joseph, 7 Hudson
Sowrley H. 713 Washington
Swift Abial, 5th st. near Av. C
Tassie James, rear 139 Forsyth
Taylor & Moore, 176 William
Trostman Anthony, 96 Sheriff
Vandewater & Healy, 82 Perry
Weaver J. C. 545 Broadway
Webb & Little, 180 Mott
Weir John, 89 King
Welsh l. 71 West Broadway

Rensselaer County.

Matthews James, rear of Boardman's Buildings　*Troy.*
Van Buskirk & Lee, 140 William
Bentley J.

Loom Makers.

Platt Christopher, 151 W. 15th
　　　　　　　　New York.

Shirlaw J. 203 20th   *New York.*
Thorn David, 187 26th

Lumber Dealers. *(See also Lumber Manufacturers; also Merchants Commission.)*

Albany County.

Warren C. 37 & 39 Water *Albany.*
Griswold, Matson & Co. 51 Water
Tyler, Bullock & Co. 48 Water
Whitlock R. 70 Water
Coffee & Brush, Water c. Spencer
Easton Charles P. 83 Water
Williams C. P. & Co. Lumber cor. Montgomery
Paddock S. jr. 127 Water
Holborn D. H. 127   do
Roger & Callender, 116 Water
Ketchum R. & Sons, 118 and 120 Water
Romaine J. P. 118 Water
Warren Clement, 69 Water
Barnes F. I. 220 Water
Sanford G North of N. Perry st.
Wilson & Meade, above   do
Clark E. C.   do
Carroll A.   do
Bloomingdale Wm. H.   do
Van Valkenbergh B. 207 Water
Cooley C. 191 Water
Ross Wm. H. 70 Pier
De Witt Wm. H. 67 Pier
Rathburn J. 67 Pier
Fassett & Washburn, (shingles) 47 Pier
Towner J. O. & Co. 37 Pier
Harbeck & Co. (staves) 31 Pier
Williams C. P. & Co. 29 Pier
King J. B. & Co. 20 Pier
Whitlock R. 16 Pier
Vaae Franklin, (shingles) 15 & 16 Pier
Van Etten J. B. 11 Pier
Grant, Freeman & Church, West Troy   *Watervliet.*
Silliman & Haswell, West Troy
Bruster O.   do
Richards A.   do
Beebe Dillon,   do
Colman Thomas,   do
Rosseau, Coffin & Eastern,   do
Babcock Edward,   do
Dauchy Philo,   do
Mackey, Wells & Co.   do
Lamport & Richards,   do
Platt & Betts,   do
Ives C. P.   do

Alleghany County.

Adams & Conklin   *Alfred.*
Parker & Simons   *Amity.*
Burrell George P.
Church P. jr.   *Angelica.*
Miner A. W.   *Bolivar.*
Ingersoll John   *Caneadea.*
Dake John C.
Smith John
Roundsville S.
Canfield J. jr.   *Ossian.*

Broome County.

M'Kinney C.   *Binghamton.*
Hart C. G.
Isbell & Way
Eldridge Hobart
Pollard & Chollar   *Maine.*
Whitmore & Dusenbury *Windsor.*

Cayuga County.

Cornell P. D. State st.   *Auburn.*
Bowen J. V. & Co. North st.
Anthony D.   *Springport.*
Everett & Winegar

Chautauque County.

Leonen J. B.   *Carroll.*
Fenton R. E. Frewsburgh

Baker Henry, Jamestown *Ellicott.*
Scott & Barrows,   do
Allen Dascum,   do
Allen Dana,   do
Lowry N. A.   do
Talcott T. D. Silver Creek   *Hanover.*
Dolloff N. Poland Centre *Poland.*
Wait & Brothers, do
Hunt H. N.
Brigham W. W. Fredonia *Pomfret.*

Chemung County.

Strang S. B.   *Elmira.*
Thurman & Ingraham
Demorest J. H.
Towner B. A.
Judson W. E.
Colburn, Andrews & Langdon
Crane Hiram
Griffin B.
Potter A. F.
Gibson W. L.
Woodward W.
Halliday Wm. & Co.
Bennett Solomon
Spalding H. C.

Columbia County.

M'Arthur C. & Son, Water st.   *Hudson.*
Rowley & Ross
Mitchell C. Diamond c. 7th
Livingston H.   *Livingston.*
Hough & Co.   *Stuyvesant.*

Delaware County.

Wheeler W.   *Hancock.*
Frisbie H.
Richards & Williams
Twaddle J. M.
Twaddle J. A.
Lakin R. G.
Smith W. P.
Landfield C.
Holloway L.

Duchess County.

Mosher L. T.   *Hyde Park.*
Collingwood & Millard, Hunt's Landing   *Poughkeepsie.*
Foster D. C. & Co. Main st. Landing
Arnold David. Upper Landing
Millard & Mills. New Hamburgh
Lee & Co. Whale Dock
Martin A., Barrytown *Red Hook.*

Erie County.

Eaton P. B. & L. L. Erie bet. Erie & ship canal   *Buffalo.*
Parsons Wm. F. (staves) 3 Coburn square
Harbeck & Co. (staves) Elk st.
Johnson David. Elk st.
Butts C. C. 4 Ohio
King W. Elk c. Michigan
Craig F. S. Elk c. Michigan
Clark & Brockelbank, Washington c. Scott
Booth John, Ohio st.
Campbell A. A. Ohio st.
Johnson Wm. & Co. Elk st.
Mixer H. M. Detroit c. Dock
Farmer & De Blaquieres, Ohio st.
Pierce C. L. Swan c. Ellicott
Dodge & Baldwin, 335 Washingt'n
Wenz J. Batavia c. Elm
Johnson Henry W. 21 Eagle
Youell Geo. Erie adj'g canal
Duthie Jas. Niagara c. Mohawk
Hotchkiss J. W. Main ab. Chippewa
Hall Joel   do   do
Monier G. F. Hanover st.
Ellis Heary, Erie c. Terrace
Vanslyke C. A. & Co. Mechanics st.
Bull J. M. Mechanics st.

Hotchkiss Wheeler, Niagara cor Pearl   *Buffalo*

Essex County.

Cutting Franklin H.   *Westport.*
Allen D. L.

Franklin County.

Wead Wm.   *Belmont.*
Brown James   *Chateaugay.*
Marks Reuben
Atwater Franklin
Buyton Joseph
Percy Gerrit
Goldsmith ——   *Harristown.*

Genesee County.

Field W. L.   *Batavia.*
Belden, Otis & Co.
Haney R.

Herkimer County.

Houghton Wm. B.   *Little Falls.*

Kings County.

Shepard J. H. Columbia c. Pacific   *Brooklyn.*
Ostrom A. P. (lath) foot of Pacific
Cantine John M. foot of Amity
Watson James H. foot of Balkb
Walterhouse, Linn & Co. Columbia c. Baltic
Fairman, Huntley & Co. Atlantic Dock
Thomas B. F. Furman n. State
Van Wagner D. H. (lath) foot of Adams
Moon John, Washington c. Water
Conklin Henry N. Pearl c. John
Studwell A. Bridge c. Plymouth
Rhodes John, Marshall c. Little
Johnson S. J. Kent Av. n Flushl'g
Church James C., Fort Hamilton   *New Utrecht.*
Brinkerhoff A. B. 142 1st   *Williamsburgh.*
Trafford A. (lath) 1st st.
Hardy & Brown, Water c. N. 1st
Lockwood & Keith, foot of N. 1st

Livingston County.

Hollister Wm.   *Dansville.*
Myers Peter
Clark Hiram
Tolfree Jas. H.
Doty Jonathan
Streeter R. R.
Adams Jas. E.
Haight D. C.
Britton & Co.
M'Bride Hugh   *Geneseo.*
Peterson Jesse   *Mount Morris.*
Spellman R. R.
Mershon E. J.
Gillett Orson
Perry C. N.
Church & Sheeman

Madison County.

Parmelee T. & Son   *Cazenovia.*
Gardner Chas. B.   *Hamilton.*
Jarvis T. N. & M. B., Canastota   *Lenox.*

Monroe County.

Fox Henry, 212 Buffalo *Rochester*
Osborn D. 15 North
Griffin George, Mount Hope Av.
Bronson Amon, Exchange st.
Hollister & Churchill,   do
Conklin J. F. 187 State
Coleman Elihu,   do
Leavenworth G. Lower Falls
Milner J. P. & Co. Oak st.
Cox J. Scottsville   *Wheatland.*

Montgomery County.

Lefferts Saml. & Son *Amsterdam.*
Smith & Co.   *Canajoharie.*

New York County.

Bailey James, 78 Lewis & 39 Mangin _New York._
Baker, Wells & Co. 344 & 350 West
Baxter W. M. Av. A. c. E. 23d
Bennett Philip, 234 Cherry
Bogert Stephen
Bridges Jonathan F. 207 West
Brinckerhoff A. B. 52 Tompkins
Broderick Edward, 711 Water
Brush B. D. & Co. 354 West
Russell George, 735 Houston
Campbell & Moody, 506 Washington & foot 36th N. River
Cantine John M. & Co. 30 Front
Carpenter Nathaniel H. 292 West
Church & Forbes, foot of 29th
Chave Wm. 12th bet. Avs. B & C
Clark & M'Cleve, 40 10th Av.
Clark & Walton, 276 Cherry
Colwell William H. Harlem
Condit Calvin, 268 Cherry
Concklin J. D. Mangin n. Stanton
Cunningham J. F. 202 & 204 Madison
Dannat James L. 248, 250 & 260 South
Dannat William H. 258 Cherry
Darling D. S. 10th Av. cor. 13th
Davis Jehoiakim, 445 West & 143 Bank
Devoe Henry F. 220 West
Dennistown Will, 651 Water
Douglass John, 217 & 215 West
Duryee Jacob & Sons, 237 Cherry
Duryee Jacob, 577 Water
Duryee & Allen, 202 Cherry & 543 Water
Eaton & Pratt, 200 6th Av.
Ferguson William, Harlem
Ferris J. M. 417 West
Farnham P. J. & Co. 85 Pearl
Finch Nehemiah, 11 Wall
Foster William M. 273 West
Foster & Van Ostrand, 570 do
Fuller Philetus, 340 do
Gouldy Francis, 356 do
Green John, 362 do
Green G. & Edward, 529 do
Gottker J. H. cor. 5th & Av. B
Hallock S. jr. W. 15th cor. 10th Av.
Hammond James. 392 West
Hoyt Gabriel P. B. 230 Cherry
Hunt Henry W. 457 West
Jacobus John. 160 Cherry
Jaycocks William. 487 W.
Johnson D. & S. 139 William
Joseph & Cummings, 18 10th Av.
Lawrence Elijah, 143 Orchard
Lowere George W. 141 Centre
Lyon James D. & J. H. 194 Cherry
Lytle Andrew. 197 Monroe
M'Clave J. bet. 29th & 30th
Martin Shelden, 223 Cherry
Martling Stephen, 459 West
Mister Mrs. W. H. 295 & 296 West
Miller & Shaurman, 402 8th
Miller & Shaurman, 371 9th & 114 Av. D
Morse Martin. 267 West
Mott Garnett S. 2 Nassau & foot of W. 54th
Moulton Theodore. 254 Cherry
Muir Sarah. 285 West
Nash J. E. 21st cor. Av. A
Nowell Darius C. 325 4th Av.
Ogden & Co. 392 Washington
Peckham Reuben, 534 West
Phelps & Wallace. 538 do
Phillips James W. 234 Cherry & 52 South
Potter & Powers. 335 West
Pugsley & Ledgerd. W. 14th cor. 10th Av.
Read C. Delancy cor. Mangin
Reeve James & Co. W. 29th st.
Rexford George R. 430 West
Roberts & Benjamin, cor. Broome & 21st
Rodman Jesse, 10 Tompkins

Rokenbaugh S. H. 57 Maiden lane _New York._
Royce Henry A. 364 West
Rudyerd William, 270 Cherry
Sanderoon & Finch, W. 29th st.
Sharp Jacob, 295 W. 18th
Sheldon Chas. & Co. 435 Water
Sheldon P. & H. A. 540 West
Sheldon Martin. 223 Cherry
Shindler Simon, 32 10th Av.
Simonson Thomas H. 384 West
Smith Milton G. 200 Av. C
Smith William & Son. Mangin st. cor. Stanton, & 12th cor. Av. C
Smith Samuel I. 24 Tompkins
Snow & Anderson, E. 18th cor. Av. A
Taylor L. 15th st. cor. 10th Av.
Titus & Co. 505 Water
Todd & Robinson. Harlem
Van Beuren D. & Co. 270 West
Vanpelt Jacob J. 12th st. bet. Avs. B & C
Wall & Peckham, 534 West
Walton & Little. 523 Delancy, 534 Water, & 260 Cherry
Waterbury and Read, cor. Delancy & Mangin
Way Evan J. 722 Water
Westervelt & Bogart, 10th Av. cor. 13th
Wood James N. foot of W. 23d
Youmans Jeremiah H. 6 Hoboken & 272 Spring

Niagara County.

Cornell N. _Lewiston._
Fitch William
Tufford Isaiah
Doty Pharis
Moore —— _Lockport._
Cooper J. D. _Newfane._
Lane Alex. Youngstown _Porter._
Wilson Luther _Wilson._

Oneida County.

Van Patten & Kimball, Canal st. _Rome._
Lawrence L. cor. Seneca & Canal Basin _Utica._
Churchill C. cor. Washington & Fayette
Downer C. & Co. cor. Fayette & Broadway
Cozzens L. Broadway
Churchill C. cor. Fayette & State
Downer C. & Co. Columbia st.
Owen Wm. & Co. Fayette st.
M'Quade & Clark, Jay st.
Wilcox T. A. M'Connellsville _Vienna._
Warner & Walt, Whitesboro _Whitestown._

Onondaga County.

Mead S. Water st. Syracuse
— _Salina._
Going Charles, do
Beamish F. do
Bradley & Trowbridge, do
Raynor & Avery do
Gifford Henry, James st. Syracuse
Leister Hovey & Co., do
Matteson H. T. Genesee st. do
Acker B. Salina st. do

Ontario County.

Saxton Stephen _Canandaigua._
Baggerly Gideon _Phelps._
Hastings & Field, Geneva _Seneca._
Jones S. L. do
Palmer H. & Co. do
Wilcox & Brace _South Bristol._
Dunton W. J.

Orange County.

Smith Stephen _Cornwall._
Conklin J. Port Jervis _Deer Park._
Farnum H. H. do
Terball & Sanford _Goshen._

Copley H. D. _Montgomery._
Luguire W. E.
Dodge and Thompson, Otisville _Mount Hope_
Bigler James _Newburgh._
Bull James, Front st.
Mapes M. D. do
Bullis Ephriam do
Foster F. H. do
Conklin S. S. South Middletown _Wallkill._
Roberts H. P. do

Orleans County.

Fanning T. C. Albion _Barre_
Harvey N. E. do
Edmonds J. _Carlton_
Hedley E. Medina _Ridgeway_

Oswego County.

Littlefield Hamilton, Smith's Cove _Oswego._
Amblers & Ells, Ames Buildings, First st.
Staats John, Front st.
Bennett Morris, Regency Block, cor. Front & Schuyler
Forward & Smith, cor. Schuyler & 2d st.

Putnam County.

Simonson J. Cold Spring _Phillipstown._

Queens County.

Peck & Fairweather _Flushing._
Peck Isaac & Sons
Davidson Alex. Rockville _Hempstead._
Covert & Green _Newtown._
Carrington James W.
Mills & Blackwell, Astoria
Kicks Wm. Roslyn _North Hempstead_

Rensselaer County.

Herrington H. foot of Adams st. _Troy_
Taylor Nathan, foot of Front st.
Whipple Wm. W. & Son, corner Front & Washington st.
Thompson C. W. Front st.
Douglass T. do
Landon & Russell, cor. Front & Liberty st.
Herrington & Avery, cor. Front & Liberty st.
Buswell John G. Front st. below Division
Landon Gardiner, cor. River & Washington
Whipple W. W. & Co. Front st.
Lee Nathaniel. 413 River
Spicer J. E. & T. C. 7 Hoosick
King F. near R. Road Bridge
Welch Wm. E. 245 4th

Richmond County.

Marfleet D. Tompkinsville _Castleton_
Bodine Wm. & Bro. Factoryville
Simpson John P. Port Richmond _Northfield._

Rockland County.

Smith D. D. & T. Nyack _Orangetown._
Miller S. Piermont

Saratoga County.

Reynolds L. A. _Moreau._
Rice J. H. Glenn's Falls
Rice & Stevens do
Conery A. do
Montgomery M. _Stillwater._

17

Scott Harvey B   *Waterford.*
Morse Elisha

Schenectady County.

Becker P. Dock st.   *Schenectady.*
Horsfall J. C. & J. 50 Green

Seneca County.

Race Whiting   *Seneca Falls.*
Johnson & Thomas
Mackey E. H. & Co.   *Waterloo.*
Vandermark Silas & Co.
Wheeler & Stevenson
Fridley Flickner

Suffolk County.

Sammis & Lockwood *Huntington.*
Penny Joseph, Greenport *Southold.*
Champion ——, do

Tioga County.

Lincoln O. & Son, New'k Valley
        Newark.

Tompkins County.

Mott Wm. 2d   *Caroline.*
Taples Peter   *Danby.*
Tyler Egbert
Jennings Samuel
Birdsley Wells
Judson Joseph
Hugg D. F. & Co. Seneca st.
  Bridge   *Ithaca.*
King A. & Co. Seneca st.
Vickery E., Inlet
Marshall H.   do
Culver & Halsey, R. R. Block

Ulster County.

Fitch E. & Co.   *Kingston.*
Hudler & Andrews, Rondout
Skeel D. W. & Co. Wilbur
Scott T.   do
Webster & Van Valkenburgh
      Saugerties.
Field John

Warren County.

Morgan & Lapham, Glenn's Falls
      Queensbury.
Flask & Kipp, Glenn's Falls
Johnson F. A.   do
Sherman Augustus, do
Cheney & Arms, do

Washington County.

Holmes Henry   *Greenwich.*
Fulding & Andrews

Wayne County.

Crosby J. S.   *Arcadia.*
Wright Benjamin
Blackmer A., Newark
Blackmer A. T. & E.   *Huron.*
Thurston E. G.   *Lyons.*
Braddish & Bourne
Cady & Stanton
Southwick & Thurber *Palmyra.*

Westchester County.

Hart Gilbert E. Peekskill
      Courtlandt.
Hought P. S. C.   do
Washburn & Denike, do
Underhill James, do
Reed David, Sing Sing *Ossining.*
Pell Stephen S.   *Pelham.*
Dock & Bush, Portchester *Rye.*
Todd & Robertson *West Farms.*
Rowland & Fitch

Yates County.

Miley Peter H. (Branchport)
      Jerusalem.
Weavers S. D. & Sons, (Branchpt.)
Platt J. F. (Penn Yan) *Milo.*
Spencer M.   do

Lumber Manufacturers.

Albany County.

Warren Clement & Co. 69 Water
      Albany.
Gibson John, (Planing) cor. Water & Spencer sts.
Hawley Henry Q. (Planing) N. of Patroon's Creek
Rathbone J.   *Bethlehem.*
Briggs Wm. S.   *Coymans.*
Ten Eyck ——
Kinney Philip
Crounse Adam   *Guilderland.*
Van Valkenburgh ——
Shell G.
Spawn E.
Williamson William   *Knox.*
Williamson George
Carpenter Zeno
Shoemaker Egbert
Gage Hyrum
Judd ——
Van Potter ——
Wetsel Philip
Crary Isaac
Lagrange Anthony *New Scotland.*
Copley C.   *Watervliet.*
Barnard J. M. West Troy
Richards A. (Planing Machine)
Rosseau, Coffin & Eastern, (Planing Machine)
Viele & Mather, Green Island
Burton William & Co. Cohoes
Verplank C. I. D.   *Westerlo.*

Alleghany County.

Black Alexander   *Alfred.*
Bundy J. & G.   *Andover.*
Hunt & Russell
Baker E.
Morse A.   *Angelica.*
Brown D.
Ranney N. C.
M'Comb J.
Van Wickle S.
Thomas, Kingsley & Co. *Belfast.*
Stoughton, Burr & Heath
Hull Stephen
Sherman J.
Risted J. & R.
Russell & Marvin   *Bolivar.*
Hosley & Wing
Ingersol Mundy, Whitney Valley
      Burns.
Whitney E. Whitney Valley
Hall & Cole   *Caneadea.*
Sweet & Co.
Parks George
Dudley & Grove
Nicholson A. S. & E.
Smith John
Walker L. P.
Horner Thomas
Brown James   *Clarksville.*
Palmer Joseph
Peckham & Keller
Southworth Asa
Robinson & Co.
Dusenbury, Wheeler & Co.
Irish George
Chamberlain Calvin T. *Cuba.*
Powers John
Green Luke
Steenrad Eben   *Friendship.*
Scott Madison
Niver William
Cross Calvin
Stebbins Jacob
Sisson Gideon & Co.
Baxter Henry
Morton Joseph   *Granger.*
Walbridge William
Fuller Ebenezer
Bullock Ephraim
Platt Joseph
Jones & VanNostrand. ShortTract
Van Nostrand Luzen   do
Thorp Montgomery   do
Crandall & Bowles, Little Genesee
      Genesee.

Fairbanks D. A. Little Genesee
      Genesee.
Langworthy J. A.   do
Potter George,   do
Crandall A. E. West Genesee
Parish & Kies,   do
Irish George,   do
Rice & Thayer   *Hume.*
Jacobs Stephen
Lapham A.
Todd John, Wiscoy
M'Graw & Co. *New Hudson.*
Smith James, Black Creek
Camford Richard, do
Spalding & Hathaway, do
Hovey & Co.   *Ossian.*
Burrell Isaac
Gould William
Roberts Benjamin
French Marcus
Baron Fletcher
Shay Lewis
Colburn Charles   *Rushford.*
Woodruff Myron
Benjamin Oliver
Colburn Seth
Warren Michael
Church, Murray & Co. *Scio.*
Barnum E. G. Wellsville
Abbot ——,   do
Van Allen John, do
Hills Justin *West Almond.*
Blinn I.
Prentiss J. G.
Sherman Samuel   *Wirt.*
Ballard J.
Richardson Harvey

Broome County.

Rogers & Co. Chenango Forks
      Barker.
Lewis H.   *Binghamton.*
Coller H. M. (Planing)
Pratt & Doolittle
Waterman T. G.
Eldridge C.
White J.   *Conklin.*
Potter T.
Adams & Randall   *Lisle.*
Pollard L.   *Maine.*
Willis A.   *Union.*
Mersereau I. P. & D.
Balch B.
Whittemore O.
Day A. P.
Reeler L. S.
Thorn & Waterman
Norton N.
La Grange J. Nanticook Mills

Cattaraugus County.

King, Rockwell & Wilson
      Ashford.
Scovy Alexander
Frank Jacob
Quackenbush John D.
Rice Abel
Smith & Benton   *Burton.*
Graves & Thompson
Hall Charles & Warren
Fox Wm. B.
Reed Charles
Blair & Robbins
Mills & Nobles
Johnson J. G.
Sheldon G. C.
Altenburgh H. & J.
Allen Seth & Orrin
Hicks C. & J.
Patterson Robert
Grimes William
Onan C. & W.
Nessell Joseph
Reynolds Elisha
Jones Ebenezer
Fuller Wm. & Hiram
Gardner & Shankland *Ellicottville.*
Colman Joseph
Stanton J. B.
Veeder J. F.
Brown Eli C. Elton   *Freedom.*

Richardson Lyman, Elton *Freedom.*
Lewis. Smith & Wilder, Sandusky
Lawton Harvey, (shingles) do
Crowell Hiram, do
Wooster Jeremy & Lucius
Great Valley.
Dunn & Morton
Williams Charles & Spencer
Nelson Wm. J.
Sears Elmore
Pemberton A.
Nelson James
Porter Salmon
Green Francis
Rowland John
Willoughby O. F.
Ellis John
Howe H. *Little Valley.*
Sherman Jason *Lynden.*
Van Dewater —— *Machias*
Peck H.
Lafferty E.
Huggins Jno. Eddyville *Mansfield.*
Cox Matthew, do
Eddy Wm. H. do
Wright S G. *New Albion.*
Barnard W.
Powell & Davis
Walt & Tubbs
Judd Harrison
Buffington J. *Otto.*
Burroughs James
Jacket William
Neye C. F.
Colvin Freeman, East Otto
Larkins Nathan, do
Matoon Calvin, do
Cook A. *Perrysburgh.*
Barker A.H.
Norton ——
Taylor J. R.
Dusenbury, Wheeler, Gregory &
Co. *Portville.*
Rice A. D.
Wheeler & Holly
Rea Walter
Middough John
Smith & Barnes
Weymouth Daniel
Bockes David
Lowry Y. M.
Smith John
Jewell Andrus & Reed
Bush A. G. *Randolph.*
Helmes C. C.
Migbells F. F.
Crowley M. A. & Co.
Burch J.
Worden Wm. *Rice.*
Davis & Farwell
Hunt & Linderman
Aiken James *South Valley.*
M'Coye Pat
Striker John I.
Striker John J.
Wadesworth William
Hall William
Covill John
Fenton John
Woodward John
Phillips Samuel & Brother
Moore F. K.
Brow Norman
Frisby & Marsh
Hotchkiss & Foster
Norton Alonzo
Barton Leonard
Flagg Eli

Cayuga County.
Slover I. Genesee st. *Auburn.*
Cowell & Rockwell *Cato.*
Rhodes J. T.
Sweetser W. *Conquest.*
Terpenning J. E. *Ira.*
Dresser —— *Sempronius.*
Winnegar & Brothers *Springport.*
Allen A.
Sanford R. *Sterling.*

Chautauque County.
Miker Henry, Jamestown *Elicott.*

Scott & Barrows, Jamestown
Elicott.
Jones Solomon, jr. do
Falconer P. do
Phillips Melvin, do
Hulet Uriah *French Creek.*
Rous James H.
Higgins Eugene
Cutting David
Jewett G. R. & Co. *Portland.*
Brown Aaron H. *Sheridan.*
Miner Justin S.
Haskins Philander
Hicks William
Brigham Haven
Usher Newell
Denney & Waits
Hilt William
Lewis F. N.
Kip & Miller *Sherman.*
Drury L. R.
Reynolds Ablather
Vincent Samson
Hill & Bloomer
Ross Charles
Willard E.
Olin George T.

Chemung County.
Thompson G. M. *Catharine.*
Beardsley S. C.
Catlin F.
Beardsley G. C. (shingles)
Mitchell John
Randall John M.
Rockwell James
Mitchell Jesse
Lyon I. M.

Chenango County.
Bennett R., Bennettsville
Bainbridge.
Corbin William, do
Watson V. *Greene.*
Stebbins S. & E. *Guilford.*
Haynes Jones
Pratt J. *North Norwich.*
Fox Daniel *Pitcher.*
Chandler Hiram
Frink Coddington *Plymouth.*
Sexton Seth
Adams Giles
Adams Alison & Brothers
Thompson Jonathan
Titus Gilbert
Peabody ——
Perley Walter
Steer Clark
Heddy Daniel
Carpenter Joel
Monroe Samuel, jr.
Taylor J.
Cooke Almond, South Plymouth
Balcom George, Oxford P.O.
Preston.
Birch L. D. *Sherburne.*

Clinton County.
Comer Samuel *Beekmantown.*
Farnsworth & Allan
Boardman M.
M'Gregor John *Black Brook.*
Duncan John T.
Potter & Richardson
Burt G. M.
Finch James M.
Bagley Alanson
Heyworth Richard *Peru.*
Barnard T. J. & Son *Plattsburgh.*
Lasell J.
Case Alfred *Saranac.*
Burdick, Cadwell & Co. Redford
Berkley Robert do

Columbia County.
Hanna & Peaslee, Malden Bridge
Chatham.
Bennett L., Chatham Four Corners
Abel E., Mellenville *Claverack.*
Wheeler Richard A. *Hillsdale.*

Williams Peter C. *Hillsdale*
Collin John F.
Stickle Wm. P.
Williams Sylvester
Lathrop G. M. & Co. *Kinderhook.*

Cortland County.
Kehoy Seth & Thomas E. *Preble.*
Philley Uriah
Crofoot David

Delaware County.
Wriant J. *Colchester.*
Dibble H.
Downs J. W.
Landfield D.
Radeker B.
Elwood H.
Dann E.
Shaver J.
Shaver H.
Bates J.
Miller E. *Davenport.*
Crawford J.
Olmstead H.
Tenyck H.
Parker W.
Bennett J.
Carpenter R., Clovesville
Middletown.
Hadley B. E., Deposit *Tompkins.*
Deveraux, Clark & Co. Deposit
Hulce M. R. do
Hotchkiss N. do
Whitaker J. O. & S. do
Gregory U. do

Duchess County.
Brett C. N., Fishkill Landing
Fishkill.
Crosby & Stevens, do
Yelverton J. H. P. G., Upper Land-
ing *Poughkeepsie.*
Arnold D. (timber) do
Swift R., Hart's Village
Washington.

Erie County.
Farnsworth A. D. & Co. *Alden.*
King J. C. & Co. Williamsville
Amherst.
Frick C. Z. do
Long Christian, do
Gets Joseph, do
Stoddard G. do
Miner Peter L. do
Gale Lockwood, Griffin's Mills
Aurora.
Robertson Findley, Spring Brook
Nortrup Lewis, do
Kyser Horace, do
Fowler Edwin, (shingles) Willink
Pond J. & J. do do
Gelston Samuel F. *Black Rock.*
Burkhart John
Townsend ——
Payne Simon *Boston.*
Abbott C.
Cooper Wm. W.
Kester Wm. H.
Fenton Cephas *Brandt.*
Butts Samuel
Ransom H. B. *Clarence.*
Ayelsworth Aaron
Eshleman John
Martin Abram
Mansfield Orange, N. Clarence
Arnold —— *Colden.*
Buffum A.
Falcom Elijah
Plumb Ralph *Collins.*
Taylor C.
Lawton Geo.
Morgan E.
Averell ——
Clark Samuel
Rice H. Gowanda, (shingles)
Freeman H., Springville *Concord.*
Clark Simeon *Eden.*
Puff John

Crower A *Eden.*
Barton & Stafford
Swan B. A.
Belknapp Porter
Belknapp John
Myers Henry
Coons John
Berland John, East Evans *Evans.*
Sheopard Matthias, do
Backus Wm. do
Earl J. & W. do
Bundy M. do
Smith Frederick, do
Candel Nehemiah, do
Gould Ruel, do
Long Isaac, Water Valley *Hamburgh.*
M'Clure David, do
M'Clure Heman, do
Austin Harmon, do
Orr Alvin *Holland.*
Rice B. F. & Co.
Callender —— *Lancaster.*
Briggs & M'Neal
Martin ——
Clark James
Clark Hiram, Town Line
Holmes B. & E. do
Simanson & Cooper, do
Davinport Horace, do
Webster S. & J. do
Bullis —— do
Harrington, Anderson & Vogdis, Akron *Newstead.*
Simpson & Woolson *Tonawanda.*
Willis G. *Wales.*
Stevens H. A.
Bart Geo. L.
Earl Elisha
Patch Oliver
Darrow Lyman
Coon W. South Wales
Pollard Benj. Wales Centre

Essex County.

Hammonds & Co. *Crown Point.*
Penfield, Harwood & Co.
Stratton, Rhoades & Brown
Noble H. R. *Elizabethtown.*
Whitcomb P. S. & Co.
Meigs Guy
Rice C. W. & L.
Glidden & Partridge
Miller Manoah
Yaw Elisha
Holcomb E. F.
Gates Willis
Post Jonathan
Heald Noah *Keene.*
Holt Harvey
Nobles Ransom & Sons *Lewis.*
Gould John
Evans W. & R. *Minerva.*
Gates D. L.
Barnes T. L.
Griffin Lorenzo D., Moriah Four Corners *Moriah.*
Sherman Samuel, Moriah Four Corners
Hendee E. P. do
Fountain Wm. do
Tarbell Daniel, do
Chapman Alpheus, do
Sprague Hiram, do
Lang Robert H. do
Hadaway Lott, do
Ensign Charles W. do
Train Richard, do
M'Kenzie Robert, do
Sherman P. do
Stiles Alonzo, do
Stiles Ephraim, do
Stone Isaac, Port Henry
Spenin J. E. do
Whitney Benj. do
Adirondac Iron Works Mill, Adirondac *Newcomb.*
Sissell Warren, Adirondac
Potter E. B., Schroon River *Schroon.*
Wyman Alonzo, do

Little Nelson, Schroon River *Schroon.*
Moore L. T. do
Knowlton Alfred, do
Lindsay R. D., Schroon Lake
Wheeler N. do
Taylor Jesse, do
Flint Jonah, do
Sturdevent A. S.
Sawyer Consnt *St. Armand.*
Skiff Daniel C.
Weed Joseph *Ticonderoga.*
Wilson & Calkins
Ross Henry H. 2d (lath)
Willsborough.
Vanderwarker Martin J.

Franklin County.

Jones James *Bangor.*
Ross William
Austin George
Spaulding Andrew
Meigs & Wood *Malone.*
Horton H.
Whipple H. W.
Bemis C.
Mason Martin
Hutchinson & Brother
Keeler George N.
Mann S. West Constable *Westville.*
Hardy Davis, do
Button H. G. do
Hadley J. P. do
Wright T. jr. do
Hyde H. do

Fulton County.

Richards O. Bleecker Falls *Bleecker.*
Bowler William, do
Burr ——, do
Foot David, do
Skiff Allen, do
Baird George B. do
Odell S. P. do
Frick Frederick, do
Chase Benjamin *Broadalbin.*
Spencer Henry W.
Edwards John *Ephratah.*
Edwards Henry
Putnam Peter
Edwards James
Empie Jacob
Devis Thomas
Newkirk G. A. *Garoga.*
Sammons & Martin
Burton Morgan
Mills William
Robinson George
Brown J.
Mead John
Stewart John D.
Curtis Hiram
Degolyer & Marcellus *Mayfield.*
Wood David
Cameron Allen
Dunning Josiah
Dixon Jacob
Wilde Jacob
O'Bryan John, Vall's Mills
Stanly Thos. Mayfield Corners
Lefever & Van Valkenburgh
Northampton.
Slocum Reuben
Corey Anson, Osborn's Bridge
Ingraham W. S. do
Thumb E. *Oppenheim.*
Cline G. H.
Brown N. J.
Smith Augustus
Flander J. & J.
Thumb Adam
Robinson John
Claus E.
Warner John
Hastings J.
Shull A. J.
Yonker L.
Brown Nathan
Galle William
Cramer S.

Cramer John *Oppenheim.*
Kellogg L. *Peck.*
Stewart William
M'Intosh John
Harriway John
Montsith John
Goodwin & Sons *Stratford.*
Crossman William

Genesee County.

Doty & Co. *Alexander.*
Loomis
Ward Henry M. *Bergen.*
Brown Daniel *Bethany.*
Fay Jonas L.
Grimes John
Wood Erastus, East Bethany
Borrass & Hoops, Linden
Terry Zeno *Byron.*
Price A. T. *Le Roy.*
Tomlinson J.
Stanley Elisha
Woodard D.
Parmelee J. H.
Gould, Willet & Co. E. *Pembroke.*

Greene County.

Strong D. B. *Ashland.*
Sherrill & Shaw *Greenville.*
Brandt & Co. *Hunter.*
Ken Robert N.
Quick Lewis L.
Connelly William A.
Douglass James
Carl James
Lane Peter
Saxe Michael
Beach N. Wm. East Kill
Farrington Asa, do
Brezee Martin, do
Williams Daniel, do
O'Brien Thomas, do
Woodworth & Howe, do
Peters George, do
Lindsley John B. do
Clune Philip P. do
Hains Jesse, do
Hains Peter B. do
Kreisted J. H. & Co. do
Hains Aaron, do
Smith James *Lexington*
Wiltsie William
Miller Justice S.
Bushnell Aaron, West Kill
Schermerhorn Uriel, do
Van Valkenburgh J. do
Fellows Philip, West Lexington
Peck James, do
Baldwin Hezekiah *New Baltimore.*
Baldwin Henry
Van Slyke Andrew
Raymond John

Hamilton County.

Whitman R. & Co. *Gilman.*
Folsom & Hawley
Bentley Edwin
Dunning David
Gilman Elias P.
Smith W. A. & Co. *Hope.*
Moore Albert
Buel Asa
Anible L.
Brownell O.
Graff John R.
Washburn E.
Moffatt Josiah *Lake Pleasant.*
Satterley John S.
Chamberlain & Ferguson *Wells.*
Overacker Michael
Chambers & Co.
Stevenson John
Copeland Leonard
Bacon Moses & Co.
Whitman R.
Dunham E. T.
Brown H. L.
Willis Nathan

Herkimer County.

Hawks Thomas *Columbia.*

Hutsen Samuel   Columbia.
Miller C. & Co.
Cooke D.
Ayres O. P. & Co.
Goalin John
Hampt Samuel   Danube.
Davis Cornelius
Jones Benj.
Moyer Jacob
Young John
West M.   Fairfield.
Parkhurst H. A.
Jackson A.
Davis J.
Phillips W.
Helmer L.
Mason Daniel   Frankfort.
Gotman Robert
Bridenbecker & Co.
Coolrage A.
Davis John
Kingsley Obadiah, West Frankfort
Crossman Wm. Frankfort Centre
Rushmore C.   do
Johnson J. Frankfort Hill
Caswell Wm.   Herkimer.
Rickettson, Bell & Davenport
Nellis Isaac
Hilts Wm.
East T.
Johnson D. S.
Skinner Wm. L   Little Falls.
Ostoragan Company
Guyvills Jacob
Ingham Harvey   Manheim.
Spafford J. D.
Ransom David
Youson J. J.
Waterman Henry   Newport.
Plants P. B, & Co.
Gray Lathan   Norway.
Western Joseph
Hine Russell
Post Chas. K.
Campbell John
Baldwin David H.   Salisbury.
Ives A. & F.
Tuttle B.
Elies Jefferson, Salisbury Centre
Lankton A.   do
Spencer G.   do
Smith S.   do
Wells John   Schuyler.
Jackson D.
Hurlbut S. C.
Shift John
Sweet V.
Baker A. & Co.
Countryman John   Stark.
Van Horn & Conklin
Miller David
Hall & Haskins, Starkville
Van Horn C. T. E. Van Hornsville
Countryman Isaac,   do
Griffin Wm.   Warren.
Lyman Fred. Jordanville
Weatherbee Alvin, Page's Corner
M'Credy Thos. Crane's Corner
Hinckley Gardner   Wilmurt.
Dodge S.   Winfield.
Clerk ——
Burgess D.
Carier & Walker, West Winfield
Hull & Guild,   do
Murdock P,   do
Willcox N.   do

Jefferson County.
Saunders W.   Adams.
Tucker M. M.
Fox & Gaylord
Butterfield & White, Redwood
    Alexandria.
Clark Jason, Plessis
Fuller John W. Alexandria Bay
Brown John E.   Brownville.
Briggs J. (Staves) Dexter
Hungerford T. B.   do
Kerby & Wood,   do
Tomlinson D. E.   do
Clark C. E.   Champion.

Crook Orrin   Champion.
Earl Lewis
Lathrop Alfred
Willis ——
Johnson S. P. Depauville Clayton.
Comee J. (shingles) Ellisburgh.
Clark C. E. Great Bond Le Ray.
Kilburn Davids, Evans' Mills
Smith Philander   Lorraine.
Gillet David
Lyman Silas
Towles Gardner
O'Nell Jacob
Putnam J. Three Mile Bay Lyme.
Leonard Charles,   do
Hamblin G.   do
Gopeley A.   do
Lamphere Wm. J. Miller's Bay
Bushnell L. Lafargeville Orleans.
Dubois W.   do
Drake Thos. E.   do
Cramer J. Watertown   Pamelia.
O'Doughty Patrick, do
Beecher & Andrews, South Rut-
    land   Rutland.
Mott S. L. Black River
Fuller Joseph,   do
Young Wm. I.   do
Felt O. A. & S. Felt's Mills
Wheeler & Carpenter, do
Fisher Archibald   Theresa.
Ranney Anson
Poole Zalmon, jr.
Seeber Wm.
Calvin Amos
Davis Michael
Hall Samuel
Boyer John L.
Snell George
Parker Horace
Guyot Bazille, Carthage Wilna.
Kimball & Cramer, do
Lathrop Alfred,   do
Willis Chester,   do
Willard Johnson, Natural Bridge

Kings County.
Bloomer John A. Pearl st. near
    Water   Brooklyn.
Lockwood & Keith, foot North 3d
    st.   Williamsburgh.

Lewis County.
Rofinob Joseph   Croghan.
Breof Francis X.
Zehr Michael
Potter John S.
Rohr Jacob
Shue Lyman
Prame Martin
Fox Abraham, Indian River
Lippencott Isaac   Diana.
Farago Chas. L. & Co.
Hunt Abel
Van Hausen William
Blanchard Sherman
Clarke Samuel & Co.
Voorhees John
Lyon L. R. Brantingham   Greig.
Reed & Shedd,   do
Northrup J. T.   do
Sand Peter J.   do
Beals Asa,   do
Beals Wheelock,   do
Williams & Greig,   do
Gellup Joshua,   do
Shedd M. & H. Lyonsdale
Garret Clark,   do
Segur & Scrafford, do
Pinney Dunham,   do
Brown George H.   do
Rogers Thomas. Port Leyden
Brown George F.   do
Booth ——,   do
Bush William H.   Harrisburgh.
Cobb N.
Edgebert F.
Dockstador S.
Knapp H.
Jones S.
Lasher & Green

Windecker J.   Harrisburgh.
Talcott Jesse   Leyden.
Thornton Philip
Kent Daniel
Coe Alvah
Walter Ezra
Hall Abijah
Merriam Ela
Post John
Clark J.
Haugh R. T.
Fox Ashbel
Roberts James   Osceola.
Baker Henry.
Hart Sylvester   Turin.
Roberts Richard
Gaylord Edwin
Danks Alvin O.
Morgan Luther
House Leonard, Houseville
Roberts Evan, Constableville
    West Turin.
Thompson S. C.   do
Crofoot Levi,   do
Stiles John,   do
Bramer G. S.   do
Readuger F.   do
Apple Frederick,   do
Western I. A.   do
Mumford W. C.   do
Broxel B.   do
Lyon L. R.   do

Livingston County.
Mather Nelson J.   Avon.
M'Kay John   Caledonia.
M'Kenzie Simon
Rockafellow & Coleman Conesus
Campbell D. T.
Triscott Solomon
Squires William   Dansville.
Fish George C. (Lath)
Dorr Samuel G.
Norris C. L. (Lath)
Stone B.
Post Parden
Brewer James
Porter M. & Son
North H. P.   Geneseo.
West E. Lakeville   Livonia.
Short Phillip,   do
Powell Elisha, Hemlock Lake
Skinner Samuel   Nunda.
Richmond B. P.
Paine C.
Bradley J.
Barker Amos
Hewett & Towsey, Hunt's Hollow
    Portage.
Slater & Nichols,   do
Pierce Luther,   do
Gearheart John,   do
Patterson James,   do
Davis Levi,   do
Brace H.   do
Messenger O. F. Oakland
Tyler Harvey S.   Springwater.
Webster ——
Wilhelm Benjamin
Passage G. Byersville
    West Sparta.
Passage John,   do
Northrip James,   do
M'Miller Isaac   York.
Allen John
Fisher Josiah, Greigville

Madison County.
Babcock P.   Brookfield.
York & Denison
Johnson E. E. & L.
Gorton V.
Burdick Clark
Babcock H.
Brightman J.
Woodward J.
Curtis Moses
Burdick G.
Osborn & Burrell
St. John H.
Hoxie L. & T. Leonardsville

Babcock Elisha, S. Brookfield
       Brookfield.
Beebe Cyrus, North do
Sweet Samuel G. do
Snow J. & Son *Cazenovia.*
Cedar Grove Mills
Williams, Ledyard & Stebbins
Billings Fletcher
Jackson George
De Clercq Peter
Winchell L.
Ward S. B
Sweetland & Brothers
Burton William
Burton William & Son
Sims & Tabor
Underwood J. L. New Woodstock
Savage William, do
Post John, do
Sutton & Sears *De Ruyter.*
Benjamin Patrick, do
Gardner D. do
Morse Ellis *Eaton.*
Harwood S. & R.
Tillinghast C. Morrisville
Shepard Nathan, do
Farwell B. F. do
De Forest A. B. do
Hecox Truman, do
Smith A. Y. Leeville
Coffee & Griffin, do
Hutchinson David *Fenner.*
Hyatt Stephen
Taylor William
Towne Phineas
Berritt William P.
Munger Rufus
Warlock Stephen
Foster H. A.
Wilber & Clay
Moseley & Hare *Georgetown.*
Isbell E.
Robie H.
Mann Erastus
Dutton William
Warren George
Wright William
Wilson George
Richardson N.
Atwood Mitchell
Eaton & Co. Poolville *Hamilton.*
Gifford T. B. do
Thompson Amos, East Hamilton
Ackley Rodney, do
Osborn & Co. do
Ackley C. R. do
Dunbar David, Hubbard's Corners
Plimpton R. *Lebanon.*
Felt Norman
Paddleford Peter
Thayer O. S.
Baker Jesse
Torrey James
Wedge M. H.
Dunham Alanson
Nash Norton
Hoppin Curtis
Morse E.
Day Marvin
Marshall & Randall, Oneida Depot
       Lenox.
Scofield N. Oneida Depot
Cobb S. E. do
Strong J. R. Canastota
Sawter Frederick, do
Shepard & Adams, Wampsville
Raymond G. do
Gorsline E. S. do
Harrington Giles, do
Allen Daniel, do
Eddy George W. do
Fox Albert, Oneida Valley
Lovejoy William, Clockville
Reynolds C. J.
Cleveland Erastus *Madison.*
Hamlen Oliver
Putnam S. & S.
Potter David
Howard James, Bouckville
Edgarton William, do
Poole Oliver, Erieville *Nelson.*
Hamilton D. A. do

Hamilton Leverett, Erieville
       Nelson.
Bumpus E. do
Whitman George, do
Daniels Orville, do
Linsley ——, do
Hammond William, Peterboro
       Smithfield.
Bump J. Peterboro
Scofield George, Siloam
Ranney George, do
Curtis ——, do
Bump Ira, do
Parmelee John H. *Stockbridge.*
Merrill & Dexter
Ranney Eben.
Parker & Burroughs
Sartwell Bela
Nelson Ebenezer
Carpenter J. & Co.
Gordon Samuel
Storms John *Sullivan.*
House J. W.
Bond Ezra
Union Mill
Spencer Wm. Chittenango
Yates John G. do
Walrath D. & R. do
Walrath John I. do
Smith A. Oneida Lake
Green & Chapman, do
Sears Alfred, Perryville
Sayles Oney, Bridgeport

Monroe County.

Hart S. R. *Brighton.*
Parsons M.
Stanley & Burns
Strong Charles *Greece.*
Johnson Spencer, Jenkins Corners
Williams H. West Henrietta
       Henrietta.
Annis J. West Mendon *Mendon.*
Houston T. Parma Corner
       Parma.
Rich Samuel *Penfield.*
Fullam N.
Rowe J. B.
Miller Samuel
Lincoln A.
Jameson & Randall, Churchville
       Riga.
Baldwin Gorden, Black Creek
Kempton Willis, Court st.
       Rochester.
Brown Sylvester, 49 N. St. Paul st
Parsons James, Water st.
Childs Jonathan, Aqueduct st.
Bronson Amon, (Planed Lumber)
 Exchange st.
Hollister & Churchill, (Planed
 Lumber) Exchange st.
Brown Sylvester, foot of Brown's
 Race
Parsons J. & S. Brown's Race
Milner J. F. & Co. Oak st.
Twitchell Lawson B. Carthage
 Flats
Jennings A. *Rush.*
Winens Theodore, West Rush
Baker S. *Webster.*
Burnett Isaac
Whitney J.
Carpenter Isaac, Scottsville
       Wheatland.

Montgomery County.

Conner Gilbert, Hagamans' Mills
       Amsterdam.
Hagaman & Mason, Hagaman's
 Mills
Wiles John I. *Canajoharie.*
Bingham Ames F. Ames
Van Deusen & Sons, Buel
Burton J. Burtonville *Charleston.*
De Graff Isaac, Minaville *Florida.*
Sander James, do
Wells J. J. do
Sweet Samuel & Leonard, Port
 Jackson

Falkner James *Glen.*
Coons W.
Jones Lynds, Fonda *Mohawk.*
Jones Abijah, do
Sammons Wm. T. Fonda
Brewer William, do
Saltsman Alexander, do
Edwards John Y. Palatine Church
       Palatine.
Gray Wm., Stone Arabia
Saltsman Peter, do
Lipe Jacob, do
Van Wie Arie, Palatine Bridge
Moyer Henry *Root.*
Covenhoven Wm. A.
Brown John
Olmstead R.
Bassett & Stagg
Yates Abraham
Pines E. M. *St. Johnsville.*
Knickerbocker John
Failing Jacob H.

New York.

Baker & Wright, rear 150 Wooster
       New York.
Bonnel Mahlon & Sons, 461 W'tr
Bussel George, 597 Washington
Colyer & Dugard, foot of West
 14th
Garno Lewis S. 450 & 516 Water
Goulding Joseph M. 115 Attorney
Hunt William S. 213 West 20th
Ingersoll & Webb, 329 5th
James Henry A. 60 Forsyth
Julian M. P. South st. cor. Govnr
Lyman & Bunnel, 10 Canal
Menzies William, foot West 13th
 N. R.
Newton Jonah, 276 5th
Price Thomas, 131 Attorney
Roach Peter R. 136 Bank
Southmayd S. G. 377 West
Wenzels Henry, 199 Attorney
Woore Edward, 115 Attorney
Wells Thomas J. West 29th st.
Wells George, foot of 12th st.

Niagara County.

Ayer Richard *Lewiston.*
Hewitt J. P.
Vanslyke Philetus, Pekin
Van Valkenburgh —— *Lockport.*
Mack C. S.
Kemp David *Newfane.*
Shaw & Vincent
Van Horn Daniel
Stahl Enoch & W
Van Horn James
Andrews Daniel
Tompkins Ira
Benedict Geo. W.
Porter A. H. *Niagara Falls.*
Thompkins & Clark
Turner O. & Co.
Whitney P.
Beals & Babcock, Youngstown
       Porter.
Fowler Joseph, do
Colwell & Sleeper, Gosport
       Royalton.
Young & Taylor *Somerset*
Paine Lewis S. Tonawanda
       Wheatfield.
Wilson Luther *Wilson.*

Oneida County.

Jarvis & Seaton *Annsville.*
Dawley N.
Baxter H.
Waterman D.
Blenis D. & Co.
Tyler J. W.
Noonin T.
Chatham A.
Mowers & White
Williams P. *Boonville.*
Tuttle M.
Marvin S. *Camden.*
Satchell N.

Scovill S. *Camden.*
Scovill H.
Cook & Hare
Barnes A. W.
Scovill M.
Babcock A M.
Matthews A.
Phelps P. & R.
Dunbar H. & E.
Raymond L.
Walworth E. Delta *Lee.*
Smith C. L.
Barnes A. West Branch
Kellogg F. *New Hartford.*
Huxford Wm.
Fuller J. S. Rome st. *Utica.*
Brown John, Bleeker st.
Rathbun S. Rathbunsville
Verona.
Smith & Norton, Durhamville
Wood W. D. M'Connellsville
Vienna.
Hazen A. do
Howel & Blake, do
Utley S. North Western *Western.*
Colman A. H. Waleeville
Whitestown.

Onondaga County.

Beach R. M. & H. G. Baldwins-
ville *Lysander.*
Bush & Savage, Baldwinsville
Cook O. F. & Co. do
Kenyan N. J. (Planing) Lock st.
Syracuse *Salina.*
Gifford Henry, (Planing) James st.

Ontario County.

Hoppough M. *Canadice.*
Doolittle M.
White S. C. *Canandaigua.*
Gallinghouse L. B. *Hopewell.*
Derr George, Larned's Corners
Gregory ——
Terry & Munson
Barlow A. *Manchester.*
Dewey E. B. Manchester Centre
Robbins T. Abram *Phelps.*
Vandermark Frederick
Vandermark Charles
Root Francis, 2d
Griffith Robert
Pierpont D. A., Honeoye
Richmond.
Sowteli M., Richmond Mills
Hastings & Field, Geneva *Seneca.*
Reed W., Seneca Castle
Garrett Hiram, Flint Creek
Van Ostrand John, do
Hill Cyrus *South Bristol.*
Nichols J. W.
Parker David
Davey H.
Parmeley James
Brown Allen
Allen & Co.

Orange County.

Dodge & Thompson *Mount Hope.*
Bigler James *Newburgh.*
Demarest D. D., New Milford
Warwick.

Orleans County.

Wilber E., Albion *Barre.*
Harrington M. A., Albion
Simons —— Barre Centre
Sturges M. D. *Clarendon.*
Smith A. & A.
Cover ——
Newton Silas *Kendall.*
Webster S. & E. K. Kendall Mills
Collins William B. do
Card & Wright *Murray.*
Brace Almanza
Balcomb Abner
Downs Judson, Sandy Creek
Arnold David, do
Warner C., Medina *Ridgeway.*
Shephard I. do

Grant & Allen *Shelby.*
Grant L. A. G. B.
Johnston S. C., Millville
Olds Edwin *Yates.*
Parsons Joel C.
Finch Titus, Lyndonville

Oswego County.

Abbott M. H. (shingles) *Albion.*
Barker Peleg
Bragdon A. B.
Coyer Sylvester
Fish W. D. (shingles)
Gurley T. N. (shingles)
Huntington S. P.
Joslin Curtiss
Jaqueth Isaac
Rice Charles
Rowell Isaac
Stillwell George W.
Salisbury Uri
Sanborn St. John B.
Simons Richard
Seamans Stephen
Seamans & Osterkirk (shingles)
Thorp Isaac J.
Taft J. L.
Nelson J. C.
Brown William *Amboy.*
Albee Judson
Patchin John E. & Co.
Cutler J. W.
Coats Walter, Amboy Centre
Carter J. & R., Carterville
Seaman Arthur, West Amboy
Garber Henry, do
Alexander Samuel *Constantia.*
Smith Samuel P.
Carter J. & R.
Farrington O. B.
Judson E. B. & Co.
Bent Jonas
Patchin R. D.
Bartlett & Hitchcock
Leigh Charles
Rhodes H. W.
Dakin George E.
Marsh N. S.
Burnet John
Bernhard J.
Dennis E. J.
Dickinson William
Forster William, Cleaveland
Brydenbecker J. G. do
Landgraff A. & Son, do
Van Bergen A. G. do
Sperry Walter, do
Hitchcock H. do
Peabody D. do
Morse & Sons, do
Willard J. E. & Co. Oswego Falls
Granby.
Dodge Alanson, Oswego Falls
Reynolds J. G. do
Mann John, do
Parker James, jr. do
Antrim Geo. (shingles) do
Skinner James *Hannibal.*
Williams & Kipp
Elliott R., Central Square
Hastings.
Goit David *Mexico.*
Guild Benjamin
Wilbur ——, Texas
Loomis, King & Brayton, Texas
Marvin O. O. *New Haven.*
Gridley C. L.
Eason R. A.
Schermerhorn C. H.
Gordon Wm. H.
Davis Albert
Goodrich Lester
Cummins L.
Mack Harmon N.
Doud Titus
Brant & Muzzy *Orwell.*
Lewis Charles
Myers Joseph, (shingles)
Potter Hiram, (shingles)
Smith George

Ames George, Ames' Block, 1st st.
Oswego.
Holbrook R. G. bet. Canal & River
Trowbridge & Miller, Smith's Cove
Bentley & Trowbridge, Crocker's
Buildings, Bridge st.
Himes Charles, (lath & shingles,)
Crocker's Buildings, Bridge st.
Webster Benjamin, (lath, posts, &
R. R. ties,) basement Washing-
ton Mills, 1st st.
Becker John *Parish.*
Storm & Young
Benson Aaron
Clapsaddle John
Ackley David P.
Owens George
Palmer Earl
Knight Solomon
Brown Daniel, Pulaski *Richland.*
Gilbert & Calkins, do
Osgood —— do
Watkins P. B. (shingles) Pulaski
Wilson Jacob, do
Filkins H. & L. do
Sharp W. & G. do
Smith & Crandall, do
Cropsey Philip, do
M'Chesney William, do
Fellows S. G. do
Miller Henry, do
Gillespie Henry, do
Harrington Adolph, Port Ontario
Stillwell G. W. do
Miles Samuel, do
Woodrough A. do
Dewey Samuel, South Richland
Pride E. P. do
Gates Sewell, do
Holmes Isaiah, do
Savage, Titus & Co. Phœnix
Schroeppel.
Hart Amasa P., Phœnix
Kendall J. G. do
Sturges Russell, do
Gilbert Hiram, Gilbert's Mills
Waugh John F. *Scriba.*
Goulding ——
Stone Erastus
Jewell Isaac
Robinson Edmond
Coe Jerome
Coon Jacob
Peck John
Jones D. & H.
Cromwell Jacob *Williamstown.*
Selden Jacob
Selden Josiah
Selden Gustavus
Humphrey & Dodge (shingles)
Humphrey George
Winsor L. B.
Hutt & West
Potts Oscar
Devereux Elijah
Crosby Samuel

Otsego County.

Rupman W. (shingles) *Middlefield.*
Gellert Daniel
Garloch John S.
Camp Jacob
Camp Henry
Rich Moses
White Gustavus
Lent Rudolphus
Walker William A.
Eckler Martin
Rice Thomas
Parshall Gellert
Pierce Benjamin
Peaks Hiram
Coffin F.
Henmann Everett
Brooks William
Richardson William *Oneonta.*
Mudge Rufus *Otego.*
Parish Ira & Reuben
Smith John
Horton Adam
Weidman & Laraway *Unadilla.*

Queens County.

Mott D. *Hempstead.*
Cornell Leonard
Sealey John, Millburn
Raynor Daniel, Raynor Town
Neal Robert, Foster's Meadow
Jamaica.
Johnson & Higbee, do
Comelee John, do

Rensselaer County.

Stevens E. *Grafton.*
Albertson P.
Baxter D. E.
Davidson P. K.
Shaver N.
Shaver J.
Snyder A.
Snyder G.
Worthington D. F.
Hayner A. P.
Tilly J.
M'Chesney J.
Maxson A. *Petersburgh.*
Knowlson, Butts & Horton
Sandlake.

Rockland County.

Eckerson J. Spring Valley
Orangetown.
Van Houtin P. P. do

St. Lawrence County.

Nevin David *Brasher.*
Nevin Benj. (shingles)
Hurlburd R. S. Brasher Falls
Buck Lemuel *Canton.*
Barrell Charles.
Parker & Jackson, Manley
Bottolph Ira, South Canton
Gibson Philo, do
Smith J. 2d, Richville *De Kalb.*
Rich M. & Co. do
Curtis Jonathan *Depeyster.*
Rushton Henry *Edwards.*
White William
Thomas A. South Edwards
Brown A. J. *Fine.*
Hosford W. D.
Fuller & Peck *Fowler.*
Sheldon & Co.
Hale Henry H.
Jenkins Calvin
Draper George
Frazier ——
Townsend John
Rose & Batchelder *Herman.*
Gardner John
Bennett ——
Evans George W.
Loop V.
Stokes J. L.
M'Collam J. D.
Hopkins I. R. *Hopkinton.*
Wilson Samuel
Peck Julius
Moon Jesse
Squier Asa
Lyman ——
Chittenden & Laughlin
Freeman Charles H.
Sprague & Culver
Briggs Henry *Lisbon.*
Flock Isaac Z.
M'Todder & Stockins
Doty B. T.
Redington G. (shingles) *Louisville.*
Kinyon Aseph L. *Macomb.*
Wicks Thomas, jr.
Houghton William P. & J.
Pope T. (shingles) Pope's Mills
Horton John, Columbia *Madrid.*
Atkinson, Osborne & Co. Wad-
dington
Chipman G. C. (shingles)
Orvis D. A. do
Orvis U. H. *Massena.*
Haskell Lemuel
Earl William A.
Robinson L. H.

Brower N. *Massena.*
Dodge William
Hitchcock William
Wheeler Sampson
Knapp O. S. (shingles)
Redington George, Lewisville
Church Wheeler *Morristown.*
Olds James
Conradt John
Robinson Eli
Vroman Simon
Krake P.
Blackstone Calvin
Webber & Co. (shingles) *Norfolk.*
Robinson & Co. do
Morgan Joel, dc
Morgan Sylvanus
Atwater & Putnam
Robinson M.
Webber J.
Brals N. F.
Hall I. E.
Hall G. J.
Fairchild E. N. (shingles) Og-
densburgh *Oswegatchie.*
Dix S. (shingles) Ogdensburgh
Adams A. & C. do do
Parish George, (shingles)
Lyon Charles
Lyon H. 2d, (planing machine)
Ogdensburgh
Northrop L. & Son, (shingles) do
Jones Ralph *Parishville.*
Allen Wm.
Woodward Lewis
Upton O.
Parish George
Cox Gardiner *Pierpont.*
Billings C. & Son (shingles)
Geer Lorenzo *Pitcairn.*
Green Asaph
Johnson Eleazer *Potsdam.*
Harmon Calvin
Hewitt Henry
Call John M.
Wilcox Abraham
Hamlin Pearl
Bibblus Erastus
Knowles Liberty, (shingles)
Bailey Alex. West Potsdam
Wright Warren, Buck's Bridge
Crary Edward, Crary's Mills
Billings Chileab, (shingles)
Smith B. *Russell.*
Robinson G.
Alger H.
Palmer J.
Whitmarsh D. (shingles)
Grandy J. *Stockholm.*
Nichols G. C.

Saratoga County.

Marvin Jas. & John *Charlton.*
Conner G. M.
Raymond J. F.
Valentine I. H. (shingles)
Callen Jas.
South Joseph
Davidson John, West Charlton
Higgins S. Jonesville *Clifton Park.*
Hagaman C. C. Vischer's Ferry
Peters Wm. A. do
Vischer Francis, do
Graves John S.
Wilson Elisha *Corinth.*
Sherman A. C. T.
Gang & English
Clother C. D.
Clother C. D. & A.
Fenton Doius
Edwards E.
Cook Ransom
Jackson Robert
Edwards John
Martin & Minor
White William B.
Ellsworth J.
Trumble E. (shingles)
Beecher Ely *Edinburgh.*
Cole A.
Hall B.

Marble Newton *Edinburgh.*
Gorden Edward W.
Barker I.
Matison H.
Mosher R. & Co. *Galway.*
Barber & Weit *Hadley*
Peck Hiram
Barber Z.
Gray Stephen
Wilkins David
M'Aran Hugh *Halfmoon.*
Usher John
Noxon Alfred
Laper & Oates
Flynn Samuel
Larkin N. West Milton *Milton*
Clute L. do
Whalen Seth, do
Taylor W. C. do
Rowland Hiram, do
Sill Enoch & Gurdon *Moreau.*
Newton D. S. & Co.
Price F.
Doty John, Gansevoort
Northumberland.
Doty Walter, Gansevoort
Banoas J. do
Ross H. do
Rose J. do
Pearsall A. H. do
Johnson William, do
Lewis Morgan, do
Vandewater W. do
Hagerdorn J *Providence.*
Fuller James
Case H. M.
Rockwell J. B.
Brown Stephen H.
Page David
Richardson John
Tabor Philip
M'Comber Allen
Hall C.
Brown James
Cadmoru George
Clark Wm. C.
Allen William
Woolsey & Co.
Cramer C. Schuylerville
Saratoga
Granger J. Victory
Rogers H. do
Arnold S. do
Savage James (Planing)
Saratoga Springs
Wing Charles *Stillwater*
Pruya Francis
Newland E.
Smith Elias

Schoharie County.

Ferguson Avery *Blenheim.*
Martin Alvin
Baldwin F.
Baldwin A.
Hyer Frederick
Hawver Henry *Broome.*
Russell John
Mattice Adam
Hiney John, jr. *Carlisle.*
Carr John
Brown J. J.
Kinakern Barney
Brown S.
Ferris Peter
Kinakern & Utman
Becker Philip
Riley A. B. *Cobleskill.*
Becker James
Becker H.
Steenburgh Marcus
Russell Nicholas
Lawyer Augustus
Bartner J.
Shaver George
Borst David
Richtmyer A. *Conesville.*
Hubbard Ira
Richtmyer Peter H. (shingles)
Foster S. Sloansville *Esperance.*
Casper William, do
Eders J. do

Buckingham James *Fulton.*
Driggs Burwell, Fultonham
Holiday Henry, do
Ferguson John, do
Driggs Alonzo, do
Burt & Ferguson, do
Haynes W. do
Haynes Henry, do
Decker Daniel, Breakabeen
Wing George, do
Bergh A. do
Bouck Lawyer, do
Sholtus John, do
Bergh Philip, do
Krum J. do
Brower B. do
Becker A. do
Bouck John, do
Haynes A. West Fulton
Billinger Jacob, do
Solsbury David, do
Spalding Samuel, do
Fox Angle, do
Watson Edward, do
Joslin Daniel, do
Harder Jacob, do
Tuttle & Son *Gilboa.*
Cornell John
Ruleffson R. W.
Shen J. H.
Whiting Charles
Matice William
Matice Peter V.
Brockaway Jesse *Jefferson.*
Hickok David
Avery John
Smith Benj.
Westover John *Richmondville.*
Mann Phillip
Fellers John
Sear Jacob
Shaver Peter T.
Smith William
Shaver Ezra
Breaker Judson
Mann David
Waldrof Jacob
Dox David
Helsinger ——
Moore John E.
Mann John
Westerhouse George
Warner J. D. & M. Warnerville
Warner Henry, do
Enders P. I. Central Bridge
 Schoharie.
Schaffur M. L & J. H.
Scharffers & Rickett
West J.
Griggs J. P.
Waterbury J. S.
Clark & Nethaway
Young Adam *Seward.*
Utman C.
Van Scoyck ——
Miller & Warner, Hyndsville
Hynds P. do
Saxton & Bly, do
Snyder Henry, do
Cropser J. *Summit.*
Baldwin Daniel
Colliton M.
Rider H. T.
Terpering D.
Herington A.
Sporbeck G. W.
Near Samuel
Boughton H. V.
Snook John
Scherry F.
Huffman Jacob
Adam W. H.
Beardsley G.
Domlack & Gordon, Gallupville
 Wright.
Becker G. do
Lampman E. do

Seneca County.

Wheeler, Bennett & Co. *Ovid.*
Bartlett Ebenezer S. *Romulus.*
Suttin Cyrus I.

Tillman A. P. *Seneca Falls.*
Klint William
Smith Isaac
Carter B. S.
Mosher & Hadley (staves & shingles) *Waterloo.*

Steuben County.

Otis F. *Avoca.*
Tilton D. & D.
Wilkinson C.
Rose H. S.
Rice O.
Squire S. W.
Waterbury S.
Tucker S. & A
Hallock & Cook *Bath.*
Rowe A.
Ellis C.
Peters H.
M'Kay T. M.
Monson, Merriman & Co. *Bradford.*
Mitchell & Co.
Hubbard A. *Cameron.*
Smith W. N.
Crocker W. R.
Hallett J. & N.
Dalrymple A.
Yost Marcy
Bates M. & A.
Brink John *Campbell.*
Fisk & Co.
Cole J.
Curtis Daniel
Taples George
Rowley John S. *Canisteo.*
Boyd R. R.
Scofield Lewis
Stevens N.
Paine L.
Crosby & Colverth
Burnham & Goff
Brown & Johnson
Breese A. B. *Caton.*
Benbee Grant
Cooley & Co.
Foster A. H.
Cleland James *Cohocton.*
Larrow & Henderson
Reynolds James
Davis M.
Hoag B. S.
Segor G. W.
Evans John
Larrowe F.
Trip Job
Haymond Daniel
Cronck Jackson
Cotton Ira *Dansville.*
Carrington Joel
Clark & Matthews
Ball & Co.
Blake G.
Perine & Locy
Cooper Judge *Erwin.*
Cobb Pliney
Corbin Alfred
Erwin Charles
Weston & Bronson
Birdsale H. H.
Beeman —— *Greenwood.*
Sevens A. H.
Davis Levi
Chadwick Joseph
Hart Charles *Hartsville.*
Ellison William
Bushkirk John
Whiting D. S.
Armstrong B. O. *Hornby.*
Morrow F. W.
Dickinson Andrew B.
Sample William
Davis Evan *Hornellsville.*
Lincoln William
Wilber Elisha
Morey & Shull
Marner & Howe
Morey & Millard
Hurlburt Christopher
Stevens J. B.
Magee H.

Mason J. *Hornellsville.*
Rice W. B. *Howard.*
Morrells T.
Goff William
Bennett M. S.
Purdy W. *Jasper.*
Brotyman A.
Graham George
Dalrymple & Co.
Ranson & Co. *Lindley.*
Smith S.
Middlebrook Morgan & Co.
Harrow B.
Merseroans J. G. & S. J.
Hutchinson Alvah *Orange.*
Vahe Joel & Co.
Butten T.
Webber Lorenzo
Miller John D.
Worden James
Snell Jacob
Hurl Uri
Hammond & Johnson *Painted Post.*
Gibson John (planing machine)
Wolcott & De Cost
Wheelock M. M.
Cutler James
Mallory Loren
Lombard J.
Stonnes Charles
French Dudley
Bailey B. F.
Bliss J. & W.
Brown Jonathan
Sly John
Mallory & Lyron (planing machine)
Gulick —— *Prattsburgh.*
Hopkins Henry
Sturtevant Joseph
Williams Ira C.
Higby Charles
Wheaton John
Williams John F. & Dinison
Avery J.
Waggoner M. *Pulteney.*
Waggoner Jacob
Hutches David
Williams James *Reading.*
Cass Mills
Baloom Lyman *Thurston.*
Rising Henry
Myer Rich
Babcock & Wheelock
Long John *Tyrone.*
Sunderlin Eli
Weller Charles
Randall Abel
Mitchell C. D.
Clark & Shefford
Randall J. & W. *Urbana.*
Baker Mrs. C.
Townsend Henry A.
Mitchell J. B. *Wayne.*
Birdseye John & Co.
Patchin Warren *Wayland.*
Whitmore A.
Hess John
Day E.
Bronson James
Stratton S. C.
Saxton Aaron
Hamlin John
Moore Chauncey
M'Cam John *West Union.*
Thorp John
Myers Peter
Dowd G. F. *Wheeler.*
Shot John
Wheeler G. H.
Smith E. H. *Woodhull.*
Parks A. & E.
Rosier S.
Hedges Isaac & W.
Hubbard Z.
Pomeroy P.
Gurnsey H.

Suffolk County.

Horton Daniel *Smithtown.*
Blydenburgh Isaac

Sullivan County.

Hill E., Hall J., & Smith S.
      Fallsburgh.
Beardsley E.
Lockwood Mrs.
Gardiner & Co. Barryville
      Lumberland.
Mills Horace, Bloomingburgh
Heart George, Burlingham

Tioga County.

Booth & Co.   *Candor.*
Sackett R. H.
Van Vleck J.
Smith W.
Robinson R. K.   *Rickford.*
Gee John H. & Co.
Cross Wm. & Co.

Tompkins County.

Sacket S. R.   *Enfield.*
Bortisk O.
Newman N
Curry S. R.
Miller Amos
Benedict A.   *Groton.*

Ulster County.

Otis S. & S.   *Shawangunk.*
Horabeck B. C.   *Wawarsing.*

Warren County.

Welch John   *Athol.*
M'Donald Alex
Adams Gardner
Cameron W. & N.
Aldrich David
Paschal Joseph
Kenyon J. S.
Barber N.
Kenyon Lyman
Frost Calvin
Hall H.
Hubell F.   *Caldwell.*
Roberts Charles
Fowler & Goodman, Chestertown
      Chester.
Weeks John H.   do
Leggatt Joseph W.   do
Thurston J. C. & S.   do
Mead H.   do
Mead L.   do
Baldwin John,   do
Green Charles S.   do
Howe & Cory, Pottersville *Hague.*
Bevins Alva
Cushman Joseph
Phillips Alonzo
Morse Alonzo
Cook Wm.
Ward Martin
Dunn John D.   *Johnsburgh.*
Armstrong Robert, jr.
Ross Hiram
Hitchcock Thomas W.
Morehouse Isaac & Samuel
Swift Sanford W.
Somervill Samuel
Roosevelt Nicholas
Washburn Joel F.
Graves Horatio
Barnes L. B.
Wells W. H.   *Luzerne.*
Spalding Alva
Furguson Joseph
Ostrum T. L.
Ferguson Wm.
Hall Ira
Foster Joseph
Van Luzen & Freeman
      Queensbury
Roberts David, Glenn's Falls
Hawley & Folsom,   do
Cheney & Arms,   do
Sherman A.   do
Wing Abraham,   do
Morgan & Eastwood do
Swartwout B. J. & Son, do

Russell & Griffin *Warrensburgh.*
Bishop J. W.
Werren N. J.
Burhans & Gray
Griffin Stephen
Richards G. & S. T.
Woodard John
Harrington Thomas
Bennett A. & C.
Millington L.
Stone Wm. B
Stone John

Washington County.

Brewster N. O. & Sons *Dresden.*
Barrett David
Pease Calvin
Burgess John
Reynolds L. A.
Barker Benajah   *Easton.*
Crandell Holder
Gale Frederick A. Galesville
Baker Amiel   *Fort Ann.*
Baker Wm.
Copeland B. & Son
Hopkins Julius
Howard John
M'Moore Chester
M'Moore Eleazer
Salmon Philander
Skinner Eli
Sloan James P.
Stevens Wm.
Stevens Wm. jr.
Stevens Wm. 2d
Thompson James
Thompson John
Vaughn Leonard
Vaughn Whitman
Washburn Adolphus
Woodruff E. & Son
Woodruff Simeon
Hodgeman F. D. *Fort Edward.*
Bradley & Underwood
Beach & Sherwood
Velie L. S. Fort Miller
Mowry William & Co. *Greenwich.*
M'Linn Aaron, Battenville
M'Neil William, East Greenwich
Allen Nathan   *Hampton.*
Reid James, W. Hebron *Hebron.*
Beverage John,   do
Zasset James,   do
Barckley William, do
Chamberlin Lewis, East Hebron
Sanford Kenyon, Parks & Co.
   Sandy Hill   *Kingsbury.*
Clark & Richards, Sandy Hill
Weeks R. H.   do
Taft Henry,   do
Baldwin J. P.   do
Kenyon Hiram,   do
Goodrich Gustavus A. *Putnam.*
Williams John   *Salem.*
Russell John & George
Stevens Henry
Law William
Martin J.

Wayne County.

Howland J.   *Arcadia.*
Van Inwagen, Fairville
Row Isaac,   do
Weaver & St. John, do
Crosine Simeon,   do
Hooker & Co.   do
Getchell E.   *Huron.*
Leighton Nathan
Merick Ira   *Lyons.*
Stanton Thomas
Hawley & Brothers
Ennis A. Alloway
Young & Moore
Boyce M.   *Marion.*
Cogdill Samuel
Wade W. G.   *Rose.*
Sergeant George   *Sodus.*
Messenger John
Sentell E. W. Sodus Point
Cook & Hill   do
Griffith David, Alton

Lawrence Isaac, Alton *Sodus*
Pierce Nathan   *Wolcott.*
Leavenworth & Hendrick

Westchester County.

Swains James P. *East Chester.*
Lee Thomas R. Croton Falls
      North Salem.
Finch Silas,   do
Copcutt John   *Yonkers.*

Wyoming County.

Yeomans Vine *Bennington.*
Delts C.
Gillett & Dudley
Brown L. Cowlesville
Potter & Matthews, do
Gilbert J.   *Covil*
Pierce G. F.
Sturdevant L
Parshall & Morse
Sprague P. C. *Covington.*
Everts Lorin
Miller W. W.
Whipple Elisha   *Eagle.*
Whaley M.
Watson J. S. Eagle Village
Williams George *Genesee Falls.*
Smith Michael
Wheeler Horace, Wyoming
      Middlebury
Mead Joseph   *Orangeville.*
Head & Butler
Griffin D.
Smith R. H.   *Perry.*
Davis G. L.
Winsor A.   *Pike.*
Griffith E. W.
Hendee ———, East Pike
Lillibridge W. East Koy
Wilder & Hodge, do
Clute N.   do
Baulky J.   *Sheldon.*
Thomas Ira
Tuttle R.
Brown Samuel, Varysburg
Raymond N. E.
Plant Ira P. Strykersville

Yates County.

Tewell & Woodmarth
      Barrington.
Lown John   *Jerusalem.*
Cole S.
Booth S. Branchport
Perry Benj. Rushville *Middlesex*
Walforce David, do
Gardner P. Yatesville *Potter.*

Macaroni & Vermicelli.

Costa John B. 69 Barclay
      New York.

Machinists, (See also Black-
smiths, also Boiler Makers,
also Iron Founders, also
Engine Builders, also
Printing Presses.)

Albany County.

Emery Horace L. 369 & 371 Bdwy.
      Albany.
Rodgers J. 33 & 35 Lumber st.
Vattell M. 4 Orange
Townsend F. & Co. cor. Hawk &
   Elk st.
Dwehle A. 15 & 17 Church
Jagger, Treadwell & Perry, 110
   Beaver
Pollard C. 160 State
Troy & Schenectady R. Road
   Machine Shop, Green Island,
   West Troy   *Watervliet.*
Rensselaer & Saratoga R. R. Ma-
   chine Shop

Alleghany County.

Morrison & Graves   *Angelica.*
Sherman D.   -   *Belfast.*

Broome County.

Overhiser B. H.   *Binghamton.*
Hotchkiss G.   *Windsor.*

Cattaraugus County.

Pope Angel, Rutledge *Conewango.*
Carter Egbert P.   *Yorkshire.*

Cayuga County.

Burdick O. H. Genesee st. *Auburn.*
Beardsley, Keeler & Curtis, State st.
Russell & Smith, State st.
Beach J. Weedsport   *Brutus.*
Carpenter R. B. do
Rockwell D.   *Cato.*
Birdsell & Stevens   *Genoa.*
Cook B.   *Ira.*
Stone & Kenyon   *Moravia.*
Keeler & Weight
Shourds & Mosher   *Venice.*

Chautauque County.

Vail H. (Engines) Mayville
   Chautauque.
Crosby T. Fredonia   *Pomfret.*
Soper D.   do

Chemung County.

Leach, Potter & Covell *Elmira.*
Sampson J. C.
Phillips & Wheeler

Chenango County.

Weller H. & Sons   *Norwich.*
Eccleston Ransom   *Oxford.*

Clinton County.

Goulding, Creen & Couse, Keeseville   *Au Sable.*

Columbia County.

Page P. E. Chatham 4 corners
   Chatham.
Wilsey J. (Sausage Cutting Machines)
Smith S. Smoky Hollow *Claverack.*
Whiting A. P. & Co. Mellenville
Perkins J. T. Hudson Machine Shop and Iron Works, cor. Columbia & Varick st.   *Hudson*
Kells P. H. Horse Power and Threshing Machines, State st.
Simonds G. B. Hudson & Berkshire R R. Repairing Shop
Reynolds R. Valatie *Kinderhook.*
Hanna & Carpenter, Valatie,

Cortland County.

Freer A. & S. D. *Cortland Village.*
Sanders Jacob   *Homer.*
Kehey Seth & Thomas E.. *Preble.*

Delaware County.

Bronson O.   *Franklin.*
Gerow J., Bloomville *Kortright.*

Duchess County.

Matteawan Mfg. Co. S. S. Howland, Pres., Wm. B. Leonard, Agt., $350,000 capital (Cotton & Woolen Machinery, Steam Engines, &c.) Matteawan *Fishkill.*
Forster R. 162 Main *Poughkeepsie.*
Adriance Coller & Barnes 234 Main
Foster C. cor. Mill & Duchess Av.
Germond E. Hart's Village
   Washington.
Swift A.   do

Erie County.

Durkee S. (Smut Machines) *Alden.*

Buffalo Steam Engine Works
   Buffalo.
Shephard John D. & Co. (Steam Engines) Ohio st.
Newman John (Boilers) Ohio st.
Monnin Chas. 42 Exchange
Bell & M'Nish, Norton st.

Essex County.

Ross Henry H. 2d *Willsborough.*

Franklin County.

Cass Wm.   *Malone.*
Lockwood A.

Fulton County.

Edwards John   *Ephratah.*
Edwards Henry

Genesee County.

Cowan & Webb   *Le Roy.*
Lay, Ganson & Co.   *Stafford.*

Greene County.

Purdy Milton A.   *Hunter.*
Lament Wilber   *Prattsville.*
Fench A. F.

Herkimer County.

Palmer Alias   *Frankfort.*
Ranney Hiram, Mohawk
   German Flats.
Tillinghast James   *Little Falls.*
Griffin W.   *Warren.*

Jefferson County.

Rogers C. W.   *Adams.*
Saunders M.
Getman Elias, Redwood
   Alexandria.
Lord William & Sons *Brownville.*
Skinner & Brothers
Forsyth James   *Cape Vincent.*
Woodruff Horace W. Watertown
   Pamelia.
Goulding George, Watertown
Howe Isaac, Black River
   Rutland.
Bastion Joseph   *Theresa.*
Wiley Nathaniel   *Watertown.*
Smith William
Scott Palmer & Son, (Iron Finishers) Carthage   *Wilna.*

Kings County.

Montgomery Robert, 30 Hamilton Av.   *Brooklyn.*
Borbeck Alexander & Son, Water near Fulton st.
Campbell Abraham, Adams near Water st.
M'Nary John, 198 Pearl
Jacobs C. S. Duffield st.
Binns James, Walworth st.
Waite Henry, N. 1st near 2d
   Williamsburgh.
Grimshaw George, 2½ North 2d

Lewis County.

Dow & Eames, Constableville
   West Turin.

Livingston County.

Sweet, Whitaker & Co. *Dansville.*
Gilman F. & M.
Late, Clement & Hudnutt
   Geneseo.
Durgee D. W. Lakeville *Livonia.*
Brown H. C.   *Mount Morris.*
Bell Alfred   *Nunda.*
Smith H. E. Fowlersville *York.*

Madison County.

Shapley M. W. & J. *Cazenovia.*
Nichols M. S.
Buel William B. (Threshing Machines)

Coin Sylvester, (Threshing Machines)   *Cazenovia.*
Cook S. S.   (do)
Ward Spencer B.   (do)
Van Zant S.   (do)
Wood E. & Co.   *Eaton.*
Grannis Henry, Morrisville
Wheaton, Kasson & Burt, Oneida Depot   *Lenox.*
Carey James (Wood Machinist)
   Sullivan.
Beebe James   (do)
Hazeltine E.   (do)
Walrath Daniel, Chittenango

Monroe County.

Smith B. F. (Woollen) Mill st.
   Rochester.
Swift Asa R. 69 S. St. Paul st.
Gordon Charles & Co. 68 S. St. Paul st.
Hitchcock S. S. (Sugar Mills) Main st.
Hall Joseph, (Manuf. Threshing Machines & Grain Separators,) Water st.
Pitts John A. (Manuf. of Pitts' Patent Premium Threshing Machine and Double Pinion Horsepower and Corn and Cobb Mill) 68 S. St. Paul st.
Snooks Thomas, (Fire Engines) Brown's Race
Duryee & Forsyth, (Manufacturers of Scales, Sugar Mills, Copying Presses & Store Trucks,) 16 Water st.
Colby John, rear 3 Buffalo st.
Braman T. & 4 Curtis Block, Main st.
Bruce Alexander, 29 Front
Lawton Wm. H. (Sash and Blind Machinery) 6 Selye Buildings
Rivers John, 8   do
Kenyon & Angell, 2 & 3 Selye Buildings, cor. Furnace & Mill
Sibley Joseph, (Manufacturer of Bradfield's Patent Bran Dusters) 4 Furnace st. Selye Buildings
Strong George, 1 Furnace st.
Jones S. C. & E. Brown's Race foot of Furnace st.
Blair James, (Threshing) Mumford   *Wheatland.*

Montgomery County.

Potter & M'Elwane   *Amsterdam.*
Chase Welcome U. & Cyrus B.
Harvey John M. & Son
Bingham Ames F., Ames
   Canajoharie.
Ehle David, Fort Plain *Minden.*
Conklin D. R. H. do
Blanchard Richard, Fonda
   Mohawk.
Hughes W. E. (Stave) do

New York County.

Alsop John, 222 W. 16th
   New York.
Atkins James, 72 Bowery
Austin Frederick J. 23 Centre
Ayres Samuel P. 174 & 176 Rivington
Baird Samuel, 57 Leonard
Ballard William, 7 Eldridge, Manufactory No. 11 Eldridge near Division
Bartholf Abm. 44 Gold
Berckhemer & Besseller, rear 96 Cliff
Bogardus James, 40 Eldridge
Brandt Lauritz, 220½ 5th
Bryant Samuel, 97 Columbia
Bullock S. W. 27 S. William
Cary Luther, 96 Forsyth
Cole A. & G. H. 129 Amos
Cook W. G. 160 Fulton
Cox William A. 43 Duane
Dunham & Browning, 100 North Moore

Esler & Bunce, 26 Washington & 17 West   *New York.*
Ewing George, 438 Broome
Fitzgerald Jesse. 79 Chrystie
Fraser John, 172½ Chambers
Freeland Aaron M. 87 Mangin
Gee George, 45 Eldridge
Gein Frederick, 105 3d Av. —
Gerow & M'Creary, 335 Stanton
Glass John. 104 Goerck
Gorden & Ray, 402 Water
Hall A. 13 Doyer
Harston George B. & Co. 58 & 60 Vesey
Henerre Wm. C. 85 Duane
Hitchings A. E. 145 10th
Hoe R. & Co. 29 Gold & Broome cor. Sheriff
Homer Henry, 90 Ann
Hooper W. G. Mangin nr. Stanton
Hunt Walter, 42 Gold
Johnson A. & H. 115 Charlton
Jones John, 54 Centre
Kingsley John L. rear 59 Ann
Leonard W. B. 66 Beaver
Lewis Charles, rear 105 Reade
Lewis W. & W. H. 142 Chatham
M'Cartney James, 8 Gold
M'Collum Henry, 40 Eldridge
Mathews John, 91 Fulton
Milligan W. E. 115 Warren
Mills John. 44 Av. D
Morgen James, 306 Stanton
Mott & Ayres, foot 25th st. N. R.
Mulden T. & J. 14 Frankfort
Nind James, 67 & 69 Forsyth
Nixon J. C. 44 Chatham
Ostrander Jonathan, r. 58 Mercer
Pease & Murphy, 506 Cherry
Perley Chas. 114 Columbia
Perret Lucien, 95 Cliff
Perry Alonzo, 230 Cherry
Perry James, 87 Eldridge
Perry Peter, rear 230 Cherry
Phillips George. 172 Chambers
Pourchot Frederick, 24 Frankfort
Prentice & Page, 119 Walker
Rogers, Ketchum & Grosvenor, 74 Broadway
Roth George, 102 Reade
Ruet Frederick, 44 Rose
St. John James, rear 97 Forsyth
Sapin Augustus, 41½ Thomas
Schenck Isaac V. 172 Elm
Schenck John A. 6 Howard
Schwingrouber Louis, 26 Reade
Seatman George, 94 Murray
Seyer Querin, 197 William
Sheridan Bernard, 45 Ann
Sherwood & Fitzgerald, 122½ Fulton
Sloan Thomas J. foot E. 25th
Smith Josiah M. 61 Elizabeth
Smith, Ransom & Co, do
Snediker Frazee E. 123 & 125 Attorney
South Charles J. 258 William
Steel John & Co. 508 Water
Stewart James, 15 Canal
Stillman, Allen & Co. foot 13th st. East River
Stone James, 290 Broadway
Taylor A. B. & Co. 3 Hague
Taylor & Moore, 176 William
Waterman Henry, 239 Cherry
Webb Philander. 59 & 61 Goerck
West & Thompson, 29 Centre
Worrall & Co. 26 & 28 Elm & 67 Duane

Niagara County

Hildreth G. W.   *Lockport.*
Pound Alexander
Cooper Wm. E.
Torrance Asher, (steam engines)
Dotey, Ford & Co. *Niagara Falls.*

Oneida County.

Alcott J. S. & A. & Oriskany Falls *Augusta.*

Wood, Dane & Co.   *Camden.*
Elmer E., Delta   *Lee.*
Rogers, Spencer & Co. (Willow Vale works, Washington Mills, cotton & woollen machinery— amount per annum $75,000, men 65)   *New Hartford.*
Pettee A. E., Clayville   *Paris.*
Miller L. & Son. (cotton & woollen machinery,) Clayville
Seymour & Adams, Dominick st.   *Rome.*
Seabury & Barnum, Waterville *Sangersfield.*
Parker G. W., South   *Trenton.*
Bushnell J. 36 Seneca   *Utica.*
Curtis Philo C. (steam engines) cor. Pine & Canal
Bagg, Roberts & Co. Cornelia st.
Bailey, Wheeler & Co. Columbia st.
Higham & Co. cor. Whitesboro & Fayette
Seymour & Brothers, Hampton- *Westmoreland.*
Terwilliger F. & Co. Whitesboro *Whitestown.*
Buel A. & Co. Walesville

Onondaga County.

Daggett E. Jordan   *Elbridge.*
Joslyn D.   *Fabius.*
Humphrey H., Baldwinsville *Lysander.*
Gaiety & Rogers,   do
Congden & Van Allen, Baldwinsville
M'Culloch & Higbee, Water st. Syracuse   *Salina.*
Deok, Herrick & Co. Washington st. Syracuse
Davis G. Water st. Syracuse
Alexander W. H. & Co. Water st. Syracuse
Olds Henry, (horse powers) Water st. Syracuse
Powell A. C., Fulton Foundry, Syracuse
Delano Howard   *Skaneateles.*

Ontario County.

Wilson Chapin   *Manchester.*
Johnson Joan R. Geneva   *Seneca.*
Burrell E. J.   do

Orange County.

Wiley A. P.   *Cornwall.*
Stanton, Clark & Co. (steam engines)   *Newburgh.*

Orleans County.

Bathgate G., Medina   *Ridgeway.*
Clenant J. & J. do

Oswego County.

Tallcott D. & Son, 1st st. *Oswego.*
Springer Wm. P. (smut machines) Crocker's Buildings, Bridge st.
Boigeal J. & Co. 2d c. Bridge
Snow & Dodge, Pulaski *Richland.*
Dewey Samuel. South Richland
Thayer A. J., Fulton   *Volney.*
Sisson Wm.   do
Dutton John E.   do

Otsego County.

Mulkins E.   *Laurens.*
Reed Jeremiah M. (threshing machines)   *Middlefield.*
Shipman O. N.   *Springfield.*
Hubbell Hiram   *Unadilla.*

Queens County.

Gerome G. F. Hempstead Branch *North Hempstead.*

Rensselaer County.

Phillips H. (threshing machines) *Brunswick.*

Wilder L. & Co.   *Hoosick.*
White & Wood
Wheeler J.   *Nassau.*
Smith Thomas
Haight H. East Nassau
Langdon John C. 9 Jacob   *Troy.*
Davis S. 9 Liberty
Rogers J. F. Adams n. River
Marshall & Tompkins, Ida Hill
Wells Z. 506 River
Hale S. River n. State dam
Richardson & Taft, do
Richmond Galen,   do

Rockland County.

N. Y. & Erie R. R. Machine shop, John Brandt Superintendent, Piermont   *Orangetown.*

St. Lawrence County.

Savage H. C.   *Canton.*
Loomis & Wright, Columbia *Madrid.*
Wickins John, Waddington
Chaney A. & Co. Ogdensburgh *Oswegatchie.*
Alden A. E. & W. C. do
Goulding Hiram   *Potsdam.*
Goulding John
Smith & Chandler

Saratoga County.

Burnham J. D.   *Halfmoon.*
Hopkins & Dix, Glenn's Falls *Moreau.*
M'Comber Joseph   *Providence.*
Platt Wm. & Co. (stock & dies & universal chuck)   *Waterford.*
Gage Geo. (printing presses)
Eddy G. W. (double pints R. R. wheel)
Button L. (fire engines)
Brooks Wm. & Co.
Gosline Wm. (rope machines)
King J. M. & Co. (stock & dies)

Schenectady County.

Pilling, Conde & Co. State st. *Schenectady.*

Schoharie County.

Gardiner Jacob J.   *Esperance.*
Westerhouse Geo., Central Bridge (threshing machines) *Schoharie.*

Seneca County.

Osgood Hiram   *Ovid.*
Pinney & Clapp, Farmer
La Fourette & Vail   *Waterloo.*

Steuben County.

Horn Lewis L.   *Addison.*
Corning & Co.   *Painted Post.*

Tompkins County.

Tremans & Brother, (Cascadilla Iron & Machine Works) Factory Hill   *Ithaca.*
Conrad V. (steam engines, &c. Aurora st.
Crequa John & Co. Trumansbur'h *Ulysses.*
Spink & Co.

Ulster County.

Baldwin J. W. & Co.   *Kingston.*
Stone D. C. Nepanock *Wawarsing.*

Washington County.

Eddy & Co. (threshing machines) Union Village   *Easton.*
Hudson River Iron Machine Co. Russell Hickok Agent, Simeon Mears Tress. (machinery of all kinds)   *Fort Edward.*
Northup N. C. & Son, Sandy Hill *Kingsbury.*

Holbrook Lyman, Sandy Hill
     Kingsbury.
Summers John,   do
Holbrook N. W.   do
Lord Samuel   *Salem.*
Seavey Robert
Darby L., North   *White Creek.*
Scott E. William st.   *Whitehall.*
Sherman S. M. & J. William st.

Wayne County.

Daggett J. Newkirk   *Arcadia.*
Olmsted Millard, Clyde   *Galen.*
Taft Newell   *Lyons.*
Barber G. S.
Brewster Henry   *Marion.*
Atwater Benjamin
Williams & Sanford, (threshing &
  carding)   *Palmyra.*
Hildreth S. (threshing & carding)
Benedict Ira,   do
Daggett D. F.   do
Holmes Myron   *Sodus.*

Westchester County.

Rikeman & Seymour, Peekskill
      Courtlandt.
Finch R. R. & Co. Peekskill

Wyoming County.

Grannis H. & Co.   *Attica.*
Otis Marvin   *Perry.*
Hicks E.
Hodge M.   *Pike.*
Hard Chester   *Warsaw.*
Norris Wm. H
Utter Isaac

Yates County.

Jones E. B. (ploughs, stoves, &c.)
     Penn Yan *Milo.*
Stebbins F. A. do   do
Cooley James, do   do
Ferrier R., Dundee   *Starkey.*
Bylington ——, do

Magazines. (*See also News-papers.*)

American Agriculturist, C. M.
  Saxton, 121 Fulton *New York.*
American Flora, Green & Spencer, 67 Bowery
American Whig Review, monthly. 118 Nassau
Baptist Memorial, Zephania P.
  Hatch, 139 Nassau.
Biblical Repository, J. M. Sherwood. 120 Nassau
Blackwood's, L. Scott & Co. publishers. 54 Gold
Braithwaite's (Medical) Retrospect, Daniel Adee, 107 Fulton
Christian Union, Rev. R. Baird, 139 Nassau
Christian Parlor Magazine, Geo.
  Pratt. 116 Nassau
Covenant, Paschal Donaldson, 1
  Spruce
Cultivator, Mark H. Newman &
  Co. 199 Broadway
Democratic Review, J. W. Moore,
  170 Broadway
Downing's Horticulturist, M. H.
  Newman & Co. 199 Broadway
Dwight's American Magazine, T.
  D. Dwight. 232 Broadway
Eclectic Magazine, William H.
  Bidwell, 20 Nassau
Edinburgh Quarterly Review, L.
  Scott & Co. publishers, 54 Gold
Evergreen, H. M. Onderdonk
  publisher, 161 Fulton
Family Circle & Parlor Annual,
  Annaiannah Newell. 126 Nassau
Godey's Ladies' Book, Dewitt &
  Davenport, 154 Nassau
Graham's Magazine, Wm. H. Graham, Brick Church Chapel

Holden's Magazine, Charles W.
  Holden. 109 Nassau *New York.*
Illustrated Natural History, Green
  & Spencer. 67 Bowery
Knickerbocker, Samuel Hueston,
  139 Nassau
Ladies' National Magazine. Dewitt & Davenport. 154 Nassau
Ladies' Wreath, Martin Neely,
  143 Nassau
London Lancet. Stringer & Townsend. 222 Broadway
London Quarterly Review. L.
  Scott & Co. publishers. 54 Gold
Massachusetts Quarterly Review,
  154 Nassau
Merchant's Magazine & Commercial Review, Freeman Hunt,
  142 Fulton
Merry's Museum, Duncan M'Donald & Co. 149 Nassau
Mothers' Journal, Robert Sewell.
  116 Nassau
Mothers' Magazine, Myron Finch,
  118 Nassau
National Preacher, J. M. Sherwood. 120 Nassau
North British Review, L. Scott &
  Co. publishers, 54 Gold
Phrenological Journal, Fowlers &
  Wells. 131 Nassau
Sartain's Union Magazine, 154
  Nassau
Scalpel. Borford & Co. Astor h.
Sears' Pictorial, Robert Sears, 128
  Nassau
Southern Literary Messenger, Dewitt & Davenport, 154 Nassau
Water Cure Journal, Fowlers &
  Wells. 131 Nassau
Westminster Review, L. Scott &
  Co. publishers. 54 Gold
World as it Moves. James L. Lockwood & Co. 459 Broadway
Youths' Cabinet, D. Austin Woodworth, 131 Nassau

Magnetic Machines.

Morehead David C. 132 Broadway
      New York.
Smith Samuel B. 293 Broadway

Magnetizer.

Hayes Geo. 111 Spring *New York.*

Mahogany Dealers. (*See also Lumber Dealers.*)

Kings County.

Duryee J. & N. W. Columbia near
  Atlantic   *Brooklyn.*
Smith E. & A. 206 Nassau
Stimmons Benjamin M. 153 1st
     Williamsburgh.

New York County.

Applegate Joseph, 154 Mulberry
      New York.
Bate John H. 118 Walker
Brower A. & J. V. 264 Washington
Bruce James, 371 Washington
Bussell George. 733 Houston
Bussell Richard, 201 Bowery
Cartereau Peter. 34 Harrison
Copcut J. & F. 348 Washington
Dawson Jacob H. 273 Cherry
Duryee Jacob, 577 Water
Duryee & Allen, 548 do
Fletcher Joseph, 93 Essex
Gilchrist J. 432 & 434 Washington
Gsell Charles. 93 Eldridge
Hawes & Graham, 176 & 178 Centre
Hollands Ferdinand, 66 Broad
Houghton E. & C. W. 90 Walker

Julian Michael F. 236 Front
      New York.
Labatut John, 137 Ludlow
Labatut J. M. J. 108 Walker
Lowerre George W. 139 Centre
Meller Peter. 263 Division
Merry Calvin H. 403 Washington
Miller Peter. 263 Division
Ogden Moses H. 43 Elizabeth
Ogden & Co. 392 Washington
Phillips J. W. 324 Cherry
Price Thomas, 129 & 131 Attorney
Roach P. R. 135 Bank
Steffen Jacob. 773 Stanton
Trimbles John. 12 3d Av.
Vanderpool Jacob. jr. 2d Cherry
Van Pelt J. W. & Co. 42 Mercer
Williams Daniel. 276 5th
Williams & Smith, 330 Washington
Williams John. 559   1o
Young Waldron, 541 Water

Tompkins County.

Demming F. 79 Owego   *Ithaca.*

Mahogany Knob Manufacturers. (*See also Knob Manufacturers.*)

M'Intire Charles H. 304 Hudson
      New York.

Maltsters.

Jones David, 125 & 127 Broome
      New York.
Kitching George. 116 Broad
Lawrence William & Co. 28th
  near 10th Av.
M'Locklan A. 30 Commerce
Mahn C. rear 78 Elizabeth
Ruppert F. 225 3d
Tweddle John. jr. 41 Barclay &
  Broome cor. Tompkins

**Manufacturers' Articles.—
Cotton and Woolen Machinery, Geerings, Findings, &c.** (*See also Machinists.*)

Andrews & Jesup, 70 Pine (see advertisement.)   *New York.*
Kennedy & Gelston, 5½ Pine
Leonard Peter A. 66 Beaver
Schenck Oscar & Co. 132 Water
Smith Clark P. 71 Liberty
Washburn Delphos, 17 Platt
Whittemore G. & H. 13 do
Whittemore John & Co. 246 Pearl

Oneida County.

Williams A. J. 215 Genesee *Utica.*
Warner J. E. & Co. 22 & 24 do

Maps and Charts.

Colton Joseph H. 86 Cedar
      New York.
Disturnell John, 102 Broadway
Ensign & Thayer, 50 Ann
Raynor Thomas, 367½ 6th Av.
Tanner Henry S. 238 Broadway
Wilson Richard J. 122   do

Map and Chart Finishers.

Dorah Thomas, 4 City Hall place
      New York.
Ensign & Thayer, 50 Ann

Marble Dealers. *(See also Marble Workers.)*

Erie County.

Belden Dexter, (see advertisement) cor. Terrace & Erie sts. *Buffalo.*
Vail George O. & Co. cor. Water & Ship Canal

New York County.

Godfrey Edward J. 384 6th *New York.*
Griffin James C. 265 West
Rice Julius H. 265 do
Robertson James, cor. Rivington & Attorney
Wakeman Hull, E. 23d bet. 3d & 4th Avs.

Saratoga County.

Hopkins H. K. L. Glaßn's Falls *Moreau.*
Rier J. H. do

Marble—Importers of.

Franklin Selim & Co. 21 New *New York.*
Mirandoli Edward, 66 Front

Marble Workers.

Albany County.

Dixon John. 36 Howard *Albany.*
Morrell R. 16 Columbia
Wall D. 64 Herkimer
Kenney T. K. 232 State
Ford H. M., W. Troy *Watervliet.*

Alleghany County.

Clark & Chaffe *Angelica.*
Byrns Henry *Belfast.*
Moore R. A.
Duff Charles *Wirt.*

Broome County.

Congden & Whiting *Binghamton.*

Cayuga County.

Keyes W. J. 31 Genesee *Auburn.*
Rajsh A. North st.

Chautauque County.

Hough N. Jamestown *Ellicott.*
Underhill Asa, do
Sikes Hiram *Westfield.*

Chenango County.

Lyon Reuben *Norwich.*
Allen A. P.
Webb George *Sherburne.*

Clinton County.

Ackley Horace *Peru.*
Lasell J. *Plattsburgh.*

Columbia County.

M'Arthur C. *Hudson.*
Nicholson William
Hitchcock E. N. Warren st.

Cortland County.

Morse Philo P. *Cortland Village.*
Sweet Eber *Virgil.*

Duchess County.

White Wm. A. (Quarries near Dover Furnace) *Dover.*
Massy E. (Preston's Marble Quarries) South Dover

Ketcham J. E. (Quarry, Dover Plains) *Dover.*
Allyn G. H. *Fishkill.*
Tilton & Nelson *Poughkeepsie.*

Erie County.

Todd A. Williamsville *Amherst.*
Belden D. (see advertisement) cor. Terrace & Erie *Buffalo.*
Thompson James. 19 East Seneca
Huntington Jacob G. 157 Main
Cleaveland Henry, 3 West Swan
Austin ——, Water Valley *Hamburgh.*

Genesee County.

Fellows & Co. *Batavia.*
Starr Orrin *Le Roy.*
Gorton C. L.

Herkimer County.

Brown J. F. Ilion *German Flats.*
Morse E. H. Mohawk

Jefferson County.

Ferrin F. M. *Adams.*
Gray M. A. Woodville *Ellisburgh.*
Stockwell E. S. *Theresa.*

Kings County.

O'Hara Peter, cor. Court & Schernerhorn sts. *Brooklyn.*
Thompson & O'Hara, 200 & 202 Atlantic
Rampper F. A. (U. S. Marble Yard) Court st. cor. Dean
Hobby & Hull, 56 Grand *Williamsburgh.*
Fisher & Brennard, (Long Island Works) 213 2d

Lewis County.

Carley Nathaniel R. *Diana.*

Livingston County.

Raish John *Dansville.*
Smith & Prussia
Manley Z. H. *Geneseo.*
Merrick J. N. *Lima.*
Stroud C. J. Hemlock Lake *Livonia.*
Sadd G. F. *Nunda.*

Madison County.

Parmelee Moses *Cazenovia.*
Case Newton *Hamilton.*

Monroe County.

Hubbard Z. & Sons, 78 South st. Paul *Rochester.*
Allen & Myrick, cor. Buffalo & Sophia
Johnson & Morgan, 94 State
Brown Wm. C. 144 State
Harmon A. Main st. Brockport *Sweden.*

Montgomery County.

Hard Cyrenias *Canajoharie.*

New York County.

Boyle & Lauder, 56 E. 13th *New York.*
Brown P. A. 9th Av. bet. 30th & 40th
Brown R. I. 354 & 360 Greenwich
Derr Henry, 602 Greenwich & 376 West
Dillaway Geo. W. 157 W. 20th;
Dudley & Sea. 594 Hudson
Eagleson T. R. 143 Division
Ferris John H. 372 Greenwich
Fisher & Bird, 297 Bowery & 79 4th

Flannelly Manus, rear 429 12th *New York.*
Flannelly Michael, 786 B'dway
Godfrey Edward J. 384 6th
Gori Ottaviano, 893 Broadway
Hart Felix, 377 6th
Hart James. jr. 106 1st Av. & 417 Greenwich
Henry & Meeghan 90 1st
Hull Wm. E. 23d st.
Lenghi Moses G. 113 E. 18th
Lippett J. F. 602 Greenwich
M'Intire Thomas, 219 6th Av.
M'Loughlin Peter, 97 & 99 6th Av.
Morris Stephen P. 24 Mercer & 166 Centre
Oatwell Joseph, 891 Broadway & E. 19th st.
O'Neil Chas. & J. 156 Greenwich
Pattison William, 417 do
Rankin William, 359 do
Raynolds John, 544 Hudson
Robertson James, 176 Rivington
Smith Daniel, 28 Attorney
Stegagnini L. rear 181½ Franklin
Swezey Nelson, 31 4th Av.
Thorp Z. & Son, 113 E. B'dway
Trowbridge A. B. foot E. 25th
Witzel William, 39 Washington
Young & Geraghty, 86 2d Av.

Niagara County.

Field & Dunkelburgh *Lockport.*

Oneida County.

Salladin J. N. *Camden.*
Crandall H. James st. *Rome.*
Crandall H. 23 Bleeker *Utica.*
Allyn & Sykes, Oriskany *Whitestown.*

Onondaga County.

Cobb I. H. Salina st. Syracuse *Salina.*
Stanton & Merritt, do
Reckley Christopher, Genesee st.

Ontario County.

Sterling Philip W. *Canandaigua.*
Sutton Daniel *Phelps.*
Fleming Amos, Geneva *Seneca.*

Orange County.

Mulligan Thomas, Salisbury Mills *Blooming Grove.*
Watson Robert *Goshen.*
Young T. S. & Co , Ridgebury *Minisink.*
Niven & Miller, Front st. *Newburgh.*
Corwin & Preston, South Middletown *Wallkill.*

Orleans County.

Field Spafford, Albion *Barre.*
Field Spafford, Medina *Ridgeway.*

Oswego County.

Stuart A. Bridge st. *Oswego.*

Otsego County.

Hull & Jennings (dealers) *Unadilla.*

Queens County.

Hall John R. *Hempstead.*
Hull Gideon *Jamaica.*

Rensselaer County.

Raiter John, 267 State *Lansingburgh.*
Golden G. D. cor. State & 5th *Troy.*
Dickerman J. 37 Ferry

St. Lawrence County.

Giles A. *Fowler.*

Whitney H. W. & Co. Washington st. Ogdensburgh *Oswegatchie.*
Woodruff & Brundage *Potsdam.*

Saratoga County.

Whipple Joel *Saratoga Springs.*
Broughton Charles *Stillwater.*

Schoharie County.

Brown Z. J. *Schoharie.*

Seneca County.

Racish A. *Seneca Falls.*

Suffolk County.

Lockwood John *Huntington.*
Hill George & Co. *Riverhead.*

Tioga County.

Shepard & Osborn *Spencer.*

Ulster County.

Pool F. W. *Kingston.*

Warren County.

Roberts David, Marble Factory, Glenn's Falls *Queensbury.*

Washington County.

Collins M. Canal st. *Whitehall.*

Wayne County.

Mead H. C. & W. W. *Lyons.*
Myrick A. G. *Palmyra.*

Wyoming County.

Farnham Freak C. *Attica.*

Yates County.

Sutton John, Penn Yan *Milo.*
Morrison B. J. do
Gustin Moses, Dundee *Starkey.*

Masons. (*See also Grate setters, also Builders.*)

Bains James, 45 Ann *New York.*
Baldwin Abner W. 173 Mulberry
Bennett William, 351 Front
Brush George F. 87 Greenwich Av.
Buckland William, 87 Hammond
Carter John, 62 Oliver
Coffin J. & J. B. 243 4th & 62 E. 14th
Collins Daniel, 42 Laurens
Cook E. L. 83 Suffolk
Crussell Walter, 279 W. 19th
Davis Thomas, 596 Grand
Davis William, 47 Roosevelt
Donahoe Andrew, 16 Orange
Eldridge Richard, 157 Duane
Feldar Robert D. 238 3d Av.
Fielding Stephen, 228 Wooster
Fitzpatrick Charles, 114 Bleecker
Fletcher P. 17 Oak
Frazee & Pierson, 193 11th
Geraghty John, rear 29 Cross
Gore Francis, 129 Orange
Hart James, 417 Greenwich
Hamilton Wm. 216 Mercer
Harrison E. C. 216 do
Huson R. 32 2d Av.
Kelly John, 140 Elizabeth
Kinsey James, 57½ Great Jones
Lane John, 80 Dey
LeCount Joseph, 133 E. B.way
Locker Thomas, 88 Division
Martin John J. 112 Av. C
Miller J. & E. 167 Greenwich
Moore W. H., E. 26th st.
Morris Peter, 112 Delancy
Moses Lorenzo, 316 W. 26th
Mulhern Thomas, 83 6th Av.
Murthar John, 296 6th Av.
Neville H. 300 8th Av.

Osborn Lewis K. 172 Orchard *New York.*
Packer John, 623 Broadway
Perine John P. 151 Varick
Post Abraham, 134 W. Broadway
Quinn E. H. 68 & 70 Nassau
Reid Simon A. 196 Greene
Secor Samuel, jr. 160 10th
Sheridan F. 6 Stanton
Timpson Thomas, jr. 8 Prince
Van Note William & Henry, 41 Greene
White A. & J. 62 M'Dougal
Wickes Thomas, 219 Cherry
Wilson & Edward, E. 16th corner Av. A
Wright William, 136 Hammond

Mats and Rugs.

Kings County.

Giles & Andrews, Kent Av. near DeKalb st. *Brooklyn.*

New York County.

Ashmore & Pierson, r. 79 Laurens *New York.*
Darragh & Law, 93 6th Av.
Dignans F., W. 20th bet. 5th & 6th Avs.
Finigan John, 496 Cherry
Law Nathaniel B. 51½ Carmine
M'Alister James, 7 Perry
Taylor William, 43 Perry

Match Makers.

Cattaraugus County.

Knapp A. *Perrysburgh.*

Chenango County.

Brown E. & D. *Oxenic.*

Essex County.

Chase Stephen, Moriah Four Corners *Moriah.*

Herkimer County.

Gates William, jr. *Frankfort.*

New York County.

Bentz Jacob, 104 Norfolk *New York.*
Golsh Alfred, 3 Cortlandt
Hyatt Theodore, 87 Barclay & 49d bet. 9th & 10th Avs.
Lacour M. 2d Av.
Partridge Charles, 2 Cortlandt
Stephens John I. 119 Attorney
Stevens John H. 114 Allen

Onondaga County.

M'Donald P. Water st. Syracuse *Salina.*

Rensselaer County.

Blass John, cor. 9th & Hoosick *Troy.*
Patrick W. 94 6th
Priest R. Fulton st.

Wyoming County.

Jennison F. *Warsaw.*

Mattress and Bed Makers.

New York County.

Baird David, 237 Hudson *New York.*
Boorman C. 116 Fulton
Brown John, 3 James
Davis H. N. 123 Fulton
Forster James, 222 & 206 Fulton

Hall Daniel K. 161½ Chatham *New York.*
Hall Moses C. 159 Chatham
Halsey Samuel F. & Co. 62 Vesey
Hotaling A. & C. K. 196 Greenwich & 344 Hudson
Irish & Hayward, 54 Mercer
Lockwood Hiram & Smith, 202 Hudson
Martin E. 195 Canal
Marten M. 99 W. Broadway
Mellen A. & Co. 1 Mott
Murphy Thos. 112 E. Broadway
Parker & Ritter, 158 Greenwich
Patterson George, 48 E. Broadway
Pomroy Harriet, 308 Division
Turner William S. 112 Chatham
Willard M. 150 Chatham
Williams & Co. 200 Pearl, (Tow & Corn Husk Depot.)

Measures—Grain.

Monroe County.

Osgood Silas, Parma Corners *Parma.*

St. Lawrence County.

Beecher George C. *Stockholm.*

Saratoga County.

Rospeth R. B. *Providence.*
Smith R. V.
Page D.

Measure Tapes.

Ashe W. A. 127 Fulton *New York.*
Eddy John W. & Geo. M. 18 Platt

Measurers—Grain.

Acker A. 86 West *New York.*
Barr M. 90 Av. B
Cahoon Robert, 15 South
Cahoon William M. 15 South
Farnham George, 126 Broad
Ferres Samuel J. 126 Broad
Geary Daniel, 21 Coenties slip
Halsted James, 21 do
King George, 21 do
Langdon Ananias, 190 Broad
Luke Andrew, 21 Coenties slip
Malthy James W. 120 Broad
Marvin Jesse, 21 Coenties slip
Miller H. A. 120 Broad
Neefus Cornelius, 196 Broad
Osborn William, 15 South
Read William B. 190 Broad
Reman Cyrus, 15 South
Rosevelt Jacob, 126 Broad
Smith Orsamus T. 15 South
Timpson T. S. 21 Coenties slip
Vaughan Richard, 15 South
Welsh A. R. 21 Coenties slip

Melting Houses.

Butchers' Melting Association, 75 & 77 1st Av. *New York.*
Hull, Wager & Son, 181 Elizabeth

Merchants—Commission.

(*See also Dry Goods Commission Merchants ; also Grocers Wholesale ; also Merchants General ; Merchants Shipping and Commission ; Merchants Importing and Commission ; Merchants Forwarding and Commission ; also Merchants Produce Commission.*)

Albany County.

Aiken E. C. (produce) 87 Quay *Albany.*
Ainsworth & Northrup, 15 State

Arthur & Lyman, 62 Quay
Albany.
Barrett & Brown, 31 & 33 Quay
Bentley C. W. (produce) 87 Quay
Bulkley & Crapo, 50 Exchange
Chapman & Savage, 121 Pier
Craft B. F. (produce) 115 Pier
Crapo Wm. & Co. 17 State
Davis William, 11 State
Dorr & Englehart. (prod.) 31 Quay
Durant E. A. & Co. do   120 Pier
French & Stevenson, do   do
Gay George. 102 Pier
Grant & Sayles. 61 Quay
Hale S. (flour) 117 Pier
Hewett H. B. & Co. (produce) 111 Pier
Higbee, Hammond & Co. (lumber) above North Ferry
Hill & Thomas, (lumber) above North Ferry
Hunt Wm. H. (lumber) 87 Water
James B. P. 105 Pier
King J. B. & Co. (lumber) 20 Pier
M'Culloch John, 12 Exchange
M'Gowen M. (lumber) 191 Water
Reed & Rawls, (produce) Pier
Root A. H. 3 & 5 Hudson
Sayles J. & G. M. 62 Quay
Schoolcraft, Raymond & Co. 14 & 16 Hudson
Schuyler T. (produce) 29 Quay
Terry O. G.   do   130 Pier
Townsley G.   do   77 Quay
Tweedle & Darlington, 86 Quay
Vanderwater & Co. 102 Pier
Vansickler R. M. & Co. (domestic) 10 Maiden Lane
Wheeler Horace R. 6 Exchange
Whitlock R. (lumber) 16 Pier
Wing & Byrne, 90 Quay
Wright & Co. 116 Pier

Cayuga County.

Pratt William. South st.   *Auburn.*
Smith A. L. Weedsport   *Brutus.*

Chemung County.

Dunn C. W. (Commission & general agency)   *Elmira.*

Columbia County.

Chrysler M. F. 282 Warren *Hudson.*

Duchess County.

Morris Henry W. 22 Market
Poughkeepsie.

Erie County.

Barney D. W. & Co. Dock cor. Lloyd   *Buffalo.*
Bement William H. 4 Ohio
Bennett D. S. & Co. 8 Cent. Wharf
Boyd R. D. 7 East Seneca
Brown Wm O. 12 Central Wharf
Brownell George. 17   do
Chard W. Long Wharf
Coit & Farnham, 56 Main and 11 & 13 Hanover
Comstock & Laing, 21 Main
Cowing H. O. & Co. Prime & Dock
Cutter A. W. Merchants' Exch.
Daw Henry, Prime & Dock
Durfee Philo & Co. cor. Ohio and Cincinnati
Evans & Dunbar, Ship canal
Fero Robert, 3 Birkhead Block, Commercial
Fish & Avery, 19 Central Wharf
Fish S. H. 5 Merchants' Exchange
Fleeharty & Hughes, Prime and Dock
Folger T. P. 16 Central Wharf
Felts & Hopkins, 1 Cent. whf.
Felts & Hopkins. foot of Main
Ford ——, 5 Birkhead Building
Hawkins Austin & Co. Merch. Ex.
Hawley M. S. 17 Cent. whf.
Hayward & Noye, Merch. Ex.

Hazard G. S. 25 Cent. whf.
Buffalo.
Hitchcock J. & C. 13 Cent. whf.
Holley & Johnson, 16 Cent. whf,
Hollister ——
Hopkins & Co. 21 Merch. Ex.
Howard H. E. Merch. Ex.
Hunter W. C. & A. A. 13 Central wharf
Lathrop S. 5 Merch. Ex.
Madison Wm. 364 Main
Marcy & Welch, 14 Webster's block
Maynard & Baldwin, 14 Seneca
Millard H. W. & Co. 10 Cent. whf.
Moore Geo. A. & Co. 42 Main
Patterson & Fitch, 9 Cent. whf.
Plimpton L. K. 50 Main
Pratt L. H. & Co. Sidway Building, Long wharf
Reynolds & Deshler, 14 & 15 Cen. whf.
Richie H. B. Merch. Ex.
Richmond Dean, Indiana c. Ohio
Rogers Geo. W. cor. Mich., Ohio & Dock
Root Edward, 16 Cent. whf.
Ruden E. 11 Cent. whf.
Sano & Stanley, 5 U. S. Hotel blk.
Settle S. W. Merch. Ex.
Seymour & Wells, Dock foot of Illinois
Stiles & Coman, Dock n. Wash.
Stimpson Wm. 14 Cent. whf.
Thayer & Co. Ohio & Dock
Tifft Geo. W. Main c. Dock
Tripp A. F. & Co. 41 Coburn sq. Ohio
Tuttle D. N. 18 Central wharf
Van Balen, 45 Genesee
Vaughan Maurice, 2 Terrace
Walbridge G. B. Washington & Dock
Walker, Clark & Co. st Niles & Wheeler's
Walker, Darrow & Co. foot of Cincinnati
Ward John E. 4 Genesee sq.
Warner J. F. & Co. 8 Merch. Ex.
Weed Elias & Co. 22 Cent. wharf
Wilkins R. P. & Co. 28 Central wharf
Wilson G. R. Ohio st.
Wright Chas. & Co. 11 Cent. whf.

Essex County.

Walker, Smith & Co. Port Kent
Chesterfield.

Jefferson County.

Hooker & Stow, Sackett's Harbor
Hounsfield.
Hall T. S.   do
Camp E. & E. B.   do
Sackett G. A. & Co. do

Kings County.

Ogden A. (domestics) 39 Henry
Brooklyn.
Walterhouse, Linn & Co. Columbia c. Baltic
Todd R. J. 88 Fulton
Campbell John, 113 Grand
Williamsburgh.
Haven Joseph W. 119 Grand

Livingston County.

Blakeslee Gad   *Caledonia.*
Wetmore C. G. & Co.   *Dansville.*
Brown L. H.
Swan Henry   *Mount Morris.*
Scott Wm. H.
Camp Moses
Bow James, Fowlersville   *York.*
Spencer John   do
M'Pherson & Austin, Piffardania
Shacelton & Colt,   do

Monroe County.

Scranton Edwin, 25 Buffalo
Rochester.
O'Donoughue James, 42 Main

Montgomery County.

Abrahams & Almy   *Canajoharie.*

New York County.

Adams Joseph, 165 Maiden lane
New York.
Adams R. W. 116 Wall
Adams & Sturgess, 16 South
Allen & Paxson, 155 Front
Arnold, Beeman & Co. 30 Broadway
Arnold E. H. 34 Beaver
Armour Paul, 93 Wall
Arms Charles & Co. 139 Pearl
Atkinson J. 93 Wall
Auchincloss & Sons. 49 Beaver
Babbidge Calvin, 168 South
Badger, Peck & Co. 120 Wall
Baxer John, jr. 154 Maiden lane
Baker Wm. L. 165 Maiden lane
Baldwin & Fox, 52 Water
Bannerman H. & Sons, 103 Broadway
Barbean Louis J. 9 Cedar
Barber & Pritchard. 41 Beaver
Barker J. W. 129 Walker
Barry S. J. W. 217 Pearl
Bartlett Asahel H. 205 Pearl
Batsele & Renwick, 163 Front
Beale, Melick & Dewitt, 110 Broad
Beals Henry C. 22 South
Bech Edw'd & Kunhardt, 69 West
Bochet Claudius C. 34 Exch. pl.
Beeckman Henry, 21 South
Bell Abraham & Son. 117 Fulton
Bennett, Hall & Co. 19 South
Benton J. B. 69 West
Bigelow Asa, jr. 46 Pine
Bingham Mason H. 47 Wall
Binns & Halsted, 85 Beaver
Blackwell Robert M. & Co. 144 Front
Blossom Benjamin, 145 Front
Blow & March, 91 Water
Bogart S. G. 99 Beaver
Bogert & Kneeland. 49 William
Bond W. L. 21 South
Bourn William B. 163 Maid. lane
Boyce John, 237 Fulton
Boyd W. L. 21 South
Braine J. H. 96 Pine
Brett & Vose, 36 South
Brewster Wm. W. 66 Front
Briscoll & Simpson, 81 John
Brookman Henry D. 37 South
Brown T. E. & Co. 47 Pearl
Brown & De Rossett, 180 Front
Branchler Fred.
Buchanan, Harris & Co. Post's Building
Bulkley George, 86 South
Bunker & Van Boskerck, 142 Front
Burgess Caleb A. 257 Front
Burgy J. Henry, 67 Wall
Burlage R. C. jr. 94 Wall
Bunham John W. 7 South
Burnham & Plumb, 43 Cedar
Burnett John, 17 Beaver
Burns G. Y. 66 Barclay
Burritt Francis, 34 Broad
Butler Henry, 115 Wall
Butler John, jr. 78 Water
Butler W. L. M. 19 Front
Caldwell Wm. H. 165 Front
Cameron A. J. 70 Pine
Cameron R. W. 104 Front
Cary & Co. 90 Pine
Castaing John M. 87 Wall
Center & Co. 20 Old slip
Chastelan & Pouvert, 67 Water
Chouteau, Merle & Sandford, 51 New
Churchman, Roberts & Co. 49 Water

Clark & Coleman, 18 South
    New York.
Coe Henry, 10 Beaver
Coit Henry, 43 South
Colt Henry A. 44 South
Colt Wm. D. 116 Wall
Cohen J. jr. 104 Wall
Colburn A. 11 Nassau
Collins & Co. 283 Pearl
Collomb Felix. 5 Hanover
Colman William A. 304 Broadway
Coman, Hopkins & Co. 60 Front
Connor David, 98 Maiden lane
Conover D. D. 83 West
Coob Jas. N. 21 South
Corey J. A. 91 Wall
Connolly C. M. 43 Water
Constantine J. B. A. 48 Broadway
Cook Francis L. & Co. 71 New
Cooley H. F. 155 Fulton
Cooper & Giraud, 138 Front
Cornell M. 259 Washington
Cotheal & Co 49 Water
Cowdrey J. H. 107 Front
Crafts & Steel, 27 Pine
Crook George C. 24 Exchange pl.
Cross Jeremy L. 243 Pearl
Cunningham James B. 103 Water
Cunningham & Osborne, 103 do
Curtis Daniel, jr. 47 South
Curtiss Stiles, 171 Front
Cuthbert George. 43 New
Dale & Wright. 42 Exchange pl.
Darby George F. 69 Wall
Darling & Johnson. 36 Water
Davenport Isaac & Co. 134 Front
Davenport & Slipper, 212 Water
Davis M. 102 William
Davis, Brooks & Co. 63 Broad
Davis S. N. & Co. 46 Broad
Day, Sherman & Co. 74 Broadway
Dawson Wm. 70 Broad
De Forest Benjamin, 185 South
Degraw A. J. S. 69 Washington
Dellinger Charles, 89 Beaver
Depew William. 124 Front
De Rahm & Moore, 24 Ex. place
Deraismes John, 88 William
Des Arts & Heuser, 78 Nassau
Dewar, Bethune & Cumming, 42
    Water
De Wolf Thomas L. 108 Broad
Diedericks R. 15 S. William & 55
    Stone
Dike H. A. 70½ Pine
Disbrow Benjamin W. 174 Front
Dollner & Potter, 166 Front
Dominguez Gregorio, 30 Coenties
    slip
Dougall James, 1 Beaver
Dow Geo. W. & Co. 7 Burling slip
Dows & Cary, 20 South
Dows & Guiteau, 119 Broad
Draper S. B. 20 Pine
Drew Thomas, jr. 165 Front
Drury Michael, 8 Beaver
Dubois & Vandervoort, 87 Water
Dudley Jonas G. & Co. 102 Pearl
Dunham E. W. & Son, 5 South
Dunn S. 187 Water
Dunn Thomas. 70 Pine
Durand C. 77 South
Durand Victor. 18 S. William
Durant, Lathrop & Co. 7 South
Emanuel Michael. 27 Depeyster
Ennis H. J. 156 Pearl
Erben Peter. jr. 28 Old slip
Ernenputsch John C. 1 Pine
Esenwein ——. 14 West
Estes G. C. 104 William
Engs Wm. & Co. 109 Water
Famer G. 3 Pine
Farnham & Co. 85 Pearl
Field Benjamin H. 127 Water
Fielder Alexander, 225 Pearl
Fitzgerald Wm. G. 63 Beaver
Fitzmaurice Henry. 85 Front
Fobes Alpheus, 36 Water
Foote Israel. 14 Pine
Fort & Lindam, 15 S. William
Foster C. M. 40 South
Foster T. R. 96 Wall

Foster & Nickerson, 25 South
    New York.
Fowler John, 50 Water
Fox B. N. 52 Water
Fox & Polhemus, 59 Broad
Frost P. H. 140 Pearl
Fry C. M. 104 Front
Furniss William P. 35 Wall
Gager I. B. 120 Wall
Gambrel John A. 104 Wall
Gamage Amory. 60 Wall
Gamage H. T. 60 Wall
Garner James G. & Co. 33 Pine
Gibson, Stockwell & Co. 35 Pearl
Gilchrist & Co. 13 Old slip
Goddard S. A. & Co. 15 Platt
Goff & Constable, 14 Water
Goodridge S. W. & Co. 10 B'way
Gordon A. R. 67 Wall
Graves E. & R. 74 Pine
Graves E. B. & Co. 112 Wall
Gray Daniel L. 165 Front
Grice Joseph, 36 Water
Griffin John. 261 Washington
Griswold J. L. & N. L. 91 Front
Habersham W. & J. R. 4 Hanover
Habicht C. Edward. 94 Wall
Halliday T. A. 109 Wall
Holt Robert. 163 Maiden lane
Harding & Roed. 6 Broadway
Harmony's P. Nephews & Co. 63½
    Broadway
Hastie Wm. J. 36 Broadway
Havens H. P. & Son, 484 Water
Haven & Co. 7 Beaver
Hawley D. 151 Fulton
Haywood G. M. 83 Exchange pla.
Hearsey, Tower & Co. 117 Broad
Hemenway Tyler, 116 South
Henry A. S. & Co. 140 Broadway
Henry H. S. 150 Water
Henshaw J. B. 161 William
Herdt Clement. 33 Old slip
Herrick S. D. 23 Water
Herick E. & W. 26 Coenties slip &
    24 South
Herckenrath & Van Damme. 29
    Beaver
Hewitt, Lees & Co. 5 Bridge
Hicks Wm. T. & Co. 149 & 151
    Front
Higginson, Day & Co. 77 Broad
Hillman Jona. 163 Maiden lane
Hincken Wm. W. 36 South
Hinrichs Carl, 114 Pearl
Hitchcock, Marshall & Co. 229
    Front
Hoadley David, 104 Wall
Hodges E. H. 65 Front
Hogan Robert, 14 Wall
Holmes & Babcock.74½ Pine
Holt & Owen, 156 South
Holcomb & Berger, 89 West
Hoppock Ely, 30 South
Horn A. F. M. 97 Wall
Houghton Fred. B. 147 Front
Howes, Godfrey & Co. 26 South
Howland B. J. 51 Exchange place
Howland Wm. H. 158 South
Hoyt A. J. M. & Sons, 176 Wash-
    ington
Hull Oliver. 145 Maiden lane
Hunter W. C. & A. A. 43 Wall
Humphrey & Merrill, 74½ Pine
Hyslop & Coffin, 43 Front
Ingalls Henry T. 85 Pearl
Jackson Thomas, 75 Pearl
Jackson & Robins, 134 Water
Jex Josiah, 22 South
Jewett J. J. 74 Broadway
Johnston Robert, 139 Cedar
Johnston J. C. & Brother
Johnson Brothers, 81 Water
Jones S. T. & Co. 49 Exchange pl.
Jones & Himrod, 3 Water
Judah Dewitt C. 7 New
Kearney Edward, 189 Front
Kearney James, 139 Front
Kellogg Ralph, 8 South William
Kelsey Chas. 74 Broadway
Kelley Samuel R. 91 Wall
Kelly & Quin, 24 Coenties slip

Kemp H. & Co. 85 Pearl
    New York.
Kemp Alfred F. 65 Broad
Kemble Wm. 79 West
Keen J. 12 Pine
Kermit Robert, 76 South & 167
    Maiden lane
Kessler Meinhard, 97 Wall
Ketchum J. & Son. 31 Front
Knight N. & Co. 180 Front
Krider & Mallett. 76 Front
Kissam George, 139 Front
Kuh Leopold, 95 Cedar
Labouisse John J. 170 Front
Lacombe & Begoden. 71 Broad
Lathers Richard, 63 Water
Lapham & Place. 260 Washington
Lahens J. & Co. 62 Wall
Lamson G. W. & Co. 7 Fletcher
Langly W. C. & Co. 25 & 27 Broad
Lassala John B. & Nephew, 12
    Broadway
Lathem & Thompson. 96 Wall
Lathors Richard, 57 Broad
Lawrence Ferd. 89 Broad
Lawrence R. P. 41 Pine
Lawrence William E. 32 Cliff
Leland Francis, 55 Water
LeRoy Daniel, 69 Wall
Leverich Ch's P. 29 Burling slip
Loverich Henry S. 29   do
Leverett J. S. 46 Broad
Lewis Ezra, 24 South
Lobach Wm. & Schepeler, 20
    Beaver
Loescher P. & Co. 74 Greenwich
Long Isaac C. 36 South
Lord J. Couper, 53 South
Lord Tobias. 30   do
Lottimer & Large, 61 Broad
Lovett Thomas E. 42 Water
Low A. A. & Brother, 115 South
Low Emory & Co. 214 Pearl
Low Seth & Co. 8 Fletcher
Lowden John W. 1 Beaver
Ludlow James. 10 Old slip
Luyster A. R. 77 South
M'Cready N. L. & Co. 36 South
M'Credy D. A. 100 South
M'Crea J. A. 168 Pearl
M'Donnell James, 7 South
M'Dougall S. T. 102 Wall & 114
    Front
M'Evors Bache, 94 Exchange pl.
Macgregor & Morris, 10 Broad'y
Mackie J. F. & Co. 85 & 87 Broad
M'Kay W. 111 South
M'Laren D. 5 Dey
Macy Josiah & Sons, 189 Front
Main T. H. 1 Coenties slip
Maitland Robert L. 16 Broad
Maitland Wm. C. 54 Wall
Maitland, Phelps & Co. 14 Stone
Makin Richard, 20 Beaver
Manly & Embury, 50 South
Mann Edward J. 12 Front
Manzanedo Jose, 123 Front
Marks & Davol, 52 Broad
Marshall Josiah T. 82 John
Martin Edward, jr. 16 Water
Mathews C. D. 61 Pearl
Maury Brothers, Post's Buildings
Mead Wm. 76 Merchants, Ex.
Meigs & Wheeler, 187 South
Meyer M. H. 139 Front
Meyer H. & F. W. 30 Cliff
Meynen H. 64 Beaver
Middleton & Co. 19 Beaver
Miller John G. 141 Front
Mills D. 151 Front
Mills L. A. & L. H. 39 Water
Mills Charles, 188 Water
Mitchill Samuel L. 194 Front
Monahad & Beers, 173 Front
Moore E. P. 90 Wall
Morgan E. D. & Co. 68 & 70 Front
Morgan M. C. & Co. 66 Dey
Moses M. 155 Fulton
Mount David H. & Co. 394 West
Mount J. W. & Co. 161 West
Muir Andrew, jr. 22 Exchange pl
Mulholland John W. 187 Pearl

18

Muller Charles C. 106 Broad
New York.
Munroe John & Co. 68 Broadway
Munroe, Osborn & Co. 68 do
Murray Christopher, 1 Beaver
Murray John B. 12 Old slip
Nathan Benj. Post's Buildings
Nathan Jonathan, Post's Buildings
Negrin Paul, 170 Front
Nesmith & Walsh, 37 South
Nevius Peter I. & Son. 11 South
Newman Richard W. 66 Broad
Newman W. H. 75 Pearl
Newcomb W. jr. 28 Broadway
Newmark Joseph, 23 Bowery
Nichols Henry G. 79 Water
Nichols Perkins, 54 Wall
Noble L. P. 147 Front
Norton J. W. 10 South
Nottebohn A. 1 Water
Oelrichs & Kruger, 73 New
Ogden M. L. 68 Cedar
Oliver & Morgan, 26 Beaver
Ormsbee John H. jr. 46 Broad
O'Reilly & Co. 157 South
Osborne Samuel, 96 Wall
Owen Thomas & Son, 156 South
Parkhurst & Adams, 87 Wall
Patrullo Andre, 84 Broad
Paul D. & S. W. & Co. 160 Pearl
Pecks & Myers, 114 Broad
Peck & Lyman, 52 Front
Peniston G. F. 6 South
Perry Theod. & Co. 92 Broad
Phillips & Aborn, 108 Broad
Platt W. H. & Co. 47 Pearl
Pollen & Colgate, 287 Pearl
Pollitz O. W. 8 Beaver
Pollock R. M. 114 Warren
Pomeroy Grove, 9 Cedar
Poppe E. & T. 50 New
Post Ralph, 38 South
Prandy Thos. 257 Front
Pratt Noah C. 170 Front
Poultney Benj. 181 Water
Powell A. H. 100 Front
Powell E. S. 104 Wall
Quincy Charles E. 16 Broad
Radcliff Augustus W. 63 Wall
Ray W. C. 84 Front
Raymond A. R. 2 Pine
Rea Samuel, 27 Water
Reed J. H. 16 South
Renard & Co. 116 Pearl
Rice John, 109 Broad
Richards Daniel, 74 Broadway
Richards Stephen, 63½ Gold
Rigney Thomas, 65 Broad
Robinson James, 81 Front
Robinson & Co. 68 Beaver
Robert & Williams, 97 & 99 W'tr
Rolker & Mollman, 96 Pearl
Ropes R. W. & Co. 44 Water
Rowland Charles N. 8.55 Water
Rowe Jacob, 6 Broadway
Rudsdale Matthew, 60 Broad
Russell Isaac, 111 Broad
Russell John, 39 Beaver
St. Jurgo Rivera, 159 Front
Sackett & Co. 60 Pearl
Sale Wm. A. jr. 124 Water
Sanborn Luke K. 96 Wall
Sandford Daniel. 163 South
Sayre David L. 74 Front
Schermerhorn John V. R. 121 Broad
Schlesinger F. S. 96 Beaver
Schmidt J. W. & Co. 56 New
Schieffelin & Fowler, 142 and 144 Front
Scrymser Robert L. 113 Wall
Scudder J. H. 12 Front
Sebring T. V. W. 112 Water
Shailer Thomas, jr. 85 Front
Shapter James S. 233 Pearl
Shaw John P. 43 Front
Shepherd Edward F. 24 Cedar
Shepard, Wright & Ripley, 37 Pine
Shepherd Henry, 17 Wall
Simes & Huffer, 15 Stone
Skaats Schuyler, 1 Water

Stark, Day & Stauffer & Co. 205 Pearl
New York.
Slate, Gardiner & Howell, 114 & 115 South
Smith Hiram, 34 Water
Smith James, 116 Wall
Smith & Boynton, 4 South
Smith O. A. & Co. 96 Broad
Smith Wm. & Son, 12th cor. Av. C
Smithers Alfred, 91 Wall
Snow G. T. 123 Water
Soule, Whitney & Co. 4 South
Soutter, Symington & Robinson, 82 Broad
Southmayd L. O. 9 West
Spaan & Hooffman, 114 Greenwich
Spence A. G. 101 Wall
Spies Francis, 80 South
Sprague, Robinson & Co. 54 Burling slip
Staples Jas. M. 18 South
Stephenson Fred. 48 Water
Stevens' Ebenezer Sons, 195 Water
Strachan & Scott, 51 William
Strybing Henry. 16 Burling slip
Sturges & Co. 6 South
Sturges, Clearman & Co. 110 Wall
Sue A. W. 87 Wall
Suydam Henry, 89 Beaver
Suydam, Sage & Co. 2 & 3 South
Swain James P. & Co. 139 Front
Talman John H. 50 South
Talman Wm. H. 50 South
Tarbox G. W. 8 Pine
Taylor A. & S. 144 Pearl
Thomes Brothers, 53 Exchange place
Thomas & Davenport, 7 & 9 Water
Thomas A. 4 Pine
Thomas & Franklin, 89 Water
Thomas Wm. H. 92 Wall
Thompson & Hunter, 22 South
Thurston F. G. & Co. 49 South
Tingle Geo. 9 Cedar
Tools Wm. H. 17 S. William
Torrance Daniel, 98 Wall
Toy Wm. 24 Cedar
Tuck Samuel B. 36 South
Tucker T. & Co. 15 Broad
Tucker & Littell, 216 Washington
Tuckeman Jos. 69 West
Uhlhorn Wm. C. 27 Old slip
Van Arsdale W. Post's Buildings
Valentine A. A. 74 Pearl
Vansyckel E. & Co. 88 West
Van Kleeck W. H. & Co. 158 & 159 West
Van Riper P. H. 6 South
Varick Jas. L. 117 West
Van Schaick P. C. & Co. 68 Front
Von Hoffman L. Post's Buildings
Victor & Duckwitz, 93 Pearl
Viets Wm. A. 30 Water
Wadsworth & Sheldon, 65 & 67 Exchange place
Walker Wm. L. 182 South
Warren, Clark & Co. 263 Washington
Waring Henry & Son, 150 Front
Waterhouse & Linn, 5 South
Watson Jas. & Co. 35 Pearl
Wells Jons. T. 117 Maiden lane
Westray Fletcher. 71 Front
Wetherbee J. 77 South
Wetmore & Cryder, 74 South
Wheeler & Van Benschoten, 110 Front
Whitaker Geo. 159 Front
White R. H. 50 Wall
White Ezra. 68 Wall
White Jos. F. 140 Nassau
Whitney Samuel, 26 Coenties slip
Wichelhausen, Recknegal and Schwab, 165 Water
Wilbur & Scott, 15 Stone
Williams John G. 186 Front
Williams J. Henry, 119 Front
Wilkinson Anthony, 15 Beaver
Wilson & Henriques, 30 Old slip
Winkle Henry, 101 Water

Winslow Isaac, jr. 76 Pearl
New York.
Wirgman C. H. 165 Front
Wissmann Frederick, 5 Hanover
Wood A. B. 27 West
Wood David, 236 Pearl
Wood Frederick, 43 Water
Wood John, 166 Pearl
Wood Silas, 107 Water
Woodward M. W. 142 Front
Wright & Holgate, 74 Pine
Young & Bonnell, 92 West
Ziegler E. G. 136 Greenwich

Oneida County.

Dugan & Willis, James st. Rome.
Backus W. W.155 Genesee Utica.
Brooks Benj. F. 133 do
Taylor & Rockwell, (wool) 86 Genesee
Clark C. D. 55 Hotel
Ray E. C. cor. Hotel & Canal
Dows & Kissam, cor. Seneca and Canal
Swift Wm. P. cor. Liberty & Hotel
Walker, Clark & Co. 17 Liberty
Culver & Co. Packet Dock
Livingston V. V. 12 Catharine
Montgomery Wm. L. Whitesboro Whitestown.

Onondaga County.

Cobb Alfred, 2 Williams' Block, Syracuse Salina.
Phinney & Winnegar, Water st.
Holmes A. T. & Co. do
Adams & Moody, do
Alden H. W., Willow st.

Ontario County.

Holley Alfred A., Geneva Seneca
Price Joseph. do
Hastings & Fields, do
Dox John, do
Bailey R. M. do

Orleans County.

Gardner Wm. G., Albion Barre.
Lee J. B. do
Warner Lewis, do
Lee & Post, do
Webb Z. do
Howard A. do
Burrell Truxton, do

Oswego County.

Platt James, foot 1st st. Oswego.
Bond & Uhlhorns, warehouse cor. 1st & Seneca—office, Bronson's Block
Cooper & Barbour, Water st.
Smyth Charles, do

Queens County.

Leech O. P. Jamaica.

Rensselaer County.

Follett R. F. 296 State Lansingburgh.
Ackley & Brother, 294 River Troy.
Priest, Allendorph & Co. 296 River

St. Lawrence County.

Angel Wm. H. Water st. Ogdensburgh Oswegatchie
Boyd & Judd, Ford st. do

Seneca County.

Freliegh G. W Ovid.
Cooley Daniel Romulus

Wayne County.

Blackmer A. T. & E. Huron.
Leach M. S. & H. J. Lyons.
Knowles J. & Brothers
Adams John & Son
Southwick & Thurber Palmyra.

Cummings J. K.   *Palmyra.*
Beecher & Gloesender
Drake William
Ferrin R. ———
Irwin Wm. P., Sodus Point *Sodus.*

**Merchants—Forwarding &
Commission.** (*See also Merchants Commission, also Merchants Forwarding.*)

Chemung County.

Thurman & Ingraham   *Elmira.*
Strang J. B.

Erie County.

Burkle & Pease   *Black Rock.*
Abell, Snow & Co. 2 Coburn sq.
      Buffalo.
Beecher H. S., Dock
Bissell John, 11 Central Wharf
Brown John G. 3 Merchants' Ex.
Carley Joseph, 9 Central Wharf
Chipman J. B. jr. & Co. near Lloyd
st. bridge
Clark & Seymour, Lloyd st. canal
& dock
Cobb A. R. & Co. 5 Wilkinson's
Block
Curtis, Mann & Co. cor. Water &
ship canal
Dart Joseph, jr. cor. ship canal &
Buffalo Creek
Davis & Sutton, Reed's warehouse
Folger & Petrie, 19 Central Wharf
Foot William, 19   do
Gelston & Evans, Water st.
Hill, Fleming & Co. 10 Central
Wharf
Holt, Palmer & Co. foot Washington st.
Hooker, Peckham & Barnard, foot
Commercial st.
Joy & Chapin, foot Lloyd st.
Joy L. & Webster, do
Kasson Wm. M. 8 & 9 Central
Wharf
Kelsey, Bowers & Talmage, foot
Washington st.
Kent & Carley, 9 Central Wharf
Kimberly, Pease & Co. Dock above
Lloyd
Kinne Henry M., Michigan Central
R. R. Dock
Maxwell & Co. 3 & 4 Coburn sq.
Meech S. L.
Monteath, Sherman & Co. 12 Main
Morrison A. & Co. 10 Central
Wharf
Nottingham J. & Co. 27 Central
Wharf
Niles & Wheeler, South Wharf
Parker Jason, Ship Canal
Perkins H. corner Commercial &
Water
Purdy Samuel & Co. Prime st.
Robinson D. N., Sidway Block
Savage E. & Co. Reed's Wharf
Sears & Griffith, cor. Long Wharf
& Ship Canal
Sternberg P. L. & Co. Long Wharf
cor. Dock
Sterling, Brothers, Ship Canal
Swan & Brainard, 26 Central Wharf
Ward & Co. 12   do
White & Thayer, 16   do
Wilkes & Co. Canada Dock

Monroe County.

Ball & Church, Spencer's Basin
      Ogden.
Cornings & Chadwick, Fairport
      Perinton.
Howard A.
Hastings Isaac, Bushnell's Basin
Rogers R. A.   *Pittsford.*
Porter E. H.
Voorhees A.
Boughton F

Brewster S. L. & J. R. 16 South
St. Paul & 72 Main *Rochester.*
Rochester N. T. & Co. 69 Exchange
Ely Abraham P. Smiths' Block,
Buffalo
Dewey J. B. 61 Buffalo
Sweet C. H. 123   do
Avery George A. 12   do
Bell & Goodman, 10   do
Sheldon O. L. & Co. 8 do
Holmes & Fish, 83 Exchange
Hickock B. E. 44   do
Smith & Perkins, 29   do
Gardiner N. H. 31   do
Hawks J. & T. 32   do
Buell E. N., Sophia near Canal
Sawyer James W. 44 State
Chapell J. cor. Fitzhugh & Canal
Fish Henry L. Washington st.
Smith l. M. foot of Platt
Smith Peter, Lower Falls
Herman, Field & Co. Brockport
      Sweden.
Smith H. Scottsville *Wheatland.*
Harmon H. & R.   do
Scofield & Shadbolt, do
Garbutt Philip, Mumford

Niagara County.

Cornell Nelson   *Lewiston.*
Harris Joel
Shuler E. D.   *Lockport.*
Kelsey & Dunlap
Cooper J. D.   *Newfane.*
Lane George, Olcott
Wright W. S.
Colwell & Sleeper, Gasport
      Royalton.
Harrington ——, Orangeport
Wilson Luther   *Wilson.*

Oswego County.

Randall, Gilbert & Co. Smith's
Cove   *Oswego.*
Smith & Post, (Lumber) do
Isaacs B. & C. cor. Water & Seneca
Merrick & Davis, Water st.
Bronson & Crocker, cor. Cayuga
& Water
Lewis & Beardsley, Market Block,
Water
Doolittle & Mollison, cor. Cayuga
& Water

Rensselaer County.

Armstrong & Squires, 277 River
      Troy.
Battershall & Weed, 311 River
Bates & Griffin, 171   do
Britton & Webb, 325   do
Dater & Carr, 299   do
Doughty S. G. & Co. 185 do
Haight & Gillespie, 269 do
Hakes & M'Donal, 327 do
Herrington Hiram, 273 do
Hillman Joseph, 173   do
Howland, Bills & Thayer, 148 do
Hunt & Baker, 187   do
Hunter & Graves, 183 do
Ide, Colt & Co. 153   do
Loveland & Swartwout, 347 do
Mather J. C. 221   do
Merritt C. H. & I. J. 253 do
Moore & Tibbitts, 145 do
Nsaro John T. 217   do
Perry A. S. & Co. 203 do
Scott & Lemon, 261   do
Shaw W. H. 159   do
Silliman & Gardiner, 239 do
Smith & Safford, 343 do
Smith & Wood, 237   do
Starbuck M. 289 & 291 do
Ten Broeck & Steen Bergh, 308 do
Tillinghast & Co. 191 do
Weed & Thurman. 349 do
Wight D. & Son, 221   do
Willard John N. 147   do
Willard Wm. T. foot of Adams
Wooster G. L. 239 River

St. Lawrence County.

Bacon Amos, Water st. Ogdensburgh *Oswegatchie.*
Allen E. B. & Sons, Ogdensburgh
Robbins & Lankton,   do
Averill James G.   do
Angel William H.   do
Humphrey & Co.   do

Schenectady County.

Benedict William F. 19 Canal
      Schenectady.
Van Vorst J. B. Liberty st.

Tompkins County.

Sage H. W. & Co. Inlet Pier
      Ithaca.
Culver & Halsey, R. R. Block
Barnard F. 7 Basin

Merchants—Forwarding.—
(*See also Freighting Agents; also
Merchants Commission; also
Merchants Forwarding and Commission.*)

Albany County.

James Thomas, 40 Quay *Albany.*
Gay George, 102 Pier
Johnson N. H.   *Coeymans.*
Lawton Willis & Colvin

Alleghany County.

Rice & Hitchcock   *Caneadea.*

Broome County.

Meloy F. W. Chenango Forks
      Barker.
M'Kinney C.   *Binghamton.*
Isbell & Way,   do

Cayuga County.

Ingraham, Havens & Co. Weedsport   *Brutus.*
Durkey & Wilson, Weedsport
Baylies A. & Co.   do
Bently T. S.   do
Havens Wm. B.   do
Ryant H.   do
Smith A. L.   do
M'Quegg & Daniels, Port Byron
      Mentz.

Chautauque County.

Lee, Snow & Co. Silver Creek
      Hanover.
Eason John   *Westfield.*
Foote Jervis

Chenango County.

Clark E. & Son   *Oxford.*
Pratt & Rexford   *Sherburne.*
Birch L. D
Crumb D.
Knapp & Briggs

Columbia County.

Hubbell, Clark & Co. Water st.
      Hudson.
Mellen L. R. & Co.   do

Duchess County.

Marshall & Co.   *Hyde Park.*
Vincent G. I. & Co. Main st. landing *Poughkeepsie.*
Hunt, Vale & Co. lower landing
Doughty, Wilkinson & Co. upper
landing
Millard & Mills. New Hamburgh
Outwater J. Tivoli *Red Hook.*
Tyler N. P. & Sons, Barrytown
Tremper, Platt & Co. *Rhinebeck.*

Erie County.
Warner J. F.   *Tonawanda.*
Wheeler John K.

Essex County.
Colvin, Allen & Co. Port Kent
   Chesterfield.

Genesee County.
Smith L. A.   *Batavia.*
Foote J.
Ganson J. & Co.
Griffin N. D.
M'Card W. & E.   *Bergen.*
Ward Henry M
Doolittle James
M'Pherson D. & Co.

Herkimer County.
Heald John M.D.   *Frankfort.*
Elwood & Folts
Bridenbecker Wm. & J. W.
Morris John, West Frankfort
Remington & Morgan, Ilion
   German Flats.
Dygert & Morgan, Ilion
Reese F. do
Mory & Devendorf, Mohawk
Root H. G. & Co. do
Brown John F. do
Ricketson & Newman, do
Priest M. W. & Co.   *Little Falls.*

Jefferson County.
Fuller & Thompson, Alexandria
   Bay   *Alexandria.*
Walton & Co. Alexandria Bay
Corlis Lyman, do
Bell Jas. & Co. Dexter *Brownville.*
Norton, M'Gunn & Beally, Dexter
Crevelin W. J. & Co. *Cape Vincent.*
Cross & Hinckley
Fellowns Joseph, Three Mile Bay
   Lyme.

Livingston County.
Hawley Wm. C.   *Caledonia.*
Welch William   *Dansville.*
Foote Wm. & Co.
Brace E. B. & Son
Bittan J. & Co.
Colt Charles   *Geneseo.*
Austin Russell
Shackleton Richard
White John, jr
Wooster Wm. W. Cuylerville
   Leicester.
Odell Lyman, do
Wilmerding & Tilton, Moscow
Deleno David B. do
Dwight Hosford, do
Jones Thomas, do
Phelps Charles, do
Swan Henry   *Mount Morris.*
Scott Wm. H.
Ketchum C. S.
Camp Moses
Bow James, Fowlersville   *York.*
Spencer John, do
M'Pherson & Austin, Piffardania
Shacelton & Colt, do

Madison County.
Lord Horace   *Hamilton.*
Page George M. Earlville
Fay Nahum, Canastota   *Lenox.*
Conley John, do
Peckham D. S. do
Gay Wm. L. do
Carter, Schuyler & Co. Chitte-
   nango   *Sullivan.*
Campbell A. & Co. Chittenango

Montgomery County.
Wood & Meyer   *Canajoharis.*
Clark, Newkirk & Hoffman
Gardner & Van Denburgh, Fulton-
   ville   *Glen.*

Clark, Newkirk & Hoffman, Fort
   Plain   *Minden.*
Spraker Daniel, Spraker's Basin
   Root.
Buel Edmund, do

New York County.
Allen Hugh, 127 Broad *New York.*
Allen John, jr. 23 Coenties slip
Benjamin Geo. B. 33 do
Brainard Leonard W. 15 South
Briggs J. & N. 40 South
Brisch Henry, 132 Washington
Brush C. W. 10 West
Brush & Co. 9 West
Caleb Madison M. & Co. 109 Broad
Campbell James W. 101 do
Canfield C. H. 7 Coenties slip
Cason William R. 7 West
Catlin Pope, 33 Coenties slip
Center Sylvester, 19 West
Clark C. V. 16 South
Clarke John F. 1 S. William
Clinton Henry P. 113 Broad
Colson Augustus, 7½ Coenties slip
Disbrow Benjamin N. 174 Front
Dwight Timothy C. 195 Broad
Eaton, Higbee & Co. 113 do
Gardiner Lathrop F. 176 B'dway
Gardiner & Vandenbergh, 8 South
Gilbert Joseph, 17 Coenties slip
Gray Morgan, 13 South
Griffith Evan, 33 Coenties slip
Griffith Walter S. 22 South
Harden William, 6 do
Hegeman Abraham, 23 Water
Higbee Isaac J. 113 Broad
Hindes R. & Co. 145 Washington
Hindes & Co. 7 West
Hollister Charles, 127 Broad
Holmes H. C. 8 South
Holt H. N. & Co. 9 Coenties slip
Hovey M. Holley, 17 do
Howell Ralph L. 121 Broad
Hulbert I. H. S. 127 Broad
Humphrey Theron M. 113 Broad
Ives E. R. & Co. 119 Broad
James & Maxwell. 119 Broad
James Charles B. 7 Coenties slip
Jennison W. H. & G. 109 Broad
Johnson Hiram, 148 West
Kimball Thomas, 8 South
Kimball & Bedient, 8 South
Leonard William F. 123 Broad
Littlejohn F. S. 100 Broad
Lockyer Thomas, 112 South
Loescher P. A. & Co. 74 G.wich
Meech Rufus, 109 Broad
Mills John W. 109 West
Munsell William A. 127 Broad
Newell & Gray, 127 Broad
Nukerck Charles C. 8 South
Oatman James, 29 Coenties slip
Ormsbe John H. jr. 46 Broad
Palmer A. W. & Co. 121 Broad
Palmer Howell & Co. 121 do
Pease E. T. 9 Coenties slip
Redfield John H. & Co. 16 South &
   82 Cortlandt
Rexford Daniel A. 7 South
Rexford Nelson C. 7 South
Rice, Clapp & Co. 31 Coenties
   slip
Saxton & Webb, 112 South
Schermerhorn John, 121 Broad
Schuyler & Co. 7 South, Old Al-
   bany line
Scovell Oliver F. 113 Broad
Saxton Stephen B. 19 West
Silliman & Gardiner, 17 Coenties
   slip
Spaulding Morrell B. 123 Broad
Stark Lucius J. N. 33 Coenties sl.
Stebbins Augustus Q. 107 Broad
Tefft Asa C. 23 Coenties slip
Thayer Seth, 106 Broad
Vandewater Robert J. 106 Broad
Warner J. L. 33 Coenties slip
Waters & Ensworth, 117 Broad
Whedon A. 8 South
Wheeler, Tracy & Co. 19 Coenties
   slip

Wilgus James H. 33 Coenties slip
   New York.
Worth John S. 23 do
Woolf & Ritchmuller, 150 Wash-
   ington
Wyckoff James S. 23 Coenties
   slip

Oneida County.
Willard J. M. Oriskany Falls
   Augusta.
Taylor A. Clinton   *Kirkland.*
Dugan & Willis, James st.
   Rome.
Edgerton & Gage, Canal st.
Leffingwell N. Hyde, do
Dows & Kissam, cor. Seneca st. &
   Canal Basin   *Utica.*
Ray E. C. cor. Hotel & Canal sts.
Swift William P. cor. Liberty and
   Hotel sts.
Culver & Co. Packet Dock
Avery E. & Co. Jay st.
Livingston V. V. 12 Catharine
Clark E. A.   *Whitestown.*
Montgomery Wm. L. Whitesboro

Onondaga County.
Rogers J. Jordan   *Elbridge*
Morris C. & Co. do
Dodge H. & Son, do
Eaton H. & Co. Warren st. Syra-
   cuse   *Salina.*
Hovey A. H. & Co. Water st.
Dickenson J. do
Hatch H. D. & Co. do
Adams & Moody, do
Alden H. W., Willow st.

Orange County.
Reeve C. W.   *Goshen.*
Thompson J. W.
Powell, Ramsdell & Co. *Newburgh.*
Carpenter B. & co
Wardrop, Smith & Co.
Crawford, Muller & Co.
Carpenter J.   *New Windsor.*

Orleans County.
Gardner Wm. G. Albion   *Barre.*
Lee J. B. do
Warner Lewis, do
Lee & Post, do
Webb Z. do
Howard A. do
Burrell Truxton, do
Britt O. E. & S. Medina *Ridgeway.*
Whalen & Parker, do
Mulls & M'Makin, Knowlesville

Oswego County.
Fitzhugh H. & Co. 1st cor. Seneca
   Oswego.
Van Derwater & Brothers, 1st cor.
   Cayuga
Crane Hunter, foot of Front and
   cor. Van Buren
Wright Henry C. Water st.
Wyman Truman, do
Fitch & Ells, Market Building
   Water st.
Forward & Smith, Schuyler c. 2d
Pettis J. J. & Co. Port Ontario
   Richland.

Rensselaer County.
Hogeboom & Schermerhorn
   Schodack
Gage H.

Saratoga County.
Vernan & Bennett   *Halfmoon*

Seneca County.
Avery John B., Farmer   *Ovid.*
Rapley & Morehouse, do
Kennedy John, do
Almy Ira do

Tracy Horace C., Farmer *Ovid.*
Swift M H. *Waterloo.*
Gay & Noyes
Kendig Daniel S.

Steuben County.

Mallory Wm. M. *Paint'd Post*
Adsett A. M. *Urbana.*

Washington County.

Travis & Co. *Whitehall.*
Eddy & Mann
Bascom O. Agent

Wayne County.

Blackner A. T. & E. *Huron.*
Southwick & Thurston *Palmyra.*
Cummings J. K.
Beecher & Glossender
Drake William
Ferrin R.
Irwin W. P., Sodus Point *Sodus.*

Wyoming County.

Stevens & Smith *Attica.*
Lyford Thomas

Yates County.

Tuttle C. G. & Co. Dundee
Starkey.

Merchants—General.

Acosta John, 76 Broad *New York.*
Arcularius John P. 100 Wall
Banks Mark, 16 Cedar
Barclay & Livingston, 24 Beaver
Bechtel & Schomburg, 90 Front
Bird & Gillilan, 40 Wall
Blanco B. 87 Front
Bloodgood William, 28 Beaver
Bowley E. I. M. & G. 165 Front
Browne Martin, 69 South
Buck Charles N. jr. 145 Front
Buckley Ralph, 272 Pearl
Burre J. P. 26 South William
Butterworth J. F. 88 Merch. Ex.
Chauncey E. N. 86 Front
Chittenden H. S. 76 Broad
Clute J. D. 60 Broadway
Collins George, 82 Wall
Cram Jacob, 115 Wall
Curtis J. L. 22 John
Danforth J. B. 61 Pearl
Davis Charles A. 74 Broadway
Dean Nicholas, 74 Broadway
Delafield H. & William, 79 Front
Denslow A. A. & Co. 69 Wall
Dixon James & Sons, 241 Pearl
Door Francis F. 14 Wall
Dortie S. C. 102 Front
Dufour, Durand & Co. 43 New
Dunning C. 8 Pearl
Fellows William, 28 Beaver
Ferguson John, 29 Whitehall
Foster Andrew & Sons, 65 South
Francia & Co. 83 Front
Furniss William P. 35 Wall
Gillander E. 61 Pearl
Gordon & Talbot, 155 Maid. Lane
Haggerty John, 75 Pine
Halliday T. A. 109 Wall
Hamilton C. K. 22 South William
Hamilton & Herriman, 67 Front
Havens R. N. 10 Wall
Haws R. T. 8 South William
Henry John & Co. 49 John
Hicks W. T. & Co. 151 Front
Holbrook D. B. 74 Broadway
Hoyt James I. 68 Wall
Ingersoll J. D. & Co. 222 Pearl
Kimball Edmund, 116 Wall
Lamar G. B. 83 Wall
Laurence, Murray & Ingate, 44 New
Lefman Henry, 232 Washington
Leland Francis, 55 Water
Lockwood Walter, 229 Greenw'h
Male Job, 74 Broadway
Major M. 5 Pearl

Manning George, 90 Wall
New York.
Mead Benjamin, 61 Water
Megrath & Hasbrouck, 5 B.way
Milbank I. & R. & Co. 82 Front
Newbold & Craft, 4 Broadway
North Brothers, 16 South William
Ogden James D. F. 74 Merch. Ex.
Owens Edward, 249 Front
Parish D. & P. 162 Pearl
Partridge W. T. 113 Wall
Peet & Simms, 9 Pine
Phipps I. L. & Co. 19 & 21 Cliff
Pigot Edward N. 120 Front
Piston Philip F. 62 Beaver
Portsons Thomas, 49 John
Post C. C. 7 Nassau
Rapelye & Purdy, 169 Front
Richard Dan. 74 Broadway
Ricketts Geo. R. A. 16 Water
Robbins E. & C. 190 Water
Robinson R. B. 251 Front
Rogers, Ketchum & Grosvenor, 74
Broadway
Rogers Sam. T. 22 South
Rolker A. & Mollmam, 96 Pearl
Rossire A. C. & Co. 12 Beaver
Ruggles Henry, 172 Front
Schnitzpahn Fred. 165 Pearl
Sheldon George, 116 Wall
Siffken & Ironside, 4 Broadway
Small, Williams & Co, 91 & 93
Washington
Smith J. E. 22 John
Squire C. 102 Nassau
Stalker & Co. 88 Front
Sturgis Russell, 78 Wall
Sturges & Co. 6 South
Suckley Rutson, 3 Nassau
Sutton Abel, 84 Wall
Sutton Effingham, 84 Wall
Suydam, Johnson & Dellicker, 164
Front
Taylor P. G. & Co. 214 Pearl
Thompson A. G. 62 Wall
Thorne R. V. W. & Co. 5 Jones
lane
Townsend Elihu, 74 Broadway
Tracy Samuel F. 6 Beaver
Tredwell Adam & Son, 168 Front
Van Wegenen R. 42 & 45 Broad
Varnum Joseph B. 165 Pearl
Wheelright G. & S. 113 Wall
White Wm. 233 Pearl
Whitney Stephen, 46 Front
Willets Joseph, 35 Pearl
Winterton W. 91 Wall
Wisners & Gale, 13 Old slip
Wood David, 4 Fulton
Young, Hawkins & Co. 41 South
Zachrisson E. 87 Wall
Zerega & Co. 86 South
Zimmerman John C. sen. 36 New

Merchants—Importing and Commission.

Aguirre & Galwey, 46 Water
New York.
Alsop & Chauncey, 42 South
Atkins A. 91 Water
Beoly Oliver, 93 Front
Bernheimer & Hausman, 38 Beaver
Bishop James & Co. 3 Beaver
Bishop Victor, 23 Malden Lane
Boonen, Graves & Co. 112 Wall
Bossange E. 99 Wall
Bougers Elie, 12 William
Buloid Robt. & Co. 102 Front
Burchard L. & W. 99 Front
Chastelan & Ponvert, 67 Water
Cottenot F. & Co. 48 Broad & 46
New
De Puga Manuel, 20 S. William
Delano Fred. A. 74 South
Fernhamp P. I. & Co. 85 Pearl
Fiedler Ernest, 22 Broadway
Fitch & Co. 43 New
Franklin Selim & Co. 21 New
Graves, Boonen & Co. 112 Wall

Hamilton C. H. 22 S. William
New York.
Hardenburgh I. D. 100 Front
Harriman William & Co. 128 Front
Heilbuth & Shultz, 39 John
Henschen & Unkart, 17 S. William
Hughes, Ward & Co. 24 Broad
Huesmann & Co. 14 Platt
Henry A. S. & Co. 142 Broadway
Kohnstamm Solomon, 1 William
Lazarus Alex. 215 Water
Le Berthon John L. 42 New
Lee James & Co. 36 New
Lilly & Racines, 109 Front
Livingston M. & W. 70 Broad
Loeschigk, Wesendonck & Co. 40
& 42 Broad
Low Seth & Co. 8 Fletcher
Luhring John & Co. 34 Beaver
M'Andrew Alexander & Co. 43
New
M'Call & Strong, 25 William
M'Monnies Wm. & Co. 83 John
Maguire & Galwey, 46 Water
Mason & Thompson, 33 Pearl
Mase C. P. 3 S. William
Metz Julius, jr. 83 Cliff
Meyer H. & F. W. 30 Cliff
Michel John, 43 New
Moller & Sand, 22 & 24 New
Morewood George B. & Co. 14 &
16 Beaver
Nathan James, 99 Pearl
Nevins & Co. 18 Broad
Olyphant & Son, 66 South
Pastacaldi Michael, 25 S. William
Pattison James, 43 & 45 Broad
Phillips Jonas & Co. 25 S. William
Richards Wm. H. 136 Front
Richardson, Watson & Co. 41 & 46
Exchange pl.
Ronth H. L. & Sons, 69 New
Rudsdale Matthew, 60 Broad
Sale Wm. A. jr. 124 Water
Sayers & Winters, 6 William
Scheitlin A. & E. 113 Pearl
Schults & Bleidorn, 76 Broad
Seaman F. A. 101 Wall
Simonsfeld, Bach & Co. 62 William
Simpson, Mayhews & Co. 12 Coenties slip
Sittenfield Ferdinand, 45 Delancy
Speyer Philip & Co. 51 Broad
Stewart Wm. George, 74 Br'dw'y
Tardy John A. 43 New
Thorne Richard V. W. & Co. 5
Jones lane
Trujillo & Barreiras, 106 Wall
Victor Theodore & Duckwitz, 98
Pearl
Waddell J. 66 Pearl
Wallerstein David, 43 William
Winston F. S. & Co. 100 Broadway
Winterhoff, Piper & Karck, 76
Broad
Wirths Edward, 18 Liberty
Wissmann Frederick, 5 Hanover
Wolfsohn E. & Seligmann, 112
William

Merchants—Produce Commission.

(*See also Flour Dealers, also Produce Dealers, also Brokers Produce, also Grain Dealers, also Provision Dealers, also Merchants Commission.*)

Abbey & Freeman, 51 Front
New York.
Adams Russell W. 116 Wall
Adams & Sturges, 19 South
Allen & Whittelsey, 21 South
Badeau & Lockwood, 209 Washington
Barker J. & Son, 212 Front
Barker J. Willard, 129 Water
Bayard, Tanner & Co. 237 Washington
Beach Henry N. 26 Front

Beals H. Channing, 22 South
    New York.
Bedle & Roberts, 23 Washington
    market
Belknapp & Haviland, 262 Washington
Bennett, Hall & Co. 19 South
Berdell Robert H. & Co. 32 Front
Bidwell J. A. & D. 34 Water
Boddy John E. 17 South
Blush Jesse, 17 Front
Bogert John M. B. 42 Stone
Bowman & Butterfield. 86 Broad
Boyd William H. 21 South
Brinckerhoff Elbert A. 259 Washington
Brock Jonathan. 30 Front
Brown & Cary, 106 Broad
Brown Thomas E. & Co. 47 Pearl
    & 34 Bridge
Brush Jesse, 17 Front
Buckley John L. & Co. 31 Front
Buffell H. & Co. 15 Front
Camp & Welles. 118 Broad
Carter Henry, 28 Moore
Cartwright, Harrison & Co. 111
    Front
Case & Freeman, 101 Front
Chenery & Johnson, 28½ Front
Clapp John F. & Co. 31 Coenties
    slip
Clark & Coleman, 18 South
Cobb James N. 21 South
Collins A. T. & J. W. 23 Coenties
    slip
Conduit & Noble, 16 Water
Cooper Charles, 9 Coenties slip
Cornell T. F. cor. Water & Coenties slip
Cowing & Co. 10 South
Cox & Truslow, 120 Broad
Darling, Albertson & Rose, 23
    Water
Darling & Johnson, 26 Water
Davis James, 2 Coenties slip
Demarest & Hoyt, 122 West
Dodge S. V. 3 Clinton market
Doremus & Crane, 20 Front
Dows & Cary, 20 South
Dows & Guiteau, 119 Broad
Dunham E. W. 5 South
Durant, Lathrop & Co. 7 South
Dwight & Johnson, 104 Broad
Elliott V. 201 Washington
Fenby Aquilla M. 36 Front
Ferguson & Sherman, 6 Front
Ferris George B. 37   do
Ferris O. L. & A. & Co. 33 Front
Fish E. & Co. 11 South
Ford & Raynolds, 80 Cortlandt
Gates P. D. 31 Coenties slip
Gibson, Stockwell & Co. 35 Pearl
Gilbert & Tomkins, 25 South
Goff & Constable, 14 Water
Gray Morgan, 15 South
Griffin John, 261 Washington
Hale & Himrod, 110 Warren
Hand James. 16 Coenties slip
Hannahs William, 32 Water
Havens H. P. & Son, 434 Water
Heaton William C. 31 Front
Heirshow C. H. 488 Cherry
Herrick Jacob B. 11 Coenties slip
Herrick Josiah & S. D. 28 Water
Herrick Stephen D. 28 Water
Herrick & Vanboskerck, 121 Broad
Higgins, Brown & Shields, 29 Front
Hillyer Vergil. 7 Coenties slip
Hinds Jesse, 7 South
Hoagland J. S. & Son, 142 Clinton
Hodges C. H. 86 Front
Hollister Charles, 197 Broad
Hotaling Samuel, 16 Front
Hubbard N. T. & Sons, 27 Front
Hulbert William & Co. 28 do
Hunter W. C. & A. A. 20 South
Hyslop & Coffin, 43 Front
Jewell, Harrison & Co. 27 Water
Johnson Dwight, 104 Broad
Johnson Leonard L. 111 Broad
Jones & Himrod, 3 Water
Keeler James R. & Co. 109 Front

Ketchum Joseph & Son, 34 Front
    New York.
Kitching John B. 47 Pearl
Lathers Richard, 57 Broad
Lawrence Ferdinand, 80 Broad
Lenthem & Thompson, 96 Wall
Leland. Adams & Co. 18 South
Ludlam & Leggett, 36 Front
M'Bride, Sheldon & Co. 102 Broad
M'Feat James, 3 Murray
Magee Thomas H. 26 S. William
Mason F. & Son, 12 Front
Mathews Charles D. 61 Pearl
Mercer W. R. cor. Coenties slip
    & Water
Mettler Enoch, 267 Front
Mills L. A. 39 Water
More D. L. & G. D. 267 W'hington
Morgan M. C. & Co. 66 Dey
Morrison & Hyde, 278 W'hington
Nason Henry, 23 Water
Nevius Peter I. & Son, 11 South
Norton John W. 10 South
Otis Austin W. & Co. 61 Pearl
Otis & Co. 14 Front
Paik Jas. S. 30 Moore
Parker & Conover, 31 Moore
Pavenstedt E. & Schumacher, 38
    New
Perry Samuel, 3 Front & 28 More
Peaks & Myers, 114 Broad
Phillips & Aborn, 108 Broad
Pickett Sears & Co. 69 Cortlandt
Pidgeon Peter, 17 Water
Platt Wm. H. & Brother, 47 Pearl
    & 24 Bridge
Powers & Fuller, 65 Dey
Powell M. M. 125 Broad
Rea Samuel, 27 Water
Reed Silas. 216 Washington
Reeve Timothy W. 30 Water
Rice J. 109 Broad
Robertson & Polhemus, 82 Beaver
Rogers Samuel T. 23 South
Rowe, Woodruff & Carter 178
    Washington
Rowland Jas. 78 Cortlandt
Schiffer I. & Brother, 184 Front
Scudder John H. 12 Front
Shotwell & Doscher, 224 Washington
Skeats Schuyler, 1 Water
Smith C. W. 116 Broad
Smith Adam & Co. 26 Front
Smith N. & J 236 Fulton
Snyder John W. 211 Washington
Snyder E. & J. A. 13 S. William
Southwick John. 38 Front
Southworth, Litchfield & Beach,
    5 Coenties slip
Stevenson & Stafford, 110 Warren
Stewart Cornelius, 64 Dey
Sturges & Co. 6 South
Sturtevant D. & A. 142 Washington
Suydam. Sage & Co. 2 & 3 South
Taylor Charles, 27 Water
Thomas & Davenport, 7 & 9 Water
Thorne John W. 118 Broad
Tompkins & Co. 23 Water
Trowbridge Timothy, 122 Front
Turnbull & Seckler, 100 Greenwich
Vail I. W. & Co. 22 Pearl
Vannortwick Wm. B. 13 Front
Wallace, Wickes & Co. 11 Front
Ward & Cady. 207 Washington
Warren, Clark & Co. 263 Washington
Waterhouse & Lynn, 5 South
Weeks & Douglass, 127 Broad
White T. R. & Co. 17 Pearl, 10
    Bridge & 15 Water
Willson & Sherman, 10 Broad
Wilson John, 439 Cherry
Williams Isaac B. 114 Warren
Winder Wm. H. 120 Broad
Wolfe N. H. 17 South
Woodward Jas. 17 Water
Work & Drake, 31 Water
Wright John B. & Co. 9 South
Wright & Losee, 18 Front

Merchants—Shipping & Commission.

(See Packet Offices, also Agents, Passenger, also Steamship companies.)

Ackerman S. H. 107 Water
    New York
Adams & Hawthorn, 51 South
Alexandre Francis, 26 South
Aranguren Antonio, 77 South
Arnold Isaac C. 259 Front
Aymar & Co. 34 South
Barstow & Pope. 98 Pine
Beach John N. 26 Front
Bectel & Dreyer. 81 Beaver
Bedel Mott. 104 Wall
Benson Alfred G. 39 South
Boeth & Edgar. 95 Front
Bossange Edouard, 99 Wall
Bostock William & James, 11
    Front
Bouchand, Thebaud & Co 25 Old
    slip
Brett & Vose, 26 South
Brigham & Carhart, 94 Front
Brower John H. 45 South
Buchanan, Harris & Co. Post's
    building
Buck Richard P. & Co. 29 South
Byrnes P. W. & Co. 83 South
Cachard Edward. 70 Broad
Chamberlin & Phelps, 103 Front
Champlin Christopher, 174 Front
Catheal & Co. 49 Water
Coe, Anderson & Co. 10 Beaver
Coffin Edwin, 28 South
Creagh & Heydecker, 24 S. Wm.
Crocker & Warren. 18 Beaver
Culbert & Finlay, 24 Old slip
Daly J. T. 106 Wall
Davis Samuel G. 43 New
Dawson William, 70 Broad
Deen & Thornton, 85 Water
De Forest William W. & Co. 82
    South
De Jonge, Brothers & Co. 102
    Wall
Delafield Henry & Wm. 79 Front
Dellinger Charles, 89 Beaver
Demill & Co. 186 Front
Doherty James, 43 New
Dowley John, 74 South
Dutilh & Cousinery, 23 S. William & 43 Stone
Eagle & Hazard, 40 South
Edes Peter, 89 Front
Eilshemius H. G. 2 Jones' lane
Elkins George B. 69 South
Elwell James W. 57 South
Eisinwein Fredk. West 13th st.
Everett & Brown. 68 South
Faber & Bierwith, 40 New
Farnham G. I. & Co. 85 Pearl
Floyd Samuel, 37 William
Foster Horatio & Co. 114 Wall
Foster & M'Kinson, 25 South
Foulke Joseph & Sons, 46 South
Fowler F. & D. 86 West
Fox & Livingston, 22 Broad
Frost & Hicks, 68 South
Goff Richard N. 37 Front
Goodhue & Co. 64 South
Grinnell, Minturn & Co. 78 South
Hargous Brothers, 33 South
Harnden & Co. 6 Wall
Hayes O. J. 174 Front
Heerdt Clement, 23 Old slip
Henschen & Ukart, 17 S. William
Hicks & Co. 80 South
Hill John S. 91 Front
Hoppock Ely, 30 South
Horn A. F. M. 97 Wall
Howes, Godfrey & Co. 26 South
Rowland William H. 186 South
Rowland & Aspinwall, 54 & 55
    South
Hunter James & Co. 153 Maiden
    lane
Hunter W. C. & A. A. 20 South
Hurlbut E. D. & Co. 84 South
Hussey & Murray, 62 South

Innes Edward S. & Co. 103 Water
   New York.
Irving Richard, 96 Front
Jeannerett James M. & Co. 94
   Wall
Jones Joshua T. 90 Wall
Johnson & Lowden, 115 Wall
Kane Pierre C. 75 Broad
Kermit Robert. 76 South
Kimball E. W. & Co. 92 Wall
Kitching John B. 47 Pearl
Kunkelmann James C. 47 New
Kursheedt Asher, 107 Water
Lawrie G. & J. & Co. 72 Merch.
   Exchange
Leland & Beach, 159 Front & 236
   South
Lewis Starks W. 24 South & 26
   Coenties slip
Lewis J. T. & Co. 82 Water
Lienau M. 2 Jones lane
M'Bride George, jr. 44 Broadway
M'Cready N. L. & Co. 36 South
M'Gaw John A. 43 South
M'Gaw Robert. 21 Front
M'Kee William J. & Brother, 42
   Front
M'Murray Joseph, 69 South
March Clement D. 4 Jones' lane
Marean Thomas, 89 Front
Marshall C. H. & Co. 38 Burling
   slip
Merian & Benard, 20 South William
Meyer & Stucken, 34 New
Milu George, 22 South William
Montgomery, Brothers & Co. 106
   Broad
Moring H. E. 97 Wall
Nelson William, 85 South
Nottebohm Augustus. 90 Front
Ogden David, 65 Wall
Ogden John. 116 Wall
Olney & Cotrell. 61 South
Phillips James W. 52 South
Pilkington Daniel, 94 Wall
Pillsbury & Sanford, 39 South
Poirier Freres, 52 New
Post Ralph. 33 South
Prulax Louis, 100 Wall
Rea William & Co. 50 Wall
Read Rufus C. 27 South
Richards Abraham, 135 Front
Richards Benjamin. 46 South
Richardson Edward & Co, 52 South
Richardson, Watson & Co. 41 & 43
   Exchange place
Robinson Robert F. 30 Moore
Robinson & Weir, 18 Beaver
Rodewald Brothers, 20 Beaver
Russell & Buck, 31 Old slip
Russell & Norton, 31 Old slip
Saul Edward, 82 South
Schmidt & Balchen, 105 & 107
   Wall
Simonds Frederick W. 43 New
Smith Isaac T. 101 Wall & 114
   Front
Smith James T. 174 Front
Southmayd Horace & Son, · 147
   Maiden lane
Spofford, Tileston & Co. 48 South
Stanton Thomas P. 55 South
Stanton & Spicer, 86 West
Tapscott W. & J. T. 86 South
Taylor John J. & Co. 41 South
Taylor Moses & Co. 44 South
Taylor & Merrill, 36 Burling slip
Thallon & Tait, 12 Old slip
Thompson Jonathan, 47 South
Thompson Samuel & Nephew, 275
   Pearl
Thompson G. W. 47 South
Thompson & Hunter, 23 South
Tooker, Smyth & Co. 57 South
Townsend George E. 165 Front
Tracy Samuel F. 6 Beaver
Trimble Geo. T. 157 Maiden lane
Trimble Merritt, 157   do
Trowbridge T. 122 Front
Trundy R. W. & Co. 27 Coenties
   slip

Tucker & Lightbourn, 22 Front
   New York.
Underwood H. 113 Wall
Wardle Thomas, 88 South
Whitlock Wm. jr. 46 South
Whitmore Isaiah C. 47 South
Williams & Guion, 40 Fulton
Wilson & Brown, 83 Beaver
Winslow Thomas S. 113 Wall
Wood Fernando, 162 South
Woodhull Albert, 87 South

Merchants—Shipping and Importing.

Atwater Elisha M. 32 Cliff
   New York.
Averill A. & Co. 47 South
Bartlett Edwin. 42 South
Bleidorn Henry, 76 Broad
Brockelmann T. & J. 38 New
Browne Martin, 69 South
Burlage Radolph C. 94 Wall
Chamberlain & Phelps, 102 Front
Corning H. K. 72 South
Crocker & Warren, 18 Beaver
Dunscomb & Beckwith, 50 Wall
Gordon & Talbot, 156 Maiden lane
Gowdy H. 56 Front
Griswold Nathaniel L. & George,
   72 South
Harbeck & Co. 60 Wall
Harmony's Peter Nephews & Co.
   63½ Broadway
Isaacs Solomon J. 215 Water
M'Crakan John L. H. 43 New
Moore John A. 77 Water
Robinson James, 81 Front
Schuchardt & Gebhard, 21 Nassau
Thurston Frederick G. & Co. 49
   South
Youngs, Hawkins & Co. 41 South

Metal Dealers.

Bruce's John M. Sons, 192 Water
   New York.
Coddington T. B. 65 Broad
Fenn G. & Co. 39 Spruce
Hart Lucius, 6 Burling slip
Hendrick & Brothers, 79 Broad
Hills & Clarke, 129 Water
Isaacs S. I. 215 Water
Miller, Coates & Youle, 275 Pearl
Moore John A. 77 Water
Phelps, Dodge & Co. 19 Cliff
Seixas Theodore J. 215 Water
Stokes, Gilbert & Co. 26 Cliff

Metal Sashes.

Coombs & Anderton, 209 Grand &
   85 Mercer   *New York.*

Military Goods. (*See also Feathers, Military & Fancy.*)

Bell Joseph T. 186 Fulton
   New York.
Boland Lewis P. 7 Dey
Cooper Garrett, 162 & 196 Fulton
Delapierre Bartholomew, 476½
   Broadway
Dingee R. & H. A. 56 Frankfort
Gratacap H. T. 392 Broadway
Horstmann, Sons & Drucker, 8
   Maiden lane
Pittman John I. 56 Frankfort
Ryer John B. 612 Broadway
Shiers Andrew M. 121 Fulton
Smith J. S. 139 Fulton
Smith Wm. H. 4 Maiden lane

Milk, Butter, &c.
(*Marked thus * deal in Milk only.*)

Kings County.

Jackson John H. 75 Jay *Brooklyn.*

Adams A. 197 Pearl   *Brooklyn.*
Rodgers M. R. 119 Bridge
Fossett J. & A. 196 Myrtle Av

New York County.

Ackerman Nicholas, 40 Cornelia
   New York.
Alexander David, 19 Prince
Archer Moses, 258 Delancy
Armstrong T. 146 W. Broadway
Aylward James, 22 Madison
Bachman John A. 336 6th
Baker George, 159 Prince
*Ball Augustus, 259 Centre
Ball Philip, 237 W. 16th
Bartlett Samuel T. 552 4th
Bigley Richard. 211 Duane
Birdsell S. C. 186 3d
Bishop John, 289 Walker
Bloom John, 267 3d
Bluderoek John, 71 Av. A
Bowron William L., E. 23d bet. 3d
   & 4th Avs.
Brave F. 166 3d
Brooks William D. 6 Walnut
Brunn Geo. 223 Houston
Bronson Thomas. 122 Orange
Bryan John, 126 Delancy
Buker George, 159 Prince
Bulkley Rebecca, 685 4th
Bush Peter, 89 Hamersley
Butts John C. 2 Clinton market'
Caldwell David. 291 W. 18th
Camp Charles, 263 Spring
Carpenter David P. 613 Greenwich
Carpenter Spencer, 72 Grove
Carr B. J. 8th Av.
Clark James H. 252 Delancy
Clifford Patrick, 38 Mott
Coleman James C. 253 Stanton
Coles J. 133 Hammond
Conger Daniel J. 70 Houston
Conselyea William, 220 Broome
Cooke Charles, 213 Stanton
Cooke Charles, 502½ Houston
Corcoran Michael, 248 Mott
Cordey Tobias, 50 Mott
Corey Peter, 100 Delancy
Coregriff Andrew, 11 Av. B
Corwin John, 27 Charles
Coyne L. 10th Av. near W. 16th
Cragan Patrick, 6 3d Av.
Cropsey H. 34 5th
Crygier G. A. 44 Broome
Cullen James, 232 5th
Curran Richard, 309 Broome
Daly P. Av. A. near E. 18th
Daly Martin, 515 Washington
Daly Michael, 469   do
Daly Thomas, 81 King
Danneman Jacob, 67 Av. A
Day Joseph, 191 Church
Degroat Abram, 154 Perry
Dennis Wm. H. 123 W. Broadway
Devine James, 90 Cannon
Devoe Joseph, 118 Greenwich Av.
Dodd Daniel, 88 Mott
Donaldson William, 83 Houston
Doscher Claus, 141 Monroe
Dowt Catharine, 140 Amos
Doyle William, 81 Ludlow
Dunahoe John. 20 Av. A
Dunn Dennis, 109 Perry
Eckerson Salome, 267 3d Av.
Emmons George, 176 Christopher
Eumons Hetty, 263 Spring
*Estrane Cornelius, 140 Orange
Farley John, 135 Houston
Farley Peter, 99 Allen
Field C. 136 8th Av.
Field William A. 346 6th Av.
Flanagan J. 10th Av. cor. W. 16th
Flanegan Martin, 478 Washington
Flood Michael. 195 Varick
Fowell William, 370 Madison
Fritz Lewis. 180 Rivington
Fuller M. 9th Av. 22d
Gaunt Mary A. 179½ Hester
Gillespie Peter, 160 W. 16th
Gordy Fred. 291 Av. A
Goth George, 500 4th

Gould Letitia, 117 Charlton
        New York.
Gowers William H. 18 Downing
Griffiths Lemuel. 378 Cherry
Graham James, 224 W. 16th
Hackett Patrick. 42 Mulberry
Haines Sarah. 133 Spring
Hamilton Mary, 144 Varick
Harrisson George, 476 Pearl
Haymes Selina. 79 6th Av.
Healy E. 159 Bowery
Heinmann George. 116 Willet
Henderson Thomas S. 327 6th
*Herring Samuel, 162 Hammond
Hosier & Hopper, 158 9th Av.
Hughes James, 16th near 10th Av.
Hughes Mathew, 469 Grand
Hughes Michael. 16 Hester
Jarvis Edmond. 517 Broome
Jarvis Henry, 96 9th Av.
Johnson Bridget. 8 Elizabeth
Keegan James, 44 Factory
Kennedy Rhode, W. 15th near 10th
        Av.
Kenney Michael. 176 Broome
Kirby Lavina, 236 Broome
Kuhn Daniel, 361 Houston
Leach John, 408 Cherry
Ledwith Christopher,131 Anthony
Leimtail David, 231 Av. B
Lester Charles, 235 Rivington
Lilly P. 14 Elm
Lotrup Maria, 43 Monroe
Lewis Edward, 13 Eldridge
Lewis William, 118 7th Av.
Lilly John, 17 Desbrosses
Lloyd Nancy, 141 Sullivan
Lynch John. 377 Broome
Lynch Walter, 272 W. 17th
M'Allister James H. 164 Suffolk
M'Avoy E. 496 Greenwich
M'Cormac Rosanna, 37 W. 13th
M'Dougal Christian B. 8 5th
*M'Dowell Alexander, 94 Henry
M'Genn Margaret, 12th bet. Avs.
        A & B.
M'Ilvoy James, W. 15th near 10th
        Av.
M'Menomy Patrick. 30 Chrystie
M'Millen John, 71 Vandam
M'Quade James, 92 Perry
Madden Francis, 242½ 7th
Madeby Edward, 89 Orange
Magnan Patrick, 121 Cherry
Mekl George, 189 Av. B
Melkenger Matthew, 161 Broome
Menk Claus, W. 15th near 10th
        Av.
Miles Benjamin J. C. 215 Greene
Moger Wm. T. 197 3d Av.
Montford Allen, 204 7th
Montross Tyson, 203 2d Av.
Mooney Daniel, 196 Varick
Moore J. 276 3d Av.
Morrow John, 80 Charlton
Morris Gouverneur, 170 9th
Morris John, 37 Elm
Munter F. 174 3d
Murphy James, 135 Clinton
Murphy Mary, 341 Madison
Murphy Timothy, 28 Leonard
Murray James, 6 Monroe
Myer John, 46 Av. B
Myers Paul C. 617 4th
Nealy Alexander, 180 W. 18th
Newman Jane, 4 Franklin
Newman Morris, 113 Av. C
Oakley Charles J. 186 2d
Odell James S. 3 Christopher
Oglesby James, 163 Varick
O'Neill Hugh, 5 Monroe
Onsted George O. 541 Hudson
Onstead John, 733 Washington
Orange Milk and Butter Associa-
        tion, 177 Reade
Ongier F. A. 5 Av. C
Pardee James A. L. 130 Suffolk
Peck Horace, 321 Spring
Peters Mary, 180½ Varick
Plumer Thomas, 119 Greene
Piatt John E. 232 Canal
Quin James, 137 Leonard

Reinhart Michael, 221 Stanton
        New York.
Rhuton Daniel A. 148 Christopher
Riebar Jacob, 95 Norfolk
Riley John, 65 Charlton
Roach Edward J. 206 Elizabeth
Roberts Robert, W. 15th n. 10th
        Av.
Robinson John H. 87 Bedford
Rogers Thomas, 84 Lewis
Rohe Henry, 196 Ridge
Ruch Jacob, Av. A. bet. E. 13th
        & E. 14th
Savage Ann, 55 Greene
Schoepps Nicholas, 67 Av A.
Seaman Elias, 145 W. 20th
Seaman Hannah, 154 Broome
Seaman Isaac, 27 Wash. mkt
Searle James, 221 Delancy
Sears David E. 69 Cortlandt
Sefton Mary, 67 Lewis
Shaughnessy Ellen, 122 Perry
Shaw David, 214 8th Av.
Shuck Fred. 239½ 3d
Shepard Richard, 347 Pearl
Sheridan Thomas, 4 M'Dougall
Sherry James, 361 Monroe
Slaight Israel L. 90 Thompson
Slote Joseph, 461 4th
Smith Charles, 71 9th Av.
Smith Horace, foot Duane N. R.
Smith W. C. & J. B. 186 8th Av.
Smith & Clark, 96 Av. D
Smith John, 199 Delancy
Springsteen John, 132 Charles
Springated Spencer, 122 Stanton
Stevens Coleman. 29 Whitehall
Stevens John, 520 Greenwich
Sturges Edward G. 84 3d Av.
Symes William, 65 W. Broadway
Talman Harriet, 125 Amity
Thomas John, 15th n. 10th Av.
Thomas Lewis, 209 W. 16th
Thompson George, 87 7th Av.
Tiebout Francis, 10th Av. n. 15th
Tompkins Noah, 178 Allen
Tranor Mary, 79 Charlton
Van Buren John, 38 M'Dougal
Watts Chas. F. 133 Washington
Welch James, 48 Ridge
Weller Wm. 51 Bedford
Wells Isaac, 31 Suffolk
Wertheimer Max. 176 Stanton
Wintermute J. 733 Washington
White Gabriel, 63 Orchard
Wolf Benjamin, 63 Suffolk
Wood Henry, 197 Reade
Wright Stephen, 127 Amos
Young Lewis, 221 Rivington

Milliners. *(See also Millinery
and Fancy Goods.)*

Albany County.

Blanchard I. W. 515 Broadway
        Albany.
Mochair Mrs. 615 Broadway
Purcell Mrs. F. 704 do
Gracie Mrs. 608   do
Mylet Mrs. M. 202   do
Burnop Miss, 30 Hudson
Davidson Miss, 46 do
Harris Mrs, 45 Greene
Braytons Misses, 47 Green
Quayle Mrs. 207 South Pearl
Porter Mrs D. 230   do
Keeler Mrs. C. 105 Lydius
Clark Mrs. R. 74 South Pearl
Gill Mrs. E. 69   do
Armington Mrs. C. 54 do
Singer Miss H. 50   do
Waterman Miss M.20   do
Tillapaugh Miss H. 18 do
Wolfey Mrs. H. E. 6½ do
Ellis Miss S. 4   do
Getty Miss E. 36½   do
M'Kinney Mrs. E. S. 44 do
Creswell Mrs. S. 12 do
Carbury Mrs. W. 88   do
Boyd Mrs. M. 31 Green
Law Miss, 88 North Pearl

Gilmore L. 27 N. Pearl   *Albany.*
Newton Miss R. 8 do
Ferguson Mrs. 48 Chapel
Kimball Miss H. 86 Washington
Chamberlain Miss, West Troy
        Waterviiet
Lenway Mrs. H. West Troy
Moe Miss, Cohoes

Alleghany County.

Van Campen Mrs.   *Almond.*
Larrabee Miss
Clark Mrs.   *Andover.*
Waggoner Mrs. Nancy *Angelica.*
Havens Miss Ann
Bullard Mrs. J. J.   *
Heath Miss   *Belfast.*
M'Dougal Miss Sarah *Clarksville.*
Coburn Mrs.   *Cuba.*
Lloyd Mrs.   *Friendship.*
Richards Miss Sarah *Rushford.*
Niver Miss L.   *Wirt.*

Broome County.

Barton Miss   *Binghamton*
Cox ——
Wells Mrs. W. H.
Westcott Mrs. S. Ann
Chamberlain Mrs.
Butler Mrs. L. A.
Crosby Miss E. Harpersville
        Colesville.

Cattaraugus County.

Wilson Betsey. Sandusky *Freedom.*
Alling Miss Julia   *New Albion.*
Curtiss Miss C. Gowanda *Persia.*
Johnson Miss Mary. do
Thompson Miss Jane,do
Olan Miss Catherine, do
Waterman Miss D.   do
King Mrs. H.   *Randolph.*
Shattuck Miss Sophia
Hollister Mrs. J.
Thorp Miss C. East Randolph
Chamberlain Mrs. B. F. do

Cayuga County.

Walter Mrs. 57 Genesee *Auburn.*
Gates Miss S. 70   do
Sheer Miss L. 68   do
Everts Mrs. J. 68   do
Gates Miss M. & Co. 77 Genesee

Chautauqua County.

Sherman Mrs. J. P. Jamestown
        Ellicott.
Ford Mrs. Milton,   do
Southland Mrs. J.   do
Avery Mrs., Irving . *Hanover*

Chemung County. .

Oliver Mrs.   *Elmira.*
Drake Miss
Kane Mrs.
Hills M. E.
Hurd Miss S. & Co.
Grover Mrs.

Chenango County.

Packard Miss A.   *Bainbridge.*
Tuncliff Miss Mary *Sherburne.*
Knapp Mrs.
Poltney Miss S.

Columbia County.

Branch Mrs. North Chatham
        Chatham.
Parker Mrs. H. H. Chatham Four
        Corners
Irish Mrs. Malden Bridge
Smith Mrs. M. A. Warren st.
        Hudson.
Edwards Miss, Warren st.
Best Mrs.   do
Tompkins Mrs. N. 319 Warren
Capron Miss, 306   do
Bostwick Miss C. W. do

Newman Mrs. A. P. 286 Warren
    Hudson
Lay Mrs. Eliza. do
Fellows Mrs. 226 do
Miller Mrs. P. do
Phillips Mrs. *Kinderhook.*
Hoxie Mrs.
Stickles Mrs.
Penniman Miss A. M. Valatie
Cowan Miss Jane, do
Bedell Mrs. E. N. *Stuyvesant.*

Cortland County.

Darling Mrs. E. *Cortland Village.*
Rose Mrs. J.
Seaman Mrs. J. M.
M'Clary Miss C.
Freer Miss I.

Delaware County.

Sullivan Misses *Davenport.*
Knapp Miss E. *Delhi.*
Gray Miss M.
Burchard Miss M. B. *Meredith.*
Jones Miss M., Hobart *Stamford.*
Burch Miss L., Deposit *Tompkins.*
Leach Miss, do
Tiffany Miss D. *Walton.*
Crawley Miss A.

Duchess County.

Brett Miss, Matteawan *Fishkill.*
Ball Mrs. Fishkill Landing
Carman Miss E. Stormville
Marshall Mrs. *Hyde Park.*
Weeks Mrs. 214 Main *Poughkeepsie.*
Schriver Mrs. 300 Main
Denton M. & M. 278 do
Woolsey Miss. 325 do
Barker Mrs. 321 do
Odell Miss, do
Stanton Mrs. E. 309½ Main
Bates Mrs. 307 Main
Hevenoe Miss H. *Red Hook.*
Nix Miss R.
Bird Miss L. & C. *Rhinebeck.*
Rockwell Miss
Tripp Miss F. *Stamford.*

Erie County.

Warner Mrs., Springville
    Concord.
Lawrence Mrs. Hamburgh Centre
    Hamburgh.

Essex County.

Kneeland Miss *Elizabethtown.*
Green Miss Mary Ann, Moriah
Four Corners *Moriah.*
Hadaway Huldah, Moriah Four
Corners
Stack Miss do

Genesee County.

Denslow J. J. *Batavia.*
Blake Mrs. A. M.
Griffith Mrs. O.
Shoreman & Halbert Misses
Clark Mrs. T. P. *Le Roy.*
Olmstead Miss L.

Greene County.

Nearings Misses *Catskill.*
Bellamy R.
Thorp A.

Herkimer County.

Lawton Mrs. *Herkimer.*
Snyders Misses, Van Hornsville
    Stark.
Bouck Miss, Jordanville *Warren.*

Jefferson County.

Allen Miss *Brownville.*
Huntington Mrs., Dexter
Timmerman Mrs. M. *Theresa.*
Lashley Miss

Newcomb Mrs. Hiram *Watertown.*
Morgan Mrs. C.
Graves Miss M. L.

Kings County.

Warwick Miss E. 131 Atlantic
    Brooklyn.
Gordon Mrs. Mary J. 179 Atlantic
Wellman Miss L. 8. 58 Atlantic
Schofield Mrs. F. 204 Atlantic
Cadley Mrs. M. J. 3 Clinton
Hawes Mrs. E. 93 Fulton
Desendorf & Co. 99 Fulton
M'Creery Mrs. 93 Main
Holmes Miss L. 243 Fulton
Tassy Miss E. 217 do
Jones Mrs. Mary, 191 do
White Misses, 181 do
Quigg Mrs. M. A.56½ Hudson Av.
Beohm Miss M. 272 Grand
    Williamsburgh.
Phillips Mrs. E. 146 Grand
Downy Ann, 2d st.

Livingston County.

Blakeslee Mrs. M. B. *Caledonia.*
Armstrong Miss E. *Dansville.*
Robinson Miss
Burns Miss
Hedges Mrs.
Stacy Mrs.
Robinson Miss Elmira C. *Geneseo.*
Bishop Miss Betsy L.
Stedman Mrs A. N.
Galaway Mrs., Cuylerville
    Leicester.
Ames & Potter Misses
    Mount Morris.
Newton Miss Sophia *Nunda.*
Sherwood Mrs. J.
Tuthill & Jones Misses
Norton Miss Lavina *Springwater.*
May Mrs. E.

Madison County.

Blood Mrs. *Cazenovia.*
Ham Miss S. G.
Osborn Miss
Matthews Miss *Eaton.*
Hatch Miss
Crandall Miss, Morrisville
Fairchild Mrs. *Hamilton.*
Shapley Mrs.
Rice Mrs.
Hall Mrs.
Mitchell Miss, Earlville
Graham Misses, Canastota *Lenox.*
Raymond Miss, do
Rice Mrs. Chittenango *Sullivan.*
Jennings Mrs. do

Monroe County.

Tobey Mrs. 14 Elm *Rochester.*
Dawson Mrs. 3 North St. Paul
Jones Mrs. 10 S. Clinton
Harris Mrs. 5 do
Sulley Mrs. cor. Chestnut & Court
Merritt Miss, 116 Main

Montgomery County.

Crabtree Miss *Amsterdam.*
Wybourn Mrs.
Hinchman Mrs.
Eagan Mrs.
Gleason Mrs. *Canajoharie.*
Burley Miss E.
Ehle Misses
Gleason Miss Almira, Fort Plain
    Minden.
Flint Mrs., Fort Plain
Ransom Mrs. do
Gross Louisa, do
Cross Mrs. Susan, Fonda *Mohawk.*
Jones Mrs. M. L. do
Beeker Miss E. do
Schenck Mrs. A. do
Snell Miss *St. Johnsville.*

New York County.

Ackenbeck Margaret, 96 Charles
    New York.
Ackerman Mary, 266 8th Av.
Ajax Rebecca. 114 Hudson
Annin C. E. 197 Christopher
Armstrong Eliza, 13 Minetta
Arnold Maria, 384 Grand
Atchinson Mrs. 145 Houston
Ayers Maria. 21 Marion
Babcock Lucinda S. 299½ B'way
Baird Miss, 559 6th Av.
Baker S. A. 113½ Division
Ball Martha. 35 Carmine
Beaks Ann, 352 Houston
Barnett Sarah. 259 & 294 Hudson
Barnum P. R. 66 White
Barr Mrs. 90 Av. B
Batschelet Mary, 30½ Carmine
Bayer George. 47 Division
Behrman Emelia. 265 Hudson
Bairne J. 157 Greenwich
Belden Mrs. 70 Gold
Binns Isaac. 309 Hudson
Binns Louisa, 564 Broadway
Bird Miss, 205 8th Av.
Blake Sophia C. 196 Bowery
Boardman Mary E. 45 Carmine
Bogle S. M. 3 Amity
Bonner Rebecca, 815 Broadway
Boosey Elizabeth, 234 Greenwich
Boughton A. 114 Orchard
Bovee Balphame, 37 Division
Boyd Susan. 23½ do
Boyle Anne, 25 Park place
Brabham Alice, 122 E. 20th
Bracher Thomas. 2 5th
Britton Mrs. 557 Hudson
Brown Peter, 16 Av. A
Brunelle Elizabeth C. 36 8th Av.
Brunner Josephine, 438 Broadway
Bryant Amanda, 466 Grand
Bugard Almira, 239 2d
Byrne Lucy A. 25 Division
Cabray Mary, 9th Av. 30th
Callaghan Ellen. 74 Henry
Calyer Phebe, 435½ Pearl
Campbell M. A. 663 Houston
Cane C. 28 Commerce
Carney Wm. H. 6 Thomas
Carpenter Cath. F. 266 Bowery
Carstang Mary, 292 6th Av.
Casllear Ann E. 190 Grand
Cass James, 227 Division
Cater Sarah, 94 11th
Chailly A. 166½ Bowery
Chevalier Josephine, 53 Av. C
Childs Mrs. 416 Grand
Church Wm. 283 & 282 Hudson
Clark Mary L. 51 Division
Claughley Almyra E. 245 Bowery
Coates Jane, 13 Carmine
Cocker Ellen, 274 Bowery
Coe Harriet, 512 Hudson
Coe Mary, 18 Greenwich Av.
Cogswell Catharine J. 262 Walker
Coleman Hester, 3 Jones
Conacher John, 239 8th Av.
Cook Amelia, 476 Grand
Cordell Orvila K. 5 Park place
Covel H. G. 78 8th Av.
Cox Almira, 66½ Division
Cox George, 286 Grand
Cranston Mary, 284 Greenwich
Cunningham Sarah, 294½ Grand
Daly C. & J. 465 Broadway
Darrow Margaret, 24½ Bowery
Davids & Hart, 160 Spring
Davidson Mrs. 131 Canal
Davis Mary, 265 3d
Deuel Caroline R. 369 Broadway
Dey Ann H. 666 Greenwich
Dickey & Mondell, 150 Spring
Donald E. 519½ Greenwich
Doom Alice, 9th Av. near 15th st.
Dorsey Louisa, 513 Broadway
Doran Mrs. 200 3d Av.
Droomgole ——. 33 Varick
Dolbeer Ann M. 463½ Hudson
Downes Anna M. 145 Spring
Downes Elizabeth, 59 Charlton

Creyfus Abraham, 63½ Division
New York.
Dryden Geo. 63 Canal
Du Bois Mary, 13 Greenwich Av.
Dudley Margaret, 179 W. 30th
Dwyer Susannah. 33 Clarkson
Edmondson Elizab. 71½ Bowery
Egan Patrick. 429 Grand
Erskine M. 213 8th Av.
Falconer Cath 151 Greenwich
Falconer Cath. 653 Broadway
Fendall Julia D. 259½ Hudson
Ferrero Jane, 339 Broadway
Finch Phebe. 17½ Division
Finiels J. 119 Grand
Flandrews J. D. 236 Bowery
Frazier Rachael, 493 Broadway
Freund Ira. 189 Houston
Furlong Nancy J. 463 Broadway
Fulton Rebecca J. 157 Houston
Gale Wm. 111 Orange
Gallaghan Mary, 130 10th Av.
Gardner E. A. 44 8th Av.
Gatfield Phebe. 457 Pearl
George Mary, 49 4th
Gibson J. 394 Bleecker
Gibney Catharine. 43½ Division
Gilbert Mary E. 445½ Pearl
Gilmore Mrs. 308 6th Av.
Gleason Jane A. 106 Perry
Godfrey Ferdinand, 349 Br'dway
Goetz Jacob, 12 Av. A
Gordon Elizabeth. 311 Broadway
Gordon Miss, 43 Carmine
Gough M. 263 6th Av.
Graham Jane A. 130 Liberty
Grange Mrs. 400 Hudson
Gray Rosaline, 36 8th Av.
Grant Caroline, 45 8th Av.
Greasley Mary, 283 Bowery
Gregory A Hoyt, 388 Grand
Gregory Mrs, 19 Lewis
Greer Robert, 260 Bleecker
Groom Elizabeth, 299½ Broadway & 50 Warren
Gruman Eliza, 249 9th Av.
Haas Wm 402½ Grand
Haddock Misses. 11 8th Av.
Haff Sarah A. 157 9th
Hall Mrs. 363 Pearl
Hall Adeline, 108½ Bowery
Halliday Margaret, 3 Catharine
Haley Mrs. 403 Pearl
Hamilton H. 519½ Greenwich
Hamilton Martha. 431 Pearl
Hammond Catharine, 441½ Pearl
Hardenbrook Henrietta, 194 Grand
Hard N. G. 311 Bowery
Harger Mary, 496 Grand
Harker Lydia, 19½ Division
Harrison V. P. 69½ Division
Hart Matilda J. 301 Broadway
Hart E. & H. 361 Bleecker
Haulenbeck Maria, 197 Madison
Haws Mrs. 371 Broadway
Haws John, 27½ Division
Hawhurst Amy, 43 Henry
Healy E. & J. 157½ Greenwich
Heather W. J. 55 Canal
Hedges Anne, 297 Hudson
Heller J. 381 Grand
Heep Misses, 363 Broadway
Henderson Catharine, 427 Grand
Henricks Esther, 190 Canal
Henricks Charlotte, 170 2d
Henrion Charlotte, 69 White
Handelbach Chas. 356 Houston
Higelow M. M. 413 Pearl
Higgins Michael, 21½ Division
Hinckley C. A. 213 3d Av.
Hitchcock Mary, 367 Broadway
Hitchins Mary, 152 9th
Hodge Margaretta D. 178 Bowery
Holmes Jemima, 439½ Pearl
Honigberger Louis, 303 Grand
Hopkins Sarah, 236 8th Av.
Hope Agnes, 361 Broadway
Horton Sarah, 369 6th Av.
Hough L. F. 189 Grand
Houdbert Josephine, 29 Warren
Hulin Mary, 75 Roosevelt
Hudson Susanna, 276 Rivington

Huntington Mary H. 565 Broom
New York.
Hyman Samuel, 23½ Division
Irvings D. E. 415 Pearl
Isaacs Lazarus. 59½ Division
Isaac Lyon, 5 Division
Jackson Abbe, 352 Houston
Jackson Rebecca A. 144 Houston
Jarvis A. F. 72 Canal
Jinnings Augusta, 189 Church
Johnson Ronea, 70 Carmine
Jones Miss, 53½ Amos
Josselyn Rachael, 243½ Grand
Joseph E. 7 Division
Kasang Margaret & Walker, 268½ Bowery
Kearns Matilda. 53½ Amos
Keep ——, 363 Broadway
Kelly Elizabeth. 193 Division
Kelly Bridget A. 54 Watts
Kessler Elizabeth, 193 Division
Kidd Witten A. 11 Carmine
King Mrs. Harlem
King Carl, 17 Division
King Maria, 29½ Division
Kingsland Adelaide, 213 W. 21st
Knapp Tamar, 447 Pearl
Knowles M. 418 Greenwich
Knox Mrs. 173 6th Av.
Lane Eleanor. 204 Spring
Lavene Madame & Co. 133½ Spring
Lawson Catherine, 17 Park place
L'Hommedi Julia, 235 3d Av.
L'Horpitalier Cath. 115 Greene
Ledwith M. 383½ Pearl
Levys Abraham, 59 Division
Lewis Margaret, 23 Division
Lichtenberg J. 264 Bowery
Lindorf L. 239 Grand
Lisle Miss, 5 Minetta lane
Lobeck Ernestine, 297½ Br'dway
Lonati Ann, 453 Pearl
Lozier Ann, 446 Hudson
Lyon Miss, 23 Amos
M'Anesple Mary, 189 7th
Mackay Louisa, 249 Hudson
M'Cafferty ——, 32 Carmine
M'Coy Michael, 231 Hudson
M'Gaw Sarah Jane, 63 Jane
M'Gready Eliza, 163 9th
M'Intyre Eliza J. 223 Greenwich
M'Kindley Mary, 76 Canal
M'Laughlin Cath. 120 Bowery
M'Lean Elizabeth. 311 Broadway
M'Quaid, Mary, 152 4th
Meguiro D. 108 Bowery
Mannaberg Nancy, 23 Carmine
Manifold Adeline, 239 West 16th
Manning Cornelia, 310 2d
Marcy Adelaide H. 214 Bowery
Marcy Lemuel, 215 Bowery
Marks Miss, 485 Pearl
Marshall Margaret, 414 Grenw'h
Mason M. 112 8th Av.
Martin Richard, 237 3d Av.
Mather Palmyra, 498½ Grand
Messier Maria, 213 Division
Metz Henry, 329 Broadway
Michelli Geswalda, 123 3d Av.
Millard Eliza, 186 6th Av.
Miller Helena, 229 Hudson
Miller S. A. 292 8th Av.
Mount Eliza, 43 Catharine
Moore & Lion, 92 Bowery
Mullin Eliza, 15 Warren
Muny John F. 51 West Broadway
Neale Eliza, 56 Carmine
Newton Sarah E. 5 Chestnut
Neymann Henrietta, 543 Bdwy.
Nicolson F. 311 Greenwich
Oakes Eliza, 98 Hester
O'Burne Jane, 157 Greenwich
Odell Mrs. 171 3d Av.
O'Hara Sarah 180 West 20th
Parsons & Co. 956 Grand
Patten Eliza B. 11 Park place
Patten W. & J. 163 Greenwich
Patterson Ann, 397 Broadway
Paulmier S. 11 Division
Peachy Miss, 301½ 4th
Pearsall Samuel, 47½ Division
Pecare Mrs. B. & Co. 86 Bowery

Perker Jane, 62 Sullivan
New York.
Perry William H. 94 Canal
Pestiaux Lucretia, 4 Astor place
Phelan Jas. 35 Carmine
Phillips Louisa, 86 Mott
Phillips ——, 1 Mercer
Phillips Samuel, 19 Division
Phillips Sarah A. & Co. 399 B'way
Pomeroy Sarah. 46 Av. D
Pool Mary, 165 9th
Post Ormenta, 124 West B'way
Post E. 419 3d Av.
Pratt Charlotte, 7 Amity
Pullen Elizabeth. 341 Bleecker
Quiggins Jane. 405 Grand
Quin Joseph, 173 8th Av.
Rallings W. 191 Spring
Ray Elizabeth, 419 Greenwich
Reeder E. 239 Greenwich
Reilley Eleanor. 63½ Division
Reid Mrs. 164 8th Av.
Richards J. 114 Grand
Ringgold Mary A. 118 6th Av.
Rion Catharine, 67½ Division
Roberts Sarah. 457 Grand
Rogers Henrietta, 210 Canal
Rogers Madame, 311½ Broadway
Rollins Eliza, 361 Greenwich
Rorke M. A. 163½ Division
Rose John, 90 Essex
Rosette Susan, 3 Mercer
Ross Caroline, 38 Barclay
Roth Minna, 115 Ridge
Roullier Francis, 381 Broadway
Schlegel George, 27 Division
Schwab Levi, 417 Grand
Schwab Michael, 379½ Grand
Scott Ann, 432 Broadway
Scott M. Ann, 165½ Division
Shaw Elizabeth, 291 2d
Sheffield Sarah, 51 Canal
Simmons Mrs. 176½ Bowery
Shepperd Maria, 56½ Carmine
Shields Rosina. 455 Pearl
Shiff Caroline, 78 Ridge
Shute Susan R. 9 W. 15th
Simmons Mrs. 176½ Bowery
Sloane Hannah, 239 Hudson
Sloanes M. 239 do
Smith Ellen, 30 Carmine
Smith Lillius, 152 7th
Sonate A. 453 Pearl
Southward Caroline, 55 Madison
Spence Jasper, 39 Division
Sproule Joseph, 3 12th
Stack Miss, 367 Broadway
Stagg Catharine, 273 Hudson
Stagg William H. 21 Division
Stevenson Hannah, 69 Division
Stevenson Mrs. 411 Greenwich
Striker C. M. 325 Broadway
Sturgis Margaret, 40 Madison
Summerhays Catharine, 439 Pearl
Synnot Ellen, 154 Canal
Tarin Madame, 449 Broadway
Tate Mary E. 311 Hudson
Taylor Jane, 368 Bowery
Thornton A. & D. 333 Broadway
Thorp Cornelia T. 95 Canal
Tibbals Lewis. 495 Broadway
Tice Mrs. 242 8th Av.
Todd S. 253 Hudson
Towers A. 58½ 3d Av.
Travers Ellen, 56 Catharine
Trudell Rachel, 128 Forsyth
Tucker Anne. 24 Carmine
Vallett H. 90½ Warren
Vannatter Ann, 70 Horatio
Van Veghten Mary, 423 Broome
Vogel S. M. 14½ Carmine
Von Vultee M. F. 175 Division
Wainwright Mrs. 163 Carmine
Walwork Mrs. 163 Division
Ward Hannah Ann. 63 Madison
Wertheim Eliza, 447½ Pearl
Wetmore Eliza, 79 Carmine
Williams Mrs. 322 Bleecker
Williams Ellen, 43 Division
Wilson Jane, 8th Av.
Wilson Charles, 61 Canal
Wilson Esther, 419 Hudson

Wilmot Alexander, 29 Division
New York.
Wood S. C. 213 Broadway
Woodfine Ann, 40 Hamilton
Woodgate Anna, 47 W. Broadway
Wolff Morris, 9 Division
Yeoman Catharine, 140 Sullivan
Zeglio Peter, 67 Division

Niagara County.

Gibbs & Hall Misses   *Lewiston.*
Seaman Miss L.
Barstow H. Pekin
Belden Mrs.   *Lockport.*
Sears Mrs.
Bowen —— Miss, *Niagara Falls.*
Pierce L. & S.
Cuddeback Mary, Youngstown
Porter.
Coleman Charlotte
Johnson Catharine, Wilson

Oneida County.

Stone Mrs. A. P.   *Camden.*
Frowd Mrs. M.
Browne Mrs. S. Clinton *Kirkland.*
Mallison Mrs. I. Dominick st.
Rome.
Baker F.   do
Hayden Miss W. James st.
Sanford Miss A. 82 Genesee *Utica.*
Fisk Mrs. M. 88   do
Myers Miss E. 77   do
Blake Mrs. E. W. 75   do
Leland Mrs. H. 73   do
Guinguigner Mrs. 162   do
O'Hara Mrs. E. 25 Catharine
Sperzell Misses M. A. & M. 21 do
Kincaid Mrs. George, 12 Broad
Williams Mrs. O. B. 6   do
Maynard Mrs. M. L. 4   do
Petheram G. & E. 2   do
Webb Miss L. A. 2   do
Jewell Mrs. M.   *Vernon.*
Northrop Mrs. N. G. Whitesboro
Whitestown.

Onondaga County.

Maibe Miss M. Arcade Building,
Syracuse   *Salina.*
Wood Miss C. A. Genesee st.
Bates Mrs. C.   do
Wheaden Mrs. C.   do
Cook Mrs. H.   do
Ellis Miss J.   do
Gregory Dorcas, Salina st.
Williams M. C.   do

Ontario County.

Abby Alta   *Canandaigua.*
Shut Miss Sarah J.
Dalley J.
Dunn Mrs.
Pardy Miss   *East Bloomfield.*
Wiley Mrs.   *Phelps.*
Morrell E. Geneva *Seneca.*
M'Kay J.   do
M'Creedie ——,   do
Beaty Mrs. Wm. do
Dorsey Mrs. U. do
Young Miss   *Victor.*
Jones Mrs.

Orange County.

Roe Miss C. P.   *Chester.*
Davis Mrs.
Barnes Miss Sarah
Spinks Mary   *Cornwall.*
Stewart Miss L. B. Port Jervis
Deer Park.
Wheat Mrs. Anna,   do
Howell Miss Sarah *Goshen.*
Drake Misses
Millspaugh Miss Frances
Warden Mrs. Eliza
Smith Mrs.
Bockover Miss M. Unionville
Minisink.
Corbin Miss S.   do

Dodge Miss E. Ridgebury *Minisink.*
Senior Mrs. L. F. *Montgomery.*
Scobey A. M.   *Monroe.*
Stanbrough L. H. 87 Water
Newburgh.
Seeley Miss E. 35   do
Pitts Miss Ellen, 12   do
Kernoshan J. Mrs. 18 do
Ryer Mrs. 20   do
Carman Miss Sarah, S. Middletown
Wallkill.
Mapes Miss,   do
Corwin Mrs.   do
Stewart Miss E. J.   do
Wheeler Miss L. A.   do
Baird Miss,   do
Travis Mrs. New Milford
Warwick.
Atwood Mrs. J. Florida

Orleans County.

Sawens Miss M. Albion   *Barre.*
Nash Mrs. C.   do
Wood Mrs. A. M. do
Wartzer Mrs. S. J. Medina
Ridgeway.
Southard Miss, Knowlesville

Oswego County.

Way Mrs. E. Pulaski *Richland.*
Smith Miss J. Phoenix *Schroeppel.*
Rice Miss   do

Otsego County.

Loper Miss R. F. Cooperstown
Otsego.
Van Namee Miss A.   do

Putnam County.

Pierce Miss A.   *Carmel.*
Hart Miss E.
Truesdell Miss L. Cold Spring
Phillipstown.
Barnes Miss,   do

Rensselaer County.

Tinslar Mrs. A. 319 State
Lansingburgh.
Dilmaire Mrs. M. 358 State
Bigwell Susan L. 172 River *Troy.*
Allen Mrs. R. 27 King
Woolworth & Walter Misses, 7
   Grand Division
Cooper & Hoyt Misses, 16 N. 2d
Washington Mrs. 139   do
Flack Miss, 86   do
Judge Mary, 36   do
Ryan Mrs. 9 3d
Stephens Mrs. S. K. 130 3d
Townsend Mrs. 130 3d
Chaapper Mrs. P. 219 4th
Lasell Mrs. 52   do
Davis Mrs. 15   do
Prime Miss E. C. 22 5th
Tobin Miss, 90   do
Marshall Mrs. 1 Albany
Flandraw Mrs. 46 State
Stevens Mrs. 47 Congress

Rockland County.

Lyons Mrs. Ann, Nyack
Orangetown.
Smith Mrs.   do

Saratoga County.

Peckham H. Ballston Spa *Milton.*
Blood A. F.   do
Harway Mrs. A. M.
Saratoga Springs.
Green Miss Caroline

Schenectady County.

Benedict Mrs. A. 86 State
Schenectady.
Doty Mrs. A. 74 State
Dunning & Hayes Misses, 70 State
Ladd Miss S. 66 State
Vanpelt Mrs. 50 do

Stryker C. M. 26 State *Schenectady.*
Northrop Mrs. 23 Ferry

Schoharie County.

Thorp Mrs.   *Schoharie.*
Best Mrs.

Seneca County.

Church Miss Emily   *Ovid.*
Barron Mrs. Jane
Gilbert Miss Mary *Seneca Falls.*
Paine & Allen Misses
Jackson Mrs. C. M.
Kinyon Mrs. C.
M'Curtis Mrs. Cornelia *Waterloo.*
Mowry Miss Caroline
Woodworth Mrs. S. E.
Townsend Mrs. S.

Steuben County.

Gould Mrs. A. R.   *Bath*
Lambert Miss
Ruggles Mrs. M.
Wheeler Mrs.   *Painted Post.*
Freeman Mrs.
Powers Mrs.

Suffolk County.

Avery Miss Bassheba, Patchogue
Brookhaven.
Graham Carrisa

Sullivan County.

Armstrong Miss Catherine, Bloom-
   ingburgh   *Mamakating.*
Bayley Miss M. Bloomingburgh
Hollister Mrs. E. Wurtsboro
Hornbeck Miss M.   do
Crane Miss A. F.   do
Wheeler Miss, Monticello
Thompson.
Smith Miss E.   do

Tompkins County.

M'Kay Miss H. Maria, 85 Owego
Ithaca.
Montgomery Miss, 90 Owego
Parker Mrs. A. 86   do
Hodson Mrs. 71   do
Kendall Mrs. 83   do

Queens County.

Rushmore Mrs. M. R. *Hempstead.*
Westlake J. A.
Covert Mrs.   *Jamaica.*
Cornwell & Higbee
Tuthill Sarah

Ulster County.

Staples Miss   *Kingston.*
Cooper Mrs. G
Davis Mrs. M. D.
Mason Miss M
Lee Mrs.
Hill E.
Young Mrs.
Westbrook S. C.
Hasbrouck Mrs. J.   *New Paltz.*
Leggett Misses M. A. & A.
Saugerties.
Post Mrs. F. J.

Washington County.

Taylor Miss Sarah J.   *Argyle.*
Stewart Miss Eliza
Bancroft Mrs. Sandy Hill
Kingsbury.
Guy Miss M.   do
Daily Mrs. Church st. *Whitehall.*
M'Conn Mrs. Canal st.
Lester Miss F. do

Wayne County.

Palmer Miss, Newark   *Arcadia.*
Southerland Mrs. do
Voorhies Mrs. Wm.   *Lyons.*
Cosart Mrs. E. S.

Belden Mrs. W.   *Lyons.*
Caswell Miss W.
Deitz Miss Jane

Westchester County.

Doty & Haight Misses, Peekskill
                    Courtlandt.
Mabie Miss, Peekskill
White Mrs. Tarrytown
                    Greenburgh.
Clark Miss, Sing Sing   *Ossining.*
Wheeler Mrs.   *White Plains.*
Anderson Mrs. W. H.   *Yonkers.*

Wyoming County.

Tinker Mrs. Horace   *Attica.*
Tobias Mrs.
Blackmer Miss, Wyoming
                    Middlebury.
Clow Miss,   do
Higgins Mrs.   *Perry.*
Sherwood Martha
Macland Miss
Hinckley Mrs. F. M.   *Pike.*
Whiton Mrs. H.
Barnes Mrs. A.
Grinald Miss Hester, Varysburg
                    Sheldon.
Stowe Mrs.   *Warsaw.*
Brundage Mrs.

Yates County.

Smith Mrs. E., Penn Yan   *Milo.*
Jacobus Mrs. S.   do
Morehouse Mrs.   do
Gilbert Mrs. S.   do
Bennett Mrs.   do
Thorp Mrs. Potter Center   *Potter.*
Bassett Miss Betsy, Rushville
Swarthout Mrs. Martha, Dundee
                    Starkey.
Hamlin W. B.   Dundee
Benham Miss S.   do

Millinery & Fancy Goods.

(See also Milliners.)

Albany County.

Gough Mrs. Teresa N. 595 B'way
                    Albany.
Hempstead Mrs. 524 Broadway
Walker Mrs. J. S. 61 Washington
Han Joseph, Cohoes   *Watervliet.*

Cayuga County.

Graham T. F. 53 Genesee st.
                    Auburn.

Duchess County.

Peterkin John, 304 Main
                    Poughkeepsie.
Harrison Mrs. 285 Main

Erie County

Putnam M. A. 273 Main   *Buffalo.*
Woodward Wm. H. 241 Main
Kimberly E. & S. 209   do
Hopkins Rebecca. 223½   do
Reilly Miss M. A. 228   do
Smith Mrs. T. 267   do
Bean Mrs. A. 183   do
Williams Mrs. B. 199   do
Jones George B. 197   do
Sargent Mrs. 263   do
Young Eliza, 293   do
Elsheimer Miss, 43 Genesee
Holiert Frances, 300 Main
Kling Francis, 302   do
Sparks Mrs. E. 323   do
Willis C. 315   do
Le Roy Mrs. 245½   do
Whitney A. S. 157   do

Genesee County.

Putnam & Shepard   *Alexander.*

Greene County.

Titus Elizabeth A.   *Athens.*
Noble C. A.

Kings County.

Bodean Wm. 59 Atlantic *Brooklyn.*
Hunter James, 282 Henry
Morse James M. 274 Hicks
Munn S. Fulton st.
Tucker A.   do
Cardery Mrs. 200 Fulton
Dewey E. (wholesale) 178 Fulton
Phillips M. 214 Fulton
Engle G. 240   do
Thompson M. 256½ Fulton
Ruggles Mrs. Julia. 262 Fulton
Verin Victor, (manufacturer) 257
    Fulton
Hall Mrs. E. 96 Bridge
Brooks Frederick, 43 Myrtle Av.
Gritman E. A. 11 High
Brooks Mrs. Jane, 263 Fulton
Newman Mrs. M. 261   do
Morrison & Deleree, 199 do
Morse J. M. 216   do
Sutton E. 173   do
Baudoine Mrs. C. L. 169 do
Mullin Daniel, 36 Hudson Av.
Martin J. 146 York
Hambridge Robert. 135½ Sands
Mason Mrs. M. 14½ Myrtle Av.
Jenkins Miss Susan, 142 4th
                    Williamsburgh.
Stenson Mrs. J. 142 Grand
Smith Miss S. J. 1st near Grand

Monroe County.

Charron V. 78 Main   *Rochester.*
Barnes Thomas. 76 State
Bair A. & Brother, 1 Front

New York County.

Aitken & Miller, 423 Broadway
                    New York.
Atwater William, 159 William
Beard Ira, 101 William
Beers Joseph, 25 John
Bennett Mrs. 201 Houston
Berly F. 15 John
Binns Isaac, 209 Hudson
Bishop N. C. 15 John
Boyer Mrs. 29 Av. D
Cuffe & Cutter, 18 John
Collis Augustus H. 32 John
Cooper Marum, 51½ Division
Curtis P. A. & J. 26 John
Donald Elizabeth J. 519½ G'wich
Ely Abner L. 65 Maiden lane
Ferrero Charles, 339 Broadway
Fisher Jacob, 271 Spring
Gough Thomas, 263 6th Av.
Greer Robert, 260 Bleecker
Gruet & Wainwright. 51 Carmine
Hamilton Ellen. 519½ Greenwich
Hart E. & H. 288 Bleecker
Higbie Aaron, 413 Pearl
Hillman & Nearing, 72 Maiden
    lane and 7 Liberty
Hinckley Charles A. 213 3d Av.
Holden Oliver S. 25 John
Homer Joseph H. 64 John
Isaacks T. E. 16 John
Isaac G. J. 34 Division
Kelly Patrick John, 641 Hudson
King Carl, 17 Division
Knox Annabella, 173 6th Av.
Lightenstein M. H. 902 Bowery
Loyd John L. 30 John
Malberbe Madame, 549½ B'way
Martin & Lawson, 24 John
Mason Mary, 112 8th Av.
Moore & Lion, 96 Canal and 92
    Bowery
Merritt A. 100 Av. D
Nicholson P. 311 Greenwich
Odell Jacob, 175 3d Av.
Pecare. Berther & Co. 86 Bowery
Perry Timothy, 54 Canal
Phelan James, 35 Carmine
Richmond George, 369 Broadway

Roberts Edwin, 457 Grand
                    New York.
Rothshilds Simon, 270 2d
Scott Mery Ann, 155½ Division
Simmons Charles W. 176½ Bwry.
Stevens L. M. & Co. 146 Pearl
Stonier T. M. 382 Bowery
Todd Sarah & Lydia, 258 Hudson
Toldbridge Barnett, 393 B'dwy
Tucker Sarah. 24 Carmine
Underhill L. & A. 6 John
Vanderburgh John J. 24 John
Wallwork Joseph, 163 Division
Wall James B. Harlem
Westheimer Bernhard, 46 Av. B
Wilcox L. A. 134 Spring
Wilson L. W. 419 Hudson

Onondaga County.

Gillmore F. H. Salina st. Syracuse
                    Salina.

Orange County.

Birdsall Mrs., Port Jervis
                    Deer Park.
Huff Mrs. M.   do
Martinau Miss Margaret, 86 Water
                    Newburgh.
Comstock Miss P. 13 Water
Adams Miss C. 28 Water
Spalding Miss, 27 Water
Minturn Miss E. C. 6 Water

Rensselaer County.

Carpenter Mrs. E. 223 State
                    Lansingburgh.
Williams Miss H. 269 State
Bigwell Susan L. 172 River *Troy.*
Keeler J. S. 185½   do
Beck James & Co. 196 do
Clark A. W. 204   do
Marshall William, 224 do
Darrows H. James, 302 do
Jones Mrs. P. H. 6 1st
Lovett Mrs. L. P. 3 Wash. square
Brown Mrs. 6 1st
Davis Mrs. 15 4th
Gay Mrs. J. 83 6th
Brownell Mrs. 8 Boardman's bld.
Clark T. 5 Albany
Saxton G. B. & Co. 8 Cannon pl.
Strout E. B. & Co. 1   do
Clements Mrs. S. C. 146 Congress

Saratoga County.

Stewart Mrs.   *Waterford.*
Alley Mrs.

Ulster County.

Johnson Miss Genett   *Saugerties.*
Heath Mrs. A.
Mundy Mrs. A. (fancy worsted)
Whitmore Mrs. R. V. Napanock
                    Wawarsing.
Samuel N., Ellenville

Westchester County.

Carpenter M.   *New Rochelle.*
Bird Mrs., Portchester   *Rye.*
Lockwood L.   do
Ackerman John   *West Farms.*

Mill—Bartlis.

Gay, Murray & Co. 522 & 524 Wa-
    ter   *New York.*

Mills—Eccentric.

Chasmer C. & E. 322 3d *New York.*

Mills—Portable.

Ross C. 126 Clinton pl. *New York.*

Millstone Manufacturers & Dealers.

Erie County.

Hayward & Noye, (millers, furnishing) 87 Main *Buffalo.*

New York County.

Morris P. & Co. 45 Duane *New York.*
Tyack Wm. 240 Washington

Oneida County.

Hart & Munson, Washington cor. Canal *Utica.*

Rensselaer County.

Crandall Ethan A. 382 River Troy.

Ulster County.

Davis Jacob, Accord *Rochester.*

Millwrights.

Alleghany County.

Lord T. C. *Friendship.*
Obert L. H.

Broome County.

Edwards C. *Lisle.*
James M. *Vestal.*

Cattaraugus County.

Rockwell N. *Ashford.*
Benson John *Conewango.*
Aikens Edward *Great Valley.*
Pierce Charles

Cayuga County.

Southwick George *Sempronius.*

Chautauque County.

Harvey Kellogg *French Creek.*

Chemung County.

M'Cartey John *Catharine.*
Frost A. R.

Chenango County.

Gifford E. *Lincklaen.*
Gifford T. M.
Foote A. *Sherburne.*
Foote A. jr.

Columbia County.

Moore P. B. *Chatham.*

Delaware County.

Gerow B. Bloomville *Kortright.*
Saunders Wm. *Meredith.*

Erie County.

Taggart Samuel *Black Rock.*
Treanor John *Eden.*
Treanor Geo.

Essex County.

Kellogg Cyrus H. *Elizabethtown.*
Leggett Wm. *Lewis.*
Jenkins Franklin
Putnam Madison, Moriah Four Corners *Moriah.*
Hicks Luth. Moriah Four Corners
Hicks Vincent, do do
Howard H. do do

Franklin County.

Cleaveland C. C. *Bangor.*
Crooks J. W.

Herkimer County.

Foote J. A. *Columbia.*

Burl Eaton *Columbia.*
Hars S. V. *Frankfort.*
Hagar Lucas
Miller H. C.
Getman Robert

Greene County.

Purdy Millon A. *Hunter.*
Patch Samuel
Purdy Erastus S.
Williams Daniel, East Kill
Turner John, Union Society *Windham.*

Jefferson County.

Bastron Joseph *Theresa.*
Barrett Isaac
Brooks Thompson

Kings County.

Binns James, Walworth st. *Brooklyn.*

Lewis County.

Church Royal T., Brantingham *Greig.*
Garrett Clark, Lyonsdale
Aldrich David *Turin.*

Livingston County.

Edgerly David, Oakland *Portage.*

Madison County.

Stillman Richard *Brookfield.*
Robie Geo. *Georgetown.*
Rector Geo. Bridgeport *Sullivan.*

Montgomery County.

Bunkle Wm. *Amsterdam.*

New York County.

Angus John, 352 Front *New York.*
Bunnell W. J. 89 Eldridge
Jones & Sterling, 44 Eldridge
Morrow A. 606 Washington
Prentiss & Page, 119 Walker

Orange County.

Racine J. *Minisink.*

Oswego County.

Ballard Wm. *Albion.*
Rich Reuben
Purmont Hyman F. (Ames' Buildings) 1st st. *Oswego.*
Taylor Samuel R. (Bates' Block, 2d story) 1st st.
Taylor James, Pulaski *Richland.*
Watkins Philo B. do
Burdick J. A. South Richland

Rensselaer County.

Allen J. *Petersburgh.*

St. Lawrence County.

Dumas Joseph *Canton.*
Dennis W. Richville *De Kalb.*
Arnott N. D. *Gouverneur.*
Sampson Jeremiah *Hopkinton.*
Briggs Henry *Lisbon.*
Power Robert *Louisville.*
Power Wm. jr.
Taggert N. Waddington *Madrid.*
Fulton Jas. do
Fulton John do
M'Dale Joseph, do
Carnathan Robert, do
Dezelle Robert, do
Bailey R. C. Ogdensburgh *Oswegatchie.*
Allen Isaac, do
Wolcott John R. *Parishville.*
Cox Gardiner *Pierpont.*
Beach Elisha W.
Smith & Chandler *Potsdam.*
Goulding John

Nichols G. C. *Stockholm.*
Nichols David R.
Nichols Lucius N.

Saratoga County.

Burnham Jonathan *Corinth.*
Burnham Julius
Burnham Spencer E.
Shippey S. Glenn's Falls *Moreau.*
Putnam G. W.

Schenectady County.

Kelley Wm. *Princetown.*

Steuben County.

Andrus Wm *Cohocton.*

Ulster County.

Kimball J. High Falls *Marbletown.*

Warren County.

Duett M. W. Chestertown *Chester.*

Washington County.

Amidon J. Sandy Hill *Kingsbury.*
Holland Park, do
Merrill E. do
Jones A. do

Wyoming County

Hunt Henry *Perry.*

Yates County.

Bartholomew Jos. *Barrington.*
Bartholomew D. B. Dundee *Starkey.*
Crippen Henry *Westfield.*

Mineral Waters. (See also Soda Water Makers.)

Clarke & Co. 10 Thames *New York.*
Delatour A. J. 25½ Wall
Eagle Wm. 194 Fulton
Southwick & Tupper, 112 Warren
Whittemore Chas. 162 Varick

Molasses—Dealers Wholesale. (See also Grocers.)

Hemenway Tyler, 116 South *New York.*
Holmes Madison, 82 Front
Patterson Holmes, 82 Front

Morocco Case Manufacturers.

Barnett Francis & Son, 182 Broadway *New York.*
Dunn Peter, 96 Fulton
Hartnett C. & J. F. 2 Courtlandt
Seele John P. 151 Fulton

Morocco Manufacturers. (See also Tanners.)

Albany County.

Covert A. & Son, 83 Dean *Albany.*
Colbyrn P. 51 Arch

New York County.

Bitter Henry, 2 Jacob *New York*
Bushnell E. L. 3 Ferry
Cammeyer & Johnson, 35 Ferry
Chambers & Burbank, 23 Ferry
Clark & Dougherty, 29 Ferry
Colgan John, 12 Jacob

Doherty James, 18 Jacob
                    New York.
Dussol John, 24 Frankfort
Eichinger & Tauscher, 135 Division
Ennis Obediah. 26 Ferry
Gallagher & Shevill, 57 Ferry
Garner Edward M. 89 Gold & rear 46 Laurens
Graves Horace F. 156 W. 17th
Griffin Philip N. & Co. 7 Ferry
Jones T. C. Washington st.
Journeymen's Co. 21 Jacob
Just John, 6 Ferry
Kerrigan J. & Son, 1 Ferry
Kerrigan & Friels, 8 Jacob
Leonard, Gallagher & Shevill, 57 Ferry
M'Colgan John & Co. 12 Jacob
M'Crodden Anthony, 92 Gold
Marshman B. 37 Spruce
Porter Jos. C. 46 Ferry
Smith Adam, 55 Ferry
Smith Jas. R. 25 Ferry
Thompson John, 53 Frankfort
Warren Horace M. 53 Ferry
Watts George, 26 Ferry

Moulders.

Kings County.

Porter, Willis & Co. 40, 42 & 44 Water   *Brooklyn.*

New York County.

Belden Amos, rear 40 Suffolk
                    New York.
Boyle & Coleman, 206 Broome
Equi G. 315 Broadway
Rigall G. 148 William

Mouldings (Wood.) (*See also Carvers.*)

Kings County.

Willis & Porter, 135 Grand
                Williamsburgh.

New York County.

Chatain H. 360 Broome *New York.*
Kneeland Wm. C. 33 Attorney
Lawrence John, 87 Elizabeth
Ritter Joseph, 31 & 33 Attorney
Servell A. T. 17 6th Av. & 87 Elizabeth
Weller P. & J. Didier, 196 Mulb'y

Musical Instrument Makers. (*See also Organs, also Piano Fortes. also Seraphines and Melodeons.*)

Albany County.

Meacham R. S. 84 State *Albany.*
Barhydt & Ballentine, 22 Union
Dwight H. 6 James
Burns F. P. 5 do
Wood & Gambel, 16 N. Pearl
Boardman & Gray, 2 & 4 do

Cayuga County.

Percival J. 78 Genesee   *Auburn.*

Chemung County.

Hayes & Laflin   *Norwich.*
Hollenbeck & King   *Greene.*

Chenango County.

Holt Nathan P.   *Guilford.*

Columbia County.

Danscher J   *Chatham.*

Duchess County.

Retter P. 353 Main *Poughkeepsie.*
Whiethen Louis, 97 Market
Anson B., Stanfordville *Stanford.*
Anson R.   do

Erie County.

Garland J. G. 148 E. Swan *Buffalo.*
Prince Geo. A. & Co. 200 Main
Benson David & Co. 196 Wash'ton

Kings County.

Cottier H. 162 Atlantic *Brooklyn.*
Gould Isaac, (guitars) 64 Adams
Bunce Charles, 11 Water
Hjousberry Lasse, 167 Fulton

Genesee County.

Elmore M.   *Bergen.*

Monroe County.

Dutton Geo. jr. 27 State *Rochester.*
Miller Michael, 196 Main
Brayley James, cor. State & Mumford
Richardson & Buzzell, Curtis' Block. Main st.
Kedzie J. & Co. 11 State
Bingham Nathaniel, 119½ Buffalo

New York County

Allovon Jean D. 111 Elm
                    New York.
Beack Edward, 61 Fulton & 72½ Chatham
Bacon & Raven, 160 Centre
Badger A. G. (flutes) 181 Broad'y
Barmore G. & H. 346 Bleecker
Bennett & Wilder, 152 Fulton
Bornhoeft John, 103 Walker
Brewer Alfred N. 289 William
Browne John F. & Co. (harps) 295 Broadway & 56 Reade
Browning Benj J. 177 Prince
Burnett Andrew, 30 Clark
Bury & Wolf, 156 4th Av.
Buttikoffer John, 102 Elm
Carhart & Needham, rear 172 Forsyth
Carr Charles, 287 Spring
Chambers Thomas H. 385 Broad'y
Chickering Jonas, 289½   do
Clearman & Bogert, 148 Elm
Daly John J. 233½ Walker
Davis William H. 67 M'Dougal
Dehoog Peter, 150 Barrow
Doyle Thomas J. 23 Canal
Dubois William H. 315 Broadway & rear 15 Crosby
Dunham John B. 87 E. 18th
Erben Henry, 172 Centre
Firth, Pond & Co. (guitars & flutes) Franklin square
Fischer J. & C. 170 Greenwich
Gale A. H. & Co. 106 3d Av.
Glen Robert & Co. 194 Fulton
Godone Caspar, 403½ Broadway
Grovesteen James H. 40 & 44 W. 18th & 122 Grand
Grow & Christopher, 111 E. 14th
Hall Wm.' & Son. 239 Broadway
Hall & Labagh, 85 & 86 Wooster
Hanley James, (harps) 232 B'way
Hardman Wm. 355 Washington
Harper John & Co. 334 Greenwich
Harrison Vivaldi F. 23 Canal
Hawkey Henry, 118 Amity
Hoffman C. T. E. rear 386 Grand
Holmes Geo. F. 14 3d Av.
Jacobs Lionel, 55 Chatham
Jardine George, 548 Pearl
Johnson Samuel, 166 William
Leocoq Jules, 133 Leonard
Lenchte Ferd. C. 111 & 115 Elm
Lindel Edward J. 36 White
Linden & Fritz, 478 Broadway
Luther John F. 116 Ludlow
Martins & Ouvrier, 83 Leonard
Mercer Charles, (violins) 44 Canal

Nunn William, 169 Fulton
                    New York.
Nunns & Clark, 257 Broadway
Nunns & Fischer, 170 Greenwich
Pethick John, 204 Bleecker
Pirsson James, 87 Leonard
Prince George A. & Co. Manuf. of the Improved Patent Melodeon. Wholesale Depot, 87 Fulton, Manufactory 200 Main st. Buffalo
Provoost Peter, 490 Hudson
Riley Frederick & Co. 297 B.way & 52 Ann
Rogers & Winant, 148 Fulton
Rohe Joseph A. 44 Maiden lane
Ronberg William, 150 Broadway
Ruck John, 114 Laurens
Schmidt Philip W. 59 Spring
Smith David & T. 222 12th
Springer John, (violins) 126 Leonard
Springer Matthew, 145 Centre
Stodart Adam. 343 Broadway
Swartz Abraham S. 6 Spring
Thompson James & Co. 7 Barclay
Thurston Joshua, 259 William
Traver & Ramsey. 46 Broadway
Valentine Dominick, 24 Madison
Van Valkenburgh Aaron,187 Pearl
Van Winkle David, rear 22 W. 10th
Wake John P. 184 Fulton
Walker J. & D. 413 Broadway
Wennerstrom & Berggvist, 40 5th Av.
Whiting Geo. A. 165 Eldridge
Worcester Horatio, 127 3d Av.
Zebisch C. A. & Sons, 179 Mott

Oneida County.

Philleo L. 52 Hotel st.   *Utica.*

Orange County.

Rider John   *Cornwall*
Traver & Ramsey   *Newburgh.*
Stanbrough & Son

Rensselaer County.

Hopkins Edward, 232 River *Troy*
Andrews J. W. 225 River
Backus A. rear Boardman's Buildings

Rockland County.

Thompson James & Co. Nyack
                Orangetown.

St. Lawrence County.

Boynton Paul   *Canton.*
Badlom E. Ford st. Ogdensburgh.
                Oswegatchie.

Tompkins County.

Akins, Hollinshead & Spencer, 104 Owego st.   *Ithaca.*

Music Stores. (*See also Musical Instrument Manufacturers.*)

Albany County.

Mayer & Collier, 512 Broadway
                    Albany.
Ilsley F. I. & Co. 525 Broadway

Broome County.

Jones J. H.   *Binghamton.*

Chautauque County.

Sackett H. S. & M. Irving
                    Hanover.

Erie County.

Prince George A. 200 Main st.
                    Buffalo.
Sheopard James D. 265 Main

Kings County.

Cottier H. 162 Atlantic st.
 Brooklyn.
Cummings J. L. 208 Fulton
Hjonsberry Lasse, 167 do
Longworth & Parsons, 120 Grand
 Williamsburgh.
Coard William, 232 1st

Monroe County

Darcus & Grant, 56 State st.
 Rochester.
Dutton George, jr. 27 State st.

Montgomery County.

Simons R. D. *Amsterdam.*

New York County

Bornhoeft John, 47 Canal
 New York.
Christman Charles G. 404 Pearl
Dubois William, 315 Broadway
Dumsday Michael, 465 Broadway
Firth, Pond & Co. 1 Franklin sq.
Geil & Jackson, 361 Broadway
Hall William & Son, 239 B.way
Henderson John Y. 549 Broadway
Hoyer Charles F. 389 Broadway
Jacobs David & Co. 102 Chatham
Jaques & Brother, 385 Broadway
Jollie Samuel C. 300 do
Kerksieg & Breusing, 421 Broad-
 way, importers of music
Millet William E 699 Broadway
Pearson Sidney, 79 Bleecker
Riley F. & Co. 297 Broadway
Rohe Joseph A. 44 Maiden lane
Scharfenberg & Luis, 463 B.way
Vanderbeck William, 479 B.way

Oneida County.

Dutton George & Son, 86 Genesee
 Utica.

Onondaga County.

Allen & Hough, Malcolm's B'ld'g
 Syracuse *Salina.*
Saul George, Salina st.

Ontario County.

Kingsland E. Geneva *Seneca.*

Oswego County

Mellen & James, 7 Eagle Block,
 1st st. *Oswego.*

Rensselaer County.

Andrews J. W. 22 River *Troy.*
Kinnicutt J. W. Boardman's Buildings

St. Lawrence County.

Searle R. D. Water st. Ogdensburgh *Oswegatchie.*

Musicians.

Allen George W. 201 Elm
 New York.
Dingle Samuel K. 67 Bowery
Dodworth Thomas, 493 Broadway
Duckworth John, 136 Spring
Ehl Augustus, 122 Church
Grafulla Claudio S. 175 Walker
Hoddick F. 12 Chrystie
Hoffman George, 104 Grand
Mern Moses, 150 Stanton
Nidds William, 465 Broadway
Plet Christian L. 85 West Broad'y
Poyer Wm. J. 23 Lispenard
Schneider George, 109½ Green
Stevens P. H. 136 Crosby
Wegner P. H. 57 Crosby
Wise F. 19 Crosby

Mustard Manufacturers.
(See also Coffee Roasters &
Spice Factors.)

Kings County

Crommelin J. R. Lafayette st.
 Brooklyn.
Crommelin F. D. P. Hudson Av.

New York County.

Freeman Nathaniel P. 21st st. cor.
 10th Av. *New York.*
Horsey Joseph. 84 Maiden lane
Ichem R. H. & J. G. 108 Front & 71
 Fulton
Mott John G. & Son. 122 Beekman
Stickney Chs. L. 178 Rivington
Van Dyk Francis, 60 Vesey
Walker Chs. & Co. 61 Elizabeth
Werbstein Conrad, 348 6th

Nail Manufacturers. *(See*
also Spike Makers.)

Clinton County

Kingsland E. & J. D. & Co. Keeseville *Au Sable.*
Rogers J. A. J. *Black Brook.*

Essex County.

Ross, Low & Gould, (900 tons annually) *Essex.*

Jefferson County.

M'Collom Hiram, Carthage *Wilna.*

Kings County.

Lange Jacob, (wrought) Myrtle
 Av. *Brooklyn.*
Kelly Patrick, (horse & wrought)
 North 5th st. cor. 2d
 Williamsburgh.

Monroe County.

Sanborn & Stratton, 6 S. St. Paul
 Rochester.
Elliott & Fitch, 23 Buffalo
Shelden Josiah, 27 Front

New York County.

Blackwells & Burr, 87 Water
 New York.
Bussing E. & J. & Co. 32 Cliff
Cebra & Cuming, 106 Pearl
Chapman John, 6th Av. between
 19th & 20th
Contos Nicholas, 549 4th
Field Jude, 80 Av. C
Gould John, 203 Pearl
Higgins Michael, 185 West 18th
Jaudons & Mason, 203 Pearl
Larkin John, 213 East 13th
M'Govarn Thomas, 240 Henry
Sweeny Edmund, rear 34 Cherry
Thompson James, 88 Monroe and
 205 Lewis
Tisdale S. T. & Co. 218 Water
Van Shaick & Heyer, 85 Maiden
 lane

Rensselaer County.

Coubrough M. C. (wrought) 364
 River *Troy.*
Hubbell N. (importer) 309 Ri-
 ver
Garrett & Feores, (wrought)
 South

Neapolitan Bonnet Makers.

Pattison, Moe & Co. 23 & 25 Delancy *New York.*

Needles and Fish Hooks—
Importers of.

Bate Thomas & Thomas H. 108
 Maiden lane *New York.*
Baylis Henry, 131 William
Barnett Thomas, 84 Cedar
Keeley James, 12 Pine
Pardow James, 95 Maiden lane
Richards R. 16 Maiden lane
Warin John, 48 Maiden lane

Needle and Fish Hook
Manufacturers.

Crowley W. & Sons, 100 William
 New York.

Newspaper and Periodi-
cal Depots.

Albany County.

Gilbert F. L. State cor. Broadway
 Albany.
Vosburgh W. H. West Troy
 Watervliet.

Columbia County.

Nash C. B. Warren st. *Hudson.*

Duchess County.

Worden R. Wappinger's Falls
 Fishkill.
Smith G H. 305 Main *Poughkeepsie.*
Colbern J. D. 277 Main
Kenworthy R. 12 Market

Erie County.

Burk Andrew, 171 Main *Buffalo.*
Hawks T. S. Washing. c. Seneca

Kings County.

Egan E. 208 Atlantic *Brooklyn.*
Green Henry. 21 Myrtle Av.
Belknap Rufus R. 5 Hudson Av.
Blanthorn James, 139 Nassau

Monroe County.

Dewy D. M. 1 & 2 Arcade Hall
 Rochester.

New York County.

Dexter & Brother, 43 Ann
 New York.
Gilbert James A. & Co. 11 Ann
Mathews Cornelius, 47 Gold

Oneida County.

Debnam W. B., Clinton *Kirkland*
Beesley G. N. Exchange Buildings, Genesee st. *Utica.*

Onondaga County.

Palmer W. L. Syracuse House,
 Syracuse *Salina.*

Orange County.

Blackman C. W. 11 Water
 Newburgh.
Callahan Wm. H. 2d st.

Rensselaer County.

Willard L. 230 River *Troy.*
Smith & Brother, 2 1st

Saratoga County.

Mundell W. A. *Saratoga Springs.*

Schenectady County.

Clare G. 133 State *Schenectady.*

Tioga County.

Reeves E. W. *Owego.*

Ulster County.

Brewer William   *Saugerties.*

Newspapers.

Albany County.

Albany Argus, Ca-well & Shaw Editors & Proprietors, (daily, weekly & semi-weekly) Exch. c. Broadway & State   *Albany.*
Albany Daily Knickerbocker. H. J. Hastings Editor & Proprietor, Museum Building   *A bany.*
Albany Daily Messenger, B. F. Romaine Editor & Proprietor, 334 Broadway   *Albany.*
Albany Evening Atlas. Vandy ke & Cassidy Editors. H. H. Van Dyke Publisher, (daily, weekly & semi-weekly) Broadway cor. Beaver   *Albany.*
Albany Morning Express, Stone & Henley Proprietors, 1 Green   *Albany.*
Albany Switch. John New Editor & Proprietor, 10 Beaver *Albany.*
American Christian Messenger. J. Hazen, Editor & Prop. 334 Broadway   *Albany.*
American Spectator, B. F. Romaine Ed. & Pro. 334 Broadway   *Albany.*
Christian Palladium, Jasper Hazen Ed. & Prop. 334 Broadway   *Albany.*
Cohoes Cataract, Silliman & Miller Eds. & Props., Cohoes   *Watervliet.*
Cultivator & Horticulturist, Luth. Tucker Ed. & Prop. 407 Broadway   *Albany.*
Evening Journal, (daily, semiweekly & weekly) Weed, Ten Eyck & Dawson Props. Weed & Dawson Eds. 61 State *Albany.*
Sunday Dutchman. Griffin & Farnsworth, Editors & Props. Broadway & Hamilton *Albany.*
Temperance Courier, J. T. Hazen Ed. & Prop. 334 Broadway *Albany.*
West Troy Advocate, W. Holland Ed. & Prop., West Troy   *Watervliet.*

Alleghany County.

Alleghany County Advertiser, E. S. Palmer. Prop.   *Angelica.*
Angelica Republican C. Horton Prop.   *Angelica.*
Republican Era, Horace E. Purdy Prop.   *Angelica.*

Broome County.

Binghamton Courier, J. T. Brodt Ed. & Prop.   *Binghamton.*
Binghamton Daily Republican, Wm. Stuart Ed., E. T. Evans Publisher   *Binghamton.*
Binghamton Democrat. H. L. Shaw Prop.   *Binghamton.*
Broome Republican, Wm. Senart Ed., E. T. Evans Publisher   *Binghamton.*
The Iris, Wm. Stuart Ed., E. T. Evans Publisher   *Binghamton.*

Cattaraugus County.

Cattaraugus Republican, R. H. Shankland Publisher   *Ellicottville.*
Cattaraugus Whig, Sill & Cary Publishers   *Ellicottville.*

Cayuga County.

Auburn Weekly Journal & Daily Advertiser, H. Montgomery &

R. W. Peck Editors, Knapp & Peck Publishers & Props. 117 Genesee   *Auburn.*
Cayuga Chief. J. W. Brown & A. Suman Eds. & Props., Genesee st.   *Auburn.*
Cayuga Democrat, W. Clark Ed. & Prop.   *Springport.*
Cayuga New Era, T. Y. How, jr. Ed., Hawes & Stone Publishers, 111 Genesee st.   *Auburn.*
Cayuga Telegraph, W. Clark Ed. & Prop.   *Springport.*
Northern Christian Advocate, Wm. Hosmer Ed., Gen. Confer. M. E. Church Props.   *Auburn.*

Chautauque County.

Jamestown Journal, F. W. Palmer & Co. Props., Jamestown   *Ellicott.*
Northern Citizen, A. Fletcher Prop. Jamestown .   *Ellicott.*

Chenango County.

Bainbridge Freeman *Bainbridge.*
Chenango Free Democrat, Alfred G. Lawyer Ed. & Publisher   *Norwich.*
Chenango Telegraph, Nelson Pellett Ed. & Publisher *Norwich.*
Chenango Union, Lafayette Lel Ed. & Publisher   *Norwich.*
New Berlin Gazette   *New Berlin.*
Oxford Times, J. B. Galpin Prop.   *Oxford.*

Clinton County.

Au Sable River Gazette, Daniel Turner, Prop., Keeseville   *Au Sable.*
Clinton County Whig, B. F. Fairman Prop.,   *Plattsburgh.*
Plattsburgh Free Democrat, —— Hart Prop.   *Plattsburgh.*
Plattsburgh Republican, R. G. Stone Prop.   *Plattsburgh.*

Columbia County.

Columbia Republican, W. Bryan Ed., Bryan & Moore Publishers, Warren st.   *Hudson.*
Columbia Washingtonian, A. N. Webb Ed., Warren st. *Hudson.*
Daily Star, A. N. Webb Ed. and Prop. Warren st.   *Hudson.*
Democratic Freeman, C. H. Collins Ed. and Prop., cor. Warren and Public Square   *Hudson.*
Hudson Gazette, P. D. Carrique, Ed. and Prop.   *Hudson.*
Kinderhook Sentinel, P. Van Schaack Ed. & Prop. *Kinderhook.*

Cortland County.

Cortlandt County Express, Benedict & Boynton Pub., M'Grawville   *Cortland Village.*
Cortland Democrat, Jas. S. Leach Ed. & Pub.   *Cortland Village.*

Delaware County.

Backwoodsman. (semi-monthly) A. C. Hills Editor, Deposit   *Tompkins.*
Delaware Express, N. Brown Ed. and Prop.   *Delhi.*
Delaware Gazette, A. M. Paine Ed. & Prop.   *Delhi.*
Deposit Courier, C. E. Wright Ed. Deposit   *Tompkins.*

Duchess County.

Democratic American, I. Tompkins Ed. & Prop. *Poughkeepsie.*
Fishkill Standard, W. R. Addington Editor and Prop.   *Fishkill Landing.*

Journal & Eagle, Platt & Schram Proprietors, 310 Main   *Poughkeepsie.*
Poughkeepsie Telegraph, E. B. Killey Ed. and Prop. 283 Main   *Poughkeepsie.*
Rhinebeck Gazette and Duchess Co. Advertiser, Wm. Suff Ed. & Prop.   *Rhinebeck.*

Erie County.

Buffalo Commercial Advertiser, (daily & tri-weekly) Thomas M. Foote Ed., C. R. Jewett & Co. Publishers, 61 Main   *Buffalo.*
Buffalo Courier, (daily, tri-weekly & weekly) W. A. Seaver, Ed. & Prop., Spaulding's Exch.   *Buffalo.*
Buffalo Medical Journal & Monthly Review, A. Flint, M. D. Ed. Jewett Thos. & Co. Publishers, 161 Main   *Buffalo.*
Buffalo Patriot & Journal, E. R. Jewett & Co. Publishers 161 Main   *Buffalo.*
Buffalo Republic (daily- & weekly) B. C. Welch & E. A. Maynard Eds., E. A. Maynard Pub. Seneca st. n. Post Office *Buffalo.*
Buffalo Telegraph, (German) Henry B. Miller, Prop. Genesee near Main   *Buffalo.*
Der Weltburgher, (German) semi-weekly & weekly) Brunck & Domedian, 346 Main *Buffalo.*
Morning Express, (daily, tri weekly & weekly) A. M. Clapp & Co. Props. Exch. Building   *Buffalo.*
Western Literary Messenger, (monthly) J. Clement Editor, Jewett Thomas & Co. Pubs. 161 Main   *Buffalo.*
Wool Grower & Magazine of Agriculture & Horticulture, (monthly) T. C. Peters Ed. & Prop. 161 Main   *Buffalo.*

Essex County.

Essex County Republican, Jonathan F. Morgan Prop. Keeseville   *Au Sable.*
Westport Courier, H. A. Sanger Ed. and Prop.   *Westport.*

Fulton County.

Fulton County Democrat, Walter N. Clark Ed. & Prop. *Johnstown.*
Fulton County Republican Geo. Henry Ed. & Prop. *Johnstown.*

Genesee County.

Le Roy Gazette, C. B. Thompson Ed. & Prop.   *La Roy.*
Republican Advocate, D. D. Walt Prop.   *Batavia.*
Spirit of the Times, Seaver & Sons, Prop.   *Batavia.*

Greene County.

Catskill Messenger, Trowbridge & Gunn Prop.   *Catskill.*
Prattsville Advocate, J. L. Hackstaff Ed. & Pub.   *Prattsville.*

Herkimer County.

Herkimer County Democrat, R. Earl Editor & Proprietor   *Herkimer.*
Herkimer Journal, O. Squires Editor & Proprietor *Little Falls.*
Mohawk Courier, H. N. Johnson Editor & Proprietor *Little Falls.*

Jefferson County.

Democratic Union, John A Haddock Ed. & Prop. *Watertown.*

Jefferson County Democrat, E. J. Clarke, Prop. *Adams*.
Northern State Journal, Ambrose W. Clark Prop. *Watertown*.
Sackett's Harbor Observer, O. H. Harris Ed. & Prop. Sackett's Harbor *Hounsfield*.
Watertown Jeffersonian, Alvin Hunt Prop. *Watertown*.

Kings County.

Brooklyn Daily Advertiser, Henry A. Lees Ed., Lees & Foulkes Props. 35 & 41 Fulton *Brooklyn*.
Brooklyn Daily Evening Star, C. B. Spooner Ed. & Pub. *Brooklyn*.
Brooklyn Eagle, (Daily & Weekly) S. G. Arnold Ed., Isaac Van Arden Pub. 30 Fulton *Brooklyn*.
Brooklyn Freeman, (Daily) Walter Whitman, jr. Ed. Fulton st. cor. Middagh *Brooklyn*.
Democratic Advocate, Robert M'Adam & Co. Props., Q. M'Adam Ed. 30 Grand *Williamsburgh*.
Long Island Star, E. B. Spooner, Ed. & Prop. *Brooklyn*.
Williamsburgh Daily Times, Bennett & Smith Pubs. & Props., E. A. Sparks Ed. 129 Grand *Williamsburgh*.
Williamsburgh Gazette, L. Darbee & Son Pubs. 145 4th *Williamsburgh*.

Lewis County.

Lewis County Democrat, Horace R. Lahe Ed. & Pub. *Turin*.

Livingston County.

Dansville Chronicle *Dansville*.
Dansville Courier *Dansville*.
Livingston Republican, C. R. Brunson Ed. & Prop. *Geneseo*.
Livingston Union, Harding & Norton Pubs. *Mount Morris*.
Trembly's Advertiser *Dansville*.

Madison County.

Chittenango Phœnix, J. P. Olmstead Ed. & Pub. Chittenango *Sullivan*.
Democratic Reflector, Waldron & Baker Publishers *Hamilton*.
Madison County Journal, C. B. Gould Editor & Proprietor *Hamilton*.
Madison County Whig, Revs. J. Coolidge Ed. & Pub. *Cazenovia*.
Madison Observer, James Norton Ed. & Pub. Morrisville *Eaton*.

Monroe County.

Advent Harbinger & Bible Advocate, Joseph Marsh Ed. & Prop. cor Buffalo & Aqueduct *Rochester*.
Brockport Watchman, Edwin T. Briggs Ed. & Prop. Brockport *Sweden*.
Christian Guardian, Revs. J. Whitney, J. Chase. S Goff, & —— Brown Eds., W. Hughes Prop. Monroe Hall, Main st. *Rochester*.
Christian Sentinel, (semi-monthly) Same Eds. & Props. as the Christian Guardian, at the same place
Daily Magnet, Wm. M. Lewis, Ed., C. R. M'Donnell & Co. 12 Buffalo *Rochester*.
Genesee Evangelist, John C. Robie, Pub. cor. Buffalo & Aqueduct *Rochester*.
Genesee Farmer, (monthly) D. D. T. Moore Pub. cor. Buffalo & Aqueduct *Rochester*.

North Star, Frederic Douglass & M. R. Delany, Eds. 25 Buffalo *Rochester*.
Rochester Advertiser, (Daily & Tri-weekly) (& Weekly Republican) Madbury & Co. Eds. & Props. cor. Buffalo & Front *Rochester*.
Rochester Daily American, Jerome & Brother Pubs. Buffalo cor. Aqueduct *Rochester*.
Rochester Democrat, (daily, tri-weekly & weekly) A. Strong & Co. Pubs. Buffalo cor. State *Rochester*.
Rochester Evening News (daily) John W. Hurn Ed. & Prop. 4 Buffalo *Rochester*.
Star of Temperance, Sam. Chipman Ed., John C. Merrill Prop. Buffalo c. Aqueduct *Rochester*.

Montgomery County.

Amsterdam Intelligencer, Jas. Riggs Ed. & Prop. *Amsterdam*.
Mohawk Valley Gazette, W. H. Riggs, Pub. *Canajoharie*.
Montgomery Union, W. S. Hawley Ed. & Pub. *Canajoharie*.
Montgomery Whig. J. W. & T. R. Horton Eds. & Props. Fultonville *Glen*.

New York County.

NEWSPAPERS—DAILY MORNING.

Bank Note Reporter, John Thompson, 12 Spruce *New York*.
Courier & Enquirer, James Watson Webb & Henry J. Raymond Editors, 70 Wall
Daily Times, O. Bradbury Editor & Proprietor, 83 Nassau
Day Book, D. Francis Bacon, Editor, 84 Nassau
Express, Jas. & Erastus Brooks, Proprietors, Express Buildings. Wall cor. Nassau
Globe, Geo. R. Haswell, Publisher, J. S. Du Solle, Editor, 162 Nassau
Journal of Commerce, Gerard Hallock. Editor. 91 Wall
Herald, James G. Bennett, 126 Fulton
Morning Bulletin, 11 Spruce, Van Winkle & Henry, Editors
Morning Star, Williams Brothers, 102 Nassau
News, W. R. James, Editor and Proprietor, 86 Nassau
Staats Zeitung, Jacob Uhl, Publisher, 11 Frankfort
Sun, Moses S. & Alfred E. Beach, Proprietors, Nassau cor. Fulton
Tribune, Horace Greeley, Editor, 154 Nassau
True Sun, 162 Nassau, George G. Gallagher, Editor

NEWSPAPERS—DAILY EVENING.

Commercial Advertiser, Francis Hall & Co. Pub. cor. William
Express, James & Erastus Brooks, Proprietors, Express Buildings, Wall cor. Nassau
Mirror, Hiram Fuller, 105 Nassau
Post, W. C. Bryant & Co. 18 Nassau cor. Pine
Tribune, Horace Greeley, Editor, Nassau cor. Spruce

NEWSPAPERS—MONTHLY.

American Agriculturist, A. B. Allen Editor, C. M. Saxton Publisher, 191 Nassau
American Missionary, Wm. Harned, Publisher, 61 John
American Temperance Recorder, Oliver & Bro., Nassau c. Fulton

Child's Companion and Youth's Friend, 147 Nassau, James C. Meeks, Agent
Christian Union. 139 Nassau, Samuel Hueston, Publisher
Chronopress, 142 Nassau, A. Honeywell, Editor
Code Reporter, John Townshend, 80 Nassau
Jewish Chronicle, A. H. Wright, 139 Nassau
Journal of the American Temperance Union, John Marsh Ed 149 Nassau
Mirror of Fashion, Genio C. Scott, 146 Broadway
Protestant Churchman, Edward Shanon. Publishing Agent, 289 Broadway
Student. Denman, Calkins & Paine, 148 Grand
Theological and Literary Journal, Franklin Knight, 140 Nassau
Youth's Cabinet. D. Austin Woodworth, 135 Nassau
Wesleyan Magazine, L. C. Matlack, Editor. 5 Spruce
Western World, Graffenberg Co. Publishers, 50 Broadway
Working Farmer, James J. Mapes Editor, Kingman & Cross Publishers, Nassau cor. Beekman

NEWSPAPERS—SEMI-ANNUAL.

Brother Jonathan. Wilson & Co. Editors, 15 Spruce

NEWSPAPERS—SEMI-MONTHLY.

Age of Reason, Peter Eckler, 21 Ann
Annalist, N. S. Davis, Proprietor and Editor, 362 Bleecker
Eureka ; A record of mechanisms, inventions, patents, science, &c. Kingley & Pireson, 5 Wall
Juvenile Wesleyan, Luther Lee, Editor. 5 Spruce
La Verdad, Miguel T. Tolon, Editor, 102 Nassau
Merchants' Association Gazette, Albert Palmer, Merchants' Exchange, first door from Hanover
Merchants' and Tradesmens' Journal. E. P. Allen, publisher and editor, 9 Spruce.
Message Bird, M. T. Brocklebank & Co. Astor House
Schnellpost, C. Winsler & C. Magnus, 77 Chatham
Sunday School Journal, James C. Meeks, 147 Nassau
Teachers' Advocate, J. M'Keen & E. P. Allen editors, 9 Spruce
Youths' Penny Gazette, James C. Meeks Agent, 147 Nassau

NEWSPAPERS—SEMI-WEEKLY.

Courier and Enquirer, James W. Webb and Henry J. Raymond, editors, 70 Wall
Express, James & Erastus Brooks prop. Express Buildings, Wall cor. Nassau
Journal of Commerce, 91 Wall
La Cronica, Anthon & San Martin, 87 Cedar
Ledger, D. Anson Pratt, 57 Wall
Path Finder, A. Franklin Bartlett, 123 Fulton
Post, W. C. Bryant & Co. 18 Nassau
Shipping and Commercial List & New York Price Current, Francis Burritt, and heirs of W. Burritt, prop. 158 Pearl
Spectator, Francis Hall & Co. 46 Pine
Tribune, Horace Greeley ed. Nassau cor. Spruce

19

NEWSPAPERS—TRI-WEEKLY.

Courier des Etats-Unis, Paul Arpin 12 Park place

NEWSPAPERS—WEEKLY.

Account and Green's National Guard, D. Francis Bacon ed., 84 Nassau

Albion, William Young, 3 Barclay

American Artisan, S. Fleet ed. 102 Nassau

Ambassador & Messenger, S. C. Bulkeley, 3 Barclay

American Railroad Journal, Henry V. Poor ed. James D. Hodge and Gen. C. T. James assistant editors. John H. Shultz & Co. publishers. 54 Wall

American Sunday School Union, James C. Meeks agent, 147 Nassau, and 28 Park row

America's Own, E. B. Child ed. 86 Chatham

Atlas, Herrick & Ropes, 111 Nassau

Bank Note List, Edmund Charles & Co. 95 Wall

Christian Advocate and Journal, Lane & Scott pub. & Rev. Geo. Peck ed. 200 Mulberry

Christian Inquirer, Rev. H.W. Bellows ed. 275 Broadway

Christian Intelligencer, John H. Bevier ed. Charles Van Wyck, prop. 103 Fulton

Churchman, Rev. William Walton, 12 John

Continental, Robt. King, 102 Nassau

Courier and Enquirer, also published for every ocean steamer, as the Morning Courier for Europe, James W. Webb & Henry J. Raymond eds. 70 Wall

Demokrat, William Schuster ed. 77 Chatham

Deutsche Schnellpost, Magnus & Bach eds. 77 Chatham

Directory and Business Bulletin, Lemuel F. Dinsmore, 123 Fulton

Dispatch, Wilson & Co. eds. 16 Spruce

Dry Goods Reporter, William Burroughs, jr. 44 William

Era, Thomas Picton, 22 Spruce

European Times, Willmer & Rogers, 42 & 44 Nassau

Examiner, Arcularius & Scoville, 113 Nassau

Express, James & Erastus Brooks prop. Express Buildings, Wall cor. Nassau

Evangelist, William H. Bidwell, 120 Nassau

Farmer & Mechanic, Starr & Alburtis. 122 Nassau

Flag of Our Union, Samuel French, 293 Broadway

Freeman's Journal, Jas. A. M'Master, 81 Marion

Gazette of the Union and Golden Rule, Crampton & Clark, 44 Ann

Herald, James Gordon Bennett, Nassau cor. Fulton

Home Journal, Morris & Willis, 107 Fulton

Horn's Rail Road Gazette, Solon Horn, 126 Nassau

Independent, J. P. Thompson, Leonard Bacon and R. S. Storrs eds., S. W. Benedict pub. 201 William

Island City, William B. Smith Ed. & Prop. 75 Chatham

Journal of Commerce, 91 Wall

Literary American, George P. Quackenbos, 105 Nassau

Literary World, E. A. & G. L. Duykinck, 157 Broadway

Merchants' Ledger, D. Anson Pratt, 87 Wall

Metropolis, Park Benjamin & Co. 16 N. William

Military & Naval Argus, John Crawley & W. Henry Levison Eds. 79 Chatham

Military Review, Van Winkle & Henry Eds. 11 Spruce

Mirror, H. Fuller Ed. & Prop. Nassau cor. Ann

Mirror of the Times, Wm. W. Wallace, 106 Broadway

Nation, Thomas D. M'Gee, 151 Fulton

National Anti-Slavery Standard, Sydney Howard Gay, 142 Nassau

National Police Gazette, George Wilkes, 106 Nassau

Ned Buntline's Own, E. Z. C. Judson, 7 Spruce

News of the World, Williams Brothers, 109 Nassau

New Y'k Presbyterian, T. Dwight Ed. 252 Broadway

Observer, Sydney E. Morse & Co. 142 Nassau

Organ, R. T. Trall & W. Oliver Eds., Oliver & Brother Pubs. 120 Fulton

People, Reilly & Robinson Eds. 5 Spruce

Post, W. C. Bryant & Co. 18 Nassau

Recorder, S. S. Cutting Ed. 15 Spruce

Scientific American, Munn & Co. 128 Fulton

Spectator, Francis Hall & Co. Pine cor. William

Spirit of the Times, John Richards Ed. 1 Barclay

Staats Zeitung. Jacob Uhl Pub. 11 Frankfort

Sun, Moses S. & Alfred E. Beach Props. Nassau cor. Fulton

Sunday Courier, Smith, Adams & Smith, 134 Nassau

Sunday Dispatch, Williamson & Burns, 61 Ann

Sunday Mercury, Paige, Nichols & Krauth, 109 Nassau

Sunday Morning News, Whitney & West, 99 Nassau

Sunday Times & Noah's Weekly Messenger, Noah, Deans & Howard Pubs. & Eds. 162 Nassau

True Wesleyan, Luther Lee, Ed. 5 Spruce

Truth Teller, Wm. Denman, Ed. 79 Chatham

Two Worlds, Lockwood & Co. Pubs. John Bailey & Wm. Ross Wallace Eds. 459 Broadway

Universe, Williamson & Burns, 61 Ann

United States Journal of Education, 143 Nassau

Volksrechte, G. Arnold & V. W. Frolick Props. 9 Elizabeth

Washingtonian. Francis D. Allen Ed. 73 Chatham

Weekly Tribune, Greeley & M'Elrath, Nassau cor. Spruce

Weekly Yankee, Oliver B. Bunce Ed. 16 N. William

Niagara County.

Iris of Niagara, George Hackstaff Ed. & Prop. *Niagara Falls.*

Niagara Cataract, Charles J. Fox Ed. & Prop. *Lockport.*

Niagara Courier, D. S Crandall Ed. & Prop. *Lockport.*

Niagara Democrat, Ballou & Campbell Props. *Lockport.*

Oneida County.

Cenhadwr (Welch) paper monthly, R. Everett Ed. & Publisher *Steuben.*

Florence Oneida Telegraph, (semi-monthly) L. Myers Ed. & Prop. *Florence.*

New York Baptist Register, D. Bennett Prop. A. M. Beebee Ed. 156 Genesee *Utica.*

Oneida Morning Herald, Daily & Weekly, Roberts & Sherman Pub. R. U. Sherman & Erastus Clark Eds. 38 & 40 Genesee *Utica.*

Oneida Whig, A. Seward Ed. R. Northway & Co. Pub. 132 Genesee *Utica.*

Roman Citizen, A. D. Griswold Ed. Sandford & Scott Pubs. Dominick st. *Rome.*

Teetotaler, W. Bailey Ed. & Prop. 42 & 44 Genesee *Utica.*

Utica Daily Gazette, Alexander Seward Editor, R. Northway & Co. Pub. 132 Genesee *Utica.*

Utica Democrat, De Witt C. Grove Ed. & Prop. 42 & 44 Genesee *Utica.*

Utica Observer, (Daily and Weekly) Kittle & Beardsley Eds. & Props. *Utica.*

Onondaga County.

Daily Star, (Daily & Weekly) Kinney & Masters Eds. & Props. *Syracuse.*

Eclectic Medical & Surgical Journal, S. H. Potter Ed. Eclectic Medical Society Pubs. *Syracuse.*

Family Companion, (semi-monthly) P. Charles & Co. Props. *Clay.*

Imperial Citizen, S. R. Ward Ed. & Prop. *Syracuse.*

Literary Union J. M. Winchell & J. Johonnot Eds. J. M. Winchell Pub. Warren st. *Syracuse.*

Onondaga Gazette, Homer & Shepherd Eds. & Pubs. Baldwinsville *Lysander.*

Onondaga Standard, Ogan & Summers Eds. & Props. *Syracuse.*

Religious Recorder, Hulin & Avery Props. G. H. Hulin Ed. Genesee st. *Syracuse.*

Reveille Daily, Palmer & Summers Eds. & Props. *Syracuse.*

Skaneateles Democrat, H. B. Dodge Ed. & Prop. *Skaneateles.*

Syracuse Daily Journal, W. W. Smith & Co. Eds. & Props. *Syracuse.*

Syracuse Democrat, William W. Green Ed. & Pub. *Syracuse.*

Temperance Protector, (Monthly) T. S. Trusir Pub. William H. Burleigh Ed. *Syracuse.*

Ontario County.

Geneva Courier, E. Van Valkenburgh Pub. Geneva *Seneca.*

Geneva Gazette, J. & S. H. Parker Pubs. Geneva *Seneca.*

Ontario Messenger, Mattison & Sandford Pubs. & Props. *Canandaigua.*

Ontario Repository, S. V. O. Mallory Ed. George L. Whiting Pub. *Canandaigua.*

Phelps Democrat, W. W. Redfield Pub. *Phelps.*

Orange County.

Banner of Liberty, (semi-monthly) G. J. Barber Ed. & Pub. *South Middletown.*

Carmichael's Literary Miscellany, (Semi-monthly) O. Carmichael Ed. & Prop. *South Middletown.*

Goshen Democrat & Whig, Mead & Webb Pubs. *Goshen.*

Highland Courier, John D. Spaulding Ed. & Prop. *Newburgh.*

Independent Republican, Clark & Montague Pubs. *Goshen.*

Middletown Advertiser, (Monthly) G. J. Beebe Ed. & Pub. *South Middletown.*
Newburgh Excelsior, Thomas George Ed. & Pub. *Newburgh.*
Newburgh Gazette, S. T. Callaham Ed. & Pub. *Newburgh.*
Newburgh Telegraph, Elias Bates Ed. & Pub. *Newburgh.*
Orange County News, J. S. Brown Ed. & Pub. *South Middletown.*
Sign of the Times, (semi-monthly) G. Beebe Ed. & Pub. *South Middletown.*

Orleans County.

Orleans American, J. & J. H. Denio Publishers, Albion *Barre.*
Orleans Republican, J. O. Wiltse Publisher, Albion *Barre.*
The Democrat, C. S. M'Connell Publisher, Albion *Barre.*

Oswego County.

Fulton Patriot, John A. Place Ed. & Pub. Fulton *Volney.*
Oswego Commercial Times, (daily & weekly) Jas. N. Brown Pub. Telegraph Block *Oswego.*
Oswego Palladium, Hatch & Mills Publishers, Woodruff's Block, cor. 1st & Cayuga *Oswego.*
Richland Courier, A. A. Mathewson Ed. & Pro. Pulaski *Richland.*

Otsego County.

Farmers' Journal Shaw & Titus Editors & Publishers *Cooperstown.*
Otsego Democrat, James J. Hendryks Editor *Cooperstown.*
Otsego Republican, A. M. Barber Editor *Cooperstown.*

Putnam County.

Putnam Democrat, S. C. Oliver, Editor *Carmel.*

Queens County.

Hempstead Inquirer and Long Island Advertiser, Seaman N. Snedeker Editor & Proprietor *Hempstead.*
Long Island Democrat, James J. Benton Editor & Publisher *Jamaica.*
Long Island Farmer, H. Willis Editor *Jamaica.*

Rensselaer County.

Family Journal and Northern New York Organ, Allen Fisk & Son Editors & Publishers, 72 1st *Troy.*
Lansingburgh Democrat, W. I. Lamb Editor & Publisher, 233 State *Lansingburgh.*
Lansingburgh Gazette, Harkness & Kirkpatrick, Editors & Publishers *Lansingburgh.*
Troy Budget, Wm. W. Whitman, Publisher, 197 River *Troy.*
Troy Daily Post, Davis & Cooper, Editors & Proprietors, 6 Cannon place *Troy.*
Troy Daily Whig, James M. Stevenson, Publisher, 149 River *Troy.*

Richmond County.

Staten Islander, F. L. Hagadorn, Editor & Publisher *Southfield.*

Rockland County.

Rockland County Messenger, Robert Marshall Editor & Proprietor *Haverstraw.*

St. Lawrence County.

Ogdensburgh Forum, Albert Tyler, Editor & Proprietor *Ogdensburgh.*
Ogdensburgh Sentinel, S. Foote Editor *Ogdensburgh.*
St. Lawrence Mercury, Wm. H. Wallace & Seth Washburn Editors & Proprietors *Potsdam.*
St. Lawrence Republican, Smith & Ornell Editors & Proprietors *Ogdensburgh.*

Saratoga County.

Ballston Democrat, T. C. Young Publisher *Ballston.*
Ballston Journal, Albert A. Moore, Publisher *Ballston.*
Saratoga Republican, John A. Corey *Saratoga Springs.*
Saratoga Whig, Geo. W. Spooner, Editor *Saratoga Springs.*

Schenectady County.

Schenectady Cabinet, S. S. Riggs, Editor & Publisher, 139 State *Schenectady.*
Schenectady Reflector *Schenectady.*

Schoharie County.

Schoharie Patriot, S. H. Mix Editor & Publisher *Schoharie.*
Schoharie Republican, Wm. H. Gallup Editor & Publisher *Schoharie.*

Seneca County.

Ovid Bee, Croydon Fairchild Editor & Proprietor *Ovid.*
Seneca County Courier, Foster & Judd Publishers *Seneca Falls.*
Seneca Observer and Union, Chas. Sentell Editor & Proprietor *Waterloo.*
The Lilly, Mrs. A. Bloomer Editor & Proprietor *Seneca Falls.*

Steuben County.

Corning Journal, Thomas Messenger Editor & Proprietor *Painted Post.*
Steuben Courier, H. H. Hall Editor & Proprietor *Bath.*
Steuben Democrat, G. H. Biddle, Editor & Proprietor *Bath.*
Steuben Farmers' Advocate, W. C. Rhodes Editor & Proprietor *Bath.*

Suffolk County.

Republican Watchman, Samuel Phillips Editor & Proprietor, Greenport *Southold.*
Suffolk Gazette, Gilbert P. Lewis Edito- & Proprietor *Riverhead.*

Sullivan County.

Sullivan County Whig, John W. Hasbrouck Editor & Proprietor *Bloomingburgh.*
Republican Watchman, Frederick A. De Voe, Editor & Proprietor, Monticello *Thompson.*

Tioga County.

Owego Advertiser, Andrew H. Calhoun, Ed. *Owego.*
Owego Gazette *Owego.*

Ulster County.

Ellenville Journal, R. Denton, Ed. & Prop. Ellenville *Wawarsing.*
Kingston Democratic Journal, W. H. Romeyn Ed. & Pub. *Kingston.*
Ulster Democrat, A. A. Bensel, Pub. *Kingston.*
Ulster Republican, R. A. Chipp, Ed. & Prop. *Kingston.*

Ulster Telegraph, S. S. Hommell, Ed. & Pub. *Saugerties.*

Warren County.

Glenn's Falls Clarion, George W. Cheney, Ed. & Prop. Glenn's Falls *Queensbury.*
Glenn's Falls Republican, Thomas J. Strong, Ed. & Pub. Glenn's Falls *Queensbury.*

Washington County.

Sandy Hill Herald, E. D. Baker, jr Ed. & Pub. Sandy Hill *Kingsbury.*
The Whitehaller, W. S. Southard, Pub. *Whitehall.*
Washington County Post, R. E. Young, Ed. & Prop. North White Creek *White Creek.*
Whitehall Chronicle, H. W. Blanchard, Pub. *Whitehall.*

Wayne County.

Lyons Gazette, S. W. Russell, Ed. & Pub. *Lyons.*
Newark Democrat, T. Creicquie, Ed. & Pub. *Arcadia.*
Palmyra Courier, F. Morley, Ed. & Pub. *Palmyra.*
Wayne Banner, M'Intire & Pain, Eds. & Props. *Wolcott.*
Wayne County Whig, W. N. Cole, Ed. & Prop. *Lyons.*
Wayne Sentinel, P. Tucker, Ed. & Prop. *Palmyra.*

Westchester County.

Bank Note List (Quarterly), Edward Sleath. Prop. *White Plains.*
Bank Note List (Quarterly), John Banta, Prop. *White Plains.*
Bank Note List (Monthly), L. C. Platt, Prop. *White Plains.*
Bank Note List (Quarterly), H. Matthias, Prop. *White Plains.*
Bank Note List (Quarterly), Sanford Savey, Prop. Sing Sing *Ossining.*
Bank Note List (Monthly), S. Edgett, Ed. & Prop. Sing Sing *Ossining.*
Eastern State Journal, Edmund G. Sutherland, Ed. & Pub. *White Plains.*
Hudson River Chronicle, Chauncy Smith, Ed. & J. Holly Platt, Pub. Sing Sing *Ossining.*
Peekskill Republican, William Richards, Peekskill *Courtlandt.*
Westchester Herald, C Roscoe, Ed. & Pub. Sing Sing *Ossining.*

Wyoming County.

Perry Democrat, C. C. Britt, Ed. & Prop. *Perry.*
Spirit of the Old Eighth, Wm. A. Siver, Pub. & Prop. *Attica.*
Western New Yorker, S. S. Blanchard, Ed. & Pub. *Warsaw.*
Wyoming County Mirror, Holly & Dudley, Pubs. *Warsaw.*

Yates County.

Dundee Record, E. Hoogland, Pub. Dundee *Starkey.*
Penn Yan Democrat, A. Reed, Ed. & Pub. Penn Yan *Milo.*
Yates County Whig, B. L. Adams, Ed. & Prop. Penn Yan *Milo.*

Nurserymen, Seedsmen, Florists, &c. (Marked thus * are Seedsmen only.)

Chemung County.

Frost Eli C. *Catharine.*

Columbia County.

Studley E. G.   *Claverack.*

Duchess County.

Lent D. B. Smith st. *Poughkeepsie.*

Kings County.

Nichols R. cor. Smith & Atlantic
sts.   *Brooklyn.*
Russell Wm., Henry cor. Amity
Davison W. (Florist) Livingston
cor. Smith
Benton R. (Florist) Henry near
Hamilton
Cadman James, Fulton st.
Reynolds John W. 87 South 7th
    Williamsburgh.
Hanfield & Hoeft, 1st nr. South 9th
Gaynor Pat. Mount Vernon Gardens, 1st near North 2d

Monroe County.

Boardman J. & Co.   *Brighton.*
Boardman S.
Boardman E.
Kelly N. *
Fisher & Moore
Sherman A.
Yale J.
*Fellows H.   *Penfield.*
Bissel. Hooker & Sloan, Rochester
Commercial Nursery, 3 East Av.
    Rochester.
Elwanger & Barry, Mount Hope
Av.
King Wm. (Ornamental Flowers)
& Monroe

New York County.

Beaver Paul, 194 West 16th
    New York.
Blake Thomas, 236 West 20th
Bloodgood Nursery, King & Ripley Proprietors, 344 Pearl
Bridgeman Alfred, 878 Broadway
and Astoria, L. I.
*Bidgeman Thomas, 874 Broadway
Brown H. 36 West 20th
Bruce James T. 60 East 17th
Buchanan Isaac, 17 West 17th
Dooley James, 11th cor. Broadway
Dunlap Thomas, 635 Broadway
Hauser J. N. 29th near 3d Av.
Hofert Herrn T. West 19th cor. 6th
Av.
Holsted Hannah, Tompkins mkt.
Monk J. 30th cor. 4th Av.
Phelan Wm. & Sons, 5th cor Av. A
*Randolph Obadiah W. F. 57
Whitehall
Reid Andrew, 799 Broadway
Reid Andrew, 163 West 11th
Shaw Joseph, 40 11th
*Smith Alexander, 336 Broadway
Thorburn James M. & Co. 15 John
Tryon E. J. 9 John
Virtue Mary, Broad'y cor 5th Av.
Vogel C. F. 64 6th Av.
Viets Wm. H. 30 Water
White Wm. M. 15th cor. 7th Av.

Oneida County.

Boyce F. W. 6 Oneida   *Utica.*

Onondaga County.

Wilson A.   *Marcellus.*

Orange County.

Brundage G. & F.   *Cornwall.*
Ferris L. M. Coldenham *Newburgh.*
Corwin Nathan H. South Middletown   *Wallkill.*

Oswego County.

Goodsell N.   *New Haven.*
Wright James H.

Queens County.

Parsons & Co. (Florists) *Flushing.*
Winter & Co.
Higgins Daniel
Doane P.   *Jamaica.*
Eagan Thomas
Marc G.(Florist) Astoria *Newtown.*
Pervo L.   do

Schenectady County.

Felthousen J. D. 141 State
    Schenectady.
Greagles C. Barret st

Wayne County.

Thomas John J. Centre *Macedon.*
Smith Wm. R.   do
Yeomans T. G.   *Walworth.*
Gardiner Wm. W

Oakum Manufacturers.

Erie County.

Green P. East Seneca st.   *Buffalo.*

Oars, Sweeps and Sculls.

Barker & Page Enoch W. 90 West
    New York.
Page Ezekiel, 20 West

Oculists.

Boudinier J. N. 537 Broadway
    New York.
Brenson C. P. 3 Warren
Brown George N. H. 362 Broome
Comstock Charles S. 17 Park place
Elliott Samuel M. 535 Broadway
Francis Isaac, 490 Broome and
Aurist
Powell James W. 261 Broadway
and Aurist
Stephenson Mark, 383 Broome
Wheeler John, 29 Greenwich, oculist & importer of French artificial eyes

Oil and Candles.

Bartlett A. 101 Front, corner of
Jones' lane, near Wall
    New York.
Bealnas Philip, 101 Broome
Barrow & Prior, 160 Wall
Dean Henry & John H. Smith, 11
Stone
Higton, Howe & M'Clenin, 263
Washington
Hatch W. T. 120 Front
Fowler Mark & Co. 184 Front
Leland & Beach, 159 Front
Litchfield & Co. 159 Front
Macy Josiah & Sons, 189 Front &
255 South
Pryer John & Co. 250 Front
Smith James A. 56 Water
Sniffen John jr. & Co. 90 Ann
Swain E. H. 165 Maiden lane

Oiled Cloth Manufacturers.
(See Oiled Floor Cloths.)

Greene County.

Mitchell Miles   *Prattsville.*

Orange County.

Young W. G.   *Newburgh.*
Gearsis George & Co.
Roe & Beers
Hawkins John

Saratoga County.

Wakeman S. Ballston Spa *Milton.*

Oiled Clothing Manufacturers.

Briggs Amos, 514 Water
    New York.
Cohen Hyam, 225 William
Reynolds Benjamin, 90 South
Roberts Samuel, 28 Fulton

Oiled Floor Cloth Manufacturers. *(See also Oiled
Cloth Manufacturers.)*

Kings County.

Van Brunt & Ellsworth, Prince
near Tillary st.   *Brooklyn.*
Wiley & Brasher, Willoughby
cor. Fleet
Woodcock Frederick, Adelphi st.
Harvey E. & Co. Bedford st.
Sparkman & Kelsey,   do
Cunningham Bernard, Walworth
Underhill James A. Bedford st.
Harvey Edward,   do

New York County.

Albro Hoyt & Co. 72 John
    New York.
Jewett John & Sons, 162 Front
Stevens Barlow, 43 Pine

Oneida County.

Pomeroy, Walker & Co. 10 Genesee   *Utica.*

Rensselaer County.

Powers D. & Sons, 32 State
    Lansingburgh.
Whipple J. E. cor. River & South
Davenport Thomas C. John st.

Oiled Silk Manufacturers.

Clark Isaac, 134 Wall & 133
Malden lane   *New York.*
Danziger Henry, 7 Suffolk

Oil Manufacturers.

Albany County.

Dey Ermand & Davis, (Linseed
Oil) 1 Broadway   *Albany.*
Wicks & Tillinghast, (Sperm Oil)
13 Hudson
Smith D.   *Bethlehem.*

Chautauque County.

Miller & Son, Fredonia *Pomfret.*
Hillard Avery   *Westfield.*

Chenango County.

Trask Almond, Centre *Guilford.*
Guernsey William G.   *Norwich.*

Columbia County.

Barnard Curtiss & Co. (Sperm &
Whale) Water st.   *Hudson.*
Humphrey & Remington (Lard
Oil)
Reed R. Allen st.

Cortland County.

Scott Ransom   *Scott.*

Franklin County.

Dickinson J. & Sons (Linseed)
    Bangor.

Fulton County.

Kellogg L. (Linseed)   *Perth.*

Genesee County.

Morgan L. G. & Wm.   *Le Roy.*

Jefferson County.

Knapp Thomas L. (Linseed)
    Brownsville.
Rawson Edward (Linseed)
    Champion.
Lathrop Alfred (Linseed)

Kings County.

Gilbert George S. (Sperm, Elephant, Whale & Lard) 125 Furman   *Brooklyn.*
Flanders & Kimball (Sperm, Elephant, Whale & Lard) Furman near Fulton
Diets, Brothers & Co. 62 Fulton
Colman & Co. 48 Fulton
Flanders Chas. N. Haxtun's Dock near Fulton
Litchfield & Co. 45 Water
Barty Joseph, Adams near Front
Rowe T. G. & A. L. (Linseed) Montauk Mills, Sand's Wharf, between Bridge & Jay
Veeder & Whittlesy (Sperm, Whale, Elephant & Lard) cor. Bridge & John
Hatch W. G. Gold cor. John
Barry H. Bedford st.

Lewis County.

Spencer Stephen, jr.   *Turin.*

Livingston County.

Stone Benjamin   *Dansville.*
Day ——

Madison County.

Knowlton E.   *Cazenovia.*
Warner Theodore , *De Ruyter.*

Monroe County.

Weddle Thomas & Sons (Linseed)
Brown's Sons   *Rochester.*

New York County.

Barnard, Curtis & Co. 111 Water
    New York.
Barrow & Prior, 109 Wall
Brown & Decker, 14 James slip
De Forest Cornel. V. 119 Clinton
Evans Robert C. 135 Amos
Frothingham & Beckwith. 140 Cedar
Hinman Elisha W. 2 Coenties slip
Howe Jas. K. 400 West
Howe A. K. & J. H. 389 & 391 West
Lambert Chas. 24 Old slip
Lewis Jas. T. & Co. 82 Water
Litchfield & Co. 159 Front
Macy Josiah & Sons. 189 Front & 266 South
Megrath & Hasbrouck, 413 West
Mitchell Richard H. 23 Fulton
Mount Alfred R. 72 Front
Pond, Champion & Co. 101 Wall
Fryer John & Co. 334 Front
Roberts John W. 97 Market
Rogers John, 283 Bowery
Smith C. E. 296 Rivington & 239 Water
Sniffen John, jr. & Co. 90 Ann
Sparrow Jas. R. 240 Front
Trussell E. D. 374 Washington
Veeder & Whittlesey, 88 Front
Williams Joseph T. 8 Peck slip

OIL MANUFACTURERS (LARD.)

Forbes John W. 14 Jacob
Howe A. K. & J. H. 389, 390 & 391 West
Megrath & Hasbrouck, 413 West & 6 Broadway

OIL MANUFACTURERS (LINSEED.)

Bridge J. 139 Front & 612 Cherry
Rowe T. G. & A. L. 198 Front

OIL MANUFACTURERS (NEATS' FOOT.)

Cooper Peter, 17 Burling slip
Cummings Chas. 2 Platt
Salter A. & Co. 100 John

OIL MANUFACTURERS (SPERM.)

Hatch W. T. 190 Front
Judd's Samuel Sons & Co. 59 Fulton, 423 Water & 139 Front
Kingsland D. & A. & Co. 55 Broad
Luckey J. N. Agent for the N. E. Whaling Co. 44 Cortlandt
Lyles & Polhamus, 262 South
Macy Josiah & Sons, 189 Front & 266 South

OIL MANUFACTURER (COD LIVER.)

Rushton. Clark & Co. 110 Br'dway
Skinner H. B. 106 Broadway

Oil Manufacturers—Continued.

Orange County

Lillburn A.   *Newburgh.*
Farrington Daniel, Front st.
Farrington D. & Son, 11 Water

Orleans County.

Coan & Chase, Medina *Ridgeway.*
Angevine E. & A. do

Oswego County

Goit David   *Mexico.*
Wright J. B. Pulaski   *Richland.*

Rensselaer County.

Reynolds & Nolton (Linseed)
    Petersburgh.
Slocum C. B. (Linseed) *Pittstown.*

Seneca County.

Knox & Purdy   *Waterloo.*
Wilson Joel

Wyoming County.

Cotton O. Attica   *Bennington.*
Hawley S. & Co   *Gainesville.*
Bailey C. F.   *Perry.*

Oil Lamps, Camphene & Burning Fluid. (See also Lamps, also Camphene.)

Kings County.

Merritt & Co. 57 Atlantic *Brooklyn.*
Diets Brother & Co. 62 Fulton
Wright George, 204 do
Butler John & Brother 112 Fulton
Pape Wm. 41 James
Bardwell Robert, 37 Hudson Av.
Wellings J. T. 221 1st
    Williamsburgh.
Licht Lewis, 491 Grand

Rensselaer County.

Rikart Jacob, 4 Franklin square
    Troy.
M'Kinney J. (Coach Lamps) 48 Albany
Leach H. 15 Congress

Oil Merchants. (See also Grocers, also Oil Manufacturers.)

Erie County.

Smith James, 66 Lloyd *Buffalo.*
Sprague & Wardwell, 10 Webster's block, Main

Kings County.

Bryant James, Plymouth st.
    Brooklyn.

Pond, Champion & Co. Haxton's dock nr. Fulton ferry *Brooklyn.*
Whitington Geo. 112 Jay

New York County.

Barnard, Curtis & Co. 111 W'tr
    New York.
Brown John A. 490 Pearl
Burke E. D. 97 1st
Cartwright, Harrison & Co. 111 Front
Clews & Williams, 3 Jones lane
Comstock Nathan, 191 Front
Elsworth Cyrus B. 110 Murray
Fish James H. 100 John
Fowler Mark, 186 Front
Gardner Zachariah B. 30 Hamilton
Haetleng Michael, 564 4th
Halsted Charles J. 44 Broome
Hughes Michael, 16 Pike
Hurlbut Samuel, 84 South
Judd's Samuel Sons & Co. 423 Water, 59 Fulton, & 139 Front
Leonard Charles H. 140 do
Lucky Joseph N. 44 Cortlandt
Lylez & Polhemus, 262 South
Macy Josiah & Sons, 266 South
Mattison & Ely, 33 Spruce
M'Donald P. 240 1st
M'Dowell Joseph T. 155 Division
M'Dowell A. 94 Henry
Lutz John, 129 Willett
Myers George. 33 Goerck
Pond, Champion & Co. 101 Wall
Quackenbush & Bamber, 172 West
Richards Stephen, 63½ Gold
Roberts John R. 97 Market
Seeley William H. & Roberts, 140 Maiden lane
Schllenbeager Kasper, 22 Av. B
Shaw Joseph, 6 10th
Slate, Gardiner & Howell, 115 South
Smith Andrew & B. 293 South
Smith B. & Co. 168 Front
Smith Charles E. 239 Water
Smith James A. 54 Water
Smith Merritt, 199 Greenwich
Taylor D. C. 28 Front
Tooker Daniel A. jr. 282 Bowery
Van Doren Jacob J. 170 G'wich
Van Voorhis E. W. & Co. 148 Front
Van Wyck Cornelius I. 34 and 40 Fletcher
Waterbery Joseph, 50 Av. D.
Wooding J. & A. 195 Spring

Oil of Peppermint—Dealers.

Wayne County.

Blackmer H. & O.   *Arcadia.*
Blackmer Abel T.
Blackmer E.
Hotchkiss H. G. & W. T. *Lyons.*

Omnibus Proprietors.

Conklin Brothers, 261 to 267 3d Av.   *New York.*
Bolster & Andrews, W. 23d bet. 6th & 7th Avs.
Hatfield & Bertine, 395 10th
Kipp & Brown, office 537 Hudson
Knickerbocker Depot, 8th Av.
Lent Charles, 7th Av. cor. W. 23d
Mackrell & Simpson, 395 & 417 19th
Marshall Jesse & J. 8th Av. cor. W. 23d
Murphy James, 90 11th
Reynolds & Weart, W. 23d cor. 6th Av.
Robbins John & Co. 547 Grand

Sudlow, Pullis & M'Lelland, 419 10th   *New York.*
Tyson William, 294 Henry

Ornithologist.

Audubon J. J. 43 Beaver *New York.*

Opticians. (*See also Spectacle Makers.*)

Albany County

Gall J. 36 Green   *Albany.*

Erie County.

Andrews R. F. & Son, 15 Webster's Block   *Buffalo.*

New York County.

Aulmann A. 228 Greenwich   *New York.*
Forster John, 222 Water
Gillmur David, 617 Hudson
Goldbacher Max & Co. 90 Division
Lewenberg Aaron, 357 4th
Lewenberg Leon, 201 Division
Moore Francis W. 68 Allen
Perry James F. 5 Dey
Pike B. & Son, 166 Broadway
Pike Benjamin, jr. 294 do
Roach John, 79 Nassau
Rosenthall Samuel, 48 Thompson
Seibold David F. 419 Pearl
Wise Marcus, 437 Broadway
Wolf John G. 98 Nassau

Organ Builders. (*See also Musical Instruments.*)

Monroe County.

Bingham N. 119½ Buffalo   *Rochester.*

New York County.

Davis William H. & Co. 67 M'Dougal   *New York.*
Erben Henry, 172 Centre
Ferris R. M. 298 Bowery
Hall & Labagh, 96 & 98 Wooster
Jackson James, 174 8th Av.
Jardine George, 648 Pearl

Rensselaer County.

Backus A. rear of Boardman's Building   *Troy.*

Tompkins County.

Akins, Hollinshead & Spencer, 104 Owego   *Ithaca.*

Ornament Makers, (Composition.)

Coffee Thomas, 57 Canal   *New York.*
Caillouette & Jackson, 136 Mercer
Farley H. C. 23 Canal
Gallier John, 648 Broadway
Kennedy & Chatterton, 134 Chatham
Searis & Williams, 57 White

Oyster Dealers.

Erie County.

Rowe & Co. 196 Main   *Buffalo.*
Blozier C. H. & Co. 151 do

Kings County.

Swift S. L. 209 Atlantic *Brooklyn.*
Inyard N. 26 Henry
Glassee William, 83 Stanton
Applegate L. & D. 153 Myrtle Av.
Seaman Gideon, 156   do
Robertson J. M. & Co. Market st.

Morgan J. & Son, Market South   *Brooklyn.*
Davis Henry, 27 Grand   *Williamsburgh.*
Oyston James, 156 Grand

Packet Offices. (*See also Merchants Shipping and Importing—also Merchants Shipping and Commission—also Steam-ship Companies.*)

Allen & Paxson, 134 Front   *New York.*
Bedell Mott, 104 Wall
Boyd & Hincken, 88 Wall
Briggs J. & N. 40 South
Brower S. H. 45   do
Bulkeley Geo. 88   do
Clanny James, 108 do
Dayton & Sprague, 107 Front
Dunham & Dimon, 67 South
Eagle & Hazard, 40   do
Elwell James W. 57   do
Frost & Hicks. 68   do
Griswold John, 70   do
Havens J. H. 39 Burling slip
Johnson Gilbert A. & F. 67 South
Jones Joshua T. 90 Wall
Kimball Thomas, 8 South
Kimball & Bedient, 8 South
Mailler & Lord, 108 Wall
M'Cready N. L. & Co. 36 South
M'Murray Joseph, 69   do
Marshall Charles H. & Co. 38 Burling slip
Murphy Richard, 76 South
Nelson William, 85   do
Pierson C. H. & W. 61 do
Platt Frederick L. 104 Wall
Powell Elzey S. 104   do
Post Ralph, 38 South
Read R. C. 27   do
Redford J. H. 16 do
Ropes R. W. & Co. 44 Water
Spofford, Tileston & Co. 48 South
Stanton Thomas P. 56   do
Sturges Clearman & Co. 110 Wall
Whitlock William, jr. 46 South

Packing Houses. (*See also Provision Dealers.*)

New York County.

Dougherty Michael, 309 W. 17th   *New York.*
Jones Lawson, 13 Marion
Larkin James, 47 Charles
Moses C. & A. 162 West & 396 Greenwich
Remsen John C. 568 Washington
Young Eben S. & Co. 76 Sullivan

Oneida County.

Jones T. E. & Co. 139 Genesee   *Utica.*
Owens D. & T. M. 10 Main
Brewer P. Broad st.

Onondaga County.

Avery & Hewlett, Syracuse *Salina.*

Pail Manufacturers.

Chenango County.

Harrington M. P. & Co.   *Pitcher.*

Erie County.

Corbin W. H. & Co. Spring Brook   *Aurora.*
Henry John L.   *Collins.*
Webster G.

Jefferson County.

Young John (butter tubs) Black River   *Rutland.*

Sleezer M. L. (tubs), Black River   *Rutland.*
Wiley Nathaniel   *Watertown.*
Button N. & D.

Livingston County.

Shelly Ezra   *Dansville.*

Monroe County.

Merick N. B. Brown's Race   *Rochester.*

Niagara County.

Patterson & Murray   *Niagara Falls.*

Oneida County.

Ray A. M'Connellsville   *Vienna.*
Watson, Ellis & Co. Whitesboro   *Whitestown.*

Ostego County.

Ellery & Holder, Cooperstown   *Otsego.*

Rensselaer County.

Kegg D. (nail kegs)   *Grafton.*

Painters, Coach and Carriage. (*See also Painters, House, Sign, and Fancy.*)

Ellis William, 74 E. Broadway   *New York.*
Marsh Joseph Y. 268 Mercer
Moriarty Albert F. 134 W. 19th
Parcells John H. 154 Delancy
Swift Charles, 105 Walker

Painters, Historical.

Brown S. 251 B'dway *New York.*
Caiyo Nicolino & Son, 131 E. 21st
Church Frederick, 497 Broadway
Doughty Thomas, 497   do
Edouart A. 607   do
Evers John, 36 Amity
Hulme J. 68½ Greene
Jarvis Charles, 3 Laight
Muller Hector B. 22 Howard
Rossiter Thomas B. 563 Broadway

Painters—House, Sign & Fancy.

Albany County.

Hart I. M. Land Side, Exchange   *Albany.*
Porter Ira, 535 Broadway
Rogers Stephen, 617 Broadway
Gladding & Morrill, 484 Broadway
Cusack M. 82 State
Gladding J. 92 State
Hurdis J. & S. 9 Church
Johnson J. W. (Coach) 90 Green
Mix Stephen, 42 Franklin
Seaton O. E. 201 S. Pearl
Vedder J. S. & Co. 106 Lydius
Haford & Scattergood, 36 S. Pearl
Camp D. H. 106 S. Pearl
Owens T. 37 Green
Gregory L. R. 22 Green
Alden S. H. 20 Beaver
Hutchins S. B. 10 Beaver
Corliss R. B. 29 Howard
Gladding F. 12 William
Brower J. H. 26 Daniel
Wilson T. & J. 3 N. Pearl
Wendren Jas. C. 28 Washington
Mills C. S. 23 Washington
Packard Wm. J. 98 Washington
Latta Jacob, Guilderland Centre, *Guilderland.*
Beaver Thomas, Dunnsville   *New Scotland.*
Pangborn J.
Weger A. West Troy *Watervliet.*
M'Allister A.   do

Benjamin Wm., West Troy
Watervliet.
Wandell S. S. do

Alleghany County.

Rose David   *Alfred.*
Green Benjamin H.
Slafter J.   *Amity.*
Goodwin E. W.   *Andover.*
Dantremont V. D.   *Angelica.*
Flynn A. L.   *Belfast.*
Lomis Harvey   *Cuba.*
Greadey Wm.
Davids Wm. B.
Mills John   *Friendship.*
Bronson Samuel
Crandall Jos. Whitesville
                          Independence.
Adams A. L.   *Rushford.*
Ellis Ephraim

Broome County.

Tupper M. F. & Co.   *Binghamton.*
Halstead Jacob
Smith L.
Tupper & Pope
Bennett E. C.

Cattaraugus County.

Gleason Wm   *Franklinville.*
Pillsbury D.   *Rice.*

Chautauque County.

Dirgley A.   *Charlotte.*
Pettis Daniel
Gray John C. Jamestown   *Ellicott.*
Arnold Henry,   do
Hanchett & Hunt,   do
Stillson B.   do
Van Deusen Samuel   *Harmony.*
Bartlett B. Fredonia   *Pomfret.*
Wilson ——,   do
Fields A.   do
Pierce H. M.   *Sherman.*

Chenango County.

Wilkins Walter S.   *Coventry.*
Blood Orson   *Guilford.*
Gregory G.   *New Berlin.*
Fisher H.
Hyde Asahel J.   *Oxford.*
Mason Jos.
Williams & Nickerson
Harrington Jas. H. Pitcher Spa
Wever L. J.   *Plicher.*
Stafford A.   *Sherburne.*

Clinton County.

Richardson R. N.   *Plattsburgh.*
Warren J. D.
Grover Wm.
Wells F.
Uran G. V.
Hare David

Columbia County.

Brown A. Spencertown *Austerlitz.*
Marshall Wm. C. Chatham Four
  Corners   *Chatham.*
Myer J. A.   *Claverack.*
Burdwin J. T. Front st.   *Hudson.*
Lisk & Decker, Columbia st.
Hildreth H. Warren st.
Stevens A. B. jr. Valatie
                             Kinderhook.
Bradley F.

Delaware County.

Williamson D.   *Delhi.*
Edwards J.
Nettle E.
Smith J. W. Deposit   *Tompkins.*
Marvis U.   do
Ogden H.   do
Allen C.   do
Eells S. D.   *Walton.*

Duchess County.

Leach D. Fishkill Landing
                              Fishkill.
Dobbs D.   *Hyde Park.*
Brant J. D.
Chamberlain L. B.   *Pine Plains.*
Wright W. T.
Pierce H. 377 Main *Poughkeepsie.*
Flower A. B. 7 Hamilton
Smith S. 7 Conklin
Culver Wm. A. 455 Main
Shield Wm. Church st.
Perkins S. H. Church st.
Pierce H.
Degriff M. S. 70 Market
Hoglen J. D. (Monochromatic) 1
  Market
Alexander & Porter, Garden st.
Wilber S. A. corner Catharine &
  Morrison
Munell R. Washington st.
Batey Jas. K. 185 Main
Elmendorf H.
Hayes C. P.
Cooper A.   *Red Hook.*
Vansteenbergh J.
Holdridge E.   *Rhinebeck.*
Varry H.   *Washington.*

Erie County.

Eggleston Almon   *Alden.*
Seward Morgan L.
Merry L.   *Black Rock.*
Gamble —— ..
Gillig L. 40 Exchange   *Buffalo.*
Braid C. Washington nr. Genesee
Chretien C. Main near Chippewa
Kirby G. W. 322 Main
Smith Jas. 66 Lloyd
Husted W. H. Niagara n. Main
Downs & Chubb (Carriage) 47 Erie
Burns & Jones, 94 Main
M'Neil John A. 60 Main
White H. G. & Co. 15 Webster's
  Block
Bunnell B.   *Clarence.*
Arnold Mortimer, Springville
                              Concord.
Tiffany Edward, Water Valley
                             Hamburgh.
Gerber Harmon   *Holland.*

Essex County.

Marvin E.M. & Co. *Elizabethtown.*
Grey Benj. F.
Stanton John
Wall Wm.
Edwards Erastus   *Essex.*
Richardson Throop

Fulton County.

Seares & Armstrong *Broadalbin.*
Cole Rufus
Derby Geo.   *Ephratah.*
Case P. W.   *Johnstown.*
Holmes J. M.
Hays Jno. M.
Bridge Jos.
Streeter & Sprague, Gloversville
Smith Lucius, Kingsboro

Genesee County.

Houghton Horace B.   *Alexander.*
Wolsey E.   *Batavia.*
Howe & Barnard
Ashling W. H.
Hollister ——   *Bergen.*
Wheeling Wm. North Bergen
Lincoln E. W.   *Bethany.*
Beede George
Howe P. W. & Brothers   *Le Roy.*
Wingate H. L.
Ball James E.
Webb Samuel C.   *Pavilion.*
Stiles Caleb   *Stafford.*

Greene County.

Wright Walker   *Cairo.*
Washburn Moses   *Catskill.*

Breasted Peter   *Catskill*
Backus Sylvanus   *Coxsackie.*
Cowles David   *Durham.*
Pierce William
Williams Chauncy   *Lexington.*

Herkimer County.

Taylor Samuel   *Frankfort.*
Fox Charles J.   *Herkimer.*
White George
Parmelee Heman   *Little Falls.*
Edgerton E. S.
Oysten Charles
Anable G. S.
Ensiga E. B.
Payne George W.   *Newport.*
Powers Charles F.

Jefferson County.

Smith J. D.   *Adams.*
Smith D. C.
Rice L. B.
Beales M.
Cass Wm. Evans' Mills   *Le Roy.*
Fassett William   *Lorraine.*
Chamberlain & Brown, Feli's
  Mills   *Rutland.*
Huntington J. L.   *Theresa.*
Robinson T.

Kings County.

Avila J. 134 Nassau   *Brooklyn.*
Bauchman Thos. 93 Myrtle Av.
Benning Thomas, 141 Atlantic
Blake Thomas, 77 Concord
Bonner William, 31 Henry
Booz James, Bond cor. State
Boyd Rufus M. 140½ York
Brown William, 132 Atlantic
Byrns Thos. 244 Gold
Coddington W. H. 80 Myrtle Av.
Cook William, 117 Atlantic
Crocker Edward, 177 Myrtle Av.
Derby Erasmus B. 183 York
Edmonds W. 2 Henry
Exner J. C. (oil and fresco) 26
  Atlantic
Graves Robert, 414 Atlantic
Grisson Samuel, 89 Tillary
Hargraves J. Hicks cor. Atlantic
Hall George, 53 Henry
Hermance C. F. 270 Hicks
Hodgkin John, 159 Court
Hudson George, 99 Fulton
Jackson G. B. 231 Fulton
Jamison George, Fulton st.
Jones J. W. 26 Hicks
Jones & Dufour, 156 Nassau
Knight J. 57½ Atlantic
Lee James, 18 Hamilton Av.
Lewis & Wood, 49 Myrtle Av.
Lyons A. Pearl near Fulton
M'Cutcheon J. 142½ Myrtle Av.
Mundell J. 116 Fulton
Parker J. 42 Fulton
Phillips Henry, 296 Henry
Robinson & Randolph, 166 Court
Smith E. W. 101 Middagh
Smith Josiah T. 86 Fulton
Williams Charles, Bond n. Fulton
Wilson Charles, 205 Fulton
Wood Charles, 7 Hicks
Yates J. 267 Washington
Brown G. Green Point *Bushwick.*
Underwood T. do
Hopkins James   *Flatbush.*
Lyon John H. 77 South 7th
                           Williamsburgh.
Hasluck T. 127 Montrose Av.
M'Devitt David, 297 South 1st
M'Lean P. C. 73 Grand
Jaynes & Bolton, 150 4th
Calmus ——, 162 Grand
Baker V. I. 168   do
Beaver Robert, 26½ do
Manjer D. 116   do
Wright Henry, (coach) 237 and
  239 1st
Weston John, 347 Grand

Lewis County.

Webb Henry   *Turin.*
Dean Geo. B. Constableville
              West Turin.

Livingston County.

White William   *Caledonia.*
Smith S. A.   *Dansville.*
Lozier Stephen
Henry M. P
Graham S.
Hunt Moses   *Geneseo.*
Stedman A. N.
French Alonzo
Robinson J. D.
Dale Thompson, Cuylerville
           Leicester.
Bristol William   *Lima.*
Dart G. W.
Murray ——   *Livonia.*
Bellman Samuel, Hemlock Lake
Remington J. E   do
Havens Smith,   do
West Perry, Lakeville
M'Arthur Arch.   *Mount Morris.*
North & M'Lane
Bard D. B.   *Nunda.*
Clark William
Holmes E. B.
Stillson Chas. L. Hunt's Hollow
           Portage.
Kendall Charles   *York.*
Smith A.

Madison County.

Babcock Leroy   *Brookfield.*
Irons & Morse   *Cazenovia.*
Jones & Partello
Keres Lorenzo D.   *Hamilton.*
Wilber J.
Gleason F., Canastota   *Lenox.*
Russell Edward,   do
Carson J. O.   do
Everts Warren A. Erieville
           Nelson.
Jones G. S. Chittenango *Sullivan.*
Barren A.   do
Doolittle Wm.   do
Hurd D. T.   do

Monroe County.

Gibson A. K., W. Mendon *Mendon.*
Halliston H., Churchville   *Riga.*
Bascom W. R. 67 South St. Paul
           Rochester.
Rich & Leslie, 10 North St. Paul
Heberd R., Ely st.
Tifft R. C. 2 Minerva
Demeeissemann J. Cayuga st.
Robinson Wm. E. 220 Buffalo
Hayes James, 140 Buffalo
Hopwood T. H. 138 & 140 Buffalo
Ethridge O. Hamlet, 10 Arcade
Van Doorn Geo. F. 12 Arcade
Van Doorn F. 12 Arcade
Peters Wm. C. 6 Spring
Green Russell, Child's Buildings,
   Exchange st.
Higgins F. 212 State
Arnold George, 66 State
Robbins Jonathan J. 10 Front
Bradley L., Mill st.
Carpenter C., Brockport *Sweden.*
Beckwith Francis X., Rochester
   c. Main, Scottsville *Wheatland.*
Quinn John,   do
Mathews John, do

Montgomery County.

Easton H. V. B.   *Amsterdam.*
Easton James
Martin Joshua
Wilson George, Tribe's Hill
Fisk C., Fultonville   *Glen.*
De Lane E. B. do
Maxfield E. B., Fonda *Mohawk.*
Dougald John W. do
White R. L. Palatine Bridge
           Palatine.

New York County.

Abberly John, 87 Madison
           New York.
Acker John B. 5 M'Dougal
Ackerman James, 102 Nassau
Adams B. 42 Water
Adams John, 28 Vandam
Adin Holbrook, 556½ Grand
Alburtis Samuel jr. 1 S. William
Allyn Peter, 28 Bridge
Ashe Wm. A., Fulton st.
Asten & Seabury, 27 Nassau
Ayres Albert, 130 Spring
Bain George, 394 Bleecker
Baker Henry P. 692 Washington
Ball Francis, Yorkville
Banker & Smith, 815 Broadway
Barlow & Gould, 318 6th
Barnard Edward H. 142 Wooster
Bathwell David, 48 1st Av.
Beatty Daniel L. 219 W. 18th
Beaver & White, 371 6th Av.
Bell J. W. 178 Fulton
Belton Patrick & John, 289 4th Av.
Benedict A. 138 Houston
Betts Wm. 36 Rutgers
Blodgett A. Tilden, 611 Hudson &
   40 Troy
Blonk Benjamin, 74 Irving pl.
Bloomer & Robinson, 85 Nassau
Bogardus & Ramsey, 137 Cedar
Bohrman Frederick, 78 Elisabeth
Bond George R. 54 Orchard
Bond Joseph N. B. 54 Orchard
Boetman & Smith, 209 Spring &
   31 Corlears
Born Philip, 160 3d
Bostwick James, 65 Bayard
Bothwell David, 348 1st Av.
Boutelle John A. 129 Av. D
Bradley Israel, 182 Hudson
Bradley P. 108 W. Broadway
Bradley & Moore, 42 5th
Breidenbah H. 58 William
Brower J. D. 120 Elizabeth
Brown Thomas, 195 Hudson
Brown & Marrenner, 155 East
   Broadway
Bunker & Smith, Broadway cor.
   12th
Cadmus Michael, 143 Canal
Carman Radcliff, 86 Barclay
Carson John C. 718 Greenwich
Chevalier John P. 59 Mercer
Chisney Thos. 305 8th Av.
Christal Timothy, 192 Varick
Clarke Andrew M. 67 Spring
Consell & Hauptman, 608 Broad-
   way
Counhoven C. D. 130 Spring
Cowley Levin N. 235 Wooster
Cragin B. F. 20 Nassau
Craig J. 4th cor. Broadway
Craig Joseph, 544 Pearl
Craig Thomas, 38 4th
Crawford R., Harlem
Crissey Lyman D. 157 12th
Daley & Reynolds, 6¼ 4th Av.
Dally Wm. 97 Bowery
Daniel Jos. S. B. r.269 Spring
Deane G. C. 14 Norfolk
Deane James, 122 Amity
Deane Michael, 109 4th Av.
Deane & Storms, 913 Broadway
Deane & Tracy, 124 Clinton pl.
Demarest Wm. R. 287½ Bleecker
Derby Edward C. 42 Water
Devin T. C. 1st Av.
Disbrow Thos. R. 108 W. B.way
Dobbs Robt. G. 619 Houston
Donnelly Bernard, 348 Greenwich
Door Joseph O. 208 Washington
Down H. 170 Centre
Drake C. & Co. 8th Av.
Dudley Richard, 161 8th Av.
Dufour Thomas, 68 Sullivan
Dunbar James, 31 Dey
Earnest James, 206 Pearl
Edwards & Son, 163 Canal
Elliott John H. 227 South and 149
   Pearl

Ellsworth W. S. 206 Allen
           New York.
Farrington John, 15 Rector
Farrington & Clark, 186 W. 21st
   & 105 8th Av.
Faulkner J. 146 Cherry
Fash Robt. (window shade) 122
   Houston
Feeny Michael, 15 Thames
Fordham George W. 73 Wall
Forster Thomas V. 24 Church
Fosdick Richard, 40 5th Av.
Foy & Bruale, 8th Av.
Franklin Henry, 36 4th Av.
Frederick Samuel R. 251 Canal
Freeland Samuel, 212 W. 16th
Fuller William B. 6 Beaver
Furbush Silas B. 190 Wooster
Gibson John, W. 25th st.
Gillett G. W. 173 10th st.
Gilroy George, 370 Hudson
Glass & Patterson, 62 Grove
Gormely John, 190 Duane
Gordon J. M. 59 Gold
Gotham David, 78 Av. B
Goulit H. 64 John
Grant Robert M. 112 Christopher
Green & Finkenaur, 361 6th Av.
Griffin John L. 173 W. 14th
Guylbert Peter, 109 Thompson &
   143 Canal
Guille & Alles, 46 Amity
Hagadorn Moses C. 236 South
Hales & Nevins, 51 Houston
Hall Archibald. 8 James slip
Hall George, 90 & 92 Grove
Hall & Little, 211 5th
Hamen E. 312 Broome
Hampson & Batigan, 446 Broadway
Henford Reuben B. 67 Vesey
Hardie John H. 156 Water
Hayes James, 172 W. Broadway
Hayes John, 162 Ludlow
Hays Charles W. & Co. 90 Eld-
   ridge
Hennion David M. 190 Houston
Hepburn William, 480 Broadway
Higge Robert W. 62 Vandam
Hill George J. 23 3d Av.
Hobbs C. 897 Broadway
Hojer George W. 282 3d Av.
Holbrook Adin, 556½ Grand
Holmes William, 181 Lewis
Horton Abram, 171 Fulton
Howe Joseph C. 101 6th Av.
Hutcheon William, 54 9th Av.
Ingram William, 125 3d Av.
Jack & Co. 110 1st Av.
Jenkins William, 163 Clinton
Jewell Presley B. 111 John
Johnson Henry, 625 Pearl
Jones E. Birmingham st.
Jones William, jr. 12 Allen
Jones S. 195 3d Av.
Journeaux Philip, 45 Carmine
Keith T. C. 252 Broadway
Kendall Joseph, 7 Perry
Kennedy Michael, 179 3d Av.
Kiffin John, 273 6th Av.
King Charles, 51 8th Av.
King & Rourke, 199 6th Av.
Kingsland Edmond, 474½ B.way
Kingsland W. & D. 207 Bleecker
Lacour William S. 340 1st Av.
Lacour John P. 276 Houston
La Fata Gaetano, 422 Broadway
Landers J. M. 32 West
Lane H. & F. M. 680 Greenwich
Laragh & Snell, 236 12th
Leach Charles, 96 3d Av.
Leonard Chancey M. 108 Warren
Leonard C. 24th st. & 9th Av.
Litton James, 207 Church
Lodewick Isaac, 118 Grand
Loewenthall C. 306 Houston
Longeill George, 4 Delancy
Lucas James, 346 6th Av.
Lugar G. C. & J. G. 94 Houston
Lush Wm. H. 95 8th Av.
Lynch Peter, 159 Water
M'Cartan Daniel, 161 1st Av.
M'Coy William, 340 1st Av.

M'Donald Randle, 191 9th
New York.
M'Glynn Oliver, 283 3d Av.
M'Kay J. S. 366 Houston
M'Leay Thomas, 116 Bleecker
M'Mahon Philip, 102 Delancy
M'Fean N. 590 Hudson
Maguffie Brothers, 83 Broad and 312 Broadway
Mahoney & Ralph, 93 Broad
Mansfield Wm., Harlem
Martin David, 11 West Broadway
Martin & Burke, 895 Broadway
Midgley Edward G. 113 Madison
Miller E. A. 86 Nassau
Miller J. W. 247 Broadway
Monroe Henry W. 48 Centre
Moores & Clark, 109 Beekman
Neil John, 241 South
Nelson & M'Peake, 28 Wooster & 520 Hudson
Neuschler Henry, 140 Ludlow
N. C Shrorager, 35 4th
O'Brien & Haynes, 16 Frankfort
Oliver & M'Glynn, 283 3d Av.
O'Connor Peter, 255 Bowery
Owens & Brophy, 49 University place
Paret William L. 347 4th
Peach James, 349 Pearl
Phillips John P. 75 Av. C
Pinckney B. P. 168 Orchard
Prankard John B. & George, 224½ Grand
Price C. W. 37 6th Av.
Pridham William, 325 Division
Pridham & Bridge, 73 East B'way
Qua Stephen F. 3 Vandam
Quarterman & Son, 114 John
Rallein P. 289 11th
Randall John, 7 Broad
Read H. Av. C
Richardson & Thompson, 20 College place
Robine David L. 68 North Moore
Rockefeller & Harris, 104 Hudson
Rodeck Hugo, 362 Broome
Rose Nathaniel, 578 Hudson
Rote Martin, 187 11th
Rowe J. W. 170 Centre
Sarach & Snell, 12th st.
Sanders J. J. 150 Broome
Schild & Zimerinader, 186 2d
Semon John G. 154 Grand
Schoonmaker A. 10 Catharine
Schottler John L. 367 Division
Schultz Fredk. 102 Reade
Sheil William & Nicholas, 271 South
Shartle D. 36 Centre
Shurrager C. G. 6th Av. cor. 20th
Shurrager N C. 35 4th
Silkman Matthias H. 172 West Broadway
Simmons & Watson, 376 G'wich
Simons Louis, 114 Prince
Smith J. L. & J. A. 280 G'wich
Spinning Edward, 230 Bowery
Squires John A. 39 Avenue D
Squires Stephen, 405 9th
Stasis R. H. & Son, 148 Elm
Stewart James, 378 Broome
Stothard James, 10 Madison
Stuckey & Keef. 100 Av. C
Swift Jonathan W. 270 Canal
Syms ——, 37½ Carmine
Tappen & Bird, 474 Grand
Tickner John, 26 Centre
Timpson G. A. 62 Market
Tindale Hezekiah M. 72 Beekman
Torboss, Chapman & Co. 92 Lbty.
Trotter John, 13 Roosevelt
Turner & Gove, 75 10th
Van Nostrand Alfred, 105 Fulton and 56 Ann
Vollmering T. 5 Norfolk
Vredenburgh William D. 6 B'ver
Walsh J. & M. 396 Bowery
Wardle Thomas, 98 6th Av.
Watson & Muckel, 73 Fulton and 385 6th Av.
Watts Josiah H. 12 Thompson

Weed Robert L. 82 Gold
New York.
Weisner Adam, 241 2d
Wentzel William, 883 Broadway
West Daniel, 233 William
White Geo. 72 3d Av.
Wilhartitz M. S. 162 Houston
Williams ——, 267 5th
Williams Samuel, 32 Old slip
Wilson Thomas S. 377 1st Av.
Winne & Howell, 10 Liberty pl.
Wolfe Charles, 82 West 20th
Wood Isaac V. 442 Hudson
Woodward & Pearse, 325 4th
Young Jacob D. 357 Bowery
Zorn Philip, 233 3d

Niagara County.

St. John L. L., Pekin   Cambria.
Churchill H.   Lewiston.
Penfold S. G.   Lockport.
Wilcox George K.
Wicker ——
Church Nathaniel   Newfane.
Whitney T. S.   Niagara Falls.
Symonds S. F.
Allen A. N.
Wheeler O. P.
Swallow Thomas, Youngstown
Porter.
Kellog F. Y., Tonawanda
Wheatfield
Whitney F. R.   Wilson.
Bishop T.
Daily M. T.

Oneida County.

Mannering E., Clinton   Kirkland.
Cole & Butler, Dominick st. Rome.
Lloyd & Smith, 179 Genesee Utica.
Thompson J. 52 Hotel
Conklin Wm. 44 Liberty
Tumbridge T. 49 Washington
Walker A. 26 Fayette
Wood D. 18 Elizabeth
Bullock & Co. 19 Broad

Onondaga County.

Coon S.   Lysander.
Cleveland P. P. Water st. Syracuse
Salina.
Cooper L. F. Genesee st.
Hall L. F. Water st
Benedict A. Warren st.
Benedict D. Genesee st.
Watkins H. W. H. Wolf st.
Wood & Brother   Scipio.

Ontario County.

Andrews & Poncett Canandaigua.
Tisdell & Munger
Kelly A. C.
Hobert Wm. C.   East Bloomfield.
Fuller E.   Phelps.
Sabin William
Earl E. P., Geneva   Seneca.
Seeley R.   do
Wilson S.   do
Anthony S.N.do
Brown & Co.   South Bristol.
Allen E.   Victor.
Deltchich C. J.

Orange County.

Fisher A. C., Port Jervis
Deer Park
Dewitt James, Unionville
Minisink.
Van Sickle Wm. do
Clark James C.   Monroe.
Jenkins I.
Comstock E. T. 119 Water
Newburgh.
Cory J. D., New Hampton
Wallkill.
Weller A., South Middletown
Baily Newell, do

Orleans County.

Goodwin E., Albion   Barre.
Bayless Armstrong, Albion
Dunham Wm. H.   do
Merriman A.   Clarendon.
Avery C. & J.   Kendall.
Spicer Henry
Vedder A. H., Medina   Ridgeway.
Peaslee Wm.   do
Vincent J.   do
Sherwood J.   do
Hanes E.   Yates.
Sherwin Cornelius, Lyndonville
Bull Howel S.   do

Oswego County.

Allen John G.   Mexico.
Carpenter & Fayette, Office Row,
Bridge st.   Oswego.
Allen Chas. F. Bridge cor. 3d
Farrel Edward, cor. 6th & Bridge
Skinner George, Bronson's Block,
Water st.
Thomas George L. 1st st.
Ricket James V. Cayuga st.
Witherel C. S. & Co. do
Backman A. P. Bronson's Block,
Water st.
Samson J. M., Pulaski   Richland.
Burch A. F.   do
Dwight A. O. Port Ontario

Otsego County.

Cook Pitman, West   Burlington.
Brewer L.   Cherry Valley.
Holmes J.
Myers M.
Ackerman Edwin R.   Edmeston.
Stillman Benj., West Edmeston
Stillman William, do
Coye J. M.   Exeter.
Collin Edward, Cooperstown
Otsego.
Bingham W. K.   do
Crandall Lewis R.   Worcester.

Putnam County.

Andrew A.   Carmel.
Livingston L. L. Cold Spring
Phillipstown.

Queens County.

Quarterman & Son   Flushing.
Travis Wm. Far Rockaway
Hempstead.
Howard Elijah P. do
Fox John, Forster's Meadow
Owen R.   Jamaica.
Conklin Lewis W.
Burtis & Mack   Newtown.
Meserole Isaac & Co. Astoria

Rensselaer County.

Hunt H., 257 State Lansingburgh.
Schermerhorn R. & Co. River st.
Barnes J.   Stephentown.
Crandall Alonzo, 96 River Troy.
Barrenger Henry, 160 River
Perry J. S. 265   do
Clark D. B. 328   do
Hogle James, 364   do
Robinson J. 317   do
Osborn H. 136 2d
Osborn M. do
Simons J. 15½ Congress
Birdsall Z. P. 68 do
Tree D. F. 71   do
Mooner Arthur, 32 Ferry.
Leach James A. 19 do
Athow B. 112 4th

Richmond County.

Standerwick T. Tompkinsville
Castleton.
Smith J. M. New Brighton

Rockland County.

Messenger A. Piermont
Orangetown.

Oliver J. H. Nyack   *Orangetown.*
Chapple C.   do
Seaman C.   do

St. Lawrence County.

Judd Orlan W.   *Canton.*
Freeman Wm.   *Hermon.*
Jenness & Rice
Clark Simeon T.
Crackett George   *Hopkinton.*
Crowley Martin P.   *Massena.*
Burney Thomas
Wallace Ralph   *Morristown.*
Coday Frederick, Ogdensburgh
    Oswegatchie.
Wilson Samuel, Ogdensburgh
Wilson Robert,
Titus S. J.   *Pitcairn.*
Scott George M.   *Potsdam.*
Levings Daniel
Cully John

Saratoga County.

Easterly William   *Edinburgh.*
Nichols & Fuller
    Saratoga Springs.
Lawrence Theodore
Savage R.   *Waterford.*
Savage M.
Cadworth J. H.

Schenectady County.

Chandler & Roney, 71 Union
    Schenectady.
Meeker Wm. 68 Union
Bradt Wm. Fonda st.

Seneca County

Fairchild Clarendon   *Ovid.*
Carman Theodore B. Farmer
Everetts Martin   *Romulus.*
Everetts John
Everetts Wm.
Cross John   *Seneca Falls.*
Wilcoxen James
Deyo G. C.   *Waterloo.*
Laing John A.
Mosher David
White Job

Suffolk County.

Case Lorenzo, East Cutchogue
    Southold.
Davis Henry,   do

Sullivan County.

Kellon C. R. Monticello
    Thompson.

Ulster County.

Du Bois Edward   *Kingston.*
Burnett Peter W.
Easton J. S. Rondout
Tyler J. T. High Falls *Marbletown.*
Warring S.   *New Paltz.*
Champlin Wm. H.   *Saugerties.*
Glennon John
Waterbury J. A.

Tompkins County.

James John T.   *Newfield.*

Warren County.

Huse Moses, Glenn's Falls
    Queensbury.
Hues Smith,   do
Knight E.   do
Purnell John   *Warrensburg.*
Burdick Lyman

Washington County.

Wells L. B.   *Cambridge.*
Rider James
Taylor Richard, Cambridge Centre
Wood Wm. H.   *Easton.*
Allen Ebin D.

Cook & Morgan   *Greenwich.*
Norton William H.
Neal George W.   *Hampton.*
Warren Squire
White Charles A. Sandy Hill
    Kingsbury.
Jackson J. C.   do
Smith William P.   do
Loomis B. M., No. White Creek
    White Creek.
Loomis E. A.   do

Wayne County.

Jenera Gilbert W.   *Arcadia.*
Perry Thomas, Newark
M'Master John, Clyde   *Galen.*
Tipling John   *Lyons.*
Bacon Charles
Wilder Luther
Ireland B. H.
Pope Samuel
West C. Macedon Centre *Macedon.*
Palmer Samuel   *Palmyra.*
Lackey S.   *Rose.*
Prosens Anson   *Sodus.*
Francisco John, South Sodus
Aldrich A.
Lawrence Mark, Alton
Higgins H.   *Williamson.*

Westchester County.

Govers G.   *New Rochelle.*
Foster D. J. Sing Sing *Ossining.*
Corran E. Portchester   *Rye.*
Carpenter Benjamin *West Farms.*
Miller Abraham
Stevens John   *Yonkers.*

Wyoming County.

Grooms A. J.   *Attica.*
Kellogg Seth   *Castile.*
Kellogg Edward
Hutchinson William
Stilson James   *Genesee Falls.*
Whiting O. H
Mitchell Levi   *Perry.*
Low A.
Snow S.
Edgerly ——
Kimberly S.   *Pike.*
Kimberly W.
Flint G.
Flint J.
Yates R. J.   *Warsaw.*
Coburn William
Osgood M. S.

Yates County.

Garrison Stephen, Belona *Benton.*
Crane Cyrus, Branchport
    Jerusalem.
Bowers E.   Penn Yan   *Milo.*
Bowers H.   do
Morey W.   do
Munger & Fowler do
Betts John,   do
Turner George, Rushville *Potter.*
Slaughter L. W. Dundee *Starkey.*
M'Collister William, do

Painters Landscape. (*See also Painters. House, Sign and Fancy.*)

Albany County.

Hart William, 46 Hudson *Albany.*

New York County.

Gignoux Regis, 74 Chambers
    New York.
Miller Wm. R. 299 Broadway
Nelson Robert, 75 11th
Parson David B. 311½   do
Talbot Jesse, Pott's Buildings
Zahner R. 74 Chambers

Rensselaer County.

Delaplace H. 64 2d   *Troy.*

Painters, Miniature. (*See also Painters Portrait.*)

Dubourjal S. E. 299 Broadway.
    New York.
Fanshaw Samuel R. 1 Cortlandt
Hite George H. 14 Warren
M'Dougall J. A. 251 Broadway
Parsall Abraham, 46 M'Dougal
Shumway H. C. 497 Broadway

Painters, Monochromatic.

Sherwood Benjamin, 311½ Broad
    way   *New York.*

Painters, Ornamental.

Ackerman James, 101 Nassau
    New York.
Ashe James H. 683 Broadway
Ashe William A. 137 Fulton
Boean L. L.
Breiding Ernest, 141 Division
Carson John C. 718 Greenwich
Corbett L. 16 King
Dorrarumo Filipo, 24 3d Av.
Dawson James, 154 E. 15th
Decker A. E. 1 Mulberry
Dryles & Co. 10 Centre
Edwards & Son, 163 Canal
Easton William W. 62 Market
Gibbs John, jr. 70 Nassau
Goulet Honore, 66 John
Hanington W. J. 364 Broadway
Hobbs C. 897   do
Hulme John, 66½ Greene
Johnson David, 465 Pearl
Johnson Henry, 526 Pearl & 105
    Chatham
Johnson Joseph H. 465 Pearl
Jones Seaman, 196 3d Av.
Kearney P. 138 Spring
Kraher John, 40 Av. B
Larrah & Snell, 235 12th
Lazarus Isaac L. 156 Broadway
Leach Charles, 98 3d Av.
Montgomery J. 145 8th Av.
Nelson & M'Peake, 28 Wooster &
    20 Hudson
Ormsbee Otis, 22 Spruce
Rosseter Seymour, 117 Fulton
Ruhl Caspar, 78 Willet
Schultz Frederick H. 108 Reade
Shultz Adolph, 163 3d Av.
Smith William A. 175 Elm
Spencer James, 123 Walker
Syms John, 37½ Carmine
Waite R. T. 78 Bank
Waller Edgar E. 21 Spruce
Watts Josiah H. 12 Thompson
Weed Robert L. 52 Gold
Weekes Warren, 58 Chatham
Williamson J. 7 Bowery
Wriley D. L. P. 7½ Bowery
Young Jacob D. 7 Nassau
Zimmermann Chas. 174 Rivington

Painters, Portrait.

Albany County.

Twitchell W. 546 Broadway
    Albany
Daggart J. 21 Douw's Buildings
Gladding T. A. 41 South Pearl
Wilkie T. 98 State

Cayuga County.

Clough George L. 63 Genesee
    Auburn
Coffin F. M. 57 Genesee

Erie County.

Nimb A. B. 190 Main *Buffalo.*
Leclere Thomas, 192 Main

Genesee County.

Staunton P. *Le Roy.*

Herkimer County.

Yale Linus, jr. *Newport.*

Kings County.

Cappel A. 122 Sands *Brooklyn.*
Herring Frederick W. 127 Atlantic
Fish James. 206 Atlantic
Lyman Sylvester S. 23 Myrtle Av.
M'George T. 198 Front
Ames Daniel F. 195 Johnson
Williamsburgh.

Livingston County.

Beecher A. D. *Avon.*
Russell A. *Nunda.*

Monroe County.

Kimble C. Stone's Block, 21 Main
Rochester.
Harris James, (Landscape) Minerva Buildings

New York County.

Ames Dan F. 181 Broadway
New York.
Andrews Ambrose, 25 Lispenard
Anelli Francis, 46 Howard
Baker George, 446 Broome
Bayer Jane, 193 Mott
Blaurett C. F. 607 Broadway
Bogle J. 74 Chambers
Boyle Ferdinand T. L. 497 B.way
Boyle James, 74 Chambers
Burlin ——, 621 Greenwich
Burns James. 449 Broadway
Carlin John, 37 W. Washington pl.
Carter D. M. 335 Broadway
Catlin Theodore B. 161 Fulton
Cogswell Wm. 607 Broadway
Colyer Vincent, 105 Bleecker
Crebassol Prosper. 396 Broadway
Cummings Thomas S. 591 Houston
Davignon Francis, 323 Broadway
Duggan Paul P 4 University pl.
Earle Joseph, 293 Broadway
Edouart A. 607 Broadway
Effie & Kholer, 673 Broadway
Elliott C. L. 497 Broadway
Fisher Alanson, 247 Grand
Flagg Jared, 396 Broadway
Flanquinet William.341 Broadway
Gray Henry P. 67 Franklin
Gercoa Joseph. 35 Howard
Hagan John, 62 White
Hall James, 460 Broome
Hansell George H. 167 Division
Harding John L. 6 Grand
Herring James, 429 Broadway
Hoffman Albert, 393 Broadway
Hoffman George W. 479 Houston
Hope Thomas W. 413 Hudson
Horn Henry J. 170 Broadway
Howard E. D. 607 Broadway
Hoxie Stansbury. 95 Clinton place
Huntington Daniel, 114 White
Inness George, 607 Broadway
Jackman William, 252 Broadway
Jarvis Charles, 3 Laight
Jenkins Charles W. 95 Bleecker
Johnston William, 66 Forsyth
Kruger Ferdinand, rear 9 Clark
Lawson Percival P. 453 Broome
Lazarus J. H. 607 Broadway
Leslie A. M. L. 120 Spring
Linen John, 669 Greenwich
Marsiglia G. 289 Broadway
Mattesop T. H. 226 Spring
May Edward H. 497 Broadway
Miller & Hillyer, 16 Rivington
Morgan Griffiths, 255 Walker
Page William, 247 Broadway

Peck John, 455 Grand *New York.*
Pratt Robert M. 74 Chambers
Radin W. H. 607 Broadway
Rogers David, 75 W. 16th
Shegogue James H. 3 Amity
Spencer Frederick R. 123 Canal
Spencer Lilly M. 72 Crosby
Stearns Edwin, 497 Broadway
Taylor Alexander H. 87 Cedar
Thompson Jerome, 102 Grand
Waldo & Jewett, 16 Warren
Wenzler A. H. 335 Bowery
Wander A. 366 Greenwich
White Edwin, 74 Chambers
Windoat William, 74 Chambers
Wright James W. 227 Broadway

Ontario County.

Leaman William T. Geneva
Seneca.

Orange County.

Tice Charles W. *Newburgh.*

Rensselaer County.

Moore A. E. 106 2d *Troy.*
Conant A. J. 3½ Albany

Saratoga County.

Eddy Franklin *Waterford.*
Savage R. A.

Schenectady County.

Sexton S. H. 25 State
Schenectady.

Suffolk County.

Mount Nelson, South *Brookhaven.*

Painters—Ship.

Bootman & Smith, 31 Corlears
New York.
Hagadown M. C. 236 South
Loonard Chancey M. 108 Warren
Nell John, 341 South
Robinson John. 120 Wall
Squires Stephen, Av. D cor. 9th

Paint Manufacturers.

Kings County.

Waldron Henry, 13 Water
Brooklyn.
Bell James, Hicks near Cole

New York County.

Blake William, 3 Broad (see advertisement) *New York.*
Seabury Jacob & James L. 168 Chrystie

Paints, Oils, &c. Artists' Colormen.

Carman Radcliff, 85 Barclay
New York.
Dechaux Edward W. 306 Broad'y
Dodge Samuel N. 189 Chatham sq.
Hawxhurst Joseph W. 107 Fulton
Marcher J. K. 28th st. bet. 9th & 10th Avs.
Rand & Co. 473 Broadway

Paints, Oil and Glass. (See also Druggists, also Grocers.)

Albany County.

Russell E. & Sons, 501 & 502 Broadway *Albany.*
Davis J. & Co. 78 State
Hurdis J. & S. 9 Church
Pringstead & Bullock, 86 Pearl

Broome County.

Tupper M. F. & Co. *Binghamton.*

Columbia County.

Tobey S. W. Warren st. *Hudson.*
Little F. B. & G. L. Warren st.
Punderson & Ham, do
Bradley F. *Kinderhook.*
Abbot & Van Slyck, Valatie

Duchess County.

Van Voorhis & Trowbridge, 219 Main *Poughkeepsie.*
Vanvalkenburgh & Coffin, (wholesale) 249 Main

Erie County.

Bond E. T. 11 E. Seneca *Buffalo.*

Greene County.

Breasted Peter *Catskill.*

Kings County

Little Charles H. 142 Atlantic
Brooklyn.
Kienzla B. (oil) 63½ Atlantic
Zeetes E. B. 16 Hamilton Av.
Prince John D. (wholesale) 89 Fulton
Dow Horace H. 67 Fulton
Gunn J. G. 206 Grand
Williamsburgh.

Monroe County.

Crombie John, 9 Buffalo *Rochester.*
Cochrane J. 26 Main
Reynolds M. F. 17 Buffalo
Avery George A. 12 do
Winslow & Young, 51 Main
Weddle Thomas & Sons, Brown's Race
Carpenter Cyrus, Brockport
Sweden.

New York County.

PAINTS, OILS, &c. RETAIL.

Abberley John, 37 Madison
New York.
Baldwin Levi, 89 Delancy
Beaver & White, 371 6th Av.
Bootman & Smith, 31 Corlears
Bunker Benj. F. 136 Chambers
Buaker & Smith, 816 Broadway
Chevalier John P. 59 Mercer
Clannon Simon, 380 Broadway
Clark Eugene J. 134 Av. C
Corson John C. 718 Greenwich
Crissey Lyman D. 167 W. 18th
Dally William, 97 Bowery
Deane Gilbert C. 14 Norfolk
Deane & Storms, 913 Broadway
Deine Michael, 199 4th Av.
Demarest Wm. R. 257½ Bleecker
Derickson & Ackerman, 317 B'ery
Devin Thos. C. 156 1st Av.
Dodge Samuel N. 189 Chatham
Easton Wm. W. 62 Market
Elliot John H. 227 South
Elsworth Cyrus B. 110 Murray
Elsworth William T. 306 Allen
Faulkner James, 146 Cherry
Fosdick Richard B. 40 5th Av.
Frederick T. R. 251 Canal
Fuller Wm. B. 6 Beaver
Gaw Alexander. 8 Amity
Gillett George W. 174 10th
Goulet Honore, 66 John
Hales & Nevins, 51 Houston
Hayes John, 182 Essex
Heineman Isaac, 266 2d
Hobbs Charles, 637 Broadway
Hopkins James, 214 Walker
Hornby Thomas, 114½ Rivington
Jack J. C. & Co. 105 & 111 North
Moore & 110 1st Av.
Kennedy & Alford, 450 Grand
Kennedy & Hill, 211 Greenwich

King & Bourke, 199 6th Av.
New York.
Kinny David, 297 Bowery
Lacour John P. 270 Houston
M'Craken Francis, 258 Spring
M'Kay John S. 23 1st Av. & 365
Houston
M'Leay Thomas, 1 Astor place &
116 Bleecker
Maguffie, Brothers, 312 Broadway
& 86 Broad
Morrison John C. 189 Greenwich
Nelson John C. 520 Hudson
O'Connor Peter. 255 Bowery
Pinckney Benj. F. 168 Orchard
Price Cyrus W. 87 6th Av.
Renoud David, 396 Bowery
Rooney Patrick, 33½ 2d Av.
Schank Alfred, 86 Division
Seabury I. & J. L. 1 Eagle Block
Chrystie st.
Squires J. A. rear Av. D cor. 9th
Vollmering John, & Norfolk
Wardle Thomas, 98 6th Av.
Weeks Josiah C. 140 Maiden lane
White George, 172 3d Av.
Wood Samuel, 423 Water

PAINTS, OILS, &C., WHOLESALE.

New York County.

Baxter C. H. & Co. 143 Maiden lane
Baxter & Clearman, 313 West
Belknap E. S. & Son, 8 Gold
Bell James J. H. 156 Front
Butler & Reynolds, 160 Water
Carle John & Co. 153 do
Crawford Samuel, 107 Broad
Dorr Joseph O. & Beesley, 308
Washington
Elsworth Edward & Co. 86 & 88
Dey & 124 West
Haydock, Corlies & Clay, 21 Pearl
Helsewood Robert, 372 W'hington
Hopkins & Crow, 169 Fulton
Jessup Benjamin, 168 Water
Levy Uriah H. 132 do
Lewis & Price, 55 Pearl
Luckey Joseph N. 44 Cortlandt
Manville J. A. 146 Maiden lane
Marsh & Northorp, 69 Pearl
Merritt & Co. 58 South
Morgan, Walker & Smith, 49 Cliff
Moss Reuben E. 542 Grand
Pentz & Co. 55 Water
Poultney Benjamin, 181 Water
Ramsey & Todd, 78 Day
Schoonmaker Samuel, 15 Doyer, 6
Chatham, & 10 Catharine
Tallmage Stephen S. 444 Broome
Talmage & Hurd, 97 Barclay & 223
Washington
Tappen & Burd, 472 Grand
Turner & Gore, 77 10th
Van Ingen Abraham, jr. 113 Canal
Waldron Henry, 180 Front

Paints, Oil & Glass—Continued.

Oneida County.

Cox D. P. & Co. Camden.
Bissell & Co. Dominick st. Rome.
Dudley & Hill, do
Merrill, Hayden & Co. James st.
Newell N. C. 111 Genesee Utica.
Greenman & Smith, 112 do

Onondaga County.

Lampman & Williams (wholesale)
Water st. Syracuse Salina.

Oswego County.

Moore & Smith, Bridge st. Oswego.
Dillworth George, Granite block,
Bridge st.
Canfield Calvert, 12 Phœnix block,
1st st.
Mead C. M. Woodruff's block,
1st st.
Bickford J. jr. cor. 1st & Bridge

Otsego County.

Ellery & Holder, Cooperstown
Otsego.
Corey E. & H. do

Rensselaer County.

Thompson J. L. & Co. 161 River
Troy.
Robinson & Griswold, 201 River
Baum & Hawley, 219 do
Dater & Brother, 245 do
Waters & Van Schaick, 271 do
Wallace G. B. 282 do
Halsted & Young, 320 do
Briggs William, 406 do
Orvis F. D. & Co, (wh'sale) 305 do
Drake R. L. & G. 221 do
Daggett J. 353 do

Schenectady County.

Chrisler P. 53 State Schenectady.
Freman E. L. 98 do

Paper Box Makers.

Bach Gustavus, 49 Fulton
New York.
Bauer & Bodine, 74 Fulton
Brower Charles P. 51 Fulton
Brower Samuel A. 329 Pearl
Brown N. 67 Canal
Cracknell Thomas, 181 William
Dobke Adolph, 181 William
Erbeg Diedrich, 160 William
Eugene & Co. 79 Fulton, manu-
facturer paper cards
Haws John, 27½ Division
Hazen J. H. 60 John
Hodes Enos, 316 Grand
Hooper John, 102 Maiden lane
Jones Henry, 115 John
Jones Silas, 48 Maiden lane
Kraft George J. 48 Maiden lane
Kralisheimer Nathan, 49 Ridge
Lesage Julius, 48 Ann
Luckner Robert, 286 Pearl
Marsh John H. 180 Pearl
Mentzel Otto, 79 Chatham
Meyer Ernest, 160 William
Miller John H. 67 Fulton
Osghahy & Worms, 181 Water
Patterson Hiram D. 71 Cannon
Pfeifer & Co. 107 Fulton
Prince Edward, 269½ Bleecker
Reiter Henry W. 54 Ann
Schorn Joseph. 209 William
Schroder O. & Co. 26 John
Schuster Ph. Frederick, 57 Maid-
en lane
Selchow Frederick, 47 Eldridge
Schultz Joseph, 106 Fulton
Sturmwald & Muller, 7 Liberty
Suckner R. 256 Pearl
Walker John, 65 Forsyth
Wenzel John H. 98 Broadway

Paper, for Designers.

Durand, Baldwin & Co. 40 Wall
New York.

Paper Hangings. (See also
Booksellers; also Dry Goods;
also Upholsterers.)

Albany County.

Steele Lemuel & Co. 360 and 362
Broadway Albany.
Irwin Wm. 338 Broadway
M'Clelland Wm. 64 Green
Richardson Wm. 6 South Pearl
Harris D. jr. 8 Green

Columbia County.

Steel W. R. (manufacturer) Warren st. Hudson.

Erie County.

Maynard & Baldwin, 14 Seneca
Buffalo.
Wilgus N. 221 Main

Kings County.

Marx E. 106 Fulton Brooklyn.
Hallam R. 216 Fulton
Barnes Reuben C. (manufacturer)
66 & 68 Schermerhorn
Gunn J. G. 206 Grand
Williamsburgh.
Cook Henry, 96 Grand

Monroe County.

Shell Jacob, 49 State Rochester.
Cochrane Wm. 11 Front
Bicknell Henry, 1 Front

New York County.

Bartol Samuel F. 175 William
New York.
Berrien Wm. 180 Bowery
Brower John, 236 Hudson
Brown Nathan, 67 Canal
Case Louis R. 234 Bowery
Childs & Smith, 449 Pearl
Christy & Constant, 60 Maiden la.
Croton Manufacturing Co. ware-
house 18 Cortlandt
Davies A. M. & R. 200 Bowery
Dawes William, 62 6th Av.
Day Thomas, 26 Carmine
Dorr & Burch, 180 Broadway
Drew T. 29 2d
Emmerich & Vils, 60 Nassau
Forbes James H. 45 Cortlandt
Gilbert, Rockland & Davis, 21
Cortlandt
Gilbert Joseph G. 215 Pearl
Greason John, 247 Greenwich
Gratacass G. P. & J. 31 Maiden la.
Hardorp John, 430 Pearl
Harpel Leo, 281 Grand
Heather W. J. 573 Broadway
Hettinger John, 86 Bowery
Hinton Wm. 43 Cortlandt
Hussey & Punter, 196 34th
Howell Martin A. 54 Maiden lane
& 29 Liberty
Janeway & Co. 100 Maiden lane
Jeffreys William, 446 Pearl
Jennings S. O. 262 & 261 Grand
Jones J. & T. & Smith, 242 & 244
West 16th, 235 Pearl cor. John,
& 365 Grand cor. Suffolk
Keith S. C. 262 Broadway
Korpke Henry, 89 Bowery
Livesay A. 750 Broadway
Lynes Samuel, 62 Liberty
Mackay Walter G. 206 Pearl
M'Collum John. 176 Canal
M'Kinney Mary B. 228 Hudson
Ormsbee Otis, 181 William
Pares Francis & Co. 370 Pearl
Partridge & Goold, 18 Cortlandt
Pehl William & Co. 436 Pearl
Phyfe James, 43 Maiden lane
Piggot Joseph, 94 Division
Pike Nicholas & Co. 173 Pearl
Pratt J. H. & J. M. 180 Pearl
Prince Edward, 269½ Bleecker
Prince Robert, 342 Pearl
Rauch Joseph, 140 Pitt
Rockwell Brothers, 21 Cortlandt
Rosted Charles, 122 Beekman
Sackett James A. 167 Pearl
Sheal William, 452 Grand
Smith Job A. 30 Carmine
Smith Robert, 399½ Pearl
Sutphen Teneyck, 1 Pine
Talmage & Burch, 151 Broadway
Thomas Cyrus B. 76 E. Broadway
Tompkins & Terry, 216 Grand
Voorhis Abm. 844 Broadway

Oneida County.

Newell N. C. 111 Genesee Utica.
Barnard H. & Son, 85 Genesee

Queens County.

Pehl V. M. (manufacturer) *Hempstead.*

Rensselaer County.

Orr A. & W. (manufacturers and importers of French paper and boards) 265 River *Troy.*

Paper Manufacturers.

Albany County.

Andrews John *Coeymans.*
Chittenden G. & Co.

Cayuga County.

West, Foot & Co. *Aurelius.*

Chautauque County.

Burnham E., Fredonia *Pomfret.*

Chenango County.

Medley C. & Co. *New Berlin.*

Clinton County.

Parks Joseph, Keeseville *Au Sable.*

Columbia County.

Wineger P. *Canaan.*
Hanna & Peaslee, (printing paper) Malden Bridge
Bristol L., *Chatham.*
Rathbun F. Chatham 4 Corners
Phillips Geo. W. & Co. Mellenville *Claverack.*
Baker A. M. & Co. Warren st. *Hudson.*
Baker A. M. & Co. *Stockport.*
Chittenden G. & Brothers
Dingman & Coventry *Stuyvesant.*
Hoes J. R.

Cortland County.

Bradford Daniel *Cortland Village.*

Delaware County.

Mann, Colburn & Co. *Franklin.*

Duchess County.

Cowman A. T. *Hyde Park.*
Judson & Co. *Rhinebeck.*
Tompkins S. P., Hull's Mills *Stanford.*
Wells P. W. & Co.

Erie County.

Bradley & Brother, Williamsville *Amherst.*

Fulton County.

Thompson J. & Brothers *Broadalbin.*
Robinson John D. (wrapping)
Brown Isaac, do
Close & Kestred *Mayfield.*

Greene County.

Austin & Brother *Catskill.*
Macomber, Hunt & Olney *Windham.*

Herkimer County.

Laflin Brothers, (letter & cap, 150 reams daily—72 Females, 22 males) *Herkimer.*
Heath Henry M. (print and wrapping) *Little Falls.*
Richmond S. M. & A. (print and wrapping)

Jefferson County.

Clark C. & C. Woodville *Ellisburgh.*
Knowlton & Rice *Watertown.*

Kings County.

Graves Robert, 414 Atlantic *Brooklyn.*

Lewis County.

Pierce & Phillips *Denmark.*
Ager & Lane, Lyonsdale *Greig.*

Livingston County.

Porter & Outerson *Dansville.*
Bradley C. & Co.
Bradley J. & L.
House J. (Wrapping, 100.000 rms. yearly) *Mount Morris.*

Madison County.

Sweetland & Brother, (Cap, Letter, Board and Wrapping) *Casenovia.*
Paddock S. D. (Straw Board) *Sullivan.*

Monroe County.

Sherwood A. West Mendon (Wrapping Paper and Book Board) *Mendon.*
Stoddart S. B. 74 State *Rochester.*
Morse C. (Printing and Wrapping Paper) Lower Falls
Ingersoll William, (Wrapping) Lower Falls
Stoddart S. B. Lower Falls

New York County.

Taylor J. W. 64 Gold *New York.*
Greele K. K. 71 Maiden lane

Niagara County.

Porter A. H. *Niagara Falls.*

Oneida County.

Savage & Moore, Sauquoit *Paris.*
Loomis & Graves, Walesville *Whitestown.*
Olmstead W. H. & Co. Walesville

Onondaga County.

Ryan & Reed, Falls *Marcellus.*
Herring J. & Sons, Falls

Orange County.

Oakley Isaac K. Salisbury Mills *Blooming Grove.*
Van Alien R. & Co. (Log and Sized Paper) Salisbury Mills
Walsh John H. (Printing) *Newburgh.*

Oswego County.

Dodge Rufus, (Fine Cap, Letter and Wrapping) Pulaski *Richland*
Smith & Stevens (Straw Board) Pulaski

Queens County.

Willitts Gilson, (Wrapping and Paste Board) Raynor Town *Hempstead.*
Valentine William, (Wrapping) Roslyn *North Hempstead.*

Rensselaer County.

Davis & Tompkins *Nassau.*
Manning & Howland, Proprietors of Mount Ida Paper Mills, Warehouse 261 River *Troy.*

Rockland County.

Dengells & Co. *Haverstraw.*
English & Cassle

St. Lawrence County.

Sturdevant N., Waddington *Madrid.*

Saratoga County.

James John W. Jamesville *Greenfield.*
Killmer & Ashman, Rock City Mills *Milton.*
Rowland H. & J. Rock City Mills
Colt & Crane, Ballston Spa
Ingalls & Brothers, do
Allen, Moshier & Wait *Stillwater.*

Schoharie County.

Boyce & Gale *Cobleskill.*
Isham A. H. *Esperance.*
Messenger & Co.
Ruff & Miller
Ingraham & Moody *Middleburgh.*

Suffolk County.

Wicks Jonas, (Straw Paper) Patchogue *Brookhaven.*
Richie Wm. *Islip.*

Ulster County.

Longbottom J. H. & Co. (Binders' Boards) Creek Locks *Rosendale.*

Washington County.

Howland, Harvey & Co. (Wrapping and Printing) Sandy Hill *Kingsbury.*
Satterly John, (Wrapping and Printing) Sandy Hill

Westchester County.

Howe Epenetus, East Salem *North Salem.*
Finch Silas, Croton Falls

Wyoming County.

Wheeler Smith *Pike*

Paper Monochromatic.

Parson David B. 310½ Broadway *New York.*

Paper Rulers.

Ireland Henry, 120 Nassau *New York.*
Parks J. B. 63 Fulton
Westlake Chas. G. 68 Fulton

Paper Stainers.

Day Thos. 26 Carmine *New York.*
DeJonge J. & L. 57 Gold
Garread John, 56 Gold
Scheffler John, 123 Fulton

Paper Warehouses.

Beebe R. 109 Fulton *New York.*
Braman & O'Connor, 5 Burling slip
Buchanan Coe S. 179 Water
Bulkley & Brother, 110 John
Bunting & Foot, 214 Pearl
Burnap & Babcock, 115 Fulton
Butler H. V. & Co. 90 John
Campbell John & Co. 110 & 112 Nassau
Carson & Hard, 281 Pearl
Clayton E. B. & Sons, 84 John
Culver Benj. H. 117 Fulton
Dawes Wm. 92 6th Av.
Ely Eugene & Co. 79 Fulton
Field Cyrus W. & Co. 11 Cliff
Forker & Brother, 2 Burling slip
Francis & Loutrel, 77 Maiden lane
Gaunt & Derrickson, 150 South
Gookin H. N. & S. W. 242 Pearl
Kingsley Simeon, 117 Maiden lane
Laggett & Brothers, 201 Pearl

Longbotham J. H. & Co. 12 Gold
New York.
M'Collum, ——, 178 Canal
O'Hara & Peeble, 105 Fulton
Persse & Brooks, 65 & 67 Nassau
Priestley John, 420 Nassau
Ripley Geo. B. & Co. 244 Pearl
Roberts John C. 102 John
Sands Daniel H. 14 Forsyth
Seymour & Co. 97 John
Son John P. 180 Fulton
Stites Apollos, 56 Gold
Thorp W. E. & Co. 188 Fulton
Thute Mathew, 18 & 28 Liberty
Travers A. & Co. 84 Maiden lane
Vernon Thos. 90 John
Warfield Preston, 4 Burling slip
White & Sheffield, 111 Fulton

Paris Green—Manufacturer of.

Schwartz T. 32 Burling slip &
47th cor. 2d Av.   New York.

Passage Offices.

Adams Forter W. 106 Barclay
New York.
Busch Henry & Co. 64 Greenwich
& 133 Washington
Bush C. W. 9 West
Centre Sylvester, 12 West
Hinds & Co. 7 West
Husted & Dorsey, 23 Albany
Kreuter Fred. 65 Greenwich
Lindsay Jas. 162 South
Lockwood R. E. 10 Battery place
Loescher P. A. 74 Greenwich
Pakker A. H. 114 Greenwich
Pride Geo. L. 3 Carlisle
Roche, Brothers & Masterson, 164
Maiden lane
Spean & Hoffman, 114 Greenwich
Thompson & Nephew, 275 Pearl
Townsend Caleb A. 2 Washington
Tyson Wm. 10 West
Wedekind F. W. C. & Co. 122 Cedar
Welden & Johnson, 148 West

Patent Medicines.

Albany County.

Herrick & Co. 6 James   Albany.

Greene County.

Keith Geo. N.   Cassackie.

Kings County.

Wallace M. T. & Co. (Granite
Block) Furman st.   Brooklyn.

Monroe County.

Morton W. D. (Stoughton's Wine
Bitters) 2 Bank Alley Rochester.

New York County.

Bachmann R. 65 Wooster
New York.
Ballard O. M. 46 Cortlandt
Barnett S. (Hodge's Bitters) 79
W. Broadway
Barry Prof. 137 Broadway
Bartine C. S. & Co. 36 Canal
Beals & Co. 183 Broadway
Blackman H. P. 75 Canal
Blake Thos. 118 Division
Boyd Wm. H.—Boyd & Wheeler's
Castor Oil and Magnesia Candy.
—Boyd & Paul, Agents, 4 Liberty
Brandreth Benj. 241 Broadway
Brandt's Indian Medicines, 106
Broadway, up stairs
Chichester C. L. 298 Madison

Clapp & Townsend, 80 & 82 Nassau
Clirehugh Vair, 179 Broadway
Comstock & Co. Brothers, 57 John
Curtis & Trall, 42 Bowery
Dalley H. 160 Pearl & 415 B'dway
Daniels John E. 333 Broadway
Dawley Wm. 152 Church
Ditchett John, 97 Roosevelt
Empire Co. 176 Broadway
Esling Joseph J. 109 Canal
Folger Robert B 161 Fulton
Fractas J. A. 42 John
Finch J. Dr. 98 Nassau
Gay Frederick A. 316 Broadway
Gough A. H. & Co, 122 Fulton
Graefenburgh Co. 50 Broadway
Harbeson James, 60 Division
Hall & Spencer, 67 Bowery
Harper T. W. 145 Broadway
Harrison M. A. F. 164 Greenwich
Hemsley & Beers, 25 John
Hibbard T. R. 96 John
Holt Washington, 168 Christopher
Hunt Phoebe, 41 Leonard
Hyatt Wm. H. 142 Bowery
Irish E. 5 3d Av.
Ivans James C. 196 Grand
Jones H. H. & A. L. Comstock, 170
Broadway
Kalb & Spencer, 67 Bowery
Kalt & Samson, 370 Broadway
Levison Uriah, 3 Division
M'Allister James, 141 Fulton
M'Munn John B. 76 Barclay
Minor Cyrus A. & Co. 286 Pearl
Moat Horatio S. 2 City Hall pl.
Moffat Wm. B. 336 Broadway
Osgood Isaac, 86 Cedar
Porter Henry H. 216 Fulton
Price Philo, 130 Fulton, Hyer's Pill
Depot
Radway & Co. 161 Fulton
Reid James, 55 6th Av. Horse and
Cattle Liniment
Reynolds Wm. D. 148 Church
Rogers George, 3 Chambers
Saxton, Armstrong & Co. 50 B'd'y
Scott & Stewart, 45 Courtlandt,
Manufacturers of the United
States Syrup
Scovill A. L. & Co. 316 Broadway,
Proprietors of Dr. Rogers' Syrup
of Liverwort, Tar, & Canchalagua
Sherman Austin, 106 Nassau
Smith G. Benjamin, 179 Green'h
Swallow J. R. 123 Fulton
Thompson, Skillman & Co. 102
Nassau
Thurston George P. 13 Platt
Tobias ——, 5 11th
Tobias Samuel I. 1¼ Murray
Tousey S. 106 Nassau
Towne Ezra, 207 Fulton
Townsend Samuel, 126 Fulton
Townshend John, 2 John
T:afton Wm. H. 123 Fulton
Wallace & Co. 106 Broadway
Washington John, 223 Broadway
Winer John & Co. 67 Maiden lane
Wright William, 288 Greenwich

Washington County.

Baker E. D. jr. Sandy Hill
Kingsbury.

Pattern Manufacturers.

Albany County.

Brown & Blanchard, 11 Church
Albany.
Gibbs S. W. 23 Green
Smith Elihu, 8 Maiden lane
Clement H. A. 6 James

Jefferson County.

Woodruff Theodore T. Watertown.

Monroe County.

Penniman Elijah T. 229 Buffalo
Rochester.
Badger A. M. 12 & 14 Hill

New York County.

Barthol Andrew, 41 Gold
New York.
Beers Nathan, 3 Allen
Bunnell Wm. J. 87 Eldridge
Concklin Jas. H. 8th Av. between
15th & 16th sts.
Quick & Beeble, 211 5th
Roberts Peter, 177 Prince
Strong & Cavanagh, r. 97 Forsyth

Oneida County.

Bettis & Shaw, Hampton
Westmoreland.

Onondaga County.

Green S. J. Water st. Syracuse
Salina.

Rensselaer County.

Green & Warren, cor. Fulton &
Mechanic   Troy.
Vedder N. S. 329 River
Simmons P. I. rear 112 4th

Paver.

Morris Peter, 112 Delancy
New York.

Pawnbrokers.

Adolphus Aaron, 423 Pearl
New York.
Barnard Henry & Co. 21 3d Av.
Bernstein Isaac, 197 Grand
Bernstein Zion, 195 Bowery
Burbank Edward, 223½ Division
Cohen Barrowy A. 269 Spring
Cohen Charles, 94 Broome
Cohen M. S. 70 6th Av.
Cudlip C. & W. 306 Hudson
Davies John M. 232 William
Ferguson Pierce, 69 W. Broadway
Fullen P. 121 Anthony
Galland A. & Co. 439 Grand
Goodman Abraham, 31 Centre
Hart H. & M. 27 Chatham
Hart Solomon I. 488 Pearl
Jackson Abram J. 56 Reade
Jackson J. 96 W. Broadway
King Bennett, 97 Canal
Koffman Louis, 8 Catharine slip
Koffmann Mendal, 75 & 77 Division
Larkin D. A. & T. Mulcahy, 206
Centre
Levy John J. 299 E. Broadway
Levy Louis, 433 Grand
Levy Saul J. 56 Wooster & 483
Broome
Moss Solomon D. 74 Catharine
Mullin Barnet, 52 Anthony
Murphy James, 68 Catharine
Phillips Jacob L. 398 Hudson
Regan Henry, 74 W. Broadway
Silver Leah, 129 Spring
Simpson J. B. & J. 25 Chatham &
19 N. William
Simpson W. & J. 265 Grand
Simpson William, 337 Broome
Shirmer John, 304 6th Av.

Pearl Barley Manufacturers.

Jefferson County.

Kimball Volney   Watertown.

Westchester County.

Miles F.   Yonkers.

Pearl Shell—Importers of.

Cotheal & Co. 49 Water
New York.

Pearl and Tortoise Shell Workers.

Kings County.

Maxon Nathaniel, 12 Remsen
Williamsburgh.

Pencil Case Makers.

Browne, Clarke & Co. 15 Beekman
New York.
Deacon Edward, 5 Liberty place
Dederick Zachariah, 16 & 18 Maiden lane
Eaton, Griffiths & Co. 72 Spring
Hague John, 12 Dutch
Hart Moses, 561 Grand
Johnston Alexander, 4 Liberty pl.
Kennedy H. P. & Co. rear 17 John
Larcombe R. J. 30 Cortlandt
Lownds Jacob J. 6 Liberty place
Manning, Mounter & Co. 59 Nassau
Magee, Hulses & Blundell, 7 Dey
Maycock Samuel, 10 N. William
Pope, North & Co. rear 7 Dey
Rauch & Co. rear 36 Cortlandt
Richardson & Son, 4 Liberty pl.
Smith, Darrow & Co. 25 Maiden l.
Stewart Isaac W. 4 Liberty place
Stewart James D. 65 Ann

Pen Makers (Gold.)

Erie County.

Brown Samuel, 146 Main *Buffalo.*

Kings County.

Brown Levi, Mechanics' Exchange, Front st. *Brooklyn.*
Woodward & Brothers, 145 Jay
Warren B. A. 122 York

New York County.

Andrews Francis L. 42 Nassau
New York.
Bagley A. G. & Co. 189 Broadway
Bard & Brothers, 191 William (see advertisement)
Beers & Clark, 25 John
Berrian A. J. & Co. rear 75 & 77 Nassau
Blakeney Thomas, 44 Nassau
Blakeney William E. 44 do
Greaton John W. 71 Cedar
Lovejoy Daniel, rear 16 Watts
Magee, Hulse & Blonder, rear 7 Dey
Munson Benjamin, 122 Fulton
Savage John Y. 92 do
Smith G. & E. M. & Co. 16 & 18 Maiden lane
Spencer & Rendell, 179 Broadway
Van Brunt T. H. 5 Dey
Wilmarth, Brother & Co. 1 Cortlandt

Onondaga County.

Benedict, Barney & Co. cor. Genesee & Salina, Syracuse
Salina.

Perfumers. (*See also Druggists.*)

Adams S. R. 298 Broadway
New York.
Ash John, 97 Fulton
Batcheler William A. 4 Wall
Benjamin W. K. 1 Cortlandt
Blackman Henry P. 77 Canal

Chilson William E. 305 Broadway
New York.
Edrehi Isaac & Co. 95 Canal
Gouraud F. Felix, 67 Walker
Hobbs Richard M. 96 Broadway
Hart H. E. 75 John
Johnson & Groser, 1 Cortlandt
Jones Thomas, 405 Broadway
Lindmark John, Mer. Exchange
Mackey James, 162 William
Mallory William H. 2 Cortlandt
Mrexec Louis, 26 William
Ramsay A. & J. 25 Maiden lane
Raphael George, 262 Pearl
Richards R. 40 Division
Saunders G. 147 Liberty & Broadway
Swift Edward, 16 Chesnut
Traphagen George H. 380 Pearl
Vidal T. C. B. 110 West
Wakeman S. H. 25 Cortlandt

Perfumers, Importing.

Brewer William, 21 Maiden lane
New York.
Bridgeman & Dey, 189 Pearl
Babitt William, 197 Water
Trapagen George H. 380 Pearl
Gilbert L. 7½ Division
Graefner Leopold, 190 William
Grandjean Auguste, 1 Barclay, Astor House
Hobbs R. M. 96 Broadway
Lanmonier Joseph, 48 Maiden la.
Peterson J. B. 34 Cliff
Peterson & Wimmer, 265 Pearl
Schmeltzer Louis, 46 New

Percussion Caps.

Sollace R. D. 19 Cortlandt

Physicians.

Albany County.

Adams H. 91 State *Albany.*
Armsby & Freeman, 669 Broad'wy
Barte L. 105 Herkimer
Barrows C. 56 Chapel
Bigelow U G. 30 Pearl
Briggs R. B. 4 Exchange
Brown J. M. 97 Herkimer
Bucklin Daniel D. 618 Broadway
Burton R. J. 68 Chapel
Cannon P. 690 Broadway
Case J. H. 86 Lydius
Cook George, 2 Norton
Coggswell M. F. 12 N. Pearl
Cox E. 71 Lydius
Dean N. S. 19 Norton
Foy H. B. 3 N. Pearl
Fonda D. F. 97 S. Pearl
Fondy John, 41 Columbia
Griffin C. C. 789 Broadway
Groghegan William, 116 Green
Hinkley J. W. 33 Hudson
Heinslus C. 44 do
Hun Thomas, 25 N. Pearl
Huyck A. 597 Broadway
Keyser W. H. 636 do
Kertin A. 64 Washington
Knapp G. A. (oculist) 496 B.way
Lockrow Van Buren, 56 Beaver
Lyon A. do
March A. 72 Hudson
Markey N. 74 Green
Martin D. 31 Columbia
M'Murdy R. S. 73 Chapel
M'Naughton P. 450 Broadway
Paine H. D. 70 Chapel
Paine Horace M. 5 Delavan House
Paine John A. do
Quackenbush J. V. P., Van Tromp & N. Pearl
Rossman J. B. 70 Lydius
Smith Thomas, 37 Columbia
Sperry R. D. 70½ N. Pearl
Staats P. P. 42 Lydius
Sheldon B. A. 185 State

Townsend H. 140 State *Albany.*
Trotter J. H. 654 Broadway
Van Antwerp A. 26 William
Van Buren P. 115 Green
Van Buren J. 3 Washington
Van Olinda. P. 77 Green
Vogal J. (oculist) 262 S. Pearl
Willard S. D. 1 Washington
Wiltse D. 5 Columbia
Wynkoop H. 29 Dean
Willard H. K. Reedville *Berne.*
Rosenkrans H. do
Babcock J. *Bethlehem.*
Springsteed David
Warren Leonard
Fredenburgh B. B. *Coymans.*
Blaisdell W.
Mosher J.
Herrick ——
Crouse F. *Guilderland.*
Wilson J. B.
M'Kown A.
Crounce C.
Wands A.
Davis Willard G. *Dunnsville.*
Johnson J. do
Chesebro I. W. *Knox.*
Crounse C. J.
Lloyd Thomas *New Scotland.*
Dixon Samuel
Ingraham Samuel, Clarksville
Wicks P. *Rensselaerville.*
Lay Z. W.
Wade G. W. *Watervliet.*
Wade M.
Burrows ——, West Troy
Van Alstyne J. T. do
Velie —— do
Fowler —— do
Brooks P. P. Cohoes
Carter Wm. F. do
Landon H. do
Sheffer J. M. do
Gibbons R. H *Westerlo.*
Lay J. W.
Barber H.
Phillips Thomas

Alleghany County.

Collins John B. *Alfred.*
Hartshorn John R.
Moxson Luke G.
Alley William *Almond.*
Robinson C. D.
Nye ——
Harmon J. J. *Andover.*
Baker Thadeus
Charles R. *Angelica.*
Todd William S.
Smith N.
Norton J. D. *Belfast.*
Saunders J. H.
Munser H. H.
Seaver C. C. *Birdsall.*
Sturgis Samuel *Bolivar.*
Dimick Martin D. *Burns.*
Woodward Horace P. Whitney Valley
Peckham George *Clarksville.*
M'Dougal John
Palmer Joseph *Cuba.*
Griffin Alfred
Maxon Stephen
Reynolds Calvin J.
Willard E. H. *Friendship.*
Dana Lorenzo
Silby J. C.
Bronson Ira
Crane N. J.
Stebbins R.
Babcock B.
Smith Reuben H. *Granger.*
Atwood Henry D.
Burton Matthias
Smith William M. Short Tract
De Camp William H. Grove Centre
Bailey William C. Little Genesee
Genesee.
Minard Isaac *Hume.*
Stewart B.

Mayboe Allen   *Hume.*
Whitney A.
Allen Calvin, Black Creek
    New Hudson.
Taylor Austin,   do
H'Call Wm   *Rushford.*
Smith Wm.
Smith R. H.
Jones George B. Wellsville *Scio.*
Sabin Orange   *West Almond.*
Truman W. M.   *Wirt.*
Green S. W.

Broome County.

Carr R. R. Chenango Forks
    Barker.
Dorr ——   do
Haines L.   do
Squires W.   do
Griswold W. S.   *Binghamton.*
Chubbuck John
Jackson T.
West S.
Bogart A.
Brooks F. B.
Burr George
Washburn C. E.
Guy E., Harpersville   *Colesville.*
Guy T., Nineveh
Sullivan J. do
Allan James, jr.   *Lisle.*
M'Call S., Centre Lisle
French T. H.   do
Ford H.   do
Hall H., Upper Lisle
Hunt S. M.   *Maine.*
Butler Wm.
Noble C. N.
Spencer Cyrenius D.   *Triangle.*
Day ——
Hemingway H. Whitney's Point
Daniels E.   *Union.*
Witherill A. A.
Peabody J. W.   *Vestal.*
Robinson E. H.
Dart ——   *Windsor.*
Bundy O. T.
Bronson A. W.
Bronson W. T.

Cayuga County.

Pitney J. T. Genesee st. *Auburn*
Hyde C. H. 72   do
Dimon D. 79   do
Boyce C. W. 101   do
Stone L. D. 114   do
Fosgate B. 92   do
Gilmore S.   do
Robinson H.   do
Bigelow L. B. 123 do
Briggs L. North st.
Abbott ——   *Aurelius.*
Cummings ——
Williams W. W.   *Brutus.*
Clark O. C.
M'Carty H.
Whitman G. H.
Ogden J.   *Cato.*
Conger D.
Palmer E. R.   *Conquest.*
Ogden W.
Baker A. jr.   *Fleming.*
Taber & Co.   *Genoa.*
Tupper ——
Luce Wm.   *Ira.*
Hedger A. M.
Martin J. V.
Benton A.
Thompson A.   *Ledyard.*
Leffingwell ——
Lacy Samuel   *Locke.*
Mead M.
May J. W., Montezuma   *Mentz.*
Griggs J. V.   do
Clarry J., Troopsville
M'Carty L.   do
Button J. D. Port Byron
Hutton W. S.   do
Elkridge H.   do
Weed ——,   do
Horton ——,   do

Powers C.   *Moravia.*
Branch ——
Cooper Wm. F   *Niles.*
Marsh H.
Rupp ——
Baker A.   *Owasco.*
Gore J. L.
Devoe B.
Strong D. O. K.
Bevier M.
Bevier D.
Fordyce B.   *Scipio.*
Pearl D. R.
Hurd F.
Cady & Son   *Sennett.*
Dodge D. & Palmer *Springport.*
Plumb S. H.   *Sterling.*
Proudfit A. H.
Jewett ——   *Summerhill.*
Fordyce B.   *Venice.*
Slawson R. K.
Hooker L.   *Victory.*

Cattaraugus County.

Phillips A. P.   *Burton.*
Egleston R. R.
Grant Henry D. Rutledge
    Conewango.
Wheeler Thomas J. do
Staunton J. B.   *Ellicottville.*
Crary Clark
Williams T. J
Arnold Isaac
Colman James L.
Stewart E.   *Farmersville.*
M'Louth Charles   *Franklinville.*
Vaernam Henry
Crandall W. J.
Mason Corydon, Sandusky
    Freedom.
Chase Dwight W.   do
Miller Horace B.   *Great Valley.*
Copp J. M.   *Machias.*
Galloway Hector, Eddyville
    Mansfield.
M'Kay D. B.   do
Alling T. L.   *New Albion.*
Goldsborough Levi   *Otto.*
Johnson Elisha
Gray H. T. B.   *Pervysburgh.*
Wilson ——
Delamatter G. C., Gowanda
    Persia.
Ellis S. G.   do
Field Seth,   do
Lake Phipps,   do
Binnie David   *Portville.*
Jackson Thomas S.
Lansing R. V. R.   *Randolph.*
Leavenworth A.
Hill I. W.
Wilcox & Borden
Jones A. P.
Cook E. G.
Babcock & Davis
Guernsey O.
Clark Aaron
Klennet Wm.
Saunders N., East Randolph
Wisner S. R.   *Rice.*
Shepherd Henry   *Yorkshire.*

Chautauqua County.

Brown S. J.   *Busti.*
Uxtell S. V.   *Carroll.*
Alvord F. L.
Van Buren R F., Frewsburgh
Pope F. A.   do
Richmond G.   *Charlotte.*
Kimball ——
North J. (Eclectic)   *Chautauque.*
W. P. Holmes, Mayville
Stedman E. P.   do
Arnold H. A., De Wittville
Phinney A. A.   *Clymer.*
Mackers ——
Daniels I.
Benedict O.   *Ellery.*
Bsnett H. W.
Gray & Hedges, Jamestown
    Ellicott.

Hazletine G. W. Jamestown
    Ellicott.
Hazletine Laban,   do
Rhodes Aseph,   do
Davis Ambrose,   do
Salisbury J. A.   do
Button William,   do
Humphrey ——,   do
Sabin Wm. P., Vermont   *Gerry.*
Eninger J. L.   do
Ward ——; Silver Creek *Hanover.*
Shaw ——,   do
Southworth ——, Irving,
Eaton S. -
Colville D. G., Forestville
Avery A. R.   do
Brown C. B., Nashville
Horton ——, Smith's Mills
Bemus Wm. F.   *Harmony.*
Elderkin Vine
Hendricks Daniel
Storer David
Sanders ——   *Mina.*
Rowe N.
Smith W. Poland Centre *Poland.*
White B., Fredonia   *Pomfret.*
Walworth B. do
Smith C.   do
Hall A.   do
Williams E., Dunkirk
Gould ——   do
Walfers A., (German)   *Portland.*
Simons M. Salem Cross Roads
Cushing Thomas, do
Tyler Horace,   do
Collins ——   *Ripley.*
Stockton ——
Aumock Amos P.   *Sheridan.*
Harriman Alanson
Hopkins Lemuel B.
Fenner James   *Sherman.*
Hall James
Pelton Sylvester
Green Thomas
Pierce ——   *Villanova.*
Walker T. G.
Spencer Silas   *Westfield.*
Spencer John
Jones Carlton
Jones Oscar
Henn Daniel
Stockton Severn

Chemung County.

Hurd Isaac H.   *Big Flats.*
Coffin James B.
Saunders William
Davis Estes   *Catharine.*
Van Vechten H.
Davie Dr.
Vanburton ——
Winton Nelson, Havana
Bailey G. D.   do
Tompkins E. A.   do
Speardown ——, do
Chase Z. F.   *Cayuta.*
Swartwood P. M.
Ford ——   *Chemung.*
Everts ——
Harendon ——
Newton J., Salubria   *Dix.*
Hewett J.   do
Slawson W. B. do
Lewis M. E.   do
Tompkins M. do
St. Croix ——, do
Booth W. E.   do
Wager ——, do
Shepard R.   do
Chubbuck H. S.   *Elmira.*
Hart Erastus
Purdy Jotham
Wilcox Boland
Beal S. T.
Aspinwall N.
Brooks T.
Reynolds J. A.
Towner D. A.
Boynton M.
Lewis J. W.
Doane W. C.
Smith Uri

Smith Norman *Elmira.*
Salsbury J.
Way W. C.
Potter A. M.
Bassett William
Woodward ——
Squires ——
Lanny ——
Payne John, Horse Heads
Jones ——, do
Gardner N. D. do
M'Millin James *Erin.*
Seaman Horace, Millport *Veteran.*
Hudson Lemuel, do
Ayres ——, do

Chenango County.

Nichols C. B. *Bainbridge.*
Banks Samuel
Corbin S. W.
Freott J. W.
Cooke J. B. South Bainbridge
Bartlett E. do
Bill B. S. Bennettsville
Haywood E. D. *Columbus.*
Perkins C.
Beardsley W. H. *Coventry.*
Willard A. *Greene.*
Purple Wm. D.
Clark John *Guilford.*
Barber ——, Guilford Centre
Jameson R. *Linchlaen.*
Beebe S. *Macdonough.*
Martin Saxton P.
Ross R. *New Berlin.*
Birch Russell B.
Loomis D.
Gibson S. C. South New Berlin
Harris J. P. do
Trusdell J. do
Beecher H. H. *North Norwich.*
Mitchell Henry *Norwich.*
Bellows Daniel
Harris Harvey
Harris Bim
Baker A. jr.
Bellows Horatio K.
Purdy Charles M.
Ford N. *Otselic.*
Wykoff ——
Clark Samuel R. *Oxford.*
Douglas George
Rouse Austin
Riddell George
Sands W. G.
Anthony J. B. *Pitcher.*
Wilbert Thomas
Bowen J. K.
Thayer O.V. (hydropathic)Pitcher Spa
Palmer Chauncey, do
Day William *Plymouth.*
Skinner William
Mason William *Preston.*
Dwight T.
White D. *Sherburne.*
Lyman E. S.
Marks B. H.
Cushman I.
Buckingham A.
Brasee W. H.
Smith B.
Clarke D. *Smithville.*
Wilder ——
Mead N. B. *Smyrna.*
Fish J. M.

Clinton County.

Adgate L.W. Keeseville *Au Sable.*
Jones Reuben. do
Talmader H. O. do
Blaisdell Jacob, do
Pollard A. do
Wiston A. do
Sawyer Asa, do
Weaver Franklin *Beekmantown.*
Fulton James
Davignon F. J. *Black Brook.*
Fitzgerald Samuel T.
Churchill J. *Champlain.*
Moore Edward J.

Loomis E. S. *Champlain.*
Fulton John S.
Dodge Daniel S.
Morian ——
Hyde Fisk, East Chazy *Chazy.*
Stevenson ——, do
Dodge & Housinger, West Chazy
Fitch Edward *Mooers.*
Soules A. W.
Cole F. H. *Peru.*
Stevenson N.
Moores B. J. *Plattsburgh.*
Kane Edward
Nelson H.
Terry Orman *Saranac.*
Terry Orville, Redford

Columbia County.

Niver C. *Ancram.*
Philips *Austerlitz.*
Bailey W. C.
Cole H. Spencertown
Reed E., do
Warner T. A. *Chatham.*
Coffin S. N.
Root H.
Peck J.
Vandyke ——
Vedder ——
Browning T. Malden Bridge
Shufelt J. T. Chatham 4 corners
Lazzell S. M. do
Conklin G. W. *Claverack.*
Cole J. H.
Jordan A.
Broadhead T. *Clermont.*
Knickerbocker P. H.
Robinson J. *Copake.*
Platner S. H.
Niver J. D. *Gallatin.*
Coburn E. L. *Ghent.*
Barnes J.
Wells G. *Hillsdale.*
Dorr J. P.
Richards ——
Mercer ——
Frary R. G. Warren st. *Hudson.*
M'Clellan J.
White G. H.
Simpson E.
Whitbeck V.
Wheeler J. P.
Benham J. C.
Cook A. F.
Doolittle R. B.
Pruyn L. *Kinderhook.*
Pruyn J. M.
Tallmadge S. G., Valatie
Abbot Alexander, do
Vanderpoel John, do
Vanderpoel S. O. do
Humphrey & Horton *Livingston.*
Jones & Smith
Bates J. *New Lebanon.*
Wright D.
Drown H. N.
Everest ——
Bedortha N. (hydropathic)
Platner R. *Taghkanic.*

Cortland County.

Eldridge Lyman *Cincinnatus.*
Davison ——
White L. B.
Ruddock A. S. *Cortland Village.*
Goodyear & Hyde
Jewett Homer O.
Deming Willard F.
Kingman C. M., M'Grawville
Kean Lorenzo, do
Riggs Lewis *Homer.*
Patterson A.
Bradford George W.
Owen Robert C.
Green Caleb S.
Patterson Josiah
Brown Wm. R. (homœopathic)
Kelley Lewis H. *Marathon.*
Havens Daniel
Barnes E. H.

Maxson Geo. W. *Scott.*
Gleason S. O. (hydropathic)
Bierce Miles H.
Cook Eli
Nelson J. C.
Smith A. B. *Truxton.*
Bronson Horace *Virgil.*
Fitch William
Ball Jay
Thomas Charles, East Virgil

Delaware County.

Peak M. T. *Andes.*
Bryant E.
Leal J. R.
Calhoun J. *Bovina.*
M'Kinzie E.
Tilford ——
Bassett P., Downsville *Colchester.*
Ostrander D. B. do
Hicks H. *Davenport.*
Ferguson J. jr.
Weterhury R. L.
Jacobs F. *Delhi.*
Steele E.
Fitch A.
Buckley H. N.
Howard C.
Sullard A. D. *Franklin.*
Wilcox S. C.
Titus L. F.
Dewey D.
Mann D. *Hamden.*
Goodrich R.
Close J.
Hotchkiss J. T. *Hancock.*
Pettingill S. C.
Appley T.
Hamilton H. R. *Harpersfield.*
M'Harge S., North *Kortright.*
Gibbs E. T., North Kortright
Foreman S., Bloomville
Ensign S. *Meredith.*
Mann A. P.
Scott H., Clovesville *Middletown.*
Allaben J. C. do
Leal ——, Margaretsville
Allaben O. M. do
Street S. *Roxbury.*
Newkirk J.
Hall A. C.
Howell O. D., Mooresville
Covell C. C. *Stamford.*
Marshall R. S., Hobart
M'Naught J. S. do
Sweet —— *Sidney.*
Smith W. A., Sidney Plains
Angell D. M., Deposit *Tompkins.*
Higgins L. D. do
Gilbert H. D. do
Eighmy B. do
Rogers T. S. do
Cotirell S., Cannonsville
M'Laury J. S. *Walton.*
Ogden T. J.
Bartlett H. E.

Duchess County.

Hunting J. M. *Amenia.*
Stanton L. W.
Payne J. C.
Chamberlain Wm. Y.
Nickerson C. A. *Beekman.*
Ring G. L.
Tallman E. W.
Cary E.
Case E. jr. *Clinton.*
Denny F. S.
Guernsey C. P.
Herrick W., Hollow
Hooker W. *Dover.*
Hammond T.
Hammond T. jr.
White B. *Fishkill.*
White L. H.
Wortman D.
Underhill A.
Smith R., Wappinger's Falls
Proal —— do
Hughson B., Hughsonville
Baxter Wm. (homœp'c,) do

20

Anthony T. V. W., Glenham
    Fishkill.
Schenck J. P., Matteawan
Guernsey E.   do
Thatcher C.   do
Vermilyea V., Fishkill Landing
Harkness J. (homœp'c.) do
Fletcher F., Stormville
Vermilyea J. R., Hopewell
Smith A. H.   *Hyde Park.*
Andrews N.
Hopkins ——   *La Grange.*
Upton ——
Lansing G. C., Lafayette Corners
    Milan.
Lasee A. T.   do
Robertson S.   *Northeast.*
Stillman S.
Crosby E.
Eastman J. R.   *Pawling.*
Cole P. S.   *Pine Plains.*
Wilber B. S.
Davis J. I. H.
Davis J. C.
Bartlett R.
Allerton C. C.
Canfield C.   *Pleasant Valley.*
Traver I. H.
Pearsell O. T., Salt Point
Cooper J. 240 Main *Poughkeepsie.*
Hughson W. 240 Main
Bockee J. 297   do
Pine P. 231   do
Barnes J. Market st.
Varrick R. Cannon st.
Hervey A. B. Main st.
Andrus C. H.   do
Barnes J. H.   do
Deyo E. Main st.
Valentine ——, Market st.
Barnes J. Main st.
Hasbrouck A. 189 Main
Bates J.   *Red Hook.*
Essletine R.
Freligh M.   *Rhinebeck.*
Kiersted J.
Platt E.
Nelson T.
Vanvielt J. & F.
Landon W. R.
Bucknum A.   *Stanford.*
Kilbourne C. J.
Campbell C. N.
Peck G.
Cook J. S. Verbank   *Union Vale.*
Dodge S.
Thorn J.   *Washington.*
Childs H. F. Lithgow
Orton H. T. Hart's Village

Erie County.

Van Pelt Wm. Williamsville
    Amherst.
Ham L. J.   do
Potter Geo.   do
Hoyt Jonathan, Willink *Aurora.*
Lapham Geo. H.   do
Allen Jabez.   do
Hoyt Horace,   do
Nedham O. H. Willink
Williams D. J. Griffin's Mills
Lewis M. G.   *Black Rock.*
Dayton Lewis O.
Davis L. L.   *Boston.*
Buxton Luther   *Brandt.*
Austin Caleb H. Erie nr. Main
    st.   *Buffalo.*
Bailey Samuel G. 144 Main
Barnes Josiah, Washington above
    Exchange
Barrett H. W. 177 Main
Barrett S. 72 Lloyd
Bently ——, 12 Mechanic
Bissell H. H. 235 Main
Brunck Francis, Niagara bet.
    Carolina & Virginia
Bunnell Bradley, 4 Ohio
Burwell Bryant, 1 East Seneca
Burwell George N.   do
Cary Walter, 148 Main
Chambers Hiram, 10 Terrace
Congar H. M. 261 Main

Davies Richard, 8 Exchange
    Buffalo.
Devening ——, 372 Main
Dellenburgh F.   do
Ehrman Frederick, (Homœopa-
    thic) 2 West Eagle
Feigemacher J. A. Batavia nr.
    Pine
Flint Austin, cor. Washington &
    Swan
Frank William, 329 Main
Frank Augustus, 351 Main
Garvin H. D. 52 Main
Geisbuch M 136 Pearl
Gray Eldred P. 145 Main
Gray P. W. (Homœopathic) East
    Seneca nr. Main
Hakstein J. J. E. Sycamore nr.
    Michigan
Hall H. L. (Eclectic) 269 Main
Hamilton Frank H. 237 W'hington
Hauenstein John, 358 Main
Hill J. D. 8 West Swan
Hill Milo W. (Botanic) 245 Main
Hubbard Silas, 21 Exchange
Jeyte John A. cor. Washington &
    Huron
King James E. cor. East Seneca
    & Main
Knolcke Adolfe, cor. Cherry and
    Michigan
Lewis Dioclesian, 278 Main
Lockwood T. T. 179 Main
Loersh Philip, (Homœopathic)
    218 East Genesee
Loomis H. N. 288 Main
Mackay Edward, 239 Main
Mann F. P. over Post-Office
Merritt Jesse, 148 South Division
Miller L. A. (Botanic) 245 Main
Mixer S. F. 140 Main
Morron Allen, 53 West Tupper
Murphy Thomas, 156 Main
Notchel ——, cor. Main & Lafay-
    ette
Nawman James M. 72 Lloyd
Norval John, Sandusky Dock
O'Hara Charles, Farmer's Hotel
Peabody Joseph, 288 Main
Pratt G. F. 8 West Swan
Pride J. B. Keeper Erie County
    Poor House
Ring William, cor. Commercial
    and Pearl
Samo James B. 180 Main
Sands Andrew J. (Homœopathic)
    290 Main
Schmid Frederick, 144 East Gen-
    esee
Scott W. K. 39 West Mohawk
Sole S. W. over Post Office
Southworth Delos W. 121 Main
Sprague A. S. 272 Main
Stearns Henry, 319 Main
Stevens C. A. over Post-Office
Stevenson J. D. G. 37 West Mo-
    hawk
Strong P. rf. 232½ Main
Theilor E. A. H. 113 Main
Thompson Wm. cor. Commerce
    & Water
Treat William, 292 Main
Trowbridge Josiah, cor. Pearl &
    Swan
Trowbridge John S. cor. Pearl &
    Swan
Wallis Erastus, cor. Main and
    East Swan
Warner N. H over Post-Office
Welch Nicholas, 276 Main
Weyland Francis J. 73 Batavia
White James P. 230 Main
Wilcox C. H. cor. Main & East
    Swan
Winne Charles, 148 Main
Witter Crandall, cor. Canal and
    State
Wyckoff C. C. 272 Main
Zimmerman William, cor. Elli-
    cott & Burton Alley
Zimmerman William, 135 East
    Genesee

Wakelee O.   *Clarence.*
Parker O. K.
Kuchler John D.
Nores Samuel C.   *Collins.*
Adams J.
Franklin ——
Bruce ——
Emmons C. Springville *Concord.*
House John,   do
Pool E. C.   do
Pratt Wm. H.   *Eden.*
Redfield Horace L.
Lathrop Geo.
Armstrong A. East Evans *Evans.*
Wheatland & Aldrich, do
Prindle Chas. Hamburgh Centre
    Hamburgh.
Knott S. E. S. H.   do
Allen ——, Water Valley
Dorland Joseph, East Hamburgh
Goodyear B.   *Holland.*
Potter Samuel   *Lancaster.*
Hosmer R. K.
Osmer O. B.
Morton Dr. Akron   *Newstead.*
Parsell Isaac,   do
Bowman P. R. do
Colgrove B. H.   *Sardinia.*
Macklush John   *Wales.*
Grovesner S. Wales Centre

Essex County.

Stearns T. Port Kent *Chesterfield.*
Hale S. E.   *Elizabethtown.*
Morse Alexander
Post Asa
Shumway Samuel   *Essex.*
Shumway Chas.
Mead Abial P.
Fuller W. D. P.   *Jay.*
Finch Wm. W.
Morse A. Upper Jay
Smith Orrin   *Lewis.*
Drury B. W. Moriah Four Corners
    Moriah.
Cheney L. P.   do
Murray J. B.   do
Goodell ——, Adirondac *Newcomb.*
Potter H. Schroon River, *Schroon.*
Rawson Clark,   do
Smith John   *Ticonderoga.*
Hall Chas. W.
Vaughn D. G.
Ramsay H. D.   *Westport.*
Holcomb Diodorus
Barton Lyman   *Willsborough.*

Franklin County.

Carpenter Christopher   *Bangor.*
Hinman Allen, jr.
Langdon Seth W.   *Bombay.*
Drummond J. B.
Mott Wm.   *Burke.*
Morse F.
Farnsworth ——   *Chateaugay.*
Goodspeed G. W.
Howe ——
Darling G. W.   *Constable.*
Daggett Wm. S.
Bates Roswell   *Fort Covington.*
Gillis Wm.
Paddock O. F.
Howard N. W.
Bates S. P.   *Malone.*
Skinner Calvin
Gay Theodore
Powell T. R.
Stevens D. H.   *Moira.*
Pettit F. H.
Mann Ebenezer   *Westville.*
Morey R. E.

Fulton County.

Barry Jas.   *Broadalbin.*
Chambers Wm.
Humphrey W.
Wood Henry   *Ephratah.*
Maxwell Samuel   *Johnstown.*
Johnson Wm. H.
Burdick Francis

Miller Jas. W.   *Johnstown.*
Smith Daniel
Mackey Ebenezer, Gloversville
Peake Wm. C. Kingsboro
Barker D. N.   *Mayfield.*
Mitchell J. R.   *Northampton.*
Marvin L. P.
Wood A.
Ayres J. S. Northville
Barker D. M.   do
Van Ness, Osborn Bridge
Ingalls C. Cranby Creek
Yoost Peter   *Oppenheim.*
Haskins L. G.
Gilbert Truman O.   *Perth.*
Scoon ——

Genesee County.

Batema L. C.   *Alabama.*
Long J.
Cox A. H. Oakfield
Tyler ——
Butler A. R. R.   *Alexander.*
Mandeville ——
Cotes John   *Batavia.*
Ganson H.
Cotes L. B.
Ford C. E.
Griswold C. D.
Fay Levi   *Bergen.*
O'Donoughue W.
Taber W. F.
Andrews Robert
Watson H.
Churchill Gilbert, East Bergen
Croff O. R.   *Bethany.*
Meacham J. G. Linden
Lynd D. J.   *Byron.*
Emory Sanford
Rayno Isaiah   *Darien.*
Billings Jonas S.   *Elba.*
Warner ——
Chamberlain D. C   *Le Roy.*
Taylor E. C.
Williams Randall
Chester & Harris
Gage J. L.
Pratt Almon
Wilcox A.
Thompson Andrew   *Oakfield.*
Bishop ——
Sprague W. M.   *Pavilion.*
Fay Warren
Owen Alanson   *Pembroke.*
Knight ——
Stoddard A. W. Corfu
Long Aaron,   do
Tomlinson ——   *Stafford.*
Haynes ——

Greene County.

Draper ——   *Ashland.*
Norbury J. F. & T. S.   *Athens.*
Wheeler John H.
King Levi   *Cairo.*
Doane John   *Catskill.*
Brace A.
Wetmore Wm. W.
Adams F. C.
Dewy & Greene, Leeds
Richards Anson   *Cassackie.*
Adams Henry
Spoor Jas. W.
Van Dyck Herman   *Durham.*
Cowles Jonathan B.
Botsford Amos   *Greenville.*
Botsford Gideon
Hamilton Erastus
Teats Philip
Ingersoll Ebenezer   *Hunter.*
Hard Amos J.
Barrett C. V. & Ogden J. G.
     Lexington.
Newman Erastus   *New Baltimore.*
Fitch Thomas   *Prattsville.*
Marsh Willard
Benham C. K.
Cramp & Van Dyck   *Windham.*
Hubbard Paul

Herkimer County.

Hannaer Luther   *Columbia.*
Hawn Peter
Easton C. L.
Devege Chas. L.
Holmes A. H.   *Danube.*
Snyder A.
Varney A. E.   *Fairfield.*
Sweet Dr.
Devendorf, D. B.   *Frankfort.*
Budlong Caleb
Parkhurst Wm. H. H.
Budlong Wm. W.
Griffith Calvin A., Mohawk
     German Flats.
Bellinger James, Mohawk
Salisbury L.   do
Pruyn Peter   *Herkimer.*
Doolittle Andrew F.
Belknapp Daniel   *Little Falls.*
Brown John R.
Belknapp Oren
Williams Nathaniel
Duffie ——
Randall O. W.   *Litchfield.*
Christie Asa   *Manheim.*
Ingham Silas
Johnson Moses   *Newport.*
Sherwood Jacob L
Philleo B.
Bushnell B. E.
Millington S. R.   *Norway.*
Hemstreet Hiram   *Ohio.*
Booth Walter   *Russia.*
Hemstreet R. J., Poland
Fenner J. G., Coldbrook
Bennett R.   do
Stebbins Wm. B.   *Salisbury.*
Hadly Hiram, Salisbury Centre
Westcott Dr.   do
Day H. B.   *Schuyler.*
Reed Z. B., Vanhornsville   *Stark.*
Munn J. D.   do
Diefendorf Edw. do
Smith A. F.
Miller Adam, Jordanville
     Warren.
Benjamin Z. W.
Crossland Wm.
Palmer D., Crane's Corner
Spencer N.   *Winfield.*
Roe G. M., West Winfield

Jefferson County.

Webb W.   *Adams*
Wetmore S.
Mann J. P.
Stow R.
Maxson E. R. Adams Centre
Hale ——   do
Hosford W. A., Plessis *Alexandria.*
Hutchins M. J.   do
Gardiner Alonzo H., Alexandria
     Bay
Conkey J. S.   *Antwerp.*
Robinson Wm.
Ayers Jesse D.   *Brownville.*
Massey Wm. P.
Wood ——, Dexter
Sackett G.   *Cape Vincent.*
Carrier J.
Potter Nelson
Bushnell Handy
Bushnell Handy, jr.
Webb Wm.
Spencer G. P.   *Champion.*
Johnson J. R.
Page ——
Whelpley ——
Winslow M. T.   *Clayton.*
Allis Amos
Jewett W. W., Depauville
France Luke E.   do
Somers A.   do
Ely A.   *Ellisburgh.*
Eastman C. W.
Sandors H. J.
Houghton S., Belleville
Jones J.   do
Veets O.   do
Barney L.   *Henderson.*

Tubbs O. A.   *Henderson.*
Harrington A. B.
Hunter D., Sackett's Harbor
     Hounsfield.
Tyler W. E.   do
Kimball D. S.   do
Smith Ira A., Evans' Mills
     Le Ray.
Comstock W. J.   do
Van Ostrand A. M. do
Jones L. E., Three Mile Bay
     Lyme.
Parker L.   do
Goodell S.   do
Rogers J. F.   do
Cillenbeck J., Lafargeville
     Orleans.
Cushman S.   do
Failing Walter W   Watertown
     Pamelia.
Carpenter James B.   *Philadelphia.*
Murdock A.
Beebe ——
Peckham ——
Jenks I.   *Rodman.*
Tuttle T.
Bates Wm S. South Rutland
     Rutland.
Dennison M.   do
Norman L F., Black River
French A. J.   *Felt's Mills.*
Helmer J. H.   *Theresa.*
Brewster Oliver
Davidson John D.
Hannah Kilborn   *Watertown.*
Goodall Reuben
Goodall Chas.
Sykes Wm. J.
Rosa Wm. V. V.
Martin Stephen
Trowbridge Amasa
Trowbridge Wm.
Rogers Alpheus
Ferguson Nelson D., Carthage
     Wilna.
West Eli,   do
French Elkanah, Natural Bridge

Kings County.

Atwater D. Remsen st.   *Brooklyn.*
Ball John, 195 Washington
Baker D. 26 Myrtle Av.
Bennett G. I. 195 Washington
Benjamin H. L. 108 Clinton
Bennett J. B. 13 Cottage pl.
Benedict W. Atlantic st.
Beers George, 102 Gold
Betts Wm. C. Myrtle Av.
Betts Wm. C. Flushing Av. near
     Kent
Beers George W. Myrtle Av.
Blackmore J. 5 Cottage pl.
Boardman J. C. 22 Myrtle Av.
Boyd Samuel, 76 Remsen
Brooks Daniel. Clinton c. Harrison
Brown W. K. Henry c. Montague
Burke A. C. Union n. Hicks
Chapman E. N. 202 Henry
Cook P. 106 Pineapple
Corson J. W. 112 Fulton
Colgan J. P. 180 Jay
Crane James, 57 Pacific
Crane J. L. 21 Myrtle Av.
Dudley Wm. H. Henry cor. State
Frink Cyrus, 114 York
Gardner Wm. H. 381 Henry
Garrison Nelson. Atlantic st.
Garrison & Enos 23 Clinton
Goodrich C. S. J. 150 Joralemon
Greene G. S. 187 Atlantic
Gullen H. J. 79 Cranberry
Guthrie C. B. 84 Hicks
Guy S. S. 74 Clinton
Hayes James, 51 Remsen
Haggerty E. Jay st.
Hibbard J. B. 64 Atlantic
Hull Aaron C. 76 State
Hutchins J. H. Myrtle Av. near
     Franklin
Hudson M. H. 261 Gold
Hurd F. W. 78 Henry
Hyde L. Henry c. Clark

Kissam D. E. Henry c. Jerome
                              Brooklyn.
Ladd John G. 79 Pacific
M'Millen Robert, 69 Nassau
Mason T. L. Clinton n. Remsen
Marvin Geo. 100 Pineapple
Marvin Geo. 79 Henry
Manley J 18 Cottage pl.
Manson James S. 150 Willoughby
Manly G. V. Navy st.
Minor James, 33 Pierpont
Mitchell C. L. Henry c. Montague
Moffat R. C. Clinton n. Baltic
O'Reilly Francis. 219 Bridge
Olmsted R. S. 28 Union pl.
Osborn Samuel J. 120 High
Ostrander E. 28 Tillary
Ostrander F. W. 69 Clark
Otterson Andrew, 147 Sands
Parker Bradley, 152 Myrtle Av.
Parker Bradley, 148 Joralemon
Palmedo U. 20 Myrtle Av.
Powers T. W. Court n. State
Price Edward E 106 High
Rea L. 87 Atlantic
Rice Edmund, 96 Prince
Rotton Otto, Fulton st.
Rowland Charles, 161 Wash.
Shaw Samuel W. 30 Nassau
Spear H. F. 135 Henry
Swaim S. J. 104 Myrtle Av.
Swift Wm. 99 Willoughby
Thiers Wm. F. J. 13 Willoughby
Thorne J. S. 43 Sands
Turney J. M. 227 Henry
Van Buren M. 56 Sands
Van Ness J. Franklin nr. Myrtle
    Av.
Vanderveer A. 280 Bridge
Wade T. A. 159 Washington
Weeks Benj. 72 Carlton Av.
Willey Sidney B. Court n. Amity
Willsher Henry, 198 Adams
Snell I. K., Green Point Bushwick.
Vanderveer Adrian   Flatbush.
Ingraham Timothy M.
Andrews H., East New York
Carpenter J.   New Utrecht.
Dubois J
Berrien J. V.
Belden & Colt, S. 7th n. 4th
                        Williamsburgh.
Belden R. 81 4th
Cooke C. L. 92 4th
Jones Algernon S. 127 S. 3d
Cox George, 4th cor. So. 3d
O'Neil M. 133 S. 2d
Bullock Francis, 128 4th
Palmer & Olcott, 127 4th
Wade S. 141 4th
Nicot Lewis, 272 Grand
Schapps C. H. 192 Grand
Costello Patrick, 138 Grand
Belden, Colt & Smith, N. 2d cor.
    Lorimer
Hooper Thomas, 82 Grand
Hahlord S. C. 440 Grand
Lorett M. Grand st.

Lewis County.

Squires C.   Denmark.
Shaw O., Copenhagen
Stanton L.   do
Bruinschwiller ——, do
Bliss John S., Brantingham Greig.
Hendee H. S.   Harrisburgh.
Olmsted Wm. J.   Leyden.
Bass Charles N.
Douglass David
Orvis C.   Martinsburgh.
Feden J. T.
Cummings Morgan L.   Turin.
Utley Henry
Budd Charles
Bliss John S.
Hannan D. B., Houseville
Gregory A., Constableville
                        West Turin.
Budd B. S.   do
Runge R.   do

Livingston County.

Salisbury Samuel, jr.   Avon.
Van Kleek J.
Parsons F.
Southworth W. T.
Butler W. C. East Avon
Wells Harlow H.   Caledonia.
Campbell Duncan
M'Arthur P. S.
M'Miller David   Conesus.
M'Miller Charles
Hovey B. L.   Dansville.
Cook L. N
Patchin E. W.
Enduss J. L.
Reynale William H.
Blake Z. H.
Davis George W.
Shepard G. W.
Townsend M. C.
Bissell Daniel H.   Geneseo.
Lauderdale Walter E.
Metcalf Elias P.
Peldon Jonathan G., Cuylerville
                         Lieester.
Allen ——,   do
Dwight Wm. C., Moscow
Peck ——,   do
Bennett G. H. & T. L.   Lima.
Dayton & Mercer
Bartlett O. C.
Reynolds H. Y.
Campbell Alex. C.
Sill Andrew   Livonia.
Clark Josiah
Meacham E. H. G. Hemlock Lake
M'Master James,   do
Salmon Edward,   do
Crandall A. jr. South Livonia
Caton P. T., Lakeville
Hoff H. D.   Mount Morris.
Thomas W. H.
Maxwell H.
Ames L. J.
Hunt S. J.
Hunt Hiram
Branch H.
Turner J. T.   Nunda.
Meachom J.
Upson S. C.
Gilmore J.
Harding Charles
Gray Amos
Wright B.
Patterson ——, Hunt's Hollow
                          Portage.
Coe Wm. L., Scottsburgh Sparta.
Joselyn ——,   do
Gray Arnold   Springwater.
Norton John B.
Bogart Gilbert, Union Corners
                        West Sparta.
Way ——, Byersville
Long J.   York.
Craig J.
Durell George J.
Stickney B., Fowlersville
Bennett Wm. Greigsville

Madison County.

Bailey Silas   Brookfield.
Saunders A. L.
Griswold N. L.
Crandall H. S., Leonardsville
Robinson Plinny,   do
Foord Alvin   Cazenovia.
Adams E. M.
Mitchell David
Potter S. M.
Chamberlain John K.
Shelden George
Rice F.
Wakeley D. M.
Goodell John, New Woodstock
Heffron Lorenzo,   do
Ballou Russell   De Ruyter.
Spencer & Clark
Whitford James
Hodgins Wm. N.
Purdy A. D.   Eaton.
Teasay D. C.

Clark Isaac   Eaton
Barnet Milton, Morrisville
Maybury F. T.   do
Mead Powers   Fenner.
Watson Jesse (Botanic)
Whitmore E.   Georgetown.
Franklin Benjamin
Beardsley H. G.   Hamilton.
Havens F. B. & Son
Babcock B. W.
Lewis B.
Green Jeremiah
Kimberly Sherman, (Botanic)
Ransom David, Earlville
Root F. W. East Hamilton
Loomis E., Oneida Depot   Lenox.
Palmer Benj.   do
Beardsley L.   do
Mason V. W., Canastota
Jarvis M. B.   do
Spooner Stillman, Wampsville
Mitchell John L., Clockville
Nott H. K. (Botanic)   do
Fowler S. F. do   do
Orton Lyman C.   Georgetown.
Baker Cyrus C.
Putnam John   Madison.
Barker D. (Homœopathic)
Root E. (Botanic)
Heffron John, Erieville   Nelson.
Greenwood L. P. do
Treat J. Siloam   Smithfield.
Powers N. C. Peterboro
Messenger E. G. do
Merrill S. B.   do
Dorrance John,   do
Frost D. H.   Stockbridge.
Sumner R. T.
Oaks William   Sullivan.
Fuller S., Chittenango
Teller I. T.   do
Arndt P. S.   do
Mead P. R., Perryville
Dideman John, do
Ramsey J. H. (Botanic) Perryville
Dunham David, Bridgeport
Ferguson ——,   do
Sweet ——, Heywood's Corners

Monroe County.

Miller Elisha   Brighton.
Brown John
Bowen Ebenezer
Lynde John, N. Chili   Chili.
Bangs Lyman, do
Powers ——,   do
Leonard A. M. Clarkson Corners
                          Clarkson.
Tozier J.   do
Clarke N. G.   do
Presbury Otis,   do
Newton A. J.   do
Carpenter A. B. Jenkin's Corner
                          Greece.
Bradley S. B.   do
Haseltine J. M. C. East Henrietta
                         Henrietta.
Browning J. East Mendon Mendon.
Smith C.   do
Hanna G. W. do
Parsons ——, do
Minor H. B. West Mendon
Allen H.   do
Smith John B.   Ogden.
Rogers R. J. Spencer's Basin
Paine Z. Parma Corners   Parma.
Cole M. S.   do
Rowley J. Parma Centre
Slayton Wm. C. do
Chappell S. G.   Penfield.
Dodge ——
Dyer M.
Durfee D. Lovett's Corners
Van Buren H. Fairport Perrinton.
Lemon R. (Eclectic) Fairport
Durand T. B. V. Bushnell's Basin
Perrine G. W.   Pittsford.
Renolds R. C.
Huntington W. M.
Camp Joseph
Carver H. (Hydropathic)

Lemoy L.   *Riga.*
Smith John R.
Barrows D. L. Churchville
Armstrong E. W. 14 North Washington   *Rochester.*
Backus Fred. F. 48 Spring
Bennett H. 45 Andrews
Bell Wm. cor. Lafayette & South Sophia
Bradley Hugh, cor. Platt & Washington
Bradley T. 25 State
Briggs M. H. 25 North St. Paul
Burt J. cor. Main & St. Paul
Church Charles E. 113 Main
De Villers J. B. 11 William
Elwood John B. 27 North St. Paul
Ely W. W. 69 South Fitzhugh
Faulkner Lewis H. 28 North
Gannane Edward, 126 Buffalo
Gilresoa B. T. 25 State
Headley Wm. W. (Eclectic) Minerva Bl'k, cor. Main & St. Paul
Harris C. G. (Eclectic) 5 Smith's Block, Buffalo st.
Haville T. 2 Bowery
Haville Thomas, 55 N. Clinton
Hurd Ewin S. 58 Andrews
Hunt Simeon, 176 Buffalo
James F. H.
Jordan J. 235 State
Langworthy Elisha P.15 Elizabeth
Langworthy Hen. H. Eagle Hotel
M'Gregor John B. 9 Minerva Bl'k, Main st.
Marter Wm. 17   do
Miller Charles C. H. 17 S. Clinton
Monroe J. S. cor. State & Water
Moore E. M. 9 State
Raymond R. C. 99 State
Rapelji A. B. 2 Minerva Bl'k, Main
Reed Wm. W. Eagle Hotel
Reichenbach T. J. 105 Main
Ripley Z. Howe, (Eclectic) 45 M'n
Rodgers M. M. 47 Main
Russell Samuel, 112 South Sophia
Schloetzer Edward, (Water Cure) 8 Atwater
Shadders Robert (Oculist)
Shipman D. J. 96 Exchange
Shipman P. G. 40 State
Smith George H., Woodside
Swinburn George, 12 Jay
Tobey P. S. 23 North St. Paul
Treat J. J. 121 Main
Valton Josiah, (Eclectic) corner Clinton and Main
Vosburgh M. L. Emporium Block, Main st.
Weybern L. D. (Eclectic) 121 Buffalo
Whitbeck J. F. Irving Hotel
Wood W. J. (Eclectic) 9 Main
Wood Wm. I. 7 Minerva Block
Smith S.   *Rush.*
Parker E. B.
Carpenter Davis, Brockport   *Sweden.*
Thatcher R.   do
Clark Horace,   do
Hicks D. M.   *Webster.*
Potter —
M'Norton D. Scottsville   *Wheatland.*
Sweeny D. (Eclectic) Scottsville
Edson Freeman,   do
M'Norton Peter,   do
Lacy Wm. G.   do

Montgomery County.

Ayes Daniel   *Amsterdam.*
Pulling Abraham
Devendorf Charles
Carroll Davis L.
Neff Henry M.
Vanderpool John
Voorhees Samuel
Coney Wm. E. Cranesville
Hull Aaron W. Tribes' Hill
Burbeck J.   *Canajoharia.*
Fox Charles J.

Wetmore J.   *Canajoharia.*
White Joseph
Stafford John
Fox J.
Marcy Simeon, Ames
Dockstader J.   do
Van Deusen Harlow A. Buel
Brownell G. H.   do
Biggams Wm.   *Charleston.*
Pangburn D. Burtonville
Belding H. H. Fort Jackson   *Florida.*
Snell J.   do
Snell J. G   do
Belding D. E.   do
Barney Z. H. Minaville
Wood G. L.   *Glen.*
Burton Thomas, Fultonville
Procter Leonard,   do
Diefendorf James, Fort Plain   *Minden.*
Snyder Morgan,   do
Phelps Elias P.   do
Riggs J. W.   do
Zinerman John N.   do
Buchbee J. J. Fonda   *Mohawk.*
Schermerhorn A. G. do
Myres Jacob,   do
Blackley George, Stone Arabia   *Palatine.*
Shibley Henry jr.   *Root.*
Snow Simeon
Leonardson Hezekiah
Ethridge F. B.   *St. Johnsville.*
Grant Gideon

New York County.

Abell Thomas, 47 Cherry   *New York.*
Adams Daniel L. 47 White
Adlam Henry R. 1 Amity
Anderson James, 167 Hudson
Anderson William, 167 Hudson
Andrews Benjamin jr. 166 Madison
Andrews Jarvis M. 46 Pearl
Andrews Josiah B. 11 Walker
Anticel —, 92 3d Av.
Archer Cornelius B. 210 Mulberry
Arden John, 30 8th st.
Arnold Edmund, 66 White
Atkinson A. 216 Greenwich
Badarous Camille, 370 Broadway
Bailey Elisha P. 204 Broome
Baldwin —, 52 6th Av.
Ball Alonzo S. 128 Bleecker
Banks Abraham. 58 Chatham
Banning E. F. 360 Broadway
Balser Henry, 183 7th
Barber J. 46 6th Av.
Barker Luke, 55 Franklin
Barlow Samuel B. 139 4th Av.
Barras —, 1 Oliver
Barrett Clement B. 170 Broadway
Barrett Thomas S. 221 Chrystie
Bartles O. S. 475 Hudson
Bathgate James, 640 Broadway
Batchelder G. H. 209 Greene
Batchelder John P. 200 Greene
Batchelder —, 104 Prince
Bayard Edward, 731 Broadway
Beach Wooster, 7 Stanton
Beadle Edward L. 42 Bleecker
Beakley Jacob, 496 Broadway
Beales John C. 543 Broadway
Beames Clare W. 512 Broadway
Beatty Thomas, 357 12th
Beck John A. 14 Leroy place, Bleecker
Beck J. W. 366 Bowery
Bedford Gunning S. 70 5th Av.
Beeker J. 154 3d st.
Belcher Elisha R. 300 Broome
Belcher George E. 419 Broome
Belden E. B. 29 E. Broadway
Belknap Daniel D. 102 Av. C
Bell Wilson F. 67 Warren
Bennett James, 139 Mott
Berdon Rudolph, 157 2d
Berger Francis E. 714 Broadway
Bergold Frederick, 37 Norfolk
Beurmann Frederick, 122 Pitt

Bigelow J. R. 92 1st   *New York*
Billings James D 95 Av. C
Bishop John, 190 Hester
Blakeman Ira B. 20 E. Broadway
Blakeman William N. 113 10th
Blankman Benjamin J. 116 Chambers
Bliss James C. 2 Leroy place
Bliss —, 2 Bleecker
Bliven Jeremiah F. 445 Grand
Blois Samuel, 320 4th
Bode T. 137 Sullivan
Bogert Cornelius R. 5 Saint Mark's place
Bolles Richard M. 294 4th
Bolton Jackson, 14 E. 14th
Bond George W. 54 Orchard
Booraem Augustus, 242 W. 22d
Borroed J. H. 68 9th
Bostwick Homer, 504 Broadway
Bouron J. S. 263 10th
Bowen William, 223 Greene
Bowers Benj. F. 113 Bleecker
Bowron John S. 263 10th
Boyd Thomas, 303 4th
Boyl James, 127 Chambers
Bradshaw Joseph W. 12 Warren
Brady John, 267 Mulberry
Brady Patrick John, 330 Broome
Brailly C. 560 Houston
Breakell R. B. 291 6th Av
Brenna David, 40 Reade
Bremon Paul, 5 W. 24th
Brooks George, 38 Walker
Brooks Orville, 19 Centre
Bronson Salmon. 70 Hamersley
Brown Edward V. 116 Eldridge
Brown H. Weeks, 12 Leroy place
Brown Robert, 174 Chambers
Brown Stephen. 12 Leroy place
Bruckman P. 308 Houston
Brundige Enoch M. 169 Bleecker
Brydges Pattendon, 3 Warren
Buck Gurdon, 775 Broadway
Budd Ben. W. 22 3d
Buel William P. 329 4th
Bulkley Henry D. 43 Bleecker
Bullus Edward, 58 7th
Burke J. 279 Houston
Burke Wm. C. 23 E. Broadway
Burnett Peter, 108 Bayard
Burrill James S. 64 Greenwich
Burtsell Thomas E. 97 Spring
Buskey J. 27 Murray
Byrne Hugh F. 76 James
Carns Robert W. 497 Hudson
Caldwell Hugh, 508 Broadway
Calvur William, 15 Centre
Calkins —, 230 Grand
Callaghan —, 54 Bleecker
Callisen Adolphe, 41 White
Cameron James, 18 N. Moore
Cameron John S. 57 3d Av.
Cammann George P. 166 Hudson
Campbell James, 41 Lispenard
Carpenter Seymour, 4 Peck slip
Carter G. S. 72 Hudson
Carter Galen, 216 4th
Carter John S. 197 W. 19th
Castle Alexander C. 512 Broadway
Cator Henry H. 610 Houston
Chabert J. X. 4 Ridge
Chalmers Thomas C. 56 Walker
Chambers Stephen. 12 Marion
Champlin Elbert H. 18 Washington place
Chapin Edward R. 3 8th Av.
Chapin J. R. & R. S. 305 3d
Chase E. P. 87 Le Roy place
Chasteney Edward, 56 Market
Chesebrough Nicholas H. 639 4th
Cheesman T. M. 473 Broadway
Cheesman John C. 473   do
Cheetham George, 8th Av.
Chichester Edward Lewis, 292 E. Broadway
Childs Samuel R. 95 Chambers
Chilton James R. 63   do
Churchill Charles W. 173 Clinton
Clark Alonzo, 566 Houston

Clark Patrick, 35 Murray
New York.
Clark Peter F. 8 Bleecker
Clarkson Cornelius, 124 Rivington
Cleaveland E. W. 144 Spring
Clement ——, 550 Houston
Clements James W. 103 Amity
Clinton Alexander, 603 Houston
Clow R. F. 7th Av.
Clussman W. H. 11 Market
Cobbett Robert, 19 Duane
Cobl C. 7 Av. A
Cochrane James, 150 Division
Cock Thomas, 15 Murray
Cock Thomas F. 15 Murray & 54 Bond
Cockey ——, 68 Lexington Av.
Cockcroft Wm. 105 E. Broadway
Colgan ——, 5 Oliver
Collett ——, 261 W. 24th
Collins Clarkson T. 70 2d Av.
Comstock Lucius 8. 70 Union pl.
Conger John, 28 E. Broadway
Conway Edward, 397 Pearl
Conway John R. 397 do
Cook Alfred. 221 5th
Cook A. B. 67½ Madison
Cook George W. 496 Broadway
Cooper Fayette. 12 9th
Cooper James 8. 259 3d Av.
Cooper John, 12 Duane
Cooper Warmuldus 8. 684 4th
Covel James. 141 Worcester
Covel John C. 130 Spring
Cox Abraham L. 8 Union place
Crane J. W. 11 Le Roy place
Crane John F. 99 Spring
Creveling Abraham. 124 White
Cunningham Thomas J. 97 Cross
Dana John W. 363 6th Av.
Daring Frederick, 367 6th Av.
Darken Edward J., West 23d bet. 6th & 7th Avs.
Davidson John M. 131 Canal
Davis John, 52 Bond
Davis N. 8. 362 Bleecker
Dayton Charles B. 87 Av. C
De Gaa C 150 Canal
Delafield Edward, 108 Bleecker
De Lancy ——, 51 Lispenard
Donslord Hermann, 564 4th
De Salm Charles F. 175 Walker
Detmold William. 192 Mercer
Dewees H. P. 513 Broadway
De Witt Gashire, 42 Charles & 1 Hammond
Dickerson Wm. W. 140 W. 20th
Dieck Augustus. 218 W. 17th
Dixon Edward H. 5 Mercer
Doane A. 8. 32 Warren
Dodd David. 47 Rutgers
Doolittle Adrastus. 141 Grand
Douglas J. Hancock, 12 Clinton pl.
Douglas Robert, 518 Broadway & 423 Greenwich
Drake ——, 141 Hudson
Draper J. W. 380 4th
Dubois Abram, 609 Houston
Duffy John, 30 Bleecker
Duggan Bryan. 99 3d Av.
Dunnel Henry, 53 Broome
Durken ——. 8th Av. 23 st.
Dwight William W. 110 Spring
Eager William B jr, 96 Hudson
Earle Edward. 79 Christopher
Edwards Joseph. 179 W. 15th
Elliott H. H. 51 3d
Farrell Jacob H. 8 Park place
Fawcett James. 51 Dey
Fell Jesse W. 173 Spring
Ferguson John T. 721 Broadway
Ferris T. T. 218 13th
Ferris Louis C. 139 Hudson
Field J. 151 10th
Fields Edward, 4 Charlton
Finley Edward, Yorkville
Finnell Thomas C. 39 Grand
Firth Henry 8. 266 Broome
Firth 8. 14 Clarkson
Fisher F. W. 30 Broadway
Fisk Lewis, 170 Delancy
Fitch H. B. 91 Greene

Fitch James, 15 Stuyvesant
New York.
Fitch Samuel 8. 707 Broadway
Fitzpatrick Charles. 82 Sheriff
Fleet Francis. 260 Hudson
Flint Clement, 178 7th
Follin Adolphus, 45 Lispenard
Forbes William R. 843 Broadway
Ford Seth P. 85 Chambers
Forrester James C. 200 Bleecker
Foster Joel, 852 Broadway
Foster Joseph H. 14 Warren
Foster Samuel, 17 Amity
Francis John W. 1 Bond
Frankel Julius, 45 Delancy
Franklin Thomas M. 11 E. 17th
Fraser Richard. 654 Broadway
Freeman Alfred. 218 E. Broadway
Gellagher John. 33 Bleecker
Gardner Augustus K. 153 Wooster
Garrish John P. 76 White
Gay H. S. 6 Market
Geer Seth, 532 Broadway
Gescheidt Anthony. 83 Walker
Gilchrest William N. 62½ Spring
Gilchrist W. 209 Elm
Gilford Jacob T. 18 Bond
Gilligan Michael, 389 8th
Gilman Chandler, 687 Houston
Glentworth Edw. H. 492 Broome
Glover Ralph, 12 Ann
Godfrey E. 349 Cherry
Goldsmith Alban, 9 Park place
Gomez Horatio. 395½ 4th
Goodrich ——, 299 Av. A
Gough John M. 22 Market
Graham ——. 27 Bleecker
Graff P. C. 48 Carmine
Gray Edward, 26 Madison
Gray Francis C. 201 W. 29d
Gray Henry M. 101 11th
Gray John F. 49 Lafayette place
Gray William M. 101 11th
Greek Charles P. 95 Greenwich
Green David. 166 Hudson
Green Horace. 12 Clinton place
Greene Isaac, 78 E. Broadway
Greenly Philo P. 191 Grand
Gregory Holly. 67½ Madison
Grey Edward. 5 Madison
Griscom John H. 223 E. Broadway
Griffin Thomas B. 68 Marion
Griswold Samuel L. 326 4th
Groef ——. 249 Stanton
Groves John, 2 12th
Guernsey Henry, 276 Madison & 287 Delancy
Guernsey Peter. 706 Houston
Guion Edward M. 63 E. 16th
Gunn Alexander N. 132 4th
Gunn George O. 107 4th
Habell 8. 543 Broadway
Hall Samuel. 119 Greene
Hallett Arnold, 120 Prince
Halleck Robert T. 174 Chambers
Hallock Lewis, 6 3d
Hallook L. 173 Cherry
Halsey William, 399 E. Broadway
Halsey William S. 564 Pearl
Halstead J. M. cor. 14th & 8th Av.
Halsted Jonathan. 18 Warren
Hammond Charles D. 86 Hudson
Hanks A. 93½ Laurens
Hanford W. H. 139 4th Av.
Hanks Azel. jr. 150 Prince
Hanners George M. 22 Chambers
Hardenbergh Theodore, 156 W. Broadway
Harriott Hampton, 144 8th Av.
Harris Elisha, 11 Walker
Harris Henry B. 96 Prince
Hart John. 30 Oliver
Hartley Francis W. 14 Greenwich
Hasbrouck Stephen, 94 Greene
Hassell John. 7 Stanton
Hassert L. 194 Hudson
Hayes G. 111 Spring
Hazelton ——, 256 Houston
Heard John 8. 53 Walker
Heine Joseph, 20 Duane
Helme John B. Harlem
Hempel Charles G. 45 Bleecker

Hendrick Thomas, 65 Ann
New York.
Henriques Aaron J. 8 Bedford
Henriques Joseph. 8 do
Henry Thomas Wilson, 76 Beekman
Henschel Charles A. 17 Murray
Herriot George. 268 Spring
Hewett J. G. 111 M'Dougal
Hewe ——, 164 2d
Heyman Ludovic, 67 Bank
Higgins E. W. 30 6th Av.
Hill Samuel A. Harlem
Hilton Joseph, 44 Oak
Hirsch Samuel, 174 2d
Hobart Wm. H. 75 Leonard
Hoexter Jacob, 628 4th
Hoffman Richard K. 201 12th and 22 Warren
Hoffman C. 197 12th
Hogan Daniel M. 5 Mott
Holden Edward H. 8. 218 Rivington
Holt D. Harlem
Holton David P. 11 Amity
Hoppe Lewis, 2 Oliver
Hopper Josiah, 20 3d
Horsfield Richard T. 269 3d Av.
Hosack Alexander E. 101 Franklin
Houke Frederick, 113 Elm
Houston ——, 71 Lexington Av.
Houghton R. 8. 51 10th st.
Hubbard Samuel T. 188 Bleecker
Hull R. M. 284 Spring
Humbert Jonas, 19 Bleecker
Hunt J. L. 232 Houston
Hunter Abraham T. 161 Hudson
Hunter Galen, 104 6th Av.
Hunter William A. 60 Church
Hunter Wm. 81 Delancy
Hurschfield H. 167 Houston
Husband George, 107 9th Av.
Husband R. J. & G. 107 9th Av. & West 40th bet. Broadway and 7th Av.
Hyslop James, 22 East Broadway
Irwin James, 347 Broome
Ives John, 8th Av.
Ing Edward, 19 Murray
Ives George W. 21 East B'dway
Jackson Charles H. 155 Grand
Jackson Francis Henry, 120 Cherry & 5 Monroe
Jackson William H. 831 B'way
Jacobson Richard 8. 68 Spring
Jennings James, 8th Av.
Jenkins Frederick W. 293 B'way
Johns Cyrus, 43 Bowery
Johnson Amos, 35 Bond
Johnson Simon, 12 Duane
Johnson William J. 84 4th
Johnston Francis U. 752 B'way
Jones Alanson 8. 148 Chambers
Jones Henry W. 120 2d Av.
Joslin Benjamin F. 113 Bleecker
Judson Hezekiah T. 135 Franklin
Kaemerer Nicholas, 74 Reade
Kaspler M. 145 Cherry
Kalt A. 370 Broadway
Kaiser C. 489½ do
Keenan Thomas, 605 Houston
Keen Stephen 8. 304 4th
Kelley J. Clawson, 259 Bowery
Kelley J. Wesley, 259 Bowery
Kiersted Chas. 22d st. 9th Av.
Kelly Patrick, 18 Prince
Kennedy Jas. 186 Duane
Kiernan ——, 8th Av.
Kiersted Christopher, 144 9th Av
Kilbourne J. Sage, 126 Franklin
King E. 8th Av.
King Andrew, 100 Bank
Kingsbury Geo. H. 266 Spring
Kinne Wm. W. 622 Broadway
Kinne W. 628 Broadway
Kinaley Hudson, 111 Amity
Kirby Stephen R. 762 Broadway
Kissam Jas. B. 7 Ludlow place
Kissam Richard 8. 654 Broc'way
Klingeman F. 205 Walker
Knapp C. 187 11th

Knight Jas. 6 Ann   *New York.*
Kuypers Sam'l S. 296 3d Av.
Lambert Lewis, 305 1st Av.
Lamberts Dr. 51 Dey
Lambright John C. 380 Broome
Lang J. 56 Greenwich
Lasher John J. 167 Duane
Lawrence Sam'l S. 246 Delancy
Leaming James R. 162 Waverley place
Leavitt Eli, 214 Division
Ledeboer B. 107 Christopher
Lee J. C. 175 Spring
Lee S. H. P. 78 Nassau
Lee T. D. 472 Grand
Leeds Gurdon J. 72 2d Av.
Leggett Robert, 265 Houston
Le Grand Henry, 87 Walker
Lehwess Rudolph, 62 Orchard
Leo-Wolf Geo. 166 Chambers
Leo-Wolf Morris, 39 Lispenard
Leveridge Benj. C. 106 E. B'dway
Levey Meyer, 109 Greene
Lindenberg Wm. 119 Hester
Lindo Stephen, 421½ Broome
Lindsay Geo. 35 6th Av.
Linsley Jared, 20 E. Broadway
Lodge Price B. 349 Cherry
Ludlow E. G. 759 Broadway
Lutenar Wm. 196 Hudson
Lyons Jas. L. 48 Hudson
M'Caffrey Chas. 280 Mulberry
M'Caffrey ——, 21 Bleecker
M'Carron ——, 184 2d Av.
M'Claurey Jas. 148 Walker
M'Clelland ——, 251 4th Av.
M'Clure J. E. 11 Warren
M'Comb John R. 165 Duane
M'Cready Benj. W. 81 Spring
M'Curley Robert, 392 4th
M'Donald Jas. 2 Amity place
M'Donnell ——, 53 Beekman
M'Donoch ——, 78 Sullivan
M'Kinzie T. 47 Cherry
M'Murray R. 221 E. Broadway
M'Vickar John A. 761 Broadway
Maclay Archibald, 464 Broome
Macneven Wm. 94 4th Av.
Maebert Edward, 233 5th Av.
Manley James, 7 Dey
Manley James R. 69 2d Av.
Marcellin Edward P. 105 4th Av.
Markoe Thomas M. 175 Greene
Marsh Charles, 906 Cherry
Marshall Benjamin, 99 Bayard
Martin Joseph, 112 Columbia
Marvin David D. 15 10th
Marvin ——, 69 Bleecker
Marx Daniel, 22½ Eldridge
Matthews ——, 202 8th Av.
Mauriceau A. M. 129 Liberty
Maxwell Wm. H. 44 Walker
Mears Hannibal H. 31 Bowery
Meier C. Ch. 164 Chambers
Meigs Joseph J. 89 Av. C
Meikleham David S. 274 W. 20th
Melver John, 186 3d Av.
Mergs J. J. 89 Av. C
Merkel Isaac H. 316 E. Broadway
Merkel John, 310   do
Metcalfe John T. 785 Broadway
Meyer Philip, 234 William
Michaelis Morris, 106 Attorney
Miller A. S. 21 Greene
Miller Francis, 106 Forsyth
Miller John, 186 E. Broadway
Miller J. S. 762 Greenwich
Miller William, 344 Broome
Miller & Van Antwerp, 788 Gr'ch
Milnor William H. 205 3d Av.
Miner William W. 37 E. Broad'y
Mitchels James, 451 Grand
Moffat Wm. B. 326 Broadway
Monroe Dennis, 147 Grand
Moor Edward, 70 6th
Moore E. 72 6th
Moore M. P. 5 Warren
Moore Samuel W. 767 Broadway
Moran Thompson, 92 Stanton
Morehead D. C. 132 Broadway
Morell ——, 61 Lexington Av.
Moreton Henry, 149 Elm

Mornes Fred. 192 Fulton *New York.*
Mornes ——, 26 8th
Morrison Patrick H. 204½ Fulton
Morris M. 268 12th
Morse Veranus, 113 E. Broadway
Mortamore Lewis, 196 William
Mortimer R. 523 Broadway
Mott H. 645   do
Mott Valentine, 152 Bleecker
Mower Thomas G. 123 Hudson
Murphy George L. 63 Gold
Murphy William, 257 2d
Murray William, 12 6th
Neilson John. 726 Broadway
Nelson James B. 16 Abington sq.
Nelson R. 66 White
Newcomb George, 14 Cherry
Newmann William, 329 Henry
Nichols Elias S. 93 Columbia
Nichols Henry W. 8th Av.
Nichols Mary S. Gove, 46 Lexington Av.
Nichterns Ponce M. 134 Liberty
Oatman Joel S. 111 Eldridge
O'Brien Thomas, 1 Mott
O'Donnell William, 41 Oliver
Ogden Benjamin, 150 Hester
O'Neal M. 50 Centre
O'Neal Michael M. 511 Pearl
O'Reilly J. 84 White
O'Reilly Joseph J. 60 Prince
O'Reilly Philip, 178 Av. B
O'Reilly Philip R. 7 Oliver
O'Reilly Walter, 306½ Mott
O'Reilly Luke, 239 6th Av.
Osborn John, 203 W. 19th
Overton J. B. 564 4th
Overton William P. 105 Av. B
Overton John B. jr. 545 4th
Owen Edward W. 390 Bowery
Paine Martin, 386 4th
Palmer Miles W. 54 Rivington
Palmer M. W. 284 3d
Palmer Walter C. 54 Rivington
Parkenson Wm. B. 19 Frankfort
Parker William, 754 Broadway
Parker W. 195 12th
Payfer Francis, 352 1st Av.
Passmore Edward E. 510 Grand
Patzott A. 579 14th
Paul James C. 31 Howard
Payton Josiah. 104 Chambers
Peirson Franklin D. 184 12th
Pentz Elias T. 131 1st Av.
Pennell Richard. 94 Chambers
Perry David, 53 Orchard
Perry Joseph S. 292 3d
Peters G. A. 251 4th Av.
Peters John C. 742 Broadway
Pfeiffer Daniel. 166 Hester
Phelps James L. 309 Mulberry
Phillips Samuel B. 415 Hudson
Pierson Charles E. 131 Franklin
Poetzold ——, 579 4th
Pond James O. 47 6th Av.
Porter J. H. 14 Warren
Porter Henry H. 216 Fulton
Post Alfred C. 4 Leroy place, Bleecker st.
Power William, 7 Carroll place
Pratt Peter, 366 Broadway
Preterre Adolphe P. 169 Bowery
Preterre Peter, 9th Av.
Prentiss Watson B. 34 Av. C
Prince Jervis, 18 Columbia
Proudfoot Lawrence, 224 12th
Purcell John, 173 Monroe
Purdy Alfred S. 421 4th
Purdy Samuel A. 16 West Washington place
Purple Samuel. 183 Hudson
Putnam A. 450 Broome
Quackenbos Henry, 527 Broadway
Quenbel J. 191 2d
Quimby Nathaniel H. 334 Broome
Quin James M. 562 Houston
Robineau Johnson, 8 Park place
Ralph Joseph E. 88 Greenwich
Rand Adoniram J. 16 W. 13th
Randolph Israel. 123 Chambers
Ranney Evander W., W. 23d bet. 8th & 9th Avs.

Rawson Edmund G. 250 3d Av.   *New York.*
Regensburger J. 42 E. Broadway
Reinecker J. T. 88 Chrystie
Remsen Robert G. 74 Broadway
Revere F. B. 3 9th
Riely L. O. 239 6th Av.
Riley James. 148 Forsyth
Roberts William C. 135 Spring
Robeson E. B. 850 Broadway
Robinson John, 156 Grand
Robson Benjamin R. 238 4th & 20 E. Broadway
Rochester Thomas, 630 Houston
Rockwell Wm. 29 & 51 E. B'dway
Rodgers J. Kearney, 112 Bleecker
Rogers Amos W. 49 E. Broadway
Root Harmon K. 225 Grand
Ross James, 70 Greenwich Av.
Ross ——, 32 Amity
Rotton Samuel, 18 Jefferson
Rotton S. 192 E. Broadway
Rowe Alon. cor. 29th st. & 10th Av.
Ruggles Edward, 673 Broadway
Russ John D. 69 E. 18th
Sabine Gustavus A. 363 4th
Sampson J. 38 Lispenard
Samson Julius, 370 Broadway
Sands David, 48 Henry
Sayre Louis A. 531 Broadway
Schallem C. R. 38 Lispenard
Schenkenberg M. 78 Warren
Scherdlin George C. 154 Mott
Schirmer William, 492 Broadway
Schmidt John W. 100 Chambers
Schulter ——, 93 Greenwich
Schultze John, 64 Mulberry
Scott John W. 1 10th
Seaman William, 69 Madison
Seiblein Dr. 123 Greenwich
Senff Henry, 107 Grand
Sewall J. O. 372 4th Av.
Shanks John, 205 W. 19th
Sharrock William, 296 Spring
Shearman J. H. 275 10th
Shepherd Horatio D. 111 Eldridge
Sheppard Henry, 190 Av. B.
Sherman Austin, 13 9th
Sherrill Hunting, 513 Hudson
Sherwood Burritt. 703 Broadway
Shook Nelson, 86 Chambers
Shower Dr. T. G. 124 Hudson
Simmons J. 113 Leonard
Sinclair James, 519 Broome
Sleight J. Wilkinson, 23 Oliver
Slevin H. 123 Mott
Smith B. J. 179 Greenwich
Smith Charles D. 50 Bleecker
Smith David, 445 Broome
Smith Gilbert, 50 Bleecker
Smith Hervy W. 29th st. 10th Av.
Smith J. Augustus, 5 Carroll place
Smith J. B. 293 Broadway
Smith Jas. M'Cune, 15 N. Moore
Smith James, 57 W. Broadway
Smith James O. 124 Prince
Smith Joseph M. 66 Bleecker
Snowden Thomas, 114 White
Southworth Malek A. 96 Av. C
Stella Nelson, 158 Grand
Stephenson Mark, 383 Broome
Stewart Jas. 3 Abington square
Stewart Jas. 75 Mulberry
Stickney Josiah D. 8 Cottage pla.
Stiles John. 299 Walker
Stillman Jacob D. B. 93 Av. D
Stillwell John E. 8 Ridge
Stillwell Wm. E. 31 Oliver
Stockbridge Thos. 127 Chambers
Stone John O. 30 Waverley place
Storer Ebenezer, 862 Broadway
Stout T. J. 49 Thompson
Stoutenburgh R. 639 Hudson
Sweeney Jas. 106 Bayard
Sweeny Hugh, 97 Elm
Sweeny Owen, 97 Elm
Sweet Hermes M. 272 Broome
Swett John A. 506 Broadway
Syme Jas. 461 Broadway
Taft Marcus L. 96 E. Broadway
Taylor J. E. 820 Broadway
Taylor Isaac E. 820 Broadway

Taylor John, 104 Spring
New York.
Tellkampf T. A. 20 Chambers
Ten Eyck ——, 7th Av.
Thayer Henry W. 168 Duane
Thomson John. 34 W. 15th
Thomson John, 354 3d Av.
Thorne Jas. G. 584 Grand
Thorp H. C. 48 8th Av.
Throckmorton S. 229 E. Br'dway
Tobias Sam'l I. 1 Murray
Tobias S. 5 11th
Townsend S. P. 87 St. Marks place
Townsend P. S. 170 E. Broadway
Trall Russell T. 15 Laight
Traphagen Geo. H. 380 Pearl
Trenor John, 1 University place
Trudeau Jas. 711 Broadway
Tully Marcus C. 215 Broome
Turner Wm. 269 10th
Tuttle John T. 216 E. Broadway
Underhill Alfred, 3 Madison
Underhill Rufus T. 300 Broadway
Upham Alfred, 195 Bowery
Van Antwerp A. 95 Bank
Van Arsdale Henry, 20 W. 11th
Van Arsdale Henry, 298 Broome
Van Arsdale Peter, 320 Broome
Van Buren ——, 200 Greene
Van Buren Wm. H. 125 Bleecker
Vanderpool Edward, 206 4th
Vandervoort John L. 53 Greene
Vanhusen D. 224 8th Av.
Vache ——, 75 Lexington Av.
Van Kleek John R. 196 E. B'way
Van Liers ——, 129 Greenwich
Vanlier A. 123 Washington
Vanlier M. A. 129 Greenwich
Van Land C. C. 43 Bank
Van Pelt Moses D. 59 W. Washington place
Van Rensselaer Jeremiah 783 Bdy.
Van Winkle Ed'd H. 574 Broome
Vanzandt Peter, 84 9th Av. & 255 West 19th
Varley Christopher D. 183 9th Av.
Vidal ——, 25 Lispenard
Vere James J. 90 Varick
Vermeule Warren, 62½ Columbia
Vlegan J. H. 477 Greenwich
Vogely Frederick G. L. 282 2d
Von Corts Charles J. 438 Broad'y
Vondersmith Eli W. 162 Bowery
Wagstaff Wm. R. 2d Av. between East 13th and East 14th
Waizenbauer Conrad, 607 4th
Walker Cornelius, 116 2d Av.
Wallace Wesley, 43 6th Av.
Wallace Wm. Clay, 82 Chambers
Walsh James, 447 Grand
Walsh H. 30 9th
Walters Wm. A. 50 Suffoll
Ward James E. 300 Spring
Ward William, 262 Broome
Warner Everardus B. 205 Ble'ker
Warner I. W. 359 3d Av.
Warner Louis T. 49 Lafayette pl.
Warren James, 342 Broadway
Washington John, 233 Broadway
Waterman & DeForest, 411 Grand
Watson John, 117 10th
Watts Robert, 65 East 14th
Weed John W. 558 Houston
Weeks Cyrus, 436 Broome
Wells Daniel, 96 Eldridge
Wells O. P. 103 9th Av.
Welsh ——, 194 Av. A.
Weltje C. 1½ Park place
Wetmore E. Walter, 10 Centre
Wheeler ——, 199 3d Av.
Whiley Charles W. 59 Murray
Whitaker John H. 510 Broadway
Whitaker Samuel P. 99 East 17th
White Ambrose L. 303 Broome
White Oliver, 50 Lispenard
White Samuel P. 721 Houston
White T. J. 33½ White
Wight Lyman L. 99 Av. C
Wilhelm ——, 84 Chrystie
Willisen ——, 93 Greenwich
Wilkes George, 26 Laight
Wilkinson Joseph, 22 Mulberry

Williams H. 35 East Broadway
New York.
Williams Murphy, 9 Av. C
Williams Merrill W. 322 Broome
Williamson John D. 91 Greene
Wilsey Ferdinand L. 596 Houston
Wilson Abel D. 42 Walker
Winnecke H. A. 67 Reade
Witherell John, 39 Oliver & 28 Hamilton
Wolf Frederick, 33 Bayard
Wolf M. Leo, 39 Lispenard
Wood Isaac, 96 E. Broadway
Wood James R. 67 do
Wood Stephen. 189 do
Wood W. G., Harlem
Woodruff Mrs. S. W. 45 W. B'way
Worster Joseph. 36 Bleecker
Wright Aaron, 145 E. Broadway
Wright Clark, 19 Amity
Wright Lucian B. 61 M'Dougal
Young John, 198 Hudson
Young William, 91 Liberty
Zerae William, 36 Bayard

Niagara County.

Kellogg Wm., Pekin   Cambria.
Kidder Isaac S. do
Eddy George P.   Lewiston.
Thomas Ambrose
Smith Oliver
Hill C.   Lockport.
Fassett & May
Shuler & Leonard
Chase R. & J.
Batty B. A. (homœopathic)
Teale ——. (botanic)
Morse Daniel
Mann George   Newfane.
Colborn Nelson
Kayner P. I.
Irons Ara, Olcott
Conger G.   Niagara Falls.
Davis W. O
Cass ——   Pendleton.
Catlin T. G., Youngstown   Porter.
Burgess C. H. do
Murphy Peter P.   Royalton.
Taylor ——, Middleport
Hurd ——, do
Brown Asa B.   Somerset.
Pratt Titus C.
Gould William B.
Lock Jesse F. Tonawanda
   Wheatfield.
Gale —— do
Hoyer J. F. do
Ware Charles, do
M'Cheaney Henry S.   Wilson.
Tabor Hiram B.
Cresswell John

Oneida County.

Beach S.   Annsville.
Nye E. O.
Trask E., Oriskany Falls Augusta.
Lord R.   Boonville.
North N.
Kellogg J. L.   Bridgewater.
Champion J. H.
Ely & Gardner   Camden.
Tawbut H. G.
Hastings H.   Deerfield.
Pell Thomas, North Gage
Griswold ——, do
Davis M. V.   Florence.
Gardner R.
Brown J. M.
Barrows C. & F. M. Clinton
   Kirkland.
Hastings S. & P. M. Clinton
Bissell Geo. (Eclectic) do
Scollard J. I. do do
Brownson G. I. do do
Frazier C.   Lee.
Ward E.
Fitch S.
Porter H. N.
Hovey I., Deansville   Marshall.

May J. S.   New Hartford.
Wiser H. A.
Clark ——
Tyler A.
Bligh A. B., Sauquoit   Paris.
Knight J. do
Budlong B., Cassville
Price E.   Remsen.
Parker G. W.
Beach H. H. Dominick st.   Rome.
Scudder S. O. do
Bergen A. do
Blair A. do
Sturdevant J. M. James st.
Pope G. W. do
Pope H. H. Dominick st.
Cobb J. V. do
Seebald L. James st.
Harris E. B., Waterville
   Sangerfield.
Cleaveland G. W., Waterville
Cleaveland Wm. P. do
Crane C. E. do
Coggeshall James S. do
Gillett A.   Steuben.
Hamilton H., Holland Patent
   Trenton.
Crane D. A. do
Gittean L. & Son, Trenton Village
Vincent ——, Prospect
Willoughby C., South Trenton
Levings O. K. 99 Genesee   Utica.
Hunt R. & Brother, Exchange Buildings, Genesee st.
M'Call J. 40 Genesee
Begg M. M. 96 do
Potter H. C. 132 do
M'Craith F. 134 do
Morris Wm. 138 do
Scott Thos. 140 do
Rathbon J. R. 54 Hotel
Newland J. F. 158 Genesee
Peckham F. B. 162 do
Meacham I. N. 178 do
Russell Wm. 106 Fayette
Bacon Dewitt C. Varick st.
Cass O. D. Columbia st.
Norton H. 44 Charlotte
Coventry & Thomas, 6 Catherine
Rudd J., New London   Verona.
Howe —— do
Stillman W., Durhamville
Lindon —— do
Whaly J. do
Whaly A. do
Shepard N. do
Frazer R., M'Connellsvill
   Vienna.
Chatfield D., South Corners
Bussey ——, Westernville
   Western.
Gillett ——, do
Hutchinson ——, do
Loomis E. Hampton Westmoreland.
Beardsley A. do
Smith W. Whitesboro Whitestown.
Henderson F. B. do
Thomas D. do
Gardner Wm. H. do
White O. W. Oriskany
Babcock & Clark, do
West J. do

Onondaga County.

Edwards G. W.   Cicero.
Marks ——, Brewerton
Kendall V.   Clay.
Loomis G. S.   De Witt.
Mervin T.   Elbridge.
Wilson ——
Williams ——
Roberts H.
Paine R. Jordan
Riggs J. do
Eddy N. P. do
Adams H.   Pobius.
Babcock ——
Rose & Pareh   La Fayette.
M'Carthy ——   Lysander.
Allen ——
Jones D. T. Baldwinsville

Hall L. B. Baldwinsville *Lysander.*
Todd J. E.   do
Carr ——   do
Schenck B. B. Plainville
Taylor Wm.   *Manlius.*
Moore H. B.
Nims H.
Briggs ——
Hyde E. Fayetteville
Shipman ——, do
Warden ——, do
Cowles A. H.   *Marcellus.*
Teft L. I.
Parsons I.
Morrell ——, Clintonville
Teft N. R. South Onondaga
      Onondaga.
Phillips ——, do
Kingsley S.   do
Needham G. Onondaga Hollow
Brewster S.   do
Smith H.   *Otisco.*
Smith W. G
Searl A.
Clark ——, Amber
Stearns J.   *Pompey.*
Candee J. Pompey Centre
Brown ——   *Salina.*
Sterling——
Trowbridge J. F.
      Genesee st.   *Syracuse*
Arnold C. Water st.   do
Matthews J. D. do   do
Parker J. B.   do   do
White M. M.   do   do
Coon H. P. James st.   do
Hubbard C. Genesee st.   do
Linsley J. B. Salina st.   do
Lovejoy W. I.   do   do
Hoyt W. H.   do   do
Stuart J C. Genesee st.   do
Lull ——, James st.   do
Shipman A. B. Arcade B'lding do
Smith Wm. M.   do
Potter S. H.   do
Brown S. Warren st.   do
Davis R. R. Genesee st.   do
Hann Abraham, do   do
Sampson P.   do   do
Spencer Thomas, Water st   do
Dunlap J. P.   do   do
Moore D. A.   do   do
Stevens R. F. (Oculist) Salina st.
Perter E. H.   *Skaneaieles.*
Benedict ——
Bartlett L.
Collins J.   *Spafford.*
Morrell I. Borodino
Kneeland J. do
Gowing G. W.   *Tully.*
Farnham S. S.
Dwinell ——
Carl D.   *Van Buren.*
Laughlin ——

Ontario County.

Simons E. W.   *Bristol.*
Durgan D.
Page ——, Bristol Centre
M'Crossen ——   *Canadice.*
Carr Edson   *Canandaigua.*
Cheney E. W.
Jacobs Nathaniel
Brown George G.
Brown A. D.
Hahn F. B.
Hickock H. P.   *East Bloomfield.*
Webster D. T.
Murphy Charles
Meschan ——
Dean ——   *Gorham.*
Potter ——
Waters ——
Buck ——
Swart W. T. Reed's Corners
Torrey Augustus   *Hopewell.*
Pratt Jonathan, Larned's Corners
Holden D. A.   do
Worts C. J.   *Manchester.*
Brown Thomas

Stafford J.   *Manchester.*
Bannister C.   *Phelps.*
Trisler John
Davis James
Thompson Albert
Jewett Harvey, Allen's Hill
      Richmond.
Paul T., Honeoye
Doolittle W. do
Kimber Wm. Geneva   *Seneca.*
Spencer T. R. do
Rhaodes & Dix, do
Graham J. S.   do
Barnes E.   do
Elmer ——   do
Goodwin F.   do
Church J. C.   do
Stevens J. L.   do
Smith ——,   do
Staats J. S.   do
Kimber Wm. jr. do
Brouwer C.   do
Crane D. O.   do
Hadley J.   do
Teele H. N.   do
Hay George C. do
Harrington ——, do
Beattie Joseph, Hall'. Corners
Woodruff E. B. Flint Creek
Ball Wm.   *Victor.*
Ball Charles
Palmer J. W.
Heli Joseph   *West Bloomfield.*
Sheldon Wm. F.

Orange County.

Sears M. Craigsville
      Blooming Grove.
Goodman A. Salisbury Mills
Mix P. Washingtonville
Carpenter S. G.   *Chester.*
Howell C. B.
Edmonson T. S.
Morrison Wm.   *Cornwall.*
Conklin Peter E.
Southgate Robert, West Point
Cuyler John M.   do
Hunter Geo.   *Crawford.*
Winfield Charles
Dale I. Port Jervis *Deer Park.*
Whitney D. B. do
Cudderback T. do
Reeve G. F.   *Goshen.*
Thompson B. W.
Ostrum J. W.
Wright B.   *Hamptonburgh.*
Vankuren James
Webb E. A. Ridgbury *Minisink.*
Halleck D. C. Slate Hill
M'Bride N. Wells' Corners
Armstrong L.   do
Church N. J.
Seymour A. A. Westown
Newkirk Wm. H. Unionville
Millspaugh F. A.   *Montgomery.*
Crawford S. M.
Millspaugh B.
Evans E.   Walden
Houghton A.   do
Millspaugh T.   do
Millspaugh G. M. do
Woodward ——   *Monroe.*
Boyd J. C.
Esray S. W.
Woodruff M. C.
Andrews J. R.
Carpenter E. B.
Stokum J. L.
Cooke A. Otisville   *Mount Hope.*
Terry Wm. C.
Gardiner S. M.   *Newburgh.*
Brown Geo.
Monell G. C.
Peck Elias
Drake Charles
Deyo N.
Edmondson D. C.
Barclay Alex.
Stevenson M.
Garrison Robert, cor. Water & 2d
Crowell Abram, Coldenham

Winfield Dr. Scotchtown *Wallkill.*
Brackner J. S.   do
Hornbeck J.   do
Lewis O. New Hampton
Young J. H.   do
Young I. S. Howell's Depot
Winfield David C. South Middle-
      town
M'Munn J. B   do
Everett R.   do
Beverea J. D.   *Warwick.*
Reyolds A.
Upson Dr.
Stevens H. B.
Townsand B. Florida
Jayne D. C. do
Holly S. D. Edenville
Wilson C. H. New Milford

Orleans County.

Nicholson & Paine, Albion *Barre.*
Noble Wm.   do
Huff M. T.   do
Sewens Willis,   do
Mills A. B.   do
Wood James   Barre Centre
Shaw D.   do
Ballou N. E.   *Carlton*
Hotalling W.
Southworth S. E.   *Clarendon.*
Lewis H.
Babcock Alfred   *Gaines*
Daniel Asahel R.
Beecher ——
Dolly ——, West Gaines
Sandford Walter R.   *Kendall*
Johnson C. C.
Titus I. W., Holley   *Murray*
Newton ——, do
Wood Erl, Sandy Creek
Nickerson Robert, do
Whaley Christopher, Medina
      Ridgeway
Frost A. M. & M. A. Medina
Grover L. C. Knowlesville
Cheeseman E.   do
Beecher H.   do
Norton Geo. H   *Shelby*
Belden A. D.
Webster ——   *Yates*
Jeffords R. B.
Phippany Horace, Lyndonville
Shaw Truman S.   do

Oswego County.

Ford ——   *Albion.*
Rosa James P.
Thomas D. V.
Manwarren James, West Amboy
      Amboy.
Haull Frederick   *Constantia.*
Slocum John O.
Allen V. Cleaveland
Yates J. A. do
Skelton J. A. Oswego Falls ——
      Granby.
Bradford ——,   do
Acker Wm. P.   *Hannibal.*
Kent Ahira
Skinner James
Rice Alfred
Earll J. B. Central Square
      Hastings.
Marble J.   do
Bowen Benjamin E.   *Mexico.*
Whaley Alex.
Snell C. D.
Dayton ——, Colosse
Brewster Sardus, Prattville
Robinson A. W.   *New Haven.*
Austin Amos J.
Gilbert Theodore   *Orwell.*
Howe ——
Colwell Justin B. Granite block,
      cor. 1st & Bridge   *Oswego*
Allen Joseph H. Hart's buildings,
      Bridge st.
Rossiter ——, Eagle block, 1st st
Scott E. 6   do
Smith N. J. foot of 1st
Hard Patrick H. Phœnix block

Van Dyck Andrew, 13th st. *Oswego.*
Dunton A. M. 1st st.
Thurber Horace K. Cayuga st.
Hart Samuel, 2d st.
Beckwith A. K. Jennings' Corner
　　　　　　　　　　　Palermo.
White Austin　　　　　*Parish.*
Green Tobias J.
Wright A. N.
Noyes Helon F., Pulaski *Richland.*
Murdock Hiram,　　do
Murdock Henry,　　do
Watson John M.　　do
Seary John. South Richland
Avery Samuel, Phœnix
　　　　　　　　　Schroeppel.
Williams Nathan, do
Hall ——, Gilbert's Mills
Baker S. J. Hinmansville
Diefendorf J.　　do
Carroll William, do
Snyder G. W.　　　*Scriba.*
Benedict Benjamin S.
Bacon Charles G. Fulton *Volney.*
Leo & Livingston,　do
Waters & Nelson,　do
Dorrance Jedediah, do
Forter Charles,　do
Bormer Lemuel,　do
Pardee Stephen, Hull's Corners
Freeman Samuel　*Williamstown.*

Otsego County.

Colburn L. Burlington Flats
　　　　　　　　　Burlington.
Robinson S. L.　　do
Stillman R. F. Burlington Green
Wing Walter　　*Butternuts.*
White M.　　　*Cherry Valley.*
Little G. W.
Stucker J.
Merritt G.
Rudd C.
Northrop J. N.　　*Decatur.*
Darrow L.
Spencer William M.　*Edmeston.*
Spencer Halsey
Russell Dwight, South Edmeston
Sprague J. S.　　*Exeter.*
Patrick David W. Schuyler's Lake
Almy A. J. Hartwick
Smith P. S.　　do
Patterson J.　　do
Almy W.　　do
Almy H.　　do
Skinner L. B.　　do
Strong A. P.　　*Laurens.*
Bassett N. T.
Hastings George, Schenevas
　　　　　　　　Maryland.
Metcalf A. E.　　*Middlefield.*
Ely Sumner
Bray E.
Beardsley ——, Middlefield Centre
Burnett I.　　　*Milford.*
Pratt E.
Spofford E. W.
Brown E. S.
Mather J. F.　　*New Lisbon.*
Wheeler G. W. T.
Tuthill A.
Crittenden ——
Case Samuel H.　　*Oneonta*
Hamilton H. A.
Boyce D. R.
Green Solomon　　*Otego.*
Stone Henry E
Saunders E. S.
Fox J. L. Cooperstown *Otsego.*
Thrall F. G.　　do
M'Names William, do
King C.　　do
Johnson P. E.　　do
Peak J. M.　　do
Hall W. B.　　*Pittsfield.*
Hackley ——　　*Plainfield.*
King ——
Manly H.　　*Richfield.*
Palmer Wheeler
Churchill A.

Powell William　　*Springfield.*
Mount ——
Westcott ——
Colwell John　　*Unadilla.*
Cone N.
Odell Evander
Drake John　　*Westford.*
Jackson E. W.
Kelley S. H.　　*Worcester.*
Bigelow A. T.
Bigelow U. Y.
Leonard Geo. H., Ea. Worcester
Stewart William, So.　do
Purple L. M.　do　　do

Putnam County.

Wales Lemuel,　　*Carmel.*
Travis A. G. Farmersville *Kent.*
Wheeler ——　　*Patterson.*
Sands A. L. Cold Spring
　　　　　　　　Phillipstown.
Johnston Wm. M. do
Young J.　　do
Tompkins G. J. S. *Putnam Valley.*
Road ——　　*Southeast.*

Queens County.

Bloodgood J.　　*Flushing.*
Hedges G.
Searing Gideon N.　*Hempstead.*
Webb Edwin
Snediker M.
Davidson J.
Baisley Robert B. Rockaway
Wheeler ——, Greenwich
Arback Julius, Rockville
Shelton Nathan　*Jamaica*
Shelton John D.
Kissam George H.
Creed Wm. C. Brushville
Stotoff Cornelius　*Newtown.*
Stevens A. H. Astoria
Bayles Hersey,　do
Sanford S. T. W. do
Strew Wm. W.　*Oyster Bay.*
Kellogg Lucius
Stoutenburgh Peter R. Norwich
Carll Selah S. Jericho
Townsend J. C.　do
Tappan De Witt,　do
Dickenson John,　do

Rensselaer County.

Hull E.　　*Berlin.*
Thomas R.
Rhodes H.
Thomas J. W.
Collins R.　　*Brunswick.*
Wheeler D.
Buckling ——
Wait R. S.　　*Grafton.*
Allen Amos
Lansing O. E.　*Greenbush.*
Parmelee ——
Mixter ——
Moseg S.　　*Hoosick.*
Sherwood L.
Fowlers M.
Frazer I. G. 153 State
　　　　　　　Lansingburgh.
Dorr J. 176 State
Leonard & Burton, 261 State
Hull A. D. 268　do
Austin J. M. 250　do
Taylor ——, 230　do
Burton ——, 203　do
Streit G. W.　　*Nassau.*
Boughton S. A.
Bassett E. D.
Beckwith M.
Haynes J. H., E. Nassau
Moses H.　　*Petersburgh.*
Hull H.
Allen A. N.
Johnson Wm.　　*Pittstown.*
May J. E.
Van Namee J.
Dyer ——
Barker L. H.　　*Poestenkill.*
Streeter L.　　*Sandlake.*

Carmichael E. W.　　*Sandlake.*
Morrell Thomas
Snyder Wm. West Sandlake
Judson B.　　do
Thomas P.　　do
Hulsapple Wm.　do
Lyon Z.　　*Schaghticoke.*
Baker E.
M'Clellan S.　　*Schodack.*
Hogeboom James
Olmstead ——
Squires J.
Graves E.　　*Stephentown.*
Dickinson Geo.
Cole ——
Cook C. R. 109 4th　*Troy*
Crandall —— 186 4th
Skilton ——, 105 4th
Blatchford ——, 48 4th
Freiot C. 23 4th
Richards ——, 13 4th
Clapp ——, 13 4th
Adams ——, 9 4th
Mattock E. J. 91 5th
Bryan ——, 3 Park pl. Congress st.
Brownell M. 13 Liberty
Cooper ——, Nail Factory
Dunlap John, 36 King
Wright ——, 47 Grand Division
Cary ——, 39　do
Thorn Dr. 88 1st
Wickes ——, 145 1st
Christie J. 116 2d
Cook S. A. Congress c. 2d
Bryan ——, 70 2d
Ruggles ——, 72 2d
Kelley & White, 48 2d
Bonteeon ——, 39 3d
Brinsmade ——, 39 3d
Wotkyns ——, 75 3d
Lawton B. F. 75 3d
Twiss Chas. S. 104 3d

Richmond County.

Smith Samuel, Tompkinsville
　　　　　　　Castleton.
Hawkwood ——, Tompkinsville
Clarke J. C., Factoryville
Eddy Wm. G. Port Richmond
　　　　　　　Northfield.
Clarke J.　　do
Finer J. H.　　do
Golder R. H., Rossville *Westfield.*
Van Hovenburgh J. O. Rossville

Rockland County.

Pratt M.　　*Haverstraw.*
Whipple Charles
Purdue John
Houghton A.
Gavan W. North Haverstraw
Oblenis B. Nyack　*Orangetown.*
Davidson ——, do
Noble W. E.　do
Howland A.　do
Bartow M. Tappan
Bartow I. H. do
Stephen J.　do
Hapson ——, Piermont
Demerest J. Spring Valley
Lake D.　　do

St. Lawrence County.

Smith I.　　*Brasher.*
Clark Darius　　*Canton.*
Baker Elijah
Raymond D. O.
Benjamin T. O.
Chandler J.　　*De Kalb.*
Morton E., Richville
Munson T. W.　*Depeyster.*
Goodnough A. B.　*Edwards.*
Burdick Charles C.　*Fowler.*
Williams P O.　*Gouverneur.*
Wait S. C.
Morris Robert　　*Hammond.*
Gregor Alexander R.
Bean John
Thatcher Seymour　*Hermon.*
Alexander James

Jerome Levi R. *Hermon.*
Sprague Gideon *Hopkinton.*
Sprague F. C.
Lawrence M. D., Lawrenceville
    Lawrence.
Burnham Milo L. do
Carpenter John F. do
Campfield Wm. A. *Lisbon.*
Carpenter Worster
Seamore Charles S. *Louisville.*
Gibson Ira
Pierce Caleb *Madrid.*
Manley Wm. J. Columbia
Jerome Milton, do
Clark Silas F. do
Storrs Lewis, Waddington
Mott James A. do
Paddock Wm. S. *Massena.*
Grinnel J H.
Whitney Ephraim
Ripley J. H.
Ransom Amos
Morgan J. P. *Morristown.*
Brown J. A.
M'Falls D.
Burns Alexander, Edwardsville
Burns Robert, do
Floyd Wm. *Norfolk.*
Ford Sylvanus
Peck Jacob
Bolan H. A.
Sherman Socrates N., Ogdens-
   burgh *Oswegatchie.*
Sherman Mason G. Ogdensburgh
Laughlin Henry D. do
Sherman Benj. F. do
Sherman Minot, do
Benjamin ——, do
Tyler Albert, do
Parker Francis *Parishville.*
Ide C. F:
Baldwin —— *Pierpont.*
Pangburn ——
M'Chesney & Ames *Potsdam.*
Marsh Samuel G.
Hewett Henry
Cole Gideon F.
Gibbons Joseph H. *Russell.*
Danton Thomas *Stockholm.*
Danton Lorenzo
Tucker ——
Maffit ——

Saratoga County.

Miller Henry J. *Charlton.*
Simpson S. W.
Finley Dr. West Charlton
Cooper Henry C. *Clifton Park.*
Higgins Seth W.
Beal George W.
Finch Morgan L., Jonesville
Sprague L. D., Vischer's Ferry
Houghton Nathaniel M. *Corinth.*
Fay J. W. *Edinburgh.*
Harris William
Pulling J. *Galway.*
Preston C.
Wells J. W.
Lewis M.
Barney Asa C. Greenfield Centre
    Greenfield.
Johnson Darius, do
Johnson George F. do
Turtellott Freeman, Jamesville
Blake John, do
Butte E. *Halfmoon.*
Boughton C.
Peters S.
Steenburgh H. W. *Malta.*
Raymond O. P.
Moore L. Ballston Spa *Milton.*
St. John E. do
Chandsey A. J. do
Culver D. W. do
Tucker George *Moreau.*
Mott O. H. *Saratoga.*
Most Walter
Brisbin Oliver
Gow A.
Preston John R.
Dimick Ira
Colby Moses H

Dean Josiah *Saratoga.*
North M. L. *Saratoga Springs.*
Freeman S.
Perry John L.
Allen R. L.
Whiting L. E.
Fletcher F.
Baxter Hiram *Stillwater.*
Bull Chauncy D.
Strang Ira
Hart Reuben H. Ketcham's Cor-
   ners
Hart Philip T. 2d *Waterford.*
Goodrich Orrin
Green T.
Westcott Joseph
Reynolds Henry *Wilton.*
Reynolds Tabor B.

Schenectady County.

Brumaghin J. *Duanesburgh.*
Woodburn A.
Delemator S. G.
Barrows Lorenzo P.
Braman J.
Sprague E. B. *Glenville.*
Young E. A.
Underhill A. K.
Ostrander ——
Miller D. O. *Niskayuna.*
Conklin J. *Rotterdam.*
Green ——
Fuller R. 125 State *Schenectady.*
Sprague L. 100 State
Van Ingen J. L. 23 State
Davis E. 42 do
Vedder A. M., Liberty st.
Dunlap Thomas, Canal
Duane William, Union st.
Swits H. A. Maiden lane
Magoffin J. C. Liberty st.
Fonda A. G. Union st.
Wheeler E. Liberty st.
Davis E. Smith st.
Tonelier P. Union st.

Schoharie County.

Burchard J. *Broome.*
Pettengell S. *Carlisle.*
Mayham J.
Kelley J.
Roscoe J. B.
Kibbee Dr. *Cobleskill.*
Flint ——
Warner ——
Lamont Wm. 2d *Conesville.*
Benham John C.
Leonard Prentice
Leonard Lorenzo J.
Dunbar Jared
Rawling Amos, Sloansville
Lawyer Moses, Fultonham *Fulton.*
Wells Lynus, Breakabeen
James T. West Fulton
Clark Peter H. do
Fanning Nelson *Gilboa.*
Cornell John, West Gilboa
Wood Alfred, do
Boyce S. E. *Jefferson.*
Flint John T.
Wells Samuel B. *Middleburgh.*
Danforth Volney
Van Gaasbeek James
Ten Eyck Jacob
Smith S. Warnerville
    Richmondville.
Van Alstine Thomas B.
Swart P. S. *Schoharie.*
Crouse J. A.
Van Dyke C. C.
Van Dyke C. H.
Chase C. Hyndsville *Seward.*
Hynds Andrew, do
Johnson Stephen, Gardinerville
Sutphen ——, do
Fox G. F. *Sharon.*
Fonda S. F. Sharon Springs
Loucks John, do
Green John, Leesville
Pettingell Dr., Sharon Centre

Havens C. W. *Summit.*
Minor P. E.
Near David
Zerr Ira, Gallupville *Wright.*
Coy Darius, do

Seneca County.

Ewens Alford *Fayette.*
Saxer Leonard L.
Wilkinson O. W.
Eastman Job L. *Lodi.*
Post Lewis
Dunn Jeremiah
Starkey W. W.
Flood F. H.
Livingston William
Sears A.
Jones Samuel *Ovid.*
Bolter Alfred
Covert Peter
Smith Amos B.
Wheeler R. K., Farmer
Watson Ethan *Romulus.*
Watson Humphrey
Didamee Henry D.
Bellows M. B. *Seneca Falls.*
Bellows James
Carson L. D.
Clark J. S.
Heath H. H.
Keeler Silas
Robinson William M.
Royston T. D.
Wells Gardner *Waterloo.*
Wells Samuel R.
Wells Landon
Wirts Peter R.
Wager J. L.
Childs Amherst
Janwasky Alexander
Evos R. S.
Patterson O. S.

Steuben County

Foot E. W. *Addison.*
Roger S. C.
Brown R. P.
Beach William
Wagner F. R.
Wallace W. A. *Avoca.*
Stewart T.
Babcock J. L. *Bath.*
Niles Addison
Dow J. D.
Morse J. C.
Higgins John D.
Rogers G. A.
De Wolf A.
Webb J C.
Lockard F. *Bradford.*
Mitchell S. *Cameron.*
Crocker W. R.
Fay H. G. *Canisteo.*
Smith Samuel H. *Caton.*
Hagadorn Stephen *Cohocton.*
Gilbert A. L. North Cohocton
Hall E. do
Ackley T. *Dansville.*
Hall R. H. *Erwin.*
Ramsey ——
Olen Samuel *Greenwood.*
Sager —— *Hartsville.*
Morrow F. W. *Hornby.*
Belden C. E. *Hornellsville.*
Wisewell Henry
Ward S. A.
Case A. B. *Howard.*
Rathburn Isaac
Robinson I. H.
Zieley H.
Hunter William *Jasper.*
Sheffield R.
Sherman Thomas *Orange.*
Barnes H. R.
Bell Robert
Terbell William *Painted Post.*
Graves J. B.
Stanley S.
Mumford O.
Harrington N. M.
Gilbert Rufus

Hyde E. E.   *Painted Post.*
Clark I. F.
Clarry Walter   *Prattsburgh.*
Look L.
Talmadge Rufus   *Pulteney.*
Skinner Milford   *Reading.*
Lockwood J.   *Tyrone.*
Gulick James
Reed John
Church Amasa   *Urbana.*
Younglove C. S.
Birdsall William   *Wayne.*
Patchin Warren   *Wayland.*
Hess H. H.
Patchin E.
Wiley F.   *Woodhull.*

Suffolk County.

Daring Thomas S. Setauket   *Brookhaven.*
Elderkin John, do
Carman William, Port Jefferson
Brown Edwin, Middle Island
Tuthill ——, Moriches
Hallock ——, do
Miller Nathaniel, do
Rice James, Patchogue
Preston William S. do
Burnell Sereno, Miller's Place
Huntington Abel   *Easthampton.*
Huntington George L.
Van Scoy David, Amagansett
Ray Joseph L.   *Huntington.*
Rhinelander J. R.
Sturges Charles
Jayne Floyd, Comac
Merriman J. Northport
Conklin George, Sweet Hollow
Scidmore F. Babylor
Thompson Abraham, do
Richmond J. Amityville
Mowbray J.   *Islip.*
Rice Charles   *Riverhead.*
Saxton N. S.
Benjamin R.
Miller George
Dayton S. D.
Bowns Josiah   *Smithtown.*
Gates ——
Bowns Josiah, jr.
Morrell J. S.
Corwin Ira   *Southold.*
Tuthill Franklin
Tuthill Seth, Orient
Carpenter Benjamin F. Cutchogue
Fanning Joshua, Greenport
Ireland Treadwell L. do
Lord Frederick W. do
Preston Shelden C. do
Skinner Ezekiel E. D. do

Sullivan County.

Turner L. S.   *Fallsburgh.*
Wales B.   *Liberty.*
Watkins John D.
Crane O. J.
Bross P. Barryville   *Lumberland.*
Perkins E. K. do
Dimmick S. G. Bloomingburgh   *Mamakating.*
Little G. S. do
Van Wyck T. C. do
Morrison J. A. Wurtsboro
Taylor John N. do
Weller Theodore, Burlingham
Robinson L.   *Neversink.*
Wheeler L.   *Rockland.*
Hamilton ——
Hasbrouck ——
Mould ——
Hamersly A. Monticello   *Thompson.*
Royce R. do
Bull A. T. do
Baker G. F. R. do

Tioga County.

Foster S. B.   *Barton.*
Knapp W.
Reed ——
Owen ——

Waldo J. T.   *Berkshire.*
Powell E.
Sutherland L.   *Candor.*
M'Key A. W.
Matthews P.
Root Royal B. Newark Valley   *Newark.*
Nelson Seth B. do
Tappin J. C. do
Everett J.   *Nichols.*
Cady G. M.
Lovejoy Ezekiel   *Owego.*
Paige Joel S.
Phelps E. B.
Arnold J. H.
Allen L. H.
Nye Frederick
Churchill & Hoyt
Frank John
Eastman H. N.
Coburn B C.
Green B. W.
Wright F. J.
Northrop George W.   *Rickford.*
Benton J. B.   *Spencer.*
Brally C.
Cook James
Maine C. J.
Earle D.   *Tioga.*
Knapp S.
Lang J.
Whitney W. E.

Tompkins County.

Williams P. A.   *Enfield.*
Miller J. S.
Sackett S. P.
White D. C.   *Hector.*
Hawes M. D.
Fish N., Mecklenburg
Nivison N. do
Brown E., Burdett
Thompson J. do
Lewis J., Searsburg
Smith H., Logan
Hawley & Morgan (Clinton House)   *Ithaca.*
Congell Chas. 18 Buffalo
Ingersoll J. O. M 53 Owego
Stevens & Sayles, 59 do
Webster H. K. 92 do
Bishop D. E. 3 Geneva
Turner Charles M   *Newfield.*
Estabrook Ralph H.
Cook Christopher C.
Sherwood A. C.

Ulster County.

Sweet T. W. Wall st.   *Kingston.*
Myer Jesse. do
Davis Wm. B. St. James st.
Nelson Thomas J. Crown st.
Hallett Arnold, Rondout
Crispell Abram. do
Wales John, do
Jourdan D. R. do
Brown J. do
Wurts M. New Paltz Landing   *Lloyd.*
Hasbrouck Q. Q. do
Oliver James   *Marbletown.*
Dewitt Matthew
Lewis H.
Wicks E. Stone Ridge
Chambers Geo. do
Knapp ——, Milton   *Marlborough.*
Gidney Wm. H. do
Fenton ——, do
Reeve I.   *New Paltz.*
Wurtz David
Hasbrouck Joseph, Tuthill
Bowman Dr. Modena   *Plattekill.*
Secor Dr. Pine Bush   *Rochester.*
Gorham M., Accord
Jewett Edwin   *Rosendale.*
Schoonmaker Simon
Budington Geo. E.
M'Ewan Neil T.
Dirker J.   *Saugerties.*
Dewitt W. C.
Dewitt A. B.

Vedder John   *Saugerties*
Davies Thos. S. Main st.
Gartz A   *Shandaken.*
Meestin J. F. Bruynswick   *Shawangunk.*
Wurey Geo. do
Jensen J. T. do
Seares S. J. Jordanville
Jordan S. T. do
Hornbeck Philip   *Wawarsing.*
Bevere B. R. Napanock
Bevere B. R. jr. do
Canline Nathaniel, Ellenville
Freer Jacob S. do
Thompson James H. do

Warren County.

Tubbs Nathan, Chestertown   *Chester.*
Mallery Alfred. do
Pritchard Morgan W. do
Shankland John   *Hague.*
Ramsey James   *Horicon.*
Cox Thomas   *Johnsburgh.*
Griswold J. H.
Lawrence James   *Luzerne.*
Shelden N. E. Glenn's Falls   *Queensbury.*
M'Niel D. do
Peck B. do
Clark Wm. J. do
Littlefield M. do
Patteson Thomas   *Warrensburg.*
Howard E. W.
M'Nult H.
Holden A. H.

Washington County.

Savage James   *Argyle.*
Proudfit Hugh P.
Kilmer Wm. H.
Gillis George
Sill John C.
Nelson Wm. G.   *Cambridge.*
Stevenson Wm.
Stevenson James
Newton E. H. jr.
Cook Oliver
Morris P. V. P. Buskirk's Bridge
Newman Roderick B. North East-on   *Easton*
Perry Asahel, South Easton
Axtell ——   *Fort Ann.*
Todd ——
Babcock ——
Corbin ——
Norton Wm. S.   *Fort Edward.*
Wright Wm.
Blois Reuben, Fort Miller
Holmes C.   *Greenwich.*
Corliss H.
Crandall S. F.
Bullions W. H.
M'Lean H. K. Battenville
Mason ——, Galesville
Stevenson John, North G'wich
Hall H.   *Hampton.*
Bliss ——
Madison John H. West Hebron   *Hebron.*
Foster James M.
Ceveland Warren
Clapp John
White Chas. J. East Hebron
Maynard William, do
Edmonds Danforth   *Kingsbury.*
Dibble H. E. Sandy Hill
Brown J. H. do
Clarke E. G. do
Haynes Samuel W.   *Putnam.*
Allen George   *Salem.*
M'Allister Archibald
Gellman Orville P.
Perry Charles
Burns George G.
Cole M.   *White Creek.*
Gray Henry
Warner K. T. White Creek Centre
Gray Henry C., N. White Creek
Sayles Cyrus, do
Hubbard L. J.   *Whitehall.*

Hall A.   *Whitehall.*
Edson O. H
Monroe N.
Porter N.
Woodward A. 7.
Wright D. S.
Wolcott W. G.

Wayne County.

Marsh   *Arcadia.*
Coventry Charles, Newark
Pomeroy Charles G. do
Vosburg William,   do
Goodrich ———   do
Rockwood C. H. do
Crandell Lyman, Fairville
Campbell C.   *Butler.*
Hendricks A. T., Clyde *Galen.*
Peck A.   do
Colvin N. P. do
Colvin D.   do
Bottom E. W., Huron
Pierce J. B.   *Lyons.*
Teachout A.
Peck Nelson
Moore Samuel
Hillman L. C.
Pollok ———
Van Sleek D. W. C., Alloway
Bullis ———, Macedon Centre
    Macedon.
Wright E. K.   *Marion.*
Green William
Dow ———
Whitcomb L. & Son, *Ontario.*
Crandall ——— *Palmyra.*
Throop Benjamin
Hoyt D. D.
M'Intire Alexander
Gallup J. C.
Dickson J. J.   *Rose.*
Valentine Peter
Van Nostrand ———
Valentine Richard S.
Wilson Duncan *Savannah.*
Olin D. S.   *Sodus.*
Gaylord Levi
Yale Asahel
Merriam & Gaylord
Ostron Henry J., Alton
Ostron Henry H. do
Usher William,   do
Graves Lewis, South Sodus
Tucker C. S.   do
Andrews E. E. do
Cook W. D. Sodus Point
Gerdner W. W. *Walworth.*
Cone E. D.
M'Llnuth John
Bennett Josiah *Williamson.*
Emerson B. H. B
Hill L. D.
Sprague L. S.
Higgins D. C., Fultneyville
Todd Asahel,   do
Wilson James M. *Wolcott.*
Johnson ———
Forst ———
Hamilton Ira, Red Creek

Westchester County.

Slanson A. H.   *Bedford.*
Keeler Walter
Trowbridge Isaac L.
Shove Seth, Mechanicsville
Bassett B., Peekskill *Courtlandt.*
Stewart P.   do
Hopkins W. G. do
Leggett ———,   do
Hammond G. B., Tarrytown
    Greenburgh.
Hasbrook Francis, do
Scribner James, do
Law James,   do
Dobias Joseph, Hastings
Lockwood James, Cross Line
    Louisborough.
Stanley William *Mamaroneck.*
Fowler J. B., Pleasantville
    Mount Pleasant.
Haight C. W.

Moulton Peter *New Rochelle.*
Voris Edgar
Finch George G. Croton Falls
    North Salem.
Brandreth B., Sing Sing *Ossining.*
Peck Levi.   do
Hoffman Adrian K. do
Sellick W.   do
Wilson James, Portchester *Rye.*
Sands Jerome, do
Mosher William, do
Nodane Charles *Westchester.*
Elder James *West Farms.*
Bayard William
Freeman N. K.
Prime A. J. *White Plains.*
Hodgson G. W.
Trask J. D.
Flagg Levi W. *Yonkers.*
Flagg Ethan
Gardiner D. P.
Gates Amos W.
Stevens ———, Croton *Yorktown.*

Wyoming County.

Roice P. A.   *Attica.*
Curtis A. P.
Dorrance Gardner
Disbro Moses
Cross Ira *Bennington.*
Holt E. C.
Potter M. E., Cowlesville
Ellenwood ———, do
Wells Gershom *Castile.*
Seaman Ezekiel
Huntington Daniel
Felch L. C.
Shedd Ira   *China.*
Higbee J. *Covington.*
Day W. W.   *Eagle.*
Amsden Elihu *Gainesville.*
Graves J.
Cyrus Warren *Genesee Falls.*
Hinds George B.
Clark Chester M.
M'Nulty James, Wyoming
    Middlebury.
Baker Merrick, do
Osborn T. J. *Orangeville.*
Huntington Jonas *Perry.*
Smith M. G.
Keeney George L.
Howard J.
Creighton ———, Perry Centre
Capron L.   *Pike.*
Abbott J. V. W.
Russell J.
Finn E. A.
Vanslyke John, East Pike
Belden Charles D. *Sheldon.*
Potter L., Varysburg
Green R.   do
Caner Peter *Warsaw.*
House Charles
Bartlett E. E.

Yates County.

Brundage G. W. *Benton.*
Wolcott O. P., Benton Centre
Baldwin A.   do
Smith E. S., Belona
Doubleday ———, Italy Hill *Italy.*
Chisom Israel, do
Wixom ———, do
Bush Wynants, Branchport
    Jerusalem.
Preston E. S. *Middlesex.*
Hawley F. C.
Harkness F., Rushville
Oliver A. F., Penn Yan *Milo.*
Soules J. Kent, do
Hammond F. M. do
Sartwell H. P. do
Oliver William, do
Nobles O. E. do
Potter F. M. do
Andrews J. B. Milo Centre
Hatmaker John, do
Preston G. H. (Eclectic) Rushville
    Potter.
Hawley Henry, do do

Bryant J. D. Rushville *Potter.*
Day F. M. do
Otis Abijah, do
Hoyt Chas. S. Potter Centre
Heemans James, do
Thomas J. R. do
Crane W. H.   do
Spence Henry *Starkey.*
Walcott Walter, Dundee
Walcott H. G do
Purdy Wm. S. do
Matley De Grasse, do
Palmer H.   do

Physicians—Botanic. (See also Physicians.)

Albany County.

Stanton W. B. 109 S. Pearl *Albany.*
Russell Andrew, 88 Beaver
Westervelt G. 71 do
Wing J. A. 1 Washington
Titus G. *Rensselaerville.*
Finch I.

Alleghany County.

Neff John *Cuba.*
Perry S. E. *Friendship.*
Pitts J.
Early James *Scio.*
Haskell ———

Broome County.

Watrous J., Harpersville
    Colesville.
Hanley T. A. *Windsor*

Cattaraugus County.

Marvin S. S. *Machias.*
Irish Luther *Otto.*

Chautauque County.

Gillis ———, Fredonia *Pomfret.*
Fuller ———, do
Chancy ———, do
Shattuck Alvin *Westfield.*

Chenango County.

Whitney J. L. *Bainbridge.*
Lee Uri *Sherburne.*
Lawrence George
Mallory ———

Columbia County.

Goodrich Walter, Warren st.
    Hudson.
Penny J. K.   do
Brown T. S. *Kinderhook.*
Waltermire D.

Delaware County.

Maltby A., Pepacton *Colchester.*
Rowe William *Davenport.*
M'Donald C. H. *Harpersfield.*
Stricklin E. S. *Meredith.*
Green G. H. Clark's Factory
    Middletown.
Searle J. O. *Walton.*

Dutchess County.

Haynes H., Union *Amenia.*
Hoag ——— *Dover.*
Kelley R. *Hyde Park.*
Hulbert P. R. 375 Main
    Poughkeepsie.
Tuthill S. 21 Academy

Erie County.

Blanchard Enos *Boston.*
Swain S.

Genesee County.

Andrews ——— *Alexander.*
Delamater J. *Batavia.*

Jefferson County.

Reynolds Wm   *Brownville.*
Nichols A. L.   *Ellisburgh.*
Cushman Darwin   *Theresa.*

Kings County.

Tobias Isaac, 196 N. 2d
                       Williamsburgh.

Livingston County.

Dean ——, East Groveland
                       Groveland.
Edson F. M.   *Mount Morris.*

Monroe County.

Thomas A. Clarkson Corner
                       Clarkson.
Eves J. H. West Mendon *Mendon.*
Vosburgh Wm. do
Sherman Howell, Parma Centre
                       Parma.
Higbie D.   *Penfield.*
Gates J. Exchange st. *Rochester.*
Duncombe C. H. 5 William
Ripley J. 47 Main
Phelps D. C. 24 Exchange
Northrop Philo   *Rush.*

Oneida County.

Wright J. S.   *Camden.*
Rudd J. C.
Tyler A., Sauquoit   *Paris.*
Tyler J.   *Rome.*
Merrill C., Holland Patent
                       Trenton.
Goodin J. T. 181 Genesee *Utica.*

Onondaga County.

Morse J. C., Jordan   *Elbridge.*
Thompson C.   *Geddes.*
Cardell Wm. Baldwinsville
                       Lysander.
Nims ——   *Manlius.*
Cobb B.   *Marcellus.*
Peterman H., South Onondaga
                       Onondaga.
Totman C. S. Clinton sq., Syracuse
                       Salina.
Barton J. James st.
Hunsicker ——   *Owasco.*

Orange County.

Jones Wm. Western Av.
                       Newburgh.
Stockwell Luther, Colden st.
Waugh John,   do
Greenleaf W. A., South Middle-
town   *Wallkill.*
Coe G.   *Warwick.*

Orleans County.

Clapp B., Albion   *Barre.*
Keith A. C.   *Clarendon.*

Oswego County.

Lenox Samuel, Lawrence Build-
ing, Bridge st.   *Oswego.*
Kingsley A. E. 1 Office Row
Dusty J. O. Office Row, Bridge st.
Kilburn Isaac, Cayuga st.
Gilbert Geo. O., Pulaski *Richland.*
Hubbard Jabez, Fulton *Volney.*
Hall Joseph   *Williamstown.*

Otsego County.

Lout O. S. West Burlington
                       Burlington.
Barker ——, Schuyler's Lake
                       Exeter.
Van Horn E. R.   *Hartwick.*
Thorn Joel   *Milford.*
Whitney Wm. H.   *Oneonta.*
French T.   *Westford.*
Chamberlin A. P.

Rensselaer County.

Mattocks John S. 34 5th *Troy.*

St. Lawrence County.

Cross J.   *Fuller.*
Sutherland German H.   *Hermon.*
Talcot G. F.   *Stockholm.*

Saratoga County.

Matthewson David, Ballston Spa
                       Milton.
Osborn Eli   *Saratoga Springs.*
Dennison J. H.
Rose Gilbert   *Wilton.*
Carr S.
King G. W.

Schenectady County.

Miller J.   *Duanesburgh.*

Schoharie County.

Nellis Jacob   *Schoharie.*

Seneca County.

Farley F. A. Farmer   *Ovid.*

Sullivan County.

Cuyler ——   *Fallsburgh.*

Tompkins County.

Woodruff Chas. Enfield Centre
                       Enfield.

Ulster County.

Smith S. A.   *Kingston.*
Friend ——, Ellenville
                       Wawarsing.

Warren County.

Parker John   *Athol.*
Cushing M. A. Glenn's Falls
                       Queensbury.

Washington County.

Cook Oliver, North *White Creek.*

Wayne County.

Smith Daniel   *Walworth.*

Westchester County.

Scofield S. Peekskill *Courtlandt.*

Wyoming County.

Woodard M. D. Wyoming
                       Middlebury.

Yates County.

Perry Levi (Penn Yan) *Milo.*

Physicians — Homœopathic
(See also Physicians.)

Albany County.

Covert I.   *Coeymans.*

Broome County.

Brown T. L.   *Binghamton.*
Hand S.
Pratt S. Centre Lisle *Lisle.*

Cayuga County.

Smith K.   *Moravia.*
Alley W.
Peterson P. H   *Springport.*

Chautauque County.

Crossveld ——, Mayville
                       Chautauque.
Parker ——, Fredonia   *Pomfret.*
Kenyon Lorenzo M.   *Westfield.*

Chenango County.

Owen J. C.   *Sherburne.*

Duchess County.

Hall ——, 25 Market *Poughkeepsie.*
Fanderburgh F.   *Rhinebeck.*
Height C. Hart's Village
                       Washington.

Genesee County.

Baker J. F.   *Batavia.*

Jefferson County.

Woodward C. Evans' Mills
                       Le Ray.
Foote G. F.   *Watertown.*

Livingston County.

Schell Thos. C.   *Genesee.*
Williams ——   *Mount Morris.*

Monroe County.

Wescott J. M. West Mendon
                       Mendon.
Lewis Geo. Ely st.   *Rochester.*
Lewis G. W. Ely st.
Ball A. R. 114 Buffalo
Schill T. C. cor. St. Paul & Main
Bennett H. cor. St. Paul & Main
Biegler A. T. 63 S. Fitzhugh
Mathews M. M. 6 Spring
Wilder L. D. V. Brockport
                       Sweden.
Reynolds Oliver   *Webster.*

Oneida County.

Bishop L. Sauquoit   *Paris.*
Monger E. D. Waterville
                       Sangerfield.
Raymond J. Waterville
Stewart S. W. 173 Genesee *Utica*
Humphreys F. 175 Genesee
Haven S. Z. 129 Genesee

Onondaga County.

Wells L. B.   *Pompey.*
Anderson B. Warren st. Syracuse
                       Salina.
Loomis J. G. Warren st.

Ontario County.

Witherell H. C.   *Canandaigua.*

Orange County.

Culbert W. A.   *Newburgh.*
Slone J. D.

Orleans County.

Blakeslee J. M. Medina *Ridgeway.*

Oswego County.

Potter & Pool, Cayuga st. *Oswego.*
Smith G. Phœnix   *Schroeppel.*
Woodbury W. L., Fulton *Volney.*

Putnam County.

Shaw Wm. Cold Spring
                       Phillipstown.

Saratoga County.

Cornell B. F.   *Moreau.*

Schoharie County.

Osborn E. B. Fultonham *Fulton.*

Seneca County.

Swift Chas. E. Farmer *Ovid.*
Ellis A. J.   do

Suffolk County.

Bryant J. Northport *Huntington.*

Tompkins County.

Sibley L. S. & B. F. 80 Owego
                       Ithaca.

Ulster County.

Garrett —— *Kingston.*
Crispell D.

Washington County.

Cole Edgar B. *Easton.*
Howe J. Sandy Hill *Kingsbury.*

Yates County.

Bardon H. (Penn Yan) *Milo.*
Nobles O. E. do
Hale T. R. Rushville *Potter.*

Piano Forte Manufacturers.

Albany County.

Meacham R. S. 84 State *Albany.*
Berbydt & Ballentine, 22 Union
Dwight H. 6 James
Burns F. P. 5 do
Wood & Gombel, 15 North Pearl
Boardman & Gray 2, 4 & 6 do

Cayuga County.

Percival J. 78 Genesee *Auburn.*

Chenango County.

Hayes & Latlin *Norwich.*
Hollenbeck & King *Greene.*

Columbia County.

Danscher J. *Chatham.*

Duchess County.

Whietpen Louis, 97 Market
Poughkeepsie.
Retter P. 363 Main
Anson B. Stanfordville *Stanford.*
Anson R. do

Erie County.

Garland J. G. 146 East Swan
Buffalo.
Benson David & Co. 196 Wash'ton

Kings County.

Bunce Charles, 11 Water
Brooklyn.
Hjousberry Lesse, 167 Fulton

Monroe County.

Miller Michael, 196 Main
Rochester.
Brayley James, cor. State & Mumford
Bingham Nathaniel. 119½ Buffalo
Dutton George, jr. 27 State

New York County.

Allovon Jean D. 111 Elm
New York.
Bacon & Raven, 160 Centre
Barmore G. & H. 248 Bleecker
Bennett & Wilder. 152 Fulton
Bornhoeft John. 103 Walker
Brewer Alfred N. 269 William
Bury & Wolff, 150 4th Av.
Buttikofer John. 102 Elm
Carr Charles, 287 Spring
Chambers Thomas H. 385 Broad'y
Chickering Jonas. 289½ do
Disbrow Wm. 334 Houston
Doyle Thomas J. 23 Canal
Dubois William. 315 Broadway
Dunham John B. 87 East 13th
Firth, Pond & Co. 1 Franklin sq.
Fischer J. & C. 170 Greenwich
Gale Adam H. & Co. 106 3d Av.
Geib & Jackson, 361 Broadway
Glenn Robert & Co. 194 Fulton
Grovesteen James H. 122 Grand & 40 & 44 West 14th
Grow & Christopher, 111 East 14th
Hall Wm. & Son, 239 Broadway

Hardman Wm. 355 Washington
New York.
Harper John & Co. 334 Greenwich
Harrison Vivaldi F. 23 Canal
Hawkey Henry, 116 Amity
Hoffman Charles F. E. rear 386 Grand
Holmes George F. 14 3d Av.
Kook Sebastian, 243 6th
Leuchte & Newton, 111 & 115 Elm
Lindell E. J. 36 White
Linden & Fritz, 478 Broadway
Luther John F. 116 Ludlow
M'Donald & Brother, 293 Bowery
Martins & Ouvrier, 83 Leonard
Nunns Wm. & Co. 300 Broadway
Nunns & Clark, 257 do
N. Y. Piano Forte Co. cor. 3d Av. & 13th st.
Pethick John, 204 Bleecker
Pirsson James, 87 Leonard
Provoost Peter, 490 Hudson
Rogers & Winant, 148 Fulton
Smith David & T. 223 12th
Stodart Adam, 343 Broadway
Thompson James & Co. 7 Barclay
Thurston Joshua, 259 William
Traver & Ramsey, 46 Broadway
Van Winkle David, r. 92 West 10th
Wake John P. 184 Fulton
Walker J. & D. 413 Broadway
Wennerstrom & Borggvist, 40 5th Av.
Whiting George A. 165 Eldridge
Worcester Horatio, 137 3d Av.

Oneida County.

Philleo L. 52 Hotel *Utica.*

Onondaga County.

Jones & Wood, Salina st. Syracuse
Salina.

Orange County.

Rider John *Cornwall.*
Traver & Ramsey *Newburgh.*
Stanbrough & Son

Rockland County.

Thompson James & Co. Nyack
Orangetown.

St. Lawrence County.

Badlam E. Ford st. Ogdensburgh
Oswegatchie.

Tompkins County.

Atkins, Hollinshead & Spencer, 104 Owego *Ithaca.*

Westchester County.

Nunns Wm. & Co. Hastings
Greenburgh.

Piano Legs.

Bancroft Wm. H. 189 9th
New York.

Piano Stool Makers.

Muchell Richard, 30 Clark
New York.
Keppert & Schmidt, 125 Canal
Pardoe Thomas, 29 & 31 Ridge

Piano Tuners.

Callaway Thomas C. 59 3d Av.
New York.
Case James, 157 East Broadway
Harper Robert, 277 6th Av.
Hill Charles, 64 Crosby
Hofman Charles, 361½ Grand
Lindell E. J. 33 West 13th

Mueller Christian G. 168 West 19th
New York.
Peek David C. 106 6th Av.
Pethick John, 204 Bleecker
Price J. E. 453 Hudson
Ratz G. 86 Grand
Searlee Jacob, 231 3d Av.
Shermer Ernest R. 274 Broome
Waldher William, 173 3d

Pickle Warehouses.

Bonnard Louis, 118 Liberty
New York.
Brady John, 67½ Ludlow
Kensett Thomas & Co. 39 Old slip
Lackey Abraham, 110 West 19th
La Rue Isaac, 55 Barclay
M'Collick Jane & Co. 98 Vesey & 101 Washington market
Raphael George, 262 Pearl
Reckhow Isaac. 142 Liberty
Scott Henry, 217 Water
Smith William D. 53 Vesey
Snyder H. & W. J. 81 Beaver
Tarou Jean, 44 Canal
Tuffs Lucian, 34 Cliff
Van Benschoten Elias H. 252 Front
Vincent E. 85 3d Av.
Wells, Miller & Provost, 217 Front & 443 Water

Picture Cleaners and Restorers.

Coleman Wm. A. 304 Broadway
New York.
M'Damott Edward, 7 Dey
Oliver John, 35 N. Moore
Rover Henry, 170 Broadway

Picture Dealers.

Flandin Pierre, 293 Broadway
New York.
Hermann L. 80½ Bleecker
Koelble Joseph, 161 3d
Lutz Valentine, 583 Bowery
Robinson F. 257 Broadway
Von Held Jacob, 566 4th

Pilots.

Hell Gates, 24 Coenties slip & South cor. Pike *New York.*
Hudson River, 308 West
Merchants, 37 South
New York, 309 Water & 179 South
Sandy Hook, 91 West & 209 Water

Plaiters and Fluters. (*See also Laundries, also Washerwomen.*)

Beaudin D. 299 Broadway
New York.
Dubourdieu Mary, 297½ Broadway
Farcy Constant, 466 do
Jones Clodine, 115½ Grand
Lefevor Julie, 493 Broadway
Lazzere Joseph, 6 Ludlow
Mandine Augustine, 406 Broadway
M'Parland Mary, 83 E. 18th
Nies Margaret, rear 111 Wooster
Reinhardt Margaret, 216 Grand
Trautwein M. 422½ Broadway

Pin Manufacturers.

Duchess County.

Fairchild, Pelton & Co. Mill st.
Poughkeepsie.

New York County.

American & Howe Pin Co. 50 Broad　　*New York.*

Pipe Manufacturers.

Kings County.

Smith J. A. 29 Hudson Av. *Brooklyn.*
Taylor Thomas, S. 6th st. *Williamsburgh.*

Piano Manufacturers.

Albany County.

Benson & Crannell, 116 State *Albany.*
Bensell & Munsell, 42 Howard

Delaware County.

Inglis A.　　*Delhi.*

Duchess County.

Sandkahl J. G. 196 Main *Poughkeepsie.*

Erie County.

White L. & I. J. 23 Ohio *Buffalo.*

Herkimer County.

Robins E.　　*Newport.*

Kings County.

Parry John S. Bridge near Fulton *Brooklyn.*
Way & Sherman, 177 1st *Williamsburgh.*

Monroe County.

Evans E. & J. cor. Main & Water *Rochester.*

New York County.

Baldwin A. & Co. 4 & 6 Gold *New York.*
Baldwin Elbridge, rear 90 Thompson
Bary Samuel S. 342½ Grand
Belch William B. rear 29 Hester, & 207 Division
Bornhoeft John, 47 Canal
Coughtry Joseph, 291 Bowery
Furr James W. 329 6th
Green Jacob, 372 Bleecker
Hannan James, 17 Suffolk
Harrow Robert, 204 Bleecker
King Josiah, 8 4th Av.
Marley Luke, 54 Centre
Merritt & Co. 58 South

Oneida County.

Reed Charles, Washington st. *Utica.*

Onondaga County.

Nolton L. Mulberry st. Syracuse *Salina.*

Rensselaer County.

Carter E. & C. 11 Ferry　*Troy.*

St. Lawrence County.

Bailey R. C. Ogdensburgh *Oswegatchie.*

Ulster County.

Styles James J., Kingston

Planing Mills. (See also Lumber Manufacturers.)

Jefferson County.

Kerby, Morgan & Wood, Dexter *Brownville.*

Kings County.

Osborn S. & Co. cor. Baltic & Columbia　*Brooklyn.*

Livingston County.

Kettle Robert　*Dansville.*
Fisk George C.

Monroe County.

Walker S. 38 Washington *Rochester.*

New York County.

Kelsey & Son, 270 5th　*New York.*
Newton Jonah, 270 5th
Serrell Alfred T. rear 87 & 89 Elizabeth
Southmayd Samuel G. 377 West
Van Hook William, 454 West
Wells George, foot 12th
Wells Thomas J., W. 29th st.
Woods Thomas W. 338 Cherry

Oneida County.

Lawrence L. cor. Seneca & Canal Basin　*Utica.*

Orleans County.

Hedley E., Medina　*Ridgeway*

Oswego County.

Ogden J. & Co. Oswego Falls *Granby.*
Littlefield Hamilton, Smith's Cove *Oswego.*
Ambler & Ells, Ames' Buildings, 1st st.

Tompkins County.

Taber I. P. (Ithaca Steam Mills) Inlet　*Ithaca.*

Rensselaer County.

Ward James K. Front cor. Division *Troy.*
Sage Norton, Adams near 1st

Schenectady County.

Horsfall J. O. & J. 50 Green *Schenectady.*

Washington County.

Finch J. C. & Co. Sandy Hill *Kingsbury*
Cook W. W.　*Whitehall.*
Bascom O.

Planished Ware Manufacturers.

Grant James, 280 Broadway *New York.*
Hodgetts, Taylor & Hodgetts, rear 168 William
Locke John D. 193 Water
Munn William A. 29 Carmine
Scovill J. M. L. & W. H. 101 Wm.
Thomas T. & Son, 63 Nassau

Plaster Cast Figures and Plaster Paris Workers.
(See also Artists Decorative.)

Ceragioli Bartholomew & Co. 215 William　*New York.*
Coffee Thomas, 57 Canal
Equi Giovanni, 315 Broadway
Fabri Lodovico, 307　do
Gaud A. 80　　do
Kolm & Kisling, 36 Great Jones
Rigali Gaetano, 148 William
Sinclair Hector, 316 Broadway

Plaster Mills.

Albany County.

Shephard & Van Zandt *Albany.*
Gibeon John, cor. Water & Spencer
Kimmey R. & J.　*Bethlehem.*
Batteman John M.　*Guilderland.*

Cayuga County.

Richardson J.　*Springport.*
Howland C. W.
Yawger P. & Brothers
Thompson J.

Chenango County.

Wheeler John H.　*Green.*
Judson Philo　*Oxford.*
Lewis Clark, jr.
Birch L. D.　*Sherburne.*
Bullock W.
Pratt & Rexford

Genesee County.

Morgan L. C. & Wm.　*Le Roy.*
Haskins W. L.
Parmelee J. H.
Fobes Enoch　*Oakfield.*
Lay, Ganson & Co.　*Stafford.*

Greene County.

Baldwin Hezekiah *New Baltimore*
Baldwin Henry
Van Slyke Andrew
Raymond John

Herkimer County.

Devendorf Jacob, Mohawk
　　　　German Flats
Ingham William　*Little Falls*
Watkins Horace, Gravesville *Russia.*

Jefferson County.

Babcock & Morgan, Dexter *Brownville.*
Waite F.　*Ellisburgh.*

Livingston County.

Williams John C. & Co. *Dansville.*
Thompson C. L.　*Mount Morris.*

Madison County.

Rice & Hamilton　*Lebanon.*
Scofield N., Wampsville *Lenox.*
Kennedy David　*Sullivan.*
Brown J. & H. (dealers only)

Monroe County.

Harmon A. & C. South Chili *Chili.*
Tracy D. (dealer)　*Pittsford.*
Garbutt P., Scottsville *Wheatland.*
Garbutt Philip, Mumford

Montgomery County.

Jones Lynds, Fonda　*Mohawk.*
Lingunfelter A. do
Wemple J. V.　do

New York County.

Ceragioli Bartholomew & Co. 215 William　*New York.*
King Jerome B. 509 West
Matthews Samuel, 36 Carmine
Seixas Theodore J. 179 & 181 11th
Wotherspoon James, W. 13th bet. 9th & 10th Avs.

Ontario County.

Pinkney T. A.　*Phelps.*

Orange County.

Racine J. Well's Corners *Minisink.*
Denton H. E. New Hampton *Wallkill.*

Little H. South Middletown *Wallkill.*
Demerest D. D. New Milford
Warwick.
Kieran J. do

Oswego County.

Ames Henry M. 1st st. *Oswego.*
Ames Leonard, Ames' Buildings

Rensselaer County.

Dunlop Robert, 347 State
Lansingburgh.
Vall. Hayner & Fellows, 151 & 153
River *Troy.*
Boutwell O. River near State Dam
Neer & Seaver, 466 River

St. Lawrence County.

Raymond Sewal *Potsdam.*
Munson Myron G.

Saratoga County.

Noxon Alfred *Half Moon*
Cronkhite George *Moreau*
Wing Charles *Stillwater.*

Seneca County.

Thompson & Howland
Seneca Falls.

Steuben County.

Hammond & Johnson *Painted Post.*

Tompkins County.

Goodwin Alfred, North Hector
Hector.

Warren County.

Conkhite George, Glenn's Falls
Queensbury.

Washington County

Gale Frederick A. Galesville
Easton.
Gamble R. G. *Greenwich.*

Platers Silver.

Albany County.

Bradley A. 95 Green *Albany.*
Wright & Co. 95 do
Scott D. I. 81½ South Pearl

Broome County.

Robothan William *Binghamton.*

Chenango County.

Goodrich H *Norwich.*

Erie County.

Taylor D. East Swan st *Buffalo.*
Pratt & Letchworth, 166 Main

Kings County.

M'Nally M. 40 Henry *Brooklyn.*
Jackson G. W 56 Myrtle Av.
White & Wittin, 85 Grand
Williamsburgh.

Monroe County.

Casey William, 17 Exchange
Rochester.

New York County.

Anderson Augustus T. 4½ Amity
New York.
Bishop A. 75 & 77 Nassau
Chalmers Thomas, 799 Broadway
Collord James, 96 Walker
Coombs & Anderton, 209 Grand &
85 Mercer
Cooper Garret, rear 196 Fulton
Crane Horace F. 54 Gold

21

Dixon James & Sons, 241 Pearl
New York.
Garvey John, 398 Bowery
Groves & Co. 183 Broadway
Harper Geo. W. 145 W. B.way
Harris James, 187 Canal
Johnstone James, r. 148 Wooster
Jones John. 180 Mott
M'Cottrey & Trosted, 36 White
Miller William, 105 Elm
Minshull Charles. 222 William
Murray & Felihee, 556 Broadway
Newman Allen G. 289 Bowery
Newman J. & Son, 379 6th Av.
Ostrander & Gable, 41 Hester
Phelps R. R. & Co. 23 Centre
Roberts Robert, 562 Broadway
Sause Edmund J. 20 Cortlandt
Smith James S. 139 Fulton

Oneida County.

Price & Dana, 92 Genesee *Utica.*
Sanders H. Franklin square

Ontario County.

Gregory S. W. *Canandaigua.*

Rensselaer County.

M'Kinney J. 28 Albany *Troy.*

Plough Manufacturers.
(See also *Founders, Iron*)

Broome County.

Bartlett J. L. *Binghamton.*
Matthews E. F.

Cayuga County.

Birsdell & Stephens *Genoa.*
Cook B. *Ira.*
Stone & Kenyan *Moravia.*
Keeler & Wright
Shourds & Mosher *Venice*

Chenango County.

Muckart N. R. & Co. *Guilford.*
Trask Almond, Guilford Centre
Avery George D. *Oxford.*

Clinton County.

Moore N. *Champlain.*
Finley & Smith
Smith, Bonner & Co. *Plattsburgh.*

Columbia County.

Spaulding M. *Gallatin.*

Duchess County.

Tier I. 354 Main *Poughkeepsie.*

Erie County.

Smith Joseph H. Terrace st.
Buffalo.
Walde L. & Co. Willink *Aurora.*

Fulton County.

Mead Ralph, Hooseville
Broadalbin.

Genesee County.

Coman & Webb *Le Roy.*

Jefferson County.

Crowner Joseph. Carthage *Wilna.*

Livingston County.

Steward David *York.*
Long Moses, Fowlersville
Smith A. C. do

Madison County.

Kellogg & Webber, Chittenango
Sullivan.

Monroe County.

King & Hitchcock, Spencer's Basin *Ogden.*
Crippin & Mott *Penfield.*
Hebbard Sterling A., Churchville
Riga.
Wright P. D. 116 State *Rochester.*
Belden A. 154 State
Tarbox H., Scottsville *Wheatland.*

Oneida County.

Wood, Dane & Co. *Camden.*

Onondaga County.

Joslyn D. *Fabius.*
Humphrey H., Baldwinsville
Lysander
Gaiety & Rogers, do
Burton B. Bear st.

Rensselaer County.

Wheeler I. *Nassau.*
Smith Thomas

St. Lawrence County.

Fletcher & Merrill *Parishville*

Washington County.

Eddy & Co. *Easton.*

Westchester County.

Finch H. R. & Co. Peekskill
Courtlandt
Minor, Horton & Co. do
Van Wart & Wildey, Tarrytown
Greenburgh.
Fowler, Horton & Co. Sing Sing
Osining.
Vredenburgh W. D. & T. Sing
Sing
Abendroth & Brothers, Portchester *Rye.*

Plumbers.

Kings County.

Hudson John, 159 Atlantic
Brooklyn.
Hudson John. 9 Hicks
Milne Peter, 55 Fulton

New York County.

Aken Joseph, 181 6th Av.
New York.
Allaire Anthony J. 616 Water
Arment Alfred A. 57 & 59 E. 14th
Armstrong Thomas S. 513 Grand
Baguely Mark, 171 William
Barkley & Wilson, 61 Hudson
Bloomfield George W. & Co. 111
Charles
Brooks & Cummings, 123 Av. D
Brower Abraham & Co. 236 Water
Brush John A. 83 Pike slip
Burnett Durant, 140 9th Av.
Burns G. B. 40 Av. C.
Butcher & Read, 244 Water
Chardavoyne Wm. & T. C. 134
Cherry
Charlock Thomas, 411 Bowery
Consall & Hauptman, 606 Broadway
Craig Joseph, 698 Broadway
Drew George S. 184 3d Av.
Duff James, 230 Water
Eagleson Alexander, 736½ Broadway
Edgar & Dickson, 437 Hudson
Eldridge, Moat & Co. 56 Vesey
Ennever Robert, 39 Anthony
Farmer John W. 346 Broome
Farr & Briggs, 30 Rector
Finch & Carter, 37 Bowery
Fulton George, 554 Broadway
Godwin Thomas. 801 Broadway
Haines John D. 551 Grand

Hanson Thomas, 153 4th Av.
New York.
Hatfield Elias, 272 Broadway
Hillsburgh Charles, 342 Water
Hitchings A. E. 146 10th
Howell George R. 32 Park Row
Hurley John J. 748 Broadway
Ingram & Cole, 327 Bowery
Ivers Alfred, 19 Dry Dock
Ivers Morton, 319 Pearl
Jones Thomas, 54 Centre
Knight Wm. 78 4th Av.
Laton Martin, 337 Bowery
Leamy Lewis W. 606 Broadway
Lent Theodore, 73 E. Broadway
Lutz Peter, 57 Av. B
M'Coy Daniel & Co. 567 Hudson
M'Kenzie Alexander, 655 Broadway
Mather John, 131½ Wooster
Meeks Wm. E. 70 4th Av.
Miller Amos, 70 Av. D
Miller, Coates & Yulee, 120 Grand & 275 Pearl
Mills Abner, 52 Av. D
Montgomery Wm. M. 121 Bowery
Neefus Peter W. 298 West
O'Hara Charles H. 642 Broadway
Pearce Edmund A. 134 8th Av.
Pearce John & Co. 11 Wall
Peckwell Wm. 119 Norfolk
Philbin J. & S. 176 Mercer & 12 & 3 Dey
Pitt Chas. & Wm. 17 3d Av.
Pryor Wm. H 378 6th Av.
Quin Joseph P. 644 Broadway
Rhodes & Patterson, 825 Br'dway
Robinson Wm. 52 8th Av.
Rochford & Worley, 82 Vesey
Sands Alfred B. 290 Water
Sawyer Nathaniel. 221 Bleecker
Simpson William P. 341 & 409 6th Av.
Sisty Benjamin P. 232 6th Av.
Smith William H. jr. & E. R. 112½ Bleecker
Stone James, 390 Broadway
Stuart James, 813 Broadway
Sweet Ezra E. 133 Canal
Trembley & Co. 136 Chrystie
Walter & Ash, 296 Broadway
Watkins Rees, 16 Roosevelt
West W. M. 123 Hudson
Whitfield G. & J. 262 Water
Wilmer John, 93 Greenwich
Williams J. T. & H. 71 4th Av.
Williams William, 163 Hudson
Zimmerman C. H. 314 Hudson

Pocket Book Manufacturers.

Chenango County.

Porter H.   *Coventry.*

New York County.

Chapman Levi, 102 William
New York.
Cholwell Geo. R. 24 Maiden lane
Collin, Mayns & Co. 90 Fulton. Manufacturers of Portemonnaies. &c.
Cook William, 96 Fulton
Doane William, 50 Nassau
Floersheim & Co. 66 Fulton, portemonnaies, bank cases, &c.
Harvey William, 194 Nassau
Hassler H. A. 90 Gold
Hine P. B. 89 William
Heussler & Rose, 1 Tryon Row
Lemon Morris, rear 88 Duane
Lockwood Reuben H. 129 Cherry
Mynce & Rice, 23 Spruce
Runnell M. & R. H. 53 Fulton
Shaw & Ireland, 240 Pearl
Seiter Andrew G. 74 Maiden lane
White Robert N., E. 21st st

Portable Houses.

Freeman Geo. & Co. 50 Broadway
New York.

Porter, Ale & Cider.

Albany County.

Hand Martha, (bottler) 9, 11, & 13 South Pearl   *Albany.*
Harris & Sons, (bottlers) 1 B'way

Erie County.

Burr & Waters. 35 & 21 East Seneca   *Buffa'o.*
Mason John. 123 Seneca
Pentland W. (wholesale) 138 Main
Williams & Stanton, 157½ Main

Kings County.

Bell Samuel, Uri Burt's Albany Cream Ale, 19 Front *Brooklyn.*
Harrou John, Agent for C. & S. Milbank's Croton Porter & Ale, 79 Main
Bartlett Theodore, 29 South 7th ,
Williamsburgh.

Monroe County.

Tyffe David, 40 Water *Rochester.*
Stroud John, Water st.
Powell H. 42 Water
Hall J. D. 6 North St. Paul
Betzel Jacob, 86 Clinton
Cutts Samuel, 10 Water

New York County.

Adams Daniel, 138 Cedar
New York.
Barber Thomas, 120 Warren
Beveridge J. & Co. 119 Warren
Bush Thomas, 23 Ann
Byrne Owen, 59 Water
Carley & Bolton, 121 Water
Coots John, 1 Roosevelt
Creighton James, 48 Anthony
Donelly A. & Co. 83 John
Eagle George, 150 Fulton
Greene Thomas D. 96 Cedar
Kelly Thomas, 376 Cherry
Lethbridge G. P. 86 & 88 Fulton
Losey William, 648 Pearl
Martin Patrick, 106 Chambers
Means Thomas, 204 Water
Murphy Edward, 211 1st Av.
Oliver J. 138 Fulton
Pollock R. M. 114 Warren
Robinson, Charlesworth & Tryner, 7 Elm
Rohlfs Henry, 205½ Fulton
Southwick Adna H. & Tupper, 112 Warren
Sullivan James, 131 Water
Taylor John & Sons, 342 G'wich
Vassar Mathew & Co. 116 Warren
White Peter, 43 Peck slip
Wintringham Sidney, 16 Wall

Porter Houses. (*See also Billiard Saloons; also Eating Houses; also Restaurants, Oyster Saloons, &c.; also Porter, Ale & Cider.*)

Albany County.

Armstrong R. 187 Montgomery
Albany.
Bartley Mrs. 156 Montgomery
Baker J. B. 7 & 9 Steuben
Bergeron M. 1 Division
Boules & Co. 82 Quay
Carroll W., Spencer cor. Montgomery
Cayle H. 29 Lumber
Chestnut Wm. 169 S. Pearl
Crannell J. 101 Pearl
Dickson J. L. 8 Steuben
Diamond Wm. M. 76 N. Pearl
Donnelly A. John cor. Quay
Driscol P. 184 Montgomery
Dunn D. 36 State
Eagan F. 81 Quay
Elmendorf —— 164 Broadway

Forrell Wm. 185 Montgomery
Albany.
Faley J. Church st.
Ferrell Thos. 25 Church
Flynn J. 3 Division
Gellipan G. Colonie st.
Gallup N. 140 Montgomery
Gaynor Thos. D. 34 Quay
Grady P. 21 Quay
Graham Wm. N. 10 Washington
Green E. 20 Washington
Hamilton Andrew, 776 Broadway
Hughs J. 48 Lydius
King K. 267 S. Pearl
Landers J. 154 Washington
Livingston Wm. 188 Montgomery
Linten ——, 196 S. Pearl
Lovel R. 62 Beaver
M'Cotten H. 10 Columbia
M'Shane F. 74 Quay
M'Callon Mrs. F. 3 Howard
M'Evely ——, 3 Howard
M'Goun Wm. 4 Beaver
Marr J. 51 Little Basin
Mayher Patrick, 78 Quay
Mulleu J. 25 Pier
Murphy E. 187 S. Pearl
Neven Isaac, 1 North Lansing
Paulus S. W. 97 Washington
Peebles J. 14 Beaver
Pendell E. 127 Arch
Putnam E. 702 Broadway
Queeny M. 199 Water
Quinn A. 4 Steuben
Quinn C. 4 Howard
Recton J. 297 S. Pearl
Rice George E. 135 Broadway
Sayles J. 2 William
Schlereth N. 146 Washington
Schwartz —, 165 S. Pearl
Shaver L. 19 Washington
Smith E. 17   do
Smith H. 161 Water
Sporborg L. 142 S. Pearl
Stern M. M. 163   do
Striker J. P. 69 Church
Swain S. R. 24 Beaver
Thayer W. B. 24 do
Tierman P. 21 Van Woert
Van Bramer D. 123 Pier
Van Horn F. 167 S. Pearl
Werhimer A. 224 do
Timmons B. West Troy *Waterville.*
Forester John, do
M'Nulty H.   do
Smith A.   do
Monecle J.   do
Bennett J. W.   do
Blass J.   do
Borton J.   do
Fass C.   do
Richards Thos. P. do

Columbia County.

Carpenter W. A.   *Hudson.*
Curtiss M. Warren st.
Lanphier W.   do
Hart A.   do
Brayman Wm. H. do

Duchess County.

Helwick H. 429 Main *Poughkeepsie.*
Stewart J. 31   do
M'Labr John, 11 Market
Marx 1. 131 Main
Ward F. Mill st.
Walsh P. do

Kings County.

M'Guire W. cor. Boerum & Fulton
Brooklyn.
M'Carty Edward. 47 Main
Gilfillan John, 25   do
Brady J. cor. Plymouth & Jay
Spouers John J. Myrtle Av. cor Lawrence st.
Hamilton W. 210 Jay
Maybury H. Bridge cor. Fulton st
Foster H. C. 203 Fulton
Benton John, 311   do

Adair John, Hudson Av. *Brooklyn.*
Conolly David. 90 do
Ackley Geo. 199 York
Christaller J. M. 200 do.
Gascoyne Thos. J. Myrtle Av.
O'Connor A. 52½ Atlantic
Wynkoop John C. 4 Hamilton Av.
Rourke Felix, 190 York
Allenbook F. East New York
        Flatbush.

New York County.

Abbott & Watt, 117 Cedar
        New York.
Abel Charles A. & George Walter,
    474 Broadway
Abelman Conrad, 110 Division
Abraham Jacob, 90 Ridge
Acker John, 55 Bayard
Acker Philip, 155½ Division
Ackerley D. 97 West
Adam John, 8th Av.
Adler Z. 146 3d
Agan E. 205 1st Av.
Aharm William, 196 Chambers
Ahern James, 440 Monroe
Ahrsburg Daniel. 92½ Sheriff
Aiken William. 464 Hudson
Aitken Ralph F. 182 South
Akerly Daniel. 97 West
Albers Hermann, 96 West
Albert James. 31 Canal
Albert William, 152 Cherry
Alden Joseph, 39 2d Av.
Allair Thomas H. 90 Perry
Allen Samuel, (Fountain Cottage)
    332 3d
Allen Samuel B. 264 Canal
Allers John A. 19 Coenties slip
Alling Alexander M. 54 West
Allison William, 9 Broadway
Alois & Muller, 116 Sheriff
Anderson Charles, 390½ Water
Andrews C. 95 Bowery
Andrews Catharine, 108 W. B'way
Ardie John, 430 Cherry
Armbruster Joseph E. 79 Chatham
Armitage Isaac, 36 Moore
Armstrong William, 134 10th Av.
Arnold David P. 15 Catharine slip
Arppen Henri, 8 Spruce
Asche Henry, 55 Fulton
Aspell & Wallace, 181 8th Av.
Assinger John. 79 Norfolk
Asten Peter, 68½ Bowery
Aubery H. F. 61 Nassau
Augustus Chas. 44 Av. C
Augustus Chas. 77 Cherry
Auld Samuel, 23 West
Austin Barclay, 238 1st Av.
Avera Patrick. 47 Roosevelt
Ayhen Geo. 37 Mulberry
Ayres Louisa, 56 Reade
Bachman Isaac, 415 Grand
Bacon Lewis S. B. 29 Peck slip
Badischen B. 224 2d
Baeder C. 123 Delancy
Baers Elias, 201 Houston
Bagan John, 213 Hester
Bagby Jas. 189 Madison
Baglan Jas. 195 W. 17th
Bailoy Jacob, 243 Stanton
Baker Chas. 454 Water
Balfe & Russell, 8th Av.
Balfe Columbus, 170 Varick
Ball John, 104 Barclay
Baltes Wilhelm, 371 Broome
Bane J. 101 Division
Barney D. J. 185 West
Barney John J. 305 Chatham
Barney S. W. & J. J. 186 West
Barker Thos. 77 Gold
Barrow Francis, 107 Spring
Barry John H. 287 Front
Barry Thos. 434 Monroe
Barry Wm. 622 Grand
Barthelemy B. E. 292 Broadway
Barwood Barnard. 37 Mulberry
Bauche John, 73 & 75 Centre
Bauer Adolph, 193 Division
Bayard Peter M. 11 State

Boyle ——, 258 Front *New York.*
Beach Ezra, 347 Spring
Beach Geo. 305 Water
Beane John, 101 Division
Beaver Joshua W. 425 West
Becher Chas. 33 Chatham
Beckor Fred. 16 Centre
Beckett Geo. 305 Water
Beddoes Thos. 153 7th
Begg Francis, 201 Stanton
Beglan James, 95 W. 17th
Behan Stephan. 75 Laurens
Behel James, 20 Cherry
Beirne Thos. 359 Water
Bell Elizabeth. 118 Fulton
Benjamin & Fuller. 94 Chatham
Benham John, 280 3d Av.
Benner Valentine, 1 Av. A
Bennet John, 89 Grand
Bennet Geo. W. 91 Roosevelt
Berger Jacob. 96 Gold
Berkele Michael, 147½ Mott
Berkimmer John. 128 Pitt
Bernard, Son & Co. 242 E. 13th
Bernard M. 6 Centre market pl.
Bernstein Bernard, 76 Allen
Berns John. 638 Greenwich
Berry Bernard, 499 Pearl
Bencking H. 51 Bowery
Bhuerie Jacob, 243 Stanton
Bick Henry, 156 Washington
Byres J. 28 Washington
Bigelow Joseph, 502 Houston
Bigelow Thomas. 16 W. Broad'y
Bilfinger Frederic, 328 Broome
Bindernagel John. 79 Bayard
Birch Henry, 149 Washington
Bird & Rushing, 17 do
Birr John. 213 1st Av.
Bischoff Charles & Co. 7 James
Blauvelt & Gold. 88 W. Broadway
Blin Sebastian, 7 Warren
Blythe Robert, 9th Av.
Bohlan Thomas. 224 13th
Bohls Henry E. 77 Walnut
Bollas John, 1 1st Av.
Bolte & Kohlstedt, 65 Greenwich
Bolton Wm. H. 217 Washington
Bork Edward, 313 Delancy
Bost Stephen, 91 Division
Bounk Michael, 175 Elizabeth
Bourke Catharine, 89 Cherry
Bowman William. 9 Howard
Boyd Thomas. 366 Hudson
Boyle John. 67 Cross
Boylen Mary, 183 Varick
Boyleu Thomas. 38 James
Bracken John. 2 3d Av.
Bracken Thomas, 126 Duane
Bradburn Thomas, 5 Little Water
Bradbury Thomas, 282 Hudson
Bradley Mary, 146 West
Brady Mary, 64 Prince
Brady Patrick, 100 Anthony
Brady Thomas, 13 Canal
Brady Thomas, 107 Elm
Brady Thomas, 129 Walker
Breidert George, 828 Pearl
Braitmayer John G. 134 Hester
Bran Henry, 22 Duane
Brandis Carl. 556 4th
Breitenstein George, 3 Albany
Brennan Dennis. 59 Cross
Brennan Matthew T. 814 Pearl &
    83 Centre
Brennan Michael, 85 Orange
Brennan Patrick, 109 Anthony
Brennan Thomas, 48½ Cherry
Brennan William, 17 Monroe
Brennen Michael, 4 Coenties slip
Brislen Dennis, 236 Mulberry
Brizolora Giacomo, 19 Spruce
Brono Charles, 38 Walnut
Brooks Joseph, 250 West
Brophy John, 106 Cherry
Brosnan Michael. 62 Centre
Brown George, 140 Prince
Brown Henry W. 150 Church
Brown James, 43 E. 13th
Brown John L. 195 South
Brown John W. cor. 26th & 2d Av.
Brown Joseph F. 13 Water

Brown Nataan, 95 Vesey
        New York.
Brown Patrick, 47 Elizabet
Brown Peter, 491 Pearl
Brown Samuel, 96 Duane
Brown William, 61 Elm
Brown William, 25 Thames
Brown ——, 65 Laurens
Brown George J. 441 Grand
Browning S. G. 26 6th
Bruce William, 208 8th Av.
Brundage Samuel, 236 Grand
Brunner Gabriel, 293 2d
Bruton Patrick, 298 1st Av.
Bryan James, 222 Centre
Buck George, 123 Greenwich
Buecking Henry, 51 Bowery
Buermeyer Ernest. 101 Broad
Buhsen Nicolaus, 42 West
Bukelmann Conrad, 123 Division
Bunce Nathaniel, 202 South
Bunn Reuben, 143 Grand
Burns John, 638 Greenwich
Bunschuh John, 24 Av. B
Bungert David, 152 3d
Burgthal ——. 14 City Hall place
Burke David, 2 6th
Burke James, 325 Water
Burke John, 15th cor. 10th Av.
Burke John, 349 Madison
Burke Patrick D. 98 Wall
Burke M. K. 7 & 9 Washington
Burke Walter, 33 James
Burleigh Giles, 591 Greenwich
Burleigh Henry, 484 Broadway
Burns Francis. 29 Madison
Burns John, 638 Greenwich
Burns John, 276 E. 13th
Burns Peter, 35 Washington
Burns Thomas, 376 Water
Burrows Michael, 366 do
Burtmer John, 274 Broome
Burt U. 7th Av. & 183 Greenwich
Burwell Sheldon, 21 Wall
Burr A. C. 334 Broadway
Bush David, 40 Clinton
Bush Thomas, (W. S. dealer) 22
    Ann
Bush J. 8 Chrystie
Bussey George E. 255 South
Butler William, 452 Broadway
Buttner John, 5 Albany
Byron John W. 34 Houston
Byrne John L. 139 Washington
Byrne Peter, 9 Hoboken
Byrnes Owen, 498 10th
Byrnes James, 24 Spruce
Cahill John, 34 Pell
Callaghan Joseph, 66 James
Callaghan Phillips, 567 Greenwich
Campbell Thos. 86 E. Broadway
Campbell John, Yorkville
Canning Bridget, 5 Catharine slip
Cannon Patrick, 179 11th
Cenoven Eliza, 179 Elm
Cantzler Henry J. 85 Greenwich
Cappelmann Otto, 10 West
Carberry B. 499 Pearl
Carl Henry, 86 Centre
Carland William, 20 Bowery
Carlisle Joseph, 59 Centre & 490
    Broome
Carroll Robert, 318 Bowery
Cartey William, 22 Madison
Case & Pollock, 136 Church
Casen Henry, 32 West
Casey Christopher, 241 11th
Casey John, 458 19th
Casey John, 53 Market
Casey Mary, 72 Hamerley
Cashana Charles, 96 James
Caspero Francis. 86 Chatham
Cassady John, 214 Elizabeth
Cassidy Nicholas, 181 Varick
Castano Louis, 31 10 Av.
Cavenagh Daniel, 47 Prince
Cavenagh James, 597 Greenwich
Chambon John B. 208 Broadway
Chance John, 72 Hamerley
Chandler A. B. 316 Greenwich
Chapman James H. 337 Hudson
Charpentier Alex. 40 Beekman

Charrington Wm. H. 132 Grand
　　New York.
Cherien Michael, 15 North Wm.
Childs Isaac, 74 East Broadway
Christensen Claus, 76 Ludlow
Christopher Mary J. 41 Walnut
Churchill Michael, 314 24th
Churchill Joseph, 186 Spring
Cisco Thomas. 565 Broadway
Clark John, 173 Av. A
Clark John, Av. A cor. East 23d
Clark Asahel, 314 Water
Clark Margaret, 483 Washington
Clark Nathaniel, 314 Water
Clark Patrick, 122 Leonard
Clarke Andrew, 176 West
Clarke A. & T. 15 Park row
Clarke Bernard. 15 Washington
Clarke James H. 265 Madison
Clear Michael, 43 Elm
Cleary Wm. 277 Walker
Clement Bridget, 5 Vandewater
Cline Simon, 63 Watts
Cling George. 142 Stanton
Clohan David. 101 James
Clough Stephen, 343 Spring
Coblenzer Emanuel, 69 Ludlow
Coffee John, 12 Roosevelt
Coffey John, 158 Maiden lane
Coffin Isaac G. & Robert A. 146
　　Division
Cogan John, 66 Orange
Coghlin John, 518 West
Cogswell Charles N. 51 Cherry
Coll Hugh, 65 King
Cook Edward, 290 Front
Coons Frederick, 39 Walnut
Cohn Hannah, 20 Grand
Colvin James, 2 Fulton
Colon George. 100 Wooster
Collins Ann, 46 Elm
Collins John, 40 Spring
Collins Michael, 36 Lispenard
Collins Wm. 3 Oak
Colly John, 119 Av. D
Comman Lawrence, 61 Cortlandt
Commins John. 31 Hamilton
Conklin John D. 61 Whitehall
Connorton Patrick, 102 Delancy
Conlan James, 143 Mulberry
Coologue Edward, 187 Duane
Connelly Edward, 222½ West 17th
Connelly Patrick, 471 Washingt'n
Connelly Daniel. 18 Canal
Conolly J. 214 West
Connolley Henry, 170 Cherry
Connolly Mary, 3 Hamilton
Connolly Michael, foot 13th N. R.
Connolly Patrick, 219 Division
Connelly Phebe, 630 Water
Connor Peter, 50 Bowery
Connor Wm. R. 183 11th
Connor Wm. West 26th st.
Conroy C. 347 3d Av.
Conroy Bridget. 139 Cedar
Conroy John, 274 W. 17th
Coogan Jas. 66 Willett
Cooks Robert, 90 Gold
Cooman L. 61 Cortlandt
Cooper Benj. F. 319 Spring & 516
　　Greenwich
Cooper Henry, 120½ Bowery
Corcoran Patrick, 211½ 1st Av.
Corles John. 290 12th
Cornelly John, 21 Prince
Corrigan Jas. 72 University place
Corson Cornelius, 162 Bowery
Cosgrove Arthur, 361 E. 21st
Cotter Ann, 93 Cherry
Coughlin Jas. 72 Oliver
Coughlin Richard, 72 Cherry
Coulter Jas. 87 11th
Cowan Thos. 315 1st Av.
Cox Andrew, 40 Orange
Cox Chas. 11 Thames
Cox Isaac T. 476 Washington
Cox Patrick, 90 Mulberry
Coyle Hugh P. 141 Chatham
Coyle John, 77 Greenwich Av.
Coyne Thos. 304 Front
Cramer J. W. West 27th st.
Craney Owen C. 294 South

Cranney Patrick, 593 Greenwich
　　New York.
Crawford Jas. H. 276 8th Av.
Crawford Robert, 2 Bridge
Crocheron Nicholas, 8 West
Croker Wm. 34 Roosevelt
Cronin Michael, 72 Centre
Crough Jas. 65 Cherry
Crowe Chas. 7 Pearl
Cudney John. 301 Division
Cullum Michael. 91 3d Av.
Cummins Jas. 373 Broadway
Cummins M. 28 City Hall place
Cummings Arthur, 155 2d
Cummings Jas. 250 2d
Cummings John, 194 Amos
Cunningham John, 45 Ann
Cunningham J. & Co. 90 Liberty
Cunningham Mary, 8 Madison
Cunningham Patrick, 194 W. 21st
Cunningham Patrick, 232 Mott
Curley Patrick, 71 Mott
Curr John. 81 Hammond
Currighan Edward, 38 5th
Curry David T. 155 Church
Curry Thos. 34 Whitehall
Curtin Patrick, 557 Pearl
Curtis Wm. 18 Cherry
Cuseck Joseph. 297 Bleecker
Dager Joseph W. 74 East B'way
Daley Daniel, 43 Laurens
Daly Michael, 383 Water
Daly Michael, 467 Washington
Darr John, 213 1st Av.
Davis Francis. 13 Dry Dock
Davis Henry, 75 Cherry
Davis James L. 23 James
Davis Robert, 295 3d Av.
Davis William, 261 8th Av.
Daw James, 66 James
Dawson Carson, 51 West
Dayton Francis, 220 Broadway
Dayton & Titus, 58 Leonard
Decker Charles, 76 Greenwich
Deick John W. 164 South
De Forest Catherine, 529 Pearl
Deleree Peter, Foot West 19th
　　N. R.
Delt George, 21 Av. B
Dennis Frederick, 123 Delancy
Denner John, 63 Attorney
Denman William F. 69 Vandam
Desmond John, 87 Cherry and 56
　　West
Desmond Margaret, 81 James
Deuel Thomas W. 151 3d Av.
Devine James, 92 Cross
Devine Michael, 84 Cross
Devlin F. 395 Cherry
Dewitt Cornelius, 398 West
Dieck Henry, 82 Gold
Dieck John W. 164 South and 268
　　Water
Diercks Henry. 117 Beekman
Dimond Nicholas, 9 Beaver
Dinan David, 91 James
Dodex Henry L. 174 W. 18th
Dolan Elizabeth. 115 Mulberry
Dolan John. 56 West Broadway
Dolen Patrick, 132 Anthony
Dolger Joseph, 41 Av. B
Dollard Matthew, 70 Duane
Doherty Anthony. 294 West
Dohn Jacob, 153 2d
Donaho Ann O. 80 Centre
Donaho Cornelius, 382 Water
Donahoe Andrew, 14 Orange
Donohoe Timothy, 262 Cherry
Donahue Patrick, 230½ 11th
Donehue F. 241 11th
Donald & Reorden, 47 Bayard
Donaldson Jas. 7th Av.
Donelevy John, 128 Anthony
Donelly Daniel, 132 West 16th
Donnelly A. & Co. 83 John
Donnelly Simon, 123 Anthony
Donnelly John, 386 6th
Donnelly Terence. 33 Whingt'n
Donohue F. West 25th st.
Donovan James, 57 Montgomery
Dooley Michael, 645 Greenwich
Doonan John, 122 West 20th

Doremus George, 106 Church
　　New York
Doran Hugh I. 7 6th
Doty Samuel H. 347 Bowery
Dougherty P. 70 Cherry
Dougherty Theodore, 76 South
Dosier A. & Fontan, 296 2d
Doyle James, 39 Oak
Doyle J. C. 474 Pearl
Dowd John. 212 Elizabeth
Dowd Martin, 211 Elizabeth
Dowd Philip, 26 Leonard
Dowdall John J. 20 Stone
Dowdell Henry, 63 Ann
Dowling John, 3 & 5 Wall
Downie James E. 9 Elm
Downey William, 237 E. 13th
Downing Samuel & J. 65 Dey
Doyle John, 346 12th
Doyle James, 39 Oak
Doyle John B. 6 Broad
Doyle James C. 474 Pearl
Dress Joseph, 166 3d
Dreyer Carsten, 109 6th Av.
Driscoll Cornelius. 31 Orange
Driscoll Daniel, 322 Water
Drin M. 13 Av. B
Drummond Anne, 446 Water
Drury John, 213 Elizabeth
Duckworth Nelson, 146 Maiden la
Duff Christopher, 415 10th
Duffy Andrew, 141 E. 16th
Duffy Bernard G. 560 4th
Duffy Felix, Av. A. between 12th
　　& East 13th
Duffy Patrick. 46 W. 14th
Duffy Peter. 98 Anthony
Duffy William, 276 Mott
Dugan L. 32 Willet
Dumser George. 234 5th
Duncan William, 4 Centre Market
　　place
Dunleavy Christopher, 7 Pitt
Dunn James, 129 Duane
Dunn Thomas A., W. 21st cor. 7th
　　Av.
Dunning Terrens, 57 Great James
Duplgnac William C. 738 Water
Duryee Francis, 391 Water
Duryee Jacob, 203 South
Duryer & Faulkner, 11 & 13 Ca-
　　tharine
Druyer John, 75 Robinson
Dutcher Joseph G. 178 Walker
Dwyer Elizabeth, 230 W. 17th
Dyckman Garret, 174 Grand
Eagle George, (dealer) 150 Fulton
Earl & Jackson, 98 Division
Eckert Adam, 225 Rivington
Eckle Frederick M. 330 Water
Edgar Theodore. 28 W. Broadway
Egan Edward, 205 1st Av.
Egan Thomas, 115 Cherry
Egbeatson Jacob, 34 Walnut
Egbert Joseph, 53 Hudson
Egner John, 45 Allen
Elekelmann Anthony, 60 Av. A
Eitel George M. 252 West
Elbert Matthew, 152 2d
Eldean James. 9 Little Water
Ellis Jane A. 39 Rose
Ellis John, 149 Leonard
Elois William. 9th Av.
Elsen C. L. 90 Nassau
Engelke George, 9 Essex
Eury Narcisse, 264 Water
Eppstein John, 224 Walker
Erbeg John, 160 William
Erford John, 64 Reade
Erley William, 155 Leonard
Esnow C. 225 West
Eulor Peter, 131 Washington
Evans William, 189 Reade
Evans William, 318 Spring
Ewens Catherine, 3 Little Water
Ewing William, 754 Washington
Fadagan Margaret, 402 Greenwich
Fagan James, 9th Av.
Fagan John, 215 1st Av.
Fairgreive William, 287 Front
Falkland & Duryee, 9 & 11 Cathar
Farley George 166 Cherry

Farley James, 845 Water
New York.
Farley John, 96 Cherry
Farley Laurence, June cor. West
Farquhar James, 25 Frankfort
Farrall Bernard, 171 Elizabeth
Farrer Charles, 91 South
Farrell Ann, 16 Doyer
Farrell James, 60 Hamersley
Farrenkopf Francis, 239 2d
Farrington J. D. cor. Montgomery & Front
Fashay John D. 101 6th Av.
Fay John. 33 Vesey
Fay Thomas, 508 Greenwich
Fay William, 895 Broadway
Fee Arthur, 61 Marion
Feldman Moses, 210 Houston
Feldmuller Zacaria, 78 Av. D
Felter Henry D. 569 Broadway
Fenegan James. 534 4th
Ferat German, 542 Pearl
Fernier John A. A. 323 Stanton
Ferrell John, Harlem
Ferrell John H. 134 Leonard
Fessler Adolphe, 128 Ridge
Fickey Henri, 21 Front
Field Robert, 813 Grand
Filk John, 91 Sheriff
Finck Johu F. & H. 86 Vesey
Finley Wm. 39 Canal
Finnagan James, 554 4th
Finnigan Matthew, 476 Water
Finnigin Thomas, 414 West
Finton Thomas & Co. 48 Cherry
Fisher Alexander, 97 Oliver
Fisher J. 560 4th & 257 Greenw'h
Fisher Nicholas, 85 Chrystie
Fitzgerald George. 77 James
Fitzgerald John. 63 Cherry
Fitzgerald Maria, 46 Catharine
Fitzgerald Mary, 21 Spring
Fitzgerald Patrick, 655 Water
Fitzpatrick John, 21 Spuce
Fitzpatrick Patrick, 479 Cherry
Fitzsimons E. 389 3d Av.
Fiseoke John F. 23 Albany & 3 Rector
Flach Francis A. 1 Carlisle
Flaak William, 26 Clark
Flagke J. F. 87 West
Flaherty Johanna, 23 Cherry
Flaherty Terence, 36 Roosevelt
Flannigan P. 66 4th Av.
Fletcher Charles, 225 Fulton
Fletcher Michael, 200 Elm
Fletcher Robert, 415 Cherry
Flood John, 3½ Marion
Flood Patrick, 48 Spring
Fliedner & Co. 82 Greenwich
Foley John, 390½ Pearl
Foley William, 64 Centre
Folz Frederick, 57 Av. A
Foot Edward G. 104 South
Foote Charles B. 25 Chambers
Forbes Maria, 148 Anthony
Ford Denis, 506 Greenwich
Ford Lewis S. 86 Nassau
Fort John, 84 W. Broadway
Foshay John D. 101 6th Av.
Foster Robert, 542 Pearl
Foster Samuel C. 47 Chatham
Fountain Cottage, (T. Allen) 323 3d
Fowkes Wm. 31st 10th Av.
Fowler Caleb, 305 West
Fox Francis, 111 Anthony
Fox Hugh, 90 Prince
Fox Richard, 277 Mott
Fox William, 159 W. Broadway
Foy John, 107 Anthony
Fraer George, 348 Bowery
Frank John, 163 Chrystie
Frapwall George, 681 Broadway
Frazer Thomas, 448 Water
Freel John, 103 Mulberry
Freshman George, 238 3d
Frickelton John, 192 Av. A
Friel Edward, 249 Mulberry
Fries John, 28 74 Essex
Fritz August, 163 Broome
Frohlich Richard, 101 Washington

Fullarton W. M. 9th Av.
New York.
Fulton James, 124 Anthony
Gaffney Michael, 14 Franklin
Gaffney William, 27 Whitehall
Gallagin Thomas, 736 Water
Galligan Michael, 126 Broome
Gambler R. 173 Houston
Geraghty John, 495 Pearl
Garde Edmond, 3 Catharine slip
Garden Anthony, 213 2d
Gardiner A. 9d st.
Gardiner Catharine, 133 Monroe
Garrick Patrick. 27 Cross
Garrick Timothy, 23 Chatham
Gartland James, 226 Stanton
Gassert John L. 198 Hester
Gatley Wm., W. 15th cor. 10th Av.
Geary Matthew, 23 Willet
Geiger Caspar, 282 3d
Geiger Valentine, 127 Ridge
Geiger & Leicken. 23 Beaver
Geiser William, 191 Av. B
Geisler Frederick, 31 Albany
Gelleg Q. 156 3d
Gellmartin John, 159 Anthony
Gemmecker Geo. & Co. 23 Av. B.
George William, 205 Varick
Geraghty John, 46 Centre & 495 Pearl
Geubharth Louis, 187 3d Av.
Geyer Jacob, 210 Houston
Gibbins Geo. 93 Bowery
Gibney Patrick, 266 E. 13th
Gilbert Chas. 22 Morris
Gill Jas. 17 4th Av.
Giller Montgom. E. 204 Bleecker
Gillfeather Mary, 39 Centre
Gilleas Owen, 127 Mott
Gilligan Peter, 174 W. 20th
Gilligan Thos. 736 Water
Gillig Geo. 156 3d
Gillman Fred. 35 Av. A
Gilmartin & Boland. 272 Henry
Gilroy Edward, 66 Cross
Gilroy John, 1st Av.
Gilroy Patrick, 164 Anthony
Gilroy Wm. 298 Av. A
Girgan John, 85 W. 18th
Glass David, 110 3d Av.
Goebill Geo. H. 140 Delancy
Gold & Blauvelt, 88 W. Br'dway
Golden B. 351 3d Av.
Goldsmith Solomon, 155 Norfolk
Good Thos. 20 5th
Goodwin John T. F. 79 Allen
Goodman Mary, 671 Hudson
Gorman Mrs. 441 Washington
Gould Geo. 32 Houston
Graaft Isaac H. 14 South
Graham E. cor. Varick & Canal
Graham John, 37 Av. D
Graham Richard, 15 Oak
Graham Wm. 80 9th Av.
Grate Herman, 135 Av. C
Grattan Jas. 109 Orange
Graves John, 343½ Water
Gray David T. 155 Duane
Gray Lawrence, 163 Leonard
Gray P. 308 3d Av.
Gredley John, 395 West
Green Catherine, 42 Walnut
Green M. D. & W. Madden, 188 Chatham
Greeman Thos. 206 W. 16th
Greene Jas. 157 Anthony
Greget Sylvester, 7 Albany
Greig Jas. jr. 407 Grand
Gress Jos. 195 3d
Gruenewald L. 8th Av.
Grundmann John F. 96 Market
Griffen Chas. 396 Water
Griffin Geo. C. 443 Hudson
Griffin Patrick, 4 N. William
Griggs Aaron H. 254 4th
Grimm Jos. 39 Av. B
Groh Martin, 101 Delancy
Gugisperg D. 66 Av. B
Gulich Adam, 79 Bowery
Gunning John, 23 4th Av.
Gunning T. 57 Great Jones
Gunter J. L. 5 Rector

Guntrum John, 194 Division
New York.
Gurlach Carl, 1 Centre market pl
Gutfleisch Leon, 445 3d
Guth Martin, 191 Rivington
Hackett John, 42 Allen
Hackett Wm. 103 6th Av.
Hadden Thos. 66 Cherry
Hadfield John, 247 Canal
Haensler Bernard, Av. A between 12th & 13th
Handley Patrick, 143 Washington
Haeys Jeremiah, 76 Henry
Haghan John, 313 8th
Haight Townsend D. 195 Bowery
Haisch M. 291 2d
Hajenbacher Fred. 68 Greenwich
Halligan James, 356 Water
Halligan Matthew, 81 6th Av.
Hallisey Patrick. 12 Washington
Hallenbeck Abraham H. 106 Warren
Hallesey Ellen, 837 Water
Halpin James C. 168 & 224 9th Av.
Halpin Michael, 19 Morris
Haley Wm. 386 Water
Hamerschmitt Martin, 13 Chrystie
Hammel Conrad, 590 Grand
Hammer John, 130 Greenwich
Hamilton Amos, Hoboken st.
Hamilton John R. 17 Coenties slip
Hamilton Wm. 647 Washington
Hammond Daniel F. 364 6th Av.
Hammond Jacob, 9th Av.
Hamsted Martin, 288 Pearl
Hanagan Michael, 244 West 16th
Handel ——, 221 3d
Hanfield Henry, 277 South
Hanlan John, 39 Laurens
Hanly Patrick, 142 Washington
Hanly William, 428 Water
Hannan John, 28 9th Av.
Hannan William, 190 East 224
Hanryt James, 273 Mott
Herman Adam, 506 Pearl
Hargrove George, 48 Roosevelt
Haring Wm. 66 Greenwich
Harknan James, 65 King
Harriot George, 111 Walker
Harrington James, 304 Mott
Harris George B. 348 Water
Harris J. 187 Canal
Harris Julia, 63 Lispenard
Harrison Arthur, 179 Chatham
Harrison Wm. 294 West
Harrison & Haal, 154 Church
Hart David B. 48 Houston
Hart Henry, 10 John
Hart Patrick, 39 Marion
Hartley Mary, 50 James
Hartman Frederick, 164 Delancy
Hartmann Herman, 119 Cedar
Hartung Philip, 157 Washington
Hasenbucker F. 68 Greenwich
Haslem Joseph, 8th Av.
Hasbell Charles, 101 Broome
Hauck Adam, 481 Broome
Hausknacht Nicholas, 185 West 19th
Havens Charles S. East c. Broome
Hawke Andrew H. 277 Front
Haydon Elizabeth, 76 Chambers
Hayes Mary, 212 Centre
Hays Ellen, 33 James
Hayward George, 187 6th Av.
Heyward John N. 602 Broadway
Heald Henry, 2 Front
Healey Michael, 697½ Greenwich
Healey Cornelius, 54 Prince
Heaney John, 42 Prince
Heaselden Elias, 122 Varick
Heckman Charles, 243 3d
Hefferns Mary H. 78 James
Heins George, 100 do
Heindl Francis J. 65 Beekman
Heller Carl, 233 Centre
Hinemen W. 155 2d
Held William, 163 2d
Heitman Henry, 2 William
Hembaier Francis, 244 Walker
Hemmons George, 124 Lewis
Hemstadt Charles, 288 Pearl

Hemstedt Marten, 288 Pearl
New York.
Hendrickson Townsend, South
cor. Clinton
Heney Bernard, 242 Cherry
Henry Patrick, 41 Centre
Henry Paul, 47   do
Heppner Joseph. 222 Stanton
Herbert Charles C. 39 Chambers
Herbert Oliver, 201 3d Av.
Herman Henry, 215 Stanton
Hermann Adam. 806 Pearl
Hethcoth Hulse, 303 Front cor.
Gouverneur
Hewlett Devine, 57 Whitehall
Hickey Owen, 8th Av
Hickman John J. 167 Chatham
Hicks John, 200 South
Higham John, 29 Vesey
Higgins John, 313 8th
Higgins Obadiah, 189 Canal
Hill James R. 21 Catharine slip
Hillebrand Francis, 170 Hester .
Hilligan M. 31 6th Av.
Billink Frederick, 143 Barrow
Hinch P. 8th Av.
Hind Thomas, 49 Clarkson & 603
Greenwich
Hines Thomas, 86 Centre
Hoeft J. & C. Olandt, 187 South
Hodgman Mrs. Harlem
Hoey John, 172 8th Av.
Hogan Felix, 194 Chambers
Hogan James, 1 Catharine
Hok August, 28 Ludlow
Holbrook Gideon, 6 Chrystie
Holland William, 246 South
Holling Charles. 115 W. 18th
Holst John H. 109 Cherry
Honey Hugh, 93 Greene
Hood Nathaniel, 111 Mulberry
Hook Benjamin, 12 South
Hook John, 270 Grand
Hoope John, 452 Broadway
Hopkins Eleazer, 87 Nassau
Horn Frantz, 13 Franklin
Horn Michael, 290 Elizabeth
Hosseus Frederick, 228 Broome
Hotta Hermenn, 128 Hester
Heuser Nicholas, 133 3d
Houston Isaac, 86 James
Howard Robert, 134 Mercer
Howell William J. 78 Ann
Howell & M'Cormick, 450 Broad-
way
Hof Jacob, 16 Centre
Hubener A. 532 Bowery
Huber Francis A. 117 Walker
Huber Joseph, 224 3d
Huber Leonard, 14 Frankfort
Hudson Augustus. 44 Houston
Hughes Daniel, 654 Water
Hughes John. 286 Av. A
Hughes John. 384 Cherry
Hughes Patrick, 86 do
Hulburt Henry P. 64 Lispenard
Hull William, 61 Bowery
Hullay Patrick, 8 6th
Humphrey Jacob B. 81 Pike slip
Humphreys William S. 43 Cham-
bers
Hunt Humphrey, 81 Broome
Hunter Mary A. 208 Centre
Hunter Robert, 375 Cherry
Huntington Chester, 31 and 33
Chambers & 209 Hudson
Hurley P. 3 6th
Hurley Dennis, 394 Water
Hurrell Elizabeth, 25 Oak
Hussey Edward M. 36 Oliver
Hussey Peter, 96 Willet
Huston James, 708 Washington
Huxley John, 10 Dey
Inglis & Dougherty, 46 Centre
Ingraham Samuel, 123 Roosevelt
Ireland John, 27 New
Irvin John. 25th st. 9th Av.
Irving Thomas, 26 do
Irwin Thomas S. 319 Water
Isinger Henry, 227 Broome
Jack John, 340 Water
Jackson John, 60 Oliver

Jacobs Henry, 37 Av. A
Jacobs William H. 326 West
Jarger J. 231 13th
Jarvis William D. 410 Grand
Jeankroh John, 231 W. 17th
Jenkins Thomas F. 190 West
Jenks Willard & E. 139 Av. D
Jennings Richard, 183 South
Jewell Peter, 288 6th Av.
Jewell W. H. 420 West
Jewell & Hubert, 247 West
Jillard John. jr. 67 Cherry
John William, 25 Av. B
Johnson Abraham P. 423 West
Johnson Charles, 94 Cherry
Johnson David, 9 Av. D
Johnson Isaac, 351 Spring
Johnson John, 877 Broadway
Johnson John, 163 Mulberry
Johnson Mary, 16 Oliver
Johnson Peter, 54 Cherry
Johnson T. 55 Bowery
Johnson William, 60 West
Johnston Oliver, 41 Market
Jones Edward, 769 Broadway
Jones Edward D. 125 Pitt
Jones George. 299 Front
Jones James, 243 Walker
Kaga John, 216 Elizabeth
Kain John, 72 Elm
Kaman Frederick, 249 South
Kamp Bernard, 34 Houston & 383
Greenwich
Kane Patrick, 13 Park Row
Kanna James, 193 Lewis
Karns Terry, 31 James
Karst A. 217 12th
Kattenstroth Henry, 93 Pine
Kautz Jacob. 23 James
Kass Anthony. 28 Av. B
Kane James, 472 Pearl
Kavanagh Jas. 597 Greenwich
Kearns Michael, 2 Franklin
Keating Thomas, 4 Cottage pl.
Keegan William, 74 Mulberry
Keeland John, 1 West
Keen Washburn A. 291 Grand
Keever John, 235½ 16th
Keenan Wm. 8th Av.
Keller John H. 355 Houston
Keller P. 63 Av. C
Kelley Edward, 181 Av. C
Kelley John, 196 Anthony
Kelley Michael, 178 Laurens
Kelley Thomas, 174 11th
Kellinger Samuel, 290 Broome
Kelly J. Constantine, 429 B'way
Kelly Daniel, 11 Dry Dock
Kelly Daniel, 481 Washington
Kelly David. 487 Washington
Kelly Dominick, 38 Hamersley
Kelly Francis, 101 Fulton
Kelly Francis. 943 11th
Kelly James. 291 West 16th
Kelly John, 197 West
Kelly John, 16 Monroe
Kelly Michael, 599 Washington
Kelly Patrick, 292 West 16th
Kelly P. 385 6th
Kelly Rose, 7 6th
Kemf Henry, 132 Greenwich
Kenley John, 944 Cherry
Kenndaly Michael, 54 Cross
Kenna Edward, 253 Washington
Kennedy Morgan, 107 Cherry
Kennedy B. 350 1st Av.
Kenney Owen, 116 Clinton pl. &
15 6th
Kenny James, 21 Duane
Kensett George, 498 Pearl
Kanny Robert, 348 4th Av.
Keough Catharine, 89 James
Keogan P. East 22d
Kern Mrs. 265 Bowery
Kerrigan Michael, 2 Centre
Kerrigan William, 202 Amos
Kersmer Joseph, 10 Walnut
Ketcham Henry. 98 Waverley pl.
Ketcham Thomas, 16 West
Kiedel Gotlieb, 103 Liberty

Kiefer Christian, 126 Greenwich
New York.
Kiernan J. 460 12th
Kiernan Margaret, 44 Elizabeth
Kiernan Thomas, 86 Sullivan
Kiernan William, 83 Cross
Kiessling Peter. 171 Av. A
Killer George. 172 6th Av.
Killigan Mary, 84 24th
Kilkenny James. 121 11th
Kinelay John, 344 Cherry
King Ebenezer A. 218 Fulton
King Michael, 7 & 9 Washington
King William, 206 Grand
King & Annan, 83 Pine
Kinney Owen, 15 6th
Kinselle Thos. cor. Goerck & 14
sts.
Kimpf John, 4 Walnut
Kipp Charles T. 535 Hudson
Kirchof Jacob, 96 W. 16th
Kirchof Peter. 120 7th Av.
Kirwin John, 235½ W. 16th
Kirwin Patrick. 264 Mott
Kisier John, 9 Walnut
Kissell N. 144 3d
Kittler John, 115 Delancy
Kivlin John, 36 Mulberry
Klearich Frederick, 107 Rivington
Kleinlein J. 187 Av. B
Kling George, 142 Stanton
Kloppenburg John, 125 Av. D
Knack Henry, 103 Washington
Knapp David S. 339 Spring
Knight Mrs. 376 Water
Knighton William, 187 Canal
Knobeloch Christian. 255 3d Av.
Knibloch Daniel, 229 Division
Koch John, 73 Ludlow
Kohlsledt ——, 65 Greenwich
Kopp John, 12 Essex
Koser Lewis, 96 Maiden lane
Kreiger Ludwig, 205 Delancy
Krollner N. 146 3d
Krusee Henry. 105 Centre
Kunz Ignotz, 66 Mott
Kyle Thomas, 526 West
La Croix F. C. 21 Coenties slip
Lager L. 281 E. 13th
Lahey Charles, 445 Washington
Lahy F. 234 12th
Lalin Charles, 53 Vesey
Lambercht Gregory, 464 Water
Lander Heary, 144 Division
Lander John, 16 Av. A
Lander Valentine, 131 Clinton
Landweber Joseph. 70 Mulberry
Lang Christian, 30 E. 20th
Langan John, 88 Cross
Langnecker Adam, 94 Albany
La Rochelle John B. 90½ Murray
Larp Thomas, 209 Elizabeth
Latham E. 102 Houston
Laity Richard, 33 Bowery
Lauxmenn John G. 20 Delancy
Lawler Mrs. 476 Greenwich
Lawler John, 60 Mulberry
Lawlor Robert, 61 Cross
Lawrence Alex. C. 158 West
Lawrence William W. 277 Water
Leach Thomas, 59 Houston
Leahy Charles, 445 Washington
Leary William. 101 W. Broadway
Lebe Henry, 24 Coenties slip
Ledwich James, 543 Houston
Ledwith James, 19th st. bet. Avs.
A & B
Lee Bernard, 343 E. 19th
Leo Hugh, 8 Elm
Lee James, 300 Greenwich
Lee John, 54 Centre
Lee J. & Co. 51 Washington
Lee Thomas, 12 Broome
Leedeman & Freudthal, 1 G'wich
Leffel Philip, 602 4th
Lefurge Catharine, 206 Canal
Leis John, 59 Crosby
Lehhlin John, 47 Av. A
Leo Daniel, 3 Whitehall
Leon A. & Co. 97 Duane
Leonard Patrick, 558 Greenwich
Leubroussart Louis, 34 3d Av.

Lester Mary, 90 Madison
New York.
Lewis Morris, 375 West
Lewis Richard, 241 South
Lewis Sarah, 4 Roosevelt
Lies Ludwig. 201 Houston
Linder Christian, 70 Av. B
Little Isaac, 426 West
Little Robert. 393 West
Lloyd Geo. H. & Cudney, 2 Gouverneur
Lochlin Thos. 39 Orange
Lockwood Timothy, 691 4th
Loflis Francis, 162 Washington
Loftus Patrick, 44 Orange
Loffel P. 602 4th
Logan Michael J. 31 Depeyster
Logue Patrick, 88 4th Av.
Longinotto Paul & Co. 489 Washington
Looke Rodney W. 59 Whitehall
Losee Albert, 232 Bowery
Lovejoy Chas. H. 143 Mercer
Lovett Robert, 279 Water
Lowe Patrick, 2 Bleecker
Low Wm. 12½ Albany
Lowerre Giles H. 58 Cherry
Lucas John, 196 Centre
Ludemann Henry, 1 Greenwich
Luna Patrick, 6 Moore
Lutz Christopher, 65 Norfolk
Lusk Bridget, 212 Mott
Lych & Bourke, 9 6th Av.
Lynch Hugh, 155 Troy
Lynch Margaret, 200 Varick
Lynch Mary A. 7 Frankfort
Lynch John, 97 James
Lynch Patrick, 222 Elizabeth
Lynch Patrick. 135 Mott
Lynch Wm. 585 Washington
Lyons Catharine, 215 Stanton
Lyons Wm 26 Prince
M'Aardle E. 502 Greenwich
M'Antee John, 199 Elm
M'Alarney ——, 141 16th
M'Aree ——, 473 Washington
M'Auley Jas. 39 Washington
M'Bride John, W. 26th st.
M'Cabe Andrew, 270 Mott
M'Cabe B. 397 3d Av.
M'Cabe Mary, 646 Water
M'Cabe Patrick, 286 E. 18th
M'Cabe Philip, 232 Elizabeth
M'Cabe Thos. 260 Mott
M'Cann C., E. 27th st.
M'Cann Bernard, 220 Mott
M'Cann John, 237 E. 13th
M'Carthy Michael, 14 Thompson
M'Carthy Thos. 388 West
M'Cartin Patrick, 224 Mulberry
M'Cay C. 44 Washington
M'Chesney Alex. 144 Walker
M'Clelland John, 165 8th Av.
M'Cluskey A. 455 1st Av.
M'Collum B. 635 Washington
M'Collum Hector, 654 Greenwich
M'Combs Margaret, 31 James
M'Connell John, 128 W. 19th
M'Cormick M. 102 Washington
M'Cormick Patrick, 244 Mott
M'Cormick Patrick, 25 Marion
M'Cormick Samuel, 17 Jacob
M'Cosker Bernard, 286 11th
M'Coy Gabriel B. 271 South
M'Dermott John T. 223 Delancy
M'Dermott ——, 66 Cherry
M'Donald Alexander, 124 Mott
M'Donald John, 533 Pearl, and 92 Centre
M'Donald Michael, 126 10th Av.
M'Donald Stephen, 87 Sheriff
M'Donald Thomas, 204 Varick
M'Donnell Peter, 130 Anthony
M'Donough Barney, 583 Wash.
M'Donough James, 151 Chatham
M'Elhill Thomas, 385 8th
M'Elroy Patrick, 422 West
M'Enroe Hugh, 194 Varick
M'Eroe John, 68 Pitt
M'Evoy Martin, 126 Broad
M'Fadden George R. 236 Division
M'Gee Michael, 345 Stanton

M'Ghan Peter, 541 Washington
New York.
M'Ginnis James, 303 Water
M'Ginney Henry, 206 7th
M'Girr James, 157 West
M'Giveny John, 30 Jay
M'Givney P. 24 Av.
M'Goirk William, 491 Pearl
M'Govern Edward, 190 Anthony
M'Govern Edward. 170 Cherry
M'Govern James, 68 E. Broadway
M'Govern William, 117 Washing.
M'Gowan Bartley, 97 Orange
M'Gowan Bridget, 29 Cross
M'Gowan Lawrence, 69 King
M'Gran Ann. 156 4th
M'Grath Frances, 352 Pearl
M'Grath John, 397 9th
M'Grath John, 66 Division
M'Groth Michael, 147 Duane
M'Guaniss ——, 152 4th
M'Guirk Andrew, 168 2d
M'Guire John. 422 9th
M'Guire John, 300 1st Av.
M'Guire John, 207 1st Av.
M'Guire Patrick, 162 Forsyth
M'Guire Thomas, 16 Spring
M'Henry James. 115 Roosevelt
M'Hugh Charles, 472 4th
M'Hugh John, 163 Anthony
M'Intyre Michael T. 47 Marion
M'Kee B. 357 Cherry
M'Keever Ann, 296 W. 17th
M'Kiernan Patrick, 294 W. 17th
M'Kiernan T. 59 9th Av.
M'Kenna James, 394 Cherry
M'Kenna Peter, 7 Howard
M'Kenna Thomas. 44 Hester
M'Kinley J. 102 Centre
M'Kenzie John, 17 10th Av.
M'Knight William, 508 Greenwich
M'Lain John. 208 Elizabeth
M'Laughlin Dennis, 197 E. 13th
M'Laughlin Eliza, 12 James
MacLin Ellen, 279 Mulberry
M'Lroy P. 422 West
M'Mahon Andrew, 76 King
M'Mahon Patrick, 453 13th
M'Millan Reynolds, 30 Old slip & 64 Cherry
M'Manus Hannah, 243 W. 16th
M'Manus Michael, 368 South
M'Nally M. 164 11th
M'Namee Owen, 96 W. 16th
M'Neckney Patrick, 90 Cherry
M'Peck Dennis, 128 4th
M'Pherson Alex. & Co. 306 Hester
M'Quinn Charles, 214 W. 16th
M'Ruith David, 47 9th Av.
M'Swinsy Edward, 710 4th
Mack John, 219 Stanton
Mack Peter, 81 Sullivan
Mack Patrick, 90 Cherry
Mackey Elbert H. 94 Vesey
Mackintaggart Edward, 42 Orange
Macrae Michael, 473 Washington
Madden John, 46 Prince
Madden & Green, 188 Chatham
Magee William & James M'Nulty, 210 Chatham
Mager Valentine, 101 Elizabeth
Magnar Patrick, 121 Cherry
Maguire Charles, 391 Greenwich
Maguire Bernard & Jas. 68 Prince
Mahaffy Francis, 90 James
Mahar Lawrence, 97 Cherry
Mahony James, 168 Greene
Mahony P. 454 12th
Maillie John P. 89 Houston
Makelm John, 299 Mott
Malone Charles, 163 Av. C
Maloney Mary, 52 Prince
Maloy James, 49 Laurens
Mangil John, 245 Front
Manjort A. 96 Duane
Mannion Dennis, 131 Liberty
Manster Henry. 145 Greenwich
Mansuy Joseph, 556 Pearl
Marchant J. 96 Crosby
Marren Patrick. 219 Centre
Marrin Philip. 335 1st Av.
Marshall George 10 Depeyster

Marshall George, 45 Spring
New York.
Marshall Henry, 391 Bowery
Marshall Square, 591 Hudson
Martens H. A. 4 Catharine slip
Marthaws Bernard, 17 Prince
Martin Aristide, 94 Church
Martin Ellen, 147 Duane
Martin Patrick, 202 Chambers
Martin Patrick, 231 W. 21st
Martin Thomas, 228 16th
Martin & Smith, 207 Duane
Martins Claus. 18 West
Mason James L. Harlem
Mason John. 49 Whitehall
Mason John, 138 Av. D
Mason Nehemiah. 104 South
Mason Robert, 26th st.
Mason & Foote. 1 South
Masterson Michael, 441 Washing.
Matthew Alexander, 364 G'wich
Matthews Thomas, 17 Laurens
Maurer & Co. 243 3d
Maurey Peter, 193 William
Mausher Hermann, 47 West
Maulton John H. 15 Sheriff
May S. & Nosbaum, 215 2d
Maybury Henry, 32 Platt
Mayer John & Co. 45 West
Mayersw B. A. 65 Barclay
Maxwell Alex. 642 Greenwich
Mead H. 76 Cherry
Medal William, 2 Gouverneur slip
Meehan Austin, 261 West
Meehan James, 12th st.
Megahey James, 514 Water
Mohan Mary, 309 West
Meinzer Jacob, 289 Rivington
Meier Caspar H. 89 Washington
Meisgerber F. 171 3d
Meir Ludwig, 104 West 17th
Meuser Henry, 76 Liberty
Melville Philip G. 38 Centre
Melvin Robert H. 299 Front
Melvin Mrs. 71 Cherry
Menge Henrick, 599½ Pearl
Merten H. A. 4 Catharine slip
Merian Louis & Co. 197 William
Merkle C. 275 6th
Meyer Dederich, 63 Vesey
Meyer Henry, 66 West
Meyer John D. South cor. Dover
Meyer & Druecker, 314 Pearl
Meyers Frederick, 149 Greenw'h
Millard Philemon. 527 Grand
Milleman Frederick, 879 Broadway
Miller Abraham, 569 Hudson
Miller A. 230 3d
Miller David, 3 Burling slip
Miller Hans, 219 Water
Miller Henry W. 28 New
Miller Isabella, 17 Spruce
Miller J. P. 89 Houston
Miller John, 116 8th
Miller Peter, 23 Rector
Miller Thos. 5 Greenwich Av.
Miles Joseph, Mott cor. Walker
Miles Mary, 236 Water
Mills John, 271½ Water
Mills John T. 7 Centre Market place & 271½ Walker
Minme John, 240 Greenwich
Mimnagns John. 145 11th
Minehy Philip, 34 Ludlow
Miner Wm. 23 Park row
Minicke Charles, 159 9th
Mitchell J D. R. 138 Cherry
Mitchell Louis, 3 Mulberry
Mitchell Peter, 19 Peck slip
Mogher John, 42 Hester
Moll Andre, W. 23d bot. 6th & 7th Avs.
Molloy Jas. 350 1st Av.
Monaghan O. 45 Washington
Monaghan Thomas, 271 Stanton
Monaghan Wm. 13 Washington
Monahan Patrick. 279 Mott
Mons Edward, 344 Monroe
Moore John, 74 Grand
Moore Wm. 27 Washington
Moorehead James, 70 Bayard
Morahan Hugh, 19 Cherry

Moran Isaac A. 167 3d Av. *New York.*
Moran John, 67 Oliver
Moran Martin, 430 Water
Morans John, 155 3d Av.
More Henry, 248 3d
Morgan Charles, 247 8th Av.
Morgan Francis, 8 Gouverneur sl.
Morgan M. 490 Water
Morgan Wm. B. 469 Broome
Moriarty Florence, 37 Stone
Morissey James, 36 Madison
Moriath Jacob, 23 Elizabeth
Moser George, 33 Pitt
Mott & Perkinson. Mangin cor. Rivington
Motz P. 176 3d
Muckleraith David, 154 Leonard
Maggieworth Wm. 26 West
Mahlhaeuser I. 231 Division
Muhren Peter, 55 Cherry
Mulaan Patrick, 54 Mulberry
Mulleder M. 469 Washington
Mullen Edward, 239 12th
Mullen Edward, 15 Peck slip
Mullen James, 45 Jay
Muller N. 220 3d
Muller Wm. 281 Liberty
Mulligan Cath. 12th bet. Avs. A & B
Mulligan M. 25th st.
Mullin Peter, 240 Cherry
Mulvey ——, 2 Front
Mulvey Elizabeth, 36½ Orange
Mulvihal Francis, 229 Elizabeth
Mulvihill Patrick, 117 Orange & 67 Mulberry
Munley Charles, 146 6th Av.
Munoz Peter L. 322 Broadway
Munson George. 17 Thomas
Murley Chas. 146 6th Av.
Murphy Ann. 119 Mulberry
Murphy D. 199 1st Av.
Murphy James, 242 1st Av.
Murphy John, 20 Roosevelt
Murphy John, 62 Cross
Murphy Martin, 24 Albany
Murphy Patrick, 155 Orange
Murphy Walter, 111 Av. D
Murray Michael, 5 Washington
Murray Owen, 245 W. 16th
Murray P. 2d Av.
Murray Richard, 30 Whitehall
Murtagh Bernard, 177 Hester
Muther Michael, 28 Prince
Myer Michael, 73 Allen
Myer Wm. 49 Nassau
Myor & Drucker, 314 Pearl
Myers Augustus, 564 Pearl
Myers Henry, 192 West
Nager John & Co. 201 2d
Nanry Charles M. 6 Depeyster
Nanston James, 640 Greenwich
Nathan Joseph, 66 Suffolk
Nawsome Elizabeth, 97 Reade
Neslis Thomas, 147 Leonard
Neary Michael, 22 Stone
Nebur Conrad, 72 W. 17th
Nealy James M. 514 Water
Nelle John F. 214 W. 21st
Nelson Charles, 105 Washington
Nelson Jane, 272 Water
Nesbit & Cornell, 72 Elm
Nesseler Joseph A. 176 Division
Neu Charles, 123 Chrystie
Neuheuser Anthony, 146 Broome
Neumager Christian, 220 Rivington
Newhall W. P. 8th Av.
Newman Abraham, 839 Bro'dway
Newsome Jacob, 320 Hudson
Newstadt & Heller, 233 Centre
Nisler Joseph, 176 Division
Nixon Abraham, 14 Washington
Noble John, 24th st.
Nolan Charles, 246 Houston
Norris L. 400 10th
Northrop Absalom, 49 Bowery
Noyes Wm. C. 43 Washington
Nugent Thomas, 57 Pike
Nusbaum Bernard, 215 2d
Nyhan John 233 Chrystie

Oakes W. 10 Mulberry *New York.*
Oakley Jacob F. 340 Pearl
Oates Patrick, 104 Anthony
Oberle A. 47 Laurens
O'Brahm Daniel, 54 Monroe
O'Brien David, 456 12th
O'Brien Dennis, 207 Elizabeth
O'Brien Isabella. 231 Stanton
O'Brien James. 162 W. Broadway
O'Brien John, 113 Washington
O'Brien John, 39 Madison
O'Brien Tarrance, 36 Spring
O'Brien Thaddeus, 922 Broadway
O'Brien Thos. 32d st. c. 16th Av.
O'Brien Thos. H. 37 Burling slip
O'Callahan Bernard, 104 Cross
Oche Joseph. 349 Grand
O'Clancy John, 9 Centre mkt
O'Conell John, E. 25th st.
O'Connell John, 314 E. 9th
O'Connor Dennis, 200 10th
O'Connor John, 106 Anthony
O'Connor Mary, 77 Cortlandt
O'Conner Mary, 83 6th Av.
O'Conor Wm. 436 Monroe
O'Donnell Bridget, 29 Washington
O'Donnel Francis B. 120 10th Av.
O'Donoheu Timothy, 362 Cherry
O'Harra ——, 37 Orange
O'Hara Stephen, 272 Mott
O'Hair Terence, 665 Washington
O'Hare Bridget, 156 W. 17th
O'Kane John, 192 Av. B
O'Keefe Henry, 100 Bayard
Olvany James. 277 Division
O'Mahoney James, 86 Centre
O'Mahony Mary, 110 Centre
O'Meary ——, 162 Elm
O'Neal James, 165 Mulberry
O'Neil Edward, 147 Orange
O'Neil John C. 20 Orange
O'Neill James. 282½ Bowery
O'Neil Jeremiah, 366 Water
O'Neil Peter, 151 Amos
O'Neil Peter. 667 Washington
O'Neil Philip, 24 4th Av.
O'Niell Daniel, 40 Prince
O'Reilly Martin, 370 Water
O'Reilly ——, 422 3d Av.
O'Rourke James F. 406 Broome
O'Sullivan D. 75 Cherry
Oram Wm. 138½ Cherry
Organ John, 23 Rose
Orpen John, 76 Centre
Orr Joseph. 467 Greenwich
Osborn Henry, 63 Whitehall
Ostrom Axel, 58 Roosevelt
Owens James, 145 Orange
Owens Thomes, 216 Centre
Ox George, 108 Delancy
Page John, 251 West
Paige David S. 293 West
Palm Adam, 7th Av.
Palmer John, 202 8th Av.
Palmer Samuel, 186 West
Papen Christopher, 19 West
Parce Sarah, 22 Walnut
Parker Patrick, 74 Cherry
Parker W. 53 Cherry
Parker Wm. 122 Greenwich Av.
Parker Wm., W. 13th cor. Greenwich Av.
Parkhurst A. 376 Water
Pastor Cornelia, 303 Broadway
Paterson Robert, 81 W. 18th
Patterson Thomes, 903 Canal
Pattulin David, 95 Duane
Paxton Joseph, 30 Spring
Peal John A. 108 Vesey
Pearsall Samuel H. 20 Houston
Pearsall Uriah, 310 Water
Pearsall & Whiley, E. 16th bet. Avs. B & C
Peeling George, 9th Av.
Peck William, 9th Av & 87 Cherry
Peitz Joseph, 13 Mott
Pelsang Martin, 241 Broome
Pender Edward, 474 Water
Perkins J. H. 56 Division
Perry Frederick, 421 Broadway
Perry John, 22 Walnut
Perry John O. 269 Grand

Peters John, 220 Division *New York.*
Peterson Hans E. 257 Water
Peterson John, 120 Church
Petrie Francis, 296 Av. A
Petit Alexander, 215 Canal
Petty Joseph, 87 Washington
Pfeffer John, 74 Ann
Pfefferkorn Frederick, 562 Pearl
Pfeifer Frederick, 106 Ludlow
Phelan John, 50 Cherry
Pheeley John, 51 Cross
Philbin Michael, 100 Centre
Picard A. 203 Houston
Pierce Richard, 15 Dover
Pierson Joseph, 50 Frankfort
Pilkington Richard, 450 Water
Pinkerton William F. 351 Water
Pittfield Charles R. 6 Amity
Place John R. 343 Spring
Platt Richard H. 35 Bowery
Plunkett P. W. 77 Washington
Plunkett Thomas, 317 Water
Poetz John C. 40 Elm
Poland Mary, 513 Water
Pollock D. 9 Chatham
Pollock John, 400½ 10th
Polte Frederick, 31 Bowery
Poosell P. 44 Vesey
Port John C. 159 Broome
Porter James, 84 W. 16th
Porter James, 25 Laurens
Potter R. W. 686 Water & 62 Walnut
Powell Mrs. Jane, Harlem
Power John, 156 Maiden lane
Powers William P. 76 Prince
Prag Marte, 231 William
Priestly John. 243 Division
Prior Hugh, 286 W. 17th
Provost William, 214 West
Pugh James. 344 Water
Pultz Morgan H. 167 Christopher
Purcell Henry, 40 Cherry
Purcell Patrick, 44 Vesey
Purdy Elijah H. 25 West
Pusseddu Pasquale, 153 Fulton
Quale Robert, 88 Oliver
Quin James, 114 Centre
Quinn John, 98 Elizabeth
Quinn Margaret, 238 1st Av.
Quirk Patrick, 37 Ann
Robertson Thomas, 44 Canal
Radley John B., W. 39th st.
Raeb Christopher, 113 Cedar
Rafter James, 401 West
Rally Christopher, 494 G.wich
Rau Adolphus, 50 Broadway
Raynolds John, 248 Mulberry
Reatter Joseph & Co. 22 do
Reddington Anthony, 68 4th Av.
Redmond Alex'r, 130 W. 15th
Regan James, 18 Whitehall
Regan J., E. 22d bet. 2d & 3d Avs.
Regan Mary, 125 Roosevelt
Reed John & Co. 201 South
Reed Robert, 569 Grand
Rees James, 11 Thames
Reichert Jacob, 256 Walker
Reil Thomas, 37 Laurens
Reilly Ann, 29 Roosevelt
Reilly Edward, 44 W. 13th
Reilly James, 37 Mulberry
Reilly Lawrence, 135½ do
Reilly M. 173 Laurens
Reilly Patrick, 114 Cedar
Reilly Thomas, 378 Houston
Reilly & O'Donnel, E. 16th cor 1st Av.
Reily Thomas, 275 Mott
Reily T. Harlem
Reineking Friedrick, 55 Mott
Reinhardt J. G. & Co. 21 Av. B
Reitschwerdt J. F. 162 Attorney
Repper Frederick, 196 Houston
Reynolds Timothy. 71 W. 17th
Rice Thomas, 31 Chatham
Richard M. cor. 8th
Richards Jane, 14 Oak
Richards John, 343 Water
Richardson Wm. 110 Perry & 781 Greenwich

Richey Robert, 165 Washington
New York.
Rickard Michael, 131 Av. C
Rickard Thomas, 576 Grand
Riley E. 44 13th
Riley James, 260 W. 17th
Riley John, 61 W. 18th
Riley Michael, 243 W. 16th
Riley M. 149 Crosby
Riley Peter, 58 W. Broadway
Riley Owen. 113 Orange
Riley Patrick. 148 2d
Riley Patrick, 108 W. 19th
Riley Terrance, 11th st. bet. Avs.
E & B
Riley Thomas, 193 Varick
Riley Thomas, 190 Church
Rily Owen, 3 Marion
Ring J. 93 Cherry & 586 Pearl
Rinz Joseph, 536   do
Robertson Alex. 106 G'wich Av.
Robertson James, 17 W. B'dway
Robertson Thomas, 44 Canal
Robinson James, 26 10th Av.
Robinson John R. 269 Front
Robinson Joseph, 200 W. 16th
Robinson T. 13 Broome
Robinson William, 62 Greenwich
Rode Frederick G. 63 James
Rodgers Benjamin, 606 Grand
Rodman Sarah. 31 Walnut
Roebuck J., W. 27th st.
Roehm H. 145 Stanton
Roff & Bernard, 100 Elizabeth
Rogers Charles, 150 Leonard
Rogers Joseph. 293 Bleecker
Rogers & Hebbeard, 181 Bowery
Rogers John, 170 Division
Rohen Patrick, 39 Vesey
Rohle Henry, 205½ Fulton
Rohn Caspar, 184 2d
Romer William, 20 Walnut
Romayne Michael, 99 Roosevelt
Roonsy John, 221 Mott
Rooney B. 13 Chambers
Rooney Thomas, 899 Broadway
Roosevelt J. W. cor. 21st st.
Rose Henry R. 339 Water
Rosener Charles, 182 Rivington
Ross J. 161 Broome
Roth Marcus, 156 2d
Rourke Patrick, 26 9th Av.
Rowe Edward, 86 Elm
Rowe Wm. 49 Av. A
Rowland J. 26th st. 9th Av.
Ruck George, 192 Greenwich
Ruef William. 44 Av. A
Rufner Sebastian, 539 Pearl
Ruble J. F. 193 Av B
Russell M. R. 187 Av. C
Russell James, 3 Barclay
Russell J. 10th Av. cor. W. 16th
Ryan Ann, 40 Whitehall
Ryan John, 155½ Chrystie
Ryan Joseph, 116 Cedar
Ryan Michael, 67 Attorney
Ryan Patrick, 350 Water
Ryan Richard, 353 Greenwich
Saddlemire George, jr. 5 4th Av.
Saeurman Philip, 13 Bayard
Samon John, 149 Crosby
Sammon James, 228 1st Av.
Sauter William, 110 Cedar
Savage William H., W. 27th st.
Scarff George, 458 Broadway
Scanlin Owen, 3 Cottage place
Scanlon John, 56 Centre
Schaaft T. 56 Chatham
Schade William, 264 West
Schafer R. 170 3d
Schafer Theobold, 403 Monroe
Scheffer F. 46th st.
Scheuer George, 187 Av. B
Scheuermann M. 38½ Chatham
Schlosser Nicholas, 5 Av. A
Schmid John, 169 7th
Schmithman Valentine, 6 Centre
Schmitt Kasper J. 111 Broome
Schneberg R. & Co. 85 Chatham
Schnell John, 207 Delancy
Schneikert A. 150 2d
Schohnhals Jacob, 121 Liberty

Schonfeld John & Co. 139 G'wich
New York.
Schrantt Michael, 255 6th
Schreier Frederick, 105 7th Av.
Schroeder Henrich, 11 West
Schnekert Augustus, 150 2d
Schade William, 263 West
Schmidt Fassert. 17¾ William
Schmidt K. J. 113 Broome
Schulken & Lane. 312 Pearl
Schultz Charles, 12 Catharine slip
Schultz Peter, 61 West
Schumann Christian, 86 Reade
Schumann Franz C. 249 William
Schwalbe Fred. W. 75 Chatham
Schwartz J. H. & Co. 20 Burl'g sl.
Schwartz George, 89 Av. A
Schwartz George, 144 2d
Schwartz J. G. 30 West
Schweyer Michael, 11 Frankfort
Schroeder Emanuel, 6 Hoboken
Scott George, 94 6th Av.
Scott James, 15 Marion
Scott Patrick, 301 Mott
Scott Sands, 5 Dey
Scott Thos. D. 770 Washington
Scott William, 121 Cedar
Seagrave P. 404 10th
Seaman Jesse W. 21 Fulton mkt.
Sears Robert, 470 Pearl
Seely J. G. 7 Cath. sl. & 259 South
Sefs Michael. 173 Division
Segor John. 129 Anthony
Segrave Patrick, 404 19th
Seim H. & Co. 237 Broome
Seinor Martha, 4 Bridge
Serr Adam, 98 Centre
Serrer Lorent. 198 Ridge
Sewell Q. 87 4th
Seymour Ellen, 17 Franklin
Shaffrey Michael, 463 Washington
Sharp Peter, 39 Av. B
Sharp Samuel, 342 Stanton
Shaw Michael, 86 6th Av.
Shaw William, 44 Bowery
Shea Edward, 39 Cherry
Shea William, 425 10th
Sheehan James, 224 12th
Sheehan Thomas, 144 Orange
Sheehen Andrew, 76 Cherry
Sheil James, 135½ Washington
Shelton & Robertson, 167 Walker
Sheridan Anthony. 225 W. 21st
Sheridan James, 129 Pitt
Sheridan Patrick, 109½ Broome
Sheridan Terry, 151½ 7th
Sheridan Thomas, 93 Greene
Sharwood Gilbert F. 163 Prince
Sherwood James, 28 Bowery
Shettle William, 68 Beekman
Shields James, 135½ Washington
Shoemaker John, 14 Canal
Shoemaker Philip, 23 Frankfort
Short Terence, 76 Hamersley
Sierk Carsten, 140 West
Sies Ludwig, 201 Houston
Siler John, 156½ Greenwich
Silva John A. 102½ Cherry
Silva Joseph V. 75 Market
Simmons D. & B. F. 141 W. B'way
Simon George, 281 Broome
Simons Patrick, 110 Mulberry
Simonson William, 24th bet. 3d &
Lexington Avs.
Skillman Edmond, 102 Centre
Slocum Daniel T. 33 Peck slip
Small John. 40 Av. B
Smith Alexander, 17th st.
Smith Andrew. 176 11th
Smith Catharine, 44 Prince
Smith Casper. 96 W. 20th
Smith Charles H. 140 Church
Smith Edward, 57 Beekman
Smith Emanuel, 374 Water
Smith Eunice. 307 West
Smith Frank & Charles, 404 8th
Smith Henry, 857 Grand
Smith Henry, (also segar dealer)
481 Cherry
Smith James C. 94 Oliver
Smith John, 216 Water
Smith John, 314 Stanton

Smith John, 117 W. 21st New York,
Smith John, 504 Washington
Smith John. cor. 15th & 1st Av.
Smith Joseph. 14 Dey
Smith Michael. 296 Av. A
Smith Oliver, 45 James
Smith Owen, 297 W. 17th
Smith Randal, 597 Broadway
Smith Thomas D. 192 Bowery
Smith & Thompson, 50 Vesey
Snell Henry, 7 James
Snow Charles E. 225 West
Snyder Henry W. 187 Houston
Sohnlein John, 47 Av. A
Somers James. 231 Mott
Sommer Solomon. 177 Broome
Southwell John. 71 Oliver
Spaeth Alois, 223 Stanton
Spafford Wm. W. 429 Hudson
Sparkes James A. 212 Bleecker
Spiker Wm. 51 West
Spohr Adam, 60 Essex
Squires Richard, 87 Walnut
Stadler Henry, 523 Pearl
Staff John, 10 & 12 Ann
Staffor Jacob, 16 Av. B
Stange Jacob & Co. 99 James
Stanley Daniel, 151 Anthony
Stapleton P. 351 Greenwich
Starck Henry, 92 Willet
Stark Archibald, 133 6th Av.
Stone James, 212 William
Stott Thomas D. 770 Washington
Story Edward, 129 Bowery
Stearns Josiah, 312 Water
Steel John, 540 Broome
Stege Cord, 340 Stanton
Stegman Conrad & Co. 23 West
Steiger Simon, 26 Essex
Steinfeldt John W. 433 10th
Stellenwerf Amos R. 195 Bleecker
Stollwagen John, 24 Duane
Stenson Michael, 61 Cherry
Stephan George S. 53 West
Stern Abram. 173 Stanton
Sternhager Hermann, 89 Essex
Stenrer Geo. 9th Av.
Stevenson John, 174 Hester
Stigeler John, 41 Duane
Stilson Michael, 61 Cherry
Strsidtman John H. 301 G'wich
Strauss Henry, 13 Delancy
Strickland H. S. 667 Grand
Strodoro E. 77 Cherry
Stukey Frau B. 151 Anthony
Sullivan Daniel, 16 Franklin
Sullivan James, 110 Centre
Summer S. 177 Broome
Susser Jacob. 103 Pitt
Saydam Israel. 33 Greenwich
Swan John, 278 Front
Sweeney Daniel, 39½ Orange
Sweeney William, 420 Water
Swezey Calvin, 29 Bowery
Tager F. 223 3d
Tanner Joseph, cor. 31st st.
Tate Thomas, 308 West
Tate William W. 58 Whitehall
Tasche Metz, 15 West
Taylor Frederick, 111 Reade
Taylor James, 123 Liberty
Taylor John, 314 1st Av.
Taylor William. 233 Stanton
Taylor & Rockett, 561 Houston
Teahen Michael, 402 West
Terney James, 42 Oak
Tetley Richard. 66 9th Av.
Tieux Peter. 190 Mercer
Tilton H. 475 Washington
Thacker John, 249 6th Av.
Thomas John. 10 Centre
Thomas & Young, 240 South
Thompson Bartholomew A. 72
East Broadway
Thompson Corlies, 248 West
Thompson James, 16 W. B'way
Thompson James A. 37 Anthony
Thompson Mary, 279 Front
Thompson John, 41 Oak
Thompson T. 118 Chatham
Tietgen Elbe, 74 Centre
Tietjen Henry, 608 Grand

Tighe P. 68 Cherry   *New York.*
Tilson Thomas. 596 Washington
Tilton Jacob, 96 Vesey
Tipper John E. 120 East B'way
Toet H. 274 Broome
Toel Patrick, 248 12th
Tohn Jacob. 188 2d
Toland Michael, 835 Greenwich
Tompson Thomas, 118 Chatham
Toms J. W. 735 Greenwich
Toomy Daniel. 24 Oak
Touton Lewis, 555 Pearl
Tovee William. 517 Pearl
Tuite Thomas, 219 Rivington
Tracy C. 352 4th Av.
Tredwell Albert, 4 Broad
Trench Joseph. 332 Broadway
Trevor Thomas, 185 Cedar
Tribken Claus. 15 Clinton
Tripp Charles. 7th Av. cor. 19th
Truex P. 190 Mercer
Tucker Frederick J. 275 3d Av.
Tucker Melvin L. 218 Hudson
Tucker E. L. 93 Bowery
Tuomey Michael, 290 Grand
Uhl John. 174 2d
Uhlin George. 89 Sheriff
Ulrich John, 231 17th
Underhill George M. K. 195 South
Underhill Wm. H. 453 Broome
Vandevoort Peter, 65 8th Av.
Valliere Henry, 80 Av. B
Van Pelt Peter. 667 Broadway
Van Pelt & Curtis, 667 do
Van Rohn Caspar. 184 2d
Van Tine John, 305 Broome
Van Varick Mary, 213 Spring
Van Valser Henry, 198 West
Vielbig Adam. 50 Chatham
Vieneburgh Jacob. 113 Walker
Vignardonne John M. 72 4th Av.
Vince Herman, 607 Water
Vogelsang H. & Co. 99½ Wash'n
Von Dohlen Allerich, 85 Pine
Vought James C. 200 West
Vroman S. 205 West
Vultee Frederick, 116 Chatham
Wack George, 94 Essex
Wadlow Charles, 194 William
Waechter August, 85 Pitt
Waesgarber F. 171 3d
Wagner Escherich & Co.13 Centre
Wagner John, 128 Liberty
Walt H. L. 33 Chambers
Walker Robert. 135 Washington
Wall Michael, 488 Cherry
Wallace Wm. 153 Cedar
Wellhauer Charles L. 27 Av. A
Walter Charles, 275 Water
Walter & Able, 474 Broadway
Walton Henry A. 39 South
Wand John, 40 Chrystie
Wangler Joseph, 107 Av. B
Wanmaker Charles, 217 3d
Wannamaker Henry, 18 Av. B
Warburton Samuel, 4 Pearl
Ward John, 54 Spring
Ward Robert, 199½ Chatham
Werk David, 40 West
Werner Reuben, 9th Av.
Warren John, 41 Duane
Warren Wm. 358 Water
Waters Edward, 71 Cross
Waterson & Magee. 60 Cherry
Watkins Charles, 29 Carmine
Watson Thomas, 150 4th Av.
Way John J. 1 State
Weaver Hamilton, 275 3d Av.
Webster James, 41 Franklin
Webster Maria. 30 Walnut
Weeks Nathaniel T. 96 Bowery
Weikersheimer H. 298 Delancy
Weinhold J. 40 Oak
Weierman John S. 69 Greenwich
Weis Frederick, 191 Pitt
Weldon James, 225 Washington
Welser Edward. 29 Canal
Wendel John, 198 Av. B
Wenz Wm. 366 Houston
Westervelt Peter J. 263 Hudson
Wheeler Edward, 456 13th
Wheeler & Drake, 2 Gouverneur

Whitaker Charles, 17 Centre
                    New York.
Whitaker John, 238 Hudson
White Cornelius, 106 Vesey
White Ezra, 40 Bowery
White Gabriel. 63 Orchard
White John, 75 Cortlandt
White Michael, 45 Elm & 589
    Greenwich
White Patrick. 41 Peck slip
White Peter, 43   do
White H. & E. 40 Bowery
Whitehead Nathan E. 113 Elm &
    14 Canal
Whitemore Ira, 401 West
Whitemore John, 496 Houston
Whitney William, 312½ Water
Wiegers Louis, 102 Bayard
Wigun Charles, 68 Harrison
Wilbur John H. 94 6th Av.
Wild Gustavus, 109 Division
Wilde William R. 380 Hudson
Wiles Patrick, 68 James
Wilkens Theodore, 84 West
Wilkes Cassady. 223   do
Wilkins James, 322 South
Will Michael, 36 Essex
Williams Henry, 279 Water
Williams John H. 8 Depeyster
Williams William, 41 Madison
Williams William, 180 Cherry
Willis Asa, 139 Washington
Willis William, 452 Broadway
Willson Ed. 281 Bowery
Willson William H. 215 do
Wilson Charles. 43 Canal
Wilson Henry, 203 West
Wilson James. 84 Walnut
Wilson I. T. 528 Pearl
Wilson Stephen, 1 Dover
Wilson Thomas. 292 Hudson
Wilson T. S. 377 1st Av.
Wilson R. 29 Washington
Wilson & Robinson, 88 7th Av.
Wilson William, Harlem
Wirth John, 173 Houston
Wise Henry, 185 Madison
Woide John, 24 Walnut
Wolcot Nelson, 535 Water & 212
    Grand
Walcott & Hays, 212 Grand
Wolfe Conrad, 29 Thames
Wolstein & Diackery, 18 Bowery
Woltman Henry, 114 Centre
Woodruff William, 206 Fulton
Woods Thomas, 486 Greenwich
Woodworth John F. 13 Dutch
Worden George P. 28 Bowery
Work David, 40 West
Wright John, 250 W. 16th
Wright Joseph. 299 Water
Wright William, 92 Ann
Wright William, 549 Pearl
Wrunger D. 243 2d
Wynn Margaret. 34 Prince
Yager Kasper, 293 3d
Yates Benjamin S. 222 3d
Youdale Jonathan, 51 Chatham
Young Charles, 5 Norfolk
Young Joseph, 226 Walker
Young Michael, 79 Orange
Young Robert, 472 Water
Zehr George, 29 Orange
Zeigler John, 184 Stanton
Zelling Henry, 109 Walker and
    147 Centre
Zerrenner Ludwig, 95 Forsyth
Ziegler L. 162 2d
Zimmer Catherine, 829 Pearl

Oneida County.

Sink A.   *Rome.*
Winn T. 49 Liberty   *Utica.*
Evans D. 83   do
Davis J. C., Whitesboro st.
Wenzel J. Culver st.
Donohoe J. 27 Catharine
M'Incrow Wm.

Onondaga County.

Owen J. Genesee st. Syracuse
                        Salina.

Harty E. & Co., Genesee st. Syra-
    cuse   *Salina.*
Williams R. C. Warren st. S'cuse
Crane D. S. Water st.   do
Cadwell P. Washington st. do
Kuntz Charles, Salina st. do

Rensselaer County.

Follett F. B. cor. Richard & State
                   Lansingburgh.
Virgo Wm. 9 Elizabeth
Dunlavey John, 256 River *Troy.*
Curley Peter, 256   do
Horton G. 292   do
Quest Edward, 8 North 4th
Brady James, 14 2d
Ghounlan Edward, 1 Franklin sq.
Hunter Wm. cor. Hill & Liberty
Tickle D. 138 4th
Copp Nathaniel, 124 4th
Hanlan Dennis, 154 5th
Heroy E. B. 36 Congress
Windsor George, 41 do
Armestrong John, 50 do
Green C.   do
M'Kena Owen, 54   do
Whiton John, 73   do
Wintermantle G. 77 do
Jordan Edward, 187 do
Purcell P. 156 4th
Lenway A. Ferryway
Carton John,   do
Sullivan Wm. O.   do
Quaids James,   do
M'Norton M.   do
Conway Daniel, Foot of Hill st.
Hollister E. cor. Adams & River
    sts.
Pendar M. 4th st.
Nauthtan P. South st.
Grace J. 189 4th
Burns Wm. 190 4th
Morgan G. Madison st.
Kimball E. Hollow road
Marr John A. Nail Factory

Richmond County.

Chambers G. W. Tompkinsville
                    Castleton.
Jones F. S.   do
Flood Patrick,   do
Meyers H.   do
Kenny N. Port Richmond
                    Northfield.
Durkan John, Stapleton *Southfield.*
Chambers J.   do

Schenectady County.

Taylor W. 4 Water *Schenectady*
M'Cann J. 15 Rotterdam
Yates G. 7   do
Van Ranken S. 169 State
Lake D.   do
Dongle J. 156   do
Lehe L. Dock st.
Benger F. do

Ulster County.

Sherer E., Rondout   *Kingston.*
Colvill John, do
Kline John, Wilber

Port Monnaie Frames Ma-
nufacturers.

Goldstein & Adler, 106 Elm
                    New York.

Port Wardens.

Story Wm. W. Master Warden
                    101 Wall
Harwood Benjamin,   do
Bunce David,   do
Field John,   do
Fash Jacob,   do
Tilyou Vincent,   do
Appointed by the Governor and
Senate of the State of New York.

Potteries.

Albany County.

Bender M. W. Westerlo & Dallius *Albany.*
Porter & Fraser, West Troy *Watervliet.*
Warner Wm. E. do

Chenango County.

Hart J. & W. C. *Sherburne.*

Columbia County.

Selby E. & Co. *Hudson.*

Duchess County.

Caire J. B. & Co. 147 Main *Poughkeepsie.*

Kings County.

M'Lees Dennis, Navy st. nr. High *Brooklyn.*
Cartridge C. & Co. Green Point *Bushwick.*

Monroe County.

Stetzmayer Frederick, 160 South Sophia *Rochester.*

New York County.

Hudson River Pottery, Edward Roche, Foot 12th N. R. bet. 9th & 10th Avs. Orders received as above by Roche, Brothers & Co. 35 Fulton *New York.*
Kinsey James, 57 Great Jones
Smith Washington, 251 West 18th

Oswego County.

Hart Samuel, Fulton *Volney.*

Saratoga County.

Harrison John *Stillwater.*

Suffolk County.

Lewis Henry, *Huntington.*
Hempstead Austin. (Flower Pots) Greenport *Southold.*
Hempstead Thomas, (Flower pots) Greenport

Ulster County.

Brandinon William & Co Ellen. ville *Wawarsing.*
Weston D. R. Ellenville

Wayne County.

Clark & Co. *Lyons.*

Yates County.

Holmes & Purdy, Dundee *Starkey.*

Poudrette.

Bommer George, 72 Greenwich *New York.*
Brinkerhoff John P. 23 Chambers
Dey James R. 51 Liberty

Poulterers.

Baldwin Moses, 6 & 8 Fulton market *New York.*
Bradley Eliphalet W. 26 Fulton market
Cassidy Cornelius, 5 Centre mkt
Danmont Augustus, 29 Bowery
Dauson John, 42 & 45 Fulton mkt
Donnelly James, 111 Washington market
Everitt John, 53 Catharine market

Forshay Mrs. Clinton market *New York.*
Flock Alfred, 616 Broadway
Garno & Son, 10 Centre market
Gotty William, 9 Washington mkt
Grady Patrick, 50 Catharine mkt
Hawkins Aaron, 816 Broadway
Hawkins A. B. 56 15th
Hedden Joseph T. & Sons, 1, 3 & 5 Jefferson market
King Susan, Tompkins market
Monfort John, 30 Fulton do
Mooney Felix, 95 Bowery
Packer Elbridge, 6 Washington market
Pittman Ann, 48½ Catharine mkt
Reed John, 54 Catharine market
Reed Mary, Essex market
Rhodes Mrs. Clinton do
Robbins A. & E. 5 & 7 Fulton mkt
Smith Ira & Daniel, 28 Fulton do
Smith John O. 47 Catharine mkt
Smith & Rogers, 9 & 11 Fulton do
Tilton David, 12 Franklin market
Thomas Margaret, 45 Catharine do
Walling, Thorn & Co. 3 Washington market
Winegar Eliza, 1 Centre market

Powder Dealers.

Hazard Powder Co. 89 Wall *New York.*
Howell Charles J. 206 Front
Kemble William, 79 West

Powder Manufacturers.

Herkimer County.

Phillips Samuel *Frankfort.*
Pearson James M.

Monroe County.

Parsons M. *Brighton.*

Rensselaer County.

Loomis, Swift & Co. *Schaghticoke.*

Ulster County.

Laflin & Smith *Saugerties.*

Westchester County.

Hawbolt E. F. Hart's Corners *Yonkers.*

Precious Stones.—Importers of.

Burdet Gros, 16 Dey *New York.*
Cottier C. 1 Cortlandt
Kortum E. F. 5 Dey
Ripley R. 32 Maiden lane

Precious Stones—(Imitation.)—Importers of.

Bishop Victor, 23 Maiden lane *New York.*
Hyde & Son J. E. 21 Maiden lane

Prepared Chalk Manufacturers.

Kings County.

Shand Elizabeth, 94 Sands *Brooklyn.*

Press (Cotton) Manufacturers.

Bullock Smith W. 37 S. William *New York.*
Gordon & Rea, 458 Water

Van Vliet H. H. 32 West *New York.*

Print Colorers.

Kellogg & Comstock, 150 Fulton *New York.*
Lawrence John, 32 Spruce
Spearing Thomas P. 183 William

Printers Book & Job. (See also Newspapers.)

Albany County.

Van Benthuysen Chas. 407 Broadway *Albany.*
Munsell J. 58 State
Stone H. D. 1 Greene
New John, 19 Beaver
Hastings H. J. 12 do
Weed, Parsons & Co. 67 State
Kilmer C. 6 James

Broome County.

Evans Edwin T. *Binghamton.*
Shaw H. L.

Cayuga County.

Finn & Rockwell, 115 Genesee *Auburn.*
Oliphant H. 94 & 96 Genesee

Chautauque County.

Palmer F. W. & Co. Jamestown *Ellicott.*
Fletcher A. Jamestown

Chenango County.

Leal & Sinclair *Norwich.*
Pellett Nelson
Lawyer Alfred G.

Clinton County.

Morgan Jonathan F. Keeseville *Au Sable.*
Turner David, do
Tuttle J. W. *Plattsburgh*
Stone R. G.

Columbia County.

Stoddard Wm. B. Warren st. *Hudson.*
Carrique P. D. do
Webb A. N. do
Collins Charles H. Public square
Bryan & Moore, Warren st.
Van Schaack F. *Kinderhook.*

Delaware County.

Paine A. M. *Delhi.*
Bowne N.
Wright C. E. Deposit *Tompkins.*

Duchess County.

Addington Wm. R. Fishkill Landing *Fishkill.*
Platt & Schram, 312 Main *Poughkeepsie.*
Tompkins I. 258 Main

Erie County.

Faxon Charles, 148 Main *Buffalo.*
Lee A. F. 136 do
Faxon James, 15 Webster's block
Reese Geo. & Co. 159 Main
Peck Charles E. 161 do
Jewett Thomas & Co.

Genesee County.

Seaver Wm. & Son *Batavia.*
Walt D. D.

Jefferson County.

Harris O. H. Sackett's Harbor *Hounsfield.*

Haddock John A. *Watertown.*
Hunt Alvin
Clark Ambrose W.
Knowlton & Rice

Kings County.

Lees & Foulkes, 35 & 41 Fulton
Brooklyn.
Wilson Peter W. 67 Concord
Brown J. B. cor. Fulton & Tillary
Darbee Levi, 146 4th cor. S. 1st
Williamsburgh.

Lewis County.

Lake Horace R. *Turin.*

Livingston County.

Stevens G. W. *Dansville.*
Richardson E. G.
Brunson C. R. *Geneseo.*
Harding & Norton *Mount Morris.*

Madison County.

Coolidge H. A. *Cazenovia.*
Norton James, Morrisville *Eaton.*
Waldron & Baker *Hamilton.*
Gould C. B.
Olmstead J. P. Chittenango
Sullivan.

Monroe County

Smith & Clough, cor. Buffalo & Exchange *Rochester.*
Hughes William, 43 Main
Morse Clarendon. 13 Front

Montgomery County.

Backus Levi S. Fort Plain *Minden.*
Whitehouse J. J. & Co. Fonda
Mohawk.

New York County.

Ackerman George H. 181 William
New York.
Adee Daniel, 107 Fulton
Allen Edward P. 9 Spruce
Allen Francis D. 73 Chatham
Alvord C. A. 1 Dutch
Angell & Engel, 1 Spruce, Tribune
buildings
Baker & Duyckinck, 158 Pearl
Barlow Benjamin R. 47 Gold
Barr Joseph K. 22 Division
Bedford Joseph D. rear 59 Ann
Belcher John, 63 Vesey
Bell Jared W. 178 Fulton
Benedict Charles W. 201 William
Benedict Seth W. 201 William &
16 Spruce
Bidwell Oliver, 12 Spruce
Biddle J. 343 Hudson
Bourne George M. 73 Liberty
Bourne William Oland. 73 Liberty
Booth Jonas, 109 Nassau
Booth Samuel, do
Bristol Hernen D. 191 Fulton
Brooks Joseph, 1 Chatham square
Brown Christian, 145 Hester
Bryant W. C. & Co. 25 Pine
Burroughs William L. 113 Fulton
Busteed & M'Coy, 163 do
Cameron John G. 23 Ann
Carpenter Robert, 44 Ann
Cassidy Hugh, 81 Nassau
Childs Casper C. 80 Vesey
Champlin L. G. 5 & 7 Spruce
Clark Jas. 122½ Fulton
Clark & Sickels, 152 Nassau
Clayton & Sons, 86 Wall
Craighead Robert, 112 Fulton
Crankasharr & Co. 184 Canal
Crawley & Levison, 79 Chatham
Crist John W. 139 Water
Crowell Jos. T. & Co. 16 Spruce
Cunningham Andr'w, 183 William
Daly & Cook. 128 Fulton
Day John, 111 8th Av.

Dean W. E. 12 Ann *New York*
Dorr Wm. S. 101 Nassau
Douglass John, 11 Spruce
Douglass & Ming, 51 Fulton
Dunham Wm. H. 138 Fulton
Egbert, Hovey & King, rear 374
Pearl
Elliott John M. 58 Nassau
Everdell & Son, 104 Fulton
Familton James B. 269 Hudson
Fanshaw Daniel. 35 Ann
Farwell J. H. & F. F. 71 Division
Fetkin Robert. 81 Cliff
Folger & Co. 118 John
Fraetas Josiah A. & Co. 7 Spruce
Gordan Geo. P. 70 Nassau
Gould Alexander S. 144 Nassau
Gray John, 104 Beekman
Gray John A. 15 Spruce
Grossman E. N. 12 Spruce
Grossman John P. 12 Spruce
Hall John, 222 Water
Hart Francis. 4 Thames
Heath Wm. 142 Fulton
Holman & Gray, 88 & 90 Fulton
Houel A. T. 111 Nassau
Hoyt Azor, 1 Spruce
Hoyt Silvanus & Co. 38 Vesey
Jackson John M. r. 203 Bowery
Jenkins Edward O. 114 Nassau
Jennings & Harrison, 122 Nassau
Kelley John C. 7 Spruce
Ketchum J. 3 Broad
King E. H. 374 Pearl
Knight & Rice, 5 Spruce
Lambert & Lane, 69 Wall
Liddle Josiah, 162 Elm
Lee Wm. W. 12 Spruce
Livezey & Brothers, 74 Fulton
Low Mrs. A. 150 Fulton
Ludwig H. & Co. 70 Vesey
MacDonald & Leo, 9 Spruce
M'Glim John. 1 Division
M'Gowan Charles. 68 Barclay
M'Gowan John R. 106 Fulton
M'Spedon & Baker, 25 Pine
Maigne George B. 5 & 7 Spruce
Marsh Joseph M. 5 Eldridge
Martin Wm. C. 109 John
Muins Wm. 90 Wall
Mearson George, 142 Fulton
Mitchell George, 265 Bowery
Mulhaeuser Jacob, 231 Division
Murphy David & Son, 153 Water
Narine & Co. 21 Wall
Nesbitt George F. 86 Wall
Norris Eugene, 135 Nassau
O'Connor Michael T. 27 Centre
Oliver & Brother, 69 Nassau &
126 Fulton
Osborn Wm. 154 Nassau
Paine Charles, 44 Nassau
Parks Hugh, 210 Chatham
Piercy Henry R. 111 Nassau
Post John, 1 Nassau
Prall John P. 9 Spruce
Pudney & Russell, 79 John
Redfield Justus S. 16 Spruce
Reed John J. 16 Spruce
Richards & Johnston, 44 Ann
Richardson Robert J. 446 Broadway
Sackett Israel, 52 Nassau
Smith Thomas, 162 Nassau
Smith W. H. B. 11 Spruce
Snowden T. 70 Wall
Sparks James A. 212 Bleecker
Spear Henry, 78 Wall
Spence Wm. J. 194 Fulton
Spring L. 142 Fulton
Sutton Thomas E. 128 Fulton
Tabele Philip, 137 W. 16th
Taylor Alexander, 9 Thames
Thomas John, 16 Spruce
Thomas Wm. 141 Delancy
Tobitt John H. 9 Spruce
Torrey James D. 121 Fulton
Townsend Andrew J. 105 Nassau
Trehern & Anderson, 141 Nassau
Trow John F. 49 & 51 Ann
Tupper Hiram, 140 Nassau
Turney Geo. W. & S. 79 Chatham

Tyler Milton, 120 4th Av.
New York.
Uhl Jacob, 11 Frankfort
Van Norden Wm. 39 William
Van Nordan & Amerman, 60 William
Van Winkle & Henry, 11 Spruce
Vinten Chas. 98 Nassau
Watson John, 58 Chatham
Westall John, 11 Spruce
Willets Charles, 152 William
Winchester Ebenezer, 44 Ann
Winser John R. r. 59 Ann
Wood George W. 16 Spruce
Wright James F. 74 Fulton
Wright & Rice, 7 Spruce

Niagara County.

Wright S. *Lockport.*
Crandall D. S.
Fox Charles S.
Ballou & Campbell
Hackstaff Geo. H. *Niagara Falls.*

Oneida County.

Pickard E. *Camden.*
Roberts & Sherman, 38 & 40 Genesee *Utica.*
Britt Wm. B. 30 Genesee
Grove Dewitt C. 42 & 44 Genesee
Curtiss H. H. Devereux Block
Bennett D. 155 Genesee
Roberts E. E. 2 Seneca

Ontario County.

Mattison & Sanford *Canandaigua*
Whitney George L.
Parker J. & S. H. Geneva *Seneca.*
Van Valkenburgh E. do
Smith Wm. H. do

Orange County.

Bebee G., S. Middletown *Wallkill*
Bebee G. J. do
Brown J. S. do

Orleans County.

Denio J. & J. H, Albion *Barre*
Wiltse J. O. do
M'Connell C. S. do

Oswego County.

Mathewson A. A., Pulaski
Richland.

Otsego County.

Avery A. S. *Butternuts*
Shaw & Titus, Cooperstown
Otsego.

Putnam County.

Blivan S. C. *Carmel.*

Queens County.

Snediker Seaman N. *Hempstead.*

Rensselaer County.

Harkness & Kirkpatrick, 265 State
Lansingburgh.
M'Arthur Chas. L. 197 River *Troy.*
Prescott & Co. 235 River
Kneeland J. C. 6 Cannen place

St. Lawrence County.

Goodrich & Wilson *Gouverneur.*
Wallace & Washburn *Potsdam.*

Saratoga County.

Davidson G. M. *Saratoga Springs*
Corey John A.
Spooner George W.
Corey A., Schuylerville *Saratoga.*
Cramer James L. do
Matchet Wm. B. *Stillwater.*

Seneca County.

Foster & Judd   *Seneca Falls.*
Sentell & Pew   *Waterloo.*

Steuben County.

Messenger Thomas   *Painted Post.*

Suffolk County.

Phillips S. Wells, Greenport
             Southold.

Tompkins County.

Andrus, Gauntlett & Co. 69 Owego
             Ithaca.
Spencer D. D. A. & S. 41 Owego

Ulster County.

Romeyn Wm. H.   *Kingston.*
Chipp R. A.

Washington County.

Curtis J. W.   *Greenwich.*
M'Call Wm.
Baker E. D. jr. Sandy Hill
             Kingsbury.
Blanchard H. W.   *Whitehall.*
Southard W. S.

Wayne County.

Cole Wm. N.   *Lyons.*
Russell S. W.

Wyoming County.

Siver Wm B.   *Attica.*
Britt C. C.   *Perry.*
Blanchard S. S.   *Warsaw.*
Holley & Dudley

Yates County.

Reed A. Penn Yan   *Milo.*
Adams R. L. do
Hoogland E., Dundee   *Starkey.*

Printers—Calico.

Arms Charles & Co. 159 Pearl
             New York.
Haggerty William C. 77 Pine
Rennie Robert, 14 Cedar

Printers—Card.

Bunce G. F. 321 Pearl *New York.*
Butler Warren C. 1 Spruce
Crowell & Co. 16 Spruce
Chapman R. 92 Fulton
Gordon George P. 10 Nassau
Hetterson C. 136 Water
Sherman Arthur N. 118 Fulton
Spring Lawrence. 142 Fulton
Starr L. W. 177 William
Sutton Thomas E. 123 Fulton

Printers—Copper Plate.

Oneida County.

Thompson A. M. 52 Hotel   *Utica.*

Kings County.

Wandall J. D. 193 5th
             Williamsburgh.

Printers' Joiners.

Clark John. 44 Av. D   *New York.*
M'Afee & Bowden. 53 Ann
Skippon John & Son. 51 Gold
Smith George W. 32 Spruce
Wilson & Clayton, rear 15 Rose

Printers—Label.

Michlin & M'Gowan, 111 Nassau
             New York

Printers' Materials.

M'Creary John D. 3 Spruce & 331
   Stanton   *New York.*
Mather George, 294 & 296 Front
Paul & Co. 632 Hudson
Wells & Webb, 18 Dutch

Printers—Music.

Ackerman G. W. rear 25 Howard
             New York.
Benedict S. W. 16 Spruce
Ackerman Samuel, 89 Nassau
Fay John O. & Co. 134 Fulton
Ferguson Robert, 22 Spruce
Roshore John, 20 Cortlandt

Printers—Plate.

Burton James R. 125 Broadway
             New York.
Chapman Robert, rear 92 Fulton
Clements & Slocum. 90 Fulton
Dalton James, 50 Mercer
Dugan Augustine, 98 Nassau
Dunnell Aaron H. 23 Chambers
Felt D. & Co. & Hosford, 50 Wall
Kelly Joseph, 141 Fulton
Lauder John, 26 Platt
M'Cune John, 92 Merch. Exch.
Merchant Henry, 206 Pearl
Miller Robert, 81 Cliff
Neale & Pate, 16 Burling slip
Thomas C. 492 Pearl
Smith Henry S. 59 Nassau
Valentine Samuel, 98 Nassau
Worts William, 56 Gold

Printers—Xylographic.

Brownson William M, 56 Gold
             New York.
Crump Samuel, 50 Nassau
Felt D. & Co. & Hosford, 50 Wall
Miller Peter & Son, 102 Broadway
Raper Bogart W. 312 Pearl
Shields Charles, 86 John

Printing Cloths.

Beach H. C. 72 Pine   *New York.*
Haggerty W. C. 77 Pine

Printing Press Makers.

(See also *Machinists.*)

Austen F. J. 23 Centre *New York.*
Hoe R. & Co. 30 & 31 Gold, and
   Broome cor. Sheriff
Sheridan Bernard, 45 Ann
Taylor A. B. & Co. 3 Hague

Printer—Silk.

Orange County.

Caldwell Robert   *Newburga.*

Produce Dealers. (See also
Grocers, also Provisions.)

Albany County.

Knapp H. 27 Quay   *Albany.*
Townsley G. 77 do
Cowel & Flaherty. 116 & 117 Quay
Chapman & Savage, 121 Pier
Terry O. G. 120   do

French & Stevens, 120 Pier ——
             Albany.
Durant E. A.   do
Reed & Rawls,   do
Craft B. F. 115   do
Goddard C. W. 98   do
Fish S. M. & Co. 84, 85, 86 do
Higgins Robert, 265 Washington

Cayuga County.

Morgan E. B.   *Ledyard.*
Smith J. C.   *Scipio.*

Chautauque County.

Gilbert A. Forestville   *Hanover.*

Chenango County.

Sutliff & Case   *Sherburne.*

Erie County.

Hun E. Terrace Market   *Buffalo.*
Weaver Jacob,   do
Murray Thomas,   do
Acton Henry,   do
Cavanagh & Peters,   do
Vanderwater James,   do
Kelly J.   do
Mills George,   do
Hoffman J. S.   do
Holdon ——   do
Turner James,   do
Western E. W   do
Wild & Kingsbury,   do
Weston & Page,   do
Dunbar & Nichols,   do
Boyd R. D. 7 E Seneca
Drake J. 4 Marvin Block, Water
Roop Henry, 72 Main
Tifft George W. foot of Main &
   Dock

Greene County.

Barker & Kirkland   *Coxsackie.*

Lewis County.

Clapp Horace, (butter and cheese)
   Houseville   *Turin.*
Bush Horace C.   do

Monroe County.

Ball, Church & Co. Spencer's
   Basin   *Ogden.*
Dewey J. B. 61 Buffalo *Rochester.*
M'Killip S. 106 & 108
Meyer J. Sebastian, 101 Main
Billings & Gilbert, 87 Main

Montgomery County.

Wood & Moyer   *Canajoharie.*
Clark, Newkirk & Hoffman

New York County.

Adams, Crowell & Co. 244 Fulton
             New York.
Barker J. S. & Son. 212 Front
Brokensha & Guyre, 15 Washing-
   ington market
Brooks Peter & Co. 1, 3 & 5 Jeffer-
   son market
Case & Freeman, 101 Front
Clancey ——, 19 Jefferson mkt.
Clark Mary. Essex   do
Elt Adam, 105 Broome
Ferris George B. 37 Front
Fish E. & Co. 11 South
Fisher & Lyon, 19 Washington
   market
Gibson James R. 142 Front
Hoagland John S. & Son, 1 Clin-
   ton market
Hobbs Francis, 86 Broad
Hoole William H. Essex mkt.
Keaney Patrick, 99 Church
M'Elroy John. Essex market
Mingay Mary L. 8 Jefferson   do
Moran Andrew. Tompkins   do
Nelson Philip, Essex   do
Pike Elizabeth, do

Plumb Borden W. 66 Broad
                        New York.
Smith Henry, 22 Washington mkt.
Strittmatter Jacob, 117 Delancy
Sturges James, Tompkins mkt.
Tappy Andrew L.   do
Tomlinson & Co. 211 Washington
Vagonal John, Essex market
Veldran R. S. & Co. 14 Washington market
Wheaton John & Co. 256 Washington

Oneida County

Moulton D.   *Floyd.*
Billings & Owens   *Remsen.*
Hunt R. W. 7 & 9 Liberty *Utica.*
Wicker J. C. cor. Liberty & Hotel
Walker, Clark & Co. 17 Liberty
Sharpsteen B. Lowell
                       Westmoreland.
Bell A. J. Lairdsville
Tompkins William, Hampton
Buell A. Walesville   *Whitestown.*

Rensselaer County.

Hogeboom & Schermerhorn
                        Schodack.
Gage H.
Ostrander J.
Deyo Daniel
Van Buren ——
Slocum Hiram, 143 River   *Troy.*
Walker J. K. 149   do
Ball Royall, (Butter & Cheese, wholesale) 279 River
Arnold A. 391   do
Stickney & Symmonds, 283 River
Merchant & Wilson, 366   do

Tompkins County.

Sage H. W. & Co. Inlet Pier *Ithaca.*
Culver & Halsey, R. R. Block
Myers Andrew   *Lansing.*

Washington County.

Taylor G. H.   *Fort Edward.*

Yates County.

Lake & Foster, Penn Yan   *Milo.*
Stewart & Tuncliff, do
Clark Alvah,   do

Provision Dealers. (*See also Grocers—also Produce Dealers.*)

Albany County.

Crook & Palmer, 9 State *Albany.*
Cary Samuel. 13   do
Stanton G. W. jr. 2 do
Peck & Joy. 8   do
Ridman & Shell, 10 do
Cushman & Co. 20 & 22 State
M'Culloch John, 12 Exchange
Crauford R. B. & Co. 8 do
Wheeler Horace R. 6 do
Carmichael James, 4 do
Sanders J. B. & Co. 72 Quay
Bergen Charles. 28   do
Cook Asher, 47   do
Rankin S. 109 South Pearl
Jennings R. 25 Green
Judson I. L. 126 Washington
Clark J. 66   do

Broome County.

Colston H. W.   *Binghamton.*
Harvey L.
Cone O.

Duchess County.

Runolds W. W. & J. R. Upper Landing   *Poughkeepsie.*

Kings County.

Lockitt Joseph, 101 Atlantic
                      Brooklyn.

Lockitt Joseph, Everett nr. Fulton
                       Brooklyn.
Sutton & Young, 77 Fulton
Fox J. W. 6 Grand *Williamsburgh.*

Madison County.

Hill & Stewart, Oneida Depot
                        Lenox.
Cobb, Stewart & Co. do
Crouse James, Chittenango
                       Sullivan.
Stewart R. & D.   do

Monroe County.

Brown John   *Pittsford.*
Quigley T. 52 Prospect *Rochester.*
Lyons D. J. c. Prospect & Adams
Osborn N. P. 11 South St. Paul
Marshall Charles, South St. Paul, cor. Court
O'Neil Wm. jr. 88 do   do
Brown John N. 100 do   do
Banker Levi, 112 Main
Kelly P. 56 Front

New York County.

Apgar Levi & Co.73 Dey *New York*
Allen U. & Co. Washington mkt.
Arnold Dudley P. 30 Water
Baker Edmund S. 183 Rivington
Barry Charles. 53 Catharine mkt.
Beach J. M. 234 Washington
Bennett Wm. W. Centre market
Benjamin John E. 77 Dey
Berry Charles & Co. 49 & 51 Catharine market
Bogert Wm. S. 50 Water
Borden Wm. D. Centre market
Boscken Henry, 26 West Broad'y
Brock J. 30 Front
Brown Albert N. 79 Dey
Brown Wm. A. 12 James slip
Brush Jesse, 17 Front
Brush & Co. 35 Front
Bullings J. D. 36 Washington
Burns Gilbert Y. 90 Barclay
Butterfield & Bowman. 86 Broad
Butts J. C. Clinton market
Cape John J. 267 Broome
Cape. Trowbridge & Co. 84 Allen
Carman Sam. S. & Co. Centre mkt.
Chamberlin Stephen S. 237 Fulton
Cheney & Johnson. 28½ Front
Clark Samuel, 146 Elizabeth
Clark. Fisk & Co. 229 Fulton
Clarke Benj. F. 234 Washington
Clearwater R. 183   do
Clinck J. W. & F. Centre market
Collius W. Washington   do
Conley & Kirk. 233 Front
Cooper & Giraud. 138 do
Cornell & Curtis. 259 Washington
Cowl Orin, 27 Coenties slip
Cragin C. A. & E. T. 152 Chrit'r
Cragin George D. 156 West
Crawford Joseph. 312 Stanton
Cruger W. 674 Washington
Darling & Johnson. 36 Water
Dean J. E. Centre market
Demarest Peter P. 7 South
Dieffenbach H. Centre market
Doremus & Crane, 30 Front
Dougherty M. 308 17th
Dougherty Wm. C. 3 Front
Earl & Bartholomew, 184 Green'h
Edwards G. W. 227 & 229 Chrystie
Emery & Co. 60 Dey
Everts Samuel P. 248 Fulton
Ferres O. L. & A. & Co. 23 Front
Gerhauszer John A. 23 Washington market
Getty Robert P. 359 West
Gibney John, 175 West
Godfrey Eliza. Essex market
Goff James, 59 Orange
Grant Gilbert W. 250 Washington
Griffin John, 261   do
Gustin Geo. W. & Co. 243 do
Haight & Tooper, (see advertisement) 97 Murray

Halsey & Gustin, 182 Washington
                        New York.
Halsted, Chamberlain & Co. 297 Bowery & 192 Forsyth
Harris, Stone & Badeau, 191 & 193 Chrystie
Harrison E. M. & Co. 144 West
Hayes John, 244 Mulberry
Hayes Wm. Centre market
Hayes W. H. Washington market
Hencken G. & Son. 236 Wash'ton
Herbell Henry, 235 Elizabeth
Herbell & Son. 1 Centre market
Hoagland & Enyard, 228 Wash'ton
Hopkins & Haring, 50 Washington market
Hopper S. H. Clinton market
Horn Peter A. 508 & 510 Wash'ton
Howell C. 182 Washington
Hunt & Smith, 197 South
Jackson J. D. Washington market
Jewell. Harrison & Co. 27 Water
Johnson Frederick, Centre market
Jones Lawson, 3   do
Jones & Wise, 233 Fulton
Kelse J. 147½ Washington
Kehol David, Centre market
Knubel Diedrick, 10 Carmine
Krider & Mallett. 27 Old slip
Lang Lewis. Washington market
Lalor Wm. Centre market
Larkin J. C. Centre market
Lawrence B.   do
Leland G. & Co. 536 Washington
Lewis John W. 532   do
Lewis Richard B. 73 Vesey
Littell A. & G. 184 Washington
Lowry James, Centre market
Loyd John B. 733 Washington
M'Ardle J. Centre market
M'Cabe T. 3 Catharine
M'Chain John & Co. 52 Marion
M'Larn & Crane, Centre market
Main R. & Son, Washington mkt
Marshall's Sons, 9 2d Av. & 3 Fulton market
Matthews P. C. & L. 83 Dey
Meyer John D. 204 Division
Miles George, 637 Washington
Miller E. S. Centre market
Mook T. H.   do
Mook William,   do
Morrison & Hyde, 278 Washington
Moseback Joseph. 7 Jefferson mkt
Moses C. & A. 162 West & 36 Greenwich
Moses D. B. & W. 94 Broad
Olmsted Wm F. 13 Clinton mkt.
Osborne A. 186 Greenwich
Palmer J. H. 351 Bowery
Park B. P. 152 Washington
Parker A. 222 Broome
Paterson Francis, 540 Washington & 48 Clinton market
Perry Theodore & Co. 90 Broad
Platt John, 25 Water
Powers & Dederick, 39 Dey
Purdy D. S. & Son. 9 Jefferson mkt.
Purdy G. R. Clinton market
Reid Jesse. 59 Cortlandt
Reid Jas. Centre market
Reid P. Centre market
Remsen John C. 568 Washington
Reynolds Jas. 181 Chrystie
Richter J. & Co. 24 West
Robbins & Patterson, 536 Washington
Robinson C. Centre market
Robinson & Co. Clinton market
Ronk Philip I. 254 Washington
Sayre J. H. 50 Essex market
Schmidt C. F. 5 Washington mkt
Schutt & Potter, 89 Barclay
Seaman J. M. Centre market
Seaman L. 27 Washington market
Sexton & Cumings. 216 Fulton
Sherlock Patrick. 163 3d Av.
Shutt & Potter, 89 Barclay
Silberhorn Wm. & Co. 34 & 36 Clinton market
Simson Jas. Centre market
Sleeman H. M. 122 Ludlow

Smith Abel S. 292 Bowery
New York.
Smith Chas. W. 116 Broad
Smith John M. & Co. 122 Broad & 59 Henry
Sparrow W. B. 76 South
Stavey E. B. 2 Jefferson market
Stevens Calvin, 13 Front
Stevens Wm. 78 Wooster
Stout J. S. & J. D. 69 Dey
Swezey N. T. & Co. 176 South
Taylor Chas. 27 Water
Terhune & Martin, 201 Chambers
Tillson Timothy C.
Tilton A. H. & Co. 690 Washington
Tompkins J. 99 Washington mkt.
Trowbridge Timothy, 122 Front
Tucker & Littell, 216 Washington
Varick Jas. L. 117 Warren & 100 Front
Van Anken B. H. & Co. 186 Washington
Van Norden's, 187 West
Van Norden B. S. Centre market
Waechter M. 10 Jefferson market
Warren Sylvanus, 127 Forsyth
Warren, Clark & Co. 268 Washington
Waters M. 550 Washington
Wawn R. 539 Broome
Weeks A. Washington market
Weeks A. & Son, 100 Washington market
Wells & Kirk, 170 West & 111 Murray
West Jesse, 546 Washington
Wheaton I. & Co. 258 Washington
Wilson T. 118 Broad
Wilson Wm. M. 23 Water
Wood Wm.
Woolsey John K. 222 Front
Wright Stephen. Essex market
Yates Fred. 28 Warren
Yates & Pepoon, 26 Warren
Young Eben S. & Co. 76 Sullivan

Oneida County.

Owens Owen, 218 Genesee *Utica.*
Thompson & Truax, Durhamville
Verona.

Onondaga County.

Smith B. (3 Williams' Block) Syracuse
Salina.
Adams H. P. Water st. Syracuse
Debney H. Centre market, do
Greenway David, Genesee st. do

Oswego County.

Crampton & Buel, Water st.
Oswego.

Rensselaer County.

Ives C. P. 341 State *Lansingburgh.*
Willard John N. 147 River *Troy.*
Hillman Joseph, 171 River
Merret H. 236 River
Deuchy & Flood, 298 River
Green H. (Meat market) 276 River
Green Henry L. 396 River
Warner E. (Salt Provisions) 307 River
Silliman & Gardiner, 339 River

Steuben County.

Additt A. M. *Urbana.*
Hastings W. & L. D.
Rose Delos

Sullivan County.

Murray & Leinham, Big Eddy
Lumberland.

Public Houses.

Albany County.

Anthony Jacob, 79 Maiden lane
Albany.
Beardsley W. 26 & 28 W'hington

Beebe E. Franklin House, 126 & 128 State *Albany.*
Bendall J. 42 & 44 Hamilton
Bertrand Jeremiah, 1 Dean
Bowers Benjamin, 815 Broadway
Cady George E., Northern Hotel, 648 Broadway
Cady H. D. & W. J. 74 W'hington
Cain J. 31 Union
Churchill A. C. 10 & 12 Hudson
Chadsey George, Saratoga House, 719 Broadway
Clark & Lawrence, 31 Dean
Colburn & Sisson, Delavan House. Broadway
Coulon & Britton, Stanwix Hall, Broadway
Cowell Royal, 354 Broadway
Duff J. A. 11 Montgomery
Gallup N., Farmers' & Mechanics' Hotel, 91 Washington
Griffin W. J. Mansion House, 470 & 472 Broadway
Hoffman T. H. 91 Church
Hollman ——, 128 Water
Holmes S. 27 Dean
House W. A. 11 Maiden lane
Huddleston George, Clinton Hotel, 19 S. Pearl
Jenkinson James, 4 Dean
Johnson George B. 264 Broadway
Joslin, City Hotel, 471 & 473 do
Krender ——, 15 Montgomery
Lacy C. E. 8 Hudson
Libresch L. 19 Hamilton
Littlejohn William, 274 & 276 Broadway
Lowe H. C. 192, 194 & 196 Water
Lockwood J. 66 Washington
M'Cardel, J. 107 Pier
Medberry Allen, 144 Broadway
Mitchell L. Congress Hall, Washington st.
Montony Wm. 15 Washington
Munger H., Lydius Street Hotel, 374 Lydius
Murphry P. 99 Church
Paff W. P. 17 Montgomery
Peterson W. A. 307 S. Pearl
Poley S. 126 do
Pond A. A. 25 Maiden lane
Raby R. City Hall Coffee House, cor. Eagle & Maiden lane
Rose J. 18 Washington
Sabin D. American Hotel, 100 State
Schmitt ——, 41 Liberty
Scovel J. 203 Washington
Schadelle F. 19 Montgomery
Shoemaker Wm. 800 Broadway
Shoemaker J. 1 Ferry
Stanford J. jr. Farmers' Hotel, 42 Washington
St. John John W. 15 & 17 Dean
Swain R. 926 Broadway
Taylor & Leslie, St. Charles Hotel, 27 Hudson
Vachon George, 294 Broadway
Wachter John. 266 do
Walden J. Welden House, 91 Quay
Wilder H. Eagle Street Hotel, 73 & 75 Eagle
Wilson Jesse P. Park House, 29 Hudson
Warmer I. C. 291 Washington
Wood Wm. H. Bull's Head, 177 Washington
Woolford W. Washington st.
Zeh J. H. 38 Hawk
Dyer B. & Sons *Berns.*
Palmer S. Reedsville
Candy Wm. do
Rainhart Wm. do
Blade N. do
Hayes R. do
Ramsey Mrs. *Bethlehem.*
Veeder L.
Dubois C. H.
Leedings J.
Tift James *Coeymans.*
Houghteling A.
Keeder F.
Whitbeck J. A. Barren Island

Steers J. R. *Guilderland.*
Foland John
Case Russell
Jewell V. D.
Brummaghim S
Jewett J. I.
Keanholts J.
M'Kown J.
Groat A.
Slingalong Dow T.
Quackenbush John I
Sloan H.
Lagrange & Frederick
Houck C. Knowerville
Foland Peter, Dunnsville
Barrows G. do
Hotaling Wm. do
Barckley H. Knox
Shutter J. do
Lee B. do
Raynsford E. *New Scotland.*
Sagee D.
Wydeman N.
M'Ewen J.
Hotaling J.
Mann A.
Reed J.
Winne J.
Bradt P. H. Clarksville
Alley J. *Rensselaerville.*
Reeve S. M.
Goff Wm.
Turner J.
Russell O.
Parker J. *Watervliet.*
Van Dewark Evert
Van Vrankin C. C.
Morris L.
Smith C. Troy & Albany Road
Dayton J. C. do
Noyes P. do
Smith Wm. do
Crane G. do
Badgely J. F. do
Segur S. do
Washburn E. W. West Troy
Shadbolt J. Tremont House
Scovill & Hart, West Troy Exchange
Powell C. Watervliet House
Gorman M. do
Miller Charles, West Troy
Collins Isaac, do
Morrison J. & R. do
Barnard A. West Troy Hotel
Nugent D., Cohoes
Bently A. C. do
Gould David *Westerlo.*
Showers Wm.
Van Luven Isaac

Alleghany County.

Burdick Amos *Alfred.*
Lamphear Joseph
Russell John
Ball —
Tracy Ira *Allen.*
Bbner Abner
Riley J. C. *Almond.*
Gernong I.
Porter D.
Helms A. *Amity.*
Ford D. *Andover.*
Hunt C. D.
Osborn A.
Hartshorn F. M. Exchange Hotel
Angelica.
Charles Andrew, Union Hotel
Oliver F. H. American House
Lawrence Wm. S. Temperance House
Scribner G. L. *Belfast.*
West John
Prothehoe Ira
Hopper E.
Stiles Samuel
Stewart N.
Ives Josiah *Birdsall.*
Kenyon George M *Bolivar.*
Houck Peter J. *Burns.*
Kuder Hiram
Bennett Daniel, Whitney Valley

Jackson James A.   *Osceola.*
Dennis William
Willard G. W.
Clark Jacob
Tewksbury D.
Fay Lambert   *Clarksville.*
King L. W.   *Friendship.*
Bradley W.
Pardy W.
Morris J. S.
Taylor D. Z.
Crooks Samuel G.   *Granger.*
Safford J. B., Short Tract
Clough Nathaniel, Grove Centre
Miel C. H.   do
Kelley Joseph.   do
Miner S. R., Little Genesee
   Genesee.
Ingham Chancy G.   *Hume.*
Dantremont Augustus
Terry Isaac
Couch Luther, Wiscoy
Withey Alanson, do
Reynolds Luther J.   *New Hudson.*
Halsey Charles
Voorhees J. & G.   *Ossian.*
Babcock E.
Gillman C.   *Rushford.*
Brooks C. Washington House
Williams A. G.
Parker Stephen
Loomis E. H.   *Scio.*
Blood Samuel F.
Wilber Thomas B.
Van Buren —, Wellsville
M'Lean   do
Woodward M.   *West Almond.*
Farnum M. J.
Watson Elijah
Stannard J. C.   *Wirt.*

Broome County.

Coles W. A., Chenango Forks
   Barker.
Willard O. H.   do
Orcutt S.   *Binghamton.*
Hall Clifton, Phœnix Hotel
M'Elwee Joseph, Binghamton House
Hart & Wells, Chenango House
Pratt E. Millville House
Way B. A. Farmers' Hotel
Whitney J. Brandywine Hotel
Colegrove G. L.   *Chenango.*
Chapman C. H.
Vaughan H.
Ogden J.
Scott W. H., Nineveh   *Colesville.*
Doolittle F., Susquehanna
Tyrell H. T., Harpersville
Poyer —, Valona Springs
Squires H.   *Conklin.*
Fowler A. W. Green Horn Hotel
Brown J.
Knapp T. G.
Weeks J. W.
Corby W.
Blakesley Z.
Jay J.
Stanley B.
Brown R.   *Lisle.*
Howland A.
Clark M., Yorkshire
Smith Silas, Upper Lisle
French R., Union Village
Hubbard G. B.   *Maine.*
Shaw Joseph, Nanticoke Springs
   Nanticoke.
De Groot C., Whitney's Point
   Triangle.
Decker M.   *Union.*
Bloomer J. F. East Union House
Cofferty J. M. Union House
Smith S. Eagle Hotel
Barney P.
Cafferty William
Norton W. A. Union Centre
Jones A. Windsor Hotel   *Windsor.*
Bragg Mrs. H. N. Village Inn
Butts S. Temperance House

Cattaraugus County.

Van Slyke John   *Ashford.*
Oyer John P.
Patterson Robert   *Burton.*
Clark Alfred
Willard S. B.
Simonds Artemas
Sears N. L.   *Carrolton.*
M'Glashan Charles, Stanley's Corners
   Conewango.
Olds James D., Stanley's Corners
Waller M., Arcade   *Ellicottville.*
Metcalf J. H. Irvine Hall
Huntley D. J. Temperance House
Gregory W. F. Gregory's Hotel
Groves J.   *Farmersville.*
Bond O.   *Franklinville.*
M'George M.
M'Cluer James I.
Beebe Hiram. Sandusky   *Freedom.*
Mason Wheaton, do
Howe Otis   *Great Valley.*
Ward Vares
Nobles Jonathan
Howe H.   *Little Valley.*
Morris James
Hickey John
Boardman John
Van Aernan William
Slocum Harry   *Lyndon.*
Hamilton M.   *Machias.*
Napier James
Randall Charles P., Eddyville
   Mansfield.
Ward R. D.   *New Albion.*
Carlisle James   *Otto.*
Cooper William   *Perrysburgh.*
Walker A. A.
Darker M. H., Gowanda   *Persia.*
Canfield W. G.   do
Pingrey Aaron   *Randolph.*
Sheldon George A.
Barrows Samuel, East Randolph
Wheeler H. N.   do
Smith Abner, Rice Hotel   *Rice.*
Aiken James   *South Valley.*
Walker Thomas B.   *Yorkshire.*
Thornton Richard B.
Woolcutt Alfred
Goodremote James
Thornton Samuel

Cayuga County.

Parmele J. National Hotel, Genesee st.   *Auburn.*
Ashby B. 3, 4 & 5 Genesee
Wood W. B. Western Exchange, Genesee st.
White J. jr. American Hotel, Genesee st.
Maxwell T. City Hotel, State st.
White A. Mansion House, 123 Genesee
Davis J. State st.
White   *Aurelius.*
Partelow A.
Twining F.
Caldwell N. D. Weedsport   *Brutus.*
Vanwee J.   do
Carpenter R. B.   do
Chase W.   *Cato.*
Wheeler V.
Timby —
Timby T. R.
Earle S.   *Conquest.*
Allen D.   *Fleming.*
Emmons F.
White Thomas   *Genoa.*
Ogden D.
Acker C.   *Ira.*
Williams G.
Carter S.
Eagle William   *Ledyard.*
Maltby L.   *Locke.*
Sutphen D.
Chipps J. K., Montezuma   *Mentz.*
Duran J. W.   do
M'Loud J.   do
Williams L., Troopeville
Lamkin H., Port Byron
Milk W. W.   do

Campbell J. Port Byron   *Mentz*
Wilkes S.   do
Bouton C.   *Moravia.*
Wood J.
Lockwood S.   *Niles*
Depuy C. W.
Powers L.   *Owasco.*
Heald A.   *Sempronius.*
Rowe S. S.
Hutchinson E.   *Scipio.*
Boughton J. D.
Freeman J.
Fellows H.   *Sennet.*
M'Master H.
Clapp Miss   *Springport.*
Cook C.
Austin & Mason   *Sterling.*
Harsha T.
Rogers ——
Day H.   *Summerhill.*
Hodge J.   *Venice.*
Doughty Thomas E.
Nesf George W.
Parker F.
Merritt H.   *Victory.*
Halsted ——
Allen G.

Chautauque County.

Johnson Nelson   *Arkwright*
Wheaton Charles, Frewsburgh
   Carroll.
Sherman Wm. Mansion House, Mayville   *Chautauque.*
Kensie Wm. New England House, Mayville
Tinkcom H. Tinkcom's Hotel, Mayville
Davis R. Ocean House, Mayville   do
Carr O. H.   do
Kent S. B.   *Cherry Creek*
Maxson M. B.
Sessions W. V.   *Clymer.*
Johnson H. L.
Hadley I. P.   *Ellery.*
Felton A. West Ellery
Scofield W. S.
Fletcher J. W. Jamestown   *Ellicott.*
Williams D. S. Allen House, Jamestown
Smith & Tinker, American Hotel, Jamestown
Van Deuser J. B. Farmers' Hotel, Jamestown
Torrey D. & J.   *Ellington.*
Durkee Orlando, French Creek
Tubbs B. Forestville   *Hanover.*
Smith H. Smith Mills
Heath Charles, Silver Creek
Keith W. W.   do
Whitney A.   do
Lanphear A.   do
Kilton —,   do
Brown Samuel   *Harmony.*
Polly Elijah, Panama
Loucks H.   *Poland.*
Cobb ——
Hunn L. C. Fredonia   *Pomfret.*
Wheeler E.   do
Wright S.   do
Pemberton S.   do
Tuttle —, do
Ward E.   do
Hull J. B.   do
More Wm. P. Dunkirk
Wilber Curtis   *Portland.*
Minton J. H. Salem Cross Roads
Fitch Russell, do   do
Huyck Richard   *Sheridan.*
Williams Alex. jr.
Ecker John J.
Ensign Seymour
Foote Gervis, Foote's Hotel
   Westfield.
Stevens C. Westfield House
Hawkins Mrs. S. S. Westfield Hotel
Smith Alex. American Hotel
Piersons Paul, jr. Eagle Hotel
Robinson Sam. Robinson's Hotel
Wright Allen, Temperance House

Chemung County.

Dunn Wm. *Big Flats.*
Mills S.
Rhodes Joseph
Cooper Peter *Catharine.*

Chenango County.

Newell D. *Bainbridge.*
Seeley N.
Corbin S. W.
Wildey E.
Ingersoll F. East Bainbridge
Stow D. South do
Long L. do do
Pollard J. D. South do
Sennett Milton, Bennettsville
Madison Richard, do
Low John *Columbus.*
Palmer G. B.
Farrell L
Miles L. *Coventry.*
Lewis Charles, Temperance Hotel
Rand Nelson, Livermore's Corners *Germana.*
Whittenhall U. Chenango House *Greene.*
Dimoe Timothy *Guilford.*
Boynton W. Guilford Centre
Ackley L. *Macdonough.*
Bunnell & Co.
Bartle Wm. East Macdonough
Gascon & Babcock *New Berlin.*
Barton John
Palmer S. South New Berlia
Atwell B. do
Owens A. & E. do
Tower J. C. *North Norwich.*
Morris & Son *Norwich.*
Lawrence D. E.
Shapley J.
Hickok & Pellett
Stokes I. *Otselic.*
Parker A.
Willis N. H.
Ford N.
Brigham Daniel *Oxford.*
Perry & Hitchcock
Perkins Alvin S.
Westcott Paul
Grant J. *Pharsalia.*
Crane L.
Blackman Charles *Pitcher.*
Locke Nathaniel
Wever Davis, Pitcher Spa
Dodge Wm. *Plymouth.*
Jones Delas, South Plymouth
Graves R. *Preston.*
Hervey U. T. Sherburne House *Sherburne.*
Irons O.
Hoyt H. B.
Hopson L. R.
Harris D.
Kelley D.
Post G. *Smithville.*
Wiles John
Merrell Enos *Smyrna.*
Kelsey Julius
West Wm.
Henry John, Temperance House

Clinton County.

Poole Thomas, Keeseville *AuSable.*
Harvey Thomas H. do
Simonds R. M. *Beekmantown.*
Hilliard J. Prison Hotel
Warden T. *Black Brook.*
North John P.
Freeman A.
Barlow A. J.
Bigelow John *Champlain.*
Fadden Joseph
Fesette F.
Gorbett Wm.
Slason Daniel, East Chazy *Chazy.*
Merrihew & Stoughton, West Chazy
Hilliker Wm. *Clinton.*
Ford Merrill
Willey James

Pratt N. W. *Moors.*
Derby T. N.
Holcomb D. G. *Peru.*
Nichols J. H.
Brewster J. K. at wharf *Plattsburgh.*
Fonqueth D. L.
Nichols John, U. S. Hotel
Demara John
Davis J.
Conway J.
M'Cann A. Village Hotel
Hart J.
Thora U. M. Turnpike House
Hillyard Freeman
Dill Edward. Cardyville
Stackpoole Paul R. *Saranac.*
Dustan Daniel, Redford

Columbia County.

Bain J. A. *Ancram.*
Rockefeller J. A.
Tyler A. B. *Austerlitz.*
Salmon G. W. Spencertown
Berry James, Railroad Hotel, Canaan 4 Corners *Canaan.*
Hoag T. *Chatham.*
Hoes A. & I. Chatham House, Chatham Four Corners
Kisselburg T. Chatham Hotel, Chatham Four Corners
Mesick J. H. Columbia Hotel, Chatham Four Corners
Brown Wm. East Chatham
Allendorph G Malden Bridge
Davis T. Temperance House, Malden Bridge
Hill H. North Chatham
Smith J. *Claverack.*
Woodworth J.
Shafelt J. I. Mansion House
Platner J. I. Smoky Hollow
Rodgers R. do
Best H. Mellenville
Waldorph J. I. Churchtown
Yager John, do
Proper J. I. *Clermont.*
M'Gill Wm. Clermont House
Bain L. Copake Hotel *Copake.*
Miller P.
Bain P. A.
Snyder J. D.
Snyder L. Jackson Corner Hotel *Gallatin.*
Chadwick W. H. Gallatinville Hotel
Weaver F. A.
Sudam J. F.
Rockefeller S. *Germantown.*
Sturgess J.
Lasher R.
Rockefeller P. D.
Perkins John, Ghent Hotel *Ghent.*
Miller A. F.
Foster S. Temperance House *Hillsdale.*
Reed Mrs. Stage House
Haggerty T. Stranger's Retreat, Franklin sq. *Hudson.*
Millard B. R. Franklin House, Franklin sq.
Miner B. Oregon House, South Front st.
Hubbard A. Hudson House
Rogers W. Columbia House, cor. Warren & 5th
Martin S. S. Eastern House
Badgley W. & Son, Mansion House, Warren st.
Miller C. H. National Hotel, Franklin sq.
De Myer B. Farmers' Hotel
Wilder A. Kinderhook Hotel
Miller S. Valatie *Kinderhook.*
Bradley W. United States Hotel, Valatie
Hoes A., Valatie
Hare H. *Livingston.*
Washburn R. & W.
Gardiner A.
Cole J.
Stall Wm. I.

Babcock L. S. Coffee House *New Lebanon.*
Holcomb Mrs. F. Lord's Hotel, New Lebanon Springs
Babcock J. W. Lebanon Springs Hotel, New Lebanon Springs
Hull H. Columbia Hall, do
Marks H. New Lebanon Centre
Bigelow H. Moffatt's Store
Hoes J. *Stockport.*
Moore J. R. Stockport House
Clapp G. *Stuyvesant.*
Hunt J. Stuyvesant Falls
Whitbeck C. *Taghkanic.*

Cortland County.

Samson Isaac M. *Cincinnatus.*
Fish C. D.
Fairchild Isaac, Eagle Tavern, *Cortland Village.*
Clark J. W. Cortland House
Etz C. Centre House
Van Renselaer John, Tioughnioga Hotel
M'Daniels ——, M'Grawville
Slocumb Calvin N. Homer Hotel, *Homer.*
Bowen Orin, Mansion House
Bishop Hiram, Exchange
Cool Giles, East Homer
Rose Luther R.
Tubbs Martin B. Little York
Burgess James *Marathon.*
Leach Mordecai
Wilcox John L. *Preble.*
Salisbury Lorenzo D.
Harrop Thomas *Scott.*
Whithey Wm.
Wheeler John *Solon.*
Wheeler Elijah
Fleming Samuel *Taylor.*
Porter B.
Westermen Peter *Truxton.*
Pierce Abijah T.
Pierce Judah
Blanchard Wm., Cuyler
Wilcox Horace *Virgil.*
More Zopher C.

Delaware County.

Hilton P. *Andes.*
Hunting E. B.
Earlle Moses W.
Shaver William, Shavertown
Wood J. East Branch, do
Kinworth J. *Bovina.*
Davis J.
Wilson James *Colchester.*
Radeker B.
Downs G. W. Downsville
Wetmore J. R. Centre Hotel *Davenport.*
Avery J.
Mackey A. Davenport House
Fenn E. B.
Grant William F. West Davenport
Barlow William do
Edgarton —— *Delhi.*
Judson C. L.
Flower J. P.
Mitchell C.
Edgarton H. Franklin Coffee House *Franklin.*
Grant J. A. Delavan House
Van Hosen P., Croton
Turnfull W. *Hamden.*
Chase G.
Brainard A. G.
Falkner J. Chechocton House *Hancock.*
Twaddle J. M.
Lanfeld C.
Reed B.
Hamilton R. H. *Harpersfield.*
Sevens S.
Jaques A. Bloomville Mansion House *Kortright.*
Edgerton G.
Hitchcock J.

22

Griffin Asa (temperance house)
Middletown.
O'Conner W., Margaretsville
Kesley D. A.   do
Osterhout D.   do
Griffin M., Clovesville
Beadle A.   do
Baldwin J. R. Delaware House,
Stamford.
Stevens S. M.
Perkins S. Eagle Hotel, Hobart
Whitmore E. S. Mansion House,
Hobart
Birdsall G. Sidney Hotel *Sidney.*
Fowler E., Sidney Plains
Sherwood E. T., Deposit
Tompkins.
Wiswell L. G.   do
Hawley Wm. Temperance Hotel,
Deposit
Salisbury A. F., Deposit
Miller A. G.   *Cannonsville.*
Smith S. W.   *Walton.*
Sprague J. O. Temperance House

Duchess County.

Butts H.   *Amenia.*
Freeman E. D.
Winchester M.
Butts H., South Amenia
Peters J.   *Beekman.*
Thomas D.
Belden C. H.   *Dover.*
Chapman W. H., South Dover
Tabor G., R. R. House, Dover
Plains
De La Vergue N., Stone Church
Hotel
Lamson R., Mansion House
Fishkill.
Bogardus Joseph, Union Hotel
Gidley A. D. Village Hotel, Wap-
pinger's Falls
Nuttal J., Wappinger's Falls
Beaver C., Hughsonville House,
Hughsonville
Sirvine A., Village Temperance
House. Hughsonville
Vanart Wm. T., Glenham
Monger ——, Low Point Hotel,
Low Point
Green J., Matteawan Hotel, Mat-
teawan
Speeding H. Eagle Hotel, Fish-
kill Landing
Vanvoorts Mrs. A. Starr Inn, Fish-
kill Landing
O'Neal J., Long Dock Hotel, Fish-
kill Landing
Tompkins J., Stormville
Yates S.. New Hackensack
Nostrandt B., Fishkill Plains
Jewell J.   do
Vandine J.   do
De Graaf M.   *Hyde Park.*
Devor C. C. Steamboat Hotel
Van Wagner J. P. Washington
Hotel
Marshall W. R. Hyde Park Hotel
Myers J. B.   *Lagrange.*
Smith J. G.
Vermelyea B.
Robinson S., Sprout Creek
Knickerbocker J., Lafayette Cor-
ner   *Milan*
Caulkins J. G., Temp. House,
North East Centre *North East.*
Hawl L.   *Pawling.*
Arnold M.
Burdock J. S.
Hageman H.   *Pine Plains.*
Myers H. E.
Farrington E., Pulver's Corners
Hotel
Keefer H. J.   do
Vails J. C.   *Pleasant Valley.*
Heerman Wm. J. Salt Point Hotel
Vails M. Independence Hall
Dickenson, C. G. Hudson River
House, Main cor. Water
Poughkeepsie.

Grant J, J. Exchange House,
Steamboat Landing *Poughkeepsie.*
Vincent G. L. & Co, Barge Ex-
change
Hepp C. Washington House, foot
Main st.
Butzer J. H. Poughkeepsie House,
245 Main
Smith & Hill, Franklin House, 227
Main
Hagaman & Ostrum, Columbian
Porter House, 219 Main
Doran C. & J., O'Connell House,
Mill st.
Gregory T. Temperance House,
Main & Catharine
Dow J. L. Mansion House, 30 Mar-
ket
Baldwin Isaac I. Northern House
Miller H. Union House, 147 Main
Phillips A. Monterey House, 139
Main
Lenty D., R. R. House, Main cor.
Clover
Howell James, 151 Main
Jewell J., New Hamburgh Hotel
Baker A.
Welling H. P.
Dolsen J.
Myer Z. V.
Hesse G., Upper Red Hook
Red Hook.
Proctor A.   do
King G. W. Steamboat Hotel, Ti-
voli
Shoemaker G. Steamboat House,
Barrytown
Jennings S. Steamboat House
Rhinebeck.
Cotting J. Long Dock
Pultz E. Rhinebeck Hotel
Pultz P.
White E.   *Stanford.*
Barlow C.
Fletcher R. N.   *Unionvale.*
Wait G. C.
Crouse B. A. & E.
Vincent R. F., Verbank
Tomlinson S., Washington Hollow
Washington.
Emigh D. P.   do
Chamberlain E. H , Mabbettsville

Erie County.

Rice E.   *Alden.*
Paddock Raymond
Perry Almond, Alden Centre
Slocum A.   *Amherst.*
Lamphere S.
Snearly Benj.
M'Allister Wm. A., Williamsville
Henshaw Joseph M., Westfall
Aurora.
Huntley George H.   do
Holmes Wm., Springbrook
Crandle James F., Willink
Sexton H. C.   do
M'Danields Michael,   do
Blakely Wm. J.   do
Angel Lloyd,   do
Lyons Step. W. Frontier House
Black Rock.
Ralph Christian, Eagle Tavern
Tilden Cyrus, Niagara House
Miller J. T. Scotts Tavern
Scott J. B. Buffalo Plains House,
Buffalo Plains
Barr A. Cold Spring House, Buf-
falo Plains
Gates George, Gates Tavern,
Buffalo Plains
Crooker Geo., Buffalo Plains
Peck Daniel   *Boston.*
Sheopard J.
Starkweather Sidney
Fuller Ira
Sprague Wm.   *Brandt.*
Field Bartholomew
Bailey & Hull. Bennett's Tempe-
rance House. (see advertise-
ment) Pearl cor. Terrace
Buffalo.

Black G. W., Mariner's Home,
Evans st.   *Buffalo*
Bonney Z., U. S. Hotel, Pearl cor
Terrace
Browning P., Lovejoy's House,
Terrace st.
Bush Isaac, jr., Farmers' Hotel,
195 Main
Claris John, Rainbow Hotel,
Swan st.
Clark G. W., Oregon House, Ohio
cor. Illinois
Cleghorn T. C., R. R. Exchange,
n. Eastern R. R. Depot
Crane & Nelson, Southern Hotel,
129 E. Seneca
Crooker E., E. Seneca st.
Crooker Wm., Pearl st. House, 17
Pearl
Dorsheimer P., Mansion House,
Main cor. Exchange
Eggers Ernst, Stadt Hanover, Ex-
change st.
Ford & Flaherty, 1st Ward House,
Washington cor. Ohio
Frost Norman, Farmers' Exch.
195 Main
Harris Wm., Elk House, Elk st.
Hodges Lewis L., Am. House,
Main st.
Horterly John, Waverly House,
S. Division st.
Huff & Thomas, Huff's Hotel,
Packet Boat Landing
Hutchins & Horton, Columbia Ho-
tel, 85 & 87 Main
Larreau A. N., Rail Road Hotel,
99 Exchange
Lawson R., Lawson's Hotel, Ohio
cor. Missouri
M'Mellen D. C., Genesee House
Main cor. Genesee
Major & Wells, Buffalo Tempe-
rance House, 41, 42 & 49 Main
Marsh Mary A. Eastern Hotel, 55
Exchange
Montague A. Evans st.
Osborn Ira, Western Hotel, Ter-
race cor. Pearl
Powell J., New England Hotel,
Carroll st.
Reif Thos., La Fayette Coffee
House, 279 Main
Rogers N.. Phelps House, Main c.
S. Division
Tunnicliff C., Rough & Ready
House, 3 & 4 Ohio Build'gs, foot
Main st.
Wasson Wm., Seneca Hydraulics
Wells Wm. Commercial st.
Wheeler Francis. Wheeler's Ho-
tel, Commercial st.
Young Peter, Huff's Hotel, 81 &
83 Main
Younglove O.. Franklin House, 44
E. Seneca
Westcott Jesse   *Cheektowaga.*
Baker A. W.
Seeley M. H.
Smith George
Heath P.   *Clarence*
Saddley J. B.
Utley George. Clarence Centre
Buffum Albert   *Colden.*
Carr David   *Collins*
Tucker Charles
Crapo Peter
Crandall C.
Hill J., Zoar
Seacous ——
Smith & Beebe, Springville *Concord*
Morton A. P. West Concord
Rockwood Reuben   *Eden.*
Lord Samuel
Langley George
Mossman Levi   *Evans*
Andrus John
Clark ——
Morgan Walter, East Evans
Colby Daniel,   do
Fisk ——   do

Thomas C. D. Water Valley
    Hamburgh.
Fish Thomas,   do
Bixler Daniel,   do
Howard ——,   do
Harvey L. P. Hamburgh Centre
Potter A. & E. East Hamburgh
Keith —— Hamburgh on the lake
Smith Joel S.   do
Stone ——,   do
Johnson Asa P.   do
Hurd William,   do
Norton Anson   *Holland.*
Paul David
Graves Waters
Morey W. L. Cazenovia Hotel
Curtis W., R. R. Hotel *Lancaster.*
Rice Harlow, Lancaster House
Rowley Abner, R. R. Exchange
George Jacob
Keiffer Peter
Kuhn Frank
Filkins Warren, Town Line
Draper Anson   *Newstead.*
Harrington S., Akron
Hastings C., Sardinia
Graham W.   do
Huff Stephen   *Tonawanda.*
Freer R.   *Wales.*
Nichols William
Jones William
Warner D. S. South Wales
Pettengill Allen, Wales Centre

Essex County.

Colvin A. Port Kent   *Chesterfield.*
Benedict Jonas A.   *Crown Point.*
Russell Samuel
Moore William
Judd David, Valley House
    Elizabethtown.
Brainard Chas. H. Essex County
  Mansion House
Bishop Lucius
Smith Abel
Swinton James M.
Fancher Charles G.   *Essex.*
Clemons Noble
Velie N., Whallonsburgh
Ritcher Alexander M.   *Jay.*
Blanchard Hiram, Temp. House
Storrs W. & Orren, Upper Jay
Downer John B.   do
Parkhurst Jas. Ausable Forks
Ford Sidney   *Keene.*
Norton Wesley
Bowman James M.   *Lewis.*
Phelps George
Burk Austin
Canary Solomon   *Minerva.*
Tappen J. Moriah Four Corners
    Moriah.
Pearse George B. Port Henry
Root R.. Schroon River *Schroon.*
Tyrrel Maaaibel, Schroon Lake
Heaton Hiram   *Ticonderoga.*
Pratt W. H. H.
Tefft James
Davis Abijah
Parsons H. J.   *Westport.*
Richards William
Hinckley Harvey   *Willsborough.*

Franklin County.

Bentley Hial   *Bangor.*
Cleaveland C. C.
Harvey Abel, North Bangor
Bonker E.   *Bombay.*
Stephens R. R.
Miner Hiram   *Burke.*
Goodspeed J. L.
Smith A. G.
Pike Reuben
Roberts Samuel   *Chateaugay.*
Derby Myron
Hilliker William
Marks Elisha
Toby ——   *Constable.*
Heath M.   *Dickinson.*
Danforth Josiah   *Duane.*
Button Schuyler   *Fort Covington.*

Paddock Oliver W. *Fort Covington.*
Spencer Joseph
Briggs Joseph
Merril John   *Franklin.*
Hatch Harry B.
Lovelin Prentice
Bigelow ——
Martin Henry   *Harrietstown.*
Martin W. F.
Miller P. B.   *Malone.*
Hosford O. T.
Harrington R.   *Moira.*
Shaw E. Brush Mills
Davis H. West Constable *Westville.*
Berry Philo

Fulton County.

Ross Mrs.   *Broadalbin.*
De Forest David
Ash R. E.
Getman Thos. Union Mills
Davis John, Hill's Corners
Moaroe Major, Hooseville
Seber A. W.   *Caroga.*
Empie Mrs.   *Ephraim.*
Fuller John K.
Cristman J. I.
Pool John, Cayadutta House
    Johnstown.
Potter George, Potter's Hotel
Johnson R. H. Johnson's Hotel
Bancroft Jas. Bancroft's Hotel
M'Intyre Peter, M'Intyre's Hotel
Thomas H. C. Gloversville Hotel
Thompson J. B. Kingsboro
Simmons T. Vails Mills *Mayfield.*
Stewart D. Mayfield Corners
Pearl Edward   *Northampton.*
Macomber Peleg, Northville
Patridge Truman,   do
Claus Mrs.   *Oppenheim.*
Lassell H. S.
Brockett C. & J. P.
Kring John
Cooke Jacob
Stewart A. Perth Hotel   *Perth.*
Allen Samuel

Genesee County.

Clark Aaron   *Alabama.*
Ames E. & Co.
Bardwell R. J.
Dusel Hiram
Rector Chas. Acid Spring House
Osmer Silas   *Alexander.*
Fargo O. T.
Norton E.
Tisdale B. G. American Hotel
    Batavia.
Bierce S. N. Genesee House
Backus I. Western Hotel
Hull E. Eagle Tavern
Frost S., R. R. House
Bischel A. Dutch Tavern
White N. A.   *Bergen.*
Hooper John
Van Dermark A. Mansion House
Gifford J. R.   *Bethany.*
Wallace Warren, East Bethany
Bennett   *Byron.*
Hovey E. S.   *Darien.*
King Stephen, Darien Centre
Carpenter P. Eagle Hotel *Le Roy.*
Ballard L. Franklin Exchange
Mills M. Cottage Inn
Hulbert A. Le Roy House
Davis L. Yellow Eagle
Olcott I.   *Oakfield.*
Lovett Jabez   *Pavilion.*
Stage Isaac N. Farmers' Hotel
    Stafford.
Watson ——, Morganville Hotel

Greene County.

Bump Ephraim   *Ashland.*
Ives John S.
Kinsley Henry
Martin Nicholas
Tuttle John
Van Hosen ——

Osborn Orrin E.   *Athens.*
Seeley Castle
Coon John
Edmonds Enos B.
Dexter Bester   *Cairo.*
Person John H.
Keith Amasa
M'Williams Jas., Acra
Guffen John   *Catskill.*
Jacobs John
Hoffman Charles
Van Burgen & Chamberlain
Beardsley Charles
Gunn Enos
Newcomb John
Paine George
Osborn Z. S.
Smith Theron
Barrett Alex. H.
Smith Silleck D. Leeds
Fitchett Isaac P.   *Cossackie.*
Vanwie Ambrose A.
Backus Charles
Livingstone Hiram
Baker Sterry
Benjamin Horace
Holcomb Abel   *Durham.*
Bell Owen
Cook Samuel W. D.
Roe Wm. '   *Greenville.*
Conkling Wm.
Hallock Benton
Ken Robert R.   *Hunter.*
Anthony Wm. East Kill
Lament Martin   *Lexington.*
Lament John M.
Van Walkenburgh L.
Corinth Eben. West Kill
Chase West, East Lexington
Mead Stephen   *New Baltimore.*
Hyatt Jeremiah
Sutherland Betuuel   *Prattsville.*
Smith Cyrus
Laraway Henry
Richards & Brandon
Osborne Henry R.   *Windham.*
French Wm. H.
Fox Hiram. Union Society
Jones Cornelius W.   do

Hamilton County.

Wadsworth D.   *Hope.*
Denny H.
Olmsted A.
Holmes John C.   *Lake Pleasant.*
Saterly Clark
Skidmore Jas.
Morehouse A. R.   *Morehouse.*
Francisco Archibald   *Wells.*
Hasley Benj.
Weld Wm. R.

Herkimer County.

Otterben John   *Columbia.*
Jacobson Henry
Shol Chas
Brown Norman
Helmer Conrad
Joyce John   *Danube.*
Ali Sylvester
Young John
Hall D.
Pickert I.
Franklin S. C.   *Fairfield.*
Christie H.
Piper N.   *Frankfort.*
Joslin C.
Ferguson S. W. West Frankfort
Wetmore Elisha, Frankfort Hill
Weller F. U. Ilion *German Flats.*
Owens R. U. Mohawk
Golden John,   do
Knapp C.   do
Taylor Ell, R. R. House *Herkimer*
Young Heman
Smith Newman
Butler Henry, Benton House
    Little Falls.
Hinchman Chas. Eagle Hotel
Able John, Canal Hotel
Moger Nicholas

Hawkins Henry   *Little Falls.*
Churchill Albert W.   *Eatonville.*
Miller C.   *Litchfield.*
Lamb G. V.   *Manheim.*
Snell Alfred
Van Valkenburgh J
Jerome C.
Strough John
Loucks Jacob
Nellis J. P.
Buckley W. S.   *Newport.*
Stacey O. L.
Pullman Elias B.   *Norway.*
Willoughby Marshall   *Ohio.*
Abub Albert
Varney J. W.   *Russia.*
Moore C. Cold Brook
Rich Henry, Postville
Potter & Arnold, Poland
Benchley Geo.   *Salisbury.*
Barrett John A. Salisbury Centre
Cool Daniel D.   do
Goodwin ——,   do
Shaver Robert,   do
Gordon Ira   *Schuyler.*
Knapp Wm. K.
Fikes Adam   *Stark.*
Ward R. R.
Lathrop Jas. Van Hornsville
Suits Thos. Starkville
Tuniclff Richard   *Warren.*
Tunnecliff Alonzo
Rathbun J.
Lyman D. T. Jordanville
Huestis C. M. Page's Corner
Petrie Jonas,   do
Hickok W.   *Winfield.*
Aldrich David
Morgan ——, West Winfield
Thomas L. G.   do

Jefferson County.

Totman C. R.   *Adams.*
Russell D. P.
Munger A. Adams Centre
Dolinger P. Redwood *Alexandria.*
Simonds Ralph, do
Paul N. C. Plessis Hotel, Plessis
Crossmen Chas. Alexandria Bay
Wescott C.   do
Pratt T. R.   *Antwerp.*
Hamblin Wm.
Brainard Enos, Ox Bow
Paul Wm. A.   do
Field Samuel W. Field's Hotel
          Brownville.
Fowler Wm.
Materson P. Dexter
Copeland Geo.
Avery Chas. B. Perch River
Edwards John W. Limerick
Gould Jas.   do
Skinner W.   *Cape Vincent.*
Ballard J.   *Champion.*
Coon ——
Benjamin S. S.   *Clayton.*
Robbins V. Depauville
Kilborn Wm.
Cook S. Woodville   *Ellisburgh.*
Chase D. Belleville
Stearns Daniel, Mannsville
Weeks S. H.   *Henderson.*
Haskins W. B. Croton House,
Sackett's Harbor   *Hounsfield.*
Dodge A. H. Exchange Hotel
Barrows L. Ontario House
Schuyler A.   do
Coon M. Graves, Great Bend
          Le Ray.
Freeman E. B.   do
Spaulding William P. Evans' Mills
Hotel, Evans' Mills
Beebe Alderson,   do
Gilman Chester   *Lorraine.*
Jones L. E. Three Mile Bay *Lyme.*
Lucas E.   do
Benson T. D.   do
Coffin F.   do
Grow F. Miller's Bay
Andrews C.   do
Richardson Stephen, Lafargeville
          Orleans.

Holloway William, Lafargeville
          Orleans.
Falling ——, Watertown *Pamelia.*
Smith ——   do
Harger ——, Pamelia 4 Corners
Mayo ——   do
Butterfield L. H   *Philadelphia.*
Lawrence H.
Warren William
Brown Samuel   *Rodman.*
Corey P. East Rodman
Howell William, South Rutland
          Rutland.
Smith T. B. Black River
Thurston P.   do
Woolson William P. Felt's Mills
Hotel   *Felt's Mills.*
Cheufty Francis   *Theresa.*
Smith John F.
Ballard & Harris, Union Hotel
Morris John
Hanson B. N. Red Tavern
Massey Baker, Eagle Tavern
          Watertown.
Gates Silas, Centre House
Buck Elijah, Empire House
Perkins Charles, Perkins's Hotel
Crowner John D.
Alexander William
Rich Henry D.
Warrington Joseph, Burrville
Hungerford Timothy, Watertown
Centre
Brown Myrick, Field's Settlement
Henry H., Carthage   *Wilna.*
Hamblen L.   do
Allen Thomas, Natural Bridge

Kings County.

Alexander H. W. 291 Fulton
          Brooklyn.
Alexander Mark, Flushing Av.
cor. Franklin
Bailey & Baldwin, Franklin
House, 15 Fulton
Bradley W. & J. 7 Hudson Av.
Bunce J. 39 Henry
Carll Selah B. Waverly House
cor. Atlantic & Furman
Carman Charles, Long Island Ho-
tel, 37 Fulton
Carll Conklin, Rio Grande House
24 Fulton
Cavanagh Dennis, 7 Atlantic
Clear Edward, Brooklyn Garden
Hotel
Centro A. Park Hotel, Hudson Av.
cor. Concord
Colgan Owen, 29 James
Colgan D. Eagle House 196 Ful-
ton
Colyer Andrew, 10 Hudson Av.
Davis John, 190 Sands
Dent Thomas, 70 Main
Doty Hiram, Fulton House, Fulton
Ferry
Duflon Alexander, 166 Myrtle Av
Dwyer John, 99 Atlantic
Gale Edwin R. Mansion House
Hicks st.
Gege Edward H. 6 Hudson Av.
Goldsmith William, Bull's Head
House, Fulton Av.
Haines David H. Montague Hall,
Court st.
Horton Mrs. Martha, Flushing Av.
cor. Grand
Joost Christopher, Stage House.
Flushing Av. cor. Classon E.
Joy William, 188 York
Jones John, American Hotel, 25
Fulton
Laird John, 43 Hudson Av.
Leach William S., Jay cor. Con-
cord
Losee Albert, 18 Atlantic
Logue A. Columbia st.
M'Clure Alexander, 1 Water cor.
Fulton
M'Dermott John, Columbia st.

M'Elhiney John, cor. Plymouth &
Bridge   *Brooklyn.*
M'Grath John, 77 Atlantic
M'Name M. 12 State cor. Furman
Mackay P. Flushing Av.
Mooney Patrick, 1 Garrison
Parker W. H. 67 Concord
Peters John, Fisherman's Hall cor.
Bond & Degraw
Post Daniel W. City Hotel, 342
Fulton
Queredo Joseph, National Hotel,
191 York
Quigley Ann, Washington corner
Front
Raynor E. Oregon House, corner
Court & Fulton
Read James, Hudson Av. corner
Nassau
Remsen George, Atlantic Hotel,
foot of Hamilton
Russell Henry, 293 Adams
Sharp William H. Myrtle Av.
Smith Daniel J. Globe Hotel, 299
Fulton
Snedeker E. V. W., Howard House,
40 Main
Sweeney Geo. 2d Ward Hotel,
York cor. Pearl
Sweeny John, U. S. Hotel, 5 At-
lantic
Teasdale John, 9 Boerum
Timmerman Lewis, cor. Kent and
Flushing Av.
Thomas J. 2d Ward House, Pros-
pect cor. Jay
Tomsey A. 29 Liberty
Van Keuren A. S. 215 Fulton
Voght Killian, 3 Atlantic
Weber Jacob, Brooklyn Hotel, 122
Hudson
White Robert, 207 Nassau
Withers Henry, 6th Ward Hotel,
Smith cor. Warren
Williams Samuel, Franklin Hotel,
Myrtle Av. cor. Division
Woodman Henry, Livingston house
cor. Atlantic & Columbia
Smith John. Green Point Hotel,
Green Point   *Bushwick.*
Randall Nathaniel, Green Point
Ferry House, Green Point
Nelson B. S. Flatbush Branch Ho-
tel   *Flatbush.*
Wiggins Henry, Flatbush Hotel
Schoonmaker J. B.
Durland William, Canarsie
          Flatlands.
Skidmore Isaac, Canarsie
Bergen John,   do
Emmons Peter V.   *Gravesend.*
Jackson Ana
Cozine James
Tappan J.
Freeman B.
Cropsey J. W. Coney Island
Wyckoff John,   do
Van Sicklen Henry,   do
Rogers M.   do
Vincent O. New Utrecht Hotel
          New Utrecht.
Brown Mrs. Ellen, Bath
Nevalle Edward, Kings Co. Hotel,
S. 7th cor. 1st   *Williamsburgh.*
Johnson & Warner, S. 7th cor. 1st
Hanfield Harmon, 1st cor. Kent Av.
Thomas Anton. Union Av.
Masset John, Leonard st.
Stury Joseph, 11 Grand
Sealy Robert, 1   do
Zaser Joseph, 285   do
Stehlio John B. 308   do
M'Mahon Michael, 196 Grand
Quin F. 160   do
Costenbader J. 6   do
Smith Obadiah, Washington House,
20 Grand
Hicks Jackson, American Hotel,
2 Grand
Cooney Philip, 1st cor. N. 2d
Hack Henry, N. 3d
Howard P. 100 No. 3d

Jennings J. M. 36 No. 3d
Williamsburgh.
Rhodes Leonard, 290 1st
Burke P. 1st. cor. N. 6th
Shipton & Jandustin, Bell Cottage 1st cor. N. 11th
Mohr M. Union Av. Hotel, 192 Union Av.
Forest John, Union Hall Hotel, Ewing st.
Lugster D. Grand near Bushwick Av.

Lewis County.

Rivet Joseph   *Croghan.*
Bent P.   *Denmark.*
Blodgett H.
Davenport A. Copenhagen
Hildreth L. C.   do
Gates Simeon   *Diana.*
Van Antwerp Adam
Blanchard Daniel H.
Harris Austin
Talcott Johnson   *Leyden.*
Talcott Ulman G.
Comstock Joel
Crofoot Isaac
Dort J. H.   *Lowville.*
Wood L. S.
House J.
Allen J. M. West Lowville
Bostwick J. R.   do
Copeland J. T.   *Martinsburgh*
Thompson E.
Harger N. N. West Martinsburgh
Woolworth George   *Turin.*
Shaffer Solomon
Van Names S. M. Houseville
Nelson B. Constableville
                    West Turin.
Miller Peter,   do
Nolen James,   do
Allen William,   do
Dexter W.   do
Hoyt Willis, Collinsville
Koohley J.   do

Livingston County.

Comstock O. Eagle Hotel   *Avon.*
Davis Samuel, Avon House
Marsh Charles
Houghton N. American House
Birdlong A. W. Knickerbocker Hall
Dunn John
Houghton N.
Wiard T. & M., E. Avon
Chadwick Josiah, S. do
Shaw James   *Caledonia.*
Hotchkin George A.
M'Vicar John   *Conesus.*
Clark L.
Keyes ——
Foster ——
Chadwick N. Dansville House
                    Dansville.
Chase H. A. American Hotel
Bingham Wm. Exchange do
Eggleston Wm. Eagle do
Jones Theron, Jones' do
Berxes Wm. Western   do
Howe H. & J. N. Junction House
Lewis Thomas J. Fountain do
Bissell Benjamin, American Hotel
                    Geneseo.
Taylor G. C. Franklin House
Van Gordon l. & H. Eagle do
Reed Morton, Farmer's Home
Benway Isaac   *Groveland.*
Wright David,National Exchange, Cuylerville   *Leicester.*
Schnart —— Cuylerville House
White William, Moscow
Watson Wilber, Genesee Valley Hotel
Hart & Co. Pine Tavern
Higgins E. C.   *Lima.*
Nash C. B.
Marten Walter   *Livonia.*
Doolittle Aaron H. Hemlock Lake
Neff Joseph, South Livonia
Doolittle Horace, Lakeville

Conger John, Lakeville *Livonia.*
Scovill Riley, Eagle Tavern
                    Mount Morris.
Kellogg H. H. American Hotel
Beach Alvah, Temperance do
Ketchum C. L.
Le Rue J.
Nicholls L. Nunda House *Nunda.*
Brown O. H. Eagle Tavern
Ryder H. A. Oakland House, Oakland,   *Portage.*
Patterson Benjamin W., Hunt's Hollow
James L.   *Sparta.*
Havens D. Scottsburgh
Williams Isaac   *Springwater.*
Herrick David
Snyder Alonzo, American House
Hitt Ray   *York.*
Bow James, Fowlersville
Angorder Simon, Greigsville
Thompson Ellis, Piffardania

Madison County.

Keith Henry   *Brookfield.*
Miner Paul B. Leonardsville
Jewell Oliver, Lincklaen House
                    Cazenovia.
Moulter Michl. Cazenovia House
Burr Wm. G., Burr's Tavern
Jones Levi
Ransom Orin
Smith A. & O. New Woodstock
Annas A. N. Annas House
                    De Ruyter.
Hull E. H.
Scott Horace
Burgess B. F.
Kellogg J. G. Exchange Hotel
                    Eaton.
Bellows J. C. Eaton Hotel
Dewey B. B., Dewey's Hotel Morrisville
Stilwell Harry, Stillwell's Exchange
Lewis R. M. & H. Madison Co House
Stone T. K. Temperance House
Temple H. Pratt's Hollow
Walden A. B. Leeville
Barritt William   *Fenner.*
Bates Ira
Mosely & Hare, Traveller's Home
                    Georgetown.
Nye T. C. Park House *Hamilton.*
Matteson J. S. Eagle Stage House
Chapham D. A. Coffee House
Dunham L. H. Earlville
Richmond Damon, Poolville
Carrier A. D. Temperance House, East Hamilton
Wood ——, Hubbard's Corners
Campbell H. A.   *Lebanon.*
Benedict Zar, Temperance House
Pope J.
Ferris B.
Cloyes Z. Lenox House *Lenox.*
Allen J. W., R. R. House, Oneida Depot
Blodgett D.   do
White E. R. Canastota House, Canastota
Montross John, Coffee House
Delano Henry, Union House
Dyer B. W. Wampsville
Johnson R.   do
Wilson H. C. Oneida Valley
Sayles Smith, Clockville
Wilcox Salmon
Curtis Isaac   *Madison.*
Priest A.
Morris Thomas, Bouckville
Hall A. G. Solsville
Smith S. & H.   *Nelson.*
Case Granville
Abbot C. H. Erieville Hotel, Erieville
Jennings C. J. Erieville
Shipman David, Peterboro Hotel, Peterboro   *Smithfield.*
Travis S. O. Peterboro

Sumner H. T.   *Stockbridge*
Vedder Fred.
French John O.   *Sullivan*
Phillips Martin, Oneida Lake
Holmes, Henry & Co. White Sulphur Springs House, Chittenango
French & Severance, Chittenango Hotel Chittenango
Campbell A. & Co. Chittenango
Russell Orimel, Harmony Hall
Daniels W. W., R. R. House
Damons E. H. Bridgeport
Shute Henry,   do
Snyder Z.   do

Monroe County.

Comer S. W. Farmers' Inn
                    Brighton.
Homan B.
Holton H.
Stickles J.
See Jacob
Rowland H.
Harford Charles, N. Chili   *Chili.*
Walbridge S., Corner *Clarkson.*
Farrer J.
Fields Luther   *Gates.*
Buck J.
Stutson J. J.   *Greece.*
Olmstead H. Traveller's Home.
Butts John
Telford T.
Andrews H. Jenkins' Corner.
Hovey H.   do
Spencer H.   do
Anthony J. East Henrietta
                    Henrietta.
Cutler J. C. West do
Swain James   *Irondequoit.*
Webster C. Farmers' Delight, East Mendon   *Mendon.*
Tuttle C. D. East Mendon
Beagle N. West do
Hyslop T.   do
Lincoln F. Eagle Hotel, Spencers' Basin   *Ogden.*
Tolford F.   *Parma.*
Honstoa I.
Gunn R. L. Parma Corner
Goodall William,   do
Knox C. A. Parma Centre
Roberts Charles,   do
M'Cormick P.   *Penfield.*
Sho craft P.
Goodrich W. H. Fairport
                    Perrinton.
Wilcox F. M.   do
Green G. W. Bushnell's Basin
Sawins Jonas,   do
Sherwood S. P. Phenix Hotel
                    Pittsford.
Wood D. Western Exchange do
Tupper Alonzo A. Rail Road Hotel, Churchville   *Riga.*
Alexander B. Kosciusko House, cor. Front & Mumford *Rochester.*
Ashley Simeon, Farmer's Hotel, 190 Main
Ashley Isaac, Clinton Hotel Exchange
Barry Garrett, St. Paul st. House
Barrer L. Jefferson House 36 Brown
Blossom Enos & Bros. Blossom Hotel 73 Main
Bonesteel Henry, Frankfort House, Frankfort st.
Botsford ——, Waverly House, cor. State & Waverly place
Bouton E. 6th Ward Hotel 141 Main
Britton A. Travellers' Inn, 166 South St. Paul
Campbell P., Campbell's Exchange, Rochester Block
Chapman J. Market Cottage, cor. Market & Front
Charles C. Temperance Hotel, Rochester Block
Charles Wm. Rochester House, Exchange st.

Benia J. Washington House, 173 Mt. Hope Av.   *Rochester.*
Dyre Russell, Spring st. House, 3 Spring
Fielding C. Cataract House, 193 State
Frost Norman, Frost's Exchange, 83 Exchange
Garrison Jacob, Union Hotel, Buffalo st.
Glemenson Wm. York House, cor. Frost & Market
Green A. Pavilion Hotel, Steamboat Landing
Haskell T. W. Irving Hotel, Buffalo st.
Jennings E. Ontario House, cor. Court & Exchange
Kellogg C. A. Arcade House, 7 Arcade
Lamson C. D. Third Ward House, cor. Sophia & Lafayette
Lux H. Rail Road Hotel, Mill st.
Lux F. Lafayette House, 40 Water
Madden Michael, Franklin House, 110 North St. Paul
Mallory H. D. 212 Main
M'Farlin B. 100 Main
M'Lean H. M'Lean House, cor. Buffalo & Fitzhugh
Meynihan A., Shamrock House, Market st.
Newcomb John, Steamboat Landing
Olmsted Zina, Cottage Inn, Lower Falls
Orson Charles, Northern Retreat, Lower Falls
Place Jas. City Hotel, 56 South St. Paul cor. Court
Propst J. A. Hunters' Home, 2 Monroe
Root L. K. Rail Road House, Mumford st.
Sherman A. California House, cor. Sophia & Layafette
Shaw J. W. 65 & 67 State
Sheehan Wm. Water St. House, 10 Water
Spencer J. T. Exchange Hotel, 120 Buffalo
Stevens H. P Congress Hall, cor. Waverly place & Mill
Tone Jas. Centre Hotel, 26 Main
Walbridge S. D Eagle Hotel, cor. Buffalo & State
Wadsworth Perry, Clifton House, 36 Exchange
Wells J. C. American House, 96 State
Davis B.   *Rush.*
Carman J. Temperance House
Hoyt E. West Rush
Hill Ira A. Eastern Hotel, Brockport   *Sweden.*
Davis W. American Hotel, Brockport
Johnson A. Main st.
Brewer Z. A.   *Webster.*
Smith A.
Moody H. West Webster
Crosby S.
Rogers Russell   *Wheatland.*
Baxter M. O. Scottsville
Hollenbeck C. Mumford
M'Naughton D.   do

Montgomery County.

Livermore J. R. Rail Road House,   *Amsterdam.*
Green J. J. American Hotel
Basset J. J. & Samplis, Bull's Head
Crane Davis, Cranesville
Manny Jas.   do
Winne P. R. Exchange Hotel   *Canajoharie.*
Bingham T. W. Canajoharie Hotel
Cory Daniel
Waits R. W.
Winsman R.
Mallett Roswell, Ames

O'Neil John, Buel   *Canajoharie.*
Lewis Morgan J. do
Fero G. L.   *Charleston.*
Potter E. L. Charleston Four Corners
M'Intosh A. Burtonville
Ripley A. M.   do
Van Hasen David   *Florida.*
Blood Jacob S. Minaville
Case E.   do
Howe Wm. H. Port Jackson
Patterson S.   do
Casey E.   do
Blood J. S.   do
Graft John, Fort Hunter
Stuart Rebecca, Phillip's Locks
Rider Priest   *Glen.*
Snyder John
Stwine Thos. Fultonville
Voorheese & Able. do
Montyne J. Smith Town
Wood David,   do
Bowen Solomon, Montgomery Hall, Fort Plain
Birge U. Harold Hall, Fort Plain
Devy Chas.   do
Pier Hiram,   do
Sands Chester L.   do
Everson J. Caughnawaga House, Fonda   *Mohawk.*
Davis & M'Intire, Franklin House, Fonda
Crosby Isaac, Republican House, Fonda
Fonda P. H. Fonda Hotel, Fonda
Quackenbush J. Cayadutta Hotel, Fonda
Prine H. L. Fonda
Van Alstine M. M. Fonda
Glacklin L. M.   do
Wagner W. Palatine Bridge   *Palatine.*
Dygert J. H.   do
Shaver Robert, Stone Arabia
Snell John J.   do
Saltaman John W.   do
Saltaman David,   do
Nestle John,   do
Nellis Stephen,   do
Van Buren Henry   *Root.*
Onderkirk Harvey
Van Buren Martin
Wessles Andrew
Sharp Jacob
Spraker E. B. Spraker's Basin
Wessless Nicholas,   do
Powell Abner   *St. Johnsville.*
Kingsbury W. & C. St. Johnsville Hotel
Starring John
Getmany Jacob
Fox Daniel

New York County.

American, Taber & Bagley, 229 Broadway   *New York.*
Astor House, Coleman & Stetson, 221 Broadway
Atlantic, William C. Anderson, 5 Broadway
Alhambra, W. Dillon, 126 Water
Albert's Hotel, Wm. Albert, 152 Cherry
Battery, Mary Pettet & Brother, 2 Battery place
Barclay St., John Patten, sen. 108 Barclay
Beekman House, Margaret Wilson, 58 Beekman
Bell Hotel, O. Higgins, 189 Canal
Benjamin & Fuller, 94 Chatham
Bernard Hotel, cor. Battery place & Washington st.
Bond St. House, Chas. Plints, 663 Broadway
Bowery Hotel, A. Northrop, 40 Bowery
Broadway Hotel, I. S. Tucker, 1 Park place
Brown & Crane, 25 Bowery
Brown Nathan, 92 Vesey

Branch Hotel, R. Platt, 36 Bowery   *New York.*
Bradbury Thos. 232 Hudson
Browning George, 29 5th
Bull's Head, Wise & Co. 3d Av. cor. 24th
Carlton House, P. H. Hodges, 389 Broadway
Carpenter's Hotel, J. W. Carpenter, 350 4th Av.
Chambers St., Wm. Humphreys, 43 Chambers
Chapman Jas. H. 337 Hudson
City Hotel, John Florence, jr. cor. Broadway & Howard
Clark Andrew, 15 Park row
Clinton, Simeon Leland, 3 Beekman
Coffee House, A. Hartmann, 29 2d Av.
Coffee House, Wm. Rowe, 96 Vesey
College Hotel, J. M. Sanderson, 28 Murray
Commercial, John Patten, jr. 13 Cortlandt
Cooper B. F. 516 Greenwich
Cox I. T. 476 Washington
Cox Charles, 11 Thames
Delmonico's, P. A. & L. Delmonico, 21, 23, 25 & 27 Broadway
Drover's Hotel, Robert Richey, 165 Washington
Dunlap's, W. G. Dunlap, 129 Fulton
Dunning's, Smith Dunning, 64 Cortlandt
Eagle, T. & M. Prenderville, 15 Greenwich
Eagle Hotel, J. P. Fensier, 35 Dey
Earle & Jackson, 98 & 100 Division
Earle's Hotel, Wm. P. Earle, 17 & 19 Park Row
East Broadway House, Kester & Sammis, 115 East Broadway
Eastern Pearl St. House, G. Seeley, 309 Pearl
Exchange, O. Clark, 196 & 197 Chambers
Farmer's Hotel, Brown & Scott, 25 Bowery
Fairfield Co. House, 31 Bowery
Fahrbeck Chas. 47 Greenwich
Fifth Ward. Thomas Riley, 135 West Broadway
Fleece Tavern, J. Huxley, 16 Dey
Florence's, Moulton & Sloat, 407 Broadway
Fountain Hotel, W. Minor, 29 Park Place
Franklin House, J. P. Treadwell, 197 Broadway
Franklin Square, Vanderveer, 236 Pearl
French's Hotel, Richard French, City Hall Square cor. Frankfort
Frost's Hotel, 84 W Broadway
Frear George B. 360 Hudson
Fulton Hotel, Johnson & Rogers, 144 Fulton
Fulton, John Murphy, 164 East Broadway
Gardner's, Settler & Rikert, 1 Washington
Globe, J. B. Pope, 66 Broadway
Gothic Hotel, Smith & Green, cor. 33d st. & 4th Av.
Gunter H. H. 147 Fulton
Harrison James, 113 West
Herbert Charles C. 59 Chambers
Hollister David M. 30 Bowery
Hollister John J. 1 Washington
Hotel De Paris, A. Vigne, 234 Broadway
Hotel Français & Espagnol, M Mondon, 57 Broadway
Hotel De Havre, 51 Dey
Howard's, Fish, Middleton & White, 176 Broadway
Hudson River Hotel, E. & J. Chamberlain, 73 Robinson
Hull Wm. W. 118 West Broadway

Hungerford F. G. 245 and 247 Washington *New York.*
Irving House, D. D. Howard, 261 Broadway
Jersey Hotel, 71 Cortlandt
Jefferson Hotel, 315 3d Av.
Jenkins Thos. F. 190 West
Jewell & Smith, 247 West
Judson's, Curtis Judson, 61 B'way
Keeland John, 1 West st. Battery Place
Krattiger John, 109 Greenwich
Ledon Jose A. 36 Beekman
Lovejoy's James S. Libby, 34 Park Row
Mansion House, William J. Bunker, 39 Broadway
Martin & Smith, 207 Duane
Merchant's, Wm. Muirheid & Co. 41 Cortlandt
Miller Abm. 671 Hudson
Murray St. House, C. S. Butts, 5 & 7 Murray
National, Seeley, 5 Cortlandt
Newsome J. 320 Hudson
New England, P. Wright, 111 Broadway
New England House, J. O. Reiley, 6 Roosevelt
New York, J. B. Monnot, 721 Broadway
North American, D. M. Hollister, 30 Bowery
Northern, James Harrison, 79 Cortlandt
North River, P. G. Maloney, 149 West
Old Staten Island Hotel, 3 Washington
Orla House, 93 & 94 Liberty & 1 Temple
Pacific. A. Flower, 162 Greenwich
Paige David S. 293 West
Pearl St. House, George Seeley, 88 Pearl
Peck Slip Hotel, W. Ames, 113 South
Pelerin Hilaire, 7 & 9 Whitehall
Pennsylvania, J. Lawton, 69 Greenwich
Philadelphia, ——, 1 West
Perkins' Hotel, —— 56 Division
Planter's, A. Isaacs, 134 G.wich
Rainbow, William Foremain, 27 Beekman
Ram's Head, Bell & Gwynn, 116 Fulton
Rathbun's, Rathbun & Clark, 163 Broadway
Ridgway & Armstrong, 163 West
Rochester, John Webster, 31 Cortlandt
Saracen's Head, N. Smith, 14 Dey
Schwartz Geo. 161 Washington
Second Ward Hotel, 87 Nassau
Sixteenth Ward Hotel, Jacob Rohr, 8th Av.
Shakespeare, E. Lievre, Duane cor. William
Seventeenth Ward Hotel, 124 1st Av.
Stoneall James C., 131 Fulton
Tammany, Howard & Brown, 168 Nassau
Taylor's Temperance, Eldad Taylor, 28 Cortlandt
Tremont Temperance House, H. Waterman, jr. 110 Broadway
Tompkins House, J. Wangler, 170 Av. B
Union, A. Sigler, 94 Greenwich
Union Place, J. C. Wheeler, 856 Broadway
United States Hotel, H. Johnson, 200 Water & Pearl cor. Fulton
Warren Hotel, ——, 7 Mercer
Washington Hotel, David Harris, 302 Greenwich
Walton House, C. H. Harris, 336 Pearl
Westchester House, C. H. Mathews, 148 Bowery

Western, Dwier & Barber, 9, 11 & 13 Cortlandt *New York.*
Woodbine Hotel, G. Hayward, 187 6th Av.
Wright House, William Wright, 22 Ann
Bathgate William, *Harlem*
Burchell Samuel, do
Cromwell Oliver, do
De Grott E. & J. do
Dodge Mrs. do
Dodge Peter, do
Dunn J. do
Ferrington John G. do
Hope Thomas, do
Jackson Thomas, do
Johnson William, do
Kuer J. do
Luf E. Red House, do
Lumindike Jacob, do
M'Guire Mrs. do
Seckett John, do
Shea Thomas, do
Shoymandike Jacob, do
Somerndyke J. do
Sparks Wm. D. Washington Hotel, Harlem
Tilden Henry, *Harlem*
Tone Mrs. do
Van Vostrum Stephen, do
Verian Alvin, do
Woodruff Isaac, do
Bryan David, Yorkville
Carter John, do
De Grott E. & J. do
Dunlap M. A. Hell's Gate
Ferry Hotel, do
Hancock William, do
Lenton Edward, do
Noakes George, do
Over G. B. Yorkville Shades
Rogers Louis
Sebastian A.
Smith William
Starr Thos. Five Mile House
Wright Samuel

Niagara County.

Pike Amos, Pekin *Cambria.*
Peck F. Eagletown *Lewiston.*
Euston James, Lewiston Hotel
Beardsley J. T. Central Hotel
Raymond C. W. Frontier House
Cornell N. American Hotel
Wadsworth Wm. Ferry House
Whitbeck & Hoag, American *Lockport.*
Nichols E. M. Eagle
Lusk Wm. Farmers' Hotel
Phillips Lyman, Farmers' Inn
Phillips J.
Patterson Arthur *Newfane.*
Rounds G. W. Wright's Corners
Cooper Wm. E. Olcott
Wood Silas. do
Whitney Gerould & Co. Cataract House *Niagara Falls.*
White H. Eagle Hotel
Fanning & Childs, Falls Hotel
Smith C. H. St. Lawrence House
Halstead D. J. Bellevue House
Clark Pendleton *Pendleton.*
Scribens A. W. Mansion House
Bentley & Fuller
Weaver Proctor B. Youngstown *Porter.*
M'Knight, Ontario House do
Barton Alexander, do
Cowan Hugh, do
Curtis Gilbert W. do
Bronson S. Reynale's Basin *Royalton.*
Smedley Elisha. Gasport
Young Sylvester *Somerset.*
Rash ——, Niagara Hotel. Tonawanda *Wheatfield.*
Chaslet ——, Commercial Hotel
Palmer Thos., Wilson
Cole J. do

Oneida County.

Gillet S. *Annsville.*
Hyde R.
Perkins J. Oriskany Falls
 Augusta.
Sergent A. do
Parker H. do
Hulbert R. *Boonville.*
Jones J.
Rich S. Alder Creek
Lewis E. *Bridgewater.*
Ringe B.
Parkhurst G.
Pierce N.
M'Cune William *Camden.*
Seymour J.
Wilson & Seymour
Phelps A.
Mellinson J. *Deerfield.*
Oster J., North Gage
Pratt Wm. H. do
Fairbanks Royal *Florence.*
Hoyt George L.
Crocker J.. Franklin *Kirtland.*
Hadcock H. do
Gallup & Budlong, Clinton
Burnham Wm. Clinton House, Clinton
Robinson Wm., Manchester
Brooks Wm. do
Lee N. *Lee.*
Clark J. A.
Higbee S.
Cornish A.
Cornish C.
Potter E. C., Stokes
Curtiss H. & D. J., Deansville
 Marshall.
Boice J. do
Hanchett N. D. do
Porter N. *New Hartford.*
Marr & Morey
Plumb H.
Chapman Wm. H.
Case J. G., Sauquoit *Paris.*
Peake R. do
Wilber Wm. do
Allen Z. E., Clayville
Willis & Holmes, Cassville
Lewis J. *Remsen.*
Fish I.
Stevens J. Dominick st. *Rome.*
Talcott & Barrett, R. R. Hotel, James st.
Jaki J., James st.
Rowe A. American Hotel, James cor. Dominick
M'Darby M. Whitestown st.
Doyle J.
Putnam H. Northern Hotel, James st.
Hawley E.
Brown G. K.
Sink M.
Tibbets J.
M'Nease ——
Harger & De Ryther, Stanwix Hall, James st.
Brown J. B. American Hotel, Waterville *Sangersfield.*
Moore S. C., Waterville
Conger Wm. E. do
Bennett C. D. do
Wheeler W. W., Holland Patent *Trenton.*
Skinner A. L. Trenton Village
Clark J. do
Wooster D. do
Moore M., Trenton Falls
White M., Prospect
Hall S. do
Hutchison J., South Trenton
Kent D. L. do
Ballou P. C. Exchange Hotel, 7 Packet Dock *Utica.*
Beston John, City Coffee House, n. R. R. Depot
Bertram S. B. & Son, Franklin House, 147 & 149 Genesee
Burdick C. L. Eagle Tavern, 139 Genesee

Churchill A., Bagg's Hotel *Utica*
Clapp J. Averell House, n. R. R. Depot
Hitchcock N. P. Chenango House, Main cor. John
Hodges L. 46 Whitesboro
Huntington R. John cor. Broad
Irons & Potter, 6 Catharine
Jones R. T. York House, 18 Whitesboro
Keiser P. Columbia st.
Lennebacker J. National Hotel, 127 Genesee
Lewis Wm. U. Fayette cor. State
Mapes J. Whitesboro st.
M'Gregor J. M'Gregor House, 13 Whitesboro
Midlam Thomas, Temperance House, 218 Genesee
Merry S. F. 37 Bleecker
Myers H. 4 Water
Owens Thomas, 73 Broad
Page Henry A. Oneida Cottage, Oneida Square
Roach J. Fayette st.
Seaman J. S. City Hotel, 219 Genesee st.
Shnelder H. 26 Seneca
Smith M. Bridge st.
Thomas A. H. Whitesboro st.
Van Pelt John, Mansion House, 25 & 27 Fayette
Vidvard P. 31 John
Waters H. Columbia st.
White A. Central Hotel, 185 & 187 Genesee
Wilson Wm. L. Globe Inn, 277 Genesee
Bushnell L. S. *Vernon.*
Couch J. P. *Verona.*
Munger Wm H.
Hess A. & D.
Parmelee M . New London
White Geo. & H. do
Vanderheyden A. Rathburnsville
Higgins C. Higginsville
Truax H., Durhamville
Borden S. do
Torney ——. do
Myers J., Pine *Vienna.*
Putnam P. R. M'Connellsville
Joslin C. do
Johnson J., North Bay
Haws ——, South Corners
Patterson D., Lowell *Westmoreland.*
Buell R., Lairdsville
Buell Jos. M., Hampton
Billington J. do
Robinson P. *Whitestown.*
Wood D. S.
Kelley J. C., Whitesboro
Chrisman & Miller, Oriskany
Kent P. H., Walesville

Onondaga County.

Warren S. *Cicero.*
Van Beamer ——
Bennett H. Brewerton
Childs P. *Clay.*
Quackenbush P., Euclid
Chambers W. W. do
Grinnell G. F. *De Witt.*
Holbrook G. W. Jamesville
Rhodes J. D. *Elbridge.*
Carson David, Clinton House, Jordan
Abrams H. Union Hall
Evans S., Peru
Ely E. *Fabius.*
Gibbs J. F. *Geddes.*
Smith S. W.
Sherwood G., Cardiff *Lafayette.*
Leonard —— do
Shaw A. B. *Lysander.*
Lutphen ——
Allen W.
Dunham L.
Lampson J. H.
Hall H. Baldwinsville
Wallace L. A. do
Davis O. W. do

Paul J. L. Plainville *Lysander.*
Spears L. *Manlius.*
Warren P & Brother
Rowley J. Fayetteville
Gilson Wm. do
Carpenter J. *Marcellus.*
Holland ——, Clintonville
Patterson A. *Onondaga.*
Hand Samuel
Norton A. jr.
Jones & Weight, South Onondaga
Billings S. *Otisco.*
Wheeler D., Amber
Snow H. Pompey Centre *Pompey.*
Candee S. do
Whitney J., Watervale
Ingersoll G. *Salina.*
Smith J.
Winton W. Globe Hotel, Salina st. Syracuse
Clark C. B. Clark's Hotel, Fayette & Salina st.
Frary N. C. Salina st.
Goodrich N. Fayette House, Fayette st.
Burrows C. & Co. Exchange Hotel, Salina st.
Gillett N. & Co. Syracuse House, Salina st.
Welch E. Coffee House, Warren
Schram W. H. do
Alvord C. California Hotel, do
Brintnall H. Brintnall's Hotel, Warren st.
June Charles, Genesee st
Schadfield A. Mulberry st.
Gerson L. do
Herbet C. Water st.
Hall J. D. Lock st. Syracuse
Warner J. B. do do
Adams T. B. Canal st.
Henderson Charles, James st.
Rust P. N. Rust's Hotel, Salina & Genesee st.
Robinson W. A. Onondaga Tem. House, Salina st.
Ogle George, do
Amos Jacob, do
Farnsworth J. do
Chappell L. do
Scott J. Salina House, Salina st.
Pohley J. do
Graff J. do
Pfohl J. do
Fay M. W. Lake House *Skaneateles.*
Lamb A. Houndeaga House
Nye J. M.
Legg Wm. W. *Spafford.*
Eddy ——, Borodino
Davis L. C. do
Hodge J. *Tully.*
Copeland Wm.
Spencer T.
Morse J.

Ontario County.

Jones E. *Bristol.*
Hicks S. C.
Baker V.
Bush M. *Canadice.*
Cogeendall Wm.
Worthington Ambrose, Canandaigua House *Canandaigua.*
Failing W. Franklin House
Powers Marvin, Ontario House
Mallory M. M. & S. S.
Fisher ——, Steamboat House
Taylor Allen *East Bloomfield.*
Pitcher —— *Gorham.*
Rogers Samuel, Reed's Corners
Warmley Jacob, Larned's Corners *Hopewell.*
Gardiner R. Chapinsville
Faronte B. *Manchester.*
Hammon B.
Park P. M. Clifton Springs
Vandroff W. Manchester Centre
Stacy ——, Port Gibson
Miller ——
Edmundson Owen *Phelps.*

Van Dusen Myron. *Phelps.*
Crandall E. F.
Swift Ralph
Starkweather Wm.
Carpenter E. G.
Quick John P. Allen's Hill *Richmond.*
Reed Silas, Richmond Mills
Bentley Seneca, Honeoye
Seeley Charles, Geneva Hotel, Geneva *Seneca.*
Borden L. S. Mansion House, Geneva
Gardner Asa. Franklin House, do
Pierce W. L. Temp. House, do
Densmore Eri, Geneva House, do
Tompkins Ira G. Tompkin's House, do
Jones Wm., R. R. House, do
Clute George, Canal House. do
Butcher Samuel, Seneca Lake House, do
Dickinson Peter, do
Tuttle J. H. do
Barden C. do
Brown Allen *South Bristol.*
Peck Henry *Victor.*
Hopkins Augustus T.
Rivers W. F.
Thompson J. P. *West Bloomfield.*
Wiggins & Gameon

Orange County.

Mullenix Tunis T. Salisbury Mills *Blooming Grove.*
Lines P. Washingtonville
Seeley M. do
Pelser S., Craigsville
Wood J., R. R. House *Chester.*
Cooper George, Stage House
Smith A. G. Washington Hotel
Smith Isaac *Cornwall.*
Syke John Y.
Davenport J.
Smith & Tannery
Lane J H. Union Hotel
O'Leary T., Eagle Valley
Mahony J. Buttermilk Falls
Cozzens ——, West Point Hotel
Rider F. West Point Hotel
Robinson S. *Cranford.*
Rouk James
Crist M.
Bull D. F., Bullville
Foster H. Delaware House, Port Jervis *Deer Park.*
Ward Mrs. E., Port Jervis
Dodder G. W. do
Hillerty D. do
M'Guire ——, do
Lewis J., R. R. Hotel, Port Jervis
Edsell J. S. *Goshen.*
Murry E. B.
Chever J. A.
Smiley W. R. Orange Hotel
Olmstead D. Washington Hotel
M'Laughlin P.
Dunn Patrick
Millspaugh William
Hurd Charles *Hamptonburgh.*
Mapes James
Dennison Mrs., Little Britain
Crist M. do
Smith Thomas, do
Green B. V.
Brown O. J. *Minisink.*
Bail S. jr. Well's Corners
Kirk A., West Town
Sargeant A. R., Unionville
Tucker C., Ridgebury
Tinney A. do
Halleck D. C. Slate Hill
Bell Wm. do
Ogden H. B., Howell's Depot
Horton E. C. *Montgomery.*
Smith Edgar
Goetchens John
Robinson John
Kent Thomas
Du Bois J., Walden
Millspaugh J D. do

Conley John A. *Monroe.*
Cuff John
Coffee John. Monroe Works
Turner F., Turner's Depot
M'Dowell T. A. *Mount Hope.*
Mills A. J.
Masters Barney, New Vernon
Boyea T. K. & J. Otisville
Stiles N. L. do
White S., Finchville
Whited R. Orange Hotel. Water st. *Newburgh.*
Whited J. J. United States Hotel, Front st.
Donadi G. Powellton House
Patton T. Temperance House, Front st.
M'Cann James. 111 Water
Fuller C. Colden st.
Du Bois J. W.
Gardiner G.
M'Kinson J. M. Colden st.
Blizzard John, Front st.
Cleary William, Mansion House, Front st.
June Jacob. Eagle Hotel, Front st.
Clark & Odell, do
Richards John. Union Hotel, do
Gallatin James, Coldenham
Johnson B. K. do
Wood William *New Windsor.*
Houston J. G., Scotchtown *Walkill.*
Marvin A. J. New Hampton
Taylor A. do
Brasted R. do
Savacool A. R. South Middletown
Sweet H., R. R. Hotel, do
Post G. G. Union House, do
Hulse J. B. do
Monell J. do
Pierson J. P. *Warwick.*
Welling J. & S. Orange Hotel
Ward T.
M'Daniel G. W., Amity
Washburn P. S. do
Sayer H. G. do
Dunn R., Edenville
Gable S. do
Gale T., New Milford
Felter T., Greenwood Lake House
Ackerman S., Sugar Loaf
Clearwater ——. do
Vail L. B., Florida
Aspell F. do

Orleans County.

Hopkins H., Mansion House, Albion *Barre.*
Remington P. Albion Hotel, Albion
Gould H. Platt House, do
Durkee W. American Hotel, do
Rowlandson E., Barre Centre
Edmonds J., Waterport *Carlton.*
Palmer L. do
Platt L. M. Platt's Hotel *Clarendon.*
Smith George *Gaines.*
Noble Harvey, West Gaines
Griswold William *Kendall.*
Perry Horace B., Holley *Murray.*
Church Calvin, Sandy Creek
Gamor S., Medina *Ridgeway.*
Alcorn John, do
Baldwin O, Knowlesville
Mason O., Oak Orchard
Tuttle Joseph, Ridgeway Corners
Deuel D. G. *Shelby.*
Johnson James, Millville
Spaulding John *Yates.*
Chamberlain Russell, Lyndonville

Oswego County.

Cole Alpheus *Albion.*
Edwards O.
Holton Arnold
Brown Warren, Carterville *Amboy.*
Gerber Henry, West Amboy
Champlin H. C. *Constantia.*
Brown J. P.
Marble Cyrus, Cleaveland
Fetter A. do
Henry Robert, do

Phillips Asa, Oswego Falls Hotel, Oswego Falls. *Granby.*
Stevens G. *Hannibal.*
Hatch Gilbert, Hannibal Centre
Barrett D. *Hastings.*
Ketchum E. P.
Whitman D.
Diffin S., Central Square
Clark M. do
Barnum O. E. do
Kelley Robert, Mexico Hotel *Mexico.*
Gillett ——, Eagle Tavern
Ayres Benjamin, Colosse House, Colosse
Fellows Hiram, Union Square
Eason Richard *New Haven.*
Goodsell T. W. Jefferson House
Thomas M. P. *Orwell.*
Engle J. Oswego Centre *Oswego.*
Ranney Neal, cor. 1st & Seneca
Burr Washington, Free Trade House, 1st st.
Sabins Collin H. Eagle Tavern, 1st st.
Garrison Ira, jr. City Hotel, (temperance) cor. 1st & Bridge
Garty Dennis, Jefferson House, cor. Bridge & 1st
Bronson Amos, 1st st.
Docktader Hiram, Ontario House, cor. 2d & Seneca
Valliant Joseph, Water st.
Leidley John, cor. Water & Schuyler
Hotchkiss Miles,Steamboat House, Water st.
Shepherd Isaac, cor. 1st & Schuyler
Beals Reuben C., Rialto House, 1st st.
Benedict Henry, Frontier House, cor 1st & Seneca
Stewart Wm. D. Welland House, cor. 1st & Cayuga
Baker J. J. 3d Ward Temperance Hotel, 1st st.
Munger Orin G. Niagara House, cor. 1st & Bridge
Jenulegs David. jr. Jennings' Hotel, Jennings' Corners *Palermo.*
Church Whitman T., Jennings' Corners
Fox George *Parish.*
Simmons Isara
Griswold H. *Redfield.*
Mathewson J. A. Pulaski House, Pulaski *Richland.*
Ford John A. Salmon River House, Pulaski
Pride Wm. Pulaski
M'Chesney James A. Steamboat Hotel, Port Ontario
Dwight A. O. do
Goodwin M. Commercial Hotel, Port Ontario
Van Patten P. J. *Phœnix Schroeppel.*
Breed A. do
Merchant David, Hinmansville
Walters Wm. do
Swift V. Scriba Centre House *Scriba.*
Brown D. J.
Woolson E.
Fetterby Robert
Gasper John, Gasper's Hotel, Fulton *Volney.*
Bean Lyman W. Fulton House, Fulton
Sabins Nelson. Fulton Exchange, Fulton
Coss John, Plank Road House, Hulls' Corners
Hough James Centre House *Williamstown.*
Fish Jesse
Tousley Hiram, Chequered House

Otsego County

Fitch O. Burlington Flats *Burlington.*

Brown H. A. Burlington Flats *Burlington.*
Day E. S. West Burlington
Slocumb J. do
Allen E. W. Burlington Green
Yates E. W. *Butternuts.*
Burgan J. S.
Corwin & Yates
Cole J. C. *Cherry Valley*
Dutcher R.
Wilkins J. R.
Wilson J. S.
Hustes ——
Potts C.
Stevens D.
Morris J.
Moak J.
Hall J. I.
Bailey T.
Lansing James E. *Decatur.*
May David C. *Edmeston.*
Waldo Erastus G
Holt Isaac N. South Edmeston
Gaskin John, West Edmeston
Chapin John, do
Edmonds H. Schuyler's Lake *Exeter.*
Palmer & Brooks, do
Conklin J. *Hartwick.*
Chapman J.
Gullett C. B.
Orlendorf P. *Laurens.*
Barton P.
Ballard S.
Straight F. & E.
Wetherby A.
Dunhan A. C. *Maryland.*
Sperrey N.
Clark Nathan. Schenevas
Lloyd Alexander *Middlefield.*
Moak Jacob
Hand Isaac B.
Aller William
Snettand Elias
Sergents H. *Milford.*
Sweet A. jr.
Sergents J.
Mumford J.
Taft T.
Aldrich D. & J. *New Lisbon.*
Herrick S.
Emmons Carter *Oneonta.*
Watkins John M.
Sullivan Silas
Sherman E. S.
H thaway Leonard
Strait Daniel P. West Oneonta
Jay Wm. *Otego.*
Bundy Gilbert S.
Shepard Ryall
Osborn J. Q.
Willoughby Z. Otsego House, Cooperstown *Otsego.*
Lewis Wm. Eagle Hotel, Cooperstown
Card A. Empire House, Cooperstown
Medbery C. H. *Pittsfield.*
Brown L. Temp. House, *Plainfield.*
Wheeler M. *Richfield.*
Vaughan J. V.
Rose ——
Angell ——
Barrows ——
Horton G. W. American Hotel, Richfield Springs
Whitney J. Springs Hotel
Groat J. *Springfield.*
Conklin G. & E.
Van Alstine A.
Brower S. T.
Heath Thomas *Unadilla.*
Kingsley Erastus
Teller Jacob
Bidlake D. *Westford.*
Palmer ——
Rues John P. *Worcester.*
Grant O. G.
Bigelow E. B. & Co. E. Worcester
Smith Jacob H. do
Burneson A. L. South Worcester

Putnam County.

Berry S. A. Mansion House
Carmel.
Baldwin R.
Monk 8.
Horton E.
Thompson N. L.
Lockwood D. Mansion House, Red Mills
Townsend H. Farmers' Mills Kent.
Doughty G. W. do
Bowne B., R. R. House, Patterson.
Aikin Mrs. S. Herviland's Corner
Penny H. Towner Station
Towner J. Towner's Corner
Stewart A. Porter House, Cold Spring Phillipstown.
Purdy H. R. Highland Hotel, Cold Spring
Simonson W. Pacific Hotel, Cold Spring
M'Cabe W. Cold Spring House, Cold Spring
Longfield Wm. Eagle Hotel, Cold Spring
M'Carty H. Breakneck Hotel, Cold Spring
Wyatt J. K. Southeast.

Queens County.

Miller H. Flushing.
Hoved & Cornell, Flushing Hotel
Hicks G. Flushing, Pavilion Hotel
Burtis James Hempstead.
Rhodes Henry E.
Curtis E. Stage House
Smith B. T. Central Hotel
Baldwin M. Temperance Inn
Hewlett Stephen, Hewlett's Hotel
Sammis H. Village Hotel
Jennings David T. Far Rockaway
Cranston Hiram, Marine Pavilion Hotel
Mott Benj. C.
Curtis J. H. & J. Rockaway
Golden M. do
Simonson Alonson, Christian Hook
Brower Sylvanus. Millburn
Edwards Michael S. Raynor Town
Raynor Daniel, do
Whaley Walton, do
Baldwin Thomas, Millburn
Lott John L., Hick's Neck
Hendrickson & Simonson, Foster's Meadow
Nostrand John, Trimming square
Gaffrey Wm. Far Rockaway
Tarrell Patrick, do
South Benjamin, Raynor Town
Moore Wm. P. Greenwich Point Hotel
Smith Zopher, Greenwich
Baldwin Wm. do
Remsen James S. Jamaica Hotel
Jamaica.
Conklin Oliver
Fleet Abraham K. Union Hotel
Conklin Henry
Hollands M. F.
Weeks Caleb, Graffe Hotel
Mott Samuel, Hickory Hotel
Brush Thos. jr. Brushville Hotel
M'Kee George C. American Hotel
Shaw Wm. I.
Durland Wm. Springfield
Mumby George W. Newtown.
Snedeker Dorus
Owens J. Main Street House, Astoria
Howe A.
Binkney James B. Roslyn
North Hempstead.
Titus & Chapman, Roslyn Village
Peters Hewlett, Little Neck
Layton Wm. Westbury
Searing J. A. Hempstead Branch
Sammis John M. Oyster Bay.
Moore Wm.
Layton John M. East Norwich
Charlick John, Jericho
Post Wm. do

Rensselaer County.

Streeter B. & Son Berlin.
Allen Ira
Livingston J. Brunswick.
Clum H. A.
Goodell J. J.
Twiss ——
Bulson A. S.
Streeter E. Grafton.
Albertson P.
Burdick J. T.
M'Chesney L.
Simmons D. L.
Fryer I. B. Greenbush.
Jordan R.
Lansing J.
Lodewick ——
Whyland John
Covert A.
Dearestyne J.
Wallace T. Hoosick.
Richmond E.
Richmond E. & W.
Mosher G.
Holmes G. F. Lansingburgh House, 147 & 149 State Lansingburgh.
Platt A. H. & L. A. Phœnix Hotel
Peets Benj. Washington House, 345 State
Cook S. V. D., State st.
Reed L. S. Stage House, State cor. Canal
Follett Joseph B. Clinton Hotel, cor. Richard & State
Haynes J. H. Temperance House, East Nassau Nassau.
Ambler S. East Nassau
Babcock N. P. Petersburgh.
Eldred P. W.
Kittle D. S. Pittstown.
Larman Wm.
Shadbolt J. & W.
Wadsworth H
Hix J.
Graves W.
Stanton E.
Thompson A. H. Sandlake.
Sliter C.
Uphams Thomas
Johnson J. A. West Sandlake
Sliter Wm. do
Grant G. W. Schaghticoke.
Aiken H
Smith A.
Downs J.
Arnold J.
Malon B.
Helmerick Joseph, Dutch Hotel, cor. Front and Ferry Troy.
Steiber Chas. North River Hotel, corner of Front & Ferry
Hamilton Alex. Empire House, 112 River
Wheeler R. City Hotel, 118 River
M'Donald Richard D. St. Charles Hotel, cor. River & Ferry
Blanchard E. York House, 252 River
Stearns Mrs., Stearns' Hotel, 332 River
Platt F. G. Northern Hotel, 392 River
Shaw D. Washington & Saratoga House, 400 River
M'Coy Luther, United States Hotel, cor. Hoosick & N. 3d
Dorion P. S. Washington Hall, cor. River & Grand Division
Colman C. S. Troy House, cor. 1st & River
Dorion E. & W. Mansion House, Washington square
Shepherd & Miller, American Hotel, 1 3d
Collamer Mrs. A. A. Eagle Hotel, 88 Congress
Worden N. Exchange Hotel, 91 Congress
Main James T., Congress Hall, 97 Congress
Loomis M. F. Ida Hill House

Smith P. P. Bull's Head Hotel, Lansingburgh road Troy.
Adams B. North Troy Hotel

Richmond County.

Dey W. C. Tompkinsville Castleton.
Kruger John, do
Reynolds J. do
Blancard ——, Pavilion House, New Brighton
Ryers D. R. Richmond Northfield.
Christopher J. Washington Hotel
Anderson George W. Port Richmond
Miller W. Stapleton Southfield.
Oakley Israel, Rossville Westfield.

Rockland County.

Oblenus Clarkstown.
Mellick W. H. New City
Clark S. New City Hotel
Ackerson T., Rockland Lake Hotel
Cook & Wood, Rockland Lake
Rand C. A. Temperance Hotel
Haverstraw.
Benson George
Benson ——, American Hotel
Westervelt W. B. Warren Hotel
Constant Lewis, Caldwell's Landing
Beard Samuel W. do
Myer A. T. Piermont Orangetown.
Mabie D. A. do
Hagan A. J. do
Blanch T. J. do
Perry Edward, York House. Nyack
Canfield J. W. Dry Dock House
De Baun J. I. Spring Valley
Van Zant E. do
Byerson H. Stone House, Tappan
Wood J. Temp. House, Spring Valley
Johnson A. Ramapo.
Carlow Mrs.
Tallman T. J.

St. Lawrence County.

Stevens John Brasher.
Young William Canton.
Foote Henry
Williams Calvin
Noble William
Whiting William
Cummings Peletah R.
Holt C. C. De Kalb.
Nottrum E. R.
Lynde T B., Richville
Mason James J. Depeyster.
Barnes Horace Edwards.
Sartwell Sylvester, S. Edwards
Clark Samuel Fowler.
Fredinburgh Peter
Hulbert William
Swem William
Spencer J. M. Gouverneur.
Van Buren P.
Fosgate William
Rice Henry Hammond.
King Henry
Smith Chauncey
Burnham Elisha Herman.
Howe Thomas L. Hopkinton.
Dunton Albert, Lawrenceville
Lawrence
Chandler Harry, Nicholville
Hathaway ——, do
Hack Rowland Lisbon.
Wells Samuel
Sheldon Peleg
Guest William
Wells Peter
Odel Abraham
Moore N. D. Louisville
Cresford Lot
Willard C. S.
Britton D.
Wilson Robert Massena.
Wright Samuel, Pope's Mills

Bartlett L. Columbia Hotel, Columbia *Madrid.*
Whiting J. Whiting's Hotel
Bssoker John, do
Louck John R. do
Edsill Richard, do
Clark William, Waddington
Marston H. *Massena.*
Wood E.
Phillips Benjamin, U. S. Hotel, Massena Springs
Moore N. D. Lewisville
Bernard H. *Morristown.*
Canfield S.
Millions John
Pohlman H. J. Edwardsville
Floyd William *Norfolk.*
Phelps S. M.
Bisbee E. M.
Nichols Ira
Johnson ——, Raymondsville Hotel
Carr D. D. T. Oswegatchie House, Lake st. Ogdensburgh *Oswegatchie.*
Seymour G. N. St. Lawrence Hotel, Ogdensburgh
Haggett John B. Tremont House, Water st. Ogdensburgh
Whitney Benjamin, Washington House, Washington st. Ogdensburgh
Bartholemew Isaac, Isabella House, Isabella, Ogdensburgh
Baldwin Jeremiah, American Hotel, Water, st. Ogdensburgh
Leonard J. S. cor. Patterson & Ford
Cox Thomas *Parishville.*
Lanphear Nathaniel *Pitcairn.*
Clark William, American Hotel *Potsdam.*
Livingston Sprague, St. Lawrence Hotel
Eldridge Homer B. Knapp House
Farmer B. West Potsdam House, West Potsdam
Smith B. *Russell.*
Taylor Caleb *Stockholm.*
Webster W. W.
Answorth A. C.
Steadman ——

Saratoga County.

Cromer Henry *Charlton.*
Cromer William
Bowlsby John, West Charlton
Smith Joseph *Clifton Park.*
Higgins Hiram. Jonesville
Graves Samuel, Graves Corners
Lansing G. G. J. Roxford Flats
Brumagen Henry, do
Hoyt Stephen *Corinth.*
Mallory Nathan
Gleason Chester
Eglin Henry *Edinburgh.*
Whitney Henry C.
Olmstead John
Morehouse E. *Galway.*
Luman D.
M'Pherson P.
Smith T.
Mitchell William, Greenfield Centre *Greenfield.*
Granger H. C. Mount Pleasant
James Perry M. Jamesville
Stewart Charles *Hadley.*
Walt John J.
M'Kinney A. *Half Moon.*
Noxon T.
Fitzgerald A.
Germond Philo
Blass M. M. ....
Cole F. Maltaville *Malta.*
Rogers George, do
Clark N. do
Riley Charles, do
Badgley George, do
Cook Lemuel *Milton.*
Medbury S. B. Ballston Spa
Chase Richard, do
Tanner Elmore, do

Jennings Joseph, Ballston Spa *Milton.*
Shepard Nelson G. do ——
Wilcox Hiram, R. R. House *Moreau.*
Griswold J. J.
Van Renselaer ——, Portville
Fine John, Gansevoort *Northumberland.*
Woodworth E. do
Ve Vey I. P. do
Woodward Isaac *Providence.*
Chase Hiram
Scribner George
Wise George
Lee Martin *Saratoga.*
M'Eackron A.
Germond P.
Tuttle George
Easton & Shaw
Carragan James *Saratoga Springs.*
Avery C. & H.
Loomis H.
Smith J. K.
Smith T.
Dedrick Hiram
Halls C. & J
Balch W. S.
Cross John
Brown W. R.
Moriaty J. D.
Stodard A.
Hart N.
Hathorn H. H.
Putnam Mrs.–
Moon C. B.——
Wilcox & Petkin
Heelin R. D. & Co.
James T. & J. –
Marvin M. & Co.
Munger Luther
Hoag F. ——
Flanagan Simon
Foot Orin
Loosee R.
Snyder P.
Hunter Andrew *Stillwater.*
Badgley Benjamin
Rudd A. H.——
Diamond Bradley
Lent Henry, Bemus Heights
Ferguson Hiram A. Ketcham's Corners *Waterford.*
Lamb David T. do
Ostrander Lewis, do
Bassett C. do
Coons D. P. do
Stiles Eli *Wilton.*
Gleason Hiram
Ballard John

Schenectady County.

Case Truman *Duanesburgh.*
Perkins ——
Wood J. D.
Bissell M.
Tulloch J.
Conklin Mrs. D.
Wasson J.
Johnson J. A.
White P.
Vedder S. S. Otsego House, Quaker Street
Swart J. M. Quaker Street
Van Ess H. *Glenville.*
House William
Pangburn J. W.
Brooks C.
Fish Sherman
Van Patten A. C.
Renwee G. B.
Dedrick P. H.
Hemstreet J. E.
Shepherd F.
Hammond H *Niskayuna.*
Gibson H. L.
Vrooman A.
Passage George *Princetown.*
M'Kay R.
Johnson ——, Temperance House
Thomas J *Rotterdam.*

Cline J. *Rotterdam.*
Thomas C.
Van Slyck D.
Bradt William H
Van Wormer F.
Timoson N.
Carroll A.
Gates D. W. 131 State *Schenectady.*
Gray E 7 do
Schuyler J. W. 54 Washington
Flansbury F. 56 do
Band R. 9 do
Freeman A. Given's Hotel, State st.
Mead R. M. Temperance House, 159 & 161 State
Barhydt Nicholas, Eagle Hotel, State st.
Vrooman R. 207 State
Van Vranken James G. American Hotel, 202 State
Livingston P. 102 State
Engleman S. 156 do
Fuller Wm. Fuller's Hotel, 126 State
Peaslee D. W. Dock st.
Brummaghim J. 30 Union
Gleason E. Malden lane
Thornton Thos. 196 Union

Schoharie County.

Shafer Geo. H. *Blenheim.*
Finck Wm.
Whiting C. *Broome.*
Parslow John
Pratt A. L.
Church C.
Griffith Orin M. *Carlisle.*
Kinskern Henry P.
Lettis Abram
Fox Geo. H.
M'Cullock David D. L.
Howe L. Cave House (See Advertisement.) *Cobleskill.*
Sternburgh Marcus
Van Dreser Aaron
Richtmyer A. *Conesville.*
Case Luther
Matice Lewis P.
Humphrey Lucian
Hare John *Esperance.*
Brown John S.
Smith Daniel W.
Lown J. E. Sloansville
Larue N. M. do
Moore Mrs. do
Holmes Geo. Fultonham *Fulton.*
Oakley John, West Fulton
Van Valkenburgh J. P. do
Burget C. Breakabeen
Parslow Henry, do
Howard David S. *Gilboa.*
Wood Edward
Matice Peter V.
Lawrence & Kibbe
Briggs ——
Merchant Reuben *Jefferson.*
Twichell Ira
M'Donald Jas. *Middleburgh.*
Snyder Abram
Becker J. L.
Tippets Geo.
Pierce J.
Mann Abram, Warnerville *Richmondville.*
Townsend John, do
Livingston Thomas C.
Cole Peter D.
Snyder P. *Schoharie.*
Hough Lorenzo
Totton Levi, Central Bridge
Davis John, do
Osterhout A. Mansion House
Schoolcraft J. jr. Schoharie House
Van Tuyl A. Eagle Hotel
Ostrum W. Hyndsville *Seward.*
Houghtail M. do
Hawes L.
Cole Peter
Butler Mrs.
Zee C.
Willer G. Sharon Centre *Sharon.*

Dimmick Geo.   *Sharon.*
Eldridge A.
Malick John, Argusville
Eldridge K. Sharon Springs
Kosboth ——, Leeville
Eldridge Nelson, Leeville
Vaughn Jas.   *Summit.*
Monk Wm. T.
Hicks E.
Ruland R Gallupville   *Wright.*

Seneca County.

Wilkin D.   *Covert.*
Whelpley ——, American House
Buchanan Geo. W.,   *Fayette.*
Shiley Jacob
Rader John
Huyler J. V. Seneca House *Lodi.*
Gorton Daniel, Eagle Hotel *Ovid.*
Wilkins Hiram, Franklin House
Bryant Andrew
Veeneece Isaac
Race Andrew, Farmer
Woodard & Woodruff, dc
Martin Wm.   *Romulus.*
Burton Chas.
Fuller J. Temperance Hotel
    Seneca Falls.
Corey T. F. Franklin House
Milk D. Clinton House
Gifford W. C. Seneca Falls House
Mousch C. Waterloo House
    Waterloo.
Horton Asa, Eagle Tavern
Scott David, National House
Sawyer Samuel, Central House

Steuben County.

Buck E. Eagle Tavern   *Addison.*
Lockerby W. Addison Hotel
Kendershot Wm. Exchange Hotel
Doolittle A.
Tucker Smith   *Avoca.*
Fox M.
Brown Richard   *Bath.*
Tayler ——
French James
Boyd A.
Vaman J.
Miner J.
Barney A. L.
Shults Geo.
Bonce Hiram
Sherman & Co.
Thorp ——
Compton J. J.   *Bradford.*
Rowles Thos.
Jones Mrs.   *Cameron.*
Pierson G. S.
Charles Henry
Reddington Thos.
Knickerbocker Henry
Yost Marcy
Clawson E.   *Campbell.*
Stewart F.
Goodwin John
Moore John D.   *Canisteo.*
Green Daniel
Stevens Elias
Stevens M. H.
Hallett Nathan
Johnson Y.
Henry Benj. D.   *Cohocton.*
Walling Jacob
Nichols A. H. North Cohocton
France Geo.   *Dansville.*
Vandusen H.
Kellogg Alex.
Beach Spencer
Savory W. J.   *Erwin.*
Young Geo. S.
Ogden Daniel
Kern Wm.
Davis Levi   *Greenwood.*
Frisby Henry   *Hartsville.*
Marrow F. W.   *Hornby.*
Magee H.   *Hornellsville.*
Morris A.
Doty C.
Hawk J.
Palmit H.

Truesdall J.   *Hornellsville.*
Ayres E.
Cary J.
Burder I.
M'Connell Asa   *Howard.*
Graves C. C.
Bennett E. N.
Howard Seymour
Taylor Stephen
Robinson Dudley
Tanner Clark
Craig Andrew   *Jasper.*
Hurd D. B.   *Orange.*
Lindeman Isaac
Shoemaker John   *Painted Post.*
Wolcott Geo.
Sly John
Jolley Dexter
Pitts ——
Somers & Clark, Corning
Wheelock & Lyon, do
Rider A.   do
Cobb R.   do
Miller S. S.   *Pulteney.*
Boyd T. W.
Boss Andrew
Hibbetts Chas.   *Reading.*
Burgess L.
Compton R.   *Tyrone.*
House A. C
Sutton R. T.
Torsher Daniel
Simons Walter
Goodwin S. C.   *Urbana.*
Cook H.
Bronson Jesse S.
Barritt S. W.
Eveland Joseph   *Wayne.*
Olmstead Aaron
Fulkerson Caleb
Patchin C. P,   *Wayland.*
Coonrod Philip
Rich Francis
Lee A.   *West Union.*
Wise Geo. C.   *Wheeler.*
Gee J.   *Woodhull.*
Sly W.
Parker John A.

Suffolk County.

Smith Richard, Temperance Hotel, Coram   *Brookhaven.*
Davies Lester H. Temperance Hotel, Coram
Carman S, Fireplace
Townsend H R. Temperance Hotel, Port Jefferson
Jayne Charles, do
Swezey Daniel D. Yaphank
Ketcham James, Patchogue
Roe Austin,   do
Scudder S. S.   *Huntington.*
Brush & Rogers
Bunce Jessie, Comac
Nichols S.   *Northport.*
Soper E.   do
King D. Temperance House, do
Snedicor Charles, Babylon
Jarvis E.   do
Higbie Samuel, do
Bodell I. sen.   do
Seaman A. Cold Springs
Sutton Samuel, Temperance Hotel
Stellengwerf Amos R.   *Islip.*
Crandell P. R.
Chapman J. T.
Snedeco Obadiah
Strong Selah, Fire Island Lights
Corwin John, jr. Suffolk Hotel
    Riverhead.
Griffing Wells, L. I. House
Hallock Thomas   *Smithtown.*
Howell Charles, Temp. House
    Southampton.
Seaman George, Good Ground
Jennings Henry, Southold Hotel
    Southold.
Terry Jeremiah, Greenport
Clark John,   do
Riggs Joel,   do

Latham Jonathan F., Orient
    Southold.
Shirley James, Mattituck
Tuthill Ira B. New Suffolk House, Cutchogue

Sullivan County.

Chamberlain & Young   *Liberty*
Dandge John
Buckley B. P.
Fields E. Big Eddy *Lumberland.*
Swartz L.   do
Horton T. Barryville
Cornwall D.   do
Vanduzer O.   *Mamakating.*
Bowen H.
Weed Wm.
Abbott A., Burlingham
Phillips W. I. Phillipsport
Langton A.   do
Sweet Stephen, Bloomingburgh
Cameron H. B.   do
Davies Wm.   do
Shons C.   do
Crance James, Temperance House, Wurtsboro
Olcott Geo. H.   do
Gumaer Samuel, do
Hunter Marcus, do
Dorrance Geo.   do
Burtis S.   *Thompson.*
Higgins Geo.   *Monticello*
Hamilton Stephen,   do
Bataford Wm. Temp. House, do

Tioga County.

Van Derhule J. D.   *Candor.*
Lincoln & Stebbins, Newark Valley House, Newark Valley
    Newark.
Wilson C. H. Newark Valley
Denio S. B. Tioga House   *Owego*
Mosher P. Central House
Gerr J. B. Mansion House
Jaggar S. H.   *Richford.*
Perkins E. A.
Giles L Willett's Hotel   *Spencer*

Tompkins County.

Ellsworth James   *Enfield.*
Vandorn Peter
Van Marten A. W., Enfield Centre
M'Coy E. R.   do
Bradford S. P.   *Hector.*
Moreland ——, Logan
Jackson Daniel, Burdett
Jones J. M.   do
Colgrove M Mecklenburg
Collins J. Reynoldsville
Russell M.   do
Sears A. P. Searsburg
Seymour T. Ithaca Hotel, cor. Owego & Aurora sts.   *Ithaca.*
Leonard & Burton, Clinton House, Cayuga st.
Phelps E. O. Tompkins House, cor. Seneca & Aurora st.
Betts K. D. Farmers' Hotel, 17 Aurora
Lucas A. M. Forest City Hotel, Cayuga st.
Livermore L. Exchange Hotel, 121 Owego
Sealey Z. Jackson House, Inlet Bridge
Gifford B. Red Lion Hotel, Inlet st.
Hall T. R. Sailor's Home, Dock Basin
Landon J. Greek Hall, 271 Owego
Martin Samuel   *Newfield.*
Casterline Geo. W.
Puff John
Harvey Charles
Stamp Jonathan
Snider James
Sanford E. Temperance House

Ulster County.

Stratton A. S.   *Hurley.*
Chapman H. West Hurley

Bristol J. West Hurley *Hurley.*
Schryver John K. Temperance House. East Front st. *Kingston.*
Clark T. Eagle Hotel, Main st.
Van Bramer Francis
Rich Mrs. M.
Cure Washington
M'Ellory W. H. Ulster Co. Hotel
Pardee I. Kingston. Crown st.
Columbus Pavilion, Kingston Lending
Hudler Wm. Santa Claus Hotel, *Rondout*
Reynolds S. Clinton Hotel, do
Rondout Hotel, do
Demming Wm. H. Eddyville
Demyer Abram S.
Lefever N. J. New Paltz Landing *Lloyd.*

Signer Jacob I. High Falls *Marbletown.*
Gillespie James, Stone Ridge
Perrine Solomon S. do
Buckley C. F. Milton *Marlborough.*
Smedes B. D. New Paltz Hotel *New Paltz.*
Johnson B.
Decker A. B. Libertyville
Sammons A. D. Tuthill
Dudrey Wm. H. *Olive.*
Coons H.
Crosby O. B.
Schoonmaker Moses I. Accord *Rochester.*
Hornbeck J. B. Pine Bush
Jeffreys M. do
Budington W. J. National Hotel *Rosendale.*
Freer A. H. Rosendale House
Schoonmaker J. L. Farmer's Hotel
Livingston Duncan, Malden *Saugerties.*
Tappan Christopher, Bristol
Turk Henry, Phœnix Hotel
Richmond A. H. Exchange House
Martin Henry D. Glasco
Griffin William *Shandaken.*
Breadstreet Mrs.
Oneil H. Temperance House
Humphrey A., Cornell
Lockwood J. do
Scott S. A. Pine Hill
Smith W. do
Maybee E. do
Decker J. *Shawangunk.*
Taylor James, Ulsterville
Johnson N., Braynswick
Schoonmaker C. T. do
Jackson J. M. *Wawarsing.*
Cortright L.
Dewitt R. C. Temperance
Schoonmaker M. J. Middleport
Gashrie Mrs. J. Port Ben
Terwilliger Eli D., Ellenville
Terwilleger Oliver A. do
Freer Aaron, do
Barlow Samuel, do
Marks J. Fountain Temperance Hotel, Napanock
Rich T. Hotel, Napanock
Snyder T. *Woodstock.*

Warren County.

Aldrich David *Athol.*
Fenton L.
Dickinson Alonzo *Caldwell.*
Thorton Joseph
Sherrill John. Lake House
Cameron J. I. Temperance House
Weatherbee John L. Chestertown *Chester.*
Potter William, Pottersville
Garfield Nathaniel *Hague.*
Davis Homer *Horicon.*
Waters George
Rockwell George G. *Luzerne.*
Wilcox J. P.
Lake Hervey
Phillips J. *Queensbury.*
Baily & Eldridge, American Hotel, Glenn's Falls

Carpenter W. L. Glenn's Falls Hotel *Queensbury*
Sternburgh D. L. Mansion House
Green Jeremiah. do
Person L. Warrensburgh Hotel *Warrensburg.*
Weatherhead H. L. Warren House
Towsley Gideon & Co.
Pratt D.

Washington County.

Rouse Joseph *Argyle.*
Dennis George C.
Clark John. North Argyle
Long Edward *Cambridge.*
Durand James A.
Milliman Elisha
Weir Hiram. Cambridge Centre
Houghton A. Buskirk's Bridge
Bartlett John C. *Easton.*
Baker Solomon
Taber Lewis, North Easton
Briggs James *Fort Ann.*
Burnell Leander N.
Brown William
Bardwell Misses
Allen W. & R., R. R. House *Fort Edward.*
Carswell Gideon, Fort Edward House
Hubbell J. S.
Elmore Ora. Temperance House
Smith William
Perkins Martin, Fort Miller
Mills Mrs. do
Roberts David, Fort Edward Centre House
Cameron John R. *Greenwich.*
Manning Jesse K.
Weir Thomas E. Centre Falls
White W. W. Battenville
Gamble R. G. Galesville
Williams Josiah *Hampton.*
Wilson L. B. West Hebron *Hebron.*
Russell Wm. North do
Button Charles N., E. Hebron
Vaughn C. B. *Kingsbury.*
Eldridge Joshua, Eagle Hotel, Sandy Hill
Sherrill Mathew D. Coffee House, Sandy Hill
Ives George M. Sandy Hill
Clark Ransom, Smith's Basin
Williamson Daniel, jr. *Putnam.*
French Solomon
Gila William *Salem.*
How John
Pratt Ira P.
Fowler D., White Creek Centre *White Creek.*
Lomis Joel, North White Creek
Comstock Hannah, do
Allen J. Phœnix Hotel *Whitehall.*
Scofield A. United States Hotel
Martin G. American Hotel
Snyder A. M. Mansion House

Wayne County.

Bently Amos *Arcadia.*
Barney V. G. Eagle Hotel, Newark
Vanderhoof A. Newark Hotel
Van Inwager Cornelius, Fairville
Lamoreaux P., Westbury *Butler.*
Wendover Thos. South Butler
Axtell Chas. Clyde Hotel, Clyde *Galen.*
Hall Bryant, Clyde
Gooldchild H. do
Boylan John, Bay Bridge House *Huron.*
Landon J. Landon's Hotel *Lyons.*
Benton Geo. Exchange Hotel
Sanford W. W., Wayne Co. Hotel
Stuver J., Alloway
Tripp Isaac, Macedon Centre *Macedon.*
Cook ——, Marion Hotel *Marion.*
Northrop R. K. *Ontario.*
Ellsworth M.
Nuttingham W. P. Palmyra Hotel *Palmyra.*

Calhoun E. Bunkerhill Hotel *Palmyra.*
Dorm Wm. Exchange House
Rortles T.
Decker & Ellenwood *Ross.*
Thayer S. W.
Housey Cruse *Savannah.*
M'Eathon H. B. Exchange Hotel *Sodus.*
Borrodaill John, Sodus Point
Young Andrew
Wood A. Mansion House, S. Point
Johnson S. P. Johnson's Hotel. do
Fowler Wm. Globe Hotel, Alton
Forbes J. Phalanx House
Craig & Babcock, South Sodus House, South Sodus
Amsden ——. Sodus Centre
Nichols Benjamin *Williamson.*
Cornwall A. A., Pultneyville
Boylen A. H. *Wolcott.*
Olmstead Jesse

Westchester County.

Miller Cyrus, Mechanicsville *Bedford.*
Betts Philo
Sarles Wesley, R. R. Hotel
Wood & Smith, Hudson R. R. Hotel. Peekskill *Courtlandt.*
Cole John O.. Peekskill
Williams John, Main st. Peekskill
Smith Charles, de
Gerrow Isaac, Atlantic Hotel, do
Taylor John *East Chester.*
Cole James
Underhill L. U., R. R. Hotel
Beaver L. T. Steamboat Hotel, Tarrytown *Greenburgh.*
Smith Martin, Tarrytown Hotel, Tarrytown
Wilson Moses H. Franklin House, Tarrytown
Vincent John, Tarrytown
Tsfergo Isaac, Hastings Hotel, Hastings
Taylor Shadrick, Dobbs' Ferry
Conway Thomas, R. R. House *Louisborough.*
Gamsey Wm., Cross Lines Hotel
Webber R. Pleasantville Hotel *Mount Pleasant.*
Hall James S., R. R. Hotel *New Castle.*
Miller Nicholas *New Rochelle.*
Rice Charles F. Neptune House
Smith Samuel P., Mile Square *North Castle.*
Bailey George, East Salem *North Salem.*
Bailey Daniel, de
Howe E. do
Bailey Lyman, Croton Falls
Reynolds A. B., Sing Sing *Ossining.*
Urmy Jackson, do
Neckerson A. E. do
Workman L. American House, Sing Sing
Tompkins Alex. Tompkins' Hotel, Sing Sing
Morgan W. Temperance House
Resseguie Oscar, Osinsing Hotel
Horton George, City Island Hotel *Pelham.*
Vansiclin Silvanus *Rye.*
Sniffin Ezra, R. R. House
Smith G. W. Pavilion Hotel, Portchester
Slater V., Portchester Hotel, Portchester
St. John Bradley, Steamboat Hotel, Portchester
Morse Isaac, Armonck Hall, Portchester
Bailey Horace, Elephant Hotel
Fowler Benj., Somerstown *Westchester.*
Fowler Lawrence, Bridge Hotel
Wilson A. Stage Hotel *West Farms*

Johnson John, Union Hotel *West Farms.*
Jessup J. H. Flag of the Union Hotel
Crowell O., R. R. House
Berrian C., R. R. House, Fordham
Valentine B., R. R. House, Williams' Bridge
Cromwell R. M. New Haven Hotel, Williams' Bridge
Tier D. do
Smith Isaac, Orawampum House *White Plains.*
Crawford Stephen H. Union Hotel
Briggs Benj.
Terboss Isaac
Bashford E. A. *Yonkers.*
Kellinger D. C. Mansion House
Bashford James, Napperkamak Hotel
Morgan P. N., R. R. Hotel, Tuckahoe
Barritt S. G., R. R. Hotel, Hart's Corners

Wyoming County.

Manger Ira M. AtticaHouse *Attica.*
Leggett & Gillett, Western Hotel
Avery Rufus G. American Hotel
Tyrrell Gideon
Polhemus Joab, Exchange Hotel
Woodford E. L. *Bennington.*
Filimen Horace, Cowlesville
Green V. do
Coats A., Attica
Dodge H. *Castile.*
Warriner Alex.
Severance N.
Rose A. H.
Davis J. M. *China.*
Miller N. E. *Covington.*
Miller David
Cooley Francis, Peoria
Tenant A. *Gainesville.*
Mix —
Town Ruel *Genesee Falls.*
Ingham Joseph, Ingham's Hotel
Providence Jno. Aqueduct House
Gillett John D. *Java.*
Waldo A. A., East Java
Lewis M., North Java
Newell Joseph, Wyoming *Middlebury.*
Wright Enos K. do
Chadburn Wm. do
Morse J. H. *Orangeville.*
Root A, East Orangeville
Walker A. B. National Hotel *Perry.*
M'Cleary Jno. Silver Lake House
Whiting D., Perry Centre
Gates J. Eagle Tavern *Pike.*
Hopson A. Pike Hotel
Knapp B., American
Flint C. Tremont House, East Pike
Wilcox A. Farmers' Exchange, East Pike
Chandler F., East Koy
Lucas L. D. *Sheldon.*
Mann A.
Bankman Augustus
Metzer George
Jackson Lyman, Strykersville
Merrill F. Varysburg
Crawford O. J. Johnsburgh
Parsons E. H. North Sheldon
M'Elwain J. A. *Warsaw.*
Frank A. Warsaw Temperance House
Stearns Willard

Yates County.

Ketcham James *Barrington.*
Tupper H. H.
Van Deventer Z. *Benton.*
Brown & Haight
Ratcliff —, Benton Centre
Smith J., Belona
Hooker F. M., Belona
Barker S. Italy Hollow *Italy.*
Felton S. do

Fox L. Italy Hollow *Italy.*
Wells R. Italy Hill
Willet William *Jerusalem.*
Paris Barney, Branchport
Blanchard John *Middlesex.*
Crouch Joseph
Mallory S. L., American, Penn Yan *Milo.*
Robbins H. C. Mansion House, Penn Yan
Cole S. M. Franklin House, Penn Yan
Murdock —, Canal House, Penn Yan
Harrison —, Travellers' Home, Penn Yen
Vanhorn D. Milo Hotel,MiloCentre
Townsend M. Milo Centre
Thomas Albert *Potter.*
Loomis C. Rushville
Tuttle Benjamin *Starkey.*
Hogaboome E. A.
Patton F. M. Dundee House *Dundee.*
Harpending S. Dundee
Bailey I. G. do
Jones B. E. do
Manso Franklin *Sherman.*

Publishers. (See also Booksellers and Stationers—also Newspapers—also Magazines.)

Adee Daniel, 107 Fulton *New York.*
Allen John, 139 Nassau
Appleton D. & Co. 200 Broadway
Baker & Scribner, 36 Park Row
Banks, Gould & Co. 144 Nassau. (See Business Register)
Barnes A. S. & Co. 51 John
Bartlett & Welford, 7 Astor House
Berford & Co. 2 do
Bidwell W. H. 120 Nassau
Cady & Burgess, 60 John
Clark, Austin & Co. 206 B.way
Carter Robert & Brother, 285 do
Colby Lewis, 122 Nassau
Collins & Brother, 254 Pearl
Coolidge Geo. F. & Brother, 323 Pearl
Currier Nathaniel, 152 Nassau
Dana Daniel, 20 John
Dean William E. 12 Ann
Dewitt & Davenport, 156 Nassau
Disturnell John, 102 Broadway
Dodd M. W. Brick Church Chapel
Doggett John, jr. 64 Liberty
Douglass Mary, 11 Spruce
Dunigan Edward & Brother, 151 Fulton
Elton Robert H. 179 William & 18 Division & 90 Nassau
Fletcher Edward H. 141 Nassau
Fowlers & Wells, 131 do
Francis C. S. & Co. 252 Broadway
French Samuel, 293 do
Gates, Stedman & Co. 116 Nassau
Graham William H. 151 do
Halsted Jacob R. 2 Wall
Harper & Brothers, 82 Cliff
Huntington & Savage, 216 Pearl
King & Greeley, 102 Nassau
Lane & Scott, 128 do
Leavitt & Co. 191 Broadway cor. of Dey
Lockwood J. L. & Co. 459 Broadway
Lockwood & Son, 411 Broadway
Long H. & Brother, 43 Ann
Martin Robert, 46 Ann
Martin J. H. 142 Nassau
Methodist Book Concern, 200 Mulberry
Nafis & Cornish, 267 Pearl
Needle J. P. 96 Nassau
Newman Mark H. & Co. 199 Broadway
Norton Charles B. 71 Chambers. (Irving House)
Pratt L. C. & H. L. 293 Broadway.

Putnam George P. 155 Broadway *New York.*
Radde William, 322 do
Redfield Justus S. 127 Nassau
Redfield N. & Co. 481 Houston
Riker John C. 129 Fulton
Saxton Charles M. 121 Fulton
Scott Leonard & Co. 54 Gold
Sears Robert, 128 Nassau
Stanford & Swords. 137 Broadway
Stringer & Townsend, 222 do
Trow John F. 49 Ann (Wilson's Business Directory)
Voorhies John S. 20 Nassau
Walker Edward, 114 Fulton
Wells J. C. 99 Nassau
Wesleyan Methodist Book Rooms, 5 Spruce
Westermann G.& B. 651 Broadway
Wilson H. 541 Pearl
Wilson & Co. 15 Spruce
Wood Richard & George, 38 Pearl
Wood Samuel & Wm. 261 Pearl

Pump and Block Makers.

Albany County.
Brainard E. 23¼ Quay *Albany*

Broome County.
Sisson B. F. *Binghamton*

Erie County.
Taff Samuel S. cor. Water & Dock *Buffalo.*
Taff Manuel, 17 Main
Ely Israel C. Water st.
Clark & Hawkins, Canada Dock

Oswego County.
Meeker F. & L. Crocker's Building, Bridge st. *Oswego.*
Lang W. E. & Co. (Blocks, Pumps and Spars) cor. Front & Van Buren

Rensselaer County.
Jaquins John. Front st. *Troy.*
Taylor John, rear 139 River
Pierson Albert M. 13 Ferry

Pump Makers. (See also Pump and Block Makers.)

Allegany County.
Olds William D. *Amboy.*
Morrison & Graves *Angelica.*

Clinton County.
Bailey T. M. *Peru.*

Columbia County.
Thayer A. Malden Bridge *Chatham.*

Dutchess County.
Palmer Hervy, 437 Main *Poughkeepsie.*

Erie County.
Wisner Joel, Willink *Aurora.*
Eddy Nathan, do
Hamilton Z. A. do
Francis Daniel, (Beer Pump) cor. Pearl & Seneca *Buffalo.*

Genesee County.
Bigelow John A. *Le Roy.*

Jefferson County.
Wilson William, Watertown *Pamelia.*

Savage Andrew, Felt's Mills
　　　　　　　　　　Rutland.
Tooker O. A.　　do
Falker Ebenezer, do

Kings County.

Ware John W. (Pumps) cor. Atlantic & Clinton st.　*Brooklyn.*
Ware J. M. 89 Livingston
Shonnard Frederick, 26 Main
Murdock James J. Pearl cor. Water
Worthington & Baker, (Steam Pumps) Kent Av. cor. Division Av.
Waterman & Burr,(Patent Blocks) Boerum near Ewing
　　　　　　　　Williamsburgh.
Drury Thomas, 192 South 1st
Holt John, 111 Grand

Livingston County.

Whitney L. (Lead Pipe)　*Geneseo.*
Sherwood J.　　　　*Nunda.*

Monroe County.

Eldridge F. (Beer Pumps) corner William & Court　*Rochester.*
Stocking D. 46 Alexander
Brainerd & Carey, (Carey's Rotary Pump) Brockport *Sweden.*
Manning John, Scottsville
　　　　　　　　Wheatland.
Markham Ransom, Mumford

Montgomery County.

Nash H. H.　　　*Amsterdam.*

Oneida County.

Dickinson M. G. Whitesboro st.
　　　　　　　　Utica.
Coffin William, Fulton st.

Orleans County.

Meade Henry, Barre Centre
　　　　　　　　Barre.
Sampson Gilbert,　do
Wyman A.　　　*Kendall.*

St. Lawrence County.

Tupper Augustus N.　*Potsdam.*
Davis Joseph N.

Seneca County.

Downs, Mynderse & Co. (See Advertisement)　*Seneca Falls.*
Seymour & Corning
Seymour & Cornell

Steuben County.

Jeffrey E. A. (Forcing Pumps)
　　　　　　　Painted Post.

Suffolk County.

Hill & Vail, Greenport　*Southold.*

Ulster County.

Fuller A. H. (Chain Pump)
　　　　　　　New Paltz.

Wyoming County.

Homes B.　　　　*Perry.*
Clute N.　　　　　*Pike.*
Buxton William　*Warsaw.*

Putty Manufacturers.

Kings County.

Phillips John F. Plymouth near Conklin's lane　*Brooklyn.*

New York County

Boyd Frederick S. 125 Bank
　　　　　　　　New York.

Bulwinkle Henry, 97 Forsyth
　　　　　　　　New York.
Hedden & Lugar 42 Av. D

Quill Manufacturers.

Cohen & De Young, 54 E. Broad'y
　　　　　　　　New York.
Trenkamp Francis, 14 Platt

Rag Dealers.　*(See also Junk Stores.)*

Beebe Samuel, 47 Gold *New York.*
Burrows Thomas, 144 Liberty
Cook John, 41 Ann
Field Cyrus W. & Co. 94 Beekman
(See Advertisement.)
Haydock John, 220 2d
Jackson Thomas, 265 Water
Kelogg Joseph L. 26 Gold
M'Bean Lachlan, 40 Spruce
Mehan James, 42 W. Broadway
Manushan James, 212 Mott
West George, 42 Duane

Railroad Offices.

Bridgeport & Housatonic, foot of Market E. R.　*New York.*
Brooklyn & Jamaica, 57 Merch's Exchange
Camden & Amboy, pier 1, N. R.
Housatonic Transfer Agency, 2 Hanover
Hudson River, 54 Wall
Naugatuck, 2 Hanover
New Haven & Northampton, 2 Hanover
New Jersey R. R. & Trans. Co. 57 Merchants' Exchange
New York & Erie, 45 Wall
New York & Harlem, 2 Hanover
New York & New Haven, 2 Hanover & 29 Canal
Norwich & Worcester, 18 Merchants' Exchange
Paterson Railroad Co. 75 Cortlandt
Sangammon & Morgan, 2 Hanover
Saratoga & Washington, 2　do

Rake Manufacturers.

Broome County.

Heath A.　　　　*Union.*
Heath & Edson

Cayuga County.

Starks I.　　　　*Genoa.*

Chautauque County.

Fenton & Willard, Jamestown
　　　　　　　　Ellicott.

Columbia County.

Dean C., New Lebanon Centre
　　　　　　　New Lebanon.

Delaware County.

Nelson A.　　　　*Franklin.*
Treadwell H. & Co.　*Croton.*

Duchess County.

Cudner P. & Co. (horse rake)
　　　　　　　Hyde Park.

Genesee County.

Tomlinson J. (horse rake) *Le Roy.*
Mills M.　　　do
Sherrell N. A.　　do

Madison County.

St. John H. (horse rake) *Brookfield.*
Beebe James　　*Sullivan.*

Ontario County.

Whitman Horace　　*Phelps*

Otsego County.

Clark J.　　　*Plainfield.*
Crumb V. C.
Williamson C. H.
St. John C.
Johnson A. D.

St. Lawrence County.

Newland Peabody (horse rake)
　　　　　　　Lawrence.

Ulster County.

Munce George, Ulsterville
　　　　　　　Shawangunk.
Steadman R., Napanock
　　　　　　　Wawarsing.

Wayne County.

Yeomans E. & T. G. (horse rake)
　　　　　　　Walworth.

Wyoming County.

Bosworth F.　　　　*Pike.*

Rattan Dealer.

Ely Smith, 79 Fulton　*New York.*

Razor Strop Manufacturers.

New York County.

Chapman Levi, 102 William
　　　　　　　New York.
Conger John, 199 William & foot of Bank
Saunders William, 336 Bowery
Saunders A. & J. 147 & 387 B'way

Rensselaer County.

Millman Isaac, 190 Congress *Troy*

Reed Makers.

Duchess County.

Carver R. D. Matteawan *Fishkill.*

Oneida County.

Warner J. E. & Co. 22 & 24 Genesee　*Utica.*

Rensselaer County.

Lairdeson John, 215 Congress
　　　　　　　　Troy.

Reflectors (R. R. Lamp.)

Monroe County.

Bidwell Salmon, 6 Selye Buildings
　　　　　　　Rochester

Refrigerators.

Barton W. B. & R. 53 10th Av.
　　　　　　　New York.
Locke John, 47 Ann
Parker Isaac, 28½ Bedford
Shay William H. 132 M'Dougal
Smith John M. 468½ Broadway
Woods William, 135 Eldridge

Restaurants,Oyster Saloons &c. (See also Eating Houses, also Porter Houses.)

Albany County.

Hagaman & Cowel,(oysters whole sale) 263 & 265 Broadway

Johnson J. 81½ South Pearl *Albany.*
Anderson J. 25   do
Strain John F. 4 Exchange
Reason P. 1   do
Van Bremer Peter, 551 Broadway
Whitecar J. 535   do
Schoonmaker I. 641   do
Slauson John, 660   do
Childs Daniel, 644   do
Remond N. 436   do
Thomas & Jones, 291   do
Veeder V. 6 N. Lansing
Adams & Welsh, 52 State
Ruso F. & F. 86   do
Anthony P. A. 96   do
Maben A. P. 130   do
Porter F. 15 Hudson
Burnham G. W. 43 Green
Anderson J. H. 62   do
Johnson H. 129½ South Pearl
Wilber A. 90   do
Osburn R. 48   do
Houck J. & P. P. 3   do
Chambers T. 79   do
Griffin S. 6 Green
M'Cardel John, 15 & 17 Beaver
Fredenrick J. 4 William
Dermody J. 10   do
Jacobs L. C. 104 Pier
Montross & Hill, (Gothic Hall) 39 Columbia
Holland C. E. 39 N. Pearl
Traber C. 19 Lodge
Wright George, 11 Washington
Carle J. F. 94   do
Harwood C., West Troy *Watervliet.*
Kelly Patrick,   do
Jook John,   do
Ellis J.   do

Alleghany County.

Waggoner Henry   *Almond.*
Van Campen Ira
Kimble L. V. & Co.

Broome County.

Rice J. F.   *Binghamton.*
Dewits ——, under Post Office
Stockwell J.
Belding E.
Whitcomb J.
Hodge F.   *Union.*
Fanning Asa

Cayuga County.

Sherwood A. 37 Genesee *Auburn.*
Leonard & Stevens, 93 do
Pulsifer J. P., State st.
Hiser H. C.   do
Howland C.   do
Miller D. C., North st.
Tabet S. T., South st.

Chenange County.

Bishop T.   *Greene.*

Columbia County.

Cornerr H., Chatham Four Corners   *Chatham.*
Cady N. J., Warren st. *Hudson.*
Bostwick E. F. cor. Warren & 7th
Hazard & Bryant. N. Front st.
Hodge J. W. (eating house) Warren st.
Miller S. (R. R. Saloon) nr. Depot

Delaware County.

Hollister J. R.   *Delhi.*
Woodruff William
Shiffer J.
M'Keever J. S.   *Hancock.*
Dean S. O., Deposit *Tompkins.*
Middlemus T. do

Duchess County.

Ransom B. E.   *Amenia.*
Member J. E. Fishkill Landing *Fishkill.*

Denton B. 284 Main *Poughkeepsie.*
Denton B. 272½ Main
Sherman Wm. A. 339 Main
Denton B. 255 Main
Brown & Leely, 249 Main
Dickenson J. P. 245 Main
Van Eck C. C. 231 & 233 Main
Myrick Thos. 349 Main
Fry J. 25 Main
Bishop John. New Hamburgh
Van Curen H. T.   *Rhinebeck.*
Fisher B.

Erie County.

Dorr John, 4 Pearl   *Buffalo.*
Knowlton T. J. 2 Packet dock
Cramer & Wentworth, 3 Packet dock
Richard Keyes, Packet dock
Bates & Dickey, 25 Pratt's Block, Commercial st.
Bastion R. C. 263 Main
Smith John, 4 & 6 E. Seneca
Thorn N. E. 10 E. Seneca
Kingman M. cor. Washington & Exchange
Robinson Wm. 43 Ohio
Brooks & Oakley, 320 Main
Dix David, 290 Main
Cotter T. Spaulding's Exchange
Coan Chas. 4½ Terrace
Elliott Jos. Commercial cor. Rock
Baker Wm. Commercial st.
Erb Peter, 6 Commercial
Becker J. G. 16 Main
Gage & Knight, 146 Main
Eaton Abraham, 100 Main
Britton Lewis, 90 Main
Stumpf John, 22 Main
M'Dougal R. 13 Main
Brown Samuel, 15 Main
Pair E. 19 Webster's Block
Mason J. W. 157 Main

Essex County.

Williams E. C.   *Elizabethtown.*
Keith Madison

Fulton County.

Ten Eycke Robert   *Broadalbin.*

Genesee County.

White N. A.   *Bergen.*

Greene County.

Freligh Henry   *Catskill.*
Ward Richard
Halsted Henry W.
Barnett Wm.
Smith & Van Steenburgh
Ely David
Eygner James
Benjamin Jesse   *Coxsackie.*
Cozine Ezekiel   *New Baltimore.*

Jefferson County.

Hubbard Wm.   *Brownsville.*
Earle O. R.
Dyer & Allen, Evans' Mills   *Le Ray.*

Kings County.

Cutting Wm. 23 Fulton *Brooklyn.*
White F. 23 James
Lane Benj. 25 James
Vanorden A. 4 Atlantic
Hurd E. (under Waverley House)
Kaufman G. H. 7 Atlantic
Brady M. 204 Fulton
Fisbeck C. & Hodge A. (under Montague Hall)
Edmonds Benj. (under Franklin House)
Boyer F. J. 61 Fulton
Stoothoof Abram, 33 James
Brown Thos. 29 Main
Davis David, 11 Prospect
O'Neil Peter, York near Main

Pouch Mrs. S. J. 35 Myrtle av *Brooklyn.*
Boman J. A. 7 Linden row
M'Bride Mrs. Mary, 195 York
Bennett Mrs. M. (Coffee) Market st.
Furman Mrs. (Coffee) Market st.
Mayne J. 19 S. 7th *Williamsburgh.*
Cox J. F. 9 S. 7th
Ackerly Alanson, 3 Grand

Livingston County.

Dimond Geo.   *Dansville.*
Curtis Wm.
Glenn & Hartman
Lerna P. S.
Goodich F. A.
Taft Samuel
Morgan Wm. C.
Best H. & Co.
Litchard H
Stacy O. D. & H.
Davis & Williams
Van Garden H. & D.   *Geneseo.*
Clark T. F.   *Lima.*
Hilliard Rufus R.   *Mount Morris.*
Terry J. & Co.   *Nunda.*
Cooley B.

Madison County.

Bishop Thos.   *Cazenovia.*
Babcock David
Hill M. C.
Wesley Geo.
Burns G. F.   *Hamilton.*
Hall L. C.
Steadman & Bentley
Bentley D. B.
Welrath Jas. J. Chittenango   *Sullivan.*
Monk H. & G.   do

Monroe County.

Cotter Jas. 11 & 12 Canal dock *Rochester.*
Miller John, cor Exchange st. & Canal Bridge
Bidwell W. 1 & 2 Canal dock
Meng Chas. 4, 5 & 6 Canal dock
Dunn J. 9 Canal dock
Campbell D. Curtis' Block, Main st.
Brown Jos. 90 Buffalo
Denny Patrick, 90 Buffalo
Damon J. B. Eagle Block, Buffalo st.
Walker Myron, 36 Buffalo
Hart J. 45 Main
Wooster & Burrows, cor. Main & St. Paul
Jackson Jasper, cor. Fitzhugh & Buffalo
Hickock Asher, 43 Exchange
Porter John, under 43 Exchange
Bischoff A. under 37 Exchange
Ardner H. N. under 39 Exchange
Smith C. B. 20 Exchange
Coon John, under 36 Exchange
Wadsworth Perry, 36 Exchange
Clark Isaac E. under Rochester House, Exchange st.
Ashley Isaac, basement Clinton Hotel, Exchange st.
Alexander B. cor. Front & Mumford
Yaky Christian, Mill st.
Delany John, cor. Front & Market
Parish Nathan   *Rush.*

Montgomery County.

Lewis Isaac   *Canajoharie.*
Stafford Job
Plant & Flint, Fort Plain *Minden.*
Saltman Peter W. Fort Plain
Dygest Stickney,   do
Wieting Jeremiah,   do
Ransom Lewis,   do
Casler David,   do
Gown H. M. Fonda   *Mohawk.*
Wires Wm. S. do
Dechstader G. M. Fonda

Davis J. J.   Fonda *Mohawk.*
Quackenbush John, do
Tappin P. S.   do

New York County.

Abel Oliver Charles, 163 Charles *New York.*
Armbruster J. E. 79 Chatham
Auld Samuel, 29 West
Au Rocher De Cancale, 15 Park row
Ayres Elihu. 33 Vesey
Babcock William F. 92 Bowery
Baker C. M. 129 do
Bardotte & Ventura, 289 B'dway
Barnswell Thomas R. 336 3d
Barnwell A. R. & P. 336 B'dway
Bassett Nathaniel, 229 W'hington
Bagley C. 100 Fulton
Bennett John, 51 8th Av.
Blohm T. Brother & Co. 94 G'wich
Bloomfield George, 30 Av. C
Bodine John, 64 Chatham
Bodine T. E. & Co. 109 Nassau
Bogart Harris, 30 6th Av.
Bohne H. & J. 74 & 125 Fulton
Bolton W. H. 217 Washington
Bond H. 148 W. Broadway
Bradcher Wm. 190 3d Av.
Braisted & Mendell, 415 B'dway
Braw H. 22 Duane
Bross Wm. H. 218 & 220 Bleecker
Brower William, 228 do
Brown J. 46 13th
Brown S. W. 424 West
Brown William E. 407 Grand
Buckridge William, 73 9th Av.
Burbridge & Morgan, 458 B'dway
Butler Henry H. 77 Catharine
Burnes T. H. 600 Broadway
Burns Francis, 39 Madison
Burns S. M. 360 Broadway
Bynner Thomas, 149 Hester
Caafe John, 596 Broadway
Cantor Nicholas, 130 Walker
Caroccioli Antonio, 160 Canal
Carstens Frederick, 110 Centre
Carstans Frederick, 156 B'dway
Carter Samuel, 153 Hester
Cartwright William, 100 Fulton
Caspare F. 38 Chatham
Chadwick Wm. 5 Catharine mkt.
Chandler Albert S. 318 Greenwich
Chapman Victor M. 897 B'dway
Chedic & Christie, foot of Dey
Childs Isaac, 74 E. Broadway
Chinery William, 6 W. do
Churchill W. 16 Broome
Cisco T. 565 Broadway
Collins Mark, 409 West
Colon Geo. 190 Wooster
Condoit Geo. 134 8th
Conelly John, 50 Bowery
Cowdry Enos, 111 Walker
Davis Francis, 13 Dry Dock
Davis Joseph, 140 9th Av.
Davis Oliver, 92 Tompkins
Deans T. 43 Canal & 417 B'dway
Decker Benj. foot of Dey N. R.
Decker Charlotte, 93 Duane
Decker David, 13 Ann
Decker F. D. & Co. 3 Hanover
Decker Joseph, 10 Franklin mkt.
Dibbin Frank, 212 Hudson
Doudan John, 201 Varick
Dow Amelie, 47 Orange
Downing George T. 590 B'dway
Downing Thomas, 5 Broad
Drewar James, 5 Clinton market
Dunford James, 29 Mulberry
Dwyer John, 90 Murray
Dwyer J. 98 Washington market
Earl & Jackson, 98 & 100 Division
Ebling J. E. 200 Bowery
Egbert J. 53 Hudson
Egbertson J. 55 Walnut
Ehrig Bruno, 11 Chatham
Ellard & Boole, 628 4th
Ettling Charles, 449 Broadway
Evans John, 158 Duane
Farrington Oliver, 285 Water

23

Feiss Henry, 117 Roosevelt *New York.*
Fenton Robert, 147 8th Av.
Fisher & Sherwood, 252 & 398 Broadway
Fletcher Nathan, 72 W. 23d
Florence Abraham, 30 Bowery
Florence Abraham. 178 Chatham
Florence John. 507 Broadway
Francis Joh.), 106 Catharine
Forsyth Joseph. 4 W'hington mkt
Forsyth R. 9 Washington market
Forsyth Wm. 5 W'hington market
Fox Wm. 159 W. Broadway
Frost William J. 498 Grand
Gallagher Ana & Co. 1 Washington market
Gorber George. 44 Orange
Gerdes Frederick, 241 Division
Gibbons John, 8 W'hington mkt
Gonsolves Joseph, 534 Grand
Graves Charles B. 347 Broadway
Green John, 319 Spring
Gulliver Samuel, 13 Canal
Hall Jonathan, 215 Doane
Harris David S. 302 Pearl
Hoit Nathaniel, 290 11th
Hellwegen & Niehaus, 129 Bow'y
Hedges & Simonson, foot of Dey
Holmes Enoch, 89 West Broad'y
Holmes Thomas, 368 Bowery
Honce David & Co. 109 Nassau
Housman Isaac, 9 & 11 Catharine
Howlett Field W. 174 Grand
Hulin Francis, 73 Roosevelt
Husted Peter, 108 Columbia
Hynes Francis, 158½ Av. A
Jayard John D. 21 Wall
Jackson & Earle, 98 & 100 Division
Jackson George, 104 Church
Jacobus John W. 109 8th Av.
Jago John, 16 West Broadway
Johnson Charles, 155 Division
Johnson Isaac, 288½ Division
Johnson John, 221 Church
Johnson William & Co. 213 West
Joseph Antoine, 63 Ludlow
Judge Thomas, 231 8th Av
Kain & Egbertson, 55 Walnut
Keefe John & Stone, 596 Broad'y
Kelly Peter, 45 Spring
Kilaby John W. 540 Hudson
Kinsey James, 144 Chatham
Knight Richard, 148 Leonard
Lassan Henry, 16 West Broadway
Lee David, 561 Pearl
Lee Robert, 44 Delancy
Lafurge William, foot of Dey
Lemonier Auguste. 60 Leonard
Leonard Patrick, 568 Greenwich
Lewis Samuel, 233 Centre
Libby Robert H. 19 Wall
Loomis H. D. cor. of 7th & Av. A
Lovegrove Hiram W. 448 Broad'y
Lynch Timothy, 100 Fulton
M'Camman Azel, 133 Spring
M'Dade ——, 261 8th Av.
M'Donald John, 129 Bowery
M'Intire John, 87 Centre
M'Kinney James, 210 Chatham
Mart Frank, 2 Catharine slip
Martin & Co. 18 West
Mason Charles, 371 4th Av.
Matern Wm. 127 Bowery
Mathieu Joseph, 111 Roosevelt
Meinberger Michael, 28 Centre
Meyer Wm. 44 Nassau
Michaels John C. 70 Barclay
Michaels John M. 217 Greenwich
Middleton Dobson. 312 Water
Monroe Oliver, foot of Dey
Montross Wm. 3 Catharine mkt.
Moore L. 455 12th
Morcer John, 150½ Greenwich
Morris Alexander, 232 West 16th
Morton L. R. 1 4th Av.
Munger Wm. H. 499 Hudson
Murphy Hugh, 59 Bayard
Palmer Daniel, 1 Catharine mkt.
Pardee Henry, 172 8th Av.
Patterson Isaac, 54 4th Av.
Perry Benjamin, 565 Grand

Pestor John C. 561 Pearl *New York.*
Pettit A. 218 Canal
Philbrick Nath'el C 142 Chatham
Philips Benj. 167 Greenwich
Phillips Francis, 134 Clinton place
Piersall Tobias, 139 Av. C
Potter Neptune. 111 Nassau
Price Amos W. 132 Walker
Purdee Henry, 172 8th Av.
Purdy E. H. 25 West
Race J. A. 499 Hudson
Reed Samuel, 4 Catharine mkt.
Reeves William, 389½ West
Ridabock Chas. 118 Water
Ring William, 244 3d Av.
Ropke John P. Exchange Retreat 78 Wall
Ross Charles, 209 Duane
Ruch Geo. 122 Greenwich
Roethenbach ——, 145 Greenwich
Ruckman Edward, foot of Dey, N. R.
Russ Parker, 480 Broome
Russell Anthony. 151 Church
Saddlemire George, jr 57 4th Av
Schwalbe F. W. 73 Chatham
Schaff T. 58 Chatham
Sembler Andrew, 98 Church
Serr Valentine, 93 Centre
Schaffner Michl. 366 Pearl
Sherwood Daniel J. 240 Broadway
Sherwood & Fisher, 252 and 398 Broadway
Shriver Charles, 474 Grand
Silva J. 4 Catharine slip
Simons William, 144½ Centre
Skillings Azel, 536 Broadway
Skinner William H. 428 Broadway
Slater L. S. 89 West Broadway
Smith Benjamin, 303 Bleecker
Smith H. 15 Center
Smith James, 47 Chatham
Smith Nathaniel. 514 Pearl
Smith Timothy, 139 Monroe
Smith William, 370 Broome
Snyder Alexander, 31 McDougal
Southard William, 2 Catharine market
Sutton Charles J. 440 Broadway
Stahl Hugo, 47 Chatham
Stallo John M. 166 Chatham
Stegman Conrad, 23 West
Stelle Peter R. 1 Ann
Story Benjamin, jr. 66 Barclay and 886 Broadway
Story Jacob, 67 University place
Shovagirl Louis, 212 8th Av.
Teneyck Joseph, 556 Broadway
Toppin H. 299 4th
Tucker Elihu L. 147 Bowery
Tyson Stephen, 363 Hudson
Vandel William, 106 Spring
Vanriper T. & L. 210 Chatham
Varnfell W. P. 145 Bowery
Vanname Henry, 132 Chatham
Vanname Isaac, 42 Bowery
Vanname William, 157 Fulton
Vanpelt Henry, 133 Walker
Vansyckle Peter, 38 Carmine
Votten Wm. H. 217 Washington
Von Roctor & Co. 12 Greenwich
Vielbig A. 50 Chatham
Vroom George W. 266 Bowery
Waderman William, 172 Canal
Walker John S. 4 Centre
Wallace Thos. 910 Canal
Walnut James A. 214 Broadway
Ward Horace, 323 Hudson
Watson William M. 564 Broadway
Wedekend Henry, 6 William
Webster G. 83 West Broadway
Wetherill J. R. & Co. foot of Dey
Wood E. A. 142 Chatham
Wood James, foot of Dey
Woolley Jacob, 62 West Broadway
Wilcox Jared, 6 Washington market
Williams Robert J. 63 Leonard
Williamson John, 112 Division
Wilson Thos. 392 Hudson
Wilt John, 153 Walker

Witherell Timothy D. foot of Dey *New York.*

Witzen John, 48 Centre

Niagara County.

Bement J. C.   *Lewiston.*
Trafford R.
Parmalee Leonard   *Lockport.*
Lewis James G.
Humphrey W. H.
Baker ———
Curtis A. H.   *Niagara Falls.*
Badgley David
Weaver P. B. Youngstown *Porter.*

Oneida County.

Amidon & Mulligan, 2 James *Rome.*

Flint Amos, James st.
Knox C.   do
Eastman J. Waterville *Sangerfield.*
Miller H. H. 27 Genesee *Utica.*
Jacobs S. C. near R. R. Depot
Green Wm. H. Devereux Block
Johnson Mrs. A. 11 Fayette
Rolin Robert, 132 Genesee
Smith T. 1, 2, 3, 4, 5, Packet Dock
Reese Thomas, 129 Genesee
Cassidy P. 2 Catharine

Ontario County.

Haskell Jeremiah *Canandaigua.*
Parshall John
Cosson Jacob & Son
Reed Joseph, Geneva *Seneca.*
Tileston C. H.   do
Ramsey H.   do
Dey M. M.   do
Donelly P.   do
Talmadge S. J.   *Victor.*
Walling J
Bushnell Fred.   *West Bloomfield.*
Wells Robert

Onondaga County.

M'Cumber Wm. Malcolm Hall, Syracuse *Salina.*
Brigham L. Salina st. Syracuse
Marlett & Co. Fruit Arcade, Salina st. Syracuse
Sacket C. D. Salina st. Syracuse
Eaton A. W.   do   do
Learned D. Genesee st.   do
Andrews F. A.   do   do
Greenman L. W. do   do
Kahn Mrs. I. Water st.   do
King D., R. R. & Warren,   do
Curtis J. Genesee st.   do
Spearpoint Wm. Water st.   do
Bowen J. W. James st.   do
Woodruff C.   do   do
Williams L. Salina st.   do
Gane G.   do   do
Abbott C. W. Wolf st.   do

Orange County.

Gatfield M.   *Chester.*
Corris I. Buttermilk Falls *Cornwall*
Foster & Lyttle, Port Jervis *Deer Park.*
Kirk J.   do
Crocker D.   do
Happock J. L.   do
Adams G. P.   do
Totten & Mirteens, do
Hart W. D.   *Goshen.*
Van Nort J. S.
M'Niece William
Clearwater P. T.   *Montgomery.*
M'Kinney James H.
Bodine C. T., Walden
Evans R. 107 Water   *Newburgh.*
Casterline J. Steamboat Office
Jones Seth, Front st.
Pennoyer J. W. Knickerbocker, 2d st.
M'Cartner Samuel, 2d st.

Murrey John & W. 3d st. *Newburgh.*
Crist William, Front st.
Ball Abram D.   do
Bickner Alex.   do
Pierce Joel F.   do
Hulse C. S. South Middletown *Wallkill.*
Crane O. M.   do
Toulon A. B.   do
Demerest P. W.   *Warwick.*
Irwin W. D.

Orleans County

Fuller M. L., Albion   *Barre.*
Hulbert M. A. do
Shadders W. P. do

Oswego County.

Ashton James W. 1st st. *Oswego.*
Knox David H. 1st st.
Earl & Hayes, Bridge st.
Lord Monroe,   do
Donohue C.   do
Fowler Wm. J. Cayuga st.
Campbell & Spencer, Water st.
Jordan Cyrus, Water st.
Peck O. & Co. Bridge st.
Coplin A. Bridge cor. Water
M'Carty Lyman, 1st st.
Hempstead C. Pulaski *Richland.*
Smith Jacob,   do
Stearns L. N.   do

Otsego County.

Short J. J. Cooperstown *Otsego.*

Putnam County.

Griffin ———, Cold Spring *Phillipstown.*
Spellman B.   do
Spellman H. S.   do
Bryant S.   do
M'Lean T   do
Ferris J.   do
Howe A.   do

Queens County.

Worden Edward   *Hempstead.*
Crossman W. H.
Bennett Mrs. Mary   *Jamaica.*
Bennett John

Rensselaer County.

Seaman G. 235 State *Lansingburgh.*
Houghton C. S. 285 State
Morris Jacob, 318 State
Follett A. 268 State
Virgo Wm. 9 Elizabeth
Walmore Wm. Front cor. Washington   *Troy.*
Riley Dennis, Water st
Brower Ransom, Front st.
Clumb John, 4 River
Holsapple D. E. 3 River
Cramer Anthony, 86 River
Troy Charles, 95 River
Cole John, River cor. Ferry
Schelleicher William, 130 River
Hilke Henry, 195 River
Rockwood E. R. 197 River
Patrick & Delany, 235 River
Potter John, 287 River
Seaman S. T. 330 River
Elliott George, 440 River
Jackson James, 481 River
Miller Harry. 375 River
Benson & Beebe, 361 River
Harris Thomas, 5 1st
Thomas Charles, 193 4th
Bennett N. 1 Franklin square
Butler R. 31 Congress
Purck John, 43½ Congress
Allen Charles, 69 Congress
Chapman Wm. 84 Congress
Barnes John C. 86½ Congress
Gregory Andrew, 92 Congress
Conner Mrs. E. 87   do
Price A. 87½   do

Woodruff John, Ida Hill   *Troy.*
Waters T. B. Front st.
Rapp John, Fulton mkt
Ayers John L. 328 River
Montgomery J. 367 River
Warner Hiram, 179 5th

Rockland County.

Gardiner B., Nyack *Orangetown.*
Brown Wm., Piermont

St. Lawrence County.

Bowman E. D. Ford st. Ogdensburgh   *Oswegatchie.*
Backer Robert & Co. Ford st. Ogdensburgh
Larkin James, State cor. Ford

Saratoga County.

Ford Amasa, Ballston Spa *Milton.*
Lockwood James H. do
Perry George,   do
Pratt Andrew   *Waterford.*
Barker Samuel

Schenectady County.

Cleary T. 149 State *Schenectady.*
Drollard N. 133 State
Onderkirk P. 67 State
Barhydt E. 152 State
Barhydt N. 139 State
Felthousen J. B. 184 Dock
Freeman A.

Schoharie County.

Moere Jacob   *Gilboa.*

Seneca County.

Burritt Sidney L.   *Seneca Falls.*
Carr Thomas
Palmer E. W.
Woodmansee A.   *Waterloo.*
Inslee C. B.

Steuben County.

Blodgett George   *Painted Post.*
Dodge ———

Sullivan County.

Fields E., Big Eddy *Lumberland.*

Tioga County.

Dewitt J. S.   *Owego.*

Tompkins County

Dierick P. T. 72 Owego   *Ithaca.*
Gregory O. H. 96 do
Brayman A. 55   do

Ulster County.

Griffin Edward   *Kingston.*
King C. C. Wall st.
Kent James
Paulding Samuel D.
Barber Luman, Rondout
Haber F.   *Saugerties.*
Richmond A. H., Empire Saloon
Hull A.
Hempsted Robert
Atkins James, Napanock *Wawarsing.*
Barlow D., Ellenville
Wilson's Saloon, do
Van Schaik G. M., Ellenville

Washington County.

White Chas., Sandy Hill *Kingsbury.*
Doubleday H. M.   do
Vaughn A. W.   do
Mead M., Smith's Basin

Wayne County.

Sabins E. W. Newark   *Arcadia.*
Torrey ———,   do
Oroke Michael,   do

Atkins J. C., Clyde   *Galen.*
Landon J.   *Lyons.*
Clark Wm.
Crandall Wm.   *Palmyra.*
Gardiner Isaac
Carter S.
Lazalare Martin   *Wolcott.*

Westchester County.

Raynor M., Peekskill *Courtlandt.*
Reed J. B.   *White Plains.*

Wyoming County.

Norton S. B.   *Warsaw.*

Yates County.

Torrance S., Branchport
    Jerusalem.
Dorman J.   do
Jacobus & Kenyon, Penn Yan
    Milo.
Bradley H. jr.   do
Brown H. & Co   do
Woodruff J. M.   do
Norris J. N.   do
Parsons A., Dundee   *Starkey.*

Reporters—Telegraph.

Jones Alexander, 3 Hanover
    New York.
Smith & Hughes, 4 Hanover

Rice Dealers.

Fowler John, 50 Water *New York.*
Leverich Henry S. 29 Burling sl.
Wheeler & Van Benschoten, 110
  Front & 111 Water

Rice Mills.

Hunt Benjamin F. 269 South
    New York.

Riggers & Stevedores.

Kings County.

Johnson Andrew, 2 Hamilton
    Brooklyn.

New York County.

Anderson George, 313 West
    New York.
Barnes & Ludlow, 24 Coenties sl.
Batty Thomas, 205 South
Bremer Henry, 25 Coenties sl.
Cabres & Co. 273 South
Conklin Benjamin F. 93 Pine
Cooper Thomas, 29 Corlears
Dorian & Junier, 260 South, & 716
  Water
Ethredge & Groves, Gouverneur
  slip cor. South
Fuller Benjamin, 162 South
Gitscho Henry. 61 West
Gray Henry, 59 West
Haggeman Joseph, 377 Broome
Hatcher & Dixon, 271 South
Hines Mark, 204 Cherry
Hynard Wm. G. 116 Wall
Lauder Alex. 110 South
Magor Thomas, 315 Front
Marshall George, 10 Depeyster
Miller Andrew, 27 Cherry
Morris & Ostrom, 164 South
Owens & Husson, 56 West
Parker Wm. B. 304 West
Peterson & Veuner, 173 South
Robinson & Adams, 90 West
Rose & Smith, 89 South
Simpson & Place, 69 Washington
Thompson John, 53 West
Van Stratton Cornelius, 258 South
Vincent Edward, 60 South
White William, 226 South
Witty Calvin, 101 Av. D

Roofers.

Kings County.

Beman & Brother, (composition)
  51 Atlantic   *Brooklyn.*
Burtis, Smith & Co. (tin) 90 Myr-
  tle Av.
Foster Joseph, (tin) Prince st.
Gillett John H. (composition) 355
  Grand   *Williamsburgh.*

New York County.

Brodie John, 625 Washington
    New York.
Crommelin Edward, 221 W. 18th
Crommelin & Ordway, 627 Wash-
  ington
Drake James H. 153 9th
Goodwin Samuel, 26 College pl.
Gordon John & Joseph, 62 Ham-
  mond
Harris E. T. 70 Av. D.
Harrison Michael, 1 Bayard
Hetzer Christopher, 192 1st Av.
Legan & Moneghan, 547 Broad'y
Martin & M'Ever, 311 Broome
Mead & Eckert, 316 Bleecker
Naylor Peter & Co. 13 Stone
O'Brian Lewis, 272 Stanton
Roberts Calvin B. 66 Christopher
  & 134 4th
Roberts Graham, 155 Spring
Stead Robert, 19 11th
Sweets Ezra B. 123 Canal
Thorp & Sinclair, 135 W. 16th
Trembley S. R. & G. W. 136
  Chrystie

**Rope and Twine Manufac-
turers.** *(See also Cordage
and Twine.)*

Chenango County.

Brown E. & D.   *Otselic.*
Brown L.
Glading J. C. & J. A.   *Pharsalia.*

Cortland County.

Caldicott Wm.   *Cortland Village.*

Fulton County.

Clark Samuel   *Broadalbin.*
Clark Walter

Kings County.

Cunningham Richard, Bedford
    Brooklyn.
Morrison John, Bedford
Ross J. & Son, (tarred rope) Nos-
  trand st. near Flushing Av.
Roth H. (rope) Bedford
Marshall John, Flushing road
    Bushwick.
Allen & Decevee, South 7th st.
    Williamsburgh.
M'Way Charles & Sons, 5th st.
Schermerhorn, Banker & Co. 2d
  st. near North 4th
Dixon James, Wither st.
Whitehill L., Maspeth Av.

Monroe County.

Church Sidney, Buffalo st.
    Rochester.

Oswego County.

Davis Chauncy, Pulaski *Richland.*

Rensselaer County.

Maly Stephen A., Lansingburgh
  road   *Troy.*
Adams N.

Saratoga County.

Fletcher Lucius   *Waterford.*

Ulster County.

Van Allen & Co. Salisbury Mills
    Blooming Grove.

Washington County.

Tilton William   *Greenwich.*

Wyoming County.

Meadon & Swain   *Castile.*

Root Beer Makers. *(See also
Soda Water Makers.)*

Abbott Daniel, jr. 103 Anthony
    New York.
Earl & Watson, 254 17th
Edwards & Rogers, 150 Leonard
Judge Patrick, 41 Orange
Ormsby Dorman L. 255 W. 16th
Pond William, 164 W. 18th
Raymond James, 226 6th
Scott Richard, 27 Broome
Watson James, 249½ Division
Winchester H. 326 6th
Whittemore Charles, 162 Varick

Rule Makers.

Belcher, Brothers, 221 Pearl
    New York.
Bragg John H. rear 53 Mercer
Burdett Charles, 10 Madison
Currie Henry, rear 53 Mercer
Gee John, 76 Division
Reynolds Jas. L. rear 53 Mercer
Walker Job & George H. 61 & 63
  Elizabeth

Saddletree Manufacturers.

Kings County.

Spencer Robert, 3 Columbia
    Brooklyn.

Wayne County.

Rempson, Polhemas & Dennis
    Lyons.

Safes.

Albany County.

Covert H. W. cor. Steuben & Water   *Albany.*
Carles J. D. 18 William

Erie County.

Prescott Wm. C. 6 Pearl *Buffalo.*

New York County.

Delano Jesse, 28 Gold *New York.*
Delano William, 29 Gold
Froelick Louis, 81 Ann
Gayler Charles J. 126 Water & 62
  Cannon
Geisler F. C. 44 Essex
Herring Silas C. 137 Water
Marvin A. S. 138½ Water. Agency
  for Rich & Co's Salamander
  safes
Moen Augustus R. 126 Water
Roff & Stearns; 249 3d

Rensselaer County.

Lillie Louis, cor. 2d & Ida *Troy.*

**Safety Fuse Manufac-
turers.**

Reynolds & Brother, 85 Liberty &
  11 Nassau   *New York.*

Sail Makers.

Erie County.

Provoost J. P. Prime st.   *Buffalo.*
Provoost David,   do
Provoost S. A. Long Wharf

New York County.

Armour & Bakewell, 163 South
        New York.
Bakewell Joseph, 85 West
Bartling Charles C. 157 South
Bennett Benjamin, 302 West
Bennett & Stewart, 302 West
Bennett & Campbell, 120 Wall
Berry Thomas J. 174 South
Blacklidge Benjamin, 44 Peck slip
Blair & Higgins, 173 West
Brayton Wm. H. 176 South
Bromley & Wilson, 112 South
Brown & Hermann. 179 South
Burdett & Co. 8 Jones lane
Burrell Alexander H. 199 South
Camerden Henry, 182 South
Carroll Joseph, 406 West
Cartwright Wm. 105 South
Clark John, 208 Houston
Cole John, 46 West
Conner John, 114 Wall
Connor John C. 39 South
Crolius Edward, 69 West
Cumiskey Daniel M. 253 South
Dougherty Henry, 171 South
Dugan Wm. T. 25 South
Durbrow Wm. 23 South
Durbrow Wm. S. 86 West
Flanders & Gerau, 86 South
Folger Robert. 67 South
Gorham James, 283 South
Graham & Barnes, 21 Coenties sl.
Haskins John B. 105 South
Hazard Wm. H. 69 South
Hemmenway & Beveridge, 263
    Front
Hendrickson Benj. S. 142 West
Hennigar James, 34 Coenties slip
Hennigar John, 91 West
Higgins Daniel C. 173 West
Hillman Wm. 16 Coenties slip
Johnson Charles, 197 Hester
King James M) 304 West
Kirk John, 121 Norfolk
Lane Robert L. 100 Pine
Laytin & Sneden, 85 South
Macy & Rich, 169 South
Maxwell John T. B. 77 South
Megie Samuel M. 27 South
Murphy Wm. D. 97 Pine
Parisen & Crystal, 191 South
Robins Wm. 100 West
Sheldon & Young, 272 South
Soltwisch George A. 241 2d
Stewart & Campbell, South st. cor.
    Wall
Sundstrom Andrew G. 56 West
Taylor Theodore, 313 West
Thorp S. S. & I. O. 162 South
Wickoff Charles, 218 Delancy
Wilson Nicholas F. 18 James slip
Work Wm. East, bet. Delancy and
    Rivington

Oswego County.

Steward W. cor. Water & Seneca
        Oswego.
Greene Robert, Water st.
Lake D. Bronson's block, Water st.

Rensselaer County.

Town B. F. 149 River   *Troy.*

Suffolk County.

Paine Alanson, Greenport
        Southold.

Washington County.

Cain William, Pier, William st.
        Whitehall.

Salt Dealers.

Broome County.

Ishbell & Way   *Binghamton.*

Erie County.

Ranney O. W. 17 Central Wharf,
        Buffalo.
Avery Thomas Y. 26   do
Filkins C. E. & Co. 9   do
Millard H. W. & Co. Canada Dock

Montgomery County.

Abraham & Almy   *Canajoharie.*

New York County.

Hotaling Samuel, 16 Front
        New York.
Ransom B. 100 Wall
Stagg Benjamin & Co. 185 & 187
    Washington
Thompson Samuel & Nephew, 275
    Pearl
Todd William W. & Co. 77 Front
Woodruff A. & Robinson, 14 Coen-
    ties slip & 44 Front

Oneida County.

Dows & Kissam, cor. State & Canal
        Utica.
Ray E. C. cor. Hotel & Canal
Willcox W. C. 19 Liberty

Onondaga County.

Mitchell. Gere & Co. 1 Williams'
    block. Syracuse   *Salina.*
Woodruff C. Water st.

Oswego County.

Crane Hunter (salt. lime & plaster)
    foot of Front & cor. of Van Buren
        Oswego.
Paddock H. (salt & lime) Front st.
Williams Ira H. Front st.
Latham Andrew J. cor. Front &
    Seneca
Carrington & Pardee, foot 1st

Salt Manufacturers.

Onondaga County.

Acketmann H.   *Geddes.*
Anthracite Salt Co. Thomas
    Spencer, Agent
Blair Wm. K.
Brewster I. G.
Brewster S. C.
Cadwell S. W.
Carpenter C.
Coykendal D. & P
Dickenson J
Dodge D. E.
Duncan H.
Earll N. H.
Fehrenz N.
Feil F.
Filkins C. E. & H.
Frazee A.
Gere R. N.
Hatch H. D. & Co.
Huntly H.
Leamey Wm.
Listman A.
Litchfield E. W.
Loreot A.
Loreot A. & Co.
M'Gurk J.
Mead S.
Nelton R. W. & Co.
Noolson A.
Oliphant E.
Paige & Hubbell
Parker J. H.
Parmelee H. S. & Co.
Pharis M. P
Pfohl J.
Power L.
Robinson Thomas

Ryan J. P. & Co.   *Geddes*
Semmons J. W.
Shauart O. C.
Shnart O. C.
Smith O.
Snyder F.
Springer F. & Co.
Stevens George
Thompson A. G.
Vroman D.
Whitney J.
White J.
White W. W.
White M. M.
Woodward J. W.
Avery B. A.   *Salina.*
Avery P. S.
Avery L. Y.
Ball J. M.
Banes W.
Bassett ——
Barrowes & Co.
Berrows F.
Burton B.
Butler W.
Carraher J.
Carraher P.
Childs N. M.
Clark G. A.
Clark W.
Clark & Alvord
Cobb A.
Cooney P. jr.
Corbin Z.
Corbin J.
Covny P.
Crippen A.
Davin J.
Dear D.
Doyle T.
Duff Wm.
Dunn W. & P.
Elton & Harranz
Farrell D.
Farrell R.
Feagan T.
Fitzgerald J
Forger J. S.
Forstell T.
Gifford H. & Co.
Gleason L.
Haskins J. P.
Hartshorn J.
Hathaway H.
Hayes J.
Hellis E. L.
Jaqueth S.
Keith J.
Kingsley A. D.
King M.
Klink A.
Lincklean L.
Luther D.
Lynch J.
Lynch D. D.
M'Carthy R. & J.
Matterly & Ford
Morell F.
Malloy F.
Newcomb A. H.
Newton V.
Nutting A. C. S.
O'Nell P.
Onondaga Co.
Paddock J.
Porter T. R.
Porter W. A.
Porter W. H.
Rouch J. N.
Ryan J.
Satterby & Ford
Savage & Titus
Sharpe J.
Shannon J.
Smith S. F.
Smith A. L.
Stamp B. F.
Stevens L. & Co.
Swansey S. & J. H.
Syracuse Coarse Salt Co
Timmerman G.
Turney C.

Williams & Babcock   Salina.
Williams C. B.
Wood N.
Woodniff J.
White W. W. & J. Warren and
Water sts. Syracuse
Stevens Geo. Warren & Water
Thompson A. Y.   do
Walton R. W. & Co.   do
Gifford H. & Co. James st.
Parker J. Willow st.
Porter W. A.
Porter T. R. Exchange st.

Sand & Emery Paper Manufacturers.

Baxter C. H. 143 Maiden la.
          New York.
Hart G. 140 Maiden la.
Isham R. H. & J. G. 102 Front &
71 Fulton
M'Intire Charles H. 304 Hudson

Sash Card Manufacturers.

Queens County.

Dickerman James   Jamaica

Saw Manufacturers.

Erie County.

Roberts John, (see advertisement)
7 Swan   Buffalo.

Kings County.

Armitage Jas.   Brooklyn.
Rhode J. A. 13 S.2d Williamsburgh.
Jacobs F. S. 73 Grand

Monroe County.

Burton D. R. 3 Buffalo Rochester.
Flint Jos. Selye Buildings

New York County.

Bakewell J. 104 Elm New York.
Burr Walter, 48 Columbia
Curtis John W. 56 Harrison
Hoe R. & Co. 29 & 31 Gold
Horner Jas. 22 Cliff
M'Clain Orlando D. 167 Spring
Thompson John, 145 Lewis
Willmott Samuel D. 3 Liberty
Wood Cortland, 5 Gold
Worrall & Co. 26 & 28 Elm & 67
Duane

Oneida County.

Partello B. 4 Catharine   Utica.

Saw Filers & Setters.

Carroll W. 99½ Oliver New York.
Crist Jacob, 146 Perry
Dyer Chas. C. 510 Greenwich
Hull John G. 176 Lewis (tool handles)
Knox Jos. 602 Grand
M'Clain Orlando D. 167 Spring
Ramsker Wm. 175 Elm
Taylor Chas. 23 1st
Tracy Caleb B. 458 Hudson

Saw Sett Manufacturer.

Herkimer County.

Stillman Abel, Cold Brook Russia.

Scales. (See also Balances and
Scales.)

Chenango County.

Avery Stephen L.   Oxford.

Monroe County.

Hitchcock S. S. 16 Aqueduct
          Rochester.

Montgomery County.

Wemple & Yates, Fonda Mohawk.

Rensselaer County.

Dorval E. Congress St. Alley
          Lansingburgh.
Groom R. 339 River   Troy.

Screw Makers.

Ballard W. 7 Eldridge New York.
Fox & Oothout, 452 Water, 157
Cherry & 12th st. bet. Avs. B & C
Hall Samuel, 131 Amos
Kemya Wm., W. 25th st.
Loomis & Lyman, 38 Broadway
Union Manfacturing Co. 36 Broadway

Westchester County.

Swaine Jas. P.   East Chester.
Russell, Birdsall & Co. Portchester   Rye.

Scroll Sawyers.

Baker & Wright, 150 Wooster
          New York.
Bernhard Augustus, 44 Eldridge
Dawson Gen. H. 17 Canal
Doughty John H. 387 Grand
Drummond & Haulenbeck, 84 6th
Av.
Dwire Wm. J. 70½ Bowery
Meschutt Jas. M. 160 Allen
Tret A. S. 13 Duane

**Sealing Wax and Wafer
Manufacturers.**

Kings County.

Hudswell W. H. 35 S. 7th
          Williamsburgh.

New York County.

Couren Wm. P. rear 15 Jacob
          New York.

Seed Stores. (See also Nurserymen.)

Albany County.

Thorburn W. 492 Broadway
          Albany.
Emory H. L. 369 & 371 Broadway

Columbia County.

Hubbel George C. cor. Water &
Ferry   Hudson.

Duchess County.

White Wm. M. & Son, 306 Main
          Poughkeepsie.

Greene County.

Nearing Ebenezer   Catskill.

Monroe County.

Fogg J. P. 38 Front   Rochester.
Rapallje & Briggs, Irving Block

Onondaga County.

Foster E. J. Water st. Syracuse
          Salina.

Rensselaer County.

Vail, Haynes & Fellows, 151 & 153
River   Troy.
Warren Henry, 215 River

Schenectady County.

Miller D. O.   Niskayuna.

Washington County.

Fenton Buel   Cambridge.
Rice R. N.

**Seraphine and Melodeon
Manufacturers.** (See also
Musical Instruments.)

Erie County.

Prince Geo. A. & Co. 200 Main
          Buffalo.

Genesee County.

Elmore M.   Bergen.

Monroe County.

Miller M. 196 Main   Rochester.

New York County.

Carhart & Needham, 77 E. 13th
          New York
Swartz Abraham S. 6 Spring
Prince G. A. & Co. 87 Fulton

St. Lawrence County.

Boynton Paul   Canton.

Wyoming County.

Brooks F. & Co. Wyoming
          Middlebury.

Shells, &c.

Felleman Moses, 65 Chatham &
25 Cortlandt   New York.

Ship Builders.

Albany County.

Kinney J. S. 74 Pier   Albany.

Duchess County.

Cramer P. Water st. Poughkeepsie.
Finch ——, Whale Dock

Erie County.

Jones Frederick N. Creek
          Buffalo.
Bidwell & Banter, Dry Dock

Essex County.

Winslow John   Essex.
Eggleston A. Port Henry Moriah.
Boynton Aikin   Willsborough.

Greene County.

Morton Wm. H.   Athens.
Mayo William   Coxsackie.
Baldwin Jedediah New Baltimore.
Baldwin Henry

Jefferson County.

Huntington & Riggs, Dexter
          Brownville.
Gober Lewis   Cape Vincent.
Merrick E. G. & Co.   Clayton.

Kings County.

Burtis & Morgan, cor. Plymouth
& Jay   Brooklyn.
Bloomfield J., John st. nr. Bridge
Whiting R. Marshall st. near Gold
Perine, Patterson & Stack, Water
st. near Grand   Williamsburgh.
Hanson Wm. Water st. cor. N. 3d
Williams Jabez & Co. 1st st near
N. 6th

New York County.

Barnaby Richard, 77 Pike slip
New York.
Bell Jacob, foot of Stanton E. R. and 134 Goerck
Bishop & Simonson, 194 Lewis
Brown Wm. H. Dry Dock cor. 12th
Brown & Englis, 127 Av. D
Cassell & Bryan, 54 West
Collyer George, foot E. 18th
Collyer T. Av. A. cor E. 13th
Collyer William, 12th cor. Av. C
Dayton John, 174 Charles
Dewey & Powless, 239 West
Dimon & Batey, 30 Water
Edsall & Bryan, 54 West & 252 South
Endershot George, 486 Water
Elliott & Guthrie, W. 29th st.
Foster W. & Co. 84 West
Hayden & Kennedy, 9 Gouverneur slip
Jones Joseph, 257 South
Lawrence & Sneden, Cherry cor. Corlears
M'Namara Peter 234 South
M'Pherson, Gray & Co. 248 South
Parsons & Co. 412 Water
Philpitt James, 1 Gouverneur slip
Pollion Cornelius & R. 234 South & 443 Water
Ruck Peter C. 49 Harrison
Secor Francis & Sons, 68 West
Smith Jacob M. 35 Depeyster
Smith & Dimon, 719 4th
Sneden & Lawrence, 26 Corlears
Webb William H. 206 Lewis
Webb, Robertson & Co. 54 West and 497 Water
Welch William, 601 Walker
Westervelt & Sons, foot of 2d E. R.
Westervelt & Mackey, Lewis cor. of 7th
Whitlock & Berrian, 346 Cherry
Wood & West, 193 South

Oswego County.

Weeks Geo. S. foot Main st.
Oswego.

Queens County.

Rhodes John P. Rockaway
Hempstead.
Rhodes Henry, Raynor Town

Rensselaer County.

Atwood James, cor. North & River *Lansingburgh.*
Weaver William, rear of Fulton market   *Troy.*

Richmond County.

Rutan William H., Rossville
Westfield.

Rockland County.

Tallman T. S., Nyack *Orangetown.*
Voris & Dickey, do
Geemer Sylvester, Nyack
Scott James,   do
Polhameus A. G.   do
Felter John I.   do

St. Lawrence County.

Demott John   *Morristown.*

Suffolk County.

Williamson Daniel M., South Brookhaven   *Brookhaven.*
Smith Jones, South Brookhaven
Hallock Ebenezer, do
Hand Silas,   do
Wells Scudder,   do
Hallock Charles D. do
Bacon William, Setauket
Hand Nehemiah,   do
Lloyd & Bailes Jas. Port Jefferson
Mather John,   do

Darling James, Port Jefferson
Brookhaven.
Brown Benjamin,   do
Darling Jeremiah,   do
Hawkins Ira,   do
Bailes Joseph, Mount Sinai
Gerard H. G., Patchogue
Prior Charles,   do
Wood Jehiol,   do
Akerly Elisha.   do
Akerly Samuel,   do
Davis & Corwin   *Riverhead.*
Post John, Greenport   *Southold.*
Bishop Hiram,   do
Bishop Harman. do
Horton Calvin, do

Ulster County.

Williams S., Rondout   *Kingston.*
Evason Morgan, do

Washington County.

Hannis William   *Whitehall.*
M'Fener A.
M'Cotter H.

Ship Chandlers.

Albany County.

Shaw L. D. 1 State   *Albany.*
Campbell J. W. 9 N. Ferry
Cole & Van Nostrand, (wholesale) 61 Quay

Erie County.

Williams, Howard & Co. corner Prime & Lloyd   *Buffalo.*
Bemis, Brothers, near foot of Commercial
Marvin & Co. Long Wharf and Water
Ely & Co. Long Wharf
Fox & Brace, 24 Central Wharf
Munger & Willard, 10 Main & 4 Central Wharf

Monroe County.

Smith & Gould, 211 Buffalo
Rochester.

New York County.

Anderson & Ritter, 59 West
New York.
Arrosmith & Wheeler, 125 Broad
Atkins Joshua & Co. 38 South
Aymar Wm. & Co. 50   do
Badger Augustus H. 191 do
Badger James W. 191   do
Banker Edward, 396 Pearl
Baxter & Clearman, 313 West
Bayles Nathaniel H. 196 South
Bloomfield S. & E. S. 13   do
Brookman Henry D. 37   do
Buhsen Nicholas, 41 & 43 West
Bulkley & Lockwood, 110 Wall
Burr, Waterman & Co. 109 South
Cadmus & Clough, 195 West
Casseboom J. C. & Co. 85 do
Coles & Thorn, 91   do
Collis & Mitchell, 175 South
Cornen Peter P. 167   do
Crosby, Crocker & Bassett, 52 South
Daniels William A. 384 Water
Duncan & Burdett, 114 Wall
Fowler F. & D. 96 West
Franklin George R. 173 West
Freeborn William A. & Co. 254 South
Gorham & Basset, 25 South
Gurnee Francis W. 400 West
Hicks James M. 68 South
Hicks & Bailey, 56 do
Howard & Wintringham, 169 South
Hulse & Van Winkle, 205 West
Hurry James, 30 South
Hutchinson Ira, 304 West
Jacobs & Rudolph, 51 Whitehall

Jenkins & Fonds, 145 West
New York.
Kemp Aaron, 116 Wall
Kindberg Andrew F. 55 West
Klots & Son, East cor. Delancy
Lassen & Petersen, 22 Rector
Lethbridge Robert & Co. 96 South
Lewis John H. 26 Coenties slip
Lewis J. B. 24 South
Logan George, 69 South
Lyon & Hall, 100 Wall
Martin & Nelson. 188 West
Maxwell John T. B. 77 South
Merritt & Co. 56 South
Merritt & Trask, 28 South
Meserole David M. 113 South
Meyerholz Henry. 57 West
Morgan Charles W. 197 Av. D
O'Brien Thomas, 37 Burling slip
Olney & Cottrell, 61 South
Perkins & Delano, 39 South
Phillips J. N. 85 Pike slip
Pratt Charles H. 85 South
Ransom Barzillai, 100 Wall
Runyon Mordecai T. Gouverneur slip cor. South
Saxton John, 164 Maiden lane
Schermerhorn, Banker & Co. 49 South
Secor Charles A. & Co. 68 West
Shermans and Stark, 29 South
Sill Horace L. 85 South
Snow & White, 22 Coenties slip
Squire Lewis L. 283 Front
Storer & Stevenson, 53 South
Sturk & Barnmans. 110 South
Tallman & Baker, 16 Coenties slip
Tapscott James T. 86 South
Terry Charles M. & Co. 106 South
Thorn Charles E. 193 Front
Tiebout & Parker, 272 South
Tyson William, 46 West
Ward James O. & Co. 27 South
Webster Benjamin C. 118 West
Wendell John, 83 South
Whitlock Augustus & Co. 87 South
Wight & Robberts, 232 South
Williams William, 135 Maiden la.
Williams & Hinman, 169 South

Oswego County.

Malcolm William S. 1st st.
Oswego
Burnam Caleb, cor. Water and Seneca st.
Cooper & Barbour, Water st.
Smyth Charles,   do

Rockland County.

Tallman T. S. Nyack *Orangetown.*

Ship Joiners.

Bell Thomas, 20 Fletcher
New York.
Bishop Cornelius, 26 Jefferson
Coger Daniel, 85 Pike slip
Conlan Michael, 292 Front
Crampton L. & H. 142 Liberty
Decker & Brown, 365 9th
De Forrest Peter, 50 West
Dennington Clement L. 400 Water
Donaldson John, 431   do
Ellsworth & Donaldson, 431 do
Farrington Darius, 38 Depeyster
Grattan John. 38   do
Hardwick James, 162 Maiden la.
Hawkins Alexander, 61 Goerck
Hawkshurst & Johnson, 44 West
Hobly Benjamin & Co. 673 Water
Huston Daniel, 58 Av. C
Jarvis Brewster, 271 South
Jarvis Jonathan, 337 9th
Jennings James E. 50 West
Judson Wm. W. 237 South
Laton Robert, 420 & 424 14th
M'Donald Hugh C. 251 South
M'Nabb James, 718 Water
Mills Andrew, 178 Lewis

Murphy & Romer, 296 Front
New York.
Place Robert, 39 Water
Purdy Johnson, 220 West
Ridgway Richard C. 101 Market
Samson & Perry, 363 5th
Sanford Nathan, 26 Houston
Simonson Charles M. 181 Lewis
Terry V. R. & Son, cor. Warren
& West sts.
Thomas Henry B. & Co. 13 Caroline & 196 West
Tobey John L. 309 West
Turner George, 36 Depeyster
Wells Jesse, 220 12th
Whitley Thomas, 52 West
Wilson Elijah, 242 South
Youngs & Cutter, 116 Cannon

Shipping Offices.

Church James C. 164 South
New York.
Clark & Co. 90 South
Clark & Deane, 37 Burling slip
Culbert & Finlay, 12 Old slip
Dickey Thomas H. & Co. 166 Maiden la.
Dill James H. 96 Wall
Munson John, 110 South
Murphy Richard, 75 South
Parisen Richard F. 113 South
Poole, Pentz & Goin, 39 Burling slip
Randall & Harris, 151 South
Seaver Zachariah, 98 Wall
Stanton & Spicer, 86 West
Taylor John B. 162 South
Woodhull Albert, 67 South
Woodward & Ryberg, 89 South

Ship Smiths. (See also Blacksmiths.)

Kings County.

Gallagher G. 20 Hamilton Av.
Brooklyn.
M'Kinney Marriott, Furman st. nr. Fulton
Yates T. Plymouth st. nr. Jay

New York County.

Anderson Jas. G. 283 Front
New York
Atkinson, Richard, 486 Water & 32 West
Browne William H. Dry Dock bet. 11th & 12th sts.
Burns Thomas I. 221 South
Carpenter Richard, 724 Water
Clark Joseph, 486   do
Dows William, 162 Maiden la.
Gregory William A. 430 10th
Hall Isaac & Co. 19 Front & 247 South
Hesketh William, 287 West
Hoyt Conkling, 33 Depeyster and 381 Rivington
Law George & Co. bet. 10th & 11th sts.
M'Donald Thomas, 36 Jay
Macy M. B. 38 Dover
Marinor George, 38 Water
Milliken James F. 26 Houston
Johnson Jeremiah & Son, 36 Depeyster & 101 Market slip
Jones H. & Son, 44 West & 257 South
Pangborn Stephen, 37 Tompkins
Place Robert S. 253 South
Roach Peter R. 138 Bank
Roberts Stephen, 212 South and 292 Front
Scott Joseph, Dry Dock bet. 11th & 12th
Thum Richard, 242 South
Trickey Samuel, 226   do
Van Blarcom & Yon 204 West & 237 South

Van Nostrand William A. 225
South   New York.
Walrond James, 327 Delaney
Waters William, Dry Dock bet. 11th & 13th
White John & Son, 61 Montgomery
Whritner Nicholas, 732 Water
Wood & Gregory, 400 Water
Wright William H. 348 South

Shirt Manufacturers. (See also Linen ready made.)

Kings County.

Filbey S. 234 Henry   Brooklyn.

Rensselaer County.

Gardiner Jefferson, 16 King Troy.
Montague O. 41 Ferry

Monroe County.

Minor Elizabeth, 78 State
Rochester.

Shoe Makers, Ladies'. (See also Boot and Shoe Makers.)

Barros John R. 17 8th Av.
New York.
Bawden Wm. T. 79 Bleecker
Bergen James, 277 Grand
Brown S K. 105 Bleecker
Burr Sidney, 15 Av. C
Cantrell Samuel, 336 Bowery
Crosby F. G. 40 East Broadway
Daily Patrick, 235 1st Av.
Davidson & Denniston, 114 8th Av.
Dupont John H. 661 Broadway
Fenton Thomas, 255 Hudson
East Josiah, 200 East Broadway
Flint & Ely, 114 Canal
Freeman J. G. 254 3d Av.
Hill Sarah, 243½ Bowery
Holmes John, 81 East Broadway
Hoyt J. W. 230 Bowery
Hunt & Hunter, 279 Grand
Jacob Martin, 73 Market
Jeffers W. H. 457 Broadway
Jones Edward, 156 6th Av.
Laboyteaux Peter, 631½ Broad'y
M'Connochie John, 671½ Broad'y
Matear John, 114 3d Av.
Mather Charles, 162 Division
Matthews ——, 243 Grand
Miller Joseph B. 134 Canal
Mitchell Wm. 261 Hudson
Newman Ward, 371 Bowery
Raymond Jacob, 138 3d Av.
Remmey Christopher, 317 5th
Rogers A. S. 409 Broadway
Rogers B. 414 Grand
Rowden Thomas W. 65 Division
Rykman R. W. & W. J. 698 B'd'y
Shaw Benjamin, 73 Canal
Smith Edward J. 71 Chambers
Stulf Simon, 307½ West
Sutherland Wm. 352½ Bowery
Totman Aaron, 42 4th Av.
Turner Charlotte, 98 3d Av.
Tyler Milton T. 120 4th Av.
Van Heynigen Nicholas, 156 Spring
Wardell Oliver T. 259 Bleecker
Whiting Winslow L. 436 Broad'y
Wilson John, 148 Houston
Windsor Francis, 120 Canal
Woods Patrick, 720 Washington
Wykes George, 29½ Thompson

Shoe Peg Manufacturers.

Erie County.

Wing H. & Co. (See advertise'nt)
6 Exchange   Buffalo.

Fulton County
Walt Joseph   Broadalbin.

Jefferson County.
Auburn Calvin   Watertown.

Monroe County.
Madden E. & Co. Curtis' Block,
Main st.   Rochester.

Montgomery County.
Marselis V   Amsterdam.

Niagara County.
Wing H. & Co.   Niagara Falls.

Oneida County.
Frenca L. North Western Western.

Shooting Galleries.

Travis John, 14 Vesey & 3½ Barclay   New York.
Weller Frederic, 96 Broadway

Shovel and Spade Manufacturers.

Chautauque County.
Waters Franklin & Co. Westfield.

New York County.
Duryea & Rhodes, 229 Pearl
New York.
Whitney Daniel W. 58 Vesey

Rensselaer County.
Kenney C. near State Dam Troy.
Trull John M.

Show Case Makers.

Barclay D. 466½ Broadway
New York.
Bertholf Gilbert, 153 Walker
Earl & Reeves, 124 Grand & 346 Broome
Frazer John H. 61 Hammond & 14 West Broadway
Purdy Hiram, 79 Elizabeth

Shower Bath Manufacturers.

New York County.
Locke John, (see advertisement)
47 Ann   New York

Oneida County.
Holbrook T. 5 Catharine Utica

Shuttle Makers.

Inglis G. 41 Hammond New York.
Sever Querin, 197 William

Silk Manufacturers.

Dale Thomas, 43 Maiden lane
New York
Dale William, 216 W. 21st
Heylin Wm. 196 W. 24th
M'Rae John, 117 Canal
Millward James, 67 Maiden lane
Tilden Joshua, 73   do
Turner P. W. & E. R. Gurley, 84 William
Zahn W. H. 56 John

Silks & Fancy Dry Goods—Importers of. (See also Dry Goods Importers.)

Artois & Denison, 35 Liberty
New York.
Blanch, Becket, Delphin & Co. 45 Beaver
Bodmer Henry, jr. 7 William
Carleton & Frothingham, 127 & 129 William
Clark & Work, 131 Broadway
Dambmann Chas. F. 62 Beaver & 199½ Pearl
Dennis, Perkins & Co. 26 Pearl
Denny Thomas. 57 Beaver
Draper, Fairchild & Co. 139 B'way
Edwards Alfred & Co 122 Pearl
Furman & Davis, 197 Pearl
Guillaume, Hemmerling & Mayet, 58 Broad
Jaffray J. R.'& Sons 73 Broadway
Loeschigk, Wesendonck & Co. 40 & 42 Broad
Mills & Co. 6 Cortlandt
Moreau & Irelin, 47 Broad
Moses Isaac & Brothers, 64 Beaver
Mussell & Whittemore, 39 Pine
Payen Charles & Co. 17 William
Petits, Bannister & Harris. 23 Nassau
Pinneo W. W. & Co. 37 & 39 Cedar & 68 William
Schmid Paul & Andrew, 63 Beaver
Stevens L M. & Co. 146 Pearl
Strange & Co. 4 William
Teterel & Blain, 134 Pearl
Thomas C. W. & A. 117 Pearl
Varet O. 13 William
Witthaus R. A. & G. H. 51 Exchange place

Silks & Fancy Dry Goods—Dealers in. (Marked thus * are Retail.)

*Arnold A. & Co. 62 Canal
New York.
*Beard Ira, 101 William
*Beekman & Cutter, 66 Canal
Blake & Brown. 71 William
Blashfield & West. 30 Cedar
Bowen & M'Namee, 112 B'way
Brodie & Bell, 61 Canal
Brown E. J. & Co. 67 William
*Brown A. & G. & H. 181 Pearl
Bruns William H. 326 Grand
Cheeseborough, Stearns & Co. 37 Nassau & 56 Liberty
Clark, Southworth & Co. 25 Nassau & 74 Cedar
*Clark, Work & M'Lean, 128 Pearl
Collis Augustus H. 32 John
Crosley Charles W. 589½ B'way
*Daley J. 465 Broadway
Davis David H. 72 Beaver
Dibblee H. E. & Co. 69 Broadway
Eastman, Sheldon & Townsend, 42 Cedar
Ely Abner L. 65 Maiden lane
Fisher, Cushing & Henderson, 10 Cortlandt
Freeman Charles P. 56 Liberty
Fuller & Hertzel, 17 Cedar
*Farnam & Davis, 197 Pearl
Hatch & Yale, 75 Cedar
Hayt James R. 63 Cedar
*Hickok & Starr, 32 Cortlandt
Hillman & Nearing, 72 Maiden lane
*Isaacs J. 34 Division
Kipling Richard, 32 Maiden lane
Lawrence Richard P. 41 Pine
*Lichtenstein M. H. 90½ Bowery
Lindsley, Cameron & Hayward, 66 Liberty
Loder & Co. 63 Cedar
Lopes & Quackinbush, 71 Liberty
*Loyd John L. 30 John
M'Arthur Wm. & Co. 72 William
M'Kenzies Edward, 61 Division

*M'Rae John, 117 Canal
New York.
*Martin & Lawson, 24 John
*Moore & Lion, 92 Bowery & 84 Canal
*Moore L. H. 45 Beaver
Myers, Suydam & Co. 149 Broadway
Neilly John R. 32 Cedar
Neustaedter Wm. 409 Broadway
Nicoleon & Wright, 54 Cedar
Peck Edwin, 79 William & 19 Liberty
Peck & Robbins, 139 Pearl & 90 Beaver
Peniman, Baxter & Faxon, 62 William
*Rankin & Burch
*Pettit, Bannister & Harris, 23 Nassau
Schmid Paul & Andreae, 63 Beaver
Smith & Lawrence, 68 Beaver
*Stewart George, 379 Broadway
Strahan John & Co. 141 Pearl
Taylor & Marks, 76 William
Terry Samuel M. 74 William
*Ubsdell & Pierson, 64 Canal
Underhill L. & A. 6 John

Silks & Ribbons—Importers of.

Guillaume, Hemmerling & Mayet, 58 Broad
New York.
Thomas C. W. & A. 117 Pearl
Von Baur Gustavus, 39 Beaver
Weed & Tingsem, 206 W. 28th

Silversmiths.

Albany County.

Johnson & Godley, 6 Liberty
Albany.
Hall, Hewson & Brower, Plain st.

Chautauque County.

M'Cain Benjamin
Westfield.

Clinton County.

Fryor J.
Plattsburgh.

Erie County.

Dubois P. 18 East Swan Buffalo.
Dubois Frederick N. 95 S. Division

Jefferson County.

Berrenger Jacob Cape Vincent.

Monroe County.

Marshall T. H. (spoons and forks) Work st.
Rochester.
Watts Charles, 72 Buffalo

New York County.

Adams William, rear 36 White
New York.
Alcock & Allen. 341 Broadway
Ahrens Christian, 63 Ann
Arnault John M. 10 Rose
Ball, Tompkins & Black, 247 Broadway
Beebe William, 102 Reade
Bostwick Zalmon, 158 William
Boyce Gerardus, rear 110 Greene
Carter, Cann & Dunn, rear 53 Mercer
Chandless William, 452 Hudson
Cole John A. 8 Liberty place
Coles Albert, 4 do
Cooper Francis W. 102 Reade
Copeland Robert, rear 83 Deane
David Henry, 10 Liberty place
Dubosy H. & W. & Co. 170 Broadway
Eoff Edward M. rear 5 Dey
Forbes William, rear 277 Spring

Gale & Hayden, 116 Fulton
New York.
Gibney Michael, 8 Reade
Gilbert P. B. 6 Liberty place
Gurnee Benjamin, rear 17 John
Gurnee Daniel, rear do
Harris T. J. jr. 177 Broadway
Hebbard Henry & Co. 86 Duane
King George, 92 Reade
Kelley G. 641½ Water
Lange William, 158 William
Merrifield James, rear 5 Dey
Moore John C. 85 Leonard
Newsam George. 389 Greenwich
Peck Gideon, jr. 30 Cortlandt
Rose William E. 37 Reade
Singer Louis, 158 William
Smith George O. & Co. 6 Liberty place
Stewart Alexander, 56 Harrison
Stewart Charles, 13 John
Van Ness Peter, 20 Cortlandt
Wood A. & W. 55 Thompson
Wood & Hughes, rear 142 Fulton

Oneida County.

Huntington R. Genesee st Utica.

Orange County.

Cornish J. & J. (spoons) Water st.
Newburgh.
Bogart James, South st.
Johnson William, New Hampton
Wallkill.

Oswego County.

Stanley A. R. Mexico.

Otsego County.

Pope S. P. Burlington Flats
Burlington.
Garratts R Butternuts.

Rensselaer County.

Fitch Dennis M. 200 River Troy.

St. Lawrence County.

Forbes John Potsdam.
Chisman Albert, State st. Ogdensburgh
Oswegatchie.

Saratoga County.

Evans Roger C. Waterford.

Steuben County.

Sedgwick William Bath.

Suffolk County.

Hammond Lewis, Port Jefferson
Brookhaven.
Wood William S. Huntington.

Sullivan County.

Benedict S. Wurtsboro.
Ketcham L. A. Monticello.

Westchester County.

Dunnerth —— , (spoons) Dobbs' Ferry Greenburgh.

Wyoming County.

Gaines Solomon Castile.

Slaters.

Albany County.

Dickson J. 65 Beaver Albany.

New York County.

Cannon C. 176 Wooster New York.
Crommelin & Ordway, 627 Washington
Dugan Daughlin & Brothers, 422 Broome

Folsy & Fyfe, 475 Broome
New York.
Lewis Thomas, 46 Rose
Phillips Samuel, rear 165 Bowery
Reed & Co. 52 White
Sinclair John, 252 Cherry and 495
Water

Rensselaer County.

Christie G. 150 4th　　　　Troy.

Slate, (Roofing,) Importers of.

Thompson Samuel & Nephew, 275
Pearl　　　　New York.

Soap & Candle Manufacturers. (See also Oil & Candles.)

Albany County.

Murphy J. 712 Broadway
Albany.
Hartness J. & Co. 58 Jackson
Wickes & Tillinghast (sperm candles) 13 Hudson
Strain Joseph, cor. Church and
Herkimer
Taylor J. & Sons. 83 Green
Ten Eyck H. M. 157 Green
Wells A. 177 Pearl
Ermand J. D. 22 Chapel
Wells H. J. 344 Bowery

Cayuga County.

Burt A. H. & J. 7 Genesee
Auburn.

Chenango County.

Smith & Sheely　　　　Norwich.

Columbia County.

Barnard Curtiss & Co. (sperm.)
Water st.　　　　Hudson.
Humphrey & Remington

Duchess County.

De Graff Jacob & Son. 192 and 194
Main　　　　Poughkeepsie.
Hill N. & Son. 367 Main
Cable Chas. & Co 157 and 159 Main

Erie County.

Person Pascal, Willink　　Aurora.
Kyser Henry,　　do
Cowles & Co. cor. Hudson and
4th　　　　Buffalo.
Horter G. & Co. 9 South Division
Hume S. Ohio st.
Wheeler I. & J. 4 Batavia
Gowans & Beard, 103 and 105
Main

Greene County.

Trowbridge Chas.　　　　Catskill.
Hanes Ward　　　　Durham.

Jefferson County.

Peck A. J.　　　　Watertown.
Napier John H. & Co.

Kings County.

Swan S. & Son, Furman near Fulton　　　　Brooklyn.
Barty Joseph, (candles) Adams
near Front
Welwood Arthur, 145 Tillary
Higgins Wm. B. (soap) between
Hamilton st. and Clinton Av.

Livingston County.

Sharp Robert　　　　Dansville.
Hayden John

Madison County.

Service John　　　　Cazenovia.
Childs W. B.
Stone E. Oneida Depot　　Lenox.

Monroe County.

Tuttle C. D. East Mendon
Mendon.
Chapin L. Court st.　　Rochester.
Anderson J. (candles) 101 Exchange
Edgell Joseph. 49 Front
McIntosh J. & W. 29 Front
Moulson Samuel, 36 Front

Montgomery County.

Warwick George　　Amsterdam.
Abrahams & Along　Canajoharie.

New York County.

Allen Hay & Co. 39 and 41 1st Av.
New York.
Alsop John, 186 Laurens
Beadel J. W. & M. 120 Front
Bleakley John F. 218 Delancy
Bogart John N. 447 Water
Boyd James. 12 Franklin
Boyd Robert, 553 Pearl
Boyd William A. 128 Orange
Brown David S. 10 Peck slip and
24 Chrystie
Buchan James, 199 Elizabeth
Clendenen Patrick, 132 Eldridge
Colgate Cornelius C. 252 Greenwich
Colgate William & Co. 6 Dutch
Dempsey Garret, 123 Stanton
Fay Patrick H. 226 Cherry and 109
and 240 Monroe
Glass W., W. 27th st.
Graboh Teaheu, rear 5 Walnut
Hall John, rear 156 Forsyth
Hamilton George G. 176 and 178
Ludlow
Hayes Saml. 227 West 17th
Higton. Howe McClenin, 263
Washington
Hein Charles A. rear 14 Roosevelt
Hull Wager & Sons. 112 Cliff
Keller Lewis, 9 Delancy
Kirkman John. 34 Catharine
Lee John D. 61 and 63 Reade
Lyman Chapin, 88 and 90 Norfolk
Mapelsden Reuben, 201 Chrystie
Morgan Enoch, 211 Washington
and 446 West
Pieper & Forester, 26 and 28 Willet
Riley John, 31 Leonard
Sexton John, 14 Desbrosses
Slater David, 136 Amos
Smith Charles W. 107 and 109
Elizabeth
Vroom & Fowler, 72 Charry
Wellwood Robt. 7 Walnut

Oneida County.

Thorn & Maynard, 21 Water
Utica.
Kirk J. S. & Co. Whitesboro st.
Maynard & Wright, Burnet st.

Onondaga County.

Orcutt O. & Co. James st. Syracuse　　　　Salina.
M'Kinstry A. Salina st.

Orange County.

Belknap A. & M. H.　　Newburgh.
M'Cutcheon R. Colden st.

Orleans County.

Woolford & Wall, Albion　Barre.

Oswego County.

Lockhart James, 1st st.　Oswego.
Heath & Powers, Bridge st.

Otsego County.

Howard H. H. (Soap)　　Unadilla.

Queens County.

Smith John W. & Co. Hempstead.

Rensselaer County.

Lansing ——, State st.
Lansingburgh.
Stanley & Hunt, 461 River　Troy.
Rankin Hugh, 455 River
Eldredge E. & M. 419 & 421 River
Barton & Fenn. 387 River
Fake J. G. H. 519 River

Saratoga County.

Blake J. R.　　　　Waterford.

Schenectady County.

Hartness J. Dock st. Schenectady.

Seneca County.

Paine Thos. J.　　Seneca Falls.
Sharpe T. B.
Webster Jas. R.　　Waterloo.

Steuben County.

Card & Greenman　Painted Post

Tompkins County.

Lee J. end of Tioga st.　Ithaca.

Ulster County.

Gibson A.　　　　Kingston.

Westchester County.

Whiting & Griffin, Peekskill
Courtlandt.
Fortmeyer F. Sing Sing Osining.

Soap Makers—Fancy.

Babbitt Wm. H. 127 Water
New York
Benjamin W. K. 1 Cortlandt
Hastings D. H. 20 Liberty
Hatch & Blauvelt. 3 Eldridge
Hult Chas. J. 1 Hamersley
Jocelyn S. S. jr. Catharine lane,
rear 344 Broadway
Johnson Wm. 55 Frankfort
Jones Stephen W. 269 W. 16th
Pinner Samuel, 112 W. 17th
Radway & Co. 161 Fulton
Williams Chas. F. 47 Gold

Soap Stone Manufacturers.

Early H. 207 Grand　New York.
Gardner A. J. 6 Sullivan
Jaens, Beebe & Co. 128 Fulton
Lynch Terence, 119 Beekman
Van Note W. & H. 41 Greene
Woolly Britian F. 115 Beekman

Soda Dealers. (See also Ashes, Pot & Pearl, and Saleratus.)

Kings County.

Tassle & Co. 96 Myrtle Av.
Brooklyn.

New York County.

Andrews Thos. 66 Washington
New York.
Dwight John & Co. W. 25th st.

Soda Water Makers.

New York County.

Boardman John & Co. rear 262
Broadway　　　New York.

Byrne Jas. 161 Bleecker *New York.*
Dearborn J. & A. 95 3d Av.
Delatour Albert J. 25¼ Wall & 87 1st Av.
Kelly J. W. & Co. 34 Beekman
M'Cullough S. & Co. 168 Mercer
Matthews John, 81 Fulton & 131 3d Av.
Murtha Edward. 211 1st Av.
Pond Wm. 164 W. 18th
Reynolds & Degnan, 105 Elizabeth
Riley Peter, 78 1st Av.
Simon Henry, 1 Congress
Smith Samuel. 164 W. 18th
Southwick Adna H. & Tupper, 112 Warren
Suydam & Dubois. 200 Chambers
Terry Thos. A. 20 Delancy
Tweddle John, jr. 41 Barclay
Whittemore Chas. 162 Varick
Williams Chas. S. 80¼ Chatham

Rensselaer County.

Blanchard D. 74½ Congress *Troy.*
Smith Samuel, 445 River

Sofa Manufacturers.

Albany County.

Moseley H. T. 17 Church *Albany.*

New York County.

Johnson C. 199 Grand   *New York.*

Sofa Spring Manufacturers.

Grotsclose John, 372 Hudson
         New York.
Oakley Wm. B. 41 King
Throp H. S. & A. & Co. 280 Pearl

Spar Makers.

Erie County.

Taff Richard, 17 Main   *Buffalo.*

New York County.

Bucknam ——, 479 Water
         New York.
Denike Abraham, 705 Water
King Geo. W. 699 & 725 Water
Taff Henry, foot of 2d st. E. R.
Winant C. foot of 8th st. E. R.

Spectacle Case Makers.

Dunn Peter, 98 Fulton *New York.*

Spectacle Makers. (*See also Opticians.*)

Bowers J. 6 Liberty pl. *New York.*
Kenney T. R. 42 Rose
Marvin John B. 78 Chrystie

Spike and Rivet Makers.

Leonard & Ash, rear 2 Gouverneur slip *New York.*
M'Farlan Henry, 75 Broad
Merritt & Co. 58 South
Price John W. 169 Lewis
Stacey Jas. 156 Allen
Thompson James, 205 Lewis & 88 Monroe

Spinning Wheels & Reels.

Franklin County.

Justin J. T. West Constable
         Westville.

St. Lawrence County.

Tilden Isaac   *Stockholm.*

Stables—Sales.

Biddleman & Arndt, 164 Washington   *New York.*
Cevin John, 140 Liberty
Gatfield John H. 31 Crosby
Hotchkiss J. B. cor. Lexington Av. & 24th st.
Miller Geo. W. 446 Broadway
Nadine E. J. & Co. 138 Amos
Richey ——, 161 Washington
Stewart Chas. 143 Liberty

Stair Builders. (*See also Carpenters.*)

Kings County.

Morgan Thos. 5 Schermerhorn
         Brooklyn.
Pearsall & Birdsall, Schermerhorn near Boerum
Lynch & Doty, 118 Livingston
Webb F. Lawrence near Tillary
Smith E. & A. 206 Nassau
Halsted Isaac, 3 Stanton
Buckelew I. C. Raymond st.
Ford T. P. Green Point *Bushwick.*
Neals Jos. 92 S. 1st *Williamsburgh.*
Trim John, 152 Union Av.

New York County.

Brady J. H. 122 Amity *New York.*
Culbert A. J., W. 13th near 7th Av.
Demarest Silas. 295 W. 19th
Gridley John V. 75 8th Av.
Hardcastle Coles D. 89 Delancy
Mandeville Henry, 29 11th
Smith Wm., E. 21st near 1st Av.
Spence & Van Vorst, rear 617 Hudson
Van Verst Garrett, 695 Hudson
Van Saun Samuel J. 3 Bethune

Stair Rod Manufacturers.

Gould M. 229 Pearl   *New York.*
Hiler Selah, 67 & 69 Forsyth

Starch Manufacturers.

Cayuga County.

Fattry J. & C., Weedsport *Brutus.*

Erie County.

Cowles & Co. Prime & Hanover
         Buffalo.

Franklin County.

Patterson D. & Co.   *Bangor.*
Dickinson J. & Sons
King William   *Malone.*
Whipple H. W.

Jefferson County.

Rice H. A. & S. E., Carthage
         Wilna.

Kings County.

Ramppen F. (pearl starch) corner Dean & Court   *Brooklyn.*

New York County.

Ayling Thomas, cor. Cherry & Gouverneur   *New York.*
Colgate William & Co. 6 Dutch
Duff John T. 148 Rivington
Gilbert Edward, 93 Fulton
Halin ——, 71 Gouverneur
Kipp Francis A. 60 Allen
Lee John D. 61 & 63 Reade

Oswego Starch Factory, T. Kingsford & Son manufacturers, Goss & Thompson agents, 196 Fulton
         New York
Waydell J. & Co. 155 Monroe

Oneida County.

Gilbert E.   *Utica.*

Queens County.

Seligman Brothers, (Pearl Starch)
         Jamaica.

St. Lawrence County.

Cox Gardiner   *Pierpont.*

Washington County.

Munson Asa E. East Hebron
         Hebron.

Stationers & Blank Book Manufacturers. (*See also Booksellers.*)

Kings County.

Dawson S. B. 96¼ Fulton *Brooklyn.*
Gimbrede Napoleon, 424 South 7th
         Williamsburgh.
Shuttleworth James, 74 Grand
Longworth & Parsons, 190 do,
Coard Wm. 232 1st

New York County.

Amburger & Stevens, 87 Wm.
         New York
Anstice Henry, 27 Nassau
Arthur & Burnet, 61 Wall,
Baker & Duyckinck, 158 Pearl
Bainbridge R. & Co. 160 Pearl
Bates Lincoln, 17 Wall
Bell & Gould, 156 Nassau, Envelope Manufacturers
Bowne & Co. Printers and Lithographers, 149 Pearl
Burtus James A. 19 Peck slip
Bunce G. H. & S. A. 31 N. Wm.
Cady & Burgess, 60 John
Cahn Joseph L. 425 Pearl
Clayton Edwin B. & Sons, 86 Wall
Coddington Robert, 366 Bowery
Cogswell H. & Co. 19 and 90 Merchants' Exchange
Cohen Lewis C. 238 William
Cohen Lewis I. 186 William
Cook George, 66 Fulton
Cornwell Wm. K. 91 Beaver
Davids & Black, 112 John & 827 8th
Doubleday U. F. & E. 40 John
Felt David & Co. 191 Pearl
Felt D. & Co. & Hosford, 56 Wall
Francis & Loutrel, (See advertisement) 77 Maiden lane
Gutch Thomas G. 204 8th Av.
Herrick J. K. 78 John
Holmes David S. 12 Av. D
Hyman L. 80¼ Bleecker
Isaacs & Solomon, 53 Nassau
Ising Charles M. 248 8th Av.
Karcheski X. 67 Forsyth
Koch & Co. 160 William
Lambert & Lane, 69 Wall
Law George. 361 6th Av.
Lawrence Benjamin, 129 William
Leman Michael L. 414 Pearl
Levison John, 196 Chatham
Lovel Wm. 98 Hudson
M'Spedon & Baker, 25 Pine
Marvin A. B. & Co. 98 William
Minns Wm. 91 Wall
Morgan & Co. 231 Pearl
Morrell Alfred, 192 Fulton
Nesbitt George F. 88 Wall
Raynor Samuel, 76 Bowery
Rich & Loutrel, 61 William
Root R. C. & Anthony, 23 William
Ross Wm. W. 19 Wall
Shaw & Ireland, 240 Pearl
Sibell & Mott, 90 Wall

Skinner H. N. 249½ Greenwich
New York.
Snell Isaac, 205 Greenwich
Strong Thomas W. 98 Nassau
Tripp Ervin H. 262 Greenwich
Turney Geo. W. & S. 76 Chatham
Van Norden & King, 45 Wall
Waterhouse T. M. & Co. 156
Greenwich
Whitlock Ephraim J. 58 Nassan

Stationery—Importers of.

Doubleday U. F. & E. 40 John
New York.
Francis & Loutrel, 77 Maiden lane
Grassie & Coffin, 43 Maiden lane
Hart Samuel & Co. 82 John
Herts H. B. & Sons. 96 John
Herrick J. H. 78 John
Jerolliman H. & Co. 134 William
Lawrence Benjamin, 122 William
Luvy Mark & Brothers, 49 Maiden
lane
Morgan James D. 221 Pearl
Small Charles, 229 Pearl
Smith & Peters, 100 John
Waterhouse J. M. & Co. 156 Green-
wich
Wheeler Wm. A. & Co. 80 Wall

Stave Makers. (See also
Coopers.)

Erie County.
Safford H. L. Black Rock.

Kings County.
Harbeck J. H. & Co. (dealers)
Hall's Dock Brooklyn.
Denniston Wm. (dealers) John st.
near Bridge

Monroe County.
Tracy D. Pittsford.
Cook & Hastings, cor. Lyell &
West Rochester.

Oswego County.
Thayer & Huntington Albion.
Church Artemas Mexico.
Buel & Taylor New Haven.
Howard Alfred
May Alanson
Gridley & Eason
Doud A. J. & T. S.
Hawley Philander
Van Buren & Snell
Goold & Hale, Phœnix Schroeppel.

New York County.
Denniston William, 451 Water
New York.
Harbeck & Co. 80 Wall
Jackson ——, 163 Goerck
Robertson & Polhemus. Jefferson
cor. Monroe & 129 Pearl

Steam Boiler Setter.

Carpenter D. (see Advertisement)
145 Nassau New York.

Steam Ship Companies.—
(See also Packet Offices.)

Baltimore & New York Co. Chas.
H. Stanton Agent New York.
British & North American R. M.
Steam Packet Co. 38 Broadway
Collins Edward K. 74 South, Agent
New York & Liverpool U. S.
Mail Steamship Company
Howard J. & Son, 24 Broadway,
Agents of the "Crescent City,"
& "Empire City," New Orleans,

Chagres & New York line Steam-
ships New York.
Howland & Aspinwall, 54 & 55
South, Agents for Pacific Mail
Steamship Company
Mitchell S. L. 194 Front, Agent for
the Havana Steamers
Ocean Steam Navigation Co. 60
Broadway
United States Mail Steamship Co.
M. O. Roberts, 116 West.

Steel and Copper Plates.

Bruce John, 24 & 26 Platt
New York.
Cail John, 183 William

Steel—Importers of.

Ash William H. 248 Pearl
New York.
Cocker S. & Son, 84 Maiden lane
Collins & Co. 283 Pearl
Rolker A. & Mollman, 96 Pearl
Turton Thomas & Sons, 248 do

Steel Manufacturers.

Adee Daniel, 107 Fulton New York.
Greaves William & Sons, 241 Pearl
Jessop William & Sons, 91 John
Kemp Alfred F. 61 Broad
Naylor & Co. 99 & 101 John
M'Farlan Henry, 75 Broad
Sanderson, Brothers & Co. 16 Cliff
Wilson, Hawksworth, Moss & Elli-
son, 74 John

Steel Pens—Importers of.

Gillott J. 91 John New York.
Herts H. B. & Sons, 86 John
Leman M. L. 414 Pearl

Steel Pen Manufacturer.

Phineas Myer, 138 William
New York.

**Stock & Die Manufac-
turers.**

Rockland County.
Suffren G. W. & Co. Ramapo.

Stocking Manufacturers.

Kings County.
Satchell Wm. 117½ Atlantic
Brooklyn.
Pinder William, Fulton st.
Canner William, 194 do
Satchell John, 200 Grand
Williamsburgh.

Monroe County.
Burgess Joseph, 43 Sophia
Rochester.

New York County.
Butler Joseph, 672 4th New York.
Garner George, 344½ Bowery
Hackett J. 31 Av. D
Hughes John, 335 Hudson
North Edward, 72 Lewis

Rensselaer County.
Clowar John, 63 4th Troy.

**Stone Cutters, Quarriers &
Dealers.**

Albany County.
Jones J. D. Herkimer st. Albany.
Taylor E. cor. Westerlo & Green
Gray Wm. Westerlo & Franklin
Conger H. (Flagging Stone)
Reedsville Berne.
Brate Wm. (Flagging Stone)
Briggs N. do Coeymans.
Powell E.
Briggs A. N.

Cayuga County.
Stanford D. L. Auburn.
Chase G. B. State st.
Comstock & Dodge Springport.

Duchess County.
Joy P. A. (Blue Stone)
Poughkeepsie.

Erie County.
Rathburn Thomas, (Dealer) Terrace st. Buffalo.

Essex County.
Riley James O. Essex.

Fulton County.
Lee B. K. Perth.

Kings County.
Murray John, cor. Columbia and
Harrison sts. Brooklyn.
Edwards Alexander, foot of De-
graw
Cummings E. foot of Degraw
Anderson Peter B. cor. Columbia
& Pacific
Linan P. cor. Amity & Hicks
Webber John. Court cor. Amity
Johnson & Anderson, Water st.
nr. Fulton
Mulford A. S. Plymouth st. nr.
Catharine Ferry
Johnson & Anderson, Water st.
nr. Adams
Leech J. & Co. Plymouth st. nr.
Bridge
Lynan Peter, Bridge st. nr. Water
Christmas Wm. 63 Bridge
Rawson B. 181 2d Williamsburgh.
Conner John C. 46 Grand
Joyce W. E. & G. North 1st st.
nr. 2d

Lewis County.
Pugh David Turin.
Jones Stephen E.

Monroe County.
Young Valentine, 2 Finney
Rochester.
Marcille & Dupont, Fitzhugh st.

New York County.
Anderson John, East 23d nr. 3d
Av. New York.
Beals & Frazer, 601 Hudson
Bell Thaddeus. 478 West
Brisley William J. 776 W'ington
Chave & Espie, East 21st st. nr.
1st Av.
Crane Thomas & Co. 309 Madison
Donaldson James, 231 Cherry
Duncan & Sheldon, 8th st. bet
Avs. C. & D
Faitoute Jonathan, 357 Monroe
Fletcher Oscar B. 29 E. B'dway
Gardner Andrew J. 6 Sullivan
Hoorhis F. P. 811 Washington
Inglis & Wasson, 13th st, cor. 10th
Av.
Joyce William, foot E. 14th
Knights M. 7th st. near Av. B
Lawrence & Owen, 764 Water

Loomis J. & Co. foot of E. 23d
New York.
Low M. P. 233 Water
M'Barron John. 74 Av. B
M'Bride Abram, foot W. 22d
M'Donald Alexander, 277 6th
M'Master David. 10th Av. cor 25th
Masterton & Smith, Av. B cor 11th
Milne & Stewart, 789 W'hington
Mulligan Michael. 180 W. 22d
Naylor J. 20 Marketfield
Norris Noah. foot W. 21st
Noyes Samuel, 8 & 47 Washington
Pettigrew R. 9th Av. cor. W. 14th
Philips.A. Irving place, c.E 19th
Rink B. 60 7th
Robinson John, 332 Rivington &
E. 23d cor. 1st Av.
Rogers Joseph. foot W. 22d
Russ & Reid, 289 Broadway
Ryan & Hearn, E. 16th bet. Av. A
& 1st Av.
Shaler A. & Co., Barrow nr. West
Sheldon & Duncan, 350 8th
Smith Abisha & Co. 425 Washington & 19th cor. 10th Av.
Smith Alfred & Co. W. 19th cor.
10th Av.
Smith & Co. 11th st. & Av. B
Stephens Nathan, 25 Reade
Trowbridge F. H. 210 Water
Wilson T., E. 21st near 1st Av
Wilson & Edwards, E. 16th cor.
Av. A
Woodruff & Reilly, foot 20th N.R.
Wright John, foot 12th N. R
Young William, 811 Washington

Niagara County.

Shuler James D. *Lockport.*
Reynale Geo.
Ransom J. B.

Oswego County.

Voorhees James L. (Proprietor of Oswego Falls stone quarry) Oswego Falls *Granby.*

Putnam County.

M'Carty H. Breakneck Cold Springs *Phillipstown.*

Rensselaer County.

Brown James, cor. Adams & 2d
Troy.
Gifford & Scott, cor. Liberty & 1st

Rockland County.

Wilkins John, Nyack *Orangetown.*
Clark D. do
Hoffman M. do
Onderdonk A. do
Onderdonk J. do

St. Lawrence County.

Hall Erastus *Canton.*

Saratoga County.

Ashley H. & W. (stone sawing)
Milton.
Hiller John, (stone sawing)

Ulster County.

Fitch E. & Co. Rondout *Kingston.*
Skeel D. W. & Co. Wilbur
M'Carthy E. J. *Saugerties.*
Kellogg & Co. Glasco
Fitch & Co. do

Washington County.

Stone Henry R. *Greenwich.*
Cook Benajah, North White Creek
White Creek.
Hoyt E. B., N. White Creek

Stone Ware Manufacturers.

Cortland County.

Woodruff Madison
Cortland Village.

Monroe County.

Clark Nathan & Co. 189 Main
Rochester.

New York County.

Christman Bernard, 59 Av. C
(Earthenware & Furnaces)
New York
Day N. S. & Co. 39 Peck slip
Pavey C. 35 Gold
Smith A. E. & Sons, 36 Peck slip
Smith Washington, 261 W. 18th

Oneida County.

White N. & Sons, Whitesboro st.
Utica.

Rensselaer County.

Thayer P. 101 State *Lansingburgh.*
Seymour I. & Son, 44 Ferry
Troy.

Storage.

Chenango County.

Wells J. *Norwich.*

Kings County.

Durkee H. H. Commercial Wharf
Brooklyn.
Johnson P., Johnson's Wharf
Verplank, Crane & Co. 32 Atlantic Dock
Shadborne James, 33 Atlantic Dock
U. S. Warehouse, Charles C. Walden. Superintendent, Atlantic Dock
Ford Hobart, Ford's Wharf, near South Ferry
Baxter & Lawrence, Furman, bet. Fulton & S. Ferry
Green W. W. Toddy's Stores, Furman st.
Waring Stephen, Waring's Wharf, Furman st.
Lyon & Haff, Pierpont Dock, Furman st.
Thompson G. W. Thompson Stores
Thorn R. V. W. & Co. Thorn's Wharf, Furman st.
Trappal M. Furman near Fulton
Leunbeer R. H. & Chadbourne, Atlantic Dock
Marston & Power, Haxtun's Dock, near Fulton Ferry
Marschalk John, Smith's Stores, Main st.
Fowler Charles B. Mitchell's Dock, John st.
Rasom & Spelman, 14 Atlantic Dock

Montgomery County.

Wood & Moyer *Canajoharie.*
Clark, Newkirk & Hoffman
Clark, Newkirk & Hoffman, Fort Plain *Minden.*

New York County.

Arnold & Beeman, 60 Broadway
New York.
Avery James, 307 Water
Bacon John, 212 South
Ball George H. 3 & 5 Bridge
Baxter & Lawrence, East bet. Delancy and Rivington
Briggs Lawson T. 578 Water and 245 Cherry
Bucklin & Crane, 53 Washington

Coe Henry, 290 Cherry & 19
Beaver *New York.*
Coggill Henry. 67 Cliff
Conklin A. T. & Co. 19 Beaver
Deforest W. W. & Co. 89 South & 37 Spruce
Dudley Jonas G. & Co. 96 and 98 Pearl
Durkee Julius A. 16 & 22 Marketfield & 78 & 90 Broad
Hall Oliver C. 286 & 290 Water
Harmony P. 83 Washington
Hicks John J. 205 South
Hobby John B. & William H. 236 & 239 South, 127 Washington & 55 West
Hobby Joseph H. 296, 298 & 309 Water & 239 South
Hunter Joseph, 253 & 255 Front & 162 & 164 South & 270 Water
Husted H. P. 214 & 221 South
Irving Louis G. 13 West and 20 Washington
Gurley & Muldrum, 5 West
Leggett William F. 286, 288 & 290 Water
Longworth David, 9 Beaver and 6 Broadway
Lyon & Haaf, 100 Water
Major M. 5 Pearl
Marston & Power, 19 South
Merle Guillaume, 268 Front and Water
Moore William S. 295 Water
Naylor Joseph, 20 Marketfield
Olney James N. 27 West
Park James S. 30 Moore
Ransom & Spellman, 100 Wall
Sayer William, 26 & 29 West
Schuyler & Gutman, 5 Broad & 54 Washington & 30 West
Staples James M. 18 South
Van Boskerk ——, 22½ Whitehall
Wadsworth W R. 4 Jones lane & 8 Beaver
Warford William K. 18 Broadway & 5 Beaver
White T. B. & Co. Hunt's Ware houses, — Bridge & 17 Pearl
Whitney J. H. 243 Water

Oswego County.

Crane Hunter, foot of Front & cor. Van Buren *Oswego.*
Government Warehouse, Water st.
Government Warehouse, corner Water & Schuyler

Steuben County.

Mallory Wm. M. *Painted Post.*

Stove and Grate Dealers.
(See also Hardware, also Tin, Sheet-Iron and Copper Workers.)

Albany County.

Blakeman E. C. 92 State *Albany.*
Fuller & Hermance, 636 Broad'y
Baker Charles, 590 & 592 do
Whitney ——, 86 Green
Hoy J. jr. 15 do
Van Warmer & M'Garvey, 14 Green
Callaman & Wilson, (wholesale) 16 Green

Cattaraugus County.

Nutting S. D. & Co. *Ellicottville.*
Colman E. S. & L. L.

Cayuga County.

Bentley T. S., Weedsport *Brutus.*
White Wm., Port Byron *Mentz.*

Chautauqua County.

Bryant Godfrey *Westfield.*

Chenango County.
Birch L. D. *Sherburne.*
Willerd & Daggett

Columbia County.
Coffin R., Front st. *Hudson.*

Erie County.
Dudley Thomas, 98 Main *Buffalo.*
Jewett & Brother, 217 Main

Essex County.
Low John H. *Westport.*

Franklin County.
Jerome M. J. *Malone.*

Kings County.
Flintoff Wm. 63 Atlantic *Brooklyn.*
Halligan J. C. Court st.
Tucker F. D. 11 & 13 S. 7th *Williamsburgh.*

Monroe County.
Ward E., Fairport *Perrinton.*
Warrants & Southworth, 18 S. St. Paul *Rochester.*
Amsden A. K. & S. St. Paul
Russell George, 74 Main
Miller Alexander, 30 do
French J. M. & Co. 42 Exchange
Cheney J. E. 24 do
Hart R. cor. Buffalo & Sophia
Backus, Fitch & Co. 50 Main, Brockport *Sweden.*

New York County.
Baker John R. 503 Grand *New York.*
Barrows Ebenezer, 228 Water
Beebe James & Co. Centre cor. Reade
Blackman Abm. 470½ Pearl
Bosworth Daniel, 56 Cliff
Ballard Thomas J. 239 Water
Carman Richard, 206 do
Chilson, Allen, Walker & Co. 351 Broadway, (warming & ventilating,) (see advertisement)
Clark & Co. 191½ Bowery
Coffin A. J. & Co. 208 Water
Cogswell & St. Amoreux, 301 Spring
Cook Charles, 133½ Division
Corrie William, 1½ Bedford
Cort Nicholas, 50 Bowery
Cort Nicholas L. 107 do
Cory Charles, 302 Division
Cox Stephan, 235 Water
Cunningham James, 268 Grand
Farmer John W. 245 Broome
Favereau Francis, 94 Cherry
Finch R. R. & Co. 231 Water
Fisk & Raymond, 209 do
Frazier Thomas, 117 Beekman
Gilhooly John, 118 Nassau
Gilhooly Thomas H. 75 Gold
Globe Stove Manufacturing Company, 127 Amos
Goggin David, 61 Centre
Goodwin Charles, 254 Water
Gregory R. A. 383 6th Av.
Grimes Joshua, 377 Houston
Guinand Charles A. 119 Beekman
Heal John, 246 Canal
Heard Thomas, 24 4th Av.
Hedenberg Francis L. 79 Division
Hine Charles S. 15 Bowery
Huse John B. 20 Greenwich Av.
Hyllier William, 50 Lewis
Kane Charles, 319 Bowery
Keyser John H. 56 Cliff & 112 Beekman
Janes, Beebe & Co. 120 Fulton
Jaquins Charles, 59 Ludlow
Kierske & Morritta, 133 Walker
Lamotte John H. 254 Water
Levi Benjamin, 186 Rivington

Liddle John, 290 Water *New York.*
Littlejohn William. 240 Water
Lockwood David, 542 Broadway
M'Michael John, 40 South
Low Michael P. & Co. 265 Water
M'Cutcheon Michael, 785 Grand
M'Pherson Guest, 233½ Water
Mason John F. 246 Greenwich
Mirbery John, 526 Grand
Merklee George F. 77 Bleecker
Merritt Frederick S. 116 Bleecker
Monsees H. W. 65 Bowery
Mott Jordan L. 264 Water
Munsell James A. 115 Beekman
Murphy John, 256 Water
Newman Jas. 290 Bowery
Peterson Richard E. & W. T. 144 Bowery
Pierce George & Co. 301 B'way
Pool Henry A. 40 3d Av.
Rea & Pollock, 160 Greenwich
Rianhard, Starling & M'Murdie 1 William
Rolhaus Philip, 250 Water
Runnells J. H. 101 Houston
Sanford W. 333 Water
Savory John & Sons, 54 Cliff
Schloss J. 3 2d
Seymour & Williams, 246 Water
Shephard & Co. 242 Water
Somerville A. & M. 11 Bowery & 260 Water
Southard Thomas, 238 Water
Stanley Adam, 41 Bowery
Stanley William J. 43 Water
Striker W. H. 242 Grand
Sumner P. 166 Greenwich
Standner E. 81 Bowery
Teets Philip, 296 Greenwich
Thorp David B. 248 Water
Tibbetts James V. 113 Beekman
Trowbridge F. H. 210 Water
Underhill David, 125 Bowery
Van Every Henry, 213 Water and 222 Greenwich
Van Every Oliver, 241 Water
Van Voorhis J. 34 West B'dway
Wands B. & Co. 211 Water
West William, 133 Hudson
Westerfield John, 739 Broadway
Whitney Washington F. 111 Beekman
Whipps Fred'k. 359 Grand
Williamson John, 256 Canal
Winchell Joseph Q. 265 Water
Wood Loftis, 237 Water

Oneida County.
Mix J. F. *Camden*
Root B. Clinton st. *Kirkland.*
Prescott J. *New Hartford.*
Giles H. G. & Co. Dominick st. *Rome.*
Wood T. H. & G. W. 40 and 41 Genesee *Utica.*
Tyrel E. & Son, 47 Genesee
Evans E. 8 Genesee

Onondaga County.
Ball, White & Co. *Marcellus.*
Tozer T. H. Clinton Square, Syracuse *Salina.*

Ontario County.
Rose P. H. *Canandaigua.*

Orange County.
Washburn Davis, Washingtonville *Blooming Grove.*
Lewis M. *Chester.*
Hare U. & Co. Port Jervis *Deer Park.*
Rowley J. M. & C.
Lee Squire *Goshen.*
Merkam & Smith
Bull B. *Montgomery.*
Newkirk C. B. *Monroe.*
Rowley J. M. & C. E. Otisville *Mount Hope.*

Gordan J. & Co. 28 Water *Newburgh.*
Lomas John, 38 Water
Finch J. L. New Hampton *Wallkill.*
Wheeler & Co. South Middletown
Moore D. F. *Warwick.*

Queens County.
Lewis & Coles *Flushing*

Rensselaer County.
Deyoe George C. 294 State *Lansingburgh.*
Taylor J. C. (stoves and tin ware) 167 River *Troy.*
Ackley P. 177 River
Edson Thomas H. 247 River
Fay & Co. (wholesale) 288 River
Viall, House & Mann. 287 River
Cox A. & Co. (wholesale) 297 River
Johnson & Cox, 297 River
Wood J. B. 365 River
Geer Gilbert, 299 River
Starbuck N. B. 313 River
Flack J. W. & Co. 323 River
Mallary & Ingalls

Suffolk County.
Brown J. Port Jefferson *Brookhaven.*

Ulster County.
Shaw Wm. H. *Kingston.*
Ross Hiram & Co. Rondout
Styles John P. *Saugerties.*
Welch John C.
Davis Jacob S.
Myer Peter K.
Washburn & Carr, Ellenville *Wawarsing.*
Jones & Shook, Napanock

Stove Manufacturers, (See also Founders—Iron.)

Albany County.
Ransom S. H. & Co. Broadway cor. Mulberry and 26 and 28 State *Albany.*
Vose & Co. South Broadway and 12 and 14 Maiden Lane
Quackenboss A. 14 State
Learned B. P. 8 Maiden Lane
McLaughlin C. 32 Hudson
Thomas & Collins cor. S. Lansing and Quay
Tremere & Wands, 21 Green
Sheer J. H. 17 and 19 Green
McCoy, Clark & Co. 13 Green
Rathburn & Co. 9 and 11 Green
Harvey F. 7 Green
Pasco E. L. 5 Green
Baker Samuel, 16 Green
Jagger, Treadwell & Perry, 129 Beaver
Potts J. C. cor. Hamilton and Grand
Orcutt & Co. 222 Hamilton
Cobb Wm. 192 Washington
Morrison & Tibbitts, Green Island, West Troy *Watervliet*

Cayuga County.
Russell & Smith, State st. *Auburn.*
Gaylord J. B. Water st.
Beach J. Weedsport *Brutus.*
Birdsell & Stevens *Genoa.*
Russell, Sittzer & Co. Port Byron *Menlz.*
Stone & Kenyan *Moravia.*
Keeler & Wright
Shoards & Mother *Venice.*

Clinton County.
Smith, Benner & Co. *Plattsburgh.*

Erie County.

Jewett & Root, 31 Main   *Buffalo.*
Dudley Thos. J. 18 Main
Wilkison & Co. 64 Main

Kings County.

Quimby Samuel, 3 Henry *Brooklyn.*
Butler Augustus, 242 Fulton
Beers N. T. 45 Fulton

Livingston County.

Chandler W. H. & S.   *Avon.*
North N. P.   *Geneseo.*
Brown H. D.   *Mount Morris.*
Long Moses, Fowlersville *York.*

Monroe County.

French John M. 87 Exchange
  Rochester.
Bristol A. G. Trowbridge st.
Seymour & Morgan, Brockport
  Sweden.
Fitch, Bang & Co. Brockport

Oneida County.

Elmer E. Delta   *Lee.*
Spencer A. W. Dominick st. *Rome.*
Seymour & Adams, Dominick st.
Berrill J. A. Waterville
  Sangerfield.
Seabury & Barnum, Waterville
Parker O. W. South Trenton
  Trenton.
Seymour & Wood, Jay st. *Utica.*
Peckham J. S. & M. 16, 18 & 20
  Catharine
Vroman C. & Co. Durhamville
  Verona.
Seymour & Brothers, Hampton
  Westmoreland.
Buel A. & Co. Walesville
  Whitestown.
Terwilliger & Co. Whitesboro

Onondaga County.

Jackson, Phelps & Co. Arcade
  Building, Syracuse *Salina.*
Walter E. & Co. Water st.
Donk, Herrick & Co. Water st.
Alexander Wm. H. Water st.
Powell A. C. Water st.
Stafford D. & Co. Warren st.
Norton, Hall & Co. Salina st
Burton B. Bear st.

Orange County.

Wheeler & Co. South Middletown
  Wallkill.

Orleans County.

King S. L. Albion   *Barre.*
Berry R. G. do

Rensselaer County.

Thatcher & Hutchins, State st.
  Lansingburgh.
Low & Hicks, 221 River *Troy.*
Edson Thos. H. 247 River
Fay & Co. 283 River
Viall, House & Mann, 287 River
Dunham A. T. & Co. 281 River
Cox A. & Co. 297 River
Johnson & Cox (Clinton Foundry)
  297 River
Geer Gilbert, 299 River
Wager, Pratt & Co, 66 6th
Pease, Keeney & Co. cor. 3d & Ida

Schenectady County.

Pilling, Conde & Co. State st.
  Schenectady.

Clute & Brothers

Seneca County.

Race W. & Co. (see advertisement) *Seneca Falls.*
Foote & Owen

Westchester County.

Finch R. R. Peekskill *Courtlandt.*
Rikeman & Seymour, Peekskill
Whitney W. S.   do
Gilbert W. T.   do
Southard Thos.   do
Van Wart & Wildey, Tarrytown
  Greenburgh.
Fowler, Horton & Co. Sing Sing
  Ossining.
Vredenburgh W. D. & F. Sing Sing
Abendroth & Brothers, Portchester *Rye.*

Straw Goods—Dealers in.

Alden & Aldrich, 63 Beaver
  New York.
Atwater Wm. 159 William
Beach J. Sterling. 243 Greenwich
Bennett Frank, 19 John
Birch Wm. N. 179 Pearl
Blake Eli C. 261 Greenwich
Blake Stephen M. 148 Pearl
Blachford Edward. 409 Pearl
Bloch Isaac, 2 William
Booth Wm. C. 194 Pearl
Booth Zalmon. 16 Cortlandt
Bostwick, Kent & Atwood, 134
  Pearl
Breck Chas. E. 258 Pearl
Bridge Edward & Co. 117 Pearl
Bridge G. 125 Pearl & 78 Beaver
Campbell & Gray. 93 William
Camp. Gilbert & Co. 148 Water
Cargill Warren, 40 John
Carrington, Orvis & Westcot, 24
  Cortlandt
Carpenter W. & Co. 54 Broad
Chapman G. M. & Co. 130 Pearl
Chapin Luther, 12 John
Clark & Vinton, 70 William
Cochran J. L. & Co. 130 Pearl
Conkling & Hawkins, 37 Nassau
Dewing. Thayer & Co. 173 Pearl
Fisher. Cushing & Henderson, 10
  Cortlandt
Flagg & Baldwin, 182 Pearl
Force & Franks, 119 Pearl
Frost B. 69 William & 37 Cedar
Frost Henry, 373 Bowery
Gault & Ballard, 149 Water
Granger D. K. 79 Cedar
Green Stafford N. 376 Bowery
Green Henry M. & Co. 144 Pearl
Haff Jas. D. 12 Pine
Hall S. D. & Co. 161 Pearl
Halladay William, 64½ Bowery &
  3 Catharine
Harley James H. 36 Maiden lane
Hawkins Samuel D. 327 Grand
Heaney John, 58 Catharine
Henderson John C. & Co. 174 and
  176 Pearl
Hills & Fisher, 136 Pearl
Hoag James D. 56 Cedar
Hubbard & Gillett, 60 Cedar
Jennings G. & Co. 158½ William
Jennings, Read & Co. 113 Pearl
Johnson A. & Co. 125 Pearl
Kirby Isaac F. 46 Cedar
Leeds Samuel, 144 Water
Leland & Mellen, 171 Pearl
Lewis William J. 146 3d Av.
Loop & Allen, 54 Cedar
Lynes Samuel, 63 Liberty
M'Namee Richard, 6 Pine
Mann, Swift & Co. 62 Cedar
Markoe & Spear, 76 Cedar
Miles Charles, 132 Water
Montgomery W. R. 3 John
Napier James, 76 William
Newell W. & Co. 71 William
Peck Gardner M. 46 Broad
Peet Munson S. 223 Greenwich
Phillips William & Co. 91 Cedar
Plimbton Charles L. 83 Beaver
Rallings William, 191 Spring
Reeder Elizabeth, 239 Greenwich
Rianhard, Starling & M'Murdie, 8
  Cortlandt

Rich & Amidon, 169 Pearl
  New York.
Richards & Cromwell, 63 Maiden
  lane
Rockwell & Barrows, 21 Cortlandt
Russell Salem T. 162 Pearl
Sammis John C. 86 Delancy
Sanger C. P. 175 Pearl
Saunders & Forman, 74 Liberty
Seaman John F. 36 John
Simmons Chas. W. 176½ Bowery
Simons William W. 60 John
Stowe & Satterlee, 94 Cedar
Sumner & Wilds, 37 Liberty
Tredwell E. L. 25 Maiden lane
Walmsley J. 21 & 54 Catharine
Wells Jonathan T. 117 Maiden la.
White John P. 131 Pearl, and 84
  Beaver
Wight John, 107 Ridge
Williams R. G. & Co. 84 Pearl
Williams & Cunningham, 194 Pearl
Young Thomas, 96 Bowery

Straw Goods—Importers.

Bostwick, Kent & Atwood, 109
  Water & 134 Pearl *New York.*
Chapman G. M & Co. 130 Pearl
Cochran & Andrews, 130 Pearl
Denny Thomas, 57 Beaver
Dord C. 90 Beaver and 139 Pearl
Draper, Clark & Co. 31 Nassau
Fort & Lindam, 15 S. William &
  55 Stone
Gault & Ballard, 120 Maiden lane
Guerber Augustus & Co. 165 Pearl
Hoguet Joseph, 10 John
Isler John, 67 Beaver
Isler & Otto, 35 Liberty
Muir A. jr. 32 Exchange place
Reynolds Thomas, 167 Pearl
Rheiner John C. 63 Beaver
Vyse & Son, 129 William
Waller A. & R. 130 Pearl
Walmsley Edward, 14 Catharine
  & 17 East Broadway
Whiting Wm. E. & Co. 122 Pearl

Sugar Refiners.

Basley O. 193 Front *New York*
Booth & Edgar, 331 West
Dohrmann Claus, r. 104 Thompson
Harris Dennis, 144 Duane
Harris & Ockerhausen, 106 Duane
Havemeyers & Mollers, 96 Front
  & 86 Vandam
Herring Silas C. 408 Washington
Meyer Henry, 196 Mott
New York Steam Sugar Company,
  331 West
Reineicke John F. 61 Chrystie
Rulheusen Hermann, 207 Cherry
Small Wm. 91 & 93 Washington
Stewart & Bussing, 418 Pearl
Stuart R. L. & A. 285 Greenwich
Swift Edwin A. 410 Washington
Swift, Briggs & Co. Washington
  cor. Laight
Swift E. H. 254 West
Turner Myron, 331 West
Woolsey & Co. 113 Wall, & South
  cor. Montgomery

Surgical & Dental Instrument Makers.

Ashmead & Hurlburt, 487 Broad'y
  New York.
Chevalier John D. 184 Broadway
  and 43 & 45 Duane
Demster James, 70½ Bowery
Dempster & Allen, 72 Bowery
Foster & Co 367 Broadway
Hernstein H. 72 Bowery
Jones, White & Co. 263 Broadway
Moeller & Kaemmerrer, 200 Division and 174 Rivington

Morson Charles F. 67 Elizabeth
New York.
Lisee Frederick, 23 Cliff
Lutz & Maxhumer, 419 Pearl
Oberlander C. F. 70 Division
Starr William O. 7 Bedford
Stockton Samuel W. 258 Broadway
Tiemann George, 63 Chatham
Ward M. & Co. 45 Ann, and 88
Maiden lane

Surveyors—Land.

Ewen D. & E. 9 Chambers
New York.
Mailler William. 186 Elm
Smith Edwin, 7 Broad
Vidal Francis P. 6 City Hall place

Surveyors—City.

Amerman Richard, 45 Bowery
New York.
Bridges E. W. 65 Ann
Bridges J. F. 65 Ann
Doughty Samuel S. 45 Bowery
Dreyer Peter H. 80 Nassau and
124 3d Av.
Ludlam Isaac. 8 James
Nicholson Francis, 174 Mercer
Pollock John, 237 West 16th
Sage Gardner A. 635 Broadway
Serrell James E. 299 Broadway &
43 West 26th
Serrell John J. 72 Murray
Smith Edwin. 113 4th Av.
Smith George W., West 23d bet.
9th & 10th Avs.
Whitlock W. H. 87 1st

Suspender Manufacturers.

Duchess County.

Briggs H. F. 294 Main
Poughkeepsie.

New York County.

Renau W. 55 Bayard   New York.
Sele & Hammond, 29 Cedar

Scythe Manufacturers.

Duchess County.

Barris S.   Pine Plains.

Franklin County.

Earle W. B.   Malone.
Beardsley & Co.

Herkimer County.

Gorton John, Poland   Russia.
Fralk J. & I., Cold Brook

Madison County.

Harwood S. & R.   Eaton.

Montgomery County.

Case, Pardee & Co.   Amsterdam.

Rensselaer County.

M'Nara David S.   Hoosick.
March Henry
Draper, Brown & Chadsey Troy.

Saratoga County.

Blood Isaiah, Ballston   Milton.
Coffin & Co.   Providence.
Newell & Clark
Barker S. S., Barkersville
Monroe S.
Hulburt Willis Saratoga Springs.

Ulster County.

Elting France   Shawangunk.

Scythe Rifle Maker.

Columbia County.

Gay H. D., New Lebanon Springs
New Lebanon.

Scythe Snath Manufacturers.

Chautauque County.

Wood Ezra, Jamestown   Ellicott.
Garfield Samuel, do

New York County.

Lamson, Goodnow & Co. 7 Gold

Tailors. (See also Tailors and
Drapers.)

Albany County.

Lee & Brothers, 471 Broadway
Albany.
Francis J. B. 626 Broadway
Topp W. H. 546   do
Chambers Wm. 3 Stanwix Hall
Boyd Isaac, 21 Quay
Jones E. 60½ State
Chatterson J. Br'dway c. Church
Lucky H. 25 Liberty
Smith R. 50 Lydius
Crow Wm. 208 S. Pearl
Mann J. V. 64   do
Hamburger J. 46 Green
Kennedy D. 22 Beaver
Stahl & Schanmaier, 3 Beaver
Fredenhall J. 16 Washington
Hall John   Guilderland.
Padmore P., West Troy Watervliet.
Bristol E. L., Cohoes
Waring & Robbins, Cohoes

Alleghany County.

Gary ——   Almond.
Rockwell I.
Hyde Wm.
Curtis ——
Shepherd D.   Amity.
Ellis N. J.   Andover.
Lisk Wm. V.
Hamer Wm. F.   Angelica.
Gardner Lewis
Simons Wm. B.
Haight T.
Bronson W. R.   Belfast.
Ford & Roscoe
Seeley Hiram
Mitchell James E., Whitney Val-
ley   Burns.
Brewer Samuel   Cuba.
Buskirk Andrew   Friendship.
Benson J. M.   Hume.
M'Can George
Northrop Samuel
White Wm., Whitesville
Independence.
Dockstader H.   Rushford.
Bullard William   New Hudson.
Hubbell John
Hume N. A.
Post John W., Wellsville   Scio.
Kenyon J. P.   Wirt.
Hanford C. W. Richburgh

Broome County.

Topping J., Chenango Forks
Barker.
Porter J. H.
White J.   Binghamton.
Stoppird J.
King J. N.
Brown G. C.
Titus J. E.
Fitzgibbons T.
O'Hara T.
Cleavwater & Lonaberg
Kelsey N., Harpersville Colesville.
Healy T. C., Nineveh
Collier P.   Conklin.
Lewis O.   Lisle.
Ball D. S.   Maine.

De Grost C., Whitney's Point
Triangle.
Armstrong A.   Union.
Mason C.
Thomas E. W.   Windsor.
Bird A. D.

Cattaraugus County.

Morton Alexander   Burton.
Church & Morris   Ellicottville.
Watson L.
Cottier J.
Bullock Adam, Sandusky Freedom
Owens Sampson W.
Westcott John R.   New Albion.
Mallbee J. B. & L. H.   Otto.
Clark A.   Perrysburgh.
Chambers Willard, Gowanda
Persia.
Hanford Zelmon,   do
Parker T. I.   do
Warner Zimri   do
Larrabee Ebenezer,   Portville.
Reid Wm.   Rundolph.
Sherman J. M.
Wheeler R. B.
Barsley T., East Randolph

Cayuga County.

Abel B.   Moravia.
Ogden J. C.   Springport.
Guest J.   Venice.
Savage Wm.

Chautauque County.

Taylor E. W. & Wm. Mayville
Chautauque.
Green Thomas, Mayville
Russell —— De Wittville
Look A.   Ellery.
Bement J. Irving   Hanover.
Fitzgerald P. Forestville
Martin James.   do
Brower N. B. Nashville
Jacops O. E. Smith's Mills
Clark H. Silver Creek
Derby John M.   Harmony
Lewis L.   Ripley.
Fuller Ebenezer   Sheridan.
Hawler Samuel T.   Sherman.
Grantier R.   Villanova.
Gates Malcolm   Westfield.
Tyler James
Fellows Levi
Sexton Wm. jr.
Tucker Darius

Chenango County.

Smith G. W.   Bainbridge.
Williams J. O.
Sheperson S.
Woolley S. W. South Bainbridge
Elderken E. J. Bennettsville
Gager Charles   Coventry.
Cornish George W.
Hicks Thomas, Guilford Centre
Guilford.
Cady N. W.
Ross D.   New Berlin.
Burrows H.
Wood W. South New Berlin
Mann & Cook   Norwich.
Duryea J. K.
Curtis & Allendorf
Sherwood N.
Couway Thomas
Grace & Bayls   Oxford.
Manahan J.
Thompson Charles
Crosier J.   Pharsalia.
York L. C.   Pitcher.
Keller J. N.   Plymouth.
Dietz John P.   Sherburne.
M'Donough P.
Kellogg W. B.   Smyrna.
Ingalls A. M.

Clinton County.

Morris Charles, Keeseville
Au Sable.

Gilberts ——, East Chazy *Chazy.*
Lloyd ——, West do
King A.   *Mooers.*
Eagan P.   *Plattsburgh.*
Dunham G.
Kennedy Thomas   *Saranac.*
Paige E. J.

Columbia County.

Shaw G. W. Spencertown
        Austerlitz.
Hotchkiss A. Canaan 4 Corners
        Canaan.
Mitchell G. North Chatham
        Chatham.
Deegan A. Chatham 4 Corners
Dunn J.   do
Merlius A. do
Carroll J. do
Willit J. W. East Chatham.
Simpson J. E. Malden Bridge
Rose R.   *Claverack.*
Shadwick F. W. *Copake.*
Hagedorn S.
Pierce D.
Hills M. L.   *Gallatin.*
Bixby J.   *Hillsdale.*
Backman Allen, Warren st.
        Hudson.
Haws H. S. do
Osborn H. P. 339 do
Nichols & Grusebeck, 300 Warren
Osborn C. B. Valatie *Kinderhook.*
Smith J. I. do
Sharp J. A. do
Pulver Wm. do
Dennis W. do
Weed J. & W. do
Sandford A. do
Hall J. J.   *Livingston.*
Jarvie G. W. New Lebanon Springs
        New Lebanon.

Cortland County.

Peck N. B.   *Cincinnatus.*
Post Cornelius
Babcock H. S. *Homer.*
Trowbridge ——
Brown Wm.
Collins Chester
Graham James N. *Marathon.*
Ward L. F.
Havens Merodoch

Delaware County.

Robinson C.   *Andes.*
Egberlston R. C. *Davenport.*
Cannon M. P.   *Delhi.*
Hughs I. J.
Sarles A.   *Franklin.*
Flynt J. H.
Scott M.
Bush A.
Ayers J. W. *Hancock.*
Webster S. S. *Meredith.*
Smith I. B.
Kidd J. Margaretsville *Middletown.*
Gillispie Wm. Clovesville
Clagur J. C. Hobart *Stamford.*
Smith D. do
Grant H. do
Cannon O. F. Sidney Plains
        Sidney.
Thomas & Radcliff, Deposit
        Tompkins.
Tailor George, do
Freeman J. H. do
Youmans P. do
Crandall J. W. do
Sawyer G. S. *Walton.*
Falling F.

Duchess County.

Thorp H. C.   *Amenia.*
Mallett N. L.
Carman J. J. Stormville *Beekman.*
Clarkson G.   *Dover.*
Northrop J. & A.
Ostrander J.   *Fishkill.*

Welcott & Smith *Fishkill.*
Hedden D. Wappingers' Falls
Monaghan P. do
Phillips J. H. Hughsonville
Browster G. B. Glenham
Pollock J. L. Matteawan
Carman J. J. Stormville
Horton W. M. Hopewell
Outwater Wm. B. *Hyde Park.*
Milroy R. Lafayette Corners
        Milan.
Holt W. R. Rook City
Perry F.   *Northeast.*
Runnell H. *Pine Plains.*
Brush A.
Turner J. *Pleasant Valley.*
De Groff B.
Cornwall J. Salt Point
Butts F. 277 Main *Poughkeepsie.*
Cross Phillip. 207 Main
Hignall C. W. New Hamburgh
M'Neil H.   *Red Hook.*
Coon A.
Smith J. I.   *Rhinebeck.*
Vansteenbergh C. L.
Barnes T.
Buel A. Stanfordville *Stanford.*
Skidmore ——, do
Bunnell E. do
Davis J. Attlebury
Florence G. Verbank *Union Vale.*
Wilber H. U. *Washington.*
Allen N. Hart's Village
Fry H. Salt Point
Wood S. R. Mabbettsvill

Erie County.

M'Guire James *Alden.*
Klitz A.. Williamsville *Amherst.*
Cossins Joseph, do
Stever Abram, do
Dunn William, Willink *Aurora.*
Knapp Charles K. do
Carr E.   *Boston.*
Wainwright Joseph
Sheppy John *Clarence.*
Walker John
Plim Christian, Clarence Centre
Hibbard Thomas S. *Collins.*
Graves Eugene, Springville
        Concord.
Zimmerman Peter *Eden.*
Phillips —— -, Hamburgh Centre
        Hamburgh.
Curtie F. W. *Holland.*
Morgan J. F., Akron *Nwstead.*
Wilder Wm. do
Price T. J. do
Lane Edward *Wales.*
Cole Isaac, Wales Centre

Essex County.

Geary John *Elizabethtown.*
Crawford John
Fortune Robert *Essex.*
Parkill Ezra
Houghton B. W., Moriah Four
  Corners   *Moriah.*
Tobin Thomas, Moriah 4 Corners
Cannon James, do
Mughan James, do
M'Rae Daniel, do
Monroe W. B. do
Santeeno Heary, Port Henry
Cann James, do
Bostwick ——, do

Franklin County.

Holbrook B. H. *Malone.*
Hall George
Thompson John
Barrie J.
Jones & Ellis
O'Sullivan M.
Parker J. W.
Millington H. *Moira.*

Fulton County.

Neugent J. R. *Broadalbin.*

Jackson Z. *Broadalbin.*
Hart Edward *Johnstown.*
Weber Frederick
Stewart Daniel
Keith Peter
Helwig M., Gloversville
Cole E. W. do
Hart James, Mayfield Corners
        Mayfield.
Foster D. C. *Northampton.*
Jackson S. B.
Hamilton N., Northville
Van Ness W. H., Osborn's Bridge
House John P. *Oppenheim.*
Booklass Wm. *Perth.*
Fell Benjamin F.

Genesee County.

Morse W. G. *Alabama.*
Hogarth   *Alexander.*
Tayler William, East Bethany
        Bethany.
Prindle D. R. do
Purdy Henry, Linden
Church P. S. *Darien.*
Milton H.
Lambert Eli, Darien Centre
Perkins O. *Le Roy.*
Keeler C. H. *Pavilion.*
Aberdean G. W. *Pembroke.*
Chappell   *Stafford.*

Greene County.

Demmick E. *Athens.*
Hill A.   *Cairo.*
Johnson David
Harris & Levy *Catskill.*
Henman Nathaniel
Bates E., Leeds
Frear William *Cossackie.*
Havens Peter
Vandenburgh Richard
Welch John
Osboon Ransom *Durham.*
Calkins Ira *Greenville.*
Green Reuben E.
Armstrong John *Hunter.*
Clowe William
Collier Albert
Rorabaek Benj. B. *Lexington.*
Lockley Thomas *New Baltimore.*
Knowles William L. *Prattsville.*
Ginnis Peter
Jordan & Jordan
Barlow James
Cowles Noble *Windham.*
Cotton John
Cole Henry, Hensonville

Herkimer County.

Hewetson T. A. *Columbia.*
Dodge James *Frankfort.*
Suits & Saltman
Schaffner M. *Herkimer.*
Hartman John
Fox P. J.
Whipple H. F. *Newport.*
Cooley Lyman
Betticher Isaac *Russia.*
Williams William
Huekans Thomas *Salisbury.*
Smith Stephen *Stark.*
Shall Daniel, Starkville
Tennant R. R., Van Hornsville
Badger   *Warren.*
Kinney G. H., Jordanville
Watrus W., West Winfield
        Winfield.
Adams & Chalder, do

Jefferson County.

Fox E. B.   *Adams.*
Wright William
Salisbury E. S.
Hubbard C., Adams Centre
Bidleman J. C., Plessis *Alexandria.*
Thompson F., Alexandria Bay
Miller P.   *Antwerp.*
Johnson H. D.
M'Carte J., Ox Bow

Bruce A. C., Dexter *Brownville.*
Colmon Joseph, do
Mackreal James, Perch River
Jennings James *Cape Vincent.*
Delany William *Clayton.*
Hudson W., Depauville
Holley T. *Ellisburgh.*
Larned S.
Ridlon J. H., Woodville
Larned A. G., Belleville
Wood A. do
Haddow M. *Henderson.*
Towsley J. G.
Nicholson & Carrier, Sackett's Harbor *Hounsfield.*
Folts G. W., Sackett's Harbor
Gladwin Geo. S. & Co. do
Peck Anthony, Evans' Mills
Le Ray.

Morse Chauncy, do *Lyme.*
Crosby William
Shall William, Three Mile Bay
Watts George W., Lafargeville
Orleans.
Howe J. W., Lafargeville
Cain M. *Philadelphia.*
Lattimer F.
Waite R., South Rutland *Rutland.*
Rogers Timothy, Felt's Mills
Morse J. W. *Theresa.*
Gale Thomas J.
Berry J.
Morrow A.

Kings County.

Flosman B. 49 Atlantic *Brooklyn.*
Lewis Robert. 8 do
Still John N. 28 do
Ryerson J. 254 do
Lynch P. Court st.
Burnett Wm. M. 61 Poplar
Brown W. 40 Hicks
Bolding John, 41 do
Callaghan J. O. 272 Hicks
Washington John J. 8 Clinton
Haide V. D. 4 Boerum
Brown Joseph, 63 Fulton
Creswell Thomas, 91 Main
Jones T. H. 92 Pearl
Wylie & Anderson, 12 Prospect
Mellard A. 93 Tillary
Storck G. P. 80 Nassau
Munro J. 38 Myrtle Av.
Winters J. 160 York
Ryan J. 104 Hudson Av.
Whelan D. 194 Nassau
Joyce T. 219 Bridge
Malks John R. *Flatbush.*
Williams John
Altenbrand L., East New York
Bill S. do
Triber Martin *New Utrecht.*
Merritt A. 257 S. 2d *Williamsburgh.*
Piper George, 123½ Grand
Filan J. 257 Grand

Lewis County.

Kidney G. *Denmark.*
Austin J.
Kellogg G. C., Copenhagen
Shepherd E. do
Wheeler C. do
Peden G. & H. H. *Martinsburgh.*
Smith D. A.
Sylvester H. West Martinsburgh
Jones John T. *Turin.*
Wilden A. S. Constableville
West Turin.
Morris R. do
Smutt Geo. do

Livingston County.

McGuire William *Avon.*
Morrison Wm.
Sayres Daniel
Whelan Maurice, East Avon
McKee William *Caledonia.*
Morrison Daniel
McGee John *Conesus.*
Boom & Thompson *Dansville.*

Rice Geo. H. *Dansville.*
Goetshall Lewis
Brockway S.
Trimmer —— *Groveland.*
Sinclair ——, Cuylerville
Leicester.
McCall Matthew, do.
Church ——, Moscow
Young Sylvenus, do
Foreman Joseph *Lima.*
Teall William N. *Livonia.*
Bernard C. F.
Warren J. C. Hemlock Lake
Davis D. do
Battorf Geo. W. Lakeville
Martin C. F. *Mount Morris.*
Teale E. N.
Carnes L. F.
Richmond B. P. *Nunda.*
Grover Silas
Clark John, Oakland *Portage.*
Hopkins O. M. Scottsburgh
Sparta.
Eply M. H. *Springwater.*
McLure James *York.*
Daggett Abram
Ford William, Greigsville

Madison County.

Gifford C. W. *Brookfield.*
Davenderf A. Leonardsville
Britton A. New Woodstock
Cazenovia.
House S. M. *De Ruyter.*
Fisher Thos.
Benedict J.
Slocum F. C. *Eaton.*
Fell D. W.
Cole L. E. Morrisville
Chambers W. H. Leeville
Griffith John, Georgetown
Fairchild Nelson *Hamilton.*
Russell Chas.
Johnson T. & Son
Wilcox R. B.
Waters E. O. Earlville
Saunders T. P. do
Mead S. W. do
Caley Edward, Poolville
Walrath J. Oneida Depot *Lenox.*
Nare Geo., Canastota
Brush & Ould, do
Pulker Chas. Clockville
Fryer H. D. *Madison.*
Ingalls Z. B.
Stevens Richard, Erieville *Nelson.*
McWilliams H. Peterboro
Smithfield.
Walrath & Colyer, Chittenango
Sullivan.
Van Valkenburgh Peter, Ch'ngo
Boardman & Harrison, do

Monroe County.

Hawkins John, North Chili *Chili.*
Anderson D. H. East Henrietta
Henrietta.
Wheeler B. West Henrietta
Woodrow B. Spencer's Basin
Ogden.
Lignean J. L. Parma Corner
Parma.
Howland G., Fairport *Perrington.*
McGuffie John, Churchville *Riga.*
Ermisse A. Ontario st. *Rochester.*
Killip W. I. N. St. Paul
McCullum Peter, 88 St. Paul
Brenin F. 17 Jackson
McLaughlin F. 19 Monroe
Hawksworth J. 118 Buffalo
Moore James, cor. State & Water
Garrett James, cor. Water & Mn.
Smith George, 106 do
Hogg William, 117 do
Cassedy Michael, 116 S. Sophia
Wilson C. G. 133 do
Jennings T. 92 Smith's Arcade
Kyle Robert, 144 State
Armstrong J. 186 do
Harrison H. 186 do
Daline S. *Rush.*

Beadle J. M. *Rush.*
Smith J. F. Main st. Brockport
Sweden.
Cotter T. do do
Veil J. O. 17 do do
Weyburn C. 15 do do
Coultis Wm. *Webster.*
Croft J. Scottsville *Wheatland.*
Dorus Daniel, Mumford

Montgomery County.

Near I. R. *Canajoharie.*
Putnam Peter
Burrill M. Ames
Gully J. B. Minaville *Florida.*
Catherward R. Port Jackson
William J. C. *Glen.*
Endor J. J.
Conyne Peter, Smithtown
Horning Alexander, Fultonville
Lynch P. do
Fox Leander, Fort Plain *Minden.*
Wagner Jeremiah, do
Dillenbach Wm. J. do
Hesler Lawrence. do
Fox Charles, do
Mayer Wm. H. do
Allen Joel, do
Bellington Henry, Fonda *Mohawk.*
Heras Benjamin, do
Leroy S. F. do
Cook B. Palatine Bridge *Palatine.*
Coppernale Elias, Stone Arabia
Vosburgh Joseph, do
Perrine Wm. *Root.*
Hart Jacob
Clemmons W.
Lampman G. H. *St. Johnsville.*
Hose David
Wagner V.
Wagner J.
Nellis Robert

Niagara County.

Leichtman Francis, Pekin
Cambria.
Phelan & Gordon *Lewiston.*
McDonald & Mayo
Pomeroy Asahel, Pekin
Thompson James E. *Lockport.*
Harrington James *Newfane.*
Jones ——
Olney Sylvester, Youngstown
Porter.
Bidleman S. Middleport *Royalton.*
Anthony Wm. Gasport
Hess Joseph *Somerset.*
Vannortwick N. B.
Warren Josiah *Wilson.*

Oneida County.

Bird W. *Camden.*
Phillips J.
Bailey A. Clinton *Kirkland.*
Hinman G. G. & C. H., Dominick st. *Rome.*
McPhee Wm. James st.
Gifford & Stantial, Waterville
Sangerfield.
Tapping I. Exchange Buildings
Utica.
Meacham & Farwell, 36 Genesee
Flanagan J. Devereux Block
Woodhull H. I. 142 Genesee
Jones J. W. 4 Seneca
Kuhn G. H. Fayette st.
Horlein J. G. do
Fowler R. Whitesboro *Whitestown.*

Onondaga County.

Smith E. R. *Geddes.*
Graff D. Genesee st. Syracuse
Salina.
Johnson W. G. do do
Hair C. James st. do
Babcock T. Salina st. do

Ontario County.

Shay John *Bristol.*
Peck Thomas

24

Burris —— *East Bloomfield.*
Rodney C. *Manchester.*
Darritie George
Addison & Draper *Phelps.*
Henry Wm.
Sholes James
Fox O. P. Honeoye *Richmond.*
Bean Wm. Geneva *Seneca.*
Hogarth J. S. do
Godfrey M. do
Bell A. do
Lazalere Jacob, Geneva

Orange County.

Benjamin N. Salisbury Mills
     Blooming Grove.
Cameron T. B. Washingtonville
Conklin W. H. *Chester.*
Winters C. Z.
Vail Wm. R.
Smith N. C.
Conklin James W. *Cornwall.*
Decker H. *Crawford.*
Jackson H. J. *Goshen.*
Smiley A.
Smith J. jr.
Saunderson J. H., Wells' Corners
     Minisink.
Gorden Z. G. West Town
Doty C. do
Elston E. R. Unionville
Howell D. T. & Co. Slate Hill
Kimbark Frederick *Montgomery.*
Smith David C.
Wood A. B. Walden
Millspaugh H. do
Mapes James, Monroe Works
     Monroe.
Hulse N.
Wiggins C. H. Otisville *Mt. Hope.*
M'Cornal M. I. do
Roe J. W.
Bogardus Abram A. Water st.
     Newburgh.
Rockaway Wm. Water st.
Chatterton S. L. 3d st.
Welling Oscar B. do
Barker Wm. New Hampton
     Wallkill.
King H. V. South Middletown
Wiggins G. O. do
Armstrong D.G. do
Randall R. F. *Warwick.*
Mable J.
Vandervoort J. W.
Wright W. A. Florida
Ackley A. A. Sugar Loaf

Orleans County.

Job H. B. Barre Centre *Barre.*
Huffman M. *Clarendon.*
Mansfield I. B.
Leach Asa W. *Kendall.*
Kendrick ——
Keyes E. H. Holley *Murray.*
Kittle A. B. Medina *Ridgeway.*
Soper I. do
Andrews ——, do
Scits ——, do
Morron H. G. Knowlesville
Clark C. do
Cane Wm. *Yates.*
Goffe J. J.
Anderson D A.
Brown N. G.
Leary Wm. Lyndonville
Porter A. D. do

Oswego County.

Reed E. S. *Albion.*
Byrns John F. *Hannibal.*
Draper John
Cooper J. *Hastings.*
Anderson W. R. Central Square
Willis W. & Co. do
Cooper Wm. *Mexico.*
Shuiter J. B.
Kilty H. J.
Nichols Job, Colosse
Cooler Daniel, do
Woodall J. *New Haven.*

Ashley Daniel D. *Orwell.*
Clark Sidney, 1st st. *Oswego.*
M'Avoy Peter, do
Little John, Empire Block, 1st st.
Smith Wm. M. do do
Abbot & Strong, do do
Cooley J. C. 1st st.
M'Elroy Geo. W. 6 Eagle Bl. do
Buckhart Wm. B. 1st st.
Mitchell Henry, Pulaski *Richland.*
Ramsdell O. L. do
June Wm. do
Phillips C. H. Phœnix *Schroeppel.*
Wright G. Hinmansville

Otsego County.

Smith W. P. *Burlington.*
Allen E. R.
Bishop J. Burlington Flats
Brazee D. L. *Butternuts.*
Little J.
Sharp J. *Cherry Valley.*
Gould A.
Nash H.
Bardin James W. *Edmeston.*
Brand James H.
Chapman John *Exeter.*
Smith C. T. *Hartwick.*
Freeland F
Merrill M.
Clark J. F. *Laurens.*
Barton P.
Lynch James J. *Middlefield.*
Westcott A. W *Milford.*
Branch W. H.
Rutherford Thomas *New Lisbon.*
Newman Samuel S. *Oneonta.*
M'Minn Charles
Evans David T.
Brazee J., Cooperstown *Otsego.*
Birge Delos L. do
Cooley R. do
Smith A. *Plainfield.*
Benedict Hiel E. *Unadilla.*
Benedict Hiram
Hunt —— *Westford.*
Nichols Henry *Worcester*

Putnam County.

Calhoun John C. *Carmel.*
Clogy G. O.
Brewer J., Farmer's Mills *Kent.*
Jacocks H., Cold Spring
     Phillipstown.

Queens County.

Howard E. *Flushing.*
Townsend R. W.
Sharp L. A. *Hempstead.*
Benton & Backus
Rider W. E.
Scott & Weeks
Baldwin Timothy, Milburn
Black Z. M. P. *Jamaica.*
Shipman H. *Newtown.*
Frost Edward, Roslyn
     North Hempstead.
Robbins Robt. L., Roslyn
Smith James W. do
Wooly Hobert S., Manhasset
Richardson Wm. *Oyster Bay.*
Backus Isaac
Remson John W. East Norwich
Campbell John, Jericho

Rensselaer County.

Cobb & Dorr, 164 River *Troy.*
Dickson John, 174 do
Randall & Leonard, 184 River
Campbell Wm. 264 do
M'Nevin Michael, 276 River
Merriam John F. & Son, 290 River
Richmond M. C. 298 do
Smith W. 300 do
Tillinghast P. D. 312 do
Miller Harry, 375 do
Hincer L. 361 do
Dunn Wm. 43 Grand Division
Raymond James, 6 1st
Brower Abraham, 96 1st

Curren James, 4 Washington sq.
     Troy
Rose & Hell, 17½ State
Wolf C. & Co. 41 Congress
Cornell James, 67 do
Haskell Peter S. 56 do
Burns J. 51 do
Jackson J. 99 do
Alien Benjamin, 144 do
Filer H. & Z. 27½ Ferry
Ashdown H. Ida Hill

Richmond County.

Alfring John, Tompkinsville
     Castleton.
O'Brien Wm. do
Smith G. do
Rossbach G do
Chute R., Port Richmond
     Northfield.
Bazer J. do
Edwards J. S. do
Hodson J., Stapleton *Southfield.*

Rockland County.

Vanderbilt A. S., Nyack
     Orangetown.
Blauvelt A. do
Fenton J. L. do
Hart Henry, Piermont
Dinan Wm. Spring Valley
Whitlaw James, do

St. Lawrence County.

Newcomb Wm. *Depeyster*
King —— *Edwards.*
Cushman M. *Gouverneur.*
Waid J.
Austin E.
Opir S. *Hammond.*
Best Thomas
Welch Robert
O'Brien Patrick
Montgomery John *Lisbon.*
Mea Thomas, Waddington
     Madrid.
Peacock John, do do
Martin James *Massena.*
Smith James
Farrell James *Morristown.*
Aston Robert
Conally James *Norfolk.*
Olmstead Barnes J. *Potsdam.*
Porter Matthew
Daley S. H. *Russell.*

Saratoga County.

Ward Benj. J. Greenfield Centre
     Greenfield.
Sessions Lyman C., Porter's Corners
Brooks J., Jamesville
Whitman J. *Saratoga.*
Curtis C.
Farley A.
Dewitt Thomas
Scofield James P.
     Saratoga Springs.
Lane Wm. H.
Shehan & Moriarty
Benedict Alfred *Stillwater*
Benedict Anson

Schenectady County.

Conant Wm. B. 100 State
     Schenectady.
Mix David, 86 State
Cahn David, 76 State
Clute F. N., State st.

Schoharie County.

Dorman D. D. *Blenheim.*
Vromer J. *Cobleskill.*
Schermerhorn John S.
Nethaway I.
Hempstead Nelson *Esperance.*
Hempstead James
Cramer J., Sloansville
Hazzard James *Gilboa.*

M'Bain James   *Middleburgh.*
Brown A.   *Schoharie.*
Farley John
Getter F.
Deyo J.
De Forrest L., Hyndsville *Seward.*
Willshaw John, Gallupville
      Wright.

Seneca County.

Harris Morgan   *Covert.*
Yakely & Buchanan   *Fayette.*
Gould A. M.   *Lodi.*
Miller George V.
Berry John   *Romulus.*

Steuben County.

Draper James   *Cohocton.*
Draper Salmon
Wample B. A., North Cohocton
Storrs Lewis B.   *Canisteo.*

Suffolk County.

Wilcox J., Patchogue *Brookhaven.*
Pearsell J.   *Huntington.*
Farre B., Northport
Brown Spafford, do
Betts John, do
Anderson James, Cold Springs
Junie Wm. Babylon
Wilson S. L. do
Brush Samuel, Comac
Hill William   *Riverhead.*
Halsey George
Edwards Daniel R.
Ruth Jacob   *Smithtown.*
Larry James   *Southampton.*

Sullivan County.

Osborn J. H. Phillipsport
      Mamakating.
Steevens Thos. Bloomingburgh
Bookstaver H. do
Jenkinson Joseph, Wurtsboro
Oakley R., Monticello *Thompson.*
Mapledoram G. do
Tidd H. do

Ulster County.

Van Buren P.   *Kingston.*
Hendrix Wm.
Post C., Rondout
Welch Wm. do
Denson G., High Falls *Marbletown.*
Ackerson F. do
Depuy Wm. Stone Ridge
Goetcheus David   *New Paltz.*
Decker John T.   *Rosendale.*
Felt Jacob   *Saugerties.*
Talcott E. C.   *Shawungunk.*
Scott L. Port Ben   *Wawarsing.*

Warren County.

Dunn J. L. Chestertown *Chester.*
Hotchkiss Wm. do
Hubbard & Peate, Glenn's Falls
      Queensbury.
Hamilton L. C. do
Williams Stephen, do
Wallace —— *Warrensburgh.*
Sentune J. C.
Smith J.

Washington County.

Clark Robert G.   *Argyle.*
Bidwell John
Sharp Cornelius
Ladd Hiram, North Argyle
Shields ——, do
Schermerhorn Alex., S. Argyle
Stackhouse Joseph   *Cambridge.*
Nobles A. S.
Edie Robertson,Cambridge Centre
Davenport T., N. Easton *Easton.*
Fox & Willard   *Fort Edward.*
Carswell D. S.
M'Intyre James
Kelley Thomas, Fort Miller

Hilson O., Battenville *Greenwich.*
Snow C. H. East Greenwich
Babcock Joseph, Lake
Burke Samuel, Galesville
Trapp Wm. North Greenwich
Osborn John   *Hampton.*
Kellogg O. D.
Ashley G., West Hebron *Hebron.*
Cary Albert, do
Acker John   *Kingsbury.*
Wilson H. S. Sandy Hill
Downs John, do
Culver James, do
Lee Stephen, do
Ferdon Jacob, do
Raymond G. A. do
Austin Abner   *Salem.*
Austin Orrin
Harrington Lewis
Bristoe Levi   *White Creek.*
Mosher H. D.
Hart Philip, White Creek Centre
Sharp A. Buskirk's Bridge
Towne E. North White Creek

Wayne County.

Kent George T.   *Lyons.*
M'Gowen E.
Stewart John   *Sodus.*
O'Keeffe Michael
Willer Jonas
Burnett C. & W., Alton
Clarey H. B., South Sodus
Freeman Franklin   *Walworth.*
Hislop ——   *Williamson.*
Griffin ——, Pultneyville
M'Lean ——   *Wolcott.*
Sheffer & Church

Westchester County.

Lockwood S. E.   *Bedford.*
Young A. Peekskill   *Courtlandt.*
Stevens R. Tarrytown *Greenburgh.*
Ayres J. E. do
Archer Thomas, Hastings
Mosier John M. Dobbs' Ferry
Keyser J. B.   *New Castle.*
Robinson I. P.   *New Rochelle.*
Barker S.
Atchinson J. A. Sing Sing
      Ossining.
Frisbee W. C. do
Kane D. do
Mack John   *Rye.*
Merritt C. B., Portchester
Wakely B. do
Merritt Alex. Y. do
Livingston James   *West Farms.*
Galloway J. S.

Wyoming County.

Starbird Samuel, Cowlesville
      Bennington.
Benedict E. M.   *Castile.*
Wing A. K.
Samson J.
Francis & Lyman   *China.*
Gledhitt S. Eagle Village *Eagle.*
De Clair Geo. do
Boland Wm   *Genesee Falls.*
Conway C. N.
Ryan Patrick
Whiteside R., Wyoming
      Middlebury.
Hedges S. do
Farmer J. B.   *Perry.*
Westlake W. J.
Walbridge John
Runyon H.   *Pike.*
M'Neal G.
Kenster John, Varysburgh
      Sheldon.
Jones Wm., Strykersville
Wilkins James   *Warsaw.*
Nicholson F.

Yates County.

Hazen H. H.   *Benton.*
Smith A., Belona
Backenstose Z., Belona

Nichols Asher   *Middlesex.*
Sprague ——, Milo Centre *Milo.*
Pierce D. C., Rushville   *Potter.*
Van Osdol James B., Rushville
Silvernail James, Potter Centre
Bander M., North Middlesex
Royce Simeon   *Starkey.*
Letts James M., Dundee
Broom Joseph, Rock Stream

Tailors & Drapers. (See also Tailors, also Clothiers.)

Albany County.

Freeman R. 481 Broadway *Albany.*
Harvey Jas. M. 468 Broadway
Sard Grange, 448 Broadway
Rolyea Peter, 446 Broadway
Newton R. N. 377 Broadway
Duncan & Jackson, 403 Broadway
Derby L. L. 373 Broadway
Shophard S. F. 313 Broadway
Brolly P. 32 Quay
Buchanan J. 196 Water
Muir W. O. 52 State
Carpenter & Kirk. 71 State
Sanders S. & Co. 21 S. Pearl
Shorn Wm. 13 Beaver
Statler John F. 5 N. Pearl
Slater F. H.   *Coeymans.*

Broome County.

Brown J. G.   *Windsor.*

Cayuga County.

Schenck S. 75 Genesee   *Auburn.*
Vananden H. A. 37 Genesee
Sherwood G. 111 Genesee
Keyes D. B. 121 Genesee
Kerman J. Weedsport   *Brutus.*
Gault O. K. & Z. W. Weedsport
Valmore J.   *Springport.*

Chautauque County.

Mason B. B. Jamestown *Ellicott.*
Butler & Westcott, do
Dimmie Jas. do
Platner Luther, do
Harrington Noah, do
Sherwood & La Due, Fredonia
      Pomfret.
Carlisle J. D. & J. H.   *Westfield.*

Chemung County.

Alexander S. S.   *Elmira.*
Davis L. & Brother
Holland David
Steele F. C.
Kane John A.
Butler & Doblin
Fish Chas.
Snell Jas. H.

Clinton County.

White John   *Plattsburgh.*

Columbia County.

Dimmick E.   *Hillsdale.*
Clark J. Warren st.   *Hudson.*
Dimmick T. Warren st
Armstrong Wm. Warren st.
Bachman & Miller, 325 Warren
Rockefeller A. 324 Warren
Lane H. W. 318 Warren

Cortland County.

Welch O. M.   *Cortland Village.*

Delaware County.

Orell J. Downsville   *Colchester.*

Duchess County.

Price & Meddaugh   *Amenia.*
O'Riley T. Wappinger's Falls
      Fishkill.
Hughson A. do
Miller H. do

Brown G. Matteawan   *Fishkill.*
Bogardus M. A. Fishkill Landing
Bogardus W. W.   do
Lester & Simonton,   do
Witham C. New Hackensack
M'Curdy J.   *Hyde Park.*
Caulkins J. G. & Co. North East
Centre   *North East.*
Spring & Goldberg, 240 Main
   Poughkeepsie.
Moses Robert, 236 Main
Fox S. 286 Main
Baker L. 317 Main
Odell J. E. 313 Main
Gemmill G. 255 Main
Smith C. D. 251 Main
Wilkenson J. 5 Market

Erie County.

Vlocher J. Williamsville *Amherst.*
Warmington Robert   *Black Rock.*
Stanbridge T.
Basket G.
Tucker & Rawson, 1 Merchant's
Hotel   *Buffalo.*
Weir Geo. jr. 7 U. S. Hotel Block,
Pearl st.
Woodhams Isaac, 12 Commercial
Cuttner & Doblin, Commercial &
104 Main
Fisher M. 13 Elm
Johnson Norman B. 261 Main
Kramer & Steyer, 12 East Seneca
Corner A. S. 272½ Main
Siebert C. 76 Eagle
Short Patrick, 5 Terrace
Kennett Thos. 182 Main
Hibbard & Torrence, 79 Lloyd
Noah N. W. 96 & 128 Main
Gietzsky J. M. 116 Main
Dodsworth ——, 106 Main
Short F. 5 Paulding's Exchange
Loebs J. L. 371 Main
Freidenburgh M. 196 Main
Nicholas Wm. 37 Main
Jennings J. H. 86 Main
Coats Wm. A. 127 Main
Satvin F. W. 147 Main
Dubois J. B. 149 Main
Healy Thos. 167 Main
Dumont Waldron, 169 Main
Jones H. P. 161 Main
Myers Isaac, 85 Main
Morgan John F. Akron *Newstead.*
Wilner W.   do

Essex County.

M'Cormick John   *Ticonderoga.*

Genesee County.

Hurlburt G. B.   *Batavia.*
Ferguson D.
Royce J. M.
Jordan J.
Allen John
Blessenger & Babcock
Smith Nathan
Morton John   *Bergen.*
Fay E.
Mann Wm.   *Oakfield.*
Matthews C.   *Cuba.*
Bronson Chas.

Greene County.

Story A. T. & Co.   *Catskill.*
Lynes Fred. S.

Herkimer County.

Fox Henry W   *Little Falls.*
Jones & Hines
Taylor Wm.
Nellis John
Sellor John
Brooks ——
Dockstader Adam   *Newport.*

Jefferson County.

Huntington & Russ   *Brownville.*

Kings County.

Moran M. 37 Atlantic *Brooklyn.*
Downes Wm. 69 Atlantic
Burns Edward, 112 Atlantic
Evans Wm. 126 Atlantic
Porter Jas. 144 Atlantic
Turner A. R. 64 Fulton
Burtis O. D. 56 Fulton
Powell S. S. 100 Fulton
Kirk Geo. 66 Henry
Luckey R. J. 196 Fulton
Perrine A. J. 166 Fulton
Hathaway Thos. 166 Fulton
Clark J. 164 Fulton
Whiting S. F. 132 Fulton
Whitney W. A. 114 Fulton
Stevens J. E. 254 Fulton
Patterson Wm. Montague Hall
Sharp Richard, 45 Fulton
Wireman John J. 57 Fulton
Bliss Wm. B. 69 Fulton
Solomon Saul, 73 Fulton
Carman T. D. 93 Fulton
Hunter T. D. 90 Fulton
Alcorn Wm. 78½ Main
Wright A. 96 Main
Quin John, 55 Myrtle Av.
Ayres Andrew, 25 Myrtle Av.
Smith M. D. 275 Fulton
Roach John C. 215 Fulton
Conner P. 213 Fulton
Park & Barr, 139 Fulton
Boues J. W. 325 Fulton
Furze Wm. 63 Hudson Av.
M'Caffry Jas. 192 York
Ceurlis & Edwards, 142 York
Forrester Wm. 136 Myrtle Av.
Price, Seaman & Co. Steuben st.
Knighton Wm. Green Point
   Bushwick.
Heiss P. & Co. 13 S. 7th
   Williamsburgh.
Wiles John, 123 Ewing
Meeks Wm. 103 Grand
Hirst Thos. 109 Grand
Suss Chas. & Co. 16 Grand
Titus John, 230 1st

Livingston County.

Brockway S.   *Dansville.*
Hassla & Maus
Boon & Thompson
Palims E. S.
Leach & Mercer   *Geneseo.*
Howes William
Patterson R. W.

Madison County.

Greenland William & Son
   Cazenovia.
Spear Martin
Ryan John
Blair & Warfield

Monroe County.

Downes E. West Mendon *Mendon.*
Burrows J.   do
Ryan Patrick, 198 Buffalo
   Rochester.
Talmadge J. A. 126 do
Cooling Martin, 70 do
Cornwall Amos, 5 Bridge
Kavanagh Joseph, 14 Main
Wille & Britenstool, 3 do
Clarkson George G. 7 Arcade
Byington George, 16 Arcade Hall
Henderson James, 11 do
Armitage W. J. 17 Reynolds' Arcade
Smith & Waterman, 41 Exchange
Stoddard S. B. 74 State
Smith H. N. 30 Main, Brockport
   Sweden.
Minot Charles, 13 Main, Brockport

Montgomery County.

Scott Alexander   *Amsterdam.*
Wooley William

Killin C. H. S.   *Amsterdam.*
Baldwin O. S.
Filmer F.   *Canajoharie.*
Brown Charles H.
Van Alstine G. P.

New York County.

Ackerman & Mixer, 106 Broadway
   New York.
Adams John, 412 Greenwich
Adler Frederick. 289 Bowery and
136 Av. C
Edward B. 174 Varick
Ahrens Frederick, 32½ Ann
Alexander Abraham, 16 Whitehall
Ambler J. 2 2d Av.
Anderson George, 44 Duane
Anderson H. 108 12th
Anderson James, 443 Greenwich
Appleton Robert, 296 Division
Armstrong Robert, 369 6th Av.
Arnoux A. & G. A. 145 Fulton
Ascher Solomon, 34 Chrystie
Asheld Thomas, 277 6th
Asser John, 162 Leonard
Atkinson A. A. 196 Beekman
Baatz Peter, 123 Varick
Bach Henry, 122 Church
Baird Robert. 73 W. 18th
Baker G. W. 345 Broome
Barguet L. W. & B. 126 Warren
Barnett Peter, 99 Greenwich Av.
Barry James T. 300½ Bowery
Bartley Stephen, 96 3d Av.
Bauer George, 7 Nassau
Beanes Henry P. 152 Fulton
Beaumont Edmond B. 203 B'dway
Beauregard Daniel, 289 do
Beck George L. 39 Elm
Becker Joseph, 84 Broadway
Beers David B. 208½ Grand
Beggs Robert, 451 Broadway
Bell & Groyn, 116 Fulton
Bell Joseph, 164 Allen
Bellamy John, 3 Park row
Benjamin Anthony, 39 Troy
Bergen James, 67 Forsyth
Bernstein Isaac, 96 Pitt
Bertram George M. 117 Grand
Bouchel George, 6 City Hall place
Bisiste F. 202 Broadway
Black Joseph, 316 Grand
Blackwell J. P. 179 Broadway
Blake Harriet M. 309 Greenwich
Bloomenbaum E. 580 Grand
Blott B., W. 28th st.
Boegler Michael, 41½ Oak
Boggy Frank, 664 4th
Bonay George, 3 Murray
Bonton E. 23 Bowery
Borger John, 73 Duane
Botmann John H. 472 Hudson
Bouton Benjamin C. 15 Maiden la.
Bouton Edwin, 47 Houston
Bradshaw John, 190 Nassau
Brennan Edward, 54 4th Av.
Britten & Parselle, 96 Fulton and
Bleecker cor. Mott
Brooks Henry, 43 West Broadway
Brooks E. S. 31 Park row
Brown Bernard, rear 134 Mott
Brown John, 172 Bleecker
Brown & Powers, 340 Broadway
Bryant William C. 123 Broadway
Bromm Christian, 70 Sullivan
Brundage James H. 164 Broadway
Buckman Louis, 63 Lewis
Bueno Francisco, 79 Chambers
Buess J. 146 Broadway
Burns Thomas, 670 Water
Bushman Frederick, 96 Browne
Busman Henry, 504 Pearl
Butler Henry J. 459 Greenwich
Butterfield William H. 222 Canal
Bysher Wm. F 417 Pearl
Caffry George W. 290 Hudson
Caffry James, 14 Walker
Cales Theodore, 306 Broadway
Cammeron John, 151 3d Av.
Cameron J. 7 1st
Campbell George, 139 Spring

Campbell Robert, 299 Madison
New York.
Canter A. 12 Elm
Cane M. 9th Av.
Cantillion Dennis, 116 Nassau
Cantwell Robert, 273 Pearl
Carroll Michael, 207 Centre
Chald James, 230 West 16th
Chadeayne A. 80½ Bowery
Chambers Miles, 406 Pearl
Cavanagh Peter, 136 9th Av.
Chichester Alonzo, 226 G'wich
Chichester F. H. 32 Maiden la.
Church William T. 48 Nassau
Clark James A. 643 Broadway
Clarke George B. 116 William
Clarke Samuel, 201 Bleecker
Clarkson George N. 62 Cortlandt
Clock & Miller, 54 Fulton
Close Jos. B. & Co. 12 Bowery
Cogswell Henry, 150 8th Av.
Cohen Hyam, 255 William
Coleman Hiram, 324 Spring
Collins & Co. 1 Rivington
Collins James, 207 Fulton
Colt Amos M. 29 Attorney
Conklin Philip F. 406 Hudson
Conklin W. L. 5 Bowery
Conley John, 42 Catharine
Conway Michael, 142 Fulton
Coon Jacob I. 56½ Carmine
Cooper Richard, 26 Varick
Corbet Alex. 137 Division
Cordell Collin M. 5½ Park pl.
Corlett Richard, 448½ Grand
Cornwell John D. 202 Grand
Corres & Co. 360 Broadway
Cortissoss Abraham, 6 Murray
Cotterell Denis, 131 West B'way
Coulter Henry, 77 Greenwich
Coyle Francis, 75 West 17th
Cox Charles, 36 Broadway
Cox A. 49½ Beekman
Craus & Besehoten, 67 Cortlandt
Craigie James, 136 Nassau
Crawford Charles T. 257 Bowery
Croney James H. 790 Broadway
Crothers John, 140 Orange
Crothers John, 282 Water
Culyer Louis, 169 Mulberry
Cummings James, 140½ Bowery
Cummings William, 367½ H'ston
Curran James, 375 Pearl
Daily James, 173 Broadway
Dall William, 6 Clarkson
Dalton Francis, 140 9th Av.
Dalous Joseph, 333 Broadway
Damm Christopher, 576 4th
Dankel Cornelius, 111½ Green'h
Dapper M. 227 Broome
Dargavel Thomas, 397 Hudson
Darley John, 146 Broadway
Davenport & Gardiner, 9 John
Davis Charles, 7 City Hall square
Davis Edward, 221 3d
Dayton C. W. & A. C. 11 John
Deckelmann Geo. 170 W. Broad'y
Deittering Frederick W. 20 New
Delmas & Co. 290 Broadway
De Long Lemuel, 177 Houston
Denjougbe Peter, 5 Dey
Denyse Ruliff V. N. 440 Hudson
Depierris V. B. & Co. 279 Broad'y
Derby, Freeman & Co. 12 Park pl.
De Yong Bernard, 88 Murray
Diesenthaler & Schafers, 196 6th
Av.
Dinon J. 192 Varick
Disch C. 31st near 8th Av.
Dischinger Lewis, 60 Av. A
Divvins John, 24 Elizabeth
Deokstader B. 96 8th Av.
Dodimead S. & Son, 501 Pearl
Deina Peter, 130 Nassau
Dolly Martin, 515 Washington
Dolsan William, 14 Bowery
Donnelly John, 123 Fulton
Donnelly Peter, 89 Wall
Denahoe Moses K. 96 Roosevelt
Donovan William, 21 West
Doris Cornelius, 628 Hudson
Dougherty John, 162 W. 16th

Dougherty & Pearson, 9 Astor
House
New York.
Dowding George, 42 Henry
Dowell M. A. 305 Bleecker
Doyle John, 127 4th Av.
Doyle M. 399 10th
Drayton Paul, 144 Centre
Drummond Peter, Harlem
Dubois Isaac, jr. 296 Grand
Dubois John, 357 Broadway
Duhm Martin, 27 Thomas
Duncan John, 15 Bridge
Dunn Richard, 7 Pell
Durando Stephen P. 155 6th Av.
Durnin Thomas, 73 Orange
Durall William S. 106 Fulton & 9
Cherry
Eales John, 829 Broadway
Edgerton Abel T. 48 Fulton
Edmonds Richard, 191 Greene
Edwards George W. 44 Av D
Eichterstreiner A. 228 Cherry
Eigler John, 43 Av. A
Eiseman Henry, 243 Centre
Elliott Andrew, 537 Washington
Elsas Joel, 19 Orange
Emddon Michael, 271 2d
Emery & Colman, 40 Fulton
Engel Anton, 114 Spring
Enste & Muler, 131 Chambers
Esler Edward, 231 8th Av.
Evans E. 70 & 72 Fulton
Evers Michael, 23½ Spruce
Farnham George W. 19 Park pl
Farrington Edgar M. 59 William
Faulkner J. C. & Son, 60 Fulton
Faytrom ——, 695 Broadway
Feldmann John G. W. 32 Hudson
Feltheim Joseph, 130 Essex
Felt & Stockbridge, 29 John
Ferber Peter, 313 Houston
Ferguson Robert J. 35 Av. C
Ferris John, 225 Varick
Finch Amos, 906 Greenwich
Finley Thomas, 59 Spring
Fischer George, 45 Greenwich
Fisher Henry W. 393 Broome
Fitzgerald Garret, 1 Av. D
Foley James, 225 W. 16th
Folwell Charles E. 94½ Fulton
Fournon Edward, 93 Cedar
Fox Alex. 62 Cortlandt
Fox Edward, 202 Broadway
Fox Geo. F. 85 Chambers
Fox & 64½ Bowery & 29 Chatham
Francis James L. 315 Bowery
Francis, Ynmand & Becker, 84
Broadway
Frank Henry, 189 Rivington
Frank J. A. 10th Av. & 26th st.
Frank Martin, 576 4th
Franklin & Wolf, 251 Canal
Frissing Lembert, 60 John
Fritter Frederick, 193 Mott
Gabel Nicholas, 103 W. 16th
Gade William, 26 New
Gallagher James, 87 Cedar
Gattmann Leonard, 59 Forsyth
Gavitt Amos T. 237 Greenwich
Gerhart Louis, 570 4th
Gibb George, rear 147 Orange
Gibbons John, 418 West
Giere Earnest, 30 Elm
Giglet John, 214 Church
Goepferrich Martin, 72 Walnut
Goettelmen George, 570 4th
Goldschmidt Jacob, 25 Rector
Goldstein, Brother & Co. 9 Bat-
tery place
Golley John, 157 Mott
Goodman John K. 23 John
Goodwin & M'Govern, 126 Nassau
Gordon Peter, 233 8th
Goubelmaun R. 17 Beekman
Gould H. A. & Co. 221 W'hington
Graham Robert, 72 Thompson
Gray Samuel A. 69 4th Av.
Gray & More, 129 Chambers
Gregory Ira W. 245 Grand
Grimm Henry, 111 John
Grimm Henry, 125 Liberty
Grisler George, 52 Walnut

Griswold Elias W. 231 Greenwich
New York.
Gross Charles G. 162½ Bowery
Grossman Moses, 206 Rivington
Grubb George, 7 West Broadway
Gueringer & Lataple, 152 Broad-
way
Guider Patrick, 87 Crosby
Guinand Francis, 84 Broadway
Gurnee Jonas, 13 Wall
Gursley W. B. 331 Broadway
Hadden E. & Co. 255½ Broadway
Haggerty John, 210 Centre
Haight Charles G. 334 Grand
Haight Elisha, 82 Bowery
Hall C. 90 Vesey
Halstead Joseph, 69½ Forsyth
Hamald James P. 154 Greenwich
Hannah & Jones, 250 Canal
Hamilton & Simons, 170 Broadway
Hand James, 250 Canal
Hanna J. A. 495 Washington
Hank John, 450 Washington
Hanson Joseph G. 149 Canal
Harbut & Cooper, 272½ Bowery
Harraday John, 1 Barclay
Harris John, 68½ Bowery
Harris John, 19 West
Harris C. N. 497 Houston
Harris J. 2 Catharine
Harrison George, 476 Pearl
Hart Peter, 2½ 3d Av.
Hascy Alonzo, 156 Fulton
Hassmann Adam, 18 Rector
Hatfield Sampson, 164 Broadway
Haviland John, 167 Broadway
Hawkins J. 45 Lispenard
Hays John, 265 Hudson
Hayden Laurence, 49 Rutgers
Healy John, 112 Church
Hearn William M. 139 9th Av.
Heckle Robert, 257 Broadway
Heckmann Frederick, 13 Thomas
Heidelberger Aaron, 51 Av. C
Hell Frederick, 97 Leonard
Heiss Carsten, 3 Pike
Helmes Bernard, 53 6th Av.
Henderson James, 96 Leonard
Hendricks John, 195½ Bowery
Henely John, 97 West Broadway
Hennill Fred'k. 234 and 236 Pearl
Henry Philip & Son, 135 Broadway
Herbeck Charles, 108 W. Broad-
way
Hern Nathan, 280 Grand
Herlehy Maurice, 24 Ann
Hermann John, 46 1st Av.
Hernes T. 160 2d
Herschberger Henry, 167 Lewis
Herwick Charles J. W. 123 Canal
Hewit & Coulson, 148 William
Heyl Daniel, 15 Forsyth
Hicks Theobald, 564 4th
Higgs Joseph, 68 Beekman
Hindhaugh William, 1 Vesey
Hingston Edward, 36 Maiden lane
Hingston Edward, 142 Centre
Hirsch Moses, 277 2d
Hitchens John, 312 9th
Hitchens John, 152 9th.
Hoelzle Henry L. 176 8th Av.
Holland Martin, 339 Washington
Holland Nicholas, 70 Suffolk
Hollermann I. H. 97 4th Av.
Holmes Thomas, 241 Walker
Hollywood Patrick, 218 Cherry
Holt Alfred F. 156 Cherry
Holt H. 35 Greenwich Av.
Honig J. 42 Stanton
Hood George A. 69 Fulton
Hopkins Edwin R. 187 Walker
Hopkins William, 3½ 9th
Hora J. K. & Co. 60½ Nassau
Horndhell & Weithart, 296 Grand
Hotmer Bernard H. 51 Pearl
Houlet & Gumbel, 32 Vestry
Housman George, 120 W. 19th
Hover Albert, 5 Vesey
Howard H. 62 John
Howlett Geo. 76 University place
Hoyt Henry N. 293 Pearl
Hoyt Geo. A. & Co. 22 Bowery

Hoyt & Knight, 46 Fulton

New York.

Huber John, 49 Av. A
Hudson & Perry, 616 Broadway
Hull Isaac P. 13 Liberty
Hume Alexander, 90 6th Av.
Humphreys J. F. & E. B. 175 Broadway
Hunolt George, 18 Madison
Husted Lawrence V. 70 Barclay & 217 Greenwich
Hutchins J. 312 9th
Hutchinson Wm. 8th Av.
Ixelheimer Isaac, 64 Willet
Ioerg Charles, 254 William
Israel Jacob, 7 Battery place
Jacobs W. H. 3 Maiden lane
Jacobs J. 288 Bowery
Jarvis Nelson, 120 Bleecker
Jeffries George C. 106 Bowery
Jenkins John. 51 Liberty
Jenkins J. 11 3d Av.
Jennings W. T. & Co. 231 B'way
Jinnings Thomas L. 167 Church
Johnston Alexander, 115½ Grand
Johnston W. 115 West Broadway
Johnston Robert, 87 Cedar
Jones Franklin L. 154 Hester
Jones Rowland, 44½ 9th Av.
Jones & Hansbergh. 137 William
Jordan Frederick, 80 James
Jordan Hugh, 17 Oak
Joseph Aaron. 14 & 16 Orange
Joyce Samuel, 378 Broadway
Juillet & Menetrier, 404 Broadway
Kaeding Charles, 3 South William
Kaiser David, 162 2d
Karsch John, 8th Av.
Kavanah Peter, 136 8th Av.
Keughran Thomas, 212 Mulberry
Keiley Philip, 11 Av. D
Kelly Luke, 273 Hudson
Kenney J. 205 3d
Kenney & Vail, 11 Greenwich Av.
Kerrigan Michael, 3 Walnut
Kirkpatrick James, 23 Madison
Kirk E. 66 Broome
Kirwan Thomas, 34 Elizabeth
Kirri & Co. 10 Centre
Kleiner Jacob, 206 Rivington
Kling Henry, 456 Grand
Knapp Wm. H. 241 Bleecker
Knight Chas. J. 46 Fulton
Knight & Gunn, 115 Chambers
Knock & Childs, 172 Broadway
Koch & Sigmann, 8th Av.
Kohler John, 506 Water
Kolb Joseph, 17 College pl.
Kopperman Wm. 95 Duane
Kracker A. 113 Elm
Kraemer & Messenkopf, 193 William
Kraft John F. 531 Pearl
Krewolf C. 9th Av. b. 24th & 25th
Krone Frederick, 50 Hudson
Kruizer Joseph, 43 Cortlandt
Kuhm Thos. B. 389 Hudson
Laibla Michael, 186 2d
L'Amie James, 59 Chambers
Lander Konrad, 218 6th Av.
Landgrebe Wm. 685 Broadway
Lane Daniel E. 532 Hudson
Lane James, 436 Broadway
Lane P. 7th Av.
Laug Morris, 153 Chrystie
Langhorst August, 80½ Eldridge
Lanphear Samuel, 46 3d Av.
Lanphier Jeremiah C. 203 Broadway
Lapine James, 63 Chambers
Leacheimer Isaac, 9 Frankfort
Laverty Moore, 79 9th Av.
Leddy B. 180 Prince
Lee H. P. 125 Christopher
Lee Joseph, 171 Fulton
Lee Joseph, 3 Nassau
Leipsegar Haeman, 15 Peck sl.
Laitheusz George, 67 Centre
Lennon Robert, 15 Reade
Leonard Wm. 186 Wooster
Leonard & Wendt, 29 Gold
Lester Charles, 88 University pl.

Leurugston H. 96 Beaver

New York.

Levy Joseph, 398 10th
Lewis John E. 184 Church
Lippiatt L. 212 Canal
Lippincott Thomas, 384 Broadway
Little James, 406 Broadway
Lockwood Gershum, 257 Broadway
Lockwood G. E. 8 John
Lockwood W.H. 257 Broadway
Lorenston J. 211 Stanton
Lorentz Samuel, 172 Bowery
Lounsbury Samuel, 27 John
Lowy Bernard, 87 Delancy
Lucas H. A. 8 John
Lutz Andrew, 166 9d
Lyons George, 306 Pearl
M'Cabe T. 333 3d Av.
M'Cay Richard, 184½ Bowery
M'Culley J. P. 97 9th Av.
M'Dowell Andrew, 307 Bleecker
M'Farlan Donald, 94 Vandam
M'Gee Thomas, 39½ Washington
M'Ginn Patrick, 128 Nassau
M'Grury T. & I. 2 University pl.
M'Guire M. N. 59 E. 14th
M'Evoy John F. & Timothy, 362 Grand
M'Ilhargy C. 530 Greenwich
M'Kechnie John, 616 Greenwich
M'Kenna C. M. Warren c. Church
M'Kenna Michael, 130½ Laurens
M'Key James, 129 Duane
M'Kinley John, 186 N. William
M'Lane Wm. 174 W. Broadway
M'Lean H. 8th Av.
M'Leish Allen, 32 9th Av.
M'Leod Roderick, 1 Cortlandt
M'Murtrie David, 782 Washington
M'Niff John, 106 8th Av.
M'Quade D. 779 Washington
M'Ready Wm. P. 71 Nassau
M'Voy Arthur P. 135 Orange
Magill James, 336 Grand
Malone Wm. 87 Cedar
Mandelbaum John, 82 Lewis
Mann Michael, 56 Oliver
Markley & Trego, 196 Greenwich
Marten Francis. 61 Attorney
Marten Jacob, 178 2d
Massabo A. 438½ Broadway
Mather Wm. L. 306 2d
Maxwell A. 144 Christopher
Maxwell John, 87 Cedar
Maxwell Wm. A. 193 Chatham
Mealey Peter, 106 Mulberry
Meara M 252 Washington
Meeker Charles W. 167 Broad'y
Melethar J. 129 Cherry
Mennot George, 26 Reade
Merschoff Theodore, 27 Ann
Meyers Alexander S. 346 Bowery
Meyer M. 214 Rivington
Mier Charles, 67 Centre
Milledge Jacob, 321 Spring
Miller Frederick, 4 City Hall pl.
Mills Wm. 399 Grand
Milne Wm. D. 9 3d Av.
Miner Edward W. 611½ Hudson
Minzesheimer Emanuel, 220½ 5th
Mitchell John, 203 Centre
Moffat John, 69 Market
Mohr John L. 164 6th Av.
Molle Hyppolite, 17 Stone
Monell Walter J. 94½ Fulton
Mooney Daniel, 245 Canal
Moore David, 191 3d Av.
Moore Henry, 673 Broadway
Moore James, 413 Hudson
Moore James, 194 Walker
Moore J. A. 109 8th Av.
Moore Thomas, 409 Grand
Morey George, 301 Madison
Morris E. R. 106 Bowery
Moseman John C. 15 North Wm.
Moseman Nash, 189 Chatham
Moss Benjamin A. 715 Washington
Moss Henry, 60 Nassau
Muir Joseph, 11 John
Mulligan P. 155 Pearl
Mulvany Patrick H. 14 Pine

Murlis Robert, 411 Broadway

New York.

Murphy Daniel, 171 Chambers
Murphy Edward. 222 1st Av.
Murphy John, 122 Nassau
Murray John, 19 Carmine
Murray Patrick, 30 Centre
Murray T. 228 Wooster
Murthe Bernard, 187 Av. C
Neuville Marks, 189 Delancy
Newman Ignoltz. 79 Greenwich
Nistle Thomas, 179 3d Av.
Noah Joseph, 67 Ann
Noe Benjamin N. 506 Broadway
Noe John C. 8 Astor House & 115 Bleecker
Nystrom Ernest, 379 6th Av.
O'Connor Thomas, 141 Madison
Gelze John, 552 4th
Oliver Sophia, 281 6th Av.
Olman A. 173 7th
Olsen E. J. 74 Bowery
Olt Henry, 35 Greenwich Av.
O'Neil Denis, 666 Water and rear 419 Cherry
O'Neil Joseph, 375 Cherry
Osborn H. P. & Brother, 476 Grand
Osborn William W. 278 Grand
O'Shannessy John, 31 Cortlandt
Ostear Philip, 49 Walnut
Owen Daniel, 354 Grand
Owen J. 30 Hubert
Ox George, 106 Delancy
Papatronesh Christian, 202 William
Papst Martin, 136 Stanton
Paterson Peter H. 26 Crosby
Patrick Alexander, 118 Elizabeth
Patrick Alexander, 11 Albany
Paulson Leonard, 14 Broadway
Payntar J. G. & Co. 203 Greenwich
Peck E. & E. 74 Chatham
Peck William C. 143 Hester
Pelton Frederick S. 432 Greenwich
Philips John D. 3 Murray
Pillath J. C. & Co. 7th Av.
Pinckney Isaac L. 176 Bowery
Pinkney William, 170 Broadway
Pinner Bernhard, 290½ Grand
Pinner Samuel, 236 Grand
Plant James. 113 Hudson
Pollery William, 327 3d Av.
Porter Augustus D. 348 Broad'w'y
Post Abraham J. 86 9th Av.
Post Peter J. 111 9th Av.
Pottebaum Herman, 107 Walker
Potter Ellis A. 91½ Canal
Potter Joseph, 156 Canal
Powell William R. 70 Liberty
Praslow Michael, 366 Grand
Price J. D. 80 Nassau
Prindle E. E. 12 John
Pringle James, 617½ Hudson
Prior Hudson L. 392½ Houston
Pullen George, 341 Bleecker
Raber Wens, 46 Av. A
Rae & Scofield, 24 Bowery
Ready William, 421 3d Av.
Reeve Samuel, 86 Division
Reckard S. B. 49 Maiden lane
Reichmann Raphael, 279 2d
Reily Peter, 236 E. 13th
Richards James, 256 Canal
Riley Charles. 76 Reade
Riley Henry C. 247 Broadway
Reilly J. 292 Av. A
Robert Sebastian, 60 Reade
Roberts Daniel A. 844 Broadway
Roberts John, 92 Warren
Roberts Thomas, 87 Cedar
Roberts William H. 200 Wooster
Rodh David, 200 Canal
Rogers F. L. 76 Fulton
Rohdt William, 167 Washington
Roffman S. & A. 296 Water
Rosenbaum & Kaufman, 238 Delancy
Rohr J. G. 260 Canal
Rolee Herman, 208 Division
Rosefeld S. 39 4th Av.
Rotacher Reuben M. 566 Grand
Roth Andrew, 86 Sullivan
Roth Geo. M. 7th Av.

Rothschild Simon, 210½ Grand
    New York.
Rourke D. O. 20 Elm
Rouse Richard W. 92 Church
Roy Peter, 476 Greenwich
Rushin Michael, 35 Day
Ryan John, rear 140 Mulberry
Ryley William, 96 Delancy
St. John Milton, 84 Broadway
St. John, Raymond & Co. 167
    Broadway
Sampson Moses, 97 Division
Samuels J. 66 Bowery
Sanford Brothers, 127 Fulton
Schachtel Adam, 133 Clinton
Schachtel Amor. 81½ Broome
Schlandorf Simon, 61 Albany
Schilling Charles, 115 Willett
Schmidt Philip W. 193 William
Schneider Henry, 199½ Division
Schnell Frederick, 160 Bowery
Scholl John, 244 6th Av.
Scholt Charles, 66 Wooster
Schreiner Joseph, 180 2d
Schurck Morritz, 101 Liberty
Schwartz Joseph. 265½ 2d
Schwartz Louis, 559 Grand
Scully Edward, 37 Pearl
See Henry P. 125 Christopher
Seidel & Couse, 61 Bleecker
Seitzinger William, 78 Vesey
Senfert John, 407 Broome
Seyms Cosby F. 60 Nassau
Shanessey John, 31 Cortland
Sherwood Bishop A. 209 Walker
Shepard James, 38 Maiden lane
Shrigley George, 37 Cedar
Silberstone Simon, 52 Orange
Sill Leonard, 138 Stanton
Sillecks E. D. C. & L. W. 66 & 68
    Fulton
Simmons Richard A. 16 W. B'way
Simon Henry, 192 Delancy
Skidmore J. H. 151 Spring
Sloan Isabella, 27 Thompson
Smith Alexander, 39 Beekman
Smith Alfred C. 2 William
Smith Amos, 85 Liberty
Smith Daniel P. 102 Fulton
Smith Frederick, 16 Walnut
Smith George, 230½ Bowery
Smith Heary, 175½ Division
Smith Richard, 231 Greenwich
Smith Thomas, 26 Clark
Smith William, 176 William
Smith & Michaels, 725 Broadway
Sneider Henry, 570 4th
Soldin Benj. 306 Grand
Souder Jos. 5 Pike
Spohr John F. 69 Attorney
Springman Anthony, 108 Delancy
Springsteen Wm. H. 134 Christo-
    pher
Staats John, 162 Fulton
Stalker Jos. 64 John
Stanley W. J. 42 Water
Staub Jos. 246 William
Stein Geo. A. 19 1st Av.
Stein Jacob, 207 Mott
Steffens Heinrick, 128 Cedar
Steen Geo. H. 19 1st Av.
Steinhauer Andreas, 206 Walker
Stinemets William H. 173 Broad-
    way
Stevens John, 426 Hudson
Stevenson Geo. 333 6th Av.
Stewart Catharine, 126 Wooster
Straus Abraham, 96 Essex
Straus H. I. 18½ Rivington
Strube Henry A. 56½ Bond
Stugard Valentine, 65 Laurens
Stull Geo. R. 36 Madison
Sufert John, 407 Broome
Sullivan Cornelius, 125 Broad
Sumner Jehn, 34th st. & 9th Av.
Sutton & Vanderbilt, 418 Broad-
    way
Taisig Edward, 231 Spring
Taylor Geo. 111½ Greenwich
Teets Ralph, 62 Fulton
Thompson R. 113 Prince

Thompson A. Harlem *New York.*
Thompson Alfred, 177 Houston
Thompson Benj. M. 223½ Bowery
Thorne & Owen, 414 Broadway
Tierney John R. 9 Henry
Tierney Patrick, 132 Mulberry
Tilley Wm. L. 42 John
Tobias D. 544 Grand
Tomme Amile, 45 Dey
Tompkins F. 286 2d Av.
Tousey & Dickson, 168 Broadway
Tracy Patrick, rear 5 Walnut
Traugott John & Co. 170 Canal
Tremper Robert B. 164 Clinton
Tryon E. W. & Co. 237 Broadway
Tucker D. N. 28 John
Ufferheide Carle, 170½ Walker
Underwood Geo. W. 344 Bowery
Vail H. C. & Gamble, 221 Centre
Van Amburgh Wm. R. 364 Green-
    wich
Vanderbilt Jacob, 212 Canal
Vanderbilt Wm. S. 419 Broadway
Van Pelt A. H. 4 Liberty place
Van Pelt Daniel, 34 6th Av.
Van Saun A. 301 Hudson
Van Valer Wm. H. 455½ Hudson
Van Voorhis J. 34 W. Broadway
Vaughn Thos. 137½ Cherry
Veith Leopold, 106 4th Av.
Vienot Fred. 42 Anthony
Vonderhale Wm. 12 Thomas
Voss Andrew, 41 Cliff
Waddington W. Church st.
Wagener John A. 296½ Bleecker
Wales Wm. 18 Centre
Wallace Chas. J. 156 Broadway
Welling S. U. 330 8th Av.
Walter John F. 267 Broadway
Walter & Weidenfeld, 267 B'way
Ward Stephen, 110 Mott
Ware John P. 192 Chatham
Wash Marks, 125 Delancy
Wasson J. C. 181 Broadway
Waters Dominick, 127 Orange
Watson James C. 181 Broadway
Watson Wm. H. 90 Bowery
Weidenfeld J. 290 Broadway
Weinrich John W. 85 Greenwich
Weinschenk Jacob, 269 2d
Welp Frederick, 15 Chambers
Wendling John, 44 1st Av.
Wendling Martin, 197 William
Westcott J. R. 62 Fulton
Weyman E. H. & Co.20 Malden la.
Wheeler Alfred, 4 Cortlandt
White Mary E. 27 Broome
White & Underhill, 118 William
Whitney Abijah, 346 Broadway
Wiley T. jr. & Co. 713 Greenwich
Wilhelm Theodore, 63 Fulton
Wilkins Isaac, 2 Pine
Wilkins Lemuel, 412 Broadway
Willey C. 1 Chatham square
William Thomas P. & Stephen G.
    170 Broadway
Williams Asa S. 94 Nassau
Williamson C. D. 96 Hudson
Willis & Saxton, 173 Broadway
Wilkinson Samuel, 158 Duane
Willmas Henry, 129 3d
Wilson & Regan, 151½ Bowery
Wilzinski Julius, 97 W. Broadway
Wilzinski Samuel, 93 Canal
Wissert Joseph, 53 Vesey
Witherspoon J. 131 Wooster
Wolbach Samuel, 203 Houston
Wolf James, 19 Laurens
Wolfe William, 40 Walnut
Wolfenstein J. & Brothers, 182
    Chatham
Wood John, 111 3d Av.
Woods Jonas, 16 Lewis
Wooley Timothy C. 370 Pearl
Wulman Wolf, 226 5th
Wumnest Conrad, 14 Mulberry
Wyant S. & G. 36 W. Broadway
Wyman & Derby, 235 Broadway
Youngs Sydney B. 144 Canal
Yung Frederick, 114 Houston
Zable Frederick, 138 Greenwich
    Av.

Niagara County.
Ballard & Thompson *Lockport.*
Place George S.
Few W. & A.
Hows I. S.
Craine J. C.
Allen A. W. *Niagara Falls.*
Harrison George

Oneida County.
Veazie H., Dominick st. *Rome.*
Walker & Chappell, do
Moss N. W., Waterville
    Sangerfield.
Lyon Z. & P. 96 Genesee *Utica.*
Manchester, Penny & Co. 102 Ge-
    nesee

Onondaga County.
Wilson W. A., Baldwinsville
    Lysander
Pierce & Wilkins, do
Agnew H., Salina st. Syracuse
    Salina.
Morris D. J., Clinton square
Smith & Baker *Skaneateles.*

Ontario County.
Wyville William *Canandaigua.*
Shafer Daniel
Woodward R. S.
Perhamus John
Mary Philip
Buxton John W
Berryhill Andrew
Buhre F.
M'Loud Hubbard *Phelps.*
Judson & Savage, Geneva *Seneca.*
Taylor Samuel, do
Murray R. E. do
Altman A. do
West George N. *Victor.*

Orange County.
Merritt Thomas B. *Cornwall.*
Mills Edward
Coleman T, N., Port Jervis
    Deer Park.
Lee P. do
Caskey H. & J. do
Sayer G. M. *Goshen.*
Kemp R. D. (clothing) 61 Water
    Newburgh.
Lawson Andrew, cor. Water & 2d
Lawson James T. 48 Water
Niven D. G. 3d st.
Tryon Geo., South Middletown
    Wallkill.
Gale B. C. do
Vandervoort J. W. *Warwick.*

Orleans County.
Smith Charles, Albion *Barre.*
Phillips E. do
Harrington C. A. & Co. Albion

Oswego County.
Temple J. F. & Co. New Block,
    1st st. *Oswego.*
Frost Morgan R. 1st st.
Abbott & Strong, cor. Bridge & 1st
Temple John F. cor. 1st & Seneca
Jefferson Thomas, do
Goulding & Klock, 1st st.
Cooper Levi, Fulton *Volney.*
Dy Remon J. H. do
Harrison John & Co. Fulton

Otsego County.
Knapp Orrs *Middlefield.*
Wilson & Graves, Cooperstown
    Otsego.
Woodruff Lloyd L. *Unadilla.*

Putnam County
Deyoe J., Cold Springs
    Phillipstown.

Queens County.

Bishop John   *Flushing.*
Waters D. S.   *Jamaica.*
Williamson C., Astoria   *Newtown.*
Swan A. T.   do

Rensselaer County.

M'Ardle G. W. 311 State
    Lansingburgh.
Clark Charles, 268 State
Seaman Alfred, 1 Hathaway's row
Kinned E. 2   do
Clark E. 228 River   *Troy.*
M'Donald Levinus, 204½ River
Cohn I. & Co. 4½ Franklin square

Richmond County.

Bender P., Tompkinsville
    Castleton.

St. Lawrence County.

Short Thomas, jr. Waddington
    Madrid.
Stocker Amos, Ford st. Ogdens-
burgh   *Oswegatchie.*
Payne Benjamin, Ford st.
Matthewson A. & H. do

Saratoga County.

Wood Hiram   *Waterford.*
Wood John

Schenectady County.

Frank & Hull, 71 State *Schenectady.*
Jacobs E. 132 State

Schoharie County.

Atchinson E. D.   *Middleburgh.*

Seneca County.

Shuts Fred. Waterloo   *Fayette.*
Stewart & Purdy   *Ovid.*
Perry Horace
Fowler Alonzo H., Farmer
Harris Morgan,   do
Keith W.   *Seneca Falls.*
Woodworth A. O.
Strong Julius C.   *Waterloo.*
Hudson J. E.
Montgomery James

Steuben County.

Smith & Graham   *Addison.*
Bailey J.

Suffolk County.

Parks T. S. Greenport   *Southold.*

Sullivan County.

Scott A. Wurtsboro, *Mamakating.*
Henderson S. do

Tompkins County.

Clark James, 101 Owego *Ithaca.*
Franks, Hischberg & Co. 105
Owego
Thompson T. C. 47 Owego
Mesick, Smith & Van Buskirk, 102
Owego
Bond H. A. 39 Owego
Goldsteing J. & S. Owego c. Pearl
Collins George H. 92 Owego
Phillips A. 71 Owego
Cheeseborough B. F. 73 Owego
Tottan W. J. 43 Owego

Ulster County

Davis P. J.   *Kingston.*
Smith John B., Rondout
Thompson James H. *Saugerties.*
Jacobs C. D.
O'Conell Benjamin
Stern Marx
Upwright G. W. Napanoch
    Wawarsing.
Marks John,   do

Hornbeck Wm. Ellenville
Ayers E.   do *Wawarsing.*

Washington County.

Naflor & Potter   *Greenwich.*
Fisher Joseph
Eggleston Jabez
Hodge J. N. North *White Creek.*
Austin A. & E. Canal st. *Whitehall.*
Connell P.   do
Lasher E.   do
Mendleson & Jacobs, Phœnix pl.
Canovan & Biggin, Canal st.

Wayne County.

Straw L. N.   *Arcadia.*
Hayes W. O. & Co. Newark
Vanbuskirk John,   do
Hankerson H. W.   do
Home A. C., Clyde   *Galen.*
Crawford G. W. do
Bancroft Luther, Macedon Centre
    Macedon.
Healer Jacob   *Marion.*
Butler B.   *Palmyra.*
Hsyck Peter P.
Chapin F.

Westchester County.

Webber B. G. Pleasantville
    Mount Pleasant.
Todd Wm. A. Portchester *Rye.*
Merritt Nelson S. do
Riley John T.   *Westchester.*
Wilson Edward
Hall William   *West Farms.*
Harbee C.   *Yonkers.*
Hobbs Bailey

Wyoming County.

Siver Jacob   *Attica.*
Burt John
Kennedy E. A.
Keith D. & W. R. Wyoming
    Middlebury.

Yates County.

Dorman J., Branchport *Jerusalem.*
Munger Lyman, do
Cooley George, Penn Yan *Milo.*
Sprague & Earl,   do
Gillett & Whitehouse, do
Stewart & Tunncliff, do
Pratt Robert,   do

Tailors' Chalk Manufacturer.

Clausen I. 256 William *New York.*

Tailors' Trimmings.

Carroll James, 46 Av. D *New York.*
Dale Thomas N. 67 Liberty
Gauley J. A. 92 Maiden lane
Halsted S. & S. 41 John
M'Cord G. 9 Cedar
Moss Henry. 60 Nassau
Packard Alanson, 66 Market
Pinkney James W. 56 William
Potts Robert E. 74 Liberty
Tanner & Burtis, 20 Liberty

Tallow.

Jay & Bogert, 447 Water
    New York.
Nottebohm Andrew, 1 Water

Tanners and Curriers.

Albany County.

Settle J. P., Reedsville *Berne.*
Canady J.   do

Waggoner C.   *Bethlehem.*
Crouuse & Waggoner, Knowers-
ville   *Guilderland.*
Crouuse J.   *Knox.*
Bellamy George *Bernedaeville.*
Potter T. K.
Snider J.   *Westerlo.*
Crandell J.

Allegany County.

Barber H. & Co.   *Alfred*
Post George
King R. K.   *Allen.*
Preston ———   *Almond.*
Preston R.   *Andover.*
Allen Richard   *Angelica.*
Allen R. jr.
Swink & Hartman
Daniels Lucius   *Bolivar.*
Smith J. Whitney Valley *Burns.*
Stevens Wm. P.   *Cuba.*
Adams Robert
Swarthout J.   *Friendship.*
Stillman M.
Hard Moses B.
Cowing & Nye   *Hume.*
Crandell & Brown, Whitesville
    Independence.
Ball Joseph   *Rushford.*
Warden Asa E.
Galt A. T.   *Scio.*
Hatch Charles & Son, Wellsville
Maxon Moses   *Wirt.*

Broome County.

Abbott J. B. & Son *Binghamton.*
Smith S.
Northrop L. & M., Harpersville
    Colesville.
Crawford J. L.   do
Jones L., Centre Lisle *Lisle.*
Burgett J., Upper Lisle
Clark A. H.   *Maine.*
Seymour G., Whitney's Point
    Triangle.
Perkins H. & G.   *Windsor*
Smith George W.

Cattaraugus County.

Hoverland John   *Ashford.*
Houes H. H., Rutledge
    Conewango.
Woodruff E. C. *Ellicottville.*
Bunce L. N.   *Franklinville.*
St. John J.
Ellethorp Jacob, Sandusky
    Freedom.
Stone Stephen B., Eddyville
    Mansfield.
Hollister Edwin,   do
Bronson E.   *New Albion.*
Borden James   *Otto.*
Ramsey Hiram, East Otto
Miner N. H.   *Perrysburgh.*
Barker A. H. & Co.
Badger Leander, Gowanda
    Persia.
Smallwood Wm.   do
Webster W. R.   do
Comstock Mark   *Portville.*
Brown A., East Randolph
    Randolph.
Freary John,   do
Pitcher Wm. C.   *Rice.*
Thomas George W. *Yorkshire.*
Wheeler Amasa
Walrath James & Co., Delavan

Cayuga County.

Watson P. T. Genesee st. *Auburn.*
Patty J. & Son, 30 Genesee
Mead L.   *Genoa.*
Dutton J. B. & Son   *Ira.*
Andrews George & Samuel
Whiston S.   *Locke.*
Little & Robinson, Port Byron
    Mentz.
Curtis H.   do
Herrington ——— *Moravia*
York J.   *Niles*

Aulgar M. *Niles.*
Brow D. *Sempronius.*
Tallman Wm. *Scipio.*
Allen ——
Wheeler B. H. *Springport.*
Cole D. S. *Starling.*
Wyman W.
Furbish I.
Barker J. A. *Venice.*

Chautauque County.

Frank J. & Son *Busti.*
Skinner & Hartwell *Charlotte.*
Hedges E. S.
Farnell O., Mayville *Chautauque.*
Walker H. S. de
Wood Elmer, De Wittville
Davison H. & J. *Cherry Creek.*
Spencer C. A.
Chapman James *Clymer.*
Fenton & Barker, Jamestown *Ellicott.*
Arnold & Hazzard do
Jones Ebenezer, do
Shaw Michael, do
Hutton G. do
Leet Lewis *Ellington.*
Waithe Geo.
Lockwood Wm. Nashville *Hanover.*
Smith R. B. & Co. Smith's Mills
Spaulding D., Silver Creek
Mathews L., Panama *Harmony.*
Green R. Fredonia *Pomfret.*
Haight & Keyes, Salem Cross Roads *Portland.*
Pierce L. *Ripley.*
Eckes & Johnson *Sheridan.*
Osborn P. S. & H. B. *Sherman.*
Gilbert R. & J.
Phelps Josiah
Stillwell Messrs.
Ramsey A. Z. *Westfield.*
Tiffeny Hiram
Peacock Thos.

Chemung County.

Cooper John T. *Catharine.*

Chenango County.

Jacobs F. *Bainbridge.*
Partridge & Foote, Bennettsville
Jones I. *Columbus.*
Foote & Hays *Coventry.*
Dibble, Russell & Son *Guilford.*
Burdick Wm. R. *Macdonough.*
Knapp T. S. *New Berlin.*
Brazee T., South New Berlin
Dibble I. do do
Hughston & Randall *Norwich.*
Moak E.
Griffing David, (morocco)
Birdleburgh P. S. *Pitcher.*
Hakes Charles, Pitcher Spa
Ballard Dennis *Plymouth.*
Lewis & Smith *Preston.*
Hall S.
Burlingham J. *Smyrna.*
Stanbro Gardiner

Clinton County.

Powers & Orleans, Keeseville *Au Sable.*
Gillorts ——, East Chazy *Chazy.*
Robinson ——, West Chazy
Ayres, Anson & Co. *Peru.*
Martin Samuel H.
Moore R. & P. *Plattsburgh.*
Haynes Samuel *Saranac.*

Columbia County.

Pitts J. W. Malden Bridge *Chatham.*
Adlet Lewis B. *Hillsdale.*
Latting Refine
Westcott S. Warren st. *Hudson.*
Wheeler M. W. (morocco) *Kinderhook.*
Williams G., New Lebanon Centre *New Lebanon.*

Cortland County.

Elder Wm. *Cortlandt Village.*
Corey David, M'Grawville
Benjamin Chas. *Harford.*
Kingsbury Wm. *Homer.*
Winnegar Lucius
Dickinson Horace *Marathon.*
Shattuck David
Crofoot Jay *Preble.*
Pierce Albert *Truxton.*
Purrington Henry W., Cuyler

Delaware County.

Kind Charles *Andes.*
Bowman J.
Haver A.
Downs, Elwood & Co. Downsville *Colchester.*
Brackney J. *Davenport.*
Reynolds L.
England H. *Delhi.*
Bartlett M. *Franklin.*
Shaw D. *Hamden.*
Dougherty J., North *Kortright.*
White S. W., Bloomville
Reynolds I. *Meredith.*
Smith G. W., Clark's Factory *Middletown.*
Schermerhorn S. Margaretville
Humphrey Robert, Clovesville
Gurgon C. Pine Hill
Moore & Howell, Mooresville *Roxbury.*
Smith D. M.
Beckly W. R. *Stamford.*
Kidney James
Deveraux, Clark & Co. Deposit *Tompkins.*
Knapp C. Deposit
Mead J. & G. S. *Walton.*

Duchess County.

Fish H. (currier) Hughsonville *Fishkill.*
Hasbrook Z. V.
Snider J. W. *Northeast.*
Gorham W. *Pawling.*
Southwick Edward C. 270 Main *Poughkeepsie.*
Boyd D. 360 Main
Hill H. & E. *Rhinebeck.*
Height & Tripp, Hart's Village *Washington.*

Erie County.

Farnsworth A. D. *Alden.*
Hutchinson John, Williamsville *Amherst.*
Lenta Reuben, do
Rumsey Aaron, G. H. Martin Agent, Griffin's Mills *Aurora.*
Heads Lysander, Willink
Spooner Dorr W. do
Clexton Samuel B. *Black Rock.*
Fowler Sumner *Boston.*
Hatch Edward X.
Potter & Co.
Case N. & Co. Carroll st. *Buffalo.*
Christopher Charles, (morocco) E. Seneca st.
Leonard H. (buckskin dresser) 2 Exchange
Baker & Co. *Clarence.*
Webster Geo. Gowande *Collins.*
Allen Alfred B.
Watkins Wm. Springville *Concord.*
Pratt Joseph O. *Eden.*
Carpenter & St. John
Janes C. & O. East Evans *Evans.*
Black & Hammond, do
Sagle Wm. Water Valley *Hamburgh.*
Morey Nathan, jr. *Holland.*
Sears, Rush & Howard *Lancaster.*
Clark John
Jackson Wm. *Newstead.*
Jackson H. D., Akron
Green F. do

Candre Joseph,

Candre Joseph, *Sardinia.*
Barker G. South Wales *Wales.*
Hall J. Wales Centre

Essex County.

Brevoort Julius C. *Crown Point.*
Gray Ozro P
Noble H. R. *Elizabethtown.*
Noble R. & Sons *Essex.*
Kidder Maynard, Moriah 4 Corners *Moriah.*
Kidder Edwin, do
Huntly John B., Port Henry
Spencer Wm. *Ticonderoga.*
Hoffnagle Edmund *Willsborough.*

Franklin County.

Wilcox Abel *Bangor.*
Clay Jonas F. *Chateaugay.*
McIlvain John
Lincoln A. *Fort Covington.*
Stevens S. *Moira*

Fulton County.

Richards O., Bleeker Falls *Bleeker*
Hopkins Patrick, do
Cornwell & Northrup *Broadalbin.*
Cornwell Enoch
Allen J. & D. C., Allenville
Newkirk G. A. *Caroga.*
Banker John *Ephratah.*
Yanney Henry
Pearson Eli *Johnstown.*
Bedford David
Vail, Buchanan & Co. Vail's Mills *Mayfield.*
Lefever & Van Valkenburgh *Northampton.*
Fay A. B.
Bacon J. Cranberry Creek
Shults J. *Oppenheim.*
Dunning Geo. *Perth.*
Bartlett Aaron & Co. *Stratford.*

Genesee County.

Geer Wm. *Alexander.*
Hutton James *East Bethany.*
Crocker —— *Byron.*
Chapin F. Darien Centre *Darien.*
Bascom Simeon *Le Roy.*
Shed & Ganson
Wilson & Brothers *Stafford.*

Greene County.

Rouse Isaac *Catskill.*
Ashley Henry
Bogardus Jacob C., *Coxsackie.*
Brandt & Co. *Hunter.*
Edwards W. H.
Kreisted J. H. & Co. East Kill
Cornish Cornelius C. *Lexington.*
Bushnell J. D. & E. P. & Co. West Hill
Bushnell Aaron
Chase Austin, West Lexington
Pratt D. & Co. East do
Brackney John B. *Prattsville.*
Snyder & White
Morse Burton C.
Pratt & Robinson *Windham.*

Hamilton County.

Smith W. A. & Co. *Hope.*

Herkimer County.

Warren P. H. *Columbia.*
Steavens T. A.
Steavens S.
Woolluber D. W.
Desvenport Benj.
Thomas G. M. *Fairfield.*
Voorhees A.
Steel W. *Frankfort.*
Countryman Peter J. *Herkimer.*
Baldy John
Myser Henry

Rust Nelson ... *Little Falls.*
Parrett Stephen S.
Kirshaw Benj. ... *Litchfield.*
Hosford Wm.
Waterman H. ... *Newport.*
Polley W. D. ... *Russia.*
Countryman P. Poland
Jones E. Postville
Knights Wm. E.
Ferguson James ... *Salisbury.*
Conoklin Jonathan, Van Horns-
ville ... *Stark.*
Weatherbee B. A. & A. E. Page's
Corners ... *Warren.*
Wheeler R. West Winfield
... *Winfield.*

Jefferson County.

Merriam & Lewis ... *Adams.*
Storm M. J., Plessis ... *Alexandria.*
Woodworth James, Alexandria
Bay
Conkey S. & J. ... *Antwerp.*
Gillett S. N. Ox Bow
Spear A. Perch River ... *Brownville.*
Powell F. ... *Cape Vincent.*
Pool Sylvanus ... *Champion.*
Smith James
Morley H. ... *Ellisburgh.*
Kilby Eben G. ... *Henderson.*
Bingham Hiram, Evans' Mills
... *Le Ray.*
Bently John ... *Lorraine.*
Bell F. Three Mile Bay ... *Lyme.*
Short James ... *Philadelphia.*
Herring H. ... *Rodman.*
Roberts O. South Rutland
... *Rutland.*
Augsbury John A. Black River
Castler John T. ... *Theresa.*
Troing Chas.
Fisk & Bates ... *Watertown.*
Farnham N. & T.
Clark Milton (morocco)
Richmond Thos. do
Gates Chancy, do
Smith James, Carthage ... *Wilna.*
Smith James W

Kings County.

Bushnell Ezra L. Gold st. near
Tillary ... *Brooklyn.*
Cammeyer & Johnaon (morocco)
Bedford Av. near Flushing Av.
Wood Joseph, Clinton Av. corner
Nassau st.
Gardiner John, Flushing Av. cor.
Wallabout Road
Green Thomas (morocco) N. 2d
st. ... *Williamsburgh.*
Vyse William, N. 9th st. near 7th.

Lewis County.

Clark Wm. Copenhagen *Denmark.*
Boynton J. do
Williams & Lindsley, Brantingham
... *Greig.*
Pratt ——, Brantingham
Bill Cyrus S. ... *Turin.*
Johnson H. Constableville
... *West Turin.*
Evans Peter, do

Livingston County.

Dinwiddie Robert ... *Caledonia.*
Leonard Thomas & Co. *Dansville.*
Keihle James
Gilbert Francis ... *Lima.*
Woodford, Coy & Co.
... *Mount Morris.*
Phelps L.
Ashley C. C. ... *Nunda.*
Daniel Hiram, Oakland ... *Portage.*
Clark G. jr. Hunt's Hollow
Hampsher Wm. K. Scottsburgh
... *Sparta.*
Pratt Samuel ... *Springwater.*

Madison County.

Jordan Samuel ... *Brookfield.*

Penilton Henry, Leonardsville
... *Brookfield.*
Edwards Benjamin, do
Allen R. & Son ... *Cazenovia.*
Phinney Gaylord
Trimbock Isaac
Loomis John C. New Woodstock
Sutton & Sears ... *De Ruyter.*
Rider Simeon
Sherrill & Orton ... *Eaton.*
Tillinghast C. Morrisville
Tillinghast Bradley, do
Richardson John ... *Fenner.*
Wormuth Benjamin
Day Ira ... *Georgetown.*
Starr A. & Son ... *Hamilton.*
Carpenter J. & S. Earlville
Merrill M. P.
Berry Richard, Poolville
Hubbard C. Hubbard's Corners
Thomson Sylvester ... *Lebanon.*
Johnson A. S. ... *Lenox.*
Smith Asa, Oneida Depot
Beecher Hamilton, Canastota
Walrath J. L. Clockville
Brigham Salmon ... *Madison.*
Barker James
Curtis Samuel, Erieville ... *Nelson.*
Hall Abner, Peterboro *Smithfield.*
Wilson J. M. ... *Stockbridge.*
Hazeltine J. D.
Spencer Wm. Chittenango
... *Sullivan.*
Riddle David, do
Richardson John, Perryville

Monroe County.

Palmer Joel, Clarkson Corner
... *Clarkson.*
Palmer Justus, do
Palmer A. H. do
Bergen C. do
Wilson Henry, West Henrietta
... *Henrietta.*
Collins J. jr. Honeoye Falls
... *Mendon.*
Ball, Church & Co. Spencer's Ba-
sin ... *Ogden.*
Tripp & Gosline, Parma Corner
... *Parma.*
Lincoln A. & Co. ... *Perrinton.*
Kaler Rufus, 2 Water *Rochester.*
Noonan Jeremiah, (morocco)
Globe Buildings Water st.
Graves D. & L. do
Trenaman Richard, do
Baker & Co. 41 Main cor. Water
Gould Geo. & Co. 16 State
Cross O. M. Lower Falls
Churchill L. & H. 2 Hill
Whiting & Martin, West Webster
... *Webster.*
Hooper Francis, Scottsville
... *Wheatland.*

Montgomery County.

Van Deusen ——, Hagaman's Mills
... *Amsterdam.*
Fisher John, Cranesville
Dawson William, do
Putnam James, Tribes Hill
Nobles Jared ... *Canajoharie.*
Tiffany Loring H. Ames
Genini John, do
Palmer B. Burtonville *Charleston.*
Johnson David, Minaville *Florida.*
Taylor R. V. do
Johnson Robert, do
Dean Wetherel, Fort Jackson
Aumac W. H. & J. ... *Glen.*
Noxon Wm. C. Fort Plain *Minden.*
Van Husen R. Fonda ... *Mohawk.*
Clark James, do
Van Dusen S. do
Vosburgh Jacob & Samuel, Stone
Arabia ... *Palatine.*
Falensby Isaac ... *Root.*
Stowes Henry J.
Averill H. & L. ... *St. Johnsville.*
Anderson H. M.
Beekman Anthony

New York County.

Angus & Stewart, (curriers) 23
Jacob ... *New York.*
Bugan John, (currier) 16½ Van-
dewater
Bowie John H. & Co. (curriers) 30
Ferry
Cauthers James, (currier) 266 2d
Fleming John, (currier) 43 Chris-
topher
Hoyt W. & O. (curriers) 17 Ferry
Moffat David, (currier) 5 Jacob
Neidhart Chas. (currier) 51 Frank-
fort
Pearson Adam, (currier) 62 do
Rogers A. (currier) 2 Jacob

Niagara County.

Fleming John ... *Dewiston.*
Eastman A. & A. H. ... *Lockport.*
Works S.
Johnson James ... *Newfane.*
Harrington James, Olcott
Kapp E. do
Clear J. do
Shoemaker Jacob ... *Royalton.*
Martin & M'Merrick *Wheatfield.*
Warren Josiah C. ... *Wilson.*
Barnard Thaddeus

Oneida County.

Worden J. & Co. ... *Annsville.*
Roberts T. J. ... *Boonville.*
Costello J. & Co. ... *Camden.*
Sliter John ... *Florence.*
Rider Lewis
Childs S. ... *New Hartford.*
Beecher M. ... *Remsen.*
Stevens & Whitmore ... *Rome.*
Merrill James
Owens William ... *Steuben.*
Sanders E. Stittsville ... *Trenton.*
Anderson ——, do
Ellis J. do
Vedder J. F. J. 43 Genesee st.
... *Utica.*
Thorn & Maynard, (morocco) 21
Water
William Thomas & Son ... *Vernon.*
Sanford ——, Durhamville
... *Verona.*
Peckham G. T. do
Tipple M. do
Utley J. Westernville ... *Western.*
Utley D. North Western
Benedict William, Whitesboro
... *Whitestown.*
Moses Richard, Whitesboro

Onondaga County.

Phillips L. S. & A. B. Baldwins-
ville ... *Lysander.*
Hickok H. Baldwinsville
Smith J. do
Stilwell & Son ... *Manlius.*
Bates A. & Pelton, Water st. Syra-
cuse ... *Salina.*
Van Buren & Clary, Water st.
Crowfoot A. ... *Tully.*

Ontario County.

Mason Jess & Co. ... *Canandaigua.*
Robinson & Co.
Munson Luther ... *East Bloomfield.*
Densmore Belden ... *Manchester.*
Arnold C. G. & Co. ... *Phelps.*
M'Michael Thomas, Honeoye
... *Richmond.*
Bishop & Moon, Honeoye
M'Gregor John, (morocco) Gene-
va ... *Seneca.*
Cromwell J. K. Geneva
Ford A. C. ... *Victor.*

Orange County.

Caldwell A. J. Salisbury Mills
... *Blooming Grove.*
Cornwall James ... *Cornwall.*
Van Ness J. West Town *Minisink.*

Bishop J. West Town   *Minisink.*
Lane J.   do
Mapes Wm. Wells' Corners
Steavens H. Slate Hill
Farnum & Jennings   *Newburgh.*
Forsyth Robert A. Front st.
Houston & Wickham, S. Middle-
  town   *Wallkill.*
Moore G.
Hulbert James
Clason S. W. New Milford
  Warwick.

Orleans County.

Clove G. & Co. Albion   *Barre.*
Fisher William, do
Clark J.   *Carlton.*
Bidleman William S.   *Gaines.*
Rutherford ———, Holley
  Murray.
Stratton Abram, Medina
  Ridgeway.
Pratt Charles, Knowlesville
Hawley Gideon   *Shelby.*
Allen William P. Millville
Dates William, Lyndonville
  Yates.

Oswego County.

Pearson, Allen & Co.   *Amboy.*
Carter J. & R. Carterville
Clifford R.   do
Phalen James,   do
Stanley H. (currier) do
Forster William, (Eagle Tannery)
  Cleaveland   *Constantia.*
Salmon Geo. & Co. Oswego Falls
  Granby.
Van Awken T. & D.   *Hannibal.*
M'Claughey John, Hannibal Cen-
  tre
Ames & Mitchell   *Mexico.*
Gregory & Merriam
Allen G. W.   *New Haven.*
Weston O.   *Orwell.*
Hubbard William O. bet. Canal &
  River st.   *Oswego.*
Allen S. & S. (morocco) bet. Canal
  and River
Hubbard J. B. & Co. (curriers) bet.
  Canal & River
Burt William R. Jennings' Corner
  Palermo.
Warn John C.   *Parish.*
Washburn Frank   *Redfield.*
Salisbury D. C. Pulaski   *Richland*
Wood Jabin, South Richland
Bentley & Hart, Phœnix
  Schroeppel.
Smith ———   do
Leslie William, Gilbert's Mills
Smith Charles,   do
Whitmarsh Jacob   *Scriba.*
Loomis A. & L. E. Fulton
  Volney.
Cromwell & Bortols *Williamstown.*
M'Kindley John

Otsego County.

Parker A. Burlington *Burlington.*
Hawkins D. R. Burlington Flats
Lull & Sons   *Butternuts.*
Matterson & Co.
Burlingame T.   *Cherry Valley.*
Barrett G.
Perkins ———
Simmons L. T.   *Edmeston.*
Pendleton Oliver, West Edmeston
Burch Orlo, Schuyler's Lake
Robinson W.   *Hartwick.*
Steere J.
Chaffee E.
Steere Rufus   *Laurens.*
Chase Geo. W.   *Maryland.*
Brown Amos H. Schenevus
Griffin E.   *Middlefield.*
Henman Everett
Shipman William
Hayden John

Eddy J.   *Milford.*
Stickney W. E.
Steere & Winsor
Steere & Cook
Hard & Palmer   *New Lisbon.*
Brown E. S.   *Oneonta.*
Waterman R. Cooperstown
  Otsego.
Barrett B.   *Springfield.*
Barrett O.
Ells Horace   *Unadilla.*
Wright Johnson
Chase Seth   *Worcester.*

Putnam County.

Fox P.   *Carmel.*
Hoight J.   *Kent.*
Fletcher C. H.   *Patterson.*
Cowler H.
Penny W.   *Phillipstown.*

Queens County.

Willetts David   *Hempstead.*
Thinnes Bernard   *Jamaica.*
Morrell Henry, Manhasset
  North Hempstead.

Rensselaer County.

Fisher H.   *Berlin.*
Hubbard E. & F.   *Brunswick.*
Hubbard D.
Fisher H.   *Petersburgh.*
Coon H.
Gregory Joseph   *Sandlake.*
Brown & Bennett   *Stephentown.*
Swan A.
Haight I. N. & L.114 Ferry Troy.
Stearns & Tanners, Hollow Road
Plum David B.   do
Swasey Edward R. Lansingburgh
  Road

Rockland County.

Hempleman Charles D. Piermont
  Orangetown.

St. Lawrence County.

Denie H. F., Helena   *Brasher.*
Page O.   *Canton.*
Guiles Reuben   *Edwards.*
Blackman F. W. A.   *Hammond.*
Soper Oscar & Co.
Goodnoe Nathaniel   *Hopkinton.*
Bancroft L.   *Louisville.*
Marsh R. D.
Graves H.
M'Clair James, Pope's Mills
  Macomb.
Dayton Edwin, Columbia *Madrid.*
Simmons Lyman. do
Cheeny Uriah   *Massena.*
Vantine M. A.
Bancroft ———, Lewisville
Pope Charlemaign   *Morristown.*
Bigsby S.   *Norfolk.*
Ketchum Alvah
Vilas Erastus, Ogdensburgh
  Oswegatchie.
Davis Darius H.   *Parishville.*
Vroman Stewart   *Pitcairn.*
Davis Orson O.   *Potsdam.*
Perrin Noah
Byington John, Bucks' Bridge
Warner A.   *Russell.*
Taylor Orrin   *Stockholm.*
Curtice C.

Saratoga County.

Ely Seldon   *Charlton.*
Reymond J. P.
Western Lloyd   *Corinth.*
Dewell A.
Reymond Henry
Hyer Alexander B.   *Edinburgh.*
Alverd Calvin
Allen H.   *Galway.*
Bowers M.
Gilbert Platt C. South Greenfield
  Greenfield.

Gifford John, Weeds' Corners
Conklin Gideon   *Hadley*
Becker Lyman   *Malta.*
Parent Sam. Ballston Spa *Milton.*
Cevert Thomas S. do
Fay Joseph   *Providence.*
Carpenter Hiram
Long George   *Saratoga.*
Green Wm.   *Wilton.*

Schenectady County.

Carrhart P.   *Niskayuna.*
Foster James G.   *Schenectady.*
Holliday & Lane
Benedict E. L.

Schoharie County.

Dickerman Hezekiah   *Blenheim.*
Morehouse Munson
Hawver Henry   *Broome.*
Kromer & Snyder   *Cobleskill.*
Richtmyer Peter H.   *Conesville.*
Deuel John L.   *Esperance.*
M'Master James, Sloansville
Reed John & Co.   *Gilboa.*
Tuttle & Son
Danforth & Hawver   *Middleburgh.*
Vroman Henry
Courter J. W. Warnerville
  Richmondville.
Babcock A.
Warner Peter
Mann P. J.   *Schoharie.*
Brownell A. & E.
Crounce Jno. Hyndsville   *Seward.*
Hartwell F.   *Summit.*
Lawrence Morgan, Gallupville
  Wright.

Seneca County.

Gross Joseph A., Farmer   *Ovid.*
Tillman Andrew P. *Seneca Falls.*
Morgan Ledyard   *Waterloo.*
Freebody Charles T.
Hendricks Samuel

Steuben County.

Otis F.   *Avoca.*
Waterbury S.
Shover & Smith
Smith Orrin   *Bath.*
Lamont D.   *Dansville.*
Cortwright & Rhodes   *Erwin.*
Mitchell Sylvester   *Greenwood.*
Knapp D.   *Jasper.*
Savage N.
Goodrich S.   *Orange.*
Roberts, Cyrus & Co.   *Reading.*
Eddy F.   *Thurston.*
Bailey David   *Urbana.*
Benham H. & J.
Berdine   *Wayne.*
Whitmore A.   *Wayland.*
Gardiner George   *Woodhull.*

Suffolk County.

Miller Enoch, Moriches
  Brookhaven.
Hammond Samuel S. Patchogue
Hawkins Wm.   do
Case David W.   do
Cooper S. W. Babylon *Huntington.*
Munsell & Mosier   *Riverhead.*

Sullivan County.

Kiersted W. & Co. Mongaup Val-
  ley   *Bethel.*
Tremain Wm. Sandburgh
  Fallsburgh.
Andrews S.   do
Palin & Flagler
Strong A. & Co.
Clements A.
Smith S. & Sons
Ludington H. R.
Ray Miles
Gildersleeve & Co.   *Liberty.*
Rickey, Stevens & Co.
Horton & Co.

Buckley D. B.   *Liberty.*
Shults J. S. & Co. Summitville
       Mamakating.
Townsley A. G. Bloomingburgh
Townsley A. Wurtsboro
Van Dozer I.   do
Dietz Michael. Burlingham
Cooke & Bushnell   *Neversink.*
Hammond & Wells
Palon A. & Co.
Johnson John
Bushnell A. & Co.
Johnson J. J. & Son
Babcock A. E.
Reynolds J.
Wells, Thompson & Co. *Thompson.*
Wells H. F. & Co.
Lyons & Burnham, Monticello

Tioga County.

Leonard S. & Son   *Berkshire.*
Lincoln, Todd & Co. Newark Valley
       Newark.
Osborne John, Newark Valley
Settle John,   do   do
Kirby George   *Nichols.*
White S. N.
Archibald & Co.   *Owego.*
Parmenter E.

Tompkins County.

Stoddard S. & E. (morocco) cor.
   Owego & Aurora sts.   *Ithaca.*
Leslie & Covert, (morocco) 21
   Aurora
Esty J. & Son,   do 29 Tioga
Hollister Horace   *Newfield.*

Ulster County.

Van Buren Tobias   *Kingston.*
Near & Teller
Freer John R. Stone Ridge
       Marbletown.
Richardson Thos.   do
Bull E. W.   do
Pratt & Sampson   *Olive.*
Morgan E.
Watson N. W., Shokan
Hasbrouck E. Kyserike
       Rochester.
Myer Peter B.   *Saugerties.*
Guigou C. Pine Hill *Shandaken.*
Smith I. Smithville
Ishams, Sherrell & Co.
Newkirk & Simpson
France E.   *Shawangunk.*
France Henry, Ulsterville
M'Kinstry F. B.   do
M'Kinstry Stephen, do
Crawford Alfred,   do
Sanford James M.   *Wawarsing.*
Cutler T. W.
Lefever & Pomeroy
Childs J. B.   *Ellenville*
Donaldson William, do
Shults A. I.   do
De Forest & Co.   *Woodstock.*

Warren County.

Archibald S. R.   *Caldwell.*
Hawley Hiram
Robertson, Fazen & Co. Chester-
   town   *Chester.*
Robertson John, Chestertown
Palmer & Mead,   do
Crandall James,   do
Palmer Alva,   do
Lanly Geo. E.   do
Sawyer & Co. Pottersville
Burhams, Gray & Pierce *Horicon.*
Barnes L. B.   *Johnsburgh.*
Crandall Josiah   *Warrensburgh.*
Burhams & Gray

Washington County.

Rowen Archibald   *Argyle.*
Robertson John   *Cambridge.*
Johnson & Culver
Perry Wm. Buskirk's Bridge

Benson Joseph, North Easton
       Easton.
Kingsley Warren B. & Co.
       Fort Ann.
Swift Willis
Robertson Thomas, Lake
       Greenwich.
Scofield Lewis, North Greenwich
Wilbur Orrin H. West Hebron
       Hebron.
Bump John H.   do
Frasier John, East Hebron
Hand Josiah, Sandy Hill
       Kingsbury.
Woodstock Wm. E.   *Putnam.*
Williamson Daniel, jr.
Buck D. M.   *White Creek.*
Taber d. & Wm. H.
Jilson J.   *Whitehall.*

Wayne County.

Pennington James W.   *Arcadia.*
Moseley Oliver, Newark
Brown Amos,   do
Perkins Rush, Clyde   *Galen.*
Rogers E. R.   *Lyons.*
Patterson Philip   *Marion.*
Hill Ira   *Ontario.*
Allen D.   *Palmyra.*
Holbrook J. L.   *Rose.*
Collier Jason, Alton   *Sodus.*
Snyder Anthony, do
Filmore Kneeland   *Walworth.*
Brown Henry W., W. Walworth
Wood W. C.   *Wolcott.*
Guild Z.

Westchester County.

Halsted Samuel, Peekskill
       Courtlandt.

Wyoming County.

Williams Joel R.   *Attica.*
Thompson C.
Scott Geo.   *Bennington.*
Whiting John, Cowlesville
Cummings T. B.   *Castile.*
Boxford E. B.   *China.*
Watson & Shay   *Eagle.*
Wiseman Noah   *Gainesville.*
Smith & Brown   *Genesee Falls.*
Fry ——, Java Village   *Java.*
De Wolfe Linus
       Middlebury.
Terry A. & Sons, Wyoming
Wheeler & Ingersoll *Orangeville.*
Foot John, Johnsburgh
Chapin W. J. & Son   *Perry.*
Olin John
Loomis & Chapin   *Pike.*
Olin N. N.
Horning J. R. East Pike
Emerick Frederick   *Sheldon.*
Gill Alfred, Strykersville
Potter James H. Varysburg
Copley H. A.   *Warsaw.*
Young Daniel
Clark John F.

Yates County.

Vail Charles, Branchport
       Jerusalem.
Benham & Henry, Penn Yan *Milo.*
Crane B. & J.   do
Hobart Wm. L.   *Potter.*
Stout James
Wright Alva, Dundee   *Starkey.*

Tassel & Fringe Manufacturers.

Kings County.

Lockitt Jos. 189 Fulton *Brooklyn.*
Cunningham M. Fulton st.
Possien C. Hudson Av.
Harris John, cor. S. 2d & 11th
       Williamsburgh.
Hobley Thos. & Sons, 44 Grand

Taxidermists.

Kings County.

Akhurst J. 11½ Prospect *Brooklyn*

New York County.

Bell J. G. 289 Br'dway *New York*

Oneida County.

Hurst J. A. 81 Genesee   *Utica.*

Tea Dealers.   (See also Grocers.—Marked thus * are wholesale.)

Erie County.

Sully Jas. 205 Main   *Buffalo.*

Kings County

Coghlan J. 144 Fulton   *Brooklyn*
M'George John, 260 Fulton
Harding Geo. & Co. 101 Fulton
Christianson F. 103 Fulton
Vandervoort B. E. 23½ Myrtle Av.
Dillon Thos. 263 Fulton
M'Brair Robert & Son, 163 Fulton
Bryant Samuel, 46 Hudson Av.
Howard Francis, 73 Hudson Av.
Plimley Wm. 160 Myrtle Av.
Billington Edward, 194 Grand
       Williamsburg
Seaich Z. 134 Grand

New York County.

Ackerman J. P. 164 Spring
       New York.
Ackland John, 160 Grand, 211
   Greenwich & 77 Barclay
Albro Benj. & Co. 106 Division
American & China Tea Co. 36
   Grand & 50 Broadway
Andrews Thos. 61 Fulton
*Baxter A. Sidney, 12 Old slip
*Beebe & Brother, 137 Front
Billings Henry S. 163 Greenwich
Brown Jas. 5 6th Av.
Burrell Dolan, 52 Catharine
Canton Tea Company, 125 Chatham
*Canton & Pekin Company, 36
   Broadway
Christianson Edw. T. 204 Greenwich & 72 Catharine
Clark Darius, 46 Av. D
Cobb E. H. 430 Broadway
Cooper Sidney A. 20 Av. D
Dixon Isaac, 328 Grand
Eallman Alex. 617 Washington
Galloway John, 185 9th Av.
Geery I. & W. 142 Walker & 719
   Broadway
Gill, Gilletis & Noyes, 31 Front
Goold A. A. 167 Bowery
Greenwood H. B. 487 Broadway
Gurnee E. 226 8th Av.
Hallett Adam F. 504½ Grand
Hallett Samuel J. 213½ and 479
   Grand & 421 Hudson
Hand Geo. 206 & 284 Bowery
Hayes Wm. B. 324 Spring
Higgins L. & J. 43 6th Av.
Hollister Reuben R. 194 Av. C
Imperial Tea Company, 176 Bowery
Lawson Gilbert, 311 Bowery
Martin C. S. 63 Front
Moody Winchester P. 141 Bowery
Munson E. & M. 189½ 6th Av.
Neilson Allan, 238 Greenwich
New York & China Tea Company,
   204 Greenwich & 73 Catharine
*Nicoll S. T. & Co. 68 Front
North American Tea Company,
   212 Pearl
Packard Elisha, 66 Lispenard
Partridge Wm. 246 Bleecker

Pekin Tea Company, Albert A. Warner, 75 Fulton *New York.*
Perkins Jacob S. 207 Fulton
Pickering Thos. 227½ 8th Av.
Powell John, 132 Lewis
Purdy Wm. M. 322 8th Av.
Rathbone —— 33 Water
Rickard Jos. W. 329 Spring & 297 2d
Roberts Daniel H. 543 Grand
Schenck G. E. 57 Cortlandt
Smith Jas. 372 Grand
Souza Theodore, 347 Hudson
Tenar Isaac, 348 6th Av.
The Imperial Pagoda Tea Company, 114 Chatham
Thompson J. & Co. 89 Catharine
*Tiers E. W. & Co. 83 Front
Todd Chas. 207 Hudson
Vail Henry E. 90 Av. B
*Vail Jas. E. 44 Water
Wakenshaw Jos. 24 Catharine
*Wardell A. W. 24 Old slip
Watson John, 178 Bowery
Watson John W. 110 6th Av.

Oneida County.

Scranton W. H. 201 Genesee *Utica.*
Turner J. F. 166 Genesee

Teas—Importers of.

Aymar & Co. 34 South *New York.*
Madden Henry, 76 Broad
Booth & Edgar, 95 & 97 Front
Bucklin & Crane, 80 Front
Cary & Co. 90 Pine
Caswell John & Co. 87 Front
Goodhue & Co. 64 South
Gordon & Talbot, 155 Maiden lane
Grinnell, Minturn & Co. 76 South
Griswold Nathaniel L. & George, 71 & 72 South
Howland & Aspinwall, 54 and 56 South
Jessup Isaac K. & Co. 179 South
Murd Hugh, 59 Water
Nicoll S. T. & Co. 69 Front
Olyphant & Son, 65 South
Tiers E. W. & Co. 83 Front
Wetmore & Cryder, 73 South
Wood Ransom E. 70 Water

Teachers.

Astronomy.

Pearce Sarah, 169 M'Dougal *New York.*

Bookkeeping.

Dixon H. 241 Broadway *New York.*
Jones Thomas, 247 Broadway
Marsh Christopher C. 88 Cedar
Renville Willis J. 269 Broadway
Wheeler Asa H. 261 Broadway

Dancing.

Bond J. N. 315 Houston *New York.*
Brooks Lawrence De G. 233 Grand
Charruaud J. 24 White
Desjardins Pauline, 74 Leonard
Dodworth Allen, 448 Broome
Parker John, 207 Bowery
Peracchio M. 36 Howard
Sarseco P. 110 Grand
Scoville J. S. 624 4th
Searing James H. 56 Bond
Whale William W. 650 Broadway & 66 6th Av.

Drawing and Painting.

Balchly Elizabeth, 9 Thompson *New York.*
Cleveland James A. 77 W. 18th
Coe Benjamin H. 105 Bleecker

French.

Allen Eden, 1 Ann *New York.*

Basset Alexander, 364 Franklin *New York.*
Bekeart Philip, 579 Broadway
Buffet Jean F. Lexington Av. near 26th
Cherbuliez D. 865 Broadway
Danneberg Carl, 44 Hudson
De St. Pierre M. D. 308 Broadway
Donzel David, 369 Broadway
Durand Manesca, 39 Walker
Foignet & Taylor, 789 Broadway
Gauvain M. A. 397 Broadway
Lagroix Dexmier, 289 Broadway
Leverett Esther S. 863 Broadway
Macadam Mary H 109 4th
Macadam Sophia N. 199 4th
Matan John, 86 4th Av.
Maurer John, 19¼ Duane
Perrin Alphonse, 865 Broadway
Rauchfuss F. 170 W. Broadway
Underhill D. C. 173 Broadway
Welchner A. 117 Bowery
Williamson Charles H. 68 Duane

German.

Ceschka William, rear 121 Forsyth *New York.*
Ertheiler M. 48 John & 43 Delancy

Guitar.

Coupa John B. 285 Broadway *New York.*
Lephonaki Numa J. 204 Broadway

Hebrew.

Nusbaum Charles, 197 Rivington *New York.*

Music.

Ayliffe J. 193 Grand *New York.*
Ayliffe Richard, 193 Grand
Ballard J. 129 Crosby
Berge William, 10 6th
Boucher Alfred, 22 Warren
Bradbury Wm. B. 199 Broadway
Bradbury & Nash, 411 Broadway
Browne Augusta. 42 Crosby
Browne David S. 42 Crosby
Brown ——, 498 Hudson
Comes Wm. D. 583 Broadway
Condon Randall M. 156 Grand
Coupa John B. 285 Broadway
Devoe William, 111 Elizabeth
Dodworth Harvey B. 498 Broadway
Doerinckel Frederick, 142 Forsyth
Dumsday M. 466 Broadway
Ehl Augustus, 129 Church
Elder R. 24 4th
Ernest Philip, 289 Broadway
Gaffray ——, 217 Walker
Heiser J. 423 6th Av.
Helfenritter Joseph, 255 Centre
Hoffman George, 104 Grand
Ives Elam, jr. 508 Broadway
Jacobs L. 55 Chatham
Johnson James A. 166 Christopher
Jones John, 304 Broadway
Kammerer Joseph, 181 Laurens
Keys Jane. 129 Mott
King Charles M. 74 6th Av.
Macadam Mary H. 109 4th
Macfarlane Miss, 61 3d Av.
Macfarren John, 115 Spring
Merpe Augustus, 56 Allen
Martin William, 168 Spring
Meyer F. 19 White
Muller George, 2 Market
Munson Reuben, 236 9th
Nash Francis H. 65 Thompson
Oakley Wm. H. 57 Bayard
Oldfield Thomas J. 121 Walker
Oton George, 51 Watts
Pearson J. 223 5th
Pearson Sidney, 296 5th
Pearson S. 367 5th
Plet Charles L. 87 W. Broadway
Poppenberg Albert, 181 Laurens
Proctor & Fenn, E. 25th nr. Lexington Av.
Rayner Wm. C. 22 1st Av.

Russell Benjamin A. 43 3d Av. *New York.*
Saar Donet, 68½ Greene
Selle Lewis, 223 Broome
Shiebel John, 3 Centre mkt. pl.
Starcke F. 405 Broome
Taylor Abraham, 183 9d
Wallace George, 242 Bowery
Warner Joseph F. 412 Broadway
Whitworth George, 130 E. Broadway
Whitworth John, 160 E. Br'dway
Wiedner M. A. 26 5th
Wiese Frederick, 19 Crosby
Williams Thomas, 172 Mulberry
Wood Wm. 679 Broadway

Navigation.

Vale George, 3 Franklin sq. *New York.*
Vale Gilbert, 3 Franklin sq.

Penmanship.

Erie County.

Rice V. M. 269 Main *Buffalo.*
Sherman N. D. 24 Commercial
Larique C. F. 323 Main

New York County.

Dixon H. 287 Broadway *New York*
Dulbear Thomas P. 335 Broadway
Goldsmith Oliver B. 289 Broadway
Hogland W. C. 521 Broadway
Metcalf J. 347 Broadway
Wheeler Asa H. 261 Broadway

Phonography.

Andrews & Boyle, 49 Ann *New York.*
Leland T. C. 49 Ann

Piano.

Behrens John F. 76 Reade *New York.*
Brown Marie L. 498 Hudson
Cooke Bridget, 9 Grand
Daniell Wm. 12 2d
De Granville Leopold, 468 Broome
Doerinckel Frederick R. 142 Forsyth
Dumsday Michael, 466 Broadway
Dyer Samuel, 24 Leroy
Elder Robert, 26 4th
Harrison Sarah E. 147 W. 16th
Jackson Samuel, 24 Leroy
Kelly R. W. 120 Liberty
Macfarlan —— 61 3d Av.
Martin William, 168 Spring
Rayner W. C. 22 1st Av.
Weidner M. A. 26 5th
Woodbury Isaac, 12 Rutgers

Stocks.

Disbrow William H. 20 4th Av *New York.*
Engel Adolph J. 156 Mercer
Hathorne Erastus, 36 University place
Jones Horace F. 127 & 129 Mercer
Merzian John, 65 Watts

Singing.

Bradbury Wm. B. 199 Broadway *New York.*
Jones J. 304 Broadway

Spanish.

Allen Eden, 1 Ann *New York.*
Morales Augustin J. 269 Broome
Rabadan Carlos, 16 Walker
Velasquez de la Cadena Mariano, 123 Troy

Telegraph Offices.

New Jersey Magnetic Telegraph Co. 8 Wall   *New York.*
New York, Albany & Buffalo, 16 Wall
New York & Boston, 5 Hanover
New York & Erie, 5 Hanover
New York & New England 29 Wall
North American, 29 Wall
Southern, 6 Hanover

Telegraph Wires—Galvanized.

Morewood George B. & Co. foot W. 12th   *New York.*

Thimble Makers.

New York County.

Platt & Brother, 6 Liberty   *New York.*
Prime, Roshore & Co, 177 Broadway
McPherson John B. 5 Dey
Van Brunt H. 5 Dey

Suffolk County.

Prince Ezra   *Huntington.*

Thread & Needle Stores.

(*See also Dry Goods Retail—also Hosiery & Gloves Retail—also Fancy Goods Retail.*)

Albany County.

Shiffer Mrs. H. H. 43 Beaver   *Albany.*

Columbia County.

Hawes Mrs. Columbia st. *Hudson.*

Kings County.

Cox Mrs. 32 Hicks   *Brooklyn.*
Hand A. T. 194 Fulton
Reed Mrs. J. A. 248 Fulton
Bodine Mrs. M. L. 345 Atlantic
Godfrey Mrs. C. 88 Main
Thompson Mrs. J. 11 Prospect
Loud George W. 53 Myrtle Av.
Pescott Mrs. J. 23 Myrtle Av.
Walker Wm. S. 86   do
Webb Mrs. E. 321 Fulton
King James, 85 Bridge
Wilson Mrs. C. 139 Nassau
Evans James, Myrtle Av.
Armstrong Wm. 134½ Grand   *Williamsburgh.*

New York County.

Adams Jane, 99½ Greenwich Av.   *New York.*
Ahern Wm. 364 Cherry
Aird Jas. 92 Av. C
Albro Wm. 455 Hudson
Alburtus Susannah, 194 Varick
Allen Dolly, 145 Forsyth
Archer Armstrong. 109 Thompson
Armstrong Edward, 227 1st Av.
Ashton Wm. 344 6th
Atkinson Wm. 310 3d Av.
Bach Solomon, 156 Stanton
Barker Alice, 28 Houston
Baker Wm. 171½ Division
Barls Mary, 132 10th Av.
Barr Ann, 42 8th Av.
Barton Josephine, 78 W. Br'dway
Bear Geo. 375 Houston
Bell Chas. 226 Bowery
Bell Fred. 194 Bowery
Bell Mary, 98 Suffolk
Bellard John, 265 Broome
Benson Alice, 128 Walker

Berry Sarah, 277 Bleecker   *New York.*
Blackman Thos. 121 3d Av.
Boardman Ludlow, 90 Ludlo
Boddy Jas. 297 Av. A
Boggs Mrs. 722½ Houston
Boggs Wm. 405½ Broadway
Boyce Maria, 279 Hudson
Brady Rosa, 77 Broome
Brannon Mary. 151 7th
Brickill Hannah, 148 Christopher
Briggs J. H. 218 Spring
Brinus Dederich, 8th Av.
Bristol Ellen. 87 Reade
Britton Geo. 559 Hudson
Browne R. W. 386 Bowery
Brown Ann, 87 King
Browning E. 307 Washington
Blackie Mrs. 275 Bleecker
Blackman Thos. 121 3d Av.
Blair David, 281 Greenwich
Buckbee Daniel, 112 Broome
Bunting Samuel, 52 Essex
Burdoch Peter, 87 Greenwich
Burcaw Catharine, 5 Av. B
Burke Edward, 313 Delancy
Caffrey Michael, 112 7th Av.
Cahill Michael, 129 E. 13th
Cain Thos. 213 Av. B
Campbell Jas. 82½ Chatham
Carley Ann, 72 3d Av.
Carlin Thos. 257 Stanton
Carpenter Thos. 95 Sheriff
Carroll Ellen, 356½ Greenwich
Carvey Mary, 1st Av. near 19th
Cassidy Peter, 70 Greene
Cern Caspar, Av. A bet. 13th & E. 14th
Chailly Alex. 166½ Bowery
Chapman Robert, 242½ Bleecker
Chichester Aaron, 90 Attorney
Clark Mary, 52 Attorney
Clark Susan, 17 Orchard
Cleary M. 19th bet. 1st & 2d Avs.
Clerk Jas. 611 Water
Cohen Jos. 368 Grand
Colemure John, 33½ 2d
Collett Eleanor, 675 Water
Collier Thos. 284 Bleecker
Collins Ellen. 2 York
Conklin E. 229 Sullivan
Conner Jas. 94 Washington
Cooke Muris L. 422½ Grand
Cooper John, 306 Bowery
Cooper Francis, 57 W. Broadway
Cope Robert, 166 W. 20th
Cororon Sarah, 25 4th Av.
Courtney Jas. 245 Broome
Cowan Sarah, 154 9th
Coyle Dennis, 36 Laurens
Craft Abel, 49 Lewis
Crean Ellen, 438 Monroe
Creighton Hugh. 161 Waverly pl.
Cronin Patrick, 29 Oak
Curran C. 171½ 6th Av.
Curran Thomas, 34 Thompson
Curry Catharine, 56 Pitt
Cunnington Samuel. 101 Green'h
Dalrymple Alex. 393½ Broadway
Darcy Margaret, 147 Chrystie
Davidson Mrs. 11½ Carmine
Davies Ann, 48 Broome
Davis Barron. 50 Roosevelt
Davis F. 397 Grand
Davis Mrs. E. 21 8th Av.
Davis Martha, 596 Grand
Day Ann, 35 White
Dazian Wolf, 4 Marion
De Faber ——, 128 Cedar
Dehrens Conrad, 335 Houston
Dennis Dennis, 109 Spring
Dexter Joseph. 235 W. 17th
Dierkes Xaverius, 68 Norfolk
Ditchett John, 67 Roosevelt
Dittenhoefer ——, 78 Bowery
Dixon Margaret, 360 10th
Donagan Ann, 177 Mott
Donovan Hannah, 34 Spring
Doran Ann, 110 3d Av.
Dornin Oscar, 7 Carmine
Douglas H. 334 Bowery
Drew Susan, 247½ Broome

Drexhagen Arend D. 214 12th   *New York*
Driou Eugene, 150 Greenwich
Drysdle Margaret, 117 Varick
Duffy Mary, 166 W. 20th
Duffey Patrick, 112 7th Av.
Duncan James. 487 Greenwich
Earl H. G. 40 4th Av.
Edmonston Peter, 187 Delancy
Egan Daniel, 136 Monroe
Eistershalmer Ab'm. 228 Cherry
Ely Caroline, 260 Spring
Embden Joseph. 121 Sheriff
Everard Jane, 96½ Broad
Eveleigh F. 148 Spring
Falconi Oscar W. 54 Vandam
Ferguson Chas. 143 W. Broadway
Filk Henry, 83 Sheriff
Finley Deborah, 26 Thompson
Firderer William, 149 Greenwich
Fitzpatrick Catharine, 4 Madison
Flandrow Joseph B. 236 Bowery
Fleekner E. 329 Bleecker
Flinn Thomas, 33 2d
Foley Mrs. 190 Av. A
Forsyth Sarah. 156 Prince
Foster Samuel, 59 Cannon
Fox Lewis, 367 Grand
Frambach Frederick, 139 Wooster
Freeman & Stone, 8th Av.
Frendrich Joseph, 60½ Willet
Gaffney James, 96 Ridge
Gallagher Ann, 40 Mulberry
Gaoghan Thomas, 85 4th
Gardiner John, 136 Laurens
Gardiner M. 142   do
Gartlane Ann, 504 Houston
Gasquet Joseph. 303 Broadway
Gearraty Winnifred, 157 Forsyth
George Martha, 68 Walnut
Gibins Francis, 170 Chrystie
Giffring Wm. H. 3 Greenwich Av.
Glassford James, 679 Broadway
Goilher Joseph, 361 6th
Golden Thomas, 85 Mulberry
Goodman Mary, 78 Delancy
Gottgetrue S. 243½ Division
Graham John S. 385 Grand
Graham W. 87 W. 18th
Green Mary Ann, 90 3d Av.
Griffin Bridget, 443 Washington
Griffith Sarah, 168 6th Av.
Griggs Jane, 37 Broome
Hagan Sarah, 390 W. 17th
Haight Elisha, 82 Bowery
Hairt James, jr. 362   do
Hall Margaret, 98 James
Hall Thomas, 133 Spring
Hallett Chloe, 56½ Broome
Handerson Robert, 236 Canal
Hanley Mary A. 136 Greenw'h Av.
Hanlon Matthew, 25 Madison
Hannor E. 122 Greenwich Av.
Hard Norman G. 314 Bowery
Hardy Alexander, 599 Greenwich
Hare Catharine, 134 Greene
Harney Richard B. 110 8th Av.
Harrington Michael, 281 2d
Harrison Charlotte, 641 Broadway
Hart James, jr. 362 Bowery
Hart Michael, 209 1st Av.
Havington Ann, 281 2d
Healey A. & J. 167½ Greenwich
Heath Lurad C. 213 Grand
Hemmings Thos. 42 W. Broadway
Hendricks Rachael, 244½ Bowery
Herdman A. & M. 30 Division
Herman Samuel, 615 Greenwich
Hetfield F. O. 449½ Hudson
Heyn E. 437½ Broadway
Hight Jeanette, 15 6th Av.
Hill Joseph, 26 Rector
Hill Mary, 221 Division
Hopwood John, 602½ Grand
Howe Hannah, 31 M'Dougal
Howland Francis, 212 Delancy
Hudson Nathaniel, 217 W. 17th
Hughes James, 106 W. Broadway
Humphrey John, 166 Monroe
Haston Jane, 58 Av. C
Ingenbeck Philip, 287 Houston
Jacobus Aaron M. 31 Goerck

Jarvis Catharine, 96 9th Av. & 164 8th Av. *New York.*
Jarvis Edmund, 253 Spring
Jenkins Samuel, 24 Christopher
Jennings Honoria, 180 Laurens
Johnson Mary, 35½ Orange
Kellock James, 367 Hudson
Kelly John, 43 Sheriff
Kelly Lawrence, 194 W. 17th
Kelly Mary, 146 Orchard
Kelly Mary, 84 7th Av.
Kennedy Patrick, 111 W. 21st
Ketcham Adeline, 80 Av. D
Ketcham E. C. 159 Division
Ketcham Rebecca, 186 Cherry
Kevlin Lacky, 38 Sheriff
Kirk Edward, 96 Broome
Kingham G. 378 Cherry
Knapp Moses, 95 Cannon
Knight C. 406 Cherry
Koch Herch, 277 Stanton
Kohlmeyer John, 23½ 2d
Latham Elizabeth, 140 Walker
Law Charles H. 538 Broome
Lawler Thomas, 8 Ludlow
Lawrence Catherine, 40 Lewis
Lawrence George, 151 Church
Leavitt Clarinda S. 214 Division
Lee Mrs. 362 Bowery
Leedy Bernard, 180 Prince
Lemon Lydia, 123 Av. D
Leonard Robert, 221 Hudson
Little Andrew, jr. 265 Greenwich
Lindsey Margaret, 541 Greenwich
Long Mary, 372 Monroe
Loudon John H. 472 Greenwich
Lydig Mary R. 55½ Thompson
Lyons David, 163 W. 18th
Lyons Patrick, 199½ W. 20th
M'Alister R. 67 Greenwich
M'Alister Arthur, 317 Rivington
M'Aviste Mary, 64 Broome
M'Cay Elizabeth, 18 Essex
M'Cormac Julia, 67 4th Av.
M'Cormick Eliza, 198 W. 16th
M'Cormick Patrick, 306½ Mott
M'Dory Alexander, 8th Av.
M'Ghee Amos D. 50 Division
M'Govern Thomas, 134 Division
M'Glinch Elizabeth, 463 Greenwich
M'Grath Daniel, 16 Corlears
M'Cabe Ann, 604 4th
M'Kenna William, 151 Greenwich
M'Keon Mary, 164 7th
M'Millen Jane, 19 Stanton
M'Neice Sarah, 211 Allen
M'Norton Ann, 606 Greenwich
M'Sorley James, 347 Houston
M'Vay Elizabeth, 429 Washington
Marceshemar Emanuel, 230 5th
Marslan Richard, 39 Frankfort
Martens Charles, 168 2d
Mestersous M. 47 Av. D
Maverick Mary, 43½ Carmine
May Charles W. 66 & 162 Bowery
Meehan Patrick, 439½ Washingt'n
Merle Henry, 156 Ludlow
Merritt Alfred, 87 9th Av.
Merryman David, 459 Hudson
Meyer Joseph, 38 Washington
Micheli G. 128 2d Av.
Miller Rosina, 99 W. 18th
Mimzesheimer Lazarus, 227 Delancy
Mitchell Robert E. 118 Clinton
Mitchell Susan, 214 Bleecker
Moore James, 120 6th Av.
Moore Margaret, 89 W. 19th
Moran Michael, 159 Lewis
Morrison David, 164 Chatham
Morrison John, 573 Broadway
Morrison John, 135 Chatham
Morrison John M. 251 Grand
Morrison W. & J. 9 Maiden lane
Morrison & Allen, 383 Broadway
Morrisay James, 48 Anthony
Morton John, 119 Canal
Mulholland Margaret, 235½ Division
Mullin Elizabeth, 118 Stanton
Mulliner William R. 240 Walker

Munsenheimer Lazarus, 178 Essex *New York.*
Munny Pauline, 61 West B'way
Murpay Ann, 63 Suffolk
Murphy Elizabeth, 105 Eldridge
Murphy John, 143 Greenwich
Murray Alexander W. 637 B'way
Murray Catharine, 247 W. 16th
Nash William, 174 Madison
Neil James, 155 8th Av.
Newell Nancy, 207 Broome
Newsam George, 339 Greenwich
Nicholson Sarah Ann, 315 Dincy.
Noble Benedick, 176 Stanton
Nusky Cornelia, 225 W. 17th
O'Connor Michael, 206 Hester
O'Donnel Mary, 162 West 16th
O'Meara Catharine, 261 G'wich
O'Neil Grace, 555 Greenwich
O'Neil Michael, 44½ Carmine
Panne Ernest H. 406 Bowery
Park & Everett, 102 Bowery
Parker Mrs. 303 Spring
Patchell Mary, 143½ 2d
Patterson & Fowler, 116 4th Av.
Pattinson John T. 567½ B'way
Paul Thomas, 455 Greenwich
Peipst Martin, 136 Stanton
Percy Mary, 187 Hester
Petrie Andrew, 312½ Grand
Pidgeon Samuel. 29 Willett
Precxler John, 296 Rivington
Proctor Wm. H. 302 Bowery
Purber William, 8 Av. A
Quig Jane, 79 Av. D
Raynor Margaret, 240½ E. 13th
Richardson A. 167 6th Av.
Road Sarah, 19½ Lewis
Reed Elizabeth. 265 Spring
Rees Hannah, 353 10th
Reilly Mary, 15 Frankfort
Reton Mary, 61 Mott
Reuter Gustavus. 105 Rivington
Rice & Smith, 727 Broadway
Riester John. 264½ Bowery
Richardson Ellen, 365 Hudson
Riggs Daniel, 207 2d Av.
Riordon Richard, 284 Av. A
Robinson Ann Eliza, 256 Pearl
Robinson Jane, 329 6th
Robinson J. 8th Av.
Robinson Maria, 390 Broome
Rosenfield M. S. 240 Bleecker
Rollason Martha, 122 Franklin
Romaine John A. 80 Mott
Ross Elizabeth, 143 Orchard
Rostron John, 111 Wooster
Rourke Patrick, 249 Greenwich
Rowland Susan, 21 Mangin
Rumsal John C. 60 Anthony
Ruthureford Christina, 91 W. 18th
Ryan John, 67 Ridge
Ryberg Charles J. 224 Bowery
Samuels Joseph, 277 Greenwich
Savage Wm. 161 11th
Sayers Ellen, 50 Prince
Schlachmer George, 297½ Division
Seeley Harriet, 177 Greenwich
Seinler E. 291 Bleecker
Seller Emanuel, 81 Essex
Shaffer T. 85 Houston
Sharpe Ann, 159 W. 15th
Shaves Wm. 83 James
Simon Abraham, 118 Willet
Simpson Harriet A. 72 Spring
Sinclair W. T. 56½ Canal
Skelly Patrick, 141 Greenwich
Skinner Ruth, 93 Delancy
Slade Charlotte, 88 Grove
Smith Edward, 407 Greenwich
Smith Hannah, 160 Rivington
Smith Julia, 15 Spring
Smith Lillius, 176 Av. A
Smith Maria, 70 W. Broadway
Smith Mary, 212½ Division
Smith Mary, 64 James
Smith Michael, 372 10th
Smyth Isabella, 361 Broome
Smyth John, 278 Delancy
Steinberger Jonas, 175 Houston

Stevenson Mary Ann, 411 Greenwich *New York.*
Stewart Robert, 271 Greenwich
Stoddard Noah, 964 Grand
Stone John N. 86 Chrystie
Stoher Felix, 128 Essex
Storms Wm. P. 230 Bleecker
Straup John, 48 Av. A
Sullivan B. 381 6th Av.
Sullivan Johanna, 265 Stanton
Sutton Thomas U. 220 Division
Swade Gertrude A. 22½ Broome
Swyen Peter, 156 Washington
Taylor Benjamin F. 444 Cherry
Taylor Mrs. 21 Av. C
Telfer David, 640 Hudson
Thom Lucinda, 57 8th Av.
Thorne Mary, 73 Ridge
Thornton Mary, 67 King
Tierney Elizabeth. 121 Suffolk
Tillman A. 1 6th Av.
Tillman Eliza, 59 Anthony
Tracy Wm. 51 Washington
Turnbull Wm. C. 254 Bowery
Turner Frances L. 23 Sullivan
Turner Mary, 131 Forsyth
Upton Harriet, 243 William
Vanderbilt W. S. 418 Broadway
Van Riper Francis, 175 7th
Van Wart Isabella. 299 6th
Voelztel W. 167 8th Av.
Volger Edward C. F. 149 Greenwich
Volkers P. 198 Division
Vignot A. 205 Canal
Wakelam Jane, 110 Anthony
Walker Margaret L. 114 Clinton
Ward Agnes J. 662 Water
Warenstadt J. 37 Carmine
Waters Elizabeth M. 223 Houston
Watkins George, 338 Bowery
Watson W. H. 92 Bowery
Weir John, 68 Vandam
Wells Eliza, 178 Christopher
West & Henry, 100 Av. D.
Wetsell Peter, 270 E. 15th
Whiand Mary, 164 Eldridge
White M. 116 Division
White Wm. 90 Canal
Whiteley G. 265 6th Av.
Willets Charles, 35 Forsyth
Williams Jane, 88½ Charlton
Woodburn John, 674 Greenwich
Woods Patrick, 25 Perry
Woolsey Charlotte, 304½ Bowery
Wright Eleanor, 44 Delancy

Orange County.

Leonard Mrs. Water st. *Newburgh.*
Ferguson Mrs. do
Cunningham Mrs. N. Broadway
King Wm S. 32½ Water
Cunningham Mrs. 5 Broadway

Thread Manufacturers.

New York County.

Fair S. & G. 220 Fulton *New York.*

Saratoga County.

Storer Peter   *Waterford.*

Threshing Machine Manufacturers. (See also Founders Iron; also Machinists.)

Duchess County.

Hall A. 370 Main   *Poughkeepsie.*

Genesee County.

Townsend Asley   *Pavilion.*

Montgomery County.

Wemple J. V. A. & Son, Fonda *Mohawk*

Niagara County.

Hildreth G. W.   *Lockport.*

Orange County.

Myers Geo. W.   *Montgomery.*

Wayne County.

Taft & Barber   *Lyons.*

Tin, Copper & Sheet Iron Workers. (*See also Hardware*)

Albany County.

M'Clure J. 627 Broadway *Albany.*
Giffin John. 715 Broadway
M'Lauglin C. 22 Hudson
Whalen Thomas, 18 Church
Austin William, 43 Green
Born J. C. 90 Green
Bailey E. 84 South Pearl
Gregory E. H. & Co. 27 Green
Tremere & Wands, 21   do
Rathburn & Co. 11   do
Pasco E. & 5   do
Clark J. H. & Co 4   · do
Roberts H. & Co. 12   do
Delehenty M. 26 Beaver
Whitney & Cluett, 18 Beaver
Smith Peter, 16 Beaver
Baker C. A. 10 Green
Roseboon J. 94 Hudson
Griffin P. H. 18 Steuben
Sager P. 44 Washington
Coughtry R. T. 33 do
Brooks D. 81   do
Roseboon G.   *Coeymans.*
Smith P. West Troy   *Watervliet.*
Luffman J. D., Cohoes

Allegany County

Grover E. C.   *Angelica.*
Anderson ——   *Belfast.*
Mead H. A.   *Cuba.*

Broome County.

Hageman & Co. Chenango Forks
                          Barker.
Overhiser I. W.   *Binghamton.*
Campbell D. & Co.
Lyttle & Co.
Olmstead S. J.
Cornell A., Harpersville *Colesville.*
Robbins E. jr.   *Union.*

Cattaraugus County.

Barre C. V.   *Franklinville.*
Dow A. G.   *Randolph.*
Green & Kan

Cayuga County.

Howe & Johnson, 84 Genesee
                         Auburn.
Foster W. H. Genesee st.

Chautauque County.

Fow & Jones, Jamestown *Ellicott.*
Williams D. S.
Baldwin J. & Co.   *Elkington.*
Webb D. Silver Creek   *Hanover.*
Farnham G. D. do
Cowden R. L, Fredonia *Pomfret.*
Gallup O. O. & W. D.   *Sherman.*
Harrington & Tinney   *Westfield.*

Chemung County.

M'Coy & Wilcox   *Elmira.*
Gridley & Davenport
Scribner & Sampson
Bixby G. M.

Chenango County.

Redfield P.   *Bainbridge.*
Northrop J. B.
Darby & Lyon   *Greene.*
Reynolds & Kinney

Root Silas   *Guilford.*
Brown & Eggleston   *Oxford.*
Phillips William
Starr N.   *Sherburne.*
Nichols N.   *Smyrna.*

Clinton County.

Matthews H. & H. O., Keeseville
                         Au Sable.
Webb C. & G. N.   *Black Brook.*
Miller F. T.   *Plattsburgh.*

Cortland County.

Murray George   *Homer.*
Newell S. B.   *Marathon.*
Carr Delevan   *Truxton.*

Columbia County.

Nash & Parsons, Spencertown
                        Austerlitz.
Allen J. R. Chatham Four Corners
                         Chatham.
Olcott E. H. Warren st.   *Hudson.*
Hunt Z. & W. 264 Warren
M'Mahan Mrs. near Public square
Thomas M. E. Warren st.
Platt I. Warren st.
Whiting C.   *Kinderhook.*
Thomas Wm. A., Valatie
Hicks H. B. New Lebanon Centre
                       New Lebanon.
Shorn S.   *Stuyvesant.*

Delaware County.

Shaver & M'Nair   *Andes.*
Hathaway N. (stoves)   *Delhi.*
Perry & Howe,   do
Taylor A. & Co. do   *Franklin.*
Noble A.   do
Doolittle W. D., Clovesville
                     Middletown.
Hanford H. (stoves) Hobart
                     Stamford.
Foot W. S.   do   do
Shaw & Burrows, (stoves) Deposit
                      Tompkins.
Palmer J. S. & C.   do Deposit
Eells H.   do *Walton.*

Dutchess County.

Fry S.   *Amenia.*
Tallman D., Dover Plains *Dover.*
Hughson Augustus   *Fishkill.*
Telford Wm., Wappinger's Falls
Jabine & Armstrong, do
Armstrong I. & A. W., Hughson-
ville
Van Kleek I. Fishkill Landing
Slate A.   *Hyde Park.*
Hall & Vanderburgh, 201 Main
                     Poughkeepsie.
Stoutenburgh R. D. C. 291 Main
Coffin A. G. & Co. 281   do
Man J. 215   do
Bradley Wm. H. 266   do
M'Niff F.   *Red Hook.*
Curtis J.
Graves O.
Curtis & Pulver, Upper Red Hook
Judson N. W. H.   *Rhinebeck.*

Erie County.

Zent P. & J., Williamsville
                        Amherst.
Britton N. S U. S. Hotel Block,
Pearl st.   *Buffalo.*
Ditmore Frederick, Genesee st.
Hubbard & Hard, 237 Main
Smith John J. & Co. 191 Main
Sangster Hugh, 41 Ohio
De Witt & Dudley, 150 Main
Flagg & Pratt, 107 Main
Candee & Wiswell. 45 Main
Booth Wm. M. 54 Main
Eaton P. G., Springville *Concord.*
French & Hill, Akron   *Newstead.*

Essex County.

Murray & Kelley   *Essex.*

Rich C. A., Port Henry   *Moriah.*
Filley & Sanders   *Ticonderoga.*
Pond A. M.
Low John H.   *Westport.*
Page Freeborn H.

Fulton County.

Demarest Samuel P.   *Broadalbin.*
Seaton Abel S.   *Johnstown.*
Gilchrist H.
Phillips & Eggleston, Gloversville
Alvord C. G. Vail's Mills *Mayfield.*
Lewis Morgan, Northville
                       Northampton.

Genesee County.

Bixby & Carpenter   *Le Roy.*
Olmsted & Howan
Grannis Samuel

Greene County.

Sander Christian   *Athens.*
Vandenburgh Peter   *Coxsackie.*
Hayes A. H.   *Durham.*
Butler Aaron   *Greenville.*
M'Cabe Hamilton J.
Kimball Elias W.   *Prattsville.*
Rowley A. W.   *Windham.*

Herkimer County.

Wolcott E. & Co.   *Frankfort.*
Johnson Chauncy, Mohawk
                     German Flats.
Buchanan R. & Co. Mohr
Fetterby Thomas   *Herkimer.*
Wheeler Wm. T.   *Little Falls.*
Bradley & Crisser
Kirk & Hilton
Cooley Martin
Lankton Joel

Jefferson County.

Childs S. J.
Lord Wm. & Son   *Brownville.*
Skinner & Brothers
Webster Ransom   *Cape Vincent.*
Angell R. G. & Co.   *Clayton.*
Ingles & Huntingdon, Depauville
Butts W.   *Ellisburgh.*
Dickinson & Bigelow, Belleville
Hughes J. Mannsville
Butts W. T.   *Henderson.*
Bowen J. H. Evans' Mills *Le Ray.*
Fellows J. Three Mile Bay *Lyme.*
Wills D. C. Lafargeville *Orleans.*
Cooper Victor   *Theresa.*
Hubbard & Hooker, Carthage
                        Wilna.
M'Collom Hiram,   do

Kings County.

Dixon W. & J. 26 Atlantic
                      Brooklyn.
Willis Jas. 141 Atlantic
M'Donald C. 106 Court
Eakin H. E. cor. Court & Bergen
Carson Wm. 135 Court
Whipple P. E. 72 Fulton
Powell & Vining, 104 Fulton
Lownes Wm. D. 28 Henry
Frazier Thos. 69 Fulton
M'Intosh R. 97 Main
Locke John D. Front near Pearl
Read John, York cor. Pearl
Williams John, 166 Jay
Nattrass Ralph, 309 Fulton
Cox Jas. 109 Bridge
Maguire Peter, 103 Hudson Av.
Gill Wm. 158 Myrtle Av.
Wilson B. 124 Myrtle Av.
Johnson Chas. Navy st.
Muenster Martyn N. Myrtle Av.
Wilson John, Flushing Av.
Case R.   *Flatbush.*
Hecox Wm. East New York
Carter E. 81 S. 7th *Williamsburgh.*
Lapp P. 183 S. 4th
Gillett J. M. 283 S. 4th
Baldinger John, 97½ Grand

Jacobs E. & R. 129½ Grand
 Williamsburgh.
Marlow Wm. 289 Grand
Lapp Philip, 289 Grand
Lowerre Wm. D. 215 1st
Many & Derundeout, 1 N. 3d
Gillett Mrs. M. (dealer) 355 Grand

Lewis County.
Coventry Shotto *Turin.*
Riggs Chas. G.
Dodge J. D. Constableville
 West Turin.

Livingston County.
Brown & Grant *Dansville.*
Wood G. G.
Reynale Geo. P. & Brother
Parker A.
North H. P. *Geneseo.*
Buell Mortimer
Roberts Luke, Hemlock Lake
 Livonia.
Hall & Summers *Mount Morris.*
Sleeper & Bingham
Long Moses *York.*

Madison County.
Stillman F. *Brookfield.*
Brown & Perkins *Cazenovia.*
Spencer & Brown
Ayres & Arnold *De Ruyter.*
Hammond S. *Eaton.*
Powers H. L. Morrisville
Durham Julius, do
Foote E. *Hamilton.*
Towne Earlville
Bennett L. Oneida Depot
 Lenox.
...d, Canastota
...rthur, do
...lter *Madison*
 Stockbridge.
...nzo, Chittenango
 Sullivan.

Monroe County.
Pride Asa, West Mendon *Mendon.*
Ward H. *Penfield.*
Parsons J. P. & J. C.
Ward E. Fairport *Perrinton.*
Warrens & Southworth, 18 South
St. Paul *Rochester.*
Woodruff R. (Tin Boxes) 3 Scio
Russell Geo. 74 Main
Hustin Cornelius, 119 Buffalo
Sharp Austin W. 180 Buffalo
Cone H. C. 122 State
Whaples Calvin, 210 State
Lockwood J. H. 31 State
Morse & Moran, 71 State
Cowles Jas. 13 Front
Bruce John, 29 Front
Miller A. (Japaned Ware) 30 Main
Parish Nathan *Rush.*
Backus, Fitch & Co. 50 Main,
Brockport *Sweden.*
Seymour & Morgan, Brockport
Slocum Geo. E. Scottsville
 Wheatland.

Montgomery County.
Gardiner L. Y. *Amsterdam.*
Warring Jeremiah
Hull A. W. Tribe's Hill
Barnes & Davis *Canajoharie.*
Ehle Charles
French David *Florida.*
Teller & Folsom, Fonda *Mohawk.*

New York County.
Adelbert E. 191 Clinton *New York.*
Abrahamson J. 147 W. Broadway
Aikin Jas. W. 367½ Cherry
Anderson David W. 71 6th Av.
Andrews Burr, 112 South
Andrews J. D. 210 Water
Andrews Robert J. 568 Houston
Armand Lewis H. 13 Thomas

25

Bailey Anthony, 82 W. Broadway
 New York.
Baker John R. 529 Grand
Beaumont Wm. 211 Fulton
Bennet Andrew H. 92 Catharine
Black Chas. 125 3d Av.
Blacklin & Stitt, 23 New
Blackman Abram, 121 Walker & 479½ Pearl
Boireau Alphonse V. 145 Fulton
Bruce John, 315 Stanton
Bruce J. M. 186 & 188 Water
Borz John, 249 Stanton
Burns John, 226 1st Av.
Caffrey John, 75 9th Av.
Cannon Cornelius, 176 Wooster
Cargill Abraham, 282 Pearl
Cargill Wm. 231 Water
Carroll Richard, 79 Mulberry
Carter Edward & Co. 213 Pearl
Chappell Wm. 86 Pike
Cherf W. S. 537 Bowery
Clark John, 168 Division
Cochran Jas. 7 Greenwich Av.
Cogswell & L'Amoureux, 301 Spring
Cook Chas. 123½ Division
Cook Ernest, 47 Pitt
Cooke Fred. 8th Av.
Cooney Patrick, 15 8th Av.
Corree ——, 3 Bedford
Corrigan Patrick, jr. 345 Houston
Cotton S. B. 86 Amity
Daniels John, 162 South
Darragh John, 366 3d Av.
Day Robert, 52 Walnut
Dean Thos. 224 Spring
Deems Henry W. 53 Carmine
Dibble John H. 196 Reade
Doughty Albert H. 40 South
Downey Patrick, 387 Grand
Drake Jas. H. 191 9th
Dunn Michael, 83 Bayard
Durlack M. 207 Houston
Evans Richard, 40 Ann
Fanley Alexander, 8½ Spring
Favereau Francis, 104 Catharine
Fefallick George F. 4 Ludlow
Felix Edward, 148 Church
Finley Aaron, 2 1st
Finley Alexander, 6 Spring
Finnegan James, 97 Broad
Foley P. 8 3d Av.
Frazer & Everitt, 36 Gold
Frilees Andrew, 242 3d
Gellaghan John, 15 4th Av
Gangloff Joseph, 46 Canal
Gasaner Morris, rear 67 Vesey
Gay James, 196 Varick
Gilmore R. 8th Av.
Gogin Michael, 44 W. Broadway
Goldsmith Henry, 59 Ludlow
Gorton Simeon, 75 4th
Gosselin E. 30 Pine
Grant James, rear 83 Duane & 280 Broadway
Greason George, 54 6th Av.
Green Timothy, 143 Houston
Gregory John, 200 8th Av.
Gregory R. A. 383 6th Av.
Gregory Samuel, 46 Madison
Gunning Martin, 722 Washington
Gustav Moses, 423 Grand
Harris Elias T. 70 Av. D
Hawley F. S. 197 Reade
Hay James, 2 Crosby
Heald John, 246 Canal
Hedderburgh F. L. 79 Division
Hersh Adolph, 264 3d
Hetsel Christian, 193 1st Av.
Hickenbolton Robert, 2 1st
Hickinbothem Wm. 267 Bowery
Hinds James, 59 Canal
Hinds William, 607 Greenwich
Hogbin Robert, 370 Madison
Hunt Hugh, 80 Centre
Huse John B. 20 Greenwich Av.
Hynes Edward, 44 Elm
Jager Andrew, 6 Av. C & 226 Houston
Jaquis Charles, 332 Greenwich
Jaquiss Thomas, 155 Grand

Johnson Robert, 119 Charles
 New York.
Kane Charles, 319 Bowery
Kierski Moritz, 423 Grand
Kissam James A. 67 Fulton
Knott John, 208 Rivington
Lancaster John, 119 Stanton
Lawrence W. B. 419 Cherry
Levi Benjamin, 264 3d
Lewis Thomas, 46 Rose
Lightbody Colin, 132 Front
Lightbody James, 85 Marke'
Lindsay David, 134 8th Av.
Lindsay John, 126 8th Av.
Loewenstein Charles, 298 Broad'y
Loewenstein John, 26 Av. B
Lorton George J. 156 Broadway
Lynch E. 128 Warren
M'Cadin B. 181 Prince
M'Connell John, 193 Greenw'h Av.
M'Donald Jeremiah, 172½ Cherry
M'Kinzie Thos. 185 6th Av.
Markewitz A. 120 Houston
Marrener Edward, 162 Grand
Martin & M'Ever, 311 Broome
Mason Francis, 248 Greenwich
Matthews John, 477 Washington
Mead Walter H. 19 8th Av.
Mead & Eckert, 316 Bleecker
Meehan Charles, 103 Cherry
Mark August, 35 Cannon
Merkle George F. 77 Bleecker
Merret F. S. 116 Bleecker
Miller, Coates & Towle, 275 Pearl
Miller D. D. 209 Water
Miller Joseph, 5 Av. B
Mills James, 56 W. Broadway
Monsees Herman W. 56 Bowery
Moore Daniel, 30 Marion
Moore Edward, 187 Houston
Moore James, 51 Spring
Moore John, 116 Mulberry
Moore William, 647 Greenwich
Moran Martin, 130 Cherry
Moubery John, 526 Grand
Mowbray R. & J. 199 Greenwich
Muckle Edmund P. 339 6th Av.
Mulane William, 95 John
Munn Wm. A. 29½ Carmine
Murphy John, 256 Water
Myers Aaron P. 236 South
Nash William, 53 Thompson
Nelson Morks, 164 Walker
Newmann James, 260 Bowery
Nicholson William, 617 Hudson
Norris William H. 81 Pine
Nott John, 30 Rivington
O'Neil Michael, 50 Madison
Parker Benjamin. 407 Hudson
Peace Alfred S. 153 3d Av.
Pearce C. 8th Av.
Peterson George, 111 Greenwich
Poole Henry A. 40 3d Av.
Porters Wm. 258 Water
Potts Wm. 72 Fulton, basement
Radley James, 5 Av. D
Rea & Pollock, 48 Cortlandt
Reiching C. 31st st. near 8th Av.
Ressenweber F. 1 Cortlandt
Richards John, 7 5th
Riedel Henry, 154 2d
Ritter Richard, 107 W. Broadway
Roberts Benjamin, 192½ Greene
Roberts G. 155 Spring
Roberts William, 90 Crosby
Robinson Anthony, 163 Greenw'h
Robinson John, 134 Beekman
Robinson Thomas, 438 Broome
Rollhaus Daniel, 312 Hudson
Rose Justus J. 195 Division
Runnells John H. 101 Houston
Rusher J. B. & G. 22 Old slip
Sander Adam, 63 4th Av.
Scherf Wolfgang, 337 Bowery
Schloss Joseph, 3 2d
Scudder Jonah, 144 3d Av.
Selberassen George, 22 Crosby
Simmon Simon, 171 Walker
Simpson Charles C. 81 Canal
Sinnefelder Leonard, 121 Chrystie
Skillman J. jr. 271 Greenwich
Skeel Geo. R.

Smith Thomas D. 147 Houston
   New York.
Smith T. & Co. 77 Fulton
Smith, Torrey & Co. 45 & 50
   Maiden lane
Somerville A. & M. 260 Water
Southwell & Roberts, 134 4th
Stanley W. J. 42 Water
Steudner Edward, 81 Bowery
Stewart William, 88 Laurens
Stouplen Charles, 87 Norfolk
Striker Wm. H. 243 Grand
Summers Alex. B. 27 Av. D
Sumner Palmer, 168 & 215 Greenwich
Swan Wm. 61 9th Av.
Taylor Edward, 544 Hudson
Teots Philip, 296 Greenwich
Thompson Robert, 179 Laurens
Tiebout N. 116 Beekman
Tompkins William, 82 Delancy
Ullman Charles A. 238 William
Underhill David, 125 Bowery
Underhill Joshua. 358 Grand
Valentine Benj. C. 227 Greene
Vanevery Henry, 222 Greenwich
Vanvoorhis J. 84 W. Broadway
Waack Thomas, 294½ Division
Watson Joseph, 63 King
Weight Peter D. 38th st. 9th Av.
Whipps Frederick, 359 Grand
White Pardon, 94 8th Av.
White Pardon, jr. 180 8th Av.
Whitlock James, 58 Oak
Williams George, 77 Charlton
Williamson George, 201½ Grand
Williamson George, 208 Spring
Williamson George, 81 Ludlow
Williamson Hugh, 3 M'Dougal
Williamson Isaac, 131 Orange
Williamson Isaac, 109 7th Av.
Williamson Isaac, 141 Varick
Williamson John, 266 Canal
Williamson John, 158 8th Av.
Williamson W. 810 8th Av.
Winchell Madison, 364 Broome
Wood Daniel, 159 11th
Wood W. 197 Reade
Woodgate Henry, 47 W. Broad'y
Woolcocks Thomas J. 107 Fulton
Woolley & Pearce, 158 3d Av.
Youngman Frederick, 5 James
Zimmerman Charles, 314 Hudson

Niagara County.

Keep C. & Co.   *Lockport.*
Mac & Flagler
Flagler H. & Co.
Bellah J. T.
Pound Alexander
Fassett & Parsons *Niagara Falls.*

Oneida County.

Hollenbeke D. *New Hartford.*
Giles H. G. & Co. Dominick st.
   Rome.
Spencer A. W.   do
Berrill J. A., Waterville
   Sangersfield.
Carton John, 132 Genesee *Utica.*
Tyrrel E. & Son, 47 do
Bright W. J. 28 Liberty
Mather S. 8 Bleeker
Desmond J. 4 Catherine
Metcalf N. F.   *Vernon.*
Clark Almond *Whitestown.*
Fennel Adin K.
Crane Hiram, Whitesboro

Onondaga County.

Marvin & Wilson, Baldwinsville
   Lysander.
Dunbar & Co. Baldwinsville
Gilmora R.   *Manlius.*
James J. W. & Co. Arcade Building, Syracuse *Salina.*
Ford J. H. Salina st.
Smith N.   *Skaneateles.*
Bench J.

Ontario County.

Frazer R. P.   *Canandaigua.*
Bradley Wm. *East Bloomfield.*
Powers S. A.   *Manchester.*
Waterman A. B.   *Phelps.*
Hayes B. S., Honeoye *Richmond.*
Snyder Richard, Geneva *Seneca.*
Gleason Joel,   do
Critchell Wm.   do
Tillman John H.   do
Proughty John S.   do
Ackley C. B. & Co. do
Dickinson A. P.   *Victor.*

Orange County.

Washburn Darius S., Washington-
   ville *Blooming Grove.*
Lewis M.   *Chester.*
Pelton H. A. & E. H., Buttermilk
   Falls *Cornwall.*
Hare U. & Co. Port Jervis
   Deer Park.
Rowley J. M. & C. do
Lomas John, 38 Water *Newburgh.*
Gordan J. & Co. 92 Water
Buchanan Geo. Colden st.
Merritt C. & Co. 16 Water
Finch J. L., New Hampton
   Wallkill.
Moore D. F.   *Warwick.*

Orleans County.

Morehouse H.. Albion *Barre.*
Hollenbake J. H. do
Jennings J., Medina *Ridgeway.*
Parsons John,   do
Morehouse Isaac, Lyndonville
   Yates.

Oswego County.

Worster Alvah *Hannibal.*
Beely & Morse, Central Square
   Hastings.
Smith & Fuller *Mexico.*
Clark S.
Merriam S. G. *New Haven.*
Jones & M'Carty, Pulaski
   Richland.
Meachams & Norton, Pulaski
Culver A. B., Phœnix *Schroeppel.*

Otsego County.

Luce Stephen, Burlington Flats
   Burlington.
Jackson & Briggs *Butternuts.*
Hotchkiss Ashby, Schenevas
   Maryland
Briggs George L. *Middlefield.*
Van Wort S.   *Oneonta.*
Johnson C.
Smith L. & Co. Cooperstown
   Otsego.
Bolles Frederick A. *Unadilla.*
Cone Lewis G.
Cone & Bolles

Putnam County.

Barnes A. I.   *Carmel.*
Pelton H. A. & E. A. Cold Spring
   Phillipstown.

Queens County.

Whitlock B.   *Flushing.*
Welsh Thomas *Hempstead.*
Carmen Coles
Halsey E. W.   *Jamaica.*
Ketcham S. A. Roslyn
   North Hempstead.
Watkins Treat, Jericho
   Oyster Bay.

Rensselaer County

Lee Jas. 275 State *Lansingburgh.*
Deyoe George C. 294 State
Filley Edwin, 6 Hoosick
Seely & Tilly, 132 River *Troy.*
Edson Thos. H. 247 do
Corss & Fay, 283 do

Aikin E. G. 374 River *Troy.*
Williamson Caleb, 365 River
Bussey Thomas, do do
Howard E. S. & Son, 25 North 3d
Swort James, 50 Congress
Joyce Wm. W. 72 do
Rogers, Crannell & Tilkins, 59
   Congress

Richmond County.

Miles W. Tompkinsville *Castleton.*
Swain John G. do
Mason J. Factoryville
Swain G. T. Port Richmond
   Northfield.
Brannin John, Stapleton *Southfield.*

Rockland County.

Myers George S. *Haverstraw.*
Craig W.
Mabie D. A. Piermont *Orangetown.*
Johnson J. M. Nyack
Eells R. P.   do

St. Lawrence County.

Parsons R. H. *Gouverneur.*
Beard & Cadwell *Herman.*
Hatch A. S. & Co. Waddington
   Madrid.
Knapp O. S.   *Massena.*
Fournier Anthony *Morristown.*
Chaney A. & Co. Water st. Ogdensburgh *Oswegatchie.*
Pitkin N. S. cor. River & Lake sts.
   Ogdensburgh
Higbee Stephen S. Isabella st. Ogdensburgh
Church Havey, Ford st. Ogdensburgh
Wilkinson Edwin *Potsdam.*

Saratoga County.

Hayes James D. *Galway.*
Beers Wm.
M'Coy Henry H. *Saratoga.*
Osborn Jacob
Collamer Daniel
Hermance Levi
Benedict John *Saratoga Springs.*
Savage James
Terwilliger S. T.
Hammond & Howland *Stillwater.*
Drummer E. & S. *Waterford.*

Schenectady County.

Smith Abel, 122 State *Schenectady.*

Schoharie County.

Lovett John *Esperance.*
Hayes Wm. B.   *Gilboa.*
Spelmidine R. *Jefferson.*
Deyo Marcus S. *Middleburgh.*
Mann Henry *Richmondville.*
Gates W. S. *Schoharie.*
Whipple & Gordon, Gallupville
   Wright.

Seneca County.

Root S. O. Farmer *Ovid.*

Steuben County.

Goddard A.   *Addison.*
Biles & Roby *Bath.*
Church L. V. & E. F.
Childs Harvey M. *Canton.*
Hodskin & Leckrider

Suffolk County.

Chadsayne Joseph, Patchogue
   Brookhaven.
Bates Charles *Riverhead.*
Brown A. & O. Greenport
   Southold.

Sullivan County.

Clark L. Monticello *Thompson.*

Tompkins County.

Whitmore George, 108 Owego
    Ithaca.
Curtis O. 87 Owego

Ulster County.

Shaw Wm. H.   *Kingston.*
Osterhout J. P.
Welch John C.   *Saugerties.*
Myer Peter K.
Davis Jacob S.
Jones & Shook, Napanock
    Wawarsing.
Washburn & Carr, Ellenville

Warren County.

Peck Noble, Glenn's Falls
    Queensbury.
Peck Harman,   do
Richards William *Warrensburgh.*

Washington County.

Gorham Issac K. & Brother
    Argyle.
Culver Oscar F.   *Cambridge.*
Robertson Joel. Galesville *Easton.*
Carrington Sidney *Fort Edward.*
Safford Jacob   *Greenwich.*
Thompson & Hooper
Bassett James H. Galesville
Doubleday Danvers, Sandy Hill
    Kingsbury.
Gordon P. North White Creek
    White Creek.
Blen H. Canal st.   *Whitehall.*
Griswold G. S. Canal st.
Merritt J. R. Chapin's Block
Parke H. N   do

Wayne County.

Pettiss Wm.   *Arcadia.*
Remson & Polhemus   *Lyons.*
Bourne & Bradish
Malone Gilson, Macedon Centre
    Macedon.
Manley E.   *Marion.*
Hart Wm.   *Palmyra.*
Clement, Hewson & Co.   *Sodus.*
Ward Henry, Pultneyville
    Williamson.
Parks James   *Wolcott.*

Westchester County.

Clark George   *Bedford.*
Sutton G. T. Peekskill *Courtlandt.*
Gallagher G. & J. P. Peekskill
Marshall & Co.   do
Clapp Benjamin A. Tarrytown
    Greenburgh.
Curtis C. Tarrytown
Wells David T.   *Mamaroneck.*
Longstaff Wm.   *New Rochelle.*
Washburn Benjamin S. Sing Sing
    Ossining.
Barlow & Jarvis, Sing Sing
Edgett A. S.   do
Pixley & Curtis, Portchester *Rye.*
White John   *White Plains.*
Gaylor George   *Yonkers.*

Wyoming County.

Fitch, Barry & Co.   *Attica.*
Matteson George, Cowlesville
    Bennington.
Davison A. P.   *Castile.*
Dillingham John   *China.*
Clark E. P.   *Perry.*
Windsor S.   *Pike.*
Woodruff Y. J. Varysburgh
    Sheldon.
Gates & Garretsee   *Warsaw.*
Hodge & Morris
Carpenter John

Yates County.

Vail Charles, Branchport
    Jerusalem.
Wolcott & White, Penn Yan *Milo.*

Morgan & Caton, Dundee *Starkey.*
Murdock N. F.   do

Tobacconists. (*See also Cigar Dealers—Also Cigar Manufacturers.*)

Albany County.

Payne & McNaughton, 7 Broadway
    Albany.
Stilwell Thomas B. 817 and 819 Broadway
Groer A. 822 Broadway
Engle John, 720 Broadway
Stavenow Julius, (cigars) 266 Broadway
Phillips H. (cigars) 80½ State
Sprague H. 54 Dean
Davis Daniel S. cor. Church and Lydius
Frank I. (cigars) 318 S. Pearl
Ridder T. B. 78 S. Pearl
Gott John, 7 James
Brown & Teelin, 35 Washington
Sweet H. M., W. Troy *Watervliet.*

Broome County.

Candee & Mason   *Binghamton.*

Cayuga County.

Coventry C. Genesee st. *Auburn.*
Baker E. North st.

Chemung County.

Nicks John J.   *Elmira.*

Columbia County.

Crego & Backus, Chatham Four Corners   *Chatham.*
Campbell Wm. (cigars) Warren st.   *Hudson.*
Mesick W. H. (cigars) Public sq.
Marcy Alex. W. do Warren st.
Marshall B. (snuff)   *Stockport.*
Ida Manufacturing Co.

Cortland Co.

Dewitt C. (cigars)
    Cortland Village.

Duchess County.

Barker J. B.   *Amenia.*
Marsh J., Glenham   *Fishkill.*
Walker J. M. 337 Main
    Poughkeepsie.
Schnapp E. 219 Main
Coldstream Wm., Main st.
Maxon S. H. 358 Main
Hendricks J. & Co.   *Red Hook.*
Reed T.   *Rhinebeck.*

Erie County.

Athearn C. & Co. (wholesale) 207 Washington   *Buffalo.*
Arkenburgh R. H.   do 5 Terrace
Vanderburgh S. (importer) 302 Main
Emigh A. & Co. 11 Webster's Block
Sever Oscar, 193 Main
Van Slyke John, 98 Main

Greene County.

Foot Alfred   *Catskill.*
Mann A. & Co.

Kings County.

Bogert Abraham L. (cigars) 16 Atlantic   *Brooklyn.*
Hattorf F. A. 17 Fulton
Blair John, 65½ Fulton
Fitch Wm. T. 47 James
Cook Alford H. 54 Main
Matthias H. 80½ Main
Beaty William, 101 Sands

Sullivan J. 175 Fulton   *Brooklyn.*
Barth Richard L. 33 Hudson Av.
Chichester Alexander, 99 Myrtle Av.
Weeks John, 163 Myrtle Av.
Henry Langlan, Flushing Av.
Bramm John, 54 Atlantic
Quimby J. L. & R. A. 100 Fulton
Kehl Charles, 91 Main
Handlen William, 84 Nassau
Miller M. & Co. Myrtle Av. near Nostrand Av.
Booz W. S. (cigars) 120 Fulton
Flexer F. M.   do   Flushing Av. near Franklin
Smith I. F.   do 43 S. 7th
    Williamsburgh.
Henry James, do 19 S. 7th
Dietrich A.   do 269 S. 4th
Vandewater Joseph H. (cigars) 103 S. 1st
Brady Bernard, (cigars) 287 Grand
Runcie Wm. & Brother, (cigars) 150 Grand
Betts W. W. (cigars) 76 Grand
Brown Joseph M. (cigars) 140 Grand
Shavel Domonick, (cigars) 129 Ewing

Monroe County.

Dwinelle John W. Phoenix Buildings rear Buffalo st.   *Rochester.*
Palmer J. H. Eagle Block, Buffalo st.
Suggett Henry, 16 Main
Hamilton Wm. 5 Arcade
Van Slyck A. 13 Exchange
Disbrow John, wholesale dealer in cut and leaf tobacco, 11 Exchange
Ketchum Richard, 48 State
Palmer J. H. (cigars) Eagle Block, Buffalo st.

Montgomery County.

Witnam A.   *Canajoharie.*
Ullman Morris. Fort Plain *Minden.*

New York County.

Acorn Margaret, 230 Canal
    New York.
Adrian M. J. 200 Division
Agnew C. 116 Water
Anderson John & Co. 106 Broadway & 4 Thames
Appleby Leonard L. F. 90 Wall & 119 Water
Appleby & Moore, 96 Wall
Bogert Abraham L. 56 Vesey
Bowen E. C. 97 Columbia
Bradenburg Samuel, 479 Broome
Burridge Thos. 431 Water
Cook C. J. 45 Canal
Cleland Henry L. 62½ Bleecker
Deen John, 78 Water
Deen John L. 78 Water
Duryee Daniel, 252 Water
Eglinger & Hess, 31½ Av. A
Finck Louis A. 47½ Pearl
Fisher J. C. 157½ Washington
Flynn John, 356 Pearl
Fossing John. 70 Thompson
Goodwin & Brother, 155 South
Goldsmith ——, 124 Canal
Guthrie John B. 245 Front
Haddock W. J. & R. 554 Hudson
Haslebarth George W. 496 Houston
Harman George, 190 Bowery
Hoffman & Schubert, 262 Division
Lear Oscar H. 560 Grand
Lemon William C. 4 Wall & 213 Duane
Lillenthal C. H. & S. 219 Washington & 78 Barclay
M'Chesney Adam, 74 Front
M'Entee Jas. 186 West 16th
M'Coy J. B. 102 Bowery
Meeker C. W. 157 Broadway
Metzger Marks, 9 Peck slip
Mickle A. H. 110 Water

Miller G. B. 110 Water *New York.*
Mitchel Lepene, 72 Division
Monal Alex. 394 10th
Newcombe G. 145 Broadway
Oakley Cornelius, 96 Water
Olmstead Joseph, 576½ Grand
Payne Jos. H. 361 Pearl
Riell Henry, 77 Front
Riker Alfred, 3 Bedford
Roome Edward, 184 Water, Ida
    Tobacco Manufacturing Co.
Sagehorn Henry, 83 Barclay &
    349 Washington
Sammanos A. A. 94 Broadway
Schott George, 177 Washington
Sears Edw. F. 38 West Broadway
Sherck Louis, 155½ Canal
Snowhill Wm. O. 2 Wall
Snyder John J. 17 Laurens
Speaights Charles, 73 Bowery
Speers W. F. 105 Water
Titus Cornelius B. 222 Bleecker
    & 11 6th Av.
Tucker W. H. 8 Peck slip
Usher Robt. jr. 44 Broadway
Van Dursen A. S. W. 137½ Division
Welle & Mayer, 15 & 17 Chrystie
Whittam Henry, 535 Water
Winser Edward, 81 9th Av.
Wilson John & Co. 104 Front
Wyre A. 438½ Broadway
Zooller T. A. 404 2d Av.

Oneida County.

Avery, Ferguson & Co. (cigars)
    James st.   *Rome.*
Miller H. T. (cigars) 6 Liberty
                          Utica.
Wilkins L. (cigars) 33 & 35
    Bleeker
Warnick & Eryan, 86 Genesee
Bushnoll H. 1. 55 Hotel
Miller H. T. 6 Liberty

Onondaga County.

Johnson & Huggins, Arcade Buildings, Syracuse   *Salina.*
Salmon D. & D. O. Genesee st.

Ontario County.

Douglas William, Geneva
                         Seneca.

Orange County.

Stimble D. H.   *Cornwall.*
Smith Alonzo   *Montgomery.*
Conger John S.
Carter Enoch, 50 Water
                       Newburgh
Hyat S. Colden st.
Dannat William E. 50 Water
M'Cullough John, Front st.
Edwards A. G. South Middletown
                        Wallkill.

Oswego County.

Swart Abram, cor. 1st & Cayuga
                          Oswego.
Lieb John, 1st bet. Canal & River
Jacobs C W. & J. M. 1st st.
Doolittle Wm. M. jr.   do

Otsego County.

Viney John, (cigars)   *Unadilla.*

Queens County.

Whollahan William   *Jamaica.*
Wood Eldred
Neat George
Fish J. J. Brushville

Rensselaer County.

Ganter Charles, (cigars) 67 State
                      Lansingburgh.
Neal Charles O. (cigars) 381½
    River   *Troy.*
Carr J. (cigars) 9th st.

Dally L. (cigars) 7 Grand Division
                          Troy.
Freeman Thomas, (cigars) 6
    Boardman Buildings
Lambert & Krutzelman, (cigars)
    19 Congress
Zimmermann Godfrey, 32 Ferry
Woodruff John. (cigars) 1da Hill
Christie John, 253 River
Neal Charles O, 381½ River
Orvis P. D. & Co., wholesale
    agents for E. Roome's, fine cut
    tobacco, 305 River
Ager William, Ida Hill
Conihe M. & Co. 137 River
Fingado Charles, 3 King
Warner Hiram, 119 5th
Lambert & Krutzelman, 19 Congress

Rockland County.

Wilson J. C. (cigars) Nyack
                    Orangetown.
Smith J. F. (cigars) Spring Valley

St. Lawrence County.

Clark C. P. Water st. Ogdensburgh
                      Oswegatchie.

Schenectady County.

Clement L. M. State st.
                    Schenectady.

Tioga County.

Wilson C. F. (cigars) Newark
    Valley   *Newark.*
Ogden & Leonard, Newark Valley
Bayette Joseph   *Richford.*

Tompkins County.

Grant H J. 98 Owego   *Ithaca.*
Brainard G. & Co. Geneva st.

Ulster County.

Cooper Gilbert   *Kingston.*
Bush Seymour, Eddyville

Westchester County.

Cox Lewis B. Peekskill *Courtland.*
Lush Richard, Portchester *Rye.*

Wyoming County.

Cooper Benjamin *Genesee Falls.*

Tobacco Warehouses.

Adams & M'Chesney, 74 Front
                      New York.
Agnew William & Sons, 284 & 286
    Front
Agnew C. 116 Water
Arkenbourgh R. H. 171 Front
Blow & March, 91 Water
Collins Peter D. & Son. 124 Front
Connolly Charles M. 45 Water
De Ma Carty G. 78 Broadway
Drew Thomas, jr. 165 Front
Dubois & Vandervoort, 37 Water
Erler Charles J. 221 Front
Esenwein Frederick, 13 West
Farish John J. 75 Broad
Farley George, 166 Cherry
Goodwin E. & Brother, 153 South
Handlen William, 21 Old slip
Hanna John, 249 Front
Hawkins & Logan. 112 Front
Holt & Palmer, 222 Front
Hopkins & Logan, 112 Front
Hoyt Thomas & Co. 256 Front
Lorillard Peter, 42 Chatham
Ludlam & Lazenby, 151 Front
Messenger T. & H. 161 Maiden la.
Messenger William H. 225 Front
Monahan & Beers, 173 Front
Mullen John, 129 Front
Oakley Cornelius, 96 Water

Patterson & Dortic, 104 Front
                      New York.
Price William M. 175 Front
Smallwood J. L. 24 South William
Smith Adam & Co. 28 Front
Speer W. F. 105 Water
Storm Charles, 93   do
Tucker William H. 8 Peck slip
Usher Robert, jr. 44 Broadway
Van Schaick F. C. & Co. commission merchants, 65 Front

Tool Stores.

Barry S. S. 242½ Grand
                      New York.
Dyer Charles C. 510 Greenwich
Fairbank Henry F 62 Chatham
Hill John, 397 Broadway
M'Clain Orlando D. 167 Spring
Rigby J. H. 60 Chatham
Searl Ashbel, 18 Horatio
Tracy C. C. 457 Hudson
Vanveghten Richard, 96 Division
Wood Thomas J. 62 Chatham

Tow Dealer.

Rensselaer County.

Smith D. River st. near Jay *Troy.*

Towing.

Anderson Wm. T. Pier No. 1 N. R.
                      New York.
Hudson River Towing Association, 15 South
Martin Joseph T. 37 South
Philips Isaac O. 65   do

Toy Stores. (*See also Fancy Goods.*)

Cayuga County.

Cooley H. H. & Co. North st.
                      Auburn.

New York County.

Allair Thomas H. 419 Broadway
                      New York
Anoae Simon, 237 Centre
Arnstein & Unger, 375½ Grand
Baptist John, 24 Grand
Blum Mrs. C. 354 Broadway
Browning Eleanor. 307 Wash'ton
Butler Hannah, 6 Crosby
Carrol Wm. 358 Greenwich
Cawley John, 19 Elm
Cuddy Elizabeth, .159 Orange
Curry John, 76 3d Av.
Dillon James, 143 Madison
Faland P. 484 Houston
Fiske Alonzo, 694 Broadway
Fitzgerald Morris, 214 Rivington
Fowler W. 30 Houston
Fudge Henry, 67 W. 21st
Goetz Christopher, 26 Division
Gordon E. 269 Greenwich
Graham J. S. 385 Grand
Hart Timothy, 24 College place
Hart & Co. 419 Broadway
Hearn Julia, 45 Centre
Higham James, 34 Av. C
Hol Adam, 302 Grand
Hovendon James B. 294 Greenw'h
Hutchinson Matthew, 75 Barclay
Jolley Oscar & Co. 330½ Grand
Kipp James, 68 Av. D
Lee Mary E. 362 Bowery
Lewin Frederick O. 216 Grand
M'Cormick —— 131 Mott
Mills Oliver, 194 6th Av.
Mose John, 144 Grand
Murphy John, 143 Greenwich
Newland James, 246 Stanton
O'Brien Julian, 441 Greenwich

O'Brien Michael, 64 Market *New York.*
O'Hearn Hugh, 95 Madison
O'Nell & Mann
Parkson Wm. 234 Greenwich
Paul Thomas, 456 Greenwich
Freudhomme E. T. 76½ Bleecker
Furver William, 8 Av. A.
Randall Jesse & S. 241 Broadway
Rinicke C. 286 Houston
Roberts William, 44 Leonard
Sondheim B. 88 Chatham
Spencer James, 10 Doyer
Stevens Sarah, 38 8th Av.
Stamp Jane, 219 Canal
Tice Matthew, 47 Av. B
Towner James, 53 Houston
Tubbs Anne, 122 4th Av.
Vickers James, 56 5d Av.
Welsh Mrs. 489 Pearl
White W. 116 Division
Wood George Alfred, 199 3d Av.

Toy Importers.

Ahrenfeldt Chas. 56 Maiden lane *New York.*
Brown William C. 63 Division
Frey Wm. H. & Brother, 62 John
Haas·J. 138 William
Montgomery C. J. 412 Pearl
Purdy & Robbins, 24 Maiden lane
Wagner William, 46 Maiden lane

Translators.

Erthellere M. 42 John *New York.*
Hayward James W. 50 Wall. Portuguese, Spanish and French languages
Smith Thomas J. jr. 76 Wall
Underhill D. C. 168 Bowery

Trap Manufacturer.

Fulton County.
Kinnicut Hiram *Mayfield.*

Trunk Makers. *(See also Saddle & Harness Makers.)*

Beck Peter S. 122 Houston & 413 Grand *New York.*
Black John, 112 Maiden lane
Blakeney J. L. 526 Broadway
Bogart Ralph, 339 Hudson
Briant Isaac H. 95 Beaver
Brock Adolph, 13 Park row
Buckmaster Thos. O. 323 Hudson & 121 Chatham
Bull J. B. & Jas. 206 Broadway
Cattnach J. 86 Broadway & 1 Wall
Chambers Richard A. 1 Murray
Cornell Viner L. 189 Broadway
Crouch & Fitzgerald, 1 Maiden lane, 176 Broadway, & 176 Chatham
Curr Jas. 201 Canal & 206 Hudson
Dawes Wm. 62 6th Av.
Donaldson & Breakley, 203 Bowery
Eston Thos. H. 14 Catharine
Farmer Edgar, 96 Maiden lane & 167 Pearl
Fick & Hucharski, 9 Bowery
Fisk Azariah, 4 Gouverneur
Gautner John, 340 6th
Gibson Wood, 160 Fulton
Hall & Wilcox, 48 & 49 Cortlandt
Halstead Geo. 210 Canal
Hamilton Jas. 2½ Cortlandt
Hand Robert H. 1 John
Hill John. 435 Hudson
Hill J. & Co. 1 Warren
Holmes Alex. B. 413 Grand
Jacques Wm. C. 135 Broadway
Johnson Jeremiah, 102 & 104 Maiden lane, 40 Fulton & 268 Pearl

Lisle H. M. 69 4th Av. & 11 3d Av. *New York.*
Loss Adolphus, 416 Broadway
Macdonald Chas J. 72 Bleecker
Macdonald & Lowry, 836 Br'dway
Macdonald R. J. East 13th cor. Broadway
Macomber Sandford L. 86 Allen
Michaels Wm. H. 111 Broadway
Milton Edward J. 403 Grand
Nodyne H. 219 Greenwich
Olssen R. H. 114 & 116 Maiden la.
Olssen R. H. & Son, 201 Pearl
Peddie & Morrison, 71 Maiden la.
Peters & Rorbach, 70 Maiden lane
Phillip H. & Son, 165 Broadway
Rampea J. F. 131½ Bowery
Reed Ephraim, 100 Broadway
Rorbach Chas. P. 9 Liberty
Selger B. M. 1 11th
Shermann Walter B. 172 Chrystie
Sked John R. 158 Fulton
Smith John, 319 Grand
Smith, Wright & Co. 129 Maiden lane
Sofield Samuel, 340 6th
Stillings Isaac I. 217 Canal
Storms C. S. 58 Fulton
Strong R. S. & W. B. 2 Peck slip
Taylor Wm. H. 280 Bleecker
Thorne John W. 18 Cedar & 105 Barrow
Tyler Chas. H. 643 Broadway
Underhill Alpheus, 196 Greene
Van Pelt, Leveridge & Co. 12 Maiden lane
Watson John, 286 2d
Wells Jas. 398 Pearl
Williams Erastus. 40 Rose
Wilson David C. 187 Pearl
Wilson John, 131 Bowery
Wilson John, 146 Walker
Wilson John, 135 Bowery
Wilson ——, 341 Pearl
Woodruff H. S. 24 Cedar & 53 Murray
Yasinake C. W. 205 Spring

Truss Makers.

Clinton County.
Babbitt L. Keeseville *Au Sable.*

Kings County.
Hathaway Mrs. Eliza, 152 Grand *Williamsburgh.*

New York County.
Acret Geo. E. 96 Broadway *New York.*
Benjamin Jos. R. 13 Beekman
Brown Letitia, 474 Greenwich
Butler Fred. M. 4 Vesay
Chamberlain Jos. 2½ Cortlandt
Goulding Wm. R. 83 Maiden lane
Hart & Co. 49 Fulton
Marsh S. N. & Co. 2 Cortlandt
Pintard Wm. 118 Sheriff
Sanderson Jos. M. 6 Barclay
Sherman Edwin W. 155 Fulton
Sherman Sylvester J. 177½ William & 41 Beekman
Stacey Elizabeth F. 234 Wooster
Wittig Louis, 67 Lispenard

Orange County.
Francks Jonathan *Newburgh.*

Turners.

Albany County.
Morrow J. & Stephens, 50 Howard *Albany.*
Pierce J. 45 Maiden lane
Mann E. Reedsville *Berne.*
Hochtrasser P. do
Barnard J. M. West Troy *Waterviet.*

Broome County.
Ransom & Flint *Maine.*

Cattaraugus County.
Lewis Ralph, Sandusky *Freslom.*

Chautauque County.
Hulet Daniel J. *French Creek.*
Delan W. (Axe Helve)

Chenango County.
Bilden Lorenzo M. *Guilford.*
Doud A. *Pilcher.*

Duchess County.
Bucknam A. J. Stanford Village *Stanford.*

Erie County.
Saris Jos. Mechanic st. *Buffalo.*
Farley D. Exchange st
Roth Conrad, 3 East Swan

Greene County.
Hitchcock Asa *Durham.*
Miller Wm S. *Lexington.*
Jones Stephen, West Kill
Moore Justin, do

Jefferson County.
Howe Jos. & T. J. Black River *Rutland.*

Kings County.
Clark J. Livingston near Bosrum *Brooklyn.*
Hollely Thos. 71 Bridge
Smith E. & A. 206 Nassau
Buckelew I. C. Raymond st.
Stinman Benj. M. 153 1st *Williamsburgh*
Wood Daniel, 10th near Grand

Madison County
West L. & M. Oneida Depot *Lenox.*
Davis & Britt, Chittenango *Sullivan.*

Monroe County.
Jameson & Randall, (iron & wood) Churchville *Riga.*
Crossman, Eaton & Co. Curtis' Block, Main st. *Rochester.*
Englhardt Chas. W. (wood, ivory & metals) 18 Lancaster
Cowles J. B. Curtis' blk., Main st.
Richardson S. (wood & iron) 1 Buffalo

Montgomery County.
Eggleston Henry *Amsterdam.*
Noxon W. C., Fort Plain *Minden*

New York County.
Atherden G. 51 Gold *New York.*
Baker & Wright, 150 Wooster
Bancroft William H. 189 9th
Bartelme Baltasar, 78 Elizabeth
Bernhardt August, 40 Eldridge
Booth James, 113 Attorney
Brann John J. 186 Orchard
Bryant & Co. 67 Forsyth
Buckland Alexander, 151 9th
Carey William E. rear 83 Varick
Cebra & Cunning, 106 Pearl
Collord John P. rear 187 Wooster
Cook Thomas, 372 Hudson
Costner William, 44 Eldridge
Craft John S. & S. B. 17 Canal
Cullin Wm. 368 Greenwich
Dean James, 562 Hudson
Dwire Wm. J. 70½ Bowery
Dwyer David, 40 Elizabeth
Fisher Daniel, 441 Pearl
Ford Frederick G. 90 Fulton

Fugmann & Staudinger, 10 Pell
New York.
Gass Lewis, 73 Chatham
Goesser T. 156 Greenwich
Gordon Charles, 390 Houston
Graser Valentine, r. 190 William
Grote F. 78 Fulton
Harrington Thomas, 194 Mercer
Hawley Henry, 56 Houston
Heckmann A. 83 Gold
Helmoth George, 24 Reade
Henderson Robert, r 147 Spring
Hill Benjamin R. 332 3d
Hill Richard, jr. 37 Greene
Hughes James, 105 W. Broadway
Hull Henry, 56 Houston
Hyde James P. 185 Church
Ingersoll & Webb, 329 5th
Jackson George. 293 Front
Jackson J. R. 33 Renwick
Jaquillard & Bocheler, 159 Orch'd
Jordan Charles, 322 Houston
Kilpatrick J. 224 West 21st
Kolp George, 75 Chatham
Larsen Henry, 16 College place
Lawson William, 62 Beach
M'Dougall Henry, 16 Doyer
Mahaney Thomas, 107 Walker
Marion Joseph, 103 Elm
Mead John H. 41 Hester
Meehan Patrick, 119 Walker
Mehler Leopold, r. 26 Chrystie
Mielke Charles, 29 John
Mosser Francis, 126 Amity
Mosser Joseph, 296 Houston
Most John, rear 18 Mulberry
Neb Stephen, 138 Crosby
Newell Darius C. foot 19th N. R.
Paffarkorn George. 125 Mott
Phyfe John, rear 19 Murray
Reinhard John, 95 Mercer
Rhode Henry, 170 Broadway
Robertson Henry B. 13 Caroline
Roeber John, 140 Suffolk
Ruthven James, rear 92 Fulton
Sawmiller Thomas, r. 282 Walker
Shardlow Samuel, 118 Fulton
Schrader & Baecker, 19 Ann
Schroll ——, 44 Elizabeth
Skippon J. & Sons, 45 Gold
Stead Robert, 19 11th
Steanhelber Jacob, 172 Hester
Strong & Kavanagh, 97 Forsyth
Suppan Gottfried, 134 Essex
Theis Frederick, rear 316 Grand
Thomann Anthony, 139 Centre
Valentine David, 363 Houston
Vandenbergh Samuel D. rear 92
Fulton
Wagener Albert H. 392 Bleecker
Webb & Ingersoll, 329 5th
Weber Francis X. 112 Ludlow
Welch Abram R. 47 Allen
Westcott Egbon, 192 Broome
Westervelt Cornelius, jr. 273 W.
18th
White Randolph, 30 Clark
Wicks George. rear 88 Division
Williams Daniel, 278 5th
Williams William. 435 10th
Williams W. L. 263 9th
Wilson Benjamin, 461 Water
Wolf Francis, 52 Fulton
Wood Daniel, 159 11th

Niagara County.

Crawford A.   *Newfane*

Oneida County.

Pease & Batchelder, Oriskany
Falls   *Augusta.*
Wheeler Charles   *Camden.*
Smith C. T. (ivory & wood) 1 Lib-
erty   *Utica.*

Ontario County.

Gillespie John   *Phelps.*
Knapp Russell D. Allen's Hill
Richmond.

Oswego County.

Willard J. E. & Co., Oswego Falls
Granby.

Otsego County

Gellert & Eckert   *Middlefield.*

Rensselaer County.

Fields J. 214 State *Lansingburgh.*
Chase B. jr. (brush handles)
Stephentown.
Potter & Doty,   do
Carpenter & Daniels, (brush han-
dles)
Doty & Clark,   do
Sherwood E. B. & Rundell, Star-
buck's Building   *Troy.*
Clum Geo. W. near 1st
Goulden Geo., Hollow Road
Carter Richard, (wood screws)
Hollow Road

Schenectady County.

Chandler & Son, 73 Union
Schenectady.

Washington County.

Gardner J.   *Whitehall.*
Moore J.
Mitchell Wm.

Wayne County.

Smallage John   *Lyons.*

Wyoming County.

Rawson & Bliss, (broom handles)
Eagle.
Prentice Alonzo,   do
Adams H. E.   *Warsaw.*

**Umbrella & Parasol Man-
ufacturers.**

Albany County.

Hunt F. 62 Broadway   *Albany.*
Adams G. 88 Hamilton

Columbia County.

Hubbard E. Water st.   *Hudson.*

Duchess County.

Power H. & Son, 299 Main
Poughkeepsie.

Erie County.

Levin L. 239 Main   *Buffalo.*
Millington & Brother, 269 Main

Kings County.

Smith Chas. E. 165 Fulton
Brooklyn.
Winkstead Richard, 161 Fulton
Fales Seth E. 191 Grand
Williamsburgh.
Saffnell Henry, 270 Grand

Monroe County.

Butt Daniel, 115 Main *Rochester.*
Jones John, 190 State
Siebert G. 77   do

New York County.

Bell Benj. 110 & 64 Canal
New York.
Bostwick, Kent & Atwood, 134
Pearl
Brady John P. 60 Anthony
Byrd George J. 142 & 144 Broad-
way
Calkins & Darrow, 28 Maid. lane
Caulkins John S. 64 Nassau
Clyde & Black, 317 Grand & 303
Broadway
Cogill John, 4 Liberty pl.

Coleman Harriet, 13 Mulberry
New York.
Cook Norman, 56½ Bowery
Cook Richard & Sons, 232 Bowery
Crossman Henry & Co. 226 Pearl
Curnich James, 8 5th
Cutter Charles N. 70 Cedar
Davis C. & J. 23 Nassau
Delahunty James. 309 Delancy
Dillo Daniel, 30 Centre
Denison & Co. 84 Pearl
Dickson John, 106 & 110 6th Av.
Dobich Frederick, 266 Stanton
Doubleday J. T. & Co. 121 Pearl
Ellis & Willis, 77 Cedar
Fancourt C. 51 13th
Ford Patrick, 164 William
Franklin Philip, 366 Pearl
Gardiner John M. 149 Laurens
Gilmour J. A. & J. 206 Greenwich
& 93 Chatham
Gilnour Thos. R. & J. 381 Broad-
way
Gilmours & Bell, 74 Canal
Gordon John, 254 W. 17th
Hall & Bohme, 29 Cedar
Hammill Wm. 62 William
Hemming & Quackenbush, 96 8th
Av.
Hillier Henry, 518 Greenwich
Houghton, Merrill & Co. 63 Wil-
liam
Johnston Wm. 166 Bowery
Keep Henry, 136 William
Kennedy Robert, 457 Hudson
Kebby William P. 71 William
King Charles, 37 Nassau
Love & Hunt, 56 Gold
Lynes Samuel, 62 Liberty
M'Namee Richard, 6 Pine
Martin Patrick, 174 Allen
Matthews George, 268½ Division
May John A. 84 Prince
Messinger Brothers, 6 Cedar
Miller W. 95 W. Broadway
Millington Samuel F. & Brothers,
266½ Bowery
Moore Wm. 68 Allen
Morris Hermon, 35 John
Palmer Thomas, 84½ Bleecker
Pomeroy H. 302 Division
Ramsden Roland, 58½ Fulton
Ransford Josiah W. 44 Division
Reiszer Lous, 35 Sullivan
Ritze John, 224 Hudson
Schmid Frederick, 123 Columbia
Sharp Robert, 146 Canal
Slaughter Mary,   60 3d Av.
Smith Andrew, 223 Bleecker
Smith Charles E. 204 Pearl
Smith Isaac & Co. 257 do
Smith James T. & S. 154 6th Av.
Smith John I. 233 Pearl
Smith Joseph. 362 do
Smith W. Willard, 36 & 38 Cedar
Spratt James H. 60½ Bowery
Stucke & Engeholm, 32 Catharine
Stuckey Philip, 48 Gold
Thomas William, 73 W. 18th
Webster Joseph E. 20 Centre
Wickstead John J. 84 Canal
Wickstead Mary, 64½ do
Wilkinson John, 201 Division
Williams & Cunningham, 194
Pearl
Witts John, 5 Oak
Wolf John, 8 Gold
Woods James, 292 Pearl
Wyatt Thomas R. 123 Fulton
Young William W. 588 Grand

Oneida County.

Pollard W. H. James st.   *Rome.*
Vines S. 196 Genesee   *Utica.*
Hall J. 90 Liberty

Onondaga County.

Heath J. C. Salina st. Syracuse
Salina.

Orange County.

Dorragh A. *Newburgh.*
Francks Jonathan, Water st.

Rensselaer County.

Hyman John, 296 River *Troy.*
Fays J. C. 58 Congress

Schenectady County.

Wise J. White st. *Schenectady.*

Washington County.

M'Nitt B. F. North White Creek
White Creek.

Umbrella Furniture.

Banks Mark. 16 Cedar *New York.*
Davis Charles & James, 30 Cedar
Lane James A. 93 Reade
Quidore Peter, rear 25 Orange
Speyer Phillip & Co. 51 Broad

Umbrella Stick Manufacturers.

Harting Frederick, 103 Oliver
New York.
M'Gowan & Barr, 21 Spruce
Wolfe John, 8 Gold

Umbrella Stick Varnisher.

Erk Christian, 83 Gold *New York.*

Undertakers. (*See also Coffin Warehouses.*)

Albany County.

Shephard A. 605 Broadway *Albany.*
Patterson George, 52 Hudson
Van Loon P. 70 Green
Lynch P. 156 do
M'Kown A. F. 86 S. Pearl
Bland J. W. West Troy
Watervliet.
Commary & Caulkins, W. Troy

Cayuga County.

Sherwood A. Genesee st. *Auburn.*

Columbia County.

Hedges D. Warren st. *Hudson.*

Duchess County.

Finch & Vandyke *Hyde Park.*

Kings County.

Van Brunt Wm. B. 133 Atlantic
Brooklyn.

Monroe County.

Allen D. W. 119 Buffalo *Rochester.*

New York County.

Beal Geo. 304 Houston *New York.*
Benedict Samuel H. 50½ Carmine
Benjamin O. T. 193 3d Av.
Bennett Richard S. 147 Canal
Blanchard Samuel, 285 Henry
Bogardus & Benjamin, 193 3d Av.
Brett G. 21 Forsyth
Brown Isaac H. 107 4th Av.
Brown Thomas, 192 Rivington
Buchanan Jacob, 149 8th Av.
Butler J. G. 8th Av.
Burrill W. B. 550 Pearl
Cantrell John. 353 Bowery
Carpenter Charles L. 39 9th Av.
Carroll Edward, 279 Division
Case Andrew J 48 4th Av.
Chandler Jonas, 117 Allen
Coapman John, 5 Cannon

Cowperthwaits John K. 14 East
Broadway *New York.*
Day Charles J. 113 8th Av.
Deal Jacob, 137 Essex
Dean John J. 116 Chrystie
Dean S. A. 351 4th Av.
Disbrow Wm. D. 16½ 4th Av.
Donaldson Thomas, 5 Marion
Donaldson Wm. 110 9th Av.
Duff James F. 7th Av. bot. 19th &
20th
Dugan John. 482 Hudson
Dugan Thomas, 470 Broadway
Duncan Alexander, 66 Grand
Dunshee James, 192 Broadway
Ferdon John B. 58 Church
Florentine Abraham, 59½ Mulberry
Gillespie Thomas D. 502 Pearl
Gilmore Francis, 11 Prince
Gorman James, 48 Prince
Greene Wm. 250 Mulberry
Hall E. F. 373 3d Av.
Hallet E. P. 243 3d Av.
Hardenbrook George W. 142 9th
Av.
Harriott Samuel, 39 Eldridge
Harrison Wm. 140 Cherry & 1
Forsyth
Heiss J. T. 581 4th
Hoffman Joseph, 23 Av. B
Horn R. W. & J. 194 Spring
Hulse Daniel, 383 Broome
Huntington John D. 196 Houston
Huyler & Bennett, 147 Canal
James J., Harlem
Jarvis George, 30 1st
Jennings T. L. 167 Church
Johnson R. J. 68 Gold
Jones Charles J. 520 Hudson
Kedey James, 83 Christopher
Keeler Lonzo M. 121 Orchard
Kehoe P. M. 357 Bowery
Klein Joseph, 14 Av. A
Leitch Baptiste, 7 1st Av.
Lewers Wm. 253 Elizabeth
M'Caddin Henry, jr. 520 Pearl
M'Graw & Taylor, 163 Bowery
M'Lean James, 569 Houston
M'Lean W. 612 Broadway
Mace John, 75 Carmine
Malone James, 496 Pearl
Maslin Wm. 17 Clarkson
Merritt Samuel, 188 W. 18th
Palmer Henry, 10 5th
Pope Charles jr. 19 Hudson
Pope Charles, 5 Anthony
Relyea Peter. 3 Willet
Ridgeway Chas. W. 360 2d
Root Milo, 21 2d
Ryers Terence R. 60 Madison
Scheffner Jacob, 8th Av.
Senior Edward H. 31 Hamersley
& 78 Carmine
Shannon George W. 14 Willet
Slevin Daniel, 176 Mulberry
Snyder Henry, 3 Av. C.
Springer Wm. 176 Duane
Stuart Charles A. 137 Grand
Thorburn James R. 93 11th
Veitch Wm. 97 Bedford
Waldron Cornelius, 268 2d
Walsh Nicholas, 8 6th Av.
White John J. 65 Greene
White Thomas, 9th Av. bet. 25th
& 26th
Willett J. W. 14 Willet
Winterbottom James, 614 Broady
Winterbottom J. & Co. 192 Spring
Young John C. 349 Broome

Rensselaer County.

Burns John. N. 2d st. Alley *Troy.*
Lovert E. 42 5th
Golden G. D. State cor. 5th
Beeker Tunis. 39 Congress
Hogan John. 3 Washington
Renouf William, 93 William

Tompkins County.

Snow Wm. Aurora st. *Ithaca.*

Upholsterers. (*See also Cabinet Makers, also Paper Hangings.*)

Albany County.

Parsons H. 586 & 588 Broadway
Albany.
Morange P. M. 500 Broadway
M'Guire Thomas, 116 State
Blair A. & Co. 36 Green

Duchess County.

Mallory David S. 359 Main
Poughkeepsie.
Woodruff C. H. 350 Main

Erie County.

Mooney G. V. 106 Main *Buffalo.*
Cameron & M'Kay, 125 Main
Cuddon James, 353 Main
Vanhouton J. H. 313 Main
Whitehead & Mooney, Stowe Bl'ck

Kings County.

Hodgkinson Thomas H. 139 Atlantic *Brooklyn.*
Riley Joseph, 26 Fulton
Prince & Willins, 56 & 107 Fulton
Bicknell D. 39 Myrtle Av.
Walters James D. 148 4th
Williamsburgh.
Crawford Alexander A. 176 Grand
Forster James, 80 Grand

Monroe County.

Lawrence & King, 119 Buffalo
Rochester.
Brewster Wm. 55 State
Cochrane Wm. 11 Front
Bicknell Henry, 1 Front
Adams W. F. 6 Front

New York County.

Baird D. 237 Hudson & 29 6th Av.
New York.
Baudoine C. A. 335 Broadway
Baumgertal Gustavus, 138 Centre
Bechet Francis L. 4 Great Jones
Bedell Elizabeth, 13 8th Av.
Blair Hannah, 63 Mott
Bower William, 11 4th Av.
Bridgeman Mark, 400 Bowery
Brown John, 91 Canal
Brown William, 161 Fulton
Burns & Trainque. 453 Broadway
Challis James, 24 4th Av.
Childs & Smith, 449 Pearl
Constantine Ellen D. 162 Fulton
Curry Hugh, 162 6th Av.
Darling Samuel, 351 Broome
Davies A. M. & R. 200 Bowery
Davies R. 165 Fulton
Deming & Bulkley, 56 Beekman
Dessoir J. 499 Broadway
De Forrest J. 300 Broadway
Dixon J. 555 Broadway
Favois Z. C. 194 Fulton
Ferguson Ellen. 188 Fulton
Fogg Wm. S. 23½ & 24 Fulton
Forster J. 206 Fulton
Frost Cyrus T. 709 Broadway
Gariepied John E. 44 Vestry
George G. L. 172 Fulton
Gratacap G. P. & J. 31 Maiden la
Green John, 353d Av.
Grundy James, 48 Ann
Hallock John H. 558 Grand
Homann E. 393 Broome
Hart John, 151 4th Av.
Heather Wm. J. 577 Broadway
Hewitt Francis, 199 Mercer
Hewitt John. jr. 90 Hudson
Hewitt & Morton, 593 Broadway
Hollis David, 60½ Vesey
Hutchings E. W. & Co. 475 Broadway
Jacobs Joseph. 114 4th Av.
Jerman E. & Co. 330 & 332 Hudson
Leprine & Marcotte, 477 Broadway

Lewis William, 452 Pearl
    New York.
Livesey Starkie, 750 Broadway
M'Auley C. & Co. 116 Hudson
M'Graw N. 455 Broadway
N'Kinney M. B. 228 Hudson
Malany James, 104 4th Av.
Martin Edward, 170 Fulton & 195 Canal
Martin Michael, 99 W. Broadway
Mason I. J. 153 W. Broadway
Mason T. 333 Broadway
Mathews Gerry, 114 Grand
Mercer Edward H. 383 Hudson
Mercier Francis, 156 4th Av.
Monaghan & Gouldburn, 890 Broadway
Moore Elsey, 23 Thomas
Moore Robert, 927 Broadway
Murphy Thomas, 39 East Broadway
Needham & Thompson, 49 Grove
Neppert Philippe, 152 Hester
Neppert & Schmidt, 125 Canal
Norwood Thomas A. 262 Bleecker
Norwood William, 112 South
O'Grady & Cassin, 13 E. Broadway
Olsen Andrew J. 501 Broadway
Parker & Ritter, 158 Greenwich
Paterson Geo. 48 E. Broadway
Pearson Marmaduke, 363 6th Av.
Phyfe Isaac M. 687 Broadway
Phyfe J. 43 Maiden lane
Piggett Joseph, 94 Division & 52 E. Broadway
Platt W. F. & Brother, 164 Fulton
Playfair John, 3 3d Av.
Puels Peter, 4 Forsyth
Quincy G. 292 6th Av.
Quirk John N. 35 Fulton
Reed J. 315½ Bowery
Reed William, 75 Chatham
Rich David A. rear 83 Duane
Ritchie Sarah, 190 Franklin
Rochefort & Skarren, 637½ Broadway
Roux Alexander, 479 Broadway
Sammis Charles A. 55 Gold
Schafer Louis S. 17 N. William
Sherdley Tobias, 44 4th Av.
Schmidt Julia. 47 6th Av.
Smith Sarah, 158 W. Broadway
Smith Job A. 30 Carmine
Sommon & Tieglensyr, 452 Broome
Solomon & Hart, 243 Broadway
Southach J. W. & C. 196 Broadway
Spiro Philip J. 72 8th Av.
Stacy George B. 234 Wooster
Stevenson Alexander, 153 9th
Stevenson James A. 127 Av. D
Stumpf David, 27 Delancy
Turcott Denis P. 26 Desbrosses
Taylor Daniel G. 492 Broadway.
Thomas C. B. 76 E. Broadway
Twamly John, 46 Broadway
Treadwell Joseph S. 683 Broadway
Vanzandt Richard D. 160 Clinton
Voorhis Abraham & Co. 344 Broadway
Waterbury Samuel, 50 Beekman
Webster J. T. 179 Church
Wemmell Peter. 79½ Canal
Williams & Co. 290 Pearl
Woodford Josiah C. 295 Broadway
Woram John, 562½ Broadway

Oneida County.

Stuart J. 34 Liberty   *Utica.*

Oswego County.

West Marmaduke, Telegraph block, 1st st.   *Oswego.*
Goodwin Richard, Bronson's block, 1st st.

Rensselaer County.

Cloyde John. 202½ River   *Troy.*
Galusha E. 246   do
Hitchins John, 339   do

St. Lawrence County.

Dunnington B. F., Division st. Ogdensburgh   *Oswegatchie.*

Variety Stores. *(See also Toy Stores; also Fancy Goods Dealers.)*

Albany County.

Mascord W. 620 Broadway *Albany.*
Pease R. H. (wholesale) Broadway
Carter Geo. T. 466 Broadway
Van Schaack Egbert (wholesale) 385 Broadway
Bow Wm. H. 60 Quay
Harris W. F. (wholesale) 81 State
Rodgers W. C. 168 South Pearl
Harley E. 229   do
Nixon R. 16½   do
Bendall H. 45   do
Jewett Miss C. 71 North Pearl
Hart J. 19   do
Lachner George, 64 Washington
Diekerman H. 55   do
Murphy Mrs. 162 State
Williams & Van Brooklin, West Troy   *Watervliet.*
Clark L. (wholesale) W. Troy

Herkimer County.

Doller A.   *Little Falls.*
Fralicks ——
Curry J. C.   *Newport.*
Borvy J. G.

Kings County.

M'Mahon Mrs. Julia, Union st.   *Brooklyn.*
Van Allen Mrs. 106 Fulton
Gillies John & Charlotte, 256 Fulton
Butler John T. 364 Fulton
Odell Mrs. L. 316 Atlantic
Miller John, 44 Main
Regan Joseph. 3 York
Cook M. 104 Bridge
Fanning Mrs. Mary, 110 York
Bradley R. 92 Jay
Skippon John, Adams cor. York
Lynch Thomas, 115 Tillary
Yeamorn Mrs. Mary, 61 Concord
Silliman Chas. 191 Fulton
Welch Elizabeth, 42 Hudson Av.
Booth Mrs. L. M. 71 Hudson Av.
Lent David. 75 Hudson Av.
Stewart Mrs. Ann, 64 Hudson Av.
Ghallegar Wm. 179 York
Flint N. 150 Hudson Av.
Merryweather George, 153 Hudson Av.
Watkins Edward, 141 Nassau
Johnston G. A. 2 Stanton
Eden N. 173 Myrtle Av.
Governeure D. 229 1st   *Williamsburgh.*

Monroe County.

Nye Caleb   *Pittsford.*
Gormly John, (wholesale) 9 Exchange   *Rochester.*

New York County.

Alexander E. 38 Bowery   *New York.*
Berhard L. 70 Catharine
Barker Mrs. 28 Houston
Behrens C. D. 335 Houston
Blessington Wm. 8th Av.
Bristol H. D. 87 Reade
Byles Ann, 155 Lewis
Campbell James, 82½ Chatham
Coleman Josephus. 45½ Carmine
Coles John, 123 Hammond
Culver Sarah, 434 Greenwich
Degray James M. 52 Houston
Delcree Wm. 368 Hudson.
Demarast H. & Co. 305 Hudson
Duffey M. 168 W. 20th

Dugan Marie, 25 W. Broadway
    New York
Dwyer M. 486 Greenwich
Elston D. 292 Hudson
Fulton Mrs. 167 Houston
Gibson Robert, 142½ Division
Gooman John, 20 6th Av.
Griffen P. 8th Av.
Hundson Robert, 236 Canal
Harrison Susannah, 130 Duane
Henley H. 348 Hudson
Hermance A. S. 215 Division
Hill M. 221 Division
Hingston Mary, 107 Bayard
Langdon E. G. 86 Hudson
Leavitt C. B. 214 Division
Levi Israel, 125 Pitt
Long S. 46½ 6th Av.
Marsden J. 20 Catharine slip
Martine Mary, 176½ Wooster
Nebs S. 138 Crosby
Regan H. 151 Bowery
Rolet Peter, 129 4th Av.
Rosenblatt Benjamin, 160 2d
Schmidt B. L. 54½ Bowery
Schneider M. 5 4th Av.
Smith Matthias, 54 3d
Southworth James, 116 Columbia
Starmond Jacob. 123 Chatham
Terrell John, 278 1st Av.
Tibbetts Geo. W. 190½ Cherry
Vanderver Cornelius, 85 West Broadway
Van Duger John, 387 Houston
Vanvilen Philip C. 159 Lewis
Welsh Ann, 487 Pearl
Walters Richard. 87 Division
Watson John, 268 2d
Wilson J. 149½ Bowery

Oneida County.

Pavey A. A. James st.   *Rome.*
Osborn J. 79 Genesee   *Utica.*
Osborn Jas. N. 174 Genesee

Orange County.

McGavah Miss H.   *Monroe.*
Gardiner Lewis W. 105 Water   *Newburgh.*
Gilliepie Wm. G. cor. Water and 2d
Travis Silas L. 39 Water
McCullough Wm. 14 Water
Adams James, 2d st.

Oswego County.

Cutter J. L. & S. T., Fulton   *Volney.*

Otsego County.

Bailey L. A., Cooperstown *Otsego.*

Rensselaer County.

Wilson David, 221 State   *Lansingburgh.*
Dummer Edward, 321 State
Knickerbocker H. 306 State
Gatchell Caroline M. 89 N. 3d   *Troy*
Adkins Mrs. 29 Jacob
Johnson Mrs. 34 2d
Woodham Mrs. M. 107 4th
Prime Mrs. E. 22 5th
Larance John. 75 5th
Tillman Wm. 155 5th
Rawson Miss. 39 Albany
Price C. 85 State
Dugdale James. 52 Congress
Teale Wm. 34 Ferry

Saratoga County.

Cox A.   *Saratoga Springs.*

Schenectady County.

Lyman Wm. 14 State *Schenectady.*
Carpenter Coles, 157 State
Bastleds J. 179 State
Van Zandt G. G
Barhydt C. W. & G. S. 140 State

Varnish—Importers of.

Routh H. L. & Sons, 69 New
New York.

Varnishers and Polishers.

Beedle Dewitt, 43 6th Av.
New York.
Clipp & Morgan, rear 87 King
Cornell Henry R. 71 Gold
Dewey James. 44 Mott
Duffy Edward, 302 1st Av.
Finger Christopher, 182 Chrystie
Fisk Willard A. 96 3d Av.
Germond George, rear 76 Elizabeth
Karg Caspar, rear 126 Amity
King C. 156 Crosby
Lane John S. 23 Catharine
Liebenau George F. 260 12th
Ludwick Solomon, 8 Spring
McDonnell Charles, 56½ 3d Av.
Mills Hugh. 10 E. Broadway
Perego Edward, 173 Elizabeth
Price William S. 51 Morton
Reed C. 234 2d
Thompson Hopkins, 32 Chrystie
Torrey Thomas, 59 Marion
Vannorden Abraham, rear 54 12th

Varnish Manufacturers.

Albany County.

Cowell & Flaherty, 116 and 117 Quay
Albany.

Kings County.

Gillespie Charles, Flushing Av.
Brooklyn.
Kissam & Keeler, N. 9th near 6th
Williamsburgh.

New York County.

Blackwell R. M. & Co. 144 Front
New York.
Blind S. & C. 283 Grand
Dupignac E. R. jr. 8 Peck slip
Dwight William R. 138 Maiden lane
Goodhue Isaac, 9th Av. between 38th and 39th
King Chas. A. 21 New
Kissam & Keller, 92 John
Lampson William. 23 E. 16th
Lindo Stephen, 422½ Broadway
Mayer Bernhard, 30 Beekman
Minett & Co. 60 Pearl. (See advertisement)
Richards Stephen, 63½ Gold
Smith, Stratton & Co. 141 Maiden lane
Thompson Hopkins, 32 Chrystie
Tilden William & Nephew, 117 Norfolk
Turner & Co. 316 Broadway

Queens County.

Smith, Stratton & Co., Astoria
Newtown.

Rockland County.

Turner & Co., Nanuet
Orangetown.

Vault Light Manufacturer.

Hyatt Thaddeus, 472 Greenwich
New York.

Velocipede Makers.

Crandall B. P. & N. T. 49 Courtlandt and 337 Stanton New York.

Vermicelli and Maccaroni.

Rey John B. 102 Front New York
Finn W. 147 3d

Vest Leather Manufacturer.

Doughty Samuel, 60 John
New York.

Veterinary Surgeons.

Banham William, 34 2d Av.
New York.
Budd R. H. 48 Mercer
Cooper John H. 28th near 3d Av.
Dixon A. H. 4 2d Av.
Drysdale Robert. 20 5th
Evans H. 294 3d Av.
Evans Thomas, 282 Stanton
Grice Charles C. 53 White
Huestiss C. 73 W. 13th
Murphy J. B. 474 Pearl
Nostrand Elbert, 112 Clinton
Petzinger Frederick, 246 3d
Williams John, 131 Chrystie

Vice and Anvil Manufacturer.

Goldie Joseph, 133 Attorney
New York.

Warehouses (Bonded.)

Erie County.

Pratt & Co. 222 Main
Buffalo.

New York County.

Diggs Edward, 88 Washington
New York.
Gurley & Mildram, 5 West
Husted H. F. 211, 212, 213 & 214 South
Jackson & Cockle, 71 Greenwich
United States Warehouse, 52 Broadway & 36, 31 & 35 West

Washing Machine Manufacturers.

Saratoga County.

Barber F.
Halfmoon.

Westchester County.

Washburn Oscar, Sing Sing
Ossining.

Watch and Clock Spring Makers.

Jacot Edward, 22 Rose New York.
Kraemer Frederick, 203 William
Quelet George, 33 Roosevelt
Rosselot Peter A. 170 William

Watch Case Makers.

Andrus C. H. rear 47 Dey
New York.
Barbier Elory, 71 Nassau
Bond Thomas, 4 Liberty place
Bowman & Ebbitt, rear 17 John
Carlier Joseph A. 89 Reade
Catting Francis, 15 W. Broadway
Clark & Andrus, rear 47 Dey
Cook Augustus, rear 371 Pearl
Droz Henry E. 92 Fulton
Ducommun & Guinant, 2 Cortl'dt
Favre Julian, 65 Ann
Favre & Voisarrd, 26 Frankfort
Glatz Lewis E. 44 Beekman
Guinand A. & Son, rear 371 Pearl

Hills Amariah M. 18 Maiden lane
New York.
Humbert & Savoye, 10 Rose
Lecour Hippolyte, 10 Rose
Lupton Charles, 18 Maiden lane
Matile Edward, 12 Rose
Matile & Grosclaude, 73 Nassau
Mercier Theodore J. 156 Fulton
Pitkin & Brother, 26 Maiden lane
Roos & Ludlam, 58 Nassau
Veyrasseatt Samuel, rear 63 Ann

Watch Case Chasers.

Brownell Benjamin B. 68 Ann
New York.
Froment Andre, 68 Ann
Guinand, Brothers, 92 Fulton
Jennings H. W. 68 Ann
Jones W. R. A. 123 Fulton
Moore Benj. F. rear 63 Ann
Thompson C. W. 73 Nassau

Watch Case Finishers.

Bon L. 47 Ann
New York.
Lecour Adolphus, r. 216 William
Watson Jesse, rear 63 Ann

Watch Case Polishers.

Bordez Jane, 92 Fulton New York.
Coulon Catharine, r. 50 Frankfort

Watch Case Spring Makers.

Bon L. 47 Ann
New York.
Pritchard Thomas J. 127 Fulton
Warner Benjamin J. 4 Liberty pl.

Watch Crystal Makers.

Kings County.

M'Guire John, State st. Brooklyn.
Robinson T. (lunette) 72 Atlantic
Berger & Walter, 90 Ewin
Williamsburgh.

New York County.

Berger & Walter, 29 Maiden lane
New York.
Brown H. 261 Bowery
Flook John, 76 & 77 Nassau
Gore John G. 34 Gold
Graydon John, 71 Nassau
M'Clean William. 195 W. 20th
Mincho Adolphe, 18 Franklin
Vogeley Charles, 206 William

Watch Dial Makers.

Burger J. & Co. 42 Ann New York.
Carliar J. 89 Reade
Gold Thomas, 51 Roosevelt
Hicks Walter, rear 47 Dey
Veyrasat Charles S. 189 Broad'y

Watches and Jewelry. (See also Jewelers, also Pencil case Makers, also Silversmiths.)

Albany County.

Jenkins Ira, 512 Broadway Albany.
Given A. 550 do
Mulford & Wendell, (importers) 480 Broadway
Simpson & Beckel, 408 Broadway
Hoyt George B. 394 do
Marsh B. 405 do
Hasoy Nelson, 34 State
Crew J. T. 38 do
Hood & Tobey, (importers) 44 State

Waterman Geo. 82 State   *Albany.*
Hascy A. R. 33   do
Magnus S. M. 95   do
Carson D. 96   do
Holliday H. 46 Westerlo
Miles E. (clocks) 164 S. Pearl
Cone J. & 1. 72   do
Harman S. 54   do
Rosengarden J. 62   do
Arms N. T. 42   do
Mix V. 14   do
Rice J. T. 21   do
Jungerman I. L. 63   do
Cutler J. N. 83 Beaver
M'Harg A. 22 Green
Mix J. jr. 24   do
Friend M. S. 7 Washington
Lewis G. H., West Troy
                        Watervliet.
Talcott Francis, Cohoes

Alleghany County.

Furman S.   *Angelica.*
Hyde Herman   *Rushford.*

Broome County.

Squires R.   *Binghamton.*
Canfield & Brother
Butler L. A.
Evans A. J.
M'Kee A.   *Windsor.*

Cattaraugus County.

Hitchcock E., Gowanda   *Persia.*
Larkin F.   *Randolph.*
Cady J. C.

Cayuga County.

Haight L. F. 51 Genesee *Auburn.*
Haight J. W. & Co. 57 do
Munger A. Genesee st.
Chedell J. H. & Co. 105 Genesee
Rice J. J. 75 Genesee
Hutchinson ——, Weedsport
                        Brutus.
Badgley H., Port Byron *Mentz.*

Chautauque County.

Kibbe F., Mayville   *Chautauque.*
Mason L., Jamestown   *Ellicott.*
Fuller F. A.   do
Bosworth H., Fredonia   *Pomfret.*
Marsh H. N.   do

Chemung County.

Hamilton D. S.   *Elmira.*
Ayres S.
Yates W. P.

Chenango County

Griswold R.   *Bainbridge.*
Slade N.
Eaton N.   *New Berlin.*
Walter H. N.   *Norwich.*
Farnham Samuel H.   *Oxford.*
Davidson P. 1.   *Sherburne.*

Clinton County.

Prescott Henry, Keeseville
                        Au Sable.

Columbia County.

Waring George, 283 Warren
                        Hudson.
Hannah William W. 287 Warren
Butler C. E. 323   do
Parkman H. D.   do
Rexford L. S.   *Kinderhook.*
Kipp William
Miller J. P. Valatie

Cortland County.

Stiles George E. *Cortland Village.*

Delaware County.

Mallory John A.   *Delhi.*

Smith William   *Franklin.*
Graves N. S. Hobart   *Stamford.*
Williams & Briggs, Deposit
                        Tompkins.
Park William, Deposit

Duchess County.

Pelham William   *Fishkill.*
Morgan William S. 322 Main
                        Poughkeepsie.
Morgan E. 298   Main
Henderson Adam. 252 do
Power H. & Son. 299 do
Van Velt B. C. 289 do
Bailey S. G. 383 do
Cramer George, 8 Liberty
Somarindyck E. 1 Garden
Wortman T.   *Rhinebeck.*
Styles William J.

Erie County.

Weber William, Springville
                        Concord.
Clark G. R. 205 Main   *Buffalo.*
Hedge Geo. 7 Birkhead Buildings,
    Commercial st.
Collette L. 6 East Seneca
Castle D. B. 189 Main
Hood G. L. 203   do
Church R. 15 East Swan
Welte F. Genesee House
Esslinger Charles, 383 Main
Rudell William, 377   do
Schimper William, 362 do
Stephenson T. & Co. (manufac-
    turers) 200 Main
Sibley O. E. 186 do
Mather & Pitkin, 196 Main
Sohlenker John M. 33 Genesee
Goodrich E. H. Commercial st.
Wheeler & Hartshorn, 2 do
Allen Philo, 164 Main
Strong & Lyon, 157 do
Walker Julius, 155 do

Essex County.

Kimball C. R. Moriah 4 Corners
                        Moriah.

Franklin County.

Moses Oren   *Malone.*
Randall A. C.

Fulton County.

Fox Reuben   *Broadalbin.*
Kibbe Thompson P.   *Johnstown.*
Settle William

Genesee County.

Clark J. A.   *Batavia.*
Dodge E. S.
Stanley H. N.   *Le Roy.*
Sampson R. L.
Lampkins A. L.

Greene County.

Willard Charles S.   *Catskill.*
Mallory Samuel
Peck Henry B.   *Coxsackie.*
Watmers Osmer C.   *Prattsville.*

Herkimer County.

Coe L. P. Mohawk *German Flats.*
Peters Jesse, do
Davis William A.   *Little Falls.*
Bosworth ——, *West Winfield.*

Jefferson County.

Whitcomb H. & Son   *Adams.*
Cook J. S. Sackett's Harbor
                        Hounsfield.
Rawson Asa, Felt's Mills *Rutland.*
Chapman & Hungerford *Theresa.*
Davis B. F. & Co.   *Watertown.*
Newcomb Hiram
Genett Washington
Perotte Adolphe, Carthage *Wilna*

Kings County.

Cochran W. D. 29 Atlantic
                        Brooklyn.
Mills Charles H. 111 Atlantic
Tice Wm. R. & Co. 127 do
Durr L. 147   do
Greiss George, 53½   do
Armstrong T. 4 Hicks
Forsyth O. C. 204 Fulton
Vanderhoff W. J. 146 do
Wise William, jr. 79 do
Lowe John. 89   do
Taylor P. L. 97   do
Shepherd B. H. cor. Main & Fulton
Snow Charles G. 62 Adams
Dayton John D. 101 Sands
Campbell Alexander, 68 Sands
Carman S. S. 267 Fulton
Chase John D. 203   do
Lowe Joseph B. 149 do
Simonds Wm. East New York
                        Flatbush.
Simonds John, East New York
Kafferer Autoy, 90 Merserole
                        Williamsburgh.
Barrett Henry D. 165 Grand
Campbell Wm. A. 78 do

Lewis County.

Bradish James S.   *Turin.*
Bennett R. Constableville
                        West Turin.

Livingston County.

Rowley David, East Avon *Avon.*
Matson N.   *Dansville.*
Wallis J. W.
Reynolds & Ripley
Fosdale R. G.
Johnson Jasper   *Genesee.*
Hager E.   *Mount Morris.*
Gilbert H.
Talcott W. O   *Nunda.*

Madison County.

Tracey & Hawley   *Cazenovia*
Burdick H. W.   *De Ruyter.*
Haughton Allen   *Eaton.*
Roys H. Morrisville
Hartshorn Asa   *Hamilton.*
Case P. N.
Chapin S. Oneida Depot *Lenox.*
Sowter I. A. Canastota
Swan L. E. Chittenango *Sullivan.*

Monroe County.

Clackner John S. 139 Franklin
                        Rochester
Charron Victor, 78 Main
Cook & Stillwell, cor. Buffalo &
    Exchange
Watts Charles, 72 Buffalo
Burr C. A. 2 State cor. Buffalo
Strasburger M. 28 Buffalo
Barron L. 81 Main
Boehnlein Geo. 99½ Main
Stanton & Brother, (importers) 9
    Exchange
Clackner A. S. 212 State
Gormly S. 54   do
Packard J. 3   do
Brinsmaid H. 5   do
Greenleaf D. C. 22 Main, Brock-
    port   *Sweden.*
Randall J. V. 13   do
Rowe Albert, Scottsville
                        Wheatland.

Montgomery County.

Shuler Lawrens   *Amsterdam.*
Pooley James
Barnes C. G.   *Canajoharie.*
Gennet A. Fort Plain   *Minden.*
Fairling John R. do

New York County.

Ackerley & Briggs, 178 Bowery
                        New York
Adams William, 198 Chatham

Adams William B. 356 Bowery
New York.
Alexander Isaac, 422 Grand
Aurich L. 72 Chatham
Badger G. J. 376 Grand
Barrow John. 159 Greenwich
Belais S. 243½ Centre
Benedict Andrew C. 28 Bowery
Benedict John J. & M. 276 do
Blanks ein M. S. 28 Division
Brown & Dwight. 10 Cortlandt
Brunner L. 84½ Chatham
Burgee & Co. 42 Ann
Butler Thomas, 145 West
Clayton E. B. 264 Grand
Cox John. 236 Bowery
Cunningham A. J. 547½ B'dway
Curtis Lemuel, 105 Av. D
Davis Jacob. 270 Bowery
Devlin John, 32 Prince
Dominick Edward H. 294 Grand
Falkenau A. 91½ Division
Faulkner James W. 356 B'dway
Fresse W. H. 56 Chatham
Gendar W. T. & T. V. 214 Greenwich
Ginochio John B. 118 Canal
Goldsmith David, 32½ Bowery
Gustien Mathieu. 81½ Broadway
Hadkins Henry & Son, 131 Sheriff, & 50 Av. D
Heitz J. F. cor. Rector & Washington
Hellrainberg E. 155 Washington
Hunter John. 239 Bleecker
Huntington D. I. 199 Greenwich
Jackson & Many. 148 Chatham
Jacobs Angel. 100 do
Jacobs Lionel. 55 do
Jacot E. E. 23 Rose
Jalumstein Zelko. 256 Bowery
Jonas Isaac A. 519 Broadway
Josephi A. 92 Bowery
Josephi Henry, 395 Broadway
Kaufman Lewis, 222½ Bowery
Kimberly Henry R. 179 Water
Knight Nicholas. 197 Waverly pl
Ladd Wm. F. 26 Wall
Ladd Geo. 441 Broadway
Lichtenberg Jacob, 264 Bowery
Lockwood Frederick. 265 Pearl
Lockwood F. H. 206 Broadway
Lyon & Cohen, 168 Chatham
Mairet & Robert. 31 Liberty
Marret. Jerry & Gaime, 391½ Broadway
Mathey A. 61 Chatham
May Lab, 170 Bowery
May Moses, 140 do
Meyers Merrick, 112½ Bowery
Moelich L. 196 Canal
Moon J. L. & Co. 42 Chatham
Murphy Richard, 262 Grand
Newman Henry & Co. 5 Peck slip
Nolan Henry, 372½ Bowery
Oertle F. 161 Division
Pachtmann F. W. 102 Canal
Peletromo & Perkins, 1 Wall
Pitkin & Brother, 26 Maiden lane
Polhumus John, 594 Grand
Price R. 63 Ann
Quelet Geo. 33 Vandewater
Reests E. 223½ Division
Ritterband Leon M. 86 Chatham
Rogers George, 14 Carmine
Rogers James, 287 Broadway
Rosenbourgh L. 450 Grand
Rossman Nathan, 171 Houston
Salisbury Henry & Co. 171 B'way
Schaap Richard, 216 Bowery
Scherpe Frederick, 305 do
Schlossheimer F. 168 Cherry
Scribner Levi. 74 Fulton
Shannon J. S. 264 Greenwich
Sharp Richard, 216 Bowery
Silverthau Leopold, 312 do
Smith W. T. 118 do
Squire & Brother, 122 Bowery & 97 Fulton
Stewart C. 565 Broadway
Stone C. J. 190 Canal
Straede G. 314 Grand

Tenny R. 251 Broadway *New York.*
Underhill William J. 141 West
Van Winkle John, 237 Bleecker
Wellin Samuel, 156 Bowery
Watson John, 178 do
Wickens Obed, 116 Canal
Winstanley H. R. 115 Roosevelt
White W. W. 63 Bowery

Niagara County.

Simmons E. *Lockport.*
Chubbuck E.
Prentiss A. T. jr.
Brown Thos. *Niagara Falls.*

Oneida County.

Bicknell F. Dominick st. *Rome.*
Delano G. W. James st.
Burman & Palmer, Dominick st.
Hughes R. Waterville
Sangersfield.
Weaver W. N. 28 Genesee *Utica.*
Roth N. 42 Genesee
Murdock & Colling. 46 Genesee
Davies & Battel, 60 Genesee
Bradley H. S. 64 Genesee
Wing S. 126 Genesee
Bailey & Brothers, 122 Genesee
Guingnigner J. 162 Genesee
Hershfield L. & A. 168 Genesee
Marsh E. Whitesboro *Whitestown.*

Onondaga County.

Becker D. Salina st. Syracuse
Salina.
Jones & Wood, Salina st. Syracuse
Willard & Hawley, Genesee st. do
Norton & Hotchkiss, do do
Judson X. Clinton square, do
Bean H. L. *Skaneateles.*

Ontario County.

Sibley O. E. *Canandaigua.*
Anderson Jas. jr.
Fraser H. N. *Phelps.*
Hall A. B. Geneva *Seneca.*
Carson T. H. do
Barnard E. do
Pepoon J. D. do

Orange County.

Tusten H. T. *Chester.*
Lockwood F. W. Port Jervis
Deer Park.
Warden D. *Goshen.*
Tindall Jos. *Montgomery.*
Haight N. 49 Water *Newburgh.*
Leonard D. G. 51 Water
Reeve Chas. 55 Water
Preston Stephen L. 66 Water
Dusenbury D. C. South Middletown *Wallkill.*

Orleans County.

Munger & Dorrance, Albion
Barre.
Cooley H. P. do
Sherman S. Medina *Ridgeway.*
Foster F. G. do

Oswego County.

Ford & Brother, Bank Building, Bridge st. *Oswego.*
Carpenter Luman, 2 Office row
Park Ass, 4 Eagle Block, 1st st.
Tallcott A. G. & Son, cor. 1st & Cayuga
Stern & Brother, Telegraph Block, 1st st.
Gaylord L. A. Pulaski *Richland.*
Mathewson A. F. do
Lee Ira, Fulton *Volney.*

Otsego County.

Smith H. *Cherry Valley.*
Burton P. C. *Oneonta.*
Holbrook ——
Tanner F. G. Cooperstown *Otsego.*

Olendorf B. F. Cooperstown
Otsego.
Annable Augustus *Unadilla.*

Queens County.

Croft H. C. *Flushing.*
Coles J. *Hempstead.*
Kinsey Edward *Jamaica.*

Rensselaer County.

Ensign H. 263 State *Lansingburgh.*
Corey Perry, 248 State
Smith S. T. 243 State
Traitee David, 199 River *Troy.*
Ensign Chas. 192 River
Hegerman Jas. 287 River
Fitch Dennis M. 200 River
Harris & Wilcox. 226 River
Hoyt Jas. A. 246 River
Goldsmith T. 2 Boardman's Buildings
Ingram Jas. 4 King
Blake I. 1 1st
Daskam Sam'l, 6 Franklin square
Champney L. C. 13 Congress
Haynes D. 21 Congress
Salmon Wm. 75 Congress
Seybert John, 73 5th

Rockland County.

Rand C. A. *Haverstraw.*
Collins W. B. Nyack *Orangetown.*

St. Lawrence County.

Iahem S. H. Waddington *Madrid.*
Strickland S. B. & F. A. Ford st. Ogdensburgh *Oswegatchie.*
Seeley & Freeman, Ford st. Ogdensburgh
Bell, John & Geo. R. Ford st. do
Ames Henry R. *Potsdam.*
Packard Lucien H.

Saratoga County.

Smith J. T. Schuylerville
Saratoga.
M'Naughton F. *Saratoga Springs.*
Young N. E.
Hood & Toby

Schenectady County.

Buell C. I. 105 State *Schenectady.*
Swartfiguer G. J. 91 State
Sanders Jas. 87 State

Schoharie County.

Messenger Storrs *Esperance.*
Willard L. *Schoharie.*
Damond C. & A. Hyndeville
Seward.

Seneca County.

Reynolds Robert L. *Ovid.*
Miller Edward B. *Romulus.*
Williams W. E. *Seneca Falls.*
Fairchild Caleb *Waterloo.*
Knight Reuben S.

Steuben County.

Waters L. M. *Addison.*
Comstock D. & Co *Painted Post.*
Edwards H. D.

Suffolk County.

Woodhull Richard *Brookhaven.*
Hawkins Samuel C. Patchogue
Walkman Wm. *Riverhead.*
Wheeler ——, Greenport *Southold.*

Tioga County.

Smith G. H. *Owego.*
Carmichael J.
Matson N.

Tompkins County.

Burritt J. & Son, 17 Aurora *Ithaca.*
Burdick W. P. jr. 64 Owego

Demming F. 70 Owego   *Ithaca.*
Place D. 70 Owego

Ulster County.

Osborn Wm.   *Kingston.*
Mullen J. N.
Vallett B. F.
Rahmer G. Rondout
Jernegan Chas. P.   *Saugerties.*
Rockwell John O. Napanock
                              Wawarsing.
Richardson Martin, Ellenville

Warren County.

Martin John, Glenn's Falls
                              Queensbury.
Rich M. C.   do

Washington County.

White Moses H.   *Greenwich.*
Levi Jacob
Horton H. V.
M'Naghten J.
Lattimer J. E. Sandy Hill
                              Kingsbury.
Bartlett Albert,   do
Bunce J. Canal st.   *Whitehall.*
Griswold H. A. Canal st.

Wayne County.

Child Sylvester, Clyde   *Galen.*
Prime Wm. D.   *Lyons.*
Allen A.
Williams T. P.   *Palmyra.*
Douglass Thomas

Westchester County.

Hanford & Son, Peekskill
                              Courtlandt.
Moses Martin,   do
Lawrence Wm. Sing Sing
                              Orinsing.
Smith Alvin, Portchester   *Rye.*
Phillips Alonzo B.   *Yonkers.*

Wyoming County.

Pratt Henry   *Attica.*
Law Andrew, Wyoming
                              Middlebury.
Willard S   *Perry.*
Hemsted E.   *Pike.*
Allen C   *Warsaw.*

Yates County.

Dunning Levi O. Penn Yan   *Milo.*
Bartwell D. S.   do
Voorhies P. Rushville   *Potter.*
Rose George P. Dundee   *Starkey.*

Watches and Jewelry—Importers of.

Allen George C. 51 Wall
                              New York.
Baldwin Samuel, 170 Broadway,
  Agent for Charles Taylor and
  Son. (See advertisement.)
Ball, Tompkins & Black, 247 Bdy.
Benedict Samuel W. 5 Wall
Bogert R. 339 Hudson
Boulier Peter, 36 Maiden lane
Brauner J. 44 Nassau
Brown & Maire, 58 Nassau
Brez Paul A. 29 Cortlandt
Bruner Joseph, 44 Nassau
Chase Samuel, 26 Maiden lane
Close Henry T. 66 Cedar
Cochran A. T. 288 Greenwich
Courvoisier Albert, 52 Dey
Courvoisier J. & Co. 119 Fulton
Conant Wm. S. 177 Pearl
Cuendet Eugene, 4 John
Davison John G. 12 Maiden lane
Delachaux A. 4 John
Descombes L. J. 156 Broadway
Dreyfous Simeon, 64 John
Dros Henry E. 92 Fulton
Dros Julien, 216 William

Dubois & Co. 61 Nassau *New York.*
Durand C. A. 1 Wall
Ducommun & Guinand, 2 Cortlandt
  and 173 Broadway
Fellows Louis S. & Schell, 21 Maid-
  en lane
Fellowes, Van Arsdale & Cooper,
  11 Maiden lane
Fellows, Wadsworth & Co. 17
  Maiden lane
Frasse Henry F. & Son, 95 Fulton
Gagnebin Charles, 6 John
Gelston & Treadwell, 4 Park pl.
Ginnel Henry, 40 Maiden lane
Glatz L. E. 44 Beekman
Grosclaude Aug'tus, 19 Beekman
Hammond S. & Co. 44 Merchants'
  Exchange
Heilbuth & Schults, 39 John
Hirschfield & Rubens, 64 John
Hoyt Seymour, 266 Pearl
Hugenin A. C. & Co. 19 Beekman
Hyde's John E. Sons, 21 Maiden l.
Jacot Courvoisier & Co. 119 Fulton
Jeanjaquet Brothers, 78 Nassau
Kayser John C. 160 Pearl
Ladd Wm. F. 26 Wall
Lamy & Martin, 177 Broadway
Lazrus J. L. 156 Broadway
Lutz Brothers, 71 Nassau
Magnin Ve J. & Guedin, 19 Maiden
  lane
Maire Henry F. 58 Nassau
Mairet & Robert, 31 Liberty
Mathez & Brother, 9 John
Mayor Augustus, 22 Maiden lane
Mott Brothers, 2 Nassau
Neustadt S. J. & Barnett, 42 Maid-
  en lane
Olcott John N. 23 Maiden lane
Platt & Brother, 20   do
Read, Taylor & Co. 9   do
Rice Leverett E. 16   do
Ritterbrand Henry M. 679½ Bdy.
Robbins Royal E. 36 John
Robert Julius H. 20 Cortlandt
Rogers Charles, 17 Wall
Rudd & Scudder, 7 Maiden lane
Samuel Morris L. & Co. 18 Platt
Salisbury H. 171 Broadway
Savoye, Crosby & Co. 41 Liberty
Schaffer Samuel, 75 Ludlow
Shreve Benjamin, 23 Maiden la.
Simons E. & H. 33 Maiden lane
Squire & Brother, 97 Fulton and
  182 Bowery
Stebbins & Co. 264 Broadway
Tarbox & Kingsley, 22 Maiden la.
Thierot Ferdinand, 130 Cortlandt
Tobias A. I. 22 Liberty
Wallis & Mathey, 4 John
Welsh & Payne, 230 Greenwich
Wennberg John F. 17 Nassau
Whalen J. A. 44 Maiden lane
Young, Redfield & Leavitt, 19
  Maiden lane

Watch Hand Makers.

Huguenin S. & Son, 81 Nassau
                              New York.

Watch Jewellers.

Austin Lavinius, 247 Broadway
                              New York.
Edouards Charles, 208 William
Hadkins John, 129 Sheriff
Harrison Eliza E. 352 Bowery
Hookey Edward N. 93 Hudson
May Moses, 140 Bowery
Meyers Merrick, 112½ Bowery
Rogers John, 6 Liberty place
Rosenbourgh Isaac, 450 Grand
Roesman Nathan, 171 Houston
Whiteford John, 6 Liberty place

Watch Makers.

Alexander Isaac, 12 Fulton
                              New York.

Abrahams Henry, 124 Stanton
                              New York.
Abry Augustus. 70 Nassau
Audemars Louis, 6 Liberty place
Auth Andre, 130 Attorney
Bachman Joseph. 326½ Grand
Baird & Graves, 16 John
Barron John. 189 Greenwich
Barrett H. 103 West Broadway
Baur John N. 119 Fulton
Beisegel J. 8th Av.
Benedict Samuel W. 5 Wall
Biggot Saml. 295 Hudson
Blakeslee R. jr. 54 John
Blankstein Moses S. 28 Division
Bogert Ralph, 339 Hudson
Bon L. & C. 65 Ann
Brunner Louis, 84½ Chatham
Burkles Joseph, 19 Rector
Butler Edward, 417 Pearl
Campbell John R. 52 John
Clark John A. 75 9th Av.
Cochrane Archibald T. 268 G'wich
Crouchley Thomas W. H. 226
  Canal
Crump Francis R. 63 Bleecker
Curtis Lemuel, 105 Av. D
Cuyningham A. J. 347½ B'way
Dodin Mensuy, 55 Av. C
Dumont Justin, 22 W. Broadway
Ederheimer ——, 131 Crosby
Eggert D. & Son. 239 Pearl
Egner Philip. 16 Av. A
Elnhaus John W. 56 Chatham
Farquhar J. 81½ 6th Av.
Fischer Fred W. 189½ Division
Fisher Richard. jr. 331 Broadway
Flemen Benedict, 92 Henry
Fox Philetus, 162 Fulton
Frost John, 287 Broome
Fry B. J. 811 Houston
Fry Nathan, 195 do
Gemmel J. & I. 502 Broadway
Germain Felix, 80 Nassau
Gernes Henry, 65 Ludlow
Giroud Victor, 394 Broadway
Goebel Henry, 391 Monroe
Gosselin & Kiddle, 88 Fulton
Gramer F. 208 William
Greffoz Julien, 272 do
Gundle L. 177 Delancy
Guy P. Adolphe, 168 3d Av.
Hammond S. & Co. 44 Merchants'
  Exchange
Harrison Wm. H. 352 Bowery
Heitz G. T. 99 Washington
Hirsch Meyers, 80 Bowery
Hobby James R. 351 Grand
Hookey Edward, 93 Hudson
Hoskay E. L. 17 Amos
Hoyt H. E. & Son, 104½ Cherry
Hoyt Seymour, 266 Pearl
Huntington David J. 199 Green'h
Imbery & Heller, 247 Grand
Jacobs Angel, 100 Chatham
Jacobs L. 204 Canal
Jennings & Lander, 94 Fulton
Jodry Leon, 33 Frankfort
Jones Robert, 322 Spring
Ketoham James, 373 Pearl
Knight Wm. N. 127 Waverly pl.
Krebs Peter, 119½ Washington
Lacour Michael, cor. 20th st. & 2d
  Av.
Landon J. E. 247 Hudson
Lange Daniel, 391 Pearl
Lewis Rees, 6 Doyer
Limburger Joseph F. 75 Wall
Linden James, 41 6th Av.
Lockwood Francis H. 206 B'way
Loomes William, 229 3d
Long William F. 105 Av. C
Maerz John, 349 Pearl
Marais John H. 194 4th Av.
Market John A. 199 6th Av.
Mathieu Gaston, 82 Broadway
Meyers George, 49 Av. B
Mercer T. J. 156 Fulton
Moir J. & W. 315 Hudson
Moore & Co. 112 Chatham
Mountjoy Thomas, 69 Centre
Mullan H. 153 Fulton

Newman H. & Co. 5 Peck slip
New York.
Niggeschmidt Ignas, 81½ Av. A
Norris Daniel S. 13 Christopher
Parsons J. C. 61 Cortlandt
Percy William, 209 1st Av.
Perkins J. P. 1 Wall
Piggot Samuel, 205 Hudson
Plain Francis. 165 6th Av
Pollitzer M. 391 Pearl
Posner Abraham, 311 Houston
Prontaut Anthony, 2 Park place
Radford Robert, 44 3d Av.
Rahmer Godfrey, 212 Rivington
Raiss F. 223 Houston
Rees Lewis, 6 Doyer
Riesle Egedius, 222½ Division
Robert Henry R. 70 Nassau
Robert Julius H. 20 Cortlandt
Rockwell S. D. 110½ Cherry
Rogers George, 3 Chambers
Rogers George. 8½ Carmine
Rogers James, 399 Hudson
Rombach Charles, 366 Houston
Rome Joseph, 96 Reade
Rudd & Scudder, 7 Maiden lane
Savage John Y. 92 Fulton
Scherpe L. F. 306 Bowery
Schlossheimer F. 168 Cherry
Scholpf P. 23 Ann
Schumann Charles W. 81 Ann
Seckel Isaac M. 176 William
Shannon Mrs. 254 Greenwich
Sharp J. 306 8th Av.
Shreve S. bet. 24th & 25th sts. 2d
Av.
Sill Horace, 214 Canal
Singleton Robert. 292 2d
Slafar Charles, 59 Av. A
Smith William S. 116 Bowery
Snider Henry, 3 Av. C
Sperry T. S. 322 Hudson
Stone H. G. 8th Av.
Thompson A. R. 165 Fulton
Van Berg Elias, 165 Washington
Vaucher Adolphe, 27 Warren
Vaughan Walter B. 129½ Fulton
Welch Benjamin D. 83 Cherry
Welch & Payne, 230 Greenwich
White I. 66 Fulton
White Wm. W. 68 Bowery
Wiekens ——, 116 Canal
Wilcox John, 137 8th Av.
Williston John T. 8 Liberty
Woolfe L. 151 Walker
Wright Alexander, 345 Hudson

Watch Makers' Tools.

Bourlier Nicholas, rear 47 Ann
New York.
Frasse Henry F. & Son. 95 Fulton
Frasse William H. 56 Chatham
Magnin Ve J. & Guedin, 19 Maiden lane
Mathey Aime, 61 Chatham

Water-Cure Establishments.

Alleghany County.

Champlin Gilbert B. Proprietor,
P. H. Hayes, M. D. Physician
Cuba.

Chenango County.

Eagle House Water-Cure, O. V.
Thayer, M.D. Physician, Pitcher
Springs *Pitcher.*

Columbia County.

New Lebanon Springs Water-
Cure Establishment, D. Cambell
& Son Proprietors, N. Bedortha
Physician.NewLebanon Springs
New Lebanon.

Cortland County.

Glen Haven Water-Cure, Jackson
& Gleason Proprietors, S. O,
Gleason M. D. Physician, Glen
Haven *Scott.*

New York County.

Nichols Mrs. M. S. 46 Lexington
Av. *New York.*
Trall R. T. 15 Laight

Oneida County.

New Graefenberg Water-Cure, R.
Holland Proprietor, Henry Foster Physician *Utica.*

Queens County.

Trall R. T. *Oyster Bay.*

Otsego County.

Rockaway Cottage Water-Cure.
Philip Roof M. D. Proprietor &
Physician, Cooperstown *Otsego.*

Tioga County.

Bethesda Water-Cure, Josiah H.
Stedman Proprietor & Physician
Richford.

Tompkins County.

Burdick J. F. *Lansing.*

Wyoming County.

Green & Fuller *Castile.*

Water Pipes.

Ball J. & Co. Reade near Centre
New York.

Weavers—Fancy.

Broome County.

Harvey J. R. & P. *Binghamton.*

Weavers—Rag Carpet.

Arthur Hugh, 580 Hudson
New York.
Boyce Joseph, 109 Bowery
Boyce R. 96 East Broadway
Boyd John, 195 Ludlow
Brown Samuel, 79 Bowery
Burman Jacob, 185 Bowery
Caldwell William, 221 G'wich
Campbell James R. 82 Fulton
Coward John, 184 Division
Dalton Patrick, 117 Bowery
Davies Ebenezer, 248 Grand
Deitch Jacob, 251 Division
Deliny James, 7 Av. C
Dilworth John, 206 Greenwich &
367 Bleecker
Duffy Patrick, 253 Delancy
Eccles Thomas, 25 Attorney
Elcock William, 308 Hudson and
140 Varick
Essig John, 169 Broome
Fair Thomas, 181 Greenwich
Gallagher James, 65, 87½, 69,
81½, 219, 221½, & 225 Bowery,
86 E. Broadway, 222 Fulton,
245 Grand, 39 Orange, 284 Hamersley, 475 Greenwich, & 204
Stanton
Gillen Robert, 41 8th Av.
Hagarty Hugh, 59 Bowery
Hamilton John, 263 Grand
Hamilton Robert, 266 Greenwich
Hemphill Francis, 155 9th Av. &
90 9th Av.
Jackson Thomas, 82 Allen

Keel Edward, 55 Bowery
New York.
Klein John, 109 Chrystie
Knox Joseph, 551 Greenwich
Laly Peter, 115 Bowery
Lamb John, 475 Greenwich
Lerp Thomas, 284 Hudson
Lettey Oliver, 241 Bleecker
M'Card Owen, 57 Bowery
M'Cauley George, 369 6th Av.
M'Clelland James, 233 & 839
Hudson & 263 Spring
M'Gilvern M. 128½ Columbia
M'Kinney Robert, 2½ Av. C
M'Mullen George, 473 G'wich
M'Murray Joseph, 90 E. B'way
M'Pherson Adam, 23 Columbia
Magivern John, 183 Houston
Martin Samuel, 196 Grand
Mathews Hugh, 336 Hudson
Maybell John. 346 Hudson
Megivern Marcus, 128½ Columbia
Melger Michael, 143 Bowery
Michael M. 143 Bowery
Miller William, 72 Vesey
Moog Charles, 77 Ludlow
Moore John, 314 Hudson
Myers Isaac, rear 86 Essex
O'Brien Thomas. 285 Bowery
Oliver James, 323 Bowery
Peoples Daniel, 34 East B'way
Purdy Elijah H. 25 West
Quin John, 205 Bowery
Regan John, 223 Bowery
Richardson Jonathan, 423 G'wich
Riley Edward, 81 Bowery
Roll George P. 231 Bowery
Ryan John, 69 Bowery
Sarsfield J. 266 Greenwich
Saarsfield Patrick, 273 G'wich
Sanders K. 244 6th
Smyth William, 551 Greenwich
Stewart David, 274 Hudson
Timmon James, 81½ Bowery
Tobias Thomas, 560 Grand
Towill J. 382 Cherry
Walker Robert, 196 Spring
White James, 9 Perry
Wilson James, 272½ Grand
Woods Peter, 121 Fulton

Webbing Makers.

Doyle Thomas, 285 W. 17th
New York.
Dupnys Noel, 216 William
Fitzpatrick William, 90 Mulberry

Weighers.

Adams & Tuthill, 148 Front
New York.
Arnold James M. 109 Wall
Baker Elijah, 127 Washington
Betts George, 86 South
Blake George W. 32 Old slip
Blackwell Thomas L. 140 Maiden
lane
Bradley L. R. 116 Wall
Burdett J. & T. W. Titus, 4 Jones
lane
Bunker Reuben, 97 Pine
Bunker R. T. 97 Pine
Bunner C. F. 22 Coenties slip
Carr William J. 147 Front
Cavanagh Patrick, 114 Broad
Cooper Obadiah, 31 Old slip
Crane Alexander P. 96 Pine
Deegan John M. 89 Front
Demarest Daniel, 39 South
Demarest John, 81 Broad
Demarest Peter, 99 South
Dixon Absalom G. 61 Water
Gardiner Charles A. 109 Wall
Guion John H. 81 Broad
Guion William H. 81 do
Halsey Gordon, 93 Wall
Higgins Cornelius, 19 South
Hillard R. B. 65 Broad

Kellogg Charles G. 111 Broad
New York.
Kuhn George C. 118 Wall
Leary William H. 81 Broad
Losee Ira, 97 Pine
Macfarland Thomas M. 81 Broad
Mead Henry W. 97 Pine
Moore John. 93 Pine
Moore Joseph, 4 Jones lane
Murray Robert, 271 Cherry
Oakley Charles S. 138 Maiden la.
Pelham Jabez C. 93 Wall
Price John, 41 South William
Puffer G. D. 101 Wall
Root William S. & Son, 50 South
Russell R. F. 30 Water
Ryer John M. 43 South
Ryer W. T. S. 40 South
Sickels Daniel, 148 Front
Smith Joseph, 148 Front
Snyder Anthony S. 106 Wall
Stoutenburgh Alfred, 81 Broad
Stoutenburgh William T. 81 do
Swan Charles, 95 Pine
Tuthill Solomon, 148 Front
Underwood Cornelius, 22 Old slip
Van Cleef Cornelius, 15 Burling
slip
Van Tuyl B. S. 168 South
Watson R. S. 97 Pine
Weekes Joseph, 138 Maiden lane
Welling James, 93 Pine
Westervelt Daniel, 81 Broad
Westervelt J. 32 Old slip
Westervelt James W. 81 Broad
White John. 109 Wall
Wood B. & J. H. 44 South

Whalebone Manufacturers.

Kings County.

Meyer & Poppenhusen, 171 1st
Williamsburgh.

New York County.

Edwards L. A. 302 West
New York.
Lottin John, 86 Frankfort
Meyer & Poppenhusen, 44 Cliff
Murphy James, rear 131 Greene
Philips L. H. 239 Pearl
Salomon & Swart, 40 Rose
Vellema Emanuel, 221 William
Whiley W. & L. & Co. 25 Cedar

Wheelwrights.

(See also Carriage Makers, also Blacksmiths.)

Anderson W. J. C. 761 Washing-
ton   *New York.*
Beveridge John, 164 Elizabeth
Bogert & Peer, 24th n. 8th Av
Boyd Wm. 24 E. 19th
Brender Chas. 4 Jones
Clark & Henry, 32 Hamersley
Clough James, 8th Av.
Coe Charles, 623 Hudson
Conboy John, 58 Mulberry
Crawford E. 16th cor. 10th Av.
Cruny H. 30th n. 3d Av.
Daggitt & Fick, 176 Laurens
Dayton & Springton, W. 31st near
6th Av.
Devoe John, 43 Harrison
Dorn John, 218 2d
Dyer John, 157 Attorney
Elderson John, 44 Crosby
Finley John, 45 & 48 Wooster
Flynn Thomas, 2d Av.
Fullmer Peter, 137 W. 19th
Gaddis Wm. 154 W. 18th
Gannon Patrick, 10 Albany
Germann John, 116 Norfolk
German Philip, 178 Chrystie
Griffin A. 542 Washington
Haok John, 218 3d

Harris William, 102 Goerck
New York.
Hunt Wm. 281 Chrystie
Jeremiah & Burger, 83 1st Av.
Kay & Barden, 267 W. 16th
Kelly Wm. 24 Goerck
Kipp Quimby, 166 Eldridge
Lacount & Ward, 166 Chrystie
Lawrence Samuel A. 168 Allen
Lawson, Allen & Synes, 39 Ham-
ersley
Long Edward, 466 Water
Lonnergen Lewis, 122 W. 17th
Lutz Peter, 123 Pitt
M'Carty John, 211 Wooster
M'Donald James, 355 Washington
M'Garr Hugh, 13th bet. 4th Av. &
Broadway
Mead Joshua, 291 3d Av.
Ming John, 8th Av.
Morgan John, 143 Mott
Morris Wm. 174 Laurens
Persall Daniel, 512 Water
Pfister George A. 122 W. 18th
Powell Benjamin, 191 Delancy
Rice D. J. & R. Pearsall, 85 Suf-
folk
Riegelman John, 254 5th
Regan Daniel, 244 Madison
Schaible Andrew, 606 Water
Schwartz Jacob, 218 2d
Scott John, 161 Attorney
Sherry P. 799 Greenwich
Smith J. 234 1st Av.
Statmiller A. 29th bet. 4th & 5th
Avs.
Stewart A. 562 6th Av.
Storms N. 256 17th
Thomas David, 346 Cherry
Thorn Joseph S. & Co. 29 Hamer-
sley
Tompkins Isaac M. 182 Eldridge
Van Buren Hector S. 137 Christo-
pher
Vanderbilt & Coe, r. 73 Laurens
Waldron George, 11th c. 7th Av.
Waldron James, 336 6th
Westfield Wm. 177 Prince
Wheeler Winthrop, 49 1st
Wilkins Harvey, 96 Sullivan
Wilson Michael, 215 Franklin
Wolcot Nelson, Water c. Jefferson
Yerman John, 104 W. 18th

Whip Manufacturers.

Erie County.

Leonard N.   *Buffalo.*
Munroe Wm. C. 35 Main

Livingston County

Guillian Wm.   *Dansville.*

Monroe County.

Fife & Bennett, Globe Building,
Main st.   *Rochester.*
Ives Theodore, 22 Adams
Strong Myron, 17 State
Wood E. G. 24 Main st. Brockport
Sweden.

New York County.

Alexander Wm. 7 Anthony
New York.
Archer Benjamin, 123½ Bowery
Marinus J. & J. H. 64 John
Stewart Charles L. 313 Pearl
Rhodo Henry, 1 Maiden lane and
174 Broadway
Thurston Edgar M. 390½ Broadway
West George, 55½ Hamersley

White Lead Manufacturers.

Jefferson County.

Knapp Thos. L.   *Brownville.*

Kings County

Waldron Hen. 12 Water *Brooklyn.*
Brooklyn White Lead Co. David
Leavitt Prest., Front st. between
Adams & Washington
Levy U. H. East Brooklyn White
Lead and Paint Works, John st.
near Adams
Union White Lead Manufacturing
Co. Front cor. Bridge
Atlantic White Lead Factory,
Robert Sherwell Supt., Marshall
near Gold

Monroe County.

Moulson Samuel, 36 Front
Rochester.

New York County.

Atlantic White Lead Company,
287 Pearl
Belleville White Lead Company,
151 Pearl
Brooklyn White Lead Company,
160 Front
Jessup Benjamin P. 158 Water
Jewett John & Sons, 182 Front
Lewis J. S. & Co. 82 Water
New York & Saugerties White
Lead Company, J. M'Cullough
Prest. 150 Front
Pollen & Colgate, 287 Pearl
Tieman Daniel F. 17 Burling slip
Ulster White Lead Manufactur-
ing Co. 163 Front
Union White Lead Manufacturing
Co. 175 Front

Richmond County.

Jewett J. & Sons, Port Richmond
Northfield.

Whiting Manufacturers.

Kings County.

Baxter Timothy, Water near Pearl
Brooklyn.
Sparkman & Truslow, South 7th
st.   *Williamsburgh.*

New York County.

Baxter T. 143 Maiden lane
New York.
Boyd Frederick S. 135 Bank
Segar F. 11th near E. R.
Sparkman & Truslow, 194 Water
Zeiger H. & Co. 11th cor. Av. C

Richmond County.

Riddle A., Stapleton   *Southfield.*

Wig & Toupee Manufac-
turers. *(See also Hair Workers; also Hair Dressers; also
Hair (Ornamental) Manufacturers.)*

Columbia County.

Green W. H. Warren st. *Hudson.*

Erie County.

Sage John, 210 Main   *Buffalo.*
Baste & Call, 204 Main

New York County.

Barker W. J. 349½ Broadway
New York.
Barry Alexander C. 130 Broadway
Batchelor William A. 4 Wall
Banyard P. 5 Frankfort
Brown William H. 222 Hudson
Carter James P. 269 Grand
Catling George, 70 Bowery
Courtois G. 250 Broadway
Dibblee William, 263 Broadway

Frost W. 114 Jane   *New York.*
Gibbins F. 92 Broadway
Hunt Elijah C. 451 Pearl
Laird James, 92 Chatham
Lind Victorine, 269 Grand
M'Kay Duncan, 399 Pearl
Martin Henry. 427 Broadway
Medhurst & Heard. 27 Maiden lane
Miniort J. 90 Broadway
Phalon Edward, 2 Dey
Quirk Thomas, 490 Broadway
Saunders Adell T. 306 Bowery

Window Shade Manufacturers.

Kings County.

Cook Henry, 98 Grand
      Williamsburgh.
Sealey Richard, 239 Lorimer

Monroe County.

Waasley Brothers, 55 Main
      Rochester.
Jennings Charles E. 66 State

New York County.

Anderson George H. 337 Grand
      New York.
Bartol Samuel F. 175 William
Berrian Wm. 180 Bowery
Briddon & Archer, 205 Chrystie
Conover Thomas, 150 Barrow
Delamano Wm. 468 Broadway
Ehrber Martin, Av. B bet. 12th &
   13th
Fasch Robert, 145 Houston
Felton Charles B. 219 6th Av.
Getty George. 293 Hudson
Godfrey Kemp, 38 Carmine
Greason John, 247 Greenwich
Hanington Wm. J. 364 Broadway
Harpell G. 251 Grand
Hinton Wm. 210 Fulton
Horn Albert, 117 West 19th
Hubbs John C. 240 Division
Hull Jonathan, 356 Hudson
Jeffreys Wm. 416 Pearl
Jeffreys ——, 705 Greenwich
Jenks Wm. O. 456 Pearl
Kelty & Riker, 131 Chatham
Koppel Sander B. 224 6th
Mac Bride Francis. 334 Hudson
M'Grorty ——, 136 William (See
   advertisement.)
Ormsbee Otis, 181 William
Parsell A. & J. H 46 M'Dougal
Seguezs Maria, 9th Av. 41st st.
Terhuen John, 71 Division
Washburn & Brother, 7½ Bowery
Woodford Josiah C. 295 Broadway
   (See advertisement.)
Woodford Oliver W. 66 Catharine

Oneida County.

Segar J. W. 42 Liberty   *Utica.*

Queens County.

Kelly & Riker, Astoria *Newtown.*

Rensselaer County.

Barrenger David P. 160 River
      Troy.

Window Shades (Wire.)

Lee & Co. 309 Bleecker *New York.*
Rossiter James, 595 Grand

Wine & Liquor Coloring.

Alston George W. 16 Roosevelt
      New York.
Crowley John, 30th st. 7th Av.

Wine and Liquor Dealers.

Albany County.

Foot & Welden, 311 Broadway
      Albany.
Knowlton H. 197   do
Fake & Todd.   do
Tracy & Edson, (wholesale) 13
   Exchange
Reid & Cushman, (wholesale) 32
   Dean.
Esmay Isaac. (wholesale) 28 Dean
Wilkinson Jacob, 27   do
Satterlee E. & E. R.
Merrin G. 7½ Hudson
Tarbell George S. 65 Quay
Moore S. B. 4 Division
Reno R. 9 South Pearl
Mascord E. 27 do
Pratt G. (wholesale) 1 William
Costigan John, (wholesale) 106 &
   108 Orange

Broome County.

Cotten & Co. (wholesale)
      Binghamton.
Morse & Gatefield, (wholesale)

Cayuga County.

M'Cabe E.W. (wholesale) North st.
      Auburn.

Erie County.

Tiphene Victor, 187 Main *Buffalo.*
Catlin Irn & Brother, 4 Packet
   Dock
Weisser Henry, 342 Main
Banrzutschky ——, 362 Main
Mosler & Yale, 10 Blosson square
Mills J. G. & W. I. Merchants' Ex.
Fero John R. 3 Birkhead's Block,
   Commercial st.
Van Duzee Wm. S. Pearl st. rear
   1st B. Church
Blancan P. C. 168 Main
Hagar Henry & Co. 62 Main
Weistbeck J. A. 40   do
Loveridge E. D. 24   do

Greene County.

Russell & Ross   *Catskill.*
Sherman Benjamin *Prattsville.*

Jefferson County

Hine N. S. Sackett's Harbor
      Hounsfield.

Kings County.

Allen W. H. (wines) 209 Atlantic
      Brooklyn.
Cornell & Mead, 2 Atlantic
Ca‑anagh John, 13   do
M'Dermott John, 3 Furman
Redding Thomas H. 74 Fulton
Watts S. C. 84   do
Schoonmaker Martence, 47½ Fulton
Gerald Thomas J. 7 Front
Shields John, 83 Main
Markey F. cor. Main & Front
Markey Andrew, cor. Plymouth &
   Pearl
M'Avoy A. 171 Jay
Donohue Hugh, 26 Hudson Av.
Fitzpatrick & Dowd, Hudson Av.
   cor. Plymouth
Robinson Wm. 52 Prince
Donnell Hugh, Hudson Av.
Donohue Hugh, Flushing Av.
Fallon James, 110 Grand
      Williamsburgh.
Brown John, 1st st. cor. North 2d
Betterman Frederick C. North 4th

Monroe County.

Osborn N. P. 11 South St. Paul
      Rochester.
Smith C. D. & Brother, 15 South
   St. Paul

Schlitger Geo. 22 South St. Paul
      Rochester.
Tracy John. 74 North St. Paul
Cutts Samuel. 10 Water
Conkey J. & E. 70 Main
Knight G. cor. Water & Main
Brackett, Averell & Co. (importers) 13 Buffalo
Mudgett Wm. jr. 69 Buffalo
Breck M. B. & Co. 67 Main
Marsh & Davis. 30 Exchange
Dawley John, 35   do
Lawrence W. T. & F. S. 20 Exchange
Rogers E. (wholesale) cor. State
   & Mumford

Montgomery County.

Clark S. B.   *Canajoharie.*
Ried Darwin E. (wholesale) Fort
   Plain   *Minden.*

New York County.

Adams J. 122 Warren *New York.*
Adema Mary. 94 Warren
Ainslie Jas. 150 Front
Alton & Co. 151 7th
Arent Arthur. 64 Essex
Armstrong Van Cleve M. 253
   Washington
Aspell & Wallace, 181 8th Av.
Assalena Leon, 97 Duane
Brant C., E. Broadway cor. Grand
Barber Jas. 261 Washington
Beal A. H. 39 Water
Bean Aaron H. 39 Water
Bechtell John, 177 Av. A.
Beddons Thos. 153½ 7th
Begg Francis, 281 Stanton
Begg Jas. 43 Hester
Begg P. & M. 71 Mulberry
Bellows Chas. 16 Broad
Benjamin Francis, jr. 138 Cedar
Bertram John A. 73 Bayard
Billinge Jas. 475 Pearl
Bininger A. M. 100 Barclay
Bininger & Cozzens, 56 Vesey
Bloodgood Nathaniel, 4 Pine
Bohde E. & Co. 204 Fulton
Borsken & Debus, 112 Houston
Boyd John, 43 Vesey
Boudy Jos. 5 1st Av.
Boylan E. 258 Front
Boylan Patrick, 63 Broome
Boylan Peter, 200 Av. A.
Brenan Mrs. 9 Elm
Browning Jos. M. 110 Warren
Bussey Geo. E. 255 South
Carpenter J. 96 Bleecker
Chapman J. & Co. 394 8th Av
Church Chas. L. 537 Hudson
Cody Jas. 143 Liberty
Cogswell, Crane & Co. 104 Wall
Connelly Robert, 83 Ludlow
Cornell Barak, 93 Houston
Cosgrove John, 56 Grand & Av. A
   cor. 21st
Coulter Jas. E. 87 11th
Daly John T. 106 Wall
Daub Louis, 91½ Bowery
David John, 4 & 6 S. William
Davis Gilbert, 45 Pine
Davis Hamilton, 56 Tompkins
Dayton & Sprague, 107 Front
De Beixcedon Edw. 59 Beekman
Deming & Tufts. 67 3d Av.
Donellan Wm. 154 Forsyth
Dowdall Luke, 17 Prince
Doyle Jas. A. 474 Pearl
Duff Henry J. 35 Vesey
Dunn Patrick, 83 9th Av.
Durand John & Co. 107 Cedar
Eagar James, 34 Cliff
Eckerson Benjamin, 175 West
Enge Philip W. & Son, 131 Front
Eury N. 284 Water
Fee Arthur, 64 Marion
Finn Hugh, 92 Centre
Fitzpatrick William, 15 Av. D
Fletcher C. 235 Fulton
Flood Conner C. & Co. 131 W. 17th

Foster Robert, 542 Pearl
New York.
Frost Zephaniah, 15 Canal
Garvin P. 8th Av.
Gavin William. 235 Bowery
Geraghty J. 493 Pearl, 45 Centre & 101 W. 18th
Gilmartin & Boland, 272 Henry
Gottsberger John G. 12 Centre
Gourreau H. 19 N. William
Grace Tobias, 130 Cedar
Graham J. H. 770 4th & 190 Lewis
Greenly & Squire, 199 Chambers
Hacket William, 193 6th Av.
Halpin James, 168 8th Av.
Halpin T. 451 1st Av.
Hart Edward, 74 James & 32 Roosevelt
Harvey Francis & Co. 121 Av. D
Holden Wm. 274 8th Av.
Hoey John, 195 do
Hott Daniel, 40 Market
Hubbard C. A. 86 Front & 36 Oliver cor. Madison
Hussey Edward M. 162 W'hington
Jackson Thomas. 42 Stone
Jacob H. 134 3d & Av. A
Jarvis & Cooper, 105 Murray
Jewett & Whitney, 136 Cedar
Johnson Jones O. C. 510 Pearl
Johnson Oliver, 41 Market
Johnson Thomas, 55 Bowery
Jones W. P. 109 Wall
Keane James, 472 Pearl
Keane John, 649 Greenwich
Kearney John, 315 Water
Keefe J. H. 100 Bayard
Keeler Joseph, 6 Centre
Kellogg E. Bruyn, 96 Barclay
Kelley D. 35 Hamersley
Kelly James, 446 12th
Kelly John, 55 Roosevelt
Kelly John, 15 Murray
Kelly J. J. 224 Front
Kelly Patrick, 74 Bayard
Kenneth & Laverty, 108 Wall
King C. A. 218 Fulton
King E. A. 218 do
Kirtland Gilbert A. 205 South
Knapp Cyrus & Co. 256 W'hington
Knowlseloch C. 255 3d Av.
Knowles J. 67 James
Laty A. 16 John
Leahy Patrick, 212 Walker
Ledwith James, 12th st. bet. A & B
Ledwith Michael, 55 G'nwich Av.
Lee J. & Co. 51 Washington
Lefman H. & Co. 232 Washington
Lehritter John A. 55 Av. A
Leuman Matthew F. 630 4th
Linders C. 70 Av. B
Lyons William, 478 Pearl
M'Carron Neil, 87 Mulberry
M'Cormick P. 219 1st Av.
M'Cormick Patrick, 266 11th
M'Cormick Patrick & Co. 31 Av. B
M'Cormick & Co. 363 3d Av.
M'Cormick & Co. cor. 6th st. & 1st Av.
M'Given P. 201 Av. B
M'Guire John, 422 10th
M'Guire & Mullen, 132 Elizabeth
M'Grugan John, 212 8th Av., 8th Ward hotel Varick cor. Dominick and hotel Grand cor. Corral
M'Kenzie John, 102 10th Av.
M'Kiernan Thomas, 59 9th Av.
M'Laughlin Michael, 494 Pearl
M'Wade A. 165 3d Av.
Mallory William, 181 South
Manson W. & Co. 232 3d Av.
Mansuy Joseph, 556½ Pearl
Matthew Alexander, 113 Warren & 354 Greenwich
Maxwell & Latham, 264 Washington
Means Thomas, 104 Water
Mercier George, 85 Fulton
Millard Royal G. 89 Barclay
Mallenhausen J. 203 3d Av.

Mullen Edward, 12th bet. 1st & Av. A *New York.*
Mullholland P. 279 Madison
Mullin Thomas. 71 W. 17th
Mulvihill Patrick, 57 Mulberry
Munro Hugh. 59 Water
Murphy James, 242 1st Av.
Murray Charles, 72 Roosevelt
Murser Henry, 76 Liberty
Nougaret Edmund. 135 Fulton
Nugent T. 95 Monroe
O'Connell Bernard, 500 Pearl
O'Donnell & Reilly, 336 1st Av.
O'Reilly John, 58 Centre
O'Reilly's & Co. 157 South
O'Rourke James F. 406 Broome
Ostheim Moritz, 116 Liberty
Papen Charles & Co. 19 West
Parker William, 132 Greenwich Av.
Pattullo David, 85 Duane
Pecker Anthony, 91 Delancy
Perry Jewett, 432 Monroe
Peters John, 280 Division
Pierson Joseph, 50 Frankfort
Powers Daniel, 31 Coenties slip
Prendergast Luke, 7 1st Av.
Prescott Henry W. 11 Wall
Radford & Co. 202 West
Raynor Richard, 448 Monroe
Read Oliver P. 63 Vesey
Reilly John M. & Co. 172 South
Riley Patrick, 148 2d
Roach John, 29 Mulberry
Robinson Reuben B. 251 Front
Rogers & Co. 109 Fulton
Reppers Frederick, 196 Houston
Russell James, 50 9th Av
Segeman John W. 51 Av. B
Samson David, 266 Washington
Sanford Daniel, 162 South
Schilling A., Av. A bet. E. 15th & E. 16th, & 184 3d
Schmadeke John, 212 Fulton
Schwoerer L. 46 Vesey
Shannon William & Co. 57 Market
Simmons & Norton, 2 3d Av.
Smith Alexander, 266 W. 17th
Smith George M. & Co. 262 Washington
Smith Isaac H. 36 Peck slip
Snyder H. & W. J. 81 Beaver
Sottan Alexander, 115 Wall
Souza Moses, 248 Washington
Sparks C. 380 3d Av.
Sparks Geo. & Co. 290 Rivington
Staples Joseph, 132 Bowery
Starin W. H. 109 Wall
Steel & Howard, 134 Cedar
Steiger Simon, 26 Essex
Stewart John, 121 Mulberry
Stirling & Walton, 119 Warren
Stoll & Armstrong, 263 W'hingtn.
Sullivan William, 82 Pike slip
Sweet Allen S. 106 Murray
Taylor George, 34 Duane
Taylor John, 314 1st Av.
Teal Lewis, 171 West
Thatcher W. B. 306 Pearl
Thomas R. 239 South
Tucker, Brooke & Co. 203 Ch'bers
Tuthill James M. & Co. 114 Warren
Twitch & Co. 231 Houston
Van Benschoten J. 157 B'way
Van Cleef Isaac, 15 Burling slip
Welford William, 76 Duane
Welch E. P. 164 3d Av.
Westfall J. & D. 194 South
White Wm. 6th Av.
Wintringham David L. 16 Wall
Woodgate John H. 213 Front
Woolsey John, 206 Front
Wright C. & F. 22 Washington

Oneida County.

Baxter & Hull, 8 Liberty *Utica.*

Onondaga County.

Given W. H. Water st. Syracuse
Salina.

Oswego County

Biddlecomb & Ayres, Water st.
Oswego
Hudson & Wilbur, cor. Water & Seneca

Queens County.

Gildersleeve Josiah *Hempstead*

Rensselaer County.

Fake & Backman, 283 State
Lambert Thomas A. 352 State
Lansingburgh
Ryan John, 212 4th *Troy*
Christie James, 43 Congress
Bennett T. J. 58 do
Jordan Thomas, 55 do
Dwyre J. 173 4th
Ten Broeck & Steenberg. 263 River
Van Derwerken J. & Son 279 do
Ash John, 131 do
Conike M. & Co. 137 do
Sage Russell, 139 do
Russell Chas. H. 141 do
Hellogg John P. 205 do
Smith & Wood (Importers) 237 do
Huddleston & Son, do 249 do
Haight & Gillespie, 269 do
Brady M. 350 do
Mahony J. 358 do
Gorman Mrs. 370 do
Sisk John, 372 do
M'Donald Alexander, 390 do
Chichester Henry S. 422 do
Bolin John, 379 do
Dater & Carr, 299 do
Murray Mrs. 79 Jacob

Richmond County.

Delvin T. Tompkinsville
Castleton.

St. Lawrence County.

Buttolph Seymour E. *Canton.*

Saratoga County.

Waterman S. S. *Waterford.*
Green J. & E. B.

Ulster County.

Anson N. & A. L. Rondout
Kingston.

Wine & Liquor Importers.

Adolphus R. 60 Broadway
New York.
Ainslie Francis V. 150 Front
Atkins A. 91 Water
Averell H. & W. J. & Co. 68 Pearl
Aymar & Co. 34 South
Bartholemy B. 292 Broadway
Barnes & Co. 281 3d
Barsalou V. & Co. 62 Water
Bayaud Theodore W. 89 Broad
Boan Aaron H. 39 Water
Beaudouin H. & Co. 57 Ann
Beers & Bogart, 177 South
Benner Valentine, 1st st. cor Av. A
Bininger A. & Co. 141 Broadway
Blackburn Edward, 10 Beaver
Bloch S. 164 Fulton
Blots & Bishop, 84 Fulton
Blow & March, 91 Water
Boker John G. & E. 93 Front
Brigham John T. 78 Broadway
Brooks & Bearns, 274 Front
Brown A. Speirs, 56 Pine
Brunel F. A. Agent for B. & S Irroy, 48 Broadway
Burdick William C. 92 Broadway
Carter Wellington A. 7 New

Cashman D. Jr. 1 Beaver
New York.
Castillou G. S. 102 Front
Caswell John & Co. 87 Front
Cazet & Astoin, 64 Water
Chambon John B. 308 Broadway
Charlick Oliver, 10 Coenties slip
Clayburn & Livingston, 132 Cedar
Conklin & Smith, 141 Front
Cooper & Vanzandt, 21 New
Courtin Napoleon, 15 Park row
Cuthbertson William D. 61 Water
Daly Kieran B. 67 Pearl
Davis Gilbert, 61 William
Disbrow A. & Co. 19 Beaver
Edgerton T. T. 84 Front
Engler Chas. 13 South
Engs Wm. & Co. 100 Water & 131 Front
Fender P. P. 102 Front
Fort & Lindam, 15 S. William
Frings Brothers, 122 Fulton
Frexes L. 102 Wall
Gibson G. C. 75 Bowery
Greenly & Squires, 199 Chambers
Hart Edward, 35 Oak
Harmony's P. Nephews & Co. 63½ Broadway
Herckenrath & Van Damme, 29 Beaver
Hilger & Co. 114 Water
Howes, Godfrey & Co. 96 South
Hubbard Cyrus A. 86 Front
Ireland Thos. S. 90 John
Irroy B. & S. 48 Broadway
Jessup & Fox, 178 South
Keefe H. O. 90 Bayard
Knechtel & Price, 178 Broadway
Keun John, 649 Greenwich
Leger Henry, 102 Wall
Lewis G. M. 81 Front
Liebmann Louis, 192 William
Lovelius J. C. C. 33 Water
M'Laughlin Michael, 494 Pearl
M'Mullen Thos. 19 Wall
March & Benson, 5 New
Martin Chauncey S. 63 Front
Meletta Chas. 47 New
Moore E. D & Co. 71 & 73 Front
Myers Lawrence & Co. 29 S. Wm
Newman Samuel, 7 New
Nielson & Anthony, 32 Beaver
Nougaret R, 135 Fulton
Oechs Adolphus, 60 New
Osborn John & Robert, 111 Wall
Pattrull David, 65 Duane
Peiffer Nicholas, 181 William
Pfirrmann C. & J. P. 119 Liberty
Prescott Henry W. 11 Wall
Quldort Eberhard F. 75 Clinton
Quitzow H. W. 50 Broadway
Renauld & Francois, 21 Beaver
Routh H. L. & Sons, 69 New
St. Amant Daniel, 41 S. William
Sattig John, 204 Broadway
Seignette A. & Co. 47 Water
Schmid Saver M 142 Fulton
Shuaderbeck & Co. 11 Spruce
Simpson Lissack H. & Son, 26 S. William & 138 W. 17th
Smith ——, 9 Coffee House Slip
Snyder H. & W. J. 81 Beaver
Soltau Alex. 115 Wall
Souza M. 248 Washington
Spencer J. 111 Wall
Stouvenel John B. 39 & 40 John
Symington & Kelly, 111 Front
Tardy John A. 13 New
Terrett Horatio N. & Co. 231 Front
Tilton & Molony, 88 Water
Tobias T. J. 43 New
Toler Henry K. 4 New
Tonnele Louis, 100 Wall
Van Rossum John P. 83 Beaver
Walter Hermann & Co. 17 Wall
Ward Willett C. 105 Front
Well & Van Benschoten, 32 Cortlandt
Will H. City Hall place corner Duane
Wilson & Henriques, 30 Old slip
Welß Udolphe 32 Beaver

Wire Cloths.

Corny J. 29 Fulton *New York.*
Dugan Thos. 502 Greenwich
Field Cyrus W. & Co. 11 Cliff (See advertisement.)
King Jas. 26th & 10th Av.

Wire Drawers.

Moore & Co. r. 47 Ann *New York.*

Wire Manufacturers.

New York County.
Crawford John, 649 Greenwich *New York.*
Dunn Simeon, 187 Water
Richardson Fred. G. 107 John
Stephens Wm. & Son, 109 John

Westchester County.
Strong & Lyon, Peekskill *Courtlandt.*
Bailey A. & Brothers, Croton *Yorktown*

Wire Workers.

Kings County.
Raber Peter (brass & copper wire cloth & iron wire sieves) Montrose Av. cor. Leonard st. *Williamsburgh.*

Monroe County.
Snow John, (screen & wire safe) Jenkins' Corner *Greece.*
Snow J. & S. (brass, copper & iron wire cloth) cor. Exchange & Buffalo *Rochester.*

New York County.
Corry Jas. 29 Fulton *New York.*
Crawford Mrs. 647 Greenwich
Gailhard Jos. B. 456 Broadway
Hink Wm. 84 3d Av.
Horler Ulrich, rear 99 Reade
Kelly Jos. 25 Fulton
Moore Thomas C. 49 Fulton & 108 Beekman
Oliver Alfred, 4 Jefferson
Oliver Henry W. 287 Division
Richardson F. G. 107 John
Rossiter Jas. 595 Grand
Stoutenborough Wm. 114 John
Williams Chas. 48 Fulton
Woods David, 45 Fulton

Onondaga County.
Herrick O. W. Baldwinsville *Lysander*

Ontario County.
Snow Marcus, Geneva *Seneca.*

Otsego County.
Smith & Richards (safes) *Edmeston.*
Smith Geo. J. (safes)

Rensselaer County.
Barclay J. (cages & traps) 336 River *Troy.*
Cook H. V. D. (wire cloth) 416 River

Washington County.
Hanks U. (sieves) *Cambridge.*

Wayne County.
Putney H. W. (screens) *Lyons.*
Griswold Lewis (screens)

Wood Dealers.

Abbott T. B. & A. B. West near Beach *New York.*
Eastbrook John C. 21st c. 1st Av.
Fisher Peter, foot 28th
Howell Nelson, 267 West
Hoyt G. & Co. foot Broome
Lozier Stephen, 21 W. Broadway
Mills & Secor, 223 & 225 Delancy
Phillips & Sheddon, 207 West
Robertson & Polhemus, 129 Pearl & 165 Monroe
Ross Sebastian & Rutger, 245 Cherry
Walton & Little, cor. East 12th
Willetts Edmond S., East b. Delancy & Rivington
Wood & Wright, Rutgers slip

Wooden Ware Dealers.

Albany County.
Williams W. H. & Co. 611 Broadway *Albany.*
Bicknell B. 397 Broadway
Wooley & Harris, 120 Washington

Duchess County.
Lillie I. W. 336 Main *Poughkeepsie.*
Beach E. 262 do

Greene County.
Edwards John *Catskill.*

Kings County.
Leech B. C. 160 Atlantic *Brooklyn.*
Ritter Thomas, (wood-mouldings and reeds) Schermerhorn near Court

New York County.
Allen Thomas E. & Son, 188 & 213 Washington *New York.*
Brandlacht C. 270 3d Av.
Barry J. 76 Catharine
Carpenter Henry, 296 Washington
Carr John, 58 Ludlow
Caverly Samuel L. 206 Greenwich & 71 Vesey
Dennis S. & D. S. 189 Washington
Dennis Wm. & Co. 192 & 194 Washington
Farnor Wm. 230 3d
Graff A. J. 142 8th Av.
Hink Wm. 48 3d Av.
Hoagland J. M. & Co. 199 Washington
Hopping A. D. & Co. 214 Wash.
Hopping & Meeker, 195 Wash
Huse J. B. Amos c. Greenwich
Jones Thos. 314 Spring
Kelly J. 164 Spring
Law H. G. 22 Fulton
Law J. F. & Co. 51½ Carmine
Laden Michael & Son, 190 Washington
Mills Wm. H. 226 Fulton
O'Brien T. 1 Centre mkt
Palmer Aaron B. & Co. 99 Cortlandt
Pauling Wm. 6th Av.
Sitgreaves John, 322 Spring
Smith Alexander W. 192 Greenwich
Smith Daniel C. 63 Houston
Stiles Robert. 81 Vesey

Onondaga County.
Graves S. & Co., Jordan *Elbridge.*

Otsego County.
Cosey E. & H., Cooperstown *Otsego.*

Queens County.

Wanzor Daniel — *Hempstead.*

Wooden Ware Manufacturers.

New York County.

Ashcroft Barbara, 239 Bowery — *New York.*
Bartholomew John, r. 11 Forsyth
Barton W. B. & R. 59 10th Av.
Brown Wm. & Co. 137 Maid. lane
Clark & Solomon, 18 Fulton
Daniel Wm. 63 Wooster
Fagan John, 743½ Greenwich
Fagin James K. 297 Spring
Jenkins John, 339 Bowery
Kelly Joseph, 154 Spring
Law Hervey G. 22 Fulton
Lockwood Cornelius, 25 Fulton
Montayne J. 186 Hester
Myers James, jr. 403 Grand
Sitgreaves John, 332 Spring
Smith George W. 17 Fulton
Smith G. H. & Co. 19 Fulton
Smith Silas C. 22 Fulton
Taggart & Gray, 18 Fulton
Taylor Wm. K. 546 Grand
Wilbur Charles, 29 Fulton
Zinc Theodore, r. 56 & 58 Attorney

Oneida County

Timan J. Columbia st. — *Utica.*

Wooden Screw Manufacturer.

Wicks George, r. 8 Division — *New York.*

Wood Type.

Nesbitt George F. 86 Wall — *New York.*

Wool Carding & Cloth Dressing.

Albany County.

Bald & Haverly, Reedsville — *Berne.*
Huick T. E. — *Coeymans.*

Alleghany County.

Burdick S. W. — *Andover.*
Hatch Silas G. — *Angelica.*
Spalding —— — *Belfast.*
Fritts H. — *Bolivar.*
Robinson G. W. — *Friendship.*
Olney J. F.
Mills, Holmes & Whitaker — *Hume.*

Broome County.

Devor J. — *Binghamton.*
Corbett S. Corbettsville — *Conklin.*
Rindge E. — *Lisle.*
Balch B. — *Union.*
Clothing H., Union Centre
Dickson D. — *Windsor.*

Cattaraugus County.

Hills C., Seeleysburgh — *Conewango.*
Haden M., Sandusky — *Freedom.*
Fallet & Farrar — *Machias.*
Payne A. S., East — *Randolph.*

Cayuga County.

Watkins J. C. Weedsport — *Brutus.*

Chautauque County.

Brown & Allen — *Charlotte.*
Hastings E. M. Jamestown — *Elliott.*
Stephenson ——, do

Nessle Joseph B. — *Ellington.*
Record S. Smith's Mills — *Hanover.*
Bly Henry — *Harmony.*
Albro J. K. Fredonia — *Pomfret.*
Jewett G. R. & Co. — *Portland.*
Kip & Miller — *Sheridan.*
Brown James L. — *Villenova.*
Parker James
Couch & Stone — *Westfield.*

Chemung County.

Johnson John A. — *Catharine.*

Chenango County.

Church E. P. Bennettsville — *Bainbridge.*
Pool —— — *Lincklaen.*
Guernsey Wm. G. — *Norwich.*
Brown William — *Plymouth.*

Clinton County.

Hartwell & Winslow — *Plattsburgh.*

Columbia County.

Gernon C. & E. Smoky Hollow — *Claverack.*
Tinker G. H. — *Gallatin.*
Dailey Wm. — *Hillsdale.*
Atkins R. — *Livingston.*

Cortland County.

Dibble Horace — *Cortlandt Village.*
Perkins Ebenezer — *Marathon.*
Jones Horatio P. — *Virgil.*

Delaware County.

Ladd W. T. & J. D. — *Andes.*
Mann H. — *Franklin.*
M'Call E.
Gibbs & Landon — *Harpersfield.*
Winslow D. — *Kortright.*
Kiff P., Bloomville
Mann A. — *Meredith.*
Doolittle G. W., Clovesville — *Middletown.*
Hulce M. R., Deposit — *Tompkins.*
Ray H. M. — *Walton.*
Townsend J.

Duchess County.

Bottomly J. — *Pine Plains.*

Erie County.

Rickert George, Williamsville — *Amherst.*
Day Timothy — *Boston.*
Plumb Ralph — *Collins.*
Akin Samuel C.
Graves Martin L. — *Eden.*
Smith F. East Evans — *Evans.*
Barton John, Water Valley — *Hamburgh.*
Rice B. T. & Co. — *Holland.*
Safford —— — *Lancaster.*
Cummings H., Akron — *Newstead.*
Gleason C. — *Sardinia.*

Essex County.

Welch Abram, Whallonsburgh — *Essex.*
Kilborn Reuben — *Keene.*
Gibbs Russell — *Lewis.*
Barton D. Moriah Four Corners — *Moriah.*

Franklin County.

Taylor Hiram — *Bangor.*

Fulton County.

Wigley Timothy, Vail's Mills — *Mayfield.*
Rice Lucius — *Northampton.*
Duncan Samuel

Genesee County.

Allen —— — *Alexander.*

Barrows S., Linden — *Bethany.*
Mills Daniel — *Elba.*
Pierce & Dean — *Pavilion.*

Greene County.

Griswold Elias W. — *Catskill.*
Harris & Levy
Miller Justice S. — *Lexington.*

Herkimer County.

Ingham Wm. — *Little Falls.*
Herendeen James — *Newport.*
Lockwood S. Gravesville — *Russia.*
Hubbard John, do
Dorr A. Starkville — *Stark*

Jefferson County.

Fulton E. — *Antwerp.*
Stacey Joel G. — *Brownville.*
Wilmott Reuben — *Champion.*
Waite F. — *Ellisburgh*
Crane I. S. Evans' Mills — *Le Ray.*
Abbey Sarelis — *Lorraine.*
Leonard Chas. Three Mile Bay — *Lyme.*
Wait —— Watertown — *Pamelia.*
Shaddock M. — *Philadelphia.*
Oakes G., Black River — *Rutland.*
Usher Wm. Felt's Mills
Collis J. C. & Co. — *Theresa.*
Lawton B. F. — *Watertown.*
Hunt W. Natural Bridge — *Wilna.*

Lewis County.

Miller James, Constableville — *West Turin.*

Livingston County.

Johnson O. B. — *Dansville.*
Dorr Samuel G.
French Arad, Oakland — *Portage.*

Madison County.

Newton Winslow — *Brookfield.*
Kellogg J. New Woodstock — *Cazenovia.*
Crandall Bailey — *De Ruyter.*
Isbell Abner, Leeville — *Eaton.*
Thompson Horace — *Fenner.*
Payne Bradford — *Georgetown.*
Ackley J. R. East Hamilton — *Hamilton.*
Powers J. W. Canastota — *Lenox.*
Day Marvin — *Lebanon.*
Britt S. Perryville — *Sullivan.*
Dunham Frederick. Bridgeport

Monroe County.

Blossom J. S. Hydraulic Buildings, Brown's Race — *Rochester.*

Montgomery County.

Van Valkinburgh James, Ames — *Canajoharie.*
M'Daniel James, Port Jackson — *Florida*
Wells J. J. Minaville
Haskel J. A. do

Niagara County.

Robbins & Comstock — *Newfane*

Oneida County.

Hart —— — *Boonville*
Wheeler Charles — *Camden.*
Tracy F. Delta — *Lee.*
Driggs J. — *Rome.*
Alder S. North Western — *Western.*

Ontario County.

Higby Elisha, Chapinsville — *Hopewell.*
Bryent William — *Manchester.*
Safford B. P. — *Phelps.*
Saulpaugh P. B.
Winegar A. Honeoye — *Richmond.*

Orange County.

Sloat A.   Crawford.
Kieram J. New Milford Warwick.

Orleans County.

Brady N. & Co. Albion   Barre.

Oswego County.

Williams & Kipp   Hannibal.
Bidwell Josiah H Centre
Eason R. A.   New Haven.
Thayer Luny   Parish.
Landon L. S. Pulaski   Richland.
Booth & Hart, Phœnix   Schroeppel.

Otsego County.

Park Avery   Burlington.
Cushman John, West Burlington
Green J.   Cherry Valley.
Finch E.
Reed Jeremiah M.   Middlefield.
Reynolds L.   Milford.
Church ——   New Lisbon.
Chamberlin Geo. A.   Oneonta.
Wilbur & Co.   Plainfield.
Conklin C.   Springfield.
Voorhees W.
Mannering J.   Westford.
Holmes Philander, East Worcester
                             Worcester.
Lake Stewart, E. Worcester

St. Lawrence County.

Ward Joseph 2d   Canton.
Smith T. K.
Winslow L. South Edwards
                             Edwards.
Giles A.   Fowler.
Cone S.   Gouverneur.
Ralph Stephen B.   Hermon.
Hyde Ezra   Hopkinton.
Doran Samuel, Waddington
                             Madrid.
Goss Alfred, Columbia
Ransom Amos   Massena.
Redington George, Lewisville
Mack Joel, on the Basin, Ogdens-
burgh   Oswegatchie.
Hart Pera   Parishville.
Cox Gardiner   Pierpont.
Miles Jacob H.
Rich B. C. & Co.   Potsdam.
Van Brocklin M.   Russell.

Saratoga County.

Peters William A. Vischer's Ferry
                             Clifton Park.
Young Divine H. Jamesville
                             Greenfield.
Peacock Willis, Porter's Corners
Foster & Co.   Providence.
Bonvoy ——
Williams William   Stillwater.

Schenectady County.

Sawyer Thomas B.   Glenville.

Schoharie County.

Riley A. B.   Cobleskill.
Brayman Henry
Cole Lewis   Esperance.
Weldren John, Breakabeen
                             Fulton.
Cook George   Gilboa.
Dies John
Patchen Lewis J.   Jefferson.
Dewey Elias
Zelle David   Middleburgh.
Waterbury J. S.   Schoharie.
Huffman & Mitchell   Summit.
Brewster E. Gallupville   Wright.

Steuben County.

Gorton J. }   Avoca.
Oxx T.
Brother & Green   Bath.
Bell & Co.   Dansville.

Capwell & Reynolds Troupsburgh.
Miller H. A.   Urbana.

Tompkins County.

Roe David C.   Caroline.
Starr Samuel H.   Groton.
Purdy Ebenezer   Newfield.

Warren County.

Thurston J. C. & S. Chestertown
                             Chester.
Burdick A.   Warrensburgh.

Washington County.

Goodfellow & Clutterbuck, Sandy
Hill   Kingsbury.
Goodrich Gustavus A.   Putnam.

Wayne County.

Daggett John, Newark   Arcadia.
Chapman & Redfield. Clyde Galen.
Sherman Gillman, East Palmyra
                             Palmyra.
Shipman James   Rose.
Drun C. Sodus Centre   Sodus.
Benedict Roswell   Wolcott.

Wyoming County.

Smith Wm. K.   Castile.
Clock ——   Java.
Wheeler E. B. Wyoming
                             Middlebury.
Smith R. H.   Perry.
Hendee George   Pike.
Davis Salem, Varysourg   Sheldon.
Naramore & Pike   Warsaw.

Yates County.

Huested Daniel   Barrington.
Higley E. Penn Yan   Milo.
Wooden Jared, Rock Stream
                             Starkey.
Wheelock E. M. Bigstream Point

**Woolen Goods Manufac-
turers.** *(See also Statistics.)*

Albany County.

Rathbone J. (satinets)   Bethlehem.
Spawn C.   Guilderland.
Batterman George C.
Conklin G.   Rensselaerville.

Alleghany County.

Crandall Silas & Co. (cassimeres &
tweeds) Whitesville
                             Independence.
Gordon & Washburn   Rushford.

Broome County.

Stevens C. A.   Binghamton.

Cattaraugus County.

Allen C. B. (12,000 yds. per an.)
                             Otto.

Cayuga County.

Winnegar & Son   Aurelius.
Midwood A.
Walker Wm.   Locke.
Simpkins ——
Goodrich D.   Moravia.
Winnegar & Brothers Springport.

Chautauque County.

Gorham W. Fredonia   Pomfret.

Chemung County.

Pratt & Co.   Elmira.

Chenango County.

Crandall J. & G. L.   Pitcher.
Jackson E. & Son   Preston.
Gurnsey & Wait
Collins J. W. & L. B.   Smyrna.

Clinton County.

Keese & Arnold, (50,000 yards an-
nually) Keeseville   Au Sable.
Morgan John M.   Peru.
Hartwell & Winslow Plattsburgh.

Columbia County.

Phillips Geo. P. & Co. (satinets &
cassimeres) Mellenville
                             Claverack.
Stotts J.   Stockport.
Vanhoosen A. W.   Stuyvesant.

Cortland County.

Andrews & Morgan   Preble.
Babcock Daniel   Scott.
Crain Almiron W.   Truxton.

Delaware County.

Wright & Everett   Davenport.
Broeck, Titus & Shaw   Hamden.

Duchess County.

Grooville Works, Glenham Co.
Glenham   Fishkill.
Dean M. Spencer Corner
                             Northeast.
Cook F.   Red Hook.
Spere J.
Gilderaleve J. Stanford Village
                             Stanford.
Wells P. W. Hull's Mills
Vale & Colwell   Unionvale.

Erie County.

Blakeley Asa & Co. West Falls
                             Aurora.
Gorton Job (cassimere & tweed)
                             Black Rock.
Plum & Ralph   Collins.
Akin Samuel C.
Cook Albert W. Springville
                             Concord.
Barton John, Water Valley
                             Hamburgh.

Essex County.

Brown, Trimble & Treadway
                             Crown Point.
Gilbert B. R.   Essex.
Treadway & Co.   Ticonderoga.

Franklin County.

Stark Luther   Fort Covington.
Briggs ——
Meigs E. L.   Malone.
Stark Russell

Fulton County.

Redish & Culbert   Broadalbin.
Casper Felix   Ephratah.
Rice Lucius   Mayfield.

Genesee County.

Fisk Levi   Byron.
Brown O.   Oakfield.

Greene County.

Harris Samuel (cassimeres.) Leeds
                             Catskill.
King Amos   Greenville.
Lord Albert S.   Prattsville.

Herkimer County.

Collis J. & W. J.   Frankfort.
Smith Henry W.   Salisbury.

Jefferson County.

Willis W. R.   Adams.
Stacey Joel G. (satinets)
                             Brownville.
Stone Solone (satinets) Dexter
White Amos (satinets) Henderson.

Lewis County.

Sheldon Wm.   Denmark.

Willard J. A. *Lowville.*
Dewey Cadwell *Turin.*

Livingston County.

Mather Norman W., Hemlock Lake *Livonia.*
Green Warren, Hemlock Lake
Elliott & Steele, do
Swain Edward & Co. (tweeds and cassimeres) *Nunda.*

Monroe County.

Gilbert & Whitney, (sheep grays, black cassimeres & broadcloths. Total amount manufactured yearly, 30.000 yds.—value $18,000—amount consumed 40.000 lbs. wool—looms 5, spindles 285, operatives. males 7, females 3.) West Mendon *Mendon.*
Sterling S. P. (amount 10,000 yds. value $8,000, capital $4,000—looms 4, operatives, males 4, females 2.) West Mendon
Duncan Levi, (goods, gray mixed —yards manufactured yearly 10,000, value $5,000, amount consumed 12,000 lb.—capital $3.000—looms 4, spindles 120, operatives, males 5, females 4) *Penfield.*
Franklin & Lewis, (sheep grays, yds. 15,000, value $9,360. capital $6,000, amount consumed 15,000 lbs.—looms 3, spindles 144, operatives, males 6, females 3.) *Perrinton.*
Baldwin & Gardinier, (broadcloths, value $14,000, amount consumed 30,000 lbs. capital $10,000—looms 4, spindles 210, operatives, males 7, females 6.) Black Creek *Riga.*
Cothrie William, 4 Selye Buildings, Furnace st. *Rochester.*

Montgomery County.

Pawting Henry, Cranesville *Amsterdam.*
Rundell A. G., Burtonville *Charleston.*
Booth John R., Fonda *Mohawk.*
Bloodough ——, Stone Arabia *Palatine.*
Winegar & Youker *St. Johnsville.*

Oneida County.

Couch Geo. W. Oriskany Falls *Augusta.*
Ostrander L. & D. B. do
Hicks Eli & Son, do
Ballard B. & Sons *Camden.*
Barton & Tracy, (cassimeres) Clinton *Kirkland.*
Bacon & Goodwin, Waterville *Sangersfield.*
Powers J. South Trenton *Trenton.*
Collins A. G. cor. Pine & Canal *Utica.*
Rathbun S., Rathbunsville *Verona.*
Dexter S. N. Agent of Oriskany manufacturing company; broadcloths—operatives 150. consume 120 tons of wool) Oriskany *Whitestown.*
Dexter Manufacturing Company, Dexter A. agent—broadcloths, shawls and tweeds—operatives 110, amount consumed, 86 tons. Pleasant Valley
Bliss N., Walesville

Onondaga County.

Miller L. *Elbridge.*
Fitch & Davis, Baldwinsville *Lysander.*
Mechan Wm. J. *Marcellus.*
Rhodes R. & Co. Marcellus Falls
Stewart S. & Gardiner R., Amber *Otisco.*
Taneyck H. & Co. Delphi *Pompey.*

Kellogg D. & Co. *Skaneateles.*
Pendleton Charles

Ontario County.

Winegar A., Honeoye *Richmond.*

Orange County.

Graham G., Wells' Corners *Minisink.*
Scofield, Capron & Co. *Montgomery.*
Andrews & Bradbury
Morrison & Ogden *New Windsor.*
Phillips H. New Hampton *Wallkill.*

Orleans County.

Cochran Wm. (tweeds, and cassimeres) *Carlton.*
Starr R. & D. (broadcloths, tweeds & cassimeres) Medina *Ridgeway.*

Oswego County.

Thayer B. (satinets) *Mexico.*
Brewster Elias, Prattville
Clark & Randall, Varick Canal *Oswego.*
Stearns & West, Pulaski *Richland.*
Fish Eler F., Fulton *Volney.*
Delany Richard R. (cassimeres & satinets) Fulton
Broadbent John (satinets) *Williamstown.*

Otsego County.

Rice & Son *Cherry Valley.*
Rockwell C. *Hartwick*
Dayton R. *Laurens.*
Otsego Woolen Company *Milford.*
King M. & Co.
Cook & Champion, East Worcester.

Queens County.

Pettit C. L. *Hempstead*
Hegeman Joseph J. (flannels and forest cloths) Roslyn *North Hempstead.*

Rensselaer County.

Bates J. W. (satinets) *Berlin.*
Green J. & Sons *Brunswick.*
Burnham ——, (shawls) *Hoosick.*
Hastings S. (satinets) *Nassau.*
Hemenway & Son, (satinets) East Nassau
Hovey Smith, (linen goods) *Petersburgh.*
Slocum L. B. *Pittstown.*
Arnold & Wight *Sandlake.*
Schermerhora C. (satinets)
Kerr J. & Co. do
Uline G. & W. (satinets) West Sandlake
Cipperly G. & A. do do
Albertson & Sons, (satinets) *Schodack.*
Schermerhorn Mrs. (satinets)
Glass George W. (flannels) *Stephentown.*

Rockland County.

Blauvelt J. C., Spring Valley *Orangetown.*
Iserman James, do

St. Lawrence County.

Merrill Joseph *Brasher.*
Berry R. M. *Louisville.*
Goss Alfred, (35,000 yds. annually) Columbia *Madrid.*
Armstrong J. & B. *Norfolk.*
Munson H. S. (satinets and cassimeres)
Beals N. F.
Rich B. C. & Co. (cassimeres) *Potsdam.*

Bicknell A. *Stockholm.*
Drake & Crane

Saratoga County.

Gray John *Corinth.*
Sisn Elias
M'Aran Hugh *Half Moon.*
Hillér John *Milton.*
Riggs J. W., Ballston
Chapman H. J. (satinets, 14 looms, 15 males, 10 females)
Hubbell J. (satinets and tweeds)
Bradford G. S. (knit shawls)
Benedict Daniel L. Glenn's Falls *Moreau.*
Williams Wm. *Stillwater.*

Schenectady County.

Green I. R. *Duanesburgh.*
Sawyer Thos. B. (satinets) *Glenville*

Schoharie County.

Riley A. B., Barnerville *Cobleskill.*
Braman Henry, do
Hutton & Co., Lawyerville
Reed John & Co. *Gilboa.*
Bradley Milo *Richmondville.*

Steuben County.

Wornbough W. jr. *Addison.*
Hothaway & Palmer *Orange.*
Day F. E. *Wayland.*

Suffolk County.

Perkins John *Riverhead.*
Blydenburgh R. & I. W. *Smithtown.*

Tioga County.

Brooks A. *Barton.*

Tompkins County.

Bushnell A. L. *Dryden.*
Whitehorn Clark. Burdett *Hector.*
Ithaca Falls Woolen Manufacturing Co., C. L. Grant, Agent, Office 100 Owego *Ithaca.*
Purdy Ebenezer *Newfield.*
Smith & Page. Trumansburgh *Ulysses.*

Ulster County.

Hasbrouck Joseph O., Tuthill *New Paltz.*
Vanderburgh John, Libertyville
Gue John, Accord *Rochester.*
Gale & Crawford, Galesville *Shawangunk.*

Washington County.

Keefer Nelson *Argyle.*
Reynolds Hart, (cassimeres and satinets. 12,000 yards yearly) Galesville *Easton.*
Lamb Samuel & Brothers *Fort Ann.*
Hall Ira
Beaman John D. *Hampton.*
Goodfellow & Clutterbuck, Sandy Hill *Kingsbury.*
Wyman John *White Creek.*
Merrill Nelson, North
Wait Wm. (carpets—13 looms, 120 spindles, 30 hands) William st. *Whitehall.*

Westchester County.

Sands Job & William. Mile Square *North Castle.*

Wyoming County.

Doty L. & K. (cassimeres) *Attica*
Robinson M., Cowlesville *Bennington.*
Mapes Ranson

Waldo H. N. (12,000 yds.) *China.*
York J. (10,000 yds.)
Hull M. A. & Co. (cassimeres and flannels) *Pike.*

Wool Dealers.

Albany County.

Newman Henry, 427 Broadway *Albany.*
Wilson J. 58 Dean
Knower J. 31 Hudson
Colburn P. 51 Arch

Broome County.

McKinney C. *Binghamton.*

Cayuga County.

Hotchkiss C. B. 34 Genesee *Auburn.*

Chenango County.

Berry Ansel *Norwich.*
Griffing D.
Sandford Augustus
Wells J.
Smith L D. *Otselic.*

Columbia County.

Niles M., Spencertown *Austerlitz.*
Anable G. H., Franklin Sq. *Hudson.*
Anable J. S., Public Sq.
Blanchard H. & Co. *Kinderhook.*
Everett F. W. *New Lebanon.*

Delaware County.

Blanchard & Woodruff *Delhi.*

Duchess County.

Kelly & Seaman, Stormville *Fishkill.*
Frost S. V. 302 Main *Poughkeepsie.*
Trowbridge & Wilkinson, 321 Main
Boyd D. 360 Main
Mills S. H., New Hamburgh
Merritt I. & Co., Hart's Village *Washington.*

Erie County.

Platt A. B. & Co. Com. st. *Buffalo.*
Mory & Welch, 14 Webster's Block
Piercival D. 24 Ohio (sheep's pelts)
Peters T. C. (Buffalo wool depot—see advertisement) cor. Washington and Exchange

Greene County.

Ashley Henry *Catskill.*

Kings County.

Cammeyer & Johnson, Bedford Av. near Flushing *Brooklyn.*
Smellen & Smith, N. 2d st. near 9th *Williamsburgh.*

Monroe County.

Erickson A. 2 Water *Rochester.*
Dundas Chas. W. & Co. Water st. Office 26 Front

New York County.

Ackerman & Myers, 412 West *New York.*
Coggill Henry & Co. 69 Broad
Chouteau, Merle & Co. 36 Broadway & 61 New
Dike Henry A. 70½ Pine
Grant R. 52 Ferry & 337 Stanton
Hoeg Harvey, 75 Pine
Johnson Jos. 97 Beekman
Kroger Bernard, 110 Pearl

Miles & Gilman, 25 Spruce *New York.*
Oakley A. 15 Beaver
Robertson & Polhemus, 129 Pearl & 62 Beaver
Spillett John, 284½ Pearl
Sprague G. H. & Co. 68 Broad
Strong Wm. K. 235 Pearl
Weed & Tingsman, 206 29th

Onondaga County.

Walter Geo. B. Genesee st. Syracuse *Salina.*
Tuttle C. Genesee st. Syracuse

Oswego County.

Allen S. & S. bet. Canal & River *Oswego.*

Otsego County.

Hemenway C. *Burlington.*
Chapin M.
Russell Dorr, Burlington Green
Root C. Cooperstown *Otsego.*

Rensselaer County.

Sweet L. jr. *Petersburgh.*
Kerr John & Co. 173 River *Troy.*
Sweetland H. K. 231 River
Herrington Hiram, 273 River
Gary Joseph, 491 River

Tompkins County.

Grant C. L. & W. G. 100 Owego *Ithaca.*
Tourtellott J. S. & Co. 94 Owego

Washington County.

Barker Stephen *White Creek.*
Hubbard M. D., N. White Creek

Wayne County.

Akenhead R. W. Alloway *Lyons.*
Gardiner Henry *Palmyra.*
Boyce Peter
Smith Edward

Woolen Yarn Manufacturers.

New York County.

Crook W. T. 22 Exchange place *New York.*
Haggerty Wm. C. 77 Pine
Whinfield Henry, 71 Liberty

Oneida County.

Collis A. G. cor. Pine & Canal *Utica.*

Worsted & Merino Goods—Dealers in.

Doubet A. 565 B'dway *New York.*
Heintzen Wilhelmine, 659 B'dway
Montgomery C. J. 412 Pearl
Wiskeman Margaret, 571 B'dway

Worsted & Merino Goods—Importers of.

Connah Jos. 46 Beaver *New York.*
Jager, Scheuch & Kimm, 38 John
Kelly A. W. & Brother, 36 John
Lawrence Brothers, 50 John
Lowitz, Becker & Cludius, 68 John
M'Clune Thos. & Co. 49 Broad
Mabee Thos. B. 81 Pine
Martine F. S. & S. A. 119 William
Van Blankensteyn & Heineman, 102 William

Yarns, Bats, Wicks, &c.
(See also Cotton Goods Manufacturers, also Domestics.)

Columbia County.

Rathburn F. Chatham Four Corners *Chatham.*

New York County.

Ennis H. J. 156 Pearl *New York.*
Fair I. & G. 230 Fulton
Hopkins O. 7th Av. bet. 26th & 27th
Insley H., W. 31st near 8th Av.
Laughlin & Avery, 32 Liberty
Waterbury Charles A. & Co. 106 Broadway
Wood John, Agent for the Phenix Wadding Mill, 156 Pearl
Whinfield Henry, 71 Liberty

Orange County.

Van Amburgh J. E. *Newburgh.*
Walsh Samuel

Rensselaer County.

Salisbury Amos (hemp yarn) Ida Hill *Troy.*

Rockland County.

Marriott Jos. (carpet yarn) Piermont *Orangetown.*

Zinc—Sheet, Sheathing & Perforated.

Kings County.

Akrill John, Kent Av. near Division Av. *Brooklyn.*

New York County.

Bishop Victor, 23 Malden lane *New York.*
La Vieille Montague Company of Liege, agency 69 Wall
Milliroux F. general agent, 69 Wall
M'Call & Strong, agents, 25 William
Rowe Jacob, 6 Broadway

Academies & Schools.

Albany County.

North Pearl st. Academy—Wm. Wrightson, Principal, 19 North Pearl *Albany.*
State Normal School.—George R. Perkins, Principal, salary, $1700. No. Teachers, 5, 4 at $800, and 2 at $700, also two females, at $500 per annum. State Annual Appropriation, $10,000. Cor. Lodge & Howard *Albany*

Alleghany County.

Alfred Academy.—Wm. C. Kenyon. Ira Sales, Jonathan Allan, J. Ford, Daniel Picket, Marvin Maxon, D. E. Maxon, Associate Principals. *Alfred.*
Angelica Union School.—Austin Niles, Principal, Miss Emily Smith & Miss E. Van Winkle. Assistants *Angelica.*
Friendship Academy.—D. E. Walker & J. Haten, Principals, Miss Hall & Miss Miner, Teachers in Female Department *Friendship.*
Richburgh Academy.—Lewis Bixbee, Mrs. Bixbee & Miss F Bixbee, Teachers *Wirt.*

Broome County.

Binghamton Academy.—A. Phelps, Principal *Binghamton.*

Female Boarding School.—Misses White & Griffin, Teachers *Binghamton.*

Female Seminary.—Miss Ruth P. Ingalls, Principal *Binghamton.*

Windsor Academy.—Rev. A. Craig, A.M. Principal, Mrs. M. E. Craig, Preceptress, Mrs. P. C. Brown, Teacher of Music *Windsor.*

Cattaraugus County.

Randolph Academy.—B. Chamberlain. A. G. Dow, J. E. Weeden, Addison Crowley, Merrick Nutting, T. S. Sheldon, & Saml. Brown, Trustees *Randolph.*

Cayuga County.

Auburn Academy.—Wm. Hopkins. Principal, 3 Teachers. 100 Pupils *Auburn.*

Genoa Academy.—M. M. Baldwin, Principal *Genoa.*

Chautauque County.

Jamestown Academy.—E. A. Dickinson, Principal, Harriet Hazeltine, Assistant, Jamestown *Ellicott.*

Jamestown Female Seminary.— Misses Wheeler & Case, Teachers, Jamestown *Ellicott.*

Westfield Academy.—Jesse E. Pillsbury, Principal Male Department, Miss Abby Coleman, Principal Female Department, Miss Kate Terry & Miss Harriet Sikes, Teachers Primary Department *Westfield.*

Chenango County.

New Berlin Academy.—Rev. S. Wright, Principal *New Berlin.*

Norwich Academy.—Rev. R. O. Page, Principal *Norwich.*

Oxford Academy.—John Abbott, Principal *Oxford.*

Smyrna Academy.———Haskell, Principal *Smyrna.*

Union School.—— Pettibone, Principal *Sherburne.*

Clinton County.

Champlain Academy.—D. D. Gorham. Principal *Champlain.*

Keeseville Academy.—Silas Arnold, Pres. John Mattocks, Secretary & Treasurer, Keeseville *Au Sable.*

Columbia County.

Claverack Academy.—I. Wortendyke, Principal *Claverack.*

Kinderhook Academy.—Alexander Watson, Principal. Miss E. Knox, Preceptress *Kinderhook.*

New Lebanon Springs Female Boarding School.—Rev. J. S. Stockwell, Principal, Miss A. Leonard, Miss M. Pierce, Teachers *New Lebanon.*

Spencertown Academy.—J. L. T. Philips, Principal, Miss S G. Olmstead, Preceptress, Spencertown *Austerlitz.*

Cortland County.

Cortland Academy.—Samuel B. Woolworth, Principal *Homer.*

Cortlandville Academy, Lemuel S. Pomeroy, Principal *Cortland Village.*

Delaware County.

Charlotte Academy.—S. I. Ferguson, Principal, Rev. S. D. Ferguson, Warden *Davenport.*

Delaware Academy.—Merritt G. M. Koon, A.M. Principal, Miss Rosamond A. Hull, Preceptress *Delhi.*

Delaware Literary Institute.—Rev. G. Kerr, A.M. Principal, M. S. Converse. F. Humphrey & Miss A. O. Buck, Assistants. 300 students per annum *Franklin.*

Deposit Academy.—Wm. B. Christopher, A.B. Principal, Mrs. L. P Christopher, Preceptress, Deposit *Tompkins.*

Hobart Select School.—D. Stewart, Principal, Hobart *Stamford.*

Hobart Seminary.—F. Henford, Principal, Hobart

Roxbury High School.—Rev. A. Trotter, A.M. Principal *Roxbury.*

Stamford Seminary.—J. G. Murphy, A.M. Principal *Stamford.*

Duchess County.

Academy of Duchess County.— Rev P. S. Burchard. A.B. Principal, James Denman, Teacher of Mathematics, A. Aweny, Teacher of Music *Poughkeepsie.*

Amenia Seminary.—Geo. G. Haven, Principal, Mrs. C. G. Randall. Preceptress *Amenia.*

Female Academy.—Miss Nye, Principal *Pine Plains.*

Female School.—Mrs. Arthuretta Van Vechten, Principal *Poughkeepsie.*

Fishkill Academy.—J. F. Pingry, Principal *Fishkill*

Mansion Square Female Seminary.—William F. Gibbons, M.D. Principal *Poughkeepsie.*

Nine Partners Boarding School.— Jarvis & Lydia Congden, Superintendents (Friends) *Washington.*

Poughkeepsie Collegiate School. —Charles Bartlett, A.M. Proprietor & Principal *Poughkeepsie.*

Poughkeepsie Female Academy. —J. C. Tooker, A.M. Principal *Poughkeepsie.*

Poughkeepsie Female Collegiate Institute.—C. H. P. M'Lellan, A.M. Principal *Poughkeepsie.*

Quintilian Seminary.—Rev. E. Fay, A.M. Principal *Poughkeepsie.*

Rhinebeck Academy.—William R. Harper, Principal, Miss Gibbons, Preceptress *Rhinebeck.*

Erie County.

Aurora Academy.—Calvin Littlefield. Principal, Mrs. C. Littlefield, Preceptress, Willink *Aurora.*

Black Rock Female Seminary.— Mrs. C. M. Steele. Principal, Miss Augusta F. Steele, Assistant, Miss Helen M. Lewis, Teacher of Music *Black Rock.*

Springville Academy.—J. W. Earl, Principal. Miss S. Johnson, Preceptress, J. Earl, Assist. Springville *Concord*

Franklin County.

Chateaugay Seminary.—H. S. Atwater, Principal *Chateaugay.*

Malone Academy.—George H. Wood, Principal *Malone.*

Genesee County.

Alexander Academy — N. F. Wright, Principal *Alexander.*

Batavia Union School.—J. B. Chase, Principal *Batavia.*

Cary Collegiate Institute *Le Roy.*

Le Roy Female Seminary.—Phi-

neas Staunton, Principal, Mrs. E. E. Staunton, Preceptress, Miss M. A. Wright, Teacher *Le Roy.*

Le Roy High School.—Joel Whitney and —— Brown, Teachers *Le Roy.*

Parochial School.—Warren Dedham, Principal *Le Roy*

Greene County.

Greenville Academy.—Lorenzo Hand, Principal *Greenville.*

Prattsville Academy.— W. L. Wood, Principal *Prattsville.*

Herkimer County.

Fairfield Academy.—Professor A. Briggs, Principal *Fairfield.*

Little Falls Academy.—J. H. Magoffin, A.M., Principal, Miss J. Noble, Preceptress *Little Falls.*

Jefferson County.

Belleville Seminary.—R. Ellis, A.M., Principal, Belleville *Ellisburgh.*

Carthage Academy.—Jacob A. Weed, Principal, Carthage *Wilna.*

Champion Academy.—H. F. Bush, Principal *Champion.*

Jefferson County Institute.—D. M. Lindsley, Principal, Allen C. Beach, Teacher Mathematics, George D. Mann, Teacher Music, Mrs. M. B. Lindsley, Preceptress, Miss A. M. Bingham, Teacher of Juvenile Department; average number of students, 100 *Watertown.*

Le Ray Academy.—B. B. Townsend, Principal *Le Ray.*

Rodman Academy.—B. Skinner, Principal *Rodman.*

Kings County.

Boarding and Day School.—Miss M. E. Selleck, Principal, 3 Blake's Buildings, Court st. *Brooklyn*

Brooklyn City High School.—Josiah T. Tubby, Principal, Prof. Charles L. Parmantier, Teacher of French, Wm. W. Carpenter, Teacher of Greek and Latin, 166 and 168 Fulton *Brooklyn.*

Brooklyn Grammar School.—J. Marsh. Principal, A. Carpenter, Teacher of Classics, B. Jones, Assistant Teacher, Prof. E. Lemee, Teacher of French and Drawing, 80 pupils per annum, 127 Atlantic *Brooklyn.*

Brooklyn High School.—Rev. B. W. Dwight, A.M., Principal, 6 assistants, 70 pupils, established March, 1846, 2 Livingston *Brooklyn.*

Brooklyn Union Institute.—H. A. Underhill. Principal, established 1843. 109 Pineapple *Brooklyn.*

Clinton St. Academy.—W. H. Bigelow, Principal, H. E. Ruggles, A. M., Assistant, 35 pupils, established 1843, Clinton near Fulton *Brooklyn.*

Female Seminary.—Miss Howland, Principal, established 1836, 4th cor. South 2d *Williamsburgh*

Grammar School.—Rev. Edward Bourns, M. A., Principal, established 1848, 30 Clinton *Brooklyn.*

Institution for Young Ladies.- Miss Maria L. Thompson, and Miss Pinkham, Teachers, 50 pupils per quarter, established 1843, 109 Pineapple *Brooklyn.*

Institution for Young Ladies.— Alfred Greenleaf, A. M. Principal, 20 pupils per annum, established in 1837, 106 Pierpont *Brooklyn.*

Jay st. Academy.—J. Davenport, Principal, 116 Jay *Brooklyn.*

Select Female School.—Misses Bunce, Principals, 39 4th *Williamsburgh.*

Select School for Children.—Mrs. G. S. Harvey, Principal, 224 Fulton *Brooklyn.*

Select School for Young Ladies.—Mrs. M. C. Fitch, Principal, 269 Atlantic *Brooklyn.*

Seminary for Young Ladies.—Miss E. A. Harvey, Principal, established 1844, 28 Johnson *Brooklyn.*

Willoughby St. Academy.—A. B. Davenport, Principal, Miss Susan L. Foster, Assistant, 50 Pupils *Brooklyn.*

Lewis County.

Denmark Academy, —— Rugg, Principal *Denmark.*

Livingston County.

Avon Academy.—Rev. George B. Eastman, Principal *Avon.*

Genesee Academy.—Rev. James H. Baird, Principal, George W. Davis, Prof. of Languages, Rev. J. C. Van Lien, Lecturer on Moral Philosophy, Miss E. M. Jackson, Principal of Female Department, Miss H. H. Jackson, Teacher of French and German *Genesee.*

Genesee Wesleyan Seminary.—James L. Alverson, Principal, Prof. H. Hoyt, Teacher of Languages, Mrs. Maria Hibbard, Principal of Female Department, Miss Anna Ross, Teacher of Music *Lima.*

Nunda Institute.—H. Winslow, Principal *Nunda.*

Nunda Union School.—Charles Bingham Principal, H. Morrison, Assistant, Miss Barnard, Assistant *Nunda.*

Madison County.

De Ruyter Institute.—J. R. Irish, Principal, G. Evans. Associate Principal *De Ruyter.*

Hamilton Academy.—Mon. Weed, Principal, Clinton Buel, Assistant, Elizabeth Newcomb, Preceptress, Mary A. Goddard, Assistant, Mrs. Crocker, Teacher of Music, 2 terms of 14 weeks each per annum *Hamilton.*

Oneida Conference Seminary.—Henry Bannister, Principal, Edward Bannister, Professor of Experimental Science, A. B. Canfield, Professor of Mathematics, A. B. Hyde, Professor of Languages, Mrs. E. M. Wymond, Preceptress, Mrs. S. Groff, Teacher of Music, 3 terms of 14 weeks each during the year, average attendance per term, 175, anniversary third week in July, diplomas conferred upon ladies who have taken a 3 years graduating course *Cazenovia.*

The Chittenango Polytechny.—Wm. Velasco, Principal. Chittenango *Sullivan.*

Monroe County.

Academy of the Sacred Heart.—J. A. Aughinburgh, Principal *Rochester.*

Brockport Collegiate Institute.—John G. K. Truair, A.M., Prin-

cipal, O. N. Gorton, A. B., Teacher of Languages, Miss H. M. Palmer, Preceptress, Miss M. Manning, Assoc. Preceptress, Mrs. Louisa Metcalf, Teacher of Music, 225 Scholars per annum. Brockport *Sweden.*

Rochester Collegiate Institute.—N. W. Benedict, A.M. Principal and Professor of the Latin and Greek Languages, Rhetoric and Moral Philosophy, Rev. C. Dewy, D.D., Professor of Mathematics, L. Wetherell, Teach. of the Engl'h Branches, Miss Delia Rogers, Preceptress of the Ladies' Department, 208 Scholars *Rochester.*

Rochester Female Academy, Miss Araminta D. Doolittle, Principal, Miss Elizabeth Hale and Miss Grace Gillett, Assistant Teachers, Miss Marion M'Gregor, Teacher of Music, 100 scholars per annum, 70 Fitzhugh *Rochester.*

Seward Female Seminary, Miss Lucelia Tracy, Principal, Miss Marilla Houghton, Assistant in the English & Classical Department, Miss Martha O. Warner, Assistant in the English Department, Miss Eugena C. Lane, Teacher of Penciling & Ornamental Needle Work, Miss Marion S. M'Gregor, Teacher of Vocal & Instrumental Music, Jas. H. Harris, Teacher of Drawing & Painting, Rev. Edward Meyer, Professor of Modern Languages & Literature, 238 students per annum, Alexander st. *Rochester.*

Montgomery County.

Amsterdam Academy, M. P. Cavert, Principal, M. L. Squires, Assistant, 3 terms per annum, 80 Pupils *Amsterdam.*

Canajoharie Academy, J. B. Steele, Principal *Canajoharie.*

Niagara County.

Lewiston Academy, —— Colton, Principal *Lewiston.*

Lockport Union School, F. R. Lord, Principal, 2 Assistants *Lockport.*

Wilson Collegiate Institute, Benj. Wilcox, Principal *Wilson.*

Oneida County.

Bridgewater Seminary, D. Smith, Principal *Bridgewater.*

Clinton Liberal Institute, T. J. Sawyer, Principal, 6 Teachers, 75 Pupils, Clinton *Kirkland.*

Domestic Seminary, H. H. Kellogg, Principal, 8 Teachers, 110 Pupils, Clinton *Kirkland.*

Whitestown Biblical School, J. J. Butler, Principal, 30 Pupils, Oriskany *Whitestown.*

Whitestown Seminary, Samuel Farnham, Principal, 4 Teachers, 120 Pupils, Oriskany *Whitestown.*

Onondaga County.

Jordan Academy, H. J. Jolly, Principal, Jordan *Elbridge.*

Monroe Academy, —— Wilson, Principal *Elbridge.*

Onondaga Academy, —— Clark, Principal *Onondaga.*

Ontario County.

Canandaigua Academy, Marcus Wilson, Principal, Geo. Wilson & Noah Clark, Assistants *Canandaigua.*

East Bloomfield Academy, Stephen W. Clark, Principal *East Bloomfield.*

Ontario Female Seminary, Edward G. Tyler, Principal, L. M. Clark & —— Pellser, Assistant Teachers *Canandaigua.*

Phelps Union School, Lewis Peck, Principal *Phelps.*

Orange County.

Chester Academy, P. Robinson, Principal *Chester.*

Farmers' Hall Academy, D. L. Tolle, Principal *Goshen.*

Ladies' Seminary, Miss S. A. Smyth, Principal *Newburgh.*

Monroe Academy, N. Campbell, Principal, Miss Smith, Preceptress *Monroe.*

Montgomery Academy, S. S. Harman, Principal, Miss Annie N. Tyler, Preceptress *Montgomery.*

Newburgh Female Academy, A. Barker. A. M. Principal, Mrs. J. A. C. Barker, Preceptress, H. P. Buchanan, Teacher of Music *Newburgh.*

Rose Hill Institute, Rev. B. R. Hall Principal *Newburgh.*

Seminary Hill Academy, Rev. Henry Connelly, Principal *Newburgh.*

Seward Institute.—Miss E. Parsons, Principal, J. Cummings, A.M. Teacher of Latin, Miss P. Stanley, Teacher of Music & Drawing, Florida *Warwick.*

Wallkill Academy.—P. M'Gregor, A.M., Principal, Miss Jane M'Gregor, Preceptress, South Middleton *Wallkill.*

Orleans County.

Albion Academy.—Perez Brown, Principal, Oliver Morehouse, Assistant, Albion *Barre.*

Gaines Academy.—W. Lovewell, Principal *Gaines.*

Holly Academy.—C. T. Ford, Principal, Holly *Murray.*

Millville Academy.—S. P. Barker, Principal, Millville *Shelby.*

Phipps Union Seminary.—Mrs. H. L. Achilles, Principal, Miss Harriet Stewart & Miss Mary Pratt, Assistant Teachers, Albion *Barre.*

Yates Academy.—W. B. Burnell, Principal *Yates.*

Oswego County.

Mexico Academy.—Abner Davidson, Principal, Miss M. F. Burnett, Proceptress, Wm. H. Gillespie, Assistant, Mrs. Helen F. Gillespie, Teacher of Music *Mexico.*

Otsego County.

Cooperstown Female Seminary.—Misses Walsh, Principals, Cooperstown *Otsego.*

Cooperstown High School.—S. J. Werting Principal, Cooperstown *Otsego.*

Hartwick Seminary.—Rev. Geo. Miller, Principal *Hartwick.*

Unadilla Seminary.—Franklin B. Wood, Principal *Unadilla.*

Putnam County.

Carmel Collegiate Institute *Carmel*

Queens County.

Classical Boarding School for Young Ladies.—Mrs. M. K Weeks, Principal, Charles O Weeks, Assistant *Hempstead*

Female Seminary.—Miss Margaret Adrian, Principal *Jamaica.*
Hempstead Seminary for Boys.—Alphonso Rollins, Principal *Hempstead.*
Union Hall Academy.—Henry Onderdonk, A.M. & John N. Brinkerhoff, A.M. Associate Principals *Jamaica.*

Rensselaer County.

Sandlake Academy.— — Schram, Principal, 8 Teachers, 75 Pupils. *Sandlake.*
Troy Academy.—J. D. E. Jones, Principal, cor. State & 7th. *Troy.*

St. Lawrence County.

Gouverneur Academy.— J. W. Armstrong, Principal *Gouverneur.*
Ogdensburgh Academy.— — Pettibone, Principal, Ogdensburgh *Oswegatchie.*
St. Lawrence Academy.—Wm. F. Bascom, Principal *Potsdam.*

Saratoga County.

Jonesville Academy.—Hiram A. Wilson Principal, Jonesville *Clifton Park.*
Select School for Gentlemen.—P. Durkee, Principal *Saratoga Springs.*
Select School for Ladies.—H. S. Hodgman, Principal, Miss Nancy Ashman. Preceptress *Saratoga Springs.*
Stillwater Academy.—Nathan W. Ayers, Principal *Stillwater.*

Schoharie County.

Gilboa Seminary.—Rev. Cornelius Bogardus, Principal *Gilboa.*
Jefferson Academy.—Joseph Hale, Principal *Jefferson.*
Schoharie Academy.—George W. Briggs, Principal, Charles H. Dann, Assistant, Miss Mary R. Whitney, Preceptress, Miss C. Landon, Teacher of Music *Schoharie.*

Seneca County.

Ovid Academy.—Geo. W. Franklin, Principal, Miss A. Jennings. Preceptress *Ovid.*
Seneca Falls Academy.—Orrin Root, Principal, Miss Frances Haskins, Preceptress *Seneca Falls.*

Steuben County.

Addison Academy.—A. W. Smith, Principal *Addison.*

Suffolk County.

Clinton Academy.—Thos. J. King, Principal *Easthampton.*
Riverhead Female Seminary.—Miss Mary E. Parsons, Principal *Riverhead.*
Southampton Academy.—Albert White, Principal *Southampton.*

Sullivan County.

Liberty Normal Institute.—J. F. Stoddard, Principal *Liberty.*
Sullivan County Institute.—H. R. Low, Principal, Monticello *Thompson.*

Tioga County.

Brookside Seminary.—F. F. Judd, Principal *Berkshire.*
Newark Valley Academy.—E. Irving Ford, Principal, Newark Valley *Newark.*

Tompkins County.

Ithaca Academy.—S. D. Carr, A.M. Principal, Mrs. Mary B. Carr, Principal female department *Ithaca.*

Ulster County.

Kingston Academy.—William M'Gregor, Principal, Miss Barbara M'Gregor, Preceptress *Kingston.*
Kingston Female Seminary.—Mrs. R. Nichols, Preceptress *Kingston.*
Rondout Seminary.—Alfred Higbee, Principal, Rondout *Kingston.*

Warren County.

Chester Academy.—Rev. R. C. Clapp, Principal *Chestertown.*
Glenn's Falls Academy.—William M'Lain, Principal, Glenn's Falls *Queensbury.*

Washington County.

Argyle Academy.—Joseph M'Cracken & Charles H. Taylor, Associate Principals, Miss Sarah A. Pettis. Assistant *Argyle.*
Boarding School.—Rev. S. B. Bostwick, Principal, Sandy Hill *Kingsbury.*
Union Academy.—Messrs. Livingston & Paddock, Principals *Greenwich.*
Whitehall Academy.—E. M. Maynard, Principal *Whitehall.*

Wayne County.

Lyons Union School.—N. Britton, Principal *Lyons.*
Marion Academy.—E. A. Noyes, Principal *Marion.*
Newark Female Seminary.—Miss Jerusha Babcock, Principal, Newark *Arcadia.*
Palmyra Union School.—— French, Principal *Palmyra.*
Walworth Academy.—Professor James Smith, Principal *Walworth.*

Westchester County.

Boarding and Select School.—William J. Lounsbury, Principal, Portchester *Rye.*
Boarding School for Boys.—John Osborne, Principal, Portchester
Boarding School for Boys, M. Churchill, Principal, and Teacher of Mathematics, H. F. Green, A.M. Teacher of Classics, Wm. S. Smith, Teacher of English Department, C. P. Boardman, Teacher of French, Miss E. C. Horton, Teacher of Music, Sing Sing
Boarding School for Girls and Boys.—Alexander Reynolds, Principal, Mechanicsville *Bedford.*
Female Boarding School.—James T. Eels, Principal *New Rochelle.*
Female Seminary.—Robert Bottom, Principal *Pelham.*
Franklin Academy.—J. D. Post, Principal, Sing Sing *Ossining.*
Hamilton Collegiate Institute.—Wm. S. Hall, Principal, Bertrand Harrison, Assistant *White Plains.*
Irving Institute Boarding School for Boys.—A. Newcombe, Principal *Greenburgh.*
Lilac Hedge Seminary for Young Ladies.—Mrs. R. B. Searles, Principal, Rev. E. S. Schenck, Teacher of Latin, A. Chemidlin,

Teacher of French, Miss Anne Searles, Teacher of Music, Drawing & Painting *White Plains.*
Locust Hill Boarding School for Boys. — G. W. Francis, A.M. Principal, Miss Mary Francis, Teacher of French, Drawing & Painting *Yonkers.*
Mount Pleasant Academy for Boys.—C. F. Maurice, A.M. Principal, 5 Assistants, Sing Sing *Ossining.*
North Salem Academy Boarding School—John Jenkins, Principal *North Salem.*
Oak Grove Seminary.—Mr. and Mrs. W. C. Foote, Associate Principals, Miss Francis Judd, Assistant, Mademoiselle Baris, Teacher of French *Yonkers.*
Paulding Institute—Boarding School for Boys.—Wm. G. Weston, Principal, Tarrytown *Greenburgh.*
Peekskill Academy & Boarding School.—Albert Wells, Principal, Rev. H. Wells, Associate, Francis H. Wells, Assistant Teacher, 70 Pupils, Peekskill *Cortlandt.*
Select Boarding School for Boys.—Rev. R. W. Harris, A.M. Principal, J. Stremmoll, A.M. Assistant, A. Chemidlin, Teacher of French *White Plains.*
Tarrytown Institute—Boarding School for Boys.—A. Newman, Principal, Tarrytown *Greenburgh.*
White Plains Institute.—John Swinburne, A. M. Principal & Chemidlin, Teacher of French & Music *White Plains.*

Wyoming County.

Wyoming Academy.—David Burbank, Principal *Middlebury.*

Yates County.

Dundee Academy.—Richard Taylor, Principal, Dundee *Starkey.*
Starkey Seminary.—Edmund Chadwick, Principal, Mrs. Adeline Chadwick, Preceptress *Starkey.*

Colleges.

Columbia College, foot of Park Place, near Broadway, New York.—Charles King, LL.D. President. Incorporated 1754. Instructors 8. Alumni 1866. Students 130. Vols. in Library, 17,000. Commencement the day after the 4th Wednesday in July.
Geneva College, Geneva, Ontario County.—Benjamin Hale, D.D., President. Founded 1825. Instructors 5. Alumni 131. Ministers 26. Students 50. Vols. in Library 5,400. Commencement 1st Wednesday in August.
Hamilton College. Clinton, Oneida County.—Simeon North, LL.D. President. Founded 1812. Instructors 6. Alumni 591. Ministers 216. Students 160. Vols. in Library 10,000. Commencement 4th Wednesday in July.
Madison University, Hamilton, Madison County.—Hon. Friend Humphrey, President of Corporation. Founded 1819. Instructors 9. Alumni 200. Students 150. Vols. in Library 7,500. Commencement 3d Wednesday in August.

St. Paul's College, College Point, Queens County.—Founded 1837. Instructors 11. Alumni 380. Students 29. Vols. in Libraries 3,800. Commencement last Thursday in June.

Union College, Schenectady. Schenectady County. — Eliphalet Nott, D.D., President. Founded 1795. Instructors 14. Alumni 2,631. Ministers 600. Vols. in Library 15,000. Commencement 4th Wednesday in July. Expenses of instruction, including room rent, $57. Students 280.

University of New York, New York.—Theodore Frelinghuysen, LL.D., President. Founded 1831. Instructors 11. Alumni 320. Students 151. Vols. in Library, 4,000. Commencement Wednesday before 4th July.

Law School.

State and National Law School, Ballston Spa, Saratoga County. —J. W. Fowler, Willis Hall, William Hay. William Odell, D. S. Manley, Professors. Terms commence on the 1st of Sept. Jan. and May, with two weeks vacation intervening.

Medical Schools.

Albany Medical College, Albany. —Founded 1839. Professors 8. Students 114. Graduates 58. Lectures commence 1st Tuesday in October.

College of Physicians and Surgeons, 67 Crosby st. New York. —Founded 1807. Professors 6. Students 219. Graduates 352. Lectures commence 1st Monday in Nov. continue 4 months. Total expense per term, $108.

Medical Department of the University of Buffalo. Buffalo, Erie County.—Charles B. Coventry, M.D., Professor of Physiology & Medical Jurisprudence. Chas. A. Lee, M.D., Prof. Pathology & Materia Medica. James Webster, M.D., Prof. Gen. & Special Anatomy. James P. White, M.D., Prof. Obstetrics and Diseases of Women and Children. Frank H. Hamilton, M.D., Prof. Principles and Practice of Surg. and Clin. Surg. Austin Flint, M.D., Prof. Principles and Practice of Med. and Clinical Med. Geo. Hadley, M.D., Prof. Chem. and Phar. Corydon La Ford, M.D., Demonstrator of Anatomy. Number of Students 62.

Med. inst. Geneva Col. Geneva.—Founded 1835. Prof. 8. Stud. 60. Graduates 96. Lectures commence 1st Tuesday in Oct.

University Medical College, 659 Broadway, New York.—Profs. Valentine Mott, G. S. Pattison, S. H. Dickson, G. S. Bedford, J. W. Draper, Martyn Paine, Wm. Darling, Demonstrator. Founded 1837. Students 421. Graduates 597. Lectures commence last Monday in October

Theological Schools.

Hamilton Literary and Theological Institute.—Hamilton, Madison County. (Baptist Denomination.) Founded 1820. Rev. John S. Maginnis, D.D., Prof.

Bib. Theo. Rev. Thomas J. Conant, D.D., Prof. Heb. & Bib. Criticism and Interpretation. Rev. Geo. W. Eaton, D.D., Prof. Ecclesiastical History. Vols. in Library 4,000.

Hartwick Seminary, Hartwick, Otsego Co.—(Lutheran Denomination.) Founded 1816. Professors 2. Volumes in Library 1250.

Theo. Sem. Asso. (Ref. Church,) Newburgh. — Founded 1836. Vols. in Library 3,200.

Theo. Sem. of Auburn (Presbyterian.)—Founded 1821. Profs. 4. Students in 1848-'9 80. Vols. in Library 6,000.

Theo. Inst. (Episcopal Church.)—New York. Founded 1817. Profs. 5. Students 64. Vols. in Library 16,000.

Union Theo. Sem.— University Place. New York, (Presb.) Rev. H. White, Prof. of Systematic Theology. Rev. Edward Robinson, Prof. of Bib. Lit. Rev. G. Shepard, Sacred Rhetoric. Rev. L. Halsey, Bible and Eccl. History. W. W. Turner, Instructor in Elements of Hebrew. Rev. L. B. Rockwood. Financial Agent. Edward Howe, jr. Instructor in Sacred Music. Founded 1836. Vols. in Library 18,000.

Insurance Companies.

Albany County.

Albany Insurance Co. 56 State st. Albany. Teunis Van Vechten, President, Stephen Groesbeck, Secretary. Capital $300,000, Shares 5,000, par value $60.

Mutual Ins. Co. of the City and County of Albany, 50 State st. Albany. Erastus Corning, President, Mathew Trotter, Sec'y, Capital $300,000.

Alleghany County.

Alleghany Mutual Ins. Co., Angelica. Thos. L. Smith, President, J. J. Rockafeller, Sec'y.

Clinton County.

Essex & Clinton Mutual Ins. Co., Keeseville, Ausable. C. D. Peabody, President, Richard Keese, Sec'y.

Duchess County.

Duchess Co. Mutual Fire Ins. Co. 10 Garden st., Poughkeepsie. James Emott, President, Owen T. Coffin, Sec'y and Treasurer.

Erie County.

Farmers' Mutual Ins. Co., Erie County, over the Post Office, Buffalo. Thos. C. Love. President, Orsamus H. Marshall, Vice Pres., Samuel Lake, Sec.

Mutual Ins. Co. of Buffalo, No. 11 Merchants' Ex. Buffalo. Dean Richmond, Pres., A. A. Eustaphieve, Sec.

Genesee County.

Genesee Mutual Ins. Co., Le Roy, A. P. Hascall, Pres., J. Summerfield, Sec.

Kings County

Kings Co. Mutual Ins. Co., 49 Fulton st. Brooklyn. Thos. Car-

penter, Pres., Adrian Kegeman, Vice Pres., Stephen Underhill, Sec.

Long Island Ins. Co., 41 Fulton st. Brooklyn. B. W. Delamater, Pres., E. C. Finn, Sec. Capital $200,000.

Brooklyn Fire Ins. Co., 43 Fulton st. Brooklyn. Wm. Ellsworth, Pres., Alfred G. Stevens, Sec.

Citizens' Fire Ins. Co., No. 18 Grand st. Williamsburgh. Daniel Burnett, Pres., James M. M'Lean, Sec. Capital $105,000.

Montgomery County.

The Montgomery Co. Mutual Ins. Co., Canajoharie. Henry Loucks Pres., Lester Wilcox, Sec. Chartered 1836. Policies issued 57,234.

New York County.

Ætna, 66 Wall, Chas. Town, Prest. Jacob Brouwer, Sec., Capital $200,000. shares 4000, par $50.

Ætna of Hartford, 89 Wall, Cap. $260,000, T. A. Alexander, Agt.

Albany, 60 Wall, Cap. $300,000, James Wright, Agent.

Albany Mutual, 60 Wall, Capital $300,000, James Wright, Agent

American, Providence, R. I. 46 Pine, Cap. $150,000, Asa Bigelow, jr. Agent.

American of Philadelphia, 121 Water, Capital $300,000, S. O Walker, Agent.

Augusta Banking & Insurance Co. (Geo.) 76 Wall, Cap. $375,000, Thos. G. Casey, Agent.

Broadway Ins. Co. 418 Broadway, Cap. $200,000, S. Halsted, Prest., John Wray, Sec.

Citizens. 67 Wall and 167 Bowery, Daniel Burtnett, Prest., J. M. M'Lean, Sec., Cap. $105,000, shares 7500, par $14.

City, 61 Wall, Cap. $210,000, Geo. S. Fox, Prest., D. F. Curry, Sec.

Columbus, (Ohio) 76 Wall, Cap. $140,000, J. Hoxie, Agent.

Eagle, 71 Wall, Cap. $300,000, A. G. Stout, Prest., Thomas Glover, Sec.

East River, 69 Wall, Cap. $150,000, John Brouwer, Prest., Chas. H. Binney, Sec.

Equitable, 58 Wall, Cap. $210,000, Richard J. Thorne, Prest., Joseph Strong, Sec.

Firemen's, Boston, Mass., 46 Pine, Cap. $300,000, Asa Bigelow, jr. Agent.

Firemen's, 59 Wall, Cap. $204,000, F. I. Luqueer, Prest., Niel Gray, Sec.

Franklin, Boston, 10 Merchants' Exchange, Cap. $300,000, Thos. Hale, Agent.

Franklin, Philadelphia, 6 Merchants' Exchange, Cap. $400,000, Chas. J. Martin, Agent.

General Mutual, 50 Wall, N. G. Rutgers, Prest., Alfred Ogden, Vice Prest., W. B. Bolles, Sec.

Greenwich, 400 Hudson, Capital $200,000, Timothy Whittemore, Prest., Joseph Torrey, Sec.

Hartford, Hartford, Conn., rear 68 Wall, Cap. $150,000, J. Neilson, jr. and Ezra White, Agents.

Howard, 66 Wall, Cap. $250,000, K. Havens, Prest. L. Phillips, Sec.

Insurance Co., N. A. Philadelphia, 60 Wall, Cap. $300,000, James Wright, Agent.

Insurance Co. State, (Pa.) Philadelphia, 66 Wall, Cap. $200,000, John S. Noble, Agent.

Jefferson, 56 Wall, Cap. $200,000, Moses Tucker, Prest., George I. Hope, Sec.

Kings County Mutual, Brooklyn, 50 Wall, F. J. Hosford, Agent.

Knickerbooker, 64 Wall, Capital $280,000, George Ireland, Prest., A. B. M'Donald, Sec.

Lexington, Ky., 76 Wall, Capital $300,000, Joseph Hoxie, Agent.

Manhattan, 68 Wall, Cap. $250,000, N. Richards, Prest., Thomas Bull, jr. Sec.

Merchants, Boston, Mass., 46 Pine, Cap. $600,000, Asa Bigelow, jr. Agent.

Manufacturer's, Boston, Mass., 46 Pine, Cap. $400,000, Asa Bigelow. jr. Agent.

Liverpool and London, 55 Wall. Cap. $10,000,000, Alfred Pell, Agent.

Nashville, Tenn., 72 Wall, Cap. $300,000, A. B. Holmes, Agent.

National, 52 Wall, Cap. $150,000, Thomas W. Thorne, Prest., W. C. Kellogg, Sec.

National, Boston, 10 Merchants' Exchange. Cap. $500,000, Thos. Hale, Agent.

Neptune, Boston, 15 Merchants' Exchange, Cap. $200,000, Thos. Hale, Agent.

New York Bowery, 124 Bowery, Cap. $300,000, Wm. Hibbard, Prest., George G. Taylor, Sec.

New York Protection, (Rome, N. Y.) 60 Wall, Cap. $150,000, Jas. Wright, Agent.

New York Fire and Marine, 72 Wall, Cap. $200,000, O. H. Jones, Prest, D. Underhill, Sec.

North American, 67 Wall, Capital $250,000, James W. Otis, Prest., R. W. Bleecker, Sec.

North River, 192 Greenwich, Cap. $350,000, P. R. Warner, Prest., John Hegeman, Sec.

North Western, Oswego, N. Y., Cap. $150,000, George Deming, Agent.

Norwich, (Conn.) 89 Wall, Cap. $150,000, I. A. Alexander, Agent.

Ohio Mutual, (Columbus, O.) 66 Wall, Cap. $250,000, William J. Boggs, Agent.

Protection, (Hartford, Conn.) Cap. $200,000, —— Clark, Agent.

The Grocers Fire Insurance Co. 81 Wall cor. of Pearl, Sampson Moore, Prest., J. Milton Smith. Sec., Cap. $200,000, shares 4000, par $50.

Trenton Mutual, 65 Wall, Capital $150,000, John S. Noble, Agent.

Union Mutual, 58 Wall, Capital $100,000, L. Suydam, Prest., F. Stagg, Sec.

United States, 69 Wall, Capital $250,000, J. S. Underhill, Prest., James Wilkie, Sec.

Oneida County.

New York Protection Insurance Co. Rome, J. Stryker, Prest., T. Jones, jr. Sec., Cap. $150,000, shares $000, par val. $50

Oswego County.

North Western Fire and Marine Insurance Co. Telegraph Block, 1st st. Oswego, George Fisher, Prest., Samuel Hawley, Sec., Cap. $150,000.

Otsego County.

Unadilla Mutual Insurance Co. Unadilla, Isaac Hayes, Prest., C. H. Noble, Sec. and Treas.

Queens County.

Glen Cove Insurance Co. Oyster Bay, J. G. Townsend. Prest., E. Valentine, Sec. and Treas.

Rensselaer County.

Mechanics Mutual Insurance Co., 10 2d Troy, Nathaniel Starbuck, Prest., Townsend M. Vail, Vice Prest., Lyman Garfield, Sec., W. D. Haight, Treas.

St. Lawrence County.

St. Lawrence County Mutual Insurance Co. Ogdensburg, Ira Wheeler, Prest., H. G. Foot, Sec. Incorporated 1836.

Schenectady County.

Schenectady Mutual Insurance Co. Schenectady, John Ohlin, Prest., T. R. Van Inger, Sec.- N. Swits, Treas.

Wayne County.

Wayne County Mutual Insurance Co. Arcadia, J. A. Miller, Sec.

Westchester County.

Westchester County Mutual Insurance Co. New Rochelle.

Life Insurance Companies.

New York City.

Albion Life (London), 69 Wall. Cap. $5,000,000, Joseph Fowler & Robert S. Buchanan, Agents.

American Mutual (New Haven), 40 Wall. Cap. $100,000, Benjamin Silliman, President, Wm. Wadsworth, Actuary.

British Commercial (London), 65 Wall. Cap. $3,000,000, Frederick Salmonson, Agent.

Commercial Mutual Life (Hartford), 54 Wall. Cap. $50,000, W. S. Dunham. Agent.

Eagle Life & Health, 40 Wall. Cap. $100,000, Shares 2000, Par $50, Geo. W. Savage, President, Richard H. Bull. Actuary

Farmer's Loan & Trust Company, 50 Wall. Cap. $300,000, Shares 40,000, Par $50, D. D. Williamson, President, R. K. Delafield, Secretary.

Lexington (Kentucky), 76 Wall. Cap. $300,000, J. Hoxie, Agent.

Liverpool & London, 46 Merchants' Exchange. Cap. $10,000,000, Alfred Pell, Agent.

Mutual Benefit, 11 Wall. Joseph L. Lord, Agent.

Mutual Life, 35 Wall. Morris Robinson. President, Samuel Hannay, Secretary.

Nashville, 72 Wall. Cap. $300,000, A. B. Holmes, Agent.

National Loan Fund (London), 71 Wall. Cap. $2,500,000, J. L. Starr, Agent.

New England Mutual (Boston) 27 Wall. Cap. $100,000, John Hopper, Agent.

New York Life Insurance & Trust, 52 Wall. Cap. $1,000,000, Shares 10,000, Par $100, David Thompson, President, Phillip R. Kearney, Secretary.

New York Life Insurance Company, 68 Wall. M. Franklin, President, Pliny Freeman, Act.

Ohio Life Insurance & Trust Company (Cincinnati), 45 Wall. Cap. $2,000,000, Chas. Stetson, President, Geo. S. Coe, Cashier.

State Mutual (Worcester, Mass.), 67 Wall. Cap. $100,000.

Tremont Mutual, 40 Wall. C. G. Imlay, Agent.

Union Mutual Life Insurance Company (Boston & New York), 37 Wall. Judd & Hollister, Agents.

United Kingdom Life Assurance Company (London), 54 Wall. Cap. $5,000,000, Wm. C. Meitland, Agent

Marine Insurance Companies.

New York City.

Astor Mutual, 36 William. Zebedee Cook, President, Edward Strong, Secretary.

Atlantic Mutual, 14 & 16 Merchants' Exchange. W. R. Jones, President, —— Smith, Secretary.

Augusta Insurance & Banking Company (Georgia), 76 Wall. Cap. $376,000, Thomas J. Casey, Agent.

Columbus (Ohio), 76 Wall. Cap. $140,000, Joseph Hoxie, Agent.

General Mutual, 50 Wall. N. G. Rutgers, President, W. B. Bolles, Secretary.

Insurance Company (N. A. Philadelphia), 60 Wall. Cap. $300,000, James Wright & W. W. Dibblee, Agents.

Lexington (Kentucky), 76 Wall. Cap. $300,000, J. Hoxie. Agent.

Mercantile Mutual, 63 Wall. Joseph Walker, President, Chas. Newcombe, Secretary.

Nashville (Tenn.), 72 Wall. Cap. $300,000, H. B. Holmes, Agent.

New York, 50 Wall. Cap. $500,000, B. M'Evers, President, J. H. Lyell, Secretary.

New York Fire & Marine. 72 Wall. Cap. $200,000, O. H. Jones, President, D. Underhill, Sec.

Protection (Hartford, Conn.) Cap. $200,000, —— Clark, Agent.

Sun Mutual, 2 & 4 Merchants' Exchange. A. B. Neilson, President, John Whitehead, Sec.

Union Mutual, 58 Wall. Lambert Suydam, President, Ferdinand Stagg, Sec.

Telegraphs.

Bain's Chemical Telegraph, Merchants' Line, Office 29 Wall st. New York.—From New York, via Stamford, Conn., New Haven, Norwich. Bridgeport, Middletown, Providence, R. 1., to Boston, Mass.

House's Printing Telegraph. Office 8 Wall st. New York.—From New York to Philadelphia, Baltimore, Washington, Pittsburgh, Cincinnati, and intermediate places South and West to New Orleans.

North American Telegraph Company. Office 29 Wall st. New York.—From New York to Philadelphia, Baltimore, Wilmington, and Washington, connecting with the O'Reilly Lines for the West at Philadelphia.

New York & Boston Magnetic Telegraph Association. Office 5 Hanover st. New York.—From Boston, via Worcester, Springfield, Hartford, New Haven, Bridgeport, New Rochelle, and Harlem, to New York.

Magnetic Telegraph Company. Office 5 Hanover st. New York. —From New York up North

River to near West Point; thence down the river to Newark. Princeton, Philadelphia, Wilmington, and Baltimore, to Washington. 340 miles.

New York, Albany, & Buffalo Telegraph Company. Office 16 Wall st. New York.—From New York to Buffalo, via Carmel, Poughkeepsie, Hudson, Troy, Albany, Schenectady, Little Falls, Utica, Rome. Syracuse, Auburn, Geneva, Canandaigua, and Rochester. 509 miles.

Erie & Michigan Telegraph Company.—From Buffalo to Milwaukee.

New York & Erie Telegraph Company. Office 5 Hanover st. New York.—From New York, via White Plains, Peekskill, Cold Spring. Newburgh, Goshen, Middletown, Honesdale, Carbondale, Moretown. Binghamton.Owego, Utica, Jefferson, Danville, & Pike, to Fredonia, where it intersects the Erie & Michigan Line. 441 miles.

Telegraph from Ithaca to Elmira. 32 miles.

From Ithaca, via Springport, Auburn. Cayuga Bridge, Seneca Falls, and Waterloo, to Palmyra. 67 miles.

From Troy to Montreal, via Bennington, Manchester, Rutland, Whitehall. Burlington, &c. 270 miles. Office Athenæum Building, 1st st. Troy.

From Syracuse to Oswego. 38 miles.

From Troy to Saratoga. 31 miles.

From Troy to Whitehall, via Schaghticoke. Union Village, Cambridge, Salem, Granville Corners, Middle Granville, and Poultney. 85 miles.

Buffalo & Canada Junction Company.—From Buffalo, via Lockport, Niagara Falls, to Queenstown, Canada West. 56 miles.

West Point Military Academy.

ACADEMIC STAFF.

Henry Brewerton, (Captain of Engineers.) Superintendent and Commandant

Dennis H. Mahan, A.M. Professor of Civil and Military Engineering

Henry L. Eustis, (2d Lieut. of Engineers.) Assistant Professor of Civil and Military Engineering

Edward B. Hunt. (2d Lieut. of Engineers.) Assistant Professor of Civil and Military Engineering

William H. C. Bartlett, LL.D. Professor of Natural and Experimental Philosophy

Joseph Roberts, (Captain 4th Artillery.) Assistant Professor of Natural and Experimental Philosophy

J. J. Reynolds, (1st Lieut. 3d Artillery.) Assistant Professor of Natural and Experimental Philosophy

F. J. Porter, (Bvt. Major 4th Artillery.) Assistant Professor of Natural and Experimental Philosophy

Wm. B. Franklin, (Bvt. 1st Lieut. Top. Engineers.) Assistant Professor of Natural and Experimental Philosophy

William P. Trowbridge, (Bvt. 2d Lieut. of Engineers,) on duty in Observatory

Albert E. Church, A.M. Professor of Mathematics

Israel Vodges, (Capt. 1st. Artillery.) Assistant Professor of Mathematics

Samuel Jones, (1st Lieut. 1st Artillery,) Assistant Professor of Mathematics

John H. Grelaud, (1st Lieut. 4th Artillery.) Assistant Professor of Mathematics

Asher R. Eddy, (1st Lieut. 1st Artillery,) Assistant Professor of Mathematics

J. L. Reno, (Bvt. Capt. Ordnance,) Assistant Professor of Mathematics

William G. Peck, (2d Lieut. Top. Engineers,) Assistant Professor of Mathematics

Jacob W. Bailey, A.M. Professor of Chemistry, Mineralogy and Geology

Francis N. Clarke, (1st Lieut. 4th Artillery.) Assistant Professor of Chemistry, Mineralogy and Geology

Edward C. Boynton, (Bvt. Capt. 1st Artillery.) Assistant Professor of Chemistry, Mineralogy and Geology

Rev. W. T. Sprole, Chaplain and Professor of Ethics and English Studies

George Deshon, (2d Lieut. Ordnance,) Assistant Professor of Ethics and English Studies

Dabney H. Maury, (Bvt. 1st Lieut. Mounted Riflemen,) Assistant Professor of Ethics and English Studies

John C. Symmes, (2d Lieut. Ordnance,) Assistant Professor of Ethics and English Studies

Robert W. Weir, N.A. Professor of Drawing

R. Somers Smith, (1st Lieut. 4th Artillery.) Assistant Professor of Drawing, Quarter Master Military Academy, and Assistant Commissary of Subsistence

James W. Abert, (2d Lieut. Top. Engineers.) Assistant Professor of Drawing

George W. Cullum, (Capt. of Engineers,) Instructor of Practical Engineering, and Commanding Company Engineer Soldiers

George B. M'Clellan, (Bvt. Capt. of Engineers,) Assistant Instructor of Practical Engineering

James C. Duane, (Bvt. 2d Lieut. of Engineers,) Assistant Instructor of Practical Engineerg

Rufus A. Roys. (Bvt. 2d Lieut. of Engineers,) Assistant Instructor of Practical Engineering

Bradford R. Alden, (Capt. 4th Infantry,) Instructor of Infantry Tactics and Commandant of Cadets

J. M. Jones, (1st Lieut. 7th Infantry,) Assistant Instructor of Infantry Tactics

Charles T. Baker, (2d Lieut. 6th Infantry,) Assistant Instructor of Infantry Tactics and Acting Adjutant

S. B. Buckner, (2d Lieut. 6th Infantry,) Assistant Instructor of Infantry Tactics

H. B. Clitz, (Bvt. 1st Lieut. 3d Infantry,) Assistant Instructor of Infantry Tactics

William M. Shover, (Bvt. Major 3d Artillery,) Instructor of Artillery and Cavalry

H. F. Clarke, (Bvt. Capt. 2d Artillery,) Assistant Instructor of Artillery

James M. Hawes, (Bvt. 1st Lieut. 2d Dragoons.) Assistant Instructor of Cavalry

H. R. Agnel, Professor of the French Language.

T. d'Orémieulx, (1st Lieut. 1st Infantry,) Assistant Professor of the French Language

Henry Coppée, A.M. (Bvt. Capt. 1st Artillery,) Assistant Professor of the French Language

P. de Janon, Instructor of the Sword Exercise

MILITARY STAFF.

Isaac S. K. Reeves, (1st Lieut. 1st Artillery,) Adjutant

Jno. M. Cuyler, M.D. Surgeon

Robert Southgate, M.D. Assistant Surgeon

B. S. Alexander, (2d Lieut. of Engineers,) Treasurer

Prisons in New York State.

Board of Inspectors.

Isaac N. Comstock, David D. Spencer, Alex. H. Wells.

AUBURN STATE PRISON, AUBURN, CAYUGA CO.

Warden, James E. Tyler. Agent, H. Underwood. Clerk, Wm. Andrews. Chaplain, F. G. Cooke. Physician, Blanchard Fosgate. Number of Guards, 20. Number of Convicts in Prison, Dec. 1st, 1849, 509. No. received during year ending Oct. 31st, 1849, 296. No. discharged in same time, as follows: By expiration of sentence, 118; Pardoned by Governor, 12; Pardoned by President, 2; Died, 7; Sent to Lunatic Asylum, 2. Contractors for Labor: Cabinet shop, Parsons, Hewson & Co.; Cooper's shop, Chester Fanning; Hame Shop, Hayden & Holmes; Carpet shop, Josiah Barber; Machine shop, Beardsley, Keeler & Co.; Shoe shop, E. P. Ross; Tool shop, Casey, Ketchel & Co.

CLINTON STATE PRISON, BEEKMANTOWN, CLINTON CO.

Agent & Warden, Geo. Throop. Salary. $1,500. Clerk, Thos. D. Gilson. Keepers, 6, Salary. $550 each. Guards, 20, Salary, $360 each. Surgeon, Geo. A. Miller, Salary, $600. Chaplain, A. Parmelee, Salary. $500. No. of Convicts, from 130 to 180. Employed in raising and separating ore, manufacturing, &c., one steam saw mill, one iron foundry; two steam engines, for raising. grinding and separating ore. The average quantity of ore raised and separated per day, from 20 to 30 tons.

SING SING STATE PRISON, OSSINING, WESTCHESTER CO. ESTABLISHED 1822.

Architect, Robert Lent. Warden. Edward L. Porter. Agent, Alfred R. Booth. Clerk, Abraham Gridley. Chaplain, Jacob Green. Physician, Wm. N. Belcher. Number of Keepers, 25. Number of Guards, 30. No. of male convicts remaining in prison, Dec. 1st, 1848, 611; No. received during the year ending Nov. 30th, 1849, 246; total,

857. Discharged during the same period, by expiration of sentence, 133 ; by pardon, 11 ; deaths, 22 ; transferred to Auburn prison, 14 ; escapes and other causes, 5 ; total, 185. Remaining in prison, Dec. 1st, 1849, 672.

Contractors for Labor : Saddlery and Hardware, Joseph J. Lewis. Railroad, Grant & Cobb. Carpets, Hotchkiss & Smith, Thos. Wetherby, John Humphries. Button Making, Albert Manville. Files, James Horner & Co. Hats, Charles Watson. Binding Hats, (females,) Chas. Watson. Lime, Henry A. Taylor. Shoes, Robert Miltze. Coopers, Henry A. Taylor.

Female Department.

Matron, Mrs. A.M. Dodge. Assistant Matrons, Mrs. E. Tompkins, Mrs. E. Green, Mrs. H. Clark, Miss M. M'Donald. No. of female convicts in prison, Dec. 1st, 1848. 83 ; No. received during the year ending Nov. 30th, 1849. 29 ; total, 112. No. discharged during the same period, as follows : by expiration of term of sentence, 32 ; by pardon, 2 ; total, 34. No. remaining Dec. 1st, 1849, 78.

State Government.

	Salary.
Hamilton Fish, New York, Governor, (term ends December 31, 1850)	$4,000
George W. Patterson, Westfield, Lieutenant-Governor, $6 per day	
*Christopher Morgan, Auburn, Sec. State & Sup't Com. Schools	2,500
*Washington Hunt, Lockport, Comptroller	2,500
*Alvah Hunt, Oxford, Treas.	1,500
Levi S. Chatfield, Attorney General	2,000
*Charles B. Stuart, State Engineer & Surveyor	2,400
*Samuel Stevens, Albany, Adjutant-General	1,000
†John Stewart, New York, Commissary-General	700
Lewis Benedict, Albany, Judge-Advocate General	
*Nelson J. Beach, Lowville, Canal Commissioner	1,700
‡Jacob Hinds, Hindsville, Canal Commissioner	1,700
‡Charles Cook, Havana, Canal Commissioner	1,700
*Isaac N. Comstock, Albany, Inspector of State Prisons	1,600
‡David D. Spencer, Ithaca, Inspector of State Prisons	1,600
‡Alexander H. Wells, Sing Sing, Inspector of State Prisons	1,600
‖David K. Abell, Albany, Canal Appraiser, $4 per day, & 5 cts. per mile for travel	
¶Gideon Hard, Albion, Canal Appraiser, $4 per day, & 5 cts. per mile for travel	
¶Elihu L. Phillips, Syracuse, Canal Appraiser, $4 per day, & 5 cts. per mile for travel	
Archibald Campbell, Albany, Dep. Sec. of State and Clerk of Commissioners of the Land Office	1,500

Philip Phelps, Albany, Dep. Comptroller	1,500
Judson W. Sherman, Albany, Dep. Treasurer	1,200
Francis H. Ruggles, Fredonia, Auditor of Canal Department	1,500
Alex'r. G. Johnson, Troy, Dep. Sup'dt. of Common Schools	1,000
Alfred B. Street, Albany, State Librarian	600
Elisha W. Skinner, Albany, Assist. Librarian	600
Robert H. Morris, Albany, Private Sec. of Governor	600

*Term expires Dec. 31, 1849.
†Term expires March 7, 1850.
‡Term expires Dec. 31, 1850.
§Term expires Dec. 31, 1851.
‖Term expires January 8, 1850.
¶Term expires April 4, 1850.

County Officers.

Albany County.

Clerk—Robert S. Lay   Westerlo.
Sheriff—Wm. Beardsley Albany.
Judge—William Parmelee
Surrogate—Lewis Benedict, jr.
District Attorney—Saml. H. Hammond
Justice of Sessions—James A. M'Kuwn   Guilderland.
Justice of Sessions—Peter F. Daw   Watervliet.
Treasurer—James Kidd Albany.

Alleghany County.

Clerk—James I. Rockafeller   Angelica.
Sheriff—Joseph B. Hughes Belfast.
Judge & Surrogate—W. G. Angel   Angelica.
District Att'y—Lucien P. Wetherbee
Justice of Sessions—Andrew A. Norton
Justice of Sessions—Henry Stevens
Treasurer—Smith Davis

Broome County.

Clerk—Erasmus D. Robinson   Chenango.
Sheriff—William Cook
Judge & Surrogate—Edward C. Kettle
District Attorney—Luther Badger   Colesville.
Justice of Sessions—E. J. Boyd   Chenango.
Justice of Sessions—Samuel M. Hunt   Maine.
Treasurer—Richard Mather   Chenango.

Cattaraugus County.

Clerk—James G. Johnson Burton.
Sheriff—Adison Crowley   Randolph.
Judge & Surrogate—R. Lamb   Machias.
District Attorney—Wm. P. Angel   Ellicottville.
Justice of Sessions—Cyrus G. M'Kay   Mansfield.
Justice of Sessions—Edwin O. Locke   Little Valley.
Treasurer—Chas. P. Washburn

Cayuga County.

Clerk—Ebenezer B. Cobb   Auburn.
Sheriff—Joseph P. Swift
Judge—William Fosgate
Surrogate—Chas. J. Hulbert

District Attorney—Ebenezer W. Arms   Aurora.
Justice of Sessions — Ezra W. Battaman   Venice.
Justice of Sessions—Samuel E. Day   Moravia.
Treasurer—Horace T. Cook   Auburn.

Chautauque County.

Clerk—Orson Stiles   Irving.
Sheriff—Noah D. Snow   Silver Creek.
Judge—Phillip S. Cottle Fredonia.
Surrogate—Abram Dixon   Westfield.
District Attorney—Abner Hazeltine   Jamestown.
Justice of Sessions—Lysander B. Brown   Dunkirk.
Justice of Sessions — Charles B. Greene   Ellington.
Treasurer—William Gifford   Mayville.

Chemung County.

Clerk—Albert F. Babcock   Millport.
Sheriff—William T. Reader   Horse Head.
Judge & Surrogate—John W. Wisner   Palmyra.
District Attorney—Erastus P. Hart   Havana.
Justice of Sessions—Nelson Hotchkiss   Big Flats.
Treasurer—Riggs Watrous   Palmyra.

Chenango County.

Clerk—Nelson Fellet   Norwich.
Sheriff—Levi H. Case   Smyrna.
Judge & Surrogate — Smith M. Purdy   Norwich.
District Attorney — James M. Banks   Bainbridge.
Justice of Sessions—Francis E. Dimmick   Smyrna.
Justice of Sessions—Harvey Hubbard   Norwich.
Treasurer—Thomas Milner

Clinton County.

Clerk—Charles H. Jones   Plattsburgh.
Sheriff—Harvey Bromley
Judge & Surrogate—Samuel Stetson   Au Sable.
District Attorney — Lorenzo B. Brock   Plattsburgh.
Justice of Sessions — John W. Havens
Justice of Sessions — Robert Berkley
Treasurer—Richard Cottrell

Columbia County.

Clerk—John R. Currie Hudson.
Sheriff—Abraham F. Miller   Ghent.
Judge—John T. Hogeboom
Surrogate—Charles B. Dutcher   Austerlitz
District Attorney—Robert E. Andrews   Livingston
Justice of Sessions — Cornelin Mesul   Ghen
Justice of Sessions — Wesley I. Gallup   Claverac
Treasurer—Silas W. Tobey   Hudsc

Cortland County.

Clerk—Rufus A. Reed   Cortland Villa,
Sheriff—James C. Pomeroy
Judge and Surrogate — Dan Hawks   Cortland Villa
District Attorney — Augustus Ballard

Justice of Sessions—Caleb Whiting *Virgil.*
Justice of Sessions — John H. Thomas
Treasurer—Justin M. Pierce *Homer.*

Delaware County.

Clerk—William M'Claughrey *Delhi.*
Sheriff—Daniel Rowland *Roxbury.*
Judge and Surrogate — Edwin More *Delhi.*
District Attorney—Amasa J. Tenbroeck
Justice of Sessions—Lewis Mills *Kortwright.*
Justice of Sessions — Robert S. Hughston *Sidney.*
Treasurer—James Elwood *Delhi.*

Duchess County.

Clerk—Joseph T. Adriance *Poughkeepsie.*
Sheriff—Alonzo H. Mory
Judge—John Rowley *Red Hook.*
Surrogate—John P. H. Tallman *Poughkeepsie.*
District Attorney — Thomas C. Campbell
Justice of Sessions—Norris Baxter *Fishkill.*
Justice of Sessions — Isaac Vail *Unionvale.*
Treasurer—Albert Vankleeck *Poughkeepsie.*

Erie County.

Clerk—Wells Brooks *Springville.*
Sheriff—Le Roy Farnham *Buffalo.*
Judge—Frederick P. Stevens
Surrogate—Peter M. Vosburg
District Attorney—Benjamin H. Austin
Justice of Sessions—John Treanor *Eden.*
Justice of Sessions—S. J. Roberts *Colden.*
Treasurer—Christian Metz. jr. *Buffalo.*

Essex County.

Clerk—George S. Nicholson *Elizabethtown.*
Sheriff—Aaron B. Mack *Westport.*
Judge and Surrogate — John E. M'Vine *Elizabethtown.*
District Attorney — Moses T. Clough *Ticonderoga.*
Justice of Sessions—Austin Hecock *Jay.*
Justice of Sessions—Geo. Brown *Crown Point.*
Treasurer—Safford E. Hale *Elizabethtown.*

Franklin County.

Clerk—Samuel C. F. Thorndike *Malone.*
Sheriff—Rufus R. Stevens
Judge and Surrogate—Joseph R. Flanders *Fort Covington.*
District Attorney — William A. Wheeler *Malone.*
Justice of Sessions—George W. Darling *Constable.*
Justice of Sessions—Samuel Manning *Moira.*
Treasurer—Samuel C. Wead *Malone.*

Fulton County.

Clerk—Stephen Wait *Johnstown.*
Sheriff—Daniel Potter
Judge and Surrogate—John Wells
District Attorney—William Wait *Vail's Mills.*
Justice of Sessions—Wm. Spencer
do   do   David Kennedy

Treasurer—Archibald Anderson *Johnstown.*

Genesee County.

Clerk—Merrill S. Soper *Batavia.*
Sheriff—Henry Monell *Elba.*
Judge and Surrogate—Horace U. Soper *Batavia.*
District Attorney—John H. Martindale
Justice of Sessions — James S. Stewart *Elba.*
Justice of Sessions—Thomas Riddle *Darien.*
Treasurer—B. Young *Batavia.*

Greene County.

Clerk—Jacob Van Arden *Catskill.*
Sheriff—George W. Halcott *Lexington.*
Judge and Surrogate — Lyman Freeman *Durham.*
District Attorney — Rufus W. Watson *Coxsackie.*
Just. of Sessions—Stephen Renne *Greenville.*
Justice of Sessions—Gilbert Merritt *Durham.*
Treasurer—Highland Hill *Catskill.*

Hamilton County.

Clerk—John C. Holmes *Lake Pleasant.*
Sheriff—Robert G. Ostrander
Judge and Surrogate—John Dunham *Wells.*
District Attorney—Richard Peck
Justice of Sessions—Joseph W. Fish *Lake Pleasant.*
Just. of Sessions—Luther Brown *Gillman.*
Treasurer—Isaiah Morristown *Wells.*

Herkimer County.

Clerk—Standish Barry *Herkimer.*
Sheriff—Daniel Hawn *Stark.*
Judge and Surrog.—Ezra Graves *Herkimer.*
District Attorney—Geo. B. Judd *Frankfort.*
Just. of Sessions—David Humphreville *Norway.*
Justice of Sessions—Morgan L. Churchill *Middletown.*
Treasurer—Robert Ethridge *German Flats.*

Jefferson County.

Clerk—Isaac Munson *Watertown.*
Sheriff—Rufus Herrick
Judge—Robert Lansing
Surrogate—Lysander H. Brown
Dist. Attorney—Joshua Moore, jr.
Justice of Sessions—Geo. Brown *Brownville.*
Treasurer—William Smith *Watertown.*

Kings County.

Clerk—Francis B. Stryker *Brooklyn.*
Sheriff—Andrew B. Hodges
Judge—Samuel E. Johnson
Surrogate—Andrew B. Hodges
District Attorney—Harmenus B. Duryea
Justice of Sessions — Samuel B. Stryker
Justice of Sessions — Nicholas Stillwell
Treasurer—Ebenezer W. Peck

Lewis County.

Clerk—Harrison Barnes *Turin.*
Sheriff—Aaron Parsons *Leyden.*

Judge & Surrogate—Francis Seger *Greig*
District Attorney—David M. Bennett *Martinsburgh*
Justice of Sessions—John Post *Leyden.*
Justice of Sessions—David T. Martin *Martinsburgh.*
Treasurer—Ela N. Merriam

Livingston County.

Clerk—Israel D. Root *Geneseo.*
Sheriff—Harvey Hill
Judge & Surrogate—Scott Lord
Dist. Attorney—Amos A. Hendee
Justice of Sessions—Harvey J. Wood *Lima.*
Justice of Sessions—Oliver Tousey *Dansville.*
Treasurer—Chauncey Metcalf *Geneseo.*

Madison County.

Clerk—Lorenzo D. Dana *Chittenango.*
Sheriff—Francis F. Stevens *Morrisville.*
Judge & Surrogate—James W. Nye *Hamilton.*
Dist. Attorney—Henry G. Goodwin *Chittenango.*
Justice of Sessions—Samuel S. Abbot *Hamilton.*
Justice of Sessions—Jonathan M. Foreman *Stockbridge.*
Treasurer—Clark Tillinghast *Morrisville.*

Monroe County.

Clerk—John T. Lacy *Chili.*
Sheriff—Octavius F. Chamberlain *Rochester.*
Judge—Patrick G. Buchan
Surrogate—Moses Sperry *Chili.*
Dist. Attorney—Wm. S. Bishop *Rochester.*
Justice of Sessions—Wm. B. Alexander
Justice of Sessions—Butler Bardwell
Treasurer—Lewis Selye

Montgomery County.

Clerk—John W. Vanderveer *Amsterdam.*
Sheriff—Barney Becker *Fort Plain.*
Judge & Surrogate—Samuel Belding, jr. *Amsterdam.*
Dist. Attorney—John A. Mitchell *St. Johnsville.*
Justice of Sessions—Perry Yates *Fonda.*
Justice of Sessions—Freeman P. Moulton *Root.*
Treasurer—Joseph W. Caldwell *Canajoharie.*

New York County.

Clerk—George W. Riblet *New York.*
Sheriff—Thomas Carnley
Judge of Court of Common Pleas—Lewis B. Woodruff
Surrogate—Alex. W. Bradford
Dist. Attorney—John M'Keon
Justice of Superior Court—Elijah Paine
Justices of Marine Court—James Lynch, Edward E. Coles

Niagara County.

Clerk—Geo. W. Gage *Lockport.*
Sheriff—Alvah Hill *Lewiston.*
Judge & Surrogate—Hiram Gardiner
Dist. Attorney—Sherburne B. Piper *Lewiston.*
Justice of Sessions—Sparrow S. Sage *Pekin.*

Justice of Sessions—Ira Race
Youngstown.
Treasurer—Thomas T. Flagler
Lockport.

Oneida County.

Clerk—Alexander Rea   Vienna.
Sheriff—John R. Jones   Vernon.
Judge—P. Sheldon Root   Utica.
Surrogate—Othniel S. Williams
Clinton.
Dist. Attorney—Calvert Comstock
Rome.
Justice of Sessions—Samuel Z.
Brooker   Floyd.
Justice of Sessions—Evan J. Ev-
ans   Boonville.
Treasurer—Sanford Adams Rome.

Onondaga County.

Clerk—Rufus Cossit   Onondaga.
Sheriff—Wm. C. Gardner   Tully.
Judge—James R. Lawrence
Syracuse.
Surrogate—Isaac T. Minard
Dist. Attorney—Hervey Shelden
Justice of Sessions—Levi Wells
Pompey.
Justice of Sessions—Jason C.
French   Amber.
Treasurer—Wheeler Truesdell
Fairmount.

Ontario County.

Clerk—Reuben Murray, jr.
Canandaigua.
Sheriff—Wm. H. Lamport Gorham.
Judge & Surrogate—Mark H. Sib-
ley   Canandaigua.
Dist. Attorney—Stephen V. Mal-
lory
Justice of Sessions—Ephraim W.
Cleveland   Naples.
Justice of Sessions—Charles J.
Folger   Geneva.
Treasurer—Henry K. Sanger
Canandaigua.

Orange County.

Clerk—Nathan Westcott Goshen.
Sheriff—John Van Etten, jr.
Deer Park.
Judge—David W. Bates Newburgh.
Surrogate—Benjamin F. Duryea
Goshen.
Dist. Attorney—Hugh B. Bull
Montgomery.
Justice of Sessions—F. A. Hoyt
Goshen.
Justice of Sessions—Charles S.
Pitts   Bloomingdale.
Treasurer—Ambrose S. Murray
Goshen.

Orleans County.

Clerk—Dan H. Cole   Albion.
Sheriff—Austin Day   Murray.
Judge & Surrogate—Henry R.
Curtis   Albion.
District Attorney—Sanford E.
Church
Justice of Sessions—Francis D.
Boardman   Medina.
Justice of Sessions—Arba Chubb
Gaines.
Treasurer—John H. Denio Albion.

Oswego County.

Clerk—Philander Rathburn
Oswego.
Sheriff—Norman Rowe
New Haven.
Judge & Surrogate—O. H. Whit-
ney   Mexico.
Dist. Attorney—Ransom H. Tyler
Fulton.
Justice of Sessions—Luna Thayer
Parish.

Justice of Sessions—Robert Elliot
Central Square.
Treasurer—Sam. H. Stone Marico.

Otsego County.

Clerk—Samuel North   Unadilla.
Sheriff—Jonas Flatner, jr.
Cherry Valley.
Judge—James Hyde   Richfield.
Surrogate—Hiram Kinney
Butternuts.
Dist. Attorney—Dewitt Bates
Cherry Valley.
Justice of Sessions—John W.
Brandon   Springfield.
Justice of Sessions—Aaron Petty
Westford.
Treasurer—John L. M'Namee
Cooperstown.

Putnam County.

Clerk—Reuben D. Barnum
Carmel.
Sheriff—James J. Smalley   Kent.
Judge & Surrogate—Azor B. Crane
Carmel.
Dist. Attorney—Charles Ga Nun
South East.
Justice of Sessions—Hart Weed
South East.
Justice of Sessions—Isaac B. Purdy
Phillipstown.
Treasurer—Thomas W. Taylor
Carmel.

Queens County.

Clerk—John C. Smith   Jamaica.
Sheriff—Robert S. Seabury
Hempstead.
Judge—Morris Fosdick   Jamaica.
Surrogate—Wm. J. Cogswell
Dist. Attorney—J. G. Lamberson
Justice of Sessions—Thomas Val-
entine   Flushing.
Justice of Sessions—Allen Hawx-
hurst   Oyster Bay.
Treasurer—Robert Cornell
Hempstead.

Rensselaer County.

Clerk—Ambrose H. Sheldon Troy.
Sheriff—Abraham Witbeck
Greenbush.
Judge—Charles C. Parmelee
Lansingburgh.
Surrogate—George T. Blair Troy.
District Attorney—A. Lottridge
Berlin.
Justice of Sessions—David S.M'Na-
mara   Hoosick.
Justice of Sessions—Charles J.
Wilbur   Schaghticoke.
Treasurer—Russell Sage   Troy.

Richmond County.

Clerk—Joshua Mersereau
Castleton.
Sheriff—Israel O. Dissosway
Southfield.
Judge & Surrogate—Henry B.
Metcalf   Castleton.
District Attorney—Lott C. Clark
Northfield.
Justice of Sessions—Wm. Shea
Westfield.
Justice of Sess.—Gilbert A. Cole
Treasurer—Stephen D. Stevens
Southfield.

Rockland County.

Clerk—Isaac A. Blauvelt
Clarkstown.
Sheriff—Haggerman Onderdonk
Orangetown.
Judge & Surrogate—William F.
Frazer   Clarkstown.
District Attorney — Horatio G.
Prall   Haverstraw.
Justice of Sessions—Isaac J. Blau-
velt   Orangetown.

Justice of Sessions—Alfred Has-
zard   Haverstraw.
Treasurer—John R. Coe Ramapo.

St. Lawrence County.

Clerk—George S. Winslow
Gouverneur.
Sheriff—Henry Barber   Canton.
Judge—Edwin Dodge Gouverneur.
Surrogate—Benjamin G. Baldwin
Potsdam.
Dist. Attorney—Charles G. Myers
Ogdensburgh.
Justice of Sess.—Joseph Barnes
Canton.
Justice of Sessions—C. Billings
Pierrepont.
Treasurer—J. L. Russell Canton.

Saratoga County.

Clerk—James W. Horton
Ballston Spa.
Sheriff—Theodore W. Sanders
Corinth.
Judge—Augustus Bockes
Saratoga Springs.
Surrogate—John C. Hulburt
Dist. Attorney—John Lawrence
Waterford.
Justice of Sessions—David W.
Wait   Half Moon.
Justice of Sessions—David Max-
well   Milton.
Treasurer—Arnold Harris
Ballston.

Schenectady County.

Clerk—D. P. Forest Schenectady.
Sheriff—John F. Clute
Judge & Surrogate—S. W. Jones
District Attorney—Benjamin F.
Potter
Justice of Sessions—Isaac Wemple
Princetown.
Justice of Sessions—Daniel Smith
Scotia.
Treasurer—Stephen Y. Vedder
Schenectady.

Schoharie County.

Clerk—Loring Andrews
Charlotteville.
Sheriff—Treat Durand
Summit Four Corners.
Judge & Surrogate—Demosthenes
Lawyer   Cobleskill.
District Attorney—Wm. H. Engle
Middleburgh.
Justice of Sessions—Chas. Watson
Fullonham.
Justice of Sess.—John E. Moore
Richmondville.
Treasurer—Ralph Brewster
Schoharie.

Seneca County.

Clerk—Ebenezer Ingalls
Waterloo.
Sheriff—Aaron R. Wheeler
Judge & Surrogate — James E.
Richardson
District Attorney—Dave Herron
Ovid.
Justice of Sessions—William T.
Johnson
Justice of Sessions—Wm. H. Bux-
ton   Waterloo.
Treasurer—Andrew Dunlop, jr.
Ovid.

Steuben County.

Clerk—Paul C. Cook   Bath.
Sheriff—Oliver Allen
Hornellsville.
Judge & Surrogate—D. M'Master
Bath.
Dist. Attorney—Alfred P. Ferris
Justice of Sess.—Arnold D. Reed

Justice of Sessions—Cephas S. Platt *Painted Post.*
Treasurer—J. R. Dudley. *Bath.*

Suffolk County.

Clerk—Benjamin T. Hutchinson *Middle Island.*
Sheriff—John Clark 3d *Greenport.*
Judge & Surrogate—Abraham T. Rose *Southampton.*
District Attorney—Wm. Wickham, jr. *Brookhaven.*
Justice of Sessions—Charles Phillips *Mount Sinai.*
Justice of Sessions—Aseph Young *Riverhead.*
Treasurer—Harvey W.Vail *Islip*

Sullivan County.

Clerk—Gad Wales *Monticello.*
Sheriff—James S. Wells
Judge & Surrogate — Alpheus Dimmick *Bloomingbu'gh.*
District Attorney—Archibald C. Niven *Monticello.*
Justice of Sessions—Harley R. Ludington *Fallsburgh.*
Justice of Sessions—George G. De Witt *Collakoon.*
Treasurer—James H. Foster *Monticello.*

Tioga County.

Clerk—Moses Stevens *Owego.*
Sheriff—Nathan H. Woodford *Candor.*
Judge & Surrogate—Charles P. Avery *Owego.*
District Attorney—Ezra S. Sweet
Justice of Sessions—Gamaliel H. Barstow *Nichols.*
Justice of Sessions—Samuel Baragar *Candor.*
Treasurer—Charles Platt *Owego.*

Tompkins County.

Clerk—Horace Mack *Ithaca.*
Sheriff—Chas. C. Howell *Danby.*
Judge & Surrogate—Alfred Wells *Ithaca.*
Dist. Attorney—Douglass Boardman

Justice of Sess.—Moses Crowell *Newfield.*
Justice of Sess.—Wm V. Penign *Ithaca.*
Treasurer—Wm. S. Hoyt

Ulster County.

Clerk—John D. L. Montague *Olive Bridge.*
Sheriff—Jacob J. Signer *Marbletown.*
Judge—James O. Linderman *Kingston.*
Surrogate—William Martin
Dist. Attorney—John Van Buren
Justice of Sess.—John P. Folland *Saugerties.*
Justice of Sessions—John Lyon *Shuwangunk.*
Treasurer—Thomas Clark *Kingston.*

Warren County.

Clerk—Thos. Archibald *Caldwell.*
Sheriff—Luther Brown *Bolton.*
Judge & Surrogate—Enoch H. Rosekrans
Dist. Attorney—George Richards
Justice of Sess.—Elisha Pendell *Athol.*
Justice of Sessions—Homer Davis *Horicon.*
Treasurer—Frederick A. Farlin *Warrensburgh.*

Washington County.

Clerk—Henry Shipherd *Argyle.*
Sheriff—Wm. A. Russell *Salem.*
Judge—Martin Lee *Granville.*
Surrogate—Joseph Boles *Greenwich.*
District Attorney—Henry B. Northrop *Kingsbury.*
Justice of Sessions—David A. Boles *Greenwich.*
Justice of Sessions—John Norton *Hartford.*
Treasurer—Edward Bulkley *North Granville.*

Wayne County.

Clerk—Alexander B. Williams *Lyons.*

Sheriff—Chester A. Ward *Clyde.*
Judge & Surrogate—George H. Middleton *Arcadia.*
District Attorney—Coles Bashford *Galen.*
Justice of Sessions—John J. Dickson *Rose.*
Justice of Sessions—Clark Mason *Newark.*
Treasurer—Bartlett R. Rogers *Lyons.*

Westchester County.

Clerk—Robert R. Oakley *White Plains.*
Sheriff—Benjamin D. Miller *Yorktown.*
Judge—Albert Lockwood *Ozinsing.*
Surrogate—Lewis C. Platt *White Plains.*
Dist. Attorney—Wm. W. Scrugham *Yonkers.*
Justice of Sessions—Cyrus Lawrence *Lewisboro.*
Justice of Sessions—James Weeks *New Castle.*
Treasurer—Elisha Horton *White Plains.*

Wyoming County.

Clerk—Ransom B. Crippen *Weatherfield*
Sheriff—Timothy H. Buxton *Warsaw.*
Judge & Surrogate—W. Riley Smith *Attica.*
District Attorney—James B. Doolittle *Warsaw.*
Justice of Sess.—Cyril Rawson *Eagle.*
Justice of Sess.—Henry O. Brown *Genesee Falls.*
Treasurer—Samuel S. Blanchard

Yates County.

Clerk—Alfred Reed *Penn Yan.*
Sheriff—George Wagener
Judge & Surrogate—A. Oliver
District Attorney—Daniel Morris
Justice of. Sessions—Samuel G. Gage *Benton Centre.*
Justice of Sessions—Geo. W. Barker *Italy.*
Treasurer—Wm. Whitney *Milo.*

TERMS OF THE SUPREME COURT, CIRCUIT COURT,

AND

COURTS OF OYER AND TERMINER,

OF THE

STATE OF NEW YORK.

THE COURTS.

The following are the times and places designated by the Judges of the eight Judicial Districts for the holding of Courts for 1850 and 1851 :

FIRST JUDICIAL DISTRICT.

CITY HALL, NEW YORK. }
November 19, 1849. {

Pursuant to section 22 of chap. 438 of the laws of 1849, the undersigned Judges of the Supreme Court in the First Judicial District, do hereby appoint the times of holding courts for the years 1850 and 1851, said courts to be held at the City Hall in the city of New York, as follows :

General Terms.—On the first Mondays of February, May, October and December.

Circuit Courts.—On the first Mondays of January, February, March, April, May, June, September, October, November and December.

Special Terms—On the first Monday of January, March, April, June, September and November, together with every Saturday for Special Motions.

Courts of Oyer and Terminer.—On the first Mondays of January, April, September and November.

S. JONES,
E. P. HURLBURT,
J. W. EDMONDS,
H. P. EDWARDS.

SECOND JUDICIAL DISTRICT.

Terms of the Supreme Court, Circuit Court and Court of Oyer and Terminer, appointed by the Justices of the Second Judicial District, to be held therein for the years 1850 and 1851.

COUNTY OF KINGS.

General Terms held by Judges of 2d district.
1850—1st Monday of May. City Hall, Brooklyn.
1st   do   October, do   do
Circuit Courts & Courts of Oyer & Terminer.
1850—1st Monday Feb. City Hall, Brooklyn, Morse.
1st   do   April,   do   do   do
1st   do   June,   do   do   do
1st   do   Sept.,   do   do   do
2d   do   Nov.,   do   do   do

COUNTY OF DUCHESS.
General Terms.
1850—1st Monday Jan. Court House, Just. of Dist.
1st   do   July,   do   do   do
Circuit Courts & Courts of Oyer & Terminer.
1850—2d Monday of March, Court House, Barculo.
3d   do   June,   do   do
3d   do   Sept.,   do   do
2d   do   Dec.,   do   do

COUNTY OF ORANGE.
Circuit Courts & Courts of Oyer & Terminer.
1850—1st Monday Feb., Co't House, Goshen, Brown.
1st   do   June,   do   Newburgh, do
1st   do   Sept.,   do   Goshen,   do
4th   do   Nov.,   do   Newburgh, do

COUNTY OF WESTCHESTER.
Circuit Courts & Courts of Oyer & Terminer.
1850—1st Mond'y Apr., C. H. White Plains, M'Coun.
1st   do   June, do   Bedford,   do
3d   do   Sept., do   White Plains,   do
4th   do   Nov., do   Bedford,   do

COUNTY OF PUTNAM.
Circuit Courts & Courts of Oyer & Terminer.
1850—3d Monday of April, Court House, Brown.
2d   do   Sept.,   do   do
3d   do   Nov.,   do   do

COUNTY OF SUFFOLK.
Circuit Courts & Courts of Oyer & Terminer.
1850—1st Monday March, Court House, M'Coun.
1st   do   Sept.,   do   do
2d   do   Dec.,   do   Brown.

COUNTY OF QUEENS.
Circuit Courts & Courts of Oyer & Terminer.
1850—3d Monday March, Court House, M'Coun.
3d   do   June,   do   do
1st   do   Nov.,   do   do

COUNTY OF RICHMOND.
Circuit Courts & Courts of Oyer & Terminer.
1850—3d Tuesday April, Court House, Barculo.
3d   do   Nov.,   do   do

COUNTY OF ROCKLAND.
Circuit Courts & Courts of Oyer & Terminer.
1850—4th Tuesday March, Court House, Barculo.
4th   do   Sept.,   do   Brown.

Special Terms are appointed to be held at the same times and places designated for holding Circuit Courts, and in addition thereto, *Special Terms* will be held on the *first* Monday of every month, as follows :

At the City Hall in Brooklyn, by Justice Morse.

At the Court House in Poughkeepsie, by Justice Barculo.

At the Court House in Newburgh, by Justice Brown.

The courts for the year 1851, are appointed to be held the same in all respects as above appointed for the year 1850, *except* that the courts appointed to be held by Justice M'Coun in 1850, will be held in 1851 by the other Justices, as follows :

Justice Morse will hold them in
    Suffolk—1st Monday of March.
    Queens—3d Monday of March.
    Westchester—3d Monday of September.
Justice Barculo will hold them in
    Westchester—1st Monday of June,
    Suffolk—1st Monday of September,
    Westchester—4th Monday of November.
Justice Brown will hold them in
    Westchester—1st Monday of April.
    Queens—3d Monday of June.
    Queens—1st Monday of November.

The foregoing appointment of courts is made by the undersigned Justices of the Second District, this 22d Nov., 1849.   W. C. M'COUN,
N. B. MORSE,
SEWARD BARCULO.

THIRD JUDICIAL DISTRICT.

Courts in the Third Judicial District for the years 1850 and 1851.

General Terms at Albany.—1st Monday of February, May, September and December.

Circuit Courts, Special Terms, & Courts of Oyer & Terminer.

Columbia—1st Monday of January.
Rensselaer—3d   do   do
Albany—1st   do   March.

Columbia—2d do April.
Rensselaer—3d do do
Ulster—4th do do
Sullivan—4th Tuesday of May.
Albany—1st Monday of June.
Schoharie—2d do do
Greene—3d do do
Sullivan—4th Tuesday of September.
Columbia—1st Monday of October.
Rensselaer—3d do do
Schoharie—3d do do
Ulster—4th do do
Greene—2d do November.
Albany—3d do do

Special Terms.

Rensselaer—3d Monday of June.
Ulster—3d do do
Columbia—4th do do
Albany—1st do July

Special Terms for hearing motions only, will be held at Albany on the last Tuesday of every month.

Pursuant to the requirements of section 22 of the Code of Procedure, the undersigned do hereby appoint the above mentioned times and places for holding the General and Special Terms, and Courts of Oyer and Terminer, in the Third Judicial District of this State, during the years 1850 and 1851. Dated November 28, 1849.

IRA HARRIS,
M. WATSON,
A. J. PARKER.

FOURTH JUDICIAL DISTRICT.

At a general term of the Supreme Court held at the Court House in the village of Ballston Spa, for the State of New York, on the 10th day of November, 1849: Present—

Hon. A. C. PAIGE,
" JOHN WILLARD,
" A. C. HAND. } Justices.

It is ordered that the general and special terms of the Supreme Court, Circuit Courts and Courts of Oyer and Terminer for the Fourth Judicial District, be held in the years 1850 and 1851, at the times and places following, to wit :

General Terms for 1850.

On the first Monday in January, at the Court House in Ballston Spa.
The first Monday in May, at the Court House in Schenectady.
The first Monday in July, at the Court House in Plattsburgh.
The first Monday in September, at the Court House in Canton.

The like for 1851.

On the first Monday in January, at the Court House in Sandy Hill.
The first Monday in May, at the Court House in Fonda.
The first Monday in July, at the Court House in Elizabethtown.
The first Monday in September, at the Court House in Canton.

Circuit Courts and Courts of Oyer and Terminer, at each of which a Special Term will be held as follows, to wit :

Essex—The third Monday in January and July, at the Court House in Elizabethtown.
Clinton—The first Monday in February and second Monday in July, at the Court House in Plattsburgh.
Franklin—Tuesday after the second Monday in February and Tuesday after the second Monday in June, at the Court House in Malone.
St. Lawrence—The third Mondays in February, June and October, at the Court House in Canton.
Saratoga—The first Monday in February, June and October, at the Court House in Ballston Spa.
Washington—In 1850, the third Monday in February and October, at the Court House in Salem, and third Monday in June, at the Court House in Sandy Hill.
In 1851, the third Mondays in February and October, at the Court House in Sandy Hill, and third Monday in June, at the Court House in Salem.
Warren—The third Tuesday in May, and Tuesday after the second Monday in October, at the Court House in Caldwell.
Montgomery—The third Monday in February, second Monday in June and fourth Monday in November, at the Court House in Fonda.

Fulton—The third Tuesday in May and last Tuesday in September, at the Court House in Johnstown.
Schenectady—The third Monday in April, and second Monday in November, at the Court House in Schenectady.

Special Terms.

The fourth Monday in January, at the Court House in Ballston Spa.
The first Tuesday in March, at the Court House in Elizabethtown.
The second Monday in March, at the Court House in Sandy Hill.
The first Tuesday in April, at the Court House in Johnstown.
The third Tuesday in July, at the Court House in Schenectady.
The first Tuesday in August, at the Court House in Caldwell.
The fourth Monday in August, at the Court House in Fonda.
The third Tuesday in September, at the Court House in Salem.
The first Monday in October, at the Court House in Plattsburgh.
The last Tuesday in October, at the Court House in Malone.
The first Tuesday in December, at the Court House in Fonda.
The second Tuesday in December, at the Court House in Ballston Spa.

And it is further ordered, that the Clerk of this Court, for the County of Saratoga, enter the foregoing appointments in the minutes of the Court, and that he transmit to the Secretary of State, a certified copy thereof, in pursuance of section 25 of the Code of Procedure.

A copy. JAMES W. HORTON,
Clerk of Saratoga County.

FIFTH JUDICIAL DISTRICT.

It is ordered that the times and places of holding the general and special terms of the Supreme Court, together with the Circuit Courts and Courts of Oyer and Terminer, in the Fifth Judicial District for the years 1850 and 1851, be appointed as follows :

General Terms for 1850 and 1851.

1st Monday of January, Academy, Utica.
1st do May, Court Room, Oswego.
1st do July, Court House, Watertown.
1st do Novr., Court Room, Syracuse.

Circuit Courts and Courts of Oyer and Terminer and Special Terms for 1850.

ONEIDA.
1st Monday of March, at Rome, Gridley.
1st do June, at Utica, do
1st do October, at Rome, Allen.

HERKIMER.
1st Monday of April, Hubbard.
1st do September, Gridley.
3d do December, Allen.

LEWIS.
3d Monday of May, Hubbard.
1st do December, Allen.

ONONDAGA.
4th Monday of February, Allen.
2d do June, Hubbard.
2d do October, Gridley.

OSWEGO.
1st Monday of February, Oswego, Gridley.
3d do June, do Allen.
3d do November, Pulaski, Hubbard.

JEFFERSON.
2d Monday of April, Gridley.
1st do September, Allen.
2d do December, Hubbard.

Circuit Courts, Courts of Oyer and Terminer and Special Terms for 1851.

ONEIDA.
1st Monday of March, at Utica, Gridley.
1st do June, at Rome, Allen.
1st do October, at Utica, Gridley.

HERKIMER.
1st Monday of April, Hubbard.
1st do September, Gridley.
3d do December, Allen.

27

LEWIS.

3d Monday of May,   Hubbard.
1st   do   December, Pratt.

ONONDAGA

4th Monday of February, Pratt.
2d   do   June,   do
2d   do   October, Allen.

OSWEGO.

1st Monday of February, Oswego, Allen.
2d   do   June,   do Gridley.
3d   do   November, Pulaski, Hubbard.

JEFFERSON.

2d Monday of April,   Pratt.
1st   do   September, Allen.
2d   do   December, Hubbard.

It is further ordered, that additional special terms be held at the Court Rooms in Utica, Syracuse, Oswego and Watertown, by the Justices residing at these places respectively, except when such Justices shall be engaged in holding courts, as follows: at Utica and Oswego on the 3d Monday of February, April, June, September and December, and at Syracuse and Watertown on the 3d Monday of January, May, July and October. Syracuse, November 14, 1849.

CHAS. GRAY
DANIEL PRATT,
PHILO GRIDLEY,
W. T. ALLEN.

SIXTH JUDICIAL DISTRICT.

Designation of the times and places of holding the general and special terms. Circuit Courts and Courts of Oyer and Terminer, and the Judges by whom they shall be held in and for the Sixth Judicial District, for two years commencing on the first day of January 1850.

COUNTY OF BROOME—Court House.
General Term.
1st Tuesday of October, 1850, Judges of District.
Circuit Courts and Courts of Oyer and Terminer and Special Terms.
1850—4th Monday of April,   J. Gray.
   4th   do   September, J. Mason.
   4th   do   December, J. Shankland.
1851—4th   do   April,   J. Shankland.
   4th   do   October,   J. Morehouse.
   4th   do   December, J. Shankland.
Special Terms.
1850—4th Tuesday of May,   J. Gray.
   4th   do   November,   do
1851—4th   do   May,   J. Shankland.
   4th   do   November,   do

COUNTY OF CHEMUNG—Court House.
General Term.
1st Tuesday of January 1850, by Justices of 6th District.
Circuit Courts, Courts of Oyer and Terminer and Special Terms.
1850—2d Tuesday of January,   J. Mason.
   1st Monday of April,   J. Gray.
   1st   do   September, J. Mason.
1851—4th   do   January,   J. Mason.
   1st   do   April,   J. Shankland.
   1st   do   October.   J. Morehouse.
Special Terms.
1850—1st Tuesday of February   J. Gray.
   3d   do   May,   do
   3d   do   July,   do
   3d   do   November,   do
1851—3d   do   February, J. Shankland.
   Last   do   October,   do

COUNTY OF CHENANGO—Court House.
General Term.
2d Tuesday of January 1851, Justices of the 6th District.
Circuit Courts and Courts of Oyer and Terminer and Special Terms.
1850—1st Monday of April,   J. Mason.
   1st   do   September, J. Gray.
   1st   do   December, J. Shankland.
1851—1st   do   April,   J. Mason.
   1st   do   October,   J. Shankland.
   1st   do   December, J. Morehouse.
Special Terms.
1850—1st Monday of February,   J. Mason.
   1st   do   June,   do

4th Monday September, J. Mason
1851—1st   do   February,   do
   1st   do   June,   do
   4th   do   September,   do

COUNTY OF CORTLAND—Court House.
Circuit Courts and Courts of Oyer and Terminer and Special Terms.
1850—1st Monday of March, J. Shankland.
   2d   do   June,   J. Morehouse.
   Last   do   September, J. Gray
1851—1st   do   March,   J. Shankland
   2d   do   June,   J. Morehouse
   Last   do   September, J. Mason
Special Terms.
Last Tuesday in June and November, in 1850 and 1851, J. Shankland.

COUNTY OF DELAWARE—Court House.
General Term.
1st Tuesday of July 1850, Justices of 6th District.

Circuit Courts and Courts of Oyer and Terminer and Special Terms.
1850—2d Monday of February, J. Morehouse
   Last   do   June,   J. Gray
   3d   do   October,   J. Shankland
1851—3d   do   February, J. Morehouse
   Last   do   June,   J. Mason
   3d   do   October,   J. Shankland
Special Terms 1850 and 1851.
Last Tuesday of May & September, J. Morehouse

COUNTY OF MADISON—Court House.
General Term.
1850—1st Monday of May, Justices of 6th District.
Circuit Courts and Courts of Oyer and Terminer and Special Terms.
1850—3d Monday of April,   J Mason
   3d   do   September, J. Gray
   3d   do   December, J. Mason
1851—3d   do   April,   J. Morehouse
   3d   do   October,   J. Mason
   3d   do   December, J. Mason
Special Terms 1850 and 1851.
2d Monday in February and June, and 4th Monday in October, J. Mason.

COUNTY OF OTSEGO—Court House.
General Term.
1st Tuesday in July 1851, Justices of 6th District
Circuit Courts and Courts of Oyer and Terminer and Special Terms.
1850—3d Monday of April,   J. Morehouse
   3d   do   September, J. Mason
   3d   do   December, J. Gray
1851—4th   do   April,   J. Morehouse
   4th   do   September, J. Shankland
   3d   do   December, J. Morehouse
Special Terms 1850 and 1851.
The last Tuesday in January, March, July and November, J. Morehouse.

COUNTY OF TIOGA—Court House.
General Term.
1st Tuesday of May 1851, Justices of 6th District.
Circuit Courts and Courts of Oyer and Terminer and Special Terms.
1850—2d Monday of April,   J. Gray
   2d   do   September, J. Mason
1851—2d   do   April,   J. Shankland
   2d   do   October,   J. Morehouse

Special Terms 1850 and 1851.
1st Tuesday in March and last Tuesday in September, J. Shankland.

COUNTY OF TOMPKINS—Court House.
General Term.
1st Tuesday of September 1851.
Circuit Courts and Courts of Oyer and Terminer and Special Terms.
1850—3d Monday of April,   J. Gray
   3d   do   September, J. Mason
   3d   do   December, J. Shankland
1851—3d   do   April,   do
   3d   do   October,   J. Morehouse
   3d   do   December, J. Mason
Special Terms 1850 and 1851.
1st Tuesday of June and 2d Tuesday of November, J. Shankland.

SEVENTH JUDICIAL DISTRICT.

Terms of the Supreme Court, Circuit Courts and Courts of Oyer and Terminer and Special Terms, in the 7th District, for the years 1850 and 1851.

General Terms.

1st Tuesday of March, City Hall, Rochester.
1st do June, do do
1st do September, do do
1st do December, do do

Circuit Courts, Courts of Oyer and Terminer and Special Terms.

MONROE.

	1850.	1851.
2d Tuesday of Feb. Rochester,	Selden.	Selden.
1st do May, do	Johnson.	Maynard.
4th Wedn'day, Nov. do	Wells.	Wells.

STEUBEN.

1st Tuesday of Feb. Bath,	Johnson.	Johnson.
3d do May, do	Wells.	Wells.
1st Wednesday, Nov. do	Johnson.	Johnson.

CAYUGA.

1st Tuesday, Feb. Auburn,	Wells.	Maynard.
1st do May, do	Selden.	Selden.
3d do Nov. do	Johnson.	Johnson.

ONTARIO.

2d Tuesday, Feb. Canandaigua,	Wells.	Wells.
3d do May, do	Selden.	Selden.
3d do Nov. do	Selden.	Maynard.

LIVINGSTON.

2d Tuesday, Jan. Geneseo,	Selden.	Selden.
3d do May, do	Johnson.	Johnson.
1st do Sep. do		Maynard.

YATES.

3d Tuesday, April, Penn Yan,	Walls.	Maynard.
3d do Oct. do	Wells.	Wells.

SENECA.

3d Tuesday, April, Waterloo,	Johnson.	Maynard.
3d do Oct. do	Wells.	Wells.

WAYNE.

3d Tuesday, April, Lyons,	Johnson.	Johnson.
3d do Oct. do	Selden.	Selden.

Additional Special Terms.

MONROE.

	1850.	1851.
1st Tuesday, Jan. Rochester,	Selden.	Selden.
1st do April, do	Selden.	Selden.
1st do Oct. do	Wells.	Maynard.

STEUBEN.

3d Tuesday, Jan. Bath,	Johnson.	Johnson.

CAYUGA.

1st Tuesday, April, Auburn,	Johnson.	Maynard.

YATES.

1st Tuesday, Jan. Penn Yan,	Wells.	Wells.

EIGHTH JUDICIAL DISTRICT.

The following schedule of course to be held in the Eighth Judicial District of the State of New York, for the years 1850 and 1851, is hereby adopted, and the courts are ordered and appointed to be held accordingly at the court houses in the respective counties named in said schedule, to wit:

General Terms of the Supreme Court.

By Justices of the 8th District

1850—In Wyoming county, 2d Monday in Feb.
Erie do 4th do April.
Orleans do 1st do Sep.
Erie do 3d do Nov.

1851—In Cattaraugus county, 2d Monday in Feb.
Erie do 4th do April.
Genesee do 3d do Sept.
Erie do 3d do Nov.

Special Terms.

IN THE COUNTY OF ERIE.

1850—On the 1st Monday in Jan. by Jus. Hoyt.
2d do April, do Sill.
4th do Aug. do Marvin.
1st do Oct. do Marvin.
1st do Dec. do Sill.

1851—On the 1st Monday in Jan. by Jus. Sill.
1st do April, do Hoyt.
4th do Aug. do Marvin.
2d do Oct. do Sill.
1st do Dec. do Marvin.

For the purpose of hearing non enumerated motions only, special terms will also be held at the same time with the January, June and September circuits in Erie county, by the Justices who shall hold said circuits.

Circuit Courts and Courts of Oyer and Terminer will be held

IN THE COUNTY OF ERIE.

1850—On the 3d Monday in Jan. by Jus. Sill.
1st do April, do Hoyt.
3d do June, do Mullett.
4th do Sept. do Sill.
1st do Dec. do Marvin.

1851—On the 3d Monday in Jan. by Jus. Hoyt.
1st do April, do Sill.
3d do June, do Marvin.
4th do Sept. do Hoyt.
1st do Dec. do Sill.

Circuit Courts, Courts of Oyer and Terminer and special terms of the Supreme Court will be held

IN THE COUNTY OF ALLEGANY.

1850—On the 3d Monday in April, by Jus. Marvin.
4th do Aug. do Hoyt.
4th do Dec. do Hoyt.

1850—On the 3d Monday in April, by Jus. Marvin.
4th do Aug. do Sill.
4th do Dec. do Hoyt.

IN THE COUNTY OF CATTARAUGUS.

1850—On the 3d Monday in Jan. by Jus. Hoyt.
1st do June, do Sill.
4th do Sept. do Mullett.

1851—On the 3d Monday in Jan. by Jus. Marvin.
4th do May, do Sill.
2d do Oct. do Hoyt.

IN THE COUNTY OF CHAUTAUQUE.

1850—On the 1st Monday in Feb. by Jus. Mullett.
3d do May, do Sill.
3d do Sept. do Marvin.

1851—On the 4th Monday in Jan. by Jus. Marvin.
3d do May, do Hoyt.
4th do Sept. do Sill.

IN THE COUNTY OF GENESEE.

1850—On the 1st Monday in March, by Jus. Mullett.
4th do June, do Marvin.
4th do Oct. do Mullett.

1851—On the 3d Monday in March, by Jus. Hoyt.
4th do June, do Sill.
1st do Oct. do Marvin.

IN THE COUNTY OF NIAGARA.

1850—On the 4th Monday in Feb. by Jus. Hoyt.
2d do June, do Marvin.
2d do Oct. do Hoyt.

1851—On the 4th Monday in Feb. by Jus. Sill.
1st do June, do Marvin.
4th do Oct. do Hoyt.

IN THE COUNTY OF ORLEANS.

1850—On the 4th Monday in Jan. by Jus. Hoyt.
3d do May, do Mullett.
4th do Sept. do Hoyt.

1851—On the 4th Monday in Jan. by Jus. Sill.
1st do June, do Hoyt.
4th do Sept. do Marvin.

IN THE COUNTY OF WYOMING.

1850—On the 4th Monday in Feb. by Jus. Marvin.
3d do June, do Sill.
3d do Oct. do Mullett.

1851—On the 4th Monday in Feb. by Jus. Hoyt.
3d do June, do Sill.
3d do Oct. do Marvin.

Buffalo, Nov. 20th, 1849.

JAMES MULLETT,
SETH E. SILL,
R. P. MARVIN.

STATE OF NEW YORK, } I have compared the preceding with the original appointments made for terms of courts, in the several judicial districts of this State for the years 1850 and 1851, on file in this office, and do certify that the same is a correct transcript therefrom and of the whole of said originals.

Given under my hand, at Albany, the 4th day of December, 1849.

CHRISTOPHER MORGAN.
Secretary of State.

UNITED STATES GOVERNMENT.

PRESIDENT,
ZACHARY TAYLOR, Louisiana.
Salary, $25,000.

VICE-PRESIDENT,
MILLARD FILLMORE, N. Y.
Salary, $5,000.

NATIONAL CABINET.
Secretary of State.
JOHN M. CLAYTON, Del. Sal. $6,000
Secretary of Treasury.
WM. M. MEREDITH, Penn. 6,000
Secretary of Interior.
THOMAS EWING, Ohio 6,000
Secretary of War.
GEORGE W. CRAWFORD, Ga. 6,000
Secretary of Navy.
WILLIAM B. PRESTON, Va. 6,000
Postmaster General.
JACOB COLLAMER, Vermont 6,000
Attorney General.
REVERDY JOHNSON, Md. 4,000

JUDICIARY OF THE UNITED STATES.
Supreme Court.
Chief Justice.
ROGER B. TANEY, Baltimore, Md.; appointed in 1836. Sal. $5,000.

Associate Justices.
John M'Lean, Cincinnati, Ohio; appointed in 1829. Salary, $4,500.
J. M. Wayne, Savannah, Ga.; appointed in 1835. 4,500
Peter V. Daniel, Richmond, Va.; appointed in 1841. 4,500
John M'Kinley, Florence, Ala. appointed in 1837. 4,500
John Catron, Nashville, Tenn. appointed in 1837. 4,500
Samuel Nelson, Cooperstown, N. Y.; appointed in 1845. 4,500
Levi Woodbury, Portsmouth. N. H.; appointed in 1845. 4,500
Robert C. Grier, Pittsburgh, Pa.; appointed in 1846. 4,500
Attorney General, Reverdy Johnson; appointed in 1849 4,000

The Supreme Court is held in the city of Washington annually, on the first Monday in December.

MEMBERS OF THE THIRTY-FIRST CONGRESS.
Assembled Monday, Dec. 3, 1849.

The Senate.
MILLARD FILLMORE, President.

Alabama.

	TERM EXPIRES.
Jeremiah Clemens,	1853
William Rufus King	1855

Arkansas.

William K. Sebastian	1853
Solon Borland	1855

Connecticut.

Roger S. Baldwin*	1851
Truman Smith*	1855

Delaware.

	TERM EXPIRES.
John Wales*	1851
Presley Spruance*	1853

Florida.

David Levy Yulee	1851
Jackson Morton*	1855

Georgia.

Jno. Macpherson Berrien*	1853
William C. Dawson*	1855

Indiana.

Jesse D. Bright	1851
James Whitcomb	1855

Illinois.

Stephen A. Douglass	1859
James Shields	1855

Iowa.

Geo. Washington Jones	1853
Augustus Caesar Dodge	1855

Kentucky.

Joseph R. Underwood*	1853
Henry Clay*	1855

Louisiana.

Solomon U. Downs	1853
Pierre Soulé	1855

Maine.

Hannibal Hamlin	1851
James W. Bradbury	1853

Massachusetts.

Daniel Webster*	1851
John Davis*	1853

Maryland.

Thomas G. Pratt*	1851
James A. Pearce*	1855

Mississippi.

Jefferson Davis	1851
Henry Stuart Foote	1853

Michigan.

Lewis Cass	1851
Alpheus Felch	1853

Missouri.

Thomas Hart Benton	1851
David R. Atchison	1855

New Hampshire.

John Parker Hale	1853
Moses Norris, jr.	1855

New York.

Daniel S. Dickinson	1851
William Henry Seward*	1855

New Jersey.

William L. Dayton*	1851
Jacob W. Miller*	1853

North Carolina.

Willie P. Mangum*	1853
George E. Badger*	1855

Ohio.

Thomas Corwin*	1851
SALMON P. CHASE.	1855

Pennsylvania.

Daniel Sturgeon	1851
James Cooper*	1855

Rhode Island.

	TERM EXPIRES.
Albert C. Greene*	1851
John H. Clarke*	1853

South Carolina.

John Caldwell Calhoun	1853
Andrew P. Butler	1855

Tennessee.

Hopkins L. Turney	1851
John Bell*	1853

Texas.

Thomas J. Rusk	1851
Samuel Houston	1853

Vermont.

Samuel S. Phelps*	1851
William Upham*	1855

Virginia.

James M. Mason	1851
Robert M. T. Hunter	1853

Wisconsin.

Henry Dodge	1851
Isaac P. Walker	1855

Whigs . . .	25
Democrats . . .	33
Free Soilers . . .	2
Total . .	60

House of Representatives.
232 Members.

HOWELL COBB, Ga., Speaker.

Alabama.
1 William J. Alston*
2 Henry W. Hilliard*
3 Samson W. Harris
4 Samuel W. Inge
5 David Hubbard
6 W'mson R. W. Cobb
7 Frank W. Bowdon

Arkansas.
1 Robert W. Johnson

California.

Connecticut.
1 Loren P. Waldo
2 WALTER BOOTH
3 Chaun. F. Cleveland
4 Thomas B. Butler*

Delaware.
1 John W. Houston*

Florida.
1 Edward C. Cabell*

Georgia.
1 —— Jackson
2 Marshall J. Welborn
3 Allen F. Owen*
4 Hugh A. Haralson
5 Thomas C. Hackett
6 Howell Cobb
7 Alex'r. H. Stevens*
8 Robert Toombs*

Illinois.
1 William H. Bissell
2 Jno. A. M'Clernand
3 Timothy R. Young
4 John Wentworth
5 Wm. A. Richardson
6 Edward D. Baker*
7 Thomas L. Harris

Indiana.

1 Nathaniel Albertson
2 Cyrus L. Dunham
3 John L. Robinson
4 GEORGE W. JULIAN
5 William J. Brown
6 Willis A. Gorman
7 Edw. W. M'Geaghey*
8 Joseph E. M'Donald
9 Graham N. Fitch
10 Andrew J. Harlan

Iowa.

1 Wm. Thompson
2 Shepherd Leffler

Kentucky.

1 Linn Boyd
2 James L. Johnson*
3 Finis E. McLean*
4 George A. Caldwell
5 John B. Thompson*
6 Daniel Breck*
7 Humphrey Marshall*
8 Charles S. Morehead*
9 John C. Mason
10 Richard H. Stanton

Louisiana.

1 Emile La Sere
2 Charles M. Conrad*
3 John M. Harmanson
4 Isaac E. Morse

Maine.

1 Elbridge Gerry
2 Nathan'l S. Littlefield
3 John Otis*
4 Rufus K. Goodenow*
5 Cullen Sawtelle
6 Charles Stetson
7 Thomas J. D. Fuller

Maryland.

1 Richard J. Bowie*
2 William T. Hamilton
3 Edward Hammond
4 Robert M. M'Lane
5 Alexander Evans*
6 John B. Kerr*

Massachusetts.

1 Robert C. Winthrop*
2 Daniel P. King*
3 James H. Duncan*
4 Vacant
5 CHARLES ALLEN
6 George Ashmun*
7 Julius Rockwell*
8 Horace Mann*
9 Orin Fowler*
10 Joseph Grinnell*

Michigan.

1 Alexander W. Buel
2 Wm. Sprague*
3 Kinsley S. Bingham

Mississippi.

1 Jacob Thompson
2 Wm. S. Featherston
3 William McWillie
4 Albert G. Brown

Missouri.

1 James B. Bowlin
2 William V. N. Bay
3 James S. Green
4 Willard P. Hall
5 John S. Phelps

New Hampshire.

1 AMOS TUCK
2 Charles H. Peaslee
3 James Wilson*
4 Harry Hibbard

New Jersey.

1 Andrew K. Hay*
2 William A. Newell*
3 Isaac Wildrick
4 John Van Dyke*
5 James G. King*

New York.

1 John A. King*
2 David A. Bokee*
3 J. Phillips Phœnix*
4 Walter Underhill*
5 George Briggs*
6 James Brooks*
7 William Nelson*
8 Ransom Halloway*
9 Thomas McKissock*
10 Herman D. Gould*
11 Peter H. Sylvester*
12 Gideon O. Reynolds*
13 John L. Schoolcraft*
14 George R. Andrews*
15 John R. Thurman*
16 Hugh White*
17 Henry P. Alexander*
18 PRESTON KING
19 Charles E. Clarke*
20 Orsamus B. Matteson*
21 Hiram Walden
22 Henry Bennett*
23 William Duer*
24 Daniel Gott*
25 Harmon S. Conger*
26 William T. Jackson*
27 William A. Sackett*
28 A. M. Schermerhorn*
29 Robert L. Rose*
30 David Rumsey*
31 Elijah Risley*
32 Elbridge G. Spalding*
33 Harvey Putnam*
34 Lorenzo Burrows*

North Carolina.

1 Thos. L. Clingman*
2 Jos. P. Caldwell*
3 Edmund Deberry*
4 Augustus H. Shepperd*
5 Abraham W. Venable
6 Wm. S. Ashe
7 John R. J. Daniel
8 Edward Stanly*
9 David Outlaw*

Ohio.

1 David T. Disney
2 L. D. CAMPBELL*
3 Robert C. Schenck*
4 Moses B. Corwin*
5 Emery D. Potter
6 Amos E. Wood
7 Jonathan D. Morris
8 John L. Taylor*
9 Edson B. Olds
10 Chas. Sweetzer
11 John K. Miller
12 Samuel F. Vinton*
13 Wm. A. Whittlesey
14 Nathan Evans*
15 W. F. HUNTER
16 Moses Hoagland
17 Jos Cable
18 David K. Carter
19 JOHN CROWELL
20 JOSHUA R. GIDDINGS
21 Jos. M. ROOT

Pennsylvania.

1 Lewis C. Levin* (N.)
2 Jos. R. Chandler*
3 Henry D. Moore*
4 John Robbins jr.
5 John Freedley*
6 Thos. Ross
7 Jesse C. Dickey*
8 Thaddeus Stevens*
9 Wm. Strong
10 Milo M. Dimmick
11 Chester Butler*
12 DAVID WILMOT

13 Jos. Casey*
14 Chas. W. Pitman*
15 Henry Nes*
16 Jas. X. M'Lanahan
17 Samuel Calvin*
18 Andrew Jackson Ogle*
19 Job Mann
20 Robert R. Reed*
21 Moses Hampton*
22 John W. Howe
23 Jas. Thompson
24 Alfred Gilmore

Rhode Island.

1 Geo. G. King*
2 Nathan F. Dixon*

South Carolina.

1 Daniel Wallace
2 Jas. L. Orr
3 Jos. A. Woodward
4 John M'Queen
5 Armistead Burt
6 Isaac E. Holmes
7 Wm. F. Colcock

Tennessee.

1 Andrew Johnson
2 Albert G. Watkins*
3 Josiah M. Anderson*
4 John H. Savage
5 Geo. W. Jones
6 Jas. H. Thomas
7 Meredith F. Gentry*
8 Andrew Ewing
9 Isham G. Harris
10 Fred. P. Stanton
11 Christopher H. Williams*

Texas.

1 David S. Kaufman
2 Volney E. Howard

Vermont.

1 Wm. Henry*
2 Wm. Hebard*
3 Jas. Meacham*
4 Lucius B. Peck

Virginia.

1 John S. Milson
2 Richard K. Meade
3 Thos. H. Averett*
4 Thos. S. Bocock
5 Paulus Powell
6 Jas. A. Seddon
7 Thos. H. Bayly
8 Alex. R. Holliday
9 Jeremiah Morton*
10 Richard Parker
11 Jas. M'Dowell
12 Henry A. Edmundson
13 Fayette M'Mullin
14 Jas. M. H. Beale
15 Thos. S. Haymond*

Wisconsin.

1 Chas. Durkee (F. S.)
2 Orsamus Cole*
3 Jas. D. Doty

Delegates.

Oregon.—S. R. Thurston

New Mexico.—Hugh Smith

Minnesota.—H. H. Sibley

Deseret.—A. W. Babbitt

[Whigs marked with * ; Democrats, without mark; Freesoilers (small caps) ; Native, (N.) The figures prefixed to the names indicate the Congressional Districts. Whigs 111. Democrats 116. Vacancy 1. Not classed 3—Messrs. Allen, Giddings and Root.]

COTTON MANUFACTURING ESTABLISHMENTS, NEW YORK.

NAME.	LOCATION.	PRESIDENT.	AGENTS.	CAP.	SH.	PAR VAL.	KIND OF GOODS.	YEARLY AMOUNT.	AMOUNT CONS'D.	Spindles.	Looms.	Males.	Females.
Albany County.													
Harmony Manufacturing Co.	Cohoes	Wm. C. Haggerty	Wm. Parsons	250,000	500	500	Print Goods	1,675,000 yds	800 bales	8,000	925	65	100
Ogden Mills	Cohoes		C. A. Olmstead	400,000	4,000	100	Sheetings and Shirting	3,500,000 yds	800 tons	11,900	490	190	280
Cayuga County.													
Nisbet R & Co	Auburn						Heavy Sheetings	624,000 yds	50 tons	9,700	72	20	40
Columbia County.													
Carpenter J	Valatie						Print Goods		11¼ tons	2,000		24	43
Hanna & Carpenter	Valatie		Criday L. Moes				Satinet Warp and Wicking		850 bales	3,306	72	30	30
Kinderhook Steam Cotton Mills	Kinderhook		Wm. P. Rathbun				Print Goods	700,000 yds				30	30
Starr Cotton Mill	Valatie	A. A. Van Allerk Co					Print Goods	3,016,000 yds	168 tons	12,000	300		
Stuyvesant Cotton Mill	Stuyvesant						Print Goods						
Wild J	Stockport						Print Goods						
Wild N	Valatie						Print Goods						
Dutchess County.													
Bloomvale Cotton Mill	Washington Hol.	Merritt & Frost		90,000			Cotton Yarn	75 tons		1,700		30	30
Burnsville Mill	Fishkill Landing	Brown & Crosby					Cotton Yarn	62¼ tons		2,000		15	30
Clinton Mill Manufacturing Co.	Wappingers falls	James Ingraham	P. McKinlay				Print Goods	2,700,000 yds	300 tons	10,000	250	100	176
Franklin Manufacturing Co.	Wappingers falls	James Ingraham	P. McKinlay				Print Goods	2,800,000 yds	320 tons	10,000	250	100	175
Hartsville Cotton Mill	Washington	Merritt & Haverland					Satinet Warp	1,300,000 yds			75	30	35
Manchester Co	Poughkeepsie	James Ingraham					Print Goods			2,900			
Mettawan Manuf. Co	Matteawan	S. S. Howland	Wm. B. Leonard	350,000			Cotton Goods						
Pleasant Valley Col. Factory	Pleasant Valley	J. Palmer & Co					Print Goods	500,000 yds	33¼ tons	3,000	75	34	61
Rochdale Cotton Manuf. Co.	Poughkeepsie	I. Taylor & Forbes					Print Goods	540,000 yds		1,650	69	60	80
Rocky Glen Co	Glenham	Russell Dart	John Vickey				Print Goods	1,500,000 yds		7,000	180	60	100
Wiccopee Co	Fishkill Landing	James Freeland	Samuel B. Leach	66,000	660		10944 Brown Sheetings	675,000 yds	227¼ tons	2,316	66	26	40
Erie County.								(900,000 yds, cl.					
Buffalo Steam Cotton Mill	Buffalo	Heywood, Joy & Webster		100,000		100	Heavy Sheetings and Batting	32 tons batt.	200 tons	3,000	75	25	75
Astoryew Mill	Little Falls		W. Herkimer	100,000	1,000		Print Goods	400,000 yds		3,254	98	31	85
New Hope Manuf Co	Van Hornsville		E. Jessman	90,000			Sheetings and 7-8 Goods	430,000 yds	55 tons	2,000	80	16	80
Jefferson County.													
Anderson & Knox	Watertown		A. W. Anderson				Col. Yarn, wicks, warp, twine & bat	10,000 yds, wick'g, 50,000 bat.		2,000		wrp 35	35
Oswego Cotton Mills	Brownville		F. W. Andrews				Coarse Sheetings	400,000 yds	141¼ tons	3,000	77	8	35
Watertown Cotton Co	Watertown		H. Holcomb				Cotton Goods	400,000 yds		1,400	40		40
Madison County.													
Chamberlain & Hamblin	Pratts Hollow						Cotton Goods						
Pierce, Cobb & Co	Eaton						Heavy Sheetings	400,000 yds	150 tons	2,000		30	35
Monroe County.													
Genesee Cotton Mills	Rochester	A. S. Cody & Co		90,000			Heavy Sheetings	600,000 yds	600 bales	4,000	78	30	90
Jones' Mill	Rochester			150,000			Heavy Sheeting	1,300,000 yds	1,000 bales	8,000	167	60	150

NAME.	LOCATION.	PRESIDENT.	AGENT.	CAP.	SH.	VAL. F.M.	KIND OF GOODS	YEARLY AMOUNT	AMOUNT CONSD.	Spls.	Loom.	Male	Fem.
Oneida County.													
America Mills	Paris		J. M. Kimball				Sheetings	370,000 yds	250 bales	2,000	30	37	34
Clark's Mill	Kirkland	E. Huntington	J. C. Wells		1,000		Sheetings			2,000	40	22	32
Clinton Cotton Mill	Clinton			40,000	1,000	4	Sheetings and Sadnet Warp	425,000 yds	460 bales			56	44
Eagle Mills	New Hartford						Sheetings	1,130,000 yds	190 tons			34	60
Franklin Manufacturing Co.	Sauquoit	N. Thompson	C. Hurlburt	100,00	1,000	10c	Sheetings and Shirtings	850,000 yds	500 bales	3,300	100	36	96
Manchester Manufacturing Co.	Manchester			60,080	600	100	Heavy Brown Sheetings	900,000 yds	960 bales	4,205	100	35	65
New Hartford Cotton Mills	New Hartford		B. S. Walcott	400,000			Coarse Sheetings	930,000 yds	640 bales	4,700	98	35	65
New York Mill	Whitestown		Wm. Walcott	1,60,000	2,000		Sheetings and Shirtings	300,000 yds	2060 bales	17,000	400	150	350
Oneida Manufacturing Society	Whitestown	Thos. H. Hubbard				50	Sheetings	1,100,000 yds	1000 bales	4,700	118	50	100
Utica Cotton Mill	New Hartford	J. A. Shearman	J. A. Shearman	100,000	1,000	100	Sheetings and Cotton Warp	1,200,000 sh, 100,000 y.wp	1072 ba.	7,000	126	60	90
Utica Steam Cotton Mill	Utica	A. Munson	Wm. Walcott	900,000	2,000	100	Cotton Goods	3,000,000 yds	3000 bales	16,000	300	150	250
Westmoreland Mill	Westmoreland	H. H. Smith					Sheetings and Wadding	200,000 y. sh, 1,000,000 y		wad-ding			
Orange County.													
Ames Barrett	Carriageville		B. Ames				Print Goods			2,600	73	25	65
Meadem Mill	New Windsor		W. B. Leonard				Cotton Yarn		100 tons	3,000		25	35
Newburgh Steam Mill	Newburgh	John Forsyth	Peter McKinly	100,000	1,000		Print Goods	2,889,000 tons	330½ tons	11,784	300	100	200
Townsend's Mill	Cornwall		I. Townsend				Print Goods			3,300	75	30	35
Oswego County.													
Oswego Cotton Mill	Oswego	Lewis, Beardsley & Wright					Cotton Goods			3,600	65		
Otsego County.													
Butternuts Woolen & Cot. Fac.	Butternuts		N. Y. Washburn	100,000		100	4-4 Sheetings	600,000 yds			100		50
Hargrave Company	Butternuts		C. H. Holbrook	100,000	100	1000	Print Goods	600,000 yds			100	25	50
Rensselaer County.													
Baxter Wm.	Mount ida						Cotton Yarns	16 tons	1 tons	216		6	4
Lawton & Greene	Mount ida						Batting and Wadding	65 tons	78 tons				
Marshall Benjamin	Mount ida						Sheeting and Ginghams	600,000 yds	390 tons	5,000	130	20	100
Marshall B.	Mount ida		Peter Booth				Cotton Goods and Tweed Warps	112,000 yds	20 tons	28	26	10	16
Robinson & Wood	Mount ida						Cotton Warps		25 tons	658		5	10
Rockland County.													
Van Riper J. & A.	Spring Valley						Sheetings	200,000 yds	25 tons	100	30	10	30
Saratoga County.													
Cook F. H.	Ballston						Print Goods	800,000 yds	75 tons	3,340	100	34	48
Cook J. M.	Ballston						Print Goods	490,000 yds	48 tons	1,658	42	17	28
Cook S. H.	Ballston						Print Goods	370,000 yds	33 tons	1,440	43	12	34
Saratoga Cotton Mill	Victory	Jared Coffin	M. Pond	280,000	830	100	Print Goods	820,000 yds		3,300	89	12	65
Victory Mill	Victory	Jared Coffin	M. Pond		1638	44	4-4 Cotton Goods	2,000,000 yds	300 tons	1,600	36	12	38
Schenectady County.													
Schenectady Manuf. Co.	Schenectady	James R. Craig	John Strang	76,920		50	Brown Sheetings	400,000 yds	70 tons	1,800	39	25	35
Seneca County.													
Waterloo Cotton Co.	Waterloo	John McAllister	Horatio Warner	40,000	900		4-4 Sheetings						
Washington County.													
Mowry & Co.	Union Village		Henry Holme				Sheetings	200,000 yds	99 tons	2,000	52	28	93
Westchester County.													
Kirbyville Cotton Factory	New Castle	L. & V. Kirby					Cotton Goods	243,300 yds		1,846	61	14	97

WOOLEN MANUFACTURING ESTABLISHMENTS, NEW YORK.

NAME.	LOCATION.	PRESIDENT.	AGENTS.	CAP.	SH.	PAR VAL.	KIND OF GOODS.	YEARLY AMOUNT.	AMOUNT CONS'D.	Spindles	Looms.	Males.	Females
Albany County.													
Tivoli Woolen Mill	Albany	Chapin & Root					Satinets and Tweeds	200,000 yds	70 tons	1,448	48	30	40
Watervliet Woolen Mill..	Watervliet	James Roy & Co					Brd Cloths,Tweeds,Sat. & Shawls			2,500	56	56	....
Allegany County.													
Hills & Morse	Angelica						Cassimeres, Flannels, and Sat's..	86,000 yds	25 t4,t3 s'ts mach-17	mach-17		29	10
Morse & Morse	Angelica						Woolen Goods	81,000 yds	24 tons 1 set do.			12	8
Cayuga County.													
Auburn Woolen Co	Auburn	J. Porter	H. G. Elsworth..	100,000	1,000	100	Broad Cloths	180,000 yds	200 t.10 st cards		54	90	80
Barber, Dennis & Co	Auburn						Carpets	180,000 yds	120 tons			110	100
Chautauque County.													
Couch & Stone	Westfield						Cassim, Tweeds,Grey, & Flannels	30,000 yds	15 tons	240	4	6	10
Steam Woolen Factory	Jamestown	Allen, Grandin & Co					Plain & Fancy Cas.TW. Gr. & Flan.	75,000 yd.	$45,000	680	14	20	16
Clinton County.													
Hartwell & Winslow	Plattsburgh						Cassimeres, Flan., Sat., & Tweeds	100,000 yds	50 tons	510	12	19	13
Delaware County.													
Delaware Woolen Factory	Delhi	Titus & Frost					Broad Cloths, Cassimeres & Flan.	30,000 y.b.cl	45 tons	600	12	10	13
Dutchess County.													
Glenham Company	Glenham	G. G. Howland	P. H. Schenck	140,000			Woolen Goods	191,000 yds	160 tons			84	65
Lagrange Woolen Manufacty	Lagrange	Titus & Sweet					Broad Cloths	40,000 yds	60 tons			35	16
Pine Grove Woolen Manuf'y	Pleasant Valley	J. Bower					Broad Cloths		5 tons				
Greene County.													
Prattsville Manufacturing Co	Prattsville	Z. Pratt	J. L. Sandford	30,000	300	100	Cassimeres and Tweeds	90,000 yds	40 tons	720	14	21	16
Herkimer County.													
Saxony Woolen Co..	Little Falls		M. W. Priest	100,000	1,000	100	Broad Cloths	60,000 yds	67¾ tons	1,200	90	42	58
Wool Growers' Manuf. Co	Little Falls		M. W. Priest	100,000	1,000	100	Broad Cloths	140,000 yds	150 tons	2,000	37	105	60
Jefferson County.													
Black River Woolen Co	Watertown		B. F. Stillman	50,000			Broad Cloths and Cassimeres	70,000 yds		1,200	24	35	42
Jefferson Woolen Co	Brownville	John Bradley	M. Lawton	20,000	560	50	Broad Cloths	100,000 yds	136 t.(7 sts	m'r'y	28	60	60
Millard & Sawyer	Watertown		Millard & Sawyer				Satinets						
Madison County.													
Beach H. H..	Eaton						Sheeps Grey		[1 set	m'r'y		7	5
Bridge Wm. & J. L.	Clockville						Woolen Goods			m'r'y			
Brooks Collin	Cazenovia						Woolen Goods		[1 set	m'r'y			
Cedar Grove Mills	Cazenovia						Cassimeres and Tweeds		60 t.[3 sets	m'r'y		26	40
Chamberlain O. & Co	Eaton						Sheeps Grey		[1 set	m'r'y		6	6
Eaton Nathan	Hamilton						Sheeps Grey			m'r'y			
Morse and Brown	Eaton						Woolen Goods	60,000 yds	[5 sets	m'r'y			
Shepard N.	Morrisville						Sheeps Grey	22,000 yds	19¾t.[1 set	m'r'y		7	5
Smith A. Y.	Leeville						Gray and Brown Cloths	105,000 vds	62¾t.[2 sts	m'r'y		15	16

NAME	LOCATION	PRESIDENT	AGENT	CAP.	SH.	PAR VAL.	KIND OF GOODS	YEARLY AMOUNT	AMOUNT CONS'D	Spin.	Loom	Males	Fem.
Stewart R. & D. & Co.	Chittenango						Broad Cloth and Cassimeres	60,000 yds	25 t. [2 sets m'r'y]	180		17	11
Ten Eyck & Curtis	Cazenovia						Cassimeres	160,000 yd	75 t. [3 sets m'r'y]			90	26
Tillinghast Clark	Morrisville						Grays and Brown Cloth	300,000 yd	130 t. [6 sets m'r'y]			24	22
Turner R. & S. C.	Brookbridge						Woolen Goods		[1 set m'r'y]				8
Williams John	Cazenovia						Satinets	36,000 yds				16	60
Williams, Ledyard & Stebbins	Cazenovia						Satinets	100,000 yds	46 t. [2 sets m'r'y]			36	
Monroe County.													
Allen Oliver	Mumford						Broad Cl. Cass. Tweeds & Flannels	18,000 yds	9 tz. wool	180	6	10	6
Coe E. B.	Rochester		W. G. Walcott				Cassimeres and Tweeds	75,000 yd	41 tz. n. wool	676	12	17	15
Dundas Chas. W. & Co.	Rochester						Broad Cloths and Medium Goods	75,000 yd	40 tz. wool	650	12	21	11
Montgomery County.													
Greene Wm. K. & Co.	Amsterdam						Ingrain Carpeting	36,000 yds			12	20	8
Sanford John & Son	Amsterdam						Carpet Yarn, Worsted Warp, 3 Ply; Ingrain & Chenief Carpets & Rugs	$133,000	$101,000	1,100	97	88	90
Oneida County.													
Van Deusen & Sons	Buel						Narrow Cloth, Satinets & Flannels			256 [3br.2in.]6			6
Clayville Mill	Clayville	I. T. Storm	F. Hollister	60,000	60t	100	Cotton Warp Broad Cloths	115,000 yds	66 t.w 14c	1,900	38	56	44
Empire Mills	Clayville	I. T. Storm	F. Hollister	100,000	1,000	100	Broad Cloths	135,000 yds	200 tons	3,185	40	96	64
Utica Globe Mills	Utica	T. S. Paxton	Samuel Churchill	100,000	1,000	100	Broad Cloths	145,000 yds	170 tons	2,400	44	90	80
Utica Steam Woolen Co.	Utica	A. S. Pond	Wm. C. Churchill	100,000	1,000	10c	Broad Cloths	145,000 yds	170 tons	2,400	44	90	80
Washington Mills	Washing'n Mills	I. T. Storm	F. Hollister	75,000	750	100	Cotton Warp Broad Cloths	135,000 yds	119 t. w.	1,600	51	76	75
Washington Steam Mills	Washing'n Mills	I. T. Storm	F. Hollister	100,000	1,000	100	Cotton Warp Broad Cloths	70,000 yds	56 t. w.	900	20	33	33
Whitestown Manufact. Co.	Walesville	S. N. Dexter	B. S. Graves	30,000	400		Twilled and Plain Flannels	130,000 yd	95 tons	550	12	18	13
Orange County.													
New Hampton Mill	New Hampton		H. Phillips				Broad Cloths and Satinets	19,250 y. b.cl / 19,375 y. sat			14	20	17
Oswego County.													
Stearns & Wet.	Pulaski						Cassimeres and Satinets	29,000 yds		248	10	14	10
St. Lawrence County.													
Guest Jacob H	Ogdensburgh						Cassimeres, Satinets, and Flannels	28,000 yds		270	6	11	7
Haskell Henry T.	Ogdensburgh						Cassimeres, Satinets, and Flannels	45,000 yds		650	12	14	15
Schenectady County.													
Schenectady Steam Mills	Schenectady	J. Cady		60,000	940	200	Carpetings	63,900 yds	78 tons	400	31	20	50
Seneca County.													
Seneca Woolen Mills	Seneca Falls	Edward Mynderse	Simon Branch	75,000	1,400	60	Black Cassimeres	195,000 yds	80 tons	1,600	38	40	80
Waterloo Woolen Manuf. Co.	Waterloo	Elijah Kimble	C. W. Cook	160,000	3,000	50	Broad Cloths and Cassimeres		[13 sets m'r'y]			50	75
Suffolk County.													
Jones J. N. & W. R. & Co.	Cold Spr. Harbor						Broad Cloths	57,000 yds	37½ tons	276	4	6	3
Wyoming County.													
Day E. D. & Co.	Warsaw						Cassimeres and Plain Cloths	94,000 yds	16 t. [1 set m'r'y]			12	6

MISCELLANEOUS MANUFACTURING ESTABLISHMENTS, NEW YORK.

NAME.	LOCATION.	PRESIDENT.	AGENTS.	CAP.	SH.	PAR VAL	KIND OF GOODS.	YEARLY AMOUNT.	AMOUNT CONSUMED.	Males.	Females.
Albany County.											
Albany Glass Works..	Albany	M. H. Myer	D. O. Fetcham	10,000	10.	100	Glass Hollow Ware	$40,000		70	..
Duchess County.											
Duchess Company	Wappingers falls	James Ingraham	Robert Williams	50,000	500	100	Calico Printing	10,000,000 ya	[140 looms]	10	..
Poughkeepsie Iron Co	Poughkeepsie	Wm. Bushnell				100	Pig Iron and all kinds of Castings				
Essex County.											
Au Sable Iron Company	Ausable Forks		J. & J. Rogers	60,000	1,000	60	Bar and Plate Iron	3000 tons			
Utica Oneida County.											
Utica Screw Company	Utica	H. Barnard	George S. Dana				Screws	$75,000		36	
Oswego County.											
Oswego Starch	Oswego	Sylvester Willard	T. Kingsford & Son	60,000			Starch	1000 tons			4
Putnam County.											
Oregon Iron Works	Putnam Valley		J. Strong				Iron Wire				
Rensselaer County.											
Albany Iron Works	Troy		Corning & Winslow				R. Road, Ship, & Boat Spikes, Cut Nails, Spring Steel and Carriage Springs, Car Axles, Boilers, &c.		[300 to 350 hands]		
Troy Iron and Nail Factory	Troy	H. Burden	P. A. Burden	90,000	500	16	Rolled and Slit Iron, Horse Shoes, Spikes, & R.R. Fasten'gs	10,000 tons		800	
Schenectady County.											
Mohawk Marble & Cement Co.	Schenectady	David Tomlinson	N. Swift	25,000	500	50	Hydraulic Cement and Plaster	15 tons		30	
Norris Locomotive Works	Schenectady		E. S. Norris	120,000			Locomotive Engines	$600,000	750 ts. pig iron, 300 ts. bar iron, 300 ts. boiler iron, 100 ts. copper	500	
Ulster County.											
Ellenville Glass Co	Wawarsing	A. B. Preston					Black Glass				
Lawrence Cement Manuf Co	Rosendale	E. W. Budington					Hydraulic Cement				
Newark Rosendale Co	Whiteport	J. H. Stevens					Hydraulic Cement				
N.Y. & Saugerties Wh. Lead Co	Saugerties	Jas. McCullough	W. R. McCullough				White Lead				
Saugerties Paper Mills	Saugerties	Joseph Kingsley					Printing Paper				
Ulster Iron Works	Saugerties	Joseph Tuckerman									

NEW YORK CITY BANKS.

NAME.	LOCATION.	PRESIDENT.	CASHIER.	DISCOUNT DAYS.	CAP.	SH.	PAR VAL.
American Exchange Bank	60 Wall st	D. Leavitt	John J. Fisk	Wednesdays and Saturdays	$1,165,400	11,544	$100
Bank of America	46 Wall st	Geo. Newbold	James Punnett	Tuesdays and Fridays	2,001,200	20,012	100
Bank of Commerce	39 Wall st	John A. Stevens	Geo. Curtis	Tuesdays and Fridays	5,000,000	50,000	100
Bank of New York	48 Wall st	John Oothout	A. P. Haley	Tuesdays and Thursdays	1,000,000	2,000	500
Bank of the State of New York	30 Wall st	C. W. Lawrence	R. Withers	Tuesdays and Thursdays	2,000,000	20,000	100
Bowery Bank	173 Bowery	D. W. Townsend	N. G. Bradford	Mondays and Thursdays	300,000	12,000	25
Broadway Bank	Corner Broadway and Anthony	F. A. Palmer	John L. Everett				
Butchers and Drovers' Bank	152 Bowery	Jacob Aims	Benedict Lewis, Jr.	Wednesdays and Saturdays	500,000	90,000	25
Chemical Bank	269 Broadway	J. Q. Jones	J. B. Desdolty	Daily	300,000	3,000	100
City Bank	52 Wall st	G. A. Worth	Robt. Strong	Mondays and Thursdays	720,000	16,000	45
Delaware and Hudson Canal Co.	31 Wall st	John Wurst	J. H. Williams				
Fulton Bank	Corner Fulton and Pearl sts	John Adams	Wm. J. Lane	Wednesdays and Saturdays	600,000	29,000	30
Greenwich Bank	402 Hudson	B. F. Wheelwright	Wm. Hawes	Tuesdays and Fridays	200,000	8,000	25
Leather Manufacturers' Bank	45 William st	F. C. Tucker	E. Platt	Tuesdays and Fridays	600,000	19,000	60
Manhattan Company	40 Wall st	C. O. Halsted	J. M. Morrison	Mondays and Thursdays	2,050,000	41,000	50
Mechanics' Banking Association	38 Wall st	Fred. Pentz	John H. Cornell	Wednesdays and Fridays	632,000	25,289	25
Mechanics' Bank	33 Wall st	S. Knapp	Francis W. Edmonds	Mondays and Thursdays	2,000,000	80,000	18
Mechanics' and Traders' Bank	570 Grand st	John Clapp	E. D. Brown	Wednesdays and Saturdays	200,000	8,000	25
Merchants' Bank	42 Wall st	John J. Palmer	O. J. Cammum	Wednesdays and Fridays	1,490,000	29,800	50
Merchants' Exchange Bank	173 Greenwich st	Jas. Van Ostrand	Wm. H. Johnson	Wednesdays and Saturdays	750,000	15,000	50
National Bank	36 Wall st	Jas. Gallatin	Frederick Dobbs	Tuesdays and Fridays	750,000	15,000	50
New York Dry Dock Company	Corner Avenue D and Tenth st	Geo. Hawley	J. Washburn	Tuesdays and Fridays	420,000	14,000	30
North River Bank	175 Greenwich st	Cha. Denison	A. Halsey	Tuesdays and Fridays	648,000	13,000	50
Ocean Bank	169 Greenwich st	Nath'l Weed	J. B. Gibbons				
Phenix Bank	45 Wall st	Thos. Tilleston	N. G. Ogden	Wednesdays and Saturdays	1,800,000	60,000	20
Seventh Ward Bank	284 Pearl st	N. G. Ogden	A. S. Fraser	Tuesdays and Fridays	500,000	10,000	50
Tradesmen's Bank	177 Chatham st	John W. Lawrence	Richard Berry	Tuesdays and Fridays	400,000	16,000	40
Union Bank	34 Wall st	W. H. Falls	D. Ebbetts	Mondays and Thursdays	1,000,000	20,000	50

COUNTRY BANKS, NEW YORK.

NAME.	LOCATION.	PRESIDENT.	CASHIER.	DISCOUNT DAYS.	CAP.	SH.	PAR VAL.
Adams Bank	Adams Village, Jefferson Co	S. D. Hungerford	N. B. Hungerford		$10,000		
Agricultural Bank of Herkimer	Herkimer, Herkimer Co	C. T. E. Van Horne	Harvey Doolittle		100,800	1,008	100
Albany City Bank	43 State st., Albany	Erastus Corning	Watts Sherman	Tuesdays and Fridays	211,000	3,110	100
Albany Exchange Bank	Albany	Geo. W. Stanton	Noah Lee	Tuesdays and Fridays	100,000		
Amenia Bank	Leedsville, Duchess Co	...J. D. Hunt, Banker			12,000		
American Bank	Mayville, Chautauque Co	Wm. Green	J. S. Doughty		200,000	4,000	50
Atlantic Bank	Brooklyn, King's Co	Daniel Embury		Tuesdays and Saturdays			
Ballston Spa Bank	Ballston, Saratoga Co	James M. Cook	E. E. Kendrick	Thursdays	240,000	5,000	50
Bank of Albany	42 State st., Albany, Albany Co	J. H. Ten Eyck	L. Burrows		100,000	2,000	50
Bank of Albion	Albion, Orleans Co	R. S. Burrows	A. J. Rich		100,000		
Bank of Attica	Spaulding's Exc., Buffalo, Erie Co	G. B. Rich	C. H. Merriam				
Bank of Auburn	Auburn	J. S. Seymour			105,000		
Bank of Bainbridge	Bainbridge, Chenango Co	D. E. Bishop	J. S. Isaacs	Every Day	110,300	1,102	100
Bank of Cayuga Lake	Ithaca, Tompkins Co	Ira Willcox	T. O. Gramm		190,000		
Bank of Central New York	Utica, Oneida Co	A. Thomas	Walter M. Conkey				
Bank of Chenango	Norwich, Chenango Co	Lester Bradner	L. C. Woodruff				
Bank of Danville	Danville, Livingston Co	W. H. Van Duzer					
Bank of the Empire State	Fairport, Chemung Co	P. L. Tracy	J. E. Robinson	Every Day	100,000	4,000	50
Bank of Genesee	Batavia, Genesee Co	C. A. Cook	W. E. Sill	Every Day	400,000	20,000	50
Bank of Geneva	Geneva, Ontario Co	Wm. Randall	Wm. B. Douglass		200,000	2,000	50
Bank of Ithaca	Ithaca, Tompkins Co	John P. Beekman	F. P. Guion	Wednesdays	125,000		10
Bank of Kinderhook	Kinderhook, Columbia Co	D. N. Barney	T. M. Janes		63,000		10
Bank of Lake Erie	Spaulding's Exc., Buffalo, Erie Co	John S. Fake	P. M. Corbin	Wednesdays	190,000	12,000	10
Bank of Lansingburgh	Lansingburgh, Rensselaer Co	L. W. Bostwick	J. L. Leonard				
Bank of Lowville	Lowville, Lewis Co	James K. Livingston	Ralph Lester	Every Day	800,000	12,000	25
Bank of Monroe	State st., Rochester, Monroe Co	John Chambers	Geo. W. Kerr	Saturdays	140,000	6,000	1750
Bank of Newburgh	Newburgh, Orange Co	D. Sayre	S. Barton				
Bank of New Rochelle	New Rochelle, Westchester Co	A. S. Murray	Thos. T. Reeve	Every Day	105,000	4,000	50
Bank of Orange County	Goshen, Orange Co	A. Ward	Thos. Clark		900,000		
Bank of Orleans	Albion, Orleans Co	W. Pumpelly	James Wright				
Bank of Oswego	Oswego, Tioga Co	L. J. Akin	G. Van Bowdud	Every Day	63,000		
Bank of Owego	Owego, Tioga Co	Thos. L. Davis	Reuben North				
Bank of Poughkeepsie	Poughkeepsie, Duchess Co	J. Seymour	H. S. Fairchild				
Bank of Rochester	Rochester, Monroe Co	John Stryker	G. B. Fairchild		100,000	2,000	50
Bank of Rome	Rome, Oneida Co	James Hasbrouck	Henry H. Reynolds	Tuesdays and Fridays	100,000	2,000	80
Bank of Rondout	Rondout, Ulster Co	D. Monroe	M. W. Bennett	Every Day	100,000	1,000	100
Bank of Salina	Salina, Onondaga Co	Thos. J. Marvin	J. S. Lambe	Every Day	140,000		
Bank of Saratoga Springs	Saratoga Springs, Saratoga Co	Geo. W. Tew	C. C. Swift		100,000		
Bank of Silver Creek	Silver Creek, Chautauque Co						

NAME	LOCATION.	PRESIDENT.	CASHIER.	DISCOUNT DAYS.	CAP.	SH.	PAR VAL.
Bank of Syracuse	Syracuse, Onondaga Co	J. Wilkinson	Horace White		$175,000	1,750	$100
Bank of Troy	Troy, Rensselaer Co	Nathan Danchy	John Paine	Tuesdays	440,000	22,000	20
Bank of Utica	Utica, Oneida Co	Thos. Walker	Wm. B. Welles		100,000		100
Bank of Utica Branch	Canandaigua, Ontario Co.	Cha. Seymour	Henry K. Sanger	Every Day	100,000	1,000	100
Bank of Vernon	Vernon, Oneida Co.	John J. Knox	T. F. Rand	Daily	54,025		
Bank of Watertown	Watertown, Jefferson Co.	Thos. C. Chittenden	H. G. Gilbert	Daily	100,000	1,250	50
Bank of Waterville	Waterville, Oneida Co.	Candee	D. R. Goodwin	Tuesdays and Fridays	30,000		
Bank of Westfield	Westfield, Chautauque Co.	Sextus H. Hungerford	J. W. Hungerford		100,000		
Bank of Whitehall	Whitehall, Washington Co.	Wm. A. Moore	H. Palmer	Mondays and Thursdays	100,000	2,400	50
Bank of Whitestown	Whitestown, Oneida Co	S. Newton Dexter	H. S. Thomas	Tuesdays and Fridays	7,500		
Black River Bank	Watertown, Jefferson Co.	S. Paddock	H. G. Gilbert	Daily	100,000	4,000	25
Brooklyn Bank	Brooklyn, King's Co.	John Bhoit	Hector Morrison	Tuesdays and Fridays	100,000	2,400	25
Broome County Bank	Binghamton, Broome Co.	C. Strong	T. R. Morgan	Wednesdays	100,000		25
Cambridge Bank	Cambridge, Washington Co.	Jacob Cornwell	W. R. Storm	Tuesdays	250,000	10,000	25
Catskill Bank	Catskill, Greene Co.	Francis N. Wilson	H. Hill		200,000	4,000	50
Cayuga County Bank	Auburn, Cayuga Co.	Nelson Beardsley					
Cayuga Lake Bank	Ithaca, Tompkins Co.	D. E. Bishop	J. N. Starin	Daily	104,000		
Cortland Bank	Cortland, Cortland Co.	David H. Little	Horatio J. Olcott			1,040	100
Champlain Bank	Cherry Valley, Otsego Co	J. B. McLane	M. Hale		157,000	1,675	100
Chautauque County Bank	Ellensburgh, Clinton Co.	Samuel Barret	Robert Newland	Daily	300,000	1,500	250
Chemung Canal Bank	Elmira, Chemung Co	Chas. Cook	John Arnol		100,000		100
Chester Bank	Chester, Orange Co.	James Wheeler	Alex. Wright	Saturdays	40,000		
City Bank	Oswego, Oswego Co	J. H. Reynolds	Delos In Wolf	Mondays and Thursdays	330,000	33,000	100
Commercial Bank	Troy, Rensselaer Co.	Elisu Plum	Fred. Leake				
Commercial Bank	40 State st., Albany, Albany Co.	J. Townsend	James Taylor				
Commercial Bank	Friendship, Allegany Co.	Luther Stowell	Cha. Colgate				
Commercial Bank	Lockport, Niagara Co	S. P. Stokes, Banker					
Commercial Bank	Rochester, Monroe Co	Asa Sprague	Geo. R. Clark				
Commercial Bank	Whitehall, Washington Co	A. H. Griswold	C. M. Davison				
Corning Bank	Painted Post, Steuben Co	H. W. Bostwick	L. Mallory				
Cortland County Bank	Cincinnatus, Cortland Co	B. Palmer			60,000		
Cuyler Bank	Palmyra, Wayne Co.	Geo. W. Cayler	S. P. Seymour		139,400	1,394	100
Delaware Bank	Delhi, Delaware Co.	H. D. Gould	W. H. Griswold	Mondays and Thursdays			
Drovers' Bank	Ogdensburgh, St. Lawrence Co.	G. W. Smith	H. Leonard				
Duchess County Bank	Amenia, Duchess Co.	H. Vail			100,000		
Essex County Bank	Keeseville, Essex Co.	Silas Arnold	Andrew Thompson	Daily	50,000		
Exchange Bank	Buffalo, Erie Co	R. Codd	Andrew Houliston		60,000		
Exchange Bank	Lockport, Niagara Co	H. S. Harvey	W. T. Rogers				
Exchange Bank of Genesee	Alexander, Genesee Co	D. W. Tomlinson	J. F. Pierpont	Daily	100,000		100
Farmers' Bank	Troy, Rensselaer Co	J. Van Schoonhoven	Philander Wells	Thursdays	278,000	6,200	40 &
Farmers' and Mechanics' Bank	Amsterdam, Montgomery Co	Cornelius Miller	Marquis Barnes	Every Day	110,000	2,200	50
Farmers' and Mechanics' Bank	Rochester, Monroe Co.	A. G. Smith	E. Huntington				
Farmers' and Drovers' Bank	Somers, Westchester Co.	Horace Bailey	E. Howland		51,400	514	
Farmers' & Mech. B'k of Genesee	Batavia, Genesee Co.	J. S. Ganson	O. Ballard	Daily	95,000		100
Farmers' Bank	Mina, Chautauque Co.	J. Relf					

NAME.	LOCATION.	PRESIDENT.	CASHIER.	DISCOUNT DAYS.	CAP.	SH.	PAR VAL.
Farmers' and Manuf. Bank	Poughkeepsie, Duchess Co.	Wm. A. Davies	F. W. Davis	Daily	$300,000	3,000	$100
Farmers' Bank	Hudson, Columbia Co.	E. Gifford	A. R. Holmes	Tuesdays	138,050	1380½	100
Fort Plain Bank	Fort Plain, Montgomery Co	J. H. Meyer	I. C. Babcock		100,000	100	100
Fort Stanwix Bank	Rome, Oneida Co.	David Utley	W. W. Nellis	Tuesdays	120,000	2,300	50
Franklin County Bank	Malone, Franklin Co.	S. C. Wead	A. B. Parmelee		80,000		
Franklin Bank	French Creek, Chautauque Co.	Wm. H. Jones, Banker	M. P. Lampson				
Genesee County Bank	Le Roy, Genesee Co.	John Lent	R. S. Ralston		100,000		
Genesee Valley Bank	Mount Morris, Lvington Co	J. B. Bond					
Herford County Bank	Hartford, Washington Co.	G. W. Wesley					
Henry Kep's Bank	Little Falls, Herkimer Co.	Henry P. Alexander	Albert G. Story	Daily	200,000	8,000	25
Henry Kep's Bank	Watertown, Jefferson Co.	Henry Kerp, Banker			10,000		
Highland Bank	Newburgh, Orange Co.	Geo. Cornwell	Alfred Post	Daily	200,000	4,000	50
Hudson River Bank	Hudson, Columbia Co	Oliver Wiswall	Aaron B. Scott	Thursdays	150,000	3,000	50
Hungerford Bank	Adams, Jefferson Co.	S. D. Hungerford, Banker					
James Bank	Jamesville, Saratoga Co	J. W. James	A. D. Grinnell	Tuesdays and Fridays	200,000		
Jefferson County Bank	Watertown, Jefferson Co	N. M. Woodruff	O. V. Brainard	Mondays and Thursdays	200,000	2,000	100
Kingston Bank	Kingston, Ulster Co.	J. H. Hasbrouck	J. S. Smith				
Kirkland Bank	Clinton, Oneida Co.	A. Gridley	W. Gridley				
Knickerbocker Bank	Genoa, Cayuga Co.	J. M. Dunning					
Lewis County Bank	Martinsburgh, Lewis Co.	L. Lyon	E. N. Merriam	Daily	100,000	1,000	100
Livingston County Bank	Geneseo, Lvington Co	Allen Ayrault	Ephraim Cone	Daily	117,000	2,350	50
Lockport Bank and Trust Co.	Lockport, Niagara Co.	I. C. Colton	J. I. B. Spooner	Wednesdays and Saturdays	300,000	6,000	50
Long Island Bank	Brooklyn, Kings Co.	Wm. S. Herriman	Geo. L. Sampson		150,000		
Luther Wright's Bank	Oswego, Oswego Co.	L. Wright	S. H. Lathrop	Daily	100,000	1,000	100
Madison County Bank	Cazenovia, Madison Co.	Jacob Ten Eyck	B. R. Wendell				
McIntyre Bank	Adirondack, Essex Co.	Andrew Porteous	Alex. Ralph				
Mechanics' and Farmers' Bank	Albany, Albany Co.	Thos. W. Olcott	Thomas Olcott	Tuesdays and Fridays	442,000	26,000	17
Mechanics' Bank	Ellery, Chautauque Co.	O. Benedict	T. Edmonds, Jr.		150,000	1,000	100
Merchants' Bank	Poughkeepsie, Duchess Co	M. J. Myers	James H. Fonda	Wednesdays	150,000		
Merchants' Bank	Buffalo, Erie Co.	E. J. Townsend	H. Johnson	Daily	86,000		
Merchants' and Farmers' Bank	Carmel, Putnam Co.	S. Washburn	Edgar Washburn	Wednesdays	250,000	6,000	50
Merchants' and Farmers' Bank	Ithaca, Tompkins Co.	J. B. Williams	Henry Hungerford	Daily	300,000	1,000	100
Merch. and Mech. Bank of Troy	Troy, Rensselaer Co.	Geo. Vail	Cha. S. Douglas	Wednesdays	100,000		
Middletown Bank	South Middletown, Orange Co	J. Davis	Wm. M. Graham		160,000		
Mohawk Bank	Schenectady, Schenectady Co	J. I. Degraf	W. B. Walton				
Mohawk Valley Bank	Mohawk Village, Montg'y Co.	Elias Root	F. E. Spinner				
New Jersey County Bank	Albany, 69 State st., Albany Co.	Rufus H. King	Ed. Wells		969,600	13,300	25
New York State Bank	Johnstown, Montgomery Co	James W. Miller	J. B. Plumb				
New York Stock Bank	Durham, Greene Co.	Platt Adams	A. Marks		60,000		
Northern Canal Bank	North Granville, Washington Co.	J. M. Pinkney					
Northern Exchange Bank	Brasher Falls, St. Lawrence Co.	C. T. Hubbard	J. T. Walsh				
Northern Bank of New York	Madrid, St. Lawrence Co.	J. Horton	A. Greenleaf		100,000	2,000	50
Ogdensburgh Bank	Ogdensburgh, St. Lawrence Co.	James Averill	John D. Judson	Tuesdays and Fridays	100,000		
Oliver Lee & Co. Bank	Buffalo, Erie Co.	F. H. Tows	H. L. Lansing	Tuesdays and Fridays	400,000	4,000	100
Oneida Bank	Utica, Oneida Co.	Alfred Munson	B. B. Lansing				

NAME.	LOCATION.	PRESIDENT.	CASHIER.	DISCOUNT DAYS.	CAP.	SH.	PAR VAL.
Onondaga County Bank	Syracuse, Onondaga Co.	Oliver Teall	H. White	Tuesdays	$150,000	3,000	50
Ontario Bank	Canandaigua, Ontario Co.	John Greig	H. B. Gibson	Fridays	500,000	10,000	50
Ontario Branch Bank	Genesee st, Utica, Oneida Co.	A. B. Johnson	James S. Lynch		300,000	6,000	50
Oswego County Bank	Granby, Oswego Co.	W. G. Young					
Otsego County Bank	Cooperstown, Otsego Co.	Henry Phinney	Henry Scott	Daily	100,000	4,000	25
Palmyra Bank	Palmyra, Wayne Co.	Pliney Saxton, Banker			15,000		
Patchin Bank	Buffalo, Erie Co.	A. D. Patchin	T. W. Patchin		100,000		
Pine Plains Bank	Pine Plains, Duchess Co.	R. W. Bostwick	J. F. Hull	Daily	100,000	1,000	100
Powell Bank	Newburgh, Orange Co.	Samuel Williams	Thos. C. Ring	Daily	93,000	936	100
Prattsville Bank	Prattsville, Greene Co.	Zadock Pratt	J. Hopkins				
Pratt Bank	Buffalo, Erie Co.	E. Pratt	T. B. Sears		50,000		
Putnam County Bank	Farmers' Mills, Putnam Co.	D. Kent	H. Townsend				
Putnam Valley Bank	Putnam Valley, Putnam Co.	A. Smith					
Rochester Bank	Exchange st, Rochester, Monroe Co.	Freeman Clark	C. W. Hardy	Daily	100,000		
Rochester City Bank	39 State st, Rochester, Monroe Co.	Thos. H. Rochester	C. T. Amsden	Wednesdays and Saturdays	400,000	4,000	100
Sackett's Harbor Bank	Sackett's Harbor, Jefferson Co.	E. G. Merrick	J. C. Dann				
Saratoga Bank	Waterford, Saratoga Co.	J. Kirkerbocker	M. S. Scott				
Security Bank	Huntsville	A. Hunt	L. D. Taylor				
Schenectady Bank	Schenectady, Schenectady Co	J. Cady	Wm. V. Goodrich		150,000	3,000	50
Seneca County Bank	Waterloo, Seneca Co	David S. Skaats	Wm. V. Mercer		200,000		
State Bank	Saugerties, Ulster Co	K. N. Isaacs	John Magee		100,000		
Suffolk County Bank	Sag Harbor, Suffolk Co	W. W. McGay	G. S. Adams				
Tanners' Bank	Catskill, Greene Co	Wm. Adams	F. Hill		100,000		
Tompkins County Bank	Ithaca, Tompkins Co.	S. S. Day	N. T. Williams	Tuesdays	250,000		
Troy City Bank	Troy, Rensselaer Co.	Herman Camp	Silas K. Stow	Mondays	200,000	6,000	80
Umadilla Bank	Umadilla, Otsego Co.	Geo. B. Warren	C. J. Hays		140,500		
Ulster County Bank	Kingston, Ulster Co.	A. B. Watson	James S. Evans	Fridays	100,000	2,000	50
Utica City Bank	Utica, Oneida Co.	Cornelius Bruyn	C. S. Wilson	Tuesdays and Fridays	200,000	4,000	50
Village Bank	Randolph, Cattaraugus Co.	Hiram Denio	J. C. Calhoun				
Warren County Bank	Johnsburgh, Warren Co	T. S. Sheldon	W. W. Watson				
Washington Bank and Loan Co.	Greenwich, Washington Co.	L. B. Barnes	Edwin Andrews				
Watertown Bank and Loan Co.	Watertown, Jefferson Co	Henry Holmes	P. V. Rogers	Daily	60,000		
Westchester County Bank	Peekskill, Westchester Co.	Geo. C. Sherman	D. F. Clapp	Mondays and Thursdays	200,000	5,000	40
White Plains Bank	White Plains, Westchester Co.	Isaac Seymour	William Williams		60,000		
White's Bank of Buffalo	Buffalo, Erie Co.	Geo. C. White					
Wooster Sherman's Bank	Watertown, Jefferson Co.	W. Sherman	John H. Rice	Daily	25,000	2,000	50
Yates County Bank	Penn Yan, Yates Co.	Asa Cole	W. M. Oliver	Wednesdays	100,000		50

KUMBEL'S PATENT
MACHINE-STRETCHED
LEATHER BANDING.

THE ONLY PATENTED BAND IN THE UNITED STATES.

Triumphant over all opposition this article has once more received the highest of all premiums, the *Gold Medal*, at the Fair of the "American Institute," in October, 1849. Awarded upon mature consideration, and severe test (in competition), of the superiority and originality of their principles of construction; thus recognizing after *thorough practical and public trial*, that rank and position which the manufacturing community has long since assigned it as the

Best Leather Band Manufactured in the United States.

This banding is made of the solid part only of the *best Oak Leather*, is thoroughly stretched, cemented and riveted, will run straight and has a perfect bearing upon the pulleys.

From the superior mode of its manufacture it possesses remarkable Strength and Durability, beyond any banding manufactured. It also excels in its running qualities any band made upon other principles or of other materials.

The Belt made of Leather is the only one that can be relied upon to perform well in all situations. It neither melts with friction, sticks to the pulleys, nor frets into shreds ; nor is it subject to sudden combustion and destruction ; all which are marked characteristics of Beltings made from Gums.

The *Patent Machine-stretched Leather Banding*, as made by the Subscriber, will stand more heat, more cold, more friction, and is far more durable than those above referred to ; and for all practical purposes, it can also be made water proof.

The best evidence of its quality is its adoption by nearly all extensive Manufacturers and Machinists throughout the city and country, the River and Sound steamers, and (with marked approbation) by the various lines of Ocean steamers. Since its introduction by the subscriber, it has revolutionized machinery to the general exclusion of gearing ; and the approval of *practical mechanics* is further emphatically expressed by the steady increase in the demand for it from year to year. Every Belt is warranted to possess all the qualities requisite for durability and good performance, or the money returned.

They can be furnished of any length and width from 1 to 24 inches, either single, double, or round. Also superior Lace Leather, with rivets, burrs, punches, setts, &c.

WILLIAM KUMBEL, Original Inventor & Manufacturer,
33 Ferry street, New York.

DESCRIPTION OF
STREVER'S FORCE PUMPS.

The two-inch Cylinder Pumps will discharge from 15 to 20 gallons per minute, and force it from 30 to 40 feet. These are calculated for Dwelling Houses, Garden Engines, and family purposes.

The three-inch Cylinder will discharge from 30 to 30 gallons per minute, and force it from 50 to 75 feet. This size discharges one and a quarter inch stream of water. These pumps can be used with equal effect with hot liquids.

The four-inch Cylinder will discharge from 40 to 60 gallons per minute, and force it from 75 to 125 feet. This size discharges a two-inch stream of water and can be worked with man, horse, water or steam power. Stroke of piston from 3 to 8 inches.

The six-inch Cylinder will discharge a three and a half inch stream of water. This size is admirably adapted for Fire-Engines, and can be worked from 4 to 10 inch stroke of piston.

The eight-inch Cylinder will discharge a four and a half inch stream of water, and is calculated to pump about 200 gallons per minute, and can be worked with horse, water, or steam power. Stroke of piston from 6 to 12 inches.

☞ These Pumps have been tested and give general satisfaction.

MANUFACTURED AND FOR SALE BY
J. H. STREVER,
120 Fulton st. near Nassau, New York.

WHO INVENTED

THE WALNUT OIL

MILITARY SHAVING SOAP?

Merchants and Traders must observe, in order to avoid Imposition, and Trickery, by a number of Manufacturers of a Spurious Article, which is palmed off as the Genuine. The following Card will satisfy any Inquirer:

A CARD.

IN order to establish the priority of my invention, and exhibit in suitable colors the several *genii* who trespass upon my prerogative, and in the vain attempt to find shelter under a mass of open violation of truth, only multiply the truth against themselves.

My first impressions respecting the WALNUT OIL SOAP, were from the celebrated Dr. Reese, Medical Hall, Piccadilly, London; and more fully matured by the aid of an officer of the highest rank in the French army, a proficient in Chemistry.

In 1844, I was manufacturing Soaps and Perfumery, when I associated myself with P. D. Vroom, whose previous occupation had been Superintendent at the Blind Asylum; consequently, he knew nothing of the business in which I was engaged. The WALNUT OIL SOAP *was then in preparation, and was peculiarly my own;* to establish which fact, I refer to Moore & Taylor, 81 Maiden Lane, who were my associates in business, at 79 Trinity Place, previous to my knowledge of Mr. Vroom—and as a further vindication of the justice of my claim, the establishing of my right, and the total refutation of Mr. Vroom's egregious pretence to the invention, allow me to state, that the Label first got up for the article, was used to a great extent, and read as follows : "JOHNSON'S Walnut Oil Soap, 79 Trinity Place, New York;" and for confirmation of this fact, I refer to W. J. Spence, printer, 194 Fulton street, who has the plate.

Another self-styled inventor, is George Banham, who was in the employ of Messrs. Johnson and Vroom ; but during his residence with us, always had the Soap in preparation, mixed in barrels by myself, previous to finishing ; to establish this fact, I refer to P. D. Vroom.

Another pretender, of the name of Gale, endeavored to purchase information from one of my workmen by the bribe of a watch. (This was before he commenced to invent the Soap.) There are other *small original Inventors,* which it is necessary the public should guard against. If they want a truly good article, mine is the only one ; and it is admitted, that since the first discovery of Soap Making by the Phœnicians, none has ever added such a laurel to the Savonic art as myself.

So far, so good. It now only remains for me to guard purchasers against a glaring counterfeit of my Soap, sold by a miserable looking man by the name of Brownell, who sells it at auction under the name of M. Johnson, bearing my address. There is no such person. It is a gross fraud. Several respectable houses have been deceived by Brownell, and have discontinued selling it. Some others, if they continue to *represent it as mine,* render themselves liable to heavy damages, which will be vigorously pursued.

Any other impositions, bearing the name of Walnut Oil, except those which bear my fac simile on each cartoon, are counterfeits of the deepest die

In order to put an end to the various controversies, I have invented

AN ENTIRE NEW ARTICLE, CALLED

JOHNSON'S MYRTLE SOAP,

The best in use, to which approved excellence, I have the highest testimonials. Also, CHRYSTALINE WASH BALLS, LAUNDRY STARCH POLISH, and every description of FANCY SOAPS.

WM. JOHNSON, ARTISTE IN SOAPS,

Soap Works, 55 Frankfort Street, New York

BUSINESS REGISTER.

AMERICAN Print Warehouse.

PRINTS ONLY.
1850.
Spring Styles.

LEE & BREWSTER,
Offer at their establishment,
44
CEDAR STREET,
New York,

AN EXTENSIVE assortment of American and Foreign PRINTED CALICOES, unsurpassed in variety and beauty of execution.

L. & B. exhibit about 1,000 Cases New Prints, comprising all desirable styles of Domestic production, and large recent importations of BRITISH and FRENCH.

The Goods now offered are printed on Cloths purchased before the late advance in prices, and are offered at *less than manufacturers' present prices*,——for Cash or the usual credit.

Agents.

CRAFTS & STELL, Purchasing Agents, Manchester, Leeds, Huddersfield, Bradford. England—Glasgow. Scotland—Belfast, Ireland—and 27 Pine st. N. Y.

PURCHASING AGENTS.
JOSH. & WM. WALKER, Commission Merchants, Leeds, England.

MABEE & WATERBURY, Agents, 11 Pine st. N. Y.

Agricult'l warehouse.

ALBANY
Agricultural Warehouse,
BY H. L. EMERY,
Manufacturer and Dealer, Wholesale and Retail, of *Agricultural Implements and Seeds,*
No. 369 & 371 Broadway,
Albany, N. Y.

Ale and Porter.

JOHN TAYLOR & SONS' Albany Imperial Pale and Amber Ale, constantly on hand, and for sale in hogsheads, barrels and half-barrels, either for city use or shipping.

BREWERY—No. 83 Green st. Albany; 342 Greenwich st. New York; and 74 Commercial st. Boston.

AGENTS—JAS. PRESTON, Charleston, S. C.; F. SHIELS, Savannah, Ga.; A. D. GRIEFF & Co. New Orleans.

JOHN TAYLOR,
JOHN R. TAYLOR,
JOSEPH B. TAYLOR.

URI BURT, Albany Pale and Amber Ale and Porter. Brewery, corner Montgomery and Colonie sts. Albany.

DEPOTS—153 Greenwich st. New York ; corner Main and Front sts. Brooklyn, N. Y.; 64 Commercial st. Boston; Lyman st. Springfield, Mass.

Argillo Works.

THE PROPRIETORS of the Albany Argillo Works manufacture for home and foreign markets, Door and Furniture Knobs, possessing the properties and beauties of polished agate. They also manufacture every description of Locks and Latches, including American and European patterns. The trade furnished at the lowest prices.

Communications addressed to
AMOS DEAN,
Argillo Works, Albany, N.Y.

Artists' Supply Store

J. W. HAWXHURST.
ARTISTS' SUPPLY STORE,
No. 107 FULTON STREET,
NEW YORK.

Attorneys.

JOHN HOPPER, Attorney and Counsellor at Law, Notary Public, and Agent of New England Mutual Life Insurance Company, of Boston, 71 Cedar st. corner of Nassau st. New York.

SMITH & VANDERPOEL, Attorneys, Counsellors, &c., Jauncey Court, 3d floor, 39 Wall st.
J. BRICK SMITH,   } New York
AARON J. VANDERPOEL. }

Bank Note List.

CHARLES & LEONORI'S Bank Note List and Counterfeit Detector and Wholesale Prices Current, published to subscribers only at $2 per annum—supplementary notices are issued and served on each subscriber immediately the failure of a Bank is known in Wall st. Mailed at newspaper rates of postage; office 35 Wall st. N. Y.

Bedsteads.

Bedsteads and Bedding.
PARKER & RITTER,
158 Greenwich st. New York. Feathers, Beds, Mattresses, and every article in the Bedding line.
R. W. PARKER,   THOS. RITTER.

Bells.

ANDREW MENEELY Keeps constantly on hand Church and other Bells, Town Clocks, Surveyors' Instruments, &c. West Troy, N. Y.

Bolting Cloths.

JOHN R. PLATT,
Importer of and Wholesale and Retail Dealer in
New Anchor Bolting Cloths,
No. 6 Spruce street,
Near the City Hall, New York.

HENRY BODMER, JR.
IMPORTER OF
Bolting Cloth and Silk Goods,
No. 7 William st. New York.

Books.

BANKS, GOULD & CO.,
No. 144 Nassau st. New York,
Law Booksellers,
Publishers & Importers,

HAVE always on hand a large and general assortment of Law Books, English and American. Booksellers and public and private Libraries supplied on liberal terms both as to price and credit.

Account Books, Paper, and Stationery.
FRANCIS & LOUTREL,
77 Maiden Lane.
Manufacturing Stationers, and Importers of all articles in their line. Sell at lowest Cash Prices.

Bookbinders.

K. S. ELLES,
BOOKBINDER.
114 Nassau st., N. Y.
Cambric Book Cases made for the trade.

BOOKBINDERS'
Furnishing Warehouse.
JOHN R. HOOLE, 194 Nassau st., N. Y. is prepared to furnish every article requisite for Binders. Lettering Stamps, Tools, & Plates from designs cut in a superior style, on the very hardest metal, with promptness and dispatch.

Boots & Shoes.

JAMES FRENCH, Manufacturer and wholesale dealer in Boots and Shoes. No. 260 Pearl st. N. Y.

CHARLES H. HOWARD, Manufacturer and wholesale Dealer in Boots and Shoes, 217 Pearl st. (up stairs) New York.

Carpets.

WILLIAM M'GRORTY,
DEALER in Carpeting and Oil Cloths, Window Shades, Druggets, Rugs, Mats, Table and Piano Covers, Stair Rods, &c., &c. No. 136 William st. opposite the Washington Stores, N. Y. and 38 Fulton st. Brooklyn.

Carriages.

CARRIAGES.
JOHN C. HAM, JR. Manufacturer and Repository; 360 Broadway, New York.

Chairs.

A. F. M‘KOWN, Manufacturer and wholesale Dealer in Chairs of every description, 86 South Pearl st Albany.

J. W. MASON, MANUFACTURER and wholesale Dealer in all kinds of Boston, Rocking, Office, Maple and Cabinet Chairs, 377 Pearl st. N. Y. Also Wash Stands, Toilet Tables, and Settees. Orders for Shipping executed at Short Notice.

Chemists.

DOREMUS & HARRIS.—Analytical and Consulting Chemists—Manufacturers of Pure Reagents, Daguerreotype Materials, &c. Importers of Chemical Apparatus of all descriptions. Chemical School, 179 Broadway. New York. R. OGDEN DOREMUS, C. TOWNSEND HARRIS.

Chocolate, &c.

CONGRESS STEAM MILLS.. JOHN CORELL. Manufacturer of Sweet and Plain Chocolate, Prepared Cocoa, Mustard, Farina, Wheaten Grits, Vermicilli, &c. Also the celebrated Portable Congress Lemonade, No. 172 Forsyth st. New York.

T. E. FULLER & CO. Dealers in Sweet & Plain Chocolate. Cocoa, Farina, Macaroni, &c. and General Commission Merchants, also Agents for the Congress Steam Mills, 118 Warren st. N. Y.

E. MENDES, MANUFACTURER OF FRENCH CHOCOLATE, WHOLESALE, No. 192 Fulton Street, NEW YORK.

Cloths.

MORTIMERS & GAWTRY. 91 John st. N. Y. Importers of Cloths, Cassimeres, Coatings. Vestings, Serges, Satins, Velvets. Trimmings, &c., and all descriptions of Goods adapted to the trade of Merchant Tailors and Clothiers.

Clothing.

D. & J. DEVLIN. 33 and 35 John st. corner of Nassau, N. Y. have on hand at all times, an immense stock of Seasonable Clothing, at Wholesale and Retail, low for Cash.

BRITTON & PARSELLS' ONE PRICE CLOTHING WAREHOUSE, 90 Fulton & 258 Bleecker, NEW YORK. Constantly on hand, a good assortment of Cloths, Cassimeres and Vestings, which will be made up at the shortest notice, on the most reasonable Terms. JOHN F. BRITTON. WM. P. PARSELLS.

Coffins.

SAMUEL A. DEARE, 351 4th Avenue, begs to inform his friends and the public, that he has on hand at all times, a superior assortment of Rosewood, Mahogany and Lead Coffins, with every other description of Goods usually supplied by Furnishing Undertakers. Should they have occasion to require his services, they will find him reasonable in his charges, and careful and prompt in the execution of their orders.

Commission Mechs.

HAIGHT & TOOPER, COMMISSION MERCHANTS. Dealers in PROVISIONS and COUNTRY PRODUCE, No. 97 Murray Street. New York.

M. CANFIELD. Nos. 80 & 82 Cedar Street, New York, Commission Merchant and Jobber of Merrimack Prints, Russia Diaper and Crash, Brown and Bleached Sheetings. Ticking, Bagging, Drills. Cotton Yarn. Carpet Warp. Bats, Wick, Twine, Wadding, &c. For Cash.

Daguerreotypes.

McDONNELL & CO. DAGUERRIAN ROOMS, No. 192 Main St. Buffalo. Daguereotype Apparatus, Chemicals. &c wholesale and retail.

O. B. EVANS' SKYLIGHT PREMIUM DAGUERRIAN GALLERY, No. 220 Main Street, Buffalo.

BRADY'S NATIONAL Collection of Daguerreotypes, 205 & 207 BROADWAY, CORNER OF FULTON STREET, N. Y., and Pennsylvania Avenue, WASHINGTON CITY, D. C.

Distillers.

JAMES ENGLE, 38 BURLING SLIP, New York. CAMPHENE. ALCOHOL, (80 and 95 per cent.,) and TURPENTINE. Factory—Williamsburgh.

Druggists.

R. B. HAVILAND & CO., (late of Haviland, Keese & Co.) Importers and Wholesale Dealers in Drugs, Medicines, Paints, Oils, Perfumery, &c. Office and Sales Room. 177 Broadway (up stairs.) Stores at Brooklyn.

WILLIAM A. WHARTON, Importer and Wholesale Dealer in Chemicals, Drugs. Medicines, Paints. Oils. Dye-Stuffs. Brushes, &c., No. 381 & 383 Broadway, Albany. N. Y.

Dry Goods.

GEORGE W. CORLIES, Wholesale Dealer in Foreign and Domestic DRY GOODS, No. 283 Pearl Street, NEW YORK.

CAMERON & BRAND, Importers of Dundee and Russia Linens, Sail Duck, &c., 42 and 44 Pine street. N. Y.

A. JOURNEAY, JR. & CO. Importers & Wholesale Dealers in FANCY AND STAPLE DRY GOODS, Cloths, Cassimeres, Carpets, Druggets, &c. No. 14 Maiden Lane. bet. Broadway and Nassau st., New York. A. JOURNEAY, JR., PARKER P. CLARK.

R. MACGREGOR & CO., Carpetings, and General Dry Goods Furnishing Store, 198 Main street. Buffalo.

WILSON & SLAUSON. Wholesale Dealers in Foreign and Domestic Dry Goods, 12 Courtlandt street, and 13 Dey street. New York.

O. LINCOLN & SON, Newark Valley, N. Y.. Dealers in Dry Goods, Groceries, Hardware. Drugs and Medicines. Paints, Oils and Dye-Stuffs. and Agents for most of the valuable Patent Medicines of the day, among which are Dr. Jayne's popular Remedies. Also Wholesale Dealers in, and Manufacturers of. Sole and Upper Leather, Buck Skin. Gloves and Mittens and Boots and Shoes. All of which are offered to the public at low prices, and terms of payment made easy.

Engravers.

R. H. CARSON, successor to E. Forbes, Rooms No. 6 Albany Exchange. Fine Book Illustrations, Seals, Certificates. Machinery, &c. &c., neatly drawn and engraved.

WEDDING, VISITING, & BUSINESS CARDS. SEALS. PAPER STAMPS, and DOOR PLATES of every description, neatly and cheaply engraved by A. DEMAREST. No. 2 Pine street, corner of Broadway. New York. Also, Manufacturer of fine Envelopes, Wholesale and Retail.

Engravings.

PRINT SELLERS AND PUBLISHERS. GOUPIL, VIBERT & CO., 289 Broadway, New York. The only Wholesale Establishment in the United States for the sale of EUROPEAN ENGRAVINGS & LITHOGRAPHS. A large and choice assortment always on hand. The usual discount allowed to the Trade.

Effervescing Com.

B. T. BABBETT & CO., 68 and 70 Washington st., Manufacturers of Effervescing Compound for raising Bread, Buckwheat Cakes. Double Refined Saleratus. pure and double strength ; warranted best in the world. Also Patent Soap Powder, for washing in hard or soft water, without rubbing, and for making soft soap. The above goods are put up in 1 oz. papers. 6 oz. boxes. Directions accompany the packages.

Fancy Goods.

GEO. W. CHOLWELL, Manufacturer and Importer, Wholesale and Retail Dealer in Pocket Books, Writing Desks, Work Boxes, Shaving and Dressing Cases, Port Folios, Manifold Writers, Bankers' Cases, Bill Books, Travelling Money-Belts, Card Cases and Needle Books of pearl, silver, ivory, velvet and leather, Ivory Tablets, Chequer and Chess Boards, Spectacle Cases, Gold Pens, Pencil Cases of gold and silver, Pen Knives, &c. &c. Rich Toilet Articles of every description. Also, Importer and Dealer in every description of French, English, and German Fancy Goods. 24 Maiden Lane.

H. SONDHEIM & CO., Importers of French and German Fancy Goods, Buttons, Trimmings, Jewelry, Perfumery, &c., Cedar st., N. Y.

KIMM & SWITZER, 116 William St., New York. IMPORTERS AND JOBBERS of BERLIN ZEPHYR WORSTED, Trimmings and Fancy Goods, Linen Tapes & Bobbins, &c., &c.

M. P. BROWN, Manufacturer of Beadwork of every description, and Importer of Beads and Fancy Goods, 17 Cedar street, New York.
☞ A very large assortment.

French China.

D. G. & D. HAVILAND, No. 47 John st. Haviland & Co., em·ges France, Importers of China of all kinds, white, gilt and decorated. A large stock.

Furnaces & Ranges.

JOHN H. KEYSER, HOT AIR FURNACES, COOKING RANGES & STOVES, McGREGOR'S PATENT. No. 56 Cliff and 113 Beekman.

Furniture.

WILLIAM H. LEE, MANUFACTORY & WAREROOMS OF Chairs & Cabinet Furniture, No. 168 Fulton St., N. Y.

THOMAS H. BEAL, FURNITURE and UPHOLSTERY Warerooms, No. 45 Vesey Street, New York.

Gilder.

A. BISHOP, Pencil Case Manufacturer, Electro Gilder and Silver Plater, in all its various branches. Nos. 75 and 77 Nassau st., New York. Rooms 37 and 46 rear building.

Glaziers' Diamonds.

JOHN DICKINSON, Importer of DIAMOND SPARKS, and Manufacturer of GLAZIERS' PATENT SWIVEL DIAMONDS, No. 33 John street, New York.

JOSHUA SHAW, GLAZIERS' SWIVEL DIAMONDS Manufacturer. No. 142 Nassau st., N. Y. No travelling agents employed.

Gold Leaf.

ROBERT COTTIER, Manufacturer of Gold and Silver Leaf, Dentists' Gold and Tin Foil, constantly on hand at New York prices. 186 Main st., Buffalo, N.Y.

BRONZE, Gold and Florence Leaf, &c. &c. Also Camphene, Pine Oil, Gas, Superior Patent Lamps, &c., for sale by WILMOT WILLIAMS, 138 Maiden Lane, New York.

Grocers.

SAM'L. P. EVERTS, Wholesale Dealer in **Fish and Provisions.** 248 Fulton street, New York.

PLATT BRUSH, Wholesale Grocer, and Dealer in Provisions, Teas, Wines, Foreign and Domestic Liquors, Segars, &c.&c., Clover, Timothy, Red Top and Orchard Grass Seeds. 160 West, cor. Robinson st., New York. HENRY P. BRUSH.

WILLIAM DAVIS, Wholesale Grocer and Commission Merchant, and Dealer in Wines, Liquors, Cigars, &c., No. 11 State street, Albany, N. Y.

Guns.

BLUNT & SYMS, **177 Broadway.** MANUFACTURERS of GUNS, RIFLES, PISTOLS, of great variety of styles. six barrelled REVOLVERS. MUSKETS, &c., &c. IMPORTERS of English and German Twist and Plain Double and Single Guns of all qualities, and in large quantities. Also Powder Flasks, Pouches, Shot-Belts, Locks, and all kinds of Gun materials for Gun Manufacturers

Hardware.

BALDWIN & MANY, Builders' Hardware, Locksmiths' and Bell Hangers' Materials. Wholesale and Retail. 34 John street, near Nassau, (corner building) N. Y.—Sole Agents for Dixon's Black Lead Crucibles.

HENRY CROMWELL, Importer & Wholesale Dealer in Hardware & Cutlery, 79 Barclay st. near Greenwich, N. Y.

JELLINGHAUS & CO., Solingen, Germany, Manufacturers of Cutlery, Edge Tools, Files and Hardware, Importers of Fancy Goods, Needles, etc. etc. WM. WALSCHEID, Agent, Office, 65 Broad st., N. Y.

J. B. WINDLE & CO., 56 Maiden Lane, Importers and Manufacturers of Table Cutlery, House and Ship Furnishing Hardware & Tinware, &c. &c.

Harps.

J. F. BROWNE & CO. Makers & Importers of Grand, Semi-Grand, and Six Octave Double Action Harps. Warerooms. 295 Broadway, next block above the Irving House.

Hides.

N. GILMAN & SON. Dealers in Putney & Spanish Hides, Leather and Oil. 72 Gold st., N. Y.

Hose.

LEATHER HOSE FOR FIRE Engines, Steamboats, Factories, Street Washers, &c., manufactured from the best oak-tanned leather, with wrought copper rivets, always on hand and for sale by JOHN H. BOWIE & CO., Curriers and Leather Dealers, 30 Ferry st.; who have also for sale, Calfskins, Wax & Grain Upper Leather, and Curried Leather of every description.

Hosiery.

JAMES KEELEY, Importer of Hosiery and Gloves, 12 Pine st., N. Y.

Hotels.

BENNET'S TEMPERANCE HOUSE, near the Liberty Pole, J. H. BAILEY, } Prop. BUFFALO. D. B. HULL, } Passengers & Baggage conveyed to and from the House, free of charge.

CLARK's VILLAGE HOTEL, Ballston Spa, by S. B. Medbery.—Livery Stable attached.

CAVE HOUSE, Howe's Cave. Cobleskill, Schoharie Co, N. Y., Lester Howe, Proprietor.

NEWARK VALLEL HOTEL, fronting the Public Square, Newark Valley, Tioga Co., N. Y., by Lincoln & Stebbins.—Stages leave daily for Owego & Cortland, connecting with N. Y. & Erie Rail Road.

WELLAND HOUSE, **W. D. STEWART,** **OSWEGO, N. Y.**

Hotel Annunciator.

A NEW INVENTION, Intended as a substitute for the usual suit of Bells in Hotels, Steamboats, Private Dwellings, &c. It is extremely simple in its construction, and may be attached to the wires used in the old arrangement of Bells.—123½ William st., New York. T. D. JACKSON & CO.

India Rubber Goods.

HEAD QUARTERS FOR GOODYEAR'S PATENT RUBBER, 19 Nassau st.
Country merchants and others are invited to look at the largest stock of Metallic or Vulcanized Rubber Goods ever offered in America;—over $100,000 in amount, and comprising about four hundred different articles, all useful and desirable. Manufactured by, and for sale at the Depot of the UNION INDIA RUBBER CO. 19 Nassau street, N. Y.
☞ Caution.—Look out for worthless imitations. Buy only those stamped "Goodyear's Patent, 1844."

INDIA RUBBER MANUFACTURER, Horace H. Day, 23 Cortlandt st., N. Y.—$100,000 Capital—20 years in the business—has built, owns, and runs 3 factories—warrants his goods, sells cheap.

METALLIC RUBBER SHOES. THE Subscriber still continues Sole Agent for L. Candee's celebrated high finished metallic RUBBER BOOTS, SHOES & GAITERS at the old stand, No. 248 Pearl st. New York.
M. J. FRISBIE.
Wholesale Commission Dealer in all kinds of Rubber Goods.

HAYWARD RUBBER CO. Manufacturers of Spring Tempered Metallic Rubber Boots and Shoes, Colchester, Conn. Stores. 20 & 22 Central st. Boston.

THE NEWARK INDIA RUBBER MANUFACTURING CO. Manufacturers, (☞ NOT AGENTS) offer to dealers all kinds of India Rubber Goods.
Their India Rubber Shoes possess qualities that give them the preference over all others. Their flexibility remains the same in all climates ; and their elegant fine jet black polish is not made by common varnish, which cracks and peals off the first time they are worn.
Dealers, know your interest ! Buy of the Manufacturers, at their Factory in Newark, N. J. or at their Store, No. 59 Maiden lane, New York. H. HUTCHINSON, President.

New York India Rubber Warehouse.
D. HODGMAN, Manufacturer and Dealer in VULCANIZED India Rubber Goods, 27 Maiden Lane, and 59 Nassau st. Factory foot of 25th st. East River. N. Y.

Iron Founders.

Williamsburgh Iron Foundry, Corner of Eighth & Ainslie sts.
Grates, Fenders, Summer Pieces, and all Ornamental Castings, made to order. Orders received at No. 7 Dutch st. New York.
JAMES RITCHIE.

WORRALL & CO. New York Iron Foundry, Printing Press and Saw Manufactory, 22, 24, 26 and 28 Elm, and 67 Duane sts.
NOAH WORRALL,
WADE B. WORRALL.

Lamps.

W. H. STARR & FELLOWES, Manufacturers of GAS FIXTURES, Chandeliers, Solar, Camphene, Burning Fluid and Phosgene LAMPS, GIRANDOLES, HALL LAMPS, &c. Manufacturers also of CAMPHENE, BURNING FLUID, AND PHOSGENE.
67 Beekman st. N. Y.

CHARLES FULLER, DEALER in Jennings' New Patent Premium Safety Gas Lamps. also, Camphene, Spirit Gas, Oil and Lard Lamps, Hall and other Lanterns, Girandoles, Chandeliers, &c. of the most approved patterns ; Britannia and Glass Ware, Cutlery and Fancy Ornaments.
ALSO CAMPHENE, Spirit Gas, Phosgene Gas, OIL, WICKS, GLASSES, &C.
No. 273 Greenwich, between Warren and Chambers sts. New York.

Lamp Wicks.

Lamp Wicks! Lamp Wicks!
NEW YORK MANUFACTURING COMPANY, Office No. 6 Broadway, New York, offer to buyers their superior Lamp Wicks, of every size and description, on accommodating terms.
HARDING & REED.

Machine Cards.

SARGENT & MORTIMER, Manufacturers of WOOLEN and COTTON MACHINE CARDS, Dealers in Woolen and Cotton Manufacturers' Articles.
Auburn, New York.

Machinery.

Matteawan Machine Works.
LOCOMOTIVE Engines, of every size and pattern. Also Tenders, Wheels, Axles, and other Railroad Machinery. Stationery Engines, Boilers, &c. arranged for Driving Cotton, Woolen and other Mills. Cotton and Woolen Machinery, of every description, embodying all the modern improvements. Mill Gearing, from probably the most extensive assortment of Patterns in this line, in any section of the country. Tools, Turning Lathes, Slabbing, Planing, Cutting, and Drilling Machines, together with all other Tools required in Machine Shops. Apply at No. 66 Beaver st. New York City, to WILLIAM B. LEONARD, Agent.

IRON FOUNDERS' FACING DUSTS, of best quality, for sale by G. O. ROBERTSON, 4 Liberty Place, Liberty st., near the Post Office, New York.

Manufctrs' Supplies.

COTTON AND WOOLEN MANUFACTURERS' SUPPLIES AND MACHINERY, of every description.
ANDREWS & JESUP.
70 Pine st., New York.

Marble Works.

DEXTER BELDEN'S MARBLE WORKS, Corner Terrace and Erie streets, Buffalo.
American and Foreign Marble Mantels, Monuments, Mural Tablets, Marble in block, slab. &c.&c.
Also, Grates, Soap Stone, Fire Brick, Plaster Paris, &c. &c., at Wholesale and Retail.

Math. Instruments.

BENJ. PIKE & SONS, Manufacturers of Mathematical and Philosophical Instruments, 166 Broadway, N. Y. Gold, Silver and Steel Spectacles.

Needles, &c.

T. BARNETT, Importer of Needles, Pins, Steel Pens. fine Cutlery, &c., No. 94 Cedar-street, near Broadway, New York.

JAMES KEELEY, Agent for Manufacturers of Needles, Fish Hooks, Threads, Bindings, Hosiery and small wares generally, No. 12 Pine street. New York.

JAMES KEELEY, Importer of Needles and Fish Hooks, No. 12 Pine-street, N. Y.

Oils.

GEORGE S. GILBERT, Manufacturer of Sperm, Elephant, Whale and Lard Oils, 124 and 126 Furman-street, (between Atlantic and Fulton Ferries. and first from the River.) Brooklyn.

NEATS-FOOT OIL, warranted PURE, and for OILING LEATHER or MACHINERY, superior to the best Sperm Oil. Also, a supply of all kinds of Glue.
PETER COOPER,
17 Burling Slip. N. Y.

Paint.

WM. BLAKE, No. 3, Broad-street, N. Y., Patentee of Blake's Patent Fire and Weather Proof Ohio Paint or Artificial Slate.

Paper Boxes.

HENRY JONES, Manufacturer of Paper Boxes, Sample Cards, Morocco Cases—Dealer in Fancy Paper and Fine Box Boards, No. 115 John-street, New York.

Paper Hangings.

ROCKWELL BROTHERS, Importers and Manufacturers of Paper Hangings and Oil Painted Window Shades, 21 Cortlandt-st., New York.

D. HARRIS, Jr., Manufacturer and Dealer in Paper Hangings, Window Shades and Paper Boxes, 8 Green-street, Albany.

L. STEELE & CO., Manufacturers and Importers of Paper Hangings, Borders, Fire Board Patterns, Window Shades, &c., Nos 360 & 362 Broadway, Albany.

Paper Warehouses.

HANNA & BEEBE, COMMISSION PAPER WAREHOUSE, No. 109 Fulton-street New York. SAMUEL HANNA, RODERICK BEEBE.

PERSE & BROOKS, Paper Manufacturers.—Warehouse 55 & 67 Nassau-street, New York.

Paris Green.

PARIS GREEN, S BRAND, Manufactured and sold by THEODORE SWARTZ, 32 Burling Slip, N. Y.

Pens.

BARD BROTHERS & CO., Manufacturers of Diamond Pointed Gold Pens and Gold and Silver Pencil Cases, 101 William-st., N. Y. and 91 Wash'tn-st.,Boston.

BLAKENEY'S GOLD PEN MANUFACTORY, 42 & 44 Nassau-street, (up stairs,) corner of Liberty, New York. Gold Pens, large, small and medium size; also, Gold and Silver Cases,

G. & E. M. SMITH, (Late of the Firm of A. G. Bagley & Co.) MANUFACTURERS OF GOLD PENS, PENHOLDERS AND PENCILS, No. 16 MAIDEN LANE, N. Y. THE Subscribers are manufacturing Gold Pens and Pencils, of the best quality. All Pens sold from our office are first proved to be perfect. The public are invited to call.
G. & E. M. SMITH, 16 Maiden Lane, N. Y.

Pianos.

BOARDMAN & GRAY, Piano Forte,(with their Patent Dolce Campana Attachment), Manufactory and Music Ware Rooms, "Old Elm Tree Corner." Nos. 4 and 6 North Pearl, near State-st., Albany.

Plumbers.

F. W. RIDGWAY, Plumber and Hydraulic Engineer. Pumps, Bathing Apparatus, Water Closets, and Hydraulic Machinery of every description. Manufacturer of Lead Retorts for Chlorine, Gas, and other Chemical Apparatus, 115 and 117 State-street, Albany. Late of New York.

Pocket Books.

COOK'S PORTE MONNAIE POCKET BOOK, and Razor Strop Manufactory, 96 Fulton st., New York.

Printers.

OLIVER & BROTHER, STEAM JOB PRINTERS, 89 NASSAU STREET, Sun Building, New York. Improved Steam Presses for all kinds of work. Yankee Card Presses. Designs and great facilities for Country Merchants. Call and see.

Publishers.

FOWLERS & WELLS, Phrenologists, No. 131 Nassau street, Clinton Hall, N. Y., Publish works on Phrenology, Physiology and Magnetism.

HALLOCK & LYON, UNIVERSALIST BOOK SELLERS and Publishers, CHRISTIAN MESSENGER, &c., 3 Astor House, Barclay st., New York.

W. F. BURGESS, Publisher & Wholesale Dealer in Cheap Publications, No. 22 Ann street, New York.

Pumps.

DOWNS. MYNDERSE & CO., Machinists and Iron Founders. Patentees, sole Manufacturers, and Wholesale Dealers in the celebrated Patent Cast Iron Revolving Spout, Well and Cistern Pumps, Seneca Falls, Seneca Co., N. Y.

Saddlery.

C. S. STORMS, Wholesale and Retail Saddle, Harness, and Trunk Manufacturer. 53 Fulton, c. Cliff st. Particular attention paid to city work and fitting horses. Military equipments conformable to the U. S. Regulations.

Saleratus.

BROWN & LAMBERT, Manufacturers of Saleratus, Super Carb. Soda, &c., Wholesale Dealers in Cream Tartar, 117 Front st. near Wall, New York.

Saws, etc.

AMERICAN STAR SAW & FILE WORKS. Samuel D. Willmott, 8 Liberty st., N. Y. Has always on hand for sale an Asortment of his approved and superior C. S. warranted SAWS & FILES, Manufactured at his Establishment at Williamsburgh, L. I.

JOHN ROBERTS, Manufacturer, Repairer & Dealer in Saws of every description, 7 Swan st. near Main, Buffalo, N. Y.

Sheetings.

STARR & BABCOCK, 76 Cedar st., N. Y., Wholesale Dealers in Bleached and Brown Sheetings. Merrimac Prints, Crash, Drills. Ticking, Bagging, Carpet-Warp, Yarn, Bats, Wick, Twine, &c., &c., for cash or city acceptance.

Shoe Findings.

H. WING & CO., Last, Boot Tree and Peg Manufacturers, No. 8 Exchange street, Buffalo, N. Y. Also, Dealers in Findings.

Silver Plating.

MURRAY & FALIHEE'S Silver Plating Establishment. 556 Broadway, New York.

Steam Boiler Setter.

D. CARPENTER, Patentee and Proprietor of Improved Plan of Setting Steam Boilers, Office. 66 Beaver street, New York.

Stoves.

W. RACE & CO., Manufacturers and Proprietors of Race's celebrated Patent Self-Regulator for Stoves—also Cast Tops and Bottoms for the same—Seneca Falls, Seneca Co., N. Y.

Threshing Machines.

WHEELER, MELICK & CO., Manufacturers of Wheeler's Patent Horse Powers, Over-Shot Separating Threshers, and other Agricultural Machines, cor. Hamilton & Liberty sts., Albany. N. Y.

Tobacco.

PAYNE & M'NAUGHTON. Manufacturers of Tobacco. Snuff, Cigars, Chocolate and Prepared Cocoa. Dealers in Pipes. Matches, Mustard, Plug Tobacco. and Imported Cigars, Snuff Boxes. &c. No. 7 Broadway, Albany, N. Y

Varnish.

MINETT & CO., MANUFACTURERS OF COACH BODY And other Copal Varnishes, 60 Pearl st. New York.

Warm'g & Ventil'g.

Chilson, Allen. Walker & Co., 351 Broadway. New York. Chilson's Air Warming and Ventilating Furnace, Dr. Clark's Ventilating Stoves, Emerson's Ventilators.

Watches.

PAUL A. BREZ, Importer of Watches, Clocks, Musical Boxes, Tools and Materials for Watchmakers, No. 29 Cortlandt st. New York.

www.ingramcontent.com/pod-product-compliance
Lightning Source LLC
Chambersburg PA
CBHW071356050326
40689CB00010B/1669